World Civilizations

The Global Experience

AP® Edition

Seventh Edition

Peter N. Stearns
George Mason University

Michael Adas
Rutgers University

Stuart B. Schwartz
Yale University

Marc Jason Gilbert
Hawaii Pacific University

PEARSON

Boston Columbus Indianapolis New York San Francisco Upper Saddle River
Amsterdam Cape Town Dubai London Madrid Milan Munich Paris Montreal Toronto
Delhi Mexico City Sao Paulo Sydney Hong Kong Seoul Singapore Taipei Tokyo

Editor-in-Chief: Dickson Musslewhite
Publisher: Charlyce Jones Owen
Project Manager: Rob DeGeorge
Program Manager: Seanna Breen
Editorial Assistant: Maureen Diana
Senior Operations Supervisor: Mary Ann Gloriande
Senior Art Director: Maria Lange
Interior Design: Red Kite Consulting
Cover Design: Depinho Design

Manager, Visual Research & Permissions: Beth Brenzel
Cover photo credit: Werner Forman/Art Resource, NY—Three women with fireworks. India. Moghul. ca. 1640.
Media Director: Brian Hyland
Media Editor: Elizabeth Roden Hall
Composition/Full-Service Project Management: SPi Global/Bruce Hobart
Printer/Binder: Courier/Kendallville
Cover Printer: Lehigh-Phoenix Color/Hagerstown

This book was set in 10/12 Minion Pro

Credits and acknowledgments borrowed from other sources and reproduced, with permission, in this textbook appear on page C-1.

Copyright © 2015, 2011, 2007 Pearson Education, Inc., publishing as Prentice Hall, 1 Lake St., Upper Saddle River, NJ 07458. All rights reserved. Manufactured in the United States of America. This publication is protected by Copyright, and permission should be obtained from the publisher prior to any prohibited reproduction, storage in a retrieval system, or transmission in any form or by any means, electronic, mechanical, photocopying, recording, or likewise. To obtain permission(s) to use material from this work, please submit a written request to Pearson Education, Inc., Permissions Department, One Lake Street, Upper Saddle River, NJ 07458.

Many of the designations by manufacturers and seller to distinguish their products are claimed as trademarks. Where those designations appear in this book, and the publisher was aware of a trademark claim, the designations have been printed in initial caps or all caps.

AP® is a trademark registered and/or owned by the College Board, which was not involved in the production of, and does not endorse, this product.

Library of Congress Cataloging-in-Publication Data on file

10 9 8 7 6 5 4 3 2 1

Student Edition: High School Binding
ISBN 10: 0-13-344770-7
ISBN 13: 978-0-13-344770-5

PearsonSchool.com/Advanced

Brief Contents

PART I

EARLY HUMAN SOCIETIES, 2.5 MILLION–600 B.C.E.: ORIGINS AND DEVELOPMENT 1

1. From Human Prehistory to the Early Civilizations 7
2. Early Civilizations, 3500–600 B.C.E. 21

PART II

THE CLASSICAL PERIOD, 600 B.C.E.–600 C.E. 48

3. Classical Civilization: China 54
4. Classical Civilization: India 74
5. Classical Civilizations in the Middle East and Mediterranean 94
6. The Classical Period: Directions, Diversities, and Declines by 500 C.E. 117

PART III

THE POSTCLASSICAL PERIOD, 600–1450: NEW FAITH AND NEW COMMERCE 149

7. The First Global Civilization: The Rise and Spread of Islam 156
8. Abbasid Decline and the Spread of Islamic Civilization to South and Southeast Asia 182
9. African Civilizations and the Spread of Islam 204
10. Civilization in Eastern Europe: Byzantium and Orthodox Europe 224
11. A New Civilization Emerges in Western Europe 241
12. The Americas on the Eve of Invasion 265
13. Reunification and Renaissance in Chinese Civilization: The Era of the Tang and Song Dynasties 287

14. The Spread of Chinese Civilization: Japan, Korea, and Vietnam 308
15. The Last Great Nomadic Challenges: From Chinggis Khan to Timur 331
16. The World in 1450: Changing Balance of World Power 351

PART IV

THE EARLY MODERN PERIOD, 1450–1750: THE WORLD SHRINKS 377

17. The World Economy 384
18. The Transformation of the West, 1450–1750 405
19. Early Latin America 425
20. Africa and the Africans in the Age of the Atlantic Slave Trade 453
21. The Rise of Russia 478
22. The Muslim Empires 493
23. Asian Transitions in an Age of Global Change 520

PART V

THE DAWN OF THE INDUSTRIAL AGE, 1750–1900 554

24. The Emergence of Industrial Society in the West, 1750–1900 561
25. Industrialization and Imperialism: The Making of the European Global Order 587
26. The Consolidation of Latin America, 1810–1920 612
27. Civilizations in Crisis: The Ottoman Empire, the Islamic Heartlands, and Qing China 639
28. Russia and Japan: Industrialization Outside the West 662

PART VI

THE NEWEST STAGE OF WORLD HISTORY: 1900–PRESENT   693

29 Descent into the Abyss: World War I and the Crisis of the European Global Order   701

30 The World between the Wars: Revolutions, Depression, and Authoritarian Response   729

31 A Second Global Conflict and the End of the European World Order   765

32 Western Society and Eastern Europe in the Decades of the Cold War   791

33 Latin America: Revolution and Reaction into the 21st Century   821

34 Africa, the Middle East, and Asia in the Era of Independence   843

35 Rebirth and Revolution: Nation-Building in East Asia and the Pacific Rim   869

36 Power, Politics, and Conflict in World History, 1990–2014   897

37 Globalization and Resistance   918

Contents

Features x

Preface xiv

Supplementary Teaching and Learning Materials xx

About the Authors xxii

Teacher to Teacher xxiii

Correlation of *World Civilizations* to the AP® Course Outline for World History xxiv

Prologue xxxii

PART I

EARLY HUMAN SOCIETIES, 2.5 MILLION–600 B.C.E.: ORIGINS AND DEVELOPMENT 1

CHAPTER 1 From Human Prehistory to the Early Civilizations 7
- Getting Started Is Always Hard 9
- Human Development and Change 10
- The Neolithic Revolution 12
- Agriculture and Change 15
- Nomadic Societies 16
- Global Connections and Critical Themes: The Early Civilizations and the World 20
- Further Readings 20
- Critical Thinking Questions 20

CHAPTER 2 Early Civilizations, 3500–600 B.C.E. 21
- Civilization 22
- Tigris-Euphrates Civilization 23
- Egyptian Civilization 27
- Egypt and Mesopotamia Compared 29
- River Valley Civilization in India 30
- China 32
- Early Civilizations in the Americas 33
- The End of the River Valley Period 35
- Global Connections and Critical Themes: The Early Civilizations and the World 38
- Further Readings 38
- Critical Thinking Questions 39
- Part I AP® Test Prep 40

PART II

THE CLASSICAL PERIOD, 600 B.C.E.–600 C.E.: Uniting Large Regions 48

CHAPTER 3 Classical Civilization: China 54
- Patterns in Classical China 56
- Political Institutions 60
- Religion and Culture 63
- Economy and Society 67
- A Distinctive Mixture 71
- Global Connections and Critical Themes: Classical China and the World 72
- Further Readings 72
- Critical Thinking Questions 73

CHAPTER 4 Classical Civilization: India 74
- The Framework For Indian History: Geography and Culture 76
- Patterns in Classical India 78
- Political Institutions 80
- Religion and Culture 82
- Economy and Society 87
- Indian Influence and Comparative Features 88
- Global Connections and Critical Themes: India and the Wider World 92
- Further Readings 93
- Critical Thinking Questions 93

CHAPTER 5 Classical Civilizations in the Middle East and Mediterranean 94
- The Persian Tradition 97
- Patterns of Greek History 99
- Patterns of Roman History 101
- Greek and Roman Political Institutions 103
- Religion and Culture 107
- Economy and Society in the Mediterranean 111
- Toward the Fall of Rome 114
- Global Connections and Critical Themes: Persia, Greece, Rome, and the World 115
- Further Readings 116
- Critical Thinking Questions 116

v

CHAPTER 6 The Classical Period: Directions, Diversities, and Declines by 500 C.E. 117

Beyond the Classical Civilizations 118

Decline in China and India 125

The Decline and Fall of the Roman Empire 129

The Development and Spread of World Religions 133

Global Connections and Critical Themes: The Late Classical Period and the World 137

Further Readings 138

Critical Thinking Questions 138

Part II AP® Test Prep 139

PART III

THE POSTCLASSICAL PERIOD, 600–1450: NEW FAITH AND NEW COMMERCE 149

CHAPTER 7 The First Global Civilization: The Rise and Spread of Islam 156

Desert and Town: The Harsh Environment of the Pre-Islamic Arabian World 158

The Life of Muhammad and the Genesis of Islam 163

The Arab Empire of the Umayyads 166

From Arab to Islamic Empire: The Early Abbasid Era 174

Global Connections and Critical Themes: Early Islam and the World 180

Further Readings 180

Critical Thinking Questions 181

CHAPTER 8 Abbasid Decline and the Spread of Islamic Civilization to South and Southeast Asia 182

The Islamic Heartlands in the Middle and Late Abbasid Eras 184

An Age of Learning and Artistic Refinements 189

The Coming of Islam to South Asia 192

The Spread of Islam to Southeast Asia 200

Global Connections and Critical Themes: Islam: A Bridge Between Worlds 202

Further Readings 202

Critical Thinking Questions 203

CHAPTER 9 African Civilizations and the Spread of Islam 204

African Societies: Diversity and Similarities 205

Kingdoms of the Grasslands 209

The Swahili Coast of East Africa 215

Peoples of the Forest and Plains 217

Global Connections and Critical Themes: Internal Development and Global Contacts 222

Further Readings 223

Critical Thinking Questions 223

CHAPTER 10 Civilization in Eastern Europe: Byzantium and Orthodox Europe 224

Civilization in Eastern Europe 225

The Byzantine Empire 227

The Split Between Eastern and Western Christianity 231

The Spread of Civilization in Eastern Europe 235

The Emergence of Kievan Rus' 235

Global Connections and Critical Themes: Eastern Europe and the World 240

Further Readings 240

Critical Thinking Questions 240

CHAPTER 11 A New Civilization Emerges in Western Europe 241

Stages of Postclassical Development 243

Western Culture in the Postclassical Era 253

Changing Economic and Social Forms in the Postclassical Centuries 257

The Decline of the Medieval Synthesis 260

Global Connections and Critical Themes: Medieval Europe and the World 263

Further Readings 263

Critical Thinking Questions 264

CHAPTER 12 The Americas on the Eve of Invasion 265

Postclassic Mesoamerica, 1000–1500 C.E. 267

Aztec Society in Transition 272

Twantinsuyu: World of the Incas 276

The Other Peoples of the Americas 282

Global Connections: The Americas and the World 285

Further Readings 285

Critical Thinking Questions 286

CHAPTER 13 Reunification and Renaissance in Chinese Civilization: The Era of the Tang and Song Dynasties 287

Rebuilding the Imperial Edifice in the Sui-Tang Era 288

Tang Decline and the Rise of the Song 295

Tang and Song Prosperity: The Basis of a Golden Age 299

Global Connections and Critical Themes: China's World Role 307

Further Readings 307

Critical Thinking Questions 307

CHAPTER 14 The Spread of Chinese Civilization: Japan, Korea, and Vietnam 308

Japan: The Imperial Age 310

The Era of Warrior Dominance 314

Korea: Between China and Japan 319

Between China and Southeast Asia: The Making of Vietnam 322

Global Connections and Critical Themes: In the Orbit of China: The East Asian Corner of the Global System 329

Further Readings   329
Critical Thinking Questions   330

CHAPTER 15   The Last Great Nomadic Challenges: From Chinggis Khan to Timur   331
The Transcontinental Empire of Chinggis Khan   333
The Mongol Drive to the West   339
The Mongol Interlude in Chinese History   343
Global Connections and Critical Themes: The Mongol Linkages   349
Further Readings   349
Critical Thinking Questions   350

CHAPTER 16   The World in 1450: Changing Balance of World Power   351
Key Changes in the Middle East   353
The Structure of Transregional Trade   354
The Rise of the West   356
Outside the World Network   362
Global Connections and Critical Themes: 1450 and the World   365
Further Readings   366
Critical Thinking Questions   366
Part III AP® Test Prep   367

PART IV

THE EARLY MODERN PERIOD, 1450–1750: THE WORLD SHRINKS   377

CHAPTER 17   The World Economy   384
The West's First Outreach: Maritime Power   385
The Columbian Exchange of Disease and Food   391
Toward A World Economy   393
Colonial Expansion   396
Global Connections and Critical Themes: The World Economy—and the World   403
Further Readings   403
Critical Questions   404

CHAPTER 18   The Transformation of the West, 1450–1750   405
The First Big Changes: Culture and Commerce, 1450–1650   407
The Commercial Revolution   412
The Scientific Revolution: The Next Phase of Change   415
Political Change   417
The West by 1750   420
Global Connections and Critical Themes: Europe and the World   424
Further Readings   424
Critical Thinking Questions   424

CHAPTER 19   Early Latin America   425
Spaniards and Portuguese: From Reconquest to Conquest   427
The Destruction and Transformation of Indigenous Societies   435
Colonial Economies and Governments   436
Brazil: The First Plantation Colony   441
Multiracial Societies   443
The 18th-Century Reforms   446
Global Connections and Critical Themes: Latin American Civilization and the World Context   451
Further Readings   451
Critical Thinking Questions   452

CHAPTER 20   Africa and the Africans in the Age of the Atlantic Slave Trade   453
Africa and the Creation of an Atlantic System   454
The Atlantic Slave Trade   456
African Societies, Slavery, and the Slave Trade   460
White Settlers and Africans in Southern Africa   467
The African Diaspora   469
Global Connections and Critical Themes: Africa and the African Diaspora in World Context   476
Further Readings   476
Critical Thinking Questions   477

CHAPTER 21   The Rise of Russia   478
Russia's Expansionist Politics under the Tsars   479
Russia's First Westernization, 1690–1790   483
Themes in Early Modern Russian History   489
Global Connections and Critical Themes: Russia and the World   492
Further Readings   492
Critical Thinking Questions   492

CHAPTER 22   The Muslim Empires   493
The Ottomans: From Frontier Warriors to Empire Builders   495
The Shi'a Challenge of the Safavids   504
The Mughals and the Apex of Muslim Civilization in India   510
Global Connections and Critical Themes: Gunpowder Empires and the Restoration of the Islamic Bridge among Civilizations   518
Further Readings   518
Critical Thinking Questions   519

CHAPTER 23   Asian Transitions in an Age of Global Change   520
The Asian Trading World and the Coming of the Europeans   522
Ming China: A Global Mission Refused   529
Fending Off the West: Japan's Reunification and the First Challenge   538

Global Connections and Critical Themes: An Age of Eurasian Proto-Globalization 542
Further Readings 542
Critical Thinking Questions 543
Part IV AP® Test Prep 544

PART V

THE DAWN OF THE INDUSTRIAL AGE, 1750–1900 554

CHAPTER 24 The Emergence of Industrial Society in the West, 1750–1900 561
Context for Revolution 562
The Age of Revolution 564
The Industrial Revolution: First Phases 569
The Consolidation of the Industrial Order, 1850–1900 571
Cultural Transformations 576
Western Settler Societies 579
Diplomatic Tensions and World War I 583
Global Connections and Critical Themes: Industrial Europe and the World 585
Further Readings 585
Critical Thinking Questions 586

CHAPTER 25 Industrialization and Imperialism: The Making of the European Global Order 587
The Shift to Land Empires in Asia 590
Industrial Rivalries and the Partition of the World, 1870–1914 597
Patterns of Dominance: Continuity and Change 601
Global Connections and Critical Themes: A European-Dominated Early Phase of Globalization 610
Further Readings 610
Critical Thinking Questions 611

CHAPTER 26 The Consolidation of Latin America, 1810–1920 612
From Colonies to Nations 614
New Nations Confront Old and New Problems 618
Latin American Economies and World Markets, 1820–1870 620
Societies in Search of Themselves 628
Global Connections and Critical Themes: New Latin American Nations and the World 637
Further Readings 637
Critical Thinking Questions 638

CHAPTER 27 Civilizations in Crisis: The Ottoman Empire, the Islamic Heartlands, and Qing China 639
From Empire to Nation: Ottoman Retreat and the Birth of Turkey 641
Western Intrusions and the Crisis in the Arab Islamic Heartlands 644

The Rise and Fall of the Qing Dynasty 650
Global Connections and Critical Themes: Muslim and Chinese Retreat and a Shifting Global Balance 660
Further Readings 660
Critical Thinking Questions 661

CHAPTER 28 Russia and Japan: Industrialization outside the West 662
Russia's Reforms and Industrial Advance 664
Protest and Revolution in Russia 670
Japan: Transformation without Revolution 673
Global Connections and Critical Themes: Russia and Japan in the World 681
Further Readings 682
Critical Thinking Questions 682
Part V AP® Test Prep 683

PART VI

THE NEWEST STAGE OF WORLD HISTORY: 1900–PRESENT 693

CHAPTER 29 Descent into the Abyss: World War I and the Crisis of the European Global Order 701
The Coming of the Great War 704
A World at War 706
Failed Peace and Global Turmoil 713
The Nationalist Assault on the European Colonial Order 714
Global Connections and Critical Themes: World War and Global Upheavals 727
Further Readings 727
Critical Thinking Questions 728

CHAPTER 30 The World between the Wars: Revolutions, Depression, and Authoritarian Response 729
The Roaring Twenties 730
Revolution: The First Waves 736
The Global Great Depression 748
The Nazi Response 751
Authoritarianism and New Militarism in Key Regions 753
Global Connections and Critical Themes: Economic Depression, Authoritarian Response, and Democratic Retreat 762
Further Readings 762
Critical Thinking Questions 764

CHAPTER 31 A Second Global Conflict and the End of the European World Order 765
Old and New Causes of a Second World War 767
Unchecked Aggression and the Coming of War in Europe and the Pacific 770
The Conduct of a Second Global War 772
War's End and the Emergence of the Superpower Standoff in the Cold War 780

Nationalism and Decolonization in South and Southeast Asia and Africa   781
Global Connections and Critical Themes: Persisting Trends in a World Transformed by War   789
Further Readings   789
Critical Thinking Questions   790

CHAPTER 32   Western Society and Eastern Europe in the Decades of the Cold War   791
After World War II: A New International Setting for the West   793
The Resurgence of Western Europe   796
Cold War Allies: The United States, Canada, Australia, and New Zealand   802
Culture and Society in the West   804
Eastern Europe After World War II: A Soviet Empire   809
Soviet Culture: Promoting New Beliefs and Institutions   812
Global Connections and Critical Themes: The Cold War and the World   819
Further Readings   819
Critical Thinking Questions   820

CHAPTER 33   Latin America: Revolution and Reaction into the 21st Century   821
Latin America After World War II   823
Radical Options in the 1950s   825
The Search for Reform and the Military Option   831
Societies in Search of Change   837
Global Connections and Critical Themes: Struggling Toward the Future in a Global Economy   841
Further Readings   842
Critical Thinking Questions   842

CHAPTER 34   Africa, the Middle East, and Asia in the Era of Independence   843
The Challenges of Independence   845
Postcolonial Options for Achieving Economic Growth and Social Justice   856
Delayed Revolutions: Religious Revivalism and Liberation Movements in Settler Societies   862
Global Connections and Critical Themes: Postcolonial Nations in the Cold War World Order   867
Further Readings   868
Critical Thinking Questions   868

CHAPTER 35   Rebirth and Revolution: Nation-Building in East Asia and the Pacific Rim   869
East Asia in the Postwar Settlements   871
The Pacific Rim: More Japans?   877
Mao's China: Vanguard of World Revolution   882
Colonialism and Revolution in Vietnam   889
Global Connections and Critical Themes: East Asia and the Pacific Rim in the Contemporary World   894
Further Readings   895
Critical Thinking Questions   896

CHAPTER 36   Power, Politics, and Conflict in World History, 1990–2014   897
The End of the Cold War   898
The Spread of Democracy   906
The Great Powers and New Disputes   908
The United States as Sole Superpower   911
Global Connections and Critical Themes: New Global Standards, New Divisions   915
Further Readings   916
Critical Thinking Questions   917

CHAPTER 37   Globalization and Resistance   918
Global Industrialization   919
Globalization: Causes and Processes   922
The Global Environment   929
Resistance and Alternatives   932
Toward the Future   936
Global Connections and Critical Themes: Civilizations and Global Forces   937
Further Readings   937
Critical Thinking Questions   938
Part VI AP® Test Prep   939

Credits   C-1

Index   I-1

Features

MAPS

1.1 The Spread of Human Populations, c. 10,000 B.C.E. 12
1.2 The Spread of Agriculture 14
2.1 Early Sumer 23
2.2 Mesopotamia in Maps 26
2.3 Egypt, Kush, and Axum, Successive Dynasties 28
2.4 India in the Age of Harappa and the Early Aryan Migrations 31
2.5 China in the Shang and Zhou Eras 33
3.1 The Era of Nomadic Incursions and Warring States 57
3.2 China from the Later Zhou Era to the Han Era 60
3.3 Ancient Capitals 69
4.1 India at the Time of Ashoka 79
4.2 The Gupta Empire 80
4.3 The Spread of Buddhism in Asia, 400 B.C.E.–600 C.E. 85
4.4 Eurasian and African Trading Goods and Routes, c. 300 B.C.E. to 300 C.E. 91
5.1 The Persian Empire in Its Main Stages 97
5.2 Greece and Greek Colonies of the World, c. 431 B.C.E. 99
5.3 Alexander's Empire and the Hellenistic World, c. 323 B.C.E. 100
5.4 The Expansion of the Roman Republic, 133 B.C.E. 102
6.1 Trade Routes at the End of the Classical Era 121
6.2 Civilizations of Central and South America 123
6.3 Germanic Kingdoms after the Invasions 131
6.4 The Mediterranean, Middle East, Europe, and North Africa, c. 500 C.E. 132
6.5 Major Religions of the Modern World 136
7.1 Arabia and Surrounding Areas Before and During the Time of Muhammad 159
7.2 The Expansion of Islamic Civilization, 622–750 168
7.3 Emergence of the Abbasid Dynasty 174
8.1 The Abbasid Empire at Its Peak 185
8.2 The Spread of Islam, 10th–16th Centuries 191
8.3 Early Islam in India 194
8.4 The Spread of Islam in Southeast Asia 201
9.1 Empires of the Western Sudan 210
9.2 The Swahili Coast; African Monsoon Routes and Major Trade Routes 216
10.1 The Byzantine Empire under Justinian 228
10.2 The Byzantine Empire, 1000–1100 233
10.3 East European Kingdoms and Slavic Expansion c. 1000 236
11.1 Charlemagne's Empire and Successor States 246
11.2 Western Europe toward the End of the Middle Ages, c. 1360 C.E. 250
11.3 Leading Trade Routes Within Western and Central Europe and to the Mediterranean 257
12.1 Central Mexico and Lake Texcoco 269
12.2 Inca Expansion 276
12.3 The Ancient Cities of Peru 278
13.1 China During the Age of Division 289
13.2 The Sui Dynasty and the Tang Dynasty 290
13.3 China in the Song and Southern Song Dynastic Periods 297
14.1 Key Centers of Civilization in East Asia in the First Millennium C.E. 309
14.2 Japan in the Imperial and Warlord Periods 311
14.3 The Korean Peninsula During the Three Kingdoms Era 320
14.4 South China and Vietnam on the Eve of the Han Conquest 323
15.1 The Transcontinental Empire of Chinggis Khan 332
15.2 The Four Khanates of the Divided Mongol Empire 340
15.3 The Mongol Empire and the Global Exchange Network 342
16.1 Polynesian Expansion 363
17.1 Spain and Portugal: Explorations and Colonies 388
17.2 French, British, and Dutch Holdings, c. 1700 391
18.1 Western Europe During the Renaissance and Reformation 410
18.2 Europe under Absolute Monarchy, 1715 412
18.3 European Population Density, c. 1600 414
19.1 Major Spanish Expeditions of Conquest in and from the Caribbean Region 429

19.2	Colonial Brazil 430		30.2	Eastern Europe and the Soviet Union, 1919–1939 735
19.3	Spanish and Portuguese South America around 1800 448		30.3	China in the Era of Revolution and Civil War 746
20.1	Portuguese Contact and Penetration of Africa 456		30.4	The Expansion of Japan to the Outbreak of World War II 758
21.1	Russian Expansion under the Early Tsars, 1462–1598 481		31.1	World War II in Europe and the Middle East 773
21.2	Russia under Peter the Great 484		31.2	Asia and the Pacific in World War II 777
21.3	Russia's Holdings by 1800 488		31.3	The Partition of Palestine After World War II 788
22.1	The Ottoman, Safavid, and Mughal Empires 496		32.1	Soviet and Eastern European Boundaries by 1948 794
22.2	The Expansion of the Ottoman Empire 497		32.2	Germany After World War II 795
22.3	The Safavid Empire 504		32.3	The European Union 799
22.4	The Growth of the Mughal Empire, from Akbar to Aurangzeb 510		33.1	U.S. Military Interventions, 1898–2000 836
23.1	Routes and Major Products Exchanged in the Asian Trading Network, c. 1500 523		34.1	The Emergence of New Nations in Africa after World War II 847
23.2	The Pattern of Early European Expansion in Asia 527		34.2	The Partition of South Asia: The Formation of India, Pakistan, Bangladesh, and Sri Lanka 848
23.3	Ming China and the Zheng He Expeditions, 1405–1433 534		34.3	The New West African Nations 856
23.4	Japan During the Rise of the Tokugawa Shogunate 539		34.4	The Middle East in the Cold War Era 859
24.1	Napoleon's Empire in 1812 567		35.1	The Pacific Rim Area by 1960 871
24.2	Industrialization in Europe, c. 1850 571		35.2	China in the Years of Japanese Occupation and Civil War, 1931–1949 882
24.3	The Unification of Italy 574		35.3	Vietnam: Divisions in the Nguyen and French Periods 889
24.4	The Unification of Germany, 1815–1871 575		35.4	North and South Vietnam 891
24.5	Early 19th-Century Settlement in the United States, Canada, Australia, and New Zealand 582		36.1	Post–Soviet Union Russia, Eastern Europe, and Central Asia by 1991 904
24.6	The Balkans After the Regional Wars, 1913 584		36.2	The Implosion of Yugoslavia, 1991–2008 909
25.1	European Colonial Territories, Before and After 1800 590		36.3	Main U.S. Overseas Military Installations by 2007 915
25.2	The Stages of Dutch Expansion in Java 591		37.1	Multinational Corporations in 2000 924
25.3	The Growth of the British Empire in India, from the 1750s to 1858 593			
25.4	The Partition of Africa Between c. 1870 and 1914 599			

DOCUMENTS

25.5 The Partition of Southeast Asia and the Pacific to 1914   600

26.1 Independent States of Latin America in 1830   618

27.1 British Egypt and the Anglo-Egyptian Sudan   649

27.2 Ottoman Empire from Late 18th Century to World War I   651

27.3 Qing Empire from Opium War of 1839–1841 to World War I   652

27.4 Coastal China and Its Hinterland in the 19th Century   655

28.1 Russian Expansion, 1815–1914   666

28.2 The Russo-Japanese War   672

28.3 Japanese Colonial Expansion to 1914   680

29.1 World War I Fronts in Europe and the Middle East   704

29.2 Africa During World War I   710

29.3 The Middle East after World War I   720

30.1 From Dominions to Nationhood: Formation of Canada, Australia, and New Zealand   734

Aryan Poetry in Praise of a War Horse   17

Hammurabi's Law Code   26

Teachings of the Rival Chinese Schools   66

A Guardian's Farewell Speech to a Young Woman About to Be Married   83

Rome and a Values Crisis   113

The Popularization of Buddhism   127

The Thousand and One Nights as a Mirror of Elite Society in the Abbasid Era   178

Ibn Khaldun on the Rise and Decline of Empires   188

The Great Oral Tradition and the Epic of Sundiata   212

Russia Turns to Christianity   237

European Travel: A Monk Visits Jerusalem   250

Aztec Women and Men   274

Ties That Bind: Paths to Power   293

Literature as a Mirror of the Exchanges among Asian Centers of Civilization 328

A European Assessment of the Virtues and Vices of the Mongols 337

Bubonic Plague 358

Western Conquerors: Tactics and Motives 398

Controversies About Women 421

A Vision from the Vanquished 433

An African's Description of the Middle Passage 471

The Nature of Westernization 485

An Islamic Traveler Laments the Muslims' Indifference to Europe 503

Exam Questions as a Mirror of Chinese Values 531

Protesting the Industrial Revolution 573

Contrary Images: The Colonizer versus the Colonized on the "Civilizing Mission" 602

Confronting the Hispanic Heritage: From Independence to Consolidation 625

Transforming Imperial China into a Nation 659

Conditions for Factory Workers in Russia's Industrialization 668

Lessons for the Colonized from the Slaughter in the Trenches 715

Socialist Realism 759

Japan's Defeat in a Global War 778

A Cold War Speech 817

The People Speak 830

Cultural Creativity in the Emerging Nations: Some Literary Samples 852

Women in the Revolutionary Struggles for Social Justice 887

Democratic Protest and Repression in China 907

Protests against Globalization 927

VISUALIZING THE PAST

Representations of Women in Early Art 11

Mesopotamia in Maps 25

Capital Designs and Patterns of Political Power 68

The Pattern of Trade in the Ancient Eurasian World 91

Political Rituals in Persia 110

Religious Geography 136

The Mosque as a Symbol of Islamic Civilization 176

The Pattern of Islam's Global Expansions 193

The Architecture of Faith 215

Women and Power in Byzantium 229

Peasant Labor 245

Archeological Evidence of Political Practices 277

Footbinding as a Marker of Male Dominance 303

What Their Portraits Tell Us: Gatekeeper Elites and the Persistence of Civilizations 326

The Mongol Empire as a Bridge Between Civilizations 342

Population Trends 357

West Indian Slaveholding 394

Versailles 417

Race or Culture? A Changing Society 444

The Cloth of Kings in an Atlantic Perspective 473

Oppressed Peasants 490

Art as a Window into the Past: Paintings and History in Mughal India 513

The Great Ships of the Ming Expeditions That Crossed the Indian Ocean 536

The French Revolution in Cartoons 566

Capitalism and Colonialism 605

Images of the Spanish-American War 634

Mapping the Decline of Two Great Empires 651

Two Faces of Western Influence 678

Trench Warfare 708

Guernica and the Images of War 754

National Leaders for a New Global Order 784

Women at Work in France and the United States 806

Murals and Posters: Art and Revolution 827

Globalization and Postcolonial Societies 866

Pacific Rim Growth 880

Symbolism in the Breakdown of the Soviet Bloc 905

Two Faces of Globalization 935

THINKING HISTORICALLY

The Idea of Civilization in World Historical Perspective 18

Women in Patriarchal Societies 29

Xunzi and the Shift from Ritual Combat to "Real" War 62

Inequality as the Social Norm 89

The Classical Mediterranean in Comparative Perspective 104

Nomads and Cross-Civilization Contacts and Exchanges 120

Civilization and Gender Relationships 172

Conversion and Accommodation in the Spread of World Religions 198

Two Transitions in the History of World Population 218

Eastern and Western Europe: The Problem of Boundaries 234

Western Civilization 253

The "Troubling" Civilizations of the Americas 279

Artistic Expression and Social Values 305

Comparing Feudalisms 316

The Global Eclipse of the Nomadic Warrior Culture 347

The Problem of Ethnocentrism 364

Causation and the West's Expansion 390

Elites and Masses 418

An Atlantic History 438

Slavery and Human Society 462

Multinational Empires 482

The Gunpowder Empires and the Shifting Balance of Global Power 506

Means and Motives for Overseas Expansion: Europe and China Compared 537

Two Revolutions: Industrial and Atlantic 580

Western Education and the Rise of an African and Asian Middle Class 595

Explaining Underdevelopment 631

Western Global Dominance and the Dilemmas It Posed for the Peoples and Societies of Africa and Asia 645

The Separate Paths of Japan and China 675

Women in Asian and African Nationalist Movements 723

A Century of Revolutions 741

Total War, Global Devastation 768

The United States and Western Europe: Convergence and Complexity 800

Human Rights in the 20th Century 834

Artificial Nations and the Rising Tide of Communal Strife 854

The Pacific Rim as a U.S. Policy Issue 881

Terrorism, Then and Now 913

How Much Historical Change? 933

Preface

World history explores the human past, around the globe, to help us understand the world we live in today. It seeks to identify how major forces have developed over time, like patterns of migration or world trade. It explores the cultures and political institutions of different regions, to help explain commonalities and differences. World history builds on a growing amount of historical scholarship, some of which has truly altered the picture of the past. It involves a rich array of stories and examples of human variety, intriguing in themselves. It helps develop skills that are vital not just to the history classroom, but to effective operation in a global society—skills like comparing different societies, appreciating various viewpoints, identifying big changes and continuities in the human experience. Always, however, it uses the past as a prologue to the present. World historians argue that no one society, past or present, can be understood without reference to other societies and to larger global forces. They argue, even more vigorously, that the present—which clearly involves relationships that embrace the whole world—cannot be grasped without a sense of the global historical record.

From its first edition, *World Civilizations: The Global Experience* has aimed at capturing a truly global approach by discussing and comparing major societies and focusing on their interactions. The goal is to present a clear factual framework while stimulating analysis about global contacts, regional patterns, and the whole process of change and continuity on a world stage. This kind of world history, focused on the development over time of the forces that shape the world today, helps students make sense of the present and prepare to meet the challenges of the future. It is hard to imagine a more important topic.

Embracing the whole world's history obviously requires selectivity and explicit points of emphasis. This text gains coherence through decisions about time, about place, and about topic. In all three cases, the book encourages analysis, relating facts to vital issues of interpretation. Through analysis and interpretation students become active, engaged learners, rather than serving as passive vessels for torrents of historical facts. Underpinning analysis, the issues of time, place, and topic are the three keys to an intelligible global past.

DECISIONS ABOUT TIME: PERIODIZATION

This text pays a great deal of attention to periodization, or the identification of major points of change in the global experience. This is an essential requirement for coherent presentation—going well beyond the one-thing-after-another type of chronology—and ultimately a precondition of relating the past to the present.

World Civilizations: The Global Experience identifies six periods in world history. Each period is determined by three basic criteria: a geographical rebalancing among major civilizational areas, an increase in the intensity and extent of contact across civilizations (or, in the case of the earliest period, cross-regional contact), and the emergence of new and roughly parallel developments in many major civilizations. The book is divided into six parts corresponding to these six major periods of world history. In each part, basic characteristics of each period are referred to in chapters that discuss the major societies in the Middle East, Africa, Asia, Europe, and the Americas, and in several cross-cutting chapters that address larger world trends. Each period offers a distinctive set of themes, or Big Concepts, that are defined in general terms and then explored in terms of particular regions. Part introductions identify the fundamental new characteristics and new levels of interaction that define each period.

Part I, *Early Human Societies, 2.5 Million–600 B.C.E.: Origins and Development*, sketches the hunting-and-gathering phase of human existence, then focuses on the rise of agriculture and the emergence of civilization in parts of Asia, Africa, Central America, and southeastern Europe—the sequence of developments that set world history in motion from the origin of the human species until about 3000 years ago.

Part II, *The Classical Period, 600 B.C.E.–600 C.E.: Uniting Large Regions*, deals with the growing complexity of major civilizations in several areas of the world. During the classical period, civilizations developed a new capacity to integrate large regions and diverse groups of people through overarching cultural and political systems. Yet many regions and societies remained unconnected to the increasingly complex centers of civilization. Coverage of the classical period of world history, then, must consider both types of societies.

The period covered in Part III, *The Postclassical Period, 600–1450: New Faith and New Commerce*, saw the emergence of new commercial and cultural linkages that brought most civilizations into contact with one another and with nomadic groups. The decline of the great classical empires, the rise of new civilizational centers, and the emergence of a network of world contacts, including the spread of major religions, are characteristics of the postclassical era.

Developments in world history over the three centuries from 1450 to 1750 mark a fourth period in world history, which is covered in Part IV, *The Early Modern Period, 1450–1750: The World Shrinks*. The rise of the West, the intensification of global contacts, the growth of trade, and the formation of new empires define this period and separate it from the preceding postclassical period.

Part V, *The Dawn of the Industrial Age, 1750–1900*, covers the period of world history dominated by the advent of industrialization in western Europe and growing European imperialism. The increase and intensification of commercial interchange, technological innovations, and cultural contacts all reflected the growth of Western power and the spread of Western influence.

The Newest Stage of World History: 1900–Present, the focus of Part VI, defines the characteristics of this period as the retreat of Western imperialism, the rise of new political systems such as communism, the surge of the United States and the Soviet Union, and a variety of economic innovations, including the achievements of Japan, China, Korea, and the Pacific Rim. Part VI deals with this most recent period of world history and some of its portents for the future.

UNDERLYING ISSUES

Two related themes and one standard historical complexity rise above the six-stage world history periodization. The first involves the interaction between tradition and change—and in recent periods, modern change. Many societies established key ideas and institutions early on, at least by the classical period. These traditions would then condition responses to change and modernity. Elements of this interplay become visible from the post-classical period onward; the tradition-change encounter remains vivid in the 21st century, though in forms very different from a thousand years ago. Each world history period involves important shifts in the interaction between change and tradition.

Theme two involves divergence and convergence. Societies emerged separately in many parts of the world, though the process was almost always affected by some wider contacts. This is part of the first phase of the human experience. Separation, or divergence, did not always mean difference, for many societies solved key problems in similar ways; but it did tend to produce separate identities. With growing contacts over time, opportunities and pressures produced various forms of imitation and convergence. The interplay between divergence and convergence is lively in the 21st century, but its shape has changed greatly over time. Here, too, each period involves a different statement of the balance between divergence and convergence.

Periodization emphasizes change, including changes in the basic frameworks in which traditions interacted with new forces and in which separate identities confronted new levels of convergence. Always, however, change must be complicated by recognition of key continuities from the past. At various points in human history, including recently, huge new forces prompt some people to claim that "everything has changed." In fact, strong traces of the past always linger. The challenge is to figure out how the balance works.

PLACE: REGIONS AND CIVILIZATIONS

Usable world history requires decisions about coherence in place as well as time. Even in the present day, and certainly in the past, key developments did not occur evenly across the whole globe: regional conditions always come into play. At the same time, not every definable society can be encompassed—early hunting-and-gathering bands of humans, after all, could number no more than sixty people. No world history survey can even approach that level of detail. World history seeks legitimate ways to define larger regions and societies that serve as the basis for meaningful contacts and reactions to global forces.

Major regions of the world depend on a combination of geography and historical developments in the form of shared institutions and beliefs. This book uses several regions as frameworks for discussing patterns of activity and larger interactions: east Asia; south and southeast Asia; the Middle East, ultimately with the addition of north Africa; sub-Saharan Africa; Europe, often with some division between eastern and western; and the Americas. Australia and key island groups, and also patterns in central Asia, must be added in as well.

In several regions, beginning in key cases several thousand years ago, major civilizations helped organize and define regional characteristics. East Asia, to take one example, would be profoundly shaped by emerging features of Chinese civilization. Civilizations used economic surpluses, beyond basic survival needs, to generate relatively elaborate political institutions, cities, and trading networks. They also emphasized particular kinds of institutional arrangements and value systems that would provide a recognizable identity, differentiating their civilization from other societies. Using, but also debating, the concept of civilization helps organize the geographical foundation of world history by introducing not only key regions but regional characteristics and identities. Civilizations provide the basis for key comparisons, with each other and in terms of regional reactions to larger forces for change. The internal developments in major civilizations, along with mutual interaction and responses to broader factors like migration or missionary religions, form much of the stuff of world history for the past 5000 years. At the same time, other types of societies, including nomadic groups, played a vital role throughout world history, particularly as they long dominated strategically vital regions like central Asia. Most of these other societies were smaller than civilizations, in terms of population, but they played crucial functions in world history and developed successful cultural and institutional forms.

Attention to the major regions of the world does more than set the stage for comparative analysis in each of the chronological periods in world history. It also promotes a sense of geographic balance that is vital to the field. Many earlier historical efforts understandably focused on developments in one's own society, assuming that the rest of the world was unimportant or somehow revolved around what was happening nearer home. Until recently, many Americans were urged to pay primary attention to the history of western Europe and the expansion of Western civilization across the Atlantic. These remain valid themes, but in the world history context they become only a part of a larger and more complicated civilizational pattern. The transition from Western to world history is still under discussion, but the global context gains ground steadily because it more accurately mirrors the world around us today. This book, paying attention to Western developments as part of the larger world story, and showing their interaction with other societies and other influences, strives to distribute appropriate attention to all the major regions and to their changing roles in the larger global story.

TOPICS AND THEMES

A final way to focus world history, intersecting with decisions about time and place, involves the kinds of human and social activities that are highlighted. The first theme follows obviously from the uses of periodization and the need to deal coherently with world history over time: *World Civilizations: The Global Experience* deals consistently with change and continuity and with the causes of basic changes in global dynamics from one period to the next.

Interactions among the major regions and societies, the second theme, focus attention on the ways individual regions and civilizations were shaped by contacts with other areas. Contacts include trade, of course, but also war, diplomacy, and international organizations from religious entities to the multinational companies and global agencies of more modern times.

A cluster of factors deal with economic activities and population patterns as they affect people, societies, and the environment. Technology has a key role here, but also population structures and disease, labor systems, migrations, plus manufacturing and agriculture. Each civilization must be discussed with these patterns in mind, as well as the broader diffusion of trade, technologies, and population exchange as they formed core parts of the larger patterns of interaction.

Each society featured characteristic social and gender structures that organized and tried to justify various systems of inequality. Dealing with how social systems changed over time and comparing them from one region to the next are core features of world history; social systems could also be affected by changing patterns of contact.

The fifth thematic area clusters around culture—belief systems, values, and artistic styles—as these emerged in religions, intellectual systems, and science. Here too, change over time and the results of interactions among societies form key elements in the cultural dynamics of world history.

Finally, politics demands emphasis: the functions and structures of states, as they formed and changed, along with ideas about politics and political identity (political culture). In modern centuries, this topic embraces the emergence of nation states and also their limitations in global context.

The topical themes of this book help organize discussions of change over time but also the possibility of developing comparisons from one society to the next. Interactions among the themes—how new trading patterns affected, and were affected by, cultural systems, for example—help structure more challenging analytical efforts.

What Is New to This Edition?

The seventh edition of *World Civilizations: The Global Experience* has been revised to reflect the latest developments in historical research and benefits from the addition of a host of new features to assist student learning. The most significant pedagogical innovation has been the seamless integration of documents, maps, videos, illustrations, and other resources from MyHistoryLab into the textbook. A new pedagogically driven design highlights a clear learning path through the material and offers a visually stunning learning experience in print or on a screen. With the Pearson eText, featuring a new streamlined design for tablet devices, students can transition directly to MyHistoryLab resources such as primary source documents, videos, and maps.

Learning Objective questions have been added to each chapter to highlight central themes and ideas. Each question is linked to one of the chapter's main sections. Critical Thinking Questions were added at the end of each chapter to reinforce important concepts covered in the chapter and to serve as possible essay or class discussion topics. Further Readings were updated in most chapters, bringing the scholarship for the new edition up-to-date. In many chapters, the authors reference cultural regions that were underrepresented in earlier editions of the book—particularly the Middle East and Oceania.

Specific changes in the content of this edition are as follows:

- Coverage of early civilizations has been greatly expanded in the form of a new chapter, Chapter 2, devoted solely to coverage of this important topic. Chapter 1 now focuses primarily on prehistory.
- Chapter 5 includes expanded treatment of Persia. Coverage of Rome's development has also been expanded.
- Chapter 6 now includes an explanation of the Mayan system of assigning dates to events. The section on the Spread of World Religions has been expanded.
- Chapter 8, the discussion of Sufis and their roles in science and philosophy has been expanded.
- Chapter 10 includes increased coverage of the Byzantine Empire. Also, there are new sections titled Cities in World History: Kiev and Global Connections and Critical Themes: Eastern Europe and the World.
- Chapter 12 features a stronger, more effective comparison of Aztecs and Incas.
- Chapter 14 includes new coverage of the importance of women in Vietnamese resistance movements and in society in general.
- In Chapter 15, the Further Readings have been expanded.
- Chapter 16 includes expanded coverage of the fifteenth century as a transition. There is a new section called The Structure of Transregional Trade. Coverage of critical themes of the Italian Renaissance has been revised. And there is new coverage of the impact of the Mongol era.
- In Chapter 18, there is expanded coverage of changes during the early modern period and an explanation of cultural changes during the 18th century.
- Chapter 19 now has added material on the Columbian exchange and the early Caribbean.
- Chapter 20 features expanded sections on slaves and sugar plantations. There is new coverage of Africans in the Americas and African actions in the era of emancipation. Data on the African slave trade has been updated.
- Chapter 21, formerly Chapter 23 in the sixth edition, has been relocated to facilitate comparison with other gunpowder empires. Also, there is expanded coverage of Russian societal changes.
- In Chapter 22, the new edition includes a greater emphasis on flourishing cities and there are further efforts to avoid the outdated Ottoman decline refrain.

- Chapter 23 has an expanded section on the Jesuits' influence with the Qing emperors and their eventual failure to convert. There is a new section on the Tokugawa system of controlling allied and vassal daimyos.
- Chapter 24 expands the definition of the Industrial Revolution and includes a discussion on the Second Industrial Revolution.
- Chapter 25 now contains more information on technology and militaries and emphasizes the role of soldiers that Europeans recruited in colonies from Vietnam to India.
- In Chapter 27, several section titles were changed to clarify or bring them into accord with recent scholarship.
- In Chapter 29, the introduction to the Document has been revised with additional information.
- Chapter 30 includes expanded information on Stalin.
- Chapter 31 features further clarification on World War II and the Cold War as well as expanded coverage of key points throughout the chapter.
- Chapter 33 has expanded coverage of leadership in Cuba and Brazil. There is also expanded coverage of female leadership in Latin America. The population table has been updated and there are updates on the political situation in Cuba, Mexico, and Brazil. Finally, there is a closer examination of Latin America's leftward swing.
- In Chapter 34, coverage of environmental factors and the impact of massive population increase and migration to urban centers has been expanded.
- Chapter 35 has a new short section on U.S. efforts to promote Japanese reconstruction in the era of the Korean and Vietnam wars as well as enhanced coverage of U.S./China relations through the present. There is expanded information on China's environment and population and the regime-made famine linked to the Great Leap Forward.
- In Chapter 36, the world events timeline has been updated and there is new coverage of the Arab Spring.
- Chapter 37 features new and expanded sections on Globalization and Global Industrialization. There are new sections on the Global Environment and Global Disease and there is new information on global environmental issues.

FEATURES

The features in *World Civilizations: The Global Experience* have been carefully constructed and honed over the course of seven editions. Our aim has been to provide students with tools to help them learn how to analyze change and continuity.

Part Introductions

Part introductions, reviewed for this edition, discuss the conditions that set the stage for the developments that define each new period in world history. They identify the characteristics of the period of world history covered in the part, and recap the continuities that exist from one period to the next. Two world maps at the beginning of each part introduction provide a graphic reference for the major changes of the period. Part timelines list the major events of the chronological period covered.

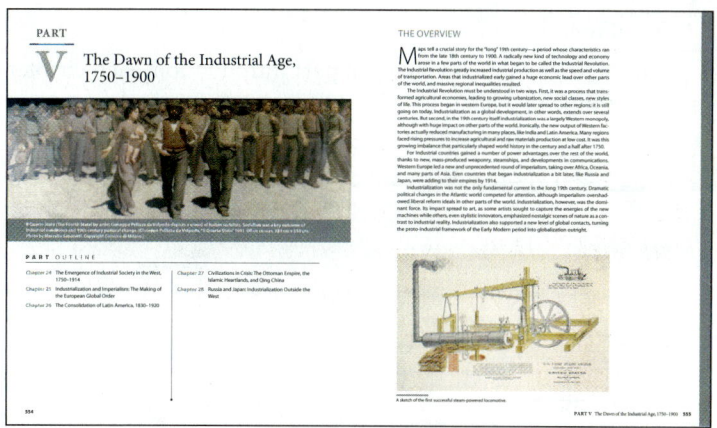

End-of-Part Analysis

Following the final chapter in each part is an essay that revisits the dominant cross-civilizational (or cross-regional) contacts and divisions that occurred during the era under examination. These sections encourage analysis of the dominant contact patterns in the period as well as the relationship to them of major individual societies.

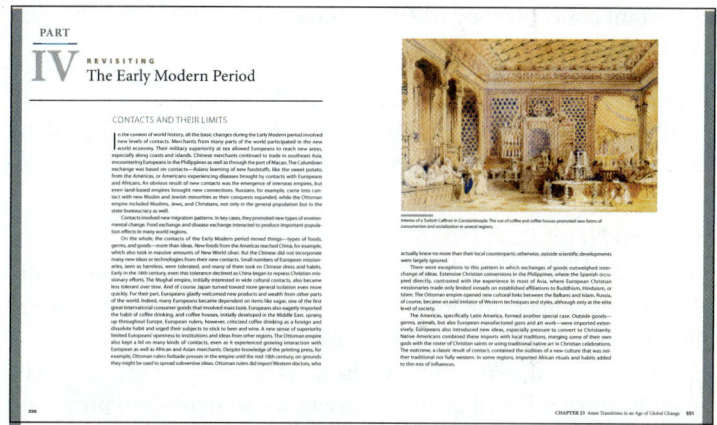

Chapter Introductions

Each chapter introduction tells a compelling story about a particular pattern, individual, or incident to spark students' interest and introduce chapter material in an engaging and dramatic way. The opening story concludes with an explanation of how the story relates to the chapter content and the key themes and analytical issues that will be examined in the chapter.

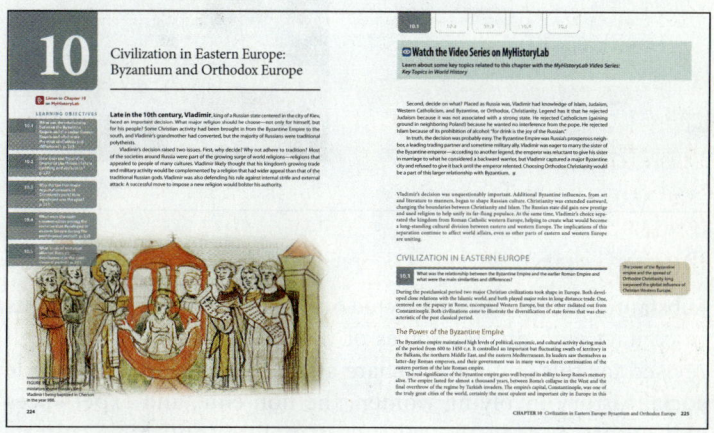

Preface **xvii**

Timelines

In addition to the timeline in each part introduction, each chapter includes a timeline that orients the student to the period, countries, and key events of the chapter.

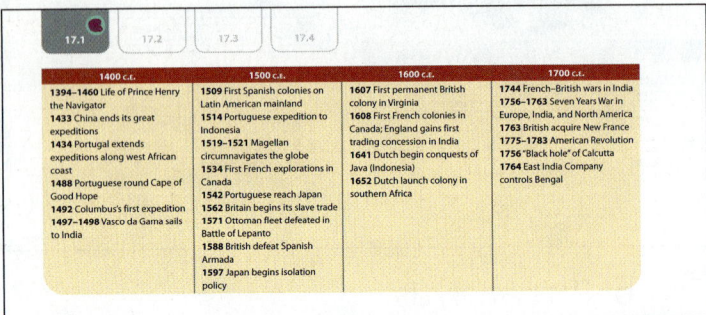

Learning Objectives

Each of the main chapter headings is followed by a Learning Objective for the section that follows. These Learning Objectives also appear on the first page of the chapter, giving students an idea of important concepts they will encounter when reading the chapter.

Section-Opening Focal Points

Focal points listed next to each of the main chapter headings identify for the student the principal points to be explored in the section.

Visualizing the Past

The Visualizing the Past feature of each chapter supports visual literacy by showing students how to read and analyze visual material such as maps, charts, graphs, tables, or photos to interpret historical patterns. Text accompanying the illustrations provides a level of analysis, and a series of questions draws the students into providing their own analyses.

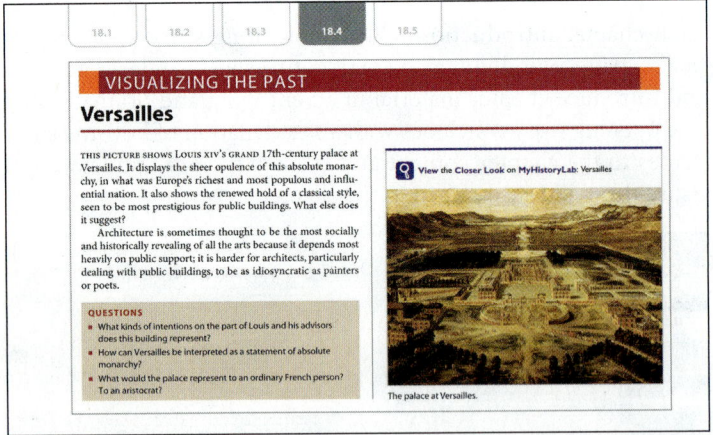

Documents

Substantial excerpts from selected original documents put students in contact with diverse voices of the past, and many have been revised for this edition. We share a firm commitment to include social history involving women, the non-elite, and experiences and events outside the spheres of politics and high culture.

Each document is preceded by a brief scene-setting narration and followed by probing questions to guide the reader through an understanding of the document and to encourage interpretive reflections and analysis.

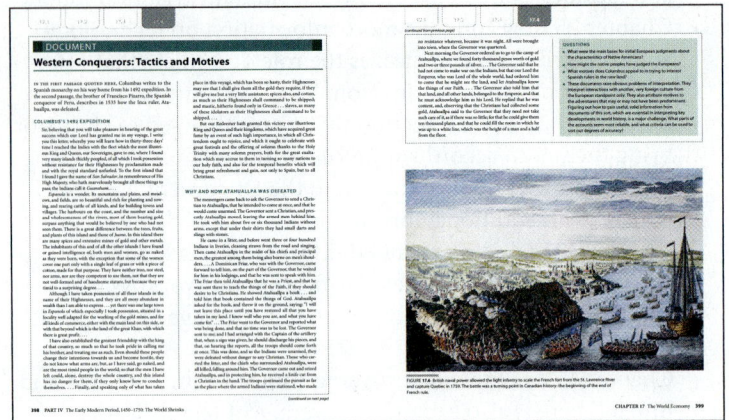

Thinking Historically

Each chapter contains an analytical essay on a topic of broad application related to the chapter's focus but extending across chronological and geographical boundaries. Critical thinking questions at the end of each essay prompt the reader to think beyond the "who, what, where, and when" of historical events and consider instead the far-reaching implications of historical developments.

Global Connections

Each chapter ends with a Global Connections section that reinforces the key themes and issues raised in the chapter and makes clear their importance not only to the areas of civilization discussed in the chapter but also to the world as a whole.

Critical Thinking Questions

Critical Thinking Questions can be found at the end of each chapter as well as at the end of each part. These questions reinforce important topics and themes explored in the text and also serve as possible essay or class discussion topics.

Further Readings

Each chapter includes several annotated paragraphs of suggested readings, substantially updated for this edition. Students receive reliable guidance on a variety of books: source materials, standards in the field, encyclopedia coverage, more readable general interest titles, and the like.

AP® Test Prep

Practice tests have been added to the end of each part to help students review content in preparation for the AP® World History exam.

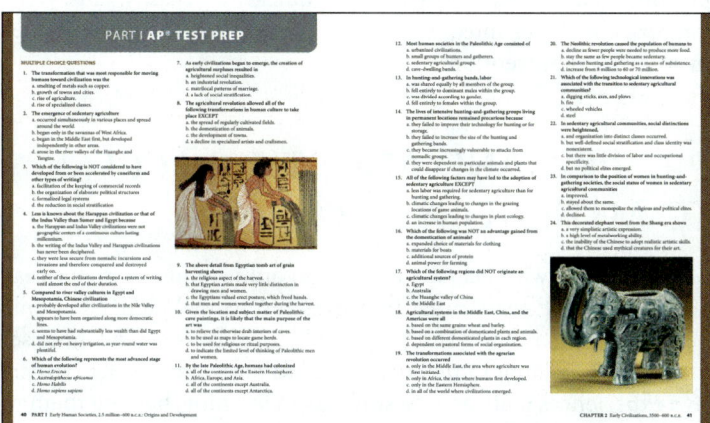

MyHistoryLab Icons

Throughout each chapter are MyHistoryLab icons paired with images, maps, and portions of the narrative that lead students to additional resources—documents, images, maps, videos, and more—found on MyHistoryLab, giving students a deeper understanding of the topics covered in the text and leading to a more thorough integration between the book and online resources.

Peter N. Stearns
Michael Adas
Stuart B. Schwartz
Marc Jason Gilbert

Supplementary Teaching and Learning Materials

MYHISTORYLAB™

A fully integrated learning program, MyHistoryLab for *World Civilizations: The Global Experience*, Seventh Edition, helps students better prepare for class, quizzes, and exams—resulting in more dynamic experiences in the classroom and improved performance in class. And, the immersive Pearson eText—with videos and interactive activities just a click away—truly engages students in their study of history, and fosters learning within and beyond the classroom.

Features of MyHistoryLab include:

Pearson eText with Audio

Contained within MyHistoryLab, the Pearson eText enables students to access their textbook online—through laptops, iPads, and tablets. Download the free Pearson eText app to use on tablets. Students may also listen to their text with the Audio eText.

New MyHistoryLibrary

The new Pearson MyHistoryLibrary contains some of the most commonly assigned primary source documents, delivered through Pearson's powerful eText platform. Each reading may also be listened to in the Audio eText companion.

MyHistoryLab Video Series: Key Topics in World History

This comprehensive video series helps students get up-to-speed on key topics. Correlated to the chapters of *World Civilizations*, each video focuses on a key topic discussed in each chapter, readying students to get the most from the text narrative. The videos feature seasoned historians reviewing the pivotal stories of our past, in a lively format designed to engage and inform.

Writing Space

Better writers make great learners—who perform better in their classes. To help you develop and assess concept mastery and critical thinking through writing, we created the Writing Space in MyHistoryLab. It's a single place to create, track, and grade writing assignments, provide writing resources, and exchange meaningful, personalized feedback with students, quickly and easily. Plus, Writing Space includes integrated access to Turnitin, the global leader in plagiarism prevention.

PREVIEW AND ADOPTION ACCESS TO MYHISTORYLAB™

MyHistoryLab with Pearson eText is an online homework, tutorial, and assessment system that improves results by helping students better master concepts and by providing educators a dynamic set of tools for gauging individual and class performance. Its immersive experiences truly engage students in learning, helping them to understand course material and improve their performance. And MyHistoryLab comes from Pearson—your partner in providing the best digital learning experiences.

Upon textbook purchase, students and teachers are granted access to MyHistoryLab with Pearson eText. High school teachers can obtain preview or adoption access for MyHistoryLab in one of the following ways:

Preview Access

- Teachers can request preview access by visiting **PearsonSchool.com/access_request**. Select Initial Access, then using Option **2**, select your discipline and title from the drop-down menu and complete the online form. *Preview Access* information will be sent to the teacher via e-mail.

Adoption Access

- With the purchase of a textbook program that offers a media resource, a *Pearson Adoption Access Card*, with student and teacher's codes and a complete Instructor's Manual, will be delivered with your textbook purchase. (ISBN: 0-13-353986-5)
- Ask your sales representative for an *Adoption Access Code Card/Instructor Manual package* (ISBN: 0-13-353986-5)

OR

- Visit **PearsonSchool.com/access_request**. Select Initial Access, then using Option **3**, select your discipline and title from the drop-down menu and complete the online form. Access information will be sent to the teacher via e-mail.

Students, ask your teacher for access.

FOR THE TEACHER

Most of the teacher supplements and resources for this text are also available electronically to qualified adopters on the Instructor Resource Center (IRC). Upon adoption or to preview, please go to **www.pearsonschool.com/access_request** and select Instructor Resource Center. You will be required to complete a brief one-time registration subject to verification of educator status. Upon verification, access information and instructions will be sent to you via e-mail. Once logged into the IRC, enter ISBN 0-13-344770-7 in the "Search our Catalog" box to locate resources.

Teacher's Resource Manual

Available at the Instructor's Resource Center (IRC), the Teacher's Resource Manual for *World Civilizations*, Seventh Edition, contains learning objectives from the text, chapter outlines, chapter summaries that cover each section in the text, key terms from the text, lecture suggestions, and class discussion questions. A full correlation of the text to the Course Outline for World History for AP® provides teachers with a helpful tool for lesson and class planning for their course. The Teacher's Resource Manual also contains Teaching Notes for class planning, with suggestions for integrating MyHistoryLab into the class.

PowerPoint Presentations

Available at the Instructor's Resource Center. Strong PowerPoint presentations make lectures more engaging for students. Correlated to the chapters of your Pearson textbook, each presentation includes a lecture outline and a wealth of images and maps from the textbook.

Test Item File

Available at the Instructor's Resource Center, the Test Item File contains a diverse set of over 2,000 multiple choice and essay questions, supporting a variety of assessment strategies. The large pool of multiple-choice questions for each chapter includes factual, conceptual, and analytical questions, so that teachers may assess students on basic information as well as critical thinking.

Test Generator

Available at the Instructor's Resource Center, this easy-to-use test generation software program provides the wealth of multiple-choice and essay questions from the test item file and allows users to add, delete, and print tests.

Instructor's Resource DVD-ROM

This DVD contains files of the Teacher's Resource Manual, Test Item File, TestGen Test Item File, PowerPoint® slides, and transparency masters that are available with the text.

Transparency Masters

Available at the Instructor's Resource Center. This set of full-color digital transparencies reproduces maps from the text.

FOR THE STUDENT

The following supplements are available for purchase.

Pearson Test Prep Series: World History

Created specifically for *World Civilizations: The Global Experience*, this student guide contains an overview of the AP® program and the World History exam for AP®. It also provides test-taking strategies, correlations between key test topics and the textbook, practice study questions, guidelines for mastering multiple-choice and free-response questions, DBQs, and two practice tests.

Reading and Note Taking Study Guide

This supplement provides a chapter-by-chapter guide to help students read their textbook effectively, using various reading and study skills and strategies for an organized approach to reading and studying.

Visual Sources in World History

This workbook provides 200 visual resources with head notes and critical thinking questions to engage students in analyzing visual documents.

Prentice Hall Atlas of World History, 2/E

Produced in collaboration with Dorling Kindersley, the leader in cartographic publishing, the updated second edition of *The Prentice Hall Atlas of World History* applies the most innovative cartographic techniques to present world history in all of its complexity and diversity.

Documents in World History

Volume I, Sixth Edition (The Great Traditions: From Ancient Times to 1500) and Volume II (The Modern Centuries: From 1500 to the Present), both edited by Peter N. Stearns, Stephen S. Gosch, Erwin P. Grieshaber, and Allison Scardino Belzer, is a collection of primary source documents that illustrate the human characteristics of key civilizations during major stages of world history.

About the Authors

PETER N. STEARNS

Peter N. Stearns is provost, executive vice president, and university professor of history at George Mason University. He received his Ph.D. from Harvard University. He has taught at Rutgers University, the University of Chicago, and Carnegie Mellon, where he won the Robert Doherty Educational Leadership Award and the Elliott Dunlap Smith Teaching Award. He has taught world history for more than 25 years. He also founded and is the editor of the *Journal of Social History*. In addition to textbooks and readers, he has written studies of gender and consumerism in a world history context. Other books address modern social and cultural history and include studies on gender, old age, work, dieting, and emotion. His most recent book in this area is *Satisfaction Not Guaranteed: Dilemmas of Progress in Modern Society*.

STUART B. SCHWARTZ

Stuart B. Schwartz was born and educated in Springfield, Massachusetts, and then attended Middlebury College and the Universidad Autonoma de Mexico. He has an M.A. and Ph.D. from Columbia University in Latin American history. He taught for many years at the University of Minnesota and joined the faculty at Yale University in 1996. He has also taught in Brazil, Puerto Rico, Spain, France, and Portugal. He is a specialist on the history of colonial Latin America, especially Brazil, and is the author of numerous books, notably *Sugar Plantations in the Formation of Brazilian Society* (1985), which won the Bolton Prize for the best book in Latin American History. He is also the author of *Slaves, Peasants, and Rebels* (1992), *Early Latin America* (1983), and *Victors and Vanquished* (1999). He has held fellowships from the Guggenheim Foundation and the Institute for Advanced Study (Princeton). For his work on Brazil he was decorated by the Brazilian government. His book *All Can Be Saved* (2008) won the Bolton Prize as well as three awards from the American Historical Association.

MICHAEL ADAS

Michael Adas is the Abraham Voorhees Professor of History and a Board of Governor's chair at Rutgers University, New Brunswick. Over the past couple of decades his teaching has focused on courses dealing with European and American colonial expansion and African and Asian responses as well as global history in the 20th century. In addition to texts on world history, Adas has written numerous books and articles on the impact of and resistance to Western colonialism and the importance of technology in those processes. His books include *Machines as the Measure of Men: Science, Technology, and Ideologies of Western Dominance*, which won the Dexter Prize in 1992, and more recently *Dominance by Design: Technological Imperatives and America's Civilizing Mission*. In 2012, he was awarded the Toynbee Prize for his lifetime contributions global history and cross-cultural understanding. He is currently working on a comparative study of the ways in which British and American soldiers' responses to the wars of attrition in the trenches of World War I and in Vietnam contributed to the decline of each of these global powers.

MARC JASON GILBERT

Marc Jason Gilbert is the holder of the National Endowment for the Humanities Endowed Chair in World History at Hawai'i Pacific University in Honolulu, Hawaii. After receiving his Ph.D from UCLA, he was for many years co-Director of Programs in South and Southeast Asia for the University System of Georgia and was recognized by that System as a Board of Regent's Distinguished Professor of Teaching and Learning. He has benefited from various fellowships which have enabled him to study in Afghanistan, Burma, Cameroon, India, Tanzania, and Yemen. He has directed world history academic conferences and workshops for teachers in Cambodia and Vietnam. He is also a past President of the World History Association and the current editor of a WHA affiliated journal, *World History Connected*. His publications explore the histories of India, Vietnam, and global cultural exchange. His most recent work is *Cross-Cultural Encounters in Modern World History* (2012), with Jon Thares Davidann.

Teacher to Teacher

The AP® World History survey encourages students to grasp concepts and patterns across a huge breadth of time and space. *World Civilizations: The Global Experience, AP® Edition* provides students with a text that helps to facilitate these global understandings and connections in the classroom. Of particular note is the emphasis on social history, allowing for greater insight and analysis into an underrepresented part of the course. The conscious attention to a broad spectrum of world history beyond political and military events is essential to the teaching of world history in the 21st century. Since, as the authors note, the book is based on "comparative work and focuses on global processes," students are able to see the history of the world as one based on multiple disciplines. The book is not regionally compartmentalized but requires an understanding of interaction and comparison through time.

Throughout the book, students are encouraged to think analytically and comparatively through the inclusion of primary sources, as well as additional special features. The Visualizing the Past sections bring out suggestions for analysis of visual images and make connections between chapters and places. The Global Connections sections allow for a broadening of context that might otherwise be lost in the detail of the chapter. This is essential for student understanding of global historical context. These sections are most effective when they are specific, mentioning specific movements of people, ideas, or goods between specific places.

No matter how good a textbook is, the AP® course description, not the textbook layout, should drive the pace of the course. This textbook allows a teacher to make the decisions about pacing and selection. The three major strengths of this text are its attention to issues of social history, including class and social structure, the modeling of good analysis, and MyHistoryLab: a fully integrated learning program with many resources and student activities. Students experience success with this text not only as they become familiar with the new scholarship and language that are part of a dynamic research field, but also as they see modeled the analytical and comparative skills necessary to apply this new knowledge.

DEBORAH SMITH JOHNSTON
Lexington High School, Lexington, Mass.

Correlation of *World Civilizations* to the AP® Course Outline for World History

The following chart is an excellent resource in preparation for topics that will be a part of the AP® World History examination. The entries in the center column show one way to break down the material into historical eras and overarching themes studied in AP® World History courses. The right column includes a detailed breakdown of chapters and page references in your *World Civilizations: The Global Experience*, AP® Edition textbook where you can learn more about those historical topics.

KEY CONCEPTS WITH CONTENT OUTLINES		PAGE REFERENCES
Period 1	Technological and Environmental Transformations, to c. 600 B.C.E.	Chapters 1–2
Key Concept 1.1	Big Geography and the Peopling of the Earth	2–19
	I. Archeological evidence indicates that during the Paleolithic era, hunting foraging bands of humans gradually migrated from their origin in East Africa to Eurasia, Australia and the Americas, adapting their technology and cultures to new climate regions.	2–12
Key Concept 1.2	The Neolithic Revolution and Early Agricultural Societies	2–6; 12–18
	I. Beginning about 10,000 years ago, the Neolithic Revolution led to the development of new and more complex economic and social systems.	12–14
	II. Agriculture and pastoralism began to transform human societies.	2–6; 12–18; 23–25
Key Concept 1.3	The Development and Interactions of Early Agricultural, Pastoral and Urban Societies	12–18; 22–36
	I. Core and foundational civilizations developed in a variety of geographical and environmental settings where agriculture flourished.	12–18; 22–36
	II. The first states emerged within core civilizations.	23–36
	III. Culture played a significant role in unifying states through laws, language, literature, religion, myths and monumental art.	23–36
Period 2	Organization and Reorganization of Human Societies, c. 600 B.C.E. to c. 600 C.E.	Chapters 3–6
Key Concept 2.1	The Development and Codification of Religious and Cultural Traditions	37; 48–55; 57–71; 74–90; 107–114; 133–137; 209–210
	I. Codifications and further developments of existing religious traditions provided a bond among the people and an ethical code to live by.	37; 74–78; 82–88
	II. New belief systems and cultural traditions emerged and spread, often asserting universal truths.	54–56; 59–60; 64–71; 74–90; 107–110; 133–137
	III. Belief systems affected gender roles. Buddhism and Christianity encouraged monastic life and Confucianism emphasized filial piety.	68–71

	IV. Other religious and cultural traditions continued parallel to the codified, written belief systems in core civilizations.	57; 63–64
	V. Artistic expressions, including literature and drama, architecture, and sculpture, show distinctive cultural developments.	74–75; 77–78; 82–84; 86–87; 107–114
Key Concept 2.2	**The Development of States and Empires**	54–71; 74–92; 94–95; 97–106; 111–114; 125–133
	I. The number and size of *key states and empires* grew dramatically by imposing political unity on areas where previously there had been competing states.	54–71; 74–92; 94–95; 97–106; 132–133
	II. Empires and states developed new techniques of imperial administration based, in part, on the success of earlier political forms.	56–63; 78–79; 94–95; 97–106; 125–133
	III. Unique social and economic dimensions developed in imperial societies in Afro-Eurasia and the Americas.	54–71; 74–92; 97–106; 111–114
	IV. The Roman, Han, Maurya and Gupta empires created political, cultural and administrative difficulties that they could not manage, which eventually led to their decline, collapse and transformation into successor empires or states.	54–71; 74–92; 99–106; 125–133
Key Concept 2.3	**Emergence of Transregional Networks of Communication and Exchange**	69–71; 77; 78–79; 84–87; 91; 97–99; 103; 111–114; 117–118; 118–122; 133–137; 145–147; 209–210
	I. Land and water routes created transregional trade, communication and exchange networks in the Eastern Hemisphere.	69–71; 87; 91; 111–114; 117–118; 118–122; 209–210
	II. New technologies facilitated long-distance communication and exchange.	69; 77; 87; 111–114; 118–122
	III. Alongside the trade in goods, the exchange of people, technology, religious and cultural beliefs, food crops, domesticated animals, and disease pathogens developed across far-flung networks of communication and exchange.	71; 78–79; 84–87; 91; 97–99; 103; 111–114; 117–118; 118–122; 133–137; 145–147
Period 3	**Regional and Transregional Interactions, c. 600 c.e. to c. 1450**	**Chapters 7–16**
Key Concept 3.1	**Expansion and Intensification of Communication and Exchange Networks**	86–87; 120–121; 125; 133; 145–155; 156–158; 161; 174–201; 201; 204–223; 235–239; 257–261; 265–269; 293–295; 298–300; 308–329; 331–349; 358–359; 361–364; 409–410; 505–507; 521–522
	I. Improved transportation technologies and commercial practices led to an increased volume of trade, and expanded the geographical range of existing and newly active trade networks.	145–155; 161; 174–201; 201; 209–216; 235–239; 257–261; 265–269; 298–300; 308–329; 331–349; 258–359; 361–362; 521–522

	II. The movement of peoples caused environmental and linguistic effects.		125; 156–158; 182–192; 215–217; 201–221; 235; 257–261; 298–300; 333–336; 361–364
	III. Cross-cultural exchanges were fostered by the intensification of existing, or the creation of new, networks of trade and communication.		86–87; 120–121; 133; 145–155; 174–201; 188–201; 204–223; 265–269; 293–295; 298–300; 308–329; 337–338; 342–346; 409–410; 505–507
	IV. There was continued diffusion of crops and pathogens throughout the Eastern Hemisphere along the trade routes.		121; 260–261; 338; 358
Key Concept 3.2	**Continuity and Innovation of State Forms and Their Interactions**		122: 128–129; 156–162; 166–202; 205–207; 218–220; 225–233; 239–243; 276–282; 287–306; 308–329; 331–349
	I. Empires collapsed and were reconstituted; in some regions new state forms emerged.		122: 128–129; 156–162; 166–202; 205–207; 218–220; 225–233; 239–243; 276–282; 287–306; 308–329; 331–349
	II. Interregional contacts and conflicts between states and empires encouraged significant technological and cultural transfers.		187–202; 252–253; 337–339; 343–349
Key Concept 3.3	**Increased Economic Productive Capacity and Its Consequences**		170–179; 186; 209; 217–218; 238–245; 257–261; 272–279; 281; 284; 287–290; 299-3–3; 309–317; 325–327; 331–347; 354; 356–363
	I. Innovations stimulated agricultural and industrial production in many regions.		175–179; 209; 217–218; 238–239; 272–273; 281; 284; 299–303; 358–359
	II. The fate of cities varied greatly, with periods of significant decline, and with periods of increased urbanization buoyed by rising productivity and expanding trade networks.		174–175; 238–239; 243–244; 257–261; 287–290; 289–290; 331–347; 356–361
	III. Despite significant continuities in social structures and in methods of production, there were also some important changes in labor management and in the effect of religious conversion on gender relations and family life.		170–173; 186; 238–245; 257–261; 272–279; 309–317; 325–327; 342–347; 354; 356; 362–363

Period 4	Global Interactions, c. 1450 to c. 1750	Chapters 17–23
Key Concept 4.1	**Globalizing Networks of Communication and Exchange**	133; 204–222; 355–356; 359–364; 377–403; 405–417; 420–422; 439–442; 453–455; 465–466; 469–475; 493–517; 533–538
	I. In the context of the new global circulation of goods, there was an intensification of all existing regional trade networks that brought prosperity and economic disruption to the merchants and governments in the trading regions of the Indian Ocean, Mediterranean, Sahara and overland Eurasia.	377–403
	II. European technological developments in cartography and navigation built on previous knowledge developed in the classical, Islamic and Asian worlds, and included the production of new tools, innovations in ship designs, and an improved understanding of global wind and currents patterns—all of which made transoceanic travel and trade possible.	361–362; 383–389
	III. Remarkable new transoceanic maritime reconnaissance occurred in this period.	355–356; 361–364; 385–389; 534–538
	IV. The new global circulation of goods was facilitated by royal chartered European monopoly companies that took silver from Spanish colonies in the Americas to purchase Asian goods for the Atlantic markets, but regional markets continued to flourish in Afro-Eurasia by using established commercial practices and new transoceanic shipping services developed by European merchants.	389–400
	V. The new connections between the Eastern and Western hemispheres resulted in the Columbian Exchange.	391–392; 533–534
	VI. The increase in interactions between newly connected hemispheres and intensification of connections within hemispheres expanded the spread and reform of existing religions and created syncretic belief systems and practices.	133; 204–222; 408–415; 439–422; 453–455; 465–466; 469–475; 493–517
	VII. As merchants' profits increased and governments collected more taxes, funding for the visual and performing arts, even for popular audiences, increased.	210–212; 359–361; 405–408; 512–514; 534
Key Concept 4.2	**New Forms of Social Organization and Modes of Production**	381–382; 392; 398; 411–412; 417–423; 428–429; 432–438; 427–450; 453–475; 497–498; 501–503; 505–512; 516–517; 529–534; 535–542; 650–658
	I. Traditional peasant agriculture increased and changed, plantations expanded, and demand for labor increased. These changes both fed and responded to growing global demand for raw materials and finished products.	381–382; 392; 411–412; 422–423; 428–429; 436–438; 427–437; 441–443; 453–466; 470–475; 533–534

	II. As new social and political elites changed, they also restructured new ethnic, racial and gender hierarchies.	398; 413–422; 432–436; 434–450; 458–472; 497–498; 501–503; 505–512; 516–517; 529–533; 535–542; 650–658
Key Concept 4.3	**State Consolidation and Imperial Expansion**	119–120; 268–270; 281; 313–319; 394–400; 410; 417–420; 426–439; 425–451; 455–460; 464–469; 493–517; 520–542; 564–568; 650–659
	I. Rulers used a variety of methods to legitimize and consolidate their power.	119–120; 268–270; 281; 313–319; 394–400; 417–420; 426–439; 427–444; 447–451; 455–457; 464–469; 493–517; 524–533; 538–540
	II. Imperial expansion relied on the increased use of gunpowder, cannons and armed trade to establish large empires in both hemispheres.	394–400; 410; 412–413; 417–420; 426–439; 425–451; 455–460; 493–517; 520–542; 564–568; 650–659
	III. Competition over trade routes, state rivalries, and local resistance all provided significant challenges to state consolidation and expansion.	400; 410; 412–413; 417–420; 446–447; 455–463; 483–485; 564–568
Period 5	Industrialization and Global Integration, c. 1750 to c. 1900	Chapters 24–28
Key Concept 5.1	**Industrialization and Global Capitalism**	423; 475; 554–583; 587–610; 618–620; 630–637; 641–660; 662–681; 837
	I. Industrialization fundamentally changed how goods were produced.	554–571; 577–578; 580–581
	II. New patterns of global trade and production developed that further integrated the global economy as industrialists sought raw materials and new markets for the increasing amount of goods produced in their factories.	554–560; 577; 579–583; 587–610; 630–637; 672–675
	III. To facilitate investments at all levels of industrial production, financiers developed and expanded various financial institutions.	423; 475; 554–560; 568–570; 677–678; 837
	IV. There were major developments in transportation and communication.	554–560; 667–670; 677–678
	V. The development and spread of global capitalism led to a variety of responses.	554–560; 568–578; 618–620; 641–660; 662–681

	VI. The ways in which people organized themselves into societies also underwent significant transformations in industrialized states due to the fundamental restructuring of the global economy.	554–560; 568–575; 593–609; 665–669; 672–673; 679–681
Key Concept 5.2	**Imperialism and Nation-State Formation**	554–560; 579–583; 587–610; 640–657; 672–680; 714–726
	I. Industrializing powers established transoceanic empires.	554–560; 579–583; 587–610; 637–638
	II. Imperialism influenced state formation and contraction around the world.	554–560; 587–610; 640–654; 672–680; 714–726
	III. New racial ideologies, especially Social Darwinism, facilitated and justified imperialism.	554–560; 587–610
Key Concept 5.3	**Nationalism, Revolution and Reform**	400; 416; 420–422; 487–488; 554–571; 572–576; 587–610; 612–681; 862
	I. The rise and diffusion of Enlightenment thought that questioned established traditions in all areas of life often preceded the revolutions and rebellions against existing governments.	400; 416; 420–422; 487–488; 554–564
	II. Beginning in the 18th century, peoples around the world developed a new sense of commonality based on language, religion, social customs and territory. These newly imagined national communities linked this identity with the borders of the state, while governments used this idea to unite diverse populations.	554–571; 587–610; 612–681
	III. The spread of Enlightenment ideas and increasing discontent with imperial rule propelled reformist and revolutionary movements.	554–571; 572–575; 587–610; 612–681; 862
	IV. The global spread of Enlightenment thought and the increasing number of rebellions stimulated new transnational ideologies and solidarities.	422; 554–560; 569–570; 575–576; 617–620; 629–630; 633–636; 669–672; 679–680
Key Concept 5.4	**Global Migration**	554–560; 564–566; 579–583; 587–610; 627–628; 633–636
	I. Migration in many cases was influenced by changes in demography in both industrialized and unindustrialized societies that presented challenges to existing patterns of living.	554–560; 556–558
	II. Migrants relocated for a variety of reasons.	554–560; 579–583; 587–610; 627–628; 633–636
	III. The large-scale nature of migration, especially in the 19th century, produced a variety of consequences and reactions to the increasingly diverse societies on the part of migrants and the existing populations.	554–560; 579; 593–594; 602–611

Period 6	Accelerating Global Change and Realignments, c. 1900 to the Present	Chapters 29–37
Key Concept 6.1	**Science and the Environment**	577–578; 587–594; 607; 693–700; 708; 715–716; 778–779; 815–818; 846–853; 861; 911–912; 923–924; 929; 929–932
	I. Researchers made rapid advances in science that spread throughout the world, assisted by the development of new technology.	577–578; 587–594; 607; 815; 923–924
	II. As the global population expanded at an unprecedented rate, humans fundamentally changed their relationship with the environment.	587–594; 929–932
	III. Disease, scientific innovations and conflict led to demographic shifts.	587–594; 708; 715–716; 778–779; 815–818; 846–853; 911–912; 929; 932
Key Concept 6.2	**Global Conflicts and Their Consequences**	402–403; 469; 583–585; 587–594; 639–643; 650–660; 670–672; 701–726; 736–748; 750–762; 765–818; 824–837; 854–867; 888–889; 889–894; 898–906; 909–915; 925
	I. Europe dominated the global political order at the beginning of the twentieth century, but both land-based and transoceanic empires gave way to new forms of transregional political organization by the century's end.	587–594; 639–643; 650–660; 670–672; 714–719; 722–724; 793–794; 891–892
	II. Emerging ideologies of anti-imperialism contributed to the dissolution of empires.	469; 714–723; 736–748; 750–762; 781–789; 857–858; 891–892; 893–894; 910–911
	III. Political changes were accompanied by major demographic and social consequences.	583–585; 587–594; 701–726; 775–776; 788–789; 854–855; 909–911; 925
	IV. Military conflicts occurred on an unprecedented global scale.	583–585; 587–594; 701–726; 736–748; 765–818; 898–906
	V. Although conflict dominated much of the 20th century, many individuals and groups—including states—opposed this trend. Some individuals and groups, however, intensified the conflicts.	402–403; 587–594; 718–719; 720–722; 755; 761–762; 782–784; 797–798; 805–806; 824–836; 856–867; 888–889; 889–894; 912–915

Key Concept 6.3	New Conceptualization of Global Economy, Society and Culture	577–578; 587–594; 611–612; 714–715; 722–724; 819–820; 797–799; 807–810; 834–835; 837–838; 852–853; 877; 887–888; 911–912; 922–939
	I. States responded in a variety of ways to the economic challenges of the twentieth century.	732–733; 750–751; 814–815; 853–862; 884–886; 903; 912; 923–925; 933
	II. States, communities, and individuals became increasingly interdependent, a process facilitated by the growth of institutions of global governance.	587–594; 714–715; 819–820; 797–799; 911–912; 922–939
	III. People conceptualized society and culture in new ways; some challenged old assumptions about race, class, gender, and religion, often using new technologies to spread reconfigured traditions.	587–594; 722–724; 807–808; 834–835; 837–838; 852–853; 887–888; 928–932; 939
	IV. Popular and consumer culture became global.	577–578; 587–594; 611–612; 809–810; 877; 923–924; 925–927

Prologue

The study of history is the study of the past. Knowledge of the past gives us perspective on our societies today. It shows different ways in which people have identified problems and tried to resolve them, as well as important common impulses in the human experience. History can inform through its variety, remind us of some human constants, and provide a common vocabulary and examples that aid in mutual communication.

The study of history is also the study of change. Historians analyze major changes in the human experience over time and examine the ways in which those changes connect the past to the present. They try to distinguish between superficial and fundamental change, as well as between sudden and gradual change. They explain why change occurs and what impact it has. Finally, they pinpoint continuities from the past along with innovations. History, in other words, is a study of human society in motion.

World history has become a subject in its own right. It involves the study of historical events in a global context. It does not attempt to sum up everything that has happened in the past. World history focuses on two principal subjects: the evolution of leading societies and the interaction among different peoples around the globe.

THE EMERGENCE OF WORLD HISTORY

Serious attempts to deal with world history are relatively recent. Many historians have attempted to locate the evolution of their own societies in the context of developments in a larger "known world": Herodotus, though particularly interested in the origins of Greek culture, wrote also of developments around the Mediterranean; Ibn Khaldun wrote of what he knew about developments in Africa and Europe as well as in the Muslim world. But not until the 20th century, with an increase in international contacts and a vastly expanded knowledge of the historical patterns of major societies, did a full world history become possible. In the West, world history depended on a growing realization that the world could not be understood simply as a mirror reflecting the West's greater glory or as a stage for Western-dominated power politics. This hard-won realization continues to meet some resistance. Nevertheless, historians in several societies have attempted to develop an international approach to the subject that includes, but goes beyond, merely establishing a context for the emergence of their own civilizations.

Our understanding of world history has been increasingly shaped by two processes that define historical inquiry: detective work and debate. Historians are steadily uncovering new data not just about particular societies but about lesser-known contacts. Looking at a variety of records and artifacts, for example, they learn how an 8th-century battle between Arab and Chinese forces in central Asia brought Chinese prisoners who knew how to make paper to the Middle East, where their talents were quickly put to work. And they argue about world history frameworks: how central European actions should be in the world history of the past 500 years, and whether a standard process of modernization is useful or distorting in measuring developments in modern Turkey or China. Through debate come advances in how world history is understood and conceptualized, just as the detective work advances the factual base.

WHAT CIVILIZATION MEANS

Humans have always shown a tendency to operate in groups that provide a framework for economic activities, governance, and cultural forms such as beliefs and artistic styles. These groups, or societies, may be quite small; hunting-and-gathering bands often numbered no more than 60 people. World history usually focuses on somewhat larger societies, with more extensive economic relationships (at least for trade) and cultures.

One vital kind of grouping is called civilization. The idea of civilization as a type of human society is central to most world history, though it also generates debate and though historians are now agreed that it is not the only kind of grouping that warrants attention. Civilizations, unlike some other societies, generate surpluses beyond basic survival needs. This in turn promotes a variety of specialized occupations and heightened social differentiation, as well as regional and long-distance trading networks. Surplus production also spurs the growth of cities and the development of formal states, with some bureaucracy, in contrast to more informal methods of governing. Most civilizations have also developed systems of writing.

Civilizations are not necessarily better than other kinds of societies. Nomadic groups have often demonstrated great creativity in technology and social relationships, and some were more vigorous than settled civilizations in promoting global contacts. Moreover, there is disagreement about exactly what defines a civilization—for example, what about cases like the Incas where there was no writing?

Used carefully, however, the idea of civilization as a form of human social organization, and an unusually extensive one, has merit. Along with agriculture (which developed earlier), civilizations have given human groups the capacity to fundamentally reshape their environments and to dominate most other living creatures. The history of civilizations embraces most of the people who have ever lived; their literature, formal scientific discoveries, art, music, architecture, and inventions; their most elaborate social, political, and economic systems; their brutality and destruction caused by conflicts; their exploitation of other species; and their degradation of the environment—a result of changes in technology and the organization of work.

The study of civilizations always involves more, however, than case-by-case detail. World history makes sense only if civilizations are compared, rather than treated separately. Equally important, civilizations (and other societies) developed important mutual contacts, which could have wide impact in reshaping several societies at the same time. And civilizations responded to still wider forces, like migration, disease, or missionary activity, that could reshape the frameworks within which they operated. Civilizations in these wider contexts—as they changed through internal dynamics, mutual interactions, and responses to broader forces—form the basic patterns of world history for the past 5000 years.

Early Human Societies, 2.5 million–600 B.C.E.: Origins and Development

PART I

These prehistoric paintings of animals, on the wall of a cave in Lascaux, France, date from 15,000 to 10,000 B.C.E. They show the centrality of the hunt in the economy and symbolism of hunting and gathering peoples.

PART OUTLINE

Chapter 1 From Human Prehistory to the Early Civilizations

Chapter 2 Early Civilizations 3500–600 B.C.E.

THE OVERVIEW

The earliest known, fully human species lived in east Africa about 2.5 million years ago. Gradually, humans developed a more erect stance and greater brain capacity. Early humans lived by hunting and gathering. Because hunting-and-gathering economies require a great deal of space—on average about 2.5 square miles per person—populations remained small, and people lived in small groups. Even a modest population increase in a hunting-and-gathering group required part of the group to migrate in search of new game. Tens of thousands of years ago, the most advanced of the human species, *Homo sapiens sapiens*, migrated from Africa into the Middle East, then into Europe and Asia, and later Australia and the Americas. Early humans developed tools, first using stones, sticks, and other natural objects. Gradually, people learned to fashion tools and weapons from stone, bone, and wood.

Domestication of animals and techniques of crop growing ultimately created alternatives to the hunting and gathering economy. Herding activities constituted one option, but agriculture was the more important innovation. Agriculture began at different times in different places, from about 10,000 years ago onward. It developed independently in at least three regions and perhaps more. The top map on the opposite page shows the early centers of food production. Gradually, agriculture spread widely, though not universally, from these initial centers.

The development of agriculture was a radical change in humans' way of life. By providing a dependable source of food, agriculture allowed people to live in larger groups. Later on, tool-making technology advanced with the discovery of metalworking, which in turn further increased agricultural production. Increased production freed some members of the society to perform other kinds of work. This in turn encouraged a further series of organizational changes we call civilization.

Early civilizations arose in several different sites, four of them along the fertile shores of great rivers. Most of these early civilizations arose independently of each other. The map of early civilizations to the right makes another point clear: Large parts of the world were not involved in these developments. Early world history focuses on agricultural civilizations, but it must also pay attention to regions that developed different kinds of economies and different organizational structures.

Big Concepts

Each of the key phases of the long period of early human history (2.5 million B.C.E.–600 B.C.E.) can be characterized by a central topic or Big Concept. The first of these is the development of human hunting skills, the adaptation of those skills to the shifting geography and climate of the Ice Age, and above all the patterns of human migration that brought humans to so many different areas. The second Big Concept is the rise of agriculture and the changes in technology associated with the Neolithic revolution (9000 and 4000 B.C.E). These changes set in motion the agricultural phase of the human experience that lasted until just a few centuries ago. The final Big Concept is the appearance of increasingly distinctive human societies through agriculture or nomadic pastoralism, and the earliest contacts among these first societies, particularly after 3500 B.C.E. when larger and more formally organized societies, often

Bone tools show the increasing intentionality of tool use among hunting and gathering peoples, as implements were shaped for various purposes.

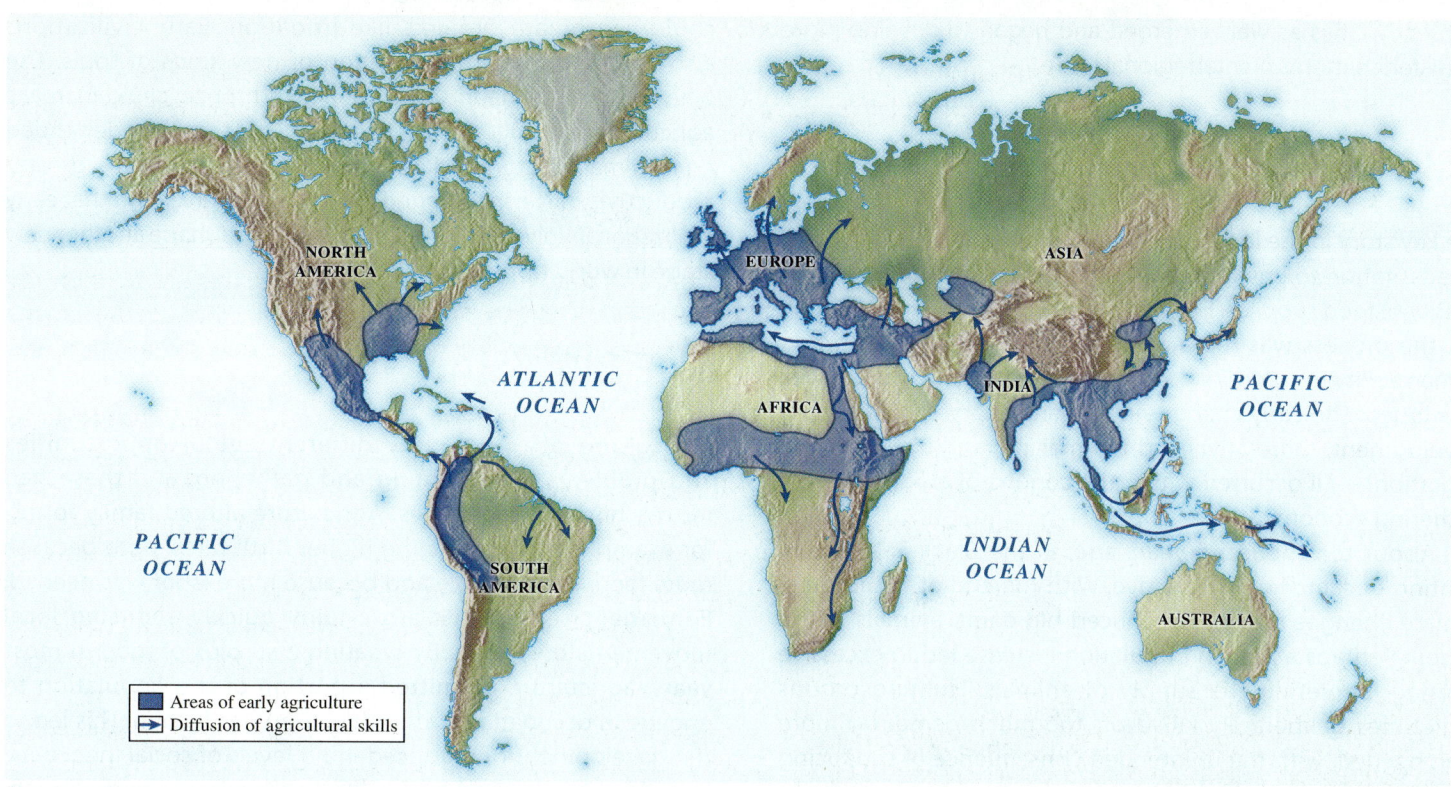

Initial Centers and Spread of Agriculture

Early Centers of Civilization

PART I Early Human Societies, 2.5 million–600 B.C.E.: Origins and Development

with early cities as well, emerged and began to develop more consistent patterns of interregional trade.

TRIGGERS FOR CHANGE

The key story in the long early phases of human history focuses on adaptation to environments, and particularly the search for adequate food supplies. Humans still react to their environment, but the process was more apparent in earlier periods, when human ability to control aspects of the environment was less well developed. The early changes in human history—evolutionary development, more advanced toolmaking, and the extensive migrations—all occurred within the context of a hunting-and-gathering economy.

About ten thousand years ago, in the Black Sea region, hunting became less productive. With the end of the ice age, climate changes may have reduced big game animals in the region. Perhaps a human population increase led to excessive hunting, depleting the supply of animals. Hunting groups sometimes deliberately killed off too much game, far more than needed, with the unintended consequence of producing a food crisis; human impact on the environment began early. Whatever the causes of the shortage, people were forced to look for new sources of food. Women, as gatherers, had undoubtedly become aware of the possibility of deliberately planting seeds and harvesting grain. Thus the rise of agriculture was under way.

Even the advent of new social organizations associated with civilization involved efforts at greater environmental control. Early civilizations provided social structures that could coordinate projects like irrigation. Early civilizations also emerged after the invention of new kinds of tools. The wheel and metal hand tools, initially of bronze, could increase agricultural production and transport. But they also depended on new manufacturing skills. Greater specialization and greater productivity alike encouraged the kind of organization that early civilization involved. New technology helped shape another new stage in world history.

THE BIG CHANGES

Agriculture offered a very different set of opportunities and problems than hunting and gathering, and these had far-reaching consequences. Agriculture altered family forms, for example, by encouraging higher birth rates, both because more food was available and because more labor was needed. Permanent settlements arose fairly quickly, reducing local movements of people. By creating a surplus of food in most years, agriculture permitted a portion of the population to engage in occupations other than food production. This led to the development of unprecedented levels of social inequality, including heightened inequality between men and women. Agriculture altered the environment, sometimes resulting in overcultivation that depleted the soil. It encouraged humans to live in larger groups, and by doing so, it created new vulnerability to communicable diseases. While agriculture clearly generated a mixture of advantages and disadvantages, its greater food production allowed more population growth. This in turn helps explain why agriculture tended to spread and why many

2.5 million B.C.E.	1.25 million B.C.E.	150,000 B.C.E.	30,000 B.C.E.	10,000 B.C.E.
2.5 million Emergence of *Homo sapiens* in eastern Africa	**1 million** Emergence of *Homo erectus*, an upright, tool-using human **600,000** Wide spread of human species across Asia, Europe, Africa; control of fire	**120,000** Emergence of *Homo sapiens sapiens*, which displaces other human species	**30,000–25,000** Passage of first people to Americas **15,000–12,000** Domestication of dogs	**8500–6500** Domestication of sheep, pigs, goats, cattle **8500–3500** Neolithic Age; development of farming in Middle East

people were willing to change basic aspects of their lives to accommodate to this new economy.

In the most fertile areas, agricultural centers ultimately developed the organizational forms associated with civilization, most notably formal political structures and cities. Not all did so: Stateless, loosely organized agricultural societies persisted in quite a few places until relatively modern times. But more formal political structures—states—plus larger urban centers—cities—as places to exchange goods and ideas could further the direction of agricultural economies. It was no accident that the first four centers of civilization developed along river valleys, with their opportunities for irrigation: Civilization resulted from the prosperity of this kind of agriculture but also responded to its organizational needs, for it took coordination to run irrigation systems. Civilizations also helped direct many of the surpluses of agricultural economies to upper-class groups—rulers, landlords, and sometimes priests. As with agriculture, although to a lesser extent, the arrival of civilizations had wider consequences. Most early civilizations, for example, developed monumental buildings often associated with religion and more formal art and culture were standard features of this final great innovation in early human history.

CONTINUITY

While the development of agriculture brought enormous changes, it is important to remember that major continuities persisted as well. Changes took place very slowly. It took thousands of years for humans to develop New Stone Age technologies such as fashioning tools rather than simply picking up suitably shaped objects, such as rocks.

The slow pace of change had two causes. First, inventing fundamentally new devices took time. In some cases, it never occurred at all: Impressive agricultural societies flourished without ever developing the wheel or metal tools. In addition, many people remained attached to old ways. Because the food supply was so precarious, the risk of innovation probably seemed dangerous. This was one reason why agriculture, although it did fan out from its initial centers, took so long to spread widely. People cherished the habits long associated with local migrations. Many men valued the challenge of hunting. Many groups held out against agriculture, even when they knew of it.

Even as change occurred, it could produce efforts to preserve older values in new ways. In hunting-and-gathering societies, men and women both had key productive roles; the roles were very different but they generated some mutual respect. With agriculture, men took on functions that probably seemed rather feminine, because they were linked to food gathering, which had been women's responsibility before. Men had far less time to hunt or to enjoy the masculine rituals associated with hunting. So men looked for ways within agriculture to emphasize manhood. One common response was to claim new levels of superiority over women. This was a key change in gender relations, but it can also be seen as a kind of compensation. To this extent, men could feel that not all traditions were being lost. Polytheistic religions in many agricultural societies also preserved older emphases, with gods and goddesses dedicated

8000 B.C.E.	6000 B.C.E.	5000 B.C.E.	4000 B.C.E.	2000 B.C.E.
7000 First town at Jericho	**5600** Beans domesticated in Western Hemisphere	**5000** Domestication of maize (corn) **5000–2000** Yangshao culture in north China	**4000–3000** Development of writing, bronze metalworking, wheel, plow in Middle East **3500–1800** Sumerian civilization **3100–1087** Founding and flowering of Egyptian civilization **2500–1500** Indus civilization in south Asia **1500** Beginning of Polynesian migrations in Pacific	**1850** Origins of Shang kingdom in China **1800** Formation of Babylonian empire in Middle East **1700–1300** Rise of village culture in Mesoamerica **1600** Beginning of Indo-European invasions of India and parts of the Mediterranean and Middle East **1600** Spread of civilization to Crete (Minoan) **1500–800** Olmec civilizations in Central America **1250** Moses and Jewish exodus from Egypt (according to Jewish belief) **1200–700** Vedas composed (India) **1122–770** Zhou Kingdom in China **900** Beginning of Maya (Central America) **850** Beginnings of Chavin culture (Andes) **800** Beginnings of Bantu migration in Africa **800** Initial Greek city states **760–600** Meroe (Kush) rules Egypt

to the hunt, even as they added rituals linked to planting and harvesting.

Once established, agriculture generated its own impulses toward continuity. Many peasant farmers clung fervently to traditional techniques and village structures, regarding further change with great suspicion. Thus, a tension between change and continuity was built into early human experience.

IMPACT ON DAILY LIFE: CHILDREN

Children are an important part of any human society. Some aspects of children's lives are doubtless natural, part of human experience at any time, in any place. But the arrival of agriculture had huge implications for children. Hunting-and-gathering societies depended on a relatively low birth rate, with few children per family. Too many children would overwhelm resources, and no family could easily transport more than one young child during migrations. So hunters and gatherers limited births, mainly by breast-feeding each child for up to four or five years, which created chemical changes in women's bodies that reduced the chances of new conception.

With agriculture, however, more children could be supported, and indeed children became a vital part of the family labor force. Infants began to be weaned at about 18 months on average, a huge change from earlier human patterns. Birth rates shot up—agricultural families usually averaged five to seven children, although some would die, as infant mortality rates were high. Childhood began to be defined in terms of work. Even young children had obligations. And by the time they were teenagers, their families depended on their labor. This was a dramatic redefinition of childhood, even as children became more numerous in the population at large.

Civilization, as an organizational form, had less impact on children, but it added its own changes. Most civilizations developed written language, although only a minority could afford the time to learn to write. As a result, the vast majority of children worked, but an elite minority were sent to school. Also, civilizations used codes of law and other prescriptions to emphasize the duties of children to their families. All agricultural civilizations emphasized the authority of parents over children and children's obligation to obey their parents. In this way, civilizations tried to instill in children a willingness to work for the benefit of their families. An early Chinese saying stated simply: "No parent is ever wrong." Children could be loved and could flourish, but there was a distinctive tone of strict discipline and obedience in agricultural civilizations that bolstered the necessity of children's labor.

Small wonder that some hunting-and-gathering or herding groups, when they encountered civilizations, were shocked at how rigorously children were handled. Many American Indians were appalled by the harsh physical discipline European immigrants dealt out to their children. Here was an example of agriculture's profound impact on daily life.

Chapter 1 focuses on the development of agriculture and the ways in which it changed the lives of early humans. It also notes the limits of these developments—the many regions that continued living by hunting and gathering as well as the different trajectory that was followed by societies whose people lived by herding animals rather than farming. Chapter 2 then shows how farming led, in several key centers, to the formation of early civilizations. ∎

From Human Prehistory to the Early Civilizations

1

Listen to Chapter 1 on MyHistoryLab

One day about 10,000 years ago, in a rock shelter near the Pecos River, an early human inhabitant of what is today West Texas inserted the bloom stalk of a yucca plant into one of several holes worn into a fire-starting stick and, holding the stalk upright, twirled it between her hands, as depicted in the artist's recreation on this page. After much effort on the part of the young woman, as shown here, the friction between the spinning stalk and the stick produced wisps of smoke, then sparks, then glowing embers. The woman used the embers to set fire to a small pile of dried yucca leaves that she had gathered nearby. Yucca leaves have thin tendrils that, when dry, catch fire readily. Carefully tended, the leaves could be used to kindle a steady fire that provided not only warmth, but the means for cooking a meal. And, importantly, stalks, fire-sticks, and leaves could easily be carried by migratory groups of early humans.

Read the Document on MyHistoryLab: A Visitor from the Neolithic Age

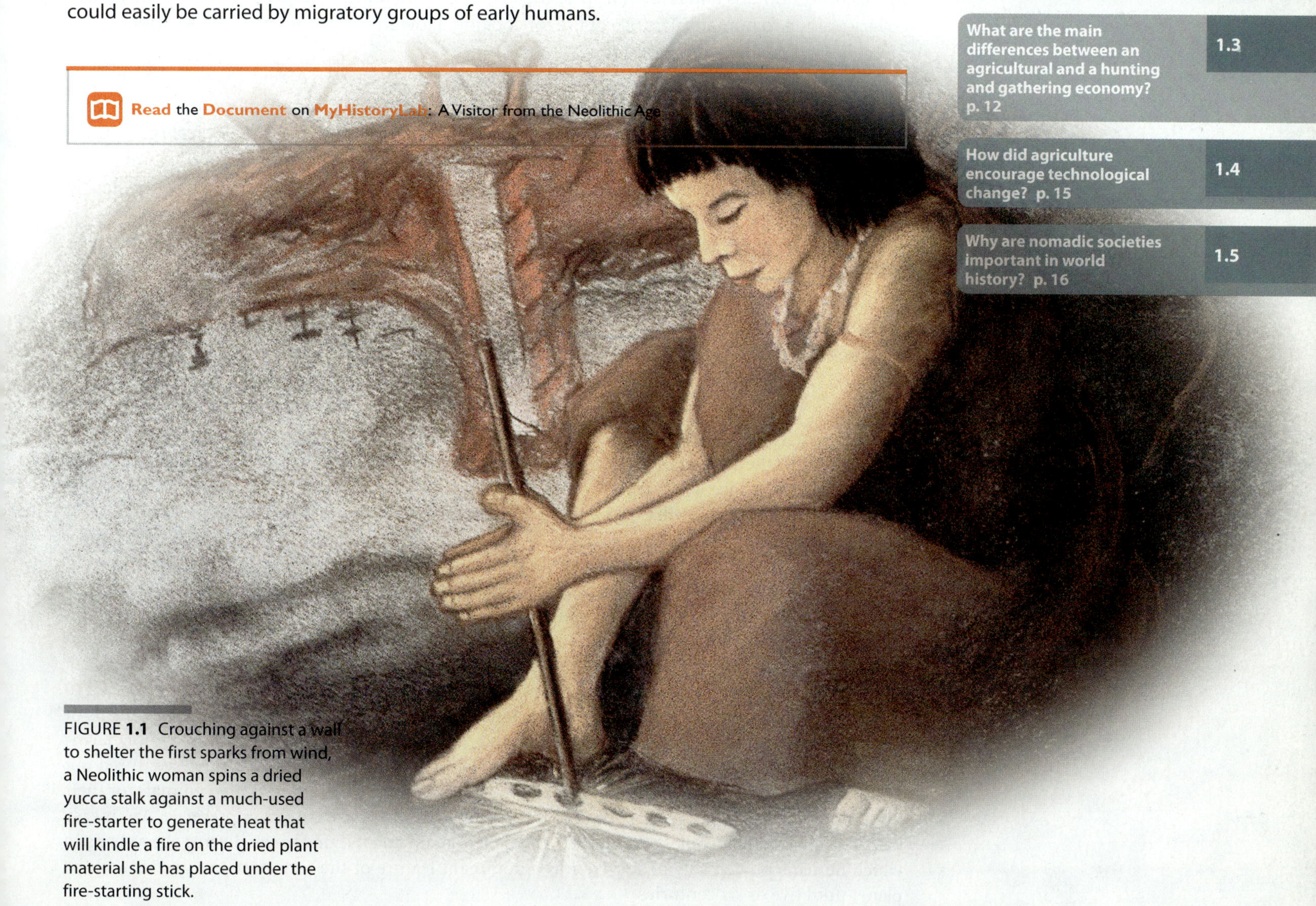

LEARNING OBJECTIVES

What are some of the main characteristics of the human species? p. 9	1.1
What were the most significant human achievements before the rise of agriculture and what were the patterns of early human migration? p. 10	1.2
What are the main differences between an agricultural and a hunting and gathering economy? p. 12	1.3
How did agriculture encourage technological change? p. 15	1.4
Why are nomadic societies important in world history? p. 16	1.5

FIGURE **1.1** Crouching against a wall to shelter the first sparks from wind, a Neolithic woman spins a dried yucca stalk against a much-used fire-starter to generate heat that will kindle a fire on the dried plant material she has placed under the fire-starting stick.

Watch the Video Series on MyHistoryLab
Learn about some key topics related to this chapter with the *MyHistoryLab Video Series: Key Topics in World History*

Several yucca-based fire-starter kits, some including bows used in the place of hands to turn the yucca stalk, have been found across the American Southwest. These Neolithic (New Stone Age) kits send us a number of messages about early world history. Most obviously, early men and women were tool users. They not only deliberately selected branches, stones, and other natural objects from the environment, they crafted them into weapons, utensils, and tools that could be used to ward off animal and human enemies, hunt, trap, fish, prepare food, and construct shelters. This capacity to fashion tools distinguishes human beings from all other animals. Although a number of other animals, including apes, are tool users, only human beings construct their tools. By this time, humans had known how to make and use fire for thousands of years—another discovery unique to humans. The use of fire for cooking allowed early humans to eat a wider variety of foods, particularly animal protein.

The toolmakers of the American Southwest lived far from eastern Africa, where human beings first evolved. Just decades ago, it was believed that the first humans migrated from northeast Asia into what is now Alaska only 12,000 years ago. Vastly improved archeological techniques have recently revealed that the crossing had been made at least as early as 25,000 B.C.E. and that the migrants spread out quickly, probably traveling both overland and by boat along the Pacific Coast, from Alaska to Chile.

Finally, we know our early ancestors could talk. Human beings had developed what some call the "speech gene" about 70,000 years earlier, vastly improving the species' capacity to communicate, beyond the sounds and gestures common to a number of animal groups. Neolithic humans were what we sometimes call "primitive," but they had already experienced a number of fundamental changes and, in some places, they were poised to introduce some more. ■

The creation of fire-starters and other tools, including weapons, proved critical to the survival of early humans and to the development of ever-larger communities and eventually whole societies. In the chapter that follows we will trace the successive stages of the early material and social development of the human species. We will explore the technological and organizational innovations that made it possible for what became the great majority of humans to move from tiny bands of wandering hunters and gatherers to sedentary village dwellers and then the builders of walled cities with populations in the thousands. More than any other factor, these transformations were made possible by the development of agriculture that increased and made more secure the supply of food by which more and more humans could be sustained.

The domestication of animals and the shift to agriculture was accompanied by major changes in the roles and relationships between men and women and patterns of childrearing. They also led to increasing social stratification, new forms of political organization, increasingly elaborate means of artistic expression, and more lethal ways of waging war. During these millennia of transition, farming communities occupied only small pockets of the earth's land area and only rarely ventured out on the sea or large rivers. Pastoral peoples who depended on herds of domesticated animals for their livelihood occupied a far greater share of the space where there was a human presence. An uneasy balance between the peoples who followed these two main adaptations to the diverse ecosystems in which humans proved able to survive was a dominant feature of the history of the species and the planet until five or six centuries.

Late Paleolithic 15,000 B.C.E.	Transition Phase 10,000 B.C.E.	Neolithic Age 8000 B.C.E.		6000 B.C.E.	Metal Age 4000 B.C.E.		2000 B.C.E.
18,000–100,000 Central Russian mammoth bone settlements **15,000–12,000** Domestication of dogs **10,500–8000** Natufian settlements	**8500** Domestication of sheep **8500–5000** Development of farming in the Middle East	**7500–6500** Domestication of pigs, goats, cattle **7000** Full-fledged town at Jericho **6250–5400** Çatal Hüyük at its peak		**5600** Beans domesticated **5000–2000** Yangshao culture in north China **5000** Domestication of maize (corn)	**4000–3000** Age of innovation in the Middle East: introduction of writing, metalworking, wheel, plow **3500** Llama domesticated **3500–2350** Civilization of Sumer **c. 3100** Rise of Egyptian civilization **2500–1500** Indus valley civilization in south Asia		**2000** Kotosh culture in Peru **c. 1766** Emergence of Shang kingdom in China **1700–1300** Rise of village culture in Mesoamerica **1000–500** Olmec civilization in Mesoamerica **400** Potatoes domesticated

GETTING STARTED IS ALWAYS HARD

1.1 What are some of the main characteristics of the human species?

> The human species developed some distinctive characteristics, and some drawbacks.

The human species has accomplished a great deal in a relatively short period of time. There are significant disagreements over how long an essentially human species, as distinct from other primates, has existed. However, a figure of about 2.5 million years seems acceptable. This is approximately 1/4000 of the time the earth has existed. If one thinks of the whole history of the earth to date as a 24-hour day, the human species began at about 5 minutes until midnight. Human beings have existed for less than 5 percent of the time mammals of any sort have lived. Yet in this brief span of time—by earth-history standards—humankind has spread to every landmass (with the exception of the polar regions) and, for better or worse, has taken control of the destinies of countless other species.

To be sure, human beings have some drawbacks as a species, compared to other existing models. They are unusually aggressive against their own kind: While some of the great apes, notably chimpanzees, engage in periodic wars, these conflicts can hardly rival human violence. Human babies are dependent for a long period, which requires some special family or childcare arrangements and often has limited the activities of many adult women. Certain ailments, such as back problems resulting from an upright stature, also burden the species. And, the distinctive human awareness of the inevitability of death imparts some unique fears and tensions.

Distinctive features of the human species account for considerable achievement as well. Like other primates, but unlike most other mammals, human beings can manipulate objects fairly readily because of the grip provided by an opposable thumb on each hand. Compared to other primates, human beings have a relatively high and regular sexual drive, which aids reproduction; being omnivores, they are not dependent exclusively on plants or on animals for food, which helps explain why they can live in so many different climates and settings; the unusual variety of their facial expressions aids communication and enhances social life. The distinctive human brain and a facility for elaborate speech are even more important: much of human history depends on the knowledge, inventions, and social contracts that resulted from these assets.

Although the rise of humankind has been impressively rapid, its early stages can also be viewed as painfully long and slow. Most of the 2 million plus years during which our species has existed are described by the term **Paleolithic**, or **Old Stone Age**. Throughout this long time span, which runs until about 14,000 years ago, human beings learned only simple tool use, mainly through employing suitably shaped rocks and sticks for hunting and warfare. Fire was tamed about 750,000 years ago. The nature of the species also gradually changed during the Paleolithic, with emphasis on more erect stature and growing brain capacity. Archeological evidence also indicates some increases in average size.

> **Paleolithic Age** The Old Stone Age ending in 12,000 B.C.E.; typified by use of crude stone tools and hunting and gathering for subsistence.

A less apelike species, whose larger brain and erect stance allowed better tool use, emerged between 500,000 and 750,000 years ago; it is called, appropriately enough, *Homo erectus*. Several species of *Homo erectus* developed and spread in Africa, then to Asia and Europe, reaching a population size of perhaps 1.5 million 100,000 years ago.

Considerable evidence suggests that more advanced types of humans killed off or displaced many competitors over time. Intermarriage also occurred. And even **Homo sapiens sapiens** coexisted with other human species in several regions for considerable periods, as recent archeological and genetic evidence suggests. Ultimately, however, the single species predominated throughout the world, rather than a number of rather similar human species, as among monkeys and apes. The newest human breed, *Homo sapiens sapiens*, of which all humans in the world today are descendants, originated about 120,000 years ago, also in Africa. The success of this subspecies means that there have been no major changes in the basic human physique or brain size since its advent.

Part of human evolution in this decisive later phase involved a probably modest genetic modification in the brain that allowed much more elaborate patterns of speech. A number of animals and birds have some power of speech, in terms of varied sounds that communicate. But with the advent of this "language gene," people became capable of a much wider variety of sounds. From this, it was possible to invent languages. Scientists have wondered what the first people who had this gene must have thought, surrounded by other people who were still confined to a series of grunts plus elaborate facial expressions.

Homo sapiens sapiens The humanoid species that emerged as most successful at the end of the Paleolithic period.

HUMAN DEVELOPMENT AND CHANGE

1.2 What were the most significant human achievements before the rise of agriculture and what were the patterns of early human migration?

Hunting-and-gathering economies dominated human history until 9000 B.C.E. These economies helped propel migration over most of the lands on earth.

Even after the appearance of *Homo sapiens sapiens*, human life faced important constraints. People who hunted food and gathered nuts and berries could not support large numbers or elaborate societies. Most hunting groups were small, and they had to roam widely for food. Two people required at least one square mile for survival. Population growth was slow, partly because women breast-fed infants for several years to limit their own fertility. On the other hand, people did not have to work very hard—hunting took about seven hours every three days on average. Women, who gathered fruits and vegetables, worked harder, but there was significant equality between the sexes based on common economic contributions.

Read the Document on MyHistoryLab: Marshall Sahlins, "The Original Affluent Society"

Read the Document on MyHistoryLab: The Toolmaker 3300 BCE.

Paleolithic people gradually improved their tool use, beginning with the crude shaping of stone and wooden implements. The development of speech allowed more group cooperation and the transmission of technical knowledge. By the later Paleolithic period, people had developed rituals to lessen the fear of death and created cave paintings to express a sense of nature's beauty and power (Figure 1.2). Goddesses often played a prominent role in the religious pantheon. Thus, the human species came to develop systems of belief that helped explain the environment and set up rules for various kinds of social behavior. The development of speech provided rich language and symbols for the transmission of culture and its growing sophistication. At the same time, different groups of humans, in different locations, developed quite varied belief systems and languages.

The greatest achievement of Paleolithic people was the sheer spread of the human species over much of the earth's surface. The species originated in eastern Africa; most of the earliest types of human remains come from this region, in the present-day countries of Tanzania, Kenya, and Uganda. But gradual migration, doubtless caused by the need to find scarce food, steadily pushed the human reach to other areas. Key discoveries, notably fire and the use of animal skins for clothing—both of which enabled people to live in colder climates—facilitated the spread of Paleolithic groups. The

FIGURE **1.2** In Lascaux, France, in 1940, four boys happened upon a long-hidden cave filled with thousands of complex and beautiful Stone Age paintings like this one. Most of the paintings are of animals, some of which were extinct by the time they were painted. No one knows for sure why Stone Age artists painted these pictures, but they remain a powerful reminder of the sophistication of so-called primitive peoples.

VISUALIZING THE PAST

Representations of Women in Early Art

THE EARLIEST WRITING SYSTEM WE KNOW of was not introduced until around 3500 B.C.E. in the civilization of Sumer in Mesopotamia (see Chapter 2). Consequently, evidence for piecing together the history of human life in the Paleolithic and Neolithic ages comes mainly from surviving artifacts from campsites and early towns. Stone tools, bits of pottery or cloth, and the remains of Stone Age dwellings can now be dated rather precisely. When combined with other objects from the same site and time period, they give us a fairly good sense of the daily activities and life cycle of the peoples who created them.

Of all the material remains of the Stone Age era, none provide better insights into the social organization and thinking of early humans than works of art. Much of what we know about gender relations, or the status of males and females and the interaction between them, has been interpreted from the study of the different forms of artistic expression of Stone Age peoples. The stone carvings and figurines reproduced here illustrate themes and impressions of women and their roles that recur in the art of many prehistoric cultures.

Some of the earliest rock carvings, such as the Venus of Laussel (c. 25,000 B.C.E.) shown in the far-right image below, depict robust pregnant women. Figurines similar to the Laussel Venus, which was found in the remains of a campsite at St.-Germain-en-Laye in France, are among the most common artifacts of early human cultures. At other early sites, including Çatal Hüyük, women are depicted as goddesses. And at Hacilar, another prehistoric town uncovered in what is today Turkey, they are represented in figurines that may well have served as images of cult veneration and paintings that suggest they may have served as oracles or cult priestesses. As in the Laussel Venus, voluptuous women predominate, and in many of the clay sculptures their roles in reproduction and nurturing are celebrated. But female figures in postures suggesting political authority, such as the woman shown sitting on what may have been a throne with animal heads, have also been found. Many of these statuettes may also have been intended to depict goddesses and have served as objects of worship.

QUESTIONS

- On the basis of the sample provided in these illustrations, which roles in early human society were closely associated with women?
- What do these representations tell us about the extent and sources of power exercised by women in prehistoric times?
- What sort of requests might those who worshiped goddesses have made through their prayers and offerings?

first people moved out of Africa about 750,000 years ago. Human remains (Peking man, Java man) have been found in China and southeast Asia dating from 600,000 and 350,000 years ago, respectively. Humans inhabited Britain 250,000 years ago. Later, migrations of *Homo sapiens sapiens* from Africa took people to Eurasia. Two strands developed once migrants had crossed into west Asia: one took people to Europe, central Asia, and south Asia and the other pushed on to east and southeast Asia. From this in turn, further migrations occurred: people first crossed to Australia 60,000 years ago, followed by another group 20,000 years later, combining to form the continent's aboriginal population.

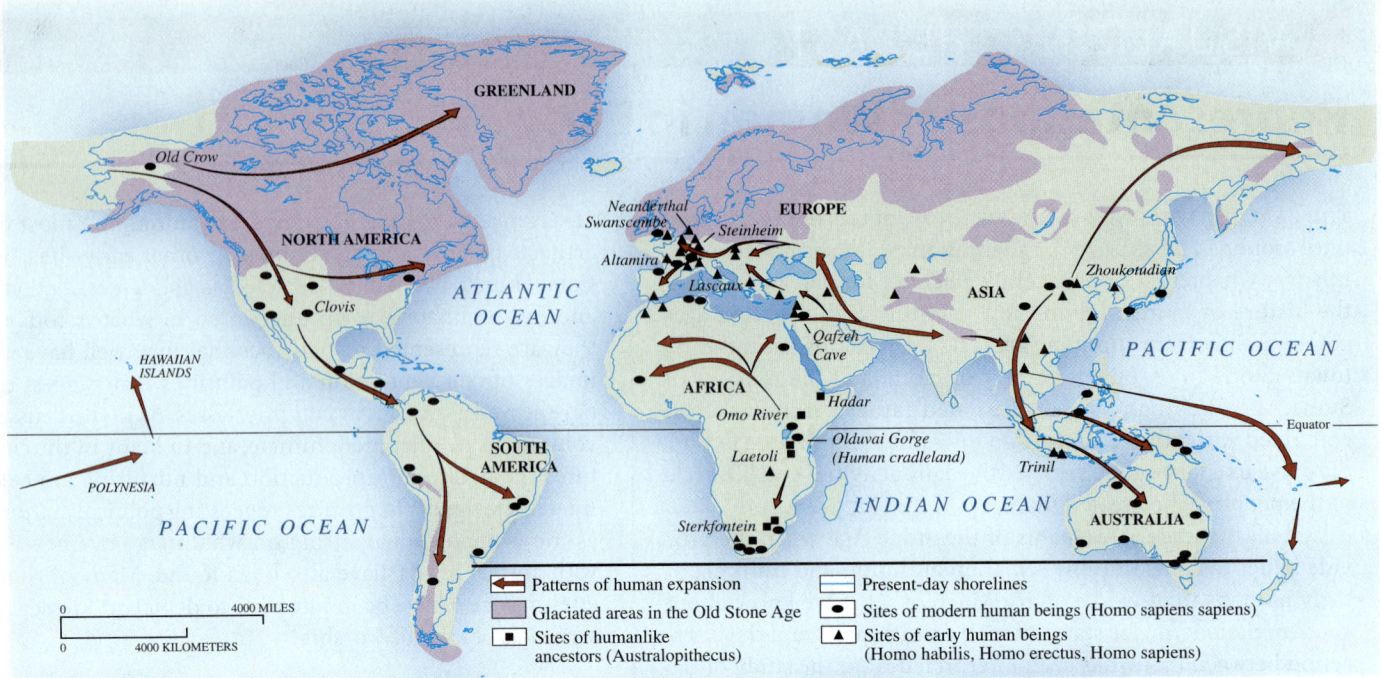

MAP **1.1 The Spread of Human Populations, c. 10,000 B.C.E.** As the map indicates, *Homo sapiens sapiens* first emerged in a single core area in east Africa and then migrated over long periods of time north to the Mediterranean and Europe, east to Asia, and then ultimately across the seas to the Americas and Oceania.

Humans crossed what was then a land bridge from Siberia to Alaska about 25,000 years ago and quickly began to spread out, reaching the tip of the South American continent possibly within a mere thousand years. Settlers from China reached Taiwan, the Philippines, and Indonesia 4500 to 3500 years ago.

In addition, soon after this time—roughly 14,000 years ago—the last great ice age ended, which did wonders for living conditions over much of the Northern Hemisphere. Human development began to accelerate. A new term, Mesolithic, or Middle Stone Age, designates a span of several thousand years, from about 12,000 to 8000 B.C.E., in which human ability to fashion stone tools and other implements improved greatly. From the Mesolithic also date the increased numbers of log rafts and dugouts, which improved fishing, and the manufacture of pots and baskets for food storage. Mesolithic people domesticated additional animals, such as cows (dogs had been tamed earlier), which again improved food supply. Population growth accelerated, which also resulted in more conflicts and wars. Skeletons from this period show frequent bone breaks and skull fractures caused by weapons.

In time, better tool use, somewhat more elaborate social organization, and still more population pressure led people in many parts of the world to the final Stone Age—the **Neolithic**, or **New Stone Age** (Map 1.1). And from Neolithic people, in turn, came several more dramatic developments that changed the nature of human existence—the invention of agriculture, the creation of cities, and other foreshadowings of civilization, which ended the Stone Age altogether throughout much of the world.

Neolithic Age The New Stone Age between 8000 and 5000 B.C.E.; period in which adaptation of sedentary agriculture occurred; domestication of plants and animals accomplished.

THE NEOLITHIC REVOLUTION

The Neolithic revolution centered on the development of agriculture.

1.3 What are the main differences between an agricultural and a hunting and gathering economy?

Human achievements during the various ages of stone are both fascinating and fundamental. What people accomplished during this long period of prehistory remains essential to human life today; our ability to make and manipulate tools depends directly on what our Stone Age ancestors invented.

Arrows actually had been invented, probably in southern Africa, 65,000 years ago, and knowledge of this advance for hunting and warfare gradually spread—although it had not reached below northern South America when Columbus made his voyage in 1492. In the Mesolithic period itself, people further refined their ability to shape stone, while also using wood and animal bones to make needles and other precise tools.

However, it was the invention of agriculture that most clearly moved the human species toward more elaborate social and cultural patterns that people today would recognize. With agriculture, human beings were able to settle in one place and focus on particular economic, political, and religious goals and activities. Agriculture also spawned a great increase in the sheer number of people in the world, a tenfold increase over several millennia.

The initial development of agriculture—that is, the deliberate planting of grains for later harvest—was probably triggered by two results of the ice age's end. First, population increases, stemming from improved climate, prompted people to search for new and more reliable sources of food. Second, the end of the ice age saw the retreat of certain big game animals, such as mastodons. Human hunters had to turn to smaller game, such as deer and wild boar, in many forested areas. Hunting's overall yield declined. Here was the basis for new interest in other sources of food. There is evidence that by 9000 B.C.E., in certain parts of the world, people were becoming increasingly dependent on regular harvests of wild grains, berries, and nuts. This undoubtedly set the stage for the deliberate planting of seeds (probably accidental to begin with) and the improvement of key grains through the selection of seeds from the best plants.

As farming evolved, new animals were also domesticated. Particularly in the Middle East and parts of Asia, by 9000 B.C.E. pigs, sheep, goats, and cattle were being raised. Farmers used these animals for meat and skins and soon discovered dairying as well. These results not only contributed to the development of agriculture, but they also served as the basis for nomadic herding societies.

Farming was initially developed in the Middle East and Black Sea regions, in an arc of territory running from present-day Turkey to Iraq and Israel. This was a very fertile area, more fertile in those days than at present. Grains such as barley and wild wheat were abundant. At the same time, this area was not heavily forested, and animals were in short supply, presenting a challenge to hunters. In the Middle East, the development of agriculture may have begun as early as 10,000 B.C.E., and it gained ground rapidly after 8000 B.C.E. Gradually, during the Neolithic centuries, knowledge of agriculture spread to other centers, including parts of India, North Africa, and Europe. Agriculture, including rice cultivation, soon developed independently in China (the second of at least three separate inventions of the new economic systems). We will see that agriculture spread later to much of Africa south of the Mediterranean coast, reaching west Africa by 2000 B.C.E., although here too there were additional developments with an emphasis on local grains and also root crops such as yams (Map 1.2). Agriculture had to be invented separately in the Americas, based on the cultivation of corn and other root crops such as potatoes, where it was also a slightly later development (about 5000 B.C.E.).

Many scholars have termed the development of agriculture a **Neolithic revolution**. The term is obviously misleading in one sense: agriculture was no sudden transformation, even in the Middle East, where the new system had its roots. Learning the new agricultural methods was difficult, and many peoples long combined a bit of agriculture with considerable reliance on the older systems of **hunting and gathering**. A "revolution" that took more than a thousand years, and then several thousands more, to spread to key population centers in Asia, Europe, and Africa, is hardly dramatic by modern standards.

The concept of revolution is, however, appropriate in demonstrating the magnitude of change involved. Early agriculture could support far more people per square mile than hunting ever could; it also allowed people to settle more permanently in one area. The system was nonetheless not easy. Agriculture required more regular work, at least of men, than hunting did. Hunting-and-gathering groups today, such as the Kung or Khoisan people of the Kalihari Desert in southwest Africa, work an average of 2.5 hours a day, alternating long, intense hunts with periods devoted to such pursuits as music, dance, and decorative art. Settled agriculture concentrated populations and encouraged the spread of disease. As much as agriculture was demanding, it was also rewarding: Agriculture supported larger populations, and with better food supplies and a more settled existence, agricultural peoples could afford to build houses and villages. Animals provided not only hides but also wool for more varied clothing.

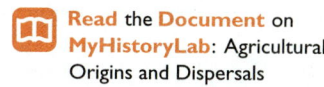

Read the **Document** on MyHistoryLab: Agricultural Origins and Dispersals

Neolithic revolution The succession of technological innovations and changes in human organization that led to the development of agriculture, 8500–3500 B.C.E.

hunting and gathering The original human economy, ultimately eclipsed by agriculture; groups hunt for meat and forage for grains, nuts, and berries.

> **Watch the Video on MyHistoryLab:** Agricultural Innovations in Ancient Africa (Jonathan T. Reynolds)

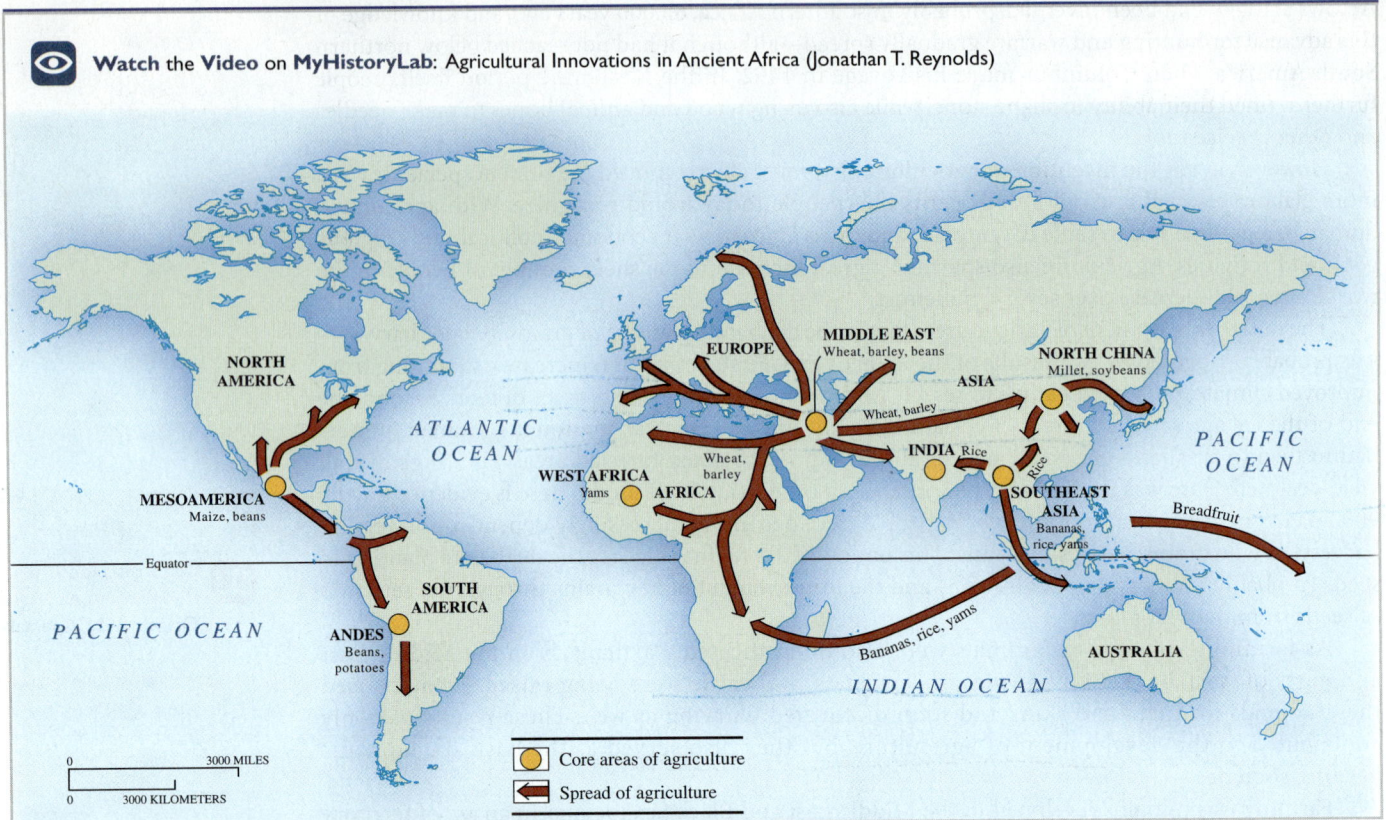

MAP **1.2 The Spread of Agriculture** Agriculture appears to have spread in ways similar to human populations, but from a Middle Eastern rather than African epicenter. And in important cases, particularly in the Americas, a wide range of staple crops were known in only some parts of the world until Columbus's voyage in the late-15th century brought together the civilizations of the Americas and Afro-Euroasia.

We know next to nothing of the debates that must have raged when people were first confronted with agriculture, but it is not hard to imagine that many would have found the new life too complicated, too difficult, or too unexciting. Most evidence suggests that many gathering and hunting peoples resisted agriculture as long as they could. Gradually, of course, agriculture did gain ground. Its success was hard to deny. And as farmers cleared new land from forests, they automatically drove out or converted many hunters. Disease played a role: Settled agricultural societies suffered from more contagious diseases because of denser population concentrations. Hunting-and-gathering peoples lacked resistance and often died when agriculturists who had developed immunities carried the diseases into new areas.

Not all the peoples of the world came to embrace the slowly spreading wave of agriculture, at least not until very recently. Important small societies in southern Africa, Australia, the islands of southeast Asia, and even northern Japan were isolated for so long that news of this economic system simply did not reach them. The white-skinned hunting tribes of northern Japan disappeared only about a hundred years ago. Northern Europeans and southern Africans converted to agriculture earlier, about 2000 years ago, but well after the Neolithic revolution had transformed other parts of their continents. Agriculture was initiated in the Americas as early as 5000 B.C.E. and developed vigorously in Central America and the northern part of South America. However, most Indian tribes in North America continued a hunting-and-gathering existence, although it was often combined with seasonal agriculture, until recent centuries. Finally, the peoples of the vast plains of central Asia long resisted a complete conversion to agriculture, in part because of a harsh climate; herding, rather than grain growing, became the basic socioeconomic system of this part of the world. From this area came waves of tough, nomadic invaders and migrants whose role in linking major civilizations was a vital force in world history until a few centuries ago.

AGRICULTURE AND CHANGE

1.4 How did agriculture encourage technological change?

Agriculture encouraged the formation of larger as well as more stable human communities than had existed before Neolithic times. A few Mesolithic groups had formed villages, particularly where opportunities for fishing were good, as around some of the lakes in Switzerland. However, most hunting peoples moved in relatively small groups, or tribes, each containing anywhere from 40 to 60 individuals, and they could not settle in a single spot without the game running out. With agriculture, these constraints changed for most of the people involved. There were advantages to staying put: Houses could be built to last, wells built to bring up water, and other "expensive" improvements afforded because they served many generations. In the Middle East, China, and parts of Africa and India, a key incentive to stability was the need for irrigation devices to channel river water to the fields. This same need helps explain why agriculture usually generated communities and not a series of isolated farms. Small groups simply could not regulate a river's flow or build and maintain irrigation ditches and sluices. Irrigation and defense encouraged villages—groupings of several hundred people—as the characteristic pattern of residence in almost all agricultural societies from Neolithic days until our own century.

One Neolithic town, **Çatal Hüyük** in southern Turkey, has been elaborately studied by archeologists (Figure 1.3). It was founded about 7000 B.C.E. and was unusually large, covering about 32 acres. Houses were made of mud bricks set in timber frameworks, crowded together, with few windows. People seem to have spent a good bit of time on their rooftops in order to experience daylight and make social contacts—many broken bones attest to frequent falls. Some houses were lavishly decorated, mainly with hunting scenes. Religious images, both of powerful male hunters and "mother goddesses" devoted to agricultural fertility, were common, and some people seem to have had special religious responsibilities. The town produced almost all the goods it consumed. Some trade was conducted with hunting peoples who lived in the hills surrounding the village, but apparently it was initiated more to keep the peace than to produce economic gain. By 5500 B.C.E., important production activities developed in the village, including those of skilled toolmakers and jewelers. With time also came links with other communities. Towns such as Çatal Hüyük ruled over smaller communities. This meant that some families began to specialize in politics, and military forces were organized. Some towns became small cities, ruled by kings who were typically given divine status. Here were developments that led to bigger changes in the organization of some agricultural societies.

The discovery of metal tools dates back to about 4000 B.C.E. Copper was the first metal with which people learned how to work, although the more resilient metal, bronze, soon entered the picture. In fact, the next basic age of human existence was the **Bronze Age.** By about 3000 B.C.E., metalworking had become so commonplace in the Middle East that the use of stone tools dissipated, and the long stone ages were over

> Agriculture generated some surplus that could support other specialist labor. By 7000 B.C.E. cities and crafts that depended on trade emerged in the Middle East.

Çatal Hüyük [cha-tal HOY-ewk] Early urban culture based on sedentary agriculture; located in modern southern Turkey; was larger in population than Jericho, had greater degree of social stratification.

Bronze Age From about 4000 B.C.E., when bronze tools were first introduced in the Middle East, to about 1500 B.C.E., when iron began to replace it.

View the **Closer Look** on MyHistoryLab: Çatal Hüyük

FIGURE **1.3** Excavation of the ancient settlement at Çatal Hüyük, in what is now southern Turkey. Movement within the settlement was mainly across the roofs and terraces of the houses. Because each dwelling had a substantial storeroom for food, the settlement was often the target of attacks by outsiders. The houses were joined together to provide protection from such attacks; when the outside entrances were barricaded, the complex was transformed into a fortress.

CHAPTER 1 From Human Prehistory to the Early Civilizations

at last—although, of course, an essentially Neolithic technology persisted in many parts of the world, even among some agricultural peoples.

Metalworking was extremely useful to agricultural or herding societies. Metal hoes and other tools allowed farmers to work the ground more efficiently. Metal weapons were obviously superior to those made from stone and wood. Agricultural peoples now supported the small number of individuals such as toolmakers, who specialized in this activity and exchanged their products with farmers for food. Specialization of this sort did not, however, guarantee rapid rates of invention; indeed, many specialized artisans seemed very conservative, eager to preserve methods that had been inherited. But specialization did improve the conditions or climate for discovery, and the invention of metalworking was a key result. Like agriculture, knowledge of metals gradually fanned out to other parts of Asia and to Africa and Europe.

Gradually, the knowledge of metal tools created further change, not only for farmers but also for manufacturing artisans, who benefited from better tools. Woodworking, for example, became steadily more elaborate as metal replaced stone, bone, and fire in the cutting and connecting of wood. We are, of course, still living in the metal ages today, although we rely primarily on iron—whose working was introduced around 1500 B.C.E. by herding peoples who moved into the Middle East from central Asia—rather than copper and bronze.

By about 4000 B.C.E., other changes began to accumulate in several agricultural centers, particularly in the Middle East, beyond metalworking and the expansion of towns. These changes depended on the extent to which agricultural production could free up a few people to specialize in craft manufacturing, initially on products used in the agriculture process, such as the manufacture of pots. Gradually, certain other inventions cropped up that could benefit agricultural production, while also spilling over into other human activities such as warfare. Around 4000 B.C.E., for example, the wheel was introduced, probably by peoples who migrated into the Middle East. Here was a vital contribution to the movement of goods and, soon, to certain kinds of fighting.

NOMADIC SOCIETIES

1.5 Why are nomadic societies important in world history?

Because it spread slowly and incompletely, agriculture was not the only economic system available to human societies, although it ultimately became the most important one. In addition to the persistence of hunting and gathering groups in some regions, nomadic herding economies created another option. Nomadic societies were more suitable to certain regions than agriculture was, and they would make their own important contribution to world history more generally.

We do not know when nomadic societies first developed, for they have left few written records and no real architectural monuments. They may have begun before the first civilizations emerged. Nomadic societies ultimately developed, particularly in the region of the huge grassy plains of central Asia, on the fringes of the Sahara desert in Africa, and also in southern Arabia. Smaller nomadic societies also developed in the Americas, in the Andes Mountains, the only place where there were relevant domesticated animals. Nomadic regions generally are characterized by rainfalls sufficient for developing grasslands but less adequate for settled agriculture.

The first groups of **nomads** to break into the historical record were the Indo-Europeans, who periodically intervened in the civilizations of the Middle East and India for a thousand years, beginning about 1500 B.C.E. Some Indo-European groups invaded civilized areas and established their own empires—such as the Hittites, who fit into the series of empire-invaders in Mesopotamia. Others, such as the Greeks, migrated into new territory and settled down, ultimately trying to fight off later groups of Indo-European invaders with whom they finally intermingled. Indo-European (Aryan) incursions into India increasingly threatened the later phases of Harappan civilization. Early Indo-Europeans used war chariots drawn by horses, but gradually they developed the equipment needed to ride horses directly.

Another early nomadic group that played an important role in larger world history, also from central Asia, was the Xiongnu, known in Europe as the Huns. The Hun invasions in China caused great devastation from the 4th century B.C.E. on. Like the Indo-Europeans before them, Hun movements

> Nomadic societies differed from hunter-gatherers and from agricultural groups, but would play a key role in world history.

nomads Cattle- and sheep-herding societies normally found on the fringes of civilized societies; commonly referred to as "barbarian" by civilized societies.

were probably initially due to droughts and internal warfare in central Asia, but then, achieving success, they took on a life of their own. Even before Hun invasions, Chinese rulers became very conscious of the nomadic peoples to their west, and sent out expeditions to meet and conciliate. They valued the nomads as a source of horses (not native to China) and also wanted to keep them happy; these were the reasons for offering gifts, such as silk, in a pattern that ultimately gave rise to a larger, interregional silk trading network—a specific example of the role nomads could play in wider historical processes.

Other early nomadic groups included reindeer herders in northern Europe (the Lapps). More important were the camel herders in Arabia and north central Africa. The camel was domesticated by 1700 B.C.E. as a pack animal. Its capacity for traveling with huge loads, for more than 20 days without new water, was ideal for nomadic life in the deserts. Cattle-raising nomads also played a role in parts of Africa.

Nomadic Society and Culture

Seasonal travel was fundamental to the nomadic way of life. Harsh weather forced movement in search of adequate food, and too much time in one place exhausted the available vegetation. Most nomadic groups usually traveled the same routes, year after year. But droughts or other hardships could promote change. While nomadic groups usually respected each other's routes, problems could cause conflicts as one group tried to muscle into the territory of another.

Animals formed the core of the cultural interests of nomadic societies, with religion usually emphasizing animal sacrifices. Size of herd was the measure of wealth in nomadic societies. Animals were also the core of the nomadic economy. Nomads traded in leather, wool, milk products, and bone sculptures.

The harshness of the nomadic environment, plus periodic warfare, often introduced a common note of violence into nomadic life. Most nomadic societies emphasized the importance of honor, or what anthropologists call courage culture. Strong, warlike men dominated, and their leadership was dependent on a willingness to meet physical challenge. Nomadic cultures valued heroic action above all other achievements. In addition to recognizing brave leaders, nomadic organization depended on kinship relations in small bands, usually of 30 to 150 people. These bands could, however, assemble into much larger groups in response to crisis.

Hospitality was another keynote of characteristic nomadic culture. Honor required that travelers be aided, a recognition of the harshness of the nomadic life. Acts of great generosity contributed to the reputation of leaders.

Nomads were outstanding fighters. Because their economic activity required much less time than that of agricultural peoples, there was more opportunity to train for battle. Easy familiarity with

---

DOCUMENT

Aryan Poetry in Praise of a War Horse

THE FOLLOWING EARLY VEDIC hymn exults in the power of a great Aryan war horse.

> Rushing to glory, to the capture of herds,
> Swooping down as a hungry falcon,
> Eager to be first, he darts amid the ranks of the chariots
> Happy as a bridegroom making a garland,
> Spurning the dust and champing at the bit.
> And the victorious steed and faithful,
> His body obedient to his driver in battle,
> Speeding on through the melee,
> Stirs up the dust to fall on his brows.
> And at his deep neigh, like the thunder of heaven,
> The foemen tremble in fear,

For he fights against thousands, and none can resist him,
So terrible is his charge.

QUESTIONS

- In what ways does this poem convey the Aryans' delight in warfare?
- What does it tell us about the way they fought their battles and their attitudes toward the herd animals that were so central to their culture?
- How does it convey the Aryans' ideals of manliness, heroism, and loyalty, and what does it say about their attitudes toward death?

horses (or other animals) made for excellent military skills as well. Nomads' ability to ride for long distances often allowed them to draw the armies of civilizations out, where, exhausted, they could later be picked off. This technique was used successfully against Persian armies in the 6th century B.C.E., in western Asia, and against the British in 19th-century Africa.

Because of their fighting skills, nomads had a reputation for cruelty. This was sometimes exaggerated, but not always. Hun invaders in China had drinking cups made from the skulls of defeated rivals. Some nomadic groups routinely killed the wives and children of leaders they defeated.

Nomadic societies were male dominated, with care of animals and skill in their use reserved for men. Marriages were arranged to promote the interests of kinship groups, although nomads liked to tell stories about great romance and love of beautiful women. Polygamy was common for wealthier men. Women's tasks, besides childrearing, involved making and breaking camp, cooking, and sewing. In a few nomadic societies, however, women held positions of greater prestige, occasionally even participating in wars and holding leadership positions.

Nomads and Civilizations

Nomads are particularly famous in history when they invade. Civilized peoples, from the Chinese to the Romans, feared and condemned nomads as offspring of evil spirits, the ultimate barbarians. Without question, nomadic invasions were important, particularly when they were part of larger migrations that could change the population structure as well as political leadership. The role of the Indo-Europeans in shaking up civilizations in the Middle East and India is obvious, and this basic pattern repeated in the classical and postclassical periods. We will discuss the unusually important impact of Mongol nomads in Chapter 15.

But nomads often had a peaceful, mutually beneficial relationship with agricultural societies, as in the exchange of goods with China, and this pattern had its own historical significance. Nomads often traded with farmers for useful goods, including vegetables, silks, and iron tools and weapons. In turn, the meat and milk products provided by the nomads could supplement meager diets for frontier farming communities. Nomads also provided warhorses for civilizations not only for China, but also for India, the Middle East, and sub-Saharan Africa.

THINKING HISTORICALLY

The Idea of Civilization in World Historical Perspective

THE BELIEF THAT THERE ARE FUNDAMENTAL differences between civilized and "barbaric" or "savage" peoples is very ancient and widespread. For thousands of years the Chinese set themselves off from cattle- and sheep-herding peoples of the vast plains to the north and west of China proper, whom they saw as barbarians. To the Chinese, being civilized was cultural, not biological or racial. If barbarians learned the Chinese language and adopted Chinese ways—from the clothes they wore to the food they ate—they were regarded as civilized.

A similar pattern of demarcation and cultural absorption was found among the American Indian peoples of present-day Mexico. Those who settled in the valleys of the mountainous interior, where they built great civilizations, lived in fear of invasions by

> **The word civilization is derived from the Latin word civilis, meaning "of the citizens."**

peoples they regarded as barbarous and called Chichimecs, meaning "sons of the dog." The latter were nomadic hunters and gatherers who periodically moved down from the desert regions of north Mexico into the fertile central valleys in search of game and settlements to pillage. The Aztecs were simply the last, and perhaps the fiercest, of a long line of Chichimec peoples who entered the valleys and conquered the urban-based empires that had developed there. But after the conquerors settled down, they adopted many of the religious beliefs and institutional patterns and much of the material culture of defeated peoples.

The word *civilization* is derived from the Latin word *civilis*, meaning "of the citizens." The term was coined by the Romans. They used it to distinguish between themselves as citizens of a

(continued on next page)

cosmopolitan, urban-based civilization and the "inferior" peoples who lived in the forests and deserts on the fringes of their Mediterranean empire. Centuries earlier, the Greeks, who had contributed much to the rise of Roman civilization, made a similar distinction between themselves and outsiders. Because the languages of the non-Greek peoples to the north of the Greek heartlands sounded like senseless babble to the Greeks, they lumped all the outsiders together as *barbarians*, which meant "those who cannot speak Greek." As in the case of the Chinese and Aztecs, the boundaries between civilized and barbarian for the Greeks and Romans were cultural, not biological. Regardless of the color of one's skin or the shape of one's nose, it was possible for free people to become members of a Greek *polis*—city-state—or to become Roman citizens by adopting Greek or Roman customs and swearing allegiance to the polis or the emperor.

Until the 17th and 18th centuries c.e., the priority given to cultural attributes (e.g., language, dress, manners) as the means by which civilized peoples set themselves off from barbaric ones was rarely challenged. But in those centuries, two major changes occurred among thinkers in western Europe. First, efforts were made not only to define the differences between civilized and barbarian but to identify a series of stages in human development that ranged from the lowest savagery to the highest civilization. Peoples such as the Chinese and the Arabs, who had created great cities, monumental architecture, writing, advanced technology, and large empires, usually won a place along with the Europeans near the top of these ladders of human achievement. Nomadic, cattle- and sheep-herding peoples, such as the Mongols of central Asia, usually were classified as barbarians. Civilized and barbarian peoples were then pitted against various sorts of savages. These ranged from the hunters and gatherers who inhabited much of North America and Australia to many peoples in Africa and Asia, whom the Europeans believed had not advanced beyond the most primitive stages of social and political development.

The second major shift in Western ideas about civilization began at the end of the 18th century but did not really take hold until a century later. In keeping with a growing emphasis in European thinking and social interaction on racial or biological differences, modes of human social organization and cultural expression were increasingly linked by historians and others to what were alleged to be the innate capacities of each human *race*. Although no one could agree on what a race was or how many races there were, most European writers argued that some races were more inventive, moral, courageous, and artistic—thus more capable of building civilizations—than others. Of course, white (or Caucasian) Europeans were considered by white European authors to be the most capable of all. The hierarchy from savage to civilized took on a color dimension, with white at the top, where the civilized peoples clustered, to yellow, red, brown, and black in descending order.

Some authors, including many prominent historians, sought to reserve all the attainments of civilization for whites, or peoples of European stock. As the evolutionary theories of thinkers such as Charles Darwin came into vogue in the late 1800s, race and level of cultural development were seen in the perspective of thousands of years of human change and adaptation rather than as being fixed in time. Nevertheless, this new perspective had little effect on the rankings of different human groups. Civilized whites were simply seen as having evolved much further than backward and barbaric peoples.

The perceived correspondence between race and level of development and the hardening of the boundaries between civilized and "inferior" peoples affected much more than intellectual discourse about the nature and history of human society. These beliefs were used to justify European imperialist expansion, which was seen as a "civilizing mission" aimed at uplifting barbaric and savage peoples across the globe. In the last half of the 19th century, virtually all non-Western peoples came to be dominated by the Europeans, who were confident that they, as representatives of the highest civilization ever created, were best equipped to govern lesser breeds of humans.

In the 21st century much of the intellectual baggage that once gave credibility to the racially embedded hierarchies of civilized and savage peoples has been discarded by most historians and other social scientists. A number of 20th-century developments, including the revolt of colonized peoples and the crimes committed by the Nazis before and during World War II in the name of racial purification, discredited racist thinking. In addition, these ideas have failed because racial supremacists cannot provide convincing proof of innate differences in mental and physical aptitude between various human groups. These trends, as well as research that has resulted in a much more sophisticated understanding of evolution, have led to the abandonment of rigid and self-serving 19th-century ideas about civilization. Historians in particular have increasingly adopted a less Eurocentric or culturally specific definition of civilization that encompasses varied cultures across the globe.

Perhaps the best way to avoid the tendency to define the term with reference to one's own society is to view civilization as we do in this world history as one of several human approaches to social organization rather than attempting to identify specific kinds of cultural achievement (e.g., writing, cities, monumental architecture). All peoples, from small bands of hunters and gatherers to farmers and factory workers, live in societies. All societies produce *cultures*: combinations of the ideas, objects, and patterns of behavior that result from human social interaction. But not all societies and cultures generate the surplus production that permits the levels of specialization, scale, and complexity that distinguish civilizations from other modes of social organization. All peoples are intrinsically capable of building civilizations, but many have lacked the resource base, historical circumstances, or desire to do so.

QUESTIONS

- Identify a society you consider civilized. What criteria did you use to determine that it was civilized?
- Can you apply those criteria to other societies?
- Can you think of societies that might not fit your criteria and yet be civilizations?
- Do the standards that you and others use reflect your own society's norms and achievements rather than neutral, more universal criteria?

Global Connections and Critical Themes

THE EARLY CIVILIZATIONS AND THE WORLD

The most important global contacts during the early periods of human history involved the spread of techniques and foods. The diffusion of agriculture and, later, the use of metals, from centers of initial invention, form the most important examples. Diffusion of this sort was usually slow, and we rarely know the precise connections involved. But foods also spread. For example, African farmers by 1000 B.C.E. were growing foods, including bananas, which originated in southeast Asia, which greatly enriched the variety available to them. Presumably this exchange occurred through Indian Ocean trade, but we do not know the mechanisms.

The most striking point about the early human experience, aside from the capacity to introduce a dramatically new economic system, involves the wide dispersion of peoples. Separate localities and regions formed, and for a long time local and regional factors shaped most of the human experience. Most polytheistic religions, for example, were local in specific beliefs and practices, even if they shared wider elements because of a common human need to explain forces of nature or the inevitability of death.

Further Readings

David Christian's *Maps of Time: An Introduction to Big History* (Berkeley, 2005) provides insight into perspectives on early human history; other rich accounts of human prehistory include John H. Morgan's *"In the Beginning—": The Paleolithic Origins of Religious Consciousness* (2007); Brian Fagan, *Peoples of the Earth* (1998 ed.); Pamela R. Willoughby, *The Evolution of Modern Humans in Africa: A Comprehensive Guide* (2007); Hawthorne Harris Wilder, *Man's Prehistoric Past* (2007); Peter S. Belwood, *The First Farmers: Origins of Agricultural Societies* (2005); and Andrew Jones, *Prehistoric Europe: Theory and Practice* (2008). See also Ronald Wright, *A Short History of Progress* (2004); John Mears, *Agricultural Origins in Global Perspective* (2000); Donald R. Kelley, "The Rise of Prehistory," *Journal of World History* (2003); www.historycooperative.org/jounals/jwh/14.1/kelley.html (2006); John Robb, *The Early Mediterranean Village: Agency, Material Culture, and Social Change in Neolithic Italy* (2007); Michael Balter, *The Goddess and The Bull: Çatalhöyük—An Archaeological Journey to the Dawn of Civilization* (2006); Marcel Mazoyer and Laurence Roudart, *A History of World Agriculture: From the Neolithic Age to the Current Crisis* (2006); Raymond Corbey and Wil Roebrocks, eds., *Studying Human Origins: Disciplinary History and Epistemology* (2001); Joy Hakim, *The First Americas* (1999); Chris Gosden, *Prehistory: A Very Short Introduction* (2003); and Steven Mithen, *After the Ice: A Global Human History, 20,000–5000 B.C.* (2004); and Barbara Sher Tinsley, *Reconstructing Western Civilization: Irreverent Essays on Antiquity* (2006).

On specific regions, see Douglas Price, *Europe's First Farmers* (2000); Ian Kuijt, *Life in Neolithic Farming Communities* (2000); R. Douglas Hurt, *Indian Agriculture in America* (1997); James Mellaart, *The Neolithic of the Near East* (1975); and Chris Scarre, ed., *Monuments and Landscape in Atlantic Europe* (2002). Jared Diamond's *Guns, Germs and Steel: The Fate of Human Societies* (1997) deals powerfully with agriculture. On debates over human nature (culture and genetics), see Matt Ridley's *Nature via Nurture* (2003). For a splendid guide to world history, from beginnings on, see Patrick Manning's *Navigating World History* (2003).

On MyHistoryLab

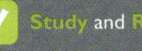

Study and Review on MyHistoryLab

Critical Thinking Questions

1. Compare nomadic societies and agricultural societies.
2. Why were people able to adapt to so many different environments?
3. What were the most significant disadvantages of agriculture?
4. Why did women not reject the imposition of patriarchal family structures?
5. Compare agriculture in the Americas to agriculture in Asia and Europe.
6. What was the impact of agriculture on the environment?

Early Civilizations, 3500–600 B.C.E.

2

Listen to Chapter 2 on MyHistoryLab

By 3000 B.C.E., Çatal Hüyük, the agricultural city discussed in Chapter 1, had become part of a civilization. Although many of the characteristics of civilization had existed by 6000 or 5000 B.C.E. in this Middle Eastern region, the origins of civilization, strictly speaking, approximately date to only 3500 B.C.E. From this point on to roughly 1000 B.C.E., the emergence of several civilization centers defined key developments in world history more generally. The first civilization arose in the Middle East along the banks of the Tigris and Euphrates rivers. Another center of civilization started soon

Read the Document on MyHistoryLab: Herodotus on the Egyptians

LEARNING OBJECTIVES

2.1 What were the main features of civilization as a form of human organization? p. 22

2.2 What did the river valley civilizations have in common? p. 23

2.3 How did Mesopotamian and Egyptian political structures compare? p. 27

2.4 How did Mesopotamian and Egyptian religions compare? p. 29

2.5 Why do we know less about Harappan civilization than about Egypt? p. 30

2.6 How does early China illustrate the main features of river valley civilizations? p. 32

2.7 How did conditions in the Americas differ from those in Asia and North Africa during the formation of early civilizations? p. 33

2.8 How and why did the early civilization period come to an end and what were the main religious changes introduced by Judaism? p. 35

FIGURE **2.1** This detail from Egyptian tomb art shows a husband and wife harvesting grain. As dictated by patriarchal values, the husband takes the lead in the work and the wife follows, but in Egypt, unlike Mesopotamia, men and women were depicted working together.

Watch the Video Series on MyHistoryLab

Learn about some key topics related to this chapter with the *MyHistoryLab Video Series: Key Topics in World History*

thereafter in northeast Africa (Egypt) (Figure 2.1), and a third by around 2500 B.C.E. along the banks of the Indus River in northwestern India. These three early centers of civilization had some interaction. The fourth early civilization center arose in China along the Yellow River, although a bit later and more separately. A fifth center would emerge in Central America, though it was not river based.

CIVILIZATION

> The emergence of civilization occurred in many, although not all, agricultural societies. Early civilizations formed in Mesopotamia, Egypt, the Indus River basin, China, and the Americas.

2.1 What were the main features of civilization as a form of human organization?

After the rise of agriculture, the introduction of **civilization** as a form of human organization was a crucial step for many people. Civilization first developed in Mesopotamia, after about 3500 B.C.E., on the heels of several changes in technology and communication. This form of human organization spread to several other places, and separately developed in China and Central America. Human organization along civilization lines did not emerge everywhere at the same time, and many regions—even some successful agricultural economies—avoided it altogether, at least until much more recently. Hunting-and-gathering and nomadic societies lacked the economic surplus necessary to develop civilization and often actively disliked the constraints they saw in civilization as well.

Civilizations normally demonstrated four distinctive features, operating powerfully in combination. First, they developed greater amounts of economic surplus, beyond subsistence needs, and they distributed this surplus unequally. This provided funds for new kinds of monuments. It also heightened social inequalities, compared to other "non-civilized" kinds of societies. Second, civilizations developed formal governments with at least small bureaucracies. Leadership thus became more specialized than in simpler agricultural or nomadic societies. Third, almost all civilizations, including all the early ones, had writing. This facilitated trade over long distances by facilitating standardized communication; it enhanced recordkeeping, which aided both commerce and bureaucracy. And fourth, they developed larger and more important urban centers as cities emerged as concentrations of populations.

In agricultural civilizations, most people lived in the countryside, and most people remained illiterate. But cities and writing were nonetheless influential in shaping societies with different characteristics from those of the earliest agricultural settlements.

There are problems with the definition of *civilization*. Some scholars prefer to use a smaller number of criteria, which would allow other societies—those that had surpluses and some formal leadership, for example, but not cities and writing—to be included as civilizations.

More serious is the common connotation of *civilization* as being better than other systems of human organization. Leaders of early civilizations often argued that their way of life was more cultivated than that of non-civilized peoples—barbarians—around them. But people in civilizations could be cruel and rude. To groups such as North American Indians, encountering Europeans in the 17th century, the behavior of the "civilized"—including drinking and violently spanking children—seemed far cruder than their own, whose habits and capacities for emotional control were often quite refined. Civilization as meaning greater impulse control should not be included in the definition of *civilization* as a form of human organization. The two meanings might, but also might very well not, overlap. Civilizations also increased human impact on the environment, another arguably "bad" result. For example, the first center of copper production in Europe, along the Danube valley, led to such deforestation that the fuel supply was destroyed, and the industry collapsed after about 3000 B.C.E. The extensive agriculture needed to support Indus river cities opened the land to erosion and flooding because of overuse of the soil and removal of trees.

civilization Societies distinguished by reliance on sedentary agriculture, ability to produce food surpluses, and existence of nonfarming elites, as well as merchant and manufacturing groups.

5000 B.C.E.	1000 B.C.E.	500 B.C.E.
5000 Plant domestication becoming widespread **4000** Maize domesticated in Mexico **c. 3000–1500** Evidence of cotton cultivation, metallurgy, ceramics **2000 B.C.E.–500 C.E.** Early cultures in southwestern United States **2000** Pottery in use in Mesoamerica **1800–1200** Ceremonial centers in the highlands of southern Mexico **1500–800** Olmec civilization flourishes	**900** Maya civilization beginnings; classic period in Mesoamerica **850–250** Early Horizon; Chavín culture flourishes **300 B.C.E.–900 C.E.** Height of Maya civilization **200 B.C.E.–500 C.E.** Nazca culture	**100** Germans in southern Germany, on Roman borders

Is the term *civilization* too misleading with its implications of progress and superiority? Is there another term that would be more accurate, while still covering the important organizational changes involved? One final caution: Areas where early civilization developed covered only a tiny portion of the inhabited parts of the world, although they were the most densely populated. The early civilizations, all clustered in key river valleys, were in a way pilot tests of the new form of social organization. Only after about 1000 B.C.E. did a more consistent process of development and spread of civilization begin. However, the great civilizations unquestionably built on the achievements of the river valley pioneers, so some understanding of this contribution to the list of early human accomplishments is essential.

> Mesopotamian civilization pioneered basic forms of civilization, from an urban economy to writing. Frequent invasions contributed to distinctive religious belief and political systems.

TIGRIS-EUPHRATES CIVILIZATION

2.2 What did the river valley civilizations have in common?

As new organizational forms, the earliest civilizations introduced innovations that most of us now take for granted—writing; formal codes of law; city planning and architecture; and institutions for trade, including the use of money. Once developed, most of these building blocks of human organization did not have to be reinvented, although in some cases they spread only slowly to other parts of the world.

It is not surprising then, given its lead in agriculture, metalworking, and village structure, that the Middle East generated the first example of human civilization. Indeed, the first civilization, founded in the valley of the Tigris and Euphrates rivers in a part of the Middle East long called **Mesopotamia** (Map 2.1), forms one of only a few cases of a civilization developed absolutely from scratch—and with no examples from any place else to imitate. (Chinese civilization and civilization in Central America also developed independently.) By 4000 B.C.E., the farmers of Mesopotamia were familiar with bronze and copper working and had already invented the wheel for transportation. They had a well-established pottery industry and interesting artistic forms. Farming in this area, because of the need for irrigation, required considerable coordination among communities, and this in turn served as the basis for complex political structures.

By about 3500 B.C.E., a people who had recently invaded this region, the **Sumerians**, developed a **cuneiform** system, the first known case of human writing (Figures 2.2 and 2.3). Their system at first used different pictures to represent various objects but soon shifted to the use of geometric shapes to symbolize spoken sounds. Early Sumerian writing may have had as many as 2000 such symbols, but this number was later reduced to about 300, as later people adapted the system for their own

Mesopotamia Literally "between the rivers"; the civilizations that arose in the alluvial plain of the Tigris and Euphrates river valleys.

Sumerians People who migrated into Mesopotamia c. 4000 B.C.E.; created first civilization within region; organized area into city-states.

cuneiform [kyoo-NAY-uh-form] A form of writing developed by the Sumerians using a wedge-shaped stylus and clay tablets.

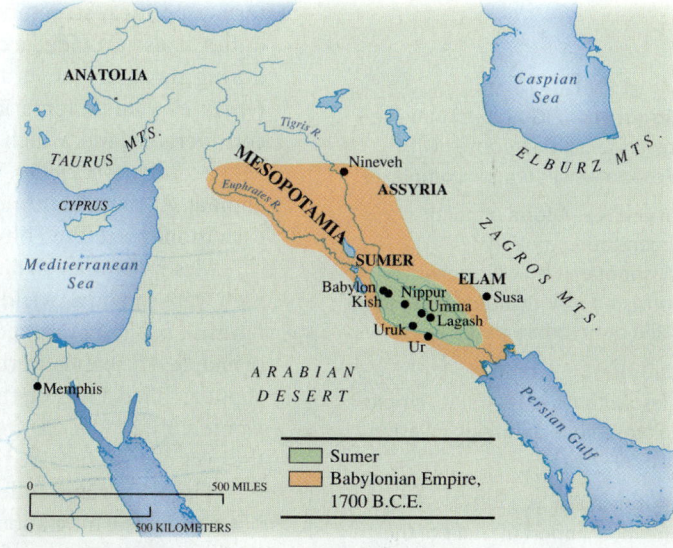

MAP 2.1 Early Sumer The civilization fanned out along the Tigris and Euphrates rivers.

CHAPTER 2 Early Civilizations, 3500–600 B.C.E. 23

FIGURE 2.2 One of the early uses of writing was to mark property boundaries. This picture shows cuneiform writing on a Mesopotamian map from about 1300 B.C.E. The map focuses on defining the king's estate, with sections for priests and for key gods such as Marduk. In what ways did writing improve property maps?

ziggurats [ZIG-uh-rats] Massive towers usually associated with Mesopotamian temple complexes.

city-state A form of political organization typical of Mesopotamian civilizations; consisted of agricultural hinterlands ruled by an urban-based king.

Babylonians Unified all of Mesopotamia c. 1800 B.C.E.; empire collapsed due to foreign invasion c. 1600 B.C.E.

Hammurabi (r. 1792–1750 B.C.E.) The most important ruler of the Babylonian empire; responsible for codification of law.

languages. Even so, writing and reading remained complex skills, which only a few had time to master. Scribes wrote on clay tablets, using styluses shaped quite like the modern ballpoint pen.

Sumerian art developed steadily as statues and painted frescoes were used to adorn the temples of the gods. Statues of the gods also decorated individual homes. Sumerian science aided a complex agricultural society, as people sought to learn more about the movement of the sun and stars—thus founding the science of astronomy—and improved their mathematical knowledge. (Astronomy defined the calendar and provided the astrological forecasts widely used in politics and religion.) The Sumerians employed a system of numbers based on units of 10, 60, and 360 that we still use in calculating circles and hours. In other words, Sumerians and their successors in Mesopotamia created patterns of observation and abstract thought about nature that a number of civilizations, including our own, still rely on, and they also introduced specific systems, such as charts of major constellations, that have been in use, at least among educated people, for 5000 years not only in the Middle East but, by later imitation, in India and Europe as well.

Sumerians developed complex religious rituals. Each city had a patron god and erected impressive shrines to please and honor this and other deities. Massive towers, called **ziggurats**, formed the first monumental architecture in this civilization. Professional priests operated these temples and conducted the rituals within. Sumerians believed in many powerful gods, for the nature on which their agriculture depended often seemed swift and unpredictable. Prayers and offerings to prevent floods as well as to protect good health were a vital part of Sumerian life. Sumerian ideas about the divine force in natural objects—in rivers, trees, and mountains—were common among early agricultural peoples; a religion of this sort, which sees gods in many aspects of nature, is known as *polytheism*. More specifically, Sumerian religious notions, notably their ideas about the gods' creation of the earth from water and about the divine punishment of humans through floods, later influenced the writers of the Old Testament and thus continue to play a role in Jewish, Christian, and Muslim cultures. Sumerian religious ideas also included a belief in an afterlife of punishment—an original version of the concept of hell.

Sumerian political structures stressed tightly organized **city-states**, ruled by a king who claimed divine authority. The Sumerian state had carefully defined boundaries, unlike the less formal territories of precivilized villages in the region. Here is a key early example of how civilization and a more formal political structure came together. The government helped regulate religion and enforce its duties; it also provided a court system in the interests of justice. Kings were originally military leaders during times of war, and the function of defense and war, including leadership of a trained army, remained vital in Sumerian politics. Kings and the noble class, along with the priesthood, controlled considerable land, which was worked by slaves. Thus began a tradition of slavery that long marked Middle Eastern societies. Warfare remained vital to ensure supplies of slaves, taken as prisoners during combat. At the same time, slavery was in a variable state of existence, and many slaves were able to earn money and even buy their freedom.

Mesopotamian civilization developed a strongly patriarchal family structure. By 3000 B.C.E., only men were shown as wielding a plow in Middle Eastern art. Laws insisted that women remain sexually faithful, but they granted greater latitude to men. Women had a few legal protections, at least in principle: Husbands were supposed to support their wives, and wives could legitimately leave if this support failed. Outside the law, customs developed, particularly in the cities, that further marked off women. By 2000 B.C.E., veiling of respectable women became common, in order to shield them from the eyes of men outside their family.

The Sumerians added to their region's agricultural prosperity not only by using wheeled carts but also by learning about fertilizers and by adopting silver as a means of exchange for buying and selling—an early form of money. However, the region was also hard to defend and proved a constant temptation to outside invaders from Sumerian times to the present. The Sumerians themselves fell to a people called the Akkadians around 2400 B.C.E. The Akkadians continued much of Sumerian culture. It was an Akkadian king, Sargon, who came to be the first identifiable figure in world history, in terms of surviving records. He unified the empire and added to Sumerian art the theme of royal victory. Sargon maintained 5400 troops, a larger professional army than had existed before. Akkadians sent troops as far as Egypt and Ethiopia.

After about 200 years, another period of decline was followed by conquest by the Babylonians, who extended their own empire and thus helped bring civilization to other parts of the Middle East. It was under Babylonian rule that the king **Hammurabi** introduced the most famous early code of law, boasting of his purpose:

> to promote the welfare of the people, me Hammurabi, the devout, god-fearing prince, to cause justice to prevail in the land, to destroy the wicked and the evil, that the strong might not oppress the weak.

Hammurabi's code established rules of procedure for courts of law and regulated property rights and the duties of family members, setting harsh punishments for crimes.

For many centuries during and after the heyday of Babylon, Middle Eastern societies were troubled by the invasions of hunting and herding groups. Indo-European peoples pressed in from the north, starting about 2100 B.C.E. In the Middle East itself, invasions by Semitic peoples from the south were more important, and Semitic people and languages increasingly dominated the region. The new arrivals adopted the culture of the conquered peoples as their own, so the key features of the civilization persisted. But large political units declined in favor of smaller city-states or regional kingdoms, particularly during the centuries of greatest turmoil, between 1200 and 900 B.C.E. Thereafter, new invaders, first the Assyrians and then the Persians, created large new empires in the Middle East.

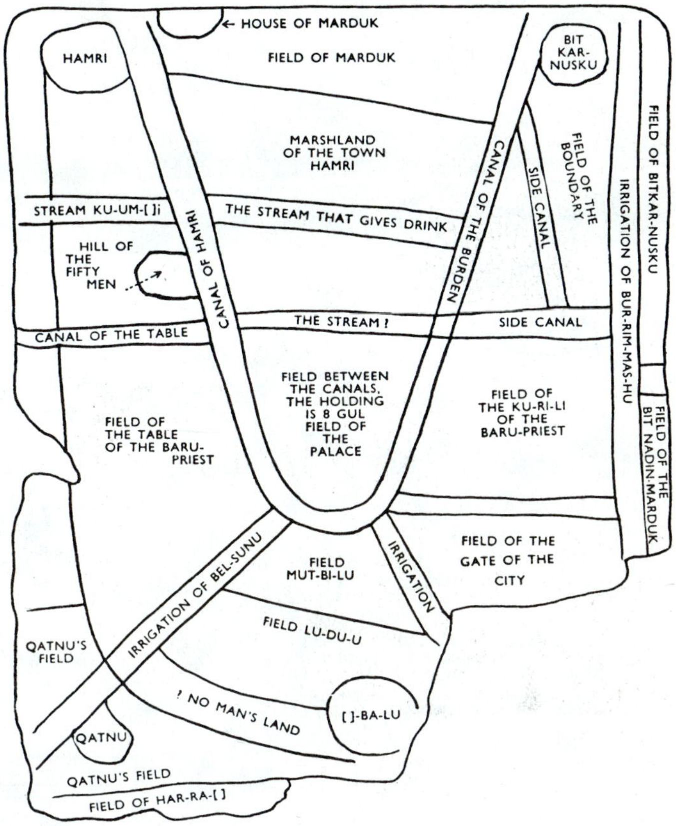

FIGURE **2.3** A translation of the map shown in Figure 2.2. (University of Pennsylvania Museum of Archaeology and Anthropology. Neg. #S4-13970)

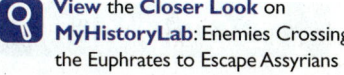
View the **Closer Look** on **MyHistoryLab**: Enemies Crossing the Euphrates to Escape Assyrians

VISUALIZING THE PAST

Mesopotamia in Maps

THE MESOPOTAMIAN CIVILIZATIONS STEADILY EXPANDED FROM their roots in the fertile valley between the Tigris and Euphrates rivers throughout their centuries of existence. Reading the maps can help explain the nature of the civilizations in the region.

This map shows the location of Sumer and two later empires in the Middle East and eastern Mediterranean.

QUESTIONS

- What do these maps suggest about the relationship between Mesopotamian civilizations and the topography of the Middle East?
- Does geography suggest reasons for invasion and political instability in this civilization center?
- Did later empires in the region have the same relationship to river valleys as did the earlier states?
- What were the potential contacts between Mesopotamia and other river valley civilization centers?
- Why has the Middle East been so significant in European, African, and Asian history?

(continued on next page)

CHAPTER 2 Early Civilizations, 3500–600 B.C.E. **25**

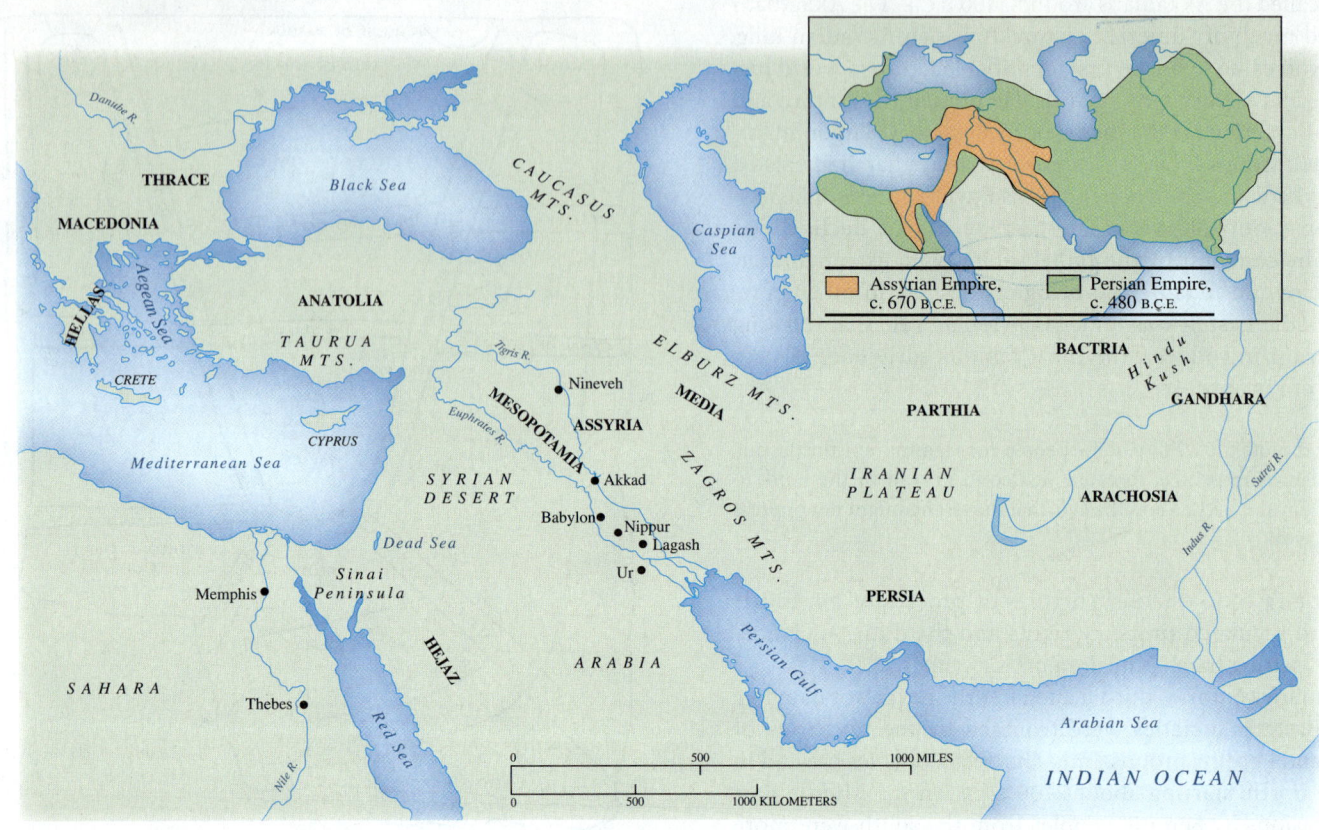

MAP 2.2 **Mesopotamia in Maps** This map shows the location of Sumer and two later empires in the Middle East and eastern Mediterranean.

DOCUMENT

Hammurabi's Law Code

HAMMURABI, AS KING OF BABYLON, UNITED MESOPOTAMIA under his rule from about 1800 to 1750 B.C.E. His law code, the earliest such compilation still in existence, was discovered on a stone slab in Iran in 1901 C.E. Not a systematic presentation, it was a collection of exemplary cases designed to set general standards of justice. The code provides vital insights into the nature of social relations and family structure in this ancient civilization. Examples of the Hammurabic code follow:

> When Marduk commanded me to give justice to the people of the land and to let [them] have [good] governance, I set forth truth and justice throughout the land [and] prospered the people.
> At that time:
> If a man has accused a man and has charged him with manslaughter and then has not proved [it against] him, his accuser shall be put to death.
>
> If a man has charged a man with sorcery and then has not proved [it against] him, he who is charged with the sorcery shall go to the holy river; he shall leap into the holy river and, if the holy river overwhelms him, his accuser shall take and keep his house; if the holy river proves that man clear [of the offense] and he comes back safe, he who has charged him with sorcery shall be put to death; he who leapt into the holy river shall take and keep the house of his accuser.
> If a man has come forward in a case to bear witness to a felony and then has not proved the statement that he has made, if that case [is] a capital one, that man shall be put to death.
> If he has come forward to bear witness to [a claim for] corn or money, he shall remain liable for the penalty for that suit.
> If a judge has tried a suit, given a decision, caused a sealed tablet to be executed, [and] thereafter varies his judgment, they shall convict that judge of varying [his] judgment and he shall pay twelvefold the claim in that suit; then they shall remove him

from his place on the bench of judges in the assembly, and he shall not [again] sit in judgment with the judges.

If a free person helps a slave to escape, the free person will be put to death.

If a man has committed robbery and is caught, that man shall be put to death.

If the robber is not caught, the man who has been robbed shall formally declare whatever he has lost before a god, and the city and the mayor in whose territory or district the robbery has been committed shall replace whatever he has lost for him.

If [it is] the life [of the owner that is lost], the city or the mayor shall pay one maneh of silver to his kinsfolk.

If a person owes money and Adad [the river god] has flooded the person's field, the person will not give any grain [tax] or pay any interest in that year.

If a person is too lazy to make the dike of his field strong and there is a break in the dike and water destroys his own farmland, that person will make good the grain [tax] that is destroyed.

If a merchant increases interest beyond that set by the king and collects it, that merchant will lose what was lent.

If a trader borrows money from a merchant and then denies the fact, that merchant in the presence of god and witnesses will prove the trader borrowed the money and the trader will pay the merchant three times the amount borrowed.

If the husband of a married lady has accused her but she is not caught lying with another man, she shall take an oath by the life of a god and return to her house.

If a man takes himself off and there is not the [necessary] maintenance in his house, his wife [so long as] her [husband is delayed] shall keep [herself chaste; she shall not] enter [another man's house].

If that woman has not kept herself chaste but enters another man's house, they shall convict that woman and cast her into the water.

If a son strikes his father, they shall cut off his forehand.

If a man has put out the eye of a free man, they shall put out his eye.

If he breaks the bone of a [free] man, they shall break his bone.

If he puts out the eye of a villain or breaks the bone of a villain, he shall pay one maneh of silver.

If he puts out the eye of a [free] man's slave or breaks the bone of a [free] man's slave, he shall pay half his price.

If a man knocks out the tooth of a [free] man equal [in rank] to him[self], they shall knock out his tooth.

If he knocks out the tooth of a villain, he shall pay one-third maneh of silver.

If a man strikes the cheek of a [free] man who is superior [in rank] to him[self], he shall be beaten with 60 stripes with a whip of ox-hide in the assembly.

If the man strikes the cheek of a free man equal to him[self in rank], he shall pay one maneh of silver.

If a man strikes the cheek of a villain, he shall pay ten shekels of silver.

If the slave of a [free] man strikes the cheek of a free man, they shall cut off his ear.

QUESTIONS
- What can you tell from the Hammurabic code about the social and family structure of Mesopotamia?
- What is the relationship between law and trade?
- Why did agricultural civilizations such as Babylon insist on harsh punishments for crimes?
- What religious and magical beliefs does the document suggest?
- Using specific examples, show how interpreting this document for significant historical meaning differs from simply reading it.

EGYPTIAN CIVILIZATION

2.3 How did Mesopotamian and Egyptian political structures compare?

A second center of civilization sprang up in northern Africa, along the Nile River. Egyptian civilization, formed by 3000 B.C.E., benefited from the trade and technological influence of Mesopotamia, but it produced quite a different society and culture. Less open to invasion, Egypt retained a unified state throughout most of its history. With some fluctuations, the kingdom lasted almost 3000 years, although its period of greatest vitality had passed by 1000 B.C.E. Farming had developed along the Nile by about 5000 B.C.E., but economic activity increased before 3200, in part because of greater trade with Mesopotamia. This acceleration provided the basis for the formation of regional kingdoms and soon a unified empire along the great river.

Because of its early unity and its cohesion along the banks of the Nile, Egypt had fewer problems with political unity than Mesopotamia did. The king, or **pharaoh**, possessed immense power. The Egyptian economy was more fully government directed than its Mesopotamian counterpart, which had a more independent business class. Government control may have been necessary because of the complexity of coordinating irrigation along the Nile. It nonetheless resulted in godlike status for the pharaohs, who built splendid tombs for themselves—the **pyramids**—from 2700 B.C.E. on. During

Egypt, in northeastern Africa, benefited from Mesopotamian trade and technology. The Egyptians developed a different, and more stable, version of civilization.

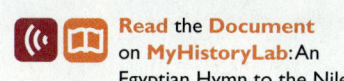
Read the Document on MyHistoryLab: An Egyptian Hymn to the Nile

pharaoh Title of kings of ancient Egypt.

pyramids Monumental architecture typical of Old Kingdom Egypt; used as burial sites for pharaohs.

MAP 2.3 **Egypt, Kush, and Axum, Successive Dynasties** As Egypt weakened, kingdoms farther up the Nile and deeper into Africa rose in importance.

Kush An African state that developed along the upper reaches of the Nile c. 1000 B.C.E.; conquered Egypt and ruled it for several centuries.

Read the Document on MyHistoryLab: Egyptian Folk Tale, c. 2000 B.C.E.

FIGURE 2.4 The statue known to the West as the *Sphinx* and to the Arabs as the *Father of Terror* has the head of a man, wearing the royal headdress of ancient Egypt, and the body of a lion. At 200 feet long and 65 feet tall, it was the largest single-stone statue in the ancient world. Exactly who built it and when is unknown, but it is believed to have been constructed as the guardian of the Necropolis at Giza (home of the Great Pyramids) and a symbol of the power of the pharaohs.

periods of weak rule and occasional invasions, Egyptian society suffered a decline, but revivals kept the framework of Egyptian civilization intact until after 1000 B.C.E (Map 2.3). At key points, Egyptian influence spread up the Nile to the area now known as Sudan, with an impact on the later development of African culture. The kingdom of **Kush** interacted with Egypt and invaded it at some points.

Neither Egyptian science nor the Egyptian alphabet was as elaborate as its Mesopotamian equal, although mathematics was more advanced in this civilization. Egyptian art was exceptionally lively; cheerful and colorful pictures decorated not only the tombs—where the belief in an afterlife made people want to be surrounded by objects of beauty—but also palaces and furnishings. Egyptian architectural forms were also quite influential, not only in Egypt but in other parts of the Mediterranean as well. Egyptian mathematics produced the idea of a day divided into 24 hours, and here too Egypt influenced the development of later Mediterranean cultures.

The most famous Egyptian art form was of course the pyramid, which the pharaohs built to house themselves and their families after death (Figure 2.4). The largest pyramids required labor forces of up to 100,000 people, and they were amazing achievements given the state of Egyptian technology. Workers rolled the huge stones, weighing more than five tons, over logs and onto Nile barges. The pyramids attested to royal power. They also illustrated Egypt's ability to generate agricultural surpluses and to command a labor force.

Egypt interacted periodically with the Middle East, but the contacts were not very influential in either direction. Egypt's interactions with the upper reaches of the Nile, deeper into Africa, were more significant. After about 1570 B.C.E., in the final main phase of the great kingdoms, Egypt also expanded trade with the islands of the eastern Mediterranean, which extended the empire's influence to southern Europe, particularly in terms of monumental art but also in the area of mathematics.

28 PART I Early Human Societies, 2.5 million–600 B.C.E.: Origins and Development

EGYPT AND MESOPOTAMIA COMPARED

2.4 How did Mesopotamian and Egyptian religions compare?

> By comparing the two first civilizations, we can highlight their differences as well as their important similarities.

Comparisons in politics, culture, economics, and society suggest that the two civilizations varied substantially because of largely separate origins and environments. The distinction in overall tone was striking, with Egypt more stable and optimistic than Mesopotamia not only in its beliefs about gods and the afterlife but also in the colorful and lively pictures the Egyptians emphasized in their decorative art. The distinction in internal history was also striking: Egyptian civilization was far less marked by disruption than its Mesopotamian counterpart.

Egypt and Mesopotamia differed in many ways, thanks to variations in geography, exposure to outside invasion and influence, and different beliefs. Despite trade and war, they did not imitate each other much. Egypt emphasized strong central authority, whereas Mesopotamian politics shifted more often over a substructure of regional city-states. Mesopotamian art focused on less monumental structures and embraced a literary element that Egyptian art lacked.

The economies differed as well. Mesopotamia developed more technological improvements because the environment was more difficult to manage than the Nile valley. Trade contacts were more wide ranging, and the Mesopotamians gave considerable attention to a merchant class and commercial law.

Social differences between the two civilizations are less obvious because we have less information on daily life for this early period. It is probable, though, that the status of women was higher in Egypt than in Mesopotamia (where women's position seems to have deteriorated after Sumer). Egyptians seem to have paid great respect to women, at least in the upper classes, in part because marriage alliances were vital to the preservation and stability of the monarchy. Vivid love poetry indicated a high regard for emotional relations between men and women. Also, Egyptian religion included more pronounced deference to goddesses as sources of creativity. Egyptians did not practice female infanticide—the killing of baby girls—which most societies used for population control.

Differences were not the whole story; as river valley civilizations, Egypt and Mesopotamia shared important features. Both emphasized social stratification, with a noble, land-owning class at the top

---

THINKING HISTORICALLY

Women in Patriarchal Societies

IN CONTRAST TO HUNTING-AND-GATHERING SOCIETIES, agricultural civilizations were generally *patriarchal*; that is, they were not only run by men but were based on the assumption that men directed political, economic, and cultural life. Furthermore, as agricultural civilizations developed and became more prosperous and more elaborately organized, the status of women increasingly deteriorated.

Patriarchal family structure rested on men's control of most or all property, starting with land. Marriage was based on property relationships, and it was assumed that marriage, and therefore subordination to men, was the normal condition for women. A revealing symptom of patriarchy in families was the fact that after marrying, a woman usually moved to the orbit (and often the residence) of her husband's family.

Characteristic patriarchal conditions developed in Mesopotamian civilization. Thus, in Sumerian law, the adultery of a wife was punishable by death, whereas a husband's adultery was treated far more lightly—a double standard characteristic of patriarchalism. Mesopotamian societies after Sumerian times began to emphasize the importance of a woman's virginity at marriage and to require women to wear veils in public to emphasize their modesty. A good portion of Mesopotamian law (such as the Hammurabic code) was devoted to prescriptions for women,

> *A good portion of Mesopotamian law (such as the Hammurabic code) was devoted to prescriptions for women, ensuring certain basic protections but clearly emphasizing limits and inferiority.*

(continued on next page)

ensuring certain basic protections but clearly emphasizing limits and inferiority.

Patriarchal conditions varied from one agricultural civilization to another. Egyptian civilization gave women, at least in the upper classes, considerable credit and witnessed several powerful queens. Nefertiti, wife of Akhenaton, seems to have been influential in the religious disputes during his reign; artistic works suggest her religious role. Some agricultural societies traced descendants from mothers rather than from fathers. This was true of Jewish law, for example. But even these matrilineal societies held women to be inferior to men; for example, Jewish law insisted that men and women worship separately, with men occupying the central temple space. These variations are important, but they usually operated within a basic framework of patriarchalism. It was around 2000 B.C.E. that an Egyptian writer, Ptah Hotep, put patriarchal beliefs as clearly as anyone in the early civilizations: "If you are a man of note, found for yourself a household, and love your wife at home, as it beseems. Fill her belly, clothe her back.... But hold her back from getting the mastery."

As agriculture improved with the use of better techniques, women's labor, though still vital, became less important than it had been in hunting-and-gathering or early agricultural societies. This was particularly true in the upper classes and in cities, where men often took over the most productive work (e.g., craft production or political leadership). The inferior position of women in the upper classes, relative to men, usually was more marked than in peasant villages, where women's labor remained essential.

Patriarchalism raises important questions about women themselves: Why did they put up with it? Many women internalized the culture of patriarchalism, holding that it was their job to obey and to serve men and accepting arguments that their aptitudes were inferior to those of men. But patriarchalism did not preclude some important options for women. In many societies, a minority of women could gain expression through religious tasks, such as prayer or service in ceremonies. These could allow them to act independently of family structures. Patriarchal laws defined some rights for women even within marriage, protecting them in theory from the worst abuses. Babylonian law, for example, gave women as well as men the right to divorce under certain conditions when the spouse had not lived up to obligations. Women could also wield informal power in patriarchal societies by their emotional hold over husbands or sons. Such power was indirect, behind the scenes, but a forceful woman might use these means to figure prominently in a society's history. Women also could form networks, if only within a large household. Older women, who commanded the obedience of many daughters-in-law and unmarried daughters, could shape the activities of the family.

Patriarchalism was a commanding theme in most agricultural civilizations from the early centuries on. Its enforcement, through law and culture, was one means by which societies tried to achieve order. In many agricultural civilizations, patriarchalism dictated that boys, because of their importance in carrying on the family name and the chief economic activities, were more likely to survive: When population excess threatened a family or a community, female infants sometimes were killed as a means of population control.

---

and masses of peasants and slaves at the bottom. A powerful priestly group also figured in the elite. Although specific achievements in science differed, both civilizations emphasized astronomy and related mathematics and produced durable findings about units of time and measurement. Both Mesopotamia and Egypt changed slowly by more modern standards. Having developed successful political and economic systems, both societies tended strongly toward conservation. Change, when it came, usually was brought by outside forces (natural disasters or invasions).

Finally, both civilizations left important heritages in their regions and adjacent territories. Several smaller civilization centers were launched under the impetus of Mesopotamia and Egypt, and some produced important innovations of their own by about 1000 B.C.E.

RIVER VALLEY CIVILIZATION IN INDIA

2.5 Why do we know less about Harappan civilization than about Egypt?

> Between about 2500 and 1600 B.C.E., the two great cities uncovered thus far and numerous towns of Harappan civilization flourished in the Indus River valley. As in the Fertile Crescent, environmental change, natural calamities, and successive nomadic migrations brought about the irretrievable decline of Harappa in the middle centuries of the 2nd millennium B.C.E.

Indus River River sources in Himalayas to mouth in Arabian Sea; location of Harappan civilization.

Harappa Along with Mohenjodaro, major urban complex of the Harappan civilization; laid out on planned grid pattern.

River valley civilizations developed in two other centers. Early civilization in the northeastern part of the Indian subcontinent—today known as Pakistan—developed impressive urban structures. Trade with the Middle East was active. The civilization ultimately did not endure, however, and for various reasons—including the inability to decipher the writing system—less is known about this society than about Egypt or Mesopotamia. Early civilization in China cropped up a bit later and is also shrouded in some mystery; but this society transmitted cultural values more directly to subsequent Chinese history than was the case in any other region, so it deserves attention.

A prosperous urban civilization emerged along the **Indus River** by 2500 B.C.E., supporting several large cities, including **Harappa** (Map 2.4). Here was another case where contacts helped support the expansion of early civilization: Harappa had extensive trade relations with Mesopotamia. Harappa featured elaborate urban facilities, with houses benefitting from running water. Toilets, in fact, connected to citywide drainage systems, were perhaps the first that humans ever invented. The important trading contacts with Mesopotamia did not prevent the development of a distinctive alphabet and artistic forms. The large cities, including Harappa itself, contained buildings that were probably for religious ceremonies or community assemblies. Public baths were also available. Governments stored grain for times of shortage and for festival days. Trade was extensive, and precious stones from China and southeast Asia have been found. Priests had great power in this civilization, serving as intermediaries between the people and the gods and goddesses who were believed to control fertility.

For all their achievements, the Harappan people seem to have been somewhat conservative. Although they used bronze, they did not keep up with the tools available in Mesopotamia, even though they had contact with this area. Notably, they did not manufacture swords, relying on bronze-tipped arrows instead. They became vulnerable to attack.

Harappa remains something of a mystery. Its ruins began to be discovered only in the mid-19th century, when it became clear that this had been a major center of ancient civilization but also rather unlike what later developed in India, for example, in terms of the styles of writing. We also do not fully know what caused the civilization to gradually decline after about 1500 B.C.E. The decline resulted from several factors, including massive flooding. Invasions and, even more, migrations by a cattle-herding people, the Indo-Europeans, probably challenged the control of the priestly group. Some violence was involved, and skeletons with crushed skulls and in postures of flight, either from invaders or from floods, have been found. Environmental changes were almost certainly a greater problem, with excessive forest-cutting leading to the creation of desert conditions and saltier soils.

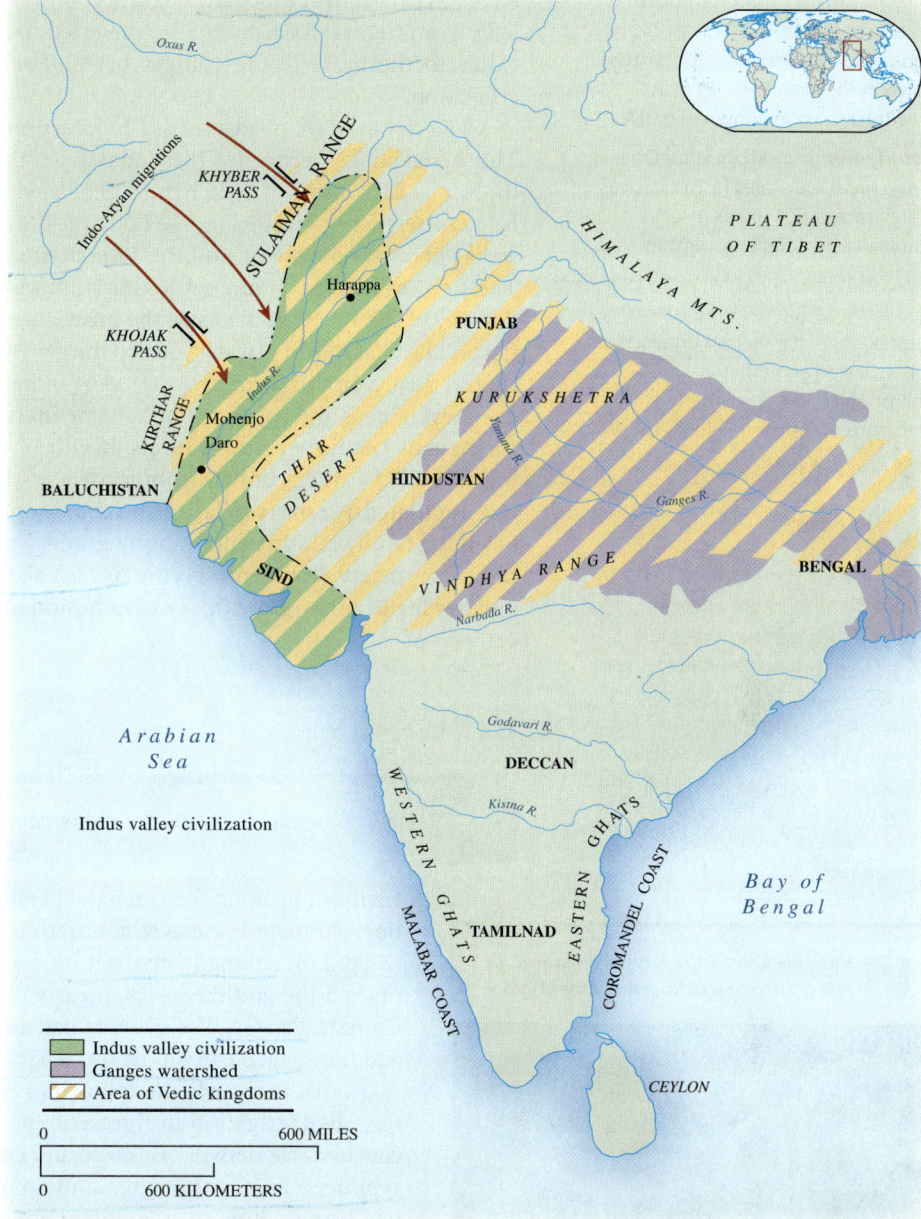

MAP 2.4 **India in the Age of Harappa and the Early Aryan Migrations** Although South Asia's first civilization was located in the Indus valley in the northwest, the Aryan invasions from southwest Asia led to extensive settlement in the Ganges valley to the east and to internal migrations that gave rise to the splendid Dravidian civilization in the Deccan and Tamilland further south.

Historians continue to debate how the factors involved compare with other cases of civilization decline. The Harappan decline resulted in such complete destruction of this culture—the Indo-Europeans were not initially interested in cities—that we know little about its nature or its subsequent influence on India. It remains true that civilization never had to be fully reinvented in India. The Indo-European migrants combined their religious and political ideas with those that had taken root in the early cities. In recent times, Indians' pride in their early civilized history has become an important part of their national identity.

After Harappa's Fall

The fall of Harappa was followed by a long transitional period in the history of the Indian subcontinent. This period is sometimes called the Vedic and Epic ages, because important cultural developments centered on the creation of elaborate epic poems. During these centuries, from about 1500 to 700

Aryans Indo-European nomadic pastoralists who replaced Harappan civilization; militarized society.

Vedas Aryan hymns originally transmitted orally but written down in sacred books from the 6th century B.C.E.

▶ Watch the Video: The Aryans in India (Howard Spodek)

CHAPTER 2 Early Civilizations, 3500–600 B.C.E. **31**

Mahabharata [muh-hah-BUH-uh-tuh] Indian epic of war, princely honor, love, and social duty; written down in the last centuries B.C.E.; previously handed down in oral form.

Ramayana [ruh-MEYE-ehn] One of the great epic tales from classical India; traces adventures of King Rama and his wife, Sita; written 4th to 2nd centuries B.C.E.

Upanishads [oo-PAHN-uh-shadz] Later books of the Vedas; contained sophisticated and sublime philosophical ideas; utilized by Brahmans to restore religious authority.

 Read the **Document** on **MyHistoryLab**: Selections from the Rig-Veda

Chinese civilization emerged from the unification of large village communities that had developed along the Yellow River. In the Shang era, which spanned much of the 2nd millennium B.C.E., existing irrigation systems were extended, and a system of writing was devised that has proved a key source of Chinese identity to the present day.

 **View** the **Closer Look** on **MyHistoryLab**: A Bronze Axe Head from the Shang Dynasty

FIGURE 2.5 This elaborately decorated bronze vessel from the Shang era shows the sophisticated artistic expression achieved very early in Chinese history. It also demonstrates a high level of metalworking ability, which carried over into Shang weapons and tools. Although the design of these ritual vessels often was abstract, mythical creatures such as dragons and sacred birds were deftly cast in bronzes that remain some of the great treasures of Chinese art.

B.C.E., **Aryan** (Indo-European) migrants poured into India. These hunting and herding peoples, originally from Central Asia, gradually converted to agriculture, extending farming from the Indus River valley to the more fertile Ganges basin. The Aryans used iron tools to clear away the dense vegetation.

The Aryans developed a series of literary epics, initially passed on orally and later written down. The sacred books were called the **Vedas**, from the Sanskrit word Veda, or "knowledge." The first epic, the Rig-Veda, consists of 1028 hymns dedicated to the Aryans gods and composed by various priests. New stories, developed during the Epic Age between 1000 and 600 B.C.E., include the **Mahabharata**, India's greatest epic poem, and the **Ramahyana**, both of which deal with real and mythical battles. These epics reflected a more settled agricultural society and better-organized political units than the Rig-Veda. The Epic Age also saw the creation of the **Upanishads**, epic poems with a more mystical flavor. The vital role of priests, but also the generation of increasingly abstract religious ideas, formed central themes in this formative period of Indian history.

Aryan ideas and social forms became increasingly influential. As they settled into agriculture, the Aryans encouraged tight levels of village organization that became characteristic of Indian history. Village chiefs, drawn from leaders of the various Aryan tribes, organized village defenses and regulated property relationships among families. In turn, patriarchal controls and tight extended family relationships among grandparents, parents, and children, solidified the local base of Indian society. As we will see, the Aryans also promoted a distinctive system of social inequality, another factor in the growing social cohesion of Indian society as it moved beyond the transitional centuries.

CHINA

2.6 How does early China illustrate the main features of river-valley civilizations?

Civilization along the Huanghe (**Yellow River**) in China developed in considerable isolation, although some overland trading contact with India and the Middle East did develop (Map 2.5). Huanghe civilization was the subject of much later Chinese legend, which praised the godlike kings of early civilization, starting with the mythic ancestor of the Chinese, Pan Gu. The Chinese had an unusually elaborate concept of their remote origins, and they began early to record a part-fact, part-fiction history of their early kings.

What is clear is the following: First, a well-organized state developed that carefully regulated irrigation in the fertile but flood-prone river valley. Early kings sponsored a considerable network of dikes and canals. Second, by about 2000 B.C.E., the Chinese had produced an advanced technology and developed an elaborate intellectual life. They had learned how to ride horses and were skilled in pottery; they used bronze well and by 1000 B.C.E. had introduced iron, which they soon learned to work with coal. Their writing progressed from knotted ropes to scratches of lines on bone to the invention of **ideographic** symbols. By 1500 B.C.E., at least 3000 pictographic characters had been devised. This standardized writing began to provide some unity to the very diverse peoples assembled in this river valley kingdom, who originally spoke a wide array of languages. Science, particularly astronomy, also arose early. Chinese art emphasized delicate designs (Figure 2.5). Because of limits on building materials in the region, the Chinese did not construct many massive monuments, choosing to live in simple houses built of mud. By about 1500 B.C.E., a line of kings called the **Shang** ruled over the Huanghe valley, and these rulers did construct some impressive tombs and palaces. Invasions disrupted the Shang dynasty and caused a temporary decline in civilization. However, there was less of a break between the river valley society and the later, fuller development of civilization in China than occurred in other regions.

River valley civilization in China generated a number of features of importance for later periods. Silk manufacturing developed. Some form of ancestor worship began. Emphasis on a strong, expansionist state, particularly under the Shang, set the basis for later Chinese politics. The Shang fought on horseback and from chariots, using conquered peoples as foot soldiers. They maintained fuller control over their armies than was characteristic of many other early societies. Shang rulers also directed important rituals, devoted to fertility. In times of famine or drought, the state provided dancers to woo the gods with their performance, and the dancers were later buried alive to calm the spirits who had caused the natural disaster. The state, in other words, took on cultural responsibilities, and this too characterized the ongoing Chinese political tradition.

The Zhou Dynasty

The collapse of the Shang dynasty did not end the early civilization period in China. It was followed by the Zhou dynasty, which initially came from the north, flourishing between 1029 and about 700 B.C.E., although technically extending beyond this point. The Zhou ruled through alliances with landed families, lacking the means to govern the whole territory directly. This was China's feudal period, with supporters asked to provide troops and tax revenues to the central government in return for grants of land. The Zhou did introduce several innovations that would connect with later Chinese history, serving as a transition from the early civilization period to the next phase. They encouraged settlers to move south, to the Yangzi river basin: This expanded China benefited from two agricultural regions (rice and wheat growing), which encouraged both population growth and trade. The Zhou emperors also claimed a "mandate of heaven"—divine support for their rule. And they promoted greater cultural unity, backing the use of the Mandarin language and discouraging more primitive religious practices, including human sacrifice, and urging more restrained ceremonies for worshipping the gods. Oral epics and stories began to be written down, further encouraging a shared culture.

MAP 2.5 **China in the Shang and Zhou Eras** As this map of early centers of Chinese civilization depicts dramatically, Chinese peoples occupied only a small portion of the area that would correspond to China from the last centuries B.C.E. to the present day.

Yellow River Also known as the Huanghe; site of development of sedentary agriculture in China.

ideographs Pictographic characters grouped together to create new concepts; typical of Chinese writing.

Shang First Chinese dynasty for which archeological evidence exists; capital located in Ordos bulge of the Huanghe; flourished 1600 to 1046 B.C.E.

The Zhou could not maintain their hold, however. After about 700 political fragmentation increased, with landlords disregarding the state and establishing their own power base. Additional nomadic peoples migrated into China, often converting to Chinese culture as they settled down. The new levels of disorder encouraged intellectuals to define a clearer Chinese value system and ultimately would provoke a more effective attempt to introduced political unity. These were the changes that ended the early civilization period more decisively.

EARLY CIVILIZATIONS IN THE AMERICAS

2.7 How did conditions in the Americas differ from those in Asia and North Africa during the formation of early civilizations?

The Olmec civilization spread certain elements of culture over the Mesoamerican region. The civilization of Chavín spread along the Peruvian coast and created a horizon of widely shared culture.

Early civilizations emerged somewhat later in the Americas than in Asia and North Africa, in part because agriculture had developed later. Many similarities arose with previous patterns in the Middle East or Harappa. But conditions in the Americas were somewhat distinctive. Few animals were available for domestication: dogs, turkeys, guinea pigs, and (in the Andes) llamas and alpacas comprised the full list. There were simply no animals to assist with heavy transportation. American societies also developed without the use of metals for tools and weapons. Finally, contact among civilization centers

CHAPTER 2 Early Civilizations, 3500–600 B.C.E. 33

was challenging in the Americas, because travel was required in a north-south direction, across climate zones, again in contrast to patterns in Asia, southern Europe and North Africa.

We have seen that people began to migrate to the Americas from Asia at least by 25,000 B.C.E., and probably earlier. Dispersal occurred fairly quickly, as small tribes fanned out in both North and South America, and a variety of different languages emerged. These early peoples were effective hunters, using Stone Age weapons, and they may have contributed to the disappearance of some large mammal species, like the mammoth, through overhunting.

Recurrent debate focuses on whether, after the migration period when the Siberian land bridge disappeared, there were any exchanges with other parts of the world. Occasional contacts may have occurred, but they did not lead to extensive borrowing. Lack of knowledge of iron technology, or the wheel, obviously continued to condition developments in the Americas. Isolation from disease exchange would also, much later on, have profound effects, for no resistance could develop to disease common to Asia, Europe, and Africa.

Agriculture developed in several regions of the Americas between 7000 and 5000 B.C.E., along with new abilities in fishing. Many groups continued to combine some agriculture with hunting, but more extensive agriculture arose in Central America, around cultivation of corn (maize), plus beans, squash, and peppers. In the Andes, the potato was also adapted for agriculture. In these centers, significant population growth occurred. More complex social and cultural forms began to emerge as well, including more elaborate artistic production. Social hierarchies included nobles and priests, as well as merchant groups. Several states arose, often from a single city center with a tribal chief as ruler.

Knowledge of many early societies in the Americas is limited by lack of evidence. Some societies did not build extensive monuments, which limits surviving archeological remains. Challenges here can be compared to problems scholars still encounter with some early civilizations elsewhere, such as Harappa.

The Olmecs

Olmecs People of a cultural tradition that arose at San Lorenzo and La Venta in Mexico c. 1200 B.C.E.; featured irrigated agriculture, urbanism, elaborate religion, beginnings of calendrical and writing systems.

Around 1500 B.C.E. a group called the **Olmecs** established the first civilization in the Americas, on a coastal area of what is now called the Gulf of Mexico. We do not know the origins of the Olmecs, and while they built upon successful village agriculture in the region, their emergence seems rather sudden.

There is no question about the apparatus they introduced: irrigation for agriculture, some early cities, and the beginnings of a writing system. Olmec religion became more complex, and monumental architecture developed. Olmec capacity to move large stones, often for many miles, was impressive and still unexplained; Olmec statuary often involved giant sculpted heads (Figure 2.6). The Olmecs also sketched a formal calendar that became the basis for all the calendar systems in Central America. The Olmec state featured a hereditary elite, while the elaborate religion governed many aspects of life. The Olmecs traded fairly widely in the region, among other things for precious jade stones that they valued for carving.

Olmec civilization declined by about 800 B.C.E., although we do not know why. Cities were abandoned or destroyed. But the legacy of the Olmecs undoubtedly affected later civilizations in the region, including the Maya. Olmec science and also artistic styles proved widely influential. It is impossible to determine whether influence reflected conquest or active trade or missionary outreach, or simply admiring imitation. But while several complex societies would later emerge in this region, for a few centuries after the Olmecs no large organizations seem to have developed.

Chavin and the Andean World

The geography of the Andes presented both challenges and opportunities. The rugged terrain complicated transportation. But different kinds of agriculture could develop at different levels, encouraging some regional trade. Farmers could grow corn (introduced from Central America) in the lower valleys, while potatoes and quinoa (a local grain) grew higher up, and llamas were pastured in higher altitudes still.

Between 1800 and 1200 B.C.E., a more complex society began to emerge. Irrigation was introduced, and large ceremonial structures were built along the coast. Pottery making

FIGURE 2.6 The origins of the Olmecs remain shrouded in mystery. Some of their enormous stone sculptures seem to have distinctively African features that indicate possible transatlantic contact. Similar features also have been found in early Khmer art from southeast Asia.

View the Closer Look on MyHistoryLab: The Basalt Olmec Heads

34 PART I Early Human Societies, 2.5 million–600 B.C.E.: Origins and Development expanded. The most important early center was **Chavín de Huantar** (850–250 B.C.E.) in the highlands of what is now Peru. Chavin contained several large temple platforms and an active craft population working in jewelry, textiles, and ceramics. Chavin artistic styles and religious beliefs spread widely in the region. Jaguars and snakes were common artistic themes, along with frequent scenes of violence. Some style resembled those of the Olmecs, leading to some speculation that both peoples may have had a common origin in the Amazonian lowlands. But, as with the Olmecs, much is not known, including the nature of the wide regional influence.

Chavin decline had occurred by about 300 B.C.E., and there followed a long period of political decentralization in the Andes. Agriculture continued to develop, however, and population grew; despite localized government, artistic production remained strong and creative.

Chavín de Huantar [SHAH-ven deh WAHN-tahr] Chavin culture appeared in highlands of Andes between 1800 and 1200 B.C.E.; typified by ceremonial centers with large stone buildings; greatest ceremonial center was Chavín de Huantar; characterized by artistic motifs.

THE END OF THE RIVER VALLEY PERIOD

2.8 How and why did the early civilization period come to an end and what were the main religious changes introduced by Judaism?

The river valley societies were widely separated, although they had trading contacts with their neighbors and, in the case of the Middle East and North Africa, an occasional military encounter. With this separation, it is not surprising that there was no single development, or even a single century, to signal the transition away from the river valley period.

Most river valley civilizations declined after about 1200 B.C.E. A number of small centers emerged in the Middle East that introduced further innovations, including the religion of Judaism.

The decline of the Olmecs, for example, seems to have been abrupt, amid circumstances that remain unclear; it had nothing to do with developments in other early civilization centers. Patterns in China were distributed in a different way. The replacement of the Shang dynasty by the Zhou led to important new developments. But it was the faltering of the Zhou dynasty, and cultural and then political reactions to growing disorder, that really ended the early period of Chinese civilization. But there was no full or decisive break, just a more gradual accumulation of basic changes.

The end of the river valley period in northwestern India was also more decisive, given the gradual but conclusive decline of Harappan society. Migrating and invading Indo-European peoples even ignored agriculture for many centuries, relying on animal herding. In the process, most traces of Harappan civilization became a dim memory. A few symbols remained, including the mother goddess and yoga positions. So did certain artistic images, including a swastika that became prominent in later Indian religious art. Agricultural techniques, including the growing of cotton, were not abandoned, and the Indo-Europeans ultimately took them over. But with the passing of Harappa, a decisive new period in Indian history clearly began.

A different set of developments took place in the Middle East and North Africa. In Egypt, we have seen that the power of the pharaohs began to weaken by around 1000 B.C.E. Invasions, including from other African peoples in the south, became more common. At times, the kingdom was divided in half. After 500 B.C.E. Persian, then Greek, then Roman invasions effectively brought an end to Egypt's independence.

In the Middle East, the pattern of outside invasion continued to 1000 B.C.E. and even beyond. As before, the new states tended to adopt Mesopotamian culture and legal forms. Around 1100 invasions by an Assyrian ruler were marked by unusual cruelty, including mass execution and the deporting of civilian populations. But the Assyrians did not maintain consistent control, although parts of their empire revived periodically. This inconsistency, and the decline of Egypt, allowed the formation of a number of smaller states for several centuries around 1000 B.C.E.

The Heritage of the River Valley Civilizations

Many accomplishments of the river valley civilizations had a lasting impact. Monuments such as the Egyptian pyramids have long been regarded as one of the wonders of the world. Other achievements, although more prosaic, are fundamental to world history even today: the invention of the wheel; the taming of the horse; the creation of usable alphabets and writing implements; the production of key mathematical concepts such as square roots; the development of well-organized monarchies, bureaucracies, and legal codes; and the invention of functional calendars and methods for other divisions of time. These basic achievements, along with the awe that the early civilizations continue to inspire, are vital legacies to the whole of human history. Almost all the major alphabets in the world today are derived from the writing forms pioneered in the river valleys, apart from the even more durable concept of writing itself. Almost all later civilizations, then, built on the massive foundations first constructed in the river valleys.

Despite these accomplishments, we have seen that most of the river valley civilizations were in decline by 1000 B.C.E. The civilizations had flourished for as many as 2500 years, although of course with periodic disruptions and revivals. But, particularly in India, the new waves of invasion did produce something of a break in the history of civilization, a dividing line between the river valley pioneers and later cultures.

This break raises one final question: Besides the vital achievements—the fascinating monuments and the indispensable advances in technology, science, and art—what legacies did the river valley civilizations leave for later ages? The question is particularly important for the Middle East and Egypt. In India, we must frankly admit much ignorance about possible links between Indus River accomplishments and what came later. In China, there is a definite connection between the first civilization and subsequent forms, as the Zhou-recorded Chinese history flowed smoothly at this point. But what was the legacy of Mesopotamia and Egypt for later civilizations in or near their centers?

Europeans, even North Americans, are sometimes prone to claim these cultures as the "origins" of "their" Western civilization. These claims should not be taken too literally. It is not altogether clear that either Egypt or Mesopotamia contributed much to later political traditions, although the Roman empire emulated the concept of a godlike king, as evidenced in the trappings of the office, and the existence of strong city-state governments in the Middle East continued to be significant. Ideas about slavery may also have been passed on from these early civilizations. Specific scientific achievements are vital, and Greek students went to Egypt to study mathematics. But scholars argue over how much of a connection exists between Mesopotamian and Egyptian science and later Greek thinking, aside from certain techniques of measuring time or charting the stars. Some historians of philosophy have asserted a basic division between a Mesopotamian and Chinese understanding of nature, which they claim affected later civilizations around the Mediterranean in contrast to China. Mesopotamians were prone to stress a gap between humankind and nature, whereas Chinese thinking developed along ideas of basic harmony. It is possible, then, that some fundamental thinking helped shape later outlooks, but the continuities here are not easy to assess. Mesopotamian art and Egyptian architecture had a more measurable influence on Greek styles, and through these, in turn, later European and Islamic cultures. The Greeks thus learned much about temple building from the Egyptians, whose culture had influenced island civilizations, such as Crete, which then affected later Greek styles.

Whatever their precise legacy, Egypt and Mesopotamia radiated a wide influence. They affected Greece, and through this not only later Western civilization but also east European civilization. Even more obviously, they influenced subsequent developments in the Middle East, including Persia, and in North Africa: Political models, but also the strong commitment to trade and vital cultural forms, including science, showed most clearly in this obvious regional transmission.

New States and Peoples around 1000 B.C.E.

There was a final connection between early and later civilizations in the form of regional cultures that sprang up under the influence of Mesopotamia and Egypt, along the eastern shores of the Mediterranean, and in northeastern Africa mainly after 1200 B.C.E. These cultures produced important innovations that affected later civilizations in Africa, the Middle East, and throughout the Mediterranean. They also created a diverse array of regional identities that continued to mark the Middle East even as other forces, such as the Roman empire or the later religion of Islam, took center stage. Several of these small cultures proved immensely durable, and in their complexity and capacity to survive, they influenced other parts of the world as well.

Kingdoms began to develop south of Egypt, for example. A kingdom in Kush emerged about 2000 B.C.E., under strong Egyptian influence. Egypt conquered the area after 1500, setting up an elaborate bureaucracy and building large temples. At this point, the population of Kush was about 100,000. Trade with southern Arabia expanded. In the 8th century, Kushites conquered Egypt, although they soon were driven out by Assyrians. Kingdoms in northeastern Africa continued to flourish, with a growing population. Local artistic styles combined with the use of Egyptian forms such as pyramids and obelisks. Much of this tradition continued in the later kingdom of Ethiopia.

Along the Mediterranean coast of the Middle East, another mixture of societies emerged. A people called the **Phoenicians**, for example, devised a greatly simplified writing system with 22 letters around 1300 B.C.E.; this alphabet, in turn, became the predecessor of Greek and Latin alphabets. The Phoenicians also improved the Egyptian numbering system. Great traders, they set up colony cities in North Africa and on the coasts of Europe. Phoenicians traded as far away as England, where they purchased tin to make bronze, and also down the Atlantic coast of Africa. Another regional group, the Lydians, first introduced coined money.

Phoenicians Seafaring civilization located on the shores of the eastern Mediterranean; established colonies throughout the Mediterranean.

Judiasm

In terms of ultimate historical impact, the most important of the smaller Middle Eastern groups were the Jews, who gave the world the first clearly developed monotheistic religion. We have seen that early religions, both before and after the beginnings of civilization, were polytheistic, claiming that many gods and goddesses worked to control nature and human destiny. The Jews, a Semitic people influenced by Babylonian civilization, settled near the Mediterranean around 1200 B.C.E. The Jewish state was small and relatively weak, retaining independence only when other parts of the Middle East were in political turmoil. What was distinctive about this culture was its firm belief that a single God, Jehovah, guided the destinies of the Jewish people. Priests and prophets defined and emphasized this belief, and their history of God's guidance of their people formed the basis for the Hebrew Bible. The Jewish religion and moral code persisted even as the Jewish state suffered domination by a series of foreign rulers, from 772 B.C.E. until the Romans seized the state outright in 63 B.C.E. Jewish **monotheism** has sustained a distinctive Jewish culture to this day; it also served as a basis for the development of both Christianity and Islam as major world religions in the Abrahamic tradition.

monotheism The exclusive worship of a single god; introduced by the Jews into Western civilization.

The innovations of Judaism involved more than the focus on a single god. Unlike many polytheistic systems, which emphasized the gods' links with nature and with each other, Judaism stressed God's focus on humankind, and injunctions for ethical behavior among people in obedience to divine commandments. While Judaism stressed appropriate forms of worship, it also stressed Jewish law, held to be derived from God, and the importance of mercy and generosity among people themselves. In gradually assembling a set of holy texts, Judaism also became a religion of the book, with a literature that would continue to inspire religious scholars as well as ordinary worshippers.

Because Judaism stressed God's special compact with the chosen Jewish people, there was no premium placed on converting non-Jews. This belief helps explain the durability of the Jewish faith itself; it also kept the Jewish people in a minority position in the Middle East as a whole. However, the elaboration of monotheism ultimately gained wider significance. In Jewish hands, the concept of god became more human focused but also less humanlike, more abstract. This represented a basic change in not only religion but also humankind's overall outlook. Jehovah had not only a power but also a rationality far different from what the traditional gods of the Middle East or Egypt possessed. These gods were whimsical and capricious; Jehovah was orderly and just, and individuals knew what to expect if they obeyed God's rules. Moral behavior was both defined and emphasized. Religion for the Jews was a way of life, not merely a set of rituals and ceremonies. The full impact of this religious transformation on Middle Eastern civilization, and beyond, was realized only later, when Jewish beliefs were embraced by other, proselytizing faiths.

Global Connections and Critical Themes:

THE EARLY CIVILIZATIONS AND THE WORLD

Mesopotamia and Egypt presented two different approaches to relationships outside the home region. Mesopotamia was flat, with few natural barriers to recurrent invasion from the north. Perhaps for this reason, Mesopotamian leaders thought in terms of expansion. Many conquering emperors expanded their territory, although within the Middle East. Many traders pushed outward, dealing either with merchants to the east or sending expeditions into the Mediterranean and beyond, and also to India. The Middle East's role as active agent in wider contact was clearly being established.

Egypt, although not isolated, was more self-contained. Here was important trade and interaction along the Nile to the south, which brought mutual influences with the peoples of Kush and Ethiopia. Trade and influence also linked Egypt to Mediterranean islands like Crete, south of Greece. A few interactions, finally, occurred with Mesopotamia. But most Egyptians, including the leaders, thought of Egypt as its own world. There was less need or desire to learn of wider horizons. Correspondingly, ancient Egypt played less of a role as intermediary among regions than did Mesopotamia.

River valley civilization in China had fewer far-reaching contacts than its counterpart in Mesopotamia. Ultimately, however, contacts with China would shape developments in Japan, Korea, and Vietnam. Already in the river valley period, the Chinese were advancing new technologies, for example, in the manufacture of silk, which would have wide influence on later interregional trade. Chinese irrigation systems became increasingly sophisticated, involving engineering principles that would gain wider scope later on.

Harappan society traded widely with Mesopotamia, but there is little evidence of significant influence. The decline of Harappan civilization also limited the civilization's impact on later developments in world history. American centers were quite isolated, although clearly some connections linked Central America and the Andes. Comparison of the early civilizations thus emphasizes quite different patterns of scope and legacy.

Further Readings

Stuart Fiedel, *Prehistory of the Americas* (1992); Charles C. Mann, *1491: New Revelations of the Americas before Columbus* (2006); Richard Burger, *Chavin and the Origins of the Andean Civilization* (1995); and Nigel Davies, *The Ancient Kingdoms of Mexico* (1991) and *The Ancient Kingdoms of Peru* (1996). See also Robert Chadwick, *First Civilizations: Ancient Mesopotamia and Ancient Egypt* (2005); Robert G. Morkot, *The Egyptians: An Introduction* (2005); Ian Shaw, *Exploring Ancient Egypt* (2003); Francis Joannès, *The Age of Empires: Mesopotamia in the First Millennium B.C.* (2004); Christiance Cesroches Noblecourt, *Gifts from the Pharaohs: How Egyptian Civilization Shaped the Modern World* (2007); John Baines, *Visual and Written Culture in Ancient Egypt* (2007); Michael D. Petraglia and Bridget Allchin, *The Evolution and History of Human Populations in Southeast Asia* (2007); Thomas E. Emerson, *Archaic Societies: Diversity and Complexity Across the Midcontinent* (2009); Mu-Chou Poo, *Enemies of Civilization: Attitudes Toward Foreigners in Ancient Mesopotamia, Egypt, and China* (2005); Kwang-chih Chang, *The Formation of Chinese Civilization: An Archaeological Perspective* (2005); Li Liu, *The Chinese Neolithic: Trajectories to Early States* (Cambridge, 2004); David N. Keightley, *The Ancestral Landscape: Time, Space, and Community in Late Shang China, ca. 1200–1045 B.C.* (Berkeley, 2000); Gregory L. Possehl, *Indus Age: The Beginnings* (1999); A. C. Pandey, *Government in Ancient India* (2000); Nicola Di Cosmo, *Ancient China and Its Enemies* (2002); and Donald B. Redford, *From Slave to Pharaoh: The Black Experience of Ancient Egypt* (Baltimore, 2004). On India, see Jayantanuja Bandyopadhyaya, *Class and Religion in Ancient India* (2008); Kiran Kumar Thaplyal, *Village and Village Life in Ancient India* (2004); and Mark Kenoyer, *Ancient Cities of the Indus Valley Civilizations* (1998).

On the environment, see I. G. Simmons, *Environmental History* (1993). On patterns of contact, see Philip D. Curtin, *Cross-Cultural Trade in World History* (1984); Xinru Liu, *Ancient India and Ancient China: Trade and Religious Exchanges* (1988); and Shereen Ratnagar, *Encounter: The Westerly Trade of the Harappan Civilization* (1981). The science and technology of the ancient world are discussed in Richard Bulliet, *The Camel and the Wheel* (1975); George Ifrah, *From One to Zero: A Universal History of Numbers* (1985); and Edgardo Marcorini, ed., *The History of Science and Technology: A Narrative Chronology* (1988). The nature and influence of early science, particularly from Egypt, is also covered in Dick Teresi's *Lost Discoveries: The Ancient Roots of Modern Science* (2002). See also M. E. Auber, *The Phoenicians and the West* (1996); Donald Redford, *Egypt, Canaan, and Israel in Ancient Times* (1995); Gay Robbins, *Women in Ancient Egypt* (1993); and J. Curtis, *Ancient Persia* (1989).

On MyHistoryLab

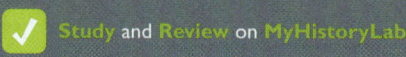 Study and Review on MyHistoryLab

Critical Thinking Questions

1. What are the main problems of evidence in dealing with early civilizations? To what extent have scholars managed to resolve some of the problems?
2. What regions of the world did not generate an early civilization?
3. Are civilizations better than other types of societies? Why, or why not?
4. Is 600 B.C.E. a good date to end the early period of world history? Are there any alternatives?
5. What major changes did Judaism introduce into the religious patterns common in early civilizations?
6. What were the main similarities and differences between early civilizations in the Americas and those in Asia and the Mediterranean?

PART I AP® TEST PREP

MULTIPLE CHOICE QUESTIONS

1. The transformation that was most responsible for moving humans toward civilization was the
   a. smelting of metals such as copper.
   b. growth of towns and cities.
   c. rise of agriculture.
   d. rise of specialized classes.

2. The emergence of sedentary agriculture
   a. occurred simultaneously in various places and spread around the world.
   b. began only in the savannas of West Africa.
   c. began in the Middle East first, but developed independently in other areas.
   d. arose in the river valleys of the Huanghe and Yangtze.

3. Which of the following is NOT considered to have developed from or been accelerated by cuneiform and other types of writing?
   a. facilitation of the keeping of commercial records
   b. the organization of elaborate political structures
   c. formalized legal systems
   d. the reduction in social stratification

4. Less is known about the Harappan civilization or that of the Indus Valley than Sumer and Egypt because
   a. the Harappan and Indus Valley civilizations were not geographic centers of a continuous culture lasting millennium.
   b. the writing of the Indus Valley and Harappan civilizations has never been deciphered.
   c. they were less secure from nomadic incursions and invasions and therefore conquered and destroyed early on.
   d. neither of these civilizations developed a system of writing until almost the end of their duration.

5. Compared to river valley cultures in Egypt and Mesopotamia, Chinese civilization
   a. probably developed after civilizations in the Nile Valley and Mesopotamia.
   b. appears to have been organized along more democratic lines.
   c. seems to have had substantially less wealth than did Egypt and Mesopotamia.
   d. did not rely on heavy irrigation, as year-round water was plentiful.

6. Which of the following represents the most advanced stage of human evolution?
   a. *Homo Erectus*
   b. *Australopithecus africanus*
   c. *Homo Habilis*
   d. *Homo sapiens sapiens*

7. As early civilizations began to emerge, the creation of agricultural surpluses resulted in
   a. heightened social inequalities.
   b. an industrial revolution.
   c. matrilocal patterns of marriage.
   d. a lack of social stratification.

8. The agricultural revolution allowed all of the following transformations in human culture to take place EXCEPT
   a. the spread of regularly cultivated fields.
   b. the domestication of animals.
   c. the development of towns.
   d. a decline in specialized artists and craftsmen.

9. The above detail from Egyptian tomb art of grain harvesting shows
   a. the religious aspect of the harvest.
   b. that Egyptian artists made very little distinction in drawing men and women.
   c. the Egyptians valued erect posture, which freed hands.
   d. that men and women worked together during the harvest.

10. Given the location and subject matter of Paleolithic cave paintings, it is likely that the main purpose of the art was
    a. to relieve the otherwise drab interiors of caves.
    b. to be used as maps to locate game herds.
    c. to be used for religious or ritual purposes.
    d. to indicate the limited level of thinking of Paleolithic men and women.

11. By the late Paleolithic Age, humans had colonized
    a. all of the continents of the Eastern Hemisphere.
    b. Africa, Europe, and Asia.
    c. all of the continents except Australia.
    d. all of the continents except Antarctica.

12. Most human societies in the Paleolithic Age consisted of
    a. urbanized civilizations.
    b. small groups of hunters and gatherers.
    c. sedentary agricultural groups.
    d. cave-dwelling bands.

13. In hunting-and-gathering bands, labor
    a. was shared equally by all members of the group.
    b. fell entirely to dominant males within the group.
    c. was divided according to gender.
    d. fell entirely to females within the group.

14. The lives of intensive hunting-and-gathering groups living in permanent locations remained precarious because
    a. they failed to improve their technology for hunting or for storage.
    b. they failed to increase the size of the hunting and gathering bands.
    c. they became increasingly vulnerable to attacks from nomadic groups.
    d. they were dependent on particular animals and plants that could disappear if changes in the climate occurred.

15. All of the following factors may have led to the adoption of sedentary agriculture EXCEPT
    a. less labor was required for sedentary agriculture than for hunting and gathering.
    b. climatic changes leading to changes in the grazing locations of game animals.
    c. climatic changes leading to changes in plant ecology.
    d. an increase in human population.

16. Which of the following was NOT an advantage gained from the domestication of animals?
    a. expanded choice of materials for clothing
    b. materials for boats
    c. additional sources of protein
    d. animal power for farming

17. Which of the following regions did NOT originate an agricultural system?
    a. Egypt
    b. Australia
    c. the Huanghe valley of China
    d. the Middle East

18. Agricultural systems in the Middle East, China, and the Americas were all
    a. based on the same grains: wheat and barley.
    b. based on a combination of domesticated plants and animals.
    c. based on different domesticated plants in each region.
    d. dependent on pastoral forms of social organization.

19. The transformations associated with the agrarian revolution occurred
    a. only in the Middle East, the area where agriculture was first initiated.
    b. only in Africa, the area where humans first developed.
    c. only in the Eastern Hemisphere.
    d. in all of the world where civilizations emerged.

20. The Neolithic revolution caused the population of humans to
    a. decline as fewer people were needed to produce more food.
    b. stay the same as few people became sedentary.
    c. abandon hunting and gathering as a means of subsistence.
    d. increase from 8 million to 60 or 70 million.

21. Which of the following technological innovations was associated with the transition to sedentary agricultural communities?
    a. digging sticks, axes, and plows
    b. fire
    c. wheeled vehicles
    d. steel

22. In sedentary agricultural communities, social distinctions were heightened,
    a. and organization into distinct classes occurred.
    b. but well-defined social stratification and class identity was nonexistent.
    c. but there was little division of labor and occupational specificity.
    d. but no political elites emerged.

23. In comparison to the position of women in hunting-and-gathering societies, the social status of women in sedentary agricultural communities
    a. improved.
    b. stayed about the same.
    c. allowed them to monopolize the religious and political elites.
    d. declined.

24. This decorated elephant vessel from the Shang era shows
    a. a very simplistic artistic expression.
    b. a high level of metalworking ability.
    c. the inability of the Chinese to adopt realistic artistic skills.
    d. that the Chinese used mythical creatures for their art.

25. The concept of "barbarians"
    a. was strictly a Chinese idea.
    b. was only developed in 19th-century European culture.
    c. was commonly used to distinguish between cosmopolitan, urban-focused cultures and nomadic peoples.
    d. was dropped in modern cultures.

26. People referred to as barbarians were often
    a. members of urbanized cultures.
    b. members of hunter-gatherer bands.
    c. sedentary agriculturalists.
    d. pastoral herdsmen.

27. The concept of civilization based on racial or biological differences was
    a. well-established in the early Chinese dynasties.
    b. developed by thinkers in western Europe in the 18th and 19th centuries.
    c. adopted by the Romans and the Greeks.
    d. never taken seriously.

28. Combinations of the ideas, objects, and patterns of behavior that result from human social interaction are referred to as
    a. culture.
    b. society.
    c. civilization.
    d. social stratification.

29. By about 7000 B.C.E., techniques of agricultural production in the Middle East had reached a level that
    a. made possible the establishment of the first towns.
    b. made possible the establishment of huge cities.
    c. forced a return to hunting and gathering.
    d. allowed most people to engage in other occupations.

30. In densely populated Middle Eastern agricultural settlements, occupational specialization and political-military elites
    a. advanced significantly.
    b. failed to develop.
    c. were retarded by the general failure of organized religion.
    d. remained at the level of hunting-and-gathering societies.

31. Which of the following developments was NOT a key ingredient of early Middle Eastern civilization?
    a. the existence of specialized nonfarming producers
    b. the existence of nonfarming political and religious elites
    c. crafts such as pottery and metalworking
    d. heavy reliance on pastoralism

32. Which of the following is true about the extensively studied site Çatal Hüyük?
    a. The town could not have sustained itself without extensive trade with the hunting people in the hills surrounding the village.
    b. By 5500 B.C.E., important production activities developed in the village, including those of skilled toolmakers and jewelers.
    c. By 5500 B.C.E., human sacrifice on a massive scale was practiced.
    d. The town became increasingly impoverished over time.

33. Which of the following was NOT a transformation associated with the 4th millennium B.C.E. (4000 to 3000 B.C.E.)?
    a. increased use of the plow
    b. widespread use of chariots
    c. use of bronze for weapons
    d. the development of writing

34. What was the "heart" of the Neolithic revolution that became the basis for the spread of human societies?
    a. innovative technologies and modes of agrarian production
    b. religion
    c. hunting
    d. architecture

35. The emergence of sedentary agriculture
    a. arose in the river valleys of the Huanghe and Yangtze.
    b. began only in the savannas of West Africa.
    c. occurred simultaneously in various places and spread around the world.
    d. started in the Middle East first but developed independently in other areas.

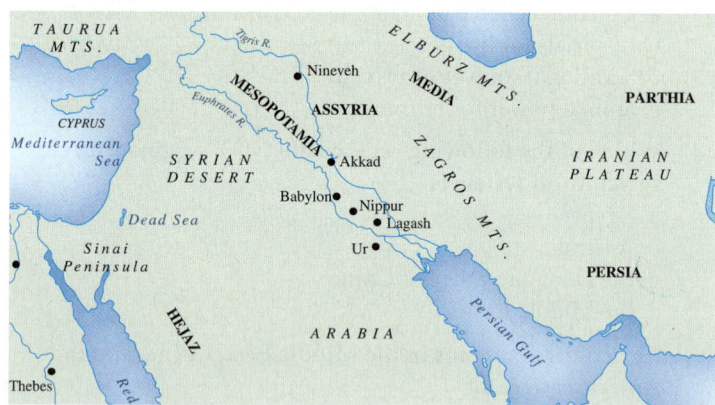

36. What do the locations of the cities on the map indicate?
    a. They shared a common religion, culture, and language.
    b. The cities had easy access to western travel and the Mediterranean Sea.
    c. They were located near sources of fresh water.
    d. They were on major trade routes to Africa.

37. Which one of the following is NOT considered a reason for the decline of the Harappan civilization after about 1500 B.C.E.?
    a. massive flooding
    b. Migrations by a cattle-herding people, perhaps the Indo-Europeans, probably challenged the control of the priestly group.
    c. Environmental changes were likely a greater problem, with excessive forest-cutting leading to the creation of desert conditions and saltier soils.
    d. earthquakes and tsunamis

38. What monumental sculptures did the Olmec civilization produce?
    a. manioc
    b. calendars
    c. stone heads
    d. stone hands

39. Which of the following statements regarding nomadic societies is true?
    a. Nomadic societies were egalitarian in terms of gender relations because care of animals was undertaken by women.
    b. Polygamy was uncommon, even for wealthier men.
    c. Hospitality was a keynote of characteristic nomadic culture and honor required that travelers be aided.
    d. Because of their cruelty, nomadic peoples never had a peaceful, mutually beneficial relationship with agricultural societies.

40. During the Neolithic Revolution, agriculture was tied to social change in which of the following ways?
    a. Agricultural productivity discouraged occupation specialization.
    b. Agricultural surpluses led to an early form of socialism in which the extra food was allocated equally to each family.
    c. Agriculture required more work leaving little time to spare on art and literature.
    d. Agricultural productivity encouraged social stratification and the formation of elites based on political and religious groups.

41. How did the actions of the Nile River influence some of the distinctive characteristics in Egyptian civilization?
    a. The river's unpredictable nature encouraged a fatalistic perspective.
    b. Devastating floods forced the creation of dikes and irrigation networks that eventually spread throughout the region, encouraging the creation of a regional empire.
    c. The river's ecosystem became the primary inspiration for the Egyptian religious pantheon.
    d. Predictable flood surges encouraged an optimistic perspective and facilitated political consolidation.

42. The features of the Jewish concept of monotheism influenced religious observance and tradition in the Middle East in all the following ways EXCEPT
    a. a more abstract notion of God that discouraged anthropomorphic representations of divinity.
    b. an emphasis on proselytizing because of the importance Jews placed on converting non-Jews.
    c. an emphasis on a strong, masculine creator god for protection and guidance that challenged animist notions of religious plurality.
    d. the links between ethical and moral conduct transformed religion from a set of rituals to a way of life.

43. Which of the following events disrupted Middle Eastern civilizations around 2100 B.C.E.?
    a. Indo-European invasions and migrations introduced new ideas and products.
    b. Competition for trade resources led to warfare between rival kingdoms, resulting in devastation and famine.
    c. plagues and diseases carried by traders from Asia and Africa
    d. Invaders from the West arrived in large numbers, captured territories, and established their own political and religious structures.

44. What appears to have been the Harappan attitude toward cross-cultural contact?
    a. ambivalent with no knowledge of other civilizations outside south Asia
    b. aggressive with active efforts to conquer and assimilate regional rivals and their innovations
    c. positive as heavy involvement in trade and political contact with other civilizations promoted acceptance of external ideas
    d. conservative and resistant to outside innovation

45. What similarities linked the Shang Chinese, Aryan, and classical Greek civilizations?
    a. All three used enslaved subject peoples as foot soldiers and forced laborers.
    b. All three possessed powerful, highly mobile military forces based on bronze-armed and armored chariots.
    c. All three were warlike, nomadic cultures.
    d. All three saw their rulers as semi-divine intermediaries between heaven and earth.

46. What invention of the Phoenicians exerted lasting influence in the Mediterranean region?
    a. a simplified trading alphabet based on Mesopotamian cuneiform
    b. navigational technology such as the sextant
    c. new ship designs that shortened travel between Africa, Asia, and Europe
    d. a trade network linking Europe, Africa, and Asia

DOCUMENT-BASED QUESTION

 Read the Document on MyHistoryLab

A practice document-based question for Part I is available on MyHistoryLab.

CONTINUITY AND CHANGE-OVER-TIME ESSAY

Analyze continuities and changes in the status of women in the Paleolithic Age with that of women in the sedentary agricultural communities of the Neolithic era.

COMPARATIVE ESSAY

Analyze similarities and differences between the Paleolithic Age (the Old Stone Age) and the Neolithic Age (the New Stone Age) in terms of means of subsistence and social organization.

PART I — REVISITING

The Early Period, 2.5 million–600 B.C.E.

CONTACTS AND THEIR LIMITS

No regular contacts among the major population centers developed during the long early phases of human history. Even at the end of the early civilization, no such patterns existed. To be sure, separate developments did not prevent many similar features. In broad outline, early civilizations developed many of the same functions, as they introduced formal governments, writing systems, and significant cities. Agriculture generated common tendencies to establish patriarchal family structures, but these developments occurred spontaneously, the result of similar needs, not because peoples in different regions learned extensively from one another. And, of course, the specifics varied considerably—the system of government and gender relations in Egypt, for example, differed from those in Mesopotamia or China.

Three kinds of contacts did exist during the early phases of human history. Their results were significant, although they were somewhat sporadic. First, local or long-distance trade could spread knowledge of new developments or products. People in one region could learn about innovations in the region next door. Local exchanges of products or symbolic gifts—the latter designed to help keep the peace—served as conduits. Through this kind of interaction, **diffusion** occurred—that is, a gradual spread of key ideas and techniques. This was the mechanism through which the knowledge of agriculture gradually spread from the areas where it was first developed to neighboring regions, and ultimately over whole subcontinents. New technologies, like metalworking, spread the same way. So did new foodstuffs: Some crops original to southeast Asia, for example, reached Africa by 1000 C.E. and gradually became staples.

These kinds of diffusion were the most important contacts in early human history. We do not always know the precise processes involved. For example, an Indian Ocean trade system existed by 1000 C.E., involving timber and perfumes; this led to southeast Asian migrations to the island of Madagascar. But we know almost nothing about the specifics of this process. It is also true that some trade contacts, like the Phoenician voyages to southern England to get tin, do not seem to have produced wider diffusion of products or technologies.

A second type of contact resulted from migration and invasion. We have seen that this combination occurred frequently in the Middle East, leading to changes in ruling dynasties, language, and the spread of new technologies. The wheel was almost certainly invented in central Asia, then brought by a migrant group to the Middle East. Migrations and invasions could be extremely disruptive, as when the Indo-Europeans moved into India. But they could also expose immigrants and local populations alike to new knowledge and technologies.

A third kind of contact involved a mix of direct trade, diplomatic relations, and military activity among two or more major early civilization centers. While Mesopotamia and Egypt developed separately for the most part, there were periods of invasion from one direction or another, some trade, and some cultural exchange. Tablets have been found, for example, whose text was written in both cuneiform and hieroglyphics, showing a need for direct translations. Egyptians and Mesopotamians both interacted with parts of Greece, including the island of Crete, which was therefore able to borrow from both societies. Some trade (although no military contact) occurred among Mesopotamia, China, and the Indus valley. Early civilizations in the Americas were much more isolated.

Contacts brought fundamental changes to the people involved, even in these early periods. Diffusion, particularly, was responsible for basic shifts in economic and therefore social systems. Most contact was sporadic, however, and did not lead to elaborate exchanges of religious or scientific ideas or political institutions. Here, the emphasis on separate patterns of development remains valid.

A Sumerian clay tablet with cuneiform characters aimed at tallying numbers of sheep and goats as part of early agriculture.

COMPLEXITIES

The early period of human history offers a great deal of variety. While the most important developments involved the Neolithic revolution and then the emergence of several early civilizations, it is vital to remember that hunting and gathering societies persisted in many places. Nomadic herding economies dominated several regions as well, presenting yet another pattern.

The substantial separation of major regions also generated huge differences in the timing of key changes. We have seen that there are at least three separate dates for the advent of agriculture: in the Middle East, in East Asia, and in the Americas. The initial foundation of civilization also varied with the region. Almost 3000 years separate the Sumerian civilization from the emergence of a complex culture in the Andes. Analysis of the early period requires comparison of patterns across a wide stretch of time.

THE END OF THE PERIOD

Regional separations also complicate decisions about when to end the early period, for there was no decisive, sweeping change that affected all of even most of the individual centers. By 600 B.C.E., some of the early civilizations did seem to be losing dynamism. Most obviously, the flourishing period of Olmec civilization had ended, and Harappan civilization had essentially disappeared. New patterns were beginning to emerge in these same areas, with the initial formation of Mayan culture in Central America and the religious changes among Aryan peoples in India that would ultimately lead to Hinduism.

In China, the Zhou dynasty, formed around 1100 B.C.E., continued, although it was after 600 that important cultural innovations took shape, particularly around the philosophy of Confucius. In the Middle East and northeast Africa, the heyday of the major early empires had passed, with Egypt in partial decline. Again, no single formula captures the variety of situations around 600 B.C.E.

Two or three changes were, however, on the horizon. Some new centers of activity were beginning to emerge, although they benefited from the legacy of the early civilizations. Mayans built on Olmec achievements. City-states arising in and around Greece would use both Egyptian and Mesopotamian heritage. Further, a number of areas were poised to introduce new cultural patterns that would ultimately provide new regional links. China's major philosophies and religions arose in the centuries after 600, and important religious developments were also taking shape in India and Persia. Finally, growing knowledge of iron technology, for tools and weapons, would gradually generate political, military, and economic changes in the Middle East, in China and other parts of Asia, and in the Mediterranean world (although not in the clearly separate societies of the Americas).

CRITICAL THINKING QUESTIONS

1. Why do some historians argue that the advent of agriculture was an unfortunate development?
2. Why was there no major protest against the emergence of patriarchal gender relations in agricultural societies?
3. Compare Olmec civilization with one of the early civilizations in Asia/North Africa. How do problems of evidence complicate the comparison?
4. What are the advantages and disadvantages of using 600 B.C.E. as an approximate date for ending the early period?

PART II The Classical Period, 600 B.C.E.– 600 C.E.: Uniting Large Regions

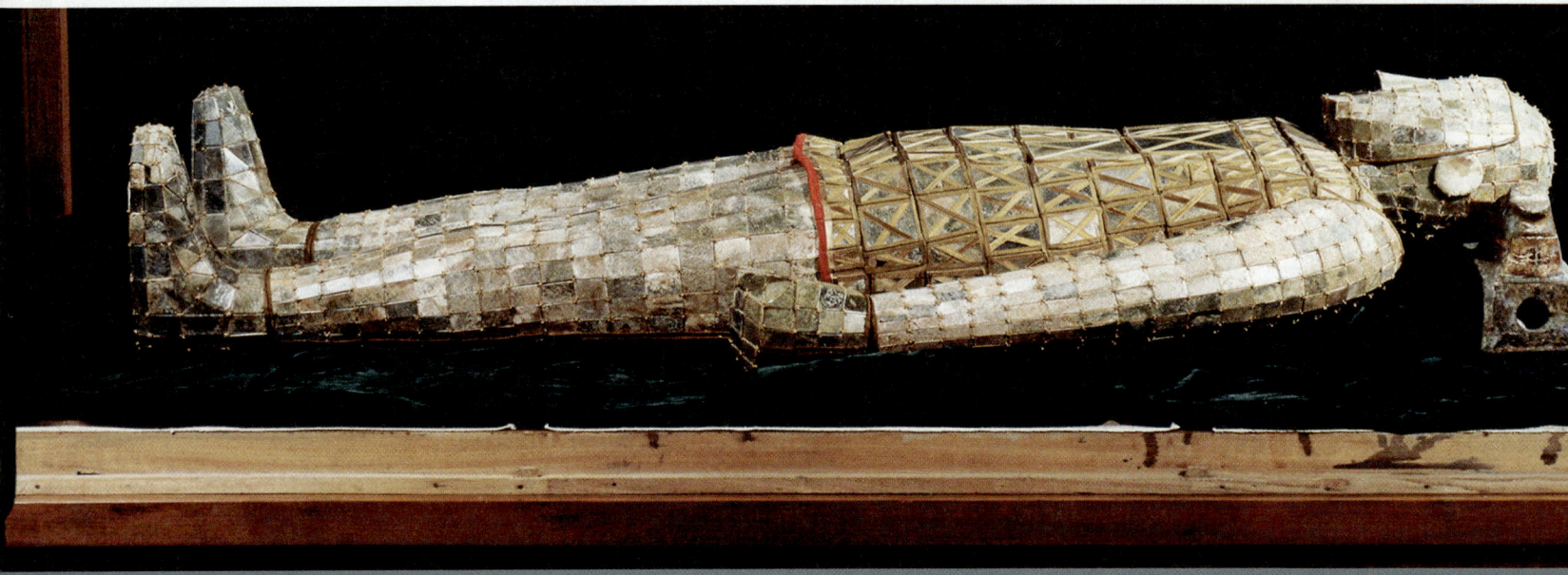

A jade funeral suit from the Western Han Dynasty, late 2nd century B.C. Chinese styles spread as the Empire expanded.

PART OUTLINE

Chapter 3 Classical Civilization: China	**Chapter 6** The Classical Period: Directions, Diversities, and Declines by 500 C.E.
Chapter 4 Classical Civilization: India	
Chapter 5 Classical Civilization in the Mediterranean: Greece and Rome	

THE OVERVIEW

The major development during the classical period of world history was the formation of large regional civilizations in China, India, the Mediterranean, the Middle East, East Africa, and Mesoamerica. These developments can be seen in the accompanying maps. The map on the top depicts the Eastern Hemisphere early in the classical period (around 800 B.C.E.); the map on the bottom shows the same area around 100 C.E. In China and the Mediterranean, what had been a set of small states—or no states at all—had been replaced by two giant empires. India also developed substantial empires at several key points in the classical centuries.

Although much of the world remained outside the main areas of civilization, these areas had by far the largest concentration of population. Furthermore, the influence of these civilizations extended into surrounding regions outside their direct control. Classical civilizations also had important relationships with nomadic groups, mostly from central Asia, who traded with them and periodically attempted invasion. Nevertheless, regions outside the world's main civilizational areas require some separate attention during this long period.

Except for brief interludes, the main civilizations did not share direct borders. Much of the development of each civilization was separate, and the establishment of distinctive cultural and institutional patterns was a key legacy of this period. Nevertheless, trade offered some contacts, as products like silk were carried from east Asia to the Mediterranean. Occasionally, interaction was more direct. The conquests of the Greek-trained warrior Alexander the Great resulted in the creation of a short-lived empire that stretched from the Mediterranean into northwestern India. This empire brought into direct contact Mediterranean, cultural Asian, Middle Eastern, and Indian societies, an encounter that yielded interesting results, some of which are clearly evident in art of the period. For example, a statue sculpted by an Indian artist depicts the beloved Buddha clothed in Greek fashions. This combination of cultural elements, called *syncretism*, is a common result of significant contact between cultures. It can have lasting implications. Syncretism was not the most common feature of the classical period, but its occurrence hinted at what would develop more fully later.

Big Concepts

The formation of the classical societies involved three striking features. First was the emergence and standardization (within each society) of key cultural and religious traditions and second, in the political real, was the development of state and empires—again, with each society producing some characteristic political forms within this category. Finally, as the period's third overarching feature, the contacts that did develop among different regions spurred trade and, to some degree, communication. All three of these features would affect world history long after the classical period had itself ended.

TRIGGERS FOR CHANGE

Despite the lack of a clear transition, the classical civilizations that began to emerge about 1000 B.C.E. were measurably different from their river valley predecessors. While they built on the earlier achievements, they grew noticeably larger in their geographic, cultural, economic, and political reach.

What allowed this greater reach was military conquest, made possible by the introduction of iron tools and weapons, beginning about 1500 B.C.E.

As larger empires developed, leaders worked to tie their territories together both commercially and culturally. New trade links emerged, sometimes encouraged by new infrastructure such as canals (China) or postal service (Persia). Religion and philosophy were formalized and disseminated as part of training a cohesive elite. New conquests, possible in part because of technological change, led to further developments intended to integrate larger regions.

Each of the classical societies ultimately declined, and great empires like the Han dynasty in China, the Gupta in India, and the western Roman empire collapsed altogether. Although these

Political Units of the World, c. 800–750 B.C.E.

Political units 800–750 BCE

Political Units of the World, c. 1–100 C.E.

Political units 1–100 CE

50 PART II The Classical Period, 600 B.C.E.–600 C.E.: Uniting Large Regions

developments did not happen at exactly the same time, together they brought the classical period to a close by 500 C.E.

THE BIG CHANGES

Each of the classical civilizations had its own social structure, religion, political system, system of science, and styles of art. Comparisons of these differences, which have continued to the present day, form a vital part of studying the classical period. To take one example: In the late 20th century the Chinese government proved reasonably effective in mandating drastic changes in birth rates. The Indian government tried and failed to enforce somewhat similar regulations. Many factors accounted for China's success and India's failure in enforcing a population policy, but an important one was the extent to which people in each country accepted as legitimate government monitoring of personal behavior. These differences in attitude can be traced back to the classical period. The civilization styles set in the classical period hardly predetermined the future, but they had, and have, undeniable influence.

The first major change, then, was the establishment of cultures that developed over time during the classical period and left durable legacies. All of the major civilizations set up vigorous internal trade that allowed considerable regional specialization—each region within a civilization produced the crops most suitable to its ecology and traded for other necessities.

Each major civilization promoted a common cultural system that would legitimate characteristic social and family customs, integrate elites, and provide bonds between ordinary people and leadership groups. This system might involve more than one component. For example, there was outright, although usually peaceful, competition between Buddhism and Hinduism in India. But the generation of powerful beliefs and their spread within each civilization was an important development in the classical period, and one that had lasting impact.

Each major civilization, at least periodically, conquered other peoples and areas and created large empires. Although empires were not new in world history, those of the classical period in world history were more powerful and widespread than any precedent.

The growth of the classical civilizations, with their impressive achievements and monuments, clearly had an impact on surrounding peoples. Some trade with neighboring regions was common. India had the widest commercial reach, extending all the way into southeast Asia, but Rome also traded with parts of Africa and Asia outside its own empire. Even more widely, nomadic peoples were often attracted toward the centers of civilization as immigrants, soldiers, or invaders. Some nomadic peoples facilitated trade between civilizations. These developments were important at the time and had implications for later patterns in world history. For example, cultural and trade contacts often prepared the way for later nomadic migrations into the classical societies.

The achievements of the major classical civilizations inspired awe, at the time and later. Great developments in philosophy, politics, and art in classical civilizations provided the foundations for subsequent civilizations. Confucianism, for example, would influence other Asian societies besides China, and a number of societies would build on the achievements of Greek science. It is for this reason that the term *classical* is commonly used to refer to this period.

CONTINUITY

While the introduction of iron helped usher in the classical period, the period itself did not witness sweeping technological developments. Most peasants continued to use traditional agricultural tools and methods. Similarly, except for the improved road systems introduced by more powerful governments, there were no great advances in transportation during this period. Rural culture remained somewhat apart from classical culture, particularly in China and the Mediterranean. Many rural people retained their traditional festivals and polytheistic religious beliefs alongside official religions and philosophies.

Interior view of the Roman baths, in Bath, England. Roman styles spread to distant parts of the empire, creating a wide area of partially shared cultures.

Patriarchal culture prevailed in each of the major civilizations of the classical period. Each culture had particular ways of defining women's roles and obligations. Comparisons among the classical civilizations are important in this area, for different styles of patriarchy would affect family life and even art, but the basic idea of patriarchal superiority had already been established. The civilizations simply related a patriarchal system to the particular cultures they developed and emphasized.

600 B.C.E.	500 B.C.E.	250 B.C.E.
600 Zoroastrian religion in Iran	**500–449** Greek wars with Persia	**221** Shi Huangdi proclaimed first emperor of China
600 Legendary ruler in Japan	**500–450** Beginnings of the Roman republic	**202 B.C.E.–9 C.E.** Former Han dynasty; development of horse collar and water mill
551–c. 233 Period of the great Chinese philosophers: Confucius, Laozi, Mencius, Legalists	**470–430** Height of Athenian culture; Socrates and Greek philosophical style	**200 B.C.E.–200 C.E.** Era of strong Buddhist influence
550 Formation of Persian empire	**431 ff.** Peloponnesian Wars; decline of Greece	**133 ff.** Decline of the Roman republic
c. 542–483 Life of the Buddha	**330** Alexander the Great	**100** Germans begin contact with Rome; Slavs migrate into eastern Europe
	327–325 Alexander's invasion of the Persion empire	
	322–185 Mauryan empire	
	300–100 Hellenistic Period	
	300 B.C.E.–900 C.E. Height of Maya civilization	
	264–140 Roman expansion in North Africa (Punic Wars) and eastern Mediterranean	

Finally, though the classical civilizations all introduced significant innovations beyond their river valley predecessors, they also retained and built on key achievements of the earlier societies. They did not have to reinvent money, the idea of codes of law, or scientific interests such as astronomy. While the classical civilizations left a heritage that shaped future developments, they also drew upon a heritage established in earlier periods.

IMPACT ON DAILY LIFE: OLD AGE

In all the classical civilizations, the achievement of old age won respect. It was seen, legitimately enough, as a sign of good habits and wisdom. Furthermore, in groups where literacy was uncommon, the elderly could be vital sources of information and cultural memory—the kinds of stories that help shape the identity of families and cultures. Respect for the elderly was a sign of good manners in all the classical societies.

But the classical civilizations also differed in their attitudes toward the elderly. Chinese Confucianism placed particular emphasis on venerating the elderly. Even older women, if they were mothers (and especially if they were widows and mothers of sons) had clear status, although officially their sons ran the household.

In Mediterranean cultures, there was greater ambivalence concerning older people. The themes of wisdom and respect were visible (although they applied much more clearly to men than to women). But the elderly also were depicted as both greedy and laughable as their capacities declined. Stories made fun of old misers or men who lusted after younger women. In the Mediterranean, more attention was paid to the physical and mental deterioration of older people, and while this sometimes produced sympathy, it could also generate scorn. The Greek dramatist Aeschylus wrote about people "old in their bones, dishonored, cut off," and the Bible offered many accounts of enfeebled, foolish elders. Societies that placed great emphasis on military prowess and youthful beauty could be harsh to people past their prime, and in the Mediterranean, there was no systematic set of beliefs, like Confucianism, to cut through these contradictions.

Did these cultural differences matter in the actual way older people were treated? Here, the evidence is sketchier; we know much more about classical value systems than about the details of daily life. What is clear is that this ambivalence toward the elderly had staying power. Even today, many argue, ambivalence about older people that goes back to Greeks, Romans, and Hebrews affects policy and outlook in the West, while in contrast, some east Asian systems write respect for the elderly into their constitutions.

TRENDS AND SOCIETIES

Initial chapters in this section describe developments in each of the major civilizations during the classical period, starting with China in Chapter 2 and India in Chapter 3. Chapter 4 returns to the Mediterranean, to take up the history of Greece and Rome. Chapter 5 returns to the main classical centers, dealing with patterns of decline and with concurrent religious innovations, including the rise of Christianity. The story of the decline of each civilization was distinct, but the overall pattern of change had some important common features. ∎

C.E.	250 C.E.	500 C.E.	750 C.E.
23–220 Later Han dynasty; invention of paper and compass	**300** Decline of Meroë	**476** Last Roman emperor in West	**800–1300** Mississippian culture
27 Augustus founds Roman empire	**300–400** Yamato claim imperial control of Japan	**527–565** Justinian Eastern emperor	**900** Polynesians to New Zealand
30 Crucifixion of Jesus	**300–700** Rise of Axum; conversion to Christianity	**580 ff.** Spread of Buddhism in Japan	**900–1200** Toltecs
88 Beginning of Han decline	**300–900** Intermediate Horizon period (Andes)	**589–618** Sui dynasty	**1000** Height of kingdom of Ghana, Africa
106 Height of Roman territory	**300–1000** Second wave of Polynesian migrations to Hawaii	**600–647** Harsha's empire	
180 Beginning of decline of Rome	**312–337** Constantine; formation of Eastern Empire; adoption of Christianity	**618** Tang dynasty	
200–500 Nasca culture (Andes)	**319–540** Gupta empire	**700 ff.** Spread of Islam; trans-Sahara trade in Africa	
200–700 Mochica culture (Andes)	**400** Chinese script imported		
200–1300 Anasazi in North America	**401 ff.** Large-scale Germanic invasions in Roman empire		
220 Last Han emperor deposed			

3

Classical Civilization: China

Listen to Chapter 3 on MyHistoryLab

LEARNING OBJECTIVES

3.1 How did the sequence of dynasties in classical China build a successful empire? p. 56

3.2 What were the distinctive features of China's political system under the Han? p. 60

3.3 What was the relationship between Confucianism and Daoism? p. 63

3.4 How did Confucianism affect Chinese social and family structure? p. 67

3.5 What were the most important complexities in classical Chinese society? p. 71

Late in the 6th century B.C.E., a brilliant middle-aged scholar-philosopher applied for a high post in the bureaucracy of the small kingdom of Lu in northeast China (Map 3.1). Perhaps because Kong Fuzi—or Confucius, as he came to be known centuries later in the West—was widely reputed to be an opinionated and outspoken person, he was denied the position for

View the map on **MyHistoryLab**: Historic Sites of Daoism and Confucianism

FIGURE 3.1 This 18th-century painting by Wang Shugu vividly illustrates the high esteem in which the philosopher Confucius has been held by the Chinese for over two millennia. Here Confucius is depicted with Laozi, another of China's great thinkers, and the Buddha, an Indian philosopher whose teachings won a widespread following in China. Confucius is clearly the pivotal figure in the painting, while Laozi is depicted as a dignified onlooker. The fact that Buddha is only a baby reflects the artist's sense of the stature of this foreign thinker compared to the two most revered figures of the Chinese intellectual tradition.

Watch the Video Series on MyHistoryLab

Learn about some key topics related to this chapter with the *MyHistoryLab Video Series: Key Topics in World History*

which he was confident he was well qualified. Angered by this rebuff, Confucius left Lu and took to the road in search of the ideal ruler, who presumably would recognize his talents and offer him employment at a suitable level of distinction at his court.

The China of Confucius's day offered abundant options for a talented political advisor. The declining power of the Zhou kingdom, which had for centuries dominated early Chinese civilization along the Yellow River, opened the way for the rise of a patchwork of rival states. Many of these competing states were ruled by nomadic peoples who had migrated from the north or west. Wars between these upstart forces and the lords of long-established households with imperial pretensions were frequent, banditry was widespread, commerce was threatened, and displaced peasants and warrior bands wandered throughout the countryside. The monarchs of some nomad kingdoms had extensively adopted the distinct culture that had been developing in the Yellow River region since the age of the Shang warrior kings. Nonetheless, Confucius and others in the emerging scholar-gentry—or shi—social strata continued to regard most of the nomads as uncouth, warlike barbarians. Convinced that he was a man with a mission, Confucius undertook a lifelong quest to become the chief advisor to a ruler who possessed the vision and skills to restore centralized control, peace, and order.

One among many wandering scholars in the late Zhou era, Confucius attracted numerous disciples, some of whom became distinguished philosophers in their own right. The master's students preserved, spread, and debated his teachings, and after his death in the early 5th century B.C.E., they compiled his wisdom in what would come to be known as the *Analects*, or collected sayings: hence, "Confucius says . . . ."

Over time, Confucius's political and social philosophy became foundational for one of humanity's greatest and most enduring civilizations (see Figure 3.1). In view of the turmoil in China when Confucian teachings were formulated, it is not surprising that they idealized strong rulers and the consolidation of political power. Confucius advocated rule by a highly educated, exclusively male elite, but one that was deemed responsible for the well-being of all of the subjects of the state. Primarily an ethical rather than a religious system, Confucianism sought to establish norms for all aspects of Chinese life, from relationships within the family that stressed respect for one's elders to the importance of art, music, and elegant calligraphy in the cultivation of scholar-bureaucrats.

Measured in terms of the acquisition of wealth and power, Confucius was a failure. He never found his ideal monarch, or even a suitable post at any of the numerous royal households that jostled for dominance across China. In fact, in the centuries following his death—often appropriately designated as the era of the warring states—political and social disintegration intensified. But the students and disciples of Confucius found a large and enthusiastic audience for his teachings in these troubled times. ∎

China generated the first of the great classical societies. The region faced periodic nomadic invasions, which encouraged an intense, and distinctive, Chinese identity. The society had a cultural heritage that stressed the basic harmony of nature: Every feature is balanced by an opposite, every *yin* by a *yang*. Thus, for hot there is cold, for male, female. According to this philosophy, an individual should seek a way, called *Dao*, to relate to this harmony, avoiding excess and appreciating the balance of opposites. Individuals and human institutions existed within this world of balanced nature, not, as in later Mediterranean philosophy, on the outside. Chinese traditions about balance, Dao, and yin/yang were

1200 B.C.E.	600 B.C.E.	400 B.C.E.	200 B.C.E.	C.E.	200 C.E.
1122–770 Former or western Zhou kingdom 770–403 Later or eastern Zhou kingdom	551–c. 233 Period of the "hundred philosophers" (including Confucius, Laozi, Mencius, Xunzi, the Legalists) 403–222 Warring States period	c. 400–320 Era of Xunzi 221–207 Qin dynasty 221 Shi Huangdi proclaimed first emperor of China 221 Great Wall completed 202–195 Reign of Liu Bang (Gaozu emperor)	200 B.C.E.–9 C.E. Former Han dynasty; development of the horse collar, stern-post rudder, and watermill 141–87 Reign of Han Wudi	23–220 Later Han dynasty; invention of paper and the compass 9–23 Interregnum of Wang Mang	2nd century Development of porcelain

intrinsic to diverse philosophies and religions established in the classical period, and they provided some unity among various schools of thought in China.

Politically, classical Chinese history begins, around 700 B.C.E., with the increasingly ineffective Zhou dynasty. Local leaders began to pull away, and there were also a number of invasions from the outside. The Zhou ruled through alliances with landed families, lacking the means to govern the whole territory directly. This was China's feudal period, with supporters asked to provide troops and tax revenues to the central government in return for grants of land. The Zhou did establish some important innovations in Chinese history, including expansion of territory. Their decline triggered cultural efforts to promote greater order—with Confucianism becoming the leading result—and ultimately a direct political response as well, under the ruthless emperor **Shi Huangdi** and the **Qin** dynasty. The Qin interlude set the conditions for the **Han** dynasty, which built the most effective bureaucracy in the premodern world. Han institutions helped build a sense of Chinese distinctiveness and identity that led the majority of Chinese to think of themselves as "sons of Han."

Despite important cultural continuities, classical China did not simply maintain earlier traditions. The formative centuries of classical Chinese history were witness to a great many changes. The religious and particularly the political habits of the Shang kingdom were substantially modified as part of building the world's largest classical empire. As a result of these new centuries of development, leading to much diversity but often painful conflict, the Chinese emerged with an unusually well-integrated system in which government, philosophy, economic incentives, the family, and the individual were intended to blend into a harmonious whole.

Shi Huangdi [shiuh-hwahng-dee] Founder of the brief Qin dynasty in 221 B.C.E.

Qin [chin] Dynasty established in 221 B.C.E. at the end of the Warring States period following the decline of the Zhou dynasty; fell in 207 B.C.E.

Han Chinese dynasty that succeeded the Qin in 202 B.C.E.; ruled for next 400 years.

PATTERNS IN CLASSICAL CHINA

3.1 How did the sequence of dynasties in classical China build a successful empire?

> The Zhou dynasty featured decentralized politics but important cultural innovations, while later dynasties emphasized order and centralization.

The Zhou Dynasty

The warfare that raged throughout China after the **Zhou** rulers lost power was a major setback for both the emerging bureaucratic elite and the ordinary people. Military skills and physical prowess were valued over the literary and ceremonial aptitudes of the scholar-administrators, or shi. Local lords whose kingdoms were constantly threatened by their neighbors (see Map 3.1) tended to concentrate power in their own hands. They put little stock in the council of men who stayed behind in the palace while they risked their lives in battle. The military leaders who wore trousers—which were widely adopted following the example of the horse-riding northern nomads—were contemptuous of the courtiers and administrators who wore robes and gowns. Rituals were neglected, and court etiquette, which had been prized in the early Zhou era, was replaced by the rough manners of nomadic invaders. Many scholar-bureaucrats found themselves without political positions and were forced to work as village schoolteachers and local scribes.

Zhou [joh] Originally a vassal family of Shang China; possibly Turkic in origin; overthrew the Shang and established second historical Chinese dynasty that flourished 1122 to 256 B.C.E.

The Zhou did, however, contribute in several ways to the development of Chinese politics and culture in their active early centuries. First, they extended the territory of China by taking over the Yangzi River valley. This new stretch of territory, from the Huanghe in the north to the Yangzi in the south, became China's core—often called the Middle Kingdom. It provided rich agricultural lands plus the benefits of two different agricultures—wheat-growing in the north, rice-growing in the south—a diversity that encouraged population growth. The territorial expansion obviously complicated the problems of central rule, for communication and transport from the capital to the outlying regions were difficult. This is why the Zhou relied so heavily on the loyalty of regional supporters.

Despite these circumstances, the Zhou actually heightened the cultural focus on the central government itself. Zhou rulers claimed direct links to the Shang rulers. They also asserted that heaven had transferred its mandate to rule China to the Zhou emperors. This political concept of a mandate from heaven remained a key justification for Chinese imperial rule from the Zhou on. Known as Sons of Heaven, the emperors lived in a world of awe-inspiring pomp and ceremony.

The Zhou worked to provide greater cultural unity in their empire. They discouraged some of the primitive religious practices of the Huanghe civilization, banning human sacrifice and urging more restrained ceremonies to worship the gods. They also promoted linguistic unity, beginning the process by which a standard spoken language, ultimately called Mandarin Chinese, prevailed over the entire Middle Kingdom. This resulted in the largest single group of people speaking the same language in the world at this time. Regional dialects and languages remained, but educated officials began to rely on the single Mandarin form. Oral epics and stories in Chinese, many gradually recorded in written form, aided in the development of a common cultural currency.

Increasing cultural unity helps explain why, when the Zhou empire began to fail, scholars were able to use philosophical ideas to lessen the impact of growing political confusion. Indeed, the political crisis spurred efforts to define and articulate Chinese culture. During the late 6th and early 5th centuries B.C.E., the philosopher known in the West as Confucius wrote an elaborate statement on political ethics, providing the core of China's distinctive philosophical heritage. Other writers and religious leaders participated in this great period of cultural creativity, which later reemerged as a set of central beliefs throughout the Middle Kingdom.

Cultural innovation did not, however, reverse the prolonged and painful Zhou downfall. Regional rulers formed independent armies, ultimately reducing the emperors to little more than figureheads. Between 402 and 201 B.C.E., a period known aptly enough as the Era of the Warring States, the Zhou system disintegrated. In reaction, new political ideas emerged, called Legalism, which urged rulers to establish order at all costs.

MAP 3.1 **The Era of Nomadic Incursions and Warring States** The fragmented state of the core areas of Chinese civilization from the 6th to the 3rd centuries B.C.E. is clearly illustrated on this map of the many states that jostled for power. The map shows the rise of the semi-nomadic kingdom of Qin in the 3rd century, which both unified politically and greatly enlarged the territory controlled by a mixture of ethnic Chinese and various nomadic peoples.

The Qin Dynasty

At this point, China might have gone the way of civilizations such as India, where centralized government was more the exception than the rule. But a new dynasty arose to reverse the process of political decay. One regional ruler deposed the last Zhou emperor and within 35 years made himself sole ruler of China. He took the title Qin Shi Huangdi, or First Emperor. The dynastic name, Qin, conferred on the whole country its name of China. Qin Shi Huangdi was a brutal ruler, but effective given the circumstances of internal disorder and supported as well by Legalist ideas. He understood that China's problem lay in the regional power of the aristocrats, and like many later centralizers in world history, he worked vigorously to undo this force. He ordered nobles to leave their regions and appear at his court, assuming control of their feudal estates. China was organized into large provinces ruled by bureaucrats appointed by the emperor; and Qin Shi Huangdi was careful to select his officials from nonaristocratic groups, so that they would owe their power to him and not dare to develop their own independent bases. Under Qin Shi Huangdi's rule, powerful armies crushed regional resistance.

The First Emperor followed up on centralization by extending Chinese territory further to the south, reaching present-day Hong Kong on the South China Sea and even influencing northern

CHAPTER 3 Classical Civilization: China 57

Read the Document on MyHistoryLab: Sima Qian, The Life of Meng Tian, Builder of the Great Wall

FIGURE 3.2 When kept in good repair and supplied with sufficient numbers of soldiers, the high walls and broad battlements of what would become the northern wall were a formidable obstacle for nomads who sought to invade China. The impressive barrier was made by joining and extending several walls that had been built by regional kingdoms in north China before they were conquered by the Qin. Among the most impressive engineering triumphs of the ancient world, the wall ran for more than 1400 miles through and above the north China plain (see Map 3.2). For more than two millennia, the wall, frequently repaired and improved as this photo illustrates, buffered the interaction between Chinese civilization and the nomadic peoples to the west and north of the Yellow River basin.

Great Wall Chinese defensive fortification intended to keep out the nomadic invaders from the north; initiated during Qin dynasty and reign of Shi Huangdi.

Vietnam. In the north, to guard against barbarian invasions, Qin Shi Huangdi built a **Great Wall**, extending more than 3000 miles, wide enough for chariots to move along its crest. This massive mud wall, probably the largest construction project in human history up to that point, was built by forced labor, conscripted by the central bureaucracy from among the peasantry (Figure 3.2).

The Qin dynasty was responsible for a number of innovations in Chinese politics and culture. To determine the empire's resources, Qin Shi Huangdi ordered a national census, which provided data for the calculation of tax revenues and labor service. The government standardized coinage, weights, and measures through the entire realm. Even the length of axles on carts was regulated to promote coherent road planning. The government also made Chinese written script uniform, completing the process of creating a single basic language in which all educated Chinese could communicate. The government furthered agriculture, sponsoring new irrigation projects, and promoted manufacturing, particularly for silk cloth. The activist government also attacked formal culture, including Confucian ideas, burning many books. Thinking, according to Qin Shi Huangdi, was likely to be subversive to his autocratic rule.

Read the Document on MyHistoryLab: Li Si and the Legalist Policies of Qin Shihuang (280–208 B.C.E.)

Although it created many durable features of Chinese government, the Qin dynasty was short-lived. Qin Shi Huangdi's attacks on intellectuals, and particularly the high taxes needed to support military expansion and the construction of the Great Wall, made him fiercely unpopular. One opponent described the First Emperor as a monster who "had the heart of a tiger and a wolf. He killed men as though he thought he could never finish, he punished men as though he were afraid he would never get around to them all." The emperor, for all his great power, grew increasingly afraid of death as he aged—partly because of various assassination attempts. He scoured the countryside seeking magic formulas to prolong life and had many books burned so that scholars would concentrate on his needs.

FIGURE **3.3** Hundreds of these clay warriors were found in the tomb of the first Chinese emperor, Shi Huangdi. Remarkably, each of the warriors has different facial features. Together with the clay horses also found in the tomb, these massed forces are striking evidence of the power of the founder of China's short-lived, first imperial dynasty. They also reflect the emperor's obsession with monumental building projects—a direct cause of the fall of the repressive Qin dynasty within a few years of Shi Huangdi's death.

Ironically, he died (in 210 B.C.E.) as a result of taking mercury pills his doctors prescribed in an effort to prolong life. Even then the drama did not end: He needed to be transported to the elaborate tomb he had constructed (Figure 3.3), but his advisers worried about a popular revolt if news of his death leaked out, so they arranged carts of rotten fish to accompany his body in order to disguise the smell. Even so, massive risings organized by aggrieved peasants broke out. One peasant leader defeated other opponents and in 202 B.C.E. established the third dynasty of classical China, the Han (see Map 3.2).

The Han Dynasty

It was the Han dynasty, which lasted more than 400 years, to 220 C.E., that rounded out China's basic political and intellectual structure. Han rulers retained the centralized administration of the Qin but sought to reduce the brutal repression of that period. Like many dynasties during the first flush of power, early Han rulers expanded Chinese territory, pushing into Korea, Indochina, and central Asia. This expansion gave rise to direct contact with India and also allowed the Chinese to develop contact with the Parthian empire in the Middle East, through which trade with the Roman empire around the Mediterranean was conducted. The most famous Han ruler, Wudi (140–87 B.C.E.), enforced peace throughout much of the continent of Asia, rather like the peace the Roman empire would bring to the Mediterranean region a hundred years later, but embracing even more territory and a larger population. Peace brought great prosperity to China itself. A Han historian conveys the self-satisfied, confident tone of the dynasty:

> The nation had met with no major disturbances so that, except in times of flood or drought, every person was well supplied and every family had enough to get along on. The granaries in the cities and the countryside were full and the government treasuries were running over with wealth. In the capital the strings of cash had stacked up by the hundreds of millions until . . . they could no longer be counted. In the central granary of the government, new grain was heaped on top of the old until the building was full and the grain overflowed and piled up outside, where it spoiled and became unfit to eat. . . . Even the keepers of the community gates ate fine grain and meat.

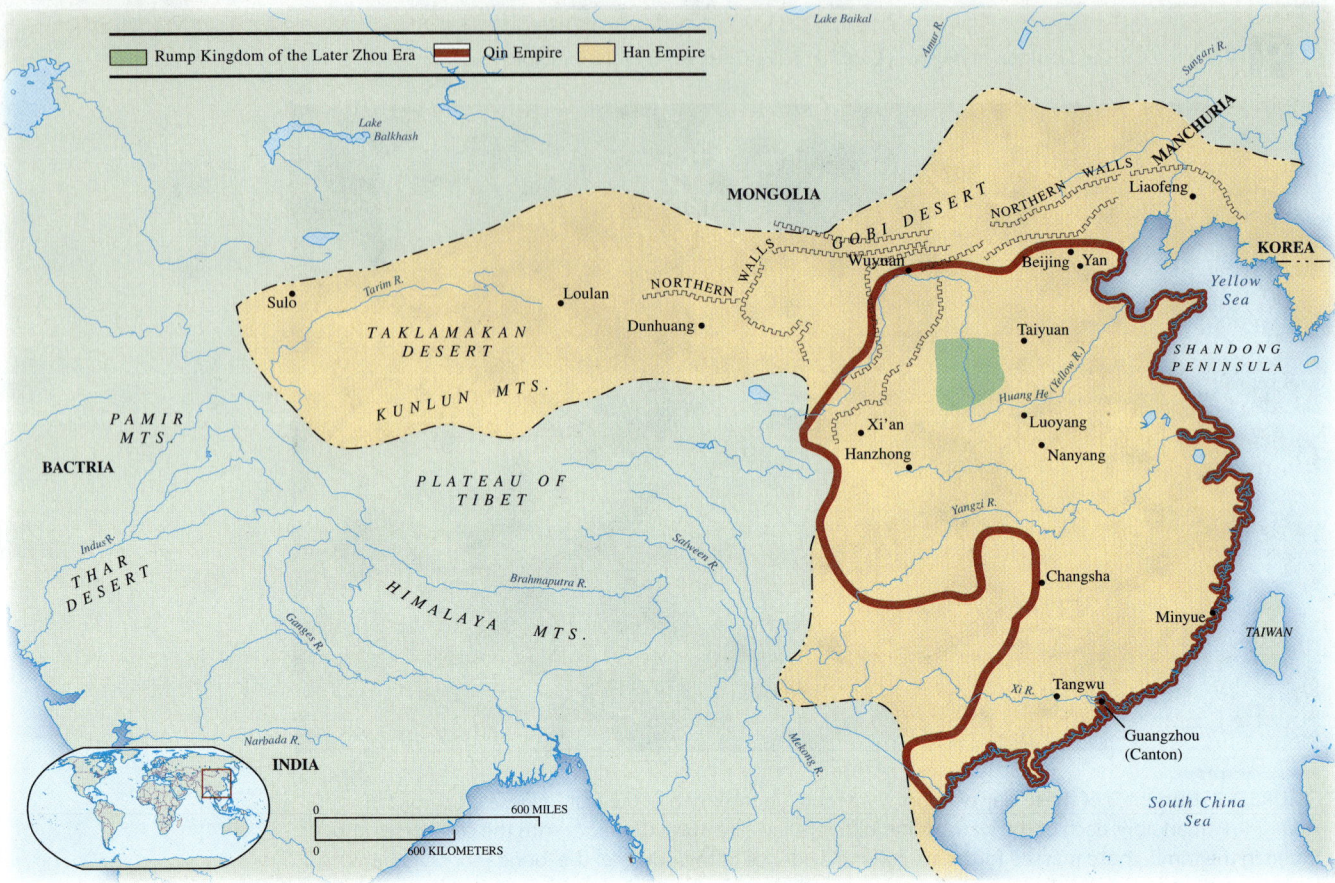

MAP 3.2 **China from the Later Zhou Era to the Han Era** As this map showing the boundaries of successive Chinese dynasties illustrates, the extent of the early Han empire greatly exceeded even that of the Qin dynasty, which was the first to effectively unify the core regions of Chinese civilization.

Under the Han dynasty, the workings of the state bureaucracy also improved, and the government was linked to formal training that emphasized the values of Confucian philosophy. Reversing the Qin dynasty's policies, Wudi urged support for Confucianism, seeing it as a vital supplement to formal measures on the government's part; shrines were established to promote the worship of the ancient philosopher as a god.

The quality of Han rule declined after about two centuries. Central control weakened, and invasions from central Asia, spearheaded by a nomadic people called the Xiongnu, who had long threatened China's northern borders, overturned the dynasty entirely. Between 220 and 589 C.E., China was in a state of chaos. Order and stability were finally restored, but by then the classical or formative period of Chinese civilization had ended. Well before the Han collapse, however, China had established distinctive political structures and cultural values of unusual clarity, capable, as it turned out, of surviving even three centuries of renewed confusion.

POLITICAL INSTITUTIONS

3.2 What were the distinctive features of China's political system under the Han?

The power of the emperor, the development of a bureaucracy, and the expansion of state functions became hallmarks of classical Chinese politics.

The Qin and Han dynasties of classical China established a distinctive, and remarkably successful, kind of government. The Qin stressed central authority, whereas the Han expanded the powers of the bureaucracy. More than any other factor, it was the structure of this government that explained how such a vast territory could be effectively ruled—for the Chinese empire was indeed the largest political system in the classical world. This structure changed after the classical period, particularly in terms of streamlining and expanding bureaucratic systems and procedures, but it never required a fundamental overhaul.

Several key elements predominated. Strong local units never disappeared. Like most successful agricultural societies, China relied heavily on tightly knit patriarchal families. Individual families were linked to other relatives in extended family networks that included brothers, uncles, and any living grandparents. Among the wealthy landowning groups, family authority was enhanced by the practice of ancestor worship, which joined family members through rituals devoted to important forebears who had passed into the spirit world. For ordinary people, among whom ancestor worship was less common, village authority surmounted family rule. Village leaders helped farming families regulate property and coordinate planting and harvest work. During the Zhou dynasty, and also in later periods when dynasties weakened, the regional power of great landlords also played an important role at the village level. Landed nobles provided courts of justice and organized military troops.

Strong local rule was not the most significant or distinctive feature of Chinese government under the Qin and Han dynasties, however. Qin Shi Huangdi not only attacked local rulers; he also provided a single law code for the whole empire and established a uniform tax system. He appointed governors to each district of his domain, who exercised military and legal powers in the name of the emperor. They, in turn, named officials responsible for smaller regions. Here indeed was a classic model of centralized government that other societies later replicated: the establishment of centralized codes and appointment of officials directly by a central authority, rather than by reliance on arrangements with numerous existing local governments. The effectiveness of a central government was further enhanced by specialization among the emperor's ministers. Some dealt with matters of finance, others with justice, others with military affairs, and so on.

Strong Bureaucracy

Han dynasty rulers not only resumed the attack on local warrior-landlords, but also realized the importance of creating a large, highly skilled bureaucracy. By the end of the Han period, China had about 130,000 bureaucrats, representing 0.2 percent of the population. The emperor Wudi established examinations for his bureaucrats—the first example of civil service tests of the sort that many governments have instituted in modern times. These examinations covered classics of Chinese literature as well as law, suggesting a model of the scholar-bureaucrat that later became an important element of China's political tradition. Wudi also established a school to train men of exceptional talent and ability for the national examinations. Although most bureaucrats were drawn from the landed upper classes, who alone had the time to learn the complex system of Chinese characters, individuals from lower ranks of society were occasionally recruited under this system. China's bureaucracy thus provided a slight check on complete upper-class rule. It also tended to limit the exercise of arbitrary power by the emperor himself. Trained and experienced bureaucrats, confident in their own traditions, could often control the whims of a single ruler, even one who, in the Chinese tradition, regarded himself as divinely appointed—the "Son of Heaven." It was no accident then that the Chinese bureaucracy lasted from the Han period until the 20th century, outliving the empire itself. Small wonder that from the classical period at least until modern times, and possibly still today, the Chinese were the most tightly governed people in any large society in the world.

Roles of the State

Government traditions established during the classical period included an impressive list of state functions. Like all organized states, the Chinese government operated military and judicial systems. Military activity fluctuated for China did not depend on steady expansion. Judicial matters—crime and legal disputes—commanded more attention by local government authorities.

The government also sponsored much intellectual life, organizing research in astronomy and the maintenance of historical records. Under the Han rulers, the government played a major role in promoting Confucian philosophy as an official statement of Chinese values and in encouraging the worship of Confucius himself. The government developed a durable sense of mission as the primary keeper of Chinese beliefs.

The imperial government was active in the economy. It directly organized the production of iron and salt. Its standardization of currency, weights, and measures facilitated trade throughout the

THINKING HISTORICALLY

Xunzi and the Shift from Ritual Combat to "Real" War

The development of classical civilizations in the Middle East, Greece, China, and India greatly advanced the business of making war. Agricultural surpluses made it possible to support specialized fighters and military commanders. Population growth made for larger armies, which needed armor, weapons, and training. Horses, and in some areas camels and elephants, were raised to carry men into battle or pull war chariots. Advances in metalworking meant steadily improving weaponry, and fortification became a major concern for early engineers and architects. Warfare came to involve more soldiers, who fought for longer periods and suffered more casualties. Frontier defenses and military campaigns became primary concerns for those who ruled civilized states.

Despite advances in weaponry and training, at least for warrior elites, warfare in most early civilizations was a combination of ritual and chaos. Wars normally were not fought during harvest times, the winter, or the monsoon season. A ruler was expected to announce his intention to attack a neighboring kingdom well in advance. Before battle, the high priests of each ruler offered sacrifices to the gods. Their readings of various sorts of omens, not strategic considerations, determined the time and place of combat. Battles consisted primarily of formal duels between trained and well-armed warriors in the midst of confused collisions of masses of poorly trained and armed foot soldiers, who were usually slaves or forcibly recruited peasants. Although often fierce, the warriors' duels were regulated by codes of honor and fair play. For example, it was unseemly for a warrior to strike from behind or to strike when his opponent had fallen.

Duels between warrior champions were the set pieces of a battle. As the great epics of early civilizations, such as the Indian *Mahabharata* and the Greek *Iliad* demonstrate, great warriors cut bloody swaths through the ranks of poorly prepared infantry and lesser fighters to get to each other and set up the hand-to-hand combats that normally determined the outcome of battle. The death of a commander, who was often the ruler of the kingdom at war or a renowned champion, usually meant the collapse of his forces and their chaotic flight from the field. Normally, the victorious army did not destroy or capture what remained of the opposing soldiers. The game had been played and won. The winners either retired with their booty to prepare for the next round or began negotiations to set the terms on which the defeated party would submit to their overlordship.

The Shang and early Zhou periods of Chinese history were filled with wars, most of which were fought according to this ritualized pattern. But by the late Zhou period, some commanders and thinkers had become highly critical of the indecisiveness and waste of the endless conflicts between the warring states. In the 4th century B.C.E., Xunzi, an advisor to one of the warring monarchs, responded to these concerns with a treatise, *The Art of War*, a classic of military theory. Xunzi proposed a vision of military conflict very different from the ritualized approach to war.

> **Xunzi argued that war was merely an extension of statecraft. Wars ought not to be games or macho contests for bragging rights; they ought to be fought only for ends that increased the territory, wealth, and power of the state.**

Xunzi argued that war was merely an extension of statecraft. Wars ought not to be games or macho contests for bragging rights; they ought to be fought only for ends that increased the territory, wealth, and power of the state. With these aims in mind, Xunzi insisted that speed was of the essence in warfare and that long wars burdened the subjects of the warring rulers and bred rebellions. He also urged that target kingdoms be captured swiftly and with as little damage as possible. Xunzi argued that war was a science, which should be the object of extensive study. Rather than brawny warriors, commanders ought to be men well versed in organization, strategy, and tactics. He proposed, and Chinese rulers set up, special schools to train officers in the art of war.

Xunzi's ideas transformed warfare in China. Rulers made every effort short of war to bring down their rivals. Bluffs, spies, threats, and saboteurs were used before armies were sent to war. Both before and after war was actually declared, substantial state resources and large bureaucracies were devoted to building and training armies and supplying them in the field. Sneak attacks were considered fair, and feints and ruses were regularly used by field commanders. Weather conditions and advantageous terrain determined the time and place of battle.

Psychological devices were strongly recommended. For example, techniques were used to make the enemy commanders angry and cause them to make foolish moves that might demoralize their armies. Discipline was needed, rather than individual heroics. This point was driven home by a ruler who had one of his commanders beheaded because the general troops attacked ahead of schedule, despite the fact that this action was the key to victory. In combat, regular formations replaced mass brawls; soldiers fought as units under the direction of a chain of commanders. Good fighters were still valued, but now as unit leaders rather than accomplished duelists. The main object of battle became the destruction of the enemy's forces as quickly as possible.

Shi Huangdi's military and political successes demonstrated how effective warfare reorganized along the lines suggested by Xunzi might be. Halfway across the globe, the Greeks were

(continued on next page)

independently developing comparable patterns of warfare. Ironically, this shift in approaches to warfare between the Greek city-states was occurring at about the same time the compilers of the *Iliad* were celebrating the contests of great heroes such as Achilles and Hector. In roughly the same era as Xunzi and Shi Huangdi, the tightly disciplined formations and training of smaller Greek armies culminated in Alexander the Great's unprecedented conquests.

But these successes did not put an end to ritual warfare between civilized peoples. Although Chinese armies tended to be organized and led according to the prescriptions of Xunzi and other theorists, the chivalric codes and battles centered on the duels of champions persisted. This was particularly true in societies that were dominated by warrior elites, such as those that later developed in India, Japan, Africa, Europe, and Mesoamerica. But conditions in the warring states and the genius of Xunzi had led to a radically new vision of what wars were about and how they were fought. The effects of this vision are still felt by civilized societies.

> **QUESTIONS**
> - What were some of the major differences between ritual warfare and the new approach proposed by Xunzi?
> - What are the main advantages and drawbacks of each approach?
> - If you were an ancient ruler, which would you tell your military commanders to use?
> - Why?

vast empire. The government additionally sponsored public works, including complex irrigation and canal systems. Han rulers even tried to regulate agricultural supplies by storing grain and rice in good times to control price increases—and potential popular unrest—when harvests were bad.

China's ambitious rulers in no sense directed the daily lives of their subjects; the technology of an agricultural society did not permit this. Even under the Han, it took more than a month for a directive from the capital city to reach the outlying districts of the empire—an obvious limit on imperial authority. A revealing Chinese proverb held that "heaven is high, and the emperor is far away." However, the power of the Chinese state did extend considerably. Its system of courts was backed by a strict code of law; torture and execution were widely employed to supplement the preaching of obedience and civic virtue. The central government taxed its subjects and also required some annual labor on the part of every male peasant—this was the source of the incredible physical work involved in building canals, roads, and palaces. No other government had the organization and staff to reach ordinary people so directly until virtually modern times, except in much smaller political units such as city-states. The power of the government and the authority it commanded in the eyes of most ordinary Chinese people help explain why its structure survived decline, invasion, and even rebellion for so many centuries. Invaders such as the Xiongnu might topple a dynasty, but they could not devise a better system to run the country, and so the system and its bureaucratic administrators endured or were soon removed.

RELIGION AND CULTURE

3.3 What was the relationship between Confucianism and Daoism?

> Chinese culture featured the development of the Confucian system, but Daoism and distinctive scientific artistic traditions complemented Confucianism.

The Chinese way of viewing the world, as this belief system developed during the classical period, was closely linked to the political structure. Upper-class cultural values emphasized a good life on earth and the virtues of obedience to the state, more than speculations about God and the mysteries of heaven. At the same time, the Chinese tolerated and often combined various specific beliefs, so long as they did not contradict basic political loyalties.

Rulers in the Zhou dynasty maintained belief in a god or gods, but little attention was given to the nature of a deity. Rather, Chinese leaders stressed the importance of a harmonious earthly life that maintained proper balance between earth and heaven. Harmony included carefully constructed rituals to unify society and prevent individual excess. Among the upper classes, people were trained in elaborate exercises and military skills such as archery. Commonly, ceremonies venerating ancestors and even marking special meals were conducted. The use of chopsticks began at the end of the Zhou dynasty; it encouraged a code of politeness at meals. Soon after this, tea was introduced, although the most elaborate tea-drinking rituals developed later on in Japan more than China.

> **Read** the **Document** on **MyHistoryLab:** Confucius: Selections from the *Analects*

FIGURE 3.4 A portrait of Confucius. Because no contemporary likenesses of Confucius have survived, the artists of each era in China's long history depicted him in ways that reflected the tastes and needs of the elites then in power. Here, for example, Confucius is shown as a kind and wise—even grandfatherly—sage. In less stable and prosperous times, he might be depicted as a stern teacher bent on restoring the moral fiber that the Chinese believed was essential to social harmony.

Confucius Also known as Kong Fuzi; major Chinese philosopher born in 6th century B.C.E.; author of *Analects*; philosophy based on need for restoration of order through advice of superior men to be found among the shi.

> **Read** the **Document** on **MyHistoryLab:** Confucian political philosophy: an excerpt from Mencius

Even before these specific ceremonies arose, however, the basic definition of a carefully ordered existence was given more formal philosophical backing. Amidst the long decline of the Zhou dynasty, many thinkers and religious prophets began to challenge Chinese traditions. From this ferment came a restatement of the traditions that ultimately reduced intellectual conflict and established a long-lasting tone for Chinese cultural and social life.

Confucianism

Confucius, or Kong Fuzi (which means Master Kong), lived from roughly 551 to 478 B.C.E. (Figure 3.4). His life was devoted to teaching, and he traveled through many parts of China preaching his ideas of political virtue and good government. Confucius was not a religious leader; he believed in a divine order but refused to speculate about it. Chinese civilization was unusual, in the classical period and well beyond, in that its dominant values were secular rather than religious.

Confucius saw himself as a spokesman for Chinese tradition and for what he believed were the great days of the Chinese state before the Zhou declined. He maintained that if people could be taught to emphasize personal virtue, which included a reverence for tradition, a solid political life would naturally result. The Confucian list of virtues stressed respect for one's social superiors—including fathers and husbands as leaders of the family. However, this emphasis on a proper hierarchy was balanced by an insistence that society's leaders behave modestly and without excess, shunning abusive power and treating courteously those people who were in their charge. According to Confucius, moderation in behavior, veneration of custom and ritual, and a love of wisdom should characterize the leaders of society at all levels. And with virtuous leaders, a sound political life would inevitably follow: "In an age of good government, men in high stations give preference to men of ability and give opportunity to those who are below them, and lesser people labor vigorously at their husbandry to serve their superiors."

Confucianism was primarily a system of ethics—do unto others as your status and theirs dictate—and a plea for loyalty to the community. It confirmed the distaste that many educated Chinese had developed for religious mysteries, as well as their delight in learning and good manners. Confucian doctrine, lovingly preserved in a book called the *Analects*, was revived under the Han emperors, who saw the usefulness of Confucian emphasis on political virtue and social order. Confucian learning was also incorporated, along with traditional literary works, into the training of aspiring bureaucrats.

Confucianism emphasized the importance of the gentleman, a member of what came to be known as the *shi* class. A superior man controlled his emotions, observed all the proper manners and rituals. He was a generalist, not a specialist, capable of serving in all sorts of government positions, capable of contributing also to art and poetry. His authority rested on his morality, not his expertise. Confucius believed that if such men ruled China, harmony would prevail forever.

For subordinates, Confucius largely recommended obedience and respect; people should know their place, even under bad rulers. However, he urged a political system that would not base rank simply on birth but would make education accessible to all talented and intelligent members of society. The primary emphasis still rested nonetheless on the obligations and desirable characteristics of the ruling class. According to Confucius, force alone cannot permanently conquer unrest, but kindness toward the people and protection of their vital interests will. Rulers should also be humble and sincere, for people will grow rebellious under hypocrisy or arrogance. Nor should rulers be greedy; Confucius warned against a profit motive in leadership, stressing that true happiness rested in doing good for all, not individual gain. Confucius projected the ideal of a gentleman, best described by his benevolence and self-control, a man always courteous and eager for service and anxious to learn.

Confucianism was accepted and amplified by many disciples. Mencius (Meng Ko) was an important figure who emphasized the goodness of human nature. People should be ruled in ways that brought out their goodness. Mencius' ideas, less hierarchical than pure Confucianism, set the basis for the belief that it was legitimate for peasants to rebel against oppressive rulers. While Confucianism spread particularly among the upper classes, ultimately encouraged by the Han dynasty, elements did spread beyond the upper classes, including a taste for ritual, although ordinary peasants also maintained an active polytheistic belief, including a host of practices designed to ward off evil spirits.

Legalism

During the Qin and early Han periods, the alternate system of political thought called Legalism sprang up in China. Legalist writers prided themselves on their pragmatism. They disdained Confucian virtues in favor of an authoritarian state that ruled by force. Human nature for the Legalists was evil and required restraint and discipline. In a proper state, the army would control and the people would labor; the idea of pleasures in educated discourse or courtesy was dismissed as frivolity. Although Legalism never captured the widespread approval that Confucianism did, it too entered the political traditions of China, where a Confucian veneer was often combined with strong-arm tactics.

Read the Document on MyHistoryLab: The Way of the State (475–221 B.C.E.)

Daoism

Classical China also produced a more religious philosophy—Daoism—which arose at roughly the same time as Confucianism, during the waning centuries of the Zhou dynasty. Daoism first appealed to many in the upper classes, who had an interest in a more elaborate spirituality. Daoism embraced traditional Chinese beliefs in nature's harmony and added a sense of nature's mystery. As a spiritual alternative to Confucianism, Daoism produced a durable division in China's religious and philosophical culture. This new religion, vital for Chinese civilization, although never widely exported, was furthered by Laozi, who probably lived during the 5th century B.C.E. Laozi stressed that nature contains inherent principles that, if not recognized, lead to strife and unhappiness. True human understanding comes in withdrawing from the world and contemplating this life force. Dao, which means "the way of nature," refers to this same basic, indescribable force:

> There is a thing confusedly formed,
> Born before heaven and earth.
> Silent and void
> It stands alone and does not change,
> Goes round and does not weary.
> It is capable of being the mother of the world.
> I know not its name,
> So I style it "the way."

Along with secret rituals, Daoism promoted its own set of ethics. Daoist harmony with nature best resulted through humility and frugal living. According to this movement, political activity and learning were irrelevant to a good life, and general conditions in the world were of little importance.

Daoism, which combined with a strong Buddhist influence from India during the chaos that followed the collapse of the Han dynasty, guaranteed that China's people were not united by a single religious or philosophical system. Individuals did come to embrace some elements from both Daoism and Confucianism, and indeed many emperors favored Daoism. They accepted its spread with little anxiety, partly because some of them found solace in Daoist belief but also because the religion, with its otherworldly emphasis, posed no real political threat. Confucian scholars disagreed vigorously with Daoist thinking, particularly its emphasis on mysteries and magic, but they saw little reason to challenge its influence. As Daoism became an increasingly formal religion, from the later Han dynasty on, it provided many Chinese with a host of ceremonies designed to promote harmony with the mysterious life force. Finally, the Chinese government from the Han dynasty on was able to persuade Daoist priests to include expressions of loyalty to the emperor in their temple services. This heightened Daoism's political compatibility with Confucianism.

Literature, Art, and Science

Confucianism and Daoism were not the only intellectual products of China's classical period, but they were the most important. Confucianism blended easily with the high value of literature and art among the upper classes. In literature, a set of Five Classics, written during the early part of the Zhou

CHAPTER 3 Classical Civilization: China   65

DOCUMENT

Teachings of the Rival Chinese Schools

THE BRIEF PASSAGES QUOTED HERE ARE taken from the writings of Confucius, Xunzi (a Legalist scholar), and Laozi. Identify the author of each passage and explain why you believe it was written by the person you chose.

CONFUCIUS:

I take no action and the people are reformed.
I enjoy peace and people become honest.
I do nothing and people become rich.
I have no desires and people return to the good and simple life.
The gentleman cherishes virtue; the inferior man cherishes possessions.
The educated man thinks of sanctions; the inferior man thinks of personal favors.

XUNZI:

The nature of man is evil; his goodness is acquired.
His nature being what it is, man is born, first, with a desire for gain.
If this desire is followed, strife will result and courtesy will disappear.
Keep your mouth closed.

LAOZI:

Be at one with the dust of the earth.
This is primal union.
Personal cultivation begins with poetry, is made firm with rules of decorum, and is perfected by music.
When it is left to follow its natural feelings, human nature will do good. That is why I say it is good. If it becomes evil, it is not the fault of man's original capability.

QUESTIONS

- Which of these ideas are most compatible?
- Which of these three cultural systems are most in conflict?
- Which of them could best be called religious?
- Which philosophers propose ideas that are best suited to people who want to build a strong and unified political order?

---

dynasty and then edited during the time of Confucius, provided an important tradition. They were used, among other things, as a basis for civil service examinations. The works provided in the Five Classics included some historical treatises, speeches, and other political materials, and a discussion of etiquette and ceremonies; in the *Classic of Songs*, more than 300 poems dealing with love, joy, politics, and family life appeared. The Chinese literary tradition developed on the basis of mastering these early works, plus Confucian writing; each generation of writers found new meanings in the classical literature, which allowed them to express new ideas within a familiar framework. In literature, poetry commanded particular attention because the Chinese language featured melodic speech and variant pronunciations of the same basic sound, a characteristic that promoted an outpouring of poetry. From the classical period on, the ability to learn and recite poetry became the mark of an educated Chinese. Finally, the literary tradition established in classical China reinforced the Confucian emphasis on human life, although the subjects included romance and sorrow as well as political values.

Chinese art during the classical period was largely decorative, stressing careful detail and craftsmanship (Figure 3.5). Artistic styles often reflected the precision and geometric qualities of the many symbols of Chinese writing. Calligraphy became an important art form. In addition, Chinese artists painted, worked in bronze and pottery, carved jade and ivory, and wove silk screens. Classical China did not produce monumental buildings, aside from the Great Wall and some imperial palaces and tombs, in part because of the absence of a single religion; indeed, the entire tone of upper-class Confucianism was such that it discouraged the notion of temples soaring to the heavens.

In science, important practical work was encouraged, rather than imaginative theorizing. Chinese astronomers had developed an accurate calendar by 444 B.C.E., based on a year of 365.5 days. Later astronomers calculated the movement of the planets Saturn and Jupiter and observed sunspots—more than 1500 years before comparable knowledge developed in Europe. The purpose of Chinese astronomy was to make celestial phenomena predictable, as part of the wider interest in ensuring harmony between heaven and earth. Chinese scientists steadily improved their instrumentation, inventing a kind of seismograph to register earthquakes during the Han dynasty. The Chinese were also active in medical research, developing precise anatomical knowledge and studying principles of hygiene that could promote longer life.

FIGURE 3.5 This painting of "The First Emperor of the Han Dynasty Entering Guandang," by Zhao Bozhu, seeks to recapture the pomp and splendor associated with the founder of the Han dynasty, one of the most powerful and long-lived in Chinese history. By the last centuries B.C.E., large, richly attired entourages, which moved about among several palaces and walled cities, were deemed essential for the emperors and regional lords who had become the dominant force in Chinese political life.

Chinese mathematics also stressed the practical. Daoism encouraged some exploration of the orderly processes of nature, but far more research focused on how things actually worked. For example, Chinese scholars studied the mathematics of music in ways that led to advances in acoustics. This focus for science and mathematics contrasted notably with the more abstract definition of science developed in classical Greece.

ECONOMY AND SOCIETY

3.4 How did Confucianism affect Chinese social and family structure?

> China's economy featured extensive internal trade and important technological innovations. China's family system stressed a rigid patriarchy.

Although the most distinctive features of classical China centered on politics and culture, developments in the economy, social structure, and family life also shaped Chinese civilization and continued to have an impact on the empire's history for a significant period of time.

As in many agricultural societies, considerable gaps developed between China's upper class, which controlled large landed estates, and the masses, farmer-peasants who produced little more than what was needed for their own subsistence. The difficulty of becoming literate symbolized these gaps, for landlords enjoyed not only wealth but also a culture denied to most common people. Prior to the Zhou dynasty, slaveholding may have been common in China, but by the time of the Zhou, the main social division existed between the landowning gentry—about 2 percent of the total population—and peasants, who provided dues and service to these lords while also controlling some of their own land. The Chinese peasantry depended on intensive cooperation, particularly in the southern rice region; in this group, property was characteristically owned and regulated by the village or the extended family, rather than by individuals. Beneath the peasantry, Chinese social structure included a group of "mean" people who performed rough transport and other unskilled jobs and suffered the lowest possible status. In general, social status was passed from one generation to the next through inheritance, although unusually talented individuals from a peasant background might be given access to an education and rise within the bureaucracy.

The Confucian Social System

Officially then and to a large extent in fact, classical China consisted of two main social groups, with the mean people and a few household slaves a third segment at the bottom of the heap. The landowning aristocracy plus the educated bureaucrats formed the top group. This top group, first known as the "shi," then the scholar-gentry, under the Han combined education and bureaucratic service with landowning. Scholar-gentry families cooperated to run the estates and also provide bureaucrats. They were marked by their special attire, including silks, which commoners were not supposed to wear. Most gentry families employed some toughs to help protect them and to make sure commoners stayed in their place, but they also received great deference from most ordinary people. Under the gentry next came the laboring masses, peasants, and also urban artisans who manufactured goods. These people, far poorer than the top group and also condemned to a life of hard manual labor, sometimes worked directly on large estates but in other cases had some economic independence. Trade became increasingly important during the Zhou and particularly the Han dynasties. Much trade focused on luxury items for the upper class, produced by skilled artisans in the cities—silks, jewelry, leather goods, and furniture. There was also food exchange between the wheat- and rice-growing regions. Copper coins began to circulate, which facilitated trade, with merchants even sponsoring commercial visits to India. Although trade and its attendant merchant class were vital, the Confucian emphasis on learning and political service led to considerable scorn for lives devoted to moneymaking. The gap between the real importance and wealth of merchants and their officially low prestige was an enduring legacy in Confucian China.

The Han Capital at Xi'an

The urban growth that had been one of the most notable social developments in the late Zhou era continued in the Han period. The new capital city at Xi'an took on the basic features of Chinese imperial cities from that time forward. Laid out on a somewhat distorted grid, Xi'an had broad roadways that gave access to and defined the main quarters of the city. Much of the city was protected by long earth and brick walls, with towers and gates at regular intervals. Estimates of Xi'an's population range from about 100,000, which probably count only people living within the walls, to 250,000, which included people living outside the walls and in neighboring villages.

VISUALIZING THE PAST

Capital Designs and Patterns of Political Power

THE DESIGN AND PHYSICAL LAYOUT OF THE CAPITAL CITIES of early civilizations can tell us a great deal about the distribution of political power and social status in different centers of the ancient world (see Map 3.3). In addition, the configurations of these pivotal cities usually manifest religious beliefs and conceptions of the cosmic order in the ways they are oriented and physically constructed. Therefore, plans of the capital centers of ancient civilizations can be read like written texts to help us understand the early history of some of humankind's greatest civilizations. Reproduced here are schematic diagrams of some of the key features of the capital cities of three of the great early civilizations of Eurasia: from Xi'an in Han China, Athens in Greece, and Harappa in India. Study and compare these diagrams for what they tell us about the kinds of elite groups that exercised political power, social stratification, and thinking about the relationship between the supernatural and human rulers in each civilization for which they served as capitals. In thinking about these issues, you may want to refer to relevant sections in Chapters 3, 4, and 5.

> **QUESTIONS**
> - Which social groups were the most powerful politically in each society?
> - How prominent was military force in the exercise of power by the elites in each civilization?
> - To what extent was political power legitimized by religious figures, ideas, and conceptions of the workings of the cosmos?
> - To what degree did the rulers and political elites seek to separate themselves from the subject population, and what evidence could you use to determine this?

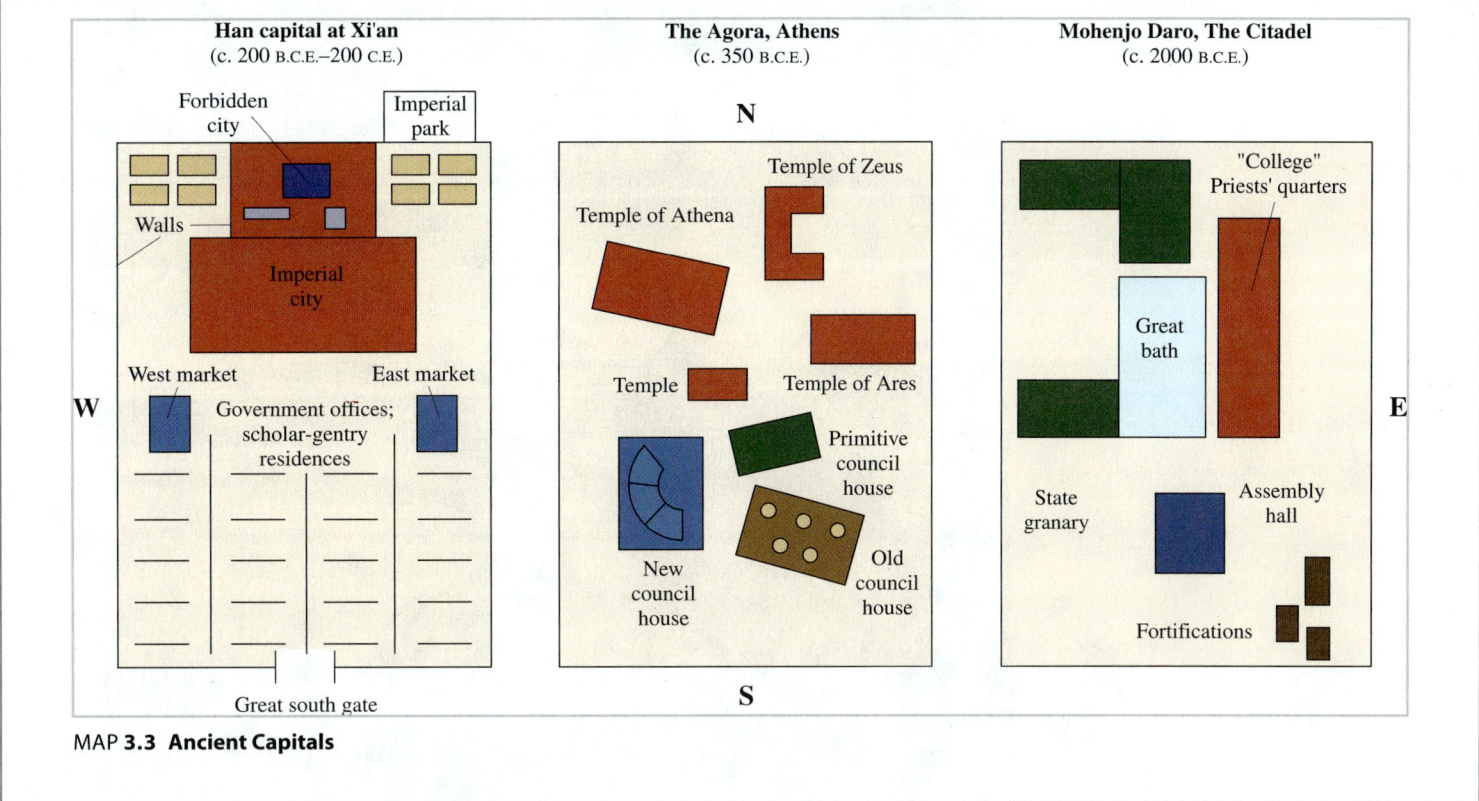

MAP 3.3 Ancient Capitals

Trade and Technology

If trade fit somewhat uncomfortably into the dominant view of society, there was no question about the importance of technological advance. Here, the Chinese excelled. Agricultural implements improved steadily. Ox-drawn plows were introduced around 300 B.C.E., which greatly increased productivity. Under the Han, a new collar was invented for draft animals, allowing them to pull plows or wagons without choking—this was a major improvement that became available to other parts of the world only many centuries later. Chinese iron mining was also well advanced, as pulleys and winding gear were devised to bring material to the surface. Iron tools and other implements such as lamps were widely used. Production methods in textiles and pottery were also highly developed by world standards. Under the Han, the first water-powered mills were introduced, allowing further gains in manufacturing. Finally, during the Han, paper was invented, which was a major boon to a system of government that emphasized the bureaucracy. In sum, classical China reached far higher levels of technical expertise than Europe or western Asia in the same period, a lead that it long maintained.

Technological improvements, emphasis on manufacturing, and the particular mastery of silk production also positioned China strongly in the world trade of the period. The quality of Chinese goods helped sustain the network of the Silk Roads.

The relatively advanced technology of classical China did not, however, steer Chinese society away from its primary reliance on agriculture (Figure 3.6). Farming technology helped increase the size of the population in the countryside; with better tools and seeds, smaller amounts of land could support more families. But China's solid agricultural base, backed by some trade in foodstuffs among key regions, did permit the expansion of cities and manufacturing. There were many towns with more than 10,000 people; China was probably the most urbanized of the classical civilizations. Nonagricultural goods were mainly produced by artisans, working in small shops or in their homes. Even though only a minority of the workforce was involved in such tasks that used manual methods for the most part, the output of tools, porcelain, and textiles increased considerably, aided in this case as well by the interest in improving techniques.

FIGURE 3.6 Han relief on a funeral tile found in the Chengdu region in Sichuan (eastern Han dynasty, 25 C.E.–220 C.E.). The hunting scene in a luxuriant landscape in the upper panel is linked with a scene (lower panel) of peasants working in the fields. Such illustrations enable historians to track the development of tool making and weapons making in ancient civilizations such as China. They also make it possible to study patterns of organization in agrarian and artisan production (for which direct evidence is sparse) as well as the leisure activities of officials and the landed elite.

Gender and Family Life

In all major social groups, tight family organization helped solidify economic and social views as well as political life. The structure of the Chinese family resembled that of families in other agricultural civilizations in emphasizing the importance of unity and the power of husbands and fathers. Within this context, however, the Chinese stressed authority to unusual extremes. Confucius said, "There are no wrongdoing parents"—and in practice, parents could punish disobedient children freely. Law courts did not prosecute parents who injured or even killed a disobedient son, but they severely punished a child who scolded or attacked a parent. In most families, the emphasis on obedience to parents, and a corresponding emphasis on wives' obedience to husbands, did not produce great friction. Chinese popular culture stressed strict control of one's emotions, and the family was seen as the center of such an orderly, serene hierarchy. Indeed, the family served as a great training ground for the principles of authority and restraint that applied to the larger social and political world. Women, although subordinate, had their own clearly defined roles and could sometimes gain power through their sons and as mothers-in-law of younger women brought into the household. The mother of a famous Confucian philosopher, Mencius, continually claimed how humble she was, but during the course of his life, she managed to exert considerable influence over him. But the basic subordination was clear. A Confucian poet stated, "A woman with a long tongue is a stepping stone to disorder. Disorder does not come down from Heaven—It is produced by women." There was even a clear hierarchical order for children, with boys superior to girls and the oldest son having the most enviable position of all. Chinese rules of inheritance, from the humblest peasant to the emperor himself, followed strict primogeniture, which meant that the oldest male child inherited property and position alike.

A DISTINCTIVE MIXTURE

3.5 What were the most important complexities in classical Chinese society?

Chinese civilization coordinated many aspects of politics, culture, and even family life, a key reason that emperors ultimately encouraged Confucianism.

Classical Chinese technology, religion, philosophy, and political structure evolved with very little outside contact. Although important trade routes did lead to India and the Middle East, most Chinese saw the world in terms of a large island of civilization surrounded by barbarian peoples with nothing to offer save the periodic threat of invasion. Nor did Chinese leaders, except to protect their central territory by exercising some control over the mountainous or desert regions that surrounded the Middle Kingdom, have any particular desire to teach the rest of the world. A missionary spirit was foreign to Chinese culture and politics. Of course, China displayed key patterns that were similar to those of the other agricultural civilizations. Further, the spread of Buddhism from India, during and after the Han decline, was a notable instance of a cultural diffusion that altered China's religious map and also its artistic styles. Nevertheless, the theme of separation and superiority, developed during the formative period of Chinese civilization, was to prove persistent in later world history—in fact, it has not entirely disappeared to this day.

Social and Cultural Links to Politics

Not surprisingly, given the close links between the various facets of their civilization, the Chinese tended to think of their society as a whole. They did not distinguish clearly between private and public sectors of activity. They did not see government and society as two separate entities. In other words, these Western concepts that we have used to define classical China and to facilitate comparisons with other societies do not really fit the Chinese view of their own world. Confucius himself, in seeing government as basically a vast extension of family relationships, similarly suggested that the component Chinese societies were intimately joined.

Complexities in Classical China

A grasp of Chinese civilization as a whole, however, should not distract us from recognizing some endemic tensions and disparities. The division in belief systems, between Confucianism and Daoism, modifies the perception of an ultimately tidy classical China. Confucianists and Daoists tolerated each other. Sometimes their beliefs coincided, so that an individual who behaved politically as a Confucianist might explore deeper mysteries through Daoist rituals. However, between both groups there was considerable hostility and mutual disdain, as many Confucianists found Daoists superstitious and overexcited. Daoism did not inherently disrupt the political unity of Chinese culture, but at times the religion did inspire attacks on established politics in the name of a mysterious divine will.

Tension in Chinese society showed in the way Confucian beliefs in mutual respect were combined with strict policing. People arrested were presumed guilty and often subjected to torture before trial. The Chinese, in fact, discovered early on the usefulness of alternating torture with benevolence, to make accused individuals confess. In the late Han period, a thief who refused to confess even under severe torture was then freed from chains, bathed, and fed, "so as to bring him in a happy mood"—whereupon he usually confessed and named his whole gang. In sum, both Confucianism and the Chinese penal system supported tight control, and the combination of the two was typically effective; however, they involved quite different approaches and quite different moral assumptions.

Global Connections and Critical Themes: Classical China and the World

The short-lived Qin dynasty and four centuries of Han rule established the basic components of the longest-lived civilization in world history. As the achievements of the classical age demonstrate, China had also become one of the most creative and influential civilizations of all human history. The strength of its agrarian base has allowed China to carry about one-fifth of the total human population from the last centuries B.C.E. to the present day. The productivity of its peasants has made it possible for some of the world's largest cities to flourish in China, and nurtured one of history's largest and most creative elites. In China's classical age, the world's largest and for much of history its best-run bureaucracy was established, and civil service exams were invented.

The Chinese also pioneered the development of a whole range of basic technologies that were later disseminated over much of Eurasia and northern Africa. These ranged from paper and compasses, which created new possibilities for human communication and cross-cultural interaction, to water mills, which provided new sources of power and food processing, to porcelain, which elevated dining to unparalleled levels of elegance and opened up exciting possibilities for artistic expression. Over the centuries, beginning in the classical period, Chinese merchants and central Asian nomads disseminated these inventions over much of the globe, and have consequently contributed to technological transformations in societies as diverse as Japan, Rome, the Middle East, and England.

Chinese products had a major influence on the patterns of world trade that developed during the classical period. Fine Chinese silk was highly prized in India, the Middle East, and even the distant Roman empire. Trade in silk and other luxury products generated a network of roads through central Asia known collectively as the Silk Road. Under the Han, the Chinese government actively encouraged trade with regions to the west. Improved roads, both in China and in the Middle East, also encouraged trade. One Chinese emissary, Zhang Qian, actually traveled to western India. Most trade along the Silk Road was carried by nomadic merchants. Until well after the classical period, no one seems to have traveled all the way from China to the Mediterranean or vice versa. But the trade was lively, spurring the development of sea routes in the Indian Ocean as well. While we do not know the volume of goods involved, the Silk Road trade was important enough to win considerable attention in upper-class and government circles, and it provided an initial framework on which global trading patterns would later be established.

China's role was greater still in the huge swath of territory from central Asia to the Pacific. Over much of central and east Asia, Chinese influence in political thought and organization, approaches to warfare, art and architecture, religion, and social norms was pervasive. For nearly 2000 years, China would serve as the "Middle Kingdom" for the diverse peoples of this vast area—the focus of their trade and the model for their often successful efforts to fashion their own variants of empire, prosperity, and sophistication.

Further Readings

Good introductions to life in China in the classical age can be found in Mark Edwards, *The Early Chinese Empire: Qin and Han* (2007), and Chun-shu Chang, *The Rise of the Chinese Empire* (2007). More detailed accounts of various aspects of the Qin-Han period have been contributed by (among others) Michael Loewe (Former Han Dynasty), Ying-shis Yü, (Foreign Relations), Patricia Ebrey and Sadao Nishijima (Economic and Social History), Robert Kramers (Confucian Thought) and Paul Demiéville (Philosophy and Religion) in Denis Twitchett and Michael Loewe, *Cambridge History of China*, vol. 1 (1986). Two works that deal extensively with the life and reign of Shi Huangdi are Arthur Cotterell's *The First Emperor of China* (1981) and Li Yu-Ning, ed. *The First Emperor of China* (1975).

A brief and clear introduction to Chinese thought is provided by Frederic Mote's *Intellectual Foundations of China* (1971). A much more detailed study that places Chinese thought in a comparative context can be found in Benjamin Schwartz's seminal *The World of Thought in Ancient China* (1983). For Confucius's teachings, see Roger Ames and Henry Rosemon, eds., *The Analects of Confucius* (1998). Michael Loewe's *Everyday Life in Early Imperial China* (1968) is excellent on Han society, as is the more detailed and scholarly work *Han Social Structure* (1972) by T'ung-Tsu Ch'u, which includes extensive quotations from Chinese texts and valuable insights into the position of women, merchants, artisans, and eunuchs. For the scholar-gentry, see Shirley Chan, *The Confucian Shi* (1993). The shifting position of women is the focus of Bret Hinsch's *Women in Early Imperial China* (2002). A detailed survey of the archeological work done on Han sites and what they tell us about Han society is provided by Wang Shongshu's *Han Civilization* (1982). Michèle Pirazzoli-t'serstevens's lavishly illustrated study *The Han Civilization of China* (1982) contains the most comprehensive, up-to-date, and readable overview of Han civilization available. Edmund Capon and William MacQuitty's *Princes of Jade* (1973) is less informative and reliable, but it also contains superb plates and illustrations.

The most authoritative and detailed account of science and technology in the Han and later dynastic periods can be found in Joseph Needham's multivolume *Science and Civilization in China* (1954). For a more recent and abbreviated survey, see Yingke Deng, *Ancient Chinese Inventors* (2005) Burton Watson's *Courtier and Commoner in Ancient China* (1974), which is a translation of portions of Ban Ku's *History of the Former Han*, includes examples and anecdotes that allow the student to gain a vivid sense of the day-to-day workings of Han society. China's trade and cultural exchanges with neighboring civilizations are treated insightfully in Xinru Liu, *Ancient India and Ancient China: Trade and Religious Exchanges, AD 1–600* (1988), and John Hill, *Through the Jade Gate to Rome* (2009). On warfare in the early classical period, see Roger Ames, ed., *Sun-Tzu: The Art of Warfare* (1993) and Stephen Turnbull, *The Fighting Ships of the Far East* (2002). For an engaging account of early China's relations with the wider world, see S. A. M. Adshead, *China in World History* (2000).

On MyHistoryLab

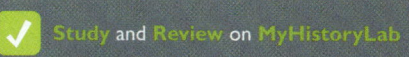

Critical Thinking Questions

1. How did classical China differ from the early civilization patterns in the region?
2. What were the most important tensions within the Chinese cultural and social systems?
3. What caused the Qin attacks on Confucianism?
4. What was the ongoing relationship between Confucian and Legalist political ideas?
5. Why were Chinese economic and technological developments important in world history more generally?

4 Classical Civilization: India

Listen to Chapter 4 on MyHistoryLab

LEARNING OBJECTIVES

4.1 How did India's geography affect the characteristics of classical society in India? p. 76

4.2 What were the main political phases in classical India? p. 78

4.3 Why was the state less important in classical India than in classical China? p. 80

4.4 What was the relationship between Hinduism and Buddhism? p. 82

4.5 What were the main features of the caste system? p. 87

4.6 What was India's trading position in the classical world? p. 88

Of the many enduring expressions of religious devotion in human history, few can match the splendid complexes of temples and monasteries carved from stone into the cliffs at Ajanta and Ellora in the western reaches of the Deccan plateau, which stretches across central India. More than 60 religious structures were carved into or out of solid rock at the two sites,

> View the Closer Look on MyHistoryLab: Gupta Sculpture: Lokanatha

FIGURE **4.1** The cave temples carved out of solid stone at Ajanta in central India provide dramatic evidence of the religious fervor that swept through south Asia in the age of the Buddha and the Hindu revival.

| 4.1 | 4.2 | 4.3 | 4.4 | 4.5 | 4.6 |

⊙ Watch the Video Series on MyHistoryLab
Learn about some key topics related to this chapter with the *MyHistoryLab Video Series: Key Topics in World History*

which are approximately 30 miles apart. These monumental religious edifices were constructed in successive stages from the last centuries B.C.E. through the 8th century C.E. This millennium of history spans an era of momentous change and creativity that in many ways culminated in the Gupta empire, which ruled most of north India from early in the 4th until the mid-6th century C.E.

The art and architecture of Ajanta and Ellora provide dramatic evidence of the intensity of the religious ferment that shaped all aspects of Indian life as a result of the challenges to the existing brahmanical order posed by the emergence of Buddhism and other popular religious alternatives in the 6th and 5th centuries B.C.E. But these monumental buildings, and particularly the exquisite sculptures and paintings they contain, also tell us a great deal about the nature of society, everyday life, and popular culture, as well as the worldview and aspirations of those who lived in what many historians consider India's golden age. The mixture, for example, of Buddhist shrines and monastic quarters and Hindu and Jain cave temples exemplifies the overwhelmingly nonviolent nature of the rivalry between these major religious systems. The blend of religions at Ajanta and Ellora also mirrored the common adoption of rituals, objects of worship, and basic beliefs by the adherents of different Indian religions in this era.

Beyond religious thought and practice, the wall paintings and stone-carved sculptures provide some of the best illustrations we have of everything from Indian ships and styles of dress at different social levels to musical instruments, weapons, and tools for farming and construction. Stone friezes decorating the walls of the shrines and temples illustrate in remarkable detail popular legends of the Buddha's life and path to enlightenment and the rich mythology that developed around the gods and goddesses propitiated by the brahman priests. One of the most celebrated temples, carved out of solid rock to be a free-standing structure, relates in stone carvings numerous episodes from the *Ramayana*, which had become one of the two great epics of Indian civilization by the last centuries B.C.E.

The kings and their consorts, brahman priests and Buddhist monks, workers and temple dancers portrayed in the Ajanta and Ellora cave temples help us to visualize more than a millennium of history that is covered in this chapter. Lasting from roughly 700 B.C.E. to 600 C.E., this era saw the rise and fall of some of India's most powerful dynasties. The brahman-dominated society that emerged in the kingdoms Aryan migrants established in the Gangetic plains was challenged in fundamental ways by the rise of Buddhism in the 6th century B.C.E. Buddhism also played a major role in the rise of the powerful Maurya dynasty and was in turn weakened by the decline of its empire. The political fragmentation in the centuries after the demise of the Mauryas was mirrored in the intense, although largely peaceful, competition among different schools of Buddhism, brahmanism, and a wide variety of other religious sects. The patronage of the rulers of the Gupta empire, which controlled much of north India from the 4th to the mid-6th centuries C.E., sparked a revival of brahmanism. These centuries comprised an age of remarkable religious effervescence, artistic creativity, and scientific breakthroughs that secured India's enduring stature as one of the core civilizations of the preindustrial world. ■

After the long period of disruption following Harappa's fall—around 1500 B.C.E.—a new civilization arose in India. India became the third great center of classical civilization, along with the Mediterranean and Middle East (Greece, Persia, and Rome) and China. India also served as a key hub of the trans-regional trading patterns that emerged in the classical period. The new foundations for Indian civilization were laid between 1500 and 500 B.C.E. by nomadic Aryans who moved into India during the centuries during and after Harappa's collapse. By the end of this period, fairly large

1600 B.C.E.	1200 B.C.E.	750 B.C.E.	500 B.C.E.	250 B.C.E.	1 C.E.
1600–1000 Aryan invasions of India **1500–1000** Vedic Age	**1200–700** Sacred Vedas composed **1000–600** Epic Age: *Mahabharata*, *Ramayana*, and *Upanishads* composed	**700–c. 550** Era of unrivaled brahman dominance **563–483** Life of the Buddha	**327–325** Alexander the Great invades India **322–298** Chandragupta Maurya rules **269–232** Reign of Ashoka	**200 B.C.E.–200 C.E.** Period of greatest Buddhist influence	**319** Gupta empire founded; one of the world's first universities established **535** Gupta empire overturned by the Huns

states, ruled by kings who claimed divine descent, controlled much of the fertile farmland of the Ganges River plains. The settlement of this vast area came at the cost of clearing the great forests that once covered it. As in northwest India and the Mediterranean, cultivation and forest-clearing on the Ganges plains contributed to significant climate change.

Buddha Creator of a major Indian and Asian religion; born in 6th century B.C.E. as son of local ruler among Aryan tribes located near Himalayas; became an ascetic; found enlightenment under bo tree; taught that enlightenment could be achieved only by abandoning desires for all earthly things.

Ritual divisions and restrictions on intermarriage between different social groups grew more rigid as an increasingly complex social hierarchy became a pervasive force in Indian life. Vedic priests, or brahmans, emerged as the dominant force in Indian society and culture. As the brahmans' power peaked, however, forces were building in Indian society that threatened to alter the course of civilized development in south Asia. By the 6th century B.C.E., many religious seers and dissenting philosophers wanted to move beyond the rituals associated with sacrifices to the gods and were weary of the power seeking and materialism of the priestly class. One of these thinkers, now known as the **Buddha**, founded one of the great world religions—a religion that provided a powerful challenge to the brahmans and many of the ancient Vedic beliefs and practices.

THE FRAMEWORK FOR INDIAN HISTORY: GEOGRAPHY AND CULTURE

Indian civilization was deeply influenced by geography and climate. Centuries of Aryan invasion and consolidation laid the foundation of classical Indian civilization.

4.1 How did India's geography affect the characteristics of classical society in India?

In the centuries that followed the Aryan incursions, the rivalry between Buddhists and brahmans played a major role in shaping gender relationships and the nature of social hierarchies as a whole in south Asia. The Buddha's teachings also contributed to the establishment of India's first genuine empire. Beginning in the late 4th century B.C.E., the rulers of a local dynasty in eastern India, the Mauryas, built what would become the largest empire in premodern India, but the Mauryan empire was short-lived. When it collapsed, it was followed by another round of nomadic invasions through the Himalayan passes in the northwest, and the subcontinent was again fragmented politically. But in the early 4th century C.E., there arose in north India a powerful new dynasty, the Gupta, that was committed to reasserting brahmans' dominance. The Gupta rulers' patronage of the religion we now know as Hinduism reaffirmed the position of the brahmans as high priests and political advisors. It also led to an age of splendid achievement in architecture, painting, sculpture, philosophy, literature, and the sciences.

The classical period of Indian history includes a number of contrasts to that of China—and many of these contrasts have proved enduring. Whereas the focus in classical China was on politics and on social structures that would support the Confucian order, the focus in classical India was on religion and social structures that would support a Hindu way of life. A political culture existed in India, of course, but it was less cohesive and less important to the larger culture than its Chinese counterpart. In religion, science, economics, and family life, the classical period generated a culture that continues to make India unique among the world's major civilizations.

While India's distinctiveness was considerable, the fact that it was an agricultural society dictated that it would be similar in many ways to China. Most people were peasant farmers, whose lives were shaped around the production of food for their family's survival. In both India and China, peasant families clustered together in villages for mutual aid and protection. This village structure gave a strong localist flavor to many aspects of life in both cultures. In addition, agriculture influenced family life. Patriarchy dictated that women seldom owned property other than their personal possessions. Although they were primarily agricultural, both China and India built great cities and engaged in extensive trade. These added to social and economic complexity and created the basis for most formal intellectual life, including schools and academies.

Formative Influences

India's distinctive culture was born of its geography and early historical experience. India was much closer to the orbit of other civilizations than China. Trading contacts with China developed late in the classical period and had little impact—China was more affected. But India was frequently open to influences from the Middle East and even the Mediterranean world. Persian empires spilled over into India at several points, bringing new artistic styles and political concepts. **Alexander the Great** invaded India, and while he did not establish a durable empire, he made possible important Indian contacts with Hellenistic culture. Periodic influences from the Middle East continued after the classical age, forcing India to react and adapt in ways that China largely avoided because it was more isolated.

In addition to links with other cultures, India's topography shaped a number of vital features of its civilization. The vast Indian subcontinent is partially separated from the rest of Asia, and particularly from East Asia, by northern mountain ranges, notably the **Himalayas**. However, important passes through the mountains, especially in the northwest, linked India to other civilizations in the Middle East. At the same time, divisions within the subcontinent made full political unity difficult. India was thus marked by greater diversity than China's Middle Kingdom. The most important agricultural regions are those along the two great rivers, the Indus and the Ganges. However, India also has mountainous northern regions, where a herding economy took root, and a southern coastal rim, separated by mountains and the Deccan plateau, where an active trading and seafaring economy arose. India's separate regions help explain not only economic diversity but also the racial and language differences that, from early times, have marked the subcontinent's populations.

Much of India is semitropical in climate. In the river valley plains, heat can rise to 120° F during the early summer. Summer also brings torrential **monsoon** rains, crucial for farming. But the monsoons vary from year to year, sometimes bringing too little rain or coming too late and causing famine-producing drought, or sometimes bringing catastrophic floods. Certain features of Indian civilization may have resulted from a need to come to terms with a climate that could produce abundance one year and grim starvation the next. In a year with favorable monsoons, Indian farmers could plant and harvest two crops and thus support a sizable population.

Brahman Culture

We have seen that, after the fall of Harappan civilization, Aryan (Indo-European) migrants increasingly penetrated the subcontinent. These migrants gradually settled down to agriculture and extend their agricultural base to the fertile Ganges river. The Aryans also developed the series of oral epics, called the Vedas and ultimately written down in **Sanskrit**, which became the literary language of the new culture. Composed by various priests, the epics provided a wealth of stories about the gods and about proper standards for human behavior. The characteristic Indian caste system also began to take shape during these formative centuries, perhaps initially as a means of establishing relationships between the Aryan invaders and the indigenous people, whom the Aryans regarded as inferior. Aryan social classes (**varnas**) partly enforced divisions familiar in agricultural societies. Thus, a warrior or governing class, the Kshatriyas (kuh-shuh-TREE-uhs), and the priestly class, or brahmans, stood at the top of the social pyramid, followed by Vaisyas, the traders and farmers, and Sudras, or common laborers. Many of the Sudras worked on the estates of large landowners. A fifth group gradually evolved, later called the **untouchables**, who were confined to a few jobs, such as transporting the bodies of the dead or hauling refuse. It was widely believed that touching these people would defile anyone from a superior class. Initially, the warrior group ranked highest, but during the Epic Age the brahmans replaced them, signaling the importance of religious links in Indian life. Thus, a law book stated, "When a brahman springs to light he is born above the world, the chief of all creatures, assigned to guard the treasury of duties, religious and civil." Gradually, the five social groups became hereditary, with marriage between castes forbidden and punishable by death; the basic castes divided into smaller subgroups, called *jati*, each with distinctive occupations and each tied to its social station by birth.

Alexander the Great Successor of Philip II; successfully conquered Persian empire prior to his death in 323 B.C.E.; attempted to combine Greek and Persian cultures.

Himalayas Mountain region marking the northern border of the Indian subcontinent; site of the Aryan settlements that formed small kingdoms or warrior republics.

monsoons Seasonal winds crossing Indian subcontinent and southeast Asia; during summer bring rains.

Sanskrit The sacred and classical Indian language.

varnas Clusters of caste groups in Aryan society; four social castes—brahmans (priests), warriors, merchants, and peasants; beneath four Aryan castes was group of socially untouchable Dasas.

untouchables Low social caste in Hindu culture; performed tasks that were considered polluting—street sweeping, removal of human waste, and tanning.

The *Rig-Veda*, the first Aryan epic, attributed the rise of the caste system to the gods:

> When they divided the original Man
> into how many parts did they divide him?
> What was his mouth, what were his arms,
> what were his thighs and his feet called?
> The brahman was his mouth, of his
> arms was made the warrior.
> His thighs became the vaisya, of
> his feet the sudra was born.

Indra Chief deity of the Aryans; depicted as a colossal, hard-drinking warrior.

The Aryans brought to India a religion of many gods and goddesses, who regulated natural forces and possessed human qualities. Thus, **Indra**, the god of thunder, was also the god of strength. Gods presided over fire, the sun, death, and so on. This system bore some resemblances to the gods and goddesses of Greek myth or Scandinavian mythology, for the very good reason that they were derived from a common Indo-European oral heritage. However, India was to give this common tradition an important twist, ultimately constructing a vigorous, complex religion that, in contrast to the Indo-European polytheistic faiths, endures to this day.

During the epic periods, the Aryans offered hymns and sacrifices to the gods. Certain animals were regarded as particularly sacred, embodying the divine spirit. Gradually, this religion became more elaborate. The epic poems reflect an idea of life after death and a religious approach to the world of nature. Nature was seen as informed not only by specific gods but also by a more basic divine force. These ideas, expressed in the mystical *Upanishads*, added greatly to the spiritual power of this early religion and served as the basis for later Hindu beliefs. By the end of the Epic Age, the dominant Indian belief system included a variety of convictions. Many people continued to emphasize rituals and sacrifices to the gods of nature; specific beliefs, as in the sacredness of monkeys and cattle, illustrated this ritualistic approach. The brahman priestly class specified and enforced prayers, ceremonies, and rituals. However, the religion also produced a more mystical strand through its belief in a unifying divine force and the desirability of seeking union with this force. Toward the end of the Epic period one religious leader, Gautama Buddha, built on this mysticism to create what became Buddhism, another major world religion.

PATTERNS IN CLASSICAL INDIA

Two major empires united large parts of India at crucial periods in classical Indian history.

4.2 What were the main political phases in classical India?

By 600 B.C.E., India had passed through its formative phase. Regional political units grew in size, cities and trade expanded, and the development of the Sanskrit language, although dominated by the priestly brahman class, furthered an elaborate literary culture. A full, classical civilization could now build on the social and cultural themes first launched during the Vedic and Epic ages.

Indian development during the classical era and beyond did not take on the convenient structure of rising and falling dynasties characteristic of Chinese history. Political eras were even less clear than in classical Greece. The rhythm of Indian history was irregular and often consisted of landmark invasions that poured in through the mountain passes of the subcontinent's northwestern border.

Toward the end of the Epic Age and until the 4th century B.C.E., the Indian plains were divided among powerful regional states. Sixteen major states existed by 600 B.C.E. in the plains of northern India, some of them monarchies, others republics dominated by assemblies of priests and warriors. Warfare was not uncommon. One regional state, Magadha, established dominance over a considerable empire. In 327 B.C.E., Alexander the Great, having conquered Greece and much of the Middle East, pushed into northwestern India, establishing a small border state called Bactria.

Chandragupta Maurya [chuhn-druh-GOOP-duh MAHR-yeh] (r. 322–298 B.C.E.) Founder of Maurya dynasty; established first empire in Indian subcontinent; first centralized government since Harappan civilization.

Mauryan [MAHR-yuhn] Dynasty established in Indian subcontinent in 4th century B.C.E. following invasion by Alexander the Great.

The Mauryan Dynasty

Political reactions to this incursion produced the next major step in Indian political history, in 322 B.C.E., when a young soldier named **Chandragupta Maurya** seized power along the Ganges River. He became the first of the **Mauryan** dynasty of Indian rulers, who in turn were the first rulers to unify much of the entire subcontinent. While it is difficult to know what, if anything, the Mauryan dynasty borrowed directly from Persian political models or the example of Alexander the Great, Chandragupta and his successors maintained large armies, with thousands of chariots and elephant-borne troops. The Mauryan rulers also developed a substantial bureaucracy, even sponsoring a postal service.

Chandragupta's style of government was highly autocratic, relying on the ruler's personal and military power. This style would surface periodically in Indian history, just as it did in the Middle East, a region with which India had important contacts. A Greek ambassador from one of the Hellenistic kingdoms described Chandragupta's life:

> Attendance on the king's person is the duty of women, who indeed are bought from their fathers. Outside the gates [of the palace] stand the bodyguards and the rest of the soldiers.... Nor does the king sleep during the day, and at night he is forced at various hours to change his bed because of those plotting against him. Of his nonmilitary departures [from the palace] one is to the courts, in which he passed the day hearing cases to the end.... [When he leaves to hunt,] he is thickly surrounded by a circle of women, and on the outside by spear-carrying bodyguards. The road is fenced off with ropes, and to anyone who passes within the ropes as far as the women, death is the penalty.

Such drastic precautions paid off. Chandragupta finally designated his rule to a son and became a religious ascetic (a person who renounces the pleasures of the material world), dying peacefully at an advanced age.

Chandragupta's grandson, **Ashoka** (269–232 B.C.E.), was an even greater figure in India's history. First serving as a governor of two provinces, Ashoka enjoyed a lavish lifestyle, with frequent horseback riding and feasting. However, he also engaged in a study of nature and was strongly influenced by the intense spiritualism not only of the brahman religion but also of Buddhism. Ashoka extended Mauryan conquests, gaining control of all but the southern tip of India through fierce fighting (Map 4.1). His methods were bloodthirsty; in taking over one coastal area, Ashoka admitted that "one hundred and fifty thousand were killed (or maimed) and many times that number later died." But Ashoka could also be compassionate. He ultimately converted to Buddhism, seeing in the belief in **dharma**, or the law of moral consequences, a kind of ethical guide that might unite and discipline the diverse people under his rule. Ashoka vigorously propagated Buddhism throughout India while also honoring Hinduism, sponsoring shrines for its worshippers. Ashoka sent Buddhist missionaries to the Hellenistic kingdoms in the Middle East, and also to Sri Lanka to the south (Figure 4.2). The "new" Ashoka urged humane behavior on the part of his officials and insisted that they oversee the moral welfare of his empire. Like Chandragupta, Ashoka also worked to improve trade and communication, sponsoring an extensive road network dotted with wells and rest stops for travelers. Stability and the sheer expansion of the empire's territory encouraged growing commerce.

The Mauryan dynasty did not, however, succeed in establishing durable roots, and Ashoka's particular style of government did not have much later impact, although a strong Buddhist current persisted in India for some time. After Ashoka, the empire began to fall apart, and regional kingdoms surfaced once again. New invaders, the **Kushans**, pushed into central India from the northwest. The greatest Kushan king, Kanishka, converted to Buddhism but actually hurt this religion's popularity in India by associating it with foreign rule.

Ashoka (r. 273–232 B.C.E.) Grandson of Chandragupta Maurya; completed conquests of Indian subcontinent; converted to Buddhism and sponsored spread of new religion throughout his empire.

dharma The caste position and career determined by a person's birth; Hindu culture required that one accept one's social position and perform occupation to the best of one's ability in order to have a better situation in the next life.

Kushans See Kush, p. 28.

Guptas Dynasty that succeeded the Kushans in the 3rd century C.E.; built empire that extended to all but the southern regions of Indian sub-continent; less centralized than Mauryan empire.

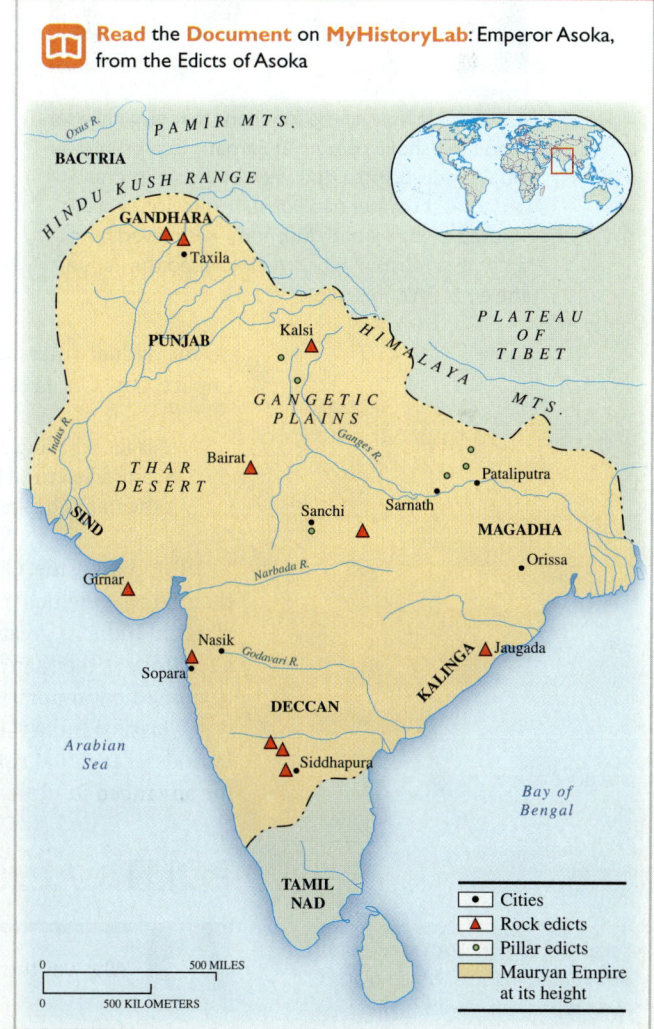

Read the **Document** on **MyHistoryLab**: Emperor Asoka, from the Edicts of Asoka

MAP 4.1 **India at the Time of Ashoka** Although, as the map shows, the Mauryan monarchs claimed to rule most of present-day South Asia, much of the subcontinent was only loosely controlled.

The Guptas

The collapse of the Kushan state, by 220 C.E., ushered in another hundred years of political instability. Then a new line of kings, the **Guptas**, established a large empire, beginning in 320 C.E. (Map 4.2). The Guptas produced

FIGURE 4.2 Two of the four lions that originally sat atop the Ashoka column at Sarnath, in present-day Uttar Pradesh, India (this view of the sculpture obscures the other two lions). This sculpture, now housed at the Sarnath Museum, was carved from a single sandstone block. Ashoka used the lions as the emblem of his rule.

MAP 4.2 **The Gupta Empire.** Not only was the territory claimed by the Gupta dynasty a good deal smaller than the empire of their Mauryan predecessors, even the area controlled was ruled to a far greater extent by local lords than the Gupta emperors.

no individual rulers as influential as the two great Mauryan rulers, but they had perhaps greater impact. One Gupta emperor proclaimed his virtues in an inscription on a ceremonial stone pillar:

> His far-reaching fame, deep-rooted in peace, emanated from the restoration of the sovereignty of many fallen royal families. . . . He, who had no equal in power in the world, eclipsed the fame of the other kings by the radiance of his versatile virtues, adorned by innumerable good actions.

Bombast aside, Gupta rulers often preferred to negotiate with local princes and intermarry with their families, which expanded influence without constant fighting. Two centuries of Gupta rule gave classical India its greatest period of political stability, although the Guptas did not administer as large a territory as the Mauryan kings had. The Gupta empire was overturned in 535 C.E. by a new invasion of nomadic warriors, the Huns.

Classical India thus alternated between widespread empires and a network of smaller kingdoms. Periods of regional rule did not necessarily suggest great instability, and both economic and cultural life advanced in these periods as well as under the Mauryas and Guptas.

POLITICAL INSTITUTIONS

> Local and regional governments dominated in India, which placed less emphasis on politics than other early civilizations.

4.3 Why was the state less important in classical India than in classical China?

Classical India did not develop the solid political traditions and institutions of Chinese civilization, or the high level of political interest that would characterize classical Greece and Rome. The most persistent political features of India, in the classical period and beyond, involved regionalism, plus considerable diversity in political forms. Autocratic kings and emperors dotted the history of classical

India, but there were also aristocratic assemblies in some regional states with the power to consult and decide on major issues.

As a result of India's diversity and regionalism, even some of the great empires had a rather shaky base. Early Mauryan rulers depended heavily on the power of their large armies, and, as we have seen, often feared betrayal and attack. Early rulers in the Gupta dynasty used various devices to consolidate support. They claimed that they had been appointed by the gods to rule, and they favored the Hindu religion over Buddhism because the Hindus believed in such gods. The Guptas managed to create a demanding taxation system, seeking up to a sixth of all agricultural produce. However, they did not create an extensive bureaucracy, rather allowing local rulers whom they had defeated to maintain regional control so long as they deferred to Gupta dominance. The Guptas stationed a personal representative at each ruler's court to ensure loyalty. A final sign of the great empire's loose structure was the fact that no single language was imposed. The Guptas promoted Sanskrit, which became the language of educated people, but this made no dent in the diversity of popular, regional languages.

The Guptas did spread uniform law codes. Like the Mauryan rulers, they sponsored some general services, such as road building. They also served as patrons of much cultural activity, including university life as well as art and literature. These achievements were more than enough to qualify the Gupta period as a golden age in Indian history.

The fact remains, however, that the political culture of India was not very elaborate. There was little formal political theory and few institutions or values other than regionalism that carried through from one period to the next. Chandragupta's chief minister, **Kautilya**, wrote an important treatise on politics, but it was devoted to telling rulers what methods would work to maintain power—somewhat like the Legalists in China. Thinking of this sort encouraged efficient authority, but it did not spread political values or a sense of the importance of political service very widely, in contrast to Confucianism in China and also to the intense interest in political ethics in Greece and Rome. Ashoka saw in Buddhism a kind of ethic for good behavior, as well as a spiritual beacon, but Buddhist leaders in the long run were not greatly interested in affairs of state. Indeed, Indian religion generally did not stress the importance of politics, even for religious purposes, but rather the preeminence of priests as sources of authority.

Kautilya [kah-TIHL-yeh] (350–275 B.C.E.) Political advisor to Chandragupta Maurya; one of the authors of *Arthashastra;* believed in scientific application of warfare.

The limitations on the political traditions developed during this period of Indian history can be explained partly by the importance of local units of government—the tightly organized villages—and particularly by the essentially political qualities of social relationships under the caste system. Caste rules, interpreted by priests, regulated many social relationships and work roles. To a great extent, the caste system and religious encouragement in the faithful performance of caste duties did for Indian life what more conventional government structures did in many other cultures, in promoting public order.

India's caste system became steadily more complex after the Epic Age, as the five initial classes subdivided into ultimately almost 300 jati (or livings), which became further divided into a multitude of subcastes—the true basis of the caste system—which defined the groups that a person could eat with or marry within. Hereditary principles grew ever stronger, so that it became virtually impossible to rise above the caste in which a person was born or to marry someone from a higher caste. It was possible to fall to a lower caste by marrying outside one's caste or by taking on work deemed inappropriate for one's caste. Upward mobility could occur within castes, as individuals might gain greater wealth through success in the economic activities appropriate to the caste. Rulers, like the Mauryans, might spring from the merchant castes, although most princes were warrior-born. It is important not to characterize the caste system in an oversimplified way, for it did offer some flexibility. Nevertheless, the system gave India the most rigid overall framework for a social structure of any of the classical civilizations.

In its origins, the caste system provided a way for India's various races, the conquerors and the conquered, to live together without perpetual conflict and without full integration of cultures and values. Quite different kinds of people could live side by side in village or city, separated by caste. In an odd way, castes promoted tolerance, and this was useful, given India's varied peoples and beliefs. The caste system also meant that extensive outright slavery was avoided. The lowest, untouchable castes were scorned, confined to poverty and degrading work, but their members were not directly owned by others.

The political consequences of the caste system derived from the detailed rules for each caste. These rules governed marriages and permissible jobs, but also social habits such as eating and drinking. For example, a person could not eat or drink with a lower-caste individual or perform any service for that person. This kind of regulation of behavior made detailed political administration less necessary. Indeed, no state could command full loyalty from subjects, for their first loyalty was to caste.

RELIGION AND CULTURE

Hinduism and Buddhism were the religions of classical India, helping also to shape distinctively Indian arts and sciences.

4.4 What was the relationship between Hinduism and Buddhism?

More of the qualities of Indian civilization rested on widely shared cultural values than was the case in China. Religion, and particularly the evolving Hindu religion as it gained ground on Buddhism under the Guptas, was the clearest cultural cement of this society, cutting across political and language barriers and across the castes. Hinduism itself embraced considerable variety, and it gave rise to important religious dissent. Nor did it ever displace important minority religions. However, Hinduism has shown a remarkable capacity to survive and is the major system of belief in India even today. It also promotes other features in Indian culture. Thus, contemporary Indian children are encouraged to indulge their imaginations longer than Western children, with less urging to test flights of fancy against external reality. It is this kind of tradition that illustrates how classical India, although not the source of enduring political institutions beyond the local level, produced a civilization that would retain clear continuity and cultural cohesiveness from this point onward—even though the subcontinent was rarely politically united, at least under indigenous rulers.

The culture of classic India was not just religious, however. Along with religion, an important tradition of rational scientific inquiry emerged. This helped sustain major initiative in higher education. It is also important to note that the Indian religions themselves were tolerant—both of other religious and of other aspects of culture. Indian governments might support religious missionaries, but they also established an openness to religious diversity. This, too, was a legacy to Indian cultures in later periods.

The Formation of Hinduism

Hinduism, the religion of India's majority, developed gradually over a period of many centuries. Its origins lie in the Vedic and Epic ages, as the Aryan religion gained greater sophistication, with concerns about an overarching divinity supplementing the rituals and polytheistic beliefs supervised by the brahman caste of priests. The *Rig-Veda* expressed the growing interest in a higher divine principle in its Creation Hymn:

> Then even nothingness was not, nor existence. There was no air then, nor the heavens beyond it. Who covered it? Where was it? In whose keeping. . . ? The gods themselves are later than creation, so who knows truly whence it has arisen?

Unlike all other world religions, Hinduism had no single founder, no central holy figure from whom the basic religious beliefs stemmed. This fact helps explain why the religion unfolded so gradually, sometimes in reaction to competing religions such as Buddhism or Islam. Moreover, Hinduism pursued a number of religious approaches, from the strictly ritualistic and ceremonial approach many brahmans preferred to the high-soaring mysticism that sought to unite individual humans with an all-embracing divine principle. Unlike Western religions or Daoism (which it resembled in part), Hinduism could also encourage political and economic goals (called artha) and worldly pleasures (called karma)—and important textbooks of the time spelled out these pursuits. Part of Hinduism's success, indeed, was the result of its fluidity, its ability to adapt to the different needs of various groups and to change with circumstance. With a belief that there are many suitable paths of worship, Hinduism was also characteristically tolerant, coexisting with several offshoot religions that garnered minority acceptance in India.

Brahman leadership reshaped Indian ideas about the gods, creating more elaborate definitions (scholars call early Hinduism *brahmanism* because of this leadership role, although Hindus always called their religion *dharma*, or moral path). Original gods of nature were altered to represent more abstract concepts. Thus, Varuna changed from a god of the sky to the guardian of ideas of right and wrong. The great poems of the Epic Age increasingly emphasized the importance of gentle and generous behavior, and the validity of a life devoted to concentration on the Supreme Spirit. The *Upanishads* particularly stressed the shallowness of worldly concerns—riches and even health were not the main point of human existence—in favor of contemplation of the divine spirit. It was in the *Upanishads* that the Hindu idea of a divine force informing the whole universe, of which each individual creature's soul is thought to be part, first surfaced clearly, in passages such as the following:

> "Fetch me a fruit of the banyan tree."
> "Here is one, sir."
> "Break it."
> "I have broken it, sir."
> "What do you see?"
> "Very tiny seeds, sir."
> "Break one."
> "I have broken it, sir."
> "What do you see now?"
> "Nothing, sir."
> "My son, . . . what you do not perceive is the essence, and in that essence the mighty banyan tree exists. Believe me, my son, in that essence is the self of all that is. That is the True, that is the Self."

However, the *Upanishads* did more than advance the idea of a mystical contact with a divine essence. They also attacked the conventional brahman view of what religion should be, a set of proper ceremonies that would lead to good things in this life or rewards after death. From the Epic Age onward, Hinduism embraced this clear tension between a religion of rituals, with fixed ceremonies and rules of conduct, and the religion of mystical holy men, seeking communion with the divine soul.

The mystics, often called **gurus** as they gathered disciples around them, and the brahman priests agreed on certain doctrines, as Hinduism became an increasingly formal religion by the first centuries of the common era. The basic holy essence, called *brahma*, formed part of everything in this world. Every living creature participates in this divine principle. The divine aspects of brahma are manifested in the forms of many gods, including **Vishnu**, the preserver, and **Shiva**, the destroyer, who could be worshipped or placated as expressions of the holy essence. The world of our senses is far less important than the world of the divine soul, and a proper life is one devoted to seeking union with this soul.

gurus Originally referred to as brahmans who served as teachers for the princes of the imperial court of the Guptas.

Vishnu The brahman, later Hindu, god of sacrifice; widely worshipped.

Shiva Hindu, god of destruction and reproduction; worshipped as the personification of cosmic forces of change.

DOCUMENT

A Guardian's Farewell Speech to a Young Woman About to Be Married

ONE OF THE GREAT PLAYS WRITTEN during the Hindu revival of the early centuries C.E. was *Shakuntala*, by Kalidasa. The play is a Cinderella-style tale about a beautiful young woman, Shakuntala, who is loved by a king, and the travails she must endure before they are happily united. In the following exchange, as Shakuntala sets out to join her husband at his palace, she is instructed by her guardians (the hermits Kashyapa and Gautami) on the proper behavior for a young wife, in a manner that recalls the famous speech by Polonius to his son, Laertes, in Shakespeare's *Hamlet*.

Kashyapa: Now you Shakuntala. Respect your superiors,

Be friendly toward the ladies of the palace.

Never be angry with your husband, no matter what happens.

Be polite with the maids;

In everything be humble.

These qualities make a woman; those without them are black sheep in their families.

What is your opinion, Gautami?

Gautami: A bride needs nothing more. Remember his advice, Shakuntala.

Shakuntala: How will I ever manage in the palace? I feel so lost. I belong here, Father.

Kashyapa: Don't worry, my child; you are privileged.

You will be his great wife;

He is noble and great.

You will give him a son, as the East gives us light.

The pain of separation will then pass.

QUESTIONS

- What does this conversation tell you about gender relationships and marriage in classical India?
- What does it say about attitudes toward women?
- How do these relationships and attitudes compare with those found in China and Greece in this era?
- How do they compare with those in our own society?

CHAPTER 4 Classical Civilization: India

reincarnation The successive attachment of the soul to some animate form according to merits earned in previous lives.

However, this quest may take many lifetimes, and Hindus stressed the principle of **reincarnation**, in which souls do not die when bodies do but pass into other beings, either human or animal. Where the soul goes, whether it rises to a higher-caste person or falls perhaps to an animal, depends on how good a life the person has led. Ultimately, after many good lives, the soul reaches full union with the soul of brahma, and worldly suffering ceases.

Hinduism provided several channels for the good life. For people who renounced this world in search of salvation, there was the meditation and self-discipline of *yoga*, which means "union," allowing the mind to be freed to concentrate on the divine spirit. For others, there were the rituals and rules of the brahmans. These included proper ceremonies in the cremation of bodies at death, appropriate prayers, and obedience to injunctions, such as treating cows as sacred animals and refraining from the consumption of beef, and following the life patterns (dharma) associated with the caste (or jati) into which one was born. Many Hindus also continued the idea of lesser gods represented in the spirits of nature, or purely local divinities, which could be seen as expressions of Shiva or Vishnu (Figure 4.3).

Hinduism also provided a basic, if complex, ethic that helped supply some unity amid the various forms of worship. The epic poems, richly symbolic, formed the key texts. They illustrated a central emphasis on the moral law of dharma as a guide to living in this world and simultaneously pursuing higher, spiritual goals. The concept of dharma directed attention to the moral consequences of action and at the same time the need to act. Each person must meet the obligations of life, serving the family, producing a livelihood and even earning money, and serving in the army when the need arises. These actions cannot damage, certainly cannot destroy, the eternal divine essence that underlies all creation. In the *Bhagavad Gita*, a classic sacred hymn, a warrior is sent to do battle against his own relatives. Fearful of killing them, he is advised by an incarnation of Brahma (Krishna) that he must carry out his duties. He will not really be killing his victims because their divine spirit will live on. This ethic urged that honorable behavior, even pleasure seeking, is compatible with spirituality and can lead to a final release from the life cycle and to unity with the divine essence. The Hindu ethic explains how devout Hindus could also be aggressive merchants or eager warriors. In encouraging honorable action, it could legitimize government and the caste system as providing the frameworks in which the duties of the world might be carried out, without distracting from the ultimate spiritual goals common to all people.

The ethical concept of dharma was far less detailed than the ethical codes associated with most other world religions, including Christianity and Islam. For certain caste groups, at certain points in their lives, dharma stresses inner study and meditation, building from the divine essence within each creature, rather than adherence to a fixed set of moral rules.

The spread of Hinduism through India, and to some other parts of Asia, had a great influence on most of southeast Asia for over a millennium and is still culturally vital and pervasive. Also it had—and still has—a major impact on Nepal, Tibet, Bhutan, Sri Lanka, and parts of Central Asia. And its impact in most of these places and in East Asia was also felt in numerous ways through its many influences on Buddhism. The religion accommodated extreme spirituality. It also provided satisfying rules of conduct for ordinary life, including rituals and a firm emphasis on the distinction between good and evil behavior, although many of the areas to which it spread did not adopt the rigid caste hierarchy. The religion allowed many people to retain older beliefs and ceremonies, which they may have derived from a more purely polytheistic religion. Through most of India, it reinforced the caste system, giving people in lower castes hope for a better time in lives to come and giving upper-caste people, including the brahmans, the satisfaction that if they behaved well, they might be rewarded by communion with the divine soul. Even though Hindu beliefs took shape only gradually and contained many ambiguities, the religion was sustained by a strong cadre of priests and through the efforts of individual gurus and mystics.

Buddhism

At times, however, the tensions within Hinduism broke down for some individuals, producing alternatives to the dominant religion. One such response, which occurred right after the Epic Age, led to a new religion closely related to Hinduism. Around 563 B.C.E. an Indian prince, Siddhartha Gautama, was born who came to question the fairness of earthly life in which so much poverty and misery

FIGURE 4.3 Perhaps the most frequently depicted Indian religious image is the god Shiva as the celestial dancer, here portrayed in a south Indian bronze. The position of the god's hands and the objects held in them each represent a different aspect of his power, which may be simultaneously creative and destructive. His left hand closest to his head, for example, is held in the posture of reassurance, and the left hand furthest away holds a drum, which signifies time. His left foot crushes the demon of ignorance, which seems to want to be destroyed by the illustrious god.

abounded. Gautama, later called Buddha or "enlightened one," lived as a Hindu mystic, fasting and torturing his body. After six years, he felt that he had found truth, then spent his life traveling and gathering disciples to spread his ideas. Buddha accepted the spiritual truth behind many Hindu beliefs, such as reincarnation, but he denied the validity of others, such as caste. He held the material world to be a snare that warped human relations and caused pain via the frustrations inherent in it: All worldly things decay, but men and women suffer and harm others as they struggle to remain attached to youth, health, and life itself, though all are destined to pass away.

Buddha maintained the possibility of spiritual rewards after life, but he saw salvation as arising from the destruction of the self, whose annihilation opens the door to a realm where suffering and decay are no more, literally a world beyond existence itself: **nirvana**. Individuals could regulate their lives and aspirations toward this goal without elaborate ceremonies. Great stress was placed on meditation and self-control: "Let a man overcome anger by love, let him overcome evil by good, let him overcome the greedy by liberalness, the liar with the truth." By arguing that a holy life could be achieved through individual effort by people at every level of society, Buddhism denied the spiritual value not only of caste and the performance of rituals, but also the absolute authority of priests. This was another sign of the complexity of Indian social life in practice.

Buddhism spread and retained coherence through the example and teachings of groups of monks, organized in monasteries but preaching throughout the world. Buddhism attracted many followers in India itself, and its growth was greatly spurred by the conversion of the Mauryan emperor Ashoka. Increasingly, Buddha himself was seen as divine. Prayer and contemplation at Buddhist holy places and works of charity and piety gave substance to the idea of a holy life on earth. Ironically, however, Buddhism did not witness a permanent following in India. Brahman opposition was strong, and it was ultimately aided by the influence of the Gupta emperors. Furthermore, Hinduism showed its adaptability by emphasizing its mystical side, thus retaining the loyalties of many Indians. Buddhism's greatest successes, aided by the missionary encouragement of Ashoka and later the Kushan emperors, came throughout Southeast Asia, including the island of Sri Lanka, off the south coast of India, and in China, Korea, and Japan (Map 4.3). Still, in some regions of South Asia, Buddhism retained a substantial following. They were joined by other dissident groups who rejected aspects of brahmanism.

nirvana The Buddhist state of enlightenment, a state of tranquility.

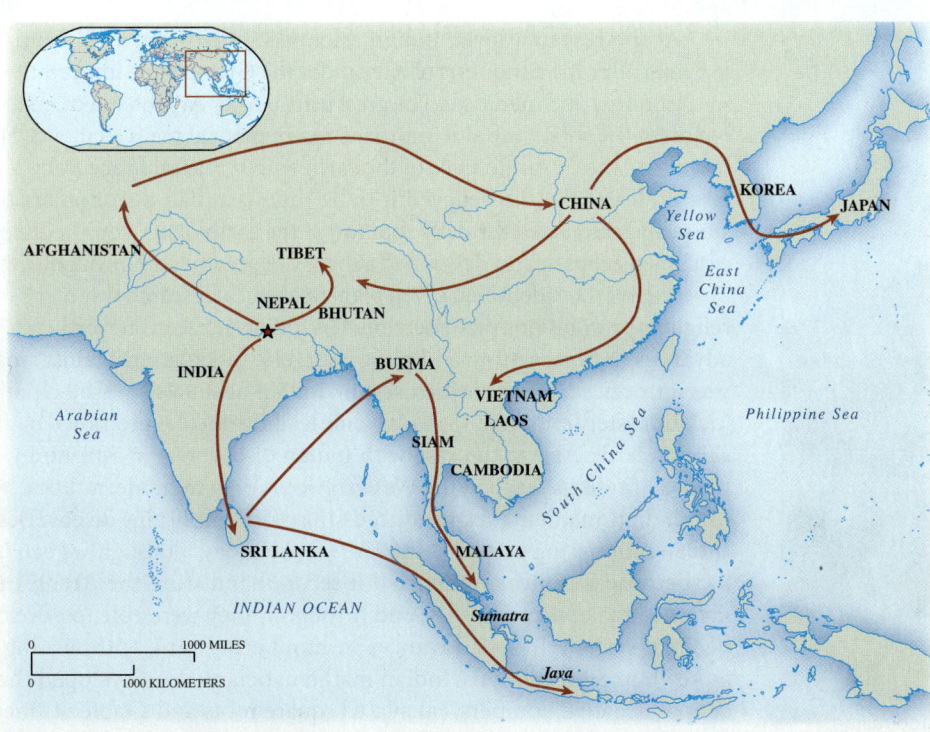

MAP 4.3 The Spread of Buddhism in Asia, 400 B.C.E.–600 C.E. In less than two centuries wandering missionaries had carried the Buddhist faith from central Asia to Sri Lanka and into China and Japan.

Thus, though "Hinduism" in its many forms grew increasingly dominant, it had to come to terms with the existence of other religions from the last centuries B.C.E..

If Hinduism, along with the caste system, formed the most distinctive and durable products of the classical period of Indian history, they were certainly not the only ones. Even aside from dissident religions, Indian culture during this period was vibrant and diverse, and religion encompassed only part of its interests. Hinduism itself encouraged many wider pursuits.

Indian thinkers wrote actively about various aspects of human life. Although political theory was sparse, a great deal of legal writing occurred. The theme of love was important also. A manual of the "laws of love," the **Kamasutra**, written in the 4th century C.E., discusses relationships between men and women.

Kamasutra [kah-muh-SOO-truh] Written by Vatsayana during Gupta era; offered instructions on all aspects of life for higher-caste males, including grooming, hygiene, etiquette, selection of wives, and lovemaking.

Arts and Sciences

Indian literature, taking many themes from the great epic poems and their tales of military adventure, stressed lively story lines. The epics were recorded in written form during the Gupta period, and other story collections, like the *Panchatantra*, which includes Sinbad the Sailor, Jack the Giant Killer, and the Seven League Boots, produced adventurous yarns now known all over the world. Classical stories were often secular, but they sometimes included the gods and also shared with Hinduism an emphasis on imagination and excitement. Indian drama flourished also, again particularly under the Guptas, and stressed themes of romantic adventure in which lovers separated and then reunited after many perils. This literary tradition created a cultural framework that still survives in India. Even contemporary Indian movies reflect the tradition of swashbuckling romance and heroic action.

stupas Stone shrines built to house pieces of bone or hair and personal possessions said to be relics of the Buddha; preserved Buddhist architectural forms.

Classical India also produced important work in science and mathematics. The Guptas supported a vast university center—one of the world's first—in the town of Nalanda that attracted students from other parts of Asia as well as Indian brahmans. Nalanda had over a hundred lecture halls, three large libraries, an astronomical observatory, and even a model dairy. Its curriculum included religion, philosophy, medicine, architecture, and agriculture.

At the research level, Indian scientists, borrowing a bit from Greek learning after the conquests of Alexander the Great, made important strides in astronomy and medicine. The great astronomer Aryabhatta calculated the length of the solar year and improved mathematical measurements. He also calculated the circumference of the earth with remarkable accuracy—which also indicates that he believed it to be round. Indian astronomers understood and calculated the daily rotation of the earth on its axis, predicted and explained eclipses, and developed a theory of gravity, and through telescopic observation they identified seven planets. Medical research was hampered by religious prohibitions on dissection, but Indian surgeons nevertheless made advances in bone setting and plastic surgery. Inoculation against smallpox was introduced, using cowpox serum. Indian hospitals stressed cleanliness, including sterilization of wounds, while leading doctors promoted high ethical standards. As was the case with Indian discoveries in astronomy, many medical findings reached the Western world only in modern times.

Indian mathematics produced still more important discoveries. The Indian numbering system is the one we use today, although we call it Arabic because Europeans imported it secondhand from the Arabs. Indians invented the concept of zero, and through it they were able to develop the decimal system. Indian advances in numbering rank with writing itself as key human inventions. Indian mathematicians also developed the concept of negative numbers, calculated square roots and a table of sines, and computed the value of pi more accurately than the Greeks did.

Finally, classical India produced lively art, although much of it perished under later invasions. Ashoka sponsored many spherical shrines to Buddha, called **stupas**, and statues honoring Buddha were also common (Figure 4.4). Under the Guptas, sculpture and painting moved away from

FIGURE 4.4 The great Buddhist stupa at Sanchi in central India. Stupas were built to house relics of the Buddha, and they became major sites of pilgrimage. The intricate carved gates and railing surrounding the stupa related incidents from the Buddha's life or displayed symbols associated with his teachings. The great dome that covered the dirt mound that formed the core of the stupa often was painted white, and it struck approaching pilgrims as a great cloud floating on the horizon.

realistic portrayals of the human form toward more stylized representation. Indian painters, working on the walls of buildings and caves, filled their work with forms of people and animals, captured in lively color. Indian art showed a keen appreciation of nature. It could pay homage to religious values, particularly during the period in which Buddhism briefly spread, but could also celebrate the joys of life.

There was, clearly, no full unity to this cultural outpouring. Religion, legalism, abstract mathematics, and art and literature coexisted. The result, however, was a somewhat distinctive overall tone, continuing, for example, with the Chinese concentration on political ethics. In various cultural expressions, Indians developed an interest in spontaneity and imagination, whether in fleshly pleasures or a mystical union with the divine essence.

ECONOMY AND SOCIETY

4.5 What were the main features of the caste system?

> The caste system structured India's social framework, but a strong emphasis on trade was also important. Family life combined patriarchy with an emphasis on affection.

The caste system shaped many key features of Indian social and economic life, as it assigned people to occupations and regulated marriages. Low-caste individuals had few legal rights, and servants were often abused by their masters, who were restrained only by the ethical promptings of religion toward kindly treatment. A brahman who killed a servant for misbehavior faced a penalty no more severe than if he had killed an animal. This extreme level of abuse was uncommon, but the caste system did unquestionably make its mark on daily life as well as on the formal structure of society. The majority of Indians living in peasant villages had less frequent contact with people of higher social castes, and village leaders were charged with trying to protect peasants from too much interference by landlords and rulers.

Family life also emphasized the theme of hierarchy and tight organization, as it evolved from the Vedic and Epic ages. The dominance of husbands and fathers remained strong. One Indian code of law recommended that a wife worship her husband as a god (see the Document on p. 83). Indeed, the rights of women became increasingly limited as Indian civilization took clearer shape. Although the great epics stressed the control of husband and father, they also recognized women's independent contributions. As agriculture became better organized and improved technology reduced (without eliminating) women's economic contributions, the stress on male authority expanded. Here India followed a common pattern in agricultural societies, as women's sphere of action was gradually circumscribed. Hindu thinkers debated whether a woman could advance spiritually without first being reincarnated as a man, and there was no consensus. The limits imposed on women were reflected in laws and literary references. A system of arranged marriage evolved in which parents contracted unions for children, particularly daughters, at quite early ages, to spouses they had never even met. The goal of these arrangements was to ensure solid economic links, with child brides contributing dowries of land or domestic animals to the ultimate family estates, but the result of such arrangements was that young people, especially girls, were drawn into a new family structure in which they had no voice.

However, the rigidities of family life and male dominance over women were often greater in theory than they usually turned out to be in practice. The emphasis on loving relations and sexual pleasure in Indian culture modified family life, since husband and wife were supposed to provide mutual emotional support as a marriage developed. The *Mahabharata* epic called a man's wife his truest friend: "Even a man in the grip of rage will not be harsh to a woman, remembering that on her depend the joys of love, happiness, and virtue." Small children were often pampered. "With their teeth half shown in causeless laughter, their efforts at talking so sweetly uncertain, when children ask to sit on his lap, a man is blessed." Families thus served an important and explicit emotional function as well as a role in supporting the structure of society and its institutions. They also, as in all agricultural societies, formed economic units. Children, after early years of indulgence, were expected to work hard. Adults were obligated to assist older relatives. The purpose of arranged marriages was to promote a family's economic well-being, and almost everyone lived in a family setting.

The Indian version of the patriarchal family was thus subtly different from that in China, although women were officially just as subordinate and later trends—as in many patriarchal societies over time—would bring new burdens. But Indian culture often featured clever and strong-willed women and goddesses, and this contributed to women's status as wives and mothers. Stories also celebrated women's emotions and beauty.

Read the **Document** on **MyHistoryLab**: Cast(e)aways? Women in Classical India (200 C.E., 6th c. C.E.)

The economy of India in the classical period became extremely vigorous, certainly rivaling China in technological sophistication and probably briefly surpassing China in the prosperity of its upper classes. In manufacturing, Indians invented new uses for chemistry, and their iron working was the best in the world. Indian capacity in ironmaking outdistanced European levels until a few centuries ago. Indian techniques in textiles were also advanced, and their cotton goods in particular were the finest in the world: hence our names for muslins, calicos, cashmeres, and pajamas. Most manufacturing was done by artisans who formed guilds and sold their goods from shops.

Indian emphasis on trade and merchant activity was far greater than in China, and indeed greater than that of the classical Mediterranean world. Indian merchants enjoyed relatively high caste status; they also traveled widely, not only over the subcontinent but by sea to the Middle East and East Asia. The seafaring peoples along the southern coast, usually outside the large empires of northern India, were particularly active. These southern Indians, the Tamils, traded cotton and silks, dyes, drugs, gold, and ivory, often earning great fortunes. From the Middle East and the Roman empire they brought back pottery, wine, metals, some slaves, and above all gold. Their trade with southeast Asia was even more active, as Indian merchants transported not only sophisticated manufactured goods but also Indian artistic and architectural styles to places like Malaysia and the larger islands of Indonesia. In addition, caravan trade developed with China.

The Indian economy remained firmly agricultural at its base. The wealth of the upper classes and the splendor of cities like Nalanda were confined to a small portion of the population, as most people lived near the margins of subsistence. But India was justly known by the time of the Guptas for its wealth as well as for its religion and intellectual life—always understanding that wealth was relative in the classical world and very unevenly divided. A Chinese Buddhist on a pilgrimage to India wrote:

> The people are many and happy. They do not have to register their households with the police. There is no death penalty. Religious sects have houses of charity where rooms, couches, beds, food, and drink are supplied to travelers.

INDIAN INFLUENCE AND COMPARATIVE FEATURES

4.6 What was India's trading position in the classical world?

> Because of its extensive trade, India's artistic and cultural influence reached many parts of the ancient world, even as India shaped a distinctive version of classical civilization.

Classical India, from the Mauryan period onward, had a considerable influence on other parts of the world. In many ways, the Indian Ocean, dominated at this point by Indian merchants and missionaries, was the most active linkage point among cultures, although admittedly, the Mediterranean, which channeled contact from the Middle East to North Africa and Europe, was a close second. Indian dominance of the waters of southern Asia, and the impressive creativity of Indian civilization itself, resulted in goods and influence traveling well beyond the subcontinent's borders. And while Indian rulers did not usually attempt political domination, dealing instead with the regional kingdoms of Burma, Thailand, Indonesia, and Vietnam, Indian travelers or settlers did bring to these locales major economic and cultural influences. Indian merchants sometimes married into local royal families. Indian-style temples were constructed and other forms of Indian art traveled widely. Buddhism spread from India to many parts of Southeast Asia, and Hinduism converted many upper-class people, particularly in several of the Indonesian kingdoms. India thus serves as an early example of a major civilization expanding its influence well beyond its own regions.

Indian influence had affected China, through Buddhism and art, by the end of the classical period. Earlier, Buddhist emissaries to the Middle East stimulated new ethical thinking that informed Greek and Roman religious and philosophical thinkers, such as the groups like the Stoics, and through them aspects of Christianity later on.

Within India itself, the classical period, starting a bit late after the Aryan invasions, lasted somewhat longer than that of China or Rome. Even when the period ended with the fall of the Guptas, an identifiable civilization remained in India, building on several key factors first established in the classical period: the religion, to be sure, but also the artistic and literary tradition and the complex social and family network. The ability of this civilization to survive, even under long periods of foreign domination, was testimony to the meaning and variety it offered.

THINKING HISTORICALLY

Inequality as the Social Norm

THE INDIAN CASTE SYSTEM IS PERHAPS the most extreme expression of a type of social organization that violates the most revered principles on which modern Western societies are based. Like the Egyptian division between a noble and a commoner and the Greek division between a freeperson and a slave, the caste system rests on the assumption that humans are inherently unequal and that their lot in life is determined by the families and social strata into which they are born. The caste system, like the social systems of all other classical civilizations, presumed that social divisions were fixed and stable and that people ought to be content with the station they had been allotted at birth.

Furthermore, all classical social systems (with the partial exception of the Greeks, at least in Athens) played down the importance of the individual and stressed collective obligations and loyalties that were centered in the family, extended kin groups, or broader occupational or social groups. Family or caste affiliation, not individual ambition, determined a person's career goals and activities.

All of these assumptions directly contradict some of the West's most cherished current beliefs. They run counter to one of the most basic organizing principles of modern Western culture, rooted in a commitment to equality of opportunity. This principle is enshrined in European and American constitutions and legal systems, taught in Western schools and churches, and proclaimed in Western media. The belief in human equality, or at least equality of opportunity, is one of the most important ideas that modern Western civilization has exported to the peoples of Africa, Asia, and Latin America.

The modern concept of equality rests on two assumptions. The first is that a person's place in society should be determined not by the class or family into which he or she is born but by personal actions and qualities. The second is that the opportunity to rise—or fall—in social status should be open to everyone and protected by law. Some of our most cherished myths reflect these assumptions: that anyone can aspire to be president of the United States, for example, or that an ordinary person has the right to challenge the actions of the politically and economically powerful.

Of course, equality is a social ideal rather than something any human society has achieved. No one pretends that all humans are equal in intelligence or talent, and there are important barriers to equality of opportunity. But the belief persists that all humans should have an equal chance to better themselves by using the brains and skills they have. In the real world, race, class, and gender differences often favor some individuals over others, and laws and government agencies often do not correct these inequities. But the citizens of modern Western societies, and increasingly the rest of the world, champion the principles of equality of opportunity and the potential for social mobility as the just and natural bases for social organization and interaction.

However, what is just and natural for modern societies would have been incomprehensible in the classical age. In fact, most human societies through most of human history have been organized on assumptions that are much closer to those underlying the Indian caste system than to those underlying modern Western norms. Ancient Egyptians and Greeks, medieval Europeans, and early modern Chinese believed that career possibilities, political power, and social privileges should be set by law according to the position of one's family in the social hierarchy. The Indian caste structure was the most rigid and complex of the systems by which occupations, resources, and status were allotted. But all classical civilizations had similar social mechanisms that determined the obligations and privileges of members of each social stratum.

In some ways, classical Chinese and Greek societies provided exceptions to these general patterns. In China, people from lowly social origins could rise to positions of great status and power, and well–placed families could fall on hard times and lose their gentry status. But "rags to riches" success stories were the exception rather than the rule, and mobility between social strata was limited. In fact, Chinese thinkers made much of the distinctions between the **scholar-gentry** elite and the common people.

Although some of the Greeks, particularly the Athenians, developed the idea of equality for all citizens in a particular city-state, most of the people of these societies were not citizens, and many were slaves. By virtue of their birth the latter were assigned lives of servitude and often drudgery. Democratic participation and the chance to make full use of their talents were limited to the free males of the city-states.

In nearly all societies, these fixed social hierarchies were upheld by creation myths and religious beliefs that proclaimed their divine origins and the danger of punishment if they were challenged. Elite thinkers stressed the importance of the established social order to human peace and well-being; rulers were duty bound to defend it. Few challenged the naturalness of the hierarchy itself; fewer still proposed alternatives to it. Each

> In nearly all societies, these fixed social hierarchies were upheld by creation myths and religious beliefs that proclaimed their divine origins and the danger of punishment if they were challenged.

(continued on next page)

person was expected to accept his or her place and to concentrate on the duties and obligations of that place rather than worry about rights or personal desires. Males and females alike were required to subordinate their individual yearnings and talents to the needs of their families, clans, communities, or social superiors. In return for a person's acceptance of his or her allotted place in the hierarchy, he or she received material sustenance and a social slot. Of course, these benefits were denied to people who fought the system. They might be outcast or exiled, physically punished, or even killed.

> **QUESTIONS**
> - What arguments did the thinkers of the classical civilizations of Greece, China, and India use to explain and justify the great differences in social status and material wealth?
> - How did those who belonged to elite groups justify their much greater status, wealth, and power compared to the peasants, artisans, and servants who made up most of the population?
> - Comparing these modes of social organization with the ideals of your own society, what do you see as the advantages and drawbacks of each?

scholar-gentry Chinese class created by the marital linkage of the local land-holding aristocracy with the office-holding shi; superseded shi as governors of China.

China and India Compared

The thrusts of classical civilization in China and India reveal the diversity generated during the classical age. The restraint of Chinese art and poetry contrasted with the more dynamic sensual styles of India. India ultimately settled on a primary religion, although with important minority expressions, that embodied diverse impulses within it. China opted for separate religious and philosophical systems that would serve different needs. China's political structures and values found little echo in India, whereas the Indian caste system involved a social rigidity considerably greater than that of China. On the other hand, the higher status of merchants in India contributed to high levels of commerce. India's cultural emphasis was, on balance, considerably more otherworldly than that of China, despite the impact of Daoism and Buddhism, which after all was an Indian import. Quite obviously, classical India and classical China created vastly different cultures. Even in science, where there was similar interest in pragmatic discoveries about how the world works, the Chinese placed greater stress on purely practical findings, whereas the Indians ventured further into the mathematical arena.

Beyond the realm of formal culture and the institutions of government, India and China may seem more similar. As agricultural societies, both civilizations relied on a large peasant class, organized in close-knit villages with much mutual cooperation. Political power rested primarily with those who controlled the land, through ownership of large estates and the ability to tax the peasant class. On a more personal level, the power of husbands and fathers in the family—the basic fact of patriarchy—encompassed Indian and Chinese families alike.

However, Indian and Chinese societies differed in more than their religion, philosophy, art, and politics. Ordinary people had cultures along with elites. Hindu peasants saw their world differently from their Chinese counterparts. They placed less emphasis on personal emotional restraint and detailed etiquette; they expected different emotional interactions with family members. Indian peasants were less constrained than were the Chinese by recurrent efforts by large landlords to gain control of their land. Although there were wealthy landlords in India, the system of village control of most land was more firmly entrenched than in China. Indian merchants played a greater role than their Chinese counterparts. There was more sea trade, more commercial vitality. Revealingly, India's expanding cultural influence was due to merchant activity above all else, whereas Chinese expansion involved government initiatives in gaining new territory and sending proud emissaries to satellite states. These differences were less dramatic, certainly less easy to document, than those generated by elite thinkers and politicians, but they contributed to the shape of a civilization and to its particular vitality, its areas of stability and instability.

Because each classical civilization developed its own unique style, in social relationships as well as in formal politics and intellectual life, exchanges between two societies like China and India involved specific borrowings, and never an effort at wholesale imitation. India and China, the two giants of classical Asia, remain subjects of comparison to our own time, because they have continued to build distinctively on their particular traditions, established before 500 C.E. These characteristics, in turn, differed from those of yet another center of civilization, the societies that sprang up on the shores of the Mediterranean during this same classical age.

VISUALIZING THE PAST

The Pattern of Trade in the Ancient Eurasian World

THE PERIOD OF MAURYA RULE IN India coincided with a great expansion in trade between the main centers of civilization in Eurasia and Africa. In the centuries that followed, a permanent system of exchange developed that extended from Rome and the Mediterranean Sea to China and Japan. The trading networks that made up this system included both those established between ports connected by ships and sea routes and those consisting of overland exchanges transmitted along the chain of trading centers that crossed central Asia and the Sudanic region of Africa. By the last centuries B.C.E., this far-flung trading system included much of the world as it was known to the peoples of the Eastern Hemisphere.

Some products produced at one end of the system, such as Chinese silks and porcelains, were carried the entire length of the network to be sold in markets at the other edge—in Rome, for example. As a general rule, products carried over these great distances tended to be high-priced luxury goods such as spices and precious jewels. But most of the exchanges, particularly in bulk goods such as metal ores or foodstuffs, were between adjoining regions. The ports of western India, for example, carried on a brisk trade with those in

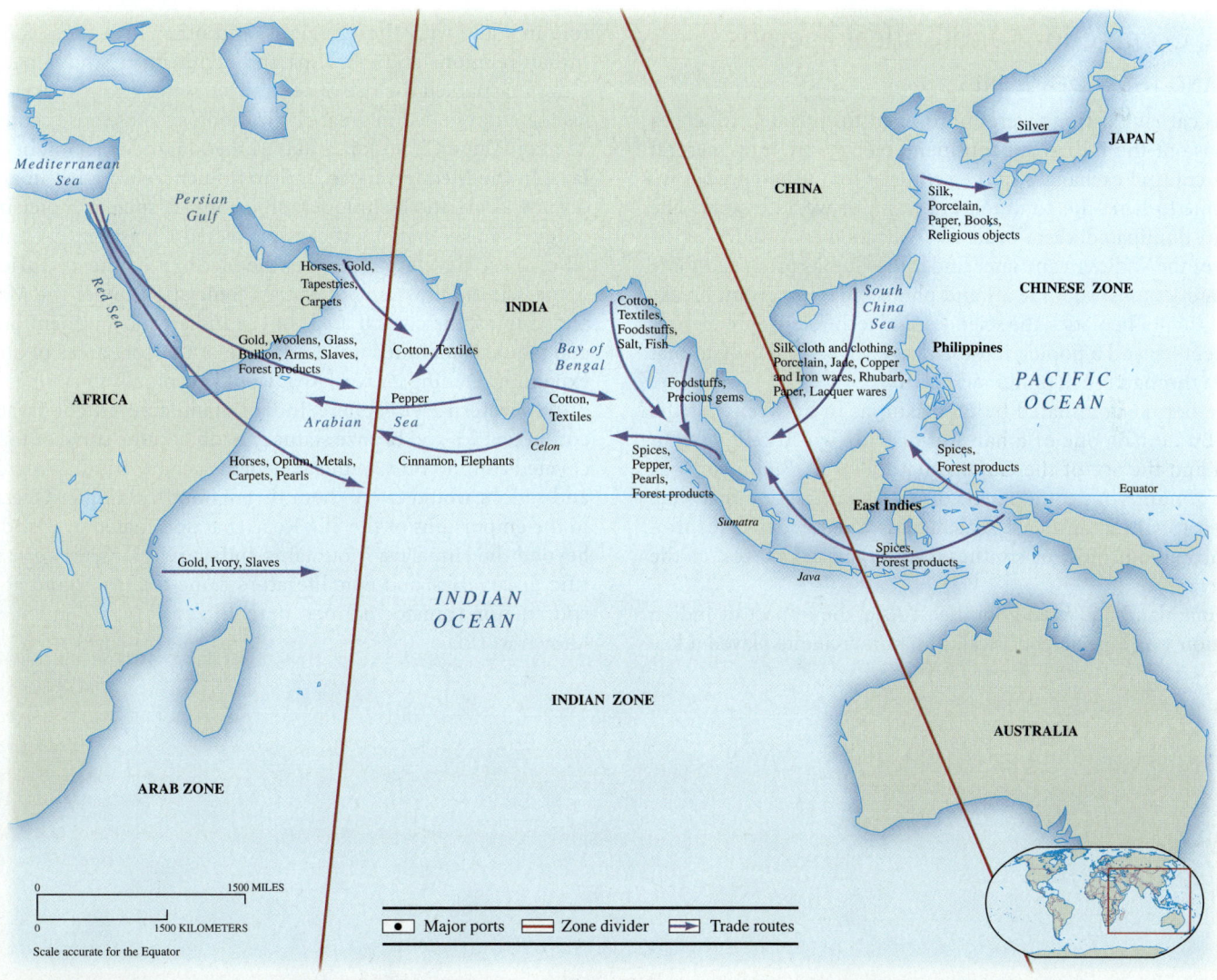

MAP 4.4 Eurasian and African Trading Goods Routes, c. 300 B.C.E. to 300 C.E. As the map above illustrates, a vibrant oceanic trading system was in place across the Afro-Eurasian continents by the last centuries B.C.E., and the Indian subcontinent was central as a producer and consumer in this vast network of contact and exchange.

(continued on next page)

(continued from previous page)

the Red Sea and Persian Gulf, while trading centers in Southeast Asia supplied China with forest products and other raw materials in exchange for the many items manufactured by China's highly skilled artisans. Although some merchants and sailors, particularly the Chinese and Arabs, could be found in ports far from their homelands, most confined their activities within regional orbits, such as the Arabian Sea, the Persian Gulf, or the South China Sea.

Map 4.4 provides an overview of this great trading network in the age of the classical civilizations, roughly the 3rd century B.C.E. to the 3rd century C.E. It shows the main centers of production, the goods exported overland and overseas, and the main directions of trade in these products. Key ports, inland trading centers, and products are shown for each of the main sectors participating in the system.

> **QUESTIONS**
> - Which civilizations or areas in the global trading network were the main centers for the production of finished products, such as cloth and pottery?
> - What major centers supplied raw materials, such as forest products or foods?
> - Why were luxury goods likely to be transported the greatest distances?
> - Why were bulk goods, especially foods, usually shipped only short distances, if at all?
> - Besides trade goods, what other things might be transmitted through the trading networks?

Global Connections and Critical Themes

INDIA AND THE WIDER WORLD

No classical civilizations were more open to outside influences than those of the Indian subcontinent. None were more central to cross-cultural exchanges in the centuries that ushered what we have come to label the common era (C.E.) of world history. The brahman-dominated, caste-ordered civilization that flourished at the end of the Vedic era and later under the Guptas produced some of humanity's most sublime art and philosophy; important breakthroughs in mathematics, the sciences, and technology; prosperous urban centers; and a population that has been second only to that of China through much of human history.

The period dominated by the Mauryas in between saw the rise of Buddhism, one of a handful of truly world religions. In this era and the age of the Guptas that followed, Buddhism was but one of numerous components of Indian civilization that were exported to China and east Asia, across the steppes of central Asia, throughout most of southeast Asia, and as far west as the Mediterranean.

In mainland and island Southeast Asia, the impact of Indian civilization was especially critical. Indian merchants played a key role in trade with these regions, and other influences followed. Indian religions and epics, art and architecture, and concepts of kingship sparked the rise of centralized states and complex societies that culminated in great civilizations, such as those centered at Angkor Wat in Cambodia and the kingdom of Majapahit in central Java. In the Mediterranean, Indian influences were felt in areas as diverse as artistic techniques, philosophies such as Stoicism, and religious ideas that significantly affected Christianity. Central to all of these developments was the fact that in the centuries that witnessed the flowering of Indian civilization under the Mauryas and Guptas, the coastal areas of the Indian subcontinent became, and would remain for millennia, one of the core areas of an ever-expanding trading network that would eventually encompass most of the Eastern Hemisphere. Indian manufactured goods, such as cotton textiles and bronze statuary, soon became some of the most coveted commodities in this system of exchange. Indian merchants and sailors would carry them throughout the Indian Ocean and to the emporiums of the Silk Road that dominated overland trade beyond the Himalaya Mountains. Indian religions, artwork, scientific discoveries, and epic literature came to enrich, and at times spur major transformations in, civilizations over much of the known world.

Further Readings

Perhaps the most readable introductions to life and society in India's classical age can be found in A. L. Basham's *The Wonder That Was India* (1963) and Jeannine Auboyer's *Daily Life in Ancient India* (2002 reprint ed.). The works of Romilla Thapar, especially *Ashoka and the Decline of the Mauryas* (1997) and *Early India: From the Origins to AD 1300* (2003), are the best on the political history of the era. See also, Milo Kearney, *The Indian Ocean in World History* (2004); Rajendra Prasad, *A Historical-Development Study of Classical Indian Philosophy of Morals* (2009); Isabel Clark-Deces, *A Companion to the Anthropology of India* (2011); and Thomas R. Traultmann, *The Aryan Debate* (2005). On the Guptas the most comprehensive recent work is Ashvini Agrawal's *Rise and Fall of the Imperial Guptas* (1989). Fine narrative histories of all aspects of Indian civilization in this period can be found in the appropriate chapters of *The History and Culture of the Indian People* (1964), edited by R. C. Majumdar, A. K. Majumdar, and D. K. Ghose. Some of the best works on the position of women and social life more generally include Pandharinath Prabhu's *Hindu Social Organization* (1940), L. K. Tripathi, *Position and Status of Women in Ancient India* (1988), and S. Tharu and K. Lalita, eds., *Women Writing in India 600 to the Present* (1991). On the development of the caste system, see B. R. Kamble, *Caste and Philosophy in Pre-Buddhist India* (1979). A wide range of other aspects of ancient Indian culture is covered in the fine essays in A. L. Basham's *A Cultural History of India* (1975).

Superb introductions to various branches of Indian religious and philosophical thinking, with well-selected portions of the appropriate texts, can be found in S. Radhakrishnan and Charles Moore, eds., *A Source Book in Indian Philosophy* (1967); and Ainslee Embree, ed., *Sources of Indian Tradition*, Vol. 1, *From the Beginning to 1800* (2nd ed., 1988). Of the many books on Buddhism, Trevor Ling's *The Buddha* (1973) is one of the more accessible, but needs to be supplemented with recent research, many of the findings of which are explored in Jonathan S. Walters, *Finding Buddhists in Global History* (1998). The spread of Indian culture to southeast Asia in this period is covered in the classic work by G. Coedés, *The Indianized States of Southeast Asia* (1964), and more recently in G. C. Pande's *India's Interaction with Southeast Asia* (2006).

S. Radhakrishnan's *Hindu View of Life* (1927) provides a useful insider's view of Hindu religious beliefs and social organization. Heinrich Zimmer's *Philosophies of India* (1956) remains a good place to begin exploring the riches and diversity of Indian mythology and religious thinking. Susan Huntington's *The Art of Ancient India* (1985) offers a stimulating and very accessible discussion of the art of this period. Benjamin Rowland's *The Art and Architecture of India* (1970), which includes southeast Asia, remains the most comprehensive work available in English on Indian art overall; J. C. Harle's *Gupta Sculpture* (1974) provides an introduction to some of the glories of the Gupta age. For a taste of Indian literature in the classical period, there are English translations of the *Ramayana* and the *Mahabharata* and P. Lal's fine translations of *Great Sanskrit Plays* (1957).

On MyHistoryLab

 Study and Review on MyHistoryLab

Critical Thinking Questions

1. What were the main similarities between classical India and classical China?
2. Compare the brahman religion with the religion of classical Greece.
3. What are some possible causes that explain the emergence of the caste system?
4. Compare the Chinese and Indian approaches to the patriarchal family.

5
Classical Civilizations in the Middle East and Mediterranean

🎧 Listen to Chapter 5 on MyHistoryLab

LEARNING OBJECTIVES

5.1 Why was the rise of Persia such an important development in the early part of the classical period? p. 97

5.2 What changes occurred between the Greek and Hellenistic periods in the eastern Mediterranean? p. 99

5.3 What were the causes of Roman expansion? p. 101

5.4 What are the main issues in defining the Greek and Roman political legacy? p. 103

5.5 What was the relationship between Greek and Roman culture? p. 107

5.6 How did the social structures of the classical Mediterranean and classical China compare? p. 111

5.7 What were the main legacies of classical Mediterranean civilization, for later societies? p. 114

It is one of the most famous stories in history: In 490 B.C.E., the Greeks, under Athenian leaders, defeated a huge Persian army at Marathon. Fear of the Persians had run strong, and news of victory was accordingly sweet. According to legend, a Greek soldier named Pheidippides ran 26 miles to bring the word to Athens and, having delivered the message, collapsed and died. The first modern Olympic Games, in 1896, featured a long-distance endurance race called the "marathon" in memory of that great feat. Pheidippides' run reminds us not only of a great military victory and strong emotion, but of the Greeks' powerful devotion to the public good of the cities they loved.

FIGURE **5.1** This famous statue depicts Pheidippides, the Athenian soldier who, according to legend, ran 26 miles to bring his fellow citizens news of victory at the Battle of Marathon and died as he made the announcement. The 26-mile endurance run was named the "marathon" to commemorate Pheidippides's heroic feat.

Watch the Video Series on MyHistoryLab

Learn about some key topics related to this chapter with the *MyHistoryLab Video Series: Key Topics in World History*

The Persian invasion of Greece began as a punishment for the revolt of several Greek city-states against Persian rule—a revolt the Persians easily put down. Immediately following the Greek victory at the Battle of Marathon, the Persians tried to attack Athens by sea, but the Athenian soldiers had hurried back to defend their city. Vowing revenge, the Persians returned to Asia.

A new Persian king, Xerxes, took personal charge of the plan to conquer the Greeks. By 480 B.C.E. he had amassed an army and fleet that outnumbered Greek forces by two to one. Many Greek states held back, assuming the Persians would win this time. Even the Greek priests, trying to foretell the future, urged surrender. To make matters worse, a Greek traitor showed the Persians a pass that would lead them to Athens, which was indefensible. Most Athenians were evacuated to an island, where they watched the Persians set fire to their temples on the hill of the Acropolis. But Themistocles, the Athenian leader, realized that the huge Persian navy could not move fast. If it could be led into a narrow strait, where its numbers did not count, it could be defeated. Themistocles sent a slave to trick Xerxes, telling him that the Greeks were quarreling among themselves. Thinking that this was their chance to finish off the Greeks, the Persians rowed into the narrow strait of Thermopylae. There, instead of the divided and weakened opponent they were expecting, they found a united force ready to fight them. Xerxes watched the battle from a hill overlooking the strait, where he had thought he would be able to see and reward the bravest of his warriors. Instead he saw his navy virtually destroyed, and he fled. ∎

History is full of might-have-beens. It is important to consider what would have happened if the normal advantage in military strength had prevailed and the Persians had won and what difference this would have made to world history.

One point is sure. The battle highlighted the developments of not one but two major civilizations in the eastern Mediterranean and Middle East. The classical civilizations that sprang up in Persia and on the shores of the Mediterranean Sea from about 800 B.C.E. until the fall of the Roman empire in 476 C.E. rivaled their counterparts in India and China in richness and impact. Two centers were involved, separately although in contact; briefly merged; then separate once more. Developments in the Middle East and the Mediterranean built directly on precedents established by the river valley civilizations not only in Mesopotamia but in Egypt. But different centers generated different emphases—the nature of Persian politics, for example, differed noticeably from that of Greece; and with Greece and Rome, civilization also extended westward, to other parts of Africa and to southern Europe. Both Persian and Mediterranean civilizations met the criteria of classical civilizations, in relying heavily on territorial expansion and empire and in founding institutions and cultural systems that would wield influence even after the classical period had ended.

A massive Persian empire developed, spurred initially by the kind of outside invasion that had earlier produced various Mesopotamian empires. But the Persian empire grew far larger, illustrating the new capacities of the classical period. Durable political and cultural traditions were established that persisted in and around present-day Iran well beyond the classical period.

Centered first in the peninsula of Greece, then in Rome's burgeoning provinces, a new Mediterranean culture centered in southern Europe. Although less significant at the time, Greece rebuffed the advance of the mighty Persian empire and established some colonies on the eastern shore of the Mediterranean, in what is now Turkey. Rome came closer to conquering the Middle East but even its empire had to contend with strong kingdoms in Persia. Nevertheless, Greece and Rome did not merely constitute a westward push of civilization from its earlier bases in the Middle East and along

2000 B.C.E.	1000 B.C.E.	500 B.C.E.	250 B.C.E.	1 C.E.	250 C.E.
1700 Indo-European invasions of Greek peninsula **1400** Kingdom of Mycenae; Trojan War	**800–600** Rise of Greek city-states; Athens and Sparta become dominant **c. 700** Homerian epics *Iliad, Odyssey*; flowering of Greek architecture **550** Cyrus the Great forms Persian empire **509** Beginnings of Roman Republic	**470–430** Athens at its height: Pericles, Phidias, Sophocles, Socrates **450** Twelve Tables of Law **431–404** Peloponnesian Wars **359–336** Philip II of Macedonia **338–323** Macedonian empire, Alexander the Great **300–100** Hellenistic period **264–146** Punic Wars	**49** Julius Caesar becomes dictator in Rome; assassinated in 44 **27** Augustus Caesar seizes power; rise of Roman empire **c. 4** Birth of Jesus	**c. 30** Crucifixion of Jesus **63** Forced dissolution of independent Jewish state by Romans **101–106** Greatest spread of Roman territory **180** Death of Marcus Aurelius; beginning of decline of Roman empire	**313** Constantine adopts Christianity **476** Fall of Rome

the Nile—although this is a part of their story. They also formed new institutions and values that reverberated in the later history of the Middle East and Europe alike.

For most Americans, and not only those who are descendants of European immigrants, classical Mediterranean culture constitutes "our own" classical past, or at least a goodly part of it. The framers of the American Constitution were extremely conscious of Greek and Roman precedents. Designers of public buildings in the United States, from the early days of the American republic to the present, have dutifully copied Greek and Roman models, as in the Lincoln Memorial and most state capitols. Plato and Aristotle continue to be thought of as the founders of the Western philosophical tradition, and skillful teachers still rely on some imitation of the Socratic method. Our sense of debt to Greece and Rome may inspire us to find in their history special meaning or links to our own world; the Western educational experience has long included elaborate explorations of the Greco-Roman past as part of the standard academic education. But from the standpoint of world history, greater balance is obviously necessary. Greco-Roman history is one of the several major classical civilizations, more dynamic than its Chinese and Indian counterparts in some respects but noticeably less successful in others. The challenge is, first, to identify leading features of Greek and Roman civilization and next to compare them with those of their counterparts elsewhere. We can then clearly recognize the connections and our own debt without adhering to the notion that the Mediterranean world somehow dominated the classical period.

Classical Mediterranean civilization is complicated by the fact that it passed through two centers during its centuries of vigor, as Greek political institutions rose and then declined and the legions of Rome assumed leadership. Roman interests were not identical to those of Greece, although the Romans carefully preserved most Greek achievements. Rome mastered engineering; Greece specialized in scientific thought. Rome created a mighty empire, whereas the Greek city-states proved rather inept in empire formation. It is possible, certainly, to see more than a change in emphases from Greece to Rome, and to talk about separate civilizations instead of a single basic pattern. And it is true that Greek influence was always stronger than Roman in the eastern Mediterranean, whereas western Europe encountered a fuller Greco-Roman mixture, with Roman influence predominating in language and law. However, Greek and Roman societies shared many political ideas; they had a common religion and artistic styles; they developed similar economic structures. Certainly, their classical heritage was used by successive civilizations without fine distinctions drawn between what was Greek and what was Roman.

For several centuries, the Persian empire far surpassed Greece in significance, certainly in the Middle East but also in the eastern Mediterranean more generally. The empire also established significant traditions that shaped a strong Persian political and cultural presence, still visible in present day Iran. And the empire generated one of the significant religions in the world history, in Zoroastrianism. The Greek tradition was largely separate, but Greek and Persian influences interacted not only in mutual warfare, but as a result of Alexander the Great's conquests and his efforts to merge cultural strands in the vast territory that briefly came under his control.

THE PERSIAN TRADITION

5.1 Why was the rise of Persia such an important development in the early part of the classical period?

After the fall of the great Egyptian and Hittite empires in the Middle East by 1200 B.C.E., much smaller states predominated the area. Then new powers stepped in, first the Assyrians and then an influx of Iranians (Persians). A great conqueror emerged by 550 B.C.E. **Cyrus the Great** established a massive Persian empire, which ran across the northern Middle East and into northwestern India. The new empire was the clearest successor to the great Mesopotamian states of the past, but it was far larger (Map 5.1). The Iranians advanced iron technology in the Middle East.

Persian politics featured several characteristics, the first of which was tolerance. The Persian empire embraced a host of languages and cultures, and the early Persian rulers were careful to grant considerable latitude for this diversity. Second, however, was a strong authoritarian streak. Darius, successor to Cyrus, worked hard to centralize laws and tax collection. The idea of wide participation in politics was rejected (Figure 5.2). Third, and related to the centralization process, Persian rulers developed a vital infrastructure for the whole empire. A major system of roads reduced travel time, although it still took 90 days to go from one end of the empire to the other. An east-west highway, largely paved, facilitated commerce and troop movement from the Indian border to the Mediterranean, and another highway reached Egypt. The Persians established the first regular postal service, and they built a network of inns along their roads to accommodate travelers. These achievements would help connect the Middle East to trade routes coming from central and eastern Asia, a vital step in the growth of new commercial connections.

The Persians worked quickly to unify their vast empire. Persia established durable political and cultural traditions.

Cyrus the Great Established massive Persian empire by 550 B.C.E.; successor state to Mesopotamian empires.

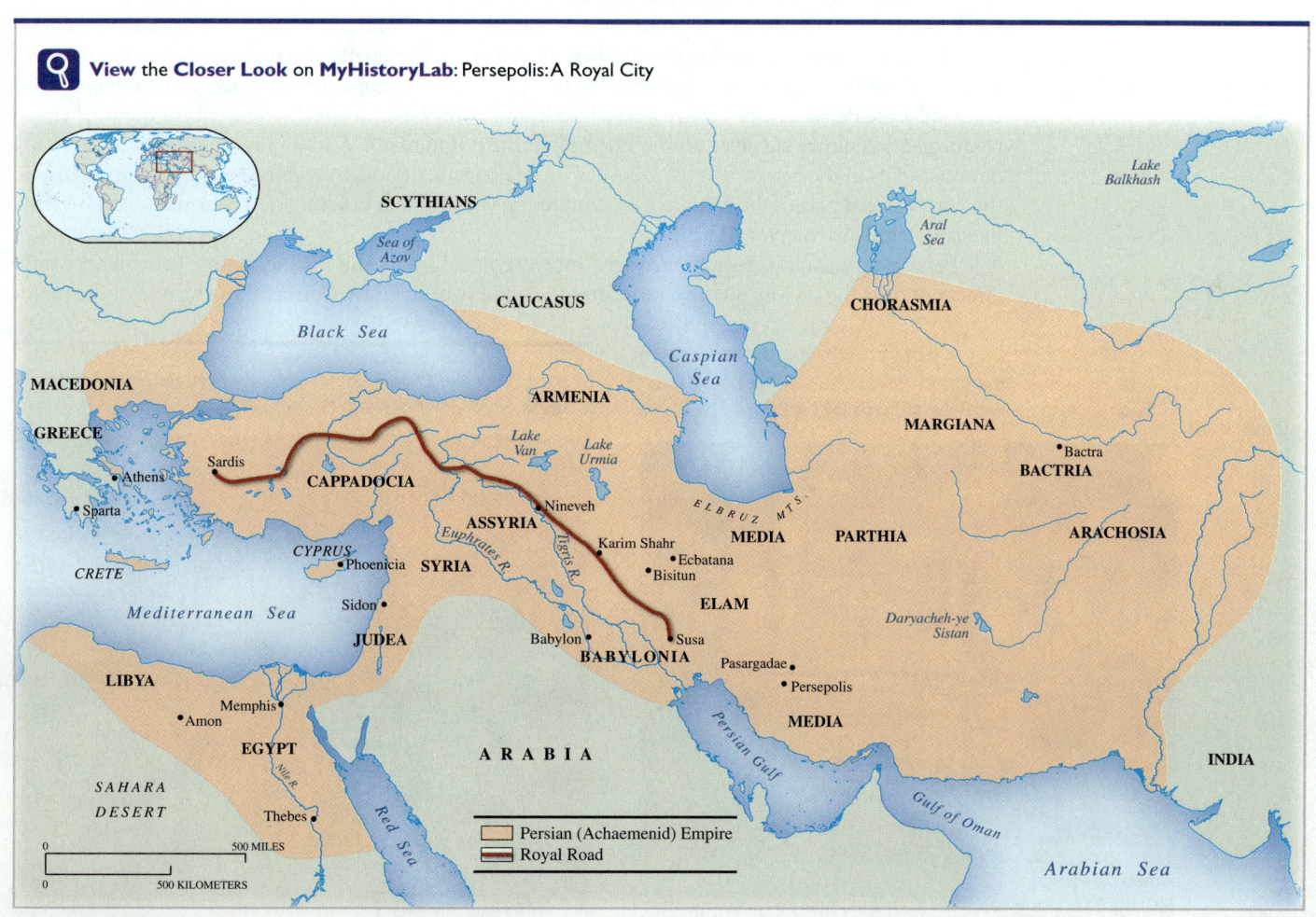

MAP 5.1 The Persian Empire in Its Main Stages At its height the Persian empire stretched through much of the Middle East to the shores of the Mediterranean, into Egypt, and into the northeast part of the Indian subcontinent.

CHAPTER 5 Classical Civilizations in the Middle East and Mediterranean 97

Zoroastrianism [zohr-oh-AS-tree-uh-NIH-zuhm] Animist religion that saw material existence as battle between forces of good and evil; stressed the importance of moral choice; righteous lived on after death in "House of Song"; chief religion of Persian empire.

Read the Document on MyHistoryLab: The "Cyrus Cylinder"

Persian emperors, particularly Darius, who worked hard not only to expand but to integrate his vast territories, developed a substantial bureaucracy. This existed alongside earlier military nobility. The central government introduced several measures to control the activities of officials assigned to distant provinces. Tax collection was carefully regulated, and spies were sent out to make sure regional officials remained loyal to the central government, rather than allying with local political forces.

Persia was also the center of a major new religion. A Zoroastrian religious leader, Zoroaster (c. 630–550 B.C.E.), revised the polytheistic religious tradition of the Sumerians through the introduction of monotheism. He banned animal sacrifice and the use of intoxicants. He introduced the idea of individual salvation through the free choice of God over the spirit of evil. Zoroaster, and the growing group of Zoroastrian priests (the *Magi*) saw life as a battle between two divine forces: good and evil. **Zoroastrianism** emphasized the importance of personal moral choice in picking one side or the other, with a Last Judgment ultimately deciding the eternal fate of each person. The righteous would live on in a heaven, the "House of Song," while the evil would be condemned to eternal pain. Zoroastrianism influenced Persia's later emperors and spread widely in the population as a whole. A Greek traveler, Herodotus, noted that the Persian religion was much more spiritual than that of the Greeks, for the Persians did not believe in humanlike gods.

Indeed, the Persian religious influence would prove far greater than that of the Greeks, although Greek culture had wide impact in other respects. Only small groups of Zoroastrians survive in the world today in Iran and through migration in a few other places, including the United States. But the religion retained a wide hold for a considerable period of time and its ideas and beliefs strongly affected Judaism, Christianity, and Islam.

Religion did not consume all of Persian cultural energies. An important artistic tradition also emerged with distinctive styles of painting and architecture (Figure 5.3).

Later kings expanded Persian holdings. They were unable to conquer Greece, but they long dominated much of the Middle East, providing an extensive period of peace and prosperity. Conquests also extended into North Africa and the Indus River valley. At its height, Persia embraced at least 14 million people. The population of Persia proper (present-day Iran), at 4 million people, had doubled under imperial rule. Ultimately, the Persian empire was toppled by Alexander the Great, a Greek-educated conqueror. Persian language and culture survived in the northeastern portion of the Middle East, periodically affecting developments in the region as a whole. After the Hellenistic period, a series of Persian empires arose in the northeastern part of the Middle East, competing with Roman holdings and later states and reviving Persian identity in many ways.

Persian political institutions strongly impressed Alexander and his successors. Persian art would affect not only the region, but also India and the wider Middle East. Zoroastrianism, one of the major

Read the Document on MyHistoryLab: Darius the Great: Ruler of Persia (522 B.C.E.)

FIGURE **5.2** Using ceremonial styles similar to those of earlier Mesopotamia, the Persian empire celebrated its powerful kings. This wall relief is on the great ceremonial stairway leading to the royal audience hall of Darius and Xerxes.

View the Closer Look on MyHistoryLab: Zoroastrianism: An Ancient Religion in Modern Times

FIGURE **5.3** Persians established a distinct artistic tradition including fine craftwork, as shown in this chariot.

98 PART II The Classical Period, 600 B.C.E.–600 C.E.: Uniting Large Regions

PATTERNS OF GREEK HISTORY

5.2 What changes occurred between the Greek and Hellenistic periods in the eastern Mediterranean?

> Greek culture reached its height during the 5th century B.C.E.; its empire spread through the empire of Alexander the Great. Rome was greatly influenced by Greek tradition as it developed its Republic and its empire.

Greece

Even as Persia developed, a new and initially much smaller civilization took shape to the west, building on a number of earlier precedents. The river valley civilizations of the Middle East and Africa had spread to some of the islands near the Greek peninsula. The island of Crete, in particular, showed the results of Egyptian influence by 2000 B.C.E., and from this the Greeks were later able to develop a taste for monumental architecture. The Greeks were an Indo-European people, like the Aryan conquerors of India, who took over the peninsula by 1700 B.C.E. An early kingdom in southern Greece, strongly influenced by Crete, developed by 1400 B.C.E. around the city of Mycenae. This was the kingdom later memorialized in Homer's epics about the Trojan War. Mycenae was then toppled by a subsequent wave of Indo-European invaders, whose incursions destabilized the peninsula until about 800 B.C.E.

The rapid rise of more complex societies in Greece between 800 and 600 B.C.E. was based on the creation of strong city-states, rather than a single political unit. Each city-state had its own government, typically either a tyranny of one ruler or an aristocratic council. The city-state served Greece well, for the peninsula was so divided by mountains that a unified government would have been difficult to establish. Trade developed rapidly under city-state sponsorship, and common cultural forms, including a rich written language with letters derived from the Phoenician alphabet, spread throughout the peninsula. The Greek city-states also joined in regular celebrations such as the athletic

MAP **5.2 Greece and Greek Colonies of the World, c. 431 B.C.E.** On the eve of the Peloponnesian War, Greek civilization had spread throughout the eastern Mediterranean.

Olympic Games One of the pan-Hellenic rituals observed by all Greek city-states; involved athletic competitions and ritual celebrations.

Pericles [PEHR-uh-kleez] Athenian political leader during 5th century B.C.E.; guided development of Athenian empire; died during early stages of Peloponnesian War.

Peloponnesian Wars [PEL-uh-poh-nee-zhun] Wars from 431 to 404 B.C.E. between Athens and Sparta for dominance in southern Greece; resulted in Spartan victory but failure to achieve political unification of Greece.

Philip of Macedonia Ruled Macedonia from 359 to 336 B.C.E.; founder of centralized kingdom; later conquered rest of Greece, which was subjected to Macedonian authority.

competitions of the **Olympic Games**. Sparta and Athens came to be the two leading city-states. The first represented a strong military aristocracy dominating a slave population; the other was a more diverse commercial state, also including the extensive use of slaves, justly proud of its artistic and intellectual leadership. Between 500 and 449 B.C.E., the two states cooperated, along with smaller states, to defeat a huge Persian invasion. It was during and immediately after this period that Greek, and particularly Athenian, culture reached its highest point. Also during this period, several city-states, and again particularly Athens, developed more colonies in the eastern Mediterranean and southern Italy, as Greek culture fanned out to create a larger zone of civilization (Map 5.2).

It was during the 5th century B.C.E. that the most famous Greek political figure, **Pericles**, dominated Athenian politics. Pericles was an aristocrat, but he was part of a democratic political structure in which each citizen could participate in city-state assemblies to select officials and pass laws. Pericles ruled not through official position, but by wise influence and negotiation. He helped restrain some of the more aggressive views of the Athenian democrats, who urged even further expansion of the empire to garner more wealth and build the economy. Ultimately, however, Pericles' guidance could not prevent a tragic war between Athens and Sparta, which depleted both sides. In the **Peloponnesian Wars** (431–404 B.C.E.) the two leading city-states, along with many allies, battled for supremacy, with both sides emerging severely damaged, although Sparta was technically the victor.

Political decline soon set in, along with widespread poverty. Ambitious kings from Macedonia, in the northern part of the peninsula, soon swept through the Greek peninsula. **Philip of Macedonia** won the crucial battle in 338 B.C.E., and then his son Alexander extended the Macedonian empire through the Middle East, across Persia to the border of India, and southward through Egypt (Map 5.3). Alexander the Great's empire was short-lived, for its creator died at the age of 33 after a mere 13 years of breathtaking conquests. However, successor regional kingdoms continued to rule much of the eastern

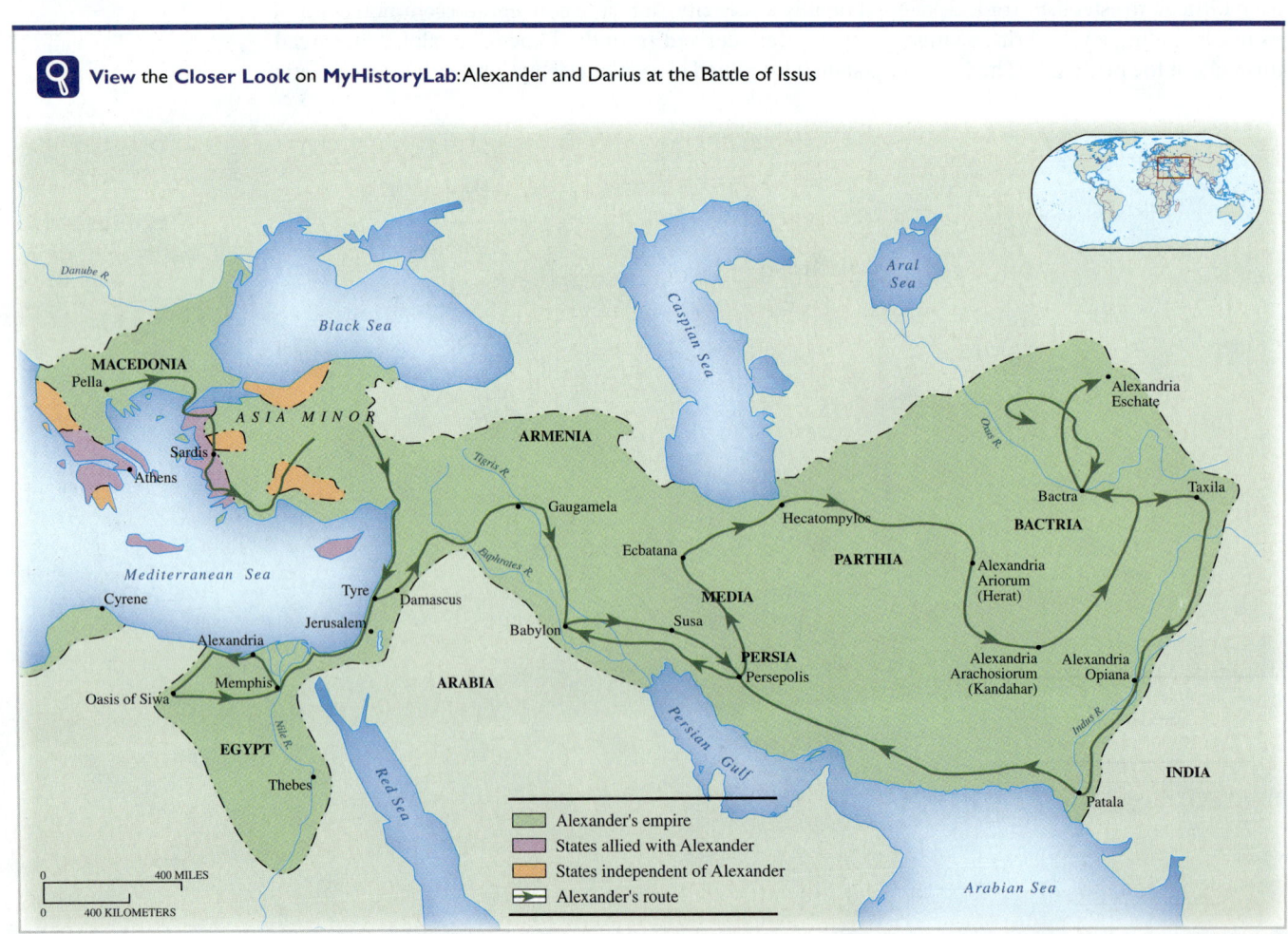

MAP **5.3 Alexander's Empire and the Hellenistic World, c. 323 B.C.E.** Note the movement through Persia and other parts of the northern Middle East, and into the Indian subcontinent and North Africa.

100 PART II The Classical Period, 600 B.C.E.–600 C.E.: Uniting Large Regions

Mediterranean for several centuries. Under their aegis, Greek art and culture merged with other Middle Eastern forms during a period called **Hellenistic**, the name derived because of the influence of the Hellenes, as the Greeks were known. Although there was little political activity under the autocratic Hellenistic kings, trade flourished and important scientific centers were established in such cities as Alexandria in Egypt. In sum, the Hellenistic period saw the consolidation of Greek civilization even after the political decline of the peninsula itself, as well as some important new cultural developments.

The Hellenistic period also provided an important opportunity for interregional contacts. Greek-Indian interactions in the kingdom of Bactria were unusual for the time. More significant was the further exchange between Greek and Persian traditions and between Greek and Egyptian as well. Alexander himself, marrying a Persian princess, hoped for a fusion of Persian and Greek politics and culture. His political achievements highlighted an authoritarian strain that meshed with Persian precedents. Art and science benefited from creative exchanges among scholars in many parts of the eastern Mediterranean. The advances in science and philosophy that resulted provided a shared intellectual legacy for the whole region, even after the Hellenistic political kingdoms collapsed.

Alexander's conquests highlight the connections between Greece and the Middle East, where a combined heritage would prove influential even under Islam. Relationships could be tense, however. Many Greek military leaders resented Alexander's policy of conciliating the Persians (Alexander even married the daughter of the last Persian emperor). In one passage, in 328 B.C.E., Alexander flew into a drunken rage against one of his best friends, Cleitus, possibly because of the Persian dispute, and actually killed him on the spot—later deeply regretting his impulse.

> **Hellenistic** That culture associated with the spread of Greek influence as a result of Macedonian conquests; often seen as the combination of Greek culture with eastern political forms.

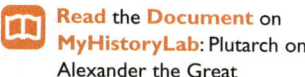
Read the Document on MyHistoryLab: Plutarch on Alexander the Great

PATTERNS OF ROMAN HISTORY

5.3 What were the causes of Roman expansion?

The rise of Rome formed the final phase of classical Mediterranean history. At the same time, Rome's advance greatly extended Mediterranean civilization to the west, over a wider stretch of southern Europe as well as North Africa. And Rome added important and distinctive contributions to the Greek and Hellenistic heritage, even as it ultimately subjugated Greece and many of the Hellenistic kingdoms.

The Roman state began humbly enough, as a local monarchy in central Italy around 800 B.C.E. Roman aristocrats succeeded in driving out the monarchy around 509 B.C.E. and established more elaborate political institutions for their city-state. The new **Roman republic** gradually extended its influence over the rest of the Italian peninsula, among other things conquering the Greek colonies in the south. Thus, the Romans early acquired a strong military orientation, although initially they may have been driven simply by a desire to protect their own territory from possible rivals. Roman conquest spread more widely during the three **Punic Wars**, from 264 to 146 B.C.E., during which Rome fought the armies of the Phoenician city of **Carthage**, situated on the northern coast of Africa. These wars included a bloody defeat of the invading forces of the brilliant Carthaginian general **Hannibal**, whose troops were accompanied by pack-laden elephants. The war was so bitter that the Romans in a final act of destruction spread salt around Carthage to prevent agriculture from surviving there. Following the final destruction of Carthage, the Romans proceeded to seize the entire western Mediterranean along with Greece and Egypt.

The politics of the Roman republic grew increasingly unstable; however, as victorious generals sought even greater power the poor of the city rebelled. Civil wars between two generals led to a victory by **Julius Caesar**, in 45 B.C.E., and the effective end of the traditional institutions of the Roman state. Caesar's grandnephew, ultimately called **Augustus Caesar**, seized power in 27 B.C.E., following another period of rivalry after Julius Caesar's assassination, and established the basic structures of the Roman empire.

For 200 years, through the reign of Emperor Marcus Aurelius in 180 C.E., the empire maintained great vigor, bringing peace and prosperity to virtually the entire Mediterranean world, from Spain and North Africa in the west to the eastern shores of the great sea. The emperors also moved northward, conquering France and southern Britain and pushing into Germany. Here was a major, if somewhat tenuous, extension of the sway of Mediterranean civilization to western Europe (Map 5.4). Rome's overall holdings obviously compare strikingly to the Han empire in China, covering almost the same amount of territory with only a slightly smaller population. Rome handled its empire somewhat differently from the Han, with less centralization, more tolerance of different local political units along with emphasis on common legal principles. In both empires, however, effective government and substantial

> Greece and Rome were ruled by aristocrats but also introduced some democratic elements. The Roman empire encompassed a huge territory and population.

Roman republic The balanced constitution of Rome from c. 510 to 47 B.C.E.; featured an aristocratic Senate, a panel of magistrates, and several popular assemblies.

Punic Wars Fought between Rome and Carthage to establish dominance in the western Mediterranean; won by Rome after three separate conflicts.

Carthage Originally a Phoenician colony in northern Africa; became a major port and commercial power in the western Mediterranean; fought the Punic Wars with Rome for dominance of the western Mediterranean.

Hannibal Great Carthaginian general during Second Punic War; successfully invaded Italy but failed to conquer Rome; finally defeated at Battle of Zama.

Caesar, Julius Roman general responsible for conquest of Gaul; brought army back to Rome and overthrew republic; assassinated in 44 B.C.E. by conservative senators.

Caesar, Augustus (63 B.C.E.–14 C.E.) Name given to Octavian following his defeat of Mark Antony and Cleopatra; first emperor of Rome.

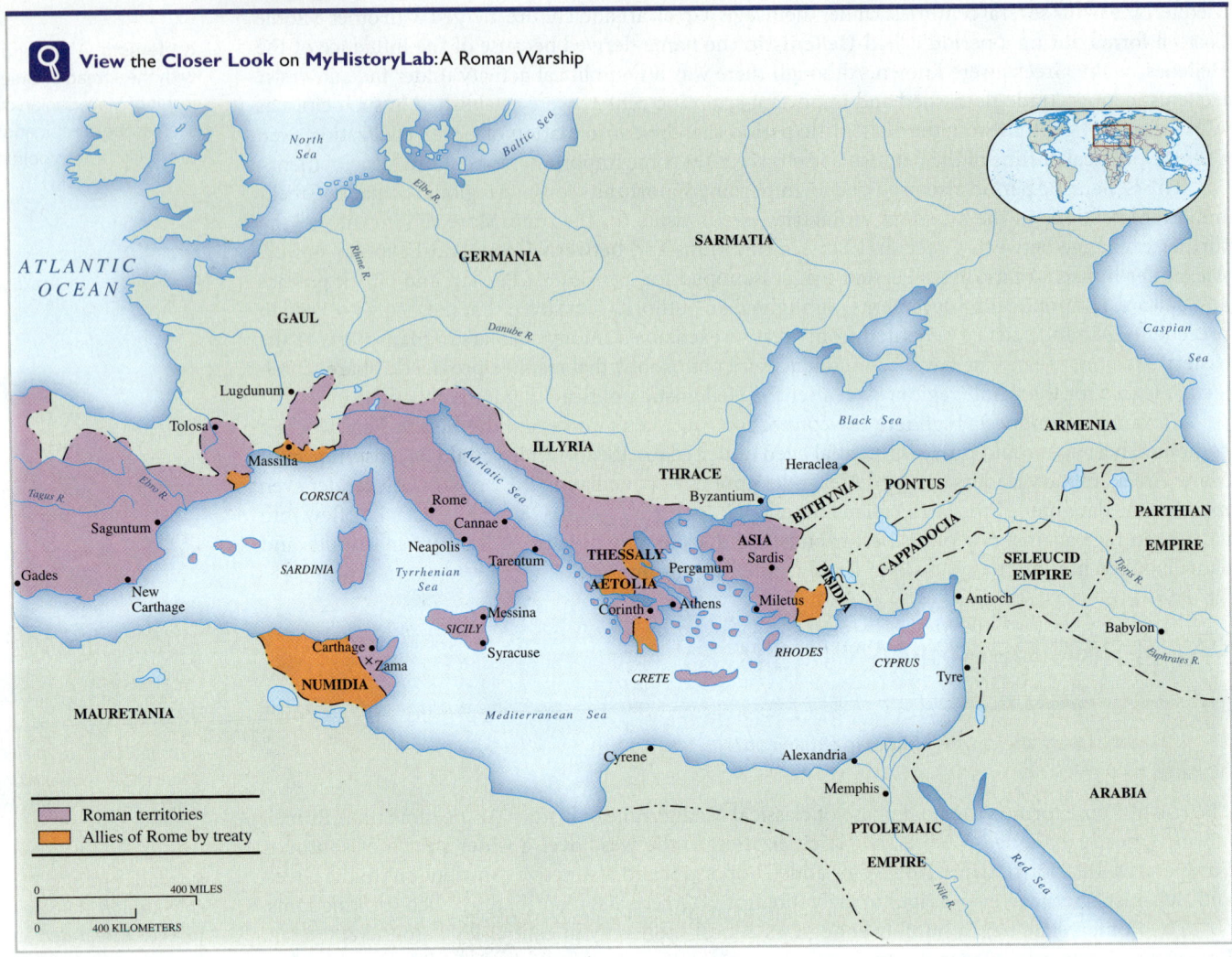

MAP 5.4 **The Expansion of the Roman Republic, 133 B.C.E.** By the end of the Punic Wars, Rome dominated much of the Mediterranean world.

military force helped assure substantial stability and prosperity, creating a striking impression at the time and in later memory.

Roman expansion brought new contacts between Persian and Mediterranean society. A Persian empire, Parthia, had emerged from the fragmentation of Alexander the Great's conquests. Rome at various points, pushing strongly into the Middle East, sought to reconquer this territory. In 113 C.E., Emperor Trajan mounted the most ambitious campaign to invade Parthia, and his victories brought Rome into Mesopotamia and also Armenia. However, internal troubles forced him to pull back and Parthia soon regained considerable territory. Wars with Parthia and its successor, the Sassanid empire, dotted the later history of the Roman empire, with mutually inconclusive results.

After 180 C.E., the Roman empire suffered a slow but decisive fall, which lasted more than 250 years, until invading peoples from the north finally overturned the government in Rome in 476 C.E. The decline manifested itself in terms of both economic deterioration and population loss: both the trade levels and the birth rate fell. Government also became generally less effective, although some strong later emperors, particularly **Diocletian** and **Constantine**, attempted to reverse the tide. It was Emperor Constantine who, in 313 C.E., adopted the then somewhat obscure religion called Christianity in an attempt to unite the empire in new ways. However, particularly in the western half of the empire, most effective government became local, as the imperial administration could no longer guarantee order or even provide a system of justice. The Roman armies depended increasingly on non-Roman recruits, whose loyalty was suspect. Then, in this deepening mire, the invasion of nomadic peoples from the north marked the end of the classical period of Mediterranean civilization—a civilization that, like its counterparts in Gupta India and Han China during the same approximate period, could no longer defend itself.

Diocletian Roman emperor from 284 to 305 C.E.; restored later empire by improved administration and tax collection.

Constantine Roman emperor from 312 to 337 C.E.; established second capital at Constantinople; attempted to use religious force of Christianity to unify empire spiritually.

To conclude: The new Mediterranean civilization built on earlier cultures along the eastern Mediterranean and within the Greek islands, taking firm shape with the rise of the Greek city-states after 800 B.C.E. These states began as monarchies but then evolved into more complex and diverse political forms. They also developed a more varied commercial economy, moving away from a purely grain-growing agriculture; this spurred the formation of a number of colonial outposts around the eastern Mediterranean and in Italy. The decline of the city-states ushered in the Macedonian conquest and the formation of a wider Hellenistic culture that established deep roots in the Middle East and Egypt. Then Rome, initially a minor regional state distinguished by political virtue and stability, embarked on its great conquests, which earned it control of the Mediterranean, with important extensions into the Middle East and into western and southeastern Europe plus the whole of North Africa. Rome's expansion ultimately overwhelmed its own republic, but the successor empire developed important political institutions of its own and resulted in two centuries of peace and glory.

GREEK AND ROMAN POLITICAL INSTITUTIONS

5.4 What are the main issues in defining the Greek and Roman political legacy?

Greece and Rome did not generate a major religion.

Politics were very important in classical Mediterranean civilization, from the Greek city-states through the early part of the Roman Empire. Indeed, the word *politics* comes from the Greek word for city-state, **polis,** which correctly suggests that intense political interests were part of life in a city-state in both Greece and Rome. Greeks who visited Persia contrasted their political values with the more authoritarian structures of their neighbor. The "good life" for an upper-class Athenian or Roman included active participation in politics and frequent discussions about the affairs of state. The local character of Mediterranean politics, whereby the typical city-state governed a surrounding territory of several hundred square miles, contributed to this intense preoccupation with politics. Citizens believed that the state was theirs, that they had certain rights and obligations without which their government could not survive. In the Greek city-states and also under the Roman republic, citizens actively participated in the military, which further contributed to this sense of political interest and responsibility. Under the Roman empire, of course, political concerns were restricted by the sheer power of the emperor and his officers. Even then, however, local city-states retained considerable autonomy in Italy, Greece, and the eastern Mediterranean—the empire did not try to administer most local regions in great detail. The minority of people throughout the empire who were Roman citizens were intensely proud of this privilege.

polis City-state form of government; typical of Greek political organization from 800 to 400 B.C.E. (pl. poleis).

Strong political ideals and interests created some similarities between Greco-Roman society and the Confucian values of classical China, although the concept of active citizenship was distinctive in the Mediterranean cultures. However, Greece and Rome did not develop a single or cohesive set of political institutions to rival China's divinely sanctioned emperor or its elaborate bureaucracy. So in addition to political intensity and localism as characteristics of Mediterranean civilization, we must note great diversity in political forms. Here the comparison extends to India, where various political forms—including participation in governing councils—ran strong. Later societies, in reflecting on classical Mediterranean civilization, did select from a number of political precedents. Monarchy was not a preferred form; the Roman republic and most Greek city-states had abolished early monarchies as part of their prehistory. Rule by individual strongmen was more common, and the word *tyranny* comes from this experience in classical Greece. Many tyrants were effective rulers, particularly in promoting public works and protecting the common people against the abuses of the aristocracy. Some of the Roman generals who seized power in the later days of the republic had similar characteristics, as did the Hellenistic kings who succeeded Alexander in ruling regions of his empire.

Greece

Democracy (the word is derived from the Greek *demos*, "the people") was another important political alternative in classical Mediterranean society. The Athenian city-state traveled furthest in this direction, before and during the Peloponnesian Wars, after earlier experiences with aristocratic rule and with several tyrants. In 5th-century Athens, the major decisions of state were made by general assemblies in which all citizens could participate—although usually only a minority attended. This was **direct democracy**, not rule through elected representatives. The assembly met every 10 days. Executive officers,

direct democracy Where people participate directly in assemblies that make laws and select leaders, rather than electing representatives.

THINKING HISTORICALLY

The Classical Mediterranean in Comparative Perspective

THE GREAT CLASSICAL CIVILIZATIONS LEND THEMSELVES to a variety of comparisons. The general tone of each differed from the others, ranging from India's otherworldly strain to China's emphasis on government centralization, although it is important to note the varieties of activities and interests and the changes that occurred in each of the three societies. Basic comparisons include several striking similarities. Each classical society developed empires. Each relied primarily on an agricultural economy. Greco-Roman interest in secular culture bears some resemblance to Confucian emphasis in China, although in each case religious currents remained as well. But Greco-Roman political values and institutions differed from the Confucian emphasis on deference and bureaucratic training. Greek definitions of science contrasted with those of India and China, particularly in the emphasis on theory. Several focal points can be used for comparison.

Each classical civilization emphasized a clear social hierarchy, with substantial distance between elites and the majority of people who did the manual and menial work. This vital similarity between the civilizations reflected common tensions between complex leadership demands and lifestyles and the limited economic resources of the agricultural economy. Groups at the top of the social hierarchy judged that they had to control lower groups carefully to ensure their own prosperity. Each classical society generated ideologies that explained and justified the great social divisions. Philosophers and religious leaders devoted great attention to this subject.

Within this common framework, however, there were obvious differences. Groups at the top of the social pyramid reflected different value systems. Confucian bureaucrats in China can be compared with the aristocrats in Greece and the Roman republic. The status of merchants varied despite the vital role commerce played in all of the classical civilizations.

Opportunities for mobility varied also. China's bureaucratic system allowed a very small number of talented people from below to rise on the basis of education, but most bureaucrats continued to come from the landed aristocracy. Mediterranean society, with its aristocratic emphasis, also limited opportunities to rise to the top, but the importance of acquired wealth (particularly in Rome) gave some nonaristocrats important economic and political opportunities. Cicero, for example, came from a merchant family. Various classes also shared some political power in city-state assemblies; the idea of citizens holding basic political rights across class lines was unusual in classical civilizations.

Each classical civilization distinctively defined the position of the lowest orders. As Greece and then Rome expanded, they relied heavily on the legal and physical compulsions of slavery to provide menial service and demanding labor. Greece and Rome gave unusual voice to farmers when they maintained their own property but tended to scorn manual labor itself, a view that helped justify and was perpetuated by slavery. Confucianism urged deference but offered more active praise for peasant work.

Finally, each classical civilization developed a different cultural glue to help hold its social hierarchy together. Greece and Rome left much of the task of managing the social hierarchy to local authorities; community bonds, as in the city-states, were meant to pull different groups into a sense of common purpose. They also relied on military force and clear legal statements that defined rights according to station. Force and legal inequalities played important roles in China and India as well, but there were additional inducements. Chinese Confucianism urged general cultural values of obedience and self-restraint, creating some agreement—despite varied religions and philosophies—on the legitimacy of social ranks by defining how gentlemen and commoners should behave.

> *Each classical civilization distinctively defined the position of the lowest orders.*

In no case did the social cement work perfectly; social unrest surfaced in all the classical civilizations, as in major slave rebellions in the Roman countryside or peasant uprisings in China. At the same time, the rigidity of classical social structures gave many common people some leeway. Elites viewed the masses as being so different from themselves that they did not try to revamp all their beliefs or community institutions.

Differences in approach to social inequality nevertheless had important results. China and, as we will see, particularly India generated value systems that might convince people in the lower classes and the upper ranks that there was some legitimacy in the social hierarchy. Greece and Rome attempted a more difficult task in emphasizing the importance of aristocracy while offering some other elements a share in the political system. This combination could work well, although some groups, including slaves and women, were always excluded. It tended to deteriorate, however, when poorer citizens lost property. Yet no sweeping new social theory emerged to offer a different kind of solace to the masses until Christianity began to spread. It is no accident, then, that Indian and Chinese social structures survived better than Mediterranean structures did, lasting well beyond the classical period into the modern era.

QUESTIONS

- Why did the classical civilizations seem to need radical social inequalities?
- What was the relationship between wealth and social position in each classical civilization?
- How did China and the Mediterranean cultures try to compensate for social inequalities?

including judges, were chosen for brief terms to control their power, and they were subject to review by the assembly. Furthermore, they were chosen by lot, not elected—on the principle that any citizen could and should be able to serve. To be sure, only a minority of the Athenian population were active citizens: Women had no rights of political participation, and half of all adult males were not citizens at all, being slaves or foreigners. This, then, was not exactly the kind of democracy we envision today. But it elicited widespread popular participation and devotion, and certainly embodied principles that we recognize as truly democratic. The Athenian leader Pericles, who led Athens during its decades of greatest glory between the final defeat of the Persians and the agony of war with Sparta, described the system this way:

> The administration is in the hands of the many and not of the few. But while the law secures equal justice to all alike in their private disputes, the claim of excellence is also recognized; and when a citizen is in any way distinguished he is preferred to the public service, not as a matter of privilege but as the reward of merit. Neither is poverty a bar, but a man may benefit his country whatever be the obscurity of his condition.

During the Peloponnesian Wars, Athens even demonstrated some of the potential drawbacks of democracy. Lower-class citizens, eager for government jobs and the spoils of war, often encouraged reckless military actions that weakened the state in its central dispute with Sparta.

Neither tyranny nor democracy, however, was the most characteristic political form in the classical Mediterranean world. The most widely preferred political framework centered on the existence of aristocratic assemblies, whose deliberations established guidelines for state policy and served as a check on executive power. Thus, Sparta was governed by a singularly militaristic aristocracy, intent on retaining power over a large slave population. Other Greek city-states, although less bent on disciplining their elites for rigorous military service, also featured aristocratic assemblies. Even Athens during much of its democratic phase found leadership in many aristocrats, including Pericles. The word *aristocracy*, which comes from Greek terms meaning "rule of the best," suggests where many Greeks—particularly, of course, aristocrats—thought real political virtue lay.

Rome

The constitution of the Roman republic, until the final decades of dissension in the 1st century B.C.E., which led to the establishment of the empire, tried to reconcile the various elements suggested by the Greek political experience, with primary reliance on the principle of aristocracy. All Roman citizens in the republic could gather in periodic assemblies, the function of which was not to pass basic laws but rather to elect various magistrates, some of whom were specifically entrusted with the task of representing the interests of the common people. The most important legislative body was the **Senate**, composed mainly of aristocrats, whose members held virtually all executive offices in the Roman state. Two **consuls** shared primary executive power, but in times of crisis the Senate could choose a dictator to hold emergency authority until the crisis had passed. In the Roman Senate, as in the aristocratic assemblies of the Greek city-states, the ideal of public service, featuring eloquent public speaking and arguments that sought to identify the general good, came closest to realization.

The diversity of Greek and Roman political forms, as well as the importance ascribed to political participation, helped generate a significant body of political theory in classical Mediterranean civilization. True to the aristocratic tradition, much of this theory dealt with appropriate political ethics, the duties of citizens, the importance of incorruptible service, and key political skills such as oratory. Roman writers such as Cicero, an active senator, expounded eloquently on these subjects. Some of this political writing resembled Confucianism, although there was less emphasis on hierarchy and obedience or bureaucratic virtues, and more on participation in deliberative bodies that make laws and judge the actions of executive officers. Classical Mediterranean writers also paid great attention to the structure of the state itself, debating the virtues and vices of the various political forms. This kind of theory both expressed the political interests and diversity of the Mediterranean world and served as a key heritage to later societies.

The Roman empire was a different sort of political system from the earlier city-states, although it preserved some older institutions, such as the Senate, which became a rather meaningless forum for debates. Of necessity, the empire developed organizational capacities on a far larger scale than the city-states; it is important to remember, however, that considerable local autonomy prevailed in many regions. Only in rare cases, such as the forced dissolution of the independent Jewish state in 63 C.E. after a major local rebellion, did the Romans take over distant areas completely. Careful organization was particularly evident in the vast hierarchy of the Roman army, whose officers wielded great political power even over the emperors.

Senate Assembly of Roman aristocrats; advised on policy within the republic; one of the early elements of the Roman constitution.

Read the Document on MyHistoryLab: Livy, The Rape of Lucretia and the Origins of the Republic

consuls Two chief executives or magistrates of the Roman republic; elected by an annual assembly dominated by aristocracy.

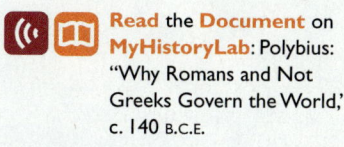
Read the Document on MyHistoryLab: Polybius: "Why Romans and Not Greeks Govern the World," c. 140 B.C.E.

In addition to considerable tolerance for local customs and religions, plus strong military organization, the Romans emphasized carefully crafted laws as the factor that would hold their vast territories together. Greek and Roman republican leaders had already developed an understanding of the importance of codified, equitable law. Aristocratic leaders in 8th-century Athens, for example, sponsored clear legal codes designed to balance the defense of private property with the protection of poor citizens, including access to courts of law administered by fellow citizens. The early Roman republic introduced its first code of law, the Twelve Tables, by 450 B.C.E. These early Roman laws were intended, among other things, to restrain the upper classes from arbitrary action and to subject them, as well as ordinary people, to some common legal principles. The Roman empire carried these legal interests still further, in the belief that law should evolve to meet changing conditions without, however, fluctuating wildly. The idea of Roman law was that rules, objectively judged, rather than personal whim should govern social relationships; thus, the law steadily took over matters of judgment earlier reserved for fathers of families or for landlords. Roman law also promoted the importance of commonsense fairness. In one case cited in the law texts of the empire, a slave was being shaved by a barber in a public square; two men were playing ball nearby, and one accidentally hit the barber with the ball, causing him to cut the slave's throat. Who was responsible for the tragedy: the barber, catcher, or pitcher? According to Roman law, the slave—for anyone so foolish as to be shaved in a public place was asking for trouble and bore the responsibility himself.

Roman law codes spread widely through the empire, and with them came the notion of law as the regulator of social life. Many non-Romans were given the right of citizenship—although most ordinary people outside Rome itself preferred to maintain their local allegiances. With citizenship, however, came full access to Rome-appointed judges and uniform laws. Imperial law codes also regulated property rights and commerce, thus creating some economic unity in the vast empire. The idea of fair and reasoned law, to which officers of the state should themselves be subject, was a key political achievement of the Roman empire, comparable in importance, although quite different in nature, to the Chinese elaboration of a complex bureaucratic structure.

The Greeks and Romans were less innovative in the functions they ascribed to government than in the political forms and theories they developed. Most governments concentrated on maintaining systems of law courts and military forces. Athens and, more durably and successfully, Rome placed great premium on the importance of military conquest. Mediterranean governments regulated some branches of commerce, particularly in the interest of securing vital supplies of grain. Rome, indeed, undertook vast public works in the form of roads and harbors to facilitate military transport as well as commerce. And the Roman state, especially under the empire, built countless stadiums and public baths to entertain and distract its subjects. The city of Rome itself, which at its peak contained more than a million inhabitants, provided cheap food as well as gladiator contests and other entertainment for the masses—the famous "bread and circuses" that were designed to prevent popular disorder. Colonies of Romans elsewhere were also given theaters and stadiums. This provided solace in otherwise strange lands such as England or Palestine. Governments also supported an official religion, sponsoring public ceremonies to honor the gods and goddesses; civic religious festivals were important events that both expressed and encouraged widespread loyalty to the state. However, there was little attempt to impose this religion on everyone, and other religious practices were tolerated so long as they did not conflict with loyalty to the state. Even the later Roman emperors, who advanced the idea that the emperor was a god as a means of strengthening authority, were normally tolerant of other religions. They only attacked Christianity, and then irregularly, because of the Christians' refusal to place the state first in their devotion.

Localism and fervent political interests, including a sense of intense loyalty to the state; a diversity of political systems together with the preference for aristocratic rule; the importance of law and the development of an unusually elaborate and uniform set of legal principles—these were the chief political legacies of the classical Mediterranean world. The sheer accomplishment of the Roman empire itself, which united a region never before or since brought together, still stands as one of the great political monuments of world history. This was a distinctive political mix. Although there was attention to careful legal procedures, no clear definition of individuals' rights existed. Indeed, the emphasis on duties to the state could lead, as in Sparta, to an essentially totalitarian framework in which the state controlled even the raising of children. Nor, until the peaceful centuries of the early Roman empire, was it an entirely successful political structure, as wars and instability were common. Nonetheless, there can be no question of the richness of this political culture or of its central importance to the Greeks and Romans themselves.

RELIGION AND CULTURE

5.5 What was the relationship between Greek and Roman culture?

> Greek and Roman economies were based on commercial agriculture, trade, and slavery. The two societies developed somewhat different versions of the patriarchal family.

The Greeks and Romans did not create a significant, world-class religion; in this, they differed from India and to some extent from China and Persia. Christianity, which was to become one of the major world religions, did of course arise during the Roman empire. It owed some of its rapid geographical spread to the ease of movement within the huge Roman empire. However, Christianity was not really a product of Greek or Roman culture, although it was ultimately influenced by this culture. It took on serious historical importance only as the Roman empire began its decline. The characteristic Greco-Roman religion was a much more primitive affair, derived from a belief in the spirits of nature elevated into a complex set of gods and goddesses who were seen as regulating human life. Greeks and Romans had different names for their pantheon, but the objects of worship were essentially the same: a creator or father god, Zeus or Jupiter, presided over an unruly assemblage of gods and goddesses whose functions ranged from regulating the daily passage of the sun (Apollo) or the oceans (Neptune) to inspiring war (Mars) or human love and beauty (Venus). Specific gods were the patrons of other human activities such as metalworking, the hunt, even literature and history. Regular ceremonies to the gods had real political importance, and many individuals sought the gods' aid in foretelling the future or in ensuring a good harvest or good health.

Aristotle (384–322 B.C.E.) Greek philosopher; teacher of Alexander the Great; knowledge based on observation of phenomena in material world.

Cicero (106–43 B.C.E.) Conservative Roman senator; Stoic philosopher; one of great orators of his day; killed in reaction to assassination of Julius Caesar.

Stoics Hellenistic group of philosophers; emphasized inner moral independence cultivated by strict discipline of the body and personal bravery.

Socrates Athenian philosopher of later 5th century B.C.E.; tutor of Plato; urged rational reflection of moral decisions; condemned to death for corrupting minds of Athenian young.

In addition to its political functions, Greco-Roman religion had certain other features. It tended to be rather human, of this world in its approach. The doings of the gods made for good storytelling; they read like soap operas on a superhuman scale. Thus, the classical Mediterranean religion early engendered an important literary tradition, as was also the case in India. (Indeed, Greco-Roman and Indian religious lore reflected the common heritage of Indo-European invaders.) The gods were often used to illustrate human passions and foibles, thus serving as symbols of a serious inquiry into human nature. Unlike the Indians, however, the Greeks and Romans became interested in their gods more in terms of what they could do for and reveal about humankind on this earth than the principles that could elevate people toward higher planes of spirituality (Figure 5.4).

This dominant religion also had a number of limitations. Its lack of spiritual passion failed to satisfy many ordinary workers and peasants, particularly in times of political chaos or economic distress. "Mystery" religions, often imported from the Middle East, periodically swept through Greece and Rome, providing secret rituals and fellowship and a greater sense of contact with unfathomable divine powers. Even more than in China, a considerable division arose between upper-class and popular belief.

The gods and goddesses of Greco-Roman religion left many upper-class people dissatisfied also. They provided stories about how the world came to be, but little basis for a systematic inquiry into nature or human society. And while the dominant religion promoted political loyalty, it did not provide a basis for ethical thought. Hence, many thinkers, both in Greece and Rome, sought a separate model for ethical behavior. Greek and Roman moral philosophy, as issued by philosophers such as **Aristotle** and **Cicero**, typically stressed the importance of moderation and balance in human behavior as opposed to the instability of much political life and the excesses of the gods. Other ethical systems were devised, particularly during the Hellenistic period. **Stoics**, for example, emphasized an inner moral independence, to be cultivated by strict discipline of the body and by personal bravery. These ethical systems, established largely apart from religious considerations, were major contributions in their own right; they also were blended with later religious thought, under Christianity.

FIGURE **5.4** After murdering his wife and children, Hercules, who became the Greeks' greatest mythical hero, was sentenced to perform 12 tasks that would have been impossible for most mortals. This vase depicts the fourth labor of Hercules, in which he was ordered to capture the Erymanthian boar and bring it to his master, Eurystheus. The frightened Eurystheus has hidden in a wine jar. (Copyright The British Museum.)

The idea of a philosophy separate from the official religion, although not necessarily hostile to it, informed classical Mediterranean political theory, which made little reference to religious principles. It also considerably emphasized the powers of human thought. In Athens, **Socrates** (born in 469 B.C.E.) encouraged his pupils to question conventional wisdom, on the grounds that the chief human duty was "the improvement of the soul."

Socrates ran afoul of the Athenian government, which thought that he was undermining political loyalty; given the choice of suicide or exile, Socrates chose the former. However, the Socratic principle of rational inquiry by means of skeptical questioning became a recurrent strand in classical Greek thinking and in its heritage to later societies. Socrates' great pupil Plato accentuated the positive somewhat more strongly by suggesting that human reason could approach an understanding of the three perfect forms—the absolutely True, Good, and Beautiful—which he believed characterized nature. Thus, a philosophical tradition arose in Greece, although in very diverse individual expressions, which tended to deemphasize the importance of human spirituality in favor of a celebration of the human ability to think. The result bore some similarities to Chinese Confucianism, although with greater emphasis on skeptical questioning and abstract speculations about the basic nature of humanity and the universe.

Greek interest in rationality carried over an inquiry into the underlying order of physical nature. The Greeks were not outstanding empirical scientists. Relatively few new scientific findings emanated from Athens, or later from Rome, although philosophers such as Aristotle did collect large amounts of biological data. The Greek interest lay in speculations about nature's order, and many non-Westerners believe that this tradition continues to inform what they see as an excessive Western passion for seeking basic rationality in the universe. In practice, the Greek concern translated into a host of theories, some of which were wrong, about the motions of the planets and the organization of the elemental principles of earth, fire, air, and water, and into a considerable interest in mathematics as a means of rendering nature's patterns comprehensible. Greek and later Hellenistic work in geometry was particularly impressive, featuring among other achievements the basic theorems of Pythagoras. Scientists, during the Hellenistic period, made some important empirical contributions, especially in studies of anatomy; medical treatises by Galen were not improved on in the Western world for many centuries. The mathematician Euclid produced what was long the world's most widely used compendium of geometry. Less fortunately, the Hellenistic astronomer Ptolemy produced an elaborate theory of the sun's motion around a stationary earth. This new Hellenistic theory contradicted much earlier Middle Eastern astronomy, which had recognized the earth's rotation; nonetheless, it was Ptolemy's theory that was long taken as fixed wisdom in Western thought.

Roman intellectuals, actively examining ethical and political theory, did not add to Greek and Hellenistic science. They did help to preserve this tradition in the form of textbooks that were administered to upper-class schoolchildren. The Roman genius was more practical than the Greek and included engineering achievements such as the great roads and aqueducts that carried water to cities large and small. Roman ability to construct elaborate arches so that buildings could carry great structural weight was unsurpassed anywhere in the world. These feats, too, left their mark, as Rome's huge edifices long served as a reminder of ancient glories. But ultimately, it was the Greek and Hellenistic impulse to extend human reason to nature's principles that resulted in the most impressive legacy.

In classical Mediterranean civilization, however, science and mathematics loomed far less large than art and literature in conveying key cultural values. The official religion inspired themes for artistic expression and the justification for temples, statues, and plays devoted to the glories of the gods. Nonetheless, the human-centered qualities of the Greeks and Romans also registered, as artists emphasized the beauty of realistic portrayals of the human form and poets and playwrights used the gods as foils for inquiries into the human condition.

All the arts received some attention in classical Mediterranean civilization. Performances of music and dance were vital parts of religious festivals, but their precise styles have unfortunately not been preserved. Far more durable was the Greek interest in drama, because plays, more than poetry, took a central role in this culture. Greek dramatists produced both comedy and tragedy, indeed making a formal division between the two approaches that is still part of the Western tradition, as in the labeling of current television shows as either form. On the whole, in contrast to Indian writers, the Greeks placed the greatest emphasis on tragedy. Their belief in human reason and balance also involved a sense that these virtues were precarious, so a person could easily become ensnared in situations of powerful emotion and uncontrollable consequences. The Athenian dramatist **Sophocles**, for example, so insightfully portrayed the psychological flaws of his hero Oedipus that modern psychology long used the term *Oedipus complex* to refer to a potentially unhealthy relationship between a man and his mother.

Sophocles (496–406 B.C.E.) Greek writer of tragedies; author of *Oedipus Rex*.

Greek literature contained a strong epic tradition as well, starting with the beautifully crafted tales of the **Iliad** and **Odyssey,** attributed to the poet Homer, who lived in the 8th century B.C.E. Roman authors, particularly the poet Vergil, also worked in the epic form, seeking to link Roman history and mythology with the Greek forerunner. Roman writers made significant contributions to poetry and to definitions of the poetic form that was long used in western literature. The overall Roman literary contribution was less impressive than the Greek, but it was substantial enough both to provide important examples of how poetry should be written and to furnish abundant illustrations of the literary richness of the Latin language.

In the visual arts, the emphasis of classical Mediterranean civilization was sculpture and architecture. Greek artists also excelled in ceramic work, whereas Roman painters produced realistic (and sometimes pornographic) decorations for the homes of the wealthy. In the brilliant age of Athens' 5th century—the age of Pericles, Socrates, Sophocles, and so many other intensely creative figures—sculptors such as Phidias developed unprecedented skill rendering simultaneously realistic yet beautiful images of the human form, from lovely goddesses to muscled warriors and athletes. Roman sculptors, less innovative, continued this heroic-realistic tradition. They molded scenes of Roman conquests on triumphal columns and captured the power but also the human qualities of Augustus Caesar and his successors on busts and full-figure statues alike.

Greek architecture, from the 8th century B.C.E. onward, emphasized monumental construction, square or rectangular in shape, with columned porticos. The Greeks devised three embellishments for the tops of columns supporting their massive buildings, each more ornate than the next: the **Doric**, the **Ionic**, and the **Corinthian**. The Greeks, in short, invented what Westerners and others in the world today still regard as "classical" architecture, although the Greeks themselves were influenced by Egyptian models in their preferences. Greece, and later Italy, provided abundant stone for ambitious temples, markets, and other public buildings. Many of these same structures were filled with products of the sculptors' workshops. They were brightly painted, although over the centuries the paint faded, so that later imitators came to think of the classical style as involving unadorned (some might say drab) stone. Roman architects adopted the Greek themes quite readily. Their engineering skill allowed them to construct buildings of even greater size, as well as new forms such as the freestanding stadium. Under the empire, the Romans learned how to add domes to rectangular buildings, which resulted in some welcome architectural diversity. At the same time, the empire's taste for massive, heavily adorned monuments and public buildings, while a clear demonstration of Rome's sense of power and achievement, moved increasingly away from the simple lines of the early Greek temples (Figure 5.5).

Classical Mediterranean art and architecture were intimately linked with the society that produced them. There is a temptation, because of the formal role of classical styles in later societies, including our own, to attribute a stiffness to Greek and Roman art that was not present in the original. Greek and Roman structures were built to be used. Temples and marketplaces and the public baths that so delighted the Roman upper classes were part of daily urban life. Classical art was also flexible, according to need. Villas or small palaces—built for the Roman upper classes and typically constructed around an open courtyard—had a light, even simple quality rather different from that of temple architecture. Classical dramas were not merely examples of high art performed for the cultural elite. Indeed, Athens lives in the memory of many humanists today as much because of the large audiences that trooped to performances of plays by authors such as Sophocles as for the creativity of the writers and philosophers themselves. Literally thousands of people gathered in the large hillside theaters of Athens and other cities for the performance of new plays and for associated music and poetry competitions. Popular taste in Rome, to be sure, seemed less elevated. Republican Rome was not an important cultural center, and many Roman leaders indeed feared the more emotional qualities of Greek art. The Roman empire is known more for monumental athletic performances—chariot races and gladiators—than for high-quality popular theater. However, the fact remains that, even in Rome, elements of classical art—the great monuments if nothing more—were part of daily urban life and the pursuit of pleasure. Roman styles also blended with Christianity during the later empire (Figure 5.6) providing another lasting expression.

Iliad Greek epic poem attributed to Homer but possibly the work of many authors; defined gods and human nature that shaped Greek mythos.

Odyssey Greek epic poem attributed to Homer but possibly the work of many authors; defined gods and human nature that shaped Greek mythos.

Doric Along with Ionian and Corinthian, distinct style of Hellenistic architecture; the least ornate of the three styles.

Ionic Along with Doric and Corinthian, distinct style of Hellenistic architecture; more ornate than Doric but less than Corinthian.

Corinthian Along with Doric and Ionian, distinct style of Hellenistic architecture; the most ornate of the three styles.

> **Read** the **Document** on **MyHistoryLab**: Vitruvius, "On Symmetry" from The Ten Books on Architecture

FIGURE **5.5** This is an artist's recreation of the Forum in imperial times. The use of decorative styles that originated in classical Greece was a central feature of Roman architecture, but as the empire grew, buildings became steadily more massive. Larger columns and greater heights reflected the Roman taste for the monumental. Ultimately, Roman architects also developed the capacity to build domed structures—a feat of engineering.
(Hypothetical reconstruction of the Roman Forum in Imperial Times. Southern part. Watercolor. Soprintendenza alle Antichita, Rome, Italy/Scala/Art Resource, NY.)

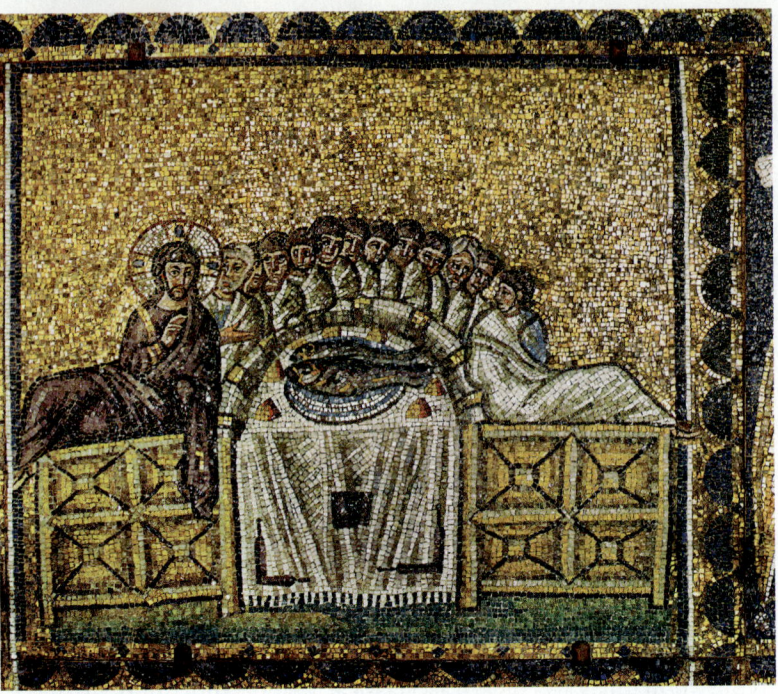

FIGURE **5.6** This mosaic from the city of Ravenna depicts the Last Supper, which took place on the night before Jesus was crucified. According to Christian belief, at this supper Jesus broke bread and drank wine with his disciples, teaching them the ritual of the Eucharist. Mosaic designs like this one were common in Roman buildings, often inlaid into floors and depicting both secular and religious scenes. The mosaic tradition continued in the Eastern empire, mainly used there to depict Christian figures, becoming ever more elegant and richly detailed.

VISUALIZING THE PAST

Political Rituals in Persia

THIS IS A RELIEF FROM THE Audience Hall of the Persian royal Palace in Persepolis, built by Darius I (522–486 B.C.E.). The scene shows court rituals in Persia. Later, when Alexander conquered Persia, he was inclined to install the same rituals, but many of his soldiers objected vigorously, and the whole issue caused great furor in the ranks. It has been speculated, however, that some of these rituals later passed to Europe, where they helped define appropriate behavior in the presence of kings.

QUESTIONS
- What kinds of rituals does this scene suggest, and what kinds of relationships between subjects and the emperor?
- Why, and on what basis, might Greeks object to this kind of behavior toward a ruler?
- Why was Alexander tempted to transfer these rituals to his own court?

ECONOMY AND SOCIETY IN THE MEDITERRANEAN

5.6 How did the social structures of the classical Mediterranean and classical China compare?

> Rome began to decline about 180 C.E., losing territory and suffering economic reversals. The legacy of the classical civilizations in the Mediterranean and Middle East was important even after this decline.

Politics and formal culture in Greece and Rome were mainly affairs of the cities—they were of intense concern only to a minority of the population. Most Greeks and Romans were farmers, tied to the soil and often to local rituals and festivals that were rather different from urban forms. Many Greek farmers, for example, annually gathered for a spring passion play to celebrate the recovery of the goddess of fertility from the lower world, an event that was seen as a vital preparation for planting and that also suggested the possibility of an afterlife—a prospect important to many people who endured a life of hard labor and poverty. A substantial population of free farmers, who owned their own land, flourished in the early days of the Greek city-states and later around Rome. However, there was a constant tendency, most pronounced in Rome, for large landlords to squeeze these farmers, forcing them to become tenants or laborers or to join the swelling crowds of the urban lower class. Tensions between tyrants and aristocrats or democrats and aristocrats in Athens often revolved around free farmers' attempts to preserve their independence and shake off the heavy debts they had incurred. The Roman republic declined in part because too many farmers became dependent on the protection of large landlords, even when they did not work their estates outright, and so no longer could vote freely.

Persia and Greece shared many social features. Persia like Greece relied heavily on agriculture. Both emphasized a military aristocracy derived originally from conquering invaders. Both also developed a strong merchant class: Persia of course encouraged land-based trade, with Athens more interested in seagoing opportunities. Both relied considerably on slavery, with many slaves captured in wars of conquest. Sparta additionally used helots, or unfree labor, as Indo-European conquerors subjected the local population and required agricultural work.

Agriculture and Trade

Farming in Greece and also in much of Italy was complicated by the fact that soil conditions were not ideal for grain growing, and yet grain was the staple of life. First in Greece, then in central Italy, farmers were increasingly tempted to shift to the production of olives and grapes, which were used primarily for cooking and wine making. These products were well suited to the soil conditions, but they required an unusually extensive conversion of agriculture to a market basis. That is, farmers who produced grapes and olives had to buy some of the food they needed, and they had to sell most of their own product in order to do this. Furthermore, planting olive trees or grape vines required substantial capital, for they did not bear fruit for at least five years after planting. This was one reason so many farmers went into debt. It was also one of the reasons that large landlords gained increasing advantage over independent farmers, for they could enter into market production on a much larger scale if only because of their greater access to capital.

The rise of commercial agriculture in Greece and then around Rome was one of the prime forces leading to efforts to establish an empire. Greek city-states, with Athens usually in the lead, developed colonies in the Middle East and then in Sicily mainly to gain access to grain production; for this, they traded not only olive oil and wine but also manufactured products and silver. Rome pushed south, in part, to acquire the Sicilian grain fields and later used much of North Africa as its granary. Indeed, the Romans encouraged such heavy cultivation in North Africa that they promoted a soil depletion, which helps account for the region's reduced agricultural fertility in later centuries.

The importance of commercial farming obviously dictated extensive concern with trade. Private merchants operated most of the ships that carried agricultural products and other goods. Greek city-states and ultimately the Roman state supervised the grain trade, promoting public works and storage facilities and carefully regulating the vital supplies. Other kinds of trade were vital also. Luxury products from the shops of urban artists or craftspeople played a major role in the lifestyle of the upper classes. There was some trade also beyond the borders of Mediterranean civilization, for goods from India and China. In this trade, the Mediterranean peoples found themselves at some disadvantage, for their manufactured products were less sophisticated than those of eastern Asia; thus, they typically exported animal skins, precious metals, and even exotic African animals for Asian zoos in return for the spices and artistic products of the east.

For all the importance of trade, merchants enjoyed a somewhat ambiguous status in classical Mediterranean civilization. Leading Athenian merchants were usually foreigners, mostly from the trading

CHAPTER 5 Classical Civilizations in the Middle East and Mediterranean peoples of the Middle East—the descendants of Lydians and Phoenicians. Merchants had a somewhat higher status in Rome, clearly forming the second most prestigious social class under the landed patricians, but here, too, the aristocracy frequently disputed the merchants' rights. Overall, merchants fared better in the Mediterranean than in China, in terms of official recognition, but worse than in India; classical Mediterranean society certainly did not set in motion a culture that distinctly valued capitalist money-making.

Slavery

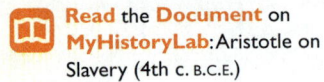
Read the Document on MyHistoryLab: Aristotle on Slavery (4th c. B.C.E.)

Slavery was another key ingredient of the classical economy. Philosophers such as Aristotle produced elaborate justifications for the necessity of slavery in a proper society. Athenians used slaves as household servants and also as workers in their vital silver mines, which provided the manpower for Athens' empire and commercial operations alike. Sparta used slaves extensively for agricultural work. Slavery spread steadily in Rome from the final centuries of the republic. Because most slaves came from conquered territories, the need for slaves was another key element in military expansion. Here was a theme visible in earlier civilizations in the eastern Mediterranean, and within later societies in this region as well, which helps explain the greater importance of military forces and expansion in these areas than in India or China. Actual slave conditions varied greatly. Roman slaves performed household tasks—including the tutoring of upper-class children, for which cultured Greek slaves were highly valued. They also worked the mines, for precious metals and for iron; as in Greece, slave labor in the mines was particularly brutal, and few slaves survived more than a few years of such an existence. Roman estate owners used large numbers of slaves for agricultural work, along with paid laborers and tenant farmers. This practice was another source of the steady pressure placed upon free farmers who could not easily compete with unpaid forced labor.

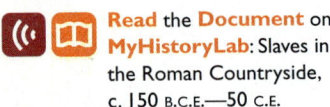
Read the Document on MyHistoryLab: Slaves in the Roman Countryside, c. 150 B.C.E.—50 C.E.

Partly because of slavery, partly because of the overall orientation of upper-class culture, neither Greece nor Rome was especially interested in technological innovations applicable to agriculture or manufacturing. The Greeks made important advances in shipbuilding and navigation, which were vital for their trading economy. Romans, less adept on the water, developed their skill in engineering to provide greater urban amenities and good roads for swift and easy movement of troops. But a technology designed to improve the production of food or manufactured goods did not figure largely in this civilization, which mainly relied on the earlier achievements of previous Mediterranean societies. Abundant slave labor probably discouraged concern for more efficient production methods. So did a sense that the true goals of humankind were artistic and political. One Hellenistic scholar, for example, refused to write a handbook on engineering because "the work of an engineer and everything that ministers to the needs of life is ignoble and vulgar." As a consequence of this outlook, Mediterranean society lagged behind both India and China in production technology, which was one reason for its resulting unfavorable balance of trade with eastern Asia.

Greek and particularly Roman economic structures had considerable environmental impact. Smoke pollution bedeviled Rome itself. Clearing of forests for fuel, construction, and expansion of agriculture led to erosion and soil depletion.

Both Greek and Roman society emphasized the importance of a tight family structure, with a husband and father firmly in control. Women had vital economic functions, particularly in farming and artisan families. In the upper classes, especially in Rome, women often commanded great influence and power within a household. But in law and culture, women were held inferior. Families burdened with too many children sometimes put female infants to death because of their low status and their potential drain on the family economy. Pericles stated common beliefs about women when he noted, "For a woman not to show more weakness than is natural to her sex is a great glory, and not to be talked about for good or for evil among men." Early Roman law stipulated, "The husband is the judge of his wife. If she commits a fault, he punishes her; if she has drunk wine, he condemns her; if she has been guilty of adultery, he kills her." (Later, however, such customs were held in check by family courts composed of members of both families.) Here was a case where Roman legal ideas modified traditional family controls. If divorced because of adultery, a Roman woman lost a third of her property and had to wear a special garment that set her apart like a prostitute. On the other hand, the oppression of women was probably less severe in this civilization than in China. Many Greek and Roman women were active in business and controlled a portion, even if only the minority, of all urban property.

DOCUMENT

Rome and a Values Crisis

ROME'S INCREASING CONTACT WITH THE EASTERN Mediterranean, particularly Greece, brought important debates about culture. Many conservatives deplored Greek learning and argued that it would corrupt Roman virtue. Cicero, a leading politician in the Senate and a major Latin writer, here defends Greek literature, using Hellenistic justifications of beauty and utility. Cicero played a major role in popularizing Greek culture during the 1st century B.C.E. His comments also reflect the concerns that Greek culture inspired a source of change.

Do you think that I could find inspiration for my daily speeches on so manifold a variety of topics, did I not cultivate my mind with study, or that my mind could endure so great a strain, did not study provide it with relaxation? I am a votary of literature, and make the confession unashamed; shame belongs rather to the bookish recluse, who knows not how to apply his reading to the good of his fellows, or to manifest its fruits to the eyes of all. But what shame should be mine, gentlemen, who have made it a rule of my life for all these years never to allow the sweets of a cloistered ease or the seductions of pleasure or the enticements of repose to prevent me from aiding any man in the hour of his need? How then can I justly be blamed or censured, if it shall be found that I have devoted to literature a portion of my leisure hours no longer than others without blame devote to the pursuit of material gain, to the celebration of festivals or games, to pleasure and the repose of mind and body, to protracted banqueting, or perhaps to the gaming-board or to ballplaying? I have the better right to indulgence herein, because my devotion to letters strengthens my oratorical powers, and these, such as they are, have never failed my friends in their hour of peril. Yet insignificant though these powers may seem to be, I fully realize from what source I draw all that is highest in them. Had I not persuaded myself from my youth up, thanks to the moral lessons derived from a wide reading, that nothing is to be greatly sought after in this life save glory and honour, and that in their quest all bodily pains and all dangers of death or exile should be lightly accounted, I should never have borne for the safety of you all the brunt of many a bitter encounter, or bared my breast to the daily onsets of abandoned persons. All literature, all philosophy, all history, abounds with incentives to noble action, incentives which would be buried in black darkness were the light of the written word not flashed upon them. How many pictures of high endeavor the great authors of Greece and Rome have drawn for our use, and bequeathed to us, not only for our contemplation, but for our emulation! These I have held ever before my vision throughout my public career, and have guided the workings of my brain and my soul by meditating upon patterns of excellence.

But let us for the moment waive these solid advantages; let us assume that entertainment is the sole end of reading; even so, I think you would hold that no mental employment is so broadening to the sympathies or so enlightening to the understanding. Other pursuits belong not to all times, all ages, all conditions; but this gives stimulus to our youth and diversion to our old age; this adds a charm to success, and offers a haven of consolation to failure. In the home it delights, in the world it hampers not. Through the night watches, on all our journeying, and in our hours of country ease, it is an unfailing companion.

If anyone thinks that the glory won by the writing of Greek verse is naturally less than that accorded to the poet who writes in Latin, he is entirely in the wrong. Greek literature is read in nearly every nation under heaven, while the vogue of Latin is confined to its own boundaries, and they are, we must grant, narrow. Seeing, therefore, that the activities of our race know no barrier save the limits of the round earth, we ought to be ambitious that whithersoever our arms have penetrated there also our fame and glory should extend; for the reason that literature exalts the nation whose high deeds it sings, and at the same time there can be no doubt that those who stake their lives to fight in honour's cause find therein a lofty incentive to peril and endeavor. We read that Alexander the Great carried in his train numbers of epic poets and historians. And yet, standing before the tomb of Achilles at Sigeum, he exclaimed, "Fortunate youth, to have found in Homer an herald of thy valor!" Well might he so exclaim, for had the *Iliad* never existed, the same mound which covered Achilles' bones would also have overwhelmed his memory.

QUESTIONS

- What kind of objections to Greek learning is Cicero arguing against?
- Which of his arguments had the most lasting appeal to those who were reshaping Roman culture?
- Can you think of similar debates about foreign culture in other times and places in history?
- How would you use this document to reconstruct the debate Cicero was participating in and why it seemed important?

Source: Cicero, *Pro Archia Poeta*. Translated by N. H. Watts. Loeb Classical Library. Cicero, *Pro Archia* (Harvard University Press, 1965), 12–14, 16, 23–24.

Because of the divisions within classical Mediterranean society, no easy generalizations about culture or achievement can be made. An 18th-century English historian called the high point of the Roman empire, before 180 C.E., the period in human history "during which the condition of the human race was most happy or prosperous." This is doubtful, given the technological accomplishments of China and India. And certainly, many slaves, women, and ordinary farmers in the

Mediterranean world might have disagreed with this viewpoint. Few farmers, for example, actively participated in the political structures or cultural opportunities that were the most obvious mark of this civilization. Many continued to work largely as their ancestors had done, with quite similar tools and in very similar poverty, untouched by the doings of the great or the bustle of the cities except when wars engulfed their lands.

We are tempted, of course, exclusively to remember the urban achievements, for they exerted the greatest influence on later ages that recalled the glories of Greece and Rome. The distinctive features of classical Mediterranean social and family structures had a less enduring impact, although ideas about slavery or women were revived in subsequent periods. However, the relatively unchanging face of ordinary life had an important influence as well, because many farmers and artisans long maintained the habits and outlook they developed during the great days of the Greek and Roman empires, and because their separation from much of the official culture posed both a challenge and opportunity for new cultural movements such as Christianity.

Pressing the Environment

Rome's economy had serious environmental consequences. In Rome itself, the burning of wood for heat but also for manufacturing created serious problems of air pollution. The accumulation of garbage was also a serious issue. Widespread use of lead, in wine production and for tableware, created extensive poisoning that, some have argued, contributed to imperial decline.

At least as serious was deforestation and inroads on natural vegetation. Trees were cut down for fuel and for construction materials, but above all to expand agriculture. Eager to promote more food production, in 111 B.C.E. the republic decreed that anyone could keep up to 20 acres of public land if it was brought into cultivation. Deforestation, particularly on hillsides, promoted erosion and loss of topsoil. Widespread grazing by herds of sheep and goats also cut into grasslands, again promoting erosion. And sheer over-farming, particularly in grain growing regions like North Africa, reduced the fertility of soil and gradually reduced productivity. Here too, historians have speculated that the results may have promoted the empire's ultimate decline.

TOWARD THE FALL OF ROME

5.7 What were the main legacies of classical Mediterranean civilization, for later societies?

Classical Mediterranean society had one final impact on world history through its rather fragmentary collapse. Unlike China, classical civilization in the Mediterranean region was not simply disrupted only to revive. Unlike India, there was no central religion, derived from the civilization itself, to serve as link between the classical period and what followed. Furthermore, the fall of Rome was not uniform; in essence, Rome fell more in some parts of the Mediterranean than it did in others. The result, among other things, was that no single civilization ultimately rose to claim the mantle of Greece and Rome. At the same time, there was no across-the-board maintenance of the classical Mediterranean institutions and values in any of the civilizations that later claimed a relationship to the Greek and Roman past. Greece and Rome lived on, in more than idle memory, but their heritage was unquestionably more complex and more selective than proved to be the case for India or China.

A Complex Legacy

Classical Greece, Persia, and their Hellenistic successors lasted for about 600 years, and Rome another 600 years beyond this. Although major political and social changes took place during this span, some durable characteristics also developed.

Greece's political legacy obviously lay more in the realm of ideas than in enduring political institutions such as China's emperor and bureaucracy, although Rome copied some Greek structures. On the whole, Greek art and philosophy formed the most lasting heritage of this classical civilization.

But, partly because they did not generate a major religion, Greek and Roman contributions to a durable popular culture were more limited than was true in China or India.

There are two final complexities in dealing with the classical civilizations of the eastern Mediterranean and the Middle East. The first involves the relationship of Greek and Roman achievements to contemporary North Americans. Classical Greece is often presented as the first phase of North Americans' own classical past. The framers of the Constitution of the United States were very conscious of Greek and Roman precedents. Designers of public buildings in the United States have copied classical Mediterranean models. The Western educational tradition has long invited elaborate explorations of the Greco-Roman past as part of the standard intellectual equipment for the educated person.

Yet this important legacy should not obscure the actual Greek and Roman record as a classical civilization. Classical ideas did not flow smoothly into a Western tradition (indeed, they had far more initial impact on the Middle East, which was where Greeks and even Romans tended to look when they thought of spreading their key achievements). Important revivals and modifications had to occur before the Greek approach to science had a fruitful impact on western Europe many centuries later. And democracy did not spread directly from Greece or Rome to other societies, although the Greek example was cited by later advocates whose passions had very different sources.

The second complexity involves Persia, an important civilization in its own right. Hellenistic conquests brought Greek cultural influence into Persia. Influences were mutual, however. Hellenistic kings imitated Persian centralization and bureaucracy. Cultural exchange also gave Zoroastrian influences a wider range. This furthered the influence these religious ideas would have on Mediterranean religions, including Judaism, and later, Christianity and Islam. The Jewish book of Daniel, for example, picked up the Zoroastrian idea that humans would be rewarded for good or bad behavior in a future life.

At the same time, there was no tidy homogenization. Persians continued to see themselves as partially distinct, and viewed Alexander's successors as foreigners. Later, more purely Persian kingdoms arose as the Hellenistic states declined. Parthians and then Sasanids revived Persian political institutions and culture in their realms to the east of the Roman empire's Middle Eastern holdings. Under Hellenism and Persia alike, the Middle East enhanced its role as a point of exchange among many different merchants and cultures.

Global Connections and Critical Themes

PERSIA, GREECE, ROME, AND THE WORLD

The Persian empire fostered trade with both Asia and with the eastern Mediterranean. Persian roads and institutions facilitated commerce from Asia to the Mediterranean. Cultural influences spread widely as well. Greeks developed wide contacts, also, but more gradually and with some definite prejudices.

Like other classical civilizations, notably China, Greeks had a definite sense of the inferiority of other peoples. Classical Greeks indiscriminately called non-Greeks "barbarians," and some Greek city-states, like Sparta, were quite closed to outside influences. But overall, the Greeks were also a trading and expansionist people. They set up Greek colonies in various parts of the Mediterranean. They traded even more widely and relied heavily on foreigners for part of this trade. Greek scholars went to Egypt to further their training in science and mathematics. Some Greeks were immensely curious about other peoples and their habits. The historian and traveler Herodotus (484–425 B.C.E.) talked enthusiastically about customs very different from his own, although he was also capable of believing wild exaggerations about how some people lived.

Greek outreach was extended by Alexander the Great, who did not have such a keen belief in Greek superiority. Alexander forged important new contacts between the eastern Mediterranean, the rest of the Middle East including Persia, and western India. He even hoped to extend his system into China, but obviously this did not occur. The system did not last, but the interest in setting up stronger links between the eastern Mediterranean and Asia remained an important concern.

Rome's world connections were in some ways more varied. The empire obviously influenced Europeans beyond the actual Roman borders, acquainting various Germanic and Celtic peoples with some Roman styles. Trade with Africa, also beyond the borders, particularly involved the northeast. Roman expeditions to India constituted an important commercial outreach. Most Roman attention, in trade as well as politics, focused on creating ties within the vast territories of the empire, but significant influence extended to other parts of the world. Some of these connections would affect trading patterns and missionary religious outreach even as the empire began to decline.

Further Readings

Important works include Xinru Liu and Lynda Norene Shaffer, *Connections Across Eurasia: Transportation, Communications and Cultural Exchange Across the Silk Roads* (2007); Lindsey Bell, *The Persian Empire* (2005); Richard A. Gabriel, *The Ancient World* (2007); Emma Bridges et al., *Cultural Responses to the Persian Wars* (2007); Peter M. Edwell, *Between Rome and Persia: The Middle Euphrates, Mesopotamia, and Palmyra Under Roman Control* (2008); George Cawkwell, *The Greek Wars: The Failure of Persia* (2005); Gene R. Garthwaite, *The Persians* (2004); Beate Dignas and Engelbert Winter, *Rome and Persia in Late Antiquity: Neighbours and Rivals* (2007); Peter Green, *The Greco-Persian Wars* (1996); John Curtis and Nigel Tallis, eds., *Forgotten Empire: The World of Ancient Persia* (2005); Nancy Demand, *A History of Ancient Greece* (1996), with a good bibliography; Waldemar Heckel, *Crossroads of History: The Age of Alexander* (2003); N. G. L. Hammond, *The Genius of Alexander the Great* (1997); Roger Brock, ed., *Alternatives to Athens: Varieties of Political Organization and Community in Ancient Greece* (2000); M. I. Finley, *Ancient Slavery and Modern Ideology* (expanded ed., 1998). See also Thomas Benediktson, *Literature and the Visual Arts in Ancient Greece and Rome* (2001); George Cawkwell, *The Greek Wars: The Failure of Persia* (New York, 2005); Gary Forsythe, *A Critical History of Early Rome: From Prehistory to the First Punic War* (2005); Alain M. Gowing, *Empire and Memory: The Representation of the Roman Republic in Imperial Culture* (2005); Callie Williamson, *The Laws of the Roman People: Public Laws in the Expansion and Decline of the Roman Republic* (2005); Richard Holland, *Augustus: Godfather of Europe* (2004); Harriet I. Flower, *The Cambridge Companion to the Roman Republic* (2004); G. E. R. Lloyd, *Ancient Worlds, Modern Reflections: Philosophical Perspectives on Greek and Chinese Science and Culture* (2004); Marilynn B. Skinner, *Sexuality in Greek and Roman Culture* (2005); I. M. Plant, *Women Writers of Ancient Greece and Rome: An Anthology* (2004); Fiona McHardy and Eireann Marshall, eds., *Women's Influence on Classical Civilization* (2004); and James I. Porter, *Classical Pasts: The Classical Traditions of Greece and Rome* (2006).

There are a number of excellent sources on classical Greece and Rome, even aside from translations of the leading thinkers and writers. Florence Dupont's *Daily Life in Ancient Rome* (1999) examines Roman ideas of space and time and honor. See M. Crawford, ed., *Sources for Ancient History* (1983); Polly Low, *Interstate Relations in Classical Greece: Morality and Power* (2007); C. Fornara, *Translated Documents of Greece and Rome* (1977); N. Lewis, *Greek Historical Documents: The Fifth Century* B.C. (1971); M. Crawford, *The Roman Republic* (1982); P. Green, *Alexander to Actium: The Historical Evolution of the Hellenistic Ages* (1990); and M. M. Austin, *The Hellenistic World from Alexander to the Roman Conquest* (1981). Important specialized works include R. Zewlnich-Abramovitz, *Not Wholly Free: The Concept of Manumission and the Status of Manumitted Slaves in the Ancient Greek World* (2005); Sarah Pomeroy, *Goddesses, Whores, Wives, and Slaves: Women in Classical Antiquity* (1975); and Renate Bridenthal and others, eds., *Becoming Visible: Women in European History* (1998). A recent book by Donald Kagan, *The Peloponnesian War* (2003), captures Greece's crisis moment. On Rome, see K. Christ, *The Romans: An Introduction to Their History and Civilization* (1984), which is eminently readable and provocative; Clifford Ando and Jorg Rupke, *Religion and Law in Classical and Christian Rome* (2006); J. Boardman et al., *Oxford History of the Classical World* (1986); and R. Saller, *The Roman Empire* (1987).

On MyHistoryLab

 Study and Review on MyHistoryLab

Critical Thinking Questions

1. How did the Persian empire illustrate major developments of the classical period?
2. What was the relationship between art and politics in the classical Mediterranean?
3. Compare the Roman empire with the Chinese empire under the Han dynasty.
4. What were the main contributions of the classical Mediterranean to Middle Eastern and to African history?
5. Can Greece, Hellenistic society, and Rome be treated as phases of a more durable Mediterranean civilization, or are separate treatments essential?
6. Compare the classical period in Mesoamerica with the classical period in the Mediterranean.

The Classical Period: Directions, Diversities, and Declines by 500 C.E.

6

Listen to Chapter 6 on MyHistoryLab

At the highpoint of the classical period, with the Han and Roman empires in full swing, the Indian Ocean provided a network of important contacts. The major civilizations did not depend on long-distance trade: Rome, China, and India were economically and culturally self-sufficient. But Roman fleets and Chinese ships regularly sailed the ocean, along with more local Persian, Arab, and Indonesian merchants. The Roman government actually arranged for archers on their convoys to beat back local pirates. Rome wanted spices and textiles from the region. The Chinese wanted exotic goods as well—one Han emperor sent a mission to India to acquire a rhinoceros.

Some types of cultural exchange also occurred in the Indian Ocean region, although historians are not sure how much. For example, Buddhism had established a number of institutions, rituals,

LEARNING OBJECTIVES

6.1 What were the main similarities and differences between Africa and the Americas by the early centuries C.E.? p. 118

6.2 What were the main differences in the process of decline in classical China and in classical India? p. 125

6.3 What were the causes of decline in the Roman empire? p. 129

6.4 How did the organization of Christianity reflect its complex relationships with the Roman empire? p. 133

Watch the Video: Symbiosis: The Exchange of Languages, Goods, and Ideas in Central Asia (Al Andrea)

FIGURE **6.1** This twelfth-century Sicilian mosaic, Christ as Pantocrator (ruler of all), depicts him as many Christian artists have, his head surrounded by a halo, representing his holiness.

117

| 6.1 | 6.2 | 6.3 | 6.4 |

Watch the Video Series on MyHistoryLab

Learn about some key topics related to this chapter with the *MyHistoryLab Video Series: Key Topics in World History*

and symbols prior to the rise of Christianity. These included the halo (technically, the nimbus) used in artistic representations of saints, the very idea of saints, monasteries, holy water, the five-chained censer to burn incense, and the hand blessing (Figure 6.1). Christianity would later develop versions of these same practices. Had these elements of Buddhism become familiar to early Christians as a result of trade (and some Buddhist missions to Persia)? We simply do not know, but the coincidences are striking. There was also movement in the other direction. Early Christians from the Middle East established at least one church for their community in India, and later Christian missionaries—including, according to legend, the apostle Thomas—went to India as well. Again, we do not know, although there is a tomb designated for Saint Thomas in southern India.

Trade and some cultural exchange raise a final question: What would happen when the decline of Rome and Han China opened the region to other initiatives? Trading opportunities still existed, but they now invited other participants. India was the first beneficiary. The Gupta empire persisted for a century or more after Rome foundered. Indian merchants fanned out from the Persian Gulf to southeast Asia, as the Guptas encouraged business. Indian elites valued gold highly, which motivated much of their trade with southeast Asia. In return, they could offer fine cotton cloth. Indian prosperity reached new levels, and many new temples were built as one result. Indian influence helped expand Hinduism and, to a greater degree, Buddhism into southeast Asia.

The Gupta dynasty finally fell. Indian trading activity continued for a time, but there were new opportunities for Persians and Greeks (from the Eastern Roman empire) to rekindle competition for trade in the Indian Ocean. China would begin to reassert itself as well. When the dust settled from the long crisis of the classical world, the Indian Ocean was open to new claimants for trade supremacy. It would be the Arabs, previously confined to lesser commercial roles, including piracy, who would first meet this postclassical challenge. ■

This chapter focuses primarily on the centers of classical civilization in Eurasia and north Africa, while sketching developments in other key regions. The end of the classical era is defined by changes in Asia, north Africa, and the Mediterranean, not the whole world. Nevertheless, the fading of the great classical empires had consequences beyond their borders. The resulting change in civilization boundaries unleashed new forces that affected sub-Saharan Africa, northern Europe, and other parts of Asia.

Three issues predominate. First, why did these civilizations decline? Invasions were an important cause. Nomadic forces accustomed to fighting on horseback had an advantage over the armies of the classical civilizations. But in their prime, the empires would have been able to turn the invaders back—so what else was going on? Second, why did different regions see different patterns of decline, with different results? And third, what was the significance of these developments—not just for the end of one period, but for the beginning of another? The rapid spread of world religions, as the empires faded, provides a vital part of the answer.

BEYOND THE CLASSICAL CIVILIZATIONS

Significant civilizations developed in the Americas and Africa outside the immediate classical orbit.

6.1 What were the main similarities and differences between Africa and the Americas by the early centuries C.E.?

Although the development of the three great civilizations is the central thread in world history during the classical period, significant changes also occurred in other parts of the world. On the borders of the major civilizations, as in northeastern Africa, Japan, and northern Europe, these changes bore some relationship to the classical world, although they were partly autonomous. Elsewhere, most notably in the Americas,

118 PART II The Classical Period, 600 B.C.E.–600 C.E.: Uniting Large Regions

new cultures continued to evolve in an entirely independent way. In all cases, changes during the classical period set the stage for more important links in world history later on. Southeast Asia gained access to civilization during the classical period mainly through its contacts with India. Regional kingdoms had already been established, and agricultural economies were familiar on the principal islands of Indonesia as well as on the mainland. Participation in wider trade patterns developed through the efforts of Indian merchants. Hindu and particularly Buddhist religion and art also spread from India. Here was a case of the outright expansion of civilization without the creation of a fully distinctive or unified culture.

Developments in Africa's Kush and Its Heritage

A similar case of expansion from an established civilization affected parts of sub-Saharan Africa; indeed, in this case the interaction had begun well before the rise of Greece and Rome. By the year 1000 B.C.E., the independent kingdom of Kush was flourishing along the upper Nile. It possessed a form of writing derived from Egyptian hieroglyphics (and which has not yet been fully deciphered) and mastered the use of iron. Briefly, around 750 B.C.E., armies from Kush conquered Egypt (Figure 6.2). Major cities were built. The Kushites seem to have established a strong monarchy, with elaborate ceremonies illustrating a belief that the king was divine. The kingdom of Kush was defeated by a rival kingdom called **Axum** by about 300 B.C.E.; Axum ultimately fell to another regional kingdom, **Ethiopia**. Axum and Ethiopia had active contacts with the eastern Mediterranean world until after the fall of Rome. They traded with this region for several centuries. The activities of Jewish merchants brought some conversions to Judaism, and a small minority of Ethiopians has remained Jewish to the present day. Greek-speaking merchants also had considerable influence, and it was through them that Christianity was brought to Ethiopia by the 4th century C.E. The Ethiopian Christian church, however, was cut off from mainstream Christianity thereafter, flourishing in isolation to modern times. And Ethiopia had the world's oldest continuous monarchy, which lasted until it was abolished in the late 20th century.

It is not clear how much influence, if any, the kingdoms of the upper Nile had on the later history of sub-Saharan Africa. Knowledge of ironworking certainly spread, facilitating the expansion of agriculture in other parts of the continent. Patterns of strong, ceremonial kingship—sometimes called divine kingship—would surface in other parts of Africa later, but whether this occurred through some contact with the Kushite tradition or independently is not known. Knowledge of Kushite writing did not spread, which suggests that the impact of this first case of civilization below the Sahara was somewhat limited.

For most of Africa below the Sahara but north of the great tropical jungles, the major development up to 500 C.E. was the further extension of agriculture. Well-organized villages arose, often very similar in form and structure to those that still exist. Farming took earliest root on the southern fringes of the **Sahara**, which was less arid than it is today. Toward the end of the classical era, important regional kingdoms were forming in western Africa, leading to the first great state in the region: Ghana. Because of the barriers of dense vegetation and the impact of African diseases on domesticated animals, agriculture spread only slowly southward. However, the creation of a strong agricultural economy prepared the way for the next, more long-lasting and influential wave of African kingdoms,

Axum Kingdom located in Ethiopian highlands; replaced Meroë in first century C.E.; received strong influence from Arabian peninsula; eventually converted to Christianity.

Ethiopia A Christian kingdom that developed in the highlands of eastern Africa under the dynasty of King Lalibela; retained Christianity in the face of Muslim expansion elsewhere in Africa.

Sahara Desert running across northern Africa; separates the Mediterranean coast from southern Africa.

FIGURE **6.2** This Egyptian wall painting portrays dark-skinned people from the rising kingdom of Kush, who interacted increasingly with Egyptian society and, for several centuries ruled Egypt directly.

1000 B.C.E.	1 C.E.	250 C.E.	500 C.E.
c. 1000 Polynesians reach Fiji, Samoa 1000 Independent kingdom of Kush 800–400 Spread of Olmec civilization: cultivation of maize (corn), potatoes; domestication of turkeys, dogs c. 300 Rise of Axum	c. 30 Crucifixion of Jesus c. 100 Root crops introduced to southern Africa through trade 100 Beginning of decline of Han dynasty 180 Rome begins to decline; population decline c. 200 Extensive agriculture practiced in Japan 227 Beginning of Sassanid empire in Persia	284–305 Reign of Diocletian c. 300 Ethiopia adopts Christianity c. 312–337 Reign of Constantine; establishment of eastern Roman empire; toleration of Christianity 330–379 Basil organizes Eastern monasticism 354–430 Life of Augustine 370–480 Nomadic invasions of western Europe c. 400 Growth of Mayan civilization c. 400 Polynesians reach Hawaii 450 Huns begin to invade India 476 Collapse of Rome	c. 500 Buddhism takes root in east and southeast Asia c. 500 Formation of Ghana c. 600 Beginning of Islam 606–647 Loose empire under Harsha in India 618 Tang dynasty in China: glorious cultural period 700 Shintoism unified into single national religion in Japan 527–565 Reign of Justinian, Eastern emperor c. 540 Collapse of Gupta dynasty 589–618 Sui dynasty

THINKING HISTORICALLY

Nomads and Cross-Civilization Contacts and Exchanges

THROUGH MUCH OF RECORDED HUMAN HISTORY, nomadic peoples have been key agents of contact between sedentary, farming peoples and town dwellers in centers of civilization across the globe. Nomadic peoples pioneered all the great overland routes that linked the civilized cores of Eurasia in ancient times and the Middle Ages. The most famous was the fabled Silk Road that ran from western China across the mountains and steppes of central Asia to the civilized centers of Mesopotamia in the last millennium B.C.E., and to Rome, the Islamic heartlands, and western Europe in the first millennium and a half C.E.

Chinese rulers at one end of these trading networks, and Roman emperors and later Islamic sultans at the other end, often had to send their armies to do battle with hostile nomads whose raids threatened to cut off the flow of trade. But perhaps more often, pastoral peoples played critical roles in establishing and expanding trading links. For periodic payments by merchants and imperial bureaucrats, they provided protection from bandits and raiding parties for caravans passing through their grazing lands. For further payments, nomadic peoples supplied animals to transport both the merchants' goods and the food and drink needed by those in the caravan parties. At times, pastoralists themselves took charge of transport and trading, but it was more common for the trading operations to be controlled by specialized merchants. These merchants were based either in the urban centers of the civilized cores or in the trading towns that grew up along the Silk Road in central Asia, the oases of Arabia, and the savanna zones that bordered on the north and south the vast Sahara desert in Africa.

Until they were supplanted by the railroads and steamships of the Industrial Revolution, the overland trading routes of Eurasia and the Americas, along with comparable networks established for sailing vessels, were the most important channels for contacts between civilizations. Religions such as Buddhism and Islam spread peacefully along the trading routes throughout central Asia, Persia, and Africa. Artistic motifs and styles, such as those developed in the cosmopolitan Hellenistic world created by Alexander the Great's conquests, were spread by trading contacts in northern Africa, northern India, and western China.

Inventions that were vital to the continued growth and expansion of the civilized cores were carried in war and peace by traders or nomadic peoples from one center to another. For example, central Asian steppe nomads who had converted to Islam clashed with the armies of China in the 8th century C.E. The victorious Muslims found craftspeople among their prisoners who knew the secrets of making paper, which had been invented many centuries earlier by the Chinese. The combination of nomadic mobility and established trading links resulted in the rapid diffusion of papermaking techniques to Mesopotamia and Egypt in the 8th and 9th centuries and across northern Africa to Europe in the centuries that followed.

Nomadic warriors also contributed to the spread of new military technologies and modes of warfare, particularly across the great Eurasian land mass. Sedentary peoples often adopted the nomads' reliance on heavy cavalry and hit-and-run tactics. Saddles, bits, and bow and arrow designs developed by nomadic herders were avidly imitated by farming societies. And defense against nomadic assaults inspired some of the great engineering feats of the preindustrial world, most notably the Great Wall of China (discussed in Chapter 2). It also spurred the development of gunpowder and cannons in China, where the threat of nomadic incursions persisted well into the 19th century.

> **Pastoral peoples played critical roles in establishing and expanding trading links.**

100 C.E.	200 C.E.	400 C.E.	600 C.E.
88 Beginning of Han decline **180 ff.** Beginning of Rome's decline; population decline **184** Daoist Yellow Turban rebellion	**220** Last Han emperor deposed; Time of Troubles begins; nomadic invasions in North China **231** First Germanic invasions of Roman empire **284–305** Reign of Diocletian emperor	**400–500** Decline of Buddhism in India; evolution of popular Hinduism **401 ff.** Increased Germanic invasions **410** Rome sacked by Visigoths under Alaric **450** Hun invasions begin **476** Last Roman emperor in West deposed **480–547** Life of Benedict, founder of Western monasticism	**618** Tang dynasty **606–647** Loose empire under Harsha in India **610** Beginning of Islam **657 ff.** Rajput (regional princes) dominant in India; periodic clashes with Islamic armies in northwest

In addition, nomadic peoples have served as agents for the transfer of food crops between distant civilized cores, even if they did not usually themselves cultivate the plants being exchanged. In a less constructive vein, nomadic warriors have played a key role in transmitting diseases. In the best-documented instance of this pattern, Mongol cavalry carried the bacterium that causes the strain of the plague that came to be known as the Black Death from central Asia to China in the 14th century. They may also have transmitted it to the West, where it devastated the port cities of the Black Sea region and was later carried by merchant ships to the Middle East and southern Europe.

QUESTIONS

- What other groups played roles as intermediaries between civilizations in early global history?
- What features of the nomads' culture and society rendered them ideal agents for transmitting technology, trade goods, crops, and diseases between different cultural zones?
- Why have the avenues of exchange they provided been open only for limited time spans and then blocked for years or decades at a time?
- What agents of transmission have taken the place of nomadic peoples in recent centuries?

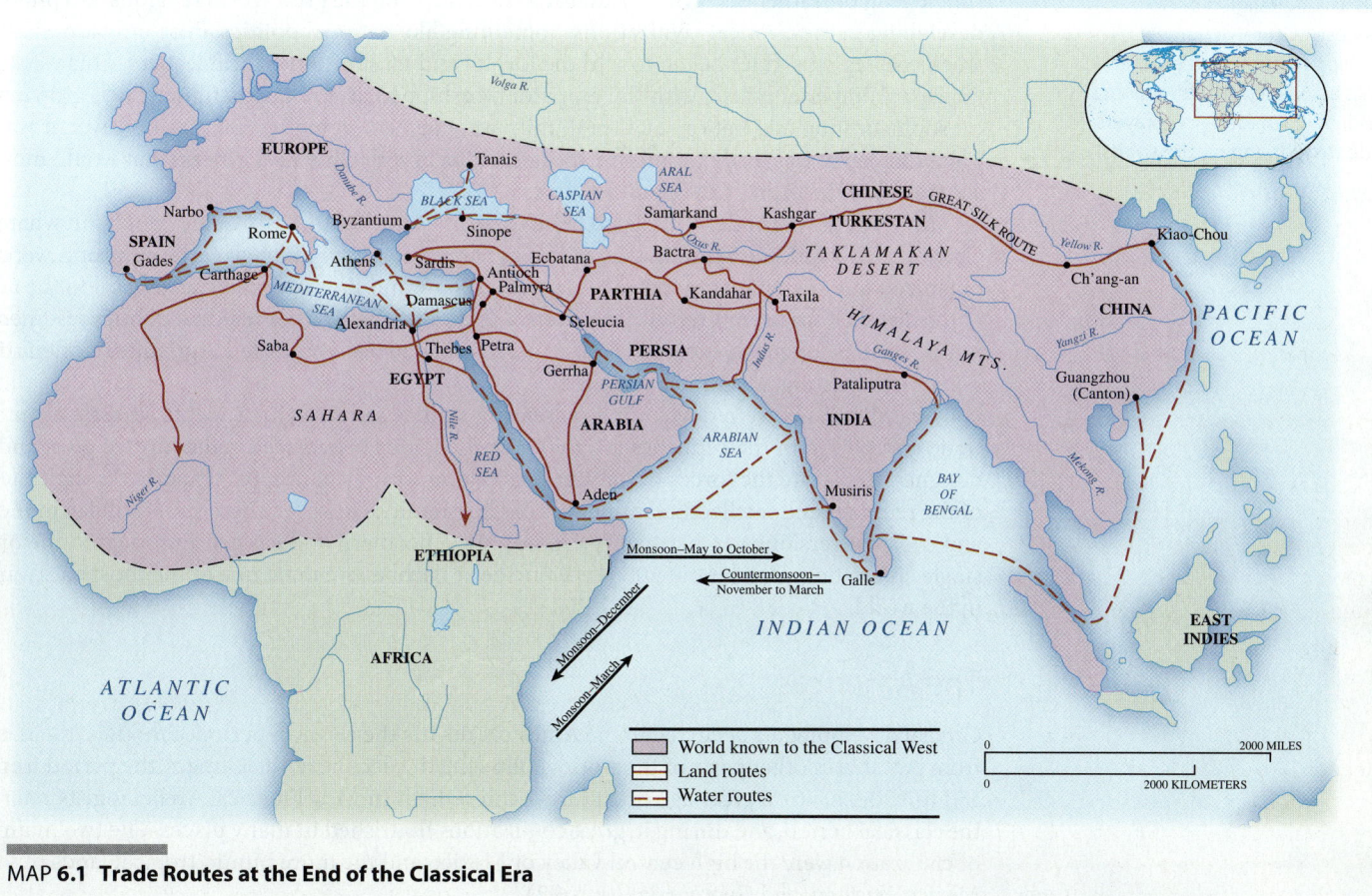

MAP 6.1 Trade Routes at the End of the Classical Era

far to the west of the Nile. New crops, including root crops and plantains introduced through trade with southeast Asia about 100 C.E., helped African farmers push into new areas.

Japan and Northern Europe

Advances in agriculture and manufacturing also occurred in other parts of the world besides sub-Saharan Africa. In northern Europe and Japan, there was no question, as yet, of elaborate contacts with the great civilizations, no counterpart to the influences that affected parts of southeast Asia and the upper Nile valley. Japan, by the year 200 C.E., had established extensive agriculture. The population of the islands had been formed mainly by migrations from the peninsula of Korea, over a 200,000-year span. These migrations had ceased by the year 200. In Japan, a regional political organization based on tribal chiefs evolved; each tribal group had its own god, thought of as an ancestor. A Chinese visitor in 297 described the Japanese as law-abiding, fond of drink, expert at agriculture and fishing; they observed strict social differences, indicated by tattoos or other body markings. Japan had also developed considerable ironworking; the Japanese seem to have skipped the stage of using bronze and copper tools, moving directly from stone tools to iron. Finally, regional states in Japan became increasingly sophisticated, each controlling somewhat larger territories. In 400 C.E., one such state brought in scribes from Korea to keep records—this represented the introduction of writing in the islands.

FIGURE **6.3** The simplicity and woodland setting of this shrine at Izumo, Japan, are characteristic of Shinto architecture, which was designed to reflect reverence for and harmony with nature.

Shintoism Religion of early Japanese culture; devotees worshipped numerous gods and spirits associated with the natural world; offers of food and prayers made to gods and nature spirits.

Japan's religion, **Shintoism**, provided for the worship of political rulers and the spirits of nature, including the all-important god of rice. Many local shrines and rituals revolved around Shinto beliefs, which became unified into a single national religion by 700 C.E. (Figure 6.3). However, this was a simple religion, rather different in ritual and doctrine from the great world religions and philosophies developing in the classical civilizations. Something like national politics arose only around 400 C.E., when one regional ruler began to win the loyalty and trust of other local leaders. This was the basis for Japan's imperial house, with the emperor worshipped as a religious figure. Such growing political sophistication and national cultural unity were just emerging by 600 C.E., however. It was at this point that Japan was ready for more elaborate contacts with China—a process that would move Japan squarely into the orbit of major civilizations.

Much of northern Europe lagged behind Japan's pace. Teutonic or Celtic peoples in what today is Germany, England, and Scandinavia, as well as Slavic peoples in much of eastern Europe, were loosely organized into regional kingdoms. Some, in Germany and England, had succumbed to the advances of the distant Roman empire, but after Rome's decline the patterns of regional politics resumed. There was no written language, except in cases where Latin had been imported. Agriculture, often still combined with hunting, was rather primitive.

Scandinavians were developing increasing skill as sailors, which would lead them into wider trade and pillage in the centuries after 600 C.E. Religious beliefs featured a host of gods and rituals designed to placate the forces of nature. This region would change, particularly through the spread of the religious and intellectual influences of Christianity. However, these shifts still lay in the future, and even conversions to Christianity did not bring northern and eastern Europe into the orbit of a single civilization. Until about 1000 C.E., northern Europe remained one of the most backward areas in the world.

The Americas

Crucial developments occurred in the Americas during the classical period, although still in isolation from patterns in other parts of the world. Following the decline of the Olmecs, the period from about 150 to 900 C.E. was a great age of cultural achievement in Mesoamerica. Archeologists refer to it as the classical period, and during it, great civilizations flourished in many places. The two main centers of civilization were the high central valley of Mexico and the more humid tropical lands of southern Mexico, Yucatan, and Guatemala (Map 6.2).

MAP 6.2 Civilizations of Central and South America Three cultural "hearths" are represented: Mesoamerica, extending from north-central Mexico to Nicaragua; the Andean region in South America, and the Intermediate zone of modern-day Colombia and Panama, which shared many characteristics with the other zones but did not build in stone.

The Valley of Mexico: Teotihuacan In central Mexico, the city of **Teotihuacan**, near modern Mexico City, emerged as an enormous urban center with important religious functions. It was supported by intensive agriculture in the surrounding region and probably by crops planted around the great lakes that dominated the central valley of Mexico. Teotihuacan's enormous temple pyramids rival those of ancient Egypt and suggest a large state apparatus with the power to mobilize many workers. Population estimates for this city, which covered 9 square miles, are as high as 200,000. This would make it greater than the cities of ancient Egypt or Mesopotamia and probably second only to ancient Rome of the cities of classical antiquity.

Certain trades and ethnic groups had their own residential districts, and there is much evidence of wide social distinctions between the priests, nobles, and common people. The many gods of Mesoamerica, still worshiped when the Europeans arrived in the 16th century, were already honored at Teotihuacan. The god of rain, the feathered serpent, the goddess of corn, and the goddess of waters all appear in the murals and decorations of the palaces and temples. In fact, almost all Teotihuacan art seems to have been religious.

The influence of Teotihuacan extended widely, and tribute probably was exacted from many regions. But by the 8th century C.E. the city was in decline, and it was finally abandoned after attacks

Teotihuacan [tay-oh-tee-wah-KAHN] Site of classic culture in central Mexico; urban center with important religious functions; supported by intensive agriculture in surrounding regions; population of as much as 200,000.

 View the **Closer Look** on MyHistoryLab: The Pyramid of the Sun in Teotihuacan

CHAPTER 6 The Classical Period: Directions, Diversities, and Declines by 500 C.E. **123**

Maya Classic culture emerging in southern Mexico and Central America contemporary with Teotihuacan; extended over broad region; featured monumental architecture, written language, calendrical and mathematical systems, highly developed religion.

probably from nomadic raiders from the north. But for centuries thereafter, the memory of Teotihuacan lived on among the peoples of Mesoamerica as a golden age of cultural achievements.

The Classic Maya Between about 300 and 900 C.E., at roughly the same time that Teotihuacan dominated the central plateau, the **Maya** peoples were developing Mesoamerican civilization to its highest point in southern Mexico and Central America. The American classic period, launched as the Old World classical civilizations were coming to an end, lasted well into the next period in history.

The Maya culture extended over a broad region that now includes parts of five different countries: Mexico, Guatemala, Belize, Honduras, and El Salvador. It included several related languages, and it had considerable regional variation, as can be seen in its art styles. The whole region shared a common culture that included monumental architecture, a written language, a calendar and mathematical system, a highly developed religion, and concepts of statecraft and social organization. Using only stone tools in an area of dense forests, plagued by insects and poor soils, as many as 50 city-states flourished. Evidence of irrigation, swamp drainage, and a system of artificially constructed ridged fields at river mouths (where intensive agriculture was practiced) seems to explain the Mayan ability to support large urban centers and a total population of perhaps 5 million. The Maya cities vary in size and layout, but almost all include large pyramids surmounted by temples, complexes of masonry buildings that served administrative or religious purposes, elite residences, a ritual ball court, and often a series of altars and memorial pillars.

The calendar system and sophisticated astronomical observations were made possible by a vigesimal system of mathematics (that is, based on 20). The Maya knew the concept of zero and used it in conjunction with the concept of place value or position. With elegant simplicity and with signs for only 1, 5 and 0, they could make complex calculations. As among all the Mesoamerican peoples, the Maya calendar was based on a concept of recurring cycles of different lengths. The Maya had a sacred cycle of 260 days divided into months of 20 days each, within which there was a cycle of 13 numbers.

A second great Maya accomplishment was the creation of a writing system. The Maya wrote on stone monuments, murals, and ceramics and in books of folded paper and deerskin, only four of which survive. Scribes were honored and held an important place in society. Although we still cannot fully decipher many inscriptions, recent advances now permit the reading of many texts. The Maya written language, like Chinese and Sumerian, was a logographic system, which combined phonetic and semantic elements. With this system and about 287 symbols, the Maya recorded complex ideas. The few surviving books are religious and astronomical texts, and many inscriptions on ceramics deal with the cult of the dead and the complex Maya cosmology, but hundreds of the inscriptions refer to the reign of kings, their victories, their accomplishments, and their lineages.

The Maya had a complex religious system with many deities, but there was a basic Mesoamerican concept of dualism—male and female, good and bad, day and night. This idea, similar to that found in some Asian religions, emphasized the unity of all things. Each god had a parallel female consort or feminine form and often an underworld equivalent as well. In addition, there were patron deities of various occupations and classes. The number of gods and goddesses in the inscriptions seems overwhelming, but they should be understood as manifestations of a more limited set of supernatural forces, much like the various incarnations of the Hindu gods.

Read the **Document** on **MyHistoryLab**: From the Popol Vuh: The Great Mythological Book of the Ancient Maya [ca. 1550]

From the historical inscriptions we know that the major Maya centers were the cores of city-states, which controlled outlying territories. There was constant warfare, and rulers such as Pacal of Palenque expanded their territories by conquest. The rulers exercised civil and probably religious power, and an elite aided their rule and performed administrative functions. A class of scribes, or perhaps priests, tended to the cult of the state and specialized in the complex calendar observations and calculations. The ruler and the scribes organized and participated in rituals of self-mutilation and human sacrifice that among the Maya, as in much of Mesoamerica, were an important aspect of religion. Also, as a form of both worship and sport, the Maya, like other Mesoamerican peoples, wagered on and played a ritual ball game on specially constructed courts in which players moved a ball with their hips or elbows. The stakes were high: Losers might forfeit their possessions or their lives. Between about 700 and 900 C.E., the Mesoamerican world was shaken by the rapid decline of the great cultural centers. The reasons for this collapse are not fully understood, but it was widespread. In the central plateau, Teotihuacan was destroyed about 650 C.E. by outside invaders, probably nomadic hunters from the north, perhaps with the help of some of the groups under the dominance of Teotihuacan. The city may have already been in decline because of increasing problems with agriculture. More mysterious was the abandonment of the Maya cities. During the 8th century C.E., Maya rulers stopped erecting

124 PART II The Classical Period, 600 B.C.E.–600 C.E.: Uniting Large Regions

commemorative stelae and large buildings, and population sizes dwindled. By 900 C.E., most of the major Maya centers has been deserted. Scholars do not agree whether this process was the result of ecological problems and climate change, agricultural exhaustion, internal revolt, or foreign pressure. The primary explanation for the collapse is agricultural exhaustion. By the 8th century, the limits of the Mayan agricultural system, given the size and density of population, may have been reached. Tikal had an estimated density of more than 300 people per square mile. Maintaining the great population centers was an increasing burden. Others believe that the peasants simply refused to bear the burdens of serving and feeding the political and religious elite and that internal rebellion led to the end of the ruling dynasties and their cities. Only after 1000 C.E. would another group, the Toltecs, revive trade and urban development in the region.

In the Andes, following the decline of Chavin culture, the Mochica state (200–700 C.E.), in the Moche (MOH-chay) valley and on the coast to the north of Chavín, mobilized workers to construct great clay brick temples, residences, and platforms. Artisans produced gold and silver jewelry and copper tools. The potter's art reached a high point; scenes on Mochica ceramics depict rulers receiving tribute and executing prisoners. Nobles, priests, farmers, soldiers, and slaves are also portrayed in remarkably lifelike ways; many vessels are clearly portraits of individual members of the elite. The Mochica also produced a great number of pottery vessels showing a variety of explicit sexual acts. These scenes are almost always in a domestic setting and indicate descriptions of everyday life rather than ritual unions.

Moche expanded its control by conquest. Mochica art contains many representations of war, prisoners, and the taking of heads as trophies. There is also archeological evidence of hilltop forts and military posts. Politically, Moche and the other regional states seem to have been military states or chiefdoms, supported by extensive irrigated agriculture and often at war. Other regional centers also emerged and one state, the Chimu (chee-MOO) expanded steadily from 800 C.E. until the rise of the **Incas**.

Polynesia A final case of isolated development featured the migration of agricultural peoples to new island territories in the Pacific. **Polynesian** peoples had reached islands such as Fiji and Samoa by 1000 B.C.E. Further explorations in giant outrigger canoes led to the first settlement of island complexes such as Hawaii by 400 C.E., where the new settlers adapted local plants, brought in new animals (notably pigs), and imported a highly stratified caste system under powerful local kings.

Overall, agriculture expanded into a number of new areas during the classical period; early civilizations, or early contacts, were also forming. These developments were not central to world history during the classical period itself, but they folded into the larger human experience thereafter.

Inca Group of clans centered at Cuzco that were able to create empire incorporating various Andean cultures; term also used for leader of empire.

Polynesia Islands contained in a rough triangle whose points lie in Hawaii, New Zealand, and Easter Island.

DECLINE IN CHINA AND INDIA

6.2 What were the main differences in the process of decline in classical China and in classical India?

Between 200 and 600 C.E., all three classical civilizations collapsed entirely or in part, first in China, then the Mediterranean, and finally in India. During this four-century span, all suffered from outside invasions, the result of growing incursions by groups from central Asia. This renewed wave of nomadic expansion was not as sweeping as the earlier Indo-European growth, which had spread over India and much of the Mediterranean region many centuries before, but it severely tested the civilized regimes. Rome, of course, fell directly to Germanic invaders, who fought on partly because they were, in turn, harassed by the fierce Asiatic Huns. The Huns swept once across Italy, invading the city of Rome amid great destruction. Another Hun group from central Asia overthrew the Guptas in India, and similar nomadic tribes had earlier toppled the Chinese Han dynasty. The central Asian nomads were certainly encouraged by a growing realization of the weakness of the classical regimes. Han China as well as the later Roman empire suffered from serious internal problems long before the invaders dealt the final blows. And the Guptas in India had not permanently resolved that area's tendency to dissolve into political fragmentation.

A combination of internal weakness and invasion led to important changes, first in China, then in India.

Decline and Fall in Han China

The deteriorations of the late Han dynasty operated on several levels. Assassinations of and by bureaucrats competing for power at the top occurred on several occasions. At a basic level, conditions among the peasantry began to deteriorate. Large landowners, always powerful under the Han, grew more

Yellow Turbans Chinese Daoists who launched a revolt in 184 C.E. in China promising a golden age to be brought about by divine magic.

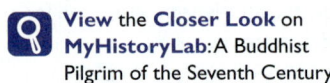

View the **Closer Look** on **MyHistoryLab**: A Buddhist Pilgrim of the Seventh Century

so, avoiding taxes and forming private armies. Taxes on peasants increased, and many farmers were forced into serfdom, where they had to provide labor and turn over much of their own produce to the landlords. Social protest increased.

Peasant unrest culminated in a great revolutionary effort led by the Daoists in 184 C.E. Leaders called the **Yellow Turbans** promised a golden age to be brought about by divine magic. Han generals suppressed this rebellion but set themselves up as regional rulers, a clear sign of the collapse of the central state. The last Han emperor was deposed in 220 C.E. China was divided into three kingdoms for several decades, but finally even these began to collapse. For several centuries, China was ruled by the land-owning class, operating beyond the control of formal government. Southern and northern China also pulled apart, with the south maintaining higher levels of economic growth and continuing to absorb tribal peoples into Chinese culture.

No firm dynasties could be established in this 350-year period, although there were short-lived regimes in the south. Northern China was pressed by invasions from central Asia. Nomadic peoples had been incorporated into Chinese armies, much as later Roman rulers tried to use Germanic troops, but as the government deteriorated the nomads broke loose and began to invade the Middle Kingdom. Several nomad-dominated states were formed, but none lasted long. Internal warfare became endemic in this unusually long breakdown in Chinese stability.

Into this chaos came the new fascination with Buddhism, which offered spiritual solace in response to political uncertainty and economic distress. Also, like Christianity in Europe, it provided cultural cohesion at a time when political links had broken down. Imported from India—the only case until modern times when China borrowed a major idea from abroad—and disseminated by silk merchants and missionaries, Buddhism spread among both the Chinese and the nomadic warriors, helping gradually to mold a common culture in which Chinese ingredients predominated. Buddhist influence also brought to China a new impetus for art and sculpture, altering the established styles and themes.

Buddhism came under periodic attack by Daoist regional rulers, but the faith reached throughout China by the 5th century C.E., and it spread rapidly for many decades (Map 6.1). Buddhist monasteries for women as well as men gained ground. Many Chinese monks made pilgrimages to India, and Buddhist literature and philosophy spread widely. Chinese Buddhists blended practices from many Indian Buddhist sects, using meditation, prayers, and devotional exercises. The Document section shows what benefits Chinese converts might expect from their new religion. The Chinese imposed some of their own values on Buddhism as well. For instance, they insisted on the importance of forming families so that the ancestral line could be preserved. Typically, as a result, only second sons became Buddhist monks, and first sons maintained the family responsibilities. Buddhists were also pressed into political loyalty, paying taxes to the government and submitting to government regulations on the formation of monasteries.

Buddhism made other adjustments in its spread in east Asia. It had a fascinating impact on women in China, among families who converted. On the face of things, Buddhism should have disrupted China's firm belief in patriarchal power, because Buddhists believed that women had souls along with men. Indeed, some individual women in China won great attention because of their spiritual accomplishments. But Chinese culture generated changes in Buddhism within the empire. Buddhist phrases like "husband supports wife" were changed to "husband controls his wife," while "the wife comforts the husband"—another Buddhist phrase from India—became "the wife reveres her husband." Finally, many men valued pious Buddhist wives, because they might benefit the family's salvation and because Buddhist activity could keep their wives busy, calm, and out of mischief. Buddhism could be meaningful to Chinese women, but it did not really challenge patriarchy. A biography of one Buddhist wife put it this way: "At times of crisis she could be tranquil and satisfied with her fate, not letting outside things agitate her mind."

The growing Buddhist influence also had an impact on Daoism, forcing greater formalization of Daoist doctrine and more efforts to reach the common people. Many Chinese found great similarities between the two faiths, although Buddhism continued to have the advantage of offering a clearer doctrine of personal salvation—the chance of holy life after death—and a firmer set of personal ethics. Daoist leaders developed a variety of practices, including meditation and dietary restrictions, which might bring immortality. Popular Daoism, mixing Daoist beliefs with an animistic pantheon of many gods, tended to hold that good or evil done in this life would be compensated by heavens or hells hereafter. Popular Daoism also provided priests and shamans who practiced faith healing to cure disease. These ramifications of Daoism appealed to the Chinese peasantry, lasting in some parts of eastern Asia even today.

Confucianism lost ground during this confused period in Chinese history, eclipsed by the more otherworldly interests. But the legacy of Chinese institutions and secular beliefs did not disappear,

DOCUMENT

The Popularization of Buddhism

CHINESE BUDDHISM, UNLIKE MOST CHINESE BELIEFS, spread among all regions and social groups. Although it divided into many sects that disagreed over details of theology and rituals by commenting on earlier Buddhist scriptures (the Sutras), many ordinary Chinese believers cared little for such details and were more concerned with direct spiritual benefits. Often they arranged to have Buddhist sermons copied, as a means of obtaining merit, while adding a note of their own. The following passages come from such notes, written mainly in the 6th century. They suggest the various reasons people might go through the challenging process of converting to a new religion.

RECORDED ON THE 15TH DAY OF THE FOURTH MONTH OF 531.

The Buddhist lay disciple Yuan Rong—having lived in this degenerate era for many years, fearful for his life, and yearning for home—now makes a donation of a thousand silver coins to the Three Jewels [the Buddha, the Law, and the Monastic Order]. This donation is made in the name of the Celestial King Vaisravana. In addition, he makes a donation of a thousand to ransom himself and his wife and children [from their earthly existence], a thousand more to ransom his servants, and a thousand more to ransom his domestic animals. This money is to be used for copying sutras. It is accompanied by the prayer that the Celestial King may attain Buddhahood; that the disciple's family, servants, and animals may be blessed with long life, may attain enlightenment, and may all be permitted to return to the capital.

DATED THE 29TH DAY OF THE FOURTH MONTH OF 550.

Happiness is not fortuitous: pray for it and it will respond. Results are not born of thin air: pay heed to causes and results will follow. This explains how the Buddhist disciple and nun Daorong—because her conduct in her previous life was not correct—came to be born in her present form, a woman, vile and unclean.

Now if she does not honor the awesome decree of Buddha, how can future consequences be favorable for her? Therefore, having cut down her expenditures on food and clothing, she reverently has had the Nirvana Sutra copied once. She prays that those who read it carefully will be exalted in mind to the highest realms and that those who communicate its meaning will cause others to be so enlightened.

She also prays that in her present existence she will have no further sickness or suffering, that her parents in seven other incarnations (who have already died or will die in the future) and her present family and close relatives may experience joy in the four realms [earth, water, fire, and air], and that whatever they seek may indeed come to pass. Finally, she prays that all those endowed with knowledge may be included within this prayer.

RECORDED ON THE 28TH DAY OF THE FIFTH MONTH OF 583.

The Army Superintendent, Song Shao, having suffered the heavy sorrow of losing both his father and mother, made a vow on their behalf to read one section each of [many] sutras. He prays that the spirits of his parents will someday reach the Pure Land [paradise] and will thus be forever freed from the three unhappy states of existence and the eight calamities and that they may eternally listen to the Buddha's teachings.

He also prays that the members of his family, both great and small, may find happiness at will, that blessings may daily rain down upon them while hardships disperse like clouds. He prays that the imperial highways may be open and free of bandits, that the state may be preserved from pestilence, that wind and rain may obey their proper seasons, and that all suffering creatures may quickly find release. May all these prayers be granted!

The preceding incantation has been translated and circulated. If this incantation is recited 7, 14, or 21 times daily (after having cleansed the mouth in the morning with a willow twig, having scattered flowers and incense before the image of Buddha, having knelt and joined the palms of the hands), the four grave sins, the five wicked acts, and all other transgressions will be wiped away. The present body will not be afflicted by untimely calamities; one will at last be born into the realm of immeasurably long life; and reincarnation in the female form will be escaped forever.

Now, the Sanskrit text has been reexamined and the Indian Vinaya monk Buddhasangha and other monks have been consulted; thus we know that the awesome power of this incantation is beyond comprehension. If it is recited 100 times in the evening and again at noon, it will destroy the four grave sins and five wicked acts. It will pluck out the very roots of sin and will ensure rebirth in the Western Regions. If, with sincerity of spirit, one is able to complete 200,000 recitations, perfect intelligence will be born and there will be no relapses. If 300,000 recitations are completed, one will see Amita Buddha face to face and will certainly be reborn into the Pure Land of tranquility and bliss.

Copied by the disciple of pure faith Sun Szu-chung on the 8th day of the fourth month of 720.

QUESTIONS

- Why did Buddhism spread widely in China by the 6th century?
- How did popular Buddhism compare with original Buddhist teachings?
- How did Chinese Buddhists define holy life?
- How do these documents suggest some of the troubles China faced after the collapse of the Han dynasty?

View the Closer Look on MyHistoryLab: A Tang Painting of the Goddess of Mercy

FIGURE 6.4 Stone relief from the tomb of the Tang emperor Taizong (7th century), showing one of his warhorses attended by a bearded "barbarian" groom. How does this relief suggest the barbarian threat was being handled after China's crisis period had ended? (Relief of Emperor T'ai Tsung's Horse, "Autumn Dew." The University Museum, University of Pennsylvania.)

and as nomadic invaders were partly converted to Chinese ways, the opportunity for political revival reemerged toward the end of the 6th century. A series of strong rulers in the north drove out nomadic bands and then merged, under a general of Chinese-Turkish background, into a new **Sui** dynasty. Under this brief dynasty, northern China was united and south China was reconquered. The government built new canals and repaired the Great Wall. Attempts to expand into Korea and central Asia brought financial collapse, along with new rebellions, and only in 618 C.E. was the more durable **Tang** dynasty established. The time of troubles had ended. New artistic works reflected renewed political integration (Figure 6.4).

The decline and fall of the Han had thus disrupted Chinese civilization and opened it to new religious influences. But old values survived as well. Even the competing landlords retained some training in Confucianism and with that training the idea of a united empire. With its greater cultural homogeneity established in the classical era, China differed markedly from the Mediterranean, where Christianity and Islam came close to displacing older philosophical concerns while challenging earlier political loyalties. Many nomadic invaders imitated Chinese styles and thus encouraged the revival of older political habits.

Sui [sway] Dynasty that succeeded the Han in China; emerged from strong rulers in northern China; united all of northern China and reconquered southern China.

Tang Dynasty that succeeded the Sui in 618 C.E.; more stable than previous dynasty.

Harsha Ruler who followed Guptas in India; briefly constructed a loose empire in northern India between 616 and 657 C.E.

Rajput [RAHJ-poot] Regional princes in western India; emphasized military control of their regions.

Devi [DAY-vee] Mother goddess within Hinduism; widely spread following collapse of Guptas; encouraged new emotionalism in religious ritual.

The End of the Guptas: Decline in India

The decline of classical civilization in India was less drastic than the collapse of Han China in that India had not depended so heavily on political structures to hold its civilization together. Yet the Gupta collapse left durable traces in later Indian history, as political unity became more difficult to achieve. The high point of Gupta rule came under Chandragupta II early in the 5th century, but his immediate successors managed to remain prosperous. India at this point probably was the most stable and peaceful area in the world. However, in 440 C.E., the nomadic Huns began a series of invasions that gradually reduced the empire's strength. The Gupta pattern of somewhat decentralized rule, whereby vassal princes were treated as partial allies rather than subject to direct central administration, made response to invasion more difficult. The Huns controlled much of northwestern India—the typical invasion route of the subcontinent—by 500 C.E. By this time, the quality of Gupta kings was also diminishing, and this added to the problem. It was a regional prince, **Harsha** Vardharna, not the Guptas themselves, who broke the hold of the Huns in the northwest about 530 C.E., and the Guptas were too weak to restore their claims. The dynasty collapsed entirely about 550 C.E.

A few echoes of Gupta splendor were heard during the 7th century. Harsha, a descendant of the Guptas through his grandmother, established a loose empire across northern India between 616 and 657. But he died without heirs, and his empire broke up again. From this point onward, until a better-organized series of outside invasions began, northern India was politically divided. Regional dynasties occasionally were powerful, but few lasted very long. A section of northern India was invaded by Tang Chinese-led Tibetan troops, who captured a young Indian prince and took him back to the Chinese capital in 648. This was the first and, until our own era, the only military clash between China and India. The northern regional princes, collectively called the **Rajput**, emphasized military prowess. Although there were many local wars, few political events had great significance.

In this localized framework, Indian culture continued to evolve. Buddhism declined steadily in India. The Guptas had preferred Hinduism, and the Hun invaders disliked the otherworldly tone of Buddhism as well. Military-minded princes had little sympathy for the Buddhist principles of calm and contemplation. Hindu beliefs gained ground, converting the Hun leaders, among other groups. Within Hinduism, worship of a mother goddess, **Devi**, spread widely, which encouraged a new popular emotionalism in religious ritual. In essence, India partially redefined its core culture by

128 PART II The Classical Period, 600 B.C.E.–600 C.E.: Uniting Large Regions

emphasizing the Hindu strain more clearly while relying heavily on cultural cohesion at a time when political life became more difficult. The reassertion of Hinduism also promoted the caste system, now spreading to southern India. The number and complexity of jati (JAH-tee), or castes, increased as invaders were assimilated into the system, but the basic principles remained.

India's economic activity also remained strong, although in periods of outright invasion there were new hardships. Here too, Indian civilization did not collapse to the extent of Han China or the western Mediterranean. Indeed, the decades after the fall of the Guptas saw new outreach in trade and even some conquest by southern Tamil kingdoms, which were trying to establish firmer strongholds along the Indian Ocean in southeast Asia.

Although Indian civilization largely maintained its position, albeit with a more diverse political lineup, another threat came after 600 C.E. from the new Middle Eastern religion of **Islam**. At first, India's contacts with this new force were limited. Arab armies, fighting under the banner of Islam, reached India's northwestern frontier during the 7th century, and although there was initially little outright conquest, Islam won some converts in the north. By the 8th century, Islamic competition also began to hit India's international economic position. Arab traders soon took control of the Indian Ocean from Tamil merchants and reduced India's commercial strength.

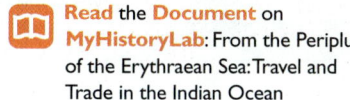

Read the **Document** on **MyHistoryLab**: From the Periplus of the Erythraean Sea: Travel and Trade in the Indian Ocean

Islam Major world religion having its origins in 610 C.E. in the Arabian peninsula; meaning literally submission; based on prophecy of Muhammad.

THE DECLINE AND FALL OF THE ROMAN EMPIRE

6.3 What were the causes of decline in the Roman empire?

Signs of decay at various levels began to emerge in the Roman empire in the late 2nd century. Population size declined, as birth rates no longer kept pace with mortality rates, and it became more difficult to recruit effective armies. Political signs included the greater brutality and arbitrariness of many later Roman emperors—victims, according to one commentator at the time, of "lustful and cruel habits." Tax collection became increasingly difficult as residents of the empire fell on hard times. The governor of Egypt complained that "the once numerous inhabitants of the aforesaid villages have now been reduced to a few, because some have fled in poverty and others have died . . . and for this reason we are in danger owing to impoverishment of having to abandon the tax-collectorship."

> Decline in Rome was complex, involving a mix of internal and external factors. The eastern and western portions of the empire developed differently after the fall of Rome.

Wide-Ranging Signs of Decline

Above all there were the human symptoms. Inscriptions on Roman tombstones increasingly ended with the motto "I was not, I was, I am not, I have no more desires," suggesting despair. As the structures of the empire deteriorated, meaning in life became harder to find, and this mood made efforts at structural revival more difficult. The signs of change in the quality of political and economic life began to emerge after about 180 C.E., at which point the empire's geographic expansion had slightly receded from its high point. Unlike Han China or Gupta India, the Roman empire had depended extensively on expansion, not only to provide prestige but to recruit the necessary slaves. With the empire's boundaries now pushed to the limits it could support, Rome had to restructure its labor policies on the great commercial estates and in the mines. This restructuring reduced economic vitality and market production.

Initially more pressing were the internal issues of politics and population. Government leadership became a problem. Growing political confusion, including disputes over how emperors should be appointed, produced a series of weak rulers and many battles over succession to the throne. Intervention of the army in the selection of emperors, as the army became an increasingly separate institution, complicated political life and contributed to the worsening of rule.

Causes of Roman Decline

The decline of the Roman state raises the question of human agency: When things go badly in a society, are weak leaders an accident, causing growing disarray, or do larger trends cause the selection of inferior rulers? Still more important in this decline was a series of plagues that swept over the empire at the end of the 2nd century C.E. These plagues decimated the population and severely disrupted economic life. Some authorities argue that Rome's urban population also suffered lead poisoning from the pipes leading from the aqueducts, which further weakened people and reduced their numbers. Lower population added to the problems of finding labor. With recruitment of troops becoming more difficult, the empire had to hire Germanic soldiers to guard its frontiers. The need to pay troops added to the demands on the state's budget, just as declining production cut into tax revenues and the absence of new conquests cut into other rewards for soldiers. Environmental deterioration in north Africa reduced grain supply and hurt the Roman tax base; overuse had reduced soil fertility and advanced desertification.

This may be the key to the process of decline: a set of general problems, including a cycle of plagues that could not be prevented, resulting in a spiral that steadily worsened, particularly as the selection of emperors deteriorated. But there is another side to Rome's downfall, although whether it was a cause or result of the initial difficulties is hard to say. Rome's upper classes became steadily more pleasure-seeking and individualistic, turning away from the concepts of civil duty that had characterized the republic and early empire. Cultural life decayed. Aside from some truly creative Christian writers, the fathers of Western theology, there was very little sparkle to the art or literature of the later empire. The Romans wrote textbooks about rhetoric instead of displaying rhetorical talent in actual political life; they wrote simple compendiums about animals or geometry that barely captured the essentials of what earlier intellectuals had known, and they often added superstitious beliefs that previous generations would have scorned. This cultural decline was not clearly caused by disease or economic collapse; it began in some ways before these larger problems hit. Something was happening to the Roman elite, perhaps because of the deadening hand of authoritarian political rule, perhaps because of a new commitment to luxuries and sensual indulgence. Military service became less attractive to the upper class, which forced the recruitment of paid soldiers from groups such as the Germanic tribes along the northern borders of the empire.

The Process of Roman Decline

As the quality of imperial rule declined and as life became more dangerous and economic survival more precarious, many farmers clustered around the protection of large landlords, surrendering full control of their plots of land, hoping for military and judicial protection. The decentralization of political and economic authority, which was greatest in the western, or European, portions of the empire, foreshadowed the manorial system of Europe in the Middle Ages. The estate system gave great political power to the landlords and could provide some local stability. But it weakened the emperor's power and tended to drive the economy away from the elaborate trade patterns of Mediterranean civilization in its heyday. Many estates attempted to produce almost everything needed on the spot. Trade and production declined further, causing tax revenues to drop and cities to shrink. The empire was locked in a vicious circle in which the responses to initial deterioration merely lessened the chances of recovery.

Diocletian Roman emperor from 284 to 305 C.E.; restored later empire by improved administration and tax collection.

Constantine Roman emperor from 312 to 337 C.E.; established second capital at Constantinople; attempted to use religious force of Christianity to unify empire spiritually.

Read the Document on MyHistoryLab: Eusebius of Caesarea, selections from Life of Constantine

Some later emperors tried to reverse the flow. **Diocletian**, who ruled from 284 to 305 C.E., tightened up the administration of the empire and tried to improve tax collection. Regulation of the dwindling economy increased. Diocletian also tried to monopolize political loyalty, increasing the pressure to worship the emperor as god. This was what prompted him to persecute Christians with particular viciousness, for they would not give Caesar preference over their god. The emperor **Constantine**, who ruled from 312 to 337, tried other experiments. He set up a second capital city, Constantinople, to regulate the eastern half of the empire more efficiently. He tried to use the religious force of Christianity to unify the empire spiritually, extending toleration and adopting it as his own faith. These measures were not without result. The eastern empire, ruled from Constantinople (formerly the Greek colony of Byzantium, now the Turkish city of Istanbul), remained an effective political and economic unit. Christianity spread under official sponsorship, although some new problems were attached to success.

But none of these measures revived the empire as a whole. Human agency could have real impact, setting new forces in motion, but it could not reverse basic trends. Division merely made the weakness of the western half worse. Attempts to regulate the economy reduced economic initiative and lowered production; ultimately, tax revenues declined once again. The army deteriorated further. When the Germanic invasions began in earnest in the 400s, there was little resistance. Many peasants, burdened by the social and economic pressures of the decaying empire, actually welcomed the barbarians. A priest noted, "In all districts taken over by the Germans, there is one desire among all the Romans, that they should never again find it necessary to pass under Roman jurisdiction." German kingdoms were set up in many parts of the empire by 425, and the last Roman emperor in the West was displaced in 476 (Map 6.3). The Germanic invaders numbered, at most, 5 percent of the population of the empire, but so great was the earlier decline that this small, uncoordinated force put an end to one of the world's great political structures.

Read the Document on MyHistoryLab: Sidonius Apollinaris, Rome's Decay and A Glimpse of the New Order

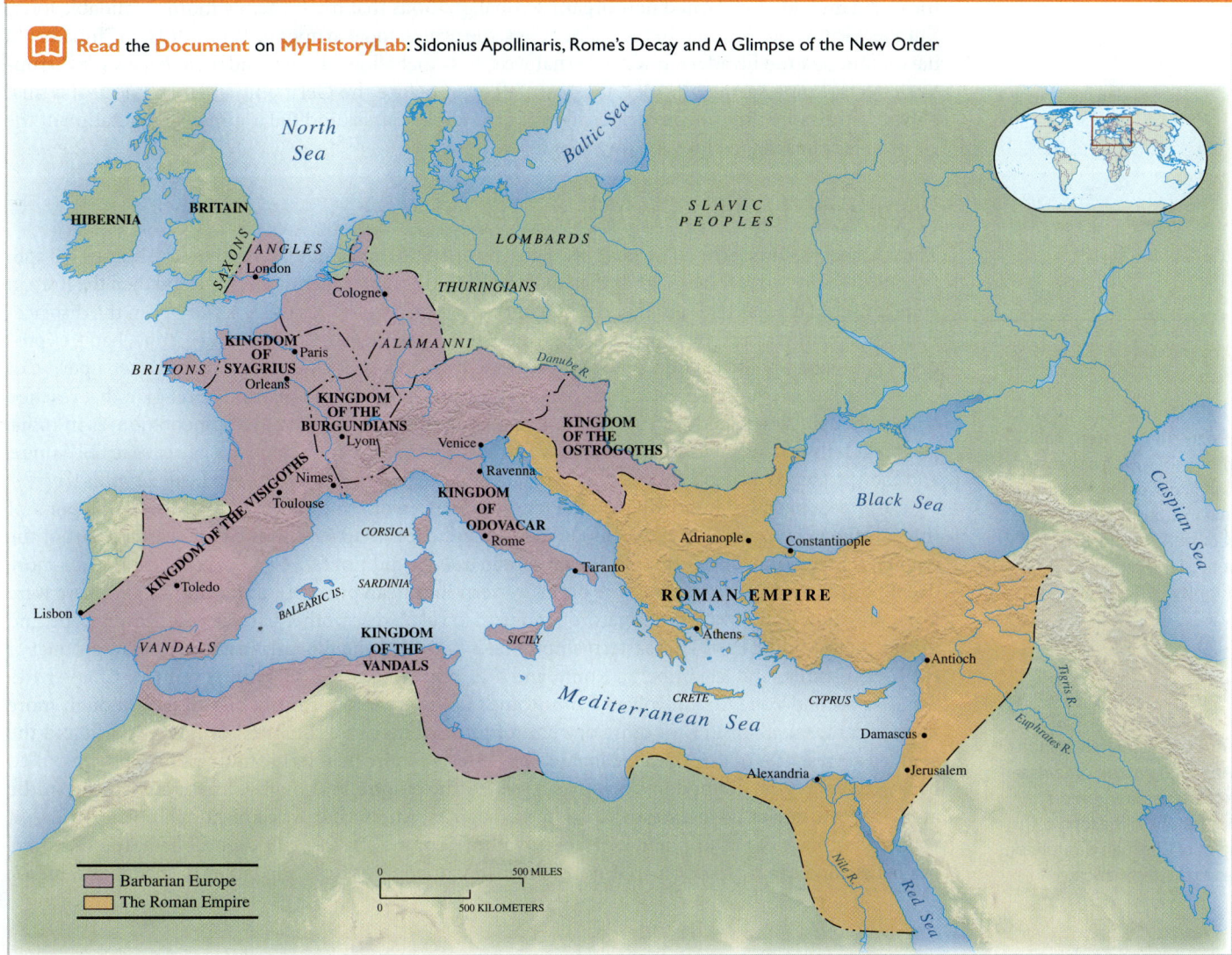

MAP 6.3 **Germanic Kingdoms After the Invasions** Nomadic tribes converged mainly on the western part of the Roman empire, invading Rome and its European outposts. Was this the cause or the result of the fact that the western portion of the empire was weaker than the eastern?

Attila the Hun

In Europe, the most famous invader was Attila the Hun, who lived from 406 to 453. Attila led the nomadic Huns, fighting with great fierceness. He organized a loose kingdom that ran from Germany to China. Known by Christians as the "scourge of God," Attila invaded what is now France in 451. Both Romans and Germanic tribes resisted him. An end run into Italy brought him to Rome, where the pope pleaded with him to spare the city—to no avail. Attila highlighted and contributed to Rome's collapse. His own kingdom fell after his death. But his success called attention to the importance of cavalry in warfare, something the Greeks and Romans, with their preference for infantry, had largely ignored.

Patterns of Decline?

The fall of Rome echoes some of the same questions that apply to China and India. Do civilizations inevitably fall, or at least undergo cycles of decline? When the collapse involves outside invading forces, does one look primarily at internal decay? Germanic or central Asian invaders had a few military advantages. Their reliance on hunting and herding gave them some skills, including excellent equestrian skills in the case of the Huns, which allowed them to overrun more populous peasant settlements where people were unaccustomed to battle. From their contacts on the Roman borders, the Germans had also learned new organizational methods that made them a more formidable force. But there is no question that in their glory days, the professional armies of Rome or Han China could have contained the invaders; it was internal weakness that allowed the invaders to have such disruptive effects. Rome seemed headed for downfall even before the Germanic intruders dealt the final blows. At the same time, the luxurious living of the upper classes and the impressive reputation of the classical empires helped lure the invaders in.

Results of the Fall of Rome

The collapse of Rome echoed through the later history of Europe and the Middle East. Rome's fall split the unity of the Mediterranean lands that had been won through Hellenistic culture and then the Roman empire itself. This was one sign that the end of the Roman empire was more serious than the displacement of the last classical dynasties in India and China. Greece and Rome, unlike China, had not produced the shared political culture and bureaucratic traditions that could allow revival after a period of chaos. Nor had Mediterranean civilization, for all its vitality, generated a common religion that reached deeply enough, or satisfied enough needs, to maintain unity amid political fragmentation, as in India. Such religions reached the Mediterranean world as Rome fell, but they came too late to save the empire, and they produced a deep rift between Christian and Muslim that has not been healed to this day.

In effect, the fall of Rome divided the Mediterranean world into three zones, the starting point of three distinct civilizations that developed in later centuries (Map 6.4). In the northeastern part of the empire, centered in Constantinople, the empire in a sense did not fall. Classical civilization was more deeply entrenched there than in some of the western European portions of the empire, and there were fewer pressures from invaders. Emperors continued to rule Greece, other parts of southeast Europe, and the northern Middle East. This eastern empire, later known as the **Byzantine empire**, was a product of the Hellenistic era and late imperial Rome, and it demonstrated great survival power (see Chapter 14).

The second zone that devolved from Rome's fall was more seriously disrupted, although more in political terms than in economic or cultural terms. This zone consisted of north Africa and the southeastern shores of the Mediterranean. The eastern empire held its ground briefly but then pulled back. Several regional kingdoms briefly succeeded the empire. Although Christianity spread in the area—indeed, one of the greatest Christian theologians, **Augustine**, was a bishop in north Africa—it was not as uniformly triumphant as in the Byzantine Empire or western Europe. Furthermore, differing beliefs and doctrines soon split north African Christianity from the larger branches, producing

Byzantine empire Eastern half of Roman empire following collapse of western half of old empire; retained Mediterranean culture, particularly Greek; later lost Palestine, Syria, and Egypt to Islam; capital at Constantinople.

Augustine (Saint) Influential church father and theologian (354–430 C.E.); born in Africa and ultimately bishop of Hippo in Africa; champion of Christian doctrine against various heresies and very important in the long-term development of Christian thought on such issues as predestination.

MAP **6.4 The Mediterranean, Middle East, Europe, and North Africa, c. 500 C.E.** Soon after the fall of Rome, the former empire split into three distinct zones.

most notably the **Coptic** Church in Egypt, which still survives as a Christian minority in that country, and another branch in Ethiopia. Soon much of north Africa was filled with the still newer doctrines of Islam and a new Arab empire.

Finally, there was the western part of the empire: Italy, Spain, and points north. Here is where Rome's fall not only shattered unities but reduced the level of civilization itself. Crude, regional Germanic kingdoms grew in parts of Italy, France, and elsewhere. The only clearly vital force in this region was not Roman tradition but the spread of Christianity. Even Christianity could not sustain sophisticated literature, art, or even theology, however. In Rome's collapse, cities and commercial activity also declined.

Coptic Christian sect in Egypt, later tolerated after Islamic takeover.

THE DEVELOPMENT AND SPREAD OF WORLD RELIGIONS

6.4 How did the organization of Christianity reflect its complex relationships with the Roman empire?

As with the period of chaos in China, Rome's decline encouraged vital new religious influences, in this case to societies around the Mediterranean. Christianity moved westward from its original center in the Middle East, just as in Asia Buddhism was spreading east from India. Although initially less significant than Buddhism in terms of numbers of converts, Christianity ultimately became one of the two largest world faiths. It played a direct role in forming the postclassical civilizations of eastern and western Europe.

The newly expanding religions (including Islam soon afterward) all emphasized intense devotion and piety, stressing the importance of spiritual concerns beyond the daily cares of life. All three offered the hope of a better existence after this life ended, and all responded to new political instability and to the growing poverty of many people in various parts of the classical world. Finally, all promoted active missionary efforts, seeking to spread their ideas of religious truth across cultural and political boundaries.

The period of classical decline saw the rapid expansion of Buddhism and Christianity. Religious change had wider cultural, social, and political implications.

Christianity and Buddhism Compared

Christianity resembled Buddhism in important ways. It could stress the unimportance of things of this world, urging a focus on spiritual destiny and divinity. Not surprisingly, Christianity, like Buddhism, produced an important monastic movement, in which people seeking holiness came together in groups to live a spiritual life and serve their religion. Christianity resembled the version of Buddhism that spread to China (and later Korea and Japan) by stressing the possibility of an afterlife and the role holy leaders could play in helping to attain it.

The Chinese version of Buddhism, called **Mahayana**, or the Greater Vehicle, placed considerable emphasis on Buddha as god or savior. Statues of the Buddha as god violated the earlier Buddhist hostility to religious images, but they emphasized the religion as a channel of salvation. Well-organized temples, with priests and rituals, also helped bring religious solace to ordinary people in east Asia. The idea developed also that Buddhist holy men, or **bodhisattvas**, built up such spiritual merit that their prayers, even after death, could aid people and allow them to achieve some holiness. These were people who had achieved enlightenment, thereby breaking the cycle of reincarnation, but chose to return to earth to help others do the same thing. Christianity in many respects moved in similar directions. It also came to emphasize salvation with well-organized rituals. Religious images, although contrary to Jewish beliefs against idol worship, helped focus popular belief in most versions of Christianity. Holy men and women, sometimes granted the title *saint* after their deaths, were revered because their spiritual attainments could lend merit to the strivings of more ordinary people. The broad similarities between Christianity and the evolving Buddhism of east Asia remind us of the common processes at work as new religions spread amid the ruins of great empires.

Mahayana Chinese version of Buddhism; placed considerable emphasis on Buddha as god or savior.

bodhisattvas [boh-dih-SAHT-vuh] Buddhist holy men and women; built up spiritual merits during their lifetimes; prayers even after death could aid people to achieve reflected holiness.

Yet Christianity had a flavor of its own. More than any of the forms of Buddhism, it emphasized church organization and structure, copying the example of the Roman empire. It also placed greater value on missionary activity and widespread conversions, believing that error must be actively opposed in God's name. More perhaps than any other major religion—certainly more than the contemplative and tolerant Buddhism—Christianity stressed its possession of exclusive truth and its intolerance of competing beliefs. Such fierce confidence was not the least of the reasons for the new religion's success.

Early Christianity

Christianity began as part of a Jewish reform movement. Initially, there seems to have been no intent to found a new religion. After Jesus' crucifixion, the disciples expected his imminent return and with it the end of the world. Only gradually, when the Second Coming did not happen, did the disciples begin to fan out and, through preaching, pick up supporters in various parts of the Roman empire.

The message of Jesus and his disciples seemed clear. There was a single God who loved humankind despite earthly sin. A virtuous life should be dedicated to the worship of God and fellowship with other believers. Worldly concerns were secondary, and a life of poverty might be most conducive to holiness. God sent **Jesus of Nazareth**, called Christ (from the Greek word *Christos*, "God's anointed"), to preach his holy word and, through his sacrifice, to prepare for the possibility of an afterlife of heavenly communion with God. Belief, good works, and discipline of fleshly concerns would lead toward heaven; rituals, such as commemorating Christ's Last Supper with wine and bread, would promote the same goal.

Jesus of Nazareth Prophet and teacher among the Jews; believed by Christians to be the Messiah; executed c. 30 C.E.

This message spread at an opportune time. The official religion of the Greeks and Romans had long seemed rather sterile, particularly to many of the poor. The Christian emphasis on the beauty of poverty and the spiritual equality of all people, plus the fervor of the early Christians and the satisfying rituals they provided, gained growing attention. The wide reach of the Roman empire made it easy for Christian missionaries to travel through Europe and the Middle East and spread the new word. Then, when conditions began to deteriorate in the empire, the solace of this otherworldly religion won even more converts.

Paul of Tarsus (c. 10–67 C.E.) was a key Christian leader. Initially a Jewish rabbi, he was hostile to Christians as heretics. But on a journey to try to round up the Christians in Damascus, a vision of Jesus came to him. He became an ardent Christian missionary and contributed to several adjustments in Christian doctrine. He spent his last years in jail, first in Roman-ruled Jerusalem, then in Rome, because of the official opposition to Christianity.

Paul One of the first Christian missionaries; moved away from insistence that adherents of the new religion follow Jewish law; use of Greek as language of Church.

The adjustments made by early Christian leaders drew even more converts. Under the guidance of Paul, Christians began to see themselves as part of a new religion rather than a Jewish reform movement, and they welcomed non-Jewish converts. Paul also encouraged more formal organization in the new church, with local groups selecting elders to govern them; soon, a single leader, or bishop, was appointed for each major city. This structure paralleled the provincial government of the empire. Finally, Christian doctrine became increasingly well organized as the writings of several disciples and others were collected into what became the New Testament of the Christian Bible.

Christianity Gains Ground

During the first three centuries after Christ, Christianity did not advance entirely smoothly. The new religion faced periodic persecution from the normally tolerant imperial government. Even so, by the time Constantine converted to the religion, Christianity had won perhaps 10 percent of the empire's population. One convert was Constantine's mother, who visited the Holy Land and founded many churches there. Constantine's favor brought some new troubles to Christianity as the state began to interfere in matters of doctrine.

Nevertheless, it became much easier to spread Christianity with official backing. Christian writers began to claim that both church and empire were works of God. At the same time, continued deterioration of the empire added to the motives to join this successful new church. In the eastern Mediterranean, where imperial rule remained strong, state control of the church became a way of life and an important motive, for certain people, for adopting Christianity in the first place. A pagan prefect of Constantinople, Cyrus of Panopolis, facing the disapproval of an imperial official in the mid-5th century, could save himself only by converting and becoming a Christian bishop. But in the west, where conditions were far more chaotic, bishops had a freer hand.

pope Bishop of Rome; head of the Christian Church in western Europe.

A centralized church organization under the leadership of the bishop of Rome, called the **pope** from the Latin word *papa*, or father, gave the western church unusual strength and independence. By the time Rome collapsed, Christianity had thus demonstrated immense spiritual power and a solid organization, although it differed from east to west. The new church faced several controversies over doctrine but managed to promote certain standard beliefs. A key tenet was a complex doctrine of the Trinity, which held that the one God had three persons, the Father, the Son (Christ), and the Holy Ghost (God as present in human spiritual experience). In 325 C.E., the church **Council of Nicaea** under imperial sponsorship, met to debate a doctrine known as Arianism, which argued that Christ was divine but not of the same nature as God the Father. Ruling against Arianism, the resultant Nicene Creed insisted

Council of Nicaea [nye-SEE-uh] Christian council that met in 325 C.E. to determine orthodoxy with respect to the Trinity; insisted on divinity of all persons of the Trinity.

on the shared divinity of all three parts of the Trinity. An important but complex decision, it showed how important unified doctrine was to Christianity, in contrast to the greater toleration of diversity in Hinduism and Buddhism. Experience in fighting heresies promoted the Christian interest in defending a single belief and strengthened its resistance to any competing doctrine or faith.

In its founding but also in its consolidation, Christianity was aided by strong individual leadership, although it can be debated how much this leadership caused religious success and how much it flowed from the religion's appeal. For example, Pope Leo I (d. 461) most clearly established the papacy as the supreme authority in western Europe. Born a Roman aristocrat, he faced the rapid collapse of the empire, negotiating with German rulers to save the city of Rome and using their backing to assert his authority over church leaders in France and elsewhere. Leo competed with the patriarch of Alexandria for spiritual primacy in Christianity, centralizing the western church and standardizing its rituals, prayers, and doctrine.

Early Christianity also produced an important formal theology through formative writers such as Augustine. This theology blended many elements of classical philosophy with Christian belief and helped the church gain respectability among intellectuals. Theologians such as Augustine grappled with such problems as freedom of the will: If God is all-powerful, can mere human beings have free will? And if not, how can human beings be justly punished for sin? By working out these issues in elaborate doctrine, the early theologians, or church fathers, provided an important role for formal, rational thought in a religion that continued to emphasize the primary importance of faith.

Like all successful religions, Christianity combined several appeals. It offered deep devotion to an all-powerful God. Christianity also developed its own complex and fascinating intellectual system. Mystical holy men and women flourished under Christian banners, particularly in the Middle East. In the West, soon after the empire's collapse, this impulse was partially disciplined through the institution of monasticism, which gained ground in Italy under **Benedict of Nursia** early in the 6th century. Benedict started a monastery to demonstrate the true holy life to Italian peasants in a region still (to Benedict's horror) worshiping the sun god Apollo. The Benedictine rule, which soon spread to many other monasteries and convents, urged a disciplined life, with prayer and spiritual development alternating with hard work in agriculture and study. Monastic movements also developed in the eastern empire, in Greece and Turkey, and in Egypt. Eastern monasticism was organized by Saint Basil in the 4th century.

Thus, Christianity tried to encourage but also to discipline intense piety and to avoid a complete gulf between the lives of saintly men and women and the spiritual concerns of ordinary people. Christianity's success and organizational strength obviously appealed to political leaders. But the new religion never became the creature of the upper classes alone, because its message of ritual and salvation continued to draw the poor. Like Hinduism in India, Christianity provided some religious unity among different social groups. It even held special interest for women. Christianity did not preach equality between men and women, but it did preach the equal importance of women's and men's souls, and unlike many other faiths it encouraged men and women to worship together.

Christianity promoted a new culture among its converts (Figure 6.5). The rituals, the otherworldly emphasis, and the interest in spiritual equality were very different from the central themes of classical Mediterranean civilization. Christianity modified classical beliefs in the central importance of the state and political loyalties. Although Christians accepted the state, they did not put it first. Christianity also worked against other classical institutions, such as slavery, in the name of brotherhood (although later Christians accepted slavery in other contexts). Western monasticism may have fostered a greater respectability for disciplined work than had been current in the aristocratic ethic of Mediterranean civilization.

Christianity preserved important classical values in addition to the interest in solid organization and some of the themes of classical philosophy. Church buildings in western Europe retained Roman architectural styles, although often with greater simplicity, if only because of the poverty of the

Read the **Document** on **MyHistoryLab**: Pope Leo I on Bishop Hilary of Arles

Benedict of Nursia Founder of monasticism in what had been the western half of the Roman Empire; established Benedictine Rule in the 6th century; paralleled development of Basil's rules in Byzantine empire.

Read the **Document** on **MyHistoryLab**: From the Rule of St. Benedict (6th c.) (Excerpt) by St. Benedict of Nursia

FIGURE **6.5** People of European background are accustomed to seeing the Madonna and child depicted as looking much like them. As this 10th-century Byzantine image demonstrates, Christians from other parts of the world developed different imagery for the major figures of their religion.

later empire and the Germanic states. Latin remained the language of the church in the West, Greek the language of most Christians in the eastern Mediterranean. Monasticism played a very valuable role in preserving classical as well as Christian learning through the patient librarianship of the monks.

The New Religious Map

The centuries after the rise of Christianity, the spread of Buddhism, and the inception of Islam (610 C.E.) saw the conversion of most of the civilized world to one or another of the great faiths. This produced a religious map that in Europe, Asia, and parts of Africa did not change greatly until our own

---

VISUALIZING THE PAST

Religious Geography

THE DISTRIBUTION OF THE WORLD'S MAJOR religions calls for knowledge both of numerical data and geography. This map and table, using contemporary data, also suggest which aspects of the world's religious distribution were beginning to solidify at the end of the late classical period and which aspects depended on developments yet to come.

QUESTIONS
- Where are the greatest concentrations of the four major religions today?
- Which aspects of modern religious geography follow from the patterns of religious dissemination under way by the end of the classical period?
- Which cannot be explained by these late classical developments?

RELIGIONS AND THEIR DISTRIBUTION IN THE WORLD TODAY

Religion	Distribution*
Christianity	2 billion
Islam	1.3 billion
Hinduism	900 million
Buddhism	360 million
Shintoism	4 million
Daoism and other Chinese traditional religions	225 million
Judaism	14 million
Non-religious	850 million

*Figures for several religions have been reduced over the past 50 years by the impact of communism in eastern Europe and parts of Asia.

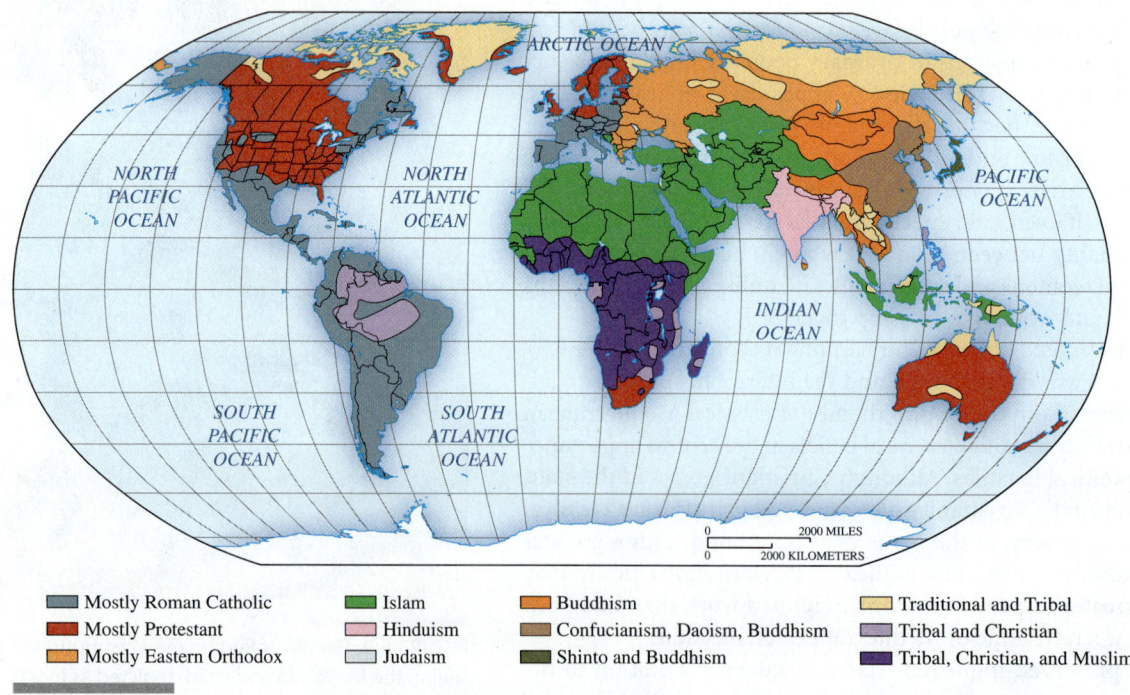

MAP **6.5 Major Religions of the Modern World** This map shows the contemporary geography of the major religions, including areas of considerable mixture like Africa.

time. The spread of the great religions caused many people in many different societies to shift their beliefs away from traditional ideas about a host of divine spirits in nature to concentration on a single divine force and on new hopes for an afterlife. Buddhism, Christianity, and Islam, plus Hinduism in a few parts of southeast Asia, provided shared beliefs that could transcend divided, bickering political units. They could indeed draw allegiance and funding away from politics. The three most widespread religions raised new social questions, because they all stressed a basic spiritual equality. The great religions could even facilitate international trade because they did not depend on local customs but on an ever-present God or divine order throughout the world; in turn, successful trade could help spread the religions. A new force was at work in world history.

In the Wake of Decline and Fall

By 600 C.E., the major civilizations looked very different from the classical world at its height, and many of the differences have never been erased. The results of classical decline went beyond the striking shifts in religious allegiance. Some areas, however, changed far more than others. China was unique in its ability to recapture so many classical ingredients. China and India shared an ability to maintain substantial cultural cohesion, based on widespread beliefs as well as restored politics in China's case. Today, Indian and Chinese civilizations are in essentially the same places where they had taken root by late classical times, and until quite recently, they still abundantly reflected the classical heritage: India in the caste system and an otherworldly cultural tone, China in Confucian beliefs and a fascination with a strong, bureaucratic state.

The case was quite different in the Mediterranean zone. The Roman empire split, in part because it had not been able to spread shared beliefs very widely. Classical Mediterranean civilization left a very real heritage, but in part because geographic unity was lost, this heritage was used by successor civilizations far more selectively than was true in eastern or southern Asia.

Another approach to the problem of decline argues that it is almost inevitable.

Global Connections and Critical Themes:
THE LATE CLASSICAL PERIOD AND THE WORLD

During most of the classical period, key developments often focused within civilizations. We have seen that there were wider contacts. Each civilization radiated trade and other influences to a larger region; thus India had contacts with other parts of south-southeast Asia, and China with Korea and Vietnam. Trade along the Silk Road through central Asia, conducted mainly by nomadic merchants, was another key connection, as were the exchanges in the Indian Ocean.

As the classical civilizations began to fail, contacts in some ways accelerated—but they also encountered new difficulties. Overland travel between China and Rome became more dangerous, because government protection faltered in both empires. This placed a new premium on using shipping connections, particularly in the Indian Ocean. On the other hand, traders, missionaries, and of course nomadic invaders began to reach out in new ways, as borders became more porous. The end of the classical period thus witnessed important new cultural exchanges across regions. These included the spread of Buddhism from India to China and to other parts of east Asia, and the spread of Christianity beyond the Roman empire into parts of northeast Africa and into Armenia. These developments set new bases for connections among various societies in Afro-Eurasia.

Further Readings

Excellent surveys of the early history of the Americas include Stuart Fiedel's *Prehistory of the Americas* (1987); Charles C. Mann, *1491* (2005); Michael Mosley, *The Incas and their Ancestors* (1992); Stephen Houston and Takeshi Inomata, *The Classic Maya* (2009), which is one of the best books on the Maya that covers the major aspects of classic Maya culture and is especially good on the debates among scholars.

The fall of the Roman empire has generated rich and interesting debate. See E. Gibbon and H. Mueller, *The Decline and Fall of the Roman Empire* (2009); Jared Diamond, *Collapse: How Societies Choose to Fail or Succeed: Revised Edition* (2011); Simon Swain and Mark Edwards, eds., *Approaching Late Antiquity: The Transformation from Early to Late Empire* (2004); James W. Ermatinger, *The Decline and Fall of the Roman Empire* (2004); Bryan Ward-Perkins, *The Fall of Rome and the End of Civilization* (2005). On barbarian attacks, J. H. G. W. Liebeschuetz, *Decline and Change in Late Antiquity: Religion, Barbarians and Their Historiography* (2006); Simon MacDowall, *Adrianopole, AD 378: The Goths Crush Rome's Legions* (2005); Peter Heather, *The Fall of the Roman Empire: A New History of Rome and the Barbarians* (2007); and Stephen Mitchell, *A History of the Later Roman Empire, AD 284–641* (2007).

For interpretation and discussion of earlier views, see A. H. M. Jones, *The Decline of the Ancient World* (1966); J. Vogt, *The Decline of Rome* (1965); and F. W. Walbank, *The Awful Revolution: The Decline of the Roman Empire in the West* (1960). On India and China in decline, worthwhile sources include R. Tharpar, *Early History of India* (2004); R. C. Majumdar, ed., *The Classical Age* (1966); Raymond Dawson, *Imperial China* (1972); and J. A. Harrison, *The Chinese Empire* (1972). See also J. R. Fairbank and E. O. Reischauer, *China: Tradition and Transformation* (1989), a fine survey with good postclassical coverage.

On the role of disease in imperial decline, W. McNeill's *Plagues and Peoples* (1977) is provocative and useful. Speculations on the causes of the rise and fall of civilizations, including those of the classical world, are addressed in Jared Diamond, *Guns, Germs, and Steel: The Fate of Human Societies* (1997); Christopher Chase-Dunn and Thomas D. Hall, *Rise and Demise: Comparing World Systems* (1997); Walter Goffart, *Barbarian Tides: The Migration Age and the Later Roman Empire* (2006); Michael Whitby, *Rome at War, AD 293–696* (2003); Joseph A. Tainter, *The Collapse of Complex Societies* (1988); and Norman Yoffee and George L. Cowgill, eds., *The Collapse of Ancient States and Civilizations* (1991).

For the rise and spread of world faiths, see Ann Heirman and Stephan Peter Bumbacher, eds., *The Spread of Buddhism* (2007); and Frederick Denny, *Atlas of the World's Religions* (2007). A good overview is Geoffrey Parinder, ed., *World Religions* (1971); see also Lewis M. Hopfe, *Religions of the World* (1997); and Jamail Ragi al Farugi, ed., *Historical Atlas of the Religions of the World* (1974). On Hinduism, see N. C. Chandhuri's *Hinduism: A Religion to Live By* (1979). Two good studies of Buddhism are N. Ross Reat, *Buddhism: A History* (1994) and A. F. Wright, *Buddhism in Chinese History* (1959). Christianity's spread is the subject of E. E. Cairns, *Christianity through the Centuries* (2009); S. Renko, *Pagan Rome and the Early Christians* (1986); and M. Hengel, *Acts and the History of Earliest Christianity* (1986). Important special topics are covered in J. Bowker, *Problems of Suffering in Religions of the World* (1975), a fascinating comparative effort; A. Sharma, ed., *Women in World Religions* (1987); and on Christianity, B. Witherington, *Women in the Earliest Churches* (1988). An important study of civilization contacts in this period and later is Jerry Bentley's *Old World Encounters: Cross-Cultural Exchanges and Contacts in Pre-Modern Times* (1993).

On MyHistoryLab

 Study and Review on MyHistoryLab

Critical Thinking Questions

1. What were the main differences in the process of decline in the four major cases: China, India, eastern Mediterranean, western Mediterranean?
2. What are some possible debates over the causes of decline at the end of the classical period?
3. What was the relationship of religious change to the process of political and economic decline?
4. What were the major adaptations of Buddhism as it spread to China? What were the main adaptations of Christianity in the later Roman empire?
5. Compare the principal features of Buddhism and Christianity as world religions.

PART II AP® TEST PREP

MULTIPLE CHOICE QUESTIONS

1. Which of the following was a result of the period of political confusion following the fall of the Zhou dynasty?
   a. Chinese civilization failed to produce another dynasty for centuries.
   b. The Shi ceased to play a significant role in Chinese government.
   c. Feudalism became the dominant form of political organization in Chinese society.
   d. Philosophers sought to find ways to end the conflict and create more permanent and unified political systems.

2. During most of his life, Kong Fuzi or Confucius
   a. served the Han emperors as their chief court advisor.
   b. advocated abolition of the "shi" as dangerous opponents of a centralized state.
   c. wandered searching for the ideal ruler.
   d. remained atop a mountain in contemplative seclusion.

3. According to Confucius, for what reason should superior men rule?
   a. to enrich their families and earn distinction
   b. to establish the glory of the emperor
   c. to establish the glory of the regional aristocracy
   d. to serve society as a whole

4. Which of the following represents the views of Xunzi, one of Confucius's disciples?
   a. Humans were by nature inclined to goodness and ought to be ruled in that fashion.
   b. Humans were inclined to be lazy and evil and ought to be ruled by authoritarian government.
   c. Humans ought to retreat from society and seek oneness with nature.
   d. Government should be rigorous and based on strict laws harshly executed.

5. Which of the following represents the philosophical viewpoint of Laozi?
   a. Humans were inclined to goodness and ought to be governed in a compassionate fashion.
   b. Humans were inclined to be lazy and evil and ought to be governed rigorously.
   c. Humans ought to retreat from society and seek oneness with nature.
   d. Government ought to be authoritarian and based on strict laws harshly executed.

6. Shi Huangdi
   a. promoted Confucian philosophy by appointing scholars to serve as legal advisers within his court.
   b. attempted to alleviate the harsher aspects of Legalist political philosophy by implementing reforms proposed by his royal council.
   c. believed in the essential goodness of humans and urged humane behavior on the part of his officials, insisting that they oversee the moral welfare of his empire.
   d. worried so much about controlling ideas in the Qin state that he proposed the burning of all books other than Legalist tracts and a few other official volumes.

7. The famous monumental structure pictured was built under which ruler?
   a. Liu Bang
   b. Wang Mang
   c. Confucius
   d. Shi Huangdi

8. Which of the following statements most accurately describes the territorial expansion of the Han dynasty?
   a. The Han were unable to expand their territories due to constant wars with the rulers of the states.
   b. The Han actually lost territories to the raids of the Xiongnu and other nomadic invaders.
   c. The Han temporarily defeated the Xiongnu and dramatically expanded Chinese territory to the east and south.
   d. The Han were able to expand their territories by conquering the Gupta civilization of India.

9. What was the status of women during the Han dynasty?
   a. Women enjoyed equal status with males during the Han dynasty.
   b. Despite the Confucian requirement for female deference to males, women had their own clearly defined roles in the family and could sometimes gain power through their sons and as mothers-in-law.
   c. Despite the Confucian requirement for male deference to females, women had less freedom than during later dynasties.
   d. The demeaned status of women meant that they were at the whim of their sons and sons-in-law, who often mistreated them.

10. Which of the following statements most accurately describes the degree of urbanization in Han China?
    a. The capital at Xianyang may have numbered as many as 250,000 people, but there were few other cities.
    b. China may have been the most urbanized civilization in the world with many large cities numbering in the thousands.
    c. As a result of the constant warfare during the Han dynasty, few cities were able to survive.
    d. Aside from walled agricultural complexes dominated by the regional aristocracy, there were few walled cities.

11. Chinese art during the Han classical period
    a. concentrated on the development of monumental sculpture.
    b. was uninspired and generally of poor quality, due to the Chinese concentration on the sciences.
    c. was most advanced in the area of painting.
    d. was largely decorative often reflecting the geometric precision of Chinese calligraphy.

12. Which of the following statements best describes the early kingdoms established in northern India?
    a. Most of them were republics ruled collectively by a council made up of the free warrior elite.
    b. Like the Greek mainland, the kingdoms were actually city-states ruled by aristocratic councils.
    c. The early kingdoms were based on a strongly centralized monarchy with well-established bureaucracies.
    d. Early political organization among the kingdoms amounted to little more than hunting-and-gathering groups.

13. What was the key function that assured the authority of the brahmans in the southern kingdoms?
    a. Only the brahmans were capable of performing the rituals and sacrifices that obliged the gods to intervene in human affairs.
    b. As the warrior elite, the brahmans controlled the military affairs of the southern kingdoms.
    c. As the commercial class of India, the brahmans were entirely responsible for the economic prosperity of the southern kingdoms.
    d. The brahman class provided the members of all of the dynasties of the southern kingdoms.

14. The period of Maurya rule in India
    a. coincided with a great expansion in trade between the main centers of civilization in Eurasia and Africa.
    b. was a period in which Buddhism was almost wiped out.
    c. was one of the longest dynastic periods in Indian history.
    d. broke up the substantial bureaucracy and existing postal service.

15. What determined a person's place within the Indian social hierarchy?
    a. wealth
    b. position within the government
    c. the degree to which the occupation was considered polluting
    d. his religious piety

16. What was the status of women in the pre-imperial period in India?
    a. Within the family they were clearly subordinate to men, but they enjoyed greater occupational opportunities than was the case by the last centuries B.C.E.
    b. Women were clearly subordinate within the household and were unable to hold any occupations outside of it.
    c. Women enjoyed great freedom within the household, but were unable to hold any occupations outside of it.
    d. Women enjoyed equality within the household, but were restricted from reading the sacred texts.

17. Which of the following was NOT a teaching of Buddha?
    a. The moment we are born we begin to die.
    b. Attachments to impermanent things of the world are the source of suffering.
    c. The road to enlightenment begins with ritual sacrifices to the gods.
    d. Once enlightenment is attained, the individual is released from suffering.

18. In addition to offering miraculous tales of Buddha's life, how did the monks devoted to Buddhism change his teachings in the years after Buddha's death?
    a. The monks equated Nirvana with heaven and stressed the salvationist qualities of the new religion.
    b. The monks sought to downplay Buddha as a deity, attempted to limit admission to the religion to the upper-caste groups, and gained the cooperation of the brahmans.
    c. The monks began to emphasize ritual sacrifices of animals as a means of gaining the confidence of the people.
    d. The monks ended the Buddha's emphasis on meditation and taught that all men were condemned to endless reincarnation.

19. How did the Mauryan empire of Chandragupta compare to the Aryan kingdoms that preceded it?
    a. Although called an empire, it was little more than a tribute-collecting patchwork of petty rulers.
    b. It retained the republican aspects of the first Aryan kingdoms with elected monarchs and warrior councils.
    c. While it did succeed in dominating most of northwestern India, it never conquered the kingdoms of southern India.
    d. It was vastly more centralized than the preceding kingdoms with a large standing army and administrators in place of the regional lords.

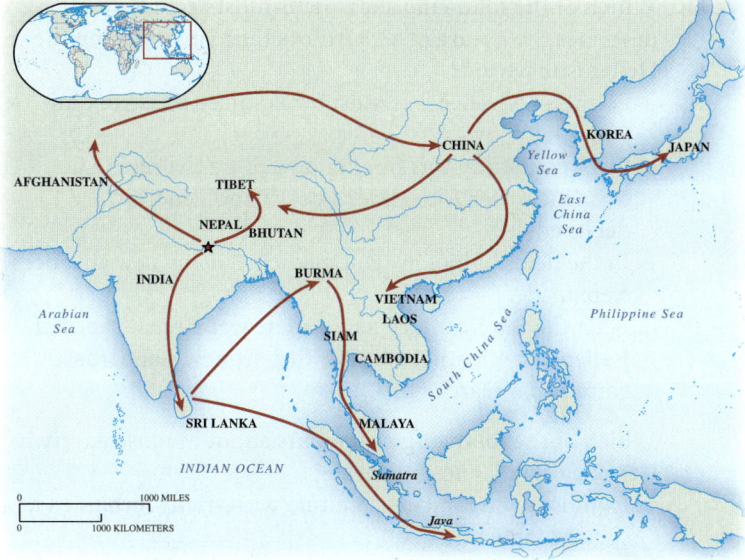

20. According to the map, what was the result of Buddhist missionary efforts during the reign of Ashoka?
    a. Despite major efforts, Buddhism failed to spread much beyond the Indian subcontinent.
    b. Through the remaining Greek influence in northwestern India, Buddhism spread to the areas affected by Greek culture.
    c. Buddhism spread to Sri Lanka and the Himalayan kingdoms and from there to central and southeastern Asia.
    d. Buddhism's spread was limited to the pastoral nomads of the central Asia steppes.

21. What economic factor weakened the hold of Buddhism on the Indian population?
    a. The improving status of the peasantry made them less likely to be interested in a salvationist religion.
    b. The untouchables were decimated by a severe famine, thus removing a class associated with Buddhism.
    c. The failure of the Rome-China trade axis weakened the merchants, who had been one of the chief benefactors of the Buddhist monasteries.
    d. The increasing wealth of all social classes reduced the strictness of social division within the caste system and undermined one of the attractions of Buddhism.

22. How was the social hierarchy of India transformed during the reign of the Guptas?
    a. In general restrictions against low-caste groups and women became harsher and more pervasive.
    b. While restrictions against untouchables became more strict, women achieved greater equality during the Gupta period.
    c. Brahmans and other upper-caste groups lost their clear social distinctiveness as Indian society became more open to social mobility.
    d. The castes were abandoned and replaced by the tripartite system of general varnas.

23. Which of the following statements is NOT true concerning the Persian religion of Zoroastrianism?
    a. It was a polytheistic.
    b. It featured a pantheon of male and female deities who acted very much like humans.
    c. The righteous lived on after death in the "House of Song."
    d. Zoroaster saw life as a struggle between two cosmic forces of good and evil.

24. The Greek governments of the period immediately after 800 B.C.E. largely consisted of
    a. regional kingdoms.
    b. a unified empire under a single ruler.
    c. city-states.
    d. feudal vassals loosely controlled by a single ruler.

25. What were the causes of the disputes that arose after 700 B.C.E. in the city-states of Greece?
    a. disagreement over the boundaries among the various city-states
    b. commercial expansion and the problems of small landowners in the new economy
    c. a decrease in the number of available slaves due to changes in the economy
    d. the imposition of a universal income tax on all Greeks

26. Which of the following statements accurately describes a difference between classical Chinese approach to politics and the approach of Hellenic Greece to politics?
    a. China placed less emphasis on hierarchy and obedience to authority than did the Greeks.
    b. Greek politics emphasized a single, centralized system of authority.
    c. The Greeks placed more emphasis on participation and less on bureaucracy.
    d. The Chinese lacked the bureaucracy that made democratic government in Greece possible.

27. In the aftermath of the Peloponnesian War, by 355 B.C.E. the political structure of Greece
    a. was completely dominated by Sparta.
    b. fell under the control of Athens and a renewed Athenian empire.
    c. had become a kingdom ruled by Philip of Macedon.
    d. had returned to a setting of independent, disorganized city-states.

28. Which of the following statements most accurately reflects Alexander's plans for his new empire?
    a. He planned to transplant Greek culture in Persia while at the same time wiping out all traces of Eastern culture.
    b. He planned to transplant Asian cultural and political institutions to Greece while at the same time wiping out all traces of Hellenic culture.
    c. As a Macedonian, Alexander disdained both Greek and Asian culture as effeminate and planned to impose Macedonian cultural values in all his domains.
    d. Alexander wanted to combine Greek culture with Asian culture to create a new, Hellenistic culture.

29. Which of the following statements most accurately compares the Greek religion to that of the Indian and Chinese civilizations?
    a. Greek religion was a vastly more sophisticated belief based on moral precepts and a strong attachment to an afterlife.
    b. Greek religion was more strongly spiritual than either the Indian or Chinese religions.
    c. The Greeks failed to develop a religion of any kind.
    d. Greek religion was derived from a belief in the spirits of nature elevated into a complex set of gods.

30. Which of the following statements best describes the function of philosophy in Greek culture?
    a. It sought to devise a system of rewards and punishments in the afterworld.
    b. It established ethical systems based on rational definitions of right and wrong.
    c. It set up ethical systems based on the struggle between the cosmic forces of good and evil.
    d. Philosophy was largely ignored in Hellenic society.

31. What does the preceding image say about Greek architecture?
    a. Greek architecture lacked almost entirely any monumental building.
    b. Most Greek monumental building was executed in bricks of standardized form with little, if any, decoration.
    c. Greek monumental architecture was almost entirely decorative and had no utilitarian purpose.
    d. Greek monumental architecture, often square or rectangular in shape and decorated with columns, was intended for a variety of public uses.

32. How did the literary production of Hellenistic Greek culture compare to that of the Hellenic period?
    a. While histories ceased to be written and the epic declined, Hellenistic Greece saw the zenith of dramatic production.
    b. For the first time since the Homeric period, new Greek epics were widely disseminated.
    c. Levels of literacy fell throughout the Greek world, and most of the Hellenic works were lost.
    d. Historical information was elaborated, and historical biography came into its own.

33. Which of the following statements most accurately describes the nature of scientific achievement during the Hellenistic period?
    a. Scientific advance was most pronounced in astronomy and geography.
    b. Scientific study was not supported by the regional dynasties after Alexander's death and generally declined.
    c. In the fields of biology and medicine, many new advances were made.
    d. After the third century B.C.E., there was a renaissance of Hellenistic scientific advance that set new standards for empirical research.

34. Which of the following statements about homosexuality in Greek culture is most accurate?
    a. Homosexuality in Greek culture was strictly forbidden as a societal taboo.
    b. Homosexual relationships often appeared between young people and their mentors, particularly among males.
    c. Homosexuality was so widely practiced among the Greeks that it detracted from their devotion to marriage and the household.
    d. Homosexuality was permitted in most parts of Greek society except among the Spartans where it was strictly forbidden among the military citizens.

35. Which of the following statements most accurately describes Cicero?
    a. He was a radical politician who supported Julius Caesar and who argued for the destruction of the republic.
    b. He was a conservative politician who favored retention of the republic.
    c. Cicero argued strongly for the exclusion of Greek influences from Roman culture and literature.
    d. Cicero supported Octavian and emerged as a major figure during the early Roman empire.

36. What was Augustus' attitude toward the republican institutions after his establishment of the empire?
    a. Augustus modeled the empire on the republic, retaining the full authority of the republican institutions.
    b. Augustus totally revised the government and eliminated all of the institutions and offices of the republic.
    c. Augustus retained the office of consul and tribune, but eliminated the Senate as a meaningful part of the empire.
    d. Augustus retained many of the institutions and offices of the republic, including the Senate, but took actual power in his own hands.

37. Which of the following was Rome's greatest political contribution?
    a. Roman law
    b. a bureaucracy selected through an examination system
    c. democracy
    d. centralized government

38. Which of the following was NOT an important aspect of Paul's contribution to Christianity?
    a. Under the guidance of Paul, Christians began to see themselves as part of a new religion that welcomed non-Jewish converts.
    b. Paul encouraged more formal organization in the new church, involving a single leader, or bishop, who was appointed for each major city.
    c. Paul's writings led to the use of Greek as the language of the Christian Church.
    d. Paul advocated for women as important leaders in the Christian Church.

39. What was the Roman imperial government's attitude toward Christianity?
    a. The Roman government systematically persecuted Christians on a constant basis until the 4th century C.E.
    b. The Roman government embraced Christianity as the official state religion in the 2nd century C.E.
    c. While some emperors chose to persecute the Christians, persecution was not constant.
    d. There were no persecutions of the Christians as the official policy of the Roman empire was religious toleration.

40. What was the cause of the deteriorating condition of the peasantry in later Han China?
    a. a lengthy drought that caused failure of the crops
    b. the growth of slavery following the introduction of Buddhism
    c. the growing power of the great landholders to tax leading to growing serfdom
    d. Confucian acceptance of the enslavement of the small farmers

41. How did the emergence of Buddhism in China affect Daoism?
    a. Daoism merged with Buddhism to create a single religious movement.
    b. Daoism rapidly disappeared following the appearance of Buddhism.
    c. The appearance of Buddhism led to greater formalization of Daoist doctrine and more efforts to reach the common people.
    d. Daoism became an illegal religion and the Chinese state moved rapidly to suppress various Daoist rituals, particularly those dealing with magic and healing.

42. What was the status of Buddhism in India following the fall of the Gupta empire?
    a. It continued to decline in the face of the Gupta preference for Hinduism and the dislike of the succeeding military rulers for Buddhist principles.
    b. Buddhism declined, but retained a presence in India as it was adopted by the Hunnic invaders.
    c. Buddhism was resurrected as a major religion in India because it was adopted by many of the regional leaders who sought to buttress their authority.
    d. Buddhism replaced Hinduism as the primary religion of the Indian population, although it was outlawed by the ruling military princes.

43. What was the impact of the reassertion of Hinduism on the caste system of India?
    a. The caste system was abolished.
    b. The caste system remained important and unchanged.
    c. The caste system was restricted to northern India.
    d. The caste system became more complex.

44. Which of the following would NOT be considered a sign of decay in the Roman empire in the late 2nd century?
    a. Population size declined as birth rates no longer kept pace with mortality rates, so it became more difficult to recruit effective armies.
    b. There was greater brutality and capriciousness on the part of many later Roman emperors, who, according to one commentator at the time, were victims of "lustful and cruel habits."
    c. Tax collection became increasingly difficult as residents of the empire fell on hard times.
    d. Roman Christians could not agree on various aspects of ritual and doctrine.

45. What occurred within the agricultural system at the end of the Roman empire?
    a. The decline of slave labor resulted in the return to primarily small independent farmsteads.
    b. The incidence of plagues drove people from the cities into the countryside and resulted in an intensification of the agricultural economy of the later Roman empire.
    c. As life became more precarious, many farmers surrendered full control of their estates and clustered around the protection of large landlords.
    d. The state undertook control of the agricultural economy and established state farms staffed by slaves.

46. Which of the following was the result of the fall of the Roman empire?
    a. Despite the collapse of classical Mediterranean civilization, the basic cultural unity of the region was retained.
    b. The collapse of the Roman empire led to cultural regression throughout the region of Mediterranean civilization.
    c. Rome's fall split the unity of the Mediterranean lands that had been won through Hellenistic culture and then the Roman empire.
    d. Rome's fall was devastating in its eastern half, but the culture of the western regions was fundamentally unaffected.

DOCUMENT-BASED QUESTION

 Read the Document on MyHistoryLab:

A practice document-based question for Part 2 is available on MyHistoryLab.

CONTINUITY AND CHANGE-OVER-TIME ESSAY

Analyze continuities and changes in time from Qin China to Han China.

COMPARATIVE ESSAY

Analyze similarities and differences between the social organization of classical Mediterranean society to that of the other classical civilizations in India and China.

PART II

REVISITING
The Classical Period, 600 B.C.E.–600 C.E.: Uniting Large Regions

CONTACTS AND THEIR LIMITS

In contrast to the early river valley civilizations, which had no regular interregional exchange system (save possibly in the Indian Ocean), reasonably systematic contacts developed during the classical period linking China, India, the Middle East, and the Mediterranean. Some goods were shipped along sea routes in the Indian Ocean, reaching as far as Egypt via the Red Sea. Important overland routes—the routes historians have labeled collectively as the Silk Road—brought goods from western China through central Asia to the Middle East, where they could also be trans-shipped to the Mediterranean. Important systems connected south Indian merchants and some Hindu and Buddhist missionaries to various parts of southeast Asia. Ethiopians in northeastern Africa traded actively with both the Mediterranean and the Middle East.

A few decades ago, archeologists, excavating the ruins of Roman Pompeii, found an ivory carving of a woman made at Taxila in what is now northwestern Pakistan. This find confirmed the importance of trade links between Rome and south Asia. Taxila had been part of the Hellenistic orbit established by Alexander

The enormous crater of Mount Vesuvius in Italy that erupted in 70 B.C.E., burying the town of Pompeii. Pompeii's ruins, later excavated, would be part of the Roman heritage to the modern world.

the Great, and exchanges with the Mediterranean continued thereafter. Taxila was also a major center along the Silk Road, serving as a link not only to the Mediterranean but also to east and southeast Asia. New levels of long-distance commerce gave many elites an active taste for goods, like silk, produced in distant places.

Improvements in technology, particularly for the fuller use of draft animals, began to contribute to transportation, along with the important road systems constructed by leaders in Persia, China, and the Mediterranean. After about 200 B.C.E., for example, the Chinese improved the harnesses used for horses, developing straps that would not choke the horse. These horse collars facilitated trade within China, but also on the routes to central Asia; ultimately, but only centuries later, knowledge of the horse collar would also reach Europe. More widely important was the growing use of saddles, with major developments from about 500 B.C.E. onward. The first saddle knob seems to have been introduced in China around 200. Bareback riding continued, but increasingly saddles provided both greater comfort and maneuverability, in turn increasing the

Three Hindu goddesses appear in an intricate carving on a temple in India. Hindu art remains an active element in Indian culture.

utility of horses for travel and military purposes alike. Not only horses, but camels and donkeys played crucial roles in overland exchange.

Contacts had some wider effects, beyond trade itself. Knowledge of South Asian crops like cotton and rice spread to the Middle East, altering agricultural patterns there. We have seen that diseases also spread, particularly from South Asia, affecting population patterns in the Mediterranean and China as part of classical decline.

Besides the trade routes, two major episodes occurred that involved direct contact between different civilizations. Alexander the Great's conquests brought Greek culture into interaction with those of Persia and India, as well as with Egypt. We have seen that Indian artists imitated Greek styles in their own work. Greeks and Indians both gained new mathematical knowledge (though it is intriguing that the Greeks did not adopt Indian numbering which, later transmitted to Europe by the Arabs, proved much superior to Greek and Roman numbering systems). Indian missionaries to the Middle East, although failing to establish Buddhism, may have influenced ethical thought in the later Roman empire and, through this, Christianity.

Interest in Asian goods also motivated Rome, although with less wide-ranging results. Once they controlled Egypt, the Romans established regular Indian Ocean expeditions from the Red Sea. Small groups of Roman merchants, located in India in particular, demonstrated a desire for more direct access to Indian spices, particularly pepper, and Chinese silks also helped motivate frequent wars with empires in Persia, although the Romans often fared badly and were unable to break through to the sources of the goods they valued. China, for its part, established regular diplomatic relations with empires in Persia, largely to further direct trade. None of these interesting interactions, however, seems to have had significant results in terms of institutional or cultural exchange.

The second major contact, toward the end of the classical period, involved China's fascination with Indian Buddhism. Chinese knowledge of Buddhism initially spread as a result of Chinese merchant ventures into India; later, religious students were sent directly. This was the only major case of successful outside influence on Chinese culture until very recent times.

These developments were exceedingly important. They also had serious limits. Interregional trade was certainly vital to some of the trading hubs in central Asia, such as Samarkand, but it had relatively little economic importance to societies like China. It was nothing compared to the growth of production for China's internal trade. There is no uncontested evidence that anyone traveled all the way from Rome to China, and Roman knowledge of China (as well as Chinese knowledge of Rome) was extremely hazy. There was trade, but no interaction between Chinese and Roman culture or technology. The two cases of direct exchange between civilizations described above are fascinating but they also stand out as unusual. And the lasting effects of the Hellenistic experience in northwestern India are questionable. Even in art, after about two centuries, Mediterranean influence seems to have disappeared, and stylistic differences once again became apparent.

So, while contacts advanced significantly in this period, the primary framework for the major societies remained internal. The classical civilizations developed largely separately. The most important kinds of contacts occurred *within* the civilizations, not among them: the careful, sometimes tense mixing of the northern Chinese with the people in the newer territories in the south; the partial extension of Greek culture to the western Mediterranean and portions of the Middle East and north Africa; the spread of Hinduism and the caste system southward on the Indian subcontinent. These contacts were vital to the formation of larger civilizational areas, which was the fundamental feature of the classical period. Clearly, far more energy went into this process than into interregional linkages at this stage in world history.

CRITICAL THEMES

The classical period added important dimensions to a number of central themes in world history. A number of social systems gained greater organization and also cultural support, beginning with the Indian caste system but extending also to Mediterranean slavery and the Confucian ideas about social order in China. State building won new attention, particularly in the construction of empires, though here too regional differences require careful comparison. More intense economic activity, including pressures applied by political leaders, contributed to environmental changes, as deforestation expanded and certain regions were over-farmed. Ultimately, probably the most important single thematic category in the period involved the elaboration of wider cultural systems—the new religions and philosophies and their links to artistic production. The systems were important at the time and proved to have tremendous durability, in many cases outlasting the classical societies themselves.

CRITICAL THINKING QUESTIONS

1. What were the main differences between the classical period and the previous period of early civilizations? What were some of the causes of change?
2. What kinds of sources help us understand gender relationships during the classical period? What kinds of additional evidence would be desirable?
3. What were the main causes of the success of Confucianism as a cultural system in classical China?
4. What were the primary limitations on contacts among the main civilization areas in the classical period?
5. What were the main similarities and differences in patterns of decline, in the main civilizations of the classical period?

The Postclassical Period, 600–1450: New Faith and New Commerce

PART III

Hagia Sophia, Istanbul, Turkey. The great cathedral symbolized the growing importance of religion.

PART OUTLINE

Chapter 7   The First Global Civilization: The Rise and Spread of Islam

Chapter 8   Abbasid Decline and the Spread of Islamic Civilization to South and Southeast Asia

Chapter 9   African Civilizations and the Spread of Islam

Chapter 10 Civilization in Eastern Europe: Byzantium and Orthodox Europe

Chapter 11 A New Civilization Emerges in Western Europe

Chapter 12 The Americas on the Eve of Invasion

Chapter 13 Reunification and Renaissance in Chinese Civilization: The Era of the Tang and Song Dynasties

Chapter 14 The Spread of Chinese Civilization: Japan, Korea, and Vietnam

Chapter 15 The Last Great Nomadic Challenges: From Chinggis Khan to Timur

Chapter 16 The World in 1450: Changing Balance of World Power

THE OVERVIEW: THE WORLD MAP CHANGES

The big changes in the period 600–1450 did not involve political boundaries. They involved the spread of the major world religions—Buddhism, Christianity, and Islam—across political and cultural borders and the development of new, more regular systems of trade that connected much of Asia, Africa, and Europe.

In some ways, an age characterized by faith and trade may seem contradictory. Indeed, many religious leaders looked down on merchants as likely to be seduced from a life of piety by the lure of wealth. But in fact the spread of trade often helped disseminate religion, and confidence in a divine order helped merchants to take risks.

The maps included here show the surge of Buddhism, Christianity, and Islam from their initial centers and the expansion of Afro-Eurasian trade around the same period. While Buddhism and Christianity started well before this period, they gained new vigor as the classical empires collapsed. Islam, which spread most rapidly, was entirely new. All three religions involved active missionary efforts. All periodically benefited from government sponsorship and sometimes from military pressure as well. For example, conquerors might impose higher taxes on those they conquered who did not convert to the conquerors' religion, or they might forcibly expel "nonbelievers" from the territory. Through a combination of persuasion and pressure, many millions of people changed their beliefs about the world around them and about the goals of life. The religious beliefs they adopted during the postclassical period established the dominant religious frameworks that still prevail in Asia, Europe, and parts of Africa today.

During the postclassical period, systematic international trade developed that went far beyond the carrying capacity of the old Silk Road. The Indian Ocean and the Mediterranean Sea were the hubs of this trade, which brought northwestern Europe, west Africa, Japan, and other regions into the existing east–west trade routes between China and Egypt. Gradually and tentatively, these connections among societies (rather than separate developments within societies) began to shape world history in important ways.

Big Concepts

Along with, and partly because of, religious change, three Big Concepts help organize the understanding of the postclassical period. First, transregional communication and exchange networks expanded with important new routes added. Missionary activity and new seafaring technologies both contributed to this. Second, forms of state organization diversified, with centralized empires now juxtaposed to a variety of looser political structures. Third, several societies—headed by China—increased their productive capacity, with social consequences extending to the emergence of new urban centers and the experimentation with different forms of labor.

Mystical conversation between Sufic sheikhs. Sufi mysticism became an important element in Islam's missionary efforts.

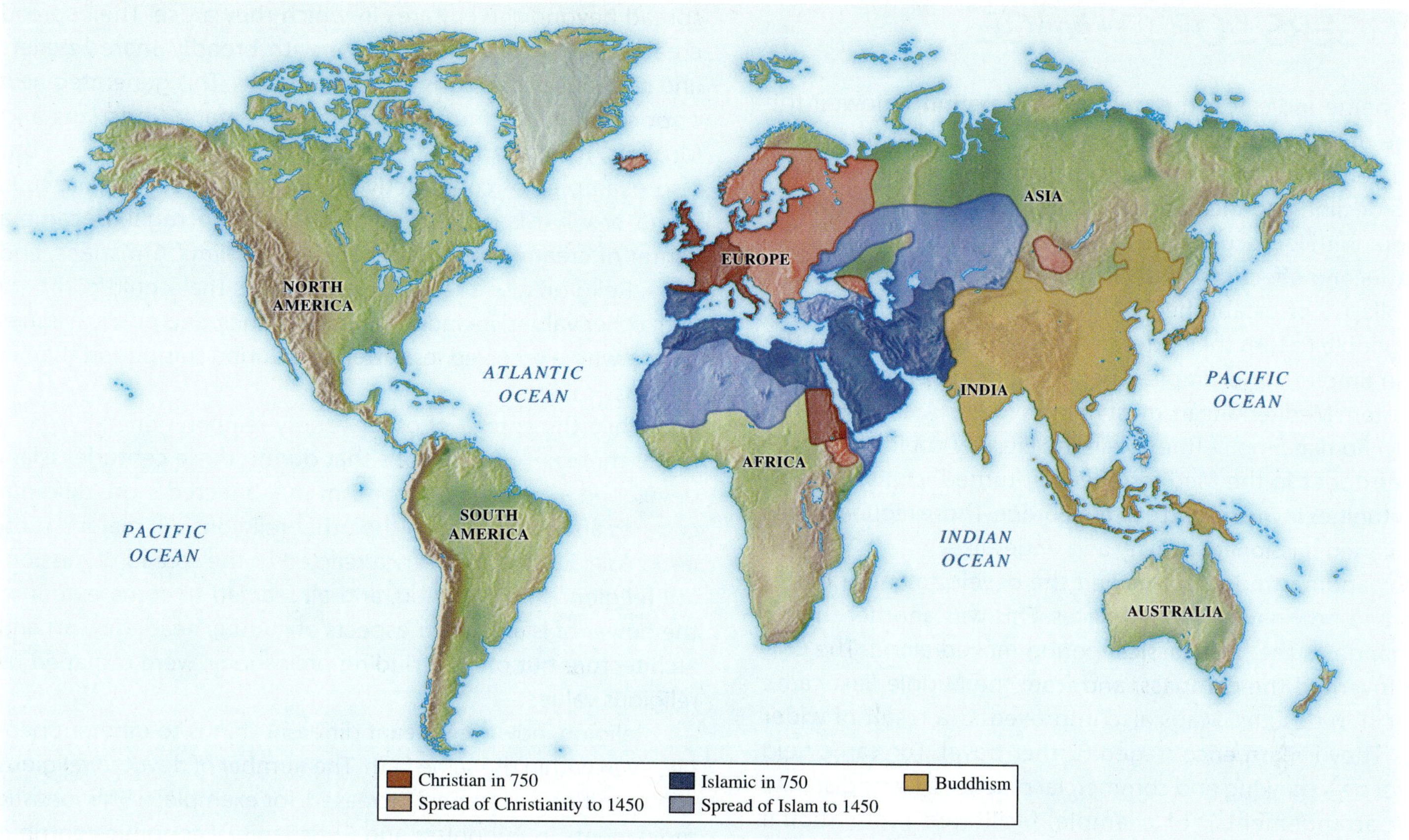

| Christian in 750 | Islamic in 750 | Buddhism |
| Spread of Christianity to 1450 | Spread of Islam to 1450 | |

Spread of Buddhism, Christianity, and Islam to c. 1450

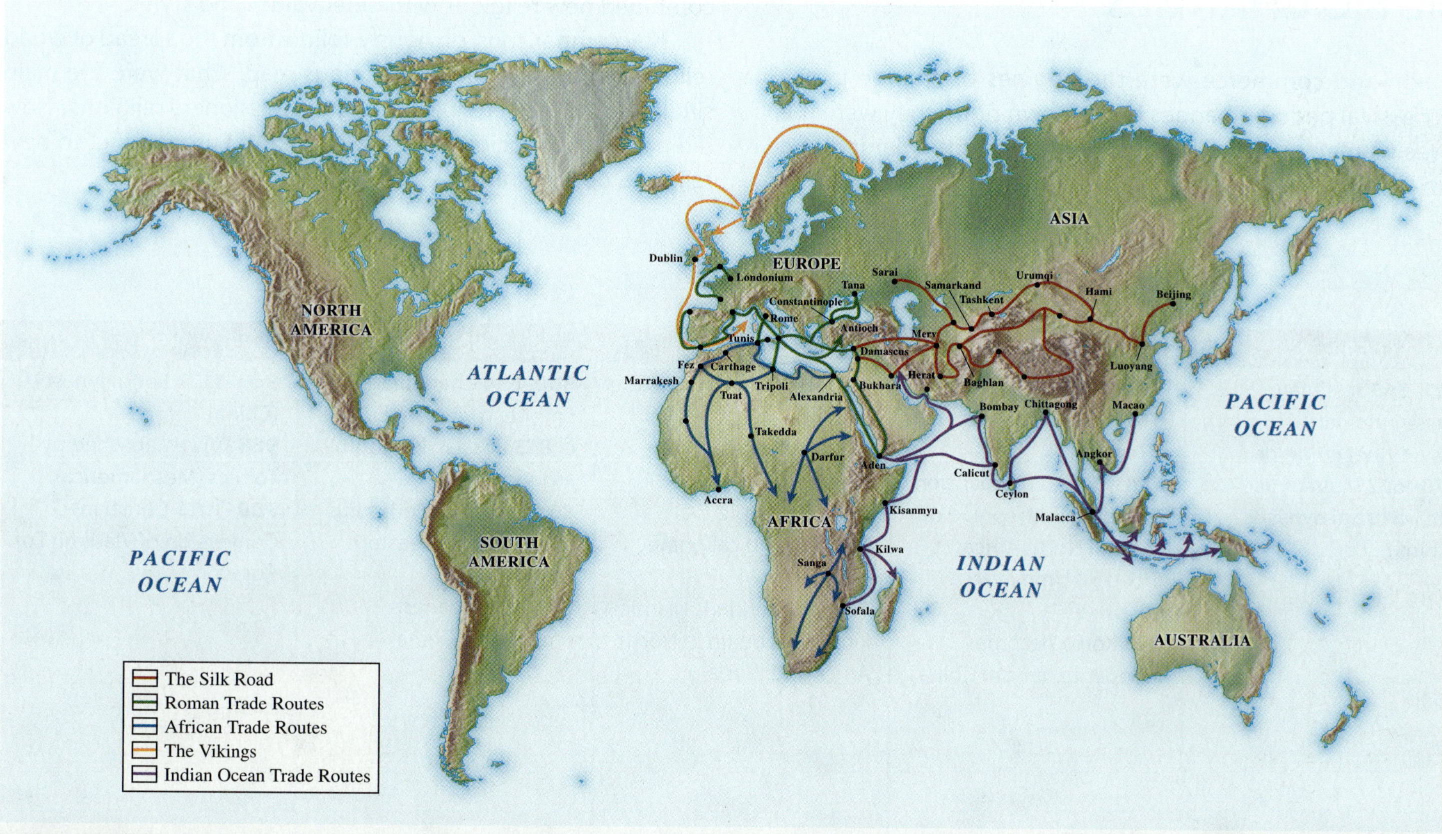

▬	The Silk Road
▬	Roman Trade Routes
▬	African Trade Routes
▬	The Vikings
▬	Indian Ocean Trade Routes

Main Routes of Afro-Eurasian Trade, c. 1250

PART III The Postclassical Period, 600–1450: New Faith and New Commerce   151

TRIGGERS FOR CHANGE

As its name indicates, the postclassical period followed the decline of the great classical empires. As areas that had previously been under the control of these empires experienced economic decline and increasing disorder, people turned toward religious faith for security, reassurance, and guidance.

A second effect of the decline of the classical empires was the collapse of established boundaries, which caused ambitious people to turn their attention to new areas. The fall of the Roman Empire, for example, opened up new opportunities in the eastern Mediterranean, most notably for the Arabs. When the Eastern Roman Empire (the Byzantine Empire) could not regain lost territories in the Mediterranean, it turned its attention to opportunities in Russia and eastern Europe. These reorientations encouraged missionary activity and trade alike.

Expanding trade encouraged the development of better ships and new navigational devices. This was another trigger for change as the postclassical period moved along. The Chinese invented the compass, and from the Middle East came better ship designs. Maps also improved as a result of wider trade. They in turn encouraged further travel. The same held true for new banking and commercial practices: Long-distance credit arrangements, for example, facilitated international exchange.

THE BIG CHANGES

Religion and commerce were the engines of change in the postclassical period. Changes in their own right, they were the causes of many other changes. Buddhism, Christianity, and Islam were the religions that showed the greatest capacity to spread beyond the cultures in which they arose. Their spread created larger groups of people with broadly shared beliefs and religious institutions than ever before. This generated new opportunities for mutual intolerance—many Christians and Muslims, particularly, developed disdain for each other—but also examples of constructive tolerance. Under Islamic rule, Iberia or what is present day Spain and Portugal, became a center of creative interaction among Muslims, Christians, and Jews. Religion also created new loyalties that could compete with other values, including political values, and political issues on the whole received less attention during this period than in the classical era.

While the spread of otherworldly religion generally was a major theme, it was obvious that during these centuries Islam developed a particular dynamism that affected more different cultures and peoples than the other religions. All major societies in Asia, Europe, and Africa reacted to the spread of missionary religions in this period, and all reacted to some extent to the power of Islam. Other aspects of culture, headed by art and architecture but often including philosophy, were reshaped by religious values.

Religion, however, meant different things to different people, even within the same faith. The number of devoted religious communities and leaders increased, for example, with monastic movements in Buddhism and Christianity. Economic contributions to religious institutions sometimes outstripped tax payments to governments. But many people combined religion with other interests, including commercial life. And most peoples combined new religions with older values and styles.

Key comparisons, obviously, follow from the spread of world religions and the changing religious map. What were the main similarities and differences among the missionary religions? How did each major society in Africa, Asia, and Europe react to new religious opportunities?

500 C.E.	600 C.E.	700 C.E.	800 C.E.	900 C.E.
527–565 Justinian, Eastern Roman (Byzantine) Emperor	**610–613** Origins of Islam	**711** First Islamic incursions into India	**800–814** Charlemagne's Empire in western Europe	**960–1127** Song dynasty (China)
570–632 Muhammad	**618–907** Tang dynasty (China)	**718** Byzantines defeat Arab attack on Constantinople	**c. 855** Russian kingdom around Kiev	**968** Tula established by Toltecs (Mesoamerica)
589–618 Sui dynasty (China)	**634–750** Arab Expansion in Middle East; spread of Islam in North Africa	**750** Abbasid caliphate founded	**864** Cyril and Methodius missionaries in eastern Europe	**980–1015** Christian Conversion of Vladimir I of Russia
	661–750 Ummayad Caliphate	**777** Independent Islamic kingdoms begin in North Africa and Iberia	**878** Last Japanese embassy to China	
	668 Korea becomes independent from China			

THE TRANSREGIONAL NETWORK

The development of regular trade created a series of interlocking trade routes that joined key parts of Asia, Africa, and Europe. These built on connections developed in the classical period, but they were more elaborate. The Arabs opened the period with new activities in the Indian Ocean, reaching from the Middle East to south and southeast Asia and to China; fairly soon, clusters of Arab traders located even in Chinese port cities. The Byzantine Empire also linked into this trade. As a result, goods like silks, porcelains, and wine traded among elite customers throughout these core regions.

But new routes linked additional regions into the network. Sub-Saharan West Africa traded overland to North Africa, and thence to the Middle East, thanks in part to improvements in the use of camels. Another route, on Africa's Indian Ocean coast, relied on regular shipping from present-day Tanzania north to the Middle East. Overland traders, using rivers in part, worked from Scandinavia down to Constantinople and the Arab centers, a third north-south route. A bit later, merchants used coastal shipping or overland and river trade to move from northwestern Europe into the Mediterranean and contacts with Arab commerce. Japan, finally, began a regular exchange with Korea and China. On the whole, the more distant regions provided less-processed goods in world trade, including gold, exotic animals, forest products, and spices.

Trade facilitated other kinds of exchanges—including, of course, missionary religions. It brought knowledge of new technologies. A number of Chinese inventions, first paper (when Islamic troops captured some papermakers in western China), then printing and explosives spread to the Middle East and on to Europe. Early in the postclassical period, this exchange was very slow (although faster than in previous centuries), but it became more rapid as time went on. At the end of the postclassical period, key Chinese inventions like printing and explosives moved westward more swiftly.

Ideas spread as well. Thanks to trade, Indian mathematics, including the numbering system, spread to the Middle East. Then Arab mathematics, blending earlier Greek and Indian achievements with Arab innovations, reached Western Europe (where people thought Arabs had invented the numbering system). Food exchange was another key development, sometimes helping to create a hint of consumer culture dependent on transregional exchange. A taste for tea developed widely in Asia. Granulated sugar, developed earlier in India and easily manufactured and transported, had already reached Persia. Arabs learned about it during their initial conquests, and spread awareness to places like North Africa and Spain. Europeans encountered it in turn—with the first English-language mention of sugar dating from 1099. The spread of disease accelerated as well. In the 14th century a new epidemic of bubonic plague—the "Black Death"—moved from China through the Middle East to Europe, killing up to a third of the population in many areas.

The interregional trade of the postclassical era was not what we think of as a global economy today. Fewer societies were involved, and the volume and range of trade were far lower. However, despite downsides like disease, the wide exchanges of the postclassical era had major effects, including new opportunities for imitation. Societies newer to interregional trade quickly realized that they could use their new contacts to copy more advanced forms, not only in technology but also in culture. The result was a major, often quite explicit, effort at borrowing that added up to another innovation in the period as a whole.

Wider patterns of trade facilitated a new breed of long-distance travelers, particularly by the final centuries of the postclassical period. These included merchants and missionaries who went from one part of Asia to another, or through the Indian Ocean basin, or into Africa or eastern Europe from centers elsewhere.

1000 C.E.	1100 C.E.	1200 C.E.	1300 C.E.	1400 C.E.
1000 Ghana Empire at its height (West Africa)	**c. 1100** Invention of explosive powder (China)	**1200** Rise of empire of Mali (West Africa)	**1320s** Europeans first use cannons in war	**1400** End of Polynesian expeditions
1054 Schism between Eastern and Western Christianity	**1150** Disintegration of Toltec Empire	**1206** Delhi sultanate in India	**1320–1340** Bubonic plague breaks out in Gobi desert and spreads to other parts of Asia and west to the Mediterranean and Europe.	**1405–1433** Chinese trading expeditions
1055 Seljuk Turks control Abbasid caliphate	**1150–1350** Spread of Gothic style; scholasticism in western Europe	**1231–1392** Mongols rule Korea		**1439** Portugal captures Azores Islands
1066 Norman conquest of England; rise of feudal monarchy in western Europe	**1185–1333** Kamakura Shogunate (Japan)	**1236** Capture of Baghdad by Mongols; end of Abbasid caliphate	**1325** Rise of Aztec Empire (Mesoamerica)	**1453** Turks capture Constantinople; end of Byzantine Empire
1096–1099 First Christian Crusade to Palestine		**1260** Death of Sundiata	**1338–1453** Hundred Years' War in Europe	**1471–1493** Peak of Inca Empire
		1265 First English parliament	**1350** Rise of Incas (Andes)	
		1279–1368 Mongol Empire in China	**1392–1910** Yi dynasty (Korea)	
		1290s Islam begins to spread to southeast Asia		

Travel reflected new contacts, with motives ranging from religious pilgrimage to simple delight in adventure, but travelers' accounts also helped motivate still further ventures. Extensive knowledge of Arabic was a key facilitator of contacts, serving as something of a first-world language. At an extreme, contacts could even lead to broader visions of a better world: a Chinese observer in the 14th century proclaimed (with a great deal of exaggeration), "civilization had spread everywhere, and no more barriers existed.... Brotherhood among peoples has certainly reached a new plane."

We live today in a period of rapidly intensifying contacts among all the world's major societies, and the process is increasingly referred to as globalization. Globalization has many new features, starting with dramatic communications technologies like the Internet. We increasingly realize, however, that contemporary globalization was prepared by previous periods in which interactions among major regions expanded. The postclassical period marked a major separation between earlier eras, in which contacts among different regions were slow or occasional, into a situation in which trade, travel and exchange created significant new, often routinized, influences on the ways individual societies developed. Defining the relationship between the systems of interaction in the postclassical period and later patterns provides a key way to map the process of change in world history.

The transcontinental network itself compelled many societies in Afro-Eurasia to decide on how to organize their participation in trade and exchange, and how to take advantage of the opportunities involved. No society responded in exactly the same way—comparing responses is an obvious assignment in analyzing the postclassical period—and some societies changed their responses over time. The spread of world religions, which created huge new areas of shared faith, but also new divisions among the religions themselves, contributed to but also complicated the evolution of the transcontinental network.

CONTINUITY AND LIMITATIONS

Change, including the formation of the transcontinental network, inevitably affected different societies to different degrees. Continuities combined with change. Even though the classical empires had collapsed, the successes of classical civilization encouraged many people to maintain or retrieve classical forms. China eagerly revived the structures of its classical age, including the empire, the bureaucracy, and Confucianism. It was touched by Islam and Buddhism, but ultimately it limited the influence of outside religions. China was not a changeless society—its growing participation in interregional trade proved its capacity to take advantage of new opportunities—but continuity remained extremely important.

The Middle East underwent great change as a result of the rise of Islam, but it also maintained continuities. Hellenistic science interacted with Islam, leading to important philosophical discussions of the relationship between science and faith. Earlier practices, such as the veiling of women in the cities, were revived. Although Islam opposed the enslavement of fellow Muslims, slavery continued to be a major component of social and labor systems over much of Afro-Eurasia, another sign of the hold of earlier traditions in the region.

Continuities also showed in the blending of traditional forms with the missionary religions. Christian architecture long used Greco-Roman styles. Buddhism adapted to Chinese values, for example, by placing more emphasis on the family loyalties of women. And there were sweeping innovations in social structures or even political forms during the postclassical centuries. The expansion of a merchant class affected social structure, but landlords remained dominant in most societies and peasants made up the bulk of the population. In key areas slavery or (in India) the caste system also maintained or revived older social institutions. Large political units developed in a few places, but outside of China and the Byzantine Empire, polities were mainly loosely organized.

Finally, major areas were still outside the system shaped by world religions and interregional trade. Most notably, the Americas and Pacific Oceania, although scenes of significant developments, operated on separate dynamics and had few if any contacts with the rest of the world.

IMPACT ON DAILY LIFE: WOMEN

The postclassical period saw an intriguing tension that affected conditions for women in many parts of Afro-Eurasia. On the one hand, the major religions all insisted that women were spiritually equal to men—that they had souls or shared in the divine essence. This was a huge innovation. And religious change was not a matter of ideals alone. Buddhist leaders in Japan argued for women's importance. Islam established new rights for women, including property ownership. Buddhism and Christianity both established religious communities for women, giving them not only new forms of expression but also new leadership roles. As these religions spread, many women gained new positions and modes of expression through religious life. On the other hand, the condition of women also deteriorated during this period. Many scholars have argued that growing trade and urban prosperity reduced women's role in political and economic life and created conditions in which upper-class women were treated as ornaments. So, although religion provided new outlets for women, the spiritual focus might also distract them from other issues such as newer gender inequalities.

Other changes were less favorable to women. Footbinding—the clearest attempt to make women more purely ornamental—spread in China. In India the practice of sati, in which some widows threw themselves on their husbands' funeral pyres to demonstrate their grief, spread somewhat, mainly within the highest castes. As Islamic society matured in the Middle East, women were increasingly secluded and excluded from active roles in public life. But in other Islamic societies, especially in Africa and southeast Asia, this was less true. At the same time, most historians conclude that the condition of women in western Europe had deteriorated by the later postclassical period, as judged, for example, by their greater exclusion from most skilled urban crafts. Thus, the postclassical period was an important one in women's history. New religions were important to many women, but new customs also limited opportunities for women to a greater degree than in the classical era. In much of the world, at least the vestiges of these limitations survive to the present day.

TRENDS AND SOCIETIES IN THE EARLY MODERN PERIOD

Chapters 7 and 8 examine the surge of Islam, first in the Middle East and then in other parts of Asia. Chapter 9 describes the expansion of trade and civilization in sub-Saharan Africa, which had various facets, but the link to Islam and the Islamic trading system was crucial. Two dynamics developed in Europe; each had contacts (both creative and hostile) with Islam and certainly with interregional trade. In eastern Europe, as detailed in Chapter 10, Byzantine culture took root, while a newer society emerged in western Europe, as described in Chapter 11. Chapter 12 describes the major cultures that developed in the Americas and the contacts among them. Chapters 13 and 14 address developments in China and the expansion of Chinese influence in Japan, Korea, and Vietnam—key parts of the network of interregional trade.

The last two centuries of the postclassical period, as Arab power declined, saw important new developments. Chapter 15 describes the Mongol conquests in the 13th and 14th centuries that, for a time, revolutionized the political map of Asia and parts of Europe, accelerating and redefining interregional trade and other exchanges. The decline of the Mongols, and the end of a brief Chinese experiment in leading world trade, left the world poised for further innovation. Chapter 16 describes a transitional moment and the complex factors that would alter world balance yet again. ■

7
The First Global Civilization: The Rise and Spread of Islam

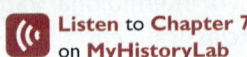
Listen to Chapter 7 on MyHistoryLab

LEARNING OBJECTIVES

7.1 What were the major ways in which the city of Mecca interacted with the bedouin tribes that lived in the desert areas around it? p. 158

7.2 Which aspects of Muhammad's religious message do you think accounted for its powerful appeal to both urban dwellers and nomadic peoples in Arabia and beyond? p. 163

7.3 What were the key factors that made possible the rapid Arab conquests in the Middle East, Central Asia, and North Africa? p. 166

7.4 In what ways was the Islamic religion a faith that elevated the status and opportunities of women, and what were the constraints on this process? p. 174

In any ranking of the greatest survivors in world history, 'Abd al-Rahman I would have to be near or at the top of the list. The grandson of the last distinguished caliph (leader of the Muslim faithful) of the Umayyad dynasty, he had barely survived the vengeful slaughter of the many male descendants of that first house of Muslim rulers by the warriors of the 'Abbasid coalition that had seized power in 749. After narrowly escaping capture and beheading on his estate on the upper Euphrates River, 'Abd al-Rahman, dodging 'Abbasid pursuers and bounty hunters alike, fled through Syria and Palestine and across north Africa. After a half decade as fugitive, he

> View the **Closer Look** on **MyHistoryLab**: The Congregational Mosque

FIGURE **7.1** The graceful "horseshoe" arches of the Great Mosque at Córdoba in southern Spain provide a striking example of the sophistication and beauty of the arts and architecture produced by the fusion of Muslim, Jewish, and Christian cultural traditions in Islamic Iberia from the 8th to the 15th centuries.

finally found uneasy sanctuary in Morocco at the western end of the lands to which Islam had spread to that point in time. In 755, the 24-year-old crossed the narrow Straits of Gibraltar that separated north Africa from the Iberian peninsula. Rallying to his cause several hundred Syrians, whose homelands had been the mainstay of the vanquished Umayyad dynasty and who had joined in earlier Arab-Berber campaigns to conquer the peninsula, 'Abd al-Rahman began his quest to become master of Iberia.

Despite continuing resistance by rivals and rebels from within and invasions plotted by Abbasid rulers in distant Baghdad, 'Abd al-Rahman steadily consolidated his control over Iberia. His early victories, particularly the capture of Córdoba in 756, secured his position as the paramount lord on the peninsula within years of his arrival. In the following decades as the capital of a flourishing Muslim kingdom, Córdoba grew rapidly into one of the most cosmopolitan and celebrated cities in the Mediterranean world. Córdoba boasted well-paved and well-lit streets, houses with running water, one of the world's finest universities, and a library with over 400,000 volumes at a time when the largest collections in Christian Europe contained a few thousand at best. But Córdoba's crowning glory was its great mosque. It was famed for its hundreds of splendid marble columns topped by ornate horseshoe arches and its elaborately decorated vaulted ceilings, shown in Figure 7.1. But even more remarkable than its distinctive architecture and decoration were the ways in which the mosque encapsulated the exceptional synergy generated by cooperation among and the blending of the diverse peoples and cultures that came together in Islamic Spain.

Like the development of Muslim civilization more generally, the construction of the great mosque of Córdoba owed much to earlier and even contemporary rival civilizations. It was built on the ruins of a Christian church, and many of the pillars that supported the signature horseshoe arches were taken from Roman ruins. And although the influence of Syrian-style Islamic architecture is apparent, the mosque's bell tower and thick walls decorated with geometric stone carvings shared key features with the Romanesque churches then found throughout Latin Christendom. Much of the mosque's stonework, and especially its intricate mosaics, were crafted by Christian Orthodox artisans from Constantinople, and its architects, laborers, and overseers were drawn from Arab and Berber Muslim migrants as well as the majority Christian population of Iberia.

The cross-cultural influences and interethnic and religious cooperation that played such vital roles in the construction of the grand mosque of Córdoba were also prominent features of Muslim Iberian society as a whole. Under the Muslims the peninsula became a key locus for the transmission of ideas, technology, and material culture between the Middle East, north Africa, and Europe. Arab and Berber migrants brought paper (originally invented, as we have seen, in China) and refined steel working to al-Andalus (the Arab name for Iberia), and their descendants carried leather working skills back to Morocco and the broader Muslim world. Muslim migrants to Iberia also introduced sophisticated irrigation systems and a wide variety of staple foods and plants, including oranges, sugar cane, and cotton.

Jews and Christians, as "people of the book," were allowed in Iberia as in the rest of the Muslim world to worship openly, to regulate their everyday lives according to their own laws, and to collaborate with Muslims in trade, scholarship, and the arts. Arab and Jewish scholars in Córdoba, Seville, and other urban centers, for example, were renowned throughout the Mediterranean for their translations of classic Greek texts. By the tenth and eleventh centuries, their collaboration had become pivotal for the recovery in Latin Christendom of the writings of the great Greek

600 C.E.	620 C.E.	640 C.E.	660 C.E.	680 C.E.
c. 570 Birth of the prophet Muhammad	**622** Muhammad's flight (hijra) from Mecca to Medina	**644–656** Rule of Caliph Uthman	**661–680** Mu'awiya	**680** Death of Ali's son Husayn at Karbala
597–626 Wars between the Byzantine and Sasanian (Persian) empires	**624–627** Wars between the followers of Muhammad and the Quraysh of Mecca	**656–661** Rule of Caliph Ali; first civil war	**661–750** Umayyad caliphate	**680–692** Second civil war
610 Muhammad's first revelations	**628** Muslim–Meccan Truce			**744–750** Third civil war; Abbasid revolt
613 Muhammad begins to preach the new faith	**630** Muhammad enters Mecca in triumph			**750** Abbasid caliphate begins
	632 Death of Muhammad			
	632–634 Rule of Caliph Abu Bakr			
	633–634 Ridda Wars in Arabia			
	634–643 Early Muslim conquests in the Byzantine Empire			
	634–644 Rule of Caliph Umar			
	637 Arab invasion and destruction of Sasanian Empire			

philosopher and scientist Aristotle in such critical areas as astronomy, mathematics, geography, and meteorology. Muslim Spain was a key source of the tradition of wandering minstrels or troubadours, who carried music, fables, and the notion of romantic love northward into Christian Europe. It was also a land where upper-class, educated Muslim, Christian, and Jewish women flourished as poets, musicians, scribes, and university students. ∎

In the chapter that follows we shall see that in many ways Muslim Iberia was a microcosm—albeit a very forward-looking one—of much of the Islamic world in its early centuries. Although spread initially mainly by nomadic camel-herding peoples of Arabia, Islam was from its inception a religion of the towns and trade. Muhammad himself was a successful caravan leader before he began to receive the divine revelations that transformed him into the founder of one of the great world religions. As in Iberia, conversion to Islam as it spread from Arabia was generally peaceful and voluntary, and in the early decades the faithful were, if anything, reluctant to recruit new believers. Even after the new faith came to undergird vast and expansive empires, such as those fashioned by the Umayyads and Abbasids, adherents of other religions based on divinely inspired scriptures—from the Jews and Christians to the Hindus—prayed and practiced their rituals openly, and their communities very often flourished economically. As was the case in Iberia, many of the most brilliant contributions of early Islamic civilization came from the openness of Arabs to borrowing from the ancient civilizations that surrounded the Arab heartlands. The Arabs' absorption and then innovations on the sciences, arts, and technologies of Greece, Rome, Byzantium, Persia, Egypt, India, and China were essential to the rise of the first genuinely global civilization in human history.

DESERT AND TOWN: THE HARSH ENVIRONMENT OF THE PRE-ISLAMIC ARABIAN WORLD

> Before the rise of Islam, Arabia was a peripheral desert wasteland whose once great trading cities had fallen on hard times. The sparse population of the Arabian peninsula was divided into rival tribes and clans that worshiped local gods.

7.1 What were the major ways in which the city of Mecca interacted with the bedouin tribes that lived in the desert areas around it?

The Arabian Peninsula (Map 7.1) was a very unlikely birthplace for the first global civilization. Much of the area is covered by some of the most inhospitable desert in the world. An early traveler wrote of the region,

MAP 7.1 Arabia and Surrounding Areas Before and During the Time of Muhammad Although much of Arabia was separated by vast deserts from surrounding classical civilizations, as the map shows it maintained contact by sea in the west and south and through camel caravans into Palestine and Syria.

All about us is an iron wilderness; a bare and black shining beach of heated volcanic stones... a vast bed and banks of rusty and basaltic bluish rocks... stubborn as heavy matter, as iron and sounding like bell metal; lying out eternally under the sand-driving desert wind.

In the scrub zones on the edges of the empty quarters, or uninhabitable desert zones, a wide variety of **bedouin** or nomadic, cultures had developed over the centuries, based on camel and goat herding. In oases like that pictured in Figure 7.2, which dotted the dry landscape, towns and agriculture flourished on a limited scale. Only in the coastal regions of the far south had extensive agriculture, sizable cities, and regional kingdoms developed in ancient times. Over much of the rest of the peninsula, the camel nomads, organized in tribes and clans, were dominant. Yet in the rocky

Bedouin [BEHD-oo-ihn] Nomadic pastoralists of the Arabian peninsula; culture based on camel and goat nomadism; early converts to Islam.

CHAPTER 7 The First Global Civilization: The Rise and Spread of Islam

FIGURE 7.2 With their supply of water, shade, and date palms, oases like this one in Egypt have long been key centers of permanent settlement and trade in the desert. Major towns usually grew around the underground springs and wells or small rivers that fed the oases. Travelers' and traders' caravans stopped at the oases to water their camels and horses and to rest and eat after their arduous treks through the desert. As points of concentration of wealth, food, and precious water, oases were tempting targets for raids by bedouin bands.

regions adjacent to the Red Sea, several trading towns had developed that played pivotal roles in the emergence of Islam.

Although the urban roots of Islam have often been stressed by writers on Muslim civilization, the bedouin world in which the religion arose shaped the career of its prophet, his teachings, and the spread of the new beliefs. In fact, key towns such as Mecca and Medina were largely extensions of the tribal culture of the camel nomads. Their populations were linked by kinship to bedouin peoples. For example, Mecca had been founded by bedouins and at the time of Muhammad was ruled by former bedouin clans. The safety of the trade routes on which the towns depended was in the hands of the nomadic tribes that lived along the vulnerable caravan routes to the north and south. In addition, the town dwellers' social organization, which focused on clan and family, and their culture—including language and religion—were much like those of the nomads.

Clan Identity, Clan Rivalries, and the Cycle of Vengeance

The harsh desert and scrub environment of Arabia gave rise to forms of social organization and a lifestyle that were similar to those of other nomadic peoples. Bedouin herders lived in kin-related clan groups in highly mobile tent encampments. Clans, in turn, were clustered in larger tribal groupings, but these were rarely congregated together and then only in times of war or severe crisis. The struggle for subsistence in the unforgiving Arabian environment resulted in a strong dependence on and loyalty to one's family and clan. Survival depended on cooperation with and support from kin. To be cut off from them or expelled from the clan encampment was in most cases fatal. The use of watering places and grazing lands, which were essential to maintaining the herds on which bedouin life depended, was regulated by clan councils. But there could be wide disparities of wealth and status within clan groups and between clans of the same tribe. Although normally elected by councils of elder advisors, the **shaykhs**, or leaders of the tribes and clans, were almost always men with large herds, several wives, many children, and numerous retainers. The shaykhs' dictates were enforced by bands of free warriors whose families made up a majority of a given clan group. Beneath the warriors were slave families, often the remnants of rival clans defeated in war, who served the shaykhs or the clan as a whole.

shaykhs [shAYks] Leaders of tribes and clans within bedouin society; usually men with large herds, several wives, and many children.

Clan cohesion was reinforced by fierce inter-clan rivalries and struggles to control vital pasturelands and watering places. If the warriors from one clan found those from another clan drawing water from one of their wells, they were likely to kill them. Wars often broke out as a result of one clan's encroaching on the pasture areas of another clan. In a culture in which one's honor depended on respect for one's clan, the flimsiest pretexts could lead to inter-clan violence. For instance, an insult to a warrior in a market town, the theft of a prize stallion, or one clan's defeat in a horse race by another clan could end in battles between clan groups. All the men of a given clan joined in these fights, which normally were won by the side that could field several champions who were famed for their strength and skill with spears or bows and arrows.

These battles were fought according to a code of chivalry that was quite common in early cultures. Although battles usually were small in terms of the numbers involved, they were hard-fought and often bloody affairs. Almost invariably the battles either initiated or perpetuated clan feuds, which could continue for hundreds of years. The deaths of the warriors of one clan required that revenge be taken on the clan that had killed them. Their deaths led in turn to reprisals. This constant infighting weakened the bedouins in relation to the neighboring peoples and empires and allowed them to be manipulated and set against each other.

Towns and Long-Distance Trade

Although bedouin herders occupied most of the habitable portions of Arabia, farmers and town dwellers carved out small communities in the western and southern parts of the peninsula in the classical era. Foreign invasions and the inroads of bedouin peoples had all but destroyed these civilizations centuries before the birth of Muhammad. But a number of cities had developed farther north as links in the transcontinental trading system that stretched from the Mediterranean to east Asia. The most important of these cities was **Mecca**, located in the mountainous region along the Red Sea on the western coast of Arabia (Map 7.1). The town had been founded by the **Umayyad** clan of the **Quraysh** bedouin tribe, and members of the clan dominated its politics and commercial economy.

Mecca City located in mountainous region along Red Sea in Arabian peninsula; founded by Umayyad clan of Quraysh; site of Ka'ba; original home of Muhammad; location of chief religious pilgrimage point in Islam.

Umayyad [oo-MY-yad] Clan of Quraysh that dominated politics and commercial economy of Mecca; clan established a dynasty under this title as rulers of Islam, 661 to 750.

Quraysh [koo-RAYSH] Tribe of bedouins that controlled Mecca in 7th century c.e.

The wealth and status of Mecca and its merchant elite were enhanced by the fact that the city was the site of the **Ka'ba**, one of the most revered religious shrines in pre-Islamic Arabia. Not only did the shrine attract pilgrims and customers for Mecca's bazaars, but at certain times of the year it was the focus of an obligatory truce in the inter-clan feuds. Freed from fears of assault by rival groups, merchants and bedouins flocked to the town to trade, exchange gossip, and taste the delights of city life.

Ka'ba Most revered religious shrine in pre-Islamic Arabia; located in Mecca; focus of obligatory annual truce among bedouin tribes; later incorporated as important shrine in Islam.

Northeast of Mecca was a town named Yathrib (Map 7.1) that later came to be known as **Medina**, or the city of the prophet Muhammad. Like most of the other towns in the peninsula, Medina was established in an oasis. Wells and springs made sedentary agriculture possible. In addition to wheat and other staples, Medina's inhabitants grew date palms, whose fruit and seeds (which were fed to camels) they traded to the bedouins. Medina was also engaged, although on a much smaller scale than Mecca, in the long-distance caravan trade that passed through Arabia. In contrast to Umayyad-dominated Mecca, control in Medina was contested by two bedouin and three Jewish clans. Their quarrels left the city a poor second to Mecca as a center of trade, and these divisions proved critical to the survival of the prophet Muhammad and the Islamic faith.

Medina Also known as Yathrib; town located northeast of Mecca; grew date palms whose fruit was sold to bedouins; became refuge for Muhammad following flight from Mecca (hijra).

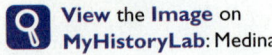

View the Image on MyHistoryLab: Medina

Marriage and Family in Pre-Islamic Arabia

Although the evidence is scant, there are several indications that women in pre-Islamic Arabian bedouin culture enjoyed greater freedom and higher status than those who lived in neighboring civilized centers, such as the Byzantine and Sasanian empires that then dominated the Middle East (Map 7.1). Women played key economic roles, from milking camels and weaving cloth to raising children. Because the men of the clan were often on the move, many tribes traced descent through the mother rather than the father. In some tribes, both men and women were allowed multiple marriage partners. To seal a marriage contract, the man was required to pay a bride-price to his prospective wife's family, rather than the woman's father sending a dowry or gift to the prospective husband. Unlike the women (especially those of elite status) in neighboring Syria and Persia, women in pre-Islamic Arabia were not secluded and did not wear veils. Their advice was highly regarded in clan and tribal councils, and they often composed poems that were the focus of bedouin cultural life in the pre-Islamic era.

Despite these career outlets, women were not by any means considered equal to men. They could not gain glory as warriors, the most prized occupation of the bedouins, and often they were little more than drudge laborers. Their status depended on the custom of individual clans and tribes rather than on legal codes. As a result, it varied widely from one clan or family to the next. Customary practices of property control, inheritance, and divorce heavily favored men. In the urban environment of trading centers such as Mecca, the rise of a mercantile elite and social stratification appear to have set back the position of women on the whole. The more stable family life of the towns led to the practice of tracing descent through the male line, and while men continued to practice polygamy, women were expected to be monogamous.

Poets and Neglected Gods

Because of the isolation of Arabia in the pre-Islamic age and the harshness and poverty of the natural environment, Arab material culture was not highly developed. Except in the far south, there was little art or architecture of worth. Even Mecca made little impression on the cosmopolitan merchants who passed through the city in caravans from the fabled cities of the ancient civilizations farther north. The main focus of bedouin cultural creativity in the pre-Islamic era was poetry, which was composed and transmitted orally because there was as yet no written language. Clan and tribal bards narrated poems that told of their kinsmen's heroics in war and the clan's great deeds. Some poets were said to have magical powers or to be possessed by demons. More than any other source, poems provide a vision of life and society in pre-Islamic Arabia. They tell of lovers spurned and passion consummated, war and vendettas, loyalty and generosity.

Bedouin religion was for most clans a blend of animism and polytheism, or the worship of many gods and goddesses. Some tribes, such as the Quraysh, recognized a supreme god named Allah. But they seldom prayed or sacrificed to **Allah**, concentrating instead on less abstract spirits who seemed more relevant to their daily lives. Both spirits and gods (for example, the moon god, Hubal) tended to be associated with night, a cool period when dew covered the earth, which had been parched by the blaze of the desert sun. Likewise, the worship of nature spirits focused on sacred caves, pure springs, and groves of trees—places where the bedouins could take shelter from the heat and wind. Religion appears to have had little to do with ethics. Rather, standards of morality and proper behavior were rooted in tribal customs and unwritten codes of honor.

How seriously the bedouins took their gods is also a matter of some doubt. Their lukewarm adherence is illustrated by the famous tale of a bedouin warrior who had set out to avenge his father's death at the hands of a rival clan. He stopped at an oracle along the way to seek advice by drawing arrows that indicated various courses of action he might take. Three times he drew arrows that advised him to abandon his quest for revenge. Infuriated by this counsel, he hurled the arrows at the idol of the oracle and exclaimed, "Accursed one! Had it been thy father who was murdered, thou would not have forbidden my avenging him."

Allah The Arab term for the high god in pre-Islamic Arabia that was adopted by the followers of Muhammad and the Islamic faith.

THE LIFE OF MUHAMMAD AND THE GENESIS OF ISLAM

7.2 Which aspects of Muhammad's religious message do you think accounted for its powerful appeal to both urban dwellers and nomadic peoples in Arabia and beyond?

In the 7th century the revelations of the prophet Muhammad provided the basis for the emergence of a new religion—Islam—in the Arabian peninsula. Although initially an Arab religion, in both beliefs and practices, Islam contained a powerful appeal that eventually made it one of the great world religions.

By the 6th century C.E., camel nomads were dominant throughout much of Arabia. The civilized centers to the south were in ruins, and trading centers such as Mecca and Medina depended on alliances with neighboring bedouin tribes to keep the caravan routes open. The constricted world of clan and kin, nomadic camp, blood feud, and local gods persisted despite the lure of the empires and cosmopolitan urban centers that stretched in a great arc to the north and east of the Arabian peninsula (see Map 7.1).

But pressures for change were mounting. Both the Byzantine and **Sasanian empires** struggled to assert greater control over the nomadic tribes of the peninsula. In addition, Arab peoples migrated into Mesopotamia and other areas to the north, where they came increasingly under foreign influence. From these regions, the influence of established monotheistic religions, especially Judaism and Christianity, entered Arabia. These new currents gave rise to a number of Arab prophets who urged the bedouin tribes to renounce idol worship and rely on a single, almighty god. The prophet **Muhammad** and the new religion that his revelations inspired in the early decades of the 7th century responded both to these influences flowing into Arabia and to related social dislocations that were disrupting Arab life.

Sasanian empires The dynasty that ruled Persia (contemporary Iran) in the centuries before the rise of Muhammad and the early decades of Islamic expansion.

The hardships of Muhammad's early life underscore the importance of clan ties in the Arabian world. He was born around 570 C.E. into a prominent clan of the Quraysh tribe, the Banu Hashim, in a bedouin encampment where he spent the first six years of his life. Because his father died before he was born, Muhammad was raised by his father's relatives. The loss of his father was compounded by the death of Muhammad's mother shortly after he went to live with her some years later. Despite these early losses, Muhammad had the good fortune to be born into a respected clan and powerful tribe. His paternal uncle, Abu Talib, was particularly fond of the boy and served as his protector and supporter through much of his early life. Muhammad's grandfather, who like other leading members of the clan was engaged in commerce, educated the young man in the ways of the merchant. With Abu Talib, Muhammad made his first caravan journey to Syria, where on this and later trips he met adherents of the Christian and Jewish faiths, whose beliefs and practices had a great impact on his teachings.

Muhammad Prophet of Islam; born c. 570 to Banu Hashim clan of Quraysh tribe in Mecca; raised by father's family; received revelations from Allah in 610 C.E. and thereafter; died in 632.

In his adolescence, Muhammad took up residence in Mecca. By his early 20s he was working as a trader for **Khadijah**, the widow of a wealthy merchant, whom he married some years later. His life as a merchant in Mecca and on the caravan routes exposed Muhammad to the world beyond Arabia and probably made him acutely aware of the clan rivalries that had divided the peoples of the region for millennia. He would also have become increasingly concerned about new forces undermining solidarity within the clans. The growth of the towns and trade had enriched some clan families and left others behind, often in poverty. It had also introduced a new source of tension between clan and tribal groupings because some clans, such as the Umayyads, grew rich on the profits from commerce, whereas others maintained their herding lifestyle.

As a trader and traveler, Muhammad would almost certainly have been aware of the new religious currents that were sweeping Arabia and surrounding areas in the early 7th century. Particularly notable among these was the spread of monotheistic ideas and a growing dissatisfaction with the old gods that had been venerated by the bedouin peoples. In Muhammad's time, several prophets had arisen, proclaiming a new faith for the Arabs.

Khadijah [kah-DEE-juh] (555–619) First wife of the prophet Muhammad, who had worked for her as a trader.

Although socially prominent, economically well off, and widely admired for his trading skills and trustworthiness, Muhammad grew increasingly distracted and dissatisfied with a life focused on material gain. He spent increasing amounts of time in meditation in the hills and wilderness that surrounded Mecca. In 610 or earlier, he received the first of many revelations, which his followers believe Allah transmitted to him through the angel Gabriel. These revelations were later written in Arabic and collected in the **Qur'an**. The teachings and injunctions of the Qur'an formed the basis of the new religion that Muhammad began to preach to his clan and the people of Mecca.

Qur'an [kuh-RAHN] Recitations of revelations received by Muhammad; holy book of Islam.

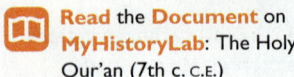
Read the Document on
MyHistoryLab: The Holy
Qur'an (7th c. C.E.)

Persecution, Flight, and Victory

At first Muhammad's following was small, consisting mainly of his wife, several members of his clan, and some servants and slaves. As his message was clarified with successive revelations, the circle of the faithful grew so that the Umayyad notables who dominated Meccan life saw him as a threat to their own wealth and power. Above all, the new faith threatened to supplant the gods of the Ka'ba, whose shrines had done so much to establish the city as a center of commerce and bedouin interchange. Although he was protected for a time by his own clan, Muhammad was increasingly threatened by the Umayyads, who plotted with other clans to murder him. It was clear that Muhammad must flee Mecca, but where was he to find refuge? Muhammad's reputation as a skillful and fair negotiator prepared the way for his successful flight from Umayyad persecution. The quarrels between the clans in the nearby city of Medina had set off increasingly violent clashes, and the oasis community was on the verge of civil war. Leaders of the bedouin clans in Medina sent a delegation to invite Muhammad, who was related to them on his mother's side, to mediate their disputes and put an end to the strife that had plagued the town.

Ali (c. 599–661) Cousin and son-in-law of Muhammad; one of orthodox caliphs; focus for Shi'a.

Clever ruses and the courage of his clansman **Ali**, who at one point took Muhammad's place and thus risked becoming the target of assassins, secured in 622 the safe passage of Muhammad and a small band of followers from Mecca to Medina. His *hijra* (HIH-jruh), or flight to Medina, marks the first year of the Islamic calendar. In Medina he was given a hero's welcome. He soon justified this warm reception by deftly settling the quarrels between the bedouin clans of the town. His wisdom and skill as a political leader won him new followers, who joined those who had accompanied him from Mecca as the core believers of the new faith.

In the eyes of the Umayyad notables, Muhammad's successes made him a greater threat than ever. Not only was he preaching a faith that rivaled their own, but his leadership was strengthening Mecca's competitor, Medina. Muslim raids on Meccan caravans provided yet another source of danger. Determined to put an end to these threats, the Quraysh launched a series of attacks in the mid-620s on Muhammad and his followers in Medina. These attacks led to several battles. In these clashes, Muhammad proved an able leader and courageous fighter.

The ultimate victory for Muhammad and his followers was signaled by a treaty with the Quraysh in 628, which included a provision granting the Muslims permission to visit the shrine at Ka'ba in Mecca during the season of truce. By then Muhammad's community had won many bedouin allies, and more than 10,000 converts accompanied him on his triumphal return to his hometown in 629. After proving the power of Allah, the single god he proclaimed, by smashing the idols of the shrine, Muhammad gradually won over the Umayyads and most of the other inhabitants of Mecca to the new faith.

Arabs and Islam

Although Islam was soon to become one of the great world religions, the beliefs and practices of the prophet Muhammad were initially adopted only by the Arab town dwellers and bedouins among whom he had grown up. There is a striking parallel here with early Christianity, which focused on Jewish converts. The new religion preached by Muhammad had much to offer the divided peoples of Arabia. It gave them a form of monotheism that belonged to no single tribe and transcended clan and class divisions. It provided a religion that was distinctly Arab in origin and yet the equal of the monotheistic faiths held by the Christians and Jews, who lived in the midst of the bedouin tribes. If anything, the monotheism preached by Muhammad was even more uncompromising than that of the Christians because it allowed no intermediaries between the individual and God. God was one; there were no saints, and angels were nothing more than messengers. In addition, there were no priests in the Christian or Jewish sense of the term.

umma Community of the faithful within Islam; transcended old tribal boundaries to create degree of political unity.

Islam offered the possibility of an end to the vendettas and feuds that had so long divided the peoples of Arabia and had undermined their attempts to throw off the domination of neighboring empires. The **umma**, or community of the faithful, transcended old tribal boundaries, and it made possible a degree of political unity undreamed of before Muhammad's time. The new religion provided a single and supernaturally sanctioned source of authority and discipline. With unity, the skills and energies that the bedouins had once channeled toward warring with each other were turned outward in a burst of conquest that is perhaps unmatched in human history in its speed and extent. From vassals, borderland warriors, or contemptible "savages" of the desert waste, the Arab bedouins were transformed into the conquerors and rulers of much of the Middle Eastern world.

The new religion also provided an ethical system that did much to heal the deep social rifts within Arabian society. Islam stressed the dignity of all believers and their equality in the eyes of Allah. It promoted a moral code that stressed the responsibility of the well-to-do and strong for the poor and weak, the aged and infirm. Payment of the **zakat**, a tax for charity, was obligatory in the new faith. In both his revelations and his personal behavior, Muhammad enjoined his followers to be kind and generous to their dependents, including slaves. He forbade the rich to exploit the poor through exorbitant rents or rates of interest for loans.

zakat Tax for charity; obligatory for all Muslims.

The prophet's teachings and the revelations of the Qur'an soon were incorporated into an extensive body of law that regulated all aspects of the lives of the Muslim faithful. Held accountable before Islamic law on earth, they lived in a manner that would prepare them for the Last Judgment, which in Islam, as in Christianity, would determine their fate in eternity. A stern but compassionate God and a strict but socially minded body of law set impressive standards for the social interaction between adherents of the new faith.

Universal Elements in Islam

Although only Arabs embraced the religion of Islam in its early years, from the outset it contained beliefs and practices that would give it a strong appeal to peoples at virtually all stages of social development and in widely varying cultural settings. Some of these beliefs—Islam's uncompromising monotheism, highly developed legal codes, egalitarianism, and strong sense of community—were the same as the attributes that had won it support among the peoples of Arabia. Its potential as a world religion was enhanced by the fact that most of the attributes of Islam were to some degree anticipated by the other Semitic religions, particularly Judaism and Christianity, with which Muhammad had contact for much of his life. He accepted the validity of the earlier divine revelations that had given rise to the Jewish and Christian faiths. He taught that the revelations he had received were a refinement of these earlier ones and that they were the last divine instructions for human behavior and worship.

FIGURE **7.3** The Ka'ba in Mecca, with masses of pilgrims. Each year tens of millions of the Muslim faithful from all around the world make the journey to the holy sites of Arabia. The rituals performed by pilgrims at Mecca and Medina are key religious duties for all who can afford to travel to the holy cities.

five pillars The obligatory religious duties of all Muslims; confession of faith, prayer, fasting during Ramadan, zakat, and hajj.

Ramadan Islamic month of religious observance requiring fasting from dawn to sunset.

hajj A Muslim's pilgrimage to the holy city of Mecca, to worship Allah at the Ka'ba.

In addition to the beliefs and practices that have given Islam a universal appeal, its **five pillars**, principles that must be accepted and followed by all believers, provided the basis for an underlying religious unity. (1) The confession of faith was simple and powerful: "There is no God but Allah, and Muhammad is his Prophet." The injunctions (2) to pray, facing the holy city of Mecca, five times a day and (3) to fast during the month of **Ramadan**, enhanced community solidarity and allowed the faithful to demonstrate their fervor. (4) The zakat, or tithe for charity, also strengthened community cohesion and won converts from those seeking an ethical code that stressed social responsibility and the unity of all believers. (5) The **hajj**, or pilgrimage to the holy city of Mecca, to worship Allah at the Ka'ba, shown in Figure 7.3, drew together the faithful from Morocco to China. No injunction did more to give Islam a universal character.

THE ARAB EMPIRE OF THE UMAYYADS

7.3 What were the key factors that account for the rapid Arab conquests in the Middle East and Central Asia and North Africa?

Despite a time of crisis after the death of the prophet Muhammad in 632 C.E., the Muslim community held together. Eventually, Muhammad's old adversaries, the Umayya clan, seized leadership of the Muslim faithful and began a sequence of stunning conquests throughout the Middle East and north Africa.

Many of the bedouin tribes that had converted to Islam renounced the new faith in the months after Muhammad's death, and his remaining followers quarreled over who should succeed him. Although these quarrels were never fully resolved, the community managed to find new leaders who directed a series of campaigns to force those who had abandoned Islam to return to the fold. Having united most of Arabia under the Islamic banner by 633, Muslim military commanders began to mount serious expeditions beyond the peninsula, where only probing attacks had occurred during the lifetime of the prophet and in the period of tribal warfare after his death. The courage, military prowess, and religious zeal of the warriors of Islam, and the weaknesses of the empires that bordered on Arabia, resulted in stunning conquests in Mesopotamia, north Africa, and Persia, which dominated the next two decades of Islamic history. The empire built from these conquests was Arab rather than Islamic. Most of it was ruled by a small Arab warrior elite, led by the Umayyads and other prominent clans. These groups had little desire to convert the subject populations, either Arab or otherwise, to the new religion.

Consolidation and Division in the Islamic Community

The leadership crisis brought on by Muhammad's death in 632 was compounded by the fact that he had not appointed a successor or even established a procedure by which a new leader would be chosen. Opinion within the Muslim community was deeply divided as to who should succeed him. In this moment of extreme danger, a strong leader who could hold the Islamic community together was urgently needed. On the afternoon Muhammad died, one of the clans that remained committed to the new faith called a meeting to select a leader who would be designated as the **caliph**, the political and religious successor to Muhammad. Several choices were possible, and a deadlock between the clans appeared likely—a deadlock that would almost certainly have been fatal to a community threatened by enemies on all sides.

caliph The political and religious successor to Muhammad.

 Read the Document on MyHistoryLab: Al-Tabari and Ibn Hisham, from "The Founding of the Caliphate"

Abu Bakr [ah-BOO BA-kuhr] The first caliph or leader of the Muslim faithful elected after Muhammad's death in 632. Renown for his knowledge of the nomadic tribes who then dominated the Islamic community.

Ridda Wars Wars that followed Muhammad's death in 632; resulted in defeat of rival prophets and some of larger clans; restored unity of Islam.

One of the main candidates, Ali, the cousin and son-in-law of Muhammad, was passed over because he was considered too young to assume a position of such great responsibility. This decision later proved to be a major source of division in the Islamic community. But in 632, it appeared that a difficult reconciliation had been won by the choice of one of Muhammad's earliest followers and closest friends, **Abu Bakr** (ah-BOO BA-kuhr) (caliph from 632 to 634). In addition to his courage, warmth, and wisdom, Abu Bakr was well versed in the genealogical histories of the bedouin tribes, which meant that he knew which tribes could be turned against each other and which ones could be enticed into alliances. Initially, at least, his mandate was very limited. He received no financial support from the Muslim community. Thus, he had to continue his previous occupation as a merchant on a part-time basis, and he only loosely controlled the military commanders.

These commanders turned out to be very able. After turning back attacks on Mecca, the Islamic faithful routed one after another of the bedouin tribes. The defeat of rival prophets and some of the larger clans in what were known as the **Ridda Wars** soon brought about the return of the Arabian tribes to the Islamic fold. Emboldened by the proven skills of his generals and the swelling ranks of the Muslim faithful, Abu Bakr oversaw raids to the north of Arabia into the sedentary zones in present-day Iraq and Syria and westward into Egypt (Map 7.1).

166 PART III The Postclassical Period, 600–1450: New Faith and New Commerce

Motives for Arab Conquests

The Arab warriors were driven by many forces. The unity provided by the Islamic faith gave them a new sense of common cause and strength. United, they could stand up to the non-Arab rulers who had so long played them against each other and despised them as unwashed and backward barbarians from the desert wastelands. It is also probable that the early leaders of the community saw the wars of conquest as a good way to release the pent-up energies of the martial bedouin tribes they now sought to lead (see Figure 7.4). Above all, the bedouin warriors were drawn to the campaigns of expansion by the promise of a share in the booty to be won in the rich farmlands raided and the tribute that could be exacted from towns that came under Arab rule. As an early Arab writer observed, the bedouins forsook their life as desert nomads not out of a promise of religious rewards, but because of a "yearning after bread and dates."

The chance to glorify their new religion may have been a motive for the Arab conquests, but they were not driven by a desire to win converts to it. In fact, other than fellow bedouin tribes of Arab descent, the invaders had good reason to avoid mass conversions. Not only would Arab warriors have to share the booty of their military expeditions with ever larger numbers if converts were made, but Muslims were exempted from some of the more lucrative taxes levied on Christian, Jewish, and other non-Muslim groups. Thus, the vision of **jihads**, or holy wars launched to forcibly spread the Muslim faith, which has long been associated with Islam in the Christian West, misrepresents the forces behind the early Arab expansion.

jihads [jih-HAHDs] Struggles; often used for wars in defense of the faith, but also a term to indicate personal quests for religious understanding.

Weaknesses of the Adversary Empires

Of the two great empires that had once fought for dominance in the Fertile Crescent transit zone, the Sasanian Empire of Persia proved the more vulnerable. Power in the extensive Sasanian domains was formally concentrated in the hands of an autocratic emperor. By the time of the Arab explosion, the emperor was manipulated by a landed, aristocratic class that harshly exploited the farmers who made up most of the population of the empire. Zoroastrianism, the official religion of the emperor, lacked popular roots. By contrast, the religion of a visionary reformer named Mazdak, which had won considerable support among the peasants, had been brutally suppressed by the Sasanian rulers in the period before the rise of Islam.

At first, the Sasanian commanders had contempt for the Arab invaders and set out against them with poorly prepared forces. By the time the seriousness of the Islamic threat was made clear by decisive Arab victories in the Fertile Crescent region and the defection of the Arab tribes on the frontier,

FIGURE 7.4 This illustration from an account of the Muslim conquest of Sicily in the 9th century C.E. is one of the earliest known artistic renderings of an Arab army at war. The camp, the armored warriors, and the siege in progress help us to envision the Muslim forces that built the first great Arab empire under the early caliphs in the 7th century C.E.

Muslim warriors had broken into the Sasanian heartland. Further Muslim victories brought about the rapid collapse of the vast empire. The Sasanian rulers and their forces retreated eastward in the face of the Muslim advance. The capital was taken, armies were destroyed, and generals were slain. When in 651 the last of the Sasanian rulers was assassinated, Muslim victory and the destruction of the empire were ensured.

Despite an equally impressive string of Muslim victories in the provinces of their empire, the Byzantines proved a stronger adversary (see Chapter 10). However, their ability to resist the Muslim onslaught was impeded by both the defection of their own frontier Arabs and the support the Muslim invaders received from the Christians of Syria and Egypt. Members of the Christian sects dominant in these areas, such as the **Copts** and **Nestorians**, had long resented the rule of the Orthodox Byzantines, who taxed them heavily and openly persecuted them as heretics. When it became clear that the Muslims would not only tolerate the Christians but tax them less heavily than the Byzantines did, these Christian groups rallied to the Arabs.

Weakened from within and exhausted by the long wars fought with Persia in the decades before the Arab explosion, the Byzantines reeled from the Arab assaults. Syria, western Iraq, and Palestine were quickly taken by the Arab invaders, and by 640 a series of probes had been made into Egypt, one of the richest provinces of the empire (Map 7.2). In the early 640s, the ancient center of learning and commerce, Alexandria, was taken, most of Egypt was occupied, and Arab armies extended their conquests into Libya to the west. Perhaps even more astounding from the point of view of the Byzantines, by the mid-640s the desert bedouins were putting together war fleets that increasingly challenged the long-standing Byzantine mastery of the Mediterranean. The rise of Muslim naval supremacy in the eastern end of the Mediterranean sealed the loss of Byzantium's rich provinces in Syria and Egypt. It also opened the way to further Muslim conquests in north Africa, the Mediterranean islands, and even southern Italy (Map 7.2 and Figure 7.4). For a time the Byzantines managed to rally their forces and stave off further inroads into their Balkan and Asia Minor heartlands. But the early triumphs of

Copts Christian sect of Egypt; tended to support Islamic invasions of this area in preference to Byzantine rule.

Nestorians A Christian sect found in Asia; tended to support Islamic invasions of this area in preference to Byzantine rule; cut off from Europe by Muslim invasions.

MAP 7.2 **The Expansion of Islamic Civilization, 622–750** Whether by land or sea, Islamic civilization expanded by both conquest and trade, while the Muslim faith was spread mainly peacefully along ancient trading routes, often by sufi holymen.

the Arab invaders had greatly reduced the strength of the Byzantine Empire. Although it survived for centuries, it was henceforth a kingdom under siege.

The Problem of Succession and the Sunni–Shi'a Split

The stunning successes of Muslim armies and the sudden rise of an Arab empire diverted attention, for a time at least, from continuing divisions within the community. Although these divisions were often generations old and the result of personal animosities, resentments had also begun to build over how the booty from the conquests should be divided among the tribal groups that made up the Islamic community. In 656, just over two decades after the death of the prophet, the growing tensions broke into open violence. The spark that began the conflict was the murder of the third caliph, **Uthman**, by mutinous warriors returning from Egypt. His death was the signal for the supporters of Ali to proclaim him as caliph. Uthman's unpopularity among many of the tribes, particularly those from Medina and the prophet's earliest followers, arose in part from the fact that he was the first caliph to be chosen from Muhammad's early enemies, the Umayyad clan. Already angered by Uthman's murder, the Umayyads rejected Ali's claims and swore revenge when he failed to punish Uthman's assassins. Warfare erupted between the two factions.

Ali was a renowned warrior and experienced commander, and his deeply committed supporters soon gained the upper hand. After his victory at the Battle of the Camel in late 656, most of the Arab garrisons shifted to his side against the Umayyads, whose supporters were concentrated in the province of Syria and the holy city of Mecca. Just as Ali was on the verge of defeating the Umayyad forces at the **Battle of Siffin** in 657, he was won over by a plea for mediation. His decision to accept mediation was fatal to his cause. Some of his most fervent supporters renounced his leadership and had to be suppressed violently. While representatives of both parties tried unsuccessfully to work out a compromise, the Umayyads regrouped their forces and added Egypt to the provinces backing their claims. In 660, **Mu'awiya**, the new leader of the Umayyads, was proclaimed caliph in Jerusalem, directly challenging Ali's position. A year later, Ali was assassinated, and his son Hasan was pressured by the Umayyads into renouncing his claims to the caliphate.

In the decades after the prophet's death, the question of succession generated deep divisions in the Muslim community. The split between the **Sunnis**, who backed the Umayyads, and the **Shi'a**, or supporters of Ali, remains to this day the most fundamental in the Islamic world. Hostility between these two branches of the Islamic faithful was heightened in the years after Ali's death by the continuing struggle between the Umayyads and Ali's second son, Husayn. After being abandoned by the clans in southern Iraq, who had promised to rise in a revolt supporting his claims against the Umayyads, Husayn and a small party were overwhelmed and killed at **Karbala** in 680. From that point on, the Shi'a mounted sustained resistance to the Umayyad caliphate.

Over the centuries, factional disputes about who had the right to succeed Muhammad, with the Shi'a recognizing none of the early caliphs except Ali, have been compounded by differences in belief, ritual, and law that have steadily widened the gap between Sunnis and Shi'a. These divisions have been further complicated by the formation of splinter sects within the Shi'a community in particular, beginning with those who defected from Ali when he agreed to arbitration.

The Umayyad Imperium

After a pause to settle internal disputes over succession, the remarkable sequence of Arab conquest was renewed in the last half of the 7th century. Muslim armies broke into central Asia, inaugurating a rivalry with Buddhism in the region that continues to the present day (Map 7.2). By the early 8th century, the southern prong of this advance had reached into northwest India. Far to the west, Arab armies swept across north Africa and crossed the Straits of Gibraltar to conquer Spain and threaten France. Although the Muslim advance into western Europe was blocked by the hard-fought victory of Charles Martel and the Franks at Poitiers in 732, the Arabs did not fully retreat beyond the Pyrenees into Spain until decades later. Muslim warriors and sailors dominated much of the Mediterranean, a position that was solidified by the conquest of key islands such as Crete, Sicily, and Sardinia in the early decades of the 9th century. By the early 700s, the Umayyads ruled an empire that extended from Spain in the west to the steppes of central Asia in the east. Not since the Romans had there been an empire to match it; never had an empire of its size been built so rapidly.

Uthman Third caliph and member of Umayyad clan; murdered by mutinous warriors returning from Egypt; death set off civil war in Islam between followers of Ali and the Umayyad clan.

Battle of Siffin Fought in 657 between forces of Ali and Umayyads; settled by negotiation that led to fragmentation of Ali's party.

Mu'awiya [moo-UH-wee-uh] (602–680) Leader of Umayyad clan; first Umayyad caliph following civil war with Ali.

Sunnis Political and theological division within Islam; supported the Umayyads.

Shi'a Also known as Shi'ites; political and theological division within Islam; followers of Ali.

Karbala Site of defeat and death of Husayn, son of Ali; marked beginning of Shi'a resistance to Umayyad caliphate.

Damascus Syrian city that was capital of Umayyad caliphate.

Although Mecca remained the holy city of Islam, under the Umayyads the political center of community shifted to **Damascus** in Syria, where the Umayyads chose to live after the murder of Uthman. From Damascus a succession of Umayyad caliphs strove to build a bureaucracy that would bind together the vast domains they claimed to rule. The empire was very much an Arab conquest state. Except in the Arabian peninsula and in parts of the Fertile Crescent, a small Arab and Muslim aristocracy ruled over peoples who were neither Arab nor Muslim. Only Muslim Arabs were first-class citizens of this great empire. They made up the core of the army and imperial administration, and only they received a share of the booty derived from the ongoing conquests. They could be taxed only for charity. The Umayyads sought to keep the Muslim warrior elite concentrated in garrison towns and separated from the local population. It was hoped that isolation would keep them from assimilating to the subjugated cultures, because intermarriage meant conversion and the loss of taxable subjects.

Converts and "People of the Book"

mawali Non-Arab converts to Islam.

jizya [JIHZ-yuh] Head tax paid by all nonbelievers in Islamic territories.

dhimmi [DIH-mee] Literally "people of the book"; applied as inclusive term to Jews and Christians in Islamic territories; later extended to Zoroastrians and even Hindus.

Umayyad attempts to block extensive interaction between the Muslim warrior elite and their non-Muslim subjects had little chance of succeeding. The citified bedouin tribes were soon interacting intensively with the local populations of the conquered areas and intermarrying with them. Equally critical, increasing numbers of these peoples were voluntarily converting to Islam, despite the fact that conversion did little to advance them socially or politically in the Umayyad period. In this era Muslim converts, **mawali**, still had to pay property taxes and in some cases the **jizya**, or head tax, levied on nonbelievers. They received no share of the booty and found it difficult, if not impossible, to get important positions in the army or bureaucracy. They were not even considered full members of the umma but were accepted only as clients of the powerful Arab clans.

As a result, the number of conversions in the Umayyad era was low. By far the greater portion of the population of the empire were the **dhimmi**, or "people of the book." As the name suggests, it was originally applied to Christians and Jews who shared the Bible with the Muslims. As Islamic conquests spread to other peoples, such as the Zoroastrians of Persia and the Hindus of India, the designation *dhimmi* was necessarily stretched to accommodate the majority groups within these areas of the empire. As the early illustration of Jewish worship in Muslim Spain in Figure 7.5 shows, the Muslim overlords generally tolerated the religions of dhimmi. Although they had to pay the jizya and both commercial and property taxes, their communities and legal systems were left intact, and they were allowed to worship as they pleased. This approach made it a good deal easier for these peoples to accept Arab rule, particularly because many had been oppressed by their pre-Muslim overlords.

FIGURE 7.5 Jews worshiping in a synagogue. As dhimmi, or "people of the book," Jews were allowed to build impressive synagogues and worship freely throughout the Muslim world. Jewish merchant families amassed great wealth, often in partnership with Muslims, and Jewish scholars were revered from Spain to Baghdad for their many contributions to learning.

Family and Gender Roles in the Umayyad Age

Broader social changes within the Arab and widening Islamic community were accompanied by significant shifts in the position of women, both within the family and in society at large. In the first centuries of Arab expansion, the greatly strengthened position of women under Islam prevailed over the seclusion and subordination that were characteristic features of women's lives through much of the rest of the pre-Islamic Middle East. Muhammad's teachings and the dictates of the Qur'an stressed the moral and ethical dimensions of marriage. The kindness and concern the prophet displayed for his own wives and daughters did much to strengthen the bonds between husband and wife and the nuclear family in the Islamic community.

Muhammad encouraged marriage as a replacement for the casual and often commercial sexual liaisons that had been widespread in pre-Islamic Arabia. He vehemently denounced adultery on the part of both husbands and wives, and he forbade female infanticide, which apparently had been widely practiced in Arabia in pre-Islamic times. Men were allowed to marry up to four wives. But the Qur'an forbade multiple marriages if the husband could not support more than one wife or treat all of his wives equally. Women could not take more than one husband. But Muhammad gave his own daughters a say as to whom they would marry and greatly strengthened the legal rights of women in inheritance and divorce. He insisted that the bride-price paid by the husband's family be given to his future wife rather than to her father.

The prophet's teachings proclaimed the equality of men and women before God and in Islamic worship. Women, most notably his wife Khadijah, were some of Muhammad's earliest and bravest followers. In the battle with the Meccans, women accompanied the forces on both sides, and a woman was the first martyr for the new faith. Many of the **hadiths**, or traditions of the prophet, which have played such a critical role in Islamic law and ritual, were recorded by women. In addition, Muhammad's wives and daughters played an important role in compiling the Qur'an.

hadiths [huh-DEETHs] Traditions of the prophet Muhammad.

Although women were not allowed to lead prayers, they played an active role in the politics of the early community. Muhammad's widow, Aisha, actively promoted the claims of the Umayyad party against Ali, while Zainab, Ali's daughter, went into battle with the ill-fated Husayn. Through much of the Umayyad period, little is heard of veiled Arab women, and women appear to have pursued a wide range of occupations, including scholarship, law, and commerce. Perhaps one of Zainab's nieces best epitomizes the independent-mindedness of Muslim women in the early Islamic era. When chided for going about without a veil, she replied that Allah in his wisdom had chosen to give her a beautiful face and that she intended to make sure that it was seen in public so that all might appreciate his grace.

Umayyad Decline and Fall

The ever-increasing size of the royal harem was just one manifestation of the Umayyad caliphs' growing addiction to luxury and soft living. Their legitimacy had been disputed by various Muslim factions since their seizure of the caliphate. But the Umayyads further alienated the Muslim faithful as they became more aloof in the early 8th century and retreated from the dirty business of war into their pleasure gardens and marble palaces. Their abandonment of the frugal, simple lifestyle followed by Muhammad and the earliest caliphs—including Abu Bakr, who made a trip to the market the day after he was selected to succeed the prophet—enraged the dissenting sects and sparked revolts throughout the empire. The uprising that proved fatal to the short-lived dynasty began among the frontier warriors who had fought and settled in distant Iran.

By the mid-8th century, more than 50,000 warriors had settled near the oasis town of Merv in the eastern Iranian borderlands of the empire (Figure 7.6). Many of them had married local women, and over time they had come to identify with the region and to resent the dictates of governors sent from distant Damascus. The warrior settlers were also angered by the fact that they were rarely given the share of the booty, which was now officially tallied in the account books of the royal treasury, they had earned by fighting the wars of expansion and

FIGURE 7.6 Muslim worshippers in modern Pakistan. Whether in a nearby mosque or in their homes and shops, Muslims are required to pray five times a day, facing the holy city of Mecca. Those congregating in a mosque, as in this photo, are oriented to Mecca by the qibla wall, which is marked by a highly ornamented inset that indicates the direction of the holy city. Men congregate in the open spaces in the center of and outside the mosque, while women pray in areas on the sides or in the back or, sometimes, in balconies above that are screened off by pillars or carved panels from the areas where the men worship.

THINKING HISTORICALLY

Civilization and Gender Relationships

WITHIN A CENTURY OF MUHAMMAD'S DEATH, the strong position women had enjoyed as a result of the teachings and example of the prophet had begun to erode. We do not fully understand all the forces that account for this decline. Ambiguities in the Qur'an and other early sources—especially the hadith, or traditions of the prophet—provide part of the answer. These sources indicate that, in both his domestic and public life, Muhammad was concerned about good treatment for women and defined certain rights, for example, to property. But early records also stipulate women's inferiority to men in key legal rights (differential punishments for adultery were a case in point). And, like their Christian counterparts, Islamic thinkers argued that women were more likely than men to be sinners. But more critical were the beliefs and practices of the urbanized, sedentary peoples in the areas the Arabs conquered and where many of them settled from the mid-7th century onward.

The example of these ancient and long-civilized peoples increasingly influenced the Arab bearers of Islam. They developed a taste for city life and the superior material and artistic culture of the peoples they ruled. In terms of gender roles, most of these influences weakened the position of women. We have seen this apparent connection between increasing political centralization and urbanization and the declining position of women in many of the ancient and classical civilizations treated thus far. In China, India, Greece, and the Middle East, women enjoyed broader occupational options and a stronger voice within the family, and in society as a whole, before the emergence of centralized polities and highly stratified social systems. In each case, the rise of what we have called civilizations strengthened paternal control within the family, inheritance through the male line, and male domination of positions of power and the most lucrative occupations. Women in these societies became more and more subjected to men—their fathers and brothers, husbands and sons—and more and more confined to the roles of homemakers and bearers of children. Women's legal rights were reduced, often sharply. In many civilizations, various ways were devised to shut women off from the world.

As we have seen, women played active and highly valued roles in the bedouin tribes of pre-Islamic Arabia. Particularly in towns such as Mecca, they experienced considerable freedom in terms of sexual and marriage partners, occupational choices (within the limited range available in an isolated pastoral society), and opportunities to influence clan decisions. The position of Muhammad's first wife, Khadijah, is instructive. Her position as a wealthy widow in charge of a thriving trading enterprise reveals that women were able to remarry and to own and inherit property. They could also pursue careers, even after their husbands died. Khadijah employed Muhammad. After he had successfully worked for her for some time, she asked him to marry her, which apparently neither surprised nor scandalized her family or Meccan society. It is also noteworthy that Khadijah was 15 years older than Muhammad, who was 25 at the time of their betrothal.

The impact of the bedouin pattern of gender roles and relationships is also clear in the teachings and personal behavior of Muhammad. Islam did much to legalize the strong but by no means equal status of women. In addition, it gave greater uniformity to their position from one tribe, town, or region to the next. For a century or two after the prophet's death, women in the Islamic world enjoyed unprecedented opportunities for education, religious expression, and social fulfillment. Then the influences of the cultures into which the Arabs had expanded began to take hold. The practices of veiling and female seclusion that were long followed by the non-Arab dwellers of Syria and Persia were increasingly adopted by or imposed upon Muslim women. Confined more and more to the home, women saw their occupational options decrease, and men served as their go-betweens in legal and commercial matters.

> *Islamic law preserved for women property, inheritance, divorce, and remarriage rights that often were denied in other civilized societies.*

Ironically, given the earlier status of women, such as Khadijah, the erosion of the position of women was especially pronounced among those who lived in the cities that became the focus of Islamic civilization. Upper-class women, in particular, felt growing restrictions on their movement and activities. In the great residences that sprang up in the wealthy administrative centers and trading towns of the Middle East, the women's quarters were separate from the rest of the household and set off by high walls and gardens. In the palaces of Islamic rulers and provincial governors, this separation was marked by the development of the *harem*, or forbidden area. In the harem, the notables' wives and concubines lived in seclusion. They were constantly guarded by the watchful eyes and sharp swords of corps of eunuchs, men castrated specifically to qualify them for the task.

When upper-class women went into the city, they were veiled from head to toe and often were carried in covered sedan chairs by servants who guarded them from the glances of the townsmen and travelers. In their homes, upper-class women were spared the drudgery of domestic chores by large numbers of female slaves. If we are to judge from stories such as those related in the *Arabian Nights* (from which excerpts are included in the Document feature on page 178), female slaves and servants were largely at the mercy

(continued on next page)

of their male masters. Although the veiling, seclusion, and other practices that limited the physical and occupational mobility of women also spread to the lower urban classes and rural areas, they were never as strictly observed there as in urban, upper-class households. Women from poorer families had to work to survive. Thus, they had to go out, "veiled but often unchaperoned," to the market or to work as domestic servants. Lower-class women also worked hard at home, not just at housekeeping but at weaving, rug-making, and other crafts that supplemented the family income. In rural areas and in towns distant from the main urban centers, veiling and confinement were observed less strictly. Peasant women worked the family or local landlord's fields, planted their own gardens, and tended the livestock.

Because of Islamic religion and law, in all locales and at all class levels the position of women in the Middle East never deteriorated to the same extent as in India, China, and many other civilized centers. Because of the need to read the Qur'an, women continued to be educated, family resources permitting, even if they rarely were able to use their learning for scholarship or artistic expression. Islamic law preserved for women property, inheritance, divorce, and remarriage rights that often were denied in other civilized societies. Thus, the strong position women had enjoyed in bedouin cultures, and that in many respects had been built into Islam, was never entirely undone by the customs and practices Muslims encountered as they came to rule the civilized centers in the rest of the Middle East.

The fact that the position of women has also been strong in other cultural areas where authority is decentralized and social organization not highly stratified, such as those in west Africa (see Chapter 9), suggests that at least in certain stages of its development, civilization works against the interests of women. Women in decentralized societies have often been able to own their own property, to engage in key economic activities, and to play important roles in religious ceremonies. The positions and status they have achieved in decentralized societies, such as those in early Arabia or much of sub-Saharan Africa and southeast Asia, suggest factors that may help explain the greater balance in gender roles and power in less centralized societies. The very immediate connection between women and agriculture and stock-raising, which are central to survival in these societies, may also account for the greater respect accorded them and for their often prominent roles in fertility rituals and religious cults. Whatever the explanation, until the present era, higher degrees of centralization and social stratification—both characteristic features of civilized societies—have almost always favored men in the allotment of power and career opportunities.

QUESTIONS

- Compare the position of upper-class women in classical Indian, Chinese, Greek, and Roman societies with regard to their ability to hold property, opportunity to pursue careers outside the home, rights in marriage and divorce, and level of education. In which of these societies were women better off, and why?
- Were differences in the position of women at lower-class levels similar between these societies?
- In what ways were women better off in decentralized pastoral or forest-farming societies?
- What advantages have they enjoyed in highly urbanized and more centralized civilizations?

---

defending the frontiers. They were contemptuous of the Umayyads and the Damascus elite, whom they saw as corrupt and decadent. In the early 740s, an attempt by Umayyad palace officials to introduce new troops into the Merv area touched off a revolt that soon spread over much of the eastern portions of the empire (Map 7.2).

Marching under the black banners of the **Abbasid** party, which traced its descent from Muhammad's uncle, al-Abbas, the frontier warriors openly challenged Umayyad armies by 747. Deftly forging alliances with dissident groups that resisted the Umayyads throughout the empire, their leader, Abu al-Abbas, the great-great-grandson of the prophet's uncle, led his forces from victory to victory. Among his most important allies were the Shi'a, who, as we have seen, had rejected Umayyad authority from the time of Ali. Also critical were the mawali, or non-Arab converts to Islam. The mawali felt that under Umayyad rule they had never been recognized as fully Muslim. In supporting the Abbasids, the mawali hoped to attain full acceptance in the community of believers.

Abbasid [uh bas id, ab uh sid] Dynasty that succeeded the Umayyads as caliphs within Islam; came to power in 750 C.E.

This diverse collection of Muslim rebels made short work of what remained of the Umayyad imperium. Persia and then Iraq fell to the rebels. In 750, the Abbasid forces met an army led by the Umayyad caliph himself in the massive **Battle of the River Zab** near the Tigris. The Abbasid victory opened the way for the conquest of Syria and the capture of the Umayyad capital.

Battle of the River Zab Victory of Abbasids over Umayyads; resulted in conquest of Syria and capture of Umayyad capital.

Wanting to eliminate the Umayyad family altogether to prevent recurring challenges to his rule, Abu al-Abbas invited many members of the clan to what was styled as a reconciliation banquet. As the Umayyads were enjoying the feast, guards covered them with carpets and they were slaughtered by Abbas's troops. An effort was then made to hunt down and kill all the remaining members of the family throughout the empire. Most were slain, but, as we have seen, the grandson of a former caliph fled to Spain and founded there what later became the Umayyad caliphate of Córdoba, which lived on for centuries after the rest of the Umayyads' empire had disappeared (see Map 7.3 and Figure 7.1).

Read the Document on MyHistoryLab: Harun al-Rashid and the Zenith of the Caliphate

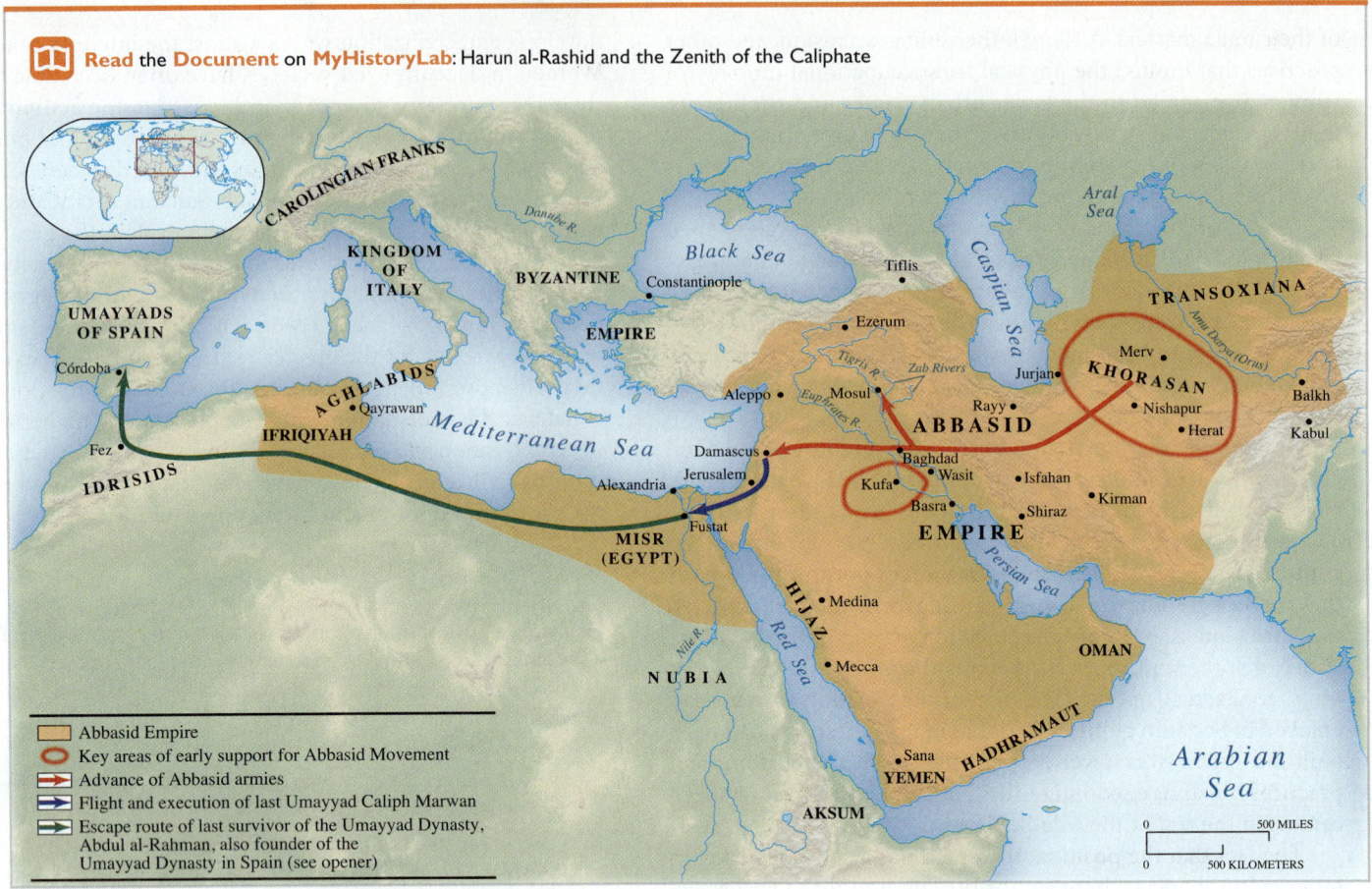

MAP 7.3 **Emergence of the Abbasid Dynasty** Frontier warriors from Khorasan far from the Umayyad capital at Damascus built a military force that overthrew the Umayyads between 747 and 750 C.E.

FROM ARAB TO ISLAMIC EMPIRE: THE EARLY ABBASID ERA

Under the Abbasids, who succeeded the Umayyads, Islam became a universal religion that spread across much of north Africa and Euro-Asia. With its capital at Baghdad, Islamic civilization flourished under the Abbasids, even as their empire began to fragment into regional power centers.

Baghdad Capital of Abbasid dynasty located in Iraq near ancient Persian capital of Ctesiphon.

7.4 In what ways was the Islamic religion a faith that elevated the status and opportunities of women, and what were the constraints on this process?

The rough treatment the Umayyad clan had received at the hands of the victorious Abbasids should have forewarned their Shi'a and mawali allies of what was to come. But the Shi'a and other dissenting groups continued the support that allowed the Abbasids to level all other centers of political rivalry. Gradually, the Abbasids rejected many of their old allies, becoming more and more righteous in their defense of Sunni Islam and increasingly less tolerant of what they called the heretical views of the various sects of Shi'ism. With the Umayyads all but eliminated and their allies brutally suppressed, the way was clear for the Abbasids to build a centralized, absolutist imperial order.

The fact that they chose to build their new capital, **Baghdad**, in Iraq near the ancient Persian capital of Ctesiphon was a clear sign of things to come. Soon the Abbasid caliphs were perched on jewel-encrusted thrones, reminiscent of those of the ancient Persian emperors, gazing down on the great gatherings of courtiers and petitioners who bowed before them in their gilt and marble audience halls. The caliphs' palaces and harems expanded to keep pace with their claims to absolute power over the Islamic faithful as well as the non-Muslim subjects of their vast empire.

The ever-expanding corps of bureaucrats, servants, and slaves who strove to translate Abbasid political claims into reality lived and worked within the circular walls of the new capital at Baghdad.

The bureaucratization of the Islamic Empire was reflected above all in the growing power of the **wazir**, or chief administrator and head of the caliph's inner councils. It was also embodied in a more sinister way in the fearful guise of the royal executioner, who stood close to the throne in the public audiences of the Abbasid rulers. The wazirs oversaw the building of an administrative infrastructure that allowed the Abbasids to project their demands for tribute to the most distant provinces of the empire. Sheer size, poor communications, and collusion between Abbasid officials and local notables meant that the farther the town or village was from the capital, the less effectively royal commands were carried out. But for more than a century, the Abbasid regime was fairly effective at collecting revenue from its subject peoples and preserving law and order over much of the empire.

wazir [wuh-ZEER] Chief administrative official under the Abbasid caliphate; initially recruited from Persian provinces of empire.

Islamic Conversion and Mawali Acceptance

The Abbasid era saw the full integration of new converts, both Arab and non-Arab, into the Islamic community. In the last decades of the Umayyad period, there was a growing acceptance of the mawali, or non-Arab Muslims, as equals. There were also efforts to win new converts to the faith, particularly among Arab peoples outside the Arabian peninsula. In the Abbasid era, when the practice of dividing booty between the believers had long been discarded, mass conversions to Islam were encouraged for all peoples of the empire, from the Berbers of north Africa to the Persians and Turkic peoples of central Asia. Converts were admitted on an equal footing with the first generations of believers, and over time the distinction between mawali and the earlier converts all but disappeared.

Read the Document on MyHistoryLab: Sunni versus Shi'a Letter from Selim I to Ismail I

Most converts were won over peacefully through the great appeal of Islamic beliefs and the advantages they enjoyed over non-Muslim peoples in the empire. Not only were converts exempt from paying the head tax, but they had greater opportunities to get advanced schooling and launch careers as administrators, traders, or judges. No group demonstrated the new opportunities open to converts as dramatically as the Persians, who, in part through their bureaucratic skills, soon came to dominate the upper levels of imperial administration. In fact, as the Abbasid rulers became more dissolute and less interested in affairs of state, several powerful Persian families close to the throne became the real locus of power in the imperial system.

dhows Arab sailing vessels with triangular or lateen sails; strongly influenced European ship design.

Read the Document on MyHistoryLab: Baghdad: City of Wonders

Town and Country: Commercial Boom and Agrarian Expansion

The rise of the mawali was paralleled in the Abbasid era by the growth in wealth and social status of the merchant and landlord classes of the empire. The Abbasid age was a time of great urban expansion that was linked to a revival of the Afro-Eurasian trading network, which had declined with the fall of the Han dynasty in China in the early 3rd century C.E. and the slow collapse of the Roman Empire in the 4th and 5th centuries. The Abbasid domains in the west and the great Tang and Song empires in the east became the pivots of the revived commercial system.

From the western Mediterranean to the South China Sea, Arab **dhows**, or sailing vessels with lateen (triangular) sails, which later influenced European ship design, carried the goods of one civilized core to be exchanged with those of another. Muslim merchants often formed joint ventures with Christians and Jews. Because each merchant had a different Sabbath, the firm could do business all week. Merchants grew rich by supplying the cities of the empire with provisions. Mercantile concerns also took charge of the long-distance trade that specialized in luxury products for the elite classes. The great profits from trade were reinvested in new commercial enterprises, the purchase of land, and the construction of the great mansions that dominated the central quarters of the political and commercial hubs of the empire. Some wealth also went to charity, as required by the Qur'an. A good deal of the wealth was spent on building and running mosques and religious schools, baths, and rest houses for weary travelers (Figure 7.7). Large donations were

FIGURE 7.7 The rulers and nobility of the Abbasid capital in Baghdad frequented baths like that shown in this Persian miniature painting. Here the caliph, Haroun al-Rashid, receives a haircut while servants prepare the steam rooms. At the baths, the Abbasid elite could relax, exchange gossip, and enjoy expert massages. (British Library, London.)

VISUALIZING THE PAST

The Mosque as a Symbol of Islamic Civilization

FROM ONE END OF THE ISLAMIC world to the other, Muslim towns and cities can be readily identified by the domes and minarets of the mosques where the faithful are called to prayer five times daily. The illustrations included here trace the development of the mosque and the refinement of mosque architecture, the crowning glory of Islamic material culture, during the early centuries of Muslim expansion. As you look at these pictures and follow the development of the mosque, consider what the functions of the mosque and the evolving style of mosque architecture can tell us about Muslim beliefs and values and the impact of earlier religions, such as Judaism and Christianity, on Islam.

Given the low level of material culture in pre-Islamic Arabia, it is not surprising that the earliest prayer houses were simple in design and construction. In fact, these first mosques were laid out along the lines suggested by Muhammad's own house. They were square enclosures with a shaded porch on one side, a columned shelter on the other, and an open courtyard in between. The outer perimeter of the earliest mosques was made of reed mats, but soon more permanent stone walls surrounded the courtyard and prayer areas. After Mecca was taken and the Ka'ba became the central shrine of the new faith, each mosque was oriented to the qibla, or Mecca wall, which always faced in the direction of the holy city.

In the last years of the prophet, his chair was located so that the faithful could see and hear him during prayer sessions. During the time of the first caliphs, the raised area became the place from

Pulpit (minbar) from which the Friday sermons are delivered throughout the Muslim world.

which sermons were delivered. From the mid-8th century, this space evolved into a genuine pulpit (*minbar* in Arabic). Somewhat earlier, the practice of building a special and often elaborately decorated niche in the qibla had developed.

Over time, mosques became more elaborate. Very often the remains of Greek or Roman temples or abandoned Christian churches formed the core of major mosques, or the ruins of these structures were mined for stone for mosque construction. In the larger cities, the courtyards of the great mosques were surrounded by columns and arches, and eventually they were enclosed by great domes such as that at the Dome of the Rock in Jerusalem.

Domes and minarets of the Shah Mosque at Isfahan, Iran.

(continued on next page)

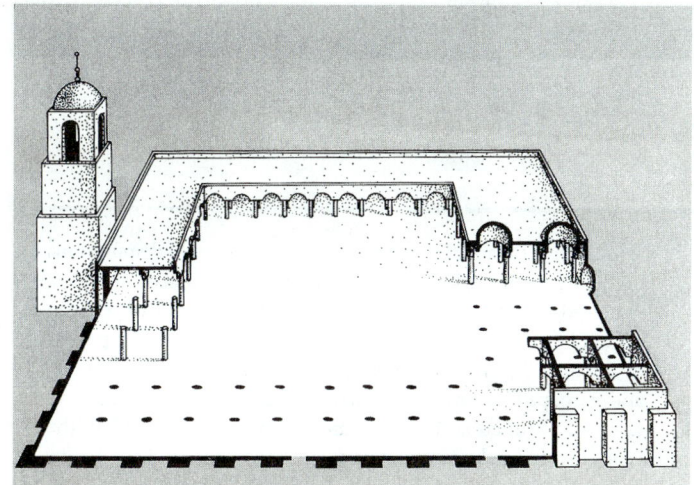

Drawing of the early mosque design.

Al-Aqsa Mosque (or Dome of the Rock) in Jerusalem, the third holiest site in Islam.

The first minarets, or towers from which the faithful were called to prayer, were added in the early 8th century and soon became a key feature of the mosque complex. As mosques grew larger and more architecturally refined, elaborate decoration in brightly colored ceramic tiles, semiprecious stones, and gold and silver filigree adorned their sides and domes. Because human and animal images were forbidden, geometric designs, passages from the Qur'an in swirling Arabic, and flower and plant motifs were favored. Nowhere were these decorations more splendid than in the mosques of Persia. Thus, in the early centuries of Islam, these great houses of worship became the focal points of Islamic cities, key places of community worship and socialization, and, with the schools that were often attached, vital intellectual and educational centers of the Islamic world.

> **QUESTIONS**
> - What do the design and decoration of Muslim mosques tell us about the Islamic view of a supreme being and the relationship between Allah and humans?
> - Discuss the Christian and Jewish influences you detect in mosque design and the pattern of religious worship conducted there. What do you think is the significance of the lavish application of color and the frequent use of floral and plant motifs and Arabic verses from the Qur'an in the decoration of mosques through much of the Muslim world?

Qibla wall with decorated section facing Mecca.

also made to hospitals, which in the numbers of their patients and the quality of their medical care surpassed those of any other civilization of that time.

The growth of Abbasid cities was also fed by a great increase in handicraft production. Both government-run and privately owned workshops expanded or were established to produce a wide range of products, from necessities such as furniture and carpets to luxury items such as glassware, jewelry, and tapestries. Although the artisans often were poorly paid and some worked in great

DOCUMENT

The Thousand and One Nights as a Mirror of Elite Society in the Abbasid Era

THE LUXURIOUS LIFESTYLE OF THE ABBASID rulers and their courtiers reflected the new wealth of the political and commercial elites of the Islamic Empire. At the same time, it intensified sectarian and social divisions in the Islamic community. As the compilation of folktales from many parts of the empire titled *The Thousand and One Nights* testifies, life for much of the elite in Baghdad and other major urban centers was luxurious and oriented to the delights of the flesh. Caliphs and wealthy merchants lived in palatial residences of stone and marble, complete with gurgling fountains and elaborate gardens, which served as retreats from the glare and heat of the southern Mediterranean climate. In the Abbasid palaces, luxurious living and ostentation soared to fantastic heights. In the Hall of the Tree, for example, there was a huge artificial tree, made entirely of gold and silver and filled with gold mechanical birds that chirped to keep the caliph in good cheer.

Because the tales were just that—tall tales—there is some exaggeration of the wealth, romantic exploits, and sexual excesses of the world depicted. But for some members of the elite classes, the luxuries, frivolities, and vices of the Abbasid age were very real. The following passages are taken from an English translation of *The Thousand and One Nights*. Each is selected to reveal a different facet of high society in the Abbasid era. The first, which describes the sumptuous interior of a mansion in Baghdad, indicates that conspicuous material consumption existed far beyond the palace.

> They reached a spacious ground-floor hall, built with admirable skill and beautified with all manner of colors and carvings, with upper balconies and groined [sharply curved] arches and galleries and cupboards and recesses whose curtains hung before them. In the midst stood a great basin full of water surrounding a fine fountain, and at the upper end on the raised dais was a couch of juniper wood set with gems and pearls, with a canopy-like mosquito curtain of red satin-silk looped up with pearls as big as filberts [hazelnuts] and bigger.

In another tale, a fallen prince details the proper upbringing and education for a person of substance:

> I am a king, son of a king, and was brought up like a prince. I learned intoning the Koran [Qur'an] according [to] the seven schools and I read all manner [of] books, and held disputations on their contents with the doctors and men of science. Moreover, I studied star lore and the fair sayings of poets, and I exercised myself in all branches of learning until I surpassed the people of my time. My skill in calligraphy [writing, in this case Arabic and perhaps Persian] exceeded that of all of the scribes, and my fame was bruited abroad over all climes and cities, and all the kings learned to know my name.

In the following passage, a stylishly dressed woman from the elite classes is described in great detail:

> There stood before him an honorable woman in a mantilla [veil] of Mosul silk broidered with gold and bordered with brocade [a rich cloth with a raised design, often of gold or silver]. Her walking shoes were also [broidered] with gold, and her hair floated in long plaits. She raised her face veil . . . showing two black eyes fringed with jetty lashes, whose glances were soft and languishing and whose perfect beauty was ever blandishing.

The woman leads a porter to a marketplace, which again reflects the opulence accessible to the rich and powerful of Abbasid society:

> She stopped at the fruiter's shop and bought from him Shami apples and Osmani quinces and Omani peaches, and cucumbers of Nile growth, and Egyptian limes and Sultani oranges and citrons, besides Aleppine jasmine, scented myrtle berries, Damascene nenuphars [water lilies], flower of privit and camomile, blood-red anemones, violets, and pomegranate bloom, eglantine [wild rose], and narcissus, and set the whole in the porter's crate.

QUESTIONS

- What objects are key symbols of wealth in Abbasid society?
- What attainments are highly valued for upper-class men?
- What do they tell us about occupations and talents that brought high status in Abbasid society, and how do they compare with career aspirations in our own?
- In comparison, what attributes of women are stressed in these passages?

workshops, they were not slaves or drudge laborers. They owned their own tools and were often highly valued for their skills. The most accomplished of the artisans formed guildlike organizations, which negotiated wages and working conditions with the merchants and supported their members in times of financial difficulty or personal crisis.

In towns and the countryside, much of the unskilled labor was left to slaves, often attached to prominent families as domestic servants. Large numbers of slaves also served the caliphs and their highest advisors. It was possible for the more clever and ambitious slaves to rise to positions of great power, and many eventually were granted their freedom or were able to buy it. Less fortunate were the slaves forced into lives of hard labor under the overseer's whip on rural estates and government projects, such as those devoted to draining marshlands, or into a lifetime of labor in the nightmare conditions of the great salt mines in southern Iraq. Most of these drudge laborers were non-Muslims captured on slaving raids in east Africa.

View the **Closer Look** on **MyHistoryLab**: Al-Hariri, Assemblies (Maqamat)

In the countryside, a wealthy and deeply entrenched landed elite called the **ayan** emerged in the early decades of Abbasid rule. Many of these landlords had been long established. Others were newcomers: Arab soldiers who invested their share of the booty in land, or merchants and administrators who funneled their profits and kickbacks into sizeable estates. In many regions, most peasants did not own the land they worked. They occupied it as tenants, sharecroppers, or migrant laborers who were required to give the greater portion of the crops they harvested to the estate owners.

ayan [ä yän] The wealthy landed elite that emerged in the early decades of Abbasid rule.

The First Flowering of Islamic Learning

In the first phase of Abbasid rule, the Islamic contribution to human artistic expression focused on the great mosques, such as those featured in the Visualizing the Past box, and great palaces. In addition to advances in religious, legal, and philosophical discourse, learning in the Muslim domains focused on the sciences and mathematics. In the early Abbasid period, the main tasks were recovering and preserving the learning of the ancient civilizations of the Mediterranean and Middle East. Beyond the works of Plato, for example, much of Greek learning had been lost to the peoples of western Europe. Thanks to Muslim and Jewish scholars, the priceless writings of the Greeks on key subjects such as medicine, algebra, geometry, astronomy, anatomy, and ethics were saved, recopied in Arabic, and dispersed throughout the empire. From Spain, Greek writings found their way into Christendom. Among the authors rescued in this manner were Aristotle, Galen, Hippocrates, Ptolemy, and Euclid.

In addition, scholars working in Arabic transmitted ideas that paralleled the rise of Arab traders and merchants as the carriers of goods and inventions. For example, Muslim invaders of south Asia soon learned of the Indian system of numbers. From India they were carried by Muslim scholars and merchants to the Middle Eastern centers of Islamic civilization. Eventually, the Indian numerical system was transmitted across the Mediterranean to Italy and from there to northern Europe. Along with Greek and Arab mathematics, Indian numbers later proved critical to the early modern Scientific Revolution in western Europe.

Global Connections and Critical Themes

EARLY ISLAM AND THE WORLD

The rise of Islamic civilization from the 7th to 9th centuries C.E. was a stunning development without precedent in human history. Not only had the largely nomadic peoples from an Arabian backwater built one of the greatest empires of the preindustrial world, they had laid the basis for the first truly global civilization if one excludes the Americas, which were unknown to the peoples of the Eastern Hemisphere. Building on earlier religious traditions, especially Christianity and Judaism, Arab culture had nurtured Islam, one of the great universal religions of humankind. The mosques, the prayer rituals and pilgrimages of the faithful, and the influence of Islamic law proclaimed the pervasive effects of this new creed in societies from Spain to eastern Indonesia and from central Asia to the savannas of west Africa.

The Arab commitment to trade and merchant activity was crucial in setting up wider connections among Asia, Africa, and Europe, with the Middle East as the hub. The region's earlier roles in commerce, in and between the Indian Ocean and Mediterranean Sea, expanded greatly.

In the arts and sciences, the Muslims initially relied heavily on the achievements of the classical civilizations of Greece and Mesopotamia. But the work of preserving and combining the discoveries of earlier peoples soon led to reformulation and innovation. As in religion and politics, Muslim peoples were soon making important contributions to learning, invention, and artistic creativity. These were carried by their armies and religious teachers to other civilizations in Europe, Africa, and Asia.

Never before had a civilization spanned so many different cultures and combined such a patchwork of linguistic groups, religions, and ethnic types. Never before had a single civilization mediated so successfully between the other centers of civilized life. Never had a civilized lifestyle so deeply affected so many of the nomadic cultures that surrounded the pools of sedentary agriculture and urban life. Ironically, the contacts Islamic mediation made possible between the civilized cores of the Eastern Hemisphere contributed much to the transformations in technology and organization that increasingly tilted the balance of power against the Muslim peoples. But those reversals were still far in the future. In the short run, Islamic conversion and contact ushered in an age of unparalleled nomadic intervention in and dominance over global history.

Further Readings

There are many accounts of Muhammad's life and the rise of Islam. The most readable is Karen Armstrong's *Muhammad: A Biography of the Prophet* (1992). A sense of the very different interpretations that have been offered to explain these pivotal developments in global history can be gained by comparing W. Montgomery Watt, *Muhammad: Prophet and Statesman* (1961); Tor Andrae, *Muhammad: The Man and His Faith* (1960); Maxime Rodinson, *Mohammad* (1971); and the more recent revisionist (and somewhat less accessible) writings of Elizabeth Crone and Michael Cook.

Despite its title, H. A. R. Gibb's *Mohammedism* (1962) remains a useful introduction to Islam as a religion. John Esposito's *Islam: The Straight Path* (1991) and Karen Armstrong's *Islam: A Short History* (2000) also provide good and updated overviews of the faith. On early Islamic expansion and civilization through the first centuries of the Abbasid caliphate, see G. E. von Grunebaum's *Classical Islam* (1970) and M. A. Shaban's *Islamic History: An Interpretation* (1971) and *The Abbasid Revolution* (1970). On nearly all of these topics, it is difficult to surpass Marshall G. S. Hodgson's brilliant analysis, *The Venture of Islam*, vol. 1 (1974), but some grounding in the history and beliefs of the Muslims is recommended before one attempts this sweeping and provocative work. More accessible, dated in some respects, but still authoritative and highly interpretive is Philip Hitti's *History of the Arabs* (1967 ed.), which can be supplemented by his very engaging *Makers of Arab History* (1968). More encyclopedic and benefiting from recent research, the surveys of Ira M. Lapidus, *A History of Islamic Societies* (1988) and Albert Hourani, *A History of the Arab Peoples* (1991) provide useful overviews.

On early Islamic society generally, see M. M. Ahsan, *Social Life Under the Abbasids* (1979). On women in Islam specifically, there is a superb essay by Guity Nashat, "Women in the Middle East, 8000 B.C.–A.D. 1800," in the collection titled *Restoring Women to History* (1988), published by the Organization of American Historians. See also the relevant portions of the essays in Lois Beck and Nikki Keddi, eds., *Women in the Muslim World* (1978); and the early chapters of Leila Ahmed, *Women and Gender in Islam* (1992). For a broad treatment of the roles and position of women in ancient civilizations more generally, see Sarah and Brady Hughes, *Women in Ancient Global History* (1998). For insights into Islamic culture and civilization from a literary perspective, a good place to begin is Eric Schroeder's delightful *Muhammad's People: A Tale by Anthology* (1955) and N. J. Dawood's translation of *Tales from the Thousand and One Nights* (1954). Of the many works on Muslim art and architecture Robert Hillenbrand's recent *Islamic Art and Architecture* (1999) is engaging, well researched, and lavishly illustrated. K. A. Creswell's *Early Muslim Architecture*, 2 vols. (1932–1940), and the more recent Markus Hattstein and Peter Delius, eds., *Islam: Art and Architecture* (2000), provide even greater detail and ample illustrations.

On MyHistoryLab

 Study and Review on MyHistoryLab

Critical Thinking Questions

1. What were the most important social bonds and status relationships in pre-Islamic society in Arabia and how did they contribute to survival in the harsh desert environment?

2. What are the five pillars of the Islamic faith and how do they make for a strong sense of identity and community within the Islamic *umma*?

3. What were the major factors that led to the Sunni—Shi'a split in the Muslim Arab community?

4. What were the major motives for converting to Islam when the *umma* opened up to non-Muslims in the Abbasid era?

8 Abbasid Decline and the Spread of Islamic Civilization to South and Southeast Asia

((•)) Listen to Chapter 8 on MyHistoryLab

LEARNING OBJECTIVES

8.1 What were the major sources contributing to the decline of the Abbasid dynasty? p. 184

8.2 Discuss the major advances in the arts and sciences that occurred in the Islamic world in the late-Abbasid period. p. 189

8.3 How did Hindu religious leaders and organizations counter the considerable appeal of Sufi missionaries and their efforts to win converts in South and Southeast Asia from the 10th through the 16th centuries? p. 192

8.4 Beyond the Sufis, who were the major agents and what were the motivations for conversions to the Islamic religion in South and South Asia in this same era? p. 200

Of all of the factors that contributed to the spread of Islamic civilization in the millennium after the prophet Muhammad received his divine revelations in the early 7th century c.e., perhaps none was as crucial—yet neglected—as the rather modest sailing vessels that plied the waters of the Red Sea and Persian Gulf. Most commonly known as *dhows* (see Chapter 7, p. 175), but appearing in numerous variations with different names and found from the Mediterranean Sea to the Indian Ocean, these ships were probably first developed along the Nile River. Compared to the great junks of China, or even many of the less-imposing trading ships in the Indian Ocean in the classical age, dhows were rather small vessels. They normally had one or two masts and planked, wooden hulls that resembled modern yachts in shape, with pointed bows and square sterns (Figure 8.1). The dhows' hull design contributed to their swiftness and maneuverability, but

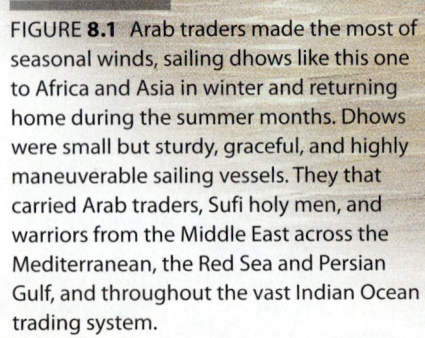

FIGURE **8.1** Arab traders made the most of seasonal winds, sailing dhows like this one to Africa and Asia in winter and returning home during the summer months. Dhows were small but sturdy, graceful, and highly maneuverable sailing vessels. They that carried Arab traders, Sufi holy men, and warriors from the Middle East across the Mediterranean, the Red Sea and Persian Gulf, and throughout the vast Indian Ocean trading system.

Watch the Video Series on MyHistoryLab

Learn about some key topics related to this chapter with the *MyHistoryLab Video Series: Key Topics in World History*

it was the configuration of their sails that have made them one of the most popular and enduring of the world's ships for two millennia. Dhows were propelled by one or two large, triangular **lateen** sails that attached to the masts by long booms or yard arms, which extended diagonally high across both the fore and aft portions of the ship.

Although their relatively shallow hulls meant that dhows could not match junks or bulkier merchant ships in cargo capacity, their slender shape gave them a considerable advantage over most other ships in speed. Their triangular sails meant that they could tack against the wind, which was very difficult in the best of conditions for square-rigged ships. Most often, however, those who sailed dhows followed a seasonal pattern set by the direction of the monsoon winds that alternated between flows to the sea or land according to the time of the year in the India Ocean and adjacent waterways. Although galleys like those of classical Greece and Rome were widely used by Arabs in the Mediterranean, from Spain to China tens of thousands of dhows were the main carriers of Muslim commerce. And along with merchants and their trade goods, many of the same ships conveyed Sufis or Muslim holy men to regions as far-flung as India, Java and Malaya, and the Philippine Islands.

Seaworthy ships like the dhows were essential to the remarkable spread of the Islamic faith and the civilizations it gave rise to in this era. In contrast to the expansion of Muslim empires, which was largely carried out by Arab armies traveling over land, lasting mass conversions of conquered peoples to the religion of Islam were mainly due to the efforts of Sufis and other spiritual leaders. These missionaries of the Islamic faith traveled by caravan into central Asia and across the Sahara or traversed the seas in sturdy dhows. In either case, those who went out to win converts to Islam also disseminated broader products of Muslim culture. These included the Arabic language; advanced technologies, such as water pumps and windmills; Muslim science, law, and philosophy; and Islamic art and architecture.

Despite their speed and dexterity, dhows did not make great warships, either before or after gunpowder was introduced into sea warfare. They were too small to provide a suitable firing platform for regular cannon, and they could not carry enough soldiers to grapple, board, and overwhelm the crews of enemy ships. Like most of the ships that sailed the seas of the Middle East, east Africa, and Asia, dhows were built for trade and not war. Designs for that purpose served the peoples of the Indian Ocean and adjoining seas well until the last years of the 15th century. But with the arrival of well-armed Portuguese fleets after 1498, neither the dhows nor any of the ships in Asia west of the South China Sea could hold back expansionist Christian warriors and seafarers. These aspiring empire builders were eager to tap into the wealth, knowledge, and technological acumen of Islamic and Chinese culture zones far more advanced in most areas of human endeavor than their own. ■

lateen Triangular sails attached to the masts of dhows by long booms, or yard arms, which extended diagonally high across the fore and aft of the ship.

Even as Muslim traders and Sufi holymen spread Islam across a great swath of Afro-Euroasia from north Africa in the west to the Philippines in the east, the Abbasid empire was crumbling from within. In many of the areas newly won to the faith, rival dynasties arose to challenge Abbasid power. These new polities and the Abbasids themselves were in turn threatened by the invasions of nomadic peoples launched by successive waves of Turkish-speakers and the Mongols from central Asia as well as Berber jihadists from Saharan Africa. Ironically, as the political hold of various Muslim rulers weakened, Islamic civilization reached new heights of creativity.

700 C.E.	800 C.E.	900 C.E.	1000 C.E.	1200 C.E.
661–750 Umayyad caliphate (Damascus) **711–713** First Muslim raids into India **750** Establishment of the Abbasid caliphate (Baghdad) **775–785** Reign of al-Mahdi **777** Independent dynasty established in Algeria **786–809** Reign of al-Rashid **788** Independent dynasty established in Morocco	**800** Independent dynasty established in Tunisia **809** First war of succession between Abbasid princes **813–833** Reign of al-Ma'mun; first mercenary forces recruited **865–925** Life of al-Razi, physician and scientist	**945** Persian Buyids capture Baghdad; caliphs become puppet rulers **973–1050** Life of al-Biruni, scientist **998** Beginning of Ghazni raids into western India	**c. 1020** Death of Firdawsi, author of the *Shah-Nama* **1055** Seljuk Turks overthrow Buyids, control caliphate **1096–1099** First Christian Crusade in Palestine **1058–1111** Life of al-Ghazali, philosopher and scientist **1038–1123** Life of Omar Khayyam, scientist and poet	**1206** Establishment of the Delhi sultanate in India **1258** Fall of Baghdad to Mongols; end of Abbasid caliphate **1290s** Beginning of the spread of Islam in southeast Asia **1291** Fall of Acre; last crusader stronghold in Middle East

As we shall see in this chapter, the Abbasid age was a time of remarkable achievements in architecture and the fine arts, in literature and philosophy, and in mathematics and the sciences. Many of these developments were enriched by the wealth, knowledge, and products exchanged among the many regions of an ever-expanding Muslim world and the non-Muslim peoples contacted in border regions from Europe to China. From the 10th to the 14th centuries, Muslim mystics, traders, and at times warriors carried the faith of Muhammad across much of the known world. In this chapter we will focus on this process in south and southeast Asia. In those that follow, north and west Africa and central Asia will be the focus of our inquiry.

THE ISLAMIC HEARTLANDS IN THE MIDDLE AND LATE ABBASID ERAS

8.1 What were the major sources contributing to the decline of the Abbasid dynasty?

The vast Abbasid empire (Map 8.1) gradually disintegrated between the 9th and 13th centuries C.E. Political decline and recurring social turmoil were fed both by the emergence of rival centers of power and the inroads of nomadic peoples attracted to the rich and fertile regions where Muslim urban life and power were centered.

As early as the reign of the third Abbasid caliph, **al-Mahdi** (r. 775–785), the courtly excesses and political divisions that eventually contributed to the decline of the empire were apparent. Al-Mahdi's efforts to reconcile the moderates among the Shi'a opposition to Abbasid rule ended in failure. This meant that Shi'a revolts and assassination attempts against Abbasid officials would plague the dynasty to the end of its days. Al-Mahdi also abandoned the frugal ways of his predecessor. In the brief span of his reign, he cultivated a taste for luxury and monumental building and surrounded himself with a multitude of dependent wives, concubines, and courtiers. These habits would prove to be an ever-greater financial drain in the reigns of later caliphs.

Perhaps most critically, al-Mahdi failed to solve the vexing problem of succession. Not only did he waver between which of his older sons would succeed him, but he allowed his wives and concubines, the mothers of different candidates, to become involved in the palace intrigues that became a standard feature of the transfer of power from one caliph to the next. Although a full-scale civil war was avoided after al-Mahdi's death, within a year his eldest son and successor was poisoned. That act cleared the way for one of the most famous and enduring of the Abbasid caliphs, **Harun al-Rashid** (r. 786–809), to ascend the throne.

al-Mahdi [al-mä dEE] (r. 775–785) Third of the Abbasid caliphs; attempted but failed to reconcile moderates among Shi'a to Abbasid dynasty; failed to resolve problem of succession.

Harun al-Rashid One of the great Islamic rulers of the Abbasid era.

Imperial Extravagance and Succession Disputes

Emissaries sent in the early 9th century to Baghdad from Charlemagne (Map 8.1), then the most powerful monarch in Christian Europe, provide ample evidence that Harun al-Rashid shared his father's taste for sumptuous living. Harun al-Rashid dazzled the Christians with the splendor of Baghdad's

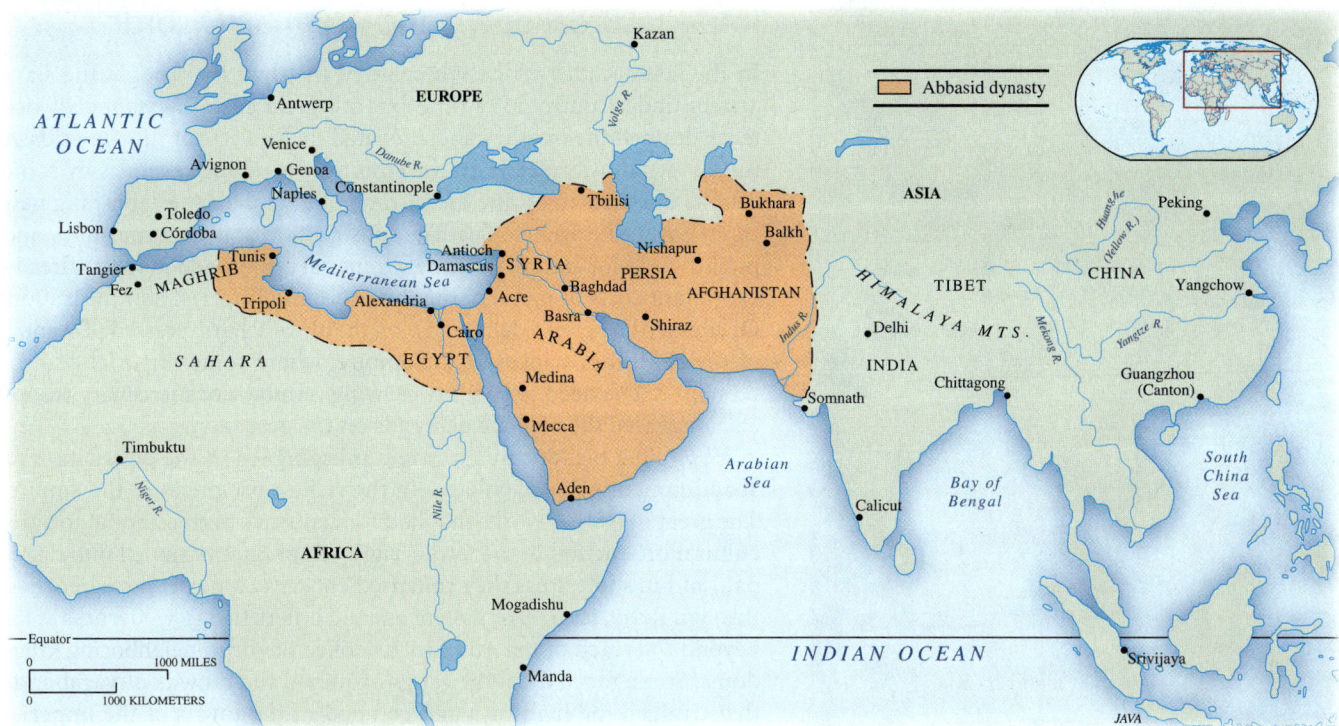

MAP 8.1 The Abbasid Empire at Its Peak

mosques, palaces, and treasure troves, which is reflected in the painting of nightlife in a palace in Figure 8.2. He also sent them back to Charlemagne with presents, including an intricate water clock and an elephant, which were literally worth a king's ransom.

The luxury and intrigue of Harun's court have also been immortalized by the tales of *The Thousand and One Nights* (see the Document in Chapter 7), set in the Baghdad of his day. The plots and maneuvers of the courtesans, eunuchs, and royal ministers related in the tales suggest yet another source of dynastic weakness. Partly because he was only 23 at the time of his accession to the throne, Harun became heavily dependent, particularly in the early years of his reign, on a family of Persian advisors. Although he eventually resisted their influence, the growth of the power of royal advisors at the expense of the caliphs became a clear trend in succeeding reigns. In fact, from the mid-9th century onward, most caliphs were pawns in the power struggles between different factions at the court.

Harun al-Rashid's death prompted the first of several full-scale civil wars over succession. In itself, the precedent set by the struggle for the throne was deeply damaging. But it had an additional consequence that would all but end the real power of the caliphs. The first civil war convinced the sons of al-Ma'mun (813–833), the winner, to build personal armies in anticipation of the fight for the throne that would break out when their father died. One of the sons, the victor in the next round of succession struggles, recruited a "bodyguard" of some 4000 slaves, mostly Turkic-speaking nomads from central Asia. On becoming caliph, he increased this mercenary force to more than 70,000.

Not surprisingly, this impressive army soon became a power center in its own right. In 846 slave mercenaries murdered the reigning caliph and placed one of his sons on the throne. In the next decade, four more caliphs were assassinated or poisoned by the mercenary forces. From this time onward, the leaders of the slave mercenary armies were often the real power behind the Abbasid throne and were major players in the struggles for control of the capital and empire. The mercenaries also became a major force for violent social unrest. They were often the catalyst for the food riots that broke out periodically when the price of everyday staples rose too sharply because of shortages or price gouging in Baghdad and other urban centers.

Imperial Breakdown and Agrarian Disorder

In the last decades of the 9th century, the dynasty brought the slave armies under control for a time, but at a great cost. Constant civil violence drained the treasury and alienated the subjects of the Abbasids. A further strain was placed on the empire's dwindling revenues by some caliphs' attempts to escape the turmoil of Baghdad by establishing new capitals near the original one. The construction of palaces, mosques, and public works for each of these new imperial centers added to the already exorbitant costs of maintaining the court and imperial administration. Of course, the expense fell heavily on the already hard-pressed peasantry of the central provinces of the empire, where some imperial control remained. The need to support growing numbers of mercenary troops also increased the revenue demands on the peasantry.

Spiraling taxation and outright pillaging led to the destruction or abandonment of many villages in the richest provinces of the empire. The great irrigation works that had for centuries been essential to agricultural production in the fertile Tigris–Euphrates basin fell into disrepair, and in some areas they collapsed entirely. Some peasants perished through flood, famine, or violent assault; others fled to wilderness areas beyond the reach of the Abbasid tax collectors or to neighboring kingdoms. Some formed bandit gangs or joined the crowds of vagabonds that trudged the highways and camped in the towns of the imperial heartland. In many cases, dissident religious groups, such as the various Shi'a sects, instigated peasant uprisings. Shi'a participation meant that these movements sought not only to correct the official abuses that had occurred under the Abbasid regime but to destroy the dynasty itself.

The Declining Position of Women in the Family and Society

The harem and the veil became the twin emblems of women's increasing subjugation to men and confinement to the home in the Abbasid era. Although the seclusion of women had been practiced by some Middle Eastern peoples since ancient times, the harem was a creation of the Abbasid court. The wives and the concubines of the Abbasid caliphs were restricted to the forbidden quarters of the imperial palace. Many of the concubines were slaves, who could win their freedom and gain power by bearing healthy sons for the rulers. The growing wealth of the Abbasid elite created a great demand for female and male slaves, who were found by the tens of thousands in Baghdad and other large cities. Most of these urban slaves continued to perform domestic services in the homes of the wealthy. One of the 10th-century caliphs is reputed to have had 11,000 eunuchs among his slave corps; another is said to have kept 4000 slave concubines.

FIGURE **8.2** The richness and vitality of urban life in the Islamic world in the Abbasid age and later eras are wonderfully captured in this 16th-century Persian illustration from the *Khamsah* (Five Poems) of Nizami. The miniature painting gives us a bird's-eye view of a typical night in one of the great palaces of Baghdad. The multiple scenes vividly capture the bustle and high artistry of the splendidly decorated rooms and gardens, from a group of musicians serenading a man who is presumably the lord of the mansion, to kitchen servants buying food and preparing to serve it to the lord and his guests.

(Attributed to Mir Sayyid 'Ali "Nighttime in a Palace." Folio from a Manuscript, c. 1539–1543. Harvard Art Museum, Arthur M. Sackler Museum, Gift of John Goelet, formerly in the collection of Louis J. Cartier, 1958.76. Katya Kallsen © President and Fellows of Harvard College.)

Most of the slaves had been captured or purchased in the non-Muslim regions surrounding the empire, including the Balkans, central Asia, and Sudanic Africa. They were sold in the slave markets found in all of the larger towns of the Abbasid realm. Female and male slaves were prized for both their beauty and their intelligence. Some of the best-educated men and women in the empire were slaves. Consequently, caliphs and high officials often spent more time with their clever and talented slave concubines than with their less-educated wives. Slave concubines and servants often had more personal liberty than freeborn wives. Slave women could go to the market, and they did not have to wear the veils and robes that were required for free women in public places.

Although women from the lower classes farmed, wove clothing and rugs, or raised silkworms to help support their families, rich women were allowed almost no career outlets beyond the home. Often married at puberty (legally set at age 9), women were raised to devote their lives to running a household and serving their husbands. But at the highest levels of society, wives and concubines cajoled their husbands and plotted with eunuchs and royal advisors to advance the interests of their sons and win for them the ruler's backing for succession to the throne. Despite these brief incursions into power politics, by the end of the Abbasid era, the freedom and influence—both within the family and in the wider world—that women had enjoyed in the first centuries of Islamic expansion had been severely curtailed.

Nomadic Incursions and the Eclipse of Caliphal Power

Preoccupied by struggles in the capital and central provinces, the caliphs and their advisors were powerless to prevent further losses of territory in the outer reaches of the empire. In addition, areas as close to the capital as Egypt and Syria broke away from Abbasid rule (Map 8.1). More alarmingly, by the mid-10th century, independent kingdoms that had formed in areas that were once provinces of the empire were moving to supplant the Abbasids as lords of the Islamic world. In 945, the armies of one of these regional splinter dynasties, the **Buyids** of Persia, invaded the heartlands of the Abbasid empire and captured Baghdad. From this point onward, the caliphs were little more than puppets controlled by families such as the Buyids. Buyid leaders took the title of *sultan* ("victorious" in Arabic), which came to designate Muslim rulers, especially in the West.

The Buyids controlled the caliph and the court, but they could not prevent the further disintegration of the empire. In just over a century, the Buyids' control over the caliphate was broken, and they were supplanted in 1055 by another group of nomadic invaders from central Asia via Persia, the **Seljuk Turks**. For the next two centuries, Turkic military leaders ruled the remaining portions of the Abbasid empire in the name of caliphs, who were usually of Arab or Persian extraction. The Seljuks were staunch Sunnis, and they moved quickly to purge the Shi'a officials who had risen to power under the Buyids and to rid the caliph's domains of the Shi'a influences the Buyids had tried to promote. For a time, the Seljuk military machine was also able to restore political initiative to the much-reduced caliphate. Seljuk victories ended the threat of conquest by a rival Shi'a dynasty centered in Egypt. They also humbled the Byzantines, who had hoped to take advantage of Muslim divisions to regain some of their long-lost lands. The Byzantines' crushing defeat also opened the way to the settlement of Asia Minor, or Anatolia, by nomadic peoples of Turkic origins, some of whom would soon begin to lay the foundations of the Ottoman Empire.

Buyids [BOO-yihds] Regional splinter dynasty of the mid-10th century; invaded and captured Baghdad; ruled Abbasid Empire under title of sultan; retained Abbasids as figureheads.

Seljuk Turks [SEHL-jook Turks] Nomadic invaders from central Asia via Persia; staunch Sunnis; ruled in name of Abbasid caliphs from mid-11th century.

The Impact of the Christian Crusades

Soon after seizing power, the Seljuks faced a very different challenge to Islamic civilization. It came from Christian crusaders, knights from western Europe (see Chapter 11) who were determined to capture the portions of the Islamic world that made up the Holy Land of biblical times. Muslim political divisions and the element of surprise made the first of the crusaders' assaults, between 1096 and 1099, by far the most successful. Much of the Holy Land was captured and divided into Christian kingdoms. In June 1099, the main objective of the Crusade, Jerusalem, was taken, and its Muslim and Jewish inhabitants were massacred by the rampaging Christian knights.

For nearly two centuries, the Europeans, who eventually mounted eight **Crusades** that varied widely in strength and success, maintained their precarious hold on the eastern Mediterranean region. But they posed little threat to the more powerful Muslim princes, whose disregard for the Christians was demonstrated by the fact that they continued to quarrel among themselves despite the intruders' aggressions. When united under a strong leader, as they were under Salah-ud-Din (known as **Saladin** in Christian Europe) in the last decades of the 12th century, the Muslims rapidly reconquered most of the crusader outposts. Saladin's death in 1193 and the subsequent breakup of his kingdom gave the remaining Christian citadels some respite. But the last of the crusader kingdoms was lost with the fall of Acre in 1291.

Undoubtedly, the impact of the Crusades was much greater on the Christians who launched them than on the Muslim peoples who had to fend them off. Because there had long been so much contact between western Europe and the Islamic world through trade and through the Muslim kingdoms in Spain and southern Italy, it is difficult to be sure which influences to attribute specifically to the Crusades. But the crusaders' firsthand experiences in the eastern Mediterranean certainly intensified European borrowing from the Muslim world that had been going on for centuries. Muslim weapons, such as the famous damascene swords (named after the city of Damascus), were highly prized and sometimes copied by the Europeans, who were always eager to improve on their methods of making war. Muslim techniques of building fortifications were adopted by many Christian rulers, as can be

Crusades Series of military adventures initially launched by western Christians to free Holy Land from Muslims; temporarily succeeded in capturing Jerusalem and establishing Christian kingdoms; later used for other purposes such as commercial wars and extermination of heresy.

Saladin Muslim leader in the last decades of the 12th century; reconquered most of the crusader outposts for Islam.

 Read the **Document** on **MyHistoryLab**: A Muslim View of the Crusades: Behâ-ed-Din, Richard I Massacres Prisoners after Taking Acre, 1191

Ibn Khaldun [i buhn kal dUn, KHUn] (1332–1406) A Muslim historian; developed concept that dynasties of nomadic conquerors had a cycle of three generations—strong, weak, dissolute.

seen in the castles built in Normandy and coastal England by William the Conqueror and his successors in the 11th and 12th centuries. Richard the Lionheart's legendary preference for Muslim over Christian physicians was but one sign of the Europeans' avid centuries-old interest in the superior scientific learning of Muslim peoples.

From Muslims and Jews in Spain, Sicily, Egypt, and the Middle East, the Europeans recovered much of the Greek learning that had been lost to northern Europe during the waves of nomadic invasions after the fall of Rome. They also mastered Arabic (properly Indian) numerals and the decimal system, and they benefited from the great advances Arab and Persian thinkers had made in mathematics and many of the sciences. The European demand for Middle Eastern rugs and textiles is demonstrated by the Oriental rugs and tapestries that adorned the homes of the European upper classes in Renaissance and early modern paintings. It is also reflected in European (and our own) names for different kinds of cloth, such as *fustian*, *taffeta*, *muslin*, and *damask*, which are derived from Persian terms or the names of Muslim cities where the cloth was produced and sold.

DOCUMENT

Ibn Khaldun on the Rise and Decline of Empires

ALTHOUGH HE LIVED IN THE CENTURY after the Abbasid caliphate was destroyed in 1258, **Ibn Khaldun** was very much a product of the far-flung Islamic civilization that the Abbasids had consolidated and expanded. He was also one of the greatest historians and social commentators of all time. After extensive travels in the Islamic world, he served as a political advisor at several of the courts of Muslim rulers in north Africa. With the support of a royal patron, Ibn Khaldun wrote a universal history that began with a very long philosophical preface called *The Muqaddimah*. Among the subjects he treated at length were the causes of the rise and fall of dynasties. The shifting fortunes of the dynasties he knew well in his native north Africa, as well as the fate of the Abbasids and earlier Muslim regimes, informed his attempts to find persistent patterns in the complex political history of the Islamic world. The following passages are from one of the most celebrated sections of *The Muqaddimah* on the natural life span of political regimes.

> We have stated that the duration of the life of a dynasty does not as a rule extend beyond three generations. The first generation retains the desert qualities, desert toughness, and desert savagery. [Its members are used to] privation and to sharing their glory [with each other]; they are brave and rapacious. Therefore, the strength of group feeling continues to be preserved among them. They are sharp and greatly feared. People submit to them.
>
> Under the influence of royal authority and a life of ease, the second generation changes from the desert attitude to sedentary culture, from privation to luxury and plenty, from a state in which everybody shared in the glory to one in which one man claims all the glory for himself while the others are too lazy to strive for [glory], and from proud superiority to humble subservience. Thus, the vigor of group feeling is broken to some extent. People become used to lowliness and obedience. But many of [the old virtues] remain in them, because they had direct personal contact with the first generation and its conditions.
>
> The third generation, then, has [completely] forgotten the period of desert life and toughness, as if it had never existed. They have lost [the taste for] group feeling, because they are dominated by force. Luxury reaches its peak among them, because they are so much given to a life of prosperity and ease. They become dependent on the dynasty and are like women and children who need to be defended [by someone else]. Group feeling disappears completely. People forget to protect and defend themselves and to press their claims. With their emblems, apparel, horseback riding, and [fighting] skill, they deceive people and give them the wrong impression. For the most part, they are more cowardly than women upon their backs. When someone comes and demands something from them, they cannot repel him. The ruler, then, has need of other, brave people for his support. He takes many clients and followers. They help the dynasty to some degree, until God permits it to be destroyed, and it goes with everything it stands for.
>
> Three generations last one hundred and twenty years. As a rule, dynasties do not last longer than that many years, a few more, a few less, save when, by chance, no one appears to attack [the dynasty]. When senility becomes preponderant [in a dynasty], there may be no claimant [for its power, and then nothing will happen] but if there should be one, he will encounter no one capable of repelling him. If the time is up [the end of the dynasty] cannot be postponed for a single hour, no more than it can be accelerated.

QUESTIONS

- What does this passage reveal about Ibn Khaldun's views of the contrasts between nomads and urban dwellers?
- Why does he see the former as a source of military power and political strength?
- What forces undermine dynasties in later generations?
- How well do these patterns correspond to the history of the Umayyad and Abbasid dynasties we have been studying?

Muslim influences affected both the elite and popular cultures of much of western Europe in this period. These included Persian and Arabic words, games such as chess, chivalric ideals and troubadour ballads, as well as foods such as dates, coffee, and yogurt. Some of these imports, namely the songs of the troubadours, can be traced directly to the contacts the crusaders made in the Holy Land. But most were part of a process of exchange that extended over centuries, and was largely a one-way process. Although Arab traders imported some manufactures, such as glass and cloth, and raw materials from Europe, Muslim peoples in this era showed little interest in the learning or institutions of the West. Nevertheless, the Italian merchant communities, which remained after the political and military power of the crusaders had been extinguished in the Middle East, contributed a good deal more to these ongoing interchanges than all the forays of Christian knights.

AN AGE OF LEARNING AND ARTISTIC REFINEMENTS

8.2 Discuss the major advances in the arts and sciences that occurred in the Islamic world in the late-Abbasid period.

> Paradoxically, even as the political power of the Abbasids declined, Islamic civilization reached new heights of achievement and entered into a phase of renewed expansion.

Although town life became more dangerous, the rapid growth and increasing prosperity that characterized the first centuries of Muslim expansion continued until late in the Abbasid era. Despite the declining revenue base of the caliphate and deteriorating conditions in the countryside, there was a great expansion of the professional classes, particularly doctors, scholars, and legal and religious experts (Figure 8.3). Muslim, Jewish, and in some areas Christian entrepreneurs amassed great fortunes supplying the cities of the empire with staples such as grain and barley, essentials such as cotton and woolen textiles for clothing, and luxury items such as precious gems, citrus fruits, and sugar cane. Long-distance trade between the Middle East and Mediterranean Europe and between coastal India and southeast Asia, in addition to the overland caravan trade with China, flourished through much of the Abbasid era (Map 8.2).

Among the chief beneficiaries of the sustained urban prosperity were artists and artisans, who continued the formidable achievements in architecture and the crafts that had begun in the Umayyad period. Mosques and palaces grew larger and more ornate in most parts of the empire. Even in outlying areas, such as Córdoban Spain, Muslim engineers and architects created some of the great architectural treasures of all time. The tapestries and rugs of Muslim peoples, most famously the Persians, were in great demand from Europe to China. To this day, Muslim rugs have rarely been matched for their exquisite designs, their vivid colors, and the skill with which they are woven. Muslim artisans also produced fine bronzes and superb ceramics.

The Full Flowering of Persian Literature

As Persian wives, concubines, advisors, bureaucrats, and (after the mid-10th century) Persian caliphs came to play central roles in imperial politics, Persian gradually replaced Arabic as the primary written language at the Abbasid court. Arabic remained the language of religion, law, and the natural sciences. Persian was favored by Arabs, Turks, and Muslims of Persian descent as the language of literary expression, administration, and scholarship. In Baghdad and major cities throughout the Abbasid empire and in neighboring kingdoms, Persian was the chief language of "high culture," the language of polite exchanges between courtiers as well as of history, poetic musings, and mystical revelations.

Written in a modified Arabic script and drawing selectively on Arabic vocabulary, the Persian of the Abbasid age was a supple language as beautiful to look at when drafted by a skilled calligrapher as it was to read aloud. Catch phrases ("A jug of wine, a loaf of bread, and Thou") from the *Rubaiyat* (ROO-bee-AHT) of Omar Khayyam (OH-mahr keye-YAHM) are certainly the pieces of Persian literature best known in the West. But other writers from this period surpassed Khayyam in profundity of thought and elegance of style. Perhaps the single most important work was the lengthy epic poem *Shah-Nama* (Book of Kings), written by Firdawsi in the late 10th and early 11th centuries. The work relates the history of Persia from the beginnings of time to the Islamic conquests, and it abounds in dramatic details of battles, intrigues, and illicit love affairs. Firdawsi's Persian has been extolled for

Shah-Nama Written by Firdawsi in late 10th and early 11th centuries; relates history of Persia from creation to the Islamic conquests.

FIGURE 8.3 The subtlety and depth attained by Muslim civilizations in the far-flung regions in which they were found is illustrated by this 17th-century watercolor painting titled *A Discourse between Muslim Sages*. The meditative figures, with scholarly books before them, surrounded by grass and trees, captures the commitment to learning and refined aesthetic sense that was cultivated by members of the elite classes throughout the Islamic world.

Read the Document on MyHistoryLab: The Rubaiyat (11th c. CE) Omar Khayyam

ulama Orthodox religious scholars within Islam; pressed for a more conservative and restrictive theology; increasingly opposed to non-Islamic ideas and scientific thinking.

al-Ghazali [al Gaz-AHL-ee] (1058–1111) Brilliant Islamic theologian; struggled to fuse Greek and Qur'anic traditions; not entirely accepted by ulama.

View the Image on MyHistoryLab: Islamic science and alchemy: page from "The Lanterns of Wisdom and the Keys of Mercy"

its grand, musical virtuosity, and portions of the *Shah-Nama* and other Persian works were read aloud to musical accompaniment. Brilliantly illustrated manuscripts of Firdawsi's epic history are among the most exquisite works of Islamic art.

In addition to historical epics, Persian writers in the Abbasid era wrote on many subjects, from doomed love affairs and statecraft to accounts of distant travels and mystical striving for communion with the divine. One of the great poets of the age, Sa'di, fuses an everyday incident with a religious one in the following relation of a single moment in his own life:

> Often I am minded, from the days of my childhood,
> How once I went out with my father on a festival;
> In fun I grew preoccupied with all the folk about,
> Losing touch with my father in the popular confusion;
> In terror and bewilderment I raised up a cry,
> Then suddenly my father boxed my ears:
> "You bold-eyed child, how many times, now,
> Have I told you not to lose hold of my skirt?"
> A tiny child cannot walk out alone,
> For it is difficult to take a way not seen;
> You too, poor friend, are but a child upon endeavour's way:
> Go, seize the skirts of those who know the way!

This blend of the mystical and commonplace was widely adopted in the literature of this period. It is epitomized in the *Rubaiyat*, whose author is much more concerned with finding meaning in life and a path to union with the divine than with extolling the delights of picnics in the garden with beautiful women.

Achievements in the Sciences

From preserving and compiling the learning of the ancient civilizations they had conquered in the early centuries of expansion, Muslim peoples—and the Jewish scholars who lived peacefully in Muslim lands—increasingly became creators and inventors in their own right. For several centuries, which spanned much of the period of Abbasid rule, Islamic civilization outstripped all others in scientific discoveries, new techniques of investigation, and new technologies. The many Muslim accomplishments in these areas include major corrections to the algebraic and geometric theories of the ancient Greeks and great advances in the use of basic concepts of trigonometry: the sine, cosine, and tangent.

Two discoveries in chemistry that were fundamental to all later investigation were the creation of the objective experiment and al-Razi's scheme of classifying all material substances into three categories: animal, vegetable, and mineral. The sophistication of Muslim scientific techniques is indicated by the fact that in the 11th century, al-Biruni was able to calculate the specific weight of 18 major minerals. This sophistication was also manifested in astronomical instruments such as those in Figure 8.4, developed through cooperation between Muslim scholars and skilled artisans. Their astronomical tables and maps of the stars were in great demand among scholars of other civilizations, including those of Europe and China.

As these breakthroughs suggest, much of the Muslims' work in scientific investigation had very practical applications. This practical bent was even greater in other fields. For example, Muslim cities such as Cairo boasted some of the best hospitals in the world. Doctors and pharmacists had to follow a regular course of study and pass a formal examination before they were allowed to practice. Muslim scientists did important work on optics and bladder ailments. Muslim traders introduced into the Islamic world and Europe many basic machines and techniques—namely, papermaking, silk-weaving, and ceramic firing—that had been devised earlier in China. In addition, Muslim scholars made some of the world's best maps, which were copied by geographers from Portugal to Poland.

Read the Document on MyHistoryLab: Ibn Battuta, selections from the Rihla

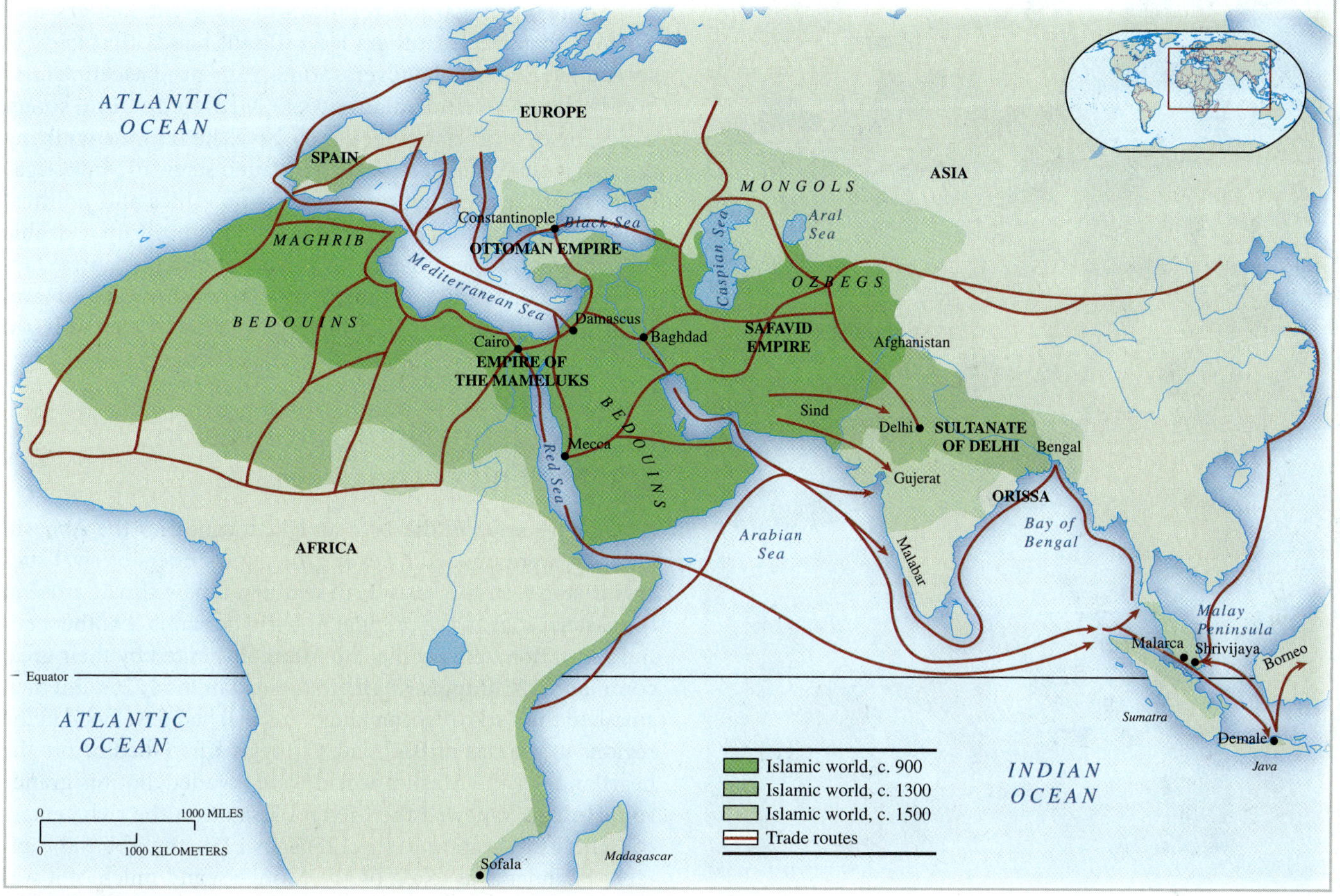

MAP 8.2 **The Spread of Islam, 10th–16th Centuries** Arrows indicate the routes by which Islam spread to south, and southeast and Central Asia, Asia Minor and the Balkans, and Sudanic Africa.

Religious Trends and the New Push for Expansion

The contradictory trends in Islamic civilization—social strife and political divisions versus expanded trading links and intellectual creativity—were strongly reflected in patterns of religious development in the later centuries of the caliphate. On one hand, a resurgence of mysticism injected Islam with a new vibrancy. On the other, orthodox religious scholars, such as the **ulama**, grew increasingly suspicious of and hostile to non-Islamic ideas and scientific thinking. The Crusades had promoted the latter trend. This was particularly true regarding Muslim borrowing from ancient Greek learning, which the ulama associated with the aggressive civilizations of Christian Europe. Many orthodox scholars suspected that the questioning that characterized the Greek tradition would undermine the absolute authority of the Qur'an. They insisted that the Qur'an was the final, perfect, and complete revelation of an all-knowing divinity. Brilliant thinkers such as **al-Ghazali** perhaps the greatest Islamic theologian, struggled to fuse the Greek and Qur'anic traditions. Their ideas were often rejected by orthodox scholars.

Much of the religious vitality in Islam in the later Abbasid period was centered on the Sufist movement. In its various guises, including both Sunni and Shi'a manifestations, Sufism was a reaction against the impersonal and abstract divinity that many ulama scholars argued was the true god of the Qur'an. Like the Indian mystics, the Sufis—whose title was derived from the woolen robes they wore—and their followers tried to see beyond what they believed to be the illusory existence of everyday life and to delight in the presence of Allah in the world. True to the strict monotheism of Islam, most Sufis insisted on a clear distinction between Allah and

Mongols Central Asian nomadic peoples; smashed Turko-Persian kingdoms; captured Baghdad in 1258 and killed last Abbasid caliph.

Chinggis Khan [JEHNG-gihs KAHN] Born in 1170s in decades following death of Kabul Khan; elected khagan of all Mongol tribes in 1206; responsible for conquest of northern kingdoms of China, territories as far west as the Abbasid regions; died in 1227, prior to conquest of most of Islamic world.

Hulegu [hoo-LAY-goo] (1217–1265) Ruler of the Ilkhan khanate; grandson of Chinggis Khan; responsible for capture and destruction of Baghdad in 1257.

Read the Document on MyHistoryLab: Science and Mathematics: Al-Ghazzali, "On the Separation of Mathematics and Religion"

humans. But in some Sufist teachings, Allah permeated the universe in ways that appeared to compromise his transcendent status.

Some Sufis gained reputations as great healers and workers of miracles; others led militant bands that tried to spread Islam to nonbelievers. Some Sufis used asceticism or bodily denial to find Allah; others used meditation, songs, drugs, or ecstatic dancing, which gave the famous whirling dervishes their name. Sufis also pursued scientific investigations as well as writing major works on ethics and political philosophy. The more accomplished Sufis built up a sizable following, and the movement as a whole was a central factor in the continuing expansion of the Muslim religion and Islamic civilization in the later centuries of the Abbasid caliphate.

New Waves of Nomadic Invasions and the End of the Caliphate

As we have seen, in the 10th and 11th centuries the Abbasid domains were divided by ever growing numbers of rival successor states. In the early 13th century, a new threat arose at the eastern edge of the original Abbasid domains. Another central Asian nomadic people, the **Mongols**, united by their great commander, **Chinggis Khan**, first raided in the 1220s and then smashed the Turko-Persian kingdoms that had developed in the regions to the east of Baghdad. Chinggis Khan died before the heartlands of the Muslim world were invaded, but his grandson, **Hulegu**, renewed the Mongol assault on the rich centers of Islamic civilization in the 1250s. In 1258, the Abbasid capital at Baghdad was taken by the Mongols, and much of it was sacked. The 37th and last Abbasid caliph was put to death by the Mongols. They then continued westward until they were finally defeated by the **Mamluks**, or Turkic slaves, who then ruled Egypt.

Baghdad never recovered from the Mongol attacks. In 1401, it suffered a second capture and another round of pillaging by the even fiercer forces of Timur or Tamerlane, another Turkic conqueror from Central Asia. Baghdad shrank for centuries from the status of one of the great cities of the world to a provincial backwater. It was gradually supplanted by Cairo to the west and then Istanbul to the north.

FIGURE **8.4** This 15th-century Persian miniature of a group of Arab scientists testing and working with a wide variety of navigational instruments conveys a strong sense of the premium placed on scientific investigation in the Muslim world in the Abbasid age and the centuries thereafter. Muslim prototypes inspired European artisans, cartographers, and scientists to develop instruments and maps, which were essential to European overseas expansion from the 14th century onward.

Mamluks Muslim slave warriors; established a dynasty in Egypt; defeated the Mongols at Ain Jalut in 1260 and halted Mongol advance.

Read the Document on MyHistoryLab: Rabi'a al-'Adawiyya, "Brothers, my peace is in my aloneness."

From the 7th century onward, Muslim invaders, traders, and migrants carried the Islamic faith and Islamic civilization to the vast south Asian subcontinent. Muslim conquests and conversions provoked a variety of Hindu responses and attempts by some followers of both religions to reconcile their differences.

THE COMING OF ISLAM TO SOUTH ASIA

8.3 How did Hindu religious leaders and organizations counter the considerable appeal of Sufi missionaries and their efforts to win converts in south and southeast Asia from the 10th through the 16th centuries?

All through the millennia when a succession of civilizations from Harappa to the brahmanic empire of the Guptas developed in south Asia, foreigners had entered India in waves of nomadic invaders or as small bands of displaced peoples seeking refuge. Invariably, those who chose to remain were assimilated into the civilizations they encountered in the lowland areas. They converted to the Hindu or Buddhist religion, found a place in the caste hierarchy, and adopted the dress, foods, and lifestyles of the farming and city-dwelling peoples of the many regions of the subcontinent. This capacity to absorb peoples moving into the area resulted from the strength and flexibility of India's civilizations and from the fact that India's peoples usually enjoyed a higher level of material culture than migrant groups entering the subcontinent. As a result, the persistent failure of Indian rulers to unite against aggressors meant periodic disruptions and localized destruction but not fundamental challenges to the existing order. All of this changed with the arrival of the Muslims in the last years of the 7th century C.E. (Map 8.2).

With the coming of the Muslims, the peoples of India encountered for the first time a large-scale influx of bearers of an outside civilization as sophisticated, if not as ancient, as their own. They were also confronted by a religious system that was in many ways the very opposite of the ones they had nurtured. Hinduism, the predominant Indian religion at that time, was open, tolerant, and inclusive of widely varying forms of religious devotion, from idol worship to meditation in search of union with the spiritual source of all creation. Islam was doctrinaire, proselytizing, and committed to the exclusive worship of a single, transcendent god.

Read the Document on MyHistoryLab: Giovanni Di Piano Carpini on the Mongols

VISUALIZING THE PAST

The Pattern of Islam's Global Expansions

THE TABLE SHOWS THE PRESENT-DAY DISTRIBUTION of Muslims in key countries from Africa to Asia. It indicates the total number of Muslims in each of the countries listed, the percentage of Muslims in the total population of that area, and the numbers and percentages of other religious groups. The table also indicates the manner in which Islam was spread to each of these areas and the key agents of that diffusion. After using the table to compare the patterns of Islamization in different areas, answer the questions that follow.

QUESTIONS
- Which areas have the highest absolute numbers of Muslims in the present day?
- Is this distribution what you would have expected, or is it surprising?
- What were the main ways that Islam was transmitted to most areas?
- What does this say about the popular notion that Islam was historically a militant religion spread primarily by forcible conversion?
- Do the statistics suggest that Islam is able to coexist with other faiths?

COMPARATIVE STATISTICS OF MODERN STATES WITH A SIZABLE MUSLIM POPULATION

	Total Population (2000 est.)	Total Number of Muslims	Percentage of Muslims	Total Number of Non-Muslims	Percentages of Other Religious Groups	Principal Agents/Modes of Conversion
Nigeria	114 million	57 million	50	57 million	40–Christian; 10–Other (African religions)	Trading Contacts Sufi Missionaries
Egypt	67 million	63 million	94	4 million	4–Christian 2–Other	Arab Migration Conquest Voluntary Mass Conversion
Iraq	22.5 million	21.8 million	97: Shi'a: 60–65; Sunni: 32–37	700,000	3–Other (Zoroastrian, Christian, Jewish)	Arab Migration Conquest Voluntary Mass Conversion
Iran	65 million	64.35 million	99: Shi'a: 89; Sunni: 10	650,000	1—Other (Zoroastrian, Bahai, Christian, Jewish)	Arab Conquest Migration Voluntary Mass Conversion
Pakistan	138 million	133.85 million	97: Shi'a 20; Sunni: 77	4.15 million	3–Other (Hindu, Christian, Buddhist)	Sufi Missionaries Voluntary Mass Conversion
India	1.001 billion	140.1 million	14	860.9 million	80–Hindu; 6–Other (Buddhist, Sikh, Christian, Jain)	Sufi Missionaries Trading Contacts Conquest Voluntary Mass Conversion
Indonesia	216 million	188 million	87	28 million	6–Protestant; 7–Other (Catholic Buddhist, etc.)	Sufi Missionaries Trading Contacts
The Phillipines	79.5 million	4 million	5	75.5 million	83–Catholic; 9–Protestant; 3–Other	Trading contacts Sufi Missionaries
Morocco	30 million	29.7 million	99	300,000	1–Other	Voluntary Mass Conversion Sufi Missionaries Conquest

NOTE: Numbers based on information from Wiesenfeld and Famighetti et al., eds., *The World Almanac and Book of Facts 2000* (Mahwah, NJ: World Almanac Books).

Socially, Islam was highly egalitarian, proclaiming all believers equal in the sight of God. In sharp contrast, Hindu beliefs validated the caste hierarchy. The latter rested on the acceptance of inborn differences between individuals and groups and the widely varying levels of material wealth, status, and religious purity these differences were believed to produce. Thus, the faith of the invading Muslims was religiously more rigid than that of the absorptive and adaptive Hindus. But the caste-based social system of India was much more compartmentalized and closed than the society of the Muslim invaders, with their emphasis on mobility and the community of believers.

Because growing numbers of Muslim warriors, traders, Sufi mystics, and ordinary farmers and herders entered south Asia and settled there, extensive interaction between invaders and the indigenous peoples was inevitable. In the early centuries of the Muslim influx, conflict, often violent, predominated. But there was also a good deal of trade and even religious interchange between them. As time passed, peaceful (if often wary) interaction became the norm. Muslim rulers employed large numbers of Hindus to govern the largely non-Muslim populations they conquered; mosques and temples dominated different quarters within Indian cities. In addition, Hindu and Muslim mystics strove to find areas of agreement between their two faiths. Nonetheless, tensions remained, and periodically they erupted into communal rioting or warfare between Hindu and Muslim rulers.

Muhammad ibn Qasim [moh-HAM-ihd ihbn HAH-sihm] (661–750) Arab general; conquered Sind in India; declared the region and the Indus valley to be part of Umayyad Empire.

Political Divisions and the First Muslim Invasions

The first and least enduring Muslim intrusion, which came in 711, resulted indirectly from the peaceful trading contacts that had initially brought Muslims into contact with Indian civilization. Since ancient times, Arab seafarers and traders had been major carriers in the vast trading network that stretched from Italy in the Mediterranean to the South China Sea. After converting to Islam, these traders continued to visit the ports of India, particularly those on the western coast. An attack by pirates sailing from Sind in western India (Map 8.3) on ships owned by some of these Arab traders prompted the viceroy of the eastern provinces of the Umayyad Empire to launch a punitive expedition against the king of Sind. An able Arab general, **Muhammad ibn Qasim** who was only 17 years old when the campaign began, led more than 10,000 horse- and camel-mounted warriors into Sind to avenge the assault on Arab shipping. After victories in several fiercely fought battles, Muhammad ibn Qasim declared the region, as well as the Indus valley to the northeast, provinces of the Umayyad empire.

In these early centuries, the coming of Islam brought little change for most inhabitants of the Indian subcontinent. In fact, in many areas, local leaders and the populace surrendered towns and districts willingly to the conquerors because they promised lighter taxation and greater religious tolerance. The Arab overlords decided to treat both Hindus and Buddhists as protected "people of the book,"

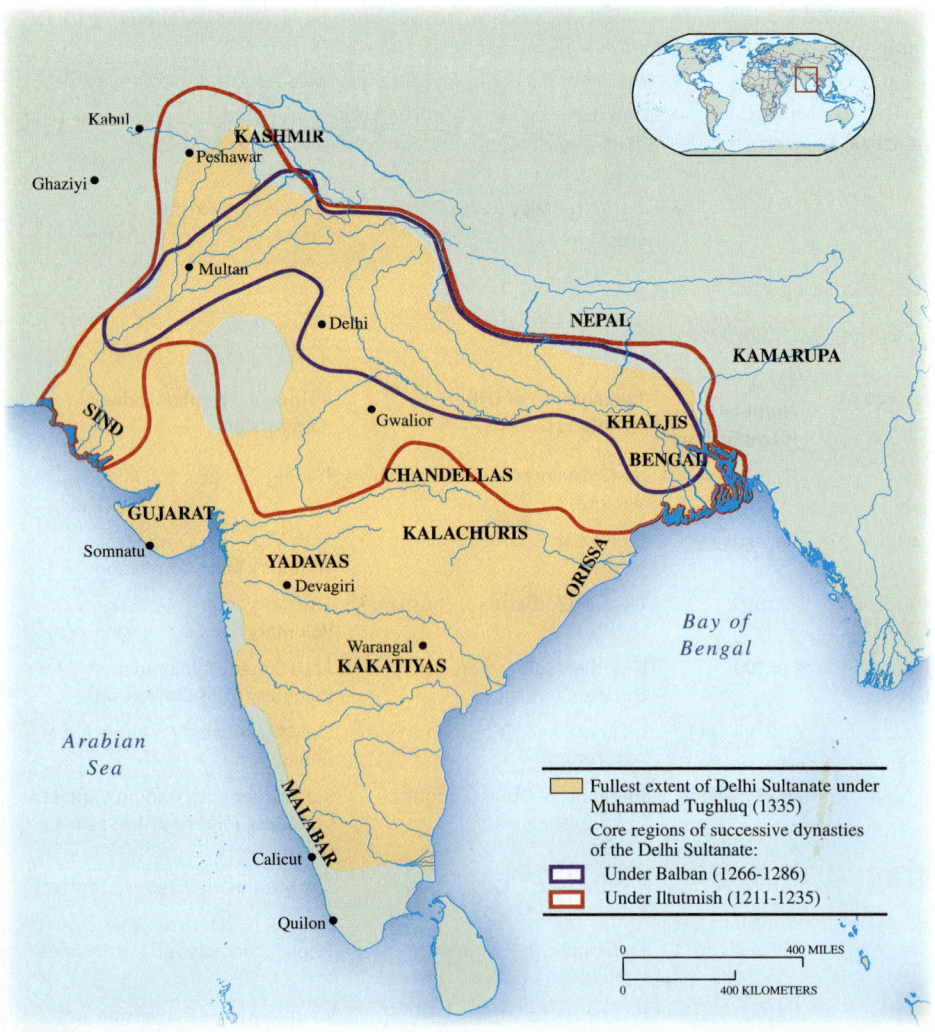

MAP 8.3 **Early Islam in India** Beginning with raids into the Indus Valley in the 8th century C.E., Muslim armies invaded and established a succession of dynasties centered on Delhi in north-central India.

despite the fact that their faiths had no connection to the Bible, the book in question. This meant that although they were obliged to pay special taxes, non-Muslims, like Jews and Christians, enjoyed the freedom to worship as they pleased.

As in other areas conquered by the Arabs, most of the local officials and notables retained their positions, which did much to reconcile them to Muslim rule. The status and privileges of the brahman castes were respected. Nearly all Arabs, who made up only a tiny minority of the population, lived in cities or special garrison towns. Because little effort was expended in converting the peoples of the conquered areas, they remained overwhelmingly Hindu or Buddhist.

Indian Influences on Islamic Civilization

Although the impact of Islam on the Indian subcontinent in this period was limited, the Arab foothold in Sind provided contacts by which Indian learning was transmitted to the Muslim heartlands in the Middle East. As a result, Islamic civilization was enriched by the skills and discoveries of yet another great civilization. Of particular importance was Indian scientific learning, which rivaled that of the Greeks as the most advanced of the ancient world. Hindu mathematicians and astronomers traveled to Baghdad after the Abbasids came to power in the mid-8th century. Their works on algebra and geometry were translated into Arabic, and their instruments for celestial observation were copied and improved by Arab astronomers.

Most critically, Arab thinkers in all fields began to use the numerals that Hindu scholars had devised centuries earlier. Because these numbers were passed on to the Europeans through contacts with the Arabs in the early Middle Ages, we call them Arabic numerals today, but they originated in India. Because of the linkages between civilized centers established by the spread of Islam, this system of numerical notation has proved central to two scientific revolutions. The first in the Middle East was discussed earlier in this chapter. The second, discussed in Chapter 18, occurred in Europe some centuries later. From the 16th century to the present, it has brought fundamental transformations to Europe and much of the rest of the world.

In addition to science and mathematics, Indian treatises on subjects ranging from medicine to music were translated and studied by Arab scholars. Indian physicians were brought to Baghdad to run the well-endowed hospitals that the Christian crusaders found a source of wonderment and a cause for envy. On several occasions, Indian doctors were able to cure Arab rulers and officials whom Greek physicians had pronounced beyond help. Indian works on statecraft, alchemy, and palmistry were translated into Arabic, and it is believed that some of the tales in the *Arabian Nights* were based on ancient Indian stories. Indian musical instruments and melodies made their way into the repertoires of Arab performers, and the Indian game of chess became a favorite of both royalty and ordinary townspeople.

Arabs who emigrated to Sind and other Muslim-ruled areas often adopted Indian dress and hairstyles, ate Indian foods, and rode on elephants just as the Hindu *rajas* (kings) did. As Figure 8.5 illustrates, the conquerors also adopted Indian building styles and artistic motifs. In this era, additional Arab colonies were established in other coastal areas, such as Malabar to the south and Bengal in the east (Map 8.3). These trading enclaves later provided the staging areas from which Islam was transmitted to island and mainland southeast Asia.

From Booty to Empire: The Second Wave of Muslim Invasions

After the initial conquests by Muhammad ibn Qasim's armies, little territory was added to the Muslim foothold on the subcontinent. In fact, disputes between the Arabs occupying Sind and their quarrels

View the **Closer Look** on MyHistoryLab: "Qutb Minar"

Read the **Document** on MyHistoryLab: A World Traveler in India (1300s) Ibn Battuta

FIGURE **8.5** The Shahi mosque, surrounded by the Hindu Kush mountains in northwestern Pakistan, is a superb example of the blending of Islamic and Hindu architectural forms, building materials, and artistic motifs.

CHAPTER 8 Abbasid Decline and the Spread of Islamic Civilization to South and Southeast Asia **195**

Mahmud of Ghazni [ma-MOOD of GAHZ-nee] (971–1030) Third ruler of Turkish slave dynasty in Afghanistan; led invasions of northern India; credited with sacking one of wealthiest of Hindu temples in northern India; gave Muslims reputation for intolerance and aggression.

Muhammad of Ghur (1173–1206) Military commander of Persian extraction who ruled small mountain kingdom in Afghanistan; began process of conquest to establish Muslim political control of northern India; brought much of Indus valley, Sind, and northwestern India under his control.

Qutb-ud-din Aibak [KUHTH-uhd-dihn ay-BAHK] Lieutenant of Muhammad of Ghur; established kingdom in India with capital at Delphi; proclaimed himself Sultan of India (r. 1206–1210).

with first the Umayyad and later the Abbasid caliphs gradually weakened the Muslim hold on the area. This was reflected in the reconquest of parts of the lower Indus valley by Hindu rulers. But the gradual Muslim retreat was dramatically reversed by a new series of military invasions, this time launched by a Turkish slave dynasty that in 962 had seized power in Afghanistan to the north of the Indus valley. The third ruler of this dynasty, **Mahmud of Ghazni**, led a series of expeditions that began nearly two centuries of Muslim raiding and conquest in northern India. Drawn by the legendary wealth of the subcontinent and a zeal to spread the Muslim faith, Mahmud repeatedly raided northwest India in the first decades of the 11th century. He defeated one confederation of Hindu princes after another, and he drove deeper and deeper into the subcontinent in the quest of ever richer temples to loot.

The raids mounted by Mahmud of Ghazni and his successors gave way in the last decades of the 12th century to sustained campaigns aimed at seizing political control in north India. The key figure in this transition was a tenacious military commander of Persian extraction, **Muhammad of Ghur**. After barely surviving several severe defeats at the hands of Hindu rulers, Muhammad put together a string of military victories that brought the Indus valley and much of north central India under his control. In the following years, Muhammad's conquests were extended along the Gangetic plain as far as Bengal, and into west and central India, by several of his most gifted subordinate commanders. After Muhammad was assassinated in 1206, **Qutb-ud-din Aibak**, one of his slave lieutenants, seized power.

Significantly, the capital of the new Muslim empire was at Delhi along the Jumna River on the Gangetic plain. Delhi's location in the very center of northern India graphically proclaimed that a Muslim dynasty rooted in the subcontinent itself, not an extension of a Middle Eastern central Asian empire, had been founded. For the next 300 years, a succession of dynasties ruled much of north and central India. Alternately of Persian, Afghan, Turkic, and mixed descent, the rulers of these imperial houses proclaimed themselves the *sultans of Delhi* (literally, princes of the heartland). They fought each other, Mongol and Turkic invaders, and the indigenous Hindu princes for control of the Indus and Gangetic heartlands of Indian civilization.

Patterns of Conversion

Although the Muslims fought their way into India, their interaction with the indigenous peoples soon came to be dominated by accommodation and peaceful exchanges. Over the centuries when much of the north was ruled by dynasties centered at Delhi, sizable Muslim communities developed in different areas of the subcontinent. The largest of these were in Bengal to the east and in the northwestern areas of the Indus valley that were the points of entry for most of the Muslim peoples who migrated into India.

Few of these converts were won forcibly. The main carriers of the new faith often were merchants, who played a growing role in both coastal and inland trade, but were most especially Sufi mystics. The latter shared much with Indian gurus and wandering ascetics in both style and message. Belief in their magical and healing powers enhanced the Sufis' stature and increased their following. Their mosques and schools often became centers of regional political power. Sufis organized their devotees in militias to fend off bandits or rival princes, oversaw the clearing of forests for farming and settlement, and welcomed low-caste and outcaste Hindu groups into Islam. After their deaths, the tombs of Sufi mystics became objects of veneration for Indian Muslims as well as Hindu and Buddhist pilgrims.

Most of the indigenous converts, who came to form a majority of the Muslims living in India, were drawn from specific regions and social groups. Surprisingly small numbers of converts were found in the Indo-Gangetic centers of Muslim political power, a fact that suggests the very limited importance of forced conversions. Most Indians who converted to Islam were from Buddhist or low-caste groups. In areas such as western India and Bengal, where Buddhism had survived as a popular religion until the era of the Muslim invasions, esoteric rituals and corrupt practices had debased Buddhist teachings and undermined the morale of the monastic orders.

This decline was accelerated by Muslim raids on Buddhist temples and monasteries, which provided vulnerable and lucrative targets for the early invaders. Without monastic supervision, local congregations sank further into orgies and experiments with magic. All of these trends opposed the Buddha's social concerns and religious message. Disorganized and misdirected, Indian Buddhism was no match for the confident and vigorous new religion the Muslim invaders carried into the subcontinent. This was particularly true when those who were spreading the new faith had the charisma and organizing skills of the Sufi mystics.

Buddhists probably made up the majority of Indians who converted to Islam. But untouchables and low-caste Hindus, as well as tribal peoples who were animists worshiping spirits found in the natural world, were also attracted to the more egalitarian social arrangements promoted by the new faith. As was the case in earlier centuries with the Buddhists, group conversions were essential because those who remained in the Hindu caste system would have little to do with those who had changed religions. Some conversions resulted from the desire of Hindus or Buddhists to escape the head tax the Muslim rulers levied on unbelievers. They were prompted by intermarriage between local peoples and Muslim migrants. Muslim migrants also swelled the size of the Islamic community in the subcontinent. This was particularly true in periods of crisis in central Asia. In the 13th and 14th centuries, for example, Turkic, Persian, and Afghan peoples retreated to the comparative safety of India in the face of the Mongol and Timurid conquests that are examined in detail in Chapter 15.

Patterns of Accommodation

Although Islam won many converts in certain areas and communities, it initially made little impression on the Hindu population as a whole. Despite military reverses and the imposition of Muslim political rule over large areas of the subcontinent, high-caste Hindus in particular saw the invaders as the bearers of an upstart religion and as polluting outcastes. Al-Biruni, one of the chief chroniclers of the Muslim conquests, complained openly about the prevailing Indian disdain for the newcomers:

> The Hindus believe that there is no country but theirs, no nation like theirs, no kings like theirs, no religion like theirs, no science like theirs. They are haughty, foolishly vain, self-conceited and stolid.

Many Hindus were willing to take positions as administrators in the bureaucracies of Muslim overlords or as soldiers in their armies and to trade with Muslim merchants. But they remained socially aloof from their conquerors. Separate living quarters were established everywhere Muslim communities developed. Genuine friendships between members of high-caste groups and Muslims were rare, and sexual liaisons between them were severely restricted.

During the early centuries of the Muslim influx, the Hindus were convinced that like so many of the peoples who had entered the subcontinent in the preceding millennia, the Muslims would soon be absorbed by the superior religions and more sophisticated cultures of India. Many signs pointed to that outcome. Hindus staffed the bureaucracies and made up a good portion of the armies of Muslim rulers. In addition, Muslim princes adopted regal styles and practices that were Hindu-inspired and contrary to the Qur'an. Some Muslim rulers proclaimed themselves to be of divine descent, and others minted coins decorated with Hindu images such as Nandi, the bull associated with a major Hindu god, Shiva.

More broadly, Muslim communities became socially divided along caste lines. Recently arrived Muslims generally were on top of the hierarchies that developed, and even they were divided depending on whether they were Arab, Turk, or Persian. High-caste Hindu converts came next, followed by "clean" artisan and merchant groups. Lower-caste and untouchable converts remained at the bottom of the social hierarchy. This may help to explain why conversions in these groups were not as numerous as one would expect given the original egalitarian thrust of Islam. Muslims also adopted Indian foods and styles of dress and took to chewing *pan*, or limestone wrapped with betel leaves.

The Muslim influx had unfortunate consequences for women in both Muslim and Hindu communities. The invaders increasingly adopted the practice of marrying women at the earlier ages favored by the Hindus and the prohibitions against the remarriage of widows found especially at the high-caste levels of Indian society. Some high-caste Muslim groups even performed the ritual of *sati*, the burning of widows on the same funeral pyres as their deceased husbands, which was found among some high-caste Hindu groups.

Islamic Challenge and Hindu Revival

Despite a significant degree of acculturation to Hindu lifestyles and social organization, Muslim migrants to the subcontinent held to their own distinctive religious beliefs and rituals. The Hindus found Islam impossible to absorb and soon realized that they were confronted by an actively proselytizing religion with great appeal to large segments of the Indian population. Partly in response to

THINKING HISTORICALLY

Conversion and Accommodation in the Spread of World Religions

ALTHOUGH NOT ALL GREAT CIVILIZATIONS HAVE produced world religions, the two tend to be closely associated throughout human history. World religions are those that spread across many cultures and societies, forge links between civilized centers, and bring civilized lifestyles to nomadic pastoral or shifting cultivating peoples. Religions with these characteristics appeared before the rise of Islam. As we have seen, India alone produced two of these faiths in ancient times: Hinduism, which spread to parts of southeast and central Asia, and Buddhism, which spread even more widely in the Asian world. At the other end of the Eastern Hemisphere, Christianity spread throughout the Mediterranean region before claiming northern and western Europe as its core area. Judaism spread not because it won converts in non-Jewish cultures but because the Jewish people were driven from their homeland by Roman persecution and scattered throughout the Middle East, north Africa, and Europe.

Because religious conversion affects all aspects of life, from the way one looks at the universe to more mundane decisions about whom to marry or how to treat others, a world religion must be broad and flexible enough to accommodate the existing culture of potential converts. At the same time, its core beliefs and practices must be well enough defined to allow its followers to maintain a clear sense of common identity despite their great differences in culture and society. These beliefs and practices must be sufficiently profound and sophisticated to convince potential converts that their own cultures can be enriched and their lives improved by adopting the new religion.

In most instances, until the 16th century, when Christianity spread through the Western Hemisphere, no world religion could match Islam in the extent to which it spread across the globe and in the diversity of peoples and cultures that identified themselves as Muslims. Given its uncompromising monotheism, very definite doctrines, and elaborate rituals and principles of social organization, Islam's success at winning converts from very different cultural backgrounds is surprising at first glance. This is particularly true if it is compared with the much more flexible beliefs and ceremonial patterns of earlier world religions such as Buddhism and Hinduism. However, closer examination reveals that Islamic beliefs and social practices, as written in the Qur'an and interpreted by the ulama, proved quite flexible and adaptable when the religion was introduced into new, non-Islamic cultures.

The fact that Islam won converts overwhelmingly through peaceful contacts between long-distance traders and the preaching and organizational skills of Sufis exemplifies this capacity for accommodation.

> **The fact that Islam won converts overwhelmingly through peaceful contacts between long-distance traders and the preaching and organizational skills of Sufis exemplifies this capacity for accommodation.**

Those adopting the new religion did not do so cause they were pressured or forced to convert but because they saw Islam as a way to enhance their understanding of the supernatural, enrich their ceremonial expression, improve the quality of their social interaction, and establish ongoing links to a transcultural community beyond their local world.

Because Islam was adopted rather than imposed, those who converted had a good deal to say about how much of their own cultures they would change and which aspects of Islam they would emphasize or accept. Certain beliefs and practices were obligatory for all true believers: the worship of a single god, adherence to the prophet Muhammad and the divine revelations he received as recorded in the Qur'an, and the observance of the five pillars of the faith. But even these were subject to reinterpretation. In virtually all cultures to which it spread, Islamic monotheism supplanted but did not eradicate the animistic veneration of nature spirits or person and place deities. Allah was acknowledged as the most powerful supernatural force, but people continued to make offerings to spirits that could heal, bring fertility, protect their homes, or punish their enemies. In such areas as Africa and western China, where the veneration of ancestral spirits was a key aspect of religious life, the spirits were retained not as powers in themselves but as emissaries to Allah. In cultures such as those found in India and southeast Asia, Islamic doctrines were recast in a heavily mystical, even magical mode.

The flexibility of Islam was exhibited in the social as well as the religious sphere. In Islamic southeast Asia and in sub-Saharan Africa, the position of women remained a good deal stronger in critical areas, such as occupation and family law, than it had become in the Middle East and India. In both regions, the male-centric features of Islam that had grown more pronounced through centuries of accommodation in ancient Middle Eastern and Persian cultures were played down. As Islam was adapted to societies where women had traditionally enjoyed more influence, both within the extended family and in occupations such as farming, marketing, and craft production. Even the caste system of India, which in principle is opposed to the strong egalitarian strain in Islam, developed among Muslim groups that migrated into the subcontinent and survived in indigenous south Asian communities that converted to Islam.

(continued on next page)

Beyond basic forms of social organization and interaction, Islam accommodated diverse aspects of the societies into which it spread. For example, the African solar calendar, which was essential for coordinating the planting cycle, was retained along with the Muslim lunar calendar. In India, Hindu-Buddhist symbols of kingship were appropriated by Muslim rulers and acknowledged by both their Hindu and Muslim subjects. In island southeast Asia, exquisitely forged knives, called *krises*, which were believed to have magical powers, were among the most treasured possessions of local rulers both before and after they converted to Islam.

There was always the danger that accommodation could go too far: that in winning converts, Islamic principles would be so watered down and remolded that they no longer resembled or actually contradicted the teachings of the Qur'an. Sects that came to worship Muhammad or his nephew Ali as godlike, for example, clearly violated fundamental Muslim principles. This danger was a key source of the periodic movements for purification and revival that have been a notable feature of nearly all Islamic societies, particularly those on the fringes of the Islamic world. But even these movements, which were built around the insistence that the Muslim faith had been corrupted by alien ideas and practices and that a return to Islamic fundamentals was needed, were invariably cast in the modes of cultural expression of the peoples who rallied to them.

QUESTIONS

- Can you think of ways in which world religions, such as Christianity, Hinduism, and Buddhism, changed to accommodate the cultures and societies to which they spread?
- Do these religions strike you as more or less flexible than Islam?
- Why?

this challenge, the Hindus placed greater emphasis on the devotional cults of gods and goddesses that earlier had proved so effective in neutralizing the challenge of Buddhism.

Membership in these **bhaktic cults** was open to all, including women and untouchables. In fact, some of the most celebrated writers of religious poetry and songs of worship were women, such as **Mira Bai**. Saints from low-caste origins were revered by warriors and brahmans as well as by farmers, merchants, and outcastes. One of the most remarkable of these mystics was a Muslim weaver named **Kabir**. In plain and direct verse, Kabir played down the significance of religious differences and proclaimed that all faiths could provide a path to spiritual fulfillment. He asked,

> O servant, where do thou seek Me?
> Lo! I am beside thee.
> I am neither in temple nor in mosque:
> Neither am I in rites and ceremonies, nor in Yoga and renunciation.

Because many songs and poems, such as those by Mira Bai and Kabir, were composed in regional languages, such as Bengali, Marathi, and Tamil, they were more accessible to the common people and became prominent expressions of popular culture in many areas.

Bhakti mystics and gurus stressed the importance of a strong emotional bond between the devotee and the god or goddess who was the object of veneration. Chants, dances, and in some instances drugs were used to reach the state of spiritual intoxication that was the key to individual salvation. Once one had achieved the state of ecstasy that came through intense emotional attachment to a god or goddess, all past sins were removed and caste distinctions were rendered meaningless. The most widely worshiped deities were the gods Shiva and Vishnu, the latter particularly in the guise of Krishna the goat herder depicted in the folk painting in Figure 8.6. The goddess Kali was also venerated in a number of different manifestations. By increasing popular involvement in Hindu worship and by enriching and extending the modes of prayer and ritual, the bhakti movement may have done much to stem the flow of converts to Islam, particularly among low-caste groups.

FIGURE 8.6 This Indian miniature painting of milkmaids serving the Hindu god Krishna reflects the highly personalized devotional worship that was characteristic of the bhakti movement. The eroticism in the milkmaids' songs, in praise of Krishna's great beauty, reveals a blending of sacred and secular, carnal and spiritual that is a recurring motif in Hindu worship and art.

bhaktic cults [BAHK-teek] Hindu groups dedicated to gods and goddesses; stressed the importance of strong emotional bonds between devotees and the god or goddess who was the object of their veneration; most widely worshipped gods were Shiva and Vishnu.

Mira Bai [MIHR-uh Bay] (1498–1547) Celebrated Hindu writer of religious poetry; reflected openness of bhaktic cults to women.

Kabir (1440–1518) Muslim mystic; played down the importance of ritual differences between Hinduism and Islam.

Stand-Off: The Muslim Presence in India at the End of the Sultanate Period

The attempts of mystics such as Kabir to minimize the differences between Hindu and Islamic beliefs and worship won over only small numbers of the followers of either faith. They were also strongly repudiated by the guardians of orthodoxy in each religious community. Sensing the long-term threat to Hinduism posed by Muslim political dominance and conversion efforts, the brahmans denounced the Muslims as infidel destroyers of Hindu temples and polluted meat-eaters. Later Hindu mystics, such as the 15th-century holy man Chaitanya, composed songs that focused on love for Hindu deities and set out to convince Indian Muslims to renounce Islam in favor of Hinduism.

For their part, Muslim ulama, or religious experts, grew increasingly aware of the dangers Hinduism posed for Islam. Attempts to fuse the two faiths were rejected on the grounds that although Hindus might argue that specific rituals and beliefs were not essential, they were fundamental for Islam. If one played down the teachings of the Qur'an, prayer, and the pilgrimage, one was no longer a true Muslim. Thus, contrary to the teachings of Kabir and like-minded mystics, the ulama and even some Sufi saints stressed the teachings of Islam that separated it from Hinduism. They worked to promote unity within the Indian Muslim community and to strengthen its contacts with Muslims in neighboring lands and the Middle Eastern centers of the faith.

After centuries of invasion and migration, a large Muslim community had been established in the Indian subcontinent. Converts had been won, political control had been established throughout much of the area, and strong links had been forged with Muslims in other lands such as Persia and Afghanistan. But non-Muslims, particularly Hindus, remained the overwhelming majority of the population of the vast and diverse lands south of the Himalayas. Unlike the Zoroastrians in Persia or the animistic peoples of north Africa and the Sudan, most Indians showed little inclination to convert to the religion of the Muslim conquerors. After centuries of Muslim political dominance and missionary activity, south Asia remained one of the least converted and integrated of all the areas Muhammad's message had reached.

THE SPREAD OF ISLAM TO SOUTHEAST ASIA

From the 13th century, traders and Sufi mystics spread Islam to island southeast Asia. As was the case in India, conversion was generally peaceful, and Islamic teachings and rituals were mixed with the animist, Hindu, and Buddhist religions long established in Malaya, Java, and other areas.

8.4 Beyond the Sufis, who were the major agents and what were the motivations for conversions to the Islamic religion in South and South Asia in this same era?

From a world history perspective, island southeast Asia had long been mainly a middle ground. It was the zone where the Chinese segment of the great Euro-Asian trading complex met the Indian Ocean trading zone to the west. At ports on the coast of the Malayan peninsula, east Sumatra, and somewhat later north Java, goods from China were transferred from east Asian vessels to Arab or Indian ships. In these same ports, products from as far west as Rome were loaded into the emptied Chinese ships to be carried to east Asia. By the 7th and 8th centuries C.E., sailors and ships from areas of southeast Asia, particularly Sumatra and Malaya, had become active in the seaborne trade of the region. Southeast Asian products had also become important exports to China, India, and the Mediterranean region. Many of these products were luxury items, such as aromatic woods from the rain forests of Borneo and Sumatra and spices such as cloves, nutmeg, and mace from the far end of the Indonesian archipelago. These trading links were to prove even more critical to the expansion of Islam in southeast Asia than they had earlier been to the spread of Buddhism and Hinduism.

From the 8th century onward, the coastal trade of India came increasingly to be controlled by Muslims from such regions as Gujarat in western India and various parts of south India. As a result, elements of Islamic culture began to filter into island southeast Asia. But only in the 13th century, after the collapse of the far-flung trading empire of **Shrivijaya**, centered on the Strait of Malacca between Malaya and the northeast of Sumatra (Map 8.4), was the way open for the widespread introduction of Islam. Indian traders, Muslim or otherwise, were welcome to trade in the chain of ports controlled by Shrivijaya. But because the rulers and officials of Shrivijaya were devout Buddhists, there was little incentive for the traders and sailors of southeast Asian ports to convert to Islam, the religion of growing numbers of the merchants and sailors from India. With the fall of Shrivijaya, incentives increased for the establishment of Muslim trading centers and efforts to preach the faith to the coastal peoples.

Shrivijaya [SHREE-vih-JAY-uh] Trading empire centered on Malacca Straits between Malaya and Sumatra; controlled trade of empire; Buddhist government resistant to Muslim missionaries; fall opened up southeastern Asia to Muslim conversion.

MAP 8.4 **The Spread of Islam in Southeast Asia** Traders and Islamic mystics were the main agents responsible for the rapid spread of Islam throughout island southeast Asia.

Trading Contacts and Conversion

As in most of the areas to which Islam spread, peaceful contacts and voluntary conversion were far more important than conquest and force in spreading the faith in southeast Asia. Throughout the islands of the region, trading contacts paved the way for conversion. Muslim merchants and sailors introduced local peoples to the ideas and rituals of the new faith and impressed on them how much of the known world had already been converted. Muslim ships also carried Sufis to various parts of southeast Asia, where they played as vital a role in conversion as they had in India. The first areas to be won to Islam in the late 13th century were several small port centers on the northern coast of Sumatra. From these ports, the religion spread in the centuries that followed across the Strait of Malacca to Malaya.

On the mainland, the key to widespread conversion was the powerful trading city of **Malacca**, whose smaller trading empire had replaced the fallen Shrivijaya. From Malacca, Islam spread along the coasts of Malaya to east Sumatra and to the trading center of **Demak** on the north coast of Java. From Demak, the most powerful of the trading states on north Java, the Muslim faith spread to other Javanese ports. After a long struggle with a Hindu-Buddhist kingdom in the interior, the rest of the island was eventually converted. From Demak, Islam was also carried to the Celebes and the Spice Islands in the eastern archipelago, and from the latter to Mindanao in the southern Philippines.

This progress of Islamic conversion shows that port cities in coastal areas were particularly receptive to the new faith. Here trading links were critical. Once one of the key cities in a trading cluster converted, it was in the best interest of others to follow suit to enhance personal ties and provide a common basis in Muslim law to regulate business deals. Conversion to Islam also linked these centers, culturally as well as economically, to the merchants and ports of India, the Middle East, and the Mediterranean.

Islam made slow progress in areas such as central Java, where Hindu–Buddhist dynasties contested its spread. But the fact that the earlier conversion to these Indian religions had been confined mainly to the ruling elites in Java and other island areas left openings for mass conversions to Islam that the Sufis eventually exploited. The island of Bali, where Hinduism had taken deep root at the popular level, remained largely impervious to the spread of Islam. The same was true of most of mainland southeast Asia, where centuries before the coming of Islam, Buddhism had spread from India and Ceylon and won the fervent adherence of both the ruling elites and the peasant masses.

Malacca Portuguese factory or fortified trade town located on the tip of the Malayan peninsula; traditionally a center for trade among the southeastern Asian islands.

Demak Most powerful of the trading states on north coast of Java; converted to Islam and served as point of dissemination to other ports.

Sufi Mystics and the Nature of Southeast Asian Islam

Because Islam was spread in many areas by Sufis from South Asia, it was often infused with mystical strains and incorporated animist, Hindu, and Buddhist elements. Just as they had in the Middle East and India, the Sufis who spread Islam in southeast Asia varied widely in personality and approach. Most were believed by those who followed them to have magical powers, and nearly all Sufis established mosque and school centers from which they traveled in neighboring regions to preach the faith.

In winning converts, the Sufis were willing to allow the inhabitants of island southeast Asia to retain pre-Islamic beliefs and practices that orthodox scholars would have found contrary to Islamic doctrine. Pre-Islamic customary law remained important in regulating social interaction, whereas Islamic law was confined to specific sorts of agreements and exchanges. Women retained a much stronger position, both within the family and in society, than they had in the Middle East and India. For example, trading in local and regional markets continued to be dominated by small-scale female buyers and sellers. In such areas as western Sumatra, lineage and inheritance continued to be traced through the female line after the coming of Islam, despite its tendency to promote male dominance and descent. Perhaps most tellingly, pre-Muslim religious beliefs and rituals were incorporated into Muslim ceremonies. Indigenous cultural staples, such as the brilliant Javanese puppet shadow plays that were based on the Indian epics of the brahmanic age, were refined, and they became even more central to popular and elite beliefs and practices than they had been in the pre-Muslim era.

Global Connections and Critical Themes

ISLAM: A BRIDGE BETWEEN WORLDS

Although problems of political control and succession continued to plague the kingdoms and empires that divided the Muslim world, the central position of Islamic civilization in global history was solidified during the centuries of Abbasid rule. Its role as the go-between for the more ancient civilizations of the Eastern Hemisphere grew as Arab trading networks expanded into new areas. More than ever, it enriched the lives of nomadic peoples, from the Turks and Mongols of central Asia to the Berbers of north Africa and the camel herders of the savanna regions south of the Sahara. Equally critically, Islam's original contributions to the growth and refinement of civilized life greatly increased. From its great cities and universities and the accomplishments generated in the fine arts, sciences, and literature to its vibrant religious and philosophical life, Islam pioneered patterns of organization and thinking that would affect the development of human societies in major ways for centuries to come.

For more than five centuries, the spread of Islam played a central role in the rise, extension, or transformation of civilization in much of the Afro-Asian world. The Islamic world also became a great conduit for the exchange of ideas, plants and medicines, commercial goods, and inventions both between centers of urban and agrarian life and between these core regions of civilization and the areas dominated by nomadic peoples that still encompassed much of the globe.

In the midst of all this achievement, however, there were tendencies that would put the Muslim peoples at a growing disadvantage, particularly in relation to their long-standing European rivals. Muslim divisions would leave openings for political expansion that the Europeans would eagerly exploit, beginning with the island southeast Asian extremities of the Islamic world and then moving across India. The growing orthodoxy and intolerance of many of the ulama, as well as the Muslim belief that the vast Islamic world contained all requirements for civilized life, caused Muslim peoples to grow less receptive to outside influences and innovations. These tendencies became increasingly pronounced at precisely the time when their Christian rivals were entering a period of unprecedented curiosity, experimentation, and exploration of the world beyond their own heartlands.

Further Readings

M. A. Shaban's *Islamic History: An Interpretation*, 2 vols. (1971), contains the most readable and thematic survey of early Islam, concentrating on the Abbasid period. Although Philip Hitti's monumental *History of the Arabs* (1967) and J. J. Saunders' *A History of Medieval Islam* (1965) are now somewhat dated, they contain much valuable information and some fine insights into Arab history. Also useful are the works of G. E. von Gruenenbaum, especially *Classical Islam* (1970), which covers the Abbasid era. On changes in Islamic religion and the makeup of the Muslim community, Marshall Hodgson's *Venture of Islam*, vol. 2 (1974), is indispensable, but it should not be tackled by the beginner. *The Cambridge History of Islam*, 2 vols. (1970); Ira Lapidus, *A History of Islamic Societies* (1988); and Albert Hourani, *A History of the Islamic Peoples* (1991), are excellent reference works for the political events of the Abbasid era and Muslim achievements in various fields. D. M. Dunlop's *Arab Civilization to A.D. 1500* (1971) also contains detailed essays on Islamic culture as well as an article on the accomplishments of Muslim women in this era.

On social history, B. F. Musallam's *Sex and Society in Islam* (1983) has material on the Abbasid period, and some of the more prominent works on urban life include Ira Lapidus's *Muslim Cities in the Later Middle Ages* (1984 ed.), Nezar al-Sayyid's *Cities and Caliphs* (1991), and Albert Hourani and S. M. Stern, eds., *The Islamic City* (1970). Two essential works on the spread of Islam to India are S. M. Ikram, *Muslim Civilization in India* (1964); and Aziz Ahmad, *Studies in Islamic Culture in the Indian Environment* (1964). For the role of the Sufis in Islamic conversion, Richard Eaton's *Sufis of Bijapur* (1978) and *The Rise of Islam and the Bengal Frontier* (1993) are particularly revealing. The best introduction to the pattern of Islamic conversion in southeast Asia is H. J. de Graaf's essay in *The Cambridge History of Islam*, vol. 2 (1976). Toby Huff's *The Rise of Early Modern Science: Islam, China, and the West* (1993) is a stimulating account of the ways in which science and technology were transmitted between these key centers of the Eastern Hemisphere and the effects of these exchanges on global history. On the exchanges among Islamic and other Eurasian civilizations more generally, see R.M. Savory, ed., *Introduction to Islamic Civilization* (1976).

On MyHistoryLab

 Study and Review on MyHistoryLab

Critical Thinking Questions

1. To what extent did Islam constitute the world's first global civilization?
2. What were the major reasons for the Sunni-Shi'a split in the Islamic *umma*?
3. What were the main motives for converting to Islam when full membership in the *umma* was opened to non-Arabs in the Abbasid Era?
4. In what ways did Muhammad's example and the teachings of the Quran make for improvements in the lives of women and what were the limits to these advances?

9
African Civilizations and the Spread of Islam

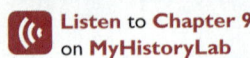 Listen to Chapter 9 on MyHistoryLab

LEARNING OBJECTIVES

9.1 Why did the Sudanic states develop in the sahel and what advantages did they have? p. 205

9.2 How did African societies accommodate Islam and what was the effect of its spread across Africa? p. 209

9.3 How integrated into international commerce were the cities of East Africa, and why? p. 215

9.4 What kinds of political organization developed in central and southern Africa? p. 217

In 1324, a great caravan of more than a hundred camels, many slaves, and a multitude of retainers crossed the arid Sahara desert and wended its way into Cairo, on the banks of the Nile. Mansa Musa, lord of the African empire of Mali, was making the *hajj*, the pilgrimage to Mecca, distributing gold with an open hand. The wealth and prodigality of the young king dazzled all who witnessed it, his polished manners and command of Arabic impressed those who met him, and his fame spread throughout the Islamic world and beyond. The chronicler al-Omari, who visited Cairo a dozen years later, reported that people still spoke of the entourage of the young king that had spent so much gold in the markets and had given so much as gifts and alms that

Read the Document on MyHistoryLab: Al-Umari describes Mansa Musa of Mali

FIGURE **9.1** In 1324, Mansa Musa, King of Mali, made a pilgrimage to Mecca that brought the attention of the Muslim world to the wealth of his kingdom. A Jewish cartographer in Spain, Abraham Cresques, depicted the trip more than 50 years later in the map shown above. Mansa Musa is depicted at the bottom right with a golden scepter and crown, symbolizing his royal power, and an enormous gold nugget, symbolizing his country's wealth.

Watch the Video Series on MyHistoryLab

Learn about some key topics related to this chapter with the *MyHistoryLab Video Series: Key Topics in World History*

the price of gold actually declined due to its ample supply. Other great caravans had made the trek from Mali across the desert before and some came after, but none had been so magnificent. Mansa Musa's caravan symbolized the wealthy potential of Africa, but even by the time he made his trip, west African gold was already well known in the world economy and Africa was already involved in contacts of vaious kinds with other areas of the world.

Mali, the kingdom of this great lord, fascinated the Muslim observers in Cairo, Damascus, and Fez. Like the earlier kingdom of Ghana, Mali was another state of the savannah country, between the desert and the forests of west Africa. Formed by the Malinke peoples, its access to gold and control of the caravan routes had promoted its rise, and its powerful army had created an empire that extended over much of the savannah from the Niger to the Senegal River. Its ruling families had converted to Islam, but the famous and cosmopolitan Moroccan traveler Abdallah Ibn Batuta, who visited Mali not long after Mansa Musa's pilgrimage, found the local customs and food less refined than those of the elegant courts to which he was accustomed and some of the practices shocking. Yet much was recognizable to him as well. Mali was an African kingdom that had become an extension of the Islamic world, and its success was tied to the trade routes that linked it to the Mediterranean and the Middle East. ■

The history of Mali underlines the fact that Africa below the Sahara was never totally isolated from the centers of civilization in Egypt, west Asia, or the Mediterranean, but for long periods the contacts were difficult and intermittent. This chapter will examine the increasing impact of a growing international network on Africa roughly in the period between 800 and 1600 C.E. Chief among those influences was the arrival of Islam, which transformed many aspects of life in some African societies and brought them through trade, politics, and cultural exchange into increasing contact. But, we must also recognize that the African societies influenced by Islam often maintained their own traditions and that other African societies remained little touched by Islam and continued to develop along their own trajectories.

African civilizations built somewhat less clearly on prior societies than did other postclassical civilizations. Some earlier themes, such as the Bantu migration and the formation of large states in the western Sudan, persisted. Overall, sub-Saharan Africa remained a varied and distinctive setting; parts of it, like the port cities of the East African coast, were drawn into new contacts with the growing world network, but much of it retained a certain isolation or cultural autonomy. The spread of universal faiths like Islam and Christianity was an important aspect of African history in this period, but much of central and southern Africa still flourished relatively unaffected by these outside influences.

AFRICAN SOCIETIES: DIVERSITY AND SIMILARITIES

9.1 Why did the Sudanic states develop in the sahel and what advantages did they have?

Like most continents, Africa is so vast and its societies so diverse that it is almost impossible to generalize about them. Differences in geography, language, religion, politics, and other aspects of life contributed to Africa's lack of political unity over long periods of time. Unlike in many parts of Asia, Europe, and north Africa, neither universal states nor universal religions characterized the history of sub-Saharan Africa. Yet universal religions, first Christianity and later Islam, did find adherents in Africa and sometimes contributed to the formation of large states and empires.

> African societies developed diverse forms, from stateless societies organized around kinship or age sets to large centralized states, and within this diversity were many shared aspects of language and beliefs. Universalistic faiths penetrated the continent and served as the basis for important cultural developments in Nubia and Ethiopia.

CHAPTER 9 African Civilizations and the Spread of Islam   205

100 C.E.	600 C.E.	1000 C.E.	1200 C.E.	1400 C.E.
100–200 Camels introduced for trade in the Sahara **300** Origins of the kingdom of Ghana	**600–700** Islam spreads across North Africa	**1000** Ghana at height of its power **1100** Almoravid movement in the Sahara	**1200** Rise of the empire of Mali **1260** Death of Sundiata; earliest stone buildings at Zimbabwe; Lalibela rules in Ethiopia; Yoruba culture flourishes at Ile-Ife **1300** Mali at its height; Kanem empire is a rival **1324** Pilgrimage of Mansa Musa	**1400** Flourishing of cities of Timbuktu and Jenne; Ethiopian Christian kingdom; Swahili cities flourish on east African coast **1417, 1431** Last Chinese trade voyages to east Africa **1500** Songhay empire flourishes; Benin at height of power

Societies With and Without States

Some African societies had rulers who exercised control through a hierarchy of officials in what can be called states, but others were **stateless societies**, organized around kinship or other forms of obligation and lacking the concentration of political power and authority we normally associate with the state. Sometimes the stateless societies were larger and more extensive than the neighboring states. Stateless societies had forms of government, but the authority and power normally exercised by a ruler and his court in a kingdom could be held instead by a council of families or by the community, with no need to tax the population to support the ruler, the bureaucrats, the army, or the nobles, as was usually the case in state-building societies. Stateless societies had little concentration of authority, and it affected only a small part of the peoples' lives. In these societies, government was rarely a full-time occupation and there was no political class. Such societies often were less hierarchical and more egalitarian.

Other alternatives to formal government were possible. Among peoples of the west African forest, secret societies of men and women controlled customs and beliefs and were able to limit the authority of rulers. Especially among peoples who had sharp rivalries between lineages or family groupings, secret societies developed that cut across the lineage divisions. Members' allegiance to these groups transcended their lineage ties. The secret societies settled village disputes. They acted to maintain stability within the community, and they served as an alternative to the authority of state institutions.

Throughout Africa many stateless societies thrived, perhaps aided by the fact that internal social pressures or disputes often could be resolved by allowing dissidents to leave and establish a new village in the sparsely populated continent. Still, stateless societies found it difficult to resist external pressures, mobilize for warfare, organize large building projects, or create stable conditions for continuous long-distance trade with other peoples. All these needs or goals contributed to the formation of states in sub-Saharan Africa.

State-building took place under a variety of conditions. For example, west Africa experienced both the cultural influence of Islam and its own internal developments. The formation of some powerful states, such as Mali and Songhay, depended more on military power and dynastic alliances than on ethnic or cultural unity. In this development and in the process of state formation itself, Africa paralleled the roughly contemporaneous developments of western Europe. The growth of city-states with strong merchant communities in west Africa and on the Indian Ocean coast bore certain similarities to the urban developments of Italy and Germany in this period. However, disparities between the technologies and ideologies of Europeans and Africans also created differences in the ways these societies developed. That was made clear with the arrival of Europeans—the Portuguese—in the 15th century whose contact drew Africans increasingly into the world economy in ways that transformed African development in the following centuries.

stateless societies African societies organized around kinship or other forms of obligation and lacking the concentration of political power and authority associated with states.

Common Elements in African Societies

Even amid the diversity of African cultures, certain similarities in language, thought, and religion provided some underlying unities. The spread of the Bantu-speaking peoples provided a linguistic base across much of Africa, so that even though specific languages differed, structure and vocabulary allowed some mutual understanding between neighboring Bantu speakers.

The same might be said of the animistic religion that characterized much of Africa. From its earliest beginnings it was a belief that a soul or spirit existed in every object, even if it was inanimate. In a future state this soul or spirit would exist as part of an immaterial soul. The spirit, therefore, was thought to be universal. Africans, like Europeans, believed that some evil, disasters, and illnesses were produced by witchcraft. Specialists were needed to combat the power of evil and eliminate the witches. This led in many societies to the existence of a class of diviners or priests who guided religious practice and helped protect the community. Above all, African religion provided a cosmology—a view of how the universe worked—and a guide to ethics and behavior.

Many African peoples shared an underlying belief in a creator deity whose power and action were expressed through spirits or lesser gods and through the founding ancestors of the group. The ancestors often were viewed as the first settlers and thus the "owners" of the land or the local resources. Through them, the fertility of the land, game, people, and herds could be ensured. Among some groups, working the land took on religious significance, so the land itself had a meaning beyond its economic usefulness.

Religion, economics, and history were thus closely intertwined. The family, lineage, or clan around which many African societies were organized also had an important role in dealing with the gods. Deceased ancestors often were a direct link between their living relatives and the spirit world. Veneration of the ancestors and gods was part of the same system of belief. Such a system was strongly linked to specific places and people. It showed remarkable resiliency even in the face of contact with monotheistic religions such as Islam and Christianity.

The economies of Africa are harder to describe in general terms than some basic aspects of politics and culture. North Africa, fully involved in the Mediterranean and Arab economic world, stands clearly apart. Sub-Saharan Africa varied greatly from one region to the next. In many areas, settled agriculture and skilled ironwork had been established before or advanced rapidly during the postclassical period. Specialization encouraged active local and regional trade, the basis for many lively markets and the many large cities that grew in both the structured states and the decentralized areas. The bustle and gaiety of market life were important ingredients of African society, and women as well as men participated actively. Professional merchants, in many cases in hereditary kinship groupings, often controlled trade. Participation in international trade increased in many regions in this period, mainly with the Islamic world and often through Arab traders.

Finally, one of the least known aspects of early African societies is the size and dynamics of their populations. This is true not only of Africa but of much of the world. Archeological evidence, travelers' reports, and educated guesses are used to estimate the population of early African societies, but in truth, our knowledge of how Africa fits into the general trends of the world population is very slight. By 1500, Africa may have had 30 to 60 million inhabitants.

The Arrival of Islam in North Africa

Africa north of the Sahara had long been part of the world of classical antiquity, where Phoenicians, Greeks, Romans, and Vandals traded, settled, built, battled, and destroyed. The Greek city of Cyrene (c. 600 B.C.E.) in modern Libya and the great Phoenician outpost at Carthage (founded c. 814 B.C.E.) in Tunisia attest to the part north Africa played in the classical world. After the age of the pharaohs, Egypt (conquered by Alexander in 331 B.C.E.) had become an important part of the Greek world and then later a key province in the Roman Empire, valued especially for its grain. Toward the end of the Roman Empire, Christianity had taken a firm hold in Mediterranean Africa, but in the warring between the Vandals and the Byzantines in north Africa in the 5th and 6th centuries C.E., great disruption had taken place. During that period, the Berber peoples of the Sahara had raided the coastal cities. As we have seen with Egypt, north Africa was linked across the Sahara to the rest of Africa in many ways. With the rise of Islam, those ties became even closer.

Ifriqiya [IHF-rih-kee-uh] The Arabic term for eastern north Africa.

Maghrib [MAH-gribb] The Arabic word for western north Africa.

Almohadis [AHL-moh-HAH-dees] A reformist movement among the Islamic Berbers of northern Africa; later than the Almoravids; penetrated into sub-Saharan Africa.

Between 640 and 700 C.E., the followers of Muhammad swept across north Africa from Suez to Morocco's Atlantic shore. By 670 C.E., Muslims ruled Tunisia, or **Ifriqiya**—what the Romans had called Africa. (The Arabs originally used this word as the name for eastern north Africa and **Maghrib** for lands to the west.) By 711, Arab and Berber armies had crossed into Spain. Only their defeat in France by Charles Martel at Poitiers in 732 brought the Muslim advance in the West to a halt. The message of Islam found fertile ground among the populations of north Africa. Conversion took place rapidly within a certain political unity provided by the Abbasid dynasty. This unity eventually broke down, and north Africa divided into several separate states and competing groups.

In opposition to the states dominated by the Arab rulers, the peoples of the desert, the Berbers, formed states of their own at places such as Fez in Morocco and at Sijilimasa, the old city of the trans-Saharan caravan trade. By the 11th century, under pressure from new Muslim invaders, a great puritanical reformist movement, whose followers were called the Almoravids (ahl-MOHR-uh-vihdz), grew among the desert Berbers of the western Sahara. Launched on the course of a *jihad*—a holy war waged to purify, spread, or protect the faith—the Almoravids moved south against the African kingdoms of the savanna and west into Spain. In 1130 another reformist group, the **Almohadis**, followed the same pattern. These north African and Spanish developments were an essential background to the penetration of Islam into sub-Saharan Africa.

Islam offered many attractions within Africa. Its fundamental teaching that all Muslims are equal within the community of believers made the acceptance of conquerors and new rulers easier. The Islamic tradition of uniting the powers of the state and religion in the person of the ruler or caliph appealed to some African kings as a way of reinforcing their authority. The concept that all members of the umma, or community of believers, were equal put the newly converted Berbers and later Africans on an equal footing with the Arabs, at least in law. Despite these egalitarian and somewhat utopian ideas within Islam, practices differed considerably at local levels. Social stratification remained important in Islamicized societies, and ethnic distinctions also divided the believers. Despite certain teachings on the equality between men and women, the fine for killing a man was twice that for killing a woman. The disparity between law and practice—between equality before God and inequality within the world—sometimes led to utopian reform movements. Groups such as the Almohadis are characteristic within Islamic history, often developing in peripheral areas and dedicated to purifying society by returning to the original teachings of Muhammad.

The Christian Kingdoms: Nubia and Ethiopia

Islam was not the first universalistic religion to take root in Africa, and the wave of Arab conquests across northern Africa had left behind it islands of Christianity. Christian converts had been made in Egypt and Ethiopia even before the conversion of the Roman Empire in the 4th century C.E. In addition to the Christian kingdom of Axum, Christian communities thrived in Egypt and Nubia, farther up the Nile. The Christians of Egypt, the Copts, developed a rich tradition in contact with Byzantium, translating the gospels and other religious literature from Greek to Coptic, their own tongue, which was based on the language of ancient Egypt. On doctrinal and political issues, they eventually split from the Byzantine connection. When Egypt was conquered by Arab armies and then converted to Islam, the Copts were able to maintain their faith; Muslim rulers recognized them as followers of a revealed religion and thus entitled to a certain tolerance. The Coptic influence had already spread up the Nile into Nubia, the ancient land of Kush. Muslim attempts to penetrate Nubia were met with such stiff resistance in the 9th century that the Christian descendants of ancient Kush were left as independent Christian kingdoms until the 13th century.

The Ethiopian kingdom that grew from Axum was perhaps the most important African Christian outpost. Cut off from Christian Byzantium by the Muslim conquest of Egypt and the Red Sea coast, surrounded by pagan neighbors, and probably influenced by pagan and Jewish immigrants from Yemen, the Christian kingdom turned inward. Its people occupied the Ethiopian highlands, living in fortified towns and supporting themselves with agriculture on terraced hillsides. Eventually, through a process of warfare, conversion, and compromise with non-Christian neighbors, a new dynasty emerged, which under King Lalibela (d. 1221) sponsored a remarkable building project in which 11 great churches were sculpted from the rock in the town that bore his name (Figure 9.2).

In the 13th and 14th centuries, an Ethiopian Christian state emerged under a dynasty that traced its origins back to the biblical marriage of Solomon and Sheba. Using the Ge'ez language of Axum as a

FIGURE 9.2 This extraordinary 13th-century church, *Bet Giorgis*, represents the power of early Christianity in Ethiopia. It was one of a great complex of eleven churches that King Lalibela believed God had commanded him to build. Dedicated to St. George, the patron saint of Ethiopia, it was cut out of the bedrock of the earth. Its roof, in the shape of an enormous cross, lies at ground level. Although it is surrounded by impassable walls and can be reached only by way of an underground tunnel carved in stone, it is still used for worship today.

religious language and Amharic as the common speech, this state maintained its brand of Christianity in isolation while facing constant pressure from its increasingly Muslim neighbors.

The struggle between the Christian state in the Ethiopian highlands and the Muslim peoples in Somalia and on the Red Sea coast shaped much of the history of the region and continues to do so today. When one of these Muslim states, with help from the Ottoman Turks, threatened the Ethiopian kingdom, a Portuguese expedition arrived in 1542 at Massawa on the Red Sea and turned the tide in favor of its Christian allies. Portuguese attempts thereafter to bring Ethiopian Christianity into the Roman Catholic church failed, and Ethiopia remained isolated, Christian, and fiercely independent.

KINGDOMS OF THE GRASSLANDS

9.2 How did African societies accommodate Islam and what was the effect of its spread across Africa?

As the Islamic wave spread across north Africa, it sent ripples across the Sahara, not in the form of invading armies but at first in the merchants and travelers who trod the dusty and ancient caravan routes toward the savanna. Africa had three important "coasts" of contact: the Atlantic, the Indian Ocean, and the savanna on the southern rim of the Sahara.

On the edge of the desert, where several resource zones came together, African states such as Ghana had already formed by the 8th century by exchanging gold from the forests of west Africa for

In the sahel grasslands, several powerful states emerged that combined Islamic religion and culture with local practices. The kingdoms of Mali and Songhay and the Hausa states were African adaptations of Islam and its fusion with African traditions.

salt or dates from the Sahara or for goods from Mediterranean north Africa. Camels, which had been introduced from Asia to the Sahara between the 1st and 5th centuries C.E., had greatly improved the possibilities of trade, but these animals, which thrived in arid and semiarid environments, could not live in the humid forest zones because of disease. Thus, the sahel, the extensive grassland belt at the southern edge of the Sahara, became a point of exchange between the forests to the south and north Africa—an active border area where ideas, trade, and people from the Sahara and beyond arrived in increasing numbers. Along the sahel, several African states developed between the trading cities, taking advantage of their position as intermediaries in the trade. But their location on the open plains of the dry sahel also meant that these states were subject to attack and periodic droughts.

Founded probably in the 3rd century C.E., Ghana rose to power by taxing the salt and gold exchanged within its borders. By the 10th century, its rulers had converted to Islam, and Ghana was at the height of its power. At a time when William the Conqueror could muster perhaps 5000 troops for his invasion of England, Muslim accounts reported that the king of Ghana could field an army many times that size. Eventually, however, Almoravid armies invaded Ghana from north Africa in 1076. The kingdom survived, but its power declined. By the beginning of the 13th century, new states had risen in the savanna to take Ghana's place of leadership.

Sudanic States

Read the Document on MyHistoryLab: Ghana and Its People in the Mid-Eleventh Century

There were several Sudanic kingdoms, and even during the height of Ghana's power, neighboring and competing states persisted, such as Takrur on the Senegal River to the west and Gao (on the Niger River) to the east. Before we deal with the most important kingdoms that followed Ghana, it is useful to review some of the elements these states had in common.

The Sudanic states often had a patriarch or council of elders of a particular family or group of lineages as leaders. Usually these states had a territorial core area in which the people were of the same linguistic or ethnic background, but their power extended over subordinate communities. These were conquest states, which drew on the taxes, tribute, and military support of the subordinate areas, lineages, and villages. The effective control of subordinate societies and the legal or informal control of their sovereignty are the usual definition of empires. The Sudanic states of Ghana, Mali, and Songhay fit that definition (Map 9.1).

juula [JOO-luh] Malinke merchants; formed small partnerships to carry out trade throughout Mali Empire; eventually spread throughout much of west Africa.

The rulers of these states were considered sacred and were surrounded by rituals that separated them from their subjects. With the conversion of the rulers of Ghana and Takrur after the 10th century, Islam was used to reinforce indigenous ideas of kingship, so that Islam became something of a royal cult. Much of the population never converted, and the Islamicized ruling families also drew on their traditional powers to fortify their rule.

Watch the Video on MyHistoryLab: West African States

Several savanna states rose among the various peoples in the Sudan. We can trace the development and culture of two of the most important, Mali and Songhay, as examples of the fusion of Islamic and indigenous African cultures within the context of trade and military expansion.

The Empire of Mali and Sundiata, the "Lion Prince"

The empire of Mali, centered between the Senegal and Niger rivers, was the creation of the Malinke peoples, who in the 13th century broke away from the control of Ghana, which was by then in decline. In Mali the old forms of kingship were reinforced by Islam. As in many of the Sudanic states, the rulers supported Islam by building mosques, attending public prayers, and supporting preachers. In return, sermons to the faithful emphasized obedience and support of the king. Mali became a model of these Islamicized Sudanic kingdoms. The economic basis of society in the Mali Empire was agriculture. This was combined with an active tradition of trade in many products, although like Ghana, Mali also depended on its access to gold-producing areas to the south. Malinke merchants, or **juula**, formed small partnerships and groups to carry out trade throughout the area. They spread beyond the borders of the empire and throughout much of west Africa.

MAP 9.1 Empires of the Western Sudan

The beginning of Malinke (also called Mandinka or Mandingo) expansion is attributed to **Sundiata** (sometimes written Sunjata), a brilliant leader whose exploits were celebrated in a great oral tradition. The **griots**, professional oral historians who also served as keepers of traditions and advisors to kings, began their epic histories of Mali with Sundiata, the "Lion Prince."

> Listen then sons of Mali, children of the black people, listen to my word, for I am going to tell you of Sundiata, the father of the Bright Country, of the savanna land, the ancestor of those who draw the bow, the master of a hundred vanquished kings.... He was great among kings, he was peerless among men; he was beloved of God because he was the last of the great conquerors.

Sundiata The "Lion Prince"; a member of the Keita clan; created a unified state that became the Mali Empire; died about 1260.

griots [grEE O, grEE O, grEE ot] Professional oral historians who served as keepers of traditions and advisors to kings within the Mali Empire.

After a difficult childhood, Sundiata emerged from a period of interfamily and regional fighting to create a unified state. Oral histories ascribed to him the creation of the basic rules and relationships of Malinke society and the outline of the government of the empire of Mali. He became the mansa, or emperor. It was said that Sundiata "divided up the world," which meant that he was considered the originator of social arrangements. Sixteen clans of free people were entitled to bear arms and carry the bow and quiver of arrows as the symbol of their status, five clans were devoted to religious duties, and four clans were specialists such as blacksmiths and griots. Such clan arrangements were traditional among the peoples of the savanna and had existed in ancient Ghana, but now Sundiata was credited with their origins. Although he created the political institutions of rule that allowed for great regional and ethnic differences in the federated provinces, he also stationed garrisons to maintain loyalty and security. Travel was secure and crime was severely punished, as **Ibn Battuta** (1304–1368 C.E.), the Arab traveler, reported: "Of all peoples," he said, "the Blacks are those who most hate injustice, and their emperor pardons none who is guilty of it." The security of travelers and their goods was an essential element in a state where commerce played so important a role.

Ibn Battuta (b. 1304) Arab traveler who described African societies and cultures in his travel records.

Sundiata died about 1260, but his successors expanded the borders of Mali until it controlled most of the Niger valley almost to the Atlantic coast. A sumptuous court was established and hosted a large number of traders. Mali grew wealthy from the trade. Perhaps the most famous of Sundiata's successors was Mansa Kankan Musa (c. 1312–1337), whose pilgrimage to Mecca in 1324 brought the attention of the Muslim world to Mali, as was described in the beginning of this chapter. Mansa Musa's trip had other consequences as well. From Mecca he brought back poet and architect Ishak al-Sahili, who came from Muslim Spain. The architect directed the building of several important mosques, and eventually a distinctive form of Sudanic architecture developed that made use of beaten clay. This can still be seen in the great mosque of Jenne.

City Dwellers and Villagers

The cities of the western Sudan began to resemble those of north Africa, but with a distinctive local architectural style. The towns were commercial and often included craft specialists and a resident foreign merchant community. The military expansion of states such as Ghana, Mali, and later Songhay contributed to their commercial success because the power of the state protected traders. A cosmopolitan court life developed as merchants and scholars were attracted by the power and protection of Mali. Malinke traders ranged across the Sudan and exploited their position as intermediaries. Cities of commercial exchange flourished, such as Jenne and **Timbuktu**, which lay just off the flood plain on the great bend in the Niger River. Timbuktu was reported to have a population of 50,000, and by the 14th century, its great Sankore mosque contained a library and an associated university where scholars, jurists, and Muslim theologians studied. The book was the symbol of civilization in the Islamic world, and it was said that the book trade in Timbuktu was the most lucrative business.

Timbuktu Port city of Mali; located just off the flood plain on the great bend in the Niger River; population of 50,000; contained a library and university.

 Read the **Document** on **MyHistoryLab**: Leo Africanus Describes Timbuktu

For most people in the empire of Mali and the other Sudanic states, life was not centered on the royal court, the great mosque, or long-distance trade but rather on the agricultural cycle and the village. Making a living from the land was the preoccupation of most people, and about 80 percent of the villagers lived by farming. This was a difficult life. The soils of the savanna were sandy and shallow. Plows were rarely used. The villagers were people of the hoe who looked to the skies in the spring for the first rains to start their planting. Rice in the river valleys, millet, sorghums, some wheat, fruits, and vegetables provided the basis of daily life in the village and supplied the caravan trade. Even large farms rarely exceeded 10 acres, and most were much smaller. Clearing land often was done communally, accompanied by feasts and competition, but the farms belonged to families and were worked

DOCUMENT

The Great Oral Tradition and the Epic of Sundiata

ORAL TRADITIONS TAKE VARIOUS FORMS. SOME are simply the shared stories of a family or people, but in many west African societies, the mastery of oral traditions is a skill practiced by *griots*. Although today's griots are professional musicians and bards, historically they held important places at the courts of west African kingdoms. The epic of Sundiata, the great ruler of Mali, has been passed down orally for centuries. In the following excerpts from a version collected among the Malinke people of Guinea by the African scholar D. T. Niane, the role of the griot and the advantages of oral traditions are outlined.

> We are now coming to the great moments in the life of Sundiata. The exile will end and another sun will rise. It is the sun of Sundiata. Griots know the history of kings and kingdoms and that is why they are the best counsellors of kings. Every king wants to have a singer to perpetuate his memory, for it is the griot who rescues the memories of kings from oblivion, as men have short memories. Kings have prescribed destinies just like men, and seers who probe the future know it. They have knowledge of the future, whereas we griots are depositories of the knowledge of the past. But whoever knows the history of a country can read its future.
>
> Other peoples use writing to record the past, but this invention has killed the faculty of memory among them. They do not feel the past any more, for writing lacks the warmth of the human voice. With them everybody thinks he knows, whereas learning should be a secret. The prophets did not write and their words have been all the more vivid as a result. What paltry learning is that which is concealed in dumb books!

The following excerpt describes the preparation for a major battle fought by Sundiata against the forces of Soumaoro, king of the Sossos, who had taken control of Mali and who is called an evil sorcerer in the epic. Note the interweaving of proverbs, the presence of aspects of Muslim and animist religion, the celebration of Sundiata's prowess, the recurring references to iron, and the high value placed on the cavalry, the key to military power in the savanna. Note how the story of Alexander the Great inspires this "African Alexander."

> Every man to his own land! If it is foretold that your destiny should be fulfilled in such and such a land, men can do nothing against it. Mansa Tounkara could not keep Sundiata back because the destiny of Songolon's son was bound up with that of Mali. Neither the jealousy of a cruel stepmother, nor her wickedness could alter for a moment the course of great destiny.
>
> The snake, man's enemy, is not long-lived, yet the serpent that lives hidden will surely die old. Djata (Sundiata) was strong enough now to face his enemies. At the age of eighteen he had the stateliness of the lion and the strength of the buffalo. His voice carried authority, his eyes were live coals, his arm was iron, he was the husband of power.
>
> Moussa Tounkara, king of Mema, gave Sundiata half of his army. The most valiant came forward of their own free will to follow Sundiata in the great adventure. The cavalry of Mema, which he had fashioned himself, formed his iron squadron. Sundiata, dressed in the Muslim fashion of Mema, left the town at the head of his small but redoubtable army. The whole population sent their best wishes with him. He was surrounded by five messengers from Mali, and Manding Bory [Sundiata's brother] rode proudly at his side. The horsemen of Mema formed behind Djata a bristling iron squadron. The troop took the direction of Wagadou, for Djata did not have enough troops to confront Soumaoro directly, and so the king of Mema advised him to go to Wagadou and take half the men of the king, Soumaba Cissé. A swift messenger had been sent there and so the king of Wagadou came out in person to meet Sundiata and his troops. He gave Sundiata half of his cavalry and blessed the weapons. Then Manding Bory said to his brother, "Djata, do you think yourself able to face Soumaoro now?"
>
> "No matter how small a forest may be, you can always find there sufficient fibers to tie up a man. Numbers mean nothing; it is worth that counts. With my cavalry I shall clear myself a path to Mali."
>
> Djata gave out his orders. They would head south, skirting Soumaoro's kingdom. The first objective to be reached was Tabon, the iron-gated town in the midst of the mountains, for Sundiata had promised Fran Kamara that he would pass Tabon before returning to Mali. He hoped to find that his childhood companion had become king. It was a forced march and during the halts the divines, Singbin Mara Cissé and Mandjan Bérété, related to Sundiata the history of Alexander the Great and several other heroes, but of all of them Sundiata preferred Alexander, the king of gold and silver, who crossed the world from west to east. He wanted to outdo his prototype both in the extent of his territory and in the wealth of his treasury.

QUESTIONS

- Can oral traditions be used like other sources?
- Even if they are not entirely true, do they have historical value?
- Judging from this epic, how did people of the Sudan define the qualities of a king?
- What aspects of the epic reveal contacts between this part of Africa and the wider world?

by them. A man with two wives and several unmarried sons could work more land than a man with one wife and a smaller family. Polygamy, the practice of having multiple wives, was common in the region, and it remains so today.

Given the difficulties of the soil, the periodic droughts, insect pests, storage problems, and the limitations of technology, the farmers of the Sudanic states—by the methods of careful cultivation, crop rotation, and in places such as Timbuktu, the use of irrigation—were able to provide for their people the basic foods that supported them and the imperial states on which they were based. The hoe and the bow became symbols of the common people of the savanna states.

The Songhay Kingdom

As the power of Mali began to wane, a successor state from within the old empire was already beginning to emerge. The people of **Songhay** dominated the middle areas of the Niger valley. Traditionally, the society of Songhay was made up of "masters of the soil," that is, farmers, herders, and "masters of the waters," or fishers. Songhay had begun to form in the 7th century as an independent kingdom, perhaps under a Berber dynasty. By 1010, a capital was established at Gao on the Niger River, and the rulers had become Muslims, although the majority of the population remained pagan. Dominated by Mali for a while, by the 1370s Songhay had established its independence again and began to thrive as new sources of gold from the west African forests began to pass through its territory. Gao became a large city with a resident foreign merchant community and several mosques. Under a dynamic leader, Sunni Ali (r. 1464–1492), the empire of Songhay was forged.

Sunni Ali was a great tactical commander and a ruthless leader. His cavalry expanded the borders and seized the traditional trading cities of Timbuktu and Jenne. The middle Niger valley fell under his control, and he developed a system of provincial administration to mobilize recruits for the army and rule the far-flung conquests. Although apparently a Muslim, he met any challenge to his authority even when it came from the Muslim scholars of Timbuktu, whom he persecuted. A line of Muslim rulers who took the military title *askia* succeeded him. These rulers, especially **Muhammad the Great**, extended the boundaries of the empire so that by the mid-16th century Songhay dominated the central Sudan.

Life in the Songhay Empire followed many of the patterns established in the previous savanna states. The fusion of Islamic and pagan populations and traditions continued. Muslim clerics and jurists sometimes were upset by the pagan beliefs and practices that continued among the population, and even more by the local interpretation of Islamic law. They wanted to impose a strict interpretation of the law of Islam and were shocked that men and women mixed freely in the markets and streets, that women went unveiled.

Songhay remained the dominant power in the region until the end of the 16th century. In 1591, a Muslim army from Morocco, equipped with muskets, crossed the Sahara and defeated the vastly larger forces of Songhay. This sign of weakness stimulated internal revolts against the ruling family, and eventually the parts of the old empire broke away.

The demise of the Songhay imperial structure did not mean the end of the political and cultural tradition of the western Sudan. Other states that combined Muslim and pagan traditions rose among the **Hausa** peoples of northern Nigeria, based on cities such as Kano and Katsina. The earliest Muslim ruler of Kano took control in the late 14th century and turned the city into a center of Muslim learning. In Kano and other Hausa cities of the region, an urbanized royal court in a fortified capital ruled over the animistic villages, where the majority of the population lived. With powerful cavalry forces these states extended their rule and protected their active trade in salt, grains, and cloth. Although these later Islamicized African states tended to be small and their goals were local, they reproduced many of the social, political, and religious forms of the great empires of the grasslands.

Beyond the Sudan, Muslim penetration came in various forms. Merchants became established in most of the major trading cities, and religious communities developed in each of these, often associated with particular families. Networks of trade and contact were established widely over the region as merchants and groups of pastoralists established their outposts in the area of Guinea. Muslim traders, herders, warriors, and religious leaders became important minorities in these segmented African societies, composed of elite families, occupational groups, free people, and slaves. Intermarriage often

---

Songhay [sohng-HEYE] Successor state to Mali; dominated middle reaches of Niger valley; formed as independent kingdom under a Berber dynasty; capital at Gao; reached imperial status under Sunni Ali (r. 1464–1492).

Muhammad the Great Extended the boundaries of the Songhay Empire; Islamic ruler of the mid-16th century.

Read the Document on MyHistoryLab: "Askia Muhammad al-Turi and Reform in Songhai"

Read the Document on MyHistoryLab: Leo Africanus' Description of Africa (1500)

Hausa Peoples of northern Nigeria; formed states following the demise of Songhay Empire that combined Muslim and pagan traditions.

took place, but Muslim influence varied widely from region to region. Nevertheless, families of traders and lineages that became known as specialists in Muslim law spread widely through the region, so that by the 18th century Muslim minorities were scattered widely throughout west Africa, even in areas where no Islamicized state had emerged.

Political and Social Life in the Sudanic States

We can generalize from these brief descriptions of Mali and Songhay about the nature of the Sudanic states. The village communities, clans, and various ethnic groups continued to organize many aspects of life in the savanna. The development of unified states provided an overarching structure that allowed the various groups and communities to coexist. The large states usually represented the political aims and power of a particular group and often of a dominant family. Many states pointed to the immigrant origins of the ruling families, and in reality the movement and fusion of populations were constant features in the Sudan. Islam provided a universalistic faith that served the interests of many groups. Common religion and law provided solidarity and trust to the merchants who lived in the cities and whose caravans brought goods to and from the savanna. The ruling families used Islamic titles, such as *emir* or *caliph*, to reinforce their authority, and they surrounded themselves with literate Muslim advisors and scribes, who aided in government administration. The Muslim concept of a ruler who united civil and religious authority reinforced traditional ideas of kingship. It is also important to note that in Africa, as elsewhere in the world, the formation of states heightened social differences and made these societies more hierarchical.

In all the Sudanic states, Islam was fused with the existing traditions and beliefs. Rulership and authority were still based on the ability to intercede with local spirits, and although Sundiata and Sunni Ali were nominally Muslim, they did not ignore the traditional basis of their rule. For this reason, Islam in these early stages in the Sudan tended to accommodate pagan practice and belief. Large proportions of the populations of Mali and Songhay never converted to Islam, and those who did convert often maintained many of the old beliefs as well.

We can see this fusion of traditions clearly in the position of women. Several Sudanic societies were matrilineal, and some recognized the role of women within the lines of kinship, contrary to the normal patrilineal customs inscribed in the **Sharia**, or Islamic law. As in the case of Songhay, north African visitors to the Sudan were shocked by the easy familiarity between men and women and the freedom enjoyed by women.

Finally, slavery and the slave trade between black Africa and the rest of the Islamic world had a major impact on women and children in these societies. Various forms of slavery and dependent labor had existed in Africa before Islam was introduced. Although we know little about slavery in central Africa in this period, slavery had been a marginal aspect of the Sudanic states. Africans had been enslaved by others before, and Nubian (African) slaves had been known in the classical world, but with the Muslim conquests of north Africa and commercial penetration to the south, slavery became a more widely diffused phenomenon, and a slave trade in Africans developed on a new scale.

In theory, Muslims viewed slavery as a stage in the process of conversion—a way of preparing pagans to become Muslims—but in reality, conversion did not guarantee freedom. Slaves in the Islamic world were used in a variety of occupations, as domestic servants and laborers, but they were also used as soldiers and administrators who, having no local ties and affiliations, were considered to be dependent on and thus trustworthy by their masters. Slaves were also used as eunuchs and concubines, hence the emphasis on enslaving women and children. The trade caravans from the sahel across the Sahara often transported slaves as well as gold, and as we shall see, other slave trade routes developed from the African interior to the east African coast.

Frequently the children of slave mothers were freed and integrated into Muslim society. Although this custom was positive in one sense, it also meant a constant demand for more slaves to replace those freed. Estimates of the volume of the trans-Saharan slave trade vary widely. One scholar places the total at 4.8 million, with another 2.4 million sent to the Muslim ports on the Indian Ocean coast. Actual figures may have been considerably lower, but the trade extended over 700 years and affected a large area. It was one more way in which Islamic civilization changed sub-Saharan Africa.

Sharia [shä rEE ä] Islamic law; defined among other things the patrilineal nature of Islamic inheritance.

VISUALIZING THE PAST

The Architecture of Faith

THE SPREAD OF ISLAM EVENTUALLY CREATED spiritual, commercial, and cultural bonds between west Africa and the Middle East and especially north Africa and Spain. The process of Islam's expansion and its local adaptation is apparent in the distinctive architectural style of west African mosques. Built usually of clay, incorporating wood beams for support and decoration, with a *mirab* tower and an open courtyard, these places of worship created spaces of simple elegance with local materials that reflect ethnic and regional differences. West African mosques vary considerably from the traditional patterns of the Middle East and south Asia. Mosques, like the simple buildings among the Dogon people or the elaborate Sankoré mosque at Timbuktu begun in 1324 by Mansa Musa and later the center of a university, reflect the integration of Islam into African life.

QUESTIONS

- The architectural styles of west African mosques differ from the classic models of the Middle East. In what way does that suggest that Islam's entry to the region was gradual and transmitted by merchants and traders?
- In what ways do the mosques of West Africa reflect local conditions and practices?
- What functions beside prayer did mosques play and how did their construction tie west Africa to a wider world?

Dogon village mosque in Kani-Kombole, Mali, west Africa.

Domed Middle Eastern mosques shown in the skyline of Yazd, Iran.

THE SWAHILI COAST OF EAST AFRICA

9.3 How integrated into international commerce were the cities of East Africa, and why?

While the kingdoms of west Africa came under the influence of Islam from across the Sahara, another center of Islamic civilization was developing on the seaboard and offshore islands of Africa's Indian Ocean coast (Map 9.2). Along that coast, extending south from the horn of Africa to modern-day Mozambique, a string of Islamicized trading cities developed that reflected their cosmopolitan contacts with trading partners from Arabia, Persia, India, and China. Islam provided the residents of these towns a universal set of ethics and beliefs that made their maritime contacts easier, but in east Africa, as in the savanna kingdoms of west Africa, Islamization was slow to reach the general population. When it did, the result often was a compromise between indigenous ways and the new faith.

A string of Islamicized African ports tied to the trade across the Indian Ocean dotted the east African coast. Although these cities were Islamicized, African customs and the Bantu Swahili language remained so strong that they represented a cultural fusion, mostly limited to the coast.

CHAPTER 9 African Civilizations and the Spread of Islam 215

The Coastal Trading Ports

View the Closer Look on MyHistoryLab: Malindi Mosque

Zenj [zehnj] Arabic term for the east African coast.

A 1st-century Greek account of the Indian Ocean, *The Periplus of the Erythraean Sea*, mentioned some ports in east Africa but was vague about whether the inhabitants were Africans or immigrants from the Arabian peninsula. From that century to the 10th century, the wave of Bantu migration had clearly reached the east African interior. Bantu-speaking herders in the north and farmers in the south mixed with older populations in the region. Other peoples were also moving to the African coast.

Contact across the Indian Ocean dated back to at least the 2nd century B.C.E. From Indonesia or Malaya, seaborne immigrants settled on the large island of Madagascar and from there introduced foods such as bananas and coconuts to the African coast. These were widely adopted and spread rapidly along the coast and into central Africa. Small coastal villages of fishers and farmers, making rough pottery and working iron, dotted this coast. By the 8th and 9th centuries, Muslim visitors and refugees from Oman and the Persian Gulf had established themselves at some of these villages, attracted by the possibilities of trade with the land of **Zenj** (zehnj), the Arabic term for the east African coast.

By the 13th century, a string of urbanized east African trading ports had developed along the coast. These towns shared the common Bantu-based and Arabic-influenced Swahili (which means "coastal") language and other cultural traits, although they were governed by separate Muslim ruling families. Towns such as Mogadishu, Mombasa, Malindi, Kilwa, Pate, and Zanzibar eventually contained mosques, tombs, and palaces of cut stone and coral. Ivory, gold, iron, slaves, and exotic animals were exported from these ports in exchange for silks from Persia and porcelain from China for the ruling Muslim families. The Arab traveler Ibn Batuta was impressed with the beauty and refinement of these towns. He described Kilwa as "one of the most beautiful and well constructed towns in the world" and was also impressed by the pomp and luxury of its ruler. Kilwa's advantage was its access to the gold coming from the interior and the fact that it was the furthest point south from which the ships sailing from India could hope to return in a single monsoon season.

From the 13th to the 15th centuries, Kilwa flourished in the context of international trade, but it was not alone; about 30 of these port towns eventually dotted the coast. They were tied to each other by an active coastal commerce and, in a few places, to the interior by a caravan trade, although it was usually Africans who brought the goods to the coast. Some Chinese ports sent goods directly to Africa in the 13th century, and as late as 1417 and 1431, large, state-sponsored expeditions sailing directly from China stopped at the east African coast to load ivory, gold, and rare woods. The Chinese discontinued such contact after 1431, and goods from China came to the coast thereafter in the ships of Arab or Indian traders.

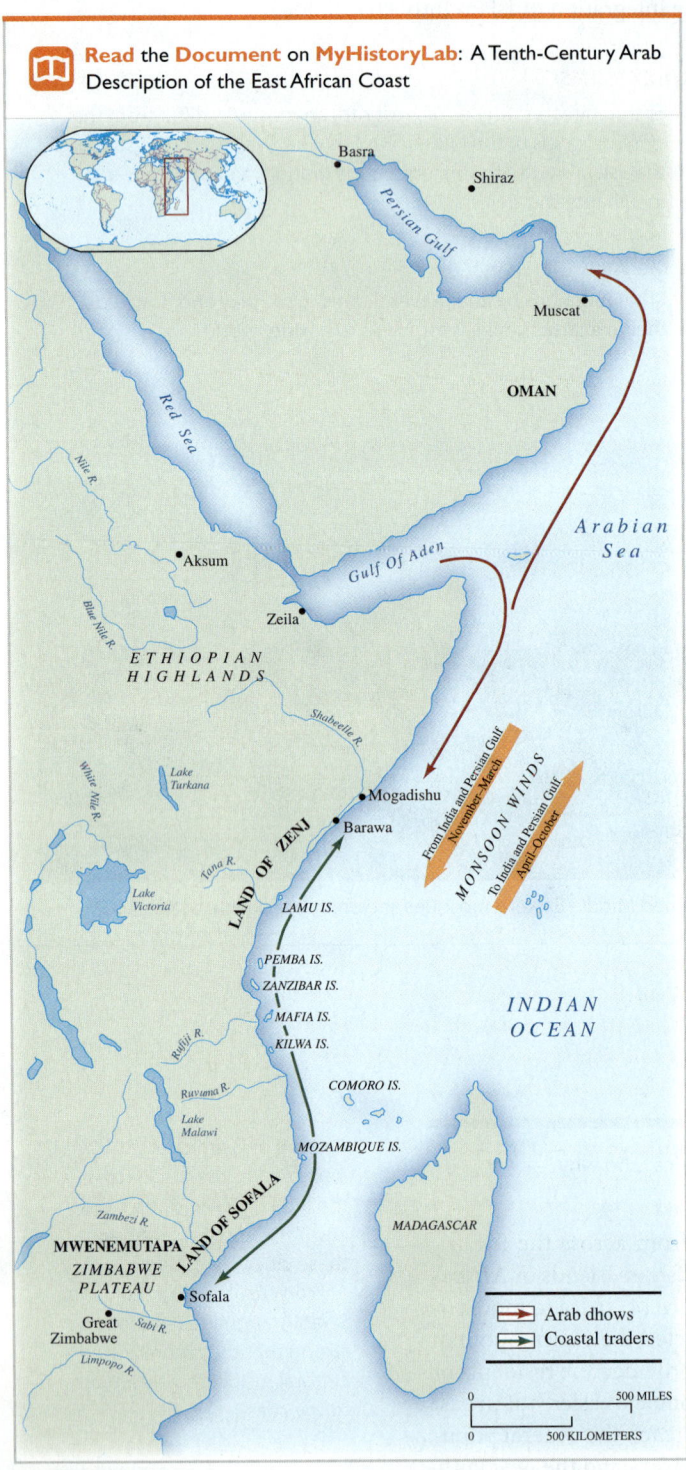

Read the Document on MyHistoryLab: A Tenth-Century Arab Description of the East African Coast

MAP 9.2 The Swahili Coast; African Monsoon Routes and Major Trade Routes

The Mixture of Cultures on the Swahili Coast

The Islamic influence in these towns promoted long-distance commerce. The 13th century was a period of great Islamic expansion, and as that faith spread eastward to India and Indonesia, it provided a religious bond of trust and law that facilitated trade throughout ports of the Indian Ocean. The ruling families in the east African trading ports built mosques and palaces; the mosque at Mogadishu was begun in 1231. Many of these ruling families claimed to be descendants of immigrants from Shiraz in Persia—a claim intended to legitimize their position and orthodoxy. In fact, some evidence indicates that the original Muslim families had emigrated to the Somali coast and from there to other towns farther south. The institutions and forms of the Muslim world operated in these cities. Whereas the rulers and merchants tended to be Muslim, the majority of the population on the east African coast, and perhaps even in the towns themselves, retained their previous beliefs and culture.

African culture remained strong throughout the area. The Swahili language was essentially a Bantu language containing a large number of Arabic words, although many of these words were not incorporated until the 16th century. The language was written in an Arabic script some time before the 13th century; the ruling families could also converse in Arabic. Islam itself penetrated very little into the interior among the hunters, pastoralists, and farmers. Even the areas of the coast near the trading towns remained largely unaffected. In the towns, the mud and thatch houses of the non-Muslim common peoples surrounded the stone and coral buildings of the Muslim elite. Islamization was to some extent class-based. Still, a culture developed that fused Islamic and traditional elements. For example, family lineage was traced both through the maternal line, which controlled property (the traditional African practice), and through the paternal line, as was the Muslim custom. Swahili culture was a dynamic hybrid, and the Swahili people spread their language and culture along the coast of east Africa.

By the time the Portuguese arrived on this coast around 1500, the Swahili culture was widely diffused. Kilwa was no longer the predominant city, and the focus of trade had shifted to Malindi and Mombasa on the Kenya coast, but the commerce across the Indian Ocean continued. Eventually, the Portuguese raided Kilwa and Mombasa in an attempt to take control of trade. Their outpost on Mozambique and their control of Sofala put much of the gold trade in their hands. Although the Portuguese built a major outpost at Fort Jesus in Mombasa in 1592, they were never able to control the trade on the northern Swahili coast. The east African patterns, as established by 1500, persisted even more than those of the Sudanic kingdoms. In some areas like the Swahili coast and the West African savanna, Islam became a dominant cultural force. In other areas such as the forest region of West Africa, Muslims remained a minority, and in other areas like the central African forests Islam hardly penetrated at all.

Read the Document on MyHistoryLab: Hans Mayr, Account of Francisco d'Almeida's attack on Kilwa and Mombasa

PEOPLES OF THE FOREST AND PLAINS

9.4 What kinds of political organization developed in central and southern Africa?

Across central Africa, kingdoms developed that were supported by complex agrarian societies capable of great artistic achievements. At Benin, in the Kongo, in the Yoruba city-states, and at Great Zimbabwe, royal authority—often considered divinely inspired—led to the creation of powerful states.

As important as the Islamic impact was on the societies of the savanna and the east African coast, other African peoples in the continent's interior and in the forests of west Africa were following their own trajectories of development. We must emphasize that African societies were diverse. By 1000 C.E., most of these societies were based on a varied agriculture, sometimes combined with herding, and most societies used iron tools and weapons. Many were still organized in small village communities. In various places, however, states had formed. Some of them began to resolve the problems of integrating large territories under a single government and ruling subject peoples. Whereas Egypt, Kush, and Ethiopia had developed writing and other areas borrowed the Arabic script, many sub-Saharan African societies were preliterate and transmitted their knowledge, skills, and traditions by oral methods and direct instruction. The presence or absence of writing has often been used as a measure of civilization by Western observers, but as in pre-Columbian Peru, various African societies made great strides in the arts, building, and statecraft, sometimes in the context of highly urbanized settings, without a system of writing.

Artists and Kings: Yoruba and Benin

In the forests of central Nigeria, terra-cotta objects of a realistic and highly stylized form have been discovered near the village of Nok. These objects, most of which date from about 500 B.C.E. to 200 C.E., reveal considerable artistic skill. The inhabitants of ancient Nok and its region practiced agriculture and used iron tools. They remain something of a mystery, but it appears that their artistic traditions spread widely through the forest areas and influenced other peoples. Nevertheless, there is a long gap in the historical and archeological record between the Nok sculptures and the renewed flourishing of artistic traditions in the region after about 1000 C.E.

CHAPTER 9 African Civilizations and the Spread of Islam **217**

FIGURE 9.3 In the 13th and 14th centuries, Ile-Ife artists worked in terra-cotta as well as bronze and produced skilled individual portraits like this one.

(The Brooklyn Museum of Art)

Benin Powerful city-state (in present-day Nigeria) which came into contact with the Portuguese in 1485 but remained relatively free of European influence; important commercial and political entity until the 19th century.

Among the Yoruba-speaking peoples of Nigeria, at the city of Ile-Ife (eel-EE-fuh), remarkable terra-cotta and bronze portrait heads of past rulers were produced in the period after 1200 C.E. The lifelike quality of these portraits and the skill of their execution place them among the greatest achievements of African art (Figure 9.3). The artists of Ile-Ife also worked in wood and ivory. Much of the art seems to be associated with kings and the authority of kingship. Ile-Ife, like other Yoruba states, seems to have been an agricultural society supported by a peasantry and dominated by a ruling family and an aristocracy. Ile-Ife was considered by many peoples in the region to be the original cultural center, and many of them traced their own beginnings to it.

Yoruba origins are obscure. Ile-Ife was seen as the holiest city of the Yoruba, their place of birth. Another legend maintained by the royal historians was that Oduduwa, a son of the king of Mecca, migrated from the east and settled in Yoruba. Modern historians have suggested that the real origins were perhaps Meroë and Nubia, or at least in the savanna south of the Sahara. In any case, the Yoruba spoke a non-Bantu language of the west African Kwa family and recognized a certain affinity between themselves and neighboring peoples, such as the Hausa, who spoke Afro-Asian languages.

The Yoruba were organized in small city-states, each controlling a radius of perhaps 50 miles. The Yoruba were highly urbanized, although many of the town inhabitants farmed in the surrounding countryside. These city-states developed under the strong authority of regional kings, who were considered divine. A vast royal court that included secondary wives, musicians, magicians, and bodyguards of soldier-slaves surrounded the king. His rule was not absolute, however. We can use the example of the Yoruba state of Oyo, which had emerged by the 14th century. Its king, the alafin, controlled subject peoples through "princes" in the provinces, drawn from local lineages, who were allowed to exercise traditional rule as long as they continued to pay tribute to Oyo. In the capital, a council of state, made up of nobles from the seven city districts, advised the ruler and limited his power, and the Ogboni, or secret society of religious and political leaders, reviewed decisions of the king and the council. The union of civil and supernatural powers in the person of the ruler was the basis of power. The highly urbanized nature of Yoruba society and the flourishing of artisan traditions within these towns bear some similarity to those of the city-states of medieval Italy or Germany.

Patterns similar to those in the Yoruba city-states could be found among Edo peoples to the east of Yoruba. A large city-state called **Benin** was formed sometime in the 14th century. Under Ewuare the Great (r. 1440–1473), Benin's control extended from the Niger River to the coast near modern Lagos. Benin City was described by early European visitors in the 16th century as a city of great population and broad avenues. The oba, or ruler, lived in a large royal compound surrounded by a great entourage, and his authority was buttressed by ritual and ceremony.

THINKING HISTORICALLY

Two Transitions in the History of World Population

AFRICA AND THE ANCIENT AMERICAS ARE two regions that make clear the difficulty of establishing the past size and structure of populations. Estimates based on fragmentary sources, the amount of available resources, and analysis of agricultural or hunting techniques have been used as rough guesses about population size. The results often are inadequate or controversial, but historians believe that the question is important. **Demography**, the study of population, has increasingly become a valued tool of historical inquiry. Clearly, unless we know the size, density, age structure, health, and reproductive capacity of a population, it is difficult to understand many aspects of its society, politics, and economy. In the contemporary world, most nations conduct periodic censuses to assess the present situation of their populations and to plan for the future. Before the mid-18th century, when census-taking became a regular procedure, population estimates and counts were sporadic and usually inaccurate. Estimating populations in the past, especially in nonliterate societies, is a highly speculative exercise in which archeological evidence and estimates of productive capacity of agricultural practices and technology are used. The earliest date

(continued on next page)

(continued from previous page)

for a population estimate with a margin of error less than 20 percent is probably 1750.

The history of human population can be divided into two basic periods: a long era—almost all of human history—of very slow growth and a very short period—about 275 years from 1750 to the present—of very rapid growth. For most of this history, the human population was very small and grew very slowly. Before agriculture was developed, the hunting-and-gathering economies of the world's populations supported 5 to 10 million people, if modern studies of such populations can be used as a guide. After about 8000 B.C.E., when plants and animals were domesticated, there was a first demographic transition as population began to increase more rapidly but still at a modest level. Agriculture provided a more secure and larger food supply, but population concentration in villages and towns may have made people more susceptible to disease and thus reduced their numbers. Other historians believe that the settled agricultural life also led to intensified warfare (because of the struggle for land and water) and increasing social stratification within societies.

Still, the Neolithic revolution and the development of agriculture stimulated population growth. It was the first major transition in the history of world population. One estimate, based on Roman and Chinese population counts and some informed guesses about the rest of the world, is an annual growth rate of about 0.36 per million. By 1 C.E., the world population may have been about 300 million people. It increased between 1 C.E. and 1750 C.E. to about 500 million people. We should bear in mind that during this period of general increase, there were always areas that suffered decline, sometimes drastic, because of wars, epidemics, or natural catastrophes. The disastrous decline of American Indian populations after contact with Europeans, caused by disease, conquest, and social disruption, is a case in point. The effect of the slave trade on Africa, although still debated, is another. Sharp population changes usually resulted in profound social and cultural adjustments. Some scholars argue that the slave trade had just such an impact on social and political patterns in Africa.

A second and extremely important transition took place between the mid-17th and the mid-18th centuries. Initially based on new food resources, this transition often is associated with the Industrial Revolution, when new sources of energy were harnessed. The growth rate greatly increased during this period in the countries most affected. Between 1750 and 1800, the world population grew at a rate of more than 4 percent a year to more than a billion people. By the mid-20th century, the world growth rate had tripled, and by 2012 world population had risen to more than 7 billion.

This **demographic transition** took place first in Europe and is still more characteristic of the developed world. Most premodern agrarian economies were characterized by a balance between the annual number of births and deaths; both were high. Life expectancy usually was less than 35 years, and the high mortality was compensated by high fertility; that is, women had many children. Improvements in medicine, hygiene, diet, and the general standard of living contributed to a decrease in mortality in the 18th century. This allowed populations to begin to grow at a faster rate. By the 19th century in most of western Europe, the decline in mortality was followed by a decline in fertility brought about by contraception. In some countries such as France, these two transitions took place at about the same time, so population growth was limited. In much of Europe, however, the decline in fertility lagged behind the decrease in mortality, so there was a period of rapid population growth. Until the 1920s, population growth in western Europe and the United States was higher than in the rest of the world, especially in the less industrialized countries. In recent times, that situation has been reversed.

Some demographers believe that demographic transition is part of the process of shifting from a basically agrarian society to an industrial, urbanized one and that the improvements in medicine, technology, and higher standards of living will necessarily result in a change to a modern demographic structure. They believe that a decreasing need for children as part of the family economic unit, laws against child labor, and state intervention in family planning will eventually lower the world birth rate and decrease the pressure of population on economic growth. This assumption remains to be proved, and responses may vary greatly from one region of the world to another because of economic conditions and cultural attitudes about proper family size.

> **At present, the world's population is growing because of a moderate rate of growth in the industrialized nations and a high rate in the developing countries.**

Finally, we should also note that responses to demographic transition can vary greatly according to historical conditions. In the 18th and 19th centuries, Europe resolved the problem of population growth with an enormous wave of emigration to the Americas, Australia, and various colonies around the globe. Present-day political circumstances make this solution less possible, although the new waves of migration in the global economy may indicate that the process is continuing.

Still, it is clear that a demographic transition has begun to take place in the developing world of Latin America, Africa, and Asia. Mortality has dropped very rapidly since 1950 because of modern medical technology, and life expectancy has doubled. To cite a single example, in Sri Lanka the mortality rate was almost cut in half between 1945 and 1952 simply by eliminating malarial mosquitoes. Fertility has declined in many places in Asia and Latin America, but in Africa, where children continue to have an important economic and social role in the extended family, it remains high. It is difficult to project what demographic transitions will take place in these areas of the world. However, all countries are faced with the problem of balancing their population's growth against the ability of the society to feed and provide an adequate standard of living to the people.

(continued on next page)

(continued from previous page)

At present, the world's population is growing because of a moderate rate of growth in the industrialized nations and a high rate in the developing countries. In the 1970s, demographer Ansley Coale pointed out that the rate of growth, about 2 percent a year, is 100 times greater than it had been for most of human history. At this rate the world's population would be multiplied by 1000 every 350 years. The results of such growth would be disastrous. Coale concluded that the present period of growth is transitory. Some people who are concerned with rapid population growth believe that the solution is to limit population growth in the developing nations by state intervention, like China's one child per family policy or through incentives to have smaller families and education about birth control. Others believe that a redistribution of resources from rich nations to poor nations would alleviate the human misery created by population pressure and eventually lead to political and social conditions that would contribute to a gradual lowering of the birth rates. Clearly, demographic questions must always be set in political, economic, and social contexts.

> **QUESTIONS**
> - Why do nations differ in their need to control population growth?
> - Why has the rate of population growth varied in different areas of the world?
> - Is overpopulation essentially a biological, social, or political problem?

demography The study of population.

demographic transition Shift to low birth rate, low infant death rate, stable population; first emerged in western Europe and United States in late 19th century.

That authority was also the theme of the magnificent artistic output in ivory and cast bronze that became characteristic of Benin. Tradition had it that Iguegha (eh-GUAY-gah), an artisan in bronze casting, was sent from Ile-Ife to introduce the techniques of making bronze sculptures. Benin then developed its own distinctive style, less naturalistic than that of Ile-Ife but no less impressive. Celebration of the powers and majesty of the royal lineage as well as objects for the rituals surrounding kingship were the subjects of much of this art. When the first Europeans, the Portuguese, visited Benin in the 1480s, they were impressed by the power of the ruler and the extent of his territory. Similarly, the artists of Benin were impressed with the Portuguese, and Benin bronzes and ivories began to include representations of Portuguese soldiers and other themes that reflected the contact with outsiders (Figure 9.4).

Central African Kingdoms

South of the rain forest that stretched across Africa almost to Lake Victoria lay a broad expanse of savanna and plain, cut by several large rivers such as the Kwango and the Zambezi. From their original home in Nigeria, the Bantu peoples had spread into the southern reaches of the rainforest along the Congo River, then southward onto the southern savannas, and eventually to the east coast. By the 5th century C.E., Bantu farmers and fishers had reached beyond the Zambezi, and by the 13th century they were approaching the southern end of the continent. Mostly beyond the influence of Islam, many of these central African peoples had begun their own process of state formation by about 1000 C.E., replacing the pattern of kinship-based societies with forms of political authority based on kingship. Whether the idea of kingship developed in one place and was diffused elsewhere or had multiple origins is unknown, but the older system based on seniority within the kinship group was replaced with rule based on the control of territory and the parallel development of rituals that reinforced the ruler's power. Several important kingdoms developed. In Katanga, the Luba peoples modified the older system of village headmen to a form of divine kinship in which the ruler and his relatives were thought to have a special power that ensured fertility of people and crops; thus, only the royal lineage was fit to rule. A sort of bureaucracy grew to administer the state, but it was hereditary, so that brothers or male children succeeded to the position. In a way, this system was a half step toward more modern concepts of bureaucracy, but it provided a way to integrate large numbers of people in a large political unit.

Kongo Kingdom, based on agriculture, formed on lower Congo River by late 15th century; capital at Mbanza Kongo; ruled by hereditary monarchy.

The Kingdoms of Kongo and Mwene Mutapa

Beginning about the 13th century, another kingdom was forming on the lower Congo River. By the late 15th century this kingdom, **Kongo**, was flourishing. On a firm agricultural base, its people also developed the skills of weaving, pottery, blacksmithing, and carving. Individual artisans, skilled in the working of wood, copper, and iron, were highly esteemed. There was a sharp division of labor between men and women. Men took responsibility for clearing the forest and scrub, producing palm oil and palm wine, building houses, hunting, and long-distance trade. Women took charge of cultivation in all its aspects, the care of domestic animals, and household duties. On the seacoast, women made salt from seawater, and they also collected the seashells that served as currency in the Kongo kingdom. The population was distributed in small family-based villages and in towns. The area around the capital, Mbanza Kongo, had a population of 60,000 to 100,000 by the early 16th century.

The kingship of the Kongo was hereditary but local chieftainships were not, and this gave the central authority power to control subordinates. In a way, the Kongo kingdom was a confederation of smaller states brought under the control of the manikongo, or king, and by the 15th century it was divided into eight major provinces. The word *mani* means "blacksmith," and it demonstrated the importance of iron and the art of working it in its association with political and ritual power.

Farther to the east, another large Bantu confederation developed among the farming and cattle-herding Shona-speaking peoples in the region between the Zambezi and Limpopo rivers. Beginning in the 9th century C.E., migrants from the west began to build royal courts in stone, to which later immigrants added more polished constructions. There were many of these zimbabwe, or stone house, sites (about 200 have been found) that housed local rulers and subchiefs, but the largest site, called **Great Zimbabwe**, was truly impressive (Figure 9.5). It was the center of the kingdom and had a religious importance, associated with the bird of God, an eagle that served as a link between the world and the spirits. The symbol of the bird of God is found at the ruins of Great Zimbabwe and throughout the area of its control. Great Zimbabwe (not to be confused with the modern nation of Zimbabwe) included several structures, some with strong stone walls 15 feet thick and 30 feet high, a large conical tower, and extensive cut-stone architecture made without the use of mortar to join the bricks together. Observers in the 19th century suspected that Phoenicians or Arabs had built these structures, mostly because their prejudices prevented them from believing that Africans were capable of erecting such buildings, but archeologists have established that a Bantu kingdom had begun construction in stone by the 11th century C.E. and had done its most sophisticated building in the 14th and 15th centuries.

FIGURE **9.4** Bronze plaque of Oba and retainers. African rulers often negotiated with the Portuguese on equal terms and incorporated them into local political and commercial networks. In this plaque, the presence of Portuguese retainers—the helmeted figures armed with muskets on each side of the main figure's head—were marks of the Oba's power.

By the 15th century, a centralized state ruled from Great Zimbabwe had begun to form. It controlled a large portion of the interior of southeast Africa all the way to the Indian Ocean. Under a king who took the title *Mwene Mutapa* (which the Portuguese later pronounced "Monomotapa"), this kingdom experienced a short period of rapid expansion in the late 15th and 16th centuries. Its dominance over the sources of gold in the interior eventually gave it great advantages in commerce, which it developed with the Arab port of Sofala on the coast. Evidence of this trade is found in the glass beads and porcelain unearthed by archeologists at Great Zimbabwe. By the 16th century, internal divisions and rebellion had split the kingdom apart, and perhaps an emphasis on cattle as a symbol of wealth led to soil exhaustion. Control of the gold fields still provided a source of power and trade. Representatives of the Mwene Mutapa called at the east-coast ports to buy Indian textiles, and their regal bearing and fine iron weapons impressed the first Europeans who saw them. As late as the 19th century, a much smaller kingdom of Mwene Mutapa survived in the interior and provided some leadership against European encroachment, but pastoralism had come to play a central role in the lives of the Shona people who descended from the great tradition.

Great Zimbabwe Bantu confederation of Shona-speaking peoples located between Zambezi and Limpopo rivers; developed after 9th century; featured royal courts built of stone; created centralized state by 15th century; king took title of Mwene Mutapa.

FIGURE **9.5** Great Zimbabwe was one of several stone settlement complexes in southeastern Africa. Added to at different times, it served as the royal court of the kingdom. In their search for traces of the non-African people they believed "must" have built these massive stone structures, European explorers and treasure-seekers stripped the site of layers of artifacts that might have told more of the story of Great Zimbabwe.

Global Connections and Critical Themes

INTERNAL DEVELOPMENT AND GLOBAL CONTACTS

This chapter has concentrated on the Sudanic states and the Swahili coast, where the impact of Islam was the most profound and where, because of the existence of written sources, it is somewhat easier to reconstruct the region's history. Sub-Saharan Africa had never been totally isolated from the Mediterranean world or other outside contacts, but the spread of Islam obviously brought large areas of Africa into more intensive contact with the global community, even though Africa remained something of an Islamic frontier. Still, the fusion of Islamic and indigenous African cultures created a synthesis that restructured the life of many Africans. Sudanic kingdoms and the Swahili coast participated in extensive borrowing and interactions with north Africa and the Middle East, similar to imitation efforts by several other societies in the postclassical period. Islamic contacts were also heavily involved in the growing integration of several parts of sub-Saharan Africa with global trade.

Although the arrival of Islam in Africa in the period from 800 to 1500 was clearly a major event, it would be wrong to see Africa's history in this period exclusively in terms of the Islamic impact. Great Zimbabwe and the Kongo kingdom, to cite only two examples, represented the development of Bantu concepts of kingship and state-building independently of trends taking place elsewhere on the continent. Similar processes and accomplishments could also be seen in Benin and among the Yoruba of west Africa. Meanwhile in Ethiopia, east Africa, and the eastern Sudan, the impact of Christianity and the pre-Islamic Mediterranean world had been long felt. The dynamic relationship between the impact of the civilizations and peoples external to Africa and the processes of development within the continent itself was a major theme in Africa's history.

Developments in Africa had their own special characteristics, and of course quite varied patterns emerged. The Sudanic kingdoms, however, warrant particular comparison with several other regions during the postclassical period. They showed the capacity to organize large, although fairly loosely structured, states.

They expanded trade and cultural contacts with other civilization centers, particularly of course in North Africa and the Middle East. They imitated aspects of their contact societies, though quite selectively. They clearly formed a vital part of the expansion of transregional trade, while constructing their own reactions to the other great theme of the period, the spread of world religions.

By the late 15th century, when the first Europeans, the Portuguese, began to arrive on the west and east coasts of Africa, in many places they found well-developed, powerful kingdoms that were able to deal with the Portuguese as equals. This was even truer in the parts of Africa that had come under the influence of Islam and through it had established links with other areas of Muslim civilization. In this period, Africa had increasingly become part of the general cultural trends of the wider world. Moreover, the intensified export trade in ivory, slaves, and especially gold from Africa drew Africans, even those far from the centers of trade, into a widening network of global relations. With the arrival of Europeans in sub-Saharan Africa in the late 15th century, the pace and intensity of the cultural and commercial contacts became even greater, and many African societies faced new and profound challenges.

Further Readings

Several books are also useful in relation to this chapter. The period covered is summarized in Robert O. Collins and James M. Burns, *A History of Sub-Saharan Africa* (2007). Essential reading on central Africa is Jan Vansina, *Paths in the Rainforests* (1990) and his *How Societies Are Born: Governance in West Central Africa* (2004). A general introduction to the grassland empires of the western Sudan is presented in David Conrad, *Empires of Medieval West Africa* (2005), while John Hunwick, *Timbuktu and the Songhay Empire* (2003) presents a translation of one of the great chronicles. On the Swahili coast, see A. Mazrui and I. Shariff, *The Swahili: Idiom and Identity of an African People* (1994) which emphasizes language; and R. L. Pouwells, *Horn and Crescent: Cultural Change and Traditional Islam on the East African Coast, 800–1900*, 2nd ed. (2002) John Middleton, *The World of the Swahili* (1992) Mark Horton and John Middleton, *The Swahili: The Social Landscape of a Mercantile Society* (2000), and Chapurukha Kusimba, *The Rise and Fall of Swahili City States* (1999) are all good introductions to the topic. On Ethiopia see Harold Marcus, *A History of Ethiopia* (1994). Stuart Munro-Hay, *The Quest for the Ark of the Covenant* (2005) delves into the Judaic and Christian origins of Ethiopia. A very good survey of the early history of Africa with interesting comments on the Nok culture is Susan Keech McIntosh and Roderick J. McIntosh's "From Stone to Metal: New Perspectives on the Later Prehistory of West Africa," *Journal of World History* 2, no. 1 (1988): 89–133. Graham Connah, *Forgotten Africa: An Introduction to Its Archaeology* (2004) reveals recent findings in that field. J. F. Ade Ajayi and Michael Crowder's *History of West Africa*, 2 vols. (1987), contains excellent review chapters by specialists. N. Levtzion's *Ancient Ghana and Mali* (1973) is still the best short introduction to these kingdoms of the sahel, but more recent are *On Islam*, David Robinson, *Muslim Societies in African History* (2004), and the essays collected in Nehemia Levtzion and Randall Pouwels, eds., *The History of Islam in Africa* (2000) are excellent starting points.

Two good books on the Kongo kingdom are Anne Hilton's *The Kingdom of the Kongo* (1992), which shows how African systems of thought accommodated the arrival of Europeans and their culture, and Georges Balandier's older *Daily Life in the Kingdom of the Kongo* (1969), which makes good use of travelers' reports and other documents to give a rounded picture of Kongo society. Joseph Vogel, *Great Zimbabwe: The Iron Age in South Central Africa* (2004) is a good starting point; David Birmingham and Phyllis Martin's *History of Central Africa*, 2 vols. (1983), is an excellent regional history.

Two multivolume general histories of Africa that provide synthetic articles by leading scholars on many of the topics discussed in this chapter are *The Cambridge History of Africa*, 8 vols. (1975–1986); and the UNESCO *General History of Africa*, 7 vols. to date (1981–).

Some important source materials on African history for this period include three translations of the Mande epic *Sundiata*: David C. Conrad and Djanta Tassey Conde's *Sunjata: A West African Epic of the Mande Peoples* (2004); D. T. Niane's *Sundiata: An Epic of Old Mali* (1986); and Bamba Suso and Banna Kanute, *Sunjata: Gambian Versions of the Mande Epic* (2000). Other sources include G. R. Crone, ed., *The Voyages of Cadamosto*, 2nd series, vol. 80 (1937), which deals with Mali, Cape Verde, Senegal, and Benin; Maylin Newitt, ed., *The Portuguese in West Africa 1415–1670* (2010) and Ross Dunn's indispensable edition of *The Adventures of Ibn Batuta: A Muslim Traveler of the 14th Century* (1990). Arab sources are translated in Nehemia Levtzion and Jay Spaulding, *Medieval West Africa: Views from Arab Scholars and Merchants* (2003).

On MyHistoryLab

 Study and Review on MyHistoryLab

Critical Thinking Questions

1. What were the products of Africa that attracted international trade and what did Africans want in return?
2. How did the expansion of Islam affect African societies?
3. Compare the advantages and disadvantages of stateless societies and those with monarchies or other forms of hereditary rule.

10
Civilization in Eastern Europe: Byzantium and Orthodox Europe

Listen to Chapter 10 on MyHistoryLab

LEARNING OBJECTIVES

10.1 What was the relationship between the Byzantine Empire and the earlier Roman Empire and what were the main similarities and differences? p. 225

10.2 How does the Byzantine Empire fit the theme of state building and expansion? p. 227

10.3 Why did the two major regional versions of Christianity part? How significant was the split? p. 231

10.4 What were the main commonalities among the societies that developed in eastern Europe during the postclassical period? p. 235

10.5 What kinds of imitation affected Russia's development in the post-classical period? p. 235

Late in the 10th century, Vladimir, king of a Russian state centered in the city of Kiev, faced an important decision. What major religion should he choose—not only for himself, but for his people? Some Christian activity had been brought in from the Byzantine Empire to the south, and Vladimir's grandmother had converted, but the majority of Russians were traditional polytheists.

Vladimir's decision raised two issues. First, why decide? Why not adhere to tradition? Most of the societies around Russia were part of the growing surge of world religions—religions that appealed to people of many cultures. Vladimir likely thought that his kingdom's growing trade and military activity would be complemented by a religion that had wider appeal than that of the traditional Russian gods. Vladimir was also defending his rule against internal strife and external attack: A successful move to impose a new religion would bolster his authority.

FIGURE **10.1** This 15th-century miniature shows Russia's King Vladimir I being baptized in Cherson in the year 988.

Watch the Video Series on MyHistoryLab

Learn about some key topics related to this chapter with the *MyHistoryLab Video Series: Key Topics in World History*

Second, decide on what? Placed as Russia was, Vladimir had knowledge of Islam, Judaism, Western Catholicism, and Byzantine, or Orthodox, Christianity. Legend has it that he rejected Judaism because it was not associated with a strong state. He rejected Catholicism (gaining ground in neighboring Poland) because he wanted no interference from the pope. He rejected Islam because of its prohibition of alcohol: "for drink is the joy of the Russian."

In truth, the decision was probably easy. The Byzantine Empire was Russia's prosperous neighbor, a leading trading partner and sometime military ally. Vladimir was eager to marry the sister of the Byzantine emperor—according to another legend, the emperor was reluctant to give his sister in marriage to what he considered a backward warrior, but Vladimir captured a major Byzantine city and refused to give it back until the emperor relented. Choosing Orthodox Christianity would be a part of this larger relationship with Byzantium. ∎

Vladimir's decision was unquestionably important. Additional Byzantine influences, from art and literature to manners, began to shape Russian culture. Christianity was extended eastward, changing the boundaries between Christianity and Islam. The Russian state did gain new prestige and used religion to help unify its far-flung populace. At the same time, Vladimir's choice separated the kingdom from Roman Catholic western Europe, helping to create what would become a long-standing cultural division between eastern and western Europe. The implications of this separation continue to affect world affairs, even as other parts of eastern and western Europe are uniting.

CIVILIZATION IN EASTERN EUROPE

10.1 What was the relationship between the Byzantine Empire and the earlier Roman Empire and what were the main similarities and differences?

During the postclassical period two major Christian civilizations took shape in Europe. Both developed close relations with the Islamic world, and both played major roles in long distance trade. One, centered on the papacy in Rome, encompassed Western Europe, but the other radiated out from Constantinople. Both civilizations came to illustrate the diversification of state forms that was characteristic of the post classical period.

> The power of the Byzantine empire and the spread of Orthodox Christianity long surpassed the global influence of Christian Western Europe.

The Power of the Byzantine Empire

The Byzantine empire maintained high levels of political, economic, and cultural activity during much of the period from 600 to 1450 C.E. It controlled an important but fluctuating swath of territory in the Balkans, the northern Middle East, and the eastern Mediterranean. Its leaders saw themselves as latter-day Roman emperors, and their government was in many ways a direct continuation of the eastern portion of the late Roman empire.

The real significance of the Byzantine empire goes well beyond its ability to keep Rome's memory alive. The empire lasted for almost a thousand years, between Rome's collapse in the West and the final overthrow of the regime by Turkish invaders. The empire's capital, Constantinople, was one of the truly great cities of the world, certainly the most opulent and important city in Europe in this

100 C.E.	600 C.E.	800 C.E.	1000 C.E.	1200 C.E.	1400 C.E.
330s Constantinople becomes capital of eastern Roman empire **527–565** Reign of Justinian	**650s** Slavic migrations into eastern Europe **718** Arab attack on Constantinople defeated	**855** Rurik king of Kievan Russia (according to legend) **864** Beginning of Christian missionary work of Cyril and Methodius in Slavic lands **870** First kingdom in what is now Czech and Slovak republics **896** Magyars settle in Hungary **c. 960** Emergence of Polish state **980–1015** Conversion of Russia to Christianity	**1018** Byzantine defeat of Bulgarian kingdom **1019–1054** Reign of Yaroslav, king of Rus' **1054** Schism between Eastern and Western Christianity **1100–1453** Byzantine decline; under growing attack by Ottomans	**1203–1204** Fourth Crusade, Westerners sack Constantinople **1237–1241** Mongols (Tatars) capture Russia	**1453** Ottoman Turks capture Constantinople; end of Byzantine empire **1480** Expulsion of Tatars from Russia

period. From Constantinople radiated one of the two major branches of Christianity: the Orthodox Christian churches that became dominant throughout most of eastern Europe.

Like the other great civilizations of the period, the Byzantine empire spread its cultural and political influence to parts of the world that had not previously been controlled by any major civilization. Just as Muslim influence helped shape civilization in parts of Africa south of the Sahara, the Byzantines began to shape civilization in the Balkans and western Russia (present-day Ukraine and Belarus as well as western Russia proper).

The empire also served as a major agent in interregional trade. It had active exchanges with the Arab world and with other parts of Asia. The empire even imported techniques of silk production from China, which reduced its dependence on foreign trade for this commodity but showed its connection to larger fashion standards. Constantinople served as a hub for goods brought in from east central Europe and Russia, to be exchanged for Arab and Byzantine products. In various ways, the empire played a key role in extending the range of contacts as part of the formation of the transcontinental network.

There were many commonalities between developments in eastern and in western Europe. In both cases, civilization spread northward partly because of the missionary appeal of the Christian religion. In both cases, polytheism gave way to monotheism, although important compromises were made, particularly at the popular level. In both cases, more northerly political units, such as Russia, Poland, Germany, and France, struggled for political definition without being able to rival the political sophistication of the more advanced societies in Asia and north Africa or in Byzantium itself. In both cases, new trading activities brought northern regions into contact with the major centers of world commerce, including Constantinople. In both cases, newly civilized areas looked back to the Greco-Roman past, as well as to Christianity, for cultural inspiration, using some of the same political ideas and artistic styles.

Yet with all these shared ingredients, the civilizations that expanded in the east and developed in the west operated largely on separate tracks. They produced different versions of Christianity that were culturally as well as organizationally separate, even hostile. The civilizations had little mutual contact. Until late in this period, commercial patterns in both cases ran south to north rather than east to west. During most of the postclassical millennium, major portions of eastern Europe were significantly more advanced than western Europe in political sophistication, cultural range, and economic vitality. Byzantium long surpassed the West in its involvement with interregional trade.

THE BYZANTINE EMPIRE

10.2 How does the Byzantine Empire fit the theme of state building and expansion?

> The Byzantine empire was shaped by the decline of the Roman empire and the rise of the Arabs. The empire weathered many attacks and flourished for several centuries, playing a major role in Asian and European trade.

The Byzantine empire in some senses began in the 4th century C.E., when the Romans set up their eastern capital in Constantinople. This city quickly became the most vigorous center of the otherwise fading imperial structure. Emperor Constantine constructed a host of elegant buildings, including Christian churches, in his new city, which was built on the foundations of a previously modest town called Byzantium. Soon, separate eastern emperors ruled from the new metropolis, even before the western portion of the empire fell to the Germanic invaders. They warded off invading Huns and other intruders while enjoying a solid tax base in the peasant agriculture of the eastern Mediterranean. Constantinople was responsible for the Balkan peninsula, the northern Middle East, the Mediterranean coast, and north Africa. Although for several centuries Latin was the court language of the eastern empire, Greek was the common tongue, and after Emperor Justinian in the 6th century, it became the official language as well. Indeed, in the eyes of the easterners, Latin became an inferior, barbaric means of communication. Knowledge of Greek enabled the scholars of the eastern empire to read freely in the ancient Athenian philosophical and literary classics and in the Hellenistic writings and scientific treatises.

The new empire benefited from the high levels of commerce long present in the eastern Mediterranean. New blood was drawn into administration and trade as Hellenized Egyptians and Syrians, long excluded from Roman administration, moved to Constantinople and entered the expanding bureaucracy of the Byzantine rulers. The empire faced many foreign enemies, although the pressure was less severe than that provided by the Germanic tribes in the West. It responded by recruiting armies in the Middle East itself, not by relying on barbarian troops. Complex administration around a remote emperor, who was surrounded by elaborate ceremonies, increasingly defined the empire's political style.

Justinian's Achievements

The early history of the Byzantine empire was marked by a recurrent threat of invasion. Eastern emperors, relying on their local military base plus able generalship by upper-class Greeks, beat off attacks by the Sassanian empire in Persia and by Germanic invaders. Then, in 533 C.E., with the empire's borders reasonably secure, a new emperor, Justinian, tried to reconquer western territory in a last futile effort to restore an empire like that of Rome (see Map 10.1). He was somber, autocratic, and prone to grandiose ideas. A contemporary historian named Procopius described him as "at once villainous and amenable; as people say colloquially, a moron. He was never truthful with anyone, but always guileful in what he said and did, yet easily hoodwinked by any who wanted to deceive him." The emperor was also heavily influenced by his power-hungry wife Theodora, a courtesan connected with Constantinople's horse-racing world. Theodora stiffened Justinian's resolve in response to popular unrest and pushed the plans for expansion.

Justinian's positive contributions to the Byzantine empire lay in rebuilding Constantinople, ravaged by earlier riots against high taxes, and systematizing the Roman legal code. Extending later Roman architecture, with its addition of domes to earlier classical styles, Justinian's builders created many new structures, the most inspiring of which was the huge new church, the **Hagia Sophia**, long one of the wonders of the Christian world. (The great church would later become a mosque and is now a museum.) This was an achievement in engineering as well as architecture, for no one had previously been able to build the supports needed for a dome of its size. Justinian's codification of Roman law reached a goal that earlier emperors had sought but not achieved, summing up and reconciling many prior edicts and decisions. Unified law not only reduced confusion but also united and organized the new empire, paralleling the state's bureaucracy. Updated by later emperors, the code ultimately helped spread Roman legal principles in various parts of Europe.

Hagia Sophia [hä juh sä FEE uh] New church constructed in Constantinople during reign of Justinian.

View the Image on MyHistoryLab: Emperor Justinian

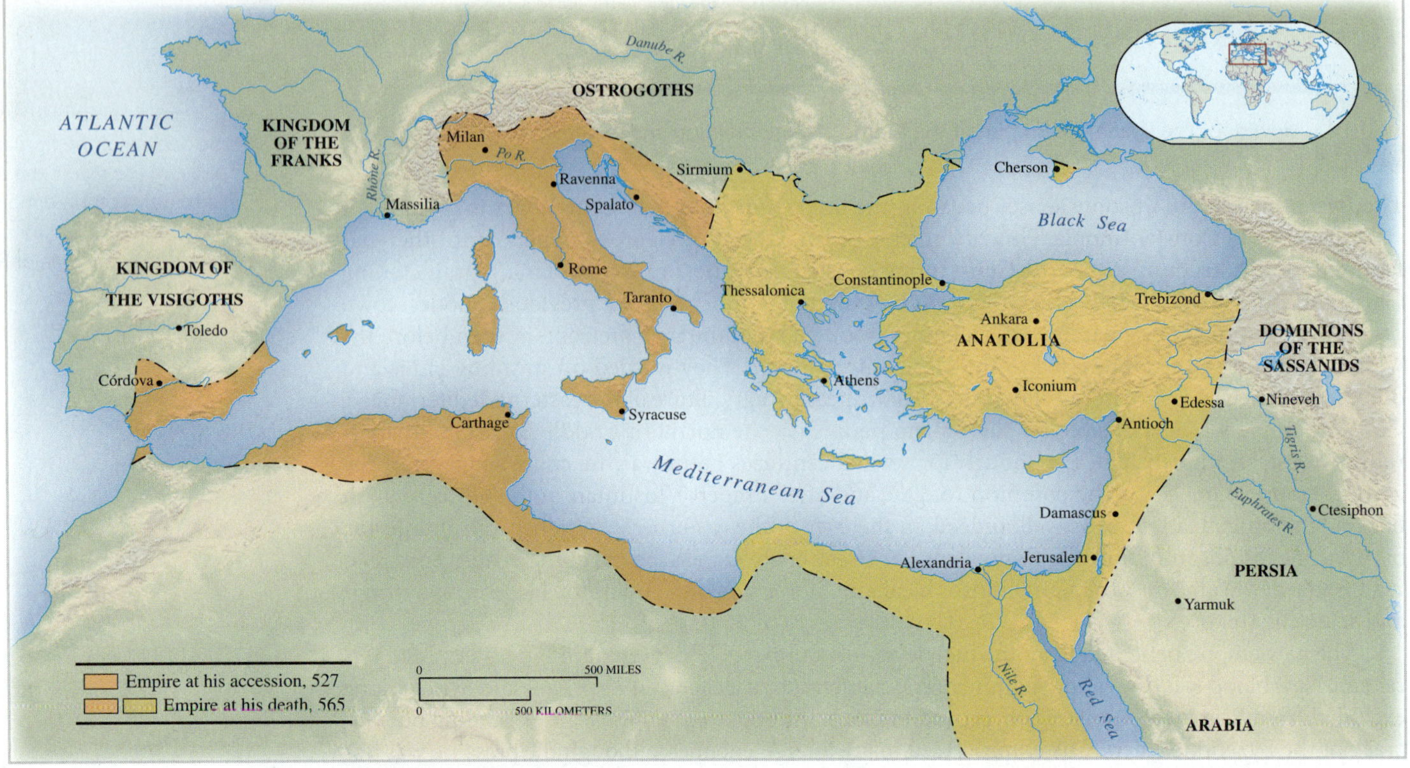

MAP **10.1** **The Byzantine Empire Under Justinian** Justinian's ambitious expansion exhausted his treasury, and the empire had lost all its holdings outside the northeastern Mediterranean within 50 years after his death.

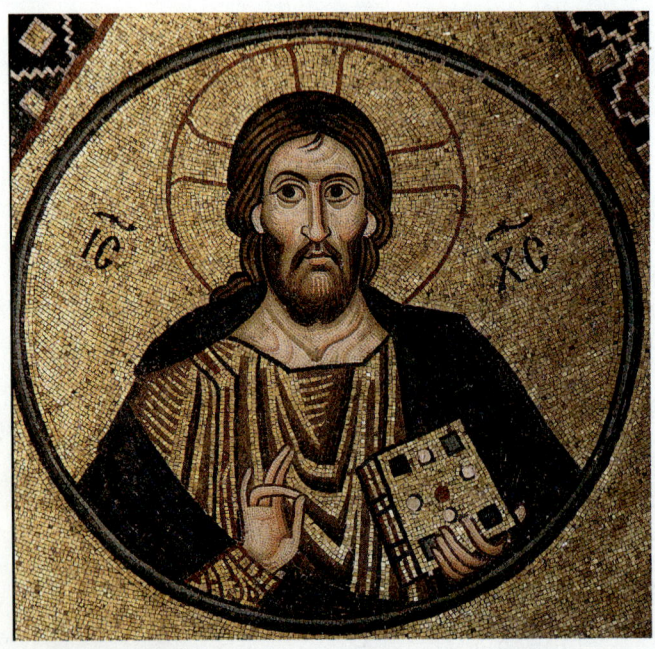

FIGURE **10.2** Dazzling mosaics from the early period of the Byzantine empire illustrate some of the highest achievements of Byzantine religious art. This mosaic features a rather militant Christ the Redeemer.

Justinian's military exploits had more ambiguous results. The emperor wanted to recapture the old Roman Empire itself. With the aid of a brilliant general, **Belisarius**, new gains were made in north Africa and Italy. Justinian's forces made their temporary capital, Ravenna, a key artistic center, embellished by some of the most beautiful Christian mosaics known anywhere in the world (Figure 10.2). But the major Italian holdings were short-lived, unable to withstand Germanic pressure, and north African territory was soon besieged as well.

Furthermore, Justinian's westward ambitions had weakened the empire in its own sphere. Persian forces attacked in the northern Middle East, while new Slavic groups, moving into the Balkans, pressed on another front (Map 10.1). Justinian finally managed to create a new line of defense and even pushed Persian forces back again, but some Middle Eastern territory was lost. Furthermore, all these wars, offensive and defensive alike, created new tax pressures on the government, and these triggered several popular revolts while forcing Justinian to exertions that contributed to his death in 565 C.E.

Arab Pressure and the Empire's Defenses

After some setbacks, Justinian's successors began to concentrate on defending the eastern empire itself. Persian advances in the northern Middle East were reversed in the 7th century, and the population was forcibly reconverted to Christianity. The resultant empire, centered in the southern Balkans and the western and central portions of present-day Turkey, was a

far cry from Rome's greatness. However, it was sufficient to amplify a rich Hellenistic culture and blend it more fully with Christianity while advancing Roman achievements in engineering and military tactics as well as law.

The Byzantine empire was also strong enough to withstand the great new threat of the 7th century, the surge of the Arab Muslims, although not without massive losses. By the mid-7th century, the Arabs had built a fleet that challenged Byzantine naval supremacy in the eastern Mediterranean while repeatedly attacking Constantinople. They quickly swallowed the empire's remaining provinces along the eastern seaboard of the Mediterranean and soon cut into the northern Middle Eastern heartland as well. Arab cultural and commercial influence also affected patterns of life in Constantinople. Byzantine territory was cut back to about half the size of the earlier eastern Roman empire.

The Byzantine empire held out nevertheless. A major siege of the capital in 717–718 C.E. was beaten back, partly because of a new weapon, a kind of napalm called **Greek fire** (a petroleum, quicklime, and sulfur mixture) that devastated Arab ships. The Arab threat was never removed entirely. Furthermore, wars with the Muslims had added new economic burdens to the empire. Invasions and taxation weakened the position of small farmers and resulted in greater aristocratic estates plus new power for aristocratic generals. The free rural population that had served the empire during its early centuries—providing military recruits and paying the bulk of the taxes—was forced into greater dependence on aristocratic landowners, often losing their land outright. Recurrent peasant risings occurred; one in 932, interestingly, involved a peasant leader posing as an aristocrat defending the people against the state.

These social changes, from the 10th century onward, weakened state revenues and military recruitment. But the empire hung on, supported in part by successful commercial activity including foreign trade. Politically, greater emphasis was given to organizing the army and navy. After the greatest Arab onslaughts had been faced, the empire was run by a dizzying series of weak and strong

Belisarius (c. 505–565) One of Justinian's most important military commanders during period of reconquest of western Europe; commanded in north Africa and Italy.

Greek fire Byzantine weapon consisting of mixture of chemicals that ignited when exposed to water; utilized to drive back the Arab fleets that attacked Constantinople.

VISUALIZING THE PAST

Women and Power in Byzantium

THIS MOSAIC, DEVELOPED BETWEEN 1034–1042, PORTRAYS the Empress Zoë, her consort, and Christ (in the center). Zoë would later rule jointly with her sister Theodora, despite their earlier struggle for power.

QUESTIONS
- What evidence does this mosaic provide about the political relationship between Zoë and her husband?
- What does it suggest about the relationship between church and state in Byzantium and about ways religion might be used to bolster political power?
- (Interpreting the haloes is a good start in answering this question.) What sense of history and religion made it reasonable to show Christ between two 11th-century people?

Istanbul, St. Sophia, Mosaic in the South Tribune: Christ with the Empress Zoë, who is presenting him with a scroll listing her donations to the church, and her consort, Monomachus, who is offering him a purse containing gold coins.

Bulgaria Slavic kingdom established in northern portions of Balkan peninsula; constant source of pressure on Byzantine empire; defeated by Emperor Basil II in 1014.

View the Closer Look on MyHistoryLab: A Holy Emperor: Basil II

emperors. Periods of vigor alternated with seeming decay. Arab pressure continued. Conquest of the island of Crete in the 9th century allowed the Muslims to harass Byzantine shipping in the Mediterranean for several centuries. Slavic kingdoms, especially **Bulgaria**, periodically pressed Byzantine territory in the Balkans, although at times military success and marriage alliances brought Byzantine control over the feisty Bulgarian kingdom. Thus, while a Bulgarian king in the 10th century took the title of *tsar*, a Slavic version of the word *Caesar*, steady Byzantine pressure through war eroded the regional kingdom. In the 11th century, the Byzantine emperor Basil II, known as *Bulgaroktonos*, or slayer of the Bulgarians, used the empire's wealth to bribe many Bulgarian nobles and generals. He defeated the Bulgarian army in 1014, blinding as many as 15,000 captive soldiers. The sight of this tragedy brought on the Bulgarian king's death. Bulgaria became part of the empire, its aristocracy settling in Constantinople and merging with the leading Greek families.

Briefly, at the end of the 10th century, the Byzantine emperor may have been the most powerful monarch on earth, with a capital city whose rich buildings and abundant popular entertainments awed visitors from western Europe and elsewhere.

Byzantine Society and Politics

The Byzantine political system had remarkable similarities to the earlier patterns in China, both serving as important examples of state building. The emperor was held to be ordained by God, head of church as well as state. He appointed church bishops and passed religious as well as secular laws. The power of the state over the church was a key feature of Orthodox Christianity, in contrast to patterns in Western Europe. Elaborate court rituals symbolized the ideals of a divinely inspired, all-powerful ruler, although they often immobilized rulers and inhibited innovative policy.

At key points, women held the imperial throne while maintaining the ceremonial power of the office. The experiences of Empress Theodora (981–1056), namesake of Justinian's powerful wife, illustrate the complex nature of Byzantine politics and the whims of fate that affected women rulers. Daughter of an emperor, Theodora was strong and austere; she refused to marry the imperial heir, who then wed her sister Zoë. Zoë was afraid of Theodora's influence and had her confined to a convent. A popular rebellion against the new emperor installed Theodora and Zoë jointly (and one assumes uneasily) as empresses. Later, Theodora managed to check unruly nobles and limit bureaucratic corruption, although her severe retaliation against personal enemies brought criticism.

Supplementing the centralized imperial authority was one of history's most elaborate bureaucracies. Trained in Greek classics, philosophy, and science in a secular school system that paralleled church education for the priesthood, Byzantine bureaucrats could be recruited from all social classes. As in China, aristocrats predominated, but talent also counted among this elite of highly educated scholars. Bureaucrats were specialized into various offices, and officials close to the emperor were mainly eunuchs. Provincial governors were appointed from the center and were charged with keeping tabs on military authorities. An elaborate system of spies helped preserve loyalty while creating intense distrust even among friends. It is small wonder that the word *byzantine* came to refer to complex institutional arrangements. Careful military organization arose as well. Byzantine rulers adapted the later Roman system by recruiting troops locally and rewarding them with grants of land in return for their military service. The land could not be sold, but sons inherited its administration in return for continued military responsibility. Many outsiders, particularly Slavs and Armenian Christians, were recruited for the army in this way. Increasingly, hereditary military leaders assumed regional power, displacing more traditional and better-educated aristocrats. One emperor, Michael II, was a product of this system and was notorious for his hatred of Greek education and his overall personal ignorance. On the other hand, the military system had obvious advantages in protecting a state recurrently under attack from Muslims of various sorts—Persians, Arabs, and later Turks—as well as nomadic intruders from central Asia. Until the 15th century, the Byzantine empire effectively blocked the path to Europe for most of these groups.

Socially and economically, the empire depended on Constantinople's control over the countryside, with the bureaucracy regulating trade and controlling food prices. Food prices were kept artificially low, to content the numerous urban lower classes, in a system supported largely by taxes on the hard-pressed peasantry. Other cities were modest in size—for example, Athens dwindled—because the focus was on the capital city and its food needs. The empire developed a far-flung trading network with Asia to the east and Russia and Scandinavia to the north. Silk production

icon An icon is an artistic representation, usually of a religious figure.

expanded in the empire, and various luxury products, including cloth, carpets, and spices, were sent north. This gave the empire a favorable trading position with less sophisticated lands. Only China produced luxury goods of comparable quality. The empire also traded actively with India, the Arabs, and east Asia while receiving simpler products from western Europe and Africa. At the same time, the large merchant class never gained significant political power, in part because of the elaborate network of government controls. In this, Byzantium again resembled China and differed notably from the looser social and political networks of the West, where merchants were gaining greater voice.

Byzantine cultural life centered on the secular traditions of Hellenism, so important in the education of bureaucrats, and on the evolving traditions of Eastern, or Orthodox, Christianity. The Byzantine strength lay in preserving and commenting on past forms more than in developing new ones. Art and architecture were exceptions; a distinct Byzantine style developed fairly early. The adaptation of Roman domed buildings, the elaboration of powerful and richly colored religious mosaics, and a tradition of **icon** paintings—paintings of saints and other religious figures, often richly ornamented—expressed this artistic impulse and its marriage with Christianity. The icons' blue-and-gold backgrounds set with richly dressed religious figures were meant to represent the unchanging brilliance of heaven.

FIGURE **10.3** A view of the interior of the Hagia Sophia, or St. Sophia—the Church of Holy Wisdom—in what is today the city of Istanbul. This magnificent church was built 532–537 C.E. under the reign of the Emperor Justinian.

THE SPLIT BETWEEN EASTERN AND WESTERN CHRISTIANITY

10.3 Why did the two major regional versions of Christianity part? How significant was the split?

> Growing divisions opened up between the two main branches of Christianity. The impact of these divisions increased when the Byzantine empire began to decline.

Byzantine culture and politics, as well as the empire's economic orientation toward Asia and northeastern Europe, helped explain the growing break between its eastern version of Christianity and the western version headed by the pope in Rome. There were many milestones in this rift. Different rituals developed as the Western church translated the Greek Bible into Latin in the 4th century. Later, Byzantine emperors deeply resented papal attempts to loosen state control over the Eastern church to make it conform more fully to their own idea of church–state relations. Contact between the two branches of Christianity trailed off, although neither the Eastern nor Western church cared to make a definitive break. The Eastern church acknowledged the pope as first among equals, but papal directives had no hold in the Byzantine church, where state control loomed larger. Religious art conveyed different styles and beliefs, as Figures 10.4 and 10.5 suggest. Even monastic movements operated according to different rules.

The Schism

Then, in 1054, an ambitious church patriarch in Constantinople raised a host of issues, including a quarrel over what kind of bread to use for the celebration of Christ's last supper in the church liturgy. The bread quarrel was an old one, relating to ritual use of bread in Christ's day, and whether communion bread must be baked without yeast. The patriarch also attacked the Roman Catholic practice, developed some centuries earlier, of insisting on celibacy for its priests; Eastern Orthodox priests could marry. Delegations of the two churches discussed these disputes, but this led only to new bitterness. The Roman pope finally excommunicated the patriarch and his followers, banishing them from

FIGURE 10.4 Just as theologians through the centuries have worked to understand Christ's message, so too have artists struggled to capture his image. This powerful mosaic of Christ at the Church of Chora in Istanbul was created in the first part of the 14th century. Notice the difference between this image and the images of Christ common in Western Christianity, which place more emphasis on suffering and less on divine majesty.

FIGURE 10.5 The Byzantine empire developed a distinctively stylized religious art, adapted from earlier Roman painting styles and conveying the solemnity of the holy figures of the faith. This illustration from a 14th-century manuscript features the holy women at the sepulchre of Christ.

Christian fellowship and the sacraments. The patriarch responded by excommunicating all Roman Catholics. Thus, the split, or schism, between the Roman Catholic church and Eastern Orthodoxy—the Byzantine or Greek, as well as the Russian Orthodox, Serbian Orthodox, and others—became formal and has endured to this day. A late-12th-century church patriarch in Constantinople even argued that Muslim rule would be preferable to that of the pope: "For if I am subject to the Muslim, at least he will not force me to share his faith. But if I have to be under the Frankish rule and united with the Roman Church, I may have to separate myself from God."

The split between the Eastern and Western churches fell short of complete divorce. A common Christianity with many shared or revived classical traditions and frequent commercial and cultural contacts continued to enliven the relationship between the two European civilizations. The division did reflect the different patterns of development the two civilizations followed during the postclassical millennium. Not only separate artistic forms and rituals, but also different ideas about the role of scholarship separated the two regions—with eastern Europe developing a less elaborate philosophical tradition in relation to religion. Differences in the role of the state in religious affairs may have contributed not just to divisions at this time, but to later distinctions in governments' claims to power between the two main European regions.

The Empire's Decline

Shortly after the split between the Eastern and Western churches, the Byzantine empire entered a long period of decline (Map 10.2). Turkish invaders who had converted to Islam in central Asia began to press on its eastern borders, having already gained increasing influence in the Muslim caliphate. In the late 11th century, Turkish troops, the Seljuks, seized almost all the Asiatic provinces of the empire, thus cutting off the most prosperous sources of tax revenue and the territories that had supplied most of the empire's food. The Byzantine emperor lost the battle of Manzikert in 1071, his larger army was annihilated, and the empire never recovered. It staggered along for another four centuries, but its doom, at least as a significant power, was sealed. The creation of new, independent Slavic kingdoms in the Balkans, such as Serbia, showed the empire's diminished power.

Eastern emperors appealed to Western leaders for help against the Turks, but their requests were largely ignored. Although the requests helped motivate Western Crusades to the Holy Land, this did not help the Byzantines. At the same time, Italian cities, blessed with powerful navies, gained increasing advantages in Constantinople, such as special trading privileges—a sign of the shift in power between East and West. Byzantium's role in world trade now attracted Western— particularly, Italian—appetites. One Crusade, in 1204, ostensibly set up to conquer the Holy Land from the Muslims, actually turned against Byzantium. Led by greedy Venetian merchants, the Crusade attacked and conquered Constantinople, briefly unseating the emperor and weakening the whole imperial structure. But the West was not yet powerful enough to hold this ground, and a small Byzantine empire was restored, able through careful diplomacy to survive for another two centuries.

Turkish settlements pressed ever closer to Constantinople in the northern Middle East—in the area that is now Turkey—and finally, in 1453, a Turkish sultan brought a powerful army, equipped with artillery purchased from Hungary, against the city, which fell after two months. By 1461, the Turks had conquered remaining pockets of Byzantine control, including most of the Balkans, bringing Islamic power farther into eastern Europe than ever before. The great eastern empire was no more.

Read the Document on MyHistoryLab: Chronicle of the Fourth Crusade (12th–13th c.) Geoffrey de Villhardouin

Read the Document on MyHistoryLab: Nestor-Iskander on the Fall of Constantinople (1450s)

MAP 10.2 The Byzantine Empire, 1000–1100 The Byzantine empire went from a major to a minor power in the period portrayed on this map. After the Turkish defeat at Manzikert in 1071, the Byzantines maintained effective control of only a small fringe of Anatolia. In the Balkans, new Serbian, Bulgarian, and Hungarian states grew powerful, despite the Byzantines' claim to control of the region.

The fall of Byzantium was one of the great events in world history, and we will deal with its impact in several later chapters. It was a vital event because the Byzantine empire had been so durable and important, anchoring a vital corner of the Mediterranean and an important segment of world trade even amid the rapid surge of Islam. The empire's commercial contacts and its ability to preserve and spread classical and Christian learning made it a vital unit throughout the postclassical period. After its demise, its legacy continued to affect other societies, including the new Ottoman empire.

THINKING HISTORICALLY

Eastern and Western Europe: The Problem of Boundaries

THE PROBLEM OF BOUNDARIES BETWEEN CIVILIZATIONS and even between states has long attracted the attention of scholars. The continuing evolution of nation states and their often self-serving desire to define themselves within larger civilizational boundaries greatly complicates the task of deciding where one civilization ends and another begins.

Defining the territory of the two related civilizations that developed in Europe is particularly difficult. A number of states sat, and still sit, on the borders of the two civilizations, sharing some characteristics of each. Furthermore, political disputes and nationalist attachments, fierce in this border territory of east central Europe during the past two centuries, make territorial definitions an emotional issue. So the question of defining Europe's civilizations is a particularly thorny case of a larger problem.

If a civilization is defined simply by its mainstream culture, then eastern and western Europe in the postclassical period divide logically according to Orthodox and Catholic territories (and use of the Cyrillic and Greek or of the Latin alphabet). By this reckoning, Poland, the Czech areas, and the Baltic states (these latter did not convert to Catholicism until the 14th century) are western, and Hungary is largely so. South Slavs are mainly but not entirely Orthodox. Russia and Ukraine are decidedly Orthodox in tradition. Religion matters. Poland and other Catholic regions have long maintained much more active ties with western Europe than Russia has. At the end of the postclassical period, a Czech religious dissenter, Jan Hus, even foreshadowed the later Protestant Reformation in his attacks on the Catholic church.

Politically, the case is more complicated. Poland, Hungary, and Lithuania formed large regional kingdoms at various times during and after the postclassical period. But these kingdoms were very loosely organized, much more so than the feudal monarchies that were developing in western Europe. Exceptionally large aristocracies in Poland and Hungary (by western or by Russian standards) helped limit these states.

Trade patterns also did not closely unite Poland or Hungary with western Europe until much later, when the two regions were clearly different in economic structure. Also, Polish and Hungarian societies often shared more features with Russia than with western Europe.

Russian expansion later pulled parts of eastern Europe, including Poland, into its orbit, although it never eliminated strong cultural identities. It is also important to remember that borders can change. The Mongol invasions that swept through Russia also conquered Poland and Hungary, but the armies did not stay there. Part of the Ukraine was also free from direct Mongol control, which helped differentiate it from Russia proper. For two centuries, at the end of the postclassical period, the divisions within eastern Europe intensified. Since 1989, many eastern European countries have again achieved full independence from Russia, and they want to claim their distinctive pasts. Not an easy border area to characterize in terms of a single civilization, east central Europe has also been a victim of many conquests interspersed with periods of proud independence.

> *Russian expansion later pulled parts of eastern Europe, including Poland, into its orbit, although it never eliminated strong cultural identities.*

QUESTIONS

- What were the main characteristics of Russian civilization as it first emerged in the postclassical period?
- In what ways did Poland, Hungary, and the Czech lands differ from these characteristics?
- Are there other civilization border areas, in the postclassical period or later, that are similarly difficult to define because of their position between two other areas?

THE SPREAD OF CIVILIZATION IN EASTERN EUROPE

10.4 What were the main commonalities among the societies that developed in eastern Europe during the postclassical period?

Long before the Byzantine decline after the 11th century, the empire had been the source of a new northward surge of Christianity. Orthodox missionaries sent from Constantinople busily converted most people in the Balkans to their version of Christianity, and some other trappings of Byzantine culture came in their wake. In 864, the Byzantine government sent the missionaries **Cyril** and **Methodius** to the territory that is now the Czech and Slovak republics. Here the venture failed, in that Roman Catholic missionaries were more successful. But Cyril and Methodius continued their efforts in the Balkans and in southern Russia, where their ability to speak the Slavic language greatly aided their efforts. The two missionaries devised a written script for this language, derived from Greek letters; to this day, the Slavic alphabet is known as Cyrillic. Thus, the possibility of literature and some literacy developed in eastern Europe along with Christianity, well beyond the political borders of Byzantium. Byzantine missionaries were quite willing to have local languages used in church services—another contrast with western Catholicism, which insisted on church Latin.

> Christian missionaries, new trade routes, and Byzantine military activity affected much of eastern Europe. Within this context, the Kievan Rus' formed the core of Russian culture and politics.

Cyril (827–869) Along with Methodius, missionary sent by Byzantine government to eastern Europe and the Balkans; converted southern Russia and Balkans to Orthodox Christianity; responsible for creation of written script for Slavic known as Cyrillic.

Methodius (826–885) Along with Cyril, missionary sent by Byzantine government to eastern Europe and the Balkans; converted southern Russia and Balkans to Orthodox Christianity; responsible for creation of written script for Slavic known as Cyrillic.

The East Central Borderlands

Eastern missionaries did not monopolize the borderlands of eastern Europe. Roman Catholicism and the Latin alphabet prevailed not only in the Czech area but also in most of Hungary (which was taken over in the 9th century by a Turkic people, the Magyars) and in Poland. Much of this region would long be an area of competition between eastern and western political and intellectual models. During the centuries after the conversion to Christianity, this stretch of eastern Europe north of the Balkans was organized in a series of regional monarchies, loosely governed amid a powerful, landowning aristocracy. The kingdoms of Poland, Bohemia, and Lithuania easily surpassed most western kingdoms in territory. This was also a moderately active area for trade and industry. For example, ironworking was more developed than in the West until the 12th century.

Eastern Europe during these centuries also received an important influx of Jews, who were migrating away from the Middle East but also fleeing intolerance in western Europe. Poland gained the largest single concentration of Jews. Eastern Europe's Jews, largely barred from agriculture and often resented by the Christian majority, gained strength in local commerce while maintaining their own religious and cultural traditions. A strong emphasis on extensive education and literacy, although primarily for males, distinguished Jewish culture not only from the rest of eastern Europe but also from most other societies in the world at this time.

THE EMERGENCE OF KIEVAN RUS'

10.5 What kinds of imitation affected Russia's development in the postclassical period?

Russia shared many features with the rest of northeastern Europe before the 15th century. As in much of eastern Europe, the centuries of Byzantine influence were an important formative period that would influence later developments, even as Russia became more important. Slavic peoples had moved into the sweeping plains of Russia and eastern Europe from an Asian homeland during the time of the Roman Empire (Map 10.3). They mixed with and incorporated some earlier inhabitants and some additional invaders, such as the Bulgarians, who adopted Slavic language and customs. The Slavs already used iron, and they extended agriculture in the rich soils of what is now Ukraine and western Russia. The Slavs maintained an animist religion with gods for the sun, thunder, wind, and fire. The early Russians also had a rich tradition of folk music and oral legends, and they developed some very loose regional kingdoms.

> Russia gradually emerged through its role in trade, growing political claims, and the decision to participate in Christianity.

CHAPTER 10 Civilization in Eastern Europe: Byzantium and Orthodox Europe

Read the Document on MyHistoryLab: Ibn Fadlan's Account of the Rus'

MAP 10.3 **East European Kingdoms and Slavic Expansion c. 1000** Beginning around the 5th century C.E., the Slavs moved in all directions from their lands around the Pripet River in what is today Ukraine and Belarus. Their migrations took them from the Baltic Sea to the Oder River and down to the Adriatic and Aegean seas. The arrival of the Hungarians in the 9th and 10th centuries prevented the Slavs from unifying. The arrival of the Hungarians in the 9th and 10th centuries complicated the Slavic holdings, tending to separate Russians and Slavs in the Balkans. Still, the various Salvic peoples dominated a vast territory in eastern Europe.

New Patterns of Trade

During the 6th and 7th centuries, traders from Scandinavia began to work through the Slavic lands, moving along the great rivers of western Russia, which run south to north, particularly the Dnieper (DNEE-puhr). Map 10.3 shows the route that led from Scandinavia to Byzantium, and the Russian territory that began to coalesce around it. Through this route the Norse traders were able to reach the Byzantine empire, and a regular, flourishing trade developed between Scandinavia and Constantinople. Luxury products from Byzantium and the Arab world traveled north in return for furs and other crude products. The Scandinavian traders, militarily superior to the Slavs, gradually set up some governments along their trade route, particularly in the city of **Kiev**. A monarchy emerged, and according to legend a man named **Rurik**, a native of Denmark, became the first prince of what came

Kiev Trade city in southern Russia established by Scandinavian traders in 9th century; became focal point for kingdom of Russia that flourished to 12th century.

Rurik Legendary Scandinavian, regarded as founder of the first kingdom of Russia based in Kiev in 855 C.E.

236 PART III The Postclassical Period, 600–1450: New Faith and New Commerce

to be called **Kievan Rus'** (KEE-eh-vehn ROOS) about 855 C.E. This principality, though still loosely organized through alliances with regional, landed aristocrats, flourished until the 12th century. It was at this time that the word *Russia* was coined, possibly from a Greek word for "red," for the hair color of many of the Norse traders.

Contacts between Kievan Rus' and Byzantium extended steadily. Kiev, centrally located, became a prosperous trading center, and from there many Russians visited Constantinople. This was the context in which Prince **Vladimir I**, a Rurik descendant who ruled from 980 to 1015, took the step of converting to Christianity, not only in his own name but on behalf of all his people. Having made his decision, Vladimir organized mass baptisms for his subjects, forcing conversions by military pressure. Early church leaders were imported from Byzantium, and they helped train a literate Russian priesthood. As in Byzantium, the king characteristically controlled major appointments, and a separate **Russian Orthodox** church soon developed.

As Kievan Rus' became Christian, it was the largest single state in Europe, although highly decentralized. Rurik's descendants managed for some time to avoid damaging battles over succession to the throne. Following Byzantine example, they issued a formal law code that reduced the severity of traditional punishments and replaced community vendettas with state-run courts, at least in principle. The last of the great Kievan princes, **Yaroslav**, issued the legal codification while building many churches and arranging the translation of religious literature from Greek to Slavic.

Kievan Rus' The predecessor to modern Russia; a medieval state that existed from the end of the 9th to the middle of the 13th century; its territory spanned parts of modern Belarus, Ukraine, and Russia.

Vladimir I Ruler of Russian kingdom of Kiev from 980 to 1015; converted kingdom to Christianity.

 View the **Closer Look** on **MyHistoryLab**: The Baptism of Vladimir

Russian Orthodoxy Russian form of Christianity imported from Byzantine empire and combined with local religion; king characteristically controlled major appointments.

Yaroslav (978–1054) Last of great Kievan monarchs; issued legal codification based on formal codes developed in Byzantium.

DOCUMENT

Russia Turns to Christianity

THIS DOCUMENT FROM A MONK'S CHRONICLE, describing King Vladimir's conversion policy, indicates what was officially believed about the power of Russian princes, Russian social structure, and the relationship between Christianity and earlier animism. These official claims are important, but they may not reflect the whole reality of this important transition in Russia history. Here is a classic case of the need to understand a particular mindset and genre of writing, to understand why particular explanations are offered without accepting their reality.

> For at this time the Russes were ignorant pagans. The devil rejoiced thereat, for he did not know that his ruin was approaching. He was so eager to destroy the Christian people, yet he was expelled by the true cross even from these very lands. . . . Vladimir was visited by Bulgars of the Mohammedan faith. . . . [He] listened to them for he was fond of women and indulgence, regarding which he heard with pleasure. But . . . abstinence from pork and wine were disagreeable to him. "Drinking," said he, "is the joy of the Russes. We cannot exist without that pleasure." [Russian envoys sent to Constantinople were astonished by the beauty of the churches and the chanting], and in their wonder praised the Greek ceremonial. . . .
>
> [Later, Vladimir was suffering from blindness; a Byzantine bishop baptized him] and as the bishop laid his hand upon him, he straightway recovered his sight. Upon experiencing this miraculous cure, Vladimir glorified God, saying, "I have now perceived the one true God." When his followers beheld this miracle, many of them were also baptized. . . . Thereafter Vladimir sent heralds throughout the whole city to proclaim that if any inhabitant, rich or poor, did not betake himself to the river [for mass baptism] he would risk the Prince's displeasure. When the people heard these words, they wept for joy and exclaimed in their enthusiasm, "If this were not good, the Prince and his nobles would not have accepted it." . . . There was joy in heaven and upon earth to behold so many souls saved. But the devil groaned, lamenting, "Woe is me. How am I driven out hence . . . my reign in these regions is at an end." . . .
>
> He [Vladimir] ordered that wooden churches should be built and established where [pagan] idols have previously stood. He founded the Church of Saint Basil on the hill where the idol of Perun and the other images had been set, and where the prince and the people had offered their sacrifices. He began to found churches, to assign priests throughout the cities and towns, and to bring people in for baptism from all towns and villages. He began to take the children of the best families and send them for instruction from books.

QUESTIONS

- In what ways might the account be simplistic in describing royal powers and popular response?
- What explanations does this religious chronicler offer for the conversion of Russians to Christianity?
- Which of the explanations are most likely, and which are the results of some kind of bias?
- What kind of church–state relationship did this kind of conversion predict?

Institutions and Culture in Kievan Rus'

Kievan Rus' borrowed much from Byzantium, but it was in no position to replicate major institutions such as the bureaucracy or an elaborate educational system. Major princes were attracted to Byzantine ceremonials and luxury and to the concept (if not yet the reality) that a central ruler should have wide powers. Many characteristics of Orthodox Christianity gradually penetrated Russian culture. Fervent devotion to the power of God and to many eastern saints helped organize worship. Churches were ornate, filled with icons and the sweet smell of incense. A monastic movement developed that stressed prayer and charity. Traditional practices, such as polygamy, gradually yielded to the Christian practice of monogamy. The emphasis on almsgiving long described the sense of obligation felt by wealthy Russians toward the poor.

The Russian literature that developed, which used the Cyrillic alphabet, featured chronicles that described a mixture of religious and royal events and showered praises on the saints and the power of God. Disasters were seen as expressions of the just wrath of God against human wickedness, and success in war followed from the aid of God and the saints in the name of Russia and the Orthodox faith. This tone also was common in western Christian writing during these centuries, but in Kievan Rus' it monopolized formal culture; a distinct philosophical or scientific current did not emerge in the postclassical period.

Russian and Ukrainian art focused on the religious also, with icon painting and illuminated religious manuscripts becoming a Kievan specialty. Orthodox churches, built in the form of a cross surmounted by a dome, similarly aped Byzantine models, although the building materials often were wood rather than stone. Domed structures adapted Byzantine themes to Russian conditions, in what proved to be a durable regional style. Religious art and music were rivaled by popular entertainments in the oral tradition, which combined music, street performances, and some theater. The Russian church unsuccessfully tried to suppress these forms, regarding them as pagan.

Just as Russia's religious culture developed separately from western Europe's, Russian social and economic patterns took distinctive shape. Russian peasants were fairly free farmers, although an aristocratic landlord class existed. Russian aristocrats, called **boyars**, had less political power than their counterparts in western Europe, although the Kievan princes had to negotiate with them.

For all its distinctiveness, Russia was not unaware of other parts of Europe. The greatest ruler of the period, Yaroslav the Wise (1019–1054), used marriages to create ties. He arranged over 30 marriages with central European royalty, including 11 with Germany, pressing six Russian princes to take German wives while inducing five German nobles to accept Russian brides. Even here, however, Yaroslav kept his main focus on Byzantium, promoting Byzantine styles in the great cathedral of Kiev and using Byzantine example as the basis for Russia's first law code.

boyars Russian aristocrats; possessed less political power than did their counterparts in western Europe.

Kiev

Kiev (or Kyiv, in Ukrainian) was the leading city of Kievan Rus', a key center for north–south trade from Scandinavia to the Middle East. Novgorod was its only main competitor along this route. The city had been founded earlier, on the site of scattered Slavic settlements. The kings who began to carve out the first Russian state adopted the city as their capital. The location was good: The main part of the city could be built on a substantial hill—as with many European cities at the time, defense against raids was a key concern. Along with city walls, a hilltop location helped. But at the base of the hill flowed the Dneiper River, a substantial artery that would facilitate trade.

Kiev quickly became a religious center. In 988, Vladimir required a mass baptism of the city's citizens in the local river, converting them to Christianity. During the following two centuries, Kiev witnessed a massive amount of church building, including the great cathedral of Saint Sophia and also a major monastery complex in the caves of Lavra. As was true of most Christian cities in the postclassical period, Kiev was dominated by religious architecture. By 1200 the city boasted 400 churches, or approximately one per 130 inhabitants, obviously a massive investment.

The city also contained eight markets, however, and an array of economic activities. In 1200 the city was the largest in Europe, with 50,000 people—by comparison, London had but 20,000 at the same point. Travelers called the city a "charming gem," and one German visitor compared it to Constantinople. But the comparison was in fact misleading: The cities of Europe outside the Byzantine empire remained tiny by Asian standards; Constantinople itself had 350,000 people at this point.

Kiev hit hard times after 1200. It was raided many times by turbulent Russian princes, and then it fell to Mongol attack. Recovery would come slowly.

Kievan Decline

The Kievan principality began to fade in the 12th century. Rival princes set up regional governments, and the royal family often squabbled over succession to the throne. Invaders from Asia whittled at Russian territory. The rapid decline of Byzantium reduced Russian trade and wealth, for the kingdom had always depended heavily on the greater prosperity and sophisticated manufacturing of its southern neighbor. The final blow in this first chapter of Russian history came in 1237–1238 and 1240–1241, when two invasions by Mongols from central Asia moved through Russia and into other parts of eastern Europe. The initial Mongol intent was to add the whole of Europe to their growing empire. The Mongols easily captured the major Russian cities, but they did not penetrate much farther west because of political difficulties in their Asian homeland. Called **Tatars** in the Russian tradition (from a Turkish word), the invaders were quickly despised but also feared—"the accursed raw-eating Tatars," as one chronicle put it.

For over two centuries much of Russia remained under Tatar control. This control further separated the dynamic of Russian history from that of western Europe. Russian literature languished under Tatar supervision. Trade lapsed in western Russia, and the vigorous north–south commerce of the Kievan period never returned. At the same time, loose Tatar supervision did not destroy Russian Christianity or a native Russian aristocratic class. As long as tribute was paid, Tatar overlords left day-to-day Russian affairs alone. Thus, when Tatar control was finally forced out in the second half of the 15th century, a Russian cultural and political tradition could reemerge, serving as a partial basis for the further, fuller development of Russian society.

Russian leaders retained an active memory of the glories of Byzantium. When Constantinople fell to the Turks in 1453, just as Russia was beginning to assert its independence from the Tatars, it was logical to claim that the mantle of east European leadership had fallen on Russia. A monk, currying favor, wrote the Russian king in 1511 that whereas heresy had destroyed the first Roman Empire and the Turks had cut down the second, Byzantium—a "third, new Rome" under the king's "mighty rule"—"sends out the Orthodox Christian faith to the ends of the earth and shines more brightly than the sun." According to the monk, "Two Romes have fallen, but the third stands, and there will be no fourth." This sense of an eastern Christian mission, inspiring a Russian resurgence, was just one result of this complicated formative period in the emergence of a separate European civilization in the Slavic lands.

Tatars Mongols; captured Russian cities and largely destroyed Kievan state in 1236; left Russian Orthodoxy and aristocracy intact.

The End of an Era in Eastern Europe

With Byzantium and Russia both under siege, eastern European civilization fell on hard times at the end of the postclassical era. These difficulties confirmed the largely separate trajectories of western and eastern Europe. Western Europe remained free from outside control and, despite some new problems, maintained a clearer vigor in politics, economy, and culture. When eastern Europe did reemerge, it was at some disadvantage to western Europe in terms of power and economic and cultural sophistication—a very different balance from that of the glory days of Byzantium and the vigor of Kievan Russia.

Tatar invasion and Byzantine collapse were profoundly disruptive. Key features of Kievan social structure disappeared in the later development of imperial Russia. Yet continuity was not entirely lost. Not only Christianity but also eastern European assumptions about political rulers and church–state relations and the pride in a lively artistic culture served as organizing threads when Russia and other Slavic societies turned to rebuilding.

Global Connections and Critical Themes

EASTERN EUROPE AND THE WORLD

The Byzantine empire and eastern Europe more generally participated actively in forging new economic connections. Byzantine trade was a central part of the transregional trading network, bringing links to Arab traders and wider opportunities in Asia as well as the Mediterranean. Kievan Rus' channeled trade from the Baltic to Constantinople, helping to link northern Europe to the larger network as well. The number of Arab coins formed along the trade routes, all the way to Scandinavia, indicates the key links.

Eastern Europe served also as a stage for major cultural change and connection. The spread of Christianity, but the rivalry between the two main versions of Christianity, were important at the time and subsequently.

State building was another obvious feature. The Byzantine state was carefully organized, in part because of military challenges in the region. Russian and other Slavic leaders were aware of the Byzantine example, but the kingdoms they created were more loosely organized.

The vitality of eastern Europe unquestionably declined during the final centuries of the postclassical era, in part because of new weaknesses in the Byzantine Empire. Under the Mongol conquest, Russia became more isolated, raising questions about what kind of contacts it would seek when, by the 15th century, it began to regain greater independence of action.

Further Readings

Recent overviews include John Rosser, *The A to Z of Byzantium* (2006); Averil Cameron, *The Byzantines* (2006); Judith Herrin, *Byzantium: The Surprising Life of a Medieval Empire* (2008); and Cyril Mango, ed., *The Oxford History of Byzantium* (2002). On early Byzantium, see Peter Sarris, *Economy and Society in the Age of Justinian* (2006), and James Allan Evans, *The Emperor Justinian and the Byzantine Empire* (2005). Byzantine Christianity is studied in G. Every, *The Byzantine Patriarchate, 451–1204* (1978) and J. M. Hussey and Andrew Louth, *The Orthodox Church in the Byzantine Empire* (2010); Derek Krueger, ed., *Byzantine Christianity* (2006); and S. Runciman, *The Byzantine Theocracy* (1977); see also D. M. Nicol, *Church and Society in the Last Centuries of Byzantium* (1979). On culture, see William Brumfield, ed., *Christianity and the Arts in Russia* (1991); Helen Evans and William Wixom, *The Glory of Byzantium: Art and Culture of the Middle Byzantine Era A.D. 843–1261* (1997); and E. Kitzinger, *Byzantine Art in the Making* (1977). Byzantine relations with the West are the main topic in H. J. Magoulias, *Byzantine Christianity: Emperor, Church and the West* (1982). On Byzantine influence in eastern Europe, D. Obolensky, *The Byzantine Commonwealth: Eastern Europe, 500–1453* (1971), remains an excellent analysis. See also Lynda Garland, ed., *Byzantine Women: Varieties of Experience 800–1200* (2006) and A. P. Kazhdan and A. W. Epstein, *Changes in Byzantine Culture in the Eleventh and Twelfth Centuries* (1985).

On Russian history, the best survey is Nicholas Riasanovsky, *A History of Russia* (1992), which has a good bibliography. See also Alfred Rambaud, *The History of Russia: From the Earliest Times to 1877* (2006); Maureen Perrie, ed., *The Cambridge History of Russia* (2006); David G. Rowley, *Exploring Russia's Past: Narrative, Sources, Images* (2006); Judith Martin, *Medieval Russia, 980–1584* (2007); and Serhii Plokhy, *The Origins of the Slavic Nations: Pre-modern Identities in Russia, Ukraine, and Belarus* (2006). Natalia Pushkareva and Eve Levin's survey *Women in Russian History: From the Tenth to the Twentieth Century* (1997) examines the place of women in early Russian history. Books dealing with early Russian culture include Mary Charmot, *Russian Painting and Sculpture* (1963); N. P. Kondakov, *The Russian Icon* (1927); J. H. Billington, *The Icon and the Axe: An Interpretive History of Russian Culture* (1966); and Arthur Voyce, *The Art and Architecture of Medieval Russia* (1967). Vladimir Volkoff, *Vladimir the Russian Viking, 960–1015* (1985), offers a unique glimpse of early Russia. Two collections are also very helpful on early Russian history: Thomas Riha, ed., *Readings in Russian Civilization*, vol. 1, *Russia Before Peter the Great, 900–1700* (1970); and especially S. A. Zenkovsky, ed. and trans., *Medieval Russia's Epics, Chronicles and Tales* (1963). The impact of the Mongols on the shaping of Russian history is examined in Robert Marshall, *Storm from the East: From Genghis Khan to Khubilai Khan* (1993), and in an older but still serviceable work, M. N. Thompson, *The Mongols and Russia* (1966).

On MyHistoryLab

 Study and Review on MyHistoryLab

Critical Thinking Questions

1. How does comparison help identify key features of eastern Europe? What were the main differences and similarities between Orthodox and Catholic (Western) Christianity?

2. How does Russian development compare with other major cases of imitation and contact during the postclassical centuries—for example, with Japanese borrowings from China?

3. What were the main changes and continuities, in the eastern Mediterranean, between patterns during the Roman empire and patterns in the postclassical period?

4. With a focus on causation, what are some of the explanations for the growing weakness of the Byzantine empire in the centuries before 1450?

A New Civilization Emerges in Western Europe

11

Listen to Chapter 11 on MyHistoryLab

LEARNING OBJECTIVES

What were the main stages of change in western Europe, from the early postclassical centuries to 1450, and what were the characteristic western political forms in each main stage? p. 243	**11.1**
What were the main cultural issues that west European intellectuals grappled with during the postclassical centuries? p. 253	**11.2**
How did growing trade fit the basic social structure of western Europe? p. 257	**11.3**
What were the basic shifts in west European characteristics at the end of the postclassical period? Was the region declining? p. 260	**11.4**

Sometimes an individual life displays the complexities of a larger society. Godric—ultimately, Saint Godric—was a 12th-century Englishman (Figure 11.1). His father was an ordinary farmer, but he early developed greater ambition. Godric started as a peddler and, according to his biographer, quickly learned how to turn a profit on cheap items. He was physically strong, and a hard worker—necessary qualities for a life of trade and travel. He soon turned to urban commerce, which was beginning to increase rapidly during the 1100s. He participated in seagoing trade with other parts of Britain and with the European continent, and clearly made a good living, acquiring a number of ships.

FIGURE **11.1** Having experienced many close calls with the weather during his years at sea, St. Godric was troubled on stormy nights for the rest of his life, thinking of the peril of sailors. He is best remembered for his extraordinary affinity for wild animals. He protected hunted animals and is said to have allowed snakes to warm themselves at his fire.

Watch the Video Series on MyHistoryLab
Learn about some key topics related to this chapter with the *MyHistoryLab Video Series: Key Topics in World History*

But he was not entirely at peace with himself. His biographer, a clergyman named Reginald of Durham, is eager to emphasize Godric's consistent Christianity. So he portrays him as content with a simple life even amid his riches, and quickly attracted to the saints and a life of God. He argues that Godric's sea voyages, undoubtedly risky, helped the future saint realize the importance of divine aid—and surely religion did often provide a sense of security to venturesome merchants. Finally, however, a purely material life did not seem sufficient.

Godric began visiting saints' shrines with increasing frequency. He began to be disturbed by the high living—feasting and drinking—of some of his merchant colleagues. He also found that some of them stole outright. He attempted to correct them but was rebuffed. Ashamed of his own materialism (and possibly of some misdeeds of his own), he went on a pilgrimage to Rome. After that, with his parents' blessing, he decided to give himself entirely to a religious life. He sold all of his goods, gave the proceeds to the poor, and spent the rest of his life wandering as a religious hermit.

Few Europeans lived lives as polarized as that of Godric, but many, particularly in growing cities, felt some tension between commercial change and religious commitment. Could someone interested in making money keep a primary devotion to God? Some, as Godric discovered, would choose commerce. Others opted for religion. Still others worked for some combination. While few made Godric's dramatic ultimate choice, many merchants gave abundantly to the splendid churches of the cities, and not a few made deathbed renunciations of their commercial pasts. ■

The postclassical period was a great age of faith in western Europe, and Christianity provided the most obvious unifying factor in the new geography of western European civilization. Christian missionary efforts led most western Europeans to convert from polytheistic faiths in the initial postclassical centuries. But there were other key developments as well, including Europe's growing participation in trade and in wider interregional contacts. Not surprisingly, it was not always easy, even for individuals, to put the pieces together.

The postclassical period in western Europe began with the fall of the Roman Empire and lasted until the 15th century. The period is known as the **Middle Ages** in European history (the adjective form is *medieval*). The period featured gradual recovery from the shock of Rome's collapse. At the same time, the forms of civilization spread northward, beyond the Roman orbit, covering the whole of western Europe. Key characteristics of western European civilization emerged from these dynamic processes.

Medieval western Europe participated in the network of expanding contacts among major societies in Asia, Europe, and parts of Africa. New tools introduced by invaders from Asia, including a new kind of plow, helped spur medieval agriculture from the 10th century onward. New crops from Africa, including new varieties of wheat, increased food production. The revival of trade in the Mediterranean, bringing contacts with the Arabs, yielded other technological gains, such as the first European paper factory. Medieval culture was at least as powerfully shaped by connections with the wider world. By the 11th and 12th centuries, contact with the Byzantines and the Arabs had taught Western scholars new lessons in mathematics, science, and philosophy. The medieval West unquestionably took more from the emerging world network than it contributed, but it was also challenged by its international position to seek new world roles.

Middle Ages The period in western European history from the decline and fall of the Roman Empire until the 15th century.

500 C.E.	800 C.E.	1000 C.E.	1150 C.E.	1300 C.E.	1450 C.E.
500–900 Recovery period after Rome's fall; Christian missionaries work in northern Europe **732** Franks defeat Muslims in France	**800–814** Charlemagne's empire **900–1000** Spread of new plows; use of horses in agriculture and transport **962** Germanic kings revive Roman empire	**1018** Beginning of Christian reconquest of Spain **1066** Norman conquest of England, strong feudal monarchy **1070–1141** Peter Abelard **1073–1085** Gregory VII, reform pope **1096–1270** Crusades	**1150–1300** Gothic style spreads **1180** University of Paris **1200–1274** Thomas Aquinas and flowering of scholasticism **1215** Magna Carta **1226–1270** Louis IX of France **1265** First English parliament	**1303** Seizure of papacy by French king **1338–1453** Hundred Years' War **1348–1380** Black Death (bubonic plague)	**1469** Formation of single Spanish monarchy

STAGES OF POSTCLASSICAL DEVELOPMENT

11.1 What were the main stages of change in western Europe, from the early postclassical centuries to 1450, and what were the characteristic western political forms in each main stage?

From about 550 C.E. until about 900, western Europe suffered from a number of problems. Rome continued to serve as the center of the growing Catholic church, in turn the most powerful institution in the West. But Italy was divided politically. Spain, another key region of the Roman Empire in the West, lay in the hands of the Muslims through much of the Middle Ages. A vibrant intellectual and economic life was focused there, and it would have an important influence on western developments later on, but it was for the time being out of the western mainstream. The center of the postclassical West lay in France, the Low Countries, and southern and western Germany, with England increasingly drawn in—areas where civilization, as a form of human organization, was new.

Frequent invasions reflected and prolonged the West's weakness, making it difficult to develop durable government or economic forms. Raids by the seagoing **Vikings** from Scandinavia periodically disrupted life from Ireland to Sicily. With weak states and little more than subsistence agriculture, it was small wonder that intellectual activity declined. The few who could read and write were concentrated in the hierarchy and the monasteries of the Catholic church, where they kept learning alive. But they could do little more than copy older manuscripts, including those of the great Christian thinkers of the later Roman Empire. By their own admission, they could not understand much of the philosophy involved, and they often apologized for their inability to write good Latin. Western Europe was still shaped by elements of the Roman heritage, but the connection was disrupted.

The Manorial System: Obligations and Allegiances

Between Rome's fall and the 10th century, effective political organization was largely local, although Germanic kings ruled some territories, such as a portion of what is France today. **Manorialism** was the system of economic and political relations between landlords and their peasant laborers. Understanding manorialism is a vital step in assessing social structures in many open cultural societies.

In European manorialism, most people were **serfs**, living on self-sufficient agricultural estates called manors. Serfs were agricultural workers who received some protection, including the administration of justice, from the landlords; in return, they were obligated to turn over part of their goods and to remain on the land. The manorial system had originated in the later Roman Empire. It was strengthened by the decline of trade and the lack of larger political structures. Serfs needed the military forces the landlords could muster for their security. Without much market economy to stimulate production and specialization, these same landlords used the serfs' produce and labor to support their own modest establishments.

> Postclassical western Europe was hard hit by the Roman collapse. However, after about 900, agriculture and trade revived, while political development advanced under the influence of feudalism and the Catholic church.

Vikings Seagoing Scandinavian raiders from Sweden, Denmark, and Norway who disrupted coastal areas of western Europe from the 8th to the 11th centuries.

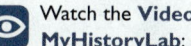 Watch the **Video** on **MyHistoryLab**: Vikings (Aberth)

manorialism System that described economic and political relations between landlords and their peasant laborers during the Middle Ages; involved a hierarchy of reciprocal obligations that exchanged labor or rents for access to land.

serfs Peasant agricultural laborers within the manorial system of the Middle Ages.

 Read the **Document** on **MyHistoryLab**: On Feudal Obligations, "Mutual Duties of Vassals and Lords" (1020) Fulbert of Chartres

moldboard Heavy plow introduced in northern Europe during the Middle Ages; permitted deeper cultivation of heavier soils; a technological innovation of the medieval agricultural system.

three-field system System of agricultural cultivation by 9th century in western Europe; included one-third in spring grains, one-third fallow.

Life for most serfs was difficult. Agricultural equipment was limited, and production was low. The available plows, copied from Mediterranean models, were too light to work the heavy soils of France and Germany effectively. In the 9th century a better plow, the **moldboard** (a curved iron plate), was introduced that allowed deeper turning of the soil. Most Western peasants early in the postclassical period also left half their land uncultivated each year to restore nutrients. This again limited productivity, although by the 9th century a new **three-field system** improved the situation. Here, only a third of the land was left unplanted each year, to regain fertility.

The obligations of the manorial system bore as heavily on most serfs as did the technological limitations. Serfs had to give their lord part of their crops in return for grazing their animals on his land or milling their grain. They also provided many days of labor repairing the lord's castle or working the lands under his control. Serfs were not slaves: They could not be bought or sold, and they retained essential ownership of their houses and lands as long as they kept up with their obligations. They could also pass their property rights on through inheritance. Nevertheless, life remained hard, particularly in the early postclassical centuries. Some serfs escaped landlord control, creating a host of wanderers who added to the disorder of the early Middle Ages.

The Church: Political and Spiritual Power

During the centuries of recovery after the Roman empire's collapse in the 6th century, the Catholic church was the only extensive example of solid organization. Here was a crucial contrast with the state's dominance over religion in the Byzantine empire. In theory, and to an extent in fact, the church copied the government of the Roman empire to administer Christendom. The pope in Rome was the top authority. Regional churches were headed by bishops, who were supposed to owe allegiance to the church's central authority; bishops, in turn, appointed and to some degree supervised local priests. The popes did not always appoint the bishops, for monarchs and local lords often claimed this right, but they did send directives and receive information. The popes also regulated doctrine, beating back several heresies that threatened a unified Christian faith. Moreover, they sponsored extensive missionary activity. Papal missionaries converted the English to Christianity. They brought the religion to northern and eastern Germany, beyond the borders of the previous Roman empire, and, by the 10th century, to Scandinavia. They were active in the border regions of eastern Europe, sometimes competing directly with Orthodox missionaries.

Clovis Early Frankish king; converted Franks to Christianity c. 496; allowed establishment of Frankish kingdom.

The interest of early Germanic kings in Christianity was a sign of the political as well as spiritual power of the church. A warrior chieftain, **Clovis**, converted to Christianity about 496 C.E. to gain greater prestige over local rivals, who were still pagan. This authority, in turn, gave him a vague dominion over the Franks, a Germanic tribe located in much of what is France today. Conversion of this sort also strengthened beliefs by Western religious leaders, particularly the popes, that they had a legitimate authority separate from and superior to the political sphere. As Figure 11.2 suggests, religious commitments continued to expand to many people.

The church also developed an important chain of monasteries during the centuries immediately after Rome's fall. Western monasteries helped discipline the intense spirituality felt by some individual Christians, people who wanted to devote themselves to prayer and religious discipline and escape the limits of ordinary material life. The most important set of monastic rules was developed by Benedict of Nursia (in Italy) in the 6th century; the spread of Benedictine monasteries promoted Christian unity in western Europe. Monasteries also served ordinary people as examples of a holy life, adding to the spiritual focus that formed part of the fabric of medieval society. Many monasteries helped improve the cultivation of the land at a time when agricultural techniques were at a low ebb. Monasteries also provided some education and promoted literacy.

FIGURE **11.2** *Last Judgment: Apocalypse of Reichenau.* This picture was part of materials to be read in religious services in the 11th century in Germany. At the bottom, the dead are rising from their tombs for the Last Judgment, summoned by angels escorted by the winds. The picture illustrates the goals Christians were urged to make paramount, focusing on life after death.

VISUALIZING THE PAST

Peasant Labor

THIS SCENE, FROM AN ILLUMINATED (ILLUSTRATED) manuscript of the 15th century, shows peasant labor and tools in France, near a stylized great palace.

QUESTIONS

- What kind of social and gender structure does the picture suggest?
- What kinds of tools were used in farming, and how productive would they be?
- The picture should be compared to earlier medieval representations, such as the representation of Charlemagne's coronation: What were the trends in medieval artistic styles, in terms of dealing with human figures and nature?

Peasants at labor.

Charlemagne and His Successors

One significant development occurred during the early postclassical centuries in the more strictly political sphere. The royal house of the Franks grew in strength during the 8th century. A new family, the **Carolingians**, took over this monarchy, which was based in northern France, Belgium, and western Germany. One founder of the Carolingian line, **Charles Martel**, or "Charles the Hammer," was responsible for defeating the Muslims in the battle of Tours in 732, although his victory had more to do with Arab exhaustion and an overextended invasion force than Carolingian strength. This defeat helped confine the Muslims to Spain and, along with the Byzantine defeat of the Arabs in the same period, preserved Europe for Christianity.

A later Carolingian ruler in this same royal line, Charles the Great, or **Charlemagne**, established a substantial empire in France and Germany around the year 800 (see Map 11.1). Briefly, it looked as if a new Roman empire might revive in the West; indeed, Charlemagne's successors in Germany continued to use the title of emperor (see Figure 11.3). Charlemagne helped to restore some church-based education in western Europe, and the level of intellectual activity began a slow recovery, in part because of these efforts. When Charlemagne died in 814, however, this empire did not long survive him. Rather, it was split into three portions as inheritance for his three grandsons: the outlines of modern France, Germany, and a middle strip consisting of the Low Countries, Switzerland, and

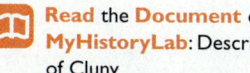 **Read** the **Document** on **MyHistoryLab**: Description of Cluny

Carolingians Royal house of Franks after 8th century until their replacement in 10th century.

Charles Martel (686–741) Carolingian monarch of Franks; responsible for defeating Muslims in battle of Tours in 732; ended Muslim threat to western Europe.

Charlemagne [SHAR-luh-mayn] Charles the Great; Carolingian monarch who established substantial empire in France and Germany c. 800.

CHAPTER 11 A New Civilization Emerges in Western Europe 245

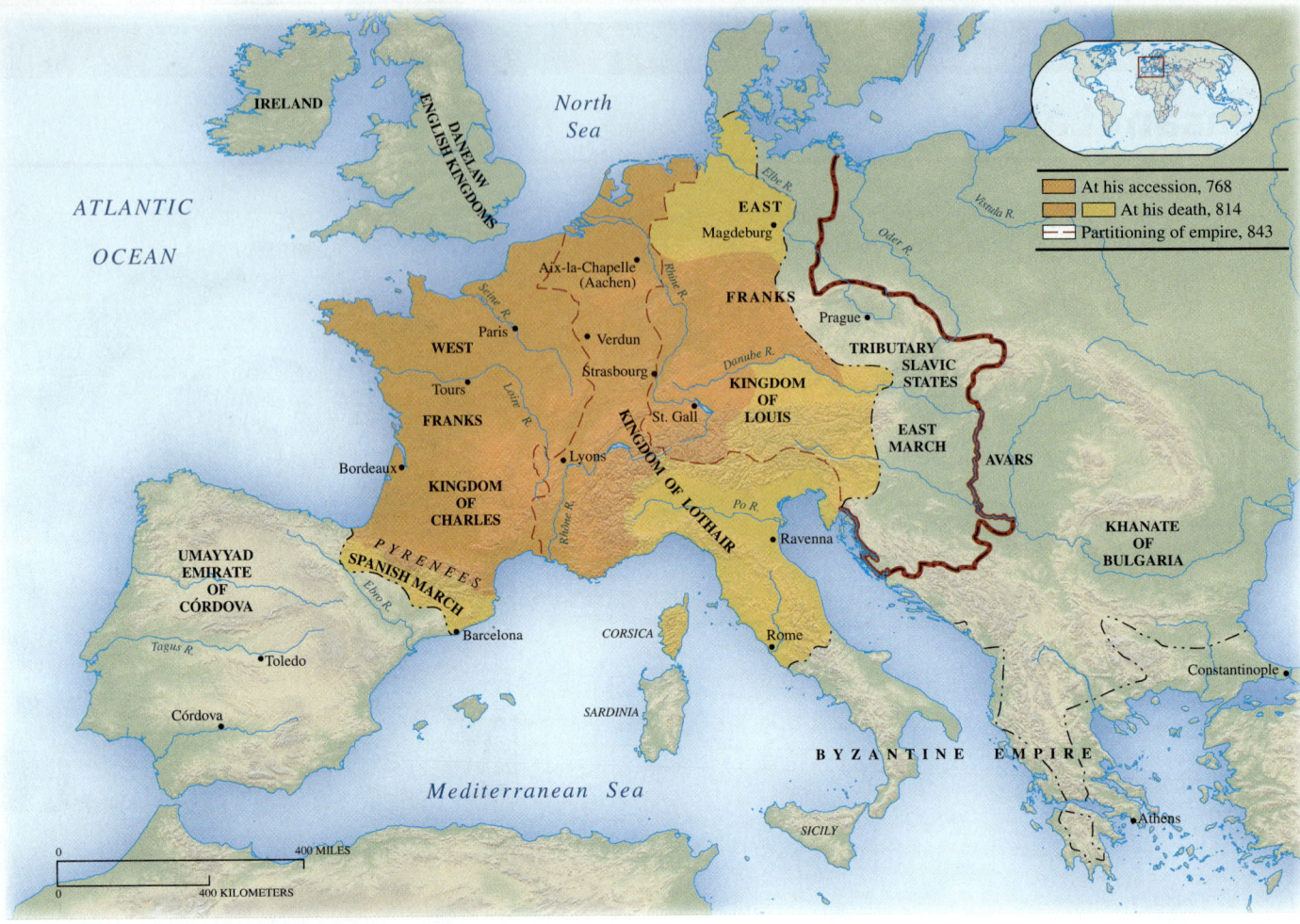

MAP 11.1 **Charlemagne's Empire and Successor States** Charlemagne gathered a wide section of western Europe under his sway, but the empire was divided among his three grandsons after his death.

northern Italy (Map 11.1). Several of Charlemagne's successors, with nicknames such as "the Bald" and "the Fat," were not great leaders even in their regional kingdoms.

From this point onward, the essential political history of western Europe consisted of the gradual emergence of regional monarchies; a durable empire proved impossible, given competing loyalties and the absence of a strong bureaucracy. The regional decentralization and frequent warfare contrasted with political patterns in China, the Arab caliphate, and the Byzantine Empire. Western Europe proved to have strong cultural unity, initially centered in Catholic Christianity, but with pronounced political divisions. No single language united this civilization, any more than did a single government. Intellectuals and the church officials used Latin, but during the Middle Ages separate spoken languages evolved, usually merging Germanic and Latin elements. These separate languages, such as French and English, in turn helped form the basis of halting national identities when political and cultural boundaries roughly coincided, which is what began to happen in key cases after the 9th century.

The royal houses of several lands gained new visibility soon after Charlemagne's empire split. At first, the rulers who reigned over Germany and northern Italy were in the strongest position. It was they who claimed the title *emperor*, beginning around the 10th century. Later they called themselves **Holy Roman emperors**, merging Christian and classical claims. By this time, however, their rule had become increasingly hollow, precisely because they relied too much on their imperial claims and did not build a solid monarchy from regional foundations. Local lords often went

Holy Roman emperors Emperors in northern Italy and Germany following split of Charlemagne's empire; claimed title of emperor c. 10th century; failed to develop centralized monarchy in Germany.

246 PART III The Postclassical Period, 600–1450: New Faith and New Commerce

their own way in Germany, while Italy was marked by the emergence of vibrant city states. For most of western Europe, however, the future lay elsewhere, with the rise of monarchies in individual states—states that ultimately would become nations.

New Economic and Urban Vigor

By 900, a series of developments began to introduce new sources of strength into Western society that ultimately had clear political and cultural repercussions. New agricultural techniques developed from contacts with eastern Europe and with Asian raiders into central Europe. The new moldboard plow and the three-field system were crucial gains; so was a new horse collar that allowed horses to be yoked without choking. The use of horse collars and stirrups also confirmed the military dominance of the lords, who monopolized fighting on horseback. The European nobility became defined by land ownership and military power. But better plows helped the ordinary people by allowing deeper working of heavy soil and the opening of new land. Monasteries also promoted better agricultural methods (in contrast to the less worldly orientation of monks in eastern Europe). During the 10th century, Viking raids began to taper off, partly because regional governments became stronger (sometimes when the Vikings themselves took over, as in the French province of Normandy) and partly because the Vikings, now Christianized, began to settle down. Greater regional political stability and improved agriculture promoted population growth, an important fact of Western history from the 10th through the 13th centuries.

Population growth encouraged further economic innovation. More people created new markets. There was a wedge here for growing trade, which in turn encouraged towns to expand, another source of demand. Landlords and serfs alike began to look to lands that had not previously been converted to agriculture. Whole regions, such as northeastern Germany, became colonized by eager farmers, and new centers sprang up throughout settled regions such as France. To woo labor to the new farms, landlords typically had to loosen the bonds of serfdom and require less outright labor service, sometimes simply charging a money rent. Harsh serfdom still existed, but most serfs gained greater independence, and some free peasants emerged. Contacts with other countries brought knowledge of new crops, such as durum wheat (from north Africa), the vital ingredient for pasta, and alfalfa (from Persia). The pace of economic life created a less rigid social structure, and more commercial, market-oriented economic motives began to coexist with earlier military and Christian ideals.

The growth of towns reflected the new vigor of western Europe's agriculture. In parts of Italy and the Low Countries, where trade and urban manufacturing were especially brisk, urban populations soared to almost 20 percent of the total by the 13th century. Overall, the townspeople made up about 5 percent of the West's population—a significant figure, although still below the often 15 percent levels of the advanced Asian civilizations. Few European cities approached a population level of 100,000 people (in contrast, China had 52 larger cities), but the rise of modest regional centers was an important development. Literacy spread in the urban atmosphere, spurring the popular languages; professional entertainers introduced new songs as well as dazzling tricks such as fire-eating and bear-baiting; urban interests spurred new forms of religious life, including city-based monastic orders dedicated to teaching or hospital work. Merchant activity and craft production expanded.

Read the Document on MyHistoryLab: Life of Charlemagne (early 9th c.) Einhard

FIGURE 11.3 The pope's coronation of the emperor Charlemagne was a vital precedent for the idea that church approval was essential for a legitimate state in western Europe. In fact, however, Charlemagne's power greatly exceeded the pope's.
(Coronation of Charlemagne at St. Peter's by Pope Leo III. Grandes Chroniques de France, fol. 106r. Musee Goya, Castres, France. Giraudon/Art Resource, NY.)

Read the Document on MyHistoryLab: Medieval Town: Customs of the Town of Chester, England 1085

Europe's economic and urban surge helped feed formal cultural life, which had already gained somewhat under Charlemagne's encouragement. By the 9th and 10th centuries, schools began to form around important cathedrals, training children who were destined for church careers. By the 11th century, there was enough demand for educated personnel to sustain the first universities. Italy offered universities to train students in medicine and law; the legal faculties profited from a growing revival in knowledge of Roman law, and medicine benefited from new learning imported from the Arabs and from revived Greek and Hellenistic science. By the 12th century, a more characteristic university was forming in Paris. It specialized in training clergy, with theology as the culminating subject but with faculties in other subjects as well. The Parisian example inspired universities in England (Oxford and Cambridge), Germany, and elsewhere. Solid educational institutions, although destined for only a small minority of Europe's population, supported increasingly diverse and sophisticated efforts in philosophy and theology. At the same time, medieval art and architecture reached a new high point, spurred by the same prosperity.

Feudal Monarchies and Political Advances

Prosperity also promoted political change, influenced by structures established in more unstable times. From the 6th century onward, the key political and military relationships in western Europe had evolved in a system called feudalism. Feudal relationships linked military elites, mostly landlords, who could afford the horses and iron weaponry necessary to fight. Greater lords provided protection and aid to lesser lords, called **vassals**; vassals in turn owed their lords military service, some goods or payments, and advice. Early feudalism after Rome's fall was very local; many landlords had armed bands of five or ten local vassals, easily converted into raiding parties. But feudal relationships could be extended to cover larger regions and even whole kingdoms. Charlemagne's empire boosted this more stable version of feudalism. He could not afford to pay his own bureaucracy, so he rewarded most of his military leaders with estates, which they quickly converted into family property in return for pledges of loyalty and service. Many German duchies were created by powerful lords with their own armies of vassals, ostensibly deferring to the Holy Roman emperor. On the whole, European feudalism inhibited the development of strong central states, but it also gradually reduced purely local warfare.

Furthermore, kings could use feudalism to build their own power. Kings of France began to win growing authority, from the 10th century onward, under the Capetian royal family. At first they mainly exploited their position as regional feudal lords in the area around Paris. They controlled many serf-stocked manors directly, and they held most other local landlords as vassals. More attentive administration of this regional base produced better revenues and armies. The kings also formed feudal links with great lords in other parts of France, often through marriage alliances, gradually bringing more territory under their control. They experimented with the beginnings of bureaucratic administration by separating their personal accounts from government accounts, thus developing a small degree of specialization among the officials who served them. Later Capetian kings sent out officials to aid in regional administration.

The growth of a strong feudal monarchy in France took several centuries. By the early 14th century, the process of cautious centralization had gone so far in France that a king could claim rights to make the church pay taxes (an issue that caused great conflict). The king could mint money and employ some professional soldiers apart from the feudal armies that still did most of the fighting.

Feudal monarchy in England was introduced more abruptly. The Duke of Normandy, of Viking descent, who had already built a strong feudal domain in his French province, invaded England in 1066. The duke, now known as **William the Conqueror**, extended his tight feudal system to his new kingdom. He tied the great lords of England to his royal court by bonds of loyalty, giving them estates in return for their military service. But he also used some royal officials, called sheriffs, to help supervise the administration of justice throughout the kingdom. In essence, he and his successors merged feudal principles with a slightly more centralized approach, including more standardized national law codes issued by the royal court.

The growth of feudal monarchy unknowingly duplicated measures taken much earlier in other societies, such as China. Developing an explicit bureaucracy, with some specialized functions, and sending emissaries to outlying provinces are examples. In Europe, kings often chose urban business or professional people to staff their fledgling bureaucracies, because unlike the feudal nobles, they would be loyal to the ruler who appointed them. Government functions expanded modestly, as kings tried to tax subjects directly and hire a small professional army to supplement feudal forces.

---

vassals Members of the military elite who received land or a benefice from a feudal lord in return for military service and loyalty.

William the Conqueror Invaded England from Normandy in 1066; extended tight feudal system to England; established administrative system based on sheriffs; established centralized monarchy.

Limited Government

Stronger monarchies did not develop evenly throughout Europe. The West remained politically divided and diverse. Germany and Italy, although nominally controlled by the Holy Roman emperor, were actually split into regional states run by feudal lords and city-states. The pope directly ruled the territory of central Italy. The Low Countries, a vigorous trade and manufacturing region, remained divided into regional units. Equally important were the limitations over the most successful feudal monarchies. Political centralization remained far short of Chinese levels. The power of the church continued to limit political claims, for the state was not supposed to intrude on matters of faith except in carrying out decisions of the popes or bishops.

Feudalism created a second limitation, for aristocrats still had a powerful independent voice and often their own military forces. The growth of the monarchy cut into aristocratic power, but this led to new statements of the limits of kings. In 1215, the unpopular English King John faced opposition to his taxation measures from an alliance of nobles, townspeople, and church officials. Defeated in his war with France and then forced down by the leading English lords, John was compelled to sign the Great Charter, or **Magna Carta**, which confirmed feudal rights against monarchical claims. John promised to observe restraint in his dealings with the nobles and the church, agreeing, for example, not to institute new taxes without the lords' permission or to appoint bishops without the church's permission. The Magna Carta showed how feudalism could generate claims of rights against the power of a king.

Late in the 13th century, this same feudal balance led to the creation of **parliaments** as bodies representing not individual voters but privileged groups such as the nobles and the church. (Even earlier, in 1000, the regional kingdom of Catalonia created a parliament.) The first full English parliament convened in 1265, with the House of Lords representing the nobles and the church hierarchy, and the Commons made up of elected representatives from wealthy citizens of the towns. As with the Magna Carta, the parliament institutionalized the feudal principle that monarchs should consult with their vassals. In particular, parliaments gained the right to rule on any proposed changes in taxation; through this power, they could also advise the crown on other policy issues. Although the parliamentary tradition became strongest in England, similar institutions arose in France, Spain, Scandinavia, and several of the regional governments in Germany. Here too, parliaments represented the key **three estates**: church, nobles, and urban leaders. They were not widely elected.

Feudal limited government was not modern limited government. People had rights according to the estate into which they were born; nobles transmitted membership in their estate to their children. There was no general concept of citizenship and certainly no democracy. Still, by creating the medieval version of representative institutions, Western feudal monarchy produced the beginnings of a distinctive political tradition. This tradition differed from the political results of Japanese feudalism, which emphasized group loyalty more than checks on central power.

Even with feudal checks, European monarchs developed more capacity for central administration during the later Middle Ages (see Map 11.2). The results clearly were uneven and by Asian standards still woefully limited. European rulers also continued to see war as a key purpose. Local battles gave way to larger wars, such as the conflicts between the proud rulers of France and England. In the 14th century, a long battle began—the **Hundred Years' War**, between the national monarchies of France and England—over territories the English king controlled in France and over feudal rights versus the emerging claims of national states.

The West's Expansionist Impulse

During the period of political development and economic advance, western Europe began to show its muscle beyond its initial postclassical borders (Map 11.2). Population growth spurred the expansionist impulse, as did the memory of Rome's lost greatness and the righteous zeal provided by Christianity. Germanic knights and agricultural settlers poured into sparsely settled areas in what is now eastern Germany and Poland, changing the population balance and clearing large areas of forest. A different kind of expansionist surge occurred in Spain. Small Christian states remained in northern Spain by the 10th century, and they gradually began to attack the Muslim government that held most of the peninsula. The "reconquest" escalated by the 11th century, as Christian forces, swelled by feudal warriors from various areas, pushed into central Spain, conquering the great Muslim center of Toledo. Full expulsion of Muslim rulers occurred only at the end of the Middle Ages in 1492, but the trend

Magna Carta Great Charter issued by King John of England in 1215; confirmed feudal rights against monarchical claims; represented principle of mutual limits and obligations between rulers and feudal aristocracy.

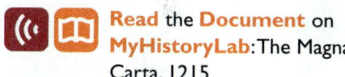 Read the Document on MyHistoryLab: The Magna Carta, 1215

parliaments Bodies representing privileged groups; institutionalized feudal principle that rulers should consult with their vassals; found in England, Spain, Germany, and France.

three estates The three social groups considered most powerful in Western countries: church, nobles, and urban leaders.

Hundred Years' War Conflict between England and France from 1337 to 1453; fought over lands England possessed in France and feudal rights versus the emerging claims of national states.

MAP 11.2 **Western Europe Toward the End of the Middle Ages, c. 1360 c.e.** Near the end of the postclassical period, strong monarchies had consolidated their holdings, and boundaries between states were coming into sharper focus.

Urban II Called for First Crusade in 1095; appealed to Christians to mount military assault to free the Holy Land from the Muslims.

of the Christian offensive was clear even earlier. During the 15th century, regional Spanish monarchies fused through the marriage of Ferdinand and Isabella, which provided the political muscle to complete the Christian "reconquesta."

At Europe's other extreme, Viking voyagers had pushed out into the northern Atlantic, establishing settlements in Iceland. By the 11th century, other voyages had pushed to Greenland and the Hudson Bay area in what is now Canada, where short-lived outposts were created. By the 13th century, Spanish and Italian seafarers entered the Atlantic from the Mediterranean, although without much initial result except several lost expeditions.

The most dramatic expansionist move involved the great Crusades against the Muslim control of the Holy Land. Pope **Urban II** called for the First Crusade in 1095, appealing to the piety of the West's rulers and common people. Crusaders were promised full forgiveness of sins if they died in battle, ensuring their entry to heaven, which obviously enhanced the religious motivations involved. The idea of attacking Islam had great appeal, as Figure 11.4 suggests. The attraction of winning spoils from the rich Arab lands added to the inducement, as did the thirst for excitement among the West's feudal warriors. Internal wars were declining in Europe, and the military values of feudalism sought outlets elsewhere. Three great armies, with tens of thousands of crusaders from various parts of the West, assembled in Constantinople in 1097, much to the distress of the Byzantine government. The Western crusaders moved toward Jerusalem, winning it from the Turkish armies that held the area by that time. For almost a century, western knights ruled the "kingdom of Jerusalem," losing it to a great Muslim general, Saladin, during the 12th century.

DOCUMENT

European Travel: A Monk Visits Jerusalem

WILLIBALD, AN ENGLISH MONK, JOURNEYED TO Jerusalem between 721 and 727 C.E. His account was written down by a German nun.

In Syria

Willibald's party had now grown to eight in number, and they became an object of suspicion to the Muslims, who, seeing that they were strangers, seized them and threw them into prison, because they knew not of what country they were, and supposed them to be spies. They carried them as prisoners before a certain rich old man, that he might examine them; and he inquired whence they came and the object of their mission; whereupon they related to him the true cause of their journey. The old man replied, "I have often seen men of the parts of the earth whence these come, traveling hither; they seek no harm, but desire to fulfil their law." And upon that they went to the palace, to obtain leave to proceed to Jerusalem.

While they were in prison it happened, by a manifest intervention of Devine Providence, that a merchant residing there was desirous, as an act of charity, and for the salvation of his soul, to purchase their deliverance, that they might pursue

(continued on next page)

(continued from previous page)

their way, but he was not allowed to carry his generous design into effect; nevertheless he sent them daily their meals, and on Wednesdays and Saturdays sent his son to them in prison, who took them out to the bath, and brought them back again. And on Sunday he took them to church through the market, that they might see the shops, and whatever they seemed to take a liking to he afterwards bought for them at his own expense. The townsmen used then to come there to look at them, because they were young and handsome, and clad in good garments.

Then, while they were still remaining in prison, a man, who was a native of Spain, came and spoke with them, and inquired earnestly who they were and from whence they came, and they told him the object of their pilgrimage. This Spaniard had a brother in the kind's palace, who was chamberlain to the king of the Muslims. . . . When [Willibald and the Spaniard] came before the king, and told him the case, he asked whence the prisoners came. And they said, "These men come from the west country, where the sun sets; and we know of no land beyond them, but water only." And the king replied, "Why ought we to punish them? they have not sinned against us: – give them leave, and let them go." And even the fine of four deniers, which the other prisoners had to pay, was remitted to them . . . .

JERUSALEM AND BETHLEHEM

On their arrival at Jerusalem, they first visited the spot where the holy cross was found, where there is now a church which is called the Place of Calvary, and which was formerly outside of Jerusalem; but when St. Helena found the cross, the place was taken into the circuit of the city. Three wooden crosses stand in this place, on the outside of the wall of the church, in memory of our Lord's cross and of those of the other persons crucified at the same time.

He next came to the place where the angel appeared to the shepherds, and thence to Bethlehem, where our Lord was born, distant seven miles from Jerusalem.

[Later, heading home they] reached Constantinople. Here repose in one altar the three saints, Andres, Timothy, and Luke the evangelist; and the sepulcher of John Chrysostome is before the altar where the priest stands when he performs mass. Willibald remained there two years, and was lodged in the church, so that he might behold daily where the saints reposed.

QUESTIONS
- What relationships between Christians and Muslims does this passage suggest, for the postclassical period?
- Why would a Spaniard play a special role in Willibald's Middle Eastern experience?
- What were Willibald's motives for travel?
- What kind of larger results did this sort of travel have, in post-classical world history?

Read the Document on MyHistoryLab: Fulcher of Chartres, The First Crusade (1100s C.E.)

FIGURE 11.4 This imaginary duel between the noble Christian champion King Richard of England and the Muslim leader Saladin clearly shows the difference between "good guys" and "bad guys." Although many actual crusaders respected Saladin as a skilled military leader, in Europe he was condemned as an infidel.

Several later Crusades attempted to win back the Holy Land, but many later efforts turned toward other goals or toward pure farce. The Third Crusade at the end of the 12th century led to the death of the German emperor and the imprisonment of the English king, although it did produce a brief truce with Saladin that facilitated Christian pilgrims' visits to Jerusalem. The Fourth Crusade was manipulated by merchants in Venice, who turned it into an attack on their commercial rivals in Constantinople.

The Crusades did not demonstrate a new western superiority in the wider world, despite brief successes. In the Middle East, they generated only a passing episode. But in expressing a combination of religious zeal and growing commercial and military vigor on the part of the knights and merchants who organized the largest efforts, the Crusades unquestionably showed the aggressive spirit of the western Middle Ages at their height. They also helped expose the West to new cultural and economic influences from the Middle East, where European invaders were impressed by urban standards of living. This was a major spur to further change, including a greater thirst for goods, like spices, available only through international trade. Simply visiting the thriving urban center of Constantinople during the Crusades could open European eyes to new possibilities. One crusader exclaimed, "Oh, what a great and beautiful city is Constantinople! How many churches and palaces it contains, fashioned with wonderful skill! Their tradesmen at all times bring by boat all the necessities of man."

Religious Reform and Evolution

As medieval society developed, the Catholic church went through several periods of decline and renewal. At times, church officials and the leading monastic groups became preoccupied with their land holdings and their political interests. The church was a wealthy institution; it was tempting for many priests and monks to behave like ordinary feudal lords in pursuit of greater worldly power. Several reform movements fought this secularism, such as the 13th-century flowering that created orders such as the Franciscans, devoted to poverty and service in Europe's bustling cities. Saint Clare of Assisi (1194–1253) exemplified this new spirit of purity and dedication to the church (Figure 11.5). She was deeply influenced by Saint Francis, also from Assisi, who had converted to a life of piety and preaching in 1205 and who founded a new monastic order. Clare refused to marry, as her parents wanted, but rather founded a women's Franciscan order (later known as the Order of Saint Clare, or the Poor Clares) with Francis's backing. Like many women in Europe, Clare found in monasticism a vital means of personal expression. In 1958 Pope Pius XII declared her the patron saint of television, for during her last illness she miraculously heard and saw on the wall of her room a Christmas mass being performed on the other side of Assisi.

In addition to monastic leaders, reform-minded popes, such as **Gregory VII** (r. 1073–1085), tried to purify the church and free it from interference by feudal lords. One technique was insistence on the particularly holy character of the priesthood. Reformers stipulated that all priests remain unmarried, to separate the priesthood from the ordinary world of the flesh. Gregory also tried to free the church from any trace of state control. He quarreled vigorously with Holy Roman Emperor Henry IV over the practice of state appointment, or **investiture**, of bishops in Germany. Ultimately, by excommunicating the emperor from the church, Gregory won his point. The emperor appealed to the pope for forgiveness on his knees in the snow of a northern Italian winter, and the investiture controversy ended, apparently in the church's favor. Gregory and several later popes made clear their beliefs that the church not only was to be free from state interference but was superior to the state in its function as a direct channel of God's word. While governments still influenced religious affairs, a network of church courts developed to rule on matters of religious law and to bring heretics to trial and occasionally to execution. This was the origin of recurrent Western beliefs in church–state separation.

The High Middle Ages

The postclassical version of Western civilization reached its high mark in the 12th and 13th centuries. Fed by the growing dynamism of western Europe's population, agriculture, and cities, the High Middle Ages were characterized by a series of creative tensions. Feudal

Gregory VII Pope during the 11th century who attempted to free church from interference of feudal lords; quarreled with Holy Roman Emperor Henry IV over practice of lay investiture.

investiture Practice of state appointment of bishops; Pope Gregory VII attempted to ban the practice of lay investiture, leading to war with Holy Roman Emperor Henry IV.

FIGURE 11.5 On the night of March 20, 1212, the Count of Sasso-Rosso's 18-year-old daughter, Clare, stole away from her father's house to dedicate herself to a life of poverty and holiness. She resisted all attempts by her father to bring her home and by the church to persuade her to accept some income as a guarantee against starvation for her order, which depended entirely on the begging of local friars for its daily bread. Clare was named abbess of a convent just three years later, and she never again left its grounds. Her sisters, her mother, and an aunt followed her into the order. She was canonized Saint Clare of Assisi in 1255.

THINKING HISTORICALLY

Western Civilization

IN RECENT YEARS, HISTORIANS HAVE BEEN critically examining the term "Western civilization," which is sometimes (wrongly) taken as self-evident.

The concept of "the West" or "western civilization" was actively used in the 20th-century cold war with the Soviet Union, yet it is hard to define. We have seen that the classical Mediterranean world did not directly identify a "Western" civilization, and this classical heritage was used most selectively by postclassical western Europe. Further, the consistent absence of political unity in western Europe complicates any definition of common structures.

Western Europeans could not have identified Western civilization in the postclassical period, but they would have recognized the concept of Christendom, along with some difference between their version of this religion and that of eastern Europe. The first definition of this civilization was primarily religious, although artistic forms associated with religion also figured in this definition. Regional cultures varied, of course, and there was no linguistic unity, but cultural developments in one area—for example, the creation of universities, which started in Italy—surfaced elsewhere fairly quickly. Supplementing culture were some reasonably common social structures—like manors and guilds—and trade patterns that increasingly joined northern and much of southern Europe. The resulting civilization was by no means as coherent as Chinese civilization; many of its members detested each other, like the English and French, who were often in conflict and sometimes engaged in name-calling (the English were "les goddams," because they swore so much, and the French were "frogs" because of what they ate). Until very recently, Europeans thought in terms of distinctive national histories, not European ones. But it is possible to define some common features that differed from those of neighboring civilizations. Even as the civilization began to change, late in the postclassical period, it preserved some common directions. Debate continues about the balance between the Western and more purely national features.

Defining Western civilization is also complicated in the postclassical period because Western leaders copied so much from other societies. They eagerly learned of new technologies from Asia. They benefited from Arab mathematics and philosophy, and they imitated Muslim commercial law on how to treat tradespeople from outside the locality. But even in imitating, most Europeans were keenly conscious of their distinctiveness as Christians. They sometimes resented the societies they copied from. Toward the end of the Middle Ages, as Europeans began to seek a new role in the world at large, the openness to imitation also began to decline, as part of the further definition of a Western or European identity.

> Defining Western civilization is also complicated... because Western leaders copied so much from other societies.

QUESTIONS
- Was there a Western civilization before the postclassical period? What were the defining features of Western civilization by the end of the postclassical period?
- How does the definition of Western civilization today compare to that of the postclassical period?

political structures, derived from local and personal allegiances, were balanced by emerging central monarchies. The unquestionable authority of the church and the cultural dominance of Christianity jostled with the intellectual vitality and diversity that formed part of university life. A social order and economy, based primarily on agriculture and the labor of serfs, now had to come to terms with important cities, merchants, and some new opportunities even for ordinary farmers.

WESTERN CULTURE IN THE POSTCLASSICAL ERA

11.2 What were the main cultural issues that West European intellectuals grappled with during the postclassical centuries?

> Christian culture dominated European philosophy and art, but it generated both change and some conflict.

During the centuries before about 1000, a small number of clergy continued the efforts of preserving and interpreting past wisdom, particularly the writings of church fathers such as Augustine, but also the work of some non-Christian Latin authors. During Charlemagne's time, a favorite practice was to gather quotations from ancient writers around key subjects. Interest in classical principles of rhetoric, particularly logic, reflected the concern for coherent organization; Aristotle, known to the Middle Ages as *the* philosopher, was valued because of his clear exposition of rational thought.

Theology: Assimilating Faith and Reason

From 1000 onward, a series of outstanding clerics advanced the logical exposition of philosophy and theology to new levels. They stressed the importance of absolute faith in God's word, but they believed that human reason could move toward an understanding of some aspects of religion and the natural order as well. Thus, according to several theologians, it was possible to prove the existence of God. Fascination with logic led some intellectuals to a certain zeal in pointing out inconsistencies in past wisdom, even in the writings of the church fathers. In the 12th century, **Peter Abelard** in Paris wrote a treatise called *Yes and No* in which he showed several logical contradictions in established interpretations of doctrine. Although Abelard protested his faith, saying, "I would not be an Aristotle if this were to part me from Christ," he clearly took an impish delight in suggesting skepticism. Here was a fascinating case of an individual's role in history. Abelard was clearly working in an established logical tradition, but his personality helped move the tradition to a new critical level. At the same time, his defiant attitudes may have drawn more attack than a softer approach would have done, which had consequences too.

The logical-rationalist current in western philosophy was hardly unopposed. A powerful monk, **Bernard of Clairvaux**, successfully challenged Abelard. Bernard, an intellectual of a different sort, stressed the importance of mystical union with God, attainable even on this earth in brief blissful glimpses, rather than rationalist endeavor. Bernard believed that reason was dangerous and that God's truth must be received through faith alone.

The debates over how and whether to combine the classical Mediterranean philosophical and scientific tradition with revealed religious faith reflected the earlier debates among Arab intellectuals during the 10th and 11th centuries. Both Christianity and Islam relied heavily on faith in a revealed word, through the Bible or Qur'an, respectively, but some intellectuals in both cultures strained to include other approaches.

Combining rational philosophy and Christian faith was the dominant intellectual theme in the postclassical West, showing the need to come to terms with both Christian and classical heritages, and with Middle Eastern learning as well. This combination of rational philosophy and Christian faith also posed formidable and fascinating problems. By the 12th century, the zeal for this kind of knowledge produced several distinctive results. It explained the intellectual vitality of most of the emerging universities, where students flocked to hear the latest debates by leading theologians. Higher education certainly benefited students through resulting job opportunities; for example, trained lawyers could hope for advancement in the growing bureaucracies of church or state. In contrast to China's institutions, however, the new universities were not directly tied into a single bureaucratic system, and the excitement they engendered during the Middle Ages was not just opportunistic. A large number of students, from the whole of western Europe, sought out the mixture of spiritual and rational understanding that leading thinkers were trying to work out.

The postclassical intellectual drive also motivated a growing interest in knowledge newly imported from the classical past and from the Arab world, and this knowledge fed the highest achievements of medieval learning. By the 12th century, Western scholars were reading vast amounts of material translated from Greek in centers in the Byzantine Empire, Italy, and Muslim Spain. They gained familiarity with the bulk of ancient Greek and Hellenistic philosophy and science. They also read translations of Arab and Jewish learning, particularly the works in which Middle Eastern scholars had wrestled with the problems of mixing human reasoning with truths gained by faith.

With much fuller knowledge of Aristotelian and Hellenistic science, plus the work of Arab rationalists such as Ibn-Rushd (IH-buhn RUSHT) (known in the West as Averroës (uh-VEHR-oh-eez), Western philosopher-theologians in the 13th century proceeded to the final great synthesis of medieval learning. The leading figure was **Thomas Aquinas**, the Italian-born monk who taught at the University of Paris. Aquinas maintained the basic belief that faith came first, but he greatly expanded the scope given to reason. Through reason alone, humans could know much of the natural order,

---

Abelard, Peter (1079–1142) Author of *Yes and No;* university scholar who applied logic to problems of theology; demonstrated logical contradictions within established doctrine.

Bernard of Clairvaux [klehr-VOH] (1090–1153) Emphasized role of faith in preference to logic; stressed importance of mystical union with God; successfully challenged Abelard and had him driven from the universities.

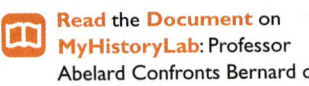

Read the Document on MyHistoryLab: Professor Abelard Confronts Bernard of Clairvaux, c. 1140

Aquinas, Thomas [Thomas ah-KWY-nuhs] (1225–1274) Creator of one of the great syntheses of medieval learning; taught at University of Paris; author of several *Summas;* believed that through reason it was possible to know much about natural order, moral law, and nature of God.

moral law, and the nature of God. Aquinas had complete confidence that all essential knowledge could be organized coherently, and he produced a host of *Summas*, or highest works, that used careful logic to eliminate all possible objections to truth as revealed by reason and faith. Essentially, this work restated in Christian terms the Greek efforts to seek a rationality in nature that would correspond to the rational capacities of the human mind. To be sure, a few philosophers carried the interest in logic to absurd degrees. After the 13th century, **scholasticism**—as the dominant medieval philosophical approach was called because of its base in the schools—sometimes degenerated into silly debates such as the one about how many angels could dance on the head of a pin. But at its height, and particularly with Aquinas, scholasticism demonstrated an unusual confidence in the logical orderliness of knowledge and in human ability to know.

scholasticism Dominant medieval philosophical approach; so called because of its base in the schools or universities; based on use of logic to resolve theological problems.

Medieval philosophy did not encourage a great deal of new scientific work. The emphasis on mastering past learning and organizing it logically could lead to overemphasis on previous discoveries rather than empirical research. Thus, university-trained doctors stressed memorization of Galen, the Hellenistic authority, rather than systematic practical experience. Toward the end of the 13th century, a current of practical science developed. In Oxford, members of the clergy, such as Roger Bacon, did experimental work with optics, pursuing research done earlier by Muslim scholars. An important by-product of this interest was the invention of eyeglasses. During the 14th and 15th centuries, experimenters also advanced knowledge in chemistry and astronomy. This early work set the stage for the flourishing of Western science.

Popular Religion

Far less is known about popular beliefs than about formal intellectual life in the Middle Ages. Christian devotion undoubtedly ran deep and may well have increased with time among many ordinary people. At least in the early medieval centuries, many people diligently followed Christian rituals yet seemed unaware of how many of their actions might contradict Christian morality. For example, Raoul de Cambrai, hero of a French epic written down in the late 12th century but orally transmitted earlier, sets fire to a convent filled with nuns, then asks a servant to bring him some food. The servant berates him for burning the convent, then reminds him that it is Lent, a time of fasting and repentance before Easter. Raoul denies that his deed was unjust, for the nuns deserved it for insulting his knights, but admits that he had forgotten Lent and goes off to distract himself from his hunger by playing chess.

Regardless of whether day-to-day morality improved, popular means of expressing religious devotion expanded over time. The rise of cities saw the formation of lay groups to develop spirituality and express their love of God. The content of popular belief evolved as well. Enthusiasm for the veneration of Mary, the mother of Jesus, expanded by the 12th century, showing a desire to stress the merciful side of Christianity, rather than the supposed sternness of God the Father, and new hopes for assistance in gaining salvation. The worship of various saints showed a similar desire for intermediaries between humanity and God. At the same time, ordinary people continued to believe in various magical rituals, and they celebrated essentially pagan festivals, which often involved much dancing and merriment. They blended their version of Christianity with great earthiness and spontaneity, some of which was conveyed by late medieval authors such as English writer Geoffrey Chaucer.

Religious Themes in Art and Literature

Religious art was another cultural area in which the medieval West came to excel, as was the case in other societies where religious enthusiasm ran strong, such as the Islamic Middle East or Hindu India. Like philosophy, medieval art and architecture were intended to serve the glory of God. Western painters used religious subjects almost exclusively. Painting mainly on wooden panels, artists in most parts of western Europe depicted Christ's birth and suffering and the lives of the saints, using stiff, stylized figures. By the 14th and 15th centuries, artists improved their ability to render natural scenes realistically and portrayed a host of images of medieval life as backdrops to their religious subjects. Stained-glass designs and scenes for churches were another important artistic expression.

Gothic An architectural style that developed during the Middle Ages in western Europe; featured pointed arches and flying buttresses as external supports on main walls.

Medieval architecture initially followed Roman models, particularly in church building, using a rectangular, or Romanesque, style sometimes surmounted by domes. During the 11th century, however, a new style took hold that was far more original, although it benefited from knowledge of Muslim design plus advances in structural engineering in the West itself. **Gothic** architects built soaring church spires and tall arched windows, as Figure 11.6 illustrates. Although their work focused on creating churches and great cathedrals, some civic buildings and palaces also picked up the Gothic motif. It is not far-fetched to see the Gothic style as representative of western postclassical culture more generally. Its spiritual orientation showed in the towers cast up to the heavens. It built also on growing technical skills and deep popular devotion, expressed in the money collected to build the huge monuments and the patient labor needed for construction that often lasted many decades. The originality of Gothic styles reflected the growing Western ability to find suitable new means of expression, just as use of Gothic styles in the later Western world showed the ongoing power of medieval models.

Medieval literature and music reflected strong religious interests. Most Latin writing dealt with points of philosophy, law, or political theory. However, alongside writing in Latin came the development of a growing literature in the spoken languages, or vernaculars, of western Europe. The pattern was not unlike that of India a few centuries earlier after the fall of the Gupta empire, when Sanskrit served as a scholarly language but increasing power was given to popular languages such as Hindi. Vernacular literature helped develop separate European languages and focused largely on secular themes. Several oral sagas, dealing with the deeds of great knights and mythic figures in the past, were written down. From this tradition came the first known writing in early English, *Beowulf*, and in French, *The Song of Roland*. Late in the Middle Ages, a number of writers created adventure stories, comic tales, and poetry in the vernacular tongues, such as Chaucer's *Canterbury Tales*. Much of their work, and also plays written for performance in the growing cities, reflected the tension between Christian values and a desire to portray the richness and coarseness of life on earth. Chaucer's narrative shows a fascination with bawdy behavior, a willingness to poke fun at the hypocrisy of many Christians, and an ability to capture some of the tragedies of human existence. In France, a long poem called *The Romance of the Rose* used vivid sexual imagery, and the poet Villon wrote, in largely secular terms, of the terror and poignancy of death.

Also using vernacular language, a series of courtly poets, or troubadours, based particularly in southern France in the 14th century, wrote hymns to the love that could flourish between men and women. Although their verses stressed platonic devotion rather than sexual love and paid homage to courtly ceremonies and polite behavior, their concern with love was the first sign of a new valuation of this emotional experience in the Western tradition.

In sum, medieval intellectual and artistic life created a host of important themes. Religion was the centerpiece, but it did not preclude a growing range of interests, from science to romantic poetry. Medieval culture was a rich intellectual achievement in its own right. It also set in motion a series of developments—in rationalist philosophy, science, artistic representations of nature, and vernacular literature—that would be building blocks for later Western thought and art.

FIGURE **11.6** The cathedral of Notre-Dame (Our Lady) at Amiens, France, is a grand example of gothic architecture, which flourished during the later Middle Ages in western Europe. The cathedral, which dwarfs the surrounding buildings, was built between 1220 and 1402 and was the tallest building in Europe at the time of its completion.

CHANGING ECONOMIC AND SOCIAL FORMS IN THE POSTCLASSICAL CENTURIES

11.3 How did growing trade fit the basic social structure of western Europe?

> While merchant capitalism gained ground in western Europe, other economic values predominated.

Although culture provided the most obvious cement for Western society during the Middle Ages, economic activity and social structure also developed common features. Here too, the postclassical West demonstrated impressive powers of innovation, for classical patterns had little hold. As trade revived by the 10th century, the West became a common commercial zone. Most regions produced primarily for local consumption, as was true in agricultural societies generally. But Italian merchants actively sought cloth manufactured in the Low Countries (present-day Belgium and the Netherlands), and merchants in many areas traded for wool produced in England or timber supplies and furs brought from Scandinavia and the Baltic lands. Great ports and trading fairs, particularly in the Low Countries and northern France, served as centers for Western exchange as well as markets for a few exotic products such as spices brought in from other civilizations (Map 11.3).

Western Europe also saw a clear expansion in productive capacity during much of the postclassical period, with gains in agriculture supporting some growth in urban manufacturing. Their achievements here did not rival those of east Asia, where the production gains and social consequences were more

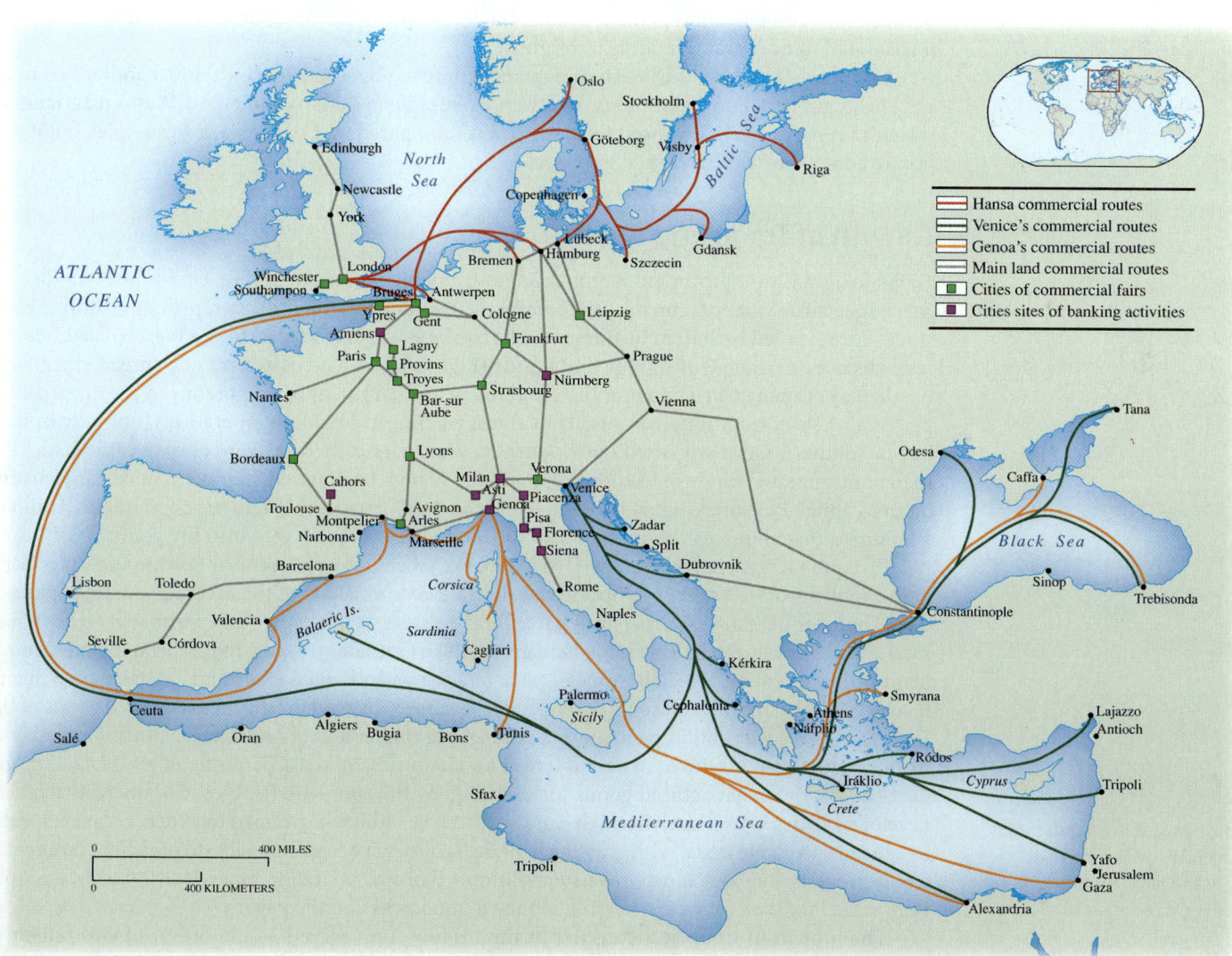

MAP **11.3** Leading Trade Routes Within Western and Central Europe and to the Mediterranean

substantial, but they did contribute important changes including a growing capacity to participate in transregional trade.

New Strains in Rural Life

The improvements in agriculture after 900 C.E. brought important new ingredients to rural life. Some peasants were able to shake off the most severe constraints of manorialism, becoming almost free farmers with only a few obligations to their landlords, although rigid manorialism remained in place in many areas. Noble landlords still served mainly military functions, for ownership of a horse and armor were prerequisites for fighting until the end of the medieval period. Although most nobles shunned the taint of commerce—like aristocrats in many societies, they found too much money-grubbing demeaning—they did use trade to improve their standard of living and adopt more polished habits. The courtly literature of the late Middle Ages reflected this new style of life.

As many lords sought improved conditions, they were often tempted to press their serfs to pay higher rents and taxes, even as serfs were gaining a new sense of freedom and control over their own land. From the late Middle Ages until the 19th century, this tension produced a recurrent series of peasant–landlord battles in Western society. Peasants sought what they viewed as their natural and traditional right to the land, free and clear. They talked of Christian equality, turning such phrases as "When Adam delved and Eve span, Who was then a gentleman?" A more complex economy clearly brought new social strains, similar to the recurrent wave of popular unrest in China or the rural uprisings in the Middle East, where religion helped prompt egalitarian sentiments as well. The gap between lord and peasant was the crucial social inequality in Europe, but it was open to change and it generated some egalitarian ideas in response.

On the whole, the lives of western peasants improved between 900 and 1300. Landlord controls were less tight than they had become in other societies, such as the Middle East. Western agriculture was not yet particularly advanced technologically (compared with east Asia, for example), but it had improved notably over early medieval levels.

Growth of Trade and Banking

Gains in agriculture promoted larger changes in medieval economic life. Urban growth allowed more specialized manufacturing and commercial activities, which in turn promoted still greater trade. Spearheaded by Italian businesspeople, banking was introduced to the West to facilitate the long-distance exchange of money and goods (Figure 11.7). The use of money spread steadily, to the dismay of many Christian moralists and many ordinary people who preferred the more direct, personal ways of traditional society. The largest trading and banking operations, not only in Italy but in southern Germany, the Low Countries, France, and Britain, were clearly capitalistic. Big merchants invested funds in trading ships and the goods they carried, hoping to make large profits on this capital. Profitmaking was not judged kindly by Christian thinkers such as Thomas Aquinas, who urged that all prices should be "just," reflecting only the labor put into the goods.

Rising trade took several forms. There were exchanges between western Europe and other parts of the known world. Wealthy Europeans developed a taste for some of the luxury goods and spices of Asia. The latter were not used merely to flavor food but were vital in preserving perishable items such as meat. Spice extracts also had great medicinal value. The Crusades played a role in bringing these products to wider attention. A Mediterranean trade redeveloped, mainly in the hands of Italian merchants, in which European cloth and some other products were exchanged for the more polished goods of the East. Commerce within Europe involved exchanges of timber and grain from the north for cloth and metal products manufactured in Italy and the Low Countries. At first an exporter of raw wool, England developed some manufactured goods for exchange by the later Middle Ages. Commercial alliances developed. Cities in northern Germany and southern Scandinavia grouped together in the **Hanseatic League** to encourage trade. With growing banking facilities, it became possible to organize commercial transactions throughout much of western Europe. Bankers, including many Jewish businesspeople, were valued for their service in lending money to monarchs and the papacy.

The growth of trade and banking in the Middle Ages served as the origin of **capitalism** in Western civilization. The greater Italian and German bankers, the long-distance merchants of the Hanseatic cities, were clearly capitalistic in their willingness to invest in trading ventures with the expectation of profit. Given the dangers of trade by land and sea, the risks in these investments were

Hanseatic League An organization of cities in northern Germany and southern Scandinavia for the purpose of establishing a commercial alliance.

capitalism Economic system based on profit-seeking, private ownership, and investment.

substantial, but profits of 100 percent or more were possible. In many cities, such as London, groups of powerful merchants banded together to invest in international trade, each buying shares in the venture and profiting or losing accordingly.

Individual merchants could amass—and lose—great fortunes. Jacques Coeur (JAHK KUR) (c. 1395–1456), one of Europe's most extraordinary merchants, demonstrated the opportunities and risks of new forms of trade. Son of a furrier, he married the daughter of a royal official and served as a tax official until he was caught minting coins with less valuable metals. He then founded a trading company that competed with Italians and Spaniards in dealing with the Middle East. He visited Damascus to buy spices, setting up a regular trade in rugs, Chinese silk, and Indonesian spices and sugar. He also became financial advisor and supplier to the French king and was ennobled. With the largest fleet ever owned by a French subject, Coeur surrounded himself with splendor, even arranging with the pope for his 16-year-old son to become an archbishop. But he had enemies, many of them nobles in debt to him, and they turned the king against him. Tortured, he admitted to various crimes, including supplying weapons to Muslims. His property was confiscated, but adventurer to the last, he died on a Greek island while serving in a papal fleet against the Turks.

By world standards this was not a totally unprecedented merchant spirit. European traders were still less venturesome and less wealthy than some of their Muslim counterparts. Nor was Western society as tolerant of merchants as Muslim or Indian societies were. Yet Western commercial endeavors clearly were growing. Because Western governments were weak, with few economic functions, merchants had a freer hand than in many other civilizations. Many of the growing cities were ruled by commercial leagues. Monarchs liked to encourage the cities as a counterbalance to the power of the landed aristocracy, and in the later Middle Ages and beyond, traders and kings typically were allied. However, aside from taxing merchants and using them as sources of loans, royal governments did not interfere much with trading activities. Merchants even developed their own codes of commercial law, administered by city courts. Thus, the rising merchant class was staking out an unusually powerful and independent role in European society.

Capitalism was not yet typical of the Western economy, even aside from the moral qualms fostered by the Christian tradition. Most peasants and landlords had not become enmeshed in the market system. In the cities, the dominant economic ethic stressed group protection, not profitmaking. The characteristic institution was not the international trading firm but the merchant or artisan guild. **Guilds** grouped people in the same business or trade in a single city, sometimes with loose links to similar guilds in other cities. These organizations were new in western Europe, although they resembled guilds in various parts of Asia but with greater independence from the state. They stressed security and mutual control. Merchant guilds thus attempted to give all members a share in any endeavor. If a ship pulled in loaded with wool, the clothiers' guild of the city insisted that all members participate in the purchase so that no one member would monopolize the profits.

Artisan guilds were made up of the people in the cities who actually made cloth, bread, jewelry, or furniture. These guilds tried to limit their membership so that all members would have work. They regulated apprenticeships to guarantee good training but also to ensure that no member would employ too many apprentices and so gain undue wealth. They discouraged new methods because security and a rough equality, not maximum individual profit, were the goals; here was their alternative to the capitalistic approach. Guilds also tried to guarantee quality so that consumers would not have to worry about shoddy quality on the part of some unscrupulous profit-seeker. Guilds played an important political and social role in the cities, giving their members recognized status and often a voice in city government. Their statutes were in turn upheld by municipal law and often backed by the royal government as well.

FIGURE **11.7** This 14th-century miniature shows views of a banking house. People might keep money in banks, seek loans, or arrange transactions with merchants in faraway centers of trade.

guilds Sworn associations of people in the same business or craft in a single city; stressed security and mutual control; limited membership, regulated apprenticeship, guaranteed good workmanship; often established franchise within cities.

Despite the traditionalism of the guilds, manufacturing and commercial methods improved in medieval Europe, although the region still lagged well behind Asia in ironmaking and textile manufacture. In a few areas, such as clockmaking—which involved both sophisticated technology and a concern for precise time initially linked to the schedule of church services—European artisans led the world. Furthermore, some manufacturing spilled beyond the bounds of guild control. Particularly in the Low Countries and parts of Italy, groups of manufacturing workers were employed by capitalists to produce for a wide market. Their techniques were simple, and they worked in their own homes, often alternating manufacturing labor with agriculture. Their work was guided not by the motives of the guilds but by the inducements of merchant capitalists, who provided them with raw materials and then paid them for their production.

Thus, by the later Middle Ages, western Europe's economy and society embraced many contradictory groups and principles. Commercial and capitalist elements jostled against the slower pace of economic life in the countryside and even against the dominant group protectionism of most urban guilds. Most people remained peasants, but a minority had escaped to the cities, where they found more excitement, along with increased danger and higher rates of disease. Medieval tradition held that a serf who managed to live in the city for a year and a day became a free person. A few prosperous capitalists flourished, but most people operated according to very different economic values, directed toward group welfare rather than individual profit. This was neither a static society nor an early model of a modern commercial society. It had its own flavor and its own tensions—the fruit of several centuries of economic and social change.

Limited Sphere for Women

The increasing complexity of medieval social and economic life may have had one final effect, which is familiar from patterns in other agricultural societies: new limits on the conditions of women. Women's work remained vital in most families. The Christian emphasis on the equality of all souls and the practical importance of women's monastic groups in providing an alternative to marriage continued to have distinctive effects on women's lives in Western society. The veneration of Mary and other female religious figures gave women real cultural prestige, counterbalancing the biblical emphasis on Eve as the source of human sin. In some respects, women in the West had higher status than their sisters under Islam: They were less segregated in religious services (although they could not lead them) and were less confined to the household. Still, women's voice in the family may have declined in the Middle Ages.

Urban women often played important roles in local commerce and even operated some craft guilds, but they found themselves increasingly hemmed in by male-dominated organizations. In contrast to Islam, women were not assured of property rights. By the late Middle Ages, a literature arose that stressed women's roles as the assistants and comforters to men, listing supplemental household tasks and docile virtues as women's distinctive sphere. Patriarchal structures seemed to be taking deeper root.

THE DECLINE OF THE MEDIEVAL SYNTHESIS

> Key characteristics of western Europe began to shift after 1300, with new problems of overpopulation and disease.

11.4 What were the basic shifts in west European characteristics at the end of the postclassical period? Was the region declining?

A major war engulfed France and England during the 14th and 15th centuries, and this proved to be both symptom and cause of larger difficulties. The Hundred Years' War, which sputtered into the mid-15th century, lasted even longer than its name and initially went very badly for France—a sign of new weakness in the French monarchy. As the war dragged on, kings reduced their reliance on the prancing forces of the nobility in favor of paid armies of their own. New military methods challenged the key monopoly of the feudal lords, as ordinary paid archers learned how to unseat armored knights with powerful bows and arrows and with crossbows (Figure 11.8). The war ended with a French victory, sparked in part by the heroic leadership of the inspired peasant woman Joan of Arc, but both its devastation and the antifeudal innovations it encouraged suggested a time of change.

Concurrently, from about 1300 onward, key sources of Western vitality threatened to disappear. Medieval agriculture could no longer keep pace with population growth: The readily available new lands had been used up, and there were no major new technological gains to compensate. The result included severe famines and a decline in population levels until the end of the century. A devastating series of plagues that persisted for several centuries, beginning with the **Black Death** in 1348, further reduced Europe's population (Figure 11.9). Plague came from Asia and the Middle East, due to trade contacts, but the results were devastating. New social disputes arose, heightening some of the tensions noted earlier between peasants and landlords, artisans and their employees. Not until the 16th century would the West begin to work out a new social structure.

The West's economy did not go into a tailspin. In some respects, as in manufacturing and mining technology, progress may even have accelerated. The 150 to 200 years after 1300 form in Western history a transition period in which the features of the Middle Ages began to blur while new problems and developments began to take center stage. Western civilization was not in a spiral of decline, but the postclassical version of this civilization was.

Signs of Strain

The decline of medieval society involved increasing challenges to several typical medieval institutions. During the 14th century, the ruling class of medieval society, the land-owning aristocracy, began to show signs of confusion. It had long staked its claim to power on its control of land and its military prowess, but its skill in warfare was now open to question. The growth of professional armies and new weaponry such as cannon and gunpowder made traditional fighting methods, including fortified castles, increasingly irrelevant. The aristocracy did not simply disappear, however. Rather, the nobility chose to emphasize a rich ceremonial style of life, featuring tournaments in which military expertise could be turned into competitive games. The idea of chivalry—carefully controlled, polite behavior, including behavior toward women—gained ground. The upper class became more cultivated. We have seen similar transformations in the earlier Chinese and Muslim aristocracy. Yet at this transitional point in Europe, some of the elaborate ceremonies of chivalry seemed rather hollow, even a bit silly—a sign that medieval values were losing hold without being replaced by a new set of purposes.

Another key area involved decisive shifts in the balance between church and state that had characterized medieval life. For several decades in the aftermath of the taxation disputes in the early 14th century, French kings wielded great influence on the papacy, which they relocated from Rome to Avignon, a town surrounded by French territory. Then rival claimants to the papacy confused the issue further. Ultimately, a single pope was returned to Rome, but the church was clearly weakened. Moreover, the church began to lose some of its grip on western religious life. Church leaders were so preoccupied with their political involvement that they tended to neglect the spiritual side. Religion was not declining; indeed, signs of intense popular piety continued to blossom, and new religious groups formed in the towns. But devotion became partially separated from the institution of the church. One result, again beginning in the 14th century, was a series of popular heresies, with leaders in places such as England and Bohemia (the present-day Czech Republic) preaching against the hierarchical apparatus of the church in favor of direct popular experience of God. Another result was an important new series of mystics, many of them women, who claimed direct, highly emotional contacts with God.

A third area in which medievalism faded was the breakdown of the intellectual and even artistic synthesis. After the work of Aquinas, church officials became less tolerant of intellectual daring, and they even declared some of Aquinas's writings heretical. The earlier blend of rationalism and religion no longer seemed feasible. Ultimately, this turned some thinkers away from religion, but this daring

FIGURE **11.8** The Siege of Paris, pictured here, took place in 1465, after the French nobility rose up against King Louis XI, whose treatment of them had left them angry and ambitious to reestablish their independence from the Crown. Calling themselves the League of Public Good, they marched on Paris, but the fighting there was indecisive and gave Louis the chance to regroup. The uprising was ended by treaty two months later. This incident was a revealing clash between feudal values and new royal ambition.

Black Death Plague that struck Europe in 14th century; significantly reduced Europe's population; affected social structure.

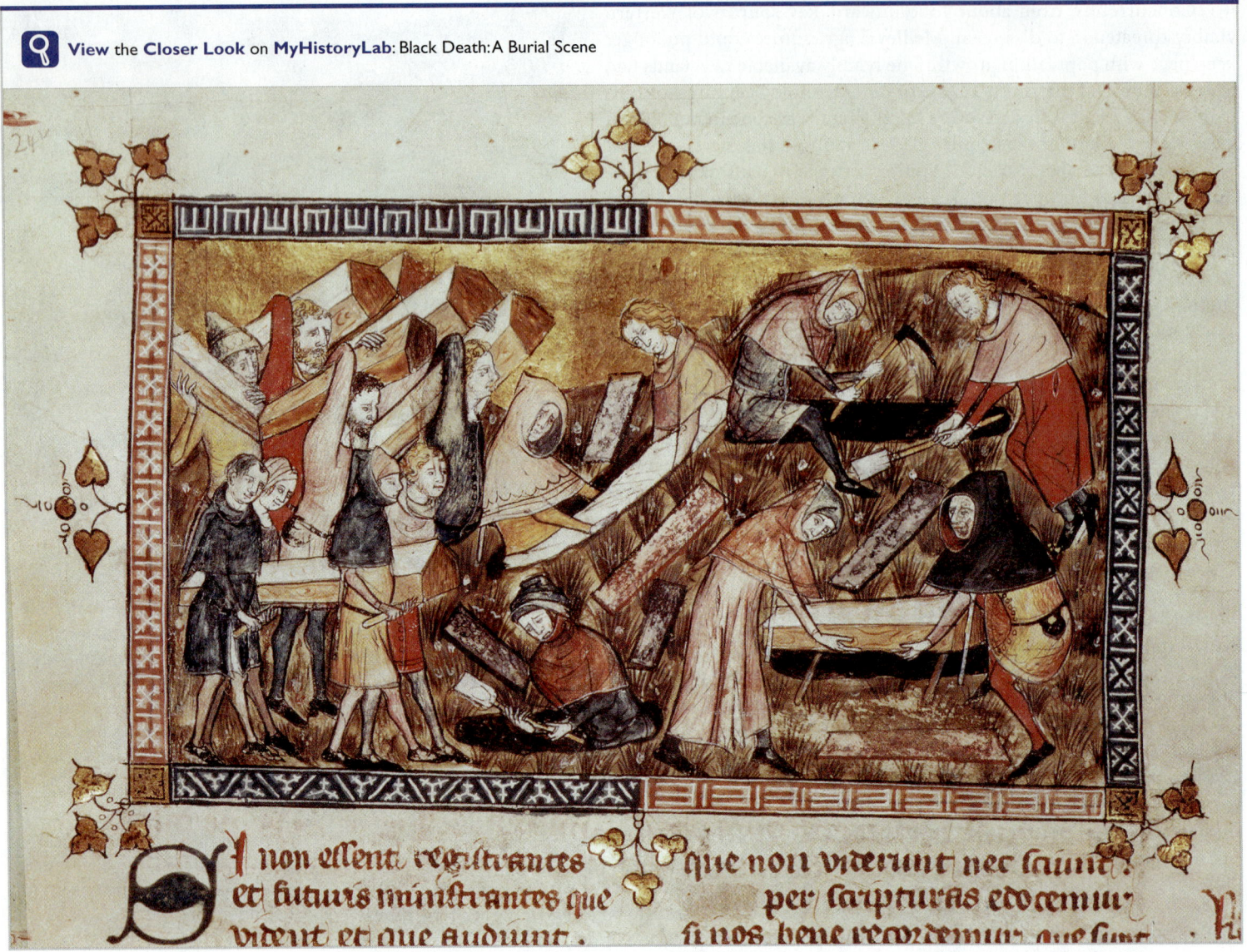

FIGURE 11.9 This painting shows survivors at Tournai placing plague victims in coffins before mass burial became the only way to keep up with the deaths. The Black Death, which killed up to a quarter of the population of Europe in just 20 years, devastated medieval society.

development took time. In art, growing interest in realistic portrayals of nature, although fruitful, suggested the beginnings of a shift away from medieval artistic standards. Religious figures became less stylized as painters grew more interested in human features for their own sake. The various constraints on forms of postclassical culture prompted many Western intellectuals to look for different emphases. In Italy most clearly, new kinds of literature and art took shape that differed from the styles and subjects of the postclassical centuries.

The Postclassical West and Its Heritage

Medieval Europe had several faces. The term *Middle Ages* implies a lull between the glories of Rome and the glitter of more modern Europe. There is some truth to this, for medieval Europe did grapple with backwardness and vulnerability.

But the Middle Ages were also a period of growing dynamism. Particularly after 900 C.E., gains in population, trade and cities, and intellectual activity created a vigorous period in European history. Key developments set a tone that would last even after the specifically medieval centuries had ended. Universities and Gothic art (often intertwined, as in the many American campuses that revived the

Gothic style for their buildings) were an enduring legacy to Western society. Distinctive ideas about government, building on Christian and feudal traditions, constituted another medieval contribution.

The medieval period was also a special moment in the relationship between Europe and the regions around it. Opportunities to advance by imitation were particularly striking, from technology to science to trade and consumption. Even the medieval university may have had Arab origins in the higher schools of the Muslim world. Europe was able to develop new contacts, but it did not reach the technological or urban levels of the leading Asian societies.

Medieval Europe warrants a particular comparison with other areas in which civilization was partially new during the postclassical period and where change and imitation proceeded rapidly. Divided political rule in Europe resembled conditions in west Africa and Japan (the only other feudal society in the period). The imitation process can be compared among Europe, Africa, Japan, and Russia. But the Crusades revealed a distinctive expansionist spirit in Europe that also warrants attention, suggesting a more aggressive interest in the wider world than the other emerging societies were demonstrating.

Global Connections and Critical Themes

MEDIEVAL EUROPE AND THE WORLD

During the Middle Ages, western Europe developed something of a love–hate relationship with the world around it. In the early Middle Ages, Europe seemed at the mercy of invasions, from the Vikings in the north or various nomadic groups pushing in from central Asia. European leaders were also keenly aware of the power of Islam, which controlled most of the Mediterranean, including Spain. Most Europeans saw Islam as a dangerously false religion and an obvious threat.

At the same time, there was much to be learned from this wider world. During the Middle Ages, Europeans actively copied a host of features from Islam, from law to science and art. They imported products and technologies from Asia. This process of imitation accelerated during the centuries of Mongol control, when European traders and travelers eagerly pushed into eastern Asia. A key question for Europe at the end of the Middle Ages involved how to gain greater control over the benefits that came from world contacts, while reducing the sense of threat. Partly through weakness, partly because of the advantages that Europeans learned from contact, the new civilization developed active growing sense of global awareness. Europe itself did not, however, become a major attraction for people in other societies, except for some of the raiders who helped keep the region off balance during the early part of the period. Neither European manufacturing nor culture was widely appealing, outside the region itself.

Further Readings

For the Middle Ages generally, Joseph Strayer's *Western Europe in the Middle Ages* (1982) is a fine survey. More recent works include Judith Bennett, *Medieval Europe: A Short History* (2010); Charles H. Parker and Jerry H. Bentley, eds., *Between the Middle Ages and Modernity: Individual and Community in the Early Modern World* (2007); Eric H. Mielants, *The Origins of Capitalism and the "Rise of the West"* (2007); and David Power, ed., *The Central Middle Ages: Europe 950–1320* (2006). Key topics are covered in Peter Reid, *Medieval Warfare: Triumph and Domination in the Wars of the Middle Ages* (2007); Huw Pryce and John Watts, eds., *Power and Identity in the Middle Ages* (2007); Isabel Davis, *Writing Masculinity in the Later Middle Ages* (2007); R. S. Lopez, *The Commercial Revolution of the Middle Ages, 950–1350* (1976); and C. H. Lawrence, *Medieval Monasticism: Forms of Religious Life in Western Europe in the Middle Ages* (1984). National histories are important for the period, particularly on political life; see J. W. Baldwin, *The Government of Philip Augustus: Foundations of French Royal Power in the Middle Ages* (1986); G. Barraclough, *The Origins of Modern Germany* (1984); Michael Alexander, *Medievalism: The Middle Ages in Modern England* (2007); and Christopher Dyer, *An Age of Transition?: Economy and Society in England in the Later Middle Ages* (2005). R. Barlett, *The Making of Medieval Europe* (1992), suggests that Western civilization was the product of cross-cultural fertilization.

Social history has dominated much recent research on the period. See P. Ariès and G. Duby, eds., *A History of Private Life*, vol. 2 (1984) and Barbara Hanawalt, *The Ties That Bound: Peasant Families in Medieval England* (1986), for important orientation in this area. David Herlihy's *Medieval Households* (1985) is a vital contribution, as is J. Chapelot and R. Fossier's *The Village and House in the Middle Ages* (1985). Margaret Schaus, *Women and Gender in Medieval Europe: An Encyclopedia* (2006) and J. Kirshner and S. F. Wemple, eds., *Women of the Medieval World* (1985), are good collections. On tensions in popular religion, see Lisa M. Bitel and Felice Lifshitz, *Gender and Christianity in Medieval Europe: New Perspectives* (2010); C. Bynum, *Jesus as Mother: Studies in the Spirituality of the High Middle Ages* (1982); and L. Little, *Religious Poverty and the Profit Economy in Medieval Europe* (1978). A highly readable account of medieval life is E. Leroy Ladurie, *Montaillou: The Promised Land of Error* (1979).

Several excellent studies take up the theme of technological change: J. Gimpel, *The Medieval Machine: The Industrial Revolution of the Middle Ages* (1977); Lynn White Jr., *Medieval Technology and Social Change* (1962); and David Landes, *Revolution in Time: Clocks and the Making of the Modern World* (1985). On environmental impact, see Roland Bechmann, *Trees and Man: The Forest in the Middle Ages* (1990).

On intellectual and artistic life, E. Gilson's *History of Christian Philosophy in the Middle Ages* (1954) is a brilliant sketch, and his *Reason and Revelation* (1956) focuses on key intellectual issues of the age. S. C. Ferruolo's *The Origins of the University* (1985) and N. Pevsner's *An Outline of European Architecture* (1963) deal with other important features; see also H. Berman's *Law and Revolution: The Formation of the Western Legal Tradition* (1983). On contacts, see Khalil Semaan, *Islam and the Medieval West: Aspects of Intercultural Relations* (1980). An intriguing classic, focused primarily on culture, is J. Huizinga, *The Waning of the Middle Ages* (1973).

On MyHistoryLab

Critical Thinking Questions

1. How do developments in European agricultural reflect the importance of new technology?
2. What were the main differences between early European capitalism and the economic ethic of the guilds?
3. How did the consequences of the Crusades compare to the initial causes?
4. What are the distinctive features of feudalism as a political system? How does the feudal system help explain patterns of political change in postclassical Europe?
5. Looking at both eastern and western Europe, what were some of the main reasons many additional people converted to Christianity in the postclassical period?
6. How did western Europe compare with sub-Saharan Africa as a participant in postclassical transregional trade? What were its comparative strengths and weaknesses?

The Americas on the Eve of Invasion

12

Listen to Chapter 12 on MyHistoryLab

LEARNING OBJECTIVES

What were the main features of the Toltec and Aztec empires? p. 267	12.1
What were the principal strengths and constraints of the Aztec economy? p. 272	12.2
What were the principal causes of the expansion of the Inca empire? p. 276	12.3
What were the characteristic economic forms of American groups outside the two great imperial territories? p. 282	12.4

If you climbed the steep stairway to the temple at its summit and looked out from atop the great pyramid at its center, you could see that the splendid city of Tenochtitlan, capital of the Aztec Empire, rose from two islands in a large lake (Figure 12.1). All around its shores were densely settled towns and cities surrounded by cultivated fields. Canoes constantly traversed the lake and entered the city through a maze of canals, large crowds trod across the causeways that linked the city and its markets to the shores, and in some marshy areas, complex farming on "floating gardens" kept thousands of peasants at work. The Mexica or Tenocha people (sometimes called the Aztecs) who built the city considered it the "foundation of Heaven." For them it was a sacred space as well as a thriving metropolis and the heart of their empire.

FIGURE **12.1** The great Aztec city-state of Tenochtitlan was established on an island in the midst of a large lake. Connected to the shores by causeways, supplied with fresh water by an aqueduct, it housed a population estimated to be over 150,000. Early Spanish observers compared its canals to Venice and were fascinated by its markets and gardens. To the Aztecs it was the center of political and spiritual power, or as they called it, "the foundation of heaven."

265

Watch the Video Series on MyHistoryLab

Learn about some key topics related to this chapter with the *MyHistoryLab Video Series: Key Topics in World History*

When the first Europeans saw Tenochtitlan in 1520, the city had a population of over 150,000 and covered about 5 square miles, making it as large as contemporary Seville or Paris. The first Europeans who saw it were amazed. Some of them compared the city and its canals to Venice. Hernán Cortés, the Spanish captain who first entered the city, reported "the stone masonry and the woodwork are equally good; they could not be bettered anywhere." His companion, the foot soldier Bernal Díaz del Castillo, a man usually given to plain speech, could not hide his admiration:

> Gazing on such wonderful sights, we did not know what to say, or whether what appeared before us was real, for on one side, on the land, there were great cities, and in the lake ever many more, and the lake was crowded with canoes, and in the causeway were many bridges at intervals, and in front of us stood the great city of Mexico.

Díaz del Castillo went on to describe the palaces and temples, the two-storied homes of the nobles, the stuccoed buildings hung with garlands of flowers, the smell of the cedar wood beams, the zoo, the aviary, the rooftop gardens, and the bustling markets filled with everything from chocolate to elaborate textiles and from parrot feathers to precious stones and slaves. The hum of the crowd in the great market, he said, could be heard miles away. Of course, there was much about the city that he did not understand, such as the fact that each city ward was controlled by a kin group that cared for its temples, shrines, and palaces. Later, he came to understand that the purpose of temples was for ceremonies of human sacrifice, which he found appalling, but his overall impression was one of admiration and wonder.

Tenochtitlan, clearly a great urban center, was the largest of about 50 such city-states that dotted central and southern Mexico. They were the heirs of the long development of civilization in the Americas, a process that seems to have taken place in relative isolation from the other centers of world history. ■

Indians Misnomer created by Columbus referring to indigenous peoples of New World; implies social and ethnic commonality among Native Americans that did not exist; still used to apply to Native Americans.

By 1500, the Americas were densely populated in many places by peoples long indigenous to the New World. These peoples were later called **Indians**. That term of course, is derived from a mistake Columbus made when he thought he had reached the Indies, what Europeans called India and the lands beyond, but the label is also misleading because it implies a common identity among the peoples of the Americas that did not exist until after the arrival of Europeans. *Indian* as a term to describe all the peoples of the Americas could have a meaning only when there were non-Indians from which to distinguish them. Still, the term has been used for so long—and is still in use by many Native Americans today—that we will continue to use it along with the term *Native Americans* to describe the early peoples of the Americas.

As should already be clear, there were many different peoples with a vast array of cultural achievements. The variety of cultural patterns and ways of life of pre-Columbian civilizations makes it impossible to discuss each in detail here, but we can focus on a few areas where major civilizations developed, based on earlier achievements. By concentrating on these regions, we can demonstrate the continuity of civilization in the Americas. This chapter examines in some detail Mesoamerica, especially central Mexico, and the Andean heartland. In both these areas great imperial states were in place when European expansion brought them into direct contact with the Old World. Discussed

900 C.E.	1150 C.E.	1300 C.E.	1450 C.E.
900 End of intermediate horizon and decline of Tihuanaco and Huari **900–1465** Chimor Empire based on Chan-Chan on north coast of Peru **968** Tula established by Toltecs **1000** Toltec conquest of Chichén Itzá and influence in Yucatan	**1150** Fall of Tula, disintegration of Toltec Empire **1200–1500** Mississippian culture flourishes	**1325** Aztecs established in central Mexico; Tenochtitlan founded **1350** Incas established in Cuzco area **1434** Creation of triple alliance **1434–1471** Great expansion under Inca Pachacuti **1434–1472** Rule of Nezhualcoyotl at Texcoco **1438** Incas dominate Cuzco and southern highlands **1440–1469** Reign of Moctezuma I	**1471–1493** Inca Topac Yupanqui increases areas under control **1493–1527** Huayna Capac expands into Ecuador; his death results in civil war **1502–1520** Reign of Moctezuma II

in less detail are a few areas influenced by the centers of civilization—and some whose development seems to have been independent of them—to provide an overview of the Americas on the eve of invasion.

POSTCLASSIC MESOAMERICA, 1000–1500 C.E.

12.1 What were the main features of the Toltec and Aztec empires?

The Toltecs and later the Aztecs were the chief civilizations that followed the fall of Teotihuacan and the abandonment of the classic Maya cities in the 8th century C.E. These new civilizations built on the accomplishments of their predecessors but rarely surpassed them except in political and military organization.

With the collapse of Teotihuacan (tay-oh-tee-wah-KAHN) in central Mexico and the abandonment of the classical Maya cities in the 8th century C.E., Mesoamerica experienced significant political and cultural change. In central Mexico, nomadic peoples from the north took advantage of the political vacuum to move into the richer lands. Among these peoples were the Toltecs, who established a capital at Tula about 968. **Toltec culture** adopted many features from the sedentary peoples and added a strongly militaristic ethic. This included the cult of sacrifice and war that is often portrayed in Toltec art. Later Mesoamerican peoples, such as the Aztecs, had some historical memory of the Toltecs and thought of them as the givers of civilization. However, the archeological record indicates that Toltec accomplishments often were fused or confused with those of Teotihuacan in the memory of the Toltecs' successors.

The Toltec Heritage

Toltec culture Succeeded Teotihuacan culture in central Mexico; strongly militaristic ethic including human sacrifice; influenced large territory after 1000 C.E.; declined after 1200 C.E.

Among the legends that survived about the Toltecs were those of **Topiltzin**, a Toltec leader and apparently a priest dedicated to the god **Quetzalcoatl** (the Feathered Serpent) who later became confused with the god himself in the legends. Apparently, Topiltzin, a religious reformer, was involved in a struggle for priestly or political power with another faction. When he lost, Topiltzin and his followers went into exile, promising to return in the future to claim his throne on the same date, within the cyclical calendar system. Supposedly, Topiltzin and his followers sailed for Yucatan; there is much evidence of Toltec influence in that region. The legend of Topiltzin/Quetzalcoatl was well known to the Aztecs and may have influenced their response when the Europeans arrived.

 View the **Closer Look** on **MyHistoryLab:** The Pyramid of the Sun in Teotihuacan

Topiltzin [toh-PEYEL-tzihn] Religious leader and reformer of the Toltecs in 10th century; dedicated to god Quetzalcoatl; after losing struggle for power, went into exile in the Yucatan peninsula.

The Toltecs created an empire that extended over much of central Mexico, and their influence spread from their capital, Tula, to areas as far away as Guatemala (Figure 12.2). About 1000 C.E., Chichén Itzá (chee-CHEHN-eet-she) in Yucatan was conquered by Toltec warriors, and it and several other cities were ruled for a long time by central Mexican dynasties or by Maya rulers under Toltec influence.

Quetzalcoatl [keht-zahl-KOH-ah-tuhl] Toltec deity; Feathered Serpent; adopted by Aztecs as a major god.

Toltec influence spread northward as well. Obsidian was mined in northern Mexico, and the Toltecs may have traded for turquoise in the American Southwest. It has been suggested that the great Anasazi adobe town at Chaco Canyon in New Mexico was abandoned when the Toltec empire fell and the trade in local turquoise ended.

FIGURE 12.2 Toltec political and cultural influence spread from its capital at Tula in northern Mexico to places as far south as Chichén Itzá in Yucatan. The colossal statues of warriors shown here served as columns that supported the roof of a great temple.

View the Closer Look on MyHistoryLab: Cahokia

How far eastward Toltec influence spread is a matter of dispute. Was there contact between Mesoamerica and the elaborate culture and concentrated towns of the Hopewell peoples of the Ohio and Mississippi valleys? Scholars disagree. Eventually, in the lower Mississippi valley from about 700 C.E., elements of Hopewell culture seem to have been enriched by external contact, perhaps with Mexico. This Mississippian culture, which flourished between 1200 and 1500 C.E., was based on maize and bean agriculture that probably spread from Mexico. Towns, usually located along rivers, had stepped temples made of earth, and sometimes large burial mounds. Some of the burial sites include well-produced pottery and other goods, and some burials seem to have been accompanied by ritual executions or sacrifices of servants or wives. This indicates social stratification in the society. Cahokia, near East St. Louis, Illinois, covered 5 square miles and may have had more than 30,000 people in and around its center. Its largest earthen pyramid, now called Monk's Mound, covers 15 acres and is comparable in size to the largest pyramids of the classic period in Mexico. Many of these cultural features seem to suggest contact with Mesoamerica.

The Aztec Rise to Power

The Toltec empire lasted until about 1150, when it apparently was destroyed by nomadic invaders from the north, who also seem to have sacked Tula about that time. The center of population and political power in central Mexico shifted to the valley of Mexico and especially to the shores of the large chain of lakes in that basin. These provided a rich aquatic environment. The shores of the lakes were dotted with settlements and towns and supported a dense population. Of the approximately 3000 square miles in the basin of the valley, about 400 square miles were under water. The lakes became the cultural heartland and population center of Mexico in the postclassic period. In the unstable world of post-Toltec Mesoamerica, various peoples and cities jockeyed for control of the lakes. The winners of this struggle, the Aztecs—or, as they called themselves, the *Mexica*—eventually built a great empire, but when they first emerged on the historical scene, they were the most unlikely candidates for power.

The Aztec rise to power and formation of an imperial state was as spectacular as it was rapid. According to some of their legends, the Mexica had once inhabited the central valley and had known agriculture and the "civilized" life but had lived in exile to the north in a place called Aztlan (AZT-lahn) (from whence we get the name *Aztec*). This may be an exaggeration by people who wanted to lay claim to a distinguished heritage. Other sources indicate that the Aztecs were simply one of the nomadic tribes that used the political anarchy, after the fall of the Toltecs, to penetrate the area of sedentary agricultural peoples. Like the ancient Egyptians, the Aztecs rewrote history to suit their purposes.

What seems clear is that the Aztecs were a group of about 10,000 people who migrated to the shores of Lake Texcoco (Map 12.1) in the central valley of Mexico around 1325. After the fall of the Toltec empire, the central valley was inhabited by a mixture of peoples: Chichimec migrants from the northwest and various groups of sedentary farmers. In this period, the area around the lake was dominated by several tribes or peoples organized into city-states. Much like medieval Europe, this was a world of political maneuvers and state marriages, competing powers and shifting alliances. These political units claimed authority on the basis of their military power and their connections to Toltec culture. Many of these peoples spoke Nahuatl (NAH-wahtl), the language the Toltecs had spoken. The Aztecs also spoke this language, a fact that made their rise to power and their eventual claims to legitimacy more acceptable.

An intrusive and militant group, the Aztecs were distrusted and disliked by the dominant powers of the area, but their fighting skills could be put to use, and this made them attractive as mercenaries or allies. For about a century the Aztecs wandered around the shores of the lake, being allowed to settle for a while and then driven out by more powerful neighbors.

In a period of warfare, the Aztecs had a reputation as tough warriors and fanatical followers of their gods, to whom they offered human sacrifices. This reputation made them both valued and feared. Their own legends held that their wanderings would end when they saw an eagle perched on a cactus with a serpent in its beak. Supposedly, this sign was seen on a marshy island in Lake Texcoco, and there, on that island and one nearby, the Mexica settled. The city of **Tenochtitlan** was founded about 1325.

From this secure base the Aztecs began to take a more active role in regional politics. Serving as mercenaries and then as allies brought prosperity to the Aztecs, especially to their ruler and the warrior nobles, who took lands and tribute from conquered towns. By 1428, the Aztecs had emerged as an independent power. In 1434, Tenochtitlan created an alliance with two other city-states that controlled much of the central plateau. In reality, Tenochtitlan and the Aztecs dominated their allies and controlled the major share of the tribute and lands taken.

The Aztec Social Contract

Aztec domination extended from the Tarascan frontier about a hundred miles north of present-day Mexico City southward to the Maya area. Subject peoples were forced to pay tribute, surrender lands, and sometimes do military service for the growing Aztec empire.

Aztec society had changed in the process of expansion and conquest. From a loose association of clans, the Mexica had become a stratified society under the authority of a supreme ruler. The histories were rewritten and the Mexica were described as a people chosen to serve the gods. Human sacrifice, long a part of Mesoamerican religion, greatly expanded into an enormous cult in which the military class played a central role as suppliers of war captives to be used as sacrificial victims. A few territories were left unconquered so that periodic "flower wars" could be staged in which both sides could obtain captives for sacrifice. Whatever the religious motivations of this cult, the Aztec rulers manipulated it as an effective means of political terror. By the time of Moctezuma II, (1502–1520) the Aztec state was dominated by a king who represented civil power and served as a representative of the gods on earth. The cult of human sacrifice and conquest was united with the political power of the ruler and the nobility.

Religion and the Ideology of Conquest

Aztec religion incorporated many features that had long been part of the Mesoamerican belief system. Religion was a vast, uniting, and sometimes oppressive force in which little distinction was made between the world of the gods and the natural world. The traditional deities of Mesoamerica—the gods of rain, fire, water, corn, the sky, and the sun, many of whom had been worshiped as far back as the time of Teotihuacan—were venerated among the Aztecs. There were at least 128 major deities, but there seemed to be many more: As in popular Hinduism each deity had a male and female form, because a basic duality was recognized in all things. Moreover, gods might have different manifestations, somewhat like the avatars of the Hindu deities. Each god had at least five aspects, each associated with one of the cardinal directions and the center. Certain gods were thought to be the patrons of specific cities, ethnic groups, or occupations.

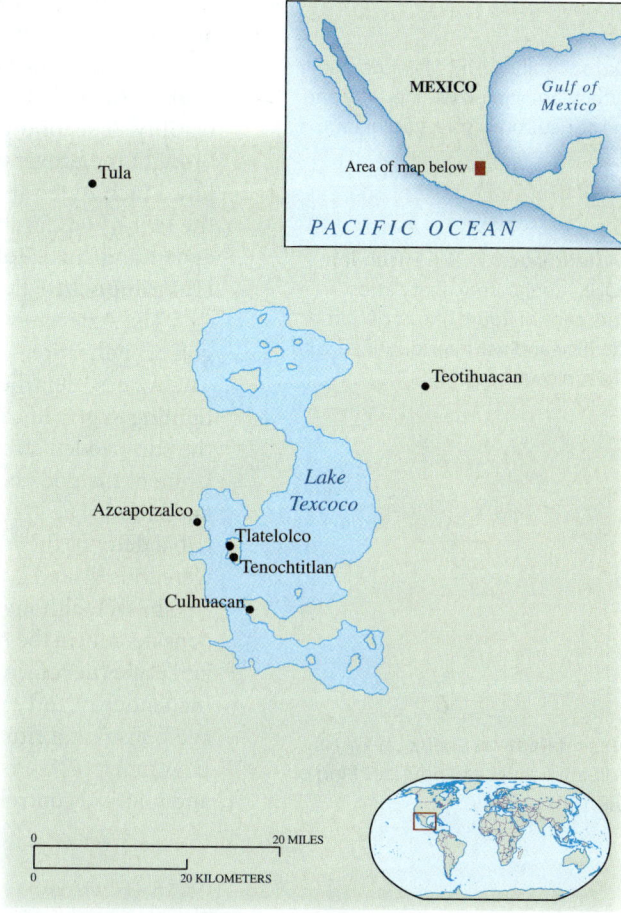

MAP 12.1 **Central Mexico and Lake Texcoco** An aquatic environment at the heart of the Aztec empire.

Tenochtitlan [teh-nahk-teet-LAHN] Founded c. 1325 on marshy island in Lake Texcoco; became center of Aztec power; joined with Tlacopan and Texcoco in 1434 to form a triple alliance that controlled most of central plateau of Mesoamerica.

Tlaloc [tlah-LOHK] Major god of Aztecs; associated with fertility and the agricultural cycle; god of rain.

Huitzilopochtli [WEE-tsuh-loh-POHKT-lee] Aztec tribal patron god; central figure of cult of human sacrifice and warfare; identified with old sun god.

Nezhualcoyotl [nehz-uh-WAHL-koh-YOH-tihl] Leading Aztec king of the 15th century.

The gods were supported by a round of yearly festivals and ceremonies that involved feasting and dancing along with penance and sacrifice. This complex array of deities can be organized into three major themes or cults. The first were the gods of fertility and the agricultural cycle, such as **Tlaloc**, the god of rain (called *Chac* by the Maya), and the gods and goddesses of water, maize, and fertility. A second group centered on the creator deities, the great gods and goddesses who had brought the universe into being. The story of their actions played a central role in Aztec cosmography. Much Aztec abstract and philosophical thought was devoted to the theme of creation. Finally, the cult of warfare and sacrifice built on the preexisting Mesoamerican traditions that had been expanding since Toltec times and, under the militaristic Aztec state, became the cult of the state. **Huitzilopochtli**, the Aztec tribal patron, became the central figure of this cult.

The Aztecs revered the great traditional deities—such as Tlaloc and Quetzalcoatl, the ancient god of civilization—so holy to the Toltecs, but their own tribal deity, Huitzilopochtli, was paramount. The Aztecs identified him with the old sun god, and they saw him as a warrior in the daytime sky fighting to give life and warmth to the world against the forces of the night. To carry out that struggle, the sun needed strength, and just as the gods had sacrificed themselves for humankind, the nourishment the gods needed most was that which was most precious: human life in the form of hearts and blood. The great temple of Tenochtitlan was dedicated to both Huitzilopochtli and Tlaloc. The tribal deity of the Aztecs and the ancient agricultural god of the sedentary peoples of Mesoamerica were thus united.

In fact, although human sacrifice had long been a part of Mesoamerican religion, it expanded considerably in the postclassic period of militarism. Warrior cults and the militaristic images of jaguars and eagles devouring human hearts were characteristic of Toltec art. The Aztecs simply took an existing tendency and carried it further. Both the types and frequency of sacrifice increased, and a whole symbolism and ritual, which included ritual cannibalism, developed as part of the cult (Figure 12.3). How much of Aztec sacrifice was the result of religious conviction and how much was a tactic of terror and political control by the rulers and priests is still open to debate.

Beneath the surface of this polytheism, there was also a sense of spiritual unity. **Nezhualcoyotl**, the king of Texcoco, wrote hymns to the "lord of the close vicinity," an invisible creative force that supported all the gods. Yet his conception of a kind of monotheism, much like that of Pharaoh Akhenaton in Egypt, appears to have been too abstract and never gained great popularity.

Although the bloody aspects of Aztec religion have gained much attention, we must also realize that the Aztecs concerned themselves with many of the same great religious and spiritual questions that have preoccupied other civilizations: Is there life after death? What is the meaning of life? What does it mean to live a good life? Do the gods really exist?

Nezhualcoyotl, whose poetry survived in oral form and was written down in the 16th century, wondered about life after death:

> Do flowers go to the land of the dead?
> In the Beyond, are we dead or do we still live?
> Where is the source of light, since that which gives life hides itself?

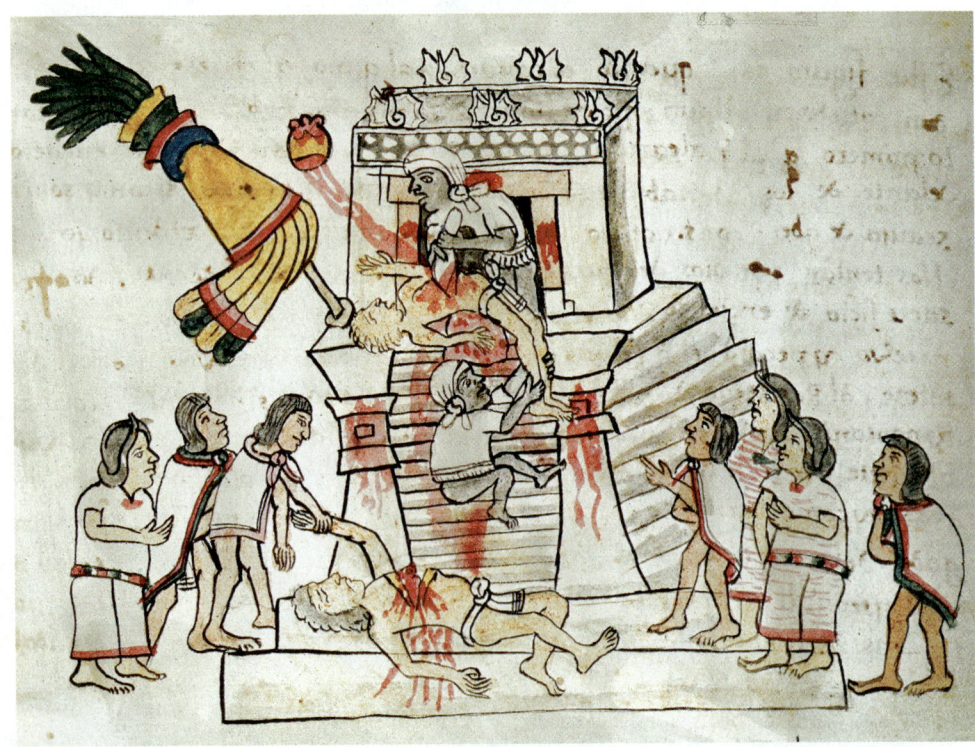

FIGURE 12.3 Human sacrifice was practiced by many Mesoamerican peoples, but the Aztecs apparently expanded its practice for political and religious reasons. This image shows Aztec priests cutting out their victims' hearts and then rolling the bodies down the steps of the pyramid.
(Ms. Magliabechiano: sacrificio umano azteco. Biblioteca Nazionale Firenze. Scala/Art Resource, NY.)

As in the Vedas of ancient India, he also wondered about the existence of the gods:

> Are you real, are you fixed?
> Only You dominate all things
> The Giver of Life.
> Is this true?
> Perhaps, as they say, it is not true.

Aztec religious art and poetry are filled with images of flowers, birds, and song, all of which the Aztecs greatly admired, as well as human hearts and blood, the "precious water" needed to sustain the gods. This mixture of images makes the symbolism of Aztec religion difficult for modern observers to appreciate.

Aztec religion depended on a complex mythology that explained the birth and history of the gods and their relationship to peoples, and on a religious symbolism that infused all aspects of life. As we have seen, the Mesoamerican calendar system was religious, and many ceremonies coincided with particular points in the calendar cycle (Figure 12.4). Moreover, the Aztecs also believed in a cyclical view of history, and that the world had been destroyed four times before and would be destroyed again. Thus, there was a certain fatalism in Aztec thought and a premonition that eventually the sacrifices would be insufficient and the gods would again bring catastrophe.

FIGURE 12.4 This Aztec stone calendar is about 12 feet across and 4 feet thick, and it weighs about 24 tons. It was unearthed accidentally by construction crews in Mexico City in 1790.

Feeding the People: The Economy of the Empire

Feeding the great population of Tenochtitlan and the Aztec confederation in general depended on traditional forms of agriculture and on innovations developed by the Aztecs. Lands of conquered peoples often were appropriated, and food sometimes was demanded as tribute. In and around the lake, however, the Aztecs adopted an ingenious system of irrigated agriculture by building **chinampas** for agriculture. These were beds of aquatic weeds, mud, and earth that had been placed in frames made of cane and rooted to the lake floor. They formed artificial floating islands about 17 feet long and 100 to 330 feet wide. This narrow construction allowed the water to reach all the plants, and willow trees were also planted at intervals to give shade and help fix the roots. Much of the land of Tenochtitlan itself was chinampa in origin, and in the southern end of the lake, more than 20,000 acres of chinampas were constructed. The yield from chinampa agriculture was high: Four corn crops a year were possible. Apparently, this system of irrigated agriculture had been used in preclassic days, but a rise in the level of the lakes had made it impossible to continue. After 1200, however, lowering water levels once again stimulated chinampa construction, which the Aztecs carried out on a grand scale.

chinampas Beds of aquatic weeds, mud, and earth placed in frames made of cane and rooted in lakes to create "floating islands"; system of irrigated agriculture utilized by Aztecs.

Production by the Aztec peasantry and tribute provided the basic foods. In each Aztec community, the local clan apportioned the lands, some of which were also set aside for support of the temples and the state. In addition, individual nobles might have private estates, which were worked by servants or slaves from conquered peoples. Each community had periodic markets—according to various cycles in the calendar system, such as every 5 and 13 days—in which a wide variety of goods were exchanged. Cacao beans and gold dust sometimes were used as currency, but much trade was done as barter. The great market at Tlatelolco (TLAT-ehl-UHL-koh) operated daily and was controlled by the special merchant class, or **pochteca**, which specialized in long-distance trade in luxury items such as plumes of tropical birds and cacao. The markets were highly regulated and under the control of inspectors and special judges. Despite the importance of markets, this was not a market economy as we usually understand it.

pochteca [pahk-TEHK-uh] Special merchant class in Aztec society; specialized in long-distance trade in luxury items.

CHAPTER 12 The Americas on the Eve of Invasion 271

The state controlled the use and distribution of many commodities and redistributed the vast amounts of tribute received from subordinate peoples. Tribute levels were assigned according to whether the subject peoples had accepted Aztec rule or had fought against it. Those who surrendered paid less. Tribute payments, such as food, slaves, and sacrificial victims, served political and economic ends. More than 120,000 mantles of cotton cloth alone were collected as tribute each year and sent to Tenochtitlan. The Aztec state redistributed these goods. After the original conquests, it rewarded its nobility richly, and the commoners received far less.

AZTEC SOCIETY IN TRANSITION

12.2 What were the principal strengths and constraints of the Aztec economy?

> Aztec society became more hierarchical as the empire grew and social classes with different functions developed, although the older organization based on clans and kinship groups never disappeared. Tribute was drawn from subject peoples, but Aztec society confronted technological barriers that made it difficult to maintain the large population of central Mexico.

Like all societies, Aztec society experienced changes over time. The Mexica were one of a number of peoples who spoke the Nahuatl language and occupied the region of central Mexico. From their humble origins as hunters and gatherers they emerged as a dominant power, and their rise created opportunities for some groups and a loss of status for others within their society. Eventually, they held sway over the 50 or so political units of the central valley of Mexico. Expansion by warfare privileged the warriors, and the religious basis for expansion made the priests and the cults of the temples a force in society. No ruler could govern without the support of these sectors of society, a support obtained and preserved by giving out rewards and benefits. But such policies transformed the nature of Aztec society.

A Widening Social Gulf

calpulli [kal-PUHL-lee] Clans in Aztec society, later expanded to include residential groups that distributed land and provided labor and warriors.

During their wanderings, the Aztecs had been divided into seven **calpulli**, or clans, a form of organization that they later expanded and adapted to their imperial position. The calpulli were no longer only kinship groups but also residential groupings, which might include neighbors, allies, and dependants. Much of Aztec local life was based on the calpulli, which performed important functions such as distributing land to heads of households, organizing labor gangs and military units in times of war, and maintaining a temple and school. Calpulli were governed by councils of family heads, but not all families were equal, nor were all calpulli of equal status.

The calpulli obviously had been the ancient and basic building block of Aztec society. In the origins of Aztec society every person, noble, and commoner had belonged to a calpulli but as Aztec power increased, the calpulli had been transformed, and other forms of social stratification had emerged. As the empire expanded, a class of nobility emerged, based on certain privileged families in the most distinguished calpulli. Originating from the lineages that headed calpulli and from marriages, military achievements, or service to the state, this group of nobles accumulated high offices, private lands, and other advantages. The most prominent families in the calpulli, those who had dominated leadership roles and formed a kind of local nobility, eventually were overshadowed by the military and administrative nobility of the Aztec state.

Although some commoners might be promoted to noble status, most nobles were born into the class. Nobles controlled the priesthood and the military leadership. In fact, the military was organized into various ranks based on experience and success in taking captives (Figure 12.5). Military virtues were linked to the cult of sacrifice and infused the whole society; they became the justification for the nobility's status. The "flowery death," or death while taking prisoners for the sacrificial knife, was the fitting end to a noble life and ensured eternity in the highest heaven—a reward also promised to women who died in childbirth. The military was highly ritualized. There were orders of warriors: The Jaguar and Eagle "Knights" and other groups each had a distinctive uniform and ritual and fought together as units. Banners, cloaks, and other insignia marked off the military ranks.

The social gulf that separated the nobility, or *pipiltin* from the commoners was widening as the empire grew. Egalitarian principles that may have existed in Aztec life disappeared, as happened among the warring Germanic tribes of early medieval Europe. Social distinctions were made apparent by the use of and restrictions on clothing, hairstyles, uniforms, and other symbols of rank. The imperial family became the most distinguished of the pipiltin families.

As the nobility broke free from their old calpulli and acquired private lands, a new class of workers almost like serfs was created to serve as laborers on these lands. Unlike the commoners attached to the land-controlling calpulli, these workers did not control land and worked at the will of others. Their status was low, but it was still above that of the slaves, who might have been war captives, criminals, or people who had sold themselves into bondage to escape hunger. Finally, there were other social groups. The scribes, artisans, and healers all were part of an intermediate group that was especially important in the larger cities. The long-distance merchants formed a sort of calpulli with their own patron gods, privileges, and internal divisions. They sometimes served as spies or agents for the Aztec military, but they were subject to restrictions that hindered their entry into or rivalry with the nobility.

It is possible to see an emerging conflict between the nobility and the commoners and to interpret this as a class struggle, but some specialists emphasize that to interpret Aztec society on that basis is to impose Western concepts on a different reality. Corporate bodies such as the calpulli, temple maintenance associations, and occupational groups cut across class and remained important in Aztec life. Competition between corporate groups often was more apparent and more violent than competition between social classes.

Overcoming Technological Constraints

Membership in society was thus defined by participation in various wider groups, such as the calpulli or a specific social class. It was also defined by gender roles. Aztec women assumed a variety of roles. Peasant women helped in the fields, but their primary domain was the household, where child-rearing and cooking took up much time. Above all, weaving skill was highly regarded. The responsibility for training young girls fell on the older women. Marriages often were arranged between lineages, and virginity at marriage was highly regarded for young women. Polygamy existed among the nobility, but the peasants were monogamous. Aztec women could inherit property and pass it to their heirs. The rights of Aztec women seem to have been fully recognized, but in political and social life their role, although complementary to that of men, remained subordinate.

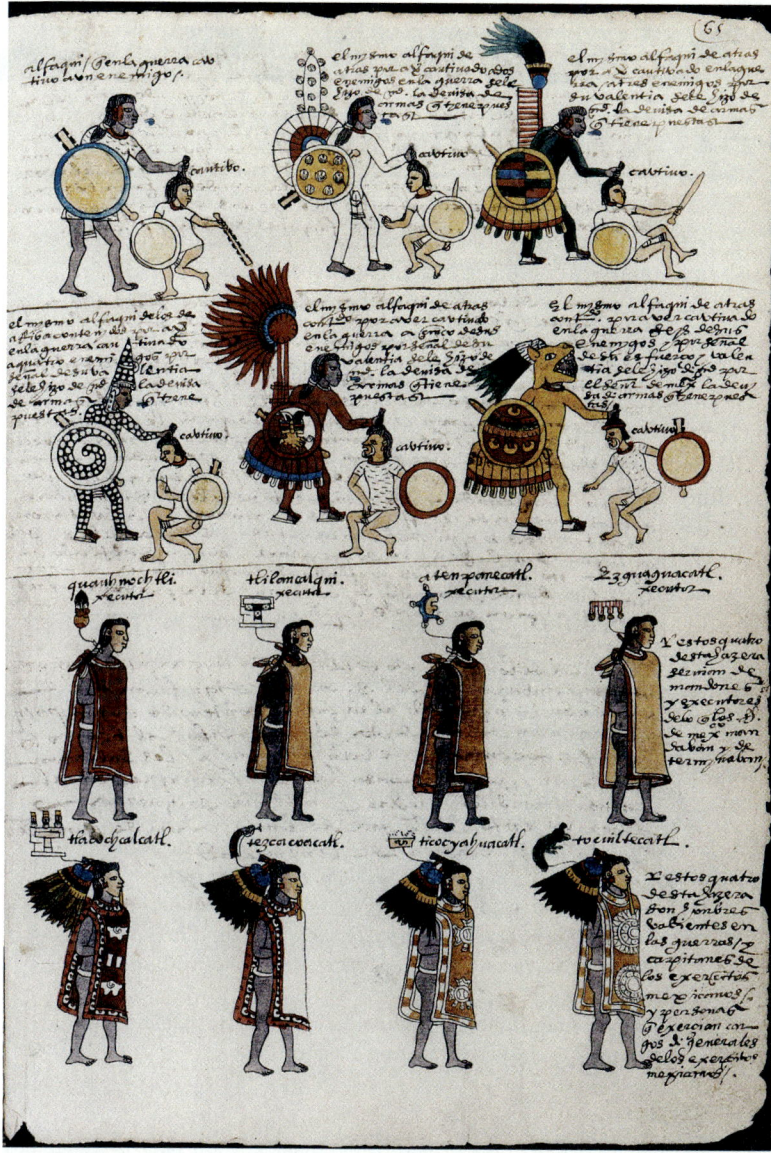

FIGURE **12.5** In the militarized society of the Aztec empire, warriors were organized into regiments and groups distinguished by their uniforms. They gained rank and respect by capturing enemies for sacrifice. Note the symbolic gripping of the defeated captives' hair as a sign of military success.

The technology of the Americas limited social development in a variety of ways. Here we can see a significant difference between the lives of women in Mesoamerica and in the Mediterranean world. In the maize-based economies of Mesoamerica, women spent six hours a day grinding corn by hand on stone boards, or *metates*, to prepare the household's food. Although similar hand techniques were used in ancient Egypt, they were eventually replaced by animal- or water-powered mills that turned wheat into flour. The miller or baker of Rome or medieval Europe could do the work of hundreds of women. Maize was among the simplest and most productive cereals to grow but among the most time-consuming to prepare. Without the wheel or suitable animals for power, the Indian civilizations were unable to free women from the 30 to 40 hours a week that went into preparing the basic food.

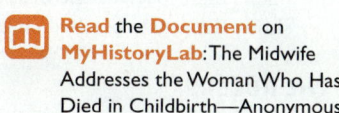 Read the Document on MyHistoryLab: The Midwife Addresses the Woman Who Has Died in Childbirth—Anonymous

Finally, we must consider the size of the population of the Aztec state. Estimates have varied widely, from as little as 1.5 million to more than 25 million, but there is considerable evidence that population density was high, resulting in a total population that was far greater than previously

CHAPTER 12 The Americas on the Eve of Invasion **273**

DOCUMENT

Aztec Women and Men

IN THE MID-16TH CENTURY, BERNARDINO DE Sahagún, a Spanish missionary, prepared an extraordinary encyclopedia of Aztec culture. His purpose was to gather this information to learn the customs and beliefs of the Indians and their language in order to better convert them. Although Sahagún hated the Indian religion, he came to admire many aspects of their culture. His *Florentine Codex: The General History of the Things of New Spain* is one of the first ethnographies and a remarkable compendium of Aztec culture. Sahagún used many Indian informants to tell him about the days before the European arrival, and even though this work dates from the postconquest era, it contains much useful information about earlier Aztec life.

In the following excerpts, the proper behavior for people in different roles in Aztec society are described by the Aztecs themselves.

FATHER

One's father is the source of lineage. He is the sincere one. One's father is diligent, solicitous, compassionate, sympathetic, a careful administrator of his household. He rears, he teaches others, he advises, he admonishes one. He is exemplary; he leads a model life. He stores up for himself; he stores up for others. He cares for his assets; he saves for others. He is thrifty; he saves for the future, teaches thrift. He regulates, distributes with care, establishes order.

The bad father is incompassionate, negligent, unreliable. He is unfeeling . . . a shirker, a loafer, a sullen worker.

MOTHER

One's mother has children; she suckles them. Sincere, vigilant, agile, she is an energetic worker—diligent, watchful, solicitous, full of anxiety. She teaches people; she is attentive to them. She caresses, she serves others; she is apprehensive for their welfare; she is careful, thrifty—constantly at work.

The bad mother is evil, dull, stupid, sleepy, lazy. She is a squanderer, a petty thief, a deceiver, a fraud. Unreliable, she is one who loses things through neglect or anger, who heeds no one. She is disrespectful, inconsiderate, disregarding, careless. She shows the way to disobedience; she expounds nonconformity.

THE RULERS

The ruler is a shelter—fierce, revered, famous, esteemed, well-reputed, renowned.

The good ruler is a protector: one who carries his subjects in his arms, who unites them, who brings them together. He rules, he takes responsibilities, assumes burdens. He carries his subjects in his cape; he bears them in his arms. He governs; he is obeyed. To him as a shelter, as refuge, there is recourse. . . .

The bad ruler is a wild beast, a demon of the air, an ocelot, a wolf—infamous, avoided, detested as a respecter of nothing. He terrifies with his gaze; he makes the earth rumble; he implants; he spreads fear. He is wished dead.

THE NOBLE

The noble has a mother, a father. He resembles his parents. The good noble is obedient, cooperative, a follower of his parents' ways, a discreet worker; attentive, willing. He follows the ways of his parents; he resembles his father; he becomes his father's successor; he assumes his lot.

One of noble lineage is a follower of the exemplary life, a taker of the good example of others, a seeker, a follower of the exemplary life. He speaks eloquently; he is soft-spoken, virtuous, deserving of gratitude. He is noble of heart, gentle of word, discreet, well-reared, well-taught. He is moderate, energetic, inquiring, inquisitive. He scratches the earth with a thorn. He is one who fasts, who starves his entrails, who parches his lips. He provides nourishment to others. He sustains one, he serves food, he provides comfort. He is a concealer [of himself], a belittler of himself. He magnifies and praises others. He is a mourner for the dead, a doer of penances, a gracious speaker, devout, godly, desirable, wanted, memorable.

The bad noble is ungrateful and forgetful, a debaser, a disparager of things, contemptuous of others, arrogant, bragging. He creates disorder, glories over his lineage, extols his own virtues.

THE MATURE COMMON WOMAN

The good mature woman is candid. She is resolute, firm of heart, constant—not to be dismayed; brave like a man; vigorous, resolute, persevering—not one to falter. She is long-suffering; she accepts reprimands calmly—endures things like a man. She becomes firm—takes courage. She is intent. She gives of herself. She goes in humility. She exerts herself.

The bad woman is thin, tottering, weak—an inconstant companion, unfriendly. She annoys others, chagrins them, shames, oppresses one. She becomes impatient; she loses hope, becomes embarrassed—chagrined. Evil is her life; she lives in shame.

THE WEAVER OF DESIGNS

She concerns herself with using thread, works with thread. The good weaver of designs is skilled—a maker of varicolored capes, an outliner of designs, a blender of colors, a joiner of pieces, a matcher of pieces, a person of good memory. She does things dexterously. She weaves designs. She selects. She weaves tightly. She forms borders. She forms the neck. . . .

The bad weaver of designs is untrained—silly, foolish, unobservant, unskilled of hand, ignorant, stupid. She tangles the thread, she harms her work—she spoils it.

(continued on next page)

THE PHYSICIAN

The physician is a knower of herbs, of roots, of trees, of stones; she is experienced in these. She is one who conducts examinations; she is a woman of experience, of trust, of professional skill: a counselor.

The good physician is a restorer, a provider of health, a relaxer—one who makes people feel well, who envelops one in ashes. She cures people; she provides them health; she lances them; she bleeds them . . . pierces them with an obsidian lancet.

QUESTIONS

- In what ways do the expectations for men and women differ in Aztec society?
- To what extent do the roles for men and women in Aztec society differ from our own?
- Did the Aztecs value the same characteristics as our own and other historical societies?

suspected. Some historical demographers estimate that the population of central Mexico under Aztec control reached over 20 million, excluding the Maya areas. This underlines the extraordinary ability of the Aztec state to intimidate and control such vast numbers of people.

A Tribute Empire

Each city-state was ruled by a speaker chosen from the nobility. The Great Speaker, the ruler of Tenochtitlan, was first among supposed equals. He was in effect the emperor, with great private wealth and public power, and was increasingly considered a living god. His court was magnificent and surrounded with elaborate rituals. Those who approached him could not look him in the eye and were required to throw dirt upon their heads as a sign of humility. In theory he was elected, but his election was really a choice between siblings of the same royal family. The prime minister held a position of tremendous power and usually was a close relative of the ruler. There was a governing council; in theory, the rulers of the other cities in the alliance also had a say in government, but in reality most power was in the hands of the Aztec ruler and his chief advisor.

During the century of greatest Aztec expansion after 1426, a social and political transformation had taken place. The position and nature of the old calpulli clans had changed radically, and a newly powerful nobility with a deified and nearly absolute ruler had emerged. The ancient cult of military virtues had been elevated to a supreme position as the religion of the state, and the double purpose of securing tribute for the state and obtaining victims for Huitzilopochtli drove further Aztec conquests.

The empire was never integrated, and local rulers often stayed in place to act as tribute collectors for the Aztec overlords. In many ways the Aztec empire was simply an expansion of long-existing Mesoamerican concepts and institutions of government, and it was not unlike the subject city-states over which it gained control. These city-states, in turn, were often left unchanged if they recognized Aztec supremacy and met their obligations of labor and tribute. Tribute payments served both an economic and a political function, concentrating power and wealth in the Aztec capital. Archeologists at the recent excavations of the Great Temple beneath the center of Mexico City have been impressed by the large number of offerings and objects that came from the farthest ends of the empire and beyond. At the frontiers, neighboring states such as that of the Tarascans of Michoacan in West Central Mexico preserved their freedom, while within the empire enclaves of independent kingdoms such as Tlaxcala (tlaks-KAHL-uh) maintained a fierce opposition to the Aztecs. There were many revolts against Aztec rule or a particular tribute burden, which the Aztecs often put down ruthlessly.

In general, the Aztec system was a success because it aimed at exerting political domination and not necessarily direct administrative or territorial control. In the long run, however, the increasing social stresses created by the rise of the nobles and the system of terror and tribute imposed on subject peoples were internal weaknesses that contributed to the Aztec empire's collapse.

The Aztecs were a continuation of the long process of civilization in Mesoamerica. The civilizations of the classic era did not simply disappear in central Mexico or among the Maya in Yucatan and Central America, but they were reinterpreted and adapted to new political and social realities. When Europeans arrived in Mexico, they assumed that what they found was the culmination of Indian civilization, when in fact it was the militarized afterglow of earlier achievements.

TWANTINSUYU: WORLD OF THE INCAS

After about 1300 C.E., the Inca empire emerged in the highlands of Peru and eventually spread its control over the whole region by integrating many ethnic groups into an extensive imperial state.

12.3 What were the principal causes of the expansion of the Inca empire?

Almost at the same time that the Aztecs extended their control over much of Mesoamerica, a great imperial state was rising in the Andean highlands, and it eventually became an empire some 3000 miles in extent (Map 12.2). The Inca empire incorporated many aspects of previous Andean cultures but fused them together in new ways. With a genius for state organization and bureaucratic control over peoples of different cultures and languages, it achieved a level of integration and domination previously unknown in the Americas.

Throughout the Andean cultural hearth, after the breakup of the large "intermediate horizon" states of Tihuanaco and Huari (c. 550–1000 C.E.), several smaller regional states continued to exercise some power. Unlike the breakdown of power that took place in postclassic Mesoamerica, in the Andean zone many large states continued to be important. Some states in the Andean highlands on the broad open areas near Lake Titicaca and the states along rivers on the north coast, such as those in the Moche valley, remained centers of agricultural activity and population density. This was a period of war between rival local chiefdoms and small states and in some ways was an Andean parallel to the post-Toltec militaristic era in Mesoamerica. Of these states, the coastal kingdom of Chimor, centered on its capital of Chan-Chan, emerged as the most powerful. Between 900 and its conquest by the Incas in 1465, it gained control of most of the north coast of Peru.

Pachacuti [PACH-uh-KOO-tee] Ruler of Inca society from 1438 to 1471; launched a series of military campaigns that gave Incas control of the region from Cuzco to the shores of Lake Titicaca.

ayllus [EYEL-lehs] Households in Andean societies that recognized some form of kinship; traced descent from some common, sometimes mythical ancestor.

The Inca Rise to Power

While Chimor spread its control over 600 miles of the coast, in the southern Andean highlands, where there were few large urban areas, ethnic groups and small states struggled over the legacy of Tihuanaco. Among these groups were several related Quechua-speaking clans, or **ayllus**, living near Cuzco, an area that had been under the influence of Huari but had not been particularly important. Their own legends stated that 10 related clans emerged from caves in the region and were taken to Cuzco by a mythical leader. Wherever their origins, by about 1350 C.E. they lived in and around Cuzco, and by 1438 they had defeated their hostile neighbors in the area. At this point under their ruler, or *inca*, **Pachacuti** (r. 1438–1471), they launched a series of military alliances and campaigns that brought them control of the whole area from Cuzco to the shores of Lake Titicaca.

Over the next 60 years, Inca armies were constantly on the march, extending control over a vast territory. Pachacuti's son and successor, Topac Yupanqui (TOH-pak YUH-pan-KEE), conquered the northern coastal kingdom of Chimor by seizing its irrigation system, and he extended Inca control into the southern area of what is now Ecuador. At the other end of the empire, Inca armies reached the Maule River in Chile against stiff resistance from the Araucanian Indians. The next ruler, Huayna Capac (WEYE-nah kah-PAHK) (r. 1493–1527), consolidated these conquests and suppressed rebellions on the frontiers. By the time of his death, the Inca Empire—or, as they called it, **Twantinsuyu**—stretched from what is now Colombia to Chile and eastward across Lake Titicaca and Bolivia to northern Argentina. Between 9 and 13 million people of different ethnic backgrounds and languages came under Inca rule, a remarkable feat, given the extent of the empire and the technology available for transportation and communication.

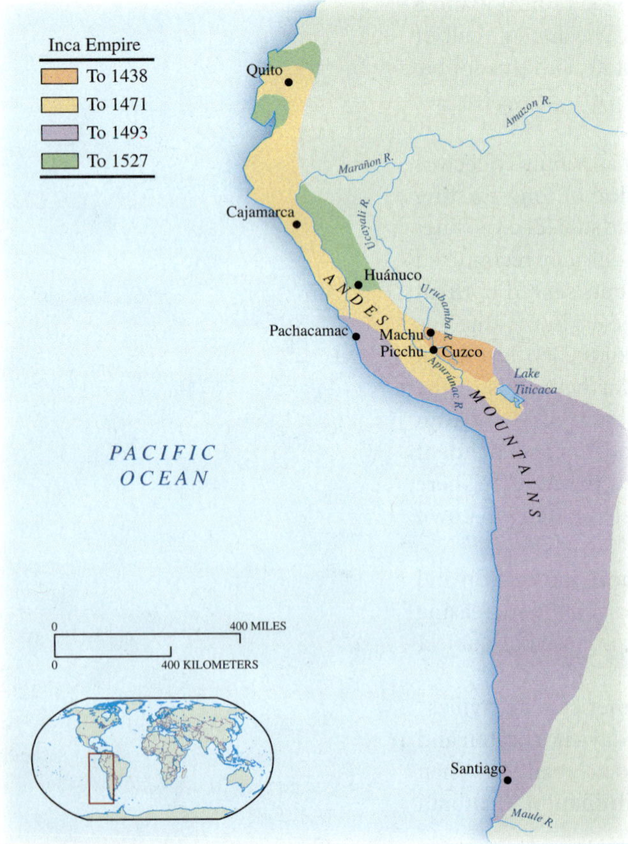

Conquest and Religion

What impelled the Inca conquest and expansion? The usual desire for economic gain and political power that we have seen in other empires is one possible explanation, but there may be others more in keeping with Inca culture and ideology. The cult of the ancestors was extremely important in Inca belief. Deceased rulers were mummified and then treated as intermediaries

MAP 12.2 **Inca Expansion** Each ruler expanded the empire in a series of campaigns to increase wealth and political control.

VISUALIZING THE PAST

Archeological Evidence of Political Practices

THE INCA SYSTEM OF SPLIT INHERITANCE probably originated in the Chimu kingdom. Chimu king lists recorded 10 rulers' names. Excavations at Chan-Chan, the Chimu capital, have revealed 10 large walled structures. Archeologists believe that each of these palatial compounds was a different king's residence and that each became a mausoleum for his mummy upon his death.

QUESTIONS
- To what extent does such evidence indicate the composite nature of Inca culture?
- What are some of the possible problems of archeological interpretation?
- To what extent can material remains be used to explain or illustrate social phenomena?

City of Chan-Chan.

Chan-Chan covered more than 2 square miles. It contained palace compounds, storehouses, residences, markets, and other structures.

---

with the gods, paraded in public during festivals, offered food and gifts, and consulted on important matters by special oracles. From the Chimor kingdom the Incas adopted the practice of royal **split inheritance**, whereby all the political power and titles of the ruler went to his successor but all his palaces, wealth, land, and possessions remained in the hands of his male descendants, who used them to support the cult of the dead Inca's mummy for eternity. To ensure his own cult and place for eternity, each new Inca needed to secure land and wealth, and these normally came as part of new conquests. In effect, the greater the number of past rulers, the greater the number of royal courts to support, and the greater the demand for labor, lands, and tribute. This system created a self-perpetuating need for expansion, tied directly to ancestor worship and the cult of the royal mummies, as well as tensions between the various royal lineages. The cult of the dead weighed heavily on the living.

Twantinsuyu [twahn-tihn-SOO-yoo] Word for Inca empire; region from present-day Colombia to Chile and eastward to northern Argentina.

split inheritance Inca practice of descent; all titles and political power went to successor, but wealth and land remained in hands of male descendants for support of cult of dead Inca's mummy.

CHAPTER 12 The Americas on the Eve of Invasion 277

Temple of the Sun Inca religious center located at Cuzco; center of state religion; held mummies of past Incas.

Inca political and social life was infused with religious meaning. Like the Aztecs, the Incas held the sun to be the highest deity and considered the Inca to be the sun's representative on earth. The magnificent **Temple of the Sun** in Cuzco was the center of the state religion, and in its confines the mummies of the past Incas were kept. The cult of the sun was spread throughout the empire, but the Incas did not prohibit the worship of local gods.

Other deities were also worshiped as part of the state religion. Viracocha (vee-reh-KOH-chuh), a creator god, was a favorite of Inca Pachacuti and remained important. Popular belief was based on a profound animism that endowed many natural phenomena with spiritual power. Mountains, stones, rivers, caves, tombs, and temples were considered *huacas*, or holy shrines. At these places, prayers were offered and animals, goods, and humans were sacrificed. In the Cuzco area, imaginary lines running from the Temple of the Sun organized the huacas into groups for which certain ayllus took responsibility. The temples were served by many priests and women dedicated to preparing cloth and food for sacrifice. The temple priests were responsible mainly for the great festivals and celebrations and for the divinations on which state actions often depended.

The Techniques of Inca Imperial Rule

The Inca were able to control their vast empire by using techniques and practices that ensured cooperation or subordination. The empire was ruled by the Inca, who was considered almost a god. He ruled from his court at Cuzco, which was also the site of the major temple; the high priest usually was a close relative. Twantinsuyu was divided into four great provinces, each under a governor, and then divided again. The Incas developed a state bureaucracy in which almost all nobles played a role. Although some chroniclers spoke of a state organization based on decimal units of 10,000, 1000, 100, and smaller numbers of households to mobilize taxes and labor, recent research reveals that many local practices and variations were allowed to continue under Inca rule. Local rulers, or *curacas*, were allowed to maintain their positions and were given privileges by the Inca in return for their loyalty. The curacas were exempt from tribute obligations and usually received labor or produce from those under their control. For insurance, the sons of conquered chieftains were taken to Cuzco for their education.

tambos Way stations used by Incas as inns and storehouses; supply centers for Inca armies on the move; relay points for system of runners used to carry messages.

mita Labor extracted for lands assigned to the state and the religion; all communities were expected to contribute; an essential aspect of Inca imperial control.

The Incas intentionally spread the Quechua (KEHCH-uh-wah) language as a means of integrating the empire. The Incas also made extensive use of colonists. Sometimes Quechua-speakers from Cuzco were settled in a newly won area to provide an example and a garrison. On other occasions, the Incas moved a conquered population to a new home. Throughout the empire, a complex system of roads was built, with bridges and causeways when needed (Map 12.3). Along these roads, way stations, or **tambos**, were placed about a day's walk apart to serve as inns, storehouses, and supply centers for Inca armies on the move. Tambos also served as relay points for the system of runners who carried messages throughout the empire. The Inca probably maintained more than 10,000 tambos.

The Inca empire extracted land and labor from subject populations. Conquered peoples were enlisted in the Inca armies under Inca officers and were rewarded with goods from new conquests. Subject peoples received access to goods not previously available to them, and the Inca state undertook large building and irrigation projects that formerly would have been impossible. In return, the Incas demanded loyalty and tribute. The state claimed all resources and redistributed them. The Incas divided conquered areas into lands for the people, lands for the state, and lands for the sun—that is, for religion and the support of priests. Also, some nobles held private estates.

With few exceptions the Incas, unlike the Aztecs, did not demand tribute in kind but rather exacted labor on the lands assigned to the state and the religion. Communities were expected to take turns working on state and church lands and sometimes on building projects or in mining. These labor turns, or **mita**, were an essential aspect of Inca control. In addition, the Inca required women to weave high-quality cloth for the court and for religious

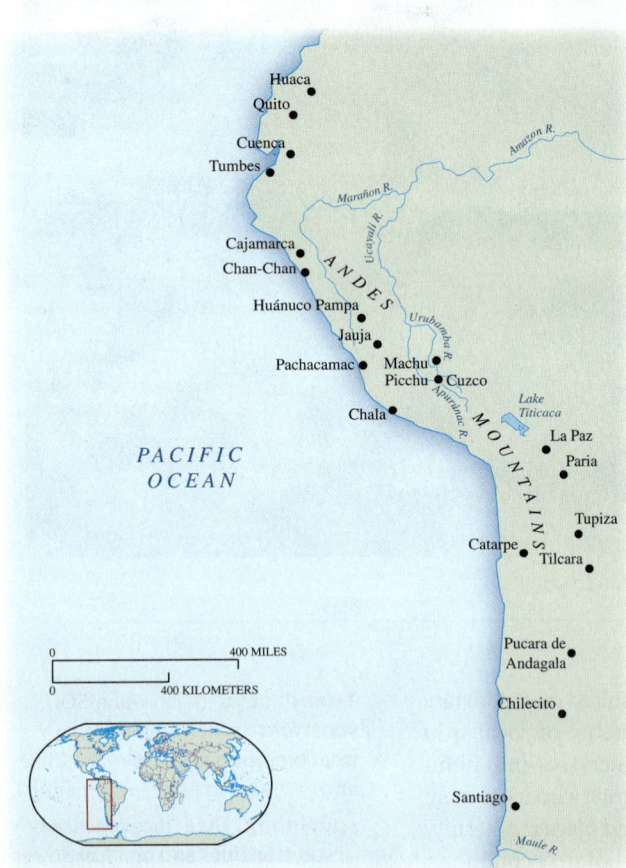

MAP 12.3 The Ancient Cities of Peru The Inca system of roads, with its series of tambos, linked major towns and cities and allowed rapid communication and troop movement.

THINKING HISTORICALLY

The "Troubling" Civilizations of the Americas

FROM THE FIRST ENCOUNTER WITH THE peoples of the Americas, European concepts and judgments about civilization, barbarism, morality, power, politics, and justice were constantly called into question. The American Indian societies had many religious ideas and practices that shocked Christian observers, and aspects of their social and familial arrangements clashed with European sensibilities. Those sensibilities often were influenced by religious and political considerations. Many of those who most condemned human sacrifice, polygamy, or the despotism of Indian rulers were also those who tried to justify European conquest and control, mass violence, and theft on a continental scale. Other European voices also were heard. Not long after the Spanish conquests in the 16th century, defenders of Indian rights came forward to argue that despite certain "unfortunate" habits, Indian civilization was no less to be admired than that of the ancient (and pagan) Romans and Greeks.

For Western civilization, evaluating and judging non-Western or past societies has always been a complex business that has mixed elements of morality, politics, religion, and self-perception along with the record of what is observed or considered to be reality. That complexity is probably just as true for Chinese, Persian, or any culture trying to understand another. Still, Western society seems to have been particularly troubled by the American civilizations, with their peculiar combination of Neolithic technology and imperial organization. At times this has led to abhorrence and rejection—as of Aztec sacrifice—but at other times it has led to a kind of utopian romanticism in which the accomplishments of the Indian past are used as a critique of the present and a political program for the future.

The existence of **Inca socialism** is a case in point. Some early Spanish authors portrayed Inca rule as despotic, but others saw it as a kind of utopia. Shortly after the conquest of Peru, Garcilaso de la Vega, the son of a Spaniard and an Indian noblewoman, wrote a glowing history of his mother's people in which he presented an image of the Inca empire as a carefully organized system in which every community contributed to the whole, and the state regulated the distribution of resources on the basis of need and reciprocity. There was some truth in this view, but it ignored some aspects of exploitation as well. In the 20th century, Peruvian socialists, faced with underdevelopment and social inequality in their country, used this utopian view of Inca society as a possible model for their own future. Their interpretation and that of historians who later wrote of Inca socialism tended to ignore the hierarchy in the Inca empire and the fact that the state extracted labor and goods from the subject communities to support the nobles, who held extensive power. The utopian view of the Incas was no less political than the despotic view. Perhaps the lesson here is that what we see in the past often depends on what we think about the present or what we want for the future.

But if Inca socialism and despotism have fascinated students of the past, Aztec religion has caught the imagination of historians and the general public. It causes us to ask how a civilization as advanced as this could engage in a practice so cruel and, to us, so morally reprehensible. Perhaps nothing challenges our appreciation of the American civilizations more than the extensive evidence of ritual torture and human sacrifice, which among the Aztecs reached staggering proportions. On some occasions thousands of people were slain, usually by having their hearts ripped out.

First, we must put these practices in perspective. Cruelty and violence can be found in many cultures, and to a world that has seen genocide, mass killings, and atomic warfare, the Aztec practices are not so different from what our own age has seen. Certain customs in many past civilizations and present cultures seem to us strange, cruel, and immoral. We find Aztec human sacrifice particularly abhorrent, but such practices also were found among the ancient Canaanites and the Celtic peoples, and the Old Testament story of Abraham and Isaac, although its message is against such sacrifice, reflects a practice known in the ancient Near East. Human sacrifice was practiced in pre-Christian Scandinavia and ancient India. Although by the time of Confucius human sacrifice of wives and retainers at the burial of a ruler was no longer practiced in China, the custom had been known. Sati, the Hindu ritual suicide of the widow on the funeral pyre of her husband, existed in India in the 19th century, although admittedly it may have been exaggerated by the British colonial authorities. The Aztecs certainly were not alone in taking human life as a religious rite. Whatever our moral judgments about such customs, it remains the historian's responsibility to understand them in the context of their own culture and time.

How have historians tried to explain or understand Aztec human sacrifice? Some defenders of Aztec culture have seen it as a limited phenomenon, greatly exaggerated by the Spanish for political purposes. Many scholars have seen it as a religious act central to the Aztec belief that humans must sacrifice that which was most precious to them—life—to receive the sun, rain, and other blessings of the gods that make life possible. Others have viewed Aztec practice as the intentional manipulation and expansion of a widespread phenomenon that had long existed among many American peoples. In other words, the Aztec rulers, priests,

> *Perhaps nothing challenges our appreciation of the American civilizations more than the extensive evidence of ritual torture and human sacrifice.*

(continued on next page)

(continued from previous page)

and nobility used the cult of war and large-scale human sacrifice for political purposes, to terrorize their neighbors and subdue the lower classes. Another possible explanation is demographic. If central Mexico was as densely populated as we believe, then the sacrifices may have been a kind of population control.

Other interpretations have been even more startling. Anthropologist Marvin Harris has suggested that Aztec sacrifice, accompanied by ritual cannibalism, was a response to a lack of protein. He argued that in the Old World, human sacrifice was replaced by animal sacrifice, but in Mesoamerica, which lacked cattle and sheep, that transformation never took place. Harris called the Aztec empire a "cannibal kingdom." Other scholars have strongly objected to Harris's interpretation of the evidence, which gave little attention to the ritual aspects of these acts. Still, human sacrifice shades all assessments of Aztec civilization.

These debates ultimately raise important questions about the role of moral judgments in historical analysis and the way in which our vision of the past is influenced by our own political, moral, ethical, and social programs. We cannot and perhaps should not abandon those programs, but we must always try to understand other times and other peoples in their own terms.

QUESTIONS
- What special features of Aztec civilization must be explained?
- Are they really distinctive?
- What explanations are most persuasive in terms of historical sensitivity and contemporary standards?
- What features of 21st-century society are similar to those of Aztec civilization and will later need to be explained?

Inca socialism A view created by Spanish authors to describe Inca society as a type of utopia; image of the Inca empire as a carefully organized system in which every community collectively contributed to the whole.

purposes. The Incas provided the wool, but each household was required to produce cloth. Woven cloth, a great Andean art form, had political and religious significance. Some women were taken as concubines for the Inca; others were selected as servants at the temples, the so-called Virgins of the Sun. In all this, the Inca had an overall imperial system but remained sensitive to local variations, so that its application accommodated regional and ethnic differences.

In theory, each community aimed at self-sufficiency and depended on the state for goods it could not acquire easily. The ayllus of each community controlled the land, and the vast majority of the men were peasants and herders. Women worked in the fields, wove cloth, and cared for the household (Figure 12.6). Roles and obligations were gender-specific and, at least in theory, equal and interdependent. Andean peoples recognized parallel descent, so that property rights within the ayllus and among the nobility passed in both the male and female lines. Women passed rights and property to daughters, men to sons. Whether in pre-Inca times women may have served as leaders of ayllus is open to question, but under the Incas this seems to have been uncommon. The Inca emphasis on military virtues reinforced the inequality of men and women.

The concept of close cooperation between men and women was also reflected in the Inca view of the cosmos. Gods and goddesses were worshiped by men and women, but women felt a particular affinity for the moon and the goddesses of the earth and corn: the fertility deities. The Inca queen, the Inca's senior wife (usually also a sister of the Inca), was seen as a link to the moon. Queen and sister of the sun, she represented imperial authority to all women. But despite an ideology of gender equality, Inca practice created a gender hierarchy that paralleled the dominance of the Inca state over subject peoples. This fact is supported, and the power of the empire over local ethnic groups is demonstrated, by the Incas' ability to select the most beautiful young women to serve the temples or be given to the Inca.

The integration of imperial policy with regional and ethnic diversity was a political achievement. Ethnic headmen were left in place, but over them were administrators drawn from the Inca nobility in Cuzco. Reciprocity and hierarchy continued to characterize Andean groups as they came under Inca rule; reciprocity between the state and the local community was simply an added level. The Inca state could provide roads, irrigation projects, and hard-to-get goods. For example, maize usually was grown on irrigated land and was particularly important as a ritual crop. State-sponsored irrigation added to its cultivation. The Inca state manipulated the idea of reciprocity to extract labor power, and it dealt harshly with resistance and revolt. In addition to the ayllu peasantry, there was also a class of people, the **yanas**, who were removed from their ayllu and served permanently as servants, artisans, or workers for the Inca or the nobility.

yanas A class of people within Inca society removed from their ayllu to serve permanently as servants, artisans, or workers for the Inca or the Inca nobility.

Members of the Inca nobility were greatly privileged, and those related to the Inca himself held the highest positions. The nobility were all drawn from the 10 royal ayllus. In addition, the residents of Cuzco were given noble status to enable them to serve in high bureaucratic posts. The nobles were distinguished by dress and custom. Only they were entitled to wear the large ear spools that enlarged the ears and caused the Spaniards to later call them *orejones*, or "big ears." Noticeably absent in most of the Inca empire was a distinct merchant class. Unlike in Mesoamerica, where long-distance trade was so important, the Incas' emphasis on self-sufficiency and state regulation of production and surplus limited trade. Only in the northern areas of the empire, in the chiefdoms of Ecuador, the last region brought under Inca control, did a specialized class of traders exist.

The Inca imperial system, which controlled an area of almost 3000 miles, was a stunning achievement of statecraft, but like all other empires it lasted only as long as it could control its subject populations and its own mechanisms of government. A system of royal multiple marriages as a way of forging alliances created rival claimants for power and the possibility of civil war. That is exactly what happened in the 1520s, just before the Europeans arrived. When the Spanish first arrived in Peru, they saw an empire weakened by civil strife.

Inca Cultural Achievements

The Incas drew on the artistic traditions of their Andean predecessors and the skills of subject peoples. Beautiful pottery and cloth were produced in specialized workshops. Inca metalworking was among the most advanced in the Americas, and Inca artisans worked gold and silver with great skill. The Incas also used copper and some bronze for weapons and tools. Like the Mesoamerican peoples, the Incas made no practical use of the wheel, but unlike them, they had no system of writing. However, the Incas did use a system of knotted strings, or **quipu**, to record numerical and perhaps other information. It worked like an abacus, and with it the Incas took censuses and kept financial records. The Incas had a passion for numerical order, and the population was divided into decimal units from which population, military enlistment, and work details could be calculated. The existence of so many traits associated with civilization in the Old World combined with the absence of a system of writing among the Incas illustrates the variations of human development and the dangers of becoming too attached to certain cultural characteristics or features in defining civilizations.

FIGURE **12.6** This Inca sculpture, made of gold, portrays one of the mamaconas, or "chosen women," who served as concubines to the Inca emperors. The wool of her cloak is woven in a classic Inca design.

quipu [KEE-poo] System of knotted strings utilized by the Incas in place of a writing system; could contain numerical and other types of information for censuses and financial records.

The Incas' genius was best displayed in their land and water management, extensive road system, statecraft, and architecture and public buildings. They developed ingenious agricultural terraces on the steep slopes of the Andes, using a complex technology of irrigation to water their crops. The empire was linked together by almost 2500 miles of roads, many of which included rope suspension bridges over mountain gorges and rivers. Inca stonecutting was remarkably accurate; the best buildings were built of large fitted stones without the use of mortar. Some of these buildings were immense. These structures, the large agricultural terraces and irrigation projects, and the extensive system of roads were among the Incas' greatest achievements, displaying their technical ability as well as their ability to mobilize large amounts of labor.

Comparing Incas and Aztecs

View the **Closer Look** on **MyHistoryLab**: Machu Picchu

The Inca and the Aztec cultures were based on a long development of civilization that preceded them. Although in some areas of artistic and intellectual achievement earlier peoples had surpassed their accomplishments, both cultures represented the success of imperial and military organization. Both empires were based on intensive agriculture organized by a state that accumulated surplus production and then controlled the circulation of goods and their redistribution to groups or social classes, although the well-developed merchant class of Mesoamerica was mostly absent in the Inca realm. In both states, older kinship-based institutions, the ayllu and the calpulli, were transformed by the emergence of a social hierarchy in which the nobility was increasingly predominant. In both areas, these nobles also were the personnel of the state, so that the state organization was almost an image of society.

Although the Incas tried to create an overarching political state and to integrate their empire as a unit (the Aztecs did less in this regard), both empires recognized local ethnic groups and political leaders and allowed variation from one group or region to another as long as Inca or Aztec sovereignty was recognized and tribute paid. Both the Aztecs and the Incas, like the Spaniards who followed them, found that their military power was less effective against nomadic peoples who lived on their frontiers. Essentially, the empires were created by the conquest of sedentary agricultural peoples and the extraction of tribute and labor from them.

We cannot overlook the great differences between Mesoamerica and the Andean region in terms of climate and geography or the differences between the Inca and Aztec civilizations. Trade and markets were far more developed in the Aztec empire and earlier in Mesoamerica in general than in the Andean world. There were differences in metallurgy, writing systems, and social definition and hierarchy. But within the context of world civilizations, it is probably best to view these two empires and the cultural areas they represent as variations of similar patterns and processes, of which sedentary agriculture is the most important. Basic similarities underlying the variations can also be seen in systems of belief and cosmology and in social structure. Whether similar origins, direct or indirect contact between the areas, or parallel development in Mesoamerica and the Andean area explains the similarity is unknown. But the American Indian civilizations shared much with each other; that factor and their isolation from external cultural and biological influences gave them their peculiar character and their vulnerability. At the same time, their ability to survive the shock of conquest and contribute to the formation of societies after conquest demonstrates much of their strength. Long after the Aztec and Inca empires had ceased to exist, the peoples of the Andes and Mexico continued to draw on these cultural traditions.

THE OTHER PEOPLES OF THE AMERICAS

12.4 What were the characteristic economic forms of American groups outside the two great imperial territories?

> The civilizations of Mesoamerica and the Andes, were high points of a Native American cultural achievement. However, the Americas continued to be occupied by a variety of peoples who lived in different ways, ranging from highly complex sedentary agricultural empires to simple kin-based bands of hunters and gatherers.

Rather than seeing a division between "primitive" and "civilized" peoples in the Americas, it is more useful to consider gradations of material culture and social complexity. Groups such as the Incas had many things in common with the tribal peoples of the Amazon basin, such as the division into clans or halves—that is, a division of villages or communities into two major groupings with mutually agreed-upon roles and obligations. Moreover, as we have seen, the diversity of ancient America forces us to reconsider ideas of human development based on Old World examples. Social complexity, for example, was not necessarily dependent on agriculture. In the Americas, some groups of fishers and hunters and gatherers, such as the peoples of the northwest coast of the United States and British Columbia, developed complex hierarchical societies. For those who see control of water for agriculture as the starting point for political authority and the state, such societies as the Pimas of Colorado and some of the chiefdoms of South America, who practiced irrigated agriculture but did not develop states, also provide exceptions to theories based on Old World evidence. Finally, archaeological finds in the Amazon now suggest that pottery and agriculture may have developed there even before it did in the Andean region.

How Many People?

A major issue that has fascinated students of the Americas for centuries is the question of population size. For years after the European conquests, many observers discounted the early descriptions of large and dense Indian populations as the exaggeration of conquerors and missionaries who wanted to make their own exploits seem more impressive. In the early 20th century, the most repeated estimate of Native American population about 1492 was 8.4 million (4 million in Mexico, 2 million in Peru, and 2.4 million in the rest of the hemisphere). Since that time, new archeological discoveries, a better understanding of the impact of disease on indigenous populations, new historical and demographic studies, and improved estimates of agricultural techniques and productivity have led to major revisions. Estimates still vary widely, and some have gone as high as 112 million at the time of contact. Most scholars agree that Mesoamerica and the Andes supported the largest populations. Table 12.1 summarizes one of the most careful estimates, which places the total figure at more than 67 million, although a Native American demographer has increased this figure to 72 million. Other scholars are still unconvinced by these estimates.

These figures should be considered in a global context. In 1500, the population of the rest of the world was probably about 500 million, of which China and India each had 75 to 150 million people and Europe had 60 to 70 million, a figure roughly equivalent to the population of the Americas (Table 12.2). If the modern estimates are valid, the peoples of the Americas clearly made up a major segment of humanity.

Differing Cultural Patterns

Although it is impossible to summarize the variety of cultural patterns and lifeways that existed in the Americas on the eve of contact with Europeans, we can describe the major patterns outside the main civilization areas. Northern South America and part of Central America were an intermediate area that shared many features with the Andes and some with Mesoamerica and perhaps served as a point of cultural and material exchange between the two regions. In fact, with the exception of monumental architecture, the intermediate zone chieftainships resembled the sedentary agriculture states in many ways.

Similar kinds of chieftainships based on sedentary agriculture were found elsewhere in the Americas. There is strong evidence of large chieftainships along the Amazon, where the rich aquatic environment supported complex and perhaps hierarchical societies. The island Arawaks or Tainos encountered by Columbus on the Caribbean island of Hispaniola were farmers organized in a hierarchical society and divided into chiefdoms. These Indian chiefdom-level societies strongly resemble the societies of Polynesia. On the bigger Caribbean islands, such as Hispaniola and Puerto Rico, chieftainships ruled over dense populations, which lived primarily on the root crop called manioc.

Agriculture was spread widely throughout the Americas by 1500. Some peoples, such as those of the eastern North American woodlands and the coast of Brazil, combined agriculture with hunting and fishing. Techniques such as slash-and-burn farming led to the periodic movement of villages when production declined. Social organization in these societies often remained without strong class divisions, craft specializations, or the demographic density of people who practiced permanent, intensive agriculture. Unlike Europe, Asia, and Africa, the Americas lacked nomadic herders. However, throughout the Americas, from Tierra del Fuego to the Canadian forests, some people lived in small, mobile, kin-based groups of hunters and gatherers. Their material culture was simple and their societies were more egalitarian.

Nowhere is Native American diversity more apparent than in North America. In that vast continent, by 1500, perhaps as many as 200 languages were spoken, and a variety of cultures reflected Indian adaptation to different ecological situations. By that time, most concentrated towns of the Mississippian mound-builder cultures had been abandoned, and only a few groups in southeastern North America still maintained the social hierarchy and religious ideas of those earlier cultures. In the Southwest, descendants of the Anasazi and other cliff dwellers had taken up residence in the adobe pueblos mostly along the Rio Grande (Figure 12.7), where they practiced terracing and irrigation to support their agriculture. Their rich religious life, their artistic ceramic and weaving traditions, and their agricultural base reflected their own historical traditions.

Elsewhere in North America, most groups were hunters and gatherers or, like the Iroquois of the northeast or the Natchez of the southeast, combined those activities with some agriculture. Sometimes an environment was so rich that complex social organization and artistic specialization could develop without an agricultural base. This was the case among the Indians of the northwest coast, who depended on the rich resources of the sea. In other cases, technology was a limiting factor. The tough prairie grasses could not be farmed easily without metal plows, nor could the buffalo be hunted effectively before Europeans introduced the horse. Thus, the Great Plains were only sparsely occupied.

TABLE **12.1** Population Estimate for the Western Hemisphere, 1492

Area	Population (thousands)
North America	4,400
Mexico	21,400
Central America	5,650
Caribbean	5,850
Andes	11,500
Lowland South America	18,500
Total	67,300

SOURCES: William M. Deneven, *The Native Population of the Americas in 1492* (1976), 289–292; John D. Durand, "Historical Estimates of World Population," *Population and Development Review* 3 (1957): 253–296; Russell Thornton, *American Indian Holocaust and Survival* (1987).

TABLE **12.2** World Population, c. 1500

Area	Population (thousands)
China	100,000–150,000
Indian subcontinent	75,000–150,000
Southwest Asia	20,000–30,000
Japan	15,000–20,000
Rest of Asia (except Russia)	15,000–30,000
Europe (except Russia)	60,000–70,000
Russia (USSR)	10,000–18,000
Northern Africa	6,000–12,000
Rest of Africa	30,000–60,000
Oceania	1,000–2,000
Americas	57,000–72,000
Total	389,000–614,000

SOURCES: William M. Deneven, *The Native Population of the Americas in 1492* (1976), 289–292; John D. Durand, "Historical Estimates of World Population," *Population and Development Review* 3 (1957): 253–296; Russell Thornton, *American Indian Holocaust and Survival* (1987).

 View the **Map** on **MyHistoryLab**: Pre-Columbian Societies of the Americas

CHAPTER 12 The Americas on the Eve of Invasion

Read the Document on MyHistoryLab: Alvar Núñez Cabeza de Vaca, "Indians of the Rio Grande"

FIGURE 12.7 Taos Pueblo, in the foothills of what is now New Mexico. The pueblos of the Rio Grande Valley were based on agriculture and the concentration of population in urban areas. This reflected a number of the traditions of the older Native American cultures of the southwestern United States.

Finally, we should note that although there was great variation among the Indian cultures, some aspects stood in contrast to contemporary societies in Europe and Asia. With the exception of the state systems of Mesoamerica and the Andes, most Indian societies were strongly kin-based. Communal action and ownership of resources, such as land and hunting grounds, were emphasized, and material wealth often was disregarded or placed in a ritual or religious context. It was not that these societies were necessarily egalitarian but rather that ranking usually was not based on wealth. Although often subordinate, women in some societies held important political and social roles and usually played a central role in crop production. Indians tended to view themselves as part of the ecological system and not in control of it, balancing their hunting or farming with existing resources. These attitudes stood in marked contrast to those of many contemporary European and Asian civilizations.

American Diversity in World Context

By the end of the 15th century, two great imperial systems had risen to dominate the two major centers of civilization in Mesoamerica and the Andes. Both empires were built on the achievements of their predecessors, and both reflected a militaristic phase in their area's development. These empires proved to be fragile, weakened by internal strains and the conflicts that any imperial system creates but also limited by their technological inferiority.

The Aztec and Inca empires were one end of a continuum of cultures that went from the most simple to the most complex. The Americas contained a broad range of societies, from great civilizations with millions of people to small bands of hunters. In many of these societies, religion played a dominant role in defining the relationship between people and their environment and between the individual and society. How these societies would have developed and what course the American civilizations might have taken in continued isolation remain interesting and unanswerable questions. The first European observers were simultaneously shocked by the "primitive" tribespeople and astounded by the wealth and accomplishments of civilizations such as that of the Aztecs. Europeans generally saw the Indians as curiously backward. In comparison with Europe and Asia, the Americas did seem strange—more like ancient Babylon or Egypt than contemporary China or Europe—except that without the wheel, large domesticated animals, the plow, and to a large extent metal tools and written languages, even that comparison is misleading. The isolation of the Americas had remained important in physical and cultural terms, but that isolation came to an end in 1492, with disastrous results.

Global Connections

THE AMERICAS AND THE WORLD

Conditions in the Americas before 1492 reveal the importance of global connections in Afro-Eurasia and the absence of such connections in the Americas. American isolation from effective global connections is exhibited by the absence of key technologies, like ironworking and the wheel, that would have been easily transmitted had contacts been available. American isolation shows in the absence of the standard range of domesticated animals. It would show, tragically, in the absence of any immunity to some of the common contagious diseases of Afro-Eurasia.

The absence of several features that had become normal in Afro-Eurasia must be stated carefully. It should not detract from the impressive economic, cultural, and political achievements of the key American Indian civilizations, including their ability (particularly in Mesoamerica) to sustain dense populations. It should not obscure the heritage of these societies to later patterns in the Americas. The comparative distinctions that resulted from lack of wider contact would count only when the Americas were forced into new global connections after 1492—but then they mattered greatly.

Further Readings

Charles C. Mann, *1491* (2005) provides a well-written overview of many aspects of Native American cultures and accomplishments. Mary Miller, *Art of Mesoamerica: From Olmec to Aztec* (2006) surveys evidence from archaeology and art history. Friedrich Katz's *The Ancient Civilizations of the Americas*, 2nd revised ed. (1997), provides the best overall survey that compares Mesoamerica and Peru. It traces the rise of civilization in both areas. Michael Coe et al., *Atlas of Ancient America* (1986), include excellent maps, illustrations, and an intelligent and comprehensive text.

The literature on the Aztecs continues to grow rapidly. Bernardino de Sahagún's *Florentine Codex: The General History of the Things of New Spain*, ed. and trans. Charles Dibble and Arthur J. O. Anderson, 12 vols. (1950–1968), is a fundamental source that most scholars still use as a starting point. Good overviews are provided by Frances Berdan's *The Aztecs of Central Mexico: An Imperial Society*, 2nd ed. (2005) and Michael E. Smith, *The Aztecs* (2012), Miguel Leon-Portilla's *Fifteen Aztec Poets* (1992) deals with religion and philosophy in a sympathetic way while David Carrasco, *Religions of Mesoamerica: Cosmovision and Ceremonial Centers* (1990) tries to integrate archaeology into an understanding of the Mesoamerican cosmology. Elizabeth Boone, *Stories in Red and Black: Pictorial Histories of the Aztecs and Mixtecs* (2000) discusses with writing systems while Ross Hassig, *Aztec Warfare* (1988), examines their military organization, and Inga Clendinnen, *The Cost of Courage in Aztec Society* (2010), provides thoughtful essays on their philosophy of war. Susan D. Gillespie, *The Aztec Kings* (1989), views Aztec history in terms of myth. Manuel Aguilar-Moreno, *Handbook to Life in the Aztec World* (2006), is a useful encyclopedia on many aspects of Aztec culture.

On Peru, a good overview through solid scholarly articles is provided in Richard W. Keatinge, ed., *Peruvian Prehistory* (1988). The article on Inca archeology by Craig Morris is especially helpful. Also useful is Michael Moseley, *The Incas and Their Ancestors* (1992). Art and archeology are the focus of Rebecca Stone Miller, *Art of the Andes from Chavín to Inca* (1995). María Rostoworowski de Diez Canseco, *History of the Inca Realm* (1996), integrates historical and archeological sources, while Juan de Betanzos, *Narrative of the Incas* (1996), makes a classic available to modern readers. Terence D'altroy, *The Incas* (2002), integrates anthropology and archaeology. John Murra's classic *The Economic Organization of the Inca State* (1980) has influenced much thinking about the Incas. J. Hyslop's *The Inca Road System* (1984) examines the building and function of the road network. The work of Gary Urton, *The History of a Myth: Pacariqtambo and the Origin of the Inka* (1990), and Frank Salomon, *The Code Keepers* (2004), on the quipus show how ethnohistory is deepening our understanding of Inca society. Interesting social history is now being done. Irene Silverblatt's *Moon, Sun, and Witches: Gender Ideologies and Class in Inca and Colonial Peru* (1987) is a controversial book on the position of women before, during, and after the Inca rise to power. Brian S. Bauer, *The Development of the Inca State* (1996), offers a new interpretation of government and rule.

In Geoffrey W. Conrad and Arthur A. Demerest's *Religion and Empire: The Dynamics of Aztec and Inca Expansionism* (1984), two archaeologists compare the political systems of the two empires and the motivations for expansion. The authors find more similarities than differences. On the native peoples who lived north of Mesoamerica there is an extensive literature. Colin G. Calloway, *One Vast Winter Count* (2003), provides an excellent and up-to-date overview while Linda Cordell, *Ancient Pueblo Peoples* (1994), and George Miner, *The Moundbuilders: Ancient Peoples of Eastern North America* (2004), provide more detail. Carroll L. Riley, *Becoming Aztlan: Mesoamerican Influence in the Greater Southwest, AD 1200–1500* (2005) weighs the evidence on the possible ties between Mesoamerica and the Anasazi and other groups. Timothy R. Pauketat, *Cahokia. Ancient America's Great City on the Mississippi* (2009), is a good starting point on Mississippian cultures that suggests inspiration from Mesoamerica. Finally, on the question of the populations of the Americas, see Noble D. Cook, *Born to Die* (1998), which tries to establish the populations when post-1492 contact took place.

On MyHistoryLab

Critical Thinking Questions

1. What were the strengths and weaknesses of the Aztec empire?
2. What were the main similarities and differences between the Aztec and Inca empires?
3. What are the key issues involved in trying to understand Aztec religious practices?
4. What were the most important differences between Central American and Andean civilizations; and the major societies of Africa, Asia and Europe during the postclassical period?

Reunification and Renaissance in Chinese Civilization: The Era of the Tang and Song Dynasties

13

Listen to Chapter 13 on MyHistoryLab

LEARNING OBJECTIVES

13.1 What were the key factors in the Sui-Tang era that made for the restoration of a strong, unified Chinese empire after centuries of division and turmoil? p. 288

13.2 Why did Buddhism become such a dominant force in the political and sociocultural life of China in the early Tang period and who led the campaigns to rein in the wealth and influence of the Buddhist monastic orders? p. 295

13.3 What innovations and socioeconomic developments account for the widespread prosperity of Chinese civilization in the Tang-Song era and what were the main social effects of those developments? p. 299

Under the aegis of two of its most celebrated dynasties, the Tang and the Song, which ruled from the early 7th century to the late 13th century C.E., Chinese society advanced in virtually all areas of human endeavor as far as any to that time. It was the largest (both in population and territory) and most prosperous empire on earth. Nowhere during these centuries were China's remarkable achievements so obvious as in the great cities found throughout the empire (see Figure 13.1), several of which exceeded a million people, surpassing those of any other civilization of the age. Although it was not the largest city, Hangzhou (hohng-joh), the capital of the Song rulers, was renowned for its beauty and sophistication.

FIGURE 13.1 This cityscape of the Song city of Bian Liang (Kaifeng), painted by Zhang Zeduan, conveys the energy and prosperity that characterized Chinese urban life in the Tang-Song eras. Like Hangzhou, Bian Liang's graceful bridges, bustling river markets, and spacious parks attracted many visitors, especially at times of festival celebrations like that depicted here.

287

Watch the Video Series on MyHistoryLab

Learn about some key topics related to this chapter with the *MyHistoryLab Video Series: Key Topics in World History*

Located between a large lake and a river in the Yangzi delta (Map 13.1), Hangzhou was crisscrossed by canals and bridges. The city's location near the Yangzi and the coast of the East China Sea allowed its traders and artisans to prosper through the sale of goods and the manufacture of products from materials drawn from throughout China as well as overseas. By late Song times, Hangzhou had more than a million and a half residents and was famed for its wealth, cleanliness, and the number and variety of diversions it offered.

A visitor to Hangzhou could wander through its ten great marketplaces, each stocked with products from much of the known world. The less consumption-minded visitor could enjoy the city's many parks and delightful gardens or go boating on the Western Lake. There the pleasure craft of the rich mingled with special barges for gaming, dining, or listening to Hangzhou's famous "singing-girls." In the late afternoon, one could visit the bath houses that were found throughout the city. At these establishments, one could also get a massage and sip a cup of tea or rice wine.

In the evening, one might dine at one of the city's many fine restaurants, which specialized in the varied and delicious cuisines of the different regions of China. After dinner, there were a variety of entertainments from which to choose. One could take in the pleasure parks, where acrobats, jugglers, and actors performed for the passing crowds. Other options included the city's ornate tea houses, an opera performance by the lake, or a viewing of landscape paintings by artists from the city's famed academy. Having spent such a day, it would be hard for a visitor to disagree with Marco Polo (a native from another beautiful city of canals, Venice) that Hangzhou was "the most noble city and the best that is in the world."

Although enjoyed mainly by elite social groups, the good life in cities like Hangzhou was made possible by the large, well-educated bureaucracy that had governed China for centuries. As we will see in this chapter, centralized control and a strong military brought long periods of peace, during which the ruling elites promoted technological innovation, agrarian expansion, and commercial enterprise at both home and overseas. Despite increasing pressure from nomadic invaders from west and north from the 11th century onward, these trends persisted. Well into the modern era, China went on to produce some of the great art of humankind and remained one of the world's most prosperous societies.

REBUILDING THE IMPERIAL EDIFICE IN THE SUI-TANG ERA

13.1 What were the key factors in the Sui-Tang era that made for the restoration of a strong, unified Chinese empire after centuries of division and turmoil?

> The emergence of the Sui dynasty at the end of the 6th century C.E. signaled a return to strong dynastic control in China. In the Tang era that followed, a Confucian revival enhanced the position of the scholar-gentry administrators and provided the ideological basis for a return to highly centralized rule under an imperial dynasty.

The initial rise of the Sui dynasty in the early 580s appeared to be just another factional struggle of the sort that had occurred repeatedly in the splinter states fighting for control of China in the centuries after the fall of the Han. Yang Jian, a member of a prominent north Chinese noble family that had long been active in these contests, struck a marriage alliance between his daughter and the ruler of the northern Zhou empire (Map 13.1). The Zhou monarch had recently defeated several rival rulers and united much of the north China plain. After much intrigue, Yang Jian seized the throne of his son-in-law and proclaimed himself emperor. Although Yang Jian was Chinese, he secured his power base by winning

200 C.E.	600 C.E.	800 C.E.	950 C.E.	1100 C.E.	1250 C.E.
220 End of the Han dynasty **220–589** Era of the Six Dynasties; political discord in China; time of great Buddhist influence **589–618** Sui dynasty; building of the Grand Canal	**618–626** Gaozu emperor **618–907** Tang dynasty **627–649** Tang Taizong emperor **688** Korean conquest; vassal state of Silla **690–705** Empress Wu; Buddhist influence in China peaks **712–756** Xuanzong emperor	**840s** Period of Buddhist persecution **907** End of the Tang dynasty	**960–1279** Song dynasty; Neo-Confucian revival **c. 1050** Invention of block printing with movable type **1067–1085** Shenzong emperor; reforms of Wang Anshi	**c. 1100** Invention of gunpowder **1115** Jurchen (Jin) kingdom in north China **1119** First reference to use of compass for sea navigation **1127–1279** Southern Song dynasty	**1279–1368** Mongol (Yuan) dynasty rules all China

the support of neighboring nomadic military commanders. He did this by reconfirming their titles and showing little desire to favor the Confucian scholar-gentry class at their expense. With their support, Yang Jian, who took the title Wendi (or Literary Emperor), extended his rule across north China. In 589 Wendi's armies attacked and conquered the weak and divided Chen kingdom, which had long ruled much of the south. With his victory over the Chen, Wendi reunited the traditional core areas of Chinese civilization for the first time in over three and a half centuries (Map 13.2).

Wendi won widespread support by lowering taxes and establishing granaries throughout his domains. Bins for storing grain were built in all of the large cities and in each village of the empire to ensure that there would be a reserve food supply in case floods or drought destroyed the peasants' crops and threatened the people with famine. Large landholders and poor peasants alike were taxed a portion of their crop to keep the granaries filled. Beyond warding off famine, the surplus grain was brought to market in times of food shortages to hold down the price of the people's staple food.

Yangdi Second member of Sui dynasty; murdered his father to gain throne; restored Confucian examination system; responsible for construction of Chinese canal system; assassinated in 618.

Sui Excesses and Collapse

The foundations Wendi laid for political unification and economic prosperity were at first strengthened even further by his son, **Yangdi**, who murdered his father to reach the throne. Yangdi extended his father's conquests and drove back the nomadic intruders who threatened the northern frontiers of the empire. He established a milder legal code and devoted resources to upgrading Confucian education. Yangdi also sought to restore the examination system for regulating entry into the bureaucracy. These legal and educational reforms were part of a broader policy of promoting the scholar-gentry in the imperial administration. But their advancement often worked to the detriment of the great aristocratic families and nomadic military commanders.

MAP **13.1 China During the Age of Division** After the collapse of the Han dynasty, China fragmented into warring kingdoms for nearly 400 years. The deep divisions of this period were captured by its designation in Chinese histories as the era of the Six Dynasties.

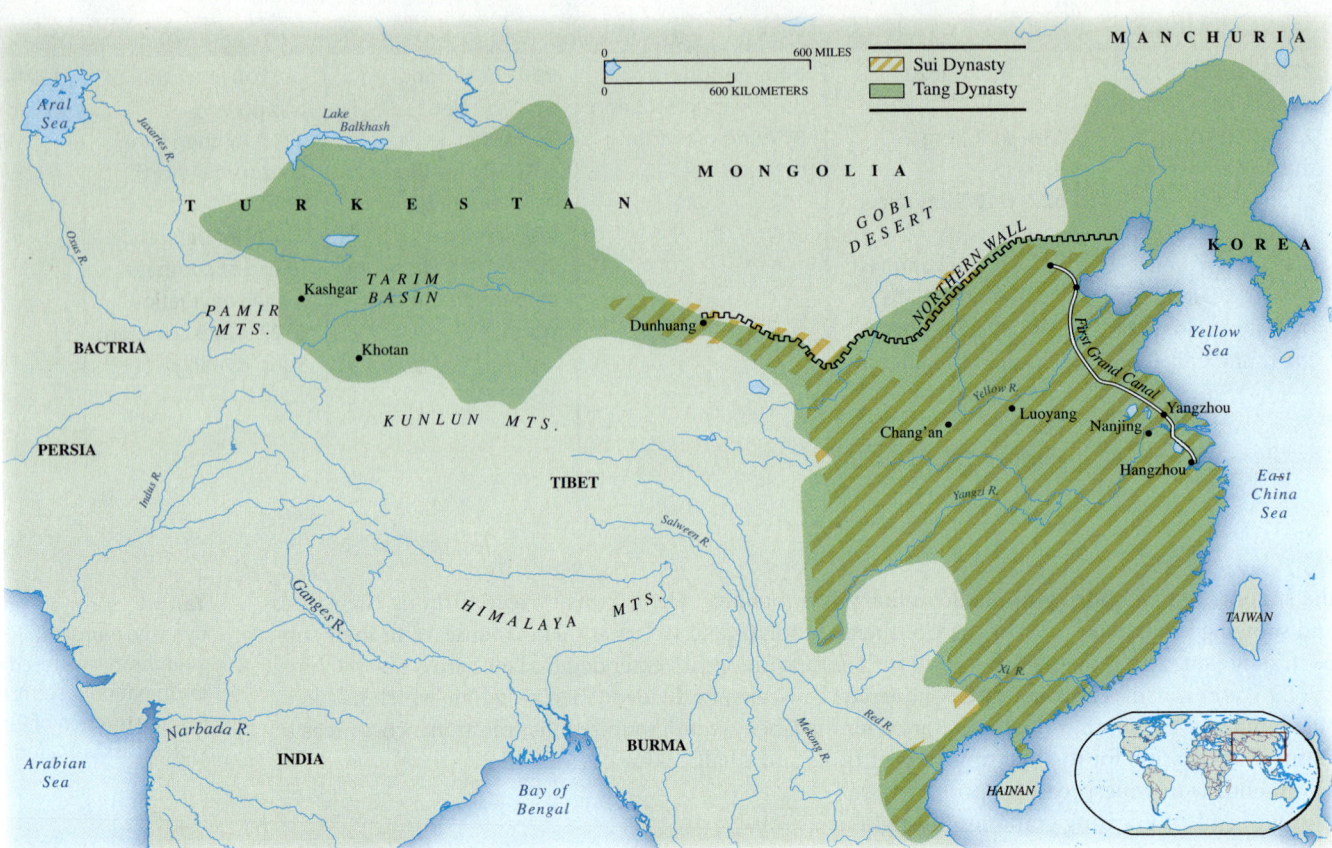

MAP 13.2 **The Sui Dynasty and the Tang Dynasty** The short-lived Sui dynasty laid the foundations for the expansive Tang. Under the latter the Chinese empire was restored on a scale not known since the Han era.

Yangdi was overly fond of luxury and extravagant construction projects. He forcibly conscripted hundreds of thousands of peasants to build palaces, a new capital city at Luoyang (lwoh-yahng) (Map 13.1), and a series of great canals to link the various parts of his empire. His demands on the people seemed limitless. In his new capital, Yangdi had an extensive game park laid out. Because there was not enough forest on the site chosen, tens of thousands of laborers were forced to dig up huge trees in the nearby hills and cart them miles to be replanted in the artificial mounds that tens of thousands of other laborers had built.

Even before work on his many construction projects was completed, Yangdi led his exhausted and angry subjects into a series of unsuccessful wars to bring Korea back under Chinese rule. His failures in the Korean campaigns between 611 and 614, and the near-fatal reverse he suffered in central Asia at the hands of Turkic nomads in 615, set in motion widespread revolts throughout the empire. Provincial governors declared themselves independent rulers, bandit gangs raided at will, and nomadic peoples again seized large sections of the north China plain. Faced with a crumbling empire, the increasingly deranged emperor retreated to his pleasure palaces in the city of Hangzhou on the Yangzi River to the south. When Yangdi was assassinated by his own ministers in 618, it looked as if China would return to the state of political division and social turmoil it had endured in the preceding centuries.

The Emergence of the Tang and the Restoration of the Empire

Li Yuan [lee wahn] (566–635) Also known as Duke of Tang; minister for Yangdi; took over empire following assassination of Yangdi; first emperor of Tang dynasty; took imperial title of Gaozu.

The dissolution of the imperial order was averted by the military skills and political savvy of one of Yangdi's officials, **Li Yuan**, the Duke of Tang. Of noble and mixed Chinese-nomadic origins, Li Yuan was for many years a loyal supporter of the Sui ruler. In fact, on one occasion Li Yuan rescued Yangdi, whose forces had been trapped by a far larger force of Turkic cavalry in a small fort that was part of the Great Wall defenses. But as Yangdi grew more and more irrational and unrest spread from one end of the empire to another, Li Yuan was convinced by his sons and allies that only rebellion could save his family and the empire. From the many-sided struggle for the throne that followed Yangdi's death and continued until 623, Li Yuan emerged the victor. Together with his second son, Tang Taizong (tahng teye-zohng), in whose favor he abdicated in 626, Li Yuan laid the basis for the golden age of the Tang.

Tang armies conquered deep into central Asia as far as present-day Afghanistan. These victories meant that many of the nomadic peoples who had dominated China in the Six Dynasties era had to submit to Tang rule. Tang emperors also completed the repairs begun by the Sui and earlier dynasties on the northern walls and created frontier armies. Partly recruited from Turkic nomadic peoples, these frontier forces gradually became the most potent military units in the empire. The sons of Turkic tribal leaders were sent to the capital as hostages to guarantee the good behavior of the tribe in question. At the Tang capital, they were also educated in Chinese ways in the hope of their eventual assimilation into Chinese culture.

The empire was also extended to parts of Tibet in the west, the Red River valley homeland of the Vietnamese in the south (see Chapter 9), and Manchuria in the north (Map 13.2). In the Tang period, the Yangzi River basin and much of the south were fully integrated with north China for the first time since the Han. In 668, under the emperor Gaozong, Korea was overrun by Chinese armies, and a vassal kingdom called Silla was established that long remained loyal to the Tang. In a matter of decades, the Tang had built an empire that was far larger than even that of the early Han empire whose boundaries in many directions extended beyond the borders of present-day China.

Rebuilding the World's Largest and Most Pervasive Bureaucracy

Crucial for the restoration of Chinese unity were the efforts of the early Tang monarchs to rebuild and expand the imperial bureaucracy. A revived scholar-gentry elite and reworked Confucian ideology played central roles in the process. From the time of the second Sui emperor, Yangdi, the fortunes of the scholar-gentry had begun to improve. This trend continued under the early Tang emperors, who desperately needed loyal and well-educated officials to govern the vast empire they had put together in a matter of decades. The Tang rulers also used the scholar-gentry bureaucrats to offset the power of the aristocracy. As the aristocratic families' control over court life and administration declined, their role in Chinese history was reduced. From the Tang era onward, political power in China was shared by a succession of imperial families and the bureaucrats of the civil service system. Members of the hereditary aristocracy continued to occupy administrative positions, but the scholar-gentry class staffed most of the posts in the secretariats and executive ministries that oversaw a huge bureaucracy.

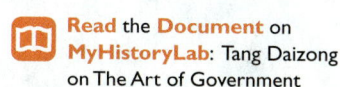

Read the Document on MyHistoryLab: Tang Daizong on The Art of Government

This bureaucracy reached from the imperial palace down to the subprefecture, or district level, which was roughly equivalent to an American county. One secretariat drafted imperial decrees; a second monitored the reports of regional and provincial officials and the petitions of local notables. The executive department, which was divided into six ministries—including war, justice, and public works—ran the empire on a day-to-day basis. In addition, there was a powerful Bureau of Censors whose chief task was to keep track of officials at all levels and report their misdeeds or failings. Finally, there was a very large staff to run the imperial household, including the palaces in the new capital at **Chang'an** and the residences of the princes of the imperial line and other dignitaries.

Chang'an [chahng-an] Capital of Tang dynasty; population of 2 million, larger than any other city in the world at that time.

Institutionalizing Meritocracy: The Growing Importance of the Examination System

Like Yangdi, the Tang emperors patronized academies to train state officials and educate them in the Confucian classics, which were thought to teach moral and organizational principles essential to effective administrators. In the Tang era, and under the Song dynasty that followed, the numbers of the educated scholar-gentry rose far above those in the Han era. In the Tang and Song periods, the examination system was greatly expanded, and the pattern of advancement in the civil service was much more regularized. This meant that in the political realm more than any previous political system (and those yet to come for centuries), the Chinese connected merit as measured by tested skills with authority and status. Several different kinds of examinations were administered by the **Ministry of Rites** to students from government schools or to those recommended by distinguished scholars.

Ministry of Rites Administered examinations to students from Chinese government schools or those recommended by distinguished scholars.

jinshi [chin shEE] Title granted to students who passed the most difficult Chinese examination on all of Chinese literature; became immediate dignitaries and eligible for high office.

The highest offices could be gained only by those who were able to pass exams on the philosophical or legal classics at the highest imperial or metropolitan level. Those who passed the latter earned the title of **jinshi**. Their names were announced throughout the empire, and their families' positions were secured by the prospect of high office that was opened up by their success. Overnight they were transformed into dignitaries whom even their former friends and fellow students addressed formally and treated with deference. Success in exams at all levels won candidates special social status. This meant that they earned the right to wear certain types of clothing and were exempt from corporal punishment. They gained access to the higher level of material comfort and the refined pleasures that were enjoyed by members of the scholar-gentry elite, some of whom are shown at play in Figure 13.2.

Even though a much higher proportion of Tang bureaucrats won their positions through success in civil service examinations than had been the case in the Han era, birth and family connections continued to be important in securing high office. Some of these relationships are clearly illustrated by the petitioner's letter printed in the Document feature. Established bureaucrats not only ensured that their sons and cousins got into the imperial academies but could pull strings to see that even failed candidates from their families received government posts. Ethnic and regional ties also played a role in staffing bureaucratic departments. This meant that although bright commoners could rise to upper-level positions in the bureaucracy, the central administration was overwhelmingly dominated by a small number of established families. Sons followed fathers in positions of power and influence, and prominent households bought a disproportionate share of the places available in the imperial academies. Many positions were reserved for members of the old aristocracy and the low-ranking sons and grandsons of lesser wives and concubines belonging to the imperial household. Merit and ambition counted for something, but birth and family influence often counted for a good deal more.

Read the Document on MyHistoryLab: An Essay Question from the Chinese Imperial Examination System

FIGURE 13.2 As shown in this ink drawing of Chinese philosophers of the Song dynasty, board games and musical recitals were highly esteemed leisure activities for the scholar-gentry class. Members of the scholar-gentry elite might also attend poetry reading or writing parties, travel to mountains to meditate amid scenic splendors, or paint the blossoming plum trees in their gardens. As in their work, members of this highly educated elite admired those who at leisure pursued a diverse array of activities.

(Handscroll "Gathering of Philosophers." The Metropolitan Museum of Art, New York, NY, U.S.A. Image copyright © The Metropolitan Museum of Art/Art Resource, NY.)

State and Religion in the Tang and Song Eras

Increasing state patronage for Confucian learning threatened not only the old aristocratic families but also the Buddhist monastic orders, which had become a major force in Chinese life in the Six Dynasties era. These tensions represent a well-documented instance of the longstanding (and still globally widespread) problem of delineating the boundaries between established religions and state systems. Many of the rulers in the pre-Tang era, particularly those from nomadic origins, were devout Buddhists and strong patrons of the Buddhist establishment. In the centuries after the fall of the Han, Buddhist sects proliferated in China. The most popular were those founded by Chinese monks, in part because they soon took on distinctively Chinese qualities. Among the masses, the salvationist **pure land** strain of Mahayana Buddhism won widespread conversions because it seemed to provide a refuge from an age of war and turmoil. Members of the elite classes, on the other hand, were more attracted to the **Chan** variant of Buddhism, or **Zen**, as it is known in Japan and the West. With its stress on meditation and the appreciation of natural and artistic beauty, Zen had great appeal for the educated classes of China.

The goal of those who followed Chan was to come to know the ultimate wisdom, and thus find release from the cycle of rebirth, through introspective meditation. The nature of this level of consciousness often was expressed in poetic metaphors and riddles, such as those in the following lines from an 8th century C.E. treatise called the *Hymn to Wisdom*:

> The power of wisdom is infinite.
> It is like moonlight reflected in a thousand waves; it can see, hear, understand, and know.
> It can do all these and yet is always empty and tranquil.

pure land Buddhism Emphasized salvationist aspects of Chinese Buddhism; popular among masses of Chinese society.

Chan Buddhism Known as Zen in Japan; stressed meditation and appreciation of natural and artistic beauty; popular with members of elite Chinese society.

Zen Buddhism Known as Chan Buddhism in China; stressed meditation and the appreciation of natural and artistic beauty.

 View the **Closer Look** on **MyHistoryLab:** A Tang Painting of the Goddess of Mercy

---

DOCUMENT

Ties That Bind: Paths to Power

THE FOLLOWING LETTER WAS INCLUDED IN a short story by Tang author Niu Su. It was sent by a local functionary named Wu Bao to a high official to whom Wu hoped to attach himself and thus win advancement in the imperial bureaucracy. What can this letter tell us about the ways in which the Chinese bureaucracy worked in the Tang and Song eras?

> To my great good fortune, we share the same native place, and your renown for wise counsel is well known to me. Although, through gross neglect, I have omitted to prostrate myself before you, my heart has always been filled with admiration and respect. You are the nephew of the Prime Minister, and have made use of your outstanding talents in his service. In consequence of this, your high ability has been rewarded with a commission. General Li is highly qualified both as a civil and a military official, and he has been put in full command of the expedition [to put down "barbarian" rebellions in the southern parts of the empire]. In his hands he unites mighty forces, and he cannot fail to bring these petty brigands to order. By the alliance of the General's heroic valor and your own talent and ability, your armies' task of subjugation will be the work of a day. I, in my youth, devoted myself to study.
>
> Reaching manhood, I paid close attention to the [Confucian] classics. But in talent I do not compare with other men, and so far I have held office only as an officer of the guard. I languish in this out-of-the-way corner beyond the Jian [mountains], close to the haunts of the barbarians. My native place is thousands of miles away, and many passes and rivers lie between. What is more, my term of office here is completed, and I cannot tell when I shall receive my next appointment. So lacking in talent, I fear I am but poorly fitted to be selected for an official post; far less can I entertain the hope of some meager salary. I can only retire, when old age comes, to some rustic retreat, and "turn aside to die in a ditch." I have heard by devious ways of your readiness to help those in distress. If you will not overlook a man from your native place, be quick to bestow your special favour on me, so that I may render you service "as a humble groom." Grant me some small salary, and a share however slight in your deeds of merit. If by your boundless favor I could take part in this triumphal progress, even as a member of the rear-most company, the day would live engraved on my memory.

QUESTIONS
- What techniques does Wu use to win the high official's favor?
- How does Wu expect the official to help him?
- What does he promise in return?
- Does birth or merit appear to be more important in his appeals?
- What dangers to the imperial system are contained in the sorts of ties that Wu argues bind him to the high official?

View the Image on MyHistoryLab: Emperor Wudi, Dunhuang, China

FIGURE 13.3 Tang era architecture at the Phoenix Pavilion in Japan. Some of the most characteristic features of this splendid style of construction are its steeply sloping tiled roofs with upturned corners, the extensive use of fine wood in the floors, walls, and ceilings, and the sliding panels that covered doors and windows in inclement weather and opened up the temples or monasteries to the natural world on pleasant days.

Empress Wu Tang ruler 690–705 C.E. in China; supported Buddhist establishment; tried to elevate Buddhism to state religion; had multistory statues of Buddha created.

Being empty means having no appearance.
Being tranquil means not having been created.
One will then not be bound by good and evil, or be seized by quietness or disturbance.
One will not be wearied by birth and death or rejoice in Nirvana.

The combination of royal patronage and widespread conversion at both the elite and mass levels made Buddhism a strong social, economic, and political force by the time of the Tang unification. The early Tang rulers continued to patronize Buddhism while trying to promote education in the Confucian classics. Emperors such as Taizong endowed monasteries, built in the style of those pictured in Figure 13.3. They also sent emissaries to India to collect texts and relics and commissioned Buddhist paintings and statuary. However, no Tang ruler matched **Empress Wu** (r. 690–705) in supporting the Buddhist establishment. At one point she tried to elevate Buddhism to the status of a state religion.

Empress Wu also commissioned many Buddhist paintings and sculptures. The sculptures are noteworthy for their colossal size. She had statues of the Buddha, which were as much as two and three stories high, carved from stone or cast in bronze. Some of these statues, such as those pictured in Figure 13.4, were carved out of the rock in the great caves near her capital at Luoyang; for cast figures at other locations, Wu had huge pagodas built. With this sort of support, it is not surprising that Buddhism flourished in the early

FIGURE 13.4 At sites such as Longmen near the Tang capital of Luoyang on the Yellow River and Yunkang far to the north, massive statues of the Buddha were carved out of rocky cliffsides beginning in the 6th century C.E. Before the age of Buddhist predominance, sculpture had not been highly developed in China, and the art at these centers was strongly influenced by that of central and even west Asia. Known more for their sheer size than for artistic refinement, the huge Buddhas of sites such as Longmen attest to the high level of skill the Chinese had attained in stone- and metalworking.

centuries of Tang rule. By the mid-9th century, there were nearly 50,000 monasteries and hundreds of thousands of Buddhist monks and nuns in China.

The Anti-Buddhist Backlash

Buddhist successes aroused the envy of Confucian and Daoist rivals. Some of these notables attacked the religion as alien, even though the faith followed by most of the Chinese was very different from that originally preached by the Buddha or that practiced in India and southeast Asia. Daoist monks tried to counter Buddhism's appeals to the masses by stressing their own magical and predictive powers. Most damaging to the fortunes of Buddhism was the growing campaign of Confucian scholar-administrators to convince the Tang rulers that the large Buddhist monastic establishment posed a fundamental economic challenge to the imperial order. Because monastic lands and resources were not taxed, the Tang regime lost huge amounts of revenue as a result of imperial grants or the gifts of wealthy families to Buddhist monasteries. The state was also denied labor power because it could neither tax nor conscript peasants who worked on monastic estates.

By the mid-9th century, state fears of Buddhist wealth and power led to measures to limit the flow of land and resources to the monastic orders. Under Emperor **Wuzong** (r. 841–847), these restrictions grew into open persecution of Buddhism. Thousands of monasteries and Buddhist shrines were destroyed, and hundreds of thousands of monks and nuns were forced to abandon their monastic orders and return to civilian lives. They and the slaves and peasants who worked their lands were again subject to taxation, and monastery lands were parceled out to taxpaying landlords and peasant smallholders.

Wuzong Chinese emperor of Tang dynasty who openly persecuted Buddhism by destroying monasteries in 840s; reduced influence of Chinese Buddhism in favor of Confucian ideology.

Although Chinese Buddhism survived this and other bouts of repression, it was weakened. Never again would the Buddhist monastic orders have the political influence and wealth they had enjoyed in the first centuries of Tang rule. The great age of Buddhist painting and cave sculptures gave way to art dominated by Daoist and Confucian subjects and styles in the late Tang and the Song dynastic era that followed. The Zen and pure land sects of Buddhism continued to attract adherents, with those of the latter numbering in the millions. But Confucianism emerged as the central ideology of Chinese civilization for most of the period from the 9th to the early 20th century. Buddhism left its mark on the arts, the Chinese language, and Chinese thinking about things such as heaven, charity, and law, but it ceased to be a dominant influence. Buddhism's fate in China contrasts sharply with its ongoing and pivotal impact on the civilizations of mainland southeast Asia, Tibet, and parts of central Asia, where it continued to spread in the centuries of Tang-Song rule.

TANG DECLINE AND THE RISE OF THE SONG

13.2 Why did Buddhism become such a dominant force in the political and sociocultural life of China in the early Tang period and who led the campaigns to rein in the wealth and influence of the Buddhist monastic orders?

The motives behind the mid-9th-century Tang assault on the Buddhist monastic order were symptomatic of a general weakening of imperial control that had begun almost a century earlier. After the controversial but strong rule between 690 and 705 by Empress Wu, who actually tried to establish a new dynasty, a second attempt to control the throne was made by a highborn woman who had married into the imperial family. Backed by her powerful relatives and a group of prominent courtiers, Empress Wei poisoned her husband, the son of Empress Wu, and placed her own small child on the throne. But Empress Wei's attempt to seize power was thwarted by another prince, who led a palace revolt that ended with the destruction of Wei and her supporters. The early decades of the long reign of this prince, who became the **Xuanzong** emperor (r. 713–756), marked the peak of Tang power and the high point of Chinese civilization under the dynasty.

Beset by internal rebellions and nomadic incursions, the Tang gave way to the Song in the early 10th century. Although the Song domains were smaller than those of the Tang, the Confucian revival flourished under the successor dynasty.

Xuanzong [shwant-song] Leading Chinese emperor of the Tang dynasty who reigned from 713 to 755, although he encouraged overexpansion.

Initially, Xuanzong took a strong interest in political and economic reforms, which were pushed by the very capable officials he appointed to high positions. But increasingly, his interest in running the vast empire waned. More and more he devoted himself to patronizing the arts and enjoying the pleasures available within the confines of the imperial city. These diversions included music, which he played himself and also had performed by the many musicians he patronized. Thousands of concubines vied in the imperial apartments for the attention of the monarch. After the death of his second

 Read the Document on MyHistoryLab: Ibn Wahab, An Arab merchant visits Tang China

FIGURE 13.5 This painting of Yang Guifei gives a vivid impression of the opulence and refinement of Chinese court life in the late Tang era. Here a very well-dressed Yang Guifei is helped by some of her servants onto a well-fed horse, presumably for a trot through the palace grounds. Two fan-bearers stand ready to accompany the now-powerful concubine on her sedate ride while other attendants prepare to lead the horse through the confined space of the royal enclosure.

Yang Guifei [yäng gwä fä] (719–756) Royal concubine during reign of Xuanzong; introduction of her relatives into royal administration led to revolt.

wife, the aged and lonely emperor became infatuated with **Yang Guifei**, a beautiful young woman from the harem of one of the imperial princes (Figure 13.5).

Their relationship was one of the most famous and illstarred romances in all of Chinese history. But it was only one of the more fateful of a multitude of interventions by powerful women at the courts of emperors and kings throughout Afro-Euroasia. Xuanzong promenaded in the imperial gardens and gave flute lessons to Yang. Soon she was raised to the status of royal concubine, and she used her new power to pack the upper levels of the government with her greedy relatives. They and Yang assumed an ever-greater role in court politics. The arrogance and excessive ambition of Yang Guifei and her family angered members of the rival cliques at court, who took every opportunity to turn Yang's excesses into a cause for popular unrest. Xuanzong's long neglect of state affairs resulted in economic distress, which fed this discontent. It also led to chronic military weaknesses, which left the government unable to deal with the disorders effectively. The deepening crisis came to a head in 755 when one of the emperor's main military leaders, a general of nomadic origins named An Lushan, led a widely supported revolt with the aim of founding a new dynasty to supplant the Tang.

Although the revolt was crushed and the Tang dynasty preserved, victory was won at a very high cost. Early in the rebellion, Xuanzong's retreating and demoralized troops mutinied, first killing several members of the Yang family and then forcing the emperor to have Yang Guifei executed. Xuanzong lived on for a time, but his grief and disillusionment rendered him incapable of continuing as emperor. None of the Tang monarchs who followed him could compare with the able leaders that the dynasty had consistently produced in the first century and a half of its rule.

Equally critical, to defeat the rebels the Tang had sought alliances with nomadic peoples living on the northern borders of the empire. They had also delegated resources and political power to regional commanders who remained loyal to the dynasty. As had happened so often in the past, in the late 8th and 9th centuries the nomads used political divisions within China to gain entry into and eventually assert control over large areas of the north China plain. At the same time, many of the allied provincial governors became in effect independent rulers. They collected their own taxes, passing little or none on to the imperial treasury. These regional lords raised their own armies and bequeathed their titles to their sons without asking for permission from the Tang court. Worsening economic conditions led to a succession of revolts in the 9th century, some of which were popular uprisings led by peasants.

The Founding of the Song Dynasty

By the end of the 9th century little remained of the once-glorious Tang Empire. By 907, when the last emperor of the Tang dynasty was forced to resign, China appeared to be entering another phase of nomadic dominance, political division, and social strife. In 960, however, a military commander emerged to reunite China under a single dynasty. **Zhao Kuangyin** had established a far-flung reputation as one of the most honest and able of the generals of the last of the Five Dynasties that had struggled to control north China after the fall of the Tang. Although a fearless warrior, Zhao was a scholarly man who collected books rather than booty while out campaigning. Amid the continuing struggles for control in the north, Zhao's subordinates and regular troops insisted that he proclaim himself emperor. In the next few years Zhao, renamed Emperor Taizu, routed all his rivals except one, thus founding the Song dynasty that was to rule most of China for the next three centuries.

Zhao Kuangyin [jaoo kwän yin] (r. 960–976) Founder of Song dynasty; originally a general following fall of Tang; took title of Taizu; failed to overcome northern Liao dynasty that remained independent.

The one rival Taizu could not overcome was the northern **Liao dynasty**, which had been founded in 907 by the nomadic **Khitan** peoples from Manchuria. This failure set a precedent for weakness on the part of the Song rulers in dealing with the nomadic peoples of the north. This shortcoming plagued the dynasty from its earliest years to its eventual destruction by the Mongols in the late 13th century. Beginning in 1004, the Song were forced by military defeats at the hands of the Khitans to sign a series of humiliating treaties with their smaller but more militarily adept northern neighbors. These treaties committed the Song to paying a very heavy tribute to the Liao dynasty to keep it from raiding and possibly conquering the Song domains. The Khitans, who had been highly *Sinified*, or influenced by Chinese culture, during a century of rule in north China, seemed content with this arrangement. They clearly saw the Song empire as culturally superior—an area from which they could learn much in statecraft, the arts, and economic organization.

Liao [lyow] **dynasty** Founded in 907 by nomadic Khitan peoples from Manchuria; maintained independence from Song dynasty in China.

Khitans [kiht-ahn] Nomadic peoples of Manchuria; militarily superior to Song dynasty China but influenced by Chinese culture; forced humiliating treaties on Song China in 11th century.

Song Politics: Settling for Partial Restoration

A comparison of the boundaries of the early Song Empire (Map 13.3) with that of the Tang domains (Map 13.2) reveals that the Song never matched its predecessor in political or military strength. The weakness of the Song resulted in part from imperial policies that were designed to ward off the conditions that had destroyed the Tang dynasty. From the outset, the military was subordinated to the civilian administrators of the scholar-gentry class. Only civil officials were allowed to be governors, thereby removing the temptation of regional military commanders to seize power. In addition, military commanders were rotated to prevent them from building up a power base in the areas where they were stationed.

At the same time, the early Song rulers strongly promoted the interests of the Confucian scholar-gentry, who touted themselves as the key bulwark against the revival of warlord influence. Officials' salaries were increased, and many perks—including additional servants and payments of luxury goods such as silk and wine—made government posts more lucrative. The civil service exams were fully routinized. They were given every three years at three levels: district, provincial, and imperial. Song examiners passed a far higher percentage of those taking the exams than the Tang examiners had, and these successful candidates were much more likely to receive an official post than their counterparts in the Tang era. As a result, the bureaucracy soon became bloated with well-paid officials who often had little to do. In this way, the ascendancy of the scholar-gentry class over its aristocratic and Buddhist rivals was fully secured in the Song era.

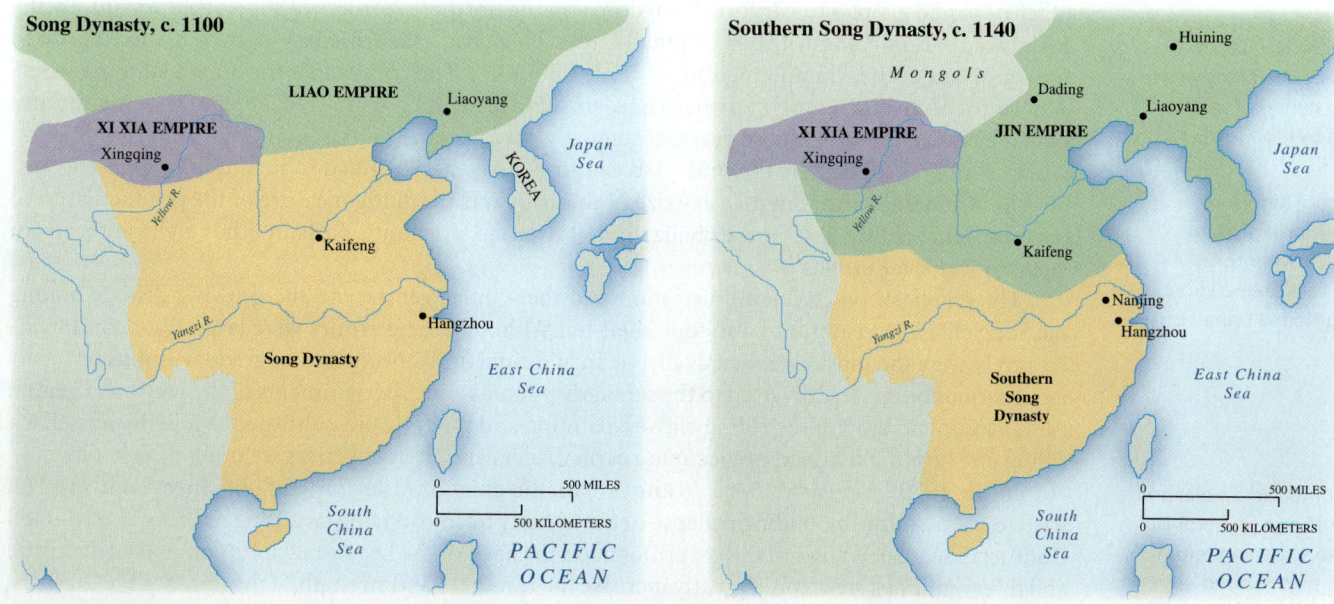

MAP 13.3 China in the Song and Southern Song Dynastic Periods A comparison of the territory controlled during the two phases of the Song dynasty clearly indicates both the growing power and pressure of nomadic peoples from the north and the weakened state of the Song rulers of China.

The Revival of Confucian Thought

The great influence of the scholar-gentry in the Song era was mirrored in the revival of Confucian ideas and values that dominated intellectual life. Many scholars tried to recover long-neglected texts and decipher ancient inscriptions. New academies devoted to the study of the classical texts were founded, and impressive libraries were established. The new schools of philosophy propounded rival interpretations of the teachings of Confucius and other ancient thinkers. They also sought to prove the superiority of indigenous thought systems, such as Confucianism and Daoism, over imported ones, especially Buddhism.

The most prominent thinkers of the era, such as **Zhu Xi**, stressed the importance of applying philosophical principles to everyday life and action. These **neo-Confucians**, or revivers of what they believed to be ancient Confucian teachings, argued that cultivating personal morality was the highest goal for humans. They argued that virtue could be attained through knowledge gained by book learning and personal observation as well as through contact with men of wisdom and high morality. In these ways, the basically good nature of humans could be cultivated, and superior men, fit to govern and teach others, could be developed. Neo-Confucian thinking had a great impact on Chinese intellectual life during the eras of all the dynasties that followed the Song. Its hostility to foreign philosophical systems, such as Buddhism, made Chinese rulers and bureaucrats less receptive to outside ideas and influences than they had been earlier. The neo-Confucian emphasis on tradition and hostility to foreign influences was one of a number of forces that eventually stifled innovation and critical thinking among the Chinese elite.

The neo-Confucian emphasis on rank, obligation, deference, and traditional rituals reinforced class, age, and gender distinctions, particularly as they were expressed in occupational roles. Great importance was given to upholding the authority of the patriarch of the Chinese household, who was compared to the male emperor of the Chinese people as a whole. If men and women kept to their place and performed the tasks of their age and social rank, the neo-Confucians argued, there would be social harmony and prosperity. If problems arose, the best solutions could be found in examples drawn from the past. They believed that historical experience was the best guide for navigating the uncertain terrain of the future.

Roots of Decline: Attempts at Reform

The means by which the Song emperors had secured their control over China undermined their empire in the long run. The weakness they showed in the face of the Khitan challenge encouraged other nomadic peoples to carve out kingdoms on the northern borders of the Song domains. By the mid-11th century, **Tangut** tribes, originally from Tibet, had established a kingdom named **Xi Xia** to the southwest of the Khitan kingdom of Liao (Map 13.3). The tribute that the Song had to pay these peoples for protection of their northern borders was a great drain on the resources of the empire and a growing burden for the Chinese peasantry. Equally burdensome was the cost of the army—numbering nearly 1 million soldiers by the mid-11th century—that the Song had to maintain to guard against invasion from the north. But the very size of the army was a striking measure of the productivity and organizational ability of Chinese civilization. It dwarfed its counterparts in other civilizations from Japan to western Europe.

The emphasis on civil administration and the scholar-gentry and the growing disdain among the Song elite for the military also took their toll. Although Song armies were large, their commanders rarely were the most able men available. In addition, funds needed to upgrade weapons or repair fortifications often were diverted to the scholarly pursuits and entertainments of the court and gentry. At the court and among the ruling classes, painting and poetry were cultivated, while the horseback riding and hunting that had preoccupied earlier rulers and their courtiers went out of fashion.

In the 1070s and early 1080s, **Wang Anshi**, the chief minister of the Song Shenzong emperor, tried to ward off the impending collapse of the dynasty by introducing sweeping reforms. A celebrated Confucian scholar, Wang ran the government on the basis of the Legalist assumption that an energetic and interventionist state could greatly increase the resources and strength of the dynasty. For 20 years, in the face of strong opposition from the conservative ministers who controlled most of the administration, Wang tried to correct the grave defects in the imperial order. He introduced cheap loans and government-assisted irrigation projects to encourage agricultural expansion. He taxed the landlord and scholarly classes, who had regularly exempted themselves from military service. Wang used the

---

Zhu Xi [ju shEE] (1130–1200) Most prominent of neo-Confucian scholars during the Song dynasty in China; stressed importance of applying philosophical principles to everyday life and action.

neo-Confucians Revived ancient Confucian teachings in Song era China; great impact on the dynasties that followed; their emphasis on tradition and hostility to foreign systems made Chinese rulers and bureaucrats less receptive to outside ideas and influences.

Tangut Rulers of Xi Xia kingdom of northwest China; one of regional kingdoms during period of southern Song; conquered by Mongols in 1226.

Xi Xia [shee-shyah] Kingdom of Tangut people, north of Song kingdom, in mid-11th century; collected tribute that drained Song resources and burdened Chinese peasantry.

Wang Anshi Confucian scholar and chief minister of a Song emperor in 1070s; introduced sweeping reforms based on Legalists; advocated greater state intervention in society.

increased revenue to establish well-trained mercenary forces to replace armies that had formerly been conscripted from the untrained and unwilling peasantry. Wang even tried to reorganize university education and reorient the examination system. His reforms stressed analytical thinking rather than the rote memorization of the classics that had long been the key to success among the scholar-gentry.

Reaction and Disaster: The Flight to the South

Unfortunately, Wang's ability to propose and enact reforms depended on continuing support from the Shenzong emperor. In 1085 that emperor died, and his successor favored the conservative cliques that had long opposed Wang's changes. The neo-Confucians came to power, ended reform, and reversed many of Wang's initiatives. As a result, economic conditions continued to deteriorate, and peasant unrest grew throughout the empire. Facing banditry and rebellion from within, an unprepared military proved no match for the increasing threat from beyond the northern borders of the empire. In 1115, a new nomadic contender, the **Jurchens**, overthrew the Liao dynasty of the Khitans and established the **Jin** kingdom north of the Song empire (Map 13.3). After successful invasions of Song territory, the Jurchens annexed most of the Yellow River basin to their Jin kingdom. These conquests forced the Song to flee to the south. With the Yangzi River basin as their anchor and their capital transferred to Hangzhou, the Song dynasty survived for another century and a half. Politically, the **Southern Song** dynasty (1167–1279) was little more than a rump state carved out of the much larger domains ruled by the Tang and northern-based Song. Culturally, its brief reign was to be one of the most glorious in Chinese history—perhaps in the history of humankind.

Jurchens [YUHR-chehns] Founders of the Jin kingdom that succeeded the Liao in northern China; annexed most of the Yellow River basin and forced Song to flee to south.

Jin Kingdom north of the Song Empire; established by Jurchens in 1115 after overthrowing Liao dynasty; ended 1234.

Southern Song Rump state of Song dynasty from 1127 to 1279; carved out of the much larger domains ruled by the Tang and northern Song; culturally one of the most glorious reigns in Chinese history.

TANG AND SONG PROSPERITY: THE BASIS OF A GOLDEN AGE

13.3 What innovations and socioeconomic developments account for the widespread prosperity of Chinese civilization in the Tang-Song era and what were the main social effects of those developments?

The attention given to canal building by the Sui emperors and the Tang rulers who followed them was driven by a major shift in the population balance within Chinese civilization. The **Grand Canal**, which Yangdi risked his throne to have built, was designed to link the original centers of Chinese civilization on the north China plain with the Yangzi River basin more than 500 miles to the south (see Maps 13.1 and 13.2). Because the great river systems that were essential to China's agrarian base ran from west to east—from the mountains of central Asia to the sea—the movement of people and goods in that direction was much easier than from north to south.

Although no major geographic barriers separated the millet-growing areas of northern China from the rice-producing Yangzi basin, overland travel was slow and difficult. The transport of bulk goods such as millet and rice was prohibitively expensive. The great increase of the Chinese population in the southern regions in the later Han and Six Dynasties periods made it necessary to improve communications between north and south once the two regions were joined by the Sui conquests. Not only did more and more of the emperor's subjects live in the southern regions, but the Yangzi basin and other rice-growing areas in the south were fast becoming the major food-producing areas of the empire. By late Tang and early Song times, the south had surpassed the north in both crop production and population.

Yangdi's Grand Canal was intended to facilitate control over the southern regions by courts, bureaucracies, and armies centered in ancient imperial centers such as Chang'an and Luoyang in the north. The canal made it possible to transport to the capital revenue collected in the form of grain from the fertile southern regions and to transfer food from the south to districts threatened by drought and famine in the north. No wonder that Yangdi was obsessed with canal construction. By the time the Grand Canal was finished, more than a million forced laborers had worked, and many had died, on its locks and embankments. The completed canal system was an engineering achievement every bit as impressive as the northern wall. Most stretches of the canal, which was nearly 1200 miles long, were 40 paces wide, and imperial highways lined with willow trees ran along the banks on both sides.

The Tang and Song eras were a time of major shifts in the population balance within China, new patterns of trade and commerce, renewed urban expansion, novel forms of artistic and literary expression, and a series of technological innovations.

Grand Canal Built in 7th century during reign of Yangdi during Sui dynasty; designed to link the original centers of Chinese civilization on the north China plain with the Yangtze river basin to the south; nearly 1200 miles long.

A New Phase of Intercontinental Commercial Expansion by Land and Sea

Tang conquests in central Asia and the building of the canal system did much to promote commercial expansion in the Tang and Song eras. The extension of Tang control deep into central Asia meant that the overland silk routes between China and Persia were reopened and protected. This intensified international contacts in the postclassical period. Tang control promoted exchanges between China and Buddhist centers in the nomadic lands of central Asia as well as with the Islamic world farther west. Horses, Persian rugs, and tapestries passed to China along these routes, while fine silk textiles, porcelain, and paper were exported to the centers of Islamic civilization. As in the Han era, China exported mainly manufactured goods to overseas areas, such as southeast Asia, while importing mainly luxury products such as aromatic woods and spices.

In late Tang and Song times, Chinese merchants and sailors increasingly carried Chinese trade overseas instead of being content to let foreign seafarers come to them. Along with the dhows of the Arabs, Chinese **junks** were the best ships in the world in this period. They were equipped with watertight bulkheads, sternpost rudders, oars, sails, compasses, bamboo fenders, and gunpowder-propelled rockets for self-defense. With such vessels, Chinese sailors and merchants became the dominant force in the Asian seas east of the Malayan peninsula.

junks Chinese ships equipped with watertight bulkheads, sternpost rudders, compasses, and bamboo fenders; dominant force in Asian seas east of the Malayan peninsula.

The heightened role of commerce and the money economy in Chinese life was readily apparent in the market quarters found in all cities and major towns (Figure 13.1). These were filled with shops and stalls that sold products drawn from local farms, regional centers of artisan production, and trade centers as distant as the Mediterranean. The Tang and Song governments supervised the hours and marketing methods in these centers, and merchants specializing in products of the same kind banded together in guilds to promote their interests with local officials and to regulate competition.

This expansion in scale was accompanied by a growing sophistication in commercial organization and forms of credit available in China. In the following millennium these innovations in instruments for economic exchange transformed domestic marketing and international commerce worldwide. The proportion of exchanges involved in the money economy expanded greatly, and deposit shops, an early form of the bank, were found in many parts of the empire. The first use of paper money also occurred in the Tang era. Merchants deposited their profits in their hometowns before setting out on trading caravans to distant cities. They were given credit vouchers, or what the Chinese called **flying money**, which they could then present for reimbursement at the appropriate office in the city of destination. This arrangement greatly reduced the danger of robbery on the often perilous journeys merchants made from one market center to another. In the early 11th century, the government began to issue paper money when an economic crisis made it clear that the private merchant banks could no longer handle the demand for the new currency.

flying money Chinese credit instrument that provided credit vouchers to merchants to be redeemed at the end of the voyage; reduced danger of robbery; early form of currency.

The expansion of commerce and artisan production was complemented by a surge in urban growth in the Tang and Song eras. At nearly 2 million, the population of the Tang capital and its suburbs at Chang'an was far larger than that of any other city in the world at the time. The imperial city, an inner citadel within the walls of Chang'an, was divided into a highly restricted zone dominated by the palace and audience halls and a section crowded with the offices of the ministries and secretariats of the imperial government. Near the imperial city but outside Chang'an's walls, elaborate gardens and a hunting park were laid out for the amusement of the emperors and favored courtiers. The spread of commerce and the increasing population also fed urban growth in the rest of China. In the north and especially the south, old cities mushroomed as suburbs spread in all directions from the original city walls. Towns grew rapidly into cities, and the proportion of the empire's population living in urban centers grew steadily. The number of people living in large cities in China, which may have been as high as 10 percent, was also far greater than that found in any civilization until after the Industrial Revolution.

Expanding Agrarian Production and Life in the Country

The movement of the population southward to the fertile valleys of the Yangzi and other river systems was part of a larger process of agrarian expansion in the Tang and Song period. The expansion of Chinese settlement and agricultural production was promoted by the rulers of both dynasties. Their officials actively encouraged peasant groups to migrate to uncultivated areas or those occupied by shifting cultivators or peoples of non-Chinese descent. The state also supported military garrisons in these areas to protect the new settlements and to complete the task of subduing non-Chinese peoples. State-regulated irrigation and embankment systems advanced agrarian expansion. For example, the great canals made it possible for peasants who grew specialized crops, such as tea, or those who cultivated silkworms to market their produce over much of the empire.

The introduction of new seeds, such as the famed Champa rice from Vietnam; better use of human, animal, and silt manures; more thorough soil preparation and weeding; and multiple cropping and improved water control techniques increased the yields of peasant holdings. Inventions such as the wheelbarrow eased the plowing, planting, weeding, and harvesting tasks that occupied much of the time of most Chinese people. The engraving shown in Figure 13.6 gives us a glimpse of rural scenes that were reproduced hundreds of thousands of times across China all through the Tang and Song centuries and much of the millennium that followed.

The rulers of both the Sui and Tang dynasties had adopted policies aimed at breaking up the great estates of the old aristocracy and distributing land more equitably among the free peasant households of the empire. These policies were designed in part to reduce or eliminate the threat that the powerful aristocracy posed for the new dynasties. They were also intended to bolster the position of the ordinary peasants, whose labors and well-being had long been viewed by Confucian scholars as essential to a prosperous and stable social order. To a point, these agrarian measures succeeded. For a time the numbers of the free peasantry increased, and the average holding size in many areas rose. The fortunes of many of the old aristocratic families also declined, thus removing many of them as independent centers of power. They were supplanted gradually in the rural areas by the gentry side of the scholar-gentry combination that dominated the imperial bureaucracy.

The extended-family households of the gentry that were found in rural settlements in the Han era increased in size and elegance in the Tang and Song. The widespread use of the graceful curved roofs, with upturned corners that one associates with Chinese civilization, dates from the Tang period. By imperial decree, curved roofs were reserved for people of high rank, including the scholar-gentry families. With intricately carved and painted roof timbers topped with glazed tiles of yellow or green, the great dwellings of the gentry left no doubt about the status and power of the families who lived in them. At the same time, their muted colors, wood and bamboo construction, and simple lines blended beautifully with nearby gardens and groves of trees.

FIGURE **13.6** The farming methods developed in the Song era are illustrated by this 17th-century engraving. Note the overseer, protected by an umbrella from the hot sun. Improved productivity, particularly of staple crops such as irrigated rice, meant that China's long-held advantages over other civilizations in terms of the population it could support increased in this era. By the early 14th century, as much as a quarter of humanity may have lived in the Chinese empire.

(© The Trustees of the British Museum/Art Resource, NY.)

Family and Society in the Tang and Song Eras

Chinese family organization at various class levels in the Tang and Song centuries closely resembled that found in earlier periods. Nonetheless, the position of women showed signs of improving under the Tang and early Song eras, and then deteriorated steadily in the late Song. As in the classical age, extended-family households were preferred, but normally they could be afforded only by the upper classes. The male-dominated hierarchy promoted by Confucius and other early thinkers held sway at all class levels. In the Tang period, the authority of elders and males within the family was buttressed by laws that prescribed beheading as a punishment for children who struck their parents or grandparents in anger, and two and one-half years of hard labor for younger brothers or sisters who hit their older siblings.

Over the centuries, a very elaborate process of forging marriage alliances developed. Professional go-betweens, almost always women, helped both families to negotiate such prickly issues as matching young men and women and the amount of the dowry to be paid to the husband's family. Brides and grooms in China, in contrast to those in India, were generally about the same age, probably because of the Confucian reluctance to mix generations.

Both within the family and in society at large, women remained clearly subordinate to men. But some evidence suggests that at least for women of the upper classes in urban areas, the opportunities for personal expression increased in the Tang and early Song. As the example of the empresses Wu and Wei and the concubine Yang Guifei make clear, Tang women could wield considerable power at the highest levels of Chinese society. That they also enjoyed access to a broad range of activities, if not career possibilities, is indicated by a surviving pottery figure from the early Tang period of a young woman playing polo.

Tang and Song law allowed divorce by mutual consent of both husband and wife. There were also laws prohibiting a husband from setting aside his wife if her parents were dead or if he had been poor when they were married and later became rich. These suggest that Chinese wives had more defenses against capricious behavior by their husbands than was the case in India at this time. A remarkable degree of independence is also indicated by the practice, reported in late Song times, of wealthy women in large cities such as Hangzhou taking lovers (or what were politely called "complimentary husbands") with the knowledge of their husbands.

The Neo-Confucian Assertion of Male Dominance

Evidence of the independence and legal rights enjoyed by a small minority of women in the Tang and Song eras is all but overwhelmed by the worsening condition of Chinese women in general. The assertion of male dominance was especially pronounced in the thinking of the neo-Confucian philosophers, who, as we have seen, became a major force in the later Song period. The neo-Confucians stressed the woman's role as homemaker and mother, particularly as the bearer of sons to continue the patrilineal family line. They advocated confining women and emphasized the importance of virginity for young brides, fidelity for wives, and chastity for widows. Like their counterparts in India, widows were discouraged from remarrying.

At the same time, men were permitted to have premarital sex without scandal, to take concubines if they could afford them, and to remarry if one or more of their wives died. The neo-Confucians attacked the Buddhists for promoting career alternatives for women, such as scholarship and the monastic life, at the expense of marriage and raising a family. They drafted laws that favored men in inheritance, divorce, and familial interaction. They also excluded women from the sort of education that would allow them to enter the civil service and rise to positions of political power. Footbinding epitomized the extent to which elite women's possibilities for self-fulfillment had been constricted by the later Song period.

View the **Closer Look** on **MyHistoryLab:** Erotic Deformity: Chinese Foot-binding

Invention, Artistic Creativity, and China's Global Impact

Perhaps even more than for political and economic transformations, the Tang and Song eras are remembered as a time of remarkable Chinese accomplishments in science, technology, literature, and the fine arts. Major technological breakthroughs and scientific discoveries were made under each dynasty. Some of them, particularly those involving the invention of new tools, production techniques, and weapons, gradually spread to other civilizations and fundamentally changed the course of human development. Until recent centuries, the arts and literature of China were not well known beyond its borders. Their impact was confined mainly to areas such as central Asia, Japan, and Vietnam, where Chinese imports had long been a major impetus for cultural change. But the poetry and short stories of the Tang and the landscape paintings of the Song are some of the most splendid artistic creations of all human history.

As we have seen, new agricultural tools and innovations such as banks and paper money contributed a great deal to economic growth and social prosperity in the Tang and Song eras. In this respect, the engineering feats of the period are particularly noteworthy. In addition to building the Grand

VISUALIZING THE PAST

Footbinding as a Marker of Male Dominance

NO ASPECT OF GENDER RELATIONS EXEMPLIFIES the degree to which women in the Tang-Song era were constricted in terms of career choices and subordinated to males as dramatically as **footbinding**. This practice may have had its origins in the delight one of the Tang emperors took in the tiny feet of his favorite dancing girls or, as has been recently argued, the fashion preference of elite women for small feet. Whatever its rationales, by the later Song era, upper-class men had developed a preference for small feet for women. This preference gradually spread to some groups further down on the social scale, including the well-to-do peasantry.

In response to male demands, on which the successful negotiation of a young woman's marriage contract might hinge, mothers began to bind the feet of their daughters as early as age five or six. The young girl's toes were turned under and bound with silk, which was wound more tightly as she grew, as shown by the accompanying photo. By the time she reached marriageable age, a young woman's feet had been transformed into the "lotus petal" or "golden lily" shapes that were presumably preferred by prospective husbands.

Bound feet were a constant source of pain for the rest of a woman's life, and they greatly limited her mobility by making it very difficult to walk even short distances. Limited mobility made it easier for husbands to confine their wives to the family compound. It also meant that women could not engage in occupations except ones that could be pursued within the extended family household, such as textile production. For this reason, the lower classes, whose households often depended on women's labor in the fields, markets, or homes of the wealthy to make ends meet, were slow to adopt the practice. But once it was in fashion among the scholar-gentry and other elite classes, footbinding became vital to winning a husband. In part, because a good marriage for their daughters was the primary goal of Chinese mothers, the practice was usually unquestioningly passed from one generation of women to the next.

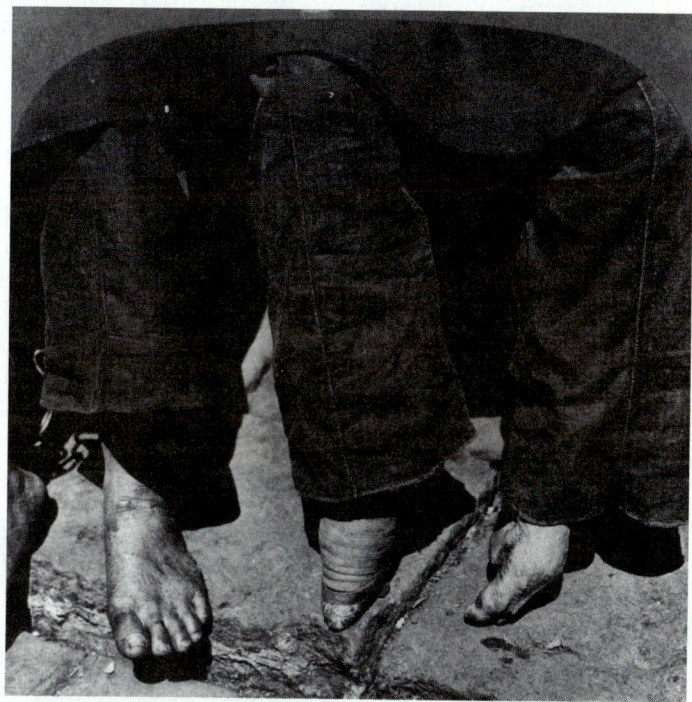

As this photograph vividly illustrates, mature women with bound feet needed special footware since they depended heavily on the very thick heel that resulted from footbinding for support when standing and walking. Little of the sole of the foot touched the ground, and toes were fused together to make a pointed foot.

QUESTIONS

- In what ways did the rise of the practice of footbinding reflect the level of prosperity achieved by China's upper classes in the Tang-Song eras and the neo-Confucian conviction that women belonged in the domestic sphere?
- Why would it be much more difficult for the laboring classes of the towns and ordinary peasant families to adopt footbinding?
- How did the structure of the family, the nature of women's extra-family links, and the sorts of pressures that could be brought to bear make it nearly impossible for women in well-to-do households to resist the imposition of the footbinding procedures?
- Beyond their lack of military training, why might the practice of footbinding make them much more vulnerable than men, especially in times of social unrest and civil war?

Canal, Tang and Song engineers made great advances in building dikes and dams and regulating the flow of water in complex irrigation systems. They also devised ingenious new ways to build bridges, long a major focus of engineering efforts in a land dominated by mountains and waterways. From arched and segmented to trussed and suspension, most of the basic bridge types known to humans were pioneered in China.

footbinding Practice in Chinese society of mutilating women's feet in order to make them smaller; produced pain and restricted women's movement; made it easier to confine women to the household.

One of the most important of the many technological advances made in the Tang era, the invention of explosive powder, at first had little impact on warfare. For centuries, the Chinese used these potent chemical mixtures mainly for fireworks, which delighted emperors and the masses alike. By the late Song, however, explosive powder was widely used by the imperial armies in a variety of grenades and bombs that were hurled at the enemy by catapults. Song armies and warships also were equipped with naphtha flamethrowers, poisonous gases, and rocket launchers. These projectiles were perhaps the most effective weapons the dynasty used in its losing struggle to check nomadic incursions. On the domestic scene, chairs modeled on those found in India were introduced into the household, the habit of drinking tea swept the empire, coal was used for fuel for the first time, and the first kite soared into the heavens.

Although the number of major inventions in the Song era was lower than in the Tang, several were pivotal for the future of all civilizations. Compasses, which had been used since the last centuries B.C.E. by Chinese military commanders and magicians, were applied to sea navigation for the first time in the Song period. The abacus, the ancestor of the modern calculator, was introduced to help merchants count their profits and tax collectors keep track of revenues. In the mid-11th century, a remarkable artisan named Bi Sheng devised the technique of printing with movable type. Although block printing had been perfected in China in the preceding centuries, the use of movable type was a great advance in the production of written records and scholarly books. Combined with paper, which the Chinese had invented in the Han period, printing made it possible for them to attain a level of literacy that excelled that of any preindustrial civilization.

Scholarly Refinement and Artistic Accomplishment

The reinvigorated scholar-gentry elite was responsible for much of the artistic and literary creativity of the Tang and Song eras. Buddhist art and architecture had been heavily patronized by the court, prosperous merchants, and wealthy monasteries in the Tang period. But scholar-administrators and Confucian teachers wrote much of the literature for which the Tang is best remembered. They also painted the landscapes that were the most sublime cultural productions of the Song era. Confucian thinkers valued skillful writing and painting, and educated people were expected to practice these arts. The Chinese educational establishment was geared to turning out generalists rather than the specialists who are so revered in our own society. A well-educated man dabbled with varying degrees of success in many fields. After a hard day at the Ministry of Public Works, a truly accomplished official was expected to spend the evening composing songs on his lute, admiring a new painting or creating his own, or sipping rice wine while composing a poem to the harvest moon. Thus, talented and often well-trained amateurs wrote most of the poems, composed much of the music, and painted the landscapes for which the Tang and Song eras are renowned (Figure 13.7).

As the Confucian scholar-gentry supplanted the Buddhists as the major producers of art and literature, devotional objects and religious homilies gave way to a growing fixation on everyday life and the delights of the natural world. Much of the short story literature was focused on the lives of the common people, popular beliefs in witchcraft and demons, ill-fated romances, and even detective stories about brutal murders. Tang poetry moved from early verses that dwelt on the "pleasant breezes that envelope[d] the emperor's chair" to a seemingly endless variety of ways of celebrating the natural world. No one was better at the latter than the most famous poet of the Tang era, **Li Bo**. His poems, like those of the great Persian authors, blend images of the everyday world with philosophical musings:

> The rain was over, green covered the land.
> One last cloudlet melted away in the clear sky.
> The east wind came home with the spring
> Bearing blossoms to sprout on the branches.
> Flowers are fading now and time will end.
> All mortal men perceive it and their sighs are deep.
> But I will turn to the sacred hills
> And learn from Tao [Dao] and from magic how to fly.

This intense interest in nature came to full artistic fruition in the landscape paintings of the Song era. Most of them were produced by the cultivated men of the scholar-gentry class, and they

Li Bo (701–762) Most famous poet of the Tang era; blended images of the mundane world with philosophical musings. The name is alternately spelled Li Po and Li Bai.

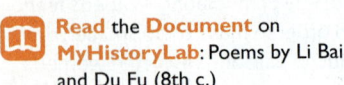
Read the Document on
MyHistoryLab: Poems by Li Bai and Du Fu (8th c.)

THINKING HISTORICALLY

Artistic Expression and Social Values

STUDYING ARTISTIC CREATIVITY IS ONE OF the most effective ways of probing the beliefs and values of a civilization. In some cases in which the civilization in question did not develop writing, or at least writing that we can now decipher, art and architecture provide much of the evidence by which we can learn about the attitudes and lifestyles of vanished peoples. Some of the most notable examples include the ancient Indus civilization of South Asia and many of the high civilizations of the Americas and sub-Saharan Africa. Even in civilizations for which written records have survived, we can learn a good deal about social structure by discovering who produced the art and for whom it was created, about technology by studying artistic techniques and materials, and about worldviews by exploring the messages the art was intended to convey. In comparing some of the major forms of artistic expression of the great civilizations, we can also identify underlying similarities and differences in the values by which the peoples who developed them organized their societies and responded to the natural and supernatural worlds.

The fact that members of the ruling political elite produced most of the landscape paintings of the Song era is unusual in the history of civilization. The sculptures that adorned the temples of India and the statues, paintings, and stained glass that graced the cathedrals of medieval Europe were created mainly by specialized and highly trained artisans whose skills were passed down over many generations. By contrast, the Song artists were often amateurs who painted in their leisure time. Even the most talented, who won enough patronage to devote themselves to painting full time, began as Confucian scholars and very often administrators. It is not just the amateur and "master of all fields" ideals that are remarkable here but the fact that so much art was produced by the men who also ran the country. In most of the other civilizations we have studied, political life has been dominated by warrior and priestly classes, not artistic scholar-bureaucrats like those who governed China.

Even in civilizations such as those of medieval Europe and Islam, where priests and religious teachers produced fine art in the form of manuscript illuminations, the people involved seldom had political responsibilities or power. Thus, the artistic creativity of China's political elite underscores the importance of the preference for civil over military leaders in Chinese society. It also tells us a good deal about the qualities the Chinese associated with a truly civilized and superior person—a person who was deemed worthy to rule the Middle Kingdom.

> [T]he artistic creativity of China's political elite underscores the importance of the preference for civil over military leaders in Chinese society.

Song landscapes expressed the reactions and ideals of individual people, whom we can identify by the distinctive seals with which they stamped their paintings. The paintings clearly were intended for the pleasure and edification of the Chinese educated classes, not for museum viewing or mass consumption. Landscape painting reinforced the identity and values of the scholarly elite across the vast spaces of the Chinese empire as well as across time. In a famous incident, the Confucian philosopher Zhu Xi remarked on the nobility and loyalty that he saw so clearly in the calligraphy of scholars from the Warring States era.

This individualism and elitism in Chinese art can be contrasted with the anonymous creation of sculptures and religious paintings in Hindu and Buddhist civilizations and medieval Europe or the mosaic decorations of the mosques of Islam. In each of these other civilizations, artistic works that adorned temples, cathedrals, and mosques were intended for a mass audience. The moral instruction for the scholarly few that was contained in the Song landscapes had a very different purpose than the religious sculptures or mosaics of other civilizations. The sculptures and mosaics were created to convey a religious message, to remind the viewers of a key event in the life of Christ or the Buddha, or to impress upon them the horrors of hell or the delights of heaven.

Thus, the highest art forms, linked to a common religion, bridged the gulf between elites and the masses in Hindu, Buddhist, Christian, and Muslim civilizations. Imported Buddhist art forms performed this function in some periods in Chinese history. But the more enduring Confucian-Daoist artistic creativity, best exemplified by landscape painting, accentuated the differences that separated the educated scholar-gentry and the common people.

QUESTIONS
- What do you think the small size of the people in Chinese landscape paintings can tell us about Chinese views on the relationship between humans and the natural world?
- Can you think of American or European politicians who have created great works of art?
- Do we expect this sort of creativity from our elected officials?
- If not, what does this tell us about the values of our own civilization?

FIGURE **13.7** The simplicity of composition, the use of empty space, and the emphasis on nature are all characteristic of Chinese landscape painting at its height in the Song era. The colors used tended to be muted; often only brown or black ink was used. Most artists stamped their work with signature seals, like the red ones in this image, and poems describing scenes related to those in the painting floated in the empty space at the top or sides.

(Ma Yuan, Chinese, 1190–1235 "Bare Willows and Distant Mountains." Photograph © 2010 Museum of Fine Arts, Boston. Special Chinese and Japanese Fund, 14.61)

pulled together diverse aspects of Chinese civilization. The brushes and techniques used were similar to those used in writing the Chinese language, which itself was regarded as a high art form. The paintings were symbolic, intended to teach moral lessons or explore philosophical ideas. The objects depicted were not only beautiful in themselves but stood for larger concepts: A crane and a pine tree, for example, represented longevity; bamboo shoots were associated with the scholar-gentry class; and a dragon could call to mind any number of things, including the emperor, the cosmos, or life-giving rain.

There was an abstract quality to the paintings that gives them a special appeal in the present day. The artists were not concerned with depicting nature accurately but rather with creating a highly personal vision of natural beauty. A premium was placed on subtlety and suggestion. For example, the winner of an imperial contest painted a lone monk drawing water from an icy stream to depict the subject announced by the emperor: a monastery hidden deep in the mountains during the winter. Song landscapes often were painted on scrolls that could be read as the viewer unfolded them bit by bit. Most were accompanied by a poem, sometimes composed by the painter, which complemented the subject matter and was aimed at explaining the artist's ideas.

Global Connections and Critical Themes

CHINA'S WORLD ROLE

The postclassical period in world history saw a vital consolidation of Chinese civilization. Although fewer fundamental changes occurred in China than those experienced in eastern and Western Europe, the Americas, and certainly the Middle East, Chinese civilization developed in important new ways. Some of these innovations, especially the technological ones, soon affected the wider world. China also consolidated its own orbit of more intense influence in eastern Asia through ongoing exchanges with central Asia, Japan, Korea, Vietnam, and elsewhere in southeast Asia. Although more isolated than the Islamic empires and India, China nevertheless contributed vitally to other regions as it flourished under two vigorous dynasties, the Tang and the Song.

From the Tang era until the 18th century, the Chinese economy was one of the world's most advanced in terms of market networks, volume of overseas trade, productivity per land area, and the sophistication of its tools and techniques of craft production. Production of luxury goods, from silks to fine ceramics, attracted traders from abroad and delighted upper-class consumers in distant lands. As a key source of both manufactured goods and cultivated consumables, such as tea and rhubarb, China contributed in major ways to the expanding Afro-Eurasian commercial system. Chinese inventions such as paper, printing, and gunpowder were also widely disseminated and fundamentally changed the course of development in all other human civilizations. Until the 18th century, the imperial dynasties of China had political power and economic resources unmatched by those of any other civilization.

By retreating to the south, the Song rulers managed to survive the assaults of the nomads from the north. But as the dynasty weakened, enduring patterns of nomadic incursions resurfaced and built to the apex of pastoral military and political expansion under the Mongols. The Song emperors could not retreat far enough to escape the onslaught of the most brilliant nomadic commander of them all, Chinggis Khan, who directed perhaps the most powerful military machine the world had seen up to that time. The Song rulers bought time by paying tribute to the Mongol Khan and making alliances with him against their common enemies. But a later Mongol leader, Kubilai Khan, launched a sustained effort to conquer the southern refuge of the Song dynasty, which was completed by 1279.

Further Readings

In addition to the general histories of China suggested in Chapter 3, several important works cover the Tang and Song eras. The recent and magisterial history of *Imperial China, 900–1800* (1999) by F. W. Mote is a superb place to start, and the volume, edited by Denis Twitchett, devoted to the Tang and Song in the *Cambridge History of China* is an essential reference work. There are detailed works on the founding of the Tang dynasty by C. P. Fitzgerald (1970) and Woodbridge Bingham (1940), but these should be read in conjunction with the more recent *Mirror to the Son of Heaven* (1974), which provides valuable correctives to the interpretations of these earlier authors. Useful insights into political and cultural life in the Tang era can be gleaned from the specialized essays in the volume *Perspectives on the Tang* (1973), edited by Arthur Wright and Denis Twitchett. On social patterns in the Tang era, see Charles Benn, *Daily Life in Traditional China: The Tang Dynasty* (2002). Until recently, the most accessible work on society and politics in the Song era was Jacques Gernet, *Daily Life in China on the Eve of the Mongol Invasion, 1250–1276* (1962), which is highly entertaining and informative. On the great social and economic transitions of the Song era, Mark Elvin, *The Pattern of the Chinese Past* (1973), is insightful, provocative, and controversial. These standard accounts can now be supplemented by P. B. Ebry, *The Aristocratic Families of Early Imperial China* (1978); Heng Chye Kiang, *Cities of Aristocrats and Bureaucrats: The Development of Medieval Chinese Cities* (1999); and D. McMullen, *State and Scholars in T'ang China* (1988). Bret Hinsch, *Women in Early Imperial China* (2002), provides a useful introduction to this subject, which is closely examined in Kathryn Bernhardt, *Women and Property in China, 960–1949* (1999), and Bettine Birge, *Women, Property and Confucian Reaction in Sung and Yüan China, 960–1368* (2002).

Of the numerous works on Chinese art and painting, perhaps the best place to start is with the standard work by Mai-mai Sze, *The Way of Chinese Painting* (1956), which quotes extensively from Chinese manuals. Of more recent works, the general survey by Laurence Sickman and Alexander Soper, as well as James Cahill's study of landscape painting, stand out. And they can be supplemented by Alfreda Murch's recent study of *Poetry and Painting in Song China* (2000). A wonderful sampler of Li Bo's poetry can be found in a volume titled *Bright Moon, Perching Bird* (1987), edited by J. P. Seaton and James Cryer.

On MyHistoryLab

 Study and Review on MyHistoryLab

Critical Thinking Questions

1. In what major ways did the relations between the Chinese and the nomadic peoples to the north and west in Central Asia shape the fortunes of Chinese dynasties in the Sui-Song eras?

2. How did the scholar-gentry become such a dominant force in Chinese politics and society from the early Tang through the Song periods?

3. How do the production, subject matter, and intended audiences of Chinese art differ from those in the Buddhist, Muslim, and Christian societies we have studied in other great civilized centers?

14

The Spread of Chinese Civilization: Japan, Korea, and Vietnam

Listen to Chapter 14 on MyHistoryLab

LEARNING OBJECTIVES

14.1 What were the key aspects of Chinese culture and organization that the Japanese imported in the early imperial era? p. 310

14.2 Why did Japan's imperial order break down beginning in the ninth century and what sort of political and social system replaced it? p. 314

14.3 What were the results of Korea's links to China? p. 319

14.4 What were the main differences in Vietnamese-Chinese relations from those in Korea and Japan? p. 322

Following a centuries-old protocol, a distinguished Vietnamese official named Ly Van Phúc entered the Chinese imperial capital at Beijing at the head of an embassy that had come to pay tribute to the Chinese ruler. Well versed in Confucian ways, Phúc was at home in the crowded streets of the great city. Because Chinese and other Asian potentates (often with good reason) regarded embassies as little more than fronts for spies, Phúc and his entourage were visiting rather than preparing to take up residence in the capital. The Vietnamese had been assigned a hostel near the Forbidden City, which housed the magnificent imperial palace where, in an elaborate ceremony, Phúc would pay homage to the Daoguang emperor (Figure 14.1).

Read the Document on MyHistoryLab: Guidelines for Tributary Missions, Qing Dynasty, 1764

FIGURE **14.1** At the height of the power and prosperity of the Qing dynasty, the emperor Qianlong, who ruled for more than 60 years, receives tribute from "the ten thousand countries" in one of his imposing palace complexes. Participation in the tribute ceremony, which had become essential for all countries—including Japan, Korea, and Vietnam—that wished to trade with China, had been established as early as the Tang dynasty in the 7th century C.E.

Watch the Video Series on MyHistoryLab

Learn about some key topics related to this chapter with the *MyHistoryLab Video Series: Key Topics in World History*

As Phúc and his countrymen approached the quarters to which they had been officially assigned, they were confronted by a placard on the building that identified it as "The Vietnamese Barbarians' Hostel." Deeply humiliated and struggling to contain his anger, Phúc ordered his companions not to enter but rather prepare an improvised campsite in the middle of the street. After commanding two of his companions to destroy the sign, he sat down and composed a strongly worded treatise entitled "On Distinguishing Barbarians." Demonstrating his admirable proficiency in Chinese calligraphy, he wrote to the Daoguang emperor, describing the insult that—whether out of ignorance or intent—the emperor's officials had directed toward the Vietnamese.

Phúc reminded the Chinese emperor (who was of Manchu descent, and thus just a few generations away from barbarian status in the Chinese view) that the Vietnamese had nurtured Chinese culture for millennia. Phúc pointed out that, like the Chinese emperor himself, the Vietnamese royal family and officials were fluent in Chinese, honored Confucian principles of governance and social organization, and organized their educational system around the classic works of Chinese civilization. As soon as it was composed, the essay was presented to Chinese officials to be delivered to the emperor. It is not certain that the very polite reprimand actually reached that exalted personage, but Vietnamese accounts of the incident expressed great satisfaction that the Chinese were most apologetic. Apparently, they even admitted their gratitude that the mistaken use of "barbarian" had been challenged and was corrected. ∎

Both the reverence for Chinese civilization and the decided ambivalence regarding the extent of its influence illustrated by the Phúc incident capture key features of centuries of interaction between China and other societies across much of central and southeast Asia. In earlier chapters we dealt in some depth with the persisting and dynamic exchanges between the Chinese and the nomadic peoples of central and northeast Asia. A similar pattern of attraction and resistance runs through the centuries when Chinese influence contributed in vital ways to the rise of complex and sophisticated societies in Japan, Korea, and Vietnam. For two millennia, China has been the premier civilization of East Asia and surrounding areas—the seedbed of technological innovation; a model for social, military, and political organization; a persisting influence on philosophical and religious thinking; and a major locus of commercial exchange (see Map 14.1).

As Phúc's obvious pride in his mastery of the Chinese language, history, and manners strikingly reveals, these influences have been particularly pervasive in agrarian-based societies, such as those that developed in neighboring Japan, Korea, and Vietnam. But Phúc's sensitivity to insults to his people and culture and his vigorous response also reflect an underlying wariness of Chinese domination that was displayed by all three of these societies. Korea and Vietnam were ruled directly by China for centuries and frequently rose in violent rebellions aimed at asserting their political independence. Japanese elites were often deeply divided about which and how much Chinese influence to introduce, and

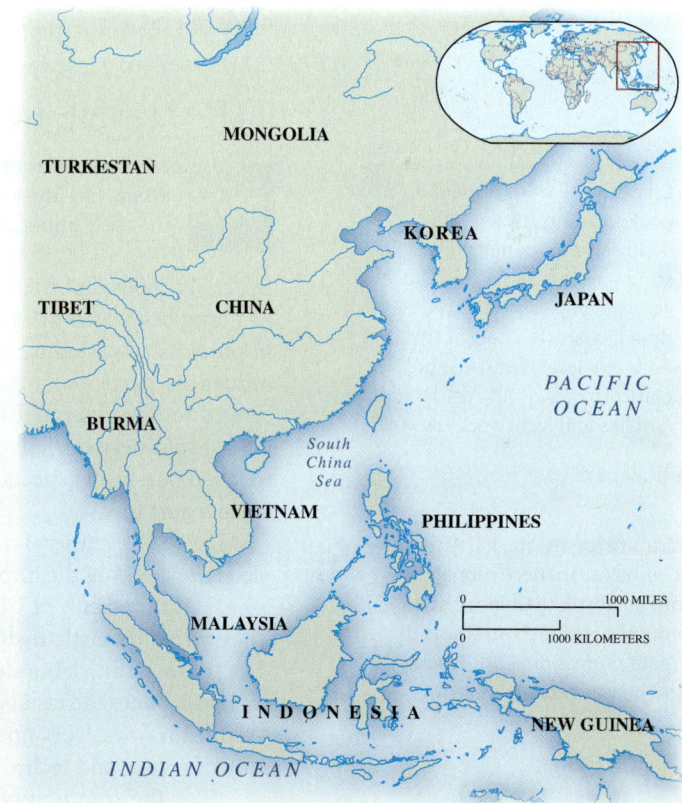

MAP **14.1 Key Centers of Civilization in East Asia in the First Millennium c.e.** Despite steady expansion over much of East Asia from the end of the last millennium b.c.e. through the first millennium c.e., the Chinese were not able to absorb three large areas on their periphery—Korea, Japan and Vietnam—into their civilization.

200 B.C.E.	600 C.E.	800 C.E.	1000 C.E.	1200 C.E.	1400 C.E.
206 B.C.E.–220 C.E. Reign of Han dynasty in China	618–907 Tang dynasty in China	838 Last Japanese embassy to China	1160–1185 Taira clan dominant in Japan	1231–1392 Mongol rule in Korea	1467–1477 Onin War in Japan
111 Vietnam conquered by China	646 Taika reforms in Japan	857–1160 Period of Fujiwara dominance in Japan	1180–1185 Gempei Wars in Japan	1279–1368 Mongol rule in China	1500 Nguyen dynasty in central/south Vietnam founded
109 Choson (Korea) conquered by China	668 Korea wins independence from Tang conquerors	918–1392 Koryo dynasty in Korea	1185–1333 Kamakura Shogunate in Japan	1392–1910 Yi dynasty in Korea	1539–1787 Trinh dynasty in Red River area (Vietnam)
39 C.E. Trung sisters revolt in Vietnam	668–918 Silla kingdom in Korea	939 Vietnam wins independence from China			1600 Founding of the Tokugawa Shogunate in Japan
222–589 Era of Division in China	710–784 Imperial Japanese capital at Nara	960–1279 Song dynasty in China			
589–618 Sui dynasty in China	794 Japanese capital shifts to Heian (Kyoto)	980–1009 Le dynasty in Vietnam			

Japanese peasants and merchants often balked at integrating Chinese imports—whether ideas or new ways of growing rice or making war—into their daily lives.

In all three cases, the tensions between the desire to emulate and borrow from China and the determination to preserve their distinctive languages, social customs, and other cultural forms profoundly shaped the nature of the highly civilized societies that developed in Japan, Korea, and Vietnam. As Phúc's confrontation with Chinese officialdom in the mid-19th century suggests, these tensions continued to shape social and political dynamics throughout east Asia well into the modern era.

JAPAN: THE IMPERIAL AGE

14.1 What were the key aspects of Chinese culture and organization that the Japanese imported in the early imperial era?

Chinese influence on Japan peaked in the 7th and 8th centuries as Japanese rulers sought to build a Chinese-style bureaucracy and society. Over time the isolated court centers at Nara and later Heian lost political control to powerful aristocratic families and local warlords.

By the late 600s C.E., the Japanese court at Nara (Map 14.2) was awash in imports from China, which had long been seen by Japan and China's other neighbors as the most advanced society in east Asia in pursuits as varied as politics, intellectual production, and material culture. Indigenous cultural influences, particularly those linked to Shinto views of the natural and supernatural world, remained central to Japanese cultural development. But in the Taika (645–710), Nara (710–784), and Heian (794–1185) periods, Japanese borrowing from China—although selective—peaked. This borrowing touched nearly all aspects of Japanese life, particularly at the level of the elites and among the people of the court towns.

Taika reforms [tai kä] Attempt to remake Japanese monarch into an absolute Chinese-style emperor; included attempts to create professional bureaucracy and peasant conscript army.

In 646 the emperor and his advisors introduced the far-reaching **Taika reforms**, aimed at completely revamping the imperial administration along Chinese lines. Japanese court scholars struggled to master thousands of Chinese characters, which bore little relationship to the language they spoke. They wrote dynastic histories patterned after those commissioned by the emperors of China, and they followed an elaborate court etiquette that somewhat uneasily combined Chinese protocol with ancient Japanese ideas about politeness and decorum. The Japanese aristocracy struggled to master Confucian ways, worshiped in Chinese-style temples, and admired Buddhist art that was Chinese in subject matter and technique.

Even the common people were affected by the steady flow of influence from the mainland. In the towns, they stared in awe at the great Buddhist temples and bowed to passing aristocrats trying to present themselves as Confucian scholars. The peasants turned to Buddhist monks for cures when they were sick or to Buddhist magic when they needed a change of luck. They had begun to mesh the worship of Buddhist deities with that of the ancient *kami*, or nature spirits, of Japan.

Read the Document on MyHistoryLab: The Seventeen Article Constitution from the Nihongi (604 C.E.)

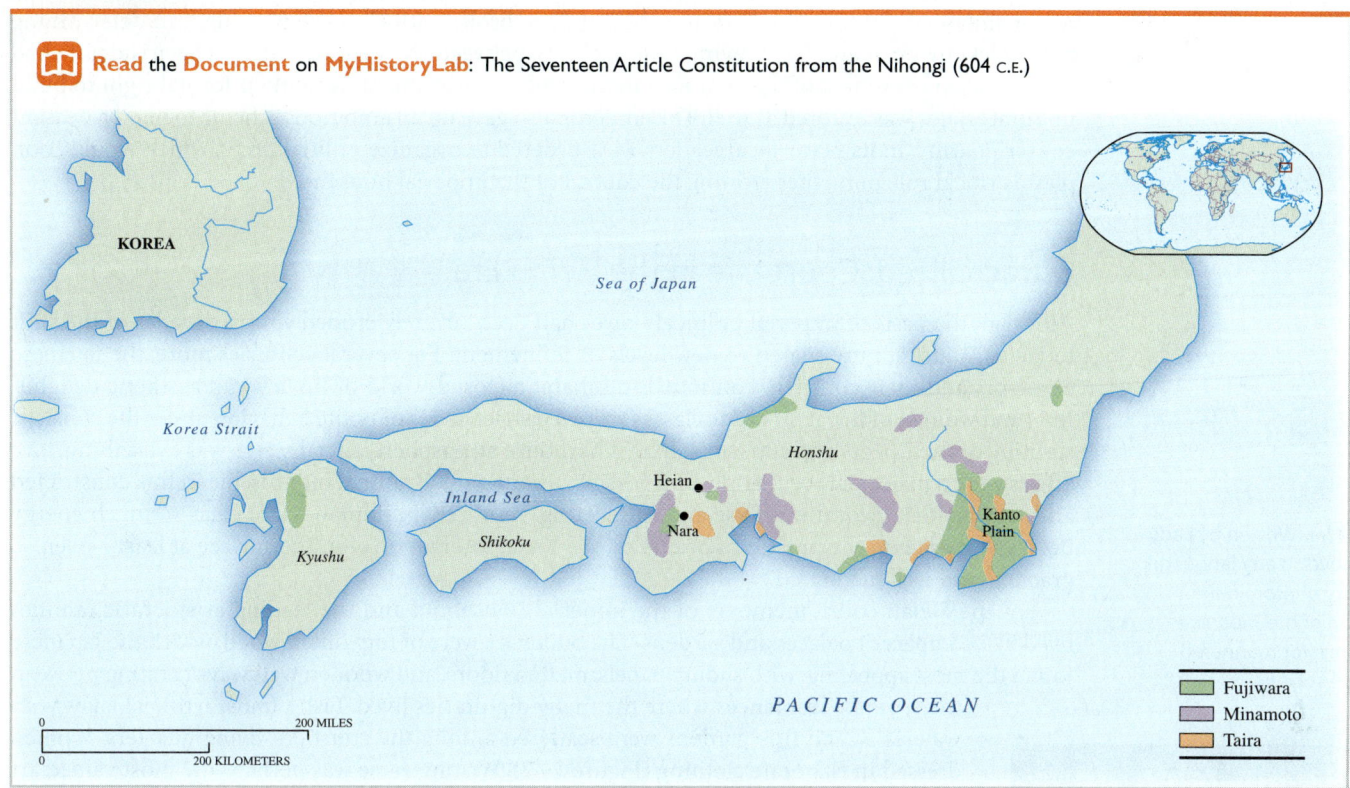

MAP 14.2 **Japan in the Imperial and Warlord Periods** Power in warlord era was concentrated in the region of the Kanto plain, which was the main rice granary of the islands and thus able to support a relatively dense population.

Crisis at Nara and the Shift to Heian (Kyoto)

If they had succeeded, the Taika reforms of 646 would have represented the culmination of centuries of Japanese borrowing from China. The central objectives of the proposed changes were to remake the Japanese monarch into an absolutist Chinese-style emperor (even to the point of adding "Son of Heaven" to the Japanese ruler's many titles). The reforms also were intended to create a genuine professional bureaucracy and peasant conscript army in Japan to match those of Han and Tang China. But the changes necessary for these goals to be achieved were frustrated by the resistance of the aristocratic families and the Buddhist monastic orders, who dominated both the emperor and the capital as a whole.

A century after the reforms were introduced, the Buddhist monks in particular had grown so bold and powerful that the court and aristocracy lived in fear of street demonstrations by "rowdy monks" and of the escalating demands of the heads of the monastic orders. Their influence even threatened to engulf the throne in the 760s, when a clever Buddhist prelate worked his way into the inner circle of the empress Koken. His schemes to marry her and become emperor were uncovered and foiled. But it was clear to the emperor's advisors that measures had to be taken to ensure that women could never rule Japan and to check the growing influence of the monastic orders at court.

Read the Document on MyHistoryLab: Buddhism in Japan: The Taika Reform Edicts

In 794 the emperor Kammu established a new capital city at Heian (hay-yan) (Map 14.2), which was later called Kyoto. Buddhists were forbidden to build monasteries in the new capital. But to get around this restriction, the monks established monasteries in the hills surrounding Heian, and they soon reemerged as a potent force at court as royal advisors.

In addition to trying to control the Buddhist monks, the emperor abandoned all pretense of continuing the Taika reforms, which had long been stalled by aristocratic and popular opposition. He fully restored the great aristocratic families, whose power the reforms had been intended to curb. The elaborate system of ranks into which the aristocrats were divided (patterned after that in China)

CHAPTER 14 The Spread of Chinese Civilization: Japan, Korea, and Vietnam 311

was maintained. But like the Koreans, the Japanese broke with Chinese precedent in determining rank solely by birth and by allowing little mobility between the various orders. The aristocrats had already taken over most of the positions in the central government. Now, their formal right to build up rural estates was restored as well. The emperor also gave up an ambitious scheme to build a peasant conscript army. In its place, local leaders were ordered to organize militia forces, which would soon play a critical role in further eroding the control of the imperial household.

Ultracivilized: Court Life in the Heian Era

Although the basis of imperial political power had been severely eroded within decades of the shift to Heian, court culture soared to new levels of refinement. For several centuries more, the Japanese emperors and their courtiers continued to inhabit a closed world of luxury and aesthetic delights. Men and women of the aristocratic classes followed strict codes of polite behavior, under the constant scrutiny of their peers and superiors. In this hothouse atmosphere, social status was everything, love affairs were a major preoccupation, and gossip was rampant. By our standards, life in this constricted and very artificial world was false and suffocating. Yet rarely in human history has so much energy been so focused on the pursuit of beauty or has social interaction—on the surface at least—been so gracious and well mannered.

At the Heian court, members of the imperial household and the leading aristocratic families lived in a complex of palaces and gardens. The buildings were of unpainted wood, which the Japanese found the most appealing, with sliding panels, matted floors, and wooden walkways running between the separate residences where the many dignitaries lived. Fish ponds, artificial lakes with waterfalls, and fine gardens were scattered among the courtiers' living quarters. Women dressed in elaborate clothing (Figure 14.2). Writing verse was perhaps the most valued art at the court. The poems were often written on painted fans or scented paper, and sometimes they were sent in little boats down the streams that ran through the palace grounds. The verse was brief and full of allusions to Chinese and Japanese classical writings. In the following couplet, a young courtier expresses his disappointment at being denied access to a pretty young woman:

> Having come upon an evening blossom
> The mist is loath to go with the morning sun.

Tale of Genji, The Written by Lady Murasaki; first novel in any language; relates life history of prominent and amorous son of the Japanese emperor; evidence for mannered style of Japanese society.

Partly to accommodate the need for literary expression of this type, the written script the Japanese had borrowed from the Chinese was simplified, making it more compatible with spoken Japanese. One result of these changes was an outpouring of poetic and literary works that were more and more distinctively Japanese. The most celebrated of these was Lady Murasaki's **The Tale of Genji**. None of the works on court life captured its charm and its underlying tensions and sadness as wonderfully as Lady Murasaki's classic, which was the first novel in any language (Figure 14.3). In the story, she relates the life history of a prominent and amorous son of the emperor and the fate of his descendants. As the story makes clear, Genji's life is almost wholly devoted to the pursuit of aesthetic enjoyment, whether in affairs with beautiful women or in musical entertainments in a garden scented with blooming flowers. Uncouth commoners and distasteful things, such as dirt, cheap pottery, and rough popular entertainments, are to be avoided at all costs. When her rivals at the court want to insult Genji's mother, for example, they leave spoiled fruit in the passages where she or her maidservants must pass. An encounter with a shriveled piece of fruit contributes to the illness that leads to her premature death.

Everyone who matters in Genji's world is obsessed with the social conventions that govern everything, from which gown is proper for a given ceremony to the composition of a suitable poem to woo a potential lover or win the emperor's favor. Although women rivaled men as poets, artists, and musicians and in their pervasive cultivation of aesthetic pleasure, it was unseemly for them to openly pursue lovers. Nonetheless, as Lady Murasaki's poignant novel makes clear, some women did court prospective lovers with great guile and passion. It was not uncommon for a high-born woman to spurn a suitor and humiliate him in front of her maidservants.

FIGURE 14.2 From this artist's impression of the elaborate dress and studied pose of a Heian courtier, one gains a vivid sense of the formality and attention to aesthetic pleasures that dominated the lives of the Japanese elite in this era. As the focus upon a woman in the painting suggests, the intense world of the Heian court provided a tiny minority of Japanese women with outlets for expressing emotion and creativity that have been denied to most women through much of civilized history.

In addition to novels such as Lady Murasaki's, some of the most elegant poetry in the Japanese language was written in this era. Again, it is sparing in words but rich in imagery and allusions to the natural world:

> This perfectly still
> Spring Day bathed in the soft light
> From the spread-out sky,
> Why do the cherry blossoms so restlessly scatter down?
> Although I am sure
> That he will not be coming
> In the evening light
> When the locusts shrilly call
> I go to the door and wait.

As the female authorship of this poem and *The Tale of Genji* clearly illustrate, women at the Heian court were expected to be as poised and cultured as men. Because they were less involved, however, with Chinese cultural imports (presumed to be a superior male preserve), they actually, for a time, played an unusually creative role in Japanese productions. They wrote poems, played flutes or stringed instruments in informal concerts, and participated in elaborate schemes to snub or disgrace rivals. Like their counterparts in China and the Islamic world, they also became involved in palace intrigues and power struggles.

The Decline of Imperial Power

While the emperor and his courtiers admired the plum blossoms and the newest fashions in court dress, some of the aristocratic families at court were busy running the rapidly shrinking imperial bureaucracy. By the mid-9th century, one of these families, the **Fujiwara**, exercised exceptional influence over imperial affairs. Not only did they pack the upper administration with family members and shape imperial policy, but they also increasingly married Fujiwaras into the imperial family. By the middle of the 10th century, one aged Fujiwara chief minister had seen four of his daughters married to emperors.

Families such as the Fujiwara used the wealth and influence of their high office to build up large estates that provided a stable financial base for their growing power. Especially in the vicinity of the capital, they had to compete in these purchases with the Buddhist monasteries. But both could work together in the steady campaign to whittle down imperial control and increase their own. As the lands under their control expanded, both the monks and the court nobility greatly increased the number of peasants and artisans they in effect ruled. Cooperation between monastic orders and court aristocrats was promoted by the introduction of the secret texts and ceremonies of esoteric Buddhism in this period. These teachings and techniques to achieve salvation through prayers and meditation, which were focused by mystical diagrams and special hand positions, were the rage among the Heian elite. As aristocrats and monks steadily built up their own power in the capital, however, they failed to reckon with the growing power of the local lords.

The Rise of the Provincial Warrior Elites

The pursuit of landed estates that increasingly preoccupied the court aristocracy was also taken up by elite families in the provinces. Some of these families had aristocratic origins, but most had risen to power as landowners, estate managers, or local state officials. These families came to control land and labor and to deny these resources to the court. They gradually carved out little kingdoms, ruled by "house" governments, in various parts of the islands. They dominated their mini-states within the larger Japanese realm from small fortresses surrounded by wooden or earthen walls and moat-like ditches. The local lord and his retainers were housed within the fortress, constantly on the alert for an attack by a neighboring lord or the forces of one of the powerful families at court. Granaries for storing the rice provided by local peasants, blacksmith forges and stables, wells for water, and even armories made the fortresses self-contained worlds.

FIGURE **14.3** This painting illustrating one of the episodes in Lady Murasaki's *The Tale of Genji* captures the inward-looking character of court life that gradually cut the emperor and his entourage off from the warriors, townspeople, and peasants they ruled. The growing isolation of the court provided opportunities for regional lords with a more military orientation and more effective links to the population as a whole to seize effective control of Japan.

Fujiwara Japanese aristocratic family in mid-9th century; exercised exceptional influence over imperial affairs; aided in decline of imperial power.

bushi Regional warrior leaders in Japan; ruled small kingdoms from fortresses; administered the law, supervised public works projects, and collected revenues; built up private armies.

samurai Mounted troops of Japanese warrior leaders (bushi); loyal to local lords, not the emperor.

Within the mini-states ruled from the forts, the warrior leaders, or **bushi**, administered law, supervised public works projects, and collected revenue—mainly for themselves, not the court. The failure of the court's plans to build conscript armies also allowed the bushi to build up their own armies. These soon became the most effective military forces in the land. The troops who served the bushi came to be called **samurai**. They were loyal to the local lords, not to the court or high aristocratic officials, even though they were increasingly called in to protect the emperor and his retainers and to keep the peace in the capital. As the imperial government's control over the country weakened in the 11th and 12th centuries, bandits freely roamed the countryside and the streets of the capital. Buddhist monasteries employed armed toughs to protect them and attack rival sects. In this atmosphere of rampant crime and civil strife, the court and high officials hired provincial lords and their samurai retainers to serve as bodyguards and to protect their palaces and mansions from robbery and arson.

These trends proved critical to the emergence of a warrior class. Counting on peasant dependants to supply them with food and other necessities, the bushi and samurai devoted their lives to hunting, riding, archery practice, and other activities that sharpened their martial skills. Until the 12th century, the main weapons of the mounted warriors were powerful longbows and spears, although they also carried straight swords. From the 12th century on, they increasingly relied on the superbly forged, curved steel swords that we commonly associate with the Japanese samurai. The bushi and the samurai warriors who served them rode into battles that increasingly hinged on the duels of great champions. These combats represented heroic warfare in the extreme. The time and location of battles were elaborately negotiated beforehand, and each side tried to demonstrate the justice of its cause and the treachery of its enemies. Before charging into battle, Japanese warriors proudly proclaimed their family lineage and its notable military exploits to their adversaries, who often missed the details because they were shouting back their own.

A warrior code developed that stressed family honor and death rather than retreat or defeat. Beaten or disgraced warriors turned to ritual suicide to prove their courage and restore their family's honor. They called this practice **seppuku**, which meant disembowelment. But it has come to be known in the West by the more vulgar expression *hara-kiri*, or belly splitting. Battles were chaotic—lots of shouting and clashing but few fatalities—and were won or lost depending on the performance of the champions on each side. Although a full chivalric code did not develop until some centuries later, Japan was steadily moving toward a feudal order that was remarkably similar to that developing in western Europe in this same postclassical period.

seppuku Ritual suicide or disembowelment in Japan; commonly known in West as hara-kiri; demonstrated courage and a means to restore family honor.

The rise of the samurai frustrated all hopes of creating a free peasantry. In fact, Japanese peasants were reduced in the next centuries to the status of serfs, bound to the land they worked and treated as the property of the local lord. They were also separated by rigid class barriers from the warrior elite, which was physically set off by its different ways of dressing and by prohibitions against the peasants carrying swords or riding horses. In their growing poverty and powerlessness, the peasants turned to popular Buddhism in the form of the salvationist pure land sect. The teachings of the pure land offered the promise of bliss in heaven for those who lived upright lives on earth. Colorful figures, such as the dancing monk Kuya, were intended to make Buddhist teachings comprehensible and appealing to both the peasantry and the artisans, who were concentrated in the fortress towns. Buddhist shrines and images became popular destinations for pilgrimages and objects of veneration.

THE ERA OF WARRIOR DOMINANCE

From the 12th century onward, Japanese history was increasingly dominated by civil wars between shifting factions of the court aristocracy and local warlords, which ended only with the rise of the Tokugawa warlord family in the early 1600s. Chinese influence declined steadily in this era, but despite strife and social dislocation, the arts and literature flourished in Japan.

14.2 Why did Japan's imperial order break down beginning in the ninth century and what sort of political and social system replaced it?

As the power of the provincial lords grew, that of the imperial household and court aristocracy declined. Powerful families at the court, such as the Fujiwara, increasingly depended on alliances with regional lords to support them in disputes with their rivals. By the 11th and 12th centuries, the provincial families had begun to pack the court bureaucracy and compete for power. By the mid-12th century, competition turned to open feuding between the most powerful of these families, the **Taira** and the **Minamoto**. For a time, the Taira gained the upper hand by controlling the emperor and dominating at court. But when rivalry turned to open warfare in the early 1180s, the Minamoto commanders and their powerful network of alliances with provincial lords in various parts of the country proved superior to the leaders or allies the Taira could muster. More importantly, the Tairas' concentration of their power-grabbing efforts in the capital led to the breakdown of critical links with rural notables, who often sided with the Minamoto in the factional struggles.

The Declining Influence of China

As the power of the imperial house weakened, the relevance of Chinese precedents and institutions diminished for the Japanese. Pretensions to a heavenly mandate and centralized power became ludicrous; the emergence of a scholar-gentry elite was stifled by the reassertion of aristocratic power and prerogatives. Grand designs for an imperial bureaucracy never materialized. Buddhism was increasingly transformed by both aristocrats and peasants into a distinctively Japanese religion. With the decline of the Tang and a return to decades of political uncertainty and social turmoil in China, the Chinese model seemed even less relevant to the Japanese. As early as 838, the Japanese court decided to discontinue its embassies to the much-reduced Tang court. Japanese monks and traders still made the dangerous sea crossing to China, but the emperor's advisors no longer deemed official visits and groveling before the Son of Heaven to be worth all the bother.

For five years, the **Gempei Wars** raged in the heartland of the main island of Honshu (Map 14.2). This conflict brought great suffering to the peasantry, whose farmlands were ravaged. At the same time, they were compelled to fight against each other. Often large numbers of poorly trained peasants were cut down by the better-armed, professional samurai warriors, who met these hapless rivals in the course of their seemingly endless ritual combats. By 1185, the Taira house faction had been destroyed. The Minamoto then established the **bakufu** (which literally means "tent"), or military government. The Minamoto capital was located at Kamakura in their base area on the Kanto plain, far to the east of the old court center at Heian (Map 14.2). The emperor and his court were preserved, but real power now rested with the Minamoto and their samurai retainers. The feudal age in Japan had begun.

The Breakdown of Bakufu Dominance and the Age of the Warlords

Yoritomo, the leader of the victorious Minamoto, gravely weakened the Kamakura regime because of his obsessive fear of being overthrown by members of his own family. Close relatives, including his brother Yoshitsune, whose courage and military genius had much to do with the Minamoto triumph over the Taira, were murdered or driven into exile. Fear of spies lent an element of paranoia to elite life under the first of the Kamakura **shoguns**, which was the title taken by the military overlords of the bakufu. Although Yoritomo's rule went unchallenged, the measures he adopted to protect his throne left him without an able heir. His death and the weakness of those who succeeded him led to a scramble on the part of the bushi lords to build up their own power and enlarge their domains. The **Hojo**, one of the warrior families that had long been closely allied to the Minamoto, soon dominated the Kamakura regime, although they were content to leave the Minamoto as the formal rulers. Thus, a curious and confusing three-tiered system arose. Real power rested in the Hojo family, who manipulated the Minamoto shoguns, who in turn claimed to rule in the name of the emperor who lived at Kyoto.

In the early 14th century, the situation became even murkier when the head of one of the branches of the Minamoto family, **Ashikaga Takuaji**, led a revolt of the bushi that overthrew the Kamakura regime and established the **Ashikaga Shogunate** (1336–1573) in its place. Because the emperor at the time of Ashikaga's seizure of power refused to recognize the usurper and tried to revive imperial power, he was driven from Kyoto to the mountain town of Yoshino. There, with the support of several warlords, the exiled emperor and his heirs fought against the Ashikaga faction and the puppet emperors they placed on the throne at Kyoto for much of the rest of the 14th century.

Although the Ashikaga were finally successful in destroying the rival Yoshino center of imperial authority, the long period of civil strife seriously undermined whatever authority the emperor had left as well as that of the shogunate. The bushi vassals of the warring factions were free to crush local rivals and to seize the lands of the peasantry, the old aristocracy, and competing warlords. As the power of the bushi warlords grew, the court aristocracy, which was impoverished by its inability to defend its estates, was nearly wiped out. The lands the warlords acquired were parceled out to their

---

Taira [teye-ruh] Powerful Japanese family in 11th and 12th centuries; competed with Minamoto family; defeated after Gempei Wars.

Minamoto Defeated the rival Taira family in Gempei Wars and established military government (bakufu) in 12th-century Japan.

Gempei Wars [gehm-pay] Waged for five years from 1180, on Honshu between Taira and Minamoto families; resulted in destruction of Taira.

bakufu Military government established by the Minamoto following the Gempei Wars; centered at Kamakura; retained emperor, but real power resided in military government and samurai.

shoguns Military leaders of the bakufu (military governments in Japan).

Hojo Warrior family closely allied with Minamoto; dominated Kamakura regime and manipulated Minamoto rulers who claimed to rule in name of Japanese emperor at Kyoto.

Ashikaga Takuaji [ah-she-kah-gah tahk-oo-ah-jee] Member of the Minamoto family; overthrew the Kamakura regime and established the Ashikaga Shogunate from 1336–1573; drove emperor from Kyoto to Yoshino.

Ashikaga Shogunate [ah-she-kah-gah shoh-guh-nayt] Replaced the Kamakura regime in Japan; ruled from 1336 to 1573; destroyed rival Yoshino center of imperial authority.

THINKING HISTORICALLY

Comparing Feudalisms

IN ONE SENSE, THE EXISTENCE OF feudalism is easily explained. Many societies generated only weak central government structures simply because they lacked the resources, shared political values, and bureaucratic experience to develop alternatives. China under the Zhou dynasty is sometimes called feudal. The Russian kings from Rurik onward exercised only loose control over powerful landlords. Kings in the divine monarchy systems of sub-Saharan Africa, which flourished from about the 9th to the 19th century in various parts of the continent, similarly relied on deals and compromises with local and regional leaders. Indeed, African historians have often noted that kingdoms such as Ghana and Mali were ruled about as effectively as were Western monarchies during the Middle Ages.

A comparison of this sort reminds us that feudal systems were in many ways early, less sophisticated versions of political societies that were gradually moving from purely local toward more centralized organization. Indeed, almost all civilizations have experienced long periods of semi-centralized rule. In all such cases, including feudal ones, the claims of central authorities are not matched by effective power. Regional leaders have armies of their own and do much of the effective administration of their localities. Kings have to make deals with such leaders, relying on personal negotiation and pledges of mutual respect, marriage alliances, negotiation, and a willingness to give the local princes free rein in practice.

The feudal systems that arose in the West and Japan differed in some respects from the many other decentralized systems they resemble. These differences make it desirable not to call all such systems feudal, thus diluting an extremely useful term beyond recognition. For example, Russia was often decentralized and often saw its rulers, whatever their grandiose claims, make concessions to regional nobles because the tsars depended on the loyalty and service of these subordinate lords. But Russia never developed a genuinely feudal political hierarchy, which is one of the features that distinguished it from the West. The same holds true for Zhou China or even the Sudanic empires of Africa.

Japan and the medieval West developed feudal systems grounded in a set of political values that embraced, however imperfectly, most of the participants in the system. The most important of these participants were the aristocratic lords, who effectively controlled the mass of the peasants. The idea of mutual ties and obligations, and the rituals and institutions that expressed them, went beyond the more casual local deals and compromises characteristic of ancient China or medieval and early modern Russia.

In both western Europe and Japan, feudalism was highly militaristic. Both the medieval West and Japan went through long centuries of unusually frequent and bitter internal warfare, based in large part on feudal loyalties and rivalries. Although this warfare was more confined to the warrior-landlord class in Europe than in Japan, in both instances feudalism summed up a host of elite military virtues that long impeded the development of more stable, centralized government. These values included physical courage, personal or family alliances, loyalty, ritualized combat, and often contempt for non-warrior groups such as peasants and merchants.

The military aura of feudalism survived the feudal era in both cases. It left Japan with serious problems in controlling its samurai class after the worst periods of internal conflict had passed in the early 17th century. In the West, the warrior ethic of feudalism persisted in the prominent belief that a central purpose of the state was to make war, thereby providing opportunities for military leaders to demonstrate their prowess. But the legacy of feudalism was not simply military. For example, the idea of personal ties between leaders or among elite groups as a foundation for political activity continued to affect political life and institutions, both in the West and in Japan, long after the feudal period ended.

The characteristics of feudalism in Japan and in the West were not identical. Western feudalism emphasized contractual ideas more strongly than did Japanese. Although mutual ties were acknowledged by members of the European warrior elite, feudal loyalties were sealed by negotiated contracts, in which the parties involved obtained explicit assurances of the advantages each would receive from the alliance. Japanese feudalism relied more heavily on group and individual loyalties, which were not confirmed by contractual agreements. Probably for this reason, the clearest ongoing legacy of feudalism in the West proved to be parliamentary institutions, where individual aristocrats (as well as townspeople and clergy) could join to defend their explicitly defined legal interests against the central monarch. (Western feudalism also helped encourage the emergence of lawyers, who have never played a comparable role in Japan.) In Japan, the legacy of feudalism involved a less institutionalized group consciousness. This approach encouraged individuals to function as part of collective decision-making teams that ultimately could be linked to the state.

> [T]he idea of personal ties between leaders or among elite groups as a foundation for political activity continued to affect political life and institutions, both in the West and in Japan, long after the feudal period ended.

(continued on next page)

(continued from previous page)

Can the common fact of a feudal heritage be used to explain another similarity between the West and Japan that emerged clearly in the 20th century? Both societies have been unusually successful in industrial development. Both have also proven adept at running capitalist economies. It is certainly tempting to point to feudalism, the medieval feature the two societies uniquely shared, as a partial explanation for these otherwise unexpected 19th- and 20th-century resemblances. The feudal legacy may also help to account for less positive aspects of western European and Japanese development in these centuries, especially their propensity for imperialist expansion and the fact that they frequently resorted to war to solve conflicts with foreign powers. In the case of Japan and Germany, recent historians have established intriguing connections between the persistence of feudalism late into the early modern era and the rise of right-wing militarist regimes in the 1930s.

When the Japanese talent for group cohesion is identified so strikingly as an ingredient in 20th-century economic success, or when Western nations win political stability through use of parliamentary forms, it surely seems legitimate to point to some persistent threads that run through the experience of the two societies. Whether the common experience of feudalism is a basis for later economic dynamism is a matter for speculation. However, it need not be excluded from a list of provocative uses of comparative analysis simply because the links are challenging.

> **QUESTIONS**
> - Do you think the characteristics of feudalism help explain the later success of Western and Japanese societies? If so, in what ways? If not, why not?
> - Which aspects of feudalism do you think had the greatest effect on these outcomes?
> - What other factors should be taken into account if we want to fully analyze these trends?

samurai retainers, who in turn pledged their loyalty and were expected to provide military support whenever their lord called on them.

The collapse of centralized authority was sharply accelerated by the outbreak of full-scale civil war, which raged from 1467 to 1477. Rival heirs to the Ashikaga Shogunate called on the warlord chiefs to support their claims. Samurai flocked to rival headquarters in different sections of Kyoto, where feuding soon broke into all-out warfare. Within a matter of years, the old imperial capital had been reduced to rubble and weed-choked fields. While the shogunate self-destructed in the capital, the provincial lords continued to amass power and plot new coalitions to destroy their enemies. Japan was divided into nearly 300 little kingdoms, whose warlord rulers were called **daimyos** rather than bushi.

daimyos [daim-yo] Warlord rulers of 300 small states following civil war and disruption of Ashikaga Shogunate; holdings consolidated into unified and bounded mini-states.

Toward Barbarism? Military Division and Social Change

Although the rituals became more elaborate, the armor heavier, and the swords more superbly forged, the chivalrous qualities of the bushi era deteriorated noticeably in the 15th and 16th centuries. In the place of mud-walled forts, there arose the massive wood and stone castles, such as that at Himeji pictured in Figure 14.4. These imposing structures dominated the Japanese landscape in the centuries that followed. Spying, sneak attacks, ruses, and timely betrayals became the order of the day. The pattern of warfare was fundamentally transformed as large numbers of peasants armed with pikes became a critical component of daimyo armies. Battles hinged less and less on the outcome of samurai combat. Victory depended on the size and organization of a warlord's forces and on how effectively his commanders used them in the field.

The badly trained and poorly fed peasant forces became a major source of the growing misery of the

View the **Closer Look** on **MyHistoryLab**: Edo Castle, Tokyo, Japan

FIGURE 14.4 Himeji Castle was one of the most formidable of the many fortresses that became focal points of much of the Japanese landscape in the era dominated by the samurai warriors. Although the inner buildings were often made of wood, these more vulnerable structures were defended by walls and long, fortified passageways made of stone. Like those of medieval Europe, each castle had wells and granaries for the storage of food that allowed its defenders to withstand long sieges by the forces of rival warlords.

CHAPTER 14 The Spread of Chinese Civilization: Japan, Korea, and Vietnam **317**

common people. As they marched about the countryside to fight the incessant wars of their overlords, they looted and pillaged. The peasantry in different areas sporadically rose up in hopeless but often ferocious revolts, which fed the trend toward brutality and destruction. It is no wonder that contemporary accounts of the era, as well as those written in later centuries, are dominated by a sense of pessimism and foreboding, a conviction that Japan was reverting from civilized life to barbarism.

Despite the chaos and suffering of the warlord period, there was much economic and cultural growth. Most of the daimyo clearly recognized the need to build up their petty states if they were to survive in the long run. The more able daimyo tried to stabilize village life within their domains by introducing regular tax collection, supporting the construction of irrigation systems and other public works, and building strong rural communities. Incentives were offered to encourage the settlement of unoccupied areas. New tools, the greater use of draft animals, and new crops—especially soybeans—contributed to the well-being of the peasantry in the better-run domains. Peasants were also encouraged to produce items such as silk, hemp, paper, dyes, and vegetable oils, which were highly marketable and thus potential sources of household income. Daimyos vied with each other to attract merchants to their growing castle towns. Soon a new and wealthy commercial class emerged as purveyors of goods for the military elite and intermediaries in trade between Japan and overseas areas, especially China. As in medieval Europe, guild organizations for artisans and merchants were strong in this era. They helped provide social solidarity and group protection in a time of political breakdown and insecurity.

Evidence reveals that the growth of commerce and the handicraft industries gave some Japanese women opportunities to avoid the sharp drop in status that most experienced in the age of the warring daimyos. Women in merchant and artisan families apparently exercised a fair degree of independence. This was reflected in their participation in guild organizations and business management and by the fact that their positions were sometimes inherited by their daughters. But the status of women in the emerging commercial classes contrasted sharply with that of women in the warrior elites. In earlier centuries, the wives and daughters of the provincial bushi households learned to ride and to use a bow and arrow, and they often joined in the hunt. By the 14th and 15th centuries, however, the trend among the daimyo families toward primogeniture, or limiting inheritance to the eldest son, dealt a heavy blow to women of the elite classes. The wives and daughters of warrior households, who had hitherto shared in the division of the family estate, now received little or no land or income.

Disinheritance was part of a larger pattern that saw women increasingly treated as defenseless appendages of their warrior fathers or husbands. They were given in marriage to cement alliances between warrior households and reared to anticipate their warrior husband's every desire. They were also taught to slay themselves rather than dishonor the family line by being raped by illicit suitors or enemy soldiers. Japanese women of all classes lost the role of the celebrant in village religious ceremonies and were replaced in Japanese theatrical performances by men specially trained to impersonate women.

Artistic Solace for a Troubled Age

Fears that the constant wars between the swaggering samurai might drag Japan back to barbarism were somewhat mollified by continuing cultivation of the arts. Zen Buddhism, which because of its stress on simplicity and discipline had a special appeal to

FIGURE **14.5** Patronage of landscape painting and the other fine arts in Japan allowed artistic expression to survive in the long centuries of political division and civil war. In paintings such as the one pictured here, Chinese aesthetic preferences and techniques were strong. In fact, Japanese artists consciously imitated the monochrome (one-colored) paintings of Song China, which they regarded as the apex of the genre. Japanese artists not only concentrated on the same themes, such as landscapes with tiny human figures, but imitated the brushstrokes that they believed had been used by the Song masters.

(Shen Zhou (Chinese 1427–1509), "Poet on a Mountain Top." The Nelson-Atkins Museum of Art, Kansas City, Missouri. Purchase: Nelson Trust, 46-51/2. Photo: Robert Newcombe.)

the warrior elite, played a critical role in securing the place of the arts in an era of strife and destruction. Zen monasteries provided key points of renewed diplomatic and trade contacts with China, which in turn led to a revival of Chinese influence in Japan, at least at the cultural level. Although much painting of the era imitated earlier Chinese work of the Song period, the monochrome ink sketches of Japanese artists were both brilliant and original. Also notable were screen and scroll paintings, such as the one in Figure 14.5, that capture the natural beauty of Japan; others provide us with invaluable glimpses into Japanese life in this period. Zen sensibilities are also prominent in some of the splendid architectural works of this period, including the Golden and Silver Pavilions that Ashikaga shoguns had built in Kyoto (Figure 14.6). Each pavilion was designed to blend into the natural setting in which it was placed to create a pleasing shelter that would foster contemplation and meditation.

This contemplative mood is also evident in the design of some of the more famous gardens of this era. One of these, at the Ryoanji Temple, consisted entirely of islands of volcanic rock set amid white pebbles, which were periodically raked into varying patterns. The influence of Shintoism and Zen Buddhism on such gardens, and the related Japanese ability to find great beauty in the rough and simple, were also present in the tea ceremony that developed in the era of warrior dominance. The graceful gestures, elaborate rituals, and subtly shaped and glazed pots and cups associated with the service of tea on special occasions all lent themselves to composure and introspection. These arts and aesthetic sensibilities were cultivated through centuries of warfare. They continued during the "long peace" of the Tokugawa shogunate that marked the last phase of the feudal period that persisted until the late-19th century.

FIGURE **14.6** The Golden Pavilion (or Kinkakuji) is one of the great architectural treasures of the age of the warring houses in Japan. Built on a small lake near Kyoto in the 15th century, the wooden, tile-roofed structure reflects the Zen and Shinto stress on simplicity typical of almost all Japanese artistic production in the centuries of the warring states. Its gold-painted exterior and the reflecting pond enhance these sensibilities.

KOREA: BETWEEN CHINA AND JAPAN

14.3 What were the results of Korea's links to China?

Of all the areas to which the Chinese formula for civilized development spread, Korea was the most profoundly influenced for the longest period of time. Despite repeated Chinese interventions, the Korean people developed a separate identity that was expressed in distinctive forms of dress, cuisine, and a unique social class system.

Because the Korean peninsula is an extension of the Chinese mainland, and because, historically, Korean kingdoms were dwarfed by their giant neighbor to the west, most observers have treated Korea as little more than an appendage of China. But lumping Korea together with China overlooks the fact that the peninsula was ruled by indigenous dynasties through most of its history, even though these dynasties often paid tribute to the reigning Chinese emperor. At an even more basic level, the peoples who occupied the Korean peninsula represented a different ethnic blend than those who, centuries earlier, had come to identify themselves as Chinese. The Koreans descended from the hunting and herding peoples of eastern Siberia and Manchuria rather than the Mongolian- and Turkic-speaking tribes to the west. By the 4th century B.C.E., the peoples who moved into the Korean peninsula had begun to acquire sedentary farming and metalworking techniques from the Chinese.

From this point onward, the Koreans played a role in the dynastic struggles that preoccupied the peoples of the north China plain. In 109 B.C.E., the earliest Korean kingdom, **Choson**, was conquered by the Han emperor Wudi. Thereafter, parts of Korea were colonized by Chinese settlers, who remained for nearly four centuries. These colonies soon became a channel by which Chinese influences began to filter into Korean culture in the critical centuries of its early development. A small Japanese enclave in the southeast of the peninsula provided contact with the islands as well, although cultural influences in this era ran overwhelmingly eastward, from China to Korea and then on to Japan.

Choson [choh-suhn] Earliest Korean kingdom; conquered by Han armies in 109 B.C.E.

CHAPTER 14 The Spread of Chinese Civilization: Japan, Korea, and Vietnam **319**

Koguryo [koh-goor-yoo] Tribal people of northern Korea; established an independent kingdom in the northern half of the peninsula in 37 B.C.E.; began a process of Sinification.

Silla Independent Korean kingdom in southeastern part of peninsula; defeated Koguryo along with their Chinese Tang allies; submitted as a vassal of the Tang emperor and agreed to tribute payment; ruled united Korea by 668.

Paekche [pah-EHK-chee] Independent Korean kingdom in southwestern part of peninsula; defeated by rival Silla kingdom and its Chinese Tang allies in 7th century.

Sinification Extensive adoption of Chinese culture in other regions; typical of Korea, Japan, and Vietnam.

Despite conquest and colonization under the Han, the tribal peoples of the peninsula, particularly the **Koguryo** in the north, soon resisted Chinese rule. As Chinese control weakened, the Koguryo established an independent state in the northern half of the peninsula that was soon at war with two southern rivals, **Silla** and **Paekche** (Map 14.3). Contacts between the splinter kingdoms that ruled north China after the fall of the Han and the Koguryo kingdom resulted in the first wave of **Sinification**—that is, the extensive adoption of Chinese culture—in Korea. As was the case in Japan, Buddhism supplied the key links between Korea and the successors of the Han dynasty in northeast China. Korean rulers patronized Buddhist artists and financed the building of monasteries and pagodas. Korean scholars traveled to China, and a select few made the long journey to the source of the Buddhist faith, India.

In addition to Sinified variants of Buddhism, Chinese writing was introduced, even though the spoken Korean language was as ill-suited for adaptation to the Chinese characters as the Japanese language had also been. The Koguryo monarch imposed a unified law code patterned after that of Han China. He established universities, where Korean youths struggled to master the Confucian classics and their teachers wrote histories of China rather than their own land. To expand his power and improve revenue collection, the Koguryo ruler also tried to put together a Chinese-style bureaucracy. But the noble families who supported him had little use for a project that posed such an obvious threat to their own power. Without their support, the monarch did not have the resources for such an ambitious undertaking. Thus, full implementation of these policies had to wait for a more powerful dynasty to emerge some centuries later.

Tang Alliances and the Conquest of Korea

Centuries of warfare between the three Korean kingdoms weakened each without giving paramount power in the peninsula to any. Internal strife also left Korea vulnerable to further attacks from the outside. In addition to the unsuccessful campaigns of the Sui (see Chapter 13), the founders of the more lasting Tang dynasty included Korea in the territories they staked out for their empire. But it was several decades before one of them could finally mount a successful invasion. The stubborn warriors of the Koguryo kingdom bore the brunt of the Tang assaults, just as they had borne those of the Sui rulers. Finally, Tang strategists hit on the idea of taking advantage of Korean divisions to bring the troublesome region into line. Striking an alliance with the rulers of the Silla kingdom to the southeast, they destroyed the Paekche kingdom and then defeated the Koguryo. Thus, the Chinese finally put an end to the long-lived dynasty that had played such a key role in Korea's early development.

The Chinese conquerors soon began to quarrel with their Silla allies over how to divide the spoils. When the Silla proved able to fight the larger Chinese forces in the peninsula to a standstill and revolts broke out in the former Paekche and Koguryo territories already conquered, the Tang decided it was time to strike a deal. In return for regular tribute payments and the Silla monarch's submission as a vassal of the Tang emperor, the Chinese withdrew their armies in 668. In so doing, they left the Silla the independent rulers of a united Korea. Despite brief lapses, the Koreans maintained this independence and roughly the same boundaries established by the Silla until the occupation of their land by the Japanese in the early 20th century.

MAP 14.3 **The Korean Peninsula During the Three Kingdoms Era** The Chinese were often able to play off the rival kingdoms that dominated Korea's early history against each other and thereby exert great influence on the political and social development of the country.

Sinification: The Tributary Link

Under the Silla monarchs, who ruled from 668 until the late 9th century, and the **Koryo** dynasty (918–1392) that followed, Chinese influences peaked and Korean culture achieved its first full flowering. The Silla rulers consciously strove to turn their kingdom into a miniature of the Tang empire. They regularly sent embassies and tribute to the Tang court, where Korean scholars collected Chinese texts and noted the latest fashions in court dress and etiquette. The Koreans' regular attendance on the Chinese emperors was a key sign of their prominent and enduring participation in the Chinese tribute system. At various times, the participants in the system included nomads from central and north Asia, the Tibetans, many of the kingdoms of southeast Asia, and the emperors of Japan. None of these participants were more committed to the tributary arrangements than the Koreans. Rather than try to conquer the Koreans and other surrounding peoples, most Chinese emperors were content to receive their embassies. These emissaries offered tribute in the form of splendid gifts and acknowledged the superiority of the Son of Heaven by their willingness to kowtow to him (kowtowing involved a series of ritual bows in which the supplicant prostrated himself before the throne).

To most of the peoples involved, this seemed a small price to pay for the benefits they received from the Middle Kingdom. Not only did submission and tribute guarantee continuing peace with the Chinese, but it brought far richer gifts than the tribute bearers offered to the Chinese ruler. In addition, the tributary system provided privileged access to Chinese learning, art, and manufactured goods. Tribute missions normally included merchants, whose ability to buy up Chinese manufactures and sell their own goods in the lucrative Chinese market hinged on their country's participation in the Chinese system. Missions from heavily Sinified areas, such as Japan, Korea, and Vietnam, also included contingents of scholars. They studied at Chinese academies or Buddhist monasteries and busily purchased Chinese scrolls and works of art to fill the libraries and embellish the palaces back home. Thus, the tribute system became the major channel of trade and intercultural exchange between China and its neighbors.

The Sinification of Korean Elite Culture

The Silla rulers rebuilt their capital at Kumsong on the Kyongju plain to look like its Tang counterpart. The streets were laid out on a regular grid; there were central markets, parks, lakes, and a separate district to house the imperial family. Fleeing the tedium of the backward rural areas and provincial capitals, the aristocratic families who surrounded the throne and dominated imperial government crowded their mansions into the areas around the imperial palace. With their large extended families and hundreds of slaves and hangers-on, they made up a large portion of the capital's population. Some aristocrats studied in Chinese schools, and a minority even submitted to the rigors of the Confucian examination system introduced under the Silla rulers. Most of the aristocracy opted for the artistic pursuits and entertainments available in the capital. They could do so because most positions in the government continued to be occupied by members of the aristocratic families by virtue of their birth and family connections rather than their knowledge of the Confucian classics.

Partly out of self-interest, the Korean elite continued to favor Buddhism over Confucianism, which was much more strongly associated with Chinese culture. They and the Korean royal family lavishly endowed monasteries and patronized works of religious art, which became major forms of Korean cultural creativity. The capital at Kumsong soon became crowded with Buddhist temples, which usually were made of wood. Buddhist monks were constantly in attendance on the ruler as well as on members of the royal family and the more powerful aristocratic households. But the schools of Buddhism that caught on among the elite were Chinese. Korean artwork and monastic design reproduced, sometimes splendidly, Chinese prototypes. Even the location of monasteries and pagodas in high places followed Chinese ideas about the need to mollify local spirits and balance supernatural forces.

Sometimes the Koreans borrowed from the Chinese and then outdid their teachers. Most notable in this regard was the pottery produced in the Silla and Koryo eras. The Koreans first learned the techniques of porcelain manufacture from the Chinese. But in the pale green-glazed celadon bowls and vases of the late Silla and Koryo, they created masterworks that even Chinese connoisseurs admired and collected. They also pioneered in making oxide glazes that were used to make the black- and rust-colored stoneware (pictured in Figure 14.7), which was characteristic of this era.

Another endeavor in which the Koreans improved on the Chinese was in the art of printing. As we have seen, the Chinese were the first to develop wood block and, later, movable metal-type printing. But after the latter was introduced into Korea, local artisans came upon an ingenious way to hold the metal type in place in the long registers in which it was assembled for printing. Using honey as a sort of glue, they were able to fix the type

Read the Document on MyHistoryLab: Preface to The Ten Diagrams of Sage Learning (1568) Yi Hwang (T'oegye)

FIGURE 14.7 Although all of the major civilized centers of east Asia produced refined ceramics, perhaps nowhere was this art as highly developed as in Korea. As the simple, yet elegant, pitcher in this photo illustrates, Korean pottery was initially crafted for household use. That which has survived from earlier periods of Korean history has become sought after by collectors of fine arts and is prominently displayed in museums.

(The Bridgeman Art Library/Detroit Institute of Arts.)

temporarily and yet disassemble it when a particular task was finished. Until the Koreans devised this technique, the Chinese had found that the metal type wore down very fast and was difficult to stabilize in the registers.

Civilization for the Few

With the exception of Buddhist sects such as the pure land that had strong appeal for the ordinary people, imports from China in this and later eras were all but monopolized by the tiny elite. The aristocratic families were divided into several ranks that neither intermarried nor socialized with each other, much less the rest of the population. They not only filled most of the posts in the Korean bureaucracy but also dominated the social and economic life of the entire kingdom. Much of Korea's trade with the Chinese and Japanese was devoted to providing these aristocrats with the fancy clothing, special teas, scrolls, and artwork that occupied such an important place in their idle lives. In return, Korea exported mainly raw materials, such as forest products and metals especially copper, which was mined by near-slaves who lived in horrendous conditions.

Members of the royal family and the aristocratic households often financed artisan production for export or to supply the court. In addition, some backed mercantile expeditions and even engaged extensively in money lending. All of this limited the activities of artisans and traders. The former were usually considered low in status and were poorly paid for their talents and labor. The latter were so weak that they did not really form a distinct class.

The aristocrats were the only people who really counted for anything in Korean society. The classes beneath them were oriented to their service. These included government functionaries, who were recognized as a separate social category. More numerous were the commoners, who were mainly peasants, and near-slaves, who were known as the "low born" and ranged from miners and artisans to servants and entertainers. Buddhist festivals periodically relieved the drudgery and monotony of the lives of the common people, and Buddhist salvationist teachings gave them hope for bliss in the afterlife.

Koryo Collapse, Dynastic Renewal

Periodically, the common people and the low born found their lot too much to bear and rose up against a ruling class that was obviously much more devoted to pursuing its own pleasures than to their well-being. Most of these uprisings were local affairs and were ruthlessly repressed by armies of the ruling class. But collectively they weakened both the Silla and Koryo regimes, and in combination with quarrels between the aristocratic households and outside invasions, they contributed to the fall of both dynasties. In the absence of real alternatives, the aristocratic families managed to survive these crises and elevated one of their number to the royal throne. After nearly a century and a half of conflict and turmoil triggered by the Mongol invasion in 1231, the **Yi** dynasty was established in 1392. Remarkably, it ruled Korea until 1910. Although there were some modifications, the Yi quickly restored the aristocratic dominance and links to China that had predominated under their predecessors. Of all of the peoples who received higher civilization from China, none were as content to live in the shadow of the Middle Kingdom as the Koreans.

Yi Korean dynasty that succeeded Koryo dynasty following period of Mongol invasions; established in 1392; ruled Korea to 1910; restored aristocratic dominance and Chinese influence.

BETWEEN CHINA AND SOUTHEAST ASIA: THE MAKING OF VIETNAM

14.4 What were the main differences in Vietnamese-Chinese relations from those in Korea and Japan?

At the end of the 2nd century B.C.E., the Han dynasty conquered the kingdom of the Nam Viet, thus beginning an effort to absorb the Vietnamese people into Chinese civilization that would span a thousand years. Although they benefited greatly from borrowings from China, the Vietnamese had a distinct identity that provided the basis for a series of rebellions and eventually produced an independent kingdom with expansionist designs against neighboring southeast Asian peoples.

The preconquest culture of the Vietnamese gave them a strong sense of themselves as a distinct people with a common heritage that they did not want to see overwhelmed by an expanding China. The Viets were well aware of the benefits they derived from the superior technology, modes of political organization, and ideas they received from China. But their gratitude was tempered by their fear of losing their own identity and becoming just another part of China's massive civilization.

Ironically, the Viets first appear in recorded history as a group of "southern barbarians" mentioned by Chinese scholars in accounts of Qin raids in south China in the 220s B.C.E. At that time, their kingdom, which the Chinese called Nam Viet, meaning "people in the south," extended along the southern coastal area of what is now China (Map 14.4). The initial raids by Qin forces left little lasting Chinese presence. But they probably gave a boost to the lively trade that had been conducted between the Viets and the peoples of south China for centuries. In exchange for silk manufactured by the Chinese, the Viets traded ivory, tortoise shells, pearls, peacock feathers, aromatic woods, and other exotic products drawn from the sea and tropical forests. Some decades after the Qin raids, the Viet rulers defeated the feudal lords who controlled the Red River valley and brought their lands under the control of the Viet kingdom. In the centuries that followed, the Viets intermarried and blended with the Mon-Khmer- and Tai-speaking peoples who occupied the Red River area. This proved to be a crucial step in the formation of the Vietnamese as a distinct ethnic group.

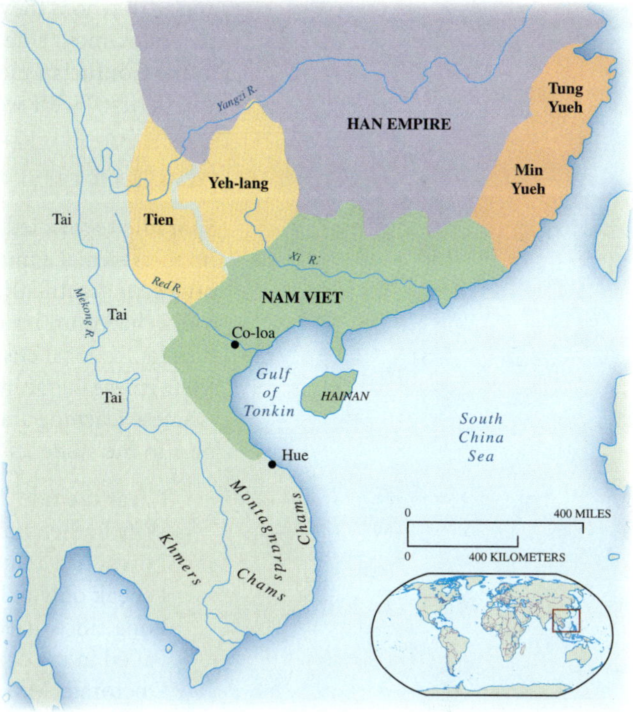

As the Viets' willingness to intermarry with ethnic groups such as the **Khmers** (today's Cambodians) and the Tais suggests (Map 14.4), before their conquest by the Han Chinese, their culture had many features characteristic of southeast Asia. Their spoken language was not related to Chinese. They enjoyed a strong tradition of village autonomy, physically symbolized by the bamboo hedges that surround northern Vietnamese villages to the present day. The Vietnamese favored the nuclear family to the extended household preferred by the Chinese, and they never developed the clan networks that have been such a prominent feature of south Chinese society. Vietnamese women have historically had greater freedom and more influence, both within the family and in society at large, than their Chinese counterparts. They were, for example, the dominant force in both local and large urban markets and the trading system more generally.

Vietnamese customs and cultural forms also differed very significantly from Chinese. The Vietnamese dressed very differently. For example, women preferred long skirts to the black pants that non-elite women wore in China. The Vietnamese delighted in the cockfight, a typical southeast Asian pastime; they chewed betel nut, which the Chinese found disgusting; and they blackened their teeth, which the Chinese considered equally repulsive. In the centuries when they were dominated by the Chinese politically, the Vietnamese managed to preserve most of these features of their society. They also became much more fervently attached at the grassroots level to Buddhism, and they developed art and literature, especially poetry, that was refined and distinct from that of the Chinese.

MAP 14.4 South China and Vietnam on the Eve of the Han Conquest As this map illustrates, Nam Viet, which formed the original core of Vietnam, could be seen as a logical extension of China and was long ruled as the southern province of Chinese empires.

Khmers [kuh-MEHRs] Indianized rivals of the Vietnamese; moved into Mekong River delta region at time of Vietnamese drive to the south.

Conquest and Sinification

As the Han rulers who succeeded the Qin tried to incorporate south China into their empire, they came into conflict with the Viets. The Han emperor initially settled for the Viet ruler's admission of his vassal status and periodic payments of tribute. But by 111 B.C.E., the Han thought it best to conquer the feisty Viets outright and to govern them directly using Chinese officials. The Red River area was garrisoned by Chinese troops, and Chinese administrators set to work co-opting the local lords and encouraging them to adopt Chinese culture. Because the Viet elite realized that they had a great deal to learn from their powerful neighbors to the north, they cooperated with the agents of the new regime. Sensing that they had found another barbarian people ripe for assimilation, the Chinese eagerly introduced essential elements of their own culture into the southern lands.

In the centuries after the Chinese conquest, the Vietnamese elite was drawn into the bureaucratic machine that the Han emperors and the shi (bureaucrats) had developed to hold together the empire won by the Qin. They attended Chinese-style schools, where they wrote in the Chinese script and read and memorized the classical Chinese texts of Confucius and Mencius. They took exams to qualify for administrative posts, whose responsibilities and privileges were defined by Chinese precedents. They introduced Chinese cropping techniques and irrigation technology, which soon made Vietnamese agriculture the most productive in southeast Asia. This meant that Vietnamese society, like that of China, could support larger numbers of people. The result was the high population density characteristic of the Red River valley and the lowland coastal areas to the south.

The Vietnamese also found that Chinese political and military organization gave them a decisive edge over the peoples to the west and south, who had adopted Indian patterns of kingship and warfare,

CHAPTER 14 The Spread of Chinese Civilization: Japan, Korea, and Vietnam

and with whom they increasingly clashed over the control of lands to settle and cultivate. Over time, the Vietnamese elite also adopted the extended family model and took to venerating their ancestors in the Confucian manner. Their Chinese overlords had every reason to assume that the Vietnamese "barbarians" were well on their way to becoming civilized—that is, like the Chinese themselves.

Roots of Resistance

Sporadic revolts led by members of the Vietnamese aristocracy, and the failure of Chinese cultural imports to make much of an impression on the Vietnamese peasantry, ultimately frustrated Chinese hopes for assimilating the Viets. Although they had learned much from the Chinese, the Vietnamese lords chafed under their rule, in part because the Chinese often found it difficult to conceal their disdain for local customs in what they considered a backward and unhealthy outpost of the empire. Vietnamese literature attests to the less than reverent attitudes felt by Vietnamese collaborators toward Chinese learning and culture. In the following poem, a teacher mocks himself and doubts his usefulness to the students he serves:

> I bear the title "Disciple of Confucius."
> Why bother with blockheads, wearing such a label?
> I dress like a museum piece:
> I speak only in learned quotations (poetry and prose);
> Long since dried out, I still strut like a peacock;
> Failed in my exams, I've been dropped like a shrivelled root.
> Doctorate, M.A.: all out of reach,
> So why not teach school, and beat the devil out of my students.

Elsewhere in Vietnamese writings, self-doubt and mockery turn to rage and a fierce determination to resist Chinese dominance, whatever the cost. The following sentiments of a Vietnamese caught up in resistance to the reimposition of rule from China by the Mongols in the 13th century provide a dramatic case in point:

> I myself often forget to eat at mealtime, and in the middle of the night I wake up and caress my pillow. My intestines hurt me incessantly, as if they had been cut off, and tears flow abundantly from my eyes. My only grief is that I have not yet succeeded in hacking apart the enemy's body, peeling off his skin, swallowing his liver, drinking his blood.

The intensity and ferocity of this passage give some sense of why the Chinese failed to assimilate the Vietnamese. They also failed because the peasantry rallied again and again to the call of their own lords to rise up and drive off the alien rulers. The most famous of these early uprisings, which broke out in 39 C.E., was led by the **Trung sisters**, who were children of a deposed local leader. Their role as rebel leaders underscores the stronger position of women in Vietnamese society, in contrast to the Chinese, and their persisting importance in Vietnamese protest movements and resistance to foreign invaders.

Vietnamese women were understandably hostile to the Confucian codes and family system that would have confined them to the household and subjected them to male authority figures. We do not know whether this resentment figured in the Trung sisters' decision to revolt. But poetry written in later centuries by female authors leaves little doubt about the reactions of Vietnamese women to Confucian norms or male dominance. One of the most famous of these writers, Ho Xuan Huong (hoo shwahn wahng), flouts Confucian decorum in the following ribald verse and mocks her male suitors:

> Careful, careful where are you going:
> You group of know-nothings!
> Come here and let your older sister teach you to write poems.
> Young bees whose stingers itch rub them in wilted flowers.
> Young goats who have nothing to do with their horns butt them against sparse shrubbery.

In another poem, "Sharing a Husband," Huong ridicules those who advocate polygamy, a practice favored by any self-respecting Confucian:

> One wife is covered by a quilted blanket, while one wife is left in the cold.
> Cursed be this fate of sharing a common husband. Seldom do you have an occasion to possess your husband,

Trung sisters Leaders of one of the frequent peasant rebellions in Vietnam against Chinese rule; revolt broke out in 39 C.E.; demonstrates importance of Vietnamese women in indigenous society.

Not even twice in one month.
You toil and endure hardships in order to earn your steamed rice, and then the rice is cold and tasteless. It is like renting your services for hire, and then receiving no wages.
How is it that I have turned out this way,
I would rather suffer the fate of remaining unmarried and living alone by myself.

Winning Independence and Continuing Chinese Influences

In addition to a strong sense of identity and motives for resistance that crossed class and gender barriers, the Vietnamese struggle for independence was assisted by the fragility of the links that bound them to China. Great distances and mountain barriers created nightmare conditions for Chinese administrators responsible for supplying military expeditions to in the far south. Only small numbers of Chinese—mostly bureaucrats, soldiers, and merchants—lived in the Red River area, and few of them did so permanently. Most critically, Chinese control over the distant Vietnamese depended on the strength of the ruling dynasties in China. The Vietnamese were quick to take advantage of political turmoil and nomadic incursions in northern China to assert their independence. After failing to completely free themselves on several occasions, they mounted a massive rebellion during the period of chaos in China after the fall of the Tang dynasty in 907.

By 939 the Vietnamese had won political independence from their northern neighbors. Although both the Mongol and Ming rulers of China later tried to reassert control, both efforts ended in humiliating retreats. From 939 until the conquests by the French in the 19th century, the Vietnamese were masters of their own land.

Although the Chinese political hold was broken, Chinese cultural exports continued to play central roles in Vietnamese society. A succession of Vietnamese dynasties beginning with the Le (980–1009), which became the source of legitimacy for the rest, built Chinese-style palaces, as in Figure 14.8, in the midst of forbidden cities patterned after those in Chang'an and Beijing. They ruled through a bureaucracy that was a much smaller copy of the Chinese administrative system, with secretariats, six main ministries, and a bureau of censors to keep graft and corruption in check. Civil service exams were reintroduced, and an administrative elite schooled in the Confucian classics sought the emperor's favor and commanded deference from the common people.

But the Vietnamese equivalent of the Chinese scholar-gentry never enjoyed as much power. For one thing, their control at the local level was much less secure than that of their Chinese counterparts. Much more than those in China, local Vietnamese officials tended to identify with the peasantry rather than with the court and higher administrators. To a much greater degree, they looked out for the interests of the peasants and served as leaders in village uprisings against the ruling dynasty when its demands on the common people became too oppressive.

The power of the scholar-bureaucrats in Vietnam was also limited in the reign of many dynasties by competition from well-educated Buddhist monks. Buddhists had much stronger links with the Vietnamese peasantry than the monastic orders had in China, which meant that the Buddhists had a good deal more popular support in their struggles with the Confucian scholars. The high esteem in which women were held in Buddhist teachings and institutions also

FIGURE 14.8 As this view of the moat and part of the palace of the Vietnamese emperors at Hue illustrates, Chinese taste and architectural styles strongly influenced the construction and decoration of the Vietnamese court. Not only were the upturned, tiled roofs and long galleries built in deliberate imitation of prototypes in Chang'an or Beijing, but they were set amid moats, ponds, and gardens patterned after those that Vietnamese envoys had seen in China. Despite this imitation, however, Vietnamese rulers were more accessible to their subjects, and their palaces and capital city made little impression on Chinese visitors, who disparaged the informality and lack of grandeur at the Hue court.

VISUALIZING THE PAST

What Their Portraits Tell Us: Gatekeeper Elites and the Persistence of Civilizations

SOME DECADES AGO, A DISTINGUISHED HISTORIAN of pre-modern China called the scholar-gentry elite the gatekeepers of Chinese civilization. In his usage, gatekeepers are pivotal elite groups that have emerged in all civilizations and proved critical to their persistence over time. Although they usually shared power with other social groups and often did not rule in their own right, gatekeepers played vital roles in shaping the dominant social values and worldviews of the most human cultures. In everything from the positions they occupied to their manners and fashions in dress, gatekeepers defined the norms and served as role models for much of the rest of society. Some gatekeeper elites, such as the scholar-gentry in China and the brahmans in India, promoted norms and ideals in written treatises on good government or the proper social order. Other gatekeepers, such as the samurai of Japan and the Aztec warriors of Tenochtitlan, embodied these ideals in their public personas and military enterprises, which at times were immortalized in songs, legends, and epics.

The illustrations shown here provide portraits of people belonging to gatekeeper elites from four of the civilizations we have considered in depth thus far. Because each of these portraits was produced by artists from the same society as the gatekeeper elite depicted here, we can assume that the portraits capture the values, symbols of legitimacy, and demeanor that these people intended to project to the viewer. Carefully examine each of these portraits, paying special attention to clothing, poses adopted, objects included in the portraits, backgrounds selected, and activities depicted.

For historical background of the civilizations that each exemplifies, see the relevant sections of Chapters 11, 12, 13, and 14.

Compare each of the portraits to the others, and then answer the questions that follow.

> **QUESTIONS**
> - What do the dress, poses, and settings of each of these portraits tell you about the values, ideals, and worldviews that each gatekeeper elite group is intended to represent?
> - With which elite groups did they share power?
> - How did they legitimize their power and privileges and to what degree is this reflected in the portraits?
> - What are comparable gatekeeper elite groups in the contemporary United States?

A samurai warrior.

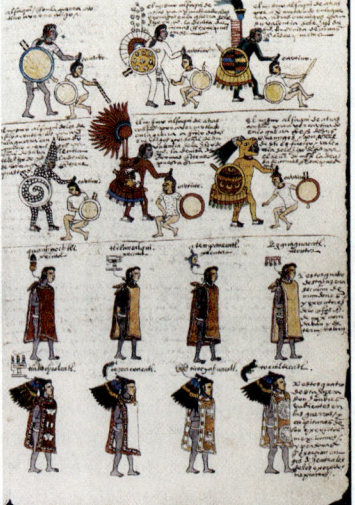

Warrior ranks from the Aztec empire.

Bankers and merchants from western Europe.

(continued on next page)

(continued from previous page)

Chinese scholars enjoying their leisure time.
(Handscroll "Gathering of Philosophers." The Metropolitan Museum of Art, New York, NY, U.S.A. Image copyright © The Metropolitan Museum of Art/Art Resource, NY.)

enhanced the popularity of the monks in Vietnam. Thus, competing centers of power and influence prevented most Vietnamese dynasties from enjoying the authority of their Chinese counterparts.

The Vietnamese Drive to the South

However watered down, the Chinese legacy gave the Vietnamese great advantages in the struggles within Indochina that became a major preoccupation of independent Vietnamese rulers. The Vietnamese refused to move into the malarial highlands that fringed the Red River area and rose abruptly from the coastal plains farther south. This meant that their main adversaries were the **Chams** and Khmers, who occupied the lowland areas to the south that the Vietnamese sought to settle themselves (Map 14.4). The Vietnamese launched periodic expeditions to retaliate for raids on their villages by the peoples in the hills. They also regularly traded with the hill dwellers for forest products. But the Vietnamese tried to minimize cultural exchange with these hunters and shifting cultivators, whom they saw as "nude savages."

As they moved out in the only direction left to them—south along the narrow plain between the mountains and the sea—the Vietnamese made good use of the larger population and superior bureaucratic and military organization that the Chinese connection had fostered. From the 11th to the 18th century, they fought a long series of generally successful wars against the Chams, an Indianized people living in the lowland areas along the coast. Eventually most of the Chams were driven into the highlands, where their descendants—in much smaller numbers—live to the present day. Having beaten the Chams and settled on their former croplands, the Vietnamese next clashed with the Khmers, who had begun to move into the Mekong delta region during the centuries of the Vietnamese drive south. Again, Indianized armies proved no match for the Chinese-modeled military forces and weapons of the Vietnamese. By the time the French arrived in force in the Mekong area in the late 18th century, the Vietnamese had occupied much of the upper delta and were beginning to push into territory that today belongs to Cambodia.

Chams Indianized rivals of the Vietnamese; driven into the highlands by the successful Vietnamese drive to the south.

Expansion and Division

As Vietnamese armies and peasant colonists moved farther and farther from the capital at Hanoi, the dynasties centered there found it increasingly difficult to control the commanders and peasants fighting and living in the frontier areas. As the southerners intermarried with and adopted some of the customs of the Chams and Khmers, differences in culture and attitude developed between them

DOCUMENT

Literature as a Mirror of the Exchanges Among Asian Centers of Civilization

THE FOLLOWING PASSAGES FROM LADY MURASAKI's classic Japanese account of court life, *The Tale of Genji* (Houghton-Mifflin, 1929 edition), and from perhaps the most popular and beloved work of Vietnamese literature, Nguyen Du's *The Tale of Kieu* (New Haven: Yale University Press, 1983 edition), are superb examples of the important and far-reaching exchanges between the civilizations of south and east Asia. Not surprisingly, Chinese influences, including many allusions to Chinese writings and historical events, are paramount, but Buddhist (hence originally Indian) themes are pervasive in both works. There is also evidence in one of these passages of significant exchanges between the satellite civilizations of China.

> . . . Kieu sensed a girl was standing by.
> And whispered she: "Your karma's still undone:
> How could you shirk your debt of grief to life"
> You're still to bear the fortune of a rose [woman]:
> you wish to quite but heaven won't allow."

> . . . . the picture of Kuei-fei, skillful though the painter might be, was but the work of a brush, and had no living fragrance. And though the poet tells us that Kuei-fei's grace was that of "the hibiscus of the Royal Lake or the willows of the Wei-yang Palace," the lady in the picture was all paint and powder and had a simpering Chinesified air.

> Now all is lost; for since she [the nun] cannot at every moment be praying for strength, there creeps into her mind the sinful thought that she did ill to become a nun and so often does she commit this sin that even Buddha must think her wickeder now than she was before she took her vows . . . . But if the *karma* of their past lives should chance to be strongly weighted against a parting, she will be found and captured before she has taken her final vows.

> He said: "You've won wide fame as lutanist:
> like Chung Tzu-ch'i I've longed to hear you play."
> . . . then she [Kieu] played.

> An air, *The Battlefield of Han and Ch'u*,
> made one hear bronze and iron clash and clang.
> The Ssu-ma tune, *A Phoenix Seeks His Mate*,
> sounded so sad, the moan of grief itself.
> Here was Chi K'ang's famed masterpiece, Kuang-ling—
> was it a stream that flowed, a cloud that roamed?
> *Crossing the Border-gate*—here was Chao-chün,
> half lonesome for her lord, half sick for home.

> She [a woman who was attracted to one of Genji's friends] sent me marvelous letters written in a very far-fetched epistolary style and entirely in Chinese characters; in return for which I felt bound to visit her, and by making her my teacher I managed to learn how to write Chinese poems. . . . Let her but be one to whom the *karma* of our past lives draws us in natural sympathy, what matter if now and again her ignorance distresses us? Come to that, even men seem to me to get along very well without much learning.

> When evil strikes, you must bow to circumstance.
> As you must weigh and choose between your love
> and filial duty, which will turn the scale?
> She [Kieu] put aside all vows of love and troth—
> A child first pays the debts of birth and care.
> Resolved on what to do, she said: "Hands off—
> I'll sell myself and Father I'll redeem."

QUESTIONS

- From these passages, can you identify Chinese precedents in terms of place names and historical personages, allusions to Chinese literary works, and attitudes toward gender or social organization that can be traced to Chinese models?
- Can you detect passages that convey Buddhist ideas about the nature of the world and human existence?
- Are additional Indian influences suggested?
- Are there ideas that are distinctively Japanese or Vietnamese, or are the authors totally caught up in Chinese precedents?

Nguyen [nhuwin] Rival Vietnamese dynasty that arose in southern Vietnam to challenge traditional dynasty of Trinh in north at Hanoi; kingdom centered on Red and Mekong rivers; capital at Hue.

Trinh Dynasty that ruled in north Vietnam at Hanoi, 1533 to 1772; rivals of Nguyen family in south.

and the northerners. Although both continued to identify themselves as Vietnamese, the northerners (much like their counterparts in the United States) came to see the Vietnamese who settled in the frontier south as less energetic and slower in speech and movement. As the hold of the Hanoi-based dynasties over the southern regions weakened, regional military commanders grew less and less responsive to orders from the north and slower in sending taxes to the court. Bickering turned to violent clashes, and by the end of the 16th century a rival dynasty, the **Nguyen**, had emerged to challenge the claims of legitimacy of the **Trinh** family that ruled the north.

The territories of the Nguyen at this time were centered on the narrow plains that connected the two great rice bowls of present-day Vietnam along the Red and Mekong rivers. Their capital was at Hue (Map 14.4), far north of the Mekong delta region that in this period had scarcely been settled by the Vietnamese. For the next two centuries, these rival houses fought for the right to rule Vietnam.

Neither accepted the division of Vietnam as permanent; each sought to unite all of the Vietnamese people under a single monarch. This long struggle not only absorbed much of the Vietnamese energies but also prevented them from recognizing the growing external threat to their homeland. For the first time in history, the danger came not from the Chinese giant to the north but from a distant land and religion about which the Vietnamese knew and cared nothing—France and the conversion-minded Roman Catholic church.

Global Connections and Critical Themes

IN THE ORBIT OF CHINA: THE EAST ASIAN CORNER OF THE GLOBAL SYSTEM

The first millennium C.E. was a pivotal epoch in the history of the peoples of east Asia. The spread of ideas, organizational models, and material culture from a common Chinese center spawned the rise of three distinct patterns of civilized development in Japan, Korea, and Vietnam. In contrast to the lands of the nomadic peoples who had long been in contact with China from the north and west, each of these regions contained fertile and well-watered lowland areas that were suited to sedentary cultivation, which was essential to the spread of the Chinese pattern of civilized development. In fact, each provided an ideal environment for the cultivation of wet rice, which was increasingly replacing millet and other grains as the staple of China.

Common elements of Chinese culture, from modes of writing and bureaucratic organization to religious teachings and art, were transmitted to each of these three areas. In all three cases, Chinese imports, with the important exception of popular Buddhism, were all but monopolized by court and provincial elite groups, the former prominent in Japan and Korea, the latter in Vietnam. In all three cases, Chinese thought patterns and modes of social organization were actively and willingly cultivated by these local elites, who knew that they were the key to a higher level of development.

One of the great world religions, Buddhism, played key roles in the transmission of Chinese civilization and the development of all three of these "satellite" societies. Because Buddhism originated in India, the layers of cross-cultural interaction in these processes are all the more complex and profound. In each case, ideas and rituals originating in India were filtered through Chinese society and culture before being passed on to Japan, Korea, and Vietnam. Buddhism also provided a critical link between the civilizations developing in Korea and Japan.

In some phases of their borrowing from China, Japan, Korea, and Vietnam shared prominent aspects of political organization, social development, and intellectual creativity. But the differing ways in which Chinese influences were transmitted to each of these very different societies resulted in very different long-term outcomes. The various combinations of Chinese-derived and indigenous elements produced distinctive variations on a common pattern of civilized life. In Korea, the period of direct Chinese rule was brief, but China's physical presence and military power were all too apparent. Thus, the need for symbolic political submission was obvious and the desire for long-term cultural dependence firmly implanted. In Vietnam, where Chinese conquest and control lasted more than a thousand years, a hard-fought struggle for political independence gave way to a growing attachment to Chinese culture as a counterbalance to the Indian influences that had brought civilization to the southeast Asian rivals of the Vietnamese.

In Japan, where all attempts by Chinese dynasties to assert direct control had failed, Chinese culture was emulated by the courtly elite that first brought civilization to the islands. But the rise of a rival aristocratic class, which was based in the provinces and championed military values that were fundamentally opposed to Chinese Confucianism, led to the gradual limitation of Chinese influence in Japan and the reassertion of Japanese traditional ways. Japanese political patterns, in particular, formed a marked contrast with the predominance of rule by a centralized bureaucracy in China. Nonetheless, in Japan as in the rest of east Asia, China remained the epitome of civilized development; Chinese ways were the standard by which all peoples in this far-flung region were judged.

Despite different patterns, the power of the Chinese model had one other important result for Korea, Japan, and to a large extent Vietnam. Contacts with other parts of the world were slight to nonexistent, because there was no sense that any other place had examples worth emulating. The intensity of interactions within the east Asian region generated tendencies toward isolation from the world beyond.

Further Readings

There are many good secondary works on early Japanese and Vietnamese history. Some older but accessible works on Korea are William Heathorn's *History of Korea* (1971), which gives some attention to the arts, and Hatada Takashi's *A History of Korea* (1969). The best new short introduction to the history of Korea is C. J. Eckert, *Korea Old and New: A History* (1980). K. B. Lee, *A New History of Korea* (1984), trans. E. Wagner et al., is quite comprehensive, while L. Kendall, *Shahmans, Housewives, and Other Restless Spirits: Women in Korean Ritual Life* (1985), offers a fresh perspective on Korean social history. The best introductory works on Japanese history and culture are the writings of E. Reischauer, especially his sections in J. K. Fairbank et al., *East Asia: The Modern Transformation* (1999); J. W. Hall's *Japan from Prehistory to Modern Times* (1970), and Mikisio Hane's superb overview, *Japan: A Historical Survey* (1972). H. Paul Varley, *Japanese Culture: A Short History* (1973), has fine sections on the arts, religion, and literature of the warlord era.

Also good on this period are Peter Duus, *Japanese Feudalism* (1969); H. Paul Varley, Ivan Morris, and Nobuko Morris, *Samurai* (1970); and George Sansom, *A History of Japan*, vols. 1 and 2 (1958, 1960).

For an understanding of the Chinese impact on Vietnam, there is no better place to begin than Alexander Woodside, *Vietnam and the Chinese Model* (1971). The best works on the earliest period in Vietnamese history are translations of the writings of French scholar Georges Coedes and the superspecialized *Birth of Vietnam* (1983) by Keith Taylor. Thomas Hodgkin's survey of Vietnamese history is highly readable and makes extensive use of Vietnamese literature. Troung Buu Lam's edited volume, *Patterns of Vietnamese Response to Foreign Intervention* (1967) and the Genji and Kieu tales cited in the Document feature of this chapter provide wonderful ways for the student to get inside Japanese and Vietnamese culture.

On MyHistoryLab

Critical Thinking Questions

1. Compare and contrast the ways in which Japan, Korea, and Vietnam interacted with China.

2. How much control did each satellite civilization have over the extent to which it borrowed from China and what factors shaped that process and the longer-term acceptance or rejection of Chinese influences?

3. What were the underlying commonalities that bound these four culture areas together and made East Asia a distinctive center of global civilization over the millennia?

4. In what ways were art and literature key elements in this East Asia cultural complex?

5. Is it more accurate to think of a common East Asian civilization by the postclassical period or to look at Japanese, Korean, and Vietnamese societies as separate cases with some interactions with China?

6. Did the spread of Chinese values to other East Asian societies suggest any particular relationship between East Asia and other parts of the world?

15

The Last Great Nomadic Challenges: From Chinggis Khan to Timur

LEARNING OBJECTIVES

The Mongol retribution came so swiftly and was so ferocious that it completely demoralized Muhammad Shah, the ruler of Khwarazm, whose arrogance brought death and destruction to his kingdom on an appalling scale. Muhammad Shah had scoffed at Chinggis Khan's demand for retribution for the plunder and slaughter of a Mongol caravan that had entered Khwarazm in 1218 (Map 15.1). Chinggis Khan had personally dispatched the caravan as a signal that he wished to establish political and commercial relations with Khwarazm. Having in effect declared war on the Mongols by ignoring their demands for just recompense, Muhammad Shah compounded his folly by quarreling with the caliph of Baghdad, who consequently had little inclination to come to his rescue.

15.1 What can the struggles Chinggis Khan faced in his youth and early career tell us about the organization and values of Mongol society? p. 333

15.2 What were the key components that made for the remarkable success of the Mongol war machine? p. 339

15.3 Compare the impact of Mongol conquest and rule in the Muslim Middle East, Russia, and China: On which area was there a greater impact, to what extent did the Mongol interlude alter the historical trajectory of each these major culture areas, and what were the similarities and differences in terms of the nature of and effects of Mongol invasions and rule? p. 343

FIGURE **15.1** A 14th-century miniature painting from Rashid al-Din's *History of the World* depicts Mongol cavalry charging into battle against retreating Persians. The speed and endurance of Mongol cavalry made it difficult for routed foes to retreat and live to fight another day. As the painting suggests, surrender or death were often the only options for those overrun by Mongol units.

(Bibliotheque Nationale de France.)

Watch the Video Series on MyHistoryLab

Learn about some key topics related to this chapter with the *MyHistoryLab Video Series: Key Topics in World History*

Caught off guard by the Mongol assault that drove deep into his empire from several directions, Muhammad Shah was at first immobilized with fear, and then in full flight, leaving his hapless subjects to fend for themselves. Columns of battle-hardened Mongol cavalry besieged, then stormed, one after another of the legendary cities that were the glory of Khwarazm. Bukhara was taken in early 1220 after its Turkish garrison was eliminated; several months later, most of the inhabitants of Samarkand, who had initially attempted to resist the invaders, were massacred. The Mongols inundated Gurganj, the former capital of Khwarazm, by opening the flood gates of a nearby river. And the ancient citadel of Bamian, where Chinggis Khan's much-loved grandson was killed by a defender's arrow, was obliterated and given the name "accursed city."

Over time the mass slaughters (often dramatized by references to pyramids of skulls) and the destruction of Khwarazm's ancient cities became defining features in accounts of the sudden emergence of the nomadic Mongols as conquerors of much of Eurasia. Until quite recently, most histories have depicted these and similar Mongol conquests as savage assaults by backward and barbaric peoples on ancient and highly developed centers of human civilization. But even the Khwarazm campaign, which was certainly one of the most violent launched by Mongol forces, provides ample illustration of another side to the Mongol imperium. Traditionally, the Mongols' contributions to cross-cultural exchange and human advance have been neglected by historians. But in many of the cities of Khwarazm, where the population resisted and was killed wholesale, skilled artisans were spared in the thousands. Some of these were sent to the Mongol capital at Karakorum. Others carried their skills throughout the empire, and both manufacturing and commerce soon thrived under the aegis of Mongol rule.

The century and a half of Mongol dominance also saw a revitalization of commerce and urban life in places like Bukara and Samarkand, along the Silk Road—the great trading network that had, for millennia, linked China and East Asia with the Middle East, India, and Europe (see the Visualizing the Past feature). Without question, the price of Muhammad Shah's treachery and the resistance that opened the way to this renewal was high—perhaps intolerably so—but it is important to take fully into account the constructive aftermath of Mongol expansionism in Khwarazm and other regions. ■

As we shall see in this chapter, the Mongols very often exhibited great curiosity and openness toward the peoples and cultures that they conquered. And perhaps none of them exemplified these qualities more than the founder of the Mongol empire, Chinggis Khan himself, who sought to attract philosophers and religious scholars from throughout Eurasia to his capital at Karakorum. He delighted in questioning them and debating the merits and drawbacks of different belief systems. In Samarkand and other cities where Muslim scholars and

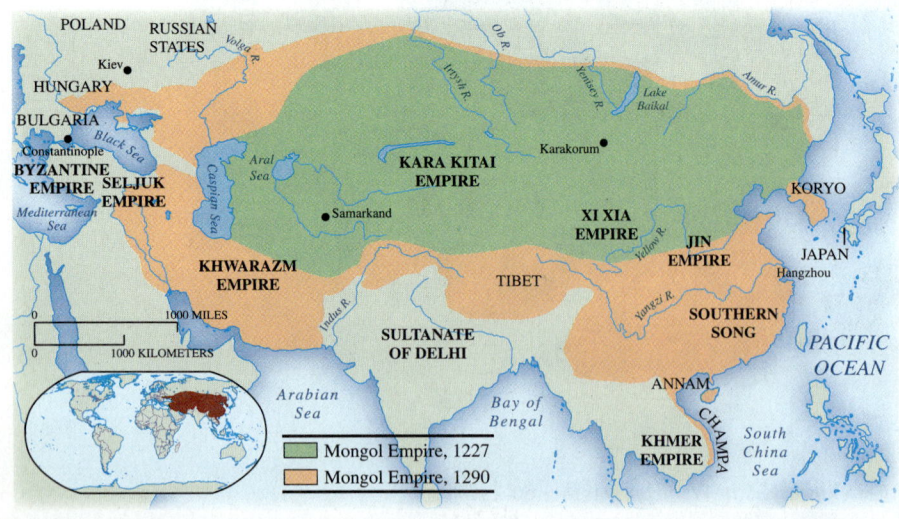

MAP 15.1 **The Transcontinental Empire of Chinggis Khan** Easily the largest empire built before the Industrial Revolution, the Mongol imperium linked most of the great Eurasian centers of civilization.

332 PART III The Postclassical Period, 600–1450: New Faith and New Commerce

900 C.E.	1100 C.E.	1200 C.E.	1250 C.E.	1300 C.E.
907–1118 Khitan conquest of north China	**1115–1234** Jurchens (Jin dynasty) rule north China	**1206** Temujin takes the name of Chinggis Khan; Mongol state founded	**1253** Mongol victory over Seljuk Turks; rise of Ottoman Turks in Middle East	**1336–1405** Life of Timur **mid-14th century** Spread of Black Death in Eurasia
1037–1194 Seljuk Turks dominate the Middle East	**1126** Song dynasty flees to south China	**1215** First Mongol attacks on north China; Beijing captured	**1258** Mongol destruction of Baghdad	
	1130–c. 1250 Almohads rule north Africa and Spain	**1219–1223** First Mongol invasions of Russia and Islamic world	**1260** Mamluk (slave) rulers of Egypt defeat Mongols at Ain Jalut; end of drive west	
		1227 Death of Chinggis Khan; Ogedei named successor	**1260–1294** Reign of Kubilai Khan in China	
		1234 Mongols take all of north China; end of Jin dynasty	**1271–1295** Journey of Marco Polo to central Asia, China, and southeast Asia	
		1235–1279 Mongol conquest of south China; end of southern Song dynasty	**1271–1368** Reign of the Yuan (Mongol) dynasty in China	
		1236–1240 Mongol conquest of Russia	**1274–1280** Failed Mongol invasions of Japan	
		1240–1241 Mongol invasion of western Europe	**1290s** First true guns used in China	

mosque attendants refused to encourage resistance, they were usually left unharmed and permitted to attend to the spiritual and physical needs of the survivors. In the aftermath of the Mongol invasions, this privileging of religious leaders was reflected in a broader tolerance on the part of these nomadic overlords for the diverse faiths and ethnic groups that had come under their rule.

As we will argue in this chapter, although the Mongols were indeed fierce fighters and capable of terrible acts of retribution against those who dared to defy them, their conquests brought much more than death and devastation. At the peak of their power, the domains of the Mongol *khans* made up a vast realm in which once-hostile peoples lived together in peace and most religions were tolerated. From the khanate of Persia in the west to the empire of the fabled Kubilai Khan in the east, the law code promulgated by Chinggis Khan gave order to human interaction. Like the far less warlike Islamic expansion that preceded it, the Mongol explosion laid the foundations for human interaction on a global scale, extending and intensifying the world network that had been building since the classical age.

THE TRANSCONTINENTAL EMPIRE OF CHINGGIS KHAN

15.1 What can the struggles Chinggis Khan faced in his youth and early career tell us about the organization and values of Mongol society?

In the early 13th century, long-standing obstacles to Mongol expansion were overcome, primarily because of the leadership of Chinggis Khan. The Mongols and allied nomadic groups built an empire that stretched from the Middle East to the China Sea.

In most ways, the Mongols epitomized nomadic society and culture. Their survival depended on the well-being of the herds of goats and sheep they drove from one pasture area to another according to the cycle of the seasons. Their staple foods were the meat and milk products provided by their herds, supplemented in most cases by grain and vegetables gained through trade with sedentary farming peoples. They also traded hides and dairy products for jewelry, weapons, and cloth made in urban centers. They dressed in sheepskins, made boots from tanned sheep hides, and lived in round felt tents made of wool sheared from their animals (Figure 15.2). The tough little ponies they rode to round up their herds, hunt wild animals, and make war were equally essential to their way of life. Mongol

Read the Document on MyHistoryLab: Excerpt from William of Rubruck's Account of the Mongols

FIGURE 15.2 This sketch shows a Mongol household on the move. The Mongols depended on sheep for food, clothing, and shelter, and they rode both horses and camels. As the drawing shows, they also used oxen to transport their housing for seasonal or longer-term migrations. The Mongols mounted their tents and other goods on enormous wagons so heavy that large teams of oxen were required to pull them. This combination of animal transport and comfortable but movable shelters made the Mongols one of the most mobile preindustrial societies.

boys and girls could ride as soon as they were able to walk. Mongol warriors could ride for days on end, sleeping and eating in the saddle.

Like the early Arabs and other nomadic peoples we have encountered, the basic unit of Mongol society was the tribe, which was divided into kin-related clans whose members camped and herded together on a regular basis. When threatened by external enemies or preparing for raids on other nomads or invasions of sedentary areas, clans and tribes could be combined in great confederations. Depending on the skills of their leaders, these confederations could be held together for months or even years. But when the threat had passed or the raiding was done, clans and tribes drifted back to their own pasturelands and campsites. At all organizational levels, leaders were elected by the free men of the group. Although women exercised influence within the family and had the right to be heard in tribal councils, men dominated leadership positions.

Courage in battle, usually evidenced by bravery in the hunt, and the ability to forge alliances and attract dependents were vital leadership skills. A strong leader could quickly build up a large following of chiefs from other clans and tribal groups. If the leader grew old and feeble or suffered severe reverses, his subordinates would quickly abandon him. He expected this to happen, and the subordinates felt no remorse. Their survival and that of their dependents hinged on attaching themselves to a strong tribal leader.

The Making of a Great Warrior: The Early Career of Chinggis Khan

Since the early millennia of recorded history, nomadic peoples speaking Mongolian languages had enjoyed moments of power and had actually carved out regional kingdoms in north China in the 4th and 10th centuries C.E. In the early 12th century, Chinggis Khan's (JEHNG-gihs kahn) great-grandfather, Kabul Khan, led a Mongol alliance that had won glory by defeating an army sent against them by the Jin kingdom of north China. Soon after this victory, Kabul Khan became ill and died. His successors could neither defeat their nomadic enemies nor hold the Mongol alliance together. Divided and beaten, the Mongols fell on hard times.

Chinggis Khan, who as a youth was named Temujin, was born in the 1170s into one of the splinter clans that fought for survival in the decades after the death of Kabul Khan. Temujin's father was an able leader who built up a decent following and negotiated a promise of marriage between his eldest son and the daughter of a stronger Mongol chief. According to Mongol accounts, just when the family fortunes seemed to be on the upswing, Temujin's father was poisoned by the agents of a rival nomadic group. Suddenly, Temujin, who was still a teenager, was thrust into a position of leadership. But most of the chiefs who had attached themselves to his father refused to follow a mere boy, whose prospects of survival appeared to be slim.

In the months that followed, Temujin's much-reduced encampment was threatened and finally attacked by a rival tribe. He was taken prisoner in 1182, locked into a wooden collar, and led in humiliation to the camp of his enemies. After a daring midnight escape, Temujin rejoined his mother and brothers and found refuge for his tiny band of followers deep in the mountains. Facing extermination, Temujin did what any sensible nomad leader would have done: He and his people joined the camp of a more powerful Mongol chieftain who had once been aided by Temujin's father. With the support of this powerful leader, Temujin avenged the insults of the clan that had enslaved him and another that had taken advantage of his weakness to raid his camp for horses and women.

These successes and Temujin's growing reputation as a warrior and military commander soon won him allies and clan chiefs eager to attach themselves to a leader with a promising future (Figure 15.3). Within a decade, the youthful Temujin had defeated his Mongol rivals and routed the forces sent to crush him by other nomadic peoples. In 1206, at a **kuriltai**, or meeting of all of the Mongol chieftains, Temujin—renamed Chinggis Khan—was elected the **khagan**, or supreme ruler, of the Mongol tribes. United under a strong leader, the Mongols prepared to launch a massive assault on an unsuspecting world.

kuriltai [KURL-tuh] Meeting of all Mongol chieftains at which the supreme ruler of all tribes was selected.

khagan [KAH-gahn] Title of the supreme ruler of the Mongol tribes.

tumens Basic fighting units of the Mongol forces; consisted of 10,000 cavalrymen; each unit was further divided into units of 1000, 100, and 10.

Building the Mongol War Machine

The men of the Mongol tribes that had elevated Chinggis Khan to leadership were natural warriors. Trained from youth not only to ride but also to hunt and fight, they were physically tough, mobile, and accustomed to killing and death. They wielded a variety of weapons, including lances, hatchets, and iron maces. None of their weapons was as devastating as their powerful short bows. A Mongol warrior could fire a quiver of arrows with stunning accuracy without breaking the stride of his horse. He could hit enemy soldiers as distant as 350 yards (the range for the roughly contemporary English longbow was 250 yards) while ducking under the belly of his pony, or leaning over the horse's rump. The fact that the Mongol armies were entirely cavalry meant that they moved so rapidly that their advances alone could be demoralizing to enemy forces.

To a people whose very lifestyle bred mobility, physical courage, and a love of combat, Chinggis Khan and his many able subordinate commanders brought organization, discipline, and unity of command. The old quarrels and vendettas between clans and tribes were overridden by loyalty to the khagan. Thus, energies once devoted to infighting were now directed toward conquest and the forcible exaction of tribute, both in areas controlled by other nomadic groups and in the civilized centers that fringed the steppes on all sides. The Mongol forces were divided into armies made up of basic fighting units called **tumens**, each consisting of 10,000 warriors. Each tumen was further divided into units of 1000, 100, and 10 warriors. Commanders at each level were responsible for training, arming, and disciplining the cavalrymen under their charge. The tumens were also divided into heavy cavalry, which carried lances and wore some metal armor, and light cavalry, which relied primarily on the bow and arrow and leather helmets and body covering. Even more lightly armed were the scouting parties that rode ahead of Mongol armies and, using flags and special signal fires, kept the main force informed of the enemy's movements.

Read the Document on MyHistoryLab: On Chinghis Khan (1270s) Marco Polo

FIGURE **15.3** In this miniature from a Persian history, Chinggis Khan is shown acknowledging the submission of a rival prince. Although he conquered a vast empire, Chinggis Khan did not live long enough to build a regular bureaucracy to govern it. His rule was dependent on vassal chieftains such as the one shown in the painting, whose loyalty in turn depended on the maintenance of Mongol military might. When the military strength of the Mongol empire began to decline, subject princes soon rose up to establish the independence of their domains.

Chinggis Khan also created a separate messenger force whose bodies were tightly bandaged to allow them to remain in the saddle for days, switching from horse to horse to carry urgent messages between the khagan and his commanders. Military discipline had long been secured by personal ties between commanders and ordinary soldiers. Mongol values, which made courage in battle a prerequisite for male self-esteem, were buttressed by a formal code that dictated the immediate execution of a warrior who deserted his unit. Chinggis Khan's swift executions left little doubt about the fate of traitors to his own cause or turncoats who abandoned enemy commanders in his favor. His generosity to brave foes was also legendary. The most famous of the latter, a man named Jebe, nicknamed the Arrow, won the khagan's affection and high posts in the Mongol armies by standing his ground after his troops had been routed and fearlessly shooting Chinggis Khan's horse out from under him.

A special unit supplied Mongol armies with excellent maps of the areas they were to invade. These were drawn largely according to the information supplied by Chinggis Khan's extensive network of spies and informers. New weapons, including a variety of flaming and exploding arrows, gunpowder projectiles, and later bronze cannons, were also devised for the Mongol forces. By the time Chinggis Khan's armies rode east and west in search of plunder and conquest in the second decade of the 13th century, they were among the best armed and trained and the most experienced, disciplined, and mobile soldiers in the world.

Conquest: The Mongol Empire Under Chinggis Khan

When he was proclaimed the khagan in 1206, Temujin probably was not yet 40 years old. At that point, he was the supreme ruler of nearly one-half million Mongols and the overlord of 1 to 2 million more nomads who had been defeated by his armies or had allied themselves with this promising young commander. But Chinggis Khan had much greater ambitions. He once said that his greatest pleasure in life was making war, defeating enemies, forcing "their beloved [to] weep, riding on their horses, embracing their wives and daughters." He came to see himself and his sons as men marked for a special destiny: warriors born to conquer the known world. In 1207, he set out to fulfill this ambition. His first campaigns humbled the Tangut (TANG-uht) kingdom of Xi Xia (shee-shyah) in northwest China (Map 15.1), whose ruler was forced to declare himself a vassal of the khagan and pay a hefty tribute. Next, the Mongol armies attacked the much more powerful Jin empire, which the Manchu-related Jurchens (YUHR-chehns) had established a century earlier in north China.

In these campaigns, the Mongol armies were confronted for the first time with large, fortified cities whose inhabitants assumed that they could easily withstand the assaults of these uncouth nomads from the steppes. Indeed, the Mongol invaders were thwarted at first by the intricate defensive works that the Chinese had perfected over the centuries to deter nomadic incursions. But the adaptive Mongols, with the help of captured Chinese artisans and military commanders, soon devised a whole arsenal of siege weapons. These included battering rams, catapults that hurled rocks and explosive balls, and bamboo rockets that spread fire and fear in besieged towns.

Chinggis Khan and the early Mongol commanders had little regard for these towns, whose inhabitants they saw as soft. Therefore, when they met resistance, the Mongols adopted a policy of terrifying retribution. Although the Mongols often spared the lives of famous scholars, whom they employed as advisors, and artisans with particularly useful skills, towns that fought back were usually sacked once they had been taken. The townspeople were slaughtered or sold into slavery; their homes, palaces, mosques, and temples were reduced to rubble. Towns that surrendered without a fight were usually spared this fate, although they were required to pay tribute to their Mongol conquerors as the price of their deliverance.

The First Assault on the Islamic World

Once they had established a foothold in north China and solidified their empire in the steppes, the Mongol armies moved westward against the Kara Khitai (KAH-rah KIHT-uh) empire, which had been established by a Mongolian-speaking people a century earlier (Map 15.1). Having overwhelmed and annexed the Kara Khitai by 1219, and, as we have seen, provoked by Muhammad Shah, Chinggis Khan led his armies in the conquest of the Khwarazm (kwahr-ahzm) empire further west. Again and again, the Mongols used their favorite battle tactic in these encounters. Cavalry were sent to attack the enemy's main force. Feigning defeat, the cavalry retreated, drawing the opposing forces out of formation in the hope of a chance to slaughter the fleeing Mongols. Once the enemy's pursuing horsemen

DOCUMENT

A European Assessment of the Virtues and Vices of the Mongols

AS WE HAVE SEEN, MUCH OF what we know about the history of nomadic peoples is based on the records and reactions of observers from sedentary cultures that were often their mortal enemies. Some of the most famous observers were those, including Marco Polo, who visited the vast Mongol domains at the height of the khans' power in the 12th and 13th centuries. Many tried to assess the strengths and weaknesses of these people, who were suddenly having such a great impact on the history of much of the known world. One of the most insightful of these observers was a Franciscan friar named Giovanni de Piano Carpini. In 1245, Pope Innocent IV sent Piano Carpini as an envoy to the "Great Khan" to protest the recent assaults by his Mongol forces on Christian Europe. The pope's protest had little effect on the Mongol decision to strike elsewhere in the following years. But Piano Carpini's extensive travels produced one of the most detailed accounts of Mongol society and culture to be written in the mid-13th century. As the following passages suggest, like other visitors from sedentary areas, he gave the Mongols a very mixed review:

> The aforesaid men (namely the Tartars) obey their lords more than anyone else in the world, whether clergymen or laymen, and they respect them greatly and do not easily lie to them. The Tartars seldom argue to the point of insult, and there are no wars, quarrels, injuries or murders among them.
>
> Each man respects his fellow and they are friendly to each other, and though food is scare among them, there is still enough to share.... When riding horses they tolerate great cold and heat. Nor are the men touchy; they do not appear jealous of their neighbors, and it seems that none are envious. No man turns another away, but instead helps him and supports him as much as possible.
>
> The Tartars are prouder than other men and despise everyone else; indeed it is as through they held outsiders for nothing whether noble or base born.... The Tartars become quite angry with other men, are indignant by nature and lie to all outsiders; almost no truth is found among them. At first they are very mild, but in the end they sting like a scorpion. The Tartars are subtle and treacherous and, if they can, they get around everything by cunning.
>
> The men are filthy with regard to their clothing, food and other things.... Drunkenness is honorable among the Tartars.... They are very jealous and greedy, demanding of favors, tenacious of what they have and stingy givers, and they think nothing of killing foreigners. In short, because their evil habits are so numerous they can hardly be set down.

QUESTIONS

- What might the qualities of the Mongols that Piano Carpini emphasizes tell us about his own society and its values or shortcomings?
- In what respects are the Mongol virtues he extols linked to the achievements of Chinggis Khan and the stunning Mongol wars of conquest?
- To what extent would they be typical of nomadic societies more generally?
- Why might his account of Mongol vices be simply dismissed as sour grapes resulting from European defeats?

had spread themselves over the countryside, the main force of Mongol heavy cavalry, until then concealed, attacked them in a devastating pincer formation. And the great cities of adversary powers fell to the new siege weapons and tactics the Mongols had perfected in their north China campaigns.

Within two years, his once flourishing cities in ruin and his kingdom in Mongol hands, Muhammad Shah, having retreated across his empire, died on a desolate island in the Caspian Sea. In addition to greatly enlarging his domains, Chinggis Khan's victories meant that he could bring tens of thousands of Turkic horsemen into his armies. By 1227, the year of his death, the Mongols ruled an empire that stretched from eastern Persia to the North China Sea.

Long Distance Trade and Cross-Cultural Exchange: Life under the Mongol Imperium

Despite their aggressiveness as warriors and the destruction they could unleash on those who resisted their demands for submission and tribute, the Mongols were remarkably astute and tolerant rulers. Chinggis Khan himself set the standard. He was a complex man, capable of gloating over the ruin of his enemies but also open to new ideas and committed to building a world where the diverse peoples of his empire could live together in peace. Although illiterate, Chinggis Khan was neither the ignorant savage nor the cultureless vandal often depicted in the accounts of civilized writers—usually those who had never met him. Once the conquered peoples had been subdued, he took a keen interest in their arts and learning, although he refused to live in their cities. Instead, he established a new capital at **Karakorum** on the steppes and summoned the wise and clever from all parts of the empire to the lavish palace of tents with gilded pillars where he lived with his wives and closest advisors.

Karakorum Capital of the Mongol empire under Chinggis Khan, 1162 to 1227.

At Karakorum, Chinggis Khan consulted with Confucian scholars about how to rule China, with Muslim engineers about how to build siege weapons and improve trade with the lands farther west, and with Daoist holy men, whom he hoped could give him an elixir that would make him immortal. Although he himself followed the *shamanistic* (focused on nature spirits) beliefs of his ancestors, all religions were tolerated in his empire. An administrative framework that drew on the advice and talents of both Muslim and Chinese bureaucrats was created. A script was devised for the Mongolian language to facilitate recordkeeping and the standardization of laws. Chinggis Khan's legal code was enforced by specially designated policemen. Much of the code was aimed at ending the divisions and quarrels that had so long plagued the Mongols and other nomadic peoples. Grazing lands were allotted to specific tribes, and harsh penalties were established for rustling livestock or stealing horses.

The Mongol conquests brought peace to much of Asia that in some areas persisted for generations. In the towns of the empire, handicraft production and scholarship flourished and artistic creativity was allowed free expression. Secure trade routes made for prosperous merchants and wealthy, cosmopolitan cities. One Muslim historian wrote of the peoples within the Mongol empire that they "enjoyed such a peace that a man might have journeyed from the land of sunrise to the land of sunset with a golden platter upon his head without suffering the least violence from anyone." Paradoxically, Mongol expansion, which sedentary chroniclers condemned as a "barbarian" orgy of violence and destruction, also became a major force for economic and social development and the enhancement of civilized life. But there was also a downside, the movement of merchants and commercial goods also facilitated the spread of disease. In fact, some historians believe that the infamous intercontinental wave of bubonic plague that came to be known as the Black Death was carried from China by the fleas on rats nesting in the saddle bags of Mongol cavalrymen across central Asia to the Black Sea and from there by ships to the Mediterranean and Europe.

The Death of Chinggis Khan and the Division of the Empire

In 1226, his wars to the west won, Chinggis Khan turned east with an army of 180,000 warriors to complete the conquest of China that he regretted having left unfinished more than a decade earlier. After routing a much larger Tangut (TANG-uht) army in a battle fought on the frozen waters of the Yellow River, the Mongol armies overran the kingdom of Xi Xia, plundering, burning, and mercilessly hunting down Tangut survivors. As his forces closed in on the Tangut capital and last refuge, Chinggis Khan, who had been injured in a skirmish some months earlier, fell grievously ill. After lecturing his sons on the dangers of quarreling among themselves for the spoils of the empire, the khagan died in August 1227.

Batu [BAH-too] Ruler of Golden Horde; one of Chinggis Khan's grandsons; responsible for invasion of Russia beginning in 1236.

Ogedei [OHGD-dih] (1186–1241) Third son of Chinggis Khan; succeeded Chinggis Khan as khagan of the Mongols following his father's death.

With one last outburst of wrath, this time directed against death itself, the Mongols carried his body back to Mongolia for burial. The Mongol forces escorting the funeral procession hunted down and killed every human and animal in its path. The vast pasturelands the Mongols now controlled were divided between Chinggis Khan's three remaining sons and **Batu**, a grandson and heir of the khagan's recently deceased son, Jochi. Towns and cultivated areas such as those in north China and parts of Persia were considered the common property of the Mongol ruling family. A kuriltai was convened at Karakorum, the Mongol capital, to select a successor to the great conqueror. In accordance with Chinggis Khan's preference, **Ogedei**, his third son, was elected khagan. Although not as capable a military leader as his brothers or nephews, Ogedei was a crafty diplomat and deft manipulator. As it turned out, these skills were much needed to keep the ambitious heads of the vast provinces of the empire from each other's throats.

For nearly a decade, Ogedei directed Mongol energies into further campaigns and conquests. The areas targeted by this new round of Mongol expansion paid the price for peace within the Mongol empire. The fate of the most important victims—Russia and Eastern Europe, the Islamic heartlands, and China—will be the focus of most of the rest of this chapter.

THE MONGOL DRIVE TO THE WEST

15.2 What were the key components that made for the remarkable success of the Mongol war machine?

Mongol commanders launched raids into Georgia and across the Russian steppe that set the stage for their conquest of the vulnerable Christian lands to the west.

Russia and Europe were added to the Mongols' agenda for world conquest. Subjugating these regions became the project of the armies of the **Golden Horde**, named after the golden tent of the early khans of the western sector of the Mongol Empire. The territories of the Golden Horde made up one of the four great **khanates** into which the Mongol Empire was divided at the time of Chinggis Khan's death (Map 15.2). Under the rule of Chinggis Khan's grandson Batu, Mongol armies began an invasion of Russia in 1236. In a very real sense, the assault on Russia was a side campaign, a chance to fine-tune the war machine and win a little booty on the way to Western Europe.

As we saw in Chapter 10, in the first half of the 13th century when the Mongol warriors first descended, Russia had been divided into numerous petty kingdoms, centered on trading cities such as Novgorod and Kiev (see Map 10.3). By this time, Kiev, which originally dominated much of central Russia, had been in decline for some time. As a result, there was no paramount power to rally Russian forces against the invaders. Despite the warnings of those who had witnessed the crushing defeats suffered by the Georgians in the early 1220s, the princes of Russia refused to cooperate. They preferred to fight alone, and they were routed individually.

In 1236, Batu led a Mongol force of more than 120,000 cavalrymen into the Russian heartlands. From 1237 to 1238 and later in 1240, these Tatars, or Tartars (meaning people from hell), as the Russians called them, carried out the only successful winter invasions in Russian history. In fact, the Mongols preferred to fight in the winter. The frozen earth provided good footing for their horses, and frozen rivers gave them access to their enemies. One after another, the Mongol armies defeated the often much larger forces of local nomadic groups and Russian princes. Cities such as Ryazan, Moscow, and Vladimir, which resisted the Mongol command to surrender, were destroyed; their inhabitants were slaughtered or led into slavery. As a contemporary Russian chronicler observed, "No eye remained to weep for the dead." Just as it seemed that all of Russia would be ravaged by the Mongols, whom the Russians compared to locusts, Batu's armies withdrew. The largest cities, Novgorod and Kiev, appeared to have been spared. Russian priests thanked God; the Mongol commanders blamed the spring thaw, which slowed the Mongol horsemen and raised the risk of defeat in the treacherous mud.

The Mongols returned in force in the winter of 1240. In this second campaign, even the great walled city of Kiev, which had reached a population of more than 100,000 by the end of the 12th century, fell. Enraged by Kievan resistance—its ruler had ordered the Mongol envoys thrown from the city walls—the Mongols reduced the greatest city in Russia to a smoldering ruin. The cathedral of Saint Sophia was spared, but the rest of the city was looted and destroyed, and its inhabitants were smoked out and slaughtered. Novgorod braced itself for the Mongol onslaught. Again, according to the Russian chroniclers, it was "miraculously" spared. In fact, it was saved largely because of the willingness of its prince, Alexander Nevsky, to submit, at least temporarily, to Mongol demands. In addition, the Mongol armies were eager to move on to the main event: the invasion of Western Europe, which they perceived as a far richer but equally vulnerable region.

Golden Horde One of the four subdivisions of the Mongol empire after Chinggis Khan's death, originally ruled by his grandson Batu; territory covered much of what is today south central Russia.

khanates [KAHN-ayts] Four regional Mongol kingdoms that arose following the death of Chinggis Khan.

Russia in Bondage

The crushing victories of Batu's armies initiated nearly two and a half centuries of Mongol dominance in Russia. Russian princes were forced to submit as vassals of the khan of the Golden Horde and to pay tribute. Mongol demands fell particularly heavily on the Russian peasantry, who had to give their crops and labor to both their own princes and the Mongol overlords. Impoverished and ever fearful of the lightning raids of Mongol marauders, the peasants fled to remote areas or became, in effect, the serfs (see Chapter 10) of the Russian ruling class in return for protection. Some Russian towns made profits on the increased trade made possible by the Mongol links. Sometimes the gains exceeded the tribute they paid to the Golden Horde. No town benefited from the Mongol presence more than Moscow. Badly plundered and partially burned in the early Mongol assaults, the city was gradually rebuilt, and its ruling princes steadily swallowed up nearby towns and surrounding villages. After 1328, Moscow also profited from its status as the tribute collector for the Mongol khans. Its princes

Read the Document on MyHistoryLab: The Mongols: An Excerpt from the Novgorod Chronicle, 1315

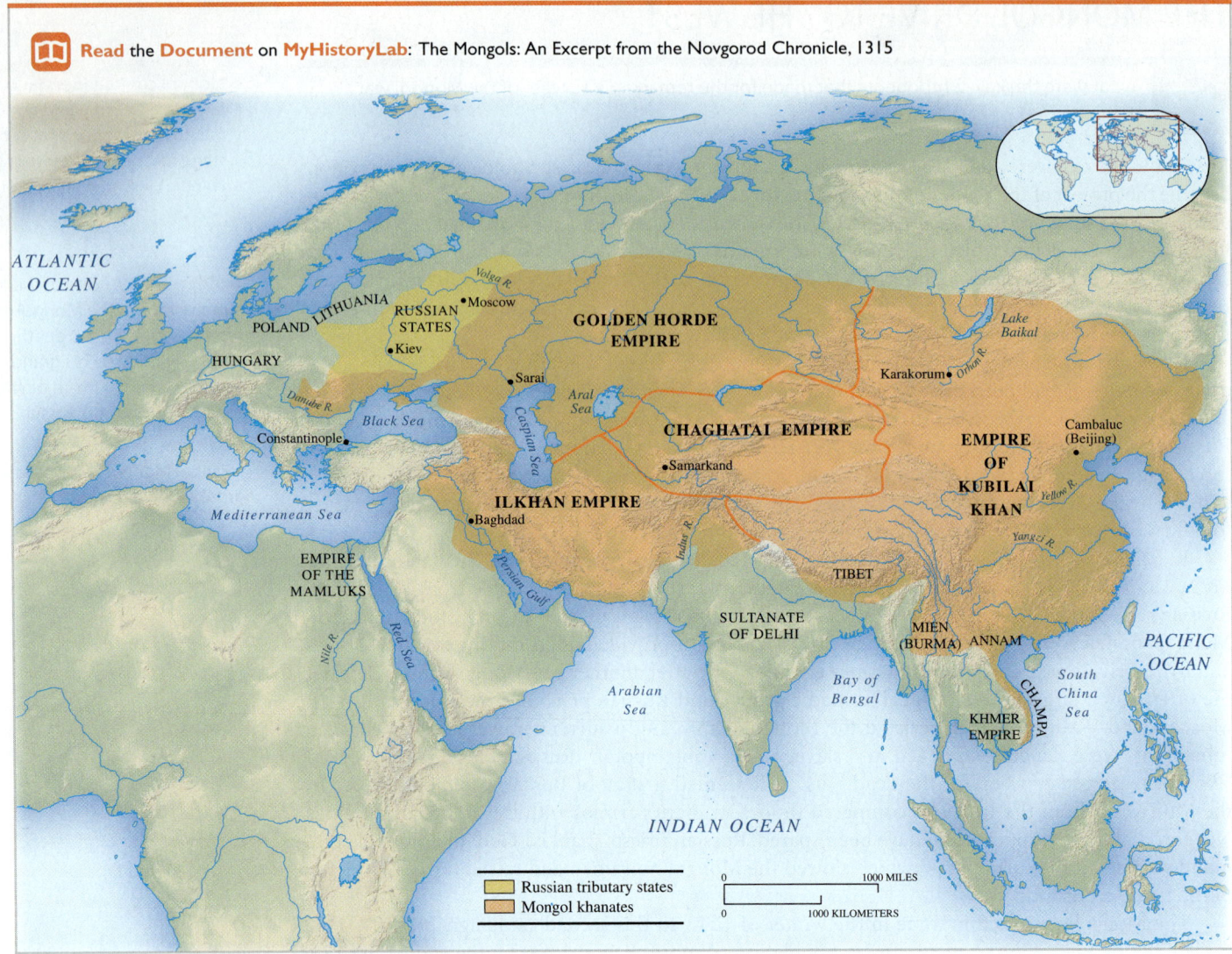

MAP 15.2 **The Four Khanates of the Divided Mongol Empire** Sheer distances and slow-moving modes of transportation made it difficult to hold together the vast domains conquered by Chinggis Khan and his immediate successors.

not only used their position to fill their own coffers but also annexed other towns as punishment for falling behind on tribute payments.

As Moscow grew in strength, the power of the Golden Horde declined. Mongol religious toleration benefited both the Orthodox Church and Moscow. The choice of Moscow as the seat of the Orthodox leaders brought new sources of wealth to its princes and buttressed its claims to be Russia's leading city. In 1380, those claims got an additional boost when the princes of Moscow shifted from being tribute collectors to being the defenders of Russia. In alliance with other Russian vassals, they raised an army that defeated the forces of the Golden Horde at the **Battle of Kulikova**. Their victory and the devastating blows Timur's attacks dealt the Golden Horde two decades later effectively broke the Mongol hold over Russia.

Although much of the Mongols' impact was negative, their conquest was a turning point in Russian history in several ways. In addition to their importance to Moscow and the Orthodox Church, Mongol contacts led to changes in Russian military organization and tactics and in the political style of Russian rulers. Claims that the Tatars were responsible for Russian despotism, either tsarist or Stalinist, are clearly overstated. Still, the Mongol example may have influenced the desire of Russian princes to centralize their control and reduce the limitations placed on their power by the landed nobility, clergy, and wealthy merchants. By far the greatest effects of Mongol rule were those resulting

Battle of Kulikova Russian army victory over the forces of the Golden Horde; helped break Mongol hold over Russia.

340 PART III The Postclassical Period, 600–1450: New Faith and New Commerce

from Russia's isolation from Christian lands farther west. On one hand, the Mongols protected a divided and weak Russia from the attacks of much more powerful kingdoms such as Poland, Lithuania, and Hungary (Map 15.2). On the other hand, in the period of Mongol rule, Russia was cut off from key transformations in western Europe that were inspired by the Renaissance and led ultimately to the Reformation.

Mongol Incursions and the Retreat from Europe

Until news of the Mongol campaigns in Russia reached European peoples such as the Germans, Poles, and Hungarians farther west, Christian leaders had been quite pleased by the rise of a new military power in central Asia. Rumors and reports from Christians living in the area, chafing under what they saw as persecution by their Muslim overlords, convinced many in western Europe that the Mongol khan was none other than **Prester John**. Prester John was the name given to a mythical rich and powerful Christian monarch whose kingdom had supposedly been cut off from Europe by the Muslim conquests of the 7th and 8th centuries. Sometimes located in Africa, sometimes in central Asia, Prester John loomed large in the European imagination as a potential ally who could strike the Muslim enemy from the rear and join up with European Christians to destroy their common adversary. The Mongol assault on the Muslim Khwarazm empire appeared to confirm the speculation that Chinggis Khan was indeed Prester John.

Prester John In legends popular from 12th to 17th century, a mythical Christian monarch whose kingdom was cut off from Europe by Muslim conquests; Chinggis Khan was originally believed to be this mythical ruler.

The assault on Christian, although Orthodox, Russia made it clear that the Mongol armies were neither the legions of Prester John nor more partial to Christians than to any other people who stood in their way. The rulers of Europe were nevertheless slow to realize the magnitude of the threat the Mongols posed to western Christendom. When Mongol envoys, one of whom was an Englishman, arrived at the court of King Bela of Hungary demanding that he surrender a group of nomads who had fled to his domains after being beaten by the Mongols in Russia, the king contemptuously dismissed them. King Bela also rebuffed Batu's demand that he submit to Mongol rule. The Hungarian monarch reasoned that he was the ruler of a powerful kingdom, whereas the Mongols were just another ragtag band of nomads in search of easy plunder. His refusal to negotiate provided the Mongols with a pretext to invade. Their ambition remained the conquest and pillage of all western Europe. That this goal was clearly attainable was demonstrated by the sound drubbing they gave to the Hungarians in 1240 and later to a mixed force of Christian knights led by the Polish ruler, King Henry of Silesia.

These victories left the Mongols free to raid and pillage from the Adriatic Sea region in the south to Poland and the German states of the north. It also left the rest of Europe open to Mongol conquest. Just as the kings and clergy of the western portions of Christendom were beginning to fear the worst, the Mongol forces disappeared. The death of the khagan Ogedei, in the distant Mongol capital at Karakorum, forced Batu to withdraw in preparation for the struggle for succession. The campaign for the conquest of Europe was never resumed. Perhaps Batu was satisfied with the huge empire of the Golden Horde that he ruled from his splendid new capital at Sarai on the Volga River in what is southern Russia today. Most certainly the Mongols had found richer lands to plunder in the following decades in the Muslim empires of the Middle East. Whatever the reason, Europe was spared the full fury of the Mongol assault. Of the civilizations that fringed the steppe homelands of the Mongols, only India was as fortunate.

The Mongol Assault on the Islamic Heartland

After the Mongol conquest of the Khwarazm empire, it was only a matter of time before they struck westward against the far wealthier Muslim empires of Mesopotamia and North Africa (see Map 8.2 and Map 15.2). The conquest of these areas became the main project of Hulegu, another grandson of Chinggis Khan and the ruler of the Ilkhan portions of the Mongol empire. As we saw in Chapter 8, one of the key results of Hulegu's assaults on the Muslim heartlands was the capture and destruction of Baghdad in 1258 (Figure 15.4). The murder of the Abbasid caliph, one of some 800,000 people who were reported to have been killed in Mongol retribution for the city's resistance, ended the dynasty that had ruled the core regions of the Islamic world since the mid-8th century. A major Mongol victory over the Seljuk Turks in 1243 also proved critical to the subsequent history of the region. It opened up Asia Minor (present-day Turkey) to conquest by a different Turkic-speaking people, the Ottomans, who would eventually become the next great power in the Islamic heartlands.

VISUALIZING THE PAST

The Mongol Empire as a Bridge Between Civilizations

CHINGGIS KHAN AND HIS SUCCESSORS ACTIVELY promoted the growth of trade and travelers by protecting the caravans that made their way across the ancient Asian silk routes. The Mongols also established rest stations for weary merchants and fortified outposts for those harassed by bandits. These measures transformed the Mongol imperium into a massive conduit between the civilizations of Europe, the Middle East, and the rest of Asia. The map illustrates a wide variety of marketable goods and inventions, as well as the agents and objects of several religions, between areas within the empire and along its lengthy borders. Study these patterns and then answer the questions that follow.

QUESTIONS

- Discuss some of the major ways in which the Mongol empire facilitated exchanges and interaction between civilizations and culture areas. What were the main centers of different kinds of products?
- What were the main directions in which ideas, goods, and new inventions flowed?
- Based on the discussions in the preceding chapters, who were some of the key agents of these exchanges?
- Why were the networks of exchange established by the Mongols so short-lived?

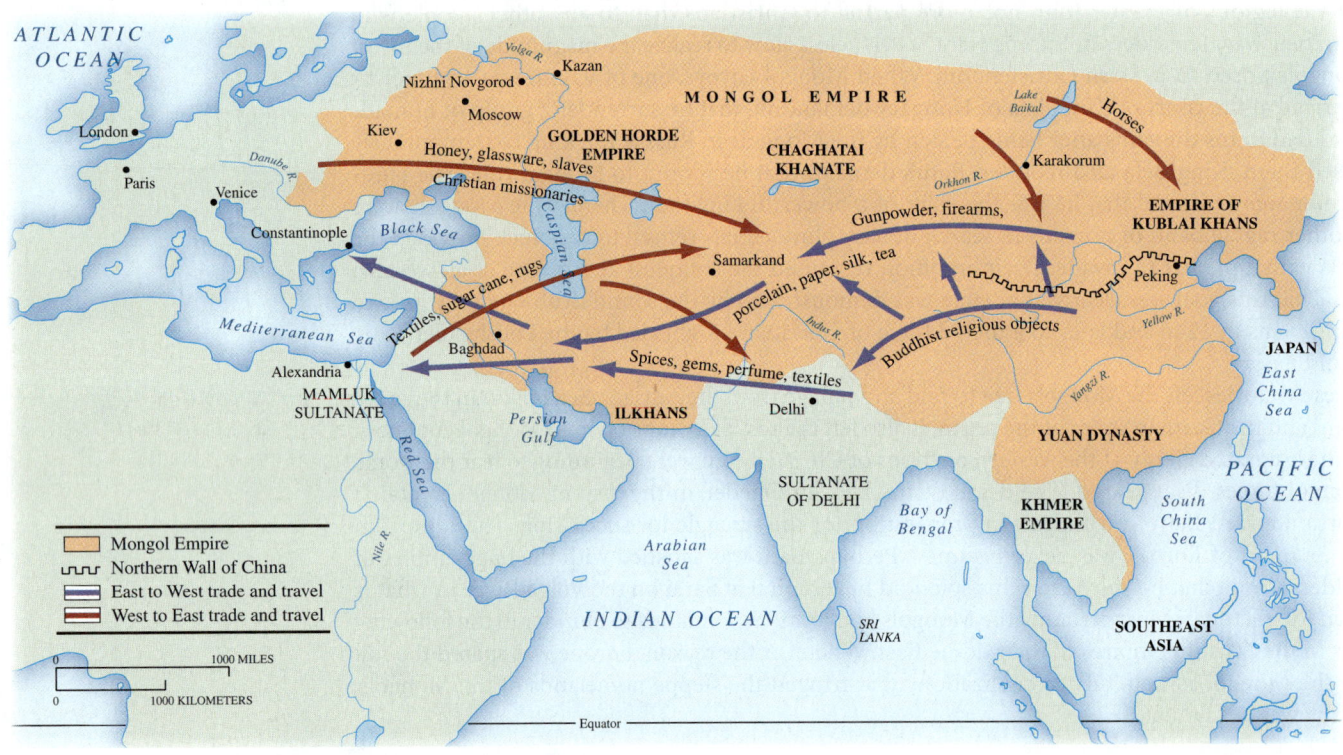

MAP 15.3 The Mongol Empire and the Global Exchange Network

Baibars [bī bars] (1223–1277) Commander of Mamluk forces at Ain Jalut in 1260; originally enslaved by Mongols and sold to Egyptians.

Berke [ber kuh] (r. 1257–1266) A ruler of the Golden Horde; converted to Islam; his threat to Hulegu combined with the growing power of Mamluks in Egypt forestalled further Mongol conquests in the Middle East.

Given the fate of Baghdad, it is understandable that Muslim historians treated the coming of the Mongols as one of the great catastrophes in the history of Islam. The murder of the caliph and his family left the faithful without a central authority. The sack of Baghdad and many other cities from central Asia to the shores of the Mediterranean devastated the focal points of Islamic civilization. One contemporary Muslim chronicler, Ibn al-Athir, found the violence the Mongols had done to his people so horrific that he apologized to his readers for recounting it and wished that he had not been born to see it. He lamented,

> In just one year they seized the most populous, the most beautiful, and the best cultivated part of the earth whose inhabitants excelled in character and urbanity. In the countries that have not yet been

overrun by them, everyone spends the night afraid that they may yet appear there, too.... Thus, Islam and the Muslims were struck, at that time by a disaster such as no people had experienced before.

Given these reverses, one can imagine the relief the peoples of the Muslim world felt when the Mongols were finally defeated in 1260 by the armies of the Mamluk, or slave, dynasty of Egypt. Ironically, **Baibars**, the commander of the Egyptian forces, and many of his lieutenants had been enslaved by the Mongols some years earlier and sold in Egypt, where they rose to power through military service. The Muslim victory was won with the rare cooperation of the Christians, who allowed Baibars's forces to cross unopposed through their much diminished crusader territories in Palestine. Christian support demonstrated how far the former crusader states had gone in accommodating their more powerful Muslim neighbors.

Hulegu was in central Asia, engaged in yet another succession struggle, when the battle occurred. Upon his return, he was forced to reconsider his plans for conquest of the entire Muslim world. The Mamluks were deeply entrenched and growing stronger; Hulegu was threatened by his cousin **Berke**, the new khan of the Golden Horde to the north, who had converted to Islam. After openly clashing with Berke and learning of Baibars's overtures for an alliance with the Golden Horde, Hulegu decided to settle for the kingdom he already ruled, which stretched from the frontiers of Byzantium to the Amu Darya (Oxus) River in central Asia (Map 15.2).

THE MONGOL INTERLUDE IN CHINESE HISTORY

15.3 Compare the impact of Mongol conquest and rule in the Muslim Middle East, Russia, and China: On which area was there a greater impact, to what extent did the Mongol interlude alter the historical trajectory of each these major culture areas, and what were the similarities and differences in terms of the nature of and effects of Mongol invasions and rule?

Soon after Ogedei was elected as the great khan, the Mongol advance into China was resumed. Having conquered the Xi Xia and Jin empires, the Mongol commanders turned to what remained of the Song Empire in south China (Maps 15.1 and 15.2). In the campaigns against the Song, the Mongol forces were directed by **Kubilai Khan** (Figure 15.5). Kubilai was one of the grandsons of Chinggis Khan, and he would play a pivotal role in Chinese history for the next half century. Even under a decadent dynasty that had long neglected its defenses, south China was one of the toughest areas for the Mongols to conquer. From 1235 to 1279, the Mongols were constantly on the march; they fought battle after battle and besieged seemingly innumerable, well-fortified Chinese cities. In 1260, Kubilai assumed the title of the great khan, much to the chagrin of his cousins who ruled other parts of the empire. A decade later, in 1271, on the recommendation of Chinese advisors, he changed the name of his Mongol regime to a Chinese-language dynastic title, the **Yuan**. Although he was still nearly a decade away from fully defeating the last-ditch efforts of Confucian bureaucrats and Chinese generals to save the Song dynasty, Kubilai ruled most of China. He now set about the task of establishing more permanent Mongol control.

As the different regions of China came under Mongol rule, Kubilai passed many laws to preserve the distinction between Mongol and Chinese. He forbade Chinese scholars to learn the Mongol script, which was used for records and correspondence at the upper levels of the imperial government. Mongols were forbidden to marry ethnic Chinese, and only women from nomadic families were selected for the imperial harem. Even friendships between the two peoples were discouraged, and Mongol

View the **Closer Look** on **MyHistoryLab**: A Mongol Passport

FIGURE 15.4 The Abbasid capital at Baghdad had long been in decline when the Mongols besieged it in 1258. The Mongols' sack of the city put an end to all pretenses that Baghdad was still the center of the Muslim world. The Mongol assault on Baghdad also revealed how vulnerable even cities with high and extensive walls were to the artillery and other siege weapons that the Mongols and Chinese had pioneered. In the centuries that followed, major innovations in fortifications, many introduced first in Europe, were made to counter the introduction of gunpowder and the new siege cannons.

(The Mongols under their chief Hülegü conquering Baghdad in 1258. From Rashid al-Din's "Jami' al-Tawarikh" (Compendium of Chronicles). Illuminated manuscript page, 14th c.e. Inv. Diez A Fol.70, image 7. Bildarchiv Preussischer/Art Resource, NY. Photo: Ruth Schacht. Oriental Division.)

After decades of hard campaigning in the mid-13th century, the Mongols gained control of the greatest prize of all, China, which they ruled for a century. Although the Chinese capacity to assimilate nomadic conquerors was evident from the outset, the Mongols managed to retain a distinct culture and social separateness.

> **Read** the **Document** on **MyHistoryLab**: Marco Polo on Chinese Society under the Mongol Rule (1270s)

FIGURE 15.5 This portrait of Kubilai Khan, by far the most important Mongol ruler of China, emphasizes his Mongol physical features, beard and hair styles, and dress. But Kubilai was determined to "civilize" his Mongol followers according to Chinese standards. Not only did he himself adopt a Chinese lifestyle, but he had his son educated by the best Confucian scholars to be a proper Chinese emperor. Kubilai also became a major patron of the Chinese arts and a promoter of Chinese culture.

Kubilai Khan [KOO-bluh KAHN] (1215–1294) Grandson of Chinggis Khan; commander of Mongol forces responsible for conquest of China; became khagan in 1260; established Sinicized Mongol Yuan dynasty in China in 1271.

Dadu Present-day Beijing; so-called when Kubilai Khan ruled China.

Chabi [CHAH-bee] Influential wife of Kubilai Khan; promoted interests of Buddhists in China; indicative of refusal of Mongol women to adopt restrictive social conventions of Chinese; died c. 1281.

military forces remained separate from the Chinese. Mongol religious ceremonies and customs were retained, and a tent encampment in the traditional Mongol style was set up in the imperial city even though Kubilai usually lived in a Chinese-style palace.

Despite his measures to ensure that the conquering Mongol minority was not completely absorbed by the culture of the defeated, Kubilai Khan had long been fascinated by Chinese civilization. Even before beginning the conquest of the Song Empire, he had surrounded himself with Chinese advisors, some Buddhist, others Daoist or Confucian. His capital at **Dadu** in the north (present-day Beijing) was built on the site occupied by earlier dynasties, and he introduced Chinese rituals and classical music into his own court. Kubilai also put the empire on the Chinese calendar and offered sacrifices to his ancestors at a special temple in the imperial city. But he rebuffed the pleas of his Confucian advisors to reestablish the civil service exams, which had been discontinued by the Jin rulers.

In the Yuan era, a new social structure was established in China, with the Mongols on top and their central Asian nomadic and Muslim allies right below them in the hierarchy. These two groups occupied most offices at the highest levels of the bureaucracy. Beneath them came the ethnic Chinese and then the minority peoples of the south. Thus, ethnic Chinese from both north and south ran the Yuan bureaucracy at the regional and local levels, but they could exercise power at the top only as advisors to the Mongols or other nomadic officials. At all levels, their activities were scrutinized by Mongol functionaries from an enlarged and much strengthened censors' bureau.

Gender Roles and the Convergence of Mongol and Chinese Culture

Mongol women remained aloof from Chinese culture—at least Chinese culture in its Confucian guise. They refused to adopt the practice of footbinding, which so limited the activities of Chinese women. They retained their rights to property and control within the household as well as the freedom to move about the town and countryside. No more striking evidence of their independence can be found than contemporary accounts of Mongol women riding to the hunt, both with their husbands and at the head of their own hunting parties. The daughter of one of Kubilai's cousins went to war, and she refused to marry until one of her many suitors was able to throw her in a wrestling match.

The persisting influence of Mongol women after the Mongols settled down in China is exemplified by **Chabi**, the wife of Kubilai Khan (Figure 15.6). She was one of Kubilai's most important confidants on political and diplomatic matters, and she promoted Buddhist interests in the highest circles of government. Chabi played a critical role in fostering policies aimed at reconciling the majority ethnic Chinese population of the empire to Mongol rule. She convinced Kubilai that the harsh treatment of the survivors of the defeated Song imperial family would only anger the peoples of north China and make them more difficult to rule. On another occasion, she demonstrated that she shared Kubilai's respect for Chinese culture by frustrating a plan to turn cultivated lands near the capital into pasturelands for the Mongols' ponies. Thus, the imperial couple was a good match of astute political skills and cosmopolitanism, tempered by respect for their own traditions and a determination to preserve those they found the most valuable.

The Mongol era was too brief and the number of influential Mongol women far too small to reverse the trends that for centuries had been lowering the position of women in Chinese society. As neo-Confucianism gained ground under Kubilai's successors, the arguments for confining women multiplied. Ultimately, even women of the Mongol ruling class saw their freedom and power reduced.

Mongol Tolerance and Foreign Cultural Influence

Like Chinggis Khan and other Mongol overlords, Kubilai and Chabi had unbounded curiosity and very cosmopolitan tastes. Their generous patronage drew scholars, artists, artisans, and office-seekers from many lands to the splendid Yuan court. Some of the most favored came from Muslim kingdoms to the east that had come under Mongol rule. Muslims were included in the second highest social grouping, just beneath the Mongols themselves. Persians and Turks were admitted to the inner circle of Kubilai's administrators and advisors. Muslims designed and supervised the building of his Chinese-style imperial city and proposed new systems for more efficient tax collection. Persian astronomers imported more advanced Middle Eastern instruments for celestial observations, corrected the Chinese calendar, and made some of the most accurate maps the Chinese had ever seen. Muslim doctors ran the imperial hospitals and added translations of 36 volumes on Muslim medicine to the imperial library.

In addition to the Muslims, Kubilai welcomed travelers and emissaries from many foreign lands to his court. Like his grandfather, Kubilai had a strong interest in all religions and insisted on toleration in his domains. Buddhists, Nestorian Christians, Daoists, and Latin Christians made their way to his court. The most renowned of the latter were members of the Polo family from Venice in northern Italy, who traveled extensively in the Mongol empire in the middle of the 13th century. Marco Polo's account of Kubilai Khan's court and empire, where Polo lived and served as an administrator for 17 years, is perhaps the most famous travel account written by a European (Figure 15.7). Polo accepted fantastic tales of grotesque and strange customs, and he may have taken parts of his account from other sources. Still, his descriptions of the palaces, cities, and wealth of Kubilai's empire enhanced European interest in Asia and helped to inspire efforts by navigators, such as Columbus, to find a sea route to these fabled lands.

Social Policies and Scholar-Gentry Resistance

Kubilai's efforts to promote Mongol adaptation to Chinese culture were overshadowed in the long run by measures to preserve Mongol separateness. The ethnic Chinese who made up the vast majority of his subjects, particularly in the south, were never really reconciled to Mongol rule. Despite Kubilai's cultivation of Confucian rituals and his extensive employment of Chinese bureaucrats, most of the scholar-gentry saw the Mongol overlord and his successors as uncouth barbarians whose policies endangered Chinese traditions. As it was intended to do, Kubilai's refusal to reinstate the examination route to administrative office prevented Confucian scholars from dominating politics. The favoritism he showed Mongol and other foreign officials further alienated the scholar-gentry.

To add insult to injury, Kubilai went to great lengths to bolster the position of the artisan classes, who had never enjoyed high standing, and the merchants, whom the Confucian thinkers had long dismissed as parasites. From the outset the Mongols had shown great regard for artisans and because of their useful skills had often spared them while killing their fellow city dwellers. During the Yuan period in China, merchants also prospered and commerce boomed, partly because of Mongol efforts to improve transportation and expand the supply of paper money. With amazing speed for a people who had no prior experience with seafaring, the Mongols developed a substantial navy, which played a major role in the conquest of the Song empire. After the conquest of China was completed, the great Mongol war fleets were used to put down pirates, who threatened river and overseas commerce. Toward the end of Kubilai's reign, the navy also launched a number of overseas expeditions of exploration and conquest, which led to attacks on Japan and a brief reoccupation of Vietnam.

FIGURE **15.6** A portrait of Chabi, the energetic and influential wife of Kubilai Khan. Kubilai's determination to adopt Chinese culture without being overwhelmed by it was bolstered by the advice and example of Chabi. Displaying the independent-mindedness and political savvy of many Mongol women, Chabi gave Kubilai critical advice on how to counter the schemes of his ambitious brother and how to handle the potentially hostile scholar-gentry elite and peasantry that came to be ruled by Mongol overlords.

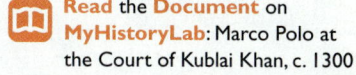
Read the Document on MyHistoryLab: Marco Polo at the Court of Kublai Khan, c. 1300

> **Read the Document on MyHistoryLab:** Mongols and Trade on the Silk Roads

FIGURE 15.7 This 15th-century manuscript illumination depicts Marco Polo and his uncle offering homage to the Great Khan. The Polos were Venetian merchants, and Marco's elders had already traveled extensively in Asia in the decade before they set off with Marco. Marco had a great facility with languages, which served him well in his journeys through Asia by land and sea. On his way home in the mid-1290s, he related his many adventures to a writer of romances while both were prisoners of the Genoese, who were fierce rivals of the Venetians. Eventually published under the title *Description of the World*, Polo's account became one of a handful of definitive sources on the world beyond Europe for the explorers of the coming age of overseas expansion.
(Paris, Bibliotheque Nationale, Ms. 2810.)

Romance of the West Chamber
Chinese drama written during the Yuan period; indicative of the continued literary vitality of China during Mongol rule.

Ironically, despite the Mongols' suspicion of cities and sedentary lifestyles, both flourished in the Yuan era. The urban expansion begun under the Tang and Song dynasties continued, and the Mongol elite soon became addicted to the diversions of urban life. Traditional Chinese artistic endeavors, such as poetry and essay writing, languished under the Mongols in comparison with their flowering in the Tang and Song eras. But popular entertainments, particularly musical dramas, flourished. Perhaps the most famous Chinese dramatic work, **Romance of the West Chamber**, was written in the Yuan period. Dozens of major playwrights wrote for the court, the rising merchant classes, and the Mongol elite. Actors and actresses, who had long been relegated by the Confucian scholars to the despised status of "mean people," achieved celebrity and social esteem. All of this rankled the scholar-gentry, who waited for the chance to restore Confucian decorum and what they believed to be the proper social hierarchy for a civilized people.

Initially, at least, Kubilai Khan pursued policies toward one social group, the peasants that the scholarly class would have heartily approved. He forbade Mongol cavalrymen from turning croplands into pasture and restored the granary system for famine relief that had been badly neglected in the late Song. Kubilai also sought to reduce peasant tax and forced-labor burdens, partly by redirecting peasant payments from local nonofficial tax farmers directly to government officials. He and his advisors also developed a revolutionary plan to establish elementary education in the villages. Although the level of learning they envisioned was rudimentary, such a project, if it had been enacted, would have been a major challenge to the educational system centered on the elite that long had dominated Chinese civilization.

The Fall of the House of Yuan

Historians often remark on the seeming contradiction between the military prowess of the Mongol conquerors and the short life of the dynasty they established in China. Kubilai Khan's long reign encompassed a good portion of the nine decades in which the Mongols ruled all of China. Already by the end of his reign, the dynasty was showing signs of weakening. Song loyalists raised revolts in the south, and popular hostility toward the foreign overlords was expressed more and more openly. The Mongol aura of military invincibility was badly tarnished by Kubilai's rebuffs at the hands of the military lords of Japan and the failure of the expeditions that he sent to punish them, first in 1274 and again in a much larger effort in 1280. The defeats suffered by Mongol forces engaged in similar expeditions to Vietnam and Java during this same period further undermined the Mongols' standing.

Kubilai's dissolute lifestyle in his later years, partly brought on by the death of his most beloved wife, Chabi, and five years later the death of his favorite son, led to a general softening of the Mongol ruling class as a whole. Kubilai's successors lacked his capacity for leadership and cared little for the tedium of day-to-day administrative tasks. Many of the Muslim and Chinese functionaries to whom they entrusted the imperial finances enriched themselves through graft and corruption. This greatly angered the hard-pressed peasantry, who bore the burden of rising taxes and demands for forced

THINKING HISTORICALLY

The Global Eclipse of the Nomadic Warrior Culture

AS THE SHOCK WAVES OF THE Mongol and Timurid explosions amply demonstrate, nomadic incursions into the civilized cores have had an impact on global history that far exceeds what one would expect, given the small numbers of nomadic peoples and the limited resources of the regions they inhabited. From the time of the great Indo-European migrations in the 3rd and 2nd millennia B.C.E. through the classical and postclassical eras, nomadic peoples periodically emerged from their steppe, prairie, and desert fringe homelands to invade, often build empires, and settle in the sedentary zones of Eurasia, Africa, and the Americas. Their intrusions have significantly changed political history by destroying existing polities and even, as in the case of Assyria, whole civilizations. They have also generated major population movements, sparked social upheavals, and facilitated critical cultural and economic exchanges across civilizations. As the Mongols' stunning successes in the 13th century illustrate, the ability of nomadic peoples to break through the defenses of the much more populous civilized zones and to establish control over much richer and more sophisticated peoples arose primarily from the nomads' advantages in waging war.

A reservoir of battle-ready warriors and mobility have proved to be the keys to success for expansion-minded nomads. Harsh environments and ongoing intertribal and interclan conflicts for survival within them produced tough, resourceful fighters who could live off the land on the march and who saw combat as an integral part of their lives. The horses and camels on which pastoral peoples in Eurasia and Sudanic Africa relied gave them a degree of mobility that confounded the sedentary peoples who tried to ward off their incursions. The mounted warriors of nomadic armies had the advantages of speed, surprise, and superior intelligence, gathered by mounted patrols. The most successful nomadic invaders, such as the Mongols, also were willing to experiment with and adapt to technological innovations. Some of these, such as the stirrup and various sorts of harnesses, were devised by the nomads themselves. Others, such as gunpowder and the siege engines—both Muslim and Chinese—that the Mongols used to smash the defenses of walled towns were borrowed from sedentary peoples and adapted to the nomads' fighting styles.

Aside from the military advantages of the nomads' lifestyles and social organization, their successes in war owed much to the weaknesses of their adversaries in the sedentary, civilized zones. Even in the best circumstances, the great empires that provided the main defense for agricultural peoples against nomadic incursions were diverse and overextended polities. Imperial control and protection diminished steadily as one moved away from the capital and core provinces. Imperial boundaries were usually fluid, and the outer provinces were vulnerable to nomadic raids and conquest.

Classical and postclassical empires, such as the Egyptian and Han and the Abbasid, Byzantine, and Song, enjoyed great advantages over the nomads in terms of the populations and resources they controlled. But their armies, almost without exception, were too slow, too low on firepower, and too poorly trained to resist large and well-organized forces of nomadic intruders. In times of dynastic strength in the sedentary zones, well-defended fortress systems and ingenious weapons—such as the crossbow, which the peasant conscripts could master fairly easily—were quite effective against nomadic incursions. Nonetheless, even the strongest dynasties depended heavily on protection payments to nomad leaders and the divisions between the nomadic peoples on their borders for their security. Even the strongest sedentary empires were shaken periodically by nomadic raids into the outer provinces. When the empires weakened or when large numbers of nomads were united under able leaders, such as the prophet Muhammad and his successors or Chinggis Khan, nomadic assaults made a shambles of sedentary armies and fortifications.

In many ways, the Mongol and Timurid explosions represented the apex of nomadic power and influence on world history. After these remarkable interludes, age-old patterns of interaction between nomads and town-dwelling peoples were transformed. These transformations resulted in the growing ability of sedentary peoples to first resist and then dominate nomadic peoples, and they mark a watershed in the history of the human community. Some of the causes of the shift were immediate and specific. The most critical of these was the devastation wrought by the Black Death on the nomads of central Asia in the 14th century. Although the epidemic was catastrophic for large portions of the civilized zones as well, it dealt the sparse nomadic populations a blow from which they took centuries to recover.

In the centuries after the Mongol conquests, the rulers of sedentary states found increasingly effective ways to centralize their political power and mobilize the labor and resources of their domains for war. The rulers of China and the empires of the Islamic belt made some improvements, but the sovereigns of the emerging states of western Europe surpassed all others in this regard. Stronger control and better organization allowed a

> **With the introduction early in the 17th century of light, mobile field artillery into the armies of the warring states of central and western Europe, the nomads' retreat began.**

(continued on next page)

growing share of steadily increasing national wealth to be channeled toward military ends. The competing rulers of Europe also invested heavily in technological innovations with military applications, from improved metalworking techniques and radical innovations in fortress construction to more potent gunpowder and firearms. From the 15th and 16th centuries, the discipline and training of European armies also improved. With pikes, muskets, exacting drill in the use of firearms, and trained commanders, European armies were more than a match for the massed nomad cavalry that had so long terrorized sedentary peoples.

With the introduction early in the 17th century of light, mobile field artillery into the armies of the warring states of central and western Europe, the nomads' retreat began. States such as Russia, which had centralized power on the western European model, as well as the Ottoman Empire in the eastern Mediterranean and the Qing in China, which had shared many of the armament advances of the Europeans, moved steadily into the steppe and desert heartlands of the horse and camel nomads. Each followed a conscious policy of settling part of its rapidly growing peasant population in the areas taken from the nomads. Thus, nomadic populations not only were brought under the direct rule of sedentary empires but saw their pasturelands plowed and planted wherever the soil and water supply permitted.

These trends suggest that the nomadic war machine had been in decline long before the new wave of innovation that ushered in the Industrial Revolution in the 18th century. But that process sealed its fate. Railways and repeating rifles allowed sedentary peoples to penetrate even the most wild and remote nomadic refuges and subdue even the most determined and fierce nomadic warriors, from the Plains Indians of North America to the bedouin of the Sahara and Arabia. The periodic nomadic incursions into the sedentary zones, which had recurred for millennia, had come to an end.

QUESTIONS
- What are some of the major ways in which nomadic peoples and their periodic expansions have affected global history?
- Which of their movements and conquests do you think were the most important?
- Why were the Mongols able to build a much greater empire than any previous nomadic contender?
- Why did the Mongol Empire collapse so rapidly, and what does its fall tell us about the underlying weaknesses of the nomadic war machine?

White Lotus Society Secret religious society dedicated to overthrow of Yuan dynasty in China; typical of peasant resistance to Mongol rule.

Zhu Yuanzhang The given name of the Hongwu emperor, the founder of the Ming dynasty.

Ming dynasty Succeeded Mongol Yuan dynasty in China in 1368; lasted until 1644; initially mounted huge trade expeditions to southern Asia and elsewhere, but later concentrated efforts on internal development within China.

Timur-i Lang Also known as Tamerlane; leader of Turkic nomads; beginning in 1360s from base at Samarkand, launched series of attacks in Persia, the Fertile Crescent, India, and southern Russia; empire disintegrated after his death in 1405.

Read the Document on MyHistoryLab: A Contemporary Describes Timur

labor. The scholar-gentry played on this discontent by calling on the people to rise up and overthrow the "barbarian" usurpers.

By the 1350s, the signs of dynastic decline were apparent. Banditry and piracy were widespread, and the government's forces were too weak to curb them. Famine hit many regions and spawned local uprisings, which engulfed large portions of the empire. Secret religious sects, such as the **White Lotus Society**, were dedicated to overthrowing the dynasty. Their leaders' claims that they had magical powers to heal their followers and confound their enemies helped encourage further peasant resistance against the Mongols. As in the past, rebel leaders quarreled and fought with each other. For a time, chaos reigned as the Yuan regime dissolved, and the Mongols who could escape the fury of the mob retreated into central Asia. The restoration of peace and order came from an unexpected quarter. Rather than a regional military commander or an aristocratic lord, a man from a poor peasant family, **Zhu Yuanzhang**, emerged to found the **Ming dynasty**, which ruled China for most of the next three centuries.

Aftershock: The Brief Ride of Timur, the Last of the Great Nomadic Conquerors

Just as the peoples of Europe and Asia had begun to recover from the upheavals caused by Mongol expansion, a second nomadic outburst from central Asia plunged them again into fear and despair. This time the nomads in question were Turks, not Mongols, and their leader, **Timur-i Lang** (Timur the Lame, or Tamerlane) was from a noble land-owning clan, not a tribal, herding background. Timur's personality was complex. On one hand, he was a highly cultured person who delighted in the fine arts, lush gardens, and splendid architecture and who could spend days conversing with great scholars, such as Muslim historian Ibn Khaldun (see the Document feature in Chapter 8). On the other, he was a ruthless conqueror, apparently indifferent to human suffering and capable of commanding his troops to commit atrocities on a scale that would not be matched in the human experience until the 20th century. Beginning in the 1360s, his armies moved out from his base at Samarkand to conquests in Persia, the Fertile Crescent, India, and southern Russia.

Although his empire did not begin to compare with that of the Mongols in size, he outdid them in the ferocity of his campaigns. In fact, Timur is remembered for little more than barbaric destruction:

His armies built pyramids of skulls with the heads of those they killed. Tens of thousands of people were slaughtered after they took the city of Aleppo in Asia Minor, and thousands of prisoners were massacred as a warning to the citizens of Delhi, in north India, not to resist his armies. In the face of this wanton slaughter, the fact that he spared artisans and scientists to embellish his capital city at Samarkand counts for little. Unlike that of the Mongols, his rule brought neither increased trade and cross-cultural exchanges nor internal peace. Fortunately, his reign was as brief as it was violent. After his death in 1405, his empire was pulled apart by his warring commanders and old enemies anxious for revenge. With his passing, the last great challenge of the steppe nomads to the civilizations of Eurasia came to an end.

Global Connections and Critical Themes

THE MONGOL LINKAGES

From the first explosion of Mongol military might from the steppes of central Asia in the early 13th century to the death of Timur in 1405, the nomads of central Asia made a stunning return to center stage in world history. Mongol invasions ended or interrupted many of the great empires of the postclassical period and also extended the world network that had increasingly defined the period. Under Chinggis Khan, the Mongols and their many nomadic neighbors were forged into the mightiest war machine the world had ever seen. With stunning rapidity the Mongols conquered central Asia, northern China, and eastern Persia (Map 15.1). Under Chinggis Khan's sons and grandsons, the rest of China, Tibet, Persia, Iraq, much of Asia Minor, and all of southern Russia were added to the vast Mongol imperium.

Although much of what the Mongols did was destructive, their forays into Europe, China, and the Muslim heartlands brought some lasting changes that were often transformative and at times beneficial. They taught new ways of making war and impressed on their Turkic and European enemies the effectiveness of gunpowder. Mongol conquests facilitated trade between the civilizations at each end of Eurasia, making possible the exchange of foods, tools, and ideas on an unprecedented scale. The revived routes brought great wealth to traders, such as those from north Italy, who set up outposts in the eastern Mediterranean, along the Black Sea coast, and as far east as the Caspian Sea.

The Mongol framework for Asian-European interactions, although short-lived, also facilitated other exchanges. It opened China to influences from Arab and Persian lands, and even to contacts with Europe. These connections came to full fruition in the centuries of indigenous Chinese revival that followed under the Ming dynasty. Europeans gained new knowledge of Chinese products and technologies that they would soon adapt back home. Explosive powder and printing were the most important examples. Regions more remote from the Mongols, such as Africa, lacked this kind of stimulus. Even the collapse of the Mongol network had an impact. Many societies had an interest in maintaining contacts, although China grew more wary of outsiders. But the Mongol decline made land-based travel more dangerous, which quickly turned attention toward sea routes. Thus, the legacy of the Mongol period was both complex and durable.

Perhaps the greatest long-term impact of the Mongol drive to the west was indirect and unintended. In recent years, a growing number of historians have become convinced that the Mongol conquests played a key role in transmitting the fleas that carried bubonic plague from south China and central Asia to Europe and the Middle East. The fleas may have hitched a ride on the livestock the Mongols drove into the new pasturelands won by their conquests or on the rats that nibbled the grain transported by merchants along the trading routes the Mongol rulers had reestablished between east and west. Whatever the exact connection, the Mongol armies unknowingly paved the way for the spread of the dreaded Black Death across the steppes to much of China, to the Islamic heartlands, and from there to most of Europe in the mid-14th century. In so doing, they unleashed possibly the most fatal epidemic in all human history. It led to mortality rates higher than 50 percent in some areas of Europe and the Middle East, and forced economic and social adjustments wherever it spread. This accidental but devastating side effect of the Mongol conquests influenced the course of civilized development in Europe, Asia, and north Africa for centuries.

Further Readings

A substantial literature has developed on the Mongol interlude in global history. The most readable and reliable biography of Chinggis Khan is René Grousset, *Conqueror of the World* (1966). Grousset has also written a broader history of central Asia, *The Empire of the Steppes* (1970). Peter Brent's more recent *The Mongol Empire* (1976) provides an updated overview and wonderful illustrations. Berthold Spuler, *History of the Mongols* (1968), supplies a wide variety of firsthand accounts of the Mongols. Timothy May's *The Mongol Art of War: Chinggis Khan and the Mongol Military System* (2000) shows that the Mongol armies had much in common with modern forces.

For the Mongols' impact on global history, see David Morgan, *The Mongols* (2006); Peter Jackson, *The Mongols and the West* (2005); and especially Thomas Allsen, *Culture and Conquest in Mongol Eurasia* (2001). Robert S. Marshall, *Storm from the East: From Genghis Khan to Khubilai Khan* (1993), and Charles J. Halperin,

Russia and the Golden Horde: The Mongol Impact on Medieval Russian History (1985), examine the Mongol impact on Russia. While George Vernadsky, *The Mongols in Russia* (1953), remains the standard work on that subject, some of its views are now contested. Morris Rossabi, *Kubilai Khan: His Life and Times* (1988), is by far the best work on the Mongols in China. George James Chambers, *The Devil's Horsemen* (1979), and Denis Sinor, *History of Hungary* (1957), contain good accounts of the Mongol incursions into eastern and central Europe. T. Allsen, *Mongol Imperialism* (1987), is the best account of the rise and structure of the empires built by Chinggis Khan and his successors. The fullest and most accessible summary of the links between Mongol expansion and the spread of the Black Death can be found in William H. McNeill, *Plagues and Peoples* (1976).

Recent works examining the broader interactions between agricultural and pastoral societies in Eurasia include Thomas J. Barfield, *The Perilous Frontier* (1992); Donald Ostrowski, *Muscovy and the Mongols: Cross-Cultural Influences on the Steppe Frontier, 1304–1589* (1998); Andrew Bell-Fialkoff, *The Role of Migration in the History of the Eurasian Steppe* (2000); and Nicola Di Cosmo, *Ancient China and Its Enemies: The Rise of Nomadic Power in East Asian History* (2004).

On MyHistoryLab

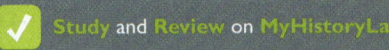
Study and Review on MyHistoryLab

Critical Thinking Questions

1. Discuss the ways in which the Mongol imperium enhanced contacts, particularly between China and the Islamic world. Which areas received the most benefit from these exchanges?

2. Why was the era of Mongol dominance so short-lived and what were some of the consequences of its disintegration?

3. What were the main effects of the Mongol period on world history? What are some of the ways that recent historical studies have forced us to rethink the nature and impact of the Mongol interlude in world history, and the roles played by nomadic peoples more generally?

The World in 1450: Changing Balance of World Power

16

Listen to Chapter 16 on MyHistoryLab

LEARNING OBJECTIVES

16.1 What were the most important changes in the Middle East between the 13th and the 15th centuries? p. 353

16.2 What caused the Chinese decision to abandon major expeditions? p. 354

16.3 What are the main issues in explaining new outreach from western Europe? What are the principal interpretations? p. 356

16.4 How did patterns in the Americas and Polynesia reflect their isolation from main transregional trade networks? p. 362

The compass is a simple enough device—something you can make yourself with an iron needle and a magnet. Yet it was also a revolutionary device, allowing sailors (and now, airplane pilots) to maintain a sense of direction no matter how dark, stormy, foggy, or unfamiliar the environment.

Although there has been debate about the origins of the compass, the instrument was clearly developed first by the Chinese. Chinese scientists may have had some knowledge of magnetic principles as early as the 1st century. Actual compasses may have been developed during the Tang dynasty. They undoubtedly originated from the discovery of naturally magnetized iron, or lodestone, that could then be used to fashion a needle that would point north. Some believe that the Chinese first used compasses in the practice of *feng shui*, which was a set of design principles by which people could align their living quarters with the forces of nature.

FIGURE **16.1** Chinese oceangoing ship from expeditions in the 16th century. This was a smaller ship than those used earlier in the great voyages of the early 15th century, whose end opened opportunities for other international traders. But the Chinese maintained active commerce even after this, particularly in maintaining contacts established in the postclassical period with the Philippines and with southeast Asia.

Watch the Video Series on MyHistoryLab

Learn about some key topics related to this chapter with the *MyHistoryLab Video Series: Key Topics in World History*

Compasses for navigation had been introduced by 1100. They were part of a growing Chinese effort to make contact with sources of spices and teas in southeast Asia. Prior to that point, Chinese seagoing had been confined to coastlines, but now it became much more venturesome. Wide-ranging Chinese expeditions introduced the compass to seafarers throughout the Indian Ocean, including Arab merchants, by the 12th century. Europeans are first known to have used the compass in 1187. Europeans may have invented the compass separately, but it is far more likely that they learned about its use as a result of contacts with Arabs or Asians.

The compass was fundamental to ambitious seagoing expeditions, like the great Chinese voyages through the Indian Ocean. Along with observation of the sun and stars, the compass provided the guidance for Columbus's travels to the Americas. It changed the shape of world history by facilitating dramatic new contacts and exchanges. By the 13th century, various seagoing peoples—Malaysians, for example, as well as Europeans—were introducing improvements in the compass, making it easier to read and more stable at sea. Italian navigators introduced the compass card, which involved placing the needle over a set of indicators. Knowledge of the compass reached Scandinavia by 1300, a further step in the long process of dissemination. ∎

In 1400 the world was undergoing a profound transition. This chapter highlights the main features of that process. The principal focus is the shifting balance among civilizations in Asia, Africa, and Europe and how these power shifts changed the nature of international contact.

This period of transition began with the decline of Arab strength—symbolized by the fall of the last Arab caliphate in 1258—and the disruptions that Mongol incursions caused elsewhere in Asia and eastern Europe. These developments created new opportunities in the Afro-Eurasian network that had been established during the postclassical centuries, initially under Arab sponsorship. Various candidates emerged to take a new international leadership role, including, for a short time, Ming China. The Chinese expeditions showed the importance transregional contacts had acquired. The end of the expeditions, however, opened the way for new alignments. Within the Middle East itself, Arab and then Mongol decline created new opportunities for Turkish conquerors and migrants. In 1453 the Ottoman Turks captured Constantinople, effectively completing the destruction of the Byzantine empire and creating a new Islamic political power. The Ottomans quickly established control around much of the Black Sea, including the Balkans, and began to push southward into Arab lands.

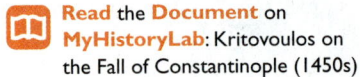
Read the Document on MyHistoryLab: Kritovoulos on the Fall of Constantinople (1450s)

While the Ottomans would play some role in transregional trade, ultimately the most dynamic new contender for leadership ultimately proved to be western Europe; the conditions that propelled Western civilization into this new position around 1400 are the second key theme of this chapter. The West was not yet a major power; it did not replace the Arabs or Chinese as international leaders quickly or easily. The first stages of the rise of the West were accompanied by important changes in Western civilization itself, which were beginning to take shape by 1400. At this point, Italy, Spain, and Portugal took the lead in western European outreach, a lead that they would hold for about two centuries.

It is also vital to note changes in societies outside the international network, in the Americas and Polynesia. New difficulties in the great American empires, in particular, would reduce their ability to respond to the challenge of contact with Europeans after 1492.

Focusing on new frameworks for international contacts, this chapter inevitably deals with the question of why individual societies reacted differently to key forces. Comparison is essential. Western Europe's response, for example, should be compared to reactions at the same time in regions like Japan or sub-Saharan Africa.

1250 C.E.	1300 C.E.	1350 C.E.	1400 C.E.	1450 C.E.
1258 Mongol conquest of Baghdad; fall of Abbasid caliphate **c. 1266–1337** Life of Giotto **1275–1292** Marco Polo in China **1290–1317** Famines in Europe **1291** First Italian expedition seeks route to Indies	**1304–1374** Life of Petrarch; development of Italian Renaissance **1320s** Spread of bubonic plague (Black Death) in Gobi desert **1320s** First European use of cannon in warfare **1330s** Black Death reaches China **1347** Black Death reaches Sicily **1348** Peak of Black Death in Middle East **1348–1375** Black Death spreads in Europe and Russia	**1368** Mongols expelled from China; Ming dynasty	**1400** End of Polynesian migrations **1405–1433** Chinese trading expeditions **1439** Portugal takes over Azores; increasing expeditions into Atlantic and along northwest African coast	**1453** Ottomans capture Constantinople, fall of Byzantine Empire **1469** Union of Aragon and Castile; rise of Spanish monarchy

Amid variations and great change, the transitions around 1450 highlighted one important continuity as well: the importance of the level of contacts that had developed through the formation of the transcontinental network. A variety of societies in Africa, Asia, and Europe depended on far-flung trade relations, and when one exchange network collapsed—as with the decline in travel security overland when the Mongol empires faded—another system quickly moved into place. Not only trade, but continued exchanges of technology and ideas continued to mark Afro-Eurasian relationships during the 15th century.

KEY CHANGES IN THE MIDDLE EAST

16.1 What were the most important changes in the Middle East between the 13th and the 15th centuries?

In 1200, the Middle East was still dominated by two powerful empires, the Byzantine in the northwest and the Islamic caliphate through much of the Middle Eastern heartland. By 1400, this structure was in disarray. The Byzantine empire still existed, but it was in rapid decline, pressed by invading Ottoman Turks. The Turkish capture of the imperial capital, Constantinople, in 1453 effectively ended the empire. Two centuries earlier, the caliphate, long sapped by increasing reliance on foreign troops and advisors, including the Turks, had fallen to Mongol invasion. Division in the Middle East, and among Arab peoples, took new forms.

> The new world order that was beginning to emerge by 1400 first involved major reshuffling in the Middle East and north Africa.

Social and Cultural Change in the Middle East

Culture shifted, along with politics, in this crucial region. An earlier tension in philosophy and the arts yielded to the predominance of the Islamic faith. The new piety associated with the rising Sufi movement, discussed in Chapter 8, contributed to a new religious emphasis. In literature, attention to secular themes, such as the joys of feasting and hunting, gave way to more strictly religious ideas. In philosophy, the rationalistic current encountered new attack. In Muslim Spain, philosopher Ibn Rushd (IH-buhn RUSHT) (Averroës) (uh-VEHR-oh-eez), espoused Greek rationalism, but his efforts were largely ignored in the Middle East. In fact, European scholars were more heavily influenced by his work. In the Middle East proper, a more typical philosopher, Al-Ghazali, in a book revealingly titled *The Destruction of the Philosophers*, now claimed to use Aristotle's logic to show that it was impossible to discover religious truth by human reason. Many Sufi scholars wrote excitedly of their mystical contacts with God and the stages of their religious passion. Islamic science continued, but its role diminished.

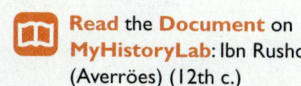
Read the Document on MyHistoryLab: Ibn Rushd (Averroës) (12th c.)

Changes in society and the economy were as telling as the shifts in politics and intellectual life. As the authority of the caliphate declined, landlords seized power over the peasantry. As a result, from about 1100 onward, Middle Eastern peasants increasingly lost their freedom, becoming serfs on large estates, providing the labor and produce landlords now sought. This loss was not the peasants' alone, for agricultural productivity suffered as a result. Landlords turned to sucking what they could from their estates rather than trying to develop a more vital agriculture. Tax revenues declined, and Arab and other Middle Eastern traders began to lose ground. Few Arab coins have been found in Europe dating from later than 1100. European merchants began to control their own turf and challenge the Arabs in other parts of the Mediterranean, gaining increasing initiative in this vital trading area.

Arab decline was gradual and incomplete. It cannot be compared with the dramatic fall of the Roman empire many centuries before. A more subtle model is needed. The reduced dynamism in trade did not take the Arabs out of major world markets, for example. Indeed, Middle Eastern commerce rebounded somewhat by 1400.

Finally, the political fragmentation of the Arab world did not produce prolonged confusion in the Middle East. The emerging Ottoman Turkish state soon mastered many of the lands of the old caliphate as well as the Byzantine corner, expanding into southeastern Europe. The new empire gave renewed vitality to Islamic politics, and it would soon be joined by two other Islamic empires, too, in Persia and India. (See Chapter 22 for the development of the new Ottoman Empire.) It is important to realize that the empire was far more powerful, politically and militarily, than the caliphate had been for many centuries. It was thus more challenging to observers in neighboring civilizations such as western Europe.

THE STRUCTURE OF TRANSREGIONAL TRADE

16.2 What caused the Chinese decision to abandon major expeditions?

Even the rise of the Ottoman empire did not restore the full international vigor that the Islamic caliphate wielded had at the height of its powers. The empire did not become the sole hub of an international network, as the caliphate had been a few centuries before. By the 15th century, merchants from many societies were competing for roles in transregional trade. In the Mediterranean, European, and particularly Italian, merchants were increasingly active; even North African pilgrims to Mecca often booked space on Italian ships. In the Indian Ocean, merchants from India and southeast Asia, most of them Muslims, rivaled Arab activity.

The big issue in the 15th century, however, involved the aftermath of the Mongol era. For 150 years, the interlocking Mongol states had facilitated overland trade between China, the Middle East, and Europe. Essentially, this Mongol system replaced earlier Arab leadership in facilitating transregional trade. But Mongol defeat in China, late in the 14th century, and new pressure on Mongol rulers in Russia and elsewhere unraveled this system. Overland travel become more difficult and dangerous without Mongol political protection. Trade and its motivations did not diminish in importance, but inevitably new emphasis focused on seagoing routes, particularly in the Indian Ocean. Two societies, first China and then Europe, sought to take advantage of the new opportunities involved.

Chinese Outreach and Reconsideration

For a brief time China asserted new leadership in international trade. This activity reflected earlier gains in Chinese shipping, and China's longstanding focus on manufacturing for export. Rebellions in China drove out the deeply resented Mongol overlords in 1368. A rebel leader from a peasant family, Zhu Yuanzhang (joo wan-jang), seized the Mongol capital of Beijing and proclaimed a new Ming— meaning "brilliant"—dynasty that was to last until 1644. The dynasty began with a burst of unusual expansionism. The initial Ming rulers pressed to secure the borders of the Middle Kingdom. This meant pushing the Mongols far to the north, to the plains of what is now Mongolia. It meant reestablishing influence over neighboring governments and winning tribute payments from states in Korea, Vietnam, and Tibet, reviving much of the east Asian regional structure set up by the Tang dynasty. Far more unusual was a new policy, adopted soon after 1400, of mounting huge, state-sponsored trading expeditions to southern Asia and beyond.

A first fleet sailed in 1405 to India, with 62 ships carrying 28,000 men. Later voyages reached the Middle East and the eastern coast of Africa, bringing chinaware and copper coinage in exchange for local goods. Chinese shipping at its height consisted of 2700 coastal vessels, 400 armed naval ships, and at least as many long-distance ships. Nine great treasure ships, the most sophisticated in the world at the time, explored the Indian Ocean, the Persian Gulf, and the Red Sea, establishing regular trade all along the way.

Between 1405 and their termination in 1433, these expeditions were commanded by the admiral **Zheng He**. A Muslim from western China, Zheng He was well suited to deal with Muslims in southeast Asia on the Indian Ocean trade route. Zheng He was also a eunuch, castrated for service at the royal court. China's Ming emperors retained a large harem of wives to ensure succession, and eunuchs were needed to guard them without threat of sexual rivalry; many gained bureaucratic powers well beyond this service. Zheng He's expeditions usually hugged the coastline, but he had an improved compass and excellent maps as well as huge vessels that contained ample supplies—even gardens—as well as goods for trade. His fleets must have impressed, even terrified, the local rulers around the Indian Ocean, many of whom paid tribute to the emperor. For even though Zheng He brought gifts, he also had well-armed troops on his expeditions. Several missions visited China from the Middle East and Africa. From Africa also came ostriches, zebras, and giraffes for the imperial zoo; the latter became the unicorns of Chinese fable. But Zheng He was resented by the Confucian bureaucrats, who refused even to write much about him in their chronicles.

Zheng He [jehng huh] Chinese Muslim admiral who commanded series of Indian Ocean, Persian Gulf, and Red Sea trade expeditions under third Ming emperor, Yunglo, between 1405 and 1433.

There is no question that the course of world history might have been changed dramatically had the Chinese thrust continued, for the tiny European expeditions that began to creep down the western coast of Africa at about the same time would have been no match for this combination of merchant and military organization. Indeed, historians wonder if one expedition might have rounded Africa to at least glimpse the Atlantic. But China's emperors called the expeditions to a halt in 1433. The bureaucrats had long opposed the new trade policy, out of rivalry with other officials such as Zheng He, but there were deeper reasons as well. The costs seemed unacceptable, given the continuing expenses of the campaigns against the Mongols and establishing a luxurious new capital city in Beijing. A new emperor also wanted to differentiate his policies from those of his predecessor.

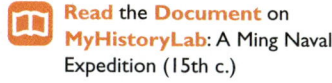

Read the Document on MyHistoryLab: A Ming Naval Expedition (15th c.)

This was a crucial shift. It reflected a preference for traditional expenditures rather than distant foreign involvements. Chinese merchant activity continued to be extensive in southeast Asia. Chinese trading groups established permanent settlements in the Philippines, Malaysia, and Indonesia, where they added to the cultural diversity of the area and maintained a disproportionate role in local and regional trading activities into the 20th century. And manufacturing levels remained high. Nonetheless, China's chance to become a dominant world trading power was lost, at least for several centuries.

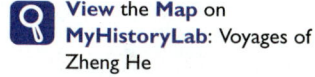

View the Map on MyHistoryLab: Voyages of Zheng He

One result, today, is an interesting challenge to interpretation. To Western eyes, accustomed to judging a society's dynamism by its ability to reach out and gain new territories or trade positions, China's decision may seem hard to understand—the precursor to decline. But to the Chinese, it was the ambitious expeditionary flurry that was unusual, not its end. Its leaders were suspicious of any policy that would unduly elevate commercial activity as opposed to rule by the scholar-gentry. Ming emperors consolidated their rule over the empire's vast territory. Internal economic development continued as well, with no need for foreign products save for goods from southeast Asia. Moreover, Chinese products continued to be highly valued in the world market. Industry expanded, with growth in the production of textiles and porcelain; ongoing trade with southeast Asia enriched the port cities; agricultural production and population increased. The end of the expeditions had no immediate downsides for China itself.

The shift in Chinese policy unintentionally cleared the way for another, in most ways less organized civilization to work toward a new international position. With the Arabs in partial eclipse and with China retreating from its brief initiative, hesitant Western expansionism, ventured before 1400, began to take on new significance. Within a century, Western explorers and traders had launched an attempt to seize international trading dominance and had expanded the international network to include parts of the Americas for the first time.

THE RISE OF THE WEST

16.3 What are the main issues in explaining new outreach from western Europe? What are the principal interpretations?

Western expansion had many causes. It must be seen as the result of growing problems as well as new strengths.

The West's gradual emergence into larger world contacts during the 15th century was surprising in many respects. Westerners remained awed by the powerful bureaucracies and opulent treasuries of empires in the traditional civilization centers such as Constantinople. Furthermore, the West was changing in some painful ways. Key features of medieval culture and society were being questioned by 1400. The church, which had long been one of the organizing institutions of Western civilization, was under new attack. Medieval philosophy had passed its creative phase. Warrior aristocrats, long a key leadership group in feudal society, softened their style of life, preferring court rituals and jousting tournaments and adopting military armor so cumbersome that real fighting was difficult.

Even more strikingly, the lives and economic activities of ordinary Europeans were in disarray. This was a time of crisis, and Europe's expanding world role could not reverse the fundamental challenges to its internal economic and demographic structure. Europeans began to suffer from recurrent famine after 1300 because population outstripped the food supply and no new food production techniques were discovered. Famine reduced disease resistance, making Europe more vulnerable to the bubonic plagues that spread from Asia.

Bubonic plague, or Black Death, surfaced in various parts of Asia in the 14th century. In China it reduced the population by nearly 30 percent by 1400. Following trade routes, it then spread into India and the Middle East, causing thousands of deaths per day in the larger cities. The plague's worst European impact occurred between 1348 and 1375, by which time 30 million people, one-third of Europe's population, died. The resulting economic dislocation produced bitter strikes and peasant uprisings.

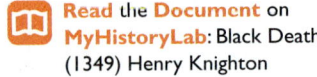
Read the Document on MyHistoryLab: Black Death (1349) Henry Knighton

Sources of Dynamism: Medieval Vitality

How, in this context, could the West be poised for a new global role? The answer to that question is complex. A number of different interpretations deserve attention, although some might be blended. First, several key advances of medieval society were not really reversed by the troubles of the decades around 1400. For example, the strengthening of feudal monarchy provided more effective national or regional governments for much of the West. The Hundred Years War between Britain and France stimulated innovations in military organization, including nonaristocratic soldiers recruited and paid directly by the royal government, that enhanced central political power. Strong regional monarchies took hold in parts of Spain and in Portugal as Christian leaders drove back the Muslim rulers of this region. The growth of cities and urban economies continued to spur the commercial side of Western society. Even the church had made its peace with such key principles of capitalism as profit-seeking. Technology continued to advance, particularly in ironwork—used for bells and weapons—and timekeeping.

In short, explaining the new Western vigor involves an understanding that some of the gains the West achieved during the postclassical period continued even as certain characteristic medieval forms wavered.

Imitation and Commercial Problems

Two additional factors affected western Europe's international position, one a clear plus, the other a growing problem. New opportunities for imitation were an obvious advantage. The Mongol empire established in Asia and eastern Europe in the late 13th and early 14th centuries provided new access to Asian knowledge and technology. Political stability and an openness to foreign visitors by the great khans helped Westerners learn of Asian technologies, ranging from printing to the compass and explosive powder. Western Europe had ideal access in the Mongol period. It was not disrupted by the Mongols, as eastern Europe and so many parts of Asia were, but it was in active contact, unlike sub-Saharan Africa. Internal European warfare and merchant zeal made western Europe an eager learner, for the Asian technologies promised to respond to both military and commercial needs.

The second international factor was the intensification of European problems in the existing world market and international arena. From the Crusades onward, Western elites had become used to increasing consumption of Asian luxury products, including spices such as cinnamon and nutmeg,

VISUALIZING THE PAST

Population Trends

PERCENTAGES OR PROPORTIONS OF TOTAL WORLD POPULATION

Continents	1000	1700	1800	1900	1975
Europe	12.2	19.6	19.7	24.0	16.3
Asia	62.9	67.6	69.3	59.8	59.2
Africa	11.2	10.0	7.8	6.8	9.9
Americas	13.4	2.1	2.7	8.9	14.0
Oceania	0.4	0.4	0.3	0.3	0.6

SOURCE: Adapted from Dennis H. Wrong, ed., *Population and Society* (1977).

QUESTIONS

The following population charts show relationships in population size, and comparative trends in population size, among the major inhabited regions of the world. Population pressure did not drive European expansion in the 15th century, because population was falling temporarily, but there were longer-term trends, from the year 1000, that might have encouraged the expansionist effort. The chart allows comparison, showing what regions experienced the greatest changes in population levels between 1000 and 1800. What might have caused these changes? Finally, the chart extends comparisons into the later 20th century.

Reading population statistics provides vital information, but it also raises questions, including ones about causation, which numbers alone cannot answer. What other data would be most helpful to put these figures in appropriate world history contexts? Which figures are more revealing: absolute numbers or percentages? Why?

POPULATION LEVELS (MILLIONS)

Continents	1000	1700	1800	1900	1975
Europe	36	120	180	390	635
Asia (includes Middle East)	185	415	625	970	2300
Africa	33	61	70	110	385
Americas	39	13	24	145	545
Oceania (includes Australia)	1.5	2.25	2.5	6.75	23
Totals	294.5	611.25	901.5	1621.75	3888

NOTE: Earlier figures are only estimates; they are fairly accurate indicators of relative size.
SOURCE: Adapted from Dennis H. Wrong, ed., *Population and Society* (1977).

---

silks, sugar, perfumes, and jewels. In exchange for the luxury items, Europeans mainly had cruder goods to offer: wool, tin, copper, honey, and salt. The value of European exports almost never equaled the value of what was imported from Asia. The resulting unfavorable balance of trade had to be made up in gold, but western Europe had only a limited gold supply. By 1400, the constant drain to Asia was creating a gold famine that threatened the whole European economy with collapse.

Furthermore, there were legitimate fears of a new Muslim threat. The Ottoman empire was taking shape, and Europeans began to fear a new Muslim surge. Even before this, the Muslim capture of the last crusader stronghold (the city of Acre in the Middle East) in 1291 gave Muslim traders, particularly Egyptians, new opportunities to act as intermediaries in the Asian trade, for there were no western-controlled ports left in the eastern Mediterranean. One response to this was a series of conquests by the city-state of Venice along the eastern coast of the Adriatic. A more important response was to begin exploring alternative routes to Asia that would bypass the Middle East and the feared and hated Muslim realms.

In sum: One explanation for Europe's new activity would emphasize the gains made in the later postclassical centuries, particularly in terms of urban and commercial growth, despite population setbacks. These gains could now be combined with new technologies learned from Asia—especially weaponry. The final ingredient was the realization that innovations were essential to meet balance of payments problems and concern about reliance on Muslim traders.

DOCUMENT

Bubonic Plague

THE SPREAD OF THE PLAGUE IN the 14th century, affecting major parts of Asia, the Middle East and Egypt, and Europe, was one of the great devastations in world history. Muslim and Christian observers described the plague and reactions to it. Ibn al-Wardi was a Muslim scholar who died of the plague in 1349; Jean de Venette was a monk who died in 1368.

IBN AL-WARDI

God is my security in every adversity. My sufficiency is in God alone. Is not God sufficient protection for His servant? Oh God, pray for our master, Muhammad, and give him peace. Save us for his sake from the attacks of the plague and give us shelter.

The plague frightened and killed. It began in the land of darkness. Oh, what a visitor! It has been current for fifteen years. China was not preserved from it nor could the strongest fortress hinder it. The plague afflicted the Indians of India. It weighted upon the Sind. It seized with its hand and ensnared even the lands of the Uzbeks. The plague destroyed mankind in Cairo. Its eye was cast upon Egypt, and behold, the people were wide-awake. It stilled all movement in Alexandria. The plague did its work like a silkworm....

Then, the plague turned to Upper Egypt. It, also, sent forth its storm to Barqah. The plague attacked Gaza, and it shook 'Asqalān severely. The plague oppressed Acre. The scourge came to Jerusalem and paid the *zakāt* [with the souls of men]. It overtook those people who fled to the al-'Aqsā Mosque, which stands beside the Dome of the Rock. If the door of mercy had not been opened, the end of the world would have occurred in a moment. It then hastened its pace and attacked the entire maritime plain. The plague trapped Sidon and descended unexpectedly upon Beirut, cunningly.

This plague is for the Muslims a martyrdom and a reward, and for the disbelievers a punishment and a rebuke. When the Muslim endures misfortune, then patience is his worship. It has been established by our Prophet: God bless him and give him peace, that the plague-stricken are martyrs. This noble tradition is true and assures martyrdom. And this secret should be pleasing to the true believer. If someone says it causes infection and destruction, say: God creates and recreates. If the liar disputes the matter of infection and tries to find an explanation, I say that the Prophet, on him be peace, said: who infected the first? If we acknowledge the plague's devastation of the people, it is the will of the Chosen Doer. So it happened again and again....

Among the benefits . . . is the removal of one's hopes and the improvement of his earthly works. It awakens men from their indifference for the provisioning of their final journey.

Nothing prevented us from running away from the plague except our devotion to the noble tradition. Come then, seek the aid of God Almighty for raising the plague, for He is the best helper. Oh God, we call You better than anyone did before. We call You to raise from us the pestilence and plague. We do not take refuge in its removal other than with You. We do not depend on our good health against the Plague but on you. We seek your protection, oh Lord of creation, from the blows of this stick.

JEAN DE VENETTE

This sickness or pestilence was called an epidemic by the doctors. Nothing like the great numbers who died in the years 1348 and 1349 has been heard of or seen or read of in times past. This plague and disease came from *ymaginatione* or association and contagion, for if a well man visited the sick he only rarely avoided the risk of death. Wherefore in many towns timid priests withdrew, leaving the exercise of their ministry to such of the religious as were more daring.... A very great number of the saintly sisters of the Hôtel-Dieu who, not fearing to die, nursed the sick in all sweetness and humility, with no thought of honor, a number too often renewed by death, rest in peace with Christ, as we may piously believe.

Some said that this pestilence was caused by infection of the air and waters, since there was at this time no famine nor lack of food supplies, but on the contrary great abundance. As a result of this theory of infected water and air as the source of the plague the Jews were suddenly and violently charged with infecting wells and water and corrupting the air. The whole world rose up against them cruelly on this account. In Germany and other parts of the world where Jews lived, they were massacred and slaughtered by Christians, and many thousands were burned everywhere, indiscriminately....

But woe is me! the world was not changed for the better but for the worse.... For men were more avaricious and grasping than before, even though they had far greater possessions. They were more covetous and disturbed each other more frequently with suits, brawls, disputes and pleas. Nor by the mortality resulting from this terrible plague inflicted by God was peace between kings and lords established. And this fact was very remarkable. Although there was an abundance of all goods, yet everything was twice as dear, whether it were utensils, victuals, or merchandise, hired helpers or peasants and serfs, except for some hereditary domains which remained abundantly stocked with everything. Charity began to cool, and iniquity with ignorance and sin to abound, for few could be found in the good towns and castles who knew how or were willing to instruct children in the rudiments of grammar....

QUESTIONS

- How did Christian and Muslim reactions compare?
- Did the reactions suggest that the plague might have different results in the Middle East and in Europe?
- How did the plague relate to other major developments toward the end of the postclassical period?

De Venette from Richard A. Newhall, ed., *The Chronicle of Jean de Venette*, pp. 51–2, Records of Civilization, Sources and Studied, No. 50. Copyright © 1953 Columbia University Press. Ibn al-Wardi from Michael Dols, "Ibn Al-Wardi's Risalha al-Naba, A translation of major sources for the history of the black death in the Middle East," in Dickran Kouymijian, ed., *Near Eastern Numismatics, Iconography, Epigraphy and History: Studies in Honor of George C. Miles*, Beirut, University of Beirut, 1974, pp. 443–55.

This explanation may not be entirely adequate, and it certainly is not the explanation preferred by most European historians. They turn—sometimes exclusively—to another set of factors: developments within Europe that would then spill outward.

Secular Directions in the Italian Renaissance

Significant changes in Europe, away from characteristic postclassical patterns, started in Italy. Medieval forms had never fully taken hold here. Cities were livelier and more independent, and institutions like feudalism did not gain ground. In 1400, Italy was in the midst of a vital cultural and political movement known as the **Renaissance**, or rebirth—referring to revival of styles and themes from classical Greece and Rome. The early phases of the Renaissance stressed more secular subjects in literature and art. Religious art remained dominant but used more realistic portrayals of people and nature, and some nonreligious themes surfaced outright (Figure 16.2). The doings of human beings deserved attention for their own sake, in the Renaissance view, not as they reflected a divine plan. Artists and writers became more openly ambitious for personal reputation and glory. Italy was the center of initial Renaissance culture because it had more contact with Roman tradition than did the rest of Europe and because by the 14th century it led the West in banking and trade.

Renaissance [REHN-uh-sahns] Cultural and political movement in western Europe; began in Italy c. 1400; rested on urban vitality and expanding commerce; featured a literature and art with distinctly more secular priorities than those of the Middle Ages.

Renaissance Culture

Although it had political and commercial roots in Italian cities, the Renaissance was first and foremost a cultural movement, launched in Florence and manifesting itself in literature and various arts (Figure 16.3). The Renaissance focused on a new interest in stylistic grace and a concern for practical ethics and codes of behavior for urban gentlemen. One leading 14th-century writer, **Francesco Petrarch**, not only took pride in his city and his age but explored the glories of personal achievement with new confidence.

Petrarch, Francesco [PEE-trahrk] (1304–1374) One of the major literary figures of the Western Renaissance; an Italian author and humanist.

FIGURE **16.2** Europe's new spirit amid old values. Dante, Italian writer of the 14th century, holds a copy of his great work, the *Divine Comedy*, with both religious (souls tormented in hell) and Renaissance (the solid, classical-style urban buildings of the city of Florence) symbolism greeting him. The painting was designed by Domenico di Michelina for the cathedral of Florence in 1465.

FIGURE **16.3** Although the nave of Florence Cathedral was completed in the fourteenth century, it was not until the fifteenth century that architect Filippo Brunelleschi was able to solve the engineering challenge presented by the plan for the massive dome. In order to eliminate the need for temporary wooden scaffolding during construction, Brunelleschi used a skeleton of eight large ribs alternated with eight pairs of thinner ribs, all tied together by nine sets of horizontal ties, all of which would be able to support the workers as the dome was raised.

Innovation flourished in the visual arts and music as well. The subject matter of art moved toward nature and people, including cityscapes and portraits of the rich and powerful, whether the themes were religious or secular. Florentine painter Giotto (gee-YAW-toh), led the way, departing from medieval formalism and stiffness. While still a young apprentice to the painter Cimabue (chee-mah-BOO-eh), Giotto painted a fly on the nose of one of Cimabue's portrait subjects, and it was so realistic that Cimabue repeatedly tried to swat it off before going back to work on the canvas. Other painters, beginning later in the 14th century, started to introduce perspective while using new colors and other materials. In architecture, favor shifted away from the Gothic to a classicism derived from the styles of Greece and Rome. Vivid, realistic statues complemented the new palaces and public buildings.

The impact of the early Renaissance must not be exaggerated. It had little influence outside of Italy. Even in Italy, it focused on high culture, not popular culture, and on the arts; there was little initial interest in science. And although it built on distinctive political and economic forms, it was not a full break from medieval tendencies.

Nevertheless, these new cultural currents were an important innovation in Western history. The full ramifications of the Renaissance feed into the next period of both world and Western history (see Chapter 18). The movement was only getting started by 1400. However, the wide range of Italian commerce and shipping proved to be one of the building blocks of European outreach. By the 15th century, ships, particularly from the western Italian city of Genoa, which was less well placed than Venice for eastern Mediterranean trade and the resultant links to Asia, were ready for new roles. Ambitious city-state governments encouraged new ventures, eager to collect more tax money and promote commerce as one of their explicit functions. A general "Renaissance spirit" could also spur innovation. Whereas people such as Petrarch defined human ambition mainly in cultural terms, other urban and commercial leaders, including seafarers such as Genoa's Christopher Columbus, might apply some of the same confidence and desire for personal glory to different areas, such as exploration or conquest.

The Iberian Spirit of Religious Mission

Along with Italy, a key center for change by the 14th century was the Iberian peninsula, where Christian military leaders had for several centuries been pressing back the boundaries of the Muslim state in Spain. Soon after 1400, major regional monarchies had been established in the provinces of **Castile** and **Aragon**, which would be united through royal marriage in 1469.

Even before the marriage between Ferdinand and Isabella, Spanish and Portuguese rulers had developed a vigorous military and religious agenda. They supported effective armies, including infantry and feudal cavalry. And they believed that government had a mission to promote Christianity by converting or expelling Arabs and Jews and by maintaining doctrinal purity within the church. Close links between church and state, portrayed in art, provided revenues and officials for the royal government. In return, the government supported church courts in their efforts to enforce moral and doctrinal purity. Later in the 15th century, this interaction led to the reestablishment of the church-run courts of the Inquisition in Spain, designed to enforce religious orthodoxy. In other words, Spain and Portugal were developing effective new governments with a special sense of religious mission and religious support. These changes promoted the West's expansion into wider world contacts.

The First Phases of Western Expansion

As early as 1291, two Italian brothers, the **Vivaldis** from Genoa, sailed with two galleys through the Straits of Gibraltar, seeking a western route to the "Indies," the spice-producing areas of south and southeast Asia. They were never heard from again. Although they were precursors of a major western thrust into the southern Atlantic, it is not even entirely clear what they meant by the "Indies." Early in the 14th century, other explorers from Genoa rediscovered the Canary Islands, in the Atlantic, populated by a hunting-and-gathering people. These islands had been known vaguely since classical times but had never been explored by Europeans. Genoese sailors also visited the Madeiras and probably reached the more distant Azores by 1351. Soon after this, ships from northeastern Spain, based in the port of Barcelona, sailed along the African coast as far south as present-day Sierra Leone.

Until 1430, technological barriers prevented further exploration for alternative routes. Without adequate navigation instruments, Europeans could not risk wider ventures into the Atlantic. They also needed better ships than the shallow-drafted, oar-propelled Mediterranean galleys. However, efforts were under way to develop an oceangoing sailing vessel. At the same time, the crucial navigational problems were met by the compass and the astrolabe, used to determine latitude at sea by reckoning from the stars. Contacts with Arab merchants and with the Chinese provided knowledge of these devices. European mapmaking, improving steadily during the 14th century, was another key innovation. Because of these advances, as well as mistaken geographic assumptions shown on the map in Figure 16.4, Europeans were ready in the decades after 1400 to undertake voyages impossible just a century before. In 1498, the Portuguese explorer **Vasco da Gama** was the first European to reach India by sea, preparing Portuguese entry into the Indian Ocean (Figure 16.5).

Castile and Aragon Regional kingdoms of the Iberian Peninsula; pressed reconquest of peninsula from Muslims and ultimately united under the Spanish monarchy.

Vivaldis Two Genoese brothers who attempted to find a western route to the "Indies"; disappeared in 1291; precursors of thrust into southern Atlantic.

da Gama, Vasco Portuguese captain who sailed for India in 1497; established early Portuguese dominance in Indian Ocean.

Henry the Navigator Portuguese prince responsible for direction of series of expeditions along the African coast in the 15th century; marked beginning of western European expansion.

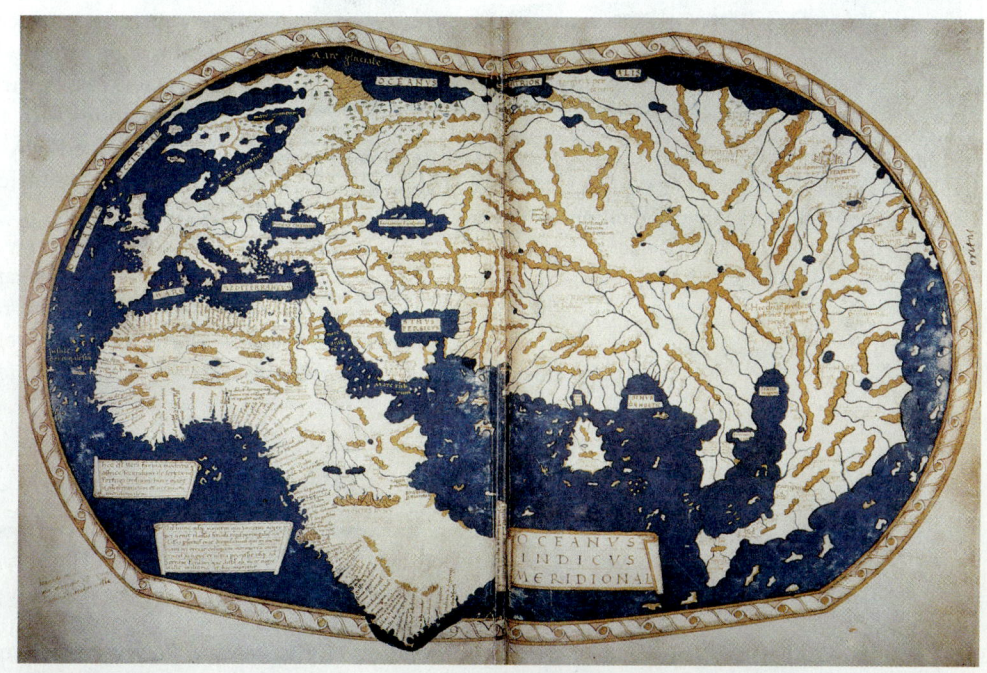

FIGURE **16.4** Columbus is supposed to have had a copy of this world map in Spain. The map, dating from about 1489, shows the Old World as Europeans were increasingly coming to know it. Note how reachable India looked to Europeans using this map—although, of course, they had to go around Africa.

Colonial Patterns

Even as these wider-ranging voyages began, westerners, led by the Spanish and Portuguese, had begun to take advantage of the new lands they had already discovered. A driving force behind both the further expeditions and the efforts to make already discovered areas economically profitable was Prince Henry of Portugal, known as **Henry the Navigator**. A student of astronomy and nautical science, Henry sponsored about a third of Portuguese voyages of exploration before his death in 1460. His mixture of motivations—scientific and intellectual curiosity, desire to spread the name of Christ to unfamiliar lands, and financial interest—reflected some of the key forces in late postclassical Europe.

Portugal by 1439 had taken control of the Azores and had granted land to colonists. Soon Spaniards and Portuguese had conquered and colonized the Madeiras and Canaries, bringing in western plants, animals, weapons, and diseases. The result was something of a laboratory for the larger European colonialism that would soon take shape, particularly in the Americas. European colonists quickly set up large agricultural estates designed to produce cash crops that could be sold on the European market. First they introduced sugar, an item once imported from Asia but now available in growing quantities from western-controlled sources. Ultimately, other crops such as cotton and tobacco were also introduced to the Atlantic islands. To produce these market crops, the new colonists brought in slaves from northwestern Africa, mainly in Portuguese ships—the first examples of a new, commercial version of slavery and the first sign that western expansion could have serious impact on other societies as well.

These developments about 1400 remained modest, even in their consequences for Africa. They illustrate mainly how quickly Western conquerors decided what to do with lands and peoples newly in their grasp. The ventures were successful enough to motivate more extensive probes into the southern Atlantic as soon as technology permitted. Indeed, voyages of exploration down the coast of Africa and across the Atlantic began to occur as the island colonies were being fully settled.

Finally, these early ventures summed up the swirl of forces that were beginning to reshape the West's role in the world: inferiorities and fears, particularly with regard to the Muslims; economic pressure from an inferior but eager position in world trade; new energies of Renaissance merchants and Iberian rulers. In final analysis, what is the best explanation for why Europe began to reach out in new ways?

Read the Document on MyHistoryLab: Excerpt from the Travel Journal of Vasco da Gama

FIGURE **16.5** This 18th-century engraving portrays Vasco da Gama's audience with the Indian ruler of Calicut in 1498. This picture was painted well after the fact. What kind of comparison does it suggest between European and Indian societies?

Read the Document on MyHistoryLab: Voyage from Lisbon

OUTSIDE THE WORLD NETWORK

Tensions in key societies in the Americas and Oceania made them vulnerable to conquest.

16.4 How did patterns in the Americas and Polynesia reflect their isolation from main transregional trade networks?

Developments in the Americas and Polynesia were not affected by the new international exchange. During the next period of world history, these regions all were pulled into a new level of international contact, but a world balance sheet in 1400 must emphasize their separateness.

At the same time, several of the societies outside the international network were experiencing some new problems during the 15th century that would leave them vulnerable to outside interference thereafter. Such problems included new political strains in the leading American civilizations and a fragmentation of the principal island groups in Polynesian culture.

Political Issues in the Americas

As we discussed in Chapter 12, the Aztec and Inca empires ran into increasing difficulties not long after 1400. Aztec exploitation of subject peoples for gold, slaves, and religious sacrifices roused great resentment. What would have happened to the Aztec empire if the Spaniards had not intervened after 1500 is not clear, but it is obvious that disunity created opportunities for outside intervention that might not have existed otherwise. The Inca system, although far less brutal than that of the Aztecs, provided ongoing tension between central leadership and local initiative. This complicated effective control of the vast expanse of the Inca domains. Here too, overextension made change likely by the 1500s—indeed, the empire was already receding somewhat—even without European intervention. At the same time, other cultures were developing in parts of the Americas that might well have been candidates for new political leadership, if American history had proceeded in isolation or if European intervention had been less sweeping.

Expansion, Migration, and Conquest in Polynesia

A second culture that was later pulled into the expanding world network involved Polynesia. Here, as in the Americas, important changes took place during the postclassical era but with no relationship to developments in societies elsewhere in the world. The key Polynesian theme from the 7th century to 1400 was expansion, spurts of migration, and conquest that implanted Polynesian culture well beyond the initial base in islands such as Tahiti, Samoa, and Fiji (Map 16.1).

One channel of migration pointed northward to the islands of Hawaii. The first Polynesians reached these previously uninhabited islands before the 7th century, traveling in great war canoes. The canoes carried all that was needed to settle on new lands, including pigs. These were to wreak some havoc on native flora and fauna in Hawaii, but at the same time Hawaiians created a land use system incorporating coastal fisheries, mid-mountain vegetable crops, and highland hunting that supported a sustainable lifestyle for centuries.

From the 7th century until about 1300 or 1400, recurrent contacts remained between the Hawaiian Islands and the larger Society Islands group, allowing periodic new migration. From about 1400 until the arrival of European explorers in 1778, Hawaiian society was cut off even from Polynesia.

Polynesians in Hawaii spread widely across the islands in agricultural clusters and fishing villages amid the volcanic mountains. Hawaiians were inventive in using local vegetation, weaving fabrics as well as making materials and fishing nets from grass. Politically, Hawaii was organized into regional kingdoms, which were highly warlike. Society was structured into a caste system with priests and nobles at the top, who reserved many lands for their exclusive use. Commoners were viewed almost as a separate people, barred from certain activities.

Thus, with a Neolithic technology and no use of metals, the Hawaiians created a complex culture on their islands. Without a written language, their legends and oral histories, tracing the genealogies of chiefly families back to the original war canoes, provided a shared set of stories and values.

Isolated Achievements by the Maori

Another group of Polynesians migrated thousands of miles to the southwest of the Society Islands, perhaps as early as the 8th century, when canoe or raft crews discovered the two large islands that today make up New Zealand. The original numbers of people were small but were supplemented over the centuries that followed by additional migrations from the Polynesian home islands. The Polynesians in New Zealand, called the Maori, successfully adapted to an environment considerably colder and harsher than that of the home islands. They developed the most elaborate of all Polynesian art and produced an expanding population that may have reached 200,000 people by the 18th century, primarily on the northern of the two islands. As in Hawaii, tribal military leaders and priests held great power in Maori society; each tribe also included a group of slaves drawn from prisoners of war and their descendants.

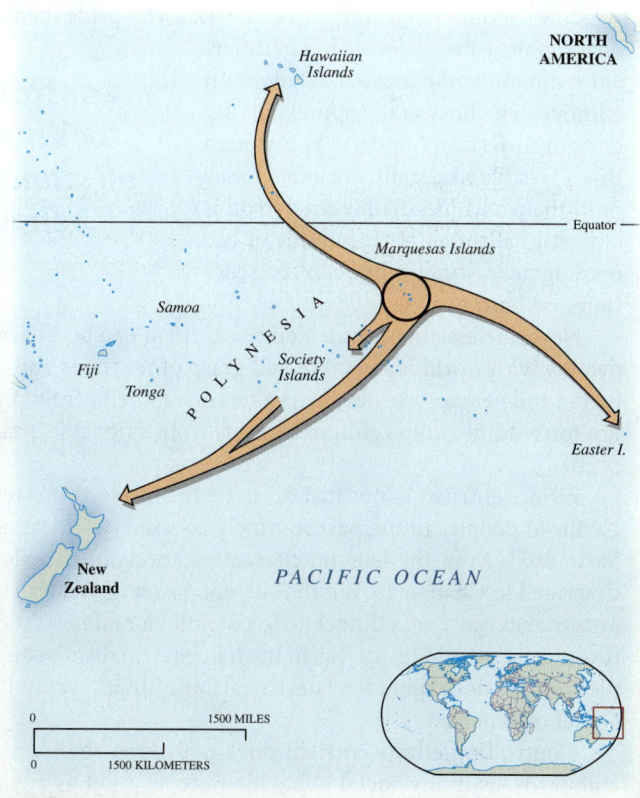

MAP **16.1 Polynesian Expansion** Starting in the 7th century, the Polynesians expanded north and south of their starting point in the Society Islands.

All these achievements were accomplished in total isolation from the rest of the world and, particularly after 1400, substantial isolation of each major island grouping from the rest of the Polynesian complex. Polynesians would be the last of the major isolated cultures to encounter the larger world currents brought forcefully by European explorers in the 18th century. When this encounter did come, it produced the same effects that it had in the Americas: vulnerability to disease, weakness in the face of superior weaponry and technology, and cultural disintegration.

THINKING HISTORICALLY

The Problem of Ethnocentrism

MANY CULTURES ENCOURAGE AN ETHNOCENTRIC OUTLOOK, and the culture of the West is certainly one of them. Ethnocentrism creates problems in interpreting world history. The dictionary definition of *ethnocentrism* is "a habitual disposition to judge foreign peoples or groups by the standards and practices of one's own culture or ethnic group"—and often finding them inferior. Most of us take pride in many of our own institutions and values, and it is tempting to move from this pride to a disapproval of other peoples when they clearly do not share our behaviors and beliefs. Many Americans have a difficult time understanding how other peoples have failed to establish the stable democratic political structure of our own country. Even liberals who pride themselves on a sophisticated appreciation of different habits in some areas may adopt an ethnocentric shock at the oppression (by current American standards) of women that is visible in certain societies today or in the past. Indeed, unless a person is almost totally alienated from his or her own society, some ethnocentric reactions are hard to avoid.

Nevertheless, unexamined ethnocentrism can be a barrier in dealing with world history. We will grasp other times and places better, and perhaps use our own values more intelligently, if we do not too readily dismiss cultures in which "objectionable" practices occur.

Ethnocentrism is not just an issue for modern Westerners. Civilized peoples in the past routinely accused outsiders of barbaric ways, as in the Islamic characterizations of the Mongols described in Chapter 15. But the current power of Western standards makes our own ethnocentric potential a real issue today in dealing with world history, as in the tendency to dismiss any people who did not exploit the latest available military technology as somehow inferior.

Controlling ethnocentrism does not mean abandoning all standards, as if any social behavior were as good as any other. It does involve a certain open-mindedness and sophistication. Reducing distracting levels of ethnocentrism can be aided by some specific procedures. It is important to realize that few cultures behave irrationally over long periods of time. They may differ from our taste, but their patterns respond to valid causes and problems. Our own values are not without complexity. We sometimes believe things about our own society that are not as true as we want, or in judging other societies, we forget about drawbacks in our own surroundings. Perspective on our own habits, including awareness of how other cultures might judge us, helps us restrain our ethnocentrism.

However, ethnocentrism may become a particularly strong impulse in dealing with some of the changes in world history taking shape about 1400. The West was gaining strength. Because many Americans identify with Western civilization, it is tempting to downplay some of the subtleties and disadvantages of this process or to exaggerate the extent to which the West began to organize world history more generally.

The balance of power among civilizations was beginning to shift about 1400, and it is legitimate—not simply ethnocentric—to note that the West's rise was one of the leading forces of this change. It is unnecessary to ignore the many other patterns continuing or emerging—including new vigor in several other societies—or to gloss over the motives and results that the West's rise entailed. The rise of the West was not just "good." It did not result simply from a triumph of progressive values. At the same time, avoiding ethnocentric impulses in evaluating this crucial transition period in world history does not require an anti-Western approach. Balance and perspective are essential—easy to say, not always easy to achieve.

> *Controlling ethnocentrism does not mean abandoning all standards, as if any social behavior were as good as any other.*

QUESTIONS

- Why can ethnocentrism complicate interpretations of world history?
- How can one balance disapproval and understanding in dealing with practices such as female infanticide?
- What are some nonethnocentric ways to interpret initial European expansion?

Adding Up the Changes

It is tempting to see some sort of master plan in the various changes that began to occur around 1400. People who emphasize an ethnocentric approach to world history, stressing some inherent superiorities in Western values, might be tempted to simplify the factors involved. However, a series of complex coincidences provides a more accurate explanation, as in other cases in which the framework of world history changed substantially. Independent developments in the Americas and elsewhere figured in, as did crucial policy decisions in places such as China. Each of the separate steps can be explained, but their combination was partly accidental.

Several elements of the world history transition deserve particular attention. Technology played a role, as opportunities to copy Asian developments were supplemented by European initiative, particularly in gunnery and ship design. The role of individuals, such as Prince Henry, must be compared with the impact of more general forces, such as Europe's international trade woes.

The overall result of change affected even societies where existing patterns persisted. Sub-Saharan Africa, for example, was not experiencing great political or cultural shifts around 1400. Regional kingdoms fluctuated: The empire of Mali fell to regional rivals, but another Muslim kingdom, Songhay, soon arose in its stead, flourishing between 1464 and 1591. African political and religious themes persisted for several centuries, but the context for African history was shifting. The decline of the Arabs reduced the vitality of Africa's key traditional contact with the international network, although African merchants remained comfortable in dealing with North Africa and the Middle East. In contrast to the Europeans, Africans had no exchange with the Mongols. Even as Africa enjoyed substantial continuity, its power balance with western Europe was beginning to change, and this became a source of further change.

Global Connections and Critical Themes

1450 AND THE WORLD

The end of the postclassical period saw both change and continuity in the contacts that affected so many societies in Asia, Africa, and Europe. Change came in the procession of societies that served as active agents for contacts. Muslim traders and missionaries from the Middle East continued to be active, particularly in the Indian Ocean and in dealing with Africa. But the period of Mongol consolidation had introduced a new set of contacts, many of them land-based and involving Asia and Europe. Mongol overlords turned out to be delighted to encounter different ideas and to use officials from many different places and cultures. Mongol decline returned attention to sea-based contacts, particularly in the Indian Ocean. This was where, for a brief time, China took an unusually active stance. The Mongol era left other impacts as well: Japan, proud of its avoidance of Mongol occupation in contrast to China, began to think in terms of greater self-sufficiency, less reliance on imitation. Russian leaders, initially around Moscow, began to gain greater independence from Mongol control; their chief goal involved further expansions of territory and they paid attention to other contacts. Overall, at a time of many regional changes the question of roles in global contacts was a vital one, and by 1450 it was in flux.

The key continuity involved the interest and dependence of many societies on interregional trade and other contacts. African merchants and leaders continued to rely heavily on interactions with the Middle East. Western Europe's involvement in contacts was intensifying. Southeast Asia was increasingly drawn in, not only to trade but also to Muslim missionary efforts. The Middle East, India, and China continued to assume the availability of goods and merchant activities beyond their own borders. The diverse advantages of Afro-Eurasian contacts were widely realized, even amid changes in trade routes and regional initiatives.

The decades around the mid-15th century both reflected and intensified the transcontinental network. On the one hand, it was clear that the level of intercontinental connections developed in the postclassical period allowed increasingly rapid imitation, in areas like technology. This gave once-backward societies, like western Europe, a chance to accelerate their economic and military development. The networks also brought sufficient advantages, in access to luxury consumer goods, that the decline of one trade system—for example, the overland Mongol routes—quickly brought forward other societies eager to develop an alternative framework—the Chinese, then the Europeans. This process, from the Mongols onward, quickened the pace of contact, from ambitious travelers like Ibn Battuta (IH-buhn BAH-too-tuh) and Marco Polo, to imaginative merchants and explorers. The stage was set for a next phase in the globalization process, in which the whole world would, for the first time, be directly involved.

Further Readings

On the world network, see Jerry Bentley, *Old World Encounters: Cross Cultural Contacts and Exchanges in Pre-Modern Times* (1993). Crucial changes in the Middle East are covered in F. Babinger, *Mehmed the Conqueror and His Times* (1978), on the Ottoman leader who captured Constantinople; and Bernard Lewis, *The Arabs in History* (1958), which offers a brisk interpretation of Arab decline. See also H. Islamoglu-Inan, ed., *The Ottoman Empire and the World Economy* (1987). On China, see D. Wu, *Footprints of foreign explorers on the Silk Road* (2006); and Charles O. Hucker, *The Ming Dynasty: Its Origins and Evolving Institutions* (1978).

An important, highly readable interpretation of the West's rise in a world context is C. Cipolla, *Guns, Sails, and Empires: Technological Innovation and the Early Phases of European Expansion, 1400–1700* (1985). See also John M. Hobson, *The Eastern Origins of Western Civilization* (2004); and K. Ciggaar and M. Metcalf, eds., *East and West in the Medieval Eastern Mediterranean* (2006). An important interpretation of new Western interests is S. W. Mintz, *Sweetness and Power: The Place of Sugar in Modern History* (1985).

On the Black Death and economic dislocation, see M. W. Dols, *The Black Death in the Middle East* (1977); W. H. McNeill, *Plagues and Peoples* (1976); and the very readable B. Tuchman, *A Distant Mirror: The Calamitous 14th Century* (1979). A provocative study of relevant western outlook is P. Ariès, *The Hour of Our Death* (1981).

J. Huizinga, *The Waning of the Middle Ages* (1973), deals with the decline of medieval forms in Europe. See also Gerald MacLean, ed., *Re-Orienting the Renaissance: Cultural Exchanges with the East* (2005). The early Renaissance is treated in D. Hay, *The Italian Renaissance* (1977); see also Walter Pater, *The Renaissance: Studies in Art and Poetry* (2011); Gary Fergusan, *Queer (re)readings of the French Renaissance* (2008); C. Hibbert, *Florence: The Biography of a City* (1993). For more cultural emphasis, see Guido Ruggiero, *Machiavelli in Love: Sex, Self, and Society in the Italian Renaissance* (2007); Manfredo Tafuri, *Interpreting the Renaissance: Princes, Cities, Architects* (2006); John Jeffries Martin, ed., *The Renaissance: Italy and Abroad* (2003); Richard Mackenney, *Renaissances: The Cultures of Italy c. 1300–c. 1600* (2005); and C. Trinkhaus, *The Scope of Renaissance Humanism* (1983). On Spain, see F. Braudel, *The Mediterranean and the Mediterranean World*, 2 vols. (1978); and E. Paris, *The End of Days* (1995), on Spanish Jews and the Inquisition. On expansion in general, see Robert Bartlett, *The Making of Europe: Conquest, Colonization, and Cultural Change* (1993).

An excellent overview of the period is Janet L. Abu-Lughod's *Before European Hegemony: The World System A.D. 1250–1350* (1989).

On MyHistoryLab

 Study and Review on MyHistoryLab

Critical Thinking Questions

1. What were the consequences of the fall of the Byzantine empire? Was this a short-term or long-term change in world history?

2. What was new about Renaissance culture? Is it possible to use a cultural change of this sort to explain innovations in trade and exploration?

3. What caused the main differences between developments in West Africa and those in western Europe during the 14th and 15th centuries?

4. Should China have maintained its commitment to great expeditions?

5. What distinctive features of Polynesian society reflected lack of contact with other major centers?

PART III AP® TEST PREP

MULTIPLE CHOICE QUESTIONS

1. What was the initial response of the Umayyads to Muhammad's new faith?
   a. They regarded him as a threat to their wealth and power as he questioned the traditional gods of the Ka'ba.
   b. They sought to protect him from a plot on his life by the Banu Hashim.
   c. The Umayyads immediately accepted Muhammad as their religious and political leader and the chief power in Mecca.
   d. The Umayyads simply ignored Muhammad as an insignificant member of a powerless clan.

2. What was Muhammad's teaching with respect to the revelations of other monotheistic religions?
   a. Muhammad accepted the earlier Christian revelations, but rejected completely any influence from Judaism.
   b. Muhammad accepted the earlier Judaic revelations, but rejected completely any influence from Christianity.
   c. Muhammad accepted the validity of earlier Christian and Judaic revelations and taught that his own revelations were a final refinement and reformulation of earlier ones.
   d. Muhammad stressed that only his own revelations had merit and that others were works of the devil.

3. Which of the following happened after Muhammad's death in 632?
   a. Many of the bedouin tribes renounced Islam.
   b. Islam ceased to exist until it was reestablished under the Umayyad dynasty at Damascus.
   c. After a lengthy period of grief, the tribes selected a new leader based on the established principle of succession in the Qu'ran.
   d. A military commander, Khalid ibn al-Walid, was chosen as leader of Islam.

4. Which of the following might be considered the most significant transformation brought about by the Abbasids' rise to power?
   a. the final defeat of the Byzantine empire
   b. the admission of the Mawali as full members of the Islamic community
   c. the destruction of absolutism within Islamic government
   d. the destruction of Sunni influences within Islam

5. What was the primary cultural contribution of the Muslims during the Abbasid period?
   a. The Muslims were able to recover and preserve the works of the ancient philosophers and mathematicians and to transmit this knowledge from one civilization to another.
   b. The Muslims became extraordinarily adept at portraiture, focusing on depictions of Muhammad and the early Caliphs.
   c. Although the material culture of the Abbasid period remained poor, Muslims were able to make some advances in music.
   d. Islamic learning was necessarily unique, as there was no access to the ancient traditions of philosophy and science.

6. Which of these was an innovation of the Abbasid court with respect to women?
   a. the expansion of the harem
   b. the legislation of multiple marriages for women
   c. the creation of Islamic nunneries
   d. legislation against concubinage and prostitution

7. What accounts for the success of the First Crusade?
   a. The overwhelming military superiority of western military technology.
   b. The contemporary emergence of the Christian Seljuk Turks in Baghdad.
   c. Muslim political fragmentation and the element of surprise.
   d. The support and cooperation of the Jewish community of the Holy Land.

8. Which answer best describes the level of trade in the Abbasid empire?
   a. Long-distance trade with Africa, the Mediterranean, India, and China continued to flourish despite periodic interruption.
   b. Trade with the East grew, but the Crusades eliminated the western trade routes.
   c. Trade with Africa and the Mediterranean continued to expand, but the wars in India disrupted the eastern trade routes.
   d. As a whole, long-distance trade along the traditional caravan routes virtually ceased during the Abbasid empire.

9. What was the difference between the Islamic invasions of India and previous incursions of the subcontinent?
   a. With the Muslims, the peoples of India encountered for the first time a large-scale influx of invaders with a civilization as sophisticated as their own.
   b. With the Muslims, the peoples of India encountered for the first time an invasion from the west rather than the east.
   c. The Muslims were rapidly able to unify all of India into a single empire.
   d. The Muslims, unlike previous invaders, bypassed the Gangetic plain in preference for southern India.

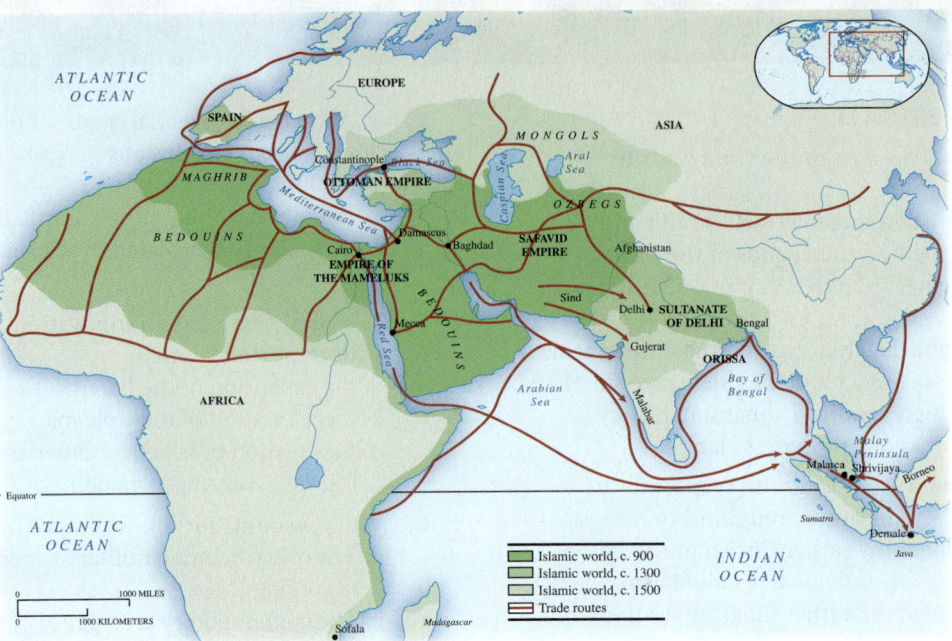

10. In general, based on the map above, how did Islam spread in southeast Asia?
    a. Port cities were points of dissemination to other links in trading networks.
    b. Most of southeast Asia was converted to Islam after the military victories of Qutb-ud-din Aibak.
    c. Islam was carried to southeast Asia from China.
    d. Trade to southeast Asia from Africa and Persia established Islamic centers on the mainland from which conversion took place.

11. Which of the following statements best describes the indigenous religion of much of sub-Saharan Africa?
    a. Much of sub-Saharan Africa was Christian.
    b. Animistic religion, belief in the power of natural forces personified as deities, characterized much of Africa.
    c. African religion prior to the arrival of the Muslims was typified by an independent form of monotheism characterized by worship in monumental temple complexes.
    d. Uniquely, African societies lacked religious principles prior to the arrival of the Christians and Muslims.

12. Which of the following best explains why Islam was so readily adopted by rulers within the Sudan?
    a. They were all conquered by overwhelming Muslim armies and forcibly converted to Islam.
    b. The Muslim concept of a ruler who united civil and religious authority reinforced traditional ideas of kingship.
    c. The Muslim concept of religious equality allowed rulers to dispose of the traditional clans and lineages of Africa.
    d. As a monotheistic religion, Islam was much like the traditional religions of Africa.

13. How did contact with the Muslim world affect the African slave trade?
    a. Because of the Muslim emphasis on equality of all believers, early Muslim rulers suppressed the slave trade.
    b. Slavery was unknown in African society until the Muslims introduced it.
    c. With the Muslim conquests of north Africa and commercial penetration to the south, slavery became a more widely diffused phenomenon and the slave trade developed rapidly.
    d. Despite the Muslim acceptance of slavery and its widespread use in Islamic society outside of Africa, Muslims generally refused to accept black slaves.

14. Which of the following statements concerning the impact of Islam on sub-Saharan Africa is most accurate?
    a. Islam cut off north Africa from the regions of sub-Saharan Africa.
    b. Although Africa had never been totally isolated from the Mediterranean, the spread of Islam brought large areas of Africa within the global community.
    c. With the conversion of regions of the continent to Islam, Africa became the center of the Islamic world.
    d. Despite widespread conversion of Africans to Islam, the continent remained outside the trading sphere of the Islamic world.

15. The preceding photograph of a mosque at Jenne on the Niger River in what is now the Republic of Mali best exemplifies which of the following historical processes?
    a. imposition of religion through military conquest
    b. spread of religion to cities of commercial exchange along trade routes
    c. abandonment of indigenous cultural styles in the face of colonization
    d. conflict between local and universalizing religions

16. Which of the following represents a difference between the spread of civilization in eastern and western Europe?
    a. The two regions produced different versions of Christianity that were culturally, as well as organizationally, separate.
    b. Only eastern Europe developed north–south commercial ties.
    c. Centralized government and well-organized bureaucracy was more a feature of western Europe than eastern Europe.
    d. Eastern Europe retained less fully the culture of the later Roman empire than did western Europe.

17. All of the following were outcomes of Justinian's wars of reconquest EXCEPT
    a. the permanent addition of Italy to the Byzantine empire.
    b. increased tax pressures on the government.
    c. military successes in north Africa and Italy.
    d. the weakening of the empire's defenses on its eastern frontiers.

18. What were the primary exports of the Byzantine empire?
    a. food products
    b. raw materials, such as metal ores from Asia Minor
    c. luxury products such as silk, cloth, and carpets
    d. The empire produced little of significance and was almost exclusively an importer of goods.

19. Which of the following issues was a cause for the split between the Roman Catholic and Orthodox churches after 1054?
    a. the Orthodox church's lack of bishops
    b. the insistence of the patriarch of Constantinople on supremacy within church councils
    c. the absence of monasticism in Roman Catholicism
    d. the Roman Catholic practice of requiring celibacy for its priests

20. Which of the following statements concerning the Tatar invasion of Russia is most accurate?
    a. Tatar control of Russia lasted for four decades.
    b. The Tatars used Russia as a springboard for their successful invasion of western Europe.
    c. Tatar supervision did not destroy Russian Christianity or a native Russian aristocracy.
    d. The Tatars rapidly devised a closely supervised local administration for the Russian cities.

21. Following the fall of Rome, where was the center of the post-classical West?
    a. in the former Roman colony of Spain
    b. in Italy, particularly Rome
    c. in the central plain of northern Europe: France, the Low Countries, and southern and western Germany
    d. Greece

22. Which of the following statements concerning the three-field rotation system is most accurate?
    a. Introduced in the 8th century, the three-field rotation added acres to production by leaving only a third of the land unplanted.
    b. The three-field system removed land from production by reserving two-thirds for fallow.
    c. The three-field system was rapidly replaced after the 8th century by the two-field system that offered greater flexibility in terms of crop rotation.
    d. The three-field system removed fallow fields and replaced them with nitrogen-bearing crops.

23. How did the introduction of feudal monarchy into England compare to the political experience of France?
    a. English feudal monarchy developed more gradually and slowly in response to the improving economy.
    b. English feudal monarchy was introduced abruptly after 1066, while French feudal monarchy developed more slowly.
    c. French feudal monarchy arose almost immediately in the 10th century as a result of the defeat of the Normans.
    d. France failed to develop feudal monarchy until the 15th century.

24. Pope Gregory VII decreed the practice of investiture invalid. What was investiture?
    a. the practice whereby aristocrats dressed in bishops' robes and attempted to rule in their place
    b. the practice of state appointment of bishops
    c. the practice of trying clerics in secular courts
    d. the state's power to tax the clergy

25. Which of the following was a result of the Hundred Years War during the 14th and 15th centuries?
    a. Kings reduced their reliance on feudal forces in favor of paid armies.
    b. An English victory at Calais would bring the conflict to final conclusion.
    c. Mounted knights continued their dominance over foot soldiers and archers.
    d. Major battles resulted in enormous loss of life over the course of the war.

26. How did the Aztecs view the cultural achievements of the Toltecs?
    a. as barbarians who lacked culture
    b. as slaves, fit only for conquest
    c. as the givers of civilization
    d. as heretics, who practiced a forbidden religion

27. **What was the Aztec view of history?**
    a. They believed in a linear view of history dedicated to the premise of Aztec superiority for eternity.
    b. Like other Mesoamerican peoples, the Aztecs believed in a cyclical pattern of repetitive destructions of the world.
    c. Unlike other Mesoamerican peoples, the Aztecs rejected the cyclical view of history for a more modern historical view based on the history of their empire.
    d. Because they lacked a calendar system, the Aztecs had no formal historical viewpoint.

28. **While the position of Aztec women in many ways paralleled that of women in other civilizations at a similar stage of development, what was the significant difference between the life of women in Mesoamerica and in the Mediterranean world?**
    a. Women in Mesoamerica participated fully in the military.
    b. There was no polygamy practiced in Mesoamerica.
    c. Aztec women were unable to inherit or to pass property on to heirs.
    d. The limited technology of Mesoamerica confined women to many more hours grinding grain for food.

29. **Which of the following was utilized in the Inca Empire, but NOT by the Aztecs?**
    a. a semi-divine emperor
    b. extensive use of colonization
    c. use of local rulers in exchange for recognition of sovereignty
    d. identification of the nobility with the administrative and military functions of the state

30. **Which of the following statements about the population of the Americas is most true?**
    a. The population of the Americas is easy to calculate.
    b. North America was more densely populated than Mesoamerica or the Andes.
    c. The population of the Americas was nearly the same as that of contemporary Europe (not including Russia).
    d. The early 20th-century estimate of 8.4 million still seems the most accurate.

31. **What made possible the rapid revival of empire under the Tang?**
    a. the abandonment of Confucianism in favor of the more widely practiced Buddhism
    b. the brevity of the period of political dislocation
    c. the willingness of the Tang to abandon traditional approaches to government
    d. the preservation in the many kingdoms of the Confucian traditions that had been central to Chinese civilization

32. **What proved to be the most damaging attack on Buddhism's popularity with the people during the early Tang dynasty?**
    a. the Buddhists' insistence on rebellion against the emperor
    b. the Confucians' successful campaign to convince the emperor that the Buddhist monastic establishment represented an economic threat
    c. the aristocracy's concern that the growing Buddhist monastic establishment was monopolizing land that otherwise would belong to them
    d. the entry of nomadic invaders who were Islamic during the 9th century

33. **What accounts for the relative weakness of the Song empire?**
    a. It never succeeded in achieving the degree of centralization that had typified the Tang empire.
    b. The scholar-gentry quickly lost influence under the Song, and the bureaucracy ceased to function effectively.
    c. Lack of agricultural productivity produced a general failure of the Chinese economy during the Song dynasty.
    d. The military was subordinated to the civilian administrators of the scholar-gentry, leaving the dynasty vulnerable to nomadic dynasties on the frontier.

34. **Why was the construction of the Grand Canal in China necessary?**
    a. Major river systems in China ran from north to south, and the canal was necessary to connect the coastal regions with the western frontier.
    b. Chinese population was increasingly concentrated along the northern plains along the Yangzi River.
    c. The canal was designed to link the original centers of Chinese civilization on the north China plain with the Yangzi River basin more than 500 miles to the south.
    d. The canal connected the Tang capitals of southern China, Changan and Loyang, with the newly acquired regions in the north.

35. **In what way did footbinding serve to diminish the independence of Chinese women by the end of the Song era?**
    a. Because footbinding could only be afforded by the elite, poorer women were assigned to a lower social status.
    b. Footbinding sufficiently crippled women to effectively confine their mobility to their household.
    c. As footbinding was required in order to practice certain professions, Chinese women found that occupational alternatives were diminished.
    d. Footbinding, although considered socially attractive, was condemned by Neo-Confucians who used the practice as a means of relegating Chinese women to subordinate roles.

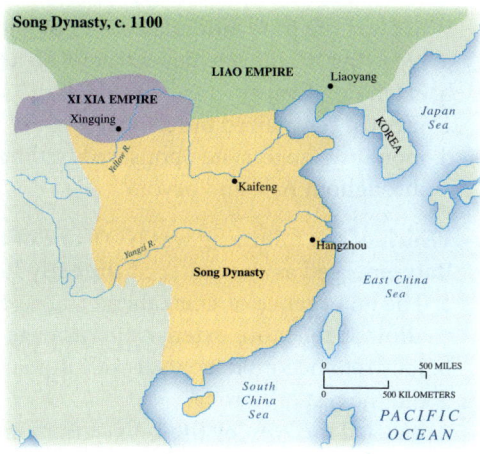
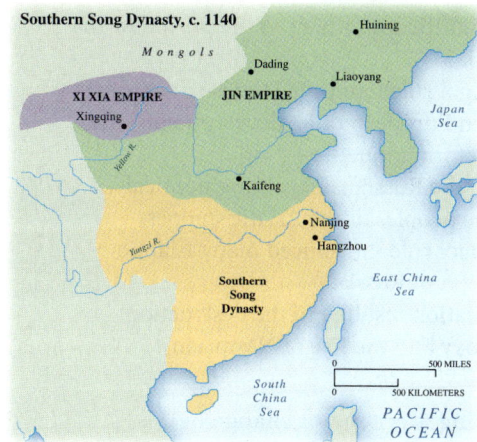

36. Based on these maps, how did the Song Dynasty compare to Southern Song Dynasty?
    a. The Southern Song Dynasty was greater in territorial extent than the Song Dynasty.
    b. The Song Dynasty and the Southern Song Dynasty were virtually identical in territorial extent.
    c. The Southern Song Dynasty was smaller in territorial extent than the Song Dynasty.
    d. Although approximately the same size, the Southern Song Dynasty extended farther north than the Song Dynasty.

37. What was the central purpose of the reforms of 646 in Japan?
    a. to remake the Japanese monarch into an absolutist Chinese-style emperor
    b. to destroy the Confucian scholar-gentry in favor of a military aristocracy
    c. to increase the power of the Buddhist monastic structure
    d. the destruction of the traditional peasant-conscript army

38. What was the impact of the rise of the samurai on the peasantry in Japan?
    a. Japanese peasants were reduced to the status of serfs bound to the land they worked.
    b. The samurai were critical to the development of a free peasantry on which the warriors depended for supplies of food and arms.
    c. The creation of the samurai created a period of great social mobility in Japan during which people rapidly moved out of the peasantry and into the class of warriors.
    d. Although separated from the warriors by rigid class barriers, the peasantry achieved greater levels of personal freedom and economic prosperity.

39. The victory of the Minamoto marks the beginning of what period in Japanese history?
    a. the centralized Confucian bureaucracy
    b. the feudal age
    c. the Onin wars
    d. the Tokugawa Shogunate

40. Which of the following statements concerning the nature of the Korean society is most accurate?
    a. Korean society is typified by equality between all classes.
    b. Koreans resented Chinese influence, and they avoided being influenced by China.
    c. A tiny elite, heavily influenced by Chinese culture, dominated the social, economic, and bureaucratic life of the entire kingdom.
    d. Korean society followed the Chinese model of a strong scholar-gentry, a weak aristocracy, and a highly regarded, though politically impotent, peasantry.

41. Which of the following statements concerning Chinggis Khan's early life is most accurate?
    a. He succeeded to the kingship of the Mongols at an early age as the only heir of his grandfather.
    b. Following the death of his father, he immediately enjoyed military success over rival clans.
    c. Following his father's death, he was abandoned by many followers and captured by a rival tribe.
    d. He fled following his father's death to the Chinese, who provided him with military support.

42. What tactic on the field of battle was employed most frequently by Chinggis Khan's forces?
    a. frontal assault by massed cavalry
    b. massed artillery barrage followed by infantry attacks on the flanks
    c. trench warfare
    d. pretended flight to draw the enemy out followed by heavy cavalry attacks on the flanks

43. Following Chinggis Khan's death, what was the provision for the administration of the empire?
    a. It was divided into four regional kingdoms, or khanates, ruled by his sons and grandsons.
    b. It was centralized with a Mongol bureaucracy located at the Chinese capital of Tatu.
    c. The empire immediately fragmented into its constituent tribes and clans.
    d. It passed as a single government with its capital at Karakorum to Chinggis Khan's oldest son.

44. **What was the most significant impact of the period of the Mongol rule on Russia?**
    a. The period of Mongol rule reinforced the isolation of Russia from western Europe and the developments of the Renaissance and Reformation.
    b. The Mongols aided the Russians in gaining political dominance over the peoples of the Asiatic steppes.
    c. The period of Mongol rule introduced many Islamic people into the region of Russia.
    d. The Mongol domination resulted in the destruction of Eastern Orthodoxy and the rise of Nestorian Christianity.

45. **Which of the following was a major change in the administration of China under the Mongols?**
    a. The central bureaucracy was dismissed and the Mongol dynasty ruled with a military elite.
    b. The Mongols discontinued the use of the examination system to keep the scholar-gentry from gaining too much power.
    c. The Mongols divided all of China into four great khanates under separate and independent rulers.
    d. Confucianism was suppressed and Daoism became the state religion of China.

46. **Which of the following statements concerning the Ottoman empire is most accurate?**
    a. Turkish rulers did not promote maritime trade as vigorously as had the Arabs.
    b. Scientific and philosophical investigations reached the level of innovation that they had enjoyed under the Abbasids.
    c. The Turks refused to patronize the traditional Persian artists and craftsmen who had dominated the later Abbasid court.
    d. The Ottomans were more interested in cultural patronage than in military organization.

47. **What was the innovation launched by the Ming dynasty?**
    a. receiving tribute payments from Korea
    b. extending their political control over Vietnam
    c. use of a centralized bureaucracy
    d. mounting huge, state-sponsored trading expeditions throughout Asia and beyond

48. **Which of the following was NOT one of the reasons that Italy emerged as the center of the early Renaissance?**
    a. The emergence of centralized states in Italy allowed for more extensive patronage of the arts.
    b. Italy retained more contact with Roman traditions than did the rest of Europe.
    c. Italy led the West by the 14th century in banking and trade.
    d. Italy had closer contacts with foreign scholars, particularly those in late Byzantium.

49. **What was unique about the development of states in the Iberian peninsula?**
    a. These governments were based on city-states rather than nation-states.
    b. Based on Castile and Aragon, the Iberian states were unique in their adoption of Islam.
    c. Spain and Portugal developed effective new governments with a special sense of religious mission and religious support.
    d. The states of Spain and Portugal were able to develop without emphasis on the military.

50. **Which of the following was NOT a result of the European contact with sub-Saharan Africa after 1500?**
    a. Trade patterns in west Africa shifted from the Mediterranean to the Atlantic.
    b. Trade shifted in west Africa from Muslim to European hands.
    c. Seizure of slaves for European use affected many regions deeply.
    d. Regional kingdoms lost all influence in west Africa and were replaced by European governments.

DOCUMENT-BASED QUESTION

 Read the Document on MyHistoryLab:

A practice document-based question for Part 3 is available on MyHistoryLab.

CONTINUITY AND CHANGE-OVER-TIME ESSAY

Analyze continuities and changes of the cultural, economic, and political impact of Islam on ONE of the following regions between 1000 C.E. and 1750 C.E. (West Africa, South Asia, or Europe).

COMPARATIVE ESSAY

Analyze similarities and differences between the Inca and Aztec empires in terms of political administration.

PART III

REVISITING

The Postclassical Period, 600–1450: New Faith and New Commerce

CONTACTS AND THEIR LIMITS

Expansion of economic systems and increasing interaction reflected crucial changes in the postclassical period. They were supported by technological shifts, particularly in shipbuilding and navigational devices, and also by expansion of manufacturing and some key improvements in agriculture. They involved many merchant families, who would send relatives to distant outposts to help facilitate exchange.

New contacts form a key part of the postclassical period. Contacts were not economic alone. Missionary exchanges as well as trade brought about new connections among people in Asia, Africa, and Europe. Southeast Asia, for example, began to contribute spice production to transcontinental trade. In turn, by the end of the postclassical period, merchants and missionaries were importing Islam into this region.

Many world historians now argue that, because of the new patterns of contact, the basic dynamic of world history was reshaped around 1000 C.E. Before that point, most societies had separate patterns of activity, and contacts with other cultures were somewhat superficial, with a few luxury goods exchanged. After that point, contact became the name of the game, and a growing number of societies vigorously sought new connections.

A key aspect of the postclassical period involved explicit efforts at imitation, another result of contact. Trade and sometimes missionary connections brought outlying parts of the Afro-Eurasian world into interaction with regions that had complex cultural, manufacturing, and urban systems. Not surprisingly, many of these societies decided to copy—selectively—in order to advance. Japan copied China; Russia copied the Byzantines; western Europe and parts of Africa borrowed widely (although differently) from Arab society. Mostly, societies imitated one another's technology and cultural forms (such as alphabets). It proved harder to copy political structures, and several ambitious efforts (particularly in Japan and western Europe) failed. Peoples in the Americas had contact with one another, but they remained isolated from Afro-Eurasia. The same was true in Polynesia. Here were important exceptions to the patterns of exchange elsewhere.

While contacts increased, they hardly homogenized Afro-Eurasia. Societies on the peripheries, like western Europe or Russia, simply lacked the manufacturing sophistication or urban wealth required to fully imitate the leading centers of Asia. In other instances, explicit decisions were made to reject foreign influences. After a brief period of enthusiasm for Chinese political institutions, for example, Japanese leaders decided they did not want to imitate some aspects of Chinese society—for example, its bureaucracy. Despite ongoing trade and important new interactions with Islam, the majority of Indians remained Hindu and lived according to its distinctive caste system. And of course Europeans, while imitating some aspects of Islamic society, had no desire for religious change—unless it involved imposing their religion on Muslims. Religion, indeed, could create new barriers among people.

The ruins of Leptis Magna, one of the three great early Roman cities, which gave Tripolitania its name. Leptis was an elaborate city with baths and ornate buildings; it was also the center of African trade.

Long-distance travel increased in the postclassical centuries. Ibn Battuta, a north African, traveled almost 80,000 miles in his lifetime, visiting various parts of Africa and Asia as well as islands in the Indian Ocean. Toward the end of this period, several western Europeans traveled widely, as did some Chinese. Greater travel was a testimony to the power of world trade and the new religious map—Ibn Battuta, for example, journeyed mainly within the Islamic world, which gave him plenty of scope.

While travel reflected and encouraged contact, it also brought people to the limits of tolerance. While he praised the piety of his hosts in sub-Saharan Africa, Ibn Battuta was appalled by the freedom that women there enjoyed. This was not his view of a fully Muslim society. European travelers to China, at the end of the period, might hope to convert the Chinese or to imitate some of their achievements—in technology, for example—but they had a strong sense of the profound differences between European and Chinese culture.

CRITICAL THEMES

New patterns of contact and changes in the religious map dominated world history during the postclassical centuries. They sometimes supported each other, when missionary and merchant expansion went hand in hand, as was often the case with Islam. But they could also create new tensions: What were merchants to do when they had to deal with people of another religion? Cultural developments and interactions can be compared with patterns of trade, but the relationships could be complex.

On the whole, social changes in the period were less significant than economic and cultural shifts. The slave trade into the Middle East and the extension of India's caste system built on earlier precedent. A number of societies deepened patriarchal gender relations, as in Chinese footbinding. Social implications of the major religions were not always translated into practice, although there was some impact.

Ibn Battuta, in Egypt. Ibn Battuta's wide travels utilized and encouraged a growing pattern of contacts.

Political developments reflected great diversity. This was a vital period for state building in areas like Japan, Russia, and West Africa. It is important to compare some of the more decentralized systems, including European and Japanese feudalism, with each other, but also to the more elaborate political forms of China, the Arab caliphate, and the Byzantine empire. This was also a period of frequent warfare. Most conflict occurred among units within regions—like western Europe, or sub-Saharan Africa. But there were a few larger military efforts, most notably the Arab military burst in the centuries after 600 and then the great Mongol conquests. A number of technological innovations accompanied warfare, such as the European crossbow and particularly the Chinese use of explosive powder.

Buddhist prayer on a scroll—earliest known printed work, 868 C.E. The image depicts the frontispiece to the world's earliest dated printed book, the Chinese translation of the Buddhist text the "Diamond Sutra." This consists of a scroll, over 16 feet long, made up of a long series of printed pages. Printed in China in 868 C.E., it was found in the Dunhuang Caves in 1907, in the northwestern province of Gansu.

All the major societies of Afro-Eurasia reacted to the key forces of the age, including the expansion of one or more of the world religions, but of course they reacted diversely; comparison remains essential. Even religious change usually offered some accommodations to older cultural patterns. Overall rates of change also varied. Some societies displayed more continuity with earlier traditions than did others.

Finally, it is vital to remember the continuing divisions in world geography during the postclassical period. Interactions in Afro-Eurasia contrast with the separate, although often impressive, trajectories of the Americas and Oceania. Deep divides in technology, animal use, and disease reflected this complexity. ∎

CRITICAL THINKING QUESTIONS

1. Pick two societies, one that changed a lot between 600 and 1450 and another that displayed more continuity. How do you compare rates of change in these two cases? What caused one society to change more than the other?
2. Should developments between 1250 and 1450 be counted as part of the postclassical period, or should they be treated as a separate period? Explain your decision.
3. What kinds of change did the rise of Islam cause? What were the major ways the world was different in 1450 from what it had been in 600, because of Islam?
4. What similarities did the "Abrahamic" religions (Judaism, Christianity, and Islam) share? How did these religions differ from Buddhism?
5. What kinds of evidence are most helpful in analyzing the impact of Islam on women?

PART IV

The Early Modern Period, 1450–1750: The World Shrinks

Explorer Vasco de Gama kneels before the king under a Portuguese flag while his ship waits in the distance. European ventures in trade and exploration helped define a new world history period.

PART OUTLINE

Chapter 17 The World Economy

Chapter 18 The Transformation of the West, 1450–1750

Chapter 19 Early Latin America

Chapter 20 Africa and the Africans in the Age of the Atlantic Slave Trade

Chapter 21 The Rise of Russia

Chapter 22 The Muslim Empires

Chapter 23 Asian Transitions in an Age of Global Change

THE OVERVIEW: THE WORLD MAP CHANGES

These maps depict two of the big changes in world history that occurred between 1450 and 1750. Over these centuries, a number of new empires came into being, replacing smaller political units characteristic of the preceding postclassical period. Several European countries acquired overseas empires, a clear first in world history. Equally important, new land-based empires arose in Asia and eastern Europe. The Russian and Ottoman empires extended over both European and Asian territory, while the new Mughal empire ruled much of the Indian subcontinent.

The second big change involved trade routes. In 1450, transregional trade focused on exchanges among Asia, Africa, and Europe across some overland routes, but also via seaways in the Indian Ocean and the Mediterranean Sea. By 1750, oceangoing routes across the Pacific and particularly the Atlantic had become increasingly important, although the Indian Ocean sea routes remained significant. For the first time, the Americas and, soon, Pacific Oceania were caught up in global exchanges, with results not only in these regions but for the rest of the world as well.

Change, of course, is never complete. Even as world geography shifted fundamentally, some political features persisted during the three Early Modern centuries. Trade routes also maintained some holdovers from the past.

Big Concepts

Three themes predominated during the Early Modern period. First, contacts with the Americas ushered in a vital series of biological exchanges—of diseases, crops, animals, and people. This Columbian Exchange led to major population shifts in many different parts of the world. It also had environmental impact, particularly in the Americas. Second, obviously, the transregional trade network was redefined, becoming global. Levels of trade increased, with major impact on economies from China to Africa to the Americas. Shipping technology improved once again, and naval contacts were transformed with the use of ships' cannon. Third, partly because of the use of guns, the various new empires formed. Several European powers staked claims in the Americas, but also in certain coastal regions and island groups in Asia. New Islamic empires were joined by the rise of Russia and also renewed political energy in China.

The Early Modern period saw important social changes, particularly in the establishment of Atlantic slavery and an intensification of serfdom in several key regions. Exploitation of labor increased in many societies, responding to new pressures to produce for global trade and also to population changes. Gender relations shifted in several societies, though there were no global patterns.

Finally, the Early Modern period did not experience systematic cultural change. Important developments occurred, but these must be explored in individual societies or through particular sets of contacts. Precisely because economic exchanges were expanding, many societies proved eager to defend a separate cultural identity.

TRIGGERS FOR CHANGE

Several developments sparked the beginning of the Early Modern period, distinguishing it from the postclassical period that preceded it. The first was the revival of empire building. A striking example of this development involved the Ottoman Turks, who conquered Constantinople, the capital of the Byzantine empire. Soon the Ottomans extended their rule over most Byzantine territories and beyond, putting a Muslim power in charge of one of the great Christian cities and territories of the past. Worried Christian leaders elsewhere in the world turned to new activities to compensate for the loss of influence and territory. The second development visible by 1450—the steady progression of explorations by Europeans along the Atlantic coast of Africa—was motivated in part by the desire to find ways to trade with east Asia that would circumvent the centers of Islamic power. New European outreach would soon have wider effects.

Model of the slave ship *Brookes*, showing plan view of slave positions. The Atlantic slave trade had major effects in four continents.

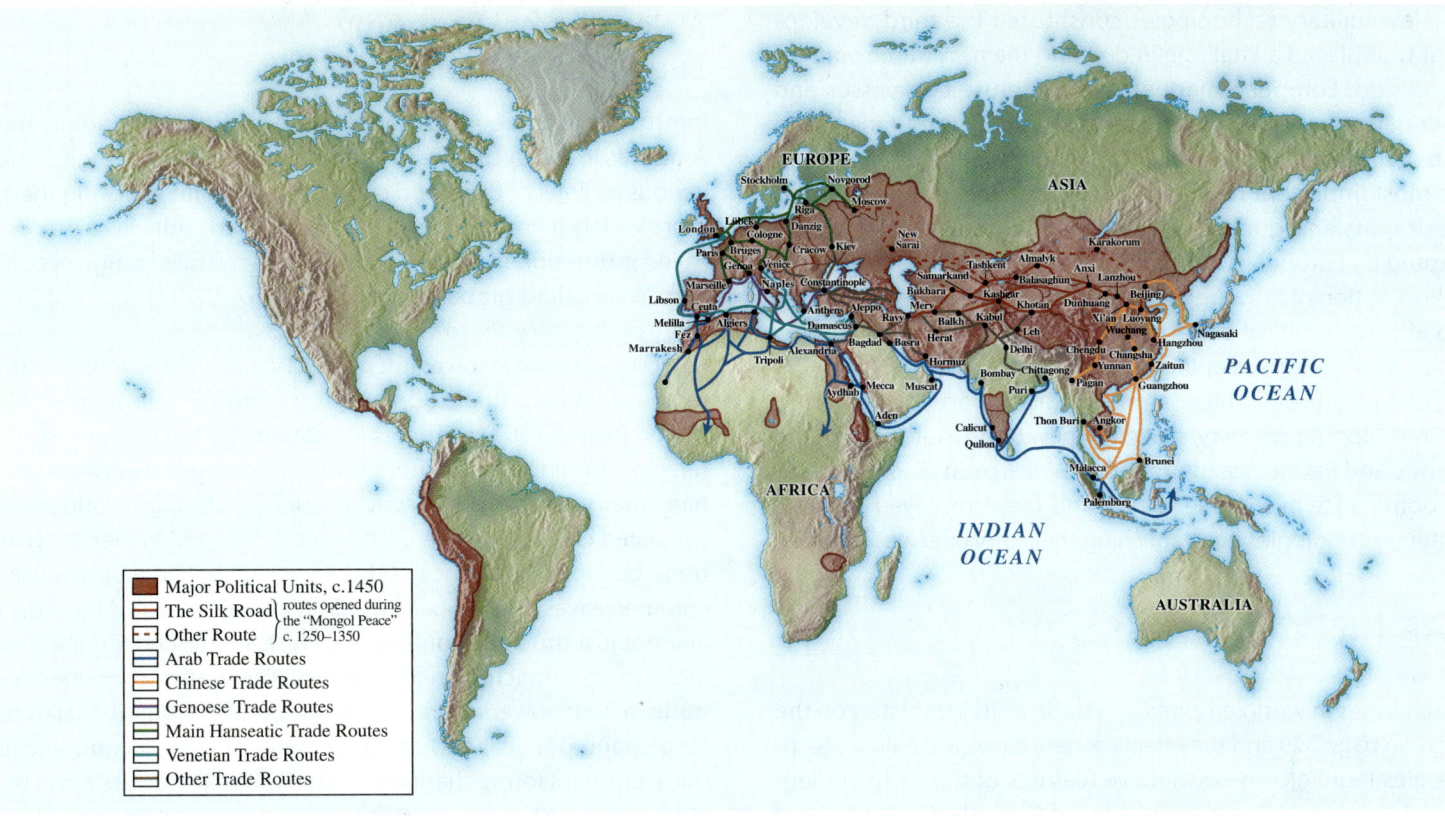

Major Political Units of the World, c. 1450

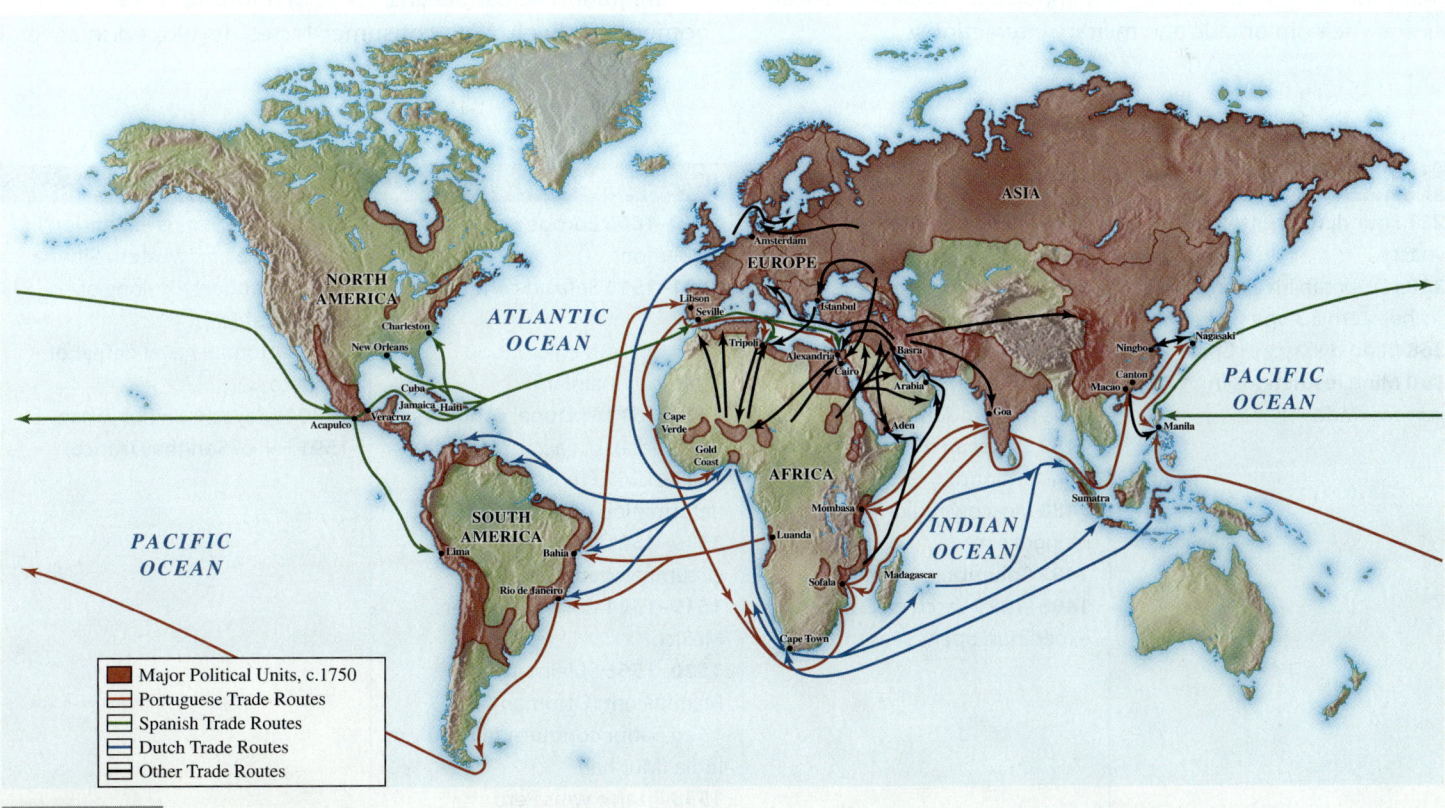

Major Political Units of the World, c. 1750

PART IV The Early Modern Period, 1450–1750: The World Shrinks

New military technologies constituted the third development that played a vital role in defining the new framework for this period. European mariners began to use compasses and other navigational devices, first introduced by the Chinese and Arabs. Europeans also learned how to design better sailing ships. The most important new military technology was the growing use of guns and gunpowder, another Chinese invention now adapted by Europeans and others. New guns played a vital role in the creation of new empires both on land and overseas. Guns also affected political patterns within Africa, Japan, and Europe, although with less sweeping results.

Larger, sturdier ships, armed with cannon and featuring greater shipping capacity, sailed the new trade routes across the Atlantic and Pacific oceans. Europeans exercised disproportionate dominance over these routes, and they employed the new military technologies in establishing their new overseas empires.

THE BIG CHANGES

The changes in world empires and trade routes depicted on the maps on page 379 and the effects of new naval and military technologies highlight the distinctive features of the Early Modern period. Every major society reacted differently, depending on world position and existing tradition. In general, however, these developments led to the three broad changes: (a) the forging of a new global economy and through this the unfolding of an initial phase of globalization; (b) new biological exchanges of food, animals, and people; and (c) the new importance of large political units and their diplomatic and military interactions.

A New Global Economy and Proto-Globalization

International trade increased, for the first time including the Americas in the exchange. This was a major step in bringing the various regions of the world closer together and exposing them more widely to international influences. The result was a process called proto-globalization—a foretaste of the fuller range of contacts now called globalization but (hence the term *proto*) in a more preliminary sense.

Globalization involves intense and varied interactions among regions that help shape human lives; proto-globalization in this period helped set this process in motion. Several changes separated proto-globalization from the transcontinental network that had emerged in the postclassical period— although world trade still relied on some of the exchanges developed earlier, such as trade between East Africa and the Middle East. Most obviously, commerce was now global, including all major parts of the world and not just the three continents of Africa, Asia, and Europe. The intensity of contacts increased as well: Trade, and production for trade, now involved more people, more effort, and it began to help shape political and social systems as well as commercial ones. Business forms changed. Major European powers now created new merchant companies, formed to organize trade with distant parts of the Americas, Asia, and Africa. These companies introduced more impersonal management structures. They depended less on kinship relations that had been true of Muslim trade during the postclassical period.

Migration across oceans, some of it forced, was a new phenomenon as well. New consumer tastes developed in several

1300 C.E.	1400 C.E.	1500 C.E.	1550 C.E.
1281 Founding of Ottoman dynasty	**1405–1433** Chinese expedition period	**1500–1600** Europe's commercial revolution	**1552** Russia begins expansion in central Asia and western Siberia
1350s Ottoman invasion of southeastern Europe	**1434–1498** Portuguese expeditions down west African coast	**1501–1510** Safavid conquest of Iran	**1570** Portuguese colony of Angola (Africa)
1368 Ming dynasty in China	**1441** Beginning of European slave trade in Africa	**1509** Spanish colonies on American mainland	**1571** Ottoman naval defeat of Lepanto
1390 Ming restrictions in overseas trade	**1453** Ottoman conquest of Constantinople	**1510–1511** Portugal conquers Goa (India), Malacca (Malaysia)	**1590** Hideyoshi unifies Japan
	1480 Moscow region free of Mongol control	**1517–1541** Protestant Reformation (Europe)	**1591** Fall of Songhay (Africa)
	1492 Columbus expeditions	**1519–1521** Magellan circumnavigates globe	
	1498–1499 Vasco da Gama expedition opens seas to Asia	**1519–1524** Cortes conquers Mexico	
		1520–1566 Suleiman the Magnificent (Ottoman)	
		1526 Babur conquest in northern India (Mughal)	
		1533 Pizarro wins Peru	
		1548 Portuguese government in Brazil	

societies that depended on goods imported from distant areas, going well beyond patterns in the earlier transcontinental network. Here, clearly, was an important step toward fuller globalization.

There was, however, still a gap between proto-globalization and the global patterns we see today. The new technologies that would revolutionize global travel and communication were still in the future. Trade contacts were important, but they had not yet reached contemporary levels. There were no internationally shared games or political standards, in contrast to the surge of cultural and political globalization that would emerge later on. Like contemporary globalization, proto-globalization brought both advantages and disadvantages, depending on the groups and regions involved. Those who profited from the new system would ultimately help prepare additional kinds of global connections.

Biological Exchange

The inclusion of the Americas global trade set in motion a number of biological exchanges of enormous consequence. Overall population leveled but also regional population balances were redefined. Foods from the Americas, like corn and the potato, began to be grown in Asia and, later, Europe. Combined with local improvements in agriculture, these new foods resulted in population increases. Europeans introduced new diseases into the Americas and Pacific island territories, decimating the native populations. Population loss encouraged new migrations, particularly from Europe and Africa, into the Americas. The massive African slave trade was in part a response to a labor shortage in the Americas. New animals, like the horse, greatly altered life in the Americas. These biological exchanges, called the "Columbian Exchange," altered many relationships among populations. New foods helped generate population increase worldwide, trumping the devastation wrought by new diseases. But new diseases and unprecedented levels of death were agonizing realities for many regions.

New Empires

The gunpowder empires formed large political units. Building and maintaining these new political structures required huge energies and huge expenses. New land-based empires in India, the Middle East, southeastern Europe, and Russia challenged political traditions in their imperial territories, while Spain, Portugal, France, England, and the Netherlands exerted pressure on their new overseas holdings.

The new empires also formed what would later be called "multinational" units, embracing different cultural and ethnic groups. The solidity of the multinational approach would be an important world history issue for the future.

The three main developments—the new global economy, the biological exchange, and the emergence of new empires—involved considerable shifts in world power. The world position of western Europe increased most obviously. Russia gained a new role as well. New masters ruled over many parts of the Americas, while portions of Africa found themselves immersed in novel orbits. Systematic patterns of inequality began to characterize some of the societies that supplied foods and raw materials to western Europe. Europe

1600 C.E.	1650 C.E.	1700 C.E.	1750 C.E.
1600 Dutch and British merchants begin activity in India	**1652** Dutch colony South Africa	**1713** New Bourbon dynasty, Spain	**1756–1763** Seven Years War
1600–1690 Scientific Revolution (Europe)	**1658–1707** Aurangzeb reign, beginning of Mughal decline	**1722** Fall of Safavid dynasty (Iran)	**1763** Britain acquires "New France"
1603 Tokugawa shogunate	**1682–1699** Turks driven from Hungary	**1759–1788** Reforms of Latin American colonial administration	**1764** British East India Company controls Bengal (India)
1607 First British colonies in North America	**1689–1725** Peter the Great (Russia)		**1770s** European–Bantu conflicts in southern Africa
1608 First French North American colonies			**1772–1795** Partition of Poland
1637 Russian pioneers to Pacific			**1775–1783** American Revolution
1640s Japan moves into isolation			**1781** Indian revolts in New Grenada and Peru (Latin America)
1641 Dutch colonies in Indonesia			**1792** Slave uprising in Haiti
1642–1727 Isaac Newton			
1644 Qing dynasty, China			

became wealthier and ever more powerful as it supplied processed goods and commercial services to these same regions. But several Asian societies, although less active in foreign trade, benefited from the new economy as well. China, the world's manufacturing leader, earned the greatest share of the silver exported from the Americas, brought by European merchants eager for Chinese goods. But India prospered also, until a major readjustment in the 18th century reduced Indian independence.

It is crucial to understand the complex balance among world regions during the Early Modern period. Western gains were important, but initiatives from several other societies helped shape both regional and global relationships.

CONTINUITY

Change is never complete. Even as world geography shifted, some political features persisted during the three centuries of the Early Modern period. Some existing trade routes continued to be important avenues of global exchange.

Many societies reacted to the big changes of the Early Modern period by preserving key features of their past. No sweeping, global cultural change occurred during this era. Although the spread of world religions was no longer a dominant theme, continued Islamic and Buddhist outreach affected parts of Asia and southeastern Europe, while the spread of Christianity to the Americas was a major development. Notable cultural innovations took place within individual societies, such as the new influence of science in western Europe or the rise of Japanese Confucianism. But cultural stability described much of the world, and global contacts did not overturn regional culture patterns.

No systematic changes occurred in gender relations in the Early Modern period. The new African slave trade affected gender balances on both sides of the Atlantic. More men than women were seized in Africa; as a result, the lack of adequate numbers of husbands encouraged African polygamy. New ideas sparked some debate over women's conditions in western Europe, although there was little real change. Relations between men and women in most other societies adhered to established patriarchal patterns.

Aside from the new developments in the military sphere, there were no technological breakthroughs until after 1750. Many societies participated only gradually in the use of guns and gunnery. Manufacturing techniques changed modestly, and little change took place in agriculture beyond the foodstuffs.

While political change, signaled by the rise of empires, was more general, several societies emphasized continuity in this realm as well. China prided itself on reviving and then maintaining its system of government. Many African societies preserved earlier traditions of divine kinship.

IMPACT ON DAILY LIFE: WORK

Changes of the Early Modern period profoundly affected ordinary people in many parts of the world. Indians in the Americas died by the thousands as European and African immigrants brought diseases like smallpox and measles. Europeans used silver to pay for desirable Chinese goods. Flush with new wealth, the Chinese government began to require that taxes be paid in silver, thus compelling ordinary Chinese to find new ways to obtain money. Often such efforts were unsuccessful, and as a result many Chinese fell ever deeper into poverty. Millions of Africans were seized from their homes and subjected to a terrifying and often deadly passage to the Americas. Those who managed to survive the voyage discovered that they were now compelled to live out their lives as slaves.

The most general social change during the Early Modern period was the growing pressure to work harder. The Early Modern world was increasingly commercial and crowded. Population increases in some regions demanded more from workers to help sustain larger families and villages. Many manufacturers and landowners tried to force their workers to increase their pace. The new forms of race-based slavery in the Americas placed greater emphasis on production. In western Europe, for example, Protestantism preached a work ethic that convinced many people that labor was a way to demonstrate God's grace.

People of all ages responded to the pressure to work harder. Child labor increased in many regions. Many European children were pressed into service as indentured laborers; for example, whole groups of orphans might be transported to work sites. By the 18th century, London orphans might be sent to work in new English factories or to North America as indentured servants. Even in old age, adults had to work if they wanted to survive. Master artisans, from makers of porcelain in China to gunsmiths in Europe, tried to compel their workers and apprentices to turn out more product. The pressure to work harder and longer was a personal side to the systemic changes that were reshaping the world.

The name commonly given to this period—Early Modern—captures complexity. The period is more recognizably modern than its predecessor. The renewed emphasis on political structures may strike a modern chord as well. But if modern, this was still early: Many features, including the continued dominance of traditional agriculture even in the most advanced economies, make it clear that there were still many changes to come in world history after 1750.

TRENDS AND SOCIETIES IN THE EARLY MODERN PERIOD

The chapters that follow examine the differing reactions to the major developments and changes of the Early Modern period. Chapter 17 offers an overview of the new global trading patterns that followed from the changes in naval technology and warfare. New trading opportunities and colonial expansion were closely related to significant changes within western Europe, the subject of Chapter 18. Chapters 19 and 20 return to the larger Atlantic world. The Early Modern era was a formative period for a new society in Latin America, born of interactions among native populations, Europeans, and Africans. Chapter 21 deals with Russia, one of the great new land-based empires of the period. Russian expansion affected not only eastern Europe, but also various parts of Asia, and complex interactions developed with western Europe as well.

Chapter 22, on the new Muslim states in the Middle East and southern Asia, concentrates on the emergence of other gunpowder empires. East Asia responded in its own, largely successful way to the new world economy. In these areas internal dynamics had more to do with developments that occurred between 1450 and 1750.

Each of the chapters in this part deals with reactions to world trade, biological exchange, and new pressures on labor. Each also highlights the diversity of patterns emerging in different parts of the world, depending on cultural orientation and shifts in positions of world power. ■

17 The World Economy

Listen to Chapter 17 on MyHistoryLab

LEARNING OBJECTIVES

17.1 Why was Western Europe able to gain a new role in world trade during the centuries after 1450? p. 385

17.2 What were the principal regional results of the Columbian Exchange? p. 391

17.3 What new kinds of regional economic inequality emerged during the period? p. 393

17.4 Did the new European colonies constitute major expansions of state power? p. 396

How did silver mined by conscripted South American Indians change China's tax system? Silver quickly became the global currency of the Early Modern period. Production and use of silver show the power of the new **world economy** emerging after 1500. Silver had long been valued, of course, but new sources of production made it a commonly traded commodity. Japanese mines raised their output, trading with Europe and China. But it was European discoveries of silver in the Americas that really turned the tide. Mexican silver mines were important, but the big find, in the mid-16th century, was at Potosi, in Bolivia, where there was an enormous vein of ore (Figure 17.1). Desperate for labor, the Spanish revived *mita*—the Inca system of drafting workers for short stints. By 1600 there were 150,000 miners at Potosi, more than a third of them conscripted through the mita system.

FIGURE **17.1** This engraving of the Potosi silver mine in 1590 shows a cut-away view of a mountain. Inside, Native American miners work by torchlight.

Watch the Video Series on MyHistoryLab

Learn about some key topics related to this chapter with the *MyHistoryLab Video Series: Key Topics in World History*

Latin American silver was a godsend to Europeans. The Spanish crown kept a fifth of the silver its colonies produced, and this was its chief gain from the American colonies. Silver allowed Spain to build massive armies and grand new public buildings. But most of the silver sent to Europe passed through Spain to merchants elsewhere. They, in turn, used silver primarily to buy Asian goods that had long been sought, such as Indian spices and Chinese porcelain and silk. The Spanish also sent considerable silver to the Philippines, where it was traded for Chinese products sent to elites in the Americas and Europe. Silver greased the wheels of international commerce, allowing Europeans to buy Asian imports that could not otherwise have been afforded.

China and India were the largest recipients of New World silver—a clear sign of Asia's dynamism in the new world economy. Silver encouraged economic growth in Asia. It began to replace paper money. Merchants required silver even for purchases of common items like food. The Ming dynasty required periodic tax payments in silver. This reduced the number of tax collections (because each payment was now more valuable)—a reform known as "one whip of the lash." Silver imports helped sustain a standard of living in China that, into the early 19th century, was superior to that of western Europe.

But there were also worries. Many Chinese observers thought that silver was creating a wider gap between rich and poor, and they pointed out that the poor had to struggle to find the silver needed to pay their taxes. A few Europeans mused about expending so much effort to obtain silver that would only be swallowed up in Asia, but most agreed that the new consumer goods were well worth the trouble. A very few Europeans, but undoubtedly lots of ordinary Latin Americans, worried about the harsh working conditions in the mines. ■

world economy Established by Europeans by the 16th century; based on control of seas, including the Atlantic and Pacific; created international exchange of foods, diseases, and manufactured products.

This chapter deals with the consequences of some key developments long celebrated in American school texts: the voyages of Columbus and other explorers and the empires built by European conquerors and missionaries. The result was a power shift in world affairs, but another set of crucial developments in world history also resulted: the redefinition of interchanges among major societies in the world.

The story is not, however, simply the familiar one. European countries did play a disproportionate role in causing global change, particularly the huge shifts affecting the Americas and Africa. But African and Asian contributions were active as well.

THE WEST'S FIRST OUTREACH: MARITIME POWER

17.1 Why was Western Europe able to gain a new role in world trade during the centuries after 1450?

European merchant fleets seized control of key international trading routes. Initial Spanish and Portuguese leadership was challenged by growing efforts from Britain, France, and Holland.

Various European leaders, particularly merchants but also some princes and clergy, had become increasingly aware of the larger world around them since 1100. The Crusades brought knowledge of the Islamic world's superior economy and the goods that could be imported from Asia. The Mongol empire, which sped up exchanges between the civilizations of Asia, also spurred European interest. The fall of the khans in China disrupted this interchange, as China became once again a land of mystery to Europeans. Europe's upper classes had by this time become accustomed to imported products

CHAPTER 17 The World Economy 385

1400 C.E.	1500 C.E.	1600 C.E.	1700 C.E.
1394–1460 Life of Prince Henry the Navigator	**1509** First Spanish colonies on Latin American mainland	**1607** First permanent British colony in Virginia	**1744** French–British wars in India
1433 China ends its great expeditions	**1514** Portuguese expedition to Indonesia	**1608** First French colonies in Canada; England gains first trading concession in India	**1756–1763** Seven Years War in Europe, India, and North America
1434 Portugal extends expeditions along west African coast	**1519–1521** Magellan circumnavigates the globe	**1641** Dutch begin conquests of Java (Indonesia)	**1763** British acquire New France
1488 Portuguese round Cape of Good Hope	**1534** First French explorations in Canada	**1652** Dutch launch colony in southern Africa	**1775–1783** American Revolution
1492 Columbus's first expedition	**1542** Portuguese reach Japan		**1756** "Black hole" of Calcutta
1497–1498 Vasco da Gama sails to India	**1562** Britain begins its slave trade		**1764** East India Company controls Bengal
	1571 Ottoman fleet defeated in Battle of Lepanto		
	1588 British defeat Spanish Armada		
	1597 Japan begins isolation policy		

from southeast Asia and India, particularly spices. These goods were transported to the Middle East in Arab ships, then brought overland, where they were loaded again onto vessels (mainly from Genoa and Venice, in Italy) for the Mediterranean trade.

Europeans entered into this era of growing contacts with several disadvantages. They remained ignorant of the wider world. Viking adventurers from Scandinavia had crossed the Atlantic in the 10th century, reaching Greenland and then North America, which they named Vinland. However, they quickly lost interest beyond establishing settlements on Greenland and Iceland, in part because they encountered indigenous warriors whose weaponry was good enough to cause them serious problems. Many Europeans were also fearful of distant voyages lest they fall off the world's edge.

As Europeans launched a more consistent effort at expansion from 1291 onward, they were pressed by new problems: fear of the strength of the emerging Ottoman empire and the lack of gold to pay for Asian imports. Initial settlements in island groups in the south Atlantic fed their hopes for further gains. However, the first expeditions were limited by the small, oar-propelled ships used in the Mediterranean trade, which could not travel far into the oceans.

New Technology: A Key to Power

During the 15th century, a series of technological improvements began to change the equation. Europeans developed deep-draft, round-hulled sailing ships for the Atlantic, capable of carrying heavy armaments. They were using and improving the compass. Mapmaking and other navigational devices improved as well. New combinations of sails, introduced on ships like the Portuguese caravel, allowed European ships to take advantage of different wind directions. Along with better ships' hulls, these innovations allowed European ships to navigate in mid-ocean, no longer dependent on coastal waters, hence not only regular trips across the Atlantic and the Pacific, but greater speed and flexibility even in the Indian Ocean.

Finally, European knowledge of explosives, another Chinese invention, was adapted into gunnery. European metalwork, steadily advancing in sophistication, allowed Western metalsmiths to devise the first guns and cannons. Although not very accurate, these weapons were awesome by the standards of the time (and terrifying to many Europeans, who had reason to fear the new destructive power of their own armies and navies). The West began to forge a military advantage over all other civilizations of the world, at first primarily on the seas—an advantage it would retain into the 20th century. With an unprecedented ability to kill and intimidate from a distance, western Europe was ready for its big push.

Portugal and Spain Lead the Pack

The specific initiative came from the small kingdom of Portugal, whose Atlantic location made it well suited for new initiatives. Portugal's rulers were drawn by the excitement of discovery, the harm they might cause to the Muslim world, and a thirst for wealth—a potent mix. A Portuguese prince, Henry the Navigator (Figure 17.2), organized a series of expeditions along the African coast and also outward to islands such as the Azores. Beginning in 1434 the Portuguese began to press down the African coast, each expedition going a little farther than its predecessor. They brought back slaves, spices such as pepper, and many stories of gold hoards they had not yet been able to find.

Later in the 15th century, Portuguese sailors ventured around the **Cape of Good Hope** in an attempt to find India, where direct contact would give Europeans easier access to luxury cloths and spices. They rounded the cape in 1488, but weary sailors forced the expedition back before it could reach India. Then, after news of Columbus's discovery of America for Spain in 1492, Portugal redoubled its efforts, hoping to stave off the new Spanish competition. Vasco da Gama's fleet of four ships reached India in 1498, with the aid of a Hindu pilot picked up in east Africa. The Portuguese mistakenly believed that the Indians were Christians, for they thought the Hindu temples were churches. They faced the hostility of Muslim merchants, who had long dominated trade in this part of the world, and they brought only crude goods for sale, like iron pots. But fortunately they had some gold as well. They managed to return with a small load of spices. A later trip involved more violence, as Europeans substituted force for their lack of attractive items for world trade. Da Gama used ships' guns to intimidate, and his forces killed or tortured many Indian merchants to set an example.

Da Gama's success set in motion an annual series of Portuguese voyages to the Indian Ocean, outlined in Map 17.1. One expedition, blown off course, reached Brazil, where it proclaimed Portuguese sovereignty. Portugal began to set up forts on the African coast and also in India—the forerunners of such Portuguese colonies as Mozambique, in east Africa, and Goa, in India. By 1514 the Portuguese had reached the islands of Indonesia, the center of spice production, and China. In 1542 one Portuguese expedition arrived in Japan, where a missionary effort was launched that met with some success for several decades.

FIGURE **17.2** Prince Henry the Navigator financed annual expeditions down the western coast of Africa in an effort to find a sea route to the Indies, establish trade with Africa, and find the fabled Christian kingdom of Prester John.

Meanwhile, only a short time after the Portuguese quest began, the Spanish reached out with even greater force. Here also was a country only reconquered from Muslim rule, full of missionary zeal and a desire for riches. The Spanish had traveled into the Atlantic during the 14th century. Then in 1492, the same year that the final Muslim fortress was captured in Spain, the Italian navigator **Christopher Columbus**, operating in the name of the newly united Spanish monarchy, set sail for a westward route to India, convinced that the round earth would make his quest possible. As is well known, he failed, reaching the Americas instead and mistakenly naming their inhabitants "Indians" (Figure 17.3). Although Columbus believed to his death that he had sailed to India, later Spanish explorers realized that they had voyaged to a region where Europeans, Africans, and Asians had not traveled previously. One expedition, headed by Amerigo Vespucci, gave the New World its name. Spain, eager to claim this new land, won papal approval for Spanish dominion over most of what is now Latin America, although a later treaty awarded Brazil to Portugal.

Finally, a Spanish expedition under **Ferdinand Magellan** set sail westward in 1519, passing the southern tip of South America and sailing across the Pacific, reaching the Indonesian islands in 1521 after incredible hardships. It was on the basis of this voyage, the first trip around the world, that Spain claimed the Philippines, which it held until 1898.

Portugal emerged from this first round of exploration with coastal holdings in parts of Africa and in the Indian port of Goa, a lease on the Chinese port of Macao, short-lived interests in trade with Japan, and finally, the claim on Brazil. Spain asserted its hold on the Philippines, various Pacific islands, and the bulk of the Americas. During the 16th century, the Spanish backed up these claims by military expeditions to Mexico and South America. The Spanish also held Florida and sent expeditions northward from Mexico into California and other parts of what later became the southwestern United States.

Cape of Good Hope Southern tip of Africa; first circumnavigated in 1488 by Portuguese in search of direct route to India.

Columbus, Christopher Genoese captain in service of king and queen of Castile and Aragon; successfully sailed to New World and returned in 1492; initiated European discoveries in Americas.

Read the **Document** on **MyHistoryLab**: Christopher Columbus, journal excerpt and letter

Magellan, Ferdinand (1480–1521) Spanish captain who in 1519 initiated first circumnavigation of the globe; died during the voyage; allowed Spain to claim Philippines.

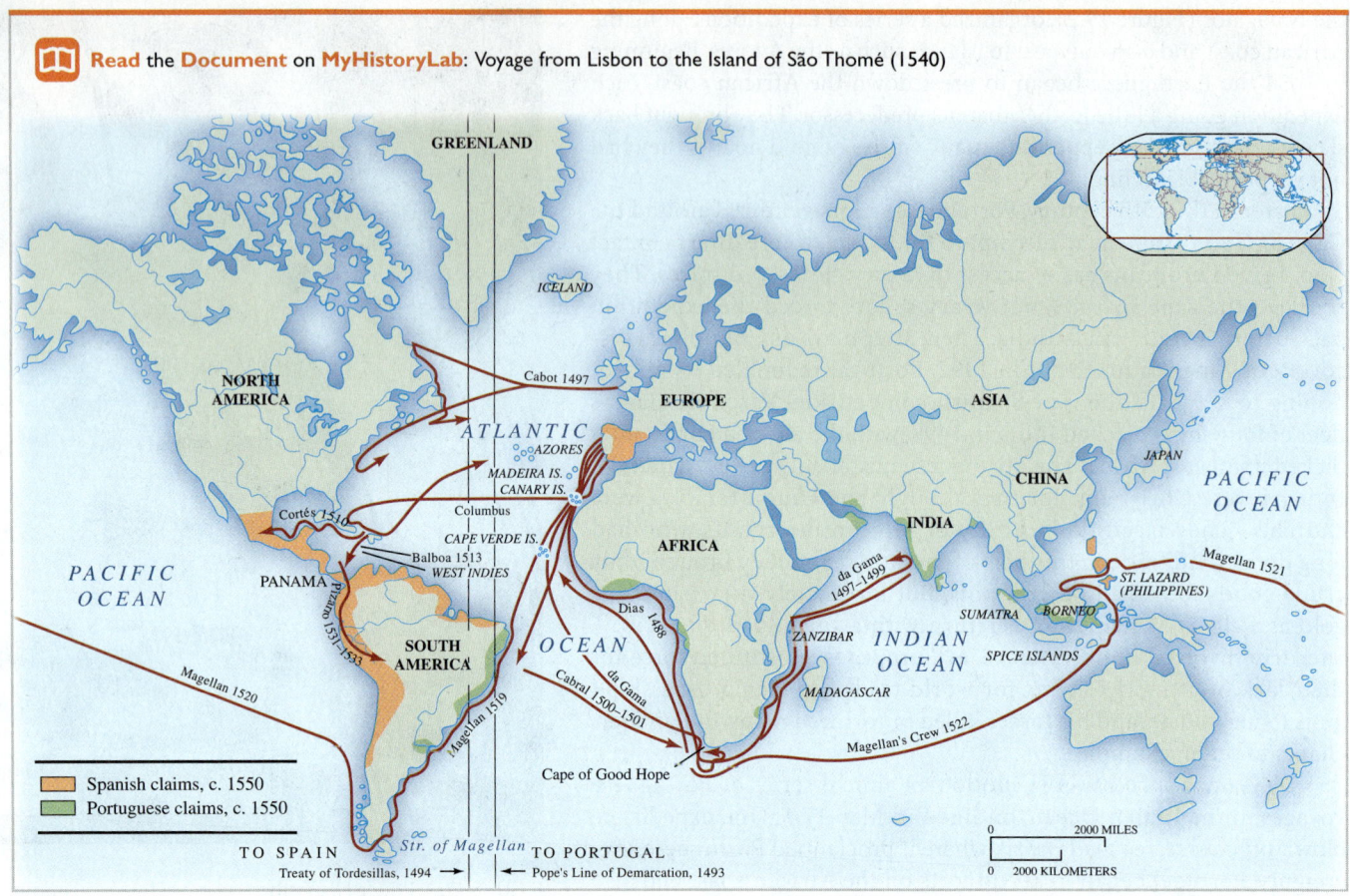

MAP 17.1 **Spain and Portugal: Explorations and Colonies** In the early years of exploration, Spanish and Portuguese voyagers surveyed much of the coast of South America and some choice ports in Africa and Asia.

Northern European Expeditions

Later in the 16th century, the lead in exploration passed to northern Europe, as newly strong monarchies, such as France and England, got into the act and zealous Protestants in Britain and Holland strove to rival Catholic gains (Map 17.2). In part this shift in dynamism occurred because Spain and Portugal were busy digesting the gains they had already made; in part it was because northern Europeans, particularly the Dutch and the British, improved the design of oceanic vessels, producing lighter, faster ships than those of their Catholic adversaries. Britain won a historic sea battle with Spain in 1588, routing the massive Spanish Armada. From this point onward, the British, the Dutch, and to some extent the French vied for dominance on the seas, although in the Americas they aimed mainly northward because they could not challenge the Spanish and Portuguese colonies. Only in the sugar-rich West Indies did northern Europe seize islands initially claimed by Spain.

The new adventurers, like their Spanish and Portuguese predecessors, appreciated the economic potential of such voyages. Britain and Holland, now Protestant countries, emphasized religious interests less than European Catholics did at this point. Two 16th-century English explorers, trying to find an Arctic route to China, were told to keep an eye out for any native populations en route, for such people would provide a perfect market for warm English woolens. And if the territory was unpopulated, it might be put to use as a source of fish for Britain. A quest for profit had become a dominant policy motive.

French explorers crossed the Atlantic first in 1534, reaching Canada, which they claimed. In the 17th century, various expeditions pressed down from Canada into the Great Lakes region and the Mississippi valley.

FIGURE 17.3 This 1505 woodcut is one of the first known European portrayals of Native Americans. It was done by an unknown German artist who had never been to America but based his drawing on the testimony of those who had. The accompanying text reported: "The people are thus naked, handsome, brown.... They also eat each other... and hang the flesh of them in the smoke. They become a hundred and fifty years of age, and have no government."

The British also turned their attention to North America, starting with a brief expedition as early as 1497. The English hoped to discover a northwest passage to spice-rich India, but they accomplished little beyond exploration of the Hudson Bay area of Canada during the 16th century. England's serious work began in the 17th century, with the colonization of the east coast of North America. Holland also had holdings in North America and, for a time, in Brazil.

The Dutch entered the picture after winning independence from Spain, and Holland quickly became a major competitor with Portugal in southeast Asia. The Dutch sent many sailors and ships to the region, ousting the Portuguese from the Indonesian islands by the early 17th century. Voyagers from the Netherlands explored the coast of Australia, although without much immediate result. Finally, toward the mid-17th century, Holland established a settlement on the southern tip of Africa, mainly to provide a relay station for its ships bound for the East Indies.

The Netherlands, Britain, and France all chartered great joint-stock trading companies, such as the **Dutch East India Company**. These companies were given government monopolies of trade in the regions designated, but they were not rigorously supervised by their own states. They had rights to raise armies and coin money on their own. Thus, semiprivate companies, amassing great commercial fortunes, long acted almost like independent governments in the regions they claimed. For some time, a Dutch trading company effectively ruled the island of Taiwan off the coast of China. The **British East India Company** played a similar role in parts of India during much of the 18th century. The companies in North America traded actively in furs.

No matter where in Europe they came from, explorers and their crews faced many hardships at sea. The work was tiring and uncertain, with voyages lasting many months or years, and diseases such as scurvy were rampant. One expedition accepted only bachelors for its crew because married men would miss their families too much. A sailor on another trip complained that "he was tired of being always tired, that he would rather die once than many times, and that they might as well shut their eyes and let the ship go to the bottom."

Dutch East India Company Joint stock company that obtained government monopoly over trade in Asia; acted as virtually independent government in regions it claimed.

British East India Company Joint stock company that obtained government monopoly over trade in India; acted as virtually independent government in regions it claimed.

Read the Document on MyHistoryLab: Jan van Linschoten on Dutch business in the Indian Ocean

THINKING HISTORICALLY

Causation and the West's Expansion

BECAUSE OF THEIR INTEREST IN SOCIAL change, historians inevitably deal with causation. What prompted the fall of Rome? Why did Islam spread so widely? What factors explain why most agricultural civilizations developed patriarchal family structures?

Historical causation differs from the kinds of causation many scientists test. When experiments or observations can be repeated, scientists can gain a fairly precise understanding of the factors that produce a phenomenon: Remove an ingredient, for example, and the product changes. Historical causation is more complex. Major developments may resemble each other, but they never happen the same way twice. Definitive proof that factor X explains 40 percent of the spread of Buddhism in east Asia is impossible. This is why historians often disagree about causation. But if precision is impossible, high probability is not. We can get a fairly good sense of why things happen, and sloppy causation claims can be disproved. Furthermore, probing causation helps us explore a phenomenon itself. We know more about the nature of Western expansion in the 15th and 16th centuries if we discuss what caused it.

Some historians and other social scientists look to a single kind of cause as the explanation of a variety of circumstances. Some anthropologists are cultural determinists. They judge that a basic set of cultural factors, usually assumed to be very durable, causes the ongoing differences between societies: Chinese and Greeks, on average, respond differently to emotional stimuli because of their different cultural conditioning. More common is a technological or economic determinism. Some historians see technological change as setting other changes in motion. Others, including Marxists, argue that economic arrangements—how the economy is structured and what groups control it—produce at least the basic framework for innovations. At another pole, some historians used to claim "great men" as the prime movers in history. The causes of change thus became Chinggis Khan or Asoka, with no need to look much further.

Various approaches to causation have been applied to the West's explorations and colonial conquests in the Early Modern period. There is room for a "great man" analysis. Many descriptive accounts that dwell on explorers and conquerors (Vasco da Gama and Cortés, for example) and on leaders who sponsored them (such as Henry the Navigator) suggest that the key cause of the West's new role stemmed from the daring and vision of exceptional individuals.

Cultural causation can also be invoked. Somehow, Europe's expansion must relate to the wonders of innovation introduced by the Renaissance. A partial link with Christian culture is even easier to prove, for a missionary spirit quickly supplemented the efforts of early explorers, leading to more voyages and settlements in Asia and the Americas. Catholic powers took a lead here; Protestant countries like Holland and Britain were less interested in missionary efforts at this point.

Political causation enters in, if not in causing the initial surge, at least in confirming it. Starting in the 16th century, rivalries between the nation-states motivated a continuing quest for new trade routes and colonies.

There is also room for a simpler, technologically determinist approach. In this view, Europe's gains came from a handful of new inventions. Benefiting from knowledge of advances in China and the Middle East, Europeans introduced naval cannons. Along with steady improvements in navigation and ship design, new techniques explain why Europe gained as it did. Except in the Americas, where they had larger technical and organizational advantages, Europeans advanced in areas they could reach by sea and dominate by ships' guns—port cities, islands, and trade routes—and not elsewhere. Put simply, Europe gained because of these few technological edges.

Like all determinisms, however, this technological approach raises as many questions as it answers. Why were Europeans so ready to adopt new inventions? (What caused the cause?) Why did other societies that were aware of Europe's innovations, such as China, deliberately decide not to imitate Western naval techniques? Here a separate culture determined a reaction different from that of the West, as the Chinese learned how to benefit from world trade in distinctive ways. Technology and culture went hand in hand. Clearly, some combined causal framework is needed in this case.

We cannot expect uniform agreement on a precise ordering of causation. However, we can expect fruitful debate—the kind of debate that has already moved our understanding beyond surface causes, such as the powerful personalities of a few people, to a grasp of more underlying contexts.

> [S]ome historians used to claim "great men" as the prime movers in history.

QUESTIONS

- If you had to choose a single determinism (cultural, technological, or economic) as basic to social change, which one would you pick? Why?
- In what ways might the professed motives of Western explorers and colonists have differed from their real motives?
- Would they necessarily have been aware of the discrepancy?

Read the Document on MyHistoryLab: Jacques Cartier: First Contact with the Indians (1534)

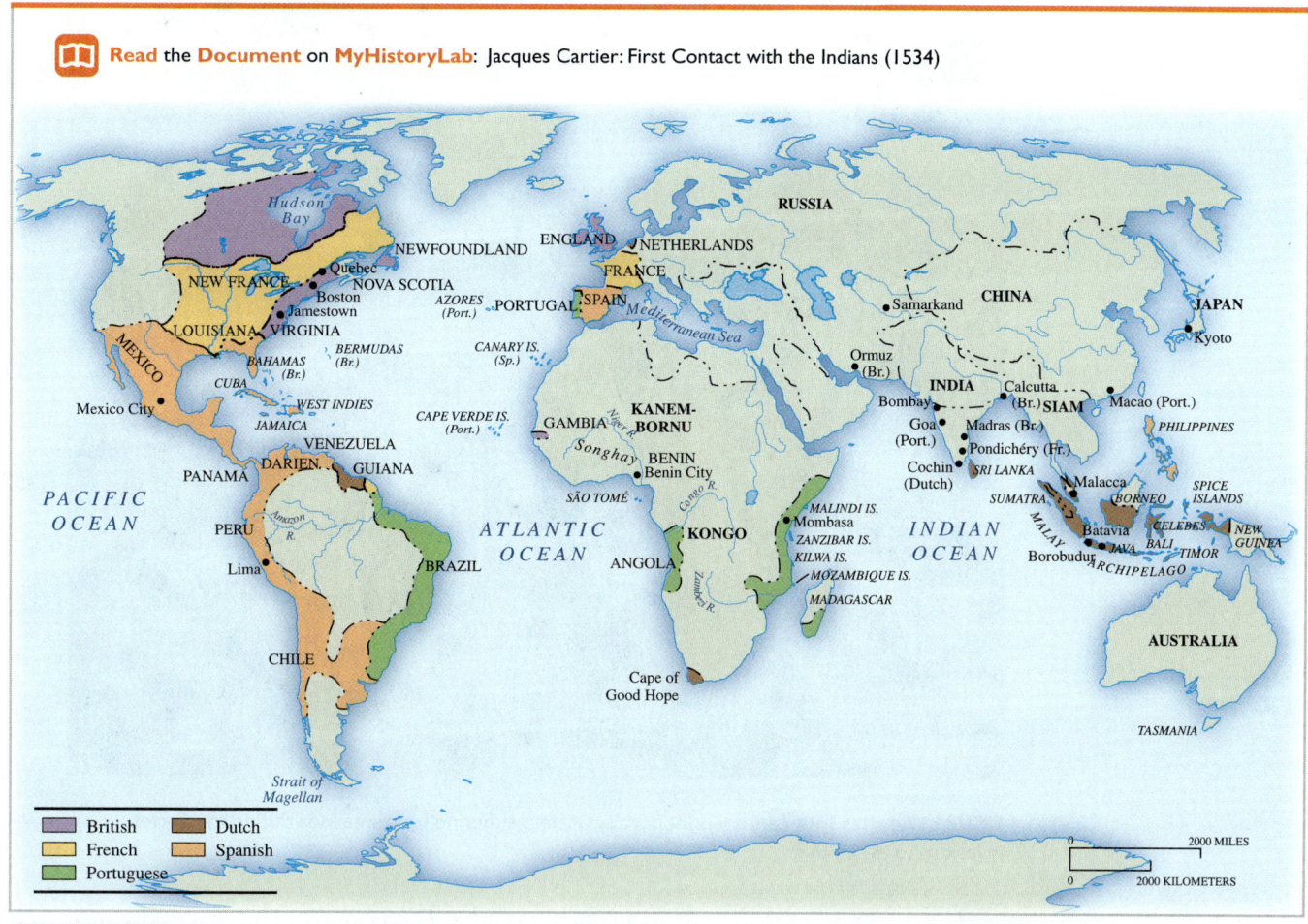

MAP 17.2 **French, British, and Dutch Holdings, c. 1700** During the 17th century, northwestern Europe took the initiative in explorations, venturing into North America and seeking convenient trading stations elsewhere.

THE COLUMBIAN EXCHANGE OF DISEASE AND FOOD

17.2 What were the principal regional results of the Columbian Exchange?

Europe's new initiatives added to existing transregional trade patterns. The range and significance of exchange began to increase steadily—a key manifestation of proto-globalization. Simply including the Americas, making exchanges truly global affected almost all major regions.

The impact of wider exchange became visible quickly. The extension of contacts across the Atlantic spread disease (see Chapter 19). The greatest victims were millions of Native Americans who had not previously been exposed to Afro-Eurasian diseases such as smallpox and measles and who therefore had no natural immunities (Figure 17.4). During the 16th and 17th centuries, they died in huge numbers. Overall, in North and South America, more than half the native population would die; some estimates run as high as 80 percent. Whole island populations in the West Indies were wiped out. This was a major blow to earlier civilizations in the Americas as well as an opportunity for Europeans to forge a partially new population of their own citizens and slaves imported from Africa. The devastation occurred over a 150-year period, although in some areas it was more rapid. When Europeans later made contact with Polynesians and Pacific Coast peoples in the 18th century, the same dreadful pattern played out, again undermining vibrant cultures.

Other exchanges were less dire. New World crops were spread rapidly via Western merchants. American corn and sweet potatoes were taken up widely in China (where merchants learned of them

> Europe's new maritime strength and new trade patterns generated wider changes, developing from the 1490s onward. One was the Columbian Exchange of foods, diseases, and people. New global economic inequalities and new overseas empires also emerged.

CHAPTER 17 The World Economy **391**

FIGURE 17.4 This 16th-century print portrays Aztecs suffering from smallpox during the Cortés invasion (1518–1519).

from Spaniards in the Philippines), the Mediterranean, and parts of Africa. In some cases these productive new crops, along with local agricultural improvements, triggered large population increases. For example, China began to experience long-term population growth in the 17th century, and new crops played a key role. When Europeans introduced the potato around 1700, major population upheaval occurred there as well.

Indeed, food played a key role in the world system created during the Early Modern period. About 30 percent of the foods consumed in the world today come from plants of American origin. Corn became a staple in the African diet. Europeans, ironically, were more conservative. Rumors spread that American foods spread disease. It took more than a century for the potato to gain ground, but fried potatoes (French fries) were being sold on the streets of Paris by the 1680s.

Animal husbandry became more similar across the world as European and Asian animals, such as horses and cattle, were introduced to the New World. The spread of basic products and diseases formed an important backdrop to world history from the 16th century on, with varying effects on population structures in diverse regions.

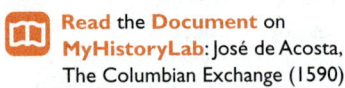

Read the Document on MyHistoryLab: José de Acosta, The Columbian Exchange (1590)

Environment and Labor

The Columbian Exchange had substantial environmental impact. Europeans ignored the environmental experience of local populations in the Americas, bent on introducing European products and expanding output. Introduction of sheep, for example, devastated local vegetation in many parts of the Americas, because of their close grazing, with increased soil erosion an obvious result. Deforestation increased in many regions, either because of population increase or, in the Americas, the desire to expand exports. By 1700 25 percent of the world's forests had been cut down, and by 1850 the percentage had risen to 50. In Latin America alone, forest clearances increased five-fold between 1650 and 1750. Hunting and fishing expanded. Many species lost ground in parts of North America thanks to the fur trade. Beginning with Spanish expeditions in the 16th century, new forms of deep-sea whaling developed, and in general extensive fishing in the North Atlantic—in part to provide cheap food for slaves—began to cut into supplies, particularly of common species like cod.

New trading opportunities and population changes generated new, or partially new, labor systems. Faced with market demand for products like sugar, now introduced to the Americas, but short of local workers thanks to disease, Europeans actively sought alternatives. Experiments with indentured servitude—with workers brought from Europe under tight contracts that controlled their labor for many years—had some success, but failed to recruit sufficient labor. The slave trade, quickly developed with Africa, proved a more important response, with millions ultimately forcibly shipped across the Atlantic. Atlantic slavery, however, was no mere imitation of earlier slave systems. Not only were greater numbers involved, but plantation owners actively strove to increase discipline and production (see Chapter 20). The Columbian Exchange thus played a major role in the general global effort to increase human labor during the Early Modern period.

TOWARD A WORLD ECONOMY

17.3 What new kinds of regional economic inequality emerged during the period?

Europeans did not displace all Asian shipping from the coastal waters of China and Japan, nor did they completely monopolize the Indian Ocean (see Chapter 23). Along the east African coast, while a few European bases were established, Muslim traders remained active, and commerce continued to move toward the Middle East. Generally, however, western Europe dominated a growing percentage of oceanic shipping, even using war ships to muscle in on trade between other societies, as between India and southeast Asia. This greatly increased Europe's overall profits, and disproportionate control by the great merchant companies increased the European ability to determine the framework for international trade. In the eastern Mediterranean, for example, a Spanish-directed fleet defeated the navy of the Ottoman empire in the battle of **Lepanto** in 1571. With this setback, any hope of successful Muslim rivalry against European naval power ended. The Turks rebuilt their fleet and continued their activity in the eastern Mediterranean, but they could not challenge the Europeans on the larger international routes.

Although western Europe did not conquer much inland territory in Africa or Asia, it did seek a limited network of secure harbors. Led by Spain and Portugal, then followed by the various northern powers, European ports spread along the west coast of Africa, several parts of the Indian subcontinent, and the islands of southeast Asia by the 17th century. Even in China, where unusually strong governments limited the Europeans' ability to seize harbors outright, the Portuguese won effective control over the island port of Macao. European-controlled ports served as areas for contact with overland traders (usually local merchants) and provided access to inland goods not directly within the reach of the West.

Where direct control was not feasible, European influence led to the formation of special western enclaves in existing cities. This was the pattern in the Ottoman empire, where Western merchants were permitted to form limited self-governing communities alongside other foreign merchants within Constantinople, and in Russia, where Western shipping agents set up first in Moscow and then in St. Petersburg. Elements of this system even emerged in Japan after a firm isolationist policy was launched about 1600, as Dutch traders were given special access to the port of Nagasaki, a privilege shared by and formerly enjoyed only by Chinese merchants. The point was obvious: International trade gained growing importance in supplementing regional economies. Because western Europe now ran began to play a larger role in trans-regional trace, its merchants often gained some new access, though Chinese traders were still dominant in most East Asian markets.

> Europe developed a network of overseas colonies, particularly in the Americas but also in a few parts of Africa and Asia. By the 18th century, growing European inroads in India marked a decisive change in south Asia.

Lepanto Naval battle between the Spanish and the Ottoman empire resulting in a Spanish victory in 1571.

Imbalances in World Trade

The most active competition in world trade emerged between European nations themselves. Spain briefly dominated, thanks to its imports of silver from the Americas. But it lacked a good banking system and could not support a full commercial surge. England, France, and Holland, where merchants had firmer status, soon pulled in the lion's share of profits from world trade. Western Europe quickly expanded its manufacturing operations, so that it could export expensive finished goods, such as guns and cloth, in return for unprocessed goods, such as silver and sugar, traded by other societies. Here was another margin for profit.

core nations Nations, usually European, that enjoyed profit from world economy; controlled international banking and commercial services such as shipping; exported manufactured goods for raw materials.

mercantilism Economic theory that stressed governments' promotion of limitation of imports from other nations and internal economies in order to improve tax revenues; popular during 17th and 18th centuries in Europe.

The dominant **core nations** in the new world system supplemented their growing economic prowess by self-serving political policies. The doctrines of **mercantilism**, which urged that a nation-state not import goods from outside its own empire but sell exports as widely as possible in its own ships, both reflected and encouraged the new world system. Tariff policies discouraged manufacturing in colonial areas and stimulated home-based manufacturing.

Beyond western Europe lay areas that were increasingly enmeshed in the world economy but as dependents to the core nations. These areas produced low-cost goods: precious metals and cash crops such as sugar, spice, tobacco, and later cotton. Human labor was a vital item of exchange. Parts of sub-Saharan Africa entered the new world economy mainly as suppliers of slaves. The earlier west African patterns of trade across the Sahara yielded to a dominant focus on the Atlantic and therefore to activities organized by Western shippers. In return for slaves and unprocessed goods, Europeans traded their manufactured items, including guns, while profiting from their control of commercial and shipping services.

A System of International Inequality

The new world economic relationships proved highly durable. Most of the areas established as dependent by the 17th century still carry some special burdens in world trade today. In dependent areas such as Latin America and the slave-supplying parts of Africa, not all people were mired in poverty. African slave traders and princes who taxed the trade might grow rich. In Latin America the silver mines and commercial estates required regional merchants and farmers to supply food. Furthermore, many peasants in Latin America and even more in Africa were not yet involved in a market economy at all—whether regional or international—but rather produced for local subsistence with traditional motives and methods. However, significant minorities were involved in production for the world market. Also, most African and Latin American merchants and landlords did not fully control their own terms of trade. They might prosper, but their wealth did not stimulate much local manufacturing or general economic advance. Rather, they tended to import European-made goods, including (in the case of American planters) art objects and luxury items.

Coercive labor systems spread. Because dependent economies relied on cheap production of unprocessed goods, there was a tendency to build a system of forced labor that would cost little even

---

VISUALIZING THE PAST

West Indian Slaveholding

THE FOLLOWING TABLE DESCRIBES THE RISE of the plantation system, and attendant slaveholding, on the British West Indian island of Antigua, where sugar growing for export gained increasing hold. Trends of the sort indicated in this table raise further analytical issues about cause and effect. What might have caused the main changes in Antigua's estate system? What do the trends suggest about the European demand for sugar and about production methods used to meet this demand?

What impact would the trends have had on slaves themselves? Laws in the British Caribbean soon began to enforce the estate system, exempting masters from murder charges when slaves died from beatings administered as punishment and fining groups such as the Quakers for daring to bring slaves to religious meetings. How do the statistical trends help explain the imposition of new laws of this sort?

QUESTIONS
- What trends in the social and economic structure of this part of Antigua during the 18th century do these figures suggest?
- Did the estate economy become more or less labor intensive, given the acreage involved and the comparative growth rates of owner and slave populations?
- What do the trends suggest about the nature of the European-born or European-derived elite of Antigua?

	1688	1706	1767
Slaveholders	16	30	65
Planters with 20+ slaves	6	16	46
Planters with 100+ slaves	0	4	22
Slaves	332	1,150	5,610
Acreage	5,811	5,660	12,350

when the overall labor supply was precarious. In the Americas, given the population loss from disease, this led to the massive importation of African slaves as well as the more limited use of indentured servants. Also, for many Native Americans and **mestizos** (people of mixed European and Native American blood), systems of estate management developed that demanded large amounts of labor. More limited examples of estate agriculture, with peasants forced into labor without the legal freedom to leave, arose for spice production in the Dutch East Indies and, by the 18th century, in British-dominated agricultural operations in India.

mestizos [mehs-TEE-zohs] People of mixed European and Indian ancestry in Mesoamerica and South America; particularly prevalent in areas colonized by Spain; often part of forced labor system.

How Much World in the World Economy?

Asia, although not sponsoring the most active merchant ventures, participated strongly, and often profitably, in the world economy. The Chinese government, having renounced large-scale international trade of its own early in the 15th century, deliberately avoided involvement with international trade on someone else's terms. It did copy some firearms manufacturing from the Europeans, but at a fairly low level. Beyond this it depended on extensive government regulation, backed up by a coastal navy, to keep European activities in check. Most of the limited trade that existed was channeled through Macao. European visitors wrote scornfully of China's disdain for military advances. A Jesuit wrote that "the military . . . is considered mean among them." The Chinese were also disparaged for adhering to tradition. One Western missionary in the 17th century described how, in his opinion, the Chinese could not be persuaded "to make use of new instruments and leave their old ones without an especial order from the Emperor to that effect. They are more fond of the most defective piece of antiquity than of the most perfect of the modern, differing much in that from us who are in love with nothing but what is new."

Read the Document on MyHistoryLab: Multatuli, Max Havelaar: Or the Coffee Auctions of the Dutch Trading Company

So China managed to avoid trying to keep up with European developments while also avoiding subservience to European merchants. Chinese manufacturing gains led to a strong export position, which is why Europeans sent a great deal of American silver to China to pay for the goods they wanted. Indeed, at the end of the 18th century, a famous British mission, appealing to the government to open the country to greater trade, was rebuffed. The imperial court, after insisting on extreme deference from the British envoy, haughtily informed him that the Chinese had no need for outside goods. European eagerness for Chinese goods—attested to by the habit adopted in the 17th century of calling fine porcelain "china"—was simply not matched by Chinese enthusiasm, but a trickle of trade continued. Westerners compensated in part by developing their own porcelain industry by the 18th century, which contributed to the early Industrial Revolution, particularly in Britain. Still, there were hopes for commercial entry to China that remained unfulfilled.

Japan, although initially attracted by Western expeditions in the 16th century, pulled back even more fully. So did Korea. The Japanese showed some openness to Christian missions, and they were fascinated by Western advances in gunnery and shipping. Artists captured the interest in exotic foreigners. Guns had particular relevance to Japan's ongoing feudal wars, for there was no disdain here for military life. Yet Japanese leaders soon worried about undue Western influence and the impact this could have on internal divisions among warring lords, as well as the threat guns posed to samurai military dominance. They encouraged a local gunmaking industry that matched existing European muskets and small cannon fairly readily, but having achieved this, they cut off most contact with any world trade. Most Japanese were forbidden to travel or trade abroad, the small Christian minority was suppressed, and from the 17th until the 19th centuries Japan entered a period of almost complete isolation except for some Chinese contact and trading concessions to the small Dutch enclave near Nagasaki.

Other societies participated variously in world trade. The rulers of India's new Mughal empire in the 16th century were interested in Western traders and even encouraged the establishment of small port enclaves. India also sold goods—not only spices but also manufactured cottons textiles and other items—in return for New World silver. Most attention, however, was riveted on internal development and land-based expansion and commerce; world trade was a sideline. The same held true for the Ottoman and Safavid empires in the Middle East through the 17th century, despite the presence of small European enclaves in key cities. Russia lay partially outside the world economic orbit until the 18th century. A largely agricultural society, Russia conducted much of its trade with nomadic peoples in central Asia, which further insulated it from west European demands.

The Expansionist Trend

The world economy was not stationary; it tended to gain ground over time, as the centerpiece of the process of proto-globalization. The process also linked to the formation of new kinds of empire. South America, the West Indies, a part of North America, and some regions in west Africa were first staked out as colonial dependencies beginning in the 16th century, and the list later expanded. Portions of southeast Asia that produced for world markets, under the dominance of the great Western trading companies, were brought into the orbit by the 17th century.

By the early 18th century, Western traders were advancing in India as the Mughal empire began to fall apart. The British and French East India Companies staked out increasing roles in internal trade and administration. Early in the 18th century, Britain passed tariffs against the import of cotton cloth made in India as a means of protecting Britain's own cotton industry. The intent was to use India as a market for British-processed goods and a source of outright payments of gold, which the British were requiring by the late 18th century. Indian observers were aware of the shifting balance. An 18th-century account noted,

> But such is the little regard which they [the British] show to the people of this kingdom, and such their apathy and indifference for their welfare, that the people under their dominion groan everywhere, and are reduced to poverty and distress.

India maintained a complex regional economy still, with much internal manufacturing and trade; it was not forced into such complete dependency as Latin America, for example. However, what had initially been a position outside the world economy was changing, to India's disadvantage. Manufacturing began to decline.

Eastern Europe also was brought into a growing relationship with the world economy and the west European core. The growth of cities in the West created a growing market for imported grains by the 18th century. Much of this demand was met by east European growers, particularly in Prussia and Poland but also in Russia. Export grains, in turn, were produced mainly on large estates by serfs, who were subjected to prolonged periods of labor service. This relationship was similar to that which prevailed in Latin America, with one exception: Outside of Poland, east European governments were much stronger than their Latin American counterparts.

COLONIAL EXPANSION

> Europe's new naval power supported the establishment of several overseas empires, particularly in the Americas. Trade patterns and the results of the Columbian exchange helped shape colonial relationships.

17.4 Did the new European colonies constitute major expansions of state power?

Opportunities to establish colonies were particularly inviting in the Americas, where European guns, horses, and iron weapons offered special advantages and where political disarray and the population losses provided openings in many cases (see Chapter 20).

The Americas: Loosely Controlled Colonies

Spain moved first. The Spanish colonized several West Indian islands soon after Columbus's first voyage, starting with Hispaniola and then moving into Cuba, Jamaica, and Puerto Rico. Only in 1509 did they begin settlement on the mainland, in search of gold. The first colony was established in what is now Panama, under an able but unscrupulous adventurer, **Vasco de Balboa**. Several expeditions fanned out in Central America, and then a separate expedition from Cuba launched the Spanish conquest of the Aztecs in Mexico. Another expedition headed toward the Inca realm in the Andes in 1531, where hard fighting was needed before ultimate victory. From this base several colonial expeditions spread to Colombia, other parts of the Andes, and portions of Argentina.

Expansion resulted from the efforts of a motley crew of adventurers, many of them violent and treacherous, like **Francisco Pizarro** (1478–1541), admittedly one of the more successful examples (Figure 17.5). Pizarro first came to the Americas in 1502 and settled on the island of Hispaniola. Later, he joined Balboa's colony in Panama, where he received a cattle ranch. Learning of wealth in Peru, he joined with an illiterate soldier and a priest, mounting two expeditions that failed. In 1528

Balboa, Vasco de (c. 1475–1519) First Spanish captain to begin settlement on the mainland of Mesoamerica in 1509; initial settlement eventually led to conquest of Aztec and Inca empires by other captains.

Pizarro, Francisco Led conquest of Inca Empire of Peru beginning in 1535; by 1540, most of Inca possessions fell to the Spanish.

he returned to Spain to gain the king's support and also his agreement that he would be governor of the new province. With these pledges and a force of about 180 men, he attacked the divided Inca empire. Capturing Emperor Atahuallpa, he accepted a large ransom and then strangled him. Several revolts followed during Pizarro's rule from Lima, a coastal city he founded. But the Spanish king ennobled Pizarro for his success. At a dinner in 1541, Pizarro was assassinated by a group of Inca rebels.

Early colonies in the Americas typically were developed by small bands of gold-hungry Europeans, often loosely controlled by colonial administrations back home. Colonial rulers often established only limited controls over native populations at first, content to exact tribute without imposing detailed administration and sometimes leaving existing leaders in place. Gradually, more formal administration spread as agricultural settlements were established and official colonial systems took shape under control of bureaucrats sent from Spain and Portugal. Active missionary efforts, designed to Christianize the native peoples, added another layer of detailed administration throughout the Spanish holdings in North and South America.

France, Britain, and Holland, although latecomers to the Americas, also staked out colonial settlements. French explorations along the St. Lawrence River in Canada led to small colonies around Quebec, from 1608 onward, and explorations in the Mississippi River basin. Dutch and English settlers moved into portions of the Atlantic coastal regions early in the 17th century. Also in the 17th century, all three countries seized and colonized several West Indian islands, which they soon involved in the growing slave trade.

British and French North America: Backwater Colonies

Colonies of European settlers developed in North America, where patterns differed in many respects from those in Latin America and the Caribbean. English colonies along the Atlantic received religious refugees, such as the Calvinists who fled religious tensions in Britain to settle in New England. Government grants of land to major proprietors such as William Penn led to explicit efforts to recruit settlers. New York began as a Dutch settlement but was taken over easily by an English expedition in 1664.

FIGURE 17.5 Francisco Pizarro.

In Canada, the first substantial European settlements were launched by the French government under Louis XIV. The initial plan involved setting up manorial estates under great lords whose rights were carefully restricted by the state. French peasants were urged to emigrate, although it proved difficult to develop an adequate labor force. However, birth rates were high, and by 1755 **New France** had about 55,000 settlers in a peasant society that proved extremely durable as it fanned out around the fortress of Quebec. Strong organization by the Catholic Church completed this partial replica of French provincial society. Britain attacked the French strongholds (Figure 17.6) as part of a worldwide colonial struggle between the two powers. In the conflict, known as the **Seven Years War**, France lost its colony under the terms of the **Treaty of Paris**, which in 1763 settled the war. France eagerly regained its West Indian sugar islands, along with trading posts in Africa, and Britain took control of Canada and the Mississippi basin. Relations between British officials and the French Canadian community remained strained as British settlements developed in eastern Canada and in Ontario. The flight of many American loyalists after the 1776 revolution added to the English-speaking contingent in Canada.

Colonial holdings along the Atlantic and in Canada were generally of modest interest to Western colonial powers in the 17th and even the 18th centuries. The Dutch were more attached to their Asian colonies. British and French leaders valued their West Indian holdings much more than their North American colonies. The value of North American products, such as timber and furs, was not nearly as great as profits from the Caribbean or Latin America, so much less attention was given to economic regulation. As a result, some merchant and manufacturing activities emerged among the new Americans.

New France French colonies in North America; extended from St. Lawrence River along Great Lakes and down Mississippi River valley system.

Seven Years War Fought both in continental Europe and also in overseas colonies between 1756 and 1763; resulted in Prussian seizures of land from Austria, English seizures of colonies in India and North America.

Treaty of Paris Arranged in 1763 following Seven Years War; granted New France to England in exchange for return of French sugar islands in Caribbean.

DOCUMENT

Western Conquerors: Tactics and Motives

IN THE FIRST PASSAGE QUOTED HERE, Columbus writes to the Spanish monarchy on his way home from his 1492 expedition. In the second passage, the brother of Francisco Pizarro, the Spanish conqueror of Peru, describes in 1533 how the Inca ruler, Atahuallpa, was defeated.

COLUMBUS'S 1492 EXPEDITION

Sir, believing that you will take pleasure in hearing of the great success which our Lord has granted me in my voyage, I write you this letter, whereby you will learn how in thirty-three days' time I reached the Indies with the fleet which the most illustrious King and Queen, our Sovereigns, gave to me, where I found very many islands thickly peopled, of all which I took possession without resistance for their Highnesses by proclamation made and with the royal standard unfurled. To the first island that I found I gave the name of *San Salvador*, in remembrance of His High Majesty, who hath marvelously brought all these things to pass; the Indians call it *Guanaham*....

Espanola is a wonder. Its mountains and plains, and meadows, and fields, are so beautiful and rich for planting and sowing, and rearing cattle of all kinds, and for building towns and villages. The harbours on the coast, and the number and size and wholesomeness of the rivers, most of them bearing gold, surpass anything that would be believed by one who had not seen them. There is a great difference between the trees, fruits, and plants of this island and those of *Juana*. In this island there are many spices and extensive mines of gold and other metals. The inhabitants of this and of all the other islands I have found or gained intelligence of, both men and women, go as naked as they were born, with the exception that some of the women cover one part only with a single leaf of grass or with a piece of cotton, made for that purpose. They have neither iron, nor steel, nor arms, nor are they competent to use them, not that they are not well-formed and of handsome stature, but because they are timid to a surprising degree....

Although I have taken possession of all these islands in the name of their Highnesses, and they are all more abundant in wealth than I am able to express... yet there was one large town in *Espanola* of which especially I took possession, situated in a locality well adapted for the working of the gold mines, and for all kinds of commerce, either with the main land on this side, or with that beyond which is the land of the great Khan, with which there is great profit....

I have also established the greatest friendship with the king of that country, so much so that he took pride in calling me his brother, and treating me as such. Even should these people change their intentions towards us and become hostile, they do not know what arms are, but, as I have said, go naked, and are the most timid people in the world; so that the men I have left could, alone, destroy the whole country, and this island has no danger for them, if they only know how to conduct themselves.... Finally, and speaking only of what has taken place in this voyage, which has been so hasty, their Highnesses may see that I shall give them all the gold they require, if they will give me but a very little assistance; spices also, and cotton, as much as their Highnesses shall command to be shipped; and mastic, hitherto found only in Greece... slaves, as many of these idolators as their Highnesses shall command to be shipped....

But our Redeemer hath granted this victory our illustrious King and Queen and their kingdoms, which have acquired great fame by an event of such high importance, in which all Christendom ought to rejoice, and which it ought to celebrate with great festivals and the offering of solemn thanks to the Holy Trinity with many solemn prayers, both for the great exaltation which may accrue to them in turning so many nations to our holy faith, and also for the temporal benefits which will bring great refreshment and gain, not only to Spain, but to all Christians.

WHY AND HOW ATAHUALLPA WAS DEFEATED

The messengers came back to ask the Governor to send a Christian to Atahuallpa, that he intended to come at once, and that he would come unarmed. The Governor sent a Christian, and presently Atahuallpa moved, leaving the armed men behind him. He took with him about five or six thousand Indians without arms, except that under their shirts they had small darts and slings with stones.

He came in a litter, and before went three or four hundred Indians in liveries, cleaning straws from the road and singing. Then came Atahuallpa in the midst of his chiefs and principal men, the greatest among them being also borne on men's shoulders.... A Dominican Friar, who was with the Governor, came forward to tell him, on the part of the Governor, that he waited for him in his lodgings, and that he was sent to speak with him. The Friar then told Atahuallpa that he was a Priest, and that he was sent there to teach the things of the Faith, if they should desire to be Christians. He showed Atahuallpa a book... and told him that book contained the things of God. Atahuallpa asked for the book, and threw it on the ground, saying: "I will not leave this place until you have restored all that you have taken in my land. I know well who you are, and what you have come for."... The Friar went to the Governor and reported what was being done, and that no time was to be lost. The Governor sent to me; and I had arranged with the Captain of the artillery that, when a sign was given, he should discharge his pieces, and that, on hearing the reports, all the troops should come forth at once. This was done, and as the Indians were unarmed, they were defeated without danger to any Christian. Those who carried the litter, and the chiefs who surrounded Atahuallpa, were all killed, falling around him. The Governor came out and seized Atahuallpa, and in protecting him, he received a knife cut from a Christian in the hand. The troops continued the pursuit as far as the place where the armed Indians were stationed, who made

(continued on next page)

(continued from previous page)

no resistance whatever, because it was night. All were brought into town, where the Governor was quartered.

Next morning the Governor ordered us to go to the camp of Atahuallpa, where we found forty thousand pesos worth of gold and two or three pounds of silver. . . . The Governor said that he had not come to make war on the Indians, but that our Lord the Emperor, who was Lord of the whole world, had ordered him to come that he might see the land, and let Atahuallpa know the things of our Faith. . . . The Governor also told him that that land, and all other lands, belonged to the Emperor, and that he must acknowledge him as his Lord. He replied that he was content, and, observing that the Christians had collected some gold, Atahuallpa said to the Governor that they need not take such care of it, as if there was so little; for that he could give them ten thousand plates, and that he could fill the room in which he was up to a white line, which was the height of a man and a half from the floor.

QUESTIONS

- What were the main bases for initial European judgments about the characteristics of Native Americans?
- How might the native peoples have judged the Europeans?
- What motives does Columbus appeal to in trying to interest Spanish rulers in the new land?
- These documents raise obvious problems of interpretation. They interpret interactions with another, very foreign culture from the European standpoint only. They also attribute motives to the adventurers that may or may not have been predominant. Figuring out how to gain useful, valid information from documents of this sort, which are essential in interpreting key developments in world history, is a major challenge. What parts of the accounts seem most reliable, and what criteria can be used to sort out degrees of accuracy?

FIGURE 17.6 British naval power allowed the light infantry to scale the French fort from the St. Lawrence River and capture Quebec in 1759. The battle was a turning point in Canadian history: the beginning of the end of French rule.

CHAPTER 17 The World Economy 399

However, the American colonies that would become the United States had a population of a mere 3 million, far smaller than the powerful colonies in Latin America. Southern colonies that produced tobacco and sugar, and then cotton, became important. Patterns there were similar to those of Latin America, with large estates based on imported slave labor, a wealthy planter class bent on importing luxury products from western Europe, and weak formal governments. Still, in world historical terms, the Atlantic colonies in North America were of limited value amid the larger colonial holdings staked out in the Early Modern centuries.

Yet European settlers did arrive. Driven by religious dissent, ambition, and other motives, Europeans, many from the British Isles, colonized the Atlantic coastal region, where native populations were quickly reduced by disease and war. The society that developed in the British colonies was far closer to west European forms than was that of Latin America. The colonies operated their own assemblies, which provided the people with political experience. Calvinist and Quaker church assemblies gave governing power to groups of elders or wider congregations. Many colonists thus had reason to share with some west Europeans a sense of the importance of representative institutions and self-government.

Colonists were also avid consumers of political theories written in Europe, such as the parliamentary ideas of John Locke. There was also wide reading and discussion of Enlightenment materials. Institutions such as the 18th-century American Philosophical Society deliberately imitated European scientific institutes, and hundreds of North Americans contributed scientific findings to the British Royal Society. The colonies remained modest in certain cultural attainments. Art was rather primitive, although many stylistic cues came from Europe. There was no question that in formal culture, North American leaders saw themselves as part of a larger Western world.

By the late 18th century, some American merchants were trading with China, their ships picking up medicinal herbs along the Pacific coast and exchanging them for Chinese artifacts and tea. Great Britain tried to impose firmer limits on this modestly thriving local economy after the Seven Years War. It hoped to win greater tax revenues and to guarantee markets for British goods and traders, but the effort came too late and helped encourage rebellion in key colonies. Unusual among the colonies, North America developed a merchant class and some stake in manufacturing in a pattern similar to that taking shape in western Europe itself.

The spread of Western values in the Atlantic colonies and in British and French settlements in Canada was facilitated by the modest impact of Native Americans in these settled areas (Figure 17.7). The native population of this part of North America had always been less dense than in Central America or the Andes region. Because few Native American groups in these regions practiced settled agriculture, instead combining hunting with slash-and-burn corn growing, European colonists found it easy to displace them from large stretches of territory. The ravages of European-imported disease reduced the indigenous population greatly. Many forest peoples were pushed westward. Some abandoned agriculture, turning to a new horse-based hunting economy on the plains (the horse was brought to Mexico by the Spaniards). Many territorial wars further distracted the Native American groups. The net result of these factors was that although European colonists interacted with Native Americans, learned from them, and feared and mistreated them, the colonists did not combine with them to forge new cultural groups like those emerging in much of Latin America.

By 1700, the importation of African slaves proved to be a more important addition to the North American experience, particularly in the southern colonies. The practice of slaveholding and interactions with

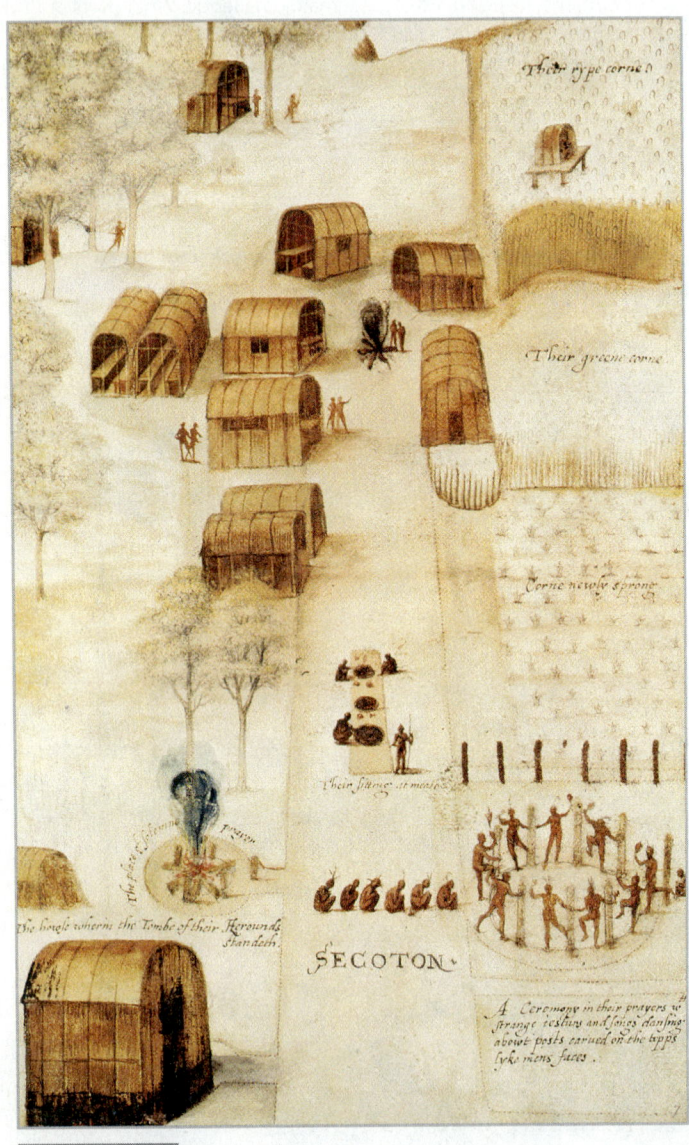

FIGURE 17.7 Watercolor by John White (c. 1590) of the Native American settlement of Secoton, Virginia. White was the governor of the pioneer colony of Roanoke, in what is now North Carolina. When he returned from a desperate voyage back to England to obtain supplies, he found the settlement abandoned. Historians have never been able to determine what happened to the men, women, and children of the "Lost Colony."

400 PART IV The Early Modern Period, 1450–1750: The World Shrinks

African culture distinguished North American life from its European counterpart. By the 18th century, 23 percent of the population of the English colonies was of African origin.

North America and Western Civilization

On balance, most white settlers intended to transplant key Western habits into their new setting. For example, family patterns were similar. American colonists were able to marry slightly earlier than ordinary western Europeans because of the greater abundance of land, and they had larger families. Still, they reproduced most features of the European-style family, including the primary emphasis on the nuclear unit. The new Americans did have unusual concern for children, if only because they depended so heavily on their work in a labor-scarce environment. European visitors commented on the child-centeredness of American families and the freedom of children to speak up. These variations, although significant, played on trends also becoming visible in Europe, such as the new emphasis on family affection.

Even when key colonies rebelled against European control, as they did in 1776, they moved in the name of Western political ideas and economic goals against the dependency the British tried to impose. They established a government that responded to the new Western political theories, implementing some key ideas for the first time.

Africa and Asia: Coastal Trading Stations

In Africa, Europeans for the most part contented themselves with small coastal fortresses, negotiating with African kings and merchants but not trying to claim large territories of their own. They sold Asian products, like Indian cotton, and European guns and decorative items in return for slaves. Generally, Europeans were deterred by climate, disease, and non-navigable rivers from trying to reach into the interior. Mostly, they dealt with West African governments and traders. There were two important exceptions. From initial coastal settlements, Portugal sent expeditions into Angola in search of slaves. These expeditions had a more direct and more disruptive impact in this part of southwestern Africa than elsewhere along the Atlantic coast. More important still was the **Cape Colony** planted by the Dutch on the Cape of Good Hope in 1652. The intent was to form another coastal station to supply Dutch ships bound for Asia. But some Dutch farmers were sent, and these **Boers** (the Dutch word for farmers) began to fan out on large farms in a region still lightly populated by Africans. They clashed with local hunting groups, enslaving some of them. Only after 1770 did the expanding Boer settlements directly conflict with Bantu farmers, opening a long battle for control of southern Africa that raged until the late 20th century in the nation of South Africa.

European colonies in Asia were also exceptional. Spain set up an administration for the Philippines and sent active Catholic missionaries. The Dutch East India company administered portions of the main islands of present-day Indonesia and also (for a time) Taiwan, off the China coast.

Colonization in Asia entered a new phase as the British and French began to struggle for control of India, beginning in the late 17th century when the Mughal empire weakened. Even before the Mughals faltered after the death in 1707 of their last great emperor, Aurangzeb, French and British forts dotted the east and west coasts, along with Portuguese Goa. As Mughal inefficiency increased, with a resultant surge of regional states ruled by Indians, portions of the subcontinent became an arena for the growing international rivalry between Britain and France.

The British East India Company had two advantages in this competition. Through negotiation with local princes, it had gained a station at **Calcutta**, which gave it some access to the great wealth of the Ganges valley. Furthermore, the company had enormous influence over the British government and, through Britain's superior navy, excellent communication on the ocean routes. Its French rivals, in contrast, had less political clout at home, where the government often was distracted by European land wars. The French also were more interested in missionary work than the British, for Protestants became deeply committed to colonial missions only in the 19th century. Before then, the British were content to leave Hindu customs alone and devote themselves to commercial profits.

French–British rivalry raged bitterly through the mid-18th century. Both sides recruited Indian princes and troops as allies. Outright warfare erupted in 1744 and then again during the Seven Years War. In 1756, an Indian ruler in Bengal attacked and captured the British base

Cape Colony Dutch colony established at Cape of Good Hope in 1652 initially to provide a coastal station for the Dutch seaborne empire; by 1770 settlements had expanded sufficiently to come into conflict with Bantus.

Boers Dutch settlers in Cape Colony, in southern Africa.

Calcutta Headquarters of British East India Company in Bengal in Indian subcontinent; located on Ganges; captured in 1756 during early part of Seven Years War; later became administrative center for all of Bengal.

at Calcutta. In the aftermath of the battle, English prisoners were placed in their own jail, where humidity and overcrowding led to perhaps as many as 120 deaths before Indian officials became aware of their plight and released them. The English used this incident, which they dubbed the "black hole of Calcutta," to rally their forces. The East India Company's army recaptured Calcutta and then seized additional Indian and French territory, aided by abundant bribes to many regional princes. French power in India was destroyed, and the East India Company took over administration of the Bengal region, which stretched inland from Calcutta. Soon after this, the British also gained the island of Ceylon (Sri Lanka) from the Dutch.

The full history of British India did not begin until late in the 18th century, when the British government took a more active hand in Indian administration, supplementing the unofficial government of the East India Company (Figure 17.8). Indeed, British control of the subcontinent was incomplete. The Mughal empire remained, although it was increasingly weak and it controlled scant territory, as did other regional kingdoms, including the Sikh state. Britain gained some new territories by force but was also content to form alliances with local princes without disturbing their internal administration.

In most colonies, European administration long remained fairly loose. Few settlers arrived, except in south Africa and the Americas. Outside the Americas, cultural impositions were slight. Missionary activity won many converts in the Philippines but not elsewhere in Asia or in Africa at this point. The main impact of colonies supplemented the more general development of the world economy: Colonial administrations pressed for economic advantage for the home country by opening markets and prompting commercial production of cheap foods and raw materials. Here, of course, the consequences to colonial peoples were very real.

Impact on Western Europe

Western Europe was hugely affected by its own colonial success, not only economically but also diplomatically. Colonial rivalries and wars added to the existing hostilities between key nation-states. England and Holland early turned against Spanish success, with great effect. The Dutch and the English competed, engaging in many skirmishes in the 17th century. Then attention turned to the growing competition between the British and the French. This contest had extensive geographic scope: the Seven Years War (1756–1763), fought in Europe, India, and North America, has been called the first world war.

FIGURE **17.8** This Indian portrait of two women in European dress illustrates the English influence in 18th-century India.
(V & A Images/Victoria and Albert Museum.)

There were also less obvious but equally dramatic effects on European society, including daily life. For example, from the mid-17th century onward, the use of colonially produced sugar spread widely. Previously, sugar had been a costly, upper-class item. Now for the first time (salt had been the one previous exception), a basic product available to ordinary people was being traded over long distances. The spread of sugar had cultural as well as social and economic significance in giving ordinary Europeans the ability to obtain pleasurable sensations in quick doses—an interesting foreshadowing of later features of Western consumer behavior. It also promoted a growing role for dentists by the 18th century.

More broadly, the profits Europeans brought in from world trade, including the African slave trade, added wealth and capital. Many Europeans turned to manufacturing operations, as owners and workers, partly because of opportunities for export in world trade. These developments enhanced Europe's commercial character, while reducing dependence on agriculture alone. They provided additional tax revenues for growing governments and their military ambitions.

The Impact of a New World Order

The development of the world economy and European colonialism had immense impact. The range of unfree labor systems to supply goods for world trade became more widespread than ever before. Slavery and serfdom deeply affected Latin America and eastern Europe, while the slave trade disrupted west Africa, and millions of individual lives as well.

Yet the world economy brought benefits as well as hardships, quite apart from the profits to Europe. New foods and wider trade patterns helped some societies deal with scarcity. Individual merchants and landowners gained new wealth virtually everywhere. China prospered from the imports of silver, although rapid population growth limited gains overall. The mixture of profits and compulsion brought more and more people and regions into the world economy network.

Global Connections and Critical Themes

THE WORLD ECONOMY—AND THE WORLD

Buoyed by its growing role in the world, western Europe unquestionably saw its economy and military power increase more rapidly than those of any other society during the Early Modern period. As the next chapter shows, Europe changed internally as well, often in dramatic ways. Because of these facts, it is tempting to see the Early Modern centuries as a European drama in which other regions either played supporting roles or watched in awe.

Yet the relationships to the world economy were in fact quite complex. They ranged from conscious isolation to controlled participation to undeniable dependency. Many societies retained vibrant political systems and internal economies. Some, although attracted to certain western features, wanted to stand apart from the values and institutions that world economic success seemed to involve.

Even societies that had changes thrust upon them, like Latin America, were hardly passive. Pressed by missionaries, Latin Americans did not simply adopt European-style Christianity, but rather blended in traditional beliefs and practices and many distinctive artistic forms. The world was growing closer, but it was not necessarily becoming simpler.

Further Readings

Excellent discussions of Western exploration and expansion are found in Kenneth Pomeranz and Steven Topik, *The World that Trade Created: Society, Culture, and the World Economy, 1400 to the Present* (2006); Carlo Cipolla, *Guns, Sails, and Empires: Technological Innovation and the Early Phases of European Expansion 1400–1700* (1997); J. H. Parry, *The Age of Reconnaissance* (1982); Richard S. Dunn, *Sugar and Slaves: The Rise of the Planter Class in the English West Indies, 1624–1713* (1972); and D. Boorstin, *The Discoverers* (1991). Other works include Alan K. Smith, *Creating a World Economy: Merchant Capital, Colonialism, and World Trade 1460–1825* (1991); and James Tracy, ed., *The Rise of Merchant Empires* (1986) and *The Political Economy of Merchant Empires* (1991). Somewhat more specific facets are treated in B. Bailyn and P. L. Denault, *Soundings in Atlantic History: Latent Structures and Intellectual Currents* (2009); Warren R. Hofstra, ed., *Cultures in Conflict: The Seven Years' War in North America* (2007); Daniel P. Barr, ed., *The Boundaries Between Us: Natives and Newcomers along the Frontiers of the Old Northwest Territory* (2006); Robert Ross, *Status and Respectability in the Cape Colony, 1750–1870: A Tragedy of Manners* (1999); Joseph E. Inikori, *Africans and the Industrial Revolution in England: A Study in International Trade and Economic Development* (2002); J. H. Parry, *The Discovery of South America* (1979); and S. Subrahmanyam, *The Portuguese Empire in Asia, 1500–1700* (1993). A vital treatment of the international results of new trading patterns of foods and disease is Alfred Crosby, *The Columbian Exchange: Biological and Cultural Consequences of 1492* (1972); see also Elinor G. Melville, *A Plague of Sheep: Environmental Consequences of the Conquest of Mexico* (1994). For a stimulating re-emphasis on Asia, see Andre Gunder Frank, *ReOrient: Global Economy in the Asian Age* (1998). See also Stephen Mosley, *Environment in World History* (2010).

On slavery and its trade, see Pamela Scully and Diana Paton, eds., *Gender and Slave Emancipation in the Atlantic World* (2005); H. S. Klein, *The Atlantic Slave Trade* (2010); Eric Williams, *Capitalism and Slavery* (1964); Orlando Patterson, *Slavery and Social Death: A Comparative Study* (1982); and D. B. Davis, *Slavery and Human Progress* (1984); the last two are important comparative and analytical statements in a major field of recent historical study. See also Philip D. Curtin, *Atlantic Slave Trade* (1972), and his edited volume, *Africa Remembered: Narratives by West Africans from the Era of the Slave Trade* (1967). A good recent survey of developments in Africa and in the period is Paul Bohannan and Philip Curtin, *Africa and Africans* (1988).

New world trading patterns, including Asia's role in them, are discussed in K. N. Chaundhuri, *Trade and Civilization in the Indian Ocean* (1985); Stephan Frederic Dale, *Indian Merchants and*

Eurasia Trade: 1600–1750 (1994); Scott Levi, *The Indian Diaspora in Central Asia and Its Trade 1550–1900* (2002); and S. Volmer, *Planting a New World: Letters and Languages of Transatlantic Botanical Exchange* (2008). A controversial theoretical statement about new trade relationships and their impact on politics and social structure is found in Immanuel Wallerstein, *The Modern World System: Capitalist Agriculture and the Origins of the European World Economy in the Sixteenth Century* (1974), and *The Modern World System: Mercantilism and the Consolidation of the European World Economy 1600–1750* (1980); see also his *Politics of the World Economy: The States, the Movements, and the Civilizations* (1984).

For discussions on where colonial North America fits in this period of world history, see Colin G. Calloway, *The Scratch of a Pen: 1763 and the Transformation of North America* (2006); Jack Greene and J. R. Pole, eds., *Colonial British America: Essays on the New History of the Early Modern Era* (1984); William J. Eccles, *France in America*, rev. ed. (1990); and Gary Nash, *Red, White, and Black: The Peoples of Early America*, rev. ed. (1982).

On MyHistoryLab

 Study and Review on MyHistoryLab

Critical Questions

1. Compare the Asian and the west European roles in the world economy that developed in the Early Modern period.
2. Did the Early Modern period see distinctive changes in human-environment interaction, or were only minor shifts involved?
3. What was the role of technological change in causing major developments during the Early Modern period?
4. Were the European settlements in North America an extension of Western civilization during the Early Modern period, or should they be seen as launching a new civilization pattern?

The Transformation of the West, 1450–1750

18

Listen to Chapter 18 on MyHistoryLab

Throughout the early modern period, Europe's growing involvement in world trade had important impacts on internal developments—on the economy, obviously, but also on government policy and even personal taste. A case in point involved the implications of brightly colored cotton cloth.

Cotton manufacturing had long been a specialty in India. Cheaper than silks, cotton fabrics could sport vivid dyes and designs. Indian cotton products had sold extensively in world trade during the postclassical period, reaching East Asia, the Middle East and, more tentatively, Europe. With Europe's new connections to India after 1498, availability of cottons, and consumer passion, both increased rapidly.

LEARNING OBJECTIVES

18.1 What was the relationship between the Renaissance and the Reformation as forces for cultural change? p. 407

18.2 How did Europe's commercial revolution affect social structure? p. 412

18.3 What were the most innovative features of Western science? p. 415

18.4 To what extent did European states begin to catch up with characteristics of effective states in various Asian societies? p. 417

18.5 In what ways did the pace of change in Europe accelerate by the 18th century? p. 420

FIGURE **18.1** This tapestry with a Tree of Life design from India dates from the early 18th century. This particular design is on cotton, but it shows the colors and artistry that made Indian fabrics such a popular global commodity in the postclassical and Early Modern periods.

Watch the Video Series on MyHistoryLab

Learn about some key topics related to this chapter with the *MyHistoryLab Video Series: Key Topics in World History*

The contrast with conventional linen and woolen fabrics, with characteristically dull colors, was marked. One European traveler to India wrote ecstatically of "cloths of the whiteness of snow, and very delicate and fine" with other fabrics "bespangled and painted with various figures." Europeans were particularly taken with floral designs, and Indian manufacturers began to target part of their production specifically for the European market. Here was one of several examples where rising levels of global trade spurred new consumer tastes, allowing new levels of personal expression through clothing. By the 17th century another observer noted that "in some things the artists of India out-do all the ingenuity of Europe" as in cotton textiles, which Europeans could not match "in their brightness and life of colour."

Portuguese traders were the first to bring cottons directly to Europe, with peddlers taking them to more northern markets. By the 17th century Danish merchants and others were traveling direct to India to seek decorative textiles for homes as well as clothing.

Royal officials in several countries worried about the impact of Indian imports on domestic production and domestic profits. There was also some chiding by moral conservatives about this kind of showy display. By the later 17th century many governments passed rules against wearing brightly colored clothing, while even more laws tried to protect European industry by banning Indian textile imports.

By this point also, however, European manufacturers themselves were beginning to wonder if they could take advantage of consumer tastes directly. In southern France, several Armenian workmen brought in new techniques in partnership with local businessmen around 1650, and Armenians also helped set up production in Amsterdam. By 1750 a factory in Switzerland, although using manual operations, employed over 1300 workers. Only by this point were European methods adequate to match the best Indian colors and designs.

By the later 18th century, dramatic new printing processes, including use of a rotary press, moved European cottons directly into the industrial revolution. By this time as well, European consumers, now seeing access to colorful cottons as a routine need, became ever more demanding of dramatic new styles each year, indulging a taste for novelty that was built into modern consumerism. What began as a deferential contact with Asia turned into an engine for European change. ∎

This chapter deals with a series of big changes in western Europe between 1450 and 1750. The specific new movements were diverse, but over the three centuries' span they added up to a novel cultural framework for intellectuals but also many ordinary people, some key political innovations, and a more commercially based social structure. In considering particular developments, it is vital to keep the larger ultimate directions of change in mind: What were the main ways western Europe in 1750 differed from western Europe in 1450? It's also important to remember that the developments occurred in a context of growing interaction with other parts of the world—even in areas as prosaic as new preferences for clothing.

During the Early Modern period major changes occurred in Europe's economy and culture, along with significant shifts in politics. Some innovations—like the idea of a nation-state or the scientific revolution—would later have global impacts. At the same time, it is important not to overdo European

1300 C.E.	1450 C.E.	1500 C.E.	1550 C.E.	1650 C.E.	1750 C.E.
1300–1450 Italian Renaissance	1450–1519 Life of Leonardo da Vinci 1450–1600 Northern Renaissance 1455 First European printing press, Mainz, Germany 1475–1514 Life of Michelangelo 1490s France and Spain invade Italian city-states; beginning of Italian decline	1500–1600 Commercial revolution 1515–1547 Reign of Francis I, France 1517 Luther's 95 theses; beginning of Protestant Reformation 1534 Beginning of Church of England 1541–1564 Calvin in Geneva 1543 Copernican revolution; Copernicus's work on astronomy	1550–1649 Religious wars in France, Germany, and Britain 1555–1603 Reign of Elizabeth I, England 1564–1642 Life of Galileo 1588 English defeat the Spanish Armada 17th century Scientific Revolution 1609 Independence of Netherlands 1618–1648 Thirty Years War 1642–1649 English Civil War 1642–1727 Life of Isaac Newton 1643–1715 Reign of Louis XIV, France; absolute monarchy 1647–1648 Culmination of popular rebellions in western Europe	1670–1692 Decline of witchcraft trials 1682–1699 Habsburgs drive Turks from Hungary 1688–1690 Glorious Revolution in Britain; parliamentary monarchy; some religious toleration; political writing of John Locke 18th century Enlightenment 1712–1786 Life of Frederick the Great of Prussia, enlightened despot 1730–1850 European population boom 1733 James Kay invents flying shuttle loom 1736 Beginnings of Methodism	1756–1763 Seven Years War: France, Britain, Prussia, and Austria 1776 Adam Smith's *Wealth of Nations* 1780–1790 Reign of Joseph II, first Habsburg emperor 1792 Mary Wollstonecraft's *Vindication of the Rights of Women*

dynamism. There were no fundamental changes, for example, in agriculture, at least until the final decades of the period, and agriculture remained basic. Furthermore, some changes saw Europe mainly catching up to achievements that many other societies had already established; not everything was really new or different, from a global perspective.

THE FIRST BIG CHANGES: CULTURE AND COMMERCE, 1450–1650

18.1 What was the relationship between the Renaissance and the Reformation as forces for cultural change?

> The Renaissance emphasized new styles and beliefs. Religious changes springing from the Protestant Reformation had an even wider impact.

The Italian writer Francesco Petrarch (1304–1374) once climbed Ventoux, a mountain in southern France. He wrote of his ascent, proud of his own skill and using the climb as a symbol of what he could achieve. There was a new spirit of individual pride expressed in this work, intended to be published, compared to the more humble and religious sentiments of the Middle Ages when individual artisans did not even put their names on the magnificent cathedrals they built. But Petrarch did not abandon religion, and in later life he talked about how he had given up poetry in favor of reading Christian texts, finding "hidden sweetness which I had once esteemed but lightly."

The Italian Renaissance

The move away from earlier European patterns began with the Renaissance, which first developed in Italy during the 14th and 15th centuries. Largely an artistic movement, the Renaissance challenged medieval intellectual values and styles. It also sketched a new, brasher spirit that may have encouraged a new Western interest in exploring strange waters or urging that old truths be re-examined.

Machiavelli, Niccolo [mak EE uh vel EE] (1469–1527) Author of *The Prince* (16th century); emphasized realistic discussions of how to seize and maintain power; one of most influential authors of Italian Renaissance.

 Read the Document on MyHistoryLab: The Prince (1519) Machiavelli

humanism Focus on humankind as center of intellectual and artistic endeavor; method of study that emphasized the superiority of classical forms over medieval styles, in particular the study of ancient languages.

 View the Closer Look on MyHistoryLab: Humanism and Renaissance Art

Northern Renaissance Cultural and intellectual movement of northern Europe; began later than Italian Renaissance (c. 1450); centered in France, Low Countries, England, and Germany; featured greater emphasis on religion than Italian Renaissance.

Francis I King of France in the 16th century; regarded as Renaissance monarch; patron of arts; imposed new controls on Catholic church; ally of Ottoman sultan against Holy Roman emperor.

Italy was already well launched in the development of Renaissance culture by the 15th century, based on its unusually extensive urban, commercial economy and its competitive city-state politics. Writers such as Petrarch and Boccaccio had promoted classical literary canons against medieval logic and theology, writing in Italian as well as the traditional Latin and emphasizing secular subjects such as love and pride. Painting turned to new realism and classical and human-centered themes. Religion declined as a central focus. The Italian Renaissance blossomed further in the 15th and early 16th centuries. This was a great age of Western art, as Leonardo da Vinci advanced the realistic portrayal of the human body and Michelangelo applied classical styles in painting and sculpture. In political theory, **Niccolo Machiavelli** emphasized realistic discussions of how to seize and maintain power. Like the artists, Machiavelli bolstered his realism with Greek and Roman examples.

Overall, Italian Renaissance culture stressed themes of **humanism**: a focus on humankind as the center of intellectual and artistic endeavor, as Francesco Petrarch's interests suggested. Religion was not attacked, but its principles were no longer predominant. Historians have debated the reasons for this change. Italy's more urban, commercial environment was one factor, but so was the new imitation of classical Greek and Roman literature and art.

These Renaissance themes had some bearing on politics and commerce. Renaissance merchants improved their banking techniques and became more openly profit-seeking than their medieval counterparts had been. City-state leaders experimented with new political forms and functions. They justified their rule not on the basis of heredity or divine guidance but more on the basis of what they could do to advance general well-being and their city's glory. Thus, they sponsored cultural activities, as states began to use art to gain greater popular support. They also tried to improve the administration of the economy. Resistance leaders developed more professional armies, for wars among the city-states were common, and gave new attention to military tactics and training. They also rethought the practice of diplomacy, introducing the regular exchange of ambassadors for the first time in the West. Clearly, the Renaissance encouraged innovation, although it also produced some dependence on classical models.

The Renaissance Moves Northward

Italy began to decline as a Renaissance center by about 1500. French and Spanish monarchs invaded the peninsula, reducing political independence. At the same time, new Atlantic trade routes reduced the importance of Mediterranean ports, a huge blow to the Italian economy.

As Renaissance creativity faded in its Italian birthplace, it passed northward. The **Northern Renaissance**—focused in France, the Low Countries, Germany, and England—began after 1450. Renaissance styles also affected Hungary and Poland in east central Europe. Classical styles in art and architecture became the rage. Knowledge of Greek and Latin literature gained ground, although many northern humanists wrote in their own languages (English, French, and so on). Northern humanists were more religious than their Italian counterparts, trying to blend secular interests with continued Christian devotion. Renaissance writers such as Shakespeare in England and Rabelais in France mixed classical themes with an earthiness—a joy in bodily functions and human passions—that maintained elements of medieval popular culture. Renaissance literature established a new set of classics for literary traditions in the major Western languages, such as the writings of Shakespeare in England and Cervantes in Spain.

The Northern Renaissance produced some political change, providing another move toward greater state powers. As their revenues and operations expanded, Renaissance kings increased their pomp and ceremony. Kings such as **Francis I** in France became patrons of the arts, importing Italian sculptors and architects to create their classical-style palaces. By the late 16th century, many monarchs were sponsoring trading companies and colonial enterprises. Interest in military conquest was greater than in the Middle Ages. Francis I was even willing to ally with the Ottoman sultan, the key Muslim leader. His goal was to distract his main enemy, the Habsburg ruler of Austria and Spain. In fact, it was an alliance in name only, but it illustrated how power politics was beginning to abandon the feudal or religious justifications that had previously clothed it in the West.

Yet the impact of the Renaissance should not be overstated, particularly outside Italy. Renaissance kings were still confined by the political powers of feudal landlords. Ordinary people were little touched by Renaissance values; the life of most peasants and artisans went on much as before. Economic life also changed little, particularly outside the Italian commercial centers. Even in the upper classes, women sometimes encountered new limits as Renaissance leaders touted men's public bravado over women's domestic roles.

Changes in Technology and Family

More fundamental changes were brewing in Western society by 1500, beneath the glittering surface of the Renaissance. Spurred by trading contacts with Asia, workers in the West improved the quality of pulleys and pumps in mines and learned how to forge stronger iron products. Printing was introduced in the 15th century when the German **Johannes Gutenberg** and other inventors introduced movable type, building on Chinese printing technology. Soon books were distributed in greater quantities in the West, which helped expand the audience for Renaissance writers and disseminated religious ideas. Literacy began to gain ground and became a fertile source of new kinds of thinking.

Family structure was also changing. A **European-style family** pattern came into being by the 15th century in the western part of the continent. This pattern involved a late marriage age and a primary emphasis on nuclear families of parents and children rather than the extended families characteristic of most agricultural civilizations. The goal was to limit family birth rates. By the 16th century, ordinary people usually did not marry until their late 20s—a marked contrast to most agricultural societies. These changes emphasized the importance of husband–wife relations. They also closely linked the family to individual property holdings, for most people could not marry until they had access to property.

Gutenberg, Johannes Introduced movable type to western Europe in 15th century; credited with greatly expanded availability of printed books and pamphlets.

 View the **Closer Look** on **MyHistoryLab:** A Renaissance Printing Press

European-style family Originated in 15th century among peasants and artisans of western Europe, featuring late marriage age, emphasis on the nuclear family, and a large minority who never married.

The Protestant and Catholic Reformations

In the 16th century, religious upheaval and a new commercial surge began to define the directions of change more fully. In 1517, a German monk named **Martin Luther** issued a document containing 95 theses, or propositions. He was publicly protesting claims made by a papal representative in selling indulgences, or grants of salvation, for money, but in fact his protest went deeper. Luther's reading of the Bible convinced him that only faith could gain salvation. Church sacraments were not the path, for God could not be manipulated. Luther's protest, which was rebuffed by the papacy, soon led him to challenge many Catholic beliefs, including the authority of the pope. Luther would soon argue that monasticism was wrong, that priests should marry (as he did), and that the Bible should be translated from Latin so ordinary people could have direct access to its teachings. Luther did not want to break Christian unity, but the church he wanted should be on his terms (or, as he would have argued, the terms of the true faith).

Luther picked up wide support for his views during the mid-16th century and beyond. Many Germans, in a somewhat nationalist reaction, resented the authority and taxes of the Roman pope. German princes saw an opportunity to gain more power. Their nominal leader, the Holy Roman emperor, remained Catholic. Thus, princes who turned Protestant could increase their independence and seize church lands. The Lutheran version of **Protestantism** (as the general wave of religious dissent was called) urged state control of the church as an alternative to papal authority, and this had obvious political appeal.

There were reasons for ordinary people to shift their allegiance as well. Some German peasants saw Luther's attack on authority as a sanction for their own social rebellion against landlords, although Luther specifically renounced this reading. Some townspeople were drawn to Luther's approval of work in the world. Because faith alone gained salvation, Lutheranism could sanction moneymaking and other earthly pursuits more wholeheartedly than did traditional Catholicism. Unlike Catholicism, Lutherans did not see special vocations as particularly holy; monasteries were abolished, along with some of the Christian bias against moneymaking.

Once Christian unity was breached, other Protestant groups sprang forward (see Map 18.1). In England, Henry VIII began to set up an **Anglican church**, initially to challenge papal attempts to enforce his first marriage, which had failed to produce a male heir. (Henry ultimately had six wives in sequence, executing two of them, a particularly graphic example of the treatment of women in power politics.) Henry was also attracted to some of the new doctrines, and his most durable successor, his daughter Elizabeth I, was Protestant outright.

Still more important were the churches inspired by **Jean Calvin**, a French theologian who established his base in the Swiss city of Geneva. Calvinism insisted on God's *predestination*, or prior determination, of those who would be saved. Calvinist ministers became moral guardians and preachers of God's word. Calvinists sought the participation of all believers in local church administration, which promoted the idea of a wider access to government. They also promoted broader popular education so that more people could read the Bible. Calvinism was accepted not only in part of Switzerland but also in portions of Germany, in France (where it produced strong

Luther, Martin (1483–1546) German monk; initiated Protestant Reformation in 1517 by nailing 95 theses to door of Wittenberg church; emphasized primacy of faith over works stressed in Catholic church; accepted state control of church.

 Read the **Document** on **MyHistoryLab:** Martin Luther's "Ninety-Five Theses," 1517

Protestantism General wave of religious dissent against Catholic church; generally held to have begun with Martin Luther's attack on Catholic beliefs in 1517; included many varieties of religious belief.

Anglican church Form of Protestantism set up in England after 1534; established by Henry VIII with himself as head, at least in part to obtain a divorce from his first wife; became increasingly Protestant following Henry's death.

Calvin, Jean French Protestant (16th century) who stressed doctrine of predestination; established center of his group at Swiss canton of Geneva; encouraged ideas of wider access to government, wider public education; Calvinism spread from Switzerland to northern Europe and North America.

Read the Document on MyHistoryLab: Calvin on Predestination (16th c.)

MAP 18.1 **Western Europe During the Renaissance and Reformation** Different Protestant denominations made inroads in much of northwestern Europe with the Reformation, but Catholicism maintained its hold on significant portions of the continent.

Catholic Reformation Restatement of traditional Catholic beliefs in response to Protestant Reformation (16th century); established councils that revived Catholic doctrine and refuted Protestant beliefs.

Jesuits A new religious order founded during the Catholic Reformation; active in politics, education, and missionary work; sponsored missions to South America, North American, and Asia.

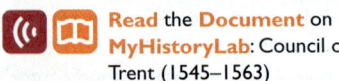
Read the Document on MyHistoryLab: Council of Trent (1545–1563)

Edict of Nantes Grant of tolerance to Protestants in France in 1598; granted only after lengthy civil war between Catholic and Protestant factions.

minority groups), in the Netherlands, in Hungary, and in England and Scotland. By the early 17th century, Puritan exiles brought it to North America.

The Catholic church did not sit still under Protestant attack. It could not restore religious unity, but it defended southern Europe, Austria, Poland, much of Hungary, and key parts of Germany for the Catholic faith. Under a **Catholic Reformation**, a major church council revived Catholic doctrine and refuted key Protestant tenets such as the idea that priests had no special sacramental power and could marry. They also attacked popular superstitions and remnants of magical belief, which meant that Catholics and Protestants alike were trying to find new ways to shape the outlook of ordinary folk. A new religious order, the **Jesuits**, became active in politics, education, and missionary work, regaining some parts of Europe for the church. Jesuit fervor also sponsored Catholic missionary activity in Asia and the Americas.

The End of Christian Unity in the West

The Protestant and Catholic Reformations had several results in Europe during the late 16th and early 17th centuries. Most obvious was an important series of bloody religious wars. France was a scene of bitter battles between Calvinist and Catholic forces. These disputes ended only with the granting of tolerance to Protestants through the **Edict of Nantes** in 1598, although in the next century French kings progressively cut back on Protestant rights. In Germany, the **Thirty Years War** broke out in 1618, pitting German Protestants and allies such as Lutheran Sweden against the Holy Roman emperor, backed by Spain. The war was so devastating that it reduced German power and prosperity

410 PART IV The Early Modern Period, 1450–1750: The World Shrinks

for a full century, cutting population by as much as 60 percent in some regions. It was ended only by the 1648 **Treaty of Westphalia**, which agreed to the territorial tolerance concept: Some princely states and cities chose one religion, some another. This treaty also finally settled a rebellion of the Protestant Netherlands against Spain, giving the former its full independence.

Religious fighting punctuated British history, first before the reign of Elizabeth in the 16th century, then in the **English Civil War** in the 1640s. Calvinists, Anglicans, and some remaining Catholics locked in combat. There was also growing tension between the claims of parliament and some strong assertions of authority by a new line of English kings. The civil war ended in 1660 (well after King Charles I had been beheaded; Figure 18.2), but full resolution came only in 1688–1689, when limited religious toleration was granted to most Protestants, although not to Catholics.

Religious issues thus dominated European politics for almost a century. The religious wars led to a grudging and limited acceptance of the idea of religious pluralism. Christian unity could not be restored, although in most individual countries the idea of full religious liberty was still in the future. The religious wars persuaded some people that religion itself was suspect; if there was no dominant single truth, why all the cruelty and carnage? Finally, the wars affected the political balance of Europe, as Map 18.2 shows. After a period of weakness during its internal strife, France was on the upswing. The Netherlands and Britain were galvanized toward a growing international role. Spain, briefly ascendant, fell back. Internally, some kings and princes benefited from the decline of papal authority by taking a stronger role in religious affairs. This was true in many Catholic and Protestant domains. In some cases, however, Protestant dissent encouraged popular political movements and enhanced parliamentary power.

The impact of religious change went well beyond politics. Popular beliefs changed most in Protestant areas, but Catholic reform produced new impulses as well. Western people gradually became less likely to see an intimate connection between God and nature. Protestants resisted the idea of miracles or other interventions in nature's course. Religious change also promoted greater concentration on family life. Religious writers encouraged love between husband and wife. As one English Protestant put it, "When love is absent between husband and wife, it is like a bone out of joint: there is no ease, no order." This promotion of the family had ambiguous implications for women. Protestantism, abolishing religious convents, made marriage more necessary for women than before;

Read the **Document** on **MyHistoryLab:** The Edict of Nantes, 1598

Thirty Years War War within the Holy Roman Empire between German Protestants and their allies (Sweden, Denmark, France) and the emperor and his ally, Spain; ended in 1648 after great destruction with Treaty of Westphalia.

Treaty of Westphalia Ended Thirty Years War in 1648; granted right to individual rulers within the Holy Roman empire to choose their own religion—either Protestant or Catholic.

English Civil War Conflict from 1640 to 1660; featured religious disputes mixed with constitutional issues concerning the powers of the monarchy; ended with restoration of the monarchy in 1660 following execution of previous king.

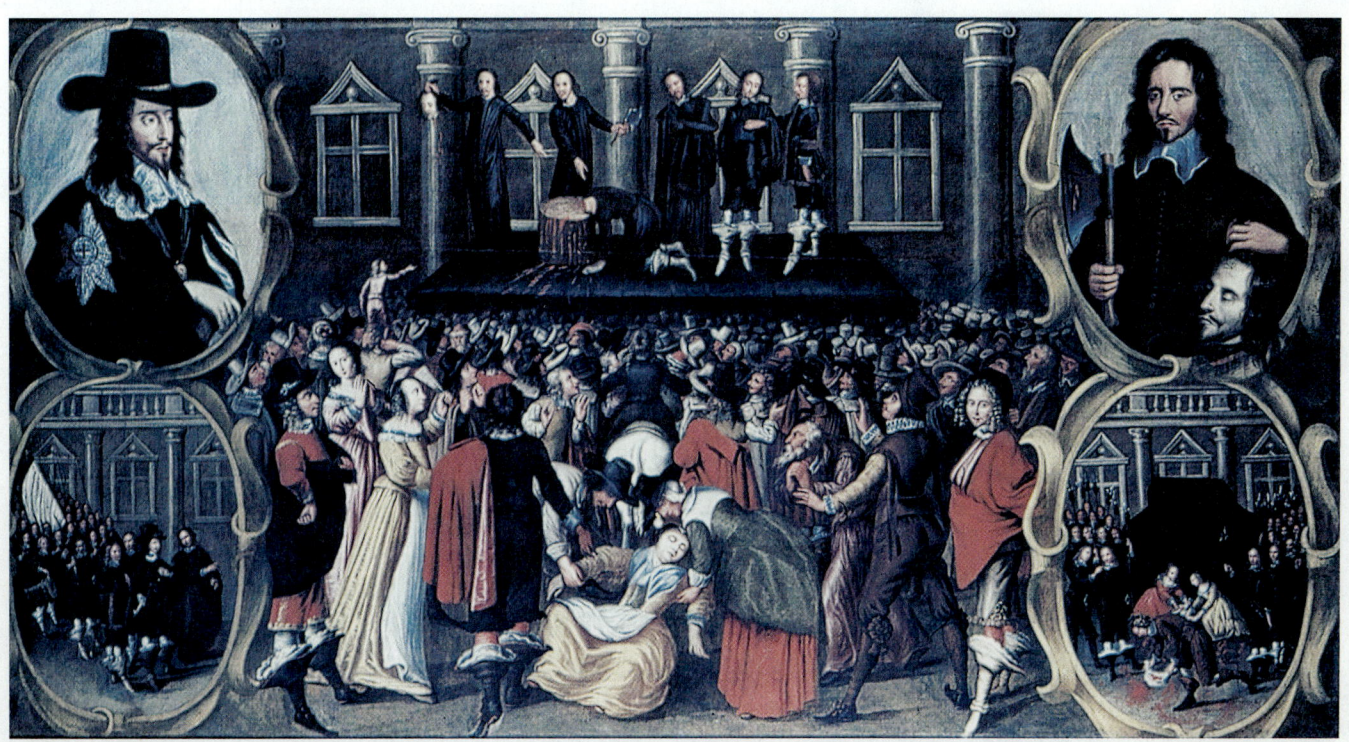

FIGURE **18.2** Civil war over religious issues and the relative power of king and parliament resulted in the beheading of Charles I in London in 1649. As this painting suggests, the regicide was one of the most controversial events in English history.

CHAPTER 18 The Transformation of the West, 1450–1750 411

MAP 18.2 **Europe Under Absolute Monarchy, 1715** The rise of absolute monarchies led to consolidation of national borders as states asserted full control of areas within their boundaries. For example, a recent study shows that villages that straddled the French–Spanish border were undifferentiated before 1600, but by 1700 they showed marked national differences because of different state policies and the greater impact of belonging to one state or another.

there were fewer alternatives for women who could not marry. Fathers were also responsible for the religious training of the children. On the other hand, women's emotional role in the family improved with the new emphasis on affection.

Religious change accompanied and promoted growing literacy along with the spread of the printing press. In the town of Durham, England, around 1570, only 20 percent of all people were literate, but by 1630 the figure had climbed to 47 percent. Growing literacy opened people to additional new ideas and ways of thinking.

Overall, the European Reformation was a fascinating case where long-run consequences did not coincide entirely with the intentions of early leaders, or with initial, short-term change. This was a very different development from the Renaissance, but ultimately, by the 17th century, the two movements could combine to an extent in their effects on politics or culture.

THE COMMERCIAL REVOLUTION

Trade and manufacturing expanded rapidly. A more commercial economy also spurred protest.

18.2 How did Europe's commercial revolution affect social structure?

Along with religious upheaval during the 16th century, the economic structure of the West was fundamentally redefined. The level of European trade rose sharply, and many Europeans had new goods available to them. Involvement with markets and merchants increased. Here was the clearest impact of the new world economy in western Europe.

The Impact of the World Economy

A basic spur to greater commercialization was the price inflation that occurred throughout western Europe during the 16th century. The massive import of gold and silver from Spain's new colonies in Latin America forced prices up. The availability of more money, based on silver supply, generated this price rise. New wealth heightened demand for products to sell, both in the colonies and in Europe, but western production could not keep pace, hence the price inflation. Inflation encouraged merchants to take new risks, for borrowing was cheap when money was losing value. A sum borrowed one year would be worth less, in real terms, five years later, so it made sense to take loans for new investments.

Inflation and the new colonial opportunities led to the formation of the great trading companies, often with government backing, in Spain, England, the Netherlands, and France. Governments granted regional monopolies to these giant concerns; thus, the Dutch East India Company long dominated trade with the islands of Indonesia. European merchants brought new profits back to Europe and developed new managerial skills and banking arrangements.

Colonial markets stimulated manufacturing. Most peasants continued to produce mainly for their own needs, but agricultural specialty areas developed in the production of wines, cheeses, wool, and the like. Some of these industries favored commercial farming and the use of paid laborers on the land. Shoemaking, pottery, metalworking, and other manufacturing specializations arose in both rural villages and the cities. Technical improvements followed in many branches of manufacture, particularly in metals and mining.

Prosperity increased for many ordinary people as well as for the great merchants. One historian has estimated that by about 1600 the average Western peasant or artisan owned five times as many "things" as his or her counterpart in southeastern Europe. A 16th-century Englishman noted that whereas in the past a peasant and his family slept on the floor and had only a pan or two as kitchenware, by the final decades of the century a farmer might have "a fair garnish of pewter in his cupboard, three or four feather beds, so many coverlets and carpets of tapestry, a silver salt, a bowl for wine . . . and a dozen spoons." It was about this time that French peasants began to enjoy wine fairly regularly rather than simply at special occasions—the result of higher productivity and better trade and transport facilities.

Social Protest

There were victims of change as well. Growing commercialization created the beginnings of a new **proletariat** in the West—people without access to wealth-producing property. Population growth and rising food prices hit hard at the poor, and many people had to sell their small plots of land. Some proletarians became manufacturing workers, depending on orders from merchant capitalists to keep their tools busy in their cottages. Others became paid laborers on agricultural estates, where landlords were eager for a more manipulable workforce to take advantage of business opportunities in the cities. Others pressed into the cities, and a growing problem of beggars and wandering poor began to affect Western society (Map 18.3). By blaming the poor for moral failings, a new, tough attitude toward poverty took shape that has lasted to some extent to the present day.

Not surprisingly, the shifts in popular economic and cultural traditions provoked important outcries. A huge wave of popular protest in western Europe developed at the end of the 16th century and extended until about 1650. Peasants and townspeople alike rose for greater protection from poverty and loss of property. The uprisings did not deflect the basic currents of change, but they revealed the massive insecurity of many workers.

The popular rebellions of the 17th century revealed social tension and new ideas of equality. Peasant songs voiced such sentiments as this: "The whole country must be overturned, for we peasants are now to be the lords, it is we who will sit in the shade." Uprisings in 1648 produced demands for a popular political voice; an English group called the Levelers gained 100,000 signatures on a petition for political rights. Elsewhere, common people praised the kings while attacking their "bad advisors" and high taxes. One English agitator said that "we should cut off all the gentlemen's heads. . . . We

proletariat Class of working people without access to producing property; typically manufacturing workers, paid laborers in agricultural economy, or urban poor; in Europe, product of economic changes of 16th and 17th centuries.

MAP 18.3 **European Population Density, c. 1600** Europe experienced new levels of population concentration in some urban areas by 1600, although by Asian standards, city size remained fairly modest.

shall have a merrier world shortly." In France, Protestant and Catholic peasants rose together against landlords and taxes: "They seek only the ruin of the poor people for our ruin is their wealth."

An unprecedented outburst against suspected witches arose in the same decades in various parts of western Europe and also in New England. Although attacks on witches had developed before, the new scale reflected intense social and cultural upheaval. Between 60,000 and 100,000 suspected witches were accused and killed. The **witchcraft persecution** reflected new resentments against the poor, who were often accused of witchcraft by communities unwilling to accept responsibility for their poverty. The hysteria also revealed new tensions about family life and the role of women, who were the most common targets of persecution. A few of the accused witches actually believed they had magical powers, but far more were accused by fearful or self-serving neighbors. The whole witchcraft experience revealed a society faced with forces of unusual complexity.

witchcraft persecution Reflected resentment against the poor, uncertainties about religious truth; resulted in death of over 100,000 Europeans between 1590 and 1650; particularly common in Protestant areas.

A Balance Sheet

Changes in Europe between 1450 and 1650 were untidy. Renaissance secular interests clashed with Reformation spiritual emphases. The confusion of change helped explain sharp reactions, like the witchcraft trials. Still, there were some basic directions to change. Europe was becoming more commercial; even some of the implications of the Reformation pushed toward higher

THE SCIENTIFIC REVOLUTION: THE NEXT PHASE OF CHANGE

18.3 What were the most innovative features of Western science?

A revolution in the nature and status of science occurred during the 17th century. The European state took on new forms and functions. This wave of change intensified after 1650.

The revolution in science, culminating in the 17th century, set the seal on the cultural reorientation of the West. Although the **Scientific Revolution** most obviously affected formal intellectual life, it also promoted changes in popular outlook. At the same time, after the political upheavals of the Reformation, a more decisive set of new government forms arose in the West, centering on the emergence of the nation-state. The functions of the state expanded. The Western nation-state was not a single form, because key variants such as absolute monarchies and parliamentary regimes emerged, but there were some common patterns beneath the surface.

Scientific Revolution Culminated in 17th century; period of empirical advances associated with the development of wider theoretical generalizations; resulted in change in traditional beliefs of Middle Ages.

Did Copernicus Copy?

This is a chapter about big changes in western Europe during the early modern period. Big changes are always complex. One key development was the rise of science in intellectual life. A key first step here was the discovery by the Polish monk **Nicolaus Copernicus**, in the 16th century, that the planets moved around the sun rather than the earth, as the Greeks had thought. This discovery set other scientific advances in motion, and more generally showed that new thinking could improve on tradition. Copernicus is usually taken as a quiet hero of western science and rationalism.

Nicolaus Copernicus Polish monk and astronomer (16th century); disproved Hellenistic belief that the earth was at the center of the universe.

Copernicus based his findings on mathematics, understanding that the Greek view of earth as central raised key problems in calculating planetary motion. Historians have recently uncovered similar geometrical findings by two Arabs, al-Urdi and al-Tusi, from the 13th and 14th centuries. Did Copernicus copy, as Westerners had previously done from the Arabs, while keeping quiet because learning from Muslims was now unpopular? Or did he discover independently? It's also worth noting that scientists in other traditions, such as Chinese, Indian, and Mayan, had already realized the central position of the sun.

Read the Document on MyHistoryLab: Galileo Galilei, "Letter to Madame Christine of Lorraine, Grand Duchesse of Tuscany"

What is certain is that based on discoveries like that of Copernicus, science began to take on more importance in Western intellectual life than had ever been the case in the intellectual history of other societies, including classical Greece. Change may be complicated but it does occur.

Science: The New Authority

During the 16th century, scientific research quietly built on the traditions of the later Middle Ages. After Copernicus, **Johannes Kepler** (1571–1630; Figure 18.3) was another important early figure in the study of planetary motion. Unusual for a major researcher, Kepler was from a poor family; his father abandoned the family outright, and his mother was once tried for witchcraft. But Kepler made his way to university on scholarship, aiming for the Lutheran ministry, but he was drawn to astronomy and mathematics. Using the work of Copernicus and his own observations, he resolved basic issues of planetary motion. He also worked on optics and, with the mixed interests so common in real intellectual life, also practiced astrology, casting horoscopes for wealthy patrons. Also around 1600, anatomical work by the Belgian Vesalius gained greater precision. These key discoveries not only advanced knowledge of the human body but also implied a new power for scientific research in its ability to test and often overrule accepted ideas.

FIGURE **18.3** Johannes Kepler, one of the leading figures in the Scientific Revolution.

Kepler, Johannes (December 27, 1571–November 15, 1630) Was an astronomer and mathematician who was a prominent figure in the Scientific Revolution.

Galileo Galilei Published Copernicus's findings (17th century); added own discoveries concerning laws of gravity and planetary motion; condemned by the Catholic church for his work.

Harvey, William English physician (17th century) who demonstrated circular movement of blood in animals, function of heart as pump.

Bacon, Francis (January 22, 1561–April 9, 1626) English philosopher, statesman, author, and scientist; an influential member of the Scientific Revolution; best known for work on the scientific method.

Descartes, René [dAY kärt] Established importance of skeptical review of all received wisdom (17th century); argued that human reason could then develop laws that would explain the fundamental workings of nature.

Newton, Isaac (1643–1727) English scientist; author of *Principia*; drew together astronomical and physical observations and wider theories into a neat framework of natural laws; established principles of motion; defined forces of gravity.

Deism Concept of God current during the Scientific Revolution; role of divinity was to set natural laws in motion, not to regulate once process was begun.

Locke, John (1632–1704) English philosopher who argued that people could learn everything through senses and reason and that power of government came from the people, not divine right of kings; offered possibility of revolution to overthrow tyrants.

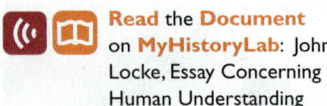 **Read** the **Document** on **MyHistoryLab**: John Locke, Essay Concerning Human Understanding

A series of empirical advances and wider theoretical generalizations extended the possibilities of science from the 1600s onward. New instruments such as the microscope and improved telescopes allowed gains in biology and astronomy. The Italian **Galileo Galilei** publicized Copernicus's discoveries while adding his own basic findings about the laws of gravity and planetary motion. Condemned by the Catholic Church for his innovations, Galileo proved the inadequacy of traditional ideas about the universe. He also showed the new pride in scientific achievement, writing modestly how he, "by marvelous discoveries and clear demonstrations, had enlarged a thousand times" the knowledge produced by "the wise men of bygone ages." Chemical research advanced understanding of the behavior of gasses. English physician **William Harvey** demonstrated the circular movement of the blood in animals, with the heart as the "central pumping station."

These advances in knowledge were accompanied by important statements about science and its impact. **Francis Bacon** urged the value of careful empirical research and predicted that scientific knowledge could advance steadily, producing improvements in technology as well. **René Descartes** established the importance of a skeptical review of all received wisdom, arguing that human reason could develop laws that would explain the fundamental workings of nature.

The capstone to the 17th-century Scientific Revolution came in 1687, when **Isaac Newton** published his *Principia Mathematica*. This work drew the various astronomical and physical observations and wider theories together in a neat framework of natural laws. Newton set forth the basic principles of all motion (for example, that a body in motion maintains uniform momentum unless affected by outside forces such as friction). Newton defined the forces of gravity in great mathematical detail and showed that the whole universe responded to these forces, which among other things explained the planetary orbits described by Kepler. Finally, Newton stated the basic scientific method in terms of a mixture of rational hypothesis and generalization and careful empirical observation and experiment. Here was a vision of a natural universe that could be captured in simple laws (although increasingly complex mathematics accompanied the findings). Here was a vision of a method of knowing that might do away with blind reliance on tradition or religious faith.

The Scientific Revolution was quickly popularized among educated westerners. Here was a key step in the cultural transformation of western Europe in the early modern period. New scientific institutes were set up, often with government aid, to advance research and disseminate the findings. Lectures and easy-to-read manuals publicized the latest advances and communicated the excitement that researchers shared in almost all parts of Europe. Beliefs in witchcraft began to decline and magistrates grew increasingly reluctant to entertain witchcraft accusations in court after about 1670. There were growing signs of a new belief that people could control and calculate their environment. Insurance companies sprang up to help guard against risk. Doctors increased their attacks on popular healers, promoting a more scientific diagnosis of illness. Newsletters, an innovation by the late 17th century, began to advertise "lost and found" items, for there was no point leaving this kind of problem to customary magicians, called "cunning men," who had poked around with presumably enchanted sticks.

By the 1680s writers affected by the new science, although not themselves scientists, began to attack traditional religious ideas such as miracles, for in the universe of the Scientific Revolution there was no room for disruption of nature's laws. Some intellectuals held out a new conception of God, called **Deism**, arguing that although there might be a divinity, its role was simply to set natural laws in motion. In England, **John Locke** argued that people could learn everything they needed to know through their senses and reason; faith was irrelevant. Christian beliefs in human sinfulness crumbled in the view of these intellectuals, for they saw human nature as basically good. Finally, scientific advances created wider assumptions about the possibility of human progress. If knowledge could advance through concerted human effort, why not progress in other domains? Even literary authorities joined this parade, and the idea that past styles set timeless standards of perfection came under growing criticism.

Science had never before been central to intellectual life. Science had played important roles in other civilizations, as in China, classical Greece, Central America, and Islam. Europe's science built in fact on continuing contacts with work in the Middle East. But while the West was not alone in developing crucial scientific ideas, it now became the leading center for scientific advance. Its key thinkers stood alone for some time in seeing science as the key to gaining and defining knowledge.

VISUALIZING THE PAST

Versailles

THIS PICTURE SHOWS LOUIS XIV'S GRAND 17th-century palace at Versailles. It displays the sheer opulence of this absolute monarchy, in what was Europe's richest and most populous and influential nation. It also shows the renewed hold of a classical style, seen to be most prestigious for public buildings. What else does it suggest?

Architecture is sometimes thought to be the most socially and historically revealing of all the arts because it depends most heavily on public support; it is harder for architects, particularly dealing with public buildings, to be as idiosyncratic as painters or poets.

QUESTIONS
- What kinds of intentions on the part of Louis and his advisors does this building represent?
- How can Versailles be interpreted as a statement of absolute monarchy?
- What would the palace represent to an ordinary French person? To an aristocrat?

View the **Closer Look** on MyHistoryLab: Versailles

The palace at Versailles.

POLITICAL CHANGE

18.4 To what extent did European states begin to catch up with characteristics of effective states in various Asian societies?

Political change from 1600 to 1750 was complicated, even as religious strife gradually calmed. A tradition of strong monarchy developed in France and elsewhere, greatly adding to the functions of the central government. But in Britain and Holland a different emphasis emerged, providing a strong parliamentary check on royal power. Both traditions proved significant in shaping Europe's political future. More effective central governments and better-trained bureaucrats helped Europe catch up to political forms that had been developed earlier in countries like China. At the same time, growing suggestions of what would come to be called the nation-state provided a new element in politics that would later spread to other parts of the world.

As feudalism declined in western Europe, new political forms gained ground. Both absolute and parliamentary monarchies emerged.

Absolute Monarchies

New political currents took shape along with the rise of science, and at times the two trends connected. The feudal monarchy—the balance between king and nobles—that had defined Western politics since the late postclassical period finally came undone in the 17th century. In most countries, after the passions of religious wars finally cooled, monarchs gained new powers, curtailing the tradition of noble pressure or revolt. At the same time, more ambitious military organization, in states that defined war as a central purpose, required more careful administration and improved tax collection.

The model for this new pattern was France, now the West's largest and most powerful nation. French kings steadily built up their power in the 17th century. They stopped convening the medieval parliament and passed laws as they saw fit, although some provincial councils remained strong. They blew up the castles of dissident nobles, another sign that gunpowder was undercutting the military basis of feudalism. They appointed a growing bureaucracy drawn from the merchants and lawyers. They sent

THINKING HISTORICALLY

Elites and Masses

WHAT CAUSED THE END OF WITCHCRAFT hysteria in the West by the later 17th century? Did wise rulers calm a frenzied populace or did ordinary people themselves change their minds? One explanation focuses on new efforts by elites, such as local magistrates, to discipline mass impulses. Authorities stopped believing in demonic disruptions of natural processes, and so forced an end to persecutions. But many ordinary people were also thinking in new ways. Without converting fully to a scientific outlook, they became open to new ideas about how to handle health problems, reducing their belief in magical remedies; they needed witches less. Potential "witches" may have become more cautious. Older women, threatened by growing community suspicion, learned to maintain a lower profile and to emphasize benign, grandmotherly qualities rather than seeking a more independent role. Without question, there was a decline both in witchcraft beliefs, once a key element in the Western mentality, and in the hysteria specifically characteristic of the 16th and 17th centuries. This decline reflected new ways of thinking about strangeness and disruption. It involved complex interactions between various segments of Western society: magistrates and villagers, scientists and priests, husbands and widows.

The transformation of Western society after 1450 raises fascinating questions about the role of elites—particularly powerful groups and creative individuals—versus the ordinary people in causing change. The growing importance of social history has called attention to ordinary people, as we have seen, but it has not answered all the questions about their actual role. This role varies by place and time, of course. Some social historians tend to see ordinary people as victims of change, pushed around by the power groups. Others tend to stress the positive historical role of ordinary people in partly shaping the context of their own lives and affecting the larger course of history.

It is easy to read the early modern transformation of western Europe as an operation created by elites, with the masses as passively watching or futilely protesting. Not only the Renaissance and Reformation but also the commercial revolution required decisive action by key leadership groups. Leading merchants spurred economic change, and they ultimately began to farm out manufacturing jobs. The resultant rise of dependent wage labor, which tore a growing minority of western Europeans away from property and so from economic control of their lives, illustrates the power disparities in Western society. Ordinary people knuckled under or protested, but they were reacting, not initiating.

The rise of science rivets our attention on the activities of extraordinarily creative individuals, such as Newton, and elite institutions, such as the scientific academies. Some historians have suggested that the rise of science opened a new gap between the ways educated upper classes and masses thought.

> *Some historians have suggested that the rise of science opened a new gap between the ways educated upper classes and masses thought.*

Yet the ordinary people of western Europe were not passive, nor did they simply protest change in the name of tradition. Widespread shifts came from repeated decisions by peasants and artisans, not just from those at the top. The steady technological improvements in manufacturing thus flowed upward from practicing artisans, not downward from formal scientists. The European-style family that had taken shape by the 16th century was an innovation by ordinary people long ignored by the elite. It encouraged new parent–child relations and new tensions between young adults and the old that might spur other innovations, including a willingness to settle distant colonies in search of property. The fact that young people often had to wait to marry until their property-owning fathers died could induce many to seek new lands or new economic methods. In other words, ordinary people changed their habits too, and these changes had wide impact.

QUESTIONS

- Did elites gain new power over the masses in early modern Western society?
- Are ordinary people more conservative by nature, more suspicious of change, than groups at the top?
- Can you describe at least two other historical cases in which it is important to determine whether change was imposed on ordinary people from above or whether ordinary people themselves produced important innovations?

---

direct representatives to the outlying provinces. They professionalized the army, giving more formal training to officers, providing uniforms and support, and creating military hospitals and pensions.

So great was the power of the monarch, in fact, that the French system became known as **absolute monarchy**. Its most glorious royal proponent, King **Louis XIV**, summed up its principles succinctly: "I am the state." Louis became a major patron of the arts, giving government a cultural role beyond any previous levels in the West. His academies not only encouraged science but also worked to standardize the French language. A sumptuous palace at Versailles was used to keep nobles busy with social functions so that they could not interfere with affairs of state.

Using the new bureaucratic structure, Louis and his ministers developed additional functions for the state. They reduced internal tariffs, which acted as barriers to trade, and created new, state-run manufacturing. The reigning economic theory, mercantilism, held that governments should promote the internal economy to improve tax revenues and to limit imports from other nations, lest money be lost to enemy states. Therefore, absolute monarchs such as Louis XIV set tariffs on imported goods, tried to encourage their merchant fleets, and sought colonies to provide raw materials and a guaranteed market for manufactured goods produced at home.

The basic structure of absolute monarchy developed in other states besides France (Map 18.2). Spain tried to imitate French principles in the 18th century, which resulted in efforts to tighten control over its Latin American colonies. However, the most important spread of absolute monarchy occurred in the central European states that were gaining in importance. A series of kings in Prussia, in eastern Germany, built a strong army and bureaucracy. They promoted economic activity and began to develop a state-sponsored school system. Habsburg kings in Austria–Hungary, although still officially rulers of the Holy Roman empire, concentrated increasingly on developing a stronger monarchy in the lands under their direct control. The power of these Habsburg rulers increased after they pushed back the last Turkish invasion threat late in the 17th century and then added the kingdom of Hungary to their domains.

Most absolute monarchs saw a strong military as a key political goal, and many hoped for territorial expansion. Louis XIV used his strong state as the basis for a series of wars from the 1680s onward. The wars yielded some new territory for France but finally attracted an opposing alliance system that blocked further advance. Prussian kings, although long cautious in exposing their proud military to the risk of major war, turned in the 18th century to a series of conflicts that won new territory.

Parliamentary Monarchies

Britain and the Netherlands, both growing commercial and colonial powers, stood apart from the trend toward absolute monarchy in the 17th century. They emphasized the role of the central state, but they also built parliamentary regimes in which the kings shared power with representatives selected by the nobility and upper urban classes. The English civil wars produced a final political settlement in 1688 and 1689 (the so-called **Glorious Revolution**) in which parliament won basic sovereignty over the king. The English parliament no longer depended on the king to convene, because regular sessions were scheduled. Its rights to approve taxation allowed it to monitor or initiate most major policies.

Furthermore, a growing body of political theory arose in the 17th century that built on these parliamentary ideas. John Locke and others argued that power came from the people, not from a divine right to royal rule. Monarchs should therefore be restrained by institutions that protected the public interest, including certain general rights to freedom and property. A right of revolution could legitimately oppose unjust rule.

Overall, western Europe developed important diversity in political forms, between absolute monarchy and a new kind of **parliamentary monarchy**. It maintained a characteristic tension between government growth and the idea that there should be some limits to state authority. This tension was expressed in new forms, but it recalled some principles that had originated in the Middle Ages.

The Nation-State

The absolute monarchies and the parliamentary monarchies shared important characteristics as nation-states. Unlike the great empires of many other civilizations, they ruled peoples who shared a common culture and language, some important minorities apart. They could appeal to a certain loyalty that linked cultural and political bonds. This was as true of England, where the idea of special rights of Englishmen helped feed the parliamentary movement, as it was of France. Not surprisingly, ordinary people in many nation-states, even though not directly represented in government, increasingly believed that government should act for their interests. Thus, Louis XIV faced recurrent popular riots based on the assumption that when bad harvests drove up food prices, the government was obligated to help people out.

In sum, nation-states developed a growing list of functions, particularly under the banner of mercantilism, whose principles were shared by monarchists and parliamentary leaders alike. They also promoted new political values and loyalties that were very different from the political traditions of other civilizations. They kept the West politically divided and often at war.

---

absolute monarchy Concept of government developed during rise of nation-states in western Europe during the 17th century; featured monarchs who passed laws without parliaments, appointed professionalized armies and bureaucracies, established state churches, imposed state economic policies.

Louis XIV (1638–1715) French monarch of the late 17th century who personified absolute monarchy.

Read the Document on MyHistoryLab: Jean Domat, On Social Order and Absolutist Monarchy

Glorious Revolution English overthrow of James II in 1688; resulted in affirmation of parliament as having basic sovereignty over the king.

parliamentary monarchy Originated in England and Holland, 17th century, with monarchs partially checked by significant legislative powers in parliaments.

THE WEST BY 1750

> **18.5** In what ways did the pace of change in Europe accelerate by the 18th century?

Key changes gained further ground in the 18th century. Most importantly, the Enlightenment expanded the range of intellectual innovation.

During the first half of the 18th century, several basic changes continued in western Europe. The impact of absolutism and the parliamentary monarchies persisted, although outright political innovation slowed. Commercial changes, however, began to have even wider results, with an important expansion of manufacturing; new agricultural developments added an important element. Europe's cultural transformation, at both elite and popular levels, continued as well, with growing implications for political and social life. The Enlightenment, building on the earlier scientific revolution, had particularly important results on Europe and, ultimately, other parts of the world.

Political Patterns

During much of the 18th century, English politics settled into a parliamentary routine in which key political groups competed for influence without major policy differences. Absolute monarchy in France changed little institutionally, but it became less effective. It could not force changes in the tax structure that would give it more solid financial footing because aristocrats refused to surrender their traditional exemptions.

Political developments were far livelier in central Europe. In Prussia, **Frederick the Great**, building on the military and bureaucratic organization of his predecessors, introduced greater freedom of religion while expanding the economic functions of the state. His government actively encouraged better agricultural methods; for example, it promoted use of the American potato as a staple crop. It also enacted laws promoting greater commercial coordination and greater equity; harsh traditional punishments were cut back. Rulers of this sort claimed to be enlightened despots, wielding great authority but for the good of society at large.

Enlightened or not, the policies of the major Western nation-states produced recurrent warfare. France and Britain squared off in the 1740s and again in the Seven Years War (1756–1763); their conflicts focused on battles for colonial empire. Austria and Prussia also fought, with Prussia gaining new land. Wars in the 18th century were not devastating, but they demonstrated the continued linkage between statecraft and war that was characteristic of the West.

Frederick the Great Prussian king of the 18th century; attempted to introduce Enlightenment reforms into Germany; built on military and bureaucratic foundations of his predecessors; introduced freedom of religion; increased state control of economy.

Enlightenment Thought and Popular Culture

In culture, the aftermath of the Scientific Revolution spilled over into a new movement known as the **Enlightenment**, centered particularly in France but with adherents throughout the Western world. Enlightenment thinkers continued to support scientific advance. Although there were no Newton-like breakthroughs, chemists gained new understanding of major elements, and biologists developed a vital new classification system for the natural species.

The Enlightenment also pioneered in applying scientific methods to the study of human society, sketching the modern social sciences. The basic idea was that rational laws could describe social as well as physical behavior and that knowledge could be used to improve policy. Thus, criminologists wrote that brutal punishments failed to deter crime, whereas a decent society would be able to rehabilitate criminals through education. Political theorists wrote about the importance of carefully planned constitutions and controls over privilege, although they disagreed about what political form was best. A new school of economists developed. In his classic book *Wealth of Nations*, Scottish philosopher **Adam Smith** set forth a number of principles of economic behavior. He argued that people act according to their self-interest but, through competition, promote general economic advance. Government should avoid regulation in favor of the operation of individual initiative and market forces. This was an important statement of economic policy and an illustration of the growing belief that general models of human behavior could be derived from rational thought.

Single individuals could sum up part of the Enlightenment's impressive range. **Denis Diderot** (1713–1784) was a multifaceted leader of the French Enlightenment, best known for his editorial work on the *Encyclopédie* that compiled scientific and social scientific knowledge. Trained initially by the Jesuits, Diderot also wrote widely on philosophy, mathematics, and the psychology of deaf-mutes and also tried his hand at literature. An active friend of other philosophers, Diderot also traveled to foreign

Enlightenment Intellectual movement centered in France during the 18th century; featured scientific advance, application of scientific methods to study of human society; belief that rational laws could describe social behavior.

Smith, Adam Established liberal economics (*Wealth of Nations*, 1776); argued that government should avoid regulation of economy in favor of the operation of market forces.

Diderot, Denis [duh-NEE DEE-duh-roh] (October 5, 1713–July 31, 1784) A French Enlightenment figure best known for his work on the first encyclopedia.

DOCUMENT

Controversies About Women

CHANGES IN FAMILY STRUCTURE AND SOME shifts in the economic roles of women, as well as ambivalent Protestant ideas about women that emphasized the family context but urged affection and respect between wives and husbands, touched off new gender tensions in Western society by the 17th century. Some of these tensions showed in witchcraft trials, so disproportionately directed against women. Other tensions showed in open debate about women's relationships to men; women not content with a docile wifeliness vied with new claims of virtue and prowess by some women. Although the debate was centered in the upper class of Protestant nations such as England, it may have had wider ramifications. Some of these ramifications, although quieter during the 18th century, burst forth again in arguments about inequality and family confinement in the 19th century, when a more durable feminist movement took shape in the West. In the selections here, the antiwoman position is set forth in a 1615 pamphlet by Joseph Swetham; the favorable view implicitly urging new rights is in a 1640 pamphlet pseudonymously authored by "Mary Tattle-Well and Ioane Hit-Him-Home, spinsters."

SWETHAM'S "ARRAIGNMENT OF WOMEN"

Men, I say, may live without women, but women cannot live without men: for Venus, whose beauty was excellent fair, yet when she needed man's help, She took Vulcan, a clubfooted Smith. . . .

For women have a thousand ways to entice thee and ten thousand ways to deceive thee and all such fools as are suitors unto them: some they keep in hand with promises, and some they feed with flattery, and some they delay with dalliances, and some they please with kisses. They lay out the folds of their hair to entangle men into their love; betwixt their breasts in the vale of destruction; and in their beds there is hell, sorrow and repentance. Eagles eat not men till they are dead, but women devour them alive. . . .

It is said of men that they have that one fault, but of women it is said that they have two faults: that is to say, they can neither say well nor do well. There is a saying that goeth thus: that things far fetched and dear bought are of us most dearly beloved. The like may be said of women; although many of them are not far fetched, yet they are dear bought, yea and so dear that many a man curseth his hard pennyworths and bans his own heart. For the pleasure of the fairest woman in the world lasteth but a honeymoon; that is, while a man hath glutted his affections and reaped the first fruit, his pleasure being past, sorrow and repentance remaineth still with him.*

*Joseph Swetnam, *The Araignment of Lewde, Idle, Froward, and Unconstant Women* (London, 1615)

TATTLE-WELL AND HIT-HIM-HOME'S "WOMEN'S SHARP REVENGE"

But it hath been the policy of all parents, even from the beginning, to curb us of that benefit by striving to keep us under and to make us men's mere Vassals even unto all posterity.

How else comes it to pass that when a Father hath a numerous issue of Sons and Daughters, the sons forsooth they must be first put to the Grammar school, and after perchance sent to the University, and trained up in the Liberal Arts and Sciences, and there (if they prove not Blockheads) they may in time be book-learned? . . .

When we, whom they style by the name of weaker Vessels, though of a more delicate, fine, soft, and more pliant flesh therefore of a temper most capable of the best Impression, have not that generous and liberal Education, lest we should be made able to vindicate our own injuries, we are set only to the Needle, to prick our fingers, or else to the Wheel to spin a fair thread for our own undoing, or perchance to some more dirty and debased drudgery. If we be taught to read, they then confine us within the compass of our Mother Tongue, and that limit we are not suffered to pass; or if (which sometimes happeneth) we be brought up to Music, to singing, and to dancing, it is not for any benefit that thereby we can engross unto ourselves, but for their own particular ends, the better to please and content their licentious appetites when we come to our maturity and ripeness. And thus if we be weak by Nature, they strive to make us more weak by our Nurture; and if in degree of place low, they strive by their policy to keep us more under.

Now to show we are no such despised matter as you would seem to make us, come to our first Creation, when man was made of the mere dust of the earth. The woman had her being from the best part of his body, the Rib next to his heart, which difference even in our complexions may be easily decided. Man is of a dull, earthy, and melancholy aspect, having shallows in his face and a very forest upon his Chin, when our soft and smooth Cheeks are a true representation of a delectable garden of intermixed Roses and Lilies. . . . Man might consider that women were not created to be their slaves or vassals; for as they had not their Original out of his head (thereby to command him), so it was not out of his foot to be trod upon, but in a medium out of his side to be his fellow feeler, his equal, and companion. . . .

Thus have I truly and impartially proved that for Chastity, Charity, Constancy, Magnanimity, Valor, Wisdom, Piety, or any Grace or Virtue whatsoever, women have always been more than equal with men, and that for Luxury, Surquidant obscenity, profanity, Ebriety, Impiety, and all that may be called bad we do come far short of them.

QUESTIONS

- What conditions prompted a more vigorous public debate about gender in the 17th century?
- How did the pro-woman argument compare with more modern views about women?
- Did the new arguments about women's conditions suggest that these conditions were improving?

courts as advisor and visiting intellectual. He visited Catherine the Great of Russia in 1773–1774, for example, to thank her for generous patronage.

More generally still, the Enlightenment produced a set of basic principles about human affairs: Human beings are good, at least improvable, and they can be educated to be better; reason is the key to truth, and religions that rely on blind faith or refuse to tolerate diversity are wrong. Enlightenment thinkers attacked the Catholic Church with particular vigor, because it seemed to support older superstitions while wielding political power. Progress was possible, even inevitable, if people could be set free. Society's goals should center on improving material and social life.

Although it was not typical of the Enlightenment's main thrust, a few thinkers applied these general principles to other areas. A handful of socialists argued that economic equality and the abolition of private property must become important goals. A few feminist thinkers, such as **Mary Wollstonecraft** (Figure 18.4) in England, argued—against the general male-centered views of most Enlightenment thinkers—that new political rights and freedoms should extend to women. Several journals written by women for women made their first appearance during this extraordinary cultural period. Madame de Beaumere took over the direction of the French *Journal des Dames* from a man, and in Germany, Marianne Ehrmann used her journal to suggest that men might be partly to blame for women's lowly position.

Wollstonecraft, Mary (1759–1797) Enlightenment feminist thinker in England; argued that new political rights should extend to women.

The popularization of new ideas encouraged further changes in the habits and beliefs of many ordinary people. Reading clubs and coffeehouses allowed many urban artisans and businessmen to discuss the latest reform ideas. Leading writers and compilations of scientific and philosophical findings, such as the *Encyclopaedia Britannica*, won a wide audience and, for a few people, a substantial fortune from the sale of books.

Other changes in popular outlook paralleled the new intellectual currents, although they had deeper sources than philosophy alone. Attitudes toward children began to shift in many social groups. Older methods of physical discipline were criticized in favor of more restrained behavior that would respect the goodness and innocence of children. Swaddling—wrapping infants in cloth so they could not move or harm themselves—began to decline as parents became interested in freer movement and greater interaction for young children. Among wealthy families, educational toys and books for children reflected the idea that childhood should be a stage for learning and growth.

mass consumerism The spread of deep interest in acquiring material goods and services below elite levels, along with a growing economic capacity to afford some of these goods. While hints of mass consumerism can be found in several pre-modern societies, it developed most clearly beginning in Western Europe from the 18th century onward.

Family life generally was changed by a growing sense that old hierarchies should be rethought and revised toward greater equality in the treatment of women and children in the home. Love between family members gained new respect, and an emotional bond in marriage became more widely sought. Change affected older children as well: Parents grew more reluctant to force a match on a son or daughter if the emotional vibrations were not right. Here was a link not only with Enlightenment ideas of proper family relations but with novels such as Richardson's *Pamela* that poured out a sentimental view of life.

Cultural changes during the 18th century were complex. They included continued religious vitality, as new groups like Methodists helped stimulate piety. Three points, however, stand out. First, mainly through the Enlightenment, many popular attitudes, as well as purely intellectual interests, were changing. Beliefs in magic, for example, began to decline. Second, in establishing a culture favorable to material progress, the Enlightenment helped set up a climate for further change in the West. And third, some Enlightenment ideas, like that notion that all people shared a fundamental rationality and human worth, had implications that spilled beyond Europe. Already in 1750, for example, new agitation began to develop against the institution of slavery, in the name of basic rights.

Ongoing Change in Commerce and Manufacturing

Ongoing economic change paralleled changes in popular culture and intellectual life. Commerce continued to spread. Ordinary Westerners began to buy processed products, such as refined sugar and coffee or tea obtained from Indonesia and the West Indies, for daily use. This was a sign of the growing importance of Europe's new colonies for ordinary life and of the beginnings of **mass consumerism** in Western society. The growing popularity of cotton textiles spread more widely, giving even relatively poor people the chance to express a sense of style. Theft of clothing increased in the 18th century, a clear indication of new consumer priorities. Another sign of change was the growing use of paid professional

FIGURE 18.4 Portrait of feminist Mary Wollstonecraft.

entertainment as part of popular leisure, even in rural festivals. Circuses, first introduced in France in the 1670s, began to redefine leisure to include spectatorship and a taste for the bizarre.

Agriculture began to change. Until the late 17th century, western Europe had continued to rely largely on the methods and techniques characteristic of the Middle Ages—a severe economic constraint in an agricultural society. The three-field system still meant that a full third of all farmland was left unplanted each year to restore fertility. First in the Netherlands and then elsewhere, new procedures for draining swamps added available land. Reformers touted nitrogen-fixing crops to reduce the need to leave land idle. Stockbreeding improved, and new techniques such as seed-drills and the use of scythes instead of sickles for harvesting increased productivity. Some changes spread particularly fast on large estates, but other changes affected ordinary peasants as well. Particularly vital in this category was the spread of the potato from the late 17th century onward.

A New World crop, the potato had long been shunned because it was not mentioned in the Bible and was held to be the cause of plagues. Enlightened government leaders, and the peasants' desire to win greater economic security and better nutrition, led to widespread use of this crop. In sum, the West improved its food supply and agricultural efficiency, leaving more labor available for other pursuits.

These changes, along with the steady growth of colonial trade and internal commerce, spurred increased manufacturing. Capitalism—the investment of funds in hopes of larger profits—also spread from big trading ventures to the production of goods. The 18th century witnessed a rapid spread of household production of textiles and metal products, mostly by rural workers who alternated manufacturing with some agriculture. Here was a key use of labor that was no longer needed for food. Hundreds of thousands of people were drawn into this domestic system, in which capitalist merchants distributed supplies and orders and workers ran the production process for pay. Although manufacturing tools were still operated by hand, the spread of domestic manufacturing spurred important technological innovations designed to improve efficiency. In 1733, John Kay in England introduced the flying shuttle, which permitted automatic crossing of threads on looms; with this, an individual weaver could do the work of two. Improvements in spinning and the mechanized printing of cotton cloth soon followed as the Western economy began to move toward a full-fledged Industrial Revolution (see Chapter 24).

Human changes accompanied and sometimes preceded technology. Around 1700, most manufacturers who made wool cloth in northern England were artisans, doing part of the work themselves. By 1720, a number of loom owners were becoming outright manufacturers with new ideas and behaviors. How were manufacturers different? They spent their time organizing production and sales rather than doing their own work. They moved work out of their homes. They stopped drinking beer with their workers. And they saw their workers as market commodities, to be treated as the conditions of trade demanded. In 1736, one such manufacturer coolly wrote that because of slumping sales, "I have turned off [dismissed] a great many of my makers, and keep turning more off weekly."

Finally, agricultural changes, commercialism, and manufacturing combined, particularly after about 1730, to produce a rapidly growing population in the West. With better food supplies, more people survived, particularly with the aid of the potato. Furthermore, new manufacturing jobs helped landless people support themselves, promoting earlier marriage and sexual relationships. Population growth, in turn, promoted further economic change, heightening competition and producing a more manipulable labor force. The West's great population revolution, which continued into the 19th century, both caused and reflected the civilization's dynamism, although it also produced great strain and confusion.

Innovation and Instability

By the 18th century, the various strands of change were increasingly intertwined in Western civilization. Stronger governments promoted agricultural improvements, which helped prod population growth. Changes in popular beliefs were fed by new economic structures; both encouraged a reevaluation of the family and the roles of children. New beliefs also raised new political challenges. Enlightenment ideas about liberty and fundamental human equality could be directed against existing regimes. New family practices might have political implications as well. Children, raised with less adult restraint and encouraged to value their individual worth through parental love and careful education, might see traditional political limitations in new ways.

There was no perfect fit, no inevitable match, in the three strands of change that had been transforming the West for two centuries or more: the commercial, the cultural, and the political. However, by 1750 all were in place. The combination had already produced an unusual version of an agricultural civilization, and it promised more upheaval in the future.

proto-globalization Proto-globalization is a term sometimes used to describe the increase of global contacts from the 16th century onward, particularly in trade, while also distinguishing the patterns from the more intense exchanges characteristic of outright globalization.

Global Connections and Critical Themes

EUROPE AND THE WORLD

In 1450, Europeans were convinced that their Christianity made them superior to other people. But they also understood that many societies were impressive in terms of cities and wealth and the strength of their governments. As Europe changed and prospered, participating strongly in the process of **protoglobalization**, its outlook toward the world changed as well. We saw in the previous chapter how Europeans began to use technology as a measure of society, arguing that other societies that were less interested in technological change were inferior. By the 18th century, criticisms of the superstitions of other people began to surface among Europeans proud of their science and rationalism.

The wider world could still provide a sense of wonder, but increasingly this was focused on natural phenomena and the strange animals being imported to European zoos. The Enlightenment generated the idea of a "noble savage"—a person uncorrupted by advanced civilization and urban ways. But this was largely a fiction designed to comment on Europe itself, not a source of real admiration for other peoples. Increasingly, European power and the rapid changes within Western civilization led to a sense that many other societies were backward, perhaps not even civilized. The idea had powerful impact not only on European attitudes but also on the ways other societies perceived themselves and reacted.

Further Readings

For an overview of developments in Western society during this period, with extensive bibliographies, see Sheldon Watts, *A Social History of Western Europe, 1450–1720* (1984); Michael Anderson, *Approaches to the West European Family* (1980); Peter N. Stearns, *Life and Society in the West: The Modern Centuries* (1988); and J. L. Roark, M. P. Johnson, P. C. Cohen, *The American Promise* (2008). Charles Tilly, *Big Structures, Large Processes, Huge Comparisons* (1985), offers an analytical framework based on major change; see also Tilly's edited volume, *The Formation of National States in Western Europe* (1975).

On more specific developments and periods, see John Man, *Gutenberg, How One Man Remade the World with Words* (2002); J. R. Hale, *The Civilization of Europe in the Renaissance* (1994); J. H. Plumb, *The Italian Renaissance* (1986); F. H. New, *The Renaissance and Reformation: A Short History* (1977); O. Chadwick, *The Reformation* (1983); Richard A. Muller, *After Calvin: Studies in the Development of a Theological Tradition* (2003); and Steven Ozment, *Protestants: The Birth of a Revolution* (1992), are fine introductions to early changes. See also John W. O'Malley, *Trent and All That: Renaming Catholicism in the Early Modern Era* (2000); H. Baron, *The Crisis of the Early Italian Renaissance* (1996), examines the place of civic life in Italian humanism. A. Vickery, *The Gentleman's Daughter: Women's Lives in Georgian England* (1998) surveys the growth or retreat of opportunities for women over time.

Later changes are sketched in Thomas Munck, *Seventeenth Century Europe: 1598–1700* (1990); C. L. Johnson, *Cultural Hierarchy in 16th-century Europe* (2011); and Jeremy Black, *Eighteenth Century Europe: 1700–1789* (1990). On England in the civil war period, see Christopher Hill, *A Nation of Change and Novelty* (1990). See also Julian Swann, *Provincial Power and Absolute Monarchy: The Estates General of Burgundy, 1661–1790* (2006). On key aspects of Enlightenment, see Darrin McMahon, *Happiness: A History* (2006); and Peter N. Stearns, *Human Rights in World History* (2012).

Key aspects of social change in this period can be approached through Gary S. De Krey, *Restoration and Revolution in Britain: A Political History of the Era of Charles II and the Glorious Revolution* (2007); Peter Burke, *Popular Culture in Early Modern Europe* (1978); Robin Biggs, *Communities of Belief: Cultural and Social Tensions in Early Modern France* (1989); Keith Thomas, *Religion and the Decline of Magic* (1971); Lawrence Stone, *The Family, Sex and Marriage in England 1500–1800* (1977); and James Sharpe, *Instruments of Darkness: Witchcraft in Early Modern England* (1997). On popular protest, see Charles Tilly, *The Contentious French* (1986); and H. A. F. Kamen, *The Iron Century: Social Change in Europe 1550–1660* (1971).

On science, Matthew L. Jones, *The Good Life in the Scientific Revolution: Descartes, Pascal, Leibniz, and the Cultivation of Virtue* (2006); John Marshall, *John Locke, Toleration and Early Enlightenment Culture: Religious Intolerance and Arguments for Religious Toleration in Early Modern and Early Enlightenment Europe* (2006); and Michael S. Reidy, Gary Kroll, and Erik M. Conway, *Exploration and Science: Social Impact and Interaction* (2007). See also N. J. G. Pounds, *A historical geography of Europe, 1500–1840* (2009).

On MyHistoryLab

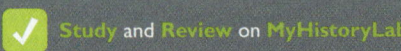
Study and Review on MyHistoryLab

Critical Thinking Questions

1. How did the Scientific Revolution compare with developments in science in other societies, during but also before the Early Modern period?
2. Amid many changes, what were two key continuities in European society during the Early Modern period?
3. What factors caused the Enlightenment in Europe?
4. Compare the institutions and assumptions of absolute versus parliamentary monarchy. Were there any similarities?

19

Early Latin America

Listen to Chapter 19 on MyHistoryLab

In September 1589 Captain Mancio Serra de Leguizamon lay dying in his bed in Cuzco, the ancient capital of the Incas in the highlands of Peru. His mind was still clear, but his body was failing, and he knew his time was approaching. He needed to set his affairs in order with his heirs, his king, and with God. He called a priest and a notary to his bedside to draw up his last will and testament.

Born in Castile like many young Spanish men, he had been attracted to the New World by its fabled wealth and opportunities for advancement. When he was 16, he sailed for the New World in search of adventure. Sometime in 1532 he joined the 168 men under the Spanish conqueror Francisco Pizarro, who were embarked on the conquest of the Inca empire. Mancio Serra claimed in his will that he was the first Spaniard to enter Cuzco when the Spaniards laid siege to the

LEARNING OBJECTIVES

19.1 What were the motivations of the Spanish conquest of the New World and how did it change the way in which Europeans viewed the world? p. 427

19.2 How were indigenous societies transformed by the conquest? p. 435

19.3 In the long run, did the mining of silver and gold stimulate the economic growth of Latin America or hold it back? p. 436

19.4 Why did the Portuguese wait so long to develop Brazil, and why did they turn to slavery to do so? p. 441

19.5 What impact did the Columbian Exchange have on the formation of New World societies? p. 443

19.6 Did reforms in the 18th century save these empires or provoke their fall? p. 446

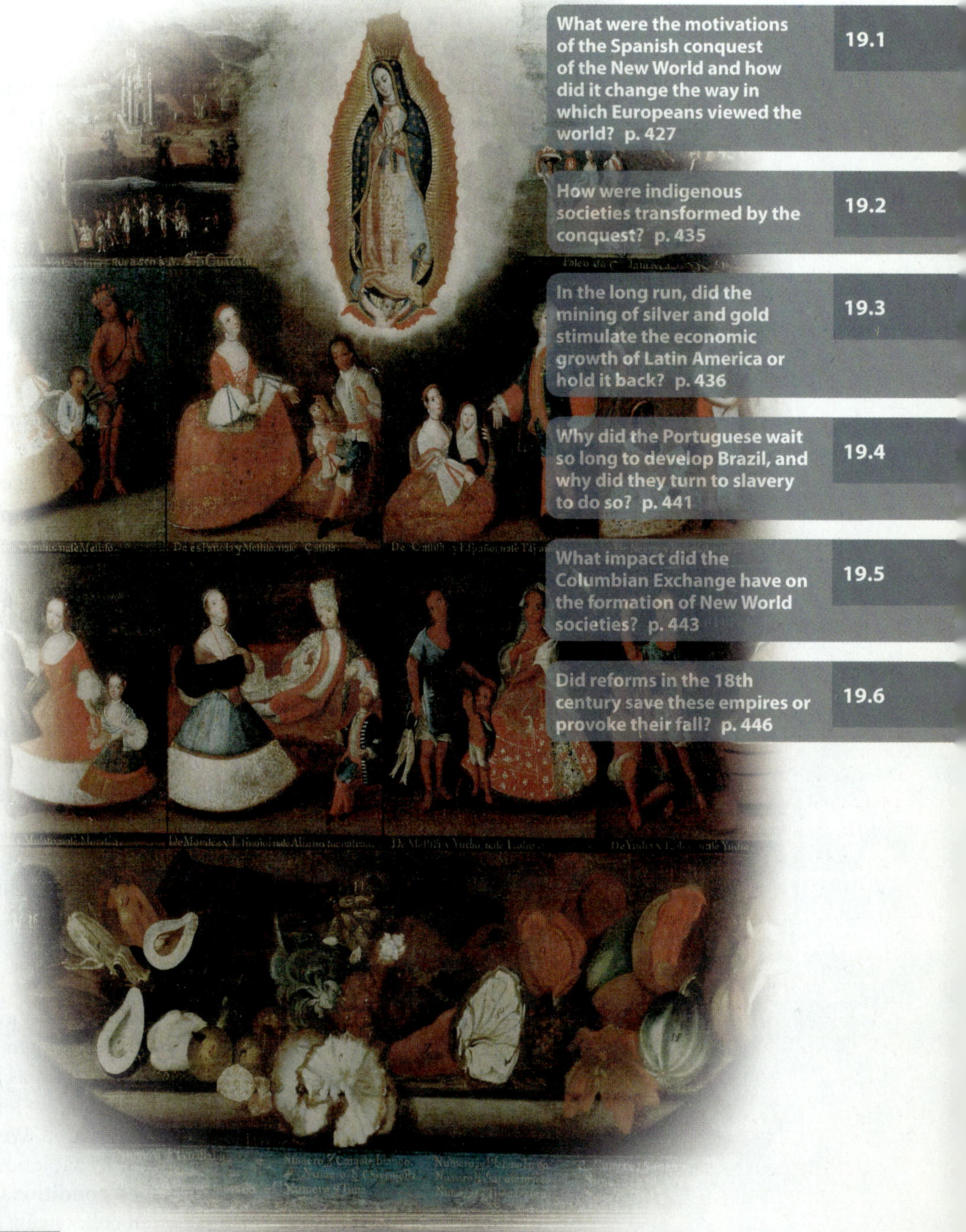

FIGURE **19.1** By the end of the 17th century, a society that fused Hispanic culture and indigenous elements had emerged in Spanish America.

Watch the Video Series on MyHistoryLab

Learn about some key topics related to this chapter with the *MyHistoryLab Video Series: Key Topics in World History*

city in 1533. Legend has it that, in the looting that followed, he seized a great golden disk representing the sun that had hung on the walls of the principal temple of the sun in Cuzco. But that very night he fell to drinking and gambling and lost the treasure. He never got over his love of gambling.

But all was not lost with the disk of gold: For his efforts, Mancio received grants of Indian laborers and a site in the city where, using an Inca stonework foundation, he built a fine home. There were more expeditions, civil wars, an Indian mistress, a marriage to an Inca noblewoman and, later, to a Spanish woman (Figure 19.1). There were numerous children, some legitimate and some not. Mancio Serra became a respected leader in Peru, for a while mayor of Cuzco, a man of substance with many servants and slaves. But unlike most of the Spaniards involved in the conquest, on his deathbed, Mancio Serra, overcome by guilt, had second thoughts about the justice of what he had done. Before assigning his property to his heirs, calling himself the last of the conquerors still alive and so the last who could give eyewitness testimony, in his will he addressed the king of Spain:

> We found these realms in such order that there was not a thief, nor a vicious man, nor an adulteress, nor were there prostitutes, nor were there immoral people, each being content and honest in their labor. And that their lands, forests, mines, pastures and dwellings and produce were regulated in such a manner that each person possessed his own property without any other seizing or occupying it. . . . I wish Your Catholic Majesty to understand the motive that moves me to make this statement is the peace of my conscience and because of the guilt I share. For we have destroyed by our evil behavior such a government as was enjoyed by these natives.
>
> (Source: Stuart Sterling, *The Last Conquistador: Mansio Sierra de Leguizamón and the conquest of the Incas* (Phoenix Mill, U.K: Sutton Publishing. 1999)

Perhaps his conscience made him romanticize Inca society, but Mancio Serra went on to say that the actions and abuses of the Spaniards had ruined the inhabitants, introduced bad habits, and reduced the ancient nobility to poverty. In an earlier will he had declared that everything produced from his grant of indigenous workers, including his landed estate, should belong to them, "since it was once their own." He had seen and lived it all, it burdened his soul and his conscience, and he believed it was a matter for the royal conscience as well. "I inform Your Majesty that there is no more I can do to alleviate these injustices other than by my words, in which I beg God to pardon me." ■

Spain and Portugal created empires in the Americas by conquest and settlement. These lands, which became Latin America, were immediately drawn into a new world economy, providing silver, gold, new crops, and other goods. They also served as a model and as an attraction for other Europeans who eventually also created an Atlantic system based on plantations, coerced labor, and the exploitation of mineral wealth that linked Europe, West Africa, and the Americas in terms of peoples, cultures, and economies, more often by violence than by persuasion. The emerging hierarchy of world economic relationships shaped conditions in this new civilization for several centuries. The peoples of Spain and Portugal, often collectively called Iberians because all came from the Iberian Peninsula in Europe, mixed with Native Americans and adopted aspects of their culture while

1450 c.e.	1500 c.e.	1600 c.e.	1750 c.e.
1492 Fall of Granada, last Muslim kingdom in Spain; expulsion of the Jews; Columbus makes landfall in the Caribbean **1493** Columbus's second expedition; beginnings of settlement in the Indies **1493–1520** Exploration and settlement in the Caribbean **1494** Treaty of Tordesillas	**1500** Cabral lands in Brazil **1519–1524** Cortés leads conquest of Mexico **1533** Cuzco, Peru, falls to Francisco Pizarro **1540–1542** Coronado explores area that is now the southwestern United States **1541** Santiago, Chile, founded **1549** Royal government established in Brazil **1580–1640** Spain and Portugal united under same rulers	**1630–1654** Dutch capture northeastern Brazil **1654** English take Jamaica **1695** Gold discovered in Brazil **1702–1713** War of the Spanish succession; Bourbon dynasty rules Spain	**1755–1776** Marquis of Pombal, prime minister of Portugal **1759** Jesuits expelled from Brazil **1756–1763** Seven Years War **1759–1788** Carlos III rules Spain; Bourbon reforms **1763** Brazilian capital moved to Rio de Janeiro **1767** Jesuits expelled from Spanish America **1781** Comunero revolt in New Granada; Tupac Amaru rebellion in Peru **1788** Conspiracy for independence in Minas Gerais, Brazil

introducing the religion, technologies, and many aspects of their culture to the indigenous peoples. Both groups were also influenced by the cultures of the slaves imported from Africa. The formative period for Latin American civilization extended from initial contacts in the 1490s through the 18th century, when colonial structures began to decline. New societies, created by the intrusion of the Iberians, especially the Castilians and the Portuguese, and by the incorporation or destruction of Native American cultures, arose throughout the American continents. Much of what the Iberians did in the Americas followed the patterns and examples of their European traditions. The Native Americans who survived, although they were battered and profoundly transformed, showed a vitality and resiliency that shaped later societies in many ways. What resulted drew on European and Native American precedents, but it was something new: the world's latest addition to the list of distinctive civilizations.

SPANIARDS AND PORTUGUESE: FROM RECONQUEST TO CONQUEST

19.1 What were the motivations of the Spanish conquest of the New World and how did it change the way in which Europeans viewed the world?

The peoples who inhabited the Iberian Peninsula had long lived at the frontier of Mediterranean Europe. During the Middle Ages their lands were a cultural frontier between Christianity and Islam. Conflicts created a strong tradition of military conquest and rule over peoples of other beliefs and customs. A number of Christian kingdoms emerged, such as Portugal on the Atlantic coast, Aragon in eastern Spain, and in the center of the peninsula, Castile, the largest of all. By the mid-15th century, the rulers **Ferdinand of Aragon** and his wife **Isabella of Castile** carried out a program of unification that sought to eliminate the religious and eventually the ethnic divisions in their kingdoms. With the fall in 1492 of Granada, the last Muslim kingdom, the cross triumphed throughout the peninsula. Moved by political savvy and religious fervor, Isabella ordered the Jews of her realm to convert or leave the country. As many as 200,000 people may have left, severely disrupting some aspects of the Castilian economy. It was also in 1492, with the Granada war at an end and religious unification established, that Isabella and Ferdinand were willing to support the project of a Genoese mariner named Christopher Columbus, who hoped to reach the East Indies by sailing westward around the globe.

> The Spaniards and Portuguese came from societies long in contact with peoples of other faiths and cultures in which warfare and conquest were well-established activities. American realities and the resistance of indigenous peoples modified these traditions, but by the 1570s, much of the Americas had been brought under Iberian control.

Ferdinand of Aragon (r. 1479–1516) Along with Isabella of Castile, monarch of largest Christian kingdoms in Iberia; marriage to Isabella created united Spain; responsible for reconquest of Granada, initiation of exploration of New World.

Isabella of Castile (1451–1504) Along with Ferdinand of Aragon, monarch of largest Christian kingdoms in Iberia; marriage to Ferdinand created united Spain; responsible for reconquest of Granada, initiation of exploration of New World.

 Read the Document on MyHistoryLab: Privileges and Prerogatives Granted by Their Catholic Majesties to Christopher Columbus: 1492

Caribbean First area of Spanish exploration and settlement; served as experimental region for nature of Spanish colonial experience; encomienda system of colonial management initiated here.

Hispaniola First island in Caribbean settled by Spaniards; settlement founded by Columbus on second voyage to New World; Spanish base of operations for further discoveries in New World.

encomienda Grant of Indian laborers made to Spanish conquerors and settlers in Mesoamerica and South America; basis for earliest forms of coerced labor in Spanish colonies.

encomendero [AYn kO mAYn dAU rO] The holder of a grant of Indians who were required to pay a tribute or provide labor. The encomendero was responsible for their integration into the church.

Iberian Society and Tradition

Like many Mediterranean peoples, the Spanish and Portuguese were heavily urban, with many peasants living in small towns and villages. That pattern was also established in America, where Europeans lived in cities and towns surrounded by a rural native population. Many commoners who came to America as conquerors sought to recreate themselves as a new nobility, with native peoples as their serfs. The patriarchal family was readily adapted to Latin America, where large estates and grants of American Indian laborers provided the framework for relations based on economic dominance. The Iberian peninsula had maintained a tradition of holding slaves—part of its experience as an ethnic frontier—in contrast to most of medieval Europe, and African slaves had been imported from the trans-Sahara trade. The extension of slavery to America built on this tradition.

The political centralization of both Portugal and Castile depended on a professional bureaucracy, usually made up of men trained as lawyers and judges. This system is worthy of comparison with the systems in China and other great empires. Religion and the church served as the other pillar of Iberian politics; close links between church and state resulted from the reconquest of the Iberian Peninsula from the Muslims, and these links, including royal nomination of church officials, were also extended to the New World.

Spanish and particularly Portuguese merchants also shaped traditions that became relevant in the American colonies. Portugal had been moving down the African coast since 1415, establishing trading posts rather than outright colonies. In the Atlantic islands, however, more extensive estates were established, leading to a slave trade with Africa and a highly commercial agricultural system based on sugar. Brazil would extend this pattern, starting out as a trade factory but then shifting, as in the Atlantic islands, to plantation agriculture.

The Chronology of Conquest

The Spanish and Portuguese conquest and colonization of the Americas falls roughly into three periods during the early modern centuries. First came an era of conquest from 1492 to about 1570 (Map 19.1), during which the main lines of administration and economy were set out. The second phase was one of consolidation and maturity from 1570 to about 1700 in which the colonial institutions and societies took their definite form. Finally, during the 18th century, a period of reform and reorganization in both Spanish America and Portuguese Brazil (Map 19.2) intensified the colonial relationship and planted the seeds of dissatisfaction and revolt.

The period from 1492 to about 1570 witnessed a remarkable spurt of human destruction and creation. During roughly a century, vast areas of two continents and millions of people were brought under European control. Immigration, commerce, and exploitation of native populations linked these areas to an emerging Atlantic economy. These processes were accompanied and made possible by the conquest and destruction of many American Indian societies and the transformation of others, as well as by the introduction in some places of African slaves. Mexico and Peru, with their large sedentary populations and mineral resources, attracted the Spaniards and became the focus of immigration and institution building. Other conquests radiated outward from the Peruvian and Mexican centers.

The Caribbean Crucible

The **Caribbean** experience served Spain as a model for its actions elsewhere in the Americas. After Columbus's first trans-Atlantic voyage in 1492, a return expedition in the next year established a colony on the island of Santo Domingo, or **Hispaniola** (Map 19.1).

In the Caribbean, the agricultural Taino people of the islands provided enough surplus labor to make their distribution to individual Spaniards feasible, and thus began what would become the encomienda, or grant of indigenous people to individual Spaniards in a kind of serfdom. The holder of an **encomienda**, an **encomendero**, was able to use the people as workers or to tax them. Gold hunting, slaving, and European diseases rapidly depopulated the islands, and within two decades little was left there to hold Spanish attention. The Spaniards occupied the larger islands like Cuba, Hispaniola, and Puerto Rico but did not settle the islands of the lesser Antilles. A few strongly fortified ports on the larger islands, such as Havana, San Juan, and Santo Domingo, guarded Spain's commercial lifeline, but on the whole the Caribbean became a colonial backwater for the next two centuries, until

428 PART IV The Early Modern Period, 1450–1750: The World Shrinks

📖 **Read the Document** on **MyHistoryLab**: Smallpox epidemic in Mexico, 1520, from Bernardino de Sahagún, Florentine Codex: General History of the Things of New Spain, 1585

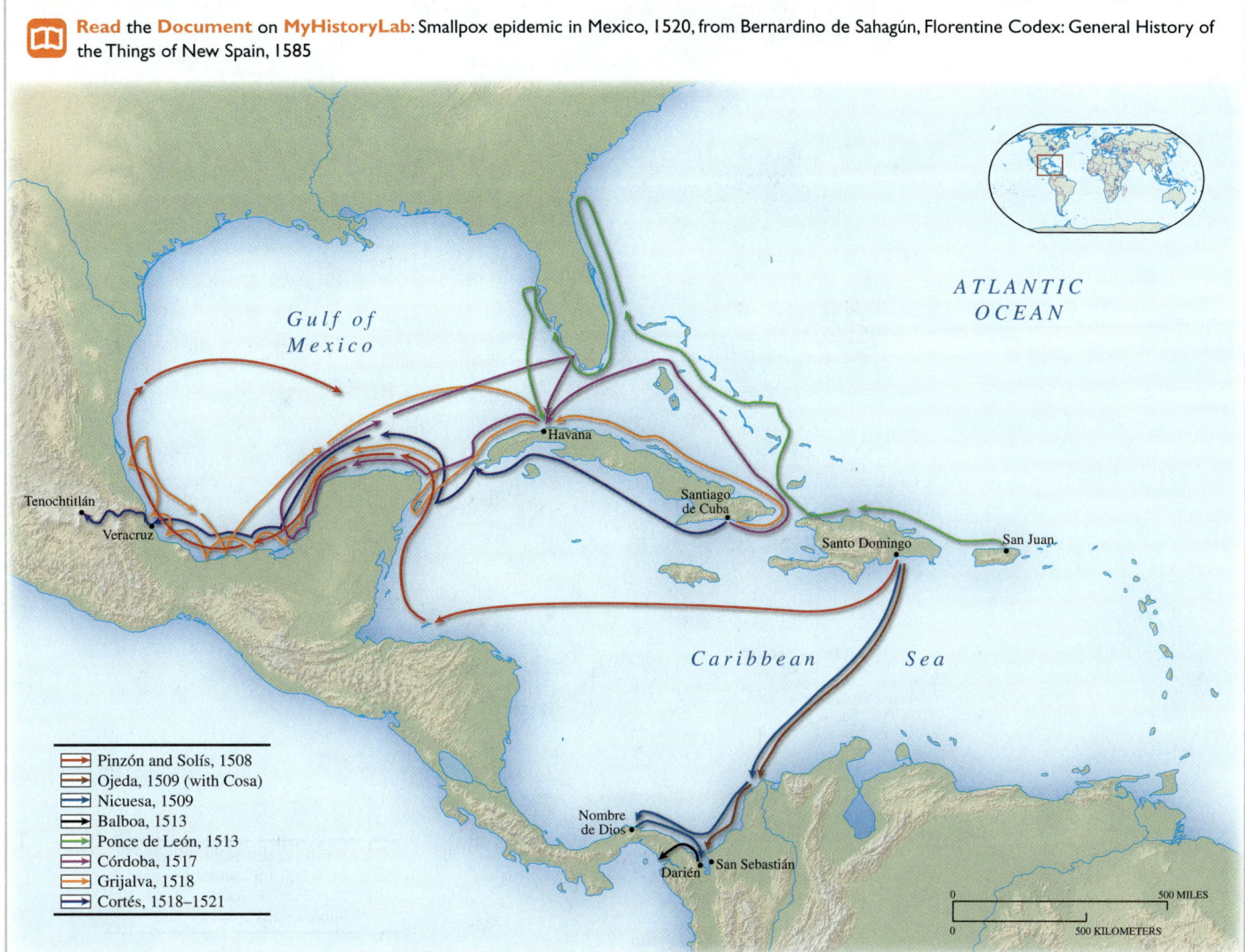

MAP 19.1 Major Spanish Expeditions of Conquest in and from the Caribbean Region The major islands and surrounding mainland coasts were explored and conquered between 1493 and c.1570. The Caribbean outposts were also the staging areas for most expeditions into the American continents, few expeditions sailed directly from Spain.

sugar and slaves became the basis of its resurgence. During the 17th century, the English, French, and Dutch began to settle the smaller islands and to compete with Spain by creating their own plantation colonies.

In the 40 years between the first voyage of Columbus and the conquest of Mexico, the Caribbean served as a testing ground. It was here that the Columbian Exchange (see Chapter 17) of peoples, crops, domesticated animals, diseases, and cultures began in earnest. The Spaniards established Iberian-style cities but had to adapt them to American realities. Hurricanes and the native peoples' resistance caused many towns to be moved or abandoned, but the New World also provided opportunities to implant new ideas and forms. Unlike cities in Europe, Spanish American cities usually were laid out according to a grid plan or checkerboard form, with the town hall, major church, and governor's palace in the central plaza (Figure 19.2). Spaniards applied Roman models and rational town planning ideas to the new situation. Conquest came to imply settlement.

To rule, Spain created administrative institutions: the governorship, the treasury office, and the royal court of appeals staffed by professional magistrates. Spanish legalism was part of the institutional transfer. Notaries accompanied new expeditions, and a body of laws was developed, based on those of

MAP 19.2 **Colonial Brazil** The Portuguese colony was mostly limited to the coast where sugar plantations thrived until the 18th century when gold discoveries attracted settlers and prospectors to the interior. The vast Amazon region was sparsely settled, mostly along the major rivers.

Castile and augmented by American experience. The church, represented at first by individual priests and then by missionaries such as the Dominicans, participated in the enterprise. By 1530, a cathedral was being built on Hispaniola, and a university soon followed.

Rumors and hopes stimulated immigration from Castile, which claimed control of the new lands, but also from the other Iberian kingdoms, and by the 1510s the immigrants included larger numbers of Spanish women. Also, Spanish and Italian merchants began to import African slaves to work on the few sugar plantations that operated on the islands. The arrival of both Spanish women and African slaves marked a shift from an area of conquest to one of settlement. The gold-hunting phase had given out in the islands by the 1520s and was replaced by the establishment of ranches and sugar plantations. The adventurous, the disappointed, and the greedy repeated the pattern as expeditions spun off in new directions.

Depopulation of the Tainos led to slaving on other islands, and in 30 years or so, most of the indigenous population had died or been killed. The people of the Lesser Antilles, or "Caribs," whom the Spaniards accused of cannibalism and who were thus always subject to enslavement, held out longer because their islands were less attractive to European settlement. To meet the labor needs of the islands, African slaves were imported. As early as 1510, the mistreatment and destruction of the American Indians led to attempts by clerics and royal administrators to end the worst abuses. The activities

FIGURE **19.2** St. Augustine, Florida. As the oldest city in the United States (founded in 1565), it was established to guard the Spanish sea route from the Caribbean that the silver fleets traveled back to Spain.

of men such as Dominican friar **Bartolomé de Las Casa**s (1484–1566; Figure 19.3), a conquistador turned priest, initiated the struggle for justice.

Expeditions leaped from island to island. Where the native peoples and cultures were more resilient, their impact on the societies that emerged was greater than in the Caribbean, but the process of contact was similar. By the time of the conquest of Mexico in the 1520s and Peru in the 1530s, all the elements of the colonial system of Latin America were in place. Even in Brazil, which the Portuguese began to exploit after 1500, a period of bartering with the Native Americans was slowly replaced by increasing royal control and development of a sugar plantation economy. There, as in the Caribbean, resistance and subsequent depopulation of the native peoples led to the importation of African laborers.

Las Casas, Bartolomé de (1484–1566) Dominican friar who supported peaceful conversion of the Native American population of the Spanish colonies; opposed forced labor and advocated Indian rights.

The Paths of Conquest

> No other race can be found that can penetrate through such rugged lands, such dense forests, such great mountains and deserts and cross such broad rivers as the Spaniards have done . . . solely by the valor of their persons and the forcefulness of their breed.

These words, written by Pedro Cieza de Leon, one of the conquistadors of Peru, underlined the Spaniards' pride in their accomplishments. In less than a century, a large portion of two continents and islands in an inland sea, inhabited by millions of people, was brought under Spanish control. Expeditions, usually comprising 50 to 500 men, provided the spearhead of conquest, and in their wake followed the women, missionaries, administrators, and artisans who began to form civil society.

The conquest was not a unified movement but rather a series of individual initiatives that usually operated with government approval. The conquest of the Americas was two pronged: one prong was directed toward Mexico; the other was aimed at South America.

We can use the well-documented campaign in Mexico as an example of a conquest. In 1519 **Hernán Cortés**, an educated man with considerable ability as a leader, led an expedition of 600 men to the coast of Mexico. After hearing rumors of a great kingdom in the interior, he began to strike inland. Pitched battles were fought with towns subject to the Aztec empire, but after gaining these victories,

Cortés, Hernán Led expedition of 600 to coast of Mexico in 1519; conquistador responsible for defeat of Aztec empire; captured Tenochtitlan.

CHAPTER 19 Early Latin America 431

Read the Document on MyHistoryLab: Bartolomè de Las Casas, "Of the Island of Hispaniola" (1542)

FIGURE 19.3 Father Bartolomé de Las Casas. This former *conquistador* became a Dominican friar and a noted theologian who spent much of his life seeking to protect the Indians from exploitation and abuse.

Moctezuma II [mok te sU mä] (1480–1520) Last independent Aztec emperor; killed during Hernán Cortés's conquest of Tenochtitlan.

Mexico City Capital of New Spain; built on ruins of Aztec capital of Tenochtitlan.

Read the Document on MyHistoryLab: The Second Letter of Hernán Cortés to King Charles V of Spain (1519) Hernán Cortés

New Spain Spanish colonial administrative unit including Central America, Mexico, and the southeast and southwest of the present-day United States.

Cortés was able to enlist the defeated peoples' support against their overlords. With the help of the Indian allies, Cortés eventually reached the great Aztec island capital of Tenochtitlan. By a combination of deception, boldness, ruthlessness, and luck, the Aztec emperor **Moctezuma II** was captured and killed (Figure 19.4). Cortés and his followers were forced to flee the Aztec capital and retreat toward the coast, but with the help of the Aztecs' traditional enemies, they cut off and besieged Tenochtitlan. Although the Aztec confederacy put up a stiff resistance, disease, starvation, and battle brought the city down in 1521. Tenochtitlan was replaced by **Mexico City**. The Aztec poets later remembered,

> We are crushed to the ground,
> we lie in ruins.
> There is nothing but grief and suffering
> in Mexico and Tlatelolco,
> where once we saw beauty and valor.

By 1535, most of central Mexico, with its network of towns and its dense, agricultural populations, had been brought under Spanish control. It became the core of the viceroyalty of **New Spain**, which eventually also included most of Central America, the islands of the Caribbean, and the Philippines and extended from the southwest of the present United States all the way to Panama.

The second trajectory of conquests led from the Caribbean outposts to the coast of northern South America and Panama. From Panama, the Spaniards followed rumors of a rich kingdom to the south. In 1532, after a false start, Francisco Pizarro led his men to the conquest of the Inca empire, which was already weakened by a long civil war. Once again, using guile and audacity, fewer than 200 Spaniards and their native Indian allies brought down a great empire. The Inca capital of Cuzco, high in the Andes, fell in 1533, but the Spanish decided to build their major city, Lima, closer to the coast. By 1540, most of Peru was under Spanish control, although an active resistance continued in remote areas for another 30 years.

From the conquests of densely populated areas, such as Mexico and Peru, where there were surpluses of food and potential laborers, Spanish expeditions spread out in search of further riches and strange peoples. They penetrated the zones of semi-sedentary and nomadic peoples, who often offered stiff resistance. From 1540 to 1542, in one of the most famous expeditions, **Francisco Vázquez de Coronado**, searching for mythical cities of gold, penetrated what is now the southwestern United States as far as Kansas. At the other end of the Americas, **Pedro de Valdivia** conquered the tenacious Araucanians of central Chile and set up the city of Santiago in 1541, although the Araucanians continued to fight long after. Buenos Aires, in the southern part of the continent, founded by an expedition from Spain in 1536, was abandoned because of resistance and was not refounded until 1580. Other expeditions penetrated the Amazon basin and explored the tropical forests of Central and South America during these years, but there was little there to attract permanent settlement to those areas. By 1570, there were 192 Spanish cities and towns throughout the Americas, one-third of which were in Mexico and Central America.

The Conquerors

The Spanish captains led by force of will and personal power. "God in heaven the king in Spain, and me here" was the motto of one captain, and sometimes, absolute power could lead to tyranny. The crown received one-fifth of all treasure. Men signed up on a shares basis; those who brought horses or who had special skills might get double shares. Rewards were made according to the contract, and premiums were paid for special service and valor. There was a tendency for leaders to reward their friends,

DOCUMENT

A Vision from the Vanquished

HISTORY USUALLY IS WRITTEN BY THE victors, so it is rare to find a detailed statement from the vanquished. In the 17th century, Guaman Poma de Ayala, an acculturated Peruvian Indian who claimed to trace his lineage to the provincial nobility of Inca times, composed a memorial outlining the history of Peru under the Incas and reporting on the current conditions under Spanish rule. Guaman Poma was a Christian and a loyal subject. He hoped that his report would reach King Philip III of Spain, who might then order an end to the worst abuses, among which were the Spanish failure to recognize the rank and status of Indian nobles. His book was not published in his lifetime and was not recovered until the 20th century.

Guaman Poma was an educated, bilingual Indian who spoke Quechua as well as Spanish and who had a profound understanding of Andean culture. His book is remarkable for its revelations of Indian life, for its detailed criticism of the abuses suffered by the Indians, and especially because Guaman Poma illustrated his memorial with a series of drawings that give his words a visual effect. The illustrations also reveal the worldview of this interesting man. The drawings and text offer a critical inside view not of the laws, but of the workings of Spain's empire in America from an Indian point of view.

MINERS

At the mercury mines of Huancavelica the Indian workers are punished and ill-treated to such an extent that they die like flies and our whole race is threatened with extermination. Even the chiefs are tortured by being suspended by their feet. Conditions in the silver-mines of Potosí and Chocllococha, or at the gold-mines of Carabaya are little better. The managers and supervisors, who are Spaniards or mestizos, have virtually absolute power. There is no reason for them to fear justice, since they are never brought before the courts.

Beatings are incessant. The victims are mounted for this purpose on a llama's back, tied naked to a round pillar or put in stocks. Their hair is cut off and they are deprived of food and water during detention.

Any shortage in the labor gangs is made an excuse for punishing the chiefs as if they were common thieves or traitors instead of the nobility of the country. The work itself is so hard as to cause permanent injury to many of those who survive it. There is no remuneration for the journey to the mines and a day's labor is paid at the rate for half a day.

PROPRIETORS

Your Majesty has granted large estates, including the right to employ Indian labor, to a number of individuals of whom some are good Christians and the remainder are very bad ones. These encomenderos, as they are termed, may boast about their high position, but in reality they are harmful both to the labor force and to the surviving Indian nobility. I therefore propose to set down the details of their life and conduct.

They exude an air of success as they go from their card games to their dinners in fine silk clothes. Their money is squandered on these luxuries, as well it may, since it costs them no work or sweat whatever. Although the Indians ultimately pay the bill, no concern is ever felt for them or even for Your Majesty or God himself.

Official posts like those of royal administrator and judge ought not to be given to big employers or mine-owners or to their obnoxious sons, because these peoples have enough to live on already. The appointments ought to go to Christian gentlemen of small means, who have rendered some service to the Crown and are educated and humane, not just greedy.

Anybody with rights over Indian labor sees to it that his own household is well supplied with servant girls and indoor and outdoor staff. When collecting dues and taxes, it is usual to impose penalties and detain Indians against their will. There is no redress since, if any complaint is made, the law always favors the employer.

The collection of tribute is delegated to stewards, who make a practice of adding something in for themselves. They too consider themselves entitled to free service and obligatory presents, and they end up as bad as their masters. All of them, and their wives as well, regard themselves as entitled to eat at the Indians' expense.

The Indians are seldom paid the few reales a day which are owed to them, but they are hired out for the porterage of wine and making rope or clothing. Little rest is possible either by day or night and they are usually unable to sleep at home.

It is impossible for servant girls, or even married women, to remain chaste. They are bound to be corrupted and prostituted because employers do not feel any scruple about threatening them with flogging, execution, or burial alive if they refuse to satisfy their master's desires.

The Spanish grandees and their wives have borrowed from the Inca the custom of having themselves conveyed in litters like the images of saints in processions. These Spaniards are absolute lords without fear of either God or retribution. In their own eyes they are judges over our people, whom they can reserve for their personal service or their pleasure, to the detriment of the community.

Great positions are achieved by favor from above, by wealth or by having relations at Court in Castile. With some notable exceptions, the beneficiaries act without consideration for those under their control. The encomenderos call themselves conquerors, but their Conquest was achieved by uttering the words: Ama mancha noca Inca, or "Have no fear. I am Inca." This false pretense was the sum total of their performance.

(continued on next page)

(continued from previous page)

> **QUESTIONS**
> - What are the main abuses Guaman Poma complains about?
> - What remedies does he recommend?
> - What relationship do his views have to traditional Inca values?
> - How might a white landlord or colonial official have answered his attacks?

View the **Closer Look** on **MyHistoryLab**: The Meeting of Cortés and Moctezuma

FIGURE 19.4 This 1519 Spanish painting, *The Meeting of Cortés and Moctezuma*, represents the Spanish view of the conquest of Mexico.

Coronado, Francisco Vázquez de (c. 1510–1554) Leader of Spanish expedition into northern frontier region of New Spain; entered what is now United States in search of mythical cities of gold.

Valdivia, Pedro de Spanish conquistador; conquered Araucanian Indians of Chile and established city of Santiago in 1541.

relatives, and men from their home province more liberally than others, so that after each conquest there was always a group of unhappy and dissatisfied conquerors ready to organize a new expedition. As one observer put it, "if each man was given the governorship, it would not be enough."

Few of the conquerors were professional soldiers; they represented all walks of Spanish life, including a scattering of gentlemen, and sometimes even former slaves and freedmen. Some of the later expeditions included a few Spanish women such as Inés Suárez, the heroine of the conquest of Chile, but such cases were rare. In general, the conquerors were men on the make, hoping to better themselves and serve God by converting the heathen at the same time. Always on the lookout for treasure, most conquerors were satisfied by encomiendas. These adventurous men, many of humble origins, came to see themselves as a new nobility entitled to dominion over a new peasantry: the American Indians.

The reasons for Spanish success were varied. Horses, firearms, and more generally steel weapons gave them a great advantage over the stone technology of the native peoples. This technological edge, combined with effective and ruthless leadership, produced remarkable results. Epidemic disease also proved to be a silent ally of the Europeans. Finally, internal divisions and rivalries within American Indian empires, and their high levels of centralization, made the great civilizations particularly vulnerable. It is no accident that the peoples who offered the stiffest and most continuous resistance were usually the mobile, tough, nomadic tribes rather than the centralized states of sedentary peasants.

By about 1570, the age of the conquest was coming to a close. Bureaucrats, merchants, and colonists replaced the generation of the conquerors as institutions of government and economy were created. The transition was not easy. In Peru a civil war erupted in the 1540s, and in Mexico there were grumblings from the old followers of Cortés. But the establishment of viceroys in the two main colonies and the creation of law courts in the main centers signaled that Spanish America had become a colony rather than a conquest.

Conquest and Morality

Conquest involved violence, domination, and theft. The Spanish conquest of the Americas created a series of important philosophical and moral questions for Europeans. Mancio Serra was not alone in questioning the conquest. Theologians and lawyers asked: Who were the Indians? Were they fully human? Was it proper to convert them to Christianity? Could conversion by force or the conquest of their lands be justified? Driven by greed, many of the conquistadors argued that conquest was necessary to spread the gospel and that control of Indian labor was essential for Spain's rule. In 1548 Juan Gines de Sépulveda, a noted Spanish scholar, basing his arguments on Aristotle, published a book claiming that the conquest was fully justified. The Spaniards had come to free the Indians from their unjust lords and to bring the light of salvation. Most importantly, he argued, the Indians were not fully human, and some peoples "were born to serve."

In 1550 the Spanish king suspended all further conquests and convoked a special commission in Valladolid to hear arguments for and against this position. Father Bartolomé de Las Casas—former conqueror and encomendero, Dominican priest, bishop of Chiapas, untiring defender of the Indians, and critic of Spanish brutality—presented the contrary opinion against Sépulveda. Las Casas had long experience in the West Indies, and he believed that the inhabitants were rational people who, unlike the Muslims, had never done harm to Christians. Thus, the conquest of their lands was unjustified. The Indians had many admirable customs and accomplishments, he said. He argued that "the Indians are our brothers and Christ has given his life for them." Spanish rule in order to spread the Christian faith was justified, but conversion should take place only by peaceful means.

The results of the debate were mixed. The crown had reasons to back Las Casas against the dangerous ambitions of the Spanish conquerors. Sépulveda's book was censored, but the conquests nevertheless continued. Although some of the worst abuses were moderated, in reality the great period of conquest was all over by the 1570s. It was too little, too late. Still, the Spanish government's concern with the legality and morality of its actions and the willingness of Spaniards such as Las Casas to speak out against abuses are also part of the story. The interests of many other conquerors and officials, however, ran in the opposite direction.

Read the Document on MyHistoryLab: Excerpt from Bartolome de las Casas' *In Defense of the Indians*

THE DESTRUCTION AND TRANSFORMATION OF INDIGENOUS SOCIETIES

19.2 How were indigenous societies transformed by the conquest?

To varying degrees, all indigenous societies suffered the effects of European conquest. Population loss was extreme in many areas. Spain worked and taxed the native peoples often disrupting their societies.

The various American peoples responded in many different ways to the invasion of their lands and the transformation of their societies. All of them suffered a severe decline of population—a demographic catastrophe. On the main islands of the Caribbean, the indigenous population had nearly disappeared by 1540 as the result of slaving, mistreatment, and disease. In Peru a similar process brought a loss from 10 million to 1.5 million between 1530 and 1590. Elsewhere in the Americas a similar but less well-documented process took place. Smallpox, influenza, and measles wreaked havoc on the American Indian population, which had developed no immunities against these diseases. In central Mexico, war, destruction, and above all disease brought the population from an estimated 25 million in 1519 to less than 2 million in 1580. That decline was matched by the rapid increase in European livestock, cattle, sheep, and horses that flourished on newly created Spanish farms or in previously unusable lands. In a shocking way, European livestock were replacing an indigenous population on the land (Figure 19.5).

Although epidemic was the major cause of depopulation, the conquest and the weakening of indigenous societies contributed to the losses. Population declines of this size disrupted native societies in many ways. For example, in central Mexico the contraction of the indigenous populations led the Spanish to concentrate the remaining population in fewer towns, and this led in turn to the seizure of former communal farming lands by Spanish landowners. Demographic collapse made maintaining traditional social and economic structures very difficult.

Exploitation of the Indians

The Spaniards did not interfere with aspects of Native American life that served colonial goals or at least did not openly conflict with Spanish authority or religion. Thus, in Mexico and Peru, while the old religions and its priestly class were eliminated, the traditional indigenous nobility remained in place, supported by Spanish authority, as middlemen between the tax and labor demands of the new rulers and the majority of the population.

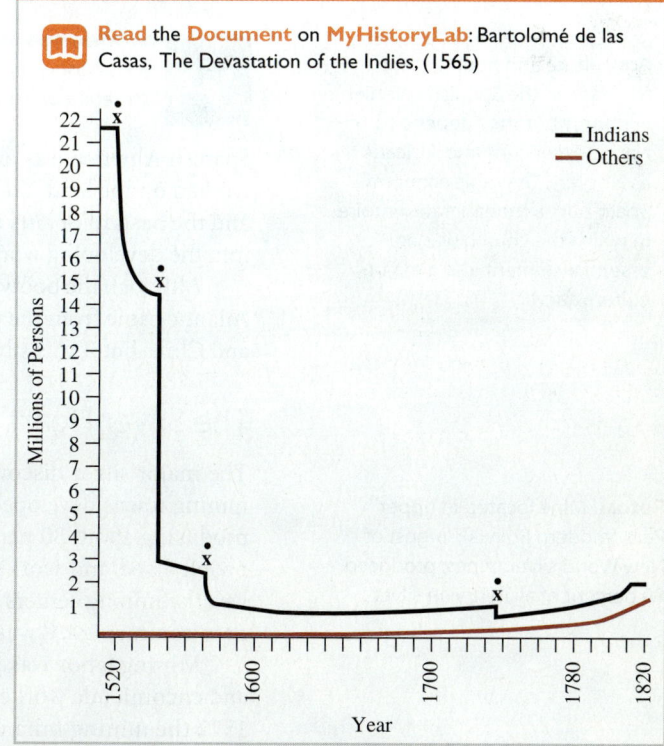

Read the Document on MyHistoryLab: Bartolomé de las Casas, The Devastation of the Indies, (1565)

FIGURE **19.5** Population decline in New Spain.

View the Image on MyHistoryLab: Medicine Man Treating Aztecs for Smallpox

The enslavement of Indians (a term the Spaniards applied to all the native peoples of the Americas), except those taken in war, was prohibited by the mid-16th century in most of Spanish America. Instead, different forms of labor or taxation were imposed. At first, encomiendas were given to the individual conquerors of a region. The holders of these grants were able to use their dependents as workers and servants or to tax them. Whereas commoners had owed tribute or labor to the state in the Inca and Aztec empires, the new demands were arbitrary, often excessive, and usually without the reciprocal obligation and protection characteristic of the indigenous societies. In general, the encomiendas were destructive. The Spanish crown, unwilling to see a new nobility arise in the New World among the conquerors with their grants of Indian serfs, moved to end the institution in the 1540s. The crown limited the inheritability of encomiendas and prohibited the right to demand certain kinds of labor from the Indians. Although encomiendas continued to exist in marginal regions at the fringes of the empire, they were all but gone by the 1620s in the central areas of Mexico and Peru. Colonists increasingly sought grants of land rather than Indians as the basis of wealth.

Meanwhile, the colonial government increasingly extracted labor and taxes from native peoples. In many places, communities were required to send groups of laborers to work on state projects, such as church construction or road building, or in labor gangs for mining or agriculture. This forced labor, called the **mita** in Peru where it was adapted from indigenous precedents, mobilized thousands of workers for the mines and on other projects. Although they were paid a wage for this work, there were many abuses of the system by the local officials, and community labor requirements often were disruptive and destructive. By the 17th century, many Indians left their villages to avoid the labor and tax obligations, preferring instead to work for Spanish landowners or to seek employment in the cities. This process eventually led to the growth of a wage labor system in which native peoples, no longer resident in their villages, worked for wages on Spanish-owned mines and farms or in the cities.

mita Labor extracted for lands assigned to the state and the religion; all communities were expected to contribute; an essential aspect of Inca imperial control.

In the wake of this disruption, Native American culture also demonstrated great resiliency in the face of Spanish institutions and forms, adapting and modifying them to indigenous ways. In Peru and Mexico, native peoples learned to use the Spanish legal system and the law courts so that litigation became a way of life. At the local level, many aspects of indigenous life remained, and Native Americans proved to be selective in their adaptation of European foods, technology, and culture.

COLONIAL ECONOMIES AND GOVERNMENTS

Agriculture and mining were the basis of the Spanish colonial economy but they depended on Native Americans and Africans as laborers. Over this economy Spain built a bureaucratic empire in which the church was an essential element and a major cultural factor.

19.3 In the long run, did the mining of silver and gold stimulate the economic growth of Latin America or hold it back?

Spanish America was an agrarian society in which perhaps 80 percent of the population lived and worked on the land. Yet in terms of America's importance to Spain, mining was the essential activity and the basis of Spain's rule in the Indies. It was precious metals that first began to fit Latin America into the developing world economy.

Although the booty of conquest provided some wealth, most of the precious metal sent across the Atlantic came from the post conquest mining industry. Gold was found in the Caribbean, Colombia, and Chile, but it was silver far more than gold that formed the basis of Spain's wealth in America.

The Silver Heart of Empire

The major silver discoveries were made in Mexico and Peru between 1545 and 1565. Great silver mining towns developed. **Potosí** in upper Peru (in what is now Bolivia) was the largest mine of all, producing about 80 percent of all the Peruvian silver. In the early 17th century, more than 160,000 people lived and worked in the town and its mine. Peru's Potosí and Mexico's Zacatecas became wealthy mining centers with opulent churches and a luxurious way of life for some. As one viceroy of Peru commented, it was not silver that was sent to Spain "but the blood and sweat of Indians."

Potosí Mine located in upper Peru (modern Bolivia); largest of New World silver mines; produced 80 percent of all Peruvian silver.

Mining labor was provided by a variety of workers. The early use of Native American slaves and encomienda workers in the 16th century gradually was replaced by a system of labor drafts. By 1572 the mining mita in Peru was providing about 13,000 workers a year to Potosí alone. Similar labor drafts were used in Mexico, but by the 17th century the mines in both places also had large numbers of wage workers willing to brave the dangers of mining in return for the good wages.

436 PART IV The Early Modern Period, 1450–1750: The World Shrinks

Although indigenous methods were used at first, most mining techniques were European in origin. After 1580, silver mining depended on a process of amalgamation with mercury to extract the silver from the ore-bearing rock. The Spanish discovery of a mountain of mercury at **Huancavelica** in Peru aided American silver production. Potosí and Huancavelica became the "great marriage of Peru" and the basis of silver production in South America.

According to Spanish law, all subsoil rights belonged to the crown, but the mines and the processing plants were owned by individuals, who were permitted to extract the silver in return for paying one-fifth of production to the government, which also profited from its monopoly on the mercury needed to produce the silver (Figure 19.6).

Mining stimulated many other aspects of the economy, even in areas far removed from the mines. Workers had to be fed and the mines supplied. In Mexico, where most of the mines were located beyond the area of settled preconquest populations, large Spanish-style farms developed to raise cattle, sheep, and wheat. The Peruvian mines high in the Andes were supplied from distant regions with mercury, mules, food, clothing, and even coca leaves, used to deaden hunger and make the work at high altitudes less painful. From Spain's perspective, mining was the heart of the colonial economy.

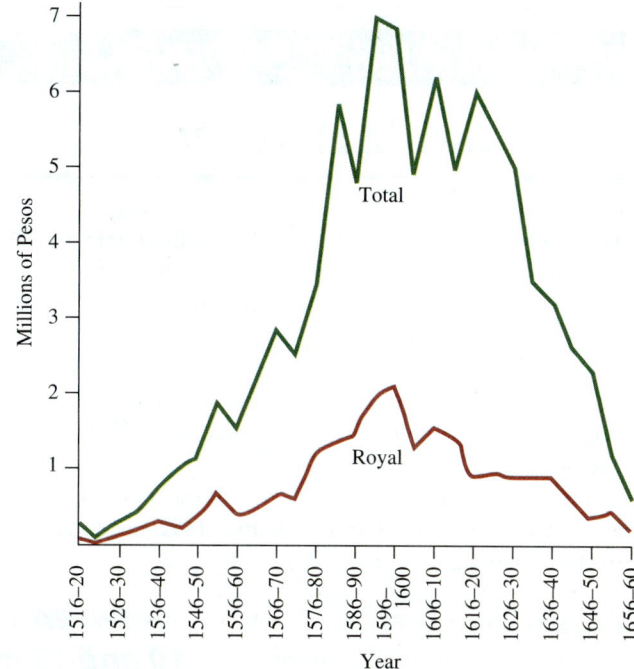

FIGURE **19.6** Silver production in Spanish America, 1516–1660.

Haciendas and Villages

Spanish America remained predominantly an agrarian economy, and wherever large sedentary populations lived, indigenous communal agriculture of traditional crops continued. As populations dwindled, Spanish ranches and farms began to emerge. The colonists, faced with declining indigenous populations, also found land ownership more attractive. Family-owned rural estates, which produced grains, grapes, and livestock, developed throughout the central areas of Spanish America. Most of the labor force on these estates came from Native Americans who had left the communities and from people of mixed Native American and European heritage. These rural estates, or **haciendas**, producing primarily for consumers in America, became the basis of wealth and power for the local aristocracy in many regions. Although some plantation crops, such as sugar and later cacao, were exported to Europe from Spanish America, they made up only a small fraction of the value of the exports in comparison with silver. In some regions where Native American communities continued to hold traditional farming lands, an endemic competition between haciendas and village communities emerged.

Huancavelica [WAHN-cah-veh-LEEK-uh] Location of greatest deposit of mercury in South America; aided in American silver production; linked with Potosí.

haciendas Rural estates in Spanish colonies in New World; produced agricultural products for consumers in America; basis of wealth and power for local aristocracy.

Industry and Commerce

In areas such as Ecuador, New Spain, and Peru, sheep raising led to the development of small textile sweatshops, where common cloth was produced, usually by women. America became self-sufficient for its basic foods and material goods and looked to Europe only for luxury items not locally available.

Still, from Spain's perspective and that of the larger world economy taking shape in the early modern centuries, the American "kingdoms" had a silver heart, and the whole Spanish commercial system was organized around that fact. Spain allowed only Spaniards to trade with America and imposed tight restrictions. Almost all American trade from Spain after the mid-16th century passed through the city of Seville and, after 1710, through the nearby port of Cadiz. A Board of Trade in Seville controlled all commerce with America, registered ships and passengers, kept charts, and collected taxes. It often worked in conjunction with a merchant guild, or **consulado**, in Seville that controlled goods shipped to America and handled much of the silver received in return. Linked to branches in Mexico City and Lima, the consulados kept tight control over the trade and were able to keep prices high in the colonies.

Other Europeans looked on the West Indies trade with envy. To discourage foreign rivals and pirates, the Spanish eventually worked out a convoy system in which two fleets sailed annually from Spain, traded their goods for precious metals, and then met at Havana, Cuba, before returning to Spain.

The fleet system was made possible by the large, heavily armed ships, called **galleons**, that were used to carry the silver belonging to the crown. Two great galleons a year also sailed from Manila in the Philippines to Mexico loaded with Chinese silks, porcelain, and lacquer. These goods were then

consulado Merchant guild of Seville; enjoyed virtual monopoly rights over goods shipped to America and handled much of the silver received in return.

galleons Large, heavily armed ships used to carry silver from New World colonies to Spain; basis for convoy system utilized by Spain for transportation of bullion.

THINKING HISTORICALLY

An Atlantic History

THE VOYAGES OF COLUMBUS AND THE subsequent Spanish and Portuguese conquest and settlement of the Americas set into motion the real beginning of a history that linked all of the lands that bordered on the Atlantic Ocean. Certainly, there had been contacts before; the Vikings had settled in Greenland, Iceland, and had reached North America by 1000 B.C.E.; the islands of the Atlantic like the Canaries and Madeira had been settled by the Spanish and Portuguese, and in the 15th century Europeans had ventured down the coast of West Africa and begun an active trade at the same time. But after 1492, the continuous and ever-increasing volume of contact, movement of populations, trade, and interaction between Europe, America, and Africa and their adjacent islands truly turned the Atlantic from being a barrier that impeded contact into a highway that connected disparate peoples and places into an increasingly interconnected and entwined history—for better or for worse.

> Between 1492 and 1850 between 10 and 15 million Africans and over five million Europeans crossed the Atlantic to the Americas in great migratory movements.

The idea of conceiving of history around a maritime space like the Atlantic is not new. The great French historian Fernand Braudel had written a classic book about the commonalities and interconnections of the Mediterranean world (1959), and other scholars had used a similar approach for the lands and peoples around the Indian Ocean. The idea of Atlantic history is more recent. Increasingly since the 1970s, historians have been trying to overcome the tendency to isolate the histories of individual continents, empires, or countries in the Atlantic basin by looking at their parallels and interconnections through a lens that makes these helpful vantage points from which to see the processes of global history. It is a way of studying contacts, comparisons, and also how different regions and peoples each responded to larger global processes. The history of the Atlantic, however, is different from these other maritime approaches because unlike the Mediterranean, which has a certain climatic and geographic unity, the Atlantic world is much larger and extends over many latitudes and a vast variety of climates, environments, and cultures. Unlike the Indian Ocean where linkages had been formed by indigenous peoples long before the arrival of Europeans, in the Atlantic firm evidence of such contacts are lacking, and if they existed were intermittent, and so Atlantic history is to some extent a direct outgrowth of the rise of European overseas empires and trade even if it has become a way to understand that history of empires from a perspective that does not necessarily celebrate the imperial powers.

What are some of the themes within a history of the Atlantic world? We can start with the movement of peoples. Between 1492 and 1850 between 10 and 15 million Africans and over five million Europeans crossed the Atlantic to the Americas in great migratory movements. These peoples carried the traditions, practices, and ideas of their homes to new situations and then maintained and adapted them to a variety of conditions and circumstances. The movement of peoples thus had both demographic and cultural results. The increasing contacts between the continents also initiated biological and ecological exchanges that changed the face of the Old World and the New and transformed the lives of their inhabitants. American products like corn and the potato and tomato transformed European diets and eventually the growth of European populations, while the introduction of horses, sheep, poultry, and cattle brought from Europe changed the nature of life for millions of people in the Americas. Regions of Africa were transformed by both the introduction of new food crops like corn and manioc and by the demands of Europeans for enslaved workers. The Atlantic slave trade had many effects; in Africa, societies were transformed, political boundaries altered, and trade routes were changed by it. For example, the former great trading empires of the sahel like Mali lost their advantage to the coastal states that had access to the new Atlantic trade. In America, the African voyagers and their descendants created new cultures and new populations, creating the basis of a Black Atlantic world while in Europe the trade brought both profits and eventually provoked the moral and religious questioning of the very nature of slavery.

Not only peoples, plants, and animals, but pathogens also crossed the Atlantic highway creating new disease environments that sometimes produced disastrous consequences such as the introduction of Old World diseases to the Americas where native peoples, lacking immunities, were devastated by epidemics. The historian Alfred Crosby has pointed out that the Columbian Exchange of peoples, plants, animals, diseases, ideas, and technologies transformed many aspects of life on the four continents of the Atlantic world.

The creation of European empires that included settlements in the Americas and slaving bases and outposts in Africa eventually linked the various parts of the Atlantic world in a series of commercial relationships. Merchants, mariners, commodities, and currencies crossed the Atlantic continually, and despite all efforts by governments to control these exchanges within national and imperial boundaries, trade between empires and interactions such as contraband, smuggling, and piracy were also part of the Atlantic world. So too was the circulation of ideas and beliefs. We could, for example, speak of a Christian Atlantic because both Protestants and Catholics shared many

(continued on next page)

common beliefs that were implanted to new settlements and colonies from Europe and because both mounted missionary activities, converting in the Americas whole populations, and in Africa, in places like the Kongo, the ruler and his court and then large sectors of the population. The challenges faced by missionaries on the far shores of the Atlantic were not as different as might first be imagined from those encountered in Europe where priests confronted with disbelief, superstition, or occult practices sometimes referred to places like southern Italy or northern Spain as the "Indies of Europe." Ideas and religions did not flow only from Europe. Africans also brought their religions which then flourished in various forms across the Atlantic as *voudon* (Haiti), *candomblé* (Brazil), or *obeah* (Jamaica). The Atlantic world became a realm of cultural creations, fusions, and adaptations.

In some ways it was the circulation of ideas that finally brought an end to the interpretative unity of Atlantic history. The circulation of the ideas of the 18th century and the emergence of local elites throughout the Atlantic world eventually led to a series of revolutions in the United States, France, Haiti, and Latin America in the late 18th and early 19th centuries that resulted in the creation of independent states and the destruction or weakening of empires. Some historians believe that with the creation of the new nations of the Americas the unities and parallels of an Atlantic history began to break down. Other scholars believe that until the end of the slave trades around 1860 or perhaps the final abolition of New World slavery in 1888 that it was still possible to speak of an Atlantic history.

Like any historical approach, Atlantic history has its problems. The Atlantic communities were tied in many ways to other areas of the world. Mexican silver flowed to China in Spanish ships, the Portuguese and the Dutch carried spices from Asia to Europe, and many of the challenges of empire confronted by the Europeans in America and Africa were also met in India, China, and east Africa. An Atlantic perspective as broad as it is, may, in fact, be too narrow for an understanding of global processes. But many scholars have increasingly found the parallels, interactions, and convergences within the Atlantic world to be a useful way to study and understand a large part of world history.

> **QUESTIONS**
> - Is the concept of *Atlantic history* too broad or too narrow?
> - How can matters like gender, ethnicity, or family be studied in an Atlantic perspective?
> - Is there a date after which the concept is no longer useful, or is the concept of *Atlantic history* really the reflection of our present global way of thinking read back onto the past?

shipped on the convoy to Spain along with the American silver. In the Caribbean, heavily fortified ports, such as Havana and Cartagena (Colombia), provided shelter for the treasure ships, while coast guard fleets cleared the waters of potential raiders. Although cumbersome, the convoys (which continued until the 1730s) were successful. Pirates and enemies sometimes captured individual ships, and some ships were lost to storms and other disasters, but only one fleet was lost—to the Dutch in 1627. While the convoy system was relatively effective, Spanish colonists in the Americas still wanted more freedom to trade, and contraband with foreigners flourished despite Spanish efforts to stop it.

In general, the supply of American silver to Spain was continuous and made the colonies seem worth the effort, but the reality of American treasure was more complicated. Much of the wealth flowed out of Spain to pay for Spain's European wars, its long-term debts, and the purchase of manufactured goods to be sent back to the West Indies. Probably less than half of the silver remained in Spain itself. The arrival of American treasure also contributed to a sharp rise in prices and a general inflation, first in Spain and then throughout western Europe during the 16th century. At no time did the American treasure make up more than one-fourth of Spain's state revenues; the wealth of Spain depended more on the taxes levied on its own population than it did on the exploitation of its Native American subjects. However, the seemingly endless supply of silver stimulated bankers to continue to lend money to Spain because the prospect of the great silver fleet was always enough to offset the falling credit of the Spanish rulers and the sometimes bankrupt government. As early as 1619, Sancho de Moncada wrote that "the poverty of Spain resulted from the discovery of the Indies." But there were few who could see the long-term costs of empire.

Ruling an Empire: State and Church

Spain controlled its American empire through a carefully regulated bureaucratic system. Sovereignty rested with the crown, based not on the right of conquest but on a papal grant that awarded the West Indies to Castile in return for its services in bringing those lands and peoples into the Christian community. Some Native Americans found this a curious idea, and European theologians agreed, but Spain was careful to bolster its rule in other ways. The **Treaty of Tordesillas** (1494) between Castile and Portugal clarified the spheres of influence and right of possession of the two kingdoms by drawing

Treaty of Tordesillas [tor duh sEEl yäs, -sEE-] Signed in 1494 between Castile and Portugal; clarified spheres of influence and rights of possession in New World; reserved Brazil and all newly discovered lands east of Brazil to Portugal; granted all lands west of Brazil to Spain.

letrados University-trained lawyers from Spain in the New World; juridical core of Spanish colonial bureaucracy; exercised both legislative and administrative functions.

Recopilación [rAY kO pEEl ä sEE On] Body of laws collected in 1681 for Spanish possessions in New World; basis of law in the Indies.

CHAPTER 19 Early Latin America 439

Council of the Indies Body within the Castilian government that issued all laws and advised king on all matters dealing with the Spanish colonies of the New World.

viceroyalties Two major divisions of Spanish colonies in New World; one based in Lima; the other in Mexico City; direct representatives of the king.

viceroys Senior government officials in Spanish America; ruled as direct representative of the king over the principal administrative units or viceroyalties; usually high-ranking Spanish nobles with previous military or governmental experience. The Portuguese also used viceroys who resided in Goa for their possessions in the Indian Ocean, and then after the mid Seventeenth century for their colony in Brazil.

audiencia Royal court of appeals established in Spanish colonies of New World; there were 16 throughout Spanish America; part of colonial administrative system; staffed by professional magistrates.

a hypothetical north–south line around the globe and reserving to Portugal the newly discovered lands (and their route to India) to the east of the line and to Castile all lands to the west. Thus, Brazil fell within the Portuguese sphere. Other European nations later raised their own objections to the Spanish and Portuguese claims.

The Spanish empire became a great bureaucratic system built on a juridical core and staffed to a large extent by **letrados**, university-trained lawyers from Spain. The modern division of powers was not clearly defined in the Spanish system, so that judicial officers also exercised legislative and administrative authority. Laws were many and contradictory at times, but the **Recopilación** (1681) codified the laws into the basis for government in the colonies.

The king ruled through the **Council of the Indies** in Spain, which issued the laws and advised him. Within the West Indies, Spain created two **viceroyalties** in the 16th century, one based in Mexico City and the other in Lima. **Viceroys**, high-ranking nobles who were direct representatives of the king, wielded broad military, legislative, and, when they had legal training, judicial powers. The viceroyalties of New Spain and Peru were then subdivided into 10 judicial divisions controlled by superior courts, or **audiencias**, staffed by professional royal magistrates who helped to make law as well as apply it. At the local level, royally appointed magistrates applied the laws, collected taxes, and assigned the work required of American Indian communities. It is little wonder that they often were highly criticized for bending the law and taking advantage of the native peoples under their control. Below them were many minor officials who made bureaucracy both a living and a way of life.

To some extent, the clergy formed another branch of the state apparatus, although it had other functions and goals as well. Catholic religious orders such as the Franciscans, Dominicans, and Jesuits carried out the widespread conversion of the Indians, establishing churches in the towns and villages of sedentary Indians and setting up missions in frontier areas where nomadic peoples were forced to settle.

Taking seriously the pope's admonition to Christianize the peoples of the new lands as the primary justification for Spain's rule, some of the early missionaries became ardent defenders of Indian rights and even admirers of aspects of indigenous culture. For example, Franciscan priest Fray Bernardino de Sahagún (1499–1590) became an expert in the Nahuatl language and composed a bilingual encyclopedia of Aztec culture, which was based on methods very similar to those used by modern anthropologists. Other clerics wrote histories, grammars, and studies of native language and culture. Some were like Diego de Landa, Bishop of Yucatán (1547), who admired much about the culture of the Maya but who so detested their religion that he burned all their ancient books and tortured many Maya suspected of backsliding from Christianity. The recording and analysis of Native American cultures were designed primarily to provide tools for conversion.

In the core areas of Peru and New Spain, the missionary church eventually was replaced by an institutional structure of parishes and bishoprics. Archbishops sat in the major capitals, and a complicated church hierarchy developed. Because the Spanish crown nominated the holders of all such positions, the clergy tended to be major supporters of state policy as well as a primary influence on it.

The Catholic Church profoundly influenced the cultural and intellectual life of the colonies in many ways. The construction of churches, especially the great baroque cathedrals of the capitals, stimulated the work of architects and artists, usually reflecting European models but sometimes taking up local themes and subjects. The printing presses, introduced to America in the early 16th century, always published a high percentage of religious books as well as works of history, poetry, philosophy, law, and language. Much intellectual life was organized around religion. Schools—such as those of Mexico City and Lima, founded in the 1550s—were run by the clergy, and universities were created to provide training primarily in law and theology, the foundations of state and society. Eventually, more than 70 universities flourished in Spanish America. A stunning example of colonial intellectual life was the nun **Sor Juana Inés de la Cruz** (1651–1695; Figure 19.7), author, poet, musician, and perceptive commentator on her society. Sor Juana was welcomed at the court of the viceroy in

FIGURE 19.7 Sor Juana Inés de la Cruz was a remarkable Mexican poet and writer whose talents won her recognition rarely given to women for intellectual or artistic achievements in colonial Latin America.

Mexico City, where her beauty and intelligence were celebrated. She eventually gave up secular concerns and her library, at the urging of her superiors, to concentrate on purely spiritual matters.

To control the morality and orthodoxy of the population, the tribunal of the Inquisition set up offices in the major capitals. Although American Indians usually were exempt from its jurisdiction, Jews, Protestants, and other religious dissenters were prosecuted and sometimes executed in an attempt to impose orthodoxy. Overall, church and state combined to create an ideological and political framework for the society of Spanish America.

de la Cruz, Sor Juana Inés (1651–1695) Author, poet, and musician of New Spain; eventually gave up secular concerns to concentrate on spiritual matters.

BRAZIL: THE FIRST PLANTATION COLONY

19.4 Why did the Portuguese wait so long to develop Brazil and why did they turn to slavery to do so?

The first official Portuguese landfall on the South American coast took place in 1500 when **Pedro Alvares Cabral**, leader of an expedition to India, made a brief and perhaps accidental landfall on the tropical Brazilian shore. There was little at first to attract European interest except for the dyewood trees that grew in the forests, and thus the Portuguese crown paid little attention to Brazil for 30 years, preferring instead to grant licenses to merchants who agreed to exploit the dyewood. Pressure from French competitors finally moved the Portuguese crown to military action. The coast was cleared of rivals and a new system of settlement was established in 1532. Minor Portuguese nobles were given strips of land along the coast to colonize and develop. The nobles who held these **captaincies** combined broad, seemingly feudal powers with a strong desire for commercial development. Most of them lacked the capital needed to carry out the colonization, and some had problems with the indigenous population. In a few places, towns were established, colonists were brought over, relations with the Native Americans were peaceful, and, most importantly, sugar plantations were established using first Native American, then African slaves.

In 1549 the Portuguese king sent a governor general and other officials to create a royal capital at Salvador. The first Jesuit missionaries also arrived. By 1600, indigenous resistance had been broken in many places by military action, missionary activity, or epidemic disease. A string of settlements extended along the coast, centered on port cities such as Salvador and Rio de Janeiro. These served roughly 150 sugar plantations, a number that doubled by 1630. The plantations were increasingly worked by African slaves. By 1600, the Brazilian colony had about 100,000 inhabitants: 30,000 Europeans, 15,000 black slaves, and the rest Native Americans and people of mixed origin.

In Brazil the Portuguese created the first great plantation colony of the Americas, growing sugar with the use of Native American and then African slaves. In the 18th century, the discovery of gold opened up the interior of Brazil to settlement and the expansion of slavery.

Cabral, Pedro Alvares Portuguese leader of an expedition to India; blown off course in 1500 and landed in Brazil.

captaincies Strips of land along Brazilian coast granted to minor Portuguese nobles for development; enjoyed limited success in developing the colony.

Sugar and Slavery

During most of the next century, Brazil held its position as the world's leading sugar producer. Sugar cane had to be processed in the field. It was cut and pressed in large mills, and the juice was then heated to crystallize into sugar. This combination of agriculture and industry in the field demanded large amounts of capital for machinery and large quantities of labor for the backbreaking work (Figure 19.8). Although there were always some free workers who had skilled occupations, slaves did most of the work. During the 17th century, about 7000 slaves a year were imported from Africa. By the end of the century, Brazil had about 150,000 slaves—about half its total population.

FIGURE **19.8** Sugar was introduced to the Caribbean in 1493, and Brazil became the greatest producer by the next century. Sugar plantations using slave labor characterized Brazil and the Caribbean.

On the basis of a single crop produced by slave labor, Brazil became the first great plantation colony and a model that later was followed by other European nations in their own Caribbean colonies. Even after the Brazilian economy became more diverse, Brazil's social hierarchy still reflected its plantation and slave origins. The white planter families became an aristocracy linked by marriage to resident merchants and to the few Portuguese bureaucrats and officials, and they dominated local institutions. At the bottom of society were the slaves, distinguished by their color and their status as property. However, a growing segment of the population was composed of people of mixed origins, the result of miscegenation between whites, Indians, and Africans who—alongside poorer whites, freed blacks, and free Indians—served as artisans, small farmers, herders, and free laborers. In many ways, society as a whole reflected the hierarchy of the plantation.

Like Spain, Portugal created a bureaucratic structure that integrated this colony within an imperial system. Two colonies were created: the State of Maranhão, the very large but sparsely populated Amazonian region in the north, and the State of Brazil comprising the rest of the territory. A governor general ruled from Salvador, but the governors in each capitaincy often acted independently and reported directly to the overseas council in Lisbon. The missionary orders were particularly important in Brazil, especially the Jesuits. Their extensive cattle ranches and sugar mills supported the construction of churches and schools as well as a network of missions with thousands of Native American residents.

As in Spanish America, royal officials trained in the law formed the core of the bureaucracy. Unlike the Spanish empire, which except for the Philippines was almost exclusively American, the Portuguese empire included colonies and outposts in Asia, Africa, and Brazil. Only gradually, in the 17th century, did Brazil become the predominant Portuguese colony. Even then, Brazil's ties to Portugal were in some ways stronger and more dependent than those between Spanish America and Spain. Unlike Spanish America, Brazil had neither universities nor printing presses. Thus, intellectual life was always an extension of Portugal, and Brazilians seeking higher education and government offices or hoping to publish their works always had to turn to the mother country. The general economic dependency of Latin America was matched by an intellectual subordination more intense in Brazil than in Spanish America.

Brazil's Age of Gold

As overseas extensions of Europe, the American colonies were particularly susceptible to changes in European politics. For 60 years (1580–1640), the Habsburg kings of Spain also ruled Portugal, a situation that promoted their cooperation and gave these rulers a truly worldwide empire. From 1630 to 1654, as part of a global struggle against Spain, the Dutch seized a portion of northeastern Brazil and controlled its sugar production. Although the Dutch were expelled from Brazil in 1654, by the 1680s the Dutch, English, and French had established their own plantation colonies in the Caribbean and were producing sugar with slave laborers. This competition, which led to a rising price for slaves and a falling world price for sugar, undercut the Brazilian sugar industry, and the colony entered into hard times. Eventually, each European nation tried to establish an integrated set of colonies that included plantations (the Caribbean, Brazil), slaving ports (Africa), and food-producing areas (New England, southern Brazil).

Although Brazil's domination of the world sugar market was lost, throughout the 17th century **Paulistas**, hardy backwoodsmen from São Paulo (an area with few sugar plantations), had been exploring the interior, capturing Indians, and searching for precious metals. These expeditions not only established Portuguese claims to much of the interior of the continent but eventually were successful in their quest for wealth. In 1695, gold strikes were made in the mountainous interior in a region that came to be called **Minas Gerais** (General Mines), and the Brazilian colony experienced a new boom.

A great gold rush began. People deserted coastal towns and plantations to head for the gold washings, and they were soon joined by waves of about 5000 immigrants a year who came directly from Portugal. Slaves provided labor in the mines, as in the plantations. By 1775, there were over 150,000 slaves (out of a total population of 300,000 for the region) in Minas Gerais. Wild mining camps and a wide-open society eventually coalesced into a network of towns such as the administrative center

Paulistas Backwoodsmen from São Paulo in Brazil; penetrated Brazilian interior in search of precious metals and slaves during 17th century.

Minas Gerais [MEE-nuhs JEH-reyes] Region of Brazil located in mountainous interior where gold strikes were discovered in 1695; became location for gold rush.

of Ouro Prêto, and the government, anxious to control the newfound wealth, imposed a heavy hand to collect taxes and rein in the unruly population. Gold production reached its height between 1735 and 1760 and averaged about 3 tons a year in that period, making Brazil the greatest source of gold in the western world.

The discovery of gold—and later of diamonds—was a mixed blessing in the long run. It opened the interior to settlement, once again with disastrous effects on the indigenous population and with the expansion of slavery. The early disruption of coastal agriculture caused by the gold strikes was overcome by government control of the slave trade, and exports of sugar and tobacco continued to be important to the colony. Mining did stimulate the opening of new areas to ranching and farming, to supply the new markets in the mining zone. **Rio de Janeiro**, the port closest to the mines, grew in size and importance. It became capital of the colony in 1763. In Minas Gerais, a distinctive society developed. The local wealth was used to sponsor the building of churches, which in turn stimulated the work of artists, architects, and composers. Like the rest of Brazil, however, the hierarchy of color and the legal distinctions of slavery marked life in the mining zones, which were populated by large numbers of slaves and free persons of color.

Finally, gold allowed Portugal to continue economic policies that were detrimental in the long run. With access to gold, Portugal could buy the manufactured goods it needed for itself and its colonies, as few industries were developed in the mother country. Much of the Brazilian gold flowed from Portugal to England to pay for manufactured goods and to compensate for a trade imbalance. After 1760, as the supply of gold began to dwindle, Portugal was again in a difficult position—it had become in some ways an economic dependency of England.

Rio de Janeiro Brazilian port; close to mines of Minas Gerais; importance grew with gold strikes; became colonial capital in 1763.

MULTIRACIAL SOCIETIES

19.5 What impact did the Columbian Exchange have on the formation of New World societies?

The conquest and settlement of Latin America created the conditions for the formation of multi-ethnic societies on a large scale. The three major groups—Indians, Europeans, and Africans—had been brought together under very different conditions: the Europeans as conquerors and voluntary immigrants, the Indians as conquered peoples, and the Africans as slaves. This situation created hierarchies of masters and servants, Christians and pagans, that reflected the relationships of power and the colonial condition. In central Mexico, where an Indian nobility had existed, aspects of preconquest social organization were maintained because they served the ends of Spanish government. In theory, there was a separation between the "republic of the Spaniards," which included all non-Indians, and the "republic of the Indians," which was supposed to have its own social rankings and its own rules and laws. This separation was never a reality, however, and the "republic of the Indians" always formed the base on which all society rested. Indians paid tribute, something not required of others in society, except the mulattos in some places.

The mixture of whites, Africans, and Indians created the basis of multiracial societies in which hierarchies of color, status, and occupation all operated. By the 18th century, the castas, people of mixed origin, began to increase rapidly and had become a major segment of the population.

The Society of Castas

Spaniards had an idea of society drawn from their own medieval experience, but American realities soon altered that concept. The key was miscegenation. The conquest had involved the sexual exploitation of Indian women and occasional alliances formed by the giving of concubines and female servants. Marriages with indigenous women, especially of the Indian nobility, were not unknown. With few European women available, especially in frontier regions, mixed marriages and informal unions were common. The result was the growth of a large population of mixed background, the so-called mestizos. Although they were always suspected of illegitimacy, their status, especially in the early years, was higher than that of Indians. More acculturated than the Indians and able to operate in two worlds, mestizos became members of an intermediate category, not fully accepted as equals to Spaniards and yet expected to live according to the standards of Spanish society and often acting as auxiliaries to it. A similar process took place in areas such as Brazil and the Caribbean coasts, where large numbers of African slaves were imported. Slave owners exploited their

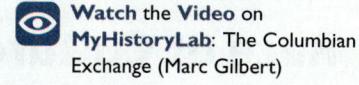

Watch the **Video** on **MyHistoryLab**: The Columbian Exchange (Marc Gilbert)

sociedad de castas American social system based on racial origins; Europeans or whites at top, black slaves or Native Americans at bottom, mixed races in middle.

FIGURE 19.9 The contact between Europeans, Africans, and Native Americans eventually produced large numbers of castas, people considered to be of mixed racial origin. By the 18th century, especially in New Spain, a genre of painting flourished that depicted a husband and wife of different racial categories and their child who would fit one of the casta designations. The purpose and public for these paintings is unclear, but they illustrate domestic relations and material culture as well as racial ideology.

female slaves or took slave women as mistresses, and then sometimes freed their mulatto children. The result was the growth of a large population of mixed background.

Throughout the Spanish Indies, European categories of noble, priest, and commoner continued, as did hierarchies based on wealth and occupation. But American realities created new distinctions in which race and place of birth also played a crucial role. This was the **sociedad de castas**, based on racial origins, in which Europeans or whites were at the top, black slaves or Native Americans were at the bottom, and the many kinds of mixes filled the intermediate categories. This accompanied the great cultural fusion in the formation of Latin America (Figure 19.9).

From the three original ethnic categories, many combinations and crosses were possible: mestizo, mulatto, and so on. By the 18th century, this segment of the population had grown rapidly, and there was much confusion and local variation in terminology. A whole genre of painting developed simply to identify and classify the various combinations. Together, the people of mixed origins were called the castas, and they tended to be shopkeepers and small farmers. In 1650 the castas made up perhaps 5 to 10 percent of the population of Spanish America, but by 1750 they made up 35 to 40 percent (see Visualizing the Past). In Brazil, still dominated by slavery, free people of color made up about 28 percent of the population—a proportion equal to that of whites. Together, however, free and slave blacks and mulattos made up two-thirds of the inhabitants of Brazil in the late 18th century.

As the mixed population grew in Spanish America, increasing restrictions were placed on them, but their social mobility could not be halted. A successful Indian might call himself a mestizo; a mestizo who married a Spanish woman might be called white. The ranks of the castas were also swelled by former slaves who had been given or had bought their freedom and by Indians who left their communities, spoke Spanish, and lived within the orbit of the Hispanic world. Thus, physical characteristics were only one criterion of rank and status, but color and ethnicity mattered, and they created a pseudoracial hierarchy. European or white status was a great social advantage. Not every person of European background was wealthy, but most

VISUALIZING THE PAST

Race or Culture? A Changing Society

THE PROCESS OF MARRIAGE OR SEXUAL contact between Spaniards, Indians, and Africans began to complicate the demographic and social structures of the American colonies. The rise of a significant number of people of mixed origin could be noted in both Peru and Mexico. These graphs point out the differences in the two areas and may imply something about the situation of the indigenous communities as well as that of the castas. We should also remember that these categories were not necessarily biological and that Indians might be classified as castas if they spoke Spanish or wore Spanish-style clothes. What seems to be precise demographic measurement may, in fact, be imprecise social definition.

QUESTION
- Do modern censuses that use cultural or "racial" labels face the same problems of definition that the early censuses in the colonial Americas confronted?

(continued on next page)

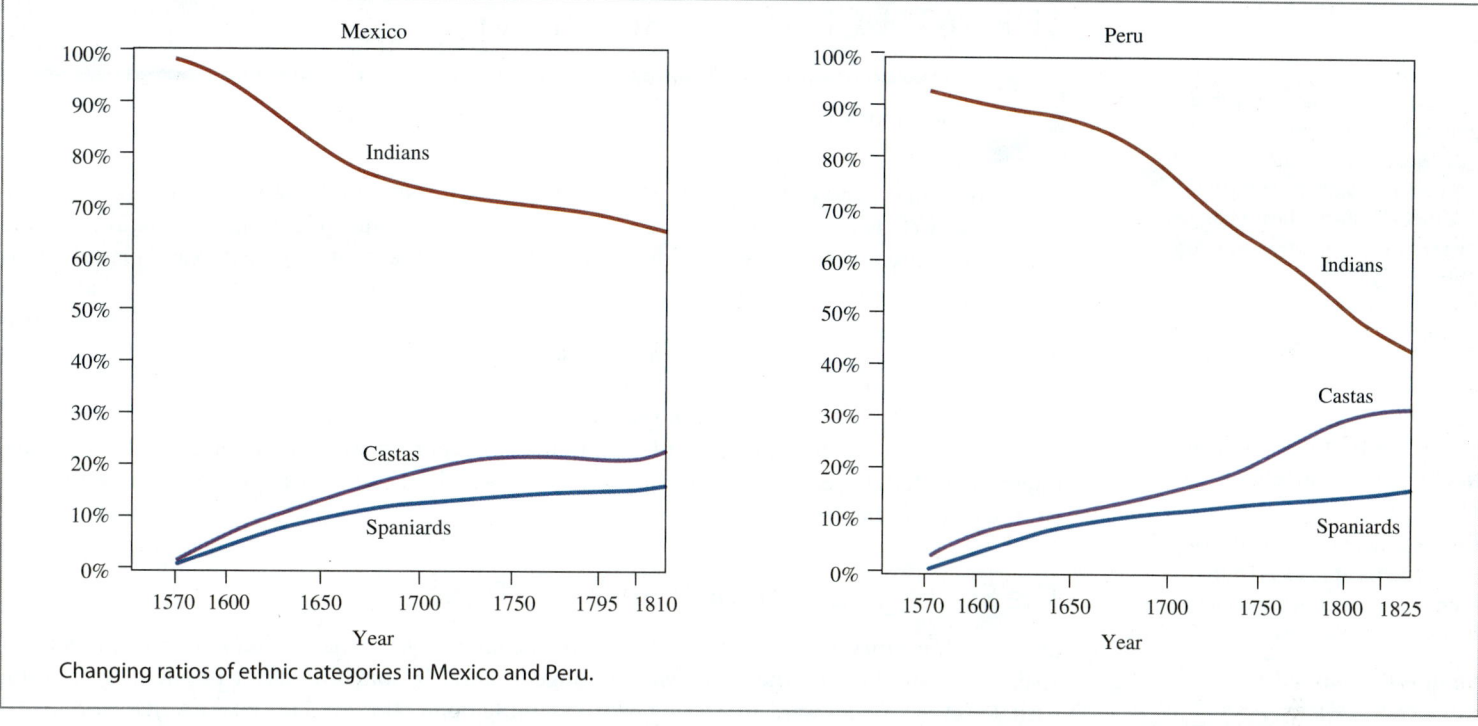

Changing ratios of ethnic categories in Mexico and Peru.

of the wealthy merchants, landowners, bureaucrats, and miners were white. As one visitor wrote, "In America, every white is a gentleman."

Originally, all whites had shared the privileged status of Spaniards regardless of the continent of their birth, but over time distinctions developed between **peninsulares**, or those actually born in Spain, and **Creoles**, or those born in the New World. Creoles thought of themselves as loyal American Spaniards, but with so many mestizos around, the shadow of a possible Indian ancestor and illegitimacy always made their status suspect as far as the Europeans were concerned. Still, Creoles dominated the local economies, held sway over large numbers of dependents at their haciendas and mines, and stood at the top of society, second only to the peninsulares. Increasingly, they developed a sense of identity and pride in their accomplishments, and they were sensitive to any suggestion of inferiority or to any discrimination because of their American birth. That growing sense of self-identity eventually contributed to the movements for independence in Latin America.

The hierarchy of race intersected with traditional Iberian distinctions based on gender, age, and class. The father of a family had legal authority over his children until they were 25. Women were in a subordinate position; they could not serve in government and were expected to assume the duties of motherhood and household (Figure 19.10). After marriage, women came under the authority of their husbands, but many a widow assumed the direction of her family's activities. Lower-class women often controlled small-scale commerce in towns and villages, worked in the fields, and labored at the looms of small factories. Marriages often were arranged and accompanied by the payment of a dowry, which remained the property of the woman throughout the marriage. Women also had full rights to inheritance. Some upper-class women who did not marry at a young age were placed in convents to prevent contacts or marriages with partners of unsuitable backgrounds.

FIGURE **19.10** Women in colonial Latin America engaged in agriculture and manufacturing, especially in textile workshops, but social ideology still reserved the household and the kitchen as the proper sphere for women, as seen in this scene of a kitchen in a large Mexican home.

THE 18TH-CENTURY REFORMS

> **19.6** Did reforms in the 18th century save these empires or provoke their fall?

Increasing attacks on the Iberian empires by foreign rivals led to the Bourbon reforms in Spanish America and the reforms of Pombal in Brazil. These changes strengthened the two empires but also generated colonial unrest that eventually led to movements for independence.

No less than in the rest of Europe, the 18th century was a period of intellectual ferment in Spain and Portugal as well as in their empires. In Spain and its colonies, small clubs and associations, calling themselves **amigos del país**, or friends of the country, met in many cities to discuss and plan all kinds of reforms. Their programs were for material benefits and improvements, not political changes. In Portugal, foreign influences and ideas created a group of progressive thinkers and bureaucrats open to new ideas in economy, education, and philosophy. Much of the change that came in both empires resulted as much from the changing European economic and demographic realities as from new ideas. The expansion of population and economy in Europe, and the increased demands for American products, along with the long series of wars in the 18th century, gave the American colonies a new importance. Both the Spanish and Portuguese empires revived, but with some long-term results that eventually led to the fall of both.

The Shifting Balance of Politics and Trade

peninsulares People living in the New World Spanish colonies but born in Spain.

Creoles Whites born in the New World; dominated local Latin American economies and ranked just beneath peninsulares.

amigos del país [uh mEE gOs, ä mEE-, del päEEs] Clubs and associations dedicated to improvements and reform in Spanish colonies; flourished during the 18th century; called for material improvements rather than political reform.

By the 18th century, it was clear that the Spanish colonial system had become outmoded and that Spain's exclusive hold on the Indies was no longer secure. To some extent the problem lay in Spain itself. Beset by foreign wars, increasing debt, declining population, and internal revolts, a weakened Spain was threatened by a powerful France and by the rising mercantile strength of England and Holland, whose Protestantism also made them natural rivals of Catholic Spain. Since the 16th century, French, Dutch, and English ship captains had combined contraband trade with raiding in the Spanish empire, and although Spain's European rivals could not seize Mexico or Peru, the sparsely populated islands and coasts of the Caribbean became likely targets. Buccaneers, owing allegiance to no nation, raided the Caribbean ports in the late 17th century. Meanwhile, the English took Jamaica in 1654, the French took control of western Hispaniola (Haiti) by 1697, and other islands fell to the English, French, and Dutch. Many of the islands turned to sugar production and the creation of slave and plantation colonies much like those in Brazil. These settlements were part of a general process of colonization, of which the English settlement of eastern North America and the French occupation of Canada and the Mississippi valley were also part. In the Caribbean new plantation colonies producing sugar, coffee, tobacco, and cotton, were created on islands like Barbados, Jamaica, and Martinique and in Guiana and Surinam on the northern coast of South America. Spain's territorial monopoly was now challenged.

Less apparent than the loss of territories, but equally important, was the failure of the Spanish mercantile and political system. The annual fleets became irregular. Silver payments from America declined, and most goods shipped to the West Indies and even the ships that carried them were non-Spanish in origin. The colonies became increasingly self-sufficient in basic commodities, and as central government became weaker, local aristocrats in the colonies exercised increasing control over the economy and government of their regions, often at the expense of the Native American and the lower-class populations. Graft and corruption were rampant in many branches of government. The empire seemed to be crumbling. What is most impressive is that Spain was able to retain its American possessions for another century.

War of the Spanish Succession Resulted from Bourbon family's succession to Spanish throne in 1701; ended by Treaty of Utrecht in 1713; resulted in recognition of Bourbons, loss of some lands, grants of commercial rights to English and French.

Even with Spain in decline, the West Indies still seemed an attractive prize coveted by other powers, and the opportunity to gain them was not long in coming. A final crisis was set in motion in 1701 when the Spanish king, Charles II, died without an heir. Other European nations backed various claimants to the Spanish throne, hoping to win the prize of the Spanish monarchy and its American colonies. Philip of Anjou, a Bourbon and thus a relative of the king of France, was named successor to the Spanish throne. The **War of the Spanish Succession** (1702–1713) ensued, and the result at the Treaty of Utrecht (1713) was recognition of a branch of the Bourbon family as rulers of Spain; the price was some commercial concessions that allowed French merchants to operate in Seville and permitted England to trade slaves in Spanish America (and even to send one ship per year to trade for silver in the Americas). Spain's commercial monopoly was now being broken not just by contraband trade but by legal means as well.

The Bourbon Reforms

The new and vigorous Bourbon dynasty in Spain launched a series of reforms aimed at strengthening the state and its economy. In this age of "enlightened despotism," the Spanish Bourbon monarchs, especially **Charles III** (r. 1759–1788), were moved by economic nationalism and a desire for strong centralized government to institute economic, administrative, and military reforms in Spain and its empire. The goal of these rulers and their progressive ministers was to revive Spain within the framework of its traditional society. Their aim was to make government more effective, more powerful, and better able to direct the economy. Certain groups or institutions that opposed these measures or stood in the way might be punished or suppressed. The Jesuit order, with its special allegiance to Rome, its rumored wealth, and its missions in the New World (which controlled almost 100,000 Indians in Paraguay alone), was a prime target. The Jesuits were expelled from Spain and its empire in 1767, as they had been from the Portuguese empire in 1759. In general, however, the entrenched interests of the church and the nobility were not frontally attacked as long as they did not conflict with the authority of the crown. The reforms were aimed at material improvements and a more powerful state, not social or political upheaval. French bureaucratic models were introduced. The system of taxation was tightened. The navy was reformed, and new ships were built. The convoy fleet system was abandoned, and in 1778 new ports were opened in Spain and America for the West Indies trade, although trade still was restricted to Spaniards or to ships sailing under Spanish license.

In the West Indies, the Bourbons initiated a broad program of reform. New viceroyalties were created in New Granada (1739) and the Rio de la Plata (1778) to provide better administration and defense to the growing populations of these regions (Map 19.3). Royal investigators were sent to the Indies. The most important of them, **José de Gálvez**, spent six years in Mexico before returning to Spain to become minister of the Indies and a chief architect of reform. His investigations, as well as reports by others, revealed the worst abuses of graft and corruption, which implicated the local magistrates and the Creole landowners and aristocracy. Gálvez moved to eliminate the Creoles from the upper bureaucracy of the colonies. New offices were created. After 1780, the *corregidores*, or local magistrates, were removed from the Indian villages, and that office was replaced by a new system of intendants, or provincial governors, based on French models. This intendancy system was introduced throughout the Indies. Such measures improved tax collection and made government more effective, but the reforms also disrupted the patterns of influence and power, especially among the Creole bureaucrats, miners, and landowners as their political power declined.

Many of the reforms in America were linked directly to defense and military matters. During the century, Spain often was allied with France, and the global struggle between England and France for world hegemony made Spain's American possessions a logical target for English attack. During the Seven Years War (1756–1763), the loss of Florida and the English seizure of Havana shocked Spain into action, particularly because when England held Havana in 1762, Cuban trade boomed. Regular Spanish troops were sent to New Spain, and militia units, led by local Creoles who were given military rank, were created throughout the empire. Frontiers were expanded, and previously unoccupied or loosely controlled regions, such as California, were settled by a combination of missions and small frontier outposts. In the Rio de la Plata, foreign competitors were resisted by military means. Spain sought every means to strengthen itself and its colonies.

During the Bourbon reforms, the government took an active role in the economy. State monopolies were established for items the government considered essential, such as tobacco and gunpowder. Whole new areas of Spanish America were opened to development. Monopoly companies were granted exclusive rights to develop certain colonial areas in return for developing the economies of those regions.

The trade of the Caribbean greatly expanded under the more liberal regulations. Cuba became another full-scale plantation and slave colony, exporting sugar, coffee, and tobacco and importing large numbers of Africans to do the work. Buenos Aires, on the Rio de la Plata, proved to be a great success story. Its population had grown rapidly in the 18th century, and by 1790 it had a booming economy based on ranching and the export of hides and salted beef. A newly prosperous merchant community in Buenos Aires dominated the region's trade.

The commercial changes were a double-edged sword. As Spanish and English goods became cheaper and more accessible, they undercut locally produced goods so that some regions that had

Charles III Spanish enlightened monarch; ruled from 1759 to 1788; instituted fiscal, administrative, and military reforms in Spain and its empire.

Gálvez, José de (1720–1787) Spanish minister of the West Indies and chief architect of colonial reform; moved to eliminate Creoles from upper bureaucracy of the colonies; created intendants for local government.

MAP 19.3 **Spanish and Portuguese South America around 1800** Bourbon reforms created new viceroyalties in order to improve defense, taxation, and administration. In Brazil, central control was enhanced from the new capital of Rio de Janeiro after 1763 while the northern Amazonian region was brought directly under Lisbon's control by strong governors.

specialized in producing cloth or other goods were unable to compete with the European imports. Links to international trade tightened as the diversity of Latin America's economy decreased. Later conflicts between those who favored free trade and those who wanted to limit imports and protect local industry often were as much about regional interests as about economic philosophy.

Finally, and most importantly, the major centers of the Spanish empire also experienced rapid growth in the second half of the 18th century. Mining inspectors and experts had been sent to Peru and New Spain to suggest reforms and introduce new techniques. These improvements, as well as the discovery of new veins, allowed production to expand, especially in New Spain, where silver output reached new heights. In fact, silver production in Mexico far outstripped that of Peru, which itself saw increased production.

All in all, the Bourbon reforms must be seen from two vantage points: Spain and America. Undoubtedly, in the short run, the restructuring of government and economy revived the Spanish empire. In the long run, the removal of Creoles from government, the creation of a militia with a Creole officer corps, the opening of commerce, and other such changes contributed to a growing sense of dissatisfaction among the elites, which only their relative well-being and the existing social tensions of the sociedad de castas kept in check. Slaves, peasants, and indigenous communities, however, were developing their own disatisfactions with colonial government.

Pombal and Brazil

The Bourbon reforms in Spain and Spanish America were paralleled in the Portuguese world during the administration of Sebastião José Carvalho e Mello, the **Marquis of Pombal** (1755–1776), Portugal's authoritarian prime minister. Pombal had lived as ambassador in England and had observed the benefits of mercantilism at firsthand. He hoped to use these same techniques, along with state intervention in the economy, to break England's hold on the Portuguese economy, especially on the flow of Brazilian gold from Portugal to England. This became crucial as the production of Brazilian gold began to decline after 1760. In another example of "enlightened despotism," Pombal brutally suppressed any group or institution that stood in the way of royal power and his programs. He developed a particular dislike for the Jesuits because of their allegiance to Rome and their semi-independent control of large areas in Brazil. Pombal expelled the Jesuits from the Portuguese empire in 1759.

Pombal made Brazil the centerpiece of his reforms. Vigorous administrators were sent to the colony to enforce the changes. Fiscal reforms were aimed at eliminating contraband, gold smuggling, and tax evasion. Monopoly companies were formed to stimulate agriculture in older plantation zones and were given the right to import large numbers of slaves. New crops were introduced. Just as in Spanish America, new regions in Brazil began to flourish. Rio de Janeiro became the capital, and its hinterland was the scene of agricultural growth. The undeveloped Amazonian region, long dominated by Jesuit missionaries, received new attention. A monopoly company was created to develop the region's economy, and it stimulated the development of cotton plantations and the export of wild cacao from the Amazonian forests. These new exports joined the traditional sugar, tobacco, and hides as Brazil's main products.

Pombal was willing to do some social tinkering as part of his project of reform. He abolished slavery in Portugal to stop the import of slaves there and to ensure a steady supply to Brazil, the economic cornerstone of the empire. Because Brazil was vast and needed to be both occupied and defended, he removed Indians from missionary control in the Amazon and encouraged whites to marry them. Immigrant couples from Portugal and the Azores were sent to colonize the Amazon basin and the plains of southern Brazil, which began to produce large quantities of wheat and cattle. Like the Bourbons in Spain, Pombal hoped to revitalize the colonies as a way of strengthening the mother country. Although new policies were instituted, little changed within the society. Brazil was just as profoundly based on slavery in the late 18th century as it had ever been: The levels of slave imports reached 20,000 a year.

Even in the long run, Pombal's policies were not fully effective. Although he reduced Portugal's trade imbalance with England during this period, Brazilian trade suffered because the demand for its products on the world market remained low. This was a classic problem for the American colonies. Their economies were so tied to the sale of their products on the European market and so controlled by policies in the metropolis that the colonies' range of action was always limited. Although Pombal's policies were not immediately successful, they provided the structure for an economic boom in the last 20 years of the 18th century that set the stage for Brazilian independence.

Marquis of Pombal Prime minister of Portugal from 1755 to 1776; acted to strengthen royal authority in Brazil; expelled Jesuits; enacted fiscal reforms and established monopoly companies to stimulate the colonial economy.

Reforms, Reactions, and Revolts

By the mid-18th century, the American colonies of Spain and Portugal, like the rest of the world, were experiencing rapid growth in population and productive capacity. By the end of the century, Spanish America had a population of almost 13 million. Between 1740 and 1800, the population of Mexico, the most populous area, increased from 3.5 million to almost 6 million, about half of whom were Indians. In Brazil the population reached about 2 million by the end of the century. This overall increase resulted from declining mortality rates, increasing fertility levels, increasing immigration from Europe, and the thriving slave trade. The opening of new areas to development and Europe's increasing demand for American products accompanied the population growth. The American colonies were experiencing a boom in the last years of the 18th century.

Reformist policies, tighter tax collection, and the presence of a more activist government in both Spanish America and Brazil disrupted old patterns of power and influence, raised expectations, and sometimes provoked violent colonial reactions. Urban riots, tax revolts, and Indian uprisings were not unknown before 1700, but serious and more protracted rebellions broke out after that date. In New Granada (present-day Colombia), popular complaints against the government's control of tobacco and liquor consumption, and rising prices as well as new taxes, led to the widespread **Comunero Revolt** in 1781. A royal army was defeated, the viceroy fled from Bogota, and a rebel army almost took the capital. Only tensions between the various racial and social groups, and concessions by the government, brought an end to the rebellion.

At the same time, in Peru, an even more threatening revolt erupted. A great Indian uprising took place under the leadership of Jose Gabriel Condorcanqui, known as **Tupac Amaru II**. A mestizo who claimed descent from the Incas, Tupac Amaru led a rebellion against "bad government." For almost three years the whole viceroyalty was thrown into turmoil while more than 70,000 Indians, mestizos, and even a few Creoles joined in rebellion against the worst abuses of the colonial regime. Tupac Amaru was captured and brutally executed, but the rebellion smoldered until 1783. It failed mostly because the Creoles, although they had their own grievances against the government, feared that a real social upheaval might take place if they upset the political balance.

This kind of social upheaval was not present in Brazil, where a government attempt to collect back taxes in the mining region led in 1788 to a plot against Portuguese control. A few bureaucrats, intellectuals, and miners planned an uprising for independence, but their conspiracy was discovered. The plotters were arrested, and one conspirator, a militia officer nicknamed Tiradentes, was hanged.

Despite their various social bases, these movements indicated that activism by governments increased dissatisfaction in the American colonies. The new prosperity of the late 18th century contributed to a sense of self-confidence and economic interest among certain colonial classes, which made them sensitive to restrictions and control by Spain and Portugal. Different groups had different complaints, but the sharp social and ethnic divisions within the colonies acted as a barrier to cooperation for common goals and tended to undercut revolutionary movements. Only when the Spanish political system was disrupted by a crisis of legitimacy at the beginning of the 19th century did real separation and independence from the mother countries become a possibility.

Comunero Revolt One of popular revolts against Spanish colonial rule in New Granada (Colombia) in 1781; suppressed as a result of divisions among rebels.

Amaru, Tupac, II (1738–1781) Mestizo leader of Indian revolt in Peru; supported by many among lower social classes; revolt eventually failed because of Creole fears of real social revolution.

Global Connections and Critical Themes

LATIN AMERICAN CIVILIZATION AND THE WORLD CONTEXT

In three centuries, Spain and Portugal created large colonial empires in the Americas. These American colonies provided a basis of power to their Iberian mother countries and took a vital place in the expanding world economy as suppliers of precious minerals and certain crops to the growing economy of Europe. By the 18th century, the weakened positions of Spain and Portugal within Europe allowed England and France to benefit directly from the Iberian trade with American colonies. To their American colonies, the Iberian nations transferred and imposed their language, laws, forms of government, religion, and institutions. Large numbers of immigrants, first as conquerors and later as settlers, came to the colonies. Eventually, the whole spectrum of Iberian society was recreated in the New World as men and women came to seek a better life, bringing with them their customs, ideas, religion, laws, and ways of life. By government and individual action, a certain homogeneity was created, both in Spanish America and in Brazil. That seeming unity was most apparent among the Europeanized population, especially in the urban areas where the networks of contact and communication were well developed.

In fact, despite the apparent continuity with Spain and Portugal and homogeneity among the various colonies, there were great variations. Latin America, with its distinct environments, its various economic possibilities, and its diverse indigenous peoples, imposed new realities. In places such as Mexico and Peru, Native American cultures emerged from the shock of conquest, battered but still vibrant. Native American communities adapted to the new colonial situation. A distinctive multiethnic and multiracial society developed, drawing on Iberian precedents but also dependent on the native population, the imported Africans, and the various mixed racial categories. Argentina with few Native Americans, Cuba with its slaves and plantations, and Mexico with its large rural indigenous populations all shared the same Hispanic traditions and laws, and all had a predominantly white elite, but their social and economic realities made them very different places. Latin America developed as a composite civilization—distinct from the West but related to it—combining European and Native American culture and society or creating the racial hierarchies of slave societies in places such as Brazil.

The empires of Spain and Portugal in Latin America bear comparison with the Russian empire that had been formed at about the same time. While Iberian expansion had been maritime and Russian expansion over land, the process of colonization and the conquest of indigenous peoples created many parallels, including the development of coerced labor. The creation of all of these empires also demonstrated the impact of gunpowder. But the cultural impact of the West was different in the Iberian and Russian empires. Whereas the Russian rulers had decided, quite selectively, what aspects of Western culture to adopt, in Latin America Western forms were often simply imposed on the populations, but not without resistance.

The American colonies of Portugal and Spain also bear comparison with those of the English, French, and Dutch who at first coveted the Iberian possessions and then created their own empires, sometimes at the expense of the Iberians, but often following their models. The empires of Portugal and Spain were global in reach, but the American colonies became part of an Atlantic system that promoted continual interchange between Africa, Europe, and America of goods, people, cultures, and ideas. This too was a pattern that other Europeans followed.

From the perspective of the world economy, despite the ultimate decline in production of precious metals, Latin American products remained in great demand in Europe's markets. As Latin Americans began to seek political independence in the early 19th century, they were confronted by this basic economic fact and by their continued dependence on trade with the developing global economy. Latin America's world economic position, with its dependent and coerced labor force and outside commercial control, revealed its colonial status, but in its often bitter history of cultural clash and accommodation a new civilization had been born.

Further Readings

Jose C. Moya, ed., *The Oxford Handbook of Latin American History* (2011) contains excellent essays on aspects of colonial history while James Lockhart and Stuart B. Schwartz, *Early Latin America* (1983), provides an interpretative overview. John Hemming, *Rivers of Gold* (2003), gives an excellent narrative of the early conquests while Henry Kamen, *Empire: How Spain Became a World Power* (2003), places the Americas in the context of Spain's other imperial holdings in Europe and Asia. John Elliott, *Empires of the Atlantic World* (2007), carefully compares English and Spanish colonization in the Americas. A view of Latin America within a comparative Atlantic perspective is provided by Christine Daniels and Michael V. Kennedy, eds., *Negotiated Empires: Centers and Peripheries in the Americas, 1500–1820* (2002), and in Jorge Cañizares-Esguerra and Erik R. Seeman, eds., *The Atlantic in Global History, 1500–2000* (2007). John R. Fisher, *The Economic Aspects of Spanish Imperialism in America, 1492–1810* (1997) is a good starting point for a discussion of commerce and government while Alejandro de la Fuente, *Havana and the Atlantic in the Sixteenth Century* (2008) does the same on a regional level.

Matthew Restall, *Seven Myths of the Spanish Conquest* (2003), provides a fresh look at that process. On the conquest period there are many excellent regional studies such as Ida Altman, *The War for Mexico's West: Indians and Spaniards in New Galicia, 1524–1550* (2010) or Susan Schroeder, *The Conquest All Over Again* (2010). The story of Mancio Serra is told in Stuart Stirling, *The Last Conquistador* (1999). An indigenous view of the conquest and of Spanish rule is found in Felipe Guaman Poma de Ayala, *The First New Chronicle and Good Government*, (2006), edited by David Frye. The conquest of Mexico can be seen from two different angles in Bernal Díaz del Castillo, *The Discovery and Conquest of Mexico*, trans. A. P. Maudsley (1956), and in James Lockhart's edition of the Nahuatl testimony gathered after the conquest by Bernardino de Sahagún, published as *We Peoples Here* (1962). Various indigenous and Spanish sources are collected in S. Schwartz, ed., *Victors and Vanquished* (2000).

The transformation of Indian societies has been studied in many books, such as Susan E. Ramírez, *The World Turned Upside Down* (1996) on Peru; Matthew Restall, *The Maya World* (1997), on Yucatan; Susan Kellogg, *Law and the Transformation of Aztec Culture, 1500–1700* (1995) on Mexico; or Kris Lane, *Quito, 1599* (2002) on Ecuador. Ward Stavig, *The World of Tupac Amaru* (1999), on 18th-century Peru; examines the transformations of the late colonial era. Other approaches to the impact of conquest are presented in Noble David Cook, *Born to Die: Disease and New World Conquest, 1492–1650* (1998), and Carolyn Dean, *Inka Bodies and the Bodies of Christ* (1999). Particularly sensitive to Indian views are Nancy Farriss, *Maya Society Under Colonial Rule* (1984), and Kenneth Mills, *Idolatry and Its Enemies* (1997).

Social and economic history have received considerable attention. The establishment of colonial economies has been studied in detail in books such as Stuart Schwartz, *Sugar Plantations and the Formation of Brazilian Society* (1985) and Peter Bakewell, *Silver Mining in Colonial Mexico* (1971). How Latin Americas commodities reached the rest of the world is revealed in Kris Lane, *Colour of Paradise. The Emerald in the Age of Gunpowder Empires* (2010). Very good social history is now being written. For example, on women there are Susan Socolow, *Women in Colonial Latin America* (2000); Susan Kellogg, *Weaving the Past* (2005), on indigenous women in general; and Karen Graubart, *With Our Labor and Sweat* (2007), on Indian women in Peru. Arnold Bauer, *Goods, Power, and History* (2001), discusses material culture. A different kind of social history that examines popular thought can be seen in Serge Gruzinski, *The Conquest of Mexico* (1993), while Ilona Katzew, *Casta Painting* (2004) brings the methods of art history to bear in an analysis of images of society in New Spain. The issue of race is studied in María Elena Martínez, *Genealogical Fictions: Limpieza de sangre, Religion, and Gender in Colonial Mexico* (2008). The newer cultural approaches can be seen in Linda Curcio-Nagy, *The Great Festivals of Colonial Mexico City* (2004). Excellent studies of the environment's impact on society and vice versa can be read in Charles Walker, *Shaky Colonialism* (2008), on the 1746 Lima earthquake, Reinaldo Funes Monzote, *From Rainforest to Cane Field in Cuba* (2008), and J. R. McNeil, *Mosquito Empires. Ecology and War in the Greater Caribbean, 1620–1914* (2010).

The best starting place on the Bourbon reforms is still David Brading, *Miners and Merchants in Bourbon Mexico* (1971). David Weber, *Bárbaros: Spaniards and Their Savages in the Age of Enlightenment* (2005), examines changing policies toward Native Americans. John R. Fisher, *Bourbon Peru, 1750–1824* (2003) provides an excellent regional study. The revolt of Tupac Amaru and other indigenous rebellions are analyzed in Sinclair Thomson, *We Alone Will Rule* (2002). On Brazil, James Wadsworth, *Agents of Orthodoxy* (2007), shows how Pombal's policies and the Enlightenment affected society and institutions while Kenneth Maxwell's *Pombal: Paradox of the Enlightenment* (1995) examines that statesman in an imperial context. Junia Furtado, *Xica da Silva* (2008), follows the life of one remarkable woman in Brazil in the late colonial era.

On MyHistoryLab

 Study and Review on MyHistoryLab

Critical Thinking Questions

1. How did the conquest and incorporation of the Americas transform the economy of the world?
2. Why did it also challenge the moral and intellectual heritage of the classical world?
3. Why did coerced labor, especially slavery become so important in its history and what were the cultural results of that importance?

20

Africa and the Africans in the Age of the Atlantic Slave Trade

Listen to Chapter 20 on MyHistoryLab

Sometimes a single, extraordinary life can represent the forces and patterns of a whole historical era. Born in the early 19th century, Mahommah Gardo Baquaqua was a young man from the trading town of Djougou in what is now the Benin Republic in west Africa. A Muslim, he could speak Arabic, Hausa, and a number of other languages, as was common among the trading peoples from which he came. At a young age, Baquaqua was captured and enslaved during a war with a neighboring African state; after gaining his freedom, he was enslaved again, and around 1845 he was sold into the Atlantic slave trade.

Baquaqua was taken first to northeastern Brazil and from there was purchased by a ship captain from Rio de Janeiro. After a number of voyages along the Brazilian coast, his ship eventually sailed for New York. After a failed attempt to use the American courts to gain his freedom (a strategy that many slaves attempted), Baquaqua fled to Boston with the help of local abolitionists.

LEARNING OBJECTIVES

20.1 What reasons impelled Europe to turn to Africa for laborers? Were racial attitudes a major cause? p. 454

20.2 How did the slave trade affect the societies and populations of Africa? p. 456

20.3 What was the cultural impact of Africans on the New World? p. 460

20.4 Compare the effects of the settler colony of South Africa to the European trading ports in West Africa. p. 467

20.5 Is "continuity" or "creative adaptation" the best way to understand the cultural importance of the African diaspora? p. 469

FIGURE **20.1** Image of African slave trade. The French artist Auguste François Biard painted this scene of the west African slave trade in 1840 in an attempt to show its cruelties. Represented here are not only the European merchants and sailors receiving the slaves but west African merchants and soldiers involved in supplying them. The painting was eventually acquired by an ardent English abolitionist.

Watch the Video Series on MyHistoryLab

Learn about some key topics related to this chapter with the *MyHistoryLab Video Series: Key Topics in World History*

In that city he was befriended by antislavery Baptist missionaries. With them, he sailed for Haiti. Eventually he learned French and English and studied at a college in upstate New York in order to prepare for missionary work in his native Africa. His life was not easy. Eventually, because of racial incidents, he moved to Canada.

Although Baquaqua had left the Baptist college, he did not abandon his desire to return to Africa, and he continued to seek ways to make that voyage. In 1854, in an attempt to get the money he needed to realize his dream, he published his autobiography, *An Interesting Narrative: Biography of Mahommah G. Baquaqua*. In it he was able to provide his personal observations on his experiences. On the slave ship, he reported:

> O the loathsomeness and filth of that horrible place will never be effaced from my memory; nay as long as my memory holds her seat in this distracted brain, will I remember that. My heart, even at this day, sickens at the thought of it. Let those *humane individuals*, who are in favor of slavery, only allow themselves to take the slave's position in the noisome hold of a slave ship, just for one trip from Africa to America, and without going into the horrors of slavery further than this, if they do not come out thorough-going abolitionists, then I have no more to say in favor of abolition.

The only place worse than the hold of a slave ship, said Baquaqua, was the place to which slave owners would be condemned in the next life (Figure 20.1). We do not know whether Baquaqua finally returned to the land of his birth, but the life of this African, while singular in many aspects, represents the stories of millions of Africans in the age of the slave trade, and these make up an important part of world history. ∎

Sub-Saharan Africa, previously linked to the Muslim world in many ways, moved at its own pace even as it was pulled in new directions during the early modern centuries. Islam remained important, and eastern Africa did trade with western Asia, but the rise of Europe and of the western-dominated world economy proved to be a powerful force in recasting the framework of African history. The strength of earlier African cultural and political traditions persisted in many places, but the impact of the West was the newest influence in Africa and in some respects an immensely powerful one. African history had its own pace, and this chapter therefore exceeds the chronological boundaries of the early modern period. The influences of Islam and the West initiated or intensified processes of religious conversion, political reorganization, and social change that persisted in some cases into the 19th century. The distinctive nature and chronology of African history should not blind us to its role in world history.

AFRICA AND THE CREATION OF AN ATLANTIC SYSTEM

> Beginning in the 16th century the Atlantic Ocean became an "inland sea" where the people, products, and ideas of Europe, Africa, and the Americas constantly moved. Africans played an essential role in this process primarily, but not exclusively, through the slave trade.

20.1 What reasons impelled Europe to turn to Africa for laborers? Were racial attitudes a major cause?

During the age of European maritime and commercial expansion, large areas of Africa were brought into the orbit of the expanding world economy and were influenced by the transformation that was taking place. Not all parts of Africa were influenced in the same way or at the same time. After 1450,

1400 C.E.	1500 C.E.	1600 C.E.	1700 C.E.	1800 C.E.
1415 Portuguese capture Ceuta (Morocco); beginning of European expansion **1441** First shipment of African slaves brought directly from Africa to Portugal **1481** Portuguese fort established at El Mina (Ghana)	**1562** Beginnings of English slave trade **1570** Portuguese establish colony in Angola **1591** Fall of Songhay Empire	**1652** Dutch establish colony at Cape of Good Hope	**1700–1717** Osei Tutu unifies the Asante kingdom **1713** English get right to import slaves to Spanish Empire **1720s** Rise of the kingdom of Dahomey **1790s** Abolitionist movement gains strength in England **1792** Slave uprising in Haiti	**1804** Usuman Dan Fodio leads Hausa expansion **1815** Cape colony comes under formal British control **1818–1828** Shaka forges Zulu power and expansion; mfecane under way **1833** Great Britain abolishes slavery in the West Indies **1834** Boers make "Great Trek" into Natal

the growing and often bitter contacts between Europeans and Africans, primarily through the slave trade, linked the destiny of Africa to the broader external trends of the emerging world economy. These contacts also resulted in a diaspora of millions of Africans to the Middle East, Europe, and especially across the Atlantic to the Americas. Not all European contact with Africa was centered on the slave trade, nor was the desire for slaves the only impulse behind European explorations, but the slave trade after 1600 overshadowed other activities until the mid-19th century. Slavery became a central feature in the links formed between the continents that bordered the Atlantic. Changing global interactions had a direct impact on certain areas of Africa, and they also made Africans an important element in the shifting balance of world civilizations. The forced movement of Africans as captive laborers and the creation of slave-based societies in the Americas were major aspects of the formation of the modern world and the growth of the economies of western Europe. This forced migration was part of the international exchange of foods, diseases, animals, and ideas that marked the era and had a profound influence on the indigenous peoples in various regions, as we saw in the case of the Americas. Moreover, in the large areas of the Americas colonized by Europeans where slavery came to be the predominant form of labor, African cultures became part of a complex mixture, contributing to the creation of new cultural forms. Although much of the analysis in this chapter emphasizes the increasing linkage between Africa and the wider world, it should be made clear at the outset that many fundamental processes of African development continued throughout this period. Almost all of Africa remained independent of outside political control, and most cultural development was autonomous as well. Although both were part of a developing Atlantic system, Africa differed profoundly from Latin America in these respects during the early modern centuries.

A variety of trends affected various parts of the sub-Saharan region. Islam consolidated its position in east Africa and the Sudan. In Ethiopia the Christian kingdom of the highlands continued to hold off its Muslim rivals. In many places in Africa, as in Europe, independent states continued to form and expand, perhaps as a result of a population expansion that followed the spread of iron tools and improved agriculture. Kingdoms spread to new areas. Scholars disagree on the extent to which these long-term developments were affected by Europeans and the rise of the Atlantic slave trade. Some argue that the enlarged political scale—the growth of large kingdoms through much of the subcontinent—was the dominant theme of the period and that slavery was one of its by-products. Others see European demand as a major impulse in political expansion. In this chapter we emphasize the impact of slavery and the slave trade because our focus in a world history is not simply the geographic region of Africa but on the Africans who, like Baquaqua, and so many others, were swept into the expanding international economy. It is important to remember that before 1800 at least twice as many Africans crossed the Atlantic than did Europeans, and so they were fundamental to creation of the Atlantic system.

Read the **Document** on **MyHistoryLab**: Leo Africanus' Description of West Africa (1500)

THE ATLANTIC SLAVE TRADE

> Early Portuguese contacts set the patterns for contact with the African coast. The slave trade expanded to meet the demand for labor in the new American colonies, and millions were exported in an organized commerce that involved both Europeans and Africans.

20.2 How did the slave trade affect the societies and populations of Africa?

Portuguese ships pushed down the west African coast and finally reached the Cape of Good Hope in 1487 (Map 20.1). Along the coast, the Portuguese established **factories:** forts and trading posts with resident merchants. The most important of these outposts was **El Mina** (1482) in the heart of the gold-producing region of the forest zone. These forts allowed the Portuguese to exercise some control with few personnel. Although the early voyagers carried out some raids, once their cannon range was exceeded the Portuguese simply were not powerful enough to enforce their will on the larger west African states. Therefore, most forts were established with the consent of local rulers, who benefited from access to European commodities and sometimes from the military support the Portuguese provided in local wars.

Africans acquired goods from the Portuguese, who sometimes provided African rulers with slaves brought from other stretches of the coast. In return, the Portuguese received ivory, pepper, animal skins, and gold. From El Mina, Accra, and other trade forts, routes led directly into the gold-producing regions of the interior, so that the Portuguese eventually traded with Mande and Soninke merchants from Mali and Songhay. Much of the Portuguese success resulted from their ability to penetrate the existing African trade routes, to which they could also add specialized items. Portuguese and African Portuguese mulatto traders struck out into the interior to establish trade contacts and collection points.

Trade was the basis of Portuguese relations with Africans, but in the wake of commerce followed political, religious, and social relations. The small states of the Senegambian coast did not impress the Portuguese, who were particularly suspicious of Muslims, their traditional enemies. When they reached the Gold Coast (modern Ghana) and found the kingdom of Benin, they were impressed both by the power of the ruler and by the magnificence of his court. Other large African states also provoked similar responses.

factories European trading fortresses and compounds with resident merchants; utilized throughout Portuguese trading empire to assure secure landing places and commerce.

El Mina Most important of early Portuguese trading factories in forest zone of Africa.

Mvemba, Nzinga [NZIHNG-uh MVEHM-buh] King of Kongo south of Zaire River from 1507 to 1543; converted to Christianity and took title Alfonso I; under Portuguese influence attempted to Christianize all of kingdom.

Missionary efforts were made to convert the rulers of Benin, Kongo, and other African kingdoms. The Portuguese contacted the Kongo kingdom south of the Zaire River about 1484. The missionaries achieved a major success in Kongo, where members of the royal family were converted. The ruler, **Nzinga Mvemba** (r. 1507–1543), with the help of Portuguese advisors and missionaries, brought the whole kingdom to Christianity. Attempts were made to "Europeanize" the kingdom. Portugal and Kongo exchanged ambassadors and dealt with each other with a certain equality in this early period, but eventually enslavement of his subjects led Nzinga Mvemba to try to end the slave trade and limit Portuguese activities. He was only partially successful because of Portugal's control of Kongo's ability to communicate with the outside world and its dominance over Kongo's trade.

These first contacts were marked by cultural preconceptions as well as by appreciation and curiosity. Africans found the newcomers strange and at first tried to fit them into their existing concepts of the spiritual and natural world. Images of Portuguese soldiers and traders began to appear in the bronzes of Benin and the carved ivory sculptures of other African peoples (Figure 20.2). The Portuguese tended to look on Africans as savages and pagans but also as capable of civilized behavior and conversion to Christianity.

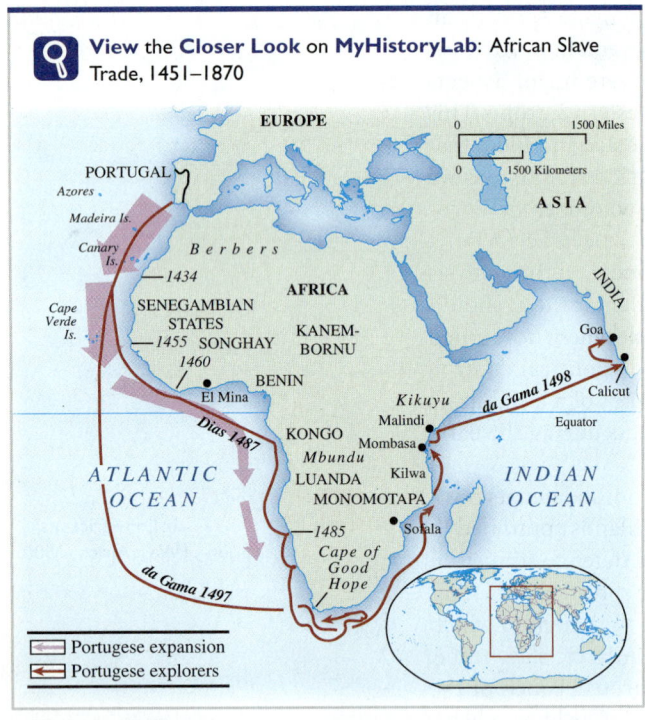

MAP 20.1 Portuguese Contact and Penetration of Africa Portuguese exploration and trade in the 15th century eventually evolved into trade, conquest, and missionary activities. In west Africa regular relations were established with a number of kingdoms like Benin and Kongo; in east Africa the Portuguese created outposts in Mozambique and along the Swahili coast, and in Ethiopia missionaries sought alliance with local Christians.

Portuguese exploration continued southward toward the Cape of Good Hope and beyond in the 16th century. Early contacts were made with the Mbundu peoples south of Kongo in the 1520s, and a more permanent Portuguese settlement was established there in the 1570s with the foundation of **Luanda** on the coast. This became the basis for the Portuguese colony of Angola. As we have already seen, the Portuguese tried to dominate the existing trading system of the African ports in the Indian

Ocean and Red Sea. They established an outpost on Mozambique Island and then secured bases at Kilwa, Mombasa, Sofala, and other ports that gave them access to the gold trade from Monomotapa (Mwenemutapa) in the interior. In east Africa, as on the west African coast, the number of permanent Portuguese settlers was minimal. The Portuguese effort was primarily commercial and military, although it was always accompanied by a strong missionary effort.

The patterns of contact established by the Portuguese were followed by others. In the 17th century, the Dutch, English, French, and others competed with the Portuguese and displaced them to some extent, but the system of fortified trading stations, the combination of force and diplomacy, alliances with local rulers, and the predominance of commercial relations continued as the principal pattern of European contact with Africa.

Although for a long time Portugal's major interest was in gold, pepper, and other products, a central element in this pattern was the slave trade. Slavery as an institution had been extensive in the Roman empire but had greatly declined in most of Europe during the Middle Ages, when it was replaced by serfdom. In the Mediterranean and in Iberia, however, where there was an active military frontier between Christians and Muslims, it had remained important. Moreover, the trans-Saharan slave trade had brought small numbers of black Africans into the Mediterranean throughout the period. The Portuguese voyages now opened a direct channel to sub-Saharan Africa. The first slaves brought directly to Portugal from Africa arrived in 1441, and after that date slaves became a common trade item. The Portuguese and later other Europeans raided for slaves along the coast, but the numbers acquired in this way were small. After initial raids, Europeans found that trade was a much more secure and profitable way to get these human cargoes. For example, the Portuguese sent about 50 slaves per year to Portugal before 1450, when raiding was prevalent, but by 1460 some 500 slaves per year arrived in Portugal as a trade with African rulers developed. Whether the victims were acquired by raiding or by trade, the effects on them were similar. An eyewitness to the unloading of slaves in Portugal in 1444 wrote,

> But what heart could be so hard as not to be pierced with piteous feelings to see that company? For some kept their heads low and their faces bathed in tears, looking one upon another; others stood groaning very dolorously, looking up to the height of heaven, fixing their eyes upon it, crying out loudly, as if asking help of the Father of Nature.

Read the Document on MyHistoryLab: Letters from the Kings of Portugal to the King of Kongo

FIGURE 20.2 African artists were impressed by the strangeness of Europeans and sometimes incorporated them in their own work, as can be seen in the headpiece of this beautifully carved ivory head of a Benin monarch. Europeans in turn employed African artisans to produce decorative luxury goods.

The slave trade was given added impetus when the Portuguese and the Spanish began to develop sugar plantations on the Atlantic islands of Madeira (Portugal) and the Canaries (Spain) and off the African coast on the Portuguese-held island of São Tomé. Sugar production demanded many workers and constant labor under difficult conditions, usually in a tropical or subtropical environment. The plantation system of organization associated with sugar, in which managers were able to direct and control laborers over long periods with little restraint, was later extended to America and then to other crops. Although the system did not depend only on Africans, they became the primary plantation laborers in the Atlantic world. The slave trade grew significantly in volume and complexity after 1550 as the American plantation colonies, especially Brazil, began to develop. By 1600, the slave trade predominated over all other kinds of trade on the African coast as Africa was pulled into an Atlantic commercial system.

Luanda Portuguese factory established in 1520s south of Kongo; became basis for Portuguese colony of Angola.

Trend Toward Expansion

Although debate and controversy surround many aspects of the history of slavery, it is perhaps best to start with the numbers. Estimates of the volume of the trade vary widely, and scholars still debate the figures and their implications, but the range of calculations has been narrowed by recent research

TABLE 20.1 SLAVE EXPORTS FROM AFRICA, 1500–1900* (IN THOUSANDS)

Area of Trade	1500–1600	Percentage (%)	1601–1700	Percentage (%)	1701–1800	Percentage (%)	1801–1900	Percentage (%)	Total
Red Sea	200	17	200	7	200	3	450	8	1,050
Trans-Sahara	550	47	700	24	700	9	1,200	22	3,150
East Africa	100	9	100	4	400	5	442	8	1,042
Trans-Atlantic	325	28	1,868	65	6,133	83	3,330	61	11,656**
Totals	1,175		2,868		7,433		5,422		16,898

*Based on Paul Lovejoy, *Transformation in Slavery: A History of Slavery in Africa* (1983). Reprinted with the permission of Cambridge University Press.
**Note: Estimates of the trans-Atlantic trade have now raised by 8% to the figure to 12,570,000 between 1501 and 1867 rather than the estmate of 11,656,000 reported here.

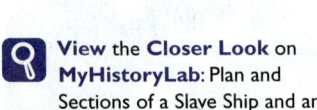

View the **Closer Look** on **MyHistoryLab**: Plan and Sections of a Slave Ship and an Illustration of a Slave Camp

Read the **Document** on **MyHistoryLab**: Job Hortop and the British Enter the Slave Trade, 1567

TABLE 20.2 ESTIMATED SLAVE IMPORTS INTO THE AMERICAS BY IMPORTING REGION, 1519–1866

Region and Country	Slaves
Brazil	3,902,000
British Caribbean	2,238,200
Spanish America	1,267,800
French Caribbean	1,092,600
Guianas*	403,700
British North America	361,100
Dutch Caribbean	129,700
Danish Caribbean	73,100
	9,468,200

*Includes Dutch, French, and British colonies, namely, Berbice, Cayenne, Demerara, Essequebo, and Suriname.

and by a large quantitative database of the slaving voyages. Between 1450 and 1850, it is estimated that about 12 million Africans were shipped across the Atlantic (Table 20.1). With a mortality rate of 10 to 20 percent on the ships, about 10 or 11 million Africans actually arrived in the Americas. How many people died in Africa as a result of the slaving wars or in the forced marches to the coast is unknown, but estimates have been as high as one-third of the total captured. The volume changed over time. In the 16th century, the numbers were small, but they increased to perhaps 16,000 per year in the 17th century. The 18th century was the great age of the Atlantic slave trade; probably more than 7 million slaves, or more than 80 percent of all those embarked, were exported between 1700 and 1800. By the latter date, about 3 million slaves lived in the Americas. Even in the 19th century, when slavery was under attack, the slave trade to some places continued. Cuba received some 700,000 slaves, and Brazil took more than 1 million in that century alone.

The high volume of the slave trade was necessary to the slave owners because, in most of the slave regimes in the Caribbean and Latin America, slave mortality was high and fertility was low (partly because more men than women were imported). Thus, over time there was usually a loss of population. The only way to maintain or expand the number of slaves was by importing more from Africa. The one exception to this pattern was the southern United States, where the slave population grew, perhaps because of the temperate climate and the fact that few worked in the most dangerous and unhealthy occupations, such as sugar growing and mining. By 1860, almost 6 million slaves worked in the Americas, about 4 million of them in the southern United States, an area that depended more on natural population growth than on the Atlantic slave trade. In terms of total population, however, slaves in British North America were never more than one-fourth of the whole population, whereas in the British and French Caribbean they made up 80 to 90 percent of the population.

The dimensions of the trade varied over time, reflecting the economic and political situation in the Americas. From 1530 to 1650, Spanish America and Brazil received the majority of African slaves, but after the English and French began to grow sugar in the Caribbean, the islands of Jamaica, Barbados, and St. Domingue (Haiti) became important terminals for the slavers. By the 18th century, Virginia and the Carolinas in North America had also become major destinations, although they never rivaled the Caribbean or Brazil (Table 20.2).

Between 1550 and 1850, Brazil alone received 3.5 to 5 million Africans, or about 42 percent of all those who reached the New World. The Caribbean islands, dedicated to sugar production, were the other major destination of Africans. The island colonies of St. Domingue and Jamaica each received more than 1 million slaves in the 18th century alone.

It should be emphasized that these figures represent only the volume in the Atlantic slave trade. The older trans-Sahara, Red Sea, and east African slave trades in the hands of Muslim traders continued throughout the period and added another 3 million people to the total of Africans exported as slaves in this period (Table 20.1). The Atlantic slave trade drew slaves from across the continent, and its concentration shifted over time. In the 16th century, the majority of slaves were exported from the Senegambia region, but by the 17th century, west central Africa (modern Zaire and

Angola) was the major supplier. Also important were the areas of the Gold Coast and the Slave Coast—Dahomey and Benin—at the end of the century, when Benin alone was exporting more than 10,000 slaves per year. In the century that followed, wars for control of the interior created the large states of Asante among the Akan peoples of the Gold Coast and Dahomey among the Fon peoples. These wars were both the cause and the result of increasing slave exports from these regions.

Demographic Patterns

The majority of the trans-Saharan slave trade consisted of women to be used as concubines and domestic servants in north Africa and the Middle East, but the Atlantic slave trade concentrated on men. To some extent this was because planters and mine owners in the Americas were seeking workers for heavy labor and were not eager to risk buying children because of the high levels of mortality. Also, African societies that sold captives into slavery often preferred to sell the men and keep the women and children as domestic slaves or to extend existing kin groups. That was especially true by the 19th century. There were regional variations, however. Far higher proportions of women were imported to the English colonies of Jamaica and Barbados than to Brazil or Cuba.

The Atlantic trade seems to have had a demographic impact on at least certain parts of west and central Africa. One estimate is that the population of about 25 million in 1850 in those regions was about one-half what it would have been had there been no slave trade. It is true that the trans-Atlantic trade carried more men than women and more women than children, but captive women and children who remained in Africa swelled the numbers of enslaved people in those societies and skewed the proportion of women to men in the African enslaving societies perhaps increasing fertility rates. Finally, as the Atlantic trade developed, new crops, such as maize and manioc introduced from the Americas provided additional food resources for the population in Africa and helped it recover from the losses to the slave trade, but African plants and botanical knowledge also moved across the Atlantic to the Americas.

Organization of the Trade

The patterns of contact and trade established by the Portuguese at first were followed by rival Europeans on the African coast. Control of the slave trade or a portion of it generally reflected the political situation in Europe. For one and a half centuries, until about 1630, the Portuguese controlled most of the coastal trade and were the major suppliers of their own colony of Brazil and the Spanish settlements in America. The growth of slave-based plantation colonies in the Caribbean and elsewhere led other Europeans to compete with the Portuguese. The Dutch became major competitors when they seized El Mina in 1637. By the 1660s, the English were eager to have their own source of slaves for their growing colonies in Barbados, Jamaica, and Virginia. The **Royal African Company** was chartered for that purpose. The French made similar arrangements in the 1660s, but not until the 18th century did France become a major carrier. Like other small European nations, even Denmark had its agents and forts on the African coast.

Royal African Company Chartered in 1660s to establish a monopoly over the slave trade among British merchants; supplied African slaves to colonies in Barbados, Jamaica, and Virginia.

Each nation established merchant towns or trade forts from which a steady source of captives could be obtained. For the Europeans stationed on the coast, Africa was also a graveyard because of the tropical diseases they encountered. Fewer than 10 percent of the employees of the Royal Africa Company who went to Africa ever returned to England, and the majority died in the first year out. European mortality among the crews of slave ships was also very high because of tropical diseases such as malaria. The slave trade proved deadly to all involved, but at least some of the Europeans had a choice, whereas for the enslaved Africans there was none.

European agents for the companies often had to deal directly with local rulers, paying a tax or offering gifts. Various forms of currency were used, such as iron bars, brass rings, and cowrie shells. The Spanish developed a complicated system in which a healthy man was called an **Indies piece**, and children and women were priced at fractions of that value. Slaves were brought to the coast by a variety of means. Sometimes, as in Angola, European military campaigns produced captives for slaves, or African and mulatto agents purchased captives at interior trade centers. In Dahomey a royal monopoly was established to control the flow of slaves. Some groups used their position to tax or control the movement of slaves from the interior to the coast. Although African and European states tried to establish monopolies over the trade, private merchants often circumvented restrictions.

Indies piece Term used within the complex exchange system established by the Spanish for African trade; referred to the value of an adult male slave.

Clearly, both Europeans and Africans were actively involved in the slave trade. It was not always clear which side was in control. One group of English merchants on the Gold Coast complained of African insolence in 1784 because in negotiations the Africans had emphasized that "the country belongs to them." In any case, the result of this collaboration was to send millions of Africans into bondage in foreign lands.

Historians have long debated the profitability of the slave trade. Some argue that the profits were so great and constant that they were a major element in the rise of commercial capitalism and, later, the origins of the Industrial Revolution. Undoubtedly, many people profited from the trade in African slaves. A single slaving voyage might make a profit of as much as 300 percent, and merchants in the ports that specialized in fitting out ships for the slave trade, such as Liverpool, England, or Nantes, France—as well as African suppliers—derived a profit from the slave trade. But the slave trade also involved risks and costs, so that in the long run, profitability levels did not remain so high. In the late 18th century, profitability in the English slave trade probably ran from 5 to 10 percent on average, and in the French and Dutch trades it was slightly lower. The slave trade was little more profitable in the long run than most business activities of the age and by itself was not a major source of the capital needed in the Industrial Revolution.

However, it is difficult to calculate the full economic importance of slavery to the economies of Europe because it was so directly linked to the plantation and mining economies of the Americas. During some periods, a **triangular trade** existed in which slaves were carried to the Americas; sugar, tobacco, and other goods were then carried to Europe; and European products were sent to the coast of Africa to begin the triangle again. Were profits from the slave trade accumulated in Liverpool invested in the textile industry of England? And if so, how important were these investments for the growth of that industry? We would need to calculate the value of goods produced in Europe for exchange in the slave trade as well as the profits derived from the colonies to measure the importance of slavery to the growth of the European economies. Still, the very persistence of the slave trade indicates its viability. The slave trade surely contributed to the formation of emerging capitalism in the Atlantic world. In Africa itself, the slave trade often drew economies into dependence on trade with Europeans and suppressed the growth of other economic activities.

It is clear that by the late 18th century, the slave trade and slavery were essential aspects of the economy of the Atlantic basin, and their importance was increasing. More than 40 percent of all the slaves that crossed the Atlantic embarked during the century after 1760, and the plantation economies of Brazil, the Caribbean, and the southern United States were booming in the early 19th century. The slave trade was profitable enough to keep merchants in it, and it contributed in some way to the expanding economy of western Europe. No one in the Atlantic world, slave or free, was entirely untouched or unaffected by it. It was also the major way in which Africa was linked to the increasingly integrated economy of the world.

triangular trade Commerce linking Africa, the New World colonies, and Europe; slaves carried to America for sugar and tobacco transported to Europe.

AFRICAN SOCIETIES, SLAVERY, AND THE SLAVE TRADE

20.3 What was the cultural impact of Africans on the New World?

Europeans in the age of the slave trade sometimes justified the enslavement of Africans by pointing out that slavery already existed on that continent. However, although forms of bondage were ancient in Africa, and the Muslim trans-Sahara and Red Sea trades already were well established, the Atlantic trade interacted with and transformed these earlier aspects of slavery.

African societies had developed many forms of servitude, which varied from a peasant status to something much more like chattel slavery in which people were considered things: "property with a soul," as Aristotle put it. African states usually were nonegalitarian, and because in many African societies all land was owned by the state or the ruler, the control of slaves was one of the few ways, if not the only way, in which individuals or lineages could increase their wealth and status. Slaves were used as servants, concubines, soldiers, administrators, and field workers. In some cases, as in the ancient empire of Ghana and in Kongo, there were whole villages of enslaved dependants who were required to pay tribute to the ruler. The Muslim traders of west Africa who linked the forest region to the savanna had slave porters as well as villages of slaves to supply their caravans.

The slave trade influenced African forms of servitude and the social and political development of African states. Newly powerful states emerged in west Africa; in the Sudan and east Africa, slavery also produced long-term effects.

In many situations, these forms of servitude were fairly benign and were an extension of lineage and kinship systems. In others, however, they were exploitive economic and social relations that reinforced the hierarchies of various African societies and allowed the nobles, senior lineages, and rulers to exercise their power. Among the forest states of west Africa, such as Benin, and in the Kongo kingdom in central Africa, slavery was already an important institution before the European arrival, but the Atlantic trade opened up new opportunities for expansion and intensification of slavery in those societies.

Despite great variation in African societies and the fact that slaves sometimes attained positions of command and trust, in most cases slaves were denied choice about their lives and actions. They were placed in dependent or inferior positions, and they were often considered aliens. It is important to remember that the enslavement of women was a central feature of African slavery. Although slaves were used in many ways in African societies, domestic slavery and the extension of lineages through the addition of female members remained important in many places. Some historians believe that the excess of women led to polygyny (having more than one wife at a time) and the creation of large harems by rulers and merchants, whose power was increased by this process, and the position of women was lowered in some societies.

In the Sudanic states of the savanna, Islamic concepts of slavery had been introduced. Slavery was viewed as a legitimate fate for nonbelievers but was illegal for Muslims. Despite the complaints of legal scholars such as Ahmad Baba of Timbuktu (1556–1627) against the enslavement of Muslims, many of the Sudanic states enslaved their captives, both pagan and Muslim. In the Niger valley, slave communities produced agricultural surpluses for the rulers and nobles of Songhay, Gao, and other states. Slaves were used for gold mining and salt production and as caravan workers in the Sahara. Slavery was a widely diffused form of labor control and wealth in Africa.

The existence of slavery in Africa and the preexisting trade in people allowed Europeans to mobilize the commerce in slaves quickly by tapping existing routes and supplies. In this venture they were aided by the rulers of certain African states, who were anxious to acquire more slaves for themselves and to supply slaves to the Europeans in exchange for aid and commodities. In the 16th-century Kongo kingdom, the ruler had an army of 20,000 slaves as part of his household, and this gave him greater power than any Kongo ruler had ever held. In general, African rulers did not enslave their own people, except for crimes or in other unusual circumstances; rather, they enslaved their neighbors. Thus, expanding, centralizing states often were the major suppliers of slaves to the Europeans as well as to societies in which slavery was an important institution.

Slaving and African Politics

As one French agent put it, "The trade in slaves is the business of kings, rich men, and prime merchants." European merchants and royal officials were able to tap existing routes, markets, and institutions, but the new and constant demand also intensified enslavement in Africa and perhaps changed the nature of slavery itself in some African societies.

In the period between 1500 and 1750, as the gunpowder empires and expanding international commerce of Europe penetrated sub-Saharan Africa, existing states and societies often were transformed. As we saw in Chapter 9, the empire of Songhay controlled a vast region of the western savanna until its defeat by a Moroccan invasion in 1591, but for the most part the many states of central and western Africa were small and fragmented. This led to a situation of instability caused by competition and warfare as states tried to expand at the expense of their neighbors or to consolidate power by incorporating subject provinces. The warrior or soldier emerged in this situation as an important social type in states such as the Kongo kingdom and Dahomey as well as along the Zambezi River. The endless wars promoted the importance of the military and made the sale of captives into the slave trade an extension of the politics of regions of Africa. Sometimes, as among the Muslim states of the savanna or the Lake Chad region, wars took on a religious overtone of believers against nonbelievers, but in much of west and central Africa that was not the case. Some authors see this situation as a feature of African politics; others believe it was the result of European demand for new slaves. In either case, the result was the capture and sale of millions of human beings. Although increasing centralization and hierarchy could be seen in the enslaving African societies, a contrary trend of self-sufficiency and anti-authoritarian ideas developed among the peoples who bore the brunt of the slaving attacks.

THINKING HISTORICALLY

Slavery and Human Society

SLAVERY IS A VERY OLD AND widespread institution. It has been found at different times all over the globe, among simple societies and in the great centers of civilization. In some of these societies, it has been a marginal or secondary form of labor, whereas in others it became the predominant labor form or "mode of production" (in the jargon of Marxist analysis). The need for labor beyond the capacity of the individual or the family unit is very old, and as soon as authority, law, or custom could be established to set the conditions for coercion, the tribe, the state, the priests, or some other group or institution extracted labor by force. Coerced labor could take different forms. There are important distinctions between indentured servants, convict laborers, debt-peons, and chattel slaves.

Although most societies placed some limits on the slaveholder's authority or power, the denial of the slave's control over his or her own labor and life choices was characteristic of this form of coercion throughout history. In most societies that had a form of chattel slavery, the slave was denied a sense of belonging in the society—the idea of kinship. The honor associated with family or lineage was the antithesis of slavery. The Old Testament figure Joseph might rise to a high position at pharaoh's court, and so might a vizier of a Turkish sultan, but as slaves they were instruments of their masters' will. In fact, because they were slaves and thus unconstrained by kinship or other ties and obligations, they could be trusted in positions of command.

Because slaves became nonpersons—or, as one modern author has put it, because they suffered a "social death"—it was always easier to enslave "others" or "outsiders": those who were different in some way. Hebrews enslaved Canaanites, Greeks enslaved "barbarians," and Muslims made slaves of nonbelievers. If the difference between slave and master was readily seen, it made enforcement of slave status that much easier. Racism as such did not cause modern slavery, but differences in culture, language, color, and other physical characteristics always facilitated enslavement. The familiarity of Europeans and Muslims with black Africans in an enslaved status contributed to the development of modern racism. To paraphrase English historian Charles Boxer, no people can enslave another for 400 years without developing an attitude of superiority.

Slavery was not only a general phenomenon that existed in many societies. Rarely questioned on any grounds, it was seen as a necessary and natural phenomenon. Slavery is accepted in the texts of ancient India, the Old Testament, and the writings of classical Greece. Aristotle specifically argued that some people were born to rule and others to serve. In Christian theology, although all people might be free in spirit in the kingdom of God, servitude was considered a necessary reality. Voices might be raised arguing for fair treatment or against the enslavement of a particular group, but the condition of servitude usually was taken as part of the natural order of the world.

In this context, the attack on slavery in western culture that grew from the Enlightenment and the social and economic changes in western Europe and its Atlantic colonies at the end of the 18th century was a remarkable turning point in world history. Some scholars believe that slavery was an outdated labor form that was incompatible with industrial capitalism and that is why it was abolished. Others hold that it was destroyed because its immorality became all too obvious. In any case, its demise was quick. In about a century and a half, the moral and religious underpinning of chattel slavery was cut away and its economic justifications were questioned seriously. Although slavery lingered in at least a few places well into the 20th century, few people were willing to defend the institution publicly.

Although slavery historically existed in many places, it has become intimately associated with Africa because of the scope of the Atlantic slave trade and the importance of slavery in forming the modern world system. There was nothing inevitable about Africa's becoming the primary source of slaves in the modern world. Europeans did use Native American and European indentured workers when they could, but historical precedents, maritime technology, and availability combined to make Africa the source of labor for the expanding plantation colonies of Europe.

African slavery obviously played an important role in shaping the modern world. The African slave trade was one of the first truly international trades, and it created an easy access to labor that enabled Europeans to exploit the Americas. Some have argued that it was an important, even a necessary feature in the rise of capitalism and the international division of labor. Others disagree. In this question, as in nearly every other question about modern slavery, controversies still abound.

In the context of African history, the interpretation of slavery is still changing rapidly. A recent and careful estimate of the volume involved in the Atlantic trade (10–12 million) has been questioned seriously, especially by African scholars, who see this new figure as an attempt to downplay the exploitation of Africa. Another debate centers on the impact of the trade on the population and societies within Africa. The slave trade was important to the economy of the Atlantic, but how important was this external trade in Africa

(continued on next page)

> **To paraphrase English historian Charles Boxer, no people can enslave another for 400 years without developing an attitude of superiority.**

itself? Reacting to the pre-abolitionist European self-justifications that the slave trade was no great crime because Africans had long become familiar with slavery and were selling already enslaved people, early researchers argued that African slavery often was an extension of kinship or other forms of dependency and was quite unlike the chattel slavery of western Europe. But further research has demonstrated that in many African societies, slavery was an integral part of the economy, and although specific conditions sometimes differed greatly from those in the Americas, the servile condition in Africa had much in common with chattel slavery. For example, the Sokoto caliphate in the 19th century had a proportion of slaves similar to that in Brazil and the southern United States. Slave societies did exist in Africa.

Controversy rages over the extent to which the development of African slavery resulted from the long-term impact of the slave trade and the European demand for captive labor. African societies did not live in isolation from the pressures and examples of the world economy into which they were drawn. The extent to which that contact transformed slavery in Africa is now in question. These controversies among historians reflect current concerns and a realization that the present social and political situation in Africa and in many places in the Americas continues to bear the burden of a historical past in which slavery played an essential role. In evaluating slavery, as in all other historical questions, what we think about the present shapes our inquiry and our interpretation of the past.

> **QUESTIONS**
> - Why did Africa become the leading source of slaves in the early modern world economy?
> - What are some of the leading issues in interpreting African slavery?
> - What were the roles of Africans and Europeans in the early modern slave trade?

One result of the presence of Europeans on the coast was a shift in the locus of power within Africa. Just as states such as Ghana and Songhay in the savanna took advantage of their position as intermediaries between the gold of the west African forests and the trans-Saharan trade routes, the states closer to the coast or in contact with the Europeans could play a similar role. Those right on the coast tried to monopolize the trade with Europeans, but European meddling in their internal affairs and European fears of any coastal power that became too strong blocked the creation of centralized states under the shadow of European forts. Just beyond the coast it was different. With access to European goods, especially firearms, iron, horses, cloth, tobacco, and other goods, western and central African kingdoms began to redirect trade toward the coast and to expand their influence. Some historians have written of a gun and slave cycle in which increased firepower allowed these states to expand over their neighbors, producing more slaves, which they traded for more guns. The result was unending warfare and the disruption of societies as the search for slaves pushed ever farther into the interior.

Asante and Dahomey

Perhaps the effects of the slave trade on African societies are best seen in some specific cases. Several large states developed in west Africa during the slave trade era. Each represented a response to the realities of the European presence and the process of state formation long under way in Africa. Rulers in these states grew in power and often surrounded themselves with ritual authority and a luxurious court life as a way of reinforcing the position that their armies had won (Figures 20.3 and 20.4).

In the area called the Gold Coast by the Europeans, the empire of **Asante** (Ashanti) rose to prominence in the period of the slave trade. The Asante were members of the Akan people (the major group of modern Ghana) who had settled in and around Kumasi, a region of gold and kola nut production that lay between the coast and the Hausa and Mande trading centers to the north. There were at least 20 small states, based on the matrilineal clans that were common to all the Akan peoples, but those of the Oyoko clan predominated. Their cooperation and their access to firearms after 1650 initiated a period of centralization and expansion. Under the vigorous **Osei Tutu** (d. 1717), the title **asantehene** was created to designate the supreme civil and religious leader. His golden stool became the symbol of an Asante union that was created by linking the many Akan clans under the authority of the asantehene but recognizing the autonomy of subordinate areas. An all-Asante council advised the ruler, and an ideology of unity was used to overcome the traditional clan divisions. With this new structure and a series of military reforms, conquest of the area began. By 1700, the Dutch on the coast realized that a new power had emerged, and they began to deal directly with it.

With control of the gold-producing zones and a constant supply of prisoners to be sold as slaves for more firearms, Asante maintained its power until the 1820s as the dominant state of the Gold

Asante empire [uh san tEE, uh sän] Established in Gold Coast among Akan people settled around Kumasi; dominated by Oyoko clan; many clans linked under Osei Tutu after 1650.

asantehene [uh-SHAHN-teh-heenuh] Title taken by ruler of Asante empire; supreme civil and religious leader; authority symbolized by golden stool.

Tutu, Osei [tU tU] (r. 1675–1717) Member of Oyoko clan of Akan peoples in Gold Coast region of Africa; responsible for creating unified Asante Empire in 1701; utilized Western firearms.

FIGURE 20.3 The annual yam harvest festival was an occasion when the power and authority of the Asante ruler could be displayed. The English observers who painted this scene were impressed by the might of this west African kingdom.

Coast. Although gold continued to be a major item of export, by the end of the 17th century, slaves made up almost two-thirds of Asante's trade.

Farther to the east, in the area of the Bight of Benin (between the Volta and Benin rivers on what the Europeans called the Slave Coast), several large states developed. The kingdom of Benin was at the height of its power when the Europeans arrived. It traced its origins to the city of Ife and to the Yoruba peoples that were its neighbors, but it had become a separate and independent kingdom with its own

FIGURE 20.4 The size of African cities and the power of African rulers often impressed European observers. Here the city of Loango, capital of a kingdom on the Kongo coast, is depicted as a bustling urban center. At this time it was a major port in the slave trade.

464 PART IV The Early Modern Period, 1450–1750: The World Shrinks

well-developed political and artistic traditions, especially in the casting of bronze. As early as 1516, the ruler, or *oba*, limited the slave trade from Benin, and for a long time most trade with Europeans was controlled directly by the king and was in pepper, textiles, and ivory rather than slaves. Eventually, European pressure and the goals of the Benin nobility combined to generate a significant slave trade in the 18th century, but Benin never made the slave trade its primary source of revenue or state policy.

The kingdom of **Dahomey**, which developed among the Fon (or Aja) peoples, had a different response to the European presence. It began to emerge as a power in the 17th century from its center at Abomey, about 70 miles from the coast. Its kings ruled with the advice of powerful councils, but by the 1720s access to firearms allowed the rulers to create an autocratic and sometimes brutal political regime based on the slave trade. In the 1720s, under King Agaja (1708–1740), the kingdom of Dahomey moved toward the coast, seizing in 1727 the port town of Whydah, which had attracted many European traders. Although Dahomey became to some extent a subject of the powerful neighboring Yoruba state of Oyo, whose cavalry and archers made it strong, Dahomey maintained its autonomy and turned increasingly to the cycle of firearms and slaves. The trade was controlled by the royal court, whose armies (including a regiment of women) were used to raid for more captives.

Dahomey Kingdom developed among Fon or Aja peoples in 17th century; center at Abomey 70 miles from coast; under King Agaja expanded to control coastline and port of Whydah by 1727; accepted western firearms and goods in return for African slaves.

As Dahomey expanded, it eliminated the royal families and customs of the areas it conquered and imposed its own traditions. This resulted in the formation of a unified state, which lasted longer than some of its neighbors. Well into the 19th century, Dahomey was a slaving state, and dependence on the trade in human beings had negative effects on the society as a whole. More than 1.8 million slaves were exported from the Bight of Benin between 1640 and 1890.

This emphasis on the slave trade should not obscure the creative process within many of the African states. The growing divine authority of the rulers paralleled the rise of absolutism in Europe. It led to the development of new political forms, some of which had the power to limit the role of the king. In the Yoruba state of Oyo, for example, a governing council shared power with the ruler. In some states, a balance of offices kept central power in check. In Asante the traditional village chiefs and officials whose authority was based on their lineage were increasingly challenged by new officials appointed by the asantehene as a state bureaucracy began to form.

The creativity of these societies was also seen in traditional arts. In many places, crafts such as bronze casting, woodcarving, and weaving flourished. Guilds of artisans developed in many societies, and their specialization produced crafts executed with great skill. In Benin and the Yoruba states, for example, remarkable and lifelike sculptures in wood and ivory continued to be produced. Often, however, the best artisans labored for the royal court, producing objects designed to honor the ruling family and reinforce the civil and religious authority of the king. This was true in architecture, weaving, and the decorative arts as well. Much of this artistic production also had a religious function or contained religious symbolism; African artists made the spiritual world visually apparent.

Europeans came to appreciate African arts and skills. In the 16th century, the Portuguese began to employ African artists from Benin, Sierra Leone, and Kongo to work local ivory into ladles, saltcellars (containers), and other decorative objects that combined African and European motifs in beautifully carved designs (Figure 20.5). Although works were commissioned by Europeans and sometimes including European religious and political symbols, African artists found ways to incorporate traditional symbols and themes from motherhood to royal power. Many of these objects ended up in the collections of nobles and kings throughout Renaissance Europe. They demonstrated the growing contact between Africa and the wider world.

View the **Closer Look** on **MyHistoryLab**: A West African View of the Portuguese

FIGURE **20.5** Portuguese soldiers serve as the base for this ivory carving done by West African craftsmen. Objects like these demonstrated the contact of European and African cultures. (Saltcellar: Portuguese Figures. Photo: Stan Reis. The Metropolitan Museum of Art, New York, NY, USA. Image Copyright © The Metropolitan Museum of Art/Art Resource, NY.)

East Africa and the Sudan

West Africa obviously was the region most directly influenced by the trans-Atlantic slave trade, but there and elsewhere in Africa, long-term patterns of society and economy continued and intersected with the new external influences. On the east coast of Africa, the Swahili trading cities continued their commerce in the Indian Ocean, adjusting to the military presence of the Portuguese and the Ottoman Turks. Trade to the interior continued to bring ivory, gold, and a steady supply of slaves. Many of these slaves were destined for the harems and households of Arabia and the Middle East, but a small number were carried away by the Europeans for their plantation colonies. The Portuguese and Indo-Portuguese settlers along the Zambezi River in Mozambique used slave soldiers to increase their territories, and certain groups in interior east Africa specialized in supplying ivory and slaves to the east African coast. Europeans did establish some plantation-style colonies on islands such as Mauritius in the Indian Ocean, and these depended on the east African slave trade.

On Zanzibar and other offshore islands, and later on the coast itself, Swahili, Indian, and Arabian merchants followed the European model and set up clove-producing plantations using African slave laborers. Some of the plantations were large, and by the 1860s Zanzibar had a slave population of about 100,000. The sultan of Zanzibar alone owned more than 4000 slaves in 1870. Slavery became a prominent feature of the east African coast, and the slave trade from the interior to these plantations and to the traditional slave markets of the Red Sea continued until the end of the 19th century.

Much less is known about the interior of eastern Africa. Large and small kingdoms were supported by the well-watered and heavily populated region of the great lakes of the interior. Bantu speakers predominated, but many peoples inhabited the region. Linguistic and archeological evidence suggests that pastoralist peoples from the upper Nile valley with a distinctive late Iron Age technology moved southward into what is today western Kenya and Uganda, where they came into contact with Bantu speakers and with the farmers and herders who spoke another group of languages called Cushitic. The Bantu states absorbed the immigrants, even when the newcomers established ruling dynasties. Later Nilotic migrations, of people who spoke languages of the Nilotic group, especially of the **Luo** peoples, resulted in the construction of related dynasties among the states in the area of the large lakes of east central Africa. At Bunyoro, the Luo eventually established a ruling dynasty among the existing Bantu population. This kingdom exercised considerable power in the 16th and 17th centuries. Other related states formed in the region. In Buganda, near Lake Victoria, a strong monarchy ruled a heterogeneous population and dominated the region in the 16th century. These developments in the interior, as important as they were for the history of the region, were less influenced by the growing contact with the outside world than were other regions of Africa.

Across the continent in the northern savanna at the end of the 18th century, the process of Islamization, which had been important in the days of the Mali and Songhay empires, entered a new and violent stage that not only linked Islamization to the external slave trade and the growth of slavery in Africa but also produced other long-term effects in the region. After the breakup of Songhay in the 16th century, several successor states had developed. Some, such as the Bambara kingdom of Segu, were pagan. Others, such as the Hausa kingdoms in northern Nigeria, were ruled by Muslim royal families and urban aristocracies but continued to contain large numbers of animist subjects, most of whom were rural peasants. In these states the degree of Islamization was slight, and an accommodation between Muslims and animists was achieved.

Beginning in the 1770s, Muslim reform movements began to sweep the western Sudan. Religious brotherhoods advocating a purifying Sufi variant of Islam extended their influence throughout the Muslim trade networks in the Senegambia region and the western Sudan. This movement had an intense impact on the **Fulani** (Fulbe), a pastoral people who were spread across a broad area of the western Sudan.

In 1804 Usuman Dan Fodio, a studious and charismatic Muslim Fulani scholar, began to preach the reformist ideology in the Hausa kingdoms. His movement became a revolution when in 1804, seeing himself as God's instrument, he preached a jihad against the Hausa kings, who, he felt, were not following the teachings of Muhammad. A great upheaval followed in which the Fulani took control of most of the Hausa states of northern Nigeria in the western Sudan. A new kingdom, based in the city of Sokoto, developed under Dan Fodio's son and brother. The Fulani expansion was driven not only by religious zeal but by political ambitions, as the attack on the well established Muslim kingdom of Bornu demonstrated. The result of this upheaval was the creation of a powerful Sokoto state under a caliph, whose authority was established over cities such as Kano and Zaria and whose rulers became emirs of provinces within the Sokoto caliphate.

By the 1840s, the effects of Islamization and the Fulani expansion were felt across much of the interior of west Africa. New political units were created, a reformist Islam that tried to eliminate pagan practices spread, and social and cultural changes took place in the wake of these changes. Literacy became more widely dispersed, and new centers of trade, such as Kano, emerged in this period. Later jihads established other new states along similar lines. All of these changes had long-term effects on the region of the western Sudan.

Luo Nilotic people who migrated from upper Nile valley; established dynasty among existing Bantu population in lake region of central eastern Africa; center at Bunyoro.

Fulani [fU lä nEE, foo lä-] Pastoral people of western Sudan; adopted purifying Sufi variant of Islam; under Usuman Dan Fodio in 1804, launched revolt against Hausa kingdoms; established state centered on Sokoto.

These upheavals, moved by religious, political, and economic motives, were affected by the external pressures on Africa. They fed into the ongoing processes of the external slave trade and the development of slavery within African societies. Large numbers of captives resulting from the wars were exported down to the coast for sale to the Europeans, while another stream of slaves crossed the Sahara to north Africa. In the western and central Sudan, the level of slave labor rose, especially in the larger towns and along the trade routes. Slave villages, supplying royal courts and merchant activities as well as a plantation system, developed to produce peanuts and other crops. Slave women spun cotton and wove cloth for sale, slave artisans worked in the towns, and slaves served the caravan traders, but most slaves did agricultural labor. By the late 19th century, regions of the savanna contained large slave populations—in some places as much as 30 to 50 percent of the whole population. From the Senegambia region of Futa Jallon, across the Niger and Senegal basins, and to the east of Lake Chad, slavery became a central feature of the Sudanic states and remained so through the 19th century.

WHITE SETTLERS AND AFRICANS IN SOUTHERN AFRICA

20.4 Compare the effects of the settler colony of South Africa to the European trading ports in West Africa.

> In southern Africa, a Dutch colony eventually brought Europeans into conflict with Africans, especially the southern Bantu-speaking peoples. One of these groups, the Zulu, created under Shaka a powerful chiefdom during the early 19th century in a process of expansion that affected the whole region.

One area of Africa little affected by the slave trade in the early modern period was the southern end of the continent. As we saw in Chapter 9, this region was still occupied by non-Bantu hunting peoples, the San (Bushmen); by the Khoikhoi (Hottentots), who lived by hunting and sheep herding; and, after contact with the Bantu, by cattle-herding peoples. Peoples practicing farming and using iron tools were living south of the Limpopo River by the 3rd century C.E. Probably Bantu speakers, they spread southward and established their villages and cattle herds in the fertile lands along the eastern coast, where rainfall was favorable to their agricultural and pastoral way of life. The drier western regions toward the Kalahari Desert were left to the Khoikhoi (KOHWEE-kohwee) and San. Mixed farming and pastoralism spread throughout the region in a complex process that involved migration, peaceful contacts, and warfare.

By the 16th century, Bantu-speaking peoples occupied much of the eastern regions of southern Africa. They practiced agriculture and herding; worked iron and copper into tools, weapons, and adornments; and traded with their neighbors. They spoke related languages such as Tswana (TSWAH-nuh) and Sotho (SOH-toh) as well as the Nguni (uhng-GOO-nee) languages such as Zulu and Xhosa (KOH-suh). Among the Sotho, villages might have contained as many as 200 people; the Nguni lived in hamlets made up of a few extended families. Men worked as artisans and herders; women did the farming and housework and sometimes organized their labor communally.

Politically, chiefdoms of various sizes—many of them small, but a few with as many as 50,000 inhabitants—characterized the southern Bantu peoples. Chiefs held power with the support of relatives and with the acceptance of the people, but there was great variation in chiefly authority. The Bantu-speaking peoples' pattern of political organization and the splitting off of junior lineages to form new villages created a process of expansion that led to competition for land and the absorption of newly conquered groups. This situation became intense at the end of the 18th century, either because of the pressures and competition for foreign trade through the Portuguese outposts on the east African coast or because of the growth of population among the southern Bantu. In any case, the result was farther expansion southward into the path of another people who had arrived in southern Africa.

In 1652 the Dutch East India Company established a colony at the Cape of Good Hope to serve as a provisioning post for ships sailing to Asia. Large farms developed on the fertile lands around this colony. The Cape Colony depended on slave labor brought from Indonesia and Asia for a while, but it soon enslaved local Africans as well. Expansion of the colony and its labor needs led to a series of wars with the San and Khoikhoi populations, who were pushed farther to the north and west. By the 1760s, the Dutch, or Boer, farmers had crossed the Orange River in search of new lands. They saw the fertile plains and hills as theirs, and they saw the Africans as intruders and a possible source of labor. Competition and warfare resulted. By about 1800 the Cape Colony had about 17,000 settlers (or Afrikaners, as they came to be called), 26,000 slaves, and 14,000 Khoikhoi.

As the Boers were pushing northward, the southern Bantu were extending their movement to the south. Matters were also complicated by European events when Great Britain seized the Cape Colony

Great Trek Movement of Boer settlers in Cape Colony of southern Africa to escape influence of British colonial government in 1834; led to settlement of regions north of Orange River and Natal.

in 1795 and then took it under formal British control in 1815. While the British government helped the settlers to clear out Africans from potential farming lands, government attempts to limit the Boer settlements and their use of African labor were unsuccessful. Meanwhile, competition for farming and grazing land led to a series of wars between the settlers and the Bantu during the early 19th century.

Various government measures, the accelerating arrival of English-speaking immigrants, and the lure of better lands caused groups of Boers to move to the north. These *voortrekkers* moved into lands occupied by the southern Nguni, eventually creating a number of autonomous Boer states. After 1834, when Britain abolished slavery and imposed restrictions on landholding, groups of Boers staged their **Great Trek** far to the north to be free of government interference. This movement eventually brought them across the Orange River and into Natal on the more fertile east coast, which the Boers believed to be only sparsely inhabited by Africans. They did not realize or care that the lack of population resulted from a great military upheaval taking place among the Bantu peoples of the region.

The Mfecane and the Zulu Rise to Power

Among the Nguni peoples, major changes had taken place. A unification process had begun in some of the northern chiefdoms, and a new military organization had emerged. In 1818 leadership fell to Shaka, a brilliant military tactician, who reformed the loose forces into regiments organized by lineage and age. Iron discipline and new tactics were introduced, including the use of a short stabbing spear to be used at close range. The army was made a permanent institution, and the regiments were housed together in separate villages. The fighting men were allowed to marry only after they had completed their service.

Shaka's own Zulu chiefdom became the center of this new military and political organization, which began to absorb or destroy its neighbors (Figure 20.6). Shaka demonstrated talent as a

FIGURE **20.6** This Zulu royal kraal, drawn in the 1830s, gives some idea of the power of the Zulu at the time that Shaka was forging Zulu dominance during the mfecane.

politician, destroying the ruling families of the groups he incorporated into the growing Zulu state. He ruled with an iron hand, destroying his enemies, acquiring their cattle, and crushing any opposition. His policies brought power to the Zulu, but his erratic and cruel behavior also earned him enemies among his own people. Although he was assassinated in 1828, Shaka's reforms remained in place, and his successors built on the structure he had created. Zulu power was still growing in the 1840s, and the Zulu remained the most impressive military force in black Africa until the end of the century.

The rise of the Zulu and other Nguni chiefdoms was the beginning of the **mfecane**, or wars of crushing and wandering. As Zulu control expanded, a series of campaigns and forced migrations led to constant fighting as other peoples sought to survive by fleeing, emulating, or joining the Zulu. Groups spun off to the north and south, raiding the Portuguese on the coast, clashing with the Europeans to the south, and fighting with neighboring chiefdoms. New African states, such as the **Swazi**, that adapted aspects of the Zulu model emerged among the survivors. One state, **Lesotho**, successfully resisted the Zulu example. It combined Sotho and Nguni speakers and defended itself against Nguni armies. It eventually developed as a kingdom far less committed to military organization, one in which the people had a strong influence on their leaders.

The whole of the southern continent, from the Cape Colony to Lake Malawi, had been thrown into turmoil by raiding parties, remnants, and refugees. Superior firepower allowed the Boers to continue to hold their lands, but it was not until the Zulu Wars of the 1870s that Zulu power was crushed by Great Britain, and even then only at great cost. During that process, the basic patterns of conflict between Africans and Europeans in the largest settler colony on the continent were created. These patterns included competition between settlers and Africans for land, the expanding influence of European government control, and the desire of Europeans to use Africans as laborers.

> **mfecane** [uhm-feh-KAH-nee] Wars of 19th century in southern Africa; created by Zulu expansion under Shaka; revolutionized political organization of southern Africa.
>
> **Swazi** New African state formed on model of Zulu chiefdom; survived mfecane.
>
> **Lesotho** [luh-SOH-toh] Southern African state that survived mfecane; not based on Zulu model; less emphasis on military organization, less authoritarian government.

THE AFRICAN DIASPORA

20.5 Is "continuity" or "creative adaptation" the best way to understand the cultural importance of the African diaspora?

The slave trade was the means by which the history of the Americas and Africa became linked and a principal way in which African societies were drawn into the world economy. The import into Africa of European firearms, Indian textiles, Indonesian cowrie shells, and American tobacco in return for African ivory, gold, and especially slaves demonstrated Africa's integration into the mercantile structure of the world. Africans involved in the trade learned to deal effectively with this situation. Prices of slaves rose steadily in the 18th century, and the terms of trade increasingly favored the African dealers. In many African ports, such as Whydah, Porto Novo, and Luanda, African or Afro-European communities developed that specialized in the slave trade and used this position to advantage.

> Despite African resistance to enslavement, the slave trade, and the horrifying Middle Passage carried millions of Africans from their original homelands. In the Americas, especially in plantation colonies, they became a large segment of the population, and African cultures were adapted to new environments and conditions.

Slave Lives

For the slaves themselves, slavery meant the destruction of their villages or their capture in war, separation from friends and family, and then the forced march to an interior trading town or to the slave pens at the coast. Conditions were deadly; perhaps as many as one-third of the captives died along the way or in the slave pens. Eventually the slaves were loaded onto the ships. Cargo sizes varied and could go as high as 700 slaves crowded into the dank, unsanitary conditions of the slave ships, but most cargoes were smaller. Overcrowding was less of a factor in mortality than the length of the voyage or the point of origin in Africa; the Bights of Benin and Biafra were particularly dangerous. The average mortality rate for slaves varied over time, but it ran at about 18 percent or so until the 18th century, when it declined somewhat. Still, losses could be catastrophic on individual ships, as on a Dutch ship in 1737, where 700 of the 716 slaves died on the voyage.

The **Middle Passage**, or slave voyage to the Americas, was traumatic. Taken from their homes, branded, confined, and shackled, the Africans faced not only the dangers of poor hygiene, dysentery, disease, and bad treatment but also the fear of being beaten or worse by the Europeans. Their situation sometimes led to suicide or resistance and mutiny on the ships. However traumatic, the Middle Passage certainly did not strip Africans of their culture, and they arrived in the Americas retaining their languages, beliefs, artistic traditions, and memories of their past.

> **Middle Passage** Slave voyage from Africa to the Americas (16th–18th centuries); generally a traumatic experience for black slaves, although it failed to strip Africans of their culture.

Africans in the Americas

The slaves carried across the Atlantic were brought mainly to the plantations and mines of the Americas. Landed estates using large amounts of labor, often coerced, became characteristic of American agriculture, at first in sugar production and later for rice, cotton, and tobacco. The plantation system already used for producing sugar on the Atlantic islands of Spain and Portugal was transferred to the New World. After attempts to use Native American laborers in places such as Brazil and Hispaniola, Africans were brought in. West Africans, coming from societies in which herding, metallurgy, and intensive agriculture were widely practiced, were sought by Europeans for the specialized tasks of making sugar. In the English colonies of Barbados and Virginia, indentured servants from England eventually were replaced by enslaved Africans when new crops, such as sugar, were introduced or when indentured servants became less available.

In any case, the plantation system of farming with a dependent or enslaved workforce characterized the production of many tropical and semitropical crops in demand in Europe, and thus the plantation became the locus of African and American life. But slaves did many other things as well, from mining to urban occupations as artisans, street vendors, and household servants. In short, there was almost no occupation that slaves did not perform, although most were agricultural laborers (Figure 20.7).

American Slave Societies

Each American slave-based society reflected the variations of its European origin and its component African cultures, but there were certain similarities and common features. Each recognized distinctions between African-born **saltwater slaves**, who were almost invariably black (by European standards) and their American-born descendants, the **Creole slaves**, some of whom were mulattos as a result of the sexual exploitation of slave women or other forms of miscegenation. In all American slave societies, a hierarchy of status evolved in which free whites were at the top, slaves were at the bottom, and free people of color had an intermediate position. In this sense, color and "race" played a role in American slavery it had not played in Africa. Among the slaves, slaveholders also created a hierarchy based on origin and color. Creole and especially mulatto slaves were given more opportunities to acquire skilled jobs on plantations or to work as house servants rather than in the fields or mines. They were also more likely to win their freedom by manumission, the voluntary freeing of

saltwater slaves Slaves transported from Africa; almost invariably black.

Creole slaves American-born descendants of saltwater slaves; result of sexual exploitation of slave women or process of miscegenation.

FIGURE **20.7** Africans performed all kinds of labor in the Americas, from domestic service to mining and shipbuilding. Most worked on plantations like this sugar mill in the Caribbean.

DOCUMENT

An African's Description of the Middle Passage

DURING THE ERA OF THE SLAVE trade, enslaved Africans by one means or another succeeded in telling their stories. These accounts, with their specific details of the injustice and inhumanities of slavery, became particularly useful in the abolitionist crusade. The autobiography of Frederick Douglass is perhaps the most famous of these accounts. The biography of Olaudah Equiano is similarly reknown. In it Equiano states that he is an Ibo from what is today eastern Nigeria on the Niger River, and he presents a personal description of enslavement in Africa and the terrors of the Middle Passage. In the story, Equiano and his sister were kidnapped in 1756 by African slave hunters and sold to British slave traders. Separated from his sister, Equiano was carried to the West Indies and later to Virginia, where he became servant to a naval officer. He traveled widely on his master's military campaigns and was later sold to a Philadelphia Quaker merchant, who eventually allowed him to buy his freedom. Later, he moved to England and became an active member in the movement to end slavery and the slave trade. His biography was published in 1789. The political uses of this kind of biography and Equiano's association with the abolitionists should caution us against accepting the account at face value. Recently questions have arisen over his place of birth, which may have been the Carolinas, so that his descriptions of Africa were based on what he heard or read rather than on his personal experience, but his book was a sensation and widely read and translated. It seemed to convey the personal shock and anguish of those caught in the slave trade.

> The first object which saluted my eyes when I arrived on the coast was the sea, and a slaveship, which was riding at anchor, and waiting for its cargo. These filled me with astonishment, which was soon converted into terror, which I am yet at a loss to describe, nor the then feelings of my mind. When I was carried on board I was immediately handled, and tossed up, to see if I were sound, by some of the crew; and I was now persuaded that I had got into a world of bad spirits, and that they were going to kill me. Their complexions too differing so much from ours, their long hair, and the language they spoke, which was very different from any I had ever heard, united to confirm me in this belief. Indeed, such were the horrors of my views and fears at that moment, that if ten thousand worlds had been my own, I would have freely parted with them all to have exchanged my condition with that of the meanest slave in my own country. When I looked round the ship too, and saw a large furnace or copper boiler, and a multitude of black people of every description chained together, every one of their countenances expressing dejection and sorrow, quite overpowered with horror and anguish, I fell motionless on the deck and fainted. When I recovered a little, I found some black people about me, who I believed were some of those who brought me on board, and had been receiving their pay; they talked to me in order to cheer me, but all in vain. I asked them if we were not to be eaten by those white men with horrible looks, red faces, and long hair. They told me I was not.... I now saw myself deprived of all chance of returning to my native country, or even the least glimpse of hope of gaining the shore, which I now considered as friendly; and I even wished for my former slavery, in preference to my present situation, which was filled with horrors of every kind, still heightened by my ignorance of what I was to undergo. I was not long suffered to indulge my grief; I was soon put down under decks, and there I received such a salutation in my nostrils as I had never experienced in my life; so that with the loathsomeness of the stench, and the crying together, I became so sick and low that I was not able to eat, nor had I the least desire to taste anything. I now wished for the last friend, death, to relieve me; but soon, to my grief two white men offered me eatables; and on my refusing to eat, one of them held me fast by the hands, and laid me across, I think, the windlass, and tied my feet while the other flogged me severely. I had never experienced anything of this kind before; and, although not being used to the water, I naturally feared that element the first time I saw it; yet, nevertheless, could I have got over the nettings, I would have jumped over the side; but I could not; and, besides the crew used to watch us very closely who were not chained down to the decks, lest we should leap into the water; and I have seen some of these poor African prisoners most severely cut for attempting to do so, and hourly whipped for not eating. This indeed was often the case with myself. In a little time after amongst the poor chained men, I found some of my own nation, which in a small degree gave ease to my mind. I inquired of them what was to be done with us? They gave me to understand we were to be carried to these white people's country to work for them. I then was a little revived, and thought, if it were no worse than working, my situation was not so desperate; but still I feared I should be put to death, the white people looked and acted, as I thought, in so savage a manner; for I had never seen among any people such instances of brutal cruelty; and this was not only shown to us blacks, but also to some of the whites themselves....
>
> At last when the ship we were in had got in all her cargo, they made ready with many fearful noises, and we were all put under deck, so that we could not see how they managed the vessel. But this disappointment was the least of my sorrow. The stench of the hold while we were on the coast was so intolerably loathsome, that it was dangerous to remain there for any time, and some of us had been permitted to stay on deck for the fresh air; but now the whole ship's cargo was confined together, it became absolutely pestilential. The closeness of the place, and the heat of the climate, added to the number in the ship, which was so crowded that each had scarcely room to turn himself, almost suffocated us. This produced copious perspirations, so that the air soon became unfit for

(continued on next page)

respiration, from a variety of loathsome smells, and brought on a sickness amongst the slaves, of which many died, thus falling victims to the improvident avarice, as I may call it, of their purchasers. This wretched situation was again aggravated by the galling of the chains, now become insupportable; and the filth of the necessary tubs, into which the children fell, and were almost suffocated. The shrieks of the women, and the groans of the dying, rendered the whole a scene of horror almost inconceivable.

QUESTIONS

- In what ways does Equiano's description contradict a previous understanding of the slave trade?
- What opportunities existed for the captives to resist?
- What effect might the experience of Africans on the slave ships have had on their perceptions of each other and of the Europeans?

slaves. Great numbers of slaves labored on large agricultural estates or plantations where work was closely regimented, hours were long, food and housing often inadequate. Sugar plantations that both grew the sugar cane and then processed it into sugar were like factories in the field and were especially demanding. As the world market for sugar and other commodities expanded, so too did the number of plantations. The continual demand for new laborers kept the trans-Atlantic slave trade alive.

This hierarchy was a creation of the slaveholders and did not necessarily reflect perceptions among the slaves. There is evidence that important African nobles or religious leaders, who for one reason or another were sold into slavery, continued to exercise authority within the slave community. Still, the distinctions between Creole and African slaves tended to divide that community, as did the distinctions between different African groups whose members maintained their ties and affiliations in America. Many of the slave rebellions in the Caribbean and Brazil were organized along African ethnic and political lines. In Jamaica there were several Akan led rebellions in the 18th century, and the largest escaped slave community in 17th-century Brazil apparently was organized and led by Angolans.

Although economic factors imposed similarities, the slave-based societies also varied in their composition. In the 18th century, on the Caribbean islands where the indigenous population had died out or had been exterminated and where few Europeans settled, Africans and their descendants formed the vast majority. In Jamaica and St. Domingue, slaves made up more than 80 percent of the population; a large proportion of them were African born. Brazil also had large numbers of imported Africans, but its more diverse population and economy, as well as a tradition of manumitting slaves and high levels of miscegenation, meant that slaves made up only about 35 percent of the population. However, free people of color, the descendants of former slaves, made up about another one-third, so that together slaves and free colored people made up two-thirds of the total population.

North American cities such as Charleston and New Orleans also developed a large slave and free African population as did Caribbean cities like Kingston and San Juan, but the southern colonies of British North America differed significantly from the Caribbean and Brazil, by depending less on imported Africans because of natural population growth among the slaves. In North America, Creole slaves predominated, but manumission was less common, and free people of color made up less than 10 percent of the total Afro-American population. The result was that slavery in North America was less influenced by Africa. By the mid-18th century, the slave population in most places in North America was reproducing itself. By 1850, fewer than 1 percent of the slaves there were African born. The combination of natural growth and the small direct trade from Africa reduced the degree of African cultural reinforcement.

The People and Gods in Exile

Africans brought as slaves to the Americas faced a peculiar series of problems. Working conditions were exhausting, and life for most slaves often was difficult and short. Family formation was made difficult because of the general shortage of female slaves; the ratio of men to women was as much as three to one in some places. To this was added the insecurity of slave status: Family members might be separated by sale or by a master's whim. Still, most slaves lived in family units, even though their marriages were not always sanctioned by the religion of their masters. Throughout the Americas,

VISUALIZING THE PAST

The Cloth of Kings in an Atlantic Perspective

THE VARIOUS ARTISTIC TRADITIONS OF WEST Africa not only attracted the attention of European traders, but also flourished as new and powerful states were formed whose monarchs and attendant courtiers demanded objects of value for rituals and the activities of daily life. Skilled artisans produced objects of wood, ivory, iron, pottery, and textiles. Among the finest examples were the kente cloths of the Asante peoples from the region of modern-day Ghana.

With the rise of a powerful Asante state in the seventeenth century, traditional weaving techniques were turned to the making of royal and sacred cloths, often incorporating sophisticated designs, geometric patterns, and vivid colors. Usually using local cotton, trade with Europeans or across the Sahara often brought silk to Ghana, which was used in the royal fabrics, and new colors were introduced with the importation of dyes from Europe and India. A traditional art form was thus amplified and expanded using materials brought by the long-distance trade. Patterns and colors conveyed symbolic meanings, blue for peacefulness, silver for purity, red for sacrifice, and certain patterns were reserved for the king alone. Over time, the traditional exclusivity diminished, and the use of kente cloth was adopted as a national symbol, although historically it was usually reserved for important occasions and ritual purposes. Kente cloth has become today one of the most recognizable traditional arts of Africa and a source of pride for people of African origin in the diaspora.

QUESTIONS

- In what way do artistic traditions depend on the patronage of those in power?
- Has this been the case in other societies in history?
- Kente was used to convey meanings, symbols, and proverbs. Do such things change over time?
- What has made kente cloth so popular today?

obeah African religious ideas and practices in the English and French Caribbean islands.

candomblé [kan dom blä] African religious ideas and practices in Brazil, particularly among the Yoruba people.

vodun African religious ideas and practices among descendants of African slaves in Haiti.

Palmares [pahl-MAHR-ehs] Kingdom of runaway slaves with a population of 8000 to 10,000 people; located in Brazil during the 17th century; leadership was Angolan.

Suriname Formerly a Dutch plantation colony on the coast of South America; location of runaway slave kingdom in 18th century; able to retain independence despite attempts to crush guerrilla resistance.

wherever Africans were brought, aspects of their language, religion, artistic sensibilities, and other cultural elements survived. To some extent, the amount of continuity depended on the intensity and volume of the slave trade from a particular area. Some slaveholders tried to mix up the slaves on their plantations so that strong African identities would be lost, but colonial dependence on slavers who consistently dealt with the same region tended to undercut such policies. In the Americas, African slaves had to adapt and to incorporate other African peoples' ideas and customs into their own lives. Moreover, the ways and customs of the masters were also imposed. Thus, what emerged as Afro-American culture reflected specific African roots adapted to a new reality. Scholars at present hotly debate the relative extent to which African identities (Yoruba, Kongo, Igbo, etc) and practices like marriage customs, political concepts, or religious beliefs continued in the New World. While some emphasize continuities, others believe that African cultures provided a framework but that emphasis should be placed on the creativity inherent in the creation of Afro-American "creole" cultures.

Religion provides an obvious example of continuity and adaptation. Slaves were converted to Catholicism by the Spaniards and the Portuguese, sometimes in Africa itself, and they showed fervent devotion as members of Black Catholic brotherhoods, some of which were organized by African origins. In North America and the British Caribbean they joined Protestant denominations. Still, African religious ideas and practices did not die out. In the English islands, **obeah** was the name given to the African religious practices, and the men and women knowledgeable in them were held in high regard within the community. In Brazilian **candomblé** (Yoruba) and Haitian **vodun** (Aja), fully developed versions of African religions, flourished and continue today, despite attempts by national governments or state churches to suppress them.

The reality of the Middle Passage meant that religious ideas were easier to transfer than the institutional aspects of religion. Without religious specialists or a priestly class, aspects of African religions were changed by contact with other African peoples as well as with colonial society. In many cases, slaves held their new faith in Christianity and their African beliefs at the same time, and tried to fuse the two. For Muslim Africans this was more difficult. In 1835 in Bahia, the largest slave rebellion in Brazil was organized by Muslim Yoruba and Hausa slaves and directed against the whites and against nonbelievers.

Resistance and rebellion were other aspects of African American history. Recalcitrance, running away, and direct confrontation were present wherever slaves were held. As early as 1508, African runaways disrupted communications on Hispaniola, and in 1527, a plot to rebel was uncovered in Mexico City. Throughout the Americas, communities of runaway slaves formed. In Jamaica, Colombia, Venezuela, Haiti, and Brazil, runaway communities were persistent and sometimes large. In Brazil during the 17th century, **Palmares**, an enormous runaways or slave kingdom with five main villages and a population of perhaps 8000 to 10,000 people, resisted Portuguese and Dutch attempts to destroy it for a century before its last king, named Zumbi, was finally killed in 1694. In Jamaica the runaway Maroons were able to gain some independence and a recognition of their freedom. So-called ethnic slave rebellions organized by a particular African group were common in the Caribbean and Brazil in the 18th century. In North America, where reinforcement from the slave trade was less continuous, resistance was also important, but it was based less on African origins or ethnicities.

Perhaps the most remarkable story of African American resistance is found in the forests of **Suriname**, a former Dutch plantation colony. There, large numbers of slaves ran off in the 18th century and mounted an almost perpetual war in the rain forest against the various expeditions sent to hunt them down. Those captured were brutally executed, but eventually a truce developed. Today about 50,000 Maroon descendants still live in Suriname and French Guiana. The Suriname Maroons maintained many aspects of their west African background in terms of language, kinship relations, and religious beliefs, but these were fused with new forms drawn from European and American Indian contacts. From this fusion, the Maroons created a truly Afro-American culture (Figure 20.8).

FIGURE **20.8** African, American, or both? In Suriname, descendants of escaped slaves maintain many aspects of African culture but have adapted, modified, and transformed them in various ways. This wooden door shows the imaginative skills of African American carvers.

The End of the Slave Trade and the Abolition of Slavery

The end of the Atlantic slave trade and the abolition of slavery in the Atlantic world resulted from economic, political, and religious changes in Europe and its overseas American colonies and former colonies. These changes, which were manifestations of the Enlightenment, the age of revolution, Christian revivalism, growing slave resistance, and the rise of a class of freed slaves and of people of mixed racial background, and perhaps the Industrial Revolution, were external to Africa, but once again they determined the pace and nature of change within Africa.

Like much else about the history of slavery, there is disagreement about the end of the slave trade. It is true that some African societies began to export other commodities, such as peanuts, cotton, and palm oil, which made their dependence on the slave trade less important, but the supply of slaves to European merchants was not greatly affected by this development. In general, the British plantation economies were booming in the period from 1790 to 1830, and plantations in Cuba, Brazil, and the southern United States flourished in the decades that followed. Thus, it is difficult to find a direct and simple link between economic self-interest and the movement to suppress the slave trade.

Opponents of slavery and the brutality of the trade had appeared in the mid-18th century, in relation to new intellectual movements in the West. Philosopher Jean-Jacques Rousseau in France and political economist Adam Smith in England both wrote against it. Whereas in ancient Rome during the spread of Christianity and Islam, and in 16th-century Europe, the enslavement of "barbarians" or nonbelievers was seen as positive—a way to civilize others—slavery during the European Enlightenment and bourgeois revolution came to be seen as backward and immoral. The slave trade was particularly criticized. It was the symbol of slavery's inhumanity and cruelty.

England, as the major maritime power of the period, was the key to the end of the slave trade. Under the leadership of religious humanitarians, such as John Wesley and **William Wilberforce**, an abolitionist movement gained strength against the merchants and the West Indies interests. After much parliamentary debate, the British slave trade was abolished in 1807. Some authors have argued that sugar earnings were already falling and that slavery was no longer profitable to Great Britain, others have disagreed and called the abolition of the trade *"econocide," a kind of economic suicide.* Whatever the truth, having set out on this course, Britain tried to impose abolition of the slave trade on other countries throughout the Atlantic. Spain and Portugal were pressured to gradually suppress the trade, and the British navy was used to enforce these agreements by capturing illegal slave ships. By the 19th century, the moral and intellectual justifications that had supported the age of the slave trade had worn thin and the movement to abolish slavery was growing in the Atlantic world. The great slave revolt in the French Caribbean that resulted in the independence of Haiti (1804) impressed both the masters and the slaves in other countries. In this process, the writings of ex-slaves like Baquaqua or Equiano also contributed to the change of opinion as did the resistance of slaves to their captivity like the shipboard revolt on the *Amistad* in 1839, a case heard by the Supreme Court of the United States that focused attention on the inherent legal contradictions of slavery. The issue was thorny, as the U.S. Civil War made clear. The full end of slavery in the Americas did not occur until 1888, when it was abolished in Brazil.

Wilberforce, William British statesman and reformer; leader of abolitionist movement in English parliament that led to end of English slave trade in 1807.

Global Connections and Critical Themes

AFRICA AND THE AFRICAN DIASPORA IN WORLD CONTEXT

Africa was drawn into the world economy in the era of the slave trade, at first slowly, but with increasing intensity after 1750. Its incorporation produced differing effects on African societies, reinforcing authority in some places, creating new states in others, and sometimes provoking social, religious, and political reactions. Although many aspects of African life followed traditional patterns, contact with the world economy forced many African societies to adjust in ways that often placed them at a disadvantage and facilitated Europe's colonization of Africa in the 19th century. Well into the 20th century, as forced labor continued in Africa under European direction, the legacy of the slave trade era proved slow to die.

Part of that legacy was the movement of millions of Africans far from their continent. Taken against their will, they and their descendants drew on the cultures and practices of Africa as they coped with slavery. Eventually, they created vibrant new cultural forms, which along with their labor and skills contributed to the growth of new societies. Africans were pulled into the developing Atlantic system of exchange of people, commodities, diseases, plants, animals, and ideas. They and their African American descendants moved between the continents not only as slaves, but also as ambassadors, soldiers, missionaries, merchants, and mariners, integral elements in a developing world economy.

Further Readings

Aside from the general books on Africa already mentioned in the Further Readings for previous chapters, some specific readings are particularly useful. Martin Hall, *The Changing Past: Farmers, Kings, and Traders in Southern Africa* (1987), discusses the use of archeological evidence in African history. D. Birmingham and Phyllis Martin, eds., *History of Central Africa*, 3 vols. (1983–98), present extended essays on a number of regions. On West Africa in the age of the slave trade, a good introduction is J. F. A. Ajayi and Michael Crowder, eds., *History of West Africa*, 2 vols. (1975), especially volume 2. On the Ashanti see Ivor Wilkes, *Forests of Gold: Essays on the Akan and the Kingdom of Assante* (1993). On southern Africa, Leonard Thompson's *A History of South Africa* (1990) presents a broad survey, while Carolyn Hamilton, *Mfecane Aftermath* (1995), looks at the long-term consequences of the Zulu expansion and Dan Wylie, *Myth of Iron: Shaka in History* (2005), is a recent interpretation of the great Zulu leader.

There are many histories of the slave trades. John Wright, *The Trans-Saharan Slave Trade* (2007), and Herbert S. Klein, *The Atlantic Slave Trade* (1999), provide up-to-date and intelligent overviews. A large general history is Hugh Thomas, *The Slave Trade* (1997). On the quantitative aspects of the slave trade, Philip Curtin, *The Atlantic Slave Trade: A Census* (1969), is the proper starting point, while David Eltis, *The Rise of African Slavery in the Americas* (2000), is an important newer study. All new quantitative studies will depend on the CD-ROM edited by David Eltis et al. entitled *The Atlantic Slave Trade* (1998) and the updated continuation edited by David Eltis and David Richardson, *Extending the Frontiers: Essays on the New Transatlantic Slave Trade Database* (2008). Indispensible is David Eltis and David Richardson, *Atlas of the TransAtlantic Slave Trade* (2011).

On Africa, Paul Lovejoy's *Transformations in Slavery: A History of Slavery in Africa*, 2nd ed. (2000) and Patrick Manning's *Slavery and African Life* (1990) provide comprehensive overviews. Robert Harms, *The Diligent: Voyage Through the Worlds of the Slave Trade* (2002), uses one voyage to examine the whole system of the Atlantic slave trade and Marcus Rediker, *The Slave Ship* (2007), uses the ships as a basis for his analysis of the system. Two good regional studies are Walter Hawthorne, *From Africa to Brazil. Culture, Identity and an Atlantic Slave Trade* (2010), on the trade to northern Brazil and Barry Boubacar's *Senegambia and the Atlantic Slave Trade* (1998). John K. Thornton, *Africa and Africans in the Making of the Atlantic World*, 2nd ed. (1998), is an excellent argument for the centrality of slavery in Africa while his *A Cultural History of the Atlantic World* (2012) places the African diaspora in a broad context. Walter Rodney's essay "Africa in Europe and the Americas," in *Cambridge History of Africa*, vol. 4, 578–622, is a succinct overview of the African diaspora. In a similar vein with a cultural emphasis is Michael Gomez, *Reversing Sail: A History of the African Diaspora* (2005), while Paul Gilroy, *Black Atlantic: Modernity and Double Consciousness* (1993), is an important statement about people of African descent in the English-speaking Atlantic world. Herbert Klein, *The Atlantic Slave Trade* (1999), and his book with Ben Vincent, *African Slavery in Latin America and the Caribbean* 2nd ed. (2007), are useful updated surveys. S. Schwartz, *Tropical Babylons* (2004), examines the early association of plantations and slavery. Excellent overviews based on the best secondary literature are Robin Blackburn's *The Making of New World Slavery* (1997) and his *The Overthrow of Colonial Slavery* (1988). On the African contribution to the Columbian Exchange, see Judith Carney and Richard N. Rosomoff, *In the Shadow of Slavery. Africa's Botanical Legacy in the Atlantic World* (2009).

On the general theoretical issues of slavery, Orlando Patterson, *Slavery and Social Death* (1982), is a broad comparative sociological study. David B. Davis, *Inhuman Bondage: The Rise and Fall of Slavery in the New World* (2006), takes a historical approach to the whole question and then places the abolitionist movement in context. Some of the best recent scholarship is collected in G. Heuman and J. Walvin, eds., *The Slavery Reader* (2003). Biography has also become an important genre in the field. See, for example, James Walvin, *The Trader, the Owner, the Slave* (2007). Vincent Carretta, *Equiano, the African: Biography of a Self-made Man* (2005), is a controversial reevaluation of Equiano's origins but still celebrates the power of the original autobiography, *The Interesting Narrative of the Life of Olaudah Equiano*, now in an easily accessible version edited by Robert J. Allison, 2nd ed. (2007). Vincent Brown, *The Reaper's Garden. Death and Power in the World of Atlantic Slavery* (2008), tries to plumb the sentiments of those who suffered slavery's burdens. On the question of African continuities vs. creolization see Michael Gomez, *Diasporic Africa: A Reader* (2006), and Linda Heywood, ed., *Central Africas and Cultural Transformations in the American Diaspora* (2002), while the creolization argument is best summarized in Richard Price and Sidney Mintz, *The Birth of Afro-American Culture* (1992). Richard Price and Sally Price, *Maroon Arts Cultural Vitality in the African Diaspora* (1999), examines the arts and crafts of maroon descendants in Suriname.

On MyHistoryLab

Critical Thinking Questions

1. Why did some African rulers and states participate in the slave trade?
2. In what ways did the plantation system transform the nature of work?
3. Slavery existed in many parts of the globe, but why did it become so important in the Atlantic world and why was it primarily in Europe that a movement to abolish the slave trade and then slavery itself?

21
The Rise of Russia

Listen to Chapter 21 on MyHistoryLab

LEARNING OBJECTIVES

21.1 How did the Russian state manage the process of territorial expansion? p. 479

21.2 What aspects of Russian society did Peter the Great NOT seek to Westernize? p. 483

21.3 What were the main causes of Russian policy toward the serfs? p. 489

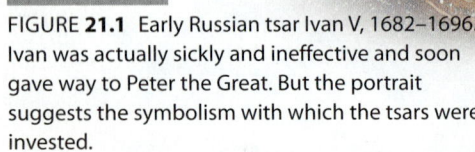

FIGURE 21.1 Early Russian tsar Ivan V, 1682–1696. Ivan was actually sickly and ineffective and soon gave way to Peter the Great. But the portrait suggests the symbolism with which the tsars were invested.

New rulers often face a special challenge of legitimacy: Why should people accept their rule and their policies? The Russian tsars of the 15th and 16th century faced just such a challenge. They claimed the right to dominate Russia and orchestrate steady expansion of territory. How could they persuade the people that their power was legitimate? Early tsars, particularly Ivan III and Ivan IV, proved particularly inventive. First, they pointed to their family tree, noting their descent from the line of Rurik, the legendary founder of Russia. Ivan IV had huge genealogy books prepared, ignoring the claims of other descendants. The early tsars also invoked the example of the Roman empire, speaking of Russia as the "third Rome"—after Byzantium and Rome itself. This had appeal: Rome was a much-admired state from the classical past, and Byzantium added an element of Christian mission. Russia could be presented as protector of the faith. Ivan IV's genealogies were thus filled with lives of the saints and church resolutions, designed to show how God's purpose, from creation onward, had been to found a truly Christian empire and how Russia was now called to fulfill this purpose. Russia's ruler was often portrayed in religious terms, as leader of the holy church and as part of a divine mission (See Figure 21.1).

Watch the Video Series on MyHistoryLab

Learn about some key topics related to this chapter with the *MyHistoryLab Video Series: Key Topics in World History*

But even this was not enough. As Ivan IV campaigned in central Asia, he also invoked the heritage of the Mongols. Russia should rule in central Asia, according to this argument, because it was the long-standing property of the Rurik dynasty (which was nonsense historically but sounded good); because it was "his duty as a Christian monarch to extirpate the rule of the infidel"; and because, having defeated the Mongols, he had become a khan himself. And sure enough, at the time and thereafter, Muslim leaders often took oaths of loyalty to the tsar on the Qur'an, and the tsar styled himself, in that region, the "khan of the north." ■

Three lessons may be taken from all this that are important for Russian and world history alike. First, tsars claimed a lot. Second, their claims embodied significant contradictions. Were they khans, claiming arbitrary authority over the masses, or were they benevolent, gentle Christians? And third, precisely because Russian expansion touched so many different regions and traditions, the new empire would inevitably be complex and multifaceted. It came to embrace many different peoples, and its size inevitably challenged the capacity of Russia's rulers. This chapter focuses strongly on Russian expansion and tsarist power, but also on social conditions that distinguished Russia during a crucial period in the nation's development.

Developments in Russia move us away from the changes in the world economy and the overseas empires that accompanied the rise of Western power. Russia was one of the growing, largely land-based empires in eastern Europe and Asia that maintained their own dynamic during the Early Modern centuries. But Russia would ultimately connect with these other global changes, altering its relationship to the West and showing some impact of larger economic relationships as well. The result is a number of comparative vantage points: as a growing power, as a "gunpowder" empire; and as an economy dependent on its own system of unfree labor.

RUSSIA'S EXPANSIONIST POLITICS UNDER THE TSARS

21.1 How did the Russian state manage the process of territorial expansion?

> Russia's Early Modern development first emphasized territorial expansion and the strengthening of tsarist rule.

The Early Modern period saw crucial changes in Russian society and a vast increase in Russia's impact on neighboring societies. Russian patterns were very different from those in the Atlantic world. Russia is best seen as a major, and very successful, example of the new land-based empires that sprang up in various parts of Eurasia. However, there were some links to developments elsewhere. One was accidental: Russia sought to develop a new system of labor controls, for both political and economic reasons, and this brought some coincidental similarities with social changes in Latin America. The other was deliberate, as Russia came to engage in active, although also quite selective, borrowings from the West.

Russia's emergence as a new power in eastern Europe and central Asia initially depended on its gaining freedom from Mongol (Tatar) control. The Duchy of Moscow was the center for the liberation effort beginning in the 14th century. Local princes began to carve out greater autonomy, and the

1450 C.E.	1600 C.E.	1750 C.E.
1462 Much of Russia freed from Tatars by Ivan III (Ivan the Great)	**1604–1613** Time of Troubles	**1762–1796** Reign of Catherine the Great
1480 Moscow region free; Russian expansion presses south	**1613–1917** Romanov dynasty	**1773–1775** Pugachev revolt
	1637 Russian pioneers to Pacific	**1772, 1793, 1795** Partition of Poland
1533–1584 Life of Ivan IV (Ivan the Terrible), first to emphasize the title of *tsar;* boyar power reduced	**1649** Law enacted making serfdom hereditary	**1785** Law enacted tightening landlord power over serfs
	1689–1725 Reign of Peter the Great	
	1700–1721 Wars with Sweden	
1552–1556 Russian expansion in central Asia, western Siberia	**1703** Founding of St. Petersburg	

effectiveness of Mongol control began to diminish. Ironically, the Moscow princes initially gained political experience as tax collectors for the Mongols, but gradually they moved toward regional independence. Under **Ivan III**—Ivan the Great (r. 1462–1505), who claimed succession from the Rurik dynasty and the old Kievan days—a large Russian territory emerged. Ivan organized a strong army, giving the new government a military emphasis it would long retain. By 1480, Moscow had been freed from any payment to the Mongols and Ivan had gained a vast kingdom running from the borders of the Polish Lithuanian kingdom to the Ural Mountains.

Russia's rise had some similarities to earlier Macedonian and Roman expansion: a new state, on the fringes of the "civilized world," suddenly and steadily gaining great power. The new Russian empire, important in its own right, also formed one of the novel varieties of empire introduced in the Early Modern period as a whole.

Ivan III Also known as Ivan the Great; prince of Duchy of Moscow; claimed descent from Rurik; responsible for freeing Russia from Mongols after 1462; took title of tsar or Caesar—equivalent of emperor.

The Need for Revival

Mongol control never reshaped basic Russian values, for the rulers were interested in tribute, not full government. Many Russian landlords adopted Mongol styles of dress and social habits. However, most Russians remained Christians, and most local administrative issues remained in the hands of regional princes, landlords, or peasant villages. In these senses, Russia was set to resume many of its earlier patterns when full independence was achieved. On the other hand, the Mongol period had reduced the vigor of Russian cultural life, lowering the levels of literacy among the priesthood, for example. Economic life deteriorated as well: With trade down and manufacturing limited, Russia had become a purely agricultural economy dependent on peasant labor. In these senses, independence brought a challenge for revival and reform.

Ivan the Great claimed an earlier tradition of centralized rule, which went back to the Rurik dynasty and Byzantine precedents, and added to it the new sense of imperial mission. He married the niece of the last Byzantine emperor, which gave him the chance to assert control over all Orthodox churches regardless of whether in Russia. The idea of Russia as a third Rome explained why Ivan called himself tsar, or caesar, the "autocrat of all the Russias."

From Ivan III onward, early modern Russia was strongly shaped by military needs. Mongol counterattacks were a legitimate concern: A Tatar group sacked Moscow as late as 1571. But Russia's rulers also pressed conquests beyond defense. They seized additional territory from the Tatars in what is now Ukraine, and also in central Asia, through the 16th century, and they also began to expand in east-central Europe, which brought them face to face with other military opponents.

To recruit soldiers, the tsars began to grant hereditary territories to military nobles; this included strict controls over the peasant serfs on these lands. Harsh conditions caused many serfs to flee to border regions, with two results. First, regulations on remaining serfs tightened, to tie them to the land lest a severe labor shortage develop. This launched a pattern of constraints on serfs that was in marked contrast to trends in western Europe at the same time, where serfdom was easing up. Peasants who fled, however, helped provide both military muscle and labor for further Russian expansion, for example, into Siberia. Cossack colonies, formed from independent peasant fighting men, played a great role in Russian success.

The powers of the aristocratic landlords, called *boyars*, also led to conflicts with the claims of the tsars, who wanted to rule without interference. These conflicts dotted Russian history in the 16th and 17th centuries, before the boyars were finally put down. This pattern, along with the deep-seated and durable pressures on the serfs, defined key developments in Russia even beyond the early modern centuries.

The next important tsar, **Ivan IV** (1533–1584), justly called Ivan the Terrible, continued the trends of Russian expansion and consolidation of power. He placed great emphasis on promoting the tsarist autocracy, earning his nickname by killing or exiling many of the Russian *boyars*, whom he suspected of conspiracy. The tsar often flew into violent rages—during one episode he killed his son and heir—followed by deep religious repentance. His conquests were largely successful, however, and there were other key gains such as the introduction of printing into Russia.

Ivan IV (1530–1584) Also known as Ivan the Terrible; confirmed power of tsarist autocracy by attacking authority of boyars (aristocrats); continued policy of Russian expansion; established contacts with western European commerce and culture.

Patterns of Expansion

Russia's creation of a vast landed empire propelled it into new importance in world history, with direct impact ultimately on Europe, East Asia, and central Asia and the Middle East. Steady territorial expansion policy was motivated by a desire to push the former Mongol overlords farther back. Russia was a country of vast plains, with few natural barriers to invasion. The early tsars turned this drawback to an advantage by pushing southward toward the Caspian Sea; they also moved east into the Ural Mountains and beyond. Both Ivan III and Ivan IV recruited peasants to migrate to the newly seized lands, particularly in the south, and the efforts to flee serfdom provided another stimulus. These peasant-adventurers, or **Cossacks**, were Russian pioneers, combining agriculture with daring military feats on horseback. The expansion territories long had a rough-and-ready frontier quality, only gradually settling down to more regular administration. The Cossack spirit provided volunteers for further expansion, for many of the pioneers—like their American counterparts in the 19th century—chafed under detailed tsarist control and were eager to move on to new settlements. During the 16th century, the Cossacks not only conquered the Caspian Sea area but also moved into western Siberia, across the Urals, beginning the gradual takeover and settlement of these vast plains, which previously had been sparsely inhabited by nomadic Asian peoples (Map 21.1).

 View the Image on MyHistoryLab: Ivan the Terrible

Cossacks Peasants recruited to migrate to newly seized lands in Russia, particularly in south; combined agriculture with military conquests; spurred additional frontier conquests and settlements.

Expansion also allowed tsars to continue to reward loyal nobles and bureaucrats by giving them estates in new territories. This practice provided new agricultural areas and sources of labor; Russia

MAP 21.1 Russian Expansion Under the Early Tsars, 1462–1598 From its base in the Moscow region, Russia expanded in three directions; the move into Siberia involved pioneering new settlements; the government encouraged Russians to push eastward. Political controls extended gradually as well.

Time of Troubles Followed death of Russian tsar Ivan IV without heir early in 17th century; boyars attempted to use vacuum of power to reestablish their authority; ended with selection of Michael Romanov as tsar in 1613.

Romanov dynasty Dynasty elected in 1613 at end of Time of Troubles; ruled Russia until 1917.

 View the Image on MyHistoryLab: Michael Romanov

Romanov, Alexis (1904–17 July 1918) The Russian heir to the throne at the time of the Russian revolution and the youngest member of the royal family at the time of their execution.

used slaves for certain kinds of production work into the 18th century. Although Russia never became as dependent on expansion for social control and economic advance as the later Roman empire or the Ottoman empire, it certainly had many reasons to continue the policy. Russia also created trading connections with its new Asian territories and their neighbors.

Russia's early expansion, along with that of the Ottoman empire to the south, eliminated independent central Asia—that age-old source of nomadic cultures and periodic invasions in both the east and the west. The same expansion, although driven by the movement of Russian peasants and landlords to new areas, also added to Russia diverse new peoples, making this a multicultural empire, like that of the Mughals and Ottomans. Particularly important was the addition of a large Muslim minority, overseen by the tsarist government but not pressed to integrate with Russian culture.

Western Contact and Romanov Policy

Along with expansion and enforcement of tsarist primacy, the early tsars added one element to their overall approach: carefully managed contacts with western Europe. The tsars realized that Russia's cultural and economic subordination to the Mongols had put them at a commercial and cultural disadvantage. Ivan III was eager to launch diplomatic missions to the leading Western

THINKING HISTORICALLY

Multinational Empires

OF ALL THE NEW MULTINATIONAL EMPIRES created in the Early Modern period, Russia's was the most successful, lasting until 1991 and to an extent beyond. In contrast, India's Mughal empire disappeared completely by the mid-19th century, and the Ottoman and Habsburg empires flickered until after World War I. All the multinational empires were reasonably tolerant of internal diversity (like the Roman and Arab empires of the past, two other multinational entities). The Russian tsar, for example, called himself "Khan of the North" to impress central Asian people and took oaths of loyalty from this region on the Qur'an. However, Russia differed from Asian empires and the Habsburgs in having a larger core of ethnic groups ready to fan out to the frontiers and establish pioneer settlements that sometimes developed into larger Russian enclaves. Russia also benefited from its willingness and ability to copy the West selectively, in contrast most obviously to the Ottoman empire in the same period. This copying provided access to new military technologies and some new organizational forms.

Ironically, the same period that saw the creation of so many new empires also confirmed the importance of the culturally more cohesive nation-state, the dominant form in western Europe. England and France, prototypical nation-states, were not culturally homogeneous; they had important pockets of minorities who differed linguistically or religiously from the majority culture. But both maintained a clear basis for joining the political unit to the cultural one to foster loyalty. Efforts by the 17th-century French kings to purify and standardize the French language, or by English parliamentarians to claim empowerment from the "rights of freeborn Englishmen," were early signs that politics and national culture were coming together.

The clash between national loyalties and multinational empires did not become serious until the 19th century, and it has continued into the 21st. In the long run, most multinational states have not been able to sustain themselves in the face of increasing demands from individual national groups. The collapse of several multinational units in the 20th century—the Ottomans in the Middle East, the Habsburgs in east central Europe, and the Russians—created new diplomatic trouble spots quite obvious in the world today, for stable nation-states have had a hard time developing in these regions.

> *The Russian tsar, for example, called himself "Khan of the North" to impress central Asian people and took oaths of loyalty from this region on the Qur'an.*

QUESTIONS
- Why have nation-states been more successful, as political units, in modern world history than multinational empires have been?
- In what ways did the Russian empire develop some nation-state characteristics?
- Amid new needs for international economic coordination in the 21st century, is it possible to build multinational organizations on some new basis?

states. During the reign of Ivan IV, British merchants established trading contacts with Russia, selling manufactured products in exchange for furs and other raw materials. Soon, Western merchants established outposts in Moscow and other Russian centers. The tsars also imported Italian artists and architects to design church buildings and the magnificent royal palace in the Kremlin in Moscow. The foreign architects modified Renaissance styles to take Russian building traditions into account, producing the ornate, onion-shaped domes that became characteristic of Russian (and other east European) churches and creating a distinctive form of classicism. A tradition of looking to the West, particularly for emblems of upper-class art and status, was beginning to emerge by the 16th century, along with some reliance on Western commercial initiative (Figure 21.2).

Ivan IV died without an heir. This led to some new power claims by the boyars—the **Time of Troubles** (1604–1613), when nobles competed with each other for power—plus Swedish and Polish attacks on Russian territory. In 1613, however, an assembly of boyars chose a member of the Romanov family as tsar. This family, the **Romanov dynasty**, was to rule Russia until the great revolution of 1917. Although many individual Romanov rulers were weak, and tensions with the claims of nobles recurred, the Time of Troubles did not produce any lasting constraints on tsarist power.

The first Romanov, Michael, reestablished internal order without great difficulty. He also drove out the foreign invaders and resumed the expansionist policy of his predecessors. A successful war against Poland brought Russia part of the Ukraine, including Kiev. In the south, Russia's boundaries expanded to meet those of the Ottoman empire. Expansion at this point was beginning to have new diplomatic implications as Russia encountered other established governments.

Alexis Romanov, Michael's successor, abolished the assemblies of nobles and gained new powers over the Russian church. He was eager to purge the church of many superstitions and errors that, in his judgment, had crept in during Mongol times. His policies resumed the Orthodox tradition of state control over the church. Dissident religious conservatives, called **Old Believers**, were exiled to Siberia or to southern Russia, where they maintained their religion and extended Russia's colonizing activities.

Measures to tightened serfdom continued, with new laws binding peasants to the land and restricting their opportunities to travel. Serf runaways were harshly punished. In 1670 a great serf revolt under Stephen Razin declared freedom from landlord control, but it was finally put down by tsarist troops.

RUSSIA'S FIRST WESTERNIZATION, 1690–1790

21.2 What aspects of Russian society did Peter the Great NOT seek to Westernize?

By the end of the 17th century Russia had become one of the great land empires, but it remained unusually agricultural by the standards of the West and the great Asian civilizations. The reign of **Peter I**, the son of Alexis and known with some justice as Peter the Great, built many new features into this framework between 1689 and 1725. In essence, Peter extended his predecessors' policies of building up tsarist control and expanding Russian territory (Map 21.2). He added a more definite interest in changing selected aspects of Russian economy and culture by imitating Western forms.

Peter's basic motives were familiar enough: He wanted to further tsarist power and enhance Russia's military strength. Early setbacks in wars with Sweden convinced him that some new departures were essential.

Peter the Great was a vigorous leader of exceptional intelligence and ruthless energy. A giant, standing 6 feet 8 inches, he was eager to move his country more fully into the Western military and cultural orbit without making it fully Western. He traveled widely in the West, incognito, seeking Western allies for a crusade against Turkish power in Europe—for which he found little enthusiasm. He also visited many Western manufacturing centers, even working as a ship's carpenter in Holland; through these activities he gained an interest in Western science and technology. He brought scores of Western artisans back with him to Russia.

View the **Closer Look** on MyHistoryLab: St. Basil's Cathedral, Moscow

FIGURE **21.2** This icon, from the 15th century, depicts Mary and the Christ Child. The Russian icon tradition used styles derived from Byzantine art. By the 17th century, under Western influence, they had become more naturalistic.

Old Believers Russians who refused to accept the ecclesiastical reforms of Alexis Romanov (17th century); many exiled to Siberia or southern Russia, where they became part of Russian colonization.

Read the **Document** on MyHistoryLab: Adan Olearius: A Foreign Traveler in Russia (early 17th c.)

Peter the Great led the first westernization effort in history. Tsarist policies encouraging Westernization focused only on particular aspects of Western society and left out large segments of the Russian population.

Peter I Also known as Peter the Great; son of Alexis Romanov; ruled from 1689 to 1725; continued growth of absolutism and conquest; included more definite interest in changing selected aspects of economy and culture through imitation of western European models.

CHAPTER 21 The Rise of Russia **483**

MAP 21.2 **Russia Under Peter the Great** From 1696 to 1725, Peter the Great allowed his country only one year of peace. For the rest of this reign he radically changed the form of his government to pursue war. By the end, he had established his much-desired "Window on the West" on the southern shores of the Baltic Sea, where he founded the new city of St. Petersburg.

Tsarist Autocracy of Peter the Great

In politics, Peter was clearly an autocrat. He put down revolts against his rule with great cruelty, in one case executing some of the ringleaders personally. He had no interest in the parliamentary features of Western centers such as Holland, seizing instead on the absolutist currents in the West at this time. Peter enhanced the power of the Russian state by using it as a reform force, trying to show that even aristocratic habits could be modified by state decree. Peter also extended an earlier policy of recruiting bureaucrats from outside aristocratic ranks and giving them noble titles to reward bureaucratic service. Here was a key means of freeing the state from exclusive dependence on aristocratic officials.

Peter imitated Western military organization, creating a specially trained fighting force that put down local militias. Furthermore, he set up a secret police to prevent dissent and to supervise the bureaucracy. Here he paralleled an earlier Chinese innovation but went well beyond the bureaucratic control impulses of Western absolutists at that time. Peter's Chancery of Secret Police survived, under different names and with changing functions, to the 1990s; it was reinstituted after 1917 by a revolutionary regime that in other respects worked to undo key features of the tsarist system.

Peter's foreign policy maintained many well-established lines (see Map 21.2). He attacked the Ottoman empire, but he won no great victories. He warred with Sweden, at the time one of the leading northern powers in Europe, and gained territory on the eastern coast of the Baltic Sea, thus reducing

Sweden to second-rate military status. Russia now had a window on the sea, including a largely ice-free port. From this time onward, Russia became a major factor in European diplomatic and military alignments. The tsar commemorated Russia's shift of interests westward by moving his capital from Moscow to a new Baltic city that he named St. Petersburg.

What Westernization Meant

Overall, Peter concentrated on improvements in political organization, on selected economic development, and on cultural change. He tried to streamline Russia's small bureaucracy and alter military structure by using Western organizational principles. He created a more well-defined military hierarchy while developing functionally specialized bureaucratic departments. He also improved the army's weaponry and, with aid from Western advisors, created the first Russian navy. He completely eliminated the old noble councils, creating a set of advisors under his control. Peter's ministers systematized law codes to extend through the whole empire and revised the tax system, with taxes on ordinary Russian peasants increasing steadily. New training institutes were established for aspiring bureaucrats and officers—one way to bring talented non-nobles into the system.

Peter's economic efforts focused on building up metallurgical and mining industries, using Russia's extensive iron holdings to feed state-run munitions and shipbuilding facilities. Without urbanizing extensively or developing a large commercial class, Peter's reforms changed the Russian economy. Landlords were rewarded for using serf labor to staff new manufacturing operations. This gave Russia the internal economic means to maintain a substantial military presence for almost two centuries.

DOCUMENT

The Nature of Westernization

PETER THE GREAT AND CATHERINE THE Great were the two chief reformist rulers in Russia before 1800. In the first of the following edicts, Peter focuses on educational change; his approach reflected a real desire for innovation, Russia's autocratic tradition in government, and its hierarchical social structure. Catherine's "Instruction" borrowed heavily from Western philosophers and was hailed by one French intellectual as "the finest monument of the century." This document also showed distinctively Russian traditions and problems. However, the reforms in law and punishment were not put into practice, and the document itself was banned as subversive by Catherine's successor, as Russia's rulers began to fear the subversive qualities of Western influence after the French Revolution.

DECREES ON COMPULSORY EDUCATION OF THE RUSSIAN NOBILITY, JANUARY 12 AND FEBRUARY 28, 1714

Send to every *gubernia* [region] some persons from mathematical schools to teach the children of the nobility—except those of freeholders and government clerks—mathematics and geometry; as a penalty [for evasion] establish a rule that no one will be allowed to marry unless he learns these [subjects]. Inform all prelates to issue no marriage certificates to those who are ordered to go to schools....

The Great Sovereign has decreed: in all *gubernias* children between the ages of ten and fifteen of the nobility, of government clerks, and of lesser officials, except those of freeholders, must be taught mathematics and some geometry. Toward that end, students should be sent from mathematical schools [as teachers], several into each *gubernia*, to prelates and to renowned monasteries to establish schools. During their instruction these teachers should be given food and financial remuneration of three altyns and two dengas per day from *gubernia* revenues set aside for that purpose by personal orders of His Imperial Majesty. No fees should be collected from students. When they have mastered the material, they should then be given certificates written in their own handwriting. When the students are released they ought to pay one ruble each for their training.

Without these certificates they should not be allowed to marry or receive marriage certificates.

FROM THE "INSTRUCTION" OF 1767

6. Russia is a European State.
7. This is clearly demonstrated by the following Observations: The Alterations which Peter the Great undertook in Russia succeeded with the greater Ease, because the Manners, which prevailed at that Time, and had been introduced amongst us by a Mixture of different Nations, and the Conquest of foreign Territories, were quite unsuitable to the Climate. Peter the First, by introducing the Manners and Customs of Europe among the European

(continued on next page)

(continued from previous page)

People in his Dominions, found at that Time such Means as even he himself was not sanguine enough to expect.

8. The Possessions of the Russian Empire extend upon the terrestrial Globe to 32 Degrees of Latitude, and to 165 of Longitude.
9. The Sovereign is absolute; for there is no other Authority but that which centers in his single Person, that can act with a Vigour proportionate to the Extent of such a vast Dominion.
10. The Extent of the Dominion requires an absolute Power to be vested in that Person who rules over it. It is expedient so to be, that the quick Dispatch of Affairs, sent from distant Parts, might make ample Amends for the delay occasioned by the great Distance of the Places.
11. Every other Form of Government whatsoever would not only have been prejudicial to Russia, but would even have proved its entire Ruin.
12. Another Reason is: That it is better to be subject to the Laws under one Master, than to be subservient to many.
13. What is the true End of Monarchy? Not to deprive People of their natural Liberty; but correct their Actions, in order to attain the supreme Good. . . .
272. The more happily a People live under a government, the more easily the Number of the Inhabitants increases. . . .

519. It is certain, that a high opinion of the *Glory* and *Power* of the Sovereign, would *increase* the *Strength* of his Administration; but a *good Opinion of his Love of Justice, will increase it at least as much.*
520. All this will never please those flatterers, who are daily instilling this pernicious Maxim into all the Sovereign on Earth, That their People are created for them only. But We think, and esteem it Our Glory to declare, "That We are created for Our People; and, of this Reason, We are obliged to Speak of Things just as they ought to be." For God forbid! That, after this Legislation is finished, any Nation on Earth should be more just; and, consequently, should flourish, more than Russia; otherwise the Intention of Our Laws would be totally frustrated; an Unhappiness which I do not wish to survive.

QUESTIONS

- In what sense did reformist measures strengthen Russian autocracy?
- What do the documents suggest about the motivations of leaders such as Peter and Catherine?
- Which Westernizer maintained a closer match between his or her claims and appearances and Russia's real conditions?

Read the Document on MyHistoryLab: On the Corruption of Morals in Russia (late 18th c.) Prince Mikhail Mikhailovich Shcherbatov

FIGURE 21.3 This contemporary Russian cartoon lampoons Peter the Great's order to his nobility to cut off their beards.

Finally, Peter was eager to make Russia culturally respectable in Western eyes. Before Peter the Great, it was a custom in upper-class marriages for the father of the bride to pass a small whip to the groom. This symbolized the transfer of male power over women. Peter, knowing that upper-class women had greater freedom in the West, abolished this practice. He also encouraged upper-class women to wear Western-style clothing and attend public cultural events. He found support among women as a result. He also reduced a source of embarrassment among Westerners in Russia, who otherwise could easily point to uncivilized treatment of women. But, as with most of his reforms, he made no move to change gender relations among the masses of Russian peasants.

Peter was eager to cut the Russian elite off from its traditions, to enhance state power, and to commit the elite to new identities. He required male nobles to shave off their beards (Figure 21.3) and wear Western clothes; in symbolic ceremonies he cut off the long, Mongol-type sleeves and pigtails that were characteristic of the boyars. Thus, traditional appearance was forcibly altered as part of Western-oriented change, although only the upper class was involved.

Cultural change supplemented bureaucratic training. Peter and his successors founded scientific institutes and academies along Western lines, and serious discussion of the latest scientific and technical findings became common. At the elite level, Peter built Russia into a Western cultural zone, and Western fads and fashions extended easily into the glittering new capital city. Ballet, initially encouraged in the French royal court, was imported and became a Russian specialty. The use of Christmas trees came from Germany.

This Westernization effort had several features that can be compared with imitation processes in other societies later on. In the first place, the changes were selective. Peter did not try to touch the ordinary people of Russia or to involve them in the technological and intellectual aspects of Westernization. In this sense Peter's reforms, which some historians see as part of a modernization program, fell well short of what modernization would later turn out to involve. New manufacturing involved serf labor that was heavily coerced, not the wage-labor spreading in the West. There was no interest in building the kind of worldwide export economy characteristic of the West. Peter wanted economic development to support military strength rather than to achieve wider commercial goals. Finally, Westernization was meant to encourage the autocratic state, not to challenge it with some of the new political ideas circulating in the West. This was real change, but it did not fold Russia into Western civilization outright. Selectivity was crucial, and there was no interest in abandoning particularly Russian goals.

Furthermore, the Westernization that did occur brought hostile responses. Many peasants resented the Westernized airs and expenses of their landlords, some of whom no longer even knew Russian but spoke only French. Elements of the elite opposed Peter's thirst for change, arguing that Russian traditions were superior to those of the West. As one priest wrote to Tsar Alexis, "You feed the foreigners too well, instead of bidding your folk to cling to the old customs." This tension continued in Russian history from this point forward, leading to important cycles of enthusiasm and revulsion toward Western values. Here was another key component of Russian development, still vivid in the early 21st century.

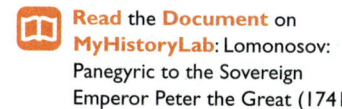

Read the Document on MyHistoryLab: Lomonosov: Panegyric to the Sovereign Emperor Peter the Great (1741)

Catherine the Great German-born Russian tsarina in the 18th century; ruled after assassination of her husband; gave appearance of enlightened rule; accepted Western cultural influence; maintained nobility as service aristocracy by granting them new power over peasantry.

Pugachev rebellion During 1770s in reign of Catherine the Great; led by Cossack Emelian Pugachev, who claimed to be legitimate tsar; eventually crushed; typical of peasant unrest during the 18th century and thereafter.

Consolidation Under Catherine the Great

The death of Peter the Great in 1724 was followed by several decades of weak rule, dominated in part by power plays among army officers who guided the selection of several ineffective emperors and empresses. The weakness of tsardom in these years encouraged new grumblings about undue Westernization and some new initiatives by church officials eager to gain more freedom to maneuver, but no major new policy directions were set. Russian territorial expansion continued, with several clashes with the Ottoman empire and further exploration and settlement in Siberia. In 1761, Peter III, nephew of Peter the Great's youngest daughter, reached the throne. He was mentally unstable, but his wife, a German-born princess who changed her name to Catherine—and was later known as **Catherine the Great** (Figure 21.4)—soon took matters in hand. Catherine II (the Great) (1729–1796) is one of the fascinating women leaders of history. Born a Prussian princess, she converted to the Orthodox faith after her marriage to the heir to the Russian throne was arranged. Her married life was miserable, with frequent threats of divorce from her husband. She also disliked her son, the future Tsar Paul I. Officers of the palace guard installed her as empress in 1762. The tsar was later murdered, possibly with Catherine's consent.

Catherine actively defended the powers of the central monarch. She put down another vigorous peasant uprising, led by Emelian Pugachev, having Pugachev himself slaughtered. She used the **Pugachev rebellion** as an excuse to extend the powers of the central government in regional affairs. Catherine's reign combined genuine reform interests with her need to consolidate power as a truly Russian ruler—a combination that explains the complexities of her policies.

Like Peter the Great, Catherine was a selective Westernizer, as her "instruction of 1767" (see the Document section) clearly demonstrated. She flirted with the ideas of the Enlightenment, importing several French philosophers for visits, and she established commissions to discuss new law codes and other Western-style measures, including reduction of traditionally severe punishments. Catherine also encouraged upper-class education and the arts and literature.

Catherine's policies were not always consistent with her image, however. She gave new powers to the nobility over their serfs, maintaining a trade-off that had been developing over the previous two centuries in Russia. In this trade-off, nobles served a strong central government and staffed it as bureaucrats and officers. They were in this sense a service

FIGURE 21.4 Catherine the Great in the costume of Minerva, the Roman goddess of wisdom, war, and the arts.

CHAPTER 21 The Rise of Russia 487

View the Closer Look on MyHistoryLab: Russian Charter of Nobility, 1785

aristocracy, not an independent force. They also accepted into their ranks newly ennobled officials chosen by the tsars. In return, however, most of the actual administration over local peasants, except for those on government-run estates, was wielded by the noble landlords. These landlords could requisition peasant labor, levy taxes in money and goods, and even impose punishments for crimes because landlord-dominated courts administered local justice. Catherine increased the harshness of punishments nobles could decree for their serfs.

Catherine patronized Western-style art and architecture, encouraging leading nobles to tour the West and even send their children to be educated there. But she also tried to avoid political influence from the West. When the great French Revolution broke out in 1789, Catherine was quick to close Russia's doors to the "seditious" writings of liberals and democrats. She also censored a small but emerging band of Russian intellectuals who urged reforms along Western lines. One of the first Western-inspired radicals, a noble named Radishev, who sought abolition of serfdom and more liberal political rule, was vigorously harassed by Catherine's police, and his writings were banned.

Catherine pursued the tradition of Russian expansion with energy and success (see Map 21.3). She resumed campaigns against the Ottoman empire, winning new territories in central Asia, including the Crimea, bordering the Black Sea. The Russian–Ottoman contest became a central diplomatic issue for both powers, and Russia became increasingly ascendant. Catherine accelerated the colonization of Russia's holdings in Siberia and encouraged further exploration, claiming the territory of Alaska in Russia's name. Russian explorers also moved down the Pacific coast of North America into what is now northern California, and tens of thousands of pioneers spread over Siberia.

Finally, Catherine pressed Russia's interests in Europe, playing power politics with Prussia and Austria, although without risking major wars. She increased Russian interference in Polish affairs. The Polish government was extremely weak, almost paralyzed by a parliamentary system that let members of the nobility veto any significant measure, and this invited interest by more powerful neighbors. Russia was able to win agreements with Austria and Prussia for the **partition of Poland**. Three partitions, in 1772, 1793, and 1795, eliminated Poland as an independent state, and Russia held the lion's share of the spoils. The basis for further Russian involvement in European affairs had obviously been created, and this would show in Russia's ultimate role in putting down the French armies of Napoleon after 1812—the first time Russian troops moved into the heartland of western Europe.

partition of Poland Division of Polish territory among Russia, Prussia, and Austria in 1772, 1793, and 1795; eliminated Poland as independent state; part of expansion of Russian influence in eastern Europe.

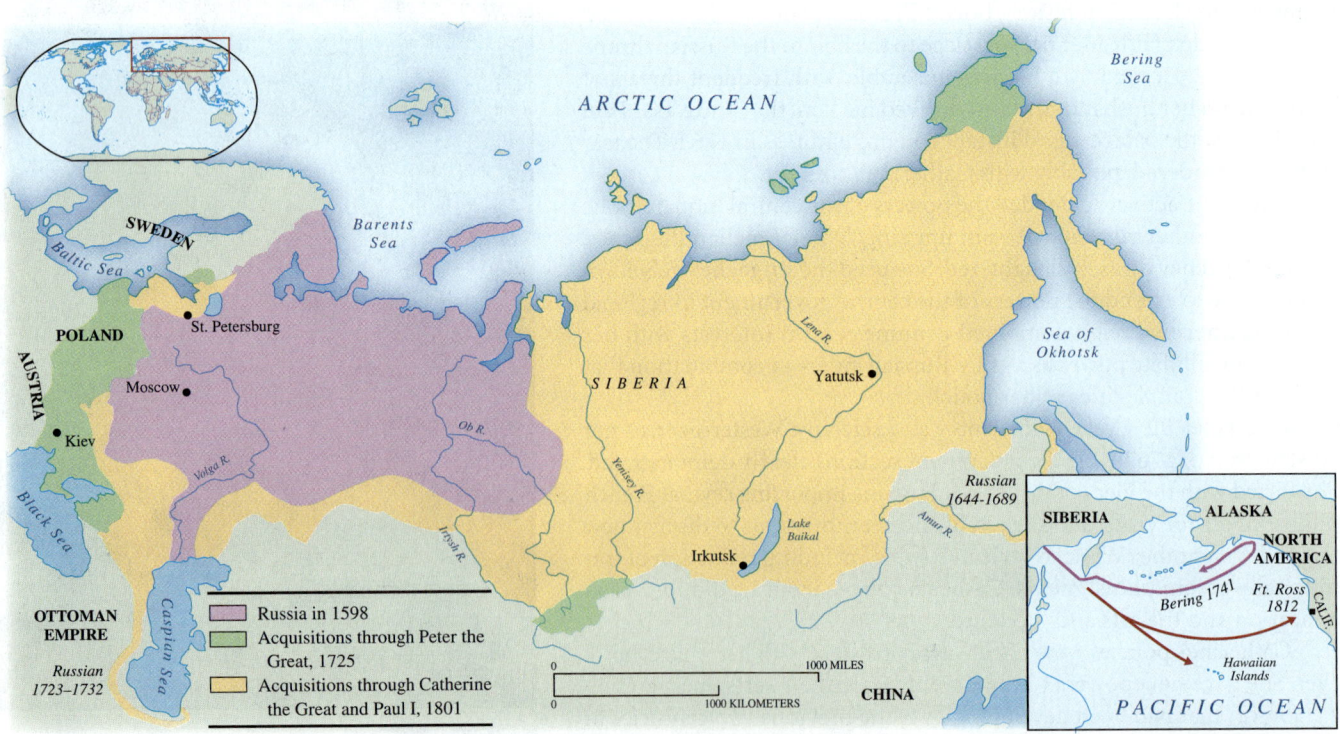

MAP 21.3 **Russia's Holdings by 1800** Expansion fluctuated from one decade to the next but persisted, bringing Russia into encounters with Europe, the Ottoman empire, and East Asia.

By the time of Catherine's death in 1796, Russia had passed through three centuries of extraordinary development. It had won independence and constructed a strong central state, although one that had to maintain a balance with the local political and economic interests of a powerful nobility. It had brought new elements into Russia's culture and economy, in part by borrowing from the West. And it had extended its control over the largest land empire in the world (Map 21.3). In the east it bordered China, where an 18th-century Amur River agreement set new frontiers. A tradition of careful but successful military aggrandizement had been established, along with a real pioneering spirit of settlement. It is no wonder that not long after 1800, a perceptive French observer, Alexis de Tocqueville, likened the expanded and increasingly important Russia to the new country emerging in the Western Hemisphere, the United States of America—the two giants of future world history.

THEMES IN EARLY MODERN RUSSIAN HISTORY

21.3 What were the main causes of Russian policy toward the serfs?

> Russian serfdom constituted a distinctive social and economic system. Its growing burdens sparked recurrent social protest.

Because of its great estates, its local political power, and its service to the state, the Russian nobility maintained a vital position in Russian society. In Russia and in eastern Europe generally, landed nobles tended to be divided between a minority of great magnates, who lived in major cities and provided key cultural patronage, and smaller landowners, whose culture was less Westernized and whose lifestyle was much less opulent.

Serfdom: The Life of East Europe's Masses

During the 17th and 18th centuries, the power of the nobility over the serfs increased steadily. Before the Mongol conquest, Russian peasants had been largely free farmers with a legal position superior to that of their medieval Western counterparts. After the expulsion of the Tatars, however, increasing numbers of Russian peasants fell into debt and had to accept servile status to the noble landowners when they could not repay. They retained access to much of the land, but not primary ownership. The Russian government actively encouraged this process from the 16th century onward. Serfdom gave the government a way to satisfy the nobility and regulate peasants when the government itself lacked the bureaucratic means to extend direct controls over the common people. As new territories were added to the empire, the system of serfdom was extended accordingly, sometimes after a period of free farming. An act of 1649 fixed the hereditary status of the serfs, so that people born to that station could not legally escape it. Laws passed during the 17th and 18th centuries tied the serfs to the land and increased the legal rights of the landlords.

Serfs on the estates of eastern Europe were also taxed, policed, and even sold by their landlords. In Russia, whole villages were sold as manufacturing labor—a process Peter the Great actively encouraged so as to spur manufacturing. Peasants were not literally slaves. They continued to use village governments to regulate many aspects of their lives, relying more heavily on community ties than their counterparts in the western countryside. Yet most peasants were illiterate and quite poor. They paid high taxes or obligations in kind, and they owed extensive labor service to the landlords or the government—a source not only of agricultural production but also of mining and manufacturing. The labor obligation tended to increase steadily. Both the economic and the legal situation of the peasantry continued to deteriorate. Although Catherine the Great sponsored a few model villages to display her enlightenment to Western-minded friends, she turned the government of the serfs over to the landlords more completely than ever before. A law of 1785 allowed landlords to punish harshly any serfs convicted of major crimes or rebellion. By 1800, half of Russia's peasantry was enserfed to the landlords, and much of the other half owed comparable obligations to the state.

Russia was setting up a system of serfdom very close to outright slavery in that serfs could be bought and sold, gambled away, and punished by their masters. The system was a very unusual case in which a people essentially enslaved many of its own members, in contrast to most slave systems, which focused on "outsiders."

Rural conditions in many other parts of eastern Europe were similar. Nobles maintained estate agriculture in Poland, Hungary, and elsewhere.

VISUALIZING THE PAST

Oppressed Peasants

THIS PAINTING IS FROM THE EARLY 20th century (1907), when revolutionary currents were swirling in Russia and the status of the peasantry was widely discussed. This raises obvious issues of interpretation. The subject of the painting, tax collection and the poor material conditions of 17th-century peasants, is valid for the 17th century, but the artist was also trying to score contemporary points.

QUESTIONS
- What aspects of the tax collector's appearance suggest that the artist was striving for an accurate rendition of the ways officials looked *before* the reforms of Peter the Great?
- Does this painting suggest early 20th-century rather than 17th-century sympathies in Russian culture?
- Given the lack of popular art from the 17th century, except religious art, does the painting provide useful material for understanding peasant conditions?

Estate Agriculture, Trade, and Dependence

In Russia, the nobility used the estate agricultural system to sustain their political power and their aristocratic status, which derived from command over land and people, not trade or commerce. This focus stifled social mobility and urbanization, which were drivers of economic growth in the West. In between serfs and landlords, there were few layers of Russian society. Cities were small, and 95 percent of the population remained rural. The manufacturing that existed took place in the countryside, so there was no well-defined artisan class. Government growth encouraged some non-noble bureaucrats and professionals. Small merchant groups existed as well, although most of Russia's European trade was handled by Westerners posted to the main Russian cities and relying on Western shipping. The nobility, concerned about potential social competition from both bureaucrats and businessmen, prevented the emergence of a substantial merchant class. The bulk of the population was increasingly composed of enserfed farmers who had little opportunity for social or economic development.

Inevitably, the intensification of estate agriculture and serf labor pursued by the nobility led to eastern Europe's growing economic subordination to the West. Coerced labor was used to produce grain surpluses purchased by Western merchants to feed the growing cities of western Europe. In return, Western merchants brought in manufactured goods, including the luxury furnishings and clothing essential to the aristocratic lifestyle. This growing dependence on Western markets and Western manufactured goods, and the reliance on serf labor to produce export goods, should be compared to patterns in Latin America (see Chapter 19). Long largely separate, Russia was being drawn into the world economy as a food and raw materials producer, dependent on cheap labor—another example of growing regional inequalities in the global system.

Russia's social and economic system worked well in some respects. It produced enough revenue to support an expanding state and empire. Russia was able to trade in furs and other commodities with areas in central Asia outside its boundaries, which meant that its export economy was not totally oriented toward the more dynamic West. It underwrote the aristocratic magnates and their glittering, Westernized culture. The system, along with Russia's expansion, yielded significant population growth: Russia's population doubled during the 18th century to 36 million. For an empire burdened by a harsh climate in most regions, this was no small achievement. Despite periodic famines and epidemics, there was no question that the overall economy had advanced.

Yet the system suffered from important limitations. Most agricultural methods were highly traditional, and there was little motivation among the peasantry for improvement because increased production usually was taken by the state or the landlord. Landlords debated agricultural improvements in their academies, but when it came time to increase production, they concentrated on squeezing the serfs. Manufacturing lagged behind Western standards, despite the important extension developed under Peter the Great.

Social Unrest

Russia's economic and social system led to protest. By the end of the 18th century, a small but growing number of Western-oriented aristocrats such as Radishev were criticizing the regime's backwardness, urging measures as far-reaching as the abolition of serfdom. Here were the seeds of a radical intelligentsia that, despite government repression, would grow with time. More significant still were the recurring peasant rebellions. Russian peasants for the most part were politically loyal to the tsar, but they harbored bitter resentments against their landlords, whom they accused of taking lands that were rightfully theirs. Periodic rebellions saw peasants destroy manorial records, seize land, and sometimes kill landlords and their officials.

Peasant rebellions had occurred from the 17th century onward, but the Pugachev rebellion of the 1770s was particularly strong. Pugachev (Figure 21.5), a Cossack chieftain who claimed to be the legitimate tsar, promised an end to serfdom, taxation, and military conscription along with the abolition of the landed aristocracy. His forces roamed over southern Russia until they were finally defeated. Pugachev was brought to Moscow in a case and cut into quarters in a public square. The triumph of Catherine and the nobility highlighted the mutual dependence of government and the upper class but did not end protest. Radishev, finding peasants barely able to work their own plots of land and sometimes tortured to work harder, thought he saw the handwriting on the wall: "Tremble, cruel hearted landlord! On the brow of each of your peasants I see your condemnation written."

FIGURE 21.5 The Cossack leader Emelian Pugachev attracted supporters by appealing to the popular belief that Peter III, Catherine's husband, was still alive. Claiming to be Peter III, he led a revolt in 1773–1774 that threatened Catherine's throne. When the revolt was defeated, Pugachev was brutally executed as an example to other potential revolutionaries.

Russia and Eastern Europe

Russian history did not include the whole of eastern Europe after the 15th century. Regions west of Russia continued to form a fluctuating borderland between western European and eastern European influences. Even in the Balkans, under Ottoman control, growing trade with the West sparked some new cultural exchanges by the 18th century, as Greek merchants, for example, picked up many Enlightenment ideas.

Areas such as present-day Poland or the Czech and Slovak regions operated more fully within the Western cultural orbit. The Polish scientist Copernicus was an early participant in fundamental discoveries in what became the Scientific Revolution. Western currents such as the Reformation also echoed in parts of east central Europe such as Hungary.

At the same time, many smaller eastern European nationalities lost political autonomy during the early modern era. Hungary, freed from the Ottomans, became part of the German-dominated Habsburg empire. This empire also took over the Czech lands, then called Bohemia. Prussian territory pushed eastward into Polish areas.

The decline of Poland was particularly striking. In 1500, Poland, formed in 1386 by a union of the regional kingdoms of Poland and Lithuania, was the largest state in eastern Europe aside from Russia. Polish cultural life, linked with the West through shared Roman Catholicism, flourished in the 16th century. By 1600, however, economic and political setbacks mounted. Polish aristocrats, charged with electing the king, began deliberately choosing weak figures. As in Russia, urban centers, and thus a merchant class, were lacking. The aristocratic parliament vetoed any reform efforts until late in the 18th century, after Poland began to be partitioned by its more powerful neighbors. The eclipse of Poland highlighted Russian emergence on the European as well as the Eurasian stage.

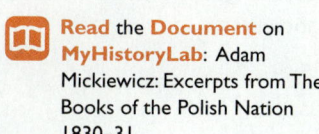

Read the Document on MyHistoryLab: Adam Mickiewicz: Excerpts from The Books of the Polish Nation 1830–31

Global Connections and Critical Themes

RUSSIA AND THE WORLD

From a world history standpoint, Russia's emergence as a key player both in Europe and in Asia was a crucial development in the Early Modern period. Today, Russia spans ten time zones, and much of this territory had been acquired by the late 18th century. By this point, Russia was affecting diplomatic and military developments in Europe, in the Middle East (through its frequent battles with the Ottoman empire), and in east Asia. It had gained a direct hold in central Asia. The spread of Russian claims to Alaska, and expeditions even to Hawaii, hinted at an even larger role. At the same time, early modern Russia did not become a major player in the process of proto-globalization. Its exports of grains and raw materials to Western Europe were significant, but it deliberately did not seek a leading commercial role. This was a different kind of empire from those that Western nations were building, but it had huge impact. Russia's expansion and political success shared many features with the land-based Asian empires of the early modern period, but here too Russia offered distinctive features that, among other things, would contribute to its durability.

Further Readings

For excellent survey coverage on this period, as well as additional bibliography, see Nicholas Riasanovsky, *History of Russia* (2005). Two excellent source collections for this vital period of Russian history are T. Riha, ed., *Readings in Russian Civilization, Vol. 2, Imperial Russia 1700–1917* (1969), and Basil Dmytryshyn, *Imperial Russia: A Sourcebook 1700–1917* (1967). On Russia's empire, see Christoph Witzenrath, *Cossacks and the Russian Empire, 1598–1725: Manipulation, Rebellion and Expansion into Siberia* (2007); John P. LeDonne, *The Grand Strategy of the Russian Empire, 1650–1831* (2004); and Williard Suderland, *Taming the Wild Field: Colonization and Empire on the Russian Steppe* (2004).

On important regimes, see P. Dukes, *The Making of Russian Absolutism: 1613–1801* (1982); J. L. I. Fennell, *Ivan the Great of Moscow* (1961); L. Hughes, *Russia in the Age of Peter the Great* (1998) and *Peter the Great and the West: New Perspectives* (2001); Isabel de Madariaga, *Ivan the Terrible: First Tsar of Russia* (2005) and *Catherine the Great: A Short History* (1990); Simon Dixon, *Catherine the Great* (2001); Simon Sebag Montefiore, *Potemkin: Catherine the Great's Imperial Partner* (2005); James Cracraft, *The Petrine Revolution in Russian Culture* (2004) and *The Revolution of Peter the Great* (2003); Paul Bushkovitch, *Peter the Great: The Struggle for Power, 1671–1725* (2001); and Inna Gorbatov, *Catherine the Great and the French Philosophers of the Enlightenment: Montesquieu, Voltaire, Rousseau, Diderot and Grim* (2006). Good studies that deal with cultural history: Richard Stites, *Serfdom Society, and the Arts in Imperial Russia: The Pleasure and the Power* (2005); W. J. Leatherbarrow and D. Offord, *A History of Russian Thought* (2010); C. R. Jensen, *Musical Cultures in 17th-century Russia* (2009); V. A. Kivelson and J. Neuberger, *Picturing Russia: Explorations in Visual Culture* (2008); and Marc Raeff, ed., *Russian Intellectual History* (1986).

For economic and social history, A. Kahan, *The Knout and the Plowshare: Economic History of Russia in the 18th Century* (1985) is an important treatment. For the vital peasant question, see Richard Hellie, *Slavery in Russia, 1450–1725* (1982). For an analytical overview, see Marc Raeff, *Understanding Imperial Russia: State and Society in the Old Regime* (1984). A very revealing comparison is Peter Kolchin, *Unfree Labor: American Slavery and Russian Serfdom* (1987). A fine survey on military and diplomatic strategy is William Fuller, *Strategy and Power in Russia, 1600–1914* (1992).

On MyHistoryLab

 Study and Review on MyHistoryLab

Critical Thinking Questions

1. Did Russia become part of Western civilization by the 18th century?
2. How did Russian conquests in Central Asia affect the role of that region in world history?
3. What were the limits on the power of the state in Russian society?
4. Compare cultural changes in Russia with those in western Europe during the Early Modern period.
5. Why did Russia not develop a more vigorous commercial economy as part of its imitation of Western patterns?

22

The Muslim Empires

Babur (or Zahar al-Din Muhammad, who was known to his troops as "The Tiger") was the first Mughal emperor of India. Claiming descent on his mother's side from Chinggis Khan and on his father's side from the ruthless Turkic conqueror Timur, he was himself a skilled warrior and a cultured man, who was known for his high spirits and love of beauty. But in April 1526, as the 44-year-old Babur led his armies into India, his future looked bleak. Although battle-hardened, his soldiers were far from their base of support, and they were headed into combat with a force that outnumbered them 10 to 1. For nearly a century the Lodis had ruled an empire that stretched across north India. Babur, in contrast, had repeatedly been defeated in his attempts to win back Ferghana, the kingdom he had inherited and lost, and he been driven from his ancestral home

Listen to Chapter 22 on MyHistoryLab

LEARNING OBJECTIVES

22.1 What were the factors that made it possible for the Ottoman Turks to conquer and control the vast empire they forged beginning in the late 13th century? p. 495

22.2 What roles did the Shi'a variant of Islam play in the rise of the Safavid dynasty and the state, society, and artistic expression that flourished in Persia under its rule? p. 504

22.3 In what major ways was the Mughal dynasty in India similar to and yet quite different from its rival Ottoman and Safavid regimes in terms of its origins and the ways in which its Indian empire was built, the composition of the subject peoples it ruled and its relationships with them, its global linkages, and the causes of its decline? p. 510

FIGURE 22.1 Babur superintending the planting of gardens in India. The rulers of each of the three great Muslim empires of the Early Modern era were lavish patrons of the arts and splendid architecture.

Watch the Video Series on MyHistoryLab

Learn about some key topics related to this chapter with the *MyHistoryLab Video Series: Key Topics in World History*

in the fabled city of Samarkand (see Map 22.1). Although in the years before his foray into India he had been able to build a small kingdom centered around Kabul in present-day Afghanistan, Babur had had little success in his attempts to recoup his earlier losses, and his plans for the conquest of Persia to the west had been foiled by the rise of the powerful Safavid dynasty in the early 1500s.

Babur decided to meet the enemy just north of the Lodi capital at Delhi, from which a succession of Muslim dynasties had dominated north India since the early 13th century. He ordered his troops to use leather strips to lash together the matchlock cannon that were positioned at the center of his army. Arrayed against them, under the command of the Lodi sultan, Ibrahim, were more than a thousand war elephants that would lead the charge to crush Babur's unimposing band of warriors. When the battle was joined at mid-morning on April 21, the roar and fire of the cannon panicked the surging elephants and they fled, trampling the Lodi soldiers marching into battle behind them. Making good use of his superior firepower—the enemy apparently had few cannons or muskets—Babur routed the massive Lodi army and went on to capture Delhi.

Babur's warriors were buoyed by their victory and the treasure seized in the capital. In the battles that followed against a Hindu alliance and an army raised by Ibrahim's brother, they effectively deployed the batteries of cannon they had arduously transported from Kabul. By the end of 1530, the Tiger was master of northern India and the founder of a new dynasty, the Mughal, which would rule varying portions of the subcontinent for nearly 300 years. ∎

Ottoman [dynasty or empire] A dynasty established beginning in the 13th century by Turkic peoples from Central Asia. Though most of their empire's early territory was in Asia Minor, the Ottomans eventually captured Constantinople and made it the capital of an empire that spanned three continents and lasted over 600 years.

Safavid dynasty Originally a Turkic nomadic group; family originated in Sufi mystic group; espoused Shi'ism; conquered territory and established kingdom in region equivalent to modern Iran; lasted until 1722.

In the chapter that follows, we will see that Babur's rapid conquest of north India displayed several key themes found in the rise of each of the three major Muslim dynasties whose empires stretched from the Mediterranean to the Bay of Bengal throughout the Early Modern phase of global history (see Map 22.1). First, like the warrior leaders who founded the **Ottoman** and **Safavid** empires to the west, Babur and his followers were from Turkic-speaking nomadic groups in central Asia. In each of the three cases, the warrior leaders who founded these dynasties took advantage of the power vacuum left by the breakup of the Mongol empire and the devastation wrought by Timur's assaults on the Islamic heartlands of the Middle East and Muslim-ruled northern India. Babur's **Mughal empire** was the last of the three Muslim empires to be established, and he drew on many of the precedents set by both the Ottomans and Safavids. But like them—and the military of all of the great Eurasian empires in the

1250 C.E.	1400 C.E.	1500 C.E.	1525 C.E.
1243 Mongol invasion of Asia Minor	**1402** Timur's invasion; Ottoman setbacks under Bayazid	**1501–1510** Safavid conquest of Persia (present-day Iran)	**1526** Battle of Panipat; Babur's conquest of India
1281 Founding of Ottoman dynasty	**c. 1450s** Shi'a influences enter Safavid teachings	**1507** Portuguese victory over Ottoman-Arab fleet at Diu in Indian Ocean	**1529** First Ottoman siege of Vienna
1334 Death of first Safavid Sufi master at Ardabil	**c. 1450s** Beginning of large-scale recruitment of Janissary troops	**1514** Ottoman victory over Safavids at Chaldiran	**1540** Babur's successor, Humayan, driven from India
1350s Ottoman invasion of Europe; conquest of much of the Balkans and Hungary	**1453** Ottoman capture of Constantinople	**1517** Ottoman capture of Syria and Egypt	**1540–1545** Humayan in exile at the Safavid court
		1520–1566 Rule of Suleyman the Magnificent; construction of Suleymaniye mosque in Constantinople	

Early Modern era—his armies relied heavily on large cannons and, increasingly, on muskets. As we shall see, in many instances the adversaries of each of the three Muslim dynasties lacked or were less skilled at deploying these weapons, which were transforming warfare across the globe. In fact, at the Battle of Khanua, Babur copied Turkish techniques in massing his muskets and cannon to defeat yet another much larger army, led by a great Hindu warrior. In contrast to the founders of the Ottoman and Safavid dynasties, Babur and the four Mughal rulers who succeeded him did not launch their conquests out of religious fervor. Like the Mughal monarchs, once in power, most of the Ottoman and Safavid rulers showed great tolerance for the faiths of the non-Muslim peoples who became their subjects. But as will become apparent in the accounts of the three dynasties that follow, the same tolerance was often not shown to rival Muslim sects. The Sunni–Shi'a split, which, as we have seen, arose early in the history of Islamic civilization, fueled often violent rivalries between the Ottomans and the Safavids. And sectarian identities frequently intensified ethnic divisions found in each of the great Muslim empires and across much of the Islamic world. Wars between the three empires and the constant need for their rulers to be attentive to shifting alliances and military innovations introduced by rival dynasties also go far toward explaining the inward-looking quality of much of Islamic society in this era.

Mughal empire Established by Babur in India in 1526; the name is taken from the supposed Mongol descent of Babur, but there is little indication of any Mongol influence in the dynasty; became weak after rule of Aurangzeb in first decades of 18th century.

THE OTTOMANS: FROM FRONTIER WARRIORS TO EMPIRE BUILDERS

22.1 What were the factors that made it possible for the Ottoman Turks to conquer and control the vast empire they forged beginning in the late 13th century?

For centuries before the rise of the Ottoman dynasty, Turkic-speaking peoples from central Asia played key roles in Islamic civilization as soldiers and administrators, often in the service of the Abbasid caliphs. But the collapse of the Seljuk Turkic kingdom of Rum in eastern Anatolia in Asia Minor (Map 22.2), after the invasion by the Mongols in 1243, opened the way for the Ottomans to seize power in their own right. The Mongols raided but did not directly rule Anatolia, which fell into a chaotic period of warfare between would-be successor states to the Seljuk sultans. Turkic peoples, both those fleeing the Mongols and those in search of easy booty, flooded into the region in the last decades of the 13th century. One of these peoples, called the Ottomans after an early leader named Osman, came to dominate the rest, and within decades they had begun to build a new empire based in Anatolia.

By the 1350s, the Ottomans had advanced from their strongholds in Asia Minor across the Bosporus straits into Europe. Thrace was quickly conquered, and by the end of the century large portions of the Balkans had been added to their rapidly expanding territories (Map 22.2). In moving into Europe in the mid-14th century, the Ottomans had bypassed rather than conquered the great city of Constantinople, long the capital of the once powerful Byzantine empire. By the mid-15th century, the Ottomans, who had earlier alternated between alliances and warfare with the Byzantines, were strong

In the 13th and 14th centuries, the Ottomans built an empire in the eastern Mediterranean that rivaled the Abbasid imperium at its height. Although the Ottomans patterned much of their empire on the ideas and institutions of earlier Muslim civilizations, in warfare, architecture, and engineering they carried Islamic civilization to new levels of attainment.

1550 C.E.	1650 C.E.	1700 C.E.
1556 Mughal empire reestablished in north India	**1657–1658** Great war of succession between sons of Shah Jahan	**1722** First Turkish-language printing press
1556–1605 Reign of Akbar	**1658–1707** Reign of Aurangzeb	**1722** Fall of the Safavid dynasty
1571 Battle of Lepanto	**1683** Last Ottoman siege of Vienna	**1730** Ottoman armies are defeated by Persian forces under Nadir Khan (later Nadir Shah, emperor of Persia)
1582 Akbar's proclamation of a new religion, designed to unite Hindus and Muslims	**1680s** Rajput and peasant revolts in north India	**1730s** First Western-modeled military schools established in Constantinople
1588–1629 Reign of Abbas I (the Great) in Persia	**1699** Treaty of Carlowitz; Ottomans cede territories in Europe	**1736–1747** Reign of Nadir Shah
		1739 Nadir Shah invades India from Persia, sacks Mughal capital at Delhi

Read the Document on MyHistoryLab: Mehmed II (15th c.)

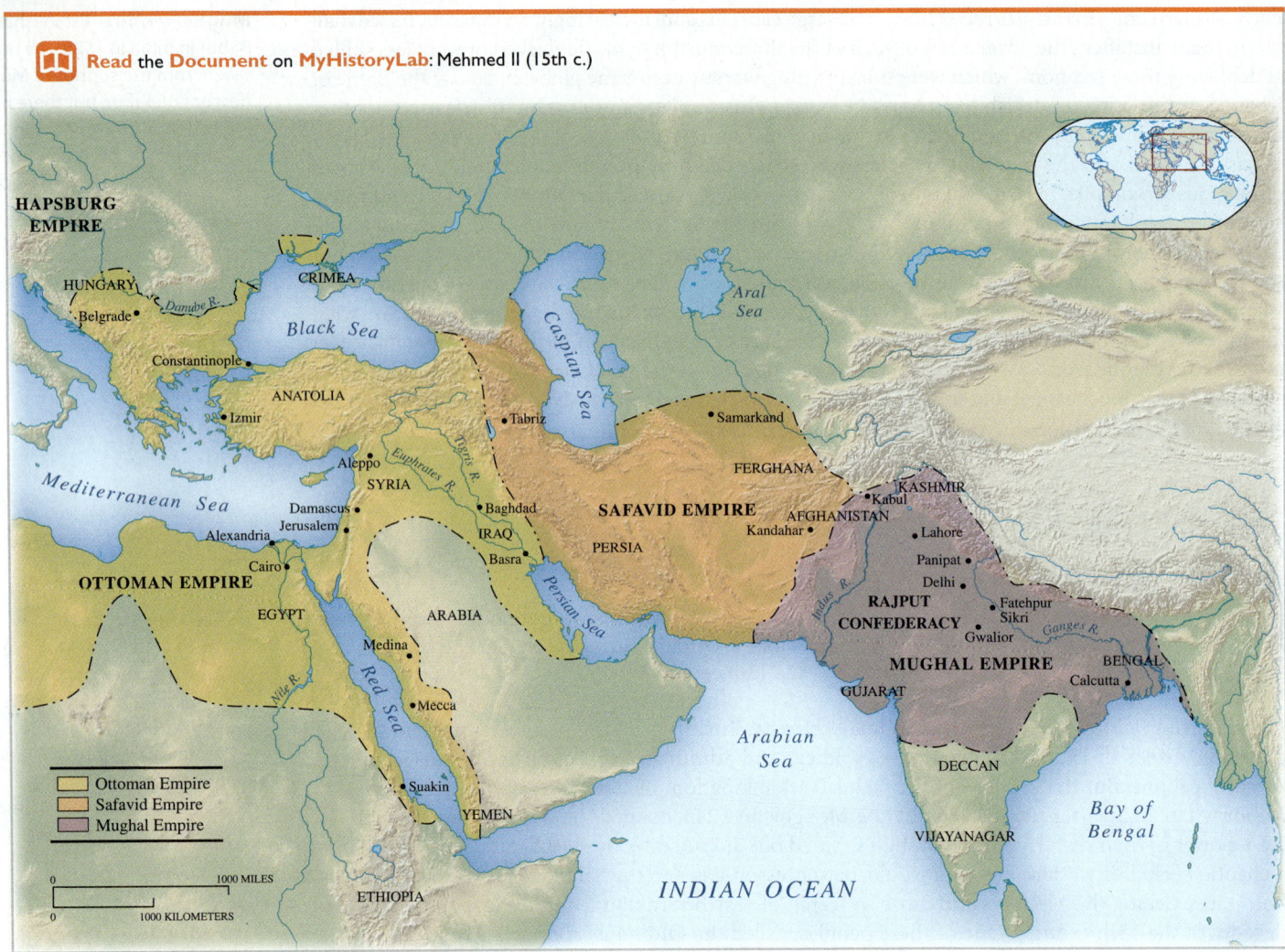

MAP 22.1 **The Ottoman, Safavid, and Mughal Empires** For several centuries the three great Muslim empires dominated the central trading and transit zones of Afro-Eurasia.

Mehmed II [me met] (1432–1481) Ottoman sultan called the "Conqueror"; responsible for conquest of Constantinople in 1453; destroyed what remained of Byzantine empire.

enough to undertake the capture of the well-fortified city. For seven weeks in the spring of 1453, the army of the Ottoman sultan, **Mehmed II**, "The Conqueror," which numbered well over 100,000, assaulted the triple ring of land walls that had protected the city for centuries (Figure 22.2). The outnumbered forces of the defenders repulsed attack after attack until the sultan ordered his gunners to batter a portion of the walls with their massive siege cannon. Wave after wave of Ottoman troops struck at the gaps in the defenses that had been cut by the guns, quickly overwhelmed the defenders, and raced into the city to loot and pillage for the three days that Mehmed had promised as their reward for victory.

In the two centuries after the conquest of Constantinople, the armies of a succession of able Ottoman rulers extended the empire into Syria and Egypt and across north Africa, thus bringing under their rule the bulk of the Arab world (Map 22.2). The empire also spread through the Balkans into Hungary in Europe and around the Black and Red seas. The Ottomans became a formidable naval power in the Mediterranean Sea. Powerful Ottoman galley fleets made possible the capture of major island bases on Rhodes, Crete, and Cyprus. The Ottoman armies also drove the Venetians and Genoese from much of the eastern Mediterranean and threatened southern Italy with invasion on several occasions. From their humble origins as frontier vassals, the Ottomans had risen to become the protectors of the Islamic heartlands and the scourge of Christian Europe. As late as 1683, Ottoman armies were able to lay siege to the capital of the Austrian Habsburg dynasty at Vienna. Even though the Ottoman empire's power relative to its rivals was weakening by this time, and the threat the assault posed to Vienna was far less serious than a previous attack in the early 16th century, the Ottomans remained a major force in European politics until the late 19th century.

MAP 22.2 **The Expansion of the Ottoman Empire** Because they were a sea as well as a land power, the Ottomans were able to conquer and rule the lands of the eastern Mediterranean and Black Sea region for half a millennium.

A State Geared to Warfare

Military leaders played a dominant role in the Ottoman state, and the economy of the empire was geared to warfare and expansion. The Turkic cavalry, chiefly responsible for the Ottomans' early conquests from the 13th to the 16th centuries, gradually developed into a warrior aristocracy. They were granted control over land and peasant producers in annexed areas for the support of their households and military retainers. From the 15th century onward, members of the warrior class also vied with religious leaders and administrators drawn from other social groups for control of the expanding Ottoman bureaucracy. As the power of the warrior aristocracy shrank at the center, they built up regional and local bases of support. These inevitably competed with the sultans and the central bureaucracy for revenue and labor control.

From the mid-15th century, the imperial armies were increasingly dominated by infantry divisions made up of troops called **Janissaries**. Most of the Janissaries had been forcibly recruited as adolescent boys in conquered areas, such as the Balkans, where the majority of the population retained its Christian faith. Sometimes the boys' parents willingly turned their sons over to the Ottoman recruiters because of the opportunities for advancement that came with service to the Ottoman sultans. Although legally slaves, the youths were given fairly extensive schooling for the time and converted to Islam. Some of them went on to serve in the palace or bureaucracy, but most became Janissaries.

Janissaries Ottoman infantry divisions that dominated Ottoman armies; forcibly conscripted as boys in conquered areas of Balkans, legally slaves; translated military service into political influence, particularly after 15th century.

Read the Document on MyHistoryLab: Venetian Observations on the Ottoman Empire late 16th c.

FIGURE 22.2 An illuminated French manuscript from the 15th century shows the Ottoman siege of Constantinople in 1453. The Muslim capture of the great eastern bastion of Christian Europe aroused fears throughout the continent, resulting in demands for new Crusades to recapture the city. The advance of the Ottomans in the east also provided impetus to the overseas expansion of nations such as Spain and Portugal on the western coasts of Europe. Both of these Catholic maritime powers saw their efforts to build overseas empires as part of a larger campaign to outflank the Muslim powers and bring areas that they controlled into the Christian camp.

Because the Janissaries controlled the artillery and firearms that became increasingly vital to Ottoman success in warfare with Christian and Muslim adversaries, they rapidly became the most powerful component in the Ottoman military machine. Their growing importance was another factor contributing to the steady decline of the role of the aristocratic cavalry. Just like the mercenary forces that had earlier served the caliphs of Baghdad, the Janissaries eventually tried to translate military service into political influence. By the late 15th century they were deeply involved in court politics; by the mid-16th century they had the power to depose sultans and decide which one of a dying ruler's sons would mount the throne.

The Sultans and Their Court

Nominally, the Ottoman rulers were absolute monarchs. But even the most powerful sultan maintained his position by playing factions in the warrior elite off each other and pitting the warriors as a whole against the Janissaries and other groups. Chief among the latter were the Islamic religious scholars and legal experts, who retained many of the administrative functions they had held under the Arab caliphs of earlier centuries. In addition to Muslim traders, commerce within the empire was in the hands of Christian and Jewish merchants, who as dhimmis, or "people of the book," were under the protection of the Ottoman rulers. Although they have often been depicted in Western writings as brutal and corrupt despots, some Ottoman sultans, especially in the early centuries of their sway, were very capable rulers. Ottoman conquest often meant effective administration and tax relief for the peoples of areas annexed to the empire.

Like the Abbasid caliphs, the Ottoman sultans grew more and more distant from their subjects as their empire increased in size and wealth. In their splendid marble palaces and pleasure gardens, surrounded by large numbers of slaves and the many wives and concubines of their harems, Ottoman rulers followed elaborate court rituals based on those of earlier Byzantine, Persian, and Arab dynasties. Day-to-day administration was carried out by a large bureaucracy headed by a grand **vizier** (*wazir* in Arabic). The vizier was the overall head of the imperial administration, and he often held more real power than the sultan. Early sultans, however, took an active role in political decisions and often personally led their armies into battle.

Like earlier Muslim dynasties, the Ottomans suffered greatly because they inherited Islamic principles of political succession that remained vague and contested. The existence of many talented and experienced claimants to the throne meant constant danger of civil strife. The death of a sultan could, and increasingly did, lead to protracted warfare among his sons. Defeated claimants sometimes fled to the domains of Christian or Muslim rulers hostile to the Ottomans, thereby becoming rallying points for military campaigns against the son who had gained the throne.

vizier [vi zEEr] Ottoman equivalent of the Abbasid wazir; head of the Ottoman bureaucracy; after 5th century often more powerful than sultan.

Constantinople Restored as the Link among Asia and Europe, the Mediterranean and the Black Sea

An empire that encompassed so many and such diverse cultures from Europe, Africa, and Asia naturally varied greatly from one province to the next in its social arrangements, artistic production, and physical appearance. But the Ottomans' ancient and cosmopolitan capital at Constantinople richly combined the disparate elements of their extensive territories. Like the Byzantine empire as a whole, Constantinople had fallen on hard times in the centuries before the Ottoman conquest in 1453. But soon after Mehmed II's armies captured and sacked the city, the Ottoman ruler set about restoring its ancient glory. He had the cathedral of Saint Sophia converted into one of the grandest mosques in the Islamic world, and new mosques and palaces were built throughout the city. This construction benefited greatly from architectural advances the Ottomans derived from the Byzantine heritage. Aqueducts were built from the surrounding hills to supply the growing population with water, markets were reopened, and the city's defenses were repaired.

Each sultan who ruled in the centuries after Mehmed strove to be remembered for his efforts to beautify the capital. The most prominent additions were further mosques that represent some of the most sublime contributions of the Ottomans to Islamic and human civilization. The most spectacular of these was the Suleymaniye, pictured in Figure 22.3. As its name suggests, the mosque was built at the behest of the most celebrated of the sultans, Suleyman the Magnificent (r. 1520–1566). Although it smacks of hometown pride, the following description by a 17th-century Ottoman chronicler of the reaction of some Christian visitors to the mosque conveys a sense of the awe that the structure still evokes:

> The humble writer of these lines once himself saw ten Frankish infidels skillful in geometry and architecture, who, when the door-keeper had changed their shoes for slippers, and had introduced them into the mosque for the purpose of showing it to them, laid their finger on their mouths, and each bit his finger from astonishment when they saw the minarets; but when they beheld the dome they tossed up their hats and cried Maria! Maria! and on observing the four arches which supported the dome . . . they could not find terms to express their admiration, and the ten . . . remained a full hour looking with astonishment on those arches. [One of them said] that nowhere was so much beauty, external and internal, to be found united, and that in the whole of Frangistan [Christian Europe] there was not a single edifice which could be compared to this.

In addition to the mosques, sultans and powerful administrators built mansions, rest houses, religious schools, and hospitals throughout the city. Both public and private gardens further beautified the capital, which Ottoman writers compared to paradise itself. The city and its suburbs stretched along both sides of the Bosporus, the narrow strait between the Mediterranean and Black seas that separates Europe from Asia (Map 22.2). Its harbors and the Golden Horn, a triangular bay that formed the northern boundary of the city, were crowded with merchant ships from ports throughout the region. Constantinople's great bazaars were filled with merchants and travelers from throughout the empire and places as distant as England and Malaya. They offered all manner of commodities, from the spices of the East Indies and the ivory of Africa to slaves and forest products from Russia

Read the Document on MyHistoryLab: An Ambassador's Report on the Ottoman Empire (1555) Ogier Ghiselin de Busbecq

FIGURE 22.3 Built in the reign of Suleyman I in the 1550s and designed by the famous architect Sinan, the Suleymaniye mosque is among the largest domed structures in the world, and it is one of the great engineering achievements of Islamic civilization. The pencil-thin minarets flanking the great central dome are characteristic of Ottoman architecture, which was quite distinct from its Safavid and Mughal counterparts.

Read the Document on MyHistoryLab: Portrait of an Ottoman Gentleman

and fine carpets from Persia. Coffeehouses—places where men gathered to drink, smoke tobacco (introduced from America in the 17th century by English merchants), gossip, do business, and play chess—were found in all sections of the city. They were pivotal to the social life of the capital. The coffeehouses also played a major role in the cultural life of Constantinople as places where poets and scholars could congregate, read their latest works aloud, and debate about politics and the merits of each other's ideas.

Beneath the ruling classes, a sizable portion of the population of Constantinople and other Ottoman cities belonged to the merchant and artisan classes. The Ottoman regime closely regulated commercial exchanges and handicraft production. Government inspectors were employed to ensure that standard weights and measures were used and to license the opening of new shops. They also regulated the entry of apprentice artisans into the trades and monitored the quality of the goods they produced. Like their counterparts in medieval European towns, the artisans were organized into guilds. Guild officers set craft standards, arbitrated disputes between their members, and provided financial assistance for needy members. They even arranged popular entertainments, often linked to religious festivals.

The early Ottomans had written in Persian, and Arabic remained an important language for works on law and religion throughout the empire's history. But by the 17th century, the Turkish language of the Ottoman court had become the preferred mode of expression for poets and historians as well as the language of the Ottoman bureaucracy. In writing as in the fine arts, the Ottomans' achievements have been somewhat overshadowed by those of their contemporary Persian and Indian rivals. Nonetheless, the authors, artists, and artisans of the Ottoman empire left a considerable legacy, particularly in poetry, miniature painting, ceramics, carpet manufacturing, and above all in architecture.

The Problem of Ottoman Decline

Much of the literature on the Ottoman empire concentrates on its slow decline from the champion of the Muslim world and the most important adversary of Christendom to the "sick man" of Europe in the 18th and 19th centuries. This approach provides a skewed view of Ottoman history as a whole. Traced from its origins in the late 13th century, the Ottoman state is one of the great success stories in human political history. Vigorous and expansive until the late 17th century, the Ottomans were able to ward off the powerful enemies who surrounded their domains on all sides for nearly four centuries. The dynasty endured for more than 600 years, a feat matched by no other in all human history.

From one perspective, the long Ottoman decline, which officials and court historians actively discussed from the mid-17th century onward, reflects the great strength of the institutions on which the empire was built. Despite internal revolts and periodic conflicts with such powerful foreign rivals as the Russian, Austrian, Spanish, and Safavid empires, the Ottomans ruled into the 20th century. Yet the empire had reached the limits of its expansive power centuries earlier, and by the late 17th century the long retreat from Russia, Europe, and the Arab lands had begun. In a sense, some contraction was inevitable. Even when it was at the height of its power, the empire was too large to be maintained, given the resource base that the sultans had at their disposal and the primitive state of transportation and communications in the preindustrial era.

The Ottoman state had been built on war and steady territorial expansion. As possibilities for new conquests ran out and lands began to be lost to the Ottomans' Christian and Muslim enemies, the means of maintaining the oversized bureaucracy and army shrank. The decline in the effectiveness of the administrative system that held the empire together was signaled by the rampant growth of corruption among Ottoman officials. The corruption and incompetence of state bureaucrats prompted regional and local officials to retain more revenue for their own purposes. Poorly regulated by the central government, many local officials, who also controlled large landed estates, squeezed the peasants and the laborers who worked their lands for additional taxes and services. At times the oppressive demands of local officials and estate owners sparked rebellions. Peasant uprisings and flight resulted in the abandonment of cultivated lands and in social dislocations that further drained the resources of the empire.

From the 17th century onward, the forces that undermined the empire from below were compounded by growing problems at the center of imperial administration. The early practice of assigning the royal princes administrative or military positions to prepare them to rule died out. Instead, possible successors to the throne were kept like hostages in special sections of the palace, where they remained until one of them ascended the throne. The other princes and potential rivals were also, in effect, imprisoned for life in the palace. Although it might have made the reigning sultan more secure, this solution to the problem of contested succession produced monarchs far less prepared to rule than those in the formative centuries of the dynasty. The great warrior-emperors of early Ottoman history gave way, with some important exceptions, to weak and indolent rulers, addicted to drink, drugs, and the pleasures of the harem. In many instances, the later sultans were little more than pawns in the power struggles of the viziers and other powerful officials with the leaders of the increasingly influential Janissary corps. Because the imperial apparatus had been geared to strong and absolute rulers, the decline in the caliber of Ottoman emperors had devastating effects on the empire as a whole. Civil strife increased, and the discipline and leadership of the armies on which the empire depended for survival deteriorated.

Military Reverses, Iberian Expansionism, and the Ottoman Retreat

Debilitating changes within the empire were occurring at a time when challenges from without were growing rapidly. The Ottomans had made very effective use of artillery and firearms in building their empire. But their reliance on huge siege guns, and the Janissaries' determination to block all military changes that might jeopardize the power they had gained within the state, caused the Ottomans to fall farther and farther behind their European rivals in the critical art of waging war. With the widespread introduction of light field artillery into the armies of the European powers in the 17th century, Ottoman losses on the battlefield multiplied rapidly, and the threat they posed for the West began to recede.

FIGURE 22.4 The clash of the galley fleets at Lepanto was one of the greatest sea battles in history. But despite devastating losses, the Ottomans managed to replace most of their fleet and go back on the offensive against their Christian adversaries within a year. Here the epic encounter is pictured in one of the many paintings devoted to it in the decades that followed. The tightly packed battle formations that both sides adopted show the importance of ramming rather than cannon fire in naval combat in the Mediterranean in this era. This pattern was reversed in the Atlantic and the other oceanic zones into which the Europeans had been expanding since the 14th century.

Read the Document on MyHistoryLab: Defeat of Ottoman Turks (1683) King John Sobieski

On the sea, the Ottomans were eclipsed as early as the 16th century. The end of their dominance was presaged by their defeat by a combined Spanish and Venetian fleet at Lepanto in 1571. The great battle is depicted in the painting in Figure 22.4. Although the Ottomans had completely rebuilt their war fleet within a year after Lepanto and soon launched an assault on North Africa that preserved that area for Islam, their control of the eastern Mediterranean had been lost. Even more ominously, in the decades before Lepanto, the Ottomans and the Muslim world more generally had been outflanked by the Portuguese seafarers who sailed down and around the coast of Africa. The failure in the early 1500s of the Ottomans and their Muslim allies in the Indian Ocean to drive the Portuguese from Asian waters proved far more harmful in the long run than Ottoman defeats in the Mediterranean.

Portuguese naval victories in the Indian Ocean revealed the decline of the Ottoman galley fleets and Mediterranean-style warships more generally. The trading goods, particularly spices, that the Portuguese carried around Africa and back to Europe enriched the Ottomans' Christian rivals. In addition, because a large portion of the flow of these products was no longer transmitted to European

502 PART IV The Early Modern Period, 1450–1750: The World Shrinks

DOCUMENT

An Islamic Traveler Laments the Muslims' Indifference to Europe

ALTHOUGH MOST OF THE TRAVELERS AND explorers in this era were Europeans who went to Africa, Asia, and the Americas, a few people from these lands visited Europe. One of these, Abu Taleb, was a scholar of Turkish and Persian descent whose family had settled in India. At the end of the 18th century, Abu Taleb traveled in Europe for three years and later wrote an account in Persian of his experiences there. Although his was one of the few firsthand sources of information about Europe available to Muslim scholars and leaders, Abu Taleb was deeply disturbed by the lack of interest shown by other Muslims in his observations and discoveries.

> When I reflect on the want of energy and the indolent dispositions of my countrymen, and the many erroneous customs which exist in all Mohammedan countries and among all ranks of Mussulmans, I am fearful that my exertions [in writing down his experiences in Europe] will be thrown away. The great and the rich intoxicated with pride and luxury, and puffed up with the vanity of their possessions, consider universal science as comprehended in the circle of their own scanty acquirements and limited knowledge; while the poor and common people, from the want of leisure, and overpowered by the difficulty of procuring a livelihood, have not time to attend to his personal concerns, much less to form desires for the acquirement of information of new discoveries and inventions, although such a person has been implanted by nature in every human breast, as an honour and an ornament to the species. I therefore despair of their reaping any fruit from my labours, being convinced that they will consider this book of no greater value than the volumes of tales and romances which they peruse merely to pass away their time, or are attracted thereto by the easiness of the style. It may consequently be concluded, that as they will find no pleasure in reading a work which contains a number of foreign names, treats on uncommon subjects, and alludes to other matters which cannot be understood at first glance, but require a little time for consideration, they will, under pretense of zeal for their religion, entirely abstain and refrain from perusing it.

QUESTIONS

- What reasons does Abu Taleb give for his fellow Muslims' indifference to his travel reports on Europe?
- What other factors can be added as a result of our study of long-standing Islamic attitudes toward Europe and conditions in the Ottoman empire in this period?
- In what ways might the Muslims' neglect of events in Europe have hindered their efforts to cope with this expansive civilization in the centuries that followed?
- Were there Western counterparts to Abu Taleb in these centuries, and how were their accounts of distant lands received in Europe?

ports through Muslim trading centers in the eastern Mediterranean, merchants and tax collectors in the Ottoman empire lost critical revenues. As if this were not enough, from the late 16th century on, large amounts of silver flowed into the Ottomans' lands from mines worked by Native American laborers in the Spanish empire in Peru and Mexico. This sudden influx of bullion into the rigid and slow-growing economy of the Ottoman empire set off a long-term inflationary trend that further undermined the finances and economic solvency of the empire.

Several able sultans took measures to shore up the empire in the 17th century. The collapse of the Safavid dynasty in Persia and conflicts between the European powers at this time also gave the Ottomans hope that their earlier dominance might be restored. But their reprieve was temporary. With the scientific, technological, and commercial transformations occurring in Europe (discussed in Chapter 18), the Ottomans were falling behind their Christian rivals in most areas. But the growing gap was most critical in trade and warfare. The Ottomans inherited from their Arab, Persian, and Turkic predecessors the conviction that little of what happened in Europe was important. This belief, which is seen as a major cause of Ottoman decline by the traveler Abu Taleb quoted in the Document feature, prevented them from taking seriously the revolutionary changes that were transforming western Europe. The intense conservatism of powerful groups such as the Janissaries, and to a lesser extent the religious scholars, reinforced this misguided attitude. Through much of the 17th and 18th centuries, these groups blocked most of the Western-inspired innovations that reform-minded sultans and their advisors tried to introduce. As a result of these narrow and potentially dangerous forces, the isolated Ottoman imperial system proved incapable of checking the weaknesses that were steadily destroying it.

THE SHI'A CHALLENGE OF THE SAFAVIDS

In the first years of the 16th century, the Safavids founded a dynasty that conquered what is now Iran. Restoring Persia (as it was then called) as a major center of political power and cultural creativity, they also established it as one of the strongest and most enduring centers of Shi'ism within the Islamic world.

22.2 What roles did the Shi'a variant of Islam play in the rise of the Safavid dynasty and the state, society, and artistic expression that flourished in Persia under its rule?

Like the Ottomans, the Safavid dynasty arose from the struggles of rival Turkic nomadic groups in the wake of the Mongol and Timurid invasions of the 13th and 14th centuries. Also like the Ottomans, the Safavids rose to prominence as the frontier warrior champions of a highly militant strain of Islam. But unlike the Ottomans, who became the champions of the Sunni majority of the Muslim faithful, the Safavids espoused the Shi'a variant of Islam. As we saw in Chapter 7, in the early decades of Muslim expansion a split developed in the community of the faithful between the Sunnis, who recognized the legitimacy of the first three successors to Muhammad (Abu Bakr, Umar, and Uthman), and the Shi'a, who believed that only the fourth successor (Ali, Mohammed's cousin and son-in-law) had the right to succeed the prophet. Over time, differences in doctrine, ritual, and law were added to the disagreements over succession that originally divided the Islamic community. Divisions have also arisen within both the Shi'a and Sunni groupings, but bitter hostility and violent conflict most often have developed along Sunni–Shi'a lines. The long rivalry between the Sunni Ottomans and the Shi'a Safavids proved to be one of the most pivotal episodes in the long history of these sectarian struggles.

The Safavid dynasty had its origins in a family of Sufi mystics and religious preachers, whose shrine center was at Ardabil near the Caspian Sea (Map 22.3). In the early 14th century, one of these Sufis, **Sail al-Din**, who gave the dynasty its name, began a militant campaign to purify and reform Islam and spread Muslim teachings among the Turkic tribes of the region. In the chaos that followed the collapse of Mongol authority in the mid-14th century, Sail al-Din and other Safavid Sufi leaders gained increasing support. But as the numbers of the **Red Heads** (as the Safavids' followers were called because of their distinctive headgear) grew, and as they began in the mid-15th century to preach Shi'a doctrines, their enemies multiplied. After decades of fierce local struggles in which three successive Safavid leaders perished, a surviving Sufi commander, **Ismâ'il**, led his Turkic followers to a string of victories on the battlefield. In 1501, Ismâ'il's armies captured the city of Tabriz, where he was proclaimed *shah*, or emperor.

Sail al-Din [sä EEl al dEEn] Early 14th-century Sufi mystic; began campaign to purify Islam; first member of Safavid dynasty.

Red Heads Name given to Safavid followers because of their distinctive red headgear.

Ismâ'il (1487–1524) Sufi commander who conquered city of Tabriz in 1501; first Safavid to be proclaimed shah or emperor.

In the next decade, Ismâ'il's followers conquered most of Persia, drove the Safavid's ancient enemies, the Ozbegs—a neighboring nomadic people of Turkic stock—back into the central Asian steppes, and advanced into what is now Iraq. The Safavid successes and the support their followers received in the Ottoman borderlands from Turkic-speaking peoples brought them into conflict with Ottoman rulers. In August 1514, at **Chaldiran** in northwest Persia, the armies of the two empires met in one of the most fateful battles in Islamic history. Chaldiran was more than a battle between the two most powerful dynasties in the Islamic world at the time. It was a clash between the champions of the Shi'a and Sunni variants of Islam. The religious fervor with which both sides fought the battle was intensified by the long-standing Safavid persecutions of the Sunnis and the slaughter of Shi'a living in Ottoman territories by the forces of the Ottoman sultan, Selim.

The battle also demonstrated the importance of muskets and field cannon in the

MAP 22.3 The Safavid Empire Surrounded by rival empires and nomadic peoples, Safavid Persia proved less enduring than its two Muslim rivals.

504 PART IV The Early Modern Period, 1450–1750: The World Shrinks

gunpowder age. Because his artillery was still engaged against enemies far to the east, Ismâ'il hoped to delay a decisive confrontation with the Ottoman forces under the Sultan Selim. When battle could not be avoided, Ismâ'il threw his cavalry against the cannon and massed muskets of the Ottoman forces. Despite desperate attempts to make up through clever maneuvers what he lacked in firepower, Ismâ'il's cavalry proved no match for the well-armed Ottomans.

The Safavids were dealt a devastating defeat, and the Ottomans' victory at Chaldiran buttressed their efforts to build the most powerful empire in the Islamic world. But the Ottomans could not follow up the battle with conquests that would have put an end to their Safavid rivals. The latter's capital at Tabriz was too far from Ottoman supply areas to be held through the approaching winter. The withdrawal of the Ottoman armies gave the Safavids the breathing space they needed to regroup their forces and reoccupy much of the territory they had originally conquered. Nonetheless, defeat at Chaldiran put an end to Ismâ'il's dreams of further westward expansion, and most critically, it checked the rapid spread of conversions to Shi'a Islam in the western borderlands that had resulted from the Safavid's recent successes in battle. The outcome at Chaldiran determined that Shi'ism would be concentrated mainly in Persia, or present-day Iran, and neighboring areas in what is today southern Iraq.

Chaldiran [chäl duh rán] Site of battle between Safavids and Ottomans in 1514; Safavids severely defeated by Ottomans; checked Western advance of Safavid empire.

 Read the **Document** on **MyHistoryLab**: Sunni versus Shi'ite: Letter from Selim I to Ismail I

Politics and War Under the Safavid Shahs

After his defeat at Chaldiran, Ismâ'il, once a courageous warrior and a popular leader, retreated to his palace and tried to escape his troubles through drink. His seclusion, along with struggles between the factions backing each of his sons for the right to succeed him, left openings for subordinate Turkic chiefs to attempt to seize power. After years of turmoil, a new shah, Tahmasp I (r. 1534–1576), won the throne and set about restoring the power of the dynasty. The Turkic chiefs were foiled in their bid for supreme power, and the Ozbegs were again and again driven from the Safavid domains. Under Shah Abbas I (r. 1587–1629), the empire reached the height of its strength and prosperity, although the territories it controlled remained roughly equivalent to those ruled by Ismâ'il and Tahmasp I.

Under Tahmasp I and his successors, repeated efforts were made to bring the Turkic chiefs under control. They were gradually transformed into a warrior nobility comparable to that in the Ottoman domains. Like their Ottoman counterparts, the Safavid warrior nobles were assigned villages, whose peasants were required to supply them and their troops with food and labor. The most powerful of the warrior leaders occupied key posts in the imperial administration, and from the defeat at Chaldiran onward they posed a constant threat to the Safavid monarchs. To counterbalance this threat, Safavid rulers recruited Persians for positions at the court and in the rapidly expanding imperial bureaucracy. The struggle for power and influence between Turkic and Persian notables was further complicated by the practice, initiated by Ismâ'il's successor, Tahmasp I, of recruiting into the bureaucracy and army slave boys who were captured in campaigns in southern Russia. Like the Janissaries in the Ottoman Empire, many of these slaves rose to positions of power. Also like the Janissaries, the slave regiments soon became a major force in Safavid political struggles.

Of all of the Safavid shahs, Abbas I, known also as **Abbas the Great**, made the most extensive use of the youths who were captured in Russia and then educated and converted to Islam. They not only came to form the backbone of his military forces but were granted provincial governorships and high offices at court. Like the Janissaries, slave regiments, which were wholly dependent on Abbas's support, monopolized the firearms that had become increasingly prominent in Safavid armies. The Persians had artillery and handguns long before the arrival of the Portuguese by sea in the early 16th century. But Abbas and his successors showed little reluctance to call on the knowledgeable but infidel Europeans for assistance in their wars with the Ottomans. Of special importance were the Sherley brothers from England. They provided instruction in the casting of cannons and trained Abbas's slave infantry and a special regiment of musketeers recruited from the Iranian peasantry. By the end of his reign, Abbas had built up a standing army of nearly 40,000 troops and an elite bodyguard. These measures to strengthen his armies and his victories on the battlefield appeared to promise security for the Safavid domains for decades to come—a promise that was not fulfilled.

Abbas the Great Safavid ruler from 1587 to 1629; extended Safavid domain to greatest extent; created slave regiments based on captured Russians, who monopolized firearms within Safavid armies; incorporated Western military technology.

State and Religion

The Safavid family was originally of Turkic stock, and early shahs such as Ismâ'il wrote in Turkish, unlike their Ottoman rivals, who preferred to write in Persian. After Chaldiran, however, Persian gradually supplanted Turkish as the language of the court and bureaucracy. Persian influences were also felt in the

THINKING HISTORICALLY

The Gunpowder Empires and the Shifting Balance of Global Power

LIKE SO MANY OF THEIR PREDECESSORS, each of the great Muslim dynasties of the premodern era came to power with the support of nomadic warrior peoples. Each based the military forces that won and sustained its empire on massed cavalry. But in each case, there was a significant divergence from past conditions. As the outcome of the critical battle of Chaldiran between the Ottomans and Safavids made clear, by the 16th century firearms had become a decisive element in armed conflict—the key to empire building. In military and political terms, global history had entered a new phase.

Although the Chinese had invented gunpowder and were the first to use it in war, the Mongols were the first to realize the awesome potential of the new type of weaponry based on explosive formulas. The Mongols continued to build their armies around swift cavalry and their skill as mounted archers. But siege cannons became critical to Mongol conquests once they ventured into the highly urbanized civilizations that bordered on their steppe homelands. Mongol successes against intricately walled and heavily fortified cities in China, Russia, and the Islamic heartlands impressed their sedentary and nomadic adversaries with the power of the new weaponry and contributed much to its spread throughout the Eurasian world in the late 13th and 14th centuries.

Innovation in the use of gunpowder spread quickly to many areas, especially Europe and the Muslim Middle East. By the late 15th century, muskets and field cannons, however heavy and clumsy the latter might be, were transforming warfare from Europe to China. In the Middle East, Janissary musketeers and heavy artillery became the driving force of Ottoman expansion. The Safavids' lack of artillery was critical to their defeat at Chaldiran. In Europe, armies were increasingly built around musket and artillery regiments. Rival states vied to attract gunsmiths who could provide them with the latest weaponry or, even better, invent guns that would give them decisive advantages over their rivals. In the Atlantic and the Mediterranean, handguns and cannons were introduced into sea warfare—an innovation that proved essential to the Europeans' ability to project their power overseas from the 16th century onward.

In many areas, the new military technology contributed to broader social and political changes. In feudal Europe and somewhat later in Japan, for example, siege cannons reduced feudal castles to rubble. In so doing, they struck a mortal blow at the warrior aristocracies that had dominated these societies for centuries. But the success of the new weaponry also drove a revolution in the design of fortifications and defense strategies. The defense systems that resulted, which were expensive and elaborate, spawned corps of professional officers and engineers, vast military supply industries, and urban centers enclosed by low-lying walls and star-shaped bastions. The cost of the field artillery, siege weapons, and new defense industries promoted state centralization, as the experience of the Muslim empires and the history of Europe and Japan in the gunpowder age demonstrate. Rulers with national or imperial ambitions had the firepower to level the fortresses of regional lords and thus more effectively control the populations and resources of their domains.

> *In feudal Europe and somewhat later in Japan ... siege cannons reduced feudal castles to rubble.*

Although the new weaponry was vital to the rise and sustenance of nation-states and empires, some political systems were more compatible than others with efforts to exploit and improve on it. At one extreme, the Chinese scholar-gentry limited innovations in gunpowder weaponry and its use in warfare because they feared that these changes would lead to the dominance of the military in Ming and later Qing society. After the early 1600s, the shoguns, or military leaders, of neighboring Japan virtually banned the firearms that had done so much to bring them to power. In this case, a military caste feared that the spread of firearms to the general populace would destroy what was left of the feudal order they had built centuries earlier.

The obstacles faced by nomadic peoples such as the Mongols were very different. Their sparse populations and arid lands simply did not generate the resources or sustained invention that would allow them to keep up with their sedentary neighbors in the expensive arms races that the new technology spawned. As the advantages of sedentary societies grew more pronounced in the 17th and 18th centuries, nomadic peoples found not only that they could no longer raid or conquer the agrarian cores but also that sedentary adversaries could advance into and occupy their homelands on the steppe and desert fringes.

Nomadic dynasties, such as the Ottomans, Safavids, and Mughals, who had won their empires in the early stages of the gunpowder revolution, did control the agrarian bases and skilled artisans needed to supply their armies with muskets and siege cannons. But they were confronted by internal conflicts and, perhaps more critically in the long run, formidable external rivals. To begin with, their military technology was far in advance of the transport and communication systems of their far-flung empires.

(continued on next page)

This fact, and their failure to build effective imperial bureaucracies, left them at the mercy of the warrior elites who brought them to power. In each of the three empires, the regional bases of the warrior classes became increasingly independent of the ruling dynasty. This meant that the rulers were denied revenue and other resources that were vital to maintaining competitive military establishments. Their fragile and overstretched administrative systems proved difficult to reform and more and more ineffective at administering the peasant populations in their charge. Internal revolts further sapped the resources of the hard-pressed Muslim dynasties.

In each Muslim empire, decline was hastened by the rise of European rivals, who proved more adept at taking advantage of the gunpowder revolution. The smaller but highly competitive nation-states of western Europe were better able to mobilize more limited human and natural resources than their Muslim counterparts. Constant struggles for survival in the multistate European system also made the elites of Spain, England, and France more receptive to technological innovation, which became a central ingredient of political success in the gunpowder era. Emulating the more advanced states of western Europe, for example, Peter the Great pushed for social reforms and military innovations that transformed a weak and backward Russia into a powerful adversary of the Ottomans and the nomadic peoples of the steppes. Thus, although it began in China and was initially spread by the Mongol nomads, the gunpowder revolution eventually tipped the global balance of power in favor of the peoples of Christian Europe. This shift was an essential condition for Europe's rise to global power in the centuries that followed.

> **QUESTIONS**
> - What advantages would gunpowder weaponry give to those who used it over those who did not in the Early Modern era?
> - Were these advantages as decisive as they were later in the industrial age?
> - Why would the use of muskets and early field cannons take a higher level of military organization and troop discipline and training than had been needed in earlier time periods?
> - What made the new military technology so expensive?
> - Why did the Europeans adopt it more readily than most other peoples, and why were they so intent on improving it?

organization of court rituals and in the more and more exalted position of the Safavid shahs. Abandoning all pretense of the egalitarian camaraderie that had marked their earlier dealings with the warrior chiefs, the Safavids took grand titles, such as *padishah*, or king of kings, often derived from those used by the ancient Persian emperors. Like the Ottoman rulers, the Safavids presided from their high thrones over opulent palace complexes crowded with servants and courtiers. The pattern of palace life was set by elaborate court rituals and social interaction governed by a refined sense of etiquette and decorum. Although the later Safavid shahs played down claims to divinity that had been set forth under Ismâ'il and his predecessors, they continued to claim descent from one of the Shi'a **imams** or successors of Ali.

imams According to Shi'ism, rulers who could trace descent from the successors of Ali.

Changes in the status accorded to the Safavid rulers were paralleled by shifts in the religious impulses that had been so critical to their rise to power. The militant, expansive cast of Shi'a ideology was modified as the faith became a major pillar of dynasty and empire. The early Safavids imported Arabic-speaking Shi'a religious experts. But later shahs came to rely on Persian religious scholars who entered into the service of the state and were paid by the government. **Mullahs**, who were both local mosque officials and prayer leaders, were also supervised by the state and given some support from it. All religious leaders were required to curse the first three caliphs and mention the Safavid ruler in the Friday sermon. Teaching in the mosque schools was also planned and directed by state religious officials.

mullahs Local mosque officials and prayer leaders within the Safavid empire; agents of Safavid religious campaign to convert all of population to Shi'ism.

Through these agents, the bulk of the Iranian population was converted to Shi'ism during the centuries of Safavid rule. Sunni Muslims, Christians, Jews, Zoroastrians, and the followers of Sufi preachers were pressured to convert to Shi'ism. Shi'a religious festivals, such as that commemorating the martyrdom of Husayn (a son of Ali) and involving public flagellation and passion plays, and pilgrimages to Shi'a shrines, such as that at Karbala in central Iraq, became the focal points of popular religion in Iran. Thus, Shi'ism not only provided ideological and institutional support for the Safavid dynasty but also came to be an integral part of Iranian identity, setting the people of the region off from most of their Arab and Turkic neighbors.

Commercial Revival, Elite Affluence, and the Art of the Mosque

Although earlier rulers had built or restored mosques and religious schools and financed public works projects, Abbas I surpassed them all. After securing his political position with a string of military victories, Abbas I set about establishing his empire as a major center of international trade and

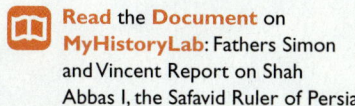 Read the Document on MyHistoryLab: Fathers Simon and Vincent Report on Shah Abbas I, the Safavid Ruler of Persia

Islamic culture. He had a network of roads and rest houses built, and he strove to make merchants and travelers safe within his domains. He set up workshops to manufacture the silk textiles and splendid Persian carpets that were in great demand both within the Safavid empire and in lands as distant as those in Europe and southeast Asia. Abbas I encouraged Iranian merchants to trade not only with their Muslim neighbors and India and China to the east but also with the Portuguese—and later the Dutch and English—whose war and merchant ships were becoming a familiar sight in the Persian Gulf and Arabian Sea.

The Splendors of Isfahan

Although Abbas I undertook building projects throughout his empire, he devoted special attention to his capital at **Isfahan**. The splendid seat of Safavid power was laid out around a great square, which was lined with two-story shops interspersed with great mosques, government offices, and soaring arches that opened onto formal gardens. Abbas I founded several colleges and oversaw the construction of numerous public baths and rest houses. He patronized workshops where intricately detailed and brilliantly colored miniatures were produced by master painters and their apprentices.

Above all, the great mosques that Abbas I had built at Isfahan were the glory of his reign (Figure 22.5). The vividly colored ceramic tiles, which Iranian builders had begun to use centuries earlier, turned the massive domes and graceful minarets of Safavid mosques and royal tombs into creations of stunning beauty. Geometric designs, floral patterns, and verses from the Qur'an written in stylized Arabic added movement and texture to the deep blue tiles that distinguished the monumental construction of the Safavid era. Gardens and reflecting pools were built near the mosques and rest houses. By combining graceful arches, greenery, and colorful designs, Persian architects and artisans created lush, cool refuges (perhaps duplicating heaven itself, as it is described in the Qur'an) in a land that is dry, dusty, and gray-brown for much of the year.

Isfahan [is fuh hän] (1592–1629) Safavid capital under Abbas the Great; planned city laid out according to shah's plan; example of Safavid architecture.

Society and Gender Roles: Ottoman and Safavid Comparisons

Although the Ottomans and Safavids were bitter political rivals and religious adversaries, the social systems that developed under the two dynasties had much in common. Both were dominated, particularly in their earliest phases, by warrior aristocracies, which shared power with the absolutist monarchs of each empire and enjoyed prestige and luxury in the capital and on rural estates. In

FIGURE **22.5** Occupying one side of the great square of the Safavid capital at Isfahan, the blue-tiled Shah Mosque was one of the architectural gems of the Early Modern era worldwide.

both cases, the warrior aristocrats gradually retreated to the estates, making life increasingly difficult for the peasants on whom they depended for the support of their grand households and many retainers. As the real power of the rulers of each empire diminished and as population increases reduced the uncultivated lands to which peasants might flee, the demands of the landlord class grew harsher. Foreign invasions, civil strife, and the breakdown in vital services once provided by the state added to the growing misery of the peasantry. The resulting spread of banditry, peasant uprisings, and flight from the land further drained the resources of both empires and undermined their legitimacy.

The early rulers of both the Ottoman and the Safavid empires encouraged the growth of handicraft production and trade in their realms. Both dynasties established imperial workshops where products ranging from miniature paintings and rugs to weapons and metal utensils were manufactured. The rulers of each empire lavishly patronized public works projects that provided reasonably well-paid work for engineers, stonemasons, carpenters, and other sorts of artisans. Some of the more able emperors of these dynasties also pursued policies that they believed would increase both internal and international trade. In these endeavors, the Ottomans gained in the short run from the fact that large-scale traders in their empire often were from minority groups, such as Christians and Jews, who had extensive contacts with overseas traders that the bazaar merchants of the Safavid realm normally lacked. Although Safavid cooperation with Portuguese traders remedied this shortcoming to some extent, the Safavid economy remained much more constricted, less market oriented, and more technically backward than that of their Ottoman rivals.

Women in Islamic societies under Ottoman or Safavid rule faced legal and social disadvantages comparable to those we have encountered in most civilized areas so far. Within the family, women were subordinated to their fathers and husbands. They seldom had political or religious power, and they had surprisingly meager outlets for artistic or scholarly expression. Even women of nomadic Turkic and Mongol backgrounds gradually lost their independence when they settled in the towns of conquered areas. There, the dictates of increasingly patriarchal codes and restrictive practices such as seclusion and veiling were imposed on women of all classes, but most strictly on those of the elite.

However, recent evidence suggests that many women in the Islamic heartlands in this era, perhaps clinging to the memory of the lives led by their nomadic predecessors, struggled against these restrictions. Travelers to Persia in the time of Abbas I remarked on the brightly colored robes worn by women in the capital and elsewhere, and noted that many women made no effort to cover their faces in public. At both the Ottoman and Safavid courts, the wives and concubines of the rulers and royal princes continued to exert influence behind the throne and remained deeply involved in palace conspiracies. More important for ordinary women in each of these societies was the fact that many were active in trade and some in money-lending. Court records also suggest that women often could invoke provisions in Islamic law that protected their rights to inheritance, decent treatment by their spouses, and even divorce in marital situations that had become intolerable.

How typical these instances of assertion and expression were is not clear. Although some women were a good deal better off than we had once thought, perhaps as well off as or even better off than their counterparts in China and India, most women probably lived unenviable lives. Limited largely to contacts with their own families and left with little more than household chores and domestic handicrafts such as embroidery to occupy their time, the overwhelming majority of women in effect disappeared from the history of two of the great centers of Islamic civilization.

The Rapid Demise of the Safavid Empire

Given the power and splendor the Safavid empire had achieved by the end of the reign of Abbas I, its collapse was stunningly rapid. Abbas's fears of usurpation by one of his sons, which were fed by plots on the part of several of his closest advisors, had led during his reign to the death or blinding of all who could legitimately succeed him. A grandson, who was weak and thus thought by high state officials to be easily manipulated, was placed on the throne after Abbas's death. From this point, the dynasty's fortunes declined. As was true of the Ottomans, the practice of confining the princes to the atmosphere of luxury and intrigue that permeated the court led to a sharp fall in the quality of Safavid rulers. Able shahs, such as Abbas II (r. 1642–1666), were too few to halt the decline of the imperial administration or to deal effectively with the many foreign threats to the empire. Factional disputes and rebellions shook the empire from within, and nomadic raiders and Ottoman and Mughal armies steadily reduced the territory the Safavids could tap for labor and revenue.

Nadir Khan Afshar (1688–1747) Soldier-adventurer following fall of Safavid dynasty in 1722; proclaimed himself shah in 1736; established short-lived dynasty in reduced kingdom.

In March 1722, Isfahan was besieged by Afghani tribes. In October, after over 80,000 of the capital's inhabitants had died of starvation and disease, the city fell and Safavid power was ended. One of the contenders who fought for the throne in the decade of war and destruction that followed claimed descent from the Safavid line. But a soldier-adventurer named **Nadir Khan Afshar** eventually emerged victorious from these bloody struggles. Although he began as a champion of Safavid restoration, Nadir Khan proclaimed himself shah in 1736. Despite the title, his dynasty and those that followed were short-lived. The area that had once made up the Safavid empire was reduced for generations to a battleground for its powerful neighbors and a tempting target for nomadic raiders.

THE MUGHALS AND THE APEX OF MUSLIM CIVILIZATION IN INDIA

In the first centuries of Mughal rule in India, Islam reached the peak of its influence as a political and cultural force in south Asian history. Under the Mughal emperors, a blend of Hindu and Islamic civilizations produced some of the world's most sublime architecture and art.

22.3 In what major ways was the Mughal dynasty in India similar to and yet quite different from its rival Ottoman and Safavid regimes in terms of its origins and the ways in which its Indian empire was built, the composition of the subject peoples it ruled and its relationships with them, its global linkages, and the causes of its decline?

Despite the fact that the founder of the Mughal dynasty, **Babur**, traced his descent on one side from the Mongol khans, the Mughal in the dynasty's name was not derived from those earlier nomadic conquerors. Babur was also descended from the Turkic conqueror Timur, and most of his followers were from Turkic or mixed nomadic origins. Unlike the Ottomans and Safavids, Babur's motives for conquest and empire building had little to do with religious fervor. Originally, he directed raids into the fertile and heavily populated plains of north India only to gain booty to support his campaigns to win back his lost kingdom, Ferghana. Although India had much greater potential as a base on which to build an empire, Babur cared little for the green and well-watered subcontinent. Even after he conquered India, he continued to long for the arid steppes and blue-domed mosques of his central Asian birthplace. But after decades of wars on the steppes that repeatedly ended in defeat, he was forced to give up his dream of reclaiming his homeland and to turn his full energies to the conquest of northern India. Within two years, his armies had conquered large portions of the Indus and Ganges plains (See Map 22.4) and he had laid the foundations for a dynasty that would last more than 300 years.

The founder of the Mughal dynasty was a remarkable man. He was a fine military strategist and fierce fighter who went into battle alongside his troops. But Babur also cultivated a taste for the arts and music over the course of the decades when he was continually fighting for survival. He wrote one of the great histories of India, was a fine musician, and designed wonderful gardens for his new capital at Delhi. But he was a better conqueror than administrator. Babur did little to reform the very ineffective Lodi bureaucracy he had taken over—a project that would have solidified the Mughals' hold on the empire he had conquered. In 1530, at the age of 48, he suddenly fell ill and died, leaving his son, **Humayan**, to inherit the newly founded kingdom. Like his father, Humayan was a good soldier; in fact, he had won his first battle at age 18. But Babur's death was the signal for his enemies to strike from all sides. One of Humayan's brothers disputed his succession, and armies from Afghanistan and the Rajput states of western India marched on his capital (Map 22.4). By 1540, with his armies shattered, Humayan was forced to flee to Persia. There he remained in exile, an uneasy guest at the Safavid court, for nearly a decade. Having gained a foothold at Kabul in 1545, Humayan launched a series of campaigns into India that restored Mughal rule to the northern plains by 1556. But Humayan did not live to savor his victory. Shortly after entering Delhi in triumph, he was hurrying down his library steps, his arms full of books, to answer the call to prayer. He stumbled and fell, hitting his head. He died within days.

MAP 22.4 **The Growth of the Mughal Empire, from Akbar to Aurangzeb** Although in its later phase the Mughal empire occupied much of South Asia, the cost of wars of expansion contributed in major ways to its rapid decline from the late 17th century.

Akbar's Religious Syncretism, Hindu Allies, and a Multicultural Empire

Humayan's sudden death once again imperiled the Mughal dynasty. His son and successor, **Akbar**, was only 13 years old, and the Mughals' enemies moved quickly to take advantage of what they saw as a very favorable turn of events. Their expectations were soon dashed because Akbar proved to be one of the greatest leaders in world history. Interestingly, Akbar's reign was contemporaneous with those of several other remarkable monarchs, including Elizabeth I of England, Philip of Spain, and the Muslim rulers Suleyman the Magnificent and Abbas I. Akbar was a match for any one of these very formidable rivals.

Like his father and grandfather, Akbar was a fine military commander with great personal courage. But unlike his predecessors, Akbar also had a vision of empire and sense of mission that hinged on uniting India under his rule. A workaholic who seldom slept more than three hours a night, Akbar personally oversaw the building of the military and administrative systems that would form the backbone of the Mughal empire for centuries. He also patronized the arts and entered into complex religious and philosophical discussions with learned scholars from throughout the Muslim, Christian, and Hindu worlds. In addition, Akbar found time to carry out social reforms and invent his own universalistic religion. Although illiterate—there had been little time for book learning when his father fought for survival in the wilderness and later at the Safavid court—Akbar had an insatiable curiosity and an incredible memory. By having others read aloud to him, he became educated in many fields.

At first with the help of senior advisors, but soon on his own, Akbar routed the enemies who had hoped to capitalize on the Mughals' misfortunes. In the decades after 1560, when he took charge of the government, Akbar's armies greatly extended the empire with conquests throughout north and central India. But it was Akbar's social policies and administrative genius that made it possible to establish the foundations of a lasting dominion in the subcontinent. He pursued a policy of reconciliation and cooperation with the Hindu princes and the Hindu majority of the population of his realm. He encouraged intermarriage between the Mughal aristocracy and the families of the Hindu Rajput rulers. Akbar also abolished the much-hated *jizya*, or head tax, that earlier Muslim rulers had levied on Hindu unbelievers. He promoted Hindus to the highest ranks in the government, ended a long-standing ban on the building of new Hindu temples, and ordered Muslims to respect cows, which the Hindu majority viewed as sacred.

Despite the success of these policies in reconciling the Hindu majority to Muslim rule, Akbar viewed tolerance as merely the first stage in a longer strategy to put an end to sectarian divisions in the subcontinent. Blending elements of the many religions with which he was familiar, he invented a new faith, the **Din-i-Ilahi**, that he believed could be used to unite his Hindu and Muslim subjects. If the adherents of India's diverse religions could be convinced to embrace this common creed, Akbar reasoned, sectarian quarrels and even violent conflict could be brought to an end.

Like their counterparts in the Ottoman and Safavid empires, the Muslim and Hindu warrior aristocrats who formed the core of the supporters of the Mughal dynasty were granted peasant villages for their support. In turn, they were required to maintain a specified number of cavalry and to be on call if the emperor needed their services. The court and the central bureaucracy were supported by revenues drawn from the tribute paid by the military retainers and from taxes on lands set aside for the support of the imperial household. Because of a shortage of administrators, in most areas local notables, many of whom were Hindu, were left in place as long as they swore allegiance to the Mughal rulers and paid their taxes on time. These arrangements left the control and welfare of the village population largely in the hands of the military retainers of the dynasty and local power brokers.

Social Reform and Attempts to Recast Gender Relations

In addition to his administrative reforms, Akbar pushed for social changes that he believed would greatly benefit his subjects. Beyond the public works typically favored by able Muslim rulers, Akbar sought to improve the calendar, to establish living quarters for the large population of beggars and vagabonds in the large cities, and to regulate the consumption of alcohol. Whatever success the latter campaign may have had in Indian society as a whole, it apparently failed in Akbar's own household, for one of his sons was reputed to drink 20 cups of double-distilled wine per day.

Babur Founder of Mughal dynasty in India; descended from Turkic warriors; first led invasion of India in 1526; died in 1530.

Humayan Son and successor of Babur; expelled from India in 1540, but restored Mughal rule by 1556; died shortly thereafter.

Akbar (1542–1605) Son and successor of Humayan; oversaw building of military and administrative systems that became typical of Mughal rule in India; pursued policy of cooperation with Hindu princes; attempted to create new religion to bind Muslim and Hindu populations of India.

Din-i-Ilahi [dEEn i i lä hee] Religion initiated by Akbar in Mughal India; blended elements of the many faiths of the subcontinent; key to efforts to reconcile Hindus and Muslims in India, but failed.

FIGURE 22.6 This engraving from a late 16th-century German traveler's account of India shows a European artist's impression of an Indian widow committing sati. Not surprisingly, this practice of burning high-caste widows in some parts of India and among certain social groups on their deceased husbands' funeral pyres often was described at great length by European visitors in this era. There was some disagreement in their accounts as to whether the women went willingly into the fire, as some early authors claimed. Later inquiries in the British period revealed that some of the widows had been drugged and others tied to the funeral pyre. It is likely that many simply caved in to pressure applied by their dead spouse's relatives and at times even their own children.

More than any of Akbar's many reform efforts, those involving the position of women demonstrated how far the Mughal ruler was in advance of his time. He encouraged widow remarriage, at that point taboo for both Hindus and Muslims, and discouraged child marriages. The latter were so widespread among the upper classes that he did not try to outlaw them, and it is doubtful that his disapproval did much to curb the practice. Akbar did legally prohibit **sati**, or the burning of high-caste Hindu women on their husbands' funeral pyres (Figure 22.6). Because this custom was deeply entrenched among the Rajput princes and warrior classes that were some of his most faithful allies, this was a risky move on Akbar's part. But he was so determined to eradicate sati, particularly in cases where the widow was pressured to agree to be burned alive, that he once personally rescued a young woman despite the protestations of her angry relatives. He also tried to provide relief for women trapped in **purdah**, or seclusion in their homes, by encouraging the merchants of Delhi and other cities to set aside special market days for women only.

sati The practice followed by small minorities, usually upper caste, of Indians of burning widows on the funeral pyres of their deceased husbands.

purdah The seclusion of Indian women in their homes.

Mughal Splendor and Early European Contacts

Despite his many successes and the civil peace and prosperity his reign brought to much of northern India, Akbar died a lonely and discouraged man. By 1605 he had outlived most of his friends and faced revolts by sons eager to claim his throne. Above all, he died knowing that Din-i-Ilahi, the religion he had created to reconcile his Hindu and Muslim subjects, had been rejected by both.

Although neither of his successors, Jahangir (r. 1605–1627) nor Shah Jahan (r. 1627–1658), added much territory to the empire Akbar had left them, in their reigns Mughal India reached the peak of its splendor. European visitors marveled at the size and opulence of the chief Mughal cities: Delhi, Agra, and Lahore. The huge Mughal armies, replete with elephant and artillery corps, dwarfed those of even the most powerful European rulers at the time. Some of the more perceptive European observers, such as François Bernier, also noted the poverty in which the lower classes in both town and countryside lived and the lack of discipline and training of most of the soldiers in the Mughal armies. Perhaps most ominously, Bernier added that in invention and the sciences, India had fallen far behind western Europe in most areas.

Nonetheless, by the late 17th century Mughal India had become one of the major overseas destinations for European traders. They brought products from throughout Asia, although little from Europe itself, to exchange for a variety of Indian manufactures, particularly the subcontinent's famed cotton textiles. The trade deficit that the demand for Indian cotton cloth and clothing had created in the Mediterranean region in Roman times persisted millennia later. The importance of the Indian textile trade to the West is suggested by the names we still use for different kinds of cotton cloth, from calico (after the Indian port city of Calicut) to chintz and muslin, as well as by our names for cotton clothes, such as pajamas.

Because they were easily washed and inexpensive, Indian textiles first won a large market among the working and middle classes in Britain and elsewhere in Europe. In the reigns of Queen Mary and Queen Anne, fine Indian cloth came into fashion at the court as well. An incident from the reign of the Mughal emperor **Aurangzeb**, who succeeded Shah Jahan, suggests just how fine the cloth in question was. Aurangzeb, a religious zealot, scolded his favorite daughter for appearing in his presence in garments that revealed so much of her body. The daughter protested that she had on three layers of fine cotton clothing. It is thus no wonder that even after industrialization had revolutionized cotton textile manufacture in England, European visitors to India continued to observe and write in great detail about the techniques Indian artisans used to weave and dye cotton cloth. The popularity of madras cloth today demonstrates that this interest has not died out.

Aurangzeb [AHR-uhng-zeb] Mughal emperor who succeeded Shah Jajan; known for his religious zealotry.

Wonders of the Early Modern World: Artistic Achievement in the Mughal Era

Both Jahangir and Shah Jahan continued Akbar's policy of tolerance toward the Hindu majority and retained most of the alliances he had forged with Hindu princes and local leaders. They made little attempt to change the administrative apparatus they had inherited from Akbar, and they fought their wars in much the same way as the founders of the dynasty had. Both mounted campaigns to crush potential enemies and in some cases to enlarge the empire. But neither was as interested in conquest and politics as in enjoying the good life. Both were fond of drink, female dancers, and the pleasure gardens they had laid out from Kashmir to Allahabad. Both were delighted by polo matches (a game invented by the princes of India), ox and tiger or elephant fights, and games of *pachisi*, which they played on life-sized boards with palace dancers as chips. Both took great pleasure in the elaborate

VISUALIZING THE PAST

Art as a Window into the Past: Paintings and History in Mughal India

IN WAYS THAT WERE SIMILAR TO China and the great Muslim empires of Asia and Africa, European states participated in the gunpowder revolution that transformed the nature of warfare and political power in the Early Modern era. But as the Iberians and somewhat later the Dutch, English, and French sailed out across the oceans, they were able to harness the firepower of cannons and hand guns mainly to establish their growing power on the seas. Except in the Americas, where millennia of isolation left the indigenous peoples without metalworking and gunpowder, once the Europeans went ashore they could not hope to dominate kingdoms with far larger armies and resources than any state in Europe in the 15th and 16th centuries. Consequently, over much of Africa and Asia, the Spanish and Portuguese and after them the northern Europeans sought for the most part to establish trading linkages, win permission to build warehouses and fortify small settlements, and pursue efforts to convert local populations from fishermen and laborers to emperors and their courtiers.

Since there were no photographs or newsreels, what we know about the interactions between Europeans and the peoples they encountered overseas in the Early Modern era comes mainly from

(continued on next page)

(continued from previous page)

different sorts of written sources. But works of art, such as the two Mughal miniatures reproduced here, can also tell us a good deal about these cross-cultural encounters.

The first depicts the Mughal armies besieging and eventually capturing the Portuguese trading post at the port of Hoogly in present-day Bengal. The second is a formal painting of the Mughal emperor, Shah Jahan, receiving homage and tribute from his vassals and foreign emissaries. And there is a connection between the two paintings—the Europeans in the lower lefthand corner of the imperial audience are Portuguese who have just lost their trading center at Hoogly.

QUESTIONS

- Study these two paintings, as well as the other artwork in this chapter that show the great naval clash (p. 502) between an allied European fleet and the Ottomans at Lepanto; a German engraving (p. 512) of an Indian woman about to be immolated on her husband's funeral pyre. What do the placement of the Europeans in relation to the Mughal court, and the postures of the Europeans and what they carry tell us about the power balance between these intruders and the rulers of the Muslim empires in this era?

- Contrast the battle at Lepanto in the Mediterranean with the Mughal siege of Hoogly in terms of the relative power between the two sides and discuss the factors that made for very different outcomes in the two clashes. And what can we learn about European attitudes towards the customs, dress, and gender positions of ordinary people and society more broadly—in this case, Hindu society in South Asia—from the German engraving of sati, or widow burning?

- Are paintings a reliable way to gain historical insights in the Early Modern era, and how do they compare to the photographs that we rely upon so heavily in the present day?

(Padshahnama: Europeans bring gifts to the Shah Jahan. The Royal Collection © 2009. Her Majesty Queen Elizabeth II.)

court ceremonies that blended Indian and Persian precedents, lavish state processions, their palaces and jewel-studded wardrobes, and the scented and sweetened ices that were rushed from the cool mountains in the north to their capitals on the sweltering plains.

Jahangir and Shah Jahan are best remembered as two of the greatest patrons of the fine arts in human history. They expanded the painting workshops that had been started by the early Mughals so that thousands of exquisite miniature paintings could be produced during their reigns. Both Jahangir and Shah Jahan also devoted massive resources to building some of the most stunning architectural works of all time. The best known of these is the **Taj Mahal** (Figure 22.7), which has become a symbol for India itself. But structures such as the audience hall in the Red Fort at Delhi, Akbar's tomb at Sikandra, and the tomb of Itimad al-Dowleh at Agra rival the Taj Mahal in design and perhaps surpass it in the beauty of their detail and decoration.

At its best, Mughal architecture blends what is finest in the Persian and Hindu traditions. It fuses the Islamic genius for domes, arches, and minarets and the balance among them with the Hindu love of ornament. In place of the ceramic tiles that the Persians used to finish their mosques and tombs, Indian artisans substituted gleaming white marble, inset with semiprecious stones arranged in floral and geometric patterns. Extensive use was also made of marble reflecting pools, the most famous of which mirrors the beauty of the Taj Mahal. When these pools were inlaid with floral patterns and provided with fountains, the rippling water appeared to give life to the stone plant forms. Like the architects and artisans of the Ottoman empire and Safavid Persia, those who served the Mughal rulers strove to create paradise on earth, an aspiration that was carved in marble on the audience hall of the Red Fort at Delhi. Around the ceiling of the great hall, it is written "If there is paradise on earth—It is here . . . it is here."

Taj Mahal Most famous architectural achievement of Mughal India; originally built as a mausoleum for the wife of Shah Jahan, Mumtaz Mahal.

 View the **Closer Look** on **MyHistoryLab:** The Mughal Emperor Jahangir Honoring a Muslim Saint over Kings and Emperors

FIGURE 22.7 Perhaps no single building has come to symbolize Indian civilization more than the Taj Mahal. The grace and elegance of the tomb that Shah Jahan built in his wife's honor provide an enduring source of aesthetic delight. The white marble of the tomb is inlaid with flowers and geometric designs cut from semiprecious stones. The windows of the central chamber, which houses the tombs of Shah Jahan and Mumtaz Mahal, are decorated with carved marble screens, which add a sense of lightness and delicacy to the structure.

Nur Jahan [NOOR juh-HAHN] (1577–1645) Wife of Jahangir; amassed power in court and created faction of male relatives who dominated Mughal empire during later years of Jahangir's reign.

Mumtaz Mahal [MUHM-tahz mah-HAHL] (1593–1631) Wife of Shah Jahan; took an active political role in Mughal court; entombed in Taj Mahal.

Court Politics and the Position of Elite and Ordinary Women

Not surprisingly, two rulers who were so absorbed in the arts and the pursuit of pleasure left most of the mundane tasks of day-to-day administration largely in the hands of subordinates. In both cases, strong-willed wives took advantage of their husbands' neglect of politics to win positions of power and influence at the Mughal court. Jahangir's wife, **Nur Jahan**, continually amassed power as he became more and more addicted to wine and opium. She packed the court with able male relatives, and her faction dominated the empire for most of the later years of Jahangir's reign. Nur Jahan was a big spender, but not only on pomp and luxury. She became a major patron of much-needed charities in the major cities.

Shah Jahan's consort, **Mumtaz Mahal**, also became actively involved in court politics. But Shah Jahan was a much more engaged and able ruler than Jahangir, and thus her opportunities to amass power behind the throne were more limited. She is remembered not for her political acumen but for the love and devotion Shah Jahan bestowed upon her, a love literally enshrined in the Taj Mahal, the tomb where she is buried. Shah Jahan's plans to build a companion tomb for himself in black marble across the Jumna River were foiled by the revolt of his sons and by his imprisonment. He was buried next to his wife in the Taj Mahal, but her tomb is central and far larger than that of her husband.

Although the position of women at the Mughal court improved in the middle years of the dynasty's power, that of women in the rest of Indian society declined. Child marriage grew more popular, and the age limit was lowered. It was not unheard of for girls to be married at age 9. Widow remarriage among Hindus nearly died out. Seclusion was more and more strictly enforced for upper-caste women, both Hindu and Muslim. Muslim women rarely ventured forth from their homes unveiled, and those who did risked verbal and even physical abuse. The governor of one of the provinces of the Mughal empire divorced his wife because she was seen scrambling for her life, unveiled, from a runaway elephant. Among upper-caste Hindus, the practice of sati spread despite Shah Jahan's renewed efforts to outlaw it. The dwindling scope of productive roles left to women, combined with the burden of the dowry that had to be paid to marry them off, meant that the birth of a girl was increasingly seen as an inauspicious event. At court as well as in the homes of ordinary villagers, only the birth of a son was greeted with feasting and celebrations.

The Beginnings of Imperial Decline

Aurangzeb, Shah Jahan's son and successor, seized control of an empire that was threatened by internal decay and growing dangers from external enemies. For decades, the need for essential administrative, military, and social reforms had been ignored. The Mughal bureaucracy had grown bloated and corrupt. The army was equally bloated and backward in weaponry and tactics. Peasants and urban workers had seen their productivity and living standards fall steadily. The Taj Mahal and other wonders of the Mughal artistic imagination had been paid for by the mass of the people at a very high price.

Although not the cruel bigot as he is often portrayed, Aurangzeb was not the man to restore the dynasty's declining fortunes. Courageous, honest, intelligent, and hard-working, he seemed an ideal successor to two rulers who had so badly neglected the affairs of state. But Aurangzeb was driven by two ambitions that proved disastrous to his schemes to strengthen the empire. He was determined to extend Mughal control over the whole of the Indian subcontinent, and he believed that it was his duty to purify Indian Islam and rid it of the Hindu influences he was convinced were steadily corrupting it.

The first ambition increased the number of the empire's adversaries, strained the allegiance of its vassals and allies, and greatly overextended its huge but obsolete military forces. By the time of his death in 1707, after a reign of nearly 50 years, Aurangzeb had conquered most of the subcontinent and extended Mughal control as far north as Kabul in what is now Afghanistan. But the almost endless warfare of his years in power drained the treasury and further enlarged an inefficient bureaucracy and army without gaining corresponding increases in revenues to support them.

Equally critically, the long wars occupied much of Aurangzeb's time and energies, diverting him from the administrative tasks and reforms essential to the dynasty's continued strength. While he was leading his massive armies in the south, there were peasant uprisings and revolts by Muslim and Hindu princes in the north. Perhaps even more harmful to the imperial system was the growing autonomy of local leaders, who diverted more and more revenue from the central administration into their own coffers. On the northern borders, incursions by Persian and Afghan warrior bands were increasing.

While Aurangzeb's military campaigns strained the resources of the empire, his religious policies gravely weakened the internal alliances and disrupted the social peace Akbar had so skillfully established. Aurangzeb continued to employ Hindus in the imperial service; in fact, he did not have sufficient Muslim replacements to do without them. But non-Muslims were given far fewer posts at the upper levels of the bureaucracy, and their personal contact with the emperor was severely restricted. Aurangzeb also took measures that he and his religious advisors felt would help rid their Muslim faith and culture of the Hindu influences that had permeated it over the centuries. He forbade the building of new temples and put an end to Hindu religious festivals at court. Aurangzeb also reinstated the hated head tax on unbelievers—a measure he hoped might prod them to convert to Islam. The tax fell heavily on the Hindu poor and in some cases drove them to support sectarian movements that rose up to resist Aurangzeb.

By the end of Aurangzeb's reign, the Mughal empire was far larger than it had been under any of the earlier emperors, but it was also more unstable. Internal rebellions, particularly those mounted by the **Marattas** in western India, put an end to effective Mughal control over large areas. The rise of new sects, such as the **Sikhs**, in the northwest, further strained the declining resources of an imperial system that was clearly overextended. The early leaders of the Sikhs originally tried to bridge the differences between Hindu and Muslim. But Mughal persecution of the new sect, which was seen as religiously heretical and a political threat to the dynasty, eventually transformed Sikhism into a staunchly anti-Muslim force within the subcontinent. In addition, Muslim kingdoms in central and east India continued to resist Mughal hegemony, and Islamic invaders waited at the poorly guarded passes through the Himalayas to strike and plunder once it was clear that the Mughals could no longer fend them off.

Marattas Western India peoples who rebelled against Mughal control early in 18th century.

Sikhs [SEEKS] Sect in northwest India; early leaders tried to bridge differences between Hindu and Muslim, but Mughal persecution led to anti-Muslim feeling.

Global Connections and Critical Themes

GUNPOWDER EMPIRES AND THE RESTORATION OF THE ISLAMIC BRIDGE AMONG CIVILIZATIONS

The formation of the Ottoman, Safavid, and Mughal dynasties warrants comparison with the steadily expanding land empires of the Russian tsars and the Ming emperors, each of which also included substantial Muslim populations. And although the emerging nation-states of western Europe expanded mainly by sea, they also shared a good deal with the vast land empires of Eurasia. All were highly centralized politically and organized around absolute and hereditary rulers. Each empire's power and capacity to expand was dependent on new military technologies and modes of military organization deployed on both land and sea. In contrast to the Muslim empires, which were established by pastoral peoples, those of Russia and China expended much of their expansive energies to contain and subdue nomadic peoples. Western Europeans confronted nomadic peoples—some of whom practiced agriculture, but most of whom were primarily hunters and gatherers—in their American and south African settler colonies.

Compared with the Abbasid era, new discoveries in the sciences dropped off during this period, but the transmission of Indian and Greco-Arab learning may have accelerated in the Muslim world. Far more impressive were the influences that the artists and architects from each of these Muslim empires exerted on each other. Contravening the Muslim prohibition of the depiction of human figures, miniature painting—typically of shahs and sultans, epic sagas, social scenes, and battles—reached a level of perfection seldom equaled. And artists, techniques, and fashions in painting were shared extensively, although regional styles could be quite distinct. Although few of the monumental buildings commissioned by Babur in India remain, all were heavily influenced by Ottoman tastes and methods of construction. In each of these fields and in every instance of emulation, borrowing, and reworking, this cross-fertilization between disparate cultures and peoples built on a tradition of exchange and innovation that had been a hallmark of Islamic civilization from its beginnings.

Changes in the position of the three great Islamic empires relative to the Russian, Chinese, and western European empires of the Early Modern era were gradual and complex. The Ottoman, Safavid, and Mughal empires retained active programs of overseas trade which, as we have seen, was a defining feature of Early Modern history worldwide. Arabs, for example, continued to interact with the peoples of the east African coast and their trade in slaves, spices, and other goods. Europeans sought luxury products both in the Middle East and in India. In fact, Indian merchants made large profits from the spices and textiles they exported and that the Europeans paid for in silver from the Americas. But the Europeans were increasingly assertive, setting up a merchant quarter in Constantinople, for example, where they followed their own laws rather than those of the Ottoman empire.

European disdain for the slower pace of scientific and technological change in the Muslim—as well as the Chinese and Russian—empires also grew as the political and military power of the dynasties that ruled these vast regions decreased. The internal causes of decline discussed in this chapter for the Early Modern Muslim empires were probably sufficient to eventually undermine these great gunpowder empires. But each was also afflicted by further weaknesses that had profound significance for Islamic civilization as a whole. Captivated by their rivalries with each other and the problems of holding together their empires, none of the dynasties took the rising threat from Europe seriously. They called on Western travelers and missionaries for advice in casting cannons or military tactics, but none of the officials of the great Islamic empires systematically monitored technological advances in Europe. Eventually, the decline of the Mughals opened the door for growing political and military intervention by Europeans in the Indian subcontinent. Leading the way were the British and French, who formed alliances with rival princes in an increasingly decentralized society. What was soon to become a British empire in India was actively forming by the end of the Early Modern centuries.

The failure to take strong measures to meet the challenges that European overseas expansion was creating for Islamic civilization was also responsible for the weakening of the economic basis of each of the empires. Key tax revenues and merchant profits were drained off by the rise of European trading empires in Asia (see Chapters 17, 18, and 23). The Europeans' gains in ways to generate wealth and economic growth meant increasing losses for Muslim societies and political systems. These setbacks eventually proved critical to the failure of Muslim efforts to compete politically and militarily with their Christian rivals.

Further Readings

The Lapidus survey suggested in the earlier chapters on Islam provides a fine introduction to each of the empires that are the focus of this chapter. For comparative explorations of the three empires, see Douglas Streusand, *Islamic Gunpowder Empires: Ottomans, Safavids, and Mughals* (2010) and Stephen Dale, *The Muslim Empires of the Ottomans, Safavids, and Mughals* (2010).

The best detailed studies of the Ottoman empire can be found in the works of Halil Inalcik, especially his chapters in *The Cambridge History of Islam* (1977). For a different perspective on the Ottomans, see Stanford Shaw's *History of the Ottoman Empire and Modern Turkey*, vol. 1 (1780–1808) (1976). For Ottoman expansionism and relations with Europe and Asia, see Palmira Brummet, *Ottoman Seapower and Levantine Diplomacy in the Age of Discovery* (1993); Giancarlo Casale, *The Ottoman Age of Exploration* (2011); and Daniel Goffman, *The Ottoman Empire and Early Modern Europe* (2002). For the most recent and approachable exploration of the origins of the Ottoman state, see C. Kafadar, *Between Two Worlds: The Construction of the Ottoman State* (1995).

G. Necipoglu, *Architecture, Ceremonial, and Power: The Topkapi Palace in the Fifteenth and Sixteenth Centuries* (1991), illuminates the potent political symbolism embedded in the Ottoman empire's greatest artistic achievement. S. S. Blair and J. Bloom, *The Art and Architecture of Islam, 1250–1800* (1994), can be used to extend this analysis across the Muslim world. Peter F. Sugar, *Southeastern Europe under Ottoman Rule, 1354–1804* (1977), is a fine account of life in the Christian portions of the empire. Afaf Lutfi al-Sayyid Marsot, *Women and Men in Late Eighteenth Century Egypt* (1995), explores gender roles in the age of the Ottomans.

R. M. Savory's writings, including *Iran under the Safavids* (1980), and his chapters in *The Cambridge History of Iran* (1986), are the most reliable of a very limited literature in English on the Safavid period. For a discussion of key themes and developments in our understanding of the Safavid period, see Colin Mitchell, *New Perspectives on Safavid Iran* (2011). Although quite specialized, Michel Mazzaoui, *The Origins of the Safavids* (1972), provides the fullest account of the beginnings and rise of the Safavid dynasty. The contributions to the volume that Savory edited on *Islamic Civilization* (1976) include good discussions of the arts and society in the Turkic and Persian sectors of the Islamic heartland. The introductory sections of Nikki Keddi's *Roots of Revolution* (1981) provide a good discussion of the relationship between religion and the state in the Safavid period.

The Ikram and Ahmad books cited in Chapter 8 on expansion of Islam in India are also good resources on the Mughals. Although specialized, the works of Irfan Habib, M. Athar Ali, Richard Eaton, and Douglas Streusand on the Mughal empire are also critical.

Perhaps the most broadly conceived recent history is provided by John Richard's *The Mughal Empire* (1996). Detailed treatment of the lives of the Mughal emperors and life at their courts can be found in Munis Faraqui, *The Princes of Mughal India, 1504–1719* (2012). Muzzafar Alam's *The Crisis of the Empire in Mughal North India* (1993) is one of a number of recent works reexamining the decline of the Mughal dynasty. Of the many works on Mughal art and architecture, Annemarie Schimmel's *The Empire of the Great Mughal: History, Art and Culture* (2006) is one of the more recent and best contextualized, and Gavin Hambly's *Mughal Cities* (1968) has some of the best color plates and an intelligent commentary.

The role of women in the Islamic gunpowder empires is addressed in several recent studies, many of which take India's Nur Jahan as their touchstone. These include Stephen P. Blake, "Contributors to the Urban Landscape: Women Builders in Safavid Isfahan and Mughal Shahjahanabad," in Gavin Hambly, ed., *Women in the Medieval Islamic World* (1998); Ellison Banks Findly, *Nur Jahan: Empress of Mughal India* (1993); Stanley K. Freiberg, *Jahanara: Daughter of the Taj Mahal* (1999); and D. Fairchild Ruggles, ed., *Women, Patronage, and Self-Representation in Islamic Societies* (2000).

Trade between the Muslim gunpowder empires is one of the issues explored in Ashin Das Gupta and M. N. Pearson, eds., *India and the Indian Ocean, 1500–1800* (1987), and in Michael Adas, ed., *Islamic and European Expansion* (1993). For a magisterial and more fully global study of state building and military/political transformations in this era, see Victor Lieberman, *Strange Parallels: Southeast Asia in Global Context*, volume two (2009).

On MyHistoryLab

Study and Review on MyHistoryLab

Critical Thinking Questions

1. What recurring patterns and factors can be seen in the decline of the three great Muslim empires of the Early Modern era?
2. Why did the Mughal empire decline earlier than the Ottoman empire?
3. Discuss the ways in which gunpowder, cannons, and muskets played critical roles in the rise, rivalries and decline of the Ottoman, Safavid, and Mughal empires, and their eclipse by the growing power of expansionist European states.
4. In what ways were the impact of Islamic beliefs and practices on politics, society, and artistic expression similar in the three empires and in what major ways did they differ?
5. In which of the empires were Islamic influences the most pervasive?
6. Under which dynasty was the influence of non-Islamic religions more prominent? In what ways and why?
7. What were some durable results of the Muslim empires?

23 Asian Transitions in an Age of Global Change

LEARNING OBJECTIVES

23.1 Where were the major centers of the Indian Ocean trading system located? Which products exchanged in this system did the Portuguese seek to use force to monopolize and ship back to Europe? How successful were they, and why? p. 522

23.2 Why were European merchants and missionaries so interested in establishing relations with and bases in China, and why were the Chinese so resistant to their overtures? p. 529

23.3 Why did the rulers of Japan initially welcome European traders and missionaries, and why did they ultimately expel all but the Dutch? p. 538

After savoring the exhilaration that only those who have made a breakthrough discovery can know, Vasco da Gama and his Portuguese crews received a number of rude shocks on the last legs of their epic voyage to India in 1498. Da Gama's exploratory probes were conducted in sailing ships that were a good deal smaller than the Portuguese merchant vessel depicted arriving in Japan a century later in the wonderful silk screen painting (Figure 23.8) on page 541. After nearly five months at sea, his tiny flotilla of four ships made its way through the treacherous waters off the Cape of Good Hope on the southern tip of Africa and sailed into the Indian Ocean.

After rounding the cape, Da Gama's expedition followed the African coastline northward in search of other Christians and a port to take on fresh supplies (Map 23.1). To their chagrin, most of the towns they encountered were controlled by Muslim Arabs. Some of the Arabs, including

FIGURE 23.1 Vasco Da Gama's arrival in Calicut on India's Malabar coast as depicted in a 16th-century European tapestry. As the pomp and splendor captured in the scene convey, Da Gama's voyage was regarded by European contemporaries as a major turning point in world history.

> **Watch the Video Series on MyHistoryLab**
>
> Learn about some key topics related to this chapter with the *MyHistoryLab Video Series: Key Topics in World History*

those at Mombasa—the largest commercial center on the coast—became hostile once they realized that the Portuguese were Christians. Conversations with the much friendlier sultan, traders, and townspeople farther north at Malindi, however, left no doubt that Da Gama's expedition had indeed discovered a sea route from Europe to the fabled Indies.

Da Gama and his compatriots were, of course, delighted and perhaps a bit awed by what they had achieved even before they crossed to India. Their very entry into the Indian Ocean meant that they had won a momentous victory over Spain. They had bested their Iberian rivals in a contest to find a sea route to the East Indies that both nations had pursued at great expense for decades. And their triumph was all the more satisfying because they had proved correct the long-standing conviction of Portuguese navigators and mapmakers that the Indian Ocean could be reached by sailing around Africa. And that in turn confirmed the Portuguese claim that Christopher Columbus's much-touted voyage across the Atlantic had been a failure. Columbus had not reached the Indies after all. He had made landfall at islands hitherto unknown to the Europeans and of undetermined value.

Learning that the goal of Da Gama's expedition was India, the sultan at Malindi generously offered the Portuguese captain general a pilot to guide his ships across the Arabian Sea to the lands of spices and gems. Nearly a month later, Da Gama's ships arrived at Calicut on India's Malabar Coast (Map 23.1). An ancient and thriving commercial emporium controlled by a Hindu ruler, whom the Portuguese at first thought might be a Christian, Calicut seemed an ideal place to conclude their long voyage from Lisbon. Da Gama and his crew scrambled ashore eager to trade for the spices, fine textiles, and other Asian products that were among the main objectives of the voyages of exploration (see Figure 23.1 above). Delighted by the fine quality and abundance of the products from all over Asia that were available in the town's great marketplace, the Portuguese were startled to learn that the local merchants had little interest in the products they had brought to trade. In fact, their cast-iron pots, coarse cloth, and glass and coral beads elicited little more than sneers from the merchants they approached.

Da Gama and his crew faced the humbling prospect of returning home to Lisbon with little proof that they had reached Asia and begun to tap its legendary wealth. Reluctantly, they concluded that they had little choice but to use the small supply of silver bullion they had brought along for emergencies. They found that the Asian merchants were quite willing to take their precious metal. But they also realized that their meager supply of bullion would not go very far toward filling the holds of their ships with Asian treasures. ■

Much of the enterprise that occupied the Europeans who went out to Asia in the 16th and 17th centuries, which is one of the major themes of the chapter that follows, was devoted to working out the implications of that first encounter in Calicut. The very fact of Da Gama's arrival demonstrated not only the seaworthiness of their **caravels** (ships) but also that the Europeans' needs and curiosity could drive them halfway around the world. Their stops at Calicut and ports on the eastern coast of Africa also confirmed reports of earlier travelers that the Portuguese had arrived in east Africa and south and southeast Asia long after their Muslim rivals. This disconcerting discovery promised resistance to Portuguese trading and empire building in Asia. It also meant major obstacles to their plans for converting the peoples of the area to Roman Catholicism. The Portuguese and the other Europeans who came after them found that their Muslim adversaries greatly outnumbered them and had long-standing and well-entrenched political and economic connections from east Africa to the

caravels Slender, long-hulled vessels utilized by Portuguese; highly maneuverable and able to sail against the wind; key to development of Portuguese trade empire in Asia.

1350 C.E.	1500 C.E.	1550 C.E.	1600 C.E.	1650 C.E.	1700 C.E.
1368 Ming dynasty comes to power in China **1368–1398** Reign of the Hongwu emperor **1390** Ming restrictions on overseas commerce **1403–1424** Reign of the Yongle emperor in China **1405–1433** Zheng He expeditions from China to southeast Asia, India, and east Africa **1498–1499** Vasco da Gama opens the sea route around Africa to Asia	**1507** Portuguese defeat combined Muslim war fleet near Diu off western India **1510** Portuguese conquest of Goa in western India **1511** Portuguese conquer Malacca on the tip of Malayan peninsula **1540s** Francis Xavier makes mass converts in India	**1573** End of the Ashikaga shogunate **1573–1620** Reign of the Wanli emperor **1580s** Jesuits arrive in China **1590** Hideyoshi unifies Japan **1592** First Japanese invasion of Korea **1597** Second Japanese invasion of Korea	**1600s** Dutch and British assault on Portuguese empire in Asia; decline of Portuguese power **1603** Tokugawa shogunate established **1614** Christianity banned in Japan **1619–1620** Dutch East India Company established at Batavia on Java **1640s** Japan moves into self-imposed isolation **1641** Dutch capture Malacca from Portuguese; Dutch confined to Deshima Island off Nagasaki **1644** End of the Ming dynasty; Manchu Qing dynasty rules China	**1662–1722** Reign of the Kangxi emperor in China	**1755–1757** Dutch become paramount power on Java; Qing conquest of Mongolia

Philippines. As we shall see, the Portuguese soon concluded that—just as the local merchants and rulers had feared—they would have to resort to military force to break into the vast Indian Ocean trading system. Although Da Gama's voyage marked a major turning point for Western Europe, its impact on Asia was much less decisive. As was the case with the Mughal and Safavid empires (see Chapter 22), the central themes in the history of Asian civilizations in the 16th and 17th centuries often had little or nothing to do with European expansion. The development of Asian states and empires emerged from long-term processes rooted in the inner workings of these ancient civilizations and in their interactions with neighboring states and nomadic peoples. Although the European presence was felt in each of the areas considered in this chapter, the impact of Europe's global expansion was of secondary importance except in the islands of southeast Asia, which were especially vulnerable to Western sea power. Most Asian rulers, merchants, and religious leaders refused to take seriously the potential threat posed by what was, after all, a handful of strangers from across the world.

THE ASIAN TRADING WORLD AND THE COMING OF THE EUROPEANS

> In the centuries following Da Gama's voyage, most European enterprise in the Indian Ocean centered on efforts to find the most profitable ways to carry Asian products back to Europe. Some Europeans went to Asia not for personal gain but to convert others to Christianity, and these missionaries, as well as some traders, settled in coastal enclaves.

23.1 Where were the major centers of the Indian Ocean trading system located? Which products exchanged in this system did the Portuguese seek to use force to monopolize and ship back to Europe? How successful were they, and why?

As later voyages by Portuguese fleets revealed, Calicut and the ports of east Africa, which Vasco da Gama had found on the initial foray into Asia, made up only a small segment of a larger network of commercial exchange and cultural interaction. This trading system stretched thousands of miles from the Middle East and Africa along all the coasts of the massive Asian continent. Both the products exchanged in this network and the main routes followed by those who sailed it had been established for centuries—in many cases, millennia.

In general, the **Asian sea trading network** can be broken down into three main zones, each of which was focused on major centers of handicraft manufacture (Map 23.1). In the west was an Arab zone anchored on the glass, carpets, and tapestries of the Islamic heartlands at the head of the Red Sea and the Persian Gulf. India, with its superb cotton textiles, dominated the central portions of the system. China, which excelled in producing paper, porcelain, and silk textiles, formed the eastern pole. In between or on the fringes of the three great manufacturing centers were areas such as Japan, the mainland kingdoms and island states of southeast Asia, and the port cities of east Africa that fed mainly raw materials—precious metals, foods, and forest products—into the trading network.

Of the raw materials circulating in the system, the broadest demand and highest prices were paid for spices, which came mainly from Ceylon (Sri Lanka in the present day) and the islands at the eastern end of what is today the Indonesian archipelago. Long-distance trade was largely in high-priced commodities such as spices, ivory from Africa, and precious stones. But silk and cotton textiles also were traded over long distances. Bulk items, such as rice, livestock, and timber, normally were exchanged among the ports within more localized networks in each of the main trading zones.

Asian sea trading network Prior to intervention of Europeans, consisted of three zones: Arab zone based on glass, carpets, and tapestries; India zone based on cotton textiles; China zone based on paper, porcelain, and silks.

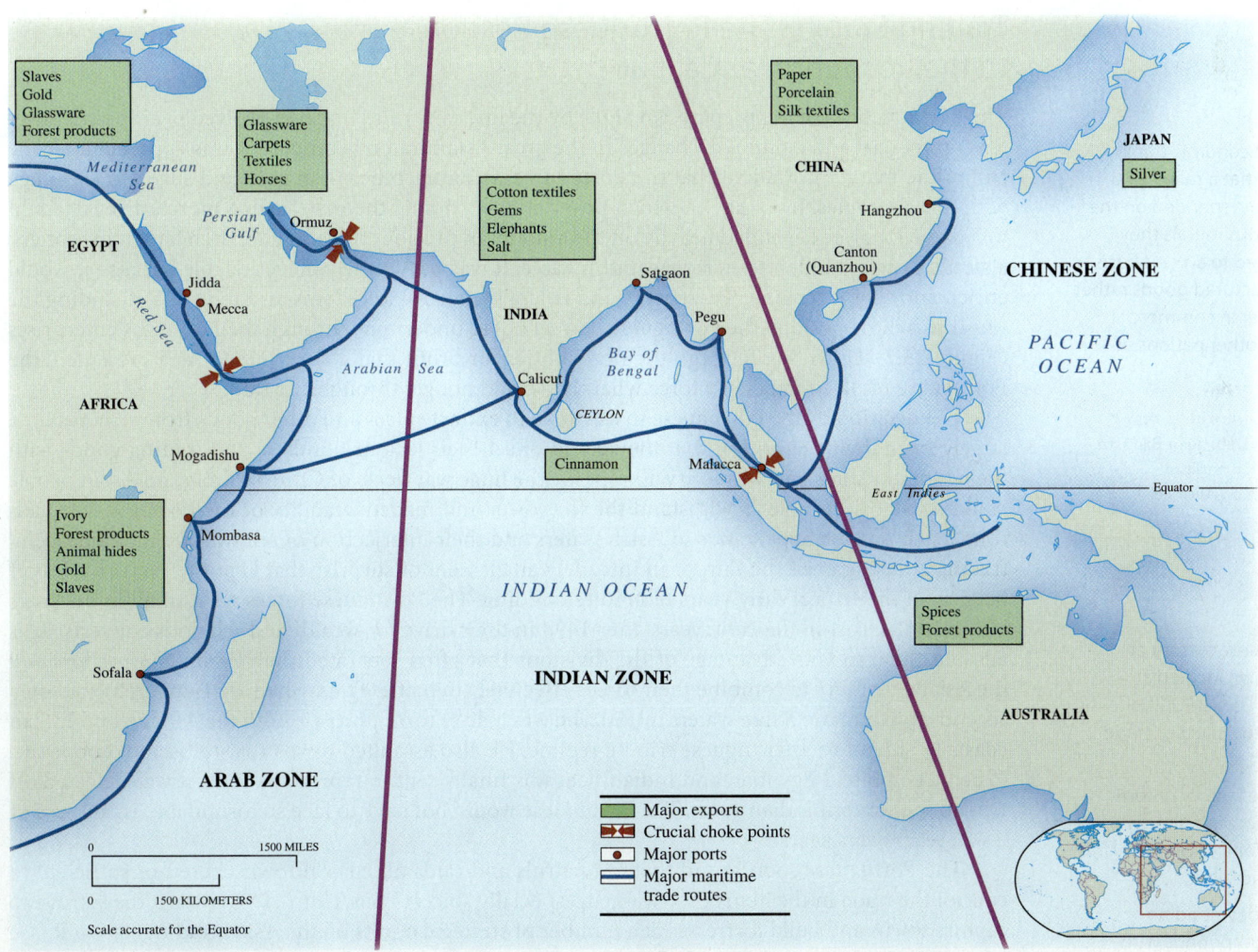

MAP 23.1 Routes and Major Products Exchanged in the Asian Trading Network, c. 1500 By the Early Modern era the ancient trading network that encompassed the Indian Ocean and neighboring seas from the Mediterranean to the North China sea had expanded greatly in the volume of shipping and goods traded from the Middle East to China as well as in the number of port cities engaged in local and intercontinental commerce.

Since ancient times, monsoon winds and the nature of the ships and navigational instruments available to sailors had dictated the main trade routes in the Asian network. Much navigation was of the coasting variety, that is, sailing along the shoreline and charting distances and location with reference to towns and natural landmarks. The Arabs and Chinese, who had compasses and large, well-built ships, could cross large expanses of open water such as the Arabian and South China seas. But even they preferred established coastal routes rather than the largely uncharted and less predictable open seas. As the Portuguese quickly learned, there were several crucial points where segments of the trade converged or where geography funneled it into narrow areas. The mouths of the Red Sea and Persian Gulf were two of these points, as were the Straits of Malacca, which separated mainland from island southeast Asia (Map 23.1).

Two general characteristics of the trading system at the time of the Portuguese arrival were critical to European attempts to regulate and dominate it. First, there was no central control. Second, military force was usually absent from commercial exchanges within it. Although Arab sailors and merchants were found in ports throughout much of the network, they had no sense of common cause. They sailed and traded to provide for their own livelihood and to make profits for the princes or merchants who financed their expeditions. The same was true for the Chinese, southeast Asian, and Indian merchants and sailors who were concentrated in particular segments of the trading complex. Because all the peoples participating in the network had something to trade for the products they wanted from others, exchanges within the system were largely peaceful. Trading vessels were lightly armed mainly for protection against attack by pirates.

Trading Empire: The Portuguese Response to the Encounter at Calicut

The Portuguese were not prepared to abide by the informal rules that had evolved over the centuries for commercial and cultural exchanges in the great Asian trading complex. It was apparent after the trip to the market in Calicut that the Portuguese had little, other than gold and silver, to exchange with Asian peoples. In an age in which prominent economic theorists, called **mercantilists**, taught that a state's power depended heavily on the amount of precious metals a monarch had in his coffers, a steady flow of bullion to Asia was unthinkable. It was particularly objectionable because it would enrich and thus strengthen merchants and rulers from rival kingdoms and religions, including the Muslims, whose position the Portuguese had set out to undermine through their overseas enterprises (Figure 23.2). Unwilling to forgo the possibilities for profit that a sea route to Asia presented, the Portuguese resolved to take by force what they could not get through fair trade.

The decision by the Portuguese to use force to extract spices and other goods from Asia resulted largely from their realization that they could offset their lack of numbers and trading goods with their superior ships and weaponry. Except for the huge war fleets of Chinese junks, no Asian people could muster fleets able to withstand the firepower and maneuverability of the Portuguese squadrons. Their sudden appearance in Asian waters and their interjection of sea warfare into a peaceful trading system gained the European intruders an element of surprise that kept their adversaries off balance in the critical early years of empire building. The Portuguese forces were small in numbers but united at least in the early years after 1498 in their drive for wealth and religious converts. This allowed them to take advantage of the divisions that often separated their Asian competitors and the Asians' inability to combine their forces effectively in battle. Thus, when Da Gama returned on a second expedition to Asian waters in 1502, he was able to force ports on both the African and Indian coasts to submit to a Portuguese tribute regime. He also assaulted towns that refused to cooperate. When a combined Egyptian and Indian fleet was finally sent in reprisal in 1509, it was defeated off Diu on the western Indian coast. The Portuguese would not have to face so formidable an alliance of Asian sea powers again.

The Portuguese soon found that sea patrols and raids on coastal towns were not sufficient to control the trade in the items they wanted, especially spices. Thus, from 1507 onward they strove to capture towns and build fortresses at a number of strategic points on the Asian trading network (see Map 23.2). In that year they took **Ormuz** at the southern end of the Persian Gulf; in 1510 they captured **Goa** on the western Indian coast. Most critical of all, in the next year they successfully stormed Malacca on the tip of the Malayan peninsula. These ports served both as naval bases for Portuguese fleets patrolling Asian waters and as **factories**, or warehouses where spices and other products could

---

mercantilists Economic thinkers who argued that a ruler's and kingdom's power depended on the amount of precious metals they controlled. This led to an emphasis on using manufactured goods rather than gold or silver in commercial exchanges with other nations or empires.

Read the Document on MyHistoryLab: Jean Baptiste Colbert, "Mercantilism: Dissertation on Alliances"

Ormuz Portuguese factory or fortified trade town located at southern end of Persian Gulf; site for forcible entry into Asian sea trade network.

Goa Portuguese factory or fortified trade town located on western India coast; site for forcible entry into Asian sea trade network.

factories European trading fortresses and compounds with resident merchants; utilized throughout Portuguese trading empire to assure secure landing places and commerce.

Read the Document on MyHistoryLab: Duarte Barbosa, Accounts of Duarte Barbosa's Journeys to Africa and India

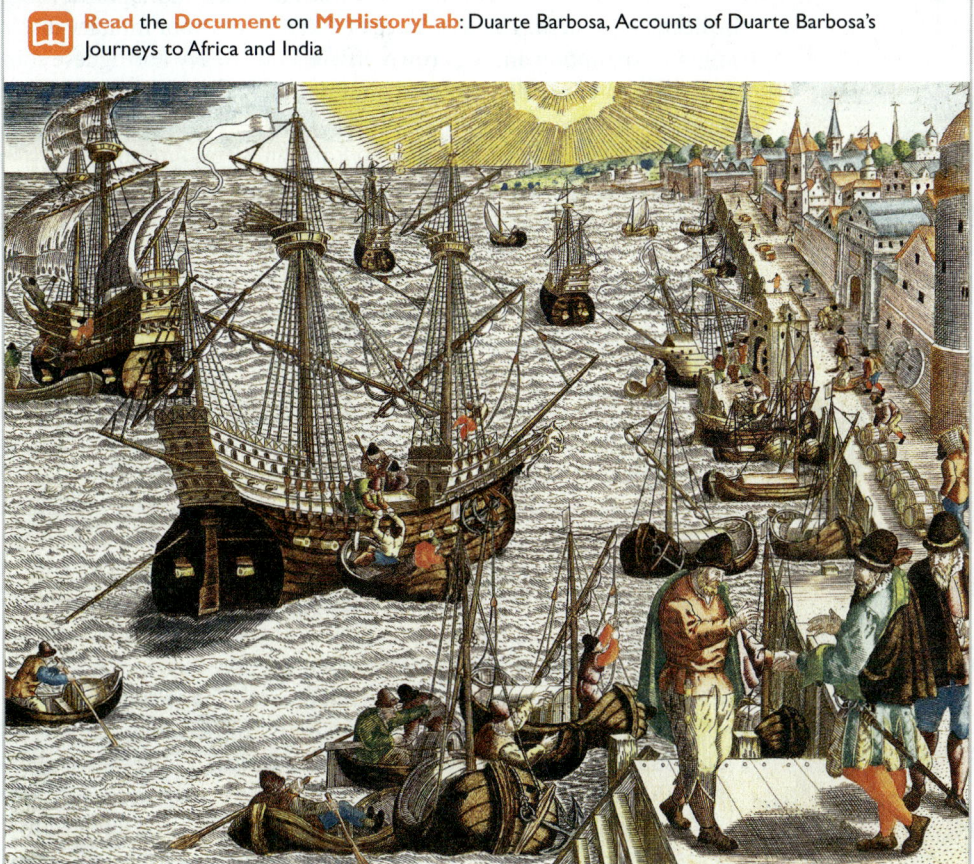

FIGURE 23.2 In the 15th and 16th centuries, the port of Lisbon in tiny Portugal was one of the great centers of international commerce and European overseas exploration. Although aspects of the early, streamlined caravel design can be detected in the ships pictured here, additional square sails, higher fore and aft castles, and numerous cannons projecting from holes cut in the ships' sides exemplify a later stage of naval development.

be stored until they were shipped to Europe or elsewhere in Asia. Ships, ports, and factories became the key components of a Portuguese trading empire that was financed and officially directed by the kings of Portugal, but often actually controlled by Portuguese in Asia and their local allies.

The aim of the empire was to establish Portuguese monopoly control over key Asian products, particularly spices such as nutmeg and cinnamon (Figure 23.3). Ideally, all the spices produced were to be shipped in Portuguese vessels to Asian or European markets. There they would be sold at high prices, which the Portuguese could dictate because they controlled the supply of these goods. The Portuguese also sought, with little success, to impose a licensing system on all merchant ships that traded in the Indian Ocean from Ormuz to Malacca. The combination of monopoly and the licensing system, backed by force, was intended to give the Portuguese control of a sizable portion of the Asian trading network.

Portuguese Vulnerability and the Rise of the Dutch and English Trading Empires

The plans for empire that the Portuguese drew up on paper never became reality. They managed for some decades to control some of the flow of spices, such as nutmeg and mace, which were grown in very limited areas. But a monopoly of the market in key condiments, such as pepper and cloves, eluded them. At times the Portuguese resorted to severe punishments such as cutting off the hands of the rival traders and ships' crews caught transporting spices in defiance of their monopoly. But they simply

FIGURE 23.3 Although today nutmeg is a minor condiment, in the Early Modern era it was a treasured and widely used spice. In this manuscript illustration from the 16th century, slices of an oversized nutmeg are being weighed in preparation for sale on the international market.

Batavia Dutch fortress located after 1620 on the island of Java.

Dutch trading empire The Dutch system extending into Asia with fortified towns and factories, warships on patrol, and monopoly control of a limited number of products.

Read the Document on MyHistoryLab: The English in south Asia and the Indian Ocean early 1600s

did not have the soldiers or the ships to sustain their monopolies, much less the licensing system. The resistance of Asian rivals, poor military discipline, rampant corruption among crown officials, and heavy Portuguese shipping losses caused by overloading and poor design had taken a heavy toll on the empire by the end of the 16th century.

The overextended and declining Portuguese trading empire proved no match for the Dutch and English rivals, whose war fleets challenged it in the early 17th century. Of the two, the Dutch emerged, at least in the short term, as the victors. They captured the critical Portuguese port and fortress at Malacca and built a new port of their own in 1620 at **Batavia** on the island of Java. Because it was much closer to the island sources of key spices (see Map 23.2), the location of Batavia indicated an improved European knowledge of Asian geography. It was also the consequence of the Dutch decision to concentrate on the monopoly control of certain spices rather than on Asian trade more generally. The English, who fought hard but lost the struggle for control of the Spice Islands, were forced to fall back to India.

The **Dutch trading empire** (Map 23.2) was made up of the same basic components as the Portuguese: fortified towns and factories, warships on patrol, and monopoly control of a limited number of products. But the Dutch had more numerous and better armed ships and went about the business of monopoly control in a much more systematic fashion. To regulate the supply of cloves, nutmeg, and mace, for example, they uprooted the plants that produced these spices on islands they did not control. They also forcibly removed and at times executed island peoples who cultivated these spices without Dutch supervision and dared to sell them to their trading rivals.

Although the profits from the sale of these spices in Europe in the mid-17th century helped sustain Holland's "golden age," the Dutch found that the greatest profits in the long run could be gained from peacefully working themselves into the long-established Asian trading system. The demand for spices declined and their futile efforts to gain control over crops such as pepper that were grown in many places became more and more expensive. In response, the Dutch came to rely mainly (as they had long done in Europe) on the fees they charged for transporting products from one area in Asia to another. They also depended on profits gained from buying Asian products, such as cloth, in one area and trading them in other areas for goods that could be sold in Europe at inflated prices. The English also adopted these peaceful trading patterns, although their enterprises were concentrated along the coasts of India and on the cotton cloth trade (discussed in Chapter 18) rather than on the spices of southeast Asia.

Going Ashore: European Tribute Systems in Asia

Their ships and guns allowed the Europeans to force their way into the Asian trading network in the 16th and 17th centuries. But as they moved inland and away from the sea, their military advantages and their ability to dominate the Asian peoples rapidly disappeared. Because the vastly superior numbers of Asian armies offset the Europeans' advantage in weapons and organization for waging war on land, even small kingdoms such as those on Java and in mainland southeast Asia were able to resist European inroads into their domains. In the larger empires such as those in China, India, and Persia, and when confronted by martial cultures such as Japan's, the Europeans quickly learned their place. That they were often reduced to kowtowing or humbling themselves before the thrones of Asian potentates is demonstrated by the instructions given by a Dutch envoy about the proper behavior for a visit to the Japanese court:

> Our ministers have no other instruction to take there except to look to the wishes of that brave, superb, precise nation in order to please it in everything, and by no means to think on anything which might cause greater antipathy to us . . . . That consequently the Company's ministers frequenting the scrupulous state each year must above all go armed in modesty, humility, courtesy, and amity, always being the lesser.

View the Image on MyHistoryLab: View of Hormuz

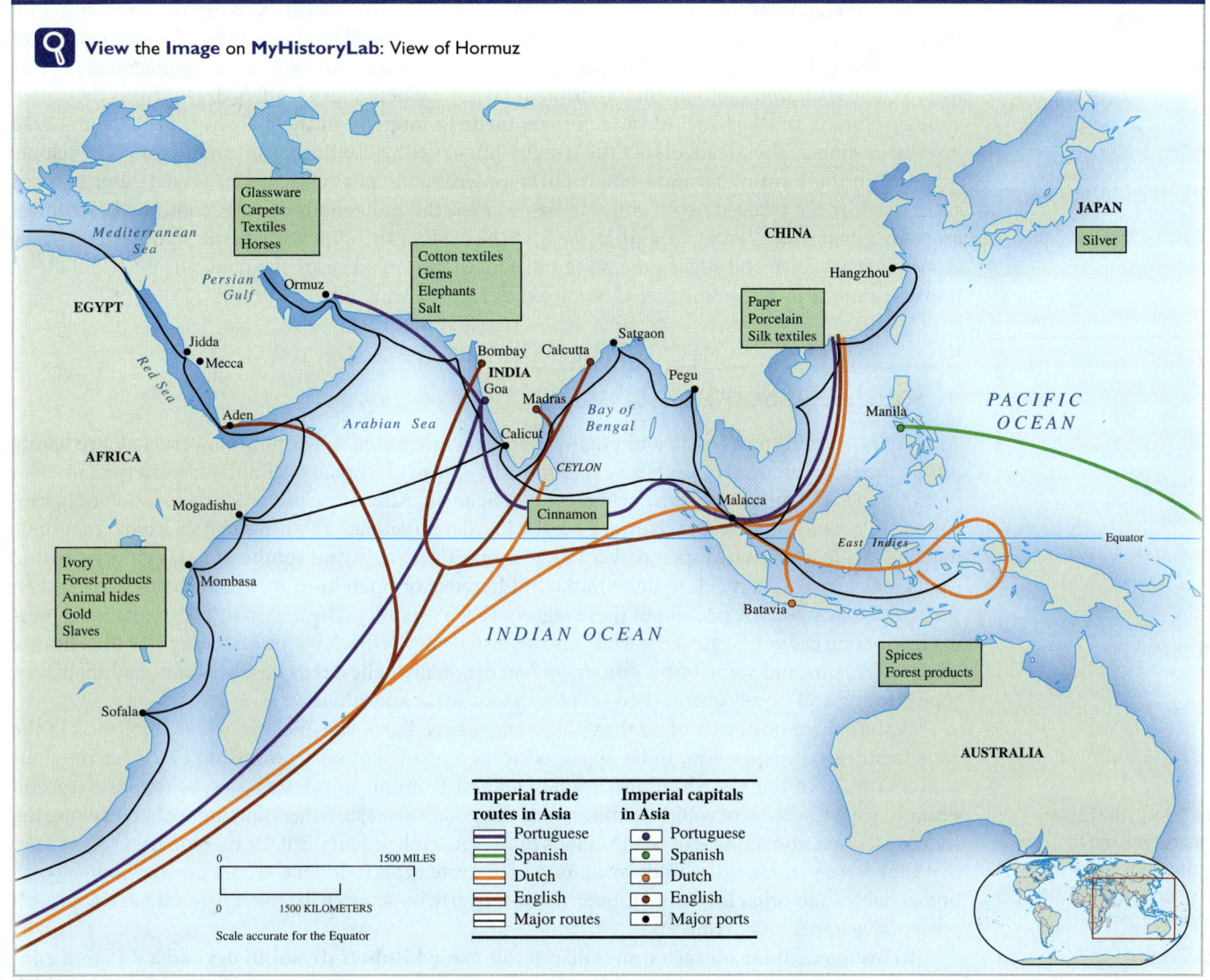

MAP 23.2 **The Pattern of Early European Expansion in Asia** The differing routes and choice of fortified outposts adopted by successive European nations as they sought to tap directly into the Indian Ocean trading network reflect the greater information regarding centers of production that latecomers, such as the Dutch and English possessed, relative to the pioneering Portuguese.

In certain situations, however, the Europeans were drawn inland away from their forts, factories, and war fleets in the early centuries of their expansion into Asia. The Portuguese, and the Dutch after them, felt compelled to conquer the coastal areas of Ceylon to control the production and sale of cinnamon, which grew in the forests of the southwest portions of that island. The Dutch moved slowly inland from their base at Batavia into the highlands of western Java. They discovered that this area was ideal for growing coffee, which was in great demand in Europe by the 17th century. By the mid-18th century, the Dutch not only controlled the coffee-growing areas but were the paramount power on Java.

The Spanish, taking advantage of the fact that the Philippine Islands lay in the half of the world the pope had given them to explore and settle in 1493, invaded the islands in the 1560s. The conquest of **Luzon** and the northern islands was facilitated by the fact that the animistic inhabitants lived in small states the Spanish could subjugate one by one. The repeated failure of Spanish expeditions to conquer the southern island of **Mindanao**, which was ruled by a single kingdom whose Muslim rulers were determined to resist Christian dominance, dramatically underscores the limits of the Europeans' ability to project their power on land in this era.

Luzon Northern island of Philippines; conquered by Spain during the 1560s; site of major Catholic missionary effort.

Mindanao Southern island of Philippines; a Muslim kingdom that was able to successfully resist Spanish conquest.

CHAPTER 23 Asian Transitions in an Age of Global Change 527

In each area where the Europeans went ashore in the early centuries of expansion, they set up tribute regimes that closely resembled those the Spanish imposed on the Native American peoples of the New World (see Chapter 20). The European overlords were content to let the indigenous peoples live in their traditional settlements, controlled largely by hereditary leaders drawn from their own communities. In most areas, little attempt was made to interfere in the daily lives of the conquered peoples as long as their leaders met the tribute quotas set by the European conquerors. The tribute was paid in the form of agricultural products grown by the peasantry under forced labor systems supervised by the peasants' own elites. In some cases, the indigenous peoples continued to harvest crops they had produced for centuries, such as the bark of the cinnamon plant. In other areas new crops, such as coffee and sugar cane, were introduced. But in all cases, the demands for tribute took into account the local peasants' need to raise the crops on which they subsisted.

Spreading the Faith: The Missionary Enterprise in South and Southeast Asia

Although the Protestant Dutch and English were little interested in winning converts to Christianity during the early centuries of overseas expansion, the spread of Roman Catholicism was a fundamental part of the global mission of the Portuguese and Spanish. After the widespread conversion of Native American peoples, the meager returns from the Iberian missionary offensive in Asia were disappointing. The fact that Islam had spread over much of maritime south and southeast Asia centuries before Da Gama's arrival had much to do with the indifference or open hostility the Portuguese met when they tried to convert the peoples of these regions to Christianity. The dream of a Christian Asia joining the Iberian crusade against the Muslims was also dealt a setback by the discovery that the Hindus, whom Da Gama and some of his entourage had originally believed to be Christians, had their own sophisticated and deeply entrenched set of religious ideas and rituals.

Despite these obstacles, of all the Asian areas where European enclaves were established in the early centuries of expansion, India appeared to be one of the most promising fields for religious conversion. From the 1540s onward, Franciscan and Dominican missionaries, as well as the Jesuit **Francis Xavier**, who were willing to minister to the poor, low-caste fishers and untouchables along the southwest coast, converted tens of thousands of the local inhabitants. But the missionaries soon found that they were making little headway among high-caste groups. In fact, taboos against contact with untouchables and other low-caste groups made it nearly impossible for the missionaries to approach prospective upper-caste converts.

To overcome these obstacles, an Italian Jesuit named **Robert di Nobili** devised a different conversion strategy in the early 1600s. He learned several Indian languages, including Sanskrit, which allowed him to read the sacred texts of the Hindus. He donned the garments worn by Indian brahmans and adopted a vegetarian diet. All these measures were calculated to win over the upper-caste Hindus in south India, where he was based. Di Nobili reasoned that if he succeeded in Christianizing the high-caste Hindus, they would then bring the lower Hindu castes into the fold. But, he argued, because the ancient Hindu religion was sophisticated and deeply entrenched, Indian brahmans and other high-caste groups would listen only to those who adopted their ways. Meat eaters would be seen as defiling; those who were unfamiliar with the Hindus' sacred texts would be considered ignorant.

Despite some early successes, di Nobili's strategy was undone by the refusal of high-caste Hindu converts to worship with low-caste groups and to give up many of their traditional beliefs and religious rituals. Rival missionary orders, particularly the Dominicans and Franciscans, denounced his approach. In assimilating to Hindu culture, they claimed, di Nobili and his co-workers, not the Indians, were the ones who had been converted. His rivals also pointed out that the refusal of di Nobili's high-caste converts to worship with untouchable Christians defied one of the central tenets of Christianity: the equality of all believers before God. His rivals finally won the ear of the pope, and di Nobili was forbidden to preach in India. Deprived of his energetic participation and knowledge of Indian ways, the mission in south India quickly collapsed, although he continued to translate Indian texts and eventually died in India.

Beyond socially stigmatized groups, such as the untouchables, the conversion of the general populace in Asia occurred only in isolated areas. Perhaps the greatest successes of the Christian missions occurred in the northern islands of the Philippines, which had not previously been exposed to a world religion such as Islam or Buddhism. Because the Spanish had conquered the island of Luzon

Xavier, Francis [zAY vyuhr] Spanish Jesuit missionary; worked in India in 1540s among the outcaste and lower caste groups; made little headway among elites.

 **Read** the **Document** on **MyHistoryLab**: Saint Francis Xavier on Conversion of the Indians

Nobili, Robert di (1577–1656) Italian Jesuit missionary; worked in India during the early 1600s; introduced strategy to convert elites first; strategy later widely adopted by Jesuits in various parts of Asia; mission eventually failed.

and the smaller islands to the south, and then governed them as part of their vast intercontinental empire, they were able to launch a major missionary effort. The friars, as the priests and brothers who went out to convert and govern the rural populace were called, became the main channel for transmitting European influences. The friars first converted local Filipino leaders. These leaders then directed their followers to build new settlements that were centered, like those in Iberia and the New World, on town squares where the local church, the residences of the missionary fathers, and government offices were located. Beyond tending to the spiritual needs of the villagers in their congregation, the friars served as government officials.

Like the Native Americans of Spain's New World empire, most Filipinos were formally converted to Catholicism. But also like the Native Americans, the Filipinos' brand of Christianity represented a creative blend of their traditional beliefs and customs and the religion preached by the friars. Because key tenets of the Christian faith were taught in Spanish for fear that they would be corrupted if put in the local languages, it is doubtful that most of the converts had a very good grasp of Christian beliefs. Many adopted Christianity because Spanish dominance and their own leaders' conversion gave them little choice. Others embraced the new faith because they believed that the Christian God could protect them from illness or because they were taken with the notion that they would be equal to their Spanish overlords in heaven.

Almost all Filipinos clung to their traditional ways and in the process seriously compromised Christian beliefs and practices. The peoples of the islands continued public bathing, which the missionaries condemned as immodest, and refused to give up ritual drinking. They also continued to commune with deceased members of their families, often in sessions that were disguised as public recitations of the rosary. Thus, even in the Asian area where European control was the strongest and pressures for acculturation to European ways the greatest, much of the preconquest way of life and approach to the world was maintained.

MING CHINA: A GLOBAL MISSION REFUSED

23.2 Why were European merchants and missionaries so interested in establishing relations with and bases in China, and why were the Chinese so resistant to their overtures?

Zhu Yuanzhang, a military commander of peasant origins who founded the Ming dynasty, had suffered a great deal under the Mongol yoke. Both his parents and two of his brothers had died in a plague in 1344, and he and a remaining brother were reduced to begging for the land in which to bury the rest of their family. Threatened with the prospect of starvation in one of the many famines that ravaged the countryside in the later, corruption-riddled reigns of Mongol emperors, Zhu alternated between begging and living in a Buddhist monastery to survive. When the neighboring countryside rose in rebellion in the late 1340s, Zhu left the monastery to join a rebel band. His courage in combat and his natural capacity as a leader soon made him one of the more prominent of several rebel warlords attempting to overthrow the Yuan dynasty. After protracted military struggles against rival rebel claimants to the throne and the Mongol rulers themselves, Zhu's armies conquered most of China. Zhu declared himself the **Hongwu** emperor in 1368. He reigned for 30 years.

Immediately after he seized the throne, Zhu launched an effort to rid China of all traces of the "barbarian" Mongols. Mongol dress was discarded, Mongol names were dropped by those who had adopted them and were removed from buildings and court records, and Mongol palaces and administrative buildings in some areas were raided and sacked. The nomads themselves fled or were driven beyond the Great Wall, where Ming military expeditions pursued them on several occasions.

Another Scholar-Gentry Revival

Because the Hongwu emperor, like the founder of the earlier Han dynasty, was from a peasant family and thus poorly educated, he viewed the scholar-gentry with some suspicion. But he also realized that their cooperation was essential to the full revival of Chinese civilization. Scholars well versed in the Confucian classics were again appointed to the very highest positions in the imperial government. The generous state subsidies that had supported the imperial academies in the capital and the regional colleges were fully restored. Most critically, the civil service examination system, which the Mongols

---

With the restoration of ethnic Chinese rule and the reunification of the country under the Ming dynasty (1368–1644), Chinese civilization enjoyed a new age of splendor. Renewed agrarian and commercial growth supported a population that was the largest of any center of civilization at the time, probably exceeding that of all Western Europe.

Hongwu First Ming emperor in 1368; originally of peasant lineage; original name Zhu Yuanzhang; drove out Mongol influence; restored position of scholar-gentry.

had discontinued, was reinstated and greatly expanded. In the Ming era and the Qing that followed, the examinations played a greater role in determining entry into the Chinese bureaucracy than had been the case under any earlier dynasty.

In the Ming era, the examination system was routinized and made more complex than before. Prefectural, or county, exams were held in two out of three years. The exams were given in large compounds, like the one depicted in Figure 23.4, that were surrounded by walls and watchtowers from which the examiners could keep an eye on the thousands of candidates. Each candidate was assigned a small cubicle where he struggled to answer the questions, slept, and ate over the several days that it took to complete the arduous exam. Those who passed and received the lowest degree were eligible to take the next level of exams, which were given in the provincial capitals every three years. Only the most gifted and ambitious went on because the process was fiercely competitive—in some years as many as 4000 candidates competed for 150 degrees. Success at the provincial level brought a rise in status and opened the way for appointments to positions in the middle levels of the imperial bureaucracy. It also permitted particularly talented scholars to take the imperial examinations, which were given in the capital every three years. Those who passed the imperial exams were eligible for the highest posts in the realm and were the most revered of all Chinese, except members of the royal family.

Reform: Hongwu's Efforts to Root Out Abuses in Court Politics

Hongwu was mindful of his dependence on a well-educated and loyal scholar-gentry for the day-to-day administration of the empire. But he sought to put clear limits on their influence and to institute reforms that would check the abuses of other factions at court. Early in his reign, Hongwu abolished the position of chief minister, which had formerly been the key link between the many ministries of the central government. The powers that had been amassed by those who occupied this office were transferred to the emperor. Hongwu also tried to impress all officials with the honesty, loyalty, and discipline he expected from them by introducing the practice of public beatings for bureaucrats found guilty of corruption or incompetence. Officials charged with misdeeds were paraded before the assembled courtiers and beaten a specified number of times on their bare buttocks. Many died of

FIGURE 23.4 A 19th-century engraving shows the cubicles in which Chinese students and bureaucrats took the imperial civil service examinations in the capital at Beijing. Candidates were confined to the cubicles for days and completed their exams under the constant surveillance of official proctors. They brought their own food, slept in the cubicles, and were disqualified if they were found talking to others taking the exams or going outside the compound where the exams were being given.

the wounds they received in the ordeal. Those who survived never recovered from the humiliation. To a certain extent, the humiliation was shared by all the scholar-gentry by virtue of the very fact that such degrading punishments could be meted out to any of them.

Hongwu also introduced measures to cut down on the court factionalism and never-ending conspiracies that had eroded the power of earlier dynasties. He decreed that the emperor's wives should come only from humble family origins. This was intended to put an end to the power plays of the consorts from high-ranking families, who built palace cliques that were centered on their influential aristocratic relatives. He warned against allowing eunuchs to occupy positions of independent power and sought to limit their numbers within the Forbidden City. To prevent plots against the ruler and fights over succession, Hongwu established the practice of exiling all potential rivals to the throne to estates in the provinces, and he forbade them to become involved in political affairs. On the darker side, Hongwu condoned thought control, as when he had some sections from Mencius's writings that displeased him deleted forever from the writings included on the imperial exams. Although many of these measures went far to keep peace at court under Hongwu and his strong successor, the Yongle emperor (r. 1403–1424), they were allowed to lapse under later, less capable rulers, with devastating consequences for the Ming empire.

A Return to Scholar-Gentry Social Dominance

Perhaps because his lowly origins and personal suffering made him sensitive to the plight of the peasantry, Hongwu introduced measures that would improve the lot of the common people. Like most strong emperors, he promoted public works projects, including dike building and the extension of irrigation systems aimed at improving the farmers' yields. To bring new lands under cultivation and

DOCUMENT

Exam Questions as a Mirror of Chinese Values

THE SUBJECTS AND SPECIFIC LEARNING TESTED on the Chinese civil service exams give us insight into the behavior and attitudes expected of the literate, ruling classes of what was perhaps the best-educated preindustrial civilization. Sample questions from these exams can tell us a good deal about what sorts of knowledge were considered important and what kinds of skills were necessary for those who aspired to successful careers in the most prestigious and potentially the most lucrative field open to Chinese youths: administrative service in the imperial bureaucracy. The very fact that such a tiny portion of the Chinese male population could take the exams and very few of those successfully pass them says a lot about gender roles and elitism in Chinese society. In addition, the often decisive role of a student's calligraphy—the skill with which he was able to brush the Chinese characters—reflects the emphasis the Chinese elite placed on a refined sense of aesthetics.

Question 1: Provide the missing phrases and elaborate on the meaning of the following:
The Duke of She observed to Confucius: "Among us there was an upright man called Kung who was so upright that when his father appropriated a sheep, he bore witness against him." Confucius said . . .

[The missing phrases are, "The upright men among us are not like that. A father will screen his son and a son his father . . . yet uprightness is to be found in that."]

Question 2: Write an eight-legged essay [one consisting of eight sections] on the following:
Scrupulous in his own conduct and lenient only in his dealings with the people.

Question 3: First unscramble the following characters and then comment on the significance of this quotation from one of the classic texts:
Beginning, good, mutually, nature, basically, practice, far, near, men's
[The correct answer is, "Men's beginning nature is basically good. Nature mutually near. Practice mutually far."]

QUESTIONS
- Looking at the content of these questions, what can we learn about Chinese society and attitudes?
- For example, where do the Chinese look for models to orient their social behavior?
- What kinds of knowledge are important to the Chinese?
- Do they stress specialist skills or the sort of learning that we associate with a broad liberal arts education?

encourage the growth of a peasant class that owned the lands it toiled so hard to bring into production, Hongwu decreed that unoccupied lands would become the tax-exempt property of those who cleared and cultivated them. He lowered forced labor demands on the peasantry by both the government and members of the scholar-gentry class. Hongwu also promoted silk and cotton cloth production and other handicrafts that provided supplemental income for peasant households.

Although these measures led to some short-term improvement in the peasants' condition, they were all but offset by the growing power of rural landlord families, buttressed by alliances with relatives in the imperial bureaucracy. Scholar-gentry households with members in government service were exempted from land taxes and enjoyed special privileges, such as permission to be carried about in sedan chairs and to use fans and umbrellas. Many scholar-gentry families engaged in moneylending on the side; some even ran lucrative gambling dens. Almost all added to their estates either by buying up lands held by peasant landholders or by foreclosing on loans made to farmers in times of need in exchange for mortgages on their family plots. Peasants displaced in these ways had little choice but to become tenants of large landowners or landless laborers moving about in search of employment.

More land meant ever larger and more comfortable households for the scholar-gentry class. They justified the growing gap between their wealth and the poverty of the peasantry by contrasting their foresight and industry with the lazy and wasteful ways of the ordinary farmers. The virtues of the scholar-gentry class were celebrated in stories and popular illustrations. The latter depicted members of scholar-gentry households hard at work weaving and storing grain to see them through the cold weather, while commoners who neglected these tasks wandered during the winter, cold and hungry, past the walled compounds and closed gates of gentry households.

At most levels of Chinese society, the Ming period continued the subordination of youths to elders and women to men that had been steadily intensifying in earlier periods. If anything, Neo-Confucian thinking was even more influential than under the late Song and Yuan dynasties. Some of its advocates proposed draconian measures to suppress challenges to the increasingly rigid social roles. For example, students were expected to venerate and follow the instructions of their teachers, no matter how muddle-headed or tipsy the latter might be. A terrifying lesson in proper decorum was drawn from an incident in which a student at the imperial academy dared to dispute the findings of one of his instructors. The student was beheaded, and his severed head was hung on a pole at the entrance to the academy. Not surprisingly, this rather unsubtle solution to the problem of keeping order in the classroom merely drove student protest underground. Anonymous letters critical of poorly prepared teachers continued to circulate among the student body.

Women were also driven to underground activities to ameliorate their subordination and, if they dared, expand their career opportunities. At the court, they continued, despite Hongwu's measures, to play strong roles behind the scenes. Even able rulers such as Hongwu were swayed by the advice of favorite wives or dowager mothers and aunts. On one occasion, Hongwu chided the empress Ma for daring to inquire into the condition of the common people. She replied that because he was the father of the people, she was the mother, and thus it was quite proper for her to be concerned for the welfare of her children.

Even within the palace, the plight of most women was grim. Hundreds, sometimes thousands of attractive young women were brought to the court in the hope that they would catch the emperor's fancy and become one of his concubines or perhaps even be elevated to the status of wife. Because few actually succeeded, many spent their lives in loneliness and inactivity, just waiting for the emperor to glance their way.

In society at large, women had to settle for whatever status and respect they could win within the family. As before, their success in this regard hinged largely on bearing male children and, when these children were married, moving from the status of daughter-in-law to mother-in-law. The daughters of upper-class families were often taught to read and write by their parents or brothers, and many composed poetry, painted, and played musical instruments (Figure 23.5).

For women from the nonelite classes, the main avenues for some degree of independence and self-expression remained becoming courtesans or entertainers. The former should be clearly distinguished from prostitutes because they served a very different clientele and were literate and often accomplished in painting, music, and poetry. Although courtesans often enjoyed lives of luxury, even the most successful made their living by gratifying the needs of upper-class men for uninhibited sex and convivial companionship.

FIGURE 23.5 The varied diversions of the wives and concubines of Ming emperors are depicted in this scene of court life. In addition to court intrigues and maneuvers to win the emperor's favor, women of the imperial household occupied themselves with dance, music, games, and polite conversation. With eunuchs, officials, and palace guards watching them closely, the women of the palace and imperial city spent most of their lives in confined yet well-appointed spaces.
(© The Trustees of the British Museum/Art Resource, NY.)

An Age of Growth: Agriculture, Population, Commerce, and the Arts

The first decades of the Ming period were an age of buoyant economic growth in China that both was fed by and resulted in unprecedented contacts with other civilizations overseas. The territories controlled by the Ming emperors were never as extensive as those ruled by the Tang dynasty. But in the Ming era, the great commercial boom and population increase that had begun in the late Song were renewed and accelerated. The peopling of the Yangzi region and the areas to the south was given a great boost by the importation, through Spanish and Portuguese merchant intermediaries, of new food crops from the Americas, particularly root crops from the Andes highlands. Three plants—maize (corn), sweet potatoes, and peanuts—were especially important. Because these crops could be grown on inferior soils without irrigation, their cultivation spread quickly through the hilly and marginal areas that bordered on the irrigated rice lands of southern China. They became vital supplements to the staple rice or millet diet of the Chinese people, particularly those of the rapidly growing southern regions.

Because these plants were less susceptible to drought, they also became an important hedge against famine. The introduction of these new crops was an important factor behind the great surge in population growth that was under way by the end of the Ming era. By 1600 the population of China had risen to as many as 150 million from 80 to 90 million in the 14th century. Two centuries later, in 1800, it had more than doubled and surpassed 300 million.

Agrarian expansion and population increase were paralleled in early Ming times by a renewal of commercial growth. The market sector of the domestic economy became ever more pervasive, and overseas trading links multiplied. Because China's advanced handicraft industries produced a wide variety of goods, from silk textiles and tea to fine ceramics and lacquerware, which were in high demand throughout Asia and in Europe, the terms of trade ran very much in China's favor. This is why China received more American silver (brought by European merchants) than any other single society in the world economy of the Early Modern period. In addition to the Arab and Asian traders, Europeans arrived in increasing numbers at the only two places—**Macao** and, somewhat later and more sporadically, **Canton**—where they were officially allowed to do business in Ming China. Despite state-imposed restrictions on contacts with foreigners, China contributed significantly to the process of proto-globalization that was intensifying cross-cultural contacts worldwide in the Early Modern era.

Not surprisingly, the merchant classes, particularly those engaged in long-distance trade, reaped the biggest profits from the economic boom. But a good portion of their gains was transferred to the state in the form of taxes and to the scholar-gentry in the form of bribes for official favors. Much of the

Macao One of two ports in which Europeans were permitted to trade in China during the Ming dynasty.

Canton One of two port cities in which Europeans were permitted to trade in China during the Ming dynasty.

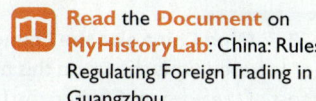

Read the Document on MyHistoryLab: China: Rules Regulating Foreign Trading in Guangzhou

merchants' wealth was invested in land rather than plowed back into trade or manufacturing, because land owning, not commerce, remained the surest route to social status in China.

Ming prosperity was reflected in the fine arts, which found generous patrons both at court and among the scholar-gentry class more generally. Although the monochromatic simplicity of the work of earlier dynasties was sustained by the ink brush paintings of artists such as Xu Wei, much of the Ming output was busier and more colorful. Portraits and scenes of court, city, or country life were more prominent. Nonetheless, the Chinese continued to delight in depicting individual scholars or travelers contemplating the beauty of mountains, lakes, and marshes that dwarf the human observers.

Whereas the painters of the Ming era concentrated mainly on developing established techniques and genres, major innovation was occurring in literature. Most notable in this regard was the full development of the Chinese novel, which had had its beginnings in the writings of the Yuan era. The novel form was given great impetus by the spread of literacy among the upper classes in the Ming era. This was facilitated by the growing availability of books that had resulted from the spread of woodblock printing from the 10th century onward. Ming novels such as *The Water Margin*, *Monkey*, and *The Golden Lotus* were recognized as classics in their own time and continue to set the standard for Chinese prose literature today.

Ming Expansion and Retreat, and the Arrival of the Europeans

The seemingly boundless energy of the Chinese in early decades of Ming rule drove them far beyond the traditional areas of expansion in central Asia and the regions south of the Yangzi. In the reign of the third Ming emperor, Yungle, they launched a series of expeditions that had no precedent in Chinese history. Between 1405 and 1433, the admiral Zheng He, one of Yongle's most trusted subordinates, led seven major expeditions overseas (see Map 23.3 and Chapter 16, p. 351). A mix of motives, including a desire to explore other lands and proclaim the glory of the Ming empire to the wider world, prompted the voyages.

The early expeditions were confined largely to southeast Asian seas and kingdoms. The last three reached as far as Persia, southern Arabia, and the east coast of Africa—distances comparable to those that would be covered by the Portuguese in their early voyages around Africa. The hundreds of great ships (see the illustrations in Visualizing the Past) deployed on these expeditions exemplified the technological sophistication, wealth, and power of China in the first centuries of Ming rule.

Nonetheless, in the decades after the last of the Zheng He expeditions in 1433, China's rulers purposely abandoned the drive to extend Ming power and prestige overseas, and increasingly sought to limit and control contacts with the outside world. The shift from an emphasis on building the impressive fleets of the Zheng He voyages to repairing and joining the northern defense works to form the Great Wall as we know it today reflected these key changes in policy and decisions about geopolitical orientation.

In the centuries that followed the suspension of overseas expeditions, the Ming war fleet declined dramatically in the number and quality of its ships, and strict limits were placed on the size and number of masts with which a seagoing ship might be fitted. This return to the long-standing priority of defending against nomadic invasions eventually left China, and the Indian Ocean world as a whole, vulnerable to European incursions by sea.

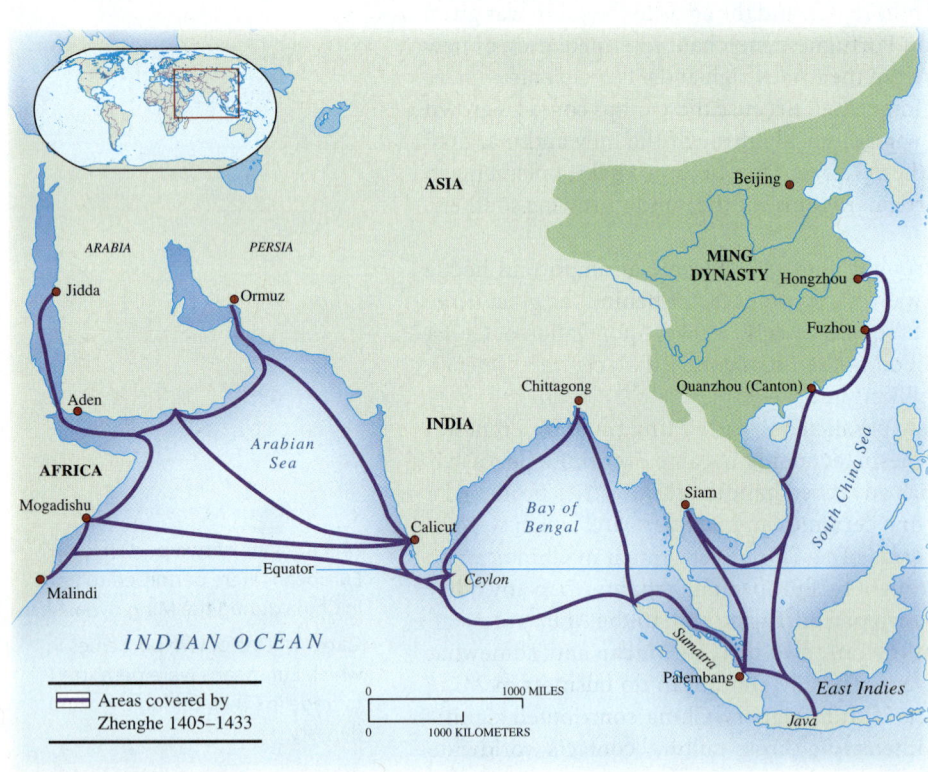

MAP 23.3 **Ming China and the Zheng He Expeditions, 1405–1433** The composite view of the Zheng He expeditions shown on this map indicate the great distances traveled as well as the fact that most of the voyages hugged the familiar coastlines of southern Asia and East Africa rather than risking navigation over large expanses of open sea.

534 PART IV The Early Modern Period, 1450–1750: The World Shrinks

While the Chinese closed themselves in, the Europeans probed ever farther across the globe and were irresistibly drawn to the most legendary of all overseas civilizations, the Middle Kingdom of China. In addition to the trading contacts noted earlier, Christian missionaries infiltrated Chinese coastal areas and tried to gain access to the court, where they hoped to curry favor with the Ming emperors. While religious orders such as the Franciscans and Dominicans toiled to win converts among the common people and made modest progress that could be counted in the tens of thousands, the Jesuits adopted the top-down strategy that di Nobili had pursued in India (Figure 23.6). In China, however, a single person, the Ming emperor, instead of a whole caste, sat at the top of the social hierarchy, and for that reason the rulers and their chief advisors became the prime targets of the Jesuit mission.

Some Chinese scholars showed interest in Christian teachings and Western thinking more generally. But the Jesuit missionaries who made their way to Beijing clearly recognized that their scientific knowledge and technical skills were the keys to maintaining a presence at the Ming court and eventually interesting the Chinese elite in Christianity. Beginning in the 1580s, a succession of brilliant Jesuit scholars, such as **Matteo Ricci** and **Adam Schall**, spent most of their time in the imperial city, correcting faulty calendars, forging cannons, and fixing clocks imported from Europe. They also managed to astound the Chinese scholar-gentry with the accuracy of their instruments and their ability to predict eclipses. They won a few converts among the elite. However, most court officials were suspicious of these strange-looking "barbarians" with large noses and hairy faces, and they tried to limit their contacts with the imperial family. Some at the court, especially the scholar-officials who were humiliated by the foreigners' corrections to their calendars, were openly hostile to the Jesuits.

Despite serious harassment, however, the later Ming emperors remained sufficiently fascinated by these very learned and able visitors that they allowed a handful to remain. When the Jesuits were able to maintain, even increase, their influence with the Qing emperors who succeeded the Ming in the middle of the 17th century, the enterprising missionaries came to believe that China was on the brink of being converted to Christianity. But the Jesuits' strategy of adopting the culture of the elites in the societies they sought to convert did them in. The critical issue was whether Chinese converts should be allowed to continue the ancestral rites that we have seen were central to Chinese family life since ancient times. After extended, and often fierce, debates with rival missionary orders, especially the Franciscans and Dominicans, the pope came down on the side of the Jesuits' rivals. When the emperor learned that a religious leader in a far off land was insisting that such a fundamental practice in Chinese culture be forbidden, he disavowed any suggestion that he or his subjects might become Christians.

Ming Decline and the Chinese Predicament

By the late 1500s, the Ming retreat from overseas involvement had become just one facet of a familiar pattern of dynastic decline. The highly centralized, absolutist political structure that had been established by Hongwu and had been run well by able successors such as Yongle became a major liability under the mediocre or incompetent men who occupied the throne through much of the last two centuries of Ming rule. Decades of rampant official corruption, exacerbated by the growing isolation of weak rulers by the thousands of eunuchs who gradually came to dominate life within the Forbidden City, eventually eroded the foundations on which the empire was built.

Read the Document on MyHistoryLab: Matteo Ricci's Journals (late 16th c.) Matteo Ricci

FIGURE 23.6 Jesuits in Chinese dress at the emperor's court. The Jesuits believed that the best way to convert a great civilization such as China was to adopt the dress, customs, language, and manners of its elite. They reasoned that once the scholar-gentry elite had been converted, they would bring the rest of China's vast population into the Christian fold.

Ricci, Matteo [rEEt chEE] (1552–1610) Along with Adam Schall, Jesuit scholar in court of Ming emperors; skilled scientist; won few converts to Christianity.

Schall, Adam (1591–1666) Along with Matteo Ricci, Jesuit scholar in court of Ming emperors; skilled scientist; won few converts to Christianity.

Read the Document on MyHistoryLab: A European View of Asia (1590)

VISUALIZING THE PAST

The Great Ships of the Ming Expeditions That Crossed the Indian Ocean

IN THE EARLY MODERN ERA CHINESE ships for canal, river, and ocean transportation improved significantly and their numbers multiplied many times. By the first decades of the Ming dynasty, some of them had also increased dramatically in size (see the image below). This trend was given great impetus by the impressive series of expeditions that were led by the eunuch Zheng He sailing through island southeast Asia and on to coastal India and east Africa beginning in 1405. Some of the dragon ships of Zheng He's fleet exceeded 400 feet in length, thus dwarfing the caravel *Niña*, one of the ships of Columbus's first voyage to the Americas (see the image below). Chinese junks in this and earlier centuries were equipped with magnetic compasses, water-tight compartments, and stern post rudders that would have allowed them to navigate the open seas rather than simply following the coastlines of the lands from which Zheng He and his crews sought to command tribute and establish direct commercial relations.

Over the course of the seven expeditions led by Zheng He, fleets of these great treasure vessels accommodated tens of thousands of sailors, merchants, and soldiers. As the illustration below clearly indicates, the largest Chinese junks were far larger than the caravels, naos, and other vessels that the Portuguese, Spanish, and rival Europeans deployed in their voyages of exploration and discovery from the 15th through the 17th century. They also dwarfed the ubiquitous and swift Arab dhows that plied the waters of the Indian Ocean and adjoining seas. With such vessels the Chinese became for much of the fifteenth century a dominant force in Asian seas east of the Malayan peninsula. The stout-walled Chinese ships also proved the only vessels in Asia that could stand up to the cannon carried by the first waves of Portuguese ships that sought to dominate the Indian Ocean trading network.

QUESTIONS
- In what ways would the dragon ships facilitate commerce both within China and overseas?
- What sorts of goods could ships of this size carry?
- Do you think that ships like these, equipped with the naval technologies described above, could have crossed the Pacific Ocean to the Americas or the Atlantic and sailed to Europe?
- If not, why not? If so, why didn't the Chinese seek to "discover" and dominate these areas?

Public works projects, including the critical dike works on the Yellow River, fell into disrepair, and floods, drought, and famine soon ravaged the land. Peasants in afflicted districts were reduced to eating the bark from trees or the excrement of wild geese. Some peasants sold their children into slavery to keep them from starving, and peasants in some areas resorted to cannibalism. Rapacious local landlords built huge estates by taking advantage of the increasingly desperate peasant population. As in earlier phases of dynastic decline, farmers who had been turned off their land and tortured for taxes, or had lost most of the crops they had grown, turned to flight, banditry, and finally open rebellion to confiscate food and avenge their exploitation by greedy landlords and corrupt officials.

THINKING HISTORICALLY

Means and Motives for Overseas Expansion: Europe and China Compared

IN THE EARLY DECADES OF THE 14th century, Chinese mariners dramatically demonstrated their capacity to mount large expeditions for overseas exploration and expansion. Because their failure to sustain these initiatives left Asian waters from the Persian Gulf to the China seas open to armed European interventions a century later, the reasons for the Chinese failure to follow up on their remarkable naval achievements merits serious examination. The explanations for the Chinese refusal to commit to overseas expansion can be best understood if they are contrasted with the forces that drove the Europeans with increasing determination into the outside world. In broad terms, such a comparison underscores the fact that although both the Europeans and the Chinese had the means to expand on a global scale, only the Europeans had strong motives for doing so.

The social and economic transformations that occurred in European civilization during the late Middle Ages and the early Renaissance had brought it to a level of development that compared favorably with China in many areas (see Chapters 11 and 13). Although the Chinese empire was far larger and more populous than tiny nation-states such as Portugal, Spain, and Holland, the European kingdoms had grown more efficient at mobilizing their more limited resources. Rivalries between the states of a fragmented Europe had also fostered a greater aggressiveness and sense of competition on the part of the Europeans than the Chinese rulers could even imagine. China's armies were far larger than those of any of the European kingdoms, but European soldiers were on the whole better led, armed, and disciplined. Chinese wet rice agriculture was more productive than European farming, and the Chinese rulers had a far larger population to cultivate their fields, build their dikes and bridges, work their mines, and make tools, clothing, and weapons. But on the whole, the technological innovations of the medieval period had given the Europeans an advantage over the Chinese in the animal and machine power they could generate—a capacity that did much to make up for their deficiencies in human power.

Despite their differences, both civilizations had the means for sustained exploration and expansion overseas, although the Chinese were ready to undertake such enterprises a few centuries earlier than the Europeans. As the voyages of Da Gama, Columbus, and Zheng He demonstrated, both civilizations had the shipbuilding and navigational skills and technology needed to tackle such ambitious undertakings. Why, then, were the impressive Zheng He expeditions a dead end, whereas the more modest probes of Columbus and Da Gama were the beginning of half a millennium of European overseas expansion and global dominance?

The full answer to this question is as complex as the societies it asks us to compare. But we can learn a good deal by looking at the groups pushing for expansion within each civilization and the needs that drove them into the outside world. There was widespread support for exploration and overseas expansion in seafaring European nations such as Portugal, Spain, Holland, and England. European rulers financed expeditions they hoped would bring home precious metals and trade goods that could be sold at great profits. Both treasure and profits could be translated into warships and armies that would strengthen these rulers in their incessant wars with European rivals and, in the case of the Iberian kingdoms, with their Muslim adversaries.

> **Why... were the impressive Zheng He expeditions a dead end, whereas the more modest probes of Columbus and Da Gama were the beginning of half a millennium of European overseas expansion and global dominance?**

European traders looked for much the same benefits from overseas expansion. Rulers and merchants also hoped that explorers would find new lands whose climates and soils were suitable for growing crops such as sugar that were in high demand and thus would bring big profits. Leaders of rival branches of the Christian faith believed that overseas expansion would give their missionaries access to unlimited numbers of heathens to be converted or would put them in touch with the legendary lost king, Prester John, who would ally with them in their struggle with the infidel Muslims.

By contrast, the Chinese Zheng He expeditions were very much the project of a single emperor and a favored eunuch, whose Muslim family origins may go a long way toward accounting for his wanderlust. Yongle appears to have been driven by little more than curiosity and the vain desire to impress his greatness and that of his empire on peoples whom he considered inferior. Although some Chinese merchants went along for the ride, most felt little need for the voyages. They already traded on favorable terms for all the products Asia, and in some cases Europe and Africa, could offer. The merchants had the option of waiting for other peoples to come

(continued on next page)

(continued from previous page)

to them, or, if they were a bit more ambitious, of going out in their own ships to southeast Asia.

The scholar-gentry were actively hostile to the Zheng He expeditions. The voyages strengthened the position of the much-hated eunuchs, who vied with the scholar-gentry for the emperor's favor and the high posts that went with it. In addition, the scholar-gentry saw the voyages as a foolish waste of resources that the empire could not afford. They believed it would be better to direct the wealth and talents of the empire to building armies and fortifications to keep out the hated Mongols and other nomads. After all, the memory of foreign rule was quite fresh.

As had happened so often before in their history, the Chinese were drawn inward, fixated on internal struggles and the continuing threat from central Asia. Scholar-gentry hostility and the lack of enthusiasm for overseas voyages displayed by Yongle's successors after his death in 1424 led to their abandonment after 1430. As the Chinese retreated, the Europeans surged outward. It is difficult to exaggerate the magnitude of the consequences for both civilizations and all humankind.

QUESTIONS

- How might history have been changed if the Chinese had mounted a serious and sustained effort to project their power overseas in the decades before Da Gama rounded the Cape of Good Hope?
- Why did the Chinese fail to foresee the threat that European expansion would pose for the rest of Asia and finally for China itself?
- Did other civilizations have the capacity for global expansion in this era?
- What prevented them from launching expeditions similar to those of the Chinese and Europeans?
- In terms of motivation for overseas expansion, were peoples such as the Muslims, Indians, and Native Americans more like the Europeans or the Chinese?

True to the pattern of dynastic rise and fall, internal disorder resulted in and was intensified by foreign threats and renewed assaults by nomadic peoples from beyond the Great Wall. One of the early signs of the seriousness of imperial deterioration was the inability of Chinese bureaucrats and military forces to put an end to the epidemic of Japanese (and ethnic Chinese) pirate attacks that ravaged the southern coast in the mid-16th century. Despite an official preoccupation with the Mongols early in the Ming era and with the Manchus to the northeast of the Great Wall in later times, the dynasty was finally toppled in 1644, not by nomads but by rebels from within. By that time, the administrative apparatus had become so feeble that the last Ming emperor, **Chongzhen**, did not realize how serious the rebel advance was until enemy soldiers were scaling the walls of the Forbidden City. After watching his wife withdraw to her chambers to commit suicide, and after bungling an attempt to kill his young daughter, the ill-fated Chongzhen emperor retreated to the imperial gardens and hanged himself rather than face capture.

Chongzhen [chohng-jehn] Last of the Ming emperors; committed suicide in 1644 in the face of a Jurchen capture of the Forbidden City at Beijing.

FENDING OFF THE WEST: JAPAN'S REUNIFICATION AND THE FIRST CHALLENGE

23.3 Why did the rulers of Japan initially welcome European traders and missionaries, and why did they ultimately expel all but the Dutch?

In the mid-16th century, the Japanese found leaders who had the military and diplomatic skills and ruthlessness needed to restore unity under a new shogunate, the Tokugawa. By the early 1600s, with the potential threat from the Europeans looming ever larger, the Tokugawa shoguns succeeded in enveloping the islands in a state of isolation that lasted nearly two and a half centuries.

By the 16th century the stalemate between the warring houses of the samurai elite was so entrenched in Japanese society that a succession of three remarkable military leaders was needed to restore unity and internal peace. **Oda Nobunaga**, the first of these leaders, was from a minor samurai household. But his skills as a military leader soon vaulted him into prominence in the ongoing struggles for power among the daimyo or regional lords. As a leader, Nobunaga combined daring, a willingness to innovate, and ruthless determination—some would say cruelty. He was not afraid to launch a surprise attack against an enemy that outnumbered him ten to one, and he was one of the first of the samurai leaders to make extensive use of the firearms that the Japanese had begun to acquire from the Portuguese in the 1540s.

In 1573 Nobunaga deposed the last of the Ashikaga shoguns, who had long ruled in name only. By 1580 he had unified much of central Honshu under his command (Map 23.4). As his armies drove against the powerful western daimyo in 1582, Nobunaga was caught off guard by one of his vassal generals and was killed when the Kyoto temple where he had taken refuge was burned to the ground.

538   PART IV   The Early Modern Period, 1450–1750: The World Shrinks

MAP 23.4 **Japan During the Rise of the Tokugawa Shogunate** As this map indicates, the main centers of population and political power in Early Modern Japan were readily accessible to the sea, which was the arena in which the Europeans could best project their military prowess and exercise their commercial prerogatives.

At first it appeared that Nobunaga's campaigns to restore central authority to the islands might be undone. But his ablest general, **Toyotomi Hideyoshi** (Figure 23.7), moved quickly to punish those who had betrayed Nobunaga and to renew the drive to break the power of the daimyo who had not yet submitted to him. Although the son of a peasant, Hideyoshi matched his master in military prowess but was far more skillful at diplomacy. A system of alliances and a string of victories over the last of the resisting daimyo made Hideyoshi the military hegemon of Japan by 1590.

The ambitious overlord had much more grandiose schemes of conquest in mind. He dreamed of ruling China and even India, although he knew little about either place. Hideyoshi also threatened, among others, the Spanish in the Philippines. Apparently as the first step toward fulfilling this vision of empire building on a grand scale, Hideyoshi launched two attacks on Korea in 1592 and 1597, each of which involved nearly 150,000 soldiers. After initial successes, both campaigns stalled. The first ended in defeat; the second was still in progress when Hideyoshi died in 1598.

Although Hideyoshi had tried to ensure that he would be succeeded by his son, the vassals he had appointed to carry out his wishes tried to seize power for themselves after his death. One of these vassals, **Tokugawa Ieyasu**, had originally come from a minor daimyo house. But as an ally of Hideyoshi, he had been able to build up a powerful domain on the heavily populated Kanto plain. Ieyasu soon emerged triumphant from the renewed warfare that resulted from Hideyoshi's death. Rather than continue Hideyoshi's campaigns of overseas expansion, Ieyasu concentrated on consolidating power at home. In 1603 he was granted the title of shogun by the emperor, an act that formally inaugurated centuries of rule by the Tokugawa shogunate.

Under Ieyasu's direction, the remaining daimyo were reorganized. Most of the lands in central Honshu were either controlled directly by the Tokugawa family, who now ruled the land from the city of **Edo** (later Tokyo), or were held by daimyo who were closely allied with the shoguns. Although many of the outlying or vassal daimyo retained their domains, they were carefully controlled and were required to pledge their personal allegiance to the shogun. To ensure their continuing loyalty, the shogun compelled them to spend half of the year in the capital city at Edo. This arrangement not only ensured that their allegiance be tested and their activities monitored, the costs involved in moving their households annually cut down on the resources they might use to become a military

Nobunaga, Oda (1534–1582) Japanese daimyo; first to make extensive use of firearms; in 1573 deposed last of Ashikaga shoguns; unified much of central Honshu under his command.

Hideyoshi, Toyotomi [tO yO tO mAY] General under Nobunaga; succeeded as leading military power in central Japan; continued efforts to break power of daimyos; constructed a series of alliances that made him military master of Japan in 1590; died in 1598.

Ieyasu, Tokugawa [toh-kuh-GAH-wah ee-YAH-soo] Vassal of Toyotomi Hideyoshi; succeeded him as most powerful military figure in Japan; granted title of shogun in 1603 and established Tokugawa shogunate; established political unity in Japan.

Edo Tokugawa capital city; modern-day Tokyo; center of the Tokugawa shogunate.

threat to the ruling dynasty. It was soon clear that the Tokugawas' victory had put an end to the civil wars and brought a semblance of political unity to the islands.

Dealing with the European Challenge

All through the decades when the three unifiers were struggling to bring the feisty daimyo under control, they also had to contend with a new force in Japanese history: the Europeans. From the time in 1543 when shipwrecked Portuguese sailors were washed up on the shore of Kyushu (the southernmost of the main Japanese islands), European traders and missionaries had been visiting Japan in increasing numbers. The traders brought the Japanese goods that were produced mainly in India, China, and Southeast Asia and exchanged them for silver, copper, pottery, and lacquerware. Perhaps more important, European traders and the missionaries who followed them to the islands brought firearms, printing presses, and other Western devices such as clocks. The firearms, which the Japanese could themselves manufacture within years and were improving in design within a generation, revolutionized Japanese warfare and contributed much to the victories of the unifiers. Commercial contacts with the Europeans also encouraged the Japanese to venture overseas to trade in nearby Formosa and Korea and in places as distant as the Philippines and Siam.

Soon after the merchants, Christian missionaries (Figure 23.8) arrived in the islands and set to work converting the Japanese to Roman Catholicism. Beginning in the outlying domains, the missionaries worked their way toward the political center that was beginning to coalesce around Nobunaga and his followers by the 1570s. Seeing Christianity as a counterforce to the militant Buddhist orders that were resisting his rise to power, Nobunaga took the missionaries under his protection and encouraged them to preach their faith to his people. The Jesuits, adopting the same top-down strategy of conversion that they had followed in India and China, converted some of the daimyo and their samurai retainers. The Jesuits were convinced that they were on the verge of winning over Nobunaga, who delighted in wearing Western clothes, encouraged his artists to copy Western paintings of the Virgin Mary and scenes from the life of Christ, and permitted the missionaries to build churches in towns throughout the islands. The missionaries were persuaded that Nobunaga's conversion would bring the whole of the Japanese people into the Christian fold. Even without it, they reported converts in the hundreds of thousands by the early 1580s.

FIGURE 23.7 In this late 16th-century portrait, Hideyoshi (1536–1598) exudes the discipline and self-confidence that made possible his campaigns to unify Japan. Although warrior skills were vital in his rise to power, he and other members of the samurai class were expected to be literate, well-mannered by the conventions of the day, and attuned to the complex and refined aesthetics of rock gardens and tea ceremonies.

Read the Document on MyHistoryLab: Tokugawa Shogunate, The Laws for the Military House, 1615

In the late 1580s, quite suddenly, the missionaries saw their carefully mounted conversion campaign collapse. Nobunaga was murdered, and his successor, Hideyoshi, although not yet openly hostile, was lukewarm toward the missionary enterprise. In part, the missionaries' fall from favor resulted from the fact that the resistance of the Buddhist sects had been crushed. More critically, Hideyoshi and his followers were alarmed by reports of converts refusing to obey their overlords' commands when they believed them to be in conflict with their newly adopted Christian beliefs. Thus, the threat that the new religion posed for the established social order was growing more apparent. That menace was compounded by signs that the Europeans might follow up their commercial and missionary overtures with military expeditions aimed at conquering the islands. The Japanese had been strongly impressed with the firearms and pugnacity of the Europeans, and they did not take threats of invasion lightly.

Japan's Self-Imposed Isolation

Growing doubts about European intentions, and fears that both merchants and missionaries might subvert the existing social order, led to official measures to restrict foreign activities in Japan, beginning in the late 1580s. First, Hideyoshi ordered the Christian missionaries to leave the islands—an

FIGURE 23.8 A number of the major forms of interaction between expansive European peoples and those of Asia are vividly illustrated in this panoramic Japanese silkscreen painting from the early 1600s. The strong impression made by the size and power of the Portuguese ship that has just arrived in harbor is evident in the artist's exaggeration of the height of its fore and aft castles. The trade goods to be unloaded, mainly Chinese silks, which are also to be sold in the marketplace at the right of the painting, but also exotic products such as peacocks and tiger skins, demonstrate the ways in which the Portuguese had become carriers between different areas in Asia, including Japan. The black-robed missionaries waiting to greet the arriving Portuguese sea captain (toward the right foreground) suggests that efforts to convert the Japanese to Christianity were in full swing, at least in this area of the kingdom.

order that was not rigorously enforced, at least at the outset. By the mid-1590s, Hideyoshi was actively persecuting Christian missionaries and converts. His successor, Ieyasu, continued this persecution and then officially banned the faith in 1614. European missionaries were driven out of the islands; those who remained underground were hunted down and killed or expelled. Japanese converts were compelled to renounce their faith; those who refused were imprisoned, tortured, and executed. By the 1630s, the persecutions, even against Christians who tried to practice their faith in secret, had become so intense that thousands of converts in the western regions joined in hard-fought but hopeless rebellions against the local daimyo and the forces of the shogun. With the suppression of these uprisings, Christianity in Japan was reduced to an underground faith of isolated communities.

Under Ieyasu and his successors, the persecution of the Christians grew into a broader campaign to isolate Japan from outside influences. In 1616 foreign traders were confined to a handful of cities; in the 1630s all Japanese ships were forbidden to trade or even sail overseas. One after another, different European nations were either officially excluded from Japan (the Spanish) or decided that trading there was no longer worth the risk (the English). By the 1640s only a limited number of Dutch and Chinese ships were allowed to carry on commerce in Japan and only at the port of Nagaskai. To prevent the spread of Christianity, Dutch traders were confined to a small island called **Deshima**, in Nagasaki Bay. The export of silver and copper was greatly restricted, and Western books were banned to prevent Christian ideas from reentering the country. Foreigners were permitted to live and travel only in very limited areas.

By the mid-17th century, Japan's retreat into almost total isolation was nearly complete. Much of the next century was spent in consolidating the internal control of the Tokugawa shogunate by extending bureaucratic administration into the vassal daimyo domains throughout the islands.

Deshima Island in Nagasaki Bay; only port open to non-Japanese after closure of the islands in the 1640s; only Chinese and Dutch ships were permitted to enter.

School of National Learning New ideology that laid emphasis on Japan's unique historical experience and the revival of indigenous culture at the expense of Chinese imports such as Confucianism; typical of Japan in 18th century.

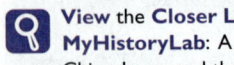 View the Closer Look on MyHistoryLab: A Meeting of China, Japan, and the West

In the 18th century, a revival of Neo-Confucian philosophy, which had marked the period of the Tokugawa's rise to power, increasingly gave way to the influence of thinkers who championed the **School of National Learning**. As its name implies, the new ideology laid great emphasis on Japan's unique historical experience and the revival of indigenous culture at the expense of Chinese imports such as Confucianism. In the centuries that followed, through contacts with the small Dutch community at Deshima, members of the Japanese elite also kept up with developments in the West. Their avid interest in European achievements contrasted sharply with the indifference of the Chinese scholar-gentry in this period to the doings of the "hairy barbarians" from the lands far to the west.

Global Connections and Critical Themes

AN AGE OF EURASIAN PROTO-GLOBALIZATION

In 1700, after two centuries of European involvement in south and southeast Asia, most of the peoples of the area had been little affected by efforts to build trading empires and win Christian converts. European sailors had added several new routes to the Asian trading network. The most important of these were the link around the Cape of Good Hope between Europe and the Indian Ocean and the connection between the Philippine Islands and Mexico in the Americas. The Europeans' need for safe harbors and storage areas led to the establishment and rapid growth of fortified trading centers such as Goa, Calicut, and Batavia. It also resulted in the gradual decline of some of the existing indigenous commercial centers, especially the Muslim cities on the east coast of Africa and somewhat later the fortress town of Malacca. The Europeans introduced the principle of sea warfare into what had been a peaceful commercial world. But the Asian trading system as a whole survived the initial shock of this innovation, and the Europeans eventually concluded that they were better off adapting to the existing commercial arrangements rather than dismantling them.

Because exchanges had been taking place between Europe and Asia for millennia, few new inventions or diseases were spread in the early centuries of expansion. This low level of major exchanges was particularly striking compared with the catastrophic interaction between Europe and the Americas. But, as in Africa, European discoveries in the long-isolated Western Hemisphere did result in the introduction of important new food plants into India, China, Java, the Philippines, and other areas from the 1600s onward. These new foods led to substantial increases in the population in the areas affected. The import of silver was also an addition to wealth and adornment in China. Otherwise, Europeans died mainly of diseases that they contracted in Asia, such as new strains of malaria and dysentery. They spread diseases only to the more isolated parts of Asia, such as the Philippines, where the coming of the Spanish was accompanied by a devastating smallpox epidemic. The impact of European ideas, inventions, and modes of social organization was also very limited during the first centuries of expansion. Key European devices, such as clocks, were often seen as toys by Asian rulers to whom they were given as presents. But the ritual-minded Chinese emperors took these superior time pieces very seriously, thereby providing the Jesuit missionaries who brought them to China with access to the court and ruler of the most powerful empire in an increasingly interconnected global system.

Except for clocks and guns, during the Early Modern period in global history, the West's surge in exploration and commercial expansion touched most of Asia only peripherally. This was particularly true of east Asia, where the political cohesion and military strength of the vast Chinese empire and the Japanese warrior-dominated states blocked all hope of European advance. Promising missionary inroads in the 16th century were stifled by hostile Tokugawa shoguns in the early 17th century. They were also carefully contained by the Ming emperors and the nomadic Qing dynasty from the mid-1600s. Strong Chinese and Japanese rulers limited trading contacts with the aggressive Europeans and confined European merchants to a few ports—Macao and Canton in China, Deshima in Japan—that were remote from their respective capitals. In its early decades, the Ming dynasty also pursued a policy of overseas expansion that had no precedent in Chinese history. But when China again turned inward in the last centuries of the dynasty, a potentially formidable obstacle to the rise of European dominance in maritime Asia was removed. China's strong position in global trade continued, in marked contrast to Japan's greater isolation. But even China failed to keep pace with changes in European technology and merchant activity, with results that would take effect mainly in the next stage of more intense global interaction.

Further Readings

The account of Da Gama's epic voyage that opens the chapter is based heavily on J. H. Parry's superb *The Discovery of the Sea* (1981). C. G. F. Simkins, *The Traditional Trade of Asia* (1968), and Anthony Reid, *Southeast Asia in the Age of Commerce, 1450–1680* (1988), provide overviews of the Asian trading network from ancient times until about the 18th century. Much more detailed accounts of specific segments of the system, as well as the impact upon it of the Dutch and Portuguese, can be found in the works of J. C. van Leur, M. A. P. Meilink-Roelofsz, K. N. Chaudhuri, Ashin Das Gupta, Sanjay Subrahmanyam, and Michael Pearson. C. R. Boxer's *The Portuguese Seaborne Empire* (1969) and *The Dutch Seaborne Empire* (1965) are still essential reading, although the latter has little on the Europeans in Asia. Boxer's *Race Relations in the Portuguese Colonial Empire, 1415–1852* (1963) provides a stimulating, if contentious, introduction to the history of European social interaction with overseas peoples in the early centuries of expansion. Important correctives to Boxer's work can be found in the more recent contributions of George Winius.

Louise Levathes, *When China Ruled the Seas: The Treasure Fleet of the Dragon Throne, 1405–33* (1994), is the most thorough account in English of China's global reach. G. B. Sansom, *The Western World and Japan* (1968), includes a wealth of information on the interaction between Europeans and, despite its title, peoples throughout Asia, and it has good sections on the missionary initiatives in both China and Japan.

The period of the Ming dynasty has been the focus of broader and more detailed studies than the dynasties that preceded it. An important early work is Charles O. Hucker, *The Censorial System of Ming China* (1966). Two essential and more recent works are Albert Chan's *The Glory and Fall of the Ming Dynasty* (1982) and Edward Dreyer's more traditional political history, *Early Ming China, 1355–1435* (1982). See also F. W. Mote and D. Twitchett, eds., *The Cambridge History of China: The Ming Dynasty 1368–1644*, vols. 6 and 7 (1988, 1998). Mote's more recent survey of *Imperial China, 900–1800* (1999) is superb on the Ming era and the early Qing that followed.

There are also wonderful insights into daily life at various levels of Chinese society in Ray Huang's very readable *1587: A Year of No Significance: The Ming Dynasty in Decline* (1981), and into the interaction between the Chinese and the Jesuits in Jonathan Spence's *The Memory Palace of Matteo Ricci* (1984). Frederic Wakeman Jr., *The Great Enterprise*, 2 vols. (1985), is essential to an understanding of the transition from Ming to Manchu rule. The early chapters of Spence's *The Search for Modern China* (1990) also provide an illuminating overview of that process.

Perhaps the best introductions to the situation in Japan in the early phase of European expansion are provided by G. B. Sansom's survey, *A History of Japan, 1615–1867* (1963) and Conrad Totman's *Politics in the Tokugawa Bakufu, 1600–1843* (1967). Numerous studies on the Europeans in Japan include those by Donald Keene, Grant Goodman, Noel Perrin, and C. R. Boxer. Intellectual trends in Japan in this era are most fully treated in H. D. Harootunian's *Toward Restoration: The Growth of Political Consciousness in Tokugawa Japan* (1970).

On MyHistoryLab

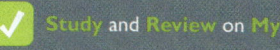

Critical Thinking Questions

1. Why were the Jesuit missionaries so successful at establishing positions at the highest levels of Chinese and Japanese society? In what ways did the reasons they failed to win each of these ancient civilizations to Christianity differ?

2. Why of all of the states and peoples of Asia were the Chinese and Japanese able to both fend off the expansion-minded European intruders and consolidate their centralized political systems and rise to even higher levels of economic productivity and cultural development?

3. What were the major ways in which the Indian/Asian trading system was transformed by the involvement of different expansion-minded European powers from the early 16th century?

4. Which of the European nations gained the most from its involvement in Asia in this era, and why? Which would dominate in the centuries to come?

PART IV AP® TEST PREP

MULTIPLE CHOICE QUESTIONS

1. Why did the initiative in early conquest and exploration pass to northern European nations in the later 16th century?
   a. Spain and Portugal were defeated in a critical war with the Ottoman empire.
   b. The Dutch and the British improved the design of oceanic vessels, producing faster ships than their Catholic rivals.
   c. Famine and disease disastrously reduced the population of the Iberian peninsula after 1588.
   d. The Spanish defeat of the English Armada cut England off from further advance in Europe and forced English attention to foreign conquest.

2. In what way were the early Dutch and British exploration and trade projects different from those of the Iberian nations?
   a. The expeditions of Spain and Portugal did not enjoy government support.
   b. Dutch and British exploration owed much to private initiative of merchant groups and the formation of chartered trading companies.
   c. Dutch and British exploratory expeditions were independent of their respective governments.
   d. The Dutch and British operated joint explorations in the names of both governments while Portugal and Spain engaged in the competition for conquest.

3. What was the impact of the introduction of American crops into Europe?
   a. The introduction of the potato led to major population growth in Europe.
   b. Fungi introduced to Europe, along with American crops, led to a severe decrease in agricultural productivity.
   c. Although American crops were introduced around the world by European traders, they were not adopted in Europe itself.
   d. Plantation agriculture fueled by slave labor became the norm in European agricultural systems.

4. Which of the following statements best accounts for the Spanish failure to hold a position of dominance in world trade?
   a. The Spanish withdrew voluntarily from the race for world trade dominance and established a policy of international isolation.
   b. The Catholic church that dominated Spanish society argued against the establishment of a commercial mentality in Spain.
   c. Spain's interests were increasingly directed toward the destruction of the Ottoman empire.
   d. Spain's internal economy and banking system were not sufficient to accommodate the bullion from the new world.

5. Which of the following statements concerning the British policies toward India in the 17th century is most accurate?
   a. Britain attempted to foster the development of the cotton manufacturing industry in India.
   b. Britain applied tariffs to destroy the cotton industry in India as a means of protecting the British cloth industry.
   c. Britain was disinterested in expanding the trade with India.
   d. The British balance of trade with India in the 17th century remained negative, as Britain was forced to exchange bullion for Indian products.

6. What was the nature of the trade between eastern and western Europe in the 17th century?
   a. Western Europe imported grain in increasing amounts from eastern Europe in return for art objects and manufactured goods.
   b. Eastern and western Europe remained economically isolated, as Russia, Poland, and Prussia extended their trade relationships with the Ottoman empire.
   c. The inability of eastern Europe to produce anything of value to the West frustrated attempts to establish trading connections between the two halves of Europe.
   d. Eastern Europe emerged as a powerful challenger to western domination of the global commercial network.

7. In which of the following regions was European settlement a significant factor in the establishment of colonies?
   a. West Indies
   b. Indonesia
   c. Dutch South Africa
   d. China

8. Which of the following statements concerning the interaction of North American colonists with the Indians is most accurate?
   a. Colonists interacted with Indians, learned from them, and mistreated them, but, for the most part, they did not forge a new cultural amalgam as that which occurred in much of Latin America.
   b. Constant warfare between the numerous sedentary agricultural tribes and the European colonists resulted in limited immigration from Europe.
   c. Rapid intermarriage between Europeans and the Native Americans resulted in the creation of a new class of people, the mestizos, who continued to play a significant role in North American colonial development.
   d. The occurrence of disease that rapidly decimated the Indian populations of Latin America did not take place in North America, thus Indian populations remained large and intermingled with the European immigrants.

9. Which of the following statements about the Renaissance is NOT accurate?
   a. The Renaissance challenged medieval intellectual values and styles.
   b. The Renaissance sketched a brasher spirit that may have helped create a new Western interest in exploring.
   c. The Renaissance failed to develop any new ideas concerning political organization.
   d. The Renaissance was built on a more commercialized economy.

10. Which of the following trends gained popularity among European families in the 15th century?
    a. extended families, early marriage ages
    b. nuclear families, early marriage ages
    c. extended families, late marriage ages
    d. nuclear families, late marriage ages

11. Which of the following was NOT a religious proposition advanced by Martin Luther?
    a. Sale of indulgence, or grants of salvation, for money was wrong.
    b. Only faith could gain salvation.
    c. Monasticism was wrong.
    d. Priests should practice celibacy.

12. Which of the following statements most accurately describes the reason why Luther picked up widespread support among the German elite?
    a. Luther proposed moving the papacy from Rome to Germany.
    b. Luther's support for a more centralized German government under the control of the Holy Roman Emperor struck a responsive chord in German nationalism.
    c. German princes who turned Protestant could increase their independence from the emperor, seize church lands, and control the church in their territories.
    d. Luther proposed that indulgences should be collected by the Holy Roman Emperor instead of the pope.

13. Which of the following reasons suggests why common people supported the Lutheran Reformation?
    a. Luther advocated the overthrow of the authority of the German princes.
    b. Lutheranism sanctioned money-making and other earthly pursuits more wholeheartedly than did traditional Catholicism.
    c. Luther's reforms meant that indulgences and other ecclesiastical means of salvation would become less expensive and more readily available to the poor.
    d. Luther advocated redistribution of land and property throughout Germany.

14. The religious wars that followed the Protestant Reformation led generally to
    a. the restoration of Catholic unity.
    b. the establishment of Protestant dominance.
    c. a limited acceptance of the idea of religious pluralism.
    d. the end of the involvement of the state in religion.

15. The monarch most associated with Versailles and absolute monarchy was
    a. Charles I of England.
    b. Frederick William of Prussia.
    c. William of Orange of the Netherlands.
    d. Louis XIV of France.

16. How did Spanish American cities differ from those of Europe?
    a. American cities were laid out in a grid plan.
    b. American cities lacked churches.
    c. There was an absence of commerce in American cities.
    d. There were no Caribbean cities.

17. What accounted for the majority of the population loss suffered by Native Americans after the European arrival?
    a. losses in warfare
    b. enslavement
    c. epidemic diseases
    d. failure of marriage patterns among the Indians

18. Why were the encomiendas discontinued by 1540s and all but gone by the 1620s?
    a. The Spanish crown was unwilling to see the growth of a new nobility in the New World.
    b. The Indians refused to continue to serve under the imperial conditions established in the 1500s and demanded a new arrangement with the Spanish crown.
    c. Despite the continued economic prosperity of the encomienda system, the Spanish crown discontinued them in order to establish a free labor system in the Americas.
    d. The viceroys of the American colonies ordered their abolition in favor of enslavement of the Indian population.

19. Which of the following statements concerning the Spanish commercial system is most accurate?
    a. The merchant guild in Seville had virtual monopoly rights over goods shipped to America and handled much of the silver received in return until the 18th century.
    b. All trade from Spain after the mid-16th century was funneled through the city of Madrid.
    c. Nearly all trade with the Spanish colonies was carried in ships built in the New World and captained by colonists.
    d. The intent of the consulado was to keep prices in the Spanish colonies low.

20. The Catholic church introduced all of the following to American life EXCEPT
    a. universities.
    b. the construction of baroque churches.
    c. the sense of independence from the state.
    d. the printing press.

21. What conditions undercut the position of the Brazilian sugar plantation economy?
    a. A demographic disaster among the Indians of Brazil resulted in a shortage of labor for the sugar plantations shortly after 1700.
    b. Competition from English, French, and Dutch plantation colonies in the Caribbean led to rising prices for slaves and falling prices for sugar.
    c. The European market was flooded with sugar supplied from Asian colonies.
    d. A series of unusually wet winters flooded the traditional sugar regions and caused Brazilian planters to seek new land for the production of sugar.

22. What was the impact of the 18th century reforms on slavery in Brazil?
    a. Slavery was abolished.
    b. The slave trade with Africa was abolished.
    c. Slave imports were restricted to encourage the elimination of the plantation economy.
    d. Brazil was just as profoundly based on slavery in the late 18th century as it had ever been.

23. Which of the following statements concerning the early Portuguese trade forts is most accurate?
    a. The Portuguese trade forts permitted the political control of much of the African interior.
    b. Where Portuguese trade forts were established, large European colonies rapidly developed.
    c. Most of the forts were established with the agreement or license of local rulers.
    d. The Portuguese trade forts were the nodal points for colonial administration on the model of the American colonies.

24. In what manner did the Portuguese seize most of the slaves that were transported from Africa?
    a. They captured them in raids into the African interior.
    b. They traded for them with African rulers.
    c. As a result of the defeat of most of the African kingdoms, the Portuguese obtained a ready supply of slaves.
    d. They purchased them from the Muslim slave traders of the east African trading cities.

Estimated Slave Imports into the Americas by Importing Region, 1519–1866

Region and Country	Slaves
Brazil	3,902,000
British Caribbean	2,238,200
Spanish America	1,267,800
French Caribbean	403,700
Guianas*	361,100
British North America	129,700
Dutch Caribbean	73,100
Danish Caribbean	9,468,200

25. Considering the preceding table, why did South America and the Caribbean import the largest number of slaves?
    a. North American cash crops did not produce wealth on par with that of Caribbean cash crops, severely limiting the purchasing power of North American slave owners.
    b. In most of the slave regimes in the Caribbean and Latin America, slave mortality was high and fertility was low, contributing to the need for increased slave imports.
    c. Growing cotton in the temperate climate of the southern U.S. was not as dangerous as the work required of slaves in the silver mines and sugar plantations of Latin America.
    d. Whereas the U.S. depended more on natural population growth, the fact that the Atlantic slave trade concentrated on men contributed to the evolution of low fertility patterns in Latin America.

26. In what way did the trans-Saharan slave trade differ from that of the Atlantic slave trade?
    a. The Atlantic slave trade was carried out almost exclusively by Muslims.
    b. The trans-Saharan slave trade was carried out in much greater volume than the Atlantic slave trade.
    c. The trans-Saharan slave trade concentrated on women, but the Atlantic slave trade concentrated on young men.
    d. The African preference for retaining young male slaves to extend kinship lines implied that primarily women were available to the Atlantic trade, while men converted to Islam were more likely trade objects for the trans-Saharan trade.

27. How did the British organize the shipment of slaves to the Americas?
    a. In Britain, unlike elsewhere, the slave trade was carried out by uncontrolled private venture.
    b. The Royal African Company was chartered for the purpose of providing a source of slaves for colonies in Barbados, Jamaica, and Virginia.
    c. The British refused to participate in the slave trade and attempted to intercept shipments of slaves to the Americas beginning in the 1660s.
    d. The British government directly participated in the slave trade through use of the Royal Navy.

28. What was the political impact of the presence of Europeans on the African coast?
    a. States were more likely to form in the savanna regions of Africa.
    b. Strong centralized states began to form on the coastline in close proximity to the European trade forts.
    c. West and central African kingdoms just inland from the forts began to redirect their trade and expand their influence.
    d. State formation in Africa took place on the Indian Ocean coast away from the trade routes established by the Europeans.

29. Why were Africans sought for plantation labor in the Americas?
    a. There was no other labor supply available in the Americas.
    b. West Africans were already familiar with metallurgy, herding, and intensive agriculture whereas Indians were not.
    c. Sugar was a crop native to Africa and exported to the Americas from there.
    d. Africans rapidly expanded their population in the Latin American colonies.

30. How were the British colonies of the southern Atlantic coast of North America different from the Latin American colonies?
    a. There was no slavery in the British colonies.
    b. Although urban slavery was common, there was no plantation agricultural system on the North American mainland.
    c. Manumission of slaves tended to be more common in the British colonies.
    d. The British colonies depended less on imported Africans because of a higher birthrate and a lower mortality rate among enslaved families in North America.

31. Ivan IV, called Ivan the Terrible,
    a. wished to confirm tsarist autocracy by attacking the authority of boyars.
    b. abandoned the principles of territorial expansion in favor of centralizing power at home.
    c. allied himself with the Russian aristocracy in a policy of political decentralization.
    d. was responsible for the incorporation of Poland into the Russian empire.

32. Politically, what aspects of Western culture did Peter the Great emulate in Russia?
    a. parliamentary government
    b. aristocratic control of the bureaucracy
    c. streamlined bureaucracy and reorganized military
    d. republicanism

33. What was the limitation of Peter the Great's policies of cultural Westernization?
    a. He made no attempt to introduce Western education, particularly in technological subjects.
    b. Westernization was limited to the elite.
    c. Peter made no attempt to enforce cultural reforms.
    d. Despite tsarist proclamations, Westernization failed to have any impact on Russian society.

34. What was Catherine the Great's attitude toward the program of Westernization?
    a. Catherine flirted vigorously with the ideas of the French Enlightenment, but failed to take steps to abolish serfdom.
    b. Catherine rejected the concepts of Westernization in favor of a distinctive Russian culture.
    c. Catherine earned the title of Enlightened Monarch by fully embracing the ideas of the French Enlightenment, including the abolition of the serfs.
    d. Catherine was eager to continue the policy of Westernization, but was unable to attract Western philosophers to backward Russia.

35. What was one of the primary differences between the social organization of the West and Russia in the 17th and 18th centuries?
    a. Russia's merchant class was more fully developed than that of the West.
    b. The West had no formal aristocracy by the 18th century, but in Russia the nobility retained their political and social function.
    c. Russia saw a progressive intensification of serfdom while the West was relaxing this institution in favor of other labor systems.
    d. The agricultural labor of the West was subject to a more restrictive form of serfdom than that of Russia.

36. A substantial merchant class in Russia during the 18th century
    a. was restricted to the cities of Moscow, Novgorod, and St. Petersburg.
    b. sprang from peasant origins.
    c. emerged among the lesser nobility within the Russian cities.
    d. failed to develop.

37. Eastern Europe shared with Russia all of the following characteristics EXCEPT
    a. the dominance of the landed aristocracy.
    b. rigid serfdom.
    c. the lack of a native commercial class and a significant urban culture.
    d. the development of empire.

38. What permitted the Janissaries to gain a position of prominence in the Ottoman empire?
    a. Their control of artillery and firearms gave them prominence over the aristocratic Turkish cavalry.
    b. Their control of the bureaucracy made them indispensable to the operation of the empire.
    c. As members of the royal family, they had access to the sultans.
    d. They rapidly gained control of the mosques of the Ottoman empire and were able to define religious orthodoxy.

39. What did the Ottomans do to Constantinople following its fall in 1453?
    a. The Ottomans destroyed the city and moved their capital to Sophia.
    b. The original city remained, but in a much reduced condition that the Ottomans did little to restore.
    c. Soon after its conquest, the Ottoman sultan undertook the restoration and beautification of Constantinople.
    d. The Ottomans rapidly abandoned Constantinople to the leaders of the Orthodox Church who were responsible for its restoration and the construction of significant churches.

40. According to the map above, the center of the Safavid empire was the modern-day state of
    a. Syria.
    b. Iraq.
    c. Jordan.
    d. Iran.

41. Why was the battle of Chaldiran in 1514 so important?
    a. The battle established the military supremacy of the Safavids over the Ottomans and marked the end to eastern expansion of the Ottoman empire.
    b. The Safavids were dealt a devastating defeat that checked the westward advance of Shi'ism and decimated the ranks of the Turkic warriors who had built the Safavid empire.
    c. The combined armies of the Safavids and Ottomans defeated the Mughal armies and ended the policy of expansion undertaken by the Mughal emperors of India.
    d. The defeat of the Safavids by a western army reduced the Islamic Empire to economic dependency on the West and military inferiority to the other Muslim empires.

42. What led to the rapid demise of the Safavid empire?
    a. Like the Ottoman empire, the lack of a principle of succession led Abbas the Great to eliminate all capable rivals, leaving no capable ruler following his death.
    b. The Safavid defeat at the battle of Panipat at the hands of a Russian army stripped the empire of its military forces just as pressure from outside enemies increased.
    c. The collapse of the Safavid economy in the 18th century diminished the revenues of the empire to the point that the central government could no longer function.
    d. The successful conquest of the Ottoman empire overextended the Safavid resources, so that the central government became increasingly inefficient.

43. Which of the following descriptions of the accomplishments of Babur is NOT accurate?
    a. He was a fine military strategist and fierce fighter who went into battle alongside his troops.
    b. He wrote one of the great histories of India and was a fine musician.
    c. He reformed the ineffective Lodi bureaucracy to create a streamlined administration.
    d. He was a fine musician and designed gardens for his new capital at Delhi.

44. Which of the following statements concerning the reign of Akbar is NOT accurate?
    a. He personally oversaw the building of the military and administrative system.
    b. He patronized the arts.
    c. He extended the Mughal conquests in central and northern India.
    d. He attempted to purify Islam by removing Hindu influences.

45. Despite their armaments, what factor convinced the Europeans that they could make little headway against the kingdoms of Asia?
    a. the inferiority of European ships
    b. the distance from European ports
    c. European lack of bullion
    d. the large populations and well-entrenched political and economic systems of Asian kingdoms

46. Why did the Chinese abandon the commercial voyages of the Zheng He expeditions?
    a. Many of the ships were lost as a result of poor ship design and inadequate sailing technology.
    b. The size of the fleets was so limited that they could not compete with the greater capacity of the European voyages.
    c. The scholar-gentry saw the voyages, which were promoted by the Emperor's eunuchs, as a foolish waste of resources that the empire could not afford.
    d. The trade with foreign regions produced a negative trade balance for China that drained bullion from imperial coffers.

47. How successful was the Portuguese monopoly on Asian products?
    a. For some decades they were able to maintain a complete monopoly over Asian products shipped to Europe.
    b. Although they managed to monopolize some spices grown in limited locales, the Portuguese lacked the manpower and ships to sustain a monopoly.
    c. The Portuguese were unable to achieve control over any Asian products due to competition from the Chinese commercial navy.
    d. The Portuguese monopoly was rigidly enforced over Asian products for almost two centuries.

48. In what way did the Dutch and English participation within the Asian sea trading network change by the middle decades of the 17th century?
    a. For both the Dutch and the English, peaceful commerce came to be more profitable than forcible control and monopolies were aimed at European rather than Asian rivals.
    b. Both northern European nations abandoned the commerce in spices in favor of cotton and silk textiles.
    c. Unlike the Portuguese and Spanish, the northern European nations undertook wholesale conversion to Protestantism of the inhabitants of the Spice Islands.
    d. As allies, the Dutch and English were able to establish a naval supremacy in Asia sufficient to monopolize all trade within the Asian sea trading network.

49. According to the map below, what was the nature of the sea routes in the Asian trading network?
    a. Well-established routes directly crossing the major oceans were maintained from ancient times.
    b. Most of the navigation was along the coastlines.
    c. Only the Chinese and Arabs practiced navigation in the Asian trading network.
    d. The only sea-going routes crossed the Indian Ocean from the Swahili ports of east Africa to India.

50. Which of the following reforms was NOT introduced by the first Ming emperor?
    a. The position of the scholar-gentry within the bureaucracy was restored.
    b. State subsidies for imperial academies and regional colleges were reinstituted.
    c. Family influence in the selection of men to the Chinese bureaucracy was eliminated.
    d. The civil service examination system was reinstated.

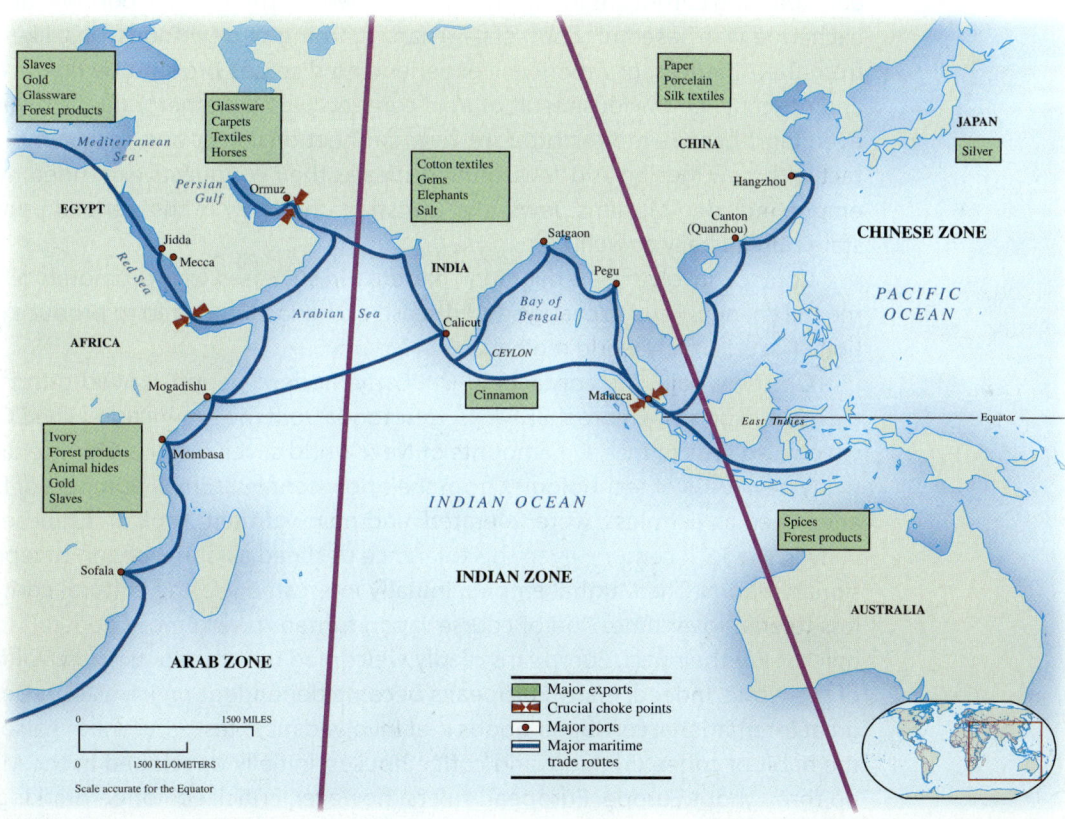

DOCUMENT BASED QUESTION

 Read the Document on MyHistoryLab:

A practice document-based question for Part 4 is available on MyHistoryLab.

CONTINUITY AND CHANGE-OVER-TIME ESSAY

Analyze continuities and changes in the Atlantic slave trade from 1450 to 1874.

COMPARATIVE ESSAY

Analyze similarities and differences between the basic structures of the three Islamic empires.

PART IV

REVISITING
The Early Modern Period

CONTACTS AND THEIR LIMITS

In the context of world history, all the basic changes during the Early Modern period involved new levels of contacts. Merchants from many parts of the world participated in the new world economy. Their military superiority at sea allowed Europeans to reach new areas, especially along coasts and islands. Chinese merchants continued to trade in southeast Asia, encountering Europeans in the Philippines as well as through the port of Macao. The Columbian exchange was based on contacts—Asians learning of new foodstuffs, like the sweet potato, from the Americas, or Americans experiencing diseases brought by contacts with Europeans and Africans. An obvious result of new contacts was the emergence of overseas empires, but even land-based empires brought new connections. Russians, for example, came into contact with new Muslim and Jewish minorities as their conquests expanded, while the Ottoman empire included Muslims, Jews, and Christians, not only in the general population but in the state bureaucracy as well.

Contacts involved new migration patterns. In key cases, they promoted new types of environmental change. Food exchange and disease exchange interacted to produce important population effects in many world regions.

On the whole, the contacts of the Early Modern period moved things—types of foods, germs, and goods—more than ideas. New foods from the Americas reached China, for example, which also took in massive amounts of New World silver. But the Chinese did not incorporate many new ideas or technologies from their new contacts. Small numbers of European missionaries, seen as harmless, were tolerated, and many of them took on Chinese dress and habits. Early in the 18th century, even this tolerance declined as China began to repress Christian missionary efforts. The Mughal empire, initially interested in wide cultural contacts, also became less tolerant over time. And of course Japan turned toward more general isolation even more quickly. For their part, Europeans gladly welcomed new products and wealth from other parts of the world. Indeed, many Europeans became dependent on items like sugar, one of the first great international consumer goods that involved mass taste. Europeans also eagerly imported the habit of coffee drinking, and coffee houses, initially developed in the Middle East, sprang up throughout Europe. European rulers, however, criticized coffee drinking as a foreign and dissolute habit and urged their subjects to stick to beer and wine. A new sense of superiority limited Europeans' openness to institutions and ideas from other regions. The Ottoman empire also kept a lid on many kinds of contacts, even as it experienced growing interaction with European as well as African and Asian merchants. Despite knowledge of the printing press, for example, Ottoman rulers forbade presses in the empire until the mid-18th century, on grounds they might be used to spread subversive ideas. Ottoman rulers did import Western doctors, who

Interior of a Turkish Caffinet in Constantinople. The use of coffee and coffee houses promoted new forms of consumerism and socialization in several regions.

actually knew no more than their local counterparts; otherwise, outside scientific developments were largely ignored.

There were exceptions to this pattern in which exchanges of goods outweighed interchange of ideas. Extensive Christian conversions in the Philippines, where the Spanish occupied directly, contrasted with the experience in most of Asia, where European Christian missionaries made only limited inroads on established affiliations to Buddhism, Hinduism, or Islam. The Ottoman empire opened new cultural links between the Balkans and Islam. Russia, of course, became an avid imitator of Western techniques and styles, although only at the elite level of society.

The Americas, specifically Latin America, formed another special case. Outside goods—germs, animals, but also European-manufactured guns and art work—were imported extensively. Europeans also introduced new ideas, especially pressure to convert to Christianity. Native Americans combined these imports with local traditions, merging some of their own gods with the roster of Christian saints or using traditional native art in Christian celebrations. The outcome, a classic result of contact, contained the outlines of a new culture that was neither traditional nor fully western. In some regions, imported African rituals and habits added to this mix of influences.

English Presbyterian missionary John Eliot addresses a gathering of Native Americans. Known as "the Apostle of the Indians," Eliot established the first church for Native Americans in Massachusetts. Missionary efforts of this sort formed a key element in shaping societies in the Americas.

CRITICAL THEMES

The point is obvious: The Early Modern period introduced many opportunities for new levels and types of contact. The results were, however, highly varied, with less widespread cultural exchange than might have been anticipated. Many peasant groups, in the interiors of Asia and Africa, experienced few new contacts of any sort. Even where trade and biological exchange penetrated, leaders and even ordinary people had some leeway about accepting other influences. Many people chose to stick to the tried and true; others, like the Japanese, launched a more internal pattern of cultural change. Americans, particularly those living along the coasts, were the great exception, but even here the native populations might modify unusual contacts and pressures to make them more recognizable and acceptable. The increased number and level of contacts of the era set new patterns in motion, but people responded to those new patterns in widely varying ways.

The multiple impacts of contacts, but also their limitations, were not the only key developments in the period. The Early Modern period offers new opportunities to examine, and compare, processes of state expansion and conflict. More empires were formed than ever before, but beneath the surface they offered various models of organization. Changes in labor systems were varied. Increasing reliance on wage labor in the West contrasted with new forms of servitude in several other societies. Figuring out the causes of key patterns invites analysis, as does the comparison of the emerging labor systems.

And while general trends of cultural change are elusive, the striking innovation in the West, with the Scientific Revolution and its aftermath, gives the Early Modern period another defining feature. Figuring out the impact of new science on other societies, already emerging by the 18th century but very gradually, become a legitimate cultural topic in world history from this point forward. ■

Bishamonten, one of the seven lucky Japanese gods. Originally from India where he is known as Tamonten Shitenno, god of treasure, war, and warriors. He wears armor, carries a spear, and also a pagoda of treasures. Historic temple, a holy site for the visually impaired. Founded in 701 C.E. by Saint Benki. Japanese cultural patterns revealed a distinctive set of contacts and local influences.

CRITICAL THINKING QUESTIONS

1. What were the most important achievements of the new Islamic empires?
2. Compare the European and the Chinese responses to the emerging world economy from 1450 to 1750.
3. Is 1750 a good date to end the Early Modern period? Are there other options worth considering?
4. What is the evidence suggests that a number of societies were becoming aware of Western science by the 18th century? What were the main causes of limited response?
5. Pick one key land-based empire and one overseas empire: Compare the functions and organization of the state in the two cases.

PART V
The Dawn of the Industrial Age, 1750–1900

Il Quarto Stato (The Fourth State) by artist Guiseppe Pellizza da Volpedo depicts a crowd of Italian socialists. Socialism was a key outcome of industrial conditions and 19th-century political change. (Giuseppe Pellizza da Volpedo, "Il Quarto Stato" 1901. Oil on canvas, 283 cm x 550 cm. Photo by Marcello Saporetti. Copyright Comune di Milano.)

PART OUTLINE

Chapter 24 The Emergence of Industrial Society in the West, 1750–1914

Chapter 25 Industrialization and Imperialism: The Making of the European Global Order

Chapter 26 The Consolidation of Latin America, 1830–1920

Chapter 27 Civilizations in Crisis: The Ottoman Empire, the Islamic Heartlands, and Qing China

Chapter 28 Russia and Japan: Industrialization Outside the West

THE OVERVIEW

Maps tell a crucial story for the "long" 19th century—a period whose characteristics ran from the late 18th century to 1900. A radically new kind of technology and economy arose in a few parts of the world in what began to be called the Industrial Revolution. The Industrial Revolution greatly increased industrial production as well as the speed and volume of transportation. Areas that industrialized early gained a huge economic lead over other parts of the world, and massive regional inequalities resulted.

The Industrial Revolution must be understood in two ways. First, it was a process that transformed agricultural economies, leading to growing urbanization, new social classes, new styles of life. This process began in western Europe, but it would later spread to other regions; it is still going on today. Industrialization as a global development, in other words, extends over several centuries. But second, in the 19th century itself industrialization was a largely Western monopoly, although with huge impact on other parts of the world. Ironically, the new output of Western factories actually reduced manufacturing in many places, like India and Latin America. Many regions faced rising pressures to increase agricultural and raw materials production at low cost. It was this growing imbalance that particularly shaped world history in the century and a half after 1750.

For Industrial countries gained a number of power advantages over the rest of the world, thanks to new, mass-produced weaponry, steamships, and developments in communications. Western Europe led a new and unprecedented round of imperialism, taking over Africa, Oceania, and many parts of Asia. Even countries that began industrialization a bit later, like Russia and Japan, were adding to their empires by 1914.

Industrialization was not the only fundamental current in the long 19th century. Dramatic political changes in the Atlantic world competed for attention, although imperialism overshadowed liberal reform ideals in other parts of the world. Industrialization, however, was the dominant force. Its impact spread to art, as some artists sought to capture the energies of the new machines while others, even stylistic innovators, emphasized nostalgic scenes of nature as a contrast to industrial reality. Industrialization also supported a new level of global contacts, turning the proto-industrial framework of the Early Modern period into globalization outright.

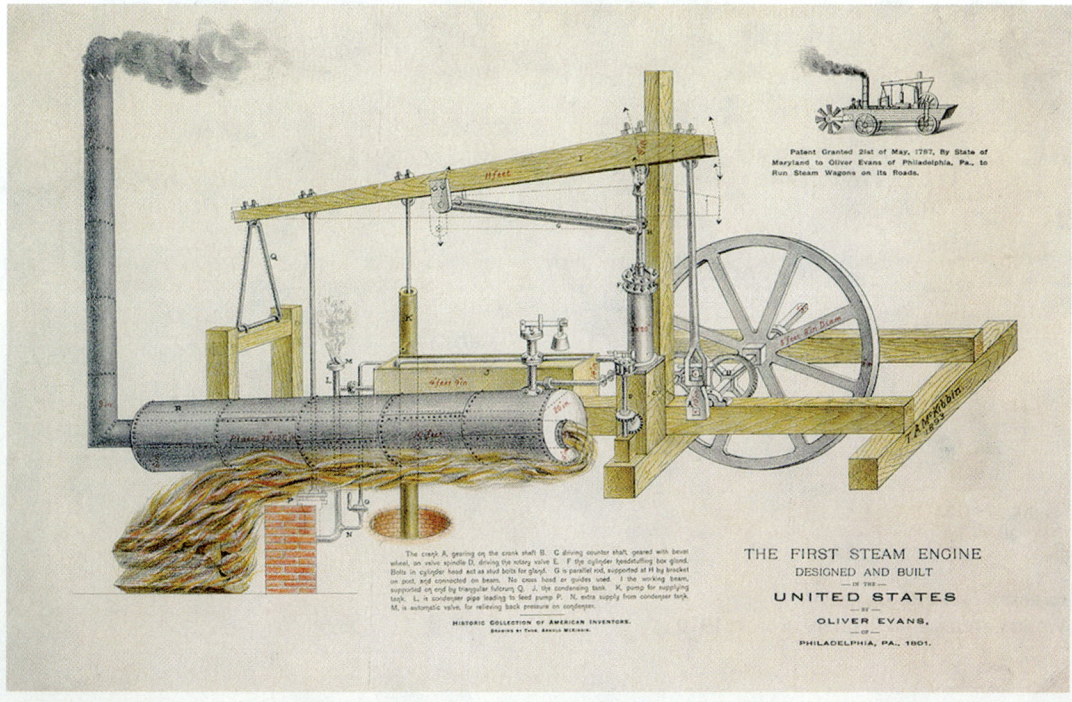

A sketch of the first successful steam-powered locomotive.

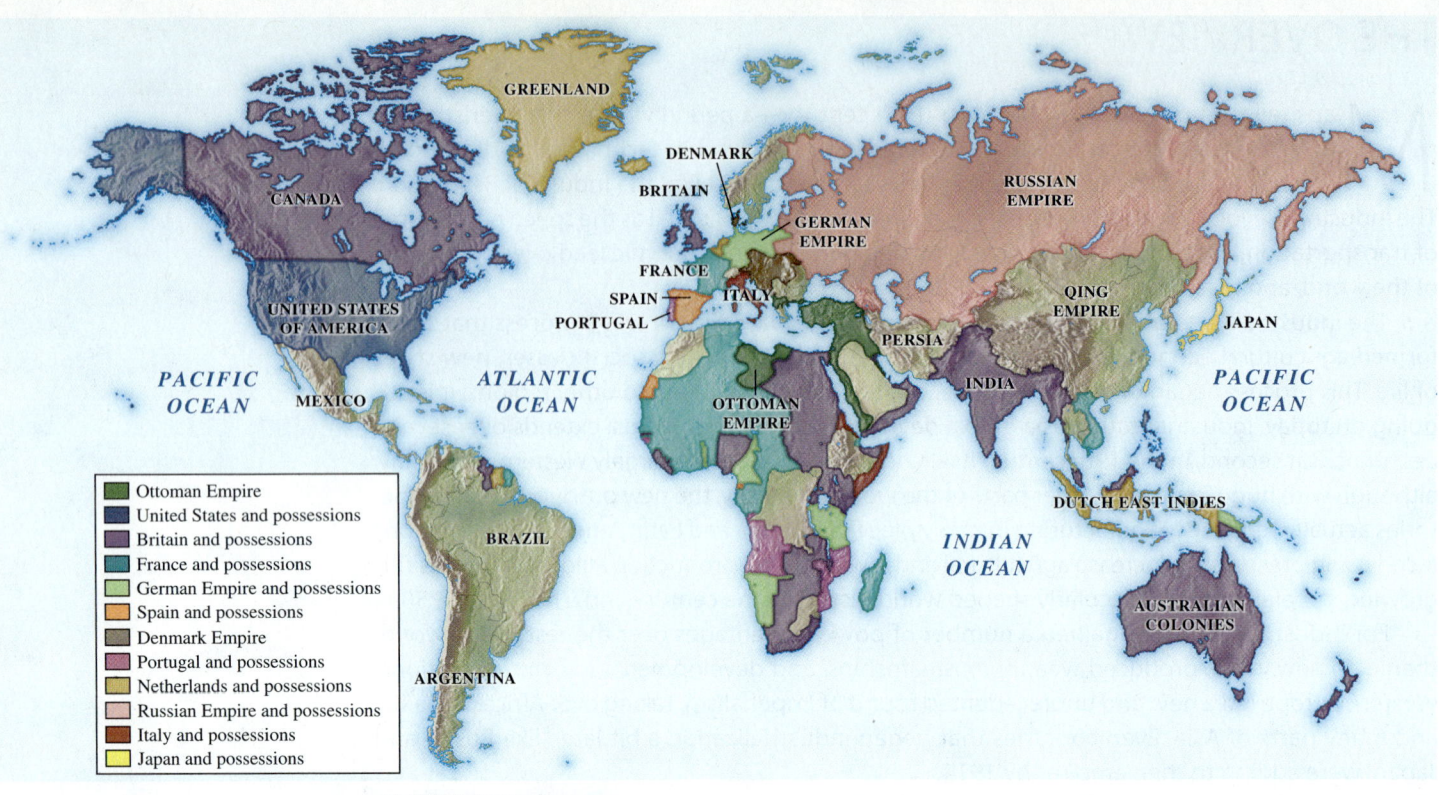

Major World Empires, c. 1910

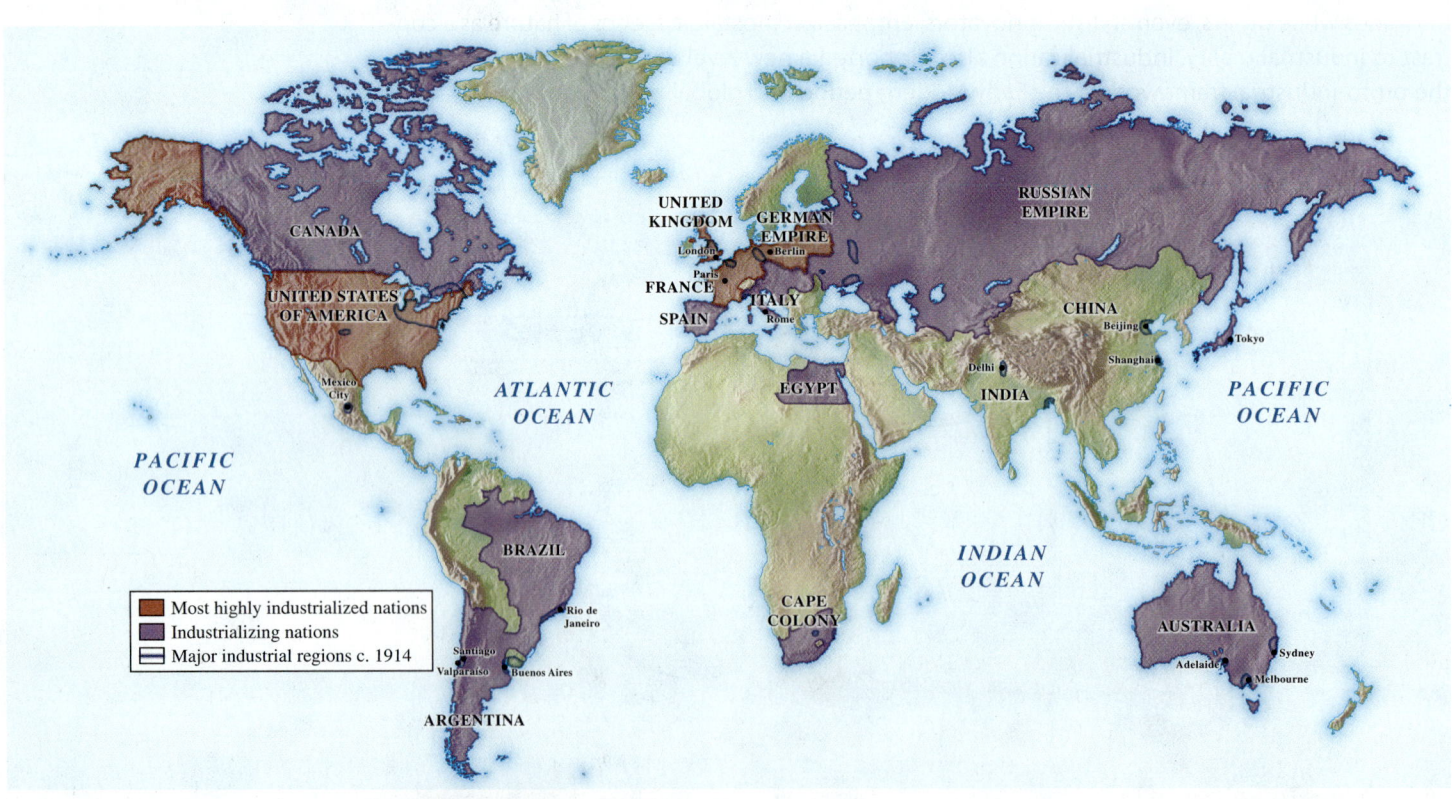

World Centers of Industrialization, c. 1910

Big Concepts

Industrialization was the dominant force in the long 19th century, but it helped spawn several more specific changes that in turn organize a series of Big Concepts. Western companies used their industrial manufacturing power, plus new systems of transportation and communication, to spread their form of capitalism on a global basis. On a global basis also, capitalists helped organize a growing segment of human labor. This was encouraged also by new patterns of global migration, reflecting population growth, new disruptions to established economies, and the changes in available global transportation. Western industrial dominance also fueled the new forms of imperialism and territorial expansion. Finally, new ideologies and political revolutions promoted reform currents of various sorts, some of them directed against the impacts of industrialization or imperialism. Industrialization and the growing globalization of capital and labor, imperialism, and the mix of new ideologies and reform currents—here were the Big Concepts that help organize a period of fundamental change.

TRIGGERS FOR CHANGE

By 1750 Europe's trading advantage over much of the rest of the world was increasing. Other gunpowder empires that had flourished during the Early Modern period were encountering difficulties; for example, the Ottoman empire began to lose territory in wars with Russia. In this context, Great Britain began to introduce revolutionary new technologies, most notably the steam engine. This core innovation soon led to further inventions that increased western Europe's economic advantage over most other parts of the world.

An impressive series of inventions emerged from Britain, France, the United States, and a few other countries at this time in world history, because Europeans knew they could make money in the world economy by selling manufactured goods to other societies in return for cheap foods and raw materials (including silver and gold). Therefore, businesses worked to accelerate the manufacturing process in order to increase their profits. European governments also began to create conditions designed to encourage industrial growth by improving roads and canals, developing new central banks, holding technology expositions, and limiting the rights of labor. In addition, about 1730, the population of western Europe began to grow very rapidly. This created new markets for goods and new workers who had no choice but to accept factory jobs. Finally, cultural changes encouraged invention and entrepreneurship. The rise of science and the European Enlightenment created an environment in which new discoveries seemed both possible and desirable. A rising appreciation of secular achievement encouraged businesspeople to undertake new ventures, and a growing number of western Europeans were interested in and could afford new goods.

Debate: The Causes of the Industrial Revolution

Historians continue to argue about what caused Europe's industrialization, including why Europe was first off the blocks in what ultimately became a global process. Industrialization caused such huge changes that explanation is clearly important, but also clearly challenging.

One explanation seeks simplicity. Great Britain in the 18th century was running short of wood for fuel. But it had abundant supplies of coal, conveniently located for transportation near rivers or the coast. Cheap, alternative fuel made it easy for manufacturers to decide to innovate. But using coal for power automatically encouraged new attention to machines to help pump water from mines as well as devices that could use coal more directly in the manufacturing process: hence the invention of the steam engine. Thanks to its success in world trade, and particularly its exploitation of American colonies, Britain also had capital to invest. Finally, once Britain got started, other Western countries could fairly quickly imitate.

Another explanation, more traditional, looks to a wider array of changes in the West. During the 18th century many Western countries worked to improve their banking systems. New economic ideas, stemming from the Enlightenment, produced new laws to promote competition. Governments began to sponsor road and canal building. All of these developments may be relevant, but several world historians have pointed out that western Europe was not measurably more advanced than China in terms of levels of wealth or new business formation. They caution against too much emphasis on a broad array of Western gains.

Recent interpretations suggest two emphases. First, while agreeing that the West was not particularly advanced across the board, historians do emphasize the importance of science and especially the Enlightenment in creating a culture open to technological and economic change. This culture helped motivate inventors and business leaders alike, and it could also encourage governments to take a supporting role. It helps explain why various countries in the West were ready quickly to follow British example.

Second, the global context may help. Europe's trading advantages and its exploitation of the Americas not only created capital for investment. They also taught Europeans the importance of manufacturing for export, as a key source of profit, and businessmen had been working for decades to discover new technologies that would allow Europe to outstrip India and China in the production of goods like printed cloth or porcelain.

Testing the various explanations for Europe's industrial revolution remains important, an ongoing challenge to careful analysis. One thing is clear: Whatever the combination of factors, once Western industrialization got going, it would have a number of further consequences, literally around the world.

THE BIG CHANGES

The Industrial Revolution had two broad results in the 19th century. First, in the industrial countries, the rise of the factory system changed many aspects of life. Work became more specialized and more closely supervised. The changes in work brought about by industrialization deeply affected families. Work moved out of the home, challenging traditional family life, in which all family members had participated in production. Although child labor was used early in the process of industrialization, increasingly childhood was redefined in industrial societies, away from work and toward schooling. Industrialization spurred the growth of cities. While new opportunities were involved, there was also great tension and, for a time, pockets of dreadful misery amid urban slums and machine-driven labor conditions.

Industrialization changed politics. New middle-class groups, expanding on the basis of industrial growth, sought a political voice. As urban workers grew restive, governments had to strengthen police forces and also, gradually, expand the right to vote among the lower classes. New nationalist loyalties involved ideological change away from primarily local and religious attachments, but they also provided identities for people whose traditional values were disrupted by industrial life and movement to the cities.

Outside the West, industrialization brought new economic imperatives. A few societies sought to industrialize early on. Egypt tried and largely failed, in the first half of the 19th century; a bit later, Japan and Russia launched industrial revolutions of their own. For most societies during the 19th century, the main effect of industrialization was to increase pressures to turn out food supplies and cheap raw materials for the industrial world, even though these societies were largely nonindustrial. Western dominance in the world economy increased, and involvement in this economy became more widespread. For Latin America this meant even more low-cost export production, with newly introduced products like coffee and increased output of resources like copper. Parts of Asia that had previously profited from the world economy were now pressed into more low-cost production. All over the world, cheap manufactured goods from Western factories put hundreds of thousands of traditional manufacturing workers, many of them women, out of a job.

While industrial transformations of the world economy exerted the greatest pressure for change, they also provided the context for European imperial expansion into many new areas. When they took over in places like Africa, Europeans moved quickly to intensify low-cost production of foods, minerals, and (sometimes) simple manufactured goods. Through outright imperialism or simply the threat of intervention, European military pressure forced literally every part of the world—including previous isolationists like Japan and Korea—into massive interaction with global trade.

Two other key changes accompanied this process of global economic change. First, the institution of slavery increasingly came under attack, a truly historic change in an old human institution. The Atlantic slave trade was legally abolished early in the 19th century. Then slave and serf systems were progressively eliminated in the Americas, Europe, Russia, and Africa. New ideas about human rights and new confidence in "free wage labor" facilitated the change. Significant population growth provided new sources of labor to replace slaves. Immigrants poured out of Europe to the Americas and Australia. Indenture systems brought massive numbers of Asians to Oceania, the Americas, and Africa. As slavery ended, harsh, low-paid "free" labor intensified in many places.

Second, the massive economic changes brought about by the Industrial Revolution impacted the environment. In industrial societies, smoke and the steady increase of chemical and urban wastes worsened regional air and water quality. The expansion of export production in other parts of the world also affected

1700 C.E.	1800 C.E.	1825 C.E.
1730–1850 Population boom in western Europe	**1805–1849** Muhammad Ali rules Egypt	**1825–1855** Repression in Russia
1770 James Watt's steam engine; beginning of Industrial Revolution	**1808–1825** Latin American wars of independence	**1826** New Zealand colonization begins
1776–1783 American Revolution	**1815** Vienna settlement	**1830, 1848** Revolutions in Europe
1786–1790 First British reforms in India	**1815** British annexation of Cape Town and region of southern Africa	**1835** English education in India
1788 Australian colonization begins	**1822** Brazil declares independence	**1838** Ottoman trade treaty with Britain
1789–1815 French Revolution and Napoleon	**1823** Monroe Doctrine	**1839–1841** Opium War between England and China
1789 Napoleon's invasion of Egypt		**1839–1876** Reforms in Ottoman empire
		1840 Semiautonomous government in Canada
		1846–1848 Mexican-American War
		1848 ff. Beginnings of Marxism

the environment in negative ways. The introduction of crops like coffee and cotton, for example, to new parts of Africa and Latin America often caused significant soil erosion.

GLOBALIZATION

Western industrial and military power, when joined with new technologies in transportation and communication, helped generate the first full emergence of globalization after the 1850s. The telegraph, railroads, and, above all, steam shipping greatly speeded the movement of goods and news around the world. Construction of the Suez Canal and then, early in the 20th century, the Panama Canal, cut massive amounts of time off oceanic shipping. Exchanges of bulk goods—wheat and meats from the Americas, metal ores, as well as expensive manufactured products—soared beyond any previous precedent.

Modern globalization differed from earlier proto-globalization not only because of the volume of goods exchanged and the impact of exports and imports on local economies from Hawaii to Mozambique to Honduras. Economic contacts were now enhanced by transnational political agreements. Some agreements related closely to economic relationships: A universal Postal Union in 1874 established international recognition of each nation's stamps, so that letters could be mailed across borders for the first time. Other efforts, however, like the new Geneva Conventions on the treatment of military prisoners, began to globalize some ideas about human rights. Additional international conventions began to implement quarantines to prevent the spread of epidemics like cholera. New levels of cultural globalization showed particularly in the clear emergence of transnational sports interests, particularly around soccer, football, and American baseball. Finally, global economic exchange began to have significant regional environmental impacts. Development of a rubber industry in Brazil, to meet needs in industrial countries, led to important levels of deforestation. The advent of globalization thus involved changes on various fronts.

Different societies participated variously in globalization, which raises important issues of comparison and continuity. New debates arose in Egypt about whether the veiling of women represented Islamic identity or an offense to global standards for women. Many countries, even though they could not resist global involvements, deplored Western dominance, and disproportionate Western benefit, from the process. Some societies, like Japan, managed to encounter globalization while preserving a sense of separate identity. The variations, and the widespread sense of resentment against too much foreign control and influence, were significant in their own right.

Political Revolutions

The long 19th century was ushered in not only by initial industrialization, but also by a series of major revolutions. The American Revolution cast off British colonial controls, while the great French Revolution had even more sweeping implications for political and social change. The revolutionary era would continue in western Europe through 1848, and it would also spur independence struggles in Latin America. A host of new ideas were nourished in the revolutionary era. Many of them, however, did not have much immediate echo outside the Atlantic world. European imperialists did not emphasize new ideas about political freedom or voting rights. The global impact of revolution was both gradual and complex, outside of the Atlantic world itself.

Revolutionary ideals did, however, play some role in the growing movement against slavery. It was from the revolutionary period also that nationalism gained new visibility. The long 19th century would see a steady spread of nationalism from its initial base in Europe and the Americas to every other major region. Indian nationalism, for example, was clearly taking shape by the

1850 C.E.	1875 C.E.	1900 C.E.
1850–1864 Taiping Rebellion in China	**1877–1878** Ottomans out of most of Balkans; Treaty of San Stefano	**1901** Commonwealth of Australia
1853 Perry expedition to Edo Bay in Japan		**1903** Construction of Panama Canal begins
1854–1856 Crimean War	**1879–1890s** Partition of west Africa	**1904–1905** Russo-Japanese War
1858 British assume control over India	**1882** British takeover of Egypt	**1905–1906** Revolution in Russia; limited reforms
1860–1868 Civil strife in Japan	**1885** Formation of National Congress Party in India	**1908** Young Turk rising
1861 Emancipation of serfs in Russia		**1910** Japan annexes Korea
1861–1865 American Civil War	**1886–1888** Slavery abolished in Cuba and Brazil	**1911–1912** Revolution in China; end of empire
1863 Emancipation of slaves in United States	**1890** Japanese constitution	**1914–1918** World War I
1864–1871 German unification	**1890s** Partition of east Africa	
1868–1912 Meiji (reform) era in Japan	**1894–1895** Sino Japanese War	
1870–1910 Acceleration of "demographic transition" in western Europe and the United States	**1895** Cuban revolt against Spain	
	1898 Formation of Marxist Social Democratic Party in Russia	
1870–1910 Expansion of commercial export economy in Latin America	**1898** Spanish-American War; United States acquires the Philippines, Puerto Rico, and Hawaii; United States intervenes in Cuba	
1871–1912 High point of European imperialism	**1898–1901** Boxer Rebellion in China	

1880s, Turkish nationalism in the following decade. Dealing with the nature and impact of this new political force is an important analytical assignment.

CONTINUITY

Industrialization's global impact and new forces of revolution did not destroy continuities from the past. In the first place, although industrialization and early globalization were indeed revolutionary, their consequences were spread out over many decades. Dramatic innovations such as department stores and ocean-going steamships should not conceal the fact that such stores controlled only about 5 percent of all retail commerce in major Western cities—the rest centered on more traditional shops, peddling, and outdoor markets.

Continuity also shows in the different ways specific groups and regions reacted to change. The need to respond to Western economic and, often, military pressure was quite real around the world. But reactions varied in part with local conditions. Japanese society adapted considerably to facilitate industrialization. The feudal system was abolished outright, but its legacy helped to shape Japanese business organizations. The absence of a comparable organizational legacy may have reduced Chinese flexibility for some time. The spread of literacy in Russia in the later 19th century—part of Russia's efforts to reform—created new opportunities for popular literature, as had occurred earlier in the West. But in contrast to Western literature, which often celebrated outlaws, Russian adventure stories always included the triumph of the state over disorder. The cultural differences illustrated by these comparisons did not necessarily persist without alteration, but they continued to influence regional patterns.

Response to change also included the "invention" of traditions. Many societies sought to compensate for disruption by appealing to apparent sources of stability that drew on traditional themes. Many Western leaders emphasized the sanctity of the family and domestic roles for women, hoping that the home would provide a "haven" amid rapid economic change. The ideas of the family as a haven and of the special domestic virtues of women were partly myths, even as both took on the status of tradition. In the 1860s the U.S. government instituted Thanksgiving as a national holiday, and many Americans assumed that this was simply an official recognition of a long-standing celebration; in fact, Thanksgiving had been only rarely and fitfully observed before this new holiday, designed to promote family and national unity, was newly established. Japanese leaders by the 1880s invented new traditions about the importance of the emperor as a divinely appointed ruler, again as a means of counterbalancing rapid change.

Even more widely, nationalism, as it spread, helped leaders in many societies talk about the importance of tradition, even as they worked for some changes that might boost national strength or establish political independence. A key appeal of nationalism was its claim to define and defend a particular identity, and traditional claims played a key part in this process. Many nationalists played up artistic traditions, or folklore, or religious values as a buffer against too much external influence.

IMPACT ON DAILY LIFE: LEISURE

The Industrial Revolution transformed leisure. Leaders in industrial centers wanted to discourage traditional festivals, because they took too much time away from work and sometimes led to rowdiness on the part of workers. Factory rules also limited napping, chatting, wandering around, and drinking on the job. In the early decades of industrialization, leisure declined at first—replaced by long and exhausting work days—just as it had when agriculture replaced hunting and gathering.

With time, however, industrial societies introduced new kinds of leisure. Professional sports began to take shape around the middle of the 19th century. A bit later, new forms of popular theater attracted many people in the cities. The idea of vacations also spread: Workers took same-day train excursions to beaches, and travel companies formed to assist the middle classes in more ambitious trips. Much of the new leisure depended on professional entertainers, with the bulk of the population turning into spectators.

While the most dramatic innovations in leisure occurred in industrial societies, here too there was quick connection to the wider world—another sign of early globalization. Many mine and plantation owners sought to curb traditional forms of leisure activity in the interests of more efficient production. Although they had less success than factory owners did, they did have some impact. New forms of leisure pioneered in western Europe or the United States also caught on elsewhere. Soccer began to win interest in Latin America by the 1860s. Baseball began to spread from the United States to the rest of the Americas and Japan by the 1890s. By the 1920s, movies had won global attention as well. While most societies retained traditional, regional leisure forms, something of a global leisure culture was beginning to emerge.

SOCIETIES AND TRENDS

Chapters in this section begin with developments in the West, where industrialization and new political ideas first emerged. The West also spawned new settler societies in the United States, Canada, Australia, and New Zealand. These developments are described in Chapter 24. Chapter 25 focuses on the world economy and imperialism, tracing the effects of Western industrialization on the nonindustrial world. Chapter 26 describes the balance between new forces within Latin America. Chapter 27 describes developments in key parts of Asia as they responded to the challenges of Western power and economic change. Chapter 28 deals with two non-Western societies, Russia and Japan, that launched ambitious plans for industrialization in the late 19th century; the comparative study of the processes of industrialization in Russia, Japan, and the West sheds new light on the varied forms this process could take. ■

The Emergence of Industrial Society in the West, 1750–1900

24

Listen to Chapter 24 on MyHistoryLab

Why did an anti-Chinese riot break out in Milwaukee in 1889 when only 16 Chinese immigrants were living in the whole state of Wisconsin? The riot occurred in March. It followed press reports that Chinese laundrymen were seducing European American girls (Figure 24.1). One paper claimed there was a sinister ring transporting girls to Chicago where they would be forced to marry Chinese men. The headlines were inflammatory: "Chinese Horrors. Twenty-two Children Are Lured into the Dens." Following accusations, police did arrest two Chinese. But court procedures were too slow for the public. Large crowds gathered, calling for lynchings, abusing

LEARNING OBJECTIVES

What changes helped prepare revolutionary upheaval in western Europe and North America? p. 562	24.1
What ideas did the French and American revolutions share? p. 564	24.2
What were the most important features of early industrialization? p. 569	24.3
What were the main changes in the nature and functions of government in the later 19th century? p. 577	24.4
What was the relationship between scientific and artistic change in the later 19th century? p. 576	24.5
Were the settler societies part of a common Western civilization, or did they differ fundamentally from western Europe? p. 579	24.6
What were the basic causes of growing diplomatic tension in Europe by 1900? p. 583	24.7

FIGURE **24.1** A Chinese laundry shop, 1855. Chinese workers began to reach the United States in the mid-19th century, part of a larger stream of Asian labor migrations to many areas in the world. The mostly uneducated and unskilled Chinese workers first came to America in response to advertising by railroad companies, who wanted cheap labor to build the Western railroads. Although the new immigrants faced resentment from American workers, both because of job competition and because of real or imagined differences in values, the Chinese managed to establish themselves in some additional types of work, especially laundries. These enterprises were attractive to the Chinese because they required little specialized skill or capital, and American men did not object to Chinese laundries, as they considered laundry to be "women's work."

Watch the Video Series on MyHistoryLab

Learn about some key topics related to this chapter with the *MyHistoryLab Video Series: Key Topics in World History*

Chinese effigies, and burning and looting Chinese stores. After a tense few days, most of the Chinese immigrants left town.

From a world history standpoint, this incident is not significant, but it is suggestive. First, it occurred after several decades of Chinese immigration into the United States, where initially many worked on western railways. This in turn was part of a larger movement of people from Asia to the Americas and elsewhere—a key migration theme for the period—as population growth in Asian nations combined with a deteriorating position in the world economy fuelled mass Asian emigration. Large Japanese populations, for example, emerged in places like Brazil and Hawaii. More than a million Chinese emigrated to various parts of the Americas in the decades before and after 1900, and there was massive movement from India, Japan, and the Philippines as well. This new migration from Asia to the Americas was a major departure in world history, and it would continue into the 21st century.

Second, of course, the Milwaukee incident illustrates the anxieties that contact with Asians caused among many Americans. The 1880s saw massive anti-Chinese rioting in the western United States, with more than 140 Chinese murdered and more than 10,000 forced to leave their homes and stores. In 1882 the first of several measures was passed to limit Chinese immigration, an exclusionary policy that would last until 1943. Anxiety focused both on Chinese competition with American labor and on accusations of predatory sexual behavior. It proved difficult, for several decades, for Chinese Americans to assimilate more fully into national life. And of course, as with many immigrants, some did not want to. For example, many Chinese spent considerable sums to send the bodies of their deceased relatives back to China, the only place, in their view, where ancestors could be properly accommodated. ■

Western history in the 19th century operates amid accelerating international contacts—of the sort that brought new Asian migration to the United States. Developments in the West, even more obviously, altered the global context in turn, through the effects of industrialization, political upheaval, and new social and cultural reforms.

For change was the name of the game in the 19th-century West—including the addition of important new settler societies in the United States and elsewhere substantially shaped by Western influences. In 1750 western Europe consisted almost entirely of monarchies. By 1914 many monarchies had been overthrown, and everywhere powerful legislatures, based on extensive voting systems, defined much of the political apparatus. Twice, in the first 15 years of the 19th century and again in the 1860s, western Europe was rocked by significant warfare, but much of the period was relatively peaceful, but by 1914 a new alliance system had emerged that was about to plunge not only Europe but other parts of the world into massive bloodshed. The rise of a new middle class, novel issues for women, substantial changes in science and popular culture—these were other areas in which tradition seemed to erode under the impact of industrialization and urban growth.

CONTEXT FOR REVOLUTION

> New ideas helped stimulate a wave of revolutions in the whole Atlantic world from the 1770s to 1848. Revolutionary patterns would gain international influence; they also interacted with the early effects of Western industrialization.

24.1 What changes helped prepare revolutionary upheaval in western Europe and North America?

Against the backdrop of intellectual challenge, commercial growth, and population pressure, the placid politics of the 18th century were shattered by the series of revolutions that took shape in the 1770s and 1780s. This was the eve of the **age of revolution**, a period of political upheaval beginning

1700 C.E.	1820 C.E.	1840 C.E.	1860 C.E.	1880 C.E.	1900 C.E.
1730 ff. Massive population rise	**1820** Revolutions in Greece and Spain; rise of liberalism and nationalism	**1840** Union act reorganizes Canada, provides elected legislature	**1860–1870** Second Maori War	**1880s ff.** High point of impressionism in art	**1901** Commonwealth of Australia creates national federation
c. 1770 James Watt's steam engine; beginning of Industrial Revolution	**1820s ff.** Industrialization in United States	**1843–1848** First Maori War, New Zealand	**1861–1865** American Civil War	**1881–1914** Canadian Pacific Railway	**1907** New Zealand gains dominion status in British Empire
1788 First convict settlement in Australia	**1823** First legislative council in Australia	**1846–1848** Mexican-American War	**1863** Emancipation Proclamation, United States	**1881–1889** German social insurance laws enacted	**1912–1913** Balkan Wars
1789 George Washington first president of the United States	**1826–1837** Active European colonization begins in New Zealand	**1848 ff.** Writings of Karl Marx; rise of socialism	**1864–1871** German unification	**1882** United States excludes Chinese immigrants	**1914** Beginning of World War I
1789–1799 French Revolution	**1829** Andrew Jackson seventh president of United States	**1848–1849** Revolutions in several European countries	**1867** British North America Act unites eastern and central Canada	**1891–1898** Australia and New Zealand restrict Asian immigration	
1790 ff. Beginning of per capita birth rate decline (United States)	**1830** Revolutions in several European countries	**1850** Australia's Colonies Government Act allows legislature and more autonomy	**1870–1879** Institution of Third Republic, France	**1893** Women's suffrage in New Zealand	
1793 First free European settlers in Australia	**1832** Reform Bill of 1832 (England)	**1852** New constitution in New Zealand; elected councils	**1870s ff.** Rapid birth rate decline	**1898** Spanish-American War; United States acquires Puerto Rico, Guam, Philippines	
1793–1794 Radical phase of French Revolution	**1837** Rebellion in Canada	**1859** Darwin's *Origin of Species*	**1870s ff.** Spread of compulsory education laws	**1898** United States annexes Hawaii	
1799–1815 Reign of Napoleon	**1837–1842** U.S.–Canada border clashes	**1859–1870** Unification of Italy	**1871–1914** High point of European imperialism	**1899** United States acquires part of Samoa	
1800–1850 Romanticism in literature and art	**1839** New British colonial policy allows legislature and more autonomy		**1879–1907** Alliance system: Germany-Austria (**1879**); Germany-Austria-Russia (**1881**); Germany-Italy-Austria (**1882**); France-Russia (**1891**); Britain-France (**1904**); Britain-Russia (**1907**)		
1803 Louisiana Purchase (United States)					
1810–1826 Rise of democratic suffrage in United States					
1815 Congress of Vienna ushers in a more conservative period in Europe					

roughly with the American Revolution in 1775 and continuing through the French Revolution of 1789 and other movements for change up to 1848. The wave of revolutions caught up many social groups with diverse motives, some eager to use revolution to promote further change and some hoping to turn back the clock and recover older values.

The same changes that rocked politics also helped establish a context for the first stages of industrialization. Early industrialization, important in its own right, would ultimately interact with political revolution, generating a final set of upheavals in 1848 that ended this revolutionary era.

age of revolution Period of political upheaval beginning roughly with the American Revolution in 1775 and continuing through the French Revolution of 1789 and other movements for change up to 1848.

Forces of Change

Three forces were working to shatter Europe's calm by the mid-18th century. The first of the forces was cultural, for intellectual ferment was running high. Enlightenment thinkers challenged regimes that did not grant full religious freedom or that insisted on aristocratic privilege, and a few called for widespread popular voice in government. Jean-Jacques Rousseau argued for government based on a general will, and this could be interpreted as a plea for democratic voting. Voltaire attacked the Church for repressing human liberty. Enlightenment thinkers collectively stood for freedoms of religion and the press and changes in government structure that would limit the powers of kings and aristocrats. They promoted their views vigorously to a growing public audience. Unquestionably, intellectual challenges played a major role in triggering eventual revolutionary outbreaks. Enlightenment thinkers also encouraged economic and technological change and policies that would promote industry; manufacturers and political reformers alike could take inspiration from these ideas.

Along with cultural change, ongoing commercialization continued to stir the economy. Businesspeople, gaining new wealth, might well challenge the idea that aristocrats alone should hold the highest political offices. They certainly were growing interested in new techniques that might spur production. Commercial practices might also draw attack, from artisans or peasant villagers who preferred older economic values. This could feed revolution as well.

population revolution Huge growth in population in western Europe beginning about 1730; prelude to Industrial Revolution; population of France increased 50 percent, England and Prussia 100 percent.

A final source of disruption was occurring more quietly at all social levels. Western Europe experienced its huge population jump after about 1730. Within half a century, the population of France rose by 50 percent; that of Britain and Prussia rose 100 percent. This **population revolution** was partly the result of better border policing by the efficient nation-state governments, which reduced the movement of disease-bearing animals. More important was improved nutrition resulting from the growing use of the potato. These factors reduced the death rate, particularly for children; instead of more than 40 percent of all children dying by age 2, the figure by the 1780s was closer to 33 percent. More children surviving also meant more people living to have children of their own, so the birth rate increased as well.

Population pressure at this level always has dramatic impact. Upper-class families, faced with more surviving children, tried to tighten their grip on existing offices. In the late 18th century, it became harder for anyone who was not an aristocrat to gain a high post in the church or state. This reaction helped feed demands for change by other groups. Above all, population pressure drove many people into the working class as they lost any real chance of inheriting property, creating new motives for protest.

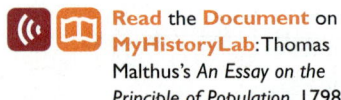

Read the Document on MyHistoryLab: Thomas Malthus's *An Essay on the Principle of Population*, 1798

The population growth of the 18th century prompted a rapid expansion of domestic manufacturing in western Europe and, by 1800, in the United States. Hundreds of thousands of people became full- or part-time producers of textile and metal products, working at home but in a capitalist system in which materials, work orders, and sales depended on urban merchants. This development has been called **proto-industrialization**, and it ultimately encouraged new technologies to expand production further because of the importance of new market relationships and manufacturing volume.

proto-industrialization Preliminary shift away from agricultural economy in Europe; workers become full- or part-time producers of textile and metal products, working at home but in a capitalist system in which materials, work orders, and ultimate sales depended on urban merchants; prelude to Industrial Revolution.

Population upheaval and the spread of a propertyless class that worked for money wages had a sweeping impact on a variety of behaviors in Western society, including North America. Many villagers began to change their dress to more urban styles; this suggests an early form of new consumer interest. Among groups with little or no property, parental authority began to decline because the traditional threat of denying inheritance had no meaning. Youthful independence became more marked, and although this was particularly evident in economic behavior as many young people looked for jobs on their own, the new defiance of authority might have had political implications as well.

THE AGE OF REVOLUTION

24.2 What ideas did the French and American revolutions share?

> The unification of Italy and Germany created new rivalries in western Europe. European countries developed new functions for governments, responding to industrial pressures, including socialism.

Overall, the spread of social tensions but also the attraction of new political ideas helped generate revolutionary political movements on both sides of the Atlantic. These Atlantic revolutions embraced independence efforts in North and later South America, a major revolution in France, and then a series of risings in various parts of western and central Europe that ran through the first half of the 19th century.

The American Revolution

When Britain's Atlantic colonies rebelled in 1775, it was primarily a war for independence rather than a full-fledged revolution. A large minority of American colonists resisted Britain's attempt to impose new taxes and trade controls on the colonies after 1763. Many settlers also resented restrictions on movement into the frontier areas. The colonists also invoked British political theory to argue that they should not be taxed without representation. The Stamp Act of 1765, imposing taxes on documents and pamphlets, particularly roused protest against British tyranny. Other grievances were involved. Crowding along the eastern seaboard led some younger men to seek new opportunities, including political office, that turned them against the older colonial leadership. Growing commerce antagonized some farmers and artisans, who looked for ways to defend the older values of greater social equality and community spirit.

With the start of the **American Revolution**, colonial rebels set up a new government, which issued the Declaration of Independence in 1776 and authorized a formal army to pursue its war. The persistence of the revolutionaries was combined with British military blunders and significant aid from the French government, designed to embarrass its key enemy. After several years of fighting, the United States won its freedom and, in 1789, set up a new constitutional structure based on Enlightenment principles, with checks and balances between the legislature and the executive branches of government, and formal guarantees of individual liberties. Voting rights, although limited, were widespread, and the new regime was for a time the most advanced in the world. Socially, the revolution accomplished less; slavery was untouched.

Read the Document on MyHistoryLab: Franklin and the British Parliament, "Proceedings Regarding The Stamp Act"

American Revolution Rebellion of English American colonies along Atlantic seaboard between 1775 and 1783; resulted in independence for former British colonies and eventual formation of United States of America.

Crisis in France in 1789

The next step in the revolutionary spiral occurred in France. It was the **French Revolution** that most clearly set in motion the political restructuring of Western Europe. Several factors combined in the 1780s in what became a classic pattern of revolutionary causation. Ideological insistence on change won increasing attention from the mid-18th century onward, as Enlightenment thinkers urged the need to limit the powers of the Catholic Church, the aristocracy, and the monarchy. Social changes reinforced the ideological challenge. Some middle-class people, proud of their business or professional success, wanted a greater political role. Many peasants, pressed by population growth, wanted fuller freedom from landlords' demands.

The French government and upper classes proved incapable of reform. Aristocrats tightened their grip in response to their own population pressure, and the government proved increasingly ineffective—a key ingredient in any successful revolution. Finally, a sharp economic slump in 1787 and 1788, triggered by bad harvests, set the seal on revolution.

The French king, **Louis XVI**, called a meeting of the traditional parliament to consider tax reform for his financially pinched regime. But middle-class representatives, inspired by Enlightenment ideals, insisted on turning this assembly (which had not met for a century and a half) into a modern parliament, with voting by head (that is, each representative with a vote, rather than a single vote for each estate) and with majority representation for nonnoble property owners. The fearful king caved in after some street riots in Paris in the summer of 1789, and the revolution was under way.

Events that summer were crucial. The new assembly, with its middle-class majority, quickly turned to devising a new political regime. A stirring ***Declaration of the Rights of Man and the Citizen*** proclaimed freedom of thought. Like the American Declaration of Independence, this document defined natural rights as "liberty, property, security, and resistance to oppression" and specifically guaranteed free expression of ideas. A popular riot stormed a political prison, the Bastille, on July 14, in what became the revolution's symbol; ironically, almost no prisoners were there. Soon after this, peasants seized manorial records and many landed estates. This triggered a general proclamation abolishing manorialism, giving peasants clear title to much land, and establishing equality under the law. Although aristocrats survived for some time, the principles of aristocratic rule were undercut. The privileges of the church were also attacked, and church property was seized. A new constitution proclaimed individual rights, including freedom of religion, press, and property. A strong parliament was set up to limit the king, and about one-half the adult male population—those with property—were eligible to vote.

French Revolution Revolution in France between 1789 and 1800; resulted in overthrow of Bourbon monarchy and old regimes; ended with establishment of French empire under Napoleon Bonaparte; source of many liberal movements and constitutions in Europe.

Read the Document on MyHistoryLab: Emmanuel Joseph Sieyès, *What Is the Third Estate?*

Louis XVI (1754–1793) Bourbon monarch of France who was executed during the radical phase of the French Revolution.

Declaration of the Rights of Man and the Citizen Adopted during the liberal phase of the French Revolution (1789); stated the fundamental equality of all French citizens; later became a political source for other liberal movements.

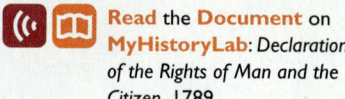

Read the Document on MyHistoryLab: *Declaration of the Rights of Man and the Citizen*, 1789

CHAPTER 24 The Emergence of Industrial Society in the West, 1750–1900

VISUALIZING THE PAST

The French Revolution in Cartoons

THIS CARTOON, TITLED *The Former Great Dinner of the Modern Gargantua with His Family*, appeared in 1791 or 1792, as the French Revolution was becoming more radical. It pictures the king as a latter-day Gargantua, referring to a French literary figure who was a notoriously great eater.

QUESTIONS

- How does the cartoon characterize the relationship between French society and economy and the monarchy?
- What conclusions might readers of the cartoon draw about what should happen to the monarchy?
- With improvements in printing and literacy, cartoons were becoming more available, and they have continued to be important into the present day. Why were they effective as a means of communicating ideas?

The French Revolution: Radical and Authoritarian Phases

By 1792 the initial push for reform began to turn more radical. Early reforms provoked massive opposition in the name of church and aristocracy, and civil war broke out in several parts of France. Monarchs in Britain, Prussia, and Austria trumpeted their opposition to the revolution, and France soon moved toward European war as well. These pressures led to a takeover by radical leaders, who wanted to press the revolution forward and to set up firmer authority in the revolution's defense. The radicals abolished the monarchy. The king was decapitated on the **guillotine**, a new device introduced, Enlightenment-fashion, to provide more humane executions, but instead it became a symbol of revolutionary bloodthirst. The radicals also executed several thousand opponents in what was named the Reign of Terror, even though by later standards it was mild.

The leader of the radical phase was Maximilien Robespierre (1758–1794), a classic example of a revolutionary ideologue. Born into a family of lawyers, he gained his law degree in 1781 and soon was publishing Enlightenment-style political tracts. The new philosophies inspired passion in Robespierre, particularly the democratic ideas of Rousseau. Elected to all the initial revolutionary assemblies, Robespierre headed the prosecution of the king in 1792 and then took over the leadership of government. He put down many factions, sponsored the Terror, and worked to centralize the government. In 1794 he set up a civic religion, the "cult of the Supreme Being," to replace Catholicism. Personally incorruptible, Robespierre came to symbolize the single-minded revolutionary. But he shied away from significant social reforms that might have drawn urban support. He was convinced that he knew the people's will. Opposition mounted, and when he called for yet another purge of moderate leaders, he was arrested and guillotined on the same day, abandoned by the popular factions that had once spurred him on.

While in power, Robespierre and his colleagues pushed revolutionary reforms. A new constitution, never fully put into practice, proclaimed universal adult male suffrage. The radicals introduced a metric system of weights and measures, the product of the rationalizing genius of the Enlightenment. Slavery was abolished in the French colonies, although this measure was reversed after the radical regime collapsed. Robespierre and his allies also proclaimed universal military conscription, arguing that men who were free citizens owed loyalty and service to the government. And revolutionary armies began to win major success. Not only were France's enemies driven out, but the regime began to acquire new territory in the Low Countries, Italy, and Germany, spreading revolutionary gains farther in western Europe.

guillotine [gil uh tEEn, gEE uh-, gil uh tEEn, gEE uh-] Introduced as a method of humane execution; utilized to execute thousands during the most radical phase of the French Revolution known as the Reign of Terror.

 View the **Closer Look** on **MyHistoryLab**: Execution of Louis XVI

A new spirit of popular **nationalism** surfaced during the revolution's radical phase. Many French people felt an active loyalty to the new regime—to a state they believed they had helped create. A new symbol was a revolutionary national anthem (the world's first), with its rousing first lines, "Come, children of the nation, the day of glory has arrived." Nationalism could replace older loyalties to church or locality.

The fall of the radicals led to four years of moderate policies. Then in 1799 the final phase of the revolution was ushered in with the victory of **Napoleon Bonaparte**, a leading general who soon converted the revolutionary republic to an authoritarian empire. Napoleon reduced the parliament to a rubber stamp, and a powerful police system limited freedom of expression. However, Napoleon confirmed other liberal gains, including religious freedom, while enacting substantial equality—although for men, not women—in a series of new law codes. To train bureaucrats, Napoleon developed a centralized system of secondary schools and universities.

Driven by insatiable ambition, Napoleon devoted most of his attention to expansion abroad (Map 24.1). A series of wars brought France against all of Europe's major powers, including Russia. At its height, about 1812, the French empire directly held or controlled as satellite kingdoms most of western Europe, and its success spurred some reform measures even in Prussia and Russia. The French empire crumbled after this point. An attempt to invade Russia in 1812 failed miserably. French armies perished in the cold Russian winter even as they pushed deep into the empire. An alliance system organized by Britain crushed the emperor definitively in 1814 and 1815. Yet Napoleon's campaigns had done more than dominate European diplomacy for one and a half decades. They had also spread key revolutionary legislation—the idea of equality under

nationalism Political viewpoint with origins in western Europe; urged importance of national unity; valued a collective identity based on culture, race, or ethnic origin.

Bonaparte, Napoleon Rose within the French army during the wars of the French Revolution; eventually became general; led a coup that ended the French Revolution; established French empire under his rule; defeated and deposed in 1815.

MAP 24.1 Napoleon's Empire in 1812 By 1812, France dominated Europe to the borders of Russia, but Napoleon's decision to invade Russia proved disastrous, as his army was soon mired in the bitter cold and deep snows of a harsh Russian winter. Defeated in 1814, Napoleon was exiled to the island of Elba (shown above) but he escaped and returned to power. After final defeat at the Battle of Waterloo (1815), he was exiled to the remote South Atlantic island of St. Helena.

CHAPTER 24 The Emergence of Industrial Society in the West, 1750–1900 **567**

the law and the attack on privileged institutions such as aristocracy, church, and craft guilds—throughout much of western Europe.

The revolution and Napoleon encouraged popular nationalism outside of France as well as within. French military success continued to draw great excitement at home. Elsewhere, French armies tore down local governments, as in Italy and Germany, which whetted appetites there for greater national unity. And the sheer fact of French invasion made many people more conscious of loyalty to their own nations; popular resistance to Napoleon, in parts of Spain and Germany, played a role in the final French defeat.

A Conservative Settlement and the Revolutionary Legacy

The allies who had brought the proud French emperor down met at Vienna in 1815 to reach a peace settlement that would make further revolution impossible. Diplomats at the **Congress of Vienna** did not try to punish France too sternly, on the grounds that the European balance of power should be restored. Still, a series of stronger powers was established around France, which meant gains for Prussia within Germany and for the hitherto obscure nation of Piedmont in northern Italy. The old map was not restored, and the realignments ultimately facilitated national unifications. Britain gained new colonial territories, confirming its lead in the scramble for empire in the wider world. Russia, newly important in European affairs, maintained its hold over most of Poland.

These territorial adjustments kept Europe fairly stable for almost half a century—a major achievement, given the crisscrossed rivalries that had long characterized Western society. But the Vienna negotiators were much less successful in promoting internal peace. The idea was to promote stability by restoring monarchy in France and linking Europe's major powers in defense of churches and kings. This was a key statement of the growing movement of **conservatives** in Europe, who defined themselves in opposition to revolutionary goals.

But political movements arose to challenge conservatism. They involved concrete political agitation but also an explosion of ideals about protecting individual rights and providing some political representation. Many of the ideals would resonate in many parts of the world during the 19th and 20th centuries. **Liberals** focused primarily on issues of political structure. They looked for ways to limit state interference in individual life and urged voting rights for propertied people. Liberals touted the importance of constitutional rule and protection for freedoms of religion, press, and assembly. Largely representing the growing middle class, many liberals also sought economic reforms, including better education, which would promote industrial growth.

Radicals accepted the importance of most liberal demands, but they also wanted wider voting rights. Some advocated outright democracy. They also urged some social reforms in the interest of the lower classes. A smaller current of socialism urged an attack on private property in the name of equality and an end to capitalist exploitation of workers. Nationalists, often allied with liberalism or radicalism, urged the importance of national unity and glory.

Political protest found support among students and among urban artisans, concerned about economic changes that might displace craft skills. Revolutions broke out in several places in 1820 and again in 1830. The 1820 revolts involved a nationalist **Greek Revolution** against Ottoman rule—a key step in gradually dismantling the Ottoman empire in the Balkans—and a rebellion in Spain. Another French Revolution of 1830 installed a different king and a somewhat more liberal monarchy. Uprisings also occurred in key states in Italy and Germany, although without durable result; the Belgian Revolution of 1830 produced a liberal regime and a newly independent nation.

Britain and the United States also participated in the process of political change, although without revolution. Key states in the United States granted universal adult male suffrage (except for slaves) and other political changes in the 1820s, leading to the election of a popular president, Andrew Jackson, in 1828. In Britain, the **Reform Bill of 1832**, a response to popular agitation, gave the parliamentary vote to most middle-class men. By the 1830s, regimes in France, Britain, Belgium, and several other countries had solid parliaments (the equivalent of Congress in the United States), some guarantees for individual rights against arbitrary state action, religious freedom not only for various Christian sects but also for Jews, and voting systems that ranged from democratic (for men) to the upper-middle class, plus aristocracy alone.

Congress of Vienna Meeting in the aftermath of Napoleonic Wars (1815) to restore political stability in Europe and settle diplomatic disputes.

conservative Political viewpoint with origins in western Europe during the 19th century; opposed revolutionary goals; advocated restoration of monarchy and defense of church.

liberal Political viewpoint with origins in western Europe during the 19th century; stressed limited state interference in individual life, representation of propertied people in government; urged importance of constitutional rule and parliaments.

radical Political viewpoint with origins in western Europe during the 19th century; advocated broader voting rights than liberals; in some cases advocated outright democracy; urged reforms in favor of the lower classes.

Greek Revolution Rebellion in Greece against the Ottoman empire in 1820; key step in gradually dismantling the Ottoman empire in the Balkans.

Reform Bill of 1832 Legislation passed in Great Britain that extended the vote to most members of the middle class; failed to produce democracy in Britain.

THE INDUSTRIAL REVOLUTION: FIRST PHASES

24.3 What were the most important features of early industrialization?

Even as political revolution gained ground, the foundations of industrialization were being laid in Britain. Causes of this change are much debated (see the Part Introduction), but there is no question that Britain had some special ingredients by the later 18th century. Domestic production spread widely, and this could encourage some inventors to think of methods to improve productivity within the system. In 1733 the flying shuttle was introduced, which automatically moved thread horizontally in a loom, almost doubling the productivity of a hand weaver. Other inventions followed for both spinning and weaving. Agricultural improvements, including seed drills but also the use of crops to replenish the soil, began to generate surpluses that could support larger urban populations. Increased attention to coal mining, the result of the need for new fuels, led to the first invention of a steam engine, in 1700, simply to pump water from the mines.

The key step was James Watt's invention of a more sophisticated steam engine, in the 1770s, that could be applied to manufacturing processes. Steam power, using fossil fuel, steadily displaced human and animal power, creating huge increases in manufacturing output in industries like cotton textiles. Additional inventions, like Edmund Cartwright's power loom in 1785, transmitted steam power to the actual manufacturing process. The new machine stimulated growth in metallurgy, alongside textiles. Steam also required factory units, grouping a large number of workers near the engine itself. Factories soon generated advantages of their own: workers could be more directly disciplined, their labor more specialized—additional gains for productivity.

Early British industrialization had wide effects. Rapid production growth fueled exports because domestic demand could not keep pace. By the 1800s Britain exported three-quarters of its textile output, with immediate impact on traditional workers in other regions. Early factories seemed to require cheap labor to compensate for large investments in equipment, so the pace of work went up, wages tended to drop, and child labor played a substantial role. Cities grew, as centers for the expanding factories: By 1850, Britain would be 50% urban, the first such level in human history. By the 1820s, introduction of steam locomotives began to spread the principles of industrialization to internal transportation.

Early industrialization had immediate environmental impact, particularly around the industrial cities themselves. Smoke could choke the air, while industrial chemicals and human sewage spilled into riverways. Early industrial cities operated in a permanent haze, blocking sunlight and promoting diseases like rickets, a bone deformity.

For all its costs, industrialization proved alluring: Businessmen sought new profits and governments saw the military advantages of the new production forms. British industrialization soon found eager imitators in Belgium, France, Germany, and the new United States. Political upheavals delayed the process somewhat, but also created governments that were more friendly to economic growth. The French Revolution, for example, by abolishing guild restrictions, facilitated technological change. Governments and businessmen alike began to copy British methods, creating a more general Western industrialization process from the 1820s onward.

A few British features were modified as industrialization spread. Use of child labor in factories, for example, prompted concern by the 1830s, not only in Britain but in the newer industrializers. Legal limits on labor, plus school requirements, began the historic conversion of childhood from a focus on work to a focus on education.

Overall, however, early industrialization promoted disruption wherever it occurred. New workers faced challenging jobs amid the pressures of crowded cities and slum housing. Older groups, like craftsmen, feared for their futures. This was a point at which, briefly, the course of early industrialization intersected with a final political outburst in western Europe.

> Dramatic changes in daily life reflected the pressures and opportunities of industrialization. Cultural changes involved steady advances in sciences and increasingly defiant innovation in the arts.

Read the **Document** on **MyHistoryLab:** James Watt on Steam Engines (mid to late 1700s)

Industrialization and the Revolutions of 1848

For by the 1830s and 1840s, industrialization was directly adding pressures to Europe's revolutionary ferment. The 1832 Reform Bill in England, for example, responded in part to growing working-class agitation, although it did not extend the vote to workers and led to further political protest. Key

Chartist movement Attempt by artisans and workers in Britain to gain the vote during the 1840s; demands for reform beyond the Reform Bill of 1832 were incorporated into a series of petitions; movement failed.

 **Read** the **Document** on **MyHistoryLab**: The Chartist Movement: British Workers Call for Political Enfranchisement, 1878

lower-class groups turned to political protest as a means of compensating for industrial change. Artisans and workers in Britain generated a new movement to gain the vote in the 1830s and 1840s, developing a charter to spell out their demands. This **Chartist movement** hoped that a democratic government would regulate new technologies and promote popular education.

The extraordinary wave of revolutions of 1848 and 1849 brought protest to a head. Paris was again the center. In the popular uprising that began in February 1848, the French monarchy was once again expelled, this time for good, and a democratic republic was established briefly. Urban artisans pressed for serious social reform—perhaps some version of socialism, and certainly government-supported jobs for the unemployed. Groups of women schoolteachers agitated for the vote and other rights for women. The social demands were far wider than those of the great uprising of 1789.

Revolution quickly spread to other centers. Major revolts occurred in Germany (Figure 24.2), Austria, and Hungary. Revolutionaries in these areas devised liberal constitutions to modify conservative monarchies, artisans pressed for social reforms that would restrain industrialization, and peasants sought a complete end to manorialism. Revolts in central Europe also pressed for nationalist demands: German nationalists worked for the unity of their country, and various nationalities in Austria–Hungary, including Slavic groups, sought greater autonomy. A similar liberal nationalist revolt occurred in various parts of Italy.

The revolutionary fires burned only briefly. The social demands of artisans and some factory workers were put down quickly; not only conservatives but middle-class liberals opposed these efforts. Nationalist agitation also failed for the moment, as the armies of Austria–Hungary and Prussia restored the status quo to central Europe and Italy. Democracy persisted in France, but a nephew of the great Napoleon soon replaced the liberal republic with an authoritarian empire that lasted until 1870. Peasant demands were met, and serfdom was fully abolished throughout western Europe. Many peasants, uninterested in other gains, supported conservative forces.

FIGURE **24.2** The 1848 revolution in Berlin. After months of maneuvering, negotiation, and street clashes, the revolutionaries agreed on a liberal constitution that would have established a constitutional monarchy. When they offered the crown under these terms to King Friedrich Wilhelm IV, who had initially given in to the demands of the crowds, he politely declined, saying in private that he could not accept a crown "from the gutter." Friedrich Wilhelm believed he ruled by divine right—not by the consent of the governed. The great difference between the king's and the reformers' views of constitutional monarchy was indicative of the chasm that existed in mid-19th-century Europe between advocates of aristocratic and democratic government.

The substantial failure of the revolutions of 1848 drew the revolutionary era in western Europe to a close. Failure taught many liberals and working-class leaders that revolution was too risky; more gradual methods should be used instead. Improved transportation reduced the chance of food crises, the traditional trigger for revolution in Western history. Bad harvests in 1846 and 1847 had driven up food prices and helped promote insurgency in the cities, but famines of this sort did not recur in the West. Many governments also installed better riot control police.

By 1850 an industrial class structure had come to predominate. Earlier revolutionary gains had reduced the aristocrats' legal privileges, and the rise of business had eroded their economic dominance. With industrialization, social structure came to rest less on privilege and birth and more on money. Key divisions by 1850 pitted middle-class property owners against workers of various sorts. The old alliances that had produced the revolutions were now dissolved.

THE CONSOLIDATION OF THE INDUSTRIAL ORDER, 1850–1900

24.4 What were the main changes in the nature and functions of government in the later 19th century?

> The expansion of settler societies strongly influenced by European institutions and values was a leading development of the 19th century.

In most respects, the 65 years after 1850 seemed calmer than the frenzied period of political upheaval and initial industrialization. Railroads and canals linked cities across Europe and spurred industrialization and urbanization (Map 24.2). City growth continued in the West; indeed, several countries, starting with Britain, passed the 50 percent mark in urbanization—the first time in human history that more than a minority of a population lived in cities. City governments began to gain ground on the pressing problems growth had created. Sanitation improved, and death rates fell below birth rates for the first time in urban history. Parks, museums, effective regulation of food and housing facilities, and more efficient police forces all added to the safety and the physical and cultural amenities of urban life. Revealingly, crime rates began to stabilize or even drop in several industrial areas, a sign of more effective social control but also of a more disciplined population.

MAP 24.2 Industrialization in Europe, c. 1850 By the mid-19th century, industrialization had spread across Europe, aided by the development of railroad links and canals that brought resources to the new factories and transported their finished goods to world markets.

The Second Industrial Revolution

In the decades after 1850, industrialization accelerated in western Europe and the United States in several ways, in a process sometimes called the second industrial revolution. New technologies like the Bessemer process, which automatically mixed alloys with molten iron, greatly increased the production of steel. Electrical and internal combustion engines added new sources of power to steam and began an expansion of oil production. A new chemicals industry took shape, with leadership from Germany and the United States. New machines expanded per worker productivity, ranging from larger mechanical looms to automatic power-drilling equipment that allowed mass production of machine parts. Finally—and here the United States took the lead—new methods of work discipline, often devised by industrial psychologists, led to greater specialization and a faster pace; these changes, soon after 1900, would generate the assembly line system. These changes slowed the growth of factory labor—fewer workers were needed for higher outputs, but these changes spurred the growth of a white-collar class of sales clerks and secretaries.

Adjustments to Industrial Life

The second industrial revolution caused new strains. It provoke higher levels of labor unrest. But in some ways people began adjusting to industrial life even so. Family life responded to industrialization. Birth rates began to drop as Western society began a demographic transition to a new system that promoted fairly stable population levels through a new combination of low birth rates and low death rates. Between 1890 and 1920, infant death rates in the West dropped from 20 to 30 percent to about 5 percent. Children were now seen as a source of emotional satisfaction and parental responsibility, not as workers contributing to a family economy. As the Document feature shows, arguments about women's special family duties gained ground.

Material conditions generally improved after 1850. By 1900 probably two-thirds of the Western population enjoyed conditions above the subsistence level. People could afford a few amenities such as newspapers and family outings, their diet and housing improved, and their health got better. The decades from 1880 to 1920 saw a real revolution in children's health, thanks in part to better hygiene during childbirth and better parental care. Infancy and death diverged for the first time in human history: Instead of one-third or more of all children dying by age 10, child death rates fell to less than 5 percent and continued to plummet. The discovery of germs by **Louis Pasteur** led by the 1880s to more conscientious sanitary regulations and procedures by doctors and other healthcare specialists; this reduced the deaths of women in childbirth. Women began to outlive men by a noticeable margin, but men's health also improved.

Pasteur, Louis French scientist who discovered relationship between germs and disease in 19th century, leading to better sanitation.

In little more than a decade, between 1860 and 1873, the number of corporations in western Europe doubled. The rise of corporations, drawing on stockholder investment funds, with new laws protecting individual investors, was a major change in business and organizational life. Important labor movements took shape among industrial workers by the 1890s, with massive strike movements by miners, metalworkers, and others from the United States to Germany. The new trade union movement stressed the massed power of workers. Hosts of labor leaders sprang up amid detested work conditions and political repression. Many workers learned to bargain for better pay and shorter hours.

In the countryside, peasant protests declined. Many European peasants gained a new ability to use market conditions to their own benefit. Some, as in Holland and Denmark, developed cooperatives to market goods and purchase supplies efficiently. Many peasants specialized in new cash crops, such as dairy products. Still more widely, peasants began to send their children to school to pick up new knowledge that would improve farming operations. The traditional isolation of rural areas began to decline.

Political Trends and the Rise of New Nations

Western politics consolidated after the failed revolutions of 1848. Quite simply, issues that had dominated the Western political agenda for many decades were largely resolved within a generation. The great debates about fundamental constitutions and government structure, which had emerged in the 17th century with the rise of absolutism and new political theory and then raged during the decades of revolution, at last grew quiet.

DOCUMENT

Protesting the Industrial Revolution

AS MACHINES WERE INTRODUCED WITH INDUSTRIALIZATION, attacks mounted. The process was called Luddism, after British protests between 1810 and 1820 in the name of a mythical leader called Ned Ludd. The following documents describing Luddism come from a wool manufacturing area around Vienne, in France, in 1819. The first document is a government source, the second a worker petition.

POLICE REPORT

We, king's attorney in the court of first instance at Vienne, acting on the information which we have just received, that the new cloth-shearing machine belonging to Messrs. Gentin and Odoard had just reached the bank of the Gère river near the building intended to house it when a numerous band of workers hastened toward the spot crying "*Down with the shearing machine*"; that some rifle shots were heard, and in general everything about this meeting of workers announced the will and the intent to pillage by force a piece of property, we immediately went to the place where the mayor and the police commissioner agreed to authorize us to use armed force and to state the nature of any crimes and their perpetrators, and to hear with us the declarations of any persons who had information to give us.

Having arrived near the shop of Messrs. Odoard and Gentin, on the right bank of the river, we saw in the steam, at a distance of about fifteen feet, a carriage without horses, its shafts in the air, loaded with four or five crates, one of which was obviously broken, and at three or four paces off in the water, an instrument of iron or some other metal of the same size as the crate, in terms of its length. Various calvary posts and policemen, on foot and mounted, placed at various distances on the two banks of the Gère and on the hills, regarded all the paths and roads; the windows which gave onto the river were partially closed.

Some minutes before our arrival . . . many individuals in short vests whom he did not know but whom he presumed to be workers, hurled themselves into the water and rushed the carriage, armed with wooden clubs and an iron instrument called a cloth-shearer, that they broke the first crate which fell into their hands and threw into the water one of the instruments which it contained.

Edlon Montal (Jean or Pierre) of Grenoble of Beaurepaire, who did his apprenticeship as cloth-shearer, is the man who provided half the strength to break the crates.

Jacques Ruffe, shearer for his cousin Dufieux, was on the carriage, breaking and throwing crates into the water.

The daughter of Claude Tonnerieux, butcher, threw stones at the dragoons and incited the workers with her shouts: "*Break it, smash it, be bold*, etc." Another woman, Lacroix, who has only one eye, shouted similar things. Marguerite Dupont, spinner for Mr. Frémy, called the lieutenant-colonel of dragoons a brigand.

Jacques Boullé, a glass worker, was noticed shouting among the first workers who came down the Saint-Martin bridge.

Basset, weaver, said, "*Let's get the machine*" and Rousset, an itinerant, expressed himself thus: "*We'll get Gentin* (one of the owners of the machine). *It's not the machine we ought to wreck*."

POSTER

Gentlemen, we are beside ourselves because of the inhumanity and hardness of your hearts, your scorn toward the poor workers who have helped you make your fortune. Seeing that we are abandoned by you, gentlemen, this alone has forced us to do what we don't want to do. We have no intention of attacking your fortunes, but if you don't arrange to give us work we can't avoid attacking you and the machines; so you have eight days to reflect. If at the end of these eight days you don't take your wool out of the machines in order to give work to four or five hundred people who are at your doors and whom you don't deign to look at, don't be surprised if you see a storm descend upon you and the machines—so much do we the poor workers suffer for ourselves and for our poor children.

We hope that you'll wish to spare us this effort which is otherwise inevitable.

QUESTIONS

- What kinds of people supported Luddism, and why?
- How did officials react to Luddism, and why?
- What effects was Luddism likely to have over the course of the Industrial Revolution?

Many Western leaders worked to reduce the need for political revolution after 1850. Liberals decided that revolution was too risky and became more willing to compromise. Key conservatives strove to develop reforms that would save elements of the old regime, including power for the landed aristocracy and the monarchy. A British conservative leader, Benjamin Disraeli, took the initiative of granting the vote to working-class men in 1867. Count Camillo di Cavour, in the Italian state of Piedmont, began even earlier to support industrial development and extend the powers of the parliament to please liberal forces. In Prussia a new prime minister, Otto von Bismarck, similarly began to work with a parliament and to extend the vote to all men (although grouping them in wealth categories

> **Read** the **Document** on **MyHistoryLab**: Fustel de Coulanges, Letter to German Historian Theodor Mommsen, 1870

MAP 24.3 The Unification of Italy The map shows the main separate states before unification, and when they added to the new nation.

American Civil War Fought from 1861 to 1865; first application of Industrial Revolution to warfare; resulted in abolition of slavery in the United States and reunification of North and South.

trasformismo Political system in late 19th-century Italy that promoted alliance of conservatives and liberals; parliamentary deputies of all parties supported the status quo.

social question Issues relating to lower classes in western Europe during the Industrial Revolution, particularly workers and women; became more critical than constitutional issues after 1870.

socialism Political movement with origins in western Europe during the 19th century; urged an attack on private property in the name of equality; wanted state control of means of production, end to capitalist exploitation of the working man.

that blocked complete democracy). Other Prussian reforms granted freedom to Jews, extended (without guaranteeing) rights to the press, and promoted mass education. The gap between liberal and conservative regimes narrowed in the West, although it remained significant.

The new conservatives also began to use the force of nationalism to win support for the existing social order. Previously, nationalism had been a radical force, challenging established arrangements in the name of new loyalties. Many liberals continued to defend nationalist causes. However, conservative politicians learned how to wrap themselves in the flag, often promoting an active foreign policy in the interest of promoting domestic calm. Thus, British conservatives became champions of expanding the empire, while in the United States, by the 1890s, the conservatives in the Republican Party became increasingly identified with imperialist causes.

The most important new uses of nationalism in the West occurred in Italy and Germany. After wooing liberal support, Cavour formed an alliance with France that enabled him to attack Austrian control of northern Italian provinces in 1858. The war set in motion a nationalist rebellion in other parts of the peninsula that allowed Cavour to unite most of Italy under the Piedmontese king (Map 24.3). This led to a reduction of the political power of the Catholic pope, already an opponent of liberal and nationalist ideas—an important part of the general reduction of church power in Western politics.

Following Cavour's example, Bismarck in Prussia staged a series of wars in the 1860s that expanded Prussian power in Germany. He was a classic diplomatic military strategist, a key example of an individual agent seizing on larger trends such as nationalism to produce results that were far from inevitable. For example, in 1863 Bismarck used the occasion of Danish incorporation of two heavily German provinces, Schleswig and Holstein, to justify the Prussian and Austrian defeat of Denmark. Then he maneuvered a pretext for a Prussian declaration of war against Austria. In 1866 Prussia emerged as the supreme German power. A final war, against France, led to outright German unity in 1871 (Map 24.4). The new German empire boasted a national parliament with a lower house based on universal male suffrage and an upper house that favored conservative state governments. This kind of compromise, combined with the dizzying joy of nationalist success, won support for the new regime from most liberals and many conservatives.

Other key political issues were resolved at about the same time. The bloody **American Civil War**—the first war based extensively on industrial weaponry and transport systems, carefully watched by European military observers—was fought between 1861 and 1865. The war resolved by force the simmering dispute over sectional rights between the North and South and also brought an end to slavery in the nation. France, after its defeat by Germany in 1870, overthrew its short-lived echo of the Napoleonic empire and established a conservative republic with votes for all men, a reduction of church power, and expansion of education, but no major social reform. Just as conservative Bismarck could be selectively radical, France proved that liberals could be very cautious.

Almost all Western nations now had parliamentary systems, usually democracies of some sort, in which religious and other freedoms were widely protected. In this system, liberal and conservative ministries could alternate without major changes of internal policy. Indeed, Italy developed a process called **trasformismo**, or transformism, in which parliamentary deputies, no matter what platforms they professed, were transformed once in Rome to a single-minded pursuit of political office and support of the status quo.

The Social Question and New Government Functions

The decline of basic constitutional disputes by the 1870s promoted the fuller development of an industrial-style state in the West. A new set of political movements emerged.

574 PART V The Dawn of the Industrial Age, 1750–1900

Government functions and personnel expanded rapidly throughout the Western world after 1870. All Western governments introduced civil service examinations to test applicants on the basis of talent rather than on connections or birth alone, thus unwittingly imitating Chinese innovations more than a thousand years before. With a growing bureaucracy and improved recruitment, governments began to extend their regulatory apparatus, inspecting factory safety, the health of prostitutes, hospital conditions, and even (through the introduction of passports and border controls) personal travel.

Schooling expanded, becoming generally compulsory up to age 12. Governments believed that education provided essential work skills and the basis for new levels of political loyalty. Many American states by 1900 began also to require high school education, and most Western nations expanded their public secondary school systems. Here was a huge addition to the ways in which governments and individuals interacted. The new school systems promoted literacy; by 1900, 90 to 95 percent of all adults in western Europe and the United States could read. Schools also encouraged certain social agendas. Girls were carefully taught about the importance of home and women's moral mission in domestic science programs. Schools also carefully propounded nationalism, teaching the superiority of the nation's language and history as well as attacking minority or immigrant cultures.

Governments also began to introduce wider welfare measures, replacing or supplementing traditional groups such as churches and families. Bismarck was a pioneer in this area in the 1880s as he tried to wean German workers from their attraction to socialism. His tactic failed, as socialism steadily advanced, but his measures had lasting importance. German social insurance began to provide assistance in cases of accident, illness, and old age. Some measures to aid the unemployed were soon added, initially in Britain. These early welfare programs were small and their utility limited, but they sketched a major extension of government power.

Overall, constitutional issues were replaced by social issues—what people of the time called the **social question**—as the key criteria for political partisanship. Socialist and feminist movements surged to the political fore, placing liberals and conservatives in a new defensive posture.

The rise of **socialism** depended above all on the power of grievances of the working class, with allies from other groups. It also reflected a redefinition of political theory by German theorist **Karl Marx**. Early socialist doctrine, from the Enlightenment through 1848, had focused on human perfectibility: Set up a few exemplary communities where work and rewards would be shared, and the evils of capitalism would end. Marx's socialism, worked out between 1848 and 1860, was tough-minded, and he blasted earlier theorists as giddy utopians. Marx saw socialism as the final phase of an inexorable march of history, which could be studied dispassionately and scientifically.

History for Marx was shaped by the available means of production and who controlled those means, an obvious reflection of the looming role of technology in the industrial world forming at that time. According to Marx, class struggle always pitted a group out of power with the group controlling the means of production; hence, in the era just passed, the middle class had battled the feudal aristocracy and its hold on the land. Now the middle class had won; it dominated production and, through this, the state and the culture as well. But it had created a new class enemy, the propertyless proletariat, that would grow until revolution became inevitable. Then, after a transitional period in which proletarian dictatorship would clean up the remnants of the bourgeois social order, full freedom would be achieved. People would benefit justly and equally from their work, and the state would wither away; the historic class struggle would at last end because classes would be eliminated.

Marx's vision was a powerful one. It clearly identified capitalist evil. It told workers that their low wages were exploitive and unjust. It urged the need for violent action but also ensured that revolution was part of the inexorable tides of history. The result would be heaven on earth—ultimately, an Enlightenment-like vision of progress.

MAP 24.4 **The Unification of Germany, 1815–1871** This map shows the stages of unification, under Prussian impetus, from 1866 to 1871.

Legend:
- Prussia, 1815–1866
- Annexed by Prussia, 1866
- Joined Prussia in forming the North German Confederation, 1867
- German Confederation, 1815–1866
- Joined with Prussia to form the German Empire, 1871
- Alsace-Lorraine ceded to German Empire by France, 1871

Marx, Karl (1818–1883) German socialist who blasted earlier socialist movements as utopian; saw history as defined by class struggle between groups out of power and those controlling the means of production; preached necessity of social revolution to create proletarian dictatorship.

Read the **Document** on **MyHistoryLab**: The Communist Manifesto (1848) Karl Marx and Friedrich Engels

revisionism Socialist movements that at least tacitly disavowed Marxist revolutionary doctrine; believed social success could be achieved gradually through political institutions.

feminist movements Sought various legal and economic gains for women, including equal access to professions and higher education; came to concentrate on right to vote; won support particularly from middle-class women; active in western Europe at the end of the 19th century; revived in light of other issues in the 1960s.

CHAPTER 24 The Emergence of Industrial Society in the West, 1750–1900 575

By the 1860s, when working-class activity began to revive, Marxist doctrine provided encouragement and structure. Marx himself continued to concentrate on ideological development and purity, but leaders in many countries translated his doctrine into practical political parties. Germany led the way. As Bismarck extended the vote, socialist leaders in the 1860s and 1870s were the first to understand the implications of mass electioneering. Socialist movements provided fiery speakers who courted popular votes. By the 1880s, socialists in Germany were cutting into liberal support, and by 1900, the party was the largest single political force in the nation. Socialist parties in Austria, France, and elsewhere followed a roughly similar course, everywhere emerging as a strong minority force.

The rise of socialism terrified many people in Western society, who took the revolutionary message literally. In combination with major industrial strikes and unionization, it was possible to see social issues portending outright social war. But socialism itself was not unchanging. As socialist parties gained strength, they often allied with other groups to achieve more moderate reforms. A movement called **revisionism** arose, which argued that Marx's revolutionary vision was wrong and that success could be achieved by peaceful democratic means. Many socialist leaders denounced revisionism but put their energies into building electoral victories rather than plotting violent revolution.

Socialism was not the only challenge to the existing order. By 1900 powerful **feminist movements** had arisen. These movements sought various legal and economic gains for women, such as equal access to professions and higher education as well as the right to vote. Feminism won support particularly from middle-class women, who argued that the very moral superiority granted to women in the home should be translated into political voice. Many middle-class women also chafed against the confines of their domestic roles, particularly as family size declined. In several countries, feminism combined with socialism, but in Britain, the United States, Australia, and Scandinavia, a separate feminist current arose that petitioned widely and even conducted acts of violence in order to win the vote. Several American states and Scandinavian countries extended the vote to women by 1914, in a pattern that would spread to Britain, Germany, and the whole United States beginning in 1918.

The new feminism, like the labor movement, was no mere abstraction but the fruit of active, impassioned leadership, largely from the middle classes. Emmeline Pankhurst (1858–1928; Figure 24.3) was typical of the more radical feminist leadership both in background and tactics. Born to a reform-minded English middle-class family, she was active in women's rights issues, as was her husband. She collaborated with Richard Pankhurst, whom she had married in 1879, to work for improvements in women's property rights, and she participated in the Socialist Fabian Society. But then she turned more radical. She formed a suffrage organization in 1903 to seek the vote for women. With her daughter Christabel, she sponsored attention-getting public disturbances, including planting a bomb in St. Paul's Cathedral. Window-smashing, arson, and hunger strikes rounded out her spectacular tactical arsenal. Often arrested, she engaged in a huge strike in 1912. The suffragists' support of the war effort in 1914 gained them public sympathy. Pankhurst moved to Canada for a time, leaving the English movement to her daughter, but returned as a respected figure to run for parliament after women had gained the vote in 1928.

FIGURE 24.3 Emmeline Goulden Pankhurst. In her 1914 autobiography, Pankhurst recalled the early stirrings of feminism in her childhood: "The education of the English boy, then as now, was considered a much more serious matter than the education of the English boy's sister.... Of course [I] went to a carefully selected girls' school, but beyond the facts that the head mistress was a gentlewoman and that all the pupils were girls of my own class, nobody seemed concerned. A girl's education at that time seemed to have for its prime object the art of 'making home attractive'—presumably to migratory male relatives. It used to puzzle me to understand why I was under such a particular obligation to make home attractive to my brothers. We were on excellent terms of friendship, but it was never suggested to them as a duty that they make home attractive to me. Why not? Nobody seemed to know."

> By the end of the 19th century, diplomatic and military tensions were escalating in Europe. Tensions reflected domestic developments, including social protest and competitive nationalisms.

CULTURAL TRANSFORMATIONS

24.5 What was the relationship between scientific and artistic change in the later 19th century?

Key developments in popular culture differentiated Western society after 1850 from the decades of initial industrialization. Better wages and the reduction of work hours gave ordinary people new opportunities. Alongside the working class grew a large white-collar labor force of secretaries, clerks, and salespeople, who served the growing bureaucracies of big business and the state. These workers, some of them women, adopted many middle-class values, but they also insisted on interesting consumption and leisure outlets. The middle class itself became more open to the idea that pleasure could be legitimate.

Emphasis on Consumption and Leisure

By this point, the maturing industrial economy demanded change. Factories could now spew out goods in such quantity that popular consumption had to be encouraged simply to keep pace with production. Widespread advertising developed to promote a sense of need where none had existed before. Product crazes emerged. The bicycle fad of the 1880s, in which middle-class families flocked to purchase the new machine, was the first of many consumer fads in modern Western history. People just had to have them. Bicycles also changed previous social habits, as women needed less cumbersome garments and young couples could outpedal chaperones during courtship.

Mass leisure culture began to emerge. Popular newspapers, with bold headlines and compelling human interest stories, won millions of subscribers in the industrial West. They featured shock and entertainment more than appeals to reason or political principle. Crime, imperialist exploits, sports, and even comics became the items of the day. Popular theater soared. Comedy routines and musical revues drew thousands of patrons to music halls. After 1900 some of these entertainment themes dominated the new medium of motion pictures. Vacation trips became increasingly common, and seaside resorts grew to the level of big business.

The rise of team sports readily expressed the complexities of the late 19th-century leisure revolution. Here was another Western development that soon had international impact. Soccer, American football, and baseball surged into new prominence at both amateur and professional levels. These new sports reflected industrial life. Although based on traditional games, they were organized by means of rules and umpires. They taught the virtues of coordination and discipline and could be seen as useful preparation for work or military life. They were suitably commercial: Sports equipment, based on the ability to mass-produce rubber balls, and professional teams and stadiums quickly became major businesses. But sports also expressed impulse and violence. They expressed irrational community loyalties and even, as the Olympic games were reintroduced in 1896, nationalist passions.

Overall, new leisure interests suggested a complex set of attitudes on the part of ordinary people in Western society. They demonstrated growing secularism. Religion still counted among some groups, but religious practice had declined as people increasingly looked for worldly entertainments. Many people would have agreed that progress was possible on this earth through rational planning and individual self-control. Yet mass leisure also suggested a more impulsive side to popular outlook, one bent on the display of passion or at least vicarious participation by spectators in emotional release.

mass leisure culture An aspect of the later Industrial Revolution; based on newspapers, music halls, popular theater, vacation trips, and team sports.

Advances in Scientific Knowledge

Science and the arts took separate paths, with influential developments in each area. The size of the intellectual and artistic community in the West expanded steadily with rising prosperity and advancing educational levels. A growing audience existed for various intellectual and artistic products. The bulk of the new activity was resolutely secular. Although new churches were built as cities grew, and missionary activity reached new heights outside the Western world, the churches no longer served as centers for the most creative intellectual life. Continuing advances in science kept alive the rationalist tradition. Universities and other research establishments increasingly applied science to practical affairs, linking science and technology in the popular mind under a general aura of progress. Improvements in medical pathology and the germ theory combined science and medicine, although no breakthrough therapies resulted yet. Science was applied to agriculture through studies of seed yields and chemical fertilizers, with Germany and then the United States in the lead.

The great advance in theoretical science came in biology with the evolutionary theory of **Charles Darwin**, whose major work was published in 1859. Darwin argued that all living species had evolved into their present form through the ability to adapt in a struggle for survival. Biological development could be scientifically understood as a process taking place over time, with some animal and plant species disappearing and others—the fittest in the survival struggle—evolving

Darwin, Charles Biologist who developed theory of evolution of species (1859); argued that all living species evolved into their present form through the ability to adapt in a struggle for survival.

from earlier forms. Darwin's ideas clashed with traditional Christian beliefs that God had fashioned humankind as part of initial creation, and the resultant debate further weakened the hold of religion. Darwin also created a more complex picture of nature than Newton's simple physical laws had suggested. In this view, nature worked through random struggle, and people were seen as animals with large brains, not as supremely rational. Darwin's ideas were also distorted in the work of Social Darwinists, who talked about struggle and survival of the fittest in order to justify European imperialism and, often, outright racism.

Developments in physics continued as well, with work on electromagnetic behavior and then, about 1900, increasing knowledge of the behavior of the atom and its major components. New theories arose, based on complex mathematics, to explain the behavior of planetary motion and the movement of electrical particles, where Newtonian laws seemed too simple. After 1900, **Albert Einstein** formalized this new work through his theory of relativity, adding time as a factor in physical measurement. Again, science seemed to be steadily advancing in its grasp of the physical universe, although it is also important to note that its complexity surpassed the understanding even of educated laypeople. Research in the social sciences and psychology expanded as well.

Einstein, Albert Developed mathematical theories to explain the behavior of planetary motion and the movement of electrical particles; after 1900 issued theory of relativity.

romanticism Artistic and literary movement of the 19th century in Europe; held that emotion and impression, not reason, were the keys to the mysteries of human experience and nature; sought to portray passions, not calm reflection.

New Directions in Artistic Expression

A second approach in Western culture developed in the 19th century. This approach emphasized artistic values and often glorified the irrational. To be sure, many novelists, such as Charles Dickens in England, bent their efforts toward realistic portrayals of human problems, trying to convey information that would inspire reform. Many painters built on the discoveries of science, using knowledge of optics and color. For example, French painter Georges Seurat was inspired by findings about how the eye processes color, applying tiny dots of paint to his canvasses so that they would blend into a coherent whole in a style aptly called pointillism.

Nevertheless, the central artistic vision, beginning with **romanticism** in the first half of the century, held that emotion and impression, not reason and generalization, were the keys to the mysteries of human experience and nature. Artists portrayed intense passions, even madness, not calm reflection. Romantic novelists wanted to move readers to tears, not philosophical debate; painters sought empathy with the beauties of nature or the storm-tossed tragedy of shipwreck (Figure 24.4). Romantics and their successors after 1850 also deliberately tried to violate traditional Western artistic standards. Poetry did not have to rhyme; drama did not necessarily need plot; painting could be evocative, not literal (Figure 24.5). (For literal portrayals, painters could now argue, use a camera.) Each generation of artists proved more defiant than the last. By 1900 painters and sculptors were becoming increasingly abstract, and musical composers worked with atonal scales that defied long-established conventions. Some artists talked of art for art's sake, arguing essentially that art had its own purposes unrelated to the larger society around it.

At neither the formal nor the popular levels, then, did Western culture produce a clear synthesis in the 19th century. New scientific discipline and rationalism warred with impulse—even with evocations of violence. The earlier certainties of Christianity and even the Enlightenment gave way to greater debate. Some observers worried that this debate also expressed tensions between different facets of the same modern mind and that these tensions could become dangerous. Perhaps the Western world was not put together quite as neatly as the adjustments and consolidations after 1850 might suggest.

FIGURE **24.4** Romantic painters delighted in evocative scenes and rural nostalgia, as depicted by John Constable in *The Cornfield*.

(John Constable (1776–1837), "The Cornfield." © The National Gallery, London, Great Britain/Art Resource, NY.)

FIGURE **24.5** Paul Cézanne's *The Large Bathers* (1898–1905). This painting illustrates the artist's abandonment of literal pictorial realism to concentrate on what he considered fundamental. This, along with his use of nudity, alienated the "respectable" public but, by the time of his death in 1906, was beginning to win him critical acclaim. Cézanne painted slowly and was wholly absorbed in his work, spending little time with friends and family. "The landscape," he said, "becomes human, becomes a thinking, living being within me. I become one with my picture. . . . We merge in an iridescent chaos."

(Paul Cezanne, "The Large Bathers." 1906. Oil on Canvas. 6′ 10″ × 8′ 2″ (2.08 × 2.49 m). The W. P. Wilstach Collection. Philadelphia Museum of Art.)

WESTERN SETTLER SOCIETIES

24.6 Were the settler societies part of a common Western civilization, or did they differ fundamentally from western Europe?

The Industrial Revolution prompted a major expansion of the West's power in the world. Western nations could pour out far more processed goods than before, which meant that they needed new markets. They also needed new raw materials and agricultural products, which spurred the development of more commercial agriculture in places such as Africa and Latin America. The vast ships and communication networks created by industrial technology spurred the intensification of the Western-led world economy (see Chapter 25).

Industrialization also extended the West's military advantage in the wider world. Steamships could navigate previously impassable river systems, bringing Western guns inland as never before. The invention of the repeating rifle and machine gun gave small Western forces superiority over masses of local troops. These new means combined with new motives: European nations competed for new colonies as part of their nationalistic rivalry, businesspeople sought new chances for profit, and missionaries sought opportunities for conversion. Haltingly before 1860, then rapidly, Europe's empires spread through Africa, southeast Asia, and parts of China and the Middle East.

Many of the same forces, and also massive European emigration, created or expanded Western settler societies overseas in areas where indigenous populations were decimated by disease. Some settler societies maintained sizable local populations, sometimes even a considerable majority. South

THINKING HISTORICALLY

Two Revolutions: Industrial and Atlantic

DURING THE LONG 19TH CENTURY, TWO major revolutionary movements launched from western Europe, with ramifications in other parts of the world. The industrial revolution began of course in Britain, and featured a fundamental economic and technological transformation, focused on new power sources, with huge implications for other aspects of society. The tide of political and social revolution that swept across the Atlantic, including the American Revolution, the French Revolution with its impacts on many other parts of Europe, the Haitian Revolution, and the Latin American wars of independence, reflected new forces of nationalism and liberalism, with strong social implications of its own.

The Atlantic revolutions were more limited in time than the industrial, ranging from the 1770s to 1849, whereas the industrial revolution, even in western Europe alone, stretched over more than a century from the 1770s until 1900. The French Revolution involved a clear sequence of events, whereas the Industrial Revolution was a more gradual set of processes that took some time to gain full momentum. Still, the two revolutions did overlap in time and (in some cases) place. What did they have to do with each other, and what was their combined impact in world history? Oddly, the question has not been explicitly addressed very often.

The two revolutions supported each other in several ways. Both reflected ideas drawn from the Enlightenment and dislocations caused by new population levels and the expansion of commerce. More directly, the principles of the Atlantic revolutions could be used to attack structures that also held back industrialization. Several European revolutions undid the guild system, whose restrictions on new technologies impeded factory industry; the broader movement against remnants of serfdom also could create a more mobile labor force. Revolutionary agendas often promoted education, which proved useful to industry. The rise of middle-class political interests, which resulted from several political revolutions, could also encourage economic change.

Other revolutionary principles, however, could be used to attack early industrialization in the name of greater social justice. The revolutions of 1848, in Europe, saw many factory workers appealing for the vote and for government assistance against harsh working conditions.

The revolutions also had many differing, even clashing implications, which is one reason it proves hard to discuss them in the same breath. The Atlantic revolutions appealed for popular rights against arbitrary authority: they focused on constitutions that would protect freedoms of the press or assembly. The industrial revolution created more authoritarian work environments, with factory managers and foremen trying to regulate the labor of ordinary employees. In its early stages, the Industrial Revolution also worked against freedom of assembly, with factory owners allying with governments to outlaw labor organizations. Even beyond these immediate tensions over authority and liberty, the revolutions moved in different directions: The Atlantic revolutions were about nationalism and political structure, the Industrial Revolution focused on increasing production and expanding manufacturing.

Not surprisingly, given these variations, the two revolutions hardly shared the same geography. Western Europe and the United States did, to be sure, undergo significant political change, along the lines of the Atlantic principles, while also industrializing in the same general time period. Even Germany, however, although industrializing fiercely, found it harder to assimilate the full implications of political revolution before 1914 or even, many would argue, before 1945. Even more obviously, the revolutionary currents in the Caribbean and Latin America, that created significant political change as part of the overall Atlantic movement, did not help generate industrialization, which would develop only much later and much more gradually (see Chapter 26). On the other hand, by the later 19th century the Industrial Revolution was spreading to other parts of the world, like Russia and Japan, that had not been deeply touched by the ideals of the Atlantic revolutions. And many parts of the world, subdued by the economic and military power of industrial Europe, saw extensive changes at the hands of Western businessmen and imperialists—but these changes bore little relationship to the glowing principles of the Atlantic revolutions.

In the long run, both revolutions would help reshape world, and not merely Western or even Atlantic history. Industrialization continues to spread even into the 21st century, along with persistent, sometimes agonizing disparities between industrial and nonindustrial economies in the global framework. Ideas derived from the Atlantic revolutions about nationalism or individual rights, have wide influence as well, although their impact is hardly uniform. Certain traditional institutions, like slavery, began to crumble even by the later 19th century under the combined impact of revolutionary ideas about human freedom and the fact that slave labor was not most suitable for industrialization.

World history requires an understanding of the workings of both the Atlantic and the industrial revolutions, over more than two centuries. It also requires recognizing that the two revolutions had complicated and extended implications, as they moved from

What did they have to do with each other, and what was their combined impact in world history?

(continued on next page)

original centers to other regions. It requires recognizing that, even today, the two movements are not entirely harmonious. Industrial societies that have also accepted elements of the political revolution let workers vote and enjoy other personal freedoms, but they also continue to regiment them strongly on the job. The changes unleashed by the long 19th century have not moved in complete unity at any point.

> **QUESTIONS**
> - How were the two revolutions interacting in Europe and the United States by the mid-19th century?
> - Which of the two revolutions has had the greater impact on ordinary people, first in the West and then worldwide?
> - Why have some societies found it easier to accept the implications of industrialization than those of the Atlantic revolutions?

Africa was a case in point, discussed in Chapter 25. But some societies filled with an overwhelming majority of immigrants, mostly of European origin, and also brought in so many institutions and beliefs from Europe that they gained a close link with Western history. Some, perhaps, were part of the West outright. The most important overseas Western nation, and the only one to become a major world force before 1914, was the United States.

All the settler societies showed massive European influence and ongoing contact. They were also shaped, however, by contacts with native peoples and frontier conditions. For the United States, particularly, many historians have long seen a pattern of exceptionalism, in which the nation must be interpreted through substantial differences from European patterns. But many trends were shared, including political and industrial revolutions, raising the question of how much the settler societies simply expanded the larger orbit of Western civilization.

Most of the older settler societies, and also Australia and New Zealand, were influenced by the results of the age of political revolution. Revolution formed the United States directly. To avoid a repetition, Britain treated other settler societies, like Canada, with greater care, facilitating the spread of parliamentary governments and liberal constitutions.

Emerging Power of the United States

The country that was to become the United States did not play a substantial role in world history in its colonial period. Its export products were far less significant than those of Latin America and the Caribbean. The American Revolution caused a stir in Europe, but the new nation emphasized internal development through the early 19th century. The Monroe Doctrine (1823) warned against European meddling in the Americas, but it was British policy and naval power that kept the hemisphere free from new colonialism. American energies were poured into elaboration of the new political system, internal commercial growth and early industrialization, and westward expansion. The Louisiana Purchase, the acquisition of Texas, and the rush to California rapidly extended the United States beyond the Mississippi River. The nation stood as a symbol of freedom to many Europeans, and it was often invoked in the revolutions of 1848, as in the earlier Latin American wars for independence. It began to receive a new stream of immigrants, particularly from Ireland and Germany, during the 1840s. Its industrialists also borrowed heavily from European investors to fund national expansion.

The crucial event for the United States in the 19th century was the Civil War. Profound differences separated the increasingly industrial North, with its growing farms, from the slaveholding South, with its export-oriented plantation economy and distinctive value system. Disputes over slaveholding led the southern states to try secession; the North opposed these actions in the interests of preserving national unity and, somewhat hesitantly, ending the slavery system. The Civil War produced an anguishing level of casualties and maimings. The North's victory brought important gains for the freed slave minority, although by the late 1870s, white politicians in the South had begun to severely constrain the political and economic rights of African Americans.

The Civil War also accelerated American industrialization. Heavy industry boomed in a push to produce for the war effort. The completion of a rail link to the Pacific opened the west to further settlement, leading to the last bitter round of wars with Native Americans. Economic expansion brought the United States into the industrial big leagues, its growth rivaling that of Germany. After the Civil War, American armaments manufacturers began to seek export markets. Other industrial producers soon followed as the United States became a major competitor worldwide. American firms, such as the Singer sewing machine company, set up branches in other countries. American agriculture, increasingly mechanized, began to pour out exports of grain and meats (the latter thanks to the development of refrigerated shipping), particularly to European markets where peasant producers could not fully compete.

American diplomacy was not particularly influential outside the Western Hemisphere, although a wave of imperialist expansion from the late 1890s onward brought American interests to the Pacific and Asia. American culture was also seen as largely parochial. Despite increasingly varied art and literature, American work had little impact abroad. Many artists and writers, such as Henry James and James McNeill Whistler, sought inspiration in European centers, sometimes becoming expatriates. Even in technology, American borrowing from Europe remained extensive, and American scientific work gained ground only in the late 19th century, partly through the imitation of German-style research universities. These developments confirmed the role of the new giant in extending many larger Western patterns.

European Settlements in Canada, Australia, and New Zealand

During the 19th century, Canada, Australia, and New Zealand filled with immigrants from Europe and established parliamentary legislatures and vigorous commercial economies that aligned them with the dynamics of Western civilization (Map 24.5). Sparse and disorganized hunting-and-gathering populations (particularly in Canada and Australia) offered little resistance. Like the United States, these new nations looked primarily to Europe for cultural styles and intellectual leadership. They also followed common Western patterns in such areas as family life, the status of women, and the extension of mass education and culture. Unlike the United States, however, these nations remained part of the British empire, although with growing autonomy.

Canada, won by Britain in wars with France in the 18th century, had remained apart from the American Revolution. Religious differences between French Catholic settlers and British rulers and settlers troubled the area recurrently, and several uprisings occurred early in the 19th century. Determined not to lose this colony as it had lost the United States, the British began in 1839 to grant increasing self-rule. Canada set up its own parliament and laws but remained attached to the larger empire. Initially, this system applied primarily to the province of Ontario, but other provinces were included,

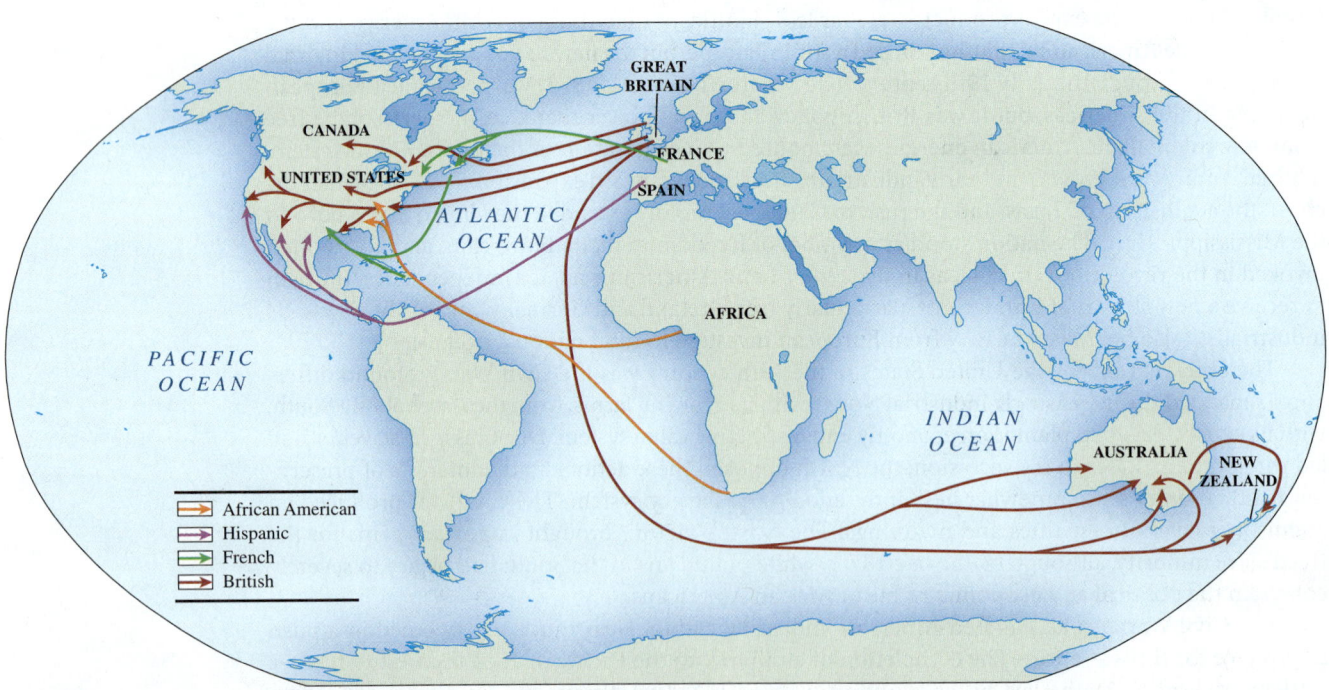

MAP 24.5 **Early 19th-Century Settlement in the United States, Canada, Australia, and New Zealand** Immigration led European settlers (and, in North America, enslaved Africans) to key areas previously populated by peoples vulnerable to imported diseases.

creating a federal system that describes Canada to this day. French hostilities were eased somewhat by the creation of a separate province, Quebec, where the majority of French speakers were located. Massive railroad building, beginning in the 1850s, brought settlement to the western territories and a great expansion of mining and commercial agriculture in the vast plains. As in the United States, new immigrants from southern and particularly eastern Europe poured in during the last decades of the century, attracted by Canada's growing commercial development.

Britain's Australian colonies originated in 1788 when a ship deposited convicts to establish a penal settlement at Sydney. Australia's only previous inhabitants had been a hunting-and-gathering people called the aborigines, and they were in no position to resist European settlement and exploration. By 1840 Australia had 140,000 European inhabitants, engaged mainly in a prosperous sheep-raising agriculture that provided needed wool for British industries. The exportation of convicts ceased in 1853, by which time most settlers were free immigrants. The discovery of gold in 1851 spurred further pioneering, and by 1861 the population had grown to more than a million. As in Canada, major provinces were granted self-government with a multiparty parliamentary system. A unified federal nation was proclaimed on the first day of the 20th century. By this time, industrialization, a growing socialist party, and significant welfare legislation had taken shape.

Finally, New Zealand, visited by the Dutch in the 17th century and explored by the English in 1770, began to receive British attention after 1814. Here the Polynesian hunting-and-gathering people, the Maoris, were well organized politically. Missionary efforts converted many of them to Christianity between 1814 and the 1840s. The British government, fearful of French interest in the area, moved to take official control in 1840, and European immigration followed. New Zealand settlers relied heavily on agriculture (including sheep raising), selling initially to Australia's booming gold-rush population and then to Britain. Wars with the Maoris plagued the settlers during the 1860s, but after the Maori defeat, generally good relations were established, and the Maoris won some representation in parliament. As in Canada and Australia, a parliamentary system was created that allowed the new nation to rule itself as a dominion of the British empire without interference from the mother country.

Canada, New Zealand, and Australia each had distinct national flavors and national issues. These new countries were far more dependent on the European, particularly the British, economy than was the United States. Industrialization did not overshadow commercial agriculture and mining, even in Australia, so that exchanges with Europe remained important. Nevertheless, despite their distinctive features, these countries followed the basic patterns of Western civilization, from political forms to key leisure activities. The currents of liberalism, socialism, modern art, and scientific education that described Western civilization to 1900 and beyond largely characterized these important new extensions.

It was these areas, along with the United States and part of Latin America, particularly Brazil and Argentina, that received new waves of European emigrants during the 19th century. Although Europe's population growth rate slowed after 1800, it still advanced rapidly on the basis of previous gains as more children reached adulthood and had children of their own. Europe's export of people helped explain how Western societies could take shape in such distant areas.

The spread of the Western settler societies also reflected the new power of Western industrialization. Huge areas could be settled quickly, thanks to steamships and rails, while remaining in close contact with western Europe.

DIPLOMATIC TENSIONS AND WORLD WAR I

24.7 What were the basic causes of growing diplomatic tension in Europe by 1900?

The unification of Germany and its rapid industrial growth profoundly altered the power balance within Europe. Bismarck was very conscious of this, and during the 1870s and 1880s, still a skilled manipulator, he built a complex alliance system designed to protect Germany and divert European attention elsewhere. France, Germany's deepest enemy, was largely isolated. But even the French concentrated on imperialist expansion in Africa and Asia.

By 1900, however, few parts of the world were available for Western seizure. Latin America was independent but under extensive U.S. influence, so a new intrusion of colonialism was impossible.

Africa was almost entirely carved up. The few final colonies taken after 1900—Morocco by France and Tripoli (Libya) by Italy—caused great diplomatic furor on the part of other colonial powers worried about the balance of forces. China and the Middle East were technically independent but were in fact crisscrossed by rivalries between the Western powers and Russia (and in China's case, Japan). No agreement was possible on further takeovers.

Yet imperialist expansion had fed the sense of rivalry between key nation-states. Britain, in particular, grew worried about Germany's overseas drive and its construction of a large navy. Economic competition between a surging Germany and a lagging Britain added fuel to the fire. France, eager to escape the Bismarck-engineered isolation, was willing to play down its traditional rivalries with Britain. The French also took the opportunity to ally with Russia, when after 1890 Germany dropped this particular alliance because of Russian–Austrian enmity.

The New Alliance System

By 1907 most major European nations were paired off in two alliance systems: Germany, Austria–Hungary, and Italy formed the **Triple Alliance**. Britain, Russia, and France formed the newer **Triple Entente**. Three against three seemed fair, but Germany grew increasingly concerned about facing potential enemies to the east (Russia) and west (France). These powers steadily built up their military arsenals in what turned out to be the first of several arms races in the 20th century. All powers save Britain had instituted peacetime military conscription to provide large armies and even larger trained reserves. Artillery levels and naval forces grew steadily—the addition of a new kind of battleship, the dreadnought, was a key escalation—and discussions about reducing armament levels went nowhere. Each alliance system depended on an unstable partner. Russia suffered a revolution in 1905, and its allies worried that any further diplomatic setbacks might paralyze the eastern giant. Austria–Hungary was plagued by nationality disputes, particularly by minority Slavic groups; German leaders fretted that a diplomatic setback might bring chaos. Both Austria and Russia were heavily involved in maneuverings in the Balkans, the final piece in what became a nightmare puzzle.

Small Balkan nations had won independence from the Ottoman empire during the 19th century; as Turkish power declined, local nationalism rose, and Russian support for its Slavic neighbors paid off. But the nations were intensely hostile to one another. Furthermore, **Balkan nationalism** threatened Austria, which had a large southern Slav population. Russia and Austria nearly came to blows on several occasions over Balkan issues. Then, in 1912 and 1913, the Balkan nations engaged in two internal wars, which led to territorial gains for several states but satisfied no one (Map 24.6).

Serbia, which bordered Austria to the south, had hoped for greater stakes. At the same time, Austria grew nervous over the gains Serbia had achieved. In 1914 a Serbian nationalist assassinated an Austrian archduke on behalf of Serbian claims. Austria vowed to punish Serbia. Russia rushed to the defense of Serbia and mobilized its troops against Austria. Germany, worried about Austria and also eager to be able to strike against France before Russia's cumbersome mobilization was complete, called up its reserves and then declared war on August 1. Britain hesitated briefly, then joined its allies. World War I had begun, and with it came a host of new problems for Western society.

Diplomacy and Society

The tensions that spiraled into major war are not easy to explain. Diplomatic maneuverings can seem quite remote from the central concerns of most people, if only because key decisions—for example, with whom to ally—are made by a specialist elite. Even as the West became more democratic, few ordinary people placed foreign affairs high on their election agendas.

The West had long been characterized by political divisions and rivalries. In comparison with some other civilizations, this was an inherent weakness of the Western political system. In a sense, what happened by the late 19th century was that the nation-state system got out of hand, encouraged by the absence of serious challenge from any other civilizations. The rise of Germany and new tensions in the Balkans simply complicated the growing nationalist competition.

Triple Alliance Alliance among Germany, Austria-Hungary, and Italy at the end of the 19th century; part of European alliance system and balance of power prior to World War I.

Triple Entente Alliance among Britain, Russia, and France at the outset of the 20th century; part of European alliance system and balance of power prior to World War I.

Balkan nationalism Movements to create independent nations within the Balkan possessions of the Ottoman empire; provoked a series of crises within the European alliance system; eventually led to World War I.

MAP **24.6** **The Balkans After the Regional Wars, 1913** The wars pushed the Ottoman empire almost entirely out of the Balkans, but left many small states dissatisfied.

This diplomatic escalation also had some links to the strains of Western society under the impact of industrialization. Established leaders in the West continued to worry about social protest. They tended to seek diplomatic successes to distract the people. This procedure worked nicely for a few decades when imperialist gains came easily. But then it backfired. Around 1914 German officials, fearful of the power of the socialists, wondered whether war would aid national unity. British leaders, beset by feminist dissent and labor unrest, failed to think through their own diplomatic options. Leaders also depended on military buildups for economic purposes. Modern industry, pressed to sell the soaring output of its factories, found naval purchases and army equipment a vital supplement. Mass newspapers, which fanned nationalist pride with stories of conquest and tales of the evils of rival nations, helped shape a belligerent popular culture.

Thus, just a few years after celebrating a century of material progress and peace, ordinary Europeans went to war almost gaily in 1914. Troops departed for the front convinced that war would be exciting, with quick victories. Their departure was hailed by enthusiastic civilians, who draped their trains with flowers. Four years later, almost everyone would agree that war had been unmitigated hell. However, the complexities of industrial society were such that war's advent seemed almost a welcome breath of the unexpected, a chance to get away from the disciplined stability of everyday life.

Global Connections and Critical Themes

INDUSTRIAL EUROPE AND THE WORLD

Europe's growing power during the 19th century transformed the world. Imperialism and the redefinition of the world economy pushed European interests to every corner of the globe. The expansion of the settler societies reflected and also expanded Western influence. It was European sponsorship and power that ushered in the process of globalization.

This same power made developments in 19th-century Europe something of a global model. Some leaders, aware of Europe's political and industrial change, found the example repellent. Russian conservatives, for example, warned against the divisiveness of parliamentary politics and the exploitation of modern industry.

Europe's revolutionary heritage, however, also won admiration, partly because it contained principles that could be used to counter European power. Liberalism, radicalism, and socialism began to spread beyond the boundaries of Europe and the settler societies. They could be directed against colonial controls or the exploitation of workers in the world economy. Nationalism spread rapidly as well, from its initial base in revolutionary Europe. Europe, in sum, was a global force in the 19th century as no society had ever been before, but its message was extremely complex.

Further Readings

On key changes see Robert B. Marks, *The Origins of the Modern World: A Global and Ecological Narrative from the Fifteenth to the Twenty-First Century* (2007); Deborah Cadbury, *Dreams of Iron and Steel: Seven Wonders of the Nineteenth Century, from the Building of the London Sewers to the Panama Canal* (2004); John Waller, *The Discovery of the Germ: Twenty Years that Transformed the Way We Think about Disease* (2002); and Nicholas Roe, ed., *Romanticism: An Oxford Guide* (2005). On Europe's industrial revolution: Kenneth Morgan, *The Birth of Industrial Britain: Social Change, 1750–1850* (2004); Stephen P. Rice, *Minding the Machine: Languages of Class in Early Industrial America* (2004); and Paul E. Rivard, *A New Order of Things: How the Textile Industry Transformed New England* (2002). For a more general survey, see Peter N. Stearns, *The Industrial Revolution in World History* (2006). On the demographic experience, see Thomas McKeown, *The Modern Rise of Population* (1977).

For the French Revolution and political upheaval, Isser Woloch's *The New Regime: Transformations of the French Civic Order, 1789–1829* (1994) is a useful introduction. See also Nigel Aston, *The French Revolution, 1789–1804: Authority, Liberty and the Search for Stability* (2004) and Suzanne Desan, *The Family on Trial in Revolutionary France* (2004). Lynn Hunt's *Politics, Culture, and Class in the French Revolution* (1984) is an important study. Other revolutionary currents are treated in *The Crowd in History: Popular Disturbances in France and England* (1981) by George Rudé and *1848: The Revolutionary Tide in Europe* (1974) by Peter Stearns.

The impact of the industrial revolution on gender relations is analyzed in L. L. Clark, *Women and Achievement in 19th-century Europe* (2008); A. Clarke, *The Struggle for the Breeches: Gender and the Making of the British Working Class* (1995); G.D. Smithers, *Science, Sexuality and Race in the United States and Australia* (2009); and Harold L. Smith, *The British Women's Suffrage Campaign, 1866–1928* (2007). Major developments concerning women and the family are covered in Steven Mintz and Susan Kellogg, *Domestic Revolutions: A Social History of American Family Life* (1989). An important age group is treated in John Gillis, *Youth and History* (1981). An influential generation receives its due in T. Hoppen, *The Mid-Victorian Generation, 1846–1886* (1998).

For an overview of social change, see Peter Stearns and Herrick Chapman, *European Society in Upheaval* (1991). On labor history, see Michael Hanagan, *The Logic of Solidarity* (1981); and Albert Lindemann, *History of European Socialism* (1983). Eugen Weber, *Peasants into Frenchmen: The Modernization of Rural France* (1976); R. D. Francis et al, *Journeys: a History of Canada* (2009); and Harvey Graff, ed., *Literacy and Social Development in the West* (1982), deal with important special topics.

On political and cultural history, see Clive Emsley, *Napoleon: Conquest, Reform and Reorganizaiton* (2003); Gordon Craig, *Germany, 1866–1945* (1978); and Isabel V. Hull, *Absolute Destruction: Military Culture and the Practices of War in Imperial Germany* (2005). J. H. Randall's *The Making of the Modern Mind* (1976) is a useful survey; see also O. Chadwick's *The Secularization of the European Mind in the Nineteenth Century* (1976) and Isidor Sadger, *Recollecting Freud* (2005). On major diplomatic developments, see D. K. Fieldhouse, *Economics and Empire, 1830–1914* (1970); and David Kaiser, *Politics and War: European Conflict from Philip II to Hitler* (1990).

The impact of these winds of change as they swept across the American sociopolitical landscape is examined in John Ferling, *Almost a Miracle: The American Victory in the War of Independence* (2007); David Armitage, *The Declaration of Independence: A Global History* (2007); Terry Bouton, *Taming Democracy: "The People," the Founders, and the Troubled Ending of the American Revolution* (2007); James M. McPherson, *This Mighty Scourge: Perspectives on the Civil War* (2007); W. Cronon, *Nature's Metropolis: Chicago and the Great West* (1991); R. M. Utley, *The Indian Frontier and the American West, 1846–1890* (1984); Robert Dahl, *How Democratic Is the American Constitution?* (2002); and S. M. Lipsett, *American Exceptionalism: A Double-Edged Sword* (1996).

On MyHistoryLab

 Study and Review on MyHistoryLab

Critical Thinking Questions

1. In what ways did political revolutions and the Industrial Revolution combine to promote change? In what ways might they clash?
2. As it began to develop by 1900, what was the nature of the industrial state, compared to states in more traditional societies?
3. What were the causes of new diplomatic tensions in the later 19th century?
4. What aspects of the settler societies differed from patterns in western Europe?

Industrialization and Imperialism: The Making of the European Global Order

25

Listen to Chapter 25 on MyHistoryLab

On January 22, 1879, at the height of its century-long reign as the paramount global power, Great Britain suffered one of the most devastating defeats ever inflicted by a non-Western people on an industrialized nation. The late-Victorian painting, shown in Figure 25.1, depicts the Battle of Isandhlwana (ihs-SAND-zwah-nuh) at which more than 20,000 Zulu soldiers outmaneuvered a much smaller but overconfident British army invading their kingdom. Taking advantage of the British commander's foolhardy decision to divide his forces, the Zulus attacked the main British encampment from all directions and, in a fiercely fought battle lasting only a couple of hours, wiped out 950 European troops and nearly 850 African irregulars. Divided and caught off guard, the British could not form proper firing lines to repel the much larger and well-led Zulu *impis*—the equivalent of a division in a Western army. The flight of the African irregulars, who made up a sizable portion of the British army, left gaps in the British force that were quickly exploited by the Zulu fighters. Soon after the main battle was joined, most of the British and mercenary

LEARNING OBJECTIVES

25.1 What were the major differences between the first burst of European global expansion from the 16th through the early 18th centuries and the era of Western imperialist dominance from the middle of the 19th century to the outbreak of World War I in 1914? p. 590

25.2 What were the major forces in Europe and overseas that pushed the European powers, and later the United States and Japan, to compete for territories over much of Africa and Asia in the half century before World War I? p. 597

25.3 How were a few thousand Europeans able to conquer and rule territories with millions, in some cases even hundreds of millions of subject peoples? p. 601

FIGURE 25.1 A romantic depiction of the 1879 Battle of Isandhlwana in the Natal province of South Africa. The battle demonstrated that, despite their superior firepower, the Europeans could be defeated by well-organized and determined African or Asian resistance forces.

Watch the Video Series on MyHistoryLab

Learn about some key topics related to this chapter with the *MyHistoryLab Video Series: Key Topics in World History*

African soldiers in the camp at Isandhlwana were dead or in desperate flight to a river nearby, where most were hunted down by impis positioned to block their retreat.

The well-drilled Zulu impis who routed the British forces at Isandhlwana skillfully wielded the cattle-hide shields and short stabbing spears, or *assegais,* which had been the Zulus' trademark for more than half a century. In the early 1800s, warriors and weapons had provided the military power for an ambitious young leader named Shaka to forge a powerful kingdom centered on Natal in the southeastern portions of what would later become the Union of South Africa (Map 25.4). The Zulus' imposing preindustrial military organization had triumphed over all African rivals and later proved the most formidable force resisting the advance of both the Dutch-descended Boers (later called Afrikaners) and British imperial armies in southern Africa.

The British defeat was shocking in large part because it seemed implausible, given the great and ever-growing disparity between the military might of the European colonial powers and the African and Asian peoples they had come to dominate in unprecedented ways. Technological innovations, including steam-powered ships and trains and mass-production, made it possible for European states to supply advanced weaponry and other war materiel to sizable naval and land forces across the globe. Set in this larger context, the aftermath of the Zulu triumph at Isandhlwana demonstrated that the British defeat was a fluke, a dramatic but short-lived exception to what had become a pervasive pattern of European (and increasingly American) political and military supremacy worldwide. Estimates of Zulu losses at Isandhlwana, for example, range from two to three times those for British units and "native" levees combined. Within hours of their utter destruction of most of the main British column, a force of some 3000 Zulu warriors was decimated in the siege of a small outpost at nearby Rorke's Drift. There a cluster of farm buildings was successfully defended by just over a hundred British soldiers, many of whom were wounded from earlier clashes.

As was the case in equally stunning massacres of the expeditionary forces of industrial powers in other colonial settings, most notably Custer's last stand in the American West, revenge for the defeat inflicted by the Zulus at Isandhlwana was massive and swift. Additional troops were drawn from throughout the far-flung British empire and, within months, a far larger British force was advancing on the Zulu capital at Ulundi. Like the coalition of Indian tribes that had joined to destroy Custer's units of the Seventh Cavalry, the Zulu impis that had turned back the first British invasion dispersed soon after the clashes at Isandhlwana and Rorke's Drift. By late August, the Zulu ruler, Cetshwayo, had surrendered to the British and been shipped into exile at Cape Town. ■

The British advances into the heart of Cetshwayo's kingdom in the last of the wars between the Europeans and the Zulus exemplified many of the fundamental shifts in the balance of world power in the turn-of-the-century decades of the great "scramble" for overseas territories that are the focus of this chapter. In important ways imperial rivalries among the European powers did much to set the stage for World War I. Like their French, Dutch, Belgian, German, Russian, Japanese, and American competitors, the British plunged deep into Africa, the Middle East, and Asia. In contrast to the earlier centuries of overseas expansion, the European powers were driven in the late-19th century mainly by rivalries with each other, and in some instances with the Japanese and Americans, rather than fears of Muslim kingdoms in the Middle East and North Africa or powerful empires in Asia.

As we shall see, in most of the areas they claimed as colonial possessions, the Europeans established direct rule, where they had once been mainly content to subjugate and control local rulers and their

1600 C.E.	1700 C.E.	1750 C.E.	1800 C.E.	1850 C.E.	1900 C.E.
1619 Dutch establish trading post at Batavia in Java	**1707** Death of Mughal emperor, Aurangzeb; beginning of imperial breakdown	**1750s** Civil war and division of Mataram; Dutch become the paramount power on Java	**1815** British annex Cape Town and surrounding area	**1850s** Boer republics established in the Orange Free State and Transvaal	**1902** Anglo-Japanese Treaty
1620s Sultan of Mataram's attacks on Batavia fail	**1739** Nadir Shah's invasion of India from Persia	**1756–1763** Seven Years War, British–French global warfare	**1830** Boers begin Great Trek in South Africa	**1853** First railway line constructed in India	**1904** Anglo-Russian crisis at Dogger Bank
1652 First Dutch settlement in South Africa at Cape Town	**1740–1748** War of Austrian Succession; global British–French struggle for colonial dominance	**1757** Battle of Plassey; British become dominant power in Bengal	**1835** Decision to give support for English education in India; English adopted as the language of Indian law courts	**1857** Calcutta, Madras, and Bombay universities founded	**1904–1905** First Moroccan crisis; Russo-Japanese War
1661 British port-trading center founded at Bombay		**1769–1770** Great Famine in Bengal		**1857–1858** "Mutiny" or Great Rebellion in north India	**1911** Second Moroccan crisis
1690 Calcutta established at center of British activities in Bengal		**1775–1783** War for independence by American colonists; another British–French struggle for global preeminence		**1858** British parliament assumes control over India from the East India Company	**1914** Outbreak of World War I
		1786–1790 Cornwallis's political reforms in India		**1867** Diamonds discovered in Orange Free State	
		1790–1815 Wars of the French Revolution and Napoleonic era		**1869** Opening of the Suez Canal	
		1798 Napoleon's invasion of Egypt		**c. 1879–1890s** Partition of west Africa	
				1879 Zulu victory over British at Isandhlwana; defeat at Rorke's Drift	
				1882 British invasion of Egypt	
				1885 Indian National Congress Party founded in India	
				1885 Gold discovered in the Transvaal	
				1890s Partition of east Africa	
				1898 British–French crisis over Fashoda in the Sudan	
				1899–1902 Anglo-Boer War in South Africa	

retainers. The 1879 Anglo-Zulu war had been precipitated by British demands, including the right to station a resident in the Zulu kingdom and the breakup of the Zulu military machine, that would have reduced Cetshwayo to the status of a vassal. Although the British and other colonizers would continue to govern through indigenous officials in many areas, their subordinates were increasingly recruited from new elites, both professional and commercial, who emerged from schools where the languages and customs of the imperial powers were taught to growing numbers of colonized peoples.

| 25.1 | 25.2 | 25.3 |

THE SHIFT TO LAND EMPIRES IN ASIA

From the mid-18th century onward, the European powers began to build land empires in Asia similar to those they had established in the Americas beginning in the 16th century. In the first phase of the colonization process, Europeans overseas were willing to adapt their lifestyles to the climates and cultures of the lands they had gone out to rule.

25.1 What were the major differences between the first burst of European global expansion from the 16th through the early 18th centuries and the era of Western imperialist dominance from the middle of the 19th century to the outbreak of World War I in 1914?

Although we usually use the term *partition* to refer to the European division of Africa at the end of the 19th century, the Western powers had actually been carving up the globe into colonial enclaves for centuries (Map 25.1). At first this process was haphazard and often quite contrary to the interests and designs of those in charge of European enterprises overseas. For example, the directors who ran the Dutch and English East India companies (which were granted monopolies of the trade between

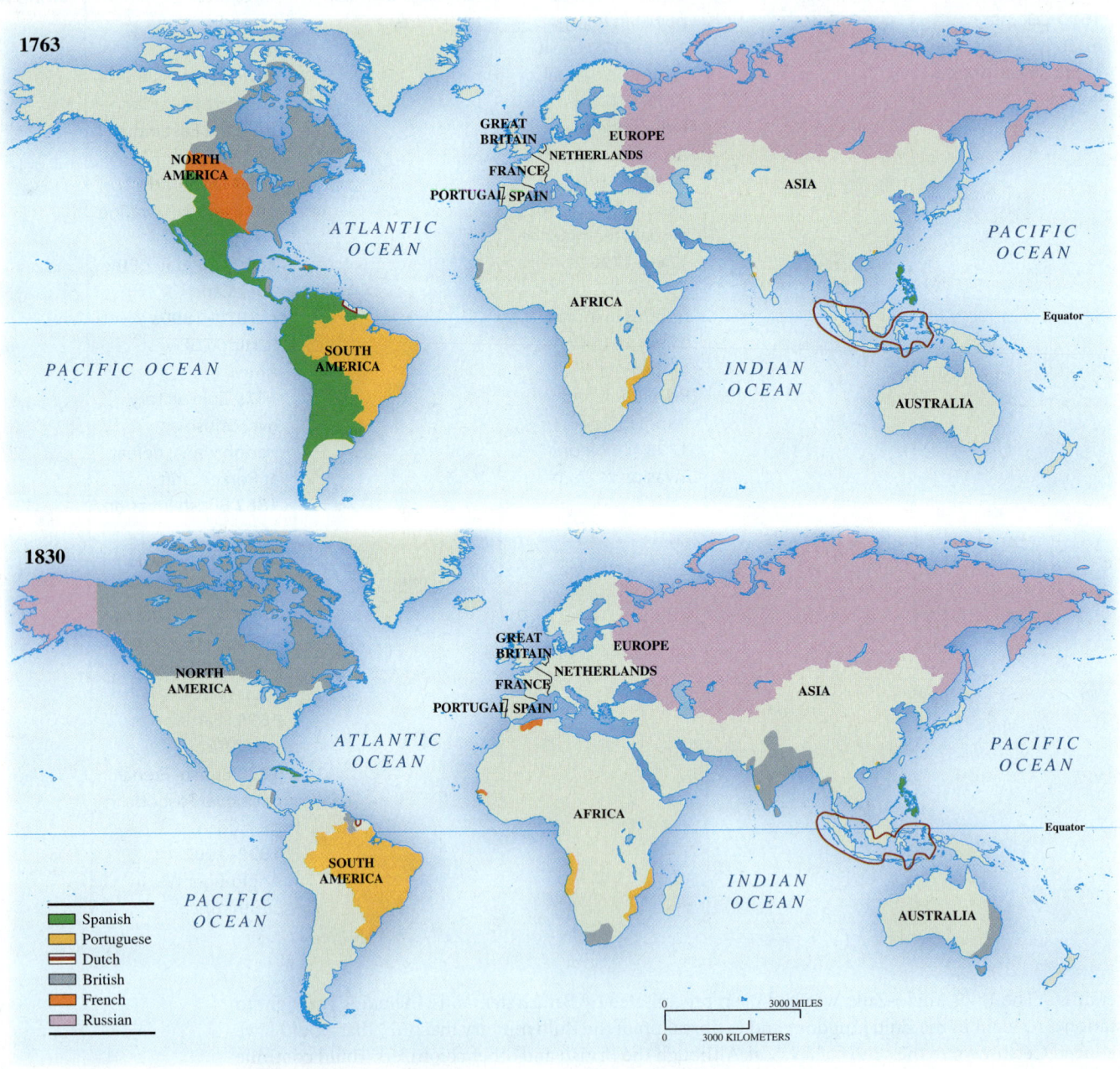

MAP 25.1 **European Colonial Territories, Before and After 1800** As a comparison of the two maps shows, the late 1700s marked a pivotal point of transition in both the contraction of colonial domination, particularly in the Americas and it's expansion in Africa, Asia, and the Pacific.

590 PART V The Dawn of the Industrial Age, 1750–1900

their respective countries and the East in the 17th and 18th centuries) had little interest in territorial acquisitions. In fact, they were actively opposed to involvement in the political rivalries of the Asian princes. Wars were expensive, and direct administration of African or Asian possessions was even more so. Both cut deeply into the profits gained through participation in the Asian trading system, and profits—not empires—were the chief concern of the Dutch and English directors.

Whatever policies company directors may have instructed their agents in Africa and Asia to pursue, these "men-on-the-spot" were often drawn into local power struggles. And before the industrial revolution produced the telegraph and other methods of rapid communication, company directors and European prime ministers had very little control over those who actually ran their trading empires. In the 18th century, a letter took months to reach Calcutta from London; the reply took many months more. Thus, commanders in the field had a great deal of leeway. They could conquer whole provinces or kingdoms before home officials even learned that their armies were on the move.

Prototype: The Dutch Advance on Java

One of the earliest empires to be built in this fashion was that pieced together in the late 17th and 18th centuries by the Dutch in Java (Map 25.2). Java was then and is now the most populous of the hundreds of islands that make up the present-day country of Indonesia. In the early years after the Dutch established their Asian headquarters at Batavia on the northwest coast of the island in 1619, it was a struggle just to survive. The Dutch were content to become the vassals of and pay tribute to the sultans of **Mataram**, who ruled most of Java. In the decades that followed, the Dutch concentrated on gaining monopoly control over the spices produced on the smaller islands of the Indonesian archipelago to the east. But in the 1670s, the Dutch repeatedly intervened in the wars between rival claimants to the throne of Mataram, and they backed the side that eventually won. As the price for their assistance, the Dutch demanded that the territories around Batavia be turned over to them to administer.

This episode was the first of a long series of Dutch interventions in the wars of succession between the princes of Mataram. Dutch armies were made up mainly of troops recruited from the island peoples of the eastern Indonesian archipelago, led by Dutch commanders. Their superior organization and discipline, even more than their firearms, made the Dutch a potent ally of whichever prince won them to his side. But the price the Javanese rulers paid was very high. Each succession dispute and Dutch intervention led to more and more land being ceded to the increasingly land-hungry Europeans. By the mid-18th century, the sultans of Mataram controlled only the south central portions of Java (Map 25.2). A failed attempt by Sultan Mangkubumi to restore Mataram's control over the Dutch in the 1750s ended with a Dutch-dictated division of the kingdom that signified Dutch control of the entire island. Java had been transformed into the core of an Asian empire that would last for 200 years.

MAP 25.2 **The Stages of Dutch Expansion in Java** The consolidation of Dutch power on Java, the center of its island Asian empire, accelerated dramatically from the late 17th century.

Mataram Kingdom that controlled interior regions of Java in 17th century; Dutch East India Company paid tribute to the kingdom for rights of trade at Batavia; weakness of kingdom after 1670s allowed Dutch to exert control over all of Java.

Keystone of World Empire: The Rise of British Rule in India

In many ways, the rise of the British as a land power in India resembled the Dutch capture of Java. The directors of the British East India Company were as hostile as the Dutch financiers to territorial expansion. But British agents of the company in India repeatedly meddled in disputes and conflicts between local princes. In these interventions, the British, adopting a practice pioneered by the French, relied heavily on Indian troops, called **sepoys** (some of whom are pictured in Figure 25.2) recruited from peoples throughout the subcontinent. As had been the case in Java, Indian princes regarded the British as allies whom they could use and control to crush competitors from within India or put down usurpers who tried to seize their thrones. As had happened in Java, the European pawns gradually emerged as serious rivals to the established Indian rulers and eventually dominated the region.

sepoys Troops that served the British East India Company; recruited mainly from various warlike peoples of India.

CHAPTER 25 Industrialization and Imperialism: The Making of the European Global Order

Partly because the struggle for India came later, there were also important differences between the patterns of colonial conquest in India and Java as well as between the global repercussions of each. In contrast to the Dutch march inland, which resulted largely from responses to local threats and opportunities, the rise of the **British Raj** (the Sanskrit-derived name for the British political establishment in India) owed much to the fierce global rivalry between the British and the French. In the 18th century, the two powers found themselves on opposite sides in five major wars. These struggles were global in a very real sense. On land and sea, the two old adversaries not only fought in Europe but also squared off in the Caribbean, where each had valuable plantation colonies; in North America; and on the coasts and bays of the Indian Ocean. With the exception of the American War of Independence (1775–1783), these struggles ended in British victories. The British loss of the American colonies was more than offset by earlier victories in the Caribbean and especially in India. These triumphs gradually gave the British control of the entire South Asian subcontinent.

Although the first victories of the British over the French and the Indian princes came in the Madras region in the south in the late 1740s, their rise as a major land power in Asia hinged on victories won in Bengal to the northeast (Map 25.3). The key battle at **Plassey** in 1757, in which fewer than 3000 British troops and Indian sepoys defeated an Indian army of nearly 50,000, is traditionally pictured as the heroic triumph of a handful of brave and disciplined Europeans over a horde of ill-trained and poorly led Asians. The battle pitted Sirāj ud-daula (sih-RAH JUHD-oh-luh), the teenage *nawab*, or ruler, of Bengal, against **Robert Clive**, the architect of the British victory in the south. The prize was control of the fertile and populous kingdom of Bengal. The real reasons for Clive's famous victory tell us a good deal about the process of empire building in Asia and Africa.

The numbers on each side and the maneuvers on the field had little to do with the outcome of a battle that in a sense was over before it began. Clive's well-paid Indian spies had given him detailed accounts of the divisions in Sirāj ud-daula's ranks in the months before the battle. With money provided by Hindu bankers, who were anxious to get back at the Muslim prince for unpaid debts and for confiscating their treasure on several occasions, Clive bought off the nawab's chief general and several of his key allies. Even the nawab's leading spy was on Clive's payroll, which somewhat offset the fact that the main British spy had been bribed by Sirāj ud-daula. The backing Clive received from the Indian bankers also meant that his troops were well paid, whereas those of the nawab were not.

Thus, when the understandably nervous teenage ruler of Bengal rode into battle on June 23, 1757, his fate was already sealed. The nawab's troops under French officers and one of his Indian commanders fought well. But his major Indian allies defected to the British or remained stationary on his flanks when the two sides were locked in combat. These defections wiped out the nawab's numerical advantage, and Clive's skillful leadership and the superiority of his artillery did the rest. The British victors had once again foiled their French rivals. As the nawab had anticipated, they soon took over the direct administration of the sizable Bengal-Bihar region. The foundations of Britain's Indian and global empire had been laid.

The Consolidation of British Rule

In the decades after Plassey, the British officials of the East India Company repeatedly went to war with Indian princes whose kingdoms bordered on the company's growing possessions (Map 25.3). These entanglements grew stronger and stronger as the Mughal empire broke down more fully in the last decades of the century. In its ruins, regional Indian princes fought to defend or expand their territories

FIGURE 25.2 Indian soldiers, or sepoys, made up a large portion of the rank-and-file troops in the armies of British India. Commanded by European officers and armed, uniformed, and drilled according to European standards, troops such as those pictured here were recruited from the colonized peoples and became one of the mainstays of all European colonial regimes.

British Raj British political establishment in India; developed as a result of the rivalry between France and Britain in India.

Plassey Battle in 1757 between troops of the British East India Company and an Indian army under Sirāj ud-daula, ruler of Bengal; British victory marked the rise of British control over northern India.

Clive, Robert (1725–1774) Architect of British victory at Plassey in 1757; established foundations of British Raj in northern India (18th century).

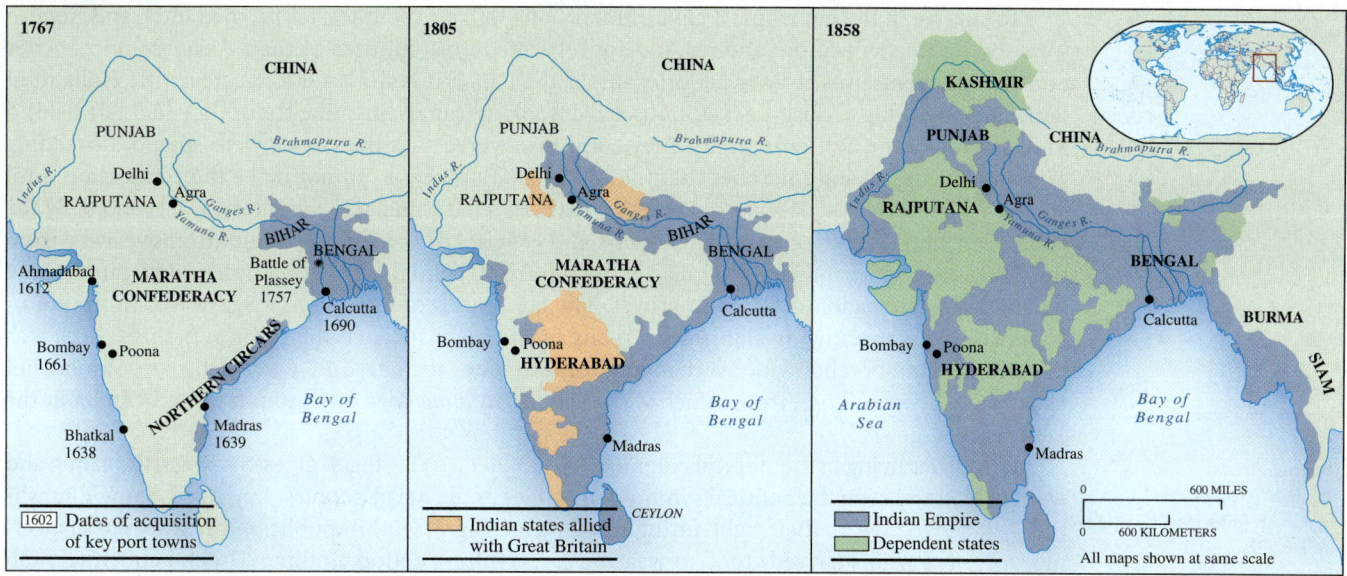

MAP 25.3 **The Growth of the British Empire in India, from the 1750s to 1858** In roughly a century between the late 1700s and the 1850s, the British had built an empire that encompassed virtually the entire subcontinent of South Asia.

at the expense of their neighbors. Interventions in these conflicts or assaults on war-weakened Indian kingdoms allowed the British to advance steadily inland from their three trading towns on the Indian coast: Madras, Bombay, and Calcutta. These cities became the administrative centers of the three **Presidencies** that eventually made up the bulk of the territory the British ruled directly in India. In many areas, the British were content to leave defeated or allied Indian rulers on the thrones of their **Princely States** and to control their kingdoms through agents stationed at the rulers' courts.

Because there was no sense of Indian national identity, it was impossible for Muslim or Hindu rulers to appeal to the defense of the homeland or the need for unity to drive out the foreigners. Indian princes continued to fear and fight with each other despite the ever-growing power of the British Raj. Old grudges and hatreds ran deeper than the new threat of the British. Many ordinary Indians were eager to serve in the British regiments, which had better weapons, brighter uniforms, and higher and more regular pay than all but a handful of the armies of the Indian rulers. By the mid-19th century, Indian soldiers in the pay of the British outnumbered British officers and enlisted men in India by almost five to one.

From the first decades of the 19th century, India was clearly the pivot of the great empire being built by Britain on a global scale. Older colonies with large numbers of white settlers, such as Canada and Australia, contributed more space to the total square miles of empire the British were so fond of calculating. But India had by far the greater share of colonized peoples. Britain's largest and most powerful land forces were the armies recruited from the Indian peoples, and these were rapidly becoming the police of the entire British Indian empire. In the mid-19th century, Indian soldiers were sent to punish the Chinese and Afghans, conquer Burma and Malaya, and begin the conquest of south and east Africa. Indian ports were essential to British sea power east of the Cape of Good Hope. As the century progressed, India became the major outlet for British overseas investments and manufactured goods as well as a major source of key raw materials.

Early Colonial Society in India and Java

Although they slowly emerged as the political masters of Java and India, the Dutch and the British were at first content to leave the social systems of the peoples they ruled pretty much as they had found them. The small numbers of European traders and company officials who lived in the colonies for any length of time simply formed a new class atop the social hierarchies that already existed in Java and different parts of India. Beneath them, the aristocratic classes and often the old ruling families were preserved. They were left in charge of the day-to-day administration at all but the very highest levels. At the highest levels, the local rulers were paired with an agent of the imperial power.

Presidencies Three districts that made up the bulk of the directly ruled British territories in India; capitals at Madras, Calcutta, and Bombay.

Princely States Domains of Indian princes allied with the British Raj; agents of East India Company were stationed at the rulers' courts to ensure compliance; made up over one-third of the British Indian empire.

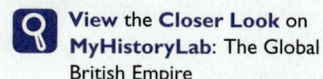

View the **Closer Look** on **MyHistoryLab**: The Global British Empire

Read the Document on MyHistoryLab: Arrival of the British in the Punjab (mid-19th c.) Prakash Tandon

To survive in the hot tropical environments of south and southeast Asia, the Dutch and English were forced to adapt to the ancient and sophisticated host cultures of their Asian colonies. After establishing themselves at Batavia, for example, the Dutch initially tried to create a little Holland in Java. They built high, close-packed houses overlooking canals, just like those they had left behind in Amsterdam and Rotterdam. But they soon discovered that the canals were splendid breeding grounds for insects and microbes that (although the Europeans did not make the connection until somewhat later) carried debilitating or lethal diseases such as malaria, dysentery, and typhoid. By the late 17th century, the prosperous merchants and officials of Batavia had begun to move away from the unhealthy center of the city to villas in the suburbs. Their large dwellings were set in gardens and separated by rice paddies and palm groves. The tall houses of the inner city gave way in the countryside to low, sprawling dwellings with many open spaces to catch the tropical breezes. Each was ringed with long porches with overhanging roofs to block the heat and glare of the sun. Similar, but usually smaller, dwellings, from which we get our term *bungalow*, came into fashion in India in the 18th century.

Europeans living in the tropical colonies also adopted, to varying degrees, the dress, the eating and work habits, and even the political symbols and styles of the Asian peoples they ruled. Some Englishmen refused to give up their tight-fitting woolen clothing, at least in public. But many (one suspects most of those who survived) took to wearing looser-fitting cotton clothing. Dutch gentlemen (and later their wives) even donned the long skirt-like sarongs of the Javanese aristocrats. British and Dutch officials learned to appreciate the splendid cuisines of India and Java—a taste that the Dutch would never lose and the British would revive at home in the post-independence era. Englishmen smoked Indian *hookahs*, or water pipes, and delighted in performances of Indian "dancing girls." Adjusting to the heat of the colonies, both the Dutch and the English worked hard in the cool of the morning, took a long lunch break (often with a siesta), and then returned to the office for the late afternoon and early evening.

Because the Europeans who went to Asia until the mid-19th century were overwhelmingly male, Dutch and British traders and soldiers commonly had liaisons with Asian women. In some cases these involved little more than visits to the local brothel. But very often European men lived with Asian women, and sometimes they married them. Before the end of the 18th century, mixed marriages on the part of prominent traders or officers were widely accepted, particularly in Java. Examples of racial discrimination against the subject peoples on the basis of their physical appearance can certainly be found during the early decades of European overseas empire. But the frequency of liaisons that cut across racial boundaries suggests a social fluidity and a degree of interracial interaction that would be unthinkable by the last half of the 19th century, when the social distance between colonizers and colonized was consciously marked in a variety of ways.

Social Reform in the Colonies

Until the early 19th century, neither the Dutch nor the British had much desire to push for changes in the social or cultural life of their Asian subjects. The British enforced the rigid divisions of the Hindu caste system, and both the British and the Dutch made it clear that they had little interest in spreading Christianity among the Indians or the Javanese. In fact, for fear of offending Hindu and Muslim religious sentiments, the British refused to allow Christian missionaries to preach in their territories until the second decade of the 19th century.

Beginning in the 1770s, however, rampant corruption on the part of company officials forced the British parliament to enact significant reforms in the administration of the East India Company and its colonies. By that time most of those who served in India saw their brief tenure as a chance to strike it rich quickly. They made great fortunes by cheating the company and exploiting the Indian peasants and artisans. The bad manners and conspicuous consumption of these upstarts, whom their peers in Great Britain scornfully called **nabobs**, were satirized by leading English novelists of the age.

When the misconduct of the nabobs resulted in the catastrophic Bengal famine of 1770, in which as much as one-third of the population of that once prosperous province died, their abuses could no longer be ignored. The British parliament passed several acts that restructured the company hierarchy and made it much more accountable to the British government. A succession of political reforms culminated in sweeping measures taken in the 1790s by the same **Lord Charles Cornwallis** whose surrender at Yorktown had sealed Britain's loss of the American colonies. By cleaning up the courts

nabobs Name given to British representatives of the East India Company who went briefly to India to make fortunes through graft and exploitation.

Cornwallis, Lord Charles Reformer of the East India Company administration of India in the 1790s; reduced power of local British administrators; checked widespread corruption.

THINKING HISTORICALLY

Western Education and the Rise of an African and Asian Middle Class

TO VARYING DEGREES AND FOR MANY of the same reasons as the British in India, all European colonizers educated the children of African and Asian elite groups in Western-language schools. The early 19th-century debate over education in India was paralleled by an equally hard-fought controversy among French officials and missionaries regarding the proper schooling for the peoples of Senegal in west Africa. The Dutch did not develop European-language schools for the sons of the Javanese elite until the mid-19th century, and many young Javanese men continued to be educated in the homes of the Dutch living in the colonies until the end of the century. Whatever their particular views on education, all colonial policymakers realized that they needed administrative assistants and postal clerks and that they could not begin to recruit enough Europeans to fill these posts. Therefore, all agreed that Western education for some segments of the colonized population was essential for the maintenance of colonial order.

One of the chief advantages of having Western-educated African and Asian subordinates—for they were always below European officials or traders—was that their salaries were much lower than what Europeans would have been paid for doing the same work. The Europeans had no trouble rationalizing this inequity. Higher pay for the Europeans was justified as compensation for the sacrifices involved in colonial service. Colonial officials also assumed that European employees would be more hardworking and efficient.

Beyond the need for government functionaries and business assistants, each European colonizer stressed different objectives in designing Western-language schools for the children of upper-class families. The transmission of Western scientific learning and production techniques was a high priority for the British in India. The goal of educational policymakers, such as Macaulay, was to teach the Indians Western literature and manners and to instill in them a Western sense of morality. As Macaulay put it, the British hoped that English-language schools would turn out brown English gentlemen, who would in turn teach their countrymen the ways of the West.

The French, at least until the end of the 19th century, went even further. Because they conceived of French nationalism as a matter of culture rather than birth, it was of prime importance that Africans and other colonial students master the French language and the subtleties of French cuisine, dress, and etiquette.

> **Western education in the colonies . . . within a generation or two would produce major challenges to European colonial dominance.**

The French also saw the process of turning colonial subjects into black, brown, and yellow French citizens as a way to increase their stagnant population to keep up with rival nations, especially Germany and Great Britain. Both of these rivals and the United States had much higher birth rates in this period.

When the lessons had been fully absorbed and the students fully assimilated to French culture, they could become full citizens of France, no matter what their family origins or skin color. Only a tiny minority of the population of any French colony had the opportunity for the sort of schooling that would qualify them for French citizenship. But by the early 20th century, there were thousands of Senegalese, Vietnamese, and Tunisians who could carry French passports, vote in French elections, and even run for seats in the French parliament. Other European colonial powers adopted either the British or the French approach to education and its aims. The Dutch and the Germans followed the British pattern, whereas the Portuguese pushed assimilation for smaller numbers of the elite classes among the peoples they colonized.

Western education in the colonies succeeded in producing clerks and railway conductors, brown Indian gentlemen, and black French citizens. It also had effects that those who shaped colonial educational policy did not intend, effects that within a generation or two would produce major challenges to European colonial dominance. The population of most colonized areas was divided into many different ethnic, religious, and language groups with separate histories and identities. Western-language schools gave the sons (and, in limited instances, the daughters) of the leading families a common language in which to communicate. The schools also spread common attitudes and ideas and gave the members of diverse groups a common body of knowledge. In all European colonial societies, Western education led to similar occupational opportunities: in government service, with Western business firms, or as professionals (e.g., lawyers, doctors, journalists). Thus, within a generation after their introduction, Western-language schools had created a new middle class in the colonies that had no counterpart in precolonial African or Asian societies.

Occupying social strata and economic niches in the middle range between the European colonizers and the old aristocracy on one hand and the peasantry and urban laborers on the other, Western-educated Africans and Asians became increasingly

(continued on next page)

aware of the interests and grievances they had in common. They often found themselves at odds with the traditional rulers or the landed gentry, who, ironically, were often their fathers or grandfathers. Members of the new middle class also felt alienated from the peasantry, whose beliefs and way of life were so different from those they had learned in Western-language schools.

For more than a generation they clung to their European tutors and employers. Eventually, however, they grew increasingly resentful of their lower salaries and of European competition for scarce jobs. They were also angered by their social segregation from the Europeans, which intensified in the heightened racist atmosphere of the late 19th century. European officials and business managers often made little effort to disguise their contempt for even the most accomplished Western-educated Africans and Asians. Thus, members of the new middle class in the colonies were caught between two worlds: the traditional ways and teachings of their fathers and the modern world of their European masters. Finding that they would be fully admitted to neither world, they rejected the first and set about supplanting the Europeans and building their own versions of the second, or modern, world.

> **QUESTIONS**
> - Why did the Europeans continue to provide Western-language education for Africans and Asians once it was clear they were creating a class that might challenge their position of dominance?
> - What advantages did Western-educated Africans and Asians have as future leaders of resistance to the European colonial overlords?
> - Do you think the European colonial rule would have lasted longer if Western-language education had been denied to colonized peoples?

and reducing the power of local British administrators, Cornwallis did much to check widespread corruption. Because of his mistrust of Indians, his measures also severely limited their participation in governing the empire.

In this same period, forces were building in both India and England that caused a major shift in British policy toward social reform among the subject peoples. The Evangelical religious revival, which had seen the spread of Methodism among the English working classes, soon spilled over into Britain's colonial domains. Evangelicals were in the vanguard of the struggle to put an end to the slave trade, and their calls for reforms in India were warmly supported by Utilitarian philosophers such as Jeremy Bentham and James Mill. These prominent British thinkers believed that there were common principles by which human societies ought to be run if decent living conditions were to be attained by people at all class levels. Mill and other Utilitarians were convinced that British society, although flawed, was far more advanced than Indian society. Thus, they pushed for the introduction of British institutions and ways of thinking in India, as well as the eradication of what they considered Indian superstitions and social abuses.

Both Utilitarians and Evangelicals agreed that Western education was the key to revitalizing an ancient but decadent Indian civilization. Both factions were contemptuous of Indian learning that was centered in *madrasas* or Islamic religious schools or Hindu *gurus* instructing individuals or small groups of students. Influential British historian Thomas Babington Macaulay put it most bluntly when he declared in the 1830s that one shelf of an English gentleman's library was worth all the writings of Asia. Consequently, the Evangelicals and the Utilitarians pushed for the introduction of English-language education for the children of the Indian elite. These officials also pushed for major reforms in Indian society and advocated a large-scale infusion of Western technology.

At the center of the reformers' campaign was the effort to put an end to sati, the ritual burning of Hindu widows on the funeral pyres of their deceased husbands (see Chapters 8 and 22). This practice, which was clearly a corruption of Hindu religious beliefs, had spread fairly widely among upper-caste Hindu groups by the era of the Muslim invasions in the 11th and 12th centuries. In fact, the wives of proud warrior peoples, such as the Rajputs, had been encouraged to commit mass suicide rather than risk dishonoring their husbands by being captured and molested by Muslim invaders. By the early 19th century, some brahman castes, and even lower-caste groups in limited areas, had adopted the practice of sati.

Bolstered by the strong support and active cooperation of Western-educated Indian leaders, such as **Ram Mohun Roy**, the British outlawed sati in the 1830s. One confrontation between the British and those affected by their efforts to prevent widow burnings illustrates the confidence of the reformers in the righteousness of their cause and the sense of moral and social superiority over the Indians that the British felt in this era. A group of brahmans complained to a British official, Charles Napier, that

Read the Document on MyHistoryLab: Edmund Burke, Speech on Fox's East India Bill

Read the Document on MyHistoryLab: T. B. Macaulay, Speech on Parliamentary Reform

Roy, Ram Mohun Western-educated Indian leader, early 19th century; cooperated with British to outlaw sati.

his refusal to allow them to burn the widow of a prominent leader of their community was a violation of their social customs. Napier replied,

> The burning of widows is your custom. Prepare the funeral pyre. But my nation also has a custom. When men burn women alive, we hang them and confiscate all their property. My carpenters shall therefore erect gibbets on which to hang all concerned when the widow is consumed. Let us all act according to our national customs.

The range and magnitude of the reforms the British enacted in India in the early 19th century marked a watershed in global history. During these years, the alien British, who had become the rulers of one of the oldest centers of civilization, consciously began to transmit the ideas, inventions, modes of organization, and technology associated with Western Europe's scientific and industrial revolutions to the peoples of the non-Western world. English education, social reforms, railways and telegraph lines were only part of a larger project by which the British tried to remake Indian society along Western lines. India's crop lands were measured and registered, its forests were set aside for "scientific" management, and its people were drawn more and more into the European-dominated global market economy. British officials promoted policies that they believed would teach the Indian peasantry the merits of thrift and hard work. British educators lectured the children of India's rising middle classes on the importance of emulating their European masters in matters as diverse as being punctual, exercising their bodies, and mastering the literature and scientific learning of the West. Ironically, the very values and ideals that the British preached so earnestly to the Indians would soon be turned against colonizers by those leading India's struggle for independence from Western political domination.

Read the Document on MyHistoryLab: An Indian Nationalist on Hindu Women and Education (early 19th c.) Ram Mohun Roy

Read the Document on MyHistoryLab: Amrita Lal Roy, English Rule in India, 1886

INDUSTRIAL RIVALRIES AND THE PARTITION OF THE WORLD, 1870–1914

25.2 What were the major forces in Europe and overseas that pushed the European powers, and later the United States and Japan, to compete for territories over much of Africa and Asia in the half century before World War I?

Although science and industry gave the Europeans power over the rest of the world, they also heightened economic competition and political rivalries between the European powers. In the first half of the 19th century, industrial Britain, with its seemingly insurmountable naval superiority, was left alone to dominate overseas trade and empire building. By the last decades of the century, Belgium, France, and especially Germany and the United States, were challenging Britain's industrial supremacy; they were also actively building (or in the case of France, adding to) colonial empires of their own. Many of the political leaders of these expansive nations saw colonies as essential to states that aspired to status as great powers. Colonies, particularly those in Africa and India, were also seen as insurance against raw material shortages and the loss of overseas market outlets to European or North American rivals.

Thus, the concerns of Europe's political leaders were both political and economic. The late 19th century was a period of recurring economic depressions in Europe and the United States. The leaders of the newly industrialized nations had little experience in handling the overproduction and unemployment that came with each of these economic crises. They were deeply concerned about the social unrest and, in some cases, what appeared to be stirrings of revolution that each phase of depression created. Some political theorists argued that as destinations to which unemployed workers might migrate, particularly white settlement colonies, such as Australia, and as potential markets for surplus goods, colonies could serve as safety valves to release the pressure built up in times of industrial slumps.

In the era of the scramble for colonial possessions, political leaders in Europe played a much more prominent role in decisions to annex overseas territories than they had earlier, even in the first half of the 19th century. In part, this was because of improved communications. Telegraphs and railways made it possible to transmit orders much more rapidly from the capitals of Europe to their representatives in the tropics. But more than politicians were involved in late 19th-century decisions to add to the colonial empires. The development of mass journalism and the extension

The spread of the Industrial Revolution from the British Isles resulted in ever higher levels of European and American involvement in the outside world. Beginning in the 1870s, the Europeans indulged in an orgy of overseas conquests that reduced much of the rest of the world to colonial possessions by the time of the outbreak of World War I in 1914.

of the vote to the lower middle and working classes in industrial Europe and the United States made public opinion a major factor in foreign policy. Although stalwart explorers might on their own initiative make treaties with local African or Asian potentates who assigned their lands to France or Germany, these annexations had to be ratified by the home government. In most cases, ratification meant fierce parliamentary debates, which often spilled over into press wars and popular demonstrations. Empires had become the property and pride of the nations of Europe and North America.

Unequal Combat: Colonial Wars and the Apex of European Imperialism

Industrial change not only justified the Europeans' grab for colonial possessions but made them much easier to acquire. By the late 19th century, scientific discoveries and technological innovations had catapulted the Europeans far ahead of all other peoples in the capacity to wage war. The Europeans could tap mineral resources that most peoples did not even know existed, and European chemists mixed ever more deadly explosives. Advances in metallurgy made possible the mass production of light, mobile artillery pieces that rendered suicidal the massed cavalry or infantry charges that were the mainstay of Asian and African armies. Advances in artillery were matched by great improvements in hand arms. Much more accurate and faster firing, breech-loading rifles replaced the clumsy muzzle-loading muskets of the first phase of empire building. By the 1880s, after decades of experimentation, the machine gun had become an effective battlefield weapon. Railroads gave the Europeans the mobility of the swiftest African or Asian cavalry and the ability to supply large armies in the field for extended periods of time. On the sea Europe's already formidable advantages (amply illustrated in Figure 25.3) were increased by industrial transformations. After the opening of the Suez Canal in 1869, steam power supplanted the sail, iron hulls replaced wooden ones, and massive guns, capable of hitting enemy vessels miles away, were introduced into the fleets of the great powers.

The dazzling array of new weaponry with which the Europeans set out on their expeditions to the Indian frontiers or the African bush made the wars of colonial conquest very lopsided. This was particularly true when the Europeans encountered resistance from peoples such as those in the

FIGURE **25.3** This striking painting captures the sleek majesty of the warships that were central to British success in building a global empire. Here the *Prince of Wales* puts ashore British soldiers in Bengal in the northeast of Britain's Indian empire.

Read the Document on MyHistoryLab: Carl Peters Calls for German Colonization of Africa, 1884.

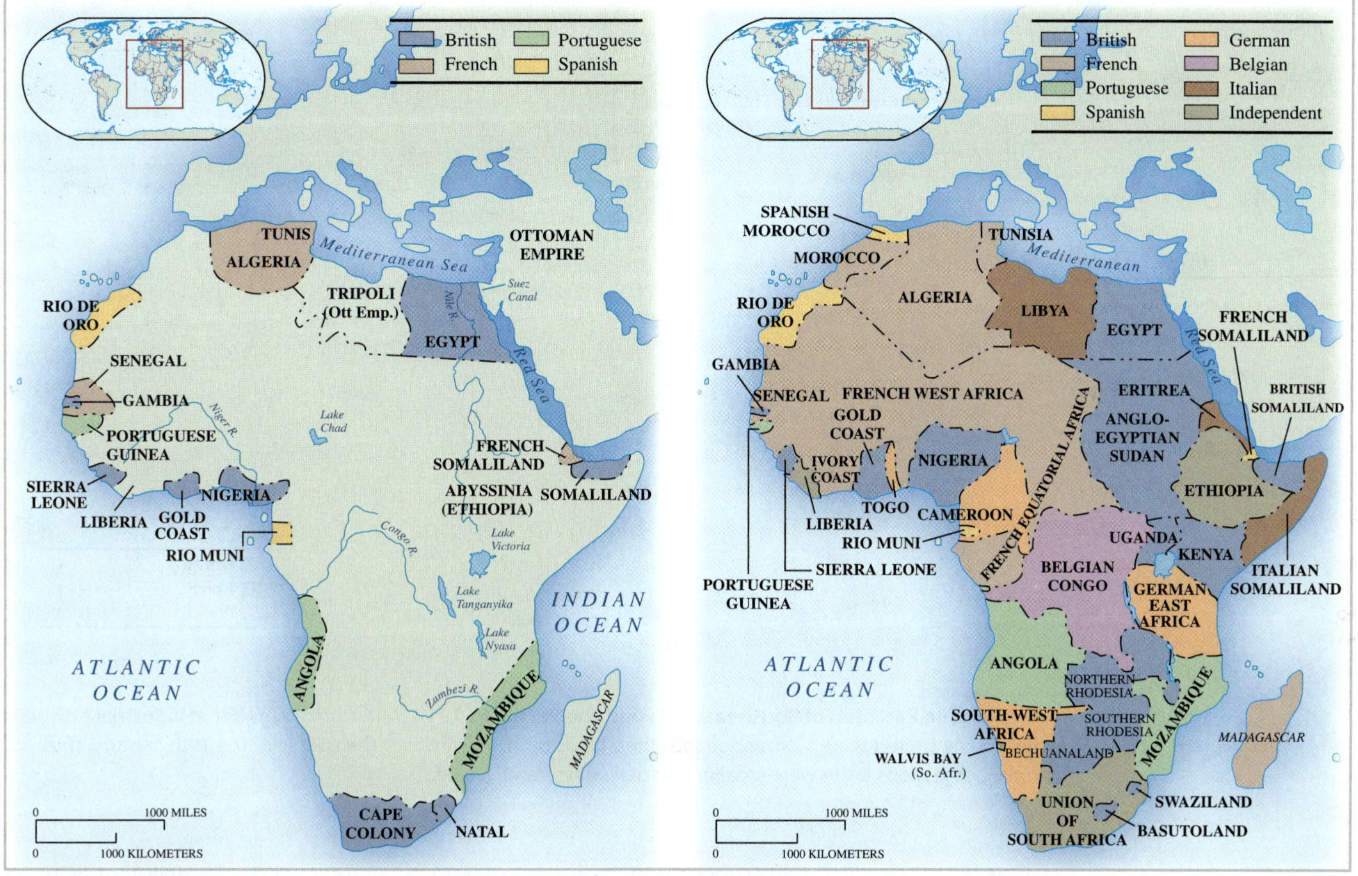

MAP **25.4 The Partition of Africa Between c. 1870 and 1914** As reflected in the patchwork that partition made of the continent, no area of the globe saw more intense rivalries between the European powers than Africa in the mid- and especially late-19th century.

interior of Africa or the Pacific islands (Maps 25.4 and 25.5). These areas had been cut off from most preindustrial advances in technology, and thus their peoples were forced to fight European machine guns with spears, arrows, and leather shields. One African leader, whose followers struggled with little hope to halt the German advance into east Africa, resorted to natural imagery to account for the power of the invaders' weapons:

> On Monday we heard a shuddering like Leviathan, the voice of many cannon; we heard the roar like waves on the rocks and rumble like thunder in the rains. We heard a crashing like elephants or monsters and our hearts melted at the number of shells. We knew that we were hearing the battle of Pangani; the guns were like a hurricane in our ears.

Not even peoples with advanced preindustrial technology and sophisticated military organization, such as the Chinese and the Vietnamese, could stand against, or really comprehend, the fearful killing devices of the Europeans. In advising the Vietnamese emperor to give in to European demands, one of his officials, who had led the fight against the French invaders, warned, "Nobody can resist them. They go where they choose. . . . Under heaven, everything is feasible to them, save only the matter of life and death."

In Vietnam, as in the rest of the colonies, the Europeans, and later the Americans and Japanese, established in the 19th century, these superior technologies were distributed to the soldiers that

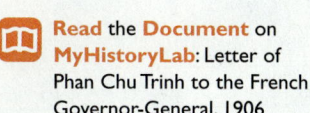

Read the Document on MyHistoryLab: Letter of Phan Chu Trinh to the French Governor-General, 1906

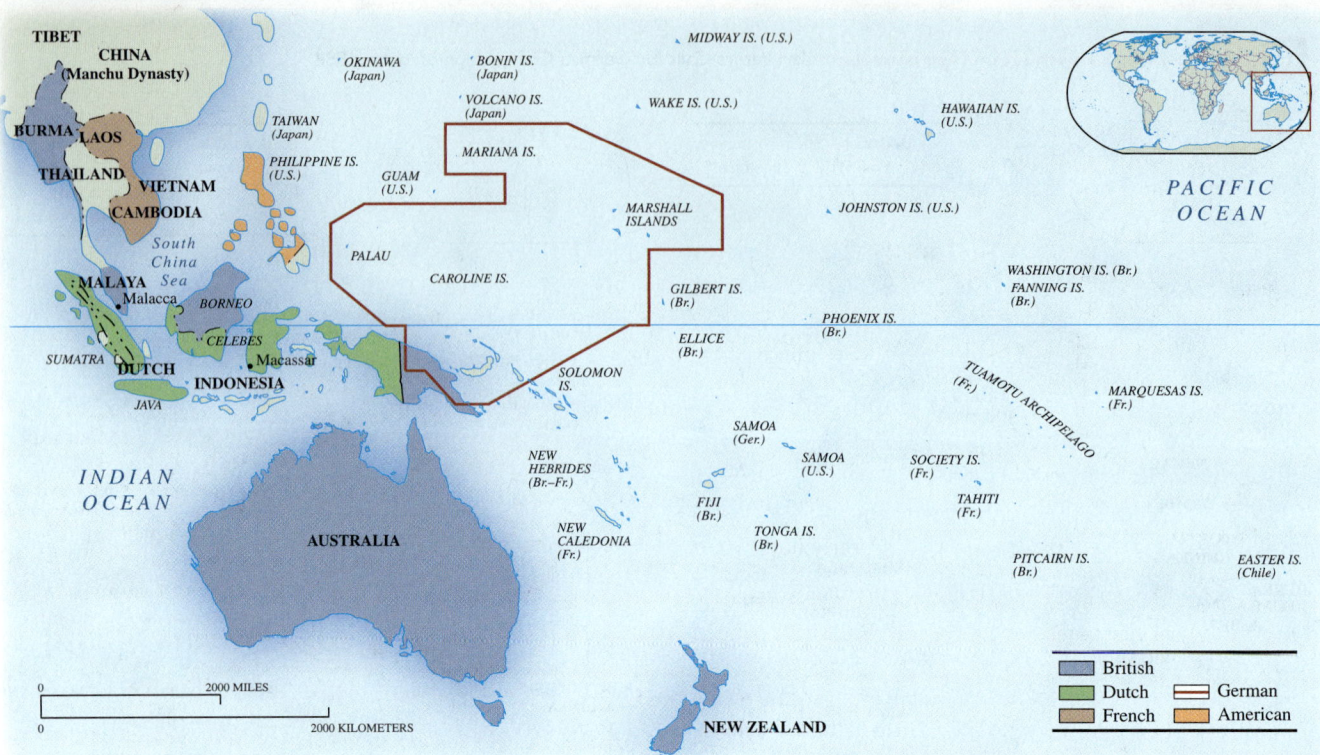

MAP 25.5 **The Partition of Southeast Asia and the Pacific to 1914** Although a number of industrial powers, including the United States, expanded into the islands of the Pacific over the course of the 19th century, the colonial possessions there were smaller and of less economic value.

each of the imperialist powers recruited from the indigenous peoples, as the English had in India in the 18th century. In fact, most of the forces that conquered and controlled European overseas empires were drawn from African and Asian peoples who had been or were being colonized. By the middle of the 19th century, the European overlords had come to view military prowess as a racial attribute. The European colonizers preferred to recruit these soldiers from ethnic and religious groups that they viewed as particularly martial. In India, for example, these included the Sikhs (pictured in Figure 25.2) and Marattas, as well as Gurkhas recruited from neighboring but independent Nepal.

Despite the odds against them, African and Asian peoples often fiercely resisted the imposition of colonial rule. West African leaders, such as Samory and Ahmadou Sekou, held back the European advance for decades. When rulers such as the Vietnamese emperors refused to fight, local officials organized guerrilla resistance in defense of the indigenous regime. Martial peoples, such as the Zulus in South Africa, had the courage and discipline to face and defeat sizable British forces in conventional battles such as that at **Isandhlwana** in 1879 (described in the chapter opener and shown in Figure 25.1). But conventional resistance eventually ended in defeat. The guerrilla bands in Vietnam were eventually run to the ground. And, as we have seen, even at Isandhlwana, many more Zulu warriors lost their lives than the British or their African allies, and the Zulu kingdom soon fell under British control. Given European advantages in conventional battles, guerrilla resistance, sabotage, and in some cases banditry proved the most effective means of fighting the Europeans' attempts to assert political control. Religious leaders were often in the forefront of these struggles, which occurred across the globe, from the revivalist Ghost Dance religion in the late 19th-century American West to the Maji Maji uprisings in German East Africa in 1907 and the Boxer Rebellion in China in 1898. The magic potions and divine assistance they offered to protect their followers seemed to be the only way to offset the demoralizing killing power of the Europeans' weapons.

Isandhlwana [EE sän dl wä nuh] Location of battle fought in 1879 between the British and Zulu armies in South Africa; resulted in defeat of British; one of few victories of African forces over western Europeans.

PATTERNS OF DOMINANCE: CONTINUITY AND CHANGE

25.3 How were a few thousand Europeans able to conquer and rule territories with millions, in some cases even hundreds of millions of subject peoples?

By the end of the 19th century, the European colonial order was made up of two different kinds of colonies. The greater portion of the European empires consisted of directly ruled **tropical dependencies** in Africa, Asia, and the South Pacific. In these colonies, small numbers of Europeans ruled large populations of non-Western peoples. The tropical dependencies were a vast extension of the pattern of dominance the British, Dutch, and French had worked out earlier in India, Java, and African enclaves such as Senegal. Most of these colonies were bought, often quite suddenly, under European rule in the late 19th and early 20th century.

Settlement colonies were the second major type of European overseas possession. But within this type there were different patterns of European occupation and indigenous response. One pattern was exhibited by colonies such as Canada and Australia, which the British labeled the **White Dominions** and are discussed in Chapter 24. These white settler colonies accounted for a good portion of the land area but only a tiny minority of the population of Britain's global empire. In these areas, as well as in some parts of Latin America, such as Chile and Argentina (see Chapter 26), descendants of European settlers made up most of the population in colonies in which relatively small numbers of native inhabitants had been decimated by diseases and wars of conquest. These patterns of European settlement and the sharp decline of the indigenous population were also found in the portions of North America that came to form the United States, which had won its independence in the late 18th century.

In some of the areas where large numbers of Europeans had migrated, a second major variation on the settlement colony developed. Both in regions that had been colonized as early as North America, such as South Africa, and in most of the areas Europeans and Americans had begun to occupy only in 19th century, including Algeria, Kenya, and Hawaii, key characteristics of tropical dependencies and the white settlement colonies were combined. Temperate climates and mild disease environments in these areas made it possible for tens or hundreds of thousands of Europeans to settle permanently. Despite the Europeans' arrival, large indigenous populations survived an initial, and sometimes steep, decline in numbers and later began to increase rapidly. As a result, in these settlement colonies, which had been brought under colonial rule for the most part in the age of industrialization, Europeans and indigenous peoples increasingly clashed over land rights, resource control, social status, and cultural differences.

Colonial Regimes and Social Hierarchies in the Tropical Dependencies

As the Europeans imposed their rule over tens of millions of additional Africans and Asians in the late 19th century, they drew heavily on precedents set in older colonies, particularly India, in establishing administrative, legal, and educational systems. As in India (or in Java and Senegal), the Europeans exploited long-standing ethnic and cultural divisions between the peoples of their new African or Asian colonies to put down resistance and maintain control. In west and east Africa in particular, they used the peoples who followed animistic religions (those that focused on nature or ancestral spirits) or who had converted to Christianity against the Muslim communities that existed in most colonies. In official reports and censuses, colonial administrators exacerbated existing ethnic differences by dividing the peoples in each colony into "tribes." The label itself, with its connotations of primitiveness and backwardness, says a great deal about general European attitudes toward the peoples of sub-Saharan Africa. In southeast Asia, the colonizers attempted to use hill-dwelling "tribal" minorities against the majority populations that lived in the lowlands. In each colonial area, favored minorities, often Christians, were recruited into the civil service and police.

As had been the case in India, Java, and Senegal, small numbers of Europeans lived mainly in the capital city and major provincial towns. From these urban centers they oversaw the administration of the African and Asian colonies, which was actually carried out at the local level mainly by hundreds

> The Europeans' sense of their own uniqueness and superiority, heightened by their unparalleled scientific and technological achievements, led them to seek to transform the lands and peoples they controlled. The demand for Western learning on the part of the elite and middle classes of colonized peoples in Africa and Asia rose sharply, eventually creating a counterforce to European domination.

tropical dependencies Colonies with substantial indigenous populations that are ruled by small European political and military minorities with the assistance of colonized bureaucrats, soldiers, clerks, and servants.

settlement colonies Areas, such as North America and Australia, that were both conquered by European invaders and settled by large numbers of European migrants who made the colonized areas their permanent home and dispersed and decimated the indigenous inhabitants.

White Dominions Colonies in which European settlers made up the overwhelming majority of the population; small numbers of native inhabitants were typically reduced by disease and wars of conquest; typical of British holdings in North America and Australia with growing independence in the 19th century.

DOCUMENT

Contrary Images: The Colonizer versus the Colonized on the "Civilizing Mission"

EACH OF THE FOLLOWING PASSAGES FROM novels written in the colonial era expresses a different view of the reasons behind European colonization in Africa and Asia and its consequences. The first is taken from an adventure story written by John Buchan titled *Prester John,* a favorite in the pre–World War I decades among English schoolboys, many of whom would go out as young men to be administrators in the colonies. Davie, the protagonist in the story, is a "tall, square-set lad ... renowned [for his] prowess at Rugby football." In the novel, Davie summarizes key elements of the "civilizing mission" credo by which so many European thinkers and political leaders tried to justify their colonization of most of the rest of the world.

> I knew then [after his struggle to thwart a "native" uprising in South Africa] the meaning of the white man's duty. He has to take all the risks, reck[on]ing nothing of his life or his fortunes and well content to find his reward in the fulfillment of his task. That is the difference between white and black, the gift of responsibility, the power of being in a little way a king; and so long as we know this and practise it, we will rule not in Africa alone but wherever there are dark men who live only for the day and their own bellies. Moreover the work made me pitiful and kindly. I learned much of the untold grievances of the natives and saw something of their strange, twisted reasoning.

The second passage is taken from René Maran's *Batouala,* which was first published in 1921 just after World War I. Although a French colonial official in west Africa, Maran was an African American, born in Martinique, who was highly sensitive to the plight of the colonized in Africa. Here his protagonist, a local African leader named Batouala, complains of the burdens rather than the benefits of colonial rule and mocks the self-important European agents of the vaunted civilizing mission.

> But what good does it do to talk about it? It's nothing new to us that men of white skin are more delicate than men of black skin. One example of a thousand possible. Everyone knows that the whites, saying that they are "collecting taxes," force all blacks of a marriageable age to carry voluminous packages from when the sun rises to when it sets.
> These trips last two, three, five days. Little matter to them the weight of these packages which are called "sandoukous." They don't sink under the burden. Rain, sun, cold? They don't suffer. So they pay no attention. And long live the worst weather, provided the whites are sheltered.
> Whites fret about mosquito bites.... They fear mason bees. They are also afraid of the "prankongo," the scorpion who lives, black and venomous, among decaying roofs, under rubble, or in the midst of debris.
> In a word, everything worries them. As if a man worthy of the name would worry about everything which lives, crawls, or moves around him.

QUESTIONS

- What sorts of roles does Davie assume that the Europeans must play in the colonies?
- What benefits accrue to colonized peoples from their rule?
- What impression does he convey of the thinking and behavior of the colonized peoples?
- In what ways do Batouala's views of the Europeans conflict with Davie's assumptions about himself and other colonizers?
- Does Batouala agree with Davie's conviction that colonial rule is beneficial for the Africans?

or thousands of African and Asian subordinates. Some of these subordinates, normally those in positions of the greatest authority, were Western educated. But most were recruited from indigenous elite groups, including village leaders, local notables, and regional lords (Figure 25.4). In Burma, Malaya, and east Africa, thousands of Indian administrators and soldiers helped the British to rule new additions to their empire.

In contrast to Java and India, where schools were heavily state supported, Western-language education in Africa was left largely to Protestant and Catholic missionaries. As a result of deep-seated racial prejudices held by nearly all the colonizers, higher education was not promoted in Africa. As a result, college graduates were few in Africa compared with India, the Dutch East Indies, or even smaller Asian colonies such as Burma and Vietnam. This policy stunted the growth of a middle class in black Africa, a consequence that European colonial officials increasingly intended. As nationalist agitation spread among the Western-educated classes in India and other Asian colonies, colonial policymakers warned against the dangers posed by college graduates. According to this argument, those with advanced educations among the colonized aspired to jobs that were beyond their capacity and were disgruntled when they could not find employment.

Changing Social Relations between Colonizers and Colonized

In both long-held and newly acquired colonies, the growing tensions between the colonizers and the rising African and Asian middle classes reflected a larger shift in European social interaction with subject peoples. This shift had actually begun long before the scramble for colonies in the late 19th century. Its causes are complex, but the growing size and changing makeup of European communities in the colonies were critical factors. As more and more Europeans went to the colonies, they tended to keep to themselves on social occasions rather than mixing with the "natives." New medicines and increasingly segregated living quarters made it possible to bring to the colonies the wives and families of government officials and European military officers (but not of the rank and file until well into the 20th century). Wives and families further closed the social circle of the colonized, and European women looked disapprovingly on liaisons between European men and Asian or African women. Brothels were off limits for upper-class officials and officers, and mixed marriages or living arrangements met with more and more vocal disapproval within the constricted world of the colonial communities and back home in Europe. The growing numbers of missionaries and pastors for European congregations in the colonies obviously strengthened these taboos.

Read the Document on MyHistoryLab: Orishatuke Faduma, "African Negro Education," 1918

FIGURE 25.4 The importance of co-opting African and Asian rulers and elite social groups for European empire building is vividly illustrated by this 1861 painting of Queen Victoria and her consort Albert presenting a Bible to an African "chief" decked out in what Victorians imagined was "native" dress attire for such a personage.

Historians of colonialism once put much of the blame on European women for the growing social gap between colonizers and colonized. But recent research has shown that male officials bore much of the responsibility. They established laws restricting or prohibiting miscegenation and other sorts of interracial liaisons. They also pushed for housing arrangements and police practices designed specifically to keep social contacts between European women and the colonized at a minimum. These measures confined European women in the colonies into an almost exclusively European world. They had many "native" servants and "native" nannies for their children. But they rarely came into contact with men or women of their own social standing from the colonized peoples. When they did, the occasions were highly public and strictly formal.

The trend toward social exclusion on the part of Europeans in the colonies and their open disdain for the culture of colonized peoples were reinforced by notions of **white racial supremacy**, which peaked in acceptance in the decades before World War I. It was widely believed that the mental and moral superiority of whites over the rest of humankind, usually divided into racial types according to the crude criterion of skin color, had been demonstrated by what were then thought to be scientific experiments. Because the non-Europeans' supposedly inferior intelligence and weak sense of morality were seen as inherent and permanent, there seemed to be little motivation for Europeans to socialize with the colonized.

There were also new reasons to fight the earlier tendency to adopt elements of the culture and lifestyle of subject peoples. As photos from the late 19th century reveal, stiff collars and ties for men and corsets and long skirts for women became obligatory for respectable colonial functionaries and their wives. The colonizers' houses were filled with the overstuffed furniture and bric-a-brac that the late Victorians loved so dearly. European social life in the colonies revolved around the infamous clubs, where the only "natives" allowed were the servants. In the heat of the summer, most of the administrators and nearly all of the colonizers' families retreated to hill stations, where the cool air and quaint architecture made it seem almost as if they were home again, or at least in a Swiss mountain resort.

white racial supremacy Belief in the inherent mental, moral, and cultural superiority of whites; peaked in acceptance in decades before World War I; supported by social science doctrines of social Darwinists such as Herbert Spencer.

 Read the Document on MyHistoryLab: Rudyard Kipling's "The White Man's Burden," 1899

Shifts in Methods of Economic Extraction

The relationship between the colonizers and the mass of the colonized remained much as it had been before. District officers, with the help of many "native" subordinates, continued to do their paternal duty to settle disputes between peasant villagers, punish criminals, and collect taxes. European planters and merchants still relied on African or Asian overseers and brokers to manage laborers and purchase crops and handicraft manufactures. But late 19th-century colonial bureaucrats and managers tried to instruct African and Asian peasants in scientific farming techniques and to compel the colonized peoples more generally to work harder and more efficiently. These efforts involved an important extension of dependent status in the Western-dominated world economy.

A wide range of incentives was devised to expand export production. Some of them benefited the colonized peoples, such as cheap consumer goods that could be purchased with cash earned by producing marketable crops or working on European plantations. In many instances, however, colonized peoples were simply forced to produce, for little or no pay, the crops or raw materials that the Europeans wanted. Head and hut taxes were imposed that could be paid only in ivory, palm nuts, or wages earned working on European estates. Under the worst of these forced-labor schemes, such as those inflicted on the peoples of the Belgian Congo in the late 19th century, villagers were flogged and killed if they failed to meet production quotas, and women and children were held hostage to ensure that the men would deliver the products demanded on time (Figure 25.5).

As increasing numbers of the colonized peoples were involved in the production of crops or minerals intended for export markets, the economies of most of Africa, India, and southeast Asia were reorganized to serve the needs of the industrializing European economies. Roads and railways were built primarily to move farm produce and raw materials from the interior of colonized areas to port centers from which they could be shipped to Europe. Benefiting from Europe's technological advances, mining sectors grew dramatically in most of the colonies. Vast areas that had previously been uncultivated or (more commonly) had been planted in food crops were converted to the production of commodities such as cocoa, palm oil, rubber, and hemp that were in great demand in the markets of Europe and, increasingly, the United States.

FIGURE **25.5** As this political cartoon of a vicious snake with Leopold II's head squeezing the life out of a defenseless African villager illustrates, an international campaign developed in the 1890s in opposition to the brutal forced-labor regime in what had become the Belgian king's personal fiefdom in the Congo after 1885. The much-publicized scandal compelled the Belgian government to take over the administration of the colony in 1906.

The profits from the precious metals and minerals extracted from Africa's mines or the rubber grown in Malaya went mainly to European merchants and industrialists. The raw materials themselves were shipped to Europe to be processed and sold or used to make industrial products. The finished products were intended mainly for European consumers. The African and Asian laborers who produced these products were generally poorly paid, if they were paid at all. The laborers and colonial economies as a whole were steadily reduced to dependence on the European-dominated global market. Thus, economic dependence complemented the political subjugation and social subordination of colonized African and Asian peoples in a world order loaded in favor of the expansionist nations of western Europe.

White Settler Colonies in South Africa and the Pacific

The settlement colonies where large numbers of Europeans migrated intending to make permanent homes exhibited many of the patterns of political control and economic exploitation found in the tropical dependencies. But the presence of substantial numbers of European settlers *and* indigenous peoples considerably altered the dynamic of political and social domination in this type of colony in comparison with societies like India or the Belgian Congo, where settlers were few and overwhelmingly outnumbered by colonized peoples. This type of settler society must be compared to the settler societies discussed in the previous chapter.

From Algeria to Argentina, settler colonies varied widely. But those established in the 19th century, with the exception of Australia, tended to be quite different from those occupied in North and

VISUALIZING THE PAST

Capitalism and Colonialism

IN THE CENTURY SINCE THE EUROPEAN powers divided up much of Africa, Asia, and the Pacific into their colonial fiefdoms, historians have often debated how much this process had to do with capitalism. They have also debated, perhaps even more intensely, over how much economic benefit the European colonial powers and the United States were able to garner from their colonies. The table shown here compares Great Britain, the premier industrialized colonial power, with Germany, Europe, the United States, and key areas of the British empire. For each Western society and colonized area, various indices of the amount or intensity of economic interaction are indicated. A careful examination of each set of statistics and a comparison among them should enable you to answer the questions that follow on the connections between capitalism and colonialism.

> **QUESTION**
> - To which areas did the bulk of British foreign investment flow?
> - With which areas did the British have the highest volume of trade?
> - On which was it the most dependent for outlets for its manufactured goods?
> - On which was it the most dependent for raw materials? Do these patterns suggest that colonized areas were more or less important than independent nations; great power rivals, such as Germany and the United States; or settler colonies, such as Canada and Australia?

BRITISH INVESTMENT ABROAD ON THE EVE OF THE FIRST WORLD WAR (1913)

Circa 1913	% of Total British Investment	% of Total British Imports	Main Products Exported to GB	% of Total British Exports	Main Products Imported fr. GB
Germany	0.17	8.98	Manufactures	9.82	Manufactures, Foodstuffs
Rest of Europe	5.64	27	Foodstuffs, Manufactures	30	Textiles, Machinery, Manufactures
"White" Dominions (ANZAC)	24.75	10.93	Wool, Foodstuffs, Ores, Textiles	12.28	Machinery, Textiles, Foodstuffs
United States of America	20.05	16.95	Manufactures, Foodstuffs	9.37	Manufactures
India (may include Ceylon)	10.07	6.30	Cotton, Jute, Narcotics, Tea, Other Comestibles	11.29	Machinery, Coal, Comestibles
Egypt	1.29	0.74	Cotton	1.25	Manufactures, Textiles, Coal
West Africa	0.99		Foodstuffs, Plant Oils, Ores, Timber		Manufactures, Textiles, Machinery
South Africa	9.84	1.60	Diamonds, Gold, Wool, Other Ores	3.79	Machinery, Textiles, Consumer Products

South America in the early centuries of European overseas expansion. In these early settler colonies, which included areas that eventually formed the nations of Canada, the United States, Argentina, and Chile, conquest and especially diseases transmitted unwittingly by incoming European migrants had devastating effects on the indigenous peoples, whose numbers in most of these regions were sparse to begin with. By the end of the 19th century in all of these areas, including Australia, which had been settled late but very thinly peopled when the Europeans arrived, the surviving indigenous peoples had been displaced to the margins both geographically and socially. As discussed in

Chapter 24, several of these older settler societies—and particularly the United States, Canada, and Australia—imported so many people, institutions, and beliefs from Europe that they now became a part of Western history.

In most of the settler colonies established in the 19th century, the indigenous peoples were both numerous when the Europeans arrived and, in north and sub-Saharan Africa at least, largely resistant to the diseases the colonizers carried with them. Even Pacific islands, such as New Zealand and Hawaii, which had been largely isolated until their first sustained contacts with the Europeans in the late-18th century, were quite densely populated by peoples who were able over time to build up immunities to the diseases the Europeans transmitted. As a result, the history of the newer settler colonies that were formed as the result of large-scale migrations from industrializing societies has been dominated by enduring competition and varying degrees of conflict between European settlers and indigenous peoples. As these divisions were hardened by ethnic, racial, and national identities, settlers also clashed with local representatives of the European powers. In many instances the settlers sought to gain independence from meddling missionaries and transient colonial officials by force.

South Africa

The initial Dutch colony at Cape Town was established to provide a way station where Dutch merchant ships could take on water and fresh food in the middle of their long journey from Europe to the East Indies. The small community of Dutch settlers stayed near the coast for decades after their arrival. But the Boers (or farmers), as the descendants of the Dutch immigrants in South Africa came to be called (see Chapters 17 and 21), eventually began to move into the vast interior regions of the continent. There they found a temperate climate in which they could grow the crops and raise the livestock they were accustomed to in Europe. Equally important, they encountered a disease environment they could withstand.

Like their counterparts in North America and Australia, the Boers found the areas into which they moved in this early period of colonization sparsely populated. Boer farmers and cattle ranchers enslaved the indigenous peoples, the *Khoikhoi* and the *San,* while integrating them into their large frontier homesteads. Extensive miscegenation between the Boers and Khoikhoi produced the sizable "colored" population that exists in South Africa today. The coloreds have historically been seen as distinct from the black African majority.

The arrival of the British overlords in South Africa in the early 19th century made for major changes in the interaction between the Boers and the indigenous peoples and transformed the nature of the settlement colony in the region. The British captured Cape Town during the wars precipitated by the French Revolution in the 1790s, when Holland was overrun by France, thus making its colonies subject to British attack. The British held the colony during the Napoleonic conflicts that followed, and they annexed it permanently in 1815 as a vital sea link to their prize colony, India. Made up mainly of people of Dutch and French Protestant descent, the Boer community differed from the British newcomers in almost every way possible. The Boers spoke a different language, and they lived mostly in isolated rural homesteads that had missed the scientific, industrial, and urban revolutions that transformed British society and attitudes. Most critically, the evangelical missionaries who entered South Africa under the protection of the new British overlords were deeply committed to eradicating slavery. They made no exception for the domestic pattern of enslavement that had developed in Boer homesteads and communities. By the 1830s, missionary pressure and increasing British interference in their lives drove a handful of Boers to open but futile rebellion, and many of the remaining Boers fled the Cape Colony.

In the decades of the Great Trek that followed, tens of thousands of Boers migrated in covered wagons pulled by oxen, first east across the Great Fish River and then over the mountains into the veld—the rolling grassy plains that make up much of the South African interior. In these areas, the Boers collided head-on with populous, militarily powerful, and well-organized African states built by Bantu peoples such as the Zulus and the Xhosa. The ever-multiplying contacts that resulted transformed the settler society in South Africa from one where the indigenous peoples were marginalized, typical of those founded in the early centuries of expansion, into a deeply contested colonial realm akin to those established in the age of industrialization. Throughout the mid-19th century, the migrating Boers clashed again and again with Bantu peoples, who were determined to resist the seizure of the lands where they pastured their great herds of cattle and grew subsistence foods.

The British followed the Boer pioneers along the southern and eastern coast, eventually establishing a second major outpost at Durban in **Natal** (see Map 25.4). Tensions between the Boers and Britain remained high, but the imperial overlords were often drawn into frontier wars against the Bantu peoples, even though they were not always formally allied to the Boers.

In the early 1850s, the hard-liners among the Boers established two **Boer Republics** in the interior, named the Orange Free State and the Transvaal, which they tried to keep free of British influence. For more than a decade, the Boers managed to keep the British out of their affairs. But when diamonds were discovered in the Orange Free State in 1867, British entrepreneurs, including most famously **Cecil Rhodes**, and prospectors began to move in, and tensions between the Boers and the British began to build anew. In 1880–1881, these tensions led to a brief war in which the Boers were victorious. But the tide of British immigration into the republics rose even higher after gold was discovered in the Transvaal in 1885.

Although the British had pretty much left the Boers to deal as they pleased with the African peoples who lived in the republics, British miners and financiers grew more and more resentful of Boer efforts to limit their numbers and curb their civil rights. British efforts to protect these interlopers and bring the feisty and independent Boers into line led to the republics' declaration of war against the British in late 1899. Boer assaults against British bases in Natal, the Cape Colony, and elsewhere initiated the **Anglo-Boer War** (1899–1902) that the British ultimately won but only at a very high cost in both lives and resources. British guilt over their brutal treatment of the Boers—men, women, and children—during the war also opened the way for the dominance of this settler minority over the black African majority that would prove to be the source of so much misery and violence in South African history through most of the 20th century.

Pacific Tragedies

The territories the Europeans, Americans, and Japanese claimed throughout the South Pacific in the 19th century were in some cases outposts of true empire and in others contested settler colonies. In both situations, however, the coming of colonial rule resulted in demographic disasters and social disruptions of a magnitude that had not been seen since the first century of European expansion into the Americas. Like the Native American peoples of the New World, the peoples of the South Pacific had long lived in isolation. This meant that, like the Native Americans, they had no immunities to many of the diseases European explorers and later merchants, missionaries, and settlers carried to their island homes from the 1760s onward. In addition, their cultures were extremely vulnerable to the corrosive effects of outside influences, such as new religions, different sexual mores, more lethal weapons, and sudden influxes of cheap consumer goods. Thus, whatever the intentions of the incoming Europeans and Americans—and they were by no means always benevolent—their contacts with the peoples of the Pacific islands almost invariably ushered in periods of social disintegration and widespread human suffering.

Of the many cases of contact between the expansive peoples of the West and the long-isolated island cultures of the South Pacific, the confrontations in New Zealand and Hawaii are among the most informative. Sophisticated cultures and fairly complex societies had developed in each of these areas. In addition, at the time of the European explorers' arrivals, the two island groups contained some of the largest population concentrations in the whole Pacific region. Both areas were subjected to European influences carried by a variety of agents, from whalers and merchants to missionaries and colonial administrators. With the great expansion of European settlement after the first decades of contact, the peoples of New Zealand and Hawaii experienced a period of crisis so severe that their continued survival was in doubt. In both cases, however, the threatened peoples and cultures rebounded and found enduring solutions to the challenges from overseas. Their solutions combined accommodation to outside influences, usually represented by the large numbers of European settlers living in their midst, with revivals of traditional beliefs and practices.

New Zealand The Maori of New Zealand actually went through two periods of profound disruption and danger. The first began in the 1790s, when timber merchants and whalers established small settlements on the New Zealand coast. Maori living near these settlements were afflicted with alcoholism and the spread of prostitution. In addition, they traded wood and food for European firearms, which soon revolutionized Maori warfare—in part by rendering it much more deadly—and upset the existing balance between different tribal groups. Even more devastating was the impact of diseases, such

---

Natal British colony in South Africa; developed after Boer trek north from Cape Colony; major commercial outpost at Durban.

Boer Republics Transvaal and Orange Free State in southern Africa; established to assert independence of Boers from British colonial government in Cape Colony in 1850s; discovery of diamonds and precious metals caused British migration into the Boer areas in 1860s.

Rhodes, Cecil British entrepreneur in South Africa around 1900; manipulated political situation in South Africa to gain entry to resources of Boer republics; encouraged Boer War as means of destroying Boer independence.

Anglo-Boer War Fought between 1899 and 1902 over the continued independence of Boer republics; resulted in British victory, but began the process of decolonization for whites in South Africa.

as smallpox, tuberculosis, and even the common cold, that ravaged Maori communities throughout the north island. By the 1840s, only 80,000 to 90,000 Maori remained of a population that had been as high as 130,000 less than a century earlier. But the Maori survived these calamities and began to adjust to the imports of the foreigners. They took up farming with European implements, and they grazed cattle purchased from European traders. They cut timber, built windmills, and traded extensively with the merchants who visited their shores. Many were converted to Christianity by the missionaries, who established their first station in 1814.

The arrival of British farmers and herders in search of land in the early 1850s, and the British decision to claim the islands as part of their global empire, again plunged the Maori into misery and despair. Backed by the military clout of the colonial government, the settlers occupied some of the most fertile areas of the north island. The warlike Maori fought back, sometimes with temporary successes, but they were steadily driven back into the interior of the island. In desperation, in the 1860s and 1870s they flocked to religious prophets who promised them magical charms and supernatural assistance in their efforts to drive out the invaders. When the prophets also failed them, the Maori seemed for a time to face extinction. In fact, some British writers predicted that within generations the Maori would die out entirely.

The Maori displayed surprising resilience. As they built up immunities to new diseases, they also learned to use European laws and political institutions to defend themselves and preserve what was left of their ancestral lands. Because the British had in effect turned the internal administration of the islands over to the settlers' representatives, the Maori's main struggle was with the invaders who had come to stay. Western schooling and a growing ability to win British colonial officials over to their point of view eventually enabled the Maori to hold their own in their ongoing legal contests and daily exchanges with the settlers. Although New Zealand was included in the White Dominions of the British empire, it was in fact a multiracial society in which a reasonable level of European and Maori accommodation and interaction has been achieved. Over time the Maori have also been able to preserve much of value in their precontact culture.

Hawaii The conversion of Hawaii to settler colony status followed familiar basic imperialist patterns but with specific twists. Hawaii did not become a colony until the United States proclaimed annexation in 1898, although an overzealous British official had briefly claimed the islands for his nation in 1843. Hawaii came under increasing Western influence from the late 18th century onward—politically at the hands of the British, and culturally and economically from the United States, whose westward surge quickly spilled into the Pacific Ocean.

Cook, Captain James Made voyages to Hawaii from 1777 to 1779 resulting in opening of islands to the West; convinced Kamehameha to establish unified kingdom in the islands.

Although very occasional contact with Spanish ships during the 16th and 17th centuries probably occurred, Hawaii was effectively opened to the West through the voyages of **Captain James Cook** from 1777 to 1779 (Figure 25.6). The Cook expedition and later British visits convinced a young Hawaiian prince, Kamehameha, that some imitation of Western ways could produce a unified kingdom under his leadership, replacing the small and warring regional units that had previously prevailed. A series of vigorous wars, backed by British weapons and advisors, won Kamehameha his kingdom between 1794 and 1810. The new king and his successors promoted economic change, encouraging Western merchants to establish export trade in Hawaiian goods in return for increasing revenues to the royal treasury.

Hawaiian royalty began to imitate Western habits, in some cases traveling to Britain and often building Western-style palaces. Two formidable queens, Keopuolani and Liliuokalani, advanced the process of change by insisting that traditional taboos subordinating women be abandoned. In this context, vigorous missionary efforts from Protestant New England, beginning in 1819, brought extensive conversions to Christianity. As with other conversion

FIGURE 25.6 One of the most famous, but ultimately tragic, cross-cultural encounters of the late 18th century was between Captain James Cook and the crew of the ship he commanded and the peoples of Hawaii. In this painting depicting his arrival in the islands, Cook, a renowned English explorer, is welcomed enthusiastically by the Hawaiians. When Cook was later killed due to less fortunate timing and misunderstandings with the Hawaiians, he was lamented throughout Europe as one of the great lost heroes of his age.

processes, religious change had wide implications. Missionaries railed against traditional Hawaiian costumes, insisting that women cover their breasts, and a new garment, the muumuu, was made from homespun American nightgowns with the sleeves cut off. Backed by the Hawaiian monarchy, missionaries quickly established an extensive school system, which by 1831 served 50,000 students from a culture that had not previously developed writing.

The combination of the political and social objectives of Hawaiian rulers and the demands and imports of Western settlers produced creative political and cultural changes, although usually at the expense of previous values. Demographic and economic trends had more insidious effects. Western-imported diseases, particularly sexually transmitted diseases and tuberculosis, had the usual tragic consequences for a previously isolated people. By 1850 only about 80,000 Hawaiians remained of a prior population of about half a million. Because of the Hawaiian population decline, it was necessary to import Asian workers to staff the estates. The first Chinese contract workers had been brought in before 1800; after 1868, a larger current of Japanese arrived. Westerners began to more systematically exploit the Hawaiian economy. Whalers helped create raucous seaport towns. Western settlers from various countries (called *haoles* by the Hawaiians) experimented with potential commercial crops, soon concentrating on sugar. Many missionary families, impatient with the subsistence habits of Hawaiian commoners, turned to leasing land or buying it outright. Most settlers did not entirely forget their religious motives for migrating to the islands, but many families who came to Hawaii to do good ended by doing well.

Formal colonization came as an anticlimax. The abilities of Hawaiian monarchs declined after 1872, in one case because of disease and alcoholism. Under a weakened state, powerful planter interests pressed for special treaties with the United States that would promote their sugar exports, and the American government claimed naval rights at the Pearl Harbor base by 1887. As the last Hawaiian monarchs turned increasingly to promoting culture, writing a number of lasting Hawaiian songs but also spending money on luxurious living, American planters concluded that their economic interests required outright U.S. control. An annexation committee persuaded American naval officers to "protect American lives and property" by posting troops around Honolulu in 1893. The Hawaiian ruler was deposed, and an imperialist-minded U.S. Congress formally took over the islands in 1898.

As in New Zealand, Western control was combined with respect for Polynesian culture. Because Hawaiians were not enslaved and soon ceased to threaten those present, Americans in Hawaii did not apply the same degree of racism found in earlier relations with African slaves or Native Americans. Hawaii's status as a settler colony was further complicated by the arrival of many Asian immigrants. Nevertheless, Western cultural and particularly economic influence extended steadily, and the ultimate political seizure merely ratified the colonization of the islands.

Global Connections and Critical Themes

A EUROPEAN-DOMINATED EARLY PHASE OF GLOBALIZATION

The Industrial Revolution not only gave the Europeans and North Americans the motives but also provided the means for them to become the agents of the first civilization to dominate the entire world. By the end of the 19th century, the Western industrial powers had directly colonized most of Asia and Africa, and (as we shall see in Chapter 27) indirectly controlled the remaining areas through the threat of military interventions or the manipulation of local elites. Political power made it possible for the Europeans to use their already well-established position in world trade to build a global economic order oriented to their industrial societies.

In many ways the first phase of globalization in the most meaningful sense of the term occurred in the four or five decades before the outbreak of World War I in 1914. The communications and commercial networks that undergirded the European colonial order made possible an unprecedented flow of foods and minerals from Africa, Asia, and Latin America to Europe and North America. Western industrial societies provided investment capital and machines to run the mines, plantations, and processing plants in colonized areas. European dominance also made it possible to extract cheap labor and administrative services from subject populations across the globe. Western culture, especially educational norms—but also manners, fashions, literary forms, and modes of entertainment—also became the first to be extensively exported to virtually all the rest of the world. No culture was strong enough to remain untouched by the European drive for global dominance in this era. None could long resist the profound changes unleashed by European conquest and colonization.

The European colonizers assumed that it was their God-given destiny to remake the world in the image of industrial Europe. But in pushing for change within colonized societies that had ancient, deeply rooted cultures and patterns of civilized life, the Europeans often aroused resistance to specific policies and to colonial rule more generally. The colonizers were able to put down protest movements led by displaced princes and religious prophets. But much more enduring and successful challenges to their rule came, ironically, from the very leaders their social reforms and Western-language schools had done so much to nurture. These Asian and African nationalists reworked European ideas and resurrected those of their own cultures. They borrowed European organizational techniques and used the communication systems and common language the Europeans had introduced into the colonies to mobilize the resistance to colonial domination that became one of the major themes of global history in the 20th century.

Further Readings

The literature on various aspects of European imperialism is vast. An analytical and thematic overview that attempts to set forth the basic patterns in different time periods is provided by David B. Abernethy, *The Dynamics of Global Dominance: European Overseas Empires 1415–1980* (2000). Useful general histories on the different empires include Bernard Porter, *The Lion's Share: A Short History of British Imperialism 1850–1970* (1975); Raymond Betts, *Tricouleur* (1978); James J. Cooke, *The New French Imperialism, 1880–1910* (1973); and Woodruff D. Smith, *The German Colonial Empire* (1978).

The best history of centuries of British involvement in South Asia is C.A. Bayly's *The Raj: India and the British, 1600–1947* (1990). The essays in R. C. Majumdar, ed., *British Paramountcy and Indian Renaissance, Part 1* (1963) provide a comprehensive, if at times somewhat dated, overview from Indian perspectives. More recent accounts of specific aspects of the rise of British power in India are available in C. A. Bayly's *Indian Society and the Making of the British Empire* (1988) and P. J. Marshall's *Bengal: The British Beachhead, 1740–1828* (1987), both part of *The New Cambridge History of India*. For the spread of Dutch power in Java and the "outer islands," see Merle Ricklets, *A History of Modern Indonesia* (1981).

Of the many contributions to the debate over late 19th-century imperialism, some of the most essential are those by D. C. M. Platt, Hans-Ulrich Wehler, William Appleman Williams, Jean Stengers, D. K. Fieldhouse, and Henri Brunschwig, as well as the earlier works by Lenin and J. A. Hobson. Winfried Baumgart's *Imperialism* (1982) provides a good overview of the literature and conflicting arguments. Very different perspectives on the partition of Africa can be found in Jean Suret-Canale's *French Colonialism in Tropical Africa, 1900–1945* (1971) and Ronald Robinson and John Gallagher's *Africa and the Victorians* (1961).

Most of the better studies on the impact of imperialism and social life in the colonies are specialized monographs, but Percival Spear's *The Nabobs* (1963) is a superb place to start on the latter from the European viewpoint, and the works of Frantz Fanon, Albert Memmi, and O. Mannoni provide many insights into the plight of the colonized. The impact of industrialization and other changes in Europe on European attitudes toward the colonized are treated in several works, including Philip Curtin, *The Image of Africa* (1964); William B. Cohen, *The French Encounter with Africans* (1980); and Michael Adas, *Machines as the Measure of Men* (1989). Ester Boserup, *Women's Role in Economic Development* (1970), provides a good overview of the impact of colonization on African and Asian women and families, but it should be supplemented by more recent monographs on the position of women in colonial settings. One of the best of these is Jean Taylor, *The Social World of Batavia* (1983). The most informative histories of social and cultural interactions in both colonies and the metropoles in the era of high imperialism include Frances Gouda's *Dutch Culture Overseas* (1995); Bernard S. Cohn, *Colonialism and Its Forms of Knowledge: The British in India* (1996); Alice Conklin, *A Mission to Civilize: The Republican Idea of Empire in France and West Africa* (1997); and for broader comparisons Scott B. Cook, *Colonial Encounters in the Age of High Imperialism* (1996).

On MyHistoryLab

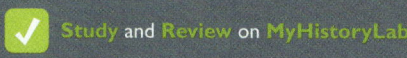

Critical Thinking Questions

1. In what ways did the balance between what the Europeans exported to societies overseas and what they imported shift between the early centuries of expansion and after the Industrial Revolution during the 19th century?

2. What roles did racial ideologies and policies play in justifying European imperial expansion and the nature of European rule in Africa and Asia, particularly in the 19th century?

3. How did gender relations both within European communities in colonized areas and between men and women in those communities and African and Asian subject populations change in the 19th century from what had existed in the early centuries of European expansion?

4. What were the fundamental differences between tropical dependencies and settler societies that made up the European colonial empires in the era of imperialist dominance?

26

The Consolidation of Latin America, 1810–1920

Listen to Chapter 26 on MyHistoryLab

LEARNING OBJECTIVES

26.1 In what ways were the Latin American independence movements part of the political and intellectual changes in 18th- and early 19th-century Europe? p. 614

26.2 Why were many of the new nations politically unstable? p. 618

26.3 How did the region fit into the world economy? p. 620

26.4 What were the positive and negative effects of its bounty of raw materials needed by an industrializing Europe? p. 628

On a rainy morning in 1867, on the Hill of Bells just outside the Mexican city of Queretaro, the handsome, erect figure of the young Austrian Archduke Maximilian stood, flanked by his loyal generals, before a Mexican firing squad. The story of his fall is a strange one. Just three years before, he and his wife, Carlota, had been sent by Carlota's grandfather, Napoleon III, to become emperor and empress of Mexico. They had replaced Benito Juárez, a reformist Mexican leader whose government had been toppled by Napoleon as a result of its refusal to pay the debts of its predecessors. Assured by Napoleon and the Conservative party of Mexico that the Mexican people enthusiastically awaited their arrival, Maximilian and Carlota believed they would bring stability to the troubled land.

FIGURE 26.1 Emperor Maximilian was finally captured after his attempt, with French help, to reestablish a monarchy in Mexico. Well meaning, he eventually lost the support of the conservatives. Juárez refused to spare his life, as a warning to other ambitious nations that Mexico would remain independent. Manet's painting of the execution of Maximilian, shown here flanked by his two loyal generals facing the firing squad reflected Europe's shock.

(Edouard Manet (1832–1883), "The Execution of Emperor Maximilian of Mexico, June 19, 1867." Oil on canvas. Location: Staedtische Kunsthalle, Mannheim, Germany. Art Resource, NY.)

Watch the Video Series on MyHistoryLab

Learn about some key topics related to this chapter with the *MyHistoryLab Video Series: Key Topics in World History*

Maximilian and Carlota were both well educated and well intentioned. They had tried to bring reforms to their adopted country and had even invited Juárez and other political opponents to join in the new government—an offer that was resolutely refused. In fact, Maximilian and Carlota had been gravely misled as to the attitude of the Mexican people toward their new rulers. Their authority rested on foreign bayonets, and their very presence was seen as an insult by the majority of Mexicans, who were determined to maintain the political independence they had won after a long and bitter struggle.

Juárez and Maximilian could not have been more different in most ways. Benito Juárez, the diminutive Zapotec Indian who had risen from poverty and obscurity to become Mexico's leading liberal politician, and Maximilian von Habsburg, the foreign-backed emperor who had blood ties to every royal house in Europe, represented two different visions of what Latin America should become. Their clash not only determined the fate of Mexico but also served as an example and a warning to other foreign states with imperialist designs.

Before the execution, Carlota had traveled all over Europe, pleading her husband's case, and numerous calls for clemency had reached Juárez's desk. But for the good of his country, Juárez refused to spare Maximilian, although he confided to friends that he could not bring himself to meet the man for fear that his determination on this point would waver. Maximilian died a tragic figure; his last words were "Long live Mexico, long live independence" (Figure 26.1). Carlota spent the next 60 years in seclusion. Even more tragically, by the time of Maximilian's death, hundreds of thousands of Mexicans had perished in the civil wars that had brought him to, and finally toppled him from, the throne. ■

In the late 18th century the former colonies of Spain and Portugal were swept by the same winds of change that transformed Europe's society and economy and led to the independence of the United States. Although at present Latin America is sometimes considered part of the developing world along with many Asian and African nations, in reality its political culture was formed in the 18th century by the ideas of the Western Enlightenment. To a large degree, both Juárez and Maximilian shared these liberal ideals.

In the early 19th century, the various regions of Latin America fought for their political independence and created new nations, often based on the old colonial administrative units. But what kind of nations were these to be? The form of government, the kind of society, the role of religion, and the nature of the economy all had to be defined in each of the new countries, and deep divisions over these questions and others created bitter political struggles. Then too, there was always the shadow of foreign interference—from the old colonial powers, from new imperialist regimes, and from neighbors seeking territory or economic advantage. Latin America in the 19th century was shaped both by its internal struggles over these questions and by the dominant international forces of the day.

Despite their many differences, most 19th-century Latin American leaders shared with Western political figures a firm belief in the virtues of progress, reform, representational and constitutional government, and private property rights. At the same time, Latin American leaders faced problems very different from those of Europe and the United States. The colonial heritage had left little tradition of participatory government. A highly centralized colonial state had intervened in many aspects of life and had created both dependence on central authority and resentment of it. Class and regional interests deeply divided the new nations, and wealth was very unequally distributed. Finally, the rise

1800 C.E.	1820 C.E.	1840 C.E.	1860 C.E.	1880 C.E.	1900 C.E.
1792 Slave rebellion in St. Domingue (Haiti)	**1821** Mexico declares independence; empire under Iturbide lasts to 1823	**1846–1848** Mexican-American War	**1862–1867** French intervention in Mexico	**1886–1888** Cuba and Brazil abolish slavery	**1903** Panamanian independence; beginning of Panama Canal (opens in 1914)
1804 Haiti declares independence	**1822** Brazil declares independence; empire established under Dom Pedro I	**1847–1855** Caste War in Yucatan	**1865–1870** War of the Triple Alliance (Argentina, Brazil, and Uruguay against Paraguay)	**1889** Fall of Brazilian empire; republic established	
1808–1825 Spanish-American wars of independence	**1823** Monroe Doctrine indicates U.S. opposition to European ambitions in the Americas	**1850s** Beginnings of railroad construction in Cuba, Chile, and Brazil	**1868–1878** Ten-year war against Spain in Cuba	**1895–1898** Cuban Spanish-American War; United States acquires Puerto Rico and Philippines	
1808 Portuguese court flees Napoleon, arrives in Brazil; French armies invade Spain	**1829–1852** Juan Manuel de Roses rules Rio de la Plata	**1854** Benito Juárez leads reform in Mexico	**1869** First school for girls in Mexico		
1810 In Mexico, Father Hidalgo initiates rebellion against Spain	**1830** Bolívar dies; Gran Colombia dissolves into separate countries of Venezuela, Colombia, and Ecuador		**1876–1911** Porfirio Díaz rules Mexico		

of European industrial capitalism created an economic situation that often placed the new nations in a weak or dependent position. These problems and tensions are the focus of our examination of Latin America in the 19th century.

FROM COLONIES TO NATIONS

A combination of internal developments and the Napoleonic wars set Latin American independence movements in motion.

26.1 In what ways were the Latin American independence movements part of the political and intellectual changes in 18th- and early 19th-century Europe?

By the late 18th century, the elites of American-born whites or Creoles (*criollos*) expressed a growing self-consciousness as they began to question the policies of Spain and Portugal. At the same time, these elites were joined by the majority of the population in resenting the increasingly heavy hand of government, as demonstrated by the new taxes and administrative reforms of the 18th century. But the shared resentment was not enough to overcome class conflicts and divisions. Early movements for independence usually failed because of the reluctance of the colonial upper classes to enlist the support of the American Indian, mestizo, and mulatto masses, who, they thought, might later prove too difficult to control. The actual movements were set in motion only when events in Europe precipitated actions in America.

Causes of Political Change

Latin American political independence was achieved as part of the general Atlantic revolution of the late 18th and early 19th centuries, and Latin American leaders were moved by the same ideas as those seeking political change elsewhere in the Atlantic world. Four external events had a particularly strong impact on political thought in Latin America. The American Revolution, from 1775 to 1783, provided a model of how colonies could break with the mother country. The French Revolution of 1789 provoked great interest in Latin America, and its slogan, "liberty, equality, and fraternity," appealed to some sectors of the population. As that revolution became increasingly radical, however, it was rejected by the Creole elites, who could not support regicide, rejection of the church's authority, and the social leveling implied by the Declaration of the Rights of Man and the Citizen. This was especially true in the regimes where slaves were a large segment of the population.

The third external event was partially an extension of the French Revolution but had its own dynamic. Torn by internal political conflict during the turmoil in France, the whites and free people of color in St. Domingue, France's great sugar colony in the Caribbean, became divided. The slaves seized the moment in 1791 to stage a general rebellion under able leadership by **Toussaint L'ouverture** and after his capture and death, by Jean Jacques Dessalines. Various attempts by France, England, and Spain to subdue the island were defeated, and in 1804 the independent republic of Haiti was proclaimed. For Latin American elites, Haiti was an example to be avoided. It was not accidental that neighboring Cuba and Puerto Rico, whose elites had plantations and slaves and were acutely aware of events in Haiti, were among the last of Spain's colonies to gain independence. For slaves, former slaves, and free people of color throughout the Americas, however, Haiti became a symbol of freedom and hope.

What eventually precipitated the movements for independence in Latin America was the confused Iberian political situation caused by the French Revolution and its aftermath. France invaded Portugal and Spain, and a general insurrection erupted in Spain in 1808, followed by a long guerrilla war. During the fighting, a central committee, or junta central (HOON-tuh sehn-TRAHL), ruled in the Spanish king's name in opposition to Napoleon's brother, whom Napoleon had appointed king.

Who was the legitimate ruler? By 1810 the confusion in Spain had provoked a crisis in the colonies. In places such as Caracas, Bogotá, and Mexico, local elites, pretending to be loyal to the deposed king Ferdinand, set up juntas to rule in his name, but they ruled on their own behalf. Soon the more conservative elements of the population—royal officials and those still loyal to Spain—opposed the movements for autonomy and independence. A crisis of legitimacy reverberated throughout the American colonies.

L'ouverture, Toussaint [TOO-san LOO-vuhr-tyuhr] (1743–1803) Leader of slave rebellion on the French island of St. Domingue in 1791 that led to creation of independent republic of Haiti in 1804.

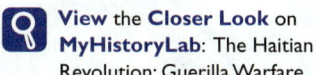
View the **Closer Look** on **MyHistoryLab**: The Haitian Revolution: Guerilla Warfare

Spanish American Independence Struggles

The independence movements divided into three major theaters of operation. In Mexico, a conspiracy among leading Creoles moved one of the plotters, the priest **Father Miguel de Hidalgo**, to call for help from the American Indians and mestizos of his region in 1810. He won a number of early victories but eventually lost the support of the Creoles, who feared social rebellion more than they desired independence. Hidalgo was captured and executed, but the insurgency smoldered in various parts of the country. Eventually, after 1820 when events in Spain weakened the king and the central government, conservative Creoles in Mexico were willing to move toward independence by uniting with the remnants of the insurgent forces. **Agustín de Iturbide**, a Creole officer at the head of an army that had been sent to eliminate the insurgents, drew up an agreement with them instead, and the combined forces of independence occupied Mexico City in September 1821. Soon thereafter, with the support of the army, Iturbide was proclaimed emperor of Mexico.

This was a conservative solution. The new nation of Mexico was born as a monarchy, and little recognition was given to the social aspirations and programs of Hidalgo and his movement. Central America was briefly attached to the Mexican empire, which collapsed in 1824. Mexico became a republic, and the Central American states, after attempting union until 1838, split apart into independent nations.

In South America and the Caribbean, the chronology of independence was a mirror image of the conquest of the 16th century. Formerly secondary areas such as Argentina and Venezuela were among the first to opt for independence and the best able to achieve it. The old colonial center in Peru and Bolivia was among the last to break with Spain. The Caribbean islands of Cuba and Puerto Rico, fearful of slave rebellion and occupied by large Spanish garrisons, remained loyal until the end of the 19th century, although there were plots for independence in that period and Cuba endured a bloody ten-year civil war.

Hidalgo, Father Miguel de [mee-GEHL duh hih-DAL-goh] Mexican priest who established independence movement among American Indians and mestizos in 1810; despite early victories, was captured and executed.

Iturbide, Agustín de [AH-guhs-tehn duh ee-tur-BEE-thay] (1783–1824) Conservative Creole officer in Mexican army who signed agreement with insurgent forces of independence; combined forces entered Mexico City in 1821; later proclaimed emperor of Mexico until its collapse in 1824.

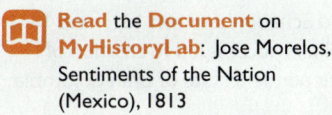
Read the **Document** on **MyHistoryLab**: Jose Morelos, Sentiments of the Nation (Mexico), 1813

Read the Document on MyHistoryLab: Simon de Bolívar, "Address to Second National Congress" (Venezuela), 1819

FIGURE 26.2 Simon Bolívar (1783–1830) led the struggle for political independence in northern South America. Son of a wealthy Creole family, he became an ardent proponent of independence and a firm believer in the republican form of government. On his deathbed, Bolívar asked his closest aide to burn all of his letters and other writings. Knowing how valuable these papers would be to future historians, the aide disobeyed the order.

Bolívar, Simon [see-MOHN BOH-lee-vahr] Creole military officer in northern South America; won series of victories in Venezuela, Colombia, and Ecuador between 1817 and 1822; military success led to creation of independent state of Gran Colombia.

Gran Colombia Independent state created in South America as a result of military successes of Simon Bolívar; existed only until 1830, at which time Colombia, Venezuela, and Ecuador became separate nations.

In northern South America, a movement for independence centered in Caracas had begun in 1810. After early reverses, **Simon Bolívar**, a wealthy Creole officer, emerged as the leader of the revolt against Spain (Figure 26.2). With considerable military skill and a passion for independence, he eventually mobilized support, and between 1817 and 1822 he won a series of victories in Venezuela, Colombia, and Ecuador. Until 1830, these countries were united into a new nation called **Gran Colombia**. Political differences and regional interests led to the breakup of Gran Colombia. Bolívar became disillusioned and fearful of anarchy. "America is ungovernable," he said, and "those who have served the revolution have plowed the sea." To his credit, however, Bolívar rejected all attempts to crown him as king, and he remained until his death in 1830 firmly committed to the cause of independence and republican government.

Meanwhile, in southern South America, another movement had coalesced under **José de San Martín** in the Rio de la Plata. Buenos Aires had become a booming commercial center in the late 18th century, and its residents, called *porteños*, particularly resented Spanish trade restrictions. Pushing for freedom of trade, they opted for autonomy in 1810 but tried to keep the outlying areas, such as Paraguay, under their control. The myth of autonomy rather than independence was preserved for a while. By 1816, however, the independence of the United Provinces of the Rio de la Plata had been proclaimed, although the provinces were far from united. Upper Peru (Bolivia) remained under Spanish control, Paraguay declared independence in 1813, and the Banda Oriental (Uruguay) resisted the central authority of Buenos Aires.

In Buenos Aires, San Martín had emerged as a military commander willing to speak and act for independence. From Argentina his armies crossed the Andes to Chile to help the revolutionary forces in that colony. After winning victories there, the patriot forces looked northward. Peru was still under Spanish control. Its upper class was deeply conservative and not attracted to the movements for independence. San Martín's forces entered Peru, and Creole adherence was slowly won after major victories like the battle of Ayacucho in 1824, where royalist forces were defeated (Figure 26.3). By 1825 all of Spanish South America had gained its political independence. Despite various plans to create some form of monarchy in many of the new states, all of them emerged as independent republics with representative governments. The nations of Spanish America were born of the Enlightenment and the ideas of 19th-century liberalism. The wars of independence became the foundational moments of their heroic birth, but the challenge of deciding what kind of governments they would have and how the disparate groups could be forged into a nation remained in most cases unanswered.

Brazilian Independence

Although the movement for independence in Brazil was roughly contemporaneous with those in Spanish America, and many of the causes were similar, independence there was achieved by a very different process. By the end of the 18th century, Brazil had grown in population and economic importance. The growth of European demand for colonial products, such as sugar, cotton, and cacao, contributed to that growth and to the increase in slave imports to the colony. Although Brazilian planters, merchants, and miners sometimes longed for more open trade and fewer taxes, they feared that any upsetting of the political system might lead to a social revolution or a Haitian-style general slave uprising. Thus, incipient movements for independence in Minas Gerais in 1788 and Bahia in 1798 were unsuccessful. As one official said, "Men established in goods and property were unwilling to risk political change."

The Napoleonic invasions provoked an outcome in Portugal different from that in Spain. When in 1807 French troops invaded Portugal, the whole Portuguese royal family and court fled

FIGURE 26.3 The battle of Maipu in April 1818 sealed the fate of the royalist forces in Chile. Jose de San Martin led the combined Chilean and Argentine insurgent forces and their victory led to the independence of Chile. Throughout South America between 1810 and 1825 the rebel forces were slowly mobilized into effective armies, but subsequently the new nations had to confront the personal and institutional power of the former commanders.

the country and, under the protection of British ships, sailed to Brazil. Rio de Janeiro became the capital of the Portuguese empire. Brazil was raised to equal status with Portugal, and all the functions of royal government were set up in the colony. As a partial concession to England and to colonial interests, the ports of Brazil were opened to world commerce, thus satisfying one of the main desires of the Brazilian elites. Unlike Spanish America, where the Napoleonic invasions provoked a crisis of authority and led Spanish Americans to consider ruling in their own name, in Brazil the transfer of the court brought royal government closer and reinforced the colonial relationship.

Until 1820, the Portuguese king, **Dom João VI**, lived in Brazil and ruled his empire from there. Rio de Janeiro was transformed into an imperial city with a public library, botanical gardens, and other improvements. Printing presses began to operate in the colony for the first time, schools were created, and commerce, especially with England, boomed in the newly opened ports. The arrival of many Portuguese bureaucrats and nobles with the court created jealousy and resentment, however. Still, during this period Brazil was transformed into the seat of empire, a fact not lost on its most prominent citizens.

Matters changed drastically in 1820 when, after the defeat of Napoleon in Europe and a liberal revolution in Portugal, the king was recalled and a parliament convoked. João VI, realizing that his return was inevitable, left his young son Pedro as regent, warning him that if independence had to come, he should lead the movement. Although Brazilians were allowed representation at the Portuguese parliament, it became clear that Brazil's new status was doomed and that it would be recolonized. After demands that the prince regent also return to Europe, Pedro refused, and in September 1822 he declared Brazilian independence. He became Dom **Pedro I**, constitutional emperor of Brazil. Fighting against Portuguese troops lasted a year, but Brazil avoided the long wars of Spanish America. Brazil's independence did not upset the existing social organization based on slavery, nor did it radically change the political structure. With the brief exception of Mexico, all of the former Spanish American colonies became republics, but Brazil became a monarchy under a member of the Portuguese ruling house.

San Martín, José de (b. 1778–d. 1850) A leader of the struggle for independence in southern South America. Born in Argentina, he served in the Spanish army but joined in the movement for independence; led the revolutionary army that crossed the Andes and helped to liberate Chile in 1817–1818, and with Simon Bolívar, Peru. For political reasons, he went into exile in Europe in 1823.

João VI [JWOW] Portuguese monarch who established seat of government in Brazil from 1808 to 1820 as a result of Napoleonic invasion of Iberian peninsula; made Brazil seat of empire with capital at Rio de Janeiro.

 View the **Closer Look** on **MyHistoryLab**: Imagining Brazilian Independence

Pedro I (1798–1834) Son and successor of João VI in Brazil; aided in the declaration of Brazilian independence from Portugal in 1822; became constitutional emperor of Brazil.

NEW NATIONS CONFRONT OLD AND NEW PROBLEMS

The new nations confronted difficult problems: social inequalities, political representation, the role of the church, and regionalism. These problems led to political fragmentation that allowed leaders having strong personal followings and representing various interests and their own ambitions, to rise to prominence.

26.2 Why were many of the new nations politically unstable?

By 1830 the former Spanish and Portuguese colonies had become independent nations. The roughly 20 million inhabitants of these nations looked hopefully to the future. Many of the leaders of independence had shared ideals: representative government, careers open to talent, freedom of commerce and trade, the right to private property, and a belief in the individual as the basis of society. There was a general belief that the new nations should be sovereign and independent states, large enough to be economically viable and integrated by a common set of laws.

On the issue of freedom of religion and the position of the church, however, there was less agreement. Roman Catholicism had been the state religion and the only one allowed by the Spanish crown. While most leaders attempted to maintain Catholicism as the official religion of the new states, some tried to end the exclusion of other faiths. The defense of the church became a rallying cry for the conservative forces.

The ideals of the early leaders of independence often were egalitarian. Bolívar had received aid from Haiti and had promised in return to abolish slavery in the areas he liberated. By 1854 slavery had been abolished everywhere except Spain's remaining colonies, Cuba and Puerto Rico, as well as in Brazil; all were places where the economy was profoundly based on it. Despite early promises, an end to American Indian tribute and taxes on people of mixed origin came much more slowly, because the new nations still needed the revenue such policies produced. Egalitarian sentiments often were tempered by fears that the mass of the population was unprepared for self-rule and democracy. Early constitutions attempted to balance order and popular representation by imposing property or literacy restrictions on voters. Invariably, voting rights were reserved for men. Although many had participated in the independence struggles, women were still disenfranchised and usually were not allowed to hold public office. The Creole elite's lack of trust of the popular classes was based on the fact that in many places the masses had not demonstrated a clear preference for the new regimes and had sometimes fought in royalist armies mobilized by traditional loyalties and regional interests.

Although some mestizos had risen to leadership roles in the wars of independence, the old color distinctions did not disappear easily. In Mexico, Guatemala, and the Andean nations, the large Indian population remained mostly outside national political life. The mass of the Latin American population—American Indians and people of mixed origins—waited to see what was to come, and they were suspicious of the new political elite, who were often drawn from the old colonial aristocracy but were also joined by a new commercial and urban bourgeoisie.

Political Fragmentation

The new Latin American nations can be grouped into regional blocks (Map 26.1). Some of the early leaders for independence had dreamed of creating a unified nation in some form, but regional rivalries, economic competition, and political divisions soon made that hope impossible. Mexico emerged as a short-lived monarchy until a republic was proclaimed in 1823, but its government remained unstable until the 1860s because of military coups, financial failures, foreign intervention, and political turmoil. Central America broke away from the Mexican monarchy and formed a union, but regional antagonisms and resentment of Guatemala, the largest nation in the region, eventually led to dissolution of the union in 1838. Spain's Caribbean colonies, Cuba and Puerto Rico, suppressed early movements for independence and remained outwardly loyal. The Dominican Republic was occupied by its neighbor Haiti, and after resisting Haiti as well as France and Spain, it finally gained independence in 1844.

MAP 26.1 **Independent States of Latin America in 1830** Despite its size, traditions, language, and religion provided certain unities. At independence a number of large states were formed out of coalitions, but these eventually divided because of regional differences and rivalries.

In South America, the old colonial viceroyalty of New Granada became the basis for Gran Colombia, the large new state created by Bolívar that included modern Ecuador, Colombia, Panama, and Venezuela. The union, made possible to some extent by Bolívar's personal reputation and leadership, disintegrated as his own standing declined, and it ended in 1830, the year of his death. In the south, the viceroyalty of the Rio de la Plata served as the basis for a state that the peoples of Argentina hoped to lead. Other parts of the region resisted. Paraguay declared and maintained its autonomy under a series of dictators. Modern Uruguay was formed by a revolution for independence against the dominant power of its large neighbors, Argentina and Brazil. It became an independent buffer between those two nations in 1828. The Andean nations of Peru and Bolivia, with their large Indian populations and conservative colonial aristocracies, flirted with union from 1829 to 1839 under the mestizo general **Andrés Santa Cruz**, but once again regional rivalries and the fears of their neighbors undermined the effort. Finally, Chile, somewhat isolated and blessed by the opening of trade in the Pacific, followed its own political course in a fairly stable fashion.

Santa Cruz, Andrés Mestizo general who established union of independent Peru and Bolivia between 1829 and 1839.

Most attempts at consolidation and union failed. Enormous geographic barriers and great distances separated nations and even regions within nations. Roads were poor and transportation rudimentary. Geography, regional interests, and political divisions were too strong to overcome. The mass of the population remained outside the political process. The problems of national integration were daunting. What is striking is not that Spanish America became 18 separate nations but that it did not separate into even more.

Caudillos, Politics, and the Church

The problems confronting the new nations were many. More than a decade of warfare in places such as Venezuela, Colombia, and Mexico had disrupted the economies and devastated wide areas. The mobilization of large armies whose loyalty to regional commanders was often based on their personal qualities, rather than their rank or politics, led to the rise of **caudillos**, independent leaders who dominated local areas by force and sometimes seized the national government itself. In times of intense division between civilian politicians, a powerful regional army commander became the arbiter of power, and thus the army sometimes made and unmade governments. Keeping the army in the barracks became a preoccupation of governments, and the amount of money spent on the military far exceeded the needs. The military had become important in the 18th century as Spain tried to shore up the defense of its empire, but it became a preserver of order.

caudillos [kow-DEE-yuhs] Independent leaders who dominated local areas by force in defiance of national policies; sometimes seized national governments to impose their concept of rule; typical throughout newly independent countries of Latin America.

Military commanders and regional or national caudillos usually were interested in power for their own sake, but they could represent or mobilize different groups in society. Many often defended the interests of regional elites, usually landowners, but others were populists who mobilized and claimed to speak for American Indians, peasants, and the poor and sometimes received their unquestioning support. A few, such as the conservative Rafael Carrera, who ruled Guatemala from 1839 to 1865, sincerely took the interest of the American Indian majority to heart, but other personalist leaders disregarded the normal workings of an open political system and the rule of law. Personalist leaders depended not on political ideology but on loyalty to help them personally.

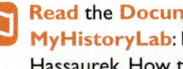 Read the Document on MyHistoryLab: Friederich Hassaurek, How to Conduct a Latin American Revolution, 1865

Other common issues confronted many of the new nations. Most political leaders were agreed on the republic as the basic form of government, but they could not agree on what kind of republic. A struggle often developed between **centralists**, who wanted to create strong, centralized national governments with broad powers, and **federalists**, who wanted tax and commercial policies to be set by regional governments. Other tensions developed between liberals and conservatives. Liberals stressed the rights of the individual and attacked the corporate (based on membership in a group or organization) structure of colonial society. They dreamed of a secular society and looked to the United States and France as models. Often they wanted a decentralized, or federalist, form of government. Conservatives believed in a strong centralized state, and they often wanted to maintain aspects of colonial society. They believed that a structure in which corporate groups (such as the American Indians), artisan guilds, or institutions (such as the church) provided the most equitable basis of social action should be recognized in law. To the conservatives, society was not based on open competition and individualism but was organic: Each group was linked to the others like parts of a body whose health depended on the proper functioning of each part. Not all conservatives resisted change, and some—such as Mexican intellectual and politician Lucas Alamán—were among the most enlightened leaders in terms of economic and commercial reforms, but as a group the conservatives were skeptical of secularism and individualism and strove to keep the Catholic Iberian heritage alive.

centralists Latin American politicians who wished to create strong, centralized national governments with broad powers; often supported by politicians who described themselves as conservatives.

federalists Latin American politicians who wanted policies, especially fiscal and commercial regulation, to be set by regional governments rather than centralized national administrations; often supported by politicians who described themselves as liberals.

The role of the church became a crucial issue in politics. It divided conservatives from the more secular liberals. In Mexico, for example, the church had played a major role in education, the economy, and politics. Few questioned its dogma, but liberals tried to limit its role in civil life. The church fought back with the aid of its pro-clerical supporters and with the power of the papacy, which until the 1840s refused to fill vacant positions in the hierarchy or to cooperate with the new governments.

Political parties, often calling themselves Liberal or Conservative, sprang up throughout Latin America. They struggled for power and tried to impose their vision of the future on society. However, their leaders usually were drawn from the same social class of landowners and urban bourgeoisie, with little to differentiate them except their position in the church or on the question of federalism versus centralization. The general population might be mobilized by the force and personality of a particular leader such as **Juan Manuel de Rosas** in Argentina or **General Antonio López de Santa Anna** in Mexico, but political ideology rarely was an issue for most of the population.

The result was political turmoil and insecurity in much of Latin America in the first 50 years after independence. Presidents came and went quickly. Written constitutions, which both liberals and conservatives thought were a positive thing, were often short-lived and were overturned with a change in government because the margin for interpretation of the constitution was slight. Great efforts were made to make constitutions precise, specific, and definitive, but this resulted in an attempt to change them each time there was a change in government. Some nations avoided the worst aspects of instability. After enacting a constitution in 1833 that gave the president broad powers, Chile established a functioning political system that allowed compromise. Brazil, with its monarchical rule, despite a period of turmoil from 1832 to 1850, was able to maintain a political system of compromise, although it was dominated by the conservatives, who were favored by the emperor. Its 1824 constitution remained in force until 1889. The issue of slavery, however, continued to gnaw at the nation's conscience, especially after 1870.

It is fair to say that in much of Latin America the basic questions of government and society remained unresolved after independence. Some observers attributed these problems to personalism, a lack of civic responsibility, and other defects in the "Latin" character. Nevertheless, the parallel experience of later emerging nations in the 20th century suggests that these problems were typical of former colonial dependencies searching for order and economic security in a world in which their options were constrained by their own potential and by external conditions.

LATIN AMERICAN ECONOMIES AND WORLD MARKETS, 1820–1870

26.3 How did the region fit into the world economy?

The former colonies of Spain and Portugal now entered the world of diplomatic relations and international commerce. The new nations sought diplomatic recognition and security. In the 1820s, while Europe was undergoing the post-Napoleonic conservative reaction and monarchies were being restored, various plans to help Spain recolonize Latin America were put forward. Great Britain generally opposed those ideas, and because Great Britain was the dominant power at sea, its recognition of Latin American sovereignty was crucial. Moreover, the newly independent United States also felt an affinity and sympathy for the new nations to the south. The **Monroe Doctrine** of 1823, discussed in Chapter 24, stated clearly that any attempt by a European power to colonize in the Americas would be considered an unfriendly act by the United States. The United States at the time probably could have done little to prevent such actions, but Britain could, and its support of Latin American independence provided needed protection.

There was a price for this support. During the turmoil of the 1820s, British foreign minister Lord Canning had once said, "Spanish America is free and if we do not mismanage our affairs sadly, she is English." He was referring to the broad economic and commercial advantages that the new nations offered. British commerce had legally penetrated the area in the 18th century, and Britain had profited from illegal trade as well. Now it could afford to offer its diplomatic recognition in exchange for the freedom to trade with the new nations. Although little capital had been invested directly in Latin

America before 1850, Latin American governments now turned to foreign governments and banks for loans. Meanwhile, Britain became a major consumer of Latin American products. In return Britain sold about £5 million worth of manufactured goods to the new nations each year, about half of which went to Brazil, where British merchants were especially strong. Although some historians argue that this was a small portion of Britain's overseas trade, it was crucial for Latin America. In some ways, Britain replaced Spain as a dominant economic force over the area in a sort of neocolonial commercial system. Although other nations, notably France and the United States, also traded with Latin America, Britain remained predominant before 1860.

Open ports and the influx of foreign goods, often of better quality and cheaper than local products, benefited the port cities that controlled customhouses and the large landowners whose hides, sugar, and other products were exported. But these policies tended to damage local industries or regions that had specialized in producing for internal markets. Latin America became increasingly dependent on foreign markets and foreign imports and thereby reinforced the old colonial economic heritage in which land was the basis of wealth and prestige.

Mid-Century Stagnation

From about 1820 to 1850, the economy of Latin America was stagnant. Wars had destroyed many industries, roads were poor, and much money was still tied up in land. Only Cuba, with its booming sugar economy, expanded, but Cuba was still a colony of Spain. After 1850, however, this situation began to change as the expansion of the European economy created new demands for Latin American products. Coffee in Brazil, hides and beef in Argentina, and minerals and grains in Chile provided the basis of growth and allowed some Latin American governments to address social issues. For example, Peru exploited enormous **guano** (bird droppings) deposits on islands off its coast. Between 1850 and 1880, exports of this fertilizer earned Peru more than £10 million, and this income allowed the government to end American Indian tribute and to abolish slavery by compensating the owners.

Latin American cities began to grow and provide good internal markets, and the introduction of steamships and railroads began to overcome the old problems of transportation. By the 1840s, steamship lines improved communication within countries and opened up new possibilities for international commerce, and by the 1860s, railroads were being built, usually to link export-producing regions to the ports. Wealth based on large land holdings and exports continued to characterize the economies of the region, as they had in the colonial era. As the levels of exports and the governments' dependence on them increased, Latin America's vulnerability to the vagaries of the world economy increased as well.

Without detailing all the complex changes within the Latin American nations during the 19th century, we can discern a few general patterns. After the turmoil of independence, liberal reformers tried to institute a series of programs in the 1820s and 1830s intended to break the patterns of the colonial heritage and to follow the main social and economic trends of western Europe by improving primary education, promoting individualism and private property, supporting small industries, and promoting secular attitudes. These ideas often were imposed on societies and economies unprepared for drastic change, especially because the strength of opposing institutions, such as the church and the army, remained intact. By the 1840s, conservatives had returned to power in many places to slow or stop the reform measures. Some of them tried to speak for the lower classes or the American Indians, who wanted to see the paternal aspects of the old colonial state reimposed to protect them from the reforms of the liberals. In some ways, an alliance between the landowners and the peasantry emerged in opposition to the changes suggested by the middle-class, urban modernizers.

Economic Resurgence and Liberal Politics

By the last quarter of the century, as the world economy entered a phase of rapid expansion, there was a shift in attitude and possibilities in Latin America. Liberals returned to power in many places in Latin America and initiated a series of changes that began to transform their nations. The ideological basis of the new liberal surge was also changing. Based on the ideas of **positivism** of the French philosopher **Auguste Comte**, who stressed observation and a scientific approach to the problems of

guano Bird droppings utilized as fertilizer; exported from Peru as a major item of trade between 1850 and 1880; income from trade permitted end to American Indian tribute and abolition of slavery.

positivism French philosophy based on observation and scientific approach to problems of society; adopted by many Latin American liberals in the aftermath of independence.

Comte, Auguste [uh-GOOST KONT] French philosopher (19th century); founder of positivism, a philosophy that stressed observation and scientific approaches to the problems of society.

society, Latin American politicians and intellectuals found a guiding set of principles and a justification of their quest for political stability and economic growth.

This shift was caused in large part by the general economic expansion of the second industrial revolution and the age of imperialism. The application of science to industry created new demands for Latin American products, such as copper and rubber, to accompany the increasing demand for its consumer products such as wheat, sugar, and coffee. The population of Latin America doubled to more than 43 million inhabitants in the 60 years between 1820 and 1880. After 1850, economies grew rapidly; the timing varied greatly, but the expansion of exports in places such as Colombia, Argentina, and Brazil stimulated prosperity for some and a general belief in the advantages of the liberal programs. The desire to participate in the capitalist expansion of the Western economy dominated the thinking of Latin American leaders. Foreign entrepreneurs and bankers joined hands with philosophical liberals, landowners, and urban merchants in Latin America to back the liberal programs, which now became possible because of the increased revenues generated by exports.

The leaders of the post-1860 governments were a new generation of politicians who had matured during the chaotic years of postindependence politics. Their inspiration came from England, France, and the United States. They were firm believers in progress, education, and free competition within a secular society, but they were sometimes distrustful of the mass of their own people, who seemed to represent an ancient "barbarism" in contrast to the "civilization" of progress. That distrust and their sometimes insensitive application of foreign models to a very different reality in their own countries—what one Brazilian author has called "ideas out of place"—prevented many from achieving the progress they so ardently desired.

Economic growth and progress were costly. Responding to international demand, landowners increased their holdings, often aided by the governments they controlled or influenced. Peasant lands were taken away by the government in Chile, Peru, and Bolivia; small farmers were displaced in Brazil and Costa Rica; church lands were seized in Mexico. Labor was needed. Immigrants from Europe flooded into Argentina and Brazil, and in other countries new forms of tenancy, peonage, and disguised servitude developed.

Mexico: Instability and Foreign Intervention

After the short monarchical experiment, a Mexican republic was established. Its constitution of 1824, based on the examples of France, the United States, and Spain, was a federalist document that guaranteed basic civil rights. Nevertheless, this constitution did not address the nation's continuing social problems and needs: the maldistribution of land, the status of the American Indians, the problems of education, and the situation of vast numbers of poor people among the approximately 7 million people in Mexico, the most populous of the new nations. Politics soon became a complicated struggle between the conservative centralists and the liberal federalists and was made even more complicated by jockeying for advantage by commercial agents of Great Britain and the United States. For a short period from 1832 to 1835, the liberals were in control and tried to institute a series of sweeping social and economic reforms, but their attack on the church led to violent reaction and the assumption of power by General Antonio López de Santa Anna.

The mercurial Santa Anna remained until his death the maker of Mexican politics. He was a typical caudillo, a personalist, autocratic leader. But Mexico's instability resulted not only from his personality. Santa Anna was merely the symptom of deeper problems.

Mexico's instability and financial difficulties made it a target for various foreign interventions. Even more threatening to the nation, Anglo-American settlers were occupying Texas, the vast area of Mexico's northern frontier. They brought their language, customs, and religion despite restrictions on the latter. Although the Texans at first sought more autonomy as federalists within the Mexican nation, as had been done in Yucatan and other Mexican provinces, ethnic and religious differences as well as Santa Anna's attempts to suppress the Texans in 1836 led to widespread fighting and the declaration of Texan independence. Santa Anna, captured for a while by the Texans, returned to dominate Mexican politics, but the question of Texas festered and became acute when in 1845 the United States, with its eye on California and **manifest destiny**—a belief that it was destined to rule the continent from coast to coast—voted to annex Texas.

The result was war. A border dispute and the breakdown of negotiations over California led to hostilities in 1846. Santa Anna, who had been in exile, returned to lead the Mexican forces, but U.S. troops seized California, penetrated northern Mexico, and eventually occupied the Mexican capital.

manifest destiny Belief of the government of the United States that it was destined to rule the continent from coast to coast; led to annexation of Texas and Mexican-American War.

 View the **Closer Look** on **MyHistoryLab**: Texas: From Mexican Province to U.S. State

Mexico was forced to sign the disadvantageous **Treaty of Guadalupe-Hidalgo** (1848), in which the United States acquired about one-half of Mexico's national territory but less than 5 percent of its population. The **Mexican-American War** and the treaty left a bitter legacy of distrust of the northern neighbor, not only in Mexico but throughout the region. For Mexico there was also a serious loss of economic potential, but the heroic battle against the better-equipped Americans produced a sense of nationalism and a desire to confront the nation's serious internal problems, which also bore some responsibility for the war and the defeat.

Politics could not revert to the prewar situation. Santa Anna did return to office for a while, more unstable and despotic than ever, but now he was opposed by a new generation of liberals: intellectuals, lawyers, and some rural leaders, many of them from middle-class backgrounds, some of them mestizos and even a few American Indians. Perhaps the most prominent of them was **Benito Juárez** (1806–1872), a Zapotec Indian of humble origins who had received a legal education and eventually become the governor of his state (Figure 26.4). He shared the liberal vision of a secular society based on the rule of law in which the old privileges of the church and the army would be eliminated as a way of promoting economic change and growth.

The liberal revolt, called **La Reforma**, began in 1854 and triumphed within a year. In a series of laws integrated into a new constitution in 1857, the liberals set the basis for their vision of society. Military and clerical privileges were curtailed, and church property was placed on sale. Indian communal lands also were restricted, and the government forced the sale of these lands to individuals—to the indigenous people themselves it was hoped. The goal of these programs was to create a nation of small independent farmers. However, speculators or big landowners often bought up the lands, and the result was that the peasants and American Indians lost what land they had. By 1910 about half of Mexico's rural population was landless. Good intentions had brought disastrous results.

The liberal program produced the expected conservative reaction. The church threatened to excommunicate those who upheld the new constitution. Civil war erupted, and in reaction Juárez, now

Treaty of Guadalupe-Hidalgo Agreement that ended the Mexican-American War; provided for loss of Texas and California to the United States; left legacy of distrust of the United States in Latin America.

Mexican-American War Fought between Mexico and the United States from 1846 to 1848; led to devastating defeat of Mexican forces, loss of about one-half of Mexico's national territory to the United States.

Juárez, Benito [beh-NEE-toh WAHR-ehz] (1806–1872) Indian governor of state of Oaxaca in Mexico; leader of liberal rebellion against Santa Anna; liberal government defeated by French intervention under Emperor Napoleon III of France and establishment of Mexican Empire under Maximilian; restored to power in 1867 until his death in 1872.

Reforma, La The liberal rebellion of Benito Juárez against the forces of Santa Anna.

FIGURE **26.4** Benito Juárez, a Zapotec Indian from southern Mexico, rose to the presidency and began a series of sweeping reforms. His uncompromising resistance to foreign intervention and monarchy made him a symbol of Mexican sovereignty and independence.

Habsburg, Maximilian von
Proclaimed Emperor Maximilian of Mexico following intervention of France in 1862; ruled until overthrow and execution by liberal revolutionaries under Benito Juárez in 1867.

president, pushed forward even more radical measures. Losing ground in the war, the conservatives turned to Europe and convinced Napoleon III of France to intervene. Attracted by possible economic advantage, dreams of empire, and a desire to please Catholics in France, Napoleon III justified French intervention by claims of a shared "Latin" culture (this was the origin of the term *Latin America*). French forces landed in 1862 and soon took the capital. At the urging of the French, **Maximilian von Habsburg**, an Austrian archduke, was convinced to take the throne of Mexico. Well intentioned but ineffective, Emperor Maximilian tried to get the support of Juárez and the liberals and even kept many of the laws of the Reforma in place, to the dismay of his conservative supporters. But Juárez absolutely rejected the idea of a foreign prince ruling Mexico. French troops and the United States' distraction with its own Civil War allowed Emperor Maximilian and his Empress Carlota to rule. When French troops were withdrawn, the regime crumbled. It was then, in 1867, that Maximilian and his loyal generals were captured and executed (as described in the chapter opening). Maximilian's death shocked Europeans. Juárez had sent a message to Europe: "Hands off Mexico."

Juárez returned to office, but his administration was increasingly autocratic—a reality that he felt was unavoidable after so long a period of instability. By his death in 1872, the force of his personality, his concern for the poor, and his nationalist position against foreign intervention had identified liberalism with nationalism in Mexico and made Juárez a symbol of the nation. By 1880 Mexico was poised on the edge of a period of strong central government and relative political stability. One of Juárez's generals, Porfirio Díaz, became president and then virtual dictator. His government witnessed rapid economic growth. Foreign companies began to invest in the exploitation of Mexican resources, and large landowners expanded their operations. Díaz, through political repression, provided a seemingly stable environment for this growth, but the seeds of revolution were also being planted.

Argentina: The Port and the Nation

Whereas Mexico and its silver had been the core of Spain's empire in America, the rolling plains, or pampas, of the Rio de la Plata in southern South America had been a colonial backwater until the 18th century, when direct trade began to stimulate its economy. The port of Buenos Aires and its merchants dominated the Rio de la Plata, but the other areas of the region had their own interests and resented the power and growth of the port city and its surrounding countryside. The United Provinces of the Rio de la Plata, which declared their independence in 1816, soon split apart, and local caudillos, able to call on the support of gauchos, dominated each region. In Buenos Aires, the liberals gained control in the 1820s and instituted a series of broad reforms in education, finance, agriculture, and immigration. These included a program of public land sales, which stimulated the growth of cattle ranches and the power of the rancher class.

As in Mexico, liberal reforms including freedom of religion produced a similar negative reaction from conservatives and the church. But the liberals' main sin was centralism, a desire to create a strong national government. Centralists (called *unitarians* in the Argentine context) provoked the reaction of the federalists, who by 1831 had taken power under Juan Manuel de Rosas, who commanded the loyalty of the gaucho employees of the ranchers.

Under Rosas, the federalist program of a weak central government and local autonomy was instituted, but Rosas's federalism favored the ranchers of the Buenos Aires province and the merchants of the great port. He campaigned against the American Indians to the south to open new lands to the cattle ranchers. Exports of hides and salted meat increased, but the revenues collected at the port were not shared with the other provinces. Although popular with the gauchos and the urban poor and remembered today as a nationalist who resisted British and French economic pressure, Rosas proved to be a despotic leader, crushing his opponents and forcing people to display his slogan: "Death to the savage, filthy unitarians." His brand of populist, authoritarian, personalist politics drove liberal opponents into exile, where they plotted his overthrow. Eventually, the liberal exiles joined forces with the caudillos jealous of the advantages Rosas's brand of federalism had given Buenos Aires province. In 1852 this coalition defeated Rosas and drove him from power.

There followed a confused decade of rival governments because the questions of federalism and the role of Buenos Aires within the nation remained unresolved. A new constitution was issued in 1853 under the influence of Juan Bautista Alberdi, an able and progressive journalist who was also a strong believer in the need to encourage immigration. This constitution incorporated the programs of the federalists but guaranteed national unity through the power of the presidency over the provincial governors. By 1862, after considerable fighting, a compromise was worked out and the new, unified nation, now called the

Argentine Republic, entered into a period of prosperity and growth under a series of liberal presidents whose programs paralleled the Reforma in Mexico. The age of the liberals was now in full swing.

Between 1862 and 1890, able and intelligent presidents like **Domingo F. Sarmiento** (1811–1888) initiated a wide series of political reforms and economic measures designed to bring progress to Argentina. Sarmiento was an archetype of the liberal reformers of the mid-century. A great admirer of England and the United States, a firm believer in the value of education, and an ardent supporter of progress, Sarmiento had been a constant opponent of Rosas and had been driven into exile. During that time, he wrote *Facundo,* a critique of the caudillo politics of the region, in which the "barbarism" of the gauchos and their leaders was contrasted to the "civilization" of the liberal reformers. (See the Document feature in this chapter.)

Now in power, Sarmiento and the other liberal leaders were able to put their programs into practice, improving the infrastructure, promoting immigration, and expanding education. They were aided by several factors. Political stability made investment more attractive to foreign banks and merchants. The expansion of the Argentine economy, especially exports of beef, hides, and wool, created the basis for prosperity. Foreign trade in 1890 was five times as great as it had been in 1860.

Argentine Republic Replaced state of Buenos Aires in 1862; result of compromise between centralists and federalists.

Sarmiento, Domingo F. (1811–1888) Liberal politician and president of Argentine Republic from 1868 to 1874; author of *Facundo,* a critique of caudillo politics; increased international trade, launched internal reforms in education and transportation.

DOCUMENT

Confronting the Hispanic Heritage: From Independence to Consolidation

SIMON BOLÍVAR (1783–1830), "THE LIBERATOR," was a man of determination and perception. His campaigns for independence were defeated on several occasions, yet he did not despair. In 1815, while in exile on the island of Jamaica, he penned a letter to a newspaper that gave his evaluation of Latin America's situation and his vision for the future for its various parts. He advocated a republican form of government and rejected monarchy, but he warned against federalism and against popular democracies that might lead to dictatorships: "As long as our countrymen do not acquire the abilities and political virtues that distinguish our brothers to the north, wholly popular systems, far from working to our advantage, will, I greatly fear, bring about our downfall." Spain had left America unprepared, and in this letter Bolívar summarized many of the complaints of Latin Americans against Spanish rule and underlined the difficulty of the tasks of liberation—political, social, and economic. The famous "Letter of Jamaica" is one of the most candid writings by a leader of Latin American independence. The following excerpts suggest its tone and content.

BOLÍVAR'S "JAMAICA LETTER" (1815)

We are a young people. We inhabit a world apart, separated by broad seas. We are young in the ways of almost all the arts and sciences, although, in a certain manner, we are old in the ways of civilized society. I look upon the present state of America as similar to that of Rome after its fall. Each part of Rome adopted a political system conforming to its interest and situation or was led by the individual ambitions of certain chiefs, dynasties, or associations. But this important difference exists: those dispersed parts later reestablished their ancient nations, subject to the changes imposed by circumstances or extent. But we scarcely retain a vestige of what once was; we are, moreover, neither Indian nor European, but a species midway between the legitimate proprietors of this country and the Spanish usurpers. In short, although Americans by birth we derive our rights from Europe, and we have to assert these rights against the rights of the natives, and at the same time we must defend ourselves against the invaders. This places us in a most extraordinary and involved situation....

The role of the inhabitants of the American hemisphere has for centuries been purely passive. Politically they were nonexistent. We are still in a position lower than slavery, and therefore it is more difficult for us to rise to the enjoyment of freedom.... States are slaves because of either the nature or the misuse of their constitutions; a people is therefore enslaved when the government, by its nature or its vices infringes on and usurps the rights of the citizen or subject. Applying these principles, we find that America was denied not only its freedom but even an active and effective tyranny....

We have been harassed by a conduct which has not only deprived us of our rights but has kept us in a sort of permanent infancy with regard to public affairs. If we could have at least managed our domestic affairs and our internal administration, we could have acquainted ourselves with the processes and mechanics of public affairs. We should also have enjoyed a personal consideration, thereby commanding a certain unconscious respect from the people, which is so necessary to preserve amidst revolutions. That is why I say we have even been deprived of an active tyranny, since we have not been permitted to exercise its functions.

Americans today, and perhaps to a greater extent than ever before, who live within the Spanish system occupy a position in society no better than that of serfs destined to labor, or at best they have no more status than that of mere consumers. Yet even

(continued on next page)

this status is surrounded with galling restrictions, such as being forbidden to grow European crops, or to store products which are royal monopolies, or to establish factories of a type the Peninsula (Spain) itself does not possess. To this add the privileges, even in articles of prime necessity, and the barriers between the American provinces, designed to prevent all exchange of trade, traffic, and understanding. In short, do you wish to know what our future held?—simply the cultivation of the fields of indigo, grain, coffee, sugar cane, cacao, and cotton; cattle raising on the broad plains, hunting wild game in the jungles; digging in the earth to mine its gold—but even these limitations could never satisfy the greed of Spain. So negative was our existence that I can find nothing comparable in any other civilized society.

By mid-century, Latin American political leaders were advocating "progress" and attempting to bring Latin America closer to the norms of life set by Europe. For liberals such as Argentine soldier, statesman, and author Domingo F. Sarmiento (1811–1888), his nation's task was to overcome the "barbarism" of rural life and implant the "civilization" of the Europeanized cities. Sarmiento saw in the bands of mounted rural workers, or *gauchos,* and their caudillo leaders an anachronistic way of life that held the nation back. His comparison of the gauchos to the Berbers of north Africa demonstrates the ancient hostility of "civilized" urban-dwellers to the nomadic way of life. In a way, Sarmiento saw the dictatorship of Juan Manuel de Rosas as a result of the persistence of the gauchos and the manipulation of the lower classes—a sort of living example of what Bolívar had warned against. The following excerpt from Sarmiento's classic *Life in the Argentine Republic in the Days of the Tyrants, or Civilization and Barbarism* (1868) demonstrates his admiration for European culture, including that of Spain, and his desire to model his nation on it. That such a program might involve economic and cultural dependency did not concern Sarmiento and others like him.

THE SEARCH FOR PROGRESS

Before 1810 two distinct, rival, and incompatible forms of society, two differing kinds of civilization existed in the Argentine Republic: one being Spanish, European, and cultivated, the other barbarous, American, and almost wholly of native growth. The revolution which occurred in the cities acted only as the cause, the impulse, which set these two distinct forms of national existence face to face, and gave occasion for a contest between them, to be ended, after lasting many years, by the absorption of one into the other.

I have pointed out the normal form of association, or want of association, of the country people, a form worse a thousand times, than that of a nomad tribe. I have described the artificial associations formed in idleness, and the sources of fame among the gauchos—bravery, daring, violence and opposition to regular law, to the civil law, that is, of the city. These phenomena of social organization existed in 1810, and still exist, modified in many points, slowly changing in others, and yet untouched in several more. These foci about which were gathered the brave, ignorant, free, and unemployed peasantry, were found by thousands through the country. The revolution of 1810 carried everywhere commotion and the sound of arms. Public life, previously wanting in this Arabo-Roman society, made its appearance in all the taverns, and the revolutionary movement finally brought about provincial, warlike associations, called montoneras [mounted gaucho guerrilla bands], legitimate offspring of the tavern and the field, hostile to the city and to the army of revolutionary patriots. As events succeed each other, we shall see the provincial montoneras headed by their chiefs; the final triumph, in Facundo Quiroga [a caudillo leader], of the country over the cities throughout the land; and by their subjugation in spirit, government, and civilization, the final formation of the central consolidated despotic government of the landed proprietor, Don Juan Manuel de Rosas, who applied the knife of the gaucho to the culture of Buenos Aires, and destroyed the work of centuries—of civilization, law, and liberty....

They [revolutions for independence] were the same throughout America, and sprang from the same source, namely, the progress of European ideas. South America pursued that course because all other nations were pursuing it. Books, events, and the impulses given by these, induced South America to take part in the movement imparted to France by North American demands for liberty, and to Spain by her own and French writers. But what my object requires me to notice is that the revolution—except in its external symbolic independence of the king—was interesting and intelligible only to the Argentine cities, but foreign and unmeaning to the rural districts. Books, ideas, municipal spirit, courts, laws, statues, education, all points of contact and union existing between us and the people of Europe, were to be found in the cities, where there was a basis of organization, incomplete and comparatively evil, perhaps, for the very reason it was incomplete, and had not attained the elevation which it felt itself capable of reaching, but it entered into the revolution with enthusiasm. Outside the cities, the revolution was a problematical affair, and [in] so far [as] shaking off the king's authority was shaking off judicial authority, it was acceptable. The pastoral districts could only regard the question from this point of view. Liberty, responsibility of power, and all the questions that the revolution was to solve, were foreign to their mode of life and to their needs. But they derived this advantage from the revolution, that it tended to confer an object and an occupation upon the excess of vital force, the presence of which among them has been pointed out, and was to add a broader base of union than that to which throughout the country districts the men daily resorted.

The Argentine Revolutionary War was twofold: first, a civilized warfare of the cities against Spain; second, a war against the cities on the part of the country chieftains with the view of shaking off all political subjugation and satisfying their hatred of civilization. The cities overcame the Spaniards, and were in their turn overcome by the country districts. This is the explanation of the Argentine Revolution, the first shot of which fired in 1810, and the last is still to be heard.

> **QUESTIONS**
> - To what extent did the leaders of independence see their problems as a result of their Hispanic heritage?
> - What would have been the reaction of the mass of the population to Sarmiento's idea of progress?
> - Were the leaders naive about Latin America's possibilities for political democracy?

The population tripled to more than 3 million as the agricultural expansion, high wages, and opportunities for mobility attracted large numbers of European immigrants. Buenos Aires became a great, sprawling metropolis. With increased revenues, the government could initiate reforms in education, transportation, and other areas, often turning to foreign models and foreign investors. There was also an increased feeling of national unity. A long and bloody war waged by Argentina, Brazil, and Uruguay against their neighbor Paraguay from 1865 to 1870 created a sense of unity and national pride.

That sense was also heightened by the final defeat of the Indians south of Buenos Aires by 1880 as more land was opened to ranching and agriculture. At about the same time as in the United States, the railroad, the telegraph, and the repeating rifle brought an end to the Indians' resistance and opened their lands to settlement. The native peoples who were pushed far to the south, and the gauchos, whose way of life was displaced by the tide of immigrants, received little sympathy from the liberal government. By 1890, Argentina seemed to represent the achievement of a liberal program for Latin America.

The Brazilian Empire

It was sometimes said that despite its monarchical form, Brazil was the only functioning "republic" in South America in the 19th century. At first glance it seemed that Brazil avoided much of the political instability and turmoil found elsewhere in the continent and that through the mediation of the emperor a political compromise was worked out. However, problems and patterns similar to those in Spanish America lay beneath that facade. The transition to nationhood was smooth, and thus the basic foundations of Brazilian society—slavery, large landholdings, and an export economy—remained securely in place, reinforced by a new Brazilian nobility created for the new empire.

fazendas Coffee estates that spread within interior of Brazil between 1840 and 1860; created major export commodity for Brazilian trade; led to intensification of slavery in Brazil.

View the **Closer Look** on **MyHistoryLab**: Coffee Plantation in Brazil

Brazilian independence had been declared in 1822, and by 1824 a liberal constitution had been issued by Dom Pedro I, the young Brazilian monarch, although not without resistance from those who wanted a republic or at least a very weak constitutional monarchy. But Dom Pedro I was an autocrat. In 1831 he was forced to abdicate in favor of his young son, Pedro (later to become Dom Pedro II), but the boy was too young to rule, and a series of regents directed the country in his name. What followed was an experiment in republican government, although the facade of monarchy was maintained.

The next decade was as tumultuous as any in Spanish America. The conflict between liberalism and conservatism was complicated by the existence of monarchist and antimonarchist factions in Brazil. A series of regional revolts erupted, some of which took on aspects of social wars as people of all classes were mobilized in the fighting. The army suppressed these movements. By 1840, however, the politicians were willing to see the young Dom Pedro II begin to rule in his own name (Figure 26.5).

Meanwhile, Brazil had been undergoing an economic transformation brought about by a new export crop: coffee. Coffee provided a new basis for agricultural expansion in southern Brazil. In the provinces of Rio de Janeiro and then São Paulo, coffee estates, or **fazendas**, began to spread toward the interior as new lands were opened. By 1840 coffee made up more than 40 percent of Brazil's exports, and by 1880 that figure reached 60 percent.

Along with the expansion of coffee growing came an intensification of slavery, Brazil's primary form of labor. For a variety of humanitarian and economic reasons, Great Britain pressured Brazil to end the slave trade from Africa during the 19th century, but the slave trade continued on an enormous scale up to 1850. More than 1.4 million Africans were imported to Brazil in the last 50 years of the trade, and even after the trans-Atlantic slave trade ended, slavery continued. At mid-century, about one-fourth of Brazil's population was still enslaved. Although some reformers were in favor of ending slavery, a real abolitionist movement did not develop in Brazil until after 1870. Brazil did not finally abolish slavery until 1888.

As in the rest of Latin America, the years after 1850 saw considerable growth and prosperity in Brazil. Dom Pedro II proved to be an enlightened man of middle-class habits who was anxious to reign over a tranquil and progressive nation, even if that tranquility was based on slave labor. The trappings of a monarchy, a court, and noble titles kept the elite attached to the regime. Meanwhile, railroads, steamships,

FIGURE **26.5** Dom Pedro II, an enlightened man of middle-class habits who was anxious to reign over a tranquil and progressive nation despite the role that slavery continued to play in its social and economic life.

and the telegraph began to change communication and transportation. Foreign companies invested in these projects as well as in banking and other activities. In growing cities such as Rio de Janeiro and São Paulo, merchants, lawyers, a middle class, and an urban working class began to exert pressure on the government. Less wedded to landholding and slavery, these new groups were a catalyst for change, even though the right to vote was still very limited. Moreover, the nature of the labor force was changing.

After 1850 a tide of immigrants, mostly from Italy and Portugal, began to reach Brazil's shores, increasingly attracted by government immigration schemes. Between 1850 and 1875, more than 300,000 immigrants arrived in Brazil; more than two-thirds of them went to work in the coffee estates of southern Brazil. Their presence lessened the dependence on slavery, and by 1870 the abolitionist movement was gaining strength. A series of laws freeing children and the aged, the sympathy of Dom Pedro II, the agitation by abolitionists (both black and white), and the efforts of the slaves (who began to resist and run away in large numbers) brought in 1888 an end to slavery in Brazil, the last nation in the Western Hemisphere to abolish it.

Support for the monarchy began to wither. The long War of the Triple Alliance against Paraguay (1865–1870) had become unpopular, and the military began to take an active role in politics. Squabbles with the church undercut support from the clergy. The planters now turned increasingly to immigrants for their laborers, and some began to modernize their operations. The ideas of positivism—the modernizing philosophy discussed above in relation to Mexico that attempted to bring about material progress by applying the scientific principles of logic and rationality to government and society—attracted many intellectuals and key members of the army. Politically, a Republican party formed in 1871 began to gather support in urban areas from a wide spectrum of the population. The Brazilian monarchy, long a defender of the planter class and its interests, could not survive the abolition of slavery. In 1889 a nearly bloodless military coup deposed the emperor and established a republic under military men strongly influenced by positivist intellectuals and Republican politicians.

But such "progress" came at certain costs in many nations in Latin America. In the harsh backlands of northeastern Brazil, for example, the change to a republic, economic hardship, and the secularization of society provoked peasant unrest. Antonio Conselheiro, a religious mystic, began to gather followers in the 1890s, especially among the dispossessed peasantry. Eventually their community, Canudos, contained thousands of followers of this messianic leader. The government feared these "fanatics" and sent four military expeditions against Canudos, Conselheiro's "New Jerusalem." The fighting was bloody, and casualties were in the thousands. Conselheiro and his followers put up a determined guerrilla defense of their town and their view of the world. The tragedy of Canudos's destruction moved journalist Euclides da Cunha to write *Rebellion in the Backlands* (*Os sertões*, 1902), an account of the events. Like Sarmiento, he saw this resistance as a struggle between civilization and barbarism. However, da Cunha maintained great sympathy for the followers of Conselheiro, and he argued that civilization could not be spread in the flash of a cannon. The book has become a classic of Latin American literature, but the problems of national integration and the disruption of traditional values in the wake of modernization and change remained unresolved. In Brazil that was especially true because of the legacy of slavery and the need to integrate the ex-slaves into the nation.

Read the Document on MyHistoryLab: Millenarianism in Late-Nineteenth-Century Brazil—Canudos

SOCIETIES IN SEARCH OF THEMSELVES

A tension in cultural life existed between European influences and the desire to express an American reality, or between elite and folk culture. Social change came very slowly for American Indians, blacks, and women, but by the end of the century the desire for progress and economic resurgence was beginning to have social effects.

26.4 What were the positive and negative effects of its bounty of raw materials needed by an industrializing Europe?

The end of colonial rule opened up Latin America to direct influences from the rest of Europe. Scientific observers, travelers, and the just plain curious—often accompanied by artists—came to see and record, and while doing so introduced new ideas and fashions. Artistic and cultural missions sometimes were brought directly from Europe by Latin American governments.

The elites of the new nations adopted the tastes and fashions of Europe. The battles and triumphs of independence were celebrated in paintings, hymns, odes, and theatrical pieces in the neoclassical style in an attempt to use Greece and Rome as a model for the present. Latin Americans followed the lead of Europe, especially France. The same neoclassical tradition also was apparent in the architecture of the early 19th century.

Cultural Expression After Independence

In the 1830s, the generation that came of age after independence turned to romanticism and found the basis of a new nationality in historical images, the American Indian, and local customs. This generation often had a romantic view of liberty. They emphasized the exotic as well as the distinctive aspects of American society. In Brazil, for example, poet António Gonçalves Dias (1823–1864) used the American Indian as a symbol of Brazil and America. In Cuba, novels sympathetic to slaves began to appear by mid-century. In Argentina, writers celebrated the pampas and its open spaces. Sarmiento's critical account of the caudillos in *Facundo* described in depth the life of the gauchos, but it was José Hernández who in 1872 wrote *Martín Fierro*, a romantic epic poem about the end of the way of the gaucho. Historical themes and the writing of history became a political act because studying the past became a way of organizing the present. Many of Latin America's leading politicians were also excellent historians and the theme of their writing was the creation of the nation.

By the 1870s, a new realism emerged in the arts and literature that was more in line with the scientific approach of positivism and the modernization of the new nations. As the economies of Latin America surged forward, novelists appeared who were unafraid to deal with human frailties such as corruption, prejudice, and greed. Chilean Alberto Blest Gana and Brazilian mulatto J. Machado de Assis (1839–1908) wrote critically about the social mores of their countries during this era.

Throughout the century, the culture of the mass of the population had been little affected by the trends and tastes of the elite. Popular arts, folk music, and dance flourished in traditional settings, demonstrating a vitality and adaptability to new situations that was often lacking in the more imitative fine arts. Sometimes authors in the romantic tradition or poets such as Hernández turned to traditional themes for their subject and inspiration, and in that way they brought these traditions to the greater attention of their class and the world. For the most part, however, popular artistic expressions were not appreciated or valued by the traditional elites, the modernizing urban bourgeoisie, or the new immigrants.

Old Patterns of Gender, Class, and Race

Although significant political changes make it appealing to deal with the 19th century as an era of great change and transformation in Latin America, it is necessary to recognize the persistence of old patterns and sometimes their reinforcement. Changes took place, to be sure, but their effects were not felt equally by all classes or groups in society, nor were all groups attracted by the promises of the new political regimes and their views of progress.

For example, women gained little ground during most of the century. They had participated actively in the independence movements. Some had taken up arms or aided the insurgent forces, and some—such as Colombian Policarpa (La Pola) Salvatierra, whose final words were "Do not forget my example"—had paid for their activities on the gallows. After independence, there was almost no change in the predominant attitudes toward women's proper role. Expected to be wives and mothers, women could not vote, hold public office, become lawyers, or in some places testify in a court of law. Although there were a few exceptions, unmarried women younger than 25 remained under the power and authority of their fathers. Once married, they could not work, enter into contracts, or control their own estates without permission of their husbands. As in the colonial era, marriage, politics, and the creation of kinship links were essential elements in elite control of land and political power, and thus women remained a crucial resource in family strategies.

Lower-class women had more economic freedom—often controlling local marketing—and also more personal freedom than elite women under the constraints of powerful families. In legal terms, however, their situation was no better—and in material terms, much worse—than that of their elite sisters. Still, by the 1870s women were an important part of the workforce.

The one area in which the situation of women began to change significantly was public education. There had already been a movement in this direction in the colonial era. At first, the idea behind education for girls and women was that because women were responsible for educating their children, they should be educated so that the proper values could be passed to the next generation. By 1842 Mexico City required girls and boys age 7 to 15 to attend school, and in 1869 the first girls' school was created in Mexico. Liberals in Mexico wanted secular public education to prepare women for an enlightened role within the home, and similar sentiments were expressed by liberal regimes elsewhere.

Public schools appeared throughout Latin America, although their impact was limited. For example, Brazil had a population of 10 million in 1873, but only about 1 million men and half that number of women were literate.

The rise of secular public education created new opportunities for women. The demand for teachers at the primary level created the need for schools in which to train teachers. Because most teachers were women, these teacher training schools gave women access to advanced education. Although the curriculum often emphasized traditional female roles, an increasing number of educated women began to emerge who were dissatisfied with the legal and social constraints on their lives. By the end of the 19th century, these women were becoming increasingly active in advocating women's rights and other political issues.

In most cases, the new nations legally ended the old society of castes in which legal status and definition depended on color and ethnicity, but in reality much of that system continued. The stigma of skin color and former slave status created barriers to advancement. Indigenous peoples in Mexico, Bolivia, and Peru often continued to labor under poor conditions and to suffer the effects of government failures. There was conflict. In Yucatan, a great rebellion broke out, pitting the Maya against the central government and the whites, in 1839 and again in 1847. Despite the intentions of governments, indigenous peoples resisted changes imposed from outside their communities and were willing to defend their traditional ways. The word *Indian* was still an insult in most places in Latin America. For some mestizos and others of mixed origin, the century presented opportunities for advancement in the army, professions, and commerce, but these cases were exceptions. The former slaves throughout Latin America sought the benefits of full citizenship, but while legal equality came with abolition, their economic condition changed slowly.

In many places, expansion of the export economy perpetuated old patterns. Liberalism itself changed during the century, and once its program of secularization, rationalism, and property rights was made law, it became more restrictive. Positivists at the end of the century still hoped for economic growth, but some were willing to gain it at the expense of individual freedoms. The positivists generally were convinced of the benefits of international trade for Latin America, and large landholdings increased in many areas at the expense of small farms and Indian communal lands as a result. A small, white Creole, landed upper class controlled the economies and politics in most places, and they were sometimes joined in the political and economic functions by a stratum of urban middle-class merchants, bureaucrats, and other bourgeois types. The landed and mercantile elite tended to merge over time to create one group that, in most places, controlled the government. Meanwhile, new social forces were at work. The flood of immigration, beginning in earnest in the 1870s, to Argentina, Brazil, and a few other nations began to change the social composition of those places. Increasingly, rapid urbanization also changed these societies. Still, Latin America, although politically independent, began the 1880s as a group of predominantly agrarian nations with rigid social structures and a continuing dependency on the world market.

The Great Boom, 1880–1920

Between 1880 and 1920, Latin America, like certain areas of Asia and Africa, experienced a tremendous spurt of economic growth, stimulated by the increasing demand in industrializing Europe and the United States for raw materials, foodstuffs, and specialized tropical crops. Mexico and Argentina are two excellent examples of the effects of these changes, but not all groups shared the benefits of economic growth. By the end of the 19th century, the United States was beginning to intervene directly in Latin American affairs.

Latin America was well prepared for export-led economic expansion. The liberal ideology of individual freedoms, an open market, and limited government intervention in the operation of the economy had triumphed in many places. Whereas this ideology had been the expression of the middle class in Europe, in Latin America it was adopted not only by the small urban middle class but also by the large landowners, miners, and export merchants linked to the rural economy and the traditional patterns of wealth and land owning. In a number of countries, a political alliance was forged between the traditional aristocracy of wealth and the new urban elements. Together they controlled the presidential offices and the congresses and imposed a business-as-usual approach to government at the expense of peasants and a newly emerging working class.

The expansion of Latin American economies was led by exports. Each nation had a specialty: bananas and coffee from the nations of Central America; tobacco and sugar from Cuba; rubber and coffee from Brazil; hennequen (a fiber for making rope), copper, and silver from Mexico; wool, wheat, and beef from Argentina; copper from Chile. In this era of strong demand and good prices, these nations made high profits. This allowed them to import large quantities of foreign goods, and it provided funds for the beautification of cities and other government projects. But export-led expansion was always risky because the world market prices of Latin American commodities ultimately were determined by conditions outside the region. In that sense, these economies were particularly vulnerable and in some ways dependent.

Also, export-led expansion could result in rivalry, hostility, and even war between neighboring countries. Control of the nitrates that lay in areas between Chile, Peru, and Bolivia generated a dispute that led to the War of the Pacific (1879–1883), pitting Chile against Bolivia and Peru. Although all were unprepared for a modern war at first, eventually thousands of troops were mobilized. The Chileans occupied Lima in 1881 and then imposed a treaty on Peru. Bolivia lost Antofagasta and its access to the Pacific Ocean and became a landlocked nation. Chile increased its size by a third and benefited from an economic boom during and after the war. In Peru and Bolivia, governments fell, and a sense of national crisis set in after the defeat in the "fertilizer war."

The expansion of Latin American trade was remarkable. It increased by about 50 percent between 1870 and 1890. Argentina's trade was increasing at about 5 percent a year during this period—one of the highest rates of growth ever recorded for a national economy. "As wealthy as an Argentine" became an expression in Paris, reflecting the fortunes that wool, beef, and grain were earning for some

THINKING HISTORICALLY

Explaining Underdevelopment

THE TERMS *UNDERDEVELOPED* AND THE MORE benign *developing* describe a large number of nations in the world with a series of economic and social problems. Because Latin America was first among what we recently called the *developing nations* to establish its independence and begin to compete in the world economy, it had to confront the reasons for its relative position and problems early and without many models to follow. The Document section of this chapter offers two visions of Latin America's early problems that are similar because both emphasize the Hispanic cultural heritage, as well as its supposed deficiencies or strengths, as a key explanation for the region's history. Such cultural explanations were popular among 19th-century intellectuals and political leaders, and they continue today, although other general theories based on economics and politics have become more popular.

At the time of Latin American independence, the adoption of European models of economy, government, and law seemed to offer great hope. But as "progress," republican forms of government, free trade, and liberalism failed to bring about general prosperity and social harmony, Latin Americans and others began to search for alternative explanations of their continuing problems as a first step in solving them. Some critics condemned the Hispanic cultural legacy; others saw the materialism of the modern world as the major problem and called for a return to religion and idealism. By the 20th century, Marxism provided a powerful analysis of Latin America's history and present reality, although Marxists themselves could not decide whether Latin American societies were essentially feudal and needed first to become capitalist or whether they were already capitalist and were ready for socialist revolution.

Throughout these debates, Latin Americans often implicitly compared their situation with that of the United States and tried to explain the different economic positions of the two regions. At the beginning of the 19th century, both regions were still primarily agricultural, and although a few places in North America were starting small industries, the mining sector in Latin America was far stronger than that of its northern neighbor. In 1850 the population of Latin America was 33 million, the population of the United States was 23 million, and the per capita income in both regions was roughly equal. By 1940, however, Latin America's population was much larger and its economic situation was far worse than in the United States. Observers were preoccupied by why and how this disparity arose. Was there some flaw in the Latin American character, or were the explanations to be found in the economic and political differences between the two areas, and how could these differences be explained? The answers to these questions were not easy

> In 19th-century Latin America... early attempts to develop industry were faced with competition from the cheaper and better products of already industrialized nations such as England and France, so a similar path to development was impossible.

(continued on next page)

to obtain, but increasingly they were sought not in the history of individual countries but in analyses of a world economic and political system.

There had long been a Marxist critique of colonialism and imperialism, but the modern Latin American analysis of underdevelopment grew from different origins. During the 1950s, a number of European and North American scholars developed the concept of *modernization,* or *westernization.* Basing their ideas on the historical experience of western Europe, they believed that development was a matter of increasing per capita production in any society, and that as development took place, various kinds of social changes would follow. The more industrialized, urban, and modern a society became, the more social change and improvement were possible as traditional patterns and attitudes were abandoned or transformed. Technology, communication, and the distribution of material goods were the means by which the transformation would take place. Some scholars also believed that as this process occurred; there would be a natural movement toward more democratic forms of government and popular participation.

Modernization theory held out the promise that any society could move toward a brighter future by following the path taken earlier by western Europe. Its message was one of improvement through gradual rather than radical or revolutionary change, and thus it tended to be politically conservative. It also tended to disregard cultural differences, internal class conflicts, and struggles for power within nations. Moreover, sometimes it was adopted by military regimes that believed imposing order was the best way to promote the economic changes necessary for modernization.

The proponents of modernization theory had a difficult time convincing many people in the "underdeveloped" world, where the historical experience had been very different from that of western Europe. In 19th-century Latin America, for example, early attempts to develop industry were faced with competition from the cheaper and better products of already industrialized nations such as England and France, so a similar path to development was impossible. Critics argued that each nation did not operate individually but was part of a world system that kept some areas "developed" at the expense of others.

These ideas were first and most cogently expressed in Latin America. After World War II, the United Nations established an Economic Commission for Latin America (ECLA). Under the leadership of Argentine economist Raul Prebisch, the ECLA began to analyze the Latin American economies. Prebisch argued that "unequal exchange" between the developed nations at the center of the world economy and those like Latin America created structural blocks to economic growth. The ECLA suggested various policies to overcome the problems, especially the development of industries that would overcome the region's dependence on foreign imports.

From the structural analysis of the ECLA and from more traditional Marxist critiques, a new kind of explanation, usually called *dependency theory,* began to emerge in the 1960s. Rather than seeing underdevelopment or the lack of economic growth as the result of failed modernization, some scholars in Latin America began to argue that development and underdevelopment were not stages but part of the same process. They believed that the development and growth of some areas, such as western Europe and the United States, were achieved at the expense of, or because of, the underdevelopment of dependent regions such as Latin America. Agricultural economies at the periphery of the world economic system always were at a disadvantage in dealing with the industrial nations of the center, and thus they would become poorer as the industrial nations got richer. The industrial nations would continually draw products, profits, and cheap labor from the periphery. This basic economic relationship of dependency meant that external forces determined production, capital accumulation, and class relations in a dependent country. Some theorists went further and argued that Latin America and other nations of the Third World were culturally dependent in their consumption of ideas and concepts. Both modernization theory and Mickey Mouse were seen as the agents of a cultural domination that was simply an extension of economic reality. These theorists usually argued that socialism offered the only hope for breaking out of the dependency relationship.

These ideas, which dominated Latin American intellectual life, were appealing to other areas of Asia and Africa that had recently emerged from colonial control. Forms of dependency analysis became popular in many areas of the world in the 1960s and 1970s. By the 1980s, however, dependency theory was losing its appeal. As an explanation of what had happened historically in Latin America, it was useful, but as a theory that could predict what might happen elsewhere, it provided little help. Marxists argued that it overemphasized the circulation of goods (trade) rather than how things were produced and that it ignored the class conflicts they believed were the driving force of history. Moreover, with the rise of multinational corporations and globalization, capitalism itself was changing and was becoming less tied to individual countries. Thus an analysis based on trade relationships between countries became somewhat outdated.

Can development be widespread, as modernization theory argues, or is the underdevelopment of some countries inherent in the capitalist world economy, as the dependency theorists believed? The issue is still in dispute. The tilt to the left in Latin American electoral politics since 2000 is evidence of growing regional dissatisfaction in two areas—with Latin America's position in the global economy and with the misdistribution of the benefits of economic growth among the population. The economic success of Chile, Colombia, and Brazil since 2005 seem to indicate that Latin America need not be condemned by its past.

QUESTIONS
- In what sense was 19th-century Latin America a dependent economy?
- Which explanation or prediction about dependency best fits world economic trends today?

in Argentina. In Mexico, an oligarchic dictatorship, which maintained all the outward attributes of democracy but imposed "law and order" under the dictator Porfirio Díaz, created the conditions for unrestrained profits. Mexican exports doubled between 1877 and 1900. Similar figures could be cited for Chile, Costa Rica, and Bolivia.

This rapidly expanding commerce attracted the interest of foreign investors eager for high returns on their capital. British, French, German, and North American businesses and entrepreneurs invested in mining, railroads, public utilities, and banking. More than half the foreign investments in Latin America were British, which alone were 10 times more in 1913 than they had been in 1870. But British leadership was no longer uncontested; Germany and, increasingly, the United States provided competition. The United States was particularly active in the Caribbean region and Mexico, but not until after World War I did U.S. capital predominate in the region.

Foreign investments provided Latin America with needed capital and services but tended to place key industries, transportation facilities, and services in foreign hands. Foreign investments also constrained Latin American governments in their social, commercial, and diplomatic policies.

Mexico and Argentina: Examples of Economic Transformation

We can use these two large Latin American nations as examples of different responses within the same general pattern. In Mexico, the liberal triumph of Juárez had set the stage for economic growth and constitutional government. In 1876, Porfirio Díaz, one of Juárez's generals, was elected president, and for the next 35 years he dominated politics. Díaz suppressed regional rebellions and imposed a strong centralized government. Financed by foreign capital, the railroad system grew rapidly, providing a new way to integrate Mexican regional economies, move goods to the ports for export, and allow the movement of government troops to keep order. Industrialization began to take place. Foreign investment was encouraged in mining, transportation, and other sectors of the economy, and financial policies were changed to promote investments. For example, United States investments expanded from about 30 million pesos in 1883 to more than $1 billion by 1911.

The forms of liberal democracy were maintained but were subverted to keep Díaz in power and to give his development plans an open track. Behind these policies were a number of advisors who were strongly influenced by positivist ideas and who wanted to impose a scientific approach on the national economy. These **científicos** set the tone for Mexico while the government suppressed any political opposition to these policies. Díaz's Mexico projected an image of modernization led by a Europeanized elite who greatly profited from the economic growth and the imposition of order under Don Porfirio.

Growth often was bought at the expense of Mexico's large rural peasantry and its growing urban and working classes. This population was essentially native, because unlike Argentina and Brazil, Mexico had received few immigrants. They participated very little in the prosperity of export-led growth. Economic expansion at the expense of peasants and American Indian communal lands created a volatile situation.

Strikes and labor unrest increased, particularly among railroad workers, miners, and textile workers. In the countryside, a national police force, the Rurales, maintained order, and the army was mobilized when needed. At the regional level, political bosses linked to the Díaz regime in Mexico City delivered the votes in rigged elections.

For 35 years, Díaz reigned supreme and oversaw the transformation of the Mexican economy. His opponents were arrested or driven into exile, and the small middle class, the landowners, miners, and foreign investors celebrated the progress of Mexico. In 1910, however, a middle-class movement with limited political goals seeking electoral reform began to mushroom into a more general uprising in which the frustrations of the poor, the workers, the peasants, and nationalist intellectuals of various political persuasions erupted in a bloody 10-year civil war, the Mexican Revolution.

At the other end of the hemisphere, Argentina followed an alternative path of economic expansion. By 1880 the American Indians on the southern pampas had been conquered, and vast new tracts of land were opened to ranching. The strange relationship between Buenos Aires and the rest of the nation was resolved when Buenos Aires was made a federal district. With a rapidly expanding economy, it became "the Paris of South America," an expression that reflected the drive by wealthy Argentines to establish themselves as a modern nation. By 1914 Buenos Aires had more than 2 million inhabitants, or about one-fourth of the national population. Its political leaders, the "Generation of

Read the Document on MyHistoryLab: Francisco García Calderón, excerpt from Latin America: Its Rise and Progress

científicos Advisors of government of Porfirio Díaz who were strongly influenced by positivist ideas; permitted Mexican government to project image of modernization.

VISUALIZING THE PAST

Images of the Spanish-American War

ALTHOUGH THE UNITED STATES HAD FOUGHT a war with Mexico in the 1840s and commercial ties were growing in the 1880s, the real push for expansion in Latin America came in 1898 with the Spanish-American War. The U.S. motives for the war were a mixture of altruism and the desire for strategic and commercial advantages. A great deal of popular support was mobilized in the United States by the popular press, not by celebrating imperial expansion but by emphasizing the oppression suffered by people still under Spain's colonial rule. Sympathy was especially strong for the Cubans who had fought a bloody rebellion for independence from 1868 to 1878. However, the U.S. press often portrayed Latin Americans as unruly children and emphasized their "racial" difference, creating an image quite typical for the period. During the war, Teddy Roosevelt's heroic feats and the American victories stimulated national pride, but the element of altruism was always part of the mix. As in Europe, the concept of a "white man's burden" could not be separated from the drive for empire.

QUESTIONS

- In what way do images convey political messages more effectively than texts?
- When do calls for moral action justify intervention in the affairs of another country?

Puck was one of the popular political magazines of the era. The two cover images shown here from the period of the Spanish-American War reflect popular sentiments and attitudes at the time.

1880," inherited the liberal program of Sarmiento and other liberals, and they were able to enact their programs because of the high levels of income the expanding economy generated.

Technological changes contributed to Argentine prosperity. Refrigerated ships allowed fresh beef to be sent directly to Europe, and this along with wool and wheat provided the basis of expansion. The flood of immigrants provided labor. Some were *golondrinas* (literally, "swallows"), who were able to work one harvest in Italy and then a second in Argentina because of the differences in seasons in the two hemispheres, but many immigrants elected to stay. Almost 3.5 million immigrants stayed in Argentina between 1857 and 1930, and unlike the Mexican population, by 1914 about one-third of the Argentine population was foreign born. Italians, Germans, Russians, and Jews came to, "hacer America"—that is, "to make America"—and remained. In a way, they really did Europeanize Argentina, as did not happen in Mexico, introducing the folkways and ideologies of the European rural and working classes. The result was a fusion of cultures that produced not only a radical workers' movement but also the distinctive music of the tango, which combined Spanish, African, and other musical elements in the cafe and red-light districts of Buenos Aires. The tango became the music of the Argentine urban working class.

As the immigrant flood increased, workers began to seek political expression. A Socialist party was formed in the 1890s and tried to elect representatives to office. Anarchists hoped to smash the political system and called for strikes and walkouts. Inspired to some extent by European ideological battles, the struggle spilled into the streets. Violent strikes and government repression characterized the decade after 1910, culminating in a series of strikes in 1918 that led to extreme repression. Development had its social costs.

The Argentine oligarchy was capable of some internal reform, however. A new party representing the emerging middle class began to organize, aided by an electoral law in 1912 that called for secret ballots, universal male suffrage, and compulsory voting. With this change, the Radical party, promising political reform and more liberal policies for workers, came to power in 1916, but faced with labor unrest it acted as repressively as its predecessors. The oligarchy made room for middle-class politicians and interests, but the problems of Argentina's expanding labor force remained unresolved, and Argentina's economy remained closely tied to the international market for its exports. On the other hand, the new political climate favored the growing calls for equality for women, and a number of feminist organizations began to emerge.

With many variations, similar patterns of economic growth, political domination by oligarchies formed by traditional aristocracies and "progressive" middle classes, and a rising tide of labor unrest or rural rebellion can be noted elsewhere in Latin America. Modernization was not welcomed by all sectors of society. Messianic religious movements in Brazil, American Indian resistance to the loss of lands in Colombia, and banditry in Mexico were all to some extent reactions to the changes being forced on the societies by national governments tied to the ideology of progress and often insensitive to its effects.

Uncle Sam Goes South

After its Civil War, the United States began to take a more direct and active interest in the politics and economies of Latin America. Commerce and investments began to expand rapidly in this period, especially in Mexico and Central America. American industry was seeking new markets and raw materials, while the growing population of the United States created a demand for Latin American products. Attempts were made to create inter-American cooperation. A major turning point came in 1898 with the outbreak of war between Spain and the United States, which began to join the nations of western Europe in the age of imperialism.

The war centered on Cuba and Puerto Rico, Spain's last colonies in the Americas. The Cuban economy had boomed in the 19th century on the basis of its exports of sugar and tobacco grown with slave labor. A 10-year civil war for independence, beginning in 1868, had failed in its main objective but had won the island some autonomy. A number of ardent Cuban nationalists, including journalist and poet José Martí, had gone into exile to continue the struggle. Fighting erupted again in 1895, and the United States joined in in 1898, declaring war on Spain and occupying Cuba, Puerto Rico, and the Philippines.

In fact, U.S. investments in Cuba had been increasing rapidly before the war, and the United States had become a major market for Cuban sugar. The **Spanish-American War** opened the door to direct U.S. involvement in the Caribbean. A U.S. government of occupation was imposed on Cuba

Spanish-American War War fought between Spain and the United States beginning in 1898; centered on Cuba and Puerto Rico; permitted American intervention in Caribbean, annexation of Puerto Rico and the Philippines.

and Puerto Rico, which had witnessed its own stirrings for independence in the 19th century. When the occupation of Cuba ended in 1902, a series of onerous conditions was imposed on independent Cuba that made it almost an American dependency—a status that was legally imposed in Puerto Rico.

For strategic, commercial, and economic reasons, Latin America, particularly the Caribbean and Mexico, began to attract American interest at the turn of the century. These considerations lay behind the drive to build a canal across Central America that would shorten the route between the Atlantic and Pacific. When Colombia proved reluctant to meet American proposals, the United States backed a Panamanian movement for independence and then signed a treaty with its representative that granted the United States extensive rights over the **Panama Canal** (Figure 26.6). President Theodore Roosevelt was a major force behind the canal, which was opened to traffic in 1914.

The Panama Canal was a remarkable engineering feat and a fitting symbol of the technological and industrial strength of the United States. North Americans were proud of these achievements and hoped to demonstrate the superiority of the "American way"—a feeling fed to some extent by racist ideas and a sense of cultural superiority. Latin Americans were wary of American power and intentions in the area. Many intellectuals cautioned against the expansionist designs of the United States and against what they saw as the materialism of American culture. Uruguayan José Enrique Rodó,

Panama Canal An aspect of American intervention in Latin America; resulted from United States support for a Panamanian independence movement in return for a grant to exclusive rights to a canal across the Panama isthmus; provided short route between Atlantic and Pacific oceans; completed 1914.

FIGURE **26.6** The drive for opening of a sea route from the Atlantic to the Pacific moved the United States to back the creation of the Panama Canal. Between 1881 and 1914 the canal, a major engineering feat, was constructed. The nation of Panama was created in the process of securing rights to the canal when the United States backed an independence movement that separated Panama from Colombia. The Panama Canal changed the nature of international maritime commerce. This image is of the Gatlin cut, which was the major excavation on the canal.

in his essay *Ariel* (1900), contrasted the spirituality of Hispanic culture with the materialism of the United States. Elsewhere in Latin America, others offered similar critiques.

Latin American criticism had a variety of origins: nationalism, a Catholic defense of traditional values, and some socialist attacks on expansive capitalism. In a way, Latin America, which had achieved its political independence in the 19th century and had been part of European developments, was able to articulate the fears and the reactions of the areas that had become the colonies and semicolonies of western Europe and the United States in the age of empire.

Global Connections and Critical Themes

NEW LATIN AMERICAN NATIONS AND THE WORLD

During the 19th century, the nations of Latin America moved from the status of colonies to that of independent nation-states. The process was sometimes exhilarating and often painful, but during the course of the century, these nations were able to create governments and begin to address many social and economic problems. These problems were inherited from the colonial era and were intensified by internal political and ideological conflicts and foreign intervention. Moreover, the Latin American nations had to revive their economies after their struggles for independence and to confront their position within the world economic system as suppliers of agricultural products and minerals and consumers of manufactured goods. Those roles also intensified certain environmental problems like deforestation, erosion, and pollution caused by the expansion of plantation crops, mining, the exploitation of forests, and increasing urbanization.

To some extent Latin America ran against the currents of global history in the 19th century. During the great age of imperialism, Latin America cast off the previous colonial controls. Swept by the same winds of change that had transformed Europe's society and economy and led to the separation of England's North American colonies, Latin American countries struggled with the problems of nation-building while, like China and Russia, holding off colonial incursions. In this sense, and also in some efforts to define a Latin American cultural identity, Latin America became a bit more isolated in the world at large.

The heritage of the past weighed heavily on Latin America. Political and social changes were many, and pressures for these changes came from a variety of sources, such as progressive politicians, modernizing military men, a growing urban population, dissatisfied workers, and disadvantaged peasants. Still, in many ways Latin America remained remarkably unchanged. Revolts were frequent, but revolutions that changed the structure of society or the distribution of land and wealth were few, and the reforms intended to make such changes usually were unsuccessful. The elite controlled most of the economic resources, a growing but still small urban sector had emerged politically but either remained weak or had to accommodate the elite, and most of the population continued to labor on the land with little hope of improvement. Latin America had a distinctive civilization, culturally and politically sharing much of the Western tradition yet economically functioning more like areas of Asia and Africa. Latin America was the first non-Western area to face the problems of decolonization, and many aspects of its history that seemed so distinctive in the 19th century proved to be previews of what would follow: decolonization and nation-building elsewhere in the world in the 20th century.

Latin America's global connections included ongoing political and cultural ties with the West. Efforts to imitate the West accelerated in some regions, for example, with the importation of sports like soccer. Growing influence and intervention from the United States was another outside force. New immigration, from southern Europe but also now from Asia, brought additional connections. But Latin America's most significant global link continued to involve its dependent economy, drawing goods, now including machinery, from the West while exporting a growing range of foods and raw materials.

Further Readings

David Bushnell and Neil Macauley, *The Emergence of Latin America in the Nineteenth Century*, 2nd ed. (1994), provides an excellent overview that is critical of the dependency thesis. A good economic analysis is found in S. Haber, *Why Latin America Fell Behind* (1997). The movements for independence and the major leaders are described in John Chasteen, *Americanos* (2007) while Jeremy Adelman, *Sovereignty and Revolution in the Iberian Atlantic* (2006), is a broad synthetic analysis of the movements for independence. Hendrik Kraay, *Race, State, and Armed Forces in Independence Era Brazil* (2001), looks at the process of creating an army in the case of Brazil.

Catherine Davies, *South American Independence: Gender, Politics, and Text* (2006), examines the role of women while Arlene Díaz, *Female Citizens, Patriarchs, and the Law in Venezuela, 1786–1904* (2004), provides a case study of how women were affected by the new states. Kenneth Andrien and Lyman Johnson, *The Political Economy of Spanish America in the Age of Revolution, 1750–1850* (1994), presents regional studies. Florencia Mallon, *Peasant and Nation* (1995), suggests a peasant origin for Latin American nationalism. Eric Van Young, *The Other Rebellion* (2001), examines Mexico's independence movement. Ricardo Salvatore, Carlos Aguirre, and Gilbert Joseph, eds. *Crime and Punishment in Latin America* (2001), has essays that show the importance of law the definition of crime in the new nations. Volumes 3 to 5 of *The Cambridge History* of Latin America (1985–1986) contain fine essays on major themes and individual countries. A good essay from the collection is Robert Freeman Smith's "Latin America, the United States, and the European Powers, 1830–1930," vol. 4, 83–120. On the complex relationship between the United States and Latin America, see the essays in G. Joseph, C. Legrand, and R. Salvatore, eds., *Close Encounters of Empire* (1998). James Dunkerley, *Americana: The Americas in the World, around 1850* (2000), provides a wonderful if idiosyncratic view of that relationship.

There are many single-volume country histories and monographs on particular topics. Richard Slatta, *Gauchos and the Vanishing Frontier* (1985); José Moya, *Cousins and Strangers: Spanish Immigrants to Buenos Aires, 1850–1930* (1998); and Jeremy Adelman, *A Republic of Capital* (1999), provide a good start on Argentina. On Brazil, Robert Levine, *A History of Brazil* (1999), and Jeffrey Needell; *Party of Order: The Conservatives, the State, and Slavery in the Brazilian Monarchy, 1831–1871* (2007), and Mark Harris, *Rebellion in the Amazon* (2010), provide excellent entry points to the literature. Michael Meyer and William Beezley, *The Oxford History of Mexico* (2000), and Herbert Klein, *A Concise History of Bolivia* (2003), are good examples of national histories. There are excellent rural histories, such as B. J. Barickman, *A Bahian Counterpoint* (1998); Charles Walker, *Smoldering Ashes: Cuzco and the Creation of Republican Peru* (1999); and Charles Berquist, *Coffee and Conflict in Colombia, 1886–1910* (1978). Nara Milanich, *Children of Fate* (2009), on Chile deals with the history of the family while Eileen J. Suarez Findlay, *Imposing Decency: The Politics of Sexuality and Race in Puerto Rico, 1870–1920* (1999), and Asunción Lavrín, *Women, Feminism, and Social Change in Argentina, Chile, and Uruguay, 1890–1940* (1995), provide good examples of the growing literature on women and gender. On the factor of race, at the regional level of analysis Greg Grandin, *The Blood of Guatemala* (2000), discusses indigenous peoples' relation to the nation in that country while Ada Ferrer, *Insurgent Cuba: Race, Nation, and Revolution, 1868–1898* (1999), discusses the intersection of politics and race in the Caribbean.

On MyHistoryLab

 Study and Review on MyHistoryLab

Critical Thinking Questions

1. What role did the unequal distribution of income from its raw materials play in Latin America's political instability?
2. What role did the secularization of society play in the rise of political liberalism?
3. How did industrialization and modernization change women's roles in Latin America?
4. What was the relationship between this region and the growing power of the United States?
5. How did the Latin American economy compare to colonial economics in 19th-century Asia and Africa?

Civilizations in Crisis: The Ottoman Empire, the Islamic Heartlands, and Qing China

27

LEARNING OBJECTIVES

27.1 What were the external pressures and the internal divisions and weaknesses that led to the breakup of much of the Ottoman Empire in the century before the outbreak of World War I in 1914? p. 641

27.2 What were the major options proposed by differing Muslim potentates and their advisors, religious leaders, and Western-educated intellectuals and politicians to counter the power and aggressive expansionism of the West? p. 644

27.3 In what ways did the rise and decline of the Qing dynasty parallel that of earlier dynasties? p. 650

Hong Xiuquan was a deeply troubled young man. One of five children from a struggling peasant family living in the Guangdong region on China's southeast coast, Hong had worked hard to excel in school so that he could take the exams that would provide entry into the lower rungs of the scholar-gentry-dominated bureaucracy. Counting on Hong's demonstrated aptitude for book learning to improve the family fortunes, his parents and kinsfolk scrimped to find the money needed to send him to school and hire tutors to prepare him for the rigorous examination process.

The pressure of such life-defining testing is invariably intense, and with the fate of his family in the balance Hong found his failures deeply humiliating. Mortification was increasingly laced with anger as he tried and failed four times to pass the exams that would earn him the lowest

FIGURE 27.1 This panoramic scene painted by a Chinese witness to the Taiping Rebellion shows the rebel forces besieging and burning an enemy town and a nearby estate house of a large landlord's family in central China.

639

Watch the Video Series on MyHistoryLab
Learn about some key topics related to this chapter with the *MyHistoryLab Video Series: Key Topics in World History*

official degree, which carried with it a modest stipend from the state and the right to wear the robes of the scholar-gentry. Perhaps to escape the shame he felt in the company of family and friends who were well aware of his failures, Hong became an avid traveler. In 1836, in Whampoa, which was close to the great port city of Canton, Hong first came into contact with Protestant missionaries from the United States. After taking up the serious study of the Bible, he came to believe that he was the younger son of Jesus and that God had given him a sword to rid the world of corrupt officials and other agents of the devil.

Hong was well educated in a society where few went to school. He was also a charismatic speaker, given to trances and speaking in tongues, and he was convinced that he had a divine mission. He began to preach in public and was soon baptizing hundreds, then thousands of converts to his growing band of "God worshipers." Often in very garbled renditions, Biblical teachings and Christian rituals were widely deployed by adherents to his sect, which became known as the Taipings (meaning "Great Peace"), after one of the Chinese titles Hong claimed for himself. As his following grew into the tens of thousands, Hong's preaching became more strident and openly directed against the ruling Qing dynasty. Hong charged that the Qing rulers were the source of all manner of earthly evils and responsible for China's recent defeats at the hands of the British. The Taiping revolutionary agenda was also aimed at the scholar-gentry and other fundamental aspects of the Confucian order. In rebel-controlled areas, ancestral tablets were smashed, land was seized from the local gentry, and the imperial examination system was abolished. The Taipings proclaimed that women were equal to men, adopted a Christian solar calendar, and sought to restore moral order by banning slavery, concubinage, arranged marriage, opium smoking, footbinding, judicial torture, and the worship of idols. After decisively defeating a Qing military force sent to put an end to the Taiping movement, Hong's followers launched one of the longest-lived and most deadly rebellions of the 19th century. ∎

Both Hong's personal crisis and the revolutionary movement his teachings launched were catalyzed by the disintegration—beginning in the early 1800s—of Confucian Chinese civilization, which had been one of the world's most advanced for thousands of years. At the other end of Asia, the Ottomans, the last of the rival Muslim dynasties that had ruled the Middle East and South Asia in the Early Modern era, had gone into decline even earlier. In both cases, the sheer size, complexity, and persisting military power of each of these empires, combined with the ongoing rivalries among the European powers, prevented them from being formally colonized like much of the rest of Asia, Africa, and the Pacific. But, as we shall see in the chapter that follows, both dynasties and the civilizations they sought to uphold came under repeated assault during the 19th century.

The Taiping Rebellion was a violent, radical variant of a succession of movements in both China and the Middle East that sought either to reform or put an end to the existing social and political order. The Taiping Rebellion and its counterpart in the Muslim Middle East, the Mahdist upheaval that raged in the Anglo-Egyptian Sudan for most of the last two decades of the century, were dedicated to bringing down an existing social order in order to replace it with a religiously inspired utopian society. At the other end of the political spectrum, Western-educated dissidents sought to build strong nation-states patterned to some extent after those of western Europe. The disruptions that resulted

1640 C.E.	1800 C.E.	1850 C.E.	1875 C.E.	1900 C.E.
1644 Manchu nomads conquer China; Qing dynasty rules **1662–1722** Reign of Kangxi emperor in China **1722** Safavid dynasty falls in Persia **1727** First printing press set up in Ottoman empire **1736–1799** Reign of Qianlong emperor in China **1768–1774** Disastrous Ottoman defeat in war with Russia **1789–1807** Reign of Ottoman Sultan Selim III **1793** British embassy to Qianlong emperor in China **1798** French invasion of Egypt; Napoleon defeats Egypt's Mamluk rulers	**1805–1849** Reign of Muhammad Ali in Egypt **1807–1839** Reign of Ottoman Sultan Mahmud II **1826** Ottoman Janissary corps destroyed **1834** Postal system established in Ottoman empire **1838** Ottoman treaty with British removing trade restrictions in the empire **1839–1841** Opium War in China **1839–1876** *Tanzimat* reforms in the Ottoman empire **1839–1897** Life of Islamic thinker al-Afghani **1849–1905** Life of Egyptian reformer Muhammad Abduh	**1850–1864** Taiping Rebellion in China **1854–1856** Crimean War **1856–1860** Anglo-French war against China **1866** First railway begun in Ottoman empire **1869** Opening of the Suez Canal **1870** Ottoman legal code reformed	**1876** Constitution promulgated for Ottoman empire **1876–1908** Reign of Ottoman Sultan Abdul Hamid **1877** Treaty of San Stefano; Ottomans driven from most of the Balkans **1882** British invasion and occupation of Egypt; failed Arabi revolt in Egypt **1883** Mahdist victory over British-led Egyptian expeditionary force at Shakyan **1889** Young Turks establish the Ottoman Society for Union and Progress in Paris **1898** British-Egyptian army defeats the Mahdist army at Omdurman **1898–1901** Boxer Rebellion and 100 Days of Reform in China	**1905** Fatherland Party established in Egypt **1908** Young Turks seize power in Istanbul

from the interventions of Western industrial powers in informally dominated areas, such as China and the Ottoman empire, often contributed to the emergence of these political movements. But growing internal divisions within the empires themselves played a far greater role in precipitating these political upheavals and determining their impact on China and the Middle East in the last half of the 19th century.

FROM EMPIRE TO NATION: OTTOMAN RETREAT AND THE BIRTH OF TURKEY

27.1 What were the external pressures and the internal divisions and weaknesses that led to the breakup of much of the Ottoman empire in the century before the outbreak of World War I in 1914?

Weakened by internal strife and unable to prevent European rivals from whittling away its territories, the Ottoman empire appeared near disintegration. But in the late 18th century, able Ottoman rulers and committed reformers devised strategies that slowed the decline of the empire and the advance of the European powers.

In part, the Ottoman crisis was brought on by a succession of weak rulers within a political and social order that was centered on the sultan at the top. Inactive or inept sultans opened the way for power struggles between rival ministers, religious experts, and the commanders of the Janissary corps. Competition between elite factions further eroded effective leadership within the empire, weakening its control over the population and resources it claimed to rule. Provincial officials colluded with the local land-owning classes, the **ayan**, to cheat the sultan of a good portion of the taxes due him, and they skimmed all the revenue they could from the already impoverished peasantry in the countryside.

At the same time, the position of the artisan workers in the towns deteriorated because of competition from imported manufactures from Europe. Particularly in the 18th and early 19th centuries, this led to urban riots in which members of artisan guilds and young men's associations often took a leading role. Merchants within the empire, especially those who belonged to minority religious

ayan [ä yän] The wealthy landed elite that emerged in the early decades of Abbasid rule.

CHAPTER 27 Civilizations in Crisis: The Ottoman Empire, the Islamic Heartlands, and Qing China

communities such as the Jews and Christians, grew more and more dependent on commercial dealings with their European counterparts. This pattern accelerated the influx of Western manufactured goods that was steadily undermining handicraft industries within the empire. In this way, Ottoman economic dependence on some of its most threatening European political rivals increased alarmingly.

With the Ottoman leaders embroiled in internal squabbles and their armies deprived of the resources needed to match the great advances in weaponry and training made by European rivals, the far-flung Ottoman possessions proved an irresistible temptation for their neighbors (see Visualizing the Past, Map 27.2, p. 651). In the early 18th century, the Austrian Habsburg dynasty was the main beneficiary of Ottoman disarray. The long-standing threat to Vienna was forever vanquished, and the Ottomans were pushed out of Hungary and the northern Balkans.

In the late 1700s the Russian empire, strengthened by Peter the Great's forced Westernization (see Chapter 19), became the main threat to the Ottomans' survival. As military setbacks mounted and the Russians advanced across the steppes toward warm-water ports on the Black Sea, the Ottomans' weakness was underscored by their attempts to forge alliances with other Christian powers. As the Russians gobbled up poorly defended Ottoman lands in the Caucasus and Crimea, the subject Christian peoples of the Balkans grew more and more restive under Ottoman rule. In 1804 a major uprising broke out in Serbia that was repressed only after years of difficult and costly military campaigns. But military force could not quell the Greek revolt that broke out in the early 1820s, and by 1830 the Greeks had regained their independence after centuries of Ottoman rule. In 1867 Serbia also gained its freedom, and by the late 1870s the Ottomans had been driven from nearly the whole of the Balkans, and thus most of the European provinces of their empire. In the decades that followed, Istanbul was repeatedly threatened by Russian armies or those of the newly independent Balkan states.

Reform and Survival

Read the Document on MyHistoryLab: The Turkish Atrocities in Bulgaria (1876) J. A. MacGahan

Despite almost two centuries of unrelieved defeats on the battlefield and steady losses of territory, the Ottoman empire somehow managed to survive into the 20th century. Its survival resulted in part from divisions between the European powers, each of which feared that the others would gain more from the total dismemberment of the empire. In fact, the British concern to prevent the Russians from controlling Istanbul—thus gaining direct access to and threatening British naval dominance in the Mediterranean—led them to prop up the tottering Ottoman regime repeatedly in the last half of the 19th century. Ultimately, the Ottomans' survival depended on reforms from within, initiated by the sultans and their advisors at the top of the imperial system and carried out in stages over most of the 19th century. At each stage, reform initiatives increased tensions within the ruling elite. Some factions advocated far-reaching change along European lines, others argued for reforms based on precedents from the early Ottoman period, and other elite groups had a vested interest in blocking change of any sort.

These deep divisions within the Ottoman elite made reform a dangerous enterprise. Although modest innovations, including the introduction of the first printing press in 1727, had been enacted in the 18th century, Sultan **Selim III** (r. 1789–1807) believed that bolder initiatives were needed if the dynasty and empire were to survive. But his reform efforts, aimed at improving administrative efficiency and building a new army and navy, angered powerful factions within the bureaucracy. They were also seen by the Janissary corps, which had long been the dominant force in the Ottoman military (see Chapter 22), as a direct threat. Selim's modest initiatives cost him his throne—he was toppled by a Janissary revolt in 1807—and his life.

Selim III Sultan who ruled Ottoman empire from 1789 to 1807; aimed at improving administrative efficiency and building a new army and navy; toppled by Janissaries in 1807.

Mahmud II (1785–1839) Ottoman sultan; built a private, professional army; fomented revolution of Janissaries and crushed them with private army; destroyed power of Janissaries and their religious allies; initiated reform of Ottoman empire on Western precedents.

Two decades later, a more skillful sultan, **Mahmud II**, succeeded where Selim III had failed. After secretly building a small professional army with the help of European advisors, in 1826 Mahmud II ordered his agents to incite a mutiny of the Janissaries. This began when the angry Janissaries overturned the huge soup kettles in their mess area. With little thought given to planning their next move, the Janissaries poured into the streets of Istanbul, more a mob than a military force. Once on the streets, they were shocked to be confronted by the sultan's well-trained new army. The confrontation ended in the slaughter of the Janissaries, their families, and the Janissaries' religious allies.

After cowing the ayan (regional landed elites) into at least formal submission to the throne, Mahmud II launched a program of much more far-reaching reforms than Selim III had attempted. Although the ulama, or religious experts, and some of Mahmud's advisors argued for self-strengthening through a return to the Ottoman and Islamic past, Mahmud II patterned his reform program mainly on Western precedents. After all, the Western powers had made a shambles of his empire. He established a diplomatic corps on Western lines and exchanged ambassadors with the European powers (Figure 27.2). The Westernization of the army was expanded from Mahmud's secret force to the whole military establishment. European military advisors, both army and navy, were imported to supervise the overhaul of Ottoman training, armament, and officers' education.

In the decades that followed, Western influences were pervasive at the upper levels of Ottoman society, particularly during the period of the **Tanzimat reforms** between 1839 and 1876. University education was reorganized on Western lines, and training in the European sciences and mathematics was introduced. State-run postal and telegraph systems were established in the 1830s, and railways were built in the 1860s. Newspapers were established in the major towns of the empire. Extensive legal reforms were enacted, and in 1876, a constitution, which was based heavily on European prototypes, was promulgated. These legal reforms greatly improved the position of minority religious groups, whose role in the Ottoman economy increased steadily.

Some groups were adversely affected by these changes, which opened the empire more and more to Western influences. This was especially true of the artisans, whose position was gravely weakened by an 1838 treaty with the British that removed import taxes and other barriers to foreign trade that had protected indigenous producers from competition from the West. Other social groups gained little from the Tanzimat reforms. This was particularly true of women. Proposals for women's education and an end to seclusion, polygamy, and veiling were debated in Ottoman intellectual circles from the 1860s onward. But few improvements in the position of women, even among the elite classes, were won until after the last Ottoman sultan was driven from power in 1908.

FIGURE 27.2 In the courtyard of the Topkapi Palace in Istanbul, Sultan Selim III receives dignitaries from throughout the Ottoman empire in the midst of a splendidly attired imperial entourage.

Tanzimat reforms Series of reforms in Ottoman empire between 1839 and 1876; established Western-style university, state postal system, railways, extensive legal reforms; resulted in creation of new constitution in 1876.

Repression and Revolt

The reforms initiated by the sultans and their advisors improved the Ottomans' ability to fend off, or at least deflect, the assaults of foreign aggressors. But they increasingly threatened the dynasty responsible for them. Western-educated bureaucrats, military officers, and professionals came increasingly to view the sultanate as a major barrier to even more radical reforms and the full transformation of society. The new elites also clashed with conservative but powerful groups, such as the ulama and the ayan, who had a vested interest in preserving as much as possible of the old order.

The Ottoman Sultan **Abdul Hamid** responded to the growing threat from Westernized officers and civilians by attempting a return to despotic absolutism during his long reign from 1878 to 1908. He nullified the constitution and restricted civil liberties, particularly the freedom of the press. These measures deprived Westernized elite groups of the power they had gained in forming imperial policies. Dissidents or even suspected troublemakers were imprisoned and sometimes tortured and killed. But the deep impact of decades of reform was demonstrated by the fact that even Abdul Hamid continued to push for Westernization in certain areas. The military continued to adopt European arms and techniques, increasingly under the instruction of German advisors. In addition, railways, including the famous line that linked Berlin to Baghdad, and telegraph lines were built between the main population centers. Western-style educational institutions grew, and judicial reforms continued.

The despotism of Abdul Hamid came to an abrupt end in the nearly bloodless coup of 1908. Resistance to his authoritarian rule had led exiled Turkish intellectuals and political agitators to found

Abdul Hamid Ottoman sultan who attempted to return to despotic absolutism during reign from 1878 to 1908; nullified constitution and restricted civil liberties; deposed in coup in 1908.

View the **Closer Look** on **MyHistoryLab:** Young Turks Overthrow Abdülhamid II, 1908

FIGURE **27.3** This photo features a group of Young Turks who ultimately survived the challenges presented by Turkey's defeat in World War I and the successful struggles of the Turks to prevent the partition of their heartlands in Asia Minor. The man in the uniform in the center is Mustafa Kemal, or Ataturk, who emerged as a masterful military commander in the war and went on to become the founder of modern Turkey.

Ottoman Society for Union and Progress Organization of political agitators in opposition to rule of Abdul Hamid; also called "Young Turks"; desired to restore 1876 constitution.

 Read the **Document** on **MyHistoryLab:** The Young Turk Revolution 1908 Halide Edib Adivar

The profound crisis of confidence brought on by successive reverses and the increasing strength of European rivals elicited a variety of responses in the Islamic world. Islamic thinkers debated the best way to reverse the decline and drive back the Europeans.

the **Ottoman Society for Union and Progress** in Paris in 1889. The Young Turks (Figure 27.3), as members of the society came to be known, professed their loyalty to the Ottoman regime and were determined to restore the 1876 constitution and resume far-reaching reforms within the empire. Clandestine printing presses operated by the Young Turks turned out tracts denouncing the regime and outlining further steps to be taken to modernize and thus save the empire. Assassinations were attempted and coups plotted, but until 1908 all were undone by a combination of divisions within the ranks of the Westernized dissidents and police countermeasures.

Sympathy within the military for the 1908 coup had much to do with its success. Perhaps even more important was the fact that only a handful of the sultan's supporters were willing to die defending the regime. Although a group of officers came to power, they restored the constitution and press freedoms and promised reforms in education, administration, and even the status of women. The sultan was retained as a political figurehead and the highest religious authority in Islam.

Unfortunately, the officers soon became embroiled in factional fights that took up much of the limited time remaining before the outbreak of World War I. In addition, their hold on power was shaken when they lost a new round of wars in the Balkans and a conflict against Italy over Libya, the Ottomans' last remaining possession in North Africa. Just as the sultans had before them, however, the Young Turk officers managed to stave off the collapse of the empire by achieving last-gasp military victories and by playing the hostile European powers against each other.

Although it is difficult to know how the Young Turks would have fared if it had not been for the outbreak of World War I, their failure to resolve several critical issues did not bode well for the future. They overthrew the sultan, but they could not bring themselves to give up the empire ruled by Turks for over 600 years. The peoples most affected by their decision to salvage what was left of the empire were the Arabs of the Fertile Crescent and coastal Arabia, who still remained under Ottoman control. Arab leaders in Beirut and Damascus had initially favored the 1908 coup because they believed it would bring about the end of their long domination by the Turks. To their dismay, the Arabs discovered that the Young Turks not only meant to continue their subjugation but were determined to enforce state control to a degree unthinkable to the later Ottoman sultans. The quarrels between the leaders of the Young Turk coalition and the growing resistance in the Arab portions of what was left of the Ottoman empire were suddenly cut short in August 1914 by the outbreak of what would soon become a global war.

WESTERN INTRUSIONS AND THE CRISIS IN THE ARAB ISLAMIC HEARTLANDS

27.2 What were the major options proposed by differing Muslim potentates and their advisors, religious leaders, and Western-educated intellectuals and politicians to counter the power and aggressive expansionism of the West?

By the early 1800s, the Arab peoples of the Fertile Crescent, Egypt, coastal Arabia, and North Africa had lived for centuries under Ottoman-Turkish rule. Although most Arabs resented Turkish domination, they could identify with the Ottomans as fellow Muslims, who were both ardent defenders of the faith and patrons of Islamic culture. Still, the steadily diminishing capacity of the Ottomans to defend the Arab Islamic heartlands left them at risk of conquest by the aggressive European powers. The European capture of outlying but highly developed Islamic states, from those in the Indonesian archipelago and India to Algeria in North Africa, engendered a sense of crisis among the Islamic faithful in the Middle Eastern heartlands. From the most powerful adversaries of Christendom, the Muslims had become the besieged. The Islamic world had been displaced by the West as the leading civilization in a wide range of endeavors, from scientific inquiry to monumental architecture.

Muhammad Ali and the Failure of Westernization in Egypt

Although it did not establish a permanent European presence in the Islamic heartlands, Napoleon's invasion of Egypt in 1798 sent shock waves across what remained of the independent Muslim world. Significantly, Napoleon's motives for launching the expedition had little to do with designs for empire in the Middle East. Rather, he saw the Egyptian campaign as the prelude to destroying British power in India, where the French had come out on the short end of earlier wars for empire (see Chapter 25, pp. 593). Whatever his calculations, Napoleon managed to slip his fleet past the British blockade in the Mediterranean and put ashore his armies in July 1798 (see Visualizing the Past). There followed one of the most lopsided military clashes in modern history. As they advanced inland, Napoleon's forces were met by tens of thousands of cavalry bent on defending the Mamluk regime, which then ruled Egypt as a vassal of the Ottoman sultans. The term *Mamluk* literally meant slave, and it suggested the Turkic origins of the regime in Egypt. Beginning as slaves who served Muslim overlords, the Mamluks had centuries earlier advanced in the ranks as military commanders and seized power in their own name. **Murad**, the head of the coalition of Mamluk households that shared power in Egypt at the time of Napoleon's arrival, dismissed the invader as a donkey boy whom he would soon drive from his lands.

Murad (1790–1820) Head of the coalition of Mamluk rulers in Egypt; opposed Napoleonic invasion of Egypt and suffered devastating defeat; failure destroyed Mamluk government in Egypt and revealed vulnerability of Muslim core.

THINKING HISTORICALLY

Western Global Dominance and the Dilemmas It Posed for the Peoples and Societies of Africa and Asia

AS WE HAVE SEEN IN OUR examination of the forces that led to the breakup of the great civilizations in human history, each civilization has a unique history. But some general patterns have been associated with the decline of civilizations. Internal weaknesses and external pressures have acted over time to erode the institutions and break down the defenses of even the largest and most sophisticated civilizations. In the preindustrial era, slow and vulnerable communication systems were a major barrier to the long-term cohesion of the political systems that held civilizations together. Ethnic, religious, and regional differences, which were overridden by the confidence and energy of the founders of civilizations, reemerged. Self-serving corruption and the pursuit of pleasure gradually eroded the sense of purpose of the elite groups that had played a pivotal role in civilized development. The resulting deterioration in governance and military strength increased social tensions and undermined fragile preindustrial economies.

Growing social unrest from within was paralleled by increasing threats from without. A major factor in the fall of nearly every great civilization, from those of the Indus valley and Mesopotamia to Rome and the civilizations of Mesoamerica, was an influx of nomadic peoples, whom sedentary peoples almost invariably saw as barbarians. Nomadic assaults revealed the weaknesses of the ruling elites and destroyed their military base. Their raids also disrupted the agricultural routines and smashed the public works on which all civilizations rested. Normally, the nomadic invaders stayed to rule the sedentary peoples they had conquered, as has happened repeatedly in China, Mesoamerica, and the Islamic world. Elsewhere, as occurred after the disappearance of the Indus valley civilization in India and after the fall of Rome, the

> *A major factor in the fall of nearly every great civilization, from those of the Indus valley and Mesopotamia to Rome and the civilizations of Mesoamerica, was an influx of nomadic peoples, whom sedentary peoples almost invariably saw as barbarians.*

(continued on next page)

vanquished civilization was largely forgotten or lay dormant for centuries. But over time, the invading peoples living in its ruins managed to restore patterns of civilized life that were quite different from, although sometimes influenced by, the civilization their incursions had helped to destroy centuries earlier.

Neighboring civilizations sometimes clashed in wars on their frontiers, but it was rare for one civilization to play a major part in the demise of another. In areas such as Mesopotamia, where civilizations were crowded together in space and time in the latter millennia B.C.E., older, long-dominant civilizations were overthrown and absorbed by upstart rivals. In most cases, however, and often in Mesopotamia, external threats to civilizations came from nomadic peoples. This was true even of Islamic civilization, which proved the most expansive before the emergence of Europe and whose rise and spread brought about the collapse of several long-established civilized centers. The initial Arab explosion from Arabia that felled Sasanian Persia and captured Egypt was nomadic. But the incursions of the Arab bedouins differed from earlier and later nomadic assaults on neighboring civilizations. The Arab armies carried a new religion with them from Arabia that provided the basis for a new civilization, which incorporated the older ones they conquered. Thus, like other nomadic conquerors, the Arabs borrowed heavily from the civilizations they overran.

The emergence of western Europe as an expansive global force radically changed long-standing patterns of interaction between civilizations as well as between civilizations and nomadic peoples. From the first years of overseas exploration, the aggressive Europeans proved a threat to other civilizations. Within decades of Columbus' arrival in 1492, European military assaults had destroyed two of the great centers of civilization in the Americas: the Aztec and Inca empires. The previous isolation of the Native American societies and their consequent susceptibility to European diseases, weapons, plants, and livestock made them more vulnerable than most of the peoples the Europeans encountered overseas. Therefore, in the first centuries of Western expansion, most of the existing civilizations in Africa and Asia proved capable of standing up to the Europeans, except on the sea. With the scientific discoveries and especially the technological innovations that transformed Europe in the 17th and 18th centuries, all of this gradually changed. The unparalleled extent of the western Europeans' mastery of the natural world gave them new sources of power for resource extraction, manufacture, and war. By the end of the 18th century, this power was being translated into the economic, military, and increasingly the political domination of other civilizations.

A century later, the Europeans had either conquered most of these civilizations or reduced them to spheres they controlled indirectly and threatened to annex. The adverse effects of economic influences from the West, and Western political domination, proved highly damaging to civilizations as diverse as those of west Africa, the Islamic heartlands, and China. For several decades before World War I, it appeared that the materially advanced and expansive West would level all other civilized centers. In that era, most leading European, and some African and Asian, thinkers and political leaders believed that the rest of humankind had no alternative (except perhaps a reversion to savagery or barbarism) other than to follow the path of development pioneered by the West. All non-Western peoples became preoccupied with coping with the powerful challenges posed by the industrial West to the survival of their civilized past and the course of their future development.

QUESTIONS

- Can you think of instances in which one preindustrial civilization was a major factor in the collapse of another?
- Why do you think such an occurrence was so rare?
- Discuss the advantages that the Native Americans' isolation from civilizations in Europe, Africa, and Asia gave the European intruders in the 16th century. What kinds of advantages did the scientific and industrial revolutions give the Europeans over all other civilized peoples from the 18th century onward?
- Is the West losing these advantages today?

Murad's contempt for the talented young French commander was symptomatic of the profound ignorance of events in Europe that was typical of the Islamic world at the time. This ignorance led to a series of crushing defeats, the most famous of which came in a battle fought beneath the pyramids of the ancient Egyptian pharaohs (see Figure 27.4). In that brief but bloody battle, the disciplined firepower of the French legions devastated the ranks of Mamluk cavalry, who were clad in medieval armor and wielded spears against the artillery Napoleon used with such devastating effect.

Because the Mamluks had long been seen as fighters of great prowess in the Islamic world, their rout was traumatic. It revealed just how vulnerable even the Muslim core areas were to European aggression and how far the Muslims had fallen behind the Europeans in the capacity to wage war. Ironically, the successful invasion of Egypt brought little advantage to Napoleon or the French. The British caught up with the French fleet and sank most of it at the Battle of Aboukir in August 1798. With his supply line cut off, Napoleon was forced to abandon his army and sneak back to Paris, where his enemies were trying to use his reverses in Egypt to put an end to his rise to power. Thus, Egypt was spared European conquest for a time. But the reprieve brought little consolation to thoughtful Muslims because the British, not Egypt's Muslim defenders, had been responsible for the French retreat.

In the chaos that followed the French invasion and eventual withdrawal in 1801, a young officer of Albanian origins named **Muhammad Ali** emerged as the effective ruler of Egypt. Deeply impressed by the weapons and discipline of the French armies, the Albanian upstart devoted his energies and the resources of the land that he had brought under his rule to building an up-to-date European-style military force. He introduced Western-style conscription among the Egyptian peasantry, hired French officers to train his troops, imported Western arms, and adopted Western tactics and modes of organization and supply. Within years he had put together the most effective fighting force in the Middle East. With it, he flouted the authority of his nominal overlord, the Ottoman sultan, by successfully invading Syria and building a modern war fleet that threatened Istanbul on a number of occasions.

Although Muhammad Ali's efforts to introduce reforms patterned after Western precedents were not confined to the military, they fell far short of a fundamental transformation of Egyptian society. To shore up his economic base, he ordered the Egyptian peasantry to increase their production of cotton, hemp, indigo, and other crops that were in growing demand in industrial Europe. Efforts to improve Egyptian harbors, particularly Alexandria, and extend irrigation works met with some success and led to modest increases in the revenues that could be devoted to the continuing modernization of the military. Attempts to reform education were ambitious, but little was actually achieved. Numerous schemes to build up an Egyptian industrial sector by setting up cotton textile factories were frustrated by the opposition of the European powers and the intense competition from imported, Western-manufactured goods.

The limited scope of Muhammad Ali's reforms ultimately checked his plans for territorial expansion and left Egypt open to inroads by the European powers. He died in 1848, embittered by the European opposition that had prevented him from mastering the Ottoman sultans and well aware that his empire beyond Egypt was crumbling. Lacking Muhammad Ali's ambition and ability, his successors were content to confine their claims to Egypt and the Sudanic lands that stretched from the banks of the upper Nile to the south. Intermarrying with Turkish families that had originally come to Egypt to govern in the name of the Ottoman sultans, Muhammad Ali's descendants provided a succession of rulers who were known as **khedives** after 1867. The khedives were the formal rulers of Egypt until they were overthrown by the military coup that brought Gamal Abdel Nasser to power in 1952.

FIGURE 27.4 Napoleon's victory in the Battle of the Pyramids led to a short-lived, but transformative, French occupation of Egypt.

Ali, Muhammad Won power struggle in Egypt following fall of Mamluks; established mastery of all Egypt by 1811; introduced effective army based on Western tactics and supply and a variety of other reforms; by 1830s was able to challenge Ottoman government in Constantinople; died in 1848.

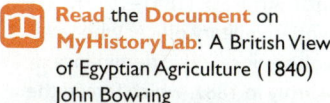 **Read** the **Document** on **MyHistoryLab**: A British View of Egyptian Agriculture (1840) John Bowring

khedives [kuh DEEVs] Descendants of Muhammad Ali in Egypt after 1867; formal rulers of Egypt despite French and English intervention until overthrown by military coup in 1952.

Bankruptcy, European Intervention, and Strategies of Resistance

Muhammad Ali's successors made a muddle of his efforts to reform and revitalize Egyptian society. While cotton production increased and the landlord class grew fat, the great majority of the peasants went hungry. The long-term consequences of these developments were equally troubling. The great expansion of cotton production at the expense of food grains and other crops rendered Egypt dependent on a single export. This meant that it was vulnerable to sharp fluctuations in demand (and thus price) on the European markets to which most of it was exported. Some further educational advances were made. But these were mainly at elite schools where French was the language of instruction.

Much of the revenue the khedives managed to collect, despite the resistance of the ayan, was wasted on the extravagant pastimes of the mostly idle elite connected to the palace. Most of what was left was squandered on fruitless military campaigns to assert Egyptian authority over the Sudanic peoples along the upper Nile. The increasing inability of the khedives to balance their books led in the mid-19th century to their growing indebtedness to European financiers. The latter lent money to the khedives and members of the Turkish elite because the financiers wanted continued access to Egypt's cheap cotton. By the 1850s, they had a second motive: a share in the potentially lucrative schemes to build a canal across the Isthmus of Suez that would connect the Mediterranean and Red seas. The completion of the **Suez Canal** in 1869 transformed Egypt into one of the most strategic places on earth. The canal soon became a vital commercial and military link between the European powers and their colonial empires in Asia and east Africa. Controlling it became one of the key objectives of their peaceful rivalries and wartime operations through the first half of the 20th century.

The ineptitude of the khedival regime and the Ottoman sultans who were their nominal overlords prompted discussion among Muslim intellectuals and political activists as to how to ward off the growing European menace. In the mid-19th century, Egypt, and particularly Cairo's ancient Muslim University of al-Azhar, became key meeting places of these thinkers from throughout the Islamic world. Some prominent Islamic scholars called for a jihad to drive the infidels from Muslim lands. They also argued that the Muslim world could be saved only by a return to the patterns of religious observance and social interaction that they believed had existed in the golden age of Muhammad.

Other thinkers, such as **Jamal al-Din al-Afghani** (1839–1897) and his disciple **Muhammad Abduh** (1849–1905), stressed the need for Muslims to borrow scientific learning and technology from the West and to revive their earlier capacity to innovate. They argued that Islamic civilization had once taught the Europeans much in the sciences and mathematics, including such critical concepts as the Indian numerals. Thus, it was fitting that Muslims learn from the advances the Europeans had made with the help of Islamic borrowings. Those who advocated this approach also stressed the importance of the tradition of rational inquiry in Islamic history. They strongly disputed the views of religious scholars who contended that the Qur'an was the source of all truth and should be interpreted literally.

Although both religious revivalists and those who stressed the need for imports from the West agreed on the need for Muslim unity in the face of the growing European threat, they could not reconcile their very different approaches to Islamic renewal. Their differences, and the uncertainties they injected into Islamic efforts to cope with the challenges of the West, remain central problems in the Muslim world today.

The mounting debts of the khedival regime and the strategic importance of the canal gave the European powers, particularly Britain and France, a growing stake in the stability and accessibility of Egypt. French and British bankers, who had bought up a good portion of the khedives' shares in the canal, urged their governments to intervene militarily when the khedives proved unable to meet their loan payments. In the early 1880s, a major challenge to the influence of foreign interests was mounted by the supporters of a charismatic young Egyptian officer named **Ahmad Arabi**. The son of a small farmer in lower Egypt, Arabi had attended Qur'anic school and studied under the reform-minded Muhammad Abduh at al-Azhar. Although a native Egyptian, Arabi had risen in the ranks of the khedival army and had become increasingly critical of the fact that the officer corps was dominated by Turks with strong ties to the khedival regime. An attempt by the khedive to save money by disbanding Egyptian regiments and dismissing Egyptian officers sparked a revolt led by Arabi in the summer of 1882. Riots in the city of Alexandria, associated with mutinies in the Egyptian armies, drove the frightened khedive to seek British assistance. After bombarding the coastal batteries set up by Arabi's troops, the British sent ashore an expeditionary force that crushed Arabi's rebellion and secured the position of the khedive.

Although Egypt was not formally colonized, the British intervention began decades of dominance both by British consuls, who ruled through the puppet khedives, and by British advisors to all high-ranking Egyptian administrators. British officials controlled Egypt's finances and foreign affairs; British troops ensured that their directives were heeded by Egyptian administrators. Direct European control over the Islamic heartlands had begun.

Jihad: The Mahdist Revolt in the Sudan

As Egypt fell under British control, the invaders were drawn into the turmoil and conflict that gripped the Sudanic region to the south. Egyptian efforts to conquer and rule the Sudan, beginning in the 1820s, were resisted fiercely. The opposition forces were led by the camel- and cattle-herding nomads who occupied the vast, arid plains that stretched west and east from the upper Nile. The sedentary peoples who worked the narrow strip of fertile land along the river were more easily dominated. Thus, Egyptian authority, insofar as it existed, was concentrated in these areas and in river towns such as **Khartoum**, which was the center of Egyptian administration in the Sudan (Map 27.1).

Even in the riverine areas, Egyptian rule was greatly resented. The Egyptian regime was notoriously corrupt, and its taxes placed a heavy burden on the peasants compelled to pay them. The Egyptians were clearly outsiders, and the favoritism they showed some of the Sudanic tribes alienated the others. In addition, nearly all groups in the Muslim areas in the northern Sudan were angered by Egyptian attempts in the 1870s to eradicate the slave trade. The trade had long been a great source of profit for both the merchants of the Nile towns and the nomads, who attacked non-Muslim peoples, such as the Dinka in the south, to capture slaves.

By the late 1870s, Egyptian oppression and British intervention had aroused deep resentment and hostility. But a leader was needed to unite the diverse and often divided peoples of the region and to provide an ideology that would give focus and meaning to rebellion. **Muhammad Ahmed** proved to be that leader. He was the son of a boat builder, and he had been educated by the head of a local Sufi brotherhood. The fact that his family claimed descent from Muhammad and that he had the physical signs—a cleft between his teeth and a mole on his right cheek—that the local people associated with the promised deliverer, or **Mahdi**, enhanced his reputation. The visions he began to experience, after he had broken with his Sufi master and established his own sectarian following, also suggested that a remarkable future was in store. What was seen to be a miraculous escape from a bungled Egyptian effort to capture and imprison Muhammad Ahmed soon led to his widespread acceptance as a divinely appointed leader of revolt against the foreign intruders.

The jihad that Muhammad Ahmed, who came to be known to his followers as the Mahdi, proclaimed against both the Egyptian heretics and British infidels was one of a number of such movements that had swept through sub-Saharan Africa since the 18th century. It represented the most extreme and violent Islamic response to what was perceived as the dilution of Islam in the African environment and the growing threat of Europe. Muhammad Ahmed promised to purge Islam of what he saw as superstitious beliefs and degrading practices that had built up over the centuries, thus returning the faith to what he claimed was its original purity. He led his followers in a violent assault on the Egyptians, whom he believed professed a corrupt version of Islam, and on the European infidels. At one point, his successors dreamed of toppling the Ottoman sultans and invading Europe.

The Mahdi's skillful use of guerrilla tactics and the confidence his followers placed in his blessings and magical charms earned his forces several stunning victories over the Egyptians. Within a few years the Mahdist forces were in control of an area corresponding roughly to the present-day nation of Sudan. At the peak of his power, the Mahdi fell ill with typhus and died. In contrast to many movements of this type, which collapsed rapidly after the death of their prophetic leaders, the Mahdists found a capable successor for Muhammad Ahmed. The **Khalifa Abdallahi** had been one of the Mahdi's most skillful military commanders. Under Abdallahi, the Mahdists built a strong, expansive state. They also sought to build a closely controlled society in which smoking, dancing, and alcoholic drink were forbidden, and theft, prostitution, and adultery were severely punished. Islamic religious and ritual practices were enforced rigorously. In addition, most foreigners were imprisoned or expelled, and the ban on slavery was lifted.

MAP 27.1 **British Egypt and the Anglo-Egyptian Sudan** Although British control over Egypt was quite secure from the time of the defeat of the Arabi revolt in 1882 until World War I, the Mahdist movement in the Sudan delayed the conquest of that vast region along the upper Nile River until 1898.

Ahmad, Muhammad Head of a Sudanic Sufi brotherhood; claimed descent from prophet Muhammad; proclaimed both Egyptians and British as infidels; launched revolt to purge Islam of impurities; took Khartoum in 1883; also known as the Mahdi.

Mahdi In Sufi belief system, a promised deliverer; also name given to Muhammad Ahmad, leader of late 19th-century revolt against Egyptians and British in the Sudan.

CHAPTER 27 Civilizations in Crisis: The Ottoman Empire, the Islamic Heartlands, and Qing China

Abdallahi, Khalifa [ab dool ä hEE] Successor of Muhammad Ahmad as leader of Mahdists in Sudan; established state in Sudan; defeated by British General Kitchener in 1898.

For nearly a decade, Mahdist armies attacked or threatened neighboring states on all sides, including the Egyptians to the north. But in the fall of 1896, the famous British General Kitchener was sent with an expeditionary force to put an end to one of the most serious threats to European domination in Africa. The spears and magical garments of the Mahdist forces proved no match for the machine guns and artillery of Kitchener's columns. At the battle of Omdurman in 1898, thousands of the Mahdist cavalry were slaughtered. Within a year the Mahdist state collapsed, and British power advanced yet again into the interior of Africa.

The 19th century was a time of severe reverses for the peoples of the Islamic world. By the century's end, it was clear that neither the religious revivalists, who called for a return to a purified Islam free of Western influences, nor the reformers, who argued that some borrowing from the West was essential for survival, had come up with a successful formula for dealing with the powerful challenges posed by the expansion-minded powers of industrial Europe. Failing to find adequate responses and deeply divided, the Islamic community grew increasingly anxious over the dangers that lay ahead. Islamic civilization was by no means defeated. But its continued viability clearly was threatened by its powerful European neighbors, which had become masters of much of the world.

THE RISE AND FALL OF THE QING DYNASTY

27.3 In what ways did the rise and decline of the Qing dynasty parallel that of earlier dynasties?

In late-18th century China, a long period of strong rule by the Qing dynasty and a high degree of social stability gave way to rampant official corruption, severe economic dislocations, and social unrest. Over the course of the 19th century, the Western powers took advantage of these weaknesses to force open China's markets and reduce its Manchu rulers to little more than puppets.

Although the Manchu nomads had been building an expansive state of their own north of the Great Wall for decades, their conquest of China was both unexpected and sudden. A local leader named **Nurhaci** (1559–1626) was the architect of unity among the quarrelsome Manchu tribes. He combined the cavalry of each tribe into extremely cohesive fighting units within eight **banner armies**, named after the flags that identified each. In the first decades of the 17th century, Nurhaci brought much of Manchuria, including a number of non-Manchu peoples, under his rule (see Visualizing the Past). Although he remained the nominal vassal of the Chinese Ming emperor, Nurhaci's forces continually harassed the Chinese who lived north of the Great Wall. During this period, the Manchu elite's adoption of Chinese ways, which had begun much earlier, was accelerated. The Manchu bureaucracy was organized along Chinese lines, Chinese court ceremonies were adopted, and Chinese scholar-officials found lucrative employment in the growing barbarian state north of the Great Wall.

Nurhaci (1559–1626) Architect of Manchu unity; created distinctive Manchu banner armies; controlled most of Manchuria; adopted Chinese bureaucracy and most ceremonies in Manchuria; entered China and successfully captured Ming capital at Beijing.

banner armies Eight armies of the Manchu tribes identified by separate flags; created by Nurhaci in early 17th century; utilized to defeat Ming emperor and establish Qing dynasty.

The weakness of the declining Ming regime, rather than the Manchus' own strength, gave the Manchus an opportunity to seize control in China. Their entry into China resulted from a bit of luck. In 1644 an official of the Ming government in charge of the northern defenses called in the Manchus to help him put down a widespread rebellion in the region near the Great Wall. Having allowed the Manchus to pass beyond the wall, the official found that they were an even greater threat than the rebels. Exploiting the political divisions and social unrest that were destroying what was left of Ming authority, the Manchus boldly advanced on the Ming capital at Beijing, which they captured within the year. It took nearly two decades before centers of Ming and rebel resistance in the south and west were destroyed by the banner armies, but the Manchus soon found themselves the masters of China.

They quickly proved that they were up to the challenge of ruling the largest empire in the world. Their armies forced submission by nomadic peoples far to the west and compelled tribute from kingdoms, such as Vietnam and Burma, to the south. Within decades, the Manchu regime, which had taken the dynastic name **Qing** (chihng) before its conquest of China, ruled an area larger than any previous Chinese dynasty with the exception of the Tang.

Qing Manchu dynasty that seized control of China in mid-17th century after decline of Ming; forced submission of nomadic peoples far to the west and compelled tribute from Vietnam and Burma to the south.

To reconcile the ethnic Chinese who made up the vast majority of their subjects, the Manchu rulers shrewdly retained much of the political system of their Ming predecessors. They added to the court calendar whatever Confucian rituals they did not already observe. They made it clear that they wanted the scholar-officials who had served the Ming to continue in office. The Manchus even

VISUALIZING THE PAST

Mapping the Decline of Two Great Empires

THROUGHOUT MUCH OF HUMAN HISTORY, THE size of the empires associated with major civilizations was usually a pretty good gauge of the extent of the political power, economic prosperity, and cultural influence they enjoyed. Civilizations on the rise were expansive and compelled even neighboring peoples who were not directly ruled to acknowledge their dominance. By contrast, civilizations in decline lost control of their borderlands to rival empires or suffered invasions—often by nomadic peoples—into the heart of the vast domains that their ruling dynasties continued to claim long after they could effectively govern them.

In the 18th and 19th centuries, two of the largest and most enduring empires in human history, the Ottoman and Qing, spiraled into decline. The plight of each of these empires is illustrated by the maps included here, which trace the advance of rival powers and the rise of internal resistance.

QUESTIONS

- Which of the empires would have been the most difficult to defend?
- Compare the timing and nature of the external threats posed for each of the empires by rival powers and other external enemies in the late 18th and 19th centuries. Why was China affected somewhat later?
- Why were the Qing rulers so much slower to respond to the outside threat compared to the Ottomans?
- Why were the Chinese more reluctant than the Ottomans to adopt the weapons and methods of their enemies?
- Which of the empires was more threatened by internal rebellions?

MAP 27.2 **Ottoman Empire from Late 18th Century to World War I** The vast territories of the Ottoman empire were lost over a period of more than two centuries to external enemies and the assertion of independence by ambitious vassals.

(continued on next page)

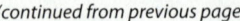

MAP 27.3 Qing Empire from Opium War of 1839–1841 to World War I Although much of the traditional Chinese territories remained intact, the Qing and later the government of the Republic of China lost control of regions distant from their capitals in the 19th and the first half of the 20th century.

pardoned many who had been instrumental in prolonging resistance to their conquest. For much of the first century of the dynasty, Chinese and Manchu officials were paired in appointments to most of the highest posts of the imperial bureaucracy, and Chinese officials predominated at the regional and local levels. Manchus, who made up less than 2 percent of the population of the Qing empire, occupied a disproportionate number of the highest political positions. But there were few limits as to how high talented ethnic Chinese could rise in the imperial bureaucracy.

Unlike the Mongol conquerors who had abolished it, the Manchus retained the examination system and had their own sons educated in the Chinese classics. The Manchu emperors styled themselves the Sons of Heaven and rooted their claims to be the legitimate rulers of China in their practice of the traditional Confucian virtues. The early Manchu rulers were generous patrons of the Chinese arts, and at least one, **Kangxi** (1661–1722), was a significant Confucian scholar in his own right. Kangxi and other Manchu rulers employed thousands of scholars to compile great encyclopedias of Chinese learning.

Kangxi [kohng-shyee] Confucian scholar and Manchu emperor of Qing dynasty from 1661 to 1722; established high degree of Sinification among the Manchus.

Economy and Society in the Early Centuries of Qing Rule

The Manchu determination to preserve much of the Chinese political system was paralleled by an equally conservative approach to Chinese society as a whole. In the early centuries of their reign, the writings of Zhu Xi that had been so influential in the preceding dynastic eras continued to dominate official thinking. Thus, long-nurtured values such as respect for rank and acceptance of hierarchy— that is: old over young, male over female, scholar-bureaucrat over commoner—were emphasized in education and imperial edicts. Among the elite classes, the extended family remained the core unit of the social order, and the state grew increasingly suspicious of any forms of social organization, such as guilds and especially secret societies, that rivaled it.

The lives of women at all social levels remained centered on or wholly confined to the household. There the dominance of elder men was upheld by familial pressures and the state. Male control was enhanced by the practice of choosing brides from families slightly lower in social status than those of the grooms. Because they were a loss to their parents' household at marriage and usually needed a sizable dowry, daughters continued to be much less desirable than sons. Despite the poor quality of the statistics relating to the practice, there are indications that the incidence of female infanticide rose in this period. In the population as a whole, males considerably outnumbered females, the reverse of the balance between the two in contemporary industrial societies.

Beyond the family compound, the world pretty much belonged to men, although women from lower-class families continued to work in the fields and sell produce in the local markets. The best a married woman could hope for was strong backing from her father and brother after she had gone to her husband's home, as well as the good luck in the first place to be chosen as the wife rather than as a second or third partner in the form of a concubine. If they bore sons and lived long enough, wives took charge of running the household. In elite families they exercised control over other women and even younger men.

Some of the strongest measures the Manchus took after conquering China were aimed at alleviating the rural distress and unrest that had become so pronounced in the last years of Ming rule. Taxes and state labor demands were lowered. Incentives such as tax-free tenure were offered to those willing to resettle lands that had been abandoned in the turmoil of the preceding decades. A sizable chunk of the imperial budget (up to 10 percent in the early years of the dynasty) was devoted to repairing existing dikes, canals, and roadways and extending irrigation works. Peasants were encouraged to plant new crops, including those for which there was market demand, and to grow two or even three crops per year on their holdings.

Given the growing population pressure on the cultivable acreage and the near disappearance in most areas of open lands that could be settled, the regime had very little success in its efforts to control the landlord classes. After several decades of holding steady, the landlord classes found that they could add to their estates by calling in loans to peasants or simply by buying them out. With a surplus of workers, tenants had less and less bargaining power in their dealings with landlords. If they objected to the share of the crop the landlords offered, they were turned off the land and replaced by those willing to accept even less. As a result, the gap between the rural gentry and ordinary peasants and laborers increased. One could not miss the old and new rich in the rural areas, as they rode or were carried in sedan chairs, decked out in silks and furs, to make social calls on their peers. To further display their superior social standing, many men of the gentry class let their nails grow long to demonstrate that they did not have to engage in physical labor.

The sector of Chinese society over which the Qing exercised the least control was also the most dynamic. The commercial and urban expansion that had begun in the Song era gained new strength in the long peace China enjoyed during the first century and a half of Manchu rule. Regional diversification in crops such as tea was matched by the development of new ways to finance agricultural and artisan production. Until the end of the 18th century, both the state and the mercantile classes profited enormously from the great influx of silver that poured into China in payment for its exports of tea, porcelain, and silk textiles. European and other foreign traders flocked to Canton, and Chinese merchants, freed from the restrictions against overseas travel of the late Ming, found lucrative market outlets overseas. Profits from overseas trade gave rise to a wealthy new group of merchants, the **compradors**, who specialized in the import-export trade on China's south coast. In the 19th century, these merchants proved to be one of the major links between China and the outside world.

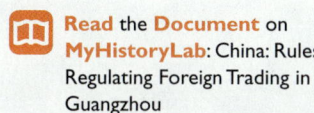

Read the Document on MyHistoryLab: China: Rules Regulating Foreign Trading in Guangzhou

compradors Wealthy new group of Chinese merchants under the Qing dynasty; specialized in the import-export trade on China's south coast; one of the major links between China and the outside world.

Rot from Within: Bureaucratic Breakdown and Social Disintegration

By the late 18th century, it was clear that like so many Chinese dynasties of the past, the Qing was in decline. The signs of decline were pervasive and familiar. The bureaucratic foundations of the Chinese empire were rotting from within. The exam system, which had done well in selecting able and honest bureaucrats in the early decades of the dynasty, had become riddled with cheating and favoritism. Despite formal restrictions, sons of high officials often were ensured a place in the ever-growing bureaucracy. Even more disturbing was the fact that nearly anyone with enough money could buy a post for sons or brothers. Impoverished scholars could be paid to take the exams for poorly educated or not-so-bright relatives. Examiners could be bribed to approve weak credentials or look the other way when candidates consulted cheat sheets while taking their exams. In one of the most notorious cases of cheating, a merchant's son won high honors despite the fact that he had spent the days of testing in a brothel hundreds of miles from the examination site.

Cheating had become so blatant by the early 18th century that in 1711 students who had failed the exams at Yangzhou held a public demonstration to protest bribes given to the exam officials by wealthy salt merchants. The growing influx of merchants' and poorly educated landlords' sons into the bureaucracy was particularly troubling because few of them had received the classical Confucian education that stressed the responsibilities of the educated ruling classes and their obligation to serve the people. Increasingly, the wealthy saw positions in the bureaucracy as a means of influencing local officials and judges and enhancing family fortunes. Less and less concern was expressed for the effects of bureaucratic decisions on the peasantry and urban laborers.

Over several decades, the diversion of revenue from state projects to enrich individual families devastated Chinese society. For example, funds needed to maintain the armies and fleets that defended the huge empire fell off sharply. Not surprisingly, this resulted in a noticeable drop in the training and armament of the military. Even more critical for the masses were reductions in spending on public works projects. Of these, the most vital were the great dikes that confined the Yellow River in northern China. Over the millennia, because of the silting of the river bottom and the constant repair of and additions to the dikes, the river and dikes were raised high above the densely populated farmlands through which they passed. Thus, when these great public works were neglected for lack of funds and proper official supervision of repairs, leaking dikes and the rampaging waters of the great river meant catastrophe for much of northeastern China.

Nowhere was this disaster more apparent than in the region of the Shandong peninsula (see Visualizing the Past, Map 27.3, p. 652). Before the mid-19th century, the Yellow River emptied into the sea south of the peninsula. By the 1850s, however, the neglected dikes had broken down over much of the area, and the river had flooded hundreds of square miles of heavily cultivated farmland. By the 1860s, the main channel of the river flowed north of the peninsula. The lands in between had been flooded and the farms wiped out. Millions of peasants were left without livestock or land to cultivate. Tens—perhaps hundreds—of thousands of peasants died of famine and disease.

As the condition of the peasantry deteriorated in many parts of the empire, further signs of dynastic decline appeared. Food shortages and landlord demands prompted mass migrations. Vagabond bands clogged the roads, and beggars crowded the city streets. Banditry, long seen by the Chinese as one of the surest signs of dynastic decline, became a major problem in many districts. As the following verse from a popular ditty of the 1860s illustrates, the government's inability to deal with the bandits was seen as a further sign of Qing weakness:

> When the bandits arrive, where are the troops?
> When the troops come, the bandits have vanished.
> Alas, when will the bandits and troops meet?

The assumption then widely held by Chinese thinkers—that the dynastic cycle would again run its course and the Manchus would be replaced by a new and vigorous dynasty—was belied by the magnitude of the problems confronting the leaders of China. The belief that China's future could be predicted from the patterns of its past ignored the fact that there were no precedents for the critical changes that had occurred in China under Manchu rule. Some of these changes had their roots in the preceding Ming era (see Chapter 23), in which, for example, food crops from the Americas, such as corn and potatoes, had set in motion a population explosion. China desperately needed innovations in technology and organization that would increase its productivity to support its rapidly increasing population at a reasonable level. The corrupt and highly conservative late

Manchu regime was increasingly an obstacle to, rather than a source of, these desperately needed changes.

Beginning in south China in the early decade of the 19th century, the British (and later other Western powers) forced their way into China's seaports and later the interior of the empire, culminating by the establishment of enclaves in the capital at Beijing by the end of the century (see Map 27.4).

Barbarians at the Southern Gates: The Opium War and After

Another major difference between the forces sapping the strength of the Manchus and those that had brought down earlier dynasties was the nature of the "barbarians" who threatened the empire from outside. Out of ignorance, the Manchu rulers and their Chinese administrators treated the Europeans much like the nomads and other peoples they saw as barbarians. But the Europeans presented a very different sort of challenge. They came from a civilization that was China's equal in sophistication and complexity. In fact, although European nation-states such as Great Britain were much smaller in population (in the early 19th century, England had 7 million people to China's 400 million), the scientific and industrial revolutions allowed them to compensate for their smaller numbers with better organization and superior technology. These advantages proved critical in the wars between China and Britain and the other European powers that broke out in the mid-19th century.

The issue that was responsible for the initial hostilities between China and the British did little credit to the latter. For centuries, British merchants had eagerly exported silks, fine porcelains, tea, and other products from the Chinese empire. Finding that they had little in the way of manufactured goods or raw materials that the Chinese were willing to take in exchange for these products, the British were forced to trade growing amounts of silver bullion. Unhappy about the unfavorable terms of trade in China, British merchants hit on a possible solution in the form of opium, which was grown in the hills of eastern India. Although opium was also grown in China, the Indian variety was far more potent and was soon in great demand in the Middle Kingdom. By the early 19th century an annual average of 4500 chests of opium, each weighing 133 pounds, were sold, either legally or illegally, to merchants on the south China coast. By 1839, on the eve of the **Opium War**, nearly 40,000 chests were imported by the Chinese.

Although the British had found a way to reverse the trade balance in their favor, the Chinese soon realized that the opium traffic was a major threat to their economy and social order. Within years, China's favorable trade balance with the outside world was reversed, and silver began to flow in large quantities out of the country. As sources of capital for public works and trade expansion decreased, agricultural productivity stagnated or declined, and unemployment spread, especially in the hinterlands of the coastal trading areas. Wealthy Chinese, who could best afford it, squandered increasing amounts of China's wealth to support their opium habits. Opium dens spread in the towns and villages of the empire at an alarming rate. It has been estimated that by 1838, 1 percent of China's more than 400 million people were addicted to the drug. Strung-out officials neglected their administrative responsibilities, the sons of prominent scholar-gentry families lost their ambition, and even laborers and peasants abandoned their work for the debilitating pleasures of the opium dens.

From the early 18th century Qing emperors had issued edicts forbidding the opium traffic, but little had been done to enforce them. By the beginning of the 19th century, it was clear to the court and high officials that the opium trade had to be stopped. When serious efforts were finally undertaken in the early 1820s, they only drove the opium dealers from Canton to nearby islands and other hidden locations on the coast. Finally, in the late 1830s, the emperor sent one of the most distinguished officials in the empire, **Lin Zexu**, with orders to use every means available to stamp out the trade. Lin, who was famous for his incorruptibility, took his charge seriously. After being rebuffed in his

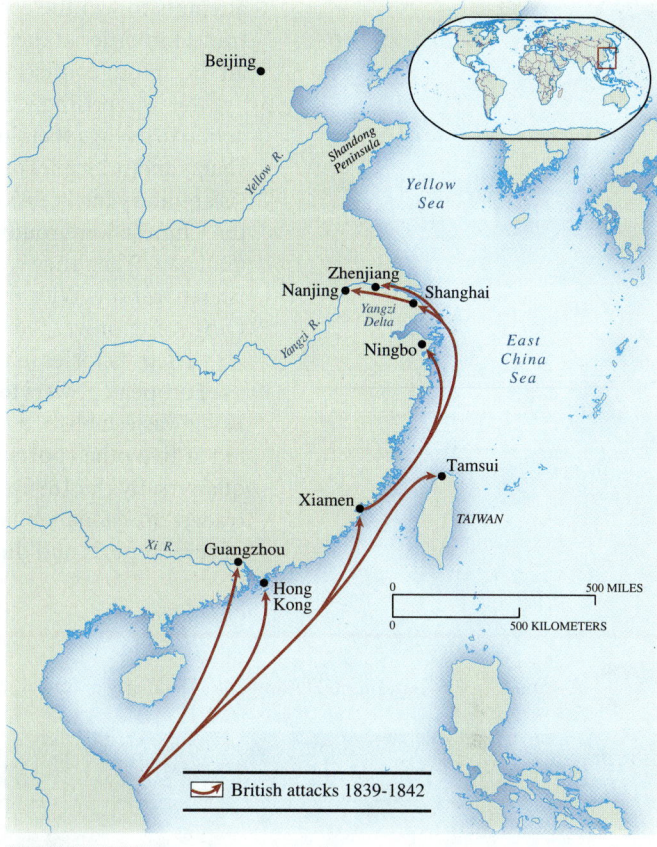

MAP 27.4 Coastal China and Its Hinterland in the 19th Century By the early 1800s, China's seaports and river deltas had become the main focus of European expansionist efforts. By the end of the century, China's southern coastal regions had also become seedbeds for nationalist resistance to Manchu rule and European domination.

Opium War Fought between the British and Qing China beginning in 1839; fought to protect British trade in opium; resulted in resounding British victory, opening of Hong Kong as British port of trade.

Lin Zexu [lihn joh-shyoo] (1785–1850) Distinguished Chinese official charged with stamping out opium trade in southern China; ordered blockade of European trading areas in Canton and confiscation of opium; sent into exile following the Opium War.

attempts to win the cooperation of European merchants and naval officers in putting an end to the trade, Lin ordered the European trading areas in Canton blockaded, their warehouses searched, and all the opium confiscated and destroyed.

Not surprisingly, these actions enraged the European merchants, and they demanded military action to avenge their losses. Arguing that Lin's measures violated both the property rights of the merchants and principles of free trade, the British ordered the Chinese to stop their anti-opium campaign or risk military intervention. When Lin persisted, war broke out in late 1839. In the conflict that followed, the Chinese were routed first on the sea, where their antiquated war junks were no match for British gunboats. Then they were soundly defeated in their attempts to repel an expeditionary force the British sent ashore. With British warships and armies threatening the cities of the Yangzi River region, the Qing emperor was forced to sue for peace and send Lin into exile in a remote province of the empire.

Their victories in the Opium War and a second conflict, which erupted in the late 1850s, allowed the European powers to force China to open trade and diplomatic exchanges. After the first war, Hong Kong was established as an additional center of British commerce. European trade was also permitted at five other ports, where the Europeans were given land to build more warehouses and living quarters. By the 1890s, 90 ports of call were available to more than 300,000 European and American traders, missionaries, and diplomats. Britain, France, Germany, and Russia had won long-term leases of several ports and the surrounding territory (Figure 27.5).

Read the Document on MyHistoryLab: The Treaty of Nanjing (1842)

FIGURE **27.5** In the second half of the 19th century, the Chinese were forced to concede port and warehouse areas, such as the one in this painting, to rival imperialist powers. These areas were, in effect, colonial enclaves. They were guarded by foreign troops, flew foreign flags, and were run by Western or Japanese merchant councils.

Although the treaty of 1842 made no reference to the opium trade, after China's defeat the drug poured unchecked into China. By the mid-19th century, China's foreign trade and customs were overseen by British officials. They were careful to ensure that European nationals had favored access to China's markets and that no protective tariffs, such as those the Americans were using at the time to protect their young industries, were established by the Chinese. Most humiliating of all for the Chinese was the fact that they were forced to accept European ambassadors at the Qing court. Not only were ambassadors traditionally (and usually quite rightly) seen as spies, but the exchange of diplomatic missions was a concession that European nations were equal in stature to China. Given the deeply entrenched Chinese conviction that their Middle Kingdom was the civilized center of the earth and that all other peoples were barbarians, this was a very difficult concession to make. European battleships and firepower gave them little choice.

A Civilization at Risk: Rebellion and Failed Reforms

Although it was not immediately apparent, China's defeat in the Opium War contributed significantly to a growing crisis that threatened not just the Qing dynasty, but Chinese civilization as a whole. Defeat and the dislocations in south China brought on by the growing commercial encroachments of the West spawned several rebellions that swept through much of south China in the 1850s and early 1860s and at one point threatened to overthrow the Qing dynasty. By far the greatest of these was the **Taiping Rebellion** led by the mentally unstable, semi-Christianized prophet **Hong Xiuquan** (see chapter opener).

By the early 1850s, Hong's talented military commanders worked his growing numbers of followers into a formidable army that included regiments of Hakka (a minority people in the southeast areas of China) women. Taiping fighters won a series of stunning victories against the demoralized and ill-disciplined Qing forces sent to destroy them. By the spring of 1853, they had captured a wide swath of territory in south-central China and established a capital at Nanjing, just west of Shanghai (see Visualizing the Past, p. 652).

With the Qing dynasty tottering on the verge of collapse, the northward drive lost its momentum, and over the next half decade it imploded. With Nanjing and a number of other prosperous cities and their hinterlands under Taiping control, the rebel leaders, including Hong, began to plot and quarrel among themselves. As some were killed and others deserted the cause, the quality of the military commanders and the training of the God Worshipers' fighters declined precipitously. Taiping policies also alienated some of their own followers and increased the numbers of the enemies arrayed against them. None of their utopian measures to provide better lives for their followers were actually implemented, and their puritanical regulations were increasingly resented by their often hostile subjects. The ban on opium smoking and Hong's bizarre variations on Christian teachings alienated the Europeans, who threw their support behind the gravely imperiled Qing dynasty.

Of all of the rebellions that threatened to topple the Qing dynasty in the 19th century, the Taiping movement posed the most serious alternative—not only to the Qing dynasty but to Confucian civilization as a whole. The Taipings not only offered sweeping programs for social reform, land redistribution, and the liberation of women, but they also attacked the traditional Confucian elite and the learning on which its claims to authority rested. In addition to smashing ancestral tablets and shrines, the Taipings sought to develop a simplified script and mass literacy, which would have undermined some of the scholar-gentry's chief sources of power.

Their attack on the scholar-gentry was one of the main causes of the Taipings' ultimate defeat. Left no option but to rally to the Manchu regime, the provincial scholar-gentry became the focus of resistance to the Taipings. Honest and able Qing officials, such as **Zeng Guofan**, raised effective, provincially based military forces just in time to fend off the Taiping assault on northern China. Zeng and his allies in the government also carried out much-needed reforms to root out corruption in the bureaucracy and revive the stagnating Chinese economy. In the late 19th century these dynamic provincial leaders were the most responsible for China's **self-strengthening movement**, which was aimed at countering the challenge from the West. They encouraged western investment in railways and factories in the areas they governed, and they modernized their armies. Combined with the breakdown of Taiping leadership and the declining appeal of a movement that could not deliver on its promises, the gentry's efforts brought about the very bloody suppression of the Taiping Rebellion. Hong died—due to illness or suicide—before his capital at Nanjing was retaken. Nearly 100,000 of his followers perished in battle or immolated themselves in mass fires.

Taiping Rebellion Broke out in south China in the 1850s and early 1860s; led by Hong Xiuquan, a semi-Christianized prophet; sought to overthrow Qing dynasty and Confucian basis of scholar-gentry.

Hong Xiuquan [hohng syoo-gwahn] (1812–1864) Leader of the Taiping rebellion; converted to specifically Chinese form of Christianity; attacked traditional Confucian teachings of Chinese elite.

Zeng Guofan [joh-syoo gwo-fan] One of the ablest scholar-gentry officials in the last half of the 19th century. Advocated the introduction of Western technologies and military reforms, and proved to be one of the staunchest defenders of the Qing dynasty.

self-strengthening movement Late 19th-century movement in China to counter the challenge from the West; led by provincial leaders.

Cixi [shur-shee] Ultraconservative dowager empress who dominated the last decades of the Qing dynasty; supported Boxer Rebellion in 1898 as a means of driving out Westerners.

Boxer Rebellion Popular outburst in 1898 aimed at expelling foreigners from China; failed because of intervention of armies of Western powers in China; defeat of Chinese enhanced control by Europeans and the power of provincial officials.

Sun Yat-sen Head of Revolutionary Alliance, organization that led 1911 revolt against Qing dynasty in China; briefly elected president in 1911, but yielded in favor of Yuan Shikai in 1912; created Nationalist party of China (Guomindang) in 1919; died in 1925.

Despite their clearly desperate situation by the late 19th century, including a shocking loss in a war with Japan in 1894–1895, the Manchu rulers stubbornly resisted the far-reaching reforms that were the only hope of saving the regime and, as it turned out, Confucian-Chinese civilization. Manchu rulers occasionally supported officials who pushed for extensive political and social reforms, some of which were inspired by the example of the West. But their efforts were repeatedly frustrated by the backlash of members of the imperial household and their allies among the scholar-gentry, who were determined to preserve the old order with only minor changes and to make no concessions to the West.

The last decades of the dynasty were dominated by the ultraconservative dowager empress **Cixi**, who became the power behind the throne. In 1898 she and her faction crushed the most serious move toward reform. Her nephew, the emperor, was imprisoned in the Forbidden City, and leading advocates for reform were executed or driven from China. On one occasion it was widely reported that Cixi defied the Westernizers by rechanneling funds that had been raised to build modern warships into the building of a huge marble boat in one of the lakes in the imperial gardens. With genuine reform blocked by Cixi and her faction, the Manchus relied on divisions among the provincial officials and among the European powers to maintain their position. Members of the Qing household also secretly backed popular outbursts aimed at expelling the foreigners from China, such as the **Boxer Rebellion** (Figure 27.6). The Boxer uprising broke out in 1898 and was put down only through the intervention of the imperialist powers in 1901. Its failure led to even greater control over China's internal affairs by the Europeans and a further devolution of power to provincial officials.

The Fall of the Qing and the Rise of a Chinese Nationalist Alternative

By the beginning of the 20th century, the days of the Manchus were numbered. With the defeat of the Taipings, resistance to the Qing came to be centered in rival secret societies such as the Triads and the Society of Elders and Brothers. These underground organizations inspired numerous local uprisings against the dynasty in the late 19th century. All of these efforts failed because of lack of coordination and sufficient resources. But some of the secret society cells became a valuable training ground that prepared the way for a new sort of resistance to the Manchus.

By the end of the 19th century, the sons of some of the scholar-gentry and especially of the merchants in the port cities were becoming more and more involved in secret society operations and other activities aimed at overthrowing the regime. Because many of these young men had received European-style educations, their resistance was aimed at more than just getting rid of the Manchus. They envisioned power passing to Western-educated, reformist leaders who would build a new, strong nation-state in China patterned after those of the West, rather than simply establishing yet another imperial dynasty. For aspiring revolutionaries such as **Sun Yat-sen**, who emerged as one of their most articulate advocates, seizing power was also seen as a way to enact desperately needed social programs to relieve the misery of the peasants and urban workers.

Although they drew heavily on the West for ideas and organizational models, the revolutionaries from the rising middle classes were deeply hostile to the involvement of the imperialist powers in Chinese affairs. They also condemned the Manchus for failing to control the foreigners. Like the Taipings, the young rebels cut off their *queues* (braided ponytails) in defiance of the Manchu order that all ethnic Chinese wear their hair in this fashion. They joined

FIGURE 27.6 China's peril in the aftermath of the Boxer Rebellion and the military interventions by the imperialist powers that it prompted are brilliantly captured in this contemporary cartoon showing the aggressive and mutually hostile great powers circling the carcass of the Qing empire.

in uprisings fomented by the secret societies or plotted assassinations and acts of sabotage on their own. Attempts to coordinate an all-China rising failed on several occasions because of personal animosities or incompetence. But in late 1911, opposition to the government's reliance on the Western powers for railway loans led to secret society uprisings, student demonstrations, and mutinies on the part of imperial troops. When key provincial officials refused to put down the spreading rebellion, the Manchus had no choice but to abdicate. In February 1912, the last emperor of China, a small boy named **Puyi**, was deposed, and one of the more powerful provincial lords was asked to establish a republican government in China.

Puyi [poo-yee] Last emperor of China; deposed as emperor while still a small boy in 1912.

The revolution of 1911 toppled the Qing dynasty, but in many ways a more important turning point for Chinese civilization was reached in 1905. In that year, the civil service exams were given for the last time. Reluctantly, even the ultraconservative advisors of the empress Cixi had concluded that solutions to China's predicament could no longer be found in the Confucian learning the exams tested. In fact, the abandonment of the exams signaled the end of a pattern of civilized life the Chinese had

DOCUMENT

Transforming Imperial China into a Nation

FACED WITH MOUNTING INTRUSIONS BY THE Western powers into China, which the Manchu dynasty appeared powerless to resist, Chinese political leaders and intellectuals debated the ways by which China could renew itself and thus survive the challenges posed by the industrialized West. As the following passages from his journal *A People Made New* (published from 1902 to 1905) illustrate, Liang Qichao, one of the main advocates of major reforms in Chinese society, recognized the need for significant borrowing from Europe and the United States. At the same time, late 19th- and early 20th-century champions of renewal such as Liang wanted to preserve the basic features of Chinese society as they had developed over two millennia of history.

> If we wish to make our nation strong, we must investigate extensively the methods followed by other nations in becoming independent. We should select their superior points and appropriate them to make up our own shortcomings. Now with regard to politics, academic learning, and techniques, our critics know how to take the superior points of others to make up for our own weakness; but they do not know that the people's virtue, the people's wisdom, and the people's vitality are the great basis of politics, academic learning, and techniques.
>
> [Those who are for "renovation"] are worried about the situation and try hard to develop the nation and to promote well-being. But when asked about their methods, they would begin with diplomacy, training of troops, purchase of arms and manufacture of instruments; then they would proceed to commerce, mining, and railways; and finally they would come, as they did recently, to officers' training, police, and education. Are these not the most important and necessary things for modern civilized nations? Yes. But can we attain the level of modern civilization and place our nation in an invincible position by adopting a little of this and that, or taking a small step now and then? I know we cannot....

> Let me illustrate this by commerce. Economic competition is one of the big problems of the world today. It is the method whereby the powers attempt to conquer us. It is also the method whereby we should fight for our existence. The importance of improving our foreign trade has been recognized by all. But in order to promote foreign trade, it is necessary to protect the rights of our domestic trade and industry; and in order to protect these rights, it is necessary to issue a set of commercial laws. Commercial laws, however, cannot stand by themselves, and so it is necessary to complement them with other laws. A law which is not carried out is tantamount to no law; it is therefore necessary to define the powers of the judiciary. Bad legislation is worse than no legislation, and so it is necessary to decide where the legislative power should belong. If those who violate the law are not punished, laws will become void as soon as they are proclaimed; therefore, the duties of the judiciary must be defined. When all these are carried to the logical conclusion, it will be seen that foreign trade cannot be promoted without a constitution, a parliament, and a responsible government....
>
> What, then, is the way to effect our salvation and to achieve progress? The answer is that we must shatter at a blow the despotic and confused governmental system of some thousands of years; we must sweep away the corrupt and sycophantic learning of these thousands of years.

QUESTIONS

- What does Liang see as the key sources of Western strength?
- What does he believe China needs most to borrow from Europe and the United States?
- Do his recommendations strike you as specific enough to rescue China from its many predicaments?
- If you were the emperor's advisor, what sorts of changes would you recommend, perhaps copying the approaches tried by the leaders of other civilizations in this era?

nurtured for nearly 2500 years. The mix of philosophies and values that had come to be known as the Confucian system, the massive civil bureaucracy, rule by an educated and cultivated scholar-gentry elite, and even the artistic accomplishments of the old order came under increasing criticism in the early 20th century. Many of these hallmarks of the most enduring civilization that has ever existed were violently destroyed.

Global Connections and Critical Themes

MUSLIM AND CHINESE RETREAT AND A SHIFTING GLOBAL BALANCE

Both Chinese and Islamic civilizations were severely weakened by internal disruptions during the 18th and 19th centuries, and each was thrown into prolonged crisis by the growing challenges posed by the West. Several key differences in the interaction between each civilization and the West do much to explain why Islam, although badly shaken, survived, whereas Chinese civilization collapsed under the burden of domestic upheavals and foreign aggression. For the Muslims, who had been warring and trading with Christian Europe since the Middle Ages, the Western threat had long existed. What was new was the much greater strength of the Europeans in the ongoing contest, which resulted from their global expansion and their scientific and industrial revolutions. For China, the challenges from the West came suddenly and brutally. Within decades, the Chinese had to revise their image of their empire as the center of the world and the source of civilization itself to take into account severe defeats at the hands of peoples they once dismissed as barbarians.

The Muslims could also take comfort from the fact that, in the Judeo-Christian and Greek traditions, they shared much with the ascendant Europeans. As a result, elements of their own civilization had played critical roles in the rise of the West. This made it easier to justify Muslim borrowing from the West, which in any case could be set in a long tradition of exchanges with other civilizations. Although some Chinese technology had passed to the West, Chinese and Western leaders were largely unaware of early exchanges and deeply impressed by the profound differences between their societies. For the Chinese, borrowing from the barbarians required a painful reassessment of their place in the world—a reassessment many were unwilling to make.

In countering the thrusts from the West, the Muslims gained from the fact that they had many centers to defend; the fall of a single dynasty or regime did not mean the end of Islamic independence. The Muslims also benefited from the more gradual nature of the Western advance. They had time to learn from earlier mistakes and try out different responses to the Western challenges. For the Chinese, the defense of their civilization came to be equated with the survival of the Qing dynasty, a line of thinking that the Manchus did all they could to promote. When the dynasty collapsed in the early 20th century, the Chinese lost faith in the formula for civilization they had successfully followed for more than two millennia. Again, timing was critical. The crisis in China seemed to come without warning. Within decades, the Qing went from being the arrogant controller of the barbarians to being a defeated and humbled pawn of the European powers.

When the dynasty failed and it became clear that the "barbarians" had outdone the Chinese in so many fields of civilized endeavor, the Chinese had little to fall back on. Like the Europeans, they had excelled in social and political organization and in mastery of the material world. Unlike the Hindus or the Muslims, they had no great religious tradition with which to counter the European conceit that worldly dominance could be equated with inherent superiority. In the depths of their crisis, Muslim peoples clung to the conviction that theirs was the true faith, the last and fullest of God's revelations to humankind. That faith became the basis of their resistance and their strategies for renewal, the key to the survival of Islamic civilization and its continuing efforts to meet the challenges of the West in the 20th and 21st centuries.

Both China and the Islamic lands of the Middle East and North Africa faced common challenges through the unavoidable intrusion of Western-dominated globalism. While their responses differed, both civilizations were only partially colonized (in contrast to Africa). Their situation also differed from that of Latin America, where connections to the West ran deeper amid an older pattern of economic dependency. They differed, finally, from two other societies, near neighbors, who retained fuller independence amid the same global pressures: Russia and Japan.

Further Readings

The more readable general introductions to the Ottoman decline and the origins of Turkey include Elisabeth Özdalga, ed., *Late Ottoman Society: The Intellectual Legacy* (2005), and Caroline Finkel, *Osman's Dream: The Story of the Ottomans* (2006), and the chapter on "The Later Ottoman Empire" by Halil Inalcik in *The Cambridge History of Islam*, vol. 1 (1973). The fall of the dynasty and the development of the Turkish republic are treated in world historical perspective in Meliha Benli Altuni-sik, *Turkey: Challenges of Continuity and Change* (2005), and Hur-I Islamo-glu-lnan, *The Ottoman Empire and the World Economy* (2004). Other recent studies on specific aspects of this process include C. V. Findley's books of Ottoman bureaucratic reform and the development of a modern civil service in what is today Turkey; Ernest Ramsaur, *The Young Turks* (1957); Stanford Shaw, *Between Old and New* (1971); and David Kusher, *The Rise of Turkish Nationalism* (1977).

On Egypt and the Islamic heartlands in this period, see P. M. Holt, *Egypt and the Fertile Crescent, 1516–1922* (1965), or P. J. Vatikiotis, *The History of Egypt* (1985). On the Mahdist movement in the Sudan, see P. M. Holt, *The Mahdist State in the Sudan* (1958), or the fine summary by L. Carl Brown in Robert Rotberg and Ali Mazrui, eds., *Protest and Power in Black Africa* (1970). The latter also includes many informative articles on African resistance to European conquest and rule. On women and changes in the family in the Ottoman realm, see Nermin Abadan-Unat, *Women in Turkish Society* (1981); in the Arab world, see Nawal el Saadawi, *The Hidden Face of Eve* (1980).

On the Manchu takeover in China, see Frederic Wakeman Jr., *The Great Enterprise* (1985), and Jonathan Spence and John E. Willis, eds., *Ming to Ch'ing* (1979). On Qing rule, among the most readable and useful works are Spence's *Emperor of China: Portrait of K'ang-hsi* (1974) and the relevant sections in his *The Search for Modern China* (1990); Susan Naquin and Evelyn Rawski, *Chinese Society in the 18th Century* (1987); and the essays in John Fairbank, ed., *The Cambridge History of China: Late Ch'ing 1800–1911* (1978). The early decades of Qing and Chinese decline are perceptively surveyed in F. W. Mote, *Imperial China, 900–1800* (1999). A good survey of the causes and course of the Opium War is provided in Hsin-pao Chang, *Commissioner Lin and the Opium War* (1964). The Taiping Rebellion is covered in Jen Yu-wen, *The Taiping Revolutionary Movement* (1973), and Jonathan D. Spence, *God's Chinese Son: Taiping Heavenly Kingdom of Hong Xiuquan* (1996). The rebellion heralding the last stage of Qing decline is examined in J. W. Esherick, *The Origins of the Boxer Uprising* (1987).

The first stages of the Chinese nationalist movement are examined in the essays in Mary Wright, ed., *China in Revolution: The First Phase* (1968). The early sections of Elisabeth Croll, *Feminism and Socialism in China* (1980), provide an excellent overview of the status and condition of women in the Qing era.

On MyHistoryLab

 Study and Review on MyHistoryLab

Critical Thinking Questions

1. Why were technological innovations so central to Ottoman attempts to defend their empire against European rivals, and which technologies did the Turks see as the most critical?

2. What were the key reasons for European interventions in the Middle East in the 18th and 19th centuries and how were they similar or different than the motives for Western advances into China in the same period?

3. What ideas, institution, and causes became the focal points of Chinese and Islamic resistance respectively to the West in the latter half of the 19th century and the first decades of the 20th?

4. Why did most of these early movements fail to stop Western advances and informal control of each of the declining empires?

28 Russia and Japan: Industrialization Outside the West

Listen to Chapter 28 on MyHistoryLab

LEARNING OBJECTIVES

28.1 How did Russian reforms help spur initial industrialization? p. 664

28.2 Why did revolutionary potential grow in Russia? p. 670

28.3 How did Meiji Japan combine fundamental change with a continuing Japanese identity? p. 673

Fukuzawa Yukichi (1834–1904) was one of the most ardent educational reformers in late 19th-century Japan. Very soon after Japan began to have greater contact with the West, he concluded that Japan needed to change. He began to travel to the United States and Europe as early as 1860. He was not uncritical—he did not like the outspokenness of Western women or divisive debates in parliaments. But he firmly believed that, in key respects, Western education surpassed Japanese. As he put it in his autobiography, in 1899: "When I compare the two . . . as to wealth, armament, and the greatest happiness for the greatest number, I have to put the Orient below the Occident" (Figure 28.1).

FIGURE **28.1** Japanese children at school. Showing children the latest in naval technology suggests the relationship between education and other aspects of Japanese development in the later 19th century.

Watch the Video Series on MyHistoryLab

Learn about some key topics related to this chapter with the *MyHistoryLab Video Series: Key Topics in World History*

The problem in Japanese education, according to Fukuzawa, was Confucianism. The Confucian tradition, he believed, undervalued science and mathematics. It also suffered from a "lack of the idea of independence." Although independence was hard to define, Fukuzawa argued that it was essential if "mankind [was] to thrive" and if Japan was to "assert herself among the great nations of the world."

Japanese conservatives were deeply offended by this enthusiasm for Western education. Fukuzawa, a member of the elite and family friend of key conservatives, was sensitive to their criticism. In a letter to one observer, he seemed to back down. He talked of his commitment to "the teaching of filial piety and brotherly harmony." He said he worried that he was not being faithful to the memory of his own parents (who had been Confucianists). He admitted that he jumped into "Western studies" at a young age and did not know as much as he should about Confucianism. He even argued that (by the late 1870s) the traditions had reconciled: "Western and Confucian teachings have now grown into one, and no contradiction is seen."

Fukuzawa's dilemma was a common one for reformers: trying to prompt real change in a Western direction without unduly offending traditionalists and without wanting to become fully Western. Russian reformers, although different from the Japanese, faced similar problems, and handled them less successfully. Fukuzawa himself bent but did not break in his reformist zeal. In his autobiography he returned to defiance: "Again and again I had to rise up and denounce the all-important Chinese influence" even though "it was not altogether a safe road for my reckless spirit to follow." ■

This chapter deals with two important nations that defied the common pattern of growing Western domination during the 19th century. By 1900 Russia and Japan had managed to launch significant programs of industrialization and to make other changes designed to strengthen their political and social systems. Russia and Japan differed from the pattern of halting reforms characteristic of China and the Middle East in the 19th century. Theirs were the only societies outside the West to begin a wholesale process of industrialization before the 1960s. In the process, Japan pulled away from other Asian societies, while Russia ultimately enhanced its power in world affairs.

Russia and Japan did have some common characteristics, which help explain why both could maintain economic and political independence during the West's century of power. They both had prior experience of imitation: Japan from China, Russia from Byzantium and then the West. They knew that learning from outsiders could be profitable and need not destroy their native cultures. Both had improved their political effectiveness during the 17th and 18th centuries, through the Tokugawa shogunate and the tsarist empire, respectively. Both nations could use the state to sponsor changes that, in the West, had rested in part with private businesses. At the same time, change took distinctive directions in each society. Russia's road to industrialization reflected its authoritarian traditions: It was marked by political repression and harsh conditions for workers that undercut social stability. Meanwhile, Japan's long experience with cultural adaptation in the face of change helped it manage the same transition from a feudal to an industrial society while retaining a great deal of political and social cohesion. Industrialization outside the West complicated economic power relationships, but it also illustrated the growing roles of global capitalism and the new forms of integrating capital and labor.

1700 C.E.	1800 C.E.	1825 C.E.	1850 C.E.	1875 C.E.	1900 C.E.
1720 End ban on Western books in Japan	**1800–1850** Growth of "Dutch Studies" in Japan	**1825** Decembrist Revolt, Russia	**1853** Perry expedition to Edo Bay	**1875–1877** Russian–Ottoman War; Russia wins new territory	**1902** Loose alliance between Japan and Britain
1762–1796 Reign of Catherine the Great	**1812** Failure of Napoleon's invasion of Russia	**1825–1855** Heightening of repression by Tsar Nicholas I	**1854** Follow-up American and British fleet visit	**1877** Final samurai rising	**1904–1905** Russo-Japanese War; Japan defeats Russia
1773–1775 Pugachev Rebellion	**1815** Russia reacquires Poland through Treaty of Vienna; Alexander I and the Holy Alliance	**1829–1878** Serbia gains increasing autonomy in Ottoman empire, then independence	**1854–1856** Crimean War	**1878** Bulgaria gains independence	**1905–1906** Russian Revolution results in peasant reforms and Duma (parliament)
1772–1795 Partitioning of Poland		**1830–1831** Polish nationalist revolt repressed	**1856** Romania gains virtual independence	**1881** Anarchist assassination of Alexander II	**1910** Japan annexes Korea
		1831 Greece wins independence after revolt against Ottomans	**1860–1868** Civil strife in Russia	**1881–1905** Growing repression and attacks on minorities in Russia	**1912** Growing party strife in Russian Duma
		1833, 1853 Russian–Ottoman wars	**1860s–1870s** Alexander II reforms	**1884–1887** New Russian gains in central Asia	**1912–1918** Balkan Wars
		1841–1843 Brief shogun reform effort	**1861** Russian emancipation of serfs	**1884–1914** Beginnings of Russian industrialization; near-completion of trans-Siberian railway (full linkage 1916)	**1914** World War I begins
			1865–1879 Russian conquests in central Asia		**1916–1918** Japan seizes former German holdings in Pacific and China
			1867 Mutsuhito, emperor of Japan		**1917** Russian Revolution leads to Bolshevik victory
			1867 Russia sells Alaska to United States	**1890** New constitution and legal code	
			1868–1912 Meiji period in Japan	**1892–1903** Sergei Witte, Minister of Finance	
			1870 Ministry of Industry established in Japan	**1894–1895** Sino-Japanese War	
			1870–1940 Population growth in Russia	**1898** Formation of Marxist Social Democratic Party, Russia	
			1872 Universal military service established in Russia		
			1872 Education Act, Japan		

RUSSIA'S REFORMS AND INDUSTRIAL ADVANCE

28.1 How did Russian reforms help spur initial industrialization?

> Before 1861, Russia stood out among European powers by the extent of its political conservatism. The nation's reform period began in 1861 with the emancipation of the serfs. Russian leaders tried to combine change with continued tsarist autocracy.

Russian rulers, beginning with Catherine the Great in her later years, sought ways to protect the country from the contagion of the French Revolution. The sense that Western policies might serve as models for Russia faded dramatically. Napoleon's 1812 invasion of Russia also led to a new concern with defense. Conservative intellectuals supported the move toward renewed isolation. In the eyes of these aristocratic writers, Russia knew the true meaning of community and stability. The system of serfdom provided ignorant peasants with the guidance and protection of paternalistic masters—an inaccurate social analysis but a comforting one.

Russia before Reform

Russia was hardly changeless. To resist Napoleon's pressure early in the 19th century, the government introduced some improvements in bureaucratic training. A new tsar, Alexander I, flirted with liberal rhetoric, but at the Congress of Vienna he sponsored the **Holy Alliance** idea. In this alliance, the conservative monarchies of Russia, Prussia, and Austria would combine in defense of religion and the established order. The idea of Russia as a bastion of sanity in a Europe gone mad was appealing, although in fact the alliance itself accomplished little.

Defending the status quo produced some important new tensions, however. Many intellectuals remained fascinated with Western progress. Some praised political freedom and educational and scientific advance. Others focused more purely on Western cultural styles. Early in the 19th century, Russia began to contribute creatively to Europe's cultural output. The poet Pushkin, for example, descended from an African slave, used romantic styles to celebrate the beauties of the Russian soul and the tragic dignity of the common people. Because of its compatibility with the use of folklore and a sense of nationalism, the romantic style took deep root in eastern Europe. Russian musical composers would soon make their contributions, again using folk themes and sonorous sentimentality within a Western stylistic context.

Holy Alliance Alliance among Russia, Prussia, and Austria in defense of religion and the established order; formed at Congress of Vienna by most conservative monarchies of Europe.

While Russia's ruling elite continued to welcome Western artistic styles and took great pride in Russia's growing cultural respectability, they increasingly censored intellectuals who tried to incorporate liberal or radical political values. A revolt of Western-oriented army officers in 1825—the **Decembrist uprising**—inspired the new tsar, Nicholas I, to still more adamant conservatism. The uprising, urging reform of tsarist autocracy, showed that liberal values had spread to elements of the Russian elite, but its failure was more significant. Repression of political opponents stiffened, and the secret police expanded. Newspapers and schools, already confined to a small minority, were tightly supervised. What political criticism there was flourished mainly in exile in places such as Paris and London; it had little impact on Russia.

Decembrist uprising Political revolt in Russia in 1825; led by middle-level army officers who advocated reforms; put down by Tsar Nicholas I.

Partly because of political repression, Russia largely avoided the wave of revolutions that spread through Europe in 1830 and in 1848. In its role as Europe's conservative anchor, Russia even intervened in 1849 to help Austria put down the nationalist revolution in Hungary—a blow in favor of monarchy but also a reminder of Russia's eagerness to flex its muscles in wider European affairs.

While turning more conservative than it had been in the 18th century, Russia maintained its tradition of territorial expansion. Russia had confirmed its hold over most of Poland at the Congress of Vienna in 1815 after Napoleon briefly sponsored a separate Polish duchy. Nationalist sentiment, inspired by the growth of romantic nationalism in Poland and backed by many Polish landowners with ties to western Europe, roused recurrent Polish opposition to Russian rule. An uprising occurred in 1830 and 1831, triggered by news of the revolutions in the West and led by liberal aristocrats and loyal Catholics who chafed under the rule of an Orthodox power. Tsar Nicholas I put down this revolt with great brutality, driving many leaders into exile.

At the same time, Russia continued its pressure on the Ottoman empire, whose weakness attracted their eager attention. A war in the 1830s led to some territorial gains. France and Britain repeatedly tried to prop up Ottoman authority in the interest of countering Russian aggression. Russia also supported many nationalist movements in the Balkans, including the Greek independence war in the 1820s; here, a desire to cut back the Turks outweighed Russia's commitment to conservatism. Overall, although no massive acquisitions marked the early 19th century, Russia continued to be a dynamic diplomatic and military force (Map 28.1).

Economic and Social Problems: The Peasant Question

Russia's economic position did not keep pace with its diplomatic aspirations. As the West industrialized and central European powers such as Prussia and Austria introduced at least the beginnings of industrialization, including some rail lines, Russia largely stood pat. This meant that it began to fall increasingly behind the West in technology and trade. Russian landlords eagerly took advantage of Western markets for grain, but they increased their exports not by improving their techniques but by tightening the labor obligations on their serfs. This was a common pattern in much of eastern Europe in the early 19th century, as Polish and Hungarian nobles also increased labor service to gain ground in the export market. In return for low-cost grain exports, Russia and other east European areas imported some Western machinery and other costly equipment as well as luxury goods for

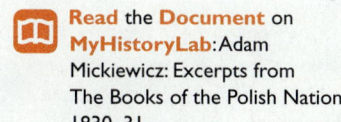

Read the Document on MyHistoryLab: Adam Mickiewicz: Excerpts from The Books of the Polish Nation 1830–31

View the Image on MyHistoryLab: The Clemency of the Russian Monster—British Cartoon, 1832

MAP 28.1 **Russian Expansion, 1815–1914** Russia continued to push to the west, south, and east. At first, its main conflicts were with the Ottoman empire. Later, however, conflicts in east Asia loomed larger.

Crimean War Fought between 1854 and 1856; began as Russian attempt to attack Ottoman empire; Russia opposed by France and Britain as well; resulted in Russian defeat in the face of western industrial technology; led to Russian reforms under Tsar Alexander II.

the great aristocrats to display as badges of cultured respectability. A few isolated factories that used foreign equipment were opened up in imitation of western European industrialization, but there was no significant change in overall manufacturing or transportation mechanisms. Russia remained a profoundly agricultural society based mainly on serf labor, but it was now a visibly stagnant society as well.

The widening gap between Russia and the West was driven home dramatically by a minor war in the Crimea between 1854 and 1856. Nicholas I provoked conflict with the Ottoman empire in 1853, arguing among other things that Russia was responsible for protecting Christian interests in the Holy Land. This time, however, France and Britain were not content with diplomatic maneuverings to limit Russian gains but came directly to the sultan's aid. Britain was increasingly worried about any great power advance in the region that might threaten its hold on India, whereas France sought diplomatic glory and also represented itself as the Western champion of Christian rights. The resultant **Crimean War** was fought directly in Russia's backyard on the Black Sea, yet the Western forces won, driving the Russian armies from their entrenched positions. (Each side lost about 250,000 troops in a truly difficult struggle.) The loss was profoundly disturbing to Russian leadership, for the Western powers won this little war not because of great tactics or inspired principles but because of their industrial advantage. They had the ships to send masses of military supplies long distances, and their artillery and other weapons were vastly superior to Russia's home-produced models. This severe blow to a regime that prided itself on military vigor was a frightening portent for the future.

The Crimean War helped convince Russian leaders, including the new tsar, Alexander II, that it was time for a change. Reform was essential, not to copy the West but to allow sufficient economic adjustments for Russia to keep pace in the military arena. First and foremost, reform meant some resolution of Russia's leading social issue, the issue that most distinguished Russian society from that of the West: serfdom. Only if the status of serfs changed could Russia develop a more vigorous and mobile labor force and so be able to industrialize. Russian concern about this issue paralleled the attacks on slavery in the Americas in the same period, reflecting a desire to meet Western humanitarian standards and a need for cheap, flexible labor.

So for two decades Russia returned to a policy of reform, based on Western standards and examples; serfdom had been abolished in western Europe after 1789 and in east central regions such as Prussia and Hungary in the aftermath of the revolutions of 1848. As before, however, the intention was not to duplicate Western measures fully but to protect distinctive Russian institutions, including the landed aristocracy and tightly knit peasant communities. The result was an important series of changes that, with tragic irony, created more grievances than they resolved while opening the way to further economic change.

View the Closer Look on MyHistoryLab: The Crimean War Recalled

emancipation of the serfs Tsar Alexander II ended rigorous serfdom in Russia in 1861; serfs obtained no political rights; were required to stay in villages until they could repay aristocracy for land.

The Reform Era and Early Industrialization

The final decision to emancipate the serfs in 1861 came at roughly the same time that the United States and Brazil decided to free slaves. Neither slavery nor rigorous serfdom suited the economic needs of a society seeking an independent position in Western-dominated world trade. While Russian reformers had specific concerns, some of them also accepted new humanitarian ideals now spreading globally, that attacked systems of unfree labor.

In some ways, the **emancipation of the serfs** was more generous than the liberation of slaves in the Americas. Although aristocrats retained part of the land, including the most fertile holdings, the serfs got most of it, in contrast to slaves, who received their freedom but nothing else. However, Russian emancipation was careful to preserve essential aristocratic power; the tsar was not interested in destroying the nobility, who remained his most reliable political allies and the source of most bureaucrats. Even more, emancipation was designed to retain the tight grip of the tsarist state. The serfs obtained no new political rights at a national level. They were still tied to their villages until they could pay for the land they were given. The redemption money went to the aristocrats to help preserve this class. Redemption payments added greatly to peasants' material hardship (Figure 28.2), and peasants thought that the land belonged to them with no need to pay for its return.

Emancipation did bring change; it helped create a larger urban labor force. But it did not spur a revolution in agricultural productivity because most peasants continued to use traditional methods on their small plots. And it did not bring contentment. Indeed, peasant uprisings became more common as hopes for a brighter future seemed dashed by the limits of change. Explosive rural unrest in Russia was furthered by substantial population growth as some of the factors that had earlier swelled the West's population now spread to Russia, including increased use of the potato. In sum, after 1861 Russia was a classic case of a society in the midst of rapid change where reform did not go far enough to satisfy key protest groups.

To be sure, the reform movement did not end with emancipation. Alexander II introduced a host of further measures in the 1860s and early 1870s. New law codes cut back the traditional punishments now that serfs were legally free in the eyes of the law (though subject to important transitional

Read the Document on MyHistoryLab: Emancipation Manifesto (1861)

FIGURE 28.2 This late 19th-century roadside scene depicts the poverty of a Russian peasant village. What forces produced such poor conditions, even after serfdom had been abolished?

zemstvoes [ZEHMST-vohs] Local political councils created as part of reforms of Tsar Alexander II (1860s); gave some Russians, particularly middle-class professionals, some experience in government; councils had no impact on national policy.

restrictions). The tsar created local political councils, the **zemstvoes**, which had a voice in regulating roads, schools, and other regional policies. Some form of local government was essential now that the nobles no longer directly ruled the peasantry. The zemstvoes gave some Russians, particularly middle-class people such as doctors and lawyers, new political experience, and they undertook important inquiries into local problems. However, the councils had no influence on national policy; the tsar resolutely maintained his own authority and that of his extensive bureaucracy. Another important area of change was the army; the Crimean War had shown the need for reform. The officer corps was improved through promotion by merit and a new organization of essential services. Recruitment was extended, and many peasants learned new skills through their military service. Some strides also were made in providing state-sponsored basic education, although schools spread unevenly.

From the reform era onward, literacy increased rapidly in Russian society. A new market developed for popular reading matter that had some similarities to the mass reading culture developing in the West. Interestingly, Russian potboiler novels, displaying a pronounced taste for excitement and exotic adventure, also attested to distinctive values. For example, Russian "bad guys" never were glorified in the end but always were either returned to social loyalty or condemned—a clear sign of the limits to individualism. Women gained new positions in this climate of change. Some won access to higher education, and, as in the West, a minority of women mainly from the upper classes began to penetrate professions such as medicine. Even sexual habits began to change, as had occurred in the West a century earlier. Fathers' control over their children's behavior loosened a bit, particularly where nonagricultural jobs were available, and sexual activity before marriage increased.

The move toward industrialization was part of the wider process of change. State support was an industrial effort, because Russia lacked a preexisting middle class and capital. State enterprises had to make up part of the gap, in the tradition of economic activity that went back to Peter the Great.

Russia began to create an extensive railroad network in the 1870s. The establishment of the **trans-Siberian railroad**, which connected European Russia with the Pacific, was the crowning achievement of this drive when it was nearly completed by the end of the 1880s. The railroad boom directly stimulated expansion of Russia's iron and coal sectors. Railroad development also stimulated the export of grain to the West, which earned foreign currency needed to pay for advanced Western machinery. The railroads also opened Siberia up to new development, which in turn brought Russia into a more active and contested Asian role.

trans-Siberian railroad Constructed in 1870s to connect European Russia with the Pacific; completed by the end of the 1880s; brought Russia into a more active Asian role.

DOCUMENT

Conditions for Factory Workers in Russia's Industrialization

RUSSIA PASSED SEVERAL LAWS PROTECTING WORKERS, but enforcement was minimal. The Ministry of Finance established a factory inspectorate in the 1880s, which dutifully reported on conditions; these reports usually were ignored. The following passages deal with a number of Moscow factories in the 1880s.

> In the majority of factories there are no special quarters for the workers. This applies to workers in paper, wool, and silk finishing. Skilled hand craftsmen like brocade weavers can earn good wages, and yet most of them sleep on or under their looms, for lack of anything else. Only in a few weaving factories are there special sleeping quarters, and these are provided not for the weavers, but for other workers—the winders and dyers, etc. Likewise, the velveteen cutters almost always sleep on the tables where they work. This habit is particularly unhealthy, since the work areas are always musty and the air is saturated with dye fumes—sometimes poisonous ones. Carpenters also generally sleep on their workbenches. In bastmatting factories, workers of both sexes and all ages sleep together on pieces and mats of bast which are often damp. Only the sick workers in these bast factories are allowed to sleep on the single stove.... Work at the mill never stops, day or night. There are two twelve-hour shifts a day, which begin at 6:00 A.M. and 6:00 P.M. The men have a half-hour for breakfast (8:30–9:00) and one hour for dinner (1:00–2:00).
>
> The worst violations of hygienic regulations were those I saw in most of the flax-spinning mills where linen is produced.... Although in western Europe all the dust-producing carding and combing machines have long been covered and well ventilated, I saw only one Russian linen mill where such a machine was securely covered. Elsewhere, the spools of these machines were completely open to the air, and the scutching apparatus is inadequately ventilated....
>
> In many industrial establishments the grounds for fines and the sizes of fines are not fixed in advance. The factory rules may

(continued on next page)

contain only one phrase like the following: "Those found violating company rules will be fined *at the discretion of the manager*."

The degree of arbitrariness in the determination of fines, and thus also in the determination of the worker's wages, was unbelievably extreme in some factories. In Podolsk, for instance, in factories No. 131 and No. 135, there is a ten-ruble forfeit for leaving the factory before the expiration of one's contract. But as applied, this covers much more than voluntary breach of contract on the worker's part. This fine is exacted from every worker who for any reason has to leave the factory. Cases are known of persons who have had to pay this fine three times. Moreover, fines are levied for so many causes that falling under a severe fine is a constant possibility for each worker. For instance, workers who for any reason came into the office in a group, instead of singly, would be fined one ruble. After a second offense, the transgressors would be dismissed—leaving behind, of course, the ten-ruble fine for breach of contract.

In factory No. 135 the workers are still treated as serfs. Wages are paid out only twice a year, even then not in full but only enough to pay the workers' taxes (other necessities are supplied by the factory store). Furthermore this money is not given to the workers directly, but is sent by mail to their village elders and village clerks. Thus the workers are without money the year around. Besides they are also paying severe fines to the factory, and these sums will be subtracted from their wages at the final year-end accounting.

Extreme regulations and regimentation are very common in our factories—regulations entangle the workers at every step and burden them with more or less severe fines which are subtracted from their often already inadequate wages. Some factory administrators have become real virtuosos at thinking up new grounds for fines. A brief description of a few of the fines in factory No. 172 is an excellent example of this variety: on October 24, 1877, an announcement was posted of new fines to be set at the discretion of the office for fourteen different cases of failure to maintain silence and cleanliness. There were also dozens of minor fines prescribed for certain individual offenses: for example, on August 4, 1883, a huge fine of five rubles was set for singing in the factory courtyard after 9:30, or at any time in any unauthorized place. On June 3, 1881, a fine was to be levied from workers who took tea and sugar, bread, or any kind of foodstuffs into the weaving building, "in order to avoid breeding any insects or vermin." On May 14, 1880, a fine was set for anyone who wrote with pencil, chalk, or anything else on the walls in the dyeing or weaving buildings.

QUESTIONS

- Were factory conditions worse than in western Europe during early industrialization, and if so in what ways and why?
- How did working conditions and management attitudes help create a revolutionary mood among Russian workers?
- Think also about the nature of this source. Why would a conservative government sponsor such a critical report?
- What do you think the results of such a report would be, in the Russian context, or indeed in any early industrial context?

By the 1880s, when Russia's railroad network had almost quintupled since 1860, modern factories were beginning to spring up in Moscow, St. Petersburg, and several Polish cities, and an urban working class was growing rapidly. Printing factories and metalworking shops expanded the skilled artisanry in the cities, and metallurgy and textile plants recruited a still newer semiskilled industrial labor force from the troubled countryside.

Under Count **Sergei Witte**, minister of finance from 1892 to 1903 and an ardent economic modernizer, the government enacted high tariffs to protect new Russian industry, improved its banking system, and encouraged Western investors to build great factories with advanced technology. As Witte put it, "The inflow of foreign capital is . . . the only way by which our industry will be able to supply our country quickly with abundant and cheap products." By 1900 approximately half of Russian industry was foreign owned and much of it was foreign operated, with British, German, and French industrialists taking the lead. Russia became a debtor nation as huge industrial development loans piled up. Russia had surged to rank fourth in the world in steel production and was second to the United States in the newer area of petroleum production and refining. Russian textile output was also impressive. Long-standing Russian economic lags were beginning to yield.

This industrial revolution was still in its early stages. Russia's world rank was a function more of its great size and population, along with its rich natural resources, than of thorough mechanization. Many Russian factories were not up to Western technical standards, nor was the labor force highly trained. Agriculture also remained backward, as peasants, often illiterate, had neither capital nor motives to change their ways.

Other reforms also produced ambiguous results. Russia remained a traditional peasant society in many ways. Beneath the official military reorganization, discipline and military efficiency were lax. Even more obvious was the absence of a large, self-confident middle class of the sort that had arisen earlier in the West. Businesspeople and professionals grew in numbers, but often they were

Witte, Sergei [vit uh] Russian minister of finance from 1892 to 1903; economic modernizer responsible for high tariffs, improved banking system; encouraged Western investors to build factories in Russia.

dependent on state initiatives, such as zemstvo employment for doctors and economic guidance for businesspeople. They were not as assertive as their Western counterparts had been (for example, in challenging aristocratic power and values).

PROTEST AND REVOLUTION IN RUSSIA

28.2 Why did revolutionary potential grow in Russia?

> Change and also the limits of change destabilized Russian society. Marxist leaders helped focus unrest.

Alexander II's reforms, as well as economic change and the greater population mobility it involved, encouraged minority nationalities to make demands of the great empire. Intellectuals explored the cultural traditions of Ukrainians and other groups. Nationalist beliefs initially were imported from western Europe, but here and elsewhere in eastern Europe, they encouraged divisive minority agitation that multinational states, such as Russia and Austria–Hungary, found very hard to handle. Nationalist pressures were not the main problem in Russia, but given Russia's mainstream nationalist insistence on the distinctive superiorities of a Russian tradition, they did cause concern.

Social protest was more vigorous still, and it was heightened not only by the limitations of reform but by industrialization itself. Recurrent famines provoked peasant uprisings. Peasants deeply resented redemption payments and taxes and often seized and burned the records that indicated what they owed.

The Road to Revolution

Along with discontent among the masses, many educated Russians, including some aristocrats, also clamored for revolutionary change. Two strands developed. Many business and professional people, although not very aggressive, began to seek a fuller political voice and new rights such as greater freedom in the schools and press; they argued for liberal reforms. At the same time, a group of radical **intelligentsia**—a Russian term for articulate intellectuals as a class—became increasingly active. As Russian universities expanded, student groups grew as well, and many were impatient with Russia's slow development and with the visible restrictions on political activity. Women students played some role in the protest current, and some specifically feminist demands (for example, toward greater professional opportunity) emerged as well.

intelligentsia [in teli jent sEE uh, gent-] Russian term denoting articulate intellectuals as a class; 19th-century group bent on radical change in Russian political and social system; often wished to maintain a Russian culture distinct from that of the West.

Some intellectuals later toned down their goals as they entered the bureaucracy or business life. But many remained inspired by radical doctrines, and more than a few devoted their lives to a revolutionary cause. This kind of intellectual alienation rested on some of the principles that had roused intellectuals in the West, but it went deeper in Russia. It was the first example of a kind of intellectual radicalism, capable of motivating terrorism, that would characterize other societies caught in tense transitions during the 20th century. The Russian intelligentsia wanted political freedom and deep social reform while maintaining a Russian culture different from that of the West, which they saw as hopelessly materialistic. Their radicalism may have stemmed from the demanding task they set themselves: attacking key Russian institutions while building a new society that would not reproduce the injustices and crippling limitations of the Western world.

anarchists Political groups seeking abolition of all formal government; formed in many parts of Europe and Americas in late 19th and early 20th centuries; particularly prevalent in Russia, opposing tsarist autocracy and becoming a terrorist movement responsible for assassination of Alexander II in 1881.

Many Russian radicals were **anarchists**, who sought to abolish all formal government. Although anarchism was not unknown in the West, it took on particular force in Russia in opposition to tsarist autocracy. Many early anarchists in the 1860s hoped that they could triumph by winning peasant support, and a host of upper-class radicals fanned out to teach the peasantry the beauties of political activism. Failure here led many anarchists to violent methods and thus to the formation of the first large terrorist movement in the modern world. Given the lack of popular support and other political outlets, assassinations and bombings seemed the only way to attack the existing order. Anarchist leader Bakunin argued that general destruction was the only real goal. He hoped for a peasant revolution, but wanted no part of reformist efforts to improve conditions of life in advance of the replacement of current social and political structures. Simply tearing down the current framework was such a huge task that there was no way, at this point, to plan what would come next.

670 PART V The Dawn of the Industrial Age, 1750–1900

Not surprisingly, the recurrent waves of terrorism merely strengthened the tsarist regime's resolve to avoid further political change in what became a vicious circle in 19th-century Russian politics.

By the late 1870s, Alexander II was pulling back from his reform interest, fearing that change was getting out of hand. Censorship of newspapers and political meetings tightened; many dissidents were arrested and sent to Siberia. Alexander II was assassinated by a terrorist bomb in 1881 after a series of botched attempts. His successors, while increasing the effort to industrialize, continued to oppose further political reform. New measures of repression also were directed against minority nationalities, partly to dampen their unrest and partly to gain the support of upper-class conservatives. The Poles and other groups were supervised carefully. Russian language instruction was forced on peoples such as Ukrainians. Persecution of the large Jewish minority was stepped up, resulting in many mass attacks—called pogroms—and seizures of property. As a consequence, many Russian Jews emigrated.

By the 1890s, the currents of protest gained new force. Marxist doctrines spread from the Western socialist movement to a segment of the Russian intelligentsia, who became committed to a tightly organized proletarian revolution. One of the most active Marxist leaders was **Vladimir Ilyich Ulyanov**, known as Lenin. Lenin, a man from a bureaucratic family whose brother was hanged after a trial following his arrest by the political police, introduced important innovations in Marxist theory to make it more appropriate for Russia. He argued that because of the spread of international capitalism, a proletariat was developing worldwide in advance of industrialization. Therefore, Russia could have a proletarian revolution without going through a distinct middle-class phase. Lenin also insisted on the importance of disciplined revolutionary cells that could maintain doctrinal purity and effective action even under severe police repression. Lenin's approach animated the group of Russian Marxists known as **Bolsheviks**, or majority party (although, ironically, they were actually a minority in the Russian Marxist movement as a whole). The approach proved ideal for Russian conditions.

Working-class unrest in the cities grew with the new currents among the intelligentsia. Russian workers became far more radical than their Western counterparts. They formed unions and conducted strikes—all illegal—but many of them also had firm political goals in mind. Their radicalism stemmed partly from the absence of legal political outlets. It arose also from rural unrest—for these new workers pulled in peasant grievances against the existing order—and from the severe conditions of early industrialization, with its large factories and frequent foreign ownership. Although many workers were not linked to any particular doctrine, some became interested in Bolshevism, and they were urged on by passionate organizers.

By 1900 the contradictory currents in Russian society may have made revolution inevitable. The forces demanding change were not united, but the importance of mass protest in both countryside and city, as well as among the radical intelligentsia, made it difficult to find a compromise. Furthermore, the regime remained resolutely opposed to compromise. Conservative ministers urged a vigorous policy of resistance and repression.

The Revolution of 1905

Military defeat in 1904 and 1905 finally lit this tinderbox. Russia had maintained its expansionist foreign policy through the late 19th century, in part because of tradition and in part because diplomatic success might draw the venom from internal unrest. It also wanted to match the imperialist strides of the Western great powers. A war with the Ottoman empire in the 1870s brought substantial gains, which were then pushed back at the insistence of France and Britain. Russia also successfully aided the creation in the Balkans of new Slavic nations, such as Serbia and Bulgaria, the "little Slavic brothers" that filled nationalist hearts with pride. Some conservative writers even talked in terms of a pan-Slavic movement that would unite the Slavic people—under Russian leadership, of course. Russia participated vigorously in other Middle Eastern and central Asian areas. Russia and Britain both increased their influence in Persia and Afghanistan, reaching some uneasy truces that divided spheres of activity early in the 20th century. Russia was also active in China. The development of the trans-Siberian railroad encouraged Russia to incorporate some northern portions of Manchuria, violating the 18th-century Amur River agreement. Russia also joined Western powers in obtaining long-term leases to Chinese territory during the 1890s.

Ulyanov, Vladimir Ilyich [VLAHD-ih-mihr IHL-lihch ool-YAH-nuhf] Better known as Lenin; most active Russian Marxist leader; insisted on importance of disciplined revolutionary cells; leader of Bolshevik Revolution of 1917.

Bolsheviks Literally, the majority party; the most radical branch of the Russian Marxist movement; led by V. I. Lenin and dedicated to his concept of social revolution; actually a minority in the Russian Marxist political scheme until its triumph in the 1917 revolution.

Read the Document on MyHistoryLab: Working Conditions of Women in the Factories (early 20th c.) M. I. Pokrovskaia

Russo-Japanese War War between Japan and Russia (1904–1905) over territory in Manchuria; Japan defeated the Russians, largely because of its naval power; Japan annexed Korea in 1910 as a result of military dominance.

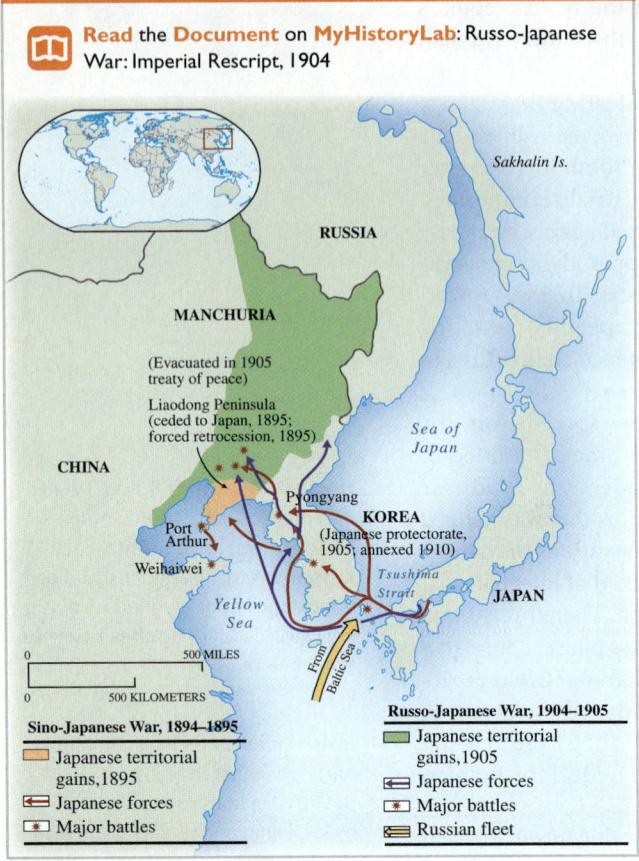

Read the Document on MyHistoryLab: Russo-Japanese War: Imperial Rescript, 1904

MAP 28.2 **The Russo-Japanese War** The Russo-Japanese war focused on disputes over Chinese territory. Japan had acquired the Liaodong peninsula after its victory over China, but Russia and others forced it out and then maneuvered for territory of their own. Japan proposed a split of Manchuria but assumed negotiations would fail, and so attacked the Russian fleet at Port Arthur, and later won over Russian armies in China as well. A Russian fleet sent from the Baltic was humiliated at Tsushima Strait, which effectively ended the war.

Duma National parliament created in Russia in the aftermath of the Revolution of 1905; progressively stripped of power during the reign of Tsar Nicholas II; failed to forestall further revolution.

Stolypin reforms Reforms introduced by the Russian interior minister Piotr Stolypin intended to placate the peasantry in the aftermath of the Revolution of 1905; included reduction in redemption payments, attempt to create market-oriented peasantry.

kulaks [KOO-laks] Agricultural entrepreneurs who utilized the Stolypin and later NEP reforms to increase agricultural production and buy additional land.

These were important gains, but they did not satisfy growing Russian ambitions, and they also brought trouble. Russia risked an overextension because its diplomatic aspirations were not backed by real increases in military power. The problem first came to a head in 1904. Increasingly powerful Japan became worried about further Russian expansion in northern China and efforts to extend influence into Korea. The **Russo-Japanese War** broke out in 1904. Against all expectations save Japan's, the Japanese won. Russia could not move its fleet quickly to the Pacific, and its military organization proved too cumbersome to oppose the more effective Japanese maneuvers (Map 28.2). Japan gained the opportunity to move into Korea as the balance of power in the Far East began to shift.

Unexpected defeat in war unleashed massive protests on the home front in the Russian Revolution of 1905 (Figure 28.3). Urban workers mounted well-organized general strikes that were designed above all for political gains. Peasants led a series of insurrections, and liberal groups also agitated. After trying brutal police repression, which only infuriated the urban crowds, the tsarist regime had to change course. It wooed liberals by creating a national parliament, the **Duma**. The interior minister Piotr Stolypin (pee-UH-tuhr STOHL-yuh-pihn) introduced an important series of reforms for the peasantry. Under the **Stolypin reforms**, peasants gained greater freedom from redemption payments and village controls. They could buy and sell land more freely. The goal was to create a stratified, market-oriented peasantry in which successful farmers would move away from the peasant masses, becoming rural capitalists. Indeed, peasant unrest did die down, and a minority of aggressive entrepreneurs, called **kulaks**, began to increase agricultural production and buy additional land. Yet the reform package quickly came unglued. Not only were a few new workers' rights withdrawn, triggering a new series of strikes and underground activities, but the Duma was progressively stripped of power. Nicholas II, a weak man who was badly advised, could not surrender the tradition of autocratic rule, and the Duma became a hollow institution, satisfying no one. Police repression also resumed, creating new opponents to the regime.

Pressed in the diplomatic arena by the Japanese advance yet eager to counter internal pressures with some foreign policy success, the Russian government turned once again to the Ottoman empire and the Balkans. Various strategies to acquire new rights of access to the Mediterranean and to back Slavic allies in the Balkans yielded no concrete results, but they did stir the pot in this vulnerable area and helped lead to World War I. And this war, in which Russia participated to maintain its diplomatic standing and live up to the billing of Slavic protector, led to one of the great revolutions of modern times.

Russia and Eastern Europe

A number of Russian patterns were paralleled in smaller eastern European states such as Hungary (joined to Austria but autonomous after 1866), Romania, Serbia, Bulgaria, and Greece. These were new nations—unlike Russia. And emerging after long Ottoman dominance, they had no access to the diplomatic influence of their giant neighbor. Most of the new nations established parliaments, in imitation of Western forms, but carefully restricted voting rights and parliamentary powers. Kings—some of them new, as the Balkan nations had set up monarchies after gaining independence from the Ottoman empire—ruled without many limits on their power. Most eastern European nations abolished serfdom either in 1848 or soon after Russia's move, but landlord power remained more extensive than in Russia, and peasant unrest followed. Most of the smaller eastern European nations industrialized much less extensively than Russia, and as agricultural exporters they remained far more dependent on Western markets.

Amid all the problems, eastern Europe enjoyed a period of glittering cultural productivity in the late 19th century, with Russia in the lead. Development of the romantic tradition and other Western styles continued. National dictionaries and histories, along with the collection of folktales and music,

View the Closer Look on MyHistoryLab: Bloody Sunday, St. Petersburg, 1905

FIGURE 28.3 Women marching in the Russian Revolution of 1905.

helped the smaller Slavic nations gain a sense of their heritage. The Russian novel enjoyed a period of unprecedented brilliance. Westernizers such as Turgenev wrote realistic novels that promoted what they saw as modern values, whereas writers such as Tolstoy and Dostoevsky tried to portray a special Russian spirit. Russian music moved from the romanticism of Tchaikovsky to more innovative, atonal styles of the early 20th century. Polish and Hungarian composers such as Chopin and Liszt also made an important mark. Russian painters began participating in modern art currents, producing important abstract work. Finally, scientific research advanced at levels of fundamental importance. A Czech scientist, Gregor Mendel, furthered the understanding of genetics, and a Russian physiologist, Ivan Pavlov, experimenting on conditioned reflexes, explained unconscious responses in human beings. Eastern Europe thus participated more fully than ever before in a cultural world it shared with the West.

JAPAN: TRANSFORMATION WITHOUT REVOLUTION

28.3 How did Meiji Japan combine fundamental change with a continuing Japanese identity?

On the surface, Japan experienced little change during the first half of the 19th century, and certainly this was a quiet time compared with the earlier establishment of the Tokugawa shogunate (see Chapter 23) or the transformation introduced after the 1850s.

Western pressure forced Japan to consider reforms beginning in the 1850s. Japan was able to combine existing strengths and traditions with significant reform.

The Final Decades of the Shogunate

During the first half of the 19th century, the shogunate continued to combine a central bureaucracy with semifeudal alliances between the regional lords, the daimyo, and the military samurai. The government repeatedly ran into financial problems. Its taxes were based on agriculture, despite the growing commercialization of the Japanese economy; this was a severe constraint. At the same time, maintaining the feudal shell was costly. The government paid stipends to the samurai in return for their loyalty. A long budget reform spurt late in the 18th century built a successful momentum for a time, but a shorter effort between 1841 and 1843 was notably unsuccessful. This weakened the shogunate by the 1850s and hampered its response to the crisis induced by Western pressure.

terakoya Commoner schools founded during the Tokugawa Shogunate in Japan to teach reading, writing, and the rudiments of Confucianism; resulted in high literacy rate, approaching 40 percent, of Japanese males.

Dutch Studies Group of Japanese scholars interested in implications of Western science and technology beginning in the 17th century; urged freer exchange with West; based studies on few Dutch texts available in Japan.

Japanese intellectual life and culture also developed under the Tokugawa regime. Neo-Confucianism continued to gain among the ruling elite at the expense of Buddhism. Japan gradually became more secular, particularly among the upper classes. This was an important precondition for the nation's response to the Western challenge in that it precluded a strong religious-based resistance to change. Various Confucian schools actively debated into the mid-19th century, keeping Japanese intellectual life fairly creative. Schools and academies expanded, reaching well below the upper class through commoner schools, or **terakoya**, which taught reading, writing, and the rudiments of Confucianism to ordinary people. By 1859 more than 40 percent of all men and over 15 percent of all women were literate—a far higher percentage than anywhere else in the world outside the West, including Russia, and on a par with some of the fringe areas of the West (including the American South).

Although Confucianism remained the dominant ideology, there were important rivals. Tensions between traditionalists and reformist intellectuals were emerging, as in Russia in the same decades. A national studies group praised Japanese traditions, including the office of emperor and the Shinto religion. One national studies writer expressed a typical sentiment late in the 18th century: "The 'special dispensation of our Imperial Land' means that ours is the native land of the Heaven-Shining Goddess who casts her light over all countries in the four seas. Thus our country is the source and fountainhead of all other countries, and in all matters it excels all the others." The influence of the national studies school grew somewhat in the early 19th century, and it would help inspire ultranationalist sentiment at the end of the century and beyond.

A second minority group consisted of what the Japanese called **Dutch Studies**. Although major Western works had been banned when the policy of isolation was adopted, a group of Japanese translators kept alive the knowledge of Dutch to deal with the traders at Nagasaki. The ban on Western books was ended in 1720, and thereafter a group of Japanese scholars interested in "Dutch medicine" created a new interest in Western scientific advances, based on the realization that Western anatomy texts were superior to those of the Chinese. In 1850, there were schools of Dutch Studies in all major cities, and their students urged freer exchange with the West and a rejection of Chinese medicine and culture. "Our general opinion was that we should rid our country of the influences of the Chinese altogether. Whenever we met a young student of Chinese literature, we simply felt sorry for him."

Just as Japanese culture showed an important capacity for lively debate and fruitful internal tension, so the Japanese economy continued to develop into the 19th century. Commerce expanded as big merchant companies established monopoly privileges in many centers. Manufacturing gained ground in the countryside in such consumer goods industries as soy sauce and silks, and much of this was organized by city merchants. Some of these developments were comparable to slightly earlier changes in the West and have given rise to arguments that economically Japan had a running start on industrialization once the Western challenge revealed the necessity of further economic change.

By the 1850s, however, economic growth had slowed—a situation that has prompted some scholars to stress Japan's backwardness compared with the West. Technological limitations constrained agricultural expansion and population increase. At the same time, rural riots increased in many regions from the late 18th century onward. They were not overtly political but rather, like many rural protests, aimed at wealthy peasants, merchants, and landlord controls. Although the authorities put down this unrest with little difficulty, the protests contributed to a willingness to consider change when they were joined by challenge from the outside.

The Challenge to Isolation

Some Japanese had become increasingly worried about potential outside threats. In 1791 a book was issued advocating a strong navy. Fears about the West's growing power and particularly Russia's Asian expansion fed these concerns in later decades. Fear became reality in 1853 when American Commodore **Matthew Perry** arrived with a squadron in Edo Bay near Tokyo and used threats of bombardment to insist that Americans be allowed to trade. The United States, increasingly an active part of the West's core economy, thus launched for Japan the same kind of pressure the Opium War had created for China: pressure from the heightened military superiority of the West and its insistence on opening markets for its burgeoning economy. In 1854 Perry returned and won the right to station an American consul in Japan; in 1856, through a formal treaty, two ports were opened to commerce. Britain, Russia, and Holland quickly won similar rights. As in China, this meant that Westerners living in Japan would be governed by their own representatives, not by Japanese law.

Perry, Matthew American commodore who visited Edo Bay with American fleet in 1853; insisted on opening ports to American trade on threat of naval bombardment; won rights for American trade with Japan in 1854.

View the Closer Look on MyHistoryLab: Japanese Views of American Naval Technology

THINKING HISTORICALLY

The Separate Paths of Japan and China

JAPAN'S ABILITY TO CHANGE IN RESPONSE to new Western pressure contrasted strikingly with the sluggishness of Chinese reactions into the 20th century. The contrast draws particular attention because China and Japan had been part of the same civilization orbit for so long, which means that some of the assets Japan possessed in dealing with change were present in China as well. Indeed, Japan turned out to benefit, by the mid-19th century, from having become more like China in key respects during the Tokugawa period. The link between Chinese and Japanese traditions should not be exaggerated, of course, and earlier differences help explain the divergence that opened so clearly in the late 19th century. The east Asian world now split apart, with Japan seizing eagerly on Chinese weakness to mount a series of attacks from the 1890s to 1945, which only made China's troubles worse.

Japan and China had both chosen considerable isolation from larger world currents from about 1600 until the West forced new openings between 1830 and 1860. Japan's isolation was the more complete. Both countries lagged behind the West because of their self-containment, which was why Western industrialization caught them unprepared. China's power and wealth roused Western greed and interference first, which gave Japan some leeway.

However, China surpassed Japan in some areas that should have aided it in reacting to the Western challenge. Its leadership, devoted to Confucianism, was more thoroughly secular and bureaucratic in outlook. There was no need to brush aside otherworldly commitments or feudal distractions to deal with the West's material and organizational power. Government centralization, still an issue in Japan, had a long history in China. With a rich tradition of technological innovation and scientific discovery in its past as well, China might have appeared to be a natural to lead the Asian world in responding to the West.

However, that role fell to Japan. Several aspects of Japanese tradition gave it a flexibility that China lacked. It already knew the benefits of imitation, which China, save for its period of attraction to Buddhism, had never acknowledged. Japan's slower government growth had allowed a stronger, more autonomous merchant tradition even as both societies became more commercial in the 17th and early 18th centuries. Feudal traditions, although declining under the Tokugawa shogunate, also limited the heavy hand of government controls while stimulating a sense of military competitiveness, as in the West. In contrast, China's government probably tried to control too much by the 18th century and quashed initiative in the process.

China was also hampered by rapid population growth from the 17th century onward. This population pressure consumed great energy, leaving scant capital for other economic initiatives. Japan's population stability into the 19th century pressed resources less severely. Japan's island status made the nation more sensitive to Western naval pressures.

Finally, China and Japan were on somewhat different paths when the Western challenge intruded in the mid-19th century. China was suffering one of its recurrent dynastic declines. Government became less efficient, intellectual life stagnated, and popular unrest surged. A cycle of renewal might have followed, with a new dynasty seizing more vigorous reins. But Western interference disrupted this process, complicating reform and creating various new discontents that ultimately overturned the imperial office.

In contrast, Japan maintained political and economic vigor into the 19th century. Whereas by the late 19th century China needed Western guidance simply to handle such bureaucratic affairs as tariff collection and repression of peasant rebellion, Japan suffered no such breakdown of authority, using foreign advisors far more selectively.

Once a different pattern of response was established, every decade increased the gap. Western exploitation of Chinese assets and dilution of government power made conditions more chaotic, while Japanese strength grew steadily after a very brief period of uncertainty. By the 20th century, the two nations were enemies—with Japan, for the first time, the stronger—and seemed to be in different orbits. Japan enjoyed increasing industrial success and had a conservative state that would yield after World War II to a more fully parliamentary form. China, after decades of revolution, finally won its 20th-century political solution: communism.

Yet today, at the onset of the 21st century, it is unclear whether east Asia was split as permanently as 19th- and early 20th-century developments had suggested. Japan's industrial lead remains, but China's economy is beginning to soar. Common cultural habits of group cooperation and decision making remind us that beneath different political systems, a fruitful shared heritage continues to operate. The heritage is quite different from that of the West but fully adaptable to the demands of economic change. And so Westerners begin to wonder whether a Pacific century is about to dawn.

> **Several aspects of Japanese tradition gave it a flexibility that China lacked.**

QUESTIONS
- What civilization features had Japan and China shared before the 19th century?
- In what ways were Japanese political institutions more adaptable than Chinese institutions?
- Why was Russia also able to change earlier and more fundamentally than 19th-century China?

The bureaucrats of the shogunate saw no alternative but to open up Japan, given the superiority of Western navies. And of course, there were Japanese who had grown impatient with strict isolation; their numbers swelled as the Dutch schools began to expand. On the other hand, the daimyo, intensely conservative, were opposed to the new concessions, and their opposition forced the shogun to appeal to the emperor for support. Soon, samurai opponents of the bureaucracy were also appealing to the emperor, who began to emerge from his centuries-long confinement as a largely religious and ceremonial figure. Whereas most daimyo defended the status quo, the samurai were more divided. Some saw opportunity in change, including the possibility of unseating the shogunate. The fact was that the complex shogunate system had depended on the isolation policy; it could not survive the stresses of foreign influence and internal reactions. The result was not immediate collapse; indeed, into the late 1850s, Japanese life seemed to go on much as before.

In the 1860s, political crisis came into the open. The crisis was spiced by samurai attacks on foreigners, including one murder of a British official, matched by Western naval bombardments of feudal forts. Civil war broke out in 1866 as the samurai eagerly armed themselves with American Civil War surplus weapons, causing Japan's aristocracy to come to terms with the advantages of Western armaments. When the samurai defeated a shogunate force, many Japanese were finally shocked out of their traditional reliance on their own superiority. One author argued that the nation, compared with the West and its technology, science, and humane laws, was only half civilized.

This multifaceted crisis came to an end in 1868 when the victorious reform group proclaimed a new emperor named Mutsuhito whose reign was commonly called "Meiji," or "Enlightened." In his name, key samurai leaders managed to put down the troops of the shogunate. The crisis period had been shocking enough to allow further changes in Japan's basic political structure—changes that went much deeper at the political level than those introduced by Russia from 1861 onward.

Industrial and Political Change in the Meiji State

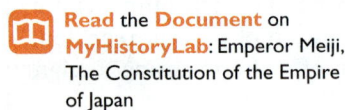

Read the Document on MyHistoryLab: Emperor Meiji, The Constitution of the Empire of Japan

The new Meiji government promptly set about abolishing feudalism, replacing the daimyo in 1871 with a system of nationally appointed prefects (district administrators carefully chosen from different regions; the prefect system was copied from French practice). Political power was effectively centralized, and from this base the Meiji rulers—the emperor and his close advisors, drawn from loyal segments of the aristocracy—began to expand the power of the state to effect economic and social change.

Quickly, the Japanese government sent samurai officials abroad, to western Europe and the United States, to study economic and political institutions and technology. These samurai, deeply impressed by what they saw, pulled back from their earlier anti-foreign position and gained increasing voice over other officials in the government. Their basic goal was Japan's domestic development, accompanied by a careful diplomatic policy that would avoid antagonizing the West.

Fundamental improvements in government finance soon followed. Between 1873 and 1876, the Meiji ministers introduced a real social revolution. They abolished the samurai class and the stipends this group had received. The tax on agriculture was converted to a wider tax, payable in money. The samurai were compensated by government-backed bonds, but these decreased in value, and most samurai became poor. This development sparked renewed conflict, and a final samurai uprising occurred in 1877. However, the government had introduced an army based on national conscription, and by 1878 the nation was militarily secure. Individual samurai found new opportunities in political and business areas as they adapted to change. One former samurai, Iwasaki Yataro (1834–1885), who started his career buying weapons for a feudal lord, set up the Mitsubishi Company after 1868, winning government contracts for railroad and steamship lines designed to compete with British companies in the region. Despite his overbearing personality, Iwasaki built a loyal management group, including other former samurai, and by his death had a stake in shipbuilding, mining, and banking as well as transportation. The continued existence of the samurai, reflecting Japan's lack of outright revolution, would yield diverse results in later Japanese history.

The process of political reconstruction crested in the 1880s. Many former samurai organized political parties. Meiji leaders traveled abroad to discover modern political forms. In 1884 they created a new conservative nobility, stocked by former nobles and Meiji leaders, that would operate a British-style House of Peers. Next, the bureaucracy was reorganized, insulated from political pressures, and opened to talent on the basis of civil service examinations. The bureaucracy began to expand rapidly; it grew from 29,000 officials in 1890 to 72,000 in 1908. Finally, the constitution, issued in 1889, ensured major prerogatives for the emperor along with limited powers for the lower house of the **Diet**, as the new parliament was called. Here, Germany provided the model, for the emperor commanded the military directly (served by a German-style general staff) and also directly named his ministers. Both the institution and its members' clothing were Western, as the Visualizing the Past feature shows. The Diet could pass laws, upon agreement of both houses, and could approve budgets, but failure to pass a budget would simply reinstate the budget of the previous year. Parliament could thus advise government, but it could not control it. Finally, the conservative tone of this parliamentary experiment was confirmed by high property qualifications set for voting rights. Only about 5 percent of Japanese men had enough wealth to be allowed to vote for representatives to the lower house.

Japan's political structure thus came to involve centralized imperial rule, wielded by a handful of Meiji advisors, combined with limited representative institutions copied from the West. This combination gave great power to a group of wealthy businesspeople and former nobles who influenced the emperor and also pulled strings within the parliament. Political parties arose, but a coherent system overrode their divisions into the 20th century. Japan thus followed its new policy of imitating the West, but it retained its own identity. The Japanese political solution compared interestingly to Russian institutions after Alexander II's reforms. Both states were centralized and authoritarian, but Japan had incorporated business leaders into its governing structure, whereas Russia defended a more traditional social elite.

Diet [DEYE-iht] Japanese parliament established as part of the new constitution of 1889; part of Meiji reforms; could pass laws and approve budgets; able to advise government, but not to control it.

Japan's Industrial Revolution

Political decisions were essential after the crisis of the 1860s, but they were soon matched by other initiatives. The new army, based on the universal conscription of young men, was further improved by formal officer training and by upgrading armaments according to Western standards. With the aid of Western advisors, a modern navy was established.

Attention also focused on creating the conditions necessary for industrialization. New government banks funded growing trade and provided capital for industry. State-built railroads spread across the country, and the islands were connected by rapid steamers. New methods raised agricultural output to feed the people of the growing cities.

The new economic structure depended on the destruction of many older restrictions. Guilds and internal road tariffs were abolished to create a national market. Land reform created clear individual ownership for many farmers, which helped motivate expansion of production and the introduction of new fertilizers and equipment.

Government initiative dominated manufacturing not only in the creation of transportation networks but also in state operation of mines, shipyards, and metallurgical plants. Scarce capital and the unfamiliarity of new technology seemed to compel state direction, as occurred in Russia at the same time. Government control also helped check the many foreign advisors needed by early Japanese industry; here, Japan maintained closer supervision than its Russian neighbor. Japan established the Ministry of Industry in 1870, and it quickly became one of the key government agencies, setting overall economic policy as well as operating specific sectors. By the 1880s, model shipyards, arsenals, and factories provided experience in new technology and disciplined work systems for many Japanese. Finally, by expanding technical training and education, setting up banks and post offices, and regularizing commercial laws, the government provided a structure within which Japan could develop on many fronts. Measures in this area largely copied established practices in the West, but with adaptation suitable for Japanese conditions; thus, well before any European university, Tokyo Imperial University had a faculty of agriculture.

Private enterprise quickly played a role in Japan's growing economy, particularly in the vital textile sector. Some businesspeople came from older merchant families, although some of the great houses had been ruined with the financial destruction of the samurai class. There were also newcomers, some rising from peasant ranks. Shuibuzawa Eiichi (SHOO-ih-buh-zah-wah EYE-ee-chee), for example, born a peasant, became a merchant and then an official of the Finance Ministry. He turned to banking in 1873, using other people's money to set up cotton-spinning mills and other textile operations.

VISUALIZING THE PAST

Two Faces of Western Influence

THESE PICTURES SHOW AN 1850S CARTOON portraying American Commodore Matthew Perry as a greedy warlord and the first meeting of the Japanese parliament in 1890.

QUESTIONS
- What kinds of attitudes toward the West does the cartoon represent?
- What does the picture of parliament convey about attitudes toward the West?
- What was the model for the design of the meeting room?
- What do the two pictures suggest about uses of costume in a time of rapid change?

zaibatsu [ZEYE-baht-soo] Huge industrial combines created in Japan in the 1890s as part of the process of industrialization.

By the 1890s huge new industrial combines, later known as **zaibatsu**, were being formed as a result of accumulations of capital and far-flung merchant and industrial operations.

By 1900 the Japanese economy was fully launched in an industrial revolution. It rested on a political and social structure different from that of Russia—one that had in most respects changed more profoundly. Japan's success in organizing industrialization, including its careful management of foreign advice and models, proved to be one of the great developments of later 19th-century history.

It is important to keep these early phases of Japanese industrialization in perspective. Pre–World War I Japan was far from the West's equal. It depended on imports of Western equipment and raw materials such as coal; for industrial purposes, Japan was a resource-poor nation. Although economic growth and careful government policy allowed Japan to avoid Western domination, Japan was newly dependent on world economic conditions and was often at a disadvantage. It needed exports to pay for machine and resource imports, and these in turn took hordes of low-paid workers. Silk production grew rapidly, the bulk of it destined for Western markets. Much of this production was based on the labor of poorly paid women who worked at home or in sweatshops, not in mechanized factories. Some of these women were sold into service by farm families. Efforts at labor organization or other means of protest were met by vigorous repression.

Social and Diplomatic Effects of Industrialization

The industrial revolution and the wider extensions of manufacturing and commercial agriculture, along with political change, had significant ramifications within Japanese culture and society. These changes also helped generate a more aggressive foreign policy. Japanese society was disrupted by massive population growth. Better nutrition and new medical provisions reduced death rates, and the upheaval of the rural masses cut into traditional restraints on births. The result was steady population growth that strained Japanese resources and stability, although it also ensured a constant supply of low-cost labor. This was one of the causes of Japan's class tensions.

The Japanese government introduced a universal education system, providing primary schools for all. This education stressed science and the importance of technical subjects along with political loyalty to the nation and emperor. Elite students at the university level also took courses that emphasized science, and many Japanese students went abroad to study technical subjects in other countries.

Education also revealed Japanese insistence on distinctive values. After a heady reform period in the 1870s, when hundreds of Western teachers were imported and a Rutgers University professor was brought in for high-level advice about the whole system, the emperor and conservative advisors stepped back after 1879. This was when reformers like Fukuzawa Yukichi began to tone down their rhetoric. Innovation and individualism had gone too far. A traditional moral education was essential, along with new skills, which would stress "loyalty to the Imperial House, love of country, filial piety toward parents, respect for superiors, faith in friends, charity toward inferiors and respect for oneself." The use of foreign books on morality was prohibited, and intense government inspection of textbooks was intended to promote social order.

Many Japanese copied Western fashions as part of the effort to become modern. Western-style haircuts replaced the samurai shaved head with a topknot—another example of the Westernization of hair in world history. Western standards of hygiene spread, and the Japanese became enthusiastic toothbrushers and consumers of patent medicines. Japan also adopted the Western calendar and the metric system. Few Japanese converted to Christianity, however, and despite Western popular cultural fads, the Japanese managed to preserve an emphasis on their own values. What the Japanese wanted and got from the West involved practical techniques; they planned to infuse them with a distinctively Japanese spirit. As an early Japanese visitor to the American White House wrote in a self-satisfied poem that captured the national mood,

> We suffered the barbarians to look upon
> The glory of our Eastern Empire of Japan.

Western-oriented enthusiasms were not meant to destroy a distinctive Japanese spirit.

Japanese family life retained many traditional emphases. The birth rate dropped as rapid population growth forced increasing numbers of people off the land. Meanwhile, the rise of factory industry, separating work from home, made children's labor less useful. This trend, developed earlier in the West, seems inseparable from successful industrialization. There were new signs of family instability as well; the divorce rate exploded until legal changes made procedures more difficult. On the more traditional side, the Japanese were eager to maintain the inferiority of women in the home. The position of Western women offended them. Japanese government visitors to the United States were appalled by what they saw as the bossy ways of women: "The way women are treated here is like the way parents are respected in our country." Standards of Japanese courtesy also contrasted with the more open and boisterous behavior of Westerners, particularly Americans. "Obscenity is inherent in the customs of this country," noted another samurai visitor to the United States. Certain Japanese religious values were also preserved. Buddhism lost some ground, although it remained important, but Shintoism, which appealed to the new nationalist concern with Japan's distinctive mission and the religious functions of the emperor, won new interest.

Traditionalism was not the only theme in the situation of Japanese women amid industrialization. As in Russia, women were widely used in the early factory labor force—and in Japan's case, also in sweatshop silk production—because their low wages were an indispensable advantage in competitive global markets. At the same time, the government carefully provided schooling for girls as part of its new commitment to mass education. And many upper-class women, as in Russia, had opportunities even for high education in secondary schools or separate universities. The tension they encountered, between assumptions that women should play subservient and domestic roles and the excitement of new educational opportunities, was particularly sharp, but not entirely different from contemporary conditions in Russia or the West. Outright feminism, however, was far less common than in either western or eastern Europe. Industrialization and urbanization made literal traditionalism impossible amid rapid economic change.

Economic change, and the tensions as well as the power it generated, also produced a shift in Japanese foreign policy. This shift was partly an imitation of Western models. New imperialism also

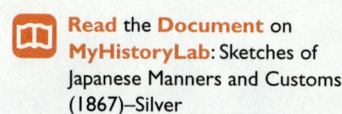
Read the Document on MyHistoryLab: Sketches of Japanese Manners and Customs (1867)–Silver

MAP 28.3 **Japanese Colonial Expansion to 1914** The map shows Japan's principal gains, but also the limitations that still frustrated Japanese nationalists.

Sino-Japanese War War fought between Japan and Qing China between 1894 and 1895; resulted in Japanese victory; frustrated Japanese imperial aims because of Western insistence that Japan withdraw from Liaodong peninsula.

relieved some strains within Japanese society, giving displaced samurai the chance to exercise their military talents elsewhere. Even more than Western countries, which used similar arguments for imperialism, the Japanese economy also needed access to markets and raw materials. Because Japan was poor in many basic materials, including coal and oil for energy, the pressure for expansion was particularly great.

Japan's quick victory over China in the **Sino-Japanese War** for influence in Korea (1894–1895) was a first step toward expansion (Map 28.2). Japan convincingly demonstrated its new superiority over all other Asian powers. Humiliated by Western insistence that it abandon the Liaodong peninsula it had just taken from China, the Japanese planned a war with Russia as a means of striking out against the nearest European state. A 1902 alliance with Britain was an important sign of Japan's arrival as an equal nation in the Western-dominated world diplomatic system. The Japanese were also eager to dent Russia's growing strength in east Asia after the development of the trans-Siberian railroad. Disputes over Russian influence in Manchuria and Japanese influence in Korea led to the Russo-Japanese War in 1904 (Map 28.3), which Japan won handily because of its superior navy. Japan annexed Korea in 1910, entering the ranks of imperialist powers.

The Strain of Modernization

Japanese achievement had its costs, including poor living standards in the crowded cities. Many Japanese conservatives resented the passion other Japanese displayed for Western fashions. Disputes between generations, with the old clinging to traditional standards and the young more interested in Western styles, were very troubling in a society that stressed the importance of parental authority.

Some tension entered political life. Political parties in Japan's parliament clashed with the emperor's ministers over rights to determine policy. The government often had to dissolve the Diet and call for new elections, seeking a more workable parliamentary majority. Political assassinations and attempted assassinations reflected grievances, including direct action impulses in the samurai tradition.

Another kind of friction emerged in intellectual life. Many Japanese scholars copied Western philosophies and literary styles, and there was enough adaptation to prevent the emergence of a full Russian-style intelligentsia. Other intellectuals expressed a deep pessimism about the loss of identity in a changing world. The underlying theme was confusion about a Japan that was no longer traditional, but not Western either. What *was* it? Thus, some writers spoke of Japan's heading for a "nervous collapse from which we will not be able to recover." Others dealt with more personal conflicts such as those in the following poem:

> Do not be loved by others; do not accept their charity, do not promise anything.... Always wear a mask. Always be ready for a fight—be able to hit the next man on the head at any time. Don't forget that when you make friends with someone you are sooner or later certain to break with him.

As an antidote to social and cultural insecurity, Japanese leaders urged national loyalty and devotion to the emperor, and with some success. The official message promoted Japanese virtues of obedience and harmony that the West lacked. School texts thus stressed,

> Our country takes as its base the family system: the nation is but a single family, the imperial family is our main house. We the people worship the unbroken imperial line with the same feeling of respect and love that a child feels toward his parents.... The union of loyalty and filial piety is truly the special character of our national polity.

Japanese nationalism built on traditions of superiority, cohesion, and deference to rulers, as well as on the new tensions generated by rapid change. It became a deep force, probably in Japan more than elsewhere, that played a unique role in justifying sacrifice and struggle in a national mission to preserve independence and dignity in a hostile world. Nationalism, along with firm police repression of dissent and the sweeping changes of the early Meiji years, certainly helps explain why Japan avoided the revolutionary pressure that hit Russia, China, and other countries after 1900.

Yet Japan's very success reminds us of how unusual it was. No other society outside the Western world was yet able to match its achievements. Russia, responding to Western example in its own way, continued its growth as a world power, but amid such social disarray that further upheaval was inevitable. Most of the rest of the world faced the more immediate concern of adjusting to or resisting Western dominance; industrialization was a remote prospect. Even today, when many societies are striving for greater industrialization, the ability to emulate the Japanese pattern of rapid change seems very limited—with other parts of east Asia, interestingly enough, leading the pack.

yellow peril Western term for perceived threat of Japanese imperialism around 1900; met by increased Western imperialism in region.

Global Connections and Critical Themes

RUSSIA AND JAPAN IN THE WORLD

Russia's world role, founded on its huge size and territorial expansion, had already been established in the Early Modern period. There were, however, new twists during the 19th century. Russian troops and diplomats periodically gained direct roles in western Europe. Russian forces entered France as part of the coalition that defeated Napoleon. A side result was the development of new restaurants in France, called bistros, based on the Russian word for *quick*. Russian armies helped put down the Hungarian revolution in 1849. Russian involvement in Middle Eastern diplomacy resulted from its steady pressure on the Ottoman empire. By the later 19th century, Russia extended its influence in eastern Asia, seizing new territories in northern China and claiming a role elsewhere, in China and Korea alike. This set the collision course with Japan. Russia also participated somewhat more broadly in the globalization of the later 19th century, participating in international conferences and contributing to "international" styles in art.

Japan's world role was much newer, and just emerging by 1900. Long isolated, Japan had experienced only one previous attempt at assertion beyond its borders, the late-16th century invasion of Korea. Now, however, ambitions increased, fueled by economic needs, growing industrial and military strength, and population pressure. It was during the Meiji era that Japanese leaders decided to open the wave of globalization, although without losing a distinctive identity, rather than trying to resist it. More specifically, Japan sought to be regarded as a great nation along Western imperialist lines. This brought the conflicts with China and Russia around 1900, and wider experiments thereafter. In the long run, it was Japan's striking economic success that would most clearly define its new place in the world. Initially, the unfolding of strength in the eastern Pacific region, along with the complex relationships to the West, marked Japan's dramatic entry as a force to be reckoned with.

The beginnings of serious industrialization in Russia and Japan, and the entry of Japan into world affairs, contributed important new ingredients to the global diplomatic picture by the end of the long 19th century. These developments, along with the rise of the United States, added to the growing sense of competition between the established Western powers. Japan's surge promoted a fear in the West of a new **yellow peril** that should be opposed through greater imperialist efforts. Outright colonial acquisitions by the new powers added directly to the competitive atmosphere, particularly in the Far East.

Further Readings

Important comparative work includes Rudra Sil, *Managing "Modernity": Work, Community, and Authority in Late-Industrialized Japan and Russia* (2002) and Kaoru Sugihara, ed., *Japan, China, and the Growth of the Asian International Economy, 1850–1949* (2005). A. Gerschenkron, *Economic Backwardness in Historical Perspective: A Book of Essays* (1962), helps define the conditions of latecomer industrialization. The best survey of Russia in this transitional period is Hans Rogger, *Russia in the Age of Modernization and Revolution, 1881–1917* (1983). See also Geoffrey Hosking, *Russia: People and Empire, 1532–1917* (1997); R. Bolton, *Russia and Europe in the Nineteenth Century* (2008); and N. B. Breyfogle, A. Schrader and W. Sunderland, *Peopling the Russian Periphery: Borderland Colonization* (2007). Russian reforms and economic change are discussed in Alexander Pulonov, *Russia in the Nineteenth Century: Autocracy, Reform and Social Change, 1814–1914* (2005); Sharon Hudgins, *The Other Side of Russia: A Slice of Life in Siberia and the Russian Far East* (2003); Patrick O'Meara, *The Decembrist Pavel Pestel: Russia's First Republican* (2003); Sidney Harcave, trans., *The Memoirs of Count Witte* (1990), includes a brief biographical sketch and his collected writings of this influential "modernizer." On social and cultural developments, see Victoria Bonnell, ed., *The Russian Worker: Life and Labor Under the Tsarist Regime* (1983); Barbara Engel, *Mothers and Daughters: Women of the Intelligentsia in Nineteenth Century Russia* (1983); and Jeffrey Brooks, *When Russia Learned to Read: Literacy and Popular Culture* (1987). On another vital area of eastern Europe, see A. Stavrianos, *The Balkans, 1815–1914* (1963).

Japan in the 19th century is viewed from a modernization perspective in R. Dore, ed., *Aspects of Social Change in Modern Japan* (1967). See also Ian Inkster, *Japanese Industrialization: Historical and Cultural Perspectives* (2001) and *The Japanese Industrial Economy: Late Development and Cultural Causation* (2001); W. W. Lockwood, *The Economic Development of Japan: Growth and Structural Change 1868–1938* (1954); J. C. Abegglen, *The Japanese Factory: Aspects of Its Social Organization*, rev. ed. (1985); Andrew Gordon, *The Evolution of Labor Relations in Japan* (1985); and Hugh Patrick, ed., *Japanese Industrialization and Its Social Consequences* (1973). E. O. Reischauer's *Japan: The Story of a Nation* (1981) remains a good general history of the period. For more closely focused works on socioeconomic change, see Masayuki Tanimoto, ed., *The Role of Tradition in Japan's Industrialization: Another Path to Industrialization* (2006); George Feifer, *Breaking Open Japan: Commodore Perry, Lord Abe, and American Imperialism in 1853* (2006); Janet Hunger, *Women and the Labour Market in Japan's Industrializing Economy: The Textile Industry before the Pacific War* (2003); Susan D. Holloway, *Women and Family in Contemporary Japan* (2010); Peter N. Stearns, *Schools and Students in Industrial Society: Japan and the West* (1997); and E. P. Tsurumi, *Factory Girls: Women in the Thread Mills of Meiji Japan* (1990). Additional studies include R. H. Myers and M. R. Beattie, eds., *The Japanese Colonial Empire 1895–1945* (1984); W. G. Beasley, *Japanese Imperialism, 1894–1945* (1987); and P. Duus, *The Abacus and the Sword: The Japanese Penetration of Korea, 1895–1910* (1995). On Japan and Russia, see Frederic A. Sharf, et al., *A Much Recorded War: The Russo-Japanese War in History and Imagery* (2005).

On MyHistoryLab

 Study and Review on MyHistoryLab

Critical Thinking Questions

1. Compare the industrialization process in Japan and Russia with early industrialization in western Europe.
2. What were the main causes of revolutionary potential in Russia by 1900? Was a major revolution inevitable by that point?
3. Through comparisons with Russia, explain why Japan managed to introduce fundamental change without provoking a revolution.
4. To what extent was Confucianism a constructive cultural framework for industrialization? What aspects of Confucianism had to change to facilitate industrial development?
5. Why did Japan do better than China in initially responding to the industrial West?

PART V AP® TEST PREP

MULTIPLE CHOICE QUESTIONS

1. Which of the following statements concerning the political philosophy of the Enlightenment is most accurate?
   a. Often aristocrats themselves, Enlightenment thinkers were firm supporters of the existing political order.
   b. Enlightenment philosophers generally conceded that organized religion was needed to ensure stability for the masses.
   c. Enlightenment thinkers were concerned that science and reason might lead people away from nature and tradition.
   d. Enlightenment authors championed the idea of progress as well as economic and technological change and policies that would promote industry.

2. Which of the following was a cause of the population revolution in 18th century Europe?
   a. improved nutrition resulting from the growing use of the potato
   b. dramatic improvements in birth control methods
   c. a cyclical decline in deadly diseases such as small pox, cholera, and tuberculosis
   d. the increasing practice of infanticide, especially against girls

3. Which of the following was NOT a cause of the French Revolution?
   a. Influential Enlightenment thinkers put forth the idea that governments should be formed on a rational basis.
   b. The Catholic church demanded greater power over the royal government.
   c. The middle class had come to feel entitled to greater political representation.
   d. Peasants resented the manorial obligations imposed on them by the landowners who controlled much of their lives.

4. Which of the following was a lasting reform passed during the initial, moderate phase of the French Revolution?
   a. universal male suffrage
   b. the introduction of Protestantism
   c. peasants were freed from all traces of manorialism
   d. universal military conscription

5. The radical phase of the French Revolution led to which of the following?
   a. The king was captured, tried, and exiled to Austria.
   b. The metric system, viewed as a symbol of the old regime, was banned as a system of weights and measures.
   c. The aristocracy and wealthy middle class were universally stripped of their property.
   d. Robespierre and his allies proclaimed universal military conscription, arguing that men who were free citizens owed loyalty and service to the government.

6. Which of the following statements concerning the impact of the French Revolution on the rest of Europe is NOT accurate?
   a. The French Revolution spread key revolutionary legislation throughout much of western Europe.
   b. The revolution encouraged popular nationalism outside of France.
   c. The French Revolution and its subsequent empire created a general consensus after the defeat of France for a more liberal Europe.
   d. The idea of equality under the law and attacks on privilege—whether aristocratic, guild, or ecclesiastical—spread throughout Europe.

7. Which of the following statements best characterizes the peace conference at Vienna following the fall of France?
   a. The allies punished France in order to make certain that no further revolution was possible.
   b. Territorial adjustments reached at Vienna kept Europe fairly stable for almost half a century.
   c. The intention of leaders of the conference, such as Metternich, was to promote democratic regimes wherever possible.
   d. Poland emerged as one of the winners in the territorial realignments that followed the wars.

8. Which of the following statements best characterizes the political philosophy of Karl Marx?
   a. Marx borrowed heavily from earlier "utopian" socialist theories.
   b. In the aftermath of the victory of the proletariat, the state would emerge permanently as a powerful dictatorship.
   c. History was shaped by the available means of production and those who controlled them.
   d. The ascension of the proletariat against the bourgeoisie would be morally superior to capitalism, but it was unlikely to happen.

9. Which of the following statements most accurately describes the relationship between science and the arts in the later 19th century?
   a. Science and art continued to follow the lines of classical and rational traditionalism.
   b. Science and art of the 19th century were freed from the traditions of classical rationalism and embarked on a radical shift that favored the emotional.
   c. Science and the arts took separate paths, with influential developments in each area.
   d. There were few scientific advances after the early stages of industrialization and little if any innovation in the field of art.

CHAPTER 28 Russia and Japan: Industrialization Outside the West

10. **How is the victory of the Americans in the revolution against Britain best explained?**
    a. The persistence of the revolutionaries was combined with British military blunders and significant aid from the French government.
    b. Americans were inspired to fight the British by their new constitutional structure based on Enlightenment principles.
    c. The British had little chance of winning because they had to rely on mercenary soldiers.
    d. The Americans had better trained soldiers and were better equipped than the British.

11. **How were British and Dutch 18th century land empires in Asia accumulated?**
    a. Through direct government intervention in the affairs of their overseas colonies, European nations managed to steer political and economic policies that would validate their continued presence.
    b. through the policy of the directors of the Dutch and British East India companies, who often used the militaries of their respective governments to bully colonial governments into relinquishing land
    c. through the initiative of overseas agents of the Dutch and British East India companies acting in the absence of instructions from the company directors
    d. No 18th century territorial acquisitions were made in Asia by Europeans, who were preoccupied with the ongoing wars and political revolutions ravaging their own continent during this period.

12. **How did the Dutch gain control of the entire island of Java?**
    a. The Dutch won a series of naval battles with forces of the sultan of Mataram.
    b. The Dutch introduced African mercenaries to Java to secure a military victory.
    c. The Dutch, using mercenary forces recruited from the people of Java, intervened in succession disputes in return for grants of land.
    d. The Dutch used the process of conversion of masses of the Javanese people as well as the elite to gain a position of supremacy on Java.

13. **Why did India become the pivot of the great 19th century empire built by Britain on a global scale?**
    a. India had by far the greatest share of colonized peoples, from which Britain's largest and most powerful land forces were recruited.
    b. India had the largest landmass of any of the areas that became part of the British empire.
    c. India became a secondary manufacturing base for British industry.
    d. The Indian navy augmented the British navy, thereby increasing its manpower and ships.

14. **Which is most true about cross-cultural gender relations between European colonizers and Asian indigenous people prior to 1850?**
    a. Though very often European men lived with Asian women, marriage was unthinkable.
    b. Before the end of the 18th century, mixed marriages on the part of prominent traders or officers were widely accepted, particularly among colonists and traders in Java.
    c. The complete lack of liaisons that cut across racial boundaries suggests a lack of social fluidity that became common by the last half of the 19th century.
    d. Women who came with their husbands had frequent liaisons with men of the local indigenous groups.

15. **Which of the following statements is most accurate?**
    a. European nations were militarily superior to African nations in the early 20th century.
    b. European nations cooperated to defeat the outmanned armies of African nations.
    c. European nations rapidly came to agreements over the territorial division of colonial holdings.
    d. The League of Nations supervised the construction of European colonial empires.

16. **Which of the following was NOT a factor in establishing the motives and in providing the means for Europeans and North Americans to become the agents of the first civilization to dominate the entire world?**
    a. Political power made it possible for Europeans to use their already well-established position in world trade in order to build a global economic order oriented to their industrial societies.
    b. The communications and commercial networks that formed the foundation of the European colonial order made possible an unprecedented flow of food and minerals from Africa, Asia, and Latin America to Europe and North America.
    c. Western industrial societies provided investment capital and machines to run the mines, plantations, and processing plants in colonized areas.
    d. Indigenous people in Asia and Africa had long hoped to be more greatly exposed to Western culture, especially the manners, fashions, literary forms, and modes of entertainment.

17. **Which of the following best describes what historians call a tropical dependency in Africa, Asia, and the South Pacific?**
    a. imperial possessions in which the numbers of European settlers and indigenous peoples were approximately equal
    b. Small numbers of Europeans came to rule large populations of people outside of the West, often quite suddenly.
    c. European settlers made up most of the population in colonies in which relatively small numbers of native inhabitants had been decimated by diseases and wars of conquest.
    d. colonies that were largely unpopulated prior to the arrival of Europeans

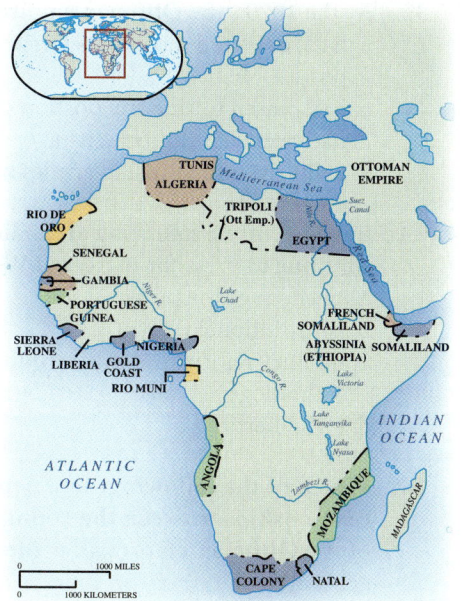
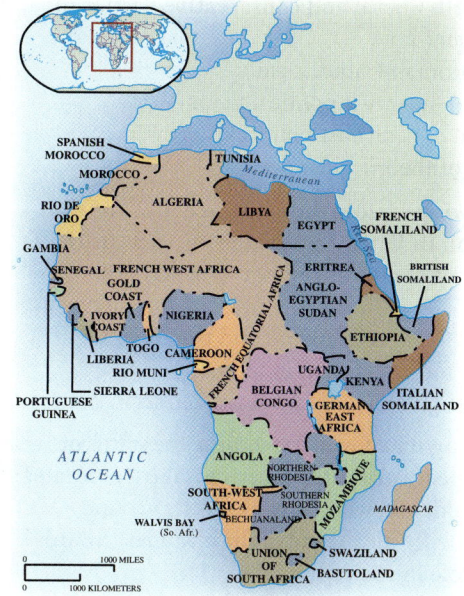

18. Referring to the maps above, which European power saw the smallest colonial gains in Africa between 1870 and 1914?
    a. British
    b. French
    c. Portuguese
    d. Spanish

19. Which of the following statements concerning the internal economies of the European colonies is most accurate?
    a. The introduction of European technology such as railways and telegraphs was intended to improve the internal economies of the colonies.
    b. Slowly, the industrial system of the West, including factories and the production of manufactured goods, was introduced into Africa and Asia.
    c. By 1914, Asian and African colonies had won economic independence from the European colonizers.
    d. Colonial economies were steadily reduced to dependence on the European-dominated global market.

20. What event set the Boer colony in South Africa on a different path than the White Dominions of Canada and Australia?
    a. the arrival of the Bantu into those regions settled by the Boers in the 1790s
    b. uprising among the Khoikhoi in 1802
    c. the annexation of the colony by the British in 1815
    d. the German invasion of southern Africa in 1902

21. Which of the following events was rejected by early 19th century Creole elites of Latin America as a model of revolution because of excessive radicalism?
    a. the American Revolution
    b. the French Revolution
    c. the independence movement in Portugal
    d. the Napoleonic Wars

22. What was the impact of the Haitian independence movement on Latin America?
    a. It served as a model for national independence movements throughout South and Central America.
    b. It demonstrated the power of Creole elites in leading revolutionary movements.
    c. It led immediately to a general abolition of slavery throughout Latin America.
    d. Creole elites viewed it with horror as an example of general social upheaval.

23. In what way was the experience of the Napoleonic wars different for Portugal than for Spain?
    a. Portugal was allied with the French emperor.
    b. The French attempted to invade Portugal, but failed.
    c. The entire royal family fled from the French to Brazil and established their capital there.
    d. Following the defeat of the Portuguese, the French took over the colonial administration of Brazil.

24. How was Brazilian independence achieved?
    a. through a rebellion led by the creole elite
    b. through a slave rebellion on the model of Haiti
    c. because the French freed the colony unilaterally
    d. Pedro, the prince regent of Brazil, declared independence

25. Which of the following statements concerning the political organization of Latin America to 1850 is most accurate?
    a. Most of Latin America was divided up into consolidated units that mirrored the colonial vice royalties.
    b. The excellent colonial road system enabled the creation of larger states after independence.
    c. Permanent consolidation and union was more typical of Central America and southern South America than elsewhere.
    d. Most attempts at consolidation and union failed.

26. In what way were both liberal and conservative parties in Latin America similar?
    a. their distrust for Roman Catholicism
    b. their acceptance of federalist political theory
    c. their endorsement of centralist political theory
    d. the social origins of their leadership

27. Which of the following factors did NOT account for the economic stagnation in Latin America from 1820 to 1850?
    a. the slow recovery of the mining sector after wars of independence
    b. the lack of a transportation network and port facilities
    c. the lack of capital for investment in industry
    d. the absence of foreign markets for raw materials

28. Which of the following statements concerning the status of women in post-independence Latin America is most accurate?
    a. Following independence, women gained little ground and there was virtually no change in the attitudes toward women's proper role in society.
    b. Because of their participation in the independence movement, women were rewarded in post-revolutionary Latin America with voting rights and access to political office.
    c. Because women in general failed to support the revolutionary movements, they were not included in the massive reforms that followed independence.
    d. The status of women actually declined after independence, as they were cut off from areas such as public education that had been available to them in colonial Latin America.

29. By 1888 the stigma of skin color and former slave status
    a. was no longer a factor in Latin American social hierarchy.
    b. was not a factor except in the former plantation colonies of the Caribbean.
    c. was not a factor for Indians, but continued to plague descendants of African slaves.
    d. continued to create barriers to social advancement throughout Latin America.

30. Which of the following statements concerning the Díaz government in Mexico is most accurate?
    a. Under Porfirio Díaz, reforms were undertaken that finally began to resolve the inequity of land distribution in Mexico.
    b. Labor unrest and political instability decreased significantly by the beginning of the 20th century.
    c. Díaz's strongly centralized government actively discouraged foreign investment in Mexican mining and transportation.
    d. Under the guise of modernization, the forms of liberal government were maintained but were subverted in order to keep Díaz in power.

31. A remarkable engineering feat, the Suez Canal created a water route between the Mediterranean Sea and the
    a. Pacific Ocean.
    b. Black Sea.
    c. Red Sea.
    d. Atlantic Ocean.

32. By the 1870s, the Ottoman empire
    a. had recovered most of its territorial losses to European powers.
    b. had ceased to rule any portion of Asia Minor.
    c. had been driven from virtually all of the Balkans.
    d. had driven the Russian armies back to the steppes.

33. In which of the following areas did Sultan Abdul Hamid continue to press for increased Westernization?
    a. freedom of the press
    b. constitutional reform
    c. military reform and the introduction of Western technology
    d. civil liberties

34. Which of the following statements concerning the relationships between the Young Turks and the Arabs of the Ottoman empire after the 1908 coup is most accurate?
    a. The Young Turks harbored resentment against the Arabs of the empire for failing to support the 1908 coup.
    b. Arab support of the 1908 coup waned when they discovered that the Young Turks had no intentions of abandoning the concept of empire.
    c. The 1908 coup resulted in the immediate independence of the Arab portions of the Ottoman empire.
    d. The close alliance between the Young Turks and the Arab leaders of the Ottoman empire continued after the 1908 coup.

35. What prevented Muhammad Ali from overthrowing the Ottoman empire?
    a. His failure to develop a modern army
    b. The lack of a navy
    c. His defeat by the Ottomans at Omdurman
    d. The opposition of European powers

36. What was the result of the rebellion by Egyptian army officers in 1882?
    a. The khedival government was overthrown by an indigenous Egyptian government.
    b. A new constitution was instituted modeled on the Ottoman constitution of 1876.
    c. The rebellion was crushed by the Turkish elements within the Egyptian army.
    d. The khedive called on the British to crush the rebellion resulting in British overlordship of Egypt.

37. What accounts for the general failure of Manchu attempts at reform?
    a. resistance on the part of the peasantry
    b. enormous population growth and the disappearance of open lands
    c. Buddhist resistance
    d. loss of territory to nomads from the Asian steppes

38. What was the impact of the British opium trade on China?
    a. Its use was restricted to the peasantry of northern China, where production of food rapidly decreased.
    b. The government was quickly able to halt the importation of opium, so that it did not have the disastrous impact on the Chinese population that was expected.
    c. Within years China's favorable balance of trade was reversed and silver began to flow out of the country.
    d. Due to the addiction of the imperial court, the British were welcomed as a valuable trade partner of China.

39. What was the outcome of the Opium War?
    a. Despite technological advantages, the British forces were overwhelmed by the Chinese numerical superiority and were unable to penetrate China's isolation.
    b. The British soon swept the seas of opposition, but were prevented from entering China by opposition from other European powers who feared Britain's overthrow of the Manchus.
    c. The British victory was so overwhelming that the Manchu dynasty was overthrown by 1850 and replaced by a republic.
    d. British victory in the Opium War allowed European powers to force China to open trade and diplomatic exchanges.

40. The conflict depicted in the cartoon above was the
    a. Boxer Rebellion.
    b. Opium War.
    c. Mahdist Revolt.
    d. Taiping Rebellion.

41. Which of the following reflects a significant similarity between Japan and Russia during the period of industrialization prior to 1914?
    a. Both experienced significant political revolutions.
    b. Both Japan and Russia had prior experience of imitation: Japan from China and Russia from Byzantium and the West.
    c. Both demonstrated remarkable political flexibility resulting in sweeping transformations of political structure.
    d. Both engaged in territorial acquisitions in the Ottoman empire.

42. Which of the following statements concerning Russian territorial expansion is most accurate?
    a. Russia's loss of Poland in the revolt of 1830 stimulated other attempts at territorial expansion.
    b. Russia actively opposed nationalist movements in the Balkans in keeping with their conservative tradition.
    c. Western powers actively aided Russia's pursuit of territories in the Ottoman empire.
    d. No massive acquisitions marked the early 19th century, but Russia continued to be an aggressive competitor for territorial expansion.

43. What accounted for the West's victory over Russia in the Crimean War?
    a. The war was fought far from Russia, necessitating lengthy lines of communication and supply.
    b. Russia was forced to fight an offensive war against entrenched positions.
    c. The war was fought almost entirely at sea where the Russians were unable to bring their numerical superiority to bear.
    d. The Western nations won not because of superior tactics or inspired principles, but because of industrial advantages.

44. Which of the following statements concerning the emancipation of the serfs in Russia is most accurate?
    a. Emancipation of the serfs destroyed the Russian aristocracy.
    b. Emancipation of the serfs loosened the grip of the tsarist state.
    c. In addition to personal freedom, the serfs were granted parcels of land, but the land was usually not the best and was subject to redemption payments.
    d. Following emancipation, peasants were free to move about Russia as they pleased, leading to massive movements of agricultural labor.

45. By 1900, how successful was the Russian industrialization program?
    a. Despite massive programs of forced labor and extensive government subsidies, the Russian program of industrialization failed.
    b. Russian industrialization progressed slowly and by 1900 had reached tenth in the world in terms of steel production.
    c. By 1900, Russia had surged to fourth rank in the world in steel production and was second to the United States in the newer area of petroleum production.
    d. Without access to plentiful raw materials, Russia was dependent on constant territorial acquisitions to fuel its lagging industrial program.

46. Which of the following statements about Russian Marxism is most accurate?
    a. Marxist insistence on careful revolutionary organization and a focus on the working class were rapidly assimilated by anarchists and peasant groups.
    b. Marxist doctrines were not imported from the West, but originated among the Russian intelligentsia.
    c. Lenin introduced important innovations in Marxist theory, including the idea that a proletarian revolution could take place without going through a middle-class phase.
    d. Lenin was dedicated to the mass electioneering typical of Western socialist parties.

47. During the final decades of the Tokugowa Shogunate
    a. more than 40 percent of all men and over 15 percent of all women were literate—a far higher percentage than anywhere else in the world outside the West.
    b. the growing commercialization of the Japanese economy gave the government a tremendous financial base for taxation, so the government could easily afford to pay stipends to the samurai in return for their loyalty.
    c. Japanese intellectual life and culture was stifled under the Tokugawa regime.
    d. the ban on Western books, begun in 1720, remained in effect.

48. Which of the following was NOT an advantage of Japan over China in the competition to assume leadership and to establish industrialization in Asia?
    a. Japan's leadership was less secular and bureaucratic than that of China.
    b. Japan already knew the benefits of imitation, which China had never acknowledged.
    c. Japan had allowed a more autonomous merchant tradition.
    d. Feudal traditions limited the heavy hand of government controls while stimulating a sense of competitiveness.

49. What was the primary difference between the reformed Japanese government and reformed Russian institutions by 1914?
    a. Japan retained an emperor at the head of government.
    b. Japan created a national parliament.
    c. Japan's government was elected by a broad majority of the population.
    d. Japan's government had incorporated business leaders into its governing structure.

50. Which is true about Western-oriented enthusiasms in late 19th century Japan?
    a. Once they saw the position Western women held in society, the Japanese were eager to elevate the position of women in Japan as well.
    b. Most Japanese copied Western fashions as part of the effort to become modern.
    c. Japanese people considered it to be effete to adopt Western hygienic practices such as brushing teeth and cutting hair.
    d. Many Japanese converted to Christianity.

DOCUMENT-BASED QUESTION

 Read the Document on MyHistoryLab:

A practice document-based question for Part 4 is available on MyHistoryLab.

CONTINUITY AND CHANGE-OVER-TIME ESSAY

Analyze continuities and changes in the relationship of the United States with Latin America from 1823 until 1910.

COMPARATIVE ESSAY

Analyze similarities and differences of the conditions leading to the overthrow of the Ottoman empire in 1908 and the Qing dynasty in 1912.

PART V

REVISITING
The Long 19th Century 1750–1900

CONTACTS AND THEIR LIMITS

The long 19th century was an age of new contacts. Steamships, railroads, and the telegraph provided unprecedented speed and volume for the movement of people, goods, and news. Interestingly, steamships initially needed coal so often that they could not travel far from the coastline, but by the 1840s they were ready for ocean crossings, with huge impact on speed and capacity alike. The opening of the Suez and Panama canals added greatly to the ease of global travel. Within this essentially technological framework, the unrelenting pressure of European merchants, missionaries, and imperialists caused people in almost every society in the world to have to react to the West. As east Asia leaders discovered, it was impossible to seek isolation. The question of what to do about Western culture and Western intrusion had become an inescapable global issue by the second half of the 19th century.

By this point, it is possible to speak of globalization as a new, more intense, and more demanding set of global contacts than had ever existed in world history. European and American corporations began setting up operations around the world, seeking raw materials and sales outlets. Many had factories in a variety of countries. By 1900, for example, Singer Sewing Machines, an American operation, was one of the largest companies in Russia.

Political globalization emerged as well, although it lagged behind international commerce. Two driving forces emerged. First, Western reformers began to take an interest in the human rights of distant peoples with whom they shared neither religion nor race but a common humanity. The origins of global human rights movements rest in the antislavery crusade of the late 18th and early 19th centuries. The World Anti-Slavery Society, still active today from its base in London, was the first international organization that depended essentially on the moral pressure of world opinion. Other movements, such as the International Red Cross and conventions about the treatment of prisoners of war, followed from humanitarian concern applied internationally. Second, economic interests saw utility in new kinds of international agreements that would facilitate commercial activity. This resulted, for example, in new conventions against piracy and the establishment of international protection for patents. Building on both impulses, the 1880s saw a flurry of new international nongovernmental organizations around issues such as labor conditions and women's rights. At the end of the 19th century, an International Court, based in the Netherlands, began operations. It was designed to deal with international disputes and, ideally, to eliminate the need for war. Many of these movements had limited impact, but they showed a clear impulse to innovate in the global political arena. There was even a reformist effort to establish a blended international language, Esperanto.

American President Theodore Roosevelt at the controls of a steam shovel during construction of the Panama Canal. The Canal greatly shortened international travel times.

Cultural globalization occurred as well. The popularity of Western sports was a case in point—for the first time popular culture spread directly from one region to the world at large. In the 1890s the Olympic Games were revived, this time as an international competition, in hopes that athletics could promote global harmony. While the level of international trade rose rapidly, there were limits to this first surge of globalization. It was clearly Western-dominated. The initial Olympics had athletes from North America and Australia joining European hosts—international, but hardly global. Global arrangements like the Universal Postal Union were truly important, but they were agreements among Western powers simply imposed on the rest of the world as part of enlightened imperialism.

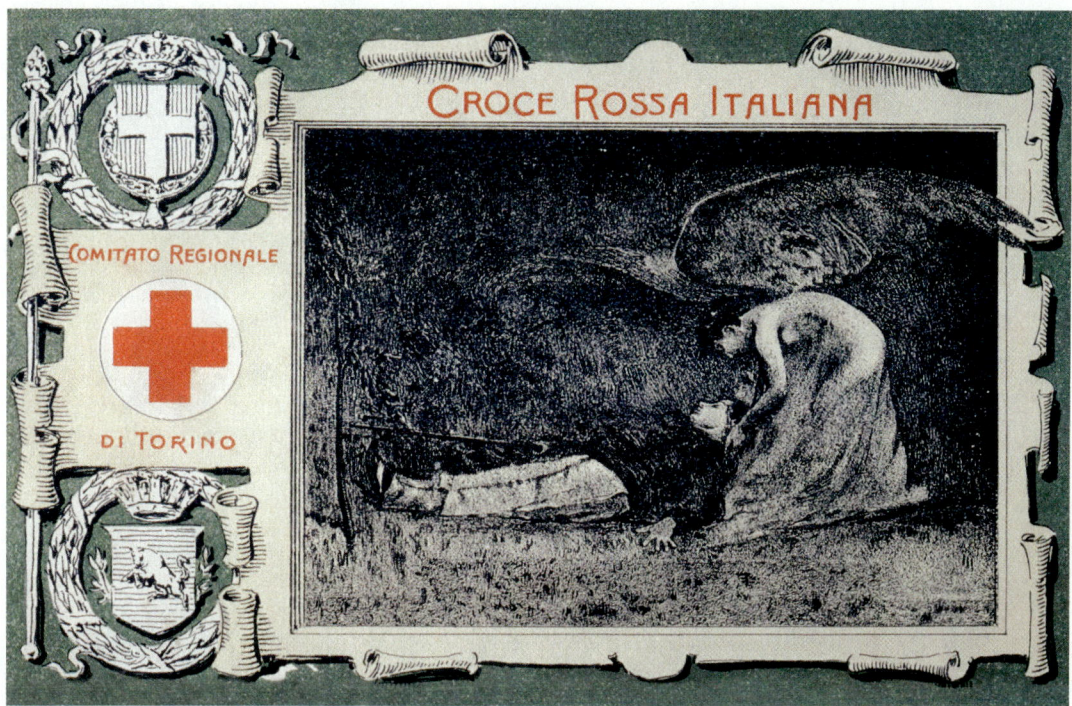

An antique Italian Red Cross poster. A winged angel bends over a fallen soldier in a frame beside the international logo. Here was a major expression of new international humanitarian impulses and political organization.

CRITICAL THEMES

Each region, including the West itself, continued to blend contacts with ongoing regional patterns in creative combinations. By 1914 the balance was clearly shifting toward globalization, but tremendous diversity persisted. The growth of Western military and economic power, plus the force of imperialism, along with globalization, must not overshadow the continued challenge of comparison among regions. Different prior experiences conditioned reactions to the basic themes of the long 19th century, as in the contrasts between Chinese and Japanese openness to imitation. Latin American efforts at state building, after independence, can be compared with Indian or African encounters with colonial administrations—even though all three areas encountered similar world economic pressures.

The growing popularity of nationalism neatly captured the complexity of the long 19th century. Here was a common force that ironically highlighted differences.

The spread of nationalism in fact permitted many regions to make new claims on real or imagined traditions as a reaction against too many concessions to global contacts. This was a new political loyalty spreading, ironically, as a result of contact; it legitimized a degree of separation and a proud assertion of the validity of specific regional traditions. Nationalism could combat Western pressure, but it could also undermine non-Western regional entities such as the Ottoman empire and, later, parts of Russia. In a world increasingly shaped by contacts, nationalism was an alternative, and largely separationist force.

Five young Japanese men have arrived in London with the aim of learning from English and Western culture. Among them are Prince Ito Hirobumi (1841–1909) (top right), who would later go on to be prime minister of the first Japanese cabinet government, and Marquis Inouye (bottom left). "Study abroad" was a key element in new levels of globalization.

CRITICAL THINKING QUESTIONS

1. What were the main differences, by 1900, between an industrial and an agricultural society?
2. Compare the colonial experiences of India and sub-Saharan Africa in the 19th century.
3. What are the main interpretive issues in explaining the causes of European industrialization?
4. Why were Japan and Russia able to respond more quickly to industrial example than many other parts of the world?
5. What were the main continuities from the Early Modern period to the long 19th century?
6. Did imperialism promote or discourage cultural interaction during the long 19th century?
7. In what respects did a new pattern of globalization emerge in the later 19th century?

PART VI

The Newest Stage of World History: 1900–Present

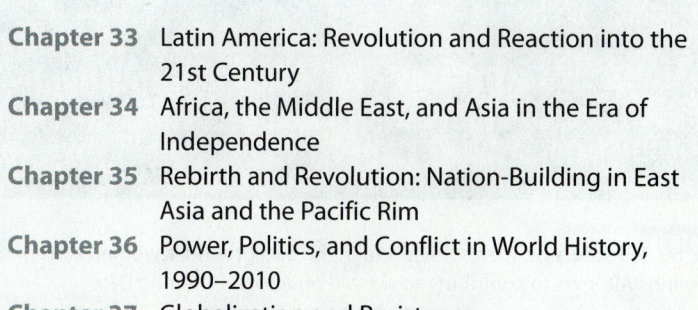

The "Occupy Wall Street" movement began in the United States in New York City as a response to the discrepancy between the banking industry—the "1 percent"—that was propped up by favorable U.S. government policies and a massive monetary bailout despite being responsible for the collapse of the world financial system in 2008, and the millions of individuals—the "99 percent"—adversely affected by the practices of these banks who received no help at all from the government. This movement quickly spread to other cities in the United States and then throughout the world. This image from an "Occupy" protest in Belfast in Northern Ireland is a great example of how local actions can quickly inspire global movements in the twenty-first century.

PART OUTLINE

Chapter 29 Descent into the Abyss: World War I and the Crisis of the European Global Order

Chapter 30 The World Between the Wars: Revolutions, Depression, and Authoritarian Response

Chapter 31 A Second Global Conflict and the End of the European World Order

Chapter 32 Western Society and Eastern Europe in the Decades of the Cold War

Chapter 33 Latin America: Revolution and Reaction into the 21st Century

Chapter 34 Africa, the Middle East, and Asia in the Era of Independence

Chapter 35 Rebirth and Revolution: Nation-Building in East Asia and the Pacific Rim

Chapter 36 Power, Politics, and Conflict in World History, 1990–2010

Chapter 37 Globalization and Resistance

THE OVERVIEW

These maps help tell two of the biggest stories of the 20th century. First, the great Western empires and the Ottoman, Austro–Hungarian, and part of the Russian empires had imploded by the end of the century. More new nations arose during the 20th century than during any other span in history. These massive boundary changes were related to other upheavals. The typical political system in 1914 was either monarchy or empire; by the early 21st century, almost every country had a different kind of government from what it had had a century before, and some societies had had multiple kinds of government. The typical social system in 1914 was still dominated by a landed aristocracy or an aristocratic and big business blend. By the beginning of the 21st century, the landed aristocracy had faded dramatically, displaced by revolution or the rise of industry. New nations were thus paralleled by new political systems and new social structures.

But political maps are not the only story. While the current phase of world history involves the rise of the nation-state, the late 20th and early 21st centuries saw new challenges to the nation-state. A variety of new regional combinations formed, the strongest being the European Union. And multinational corporations often possessed powers far greater than any but the largest nations.

The age of empire has passed. But its replacement is less clear. Will it be a welter of new nations, each with a stake in its separate identity, or will it be new organizations associated with globalization? A period of world history has passed. The 19th century has ended far more than chronologically. But defining the new period is an ongoing challenge. The problem is perspective: For past periods we know what the dominant trends and factors were, because we know the end of the story. For the current phase of world history, picking out the key themes amid the specific changes must be more tentative. Several clear conclusions must be mixed with several open questions.

Starting the contemporary period around 1900 picks up several shifts away from the dominant themes of the long 19th century. By 1900 European empires had almost reached their limits and would soon begin to retreat around new European weakness and nationalist pressures. Ongoing industrialization in Russia and Japan made it increasingly clear that the Western monopoly over modern industrial

Poster showing a German soldier, and in the background, a woman surrounded by her children. Text reminds Altoners to contribute to war aid on Altona's Offering Day.

Political Map of the World in 1914

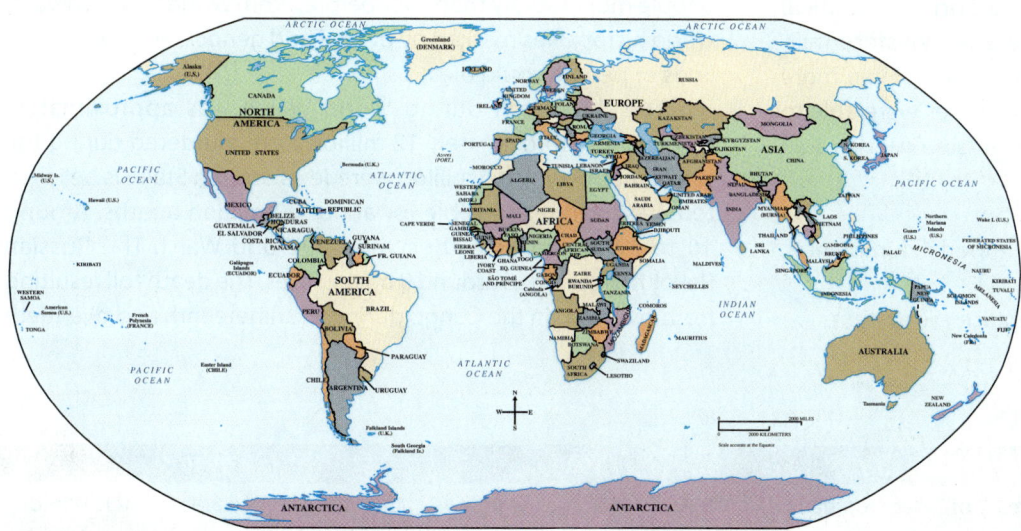

Political Map of the Present-Day World

would come to an end. A first series of revolutions—Russia in 1905, Mexico 1910, and China 1911—suggested that older social and political forms, like monarchy, would be under new challenge. Thanks to the spread of new public health measures, global populations began growing more rapidly. Finally, World War I, breaking out in 1914, seriously damaged Europe, while promoting political changes elsewhere. And the conflict, applying industrial technology to warfare, opened new levels of violence that would recurrently mark the century that followed. This was not the 19th-century world.

BIG CONCEPTS

The contemporary period in world history organizes around several global themes. A key concept involves the dissolution of global empires through decolonization. This was a major change, extending particularly from the 1920s through the 1970s, that in some ways pushed back global forces in favor of new levels of nationalism and regional assertion. The contemporary era also, from 1914 onward, saw new global wars and conflicts—including the recent global tensions associated with terrorism, another Big Concept for the period as a whole. New global institutions also emerged, at various points, in business, politics, finance, and even culture. Finally, particularly from the late 1940s onward and increasingly fueled by new technologies and explicit policies alike, a heightened level of global contacts form the final Big Concept for world history's newest period.

TRIGGERS FOR CHANGE

The world of European dominance began to come crashing down with World War I, and the destruction accelerated with the worldwide economic depression and then World War II. The two world wars were, in part, European civil wars, which caused massive loss of economic, demographic, and political vitality. It became impossible to cling to exclusive economic dominance, much less to overseas empires. Add the growing strength and effectiveness of anticolonial nationalisms, and the political order of the 19th century had to crumble. Even Western military supremacy was shaken. New challenges arose. Even more pervasively, a large number of the former colonies were able to develop sufficient military arsenals to make outside intervention dauntingly expensive.

Trigger 1: The collapse of European imperial dominance and decolonization.
Question 1: What framework will replace the system?

Initially the cold war rivalry between the United States and the Soviet Union provided a political, economic, and policy framework. This ended too, and the United States emerged as sole superpower, but this was unlikely to provide a durable pattern either. Would the next phase of world history see some other dominant civilization, playing the role that the Islamic Middle East and then the West had maintained for significant stretches of world history? Would world history be framed by a number of centers of political, military, and economic strength, with no absolute top dog?

New methods of transportation and communication provided another defining feature and ushered in another stage in the capacity to move people, goods, and ideas worldwide. Radio, satellite transmissions, and the Internet shrunk the world as never before. New technology also redefined military life. From World War I onward, the destructive power of warfare steadily grew, boundaries between military personnel and civilians blurred, and even outside of outright war it became possible to kill more people more rapidly than ever before. From World War II onward, world history was marked by purges and genocides in which millions of people could die.

The death toll during World War II was approximately 66 million. Approximately 12 million were murdered during the Holocaust, of which 6 million were Jews. Joseph Stalin is believed to have been responsible for about 20 million deaths. Around 10 to 12 million lost their lives in World War I. The Russian Revolution claimed around 9 million lives. The death toll resulting from civil strife in the Congo during the nineteenth and twentieth

1910 C.E.	1920 C.E.	1930 C.E.	1940 C.E.
1910–1920 Mexican Revolution	**1920** Treaty of Sèvres reorganizes Middle East	**1930–1945** Vargas regime in Brazil	**1941** United States enters World War II
1912 African National Congress party formed in South Africa	**1921** Foundation of Chinese Communist party	**1931** Japan invades Manchuria	**1942–1945** Holocaust
1912 Fall of Qing dynasty in China; beginning of Chinese Revolution	**1927–1928** Stalin takes power in Soviet Union; initiates five-year plans and collectivization	**1931–1947** Gandhi-led resistance in India	**1945** Formation of United Nations
1914–1918 World War I	**1929–1933** Height of Great Depression	**1933** Nazis rise to power in Germany	**1945** Atomic bombs dropped on Japan
1916 Arab revolts against Ottomans	**1920s** Gandhian resistance continues.	**1933–1939** New Deal in United States	**1945** Communists proclaim Vietnam independence
1917 United States enters World War I		**1934–1940** Cárdenas reform period in Mexico	**1945–1948** Soviet takeover of eastern Europe
1917 Russian Revolution		**1935** German rearmament; Italy captures Ethiopia	**1946** Philippine independence from the United States
1917 Balfour Declaration promises Jews a homeland in Palestine		**1937** Army officers in power in Japan; invasion of China	**1947** Peronism in Argentina
1919 Versailles peace settlement, League of Nations		**1939–1945** World War II	**1947** India and Pakistan gain independence
1919 Revolt in Egypt, first Pan-African Nationalist Congress, non-violent protest in India.		**1939** Nazi–Soviet Pact	**1947–1949** Marshall Plan for Western Europe
1919 Gandhian resistance begins.			**1948** Division of Korea
			1948 Israel–Palestine partition; first Arab–Israeli war
			1949 Formation of NATO
			1949 Communist victory in China

centuries is approximately 8 million. And around 40 million died prematurely in Maoist China.

Trigger 2: Massive technological innovation.
Question 2: Which aspect—military capacity or global communications networks—should be emphasized?

Tremendous population growth provided a third defining feature of the new period in world history. New public health measures, introduced beginning in the 19th century, explain most of the growth. Improvements in food supply for the most part kept pace, although some regions experienced devastating famines. In many regions, population growth was accompanied by massive urbanization, often in advance of industrial growth, and new patterns of urban poverty played their own role, not just in regional but also in world history. In 2007, half of the world's population lived in cities—a world history first.

Massive population growth also fed new patterns of immigration, bringing people over long distances, mainly from less industrial to more industrial areas. This immigration mixed culture groups, created new opportunities, and frequently generated new tensions. Population growth and urban expansion at contemporary levels pressed the environment, one of the reasons environmental conditions degraded at a rapid rate during the contemporary period. Ultimately, population growth led many families and societies to seek to put the brakes on, through lower birth rates (along with lower child death rates), leading to major changes in population structure. These new population patterns arose in the West by 1920, in Japan by 1950, in China and Latin American by the 1970s and 1980s.

Trigger 3: The demographic explosion.
Question 3: Will historians look back on this as a framework for disaster, inevitably leading to exhaustion of resources, battles for space, and pollution; or will the new population levels prove manageable and self-correcting, as the rapid declines in birth rates by 2000 might suggest?

How should the story of the current period of world history be written? As some combination of military technology, population pressure, and environmental crises creating a catastrophe simply waiting to happen? Or as new global linkages, restraint in the use of military technology, and successful responses to population growth leading to change but also to new opportunities?

THE BIG CHANGES

Economic, political, and social changes marked the new period in world history; trends in culture were less clear, but there was new debate and conflict. Several factors spurred change. New international contacts, with the West but also communist Russia, provided examples of innovation and challenged traditional arrangements. Outright revolution played a key role. The growth of city populations and manufacturing also put pressure on older systems. In the process, age-old arrangements, like monarchy, the dominance of landed aristocracy, and even patriarchal gender

1950 C.E.	1960 C.E.	1970 C.E.	1980 C.E.	1990 C.E.
1950–1953 Korean War	**1960s** Civil rights movement in United States; revival of feminism	**1972, 1979** Oil crises; height of OPEC power	**1980–1988** Iran–Iraq War	**1990** Reunification of Germany
1955 Warsaw Pact		**1973** Third Arab–Israeli War	**1985 ff.** Gorbachev heads Soviet Union; reforms and unrest through eastern Europe	**1990–1991** Iraq invades Kuwait; Persian Gulf crisis; U.S.–Allied defeat of Iraq
1955 Bandung conference; nonaligned movement	**1962** Algeria declares independence, Cuban Missile Crisis	**1975** Communist victory in Vietnam		
1956 Partial end of Stalinism	**1963–1973** U.S. military intervention in Vietnam	**1975–1998** Democratic regimes spread in Latin America	**1989** Reform movement in South Africa	**1992** Full economic integration of Common Market
1957 European Economic Community (Common Market)	**1965–1968** Cultural revolution in China	**1976** Death of Mao; new reform pattern in China	**1989** New regimes throughout eastern Europe	**1994** Oslo Accords between Palestinians and Israelis; Full democracy in South Africa, Nelson Mandela President
1957 Ghana becomes first independent African nation!	**1967** Second Arab-Israeli War; Israeli occupation of the West Bank, the Arab quarter of Jerusalem, Gaza, the Sinai, and Golan Heights	**1979** Iranian Revolution	**1991** Collapse of the Soviet Union	
1959 Cuban Revolution	**1968–1973** Student protests in West			**2003** U.S.–British war invasion of Iraq

relations were newly challenged and, often, replaced. New structures replaced many characteristic staples of agricultural society.

Several shifts were quite stark. In 1914, the dominant social class in most of the world's societies was the landed aristocracy. By 2009, it was an upper middle class of educated managers and big-business owners, a huge change. In 1914, most political regimes were empires or monarchies. By 2009, monarchy, except for figurehead rulers, was quite rare, and multinational empires had largely disappeared. Concerning gender, while men and women were still unequal by the 21st century, patriarchal conventions had been seriously modified, almost everywhere, by voting rights for women, new educational access, and other legal and social changes. By the end of the 20th century, rapidly declining birth rates added another dimension to the changing lives of women.

The various core challenges to the traditions of agricultural societies did not produce uniform responses. Monarchies might be largely gone, but there was massive divergence between democratic and authoritarian replacements. Woman had new rights almost everywhere, but their economic conditions and even their gender goals varied widely. Finally, the method of innovation varied from one place to the next. Huge revolutions spurred changes in some cases, not only in social structure and politics but also (at least in principle) in women's condition. In other places, new kinds of contacts and the process of decolonization set the contexts for innovation, although with less sweeping drama.

With greater political independence and new political regimes, many parts of the world made systematic efforts to improve their position in the world economy. A few regions such as Japan and the Pacific Rim joined western Europe and the United States as advanced industrial societies at the top of the economic heap. A larger number of societies won a greater voice at the global economic table. Some, like the oil-producing states, took advantage of their control over vital global resources. Some focused on replacing excessive reliance on the leading economic nations with local manufacturing through a process called import substitution. Others began to develop modern export sectors. Here, the biggest changes occurred from the 1970s onward. Beginning in the 1980s China became a global manufacturing powerhouse. India enhanced its exports and developed as a center for the outsourcing of services. Brazil became the world's fourth largest computer exporter. Economic change and the advance of modern manufacturing were widespread. The result was a more complex world economy than that of the 19th century. Before 1914, only about 20 percent of the world's population had been directly involved in industrialization; by 2009, the figure was passing 60 percent. Great economic inequalities persisted around the world, but the shift to more industrial economies was widespread, helping to explain other aspects of change as well.

In the cultural field, change also occurred, but here amid far greater dispute and resistance. Three cultural forces encouraged new secular loyalties. Nationalism won allegiance from most of humanity. Marxism was a persuasive belief system for many of the world's peoples during the 20th century. From the West and Japan came an emphasis on consumer values and faith in science. The cold war brought worldwide competition between Marxism and Western consumerism. Many people changed or modified their beliefs during the 20th and 21st centuries. But the major religions retained powerful support as well. Missionary activities—Christian and Islamic—were successful in Africa and elsewhere. From the 1970s onward, a strong commitment to what many argued were fundamentalist religious values gained ground, often making use of new technology to get the message across and characterized by new levels of intolerance. The result was a real contest for cultural preferences within societies such as the Middle East, India, Russia, and the United States.

A new round of globalization occurred in the second half of the 20th century. During the middle decades of the 20th century, globalization had receded. In the 1920s and 1930s, the Soviet Union pulled out of the international economic and political system, as did Nazi Germany and authoritarian Japan. China withdrew during the early decades of the cold war, as did the United States partially, during its two decades of isolationism. The technologies promoting further contacts continued to accelerate, however, and key societies shifted position in the decades after World War II. Japan, Germany, and the United States became active global players. China reentered the global system after 1978, Russia after 1985. Not surprisingly, this second round of globalization proved even more intense than the first. Multinational corporations, for example, depended on much closer global integration than earlier international corporations. From the 1970s onward, a massive network of international nongovernmental organizations emerged, which sought to deal with an array of issues from human rights and the environment to sweatshop labor. Global cultural change, linked to consumerism, became more extensive than ever before. Population growth encouraged new forms of migration that brought people from Africa, Asia, and Latin America to industrial centers in the United States, western Europe, and to some extent Japan. Many migrants now went back and forth frequently, encouraging further cultural contact between their societies of origin and their new homes.

Globalization began also to involve new kinds of environmental change. The human impact on the environment had been largely regional. Now it took on international dimensions. Multinational corporations were responsible for recurrent pollution crises, including oil spills and chemical disasters. Air pollution from industrial regions brought acid rain to forests hundreds of miles away. Most scientists became convinced by the early 21st century that air pollution and the destruction of tropical rain forests were creating global warming, which had implications for the entire planet. And while policymakers struggled to find global responses, there was a lag between economic globalization and the political will to solve the problems it created.

Four themes, then, organize many of the specific developments in the contemporary period: the end of empires and the relative decline of the West; the population explosion and its consequences; the redefinition of traditional political and social forms and the global expansion of industrialization; and the acceleration of globalization itself. Some historians would advance a fifth theme: the increase incidence of devastating war and civil strife, one of the darkest sides of the contemporary period.

CONTINUITY

In the late 20th century, many people believed that change was accelerating more rapidly than at any previous point in world history. It was important, nevertheless, to recognize continuities. These fell into three related categories. While a number of regions advanced industrialization, others continued to focus on low-cost production of raw materials and foods. During much of the 20th century industrial countries intensified their control over most African exports. Parts of Latin America and southeast Asia were also still dominated by older constraints in the world economy. Even within changing societies, such as India, rural regions often maintained older economic and social forms. Worldwide, by 2005, fewer than 30 percent of the world's people had access to the Internet—this was a huge minority, of course, and an impressive sign of change; but also a reminder of ongoing limitations. Overall, many economic inequalities had worsened by the early 21st century, both within regions and among them, and most of these gaps reflected older historical patterns.

There was great resistance to change in many parts of the world. Many societies hesitated to redefine gender relation. This was one reason why, in places like Africa and the Middle East, girls continued to be less likely to receive primary education than boys. The increased influence of fundamentalist religions both reflected and encouraged resistance to many kinds of change, including in some instances the inroads of consumer culture. Even aside from outright resistance, many regions attempted to discipline change by combining it with older traditions. Early in the 21st century, in the southern Indian state of Kerala, for example, leaders attempted to organize beauty contests in which prizes would go to women with the best command of Keralan language and culture. This was an intriguing effort to use a new and popular aspect of global consumerism to revive regional tradition. The food chain McDonald's, even as it built a worldwide empire, accepted essential adjustments to local customs. McDonald's provided wine and beer in its European outlets, more vegetarian fare in India, and teriyaki burgers in Japan. Globalization did not entirely override continuity or opposition in the name of continuity.

Finally, even as they responded to change, many societies retained broader orientations derived from their past. Early in the 21st century it was clear that the United States continued to be extremely suspicious of participating in international agreements that might limit its sovereignty. Hence, it rejected several pacts, including those on the environment, on punishing war criminals, and on banning land mines. China changed mightily during the 20th century, but it continued to place an unusual emphasis on order and conformity. Government attacks on a Buddhist-derived religious movement, the Falun Gong, were uncannily similar to the repression of Buddhism itself under the Tang dynasty. Russia's return to greater authoritarianism in the early 21st century reminded many observers of the strong continuities between tsarist political systems, communism, and the new leadership—all intolerant of internal opposition and critique. Thus, a key use of world history involves interpreting contemporary conditions to understand how older regional or civilizational traditions continue to shape responses to current problems. The hand of the past does not prevent dramatic change, but it usually colors that change.

Impact on Daily Life: Emotions and Behavior

Key developments in the 20th and 21st centuries affected people's emotions and behavior. Emotions are to some extent hardwired and not subject to historical change. Many emotional and behavioral formulations reflect individual personality or particular cultures. And some emotional and behavioral standards continued to characterize specific civilizations in the 20th century. Thus Tahitians, according to anthropologists, were slower to anger than most people. Societies around the Mediterranean maintained traditions of angry or jealous responses to offenses.

Nevertheless, three kinds of change reflected and furthered the larger currents of world history. In many societies, efforts to destroy social inequality involved attempts to reverse emotional passivity. Mao Zedong, leader of the communist upheaval in China, urged peasants to cast off their traditional reluctance to show anger. Civil rights leaders in the United States wrote childrearing manuals to show African American parents how to instill new assertiveness in their children rather than more traditional deference.

Demographic changes had emotional and behavioral implications. When families drastically lowered their birth rates, emotional attachments to individual children increased. American families in the 20th century could rarely survive the death of a child without divorce. By the 1990s Chinese educators were noting growing debates with school officials over the proper treatment of particular children by teams of parents and grandparents, now focused intensely on the fate of a single child.

The spread of global consumerism affected some behaviors. When McDonald's set up its first restaurants in Soviet Russia, it had to teach workers to smile and pretend to be cheerful, a marked contrast to the surly style that had been common among salespeople in the Soviet system. Flight attendants on international airlines received similar training in cheerfulness and service. Many consumer pitches played up emotions like romantic love and played down emotions like grief. Revealingly, when China opened up to the global economy after 1978, public expressions of romantic love increased, as did imports of foreign items that seemed to express loving care.

Saudis place their orders at a McDonald's restaurant in this photo taken Friday, Oct. 31, 2003, in a shopping mall in Riyadh, Saudi Arabia. Here was an intriguing aspect of globalization, where shared patterns and regional distinctions combined.

Emotions and behaviors hardly homogenized worldwide. Older distinctions persisted. New trends often contradicted each other. There were big differences, for example, between anger-fueled protest and the emotions suitable for consumerism. But there were some wider patterns nevertheless. A growing number of people, such as global businesspeople and immigrants who traveled back and forth between their old and new countries, learned a variety of behavioral rules depending on their setting, becoming fluent in global manners and also in the languages and habits of particular societies.

SOCIETIES AND TRENDS

The section begins with Chapter 29 on World War I, in which some of the key trends of the 19th century were brutally reversed. The chapter covers not only the war, but the flawed peace settlement and the growing attacks on European imperialism around the world. Chapter 30 deals with other major developments between the two world wars, including dramatic new regimes in Russia, Germany, China, and Italy, and the global impact of economic depression. Chapter 31 describes World War II and the ensuing surge of decolonization, which definitively ended the European order. Chapter 32 focuses on changes both in Western society and in eastern Europe during the cold war. Chapter 33 treats Latin America into the 21st century. Chapter 34 deals with the impacts of decolonization and ensuing developments in Africa, the Middle East, and south and southeast Asia. Chapter 35 focuses on east Asia and the Pacific Rim, where complex developments and divisions had major effects on the world at large. Chapters 36 and 37 describe key changes in the transition from the 20th to the 21st century.

Taken together, the chapters in this section illustrate the larger themes of this new period in world history. But they also recognize key stages within the past century: the world wars and interwar period as a time of transition; postwar developments dominated by the cold war and decolonization; and a third phase—our current phase—in which new alignments, within a framework of accelerating global contacts, hold pride of place. ■

Descent into the Abyss: World War I and the Crisis of the European Global Order

29

Listen to Chapter 29 on MyHistoryLab

The British overlords were staggered and even some Egyptian nationalist leaders were taken aback by the thousands of women—young and old—who joined the mass demonstrations in the spring of 1919. Spreading from Cairo to towns and villages throughout the Protectorate, the protests shook the global British imperial edifice to its very foundations. Most accounts of the demonstrations, which in many instances turned into violent clashes, stressed the role of students and working-class men. The participation of women was often mentioned. But most narratives dealt only with elite women—some of whom are captured in the photograph here—who marched in the streets veiled to signal their defiance of the British colonizers. Predictably, we know a good deal about the backgrounds of these elite protesters and the causes they espoused. Little attention, however, has been given to working-class women who—although they have remained largely anonymous—marched in far larger numbers alongside the students and working-class men, and who took on much more aggressive roles during the political upheavals of the early 1920s.

LEARNING OBJECTIVES

29.1 What were the crises and motivations that led to the formation of the opposing European alliances and the factors that brought the two alliances to war in 1914? p. 704

29.2 What were the major factors, particularly in Europe, that contributed to the catastrophic levels of casualties and general destructiveness of World War I? p. 706

29.3 How did the fallout from the conflict alter gender and racial attitudes and interactions both in wartime and especially in the decades after the war? p. 713

29.4 What were the major grievances that drove the resistance and rebellions that African, Middle Eastern, and Asian peoples mounted during and after World War I? p. 714

FIGURE **29.1** In late May 1919, large numbers of veiled women joined the mass protests in Cairo and other Egyptian cities and towns that were sparked by the harsh wartime conditions that British demands had exacerbated and by the colonizers' refusal to give Egyptian leaders a hearing at the peace conference in Paris.

Watch the Video Series on MyHistoryLab

Learn about some key topics related to this chapter with the *MyHistoryLab Video Series: Key Topics in World History*

It is not likely that young working-class women, such as Shafika Muhammad and Hamida Khalil, gave much thought to what contemporary reporters or later historians would write about their activities during the tumultuous months from 1919 to 1922 in Egypt. They were too deeply engaged in the tense demonstrations, which held the constant threat of serious injury or even death as Egyptians became more and more aggressive in their resistance to British attempts to crush the mounting popular protest. If they had known, however, that they would be lumped together with unveiled and scantily clad prostitutes in a report on the nationalist risings by a widely read British journalist, the young women would have been outraged. For even though they too marched in the streets unveiled, it was not a reflection of their lack of modesty. In contrast to the veiled well-to-do women from prominent families who had dominated the nationalist movement for decades, women who labored in the processing plants and farmlands of Egypt could not work effectively if restricted by veils and had never made much use of them. But unlike the prostitutes, working-class women made certain that their bodies were well covered, even if that meant wearing loose-fitting pants for some of the more dangerous revolutionary endeavors many were willing to undertake.

In important ways the grievances that sparked the popular risings all along the Nile Valley had much more to do with the lives of the working women than with the concerns of their elite counterparts. The former had always labored long hours at arduous tasks in the sweatshops or fields to earn meager wages or grow a little more food to share with their families. But the demands of the hard-pressed British rulers during World War I had proved devastating for the women and other ordinary Egyptians, who had begun to feel the effects of the global conflict within months of its outbreak in early August 1914.

The war triggered an export boom, especially in cotton, which was in great demand for uniforms, medical supplies, and many other wartime uses. For poor women like Shafika and Hamida, that meant jobs in the factories. And employment opportunities for women increased as the war dragged on, fed by the British decision to conscript Egyptian men in the tens of thousands. Most of the Egyptians worked as bearers, animal tenders, and purveyors of all sorts of services for the influx of British, Australian, and New Zealand armed forces that used Egypt as a staging area for attacks on Turkey and to check German and Turkish threats to the Suez Canal. But the poorly paid and often dangerous jobs that became available to women like Shafika and Hamida could not begin to make up for the runaway inflation that plagued Egypt during the war years. Ordinary Egyptians were affected by sharply rising prices for all manner of household necessities, from bread to clothing to kerosene for lamps and cooking. The demands of garrisoning tens of thousands of soldiers from throughout the empire placed increasing demands on the already overstretched food supply of the Egyptian people, some of whom perished of malnutrition linked to the war. And widespread British confiscations of draft animals belonging to Egyptians enraged peasants and urban workers, both of whom depended on these animals for survival.

Although these and other abuses contributed to the buildup of social and political pressures during the war years, the British underestimated growing signs that a revolt was in the making, because they had long regarded the Egyptians as passive and pliable. Colonial officials were consequently ill-prepared to deal with the literal explosions of popular risings that occurred in the spring of 1919. When the British refused to let Egyptian nationalist leaders travel to France

1870 C.E.	1890 C.E.	1900 C.E.	1910 C.E.	1920 C.E.
1870–1890 Cycle of economic depressions in Europe and the United States	**1890** End of the Three Emperors' Alliance (Russia, Austria–Hungary, Germany) **1894** Franco-Russian alliance **1899–1901** Anglo-Boer war in South Africa	**1904–1905** Japanese victory over Russia **1906** Dinshawai incident in Egypt **1909** Morley-Minto reforms in India	**1910** Union of South Africa formed **1914–1918** World War I **1916** Beginning of Arab revolt against Ottoman empire **1917** Russian Revolution **1917** United States enters World War I **1918** Treaty of Brest-Litovsk; Russia withdraws from war **1919** Treaty of Versailles; League of Nations established **1919** Gandhi leads first nonviolent protest movements in India; revolt in Egypt; Rowlatt Act in India	**1922** French and British mandates set up in Middle East **1920s** Pan-African Congresses in Paris **1923** Treaty of Lausanne recognizes independence of Turkey

to make the case for Egyptian independence at the Versailles peace conference. Mass protest spread like wildfire throughout the colony. And none of the colonial officials could figure out how to handle either the elite or the working-class women who displayed great aptitude for political organization, dramatizing their causes and fearlessly confronting the police and armed forces. Working-class women even became involved in bombings and armed assaults directed against railways, telegraph stations, and government buildings. And, like Shafika Muhammad, who was killed by British soldiers when they fired on crowds of unarmed demonstrators on March 14, 1919, some became martyrs of the national liberation movement. They were revered by ordinary Egyptians at the time (if neglected by subsequent historians), and for decades by the leaders of the nationalist movement. ■

Although far removed from the massive slaughter of young men in the trench warfare of Europe that we normally associate with World War I, the risings in Egypt and the emergence of women as a major force in resistance to continuing colonial domination underscore the importance of seeing the conflict as a truly global phenomenon. It had profound and far-reaching repercussions for peoples and societies across much of Europe, the Middle East, Africa, Asia, North America, and the Pacific—especially Australia and New Zealand. The fact that the three main adversaries in the war—Great Britain, France, and Germany—were colonial powers meant that when they plunged into war, they pulled their empires into the abyss with them.

Because the British controlled the sea approaches to Europe, they and their French allies were able to draw soldiers, laborers, raw materials, loans, and donations from their colonial possessions, and these proved critical to their ability to sustain the long war of attrition against Germany. In addition, there were major theaters of combat in the Middle East and Africa as well as clashes in China and the Pacific. The years of increasingly senseless slaughter on the Western Front made a mockery of European claims of superior rationality and a racially ingrained capacity to rule. Pressed by a shortage of trained officials, Europeans were willing to give Western-educated Africans and Indians roles in governance that would have been unimaginable without the war. When the British and French victors sought to renege on promises made to these elites and restore their prewar political prerogatives, the first wave of decolonization was set in motion in Egypt, India, Vietnam, and other colonial societies. World War I, a huge event in itself, gave rise to a troubled peace and to varied attacks on European imperialism in the ensuing decades.

THE COMING OF THE GREAT WAR

> By 1914 diplomatic tensions among the major European powers had been escalating steadily for a generation. Colonial rivalries and arms races had led to the formation, beginning in the 1890s, of two increasingly hostile alliances.

29.1 What were the crises and motivations that led to the formation of the opposing European alliances and the factors that brought the two alliances to war in 1914?

Fear of Germany's growing economic and military power had driven autocratic Russia to ally first with republican France and then with the even more democratic Britain (Map 29.1). Germany's growing power also menaced its neighbor to the west, France. From the early 1890s, the arrogance and aggressive posturing of Germany's new ruler, Kaiser Wilhelm II, only magnified the threat the emerging colossus seemed to pose for the rest of Europe. The French hoped that their alliance with Russia would lead to a two-front war that would check Germany's rising supremacy and allow France to recover the provinces of Alsace and Lorraine, which France had lost to Germany due to its defeat in the Franco-Prussian War of 1870. Eclipsed by Germany economically, and increasingly threatened

MAP **29.1 World War I Fronts in Europe and the Middle East** In contrast to the large swaths of territory caught up in the war on the eastern front, the area contested and the battle lines in the west were confined largely to a corner of Belgium and northernmost France.

overseas by a growing German navy, Britain joined with Russia and France to form the Triple Entente in the early 1900s.

In the same decade the Triple Entente powers increasingly confronted a counteralliance consisting of Germany, Austria–Hungary, and (nominally at least) Italy that would become known as the Central Powers. After Wilhelm II became emperor (or Kaiser), Germany moved away from a defensive triple alliance with Russia and Austria–Hungary to a growing dependence on the latter alone. The German had also sought to draw the Italians into the coalition with promises of support for the Italian's schemes for colonial expansion. But Italian hostility to Austria–Hungary, which still controlled lands the Italians claimed as their own, kept Italy's role as one of the Central Powers tentative and liable to shift with changing international circumstances. Italian ambivalence became all too clear after the outbreak of war when Italy not only refused to support Germany and Austria–Hungary but in 1915 entered the conflict on the side of the Triple Entente.

Read the Document on MyHistoryLab: Carl Peters Calls for German Colonization of Africa, 1884

The alliance system, although menacing in itself, was embittered by the atmosphere generated by imperial rivalries that were played out over most of the globe. In the decades leading up to World War I, most of the European powers had been involved in empire-building overseas, and they came to equate the prestige of "great power" status with the possession of colonies. Their rivalries heightened nationalist sentiments in each country. But by 1900 most of the world's available territories had been colonized by one or another of the states in the two alliance systems. As a result, the scramble in the early 1900s for the few areas as yet unclaimed produced ever greater tensions in the European diplomatic system. The French maneuvered to annex Morocco to their North African colonies, which already included Algeria and Tunisia (Map 29.1). Germany twice threatened war if the French advance continued, only to back off when it was clear that none of the other European powers would support it. In the second of the international crises over Morocco in 1911, the Germans had to be bought off by a French concession of territory from their possessions in central Africa.

View the Closer Look on MyHistoryLab: The French in Morocco

Imperialist rivalries solidified the growing divisions between the two alliances and fed the jingoism (warlike nationalist sentiments that spread widely among the middle and working classes throughout Europe) that had much to do with the coming of the war. Most European leaders of both the great powers and smaller states, such as those in the Balkans, were eager to vie for increased territories and obsessed with keeping their rivals from advancing at their own country's expense (Figure 29.2).

Imperialism and the alliance system were both linked to ever more intense and costly arms races. Naval rivalry was the most apparent and fiercely contested. The Germans' decision to build a navy that could threaten Great Britain's long-standing control of the world's oceans was one of the key reasons for Britain's move for military cooperation with France and (more grudgingly) Russia. It also touched off the greatest arms race in all of history to that time. Huge new warships, such as the *Dreadnought* battleship launched in 1906 and the German ships built in response, kept the naval rivalry at fever pitch. Serious hopes for arms limitations, much less reductions, faded. Armies grew steadily in size and firepower, and they practiced massive maneuvers that national leaders were prepared to implement in the event of the outbreak of a general war. Not surprisingly, the military buildup helped pave the way to war, as some in the German military in particular pushed for a preemptive strike before army reforms in Russia made it too powerful to overcome.

Diplomatic and military competition tied foreign policy to spiraling domestic tensions. All of the major industrial nations, and those in the process of industrializing like Russia, faced growing labor unrest after 1900. Strikes, the growth of trade unions, and votes for socialist parties

FIGURE **29.2** This U.S. poster drumming up financial support for the war effort epitomizes the paranoia and extreme stereotyping of adversary peoples and powers that poisoned international relations in the decades leading up to the war and drove the continuing slaughter on all fronts from 1914 to 1918.

mounted steadily in the decade and a half before 1914. The business classes and the political elites were alarmed by these challenges to their dominance. They sought diplomatic successes and confrontations with rival powers to distract their subjects from social problems at home. British ministers and the German kaiser, for example, appealed for labor peace in the name of national unity in the face of the threat of attack by powerful rivals. Those in power also supported military buildups because they provided employment for the working classes and huge profits to industrialists who were pillars of support for each of the European regimes.

The Outbreak of the War

In the years just before 1914, decades of rivalry and mounting tensions within the European state system were increasingly centered on the Balkans, where Russia sought to back Serbia in its determined resistance to the steady advance of the Austro–Hungarian empire (see Map 29.1). The complex ethnic divisions and interstate rivalries of the Balkans region mirrored the growing crisis of Europe as a whole. It was not surprising then, that the event that precipitated World War I occurred in the Balkans. In July 1914, a Serbian nationalist, Gavriel Princip, assassinated the heir apparent to the Austro–Hungarian throne, **Archduke Franz Ferdinand** and his wife in **Sarajevo**, which was the administrative center of the Bosnian province of the Austrian empire. Bolstered by the infamous "blank check" promised by the kaiser for reprisals against Serbia, the Austro–Hungarians drew up a list of demands that it was impossible for the Serbs to accede to without surrendering their nation's sovereignty. The ruling circles of Austria–Hungary were determined to put an end to decades of Serbian challenges to their control over portions of the Balkans, and thus they were clearly intent on forcing a war.

When the Russians vowed to support their Slavic brethren in Serbia should war break out with the Austrians, the alliance systems that had been forged in the preceding decades quickly came into play. Within months the confrontation of the two blocs had transformed what might have been a regional war among the Balkan states and their Austrian or Russian backers into the threat of a general European war. Inept diplomacy and a widespread sense of resignation to the eventual outbreak of war, which some believed would sort out the quarrels and tensions that had been building for decades, led to the mobilization of the armies of the great powers in late July 1914.

Although the leaders of most of the powers had long regarded mobilization as a way of applying diplomatic pressure, for the Germans mobilization meant war. Because they had faced the possibility of massive combat on two fronts since the 1890s, the Germans had devised an intricate plan to first attack in the west and defeat France before turning to the more backward, and thus slower to mobilize, Russians in the east. Once Russia mobilized against Germany, and the German armies moved to mobilize in retaliation according to a rigid railway timetable that plotted an invasion of neutral Belgium on the way to an all-out assault on France, the alliance systems were locked into a massive war. When the British entered the conflict, officially to defend tiny Belgium, which they had long before pledged to protect, a European conflict was transformed into a global one. Britain's naval ally Japan quickly jumped into the fray. British-ruled colonial territories, from the White Dominions of Canada, Australia, and New Zealand to Britain's extensive imperial possessions in India and across Africa and Southeast Asia, were brought directly into the war. After nearly a century's lapse, Europe was again consumed by a general war that rapidly spread to other parts of the world.

A WORLD AT WAR

29.2 What were the major factors, particularly in Europe, that contributed to the catastrophic levels of casualties and general destructiveness of World War I?

Perhaps more than any other single factor, the failure of Germany's ambitious plan for a quick victory over France ensured that there would be a long war of stalemate and attrition. German political and military leaders counted on their country's superb railway system and huge armies to overwhelm the Belgians and defeat the French before they could even fully mobilize. The French obliged them by launching offensives against deeply entrenched German forces in Alsace-Lorraine that ended in the near destruction of some of France's best armies. But the Belgians resisted bravely, slowing the German goliath, and the small but superbly trained British army suddenly appeared to contest the momentum of three German armies—each of which was larger than the total British forces. By

---

Ferdinand, Archduke Franz (1863–1914) Heir apparent to the Austro-Hungarian throne whose assassination in Sarajevo set in motion the events that started World War I.

Sarajevo Administrative center of the Bosnian province of Austrian empire; assassination there of Archduke Ferdinand in 1914 proved to be the spark that started World War I.

Read the Document on MyHistoryLab: The Murder of Archduke Franz Ferdinand at Sarajevo 1914 Borijove Jevtic

Part of the reason that Europeans let their nations blunder into war in 1914 was that most of them expected the conflict to be brief and decisive. But after only a month, it was beginning to be clear that the world had been plunged into a conflict that was likely to go on for a good deal longer.

the time they reached the frontiers of northern France, the German soldiers were tired and, having left the railways behind in southern Belgium, growing short of boots, food, and ammunition. Reeling from their defeats by the Germans in Alsace-Lorraine, the French forces retreated toward Paris, where they regrouped, were reinforced (in part by a famous convoy of Parisian cab drivers), and prepared for the German onslaught. During a five-day battle along the Marne River in early September, the German advance was halted; then thrown back. Paris had been saved and the stage set for over three years of bloody stalemate on the **Western Front**.

To protect themselves from the withering firepower of the artillery and machine guns of the opposing armies, British and German soldiers began to dig into the ground during and after the clashes along the Marne. Soon northern and western France was crisscrossed by miles and miles of entrenchments that frustrated—with staggering levels of dead and wounded—all attempts to break the stalemate between the opposing forces until well into 1918. The almost unimaginable killing power of the industrial technology wielded by the opposing European armies favored the defensive. Devastating artillery, the withering fire of machine guns, barbed-wire barriers, and the use of poison gas turned the Western Front into a killing ground that offered no possibility of decisive victory to either side. The carnage reached unimaginable levels, with the Germans losing 850,000 troops, the French 700,000, and the British over 400,000 in the single year of 1916 on just the Western Front.

Western Front Front established in World War I; generally along line from Belgium to Switzerland; featured trench warfare and horrendous casualties for all sides in the conflict.

By the millions, the youths of Europe were killed, maimed, and driven insane, or they waited for the next offensive catastrophe in rat- and lice-infested trenches. Like the so-called primitive peoples the Europeans had come to dominate overseas, soldiers were exposed to rain and cold and deprived of virtually all of the material comforts that large sections of western European societies had come to regard as their birthright. A German soldier, and later novelist, captured the constant fear, the almost unendurable anxiety the soldiers experienced:

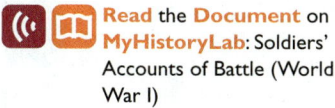
Read the Document on MyHistoryLab: Soldiers' Accounts of Battle (World War I)

> The front is a cage in which we must await fearfully whatever may happen. We lie under the network of arching shells and live in a suspense of uncertainty. Over us chance hovers.

In so many ways, the war in Europe was centered on the ongoing and senseless slaughter in the trenches. Levels of dead and wounded that would have been unimaginable before the war rose ever higher between 1915 and 1918. They were all the more tragic because neither side could break the stalemate; hundreds of thousands were killed or maimed to gain small patches of ground that were soon lost in counterattacks. Years of carnage made all too evident the lack of imagination and utter incompetence of most of the generals on both sides of the conflict. Few understood that mass assaults on mechanized defenses had become suicidal at this point in the industrial age. The aged officers in the higher commands and overmatched politicians on the home fronts soon demoted or dismissed those who sought to find creative ways out of the trench morass. As the years passed, as a British war poet observed:

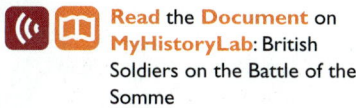
Read the Document on MyHistoryLab: British Soldiers on the Battle of the Somme

> Neither [side] had won or could win the war
> The war had won and would go on winning.

The War in Eastern Europe and Italy

In the first weeks of the conflict, the Germans were alarmed by the rapidity with which the Russians were able to mount major offensives against both the Austro–Hungarians and eastern Germany. Having committed most of their forces to their own offensives against France, the German high command felt obliged to divert critical resources and manpower to check the advancing Russian armies. In late August the reorganized German forces virtually destroyed an entire Russian army (and sent a second into headlong retreat). In defeat, the Russian forces exhibited many of the weaknesses that resulted in, by far, the highest levels of casualties of any of the combatants and the ultimate and utter defeat of the tsarist armies. Aristocratic generals dispatched millions of mostly illiterate and poorly trained peasants to certain death in repeated assaults on better-armed and led German forces. Commands in critical battles were sent in uncoded format and readily picked up by their adversaries. Russian artillery, manned by upper-class personnel, usually provided little cover for massed peasant forces, which were reduced to little more than cannon and machine-gun fodder in assaults on the entrenched Germans.

Although the lines shifted over large areas in the east, they inexorably, with horrific human cost, moved east into the provinces of the Russian empire. The poor showing of the Russian commanders,

VISUALIZING THE PAST

Trench Warfare

THIS WORLD WAR I PAINTING HIGHLIGHTS soldiers in the trench fighting that dominated the conflict on the Western Front.

QUESTIONS
- What were the trenches like?
- Can the expressions and poses of the soldiers be read to suggest what war meant to them?
- How did life in the trenches compare with their previous lives in industrial society and with expectations in an age that had placed a premium on manliness and nationalism?
- Does the painting raise issues of bias or staging on the part of the artist, or is it a neutral piece of evidence?

Nicholas II Tsar of Russia 1894–1917; forcefully suppressed political opposition and resisted constitutional government; deposed by revolution in 1917.

including the hapless tsar **Nicholas II**, who insisted on taking control at the front, did much to spark the mutinies and peasant revolts that were critical forces in the revolutionary waves that destroyed the tsarist regime in 1917.

The Russians fared somewhat better on the Austro–Hungarian front (Map 29.1), where they faced even more inept generals than their own and multiethnic armies whose soldiers' loyalty to the Austrian emperor was often lukewarm or nonexistent. But the Russians could not prevent the Austrians from crushing Serbia, which held out until the end of 1915. Thanks largely to timely interjections of German soldiers, the Austro–Hungarians managed, again at the cost of millions of casualties, to check repeated Russian offensives. The Austrian forces generally fought much better against the Italians, who entered the war in May 1915. Nine months earlier, Italian leaders had declined to march to war with their Central Power allies, who the Italians claimed had attacked first and thus nullified what was a defensive treaty. Having wrested British promises of substantial territorial gains, mostly at Austria–Hungary's expense, the Italians launched a series of offensives against the Austrians.

With the Austrians enjoying the high ground in the eastern Alps, the assaults all ended in disaster. Incompetent and corrupt generals, soldiers increasingly disgusted by costly campaigns that went nowhere, and venal politicians double-dealing behind the lines resulted in the near collapse of the

Italian front in 1917. Although British and French reinforcements rushed from the Western Front eventually stalled the Austrian advance, Italian soldiers deserted in droves and the war plunged Italy into social and political turmoil. One of the Italian soldiers who was briefly at the front and slightly wounded, Benito Mussolini, would soon exploit this unrest to the fullest in his postwar drive to impose a fascist dictatorship on Italy.

The Home Fronts in Europe

As the war dragged on without any sign that decisive victories could be won by either side, soldiers at the fronts across Europe grew resentful of the civilians back home. Their anger was focused on political leaders who cheered them on from the safety of the sidelines far to the rear. But the soldiers were also disturbed more generally by the patriotic zeal and insensitivity of the civilian populace, which had little sense of the horrors that were endured at the front. In fact, in the soldiers' view the civilians behind the lines often had a stronger commitment and more pronounced hatred for the enemy than did the soldiers in combat. Each of the powers remained able to mobilize ever larger numbers of soldiers and military resources, despite growing food shortages and privations on the home fronts. Governments responded by rationing resources and regulating production to head off potentially crippling labor disputes.

Whole industrial sectors, such as railways, were administered directly by the state. Executive branches of the combatants' governments gradually took over the power of elected parliaments—particularly in Germany, where by late 1916 the General Staff virtually ran the country. Dissent was suppressed, often by force, and newspapers and other media outlets (as well as the letters of the soldiers) were strictly censored. Governments developed propaganda departments that grew more sophisticated and strident as the war dragged on. The British proved the most adept at propaganda. Much of this was aimed at the United States in the hope that the Americans would be drawn into the war. British and American citizens were bombarded with stories of German atrocities. As the war went into its second and third years, news of severe setbacks was increasingly hidden from the German people. As a consequence, most Germans were stunned by what seemed their sudden defeat in 1918. The extent of the involvement of the civilian population (in some cases as targets of bombardments and aerial assaults) and the power of governments to mobilize millions of men and women and control the information they received about the conflict made "the Great War" truly the first total war in human history.

The war sped up many developments already visible in industrial societies. The power of organization increased, particularly through the new interventions of governments. To maintain unified backing of the civilian population, socialists and trade union chiefs were given new recognition and allowed to serve on governing boards in charge of industrial production and negotiate improved working conditions. As their leaders became ever more drawn into the existing governmental system, some labor groups rejected their leadership and became ever more vocal critics of the war. As the war lumbered on, seemingly out of control, these trends became more pronounced, particularly in Russia and Germany. Labor protests in Moscow and St. Petersburg gave powerful momentum to the wave of discontent and mass protest that brought down the tsarist regime in February 1917 and propelled the Bolsheviks to power in October of the same year (see Chapter 30). In Germany, labor agitation, very often sparked by growing shortages of food and fuel that were intensified by the British naval blockade, also loomed as a threat to the military commanders who ran the country in the last years of the conflict. As the German front in France and Belgium collapsed in the early summer of 1918, leftist leaders and angry laborers pushed the nation to the brink of revolution in late 1918 and 1919.

As a direct consequence of the war, women's participation in the labor force increased greatly, particularly in Germany, Britain, and the United States. Defying prevailing prewar notions about the "natural" gender roles, women proved very able to work even in heavy industry, where many were engaged in the very dangerous production of munitions (Figure 29.3). Better wages and the confidence they gained from their mastery of such demanding and critical roles as factory workers and nurses at

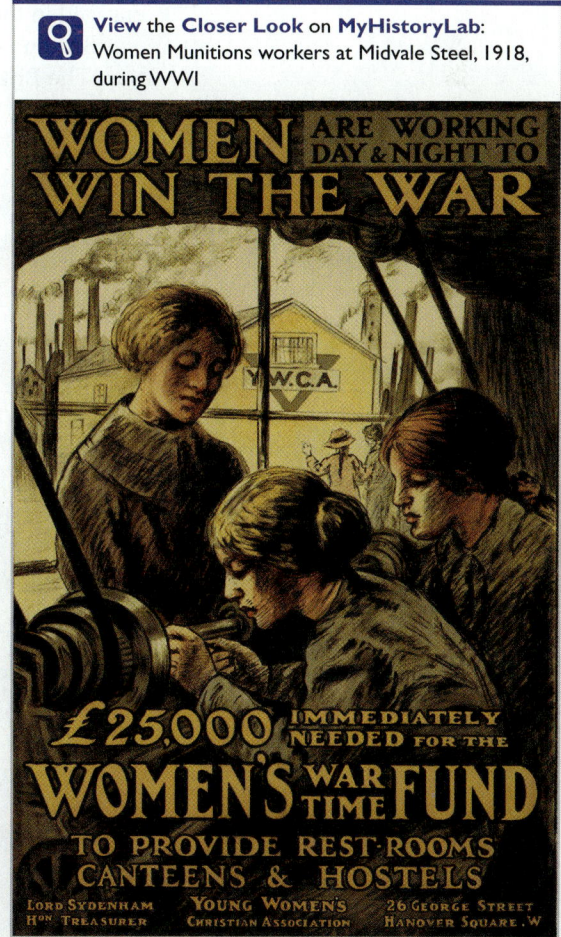

FIGURE 29.3 As this British recruiting poster illustrates, the drastic shortage of farm and factory workers caused by the insatiable military manpower needs of World War I generals provided abundant, but often dangerous, job opportunities for women.

the front sparked a broader liberation for women during the war years. From the rising hemlines of their dresses and their license to smoke in public to unchaperoned dating and greatly increased political activism, many women sought to recast gender roles and improve their social status. At war's end many women lost their jobs to men returning from the front as well as government programs consciously designed to force them back into the home. But in Britain, Germany, and the United States, they gained the vote, which they had struggled to win in the decades before 1914. Particularly in Germany, food shortages and growing anti-war sentiment compelled tens of thousands of women to engage in political agitation and disruptive protests to an extent almost inconceivable before the war. The visibility and influence of the career-oriented and sophisticated "new women" of the 1920s, although a small minority even in Germany and the United States, gave promise of broader advances in the decades to come.

The War Beyond Europe

Except for Austria–Hungary, all of the major powers that went to war in 1914 had colonies outside Europe. When it became clear that the war was not to be the quick and decisive clash that most observers had anticipated, the manpower and resources of these imperial possessions were increasingly sucked into the spreading conflict. By 1915 fighting had spread to the Middle East, west and east Africa, across most of the seas and oceans of the world, and even to China and the islands of the Pacific. Troops from Canada, Australia, New Zealand, India, and throughout much of Africa had been recruited, mainly to fight for the Triple Entente allies (Map 29.2). By 1917 the United States had entered the war, leaving only the nations of South America alone of all the continents not directly engaged in the struggle.

Britain's participation, more than that of any other power, contributed to the war's globalization. The British navy not only cut off Germany from its colonies in Africa, China, and the Pacific islands, but it hunted down German ships still on the high seas at the outbreak of war. Perhaps most critically, British naval supremacy meant that an effective blockade could be maintained that would deprive the Central Powers of supplies of food and raw materials from overseas throughout the war. Because the British also controlled trans-Atlantic cable links, they could easily outdo the Germans in propaganda efforts to convince the neutral United States to side with them in the war. The expensive and highly touted German navy fully engaged the British grand fleet only once during the war, in 1916 off Jutland in Denmark. Although the Germans sank more ships and killed more British sailors, the high seas fleet was driven back into port and proved of little use to the larger German effort for the rest of the war.

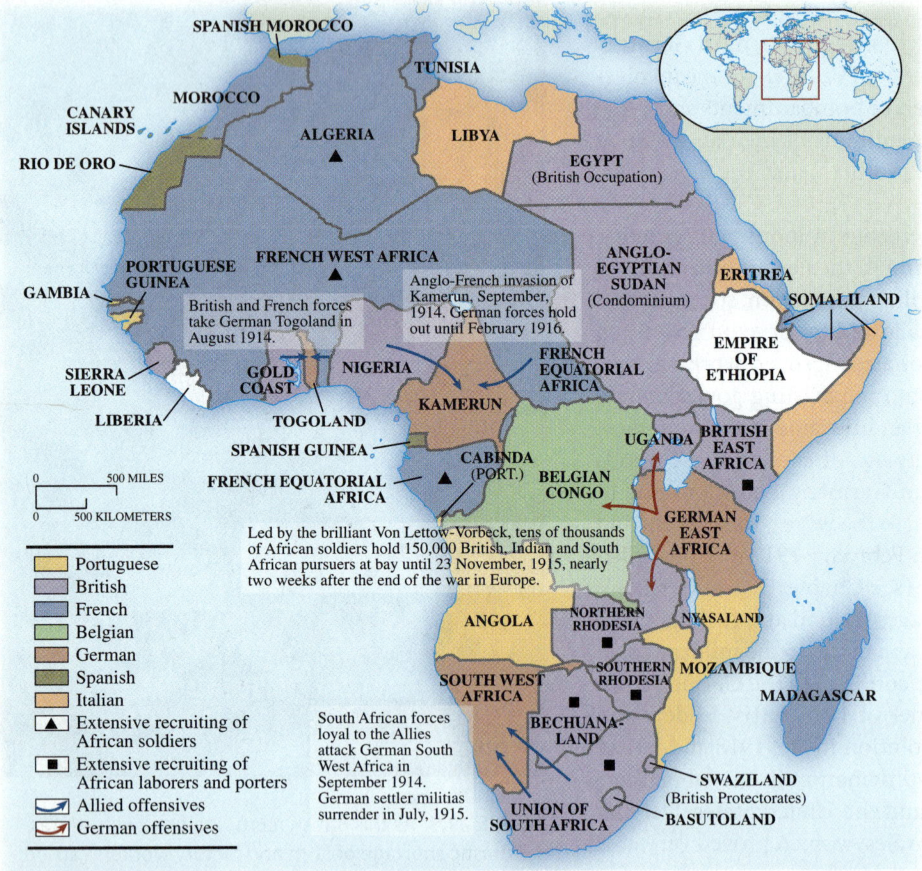

The British entry into the war also meant that its empire and allies were drawn into the fray. Japan, which had joined Britain in a naval pact in 1902, eagerly attacked German colonies in China and the Pacific. These acquisitions, especially the seizure of the Shandong peninsula, would provide great impetus to Japan's imperialist aspirations in China in the 1930s. The islands they captured from the Germans in World War I became part of the defense perimeter the Japanese sought to build across the Pacific during World War II.

The British Dominions—Canada, Australia, and New Zealand—quickly marshaled considerable resources to support the war effort. These

MAP 29.2 Africa During World War I Not only was Africa the site of significant combat in World War I, but from Algeria in the north to the Union of South Africa it was a recruiting ground for tens of thousands of Arab-Berber and African soldiers and bearers and other laborers.

settler societies not only supplied food and critical raw materials, but in defiance of the German U-boat fleet in the Atlantic, they swelled the initially meager ranks of Britain's armed forces. Dominion troops were a mainstay of British operations in the Middle East, including the defense of the vital Suez Canal link and the ill-fated 1915 assault at **Gallipoli**, a peninsula in Turkey south of Istanbul. They fought valiantly on the Western Front throughout the war, at times bolstering British lines that were crumbling under massive German assaults. White settler colonials in South Africa also joined those from the Dominions in support of the British. But siding with the British had to overcome bitter opposition from some segments of the Afrikaner population, which had suffered so greatly as a result of draconian British repression in the Anglo-Boer war just over a decade earlier.

Gallipoli Peninsula south of Istanbul; site of decisive 1915 Turkish victory over Australian and New Zealand forces under British command during World War I.

The British and the French also received vital assistance from their non-settler colonies in Africa, India, and Southeast Asia. The massive army that the British had recruited in India for over a century and a half did much of the fighting in sub-Saharan Africa and the Middle East. The French deployed tens of thousands of non-European soldiers, recruited mainly in North and West Africa, on the Western Front, where many served with distinction but with scant reward. Unlike the British, who turned mainly to women to replace the millions of farmers and factory workers who went off to war, the French relied heavily on laborers recruited in their colonies from Africa to Vietnam.

Although the Germans quickly lost most of their colonies in Africa and the Far East, superbly led African soldiers recruited and trained in German East Africa (Tanzania today) held off hundreds of thousands of British-led Indian and South African troops until two weeks after the end of hostilities in Europe. But Germany's main support outside Europe came from the Ottoman empire (Map 29.1), which entered the war in the fall of 1915. After the Young Turk leaders consolidated their power in Istanbul in the decade leading up to the war (see Chapter 27), they continued the Ottoman reliance on German military advisors and financiers. Having fended off the British-led campaign to capture the Gallipoli, the Turks opened up fronts in southern Russia, where they suffered severe defeats, and the Middle East, where their fortunes were more mixed. They remained for years a threat to the British in Egypt and the Suez Canal zone.

The Young Turk leaders sought to transfer blame for the reverses on the Russian front to the Christian Armenian minority, which was concentrated in areas that spanned the two empires in eastern Anatolia and the Caucasus. In fact, remembering earlier pogroms launched by the Turks against them, some of the Armenians living in Turkish areas had backed the Russians. But most of the minority ethnic group was loyal or neutral, and poor generalship and bad planning were the main causes of the Turkish military disasters. Struggling to cover their blunders, the Young Turk leaders launched an assault in 1915 against the Armenians. The ensuing **Armenian genocide** claimed as many as a million lives and sent hundreds of thousands of Armenians in flight to Russia and the Middle East.

Armenian genocide Assault carried out by mainly Turkish military forces against Armenian population in Anatolia in 1915; over a million Armenians perished and thousands fled to Russia and the Middle East.

The last major combatant to enter the global conflagration was the United States, which declared war on Germany in the spring of 1917. The war made the United States into a major global power, culminating developments that had been underway for decades. By 1914 the United States had become an active force in international diplomacy and power politics. It had built a modest Pacific empire, centering on Hawaii and the Philippine islands, and had become increasingly forceful in its interventions in Central America and the Caribbean. The outbreak of the war was greeted with considerable ambivalence on the part of American leaders and the citizenry more generally. Distant from the battlefields, Americans disagreed over which side was in the right and whether they should intervene in quarrels that seemed to have little to do with them. But American businesses profited greatly from the war by selling food, raw materials, and eventually weapons, mainly (due to the British blockade) to the Entente allies. American mercantile interests, like their counterparts in Japan, also took advantage of the Europeans' need to concentrate their industrial production on the war effort by taking over new markets in Latin America and Asia. Rapidly rising exports, combined with huge loans to Britain, France, and Russia, which all needed credit to buy American goods, transformed the United States from an international debtor into the world's largest creditor and strongest economy.

 Read the **Document** on **MyHistoryLab**: A Turkish Officer Describes the Armenian Genocide (1915–1916)

Despite all of the gains that the United States had accrued through neutrality, American leadership and a majority of the American public was pro-British. British successes in the propaganda war and ever-growing economic ties to the Entente allies did much to explain this sentiment. But clumsy German attempts to influence American opinion and, most critically, the German need to use submarines to counter the British blockade and control sea access to Europe did much to drive the United States into the war. Following the resumption of unrestricted submarine warfare in the Atlantic, which President Woodrow Wilson had earlier warned would force military retaliation, America entered

View the **Closer Look** on MyHistoryLab: Mobilizing the home front

the conflict in April 1917. American warships joined with the British to create a convoy system that eventually offset an intensified German submarine campaign designed to starve the British Isles into submission.

For much of 1917, the number of American troops sent to Europe was small and largely symbolic. But by early 1918, millions of young Americans were in training and hundreds of thousands arrived in Europe each week. The growing buildup of American reinforcements, and American-produced arms and supplies, convinced the German high command that they must launch a massive strike for a quick victory, before the full manpower and resources of the United States could be brought to bear against their weary soldiers.

Endgame: The Return of Offensive Warfare

For several weeks in March and April 1918, the massive offensives launched by the Germans on the Western Front looked as if they might bring victory to the Central Powers. An entire British army had been shattered and another was in full retreat; the already demoralized French forces were also falling back toward Paris. Nearly a million German soldiers transferred from the **Eastern Front** after Russia was knocked out of the war, and new assault tactics and the deployment of storm troopers had restored the offensive and broken three long years of bloody stalemate. But just as Paris was again within the range of the great German guns, the advance slowed. Mounting casualties and sheer fatigue on the German side, counteroffensives, new weapons like tanks, and a rapidly increasing influx of fresh and enthusiastic American soldiers stalled the German drive. Soon the reinforced Entente forces began to push the German armies out of northern France. At the same time, the Austrian fronts broke down in both northeast Italy and the Balkans. The Austro–Hungarian empire fragmented along national lines, and the heir to the Habsburg throne abdicated as separate republics in Austria and Hungary sued the Entente allies for peace.

Fearing that their armies were on the verge of collapse and menaced by widespread rebellions at home, the German commanders agreed to an armistice on November 11, 1918. The generals sought to shift the blame for defeat to a civilian government that they had abruptly installed in Berlin. Made up of members of the Center and Socialist parties, Germany's new government was both forced to sue the Entente allies for peace and to consent to an armistice agreement delivered fittingly by two British admirals and two French generals. Having anticipated that their armies were on the verge of victory just months before, the German people were stunned by the sudden reversal. Many accepted the myth that Germany had been betrayed by socialist and Jewish politicians, whose alleged "stab in the back" would become a rallying cry for **Adolf Hitler** and the Nazis' drive for power from the early 1920s.

After four years of slaughter, the casualty totals were staggering (see Table 29.1). At least 10 million soldiers were dead and 20 million more wounded. The losses were, by far, the heaviest among the great powers of Europe who had been the main adversaries in the conflict. From France to Russia, virtually every European family had a death to mourn. As the fighting ended, an additional calamity struck. Hundreds of thousands of soldiers and millions of civilians died in an influenza pandemic that began in Asia and spread like wildfire around the globe. Although the direct costs of the long and widespread war and the indirect economic losses it inflicted are almost impossible to calculate with

Eastern Front Most mobile of the fronts established during World War I; after early successes, military defeats led to downfall of the tsarist government in Russia.

Hitler, Adolf Nazi leader of Nazi Germany from 1933 to his suicide in 1945; created a strongly centralized state in Germany; eliminated all rivals; launched Germany on aggressive foreign policy leading to World War II; responsible for genocide of European Jews.

TABLE 29.1 WORLD WAR I LOSSES

	Dead	Wounded	Prisoner
Great Britain	947,000	2,122,000	192,000
France	1,385,000	3,044,000	446,000
Russia	1,700,000	4,950,000	500,000
Italy	460,000	947,000	530,000
United States	115,000	206,000	4,500
Germany	1,808,000	4,247,000	618,000
Austria–Hungary	1,200,000	3,620,000	200,000
Turkey	325,000	400,000	

NOTE: The number of known dead (round numbers) was placed at about 10 million and the wounded at about 20 million, distributed among chief combatants.

certainty, both totals reached hundreds of billions of dollars. In Belgium, northern France and Italy, and across east central Europe, extensive swaths of fertile farmlands and bustling cites were reduced to smoldering ruins. This devastation and a postwar economic downturn that followed the armistice dislocated economies across the globe until well into the mid-1920s and fed into the Great Depression that was to follow a decade later.

FAILED PEACE AND GLOBAL TURMOIL

29.3 How did the fallout from the conflict alter gender and racial attitudes and interactions both in wartime and especially in the decades after the war?

The widespread bitterness evoked by the war's unprecedented cost in lives and destruction was redoubled by the utter failure of the peace conference convened by the victorious allies in Paris.

While the Italians and Japanese scrambled to obtain maximum advantage from their support of the Entente forces during the war, the French insisted that they had suffered the most and their losses had to be avenged. **Georges Clemenceau**, the French premier, pushed for the peace conference to brand the Germans the aggressors and thus force them to pay huge reparations to France and the other nations assaulted. He also worked to cut down the size of Germany and funnel its resources to France and the other powers.

Fearing that a reduced Germany would prove fertile ground for the spread of communist revolution, **David Lloyd George**, the British prime minister, attempted with little success to mediate between Clemenceau and Woodrow Wilson and to win enough reparations to satisfy a disgruntled electorate at home. All of the leaders of the victorious Entente powers, including Wilson, soon closed ranks against the demands welling up from peoples in colonized areas, from the Middle East to Vietnam (Figure 29.4). Dashing the expectations that he had aroused by his ringing call for the right of peoples to **self-determination**, Wilson soon made it clear that the peoples he had in mind were

Clemenceau, Georges French premier in last years of World War I and during Versailles Conference of 1919; pushed for heavy reparations from Germans.

 Read the **Document** on MyHistoryLab: George Clemenceau, "French Demands at the Peace Conference"

Lloyd George, David Prime minister of Great Britain who headed a coalition government through much of World War I and the turbulent years that followed.

self-determination Right of people in a region to choose their own political system and its leaders.

FIGURE **29.4** At the Paris peace conference of 1919, the Arabs sought a new voice. The Arab representatives included Prince Feisal, later king of Iraq, and an Iraqi general. A British delegation member, T. E. Lawrence (third from the right), was a longtime friend of the Arabs. The Arabs did not win national self-determination for their homelands, as the British had promised during the war.

CHAPTER 29 Descent into the Abyss: World War I and the Crisis of the European Global Order 713

white ethnic groups like the Poles, not Arabs or Vietnamese. With Wilson's blessing, the British and French set about shoring up, and in fact expanding, their battered empires, while the Japanese solidified their beachhead in China and island enclaves in the western Pacific. The triumvirate of Wilson, Lloyd George, and Clemenceau, which dominated the proceedings at Versailles, also made certain that a mild antiracist clause, which was proposed by the Japanese, never made it into the final draft of the treaty.

The Versailles Treaty, which was the most important of a series of treaties that emerged from the gathering at Versailles, was nothing less than the *diktat* (dictated peace, without negotiations) that German politicians across the political spectrum sought to reverse in the postwar era. The German delegation was allowed no part in drafting the treaty, and they were given no opportunity to amend or refuse it. The German representatives were even humiliated by being brought in by the servants' entrance for the signing and being required to stand for hours while the entire draft of the treaty was read aloud before the assembled delegates. The Germans' main allies—the Austrians—were also major targets of the treaties that emerged from the conference. The Austro–Hungarian empire was dismembered, as nationalist groups carved out the new nations of Czechoslovakia, Hungary, and Yugoslavia. Poland was also reborn, and like Czechoslovakia, it was given substantial chunks of what had been German territory before the war. This left a somewhat fragile Germanic Austria, cut off from its traditional markets, as one of many weak countries between a smaller Germany and a massive Soviet Union to the east.

The fatal flaws of the peace process extended far beyond deliberate insults aimed at the Germans. The new Bolshevik leaders of Russia, who would be treated as pariahs for decades, were not even invited to the conference. Wartime promises to the Arabs in return for their support for the Entente in the war were forgotten as Britain and France divided the Arab heartlands of the Middle East between themselves. China's pleas for protection from Japanese occupation of the Shandong peninsula were dismissed, and a youthful Ho Chi Minh, the future leader of Vietnam, was rudely refused an audience with Woodrow Wilson. Denied their demand that Germany be permanently partitioned, French leaders turned inward on each other and waited despondently for the next German assault they were convinced was inevitable.

Even the Americans, whose President Wilson had opened the peace conference with such exuberant expectations, repudiated what had been wrought at Versailles. Despite Wilson's literally near-fatal efforts to win popular support for the treaty, the United States Congress voted down the critical clauses establishing the **League of Nations** and later made a separate peace with Germany. Even as the delegates were still at work, it was clear to knowledgeable observers that Versailles was a disaster. One of the most perceptive chroniclers of the war years and their aftermath, Vera Brittain, wrote as the terms of the treaty began to be made public in the press:

> The Big Four were making a desert and calling it peace. When I thought about these negotiations... they did not seem to me to represent at all the kind of "victory" that the young men whom I had loved would have regarded as sufficient justification for their lost lives.

League of Nations International diplomatic and peace organization created in the Treaty of Versailles that ended World War I; one of the chief goals of President Woodrow Wilson of the United States in the peace negotiations; the United States was never a member.

THE NATIONALIST ASSAULT ON THE EUROPEAN COLONIAL ORDER

29.4 What were the major grievances that drove the resistance and rebellions that African, Middle Eastern and Asian peoples mounted during and after World War I?

Four long years of intra-European slaughter severely disrupted the systems of colonial domination that had been expanded and refined in the century leading up to World War I. The conflict also gave great impetus to the forces of resistance that had begun to well up in the decades before the war.

Although the European colonizers had frequently quarreled over colonial possessions in the late 19th century, during World War I they actually fought each other in the colonies for the first time. African and Asian soldiers and laborers in the hundreds of thousands served on the Western Front and in the far-flung theaters of war in Egypt, Palestine, Mesopotamia, and East Africa (Maps 29.2 and 29.3). The colonies also supplied food for the home populations of the Triple Entente powers, as well as vital raw materials such as oil, jute, and cotton. Contrary to long-standing colonial policy, the hard-pressed British even encouraged a considerable expansion of industrial manufacturing production in India to supplement the output of their overextended home factories. Thus, the war years contributed to the development in India of the largest industrial sector in the colonized world.

World War I presented the subjugated peoples of Africa and Asia with the spectacle of the self-styled civilizers of humankind sending their young men by the millions to be slaughtered in the horrific and barbaric trench stalemate on the Western Front. For the first time, African and Asian soldiers were ordered by their European officers to kill other Europeans. In the process the vulnerability of the seemingly invincible Europeans and the deep divisions between them were starkly revealed. During the war years, European troops in the colonies were withdrawn to meet the need for manpower on the many war fronts. The garrisons that remained were dangerously understaffed. The need to recall administrative personnel from British and French colonies meant that colonial officials were compelled to fill their vacated posts with African and Asian administrators, many of whom enjoyed real responsibility for the first time.

To maintain the loyalty of their traditional allies among the colonized and to win the support of the Western-educated elites or new allies, such as the Arabs, the British and French made many promises regarding the postwar settlement. Because these concessions often seriously compromised their prewar dominance or their plans for further colonial expansion, the leaders of the victorious allies repeatedly reneged on them in the years after the war. The betrayal of these pledges understandably did a great deal to spark postwar agitation against the continuance and spread of European colonial domination.

DOCUMENT

Lessons for the Colonized from the Slaughter in the Trenches

THE PROLONGED AND SENSELESS SLAUGHTER OF the youth of Europe in the trench stalemate on the Western Front seriously eroded the image of Europeans as superior, rational, and more civilized beings that they had worked hard to propagate among the colonized peoples in the decades before the Great War. The futility of the seemingly endless slaughter cast doubts on the Europeans' rationality and fitness to rule themselves, much less the rest of the world. The destructive uses to which their science and technology were put brought into question the Europeans' long-standing claims that these material advancements tangibly demonstrated their intellectual and organizational superiority over all other peoples. The excerpts below, taken from the writings of some of the leading thinkers and political leaders of the colonized peoples of Africa and Asia, reflect their disillusionment with the West as a result of the war and the continuing turmoil in Europe in the postwar era.

RABINDRANATH TAGORE

Bengali poet, playwright, and novelist Rabindranath Tagore was one of the earliest non-European recipients of the Nobel Prize for literature. He wrote:

> Has not this truth already come home to you now when this cruel war has driven its claws into the vitals of Europe? When her hoard of wealth is bursting into smoke and her humanity is shattered on her battlefields? You ask in amazement what she has done to deserve this? The answer is, that the West has been systematically petrifying her moral nature in order to lay a solid foundation for her gigantic abstractions of efficiency. She has been all along starving the life of the personal man into that of the professional.

From: *Nationalism* (1917)

MOHANDAS GANDHI

In the years after World War I, Mohandas Gandhi emerged as India's leading nationalist figure. The Mahatma challenged the widely held assumption that the trajectory of the industrial West would inevitably be followed by the rest of human societies:

> India's destiny lies not along the bloody way of the West, but along the bloodless way of peace that comes from a simple and godly life. India is in danger of losing her soul.... She must not, therefore, lazily and helplessly say, "I cannot escape the onrush from the West." She must be strong enough to resist it for her own sake and that of the world. I make bold to say that the Europeans themselves will have to remodel their outlooks if they are not to perish under the weight of the comforts to which they are becoming slaves.

From: *Young India* (1926)

LÉOPOLD SÉDAR SENGHOR

Senegalese poet and political leader Léopold Sédar Senghor is widely regarded as one of the 20th century's finest writers in the French language. Many of his most powerful poems mocked the

(continued on next page)

French conceit of their mission to civilize the peoples of Africa and Asia:

> Lord, the snow of your Peace is your proposal to a divided world
> to a divided Europe
> To Spain torn apart.
> And I forget
> White hands that fired the shots which brought the empires crumbling
> Hands that flogged the slaves, that flogged You [Jesus Christ]
> Chalk-white hands that buffeted You, powdered painted hands that buffeted me
> Confident hands that delivered me to solitude to hatred
> White hands that felled the forest of palm trees once commanding Africa, in the heart of Africa.

From *Snow upon Paris* (1938)

AIMÉ CÉSAIRE

West Indian poet Aimé Césaire was a founder of the négritude movement, which asserted black culture in the late 1920s. Césaire celebrated qualities European colonizers viewed as signs of African racial inferiority:

> Heia [Praise] for those who have never invented anything
> those who never explored anything
> those who never tamed anything
> those who give themselves up to the essence of all things
> ignorant of surfaces but struck by the movement of all things.

From *Return to My Native Land* (1938)

QUESTIONS

- On the basis of these samples, what aspects of the West's claims to superiority would you say were called into question by the suicidal conflict of the leading powers within European civilization?
- What aspects of their own civilizations do these writers, both implicitly and explicitly, champion as alternatives to the ways of the West?
- Are these writers in danger of stereotyping both the West and their own civilizations?

For intellectuals and political leaders throughout Africa and Asia, the appalling devastation of World War I cast doubt on the claims that the Europeans had made for over a century that they were, by virtue of their racial superiority, the fittest of all peoples to rule the globe. The social and economic disruptions caused by the war in key colonies, such as Egypt, India, and the Ivory Coast, made it possible for nationalist agitators to build a mass base for their anticolonial movements for the first time. But in these and other areas of the colonized world, the war gave added impetus to movements and processes already underway, rather than initiating new responses to European global domination. Therefore, it is essential to place wartime developments in the colonies and the postwar surge in anticolonial resistance in a longer-term context that takes into account African and Asian responses that extend in some cases back to the last decades of the 19th century. Since it is impossible to relate the history of the independence struggles in all of the European colonies, key movements, such as those that developed in India, Egypt, and British and French West Africa, will be considered in some depth. These specific movements will then be related to broader patterns of African and Asian nationalist agitation and the accelerating phenomenon of decolonization worldwide.

India: The Makings of the Nationalist Challenge to the British Raj

Because India and much of southeast Asia had been colonized long before Africa, movements for independence arose in Asian colonies somewhat earlier than in their African counterparts. By the last years of the 19th century, the Western-educated minority of the colonized in India and the Philippines had been organized politically for decades. Their counterparts in Burma and the Netherlands Indies were also beginning to form associations to give voice to their political concerns. Because of India's size and the pivotal role it played in the British empire (by far the largest of the European imperialist empires), the Indian nationalist movement pioneered patterns of nationalist challenge and European retreat that were later followed in many other colonies. Although it had been under British control for only a matter of decades, Egypt also proved an influential center of nationalist organization and resistance in the pre–World War I era.

Local conditions elsewhere in Asia and in Africa made for important variations on the sequence of decolonization worked out in India and Egypt. But key themes—such as the lead taken by Western-educated elites, the importance of charismatic leaders in the spread of the anticolonial struggle to the peasant and urban masses, and a reliance on nonviolent forms of protest—were repeated again and again in other colonial settings.

The **National Congress party** led the Indians to independence and governed through most of the early decades of the postcolonial era. It grew out of regional associations of Western-educated Indians that were originally more like study clubs than political organizations in any meaningful sense of the term. These associations were centered in the cities of Bombay, Poona, Calcutta, and Madras (see Map 29.3). The Congress party that Indian leaders formed in 1885 had the blessing of a number of high-ranking British officials. These officials viewed it as a forum through which the opinions of educated Indians could be made known to the government, thereby heading off potential discontent and political protest.

For most of its first decades, the Congress party served these purposes quite well. The organization had no mass base and very few ongoing staff members or full-time politicians who could sustain lobbying efforts on issues raised at its annual meetings. Some members of the Congress party voiced concern for the growing poverty of the Indian masses and the drain of wealth from the subcontinent to Great Britain. But the Congress party's debates and petitions to the government were dominated by elite-centric issues, such as the removal of barriers to Indian employment in the colonial bureaucracy and increased Indian representation in all-Indian and local legislative bodies. Most of the members of the early Congress party were firmly loyal to the British rulers and confident that once their grievances were made known to the government, they would be remedied.

Many Western-educated Indians were increasingly troubled, however, by the growing virulence of British racism. This they were convinced had much to do with their poor salaries and limited opportunities for advancement in the colonial administration. In their annual meetings, members of the Congress, who were now able to converse and write in a common English language, discovered that no matter where they came from in India, they were treated in a similar fashion. The Indians' shared grievances, their similar educational and class backgrounds, and their growing contacts through the Congress party gave rise to a sense of common Indian identity that had never before existed in a south Asian environment that was more diverse linguistically, religiously, and ethnically than the continent of Europe.

National Congress party Grew out of regional associations of Western-educated Indians; originally centered in cities of Bombay, Poona, Calcutta, and Madras; became political party in 1885; focus of nationalist movement in India; governed through most of postcolonial period.

Social Foundations of a Mass Movement

By the last years of the 19th century, the Western-educated elites had begun to grope for causes that would draw a larger segment of the Indian population into their growing nationalist community. More than a century of British rule had generated in many areas of India the social and economic disruptions and the sort of discontent that produced substantial numbers of recruits for the nationalist campaigns. Indian businessmen, many of whom would become major financial backers of the Congress party, were angered by the favoritism the British rulers showed to British investors in establishing trade policies in India. Indian political leaders increasingly stressed these inequities and the more general loss to the Indian people resulting from what they termed the "drain" of Indian resources under colonial rule. Although the British rebuttal was that a price had to be paid for the peace and good government that had come with colonial rule, nationalist thinkers pointed out that the cost was too high.

A large portion of the government of India's budget went to cover the expenses of the huge army that mainly fought wars elsewhere in the British empire. The Indian people also paid for the generous salaries and pensions of British administrators, who occupied positions that the Indians were qualified to assume. Whenever possible, as in the purchase of railway equipment or steel for public works projects, the government bought goods manufactured in Great Britain. This practice served to buttress a British economy that was fast losing ground to the United States and Germany. It also ensured that the classic colonial relationship between a manufacturing European colonizer and its raw-material-producing overseas dependencies was maintained.

In the villages of India, the shortcomings of British rule were equally apparent by the last decades of the 19th century. The needs of the British home economy had often dictated policies that pushed the Indian peasantry toward the production of cash crops such as cotton, jute, and indigo. The decline in food production that invariably resulted played a major role in the regional famines that struck repeatedly in the pre–World War I era. Radical Indian nationalists frequently charged that the British were callously indifferent to the suffering caused by food shortages and outbreaks of epidemic disease and that they did far too little to alleviate the suffering that resulted. In many areas, landlessness and chronic poverty, already a problem before the establishment of British rule, increased markedly. In most places, British measures to control indebtedness and protect small landholders and tenants were too little and came too late.

The Rise of Militant Nationalism

Some of the issues that Indian nationalist leaders stressed in their early attempts to build a mass base had great appeal for devout Hindus. This was particularly true of campaigns for the protection of cows, which have long had a special status for the Hindu population of South Asia. But these religious-oriented causes often strongly alienated the adherents of other faiths, especially the Muslims. Not only did Muslims eat beef, and thus slaughter cattle, but they made up nearly one-fourth of the population of the Indian empire. Some leaders, such as **B. G. Tilak**, were little concerned by this split. They believed that since Hindus made up the overwhelming majority of the Indian population, nationalism should be built on appeals to Hindu religiosity. Tilak worked to promote the restoration and revival of what he believed to be the ancient traditions of Hinduism. On this basis, he opposed women's education and raising the very low marriage age for women. Tilak turned festivals for Hindu gods into occasions for mass political demonstrations. He broke with more moderate leaders of the Congress party by demanding the boycott of British-manufactured goods. Tilak also sought to persuade Indians to refuse to serve in the colonial administration and military. Tilak demanded full independence, with no deals or delays, and threatened violent rebellion if the British failed to comply.

Tilak, B. G. (1856–1920) Believed that nationalism in India should be based on appeals to Hindu religiosity; worked to promote the restoration and revival of ancient Hindu traditions; offended Muslims and other religious groups; first populist leader in Indian nationalist movement.

Tilak's oratorical skills and religious appeal made him the first Indian nationalist leader with a genuine mass following. Nonetheless, his popularity was confined mainly to his home base in Bombay and in nearby areas in western India. At the same time, his promotion of a very reactionary sort of Hinduism offended and frightened moderate and progressive Hindus, Muslims, and followers of other religions, such as the Sikhs. When evidence was found connecting Tilak's writings to underground organizations that advocated violent revolt, the British, who had grown increasingly uneasy about his radical demands and mass appeal, arrested and imprisoned him. Six years of exile in Burma for Tilak had a dampening effect on the mass movement he had begun to build among the Hindu population.

The other major threat to the British in India before World War I came from Hindu communalists who advocated the violent overthrow of the colonial regime. But unlike Tilak and his followers, those who joined the terrorist movement favored clandestine operations over mass demonstrations. Although terrorists were active in several parts of India by the last decade of the 19th century, those in Bengal built perhaps the most extensive underground network. Considerable numbers of young Bengalis, impatient with the gradualist approach advocated by moderates in the Congress party, were attracted to underground secret societies. These were formed by quasi-religious, guru-style leaders who exhorted their followers to build up their physiques with Western-style calisthenics and learn how to use firearms and make bombs. British officials and government buildings were the major targets of terrorist assassination plots and sabotage. On occasion the young revolutionaries also struck at European civilians and collaborators among the Indian population. But the terrorists' small numbers and limited support from the colonized populace as a whole rendered them highly vulnerable to British repressive measures. The very considerable resources the British devoted to crushing these violent threats to their rule had removed the terrorist threat by the outbreak of World War I.

Morley-Minto reforms Provided educated Indians with considerably expanded opportunities to elect and serve on local and all-India legislative councils.

Tilak's exile and the repression campaigns against the terrorists strengthened the hand of the more moderate politicians of the Congress party in the years before the war. Western-educated Indian lawyers became the dominant force in nationalist politics, and—as the careers of Gandhi, Jinnah, and Nehru demonstrate—they would provide many of the movement's key leaders throughout the struggle for independence. The approach of those who advocated a peaceful, constitutionalist route to decolonization was given added appeal by timely political concessions on the part of the British. The **Morley-Minto reforms** of 1909 provided educated Indians with considerably expanded opportunities both to vote for and serve on local and all-India legislative councils.

The Emergence of Gandhi and the Spread of the Nationalist Struggle

In the months after the outbreak of World War I, the British could take great comfort from the way in which the peoples of the empire rallied to their defense. Of the many colonies among the tropical dependencies, none played as critical a role in the British war effort as India. The Indian princes offered substantial war loans; Indian soldiers bore the brunt of the war effort in East Africa and the Middle East; and nationalist leaders, including Gandhi and Tilak, toured India selling British war bonds. But as the war dragged on and Indians died on the battlefields or went hungry at home to sustain a conflict that had little to do with them, signs of unrest spread throughout the subcontinent.

Wartime inflation had adversely affected virtually all segments of the Indian population. Indian peasants were angered at the ceilings set on the price of their market produce, despite rising costs. They were also often upset by their inability to sell what they had produced because of shipping shortages linked to the war. Indian laborers saw their already meager wages drop steadily in the face of rising prices. At the same time, their bosses grew rich from profits earned in war production. Many localities suffered from famines, which were exacerbated by wartime transport shortages that impeded relief efforts.

After the end of the war in 1918, moderate Indian politicians were frustrated by the British refusal to honor wartime promises. Hard-pressed British leaders had promised the Indians that if they continued to support the war effort, India would move steadily to self-government within the empire once the conflict was over. Indian hopes for the fulfillment of these promises were raised by the **Montagu-Chelmsford reforms** of 1919. These measures increased the powers of Indian legislators at the all-India level and placed much of the provincial administration of India under their control. But the concessions granted in the reforms were offset by the passage later in the same year of the **Rowlatt Act**, which placed severe restrictions on key Indian civil rights, such as freedom of the press. These conditions fueled local protest during and immediately after the war. At the same time, **Mohandas Gandhi** emerged as a new leader who soon forged this localized protest into a sustained all-India campaign against the policies of the colonial overlords.

Gandhi's remarkable appeal to both the masses and the Western-educated nationalist politicians was due to a combination of factors. Perhaps the most important was the strategy for protest that he had worked out a decade earlier as the leader of a successful movement of resistance to the restrictive laws imposed on the Indian migrant community in South Africa. Gandhi's stress on nonviolent but quite aggressive protest tactics endeared him both to the moderates and to more radical elements within the nationalist movement. His advocacy of peaceful boycotts, strikes, noncooperation, and mass demonstrations—which he labeled collectively **satyagraha**, or truth force—proved an effective way of weakening British control while limiting opportunities for violent reprisals that would allow the British to make full use of their superior military strength.

It is difficult to separate Gandhi's approach to mass protest from Gandhi as an individual and thinker. Although physically unimposing, he possessed an inner confidence and sense of moral purpose that sustained his followers and wore down his adversaries. He combined the career of a Western-educated lawyer with the attributes of a traditional Hindu ascetic and guru. The former had given him considerable exposure to the world beyond India and an astute understanding of the strengths and weaknesses of the British colonizers. These qualities and his soon legendary skill in negotiating with the British made it possible for Gandhi to build up a strong following among middle-class, Western-educated Indians, who had long been the dominant force behind the nationalist cause. But the success of Gandhi's protest tactics also hinged on the involvement of ever-increasing numbers of the Indian people in anticolonial resistance. The image of a traditional mystic and guru that Gandhi projected was critical in gaining mass support from peasants and laborers alike. Many of these "ordinary" Indians would walk for miles when Gandhi was on tour. Many did so in order to honor a saint rather than listen to a political speech. Gandhi's widespread popular appeal, in turn, gave him even greater influence among nationalist politicians. The latter were very much aware of the leverage his mass following gave to them in their ongoing contests with the British overlords. Under Gandhi's leadership, nationalist protest surged in India during the 1920s and 1930s.

Montagu-Chelmsford reforms Increased the powers of Indian legislators at the all-India level and placed much of the provincial administration of India under local ministries controlled by legislative bodies with substantial numbers of elected Indians; passed in 1919.

Rowlatt Act Placed severe restrictions on key Indian civil rights such as freedom of the press; acted to offset the concessions granted under Montagu-Chelmsford reforms of 1919.

Gandhi, Mohandas (1869–1948) Led sustained all-India campaign for independence from British empire after World War I; stressed nonviolent but aggressive mass protest.

satyagraha [suh-TYAH-grah-huh] Literally, "truth-force"; strategy of nonviolent protest developed by Mohandas Gandhi and his followers in India; later deployed throughout the colonized world and in the United States.

Egypt and the Rise of Nationalism in the Middle East

Egypt is the one country in the Afro-Asian world in which the emergence of nationalism preceded European conquest and domination (Map 29.3). Risings touched off by the mutiny of Ahmad Arabi and other Egyptian officers (see Chapter 27), which led to the British occupation in 1882, were aimed at the liberation of the Egyptian people from their alien Turkish overlords as well as the meddling Europeans. British occupation meant, in effect, double colonization for the Egyptian people by the Turkish khedives (who were left in power) and their British advisors.

MAP 29.3 **The Middle East after World War I** Despite promises to the Arab peoples who supported them in the war to let them decide their own postwar political fate, the victorious British and French allies divided much of the Middle East into what in effect were new colonial enclaves.

Cromer, Lord (1841–1917) British Consul-General in khedival Egypt from 1883 to 1907; pushed for economic reforms that reduced but failed to eliminate the debts of the khedival regime.

effendi Class of prosperous business and professional urban families in khedival Egypt; as a class generally favored Egyptian independence.

Dinshawai incident [din shä wAY] Clash between British soldiers and Egyptian villagers in 1906; arose over hunting accident along Nile River where wife of prayer leader of mosque was accidentally shot by army officers hunting pigeons; led to Egyptian protest movement.

In the decades following the British conquest, government policy was dominated by the strong-willed and imperious **Lord Cromer**. As Consul-General of Egypt, he pushed for much-needed economic reforms that reduced but could not eliminate the debts of the puppet khedival regime. Cromer also oversaw sweeping reforms in the bureaucracy and the construction of irrigation systems and other public works projects. But the prosperity the British congratulated themselves for having brought to Egypt by the first decade of the 20th century was enjoyed largely by tiny middle and elite classes, often at the expense of the mass of the population. The leading beneficiaries included foreign merchants, the Turco-Egyptian political elite, a small Egyptian bourgeoisie in Cairo and other towns in the Nile delta, and the ayan, or the great landlords in the rural areas.

The latter were clearly among the biggest gainers. The British had been forced to rely heavily on local, estate-owning notables in extending their control into the rural areas. As a result, the ayan, not the impoverished mass of rural cultivators and laborers, received most of the benefits of the new irrigation works, the building of railways, and the increasing orientation of Egyptian agriculture to the production of raw cotton for the export market. Unfettered by legal restrictions, the ayan greedily amassed ever-larger estates by turning smallholder owners into landless tenants and laborers. As their wealth grew, the contrast between the landlords' estate houses and the thatch and mud-walled villages of the great mass of the peasantry became more and more pronounced. Bored by life in the provinces, the well-heeled landed classes spent most of their time in the fashionable districts of Cairo or in resort towns such as Alexandria. Their estates were run by hired managers, who were little more than rent collectors as far as the peasants were concerned.

With the khedival regime and the great landlords closely allied to the British overlords, resistance to the occupation was left mainly to the middle class. Since the middle of the 19th century, this relatively new and small social class had been growing in numbers and influence, mainly in the towns in the Nile delta. With the memory of Arabi's revolt in 1882 still fresh, the cause of Egyptian independence was taken up mainly by the sons of the **effendi**, or the prosperous business and professional families that made up much of this new middle class. Even nationalist leaders who came from rural ayan families built their following among the urban middle classes. In contrast to India, where lawyers predominated in the nationalist leadership, in Egypt, journalists (a number of them educated in France) led the way.

In the 1890s and early 1900s, numerous newspapers in Arabic (and to a lesser extent French and English) vied to expose the mistakes of the British and the corruption of the khedival regime. Egyptian writers also attacked the British for their racist arrogance and their monopolization of well paying positions in the Egyptian bureaucracy. Like their Indian counterparts, Egyptian critics argued that these could just as well have been filled by university-educated Egyptians. In the 1890s the first nationalist party was formed. But again in contrast to India, where the Congress party dominated the nationalist movement from the outset, a variety of rival parties proliferated in Egypt. There were three main alternatives by 1907, but none could be said to speak for the great majority of the Egyptians, who were illiterate, poorly paid, and largely ignored urban laborers and rural farmers.

In the years before the outbreak of World War I in 1914, heavy-handed British repression on several occasions put down student riots or retaliated for assassination attempts against high British and Turco-Egyptian officials. Despite the failure of the nationalist parties to unite or build a mass base in the decades before the war, the extent of the hostility felt by the Egyptian masses was demonstrated by the **Dinshawai incident** in 1906 (see Figure 29.5). This confrontation between the British and their Egyptian subjects exemplified the racial arrogance displayed by most of the European colonizers. Although the incident at Dinshawai was seemingly a small clash resulting in only limited numbers of fatalities, the excessive British response to it did much to undermine whatever support remained for their continued presence in Egypt.

Most Egyptian villages raised large numbers of pigeons, which served as an important supplement to the meager peasant diet. Over the years, some of the British had turned the hunting of the pigeons of selected villages into a holiday pastime. A party of British officers on leave was hunting the pigeons of the village of Dinshawai in the Nile delta when they accidentally shot the wife of the prayer leader of the local mosque. The angry villagers mobbed the greatly outnumbered shooting party, which in panic fired on the villagers. Both the villagers and the British soldiers suffered casualties in the clashes that followed. In reprisal for the death of one of the officers, the British summarily hung four of the villagers. Although the actual hanging was not photographed, the building of the scaffolding was captured in a photo (Figure 29.5). The British also ordered that other villagers connected to the incident be publicly flogged or sentenced to varying terms of hard labor.

The harsh British reprisals aroused a storm of protest in the Egyptian press and among the nationalist parties. Some Egyptian leaders later recounted how the incident convinced them that cooperation with the British was totally unacceptable and fixed their resolve to agitate for an end to Egypt's occupation. Popular protests in several areas, and the emergence of ayan support for the nationalist cause, also suggested the possibility of building a mass base for anti-British agitation. More than anything else, the incident at Dinshawai had galvanized support for popular protest across the communal and social boundaries that had so long divided the peoples of Egypt.

By 1913 the British had been sufficiently intimidated by the rising tide of Egyptian nationalism to grant a constitution and representation in a parliament elected indirectly by the men of wealth and influence. World War I and the British declaration of martial law put a temporary end to nationalist agitation. But, as in India, the war unleashed forces in Egypt that could not be stopped and that would soon lead to the revival of the drive for independence with even greater strength than before.

Read the Document on MyHistoryLab: Gandhi on Civil Disobedience (1910s)

FIGURE 29.5 This photograph, probably taken without the knowledge of the British authorities, shows the construction of the gallows that were used to hang the four peasants who were executed in reprisal for the attacks on British soldiers at Dinshawai in 1906. The Dinshawai incident exemplified the colonizers' tendency to overreact to any sign of overt resistance on the part of the colonized.

War and Nationalist Movements in the Middle East

In the years after World War I, resistance to European colonial domination, which had been confined largely to Egypt in the prewar years, spread to much of the rest of the Middle East. Having sided with the Central Powers in the war, the Turks now shared in their defeat. The Ottoman empire disappeared from history, as Britain and France carved up the Arab portions that had revolted against the Young Turk regime during the war. Italy and Greece attacked the Turkish rump of the empire around Istanbul and in Anatolia (Asia Minor) with the intent of sparking a partition of these areas in concert with the other Entente allies. But a skilled military commander, Mustafa Kemal, or **Ataturk**, had emerged from the Turkish officer corps during the war years. Ataturk rallied the Turkish forces and gradually drove back the Greek armies intent on colonizing the Turkish homeland.

By 1923 an independent Turkish republic had been established, but at the cost of the expulsion of tens of thousands of ethnic Greeks. As an integral part of the effort to establish a viable Turkish nation, Ataturk launched a sweeping program of reforms. Many of the often radical changes his government introduced in the 1920s and 1930s were modeled on Western precedents, including a new Latin alphabet, women's suffrage, and criticism of the veil. But in important ways his efforts to secularize and develop Turkey also represented the culmination of transformations made under the Ottomans over the preceding century (see Chapter 27).

With Turkish rule in the Arab heartlands ended by defeat in the war, Arab nationalists in Beirut, Damascus, and Baghdad turned to face the new threat presented by the victorious Entente powers,

Ataturk Also known as Mustafa Kemal; leader of Turkish republic formed in 1923; reformed Turkish nation using Western models.

Hussein Sherif of Mecca from 1908 to 1917; used British promise of independence to convince Arabs to support Britain against the Turks in World War I; angered by Britain's failure to keep promise; died 1931.

mandates Governments entrusted to European nations in the Middle East in the aftermath of World War I; Britain and France assumed control in Syria, Iraq, Lebanon, and Palestine after 1922.

Zionism Movement originating in eastern Europe during the 1860s and 1870s whose leaders argued that the Jews must return to a Middle Eastern holy land; eventually identified with the settlement of Palestine.

Balfour Declaration British minister Lord Balfour's promise of support for the establishment of Jewish homeland in Palestine issued in 1917.

Pinsker, Leon (1821–1891) European Zionist who believed that Jewish assimilation into Christian European nations was impossible; argued for return to Middle Eastern Holy Land.

Herzl, Theodor [hûrt suhl] Austrian journalist and Zionist; formed World Zionist Organization in 1897; promoted Jewish migration to Palestine and formation of a Jewish state.

Dreyfus, Alfred (1859–1935) French Jew falsely accused of passing military secrets to the Germans; his mistreatment and exile to Devil's Island provided flash-point for years of bitter debate between the left and right in France.

World Zionist Organization Founded by Theodor Herzl to promote Jewish migration to and settlement in Palestine to form a Zionist state.

France and Britain. Betraying promises to preserve Arab independence that the British had made in 1915 and early 1916, French and British forces occupied much of the Middle East in the years after the war. **Hussein**, the sherif of Mecca, had used these promises to convince the Arabs to rise in support of Britain's war against the Turks, despite the fact that the latter were fellow Muslims. Consequently, the allies' postwar violation of these pledges humiliated and deeply angered Arabs throughout the Middle East. The occupying European powers faced stiff resistance from the Arabs in each of the **mandates** they carved out in Syria, Iraq, and Lebanon under the auspices of the League of Nations. Nationalist movements in these countries gained ground during the 1920s and 1930s. The Arabs' sense of humiliation and anger was greatly intensified by the disposition of Palestine, where British occupation was coupled with promises of a Jewish homeland.

The fact that the British had appeared to promise Palestine, for which they received a League of Nations mandate in 1922, to both the Jewish **Zionists** and the Arabs during the war greatly complicated an already confused situation. Despite repeated assurances to Hussein and other Arab leaders that they would be left in control of their own lands after the war, Lord Balfour, the British foreign secretary, promised prominent Zionist leaders in 1917 that his government would promote the establishment of a Jewish homeland in Palestine after the war. This pledge, the **Balfour Declaration**, fed existing Zionist aspirations for the Hebrew people to return to their ancient Middle Eastern lands of origin, which had been nurtured by the Jews of the diaspora for millennia. In the decades before World War I, these dreams led to the formation of a number of organizations. Some of these were dedicated to promoting Jewish emigration to Palestine; others were committed to the eventual establishment of a Jewish state there.

These early moves were made in direct response to the persecution of the Jews of eastern Europe in the last decades of the 19th century. Particularly vicious *pogroms*, or violent assaults on the Jewish communities of Russia and Romania in the 1860s and 1870s, convinced Jewish intellectuals such as **Leon Pinsker** that assimilation of the Jews into, or even acceptance by, Christian European nations was impossible. Pinsker and other thinkers called for a return to the Holy Land. Like-minded individuals founded Zionist organizations, such as the Society for the Colonization of Israel, to promote Jewish migration to Palestine in the last decades of the 19th century. Until World War I, the numbers of Jews returning to Palestine were small—in the tens of thousands—although Zionist communities were established on lands purchased in the area.

Until the late 1890s, the Zionist effort was generally opposed by Jews in Germany, France, and other parts of western Europe who enjoyed citizenship and extensive civil rights. In addition, many in these communities had grown prosperous and powerful in their adopted lands. But a major defection to the Zionists occurred in 1894. **Theodor Herzl**, an established Austrian journalist, was stunned by French mobs shouting "Death to the Jews" as they taunted the hapless army officer **Alfred Dreyfus**. Dreyfus was a French Jew who had been falsely accused of passing military secrets to the Germans. His subsequent mistreatment, including exile to the infamous penal colony on Devil's Island, became the flashpoint for years of bitter debate between the left and right in France. Soon after this incident in 1897, Herzl and a number of other prominent western European Jews joined with Jewish leaders from eastern Europe to form the **World Zionist Organization**. As Herzl made clear in his writings, the central aim of this increasingly well-funded organization was to promote Jewish migration to and settlement in Palestine until a point was reached when a Zionist state could be established in the area. Herzl's nationalist ambitions, as well as his indifference to the Arabs already living in the area, were captured in the often-quoted view of one of his close associates that Palestine was "a land without people for a people [the Jews] without a land."

Lord Balfour's promises to the Zionists and the British takeover of Palestine struck the Arabs as a double betrayal of wartime assurances that Arab support for the Entente powers against the Turks would guarantee them independence after the war. This sense of betrayal was a critical source of the growing hostility the Arabs felt toward Jewish emigration to Palestine and their purchase of land in the area. Rising Arab opposition convinced many British officials, especially those who actually administered Palestine, to severely curtail the rather open-ended pledges that had been made to the Zionists during the war. This shift led in turn to Zionist mistrust of British policies and open resistance to them. It also fed the Zionists' determination to build up their own defenses against the increasingly violent Arab resistance to the Jewish presence in Palestine. But British attempts to limit Jewish emigration and settlement were not matched by efforts to encourage, through education and consultation, the emergence of strong leadership among the Arab population of Palestine. Consequently, in the critical struggles and diplomatic maneuvers of the 1930s and 1940s, the Arabs of Palestine were rarely able to speak for themselves. They were represented by Arab leaders from neighboring lands, who did not always understand Palestinian needs and desires. These non-Palestinian spokespersons also often acted more in the interests of Syrian or Lebanese Arabs than those of the Christian and Muslim Arab communities in Palestine.

Revolt in Egypt, 1919

Because Egypt was already occupied by the British when the war broke out, and it had been formally declared a protectorate in 1914, it was not included in the promises made by the British to the sherif Hussein. As a result, the anticolonial struggle in Egypt was rooted in earlier agitation and the heavy toll the war had taken on the Egyptian people, particularly the peasantry. During the war, the defense of the Suez Canal was one of the top priorities for the British. To guard against possible Muslim uprisings in response to Turkish calls for a holy war, martial law was declared soon after hostilities began. Throughout the war, large contingents of Entente and empire forces were garrisoned in Egypt. These created a heavy drain on the increasingly scarce food supplies of the area. Forced labor and confiscations by the military of the precious draft animals of the peasantry also led to widespread discontent. As the war dragged on, this unrest was further inflamed by spiraling inflation as well as by food shortages and even starvation in some areas.

By the end of the war, Egypt was ripe for revolt. Mass discontent strengthened the resolve of the educated nationalist elite to demand a hearing at Versailles, where the victorious Allies were struggling to reach a postwar settlement. When a delegation (*wafd* in Arabic) of Egyptian leaders was denied permission to travel to France to put the case for Egyptian self-determination to the peacemakers at Versailles, most Egyptian leaders resigned from the government and called for mass demonstrations. What followed shocked even the most confident British officials. Student-led riots touched off outright insurrection over much of Egypt. At one point, Cairo was cut off from the outside world, and much of the countryside was hostile territory for the occupying power. Although the British army was able, at the cost of scores of deaths, to restore control, it was clear that some hearing had to be given to Egyptian demands. The emergence of the newly formed **Wafd party** under its hard-driving leader **Sa'd Zaghlul** provided the nationalists with a focus for unified action and a mass base that far excelled any they had attracted in the prewar decades.

Wafd party [wäft] Egyptian nationalist party that emerged after an Egyptian delegation was refused a hearing at the Versailles treaty negotiations following World War I; led by Sa'd Zaghlul; negotiations eventually led to limited Egyptian independence beginning in 1922.

Zaghlul, Sa'd [SAHD ZAG-luhl] Leader of Egypt's nationalist Wafd party; their negotiations with British led to limited Egyptian independence in 1922.

THINKING HISTORICALLY

Women in Asian and African Nationalist Movements

ONE IMPORTANT BUT OFTEN NEGLECTED DIMENSION of the liberation struggles that Asian and African peoples waged against their colonial overlords was the emergence of a stratum of educated, articulate, and politically active women in most colonial societies. In this process, the educational opportunities provided by the European colonizers often played as vital a role as they had in the formation of male leadership in nationalist movements. Missionary girls' schools were confined in the early stages of European involvement in Africa and Asia to the daughters of low-class or marginal social groups. But by the end of the 19th century these schools had become quite respectable for women from the growing Westernized business and professional classes. In fact, in many cases, some degree of Western education was essential if Westernized men were to find wives with whom they could share their career concerns and intellectual pursuits.

As nationalist leaders moved their anticolonial campaigns into the streets, women became involved in mass demonstrations.

The seemingly insurmountable barriers that separated Westernized Asian and African men from their traditional—and thus usually without formal education—wives became a stock theme in the novels and short stories of the early nationalist era. This concern was perhaps best exemplified by the works of Rabindranath Tagore. The problem was felt so acutely by the first generation of Indian nationalist leaders that many took up the task of teaching their wives English and Western philosophy and literature at home. Thus, for many upper-class Asian and African women,

(continued on next page)

colonization proved a liberating force. This trend was often offset by the male-centric nature of colonial education and the domestic focus of much of the curriculum in women's schools.

Women usually played supporting roles in the early, elitist stages of Asian and African nationalist movements. But they frequently became more and more prominent as the early study clubs and political associations reached out to build a mass base. In India, women who had been exposed to Western education and European ways, such as Tagore's famous heroine in the novel *The Home and the World*, came out of seclusion and took up supporting roles, although they were still usually behind the scenes. Gandhi's campaign to supplant imported, machine-made British cloth with homespun Indian cloth, for example, owed much of whatever success it had to female spinners and weavers. As nationalist leaders moved their anticolonial campaigns into the streets, women became involved in mass demonstrations. Throughout the 1920s and 1930s, Indian women braved the *lathi*, or billy club, assaults of the Indian police, suffered the indignities of imprisonment, and launched their own newspapers and lecture campaigns to mobilize female support for the nationalist struggle.

In Egypt, the British made special note of the powerful effect that the participation of both veiled women and more Westernized upper-class women had on mass demonstrations in 1919 and the early 1920s. These outpourings of popular support did much to give credibility to the Wafd party's demands for British withdrawal. In both India and Egypt, female nationalists addressed special appeals to British and American suffragettes to support their peoples' struggles for political and social liberation. In India in particular, their causes were advanced by feminists such as the English champion of Hinduism, Annie Besant, who became a major figure in the nationalist movement before and after World War I.

When African nationalism became a popularly supported movement in the post–World War II period, women, particularly the outspoken and fearless market women in west Africa, emerged as a major political force. In settler colonies, such as Algeria and Kenya, where violent revolt proved necessary to bring down deeply entrenched colonial regimes, women took on the dangerous tasks of messengers, bomb carriers, and guerrilla fighters. As Frantz Fanon argued decades ago, and as was later beautifully dramatized in the film *The Battle of Algiers*, this transformation was particularly painful for women who had been in seclusion right up to the time of the revolutionary upsurge. Cutting their hair and wearing lipstick and Western clothes often alienated them from their fathers and brothers, who equated such practices with prostitution.

In many cases, women's participation in struggles for the political liberation of their people was paralleled by campaigns for female rights in societies that, as we have seen, were dominated by males. Upper-class Egyptian women founded newspapers and educational associations that pushed for a higher age of marriage, educational opportunities for women, and an end to seclusion and veiling. Indian women took up many of these causes and also developed programs to improve hygiene and employment opportunities for lower-caste women. These early efforts, as well as the prominent place of women in nationalist struggles, had much to do with the granting of basic civil rights to women. These included suffrage and legal equality, which were key features of the constitutions of many newly independent Asian and African nations. The great majority of women in the new states of Africa and Asia have yet to enjoy most of these rights. Yet their inclusion in constitutions and post-independence laws provides crucial backing for the struggles for women's liberation in the nations of the postcolonial world.

QUESTIONS
- In what ways do you think measures to "modernize" colonial societies were oriented to males?
- Can you think of women who have been or are major political figures in contemporary Africa and Asia?
- What sorts of traditional constraints hamper the efforts of women to achieve economic and social equality and major political roles in newly independent nations?

When a special British commission of inquiry into the causes of the upheaval in Egypt met with widespread civil disobedience and continuing violent opposition, it recommended that the British begin negotiations for an eventual withdrawal from Egypt. Years of bargaining followed, which led to a highly qualified independence for the Egyptians. The British departure occurred in stages, beginning in 1922 and culminating in the British withdrawal to the Suez Canal zone in 1936. But although they pulled out of Egypt proper, the khedival regime was preserved and the British reserved the right to reoccupy Egypt should it be threatened by a foreign aggressor.

Although they had won a significant degree of political independence, the Egyptian leaders of the Wafd party, as well as its rivals in the Liberal Constitutionalist and Union parties, did little to relieve the increasing misery of the great majority of the Egyptian people. Most Egyptian politicians regarded the winning of office as an opportunity to increase their own and their families' fortunes. Many politicians from ayan households and from the professional and merchant classes used their influence and growing wealth to amass huge estates, which were worked by landless tenants and laborers. Locked in personal and interparty quarrels, as well as the ongoing contest with the khedival regime for control of the government, few political leaders had the time or inclination to push for the land reforms and public works projects that the peasantry so desperately needed.

The utter social bankruptcy of the 40 years of nationalist political dominance that preceded the military coup and social revolution led by Gamal Abdul Nasser in 1952 is suggested by some revealing statistics compiled by the United Nations in the early 1950s. By that time, nearly 70 percent of Egypt's cultivable land was owned by 6 percent of the population. Some 12,000 families alone controlled 37 percent of the farmland. As for the mass of the people, 98 percent of the peasants were illiterate, malnutrition was chronic among both the urban and rural population, and an estimated 95 percent of rural Egyptians suffered from eye diseases. Such was the legacy of the very unrevolutionary process of decolonization in Egypt.

The Beginnings of the Liberation Struggle in Africa

Most of Africa had come under European colonial rule only in the decades before the outbreak of World War I. Nonetheless, precolonial missionary efforts had produced small groups of Western-educated Africans in parts of west and south central Africa by the end of the 19th century. Like their counterparts in India, most Western-educated Africans were staunchly loyal to their British and French overlords during World War I. With the backing of both Western-educated Africans and the traditional rulers, the British and especially the French were able to draw on their African possessions for manpower and raw materials throughout the war. But this reliance took its toll on their colonial domination in the long run. In addition to local rebellions in response to the forcible recruitment of African soldiers and laborers, the war effort seriously disrupted newly colonized African societies (Figure 29.6). African merchants and farmers suffered from shipping shortages and the sudden decline in demand for crops, such as cocoa. African villagers were not happy to go hungry so that their crops could feed the armies of the allies. As Lord Lugard, an influential colonial administrator, pointed out, the desperate plight of the British and French also forced them to teach tens of thousands of Africans:

> how to kill white men, around whom [they had] been taught to weave a web of sanctity of life. [They] also know how to handle bombs and Lewis guns and Maxims . . . and [they have] seen the white men budge when [they have] stood fast. Altogether [they have] acquired much knowledge that might be put to uncomfortable use someday.

FIGURE **29.6** Soldiers, like those captured in this photograph, were extensively recruited by the French in their colonies in North and West Africa, and to a lesser extent, Vietnam to bolster their defenses on the Western Front in France and battle the Germans in colonized Africa.

Garvey, Marcus African American political leader; had a major impact on emerging African nationalist leaders in the 1920s and 1930s.

Du Bois, W. E. B. One of the most influential African American intellectuals and spokesmen of the 20th century. His extensive and widely-read writings on the plight of blacks in American society and critiques of racism were foundational to both civil rights movements in the United States and African resistance to colonialism.

pan-African Organization that brought together intellectuals and political leaders from areas of Africa and African diaspora before and after World War I.

négritude Literary movement in Africa; attempted to combat racial stereotypes of African culture; celebrated the beauty of black skin and African physique; associated with origins of African nationalist movements.

Senghor, Léopold Sédar (1906–2001) One of the post–World War I writers of the négritude literary movement that urged pride in African values; president of Senegal from 1960 to 1980.

The fact that the Europeans kept few of the promises of better jobs and public honors, which they had made during the war to induce young Africans to enlist in the armed forces or serve as colonial administrators, contributed a good deal to the unrest of the postwar years. This was particularly true of the French colonies, where opportunities for political organization, much less protest, were severely constricted before, during, and after the war. Major strikes and riots broke out repeatedly in the postwar years. In the British colonies, where there was considerably more tolerance for political organization, there were also strikes and a number of outright rebellions. Throughout colonized Africa, protest intensified in the 1930s in response to the economic slump brought on by the Great Depression.

Although Western-educated politicians did not link up with urban workers or peasants in most African colonies until the 1940s, disenchanted members of the emerging African elite began to organize in the 1920s and 1930s. In the early stages of this process, charismatic African American political figures, such as **Marcus Garvey** and **W. E. B. Du Bois**, had a major impact on emerging African nationalist leaders. In the 1920s much effort was placed into attempts to arouse all-Africa loyalties and build **pan-African** organizations. However, the leadership of these organizations was mainly African American and West Indian, and the delegates from colonized areas in Africa faced very different challenges under different colonial overlords. Although these differences had much to do with the fact that pan-Africanism proved unworkable in Africa itself, its well-attended conferences, especially the early ones in Paris, did much to arouse anticolonial sentiments among Western-educated Africans.

By the mid-1920s, nationalists from French and British colonies were pretty much going separate ways. Because of restrictions in the colonies, and because small but well-educated groups of Africans were represented in the French parliament, French-speaking west Africans concentrated their organizational and ideological efforts in Paris in this period. The **négritude** literary movement nurtured by these exiles did much to combat the racial stereotyping that had so long held the Africans in psychological bondage to the Europeans. Writers such as the Senegalese poet **Léopold Sédar Senghor** and Léon Damas from French Guiana, and the West Indian Aimé Césaire celebrated the beauty of black skin and the African physique. They argued that in the precolonial era, African peoples had built societies where women were freer, old people were better cared for, and attitudes toward sex were far healthier than they had ever been in the so-called civilized West.

Except in settler colonies, such as Kenya and Rhodesia, Western-educated Africans in British territories were given greater opportunities to build political associations within Africa. In the early stages of this process, African leaders sought to nurture organizations that linked the emerging nationalists of different British colonies, such as the National Congress of British West Africa. By the late 1920s, these pan-colony associations gave way to political groupings concerned primarily with issues within individual colonies, such as Sierra Leone, the Gold Coast, or Nigeria. After the British granted some representation in colonial advisory councils to Western-educated Africans in this period, emphasis on colony-specific political mobilization became even more pronounced. Although most of these early political organizations were too loosely structured to be considered true political parties, there was a growing recognition by some leaders of the need to build a mass base. In the 1930s a new generation of leaders made much more vigorous attacks on the policies of the British. Through their newspapers and political associations, they also reached out to ordinary African villagers and the young, who had hitherto played little role in nationalist agitation. Their efforts to win a mass following would come to full fruition only after European divisions plunged humanity into a second global war.

Global Connections and Critical Themes

WORLD WAR AND GLOBAL UPHEAVALS

World War I—or the Great War, as it was called by those who lived through it and did not know a second conflict of this magnitude lay in their future—was one of several key turning points of world history in the 20th century. The long conflict, particularly the horrific and draining stalemate in the trenches, did much to undermine Europe's prewar position of global dominance. The war severely disrupted Europe's economy and bolstered already emerging rivals, especially the United States and Japan, for preeminence in world trade and finance. Over much of Europe, the hardships endured by the civilian populations on the home front reignited long-standing class tensions. In Russia, but also elsewhere in east central Europe, growing social divisions sparked full-scale revolutions. In Britain, France, Germany, and other liberal democracies in western Europe, labor parties, some socialist or communist, emerged with much greater power after the conflict. Many shared power, both in coalitions with center parties or in their own right in the 1920s and 1930s. The war saw major changes in gender roles in spheres ranging from employment and marriage to sex and fashion. It also generated growing challenges to the rigid racial hierarchies that had dominated both scientific theorizing and popular attitudes in the decades leading up to the conflict.

The victorious Entente allies, especially the British and French but also the Belgians and Japanese, managed to hold on to, and in fact enlarge, their empires. But the hardships endured by colonized peoples and the empty promises made by their desperate colonial overloads during the war gave great impetus to resistance to their empires that spread from the Middle East and India to Vietnam and China. For African and Asian intellectuals at least, the psychological advantage that racial thinking and scientific and technological superiority had given the Europeans began to dissipate. Nationalist leaders like Gandhi gave them and their ideologies of liberation access to ever larger numbers of colonized peoples. In the postwar decades, mass civil disobedience campaigns in India and Egypt, and peasant risings in Vietnam and China, established the protest techniques and demands that would ultimately bring down all of the European colonial empires. The revolutionary regime in Russia, which had come to power as a direct consequence of the war, actively abetted efforts to advance the cause of decolonization around the world. Two other industrial nations whose power had been greatly enhanced by the war, the United States and Japan, sought in different ways both to supplant the European colonizers and replace them as the economic and political power centers of the 20th century.

Further Readings

There is a vast literature on the origins of World War I. A somewhat dated, but still very readable, introduction is Laurence Lafore, *The Long Fuse* (1965). James Joll, *The Origins of the First World War* (1984), includes a much more detailed treatment of the many and highly contested interpretations of the causes of the conflict. Fritz Fisher, *Germany's Aims in the First World War* (1967), stirred great controversy by arguing that Germany's leaders purposely provoked the conflict, while Paul Kennedy, *The Rise of the Anglo-German Antagonism, 1860–1914* (1980), covers one of the key rivalries and especially the naval race with a good deal more balance. The impact of colonial disputes on the coming of the war is concisely and convincingly treated in L. F. C. Turner, *Origins of the First World War* (1970).

Of the many general histories of the war on land and sea, the more reliable and readable include *The World in the Crucible, 1914–1919* (1984) by Bernadotte Schmitt and Harold Vedeler, and most recently John Keegan's *The First World War* (1999). Marc Ferro's *The Great War* (1973) remains one of the most stimulating analyses of the conduct of the war. Three of the most successful attempts to understand the war from the participants' perspectives are Paul Fussell's *The Great War and Modern Memory* (1975) and John Cruickshank's *Variations on Catastrophe* (1982), which draw on literary works and memoirs, and Richard Cork's magisterial exploration of artistic images of the conflict in *A Bitter Truth: Avant-Garde Art and the Great War* (1994). Some of the better accounts by the participants include Erich Remarque, *All Quiet on the Western Front* (1929); Frederic Manning, *The Middle Parts of Fortune* (1929); Vera Brittain, *Testament of Youth* (1933); and Wilfred Owen, *Poems* (1920) reprinted as *The Collected Poems of Wilfred Owen* (1964).

The disasters at Versailles and some of their consequences are also chronicled in numerous books and articles. Two of the most readable are Harold Nicholson's *Peace Making, 1919* (1965) and Charles L. Mee Jr.'s *The End of Order: Versailles, 1919* (1980). Samples of varying views on the many controversies surrounding the conference can be found in Ivo J. Lederer, ed., *The Versailles Settlement* (1960). Margaret Macmillan's *Paris 1919* (2003) provides a spirited, but often problematic, defense of the Wilson and other peacemakers at Versailles. The best book on the wider ramifications of the decisions made at or in connection with the conference is Arno Mayer, *Politics and Diplomacy of Peace-Making, 1918–1919* (1967).

The best surveys of the conduct and impact of the war beyond Europe are John Morrow's *The Great War: An Imperial History* (2004) and Hew Strachan, *The First World War* (2005).

A good general historical narrative of the impact of the war on the struggle for Indian independence can be found in Sumit Sarkar, *Modern India, 1885–1947* (1983). A closer analysis is offered in the essays in DeWitt C. Elinwood and S. D. Pradhan, eds., *India and World War I* (1978). The war also figures importantly in the early sections of Mohandas Gandhi's autobiographical *The Story of My Experiments with Truth* (1927). Louis Fischer's *Gandhi* (1950) still yields valuable insights into the personality of one of the great nationalist leaders and the workings of nationalist politics. Judith Brown's studies of Gandhi as a political leader, including *Gandhi's*

Rise to Power (1972), and her recent biography of his life and career provide an approach more in tune with current research. The poems and novels of Rabindranath Tagore yield wonderful insights into the social and cultural life of India through much of this era.

P. J. Vatikiotis, *The History of Egypt* (especially the 1985 edition), has excellent sections on the war and early nationalist era in that country. Interesting but often less reliable is Jacques Berque, *Colonialism and Nationalism in Egypt* (1972). Leila Ahmed, *Women and Gender in Islam* (1992), has excellent chapters on the role of women at various stages of the nationalist struggle and in the postindependence era. Beth Baron's *The Women's Awakening in Egypt: Culture, Society, and the Press* (1997) is the best account of women's involvement in the early stages of the Egyptian nationalism movement. A comprehensive treatment of working-class women protesters in Egypt is provided by Nawal El Saadawi, *The Hidden Face of Eve* (1980). George Antonius, *The Arab Awakening* (1946), is essential reading on British double dealing in the Middle East during the war, especially as this affected the Palestine question. Alternative perspectives are provided by Aaron Cohen, *The Arabs and Israel* (1970). David Fromkin, *A Peace to End All Peace* (1989), provides a more recent and superb account of wartime and postwar events in the Middle East as a whole.

The early stages of the nationalist struggle, including the war years, in West Africa are well covered by Michael Crowder, *West Africa under Colonial Rule* (1982). A narrative of the history of World War I as a whole in sub-Saharan Africa can be found in Byron Farwell, *The Great War in Africa* (1986). The continued advance of European colonialism in the Middle East and Africa in the postwar years is analyzed in *France Overseas* (1981) by Christopher Andrew and A. S. Kanya-Forstner.

On MyHistoryLab

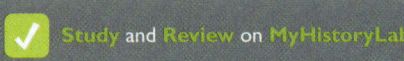

Critical Thinking Questions

1. In what ways did the obsession of the great powers of Europe with building or expanding colonial empires prove to be major factors leading to World War I?
2. How did the long, costly, and basically indecisive conflict undermine the attitudes, ideas, and methods the Europeans had deployed to dominate the African and Asian peoples whom they sought to rule?
3. What were some of the most serious flaws in the treaties and settlements that were supposed to end World War I?
4. What would you argue were the three most important effects World War I had on the history of the twentieth century that followed?

The World between the Wars: Revolutions, Depression, and Authoritarian Response

30

LEARNING OBJECTIVES

Russia's communist revolution in 1917 produced a regime that declared its commitment to workers. It was understandably less clear about its commitment to consumers. Department stores had spread in prerevolutionary Russia, almost exclusively for the rich. It was easy for the new communist rulers to decide to seize the stores. In their place, the government set up state department stores, headed by the chain called GUM (an acronym for State Universal Store, pronounced *goom*), with a flagship store right on Red Square in Moscow (Figure 30.1). It was also easy to proclaim that department stores were now available to all the people. GUM advertisements featured weathered peasants pondering new leather coats, and slogans trumpeted "Everything for Everybody" and "We Have Everything You Need at GUM."

There were, however, three problems. First, this was a poor society, and leaders were spending massive amounts of money on further industrialization and agricultural reform. There was not much left for abundant consumer goods. Second, communists were ambivalent about consumerism anyway. Sometimes they wanted consumerism for everybody, but sometimes they worried

30.1 How do short-term and long-term changes relate in analyzing the 1920s? p. 730

30.2 What were the common patterns of early 20th-century revolutions, and what were the major differences among Mexico, China, and the Soviet Union? p. 736

30.3 What were the principal regional differences in the impact of and response to the Great Depression? p. 748

30.4 What were the main features of the Nazi state? p. 751

30.5 Did global developments in the 1930s make another world war inevitable? p. 753

FIGURE **30.1** The most famous link in the chain of Russian department stores known as GUM is the palatial pre-Communist era building on the right of this 1935 photograph of Red Square, Moscow.

Watch the Video Series on MyHistoryLab

Learn about some key topics related to this chapter with the *MyHistoryLab Video Series: Key Topics in World History*

that consumerism was foreign, "bourgeois," and trivial. (Even in Western countries, Communist parties took some time to adjust to consumerism.) Third, the desire arose to protect workers in the stores from what the communists perceived as the demeaned status of those who "wait on" customers. The government stopped calling them clerks or salespeople, instead using the term "workers of the counter." They sought to protect these workers from the subservience Western sales clerks had to endure. Unfortunately, this led to clerks taking a surly attitude toward customers (now simply called "consumers").

The result of all this was that GUM stores became notorious for poor supplies and bad service. Customers were free to complain, and they often did, but government representatives rejected almost all the complaints with phrases like "does not correspond to reality." Communism and consumerism were both realities of the 20th century. Both movements could claim successes, but the two were not easy to combine. Russia's department stores and their poor-quality goods and service became a symbol of communist inadequacy to many Western observers, particularly after World War II amid the competitive pressures of the cold war. But comparisons with Western standards could be misleading, because communist leaders were seeking different goals. Along with shoddy consumer goods came not only the huge advance in heavy industry and military production but also other, more personal gains like extensive vacation opportunities for workers. This was a different kind of industrial society, and the two decades between the wars were its seedbed. ■

The 1920s and 1930s—the interwar period—featured several crucial developments in addition to the immediate postwar adjustments around the flawed peace settlement and the rise of nationalist protest against European colonialism. The 1920s featured many innovations in industrial societies, but also a combination of structural weakness and misleading illusion. The key dynamics of the interwar period revolved around a wave of major revolutions, a global economic depression, and new authoritarian regimes spearheaded by German Nazism.

THE ROARING TWENTIES

30.1 How do short-term and long-term changes relate in analyzing the 1920s?

In the West and Japan, consumerism and changes in women's roles gained ground, along with new political tensions. New authoritarian movements surfaced in eastern Europe and Italy.

The postwar challenges to western European society were immense. Massive war deaths—over 10 million Europeans had died—combined with widespread injuries and tremendous blows to morale. Property damage and economic dislocation added to the problems: Because wartime governments had printed new money rather than raise taxes, an unprecedented postwar inflation occurred, wiping out savings for many groups.

1910 C.E.	1920 C.E.	1930 C.E.
1917 Tsarist regime overthrown in February; Bolshevik revolution in October; Mexican constitution includes revolutionary changes **1918** Armistice ends World War I in November **1919** Versailles conference; Peace of Paris; leftist revolution defeated in Germany; May Fourth movement in China	**1920–1940** Muralist movement in Mexico **1921** Albert Einstein wins the Nobel Prize; Chinese Communist party founded; Lenin's New Economic Policy begins in U.S.S.R. **1922** Mussolini and the Fascists seize power in Italy; first commercial radio station in Pittsburgh **1923–1924** Hyperinflation in Germany **1923** Defeat of Japanese bill for universal suffrage; Tokyo earthquake **1927** Charles Lindbergh's solo trans-Atlantic flight; Guomindang (Nationalists) capture north China, purge Communist party **1927–1928** Stalin pushes the first five-year plan in the Soviet Union, collectivization begins; agricultural slump in United States **1928–1929** Skyscraper craze in New York **1929** Stock market crash	**1930** U.S. Congress passes the Smoot-Hawley tariff; economic downturn in western Europe and throughout European colonial empires; rapid rise of Nazi party in Germany **1931** Statute of Westminster gives full autonomy to British Dominions of Canada, Australia, New Zealand, South Africa, and the Irish Free State; failed rebellion against Japanese rule in Korea; poor harvests and severe economic dislocations in Japan; Japanese invasion of Manchuria **1932** Franklin Roosevelt begins four-term tenure as U.S. president and launches the New Deal **1932–1934** Height of forced collectivization in U.S.S.R.; genocidal famine inflicted on the Ukraine and other areas **1933** Adolf Hitler becomes chancellor of Germany **1934–1940** Lázaro Cárdenas president of Mexico, extensive land reform **1935** Nuremberg laws deprive Jews of German citizenship; Mussolini's armies invade Ethiopia; outbreak of civil war in Spain **1936** Popular Front government formed in France; junior army officers revolt in Japan, key political leaders assassinated **1936–1938** Height of Stalinist purges in U.S.S.R. **1937** Full-scale Japanese invasion of China **1938** *Kristallnacht* begins intensification of attacks on Jews in Germany; Munich agreement allows Hitler to begin destruction of Czechoslovakia **1938** Japan's military leaders impose state control over economy and social system, Diet approves war budget **1939** Hitler invades Poland, leading to outbreak of World War II

Bouncing Back?

Superficially, however, a more buoyant attitude resumed by the middle of the decade. A new, democratic republic in Germany made some positive strides, despite the burdensome reparations payments the World War I victors had required. Artistic creativity included the **cubist movement**, led by Pablo Picasso, that rendered familiar objects in geometrical shapes, as in Figure 30.2. Writers and composers also challenged stylistic traditions. Modern design in architecture and furnishing gained ground (Figure 30.3). Important achievements in science included further work on Albert Einstein's groundbreaking theories of relativity in physics. Knowledge of atomic structure and also of genetics advanced.

cubist movement 20th-century art style; best represented by Spanish artist Pablo Picasso; rendered familiar objects as geometrical shapes.

FIGURE **30.2** Marcel Duchamp's *Nude Descending a Staircase, No. 2* (1912). Using a modified cubist style, Duchamp achieved a dramatic visual effect in an approach characteristic of Western art from the 1920s onward.

(Marcel Duchamp (American, b. France 1887–1968), "Nude Descending a Staircase, No. 2," 1912. Philadelphia Museum of Art: The Louise and Walter Arensberg Collection. 1950-134-59. © 2009 Artists Rights Society (ARS), New York/ADAGP, Paris/Succession Marcel Duchamp.)

FIGURE **30.3** The skyscraper, developed first in the United States, became a major expression of artistic innovation and was the result of the use of new structural materials that allowed for unprecedented heights and dramatic effects. Buildings like this one—the Wrigley Building in Chicago—combined the new technology with elements of gothic architecture that recalled the great cathedrals of the Middle Ages, earning them the nickname "Cathedrals of Commerce."

Read the Document on MyHistoryLab: Advertisements (1925, 1927)

New mass consumption items, like the radio, were important as well. Middle-class women gained new participation in popular culture, some of them going to nightclubs, smoking, and participating in dance crazes that often originated in the United States or Latin America (Figure 30.4). In several countries—Germany, Great Britain, the United States, and Turkey headed the list—women also gained the right to vote.

Aspects of the new culture, however, seemed frenzied, and certainly disturbed traditionalists. Key economic sectors—like agricultural and coal mining—did not really recover prosperity, and much of the British economy overall remained sluggish. Western Europe did not regain export markets that had been taken over by the United States or Japan. Most western European countries also faced increasing political extremism. New communist parties on the left were matched by right-wing movements, often supported by many war veterans.

Other Industrial Centers

Canada, Australia, and New Zealand gained rewards for their loyal participation in World War I. Australia, newly independent in 1901, gained particular pride in its military role. Several conferences in the 1920s confirmed the independence of the Dominions and their co-equal status with Britain (Map 30.1). The British Commonwealth of Nations was a free association of members, as British representation in the three Dominions became purely symbolic. The Dominions also registered solid export growth and population gains from immigration. Australia introduced extensive welfare measures, responding to a strong labor movement, and considerable economic planning.

U.S. economic and popular cultural initiatives advanced rapidly during the 1920s. The economy boomed throughout much of the decade. Corporations expanded and innovated—for example, adding research and development operations to their portfolios. Organization of work systems changed. Henry Ford had introduced the assembly line for automobile production in 1913, using conveyor belts to move parts past semi-skilled workers doing small, repetitive tasks as each automobile was completed. During the 1920s industrial psychologists studied how to increase output further—for example, by piping in music. These production changes were widely imitated in Europe, Japan, and the Soviet Union. The United States also increased its popular cultural exports. Jazz spread from African American centers in the South to performances in Europe. Hollywood became the global film capital by 1920, and Hollywood stars, many of them foreign, became international staples.

The role of the United States worldwide had new complexities, however. The U.S. Senate rejected the Versailles treaty, refusing to enter the League of Nations. Diplomatically, the United States pursued an isolationist policy for two decades, refusing foreign alliances. Fear of communism also ran unusually high in the United States, with a "Red Scare" early in the decade heightening resistance to outside influences.

Japan entered a new phase of industrialization during the 1920s. Agricultural output improved with greater use of fertilizers and mechanical equipment. This freed labor for expanding factories. Japan rapidly augmented its heavy industrial sector, in metallurgy, shipbuilding, and electrical power, organized mainly by large industrial combines—the zaibatsu—linked to the state. Japan still depended heavily on cheap exports to the West, because it needed foreign earnings to cover the import of fuel and raw materials and to support rapid population growth. (A population of 45 million in 1900 had increased to 70 million by 1940.) Politically, tensions between Japan's military leaders and the civilian government increased during the decade. Military leaders, trained separately and reporting directly to the emperor, resented political controls that periodically reduced their budgets. Liberal politicians expanded voting rights to all adult males, but there was no full agreement on the appropriate political structure. The military, suspicious of growing consumerism in Japan, regarded itself as a guardian of tradition. It also exercised considerable independence in diplomacy, particularly concerning growing Japanese involvement in China.

FIGURE **30.4** The interwar decades saw the rise of a succession of dance crazes. Adults as well as young people were caught up in dancing to the new big bands.

Read the **Document** on **MyHistoryLab**: Frederick Winslow Taylor, Employees and Productivity, from Scientific Management, (1919)

New Authoritarianism: The Rise of Fascism

Explicit hostility to liberal and democratic political systems emerged first on the fringes of western Europe. In 1919 a former socialist and (very briefly) former soldier, **Benito Mussolini**, formed the *fascio di combattimento*, or "union for struggle," in Italy. Italian fascists vaguely advocated a corporate state that would replace both capitalism and socialism with a new national unity. They pointed to the need for an aggressive, nationalistic foreign policy. Above all, fascists worked to seize power by any means and to build a strong state under a strong leader. They violently attacked rival political groups, seeking to promote an atmosphere of chaos.

Fascism had its roots in the late 19th century, with groups disenchanted with liberal, parliamentary systems and with social conflict. Various intellectuals, in many countries, began to urge the need for new, authoritarian leadership and devotion to nationalist values over capitalist profit-seeking and socialist class struggle.

Conditions in postwar Italy gave these impulses a huge boost. Nationalists resented the fact that Italy had gained so little new territory in World War I. Veterans often felt abandoned by civilian society, and some thirsted for new action. Labor unrest increased, which convinced some conservatives that new measures were essential against ineffective liberal leadership. The Italian parliament seemed incapable of decisive measures, as political factions jockeyed for personal advantage. In these conditions Mussolini, fascism's leading exponent, could make his mark even with a minority of direct supporters.

Mussolini, Benito Italian fascist leader after World War I; created first fascist government (1922–1943) based on aggressive foreign policy and new nationalist glories.

fascism Political philosophy that became predominant in Italy and then Germany during the 1920s and 1930s; attacked weakness of democracy, corruption of capitalism; promised vigorous foreign and military programs; undertook state control of economy to reduce social friction.

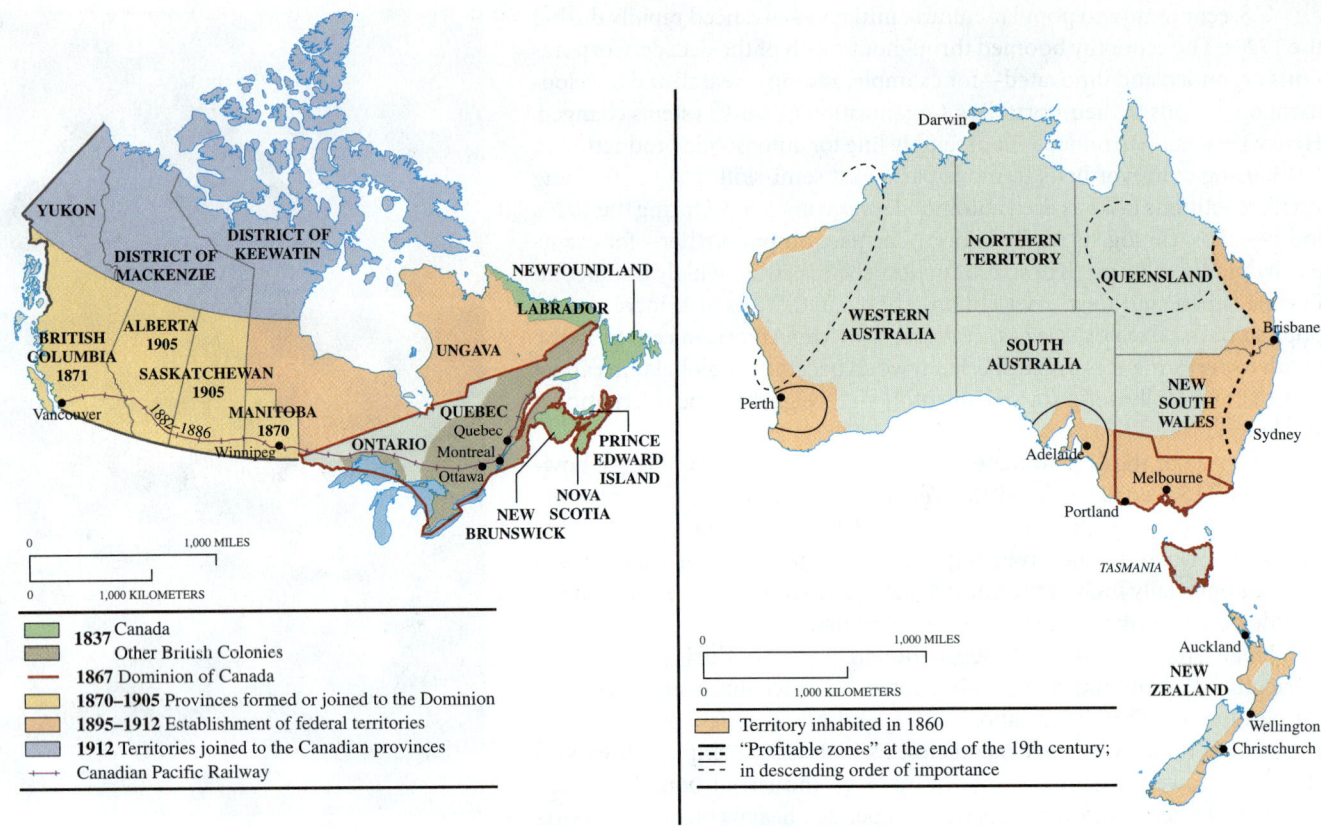

MAP 30.1 **From Dominions to Nationhood: Formation of Canada, Australia, and New Zealand** The new states of key settler societies were an important development.

Read the Document on MyHistoryLab: Benito Mussolini, "The Political and Social Doctrine of Fascism"

FIGURE 30.5 One of the most ominous acts of Mussolini's fascist regime was the burning of books and other literature deemed "subversive."

Amid growing political divisions and a rising threat from the working-class left, in 1922 the Italian king called on Mussolini to form a new government. Although the fascists had only limited popular support, they seemed the only hope to stem left-wing agitation and parliamentary ineptitude. Once in power, Mussolini eliminated most opposition (Figure 30.5), suspending elections outright in 1926, while seeking greater state direction of the economy and issuing strident propaganda about the glories of military conquest. This first fascist regime moved with some caution, fitting into the briefly hopeful negotiations among European states in the 1920s, but the principles it espoused suggested how far European politics had been unseated from the widespread prewar agreements on parliamentary rule.

The New Nations of East Central Europe

Authoritarian regimes also took root in east central Europe during the 1920s, although they were not explicitly fascist. New nations in this region, created by the Versailles Treaty, began with Western-style parliaments, but most could not maintain them amid economic difficulties.

MAP **30.2 Eastern Europe and the Soviet Union, 1919–1939** The Soviet Union regained some territory ceded to Germany in the 1918 peace treaty, but it lost ground to a number of east European states.

Most of the new nations, from the Baltic states to Yugoslavia, were consumed by nationalist excitement at independence but also harbored intense grievances about territories they had not acquired. Hence there were bitter rivalries among the small eastern European states, which weakened them both diplomatically and economically (Map 30.2). Authoritarianism arrived either through a dictator (as in Poland) or by a monarch's seizure of new power (as in Yugoslavia, the new nation expanded from Serbia). This political pattern resulted from more underlying social tensions. Most eastern European countries remained primarily agricultural, heavily dependent on sales to western Europe. They were hard hit by the collapse of agricultural prices in the 1920s and then further damaged by the Depression. Furthermore, most countries refused to undertake serious land reform, despite widely professed intentions. Aristocratic estate owners thus sought desperately to repress peasant movements, which brought them to support authoritarian regimes, which often had vaguely fascist trappings. Peasant land hunger and continued problems of poverty and illiteracy were simply not addressed in most cases.

A Balance Sheet

Changes in Europe, other Western societies, and Japan during the 1920s were complex. Democratic and parliamentary political forms took further root in Germany and in places like Canada and Japan. Significant industrial and social change combined with signs of creativity in culture, in sciences and the arts. On the other hand, challenges to democracy arose in Italy and in much of east central Europe, while Japanese politics became less stable. The United States tried to isolate itself from world politics. Events would soon prove that the economic foundations of the major industrial powers were shaky as well. Even in the 1920s the economy of western Europe was newly challenged by the greater vigor of the United States and Japan.

REVOLUTION: THE FIRST WAVES

Major revolutions broke out in Mexico, Russia, and China before or during World War I. All three revolutions challenged Western dominance to some degree, and all reflected concerns about world economic relationships.

30.2 What were the common patterns of early 20th-century revolutions, and what were the major differences among Mexico, China, and the Soviet Union?

A variety of social tensions affected Latin America early in the 20th century. Many countries continued to depend on a key export crop, like coffee. These crops provided profits to owners while Western demand was high, but they also depended on low wages for workers. During World War I, European manufactured goods were diverted. Several Latin American countries expanded their industrial output, in a process called import substitution. This mainly involved light industry, and the initiative receded after the war, leading to further poverty.

These developments did stimulate some political change. In Argentina a new 1912 election law gave voice to the middle classes. Labor agitation increased, some of it under the banners of **syndicalism**, which sought to use a general strike to seize power. Major strikes occurred from 1907 onward, usually brutally repressed by the state. An atmosphere of class conflict intensified. Only in Mexico, however, was there outright revolution.

Mexico's Upheaval

Several cataclysmic events launched Latin America into the 20th century and set in motion trends that would determine much of the region's subsequent history. The first of these events was the 10-year civil war and political upheaval of the **Mexican Revolution**, caused primarily by internal forces. Eventually, the Mexican Revolution was also influenced by another major event: the outbreak of World War I. Although most Latin American nations avoided direct participation in the Great War, as World War I was called at the time, the disruption of traditional markets for Latin American exports and the elimination of European sources of goods caused a realignment of the economies of several nations in the region. They were forced to rely on themselves. A spurt of manufacturing continued the process begun after 1870, and some small steps were taken to overcome the traditional dependence on outside supply. Finally, at the end of World War I, the United States emerged as the dominant foreign power in the region, replacing Great Britain in both economic and political terms. That position created a reality that Latin Americans could not ignore and that greatly influenced the economic and political options in the region.

The regime of **Porfirio Díaz** had been in power since 1876 and seemed unshakable. During the Díaz dictatorship, tremendous economic changes had been made, and foreign concessions in mining, railroads, and other sectors of the economy had created a sense of prosperity among the Mexican elite. However, this progress had been bought at considerable expense. Foreigners controlled large sectors of the economy. The hacienda system of extensive landholdings by a small elite dominated certain regions of the country. The political system was corrupt, and any complaint was stifled. The government took repressive measures against workers, peasants, and American Indians who opposed the loss of their lands or the unbearable working conditions. Political opponents often were imprisoned or forced into exile. In short, Díaz ruled with an iron fist through an effective political machine.

Mexico nevertheless faced major issues. The economy, increasingly dependent on exports, lacked adequate investment funds. U.S. concerns owned 20 percent of the nation's territory. Growing nationalist resentment was similar to other reactions to widespread foreign control—a major spur to the revolutionary wave in general.

By 1910, moreover, Díaz was 80 years old, newly vulnerable to political opposition. **Francisco Madero**, a wealthy son of an elite family, proposed to run against Díaz. Madero believed that some moderate democratic political reforms would relieve social tensions and allow the government to continue its economic development with a minimum of popular unrest. This was more than Díaz could stand. Madero was arrested, a rigged election put Díaz back in power, and things returned to normal. When Madero was released from prison, he called for a revolt.

A general rebellion developed. In the north, small farmers, railroaders, and cowboys coalesced under the colorful former bandit and able commander **Pancho Villa**. In the southern province of Morelos, an area of old conflicts between American Indian communities and large sugar estates, a peasant-based guerrilla movement began under **Emiliano Zapata**, whose goal of land reform was

---

syndicalism Economic and political system based on the organization of labor; imported in Latin America from European political movements; militant force in Latin American politics.

Mexican Revolution Fought over a period of almost ten years from 1910; resulted in ouster of Porfirio Díaz from power; opposition forces led by Pancho Villa and Emiliano Zapata.

Díaz, Porfirio One of Juárez's generals; elected president of Mexico in 1876; dominated Mexican politics for 35 years; imposed strong central government.

Madero, Francisco (1873–1913) Moderate democratic reformer in Mexico; proposed moderate reforms in 1910; arrested by Porfirio Díaz; initiated revolution against Díaz when released from prison; temporarily gained power, but removed and assassinated in 1913.

Villa, Pancho [vEE uh] (1878–1923) Mexican revolutionary and military commander in northern Mexico during the Mexican Revolution; succeeded along with Emiliano Zapata in removing Díaz from power in 1911; also participated in campaigns that removed Madero and Huerta.

Zapata, Emiliano Mexican revolutionary and military commander of peasant guerrilla movement after 1910 centered in Morelos; succeeded along with Pancho Villa in removing Díaz from power; also participated in campaigns that removed Madero and Huerta; demanded sweeping land reform.

expressed in his motto "Tierra y Libertad" (Land and Liberty). Díaz was driven from power by this coalition of forces, but it soon became apparent that Madero's moderate programs would not resolve Mexico's continuing social problems. Zapata rose in revolt, demanding a sweeping land reform, and Madero steadily lost control of his subordinates. In 1913, with at least the tacit agreement of the U.S. ambassador in Mexico, who wanted to forestall revolutionary changes, a military coup removed Madero from government and he was then assassinated.

General **Victoriano Huerta** sought to impose a Díaz-type dictatorship supported by the large landowners, the army, and the foreign companies, but the tide of revolution could not be stopped so easily. Villa and Zapata rose again against the government and were joined by other middle-class political opponents of Huerta's illegal rule. By 1914 Huerta was forced from power, but the victorious leaders now began to fight over the nature of the new regime and the mantle of leadership. An extended period of warfare followed, and the tides of battle shifted constantly. The railroad lines built under Díaz now moved large numbers of troops, including *soldaderas*, women who sometimes shouldered arms. Matters were also complicated by clumsy U.S. intervention, aimed at bringing order to the border regions, and by diplomatic maneuverings after the outbreak of World War I in Europe.

Villa and Zapata remained in control in their home territories, but they could not wrest the government from the control of the more moderate political leaders in Mexico City. **Alvaro Obregón**, an able general who had learned the new tactics of machine guns and trenches from the war raging in Europe and had beaten Villa's cavalry in a series of bloody battles in 1915, emerged as leader of the government.

By 1920 the civil war had ended and Mexico began to consolidate the changes that had taken place in the previous confused and bloody decade. Obregón was elected president in that year. He was followed by a series of presidents from the new "revolutionary elite" who tried to consolidate the new regime. There was much to be done. The revolution had devastated the country; 1.5 million people had died, major industries were destroyed, and ranching and farming were disrupted. But there was great hope because the revolution also promised (although it did not always deliver) real changes.

What were some of these changes? The new **Mexican Constitution of 1917** promised land reform, limited the foreign ownership of key resources, and guaranteed the rights of workers. It also placed restrictions on clerical education and church ownership of property, and promised educational reforms. The workers who had been mobilized were organized in a national confederation and were given representation in the government. The promised land reforms were slow in coming, though later, under President Lázaro Cárdenas (1934–1940), more than 40 million acres were distributed, most of it in the form of *ejidos* (eh-HEE-dos), or communal holdings. The government launched an extensive program of primary and especially rural education.

Culture and Politics in Postrevolutionary Mexico

Nationalism and *indigenism*, or the concern for the indigenous peoples and their contribution to Mexican culture, lay beneath many reforms. Having failed to integrate the American Indians into national life for a century, Mexico now attempted to "Indianize" the nation through secular schools that emphasized nationalism and a vision of the Mexican past that glorified its American Indian heritage and denounced Western capitalism. Artists such as **Diego Rivera** and **José Clemente Orozco** recaptured that past and outlined a social program for the future in stunning murals on public buildings designed to inform, convince, and entertain at the same time. The Mexican muralist movement had a wide impact on artists throughout Latin America even though, as Orozco himself stated, it sometimes created simple solutions and strange utopias by mixing a romantic image of the American Indian past with Christian symbols and communist ideology.

Novelists, such as Mariano Azuela, found in the revolution a focus for the examination of Mexican reality. Popular culture celebrated the heroes and events of the revolution in scores of ballads (*corridos*) that were sung to celebrate and inform. In literature, music, and the arts, the revolution and its themes provided a stimulus to a tremendous burst of creativity, as in the following lines of poetry:

> Gabino Barrera rose in the mountains
> his cause was noble,
> protect the poor and give them the land.
> Remember the night he was murdered

Huerta, Victoriano Attempted to reestablish centralized dictatorship in Mexico following the removal of Madero in 1913; forced from power in 1914 by Villa and Zapata.

Obregón, Alvaro (1880–1928) Emerged as leader of the Mexican government in 1915; elected president in 1920.

Mexican Constitution of 1917 Promised land reform, limited foreign ownership of key resources, guaranteed the rights of workers, and placed restrictions on clerical education; marked formal end of Mexican Revolution.

Rivera, Diego [ri vär uh] (1886–1957) Mexican artist of the period after the Mexican Revolution; famous for murals painted on walls of public buildings; mixed romantic images of the Indian past with Christian symbols and Marxist ideology.

Orozco, José Clemente (1883–1949) Mexican muralist of the period after the Mexican Revolution; like Rivera's, his work featured romantic images of the Indian past with Christian symbols and Marxist ideology.

three leagues from Tlapehuala;
22 shots rang out
leaving him time for nothing.
Gabino Barrera and his loyal steed
fell in the hail of rounds,
the face of this man of the Revolution
finally rested, his lips pressed to the ground.

The gains of the revolution were not made without opposition. Although the revolution preceded the Russian Revolution of 1917 and had no single ideological model, many of the ideas of Marxist socialism were held by leading Mexican intellectuals and a few politicians. The secularization of society and especially education met strong opposition from the Catholic Church and the clergy, especially in states where socialist rhetoric and anticlericalism were extreme. In the 1920s, a conservative peasant movement backed by the church erupted in central Mexico. These **Cristeros**, backed by conservative politicians, fought to stop the slide toward secularization. The fighting lasted for years until a compromise was reached.

The United States intervened diplomatically and militarily during the revolution, motivated by a desire for order, fear of German influence on the new government, and economic interests. An incident provoked a short-lived U.S. seizure of Veracruz in 1914, and when Pancho Villa's forces raided across the border, the United States sent an expeditionary force into Mexico to catch him. The mission failed. For the most part, however, the war in Europe dominated U.S. foreign policy efforts until 1918. The United States was suspicious of the new government, and a serious conflict arose when U.S.-owned oil companies ran into problems with workers.

As in any revolution, the question of continuity arose when the fighting ended. The revolutionary leadership hoped to institutionalize the new regime by creating a one-party system. This organization, called the Party of the Institutionalized Revolution (**PRI**), developed slowly during the 1920s and 1930s into a dominant force in Mexican politics. It incorporated labor, peasant, military, and middle-class sectors and proved flexible enough to incorporate new interest groups as they developed. Although Mexico became a multiparty democracy in theory, in reality the PRI controlled politics and, by accommodation and sometimes repression, maintained its hold on national political life. Some presidents governed much like the strongmen in the 19th century had done, but the party structure and the need to incorporate various interests within the government coalition limited the worst aspects of caudillo, or personalist, rule. The presidents were strong, but the policy of limiting the presidency to one six-year term ensured some change in leadership. The question of whether a revolution could be institutionalized remained in debate. By the end of the 20th century, many Mexicans believed that little remained of the principles and programs of the revolutionaries of 1910.

Revolution in Russia: Liberalism to Communism

In March 1917, strikes and food riots broke out in Russia's capital, St. Petersburg. The outbursts were spurred by wartime misery, including painful food shortages. They also and more basically protested the conditions of early industrialization set against incomplete rural reform and an unresponsive political system. And they quickly assumed revolutionary proportions. The rioters called not just for more food and work but for a new political regime as well. The tsar's forces struck back brutally but unsuccessfully. A council of workers, called a soviet, took over the city government and arrested the tsar's ministers. Unable to rely on his own soldiers, the tsar abdicated, thus ending the long period of imperial rule.

For eight months a liberal provisional government struggled to rule the country. Russia seemed thus to launch its revolution on a basis similar to France in 1789, where a liberal period set change in motion. Like Western liberals, Russian revolutionary leaders, such as **Alexander Kerensky**, were eager to see genuine parliamentary rule, religious and other freedoms, and a host of political and legal changes. But liberalism was not deeply rooted in Russia, if only because of the small middle class, so the analogies with the first phase of the French revolution cannot be pressed too far. Furthermore, Russia's revolution took place in much more adverse circumstances, given the pressures of participation in World War I. The initial liberal leaders were eager to maintain the war effort, which linked them with democratic France and Britain. Yet the nation was desperately war weary, and prolongation drastically worsened economic conditions while public morale plummeted. Liberal leaders also

---

Cristeros Conservative peasant movement in Mexico during the 1920s; most active in central Mexico; attempted to halt slide toward secularism; movement resulted in armed violence.

Kerensky, Alexander (1881–1970) Liberal revolutionary leader during the early stages of the Russian Revolution of 1917; sought development of parliamentary rule, religious freedom.

held back from the massive land reforms expected by the peasantry, for in good middle-class fashion they respected existing property arrangements and did not wish to rush into social change before a legitimate new political structure could be established. Hence serious popular unrest continued, and in November (October, by the Russian calendar) a second revolution took place, which expelled liberal leadership and soon brought to power the radical, Bolshevik wing of the Social Democratic party, soon renamed the Communist party, and Lenin, their dynamic chief (Figure 30.6).

The revolution was a godsend to Lenin. This devoted revolutionary had long been writing of Russia's readiness for a communist revolt because of the power of international capitalism and its creation of a massive proletariat, even in a society that had not directly passed through middle-class rule. Lenin quickly gained a strong position among the urban workers' councils in the major cities. This corresponded to his deeply rooted belief that revolution should come not from literal mass action but from tightly organized cells whose leaders espoused a coherent plan of action.

Once the liberals were toppled, Lenin and the Bolsheviks faced several immediate problems. One, Russia's continued involvement in World War I, they handled by signing a humiliating peace treaty with Germany and giving up huge sections of western Russia in return for an end of hostilities. This treaty was soon nullified by Germany's defeat at the hands of the Western allies, but Russia was ignored at the Versailles peace conference—treated as a pariah by the fearful Western powers. Much former territory was converted into new nation-states. A revived Poland built heavily on land Russia had controlled for more than a century, and new, small Baltic states cut into even earlier acquisitions. Still, although Russia's deep grievances against the Versailles treaty would later help motivate renewed expansionism, the early end to the war was vital to Lenin's consolidation of power.

Although Lenin and the Bolsheviks had gained a majority role in the leading urban soviets, they were not the most popular revolutionary party, and this situation constituted the second problem faced at the end of 1917. The November seizure of power had led to the creation of the Council of People's Commissars, drawn from soviets across the nation and headed by Lenin, to govern the state. But a parliamentary election had already been called, and this produced a clear majority for the Social

Read the Document on MyHistoryLab: Bolshevik Seizure of Power, 1917

FIGURE 30.6 Moscow workers guard the Bolshevik headquarters during the Russian Revolution of 1917.

Revolutionary party, which emphasized peasant support and rural reform. Lenin, however, shut down the parliament, replacing it with a Bolshevik-dominated Congress of Soviets. He pressed the Social Revolutionaries to disband, arguing that "the people voted for a party which no longer existed." Russia was thus to have no Western-style, multiparty system but rather a Bolshevik monopoly in the name of the true people's will. Indeed, Communist party control of the government apparatus persisted from this point to 1989, a record for continuity much different from the fate of revolutionary groups earlier in the Western past.

Russia's revolution produced a backlash that revolutionaries in other eras would have recognized quite easily: foreign hostility and, even more important, domestic resistance. The world's leading nations—aside from Germany, now briefly irrelevant—were appalled at the communist success, which threatened principles of property and freedom they cherished deeply. As settled regimes, they also disliked the unexpected, and some were directly injured by Russia's renunciation of its heavy foreign debts. The result was an attempt at intervention, recalling the attacks on France in 1792. Britain, France, the United States, and Japan all sent troops. But this intervention, although it heightened Russian suspicion of outsiders, did relatively little damage. The Western powers, exhausted by World War I, pulled out quickly, and even Japan, although interested in lingering in Asiatic Russia, stepped back fairly soon.

The internal civil war, which foreign troops slightly abetted, was a more serious matter, as it raged from 1918 to 1921. Tsarist generals, religiously faithful peasants, and many minority nationalities made common cause against the communist regime. Their efforts were aided by continuing economic distress, the normal result of revolutionary disarray, but also heightened by earlier communist measures. Lenin had quickly decreed a redistribution of land to the peasantry and also launched a nationalization, or state takeover, of basic industry. Many already landed peasants resented the loss of property and incentive, and in reaction they lowered food production and the goods sent to markets. Industrial nationalization somewhat similarly disrupted manufacturing. Famine and unemployment created more economic hardship than the war had generated, which added fuel to the civil war fires. Even workers revolted in several cities, threatening the new regime's most obvious social base as well as its ideological mainstay.

Stabilization of Russia's Communist Regime

Order was restored after the revolution on several key foundations. First, the construction of the powerful new army under the leadership of Leon Trotsky recruited able generals and masses of loyal conscripts. This **Red Army** was an early beneficiary of two ongoing sources of strength for communist Russia: a willingness to use people of humble background but great ability who could rise to great heights under the new order but who had been doomed to immobility under the old system, and an ability to inspire mass loyalty in the name of an end to previous injustice and a promise of a brighter future. Next, economic disarray was reduced in 1921 when Lenin issued his **New Economic Policy**, which promised considerable freedom of action for small business owners and peasant landowners. The state continued to set basic economic policies, but its efforts were now combined with individual initiative. Under this temporary policy, food production began to recover, and the regime gained time to prepare the more durable structures of the communist system.

By 1923 the Bolshevik revolution was an accomplished fact. There was a new capital: Moscow. And a new constitution set up a federal system of socialist republics. This system recognized the multinational character of the nation, which was called the **Union of Soviet Socialist Republics**. The dominance of ethnic Russians was preserved in the central state apparatus, however, and certain groups, notably Jews, were given no distinct representation. Since the separate republics were firmly controlled by the national Communist party and since basic decisions were as firmly centralized, the impact of the new nationalities policy was somewhat mixed; yet it was also true that direct nationalities' protests declined notably from the 1920s until the late 1980s.

Red Army Military organization constructed under leadership of Leon Trotsky, Bolshevik follower of Lenin; made use of people of humble background.

New Economic Policy Initiated by Lenin in 1921; state continued to set basic economic policies, but efforts were now combined with individual initiative; policy allowed food production to recover.

Union of Soviet Socialist Republics Federal system of socialist republics established in 1923 in various ethnic regions of Russia; firmly controlled by Communist party; diminished nationalities protest under Bolsheviks; dissolved 1991.

THINKING HISTORICALLY

A Century of Revolutions

NOT SINCE THE LATE 18TH AND early 19th centuries had there been a succession of revolutions like those in the early decades of the 20th century. In contrast to the revolutionary movements of the earlier period, however, the early 20th-century upheavals were just the first waves of a revolutionary tide that struck with renewed fury after 1945. A number of factors account for the successive surges of revolution in the 20th century. Rural discontent was crucial, for peasants provided vital contributions to 20th-century revolutions everywhere they occurred. Peasants were newly spurred by pressures of population growth, combined with resentment against big landowners. Modern state forms tended to increase taxes on the peasantry, while making traditional protests, like banditry, more difficult.

Equally fundamentally, the rise of revolutionary movements was fed by the underlying disruptions caused by the spread of the Industrial Revolution and the Western-centered, global market system. Handicraft producers thrown out of work by an influx of machine-manufactured goods, and peasants, such as those in central Mexico who lost their land to moneylenders, frequently rallied to calls to riot and, at times, ultimately became caught up in revolutionary currents. In the colonies, unemployed Western-educated African and Asian secondary school and college graduates became deeply committed to struggles for independence that promised them dignity and decent jobs. Urban laborers, enraged by the appalling working and living conditions that were characteristic of the early stages of industrialization in countries such as Russia and China, provided key support for revolutionary parties in many countries.

Although global economic slumps did much to fire the revolutionaries' longings, world wars proved even more fertile seedbeds of revolution. Returning soldiers and neglected veterans provided the shock troops for leftist revolutionaries and fascist pretenders alike. Defeated states witnessed the rapid erosion of their power to suppress internal enemies and floundered as their armies refused to defend them or joined movements dedicated to their overthrow. In this regard, the great increase in global interconnectedness in the 20th century was critical. The economic competition and military rivalries of the industrial powers drew them into unwanted wars that they could not sustain without raw materials and manpower drawn from their colonies and other neutral states.

Another key factor that contributed to the sharp rise in the incidence of revolutions in the 20th century was the underlying intellectual climate. Notions of progress and a belief in the perfectibility of human society, which were widely held in the 19th century, deeply influenced such communist theorists as Marx, Lenin, Mao Zedong, and Ho Chi Minh. These and other revolutionary ideologues sought, in part, to overthrow existing regimes that they viewed as exploitive and oppressive. But they were also deeply committed to building radically new societies that would bring justice and a decent livelihood to previously downtrodden social groups, especially the working classes, peasantry, and urban poor. Visions of the good life in peasant communes or workers' utopias were a powerful driving force for revolutionary currents throughout the century from Mexico to China. One measure of their influence is the extent to which highly competitive capitalist societies developed social welfare programs to curb social discontent that could spiral into active protest, and perhaps even revolutionary challenges to the existing social order.

A final common ingredient of 20th-century revolutions was the need to come to terms with Western influence and often to reassert greater national autonomy. Mexico, Russia, and China all sought to reduce Western economic control and cultural influence, seeking alternative models. Many revolutions involved active anti-Western sentiment and attacks on Western investments. In Russia, Stalinism went on the attack against "decadent" Western cultural influences.

> *Visions of the good life in peasant communes or workers' utopias were a powerful driving force for revolutionary currents throughout the century from Mexico to China.*

QUESTIONS

- What internal and external forces weakened the governments of Mexico and China in the opening decades of the 20th century and unleashed the forces of revolution?
- What key social groups were behind the revolutions in Mexico, China, and Russia, and why were they so important in each case?
- What similarities and differences can you identify among these three early revolutions in the 20th century?

Supreme Soviet Parliament of Union of Soviet Socialist Republics; elected by universal suffrage; actually controlled by Communist party; served to ratify party decisions.

The apparatus of the central state was another mixture of appearance and reality. The **Supreme Soviet** had many of the trappings of a parliament and was elected by universal suffrage. But competition in elections was normally prohibited, which meant that the Communist party easily controlled the body, which served mainly to ratify decisions taken by the party's central executive. Parallel systems of central bureaucracy and party bureaucracy further confirmed the Communists' monopoly on power and the ability to control major decisions from the center. The Soviet political system was elaborated over time. A new constitution in the 1930s spoke glowingly of human rights. In fact, the Communists had quickly reestablished an authoritarian system, making it more efficient than its tsarist predecessor had been, complete with updated versions of political police to ensure loyalty.

Soviet Experimentation

The mid-1920s constituted a lively, experimental period in Soviet history, partly because of the jockeying for power at the top of the power pyramid. Despite the absence of Western-style political competition, a host of new groups found a voice. The Communist party, although not eager to recruit too many members lest it lose its tight organization and elite status, encouraged all sorts of subsidiary organizations. Youth movements, women's groups, and particularly organizations of workers all actively debated problems in their social environment and directions for future planning. Workers were able to influence management practices; women's leaders helped carve legal equality and new educational and work opportunities for their constituents.

One key to the creative mood of these years was the rapid spread of education promoted by the government, as well as educational and propaganda activities sponsored by various adult groups. Literacy gained ground quickly. The new educational system was also bent on reshaping popular culture away from older peasant traditions and, above all, religion, and toward beliefs in Communist political analysis and science. Access to new information, new modes of inquiry, and new values encouraged controversy.

The Soviet regime grappled with other key definitional issues in the 1920s. Rivalries among leaders at the top had to be sorted out. Lenin became ill and then died in 1924, creating an unexpected leadership gap. (St. Petersburg was renamed Leningrad in his honor, a name it retained until 1991.) A number of key lieutenants jostled for power, including the Red Army's flamboyant Trotsky and a Communist party stalwart of worker origins who had taken the name **Stalin**, meaning *steel*. After a few years of jockeying, Joseph Stalin emerged as undisputed leader of the Soviet state, his victory a triumph also for party control over other branches of government.

Stalin, Joseph Successor to Lenin as head of the U.S.S.R.; strongly nationalist view of communism; represented anti-Western strain of Russian tradition; crushed opposition to his rule; established series of five-year plans to replace New Economic Policy; fostered agricultural collectivization; led U.S.S.R. through World War II; furthered cold war with western Europe and the United States; died in 1953.

Stalin's accession was more than a personal bureaucratic issue, however. Stalin represented a strongly nationalist version of communism, in contrast to the more ideological and international visions of many of his rivals. At the revolution's outset Lenin had believed that the Russian rising would be merely a prelude to a sweeping communist upheaval throughout the Western industrial world. Many revolutionary leaders actively encouraged communist parties in the West and set up a **Comintern**, or Communist International office, to guide this process. But revolution did not spill over, despite a few brief risings in Hungary and Germany right after World War I. Under Stalin, the revolutionary leadership, although still committed in theory to an international movement, pulled back to concentrate on Russian developments—building "socialism in one country," as Stalin put it. Stalin in many ways represented the anti-Western strain in Russian tradition, although in new guise.

Comintern International office of communism under U.S.S.R. dominance established to encourage the formation of Communist parties in Europe and elsewhere.

Stalin also instituted a new level of police repression that ultimately led to the deaths of millions of Russian dissidents, from peasants to intellectuals. Rival leaders were killed or expelled, rival visions of the revolution downplayed. Stalin would also accelerate industrial development while attacking peasant land ownership with a new **collectivization** program (Figure 30.7).

collectivization Creation of large, state-run farms rather than individual holdings; allowed more efficient control over peasants, although often lowered food production; part of Stalin's economic and political planning; often adopted in other communist regimes.

The Russian Revolution was one of the most successful risings in human history, at least for several decades. Building on widespread if diverse popular discontent and a firm belief in centralized leadership, the Bolsheviks beat back powerful odds to create a new, although not totally unprecedented, political regime. They used features of the tsarist system but managed to propel a wholly new leadership group to power not only at the top but also at all levels of the bureaucracy and army. The tsar and his hated ministers were gone, mostly executed, but so was the overweening aristocratic class that had loomed so large in Russian history for centuries.

Read the Document on MyHistoryLab: Stalin Demands Rapid Industrialization of the USSR (1931)

FIGURE 30.7 Russian children help carry the propaganda for Stalin's campaign for collectivization of agriculture. The banner reads, "Everybody to the collective farms!" These happy faces belie the tragedy resulting from the collectivization program, in which millions fell victim to slaughter or starvation.

Toward Revolution in China

The abdication of Puyi, the Manchu boy-emperor in 1912, marked the end of a century-long losing struggle on the part of the Qing dynasty to protect Chinese civilization from foreign invaders and revolutionary threats from within, such as the massive Taiping movement (see Chapter 27). The fall of the Qing opened the way for an extended struggle over which leader or movement would be able to capture the mandate to rule the ancient society that had for millennia ordered the lives of at least one-fifth of humankind. Contenders included regional warlords; the loose alliance of students, middle-class politicians and secret societies, many of them attracted to a Western political model; and soon, Japanese intruders and a new communist movements as well. Internal divisions and foreign influences paved the way for the ultimate victory of the Chinese Communist party under Mao Zedong.

After the fall of the Qing dynasty, the best-positioned of the contenders for power were regionally based military commanders or warlords, who would dominate Chinese politics for the next three decades. Many of the warlords combined in cliques or alliances to protect their own territories and to crush neighbors and annex their lands. The most powerful of these cliques, centered in north China, was headed by the unscrupulous **Yuan Shikai**, who hoped to seize the vacated Manchu throne and found a new dynasty. By virtue of their wealth, the merchants and bankers of coastal cities like Shanghai and Canton made up a second power center in post-Manchu China. Their involvement in politics resulted from their willingness to bankroll both favored warlords and Western-educated, middle-class politicians like Sun Yat-sen.

Sometimes supportive of the urban civilian politicians and sometimes wary of them, university students and their teachers, as well as independent intellectuals, provided yet another factor in the complex post-Qing political equation. Although the intellectuals and students played critical roles in shaping new ideologies to rebuild Chinese civilization, they were virtually defenseless in a situation

Yuan Shikai [yoo-ahn shur-geye] Warlord in northern China after fall of Qing dynasty; hoped to seize imperial throne; president of China after 1912; resigned in the face of Japanese invasion in 1916.

in which force was essential to those who hoped to exert political influence. Deeply divided, but very strong in some regions, secret societies represented another contender for power. Like many in the military, members of these societies envisioned the restoration of monarchical rule, but under a Chinese dynasty, not a foreign one. As if the situation were not confused enough, it was further complicated by the continuing intervention of the Western powers, eager to profit from China's divisions and weakness. Their inroads, however, were increasingly overshadowed by the entry into the contest for the control of China by the newest imperialist power, Japan. From the mid-1890s, when the Japanese had humiliated their much larger neighbor by easily defeating it in war, until 1945, when Japan's surrender ended World War II, the Japanese were a major factor in the long and bloody contest for mastery of China.

China's May Fourth Movement and the Rise of the Marxist Alternative

Sun Yat-sen headed the Revolutionary Alliance, a loose coalition of anti-Qing political groups that had spearheaded the 1911 revolt. After the Qing were toppled, Sun claimed that he and the parties of the alliance were the rightful claimants to the mandate to rule all of China. But he could do little to assert civilian control in the face of warlord opposition. The Revolutionary Alliance had little power and virtually no popular support outside the urban trading centers of the coastal areas in central and south China. Even in these areas, they were at the mercy of the local warlords. The alliance formally elected Sun president at the end of 1911, set up a parliament modeled after those in Europe, and chose cabinets with great fanfare. But their decisions had little effect on warlord-dominated China.

Sun Yat-sen conceded this reality when he resigned the acting presidency in favor of the northern warlord Yuan Shikai in 1912. As the most powerful of the northern clique of generals, Yuan appeared to have the best chance to unify China under a single government. He at first feigned sympathy for the democratic aims of the alliance leaders but soon revealed his true intentions. He took foreign loans to build up his military forces and buy out most of the bureaucrats in the capital at Beijing. When Sun and other leaders of the Revolutionary Alliance called for a second revolution to oust Yuan in the years after 1912, he made full use of his military power and more underhanded methods, such as assassinations, to put down their opposition. By 1915 it appeared that Yuan was well on his way to realizing his ambition of becoming China's next emperor. His schemes were foiled, however, by the continuing rivalry of other warlords, republican nationalists like Sun, and the growing influence of Japan in China. The latter increased dramatically as a result of World War I.

As England's ally according to terms of a 1902 treaty, Japan immediately entered the war on the side of the Entente, or Western allied powers. Moving much too quickly for the comfort of the British and the other Western powers, the Japanese seized German-held islands in the Pacific and occupied the Germans' concessionary areas in China. With all the great powers except the United States embroiled in war, the Japanese sought to establish a dominant hold over their giant neighbor. In early 1915, they presented Yuan's government with Twenty-One Demands, which, if accepted, would have reduced China to the status of a dependant protectorate. Although Sun and the Revolutionary Alliance lost much support by refusing to repudiate the Japanese demands, Yuan was no more decisive. He neither accepted nor rejected the demands but concentrated his energies on an effort to trump up popular enthusiasm for his accession to the throne. Disgusted by Yuan's weakness and ambition, one of his warlord rivals plotted his overthrow. Hostility to the Japanese won Yuan's rival widespread support, and in 1916, Yuan was forced to resign the presidency. His fall was the signal for a free-for-all power struggle between the remaining warlords for control of China.

As one of the victorious allies of World War I, Japan managed to solidify its hold on northern China by winning control of the former German concessions in the peace negotiations at Versailles in 1919. But the Chinese had also allied themselves to the Entente powers during the war. Enraged by what they viewed as a betrayal by the Entente powers, students and nationalist politicians organized mass demonstrations in numerous Chinese cities on May 4, 1919. The demonstrations began a prolonged period of protest against Japanese inroads. This protest soon expanded from marches and petitions to include strikes and mass boycotts of Japanese goods.

The fourth of May, 1919, the day when the resistance began, gave its name to a movement in which intellectuals and students played a leading role. Initially at least, the **May Fourth movement** was aimed at transforming China into a liberal democracy. Its program was enunciated in numerous

May Fourth movement Resistance to Japanese encroachments in China began on this date in 1919; spawned movement of intellectuals aimed at transforming China into a liberal democracy; rejected Confucianism.

speeches, pamphlets, novels, and newspaper articles. Confucianism was ridiculed and rejected in favor of a wholehearted acceptance of all that the Western democracies had to offer. Noted Western thinkers, such as Bertrand Russell and John Dewey, toured China, praising democracy and basking in the cheers of enthusiastic Chinese audiences. Chinese thinkers called for the liberation of women (including the abolition of footbinding), the simplification of the Chinese script in order to promote mass literacy, and the promotion of Western-style individualism. Many of these themes are captured in the literature of the period. In the novel *Family* by Ba Jin, for example, a younger brother audaciously informs his elder sibling that he will not accept the marriage partner the family has arranged for him. He clearly sees his refusal as part of a more general revolt of the youth of China against the ancient Confucian social code.

> Big Brother, I'm doing what no one in our family has ever dared do before—I'm running out on an arranged marriage. No one cares about my fate, so I've decided to walk my own road alone. I'm determined to struggle against the old forces to the end. Unless you cancel the match, I'll never come back. I'll die first.

However enthusiastically the program of the May Fourth movement was adopted by the urban youth of China, it was soon clear that mere emulation of the liberal democracies of the West could not provide effective solutions to China's prodigious problems. Civil liberties and democratic elections were meaningless in a China that was ruled by warlords. Gradualist solutions and parliamentary debates were folly in a nation where the great mass of the peasantry was destitute, much of them malnourished or dying of starvation. It soon became clear to many Chinese intellectuals and students, as well as to some of the nationalist politicians, that more radical solutions were needed. In the 1920s, this conviction gave rise to the communist left within the Chinese nationalist movement.

The Bolshevik victory and the programs launched to rebuild Russia prompted Chinese intellectuals to give serious attention to the works of Marx and other socialist thinkers and the potential they offered for the regeneration of China. But the careful study of the writings of Marx, Engels, Lenin, and Trotsky in the wake of the Russian Revolution also impressed a number of Chinese intellectuals with the necessity for major alterations in Marxist ideology if it was going to be of any relevance to China or other peasant societies. Marx, after all, had focused on advanced industrial societies and had regarded peasants as conservative or even reactionary. Taken literally, Marxism offered discouraging prospects for revolution in China.

The most influential of the thinkers who called for a reworking of Marxist ideology to fit China's situation was **Li Dazhao**. Li was from peasant origins, but he had excelled in school and eventually become a college teacher. He headed the Marxist study circle that developed after the 1919 upheavals at the University of Beijing. His interpretation of Marxist philosophy placed heavy emphasis on its capacity for promoting renewal and its ability to harness the energy and vitality of a nation's youth. In contrast to Lenin, Li saw the peasants, rather than the urban workers, as the vanguard of revolutionary change. He justified this shift from the orthodox Marxist emphasis on the working classes, which made up only a tiny fraction of China's population at the time, by characterizing the whole of Chinese society as proletarian. All of China, he argued, had been exploited by the bourgeois, industrialized West. Thus, the oppressed Chinese as a whole needed to unite and rise up against their exploiters.

Li Dazhao [lee duh-JOH] (1888–1927) Chinese intellectual who gave serious attention to Marxist philosophy; headed study circle at the University of Beijing; saw peasants as vanguard of revolutionary communism in China.

Li's version of Marxism, with alterations or emphasis on elements that made it suitable for China, had great appeal for the students, including the young **Mao Zedong**, who joined Li's study circle. They, too, were angered by what they perceived as China's betrayal by the imperialist powers. They shared Li's hostility (very much a throwback to the attitudes of the Confucian era) to merchants and commerce, which appeared to dominate the West. They, too, longed for a return to a political system, like the Confucian, in which those who governed were deeply committed to social reform and social welfare. They also believed in an authoritarian state, which they felt ought to intervene constructively in all aspects of the peoples' lives. The Marxist study club societies that developed as a result of these discoveries soon spawned a number of more broadly based, politically activist organizations.

Mao Zedong [mow dzuh-doong] (1893–1976) Communist leader in revolutionary China; advocated rural reform and role of peasantry in Nationalist revolution; influenced by Li Dazhao; led Communist reaction against Guomindang purges in 1920s, culminating in Long March of 1934; seized control of all of mainland China by 1949; initiated Great Leap Forward in 1958.

In the summer of 1921, in an attempt to unify the growing Marxist wing of the nationalist struggle, a handful of leaders from different parts of China met in secret in the city of Shanghai. At this meeting, closely watched by the agents of the local warlord and rival political organizations, the Communist party of China was born. The party was minuscule in terms of the numbers of their supporters, and at this time it was still dogmatically fixed on a revolutionary program oriented to the small and scattered working class. But the communists at least offered a clear alternative to fill the ideological and institutional void left by the collapse of the Confucian order.

The Seizure of Power by China's Guomindang

In the years when the communist movement in China was being put together by urban students and intellectuals, the **Guomindang**, or Nationalist party, which was to prove the communists' great rival for the mandate to rule in China, was struggling to survive in the south. Sun Yat-sen, who was the acknowledged head of the nationalist struggle from the 1911 revolution until his death in early 1925, had gone into temporary exile in Japan in 1914, while warlords such as Yuan Shikai consolidated their regional power bases. After returning to China in 1919, Sun and his followers attempted to unify the diverse political organizations struggling for political influence in China by reorganizing the revolutionary movement and naming it the Nationalist party of China (the Guomindang).

The Nationalists began the slow process of forging alliances with key social groups and building an army of their own, which they now viewed as the only way to rid China of the warlord menace (Map 30.3). Sun strove to enunciate a nationalist ideology that gave something to everyone. It stressed the need to unify China under a strong central government, to bring the imperialist intruders under control, and to introduce social reforms that would alleviate the poverty of the peasants and the oppressive working conditions of laborers in China's cities. Unfortunately for the great majority of the Chinese people, for whom social reforms were the main concern, the Nationalist leaders concentrated on political and international issues, such as relations with the Western powers and Japan, and failed to implement most of the domestic programs they proposed, most especially land reform.

In this early stage Sun and the Nationalists built their power primarily on the support provided by urban businesspeople and merchants in coastal cities such as Canton. Sun forged an alliance with the communists that was officially proclaimed at the first Nationalist party conference in 1924. For

Guomindang [gwoh-mihn-dohng] Chinese Nationalist party founded by Sun Yat-sen in 1919; drew support from local warlords and Chinese criminal underworld; initially forged alliance with Communists in 1924; dominated by Chiang Kai-shek after 1925.

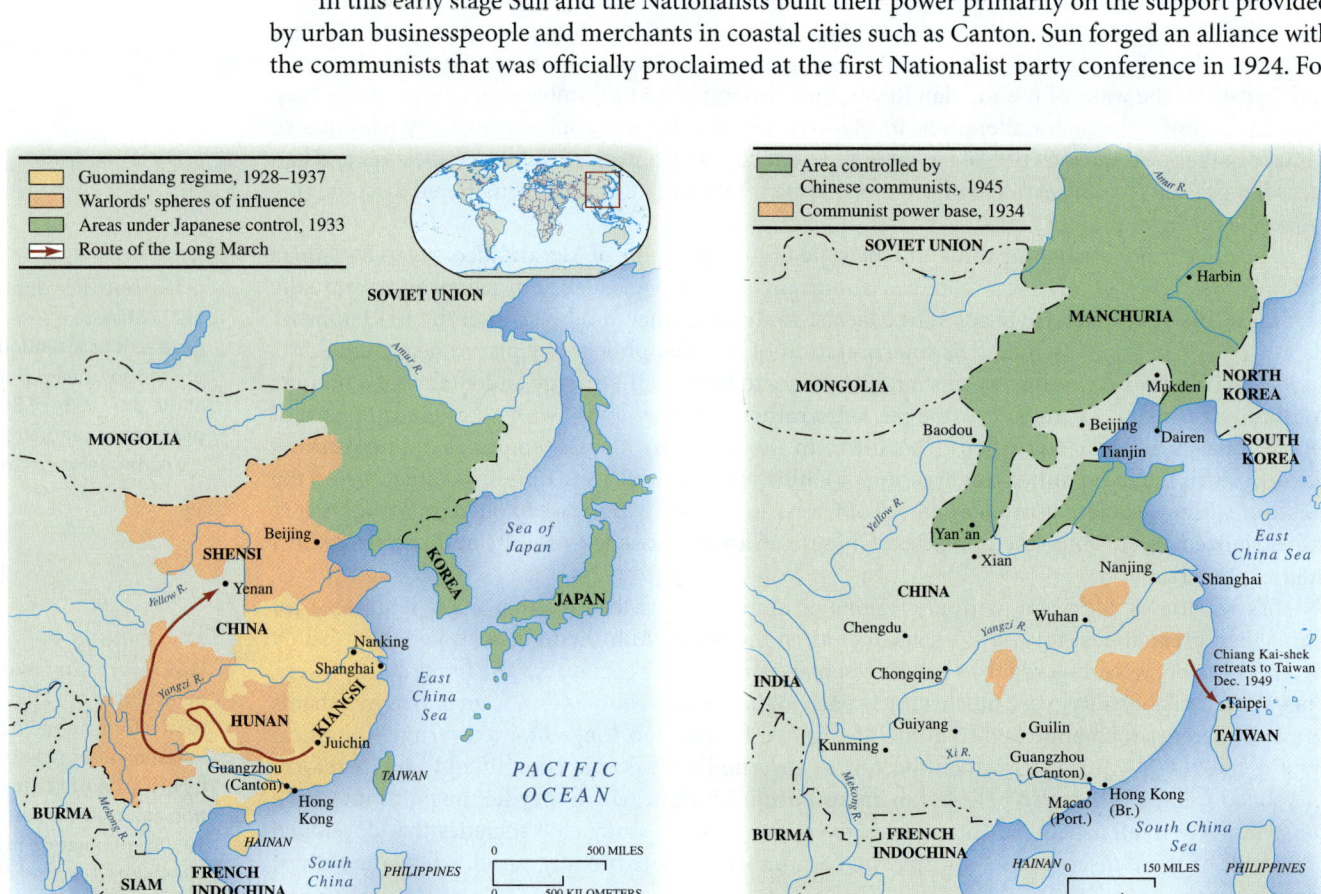

MAP **30.3 China in the Era of Revolution and Civil War** Political reform was constrained by the nationalist-communist dispute and by Japanese invasion.

the time being at least, the Nationalist leaders were content to let the communists serve as their major link to the peasants and the urban workers. Nationalist leaders also turned to Soviet Russia, and the Bolsheviks sent advisors and gave material assistance.

In 1924 the **Whampoa Military Academy** was founded with Soviet help and partially staffed by Russian instructors. The academy gave the Nationalists a critical military dimension to their political maneuvering. The first head of the academy was an ambitious young military officer named **Chiang Kai-shek**. The son of a poor salt merchant, Chiang had made his career in the military and by virtue of connections with powerful figures in the Shanghai underworld. He had received some military training in Japan and managed by the early 1920s to work his way into Sun Yat-sen's inner circle of advisors. Chiang was not happy with the communist alliance. But he was willing to bide his time until he had the military strength to deal with both the communists and the warlords, who remained the major obstacles to the Nationalist seizure of power.

Political tensions distracted the Nationalist leaders from the growing deterioration of the economy. The peasantry, 90 percent of the population, suffered increasing misery following a long period of government ineffectiveness and depredations by the landlords. Famine and disease stalked the countryside, while irrigation systems deteriorated. Many peasants could not even bury their deceased parents, whose bodies were left for animals to devour.

Sun gave lip service to the Nationalist party's need to deal with the peasant problem. But his abysmal ignorance of rural conditions was revealed by statements in which he denied that China had exploitive landlords and his refusal to believe that there were "serious difficulties" between the great mass of the peasantry and the landowners.

Whampoa Military Academy Founded in 1924; military wing of the Guomindang; first head of the academy was Chiang Kai-shek.

Chiang Kai-shek [jee-ahng keye-shehk] A military officer who succeeded Sun Yat-sen as the leader of the Guomindang or Nationalist party in China in the mid-1920s; became the most powerful leader in China in the early 1930s, but his Nationalist forces were defeated and driven from China by the Communists after World War II.

Mao and the Peasant Option

Although the son of a fairly prosperous peasant, Mao Zedong had rebelled early in his life against his father's exploitation of the tenants and laborers who worked the family fields. Receiving little assistance from his estranged father, Mao was forced to make his own way in the world. Through much of his youth and early adulthood, he struggled to educate himself in the history, philosophy, and economic theory that most other nationalist and revolutionary leaders mastered in private schools. Having moved to Beijing in the post–May Fourth era, Mao came under the influence of thinkers such as Li Dazhao, who placed considerable emphasis on solutions to the peasant problem as one of the keys to China's survival. In his early writings, Mao indicated almost from the outset his commitment to revolutionary solutions that depended on peasant support. Mao viewed revolution as a violent act in which one social class overthrows another. According to Mao, in the countryside, a revolution involves peasants overthrowing the power of the landlord class and the feudal system. If they do not use extreme force, Mao believed, peasants cannot displace the power of the landlords, which had existed for thousands of years and which had very deep roots in Chinese society.

The Nationalists' successful drive for national power began only after Sun Yat-sen's death in 1925, which opened the way for Chiang Kai-shek and his warlord allies to seize control of the party. After winning over or eliminating the military chiefs in the Canton area, Chiang marched north with his newly created armies. His first campaign culminated in the Nationalists' seizure of the Yangzi River valley and Shanghai in early 1927. Later his forces also captured the capital at Beijing and the rest of the Yellow River basin. The refusal of most of the warlords to end their feuding meant that Chiang could defeat them or buy them out, one by one. By the late 1920s, he was the master of China in name and international standing, if not in actual fact. He was, in effect, the head of a warlord hierarchy. But most political leaders within China and in the outside world recognized him as the new president of China.

 Read the **Document** on **MyHistoryLab**: Mao Zedong, "A Single Spark Can Start a Prairie Fire," 1953

Long March Communist escape from Hunan province during civil war with Guomindang in 1934; center of Communist power moved to Shanxi province; firmly established Mao Zedong as head of the Communist party in China.

Chiang quickly turned against the communists, attacking them in various places. A brutal massacre occurred in Shanghai in 1927, with many workers gunned down or beheaded. Chiang carefully wooed support from western Europe and the United States, while lining up most police and landlord leaders at home. The offensive propelled Mao Zedong to leadership. An attack on the communist rural stronghold in south central China, supported by German advisors, caused Mao to spearhead a **Long March** of 90,000 followers in 1934, across thousands of miles to the more remote northwest. Here, in Shanxi, where some peasant communes had already been established, the new communist center took shape (Map 30.3).

While the Long March solidified Mao's leadership of Chinese communism and gave many followers a sense that they could not be defeated, it was the Japanese invasions of China in the 1930s that would begin to give communists a new advantage. Chiang had to ally with communists to fight the Japanese threat, while his own power base, along the coast, was eroded by the powerful Japanese advance. The Chinese revolution was far from over.

THE GLOBAL GREAT DEPRESSION

30.3 What were the principal regional differences in the impact of and response to the Great Depression?

> Several weaknesses in the world economy led to a major collapse, beginning in 1929. Massive economic and personal dislocation affected many regions, and responses to the crisis were mixed. The results deepened divisions in the world as a whole.

Great Depression International economic crisis following World War I; began with collapse of American stock market in 1929; actual causes included collapse of agricultural prices in 1920s, collapse of banking houses in the United States and western Europe, massive unemployment; contradicted optimistic assumptions of 19th century.

Coming barely a decade after the turmoil of World War I, the onset of global economic depression constituted a crucial next step in the mounting spiral of international crises. The crash of the New York stock market hit the headlines in 1929, but in fact the **Great Depression** had begun, sullenly, in many parts of the world economy even earlier. The Depression resulted from new problems in the industrial economy of Europe and the United States, combined with the long-term weakness in economies, like those of Latin America, that depended on sales of cheap exports in the international market. The result was a worldwide collapse that spared only a few economies and brought political as well as economic pressures on virtually every society.

Causation

Structural problems affected many industrial societies during the 1920s, even after postwar recovery. Farmers throughout much of the Western world, including the United States, faced almost chronic overproduction of food and resulting low prices. Food production had soared in response to wartime needs; during the postwar inflation many farmers, both in western Europe and in North America, borrowed heavily to buy new equipment, overconfident that their good markets would be sustained. But rising European production combined with large imports from the Americas and New Zealand sent prices down, which lowered earnings and made debts harder to repay. One response was continued population flight from the countryside as urbanization continued. Remaining farmers were hard pressed and unable to sustain high demand for manufactured goods.

Thus, although economies in France and Germany seemed to have recovered by 1925, problems continued: The fears that massive postwar inflation had generated limited the capacity of governments to respond to other problems. Much of the mid-decade prosperity rested on exceedingly fragile grounds. Loans from U.S. banks to various European enterprises helped sustain demand for goods but on condition that additional loans pour in to help pay off the resultant debts.

Furthermore, most of the dependent areas in the world economy, colonies and noncolonies alike, were suffering badly. Pronounced tendencies toward overproduction developed in the smaller nations of eastern Europe, which sent agricultural goods to western Europe, as well as among tropical producers in Africa and Latin America. Here, continued efforts to win export revenue pressed local estate owners to drive up output in coffee, sugar, and rubber. As European governments and businesses organized their African colonies for more profitable exploitation, they set up large estates devoted to goods of this type. Again, production frequently exceeded demand, which drove prices and earnings down in both Africa and Latin America. This meant, in turn, that many colonies and dependant economies were unable to buy many industrial exports, which weakened demand for Western products precisely when output tended to rise amid growing U.S. and Japanese competition. Several food-exporting regions, including many of the new eastern European nations, fell into a depression, in terms of earnings and employment, by the mid-1920s, well before the full industrial catastrophe.

Governments of the leading industrial nations provided scant leadership during the emerging crisis of the 1920s. Most Western leaders had only a feeble grasp of economics. Nationalistic selfishness predominated. Western nations were more concerned about insisting on repayment of any debts owed to them or about constructing tariff barriers to protect their own industries than about facilitating balanced world economic growth. Protectionism, in particular, as practiced even by traditionally free-trade Great Britain and by the many nations in eastern Europe, simply reduced market opportunities and made a bad situation worse. By the later 1920s employment in key Western industrial sectors—coal (also beset by new competition from imported oil), iron, and textiles—began to decline, the foretaste of more general collapse.

The Debacle

The formal advent of the Depression occurred in October 1929, when the New York stock market collapsed. Stock values tumbled as investors quickly lost confidence in prices that had been pushed ridiculously high. Banks, which had depended heavily on their stock investments, rapidly echoed the financial crisis, and many institutions failed, dragging their depositors along with them. Even before this crash, Americans had begun to call back earlier loans to Europe. Yet the European credit structure depended extensively on U.S. loans, which had fueled some industrial expansion but also less productive investments, such as German reparations payments and the construction of fancy town halls and other amenities. In Europe, as in the United States, many commercial enterprises existed on the basis not of real production power but of continued speculation. When one piece of the speculative spiral was withdrawn, the whole edifice quickly collapsed. Key bank failures in Austria and Germany followed the U.S. crisis. Throughout most of the industrial West, investment funds dried up as creditors went bankrupt or tried to cut their losses.

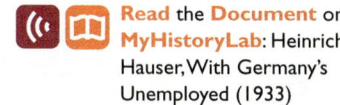

Read the Document on MyHistoryLab: Heinrich Hauser, With Germany's Unemployed (1933)

With investment receding, industrial production quickly began to fall, beginning with the industries that produced capital goods and extending quickly to consumer products fields. Falling production—levels dropped by as much as one-third by 1932—meant falling employment and lower wages, which in turn withdrew still more demand from the economy and led to further hardship. Unemployed and underpaid workers could not buy goods whose production might give other workers jobs. The existing weakness of some markets, such as the farm sector or the nonindustrial world, was exacerbated as demand for foods and minerals plummeted. New and appalling problems developed among workers, now out of jobs or suffering from reduced hours and reduced pay (Figure 30.8), as well as among the middle classes. The Depression, in sum, fed on itself, growing steadily worse from 1929 to 1933. Even countries initially less hard hit, such as France and Italy, saw themselves drawn into the vortex by 1931.

Read the Document on MyHistoryLab: The Great Depression: An Oral Account (1932)

In itself the Great Depression was not entirely unprecedented. Previous periods had seen slumps triggered by bank failures and overspeculation, yielding several years of falling production, unemployment, and hardship. But the intensity of the Great Depression had no precedent in the brief history of industrial societies. Its duration was also unprecedented; in many countries, full recovery came only after a decade and only with the forced production schedules provoked by World War II. Unlike earlier depressions, this one came on the heels of so much other distress—the economic hardships of war, for example, and the catastrophic inflation of the 1920s—and caught most governments totally unprepared.

The Depression was more, of course, than an economic event. It reached into countless lives, creating hardship and tension that would be recalled even as the crisis itself eased. Loss of earnings, loss of work, or simply fears that loss would come devastated people at all social levels. The suicides of ruined investors in New York were paralleled by the vagrants' camps and begging that spread among displaced workers. The statistics were grim: Up to one-third of all blue-collar workers in the West lost their jobs for prolonged periods. White-collar unemployment, although not quite as severe, was also unparalleled. In Germany 600,000 of 4 million white-collar workers had lost their jobs by 1931. Graduating students could not find work or had to resort to jobs they regarded as insecure or demeaning. Six million overall unemployed in Germany and 22 percent of the labor force unemployed in Britain were statistics of stark misery and despair. Families were disrupted; men felt emasculated at their inability to provide, and women and children were disgusted with authority figures whose

FIGURE **30.8** This famous photograph of a tenant farmer and her children in the American South was published in the book *Let Us Now Praise Famous Men*. It exemplifies the hardship and poverty endured by many during the Great Depression.

View the **Closer Look** on MyHistoryLab: Bread line, 1930s

authority was now hollow. In some cases wives and mothers found it easier to gain jobs in a low-wage economy than their husbands did, and although this development had some promise in terms of new opportunities for women, it could also be confusing for standard family roles. For many, the agony and personal disruption of the Depression were desperately prolonged, with renewed recession around 1937 and with unemployment still averaging 10 percent or more in many countries as late as 1939.

The Depression, like World War I, was an event that blatantly contradicted the optimistic assumptions of the later 19th century. To many it showed the fragility of any idea of progress, while to others it seemed to condemn the system of parliamentary democracy. Because it was a second catastrophic event within a generation, the Depression led to even more extreme results than the war had done—more bizarre experiments, more paralysis in the face of deepening despair. To be sure, there were some escapist alternatives: Hollywood movies put up a cheerful front, and in 1938 a new American comic book figure, Superman, provided an alternative to the constraints of normal life. But these were modest alternatives at best.

For most of the world outside the West, moreover, the Depression worsened an already bleak economic picture. Western markets could absorb fewer commodity imports as production fell and incomes dwindled. Hence the nations that produced foods and raw materials saw prices and earnings drop even more than before. Unemployment rose rapidly in the export sectors of the Latin American economy, creating a major political challenge not unlike that faced by the Western nations. Japan, a new industrial country, still heavily depended on export earnings for financing its imports of essential fuel and raw materials. The Japanese silk industry, an export staple, was already suffering from the advent of artificial silklike fibers produced by Western chemical giants. Now Western luxury purchases collapsed, leading to severe unemployment in Japan and a crucial political crisis. Between 1929 and 1931, the value of Japanese exports plummeted by 50 percent. Workers' real income dropped by almost one-third, and more than 3 million people were unemployed. Depression was compounded by poor harvests in several regions, leading to rural begging and near starvation. The Great Depression, although most familiar in its Western dimensions, was a truly international collapse.

Responses to the Depression in Western Europe

Western governments, already weakened, responded to the onset of the economic catastrophe counterproductively. National tariffs were raised to keep out the goods of other countries, but this merely worsened the international economy and curbed sales for everyone. Most governments tried to cut spending, reflecting the decline in revenues that accompanied falling production. They were concerned about avoiding renewed inflation, but in fact their measures further reduced economic stimulus and pushed additional workers—government employees—out of jobs. Confidence in the normal political process deteriorated. In many countries the Depression heightened political polarization. People sought solutions from radical parties or movements, both on the left and on the right. Support for communist parties increased in many countries, and in important cases the authoritarian movement on the right gained increased attention. Even in relatively stable countries, such as Britain, battles between the Conservative party and the labor movement made decisive policy difficult. Class conflict rose to new levels, in and out of politics.

In key cases, the Great Depression led to one of two effects: either a parliamentary system that became increasingly incapacitated, unable to come to grips with the new economic dilemma and too divided to take vigorous action, even in foreign policy, or the outright overturning of the parliamentary system.

France was a prime example of the first pattern. The French government reacted sluggishly to the Depression. Voters responded by moving toward the political extremes. Socialist and then communist parties expanded. Rightist movements calling for a strong leader and fervent nationalism grew, their adherents often disrupting political meetings in order to discredit the parliamentary system by making orderly debate impossible. In response liberal, socialist, and communist parties formed the **Popular Front** in 1936 to win the election. The Popular Front government, however, was unable to take strong measures of social reform because of the ongoing strength of conservative republicans hostile to change and the authoritarian right that looked to forceful leadership to contain the lower classes. The same paralysis crept into foreign policy, as Popular Front leaders, initially eager to support the new liberal regime in Spain that was attacked by conservative army leaders in the Spanish Civil War, found themselves forced to pull back. The Popular Front fell in 1938, but even before this France was close to a standstill.

Popular Front Combination of socialist and communist political parties in France; won election in 1936; unable to take strong measures of social reform because of continuing strength of conservatives; fell from power in 1938.

There were more constructive responses. Scandinavian states, most of them directed by moderate socialist parties, increased government spending, providing new levels of social insurance against illness and unemployment. This foreshadowed the welfare state. British policy was more tentative, but new industrial sectors emerged under the leadership of innovative businesspeople. The world's first television industry, for example, took shape in southern England in the late 1930s, although it was too small to break the hold of the Depression.

The New Deal

After a few years of floundering, the United States generated another set of creative responses. Initial American policies, under President Herbert Hoover, resembled those of western Europe, in seeking higher tariffs and attempting to cut spending in reaction to falling revenues. The United States also sought to accelerate war debt repayments from Europe, which also made matters worse internationally. In 1933 a new administration took over, under Franklin Roosevelt, offering a "new deal" to the American people.

New Deal policies, as they unfolded during the 1930s, offered more direct aid to Americans at risk, through increased unemployment benefits and other measures. Many unemployed people were given jobs on public works projects. A crucial innovation was the Social Security system, based on contributions from workers and employers and designed to provide protection in unemployment and old age. The New Deal also undertook some economic planning and stimulus, for both industry and agriculture, while installing new regulations on banking.

The New Deal ushered in a period of rapid government growth, a watershed in American history particularly as it was followed by the massive expansion of military operations in World War II. The regime did not solve the Depression, which sputtered on until wartime spending ended it in the early 1940s. It also did not install a full welfare state, holding back, for example, from plans to offer a health insurance system. But the New Deal did restore the confidence of most Americans in their political system, preempting more extremist political movements and minimizing the kind of paralysis that afflicted Britain and France in the same years.

 Watch the **Video** on **MyHistoryLab**: Responding to the Great Depression: Whose New Deal? (James Fraser)

New Deal President Franklin Roosevelt's precursor of the modern welfare state (1933–1939); programs to combat economic depression enacted a number of social insurance measures and used government spending to stimulate the economy; increased power of the state and the state's intervention in U.S. social and economic life.

THE NAZI RESPONSE

30.4 What were the main features of the Nazi state?

German patterns differed markedly from the wavering responses of Germany's neighbors and from democratic welfare innovation as well. In Germany the impact of the Depression led directly to a new fascist regime. Germany had suffered the shock of loss in World War I, enhanced by treaty arrangements that cast primary blame for the war on the German nation, which had only recent and shaky parliamentary traditions. A number of factors, in sum, combined to make Germany a fertile breeding ground for fascism, although it took the Depression to bring this current to the fore.

> The Great Depression was centered in the West but had global roots and impact. Western responses to the Depression varied, but none succeeded in ending the crisis.

The Rise of Nazism

While Germany introduced the sharpest political changes in response to the depression and to nationalist pattern, important political change also affected Japan, the Soviet Union, and later America. Western-style democracies were in substantial retreat.

Fascism in Germany, as in Italy, was a product of the war. The movement's advocates, many of them former veterans, attacked the weakness of parliamentary democracy and the corruption and class conflict of Western capitalism. They proposed a strong state ruled by a powerful leader who would revive the nation's forces through vigorous foreign and military policy. While fascists vaguely promised social reforms to alleviate class antagonisms, their attacks on trade unions as well as on socialist and communist parties pleased landlords and business groups. Although fascism won outright control only in Italy in the movement's early years, fascist parties complicated the political process in a number of other nations during the 1920s and beyond. But it was the advent of the National Socialist, or Nazi, regime in Germany under Adolf Hitler that made this new political movement a major force in world history. Here, a Western commitment to liberal, democratic political forms was challenged and reversed.

In his vote-gathering campaigns, in the later 1920s and early 1930s, Hitler repeated standard fascist arguments about the need for unity and the hopeless weakness of parliamentary politics. The state should provide guidance, for it was greater than the sum of individual interests, and the leader should guide the state. Hitler promised many groups a return to more traditional ways; thus many artisans voted for him in the belief that preindustrial economic institutions, such as the guilds, would be revived. Middle-class elements, including big-business leaders, were attracted to Hitler's commitment to a firm stance against socialism and communism. Hitler also focused grievances against various currents in modern life, from big department stores to feminism, by attacking what he claimed were Jewish influences in Germany. He promised a glorious foreign policy to undo the wrongs of the Versailles treaty. Finally, Hitler represented a hope for effective action against the Depression. Although the Nazis never won a majority vote in a free election, his party did win the largest single slice in 1932, and this enabled Hitler to make arrangements with other political leaders for his rise to power legally in 1933.

Once in power, Hitler quickly set about constructing a **totalitarian state**—a new kind of government that would exercise massive, direct control over virtually all the activities of its subjects. Hitler eliminated all opposition parties; he purged the bureaucracy and military, installing loyal Nazis in many posts. His secret police, the **Gestapo**, arrested hundreds of thousands of political opponents. Trade unions were replaced by government-sponsored bodies that tried to appease low-paid workers by offering full employment and various welfare benefits. Government economic planning helped restore production levels, with particular emphasis on armaments construction. Hitler cemented his regime by continual, well-staged propaganda bombardments (Figure 30.9), strident nationalism, and an incessant attack on Germany's large Jewish minority.

Hitler's hatred of Jews ran deep; he blamed them for various personal misfortunes and also for socialism and excessive capitalism—movements that in his view had weakened the German spirit. Obviously, anti-Semitism served as a catchall for a host of diverse dissatisfactions, and as such it

totalitarian state A new kind of government in the 20th century that exercised massive, direct control over virtually all the activities of its subjects; existed in Germany, Italy, and the Soviet Union.

Gestapo Secret police in Nazi Germany, known for brutal tactics.

Read the Document on MyHistoryLab: Adolf Hitler, Mein Kampf (1923)

FIGURE **30.9** The adulation that the German masses felt for Adolf Hitler in the mid-1930s is evident in this rally photo. Hitler's popularity rested primarily on his promises to rebuild Germany's deeply depressed economy and restore its world power status by reversing the 1919 treaty ending World War I.

appealed to many Germans. Anti-Semitism also played into Hitler's hands by providing a scapegoat that could rouse national passions and distract the population from other problems. Measures against Jews became more and more severe; they were forced to wear special emblems, their property was attacked and seized, and increasing numbers were sent to concentration camps. After 1940 Hitler's policy insanely turned to the literal elimination of European Jewry, as the Holocaust raged in the concentration camps of Germany and conquered territories (see Chapter 31).

Hitler's foreign and military policies were based on preparation for war. He wanted to not only recoup Germany's World War I losses but also create a land empire that would extend across much of Europe, particularly toward the east against what he saw as the inferior Slavic peoples. Progressively Hitler violated the limits on German armaments and annexed neighboring territories, provoking only weak response from the Western democracies.

AUTHORITARIANISM AND NEW MILITARISM IN KEY REGIONS

30.5 Did global developments in the 1930s make another world war inevitable?

> European fascism expanded in response to the new crisis as Nazism took hold in Germany. New authoritarian regimes gained ground in Latin America, Japan, and the Soviet Union.

The Spread of Fascism and the Spanish Civil War

Nazi triumph in Germany inevitably spurred fascism in other parts of Europe. Many east central states, already authoritarian, took on fascist trappings. Explicit fascist movements emerged in Hungary and Romania. Fascism in Austria was vindicated when Hitler proclaimed the union of Austria and Germany in 1938, quickly spreading the apparatus of the Nazi party and state.

Hitler's advent galvanized the authoritarian regime of a nearby power, Italy, where a fascist state had been formed in the 1920s, led by Benito Mussolini. Like Hitler, Mussolini had promised an aggressive foreign policy and new nationalist glories, but his first decade had been rather moderate diplomatically. With Hitler in power, Mussolini began to experiment more boldly, if only to avoid being overshadowed completely.

In 1935 Mussolini attacked Ethiopia, planning to avenge Italy's failure to conquer this ancient land during the imperialist surge of the 1890s. The League of Nations condemned the action, but neither it nor the democratic powers in Europe and North America took action. Consequently, after some hard fighting, the Italians won their new colony. Here, then, was another destabilizing element in world politics.

Fascism also spread into Spain, leading to the **Spanish Civil War**. Here, forces supporting a parliamentary republic plus social reform had feuded since 1931 with advocates of a military-backed authoritarian state. In 1936 outright civil war broke out. Spanish military forces, led by General Francisco Franco, were backed by an explicitly fascist party, the Falange (feh-LAHNJ), as well as more conventionally conservative landowners and Catholic leaders.

Spanish Civil War War pitting authoritarian and military leaders in Spain against republicans and leftists between 1936 and 1939; Germany and Italy supported the royalists; the Soviet Union supported the republicans; led to victory of the royalist forces.

Republican forces included various groups, with support from peasants and workers in various parts of the country. Communists and a large anarchist movement played a crucial role. They won some support also from volunteers from the United States and western Europe, and from the Soviet Union.

Bitter fighting consumed much of Spain for three years. German and Italian forces bombed several Spanish cities, a rehearsal for the bombing of civilians in World War II. This was another example of how civilian and military lines were now blurring in the application of force. France, Britain, and the United States made vague supporting gestures to the republican forces but offered no concrete aid, fearful of provoking a wider conflict and paralyzed by internal disagreements about foreign policy. Franco's forces won in 1939. The resultant regime was not fully fascist, but it maintained authoritarian controls and catered to landlords, church, and army for the next 25 years.

Economic and Political Changes in Latin America

In the 1920s and 1930s, the limitations of liberalism became increasingly apparent in Latin America. A middle class had emerged and had begun to enter politics, but unlike its western European counterpart, it gained power only in conjunction with the traditional oligarchy or the military. In Latin

America, the ideology of liberalism was not an expression of the strength of the middle class but rather a series of ideas not particularly suited to the realities of Latin America, where large segments of the population were landless, uneducated, and destitute. Increasing industrialization did not dissolve the old class boundaries, nor did public education and other classic liberal programs produce as much social mobility as had been expected.

Disillusioned by liberalism and World War I, artists and intellectuals who had looked to Europe for inspiration turned to Latin America's own populations and history for values and solutions to Latin American problems. During the 1920s intellectuals complained that Latin America was on a race to nowhere. In literature and the arts, the ideas of rationality, progress, and order associated with liberalism and the outward appearances of democracy were under attack.

Ideas of reform and social change were in the air. University students in Córdoba, Argentina, began a reform of their university system that gave the university more autonomy and students more power within it. This movement soon spread to other countries. There were other responses as well. Socialist and communist parties were formed or grew in strength in several Latin American nations

VISUALIZING THE PAST

Guernica and the Images of War

THIS PAINTING, PROBABLY THE MOST FAMOUS work of art of the 20th century, was Spanish artist Pablo Picasso's protest against the bombing of the village of Guernica during the Spanish Civil War. On April 27, 1937, German and Italian planes bombarded the city for three hours. Guernica burned for three days, and more than 1500 people were killed.

QUESTIONS

- What was Picasso trying to say through the painting?
- Why did it have such a strong impact?
- Picasso, a Cubist artist, was working in a nonrepresentational style of art. Can you think of other works of art, including photographs, that have helped capture the notion of modern war?
- Does art make a difference where war is concerned?

Pablo Picasso's *Guernica*. (Pablo Picasso (1881–1973), "Guernica," 1937. Museo Nacional Centro de Arte Reina Sofia, Madrid, Spain. © 2010 Estate of Pablo Picasso/Artists Rights Society (ARS), New York. John Bigelow Taylor / Art Resource, NY.)

in this period, especially after the Russian Revolution of 1917. The strength of these parties of the left originated in local conditions but sometimes was aided by the international communist movement. Although criticism of existing governments and of liberalism as a political and economic philosophy came from these left-leaning parties, it also came from traditional elements in society such as the Roman Catholic Church, which disliked the secularization represented by a capitalist society.

The Great Crash and Latin American Responses

The economic dependency of Latin America and the internal weaknesses of the liberal regimes were made clear by the great world financial crisis. Export sales dropped rapidly. Amid growing poverty, reform movements gained momentum. More important, however, was the rise of a conservative response, hostile to class conflict and supported by church and military leaders. A corporatist movement, aimed at curbing capitalism while avoiding Marxism, won growing attention. **Corporatism** emphasized the organic nature of society, with the state as a mediator adjusting the interests of different social groups; the ideology appealed to conservative groups and the military, in European as well as Latin American societies. Some corporatist leaders sympathized with aspects of Italian and German fascism.

New regimes, as well as a new concern with social problems, characterized much of Latin America in the 1930s. One such reforming administration was that of President **Lázaro Cárdenas** (1934–1940) in Mexico, when land reform and many of the social aspects of the revolution were initiated on a large scale. Cárdenas distributed more than 40 million acres of land and created communal farms and a credit system to support them. He expropriated foreign oil companies that refused to obey Mexican law and created a state oil monopoly. He expanded rural education programs. These measures made him broadly popular in Mexico and seemed to give substance to the promise of the revolution.

Cárdenas in Mexico was perhaps the most successful example of the new political tide that could be seen elsewhere in Latin America. In Cuba, for example, the leaders of a nationalist revolution aimed at social reform and breaking the grip of the United States took power in 1933, and although their rule soon was taken over by moderate elements, important changes and reforms did take place. To some extent, such new departures underlined both the growing force of nationalism and the desire to integrate new forces into the political process. Nowhere was this more apparent than in the populist Vargas regime of Brazil.

corporatism Political ideology that emphasized the organic nature of society and made the state a mediator, adjusting the interests of different social groups; appealed to conservative groups in European and Latin American societies and to the military.

Cárdenas, Lázaro President of Mexico from 1934 to 1940; responsible for redistribution of land, primarily to create *ejidos*, or communal farms; also began program of primary and rural education.

The Vargas Regime in Brazil

In Brazil, a contested political election in 1929, in which the state elites could not agree on the next president, resulted in a short civil war and the emergence of **Getúlio Vargas** (1872–1954) as the new president. The Brazilian economy, based on coffee exports, had collapsed in the 1929 crash. Vargas had promised liberal reforms and elimination of the worst abuses of the old system. Once in power, he launched a new kind of centralized political program, imposing federal administrators over the state governments. He held off attempted coups by the communists in 1935 and by the green-shirted fascist "Integralists" in 1937. With the support of the military, Vargas imposed a new constitution in 1937 that established the *Estado Novo* (New State), based on ideas from Mussolini's Italy. It imposed an authoritarian regime within the context of nationalism and economic reforms, limiting immigration and eliminating parties and groups that resisted national integration or opposed the government.

For a while, Vargas played off Germany and the Western powers in the hope of securing armaments and favorable trade arrangements. Despite Vargas's authoritarian sympathies, he eventually joined the Allies during World War II, supplied bases to the United States, and even sent troops to fight against the Axis powers in Italy. In return, Brazil obtained arms, financial support for industrial development, and trade advantages. Meanwhile, Vargas ran a corporatist government, allowing some room for labor negotiations under strict government supervision. Little open opposition to the government was allowed. The state organized many other aspects of the economy. Opposition to Vargas and his repressive policies was building in Brazil by 1945, but by then he was turning increasingly to the left, seeking support from organized labor and coming to terms with the Communist party leaders whom he had imprisoned.

Vargas, Getúlio [vär guhs] Elected president of Brazil in 1929; launched centralized political program by imposing federal administrators over state governments; held off coups by communists in 1935 and fascists in 1937; imposed a new constitution based on Mussolini's Italy; leaned to communists after 1949; committed suicide in 1954.

Under criticism from both the right and the left, Vargas committed suicide in 1954. His suicide note emphasized his populist ties and blamed his death on Brazil's enemies:

> Once more the forces and interests which work against the people have organized themselves again and emerge against me. . . . I was a slave to the people, and today I am freeing myself for eternal life. But this people whose slave I was will no longer be slave to anyone. My sacrifice will remain forever in their souls and my blood will be the price of their ransom.

Much of Brazilian history since Vargas has been a struggle over his mantle of leadership. In death, Vargas became a martyr and a nationalist hero, even to those groups he had repressed and imprisoned in the 1930s.

Argentina: Populism, Perón, and the Military

Argentina was something of an anomaly. There, the middle-class Radical party, which had held power during the 1920s, fell when the economy collapsed in 1929. A military coup backed by a strange coalition of nationalists, fascists, and socialists seized power, hoping to return Argentina to the golden days of the great export boom of the 1890s. The coup failed. Argentina became more dependent as foreign investments increased and markets for Argentine products declined. However, industry was growing, and with it grew the numbers and strength of industrial workers, many of whom had migrated from the countryside. By the 1940s the workers were organized in two major labor federations. Conservative governments backed by the traditional military held power through the 1930s, but in 1943 a military group once again took control of the government.

The new military rulers were nationalists who wanted to industrialize and modernize Argentina and make it the dominant power of South America. Some were admirers of the fascist powers and their programs. Although many of them were distrustful of the workers, the man who became the dominant political force in Argentina recognized the need to create a broader basis of support for the government. Colonel **Juan D. Perón** (1895–1974) emerged as a power in the government. Using his position in the Ministry of Labor, he appealed to workers, raising their salaries, improving their benefits, and generally supporting their demands. Attempts to displace him failed, and he increasingly gained popular support, aided by his wife, Eva Duarte, known as Evita, a fascinating woman from the provincial lower classes. She became a public spokesperson for Perón among the lower classes. During World War II, Perón's admiration for the Axis powers was well known. In 1946, when the United States tried to discredit him because of his fascist sympathies, he turned the attempt into nationalist support for his presidential campaign.

As president, Perón forged an alliance among the workers, the industrialists, and the military. Like Vargas in Brazil, he learned the effectiveness of the radio, the press, and public speeches in mobilizing public support. He depended on his personal charisma and on repression of opponents to maintain his rule. The Peronist program was couched in nationalistic terms. The government nationalized the foreign-owned railroads and telephone companies, as well as the petroleum resources. The foreign debt was paid off, and for a while the Argentine economy boomed in the immediate postwar years. But by 1949 there were economic problems again. Meanwhile, Perón ruled by a combination of inducements and repression, while Evita Perón became a symbol to the *descamisados*, or the poor and downtrodden, who saw in Peronism a glimmer of hope. Her death in 1952 at age 33 caused an outpouring of national grief.

Perón's regime was a populist government with a broader base than had ever been attempted in Argentina. Nevertheless, holding the interests of the various components of the coalition together became increasingly difficult as the economy worsened. A democratic opposition developed and complained of Perón's control of the press and his violation of civil liberties. Industrialists disliked the strength of labor organizations. The military worried that Perón would arm the workers and cut back on the military's gains. The Peronist party became more radical and began a campaign against the Catholic Church. In 1955, anti-Perón military officers drove him into exile.

Argentina spent the next 20 years in the shadow of Perón. The Peronist party was banned, and a succession of military-supported civilian governments tried to resolve the nation's economic problems and its continuing political instability. But Peronism could survive even without Perón, and the mass of urban workers and the strongly Peronist unions continued to agitate for his programs, especially as austerity measures began to affect the living conditions of the working class. Perón and his new wife,

---

Perón, Juan D. Military leader in Argentina who became dominant political figure after military coup in 1943; used position as Minister of Labor to appeal to working groups and the poor; became president in 1946; forced into exile in 1955; returned and won presidency in 1973.

Isabel, returned to Argentina in 1973, and they won the presidential election in that year—she as vice president. When Perón died the next year, however, it was clear that Argentina's problems could not be solved by the old formulas. Argentina slid once more into military dictatorship.

The Militarization of Japan

Authoritarian military rule took over in Japan even earlier than in the West. Not fascist outright, it had some clear affinities with the new regimes in Europe, including its aggressive military stance. As early as 1931, as the Depression hit Japan hard, military officials completed a conquest of the Chinese province of Manchuria, without the backing of the civilian government (Map 30.3).

As political divisions increased in response to the initial impact of the Depression, a variety of nationalist groups emerged, some advocating a return to Shintoist or Confucian principles against the more Western values of urban Japan. This was more than a political response to economic depression. As in Germany, a variety of groups used the occasion for a more sweeping protest against parliamentary forms; nationalism here seemed a counterpoise to alien Western values. Older military officers joined some bureaucrats in urging a more authoritarian state that could ignore party politics; some wanted further military expansion to protect Japan from the uncertainties of the world economy by providing secure markets and sources of raw materials.

In May 1932 a group of younger army officers attacked key government and banking officers and murdered the prime minister. They did not take over the state directly, but for the next four years moderate military leaders headed the executive branch, frustrating both the military firebrands and the political parties. Another attempted military coup in 1936 was put down by forces controlled by the established admirals and generals, but this group, including General Tojo Hideki, increasingly interfered with civilian cabinets, blocking the appointment of most liberal bureaucrats. The result, after 1936, was a series of increasingly militaristic prime ministers.

The military superseded civilian politics, particularly when renewed wars broke out between Japan and China in 1937. Japan, continuing to press the ruling Chinese government lest it gain sufficient strength to threaten Japanese gains, became involved in a skirmish with Chinese forces in the Beijing area in 1937. Fighting spread, initially quite unplanned. Most Japanese military leaders opposed more general war, arguing that the nation's only interest was to defend Manchuria and Korea. However, influential figures on the General Staff held that China's armies should be decisively defeated to prevent trouble in the future. This view prevailed, and Japanese forces quickly occupied the cities and railroads of eastern China. Several devastating bombing raids accompanied this invasion.

Although Japanese voters had continued to prefer more moderate policies, their wishes were swept away by military leaders in a tide of growing nationalism. By the end of 1938 Japan controlled a substantial regional empire, including Manchuria, Korea, and Taiwan (Formosa), within which the nation sold half its exports and from which it bought more than 40 percent of all imports, particularly food and raw materials. Both the military leadership, eager to justify further modernization of Japan's weaponry and to consolidate political control, and economic leaders, interested in rich resources of other parts of Asia—such as the rubber of British Malaya or the oil of the Dutch East Indies—soon pressed for wider conquests as Japan surged into World War II (Map 30.4).

As war in Asia expanded, well before the formal outbreak of World War II, Japan also tightened its hold over its earlier empire, particularly in Korea. Efforts to suppress Korean culture were stepped up, and the Japanese military brutally put down any resistance. Japanese language and habits were forced on Korean teachers. Japanese industrialists dominated Korean resources, while peasants were required to produce rice for Japan at the expense of nutrition in Korea itself. Young men were pressed into labor groups, as the population was exhorted to join the Japanese people in "training to endure hardship."

Industrialization and Recovery

Japan's policies in the 1930s quelled the effects of the Depression for Japan even more fully than Hitler's policies were able to do for Germany. While the Depression initially hit Japan hard—half of all factories were closed by 1931, children in some areas were reduced to begging for food from passengers on passing trains, and farmers were eating tree bark—active government policies quickly responded. As a result, Japan suffered far less than many Western nations did during the Depression decade as a whole. Under the 1930s minister of finance, Korekiyo Takahashi, the government increased its spending to provide jobs, which in turn generated new demands for food and manufactured items,

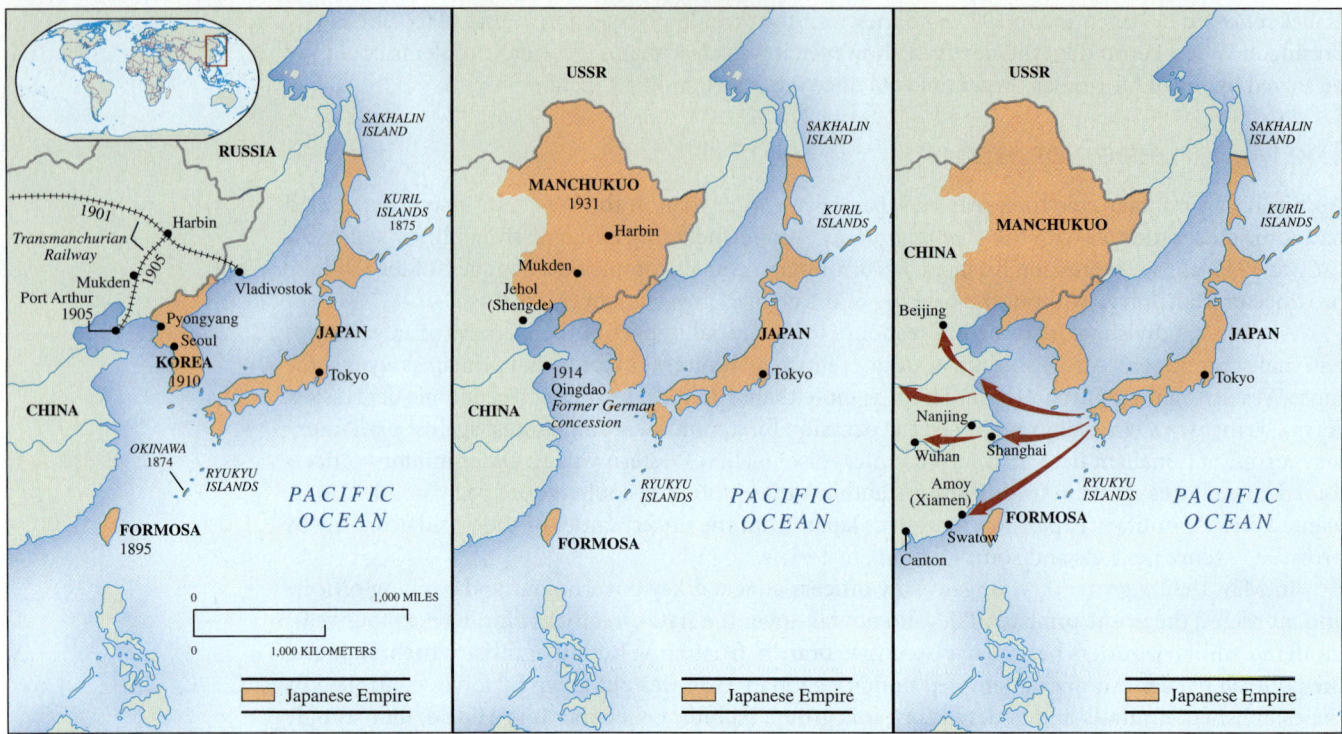

MAP 30.4 **The Expansion of Japan to the Outbreak of World War II** Two stages of Japan's attacks on China are clearly shown.

yielding not only the export boom but also the virtual elimination of unemployment by 1936. The same policy helped support government military purchasing, but it is not clear that this constituted an essential response.

Indeed, Japan made a full turn toward industrialization after 1931, its economy growing much more rapidly than that of the West and rivaling the surge of the Soviet Union. Production of iron, steel, and chemicals soared. The spread of electric power was the most rapid in the world. The number of workers, mainly men, in the leading industries rose sevenfold during the 1930s. Quality of production increased as assembly-line methods were introduced, and Japanese manufacturing goods began to rival those of the West. As the level of Japanese industrial goods rose, the first Western outcry against Japanese exports was produced—even though in 1936 the Japanese controlled only 3.6 percent of world trade.

Japan also initiated a series of new industrial policies designed to stabilize the labor force and prevent social unrest. These paralleled the growing emphasis on mass patriotism and group loyalty developed by the government. Big companies began to offer lifetime contracts to a minority of skilled workers and to develop company entertainments and other activities designed to promote hard work and devotion. These distinctive Japanese policies, not part of its initial industrialization, proved to be a durable feature of Japanese society.

By 1937 Japan boasted the third largest and the newest merchant marine in the world. The nation became self-sufficient in machine tools and scientific equipment, the fruit of the growth in technical training. The basis had been set for the more significant economic expansion of the later 20th century, delayed by Japan's dash into World War II.

Stalinism in the Soviet Union

The Soviet Union was buffered from the Depression by its separate economy. Soviet leaders made much of the nation's ongoing industrial growth, even as Western economies collapsed. But the 1930s saw a tightening of the communist system under Stalin in ways that echoed authoritarian responses in other societies.

Stalin devoted himself to a double task: to make the Soviet Union a fully industrial society and to do so under full control of the state rather than through private initiative and individual ownership of producing property. He reversed the more experimental mood of the 1920s, including tolerance for small private businesses and wealthy peasant farmers. In essence, Stalin wanted modernization but with a revolutionary, noncapitalist twist. Although he was willing to borrow Western techniques and advice, importing a small number of foreign engineers, for example, he insisted on Soviet control and substantial Soviet isolation.

Stalin was ruthless in applying his policies, attacking groups like wealthy peasants and other possible sources of opposition. Twenty million people were killed outright, one of the most brutal episodes in a brutal century.

Economic Policies

A massive program to collectivize agriculture began in 1928. Collectivization meant the creation of large, state-run farms, rather than individual holdings as in the West. Communist party agitators pressed peasants to join in collectives. In addition to being distinctly socialistic, the collectives movement also further offered, at least in theory, the chance to mechanize agriculture most effectively, as collective farms could group scarce equipment, such as tractors and harvesters. Collectivization also allowed more efficient control over peasants, reflecting, although in radical new form, a traditional reluctance to leave peasants to their own devices. Government and party control was desirable not only for political reasons, but also because Stalin's hopes for a speedup of industrialization required that resources be taken from peasants, through taxation, in order to provide capital for industry.

The peasantry responded to collectivization with a decidedly mixed voice. Many laborers, resentful of kulak wealth, initially welcomed the opportunity to have more direct access to land. But most kulaks refused to cooperate voluntarily, often destroying livestock and other property rather than submit to collectivization. Devastating famine resulted from Stalin's insistence on pressing forward. In addition, millions of kulaks were killed or deported to Siberia during the early 1930s. Gradually, rural resistance collapsed and production began to increase once again; the decimation of the kulaks may indeed have weakened opportunities to oppose Stalin's increasingly authoritarian hold for a generation or two. But collectivization, although increasingly thorough, was not a smash success, for even those peasants who participated often seemed fairly unmotivated. Although the collective farms allowed peasants small plots of their own, as well as job security and considerable propagandizing by the omnipresent Communist party members, they created an atmosphere of factory-like discipline and rigid planning from above that antagonized many peasants. The centralized planning process allowed few incentives for special efforts and often complicated a smooth flow of supplies and equipment, a problem also exacerbated by the Stalinist regime's priority concentration on the industrial sector. Agricultural production remained a major weakness in the Soviet economy, demanding a higher percentage of the labor force than was common under industrialization.

DOCUMENT

Socialist Realism

ONE OF THE MOST FASCINATING FEATURES of the Soviet system was the attempt to create a distinctive art, different from the art of Western cultures (seen as decadent) and appropriate to the communist mission. This effort involved censorship and forced orthodoxy, but it also was an attempt to resolve earlier Russian problems of relating formal culture to the masses and trying to preserve a national distinctiveness amid the seductions of Western influence. The following effort to define Soviet artistic policy was written by Andrey Zhdanov in 1934, the year Stalin made him the party's spokesperson at the Congress of Soviet Writers.

> There is not and never has been a literature making its basic subject-matter the life of the working class and the peasantry and their struggle for socialism. There does not exist in any country in the world a literature to defend and protect the equality of rights of the working people of all nations and the equality of rights of women. There is not, nor can there be in any bourgeois

(continued on next page)

country, a literature to wage consistent war on all obscurantism, mysticism, hierarchic religious attitudes, and threats of hell-fire, as our literature does.

Only Soviet literature could become and has in fact become such an advanced, thought-imbued literature. It is one flesh and blood with our socialist construction....

What can the bourgeois writer write or think of, where can he find passion, if the worker in the capitalist countries is not sure of his tomorrow, does not know whether he will have work, if the peasant does not know whether he will be working on his bit of land or thrown on the scrap heap by a capitalist crisis, if the working intellectual is out of work today and does not know whether he will have work tomorrow?

What can the bourgeois author write about, what source of inspiration can there be for him, when the world, from one day to the next, may be plunged once more into the abyss of a new imperialist war?

The present position of bourgeois literature is such that it is already incapable of producing great works. The decline and decay of bourgeois literature derives from the decline and decay of the capitalist system and are a feature and aspect characteristic of the present condition of bourgeois culture and literature. The days when bourgeois literature, reflecting the victories of the bourgeois system over feudalism, was in the heyday of capitalism capable of creating great works, have gone, never to return. Today a degeneration in subject matter, in talents, in authors and in heroes, is in progress....

A riot of mysticism, religious mania, and pornography is characteristic of the decline and decay of bourgeois culture. The "celebrities" of that bourgeois literature which has sold its pen to capital are today thieves, detectives, prostitutes, pimps, and gangsters....

The proletariat of the capitalist countries is already forging its army of writers and artists—revolutionary writers, the representatives of whom we are glad to be able to welcome here today at the first Soviet Writers' Congress. The number of revolutionary writers in the capitalist countries is still small but it is growing and will grow with every day's sharpening of the class struggle, with the growing strength of the world proletarian revolution.

We are firmly convinced that the few dozen foreign comrades we have welcomed here constitute the kernel, the embryo, of a mighty army of proletarian writers to be created by the world proletarian revolution in foreign countries....

Comrade Stalin has called our writers "engineers of the human soul." What does this mean? What obligations does such an appellation put upon you?

It means, in the first place, that you must know life to be able to depict it truthfully in artistic creations, to depict it neither "scholastically" nor lifelessly, nor simply as "objective reality," but rather as reality in its revolutionary development. The truthfulness and historical exactitude of the artistic image must be linked with the task of ideological transformation, of the education of the working people in the spirit of socialism. This method in fiction and literary criticism is what we call the method of socialist realism.

Our Soviet literature is not afraid of being called tendentious, for in the epoch of class struggle there is not and cannot be "apolitical" literature.

And it seems to me that any and every Soviet writer may say to any dull-witted bourgeois, to any philistine or to any bourgeois writers who speak of the tendentiousness of our literature: "Yes, our Soviet literature is tendentious and we are proud of it, for our tendentiousness is to free the working people—and the whole of mankind—from the yoke of capitalist slavery."

To be an engineer of the human soul is to stand four-square on real life. And this in turn means a break with old-style romanticism, with the romanticism which depicted a nonexistent life and nonexistent heroes, drawing the reader away from the contradictions and shackles of life into an unrealizable and utopian world. Romanticism is not alien to our literature, a literature standing firmly on a materialistic basis, but ours is a romanticism of a new type, revolutionary romanticism. We say that socialist realism is the fundamental method of Soviet fiction and literary criticism, and this implies that revolutionary romanticism will appear as an integral part of any literary creation, since the whole life of our Party, of the working class and its struggle, is a fusion of the hardest, most matter-of-fact practical work, with the greatest heroism and the vastest perspectives. The strength of our Party has always lain in the fact that it has united and unites efficiency and practicality with broad vision, with an incessant forward striving and the struggle to build a communist society.

Soviet literature must be able to portray our heroes and to see our tomorrow. This will not be utopian since our tomorrow is being prepared by planned and conscious work today.

QUESTIONS
- How did Soviet cultural leaders analyze Western intellectual life?
- What were the proper tasks of an artist in Soviet society?
- How were these tasks expressed in socialist realism?
- What would the Soviet response be to Western intellectuals who claimed objectivity for their work?

The collective farms did, however, allow normally adequate if minimal food supplies once the messy transition period had ended, and they did free excess workers to be channeled into the ranks of urban labor. The late 1920s and early 1930s saw a massive flow of unskilled workers into the cities, as the Soviet Union's industrialization, already launched, shifted into high gear.

If Stalin's approach to agriculture had serious flaws, his handling of industry was in many ways a stunning success. A system of **five-year plans** under the state planning commission began to set clear priorities for industrial development, including expected output levels and new facilities. The government constructed massive factories in metallurgy, mining, and electric power to make the Soviet Union an industrial country independent of Western-dominated world banking and trading patterns. There was more than a hint of Peter the Great's policies here, in updating the economy without really

five-year plans Stalin's plans to hasten industrialization of U.S.S.R.; constructed massive factories in metallurgy, mining, and electric power; led to massive state-planned industrialization at cost of availability of consumer products.

Westernizing it, save that industrialization constituted a more massive departure than anything Peter had contemplated. The focus, as earlier, was on heavy industry, which built on the nation's great natural resources and also served to prepare for possible war with Hitler's anticommunist Germany.

This distinctive industrialization, which slighted consumer goods production, was to remain characteristic of the Soviet version of industrial society. Further, Stalin sought to create an alternative not simply to private business ownership but also to the profit-oriented market mechanisms of the West. Thus he relied not on price competition but on formal, centralized resource allocation to distribute equipment and supplies. This led to many bottlenecks and considerable waste, as quotas for individual factories were set in Moscow, but there was no question that rapid industrial growth occurred. During the first two five-year plans, to 1937—that is, during the same period that the West was mired in the Depression—Soviet output of machinery and metal products grew 14-fold. The Soviet Union had become the world's third industrial power, behind only Germany and the United States. A long history of backwardness seemed to have ended.

Toward an Industrial Society

For all its distinctive features, the industrialization process in the Soviet Union produced many results similar to those in the West. Increasing numbers of people were crowded into cities, often cramped in inadequate housing stock. Factory discipline was strict, as communist managers sought to instill new habits in a peasant-derived workforce. Incentive procedures were introduced to motivate workers to higher production. Particularly capable workers received bonuses and also elaborate public awards for their service to society. At the same time, communist policy quickly established a network of welfare services, surpassing the West in this area and reversing decades of tsarist neglect. Workers had meeting houses and recreational programs, often including vacations on the Black Sea, as well as protection in cases of illness and old age. Soviet industrial society provided only modest standards of living at this point, but a host of collective activities compensated to some degree.

Finally, although Soviet industry was directed from the top, with no legal outlet for worker grievances—strikes were outlawed, and the sole trade union movement was controlled by the party—worker concerns were studied, and identified problems were addressed. The Soviet Union under Stalin used force and authority, but it also recognized the importance of maintaining worker support—so, informally, laborers were consulted as well.

socialist realism Attempt within the U.S.S.R. to relate formal culture to the masses in order to avoid the adoption of western European cultural forms; begun under Joseph Stalin; fundamental method of Soviet fiction, art, and literary criticism.

Totalitarian Rule

Stalinism instituted new controls over intellectual life. In the arts, Stalin insisted on uplifting styles that differed from the nonrepresentational modern art themes of the West, which he condemned as capitalist decadence. (Hitler and Stalin, bitter enemies, both viewed contemporary Western culture as dangerous.) Artists and writers who did not toe the line risked exile to Siberian prison camps, and party loyalists in groups like the Writers Union helped ferret out dissidents. **Socialist realism** was the dominant school, emphasizing heroic idealizations of workers, soldiers, and peasants (Figure 30.10). Science was also controlled. Stalin clamped down hard on free scientific inquiry, insisting, for example, that evolutionary biology was wrong because it contradicted Marxism. A number of scientists were ruined by government persecution.

Stalin also combined his industrialization program with a new intensification of government police procedures; he used party and state apparatus to monopolize power, even more thoroughly than Hitler's totalitarian state attempted. Real and imagined opponents of his version of communism were executed, in one of the great bloodbaths of the 20th century. During the great purge of party leaders that culminated in 1937–1938, hundreds of people were intimidated into confessing imaginary crimes against the state, and most of them were then put to death. Many thousands more were sent to Siberian labor camps. News

FIGURE **30.10** In his 1949 painting *Creative Fellowship*, Soviet artist Shcherbakov shows the cooperation of scientists and workers in an idealized factory setting. The painting exemplifies the theories and purposes of socialist realism.

Politburo Executive committee of the Soviet Communist party; 20 members.

outlets were monopolized by the state and the party, and informal meetings also risked a visit from the ubiquitous secret police, renamed the MVD in 1934. Party congresses and meetings of the executive committee, or **Politburo**, became mere rubber stamps. An atmosphere of terror spread.

Stalin's purges, which included top army officials, ironically weakened the nation's ability to respond to growing foreign policy problems, notably the rising threat of Hitler. Soviet diplomatic initiatives after the 1917 revolution had been unwontedly modest, given the nation's traditions, largely because of the intense concentration on internal development. Diplomatic relations with major nations were gradually reestablished as the fact of communist leadership was accepted, and the Soviet Union was allowed into the League of Nations. A few secret military negotiations, as with Turkey in the early 1920s, showed a flicker of interest in more active diplomacy, and of course the nations continued to encourage and often guide internal Communist party activities in many other countries.

Hitler's rise was a clear signal that more active concern was necessary. A strong Germany was inevitably a threat to Russia from the west, and Hitler was vocal about his scorn for Slavic peoples and communism, and about his desire to create a "living room" for Germany to the east. Stalin initially hoped that he could cooperate with the Western democracies in blocking the German threat. The Soviet Union thus tried to participate in a common response to German and Italian intervention during the Spanish Civil War, in 1936–1937. But France and Britain were incapable of forceful action and were in any event almost as suspicious of the Soviets as of the Nazis. So the Soviet Union, unready for war and greatly disappointed in the West, signed a historic agreement with Hitler in 1939. This pact bought some time for greater war preparation and also enabled Soviet troops to attack eastern Poland and Finland in an effort to regain territories lost in World War I. Here was the first sign of a revival of Russia's long interest in conquest, which would be intensified by the experience of World War II.

Global Connections and Critical Themes

ECONOMIC DEPRESSION, AUTHORITARIAN RESPONSE, AND DEMOCRATIC RETREAT

The Great Depression of the 1930s promoted a growing wave of nationalist reactions and further weakened global ties. Western European countries and the United States increased their tariffs and refused to collaborate in measures that might have alleviated economic dislocation. Their narrow policies made economic collapse even worse. Japan, badly hurt by a new U.S. tariff that cut into silk exports, increased its own nationalism; here was the context for the growing power of younger army officers pushing for overseas expansion. Japan began to think of its own new empire in east Asia that could shield it from worldwide economic trends. Nazi Germany also pulled out of the international community, seeking to make Germany as economically self-sufficient as possible. The Soviet Union still mouthed communist commitment to internationalism, but in fact Stalin concentrated on standing alone, in a nationalist and isolationist version of the great Russian Revolution. The world was falling into pieces, and no society, certainly not the beleaguered West, seemed capable of putting it back together.

Further Readings

Sally Marks, *The Ebbing of European Ascendancy: An International History of the World: 1914–1945* (2002), is a good standard introduction to the diplomacy of the period. See also Bernard Wasserstein, *Barbarism and Colonization: A History of Europe in Our Times* (2007); C. H. Feinstein, P. Temin, and G. Toniolo, *The World Economy Between the World Wars* (2008); B. Lazier, *God Interrupted: Heresy and the European Imagination Between the World Wars* (2008); A. Dawahare, *Nationalism, Marxism and African American Literature Between the Wars* (2007); and Allan Todd, *The European Dictatorships: Hitler, Stalin, Mussolini* (2002). Good overall studies of the political revolutions of the period include Eric Wolf, *Peasant Wars of the Twentieth Century* (1965); Theda Skocpol, *States and Social Revolutions* (1970); and John Dunn, *Modern Revolutions* (1972). Mark N. Katz, *Reflections on Revolutions* (1999), is an accessible survey of historical theories of revolution. See also Michael J. Gonzales, *The Mexican Revolution, 1910–1940* (2002); Thomas Kampen, *Mao Zedong, Zhou Enlai and the Evolution of the Chinese Communist Leadership* (2000); Xiaoyuan Liu, *Frontier Passages: Ethnopolitics and the Rise of Chinese Communism, 1921–1945* (2004). Two studies of the Long March that make superior use of eyewitnesses accounts are Andrew McEwen and Ed Jocelyn, *The Long March: The True Story Behind the Legendary March that Made Mao's China*, and Sun Shuyun, *The Long March: The True History of Communist China's Founding Myth*, both 2006.

On the Russian Revolution, Sheila Fitzpatrick, *The Russian Revolution* (1994), is an overview with a rich bibliography. See also Ian D. Thatcher, ed., *Reinterpreting Revolutionary Russia* (2006) and S. A. Smith, *The Russian Revolution: A Very Short Introduction* (2002). Rex Wade, *The Russian Revolution, 1917* (2005), is a comprehensive social and political history of the revolution's early years.

On specific social groups, see John Keep, *The Russian Revolution: A Study in Mass Mobilization* (1976); and Victoria Bonnell, *Roots of Rebellion: Workers' Politics and Organizations in St. Petersburg and Moscow, 1900-1914* (1983). Leon Trotsky's *History of the Russian Revolution*, a gripping narrative by a participant, surveys social, economic, and political dimensions of the revolution.

On fascism in Italy, see R. J. B. Bosworth, *The Italian Dictatorship: Problems and Perspectives in the Interpretation of Mussolini and Fascism* (1998) and *Mussolini's Italy: Life under the Dictatorship, 1915-1945* (2006). Philip Morgan, *Italian Fascism, 1919-1945* (1995), provides a general overview. Emilio Gentile, *The Sacralization of Politics in Fascist Italy*, trans. Keith Botsford (1996), examines popular political culture. See also Anthony L. Cardoza, *Benito Mussolini: The First Fascist* (2006).

The economic history of Latin America is summarized in the classic by Brazilian economist Celso Furtado, *Economic Development of Latin America* (1976), and in John Sheahan, *Patterns of Development in Latin America* (1987). There are many good studies of Latin American politics, but Guillermo O'Donnell's *Modernization and Bureaucratic Authoritarianism* (1973) has influenced much recent scholarship. Also useful are Alan Knight's *The Mexican Revolution*, 2 vols. (1986) and John M. Hart's *Revolutionary Mexico* (1987), which provide excellent analyses of that event. Freidrich Katz, *The Life and Times of Pancho Villa* (1998), is an outstanding biography.

On the cultural aspects of the U.S. influence on Latin America there is Gilbert Joseph et al., eds., *Close Encounters Empire* (1998). The role of the United States is discussed in Abraham Lowenthal, *Partners in Conflict: The United States and Latin America* (1987). Lester D. Langley's *The United States and the Caribbean in the Twentieth Century* (1989) gives a clear account of the recent history of that region, and Walter La Feber's *Inevitable Revolutions* (1984) is a critical assessment of U.S. policy in Central America.

For the United States, Niall Palmer, *The Twenties in America: Politics and History* (2006); Carrie A. Meyer, *Days on the Family Farm: From the Golden Age through the Great Depression* (2007); Ronald Allen Goldberg, *America in the Twenties* (2003); and David Joseph Goldberg's *Discontented America: The United States in the 1920s* (1999) are useful introductions. Robert Cruden, *Body and Soul: The Making of American Modernism* (2000), and Lynn Dumenil and Eric Foner, *The Modern Temper: American Culture and Society in the 1920s* (1995), offer intriguing analyses of the period. Robert Stern, Gregory Gilmartin, and Thomas Mellins, *New York: 1930* (1987), examine American architecture and urbanism between the two world wars. Steve Watson, *The Harlem Renaissance* (1995), is unsurpassed as a general study of African American culture and society in the "Roaring Twenties." Paula Fass, *The Damned and the Beautiful: American Youth in the 1920's* (1977), remains the best introduction to the "Lost Generation."

Some of the best general studies on China in the early 20th century include Lucian Bianco, *The Communist Revolution in China* (1967); C. P. Fitzgerald, *Birth of Communist China* (1964); Wolfgang Franke, *A Century of Chinese Revolution, 1851-1949* (1970); and Jonathan Spence, *The Search for Modern China* (1990). For first-hand accounts of conditions in the revolutionary era, see especially Graham Peck, *Two Kinds of Time* (1950); Edgar Snow, *Red Star over China* (1938); and Theodore White and Analee Jacoby, *Thunder out of China* (1946).

On the causes and onset of the Great Depression, Amity Shlaes, *The Forgotten Man: A New History of the Great Depression* (2007) and Mary C. McComb, *Great Depression and the Middle Class: Experts, Collegiate Youth and Business Ideology, 1929-1941* (2006) are solid introductions. See also J. Galbraith, *The Great Crash: 1929* (1980), and, for a useful collection of articles, W. Lacquer and G. L. Mosse, eds., *The Great Depression* (1970). Japan's experience is covered in I. Morris, ed., *Japan, 1931-1945: Militarism, Fascism, Japanism?* (1963).

Ronald Edsforth, *The New Deal: America's Response to the Great Depression* (2000), is a readable introduction to the political history of the New Deal. For a case study of social and political change in the United States during the period, see Lizabeth Cohen, *Making a New Deal: Industrial Workers in Chicago, 1919-1939* (1990). See also William Chafe, *Women and Equality: Changing Patterns in American Culture* (1984).

Alan Bullock's *Hitler: A Study in Tyranny* (1964) remains the best introduction to the Nazi leader. The methods and manner of the rise of German fascism are explored in William S. Allen, *Nazi Seizure of Power in a Single Town, 1930-1935* (1969); Russell G. Lemmons, *Goebbels and Der Angriff: Nazi Propaganda, 1927-1933* (1994); David Schoenbaum, *Hitler's Social Revolution: Class and Status in Nazi Germany* (1997); and Samuel W. Mitchum Jr., *Why Hitler? The Genesis of the Nazi Reich* (1996).

For a standard analysis of the Spanish Civil War, see Hugh Thomas, *The Spanish Civil War* (1977); Paul Preston, *The Spanish Civil War, 1936-1939* (1994); and Raymond Carr, *The Spanish Tragedy: The Civil War in Perspective* (1993). Peter Carroll's *The Odyssey of the Abraham Lincoln Brigade: Americans in the Spanish Civil War* (1994) deals with one of the civil war's many international aspects.

For the career of Juan Perón and Peronism, there is Frederick C. Turner, *Juan Peron and the Reshaping of Argentina* (1983). Robert M. Levine, *Getúlio Vargas: Father of the Poor* (1998), explores Brazil's corporatist state. Luis Aguilar, *Cuba 1933: Prologue to Revolution* (1972), demonstrates that, as in so many Asian and Latin American countries, the post–World War II revolutionary movement in Cuba led by Fidel Castro was rooted in the events of the 1930s. Irwin Gellman's *Good Neighbor Diplomacy: United States Policy in Latin America, 1933-1945* (1980) and *Roosevelt and Batista: Good Neighbor Policy in Cuba, 1933-1945* (1973) address the U.S. role in shaping the regimes that were challenged by those later revolutionary movements.

On the Stalinist era, Robert Conquest's *The Great Terror: A Reassessment* (1990) and Roy Medvedev's *Let History Judge: The Origins and Consequences of Stalinism* (1989) are important studies of the period. Stephen Kotkin, *Magnetic Mountain: Stalinism as Civilization* (1995), assesses the cultural, social, and political impact of Stalin's industrialization program by looking at the experience of a planned industrial city. Sarah Davies, *Popular Opinion in Stalin's Russia: Terror, Propaganda, and Dissent, 1934-1941* (1997), offers a revealing portrayal of everyday cultural life under Stalin. Alan Bullock, *Hitler and Stalin: Parallel Lives* (1993), offers a comparative biography of the two totalitarian leaders.

On MyHistoryLab

Critical Thinking Questions

1. What were the causes of the widespread abandonment of liberal democracy during the interwar decades?
2. Compare the Mexican and Russian revolutions in terms of causes and results.
3. What were the main social changes in Russia under communism?
4. Why was China unable to repel Japanese invasion?
5. How did the impact of Depression in the West compare to its impact elsewhere?

A Second Global Conflict and the End of the European World Order

31

Listen to Chapter 31 on MyHistoryLab

FOCUS QUESTIONS

Would it be fair to argue that World War II began with the Japanese invasions of Manchuria in 1931 and China in 1937 rather than with the German invasion of Poland in 1939? p. 767	**31.1**
What were the key factors in the early success of Japanese and German military aggression? p. 770	**31.2**
What combination of forces led to the equally rapid demise of the empires that each of these expansionist powers had built? p. 772	**31.3**
How did the cold war emerge from the end of World War II? p. 780	**31.4**
Were the roles played by colonized peoples more or less important in World War II than they had been in World War I, and in what ways was the second conflict more truly global? p. 781	**31.5**

Because the Japanese forces had taken Padang on the coast of Sumatra in the Dutch East Indies so swiftly and had routed the Dutch defenders so thoroughly, Sukarno felt comfortable taking a walk through the town the morning after it had been captured. As the European global order in Asia came tumbling down in late 1941 and the first weeks of 1942, he explained to his young friend, Waworuntu, why the Japanese invaders ought to be seen as the liberators of the peoples of what was soon to be the nation of Indonesia, as well as much of the rest of southeast Asia. As he later recalled in an autobiographical account of his life related to an American reporter, Sukarno denounced the Dutch because they had long humiliated and exploited the colonized

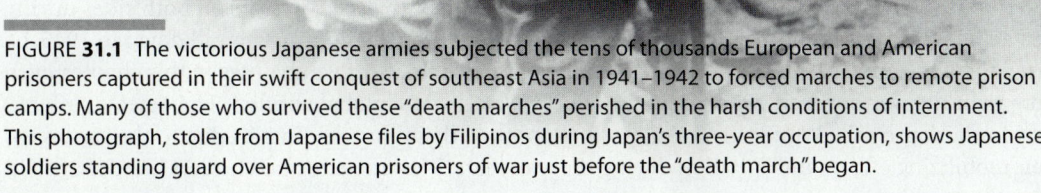

FIGURE 31.1 The victorious Japanese armies subjected the tens of thousands European and American prisoners captured in their swift conquest of southeast Asia in 1941–1942 to forced marches to remote prison camps. Many of those who survived these "death marches" perished in the harsh conditions of internment. This photograph, stolen from Japanese files by Filipinos during Japan's three-year occupation, shows Japanese soldiers standing guard over American prisoners of war just before the "death march" began.

Watch the Video Series on MyHistoryLab

Learn about some key topics related to this chapter with the *MyHistoryLab Video Series: Key Topics in World History*

peoples of Indonesia. In addition, after posturing for centuries as a superior race, the Dutch had fled or stood by passively as the Japanese took their place as rulers of the archipelago.

In tandem with the successful Japanese sneak attack on Pearl Harbor in Hawaii, the Japanese navy and army had swept down into Malaya, Borneo, the Philippines, the Dutch East Indies (later Indonesia), and Burma (Map 31.2, p. 777). In a matter of weeks, the armed forces of the Western colonial powers—Britain, the Netherlands, and the United States—which had colonized these areas decades or in some cases centuries earlier, had been defeated. Like Sukarno and his fellow Indonesians, peoples across southeast Asia watched as bedraggled European and American soldiers, nurses, bureaucrats, and merchants were herded on long marches to prison camps. Many died on the way and many more died in captivity. The Japanese intentionally staged marches, such as that depicted in Figure 31.1, to break the psychological hold "whites" had striven for centuries to establish over colonized peoples. And as they vanquished and discredited the former overlords, the Japanese sought to pass themselves off as liberators—fellow Asians whose rule would soon bring a new order and better lives to peoples so long subjected to alien rule.

Recalling this moment of profound transition decades later, Sukarno claimed that he saw through the Japanese propaganda. He claimed that he knew they were "fascists" and would be little better as rulers than the Western imperialists. Regardless of whether he had actually seen this outcome at the time, his prediction was correct. The Indonesians and other peoples now colonized by the Japanese soon came to realize that their new masters were going to be far more demanding and brutal than the Dutch, British, or Americans. The Japanese soon alienated the peasants and workers who made up the great majority of their subject peoples by introducing often brutal forced labor systems (romusha) to extract the raw materials they so desperately needed to fight the Pacific war. As the conflict began to turn against the Japanese in mid-1942, they recruited nationalist leaders like Sukarno to mobilize colonized peoples to work and fight for their self-styled Japanese "liberators." Sukarno was later branded by some among the Allied leadership as a collaborator for becoming a front man for these campaigns. But a good deal of evidence bears out his impassioned insistence after the war that he was actually working to revitalize nationalist resistance to both the Japanese and Western colonizers.

A highly charismatic speaker, Sukarno cleverly foiled the intelligence officers who shadowed him at every step as he spoke at mass rallies and to paramilitary forces being trained by the Japanese. He packed his speeches with stories from the *wayang* shadow puppet plays based on the great Indian epics, the *Mahabharata* and the *Ramayana*, which had for centuries been central elements of Indonesian culture. Sukarno spoke in Javanese or Indonesian, so his Japanese handlers would not understand what he said. In a spirited oratorical style that suited the shadow dramas, he mocked the Japanese pretense that they were benevolent overlords by equating them with cruel rulers or treacherous characters from the epics. ■

Like many of the leaders of the decolonization movements that swept Asia and Africa after 1945, Sukarno used the power vacuum created by the weakening of the great powers on both sides during the Pacific war to arouse and organize nationalist resistance. As the fighting wound down in 1945, he seized the opportunity to declare Indonesia's independence. Thus, as we shall see in this chapter, even more than the war between 1914 and 1918, World War II was a global conflict. The defeats suffered early in the war by the Western colonial powers doomed their empires. In part due to the success of their mobilizing efforts and agitation during the war years, Western-educated leaders like Sukarno in

1930 C.E.	1940 C.E.	1950 C.E.	1960 C.E.
1930s Great Depression	**1941** Japanese attack Pearl Harbor; United States enters World War II	**1954** Anti-French rebellion breaks out in Algeria	**1960** Congo granted independence from Belgian rule
1931 Japan invades Manchuria	**1941** German invasion of the Soviet Union	**1954** French armies defeated and withdraw from Vietnam	**1961** Afrikaner-dominated parliament votes for complete South African independence from Great Britain
1933 Nazis come to power in Germany	**1942** Fall of Singapore to the Japanese	**1957** Ghana established as first independent African nation	
1935 Government of India Act	**1942** Cripps mission to India; Quit India movement	**1958** Afrikaner Nationalist party declares independence of South Africa	**1962** Algeria wins independence
1935 Italy invades Ethiopia	**1945** Atomic bomb dropped on Japan; World War II ends; United Nations established	**1958** Charles de Gaulle returns to power in France	
1936–1939 Spanish Civil War			
1936–1939 Arab uprisings in Palestine			
1937 Japan invades China	**1947** India and Pakistan gain independence, leading to wider decolonization		
1938 Germany's union (Anschluss) with Austria; Munich conference; German armies occupy the Sudetenland	**1947** Cold war heats up		
1939 Nazi-Soviet Pact	**1948** Israel-Palestine partition, first Arab-Israeli war; beginning of apartheid legislation in South Africa		
1939 Nazi armies invade Poland; World War II in Europe begins			

many cases inherited political power in the new nations that emerged from the fallen empires. Like Sukarno, many of these leaders lacked the skills and political base to deal effectively with the problems that faced their new states, which were often artificially patched together, ethnically and religiously divided, and economically disadvantaged. And many of these leaders shared Sukarno's fate, as his failures and the machinations of the superpowers locked in cold war rivalries led to his overthrow by military leaders who often seized power in nations emerging from colonial rule.

The war itself was a searing event, adding to the destructive potential of contemporary conflict and blurring the lines between civilians and the military. The war's consequences included another complex and flawed settlement, which led directly to the struggles of the cold war, and to the global unfolding of the decolonization movement across Asia and Africa.

OLD AND NEW CAUSES OF A SECOND WORLD WAR

31.1 Would it be fair to argue that World War II began with the Japanese invasions of Manchuria in 1931 and China in 1937 rather than with the German invasion of Poland in 1939?

The gradual militarization of Japan proceeded despite the solid majorities that moderate political parties continued to win until the end of the 1930s. And it developed in the context of a succession of regional diplomatic crises. During the later 1920s, nationalistic forces in China began to get the upper hand over the regional warlords who had dominated Chinese politics since the early 1900s. At the head of the Guomindang (or Nationalist) party, General Chiang Kai-shek in particular was able to win the support of intellectuals, students, the business classes, the rural gentry, and even members of the largely discredited Confucian elites and rival military leaders. His military successes against first the southern and later the northern warlords seemed destined to unify China under a strong central government for the first time in decades.

The success of the Guomindang worried Japan's army officers, who feared that a reunited China would move to resist the informal control the Japanese had exerted over Manchuria since their victory in the Russo-Japanese war in 1905. Fearful of curbs on their expansionist aims on the mainland and unimpeded by weak civilian governments at home, the Japanese military seized Manchuria in 1931 and proclaimed it the independent state of Manchukuo. The international crisis that resulted worked to the military's advantage because civilian politicians were reluctant to raise objections that might weaken Japan in negotiations with the United States and the other powers or undermine its armies of occupation in Manchuria and Korea, which the Japanese had declared a colony in 1910.

> The path to World War II was paved in large part by major social and political upheavals in several of the nations that had fought in World War I. Grievances related to World War I were compounded in each case by the economic havoc and resulting social tensions brought on by the Great Depression.

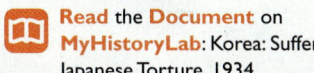
Read the Document on MyHistoryLab: Korea: Suffering Japanese Torture, 1934

Rehearsals: Dictators, Militarism, and the Agony of the Spanish Civil War

In contrast to the gradual shift of power to the military in Japan, the change of regimes in Germany was more abrupt and more radical. Parliamentary government in the Weimar era had been under siege from the time its civilian leaders had agreed to the armistice in 1918, and even more so after they signed the punitive treaty at Versailles. Weimar had survived these humiliations, civil war, and the hyperinflation of the mid-1920s, but just as economic recovery appeared to be gaining real momentum, the Great Depression struck. In the social discontent and political turmoil that followed, Adolf Hitler and the **National Socialist (Nazi) party** captured a steadily rising portion of the votes and parliamentary seats in a rapid succession of elections.

The Nazis promised to put the German people back to work, restore political stability, and set in motion a remilitarization program that would allow Germany to throw off the shackles of what Hitler branded the diktat of Versailles. Hitler also promised to turn back the communist bid to capture power in Germany that had grown more and more serious as the Depression deepened. The threat of the communists within was linked to that from the Soviet Union to the east. From the early 1920s, Hitler and his lieutenants had stressed the need to invade and destroy the Soviet empire, and a *central* part of Hitler's racist vision for the future was to reduce the Russians and other Slavic peoples to virtual slaves in the service of the Aryan master race.

As we have seen in Chapter 30, a priority of the Nazis' political agenda once in power was a systematic dismantling of the political and diplomatic system created by the Versailles settlement. Beginning with rearmament from 1935, the militarization of the Rhineland in 1936, and a forced union with Austria in 1938, the Nazis had fulfilled key aspects of this promise. The seizure in the latter half of 1938 of areas in Czechoslovakia where German-speakers were in the majority, and the occupation

National Socialist party Also known as the Nazi party; led by Adolf Hitler in Germany; picked up political support during the economic chaos of the Great Depression; advocated authoritarian state under a single leader, aggressive foreign policy to reverse humiliation of the Versailles treaty; took power in Germany in 1933.

THINKING HISTORICALLY

Total War, Global Devastation

WAR HAD CHANGED RADICALLY LONG BEFORE the 20th century. With state centralization, war lost its ritual characteristics. It became more commonly an all-out battle, using any tactics and weapons that would aid in victory. In other words, war became less restrained than it had been among less bureaucratized peoples who often used bluff and scare tactics more than all-out violence.

The 20th century most clearly saw the introduction of a fundamentally new kind of war, total war, in which vast resources and emotional commitments of the belligerent nations were marshaled to support military effort. The two world wars were thus novel not only in their geographic sweep, but in their mobilization of the major combatants. The features of total war also colored other forms of struggle, helping to explain brutal guerrilla and terrorist acts by groups not powerful enough to mount total wars but nonetheless affected by their methods and passions.

Total war resulted from the impact of industrialization on military effort, reflecting both the technological innovation and the organizational capacity that accompanied industrial economies. Key steps in the development of total war emerged in the West at the end of the 18th century. The French Revolution, building new power for the state in contact with ordinary citizens, introduced mass conscription of men, forming larger armies than had ever before been possible. New citizen involvement was reflected in incitements to nationalism and stirring military songs, including aggressive national anthems—a new idea in itself. Industrial technology was first applied to war on a large scale in the U.S. Civil War. Railroads allowed wider movement of mass armies. Mass-produced guns and artillery made a mockery of earlier cavalry charges and redefined the kind of personal bravery needed to fight in war.

However, it was World War I that fully revealed the nature of total war. Steadily more destructive technology included battleships, submarines, tanks, airplanes, poison gas (which had been banned by international agreement before the war), machine

> [O]ne defining measure of total war was a blurring of the distinction between military and civilians, a distinction that had often limited war's impact earlier in world history.

(continued on next page)

guns, and long-range artillery. Organization for war included not only massive, compulsory recruitment—the draft—but also government control of economic activity via obligatory planning and rationing. Another factor was the unprecedented control of media, not only through effective censorship and the containment of dissidents but through powerful propaganda designed to incite passionate, all-out commitment to the national cause and deep, unreasoned hatred of the enemy. Vivid posters, inflammatory speeches, and outright falsehood were combined in the emotional mobilization effort. All of these features returned with a vengeance in World War II, from the new technologies for aerial bombing, rocketry, and ultimately the atomic bomb to the enhanced economic mobilization organized by government planners.

The people most affected by the character of total war were the troops, who directly endured—bled and died from—the new weaponry. But one defining measure of total war was a blurring of the distinction between military and civilians, a distinction that had often limited war's impact earlier in world history. Whole civilian populations, not just those unfortunate enough to be near the front lines, were forced into certain types of work and urged to certain types of beliefs. The bombing raids, including the German rockets directed against British cities late in World War II, subjected civilians to some of the most lethal weapons available. By the early 20th century belligerents deliberately focused their attacks on densely populated cities. Correspondingly, psychological suffering, although less common among civilians than among frontline soldiers, spread throughout the populations involved in war.

Total war, like any major historical development, had mixed results. Greater government economic direction often included new measures to protect workers and give them a voice on management boards. Mobilization of the labor force often produced at least temporary breakthroughs for women. Intense efforts to organize technological research often produced side effects of more general economic benefit, such as the invention of synthetic rubber and the production of nitrites in chemistry labs.

Still, total war was notable especially for its devastation. The idea of throwing all possible resources into a military effort made war more economically disruptive than had been the case before. The emotions unleashed in total war produced embittered veterans who might vent their anger by attacking established political values. It certainly made postwar diplomacy more difficult. One result of total war was a tendency for the victor to be inflexible in negotiations at war's end. People who fought so hard and had suffered extensive civilian casualties and deprivations found it difficult to treat enemies generously. The results of a quest for vengeance often produced new tensions that led directly, and quickly, to further conflict. War-induced passions and disruptions could also spark new violence at home; crime rates often soared not only right after the war ended (a traditional result) but for longer periods of time. Children's toys started to reflect the most modern weaponry. Thus, much of the nature of life in the 20th and 21st centuries has been determined by the consequences of total war.

QUESTIONS
- How did the experience of total war affect social and political patterns after World War II?
- Why do many historians believe that total war made rational peacetime settlements more difficult than did earlier types of warfare?

of the rest of the Czechoslovak republic the following year, made a shambles of the agreements that had ended World War I. Hitler's successes emboldened Mussolini to embark on military adventures of his own, most infamously in Ethiopia. During the invasion Italian pilots bombed defenseless cities and highly mechanized armies made extensive use of poisonous gases against resistance forces armed with little more than rifles. The fascists stunned much of the rest of the world by routinely unleashing these weapons on a civilian population that had no means of defending itself.

Hitler and Mussolini also intervened militarily in the Spanish Civil War in the mid-1930s in the hope of establishing an allied regime. Once again, Mussolini's mechanized forces proved effective, this time against the overmatched, left-leaning armed forces of the Spanish republic. Both the Italian and German air forces used the Spanish conflict as a training ground for their bomber pilots in the absence of enemy planes or pilots. But their main targets were ground forces and, ominously, civilians in Spain's cities and villages. Support from Mussolini and Hitler was critical to Franco's destruction of the elected republican government and seizure of power, particularly since the Western democracies had refused to counter the Nazi and fascist interventions.

Excepting volunteer forces recruited in England, France, the United States, and other democracies, only the Soviet Union sought to provide military aid to Spain's republicans. Although valiant, these relief attempts proved futile in the face of relentless assaults by Franco's well-supplied legions and both Nazi and Fascist forces. Despite the critical assistance provided by his fellow fascists, Franco refused to join them in the global war that broke out soon after he had crushed the republic and begun a dictatorial rule in Spain that would last for decades.

UNCHECKED AGGRESSION AND THE COMING OF WAR IN EUROPE AND THE PACIFIC

31.2 What were the key factors in the early success of Japanese and German military aggression?

By the late 1930s, the leaders of the new totalitarian states acted on the lesson that international rivalries in the preceding decades seemed to offer—that blatant aggression would succeed and at little cost.

According to standard histories, World War II began on September 1, 1939, with the German invasion of Poland. But a succession of localized clashes, initiated by the Japanese seizure of Manchuria in 1931, can be seen as part of a global conflict that raged for well over a decade between 1930 and 1945. In contrast to the coming of World War I, which, as we have seen, the leaders of Europe more or less blundered into, World War II was provoked by the deliberate aggressions of Nazi Germany and a militarized and imperialist Japan. The failure of the Western democracies and the Soviet Union to respond resolutely to these challenges simply fed the militarist expansionism of what came to be called the Axis powers, in reference to the linkages, both real and imagined, between Berlin, Rome, and Tokyo.

Hitler and Mussolini discovered that Britain and France, and even more so the increasingly isolated United States, were quite willing to sacrifice small states, such as Spain and Czechoslovakia, in the false hope that fascist and especially Nazi territorial ambitions would be satisfied and thus war averted. Leaders like **Winston Churchill**, who warned that a major war was inevitable given Hitler's insatiable ambitions, were kept from power by voters who had no stomach for another world war. Rival politicians, such as Neville Chamberlain and the socialist leaders of France, also feared correctly that rearming as Churchill proposed would put an end to their ambitious schemes to build welfare states as an antidote to further economic depressions. But in the late 1930s, another round of provocative aggressions pushed the democracies into a war that none had the stomach for or was prepared at that point to fight.

Churchill, Winston (1874–1965) British prime minister during World War II; responsible for British resistance to German air assaults.

Read the Document on MyHistoryLab: Transcript of the Rape of Nanjing Sentencing

The Japanese Invasion of China

Although Nazi aggressions traditionally have been stressed as the precipitants of World War II, the Japanese military actually moved first. In the second half of 1937, from their puppet state, Manchukuo, which had been carved out of Manchuria, they launched a massive invasion of China proper. Exploiting a trumped-up incident in early July that led to a fire fight between Japanese and Chinese troops, the army launched an ill-advised campaign to conquer the whole of China. Prominent naval leaders and civilian politicians had deep misgivings about this massive escalation of the war in China and were uneasy about American and British reactions to yet another major round of Japanese aggression. But they were largely cowed into silence by the threat of assassination by fanatical junior army officers and renewed appeals to patriotic solidarity in a situation where Japanese soldiers were at risk.

At first, the advancing Japanese forces met with great success, occupying most of the coastal cities, including Shanghai and, by the end of 1938, Canton as well as the hinterlands behind cities in the north. The Japanese deployed extensive aerial bombing against Guomindang forces and especially the civilian population in the coastal cities. As Chinese resistance stiffened in some areas, Japanese soldiers resorted to draconian reprisals against both the Chinese fighters and civilians. In many instances, most infamously in the capture in December 1937 of the city of Nanjing, the evacuated Guomindang capital, Japanese forces took out their frustrations on retreating Chinese troops and the civilian population (Figure 31.2). The wanton destruction and pillage, murder of innocent civilians, and rape of tens of thousands of undefended Chinese women that accompanied the Japanese occupation of the ancient city was but a prelude to the unparalleled human suffering of the world war that had now begun.

Deprived of the coastal cities and provinces that were the main centers of their power, Chiang and the Guomindang forces retreated up the Yangzi

FIGURE **31.2** As Chinese resistance to Japanese invasion in 1937 and 1938 stiffened, the invading armies resorted to random, mass executions to cow Chinese soldiers and civilians into submission.

River, deep into the interior to the city of Chongqing, which became the nationalist capital for the rest of the war. Thus, long before the Japanese attacks on Pearl Harbor and Western colonies throughout southeast Asia in late 1941 that greatly expanded the war in Asia, Japan and China were engaged in a massive and deadly contest for control of all of east Asia.

The Partition of Poland and Nazi Preparations for War in the West

The Japanese had plunged into war without coordination, or even serious consultation with their likely allies, Germany and Italy. In fact, the Tripartite Pact, which joined the three expansive Axis states in a loose alliance, was not signed until September 1940, when the war was well under way in both Europe and east Asia. Ironically, Nazi military advisors had contributed greatly to the training of the Guomindang officers and troops that fought to contain the Japanese invasion of China.

With a pause to consolidate Germany's stunning gains in central Europe from 1936 to 1938, Hitler now concentrated his forces on the drive to the Slavic east, which he had long staked out as the region that would provide living space for the Germanic master race. He bought time to prepare the way for the assault on the main target, the Soviet Union, by signing a nonaggression pact with Stalin in August 1939. Military emissaries of the two dictators negotiated a division of the smaller states that separated their empires, and Stalin swallowed short-term disappointments, such as the division of Poland, to prepare the Soviet Union for the invasion that most observers were now convinced was inevitable. Within days of signing the agreement, Hitler ordered the Wehrmacht, or Nazi armies, to overrun western Poland; the Soviets then occupied the eastern half of the country, which had been promised to them in the cynical pact just concluded with the Nazis.

The brutal Nazi invasion of Poland on September 1, 1939, put an end to any lingering doubts about Hitler's contempt for treaties and repeated assurances that Germany's territorial ambitions had been satisfied by the absorption of Czechoslovakia into the Nazi Reich (Figure 31.3). Although they

Read the Document on MyHistoryLab: Adolf Hitler, "The Obersalzberg Speech"

FIGURE 31.3 Sober-faced and weeping Czechs watch the entry of the Nazi armies into Prague in the spring of 1939, as Hitler completes the takeover of the tiny democracy that was betrayed by the duplicity and cowardice of Allied leaders.

were helpless to assist the overmatched Poles in their futile efforts to oppose the German advance, the British and French had no choice but to declare war on Germany. But the armies of both powers simply dug in along the defensive lines that had been established in eastern France in the late 1920s. There they waited for the Nazis to turn to the west for further conquests and prepared for another defensive war like the one they had managed to survive, at such horrific cost, between 1914 and 1918. But a second major theater of what rapidly developed into a second world war had been opened, and this conflict would prove radically different in almost all major respects from the one to which the new configuration of powers in Europe and the Pacific believed they were committing themselves.

THE CONDUCT OF A SECOND GLOBAL WAR

31.3 What combination of forces led to the equally rapid demise of the empires that each of these expansionist powers had built?

> The forces that gave rise to World War II meant that there would be more of a balance than in the Great War between a number of theaters spread across Europe, north Africa, and Asia. The largest and most costly fronts in lives lost and physical destruction resulted from the Nazi invasion of the vast expanses of the Soviet Union and the Japanese invasion of China, and later Southeast Asia and the Pacific after the attack on the U.S. fleet at Pearl Harbor.

The reluctance to rearm and react decisively displayed by both the Western democracies and the Soviet Union in the 1930s made possible crushing and almost unremitting victories and rapid territorial advances on the part of the main Axis powers, Germany and Japan, early in the war. But once the Nazis became bogged down in the expanses of the Russian steppes and the United States entered the war, the tide shifted steadily in favor of the Allies. Once the initial momentum of the Axis war machine was slowed, it became increasingly clear that the Anglo-American and Soviet alliance was decidedly more powerful in terms of population size, potential industrial production, technological innovation, and military capacity on land, in the seas, and in the air.

Nazi Blitzkrieg, Stalemate, and the Long Retreat

As the Japanese bogged down in China and debated the necessity of tangling with the United States and the European colonial powers, the Nazi war machine captured France and the Low Countries with stunning speed, forced the British armies to beat a fast retreat to their island refuge, and then rolled over eastern Europe and drove deep into the Soviet Union (Map 31.1). Germany appeared unstoppable, and the fate of a large chunk of humanity seemed destined for a long period of tyrannical Nazi rule. From the outset, German strategy was centered on the concept of **blitzkrieg**, or "lightning war," which involved the rapid penetration of enemy territory by a combination of tanks and mechanized troop carriers, backup infantry, and supporting fighter aircraft and bombers. The effective deployment of these forces overwhelmed the Poles in 1939, and more critically routed the French and British within a matter of days in the spring of 1940, thereby accomplishing what the kaiser's armies failed to do through four long years of warfare between 1914 and 1918. German willingness to punish adversaries or civilian populations in areas that refused to yield greatly magnified the toll of death and destruction left in the wake of Hitler's armies. In early 1940, for example, the Dutch port of Rotterdam was virtually leveled by Nazi bombers, killing over 40,000 civilians.

blitzkrieg German term for lightning warfare; involved rapid movement of airplanes, tanks, and mechanized troop carriers; resulted in early German victories over Belgium, Holland, and France in World War II.

The rapid collapse of France was, in part, a consequence of the divided and weak leadership the republic had displayed in the successive crises of the 1930s. Governments had come and gone as if, contemporaries quipped, they were moving through revolving doors. Left and right quarreled and stalemated over rearming, responding to the Nazis, and allying with the British and the Soviets. When the war broke out, the citizenry of France was thoroughly demoralized, and the nation's defenses were outdated and extremely susceptible to the Wehrmacht's blitzkrieg offensives. By the summer of 1940 all of north and central France was in German hands; in the south, a Nazi puppet regime, centered on the city of **Vichy** (VEE-shee), was in charge. With the Nazi occupations of Norway and Denmark in the preceding months, Britain alone of the Western democracies in Europe survived. But what remained of the British armies had been driven from the continent. Britain's people and cities were under heavy assault by a markedly superior German air force, which strove to open the way to cross-channel invasion by the much larger and more powerful land forces of the steadily growing Nazi empire.

Vichy French collaborationist government established in 1940 in southern France following defeat of French armies by the Germans.

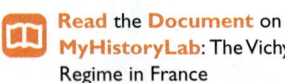
Read the Document on MyHistoryLab: The Vichy Regime in France

Remarkably, under the courageous leadership of Winston Churchill, the British people weathered what their new prime minister had aptly pronounced the nation's "darkest hour." A smaller British air force proved able to withstand the Nazi air offensive, including saturation bombing of London

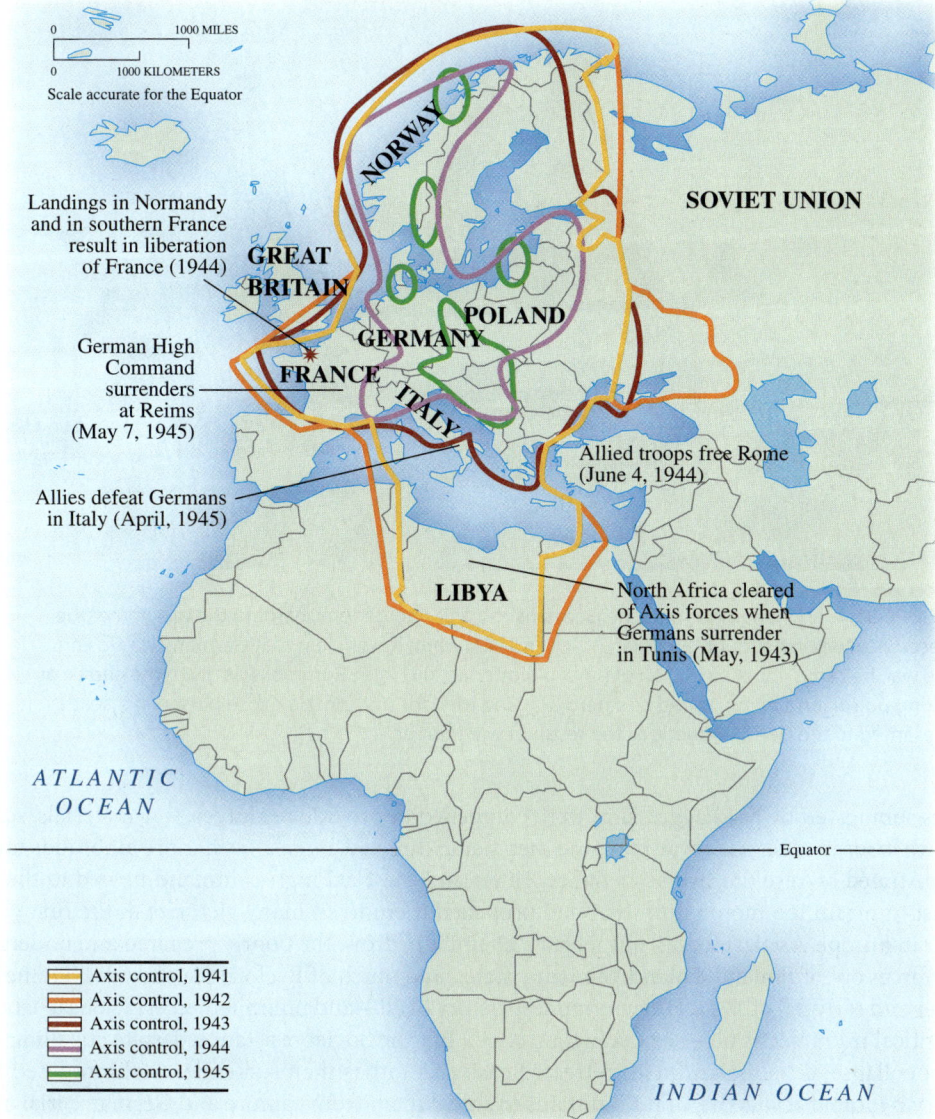

MAP 31.1 **World War II in Europe and the Middle East** The Nazi empire in Europe and the Middle East both rose and fell with remarkable speed but at the cost of tens of millions of lives.

and other British cities. Victory in what came to be known as the **Battle of Britain** was due to a mix of strong leadership by Churchill and a very able coalition cabinet, and innovative air tactics made possible by the introduction of radar devices for tracking German assault aircraft. The ability to withstand the Nazi onslaught also owed much to the bravery of Britain's royal family and the high morale of the citizenry as a whole that the bombing raids seemed only to enhance. Unable to destroy Britain's air defenses or break the resolve of its people, Hitler and the Nazi high command had to abandon their plans for conquest of the British Isles. Without air superiority, the Germans could not prevent the Royal Navy from entering the channel and destroying the huge flotilla of landing craft that would be needed to carry the Nazi forces across the narrow but turbulent straits that had for nearly a millennium shielded Britain from outside invasion.

By mid-1941 the Germans controlled most of the continent of Europe and much of the Mediterranean. They had rescued the Italians' floundering campaign to conquer Albania and overrun Yugoslavia and Greece. They had conquered, or in the case of Sweden forced the neutralization of, the Scandinavian countries. They continued on to capture most of the islands of the Mediterranean and launched motorized offensives under the soon-to-be legendary commander Erwin Rommel (Figure 31.4) across north Africa and on to Egypt. These campaigns were designed to seize the Suez Canal, thus cutting Britain off from its Asian empire. Once conquered, the hundreds of millions of

Battle of Britain The 1940 Nazi air offensive including saturation bombing of London and other British cities, countered by British innovative air tactics and radar tracking of German assault aircraft.

 Read the **Document** on **MyHistoryLab:** Winston Churchill Rallies the British People to Fight the Nazis, 1940

CHAPTER 31 A Second Global Conflict and the End of the European World Order **773**

FIGURE **31.4** Erwin Rommel was the Germans' most daring general, earning the nickname "the Desert Fox" when he fought in north Africa. In 1944, when it was clear that Germany was losing the war, he came under suspicion of having plotted to kill Hitler. Rommel was given the choice of taking poison and being buried as a hero or being tried for treason. He chose poison; his death was presented to the German public as the result of war injuries.

peoples subjugated by Nazi aggression were compelled to provide resources, war materials, soldiers, and slave labor to a German war machine then being directed against even more ambitious targets.

Frustrated by resolute British defiance, Hitler and the Nazi high command turned to the south and east to regain the momentum that had propelled them to so many victories in the first years of the war in Europe. As Nazi forces, numbering 3.5 million, drove the poorly prepared and understaffed Soviet forces out of Finland, Poland, the Baltic states, and much of Byelorussia and the Ukraine in the summer and early fall of 1941, Hitler's grandest victory of all—and unlimited access to cheap labor and such critical resources as oil—seemed within reach. But the Soviet resistance, despite appalling losses, did not collapse; the Russian forces retreated eastward rather than surrender. Stalin ordered Soviet industry relocated across the Ural Mountains to shield them from capture and German aerial attacks.

As with Napoleon's invasion nearly a century and a half earlier, Russian resistance stiffened as winter approached, and the German drive east stalled on the outskirts of Moscow and Leningrad. The harsh winter caught the German forces unprepared while their Russian adversaries used terrain and weather conditions they knew well to counterattack with ferocity on a wide front. The Nazis' mass killings and harsh treatment of the Slavic peoples aroused guerrilla resistance by tens then hundreds of thousands of partisans. These irregular forces fought behind German lines throughout the rest of the war. Many of the Ukrainians in particular were initially at least predisposed to back the Germans, but Nazi brutality proved a major obstacle to the conquest of the Soviet Union.

Renewed German offensives in the spring of 1942 again drove deep into Russia but failed a second time to capture key cities like Moscow, Leningrad, and Stalingrad, and perhaps as critically the great Baku oil fields in the southern steppes. The two sides clashed in some of the greatest battles of the entire war—in fact of all human history—including Kursk, which featured thousands of tanks deployed (and destroyed) by each of the adversaries. As another winter approached, the Germans were further away from knocking the Soviets out of the war than the year before. In fact, the failed Nazi attempt to capture Stalingrad in the bitter winter of 1942 and 1943 ended in the destruction of an entire German army and proved a decisive turning point in the war in the east.

In 1943 the Soviet armies went on the offensive at numerous points along the overextended, undermanned, and vulnerable German front. With staggering losses in lives and equipment, the Nazi forces, despite Hitler's rantings that they die in place, began the long retreat from the Soviet Union. By late 1944, Red armies had cleared the Soviet Union of Nazi forces and captured Poland and much of east central Europe southward into the Balkans. As the Soviet forces advanced inexorably toward

Germany, it was clear that the destruction of Hitler's "thousand-year reich" was only months away. It was also apparent that the almost unimaginable sacrifices and remarkable resilience of Russian soldiers, which included many women, had contributed mightily to the destruction of the once imposing Nazi armed forces.

From Persecution to Genocide: Hitler's War Against the Jews

As the Nazi war machine bogged down in Russia, Hitler and his Nazi henchmen stepped up their vendetta against Gypsies, leftist politicians, homosexuals, and especially Jews. Jews, Polish intellectuals, and communists had been rounded up and killed in mass executions during the German offensives into eastern Europe and Russia in the early 1940s. But after a "final solution" for the "Jewish problem" was decided upon by prominent Nazi officials at the Wannsee Conference in February 1942, the regime directed its energies explicitly and systematically to genocide. The destruction, rather than the removal, of the Jewish people became the official policy of the Reich. The concentration camps that had been set up in the 1930s to incarcerate political enemies and groups branded as racially inferior—thus polluting to the Aryan people—were transformed into factories for the mass production of death.

The more the war turned against Hitler and the Nazi high command, the more they pressed the genocidal campaign against the largely defenseless Jewish peoples of Europe. Vital resources were regularly diverted from the battle fronts for transportation, imprisonment, and mass murder in the camps, where the destruction of human life reached a frenetic pace in the last years of the regime. Jews and other "undesirables" were identified and arrested throughout the Nazi empire. Shipped to the camps in the east, those deemed physically fit were subjected to harsh forced labor that took a heavy toll in lives. The less fortunate, including the vast majority of the women and children, were systematically murdered, sometimes in experiments carried out by German physicians with the callous disregard for human suffering and humiliation that was a hallmark of the Nazi regime.

As many as 12 million people were murdered in the massive and systematic genocide that has come to be known as the **Holocaust**, which will almost certainly be remembered more than anything else about the brutal and ruthless Nazi regime. Of these, at least 6 million were Jews, and many millions of others were Slavic peoples mercilessly slaughtered on the Eastern Front. Without question, the Holocaust was by far the most costly genocide of the 20th century, which had begun with the Armenian massacres in 1915, and had the horrors of Kampuchea, Rwanda, Bosnia, and Kosovo yet to come. With the possible exceptions of the massacres in the Soviet Ukraine in the 1930s and those carried out in the 1970s by the Khmer Rouge, more than any of the other major episodes of the 20th-century genocide, the Holocaust was notable for the degree to which it was premeditated and systematic. It was carried out by the Nazi state apparatus and German functionaries, who until the very end kept precise and detailed records of their noxious deeds. The Holocaust was at least passively abetted by denial on the part of the people of Germany and the occupied countries, although the Danes and Italians were notable for their resistance to Nazi demands that they turn over "their" Jews for incarceration.

The plight of the Jews of Europe was also greatly exacerbated by the refusal of the Western Allies to accept as immigrants any but the most affluent or skilled Jews fleeing Nazi atrocities. Those same Allies also failed to use their military assets to strike at the railway lines and killing chambers they clearly knew were in operation by the last months of the war. These responses to the Nazi horror only steeled the resolve of Zionist leaders in Palestine and elsewhere to facilitate, by negotiations with the hated Nazis if necessary, the flight of the European Jews. It also intensified their determination to establish a Jewish state in Palestine to ensure that there could never be another Holocaust.

Anglo-American Offensives, Encirclement, and the End of the 12-Year Reich

For nearly two years, the British were so absorbed in their own struggle for survival that they could provide little relief for their Soviet allies, hard-pressed as Hitler's foolhardy invasion of Russia. Even before the attack on Pearl Harbor in December 1941, the United States was providing substantial assistance, including military supplies, to beleaguered Britain. Franklin Roosevelt was quite openly sympathetic to the British cause and soon established a good working relationship with Churchill. Similar to World War I, American forces first entered the war in a major way in the campaigns to counter German U-boat

Holocaust Term for Hitler's genocide of European Jews during World War II; resulted in deaths of 6 million Jews.

attacks on shipping crossing the Atlantic. Then American tank divisions and infantry joined the British in reversing Rommel's gains in North Africa in 1942 and 1943. Having all but cleared Nazi forces from Africa and the Middle East, Anglo-American armies next struck across the Mediterranean at Sicily and then Italy proper. Their steady, but often costly, advance up the peninsula lasted into early 1945 but eventually toppled the fascist regime and prompted a Nazi takeover of northern Italy. Mussolini and the last of his many mistresses were captured and shot by partisans and enraged civilians, and hung upside down on a lamp post near Lake Bellagio.

With significant German forces tied down on the Eastern Front and in Italy, the Allied high command, with General Dwight Eisenhower at its head, prepared landings in northern France. These were intended to carry the war into the fortress the Nazis had been building in occupied Europe ever since their defeat in the Battle of Britain in 1940. In early June, against fierce resistance, the Allies established beachheads at Normandy, from which they launched liberation campaigns into the Low Countries and the rest of France. Despite Hitler's last-ditch effort to repel the invading Allied armies in what became known as the **Battle of the Bulge** in the winter of 1944–1945, by early in 1945, the Allies had invaded Germany from the west, while the Red armies were pouring in from the east.

In late April, Russian and American troops linked up at the Elbe River, where they became caught up in spontaneous celebrations. The genuine camaraderie and mutual respect widely displayed by troops on both sides would soon be lost in high-stakes maneuvers by the political leaders in each camp to shape the postwar world order. On April 30, after haranguing his closest advisors for his betrayal by the German people, Adolf Hitler committed suicide in his Berlin bunker. Less than two weeks later, German military leaders surrendered their forces, putting an end to the war in the European and Mediterranean theaters. But the contest between the Anglo-American and Soviet allies for control of Germany had already commenced, and it would soon be extended to Europe as a whole and the rest of the world.

Battle of the Bulge Hitler's last-ditch effort to repel the invading Allied armies in the winter of 1944–1945.

The Rise and Fall of the Japanese Empire in the Pacific War

Long before their attack on **Pearl Harbor** on December 7, 1941 (Figure 31.5), the Japanese had been engaged in a major war on the Chinese mainland. Even after Pearl Harbor, roughly one-third of all Japanese military forces would remain bogged down in China, despite the sudden extension of the Japanese empire over much of southeast Asia and far out into the Pacific (Map 31.2). With the American Pacific fleet temporarily neutralized by the attack, Japan's combined air, sea, and army assaults quickly captured the colonial territories of the British in Hong Kong in south China as well as Malaya and Burma. They also overran the Dutch East Indies and the Philippines—despite more determined resistance—and completed the takeover of French Indochina. The Thais managed to stave off the invasion and occupation of Siam by retreating into neutrality and cooperating with the ascendant Japanese. Although Great Britain remained a major combatant, and Australia and New Zealand provided important support, the United States soon emerged as the major counterforce to Japan's ever-expanding Asian empire.

View the **Closer Look** on MyHistoryLab: The Japanese Raid on Pearl Harbor, December 7, 1941

FIGURE **31.5** U.S. warships in flames at the American base at Pearl Harbor following a Japanese attack on December 7, 1941. The attack brought the United States into World War II.

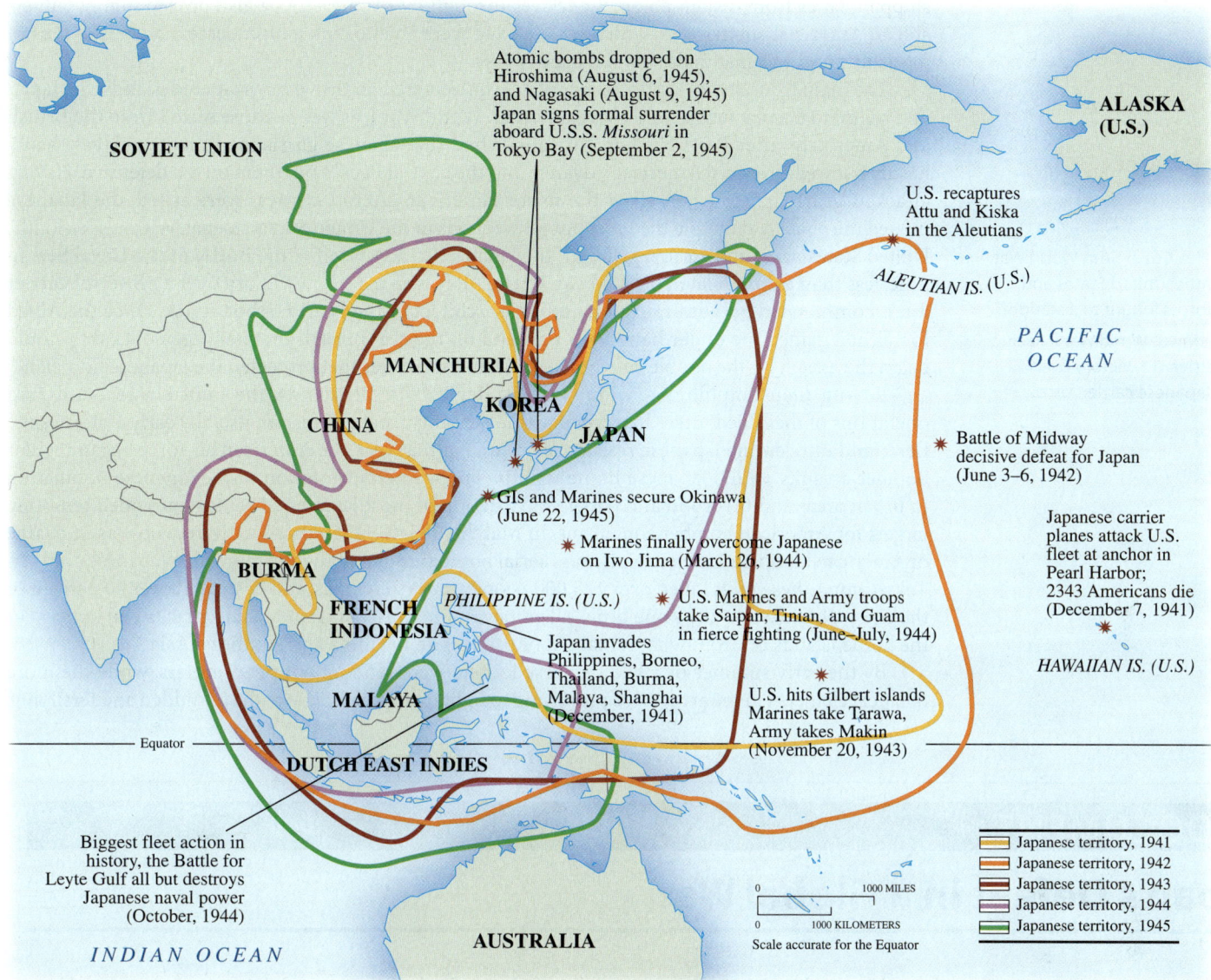

MAP 31.2 **Asia and the Pacific in World War II** Although the human cost in this theatre of the war was the highest in China, the decisive battles were fought on the seas and islands of the vast Pacific Ocean.

Although impressive in size and the speed with which it was formed, the Japanese empire soon proved highly vulnerable to the Allied forces committed to its destruction. The Japanese had risked alienating virtually all of the European colonial powers by their seizure of much of southeast Asia. They did so because they calculated that since the European metropoles had been overrun or were hard-pressed by the Nazis, the Europeans would not be able to reinforce their colonial enclaves. The Japanese leadership was also aware that their homeland's wartime economy was in desperate need of critical raw materials, including oil and staple foods that could be imported from southeast Asia. But in their efforts to extract those resources, the Japanese imposed colonial regimes on the peoples of southeast Asia that were a good deal more brutally oppressive than those of any of the displaced Western colonizers. Over time, these demands produced growing resistance movements from Burma to the Philippines, which drew Japanese soldiers and substantial resources from the war in the Pacific against the advancing Allied forces.

Resistance fighters also cooperated with British and American forces pushing into the area in the latter stages of the war. Southeast Asian guerrilla forces, which often had communist affiliations, played significant roles in sabotaging occupying forces and harassing retreating Japanese armies. The

Pearl Harbor American naval base in Hawaii; attack by Japanese on this facility in December 1941 crippled American fleet in the Pacific and caused entry of United States into World War II.

CHAPTER 31 A Second Global Conflict and the End of the European World Order **777**

shipping lanes from distant colonial enclaves throughout southeast Asia also proved highly vulnerable to American submarines, which by late 1944 were able to sink a high percentage of the tons of foodstuffs and war materials shipped back to Japan.

The main front of the Pacific theater of the war centered on the widely scattered islands that Japan had begun to occupy before, and especially after, World War I, as well as those seized from the British and Americans after Pearl Harbor. No sooner had the Japanese garrisoned these enclaves than a hastily but well-prepared American advance into the central Pacific put them on the defensive. Having attacked Pearl Harbor when all of the major American aircraft carriers were at sea, the Japanese missed the chance to cripple the most potent weapons in the United States arsenal. Within six months United States naval and air forces fought the Japanese to a standoff at the **Battle of the Coral Sea**. In June, less than a month later, off **Midway Island**, they won a decisive victory over a powerful carrier force, commanded by Admiral Yamamoto, the architect of the Pearl Harbor attack. Once the Allied forces had gained the upper hand in the air and on the sea through these engagements, they could begin the assault on the double ring of Pacific island fortresses that protected the Japanese homeland.

Keying their amphibious assaults on strategically vital islands, the joint air, sea, and land operations of the Allied forces had come within striking distance of Japan itself by early 1944, despite fierce and unrelenting Japanese resistance. In June of that year, the American air force began regular bomber assaults on the Japanese home islands. The high concentration of the Japanese population in urban areas and the wood and paper construction of most Japanese dwellings provided tempting targets for American bomber squadrons. In March 1945, General Curtis Le May, who was in charge of American air operations, ordered mass aerial bombardment of highly vulnerable Japanese cities. In Tokyo alone, these raids killed over 125,000 people, mostly civilians, and destroyed over 40 percent of the city within days. At the same time, Allied naval superiority and submarine attacks had largely cut the home islands off from what remained of the empire in China and southeast Asia.

By the early summer of 1945, Japanese leaders were sending out peace feelers, while the more fanatical elements in the army were promising to fight to the death. The end was sudden and terrifying.

Battle of the Coral Sea World War II Pacific battle; United States and Japanese forces fought to a standoff.

Midway Island World War II Pacific battle; decisive U.S. victory over powerful Japanese carrier force.

DOCUMENT

Japan's Defeat in a Global War

JAPAN'S DEFEAT IN WORLD WAR II brought moral and material confusion. The government was so uncertain of the intentions of the victorious Americans that it evacuated its female employees to the countryside. The following excerpt from the 1945 diary of Yoshizawa Hisako (who became a writer on home economics) reveals more popular attitudes and the mixed ingredients that composed them. The passage also suggests how the American occupation force tried to present itself and the reception it received.

August 15. As I listened to the Emperor's voice announcing the surrender, every word acquired a special meaning and His Majesty's voice penetrated my mind. Tears streamed down my cheeks. I kept on telling myself that we must not fight ourselves and work hard for our common good. Yes, I pledged myself, I must work [for Japan's recovery].

The city was quiet.

I could not detect any special expression in people's faces. Were they too tired? However, somehow they seemed brighter, and I could catch an expression showing a sign of relief. It could have been a reflection of my own feelings. But I knew I could trust what I saw . . .

The voluntary fighting unit was disbanded, and I was no longer a member of that unit. Each of us burned the insignia and other identifications.

I cannot foresee what kind of difficulty will befall me, but all I know is that I must learn to survive relying on my health and my will to live.

August 16. People do not wear expressions any different from other days. However, in place of a "good morning" or "good afternoon," people are now greeting each other with the phrase "What will become of us?"

During the morning, the city was still placed under air-raid alert.

My company announced that until everything becomes clearer, no female employees were to come to work and urged all of us to go to the countryside, adding that we should leave forwarding addresses. This measure was taken to conform to the step already taken by governmental bureaus. Are they thinking that the occupation army will do something to us girls? There

(continued on next page)

are so many important questions we have to cope with, I cannot understand why governmental officials are so worried about these matters.

We did not have enough power and lost the war.

The Army continued to appeal to the people to resist the enemy to the end. This poses a lot of problems. People can show their true colors better when they are defeated than when they win. I just hope we, as a nation, can show our better side now.

Just because we have been defeated, I do not wish to see us destroying our national characteristics when we are dealing with foreign countries.

August 17. It was rumored that a number of lower echelon military officers were unhappy with the peace, and were making some secret moves. There were other rumors, and with the quiet evacuation of women and children from the cities, our fear seemed to have intensified. After all we have never experienced a defeat before. Our fear may simply be the manifestation of fear of the unknown.

Our airplanes dropped propaganda leaflets.

One of the leaflets was posted at the Kanda Station which said: "Both the Army and Navy are alive and well. We expect the nation to follow our lead." The leaflet was signed. I could understand how those military men felt. However, we already have the imperial rescript to surrender. If we are going to rebuild, we must open a new path. It is much easier to die than to live. In the long history of our nation, this defeat may become one of those insignificant happenings. However, the rebuilding after the defeat is likely to be treated as a far more important chapter in our history.

We did our best and lost, so there is nothing we have to say in our own defense. Only those people who did not do their best may now be feeling guilty, though.

Mr. C. said that everything he saw in the city was so repugnant that he wanted to retreat to the countryside. I was amazed by the narrowness of his thought process. I could say that he had a pure sense of devotion to the country, but that was only his own way of thinking. Beautiful perhaps, but it lacked firm foundation. I wish men like him would learn to broaden their perspectives.

August 18. Rationed bread distribution in the morning. I went to the distribution center with Mrs. A.

August 21. We heard that the Allied advance units will be airlifted and arrive in Japan on the 26th. And the following day, their fleet will also anchor in our harbors. The American Army will be airlifted and land in Atsugi airport.

According to someone who accompanied the Japanese delegation which went to accept surrender conditions, the Americans behaved like gentlemen. They explained to the Americans that certain conditions were unworkable in light of the present situation in Japan. The Americans immediately agreed to alter those conditions. They listened very carefully to what the Japanese delegation had to say.

An American paper, according to someone, reported that meeting as follows: "We cooked thick beefsteak expecting seven or eight Japanese would appear. But seventeen of them came, so we had to kill a turkey to prepare for them. We treated them well before they returned." . . . When I hear things like this, I immediately feel how exaggerated and inefficient our ways of doing things are. They say that Americans will tackle one item after another at a conference table, and do not waste even 30 seconds. . . .

In contrast, Japanese administration is conducted by many chairs and seals. For example when an auxiliary unit is asked to undertake a task for a governmental bureau, before anything can be done, twenty, or thirty seals of approval must be secured. So there is no concept of not wasting time. Even in war, they are too accustomed to doing things the way they have been doing and their many seals and chairs are nothing but a manifestation of their refusal to take individual responsibilities.

The fact of a defeat is a very serious matter and it is not easy to accept. However, it can bring some positive effects, if it can inculcate in our minds all the shortcomings we have had. I hope this will come true some day, and toward that end we must all endeavor. Even if we have to suffer hunger and other tribulations we must strive toward a positive goal.

QUESTIONS

- How did Japanese attitudes in defeat help prepare Japan for postwar redevelopment?
- Did defeat produce new divisions in attitudes among the Japanese?
- What other kinds of reactions might have been expected?
- How would you explain the rather calm and constructive outlook the passage suggests?
- Would American reactions to a Japanese victory have been similar?

On August 6 and three days later on August 9, atomic bombs were dropped on Hiroshima and Nagasaki, respectively. In moments these cities, which to this point had been spared bombing, were reduced to ashes. Short-term casualties in both cities were well over 100,000, and deaths from radiation sickness increased this total greatly in the years, and even decades, that followed. Even more than in the European theater, the end of the long and most destructive war in human history came swiftly. As they had in dealing with Germany, the Allies demanded unconditional surrender by the Japanese. With the exception of retaining the emperor, which was finally allowed, the Japanese agreed to these terms and began to disarm. With the division of Germany that had begun some months earlier, the Allied occupation of the islands set the stage for the third main phase of the 20th century, which would be dominated by the cold war between the Soviet and American superpowers that would be waged amid the collapse of the European colonial order.

WAR'S END AND THE EMERGENCE OF THE SUPERPOWER STANDOFF IN THE COLD WAR

31.4 How did the cold war emerge from the end of World War II?

The final stages of World War II quickly led to a tense worldwide half-century of confrontation between the United States and the Soviet Union, each of which headed hostile alliances anchored in nations that had been major combatants during the war.

United Nations (UN) International organization formed in the aftermath of World War II; included all of the victorious Allies; its primary mission was to provide a forum for negotiating disputes.

World War II did not produce the sweeping peace settlements, misguided as most of them turned out to be, that had officially ended World War I. The leaders of the Allies opposed to the Axis powers met on several occasions in an attempt to build the framework for a more lasting peace free of the vindictiveness that was so prominent at the Versailles gathering. A key result of Allied discussions was agreement on establishing the **United Nations (UN)**. From the outset this new international organization was more representative of the world's peoples, in both large and small nations, than the League of Nations. The United States pledged to join, played a major role in the United Nations' planning and finance, and provided a site on the East River in Manhattan for the organization's permanent headquarters. The Soviet Union was also a charter member, along with long-standing great powers, such as Britain and France. China, represented in the first decades after 1945 by the Guomindang, was grouped with these other global powers as a permanent member of the Security Council, the steering committee for United Nations operations. In the decades after the end of the war, the vanquished Axis powers were eventually granted membership, as were the former colonies, soon after each of them gained independence.

With the successful establishment of the United Nations, international diplomacy and assistance moved beyond the orbit of the Western powers that had all but monopolized them for centuries. But through their vetoes in the Security Council they retained considerable control. The United Nations' primary mission was to provide a forum for negotiating international disputes. It also took over the apparatus of more specialized international agencies, including the World Court of Justice and those concerned with human rights. The UN also coordinated programs directed at specific groups and problems, ranging from labor organization and famine relief to agricultural development and women's concerns. Although UN interventions to preserve or restore peace to numerous regions have encountered much resistance by both the great powers and regional political leaders, they have repeatedly proved vital to reducing violent conflict and providing refugee relief throughout the globe. The United Nations has also sponsored initiatives, including critical international conferences, which have proved highly influential in shaping policies and programs affecting child labor, women's rights, and environmental protection.

From Hot War to Cold War

The cold war would last until the 1980s, with various points of crisis and confrontation. Direct conflict between the two superpowers did not occur, despite dire forebodings. Much of world history, however, was shaped by cold war maneuvering for over four decades. The U.S.-Soviet confrontation began when the World War II allies turned, in the war's final conferences, to debate the nature of the postwar settlement. It quickly became apparent that the Soviet Union expected massive territorial gains and that Britain and the United States intended to limit these gains through their own areas of influence. Unresolved disputes then led to a steady expansion of the cold war between 1945 and 1949.

Tehran Conference Meeting among leaders of the United States, Britain, and the Soviet Union in 1943; agreed to the opening of a new front in France.

Yalta Conference Meeting among leaders of the United States, Britain, and the Soviet Union in 1945; agreed to Soviet entry into the Pacific war in return for possessions in Manchuria, organization of the United Nations; disputed the division of political organization in the eastern European states to be reestablished after the war.

Tensions had clearly surfaced during the 1944 **Tehran Conference**, when the allies agreed on the invasion of Nazi-occupied France. The decision to focus on France rather than moving up from the Mediterranean gave the Soviet forces a free hand to move through the smaller nations of eastern Europe as they pushed the Nazi armies back. Britain negotiated separately with the Soviets to ensure Western preponderance in postwar Greece as well as equality in Hungary and Yugoslavia, with Soviet control of Romania and Bulgaria. But the United States resisted this kind of un-Wilsonian scorn for the rights of small nations.

The next settlement meeting was the **Yalta Conference** in the Soviet Crimea early in 1945. President Franklin Roosevelt of the United States was eager to press the Soviet Union for assistance against Japan and to this end promised the Soviets important territorial gains in Manchuria and the northern Japanese islands. The organization of the United Nations was confirmed. As for Europe, however, agreement was more difficult. The three powers arranged to divide Germany into four occupation zones (liberated France getting a chunk), which would be disarmed and purged of Nazi influence. Britain, however, resisted Soviet zeal to eliminate German industrial power, seeing a viable

780 PART VI The Newest Stage of World History: 1900–Present

Germany as a potential ally in a subsequent Western–Soviet contest. Bitter dispute also raged over the smaller nations of eastern Europe. No one disagreed that they should be friendly to their Soviet neighbor, but the Western leaders also wanted them to be free and democratic. Stalin, the Soviet leader, had to make some concessions by including noncommunist leaders in what was already a Soviet-controlled government in liberated Poland—concessions that he soon violated.

The final postwar conference occurred in the Berlin suburb of **Potsdam** in July 1945. Russian forces now occupied not only most of eastern Europe but eastern Germany as well. This de facto situation prompted agreement that the Soviet Union could take over much of what had been eastern Poland, with the Poles gaining part of eastern Germany in compensation. Germany was divided pending a final peace treaty (which was not to come for more than 40 years). Austria was also divided and occupied, gaining unity and independence only in 1956, on condition of neutrality between the United States and the Soviet Union. Amid great difficulty, treaties were worked out for Germany's other allies, including Italy, but the United States and later the Soviet Union signed separate treaties with Japan.

Potsdam Conference Meeting among leaders of the United States, Britain, and the Soviet Union just before the end of World War II in 1945; Allies agreed upon Soviet domination in eastern Europe; Germany and Austria to be divided among victorious Allies.

All these maneuvers had several results. Japan was occupied by the United States and its wartime gains stripped away. Even Korea, taken earlier, was freed but was divided between U.S. and Soviet zones of occupation (the basis for the North Korea–South Korea division still in effect today). Former Asian colonies were returned to their old "masters," although often quite briefly, as continuing and new independence movements quickly challenged the control of the weakened imperialist powers. China regained most of its former territory, although here, too, stability was promptly challenged by renewed fighting between communist and nationalist forces within the nation, aided by the Soviet Union and the United States, respectively.

The effort to restore old colonial regimes applied also to the Middle East, India, and Africa. Indian and African troops had fought for Britain during the war, as in World War I, although Britain imprisoned key nationalist leaders and put independence plans on hold. African leaders had participated actively in the French resistance to its authoritarian wartime government. The Middle East and North Africa had been shaken by German invasions and Allied counterattacks. Irritability increased, and so did expectations for change. With Europe's imperial powers further weakened by their war effort, adjustments seemed inevitable, just as they had been in those parts of Asia invaded by the Japanese.

In Europe the boundaries of the Soviet Union pushed westward, with virtually all the losses after World War I erased. Independent nations created in 1918 were for the most part restored (although the former Baltic states of Latvia, Lithuania, and Estonia became Soviet provinces because they had been Russian provinces before World War I). Except for Greece and Yugoslavia, the new nations quickly fell under Soviet domination, with communist governments forced on them and Soviet troops in occupation. The nations of western Europe were free to set up or confirm democratic regimes, but most of them lived under the shadow of growing U.S. influence, manifested in continued presence of U.S. troops, substantial economic aid and coordination, and no small amount of outright policy manipulation.

View the **Closer Look** on **MyHistoryLab**: Major Cold War European Alliance Systems (Map)

The stage was set, in other words, for two of the great movements that would shape the ensuing decades in world history. The first comprised challenges by subject peoples to the tired vestiges of control by the great European empires—the movement known as "decolonization" that in a few decades would create scores of new nations in Asia, Africa, and the West Indies. The second great theme was the confrontation between the two superpowers that emerged from the war—the United States and the Soviet Union, each with new international influence and new military might. Many believed that this cold war would soon become a war in a more literal and devastating sense. That these trends constituted a peace settlement was difficult to imagine in 1945 or 1947, yet they seemed the best that could be done.

NATIONALISM AND DECOLONIZATION IN SOUTH AND SOUTHEAST ASIA AND AFRICA

31.5 Were the roles played by colonized peoples more or less important in World War II than they had been in World War I, and in what ways was the second conflict more truly global?

A second global conflict between the industrial powers proved fatal to the already badly battered European colonial empires. From the Philippines to west Africa, independence was won in most of the nonsettler colonies with surprisingly little bloodshed and remarkable speed; the opposite was true in colonies with large settler communities, where liberation struggles were usually violent and prolonged.

The Nazi rout of the French and the stunningly rapid Japanese capture of the French, Dutch, British, and U.S. colonies in southeast Asia put an end to whatever illusions the colonized peoples of Africa and Asia had left about the strength and innate superiority of their colonial overlords. Because the Japanese were non-Europeans, their early victories over the Europeans and Americans played a particularly critical role in destroying the myth of the white man's invincibility. The fall of the "impregnable" fortress at Singapore on the southern tip of Malaya and the Americans' reverses at Pearl Harbor and in the Philippines proved to be blows from which the colonizers never quite recovered, even though they went on to eventually defeat the Japanese. The sight of tens of thousands of British, Dutch, and American troops, struggling under the supervision of the victorious Japanese to survive the "death marches" to prison camps in their former colonies, left an indelible impression on the Asian villagers who saw them pass by. The harsh regimes and heavy demands the Japanese conquerors imposed on the peoples of southeast Asia during the war further strengthened the determination to fight for self-rule and to look to their own defenses after the conflict was over.

The devastation of World War II—a **total war** fought in the cities and countryside over much of Europe—drained the resources of the European powers. This devastating warfare also sapped the will of the European populace to hold increasingly resistant African and Asian peoples in bondage. The war also greatly enhanced the power and influence of the two giants on the European periphery: the United States and the Soviet Union. In Africa and the Middle East, as well as in the Pacific, the United States approached the war as a campaign of liberation. American propagandists made no secret of Franklin Roosevelt's hostility to colonialism in their efforts to win Asian and African support for the Allied war effort. In fact, American intentions in this regard were enshrined in the **Atlantic Charter of 1941**. This pact sealed an alliance between the United States and Great Britain that the latter desperately needed to survive in its war with Nazi Germany. In it Roosevelt persuaded a reluctant Churchill to include a clause that recognized the "right of all people to choose the form of government under which they live." The Soviets were equally vocal in their condemnation of colonialism and were even more forthcoming with material support for nationalist campaigns after the war. In the cold war world of the superpowers that emerged after 1945, there was little room for the domination that the much-reduced powers of western Europe had once exercised over much of the globe.

The Winning of Independence in South and Southeast Asia

The outbreak of World War II soon put an end to the accommodation between the Indian National Congress and the British in of the late 1930s. Congress leaders offered to support the Allies' war effort if the British would give them a significant share of power at the all-India level and commit themselves to Indian independence once the conflict was over. These conditions were staunchly rejected both by the viceroy in India and at home by Winston Churchill, who headed the coalition government that led Britain through the war. Labour members of the coalition government, however, indicated that they were quite willing to negotiate India's eventual independence. As tensions built between nationalist agitators and the British rulers, Sir Stafford Cripps was sent to India in early 1942 to see whether a deal could be struck with the Indian leaders. Indian divisions and British intransigence led to the collapse of Cripps's initiative and the renewal of mass civil disobedience campaigns under the guise of the **Quit India movement**, which began in the summer of 1942.

The British responded with repression and mass arrests, and for much of the remainder of the war, Gandhi, Nehru, and other major Congress politicians were imprisoned (Figure 31.6). Of the Indian nationalist parties, only the Communists—who were committed to the antifascist alliance—and, more ominously, the **Muslim League** rallied to the British cause. The League, now led by a former Congress party politician, the dour and uncompromising **Muhammad Ali Jinnah**, won much favor from the British for its wartime support. As their demands for a separate Muslim state in the subcontinent hardened, the links between the British and Jinnah and other League leaders became a key factor in the struggle for decolonization in south Asia.

World War II brought disruptions to India similar to those caused by the earlier global conflict. Inflation stirred up urban unrest, while a widespread famine in 1943 and 1944, brought on in part by wartime transport shortages, engendered much bitterness in rural India. Winston Churchill's defeat in the first postwar British election in 1945 brought a Labour government to power that was ready to deal with India's nationalist leaders. With independence in the near future tacitly conceded, the process of decolonization between 1945 and 1947 focused on what sort of state or states would be carved out of the subcontinent after the British withdrawal. Jinnah and the League had begun to build a mass following among the Muslims. In order to rally support, they played on widespread anxieties among the Muslim minority that a single Indian nation would be dominated by the Hindu majority, and that the Muslims would become the targets of increasing discrimination. It was therefore essential,

---

total war Warfare of the 20th century; vast resources and emotional commitments of belligerent nations were marshaled to support military effort; resulted from impact of industrialization on the military effort reflecting technological innovation and organizational capacity.

Atlantic Charter of 1941 World War II alliance agreement between the United States and Britain; included a clause that recognized the right of all people to choose the form of government under which they live; indicated sympathy for decolonization.

Quit India movement Mass civil disobedience campaign that began in the summer of 1942 to end British control of India.

Muslim League Founded in 1906 to better support demands of Muslims for separate electorates and legislative seats in Hindu-dominated India; represented division within Indian nationalist movement.

Jinnah, Muhammad Ali (1876–1948) Muslim nationalist leader in India; originally a member of the National Congress party; became leader of Muslim League; traded Muslim support for British during World War II for promises of a separate Muslim state after the war; first president of Pakistan.

they insisted, that a separate Muslim state called Pakistan be created from those areas in northwest and east India where Muslims were the most numerous.

As communal rioting spread throughout India, the British and key Congress party politicians reluctantly concluded that a bloodbath could be averted only by partition—the creation of two nations in the subcontinent: one secular, one Muslim. Thus, in the summer of 1947, the British handed power over to the leaders of the majority Congress party, who headed the new nation of India, and to Jinnah, who became the first president of Pakistan.

In part because of the haste with which the British withdrew their military forces from the deeply divided subcontinent, a bloodbath occurred anyway. Vicious Hindu–Muslim and Muslim–Sikh communal rioting, in which neither women nor children were spared, took the lives of hundreds of thousands in the searing summer heat across the plains of northwest India. Whole villages were destroyed; trains were attacked and their passengers hacked to death by armed bands of rival religious adherents. These atrocities fed a massive exchange of refugee populations between Hindu, Sikh, and Muslim areas that may have totaled 10 million people. Those who fled were so terrified that they were willing to give up their land, their villages, and most of their worldly possessions. The losses of partition were compounded by the fact that there was soon no longer a Gandhi to preach tolerance and communal coexistence. On January 30, 1948, on the way to one of his regular prayer meetings, he was shot by a Hindu fanatic.

In granting independence to India, the British, in effect, removed the keystone from the arch of an empire that spanned five continents. Burma (known today as Myanmar) and Ceylon (now named Sri Lanka) won their independence peacefully in the following years. India's independence and Gandhi's civil disobedience campaigns, which had done so much to win a mass following for the nationalist cause, also inspired successful struggles for independence in Ghana, Nigeria, and other African colonies in the 1950s and 1960s.

The retreat of the most powerful of the imperial powers could not help but contribute to the weakening of lesser empires such as those of the Dutch, the French, and the Americans. In fact, the process of the transfer of power from U.S. officials to moderate, middle-class Filipino politicians was well under way before World War II broke out. The loyalty to the Americans that most Filipinos displayed during the war, as well as the stubborn guerrilla resistance they put up against the Japanese occupation, did much to bring about the rapid granting of independence to the Philippines once the war ended. The Dutch and French were less willing to follow the British example and relinquish their colonial possessions in the postwar era. From 1945 to 1949, the Dutch fought a losing war to destroy the nation of Indonesia, which nationalists in the Netherlands Indies had established when the Japanese hold over the islands broke down in mid-1945. The French struggled to retain Indochina. Communist revolutions in East Asia also emerged victorious in the postwar period. No sooner had the European colonizers suffered these losses than they were forced to deal with new threats to the last bastions of the imperial order in Africa.

Read the Document on MyHistoryLab: Jinnah, the "Father" of Pakistan

FIGURE **31.6** In 1931 Mahatma Gandhi returned to Great Britain for the first time since his student days in 1915. Although his attempts to negotiate with British leaders came to little, he was a great hit with the British public, in part because of his sly sense of humor. When asked on another occasion, after he had an audience with King George V, if he was embarrassed to meet His Royal Highness in the scant khadi-cloth apparel he wears in this photo, Gandhi quipped that the king-emperor had on enough clothes for the both of them.

The Liberation of Nonsettler Africa

World War II proved even more disruptive to the colonial order imposed on Africa than the first global conflict of the European powers. Forced labor and confiscations of crops and minerals returned, and inflation and controlled markets again cut down on African earnings. African recruits in the hundreds of thousands were drawn once more into the conflict and had even greater opportunities to use the latest European weapons to destroy Europeans. African servicemen had witnessed British and French defeats in the Middle East and southeast Asia, and they fought bravely only to experience renewed racial discrimination once they returned home. Many were soon among the staunchest supporters of postwar nationalist campaigns in the African colonies of the British and French. The swift and humiliating rout of the French and Belgians by Nazi armies in the spring of 1940 shattered whatever was left of the colonizers' reputation for military prowess. It also led to a bitter and, in the circumstances, embarrassing struggle between the forces of the puppet Vichy regime and those of de Gaulle's Free French, who continued fighting the Nazis mainly in France's North and West African colonies.

The wartime needs of both the British and the Free French led to major departures from long-standing colonial policies that had restricted industrial development throughout Africa. Factories

VISUALIZING THE PAST

National Leaders for a New Global Order

THROUGHOUT AFRICA AND ASIA, STRUGGLES FOR decolonization and national independence often led to the emergence of leaders with exceptional mass appeal and political skills. But the personal qualities, visions of the future, and leadership styles that made for widespread loyalty to these individuals varied widely depending on the cultures and social settings from which they emerged as well as the nature of the political contests that led to the colonizers' retreat and the establishment of new nations. The following are photos of four of the most charismatic and effective leaders of independence movements in Africa and Asia. Study these photos and the background information on each of these individuals that is provided in earlier sections of this chapter and the relevant sections of Chapters 29 and 34, and answer the questions about leadership styles and images that follow.

QUESTIONS

- What do the dress and poses of these leaders tell us about the image each projected?
- Why did the style and approach each adopted win widespread popular support in each of the very different societies in which they emerged as pivotal leaders in the struggles for independence?
- How well do you think that each of their approaches to leadership served them in dealings with the European colonizers and contests with the rival leaders and political parties they faced in each of the societies in which they arose?
- What did charisma mean in each of these settings?

Mohandas Gandhi, India.

Léopold Sédar Senghor, Senegal.

Gamal Abdul Nasser, Egypt.

Kwame Nkrumah, Ghana.

were established to process urgently needed vegetable oils, foods, and minerals in western and south central Africa. These in turn contributed to a growing migration on the part of African peasants to the towns and a sharp spurt in African urban growth. The inability of many of those who moved to the towns to find employment made for a reservoir of disgruntled, idle workers that would be skillfully tapped by nationalist politicians in the postwar decades.

There were essentially two main paths to decolonization in nonsettler Africa in the postwar era. The first was pioneered by Kwame Nkrumah (KWAH-mee ehn-KROO-muh) and his followers in the British Gold Coast colony, which, as the independent nation of Ghana, launched the process of decolonization in Africa. Nkrumah epitomized the more radical sort of African leader that emerged throughout Africa after the war (see Visualizing the Past feature). Educated in African missionary schools and the United States, he had established wide contacts with nationalist leaders in both British and French West Africa and civil rights leaders in America prior to his return to the Gold Coast in the late 1940s. He returned to a land in ferment. The restrictions of government-controlled marketing boards and their favoritism for British merchants had led to widespread, but nonviolent, protest in the coastal cities. But after the police fired on a peaceful demonstration of ex-servicemen in 1948, rioting broke out in many towns.

Although both urban workers and cash crop farmers had supported the unrest, Western-educated African leaders were slow to organize these dissident groups into a sustained mass movement. Their reluctance arose in part from their fear of losing major political concessions, such as seats on colonial legislative councils, which the British had just made. Rejecting the caution urged by more established political leaders, Nkrumah resigned his position as chair of the dominant political party in the Gold Coast and established his own **Convention People's Party (CPP)**. Even before the formal break, he had signaled the arrival of a new style of politics by organizing mass rallies, boycotts, and strikes.

In the mid-1950s, Nkrumah's mass following, and his growing stature as a leader who would not be deterred by imprisonment or British threats, won repeated concessions from the British. Educated Africans were given more and more representation in legislative bodies, and gradually they took over administration of the colony. The British recognition of Nkrumah as the prime minister of an independent Ghana in 1957 simply concluded a transfer of power from the European colonizers to the Western-educated African elite that had been under way for nearly a decade.

The peaceful devolution of power to African nationalists led to the independence of the British nonsettler colonies in black Africa by the mid-1960s. Independence in the comparable areas of the French and Belgian empires in Africa came in a somewhat different way. Hard-pressed by costly military struggles to hold on to their colonies in Indochina and Algeria, the French took a much more conciliatory line in dealing with the many peoples they ruled in west Africa. Ongoing negotiations with such highly Westernized leaders as Senegal's Léopold Sédar Senghor and the Ivory Coast's Felix Houphouât-Boigny (hoh-FOO-aht BWAHN-yay) led to reforms and political concessions.

The slow French retreat ensured that moderate African leaders, who were eager to retain French economic and cultural ties, would dominate the nationalist movements and the postindependence period in French west Africa. Between 1956 and 1960, the French colonies moved by stages toward nationhood—a process that sped up after de Gaulle's return to power in 1958. By 1960 all of France's west African colonies were free.

In the same year, the Belgians completed a much hastier retreat from their huge colonial possession in the Congo. Their hasty abandonment of the colony was epitomized by the fact that there was little in the way of an organized nationalist movement to pressure them into concessions of any kind. In fact, by design there were scarcely any well-educated Congolese to lead resistance to Belgian rule. At independence in 1960, there were only 16 African college graduates in a Congolese population that exceeded 13 million. Although the Portuguese still clung to their impoverished and scattered colonial territories, by the mid-1960s the European colonial era had come to an end in all but the settler societies of Africa.

Convention People's Party (CPP) Political party established by Kwame Nkrumah in opposition to British control of colonial legislature in Gold Coast.

Repression and Guerrilla War: The Struggle for the Settler Colonies

The pattern of relatively peaceful withdrawal by stages that characterized the process of decolonization in most of Asia and Africa proved unworkable in most of the settler colonies (see Map 25.1, p. 590). These included areas like Algeria, Kenya, and Southern Rhodesia, where substantial numbers of Europeans had gone intending to settle permanently in the 19th and early 20th centuries. South Africa provided few openings for nationalist agitation except that mounted by the politically and economically dominant colonists of European descent. In each case, the presence of European settler communities, varying in size from millions in South Africa and Algeria to tens of thousands in Kenya and Southern Rhodesia, blocked both the rise of indigenous nationalist movements and concessions on the part of the colonial overlords.

Because the settlers regarded the colonies to which they had emigrated as their permanent homes, they fought all attempts to turn political control over to the African majority or even to grant them civil rights. They also doggedly refused all reforms by colonial administrators that required them to give up any of the lands they had occupied, often at the expense of indigenous African peoples. Unable to make headway through nonviolent protest tactics—which were forbidden—or negotiations with British or French officials, who were fearful of angering the highly vocal settler minority, many African leaders turned to violent, revolutionary struggles to win their independence.

The first of these erupted in Kenya in the early 1950s. Impatient with the failure of the nonviolent approach adopted by **Jomo Kenyatta** and the leading nationalist party, the **Kenya African Union (KAU)**, an underground organization coalesced around a group of more radical leaders. After forming the **Land and Freedom Army** in the early 1950s, the radicals mounted a campaign of terror and guerrilla warfare against the British, the settlers, and Africans who were considered collaborators. At the height of the struggle in 1954, some 200,000 rebels were in action in the capital at Nairobi and in the forest reserves of the central Kenyan highlands. The British responded with an all-out military effort to crush the guerrilla movement, which was dismissed as an explosion of African savagery and labeled the "Mau Mau" by the colonizers, not the rebels. In the process, the British, at the settlers' insistence, imprisoned Kenyatta and the KAU organizers, thus eliminating the nonviolent alternative to the guerrillas.

The rebel movement had been militarily defeated by 1956 at the cost of thousands of lives. But the British were now in a mood to negotiate with the nationalists, despite strong objections from the European settlers. Kenyatta was released from prison, and he emerged as the spokesperson for the Africans of Kenya. By 1963 a multiracial Kenya had won its independence. Under what was, in effect, Kenyatta's one-party rule, it remained until the mid-1980s one of the most stable and more prosperous of the new African states.

The struggle of the Arab and Berber peoples of Algeria for independence was longer and even more vicious than that in Kenya. Algeria had for decades been regarded by the French as an integral part of France—a department just like Provence or Brittany. The presence of more than a million European settlers in the colony only served to bolster the resolve of French politicians to retain it at all costs. But in the decade after World War II, sporadic rioting grew into sustained guerrilla resistance. By the mid-1950s, the **National Liberation Front (FLN)** had mobilized large segments of the Arab and Berber population of the colony in a full-scale revolt against French rule and settler dominance. High-ranking French army officers came to see the defeat of this movement as a way to restore a reputation that had been badly tarnished by recent defeats in Vietnam (see Chapter 35). As in Kenya, the rebels were defeated in the field. But they gradually negotiated the independence of Algeria after de Gaulle came to power in 1958. The French people had wearied of the seemingly endless war, and de Gaulle became convinced that he could not restore France to great power status as long as its resources continued to be drained by the Algerian conflict.

In contrast to Kenya, the Algerian struggle was prolonged and brutalized by a violent settler backlash. Led after 1960 by the **Secret Army Organization (OAS)**, settler violence was directed against Arabs and Berbers as well as French who favored independence for the colony. With strong support from elements in the French military, earlier resistance by the settlers had managed to topple the government in Paris in 1958, thereby putting an end to the Fourth Republic. In the early 1960s, the OAS came close to assassinating de Gaulle and overthrowing the Fifth Republic, which his accession to power had brought into existence. In the end, however, the Algerians won their independence in 1962 (Figure 31.7). After the bitter civil war, the multiracial accommodation worked out in Kenya appeared out of the question as far as the settlers of Algeria were concerned. Over 900,000 left the new nation within months after its birth. In addition, tens of thousands of harkis, or Arabs and Berbers who had sided with the French in the long war for independence, fled to France. They, and later migrants, formed the core of the substantial Algerian population now present in France.

The Persistence of White Supremacy in South Africa

In southern Africa, violent revolutions put an end to white settler dominance in the Portuguese colonies of Angola and Mozambique in 1975 and in Southern Rhodesia (now Zimbabwe) by 1980. Only in South Africa did the white minority manage to maintain its position of supremacy. Its

---

Kenyatta, Jomo (1946–1978) Leader of the nonviolent nationalist party in Kenya; organized the Kenya Africa Union (KAU); failed to win concessions because of resistance of white settlers; came to power only after suppression of the Land Freedom Army, or Mau Mau.

Kenya African Union (KAU) Leading nationalist party in Kenya; adopted nonviolent approach to ending British control in the 1950s.

Land and Freedom Army Radical organization for independence in Kenya; frustrated by failure of nonviolent means, initiated campaign of terror in 1952; referred to by British as the Mau Mau.

National Liberation Front (FLN) Radical nationalist movement in Algeria; launched sustained guerilla war against France in the 1950s; success of attacks led to independence of Algeria in 1958.

Secret Army Organization (OAS) Organization of French settlers in Algeria; led guerrilla war following independence during the 1960s; assaults directed against Arabs, Berbers, and French who advocated independence.

ability to do so rested on several factors that distinguished it from other settler societies. To begin with, the white population of South Africa, roughly equally divided between the Dutch-descended Afrikaners and the more recently arrived English speakers, was a good deal larger than that of any of the other settler societies. Although they were only a small minority in a country of 23 million black Africans and 3.5 million East Indians and coloreds (mulattos, in American parlance), by the mid-1980s, South Africa's settler-descended population had reached 4.5 million.

Unlike the settlers in Kenya and Algeria, who had the option of retreating to Europe as full citizens of France or Great Britain, the Afrikaners in particular had no European homeland to fall back upon. They had lived in South Africa as long as other Europeans had in North America, and they considered themselves quite distinct from the Dutch. Over the centuries, the Afrikaners had also built up what was for them a persuasive ideology of white racist supremacy. Although crude by European or American standards, Afrikaner racism was far more explicit and elaborate than that developed by the settlers of any other colony. Afrikaner ideology was grounded in selected biblical quotations and the celebration of their historic struggle to "tame a beautiful but hard land" in the face of opposition from both the African "savages" and the British "imperialists."

Ironically, their defeat by the British in the Boer War from 1899 to 1902 also contributed much to the capacity of the white settler minority to maintain its place of dominance in South Africa. A sense of guilt, arising especially from their treatment of Boer women and children during the war—tens of thousands of whom died of disease in what the British called concentration camps—led the victors to make major concessions to the Afrikaners in the postwar decades. The most important of these was internal political control, which included turning over the fate of the black African majority to the openly racist supremacist Afrikaners. Not surprisingly, the continued subjugation of the black Africans became a central aim of the Afrikaner political organizations that emerged in the 1930s and 1940s, culminating in the **Afrikaner National Party**. From 1948, when it emerged as the majority party in the all-white South African legislature, the National party devoted itself to winning complete independence from Britain (which came without violence in 1961). The Afrikaners also strove to complete a decades-long quest to establish white domination over the political, social, and economic life of the new nation.

A rigid system of racial segregation (which will be discussed more fully in Chapter 34), called **apartheid** by the Afrikaners, was established after 1948 through the passage of thousands of laws. Among other things, this legislation reserved the best jobs for whites and carefully defined the sorts of contacts permissible between different racial groups. The right to vote and political representation were denied to the black Africans, and ultimately to the coloreds and Indians. It was illegal for members of any of these groups to hold mass meetings or to organize political parties or labor unions. These restrictions, combined with very limited opportunities for higher education for black Africans, hampered the growth of black African political parties and their efforts to mobilize popular support for the struggle for decolonization. The Afrikaners' establishment of a vigilant and brutal police state

FIGURE 31.7 Algerians celebrate after independence was announced in July 1962. Inhabitants of the city stand in triumph atop the motorcade of the PGAR (Provisional Government of the Algerian Republic), which negotiated the terms of independence with the French government. Before independence, barricades had been erected throughout the colony to keep European residential areas off limits to the Arabs and Berbers, who made up the overwhelming majority of the population.

Afrikaner National Party Emerged as the majority party in the all-white South African legislature after 1948; advocated complete independence from Britain; favored a rigid system of racial segregation called apartheid.

apartheid Policy of strict racial segregation imposed in South Africa to permit the continued dominance of whites politically and economically.

Conflicting Nationalisms: Arabs, Israelis, and the Palestinian Question

Haganah Zionist military force engaged in violent resistance to British presence in Palestine in the 1940s.

Along with Egypt, several Middle Eastern states, including Iraq and Syria, had technically gained independence between the world wars, although European influence remained strong. With World War II, independence became more complete, although it was not until the 1970s that governments were strong enough to shake off Western dominance of the oil fields. Egypt's 1952 revolt and independence movements in the rest of north Africa gained ground, although the struggle against France in Algeria was bitter and prolonged. Although virtually all Arab peoples who were not yet free by the end of World War II were liberated by the early 1960s, the fate of Palestine continued to present special problems. Hitler's campaign of genocide against the European Jews had provided powerful support for the Zionists' insistence that the Jews must have their own homeland, which more and more was conceived in terms of a modern national state. The brutal persecution of the Jews also won international sympathy for the Zionist cause. This was in part due to the fact that the leaders of many nations, including the United States and Great Britain, were reluctant to admit Jews fleeing the Nazi terror into their own countries. As Hitler's henchmen stepped up their race war against the Jews, the tide of Jewish immigration to Palestine rose sharply. But growing Arab resistance to Jewish settlement and land purchases in Palestine, which was often expressed in communal rioting and violent assaults on Zionist communities, led to increasing British restrictions on the entry of Jews into the colony.

A major Muslim revolt swept Palestine between 1936 and 1939. The British managed to put down this rising but only with great difficulty. It both decimated the leadership of the Palestinian Arab community and further strengthened the British resolve to stem the flow of Jewish immigrants to Palestine. Government measures to keep out Jewish refugees from Nazi oppression led in turn to violent Zionist resistance to the British presence in Palestine. The Zionist assault was spearheaded by a regular Zionist military force, the **Haganah**, and several underground terrorist organizations.

By the end of World War II, the major parties claiming Palestine were locked into a deadly stalemate. The Zionists were determined to carve out a Jewish state in the region. The Palestinian Arabs and their allies in neighboring Arab lands were equally determined to transform Palestine into a multireligious nation in which the position of the Arab majority would be ensured. Having badly bungled their mandatory responsibilities, and under attack from both sides, the British wanted more than anything else to scuttle and run. The 1937 report of a British commission of inquiry supplied a possible solution: partition. The newly created United Nations provided an international body that could give a semblance of legality to the proceedings. In 1948, with sympathy for the Jews running high because of the postwar revelations of the horrors of Hitler's Final Solution, the member states of the United Nations—with the United States and the Soviet Union in rare agreement—approved the partition of Palestine into Arab and Jewish countries (Map 31.3).

MAP 31.3 The Partition of Palestine After World War II The areas granted to the Palestinian people by the 1948 UN Partition were quickly occupied by the warring states of Israel and Egypt, Jordan and Syria.

The Arab states that bordered the newly created nation of Israel had vehemently opposed the UN action. Soon the two sides were engaged in all-out warfare. Although heavily outnumbered, the Zionists proved better armed and much better prepared to defend themselves than almost anyone could have expected. Not only did they hold onto the tiny, patchwork state they had been given by the United Nations, but they expanded it at the Arabs' expense. The brief but bloody war that ensued created hundreds of thousands of Palestinian Arab refugees. It also sealed the persisting hostility between Arabs and Israelis that has been the all-consuming issue in the region and a major international problem to the present day. In Palestine, conflicting strains of nationalism had collided. As a result, the legacy of colonialism proved even more of a liability to social and economic development than in much of the rest of newly independent Africa and Asia.

Global Connections and Critical Themes

PERSISTING TRENDS IN A WORLD TRANSFORMED BY WAR

Given the fragile foundations on which it rested, the rather rapid demise of the European colonial order is not really surprising. World War II completed the process that World War I and anticolonial nationalism had begun; the end of Western imperialism came quickly. In this sense, the global framework was transformed. However, the winning of political freedom in Asia and Africa also represented less of a break with the colonial past than the appearance of many new nations on the map of the world might lead one to assume.

The decidedly nonrevolutionary, elite-to-elite transfer of power that was central to the liberation process in most colonies, even those where there were violent guerrilla movements, limited the extent of the social and economic transformation that occurred. The Western-educated African and Asian classes moved into the offices and took the jobs—and often the former homes—of the European colonizers. But social gains for the rest of the population in most new nations were minimal or nonexistent. In Algeria, Kenya, and Zimbabwe (formerly Southern Rhodesia), abandoned European lands were distributed to Arab and African peasants and laborers. But in most former colonies, especially in Asia, the big landholders that remained were indigenous, and they have held on tenaciously to their holdings. Educational reforms were carried out to include more sciences in school curricula and the history of Asia or Africa rather than Europe. But Western cultural influences have remained strong in almost all of the former colonies. Indians and many west Africans with higher education continue to communicate in English and French.

The liberation of the colonies also did little to disrupt Western dominance of the terms of international trade or the global economic order more generally. In fact, in the negotiations that led to decolonization, Asian and African leaders often explicitly promised to protect the interests of Western merchants and businesspeople in the postindependence era. These and other limits that sustained Western influence and often dominance, even after freedom was won, greatly reduced the options open to nationalist leaders struggling to build viable and prosperous nations. Although new forces have also played important roles, the postindependence history of colonized peoples cannot be understood without a consideration of the lingering effects of the colonial interlude in their history.

Further Readings

Three of the most genuinely global histories of World War II, which also include extensive accounts of the origins of the war in both Europe and the Pacific, are Gerhard L. Weinberg, *A World at Arms: A Global History of World War II* (1994); Peter Calvocoressi and Guy Wint, *Total War: Causes and Courses of the Second World War* (1972); and more recently Anthony Beevor's *The Second World War* (2012). Richard Overy's many works on World War II and 20th century conflicts more generally are among the most original and engaging in a very extensive literature on modern warfare. For a good overview of the coming of the war in Europe from the British perspective, see Christopher Thorne, *The Approach of War 1938–1939* (1967), and from the German viewpoint, Gerhard L. Weinberg, *Germany, Hitler, and World War II* (1995). A fine analysis of the underlying patterns in the European theater can be found in Gordon Wright, *The Ordeal of Total War, 1939–1945* (1968).

From a prodigious literature on the Holocaust, some good works to begin with are Hannah Arendt's brilliant *Eichmann in Jerusalem* (1963) and Raul Hilberg's *Destruction of the European Jews* (1985). Christopher Browning's *Ordinary Men* (1992) provides a chilling account of some of those who actually carried out the killings, while Viktor Frankl's *Man's Search for Meaning* (1959) is one of the most poignant of the numerous autobiographical accounts of the concentration camps. Omer Bartov provides a thoughtful meditation on the wider meanings of the Holocaust for 20th-century history in *Murder in Our Midst* (1996).

On the causes of the Pacific war, see Michael Barnhart, *Japan Prepares for Total War* (1987), and William O'Neill, *A Democracy at War* (1993). Sukarno's reactions to the Japanese invasion of the

Netherlands Indies can be found in his *Autobiography* (1965) as related to Cindy Adams, which should be balanced by John Legge's *Sukarno: A Political Biography* (1972). On the course of the war in the Pacific from differing perspectives, see Ronald Spector, *Eagle Against the Sun* (1985); Saburò Ienaga, *The Pacific War, 1931–1945* (1978); and John Dower, *War Without Mercy: Race and Power in the Pacific War* (1986). On the end of the war and the forces that led to the cold war, see Martin Sherwin, *A World Destroyed: The Atomic Bomb and the Grand Alliance* (1975); William Craig, *The Fall of Japan* (1967); Herbert Feis, *From Trust to Terror: The Onset of the Cold War, 1945–1950* (1970); and Melvyn Leffler, *A Preponderance of Power: National Security, the Truman Administration, and the Cold War* (1992).

A thoughtful overview of the process of decolonization in the British empire as a whole can be found in the works of John Darwin. In addition to P. J. Vatikiotis's general *History of Egypt*, Jacques Berque's *Egypt: Imperialism and Revolution* (1972) and Peter Mansfield's *The British in Egypt* (1971) provide detailed accounts of the nationalist revolt and early years of quasi-independence. The struggles for decolonization in Africa are surveyed by Ali A. Mazrui and Michael Tidy in *Nationalism and New States in Africa* (1984); J. D. Hargreaves, *Decolonization in Africa* (1988); and W. R. Louis and P. Gifford, eds., *Decolonization in Africa* (1984).

From the very substantial literature on the rise of nationalism in settler societies, some of the best studies include C. Roseberg and J. Nottingham, *The Myth of "Mau Mau"* (1966), on Kenya; the writings of Terrence Ranger on Rhodesia; and Alastair Horne, *A Savage War of Peace* (1977), on Algeria. Of the many works on South Africa, the general histories of S. Throup, B. Bunting, T. D. Moodie, and Leonard Thompson provide a good introduction to the rise of Afrikaner power. The period of the partition and the first Arab-Israeli conflict have been the subject of much revisionist scholarship in recent years. Some of the best of this is included in important books by Avi Schleim, Walid Khalidi, Ilan Pappé, and Tom Segev.

On the United States in the cold war decades, see Walter Lafeber, *America, Russia, and the Cold War, 1945–2004* (2004). Ronald Powaski, *The Cold War: The United States and the Soviet Union, 1917–1991* (1998), is a reliable and readable standard political history that synthesizes the historiography of the cold war. Ellen Schrecker, *Many Are the Crimes: McCarthyism in America* (1998), has a broad social history of the political and cultural legacy of the Red Scare. T. H. Etzold and J. L. Gaddis, eds., *Containment: Documents on American Policy and Strategy, 1945–1950* (1978), provides primary source material on the political history of the early cold war.

On MyHistoryLab

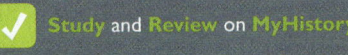

Critical Thinking Questions

1. In what ways did the causes of World War II differ from those that led to World War I?
2. Discuss the sociopolitical, economic, and military developments that led to the global transformation of warfare in the 19th and 20th centuries.
3. In what ways did the total war fought between 1914 and 1918 carry to even more brutal and indiscriminate extremes in the global conflict that followed between 1937 and 1945?
4. What was novel about the cold war, compared to diplomatic and military relations before World War II?
5. How did a second, 20th-century global conflict intensify and add to the forces that weakened and ultimately negated the ideological, political-military, and economic underpinnings of the European colonial empires?

Western Society and Eastern Europe in the Decades of the Cold War

32

Listen to Chapter 32 on MyHistoryLab

LEARNING OBJECTIVES

How did the cold war and decolonization alter the international framework for the West? p. 793	**32.1**
What were the main changes in western Europe, compared to patterns during the 1920s and 1930s? p. 796	**32.2**
How did postwar developments in the United States compare to those in western Europe? p. 802	**32.3**
What caused the changes in the roles and motivations of women in western Europe and the United States? p. 804	**32.4**
What were the main goals of the Soviet Union in Europe after World War II? p. 809	**32.5**
What were the main shifts in Soviet society and policy between World War II and the 1980s? p. 812	**32.6**

In 1954, the United States tested a nuclear weapon in the Marshall Islands that caused radioactive fallout to shower a Japanese fishing boat, ultimately killing one crew member and hospitalizing many others. International outrage ensued. Both the United States and the Soviet Union were conducting aboveground nuclear tests, and they would soon be joined by France and Britain. All sorts of people, in all sorts of places, rallied against these tests, in a striking manifestation of what media were beginning to label "world opinion."

Church groups, from Quakers to Roman Catholics, protested the tests. Buddhist voices were also strong. Japanese leadership was crucial; given the nation's experience at the end of World War II, it was hardly surprising that 86 percent of Japanese opposed nuclear testing. Australia and New Zealand vigorously objected to the use of the Pacific for tests, while Egypt and other Middle Eastern countries resisted French use of the Sahara. In Germany, with a new passion against war, hundreds of thousands of demonstrators marched before the U.S. embassy. African and Indian voices were also strong. In the United States many women joined protest

FIGURE 32.1 This 1958 Russian poster depicts a woman shielding her eyes from the light of a mushroom cloud and holding her hand up in a universal gesture of opposition. The lettering says "No!" The palm trees make clear that the reference is to testing in the Pacific. Why might the Soviets, who had themselves done aboveground nuclear testing, publish such a poster?

791

Watch the Video Series on MyHistoryLab

Learn about some key topics related to this chapter with the *MyHistoryLab Video Series: Key Topics in World History*

groups—there was widespread concern that testing would lead to nuclear contamination of milk that would threaten the health of children.

The governments that were doing the testing initially resisted attempts to outlaw it. Many American leaders claimed the protests were a communist plot, and it was true that Soviet groups tried to use the rallies to their advantage (Figure 32.1). But finally the great powers reconsidered. In 1958 President Dwight Eisenhower, told by a scientist that further tests would create still more awesome bombs, replied: "The new thermonuclear weapons are tremendously powerful; however they are not as powerful as is world opinion today in obliging the United States to follow certain lines of policy." A testing moratorium was declared in 1958, and an initial test ban treaty was negotiated in 1963. ■

Both western and eastern Europe had been devastated by World War II. Yet the Soviet Union emerged within a few years with a new European empire and status as a world superpower, rivaling the United States and its allies. Western Europe bounced back as well, although it did not recover its prewar world dominance. The United States, defying its earlier traditions, became very active in international affairs, maintaining a strong international presence and making massive military expenditures.

While the cold war and the rise of nuclear weapons set the framework for developments in the West and in eastern Europe, other changes may have been more important for the longer run. In the West, democratic political forms gained new vitality, along with rising consumer prosperity. In eastern Europe, dominated by the Soviet Union, the desire for economic development and cultural change vied with the goal of maintaining superpower status. Both the West and the Soviet bloc emphasized industrial growth and related social and family structures, and both emphasized science. Along the cold war tensions, these parallels had important effects on the rest of the world.

1940 C.E.	1950 C.E.	1960 C.E.
1945 End of World War II	**1953** Stalin's death	**1960s** Civil rights and feminist movements in United States
1945–1948 Soviet takeover of eastern Europe; new constitutions in Italy, Germany, and France; Labour Party victory in Britain; growth of welfare states in western Europe	**1955** Formation of Warsaw Pact	**1961** Berlin Wall erected
	1956 Khrushchev breaks with Stalinism	**1962** Cuban missile crisis
	1956 Hungarian revolt and its suppression	**1968** Czechoslovakian revolt suppressed; Brezhnev Doctrine proclaims right to intervene in any socialist country
1947 Marshall Plan	**1957** Establishment of European Economic Community or Common Market (basis of later European Union)	
1947–1960s Cold war begins and reaches its peak	**1958** De Gaulle's Fifth Republic in France	**1968–1973** Massive student protests in West
1949 Separate East and West German regimes established		
1949 Soviet Union develops atomic bomb; North Atlantic Treaty Organization established		

AFTER WORLD WAR II: A NEW INTERNATIONAL SETTING FOR THE WEST

32.1 How did the cold war and decolonization alter the international framework for the West?

World War II left western Europe in shambles. The sheer physical destruction caused problems with housing and transportation. Downed bridges and rail lines complicated food shipments, leaving many people in France and Germany ill-fed and unable to work at full efficiency. Nazi Germany's use of forced foreign labor, as well as the many boundary changes resulting from the war, generated hundreds of thousands of refugees trying to return home or find new homes. For at least two years after 1945 it was unclear that recovery would be possible—mere survival proved difficult enough. Europe's postwar weakness after three decades of strife helped trigger a crescendo of nationalist sentiment in areas the West had colonized, as well as the fuller emergence of the United States and the Soviet Union, whose size and growing industrial strength now overshadowed Europe's proud nation-states.

> Western Europe had to adjust to its loss of world dominance after the war. Western European countries lost their colonies and became secondary players in the cold war between the superpowers.

Europe and Its Colonies

The two larger changes provoked by the war—decolonization and the cold war—quickly intruded on the West. We have seen that colonies outside Europe, roused by the war, became increasingly restive. When the British returned to Malaya and the Dutch to Indonesia—areas from which they had been dislodged—they found a more hostile climate, with well-organized nationalist resistance. It was soon clear that many colonies could be maintained only at great cost, and in the main the European nations decided that results were not worth the effort. A few cases proved messy. France tried to defend its holdings in Vietnam against communist guerrillas, yielding only in 1954 after some major defeats. The French clung even more fiercely to Algeria, the oldest African colony and one with a large European minority. The French military joined Algerian settlers in insisting on a war to the death against nationalist forces, and bitter fighting went on for years. The tension even threatened civil war in France, until a new president, Charles de Gaulle, realized the hopelessness of the struggle and negotiated Algeria's independence in 1962.

Overall, decolonization proceeded more smoothly than this between the late 1940s and the mid-1970s, without prolonged fighting that might drain the Western nations. Kenya, Vietnam, and the Algerian morass were bitter exceptions. Western governments typically retained important cultural relations with their former colonies and sometimes provided administrative and military help as well. Both France and Belgium, for example, frequently intervened in Africa after decolonization was officially complete. Finally, Western economic interests remained strong in most former colonies—particularly in Africa, where they exploited mineral and agricultural resources in a pattern of trade not radically different from that of colonial days.

1970 C.E.	1980 C.E.	1990 C.E.	2000 C.E.
1970s Democratic regimes in Spain, Portugal, and Greece	**1981–1988** Reagan president in United States	**1992** End of economic restrictions within Common Market	**2001** Euro currency introduced
1973, 1977 Oil crises	**1985–1991** Gorbachev heads Soviet Union	**1993** Division of Czechoslovakia; Clinton inauguration ends three-term Republican tenure in White House	**2001** Growing concern about terrorism
1979 Uprisings in Poland and their suppression; Thatcher and new conservatism in Britain; Soviet invasion of Afghanistan; significant economic recession	**1989** Berlin Wall division ends; new regimes throughout eastern Europe		**2003** U.S. invasion of Iraq
			2005 Expansion of European Union in eastern Europe

cold war The state of relations between the United States and its allies and the Soviet Union and its allies between the end of World War II and 1990; based on creation of political spheres of influence and a nuclear arms race rather than actual warfare.

eastern bloc Nations favorable to the Soviet Union in eastern Europe during the cold war—particularly Poland, Czechoslovakia, Bulgaria, Romania, Hungary, and East Germany.

Truman, Harry American president from 1945 to 1952; less eager for smooth relations with the Soviet Union than Franklin Roosevelt; authorized use of atomic bomb during World War II; architect of American diplomacy that initiated the cold war.

iron curtain Phrase coined by Winston Churchill to describe the division between free and communist societies taking shape in Europe after 1946.

The impact of decolonization on the West should not, however, be minimized. Important minorities of former settlers and officials came home embittered, although, except briefly in France, they were not a significant political force. Europe's overt power in the world was dramatically reduced. Efforts by Britain and France to attack independent Egypt in 1956, to protest Egypt's nationalization of the Suez Canal, symbolized the new state of affairs. The United States and the Soviet Union forced a quick end to hostilities, and what was once a colonial lifeline came into non-Western hands. Yet although decolonization was a powerful change in world affairs, it did not, at least in the short run, overwhelm the West, as neither economic growth nor internal political stability suffered greatly.

The Cold War

The final new ingredient of Europe's diplomatic framework, the **cold war** between the United States and the Soviet Union, had a more durable ongoing influence on politics and society within the West. The conflict took shape between 1945 and 1947. The last wartime meetings among the leaders of Britain, the United States, and the Soviet Union had rather vaguely staked out the boundaries of postwar Europe, which were certainly open to varied interpretations. By the war's end, Soviet troops firmly occupied most eastern European countries, and within three years the Soviets had installed communist regimes to their liking, while excluding opposition political movements. Thus an **eastern bloc** emerged that included Poland, Czechoslovakia, Bulgaria, Romania, and Hungary. And Soviet boundaries themselves had pushed west, reversing the decisions of the post–World War I Versailles conference. The Baltic states disappeared, and Poland lost territory to Russia, gaining some former German lands as compensation. Finally, Soviet occupation of the eastern zone of Germany gave Russia a base closer toward the heart of Europe than the tsars had ever dreamed possible (Map 32.1).

Offended by the Soviet Union's heavy-handed manipulation of eastern Europe, including its zone in eastern Germany, U.S. and British policymakers tried to counter. The new American president, **Harry Truman**, was less eager for smooth relations with the Soviets than Franklin Roosevelt had been; Truman was emboldened by the U.S. development of the atomic bomb in 1945. Britain's wartime leader, Winston Churchill, had long feared communist aggression; it was he who in 1946 coined the phrase **iron curtain** to describe the division between free and repressed societies that he saw taking shape in Europe. But Britain frankly lacked the power to resist Soviet pressure, and under the Labour government it explicitly left the initiative to the United States.

The United States responded to Soviet rivalry with vigor. It criticized Soviet policies and denied Soviet applications for reconstruction loans. It bolstered regimes in Iran, Turkey, and Greece that were under Soviet pressure. Then in 1947 the United States proclaimed its **Marshall Plan**, designed to provide loans to help Western nations rebuild from the war's devastation. In Soviet eyes the Marshall Plan was a vehicle for U.S. economic dominance, and indeed there is little question that in addition to humanitarian motives the United States intended to beat back domestic communist movements in countries such as France and Italy by promoting economic growth.

The focal point of the cold war in these early years was Germany: The question of what to do about Germany, which had played such a great role in European affairs since 1870, took a new form. After 1944 the nation was divided into four zones administered by the United States, Britain, France, and the Soviet Union (Map 32.2). Soviet policy in Germany initially concentrated on seizing goods and factories as reparation. The Western Allies soon prevented Soviet intervention in their own zones and turned to some rebuilding efforts in the interests of playing a modest "German card" against growing Soviet strength in the East. That is, although the West, led by the United States, did not intend to resurrect a powerful Germany, it soon began to think in terms of constructing a

MAP 32.1 Soviet and Eastern European Boundaries by 1948 The new communist empire was joined in the Warsaw Pact, formed to respond to the West's North Atlantic Treaty Organization (itself formed in response to a perceived communist threat).

viable political and economic entity. Allied collaboration started building a unified West Germany in 1946, and local political structures followed by more national ones were established through elections. When in 1947 the West moved to promote German economic recovery by creating a stable currency, the Soviet Union responded by blockading the city of Berlin, the divided former capital that sat in the midst of the Soviet zone. The United States responded with a massive airlift to keep the city supplied, and the crisis finally ended in 1948, with two separate Germanies—East and West—beginning to take clear shape along a tense, heavily fortified frontier.

Cold war divisions spread from Germany to Europe more generally with the formation of two rival military alliances. The **North Atlantic Treaty Organization (NATO)** was formed in 1949, under U.S. leadership, to group most of the western European powers and Canada in a defensive alliance against possible Soviet aggression. The NATO pact soon legitimated some rearmament of West Germany in the context of resistance to communism, as well as the continued maintenance of a substantial U.S. military presence in Germany and in other member nations. In response, the Soviet Union organized the **Warsaw Pact** among its eastern European satellites. When in 1949 the Soviets developed their own nuclear capability, the world—particularly the European world—seemed indeed divided between two rival camps, each in turn dominated by its own superpower. Numerous U.S. and Soviet military units were permanently stationed in Europe on either side of the cold war divide.

The cold war had a number of implications for western Europe. It brought new influences from the United States on internal as well as foreign policy. Through the 1950s and beyond, the United States pressed for acceptance of German rearmament (although under some agreed-on limits); it lobbied for higher military expenditures in its old allies France and Britain; and it pressed for acceptance of U.S. forces and weapons systems. The Americans' wishes were not always met, but the United States had vital negotiating leverage in the economic aid it offered (and might withdraw), in the troops it stationed in Europe, and in the nuclear "umbrella" it developed (and might, in theory, also withdraw). Nuclear weapons seemed to offer the only realistic protection should the Soviet Union venture direct attack. The Soviets, for their part, influenced western Europe not only through perceived aggressive intent but also by funding and supporting substantial communist movements in France and Italy, which in turn affected but did not overwhelm the political process.

The cold war did not maintain within Europe the intensity it reached in the initial years. Centers of conflict shifted in part outside Europe as Korea, then Vietnam, and recurrently the Middle East became centers of tension. After 1958 France became more and more restless under what it viewed as Anglo-U.S. dominance of NATO, and it finally withdrew its forces from the joint NATO command, requiring also that U.S. troops leave French soil. In the 1970s Germany opened new negotiations with the Soviet Union and eastern bloc countries, wanting increased export opportunities and lower diplomatic tension. Nevertheless, the cold war and the resultant alliance system continued to describe much of the framework of East–West relations in Europe and elsewhere in the world.

The shifting balance between the United States and Europe produced a crisscrossing of military relationships, whatever the larger implications of the shift. As western Europe abandoned military preeminence, the United States, never before a major peacetime military power, devoted growing resources to its military capacity and gave an increasing voice to its military leaders. Regardless of the political party in power, the percentage of the U.S. government budget going to the military remained stable from the 1950s to the 1980s—when it went up as a new American president put greater pressure on the Soviet Union. In contrast, some European leaders boasted that their societies had made a transition toward preeminence of civilian values and goals. Although U.S. and European values and institutions became more similar in key respects after World War II, the difference in military roles signaled ongoing distinctions within Western society.

MAP 32.2 **Germany After World War II** Initial divisions of Germany and Berlin into occupied zones turned into a division between western and Soviet regimes.

Marshall Plan Program of substantial loans initiated by the United States in 1947; designed to aid Western nations in rebuilding from the war's devastation; vehicle for American economic dominance.

North Atlantic Treaty Organization (NATO) Created in 1949 under U.S. leadership to group most of the western European powers plus Canada in a defensive alliance against possible Soviet aggression.

Warsaw Pact Alliance organized by Soviet Union with its eastern European satellites to balance formation of NATO by Western powers in 1949.

THE RESURGENCE OF WESTERN EUROPE

Western Europeans introduced striking innovations in politics and the economy, sustaining a strong global role. Strides toward European unity cut through traditional enmities.

32.2 What were the main changes in western Europe, compared to patterns during the 1920s and 1930s?

A new set of leaders emerged in many European countries, some from wartime resistance movements against Nazi occupation, eager to avoid the mistakes that had led to economic depression and war. Their vision was not always realized, but from 1945 onward, western Europe did move forward on three important fronts: the extension of democratic political systems, a modification of nation-state rivalries within Europe, and a commitment to rapid economic growth that reduced previous social and gender tensions.

The Spread of Liberal Democracy

In politics, defeat in war greatly discredited fascism and other rightist movements that had opposed parliamentary democracy. Several new political movements surfaced in western Europe, notably an important Christian Democratic current, which was wedded to democratic institutions and moderate social reform. Communist as well as socialist leaders largely accepted democratic procedures. Western Europe experienced a shift in the political spectrum toward fuller support for democratic constitutions and greater agreement on the need for government planning and welfare activities.

New regimes had to be constructed in Germany and Italy after the defeat of fascist and Nazi leadership. France established a new republic once occupation ended. In Germany, political reconstruction was delayed by the division of the nation by the victorious Allies. As the cold war took shape, however, France, Britain, and the United States progressively merged their zones into what became the Federal Republic of Germany (West Germany), encouraging a new constitution that would avoid the mistakes of Germany's earlier Weimar Republic by outlawing extremist political movements. Italy established a constitutional democracy. Women's voting rights spread throughout the region as well.

Western Europe's movement toward more consistent democracy continued in the 1970s, when Spain and Portugal moved from their authoritarian, semifascist constitutions (following the deaths of longtime strongmen) to democratic, parliamentary systems. Greece, increasingly linked to the West, followed the same pattern. By the 1980s western Europe had become more politically uniform than ever before in history.

The Welfare State

welfare state New activism of the western European state in economic policy and welfare issues after World War II; introduced programs to reduce the impact of economic inequality; typically included medical programs and economic planning.

The consolidation of democracy also entailed a general movement toward a **welfare state**. Wartime resistance ideas and the shift leftward of the political spectrum helped explain the new activism of the state in economic policy and welfare issues. Wartime planning in the British government had pointed to the need for new programs to reduce the impact of economic inequality and to reward the lower classes for their loyalty (Figure 32.2). Not surprisingly, the governments that emerged at the war's end—Britain's Labour party and the Communist-Socialist-Christian Democrat coalitions in France and Italy—quickly moved to set up a new government apparatus that would play a vigorous role in economic planning and develop new social activities. By 1948 the basic nature of the modern welfare state had been established throughout western Europe, as not only the new regimes but also established reformists (as in Scandinavia) extended a variety of government programs. The United States, although somewhat more tentative in welfare measures, added to its New Deal legislation through President Lyndon Johnson's Great Society programs in the 1960s, creating medical assistance packages for the poor and the elderly. Canada enacted an even more comprehensive medical insurance plan.

The welfare state elaborated a host of social insurance measures. Unemployment insurance was improved. Medical care was supported by state-funded insurance or, as in Britain where it became a centerpiece to the new Labour program, the basic healthcare system was nationalized. State-run medical facilities provided free care to the bulk of the British population from 1947 onward, although some small fees were later introduced. Family assistance was another category, not entirely new, that was now greatly expanded. All western European governments provided payments to families with

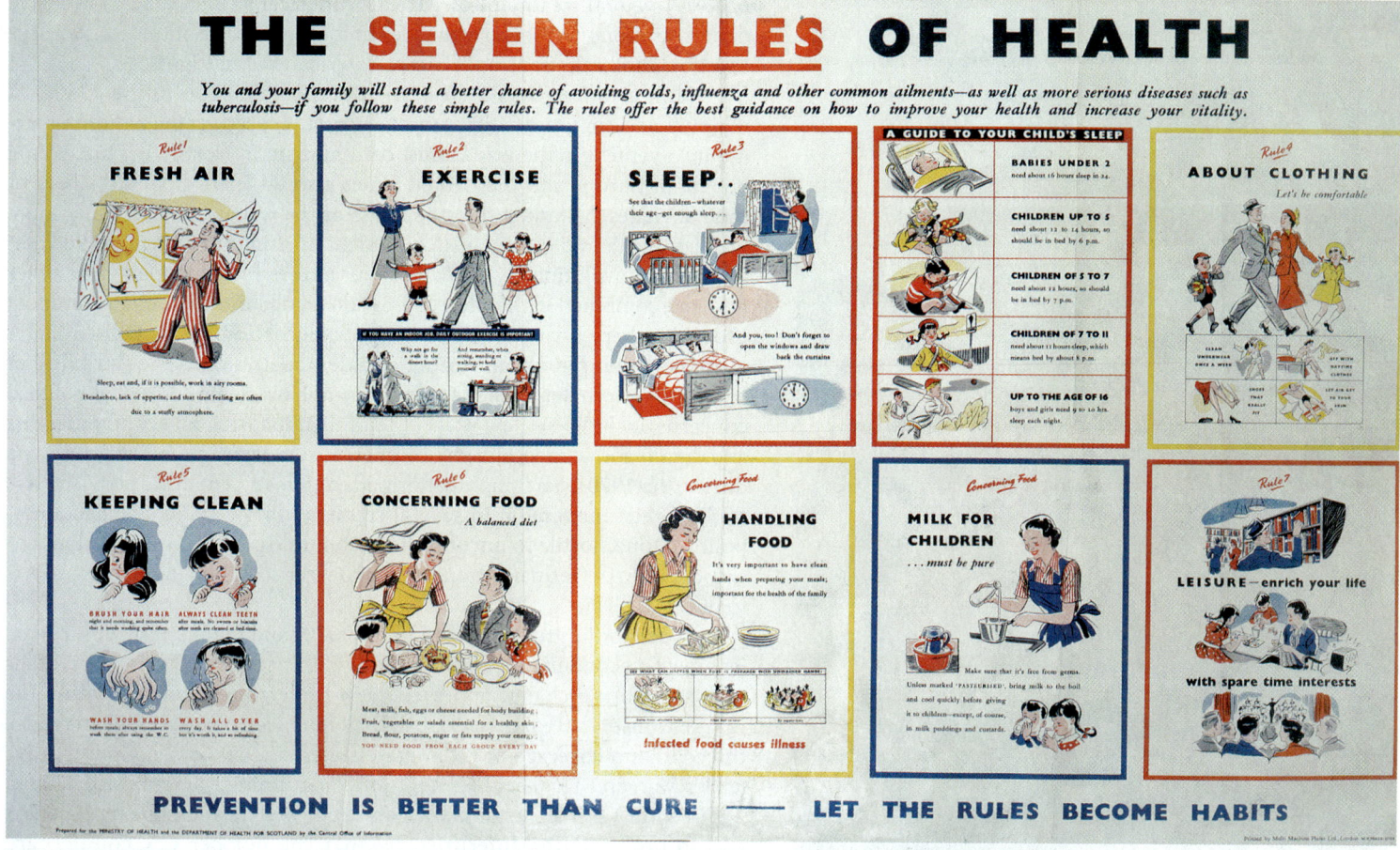

FIGURE 32.2 This poster, published by the British Ministry of Health during the 1950s, was intended to increase public awareness of good health practices. Campaigns like these were part of a major shift in thinking about the role of government in Western societies: After World War II, most western European nations established "welfare states," intended to provide social services and economic assistance for citizens "from the cradle to the grave."

several children, the amount increasing with family size. In the 1950s a French worker family with low earnings and five children could improve its income by as much as 40 percent through family aid. Governments also became more active in the housing field—a virtual necessity, given wartime destruction and postwar population growth. By the 1950s over one-fourth of the British population was housed in structures built and run by the government. The welfare state cushioned citizens against major expenses and unusual hardships, although it did not rearrange overall social structure.

The welfare state was undeniably expensive. It greatly enlarged government bureaucracies, in addition to channeling tax monies to new purposes. A new breed of bureaucrat, often called a **technocrat** because of intense training in engineering or economics and because of a devotion to the power of national planning, came to the fore in government offices. By the 1950s up to 25 percent of the gross national product of France and Holland was going to welfare purposes, and the figure tended to rise with time. As military expenses began to stabilize, welfare commitments became far and away the largest component of Western government budgets outside the United States. Here was a clear indication of the extent to which the western European state had altered its relationship to the wider society.

technocrat New type of bureaucrat; intensely trained in engineering or economics and devoted to the power of national planning; came to fore in offices of governments following World War II.

New Challenges to Political Stability

The Western pattern of political compromise around the mechanisms of parliamentary democracy and the welfare state were severely jolted by a series of student protests that developed in the late 1960s. Even before this, in the United States a vigorous civil rights movement had developed to

📖 Read the Document on MyHistoryLab: John Lewis, Address at the March on Washington (1963)

FIGURE 32.3 The great civil rights rally drew more than 250,000 people to Washington, DC, in August 1963. The large numbers and high feelings expected at this rally caused much worry about civil unrest—liquor sales were suspended, thousands of troops were put on alert, police were brought in from other cities, and the public address system was set up so that government officials could shut it down if they thought it necessary—but the day was entirely peaceful.

Green movement Political parties, especially in Europe, focusing on environmental issues and control over economic growth.

European Union Began as European Economic Community (or Common Market), an alliance of Germany, France, Italy, Belgium, Luxembourg, and the Netherlands to create a single economic entity across national boundaries in 1958; later joined by Britain, Ireland, Denmark, Greece, Spain, Portugal, Sweden, Austria, Finland, and other nations for further European economic integration.

protest unequal treatment of African Americans (Figure 32.3). Massive demonstrations, particularly in cities in the American South, attacked segregation and limitations on African American voting rights.

Campus unrest was a Western-wide phenomenon in the 1960s. At major American universities, campus unrest focused on the nation's growing involvement in the war against communism in North Vietnam. Young people in Europe and the United States also targeted the materialism of their societies, including the stodginess of the welfare state, seeking more idealistic goals and greater justice. Student uprisings in France in 1968 created a near revolution. By the early 1970s new rights for students and other reforms, combined with police repression, ended the most intense student protests, whereas passage of civil rights legislation in the United States ultimately reduced urban rioting and demonstrations. The flexibility of postwar Western democracy seemed triumphant. Some additional political concerns, including a new wave of feminism focusing on economic rights and dignity for women, and environmentalist movements entered the arena during the 1970s, partly as an aftermath of the student explosion. The rise of the **Green movement** in several countries in the 1970s signaled a new political tone, hostile to uncontrolled economic growth. Green parliamentary deputies in Germany even refused to wear coats and ties in their efforts to defy established political habits.

As economic growth slowed in the 1970s and the Western world faced its greatest economic recession since the immediate postwar years, other signs of political change appeared. New leadership sprang up within the British Conservative party and the U.S. Republican party, seeking to reduce the costs and coverage of the welfare state. In 1979 British Conservative leader Margaret Thatcher began the longest-running prime-ministership in 20th-century British history, working to cut welfare and housing expenses and to promote free enterprise. Neither she nor her U.S. counterpart, Ronald Reagan, fully dismantled the welfare state, but they did reduce its impact. Despite important adjustments, however, the main line of postwar government in the West persisted into the 21st century.

Toward Greater European Unity

Along with the extension of democracy and the development of the welfare state, the West showed postwar vigor in addressing some traditional diplomatic problems, notably recurrent nationalistic rivalry, as well as specific manifestations, such as French–German enmity. U.S. guidance combined with innovative thinking in the new European governments.

During the war, many resistance leaders had tempered their hatred of Nazism with a plea for a reconstruction of the European spirit. The Christian Democratic movement, particularly, produced important new advocates of harmony among European nations. By 1947 U.S. leaders were also eager to spur western Europe's economic recovery, for which they judged coordination across national boundaries an essential precondition. Thus the Marshall Plan required discussion of tariffs and other development issues among recipient nations. With simultaneous U.S. insistence on the partial rearmament of West Germany and West German participation in NATO, the framework for diplomatic reform was complete.

Faced with these pressures and aware of the failure of nationalistic policies between the wars, France initiated coordination with Germany as a means of setting up a new Europe. The nations of the Low Countries and Italy were soon linked in these activities. The idea was to tie German economic activity to an international framework so that the nation's growing strength would not again threaten European peace. Institutions were established to link policies in heavy industry and later to develop atomic power. A measure to establish a united European military force proved too ambitious and collapsed under nationalist objections. But in 1957 the six western European nations (West Germany, France, Italy, Belgium, Luxembourg, and the Netherlands) set up the European Economic Community, or Common Market—later called the **European Union**—to begin to create a single economic entity

Read the Document on MyHistoryLab: A Common Market and European Integration (1960)

MAP 32.3 **The European Union** The Union, originally called the Common Market, expanded notably from its 1957 origins, particularly after the end of the cold war.

across national political boundaries (Map 32.3). Tariffs were progressively reduced among the member nations, and a common tariff policy was set for the outside world. Free movement of labor and investment was encouraged. A Common Market bureaucracy was established, ultimately in Brussels, to oversee these operations. The Common Market set up a court system to adjudicate disputes and prevent violations of coordination rules; it also administered a development fund to spur economic growth in such laggard regions as southern Italy and western France.

THINKING HISTORICALLY

The United States and Western Europe: Convergence and Complexity

THE RELATIONSHIP BETWEEN THE UNITED STATES and western Europe has been important both historically and analytically for at least two centuries. Many people in the United States have tried to establish a distinctive identity while acknowledging special relationships with Europe; isolationism was one response earlier in this century. Europeans, for their part, have groped for definition of their U.S. "cousins," particularly as U.S. military and cultural influence grew in the 20th century. Were U.S. innovations to be welcomed, as stemming from a kindred society with a special flair for technology and modern mass taste, or should they be resisted as emblems of a superficial, degenerate, and essentially un-European society? Comparison is vital to understand both societies.

The relationship between the United States and western Europe has not been constant. Over time, and particularly since 1945, U.S. and European societies have in many important respects converged. Because of heightened imitation and shared advanced industrial economies, some earlier differences have receded.

Western Europe, for example, no longer has a very distinct peasantry. Its farmers, although smaller scale than their U.S. agribusiness counterparts, are commercialized and simply so few in numbers that they no longer set their society apart. European workers, although less likely than those in the United States to call themselves middle class, are now relatively prosperous. They have moved away from some of the political radicalism that differentiated them from their U.S. counterparts earlier in the 20th century. Europe does not have as deep-seated a racial issue as the United States inherited from slavery, but the growing influx of people from the West Indies, north Africa, and Asia has duplicated in Europe some of the same racial tensions and inner-city problems that bedevil the United States. At the other end of the social scale, trained managers and professionals now form a similar upper class in both societies, the fruit of systems of higher education that differ in particulars but resemble each other in producing something of a meritocratic elite.

A shared popular culture has certainly emerged. Although it stemmed mainly from U.S. innovations before World War II, more recently it has involved mutual borrowing. The United States, for example, embraced miniskirts and rock groups from Britain in the 1960s, and not only British but also French youth raced to buy the latest style in blue jeans.

Differences remain, some of them going back to earlier historical traditions. The United States has relied more fully on free-market capitalism than did western Europe, with the United States possessing less complete planning, fewer environmental regulations, and a more modest welfare apparatus. The difference was heightened during the 1990s. The United States proved much more religious than did western Europe. Only a minority of people in most western European countries professed religious belief by the 1990s, with less than 10 percent in most cases attending church with any regularity. In contrast the United States remains highly religious, with up to 40 percent regular church attendance, and 70 to 80 percent of its people professing religious belief. The United States made a less complete conversion to a new leisure ethic after World War II than did western Europe; European vacation time advanced toward more than a month a year, whereas the average in the United States remained two weeks or less. Europeans were franker about teenage sexuality, following the 1960 sexual revolution. They distributed birth control materials to adolescents much more commonly than did their more prudish U.S. counterparts, reducing rates of teenage pregnancy in the process.

> [T]he United States constituted a more traditional society, in terms of values, in the later 20th century than did western Europe.

In certain important respects, then, the United States constituted a more traditional society, in terms of values, in the later 20th century than did western Europe. Some of the variation between the two societies related to long-established distinctions (as in the degree of suspicion of government power); others emerged for the first time, sometimes surprisingly, after World War II.

The biggest distinctions between the two societies in recent decades, however, followed from their increasingly divergent world roles. Western Europe, although still highly influential in culture and trade on a global scale, concentrated increasingly on its own regional arrangements, including the European Union trading bloc, and decreasingly on military development. The United States moved in the opposite direction. Thus a traditional distinction was reversed; the United States became the more military (and some would argue militaristic) society, and many Europeans became committed to more strictly civilian goals.

QUESTIONS
- Why did the United States and western Europe converge in new ways during the 20th century?
- Do the two societies remain part of a common civilization?
- What are the most important issues to resolve in making this judgment?

The Common Market did not move quickly toward a single government. Important national disputes limited the organization's further growth. France and Germany, for example, routinely quarreled over agricultural policy, with France seeking more payments to farmers as a matter of obvious self-interest. But although the European Union did not turn into full integration, on the whole it contributed to economic growth. It even established an advisory international parliament, ultimately elected by direct vote. Further, in the 1980s firm arrangements were made to dismantle all trade and currency exchange barriers among member states in 1992, creating essentially complete economic unity. A single currency, the euro, was set up in many member countries by 2001. The European Union's success expanded its hold within western Europe. After long hesitations Britain, despite its tradition of proud island independence, decided to join, as did Ireland, Denmark, and later Greece, Spain, Portugal, Austria, Sweden, and Finland. By 2005 nine other nations, mostly in central Europe, were admitted to membership.

Nationalist tensions within Europe receded to a lower point than ever before in modern European history. After the worst scares of the cold war, focused mainly on the division between communist East and semicapitalist West, Europe became a diplomatically placid continent, enjoying one of the longest periods of substantial internal peace in its history.

Economic Expansion

After a surprisingly short, if agonizing, postwar rebuilding, striking economic growth accompanied political and diplomatic change. The welfare state and the European Union may have encouraged this growth by improving purchasing power for the masses and facilitating market expansion across national boundaries; certainly economic growth encouraged the success of new political and diplomatic systems.

There was no question that by the mid-1950s western Europe had entered a new economic phase. Agricultural production and productivity increased rapidly as peasant farmers, backed by technocrats, adopted new equipment and seeds. European agriculture was still less efficient than that of North America, which necessitated some much-resented tariff barriers by the Common Market. But food production easily met European needs, often with some to spare for export. Retooled industries poured out textiles and metallurgical products. Expensive consumer products, such as automobiles and appliances, supported rapidly growing factories. Western Europe also remained a leading center of weapons production, trailing only the United States and the Soviet Union in exports. Overall growth in gross national product surpassed the rates of any extended period since the Industrial Revolution began; it also surpassed the growth rates of the U.S. economy during the 1950s and 1960s.

By this point French, German, and Italian economies were growing between 6 percent and 11 percent annually. These growth rates depended on rapid technological change. Europe's rising food production was achieved with a steadily shrinking agricultural labor force. France's peasant population—16 percent of the labor force in the early 1950s—fell to 10 percent two decades later, but overall output was much higher than before. During the 1950s the industrial workforce grew as part of factory expansion, but by the 1960s the relative proportion of factory workers also began to drop, despite rising production. Workers in the service sector, filling functions as teachers, clerks, medical personnel, insurance and bank workers, and performers and other "leisure industry" personnel, rose rapidly in contrast. In France half of all paid workers were in the service sector by 1968, and the proportion rose steadily thereafter.

Another key change involved immigration. Many parts of the continent experienced a labor shortage and had to seek hundreds of thousands of workers from other areas—first from southern Europe, then, as this region industrialized, from Africa, the Middle East, and parts of Asia. The rise of immigrant minorities was a vital development in western Europe and also the United States, where the influx of Asian and Latin American

Read the Document on MyHistoryLab: The Teenage Consumer, *Life* (1959)

FIGURE 32.4 In the United States, as well as in Japan and western Europe, advertisements increasingly tried to create the sense that a good life could be achieved by buying the right goods. Here, a new car was associated with a prosperous home, a loving family, and even happy pets.

immigrants stepped up markedly. By 2000, countries like France had Muslim minorities of up to 10 percent of the population while in the United States Latinos became the largest ethnic minority.

Unprecedented economic growth and low unemployment meant unprecedented improvements in incomes, even with the taxation necessary to sustain welfare programs. New spending money rapidly translated into huge increases in the purchase of durable consumer goods, as virtually the whole of Western civilization became an "affluent society."

Ownership of standard consumer goods like televisions and cars spread widely. Shopping malls and supermarkets migrated across the Atlantic. Advertising was not quite as ubiquitous in Europe as in the United States. But promptings to buy, to smell good, to look right, to express one's personality in the latest car style began quickly to describe European life (Figure 32.4). The frenzy to find good vacation spots grew intense. Millions of Germans poured annually into Italy and Spain, seeking the sun. Britons thronged to Spanish beaches. Europeans were bent on combining efficient work with indulgent leisure.

The West's economic advance was not without some dark spots. Many immigrant workers from Turkey, north Africa, Pakistan, and the West Indies suffered very low wages and unstable employment. These immigrants, euphemistically labeled "guest workers," were often residentially segregated and victims of discrimination by employers and police.

By the 1990s slower economic growth raised new unemployment problems in western Europe. Economic inequality increased throughout the West, although particularly in the United States. Nevertheless, the West's economic vitality, a marked contrast to the interwar decades, underpinned vital social transformations and played a major role in the global economic framework as well.

COLD WAR ALLIES: THE UNITED STATES, CANADA, AUSTRALIA, AND NEW ZEALAND

32.3 How did postwar developments in the United States compare to those in western Europe?

> Many changes in the non-European West paralleled those in Europe, including the welfare state. The United States took a distinctive role, particularly because of its new position as a military superpower.

Developments in the so-called overseas West in many ways paralleled those in western Europe, but without the sense of grappling with prior collapse. The sheer level of innovation in domestic policy was less great, in part because the crises of the first half of the 20th century had been less severe. Crucial adjustments occurred, however, in foreign policy. The United States led the way in making the changes in its own tradition that were necessary to develop a massive peacetime military force and a global set of alliances. With the decline of European, and particularly British, international power and the emergence of the cold war context, Australia, New Zealand, and Canada tightened their links with the United States and developed new contacts with other areas of the world.

The Former Dominions

Canada forged ahead in welfare policies after World War II, establishing a greater stake in economic planning and state-run medical insurance than did the United States. At the same time, however, Canadian economic integration with the United States continued, with U.S. investments in Canadian resources and mutual exports and imports soaring steadily into the 1970s. By 1980 the Canadian government took some measures to limit further U.S. penetration, and a sense of Canadian nationalism sparked resentment of the giant to the south. In 1988, however, the two nations signed a free-trade agreement, creating a North American trading bloc at a time when European unity was increasing rapidly.

Continued emigration to Canada pointed in new directions also, with growing numbers of people arriving from various parts of Asia. Canada's most distinctive issue, however, involved growing agitation by French Canadians in Quebec for regional autonomy or even national independence. A new separatist party, founded in 1967, took control of the provincial government during the 1970s. Subsequent legislation limited the use of the English language in Quebec's public and commercial life, although referendums for full independence failed during the 1980s. A new Canadian constitution in

1982, however, granted greater voice to the provinces, both to counter French Canadian demand and also to recognize the growing economic strength of the resource-rich western provinces. Separatist tensions continue to simmer, however, into the 21st century.

From 1945 onward Australia and New Zealand moved steadily away from their traditional alignment with Great Britain and toward horizons around the Pacific. The two commonwealths joined a mutual defense pact with the United States in 1951, directed against potential communist aggression in the Pacific. Both nations cooperated with the United States in the Korean War, and Australia backed U.S. intervention in Vietnam. In 1966 the Australian prime minister declared, "Wherever the United States is resisting aggression . . . we will go a-waltzing Matilda with you." In the later 1970s and 1980s Australia and especially New Zealand began to distance themselves somewhat from U.S. foreign policy. New Zealand barred U.S. nuclear-armed vessels in 1985.

Economically, Australian and New Zealand exports were increasingly directed toward other Pacific nations, notably Japan and later China, with investment capital coming mainly from the United States and Japan. Indeed, Australia became Japan's chief raw-materials supplier aside from oil. Asian emigration also increasingly altered the population mix, again particularly in Australia. The Australian government had to back down from a long-held whites-only immigration policy, permitting growing regional emigration, particularly from Indochina. By 1983 Asians accounted for 60 percent of the total immigrant population in Australia.

The "U.S. Century"?

Amid a host of domestic issues, the big news in U.S. history after 1945 was its assumption—in many ways, its eager assumption—of the superpower mantle, opposing the Soviet Union and serving as the world's leading defender of democratic and capitalistic values. The United States hesitated briefly after 1945, demobilizing its World War II forces rather quickly with some hope that world peace would provide some respite from further international engagement. However, Great Britain's inability to continue to police the world for the West, together with rapid Soviet successes in installing communist governments in eastern Europe, prompted a decisive U.S. stance. In 1947 President Harry Truman promised support for "free peoples who are resisting subjugation by armed minorities or by outside pressures." The doctrine was specifically directed against communist pressures on Greece and Turkey. It was soon extended into the elaboration of Marshall Plan aid to rebuild the economies of western Europe against the possibility of communist subversion in these war-torn countries.

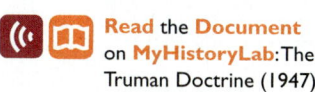

Read the Document on MyHistoryLab: The Truman Doctrine (1947)

The plunge into the cold war took a toll on the home front. The United States entered a period of intense, even frenzied concern about internal communist conspiracies, ferreting out a host of suspected spies and subjecting people in many fields to dismissal from their jobs on grounds of suspected radical sympathies.

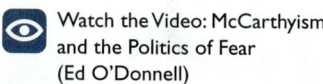

Watch the Video: McCarthyism and the Politics of Fear (Ed O'Donnell)

Cold war engagement prompted other policy changes in the federal government. The Defense Department was set up in 1947 to coordinate military policy, and the Central Intelligence Agency was established to organize a worldwide information-gathering and espionage network. Military spending increased considerably, with the formation of the Strategic Air Command to stand in constant readiness in case of a Soviet bombing attack. A massive U.S. airlift thwarted Soviet pressure on the western sectors of occupied Berlin. The United States resisted the invasion of South Korea by the communist North, beginning in the 1950s; U.S. troops stationed in Japan were sent in to support the South Koreans. Under General Douglas MacArthur and backed by several allies under a hastily arranged United Nations mandate, the North Korean invasion was repulsed within a few months. The United States then authorized an invasion into North Korea, which brought a retaliatory intervention from communist China. The United States was pushed back, and more than two years of additional fighting ensued before peace was negotiated in 1953—with the new boundary line between the two Koreas relatively close to the previous line. In the meantime annual U.S. spending on the military had increased from $13.5 billion to $50 billion.

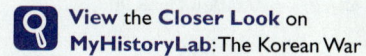

View the Closer Look on MyHistoryLab: The Korean War

During the 1950s, under the presidency of Dwight Eisenhower, the United States settled into a policy of containment of the Soviet Union, which involved maintenance of large peacetime military forces. The United States also arranged alliances not only with western Europe, in NATO, but also with Australia and New Zealand, with several southeast Asian nations, and with several nations in the Middle East; this alliance system virtually surrounded the Soviet Union. Less novel was recurrent U.S. intervention in Central America against suspected communist movements; thus U.S. aid toppled a new Guatemalan government in 1954. The United States was unable to prevent a takeover in Cuba that propelled Cuba into the communist camp, despite a U.S.-backed invasion attempt by anticommunist Cuban rebels. Nonetheless, the United States maintained its policy of vigilance (under President John Kennedy in 1962) by forcing the Soviet Union to withdraw its missile sites on the island.

The U.S. containment policy yielded a final test that took shape during the 1960s, when intervention against communist revolutionaries in South Vietnam gradually escalated. The U.S. Air Force began bombing communist North Vietnam in 1965. Later that year American troops were sent in, reaching a total of 550,000 by 1968. By this time the United States was spending $2 billion a week on a war that never produced convincing success and gradually bogged down in horrendous bloodshed on both sides. By 1970 more bombs had been dropped on Vietnam than had been dropped by anyone, anywhere previously in the 20th century. By 1968 domestic pressure against the war, centered particularly on U.S. college campuses, began to force changes in strategy. A new U.S. president, Richard Nixon, tried to expand the war to other parts of Indochina, to increase pressure on North Vietnam. Simultaneously, peace negotiations with North Vietnam were launched, resulting finally in an agreement on a cease-fire, in 1973. By 1975, as the United States speedily withdrew, all Vietnam lay in communist hands.

View the **Closer Look** on MyHistoryLab: October 1967 March on the Pentagon

Furor over the Vietnam War led to agonizing policy reassessments in the United States. Some observers judged that new directions might be forged, as the United States had discovered that its massive military might could be stalemated by fervent guerrilla tactics. Both the U.S. military and the public grew more wary of regional wars. Although the national mood sobered, decisive policy changes did not ensue. A socialist government in Chile, for example, was ousted with the aid of covert U.S. pressure even as the Vietnam conflict wound down. The socialist government was replaced by a brutal military regime.

In 1980 the United States overwhelmingly elected a new president, Ronald Reagan, who combined conservative domestic policies with a commitment to bolster military spending and make sure that the United States would "ride tall" again in world affairs. The 1980s saw no major new international involvements, but several punitive raids were conducted against suspected terrorists in the Middle East, and the small West Indian island of Grenada was invaded to topple a leftist regime. President Reagan sponsored a number of expensive new weapons systems, which helped press an afflicted Soviet economy to virtual collapse as its leaders attempted to keep pace. The next president, George Bush, continued an interventionist policy by sending U.S. troops into Panama to evict and arrest an abrasive dictator and then by spearheading a Western and moderate Arab alliance against Iraq's invasion of Kuwait, during 1990–1991. Under President Bill Clinton, the United States led participation in military action against forces in the Balkans in the 1990s.

By this point, with the cold war over, the United States emerged as "the world's only superpower." Its annual military spending outstripped that of the next 20 nations combined. This unrivaled military power enabled it to take over and expand many of the international policing functions once held by Western nations like Britain. Other Western states sometimes resented American leadership, but they generated no clear alternative and usually supported U.S. initiatives.

CULTURE AND SOCIETY IN THE WEST

The expansion of consumer culture marked recent Western history. Dramatic changes in gender relations also defined Western society.

32.4 What caused the changes in the roles and motivations of women in Western Europe and the United States?

Political and economic changes in Western society progressively altered the contours of earlier industrial development. The West became the first example of an advanced industrial society, especially from the 1950s onward, and both the United States and western Europe shared in leading facets of change.

Social Structure

Economic growth, bringing increasing prosperity to most groups, eased some earlier social conflicts throughout the West. Workers were still propertyless, but they had substantial holdings as consumers, and their sense of social inferiority often declined as a result. Social lines were also blurred by increasing social mobility, as educational opportunities opened further and the size of the white-collar sector expanded. Much unskilled labor was left to immigrants. Economic and political change also altered conditions for western Europe's peasantry, and not only by cutting its size. Peasants became increasingly commercial, eager for improvements in standards of living, and participants, through car trips and television, in urban culture. They also became more attuned to bureaucracies, as state regulations pushed them into cooperative organizations.

Social distinctions remained. Middle-class people had more abundant leisure opportunities and a more optimistic outlook than did most workers. Signs of tension continued. Crime rates went up throughout Western society after the 1940s, although the levels were particularly high in the United States. Race riots punctuated U.S. life in the 1950s and 1960s and exploded in immigrant sections of British cities in the 1980s and Germany in the early 1990s.

The Women's Revolution

A key facet of postwar change involved women and the family, and again both western Europe and the United States participated fully in this upheaval. Although family ideals persisted in many ways—with workers, for example, urging that "a loving family is the finest thing, something to work for, to look to and to look after"—the realities of family life changed in many ways. Family leisure activities expanded. Extended-family contacts were facilitated by telephones and automobiles. More years of schooling increased the importance of peer groups for children, and the authority of parents undoubtedly declined.

The clearest innovation in family life came through the new working patterns of women. World War II brought increased factory and clerical jobs for women, as the earlier world war had done. After a few years of downward adjustment, the trends continued. From the early 1950s onward, the number of working women, particularly married women, rose steadily in western Europe, the United States, and Canada. (See Visualizing the Past feature.) Women's earlier educational gains had improved their work qualifications; the growing number of service jobs created a need for additional workers—and women, long associated with clerical jobs and paid less than men, were ideal candidates. Many women also sought entry into the labor force as a means of adding to personal or family income, to afford some of the consumer items now becoming feasible but not yet easy to buy, or as a means of personal fulfillment in a society that associated worth with work and earnings.

The growing employment of women, which by the 1970s brought the female segment of the labor force up to 44 percent of the total in most Western countries, represented particularly the employment of adult women, most of them married and many with children. Teenage employment dropped as more girls stayed in school, but long-term work commitments rose steadily. This was not, to be sure, a full stride to job equality. Women's pay lagged behind men's pay. Most women were concentrated in clerical jobs rather than spread through the occupational spectrum, despite a growing minority of middle-class women entering professional and management ranks. Clearly, however, the trends of the 19th-century Industrial Revolution, to keep women and family separate from work outside the home, had yielded to a dramatic new pattern.

Other new rights for women accompanied this shift. Where women had lacked the vote before, as in France, they now got it; of the western European nations, only Switzerland doggedly refused this concession at the national level until 1971. Gains in higher education were considerable, although again full equality remained elusive. Women constituted 23 percent of German university students in 1963, and under socialist governments in the 1970s the figure rose. Preferred subjects, however, remained different from those of men, as most women stayed out of engineering, science (except medicine), and management.

Family rights improved, at least in the judgment of most women's advocates. Access to divorce increased, which many observers viewed as particularly important to women. Abortion law eased, although more slowly in countries of Catholic background than in Britain or Scandinavia; it became increasingly easy for women to regulate their birth rate. Development of new birth control methods, such as the contraceptive pill introduced in 1960, as well as growing knowledge and acceptability of birth control, decreased unwanted pregnancies. Sex and procreation became increasingly separate considerations. Although women continued to differ from men in sexual outlook and behavior—more than twice as many French women as men, for example, hoped to link sex, marriage, and romantic love, according to 1960s polls—more women than before tended to define sex in terms of pleasure.

VISUALIZING THE PAST

Women at Work in France and the United States

A STATISTICAL TABLE OF THE SORT presented here is essentially descriptive. Several questions help elicit clearer meaning. What patterns are described? Is there a major change, and how can it be defined? What are the main differences between these two nations? Were they converging, becoming more similar, in 1962? In 1982? Do they end up in a similar situation with regard to women's work roles, or are they more different in 1982 than they were in 1946?

> **QUESTIONS**
> - From description, questions of causation arise. Statistical patterns provide a precise framework for a challenging analysis. Why were the United States and France so different in 1946?
> - What might have caused the changes in patterns (for example, in the United States during the 1950s)?
> - What was the role of new feminist demands in 1963?
> - What might have caused the differences in the timing of trends in France and the United States?

WOMEN AT WORK: THE FEMALE LABOR FORCE IN FRANCE AND THE UNITED STATES

	France		United States	
	Women Workers (thousands)	Percentage of Total Force	Woman Workers (thousands)	Percentage of Total Force
1946	7,880	37.90	16,840	27.83
1954	6,536	33.93	19,718	29.43
1962	6,478	33.23	24,047	32.74
1968	6,924	34.62	29,242	35.54
1975	7,675	36.48	37,553	39.34
1982	8,473	39.46	47,894	42.81

SOURCES: B. R. Mitchell, *International Historical Statistics: Europe, 1750–1988*; U.S. Bureau of the Census, *Historical Statistics of the United States, Colonial Times to 1970, Bicentennial Edition, Part 1*; U.S. Bureau of the Census, *Statistical Abstract of the United States: 1984*.

Predictably, of course, changes in the family, including the roles of women, brought new issues and redefined ideals of companionship. The first issue involved children. A brief increase in the Western birth rate ended in the early 1960s and a rapid decline ensued. Women's work and the desire to use income for high consumer standards mitigated against children, or very many children, particularly in the middle class, where birth rates were lowest. Those children born were increasingly sent, often at an early age, to daycare centers, one of the amenities provided by the European welfare state and particularly essential where new fears about population growth began to surface. European families had few hesitations about replacing maternal care with collective care, and parents often claimed that the result was preferable for children. At the same time, however, some observers worried that Western society, and the Western family, were becoming indifferent to children in an eagerness for adult work and consumer achievements. American adults, for example, between the 1950s and 1980s, shifted their assessment of family satisfaction away from parenthood by concentrating on shared enjoyments between husbands and wives.

New cracks also opened in family stability. Pressures to readjust family roles, women working outside the family context, and growing legal freedoms for women caused men and women alike to turn more readily to divorce. In 1961, 9 percent of all British marriages ended in divorce; by 1965 the figure was 16 percent and rising. By the late 1970s, one-third of all British marriages ended in divorce, and the U.S. rate was higher still.

The development of a new surge of feminist protest, although it reflected much wider concerns than family life alone, showed the strains caused by women's new activities and continued limitations. Growing divorce produced many cases of impoverished women combining work and childcare. New work roles revealed the persistent earnings gap between men and women. More generally, many women sought supporting values and organizations as they tried to define new identities less tied to the domestic roles and images of previous decades.

A **new feminism** began to take shape with the publication in 1949 of *The Second Sex* by the French intellectual Simone de Beauvoir. Echoed in the 1950s and 1960s by other works, such as *The Feminine Mystique*, by Betty Friedan of the United States (Figure 32.5), a new wave of women's rights agitation rose after three decades of relative calm. The new feminism tended to emphasize a more literal equality that would play down special domestic roles and qualities; therefore, it promoted not only specific reforms but also more basic redefinitions of what it meant to be male and female.

The new feminism did not win all women, even in the middle class, which was feminism's most avid audience. It also did not cause some of the most sweeping practical changes that were taking place, as in the new work roles. But it did support the revolution in roles. From the late 1960s onward it pressed Western governments for further change, raising issues that were difficult to fit into established political contexts. The movement both articulated and promoted the gap between new expectations and ongoing inequalities in gender. And the new feminism expressed and promoted some unanswered questions about family functions. In a real sense, later 20th-century feminism seemed to respond to the same desire for individuality and work identity in women that had earlier been urged on men as part of the new mentality suitable for a commercialized economy. Family remained important in the evolving outlook of women, although some feminist leaders attacked the institution outright as hopelessly repressive. Even for many less ideological women, however, family goals were less important than they had been before.

new feminism New wave of women's rights agitation dating from 1949; emphasized more literal equality that would play down domestic roles and qualities for women; promoted specific reforms and redefinition of what it meant to be female.

FIGURE 32.5 In Houston, in November 1977, the U.S. government sponsored a National Women's Conference. In order to symbolize the direct link between earlier American feminists and the women at the Conference, a torch was lit in Seneca Falls, New York—seat of the famous women's right convention of 1848—and carried 2600 miles by relay runners to Houston. In this photograph, feminist leaders accompany the torch and its three bearers on the last mile of the journey. Here, from left to right, are Susan B. Anthony II, Representative Bella Abzug, Sylvia Ortiz, Peggy Kokernot, and Michele Cearcy (the torch bearers), and Betty Friedan.

Western Culture

Amid great innovations in politics, the economy, and social structure—including some pressing new problems—Western cultural life in many respects proceeded along established lines. A host of specific new movements arose, and a wealth of scientific data was assimilated, although basic frameworks had been set earlier, often in the more turbulent but intellectually creative decades of the early 20th century.

One key development was a shift of focus toward the United States. Greater political stability in the United States during the 1930s and 1940s, as well as Hitler's persecutions, had driven many prominent intellectuals to U.S. shores, where they often remained even as western Europe revived. As U.S. universities expanded, their greater wealth fueled more scientific research; what was called a "brain drain," based on dollar power, drew many leading European scientists to the United States even during the 1950s and 1960s. European science remained active, but the costliness of cutting-edge research produced a durable U.S. advantage. Money also mattered in art, as patronage became increasingly important, and thus New York replaced Paris as the center of international styles.

Europeans did participate in some of the leading scientific advances of the postwar years. Francis Crick, of Cambridge University in England, shared with the American James Watson key credit for the discovery of the basic structure of the genetic building block deoxyribonucleic acid (DNA), which in turn opened the way for rapid advances in genetic knowledge and industries based on artificial synthesis of genetic materials. By 2000 work on the human genome project was proceeding rapidly on both sides of the Atlantic. Europeans also participated in nuclear research, often through laboratories funded by the European Union or other inter-European agencies. European space research, slower to develop than Soviet or U.S. initiatives, nevertheless also produced noteworthy achievements by the 1970s, and again there were important commercial spin-offs in communications satellites and other activities.

Developments in the arts maintained earlier 20th-century themes quite clearly. Most artists continued to work in the "modern" modes set before World War I, which featured unconventional self-expression and a wide array of nonrepresentational techniques. The clearest change involved growing public acceptance of the modern styles. The shock that had greeted earlier innovations disappeared, and the public, even when preferring older styles displayed in museums or performed by symphony orchestras devoted to the classics, now seemed reconciled to the redefinition of artistic standards

Europeans retained clearer advantages in artistic films. Italian directors produced a number of gripping, realistic films in the late 1940s, portraying both urban and peasant life without frills. Italy, France, and Sweden became centers of experimental filmmaking again in the 1960s. Jean-Luc Godard and Michelangelo Antonioni portrayed the emptiness of urban life, and Swedish director Ingmar Bergman produced a series of dark psychological dramas. Individual directors in Spain, Britain, and Germany also broke new ground, as Europeans remained more comfortable than their U.S. counterparts in producing films of high artistic merit, relatively free from commercial distractions.

A Lively Popular Culture

Western society displayed at least as much vitality in its popular culture as in formal intellectual life, which reflected the results of economic and social change. As European economies struggled to recover from the war and as U.S. military forces spread certain enthusiasms more widely than before, some observers spoke of a U.S. "Coca-colonization" of Europe. U.S. soft drinks, blue-jean fashions, chewing gum, and other artifacts became increasingly common. U.S. films continued to wield substantial influence, although the lure of Hollywood declined somewhat. More important was the growing impact of U.S. television series. Blessed with a wide market and revenues generated from advertising, American television was quite simply "slicker" than its European counterparts, and the western drama *Bonanza*, the soap opera *Dallas*, and many other shows appeared regularly on European screens to define, for better or worse, an image of the United States.

In contrast to the interwar decades, however, European popular culture had its own power, and it even began to influence the United States. The most celebrated figures of popular culture in the 1960s were unquestionably the Beatles, from the British port city of Liverpool. Although they adopted popular music styles of the United States, including jazz and early rock, the Beatles added an authentic working-class touch in their impulsiveness and their mockery of authority. They also expressed a good-natured desire to enjoy the pleasures of life, which is a characteristic of modern Western popular culture regardless of national context. British popular music groups continued to set standards in the 1970s and had wide impact on western Europe more generally.

Other facets of popular culture displayed a new vigor. Again in Britain, youth fashions, separate from the standards of the upper class, showed an ability to innovate and sometimes to shock. Unconventional uses of color and cut, as in punk hairstyles of the later 1970s, bore some resemblance to the anti-conventional tone of modern painting and sculpture.

Sexual culture also changed in the West, building on earlier trends that linked sex to a larger pleasure-seeking mentality characteristic of growing consumerism and to a desire for personal expression. Films and television shows demonstrated increasingly relaxed standards about sexual display. In Britain, Holland, and Denmark, sex shops sold a wide array of erotic materials and products.

Both the United States and western Europe experienced important changes in sexual behavior starting around 1960, particularly among young people. Premarital sex became more common. The average age of first sexual intercourse began to go down. Expressive sexuality in western Europe was also evident in the growing number of nude bathing spots, again in interesting contrast to more hesitant initiatives in the United States. Although the association of modern popular culture with sexuality and body concern was not novel, the openness and diversity of expression unquestionably reached new levels and also demonstrated western Europe's new confidence in defining a vigorous, nontraditional mass culture of its own.

Critics of Western popular culture worried about its superficiality and its role in distracting ordinary people from ongoing problems such as social inequality. But there were no huge reactions, like those of Nazism against the cultural trends of the 1920s. Western popular culture played a major role in setting global cultural standards, enhancing the West's international influence even as its formal political dominance declined.

EASTERN EUROPE AFTER WORLD WAR II: A SOVIET EMPIRE

32.5 What were the main goals of the Soviet Union in Europe after World War II?

> Soviet Russia expanded its effective empire. Amid new challenges, the Soviet system maintained distinctive political controls.

By 1945 Soviet foreign policy had several ingredients. Desire to regain tsarist boundaries (although not carried through regarding Finland) joined with traditional interest in expansion and in playing an active role in European diplomacy. Genuine revulsion at Germany's two invasions prompted a feverish desire to set up buffer zones under Soviet control, to prevent any repetition. As a result of Soviet industrialization and its World War II push westward, the nation also emerged as a world power, like the newcomer United States. Continued concentration on heavy industry and weapons development, combined with strategic alliances and links to communist movements in various parts of the world, helped maintain this status.

The Soviet Union as Superpower

Soviet participation in the late phases of the war against Japan provided an opportunity to seize some islands in the northern Pacific. The Soviet Union established a protectorate over the communist regime of North Korea, to match the U.S. protectorate in South Korea. Soviet aid to the victorious Communist party in China brought new influence in that country for a time, and in the 1970s the Soviet Union gained a new ally in communist Vietnam, which provided naval bases for the Soviet fleet. Its growing military and economic strength gave the postwar Soviet Union new leverage in the Middle East, Africa, and even parts of Latin America; alliance with the new communist regime in Cuba was a key step here, during the 1960s. The Soviet Union's superpower status was confirmed by its development of the atomic and then hydrogen bombs, from 1949 onward, and by its deployment of missiles and naval forces to match the rapid expansion of U.S. arsenals. The Soviet Union had become a world power.

The New Soviet Empire in Eastern Europe

As a superpower the Soviet Union developed increasing worldwide influence, with trade and cultural missions on all inhabited continents and military alliances with several Asian, African, and Latin American nations. But the clearest extension of the Soviet sphere developed right after World War II, in eastern Europe (Map 32.1). Here the Soviets made it plain that they intended to stay, pushing the Soviet effective sphere of influence farther to the West than ever before in history. Soviet insistence on this empire helped launch the cold war, as the Soviet Union preferred to confront the West rather than relax its grip.

The small nations of eastern Europe, mostly new or revived after World War I, had gone through a troubled period between the world wars. Other than democratic Czechoslovakia, they had failed to establish vigorous, independent economies or solid political systems. Then came the Nazi attack and ineffective Western response, as Czechoslovakia, Poland, and Yugoslavia were seized by German or Italian forces. Eastern Europe fell under Nazi control for four years. Although anti-Nazi governments formed abroad, only in Yugoslavia was a resistance movement strong enough to seriously affect postwar results.

By 1945 the dominant force in eastern Europe was the Soviet army, as it pushed the Germans back and remade the map. Through the combination of the Soviet military might and collaboration with local communist movements in the nations that remained technically independent, opposition parties were crushed and noncommunist regimes forced out by 1948. The only exceptions to this pattern were Greece, which moved toward the Western camp in diplomatic alignment and political and social systems; Albania, which formed a rigid Stalinist regime that ironically brought it into disagreement with Soviet post-Stalinist leaders; and Yugoslavia, where a communist regime formed under the resistance leader Tito quickly proclaimed its neutrality in the cold war, resisting Soviet direction and trying to form a more open-ended, responsive version of the communist economic and social system.

After what was in effect the Soviet takeover, a standard development dynamic emerged throughout most of eastern Europe by the early 1950s. The new Soviet-sponsored regimes attacked possible rivals for power, including, where relevant, the Roman Catholic Church. Mass education and propaganda outlets were quickly developed. Collectivization of agriculture ended the large estate system, without creating a property-owning peasantry. Industrialization was pushed through successive five-year plans, though with some limitation due to Soviet insistence on access to key natural resources (such as Romanian oil) on favorable terms. Finally, a Soviet and eastern European trading zone became largely separate from the larger trends of international commerce.

After the formation of NATO in western Europe, the relevant eastern European nations were enfolded in the Warsaw Pact defense alliance and a common economic planning organization. Soviet troops continued to be stationed in most eastern European states, both to confront the Western alliance and to ensure the continuation of the new regimes and their loyalty to the common cause.

Although it resolved certain social problems in the smaller nations of eastern Europe, as well as responding to the Soviet desire to expand its influence and guard against German or more general Western attack, the new Soviet system created obvious tensions. Particularly tight controls in East Germany brought a workers' rising there in 1953, vigorously repressed by Soviet troops. Faced with a widespread exodus to West Germany, the East German regime built the **Berlin Wall** in 1961 to stem the flow. All along the new borders of eastern Europe, barbed-wire fences and armed patrols kept the people in.

In 1956 a relaxation of Stalinism within the Soviet Union created new hopes that controls might be loosened. More liberal communist leaders arose in Hungary and Poland, with massive popular backing, seeking to create states that, although communist, would permit greater diversity and certainly more freedom from Soviet domination. In Poland the Soviets accepted a new leader more popular with the Polish people. Among other results, Poland was allowed to halt agricultural collectivization, establishing widespread peasant ownership in its place, and the Catholic Church, now the symbol of Polish independence, gained greater tolerance. But a new regime in Hungary was cruelly crushed by the Soviet army and a hard-line Stalinist leadership set up in its place (Figure 32.6).

Yet Soviet control over eastern Europe did loosen slightly overall, for the heavy-handed repression cost considerable prestige. Eastern European governments were given a freer hand in economic policy and were allowed limited room to experiment with greater cultural freedom. Several countries thus began to outstrip the prosperity of the Soviet Union itself. Contacts with the West expanded in several cases, with greater trade and tourism. Eastern Europe remained with the Soviet Union as a somewhat separate economic bloc in world trade, but there was room for limited diversity. Individual

Berlin Wall Built in 1961 to halt the flow of immigration from East Berlin to West Berlin; immigration was in response to lack of consumer goods and close Soviet control of economy and politics; torn down at end of cold war in 1991.

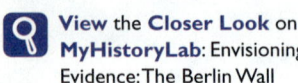
View the **Closer Look** on **MyHistoryLab**: Envisioning Evidence: The Berlin Wall

FIGURE **32.6** As Soviet troops moved into Hungary to crush the revolt of 1956, freedom fighters in Budapest headed for the front with whatever weapons they could find. This truckload of supporters is being urged on by the crowd.

nations, such as Hungary, developed new intellectual vigor and experimented with slightly less centralized economic planning. The communist political system remained in full force, however, with its single-party dominance and strong police controls; diplomatic and military alignment with the Soviet Union remained essential.

The limits of experimentation in eastern Europe were brought home again in 1968, when a more liberal regime came to power in Czechoslovakia. Again the Soviet army responded, expelling the reformers and setting up a particularly rigid leader. A challenge came from Poland once more in the late 1970s, in the form of widespread Catholic unrest and an independent labor movement called **Solidarity**, all against the backdrop of a stagnant economy and low morale. Here response was slightly more muted, although key agitators were arrested; the Polish army took over the state, under careful Soviet supervision.

By the 1980s eastern Europe had been vastly transformed by several decades of communist rule. Important national diversity remained, visible both in industrial levels and in political styles. Catholic Poland thus differed from hard-line, neo-Stalinist Bulgaria or Romania. Important discontents remained as well. Yet a communist-imposed social revolution had brought considerable economic change and real social upheaval. The once-dominant aristocracy had been abolished and the lives of ordinary people had changed greatly through new systems of mass education and industrial, urban growth. Earlier cultural ties with the West, although still greater than in the Soviet Union itself, had been lessened; Russian, not French or English, was the first foreign language learned.

The expansion of Soviet influence answered important Soviet foreign policy goals, both traditional and new. The Soviets retained a military presence deep in Europe, which among other things reduced very real anxiety about yet another German threat. Eastern European allies aided Soviet ventures in other parts of the world, providing supplies and advisors for activities in Africa, Latin America, and elsewhere. Yet the recurrent unrest in eastern Europe served as something of a check on Soviet policy as well. The need for continued military presence may have diverted Soviet leaders from emphasizing expansionist ambitions in other directions, particularly where direct commitment of troops might be involved.

Solidarity Polish labor movement formed in 1970s under Lech Walesa; challenged U.S.S.R.-dominated government of Poland.

Evolution of Domestic Policies

Within the Soviet Union the Stalinist system remained intact during the initial postwar years. The war encouraged growing use of nationalism as well as appeals for communist loyalty, as millions of Russians responded heroically to the new foreign threat. Elements of this mood were sustained as the cold war with the United States developed after 1947, with news media blasting the United States as an evil power and a distorted society. Many Soviets, fearful of a new war that U.S. aggressiveness seemed to them to threaten, agreed that strong government authority remained necessary. This attitude helped sustain the difficult rebuilding efforts after the war, which proceeded rapidly enough for the Soviet Union to regain its prewar industrial capacity and then proceed, during the 1950s, to impressive annual growth rates. The attitude also helped support Stalin's rigorous efforts to shield the Soviet populations from extensive contact with foreigners or foreign ideas. Strict limits on travel, outside media, or any uncensored glimpse of the outside world kept the Soviet Union unusually isolated in the mid-20th-century—its culture, like its economy, largely removed from world currents.

Stalin's political structure continued to emphasize central controls and the omnipresent party bureaucracy. Stalin himself insisted on increasing adulation, and he also grew more suspicious of possible plots against him. Moscow-based direction of the national economy, along with the steady extension of education, welfare, and police operations, expanded the bureaucracy both of the government and of the parallel Communist party. Recruitment from the ranks of peasant and worker families continued into the 1940s, as educational opportunities, including growing secondary school and university facilities, allowed talented young people to rise from below. Party membership, the ticket to bureaucratic promotion, was deliberately kept low, at about 6 percent of the population, to ensure selection of the most dedicated elements. New candidates for the party, drawn mostly from the more broadly based communist youth organizations, had to be nominated by at least three party members. Party members vowed unswerving loyalty and group consciousness.

SOVIET CULTURE: PROMOTING NEW BELIEFS AND INSTITUTIONS

> Rapid industrialization caused significant social change in eastern Europe. Tensions increased over relationships with Western culture.

32.6 What were the main shifts in Soviet society and policy between World War II and the 1980s?

The Soviet government was an impressive new product, not just a renewal of tsarist autocracy. It carried on a much wider array of functions than the tsars had ventured, not only in fostering industrialization but also in reaching out for the direct loyalties of individual citizens. The government and the party also maintained an active cultural agenda, and although this had been foreshadowed by the church and state links of tsarist days, it had no full precedent. The regime declared war on the Orthodox church and other religions soon after 1917, seeking to shape a secular population that would maintain a Marxist, scientific orthodoxy; limited church activities remained but under tight government regulation. Artistic and literary styles, as well as purely political writings, were carefully monitored to ensure adherence to the party line. The educational system was used not only to train and recruit technicians and bureaucrats but also to create a loyal, right-thinking citizenry. Mass ceremonies, such as May Day parades, stimulated devotion to the state and to communism.

Although the new regime did not attempt to abolish the Orthodox church outright, it greatly limited the church's outreach. Thus the church was barred from giving religious instruction to anyone under 18, and state schools vigorously preached the doctrine that religion was mere superstition. Although loyalties to the church persisted, they now seemed concentrated in a largely elderly minority. The Soviet regime also limited freedom of religion for the Jewish minority, often holding up Jews as enemies of the state in what was in fact a manipulation of traditional Russian anti-Semitism. The larger Muslim minority was given greater latitude, on condition of careful loyalty to the regime. On the whole, the traditional religious orientation of Soviet society declined in favor of a scientific outlook and Marxist explanations of history in terms of class conflict. Church attendance dwindled under government repression; by the 1950s only the elderly seemed particularly interested.

The Soviet state also continued to attack modern Western styles of art and literature, particularly when they involved abstract forms regarded as decadent, but maintained some earlier Western styles, which were appropriated as Russian. Thus Russian orchestras performed a wide variety of classical music, and the Russian ballet, although rigid and conservative by 20th-century Western norms, commanded wide attention and enforced rigid standards of excellence. In the arts, socialist realist principles spread to eastern Europe after World War II, particularly in public displays and monuments. With some political loosening and cold war thaw after 1950, however, Soviet and eastern European artists began to adopt Western styles to some extent. At the popular level, jazz and rock music bands began to emerge by the 1980s, although official suspicion persisted.

Literature in the Soviet Union remained diverse and creative, despite official controls sponsored by the communist-dominated Writers' Union. Leading authors wrote movingly of the travails of World War II, maintaining the earlier tradition of sympathy with the people, great patriotism, and concern for the Russian soul. The most imaginative Soviet artists, particularly the writers, often skirted a fine line between conveying some of the sufferings of the Russian people in the 20th century and courting official disapproval. Their freedom also depended on leadership mood; censorship eased after Stalin and then tightened again somewhat in the late 1960s and 1970s, although not to previous levels. Yet even authors critical of aspects of the Soviet regime maintained distinctive Russian values. **Aleksandr Solzhenitsyn** for example, exiled to the United States after the publication of his trilogy on Siberian prison camps, *The Gulag Archipelago*, found the West too materialistic and individualistic for his taste. Although barred from his homeland, he continued to seek an alternative both to communist policy and to Westernization, with more than a hint of a continuing belief in the durable solidarity and faith of the Russian common people and a mysterious Russian national soul.

Solzhenitsyn, Aleksandr [sohl-zuh-NEET-suhn] (b. 1918) Russian author critical of the Soviet regime but also of Western materialism; published trilogy on the Siberian prison camps, *The Gulag Archipelago* (1978).

Along with interest in the arts and a genuine diversity of expressions despite official party lines, Soviet culture continued to place great emphasis on science and social science. This was a major component in the global expansion of science in the contemporary period. Scientists enjoyed great prestige and wielded considerable power. Social scientific work, heavily colored by Marxist theory, nonetheless produced important analyses of current trends and of history. Scientific research was even more heavily funded, and Soviet scientists generated a number of fundamental discoveries in physics, chemistry, and mathematics. At times scientists felt the heavy hand of official disapproval. Biologists and psychiatrists, particularly, were urged to reject Western theories that called human rationality and social progress into question, although here as in other areas controls were most stringent in the Stalinist years. Thus Freudianism was banned, and under Stalin, biologists who overemphasized genetics were jailed. Too much emphasis on the unconscious, as with Freud, or genetic determinism, contradicted the idea that the revolutionary states could control human destiny. But Soviet scientists overall enjoyed considerable freedom and great prestige. As in the West, their work was often linked with advances in technology and weaponry. After the heyday of Stalinism, scientists gained greater freedom from ideological dictates, and exchanges with Western researchers became more common in what was, at base, a common scientific culture.

Shaped by substantial state control, 20th-century Soviet culture overall proved neither traditional nor Western. Considerable ambivalence about the West remained, as Soviets continued to utilize many art forms they developed in common with the West, while instilling a comparable faith in science. Fear of cultural pollution—particularly through non-Marxist political tracts but also through modern art forms—remained lively, as Soviet leaders sought a culture that would enhance their goals of building a socialist society separate from the capitalist West (Figure 32.7).

FIGURE **32.7** Work incentives were a problem in collectivized agriculture. This 1947 poster was designed to spur Soviet farm workers to greater productivity. It proclaims, "Work hard and abundant bread will be your reward."

Economy and Society

The Soviet Union became a fully industrial society between the 1920s and the 1950s. Rapid growth of manufacturing and the rise of urban populations to more than 50 percent of the total were measures of this development. Most of the rest of eastern Europe was also fully industrialized by the 1950s. Eastern European modernization, however, had a number of distinctive features. State control of virtually all economic sectors was one key element; no other industrialized society gave so little leeway to private initiative. The unusual imbalance between heavy industrial goods and consumer items was another distinctive aspect. The Soviet Union lagged in the priorities it placed on consumer goods—not only such Western staples as automobiles but also housing construction and simple items, such as bathtub plugs. Consumer-goods industries were poorly funded and did not achieve the advanced technological level that characterized the heavy-manufacturing sector.

The Soviet need to amass capital for development in a traditionally poor society helped explain the inattention to consumer goods; so did the need to create, in a society that remained poorer overall, a massive armaments industry to rival that of the United States. Soviet fears of resurgent Germany also motivated its military goals. Thus despite an occasional desire to beat the West at its own affluent-society game, communist eastern Europe did not develop the kind of consumer society that came to characterize the West. Living standards improved and extensive welfare services provided security for some groups not similarly supported in the West, but complaints about poor consumer products and long lines to obtain desired goods remained a feature of Soviet life.

Soviet industrialization also caused an unusual degree of environmental damage. The drive to produce at all costs created bleak zones around factories, where waste was dumped, and in agricultural and mining areas. Up to one-quarter of all Soviet territory (and that of the eastern bloc) was environmentally degraded, often leading to severe health problems for people in the affected areas. Ultimately, environmental damage constrained Soviet industry as well.

The communist system throughout eastern Europe also failed to resolve problems with agriculture. Capital that might have gone into farming equipment was often diverted to armaments and heavy industry. The arduous climate of northern Europe and Asia was a factor as well, dooming a number of attempts to spread grain production to Siberia, for example. But it seemed clear that the eastern European peasantry continued to find the constraints and lack of individual incentive in collectivized agriculture deterrents to maximum effort. Thus eastern Europe had to retain a larger percentage of its labor force in agriculture than was true of the industrial West, but it still encountered problems with food supply and quality.

Despite the importance of distinctive political and economic characteristics, the communist states of eastern Europe echoed a number of the themes of contemporary Western social history—simply because of the shared fact of industrial life. Work rhythms, for example, became roughly similar. Industrialization brought massive efforts to speed the pace of work and to introduce regularized supervision. The incentive systems designed to encourage able workers resembled those used in Western factories. Along with similar work habits came similar leisure activities. For decades, sports have provided excitement for the peoples of eastern Europe, as have films and television. Family vacations to the beaches of the Black Sea became cherished respites. Here, too, there were some distinctive twists, as the communist states sponsored a massive sports apparatus as part of their political program (in contrast to the Western view of sports as a combination of leisure and commercialism). East Germany, along with the Soviet Union, developed particularly extensive athletic agendas under state guidance, from training programs for talented children to substantial rewards for successful adult competitors, winning international competitions in a host of fields.

Eastern European social structure also grew closer to that of the West, despite the continued importance of the rural population and despite the impact of Marxist theory. Particularly interesting was a tendency to divide urban society along class lines—between workers and a better-educated, managerial middle class. Wealth divisions remained much less great than in the West, to be sure, but the perquisites of managers and professional people—particularly for Communist party members—set them off from the standard of living of the masses.

Finally, the Soviet family reacted to some of the same pressures of industrialization as did the Western family. Massive movements to the cities and crowded housing enhanced the nuclear family unit, as ties to a wider network of relatives loosened. The birth rate dropped. Official Soviet policy on birth rates varied for a time, but the basic pressures became similar to those in the West. Falling infant death rates, with improved diets and medical care, together with increasing periods of schooling and some increase in consumer expectations, made large families less desirable than before. Wartime dislocations contributed to birth rate decline at points as well. By the 1970s the Soviet growth rate was about the same as that of the West. As in the West, some minority groups—particularly Muslims in the southern Soviet Union—maintained higher birth rates than the majority ethnic group—in this case, ethnic Russians—a differential that caused some concern about maintaining Russian cultural dominance.

Patterns of childrearing showed some similarities to those in the West, as parents, especially in the managerial middle class, devoted great attention to promoting their children's education and ensuring good jobs for the future. At the same time children were more strictly disciplined than in the West, both at home and in school, with an emphasis on authority that had political implications as well. Soviet families never afforded the domestic idealization of women that had prevailed in the West during industrialization. Most married women worked, an essential feature of an economy struggling to industrialize and offering relatively low wages to individual workers. As had been true for peasants in the past, women performed many heavy physical tasks. They also dominated some professions, such as medicine, although these professionals remained lower in status than were their male-dominated counterparts in the West. Soviet propagandists took pride in the constructive role of women and their official equality, but there were signs that many women were suffering burdens from demanding jobs with little help from their husbands at home.

De-Stalinization

The rigid government apparatus created by Stalin and sustained after World War II by frequent arrests and exiles to forced labor camps was put to a major test after Stalin's death in 1953. The results gradually loosened, without totally reversing, Stalinist cultural isolation. Focus on one-man rule might have created immense succession problems, and indeed frequent jockeying for power did develop among aspiring candidates. Yet the system held together. Years of bureaucratic experience had given most Soviet leaders a taste for coordination and compromise, along with a reluctance to strike out in radical new directions that might cause controversy or arouse resistance from one of the key power blocs within the state. Stalin's death was followed by a ruling committee that balanced interest groups, notably the army, the police, and the party apparatus. This mechanism encouraged conservatism, as each bureaucratic sector defended its existing prerogatives, but it also ensured fundamental stability.

In 1956, however, **Nikita Khrushchev** emerged from the committee pack to gain primary power, although without seeking to match Stalin's eminence. Indeed, Khrushchev attacked Stalinism for its concentration of power and arbitrary dictatorship. In a stirring speech delivered to the Communist party congress, Khrushchev condemned Stalin for his treatment of political opponents, for his narrow interpretations of Marxist doctrine, even for his failure to adequately prepare for World War II. The implications of the de-Stalinization campaign within the Soviet Union suggested a more tolerant political climate and some decentralization of decision making. In fact, however, despite a change in tone, little concrete institutional reform occurred. Political trials became less common, and the most overt police repression eased. A few intellectuals were allowed to raise new issues, dealing, for example, with the purges and other Stalinist excesses. Outright critics of the regime were less likely to be executed and more likely to be sent to psychiatric institutions or, in the case of internationally visible figures, exiled to the West or confined to house arrest. Party control and centralized economic planning remained intact. Indeed, Khrushchev planned a major extension of state-directed initiative by opening new Siberian land to cultivation; his failure in this costly effort, combined with his antagonizing many Stalinist loyalists, led to his quiet downfall.

Khrushchev, Nikita [kroosh chef, chof, krUsh-] Stalin's successor as head of U.S.S.R. from 1953 to 1964; attacked Stalinism in 1956 for concentration of power and arbitrary dictatorship; failure of Siberian development program and antagonism of Stalinists led to downfall.

After the de-Stalinization furor and Khrushchev's fall from power, patterns in the Soviet Union remained stable into the 1980s, verging at times on stagnant. Economic growth continued but with no dramatic breakthroughs and with recurrent worries over sluggish productivity and especially over periodically inadequate harvests, which compelled expensive grain deals with Western nations, including the United States. A number of subsequent leadership changes occurred, but the transitions were handled smoothly.

Cold war policies eased somewhat after Stalin's death. Khrushchev vaunted the Soviet ability to outdo the West at its own industrial game, bragging on a visit to the United States that "we will bury you." The Khrushchev regime also produced one of the most intense moments of the cold war with the United States, as he probed for vulnerabilities. The Soviets installed missiles in Cuba, yielding only to a firm U.S. response in 1962 by removing their missiles but not their support of the communist regime on the island. Khrushchev had no desire for war, and overall he promoted a new policy of peaceful coexistence. He hoped to beat the West economically and actively expanded the Soviet space program; *Sputnik*, the first space satellite, was sent up in 1957, well in advance of its U.S. counterpart. Khrushchev maintained a competitive tone, but he shifted away from an exclusive military emphasis. Lowered cold war tensions with the West permitted a small influx of Western tourists by the 1960s as well as greater access to the Western media and a variety of cultural exchanges, which gave some Soviets a renewed sense of contact with a wider world and restored some of the earlier ambiguities about the nation's relationship to Western standards.

At the same time, the Soviet leadership continued a steady military buildup, adding increasingly sophisticated rocketry and bolstered by its unusually successful space program (Figure 32.8). The Soviets maintained a lead in manned space flights into the late 1980s. Both in space and in the arms race, the Soviet Union demonstrated great technical ability combined with a willingness to settle for somewhat simpler systems than those the United States attempted, which helped explain how it could maintain superpower parity even with a less prosperous overall economy. An active sports program, resulting in a growing array of victories in Olympic Games competition, also showed the Soviet Union's new ability to compete on an international scale and its growing pride in international achievements.

The nation faced a number of new foreign policy problems, even though it maintained superpower status. From the mid-1950s onward the Soviet Union experienced a growing rift with China, a communist nation with which it shared a long border. Successful courtship of many other nations—such as Egypt, a close diplomatic friend during the 1960s—often turned sour, although these developments were often balanced by new alignments elsewhere. The rise of Muslim awareness in the 1970s was deeply troubling to the Soviet Union, with its own large Muslim minority. This prompted a 1979 invasion of Afghanistan, to promote a friendly puppet regime, which bogged down amid guerrilla warfare into the late 1980s. On balance, the Soviet Union played a normally cautious diplomatic game, almost never engaging directly in warfare but maintaining a high level of preparedness (Figure 32.9).

Problems of work motivation and discipline loomed larger in the Soviet Union than in the West by the 1980s, after the heroic period of building an industrial society under Stalinist exhortation and threat. With highly bureaucratized and centralized work plans and the absence of abundant consumer goods, many workers found little reason for great diligence. High rates of alcoholism, so severe as to

FIGURE **32.8** This Soviet postcard proclaims, "Glory! The world's first group flight in space, August, 1962," and depicts cosmonauts A. G. Nikolaev and P. R. Popovich. ("CCCP" on the cosmonauts' helmets is Cyrillic lettering meaning "U.S.S.R.") Soviet advances in science and technology both surprised and threatened the United States and western Europe.

DOCUMENT

A Cold War Speech

U.S. PRESIDENT DWIGHT EISENHOWER, A FORMER military leader during World War II, delivered this speech in 1961, right before stepping down from office. The speech was widely noted for its focus on the American "military-industrial complex," a point highlighted in many journalists' accounts.

Crises there will continue to be. In meeting them, whether foreign or domestic, great or small, there is a recurring temptation to feel that some spectacular and costly action could become the miraculous solution to all current difficulties. A huge increase in newer elements of our defense; development of unrealistic programs to cure every ill in agriculture; a dramatic expansion in basic and applied research—these and many other possibilities, each possibly promising in itself, may be suggested as the only way to the road we wish to travel.

But each proposal must be weighed in the light of a broader consideration: the need to maintain balance in and among national programs—balance between the private and the public economy, balance between cost and hoped for advantage—balance between the clearly necessary and the comfortably desirable; balance between our essential requirements as a nation and the duties imposed by the nation upon the individual; balance between actions of the moment and the national welfare of the future. Good judgment seeks balance and progress; lack of it eventually finds imbalance and frustration.

The record of many decades stands as proof that our people and their government have, in the main, understood these truths and have responded to them well, in the face of stress and threat. But threats, new in kind or degree, constantly arise. I mention only two.

A vital element in keeping the peace is our military establishment. Our arms must be mighty, ready for instant action, so that no potential aggressor may be tempted to risk his own destruction.

Our military organization today bears little relation to what known by any of my predecessors in peacetime, or indeed by the fighting men of World War II or Korea.

Until the latest of our world conflicts, the United States had no armaments industry. American makers of plowshares could, with time and as required, make swords as well. But now we can no longer risk emergency improvisation of national defense; we have been compelled to create a permanent armaments industry of vast proportions. Added to this, three and a half million men and women are directly engaged in the defense establishment. We annually spend on military security more than the net income of all United States corporations.

This conjunction of an immense military establishment and a large arms industry is new in the American experience. The total influence—economic, political, even spiritual—is felt in every city, every State house, every office of the Federal government. We recognize the imperative need for this development. Yet we must not fail to comprehend its grave implications. Our toil, resources, and livelihood are all involved; so is the very structure of our society.

In the councils of government, we must guard against the acquisition of unwarranted influence, whether sought or unsought, by the military industrial complex. The potential for the disastrous rise of misplaced power exists and will persist.

We must never let the weight of this combination endanger our liberties or democratic processes. We should take nothing for granted. Only an alert and knowledgeable citizenry can compel the proper meshing of the huge industrial and military machinery of defense with our peaceful methods and goals, so that security and liberty may prosper together.

Akin to, and largely responsible for the sweeping changes in our industrial-military posture, has been the technological revolution during recent decades.

In this revolution, research has become central; it also becomes more formalized, complex and costly. A steadily increasing share is conducted for, by, or at the direction of, the Federal government.

Today, the solitary inventor, tinkering in his shop, has been overshadowed by task forces of scientists in laboratories and test fields. In the same fashion, the free university, historically the fountainhead of free ideas and scientific discovery, has experienced a revolution in the conduct of research. Partly because of the huge costs involved, a government contract becomes virtually a substitute for intellectual curiosity. For every old blackboard there are now hundreds of new electronic computers.

The prospect of domination of the nation's scholars by Federal employment, project allocations, and the power of money is ever present and is gravely to be regarded. Yet, in holding scientific research and discovery in respect, as we should, we must also be alert to the equal and opposite danger that public policy could itself become the captive of a scientific-technological elite.

It is the task of statesman to mold, to balance, and to integrate these and other forces, new and old, within the principles of our democratic system—ever aiming toward the supreme goals of our free society.

QUESTIONS

- What kinds of changes was Eisenhower identifying, and how might they seem to clash with American or Western traditions?
- Were the two changes related?
- Did the speech have much impact on American policies since the early 1960s?

FIGURE **32.9** May Day in the Soviet Union was an occasion for massive military parades including troops, missiles, jets, and tanks, showcasing the country's military power, and for glorification of the state and its leaders, past and present. Enormous banners with portraits of Marx, Engels, and Lenin were stretched high over Red Square, suggesting the current leadership's connection with these giants. In this photo of the 1947 May Day parade, top Soviet leaders watch from reviewing stands in front of Lenin's tomb. Behind them is the wall of the Kremlin.

cause an increase in death rates, particularly among adult males, also burdened work performance and caused great concern to Soviet leaders. More familiar were problems of youth agitation. Although Soviet statistics tended to conceal outright crime rates, it is clear that many youth became impatient with the disciplined life and eager to have greater access to Western culture, including rock music and blue jeans.

Most observers thought the Soviet Union remained firmly established in the early 1980s, thanks to careful police control, vigorous propaganda, and real, popular pride in Soviet achievements. Although even the U.S. Central Intelligence Agency failed to see major problems, however, economic conditions were in fact deteriorating rapidly, and the whole Soviet system would soon come unglued. Yet its collapse was all the more unsettling because of communism's huge success for many decades. At great cost to many people, the Soviet Union had attained world power. Many rejoiced in its fall, but many were also disoriented by it. What could and should replace a system that had dominated huge stretches of Europe and Asia for so long?

Global Connections and Critical Themes

THE COLD WAR AND THE WORLD

The massive competition between the West and the Soviet alliance dominated many aspects of world history between 1945 and 1992. It played a key role in other major global themes, such as decolonization and nationalism. But the competition also gave other parts of the world some breathing room, as they could play one side against the other—a contrast to previous decades in which Western imperialism had dominated.

At the same time, Western and Soviet influences were not entirely contradictory. While Western consumerism and Soviet communism were quite different, both were largely secular. Both societies emphasized science. Both societies challenged key social traditions, including purely traditional roles for women. Both, although in different ways, embraced a vision of globalization, trying to organize wiser international. These shared features helped shape world history for a crucial half-century.

Further Readings

Important overviews of recent European history are Walter Laqueur, *Europe Since Hitler* (1982); John Darwin, *Britain and Decolonization* (1988); Helen Wallace et al., *Policy-Making in the European Community* (1983); and Alfred Grosser, *The Western Alliance* (1982).

On the Cold War, see Jeffrey A. Engel, *Cold War at 30,000 Feet: The Anglo-American Fight for Aviation Supremacy* (2007); Wilson D. Miscamble, *From Roosevelt to Truman: Potsdam, Hiroshima, and the Cold War* (2007); Hal M. Friedman, *Governing the American Lake: The US Defense and Administration of the Pacific, 1945–1947* (2007); Robert David Johnson, *Congress and the Cold War* (2006); Elizabeth Edwards Spalding, *The First Cold Warrior: Harry Truman, Containment, and the Remaking of Liberal Internationalism* (2006); Kenneth Osgood, *Total Cold War: Eisenhower's Secret Propaganda Battle at Home and Abroad* (2006); David Reynolds, *From World War to Cold War: Churchill, Roosevelt, and the International History of the 1940s* (2006); Yale Richmond, *Cultural Exchange & the Cold War: Raising the Iron Curtain* (2003); Scott W. Palmer, *Dictorship of the Air: Aviation Culture and the Fate of Modern Russia* (2006); and Rana Mitter and Patrick Major, eds., *Across the Blocs: Cold War Cultural and Social History* (2004).

Some excellent national interpretations provide vital coverage of events since 1945 in key areas of Europe, including A. F. Havighurst's *Britain in Transition: The Twentieth Century* (1982) and John Ardagh's highly readable *The New French Revolution: A Social and Economic Survey of France* (1968) and *France in the 1980s* (1982). Volker Berghahn, *Modern Germany: Society, Economy, and Politics in the 20th Century* (1983), is also useful.

On post–World War II social and economic trends, see C. Kindleberger, *Europe's Postwar Growth* (1967); V. Bogdanor and R. Skidelsky, eds., *The Age of Affluence, 1951–1964* (1970); R. Dahrendorf, ed., *Europe's Economy in Crisis* (1982); and Peter Stearns and Herrick Chapman, *European Society in Upheaval* (1991). On the welfare state, see Stephen Cohen, *Modern Capitalist Planning: The French Model* (1977), and E. S. Einhorn and J. Logue, *Welfare States in Hard Times* (1982).

On Commonwealth nations, see Charles Doran, *Forgotten Partnership: U.S.-Canada Relations Today* (1983); Edward McWhinney, *Canada and the Constitution, 1979–1982* (1982); and Stephen Graubard, ed., *Australia: Terra Incognita?* (1985).

Postwar Soviet history is treated in Richard Barnet, *The Giants: Russia and America* (1977); A. Rubinstein, *Soviet Foreign Policy Since World War II* (1981); Alec Nove, *The Soviet Economic System* (1980); Stephen Cohen et al., eds., *The Soviet Union Since Stalin*; and Ben Eklof, *Gorbachev and the Reform Period* (1988).

On Soviet culture, Matthew Lenoe, *Closer to the Masses: Stalinist Culture, Social Revolution and Soviet Newspapers* (2004); Jeffrey Brooks, *Thank You, Comrade Stalin! Soviet Public Culture from Revolution to Cold War* (2000), is a cultural history of the communist press. James von Geldern and Richard Stites, eds., *Mass Culture in Soviet Russia: Tales, Poems, Songs, Movies, Plays, and Folklore, 1917–1953* (1995), is a valuable repository of primary cultural texts and documents.

Postwar eastern Europe is treated in H. Setson Watson, *Eastern Europe Between the Wars* (1962); F. Fetjo, *History of the People's Democracies: Eastern Europe Since Stalin* (1971); J. Tampke, *The People's Republics of Eastern Europe* (1983); Timothy Ash, *The Polish Revolution: Solidarity* (1984); H. G. Skilling, *Czechoslovakia: Interrupted Revolution* (1976) (on the 1968 uprising); and B. Kovrig, *Communism in Hungary from Kun to Kadar* (1979).

A major interpretation of the communist experience is T. Skocpol's *States and Social Revolutions* (1979). On women's experiences, see Barbara Engel and Christine Worobec, eds., *Russia's Women: Accommodation, Resistance, Transformation* (1990).

On the early signs of explosion in eastern Europe, see K. Dawisha, *Eastern Europe, Gorbachev, and Reform: The Great Challenge* (1988). Bohdan Nahaylo and Victor Swoboda's *Soviet Disunion: A History of the Nationalities Problem in the USSR* (1990) provides important background. See also Rose Brady, *Kapitalizm: Russia's Struggle to Free Its Economy* (1999). Joseph Rothschild, *Return to Diversity: A Political History of East Central Europe Since World War II* (2000), stands as the authoritative political history. Sabrina Ramet, ed., *Eastern Europe: Politics, Culture, and Society Since 1939* (1998), presents a cultural and social history survey through each country and includes a relevant bibliography.

James T. Patterson, *Grand Expectations: The United States, 1945–1974* (1996), offers a useful overview of the period. Trends in the postwar United States include the civil rights movement, movingly described in David J. Garrow, *Bearing the Cross: Martin Luther King Jr. and the Southern Leadership Conference, 1955–1968* (1986).

The transformation of America's cities is traced by Kenneth T. Jackson, *Crabgrass Frontier: The Suburbanization of the United States* (1985), and the growth of popular culture analyzed in R. Maltby, ed., *The Passing Parade: A History of Popular Culture in the Twentieth Century* (1989), and Lewis MacAdams, *The Birth of Cool: Beat, Bebop, and the American Avant-Garde* (2001). Arthur M. Schlesinger Jr., *A Thousand Days: John F. Kennedy in the White House* (1965); Doris Kearns, *Lyndon Johnson and the American Dream* (1976); and David Stockman, *The Triumph of Politics: Inside Story of the Reagan Revolution* (1987), offer accounts of American political aspirations during three key presidential administrations by authors closely identified with their subjects.

On MyHistoryLab

Critical Thinking Questions

1. Was one side more at fault than the other in causing the cold war? What kinds of evidence would be most helpful in answering this question?
2. Compare the major similarities and differences in the industrial societies of the West and the Soviet bloc after World War II.
3. As formal Western imperialism declined after World War II, what features of the West continued to wield global influence, and why?
4. Judging by European, Russian, and American experience, why do families in industrial societies usually have low birth rates?
5. Along with massive change, what features of Soviet society reflected some continuities with earlier Russian traditions?

Latin America: Revolution and Reaction into the 21st Century

33

Listen to Chapter 33 on MyHistoryLab

In the late summer of 1973, everyone in Chile knew that a coup against the government was being hatched, but no one was quite sure whether it would come from the right-wing military or from the radical left. People turned on the radio each morning to learn whether the coup had taken place during the night. The country was almost at a standstill; the currency had no international value, public transportation did not function, and soldiers armed with machine guns guarded banks and gas stations. The atmosphere was tense; a political storm was coming. Since 1964 the military forces in various Latin American countries (Brazil, 1964; Argentina, 1966; Peru, 1968) had decided to take over their governments. Latin America, like much of the world, seemed divided between the backers of radical revolutionary change and those who wished to keep the status quo or to move very slowly toward any change.

LEARNING OBJECTIVES

33.1 In what ways was Latin America drawn into the Cold War as a participant and as a battleground? p. 823

33.2 Why did social revolution appeal to so many people in Latin America in the post-World War II era and what forces opposed it? p. 825

33.3 What have been the tensions between nationalism and the development of the global economy? p. 831

33.4 How did urbanization in Latin America compare to the rest of the developing world and how did it alter the lives of its people? p. 837

FIGURE 33.1 Soldiers under the command of Gen. Augusto Pinochet surround the Chilean Presidential Palace on September 11, 1973, and take cover while it is bombed in a coup against the elected President Salvador Allende. Allende apparently committed suicide rather than be taken prisoner. Once in control, Pinochet and the military remained in power rather than holding elections and returning control to the civilian legislature.

Watch the Video Series on MyHistoryLab

Learn about some key topics related to this chapter with the *MyHistoryLab Video Series: Key Topics in World History*

The president of Chile at the time was Salvador Allende, a socialist politician who had been elected by a plurality in 1970 and who had begun to push through a series of reforms, including land redistribution and allowing workers to take control of their factories. He was pledged to peaceful change and respect for the Chilean constitution, but his political supporters in the "Popular Unity" movement were awash with enthusiasm. For them it seemed like a new era and their motto "A people united will never be defeated" became a rallying cry for the Left all over Latin America. Such a program would have generated enthusiasms and fears at any time, but this was the era of the cold war and the nations of Latin America were pulled into the struggle between the capitalist West aligned with the United States and the communist countries aligned with the Soviet Union. The United States did its best to destabilize and undercut the Allende regime. Allende's programs and the encouragement he received from Fidel Castro provoked conservative and middle-class elements in Chile. His insistence on remaining within the limits of the constitution bothered impatient radicals who wanted a government-led socialist revolution (Figure 33.1).

On the morning of September 11, 1973, it was the military, backed by conservative and anti-communist forces, that took action and seized the presidential palace. Allende died in the palace. His wife went into exile. The military crushed any resistance and imposed a regime of authoritarian control under General Augusto Pinochet. What followed next was almost two decades of repression. About 3000 people were killed or "disappeared," more than 80,000 people were arrested for political reasons, and more than 200,000 Chileans went into exile. This was an example of the kind of "dirty war" that could be seen elsewhere in Latin America in this era; it was the internalization of the ideological and political struggles of the cold war. During this period, however, neoliberal economics also restored economic stability to the country. The country returned to democracy in 1990, but the wounds on the nation's psyche were still fresh.

In 1998 General Augusto Pinochet, the elderly former commander in chief of the Chilean army and virtual dictator of his country from 1974 to 1990, was arrested in London on charges of crimes against humanity during his years in power. Pinochet and his supporters claimed he had no personal role in the abuses and that he had saved the country from anarchy and restored economic prosperity. His opponents looked on his regime as one of brutal oppression. The arrest became an international incident, and even though Pinochet was eventually released and for "reasons of health" was not forced to stand trial, some Chileans believed that at least a message had been sent to such dictators that crimes of oppression would not be tolerated or forgotten. But many Chileans—and Latin Americans in general—remained divided over what to do about the political struggles of the past. ■

From the second half of the 20th and into the 21st century, Latin America continued to hold an intermediate position between the nations of the North Atlantic and the developing countries of Asia and Africa. Although Latin America shared many problems with these other developing areas, its earlier political independence and its often more Western social and political structures placed it

1940 C.E.	1960 C.E.	1980 C.E.	1990 C.E.	2000 C.E.
1942 Brazil joins Allies in World War II, sends troops to Europe **1944–1954** Arevalo and Arbenz reforms in Guatemala **1947** Juan Perón elected president of Argentina **1952–1964** Bolivian revolution **1954** Arbenz overthrown with help from United States **1959** Castro leads revolution in Cuba	**1961** U.S.-backed invasion of Cuba is defeated **1964** Military coup topples Brazilian government **1970–1973** Salvador Allende's socialist government in Chile; Allende overthrown and assassinated by the military in 1973 **1979** Sandinista revolution in Nicaragua	**1982** Argentina and Great Britain clash over Falkland Islands (Islas Malvinas) **1983** United States invades Grenada **1989** Sandinistas lose election in Nicaragua **1989** United States invades Panama, deposes General Noriega	**1994** Brazil stabilizes economy with new currency: the *real* **1994** Zapatista uprising in Chiapas, Mexico **1996** Return to civilian government in Guatemala **1998** Colombian government initiates negotiations with FARC guerrillas but kidnappings and drug trade continue **1998** Colonel Hugo Chávez elected president in Venezuela and new constitution approved in 1999	**2000** PRI loses presidency of Mexico; Vicente Fox elected **2001** Economic collapse of Argentina **2002** "Lula" and Workers' party win Brazilian elections **2003** Néstor Kirchner elected president of Argentina; one wing of the Peronist party returns to power **2005** Lula's government faces major corruption scandal **2005** Hugo Chávez, using nationalist rhetoric, opposes U.S.-sponsored free trade policies

in a distinct category. After 1945, and particularly from the 1970s onward, the Latin American elites led their nations into closer ties with the growing international capitalist economy over increasing objections from critics within their nations. Investments and initiative often came from Europe and the United States, and Latin American economies continued to concentrate on exports. As a result, Latin America became increasingly vulnerable to changes in the world financial system. For many Latin Americans, the economic decisions made outside the region were also reflected in a political and even cultural dependency on foreign models and influences.

Throughout the 20th century, Latin Americans grappled with the problem of finding a basis for social justice, cultural autonomy, and economic security by adopting ideologies from abroad or by developing a specifically Latin American approach. Thus, in Latin America the struggle for decolonization has been primarily one of economic disengagement and a search for political and cultural forms appropriate to Latin American realities rather than a process of political separation and independence, as in Asia and Africa.

New groups began to appear on the political stage. Although Latin America continued its 19th-century emphasis on agricultural and mineral production, an industrial sector also grew in some places. As this movement gathered strength, workers' organizations began to emerge as a political force. Industrialization was accompanied by some emigration and by explosive urban growth in many places. A growing urban middle class linked to commerce, industry, and expanding state bureaucracies also began to play a role in the political process.

LATIN AMERICA AFTER WORLD WAR II

33.1 In what ways was Latin America drawn into the Cold War as a participant and as a battleground?

With variations from country to country, in Latin America overall the economy and the political process were subject to a series of broad shifts. There was a pattern to these shifts, with economic expansion (accompanied by conservative regimes that, although sometimes willing to make gradual

After World War II, the cold war helped stimulate new revolutionary agitation in Latin America, partly under Marxist inspiration and with some Soviet backing. Although Latin America had been independent of foreign rule for more than a century, the third world decolonization movement encouraged restiveness about continued economic dependency.

reforms, hoped to maintain a political status quo) alternating with periods of economic crisis during which attempts were made to provide social justice or to break old patterns. Thus, the political pendulum swung broadly across the region and often affected several countries at roughly the same time, indicating the relationship between international trends and the internal events in these nations.

Latin Americans have long debated the nature of their societies and the need for change. Although much of the rhetoric of Latin America stressed radical reform and revolutionary change in the 20th century, the region has remained remarkably unchanged. Revolutionaries have not been lacking since 1945, but the task of defeating the existing political and social order and creating a new one on which the majority of the population will agree is difficult, especially when this must be done within an international as well as a national context. Thus, the few revolutionary political changes that have had long-term effects stand in contrast to the general trends of the region's political history. At the same time, however, significant improvements in education, social services, the position of women, and the role of industry have taken place over the past several decades and have begun to transform many areas of Latin American life.

In 1945 several key Latin American countries were still dominated by authoritarian reformers who had responded to the impact of the Great Depression. Getúlio Vargas returned to power in Brazil in 1950 with a program of populist nationalism; the state took over the petroleum industry. Juan Perón (Figure 33.2) ruled in Argentina, again with a populist platform combined with severe political repression. A military group drove Perón from power in 1955, but the popularity of Peronism, particularly among workers, continued for two decades. This encouraged severe political measures by the military dictators, including torture and execution of opponents in what was called the "dirty war." The military government involved Argentina in a war with Britain in 1982, over the Islas Malvinas, or Falkland Islands, which Britain controlled and Argentina claimed. The rulers hoped to gain nationalist support, but they lost the war and the regime was discredited.

FIGURE 33.2 The populist politics of Juan Perón and his wife Evita brought new forces, especially urban workers, into Argentine politics. Their personal charisma attracted support from groups formerly excluded from politics but eventually led to opposition from the Argentine military and Perón's overthrow in 1955.

PRI Party of the Institutionalized Revolution; dominant political party in Mexico; developed during the 1920s and 1930s; incorporated labor, peasant, military, and middle-class sectors; controlled other political organizations in Mexico.

Zapatistas Guerrilla movement named in honor of Emiliano Zapata; originated in 1994 in Mexico's southern state of Chiapas; government responded with a combination of repression and negotiation.

Mexico and the PRI

From the 1940s until a historic change in the 2000 election, Mexico was controlled by the Party of the Institutionalized Revolution, or **PRI** (Figure 33.3). By the last decades of the 20th century, the stability provided by the PRI's control of politics was undercut by corruption and a lack of social improvement. Many Mexicans believed that little remained of the revolutionary principles of the 1910 revolution. Charges of corruption and repression mounted for several decades. In 1994 an armed guerrilla movement burst forth in the heavily Indian southern state of Chiapas (Figure 33.4). Calling themselves **Zapatistas** in honor of Emiliano Zapata, the peasant leader in the 1910 revolution, the movement showed how key social issues remained unresolved. The Mexican government responded with a combination of repression and negotiation (Figure 33.4).

Also in the 1990s the government joined in negotiations for the North American Free Trade Agreement (NAFTA), hoping to spur Mexican industry. Results have remained unclear, although trade with the United States has increased, and Mexico has become the second largest U.S. trade partner. Mexico is preoccupied with fears of the loss of economic control and a growing gap between a sizable middle class and the very poor, including most of Mexico's Indians. NAFTA has also drawn Mexico into closer political and economic ties with the United States, but by 2008 the increasing flow of illegal immigration to the United States, in response to economic conditions in Mexico and opportunities in the United States, had become a contentious issue between the two countries.

In 2000 a national election ended the PRI political monopoly. Vicente Fox, leader of the conservative National Action party (PAN), became president on a platform of cleaning up corruption and improving conditions for Mexican workers in the United States. That party won again in a hotly contested election in 2006, but the peaceful settlement of the electoral dispute, despite irregularities, was a testimony to the nation's desire for democratic government. In 2012 the Mexican electorate, exhausted by the growing violence of the drug cartels and corruption brought the PRI back to power, hoping that it would be faithful to its pledge to democratic principles and to policies that would bring security and stability to the country.

FIGURE 33.3 On July 2, 2000, joyful supporters of the new Mexican president, Vicente Fox, celebrated their victory in electing an opposition candidate for the first time in more than a century.

RADICAL OPTIONS IN THE 1950s

33.2 Why did social revolution appeal to so many people in Latin America in the post–World War II era and what forces opposed it?

The Argentine and Brazilian changes begun by Perón and Vargas were symptomatic of the continuing problems of Latin America, but their populist authoritarian solutions were only one possible response. By the 1940s, pressure for change had built up through much of Latin America. Across the political spectrum there was a desire to improve the social and economic conditions throughout the region and a general agreement that development and economic strength were the keys to a better future. How to achieve those goals remained in question. In Mexico, as we have seen, one-party rule continued, and the "revolution" became increasingly conservative and interested in economic growth rather than social justice. In a few countries, such as Venezuela and Costa Rica, reform-minded democratic parties were able to win elections in an open political system. In other places, such a solution was less likely or less attractive to those who wanted reform. Unlike the Mexican revolutionaries of 1910–1920, those seeking change in the post–World War II period could turn to the well-developed political philosophy of Marxian socialism as a guide. However, such models were fraught with dangers because of the context of the cold war and the ideological struggle between western Europe and the Soviet bloc.

> After World War II, a surge of radical unrest in several smaller countries quickly brought cold war tensions into play. In Bolivia, Guatemala, and Cuba, revolutionaries tried to change the nature of government and society, but they had to accommodate the realities of the cold war and the interests of the United States.

FIGURE 33.4 On January 1, 1994, the North American Free Trade Agreement (NAFTA) went into effect. On that day, Zapatista rebels in Chiapas, Mexico, seized control of several towns, announcing their opposition to NAFTA, seizing weapons, and freeing prisoners from jail. Although its natural resources are great, the people of Chiapas are among the poorest in Mexico. Their declaration read, in part: "We have nothing to lose, absolutely nothing, no decent roof over our heads, no land, no work, poor health, no food, no education, no right to freely and democratically choose our leaders, no independence from foreign interests, and no justice for ourselves or our children. . . . We are the descendants of those who truly built this nation, we are the millions of dispossessed, and we call upon all of our brethren to join our crusade, the only option to avoid dying of starvation!" In this photo, Zapatista rebels exercise near one of their bases in April 1994.

Throughout Latin America, the failures of political democratization, economic development, and social reforms led to consideration of radical and revolutionary solutions to national problems. In some cases, the revolutions at first were successful but ultimately were unable to sustain the changes. In predominantly Indian Bolivia, where as late as 1950 90 percent of the land was owned by 6 percent of the population, a revolution erupted in 1952 in which miners, peasants, and urban middle-class groups participated. Although mines were nationalized and some land redistributed, fear of moving too far to the left brought the army back into power in 1964, and subsequent governments remained more interested in order than in reform.

Guatemala: Reform and U.S. Intervention

The first place where more radical solutions were tried was Guatemala. This predominantly Indian nation had some of the worst of the region's problems. Its population was mostly illiterate and suffered poor health conditions and high mortality rates. Land and wealth were distributed very

VISUALIZING THE PAST

Murals and Posters: Art and Revolution

PUBLIC ART FOR POLITICAL PURPOSES HAS been used since ancient Egypt, but with the development of lithography (a color printing process), the poster emerged as a major form of communication. First developed in the late 19th century as a cheap form of advertising using image and text to sell soap, wine, or chocolate or to advertise dance halls and theaters, by the 1880s posters were adapted to political purposes, and in World War I all the major combatants used them. But those opposed to governments could also use posters to convey a revolutionary message to a broad public. In Latin America, the Mexican Revolution made use of public art in great murals, but these were often expensive and took a long time to complete. The Cuban revolutionaries of the 1960s and the Nicaraguan revolutionaries of the 1980s turned to the poster as a way to convey their policies and goals to a broad public.

> **QUESTIONS**
> - What are the advantages of the poster over the mural, and vice versa?
> - Is poster art really art?
> - Why are images of the past often the subjects of revolutionary art?
> - To whom is political art usually directed?

(David Alfaro Siqueiros. Detail from the mural, "For the Complete Safety of All Mexicans at Work." 1952–54. Art Resource, NY. © 2009 Artists Rights Society (ARS), New York/SOMAAP, Mexico City. Reproduction authorized by the Instituto Nacional de Bellas Artes and Literature.)

unequally, and the whole economy depended on the highly volatile prices for its main exports of coffee and bananas. In 1944 a middle-class and labor coalition elected reformer **Juan José Arevalo** as president. Under a new constitution, he began a series of programs within the context of "spiritual socialism" that included land reform and an improvement in the rights and conditions of rural and industrial workers. These programs and Arevalo's sponsorship of an intense nationalism brought the government into direct conflict with foreign interests operating in Guatemala, especially the **United Fruit Company**, the largest and most important foreign concern there.

In 1951, after a free election, the presidency passed to Colonel Jacobo Arbenz, whose nationalist program was more radical. Arbenz announced several programs to improve or nationalize the transportation network, the hydroelectric system, and other areas of the economy. A move to expropriate unused lands on large estates in 1953 provoked opposition from the large landowners and from United Fruit, which eventually was threatened with the loss of almost half a million acres of reserve land. The U.S. government, fearing "communist" penetration of the Arbenz government and under

Arevalo, Juan José [WAHN hoh-ZAY ahr-uh-VAHL-oh] Elected president of Guatemala in 1944; began series of socialist reforms including land reform; nationalist program directed against foreign-owned companies such as United Fruit Company.

United Fruit Company Most important foreign economic concern in Guatemala during the 20th century; attempted land reform aimed at United Fruit caused U.S. intervention in Guatemalan politics leading to ouster of reform government in 1954.

considerable pressure from the United Fruit Company, denounced the changes and began to impose economic and diplomatic restrictions on Guatemala. At the same time, the level of nationalist rhetoric intensified, and the government increasingly received the support of the political left in Latin America and in the socialist bloc.

In 1954, with the help of the U.S. Central Intelligence Agency, a dissident military force was organized and invaded Guatemala. The Arbenz government fell, and the pro-American regime that replaced it turned back the land reform and negotiated a settlement favorable to United Fruit. The reform experiment was thus brought to a halt. By the standards of the 1960s and later, the programs of Arevalo and Arbenz seem rather mild, although Arbenz's statements and supposedly his acceptance of arms from eastern Europe undoubtedly contributed to U.S. intervention.

The reforms promised by the U.S.-supported governments were minimal. Guatemala continued to have a low standard of living, especially for its Indian population. After the coup the series of military governments failed to address the nation's social and economic problems. That failure led to continual violence and political instability. Political life continued to be controlled by a coalition of coffee planters, foreign companies, and the military. A guerrilla movement grew and provoked brutal military repression, which fell particularly hard on the rural Indian population. Guatemala's attempt at radical change, an attempt that began with an eye toward improving the conditions of the people, failed because of external intervention. The failure was a warning that change would not come without internal and foreign opposition.

The Cuban Revolution: Socialism in the Caribbean

The differences between Cuba and Guatemala underline the diversity of Latin America and the dangers of partial revolutions. The island nation had a population of about 6 million, most of whom were the descendants of Spaniards and the African slaves who had been imported to produce the sugar, tobacco, and hides that were the colony's mainstays. Cuba had a large middle class, and its literacy and healthcare levels were better than in most of the rest of the region. Rural areas lagged behind in these matters, however, and there the working and living conditions were poor, especially for the workers on the large sugar estates. Always in the shadow of the United States, Cuban politics and economy were rarely free of American interests. By the 1950s, about three-fourths of what Cuba imported came from the United States. American investments in the island were heavy during the 1940s and 1950s. Although the island experienced periods of prosperity, fluctuations in the world market for Cuba's main product, sugar, revealed the tenuous basis of the economy. Moreover, the disparity between the countryside and the growing middle class in Havana underlined the nation's continuing problems.

From 1934 to 1944, **Fulgencio Batista**, a strong-willed, authoritarian reformer who had risen through the lower ranks of the army, ruled Cuba. Among his reforms were a democratic constitution of 1940 that promised major changes, nationalization of natural resources, full employment, and land reform. However, Batista's programs of reform were marred by corruption, and when in 1952 he returned to the presidency, there was little left of the reformer but a great deal of the dictator. Opposition developed in various sectors of the society. Among the regime's opponents was **Fidel Castro**, a young lawyer experienced in leftist university politics who was an ardent critic of the Batista government and of the ills of Cuban society. On July 26, 1953, Castro and a few followers launched an unsuccessful attack on some military barracks. Captured, Castro faced a trial, an occasion he used to expound his revolutionary ideals, aimed mostly at a return to democracy, social justice, and the establishment of a less dependent economy.

Released from prison, Castro fled to exile in Mexico where, with the aid of **Ernesto "Che" Guevara**, a militant Argentine revolutionary, he gathered a small military force. They landed in Cuba in 1956 and slowly began to gather strength in the mountains. By 1958 the "26th of July Movement" had found support from students, some labor organizations, and rural workers and was able to conduct operations against Batista's army. The bearded rebels, or *barbudos*, won a series of victories. The dictator, under siege and isolated by the United States (which because of his abuses of power and

Batista, Fulgencio Dictator of Cuba from 1934 to 1944; returned to presidency in 1952; ousted from government by revolution led by Fidel Castro.

Castro, Fidel Cuban revolutionary; overthrew dictator Fulgencio Batista in 1958; initiated series of socialist reforms; came to depend almost exclusively on Soviet Union.

Guevara, Ernesto "Che" [gay-VAHR-uh] Argentine revolutionary; aided Fidel Castro in overthrow of Fulgencio Batista regime in Cuba; died while directing guerrilla movement in Bolivia in 1967.

use of violence refused to support him any longer), fled into exile, and the rebels took Havana amid wild scenes of joy and relief (Figure 33.5).

What happened next is highly debatable, and Castro himself has offered alternative interpretations at different times. Whether Castro was already a Marxist-Leninist and had always intended to introduce a socialist regime (as he now claims) or whether the development of this program was the result of a series of pragmatic decisions is in question. Rather than simply returning to the constitution of 1940 and enacting moderate reforms, Castro launched a program of sweeping change. Foreign properties were expropriated, farms were collectivized, and a centralized socialist economy was put in place. Most of these changes were accompanied by a nationalist and anti-imperialist foreign policy. Any resistance to these changes was suppressed, and the press was stifled. Relations with the United States were broken off in 1961, and Cuba increasingly depended on the financial support and arms of the Soviet Union to maintain its revolution. With that support in place, Castro was able to survive the increasingly hostile reaction of the United States. That reaction included a disastrous U.S.-sponsored invasion by Cuban exiles in 1961 and a U.S. embargo on trade with Cuba. Increasing Cuban economic and political dependence on the Soviet Union led to a crisis in 1962, when Soviet nuclear missiles were discovered and a confrontation between the superpowers ensued. Despite these problems, to a large extent the Cuban revolution survived because of the global context. The politics of the cold war provided Cuba with a protector and a benefactor, the Soviet Union.

FIGURE 33.5 Fidel Castro and his "barbudos" (bearded) guerillas brought down the Batista government in January 1959 to the wild acclaim of many Cubans. Castro initiated sweeping reforms in Cuba that eventually led to the creation of a socialist regime and a sharp break with the United States.

The results of the revolution have been mixed. The social programs were extensive. Education, health, and housing have improved greatly and rank Cuba among the world's leaders—quite unlike most other nations of the region. This is especially true in the long-neglected rural areas. A wide variety of social and educational programs have mobilized all sectors of the population. The achievements have been accompanied by severe restrictions of basic freedoms.

Attempts to diversify and strengthen the economy have been less successful. An effort to industrialize in the 1960s failed, and Cuba turned again to its ability to produce sugar. The world's falling sugar and rising petroleum prices led to disaster. Only by subsidizing Cuban sugar and supplying petroleum below the world price could the Soviet Union maintain the Cuban economy. After the breakup of the Soviet Union in the 1990s, the Cuban situation deteriorated as Castro adhered to an inflexible socialist economic policy. Increasingly isolated, in 2008, Castro, in failing health, turned government over to his brother Raúl Castro, who was a more efficient administrator, but without much-needed Soviet aid and still constrained by U.S. trade restrictions, Cuba faced an uncertain future. Despite these problems, the Cuban revolution offered an example that proved attractive to those seeking to transform Latin American societies. Early direct attempts to spread the model of the Cuban revolution, such as Che Guevara's guerrilla operation in Bolivia, where he lost his life in 1967, were failures. But the Cuban example and the island's ability to resist the pressure of a hostile United States proved an attractive model for other nations in the Caribbean and Central America, such as Grenada and Nicaragua, that also exercised the revolutionary option. U.S. reaction to such movements has been containment or intervention but after 2005 the growing number of populist leaders and left of center regimes in Venezuela, Brazil, Ecuador, and Bolivia has diminished Cuba's isolation within the region.

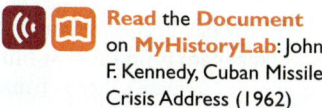

Read the Document on MyHistoryLab: John F. Kennedy, Cuban Missile Crisis Address (1962)

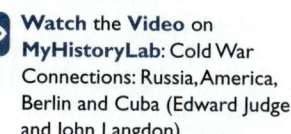

Watch the Video on MyHistoryLab: Cold War Connections: Russia, America, Berlin and Cuba (Edward Judge and John Langdon)

DOCUMENT

The People Speak

Scholarly analysis of general trends often fails to convey the way in which historical events and patterns affect the lives of people or the fact that history is made up of the collective experience of individuals. It is often very difficult to know about the lives of common people in the past or to learn about their perceptions of their lives. In recent years in Latin America, however, a growing literature of autobiographies, interpreted autobiographies (in which another writer puts the story down and edits it), and collections of interviews have provided a vision of the lives of common people. These statements, like any historical document, must be used carefully because their authors or editors sometimes have political purposes, because they reflect individual opinions, or because the events they report may be atypical. Nevertheless, these personal statements put flesh and blood on the bones of history and provide an important perspective from those whose voice in history often is lost.

A BOLIVIAN WOMAN DESCRIBES HER LIFE

Domitila Barrios de Chungara was a miner's wife who became active in the mine workers' political movement. Her presence at the United Nations–sponsored International Woman's Year Tribunal in 1975 moved a Brazilian journalist to organize her statements into a book about her life. This excerpt provides a picture of her everyday struggle for life.

> My day begins at four in the morning, especially when my compañero is on the first shift. I prepare his breakfast. Then I have to prepare salteñas [small meat pastries] because I make about one hundred salteñas every day and I sell them on the street. I do this in order to make up for what my husband's wage doesn't cover in terms of our necessities. The night before, we prepare the dough and at four in the morning I make the salteñas while I feed the kids. The kids help me.
>
> Then the ones that go to school in the morning have to get ready, while I wash the clothes left soaking over night.
>
> At eight I go out to sell. The kids that go to school in the afternoon help me. We have to go to the company store and bring home the staples. And in the store there are immensely long lines and you have to wait there until eleven in order to stock up. You have to line up for meat, for vegetables, for oil. So it's just one line after another. Since everything is in a different place, that's how it has to be.
>
> From what we earn between my husband and me, we can eat and dress. Food is very expensive: 28 pesos for a kilo of meat, 4 pesos for carrots, 6 pesos for onions.... Considering that my compañero earns 28 pesos a day, that's hardly enough is it?
>
> We don't ever buy ready made clothes. We buy wool and knit. At the beginning of each year, I also spend about 2000 pesos on cloth and a pair of shoes for each of us. And the company discounts some of that each month from my husband's wage. On the pay slips that's referred to as the "bundle." And what happens is that before we finish paying the "bundle" our shoes are worn out. That's how it is.
>
> Well, from eight to eleven in the morning I sell the salteñas. I do the shopping in the grocery store, and I also work at the Housewives Committee talking with the sisters who go there for advice.
>
> At noon, lunch has to be ready because the rest of the kids have to go to school.
>
> In the afternoon I have to wash clothes. There are no laundries. We use troughs and have to get the water from a pump.
>
> I've got to correct the kids' homework and prepare everything I'll need to make the next day's salteñas.

FROM PEASANT TO REVOLUTIONARY

Rigoberta Menchú, a Quiché Indian from the Guatemalan highlands, came from a peasant family that had been drawn into politics during the repression of Indian communities and human rights in the 1970s. In these excerpts, she reveals her disillusionment with the government and her realization of the ethnic division between Indians and ladinos, or mestizos, that complicates political action in Guatemala.

> The CUC [Peasant Union] started growing; it spread like wildfire among the peasants in Guatemala. We began to understand that the root of all our problems was exploitation. That there were rich and poor and that the rich exploited the poor—our sweat, our labor. That's how the rich got richer and richer. The fact that we were always waiting in offices, always bowing to the authorities was part of the discrimination that we Indians suffered.
>
> The situation got worse when the murderous generals came to power although I did not actually know who was the president at the time. I began to know them from 1974 when General Kjell Langerud came to power. He came to our region and said: "We're going to solve the land problem. The land belongs to you. You cultivate the land and I will share it out among you." We trusted him. I was at the meeting when [he] spoke. And what did he give us? My father tortured and imprisoned.
>
> Later I had the opportunity of meeting other Indians. Achi Indians, the group that lives closest to us. And I got to know some Mam Indians too. They all told me: "The rich are bad. But not all ladinos are bad." And I started wondering: Could it be that not all ladinos are Achi Indians, the group that lives closest to us? And I know some Mam Indians too. They all told me: "The rich are bad." ... There were poor ladinos as well as rich ladinos, and they were exploited as well. That's when I began recognizing exploitation. I kept on going to the finca [large farm] but now I really wanted to find out, to prove if that was true and

(continued on next page)

learn the details. There were poor ladinos on the finca. They worked the same, and their children's bellies were swollen like my little brother's. . . . I was just beginning to speak a little Spanish in those days and I began to talk to them. I said to one poor ladino: "You are a poor ladino, aren't you?" And he nearly hit me. He said: "What do you know about it, Indian!" I wondered: "Why is that when I say poor ladinos are like us, I'm spurned?" I didn't know then that the same system which tries to isolate us Indians also puts barriers between Indians and ladinos. . . . Soon afterwards, I was with the nuns and we went to a village in Uspantán where mostly ladinos live. The nun asked a little boy if they were poor and he said: "Yes, we're poor but we're not Indians." That stayed with me. The nun didn't notice, she went on talking. She was foreign, she wasn't Guatemalan. She asked someone else the same question and he said: "Yes, we're poor but we're not Indians." It was very painful for me to accept that an Indian was inferior to a ladino. I kept on worrying about it. It's a big barrier they've sown between us, between Indian and ladino. I didn't understand it.

QUESTIONS

- What was distinctive about lower-class life and outlook in late 20th-century Latin America?
- How had lower-class life changed since the 19th century?

THE SEARCH FOR REFORM AND THE MILITARY OPTION

33.3 What have been the tensions between nationalism and the development of the global economy?

The revolutionary attempts of the 1950s, the durability of the Cuban revolution, and the general appeal of Marxist doctrines in developing nations underlined Latin America's tendency to undertake revolutionary change that left its economic and social structures unchanged. How could the traditional patterns of inequality and international disadvantage created by Latin America's dependence on the world consumption of its raw materials be overcome? What was the best path to the future?

For some, the answer was political stability, imposed if necessary, to promote capitalist economic growth. The one-party system of Mexico demonstrated its capacity for repression when student dissidents were brutally killed during disturbances in 1968. Mexico enjoyed some prosperity from its petroleum resources in the 1970s, but poor financial planning, corruption, and foreign debt again caused problems by the 1980s, and the PRI lost its ability to maintain control of Mexican politics.

For others, the church, long a power in Latin America, provided a guide. Christian Democratic parties formed in Chile and Venezuela in the 1950s, hoping to bring reforms through popularly based mass parties that would preempt the radical left. The church often was divided politically, but the clergy took an increasingly engaged position and argued for social justice and human rights, often in support of government opponents. A few, such as Father Camilo Torres in Colombia, actually joined armed revolutionary groups in the 1960s.

More common was the emergence within the church hierarchy of an increased concern for social justice (Figure 33.6). By the 1970s, a **liberation theology** combined Catholic theology and socialist principles or used Marxist categories for understanding society in an effort to improve conditions for the poor. Liberation theologians stressed social equality as a form of personal salvation. When criticized for promoting communism in his native Brazil, Dom Helder da Camara, archbishop of Pernambuco, remarked, "The trouble with Brazil is not an excess of communist doctrine but a lack of Christian justice." The position of the Catholic Church in Latin American societies was changing, but there was no single program for this new stance or even agreement among the clergy about its validity. Still, this activist position provoked attacks against clergy such as the courageous Archbishop Oscar Romero of El Salvador, who was assassinated in 1980 for speaking out for social reform, and even against nuns involved in social programs. The church, however, played an important role in the fall of the Paraguayan dictatorship in 1988.

Out of the Barracks: Soldiers Take Power

The success of the Cuban revolution impressed and worried those who feared revolutionary change within a communist political system. The military forces in Latin America had been involved in politics since the days of the caudillos in the 19th century, and in several nations military interventions

---

Latin Americans continued to seek solutions to their problems using Catholic, Marxist, and capitalist doctrines. In the 1960s and 1970s nationalistic, pro-capitalist military governments created new "bureaucratic authoritarian" regimes. By the 1980s, a new wave of democratic regimes was emerging.

Read the **Document** on **MyHistoryLab:** Camilo Torres and Liberation Theology (1950s)

liberation theology Combined Catholic theology and socialist principles in effort to bring about improved conditions for the poor in Latin America in 20th century.

FIGURE 33.6 In September 1999, thousands of Brazilians attended a mass to celebrate the "Cry of the Excluded," a protest against the social and economic degradation of the nation's poor, who make up more than a third of the population.

had been common. As the Latin American military became more professionalized, however, a new philosophy underlay the military's involvement in politics. The soldiers began to see themselves as above the selfish interests of political parties and as the true representatives of the nation. With technical training and organizational skills, military officers by the 1920s and 1930s believed that they were best equipped to solve their nations' problems, even if that meant sacrificing the democratic process and imposing martial law.

In the 1960s, the Latin American military establishments, made nervous by the Cuban success and the swing to leftist or populist regimes, began to intervene directly in the political process, not simply to clean out a disliked president or party, as they had done in the past, but to take over government itself. In 1964 the Brazilian military (with the support of the United States and the Brazilian middle class) overthrew the elected president after he threatened to make sweeping social reforms. In Argentina, growing polarization between the Peronists and the middle class led to a military intervention in 1966. In 1973 the Chilean military, which until then had remained for the most part out of politics, overthrew the socialist government of President **Salvador Allende**, as described in the chapter opening.

The soldiers in power imposed a new type of bureaucratic authoritarian regime. Their governments were supposed to stand above the competing demands of various sectors and establish economic stability. Now, as arbiters of politics, the soldiers believed that they would place the national interest above selfish interests by imposing dictatorships. Government was essentially a presidency, controlled by the military, in which policies were formulated and applied by a bureaucracy organized like a military chain of command. Political repression and torture were used to silence critics, and stringent measures were imposed to control inflation and strengthen the countries' economies. In Argentina, violent opposition to military rule led to a counteroffensive and the "dirty war" in which thousands of people "disappeared."

Government economic policies fell heaviest on the working class. The goal of the military in Brazil and Argentina was development. To some extent, in Brazil at least, economic improvements were achieved, although income distribution became even more unequal than it had been. Inflation was

Allende, Salvador [ä yAHn dAY, ä yen dEE] President of Chile; nationalized industries and banks; sponsored peasant and worker expropriations of lands and foreign-owned factories; overthrown in 1973 by revolt of Chilean military with the support of the United States.

reduced, industrialization increased, and gains were made in literacy and health, but basic structural problems such as land ownership and social conditions for the poorest people remained unchanged.

There were variations within these military regimes, but all were nationalistic. The Peruvian military tried to create a popular base for its programs and to mobilize support among the peasantry. It had a real social program, including extensive land reform, and was not simply a surrogate for the conservatives in Peruvian society. In Chile and Uruguay, the military was fiercely anticommunist. In Argentina, nationalism and a desire to gain popular support in the face of a worsening economy led to a confrontation with Great Britain over the Falkland Islands (Islas Malvinas), which both nations claimed. The war stimulated pride in Argentina and its soldiers and sailors, but defeat caused a loss of the military's credibility.

The New Democratic Trends

In Argentina and elsewhere in South America, by the mid-1980s the military had begun to return government to civilian politicians. Continuing economic problems and the pressures of containing opponents wore heavily on the military leaders, who began to realize that their solutions were no more destined to success than those of civilian governments. Moreover, the populist parties, such as the Peronists and Apristas, seemed less of a threat, and the fear of Cuban-style communism had diminished. Also, the end of the Cold War meant that the United States was less interested in sponsoring regimes that, although "safe," were also repressive. In Argentina, elections were held in 1983. Brazil began to restore democratic government after 1985 and in 1989 chose its first popularly elected president since the military takeover. The South American military bureaucrats and modernizers were returning to their barracks.

Read the Document on MyHistoryLab: Brazil's Constitution of 1988

The process of redemocratization was not easy, nor was it universal. In Peru, *Sendero Luminoso* (Shining Path), a long-sustained leftist guerrilla movement, controlled areas of the countryside and tried to disrupt national elections in 1990. In Central America, the military cast a long shadow over the government in El Salvador, but return to civilian government took place in 1992. In Nicaragua, the elections of 1990, held under threat of a U.S. embargo, removed the **Sandinista party** from control in Nicaragua. In subsequent elections the party of the Sandinistas could still muster much support, but it did not win back the presidency until 2006. The trend toward a return to electoral democracy could be seen in Guatemala as well. By 1996 civilian government had returned to Guatemala as the country struggled to overcome the history of repression and rebellion and the animosities they had created. The United States had demonstrated its continuing power in the region in its 1989 invasion of Panama and the arrest of its strongman leader, Manuel Noriega.

Sandinista party Nicaraguan socialist movement named after Augusto Sandino; successfully carried out a socialist revolution in Nicaragua during the 1980s.

Latin American governments in the last decades of the 20th century faced tremendous problems. Large foreign loans taken in the 1970s for the purpose of development had created a tremendous level of debt that threatened the economic stability of countries such as Brazil, Peru, and Mexico. In 2002 the Argentine government defaulted on its debt and faced economic crisis. High rates of inflation provoked social instability as real wages fell. Pressure from the international banking community to curb inflation by cutting government spending and reducing wages often ignored the social and political consequences of such actions. An international commerce in drugs, which produced tremendous profits, stimulated criminal activity and created powerful international cartels that could even threaten national sovereignty. In Colombia a leftist guerrilla movement controlled large areas of the country and funded itself from the drug trade. It destabilized the country and the government's legitimacy. In countries as diverse as Cuba, Panama, and Bolivia, the narcotics trade penetrated the highest government circles.

But despite the problems, the 1990s seemed to demonstrate that the democratic trends were well established. In Central America there was a return to civilian government. In Venezuela and Brazil, corruption in government led to the fall of presidents and, as we have mentioned, led to a major political change in Mexico in 2000. But dissatisfaction with NAFTA and continuing economic problems continued. In Brazil a leftist working-class presidential candidate, Lula (Luiz Inacio Lula da Silva), was elected in 2002, and despite charges of corruption his policies began to eliminate social inequalities and enlarge the middle class. His PT (Workers Party) gained widespread support, and helped by the discovery of new offshore oil reserves, the economy boomed. More radical options were also still possible. In Colombia the insurgency supported by ties to the drug trade continued to threaten the nation's stability. In neighboring Venezuela a populist military leader, Hugo Chávez, had

THINKING HISTORICALLY

Human Rights in the 20th Century

IN LATIN AMERICA, THE QUESTION OF human rights became a burning issue in the 1960s and continued thereafter. The use of torture by repressive governments, the mobilization of death squads and other vigilante groups with government acquiescence, and the use of terrorism against political opponents by the state and by groups opposed to the state became all too common in the region. Latin America's record on the violation of human rights was no worse than that of some other areas of the world. However, the demonstrations by the Argentine "Mothers of the Plaza del Mayo" to focus attention on their disappeared children; the publication of prison memoirs recounting human rights violations in Brazil, Cuba, and Argentina; and films dramatizing events such as the assassination of Archbishop Oscar Romero in El Salvador have all focused attention on the problem in Latin America. Moreover, because Latin America shares in the cultural heritage of Western societies, it is difficult to make an argument that human rights there have a different meaning or importance than in Europe or North America.

The concept of human rights—that is, certain universal rights enjoyed by all people because they are justified by a moral standard that stands above the laws of any individual nation—may go back to ancient Greece. The concept of natural law and the protection of religious or ethnic minorities also moved nations in the 19th century toward a defense of human rights. To some extent, the international movement to abolish the slave trade was an early human rights movement. In modern times, however, the concept of human rights has been strongly attached to the foundation of the United Nations. In 1948 that body, with the experience of World War II in mind, issued a Universal Declaration of Human Rights and created a commission to oversee the human rights situation. The Universal Declaration, which guaranteed basic liberties and freedoms regardless of color, sex, or religion, proclaimed that it should be the "common standard for all peoples and nations." However, one critic has stated that of the 160 nations in the United Nations, only about 30 have a consistently good record on human rights.

A major problem for the international community has been enforcing the Universal Declaration. The United Nations commission did not have any specific powers of enforcement, and much debate has taken place on the power of the United Nations to intervene in the internal affairs of any nation. More recently, various regional organizations have tried to establish the norms that should govern human rights and to create institutions to enforce these norms.

> **Whereas developing nations view the right to development as a human right, it is viewed as a political and economic demand in wealthier nations of the West.**

One specialist has claimed that "human rights is the world's first universal ideology." The defense of human rights seems to be a cause that most people and governments can accept without hesitation, but the question is complex. Although the rights to life, liberty, security, and freedom from torture or degrading punishment are generally accepted in principle by all nations, other rights remain open to question. What is a right, and to what extent are definitions of rights determined by culture?

The question of universality versus relativism emerged quickly in the debate over human rights. What seemed to be obvious human rights in Western societies were less obvious in other parts of the world, where other priorities were held. For example, laws prohibiting child labor were enforced by most Western societies, but throughout the world perhaps 150 million children worked, often in unhealthy and exploitive conditions. They worked because of economic necessity in many cases, but in some societies such labor was considered moral and proper. Such cultural differences have led to a position of relativism, which recognizes that there are profound cultural variations in what is considered moral and just. Critics of the original Universal Declaration contend that its advocacy of the right to own property and the right to vote imposed Western political and economic values as universals. Cultural relativism had the advantage of recognizing the variety of cultures and standards in the world, but it has also been used as a shield to deflect criticism and to excuse the continued violation of human rights.

The definition of human rights is also political. The West emphasizes the civil and political rights of the individual. The socialist nations placed social and economic justice above individual rights, although by the 1990s movements in eastern Europe and China indicated that there was pressure to modify this approach. In the developing nations, an argument for peoples' rights has emerged in which the "right to development," which calls for a major structural redistribution of the world's resources and economic opportunities, is a central concept. As Léopold Senghor of Senegal put it, "Human rights begin with breakfast"; or as a report on Ghana stated, "'One man, one vote' is meaningless unless accompanied by the principle of 'one man, one bread.'" Whereas developing nations view the right to development as a human right, it is viewed as a political and economic demand in wealthier nations of the West.

Another dimension of human rights is the extent to which it influences national foreign policies. Governments may make statements pledging respect for human rights in their foreign

(continued on next page)

policies, but considerations of national defense, security, sovereignty, war against terrorism, or other goals often move human rights concerns into a secondary position. Disputes over the role of human rights in foreign policy sometimes are posed as a conflict between "moralistic utopians" who see the world as it should be and "pragmatists" who see the world as it is. Neither approach necessarily denies the importance of human rights, but there are differences in priority and strategy. Pragmatists might argue that it is better to maintain relations with a nation violating human rights in order to be able to exercise some influence over it in the future, or that other policy considerations must be weighed along with those of human rights in establishing foreign policy. Moralists would prefer to bring pressure by isolating and condemning a nation that violates international standards.

These different approaches have been reflected in the U.S. policy shifts toward Latin America. In the 1950s, human rights considerations were secondary to opposing the spread of communism in the hemisphere, and the United States was willing to support governments that violated human rights as long as they were anticommunist allies. During the 1960s, this policy continued, but increasing and systematic abuses by military regimes in Brazil, Uruguay, Chile, Nicaragua, and elsewhere in Latin America began to elicit some changes. In 1977 President Carter initiated a new policy in which human rights considerations would be given high priority in U.S. foreign policy. This weakened some regimes and stimulated resistance to human rights violations in Latin America, but by the 1980s a more pragmatic approach had returned to U.S. policy. Criticism of human rights violations sometimes was made selectively, and abuses in "friendly" governments were dismissed. The extent to which human rights concerns must be balanced against issues such as security, the maintenance of peace, and nonintervention continues to preoccupy policymakers. The issue became particularly thorny in the United States in the aftermath of the terrorist attack of September 11, 2001, when in 2004 the United States suspended normal legal protections and restraints against torture in the treatment of military prisoners from the wars in Iraq and Afghanistan and in dealing with potential terrorists at home. Problems of definition still remain, and there is no universal agreement on the exact nature of human rights. Controversy on the weight of political and civil rights and social, cultural, and economic rights continues to divide richer and poorer nations. Still, the United Nations Declaration of Human Rights, to which 160 nations are signatories, provides a basic guide and an outline for the future.

QUESTIONS

- Why might various regimes oppose human rights, and on what basis?
- Is the human rights movement a Western replacement for imperialism as a way to exert international political influence?
- Have international human rights movements produced political change?

come to power in a 1998 election. He survived a coup in 2002 and threatened to move the country toward a more independent foreign policy by rejecting Washington's economic plans and by joining forces with other opponents of U.S. policies. By 2009 he had removed restrictions on his continuation in office and mobilized support among other nations in Latin America. In other countries the military was sometimes troublesome, but a commitment to a more open political system in most of the region seemed firm.

The United States and Latin America: Continuing Presence

As a backdrop to the political and economic story we have traced thus far stands the continuing presence of the United States. After World War I, the United States emerged as the predominant power in the hemisphere, a position it had already begun to assume at the end of the 19th century with the Cuban–Spanish–American war and the building of the Panama Canal. European nations were displaced as the leading investors in Latin America by the United States. In South America, private investments by American companies and entrepreneurs, as well as loans from the American government, were the chief means of U.S. influence. U.S. investments rose to more than $5 billion by 1929, or more than one-third of all U.S. investments abroad.

Cuba and Puerto Rico experienced direct U.S. involvement and almost a protectorate status. But in the Caribbean and Central America, the face of U.S. power, economic interest, and disregard for the sovereignty of weaker neighbors was most apparent. Military interventions to protect U.S.-owned properties and investments became so common that there were more than 30 before 1933 (Map 33.1). Haiti, Nicaragua, the Dominican Republic, Mexico, and Cuba all experienced direct interventions by U.S. troops. Central America was a peculiar case because the level of private investments by U.S. companies such as United Fruit was very high and the economies of these countries were so closely tied to the United States. Those who resisted the U.S. presence were treated as bandits by expeditionary

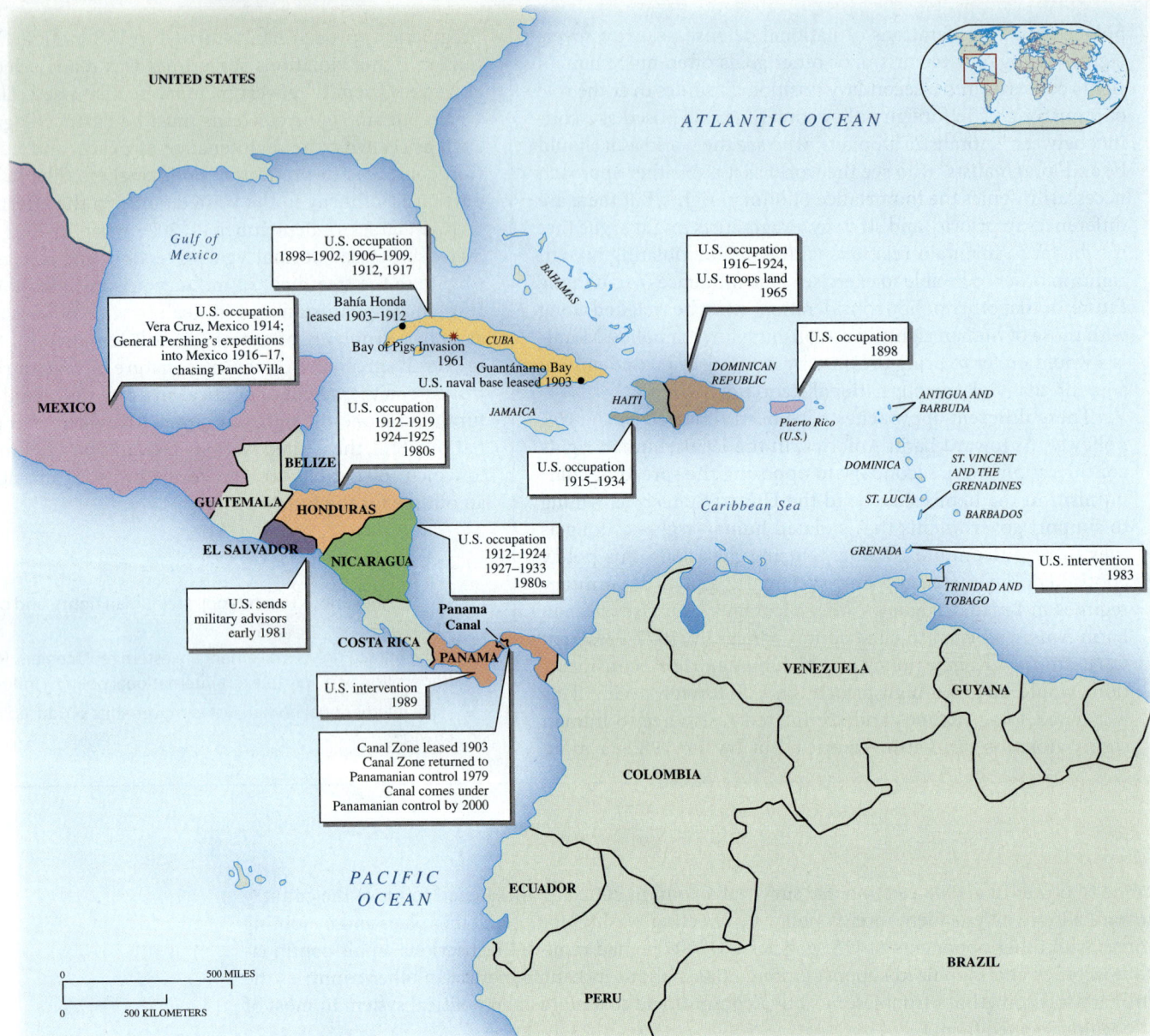

MAP 33.1 **U.S. Military Interventions, 1898–2000** Moved by strategic, economic, and political considerations, the United States repeatedly intervened militarily in the Caribbean and also used its political influence to support regimes that assured "stability" and protected U.S. interests. After 1945 and especially after Castro's alliance with the Soviet Union, cold war considerations also affected U.S. policy.

banana republics Term given to governments supported or created by the United States in Central America; believed to be either corrupt or subservient to U.S. interests.

Sandino, Augusto Led a guerrilla resistance movement against U.S. occupation forces in Nicaragua; assassinated by Nicaraguan National Guard in 1934; became national hero and symbol of resistance to U.S. influence in Central America.

forces. In Nicaragua, **Augusto Sandino** led a resistance movement against occupying troops until his assassination by the U.S.-trained Nicaraguan National Guard in 1934. His struggle against U.S. intervention made him a hero and later the figurehead of the Sandinista party, which carried out a socialist revolution in Nicaragua in the 1980s.

The grounds for these interventions were economic, political, strategic, and ideological. The direct interventions usually were followed by the creation or support of conservative governments, often dictatorships that would be friendly to the United States. These became known as **banana republics**, a reference not only to their dependence on the export of tropical products but also to their often subservient and corrupt governments.

Foreign interventions contributed to a growing nationalist reaction. Central America with its continuing political problems became a symbol of Latin America's weakness in the face of foreign influence and interference, especially by the United States. The Nobel Prize–winning Chilean communist poet Pablo Neruda, in his poem "The United Fruit Co.," (1950) spoke of the dictators of Central

America as "circus flies, wise flies, learned in tyranny" who buzzed over the graves of the people. He wrote the following lines with passion:

> When the trumpet sounded, everything
> on earth was prepared
> and Jehovah distributed the world
> to Coca Cola Inc., Anaconda,
> Ford Motors and other entities:
> The Fruit Company Inc.
> the central coast of my land,
> the sweet waist of America.
> It re-baptized the lands
> "Banana Republics"

The actions of the United States changed for a time after 1937. In that year, President Franklin D. Roosevelt introduced the **Good Neighbor Policy**, which promised to deal more fairly with Latin America and to stop direct interventions. After World War II, however, the U.S. preoccupation with containment of the Soviet Union and communism led to new strategies in Latin America. They included participation in regional organizations, the support of governments that at least expressed democratic or anticommunist principles, the covert undermining of governments considered unfriendly to U.S. interests, and when necessary, direct intervention. Underlying much of this policy was also a firm belief that economic development would eliminate the conditions that contributed to radical political solutions. Thus, U.S. programs such as the **Alliance for Progress**, begun in 1961, aimed to develop the region as an alternative to those solutions. The alliance had limited success despite good intentions and more than $10 billion in aid, but many Latin Americans perceived that it benefited the elites rather than the poor. Because of its record, Latin Americans and North Americans both began to question the assumption that development was basically a problem of capital and resources and that appropriate strategies would lead to social and economic improvement, which in turn would forestall revolution.

During the 1970s and 1980s, U.S. policy often was pragmatic, accepting Latin America as it was, which meant dealing on friendly terms with the military dictatorships as part of a cold war strategy. President Jimmy Carter made a new initiative to deal with Latin America and to influence governments there to observe civil liberties. Most significantly, a treaty was signed with Panama that ceded to that nation eventual control of the Panama Canal. In 1979, he also received the Sandinista rebels who had overthrown the dictator of Nicaragua and offered them financial aid. But increasing violence in Central America in the 1980s and the more conservative presidencies of Ronald Reagan and George H. Bush led the United States back to policies based on strategic, economic, and defense considerations in which direct intervention or support of counterrevolutionary forces such as the Contras in Nicaragua played a part. Thus, in 1989 and 1990, the United States toppled a government in Panama that was authoritarian, defied U.S. policies, and promoted drug smuggling, replacing it with a cooperative regime backed by American troops.

After 2000, U.S. concerns with Latin America continued to focus on the issues of commerce, immigration, the drug trade, and political stability. Militarization of the campaign against drugs and increasing concern with terrorism meant that by 2003 almost 60 percent of U.S. aid to Latin America was pledged to military purposes. Globalization for Latin America did increase national economic growth, but free trade arrangements did not protect workers and well over 30 percent of the region's population still fell below the poverty line. That fact contributed to the growing tide of Latin American migration—legal and illegal—to the United States. By 2013 there were 52 million Hispanics in the United States, about 35 percent of them immigrants.

Good Neighbor Policy Established by Franklin D. Roosevelt for dealing with Latin America in 1933; intended to halt direct intervention in Latin American politics.

Alliance for Progress Begun in 1961 by the United States to develop Latin America as an alternative to radical political solutions; enjoyed only limited success; failure of development programs led to renewal of direct intervention.

Read the Document on MyHistoryLab: Ronald Reagan, Support for the Contras (1984)

SOCIETIES IN SEARCH OF CHANGE

33.4 How did urbanization in Latin America compare to the rest of the developing world and how did it alter the lives of its people?

Despite frustrated Latin American attempts at profound reform, there were great changes during the 20th century. Social and gender relations changed during the century. We have already seen how countries such as Mexico, Peru, and Bolivia sought to enfranchise their Indian populations during this

Social relations changed slowly in Latin America. Population growth, urbanization, and the migration of workers continued to challenge the region.

century in different ways and with differing degrees of success. National ideologies and actual practice often are not the same, and discrimination on the basis of ethnicity continues. To be called "Indian" is still an insult in many places in Latin America. Although ethnic and cultural mixture characterizes many Latin American populations and makes Indian and African elements important features of national identity, relations with Indian populations often continue to be marked by exploitation and discrimination in nations as diverse as Brazil, Nicaragua, and Guatemala.

Slow Change in Women's Roles

The role of women has changed slowly. After World War I, women in Latin America continued to live under inequalities in the workplace and in politics. Women were denied the right to vote anywhere in Latin America until Ecuador enfranchised women in 1929 and Brazil and Cuba did the same in 1932. Throughout most of the region, those examples were not followed until the 1940s and 1950s. In some nations, the traditional associations of women with religion and the Catholic Church in Hispanic life made reformers and revolutionaries fear that women would become a conservative force in national politics. This attitude, combined with traditional male attitudes that women should be concerned only with home and family, led to a continued exclusion of women from political life. In response, women formed various associations and clubs and began to push for the vote and other issues of interest to them.

Feminist organizations, suffrage movements, and international pressures eventually combined to bring about change. In Argentina, 15 bills for female suffrage were introduced in the senate before the vote was won in 1945. Sometimes the victory was a matter of political expediency for those in power: In the Dominican Republic and some other countries, the enfranchisement of women was a strategy used by conservative groups to add more conservative voters to the electorate in an effort to hold off political change. In Argentina, recently enfranchised women became a major pillar of the Peronist regime, although that regime also suppressed female political opponents such as Victoria Ocampo, editor of the important literary magazine *Sur*.

Women eventually discovered that the ability to vote did not in itself guarantee political rights or the ability to have their specific issues heard. After achieving the vote, women tended to join the national political parties, where traditional prejudices against women in public life limited their ability to influence political programs. In Argentina, Brazil, Colombia, and Chile, for example, the integration of women into national political programs was slow, and women did not participate in proportion to their numbers. In a few cases, however, women played a crucial role in elections (Figure 33.7).

Some of the earliest examples of mobilization of women and their integration into the national labor force of various Latin American nations came in the period just before World War I and continued thereafter. The classic roles of women as homemakers, mothers, and agricultural workers were expanded as women entered the industrial labor force in growing numbers. By 1911 in Argentina, for example, women made up almost 80 percent of the textile and clothing industry's workers. But women found that their salaries often were below those of comparable male workers and that their jobs, regardless of the skill levels demanded, were considered unskilled and thus less well paid. Under these conditions, women, like other workers, joined the anarchist, socialist, and other labor unions and organizations.

Labor organizations are only a small part of the story of women in the labor force. In countries such as Peru, Bolivia, and Ecuador, women working in the markets control much small-scale commerce and have become increasingly active politically. In the growing service sectors, women have also become an important part of the labor force. Shifts in attitudes about women's roles have come more slowly than political and economic changes. Even in revolutionary Cuba, where a Law of the Family guaranteed equal rights and responsibilities within the home, enforcement has been difficult.

By the mid-1990s, the position of women in Latin America was closer to that in western Europe and North America than to the other areas of the world. Women like Violeta Chamorro (Nicaragua, 1990–1997), Cristina Kirchner (Argentina, 2007–) and Dilma Rouseff (Brazil, 2011–) were elected to the presidency of their countries, and by 2012 women held 25 percent of the ministerial posts in Latin American governments. In terms of demographic patterns, health, education, and place in the workforce, the comparative position of women reinforced Latin America's intermediate position between industrialized and developing nations.

FIGURE 33.7 President Dilma Rouseff of Brazil visits China, emphasizing the growing economic power of Asian and Latin American economies. Rouseff, Brazil's first female president and the political successor of Lula's Worker's Party, symbolized to many an increasing influence of women in Latin American politics and Brazil's efforts to combine social programs with economic development. The increasing participation of women in the political process has been noted throughout the region.

The Movement of People

In 1950 the populations of North America (United States and Canada) and Latin America were both about 165 million, but by 1985 North America's population was 265 million, while Latin America's had grown to more than 400 million. Declining mortality and continuing high fertility were responsible for this situation.

At the beginning of the 20th century, the major trend of population movement was immigration to Latin America, but the region has long experienced internal migration and the movement of people within the hemisphere. By the 1980s, this movement had reached significant levels, fed by the flow of workers seeking jobs, the demands of capital for cheap labor, and the flight of political refugees seeking basic freedoms. During World War II, government programs to supply laborers were set up between the United States and Mexico, but these were always accompanied by extralegal migration, which fluctuated with the economy. Conditions for migrant laborers often were deplorable, although the extension of social welfare to them in the 1960s began to address some of the problems. By the 1970s, more than 750,000 illegal Mexican migrants a year were crossing the border—some more than once—as the United States continued to attract migrants.

This internationalization of the labor market was comparable in many ways with the movement of workers from poorer countries such as Turkey, Morocco, Portugal, and Spain to the stronger economies of West Germany and France. In Latin America it also reflected the fact that industrialization in the 20th century depended on highly mechanized industry that did not create enough new jobs to meet the needs of the growing population. Much of the migration has been to the United States, but there has also been movement across Latin American frontiers: Haitians migrate to work in the Dominican Republic, and Colombians illegally migrate to Venezuela. By the 1970s, about 5 million people per year were migrating in Latin America and the Caribbean.

Politics has also been a major impulse for migration. Haitians fleeing political repression and abysmal conditions have risked great dangers in small open boats to reach the United States. The Cuban revolution caused one of the great political migrations of the century. Beginning in 1959, when the Cuban middle class fled socialism, and continuing into the 1980s with the flight of Cuban workers, almost 1 million Cubans left the island. The revolutionary upheaval in Nicaragua, political violence in Central America, and poverty in Haiti have contributed to the flight of refugees. Often, it is difficult to

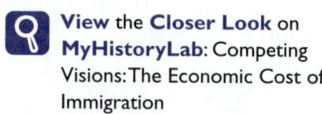

View the **Closer Look** on **MyHistoryLab**: Competing Visions: The Economic Cost of Immigration

TABLE 33-1 POPULATION OF CAPITAL CITIES AS A PERCENTAGE OF TOTAL POPULATION IN 10 LATIN AMERICAN NATIONS

Nation	Capital	1880	1930	1960	1983	2012
Argentina	Buenos Aires	12	20	32	34	32
Brazil	Rio de Janeiro	3	4	7	4*	3*
Chile	Santiago	6	13	22	37	31
Colombia	Bogotá	1	2	8	11	15
Cuba	Havana	13	15	18	20	20
Mexico	Mexico City	3	5	15	20	16
Panama	Panama City	7	16	25	20	12
Peru	Lima	3	5	19	27	27
Uruguay	Montevideo	12	28	31	40	40
Venezuela	Caracas	3	7	20	18	7

*No longer the capital city.
SOURCES: From J. P. Cole, *Latin America: An Economic and Social Geography* (1965), 417; and http://www.world-gazetteer.com.

separate political and economic factors in the movement of people from their homelands.

International migration is only part of the story. During the 20th century, there was a marked movement in Latin America from rural to urban areas (Table 33.1). Whereas in the 19th century Latin America was an agrarian region, by the 1980s about one-half of the population lived in cities of more than 20,000, and more than 25 of these cities had populations of more than 1 million. Some of these cities had reached enormous size. By 2012 Mexico City had more than 20 million inhabitants, São Paulo had over 18 million, and Buenos Aires had over 13 million. Latin America was by far the most urbanized area of the developing world and only slightly less urbanized than western Europe.

The problem is not simply size but rate of growth. The urban populations grew at a rate about three times that of the population as a whole, which itself has grown rapidly. Urban economies have not been able to create enough jobs for the rapidly increasing population. Often recent migrants lived in marginal neighborhoods or in shantytowns, which have become characteristic of the rapidly growing cities of Latin America. These *favelas*, to use the Brazilian term, have created awful living conditions, but over time some have become poorer neighborhoods within the cities, and community cooperation and action within them have secured basic urban services. More recently, the rate of urban growth has slowed, but the social problems in the cities remain a major challenge.

Although Latin American urbanization increased rapidly after 1940, the percentage of its people living in cities is still less than in western Europe but more than in Asia and Africa. Unlike the 19th-century European experience, the lack of employment in Latin American cities has kept rural migrants from becoming part of a laboring class with a strong identification with fellow workers. Those who do succeed in securing industrial jobs often join paternalistic labor organizations that are linked to the government. Thus, there is a separation between the chronically underemployed urban lower class and the industrial labor force. Whereas industrialization and urbanization promoted strong class solidarity in 19th-century Europe, which led to the gains of organized labor, in contemporary Latin America nationalist and populist politics have weakened the ability of the working class to operate effectively in politics.

Cultural Reflections of Despair and Hope

Latin America remains an amalgamation of cultures and peoples trying to adjust to changing world realities. Protestant denominations have made some inroads, but the vast majority of Latin Americans are still Catholic. Hispanic traditions of family, gender relations, business, and social interaction influence everyday life and help to determine responses to the modern world.

Latin American popular culture remains vibrant. It draws on African and Indian traditional crafts, images, and techniques but arranges them in new ways. Music is also part of popular culture. The Argentine tango of the turn of the century began in the music halls of lower-class working districts of Buenos Aires and became an international craze. The African-influenced Brazilian samba and the Caribbean salsa have spread widely. They are a Latin American contribution to world civilization.

The struggle for social justice, economic security, and political formulas in keeping with the cultural and social realities of their nations has provided a dynamic tension that has produced tremendous artistic achievements. Latin American poets and novelists have gained worldwide recognition. We have already noted the artistic accomplishments of the Mexican Revolution. In 1922 Brazilian artists, composers, and authors staged a Modern Art Week in São Paulo, which emphasized a search for a national artistic expression that reflected Brazilian realities.

That theme also preoccupied authors elsewhere in Latin America. The social criticism of the 1930s produced powerful realist novels, which revealed the exploitation of the poor, the peasantry, and the Indians. Whether in the heights of the Andes or in the dark streets of the growing urban slums, the plight of the common folk provided a generation of authors with themes worthy of their effort. Social and political criticism has remained a central feature of Latin American literature and art and has played an important role in the development of newer art forms such as film.

The inability to bring about social justice or to influence politics has also sometimes led Latin American artists and intellectuals to follow other paths. In the 1960s a wave of literature took place in which novels that mixed the political, the historical, the erotic, and the fantastic were produced by a generation of authors who used "magical realism" because they found the reality of Latin America too absurd to be described by the traditional forms or logic. Writers such as the Argentine Jorge Luis Borges (1899–1980) and the Colombian Gabriel García Marquez (b. 1928) won acclaim throughout the world. García Marquez's *One Hundred Years of Solitude* (1967) used the history of a family in a mythical town called Macondo as an allegory of Latin America and traced the evils that befell the family and the community as they moved from naive isolation to a maturity that included oppression, exploitation, war, revolution, and natural disaster but never subdued the spirit of its people. This literary "boom" of the 1960s has been followed by a subsequent generation of novels that has emphasized emotions and personal fulfillment and by "testimonial" books that have sometimes mixed autobiography with fiction as a way to bring the reality of Latin American life and politics to a personal level.

Global Connections and Critical Themes

STRUGGLING TOWARD THE FUTURE IN A GLOBAL ECONOMY

As Latin America entered the 21st century, it continued to search for economic growth, social justice, and political stability. No easy solutions were available. In many ways, Latin American societies remained "unrevolutionary"—unable to bring about needed changes because of deeply entrenched class interests, international conditions, or power politics. However, the struggle for change had produced some important results. Between 1900 and 2000 literacy rates and life expectancy doubled in the region and the standard of living improved in many countries, especially after 1950. The Mexican and Cuban revolutions brought profound changes in those countries and had a broad impact on the rest of the hemisphere, either as models to copy or as dangers to be avoided. Other nations, such as Bolivia, Peru, and Nicaragua, attempted their own versions of radical change with greater or lesser success. New forms of politics, sometimes populist and sometimes militarist, were tried. New political and social ideas, such as those of liberation theology, grew out of the struggle to find a just and effective formula for change. Latin American authors and artists served as a conscience for their societies and received worldwide recognition for their depiction of the sometimes bizarre reality they observed. Although tremendous problems continued to face the region, Latin America remained the most advanced part of the developing world. Levels of literacy, for example, easily surpassed those in most of Asia and in Africa.

In the age of globalization, Latin America faces new challenges. The new world economy has created opportunities for expansion, and in the 1990s Latin American economies grew considerably, but this growth has made the problems of the distribution of wealth in Latin America even more acute. Other problems also result from economic changes. The northern part of Mexico near the border with the United States has benefited from new trade opportunities while southern Mexico has gotten poorer. Then too, integration into the world economy often threatens traditional cultures. Since the 1980s, various indigenous peoples' political movements have sought to protect traditional cultures while seeking political and economic opportunities. Frustrated by continuing social problems and its disadvantages in the global economy of free trade and privatization, Latin America moved toward the left. By 2008, Leftist presidents had been elected in Chile, Nicaragua, Ecuador, Peru, and Bolivia, joining those already in power in Cuba, Venezuela, Brazil, Argentina, and Uruguay. This trend revealed collective discontent and sometimes a strident rhetoric of opposition to U.S. policies, but it also demonstrated that democratic politics were functioning through much of the region as countries sought policies designed to overcome extreme inequalities of wealth. When in 2007 Venezuelan president Chávez sought by referendum to broaden his presidential powers and hold the office for life, he was defeated. He accepted the vote and later succeeded in 2008. A new political leadership was emerging. Chile elected its first woman president in 2006, and in Bolivia, Evo Morales was the first president of Native American background to be elected. Some, like Chávez and Morales, joined Cuba's ailing Castro in open opposition of U.S. policies. Others like Brazil's Lula, a former factory worker, sought better trade relations. Despite the differences among these new leaders, they represented Latin American concern for the region's place in the emerging global order.

Cultural issues remain unresolved as well. Partly reflecting divisions in wealth and urbanism, Latin Americans have participated variously in global consumer currents. Middle-class Mexicans, for example, began to copy U.S. patterns in celebrating Halloween (previously an important traditional holiday focused on the forces of death) and Christmas. To some Mexican intellectuals, this represented a crucial abandonment of identity, and to others the new interests seemed either alien or unobtainable. The spread of new religious movements, including fundamentalist Protestantism, signaled an attempt to provide alternatives to global culture, particularly among urban slum-dwellers. About 10 percent of Latin Americans are now members of Protestant denominations. At the same time, Latin American filmmakers, artists, and popular musicians have contributed directly to global culture, often incorporating traditional elements in the process and joining them to hip-hop and other international music styles. Latin America's global position has become increasingly complex.

Further Readings

A considerable literature in many disciplines deals with Latin America as a whole, and there are many country-specific studies. A good introductory text, which presents a variation of the "dependency" interpretation, is Thomas E. Skidmore and Peter H. Smith, *Modern Latin America* (1989). John Charles Chasteen, *Born in Fire and Blood* (2001), and Peter Winn, *Americas: The Changing Face of Latin America and the Caribbean*, 3rd ed. (2006) gives up-to-date overviews.

The economic history of Latin America is summarized ably in Victor Bulmer-Thomas, *The Economic History of Latin America Since Independence* (1994). An overview is provided by Richard Salvucci, ed., in *Latin America and the World Economy* (1996).

Charles Berquist, *Labor in Latin America* (1986), provides a good overall starting point, and there are excellent case studies like John French, *Drowning in Laws: Labor Law and Brazilian Political Culture* (2004); Peter Winn, *Victims of the Chilean Miracle: Workers and Neoliberalism in the Pinochet Era, 1973–2002* (2004); and Ann Farnsworth-Alvear, *Dulcinea in the Factory: Myths, Morals, Men, and Women in Colombia's Industrial Experiment, 1905–1960* (2000). Recent approaches are analyzed in Maria Lorena Cook, *The Politics of Labor Reform* (2007).

There are many good studies of Latin American politics, but Guillermo O'Donnell, *Modernization and Bureaucratic Authoritarianism* (1973), influenced a generation of scholars. The role of the United States is discussed in Brian Loveman, *No Higher Law: American Foreign Policy and the Western Hemisphere since 1776* (2010). John Coatsworth, *Central America and the United States* (1994), is a critical assessment of U.S. policy in that region. Greg Grandin, *Empire's Workshop: Latin America, the United States and the Rise of the New Imperialism* (2006) argues that U.S. policies in Latin America were later applied in other regions. Recent scholarship has emphasized the cultural dimensions of this relationship. Frederick Pike, *The United States and Latin America: Myths and Stereotypes of Civilization and Nature* (1992), set the outlines of cultural relations. Gilbert Joseph et al., eds., *Close Encounters of Empire* (1998), presents suggestive essays. Lars Schoultz, *Human Rights and United States Policy Toward Latin America* (1981), details the influence of human rights on foreign policy and the challenges of setting consistent policies. Steve Stern's trilogy, *Remembering Pinochet's Chile* (2004), *Battling for Hearts and Minds* (2006), and *Reckoning with Pinochet* (2010) discusses the difficulty of national reconciliation when those rights are violated.

The high level of scholarship on Latin America is demonstrated by books like. Alan Knight, *The Mexican Revolution*, 2 vols. (1990) which provides an excellent analysis of that event; Friedrich Katz, *The Life and Times of Pancho Villa* (1998), an outstanding biography; and Florencia Mallon, *The Defense of Community in Peru's Central Highlands* (1983) that looks at national change from a community perspective. The Cuban revolution and its implications are treated in Louis Perez, *On Becoming Cuban: Identity, Nationality, and Culture* (1999), and Aviva Chomsky, *A History of the Cuban Revolution* (2011). David Kunzle et al. examine the role of Che Guevara in the Cuban revolution and its legacy for the wider world in *Che Guevara: Icon, Myth, and Message* (2002).

Frank McCann, *Soldiers of the Patria* (2004), on the military in Brazil, is one of the most in-depth studies of a Latin American military establishment, and Richard Gott, *Guerrilla Movements in Latin America* (1972), is, despite its age, a valuable book that presented analysis and documents on the movements seeking revolutionary change at that time. On some of the major themes of the 21st century, there are Juan Gonzalez, *Harvest of Empire: A History of Latinos in America* (2000); Michael Coniff, ed., *Populism in Latin America* (1999); Steve Ellner and Daniel Hellinger, *Venezuela Politics in the Chávez Era* (2003); and Carol Wise, ed., *The Post-NAFTA Political Economy: Mexico and the Western Hemisphere* (1998). Fernando-López-Alves and Diana E. Johnson, *Globalization and Uncertainty in Latin America* (2007), look at the future economic and political challenges, and Kurt Weyland, R. Madrid, and W. Hunter, *Leftist Governments in Latin America. Successes and Shortcomings* (2010), examine the recent political swing away from neo-liberalism. Finally, a new interest in environmental history can be seen in Reinaldo Funes Monzote, *From Rainforest to Cane Field in Cuba* (2008); John McNeil, *Mosquito Empires. Ecology and War in the Greater Caribbean, 1620–1914* (2010); and Shawn William Miller, *An Environmental History of Latin America* (2007).

On MyHistoryLab

 Study and Review on MyHistoryLab

Critical Thinking Questions

1. Why has it been so difficult to bring about structural change in most of Latin America? How has Latin America's role in the global economy improved the life of its citizens?

2. What role has Latin America's relationship to the United States played in its economic and political life; and what role is it likely to play in the future?

Africa, the Middle East, and Asia in the Era of Independence

34

Listen to Chapter 34 on MyHistoryLab

As she had so often in the past, Indira Gandhi refused to heed those who urged her to be cautious. She had audaciously ordered the army to drive the extreme separatist Sikhs from the sacred grounds of the Golden Temple in Amritsar in northwest India. Indian troops had carried out her orders all too well. They had evicted the Sikh radicals, who demanded an independent state, which they called Khalistan. But in the process the troops had killed thousands of Sikhs inside the temple grounds and destroyed or badly damaged many revered shrines, including the library housing the Sikhs' holy scriptures. Now her advisors pleaded with her to replace her Sikh bodyguards with elite army units that had no religious or kinship ties to the aggrieved Sikh community. But Prime Minister Gandhi insisted that the Sikh units that had traditionally guarded her—and her father and British colonial rulers before him—remained loyal and placed their honor

LEARNING OBJECTIVES

34.1 Which of the challenges facing post-colonial nations after 1945 do you think were the most critical and why? p. 845

34.2 Which, if any, of the postcolonial paths to political stability and socioeconomic development do you think was the most successful and what factors were the most important in shaping positive outcomes? p. 856

34.3 How did religious revivalist movements, most especially the one led by Ayatollah Khomeini in Iran, differ from other twentieth century revolutions, and why was decolonization delayed in almost all settler colonial societies, such as South Africa? p. 862

FIGURE **34.1** As this photograph of Indian Prime Minister Indira Gandhi strikingly reveals, she reveled in direct contact with the ordinary people of India. Seeing herself as the champion of the poor and defenseless, she refused to be isolated by the phalanxes of bodyguards commonly associated with national leaders across the globe.

843

Watch the Video Series on MyHistoryLab

Learn about some key topics related to this chapter with the *MyHistoryLab Video Series: Key Topics in World History*

as soldiers and duty to the nation above whatever sympathy they might feel for radical elements among the Sikh faithful.

So Sikh soldiers were on guard several months later as Indira Gandhi walked from her home through a beloved garden to her nearby office. As she approached the garden gate, she was challenged by two of her most trusted protectors, both Sikhs, who opened fire at close range and riddled her body with bullets. The assassination sparked anti-Sikh riots across India's capital that left thousands dead and sections of the city smoldering ruins. Her son Rajiv, who had only recently taken up a political career, was soon sworn in as her successor. But across the world's largest democracy, Indira was mourned as the lost "mother of the nation" and a relentless champion of the poor and powerless.

Few Indian politicians expected Indira Gandhi to be a forceful, dynamic prime minister with a vision of her own when she first came to power in January 1966. As the daughter of Jawaharlal Nehru, who was second only to Gandhi among those who fashioned the nationalist revolt and one of the most influential leaders of the early cold war decades, Indira Gandhi inherited close links to the powerful. But although she became her father's confidante and close companion, she was regarded by India's numerous time-tested and ambitious politicians as a shy young woman who was content to be her father's helpmate. Seeing her as someone they could control, several of the power brokers of the Congress party backed her as the successor to Lal Bahadur Shastri. Shastri, who had become prime minister on the death of her father two years before, only to die suddenly himself of a heart attack in the first days of 1966.

Indira Gandhi soon made it clear that she was as strong-willed as her father and as determined to pursue her own agenda for the uplift of India's peoples and extending the nation's influence in international affairs. Perhaps even more than her famous father, she was a rousing speaker, able to energize party loyalists and supporters as well as frustrate the ambitions of rival leaders within the Congress Party and the attacks of opposition politicians. She successfully led India in war against Pakistan and oversaw the birth of the nation of Bangladesh that had formerly made up the eastern half of the Pakistani state. Although she pursued a populist, reformist agenda in domestic politics, she maintained India's neutrality through some of the more turbulent decades

1910 C.E.	1920 C.E.	1930 C.E.	1940 C.E.	1950 C.E.
1912 African National Congress party formed **1919** First Pan-African Nationalist Congress	**1928** Founding of the Muslim Brotherhood in Egypt	**1930s** Free Officers movement develops in Egypt	**1947** India and Pakistan achieve independence **1948** First Arab-Israeli War; Afrikaner Nationalist party comes to power in South Africa, bringing the beginning of apartheid **1949** Hassan al-Banna assassinated in Egypt	**1951** India's first five-year plan for economic development launched **1952** Farouk and khedival regime overthrown in Egypt; Nasser and Free Officers come to power **1955** Bandung Conference; beginning of nonaligned movement **1956** Aborted British-French-Israeli intervention in Suez **1958** South Africa completely independent of Great Britain

of the cold war. Her nationalization policies and moves to restrict the powers of her adversaries in the legislature were seen by many at the time as harmful to India's fledgling democracy. But in the face of a country deeply divided religiously and ethnically, in which famine and poverty remained pervasive problems, Indira Gandhi preserved the independent judiciary, multiparty competition and free elections that are the hallmarks of India to the present day. With the exception of a three-year hiatus after she had been defeated in national elections in 1977, she dominated Indian politics from 1966 until her assassination in 1984. ∎

The prodigious challenges faced by activist postcolonial leaders, such as Indira Gandhi, and the often very different strategies for tackling them adopted by different African and Asian leaders are the focus of this chapter. On a resource base depleted by millennia of use, Prime Minister Gandhi sought to find ways first to feed the people and then to improve the living standards of one of the poorest and most populous nations on earth. Like other leaders of developing nations, she had to find a way to balance the demands of the U.S. and Soviet superpowers while maintaining India's nonaligned status in a world threatened by nuclear conflagration. And as demonstrated by the confrontation with the Sikh separatists—only one of a number of highly inflammatory ethno-religious divisions she had to deal with—like other leaders in the emerging nations, Indira Gandhi spent a great deal of her energy and political capital just holding the country together.

Like the majority of postcolonial heads of state in the developing world, Gandhi sought to centralize power in her own hands, and she resorted at times to preemptive strikes against her political opponents or used force to put down what she perceived as enemies of the new nation. And like so many of her counterparts in the often artificial and unstable political entities carved out of the Euro-American colonial empires, she was violently removed from power. Indira Gandhi's regime ended with her assassination by loyalists turned into implacable enemies by her violent attempt to suppress separatist forces similar to those that have threatened at one time or other to pull apart virtually all of the new nations of the developing world.

THE CHALLENGES OF INDEPENDENCE

34.1 Which of the challenges facing post-colonial nations after 1945 do you think were the most critical and why?

The nationalist movements that won independence for most of the peoples of Africa, the Middle East, and Asia usually involved some degree of mass mobilization. Peasants and working-class townspeople, who hitherto had little voice in politics beyond their village boundaries or local labor associations,

In the early decades of independence, the very existence of the nation-states that were carved out of the Western colonial empires was often challenged by internal rivalries between different social and ethnic groups. Economic growth was hampered by unprecedented rates of population increase, the structure of the international market, and the underdeveloped state of most colonial economies at the time of independence.

1960 C.E.	1970 C.E.	1980 C.E.	1990 C.E.
1960 Sharpeville shootings in South Africa	**1970s** Peak period for OPEC cartel	**1980–1988** Iran-Iraq War	**1990** Nelson Mandela released from South African prison; Iraqi invasion of Kuwait
1966 Nkrumah overthrown by military coup in Ghana	**1971** Bangladesh revolt against West Pakistan; Indo-Pakistani War	**1989** De Klerk charts path of peaceful reform in South Africa	**1991** Persian Gulf War
1966–1970 Biafran secessionist war in Nigeria	**1972** Bangladesh becomes independent nation		**1994** First democratic elections in South Africa
1967 Six-Day War between Israel and Arab nations	**1973** Third Arab-Israeli War		
	1979 Shah of Iran overthrown; Islamic republic declared		

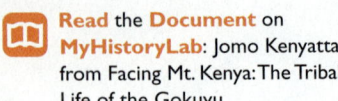

Read the Document on MyHistoryLab: Jomo Kenyatta, from Facing Mt. Kenya: The Tribal Life of the Gokuyu

were drawn into political contests that toppled empires and established new nations. To win the support of these groups, nationalist leaders promised jobs, civil rights, and equality once independence was won. The leaders of many nationalist movements nurtured visions of post-independence utopias in the minds of their followers. The people were told that once the Europeans, who monopolized the best jobs, were driven away and their exploitive hold on the economy was brought to an end, there would be enough to give everyone a good life.

Unfortunately, post-independence realities in almost all of the new nations made it impossible for nationalist leaders to fulfill the expectations they had aroused among their followers and, in varying degrees, among the colonized populace at large. Even with the Europeans gone and the terms of economic exchange with more developed countries somewhat improved, there was simply not enough to go around. Thus, the socialist-inspired ideologies that nationalist leaders had often embraced and promoted were misleading. The problem was not just that goods and services were unequally distributed, leaving some people rich and the great majority poor. The problem was that there were not enough resources to take care of everybody, even if it was possible to distribute them equitably.

When utopia failed to materialize, personal rivalries and long-standing divisions between different classes and ethnic or religious groups, which had been muted by the common struggle against the alien colonizers, resurfaced or intensified. The European colonizers had established arbitrary boundaries (Maps 34.1 and 34.2), sometimes combining hostile ethnic or religious groups. In almost all the new states, these rivalries and differences became dominant features of political life. They produced political instability and often threatened the viability of the nations themselves, as with East and West Pakistan, where extreme contrasts of topography and culture led to violence and the secession of the area that became **Bangladesh**. The recurring problems of famine and pervasive malnutrition in parts of Asia and Africa have stemmed from human conflicts as much as natural disasters (Figure 34.2). Rivalries and civil wars in many of the newly decolonized nations consumed resources that might have been devoted to economic development. They also blocked—in the name of the defense of subnational interests—measures designed to build more viable and prosperous states. Absorbed by the task of just holding their new nations together, politicians neglected problems—such as soaring population increases, uncontrolled urban growth, rural landlessness, and environmental degradation—that soon formed as large a threat as political instability to their young nations.

Bangladesh Founded as an independent nation in 1972; formerly East Pakistan.

The Population Bomb

The nationalist leaders who led the colonized peoples of Africa and Asia to independence had firmly committed themselves to promoting rapid economic development once colonial restraints were removed. In keeping with their Western-educated backgrounds, most of these leaders saw their nations following the path of industrialization that had brought national prosperity and international power to much of western Europe and the United States. This course of development was also fostered by representatives of the Soviet bloc, who had emphasized heavy industry in their state-directed drives to modernize their economies and societies. Of the many barriers to the rapid economic breakthroughs postcolonial leaders hoped for, the most formidable and persistent were the spiraling population increases that often overwhelmed whatever economic advances the peoples of the new nations managed to make (Figure 34.3).

Factors making for sustained population increases in already densely populated areas of Asia and Africa had begun to take effect even before the era of high colonialism. Food crops, mostly from the New World, contributed to dramatic population growth in China, India, and Java as early as the 17th century. They also helped sustain high levels of population in areas such as the Niger delta in West Africa, despite heavy losses as a result of the slave trade. The coming of colonial rule reinforced these upward trends in a number of ways. It ended local warfare that had caused population losses and, perhaps more significantly, had indirectly promoted the spread of epidemic diseases and famine. The new railroad and steamship links established by the colonizers to foster the spread of the market economy also cut down on the regional famines that had been a major check against sustained population increase since ancient times. Large amounts of food could be shipped from areas where harvests were good to those where drought or floods threatened the local inhabitants with starvation.

With war and famine—two of the main barriers to population increase—much reduced, growth began to speed up. This was particularly true in areas such as India and Java that had been under

MAP 34.1 The Emergence of New Nations in Africa after World War II A comparison of this map with Map 25.4 on page 599 quickly reveals the pronounced overlap between the boundaries drawn by the European imperialist powers and the postcolonial nations that emerged after 1945.

European control in some cases for centuries. Death rates declined, but birth rates remained much the same, leading to increasingly larger net increases. Improved hygiene and medical treatment played little part in this rise until the early 20th century. From that time, efforts to eradicate tropical diseases, as well as global scourges such as smallpox, and to improve sewage systems and purify drinking water have led to further population increases.

CHAPTER 34 Africa, the Middle East, and Asia in the Era of Independence 847

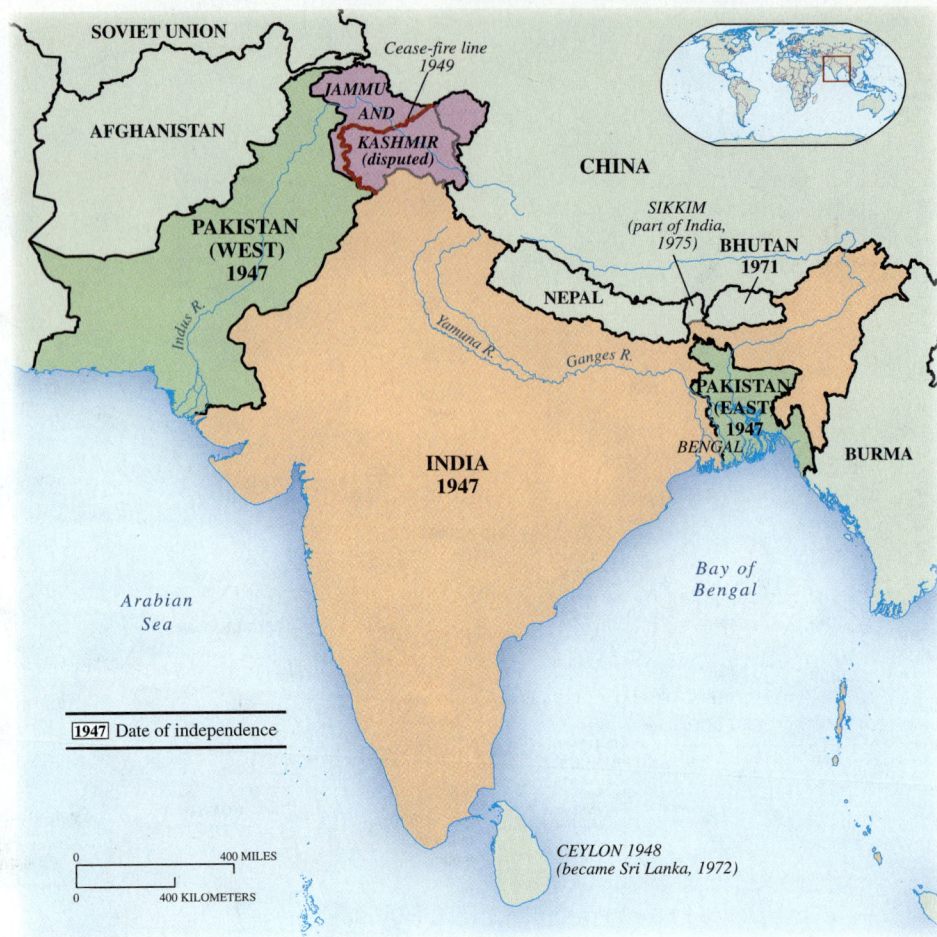

MAP 34.2 **The Partition of South Asia: The Formation of India, Pakistan, Bangladesh, and Sri Lanka** Religious fault lines largely explain the fragmentation of the South Asian empire that the British had forged in the 18th and early 19th centuries.

Nearly all leaders of the emerging nations headed societies in which population was increasing at unprecedented levels. This increase continued in the early years of independence. In much of Asia, it has begun to level off in recent decades. But in most of Africa, population growth continues at very high rates. In some cases, most notably south Asia, moderate growth rates have produced huge total populations because they were adding to an already large base. Population experts predicted in the 1970s that south Asia's population of more than 600 million would more than double by the year 2000. With more than 1 billion people in India alone at present, the prophecy has more than been fulfilled.

In Africa, by contrast, which began with low population levels relative to its large land area, very high birth rates and diminished mortality rates have resulted in very steep population increases in recent decades. Some population experts predict that if present growth rates continue, by the mid-21st century Nigeria will have a population equal to that of present-day China. In view of the AIDS epidemic that has spread through much of central and eastern Africa since the 1980s, some of the estimates for population increases in the continent as a whole may have to be revised downward. But recent measures of African productivity and per capita incomes suggest that even more moderate increases in population may be difficult to support at reasonable living standards. This prospect is underscored by estimates that the 400 million people of Africa are supported by a continental economy with a productive capacity equal to just 6 percent of that of the United States, or roughly equal to that of the state of Illinois.

On the face of it, the conquest of war, disease, and famine was one of the great achievements of European colonial regimes. It was certainly an accomplishment that colonial officials never tired of citing in defense of continued European dominance. But the European policy of limiting industrialization in their colonial dependencies meant that one of the key ways by which Europe had met its own population boom in the 19th and early 20th centuries was not available to the new nations. They lacked the factories to employ the exploding population that moved to the cities from the rural areas, as well as the technology to produce the necessities of life for more and more people. Unlike the Europeans and the Americans, the emerging nations found it difficult to draw food and mineral resources from the rest of the world to feed this growing population. In fact, these were the very things the colonized peoples had been set up to sell to the industrialized nations. Even in countries such as India, where impressive advances in industrialization were made in the postcolonial era, gains in productivity were swallowed up rapidly by the population explosion.

In most African and Asian countries, there has been resistance to birth control efforts aimed at controlling population growth. Some of this resistance is linked to deeply entrenched social patterns and religious beliefs. In many of these societies, procreation is seen as a sign of male virility. In addition, the capacity to bear children, preferably male children, continues to be critical to the social standing of women. In some cases, resistance to birth control is linked to specific cultural norms. For example, Hindus believe that a deceased man's soul cannot begin the cycle of rebirth until his eldest son has performed special ceremonies over his funeral pyre. This belief increases the already great pressure on Indian women to have children, and it encourages families to have several sons to ensure that at least one survives the father.

In Africa, children are seen as indispensable additions to the *lineage*: the extended network of relatives (and deceased ancestors) that, much more than the nuclear family, makes up the core social group over much of the subcontinent. As in India, sons are essential for continuing the patrilineal family line and performing burial and ancestral rites. The key roles played by women in agricultural production and marketing make girls highly valued in African societies. This is not true in many Asian societies, where high dowries and occupational restrictions limit their contribution to family welfare.

Before the 20th century, the high rates of stillbirths and infant mortality meant that mothers could expect to lose many of the children they conceived. Ten or 12 deaths of 15 or 16 children conceived was not unheard of. Beyond the obvious psychological scars left by these high death rates, they also fostered the conviction that it was necessary to have many children to ensure that some would outlive the parents. In societies where welfare systems and old-age pensions were meager or unknown, surviving children took on special urgency because they were the only ones who would care for parents who could no longer work for themselves. The persistence of these attitudes in recent decades, when medical advances have greatly reduced infant mortality, has been a major factor contributing to soaring population growth.

In the early decades after independence, many African and Asian leaders were deeply opposed to state measures to promote family planning and birth control. Some saw these as Western attempts to meddle in their internal affairs; others proudly declared that the socialist societies they were building would be able to take care of the additional population. As it has become increasingly clear that excessive population increase makes significant economic advances impossible, many of these leaders have begun to reassess their attitudes toward birth control. A particular cause for alarm is the fact that in many developing countries a high percentage of the population is under age 15 (as high as 40 percent in some areas) and thus dependent on others for support. But even for those who now want to promote family planning, the obstacles are staggering. In addition to the cultural and social factors just discussed, leaders often find they lack sufficient resources and the educated personnel needed to make these programs effective. High rates of illiteracy, particularly among women, must be overcome, but education is expensive. Perhaps no form of financial and technical assistance from the industrialized to the developing world will be as critical in the coming decades as that devoted to family planning.

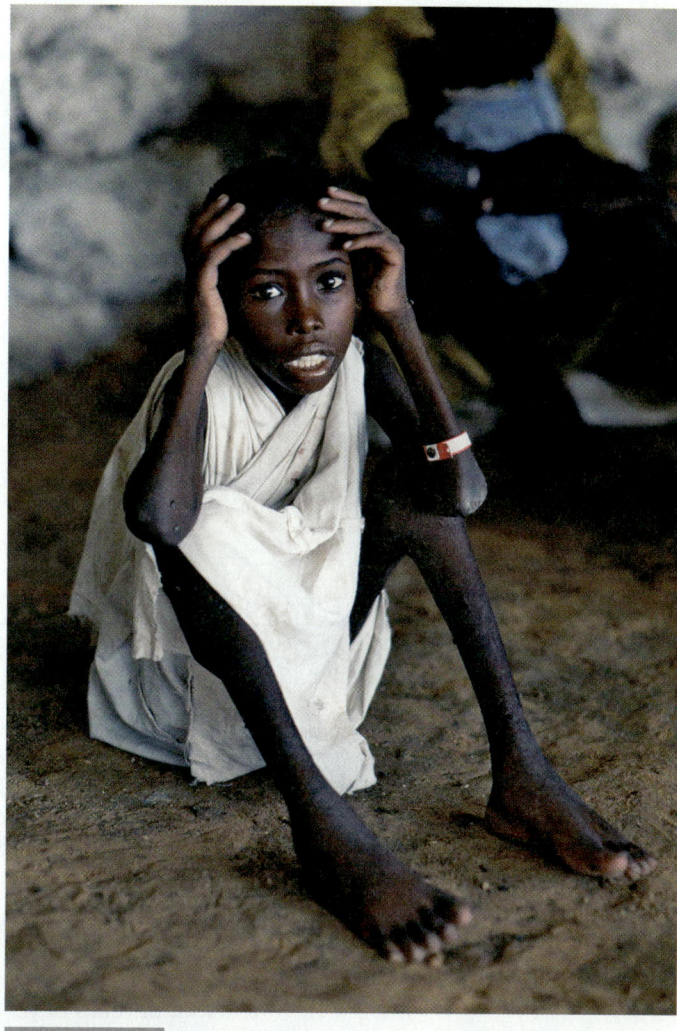

FIGURE **34.2** Since independence, famine has stalked much of the formerly colonized world, particularly in sub-Saharan Africa. Often, as in the case of these young refugees from the Nigerian civil war photographed in the late 1960s, starvation has been caused by human conflicts rather than natural disasters.

Read the Document on MyHistoryLab: Nelson Mandela, Closing Address at the 13th International AIDS Conference, July 2000

Read the Document on MyHistoryLab: Indian Declaration of Independence (1930)

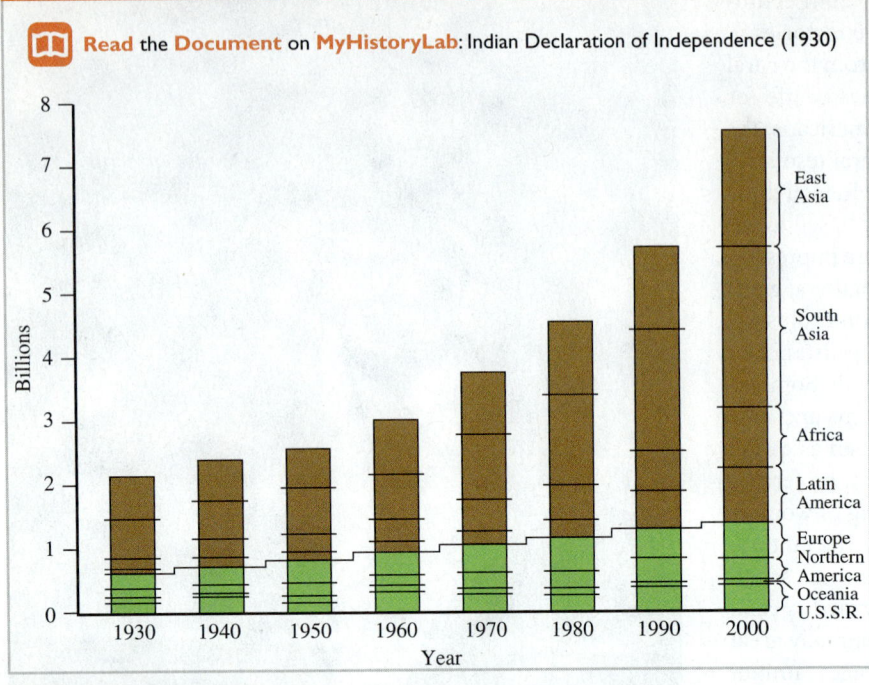

FIGURE 34.3 This graph shows the growth of the world population by major global geographic areas between 1930 and 2000. It illustrates the near-stabilization of the upswing in populations of the West and the states of the former Soviet Union that began with industrialization in the 18th century. It charts the explosion that occurred in recent decades in the areas of the globe that were colonized, both formally and informally, by the industrial powers in the 19th and early 20th centuries. These increases surpass those of any other epoch in human history.

Parasitic Cities and Endangered Ecosystems

As population increase in the rural areas of emerging nations outstripped the land and employment opportunities available to the peasantry, mass migrations to urban areas ensued. The massive movement of population from overcrowded villages to the cities was one of the most dramatic developments in the postcolonial history of most new nations. This influx, and more modest rural to urban and international emigration to the already large cities of the industrial nations, pushed the numbers of humans living in cities worldwide over 50 percent for the first time in history.

Ambitious youths and the rural poor have crowded into port centers and capital cities in search of jobs and a chance to find the "good life" that the big hotels and restaurants and the neon lights of the city center appeared to offer to all comers. But because most of these cities lacked the rapidly expanding industrial sectors that had made possible the absorption of a similar migrant influx earlier in the West, they were often dead ends for migrants from the rural areas. There were few jobs, and heavy competition for them ensured that wages would remain low for most workers. The growing numbers of underemployed or unemployed migrants turned to street vending, scavenging, huckstering, begging, or petty crime to survive.

The urban poor have become a volatile factor in the political struggles of the elite. They form the crowds willing for a price to cheer on one contender or jeer down another, and they are ready to riot and loot in times of government crisis. In deeply divided societies, the poor, working-class, or idle youths of the urban areas often form the shock troops in communal clashes between rival ethnic and religious groups. Fear of outbursts by urban "mobs" has forced Asian, Middle Eastern, and African regimes to spend scarce resources to subsidize and thus keep low the price of bread, kerosene, and other necessities.

The sudden population influx from the rural areas to cities without sufficient jobs or the infrastructure to support them has greatly skewed urban growth in the emerging nations. Within decades Asian cities have become some of the largest in the world, and Middle Eastern and African urban areas have sprawled far beyond their modest limits in colonial times. As Figure 34.4 dramatically illustrates, the wealth of the upper- and middle-class areas, dominated by glitzy hotels and high-rises, contrasts disturbingly with the poverty of the vast slums that stretch in all directions from the city centers. Little or no planning was possible for the slum quarters that expanded as squatters erected makeshift shelters wherever open land or derelict buildings could be found. Originally, most of the slum areas lacked electricity, running water, or even the most basic sewage facilities. As shanties were gradually converted into ramshackle dwellings, many governments scrapped plans to level slum settlements and instead tried to provide them with electrical and sanitary systems. As an increasing number of development specialists have reluctantly concluded, slums often provide the only housing urban dwellers are likely to find for some time to come.

These conditions have burdened many postcolonial societies with parasitic rather than productive cities. This means that they are heavily dependent for survival on food and resources drawn from their own countryside or from abroad. In contrast to the cities of western Europe and North America, even during the decades of rapid urban expansion in the 19th century, few cities of the emerging nations have had the manufacturing base needed to generate growth in their surrounding regions or the nation as a whole. They take from the already impoverished countryside, but they are able to give little in return. Urban dependence on the countryside further stretches the already overextended resources of the rural areas.

Rural overpopulation in the decades after independence has led to soil depletion in many areas that have been worked for centuries or millennia. It has also resulted in an alarming rate of deforestation throughout Africa and Asia. Peasant villagers cut trees for fuel or clear land for farming and livestock grazing. Logging firms, which are often owned by multinational corporations centered in Europe, North America, Japan, and increasingly China, clear cut large swaths of rain forests to harvest widely dispersed, specialty hardwood trees, such as ebony, which bring high prices in the global marketplace. Deforestation and overgrazing not only pose major threats to wild animal life but also upset the balance in fragile tropical ecosystems, producing further soil depletion and erosion and encouraging desertification, which by the 1980s had spread to areas in Africa twice the size of all of India. Wildlife is also threatened by poachers who slaughter elephants for just their ivory tusks or kill gorillas to fashion trophy ashtrays from their severed hands. Hunting and the destruction of wildlife habitats have led to rates of animal species extinction unequaled since the end of the age of the dinosaurs. In 1989, for example, UN agencies estimated that 3800 species of plants and animals faced extinction worldwide.

Environmental degradation is intensified by industrial pollution—including the waste runoff and spills from mines and oil fields—which is pervasive in both the developed countries and the emerging nations. Although the industrial sectors in the latter are small, pollution tends to be proportionally greater than in the developed world because developing nations rarely can afford the antipollution technology introduced over the last few decades in western Europe, Japan, North America, and increasingly China. Many of the larger cities of the developing world, such as Mexico City, Jakarta, and Beijing, are shrouded for much of the year by killer smog that is also produced by the burning of the rain forests and in some years has spread across areas as vast as southeast Asia from Thailand and Malaya across the Indonesian archipelago.

The Subordination of Women and the Nature of Feminist Struggles in the Postcolonial Era

The example of both the Western democracies and the communist republics of eastern Europe, where women had won the right to vote in the early- and mid-20th century, encouraged the founders of many emerging nations to write female suffrage into their constitutions. The very active part women played in many nationalist struggles was perhaps even more critical to their earning the right to vote and run for political office. Women's activism also produced some semblance of equality in legal rights, education, and occupational opportunities under the laws of many new nations.

However, the equality that was proclaimed on paper often bore little resemblance to the actual rights that most women could exercise. It also had little bearing on the conditions under which they lived their daily lives. Even the rise to power of individual women such as **Indira Gandhi**, whose career and downfall were profiled in the opening section, or **Corazon Aquino**, president of the Philippines in the post-Marcos era of the late 1980s, is deceptive. In most instances, female heads of state in the emerging nations entered politics and initially won political support because they were connected to powerful men. As we have seen, Indira Gandhi was the daughter of **Jawaharlal Nehru**, India's first prime minister. Corazon Aquino's husband was the martyred leader of the Filipino opposition to Ferdinand Marcos. **Benazir Bhutto**, a prime minister of Pakistan, was the daughter of a domineering Pakistani prime minister who had been toppled by a military coup and executed in the late 1970s. Lacking these sorts of connections, most African, Middle Eastern, and Asian women

FIGURE 34.4 In the urban areas of undeveloped nations, the contrast between the wealth of the few and the poverty of the majority is revealed by the juxtaposition of the high-rise apartments of the affluent middle classes and the shantytowns of the urban poor. The city centers in emerging nations are much like those of the industrial West or Japan. But the cities as a whole often are more like collections of large villages than integrated urban units. Many of these villages are vast shantytowns with varying levels of basic services such as running water, sewer systems, and transportation networks to the city center.

Gandhi, Indira (1917–1984)
Daughter of Jawaharlal Nehru (no relation to Mahatma Gandhi); installed as a figurehead prime minister by the Congress party bosses in 1966; a strong-willed and astute politician, she soon became the central figure in India politics, a position she maintained through the 1970s and passed on to her sons.

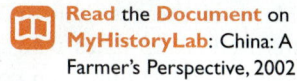 Read the Document on MyHistoryLab: China: A Farmer's Perspective, 2002

Read the **Document** on **MyHistoryLab**: Winona LaDuke, The Indigenous Women's Network, Our Future, Our Responsibility (1995)

Aquino, Corazon (b. 1933) First president of the Philippines in the post-Marcos era of late 1980s; she served from 1986 to 1992; Aquino, whose husband was assassinated by thugs in the pay of the Marcos regime, was one of the key leaders in the popular movement that toppled the dictator.

Nehru, Jawaharlal [juh-WAH-huhr-lahl NAY-roo] (1889–1964) One of Gandhi's disciples; governed India after independence (1947); committed to program of social reform and economic development; preserved civil rights and democracy.

Bhutto, Benazir [BEH-nah-zeer BOO-toh] Twice prime minister of Pakistan in the 1980s and 1990s; first ran for office to avenge her father's execution by the military clique then in power.

religious revivalism An approach to religious belief and practice that stresses the literal interpretation of texts sacred to the religion in question and the application of their precepts to all aspects of social life; increasingly associated with revivalist movements in a number of world religions, including Christianity, Islam, Judaism, and Hinduism.

have been at best relegated to peripheral political positions and at worst allowed no participation in the political process.

The limited gains made by women in the political sphere are paralleled by the second-class position to which most are consigned in many societies. In some respects, their handicaps are comparable to those that constrict women in the industrialized democracies and communist nations. But the obstacles to female self-fulfillment, and in many cases mere survival, in emerging nations are usually much more blatant and fundamental than the restrictions women have to contend with in developed societies. To begin with, early marriage ages for women and large families are still the norm in most African, Middle Eastern, and Asian societies. This means that women spend their youthful and middle-age years having children. There is little time to think of higher education or a career.

Because of the low level of sanitation in many postcolonial societies and the scarcity of food, all but elite and upper-middle-class women experience chronic anxiety about such basic issues as adequate nutrition for their children and their susceptibility to disease. The persistence of male-centric customs directly affects the health and life expectancy of women. For example, the Indian tradition that dictates that women first serve their husbands and sons and then eat what is left has obvious disadvantages. The quantity and nutritional content of the leftovers is likely to be lower than that of the original meals, and in tropical environments flies and other disease-bearing insects are more likely to have fouled the food.

The demographic consequences of these social patterns can be dramatic. In the 1970s, for example, it was estimated that as much as 20 percent of the female population of India was malnourished and that another 30 percent had a diet that was well below acceptable United Nations levels. In sharp contrast to the industrial societies of Japan, the United States, and Europe, where women outnumber (because on the average they outlive) men, in India there are only 930 females for every 1000 males.

Although the highly secular property and divorce laws many new states passed after independence have given women much greater legal protection, many of these measures are ignored in practice. Very often, women have neither the education nor the resources to exercise their legal rights. The spread of **religious revivalism** in many cases has further eroded these rights, even though advocates of a return to tradition often argue that practices such as veiling and stoning for women (but not men) caught in adultery actually enhance their dignity and status. Most Asian, Middle Eastern, and African women continue to be dominated by male family members, are much more limited than men in their career opportunities, and are likely to be less well fed, educated, and healthy than men at comparable social levels.

DOCUMENT

Cultural Creativity in the Emerging Nations: Some Literary Samples

DESPITE, OR PERHAPS BECAUSE OF, POLITICAL instability and chronic economic difficulties, postcolonial societies have generated a high level of artistic creativity over the past four or five decades. Nowhere has this creativity been more prominent and brilliant than in literary works for which African, Middle Eastern, and Asian writers have earned Nobel prizes and won a wide readership far beyond their own nations. The selections that follow are only a small sample of the vast and varied works of these talented writers, from poetry and drama to novels and short stories.

Many of these writers focus on the predicament of the Western-educated elites who dominate the new nations that emerged from the European colonial empires. In the following stanza from the poem "I Run Around with Them," Indonesian poet Chairil Anwar reflects on the lack of purpose and malaise he believed to be widespread among the children of these elite groups.

I run around with them, what else can I do, now—
Changing my face at the edge of the street, I use their eyes
And tag along to visit the fun house:
These are the facts as I know them
(A new American flic at the Capitol,
The new songs they dance to).
We go home: there's nothing doing
Though this kind of Death is our neighbor, our friend, now.

(continued on next page)

Hanging around at the corner, we wait for the city bus
That glows night to day like a gold tooth;
Lame, deformed, negative, we
Lean our bony asses against lamp poles
And jaw away the years.

In the next quotation, from the novel *No Longer at Ease*, widely read Nigerian author Chinua Achebe identifies another dilemma: the pull between Western culture and the ancient civilization of one's own land.

Nothing gave him greater pleasure than to find another Ibo-speaking student in a London bus. But when he had to speak in English with a Nigerian student from another tribe he lowered his voice. It was humiliating to have to speak to one's countryman in a foreign language, especially in the presence of the proud owners of that language. They would naturally assume that one had no language of one's own. He wished they were here today to see. Let them come to Umuofia [the protagonist's home village] now and listen to the talk of men who made a great art of conversation. Let them come and see men and women and children who knew how to live, whose joy of life had not yet been killed by those who claimed to teach other nations how to live.

Like many of the more famous novelists of the emerging nations, V. S. Naipaul is an expatriate, born in the Caribbean and now living in rural England. In his moving and controversial account of his return to his Indian ancestral home, titled *An Area of Darkness*, Naipaul confronts the problem of massive poverty and the responses of foreigners and the Indian elite to it.

To see [India's] poverty is to make an observation of no value; a thousand newcomers to the country before you have seen and said as you. And not only newcomers. Our own sons and daughters, when they return from Europe and America, have spoken in your very words. Do not think that your anger and contempt are marks of your sensitivity. You might have seen more: the smiles on the faces of the begging children, that domestic group among the pavement sleepers waking in the cool Bombay morning, father, mother and baby in a trinity of love, so self-contained that they are as private as if walls had separated them from you; it is your gaze that violates them, your sense of outrage that outrages them. . . . It is your surprise, your anger that denies [them] humanity.

QUESTIONS
- Can you think of parallels in U.S. history or contemporary society to the situations and responses conveyed in these passages from recent postcolonial writings?
- Do they suggest that it is possible to communicate even intimate feelings across cultures, or do you find them alien, different?
- What other issues would you expect African, Middle Eastern, and Asian postcolonial artists to deal with in their work?

Neocolonialism, Cold War Rivalries, and Stunted Development

The schemes of nationalist leaders aimed at building an industrial base that would support the rapidly increasing populations of their new nations soon yielded to the economic realities of the postcolonial world. Not only did most of the nations that emerged from colonialism have little in the way of an industrial base, but their means of obtaining one were meager. To buy the machines and hire or train the technical experts that were essential to get industrialization going, the new nations needed to earn capital they could invest for these ends. Some funds could be accumulated by saving a portion of the state revenues collected from the peasantry. In most cases, however, there was little left once the bureaucrats had been paid, essential public works and education had been funded, and other state expenses had been met. Thus, most emerging nations have relied on the sale of cash crops and minerals to earn the money they need to finance industrialization. As their leaders soon discovered, the structure of the world market worked against them.

The pattern of exchange promoted in the colonial era left most newly independent countries dependent on the export production of two or three food crops or industrial raw materials. The former included cocoa, palm oil, coffee, jute, and hemp. Key among the latter were minerals, such as copper, bauxite, and oil, for which there was a high demand in the industrialized economies of Europe, North America, Japan, and more recently China. Since World War II, the prices of these exports—which economists call **primary products**—have not only fluctuated widely but have declined steadily compared to the prices of most of the manufactured goods emerging nations usually buy from the industrialized world. Price fluctuations have created nightmares for planners in developing nations. Revenue estimates from the sale of coffee or copper in years when the price is high are used to plan government projects for building roads, factories, and dams. Market slumps can wipe out these critical funds, thereby retarding economic growth and throwing countries deeply into debt.

African, Middle Eastern, and Asian leaders have been quick to blame the legacy of colonialism and what they have called the **neocolonial economy**—the global economy that has been dominated

primary products Food or industrial crops for which there is a high demand in industrialized economies; prices of such products tend to fluctuate widely; typically the primary exports of Third World economies.

 View the Image on MyHistoryLab: Cocoa harvesting in Ghana

neocolonial economy Industrialized nations' continued dominance of the world economy; ability of the industrialized nations to maintain economic colonialism without political colonialism.

THINKING HISTORICALLY

Artificial Nations and the Rising Tide of Communal Strife

AGAIN AND AGAIN IN THE POSTCOLONIAL era, new states have been torn by internal strife. Often much of what we in the industrialized West know of these areas in Africa, the Middle East, and Asia is connected to the breakdown of their political systems and the human suffering that has resulted. In just the last few years, for example, international news reports have featured descriptions of famines generated by civil wars in Somalia, the Sudan, and Mozambique; by harrowing images of refugees fleeing for their lives from Rwanda, Angola, and Cambodia; by religious riots in India and mass slaughter in Timor. In the first decades of the post-cold war era, ethnic and religious divisions have played major roles in revolutionary movements in Syria, the failed U.S. occupation of Iraq from 2003 to 2012, and ongoing strife in Afghanistan. Western observers are often tempted to take this instability and the conflicts that often result as proof that the people of these decolonized areas are unfit to rule themselves, that they are incapable of building viable political systems.

Although these responses are understandable given the crisis-focused coverage of the emerging nations by international news agencies, they fail to take into account the daunting obstacles that have confronted African, Middle Eastern, and Asian nation-builders. They ignore the important ways in which Western colonialism contributed to the internal divisions and political weaknesses of newly independent states. They also overlook the deep, often highly disruptive social divisions within Western societies (the long history of racial conflict in the United States, for example, or the vicious civil war in the former European nation of Yugoslavia). Any analysis of the recurring political crises of Africa, the Middle East, and Asia should begin with the realization that nearly all the nations that emerged from decolonization were artificial creations. The division of Africa and Asia by the Western imperialist powers was arbitrary (see, for example, Maps 34.1 and 34.2). Some colonial boundaries cut peoples apart: the Shans of southeast Asia, the Kurds of the Middle East, the Somalis of the horn of east Africa. Some imposed boundaries that tossed together tens, sometimes hundreds, of very different and often hostile ethnic or religious groups. The roads and railways built by the colonizers, the marketing systems they established, and the educational policies they pursued all hardened the unnatural boundaries and divisions established in the late 19th century. It was these artificial units, these motley combinations of peoples that defied the logic of history and cultural affinity that African, Middle Eastern, and Asian nationalist leaders had to try to meld into nations after World War II.

> *Any analysis of the recurring political crises of Africa, the Middle East, and Asia should begin with the realization that nearly all the nations that emerged from decolonization were artificial creations.*

The point is not that there was perfect harmony or unity among the peoples of these areas before the coming of colonial rule. As we have seen, there was a great diversity of ethnicity, languages, and religions among the peoples who built civilizations in these areas in the precolonial era. Intense competition, communal conflict, and countless wars occurred between different ethnic and religious groups. European colonization worsened these divisions while suppressing violent confrontations between different communities. In fact, European colonial regimes were built and maintained by divide-and-rule tactics. Very often the colonizers selectively recruited minority ethnic or religious groups into their armies, bureaucracies, and police forces. For example, the Tutsi minority in strife-torn Rwanda and Burundi was much favored by first the Belgians and later the French. In the colonial period, the Tutsis had greater access than the Hutu majority to missionary education, military training, and government positions. These advantages gained a disproportionate share of political power and social standing for the Tutsis after independence. But they also made them the obvious target for persecution by disgruntled Hutus. Rivalry and violent conflict between the two groups has often made a shambles of nation-building initiatives in Rwanda and Burundi over the past several decades and reached catastrophic levels in the mid-1990s. It has continued to simmer in the years since often spilling over into political struggles in neighboring states such as Congo.

The inequities of the colonial order were compounded by the increasingly frequent use of divide-and-rule policies by European officials in the last years of their rule. In addition, the colonizers' desire to scuttle and run from their colonial responsibilities when it was clear that the days of colonial rule were numbered opened the way for ethnic and religious strife. Communal violence in turn prompted the exodus of refugees that accompanied the winning of independence in many colonies, most notably in south Asia, Nigeria, the Belgian Congo, and Palestine. The Western-educated leaders who came to power in these and other newly independent states soon realized that only a small portion of the population was committed to an overarching nationalist identity. Even among the Westernized elite classes, which had led the decolonization struggle, national loyalties were often shallow and overridden by older, subnational ethnic and religious identities. As a result, many of the new nations of Africa and Southeast Asia have been threatened by secessionist movements.

The most spectacular collapse of a new state came in Pakistan, the unwieldy patchwork of a nation the British threw together at

(continued on next page)

(continued from previous page)

the last minute in 1947 to satisfy Jinnah's demands for majority rule in Muslim areas of the Indian subcontinent (Map 34.2). A glance at the map reveals the vulnerability of Pakistan, split into two parts: West and East Pakistan, separated by India's more than 1000 miles of hostile territory. East and West Pakistan also differed greatly in their natural environments and in the ethnic makeup of their peoples and the languages they used. They even differed in their approaches to the Islamic faith that had justified including them in the same country in the first place.

Fragile national ties were eroded rapidly by the East Pakistanis' perception that they had been in effect recolonized by West Pakistan. West Pakistanis held highly disproportionate shares of government jobs and military positions, and West Pakistan received the lion's share of state revenues although East Pakistan generated most of the new nation's foreign earnings. By the early 1970s, East and West Pakistan were locked in a bloody civil war, which ended with the creation of the nation of Bangladesh from East Pakistan in 1972.

India, which relished the chance to contribute to the breakup of Pakistan, has itself been repeatedly threatened by civil strife between different linguistic, religious, and ethnic groups. In the early 1980s, Sikh guerrillas carried on a violent campaign for separation in the north, and the Indian government was forced to intervene militarily in the violent struggle between different ethnic and religious groups in Sri Lanka (Ceylon), its neighbor to the south. In 1997 an avowedly Hindu communalist party came to power in New Delhi, in defiance of the staunch adherence to the principle of a secular state upheld by leading Indian nationalist figures in the colonial era and all of the earlier postindependence governments. The victory of the Bharatya Janata party (BJP) intensified the anxieties of the large Muslim minority and other non-Hindu religious groups about the possibility of discrimination and even open persecution.

In Africa, where there was even less of a common historical and cultural basis on which to build nationalism than in south or southeast Asia, separatist movements have been a prominent feature of the political life of new states. Secessionist movements have raged from Morocco in the northwest to Ethiopia in the east and Angola in the south (Map 34.1). Civil wars, such as the struggle of the non-Muslim peoples of the southern Sudan against the Muslim rulers from the northern parts of that country, have also abounded. Thus far, few of the secessionist movements have succeeded, although Somalia has fragmented and the secession movement in southern Sudan has ended with the division of the country into two states. In all cases, the artificial nature of the new nations of Africa, the Middle East, and Asia has proved costly. In addition to internal divisions, boundary disputes between newly independent nations have often led to border clashes and open warfare. India and Pakistan have fought three such wars since 1947. Iraq's Saddam Hussein justified his 1990 annexation of Kuwait with the argument that the tiny but oil-rich Arab "sheikhdom" was an artificial creation of the British colonizers, who had carved Kuwait out of land that historically had been part of Iraq.

Democracy has often been one of the main victims of the tensions between rival ethnic groups within many emerging nations and threats from neighbors without. Politicians in nearly all the new states have been quick to play on communal fears as well as on ethnic and religious loyalties to win votes. As a result, freely elected legislatures have often been dominated by parties representing these special interests. Suspicions that those in power were favoring their own or allied groups has led to endless bickering and stalemates in national legislatures, which have become tempting targets for coup attempts by military strongmen. One of the more predictable reasons these usurpers have given for dictatorial rule has been the need to contain the communal tensions aroused by democratic election campaigns.

QUESTIONS
- How might colonial policies have been changed to reduce the tensions between different ethnic and religious communities?
- Why were these measures not taken?
- What can be done now to alleviate these divisions?
- Should the United Nations or industrialized nations such as the United States or Japan intervene directly to contain communal clashes or civil wars in Africa and Asia?
- What is to be done with the rapidly growing refugee populations created by these conflicts?

by the industrialized nations—for the limited returns yielded thus far by their development schemes. Although there is much truth to these accusations, they do not tell the whole story. These leaders must also share the responsibility for the slow pace of economic growth in much of the developing world. The members of the educated classes that came to dominate the political and business life of newly independent nations often used their positions to enrich themselves and their relatives at the expense of their societies as a whole. Corruption has been notoriously widespread in most of the new nations. Government controls on the import of goods such as automobiles, television sets, and stereos, which are luxury items beyond the reach of most of the people, have often been lax. As a result, tax revenues and export earnings that could have fueled development have often gone to provide the good life for small minorities within emerging nations. The inability or refusal of many regimes to carry out key social reforms, such as land redistribution, which would spread the limited resources available more equitably over the population, has contributed vitally to the persistence of these patterns.

Badly strapped for investment funds and essential technology, emerging African, Middle Eastern, and Asian nations have often turned to international organizations, such as the World Bank and the International Monetary Fund, or to industrial nations for assistance. Although resources for development have been gained in this way, the price for international assistance has often been high. The industrialized nations have demanded major concessions in return for their aid. These have ranged from commitments to buy the products of, and favor investors from, the lending countries to entering into alliances and permitting military bases on the territory of the client state.

Loans from international lending agencies almost invariably have been granted only after the needy nation agreed to structural adjustments. These are regulations that determine how the money is to be invested and repaid, and they usually involve promises to make major changes in the economy of the borrowing nation. These promises often included a commitment to remove or reduce state subsidies on food and other essential consumer items. State subsidies were designed to keep prices for staple goods at a level that the urban and rural poor—the great majority of the people in almost all emerging nations—could afford. When carried out, subsidy reductions often have led to widespread social unrest, riots, and the collapse or near collapse of postcolonial regimes.

> The leaders of the new nations of Africa, the Middle East, and Asia soon felt the need to deliver on the promises of social reform and economic well-being that had rallied support to the nationalist cause. Strategies ranged from populism to dictatorship to rejection of the West.

POSTCOLONIAL OPTIONS FOR ACHIEVING ECONOMIC GROWTH AND SOCIAL JUSTICE

34.2 Which, if any, of the postcolonial paths to political stability and socioeconomic development do you think was the most successful and what factors were the most important in shaping positive outcomes?

Depending on their own skills, the talents of their advisors and lieutenants, and the resources at their disposal, leaders in the emerging nations have tackled the daunting task of development with varying degrees of success. Ways have been found to raise the living standards of a significant percentage of the population of some of the emerging nations. But these strategies have rarely benefited the majority. It may be too early to judge the outcomes of many development schemes. But so far, none has proved to be the path to the social justice and general economic development that nationalist leaders proclaimed as the ultimate goals of struggles for decolonization. Although some countries have done much better than others, successful overall strategies to deal with the challenges facing emerging nations have yet to be devised.

Charismatic Populists and One-Party Rule

One of the least successful responses on the part of leaders who found their dreams for national renewal frustrated has been a retreat into authoritarian rule. This approach has often been disguised by calculated, charismatic appeals for support from the disenfranchised masses. Perhaps the career of Kwame Nkrumah, the leader of Ghana's independence movement, illustrates this pattern best. There is little question that Nkrumah was genuinely committed to social reform and economic uplift for the Ghanaian people during the years of his rise to become the first prime minister of the newly independent west African nation of Ghana in 1957 (Map 34.3). After assuming power, he moved vigorously to initiate programs that would translate his high aspirations for his people into reality. But his ambitious schemes for everything from universal education to industrial development soon ran into trouble.

Rival political parties, some representing regional interests and ethnic groups long hostile to Nkrumah, repeatedly challenged his initiatives and tried to block the efforts to carry out his plans. His leftist leanings won support from the Soviet bloc but frightened away Western investors, who had a good deal more capital to plow into Ghana's economy. They also led to growing hostility on the part of the United States, Great Britain, and other influential noncommunist countries. Most devastatingly, soon after independence, the price of cocoa—by far Ghana's largest export crop—began

MAP 34.3 The New West African Nations Ghana was one of many ethnically fragmented, new African states that came to be dominated by charismatic leaders and then military dictatorships in the cold war era.

to fall sharply. Tens of thousands of Ghanaian cocoa farmers were hard hit and the resources for Nkrumah's development plans suddenly dried up.

Nkrumah's response to these growing problems was increasingly dictatorial. He refused to give up or cut back on his development plans. As a result, most of these schemes failed miserably due to the lack of key supplies and official mismanagement. In the early 1960s, Nkrumah forcibly crushed all political opposition by banning rival parties and jailing other political leaders. He assumed dictatorial powers and ruled through functionaries in his own Convention People's Party.

Nkrumah also sought to hold on to the loyalty of the masses and mobilize their energies by highly staged "events" and the manipulation of largely invented symbols and traditions that were said to be derived from Ghana's past. Thus, he tried to justify his policies and leadership style with references to a uniquely African brand of socialism and the need to revive African traditions and African civilization. Even before independence, he had taken to wearing the traditional garb of the Ghanaian elite. The very name *Ghana*, which Nkrumah himself proposed for the new nation that emerged from the former Gold Coast colony, had been taken from an ancient African kingdom. The original Ghanaian kingdom actually was centered much farther to the north and had little to do with the peoples of the Gold Coast.

Nkrumah went about the country giving fiery speeches, dedicating monuments to the "revolution," which often consisted of giant statues of himself (Figure 34.5). He also assumed a prominent role in the nonaligned movement that was then sweeping the newly independent nations. His followers' adulation knew no bounds. Members of his captive parliament compared him to Confucius, Muhammad, Shakespeare, and Napoleon and predicted that his birthplace would serve as a "Mecca" for all of Africa's leaders. But his suppression of all opposition and his growing ties to the Communist party, coupled with the rapid deterioration of the Ghanaian economy, increased the ranks of his enemies, who waited for a chance to strike. That chance came early in 1966, when Nkrumah went off on one of his many trips, this time a peace mission to Vietnam. In his absence, he was deposed by a military coup. Nkrumah died in exile in 1972, and Ghana moved in a very different direction under its new military rulers.

Military Responses: Dictatorships and Revolutions

Given the difficulties that leaders such as Nkrumah faced after independence and the advantages the military have in crisis situations, the proliferation of coups in the emerging nations is not surprising. Armed forces have at times been divided by the religious and ethnic rivalries that have been so disruptive in new nations. But the regimentation and emphasis on discipline and in-group solidarity in military training often render soldiers more resistant than other social groups to these forces. In conditions of political breakdown and social conflict, the military possesses the monopoly—or near monopoly—of force that is often essential for restoring order. Their occupational conditioning makes soldiers not only more ready than civilian leaders to use the force at their disposal but less concerned with its destructive consequences. Military personnel also tend to have some degree of technical training, which was usually lacking in the humanities-oriented education of civilian nationalist leaders. Because most military leaders have been staunchly anticommunist, they have often attracted covert technical and financial assistance from Western governments.

Once in control, military leaders have banned civilian political parties and imposed military regimes of varying degrees of repression and authoritarian control. Yet the ends to which these regimes have put their dictatorial powers have differed greatly. At their worst, military regimes—such as those in Uganda (especially under Idi Amin), Myanmar (formerly Burma), and Congo—have quashed civil liberties while making little attempt to reduce social inequities or improve living standards. These regimes have existed mainly to enrich the military leaders and their allies. Military governments of this sort have been notorious for official corruption and for

View the **Closer Look** on MyHistoryLab: Kwame Nkrumah and Julius Nyerere

FIGURE **34.5** Many monumental statues of Kwame Nkrumah, such as this one, rose in the towns and villages of Ghana as he tried to cover the failure of his socialist-inspired development programs with dictatorial rule and self-glorification. Although Nkrumah's efforts to cover his regime's failures through self-glorifying displays and pageantry were extreme, they were not unique. The many images of the "great leader" of the moment that one finds in many developing nations are a variation on Nkrumah's tactics. These state campaigns to glorify the dictatorial figures are reminiscent of those mounted by the leaders of the communist revolutions in Russia, China, and Cuba.

Nasser, Gamal Abdel (1918–1970) Took power in Egypt following a military coup in 1952; enacted land reforms and used state resources to reduce unemployment; ousted Britain from the Suez Canal zone in 1956.

Free Officers movement Military nationalist movement in Egypt founded in the 1930s; often allied with the Muslim Brotherhood; led coup to seize Egyptian government from khedive in July 1952.

Muslim Brotherhood Egyptian nationalist movement founded by Hasan al-Banna in 1928; committed to fundamentalist movement in Islam; fostered strikes and urban riots against the khedival government.

imprisoning, torturing, or eliminating political dissidents. Understandably uneasy about being overthrown, these regimes have diverted a high proportion of their nations' meager resources, which might have gone for economic development, into expenditures on expensive military hardware. Neither the Western democracies nor the countries of the Soviet bloc have hesitated to supply arms to these military despots.

In a few cases, military leaders have been radical in their approaches to economic and social reform. Perhaps none was more so than **Gamal Abdel Nasser** (Figure 34.6), who took power in Egypt after a military coup in 1952. As we have seen in Chapter 29, the Egyptians won their independence in the mid-1930s except for the lingering British presence in the Suez Canal zone (Map 34.4). But self-centered civilian politicians and the corrupt khedival regime had done little to improve the standard of living of the mass of the Egyptian people. As conditions worsened and Egypt's governing parties did little but rake in wealth for their elitist memberships, revolutionary forces emerged in Egyptian society.

The radical movement that succeeded in gaining power, the **Free Officers movement**, evolved from a secret organization established in the Egyptian army in the 1930s. Founded by idealistic young officers of Egyptian rather than Turco-Egyptian descent, the secret Revolutionary Command Council studied conditions in the country and prepared to seize power in the name of a genuine revolution. For decades, it was loosely allied to the **Muslim Brotherhood**, another revolutionary alternative to the khedival regime.

The brotherhood was founded by Hasan al-Banna (Figure 34.7) in 1928. Al-Banna was a schoolteacher who had studied in his youth with the famous Muslim reformer Muhammad Abduh. While at Al-Azhar University in Cairo in the years after World War I, al-Banna had combined a deep interest in scientific subjects with active involvement in student demonstrations in support of Wafd demands for Egyptian independence. In this period, like many other Egyptian students, al-Banna developed contempt for the wealthy minority of Egyptians and Europeans who flourished in the midst of the appalling poverty of most of his people.

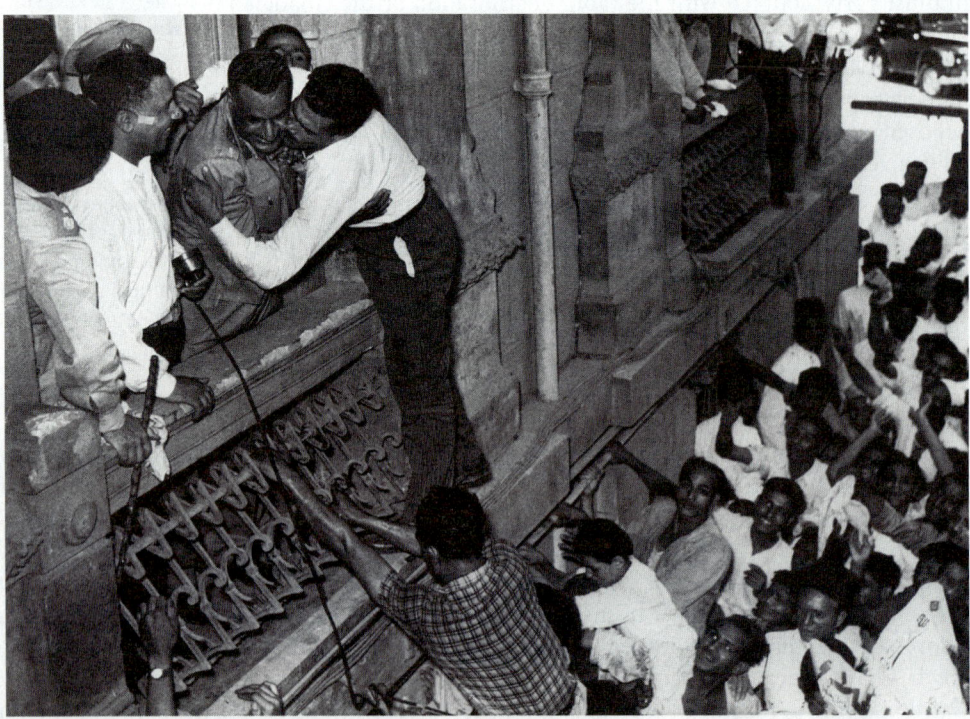

FIGURE **34.6** After the Free Officers seized power in the 1952 coup, a young general named Nasser emerged as the most charismatic and able of a number of rivals for power. Here cheering crowds climb toward a balcony where the new leader of Egypt has been addressing them, and Nasser is embraced by one enthusiastic supporter.

MAP 34.4 The Middle East in the Cold War Era As in Africa and over much of Asia, the new states of the Middle East were very often based on the colonies established by the different European powers in the age of high imperialism.

To remedy these injustices and rid Egypt of its foreign oppressors, al-Banna founded the Muslim Brotherhood in 1928. Although members of the organization were committed to a revivalist approach to Islam, the brotherhood's main focus, particularly in the early years, was on a program of social uplift and sweeping reforms. The organization became involved in a wide range of activities, from promoting trade unions and building medical clinics to educating women and pushing for land reform. By the late 1930s, the brotherhood's social services had become highly politicized. Al-Banna's followers fomented strikes and urban riots and established militant youth organizations and paramilitary assassination squads. Despite the murder of al-Banna by the khedive Farouk's assassins in 1949, the members of the brotherhood continued to expand its influence in the early 1950s among both middle-class youths and the impoverished masses.

After Egypt's humiliating defeats in the first Arab-Israeli War of 1948 and in a clash with the British over the latter's continuing occupation of the Suez Canal zone in 1952, mass anger with a discredited khedival and parliamentary regime gave the officers their chance. In July 1952, an almost bloodless military coup toppled the corrupt khedive Farouk from his jewel-encrusted throne (Figure 34.8). The revolution had begun. The monarchy was ended, and with the installation of Nasser and the Free Officers, Egyptians ruled themselves for the first time since the 6th century B.C.E. By 1954

CHAPTER 34 Africa, the Middle East, and Asia in the Era of Independence

FIGURE 34.7 Hasan al-Banna, the founder of the Muslim Brotherhood, an opposition group in Egypt that established medical clinics and promoted unions, land reform, and women's education.

all political parties had been disbanded, including the Muslim Brotherhood, which had clashed with its former allies in the military and had been suppressed after an attempt on Nasser's life. Nasser was only one of several officers at the head of the Free Officers movement, and by no means was he initially the most charismatic. But after months of internal power struggles in the officer corps, he emerged as the head of a military government that was deeply committed to revolution.

Nasser and his fellow officers used the dictatorial powers they had won in the coup to force through programs that they believed would uplift the long-oppressed Egyptian masses. They were convinced that only the state had the power to carry out essential social and economic reforms, and thus they began to intervene in all aspects of Egyptian life. Land reform measures were enacted: Limits were placed on how much land an individual could own, and excess lands were seized and redistributed to landless peasants. State-financed education through the college level was made available to Egyptians. The government became Egypt's main employer; by 1980, more than 30 percent of Egypt's workforce was on the state payroll. State subsidies were used to lower the price of basic food staples, such as wheat and cooking oil. State-controlled development schemes were introduced that emphasized industrial growth, modeled after the five-year plans of the Soviet Union.

To establish Egypt's economic independence, stiff restrictions were placed on foreign investment. In some cases foreign properties were seized and redistributed to Egyptian investors. Nasser also embarked on an interventionist foreign policy that stressed the struggle to destroy the newly established Israeli state, forge Arab unity, and foment socialist revolutions in neighboring lands. His greatest foreign policy coup came in 1956, when he rallied international opinion to finally oust the British and their French allies from the Suez Canal zone. Despite the setbacks suffered by Egyptian military forces, Nasser made good use of the rare combined backing of the United States and the Soviet Union to achieve his aims in the crisis.

However well intentioned, many of Nasser's initiatives misfired. Land reform efforts were frustrated by bureaucratic corruption and the clever strategies devised by the landlord class to hold on to their estates. State development schemes often lacked proper funding and failed because of mismanagement and miscalculations. Even the Aswan Dam project, the cornerstone of Nasser's development drive, was a fiasco. Egypt's continuing population boom quickly canceled out the additional cultivable lands the dam produced. The dam's interference with the flow of the Nile resulted in increasing numbers of parasites that cause blindness. It also led to a decline in the fertility of farmlands in the lower Nile delta, which were deprived of the rich silt that normally was washed down by the river. Foreign investment funds from the West, which Egypt desperately needed, soon dried up. Aid from the much poorer Soviet bloc could not begin to match what was lost, and much of this assistance was military.

In the absence of sufficient foreign investment and with Egypt's uncontrolled population rising at an alarming rate, the state simply could not afford all the ambitious schemes to which Nasser and the revolutionary officers had committed it. The gap between aspirations and means was increased in the later years of Nasser's reign (in the 1960s) by the heavy costs of his mostly failed foreign adventures, including the disastrous Six-Day War with Israel in 1967.

Although he had to move slowly at first, Nasser's successor, **Anwar Sadat**, had little choice but to dismantle the massive state apparatus that had been created. He favored private rather than state initiatives. During Sadat's tenure in office, the middle class, who had been greatly restricted by Nasser, emerged again as a powerful force. After fighting the Israelis to a stalemate in 1973, Sadat also moved to end the costly confrontation with Israel as well as Egypt's support for revolutionary movements in the Arab world. He expelled the Russians and opened Egypt to aid and investment from the United States and western Europe.

Sadat's shift in direction was continued by his successor, **Hosni Mubarak**. But neither the attempt at genuine revolution led by Nasser nor the move to capitalism and more pro-West positions under his successors has done much to check Egypt's alarming population increases and the corruption of its bloated bureaucracy. Neither path to development has had much effect on the glaring gap between the living conditions of Egypt's rich minority and its impoverished masses. No better gauge of the discontent that is bred by these inequities can be found than the proliferation of Muslim fundamentalist movements. One of these succeeded in assassinating Sadat; others mounted legal campaigns and underground movements aimed at overthrowing the Mubarak regime. This resistance peaked in the protests of what was dubbed the "Arab Spring" in 2011, which brought an abrupt end to the Mubarak regime and

Sadat, Anwar [AHN-wahr suh-DAHT] Successor to Gamal Abdel Nasser as ruler of Egypt; acted to dismantle costly state programs; accepted peace treaty with Israel in 1973; opened Egypt to investment by western nations.

Mubarak, Hosni [HOHZ-nee MOO-bahr-uhk] President of Egypt from 1981, to 2011 succeeding Anwar Sadat and continuing his policies of cooperation with the West.

eventually carried the reform-minded Muslim Brotherhood to a brief stint in power, which was abruptly ended mid-summer 2013 by a military coup.

The Indian Alternative: Development for Some of the People

Although the approach to nation-building and economic development followed by the leaders of independent India has shared the Nasserite emphasis on socialism and state intervention, India's experience has differed from Egypt's in several significant ways. To begin with, the Indians have managed to preserve civilian rule throughout more than half a century since they won their independence from Great Britain. In fact, in India the military has consistently defended secular democracy against religious extremism and other would-be authoritarian trends. In addition, although India, like Egypt, has been saddled with a crushing burden of overpopulation, it came to independence with a larger industrial and scientific sector, a better communication system and bureaucratic grid, and a larger and more skilled middle class in proportion to its total population than most other emerging nations.

During the first decades of its freedom, India had the good fortune to be governed by leaders such as Jawaharlal Nehru and his allies in the Congress party, who were deeply committed to social reform and economic development as well as the preservation of civil rights and democracy. India's success at the latter has been remarkable. Despite continuous threats of secession by religious and linguistic minorities, as well as poverty, unemployment, and recurring natural disasters, India remains the world's largest functioning democracy. Except for brief periods of rule by coalitions of opposition parties, the Congress party has either ruled or played key roles in governing at the center for most of the independence era. But opposition parties have controlled many state and local governments, and they remain vocal and active in the national parliament. Civil liberties, exemplified by a very outspoken press and free elections, have been upheld to an extent that sets India off from much of the rest of the emerging nations.

Nehru's approach to government and development also differed from Nasser's in his more moderate mix of state and private initiatives. Nehru and his successors pushed state intervention in some sectors but also encouraged foreign investment from countries in both of the rival blocs in the cold war. As a consequence, India has been able to build on its initial advantages in industrial infrastructure and its skilled managerial and labor endowment. Its significant capitalist sector has encouraged ambitious farmers, such as those in the Punjab in the northwest, to invest heavily in the **Green Revolution**—the introduction of improved seed strains, fertilizers, and irrigation as a means of producing higher crop yields. Industrial and agrarian growth has generated the revenue necessary for the Indian government to promote literacy and village development schemes, as well as family planning, village electrification, and other improvement projects in recent decades. Indians have also developed one of the largest and most sophisticated high-tech sectors in the postcolonial world, including its own "silicon valleys" in cities like Bangalore in southern India. From the late 1980s India also provided tens of thousands of computer and Internet experts for advanced industrial societies such as those found in the United States and Europe.

Despite its successes, India has suffered from the same gap between needs and resources that all developing nations have had to face. Whatever the government's intentions—and India has been hit by corruption and self-serving politicians like most nations—there have simply not been the resources to raise the living standards of even a majority of its huge population. The middle class has grown, perhaps as rapidly as that of any postcolonial nation. Its presence is striking in the affluent neighborhoods of cities such as Mumbai and Delhi and is proclaimed by the Indian film industry, the world's largest, and in many sitcoms and dramas about the lives of Indian-style yuppies. But as much as 50 percent of India's people has gained little from the development plans and economic growth that have occurred since independence.

Read the Document on MyHistoryLab: Gamal Abdel Nasser, Speech on the Suez Canal (Egypt), 1956

FIGURE 34.8 Growing Egyptian resistance to the British occupation of the Suez Canal zone was expressed in this effigy of a British soldier that was strung up on a Cairo street corner in January 1952. The Arabic banner that accompanies the mock hanging reminds Egyptians of the Dinshawai incident, discussed in Chapter 29, and the need to sustain resistance to British domination. Within months of this protest, mass demonstrations and a military coup freed the Egyptian people from both the British occupation and the repressive khedival regime.

Read the Document on MyHistoryLab: Jawaharlal Nehru, "Why India is Non-Aligned" (India), 1956

Green Revolution Introduction of improved seed strains, fertilizers, and irrigation as a means of producing higher yields in crops such as rice, wheat, and corn; particularly important in the densely populated countries of Asia.

In part, this is because population growth has offset economic gains. But social reform has been slow in most areas, both rural and urban. Groups such as the wealthy landlords, who supported the nationalist drive for independence, have continued to dominate the great mass of tenants and landless laborers, just as they did in the precolonial and colonial eras. Some development measures, most notably those associated with the Green Revolution, have greatly favored cultivators with the resources to invest in new seeds and fertilizer. They have increased the gap between rich and poor people over much of rural India and often contributed in major ways to the deterioration of India's environment. Thus, the poor have paid and will continue to pay the price for Indian gradualism.

DELAYED REVOLUTIONS: RELIGIOUS REVIVALISM AND LIBERATION MOVEMENTS IN SETTLER SOCIETIES

34.3 How did religious revivalist movements, most especially the one led by Ayatollah Khomeini in Iran, differ from other twentieth century revolutions, and why was decolonization delayed in almost all settler colonial societies, such as South Africa?

> Although societies like Iran and South Africa remained independent or broke free from European colonial control in the post–World War II era, the liberation of the majority of their populations was delayed. Rather, in these instances, different sorts of revolutions than those that had brought decolonization to most of Africa, Asia, and the Middle East were required.

As we saw in Chapter 27, not all African, Middle Eastern or Asian states were conquered and ruled outright by colonizing Western nations in the 19th century. Like Turkey and China, Iran escaped direct colonial domination. But in the late-19th and the first half of the 20th centuries, Iran was reduced to a buffer state between first the British and Russian and later the Soviet and Anglo-American great powers. Partly in response to these external threats, regional strongmen emerged to claim national leadership, such as the self-styled shahs of the Pahlavi dynasty. The second of these shahs in particular, Muhammad Reza, whose throne was rescued by covert interventions by the United States in 1953, ruled the country as an absolutist monarch with a vast secret security force repressing all serious opposition. By the late 1970s, most segments of the population had become dissatisfied with his rule and supportive of the efforts of the Ayatollah Khomeini and his supporters to carry out a religiously based Shi'a revolution.

In South Africa, a rather different sort of popular resistance had been struggling to overthrow the minority-run apartheid regime through the same post–World War II decades. Locked out of political power and exploited and impoverished economically by the ruling, European-descended Afrikaner settlers, the black African majority, and their colored and Indian allies risked prison, torture, and execution in a struggle for social justice and the right to vote and hold office. Their liberation struggle lasted decades longer than the Iranians' overthrow of the shah and arose from rather different forms of oppression. It also led to the establishment of a genuine democracy, which was ultimately denied to the Iranians, who despite periodic elections have been governed by a theocratic regime.

Iran: Religious Revivalism and the Rejection of the West

With the exception of the Peoples' Republic of China, no path of development adopted by a postcolonial society has provided more fundamental challenges to the existing world order than revolutionary Iran under the direction of the **Ayatollah Ruhollah Khomeini**. In many respects, the Khomeini revolution of 1979 was a throwback to the religious fervor of such anticolonial resistance movements as that led by the Mahdi of the Sudan in the 1880s. Core motivations for the followers of both movements were provided by the emphasis on religious purification and the rejoining of religion and politics, which leaders such as the Mahdi and Khomeini have seen as central to the Islamic tradition. The call for a return to the kind of society believed to have existed in the past "golden age" of the prophet Muhammad was central to the policies pursued by both the Mahdist and Iranian regimes once they had gained power. Both movements were aimed at toppling Western-backed governments: the Mahdists' the Anglo-Egyptian presence in the Sudan, Khomeini's the autocratic Iranian shah and the Pahlavi dynasty.

Although they came from the Sunni and Shi'a religious traditions, respectively, both the Mahdi and Khomeini claimed to be divinely inspired deliverers. Each promised to rescue the Islamic faithful from imperialist Westerners and from corrupt and heretical leaders within the Muslim world. Both leaders promised their followers magical protection and instant paradise should they fall while waging the holy war against the heretics and infidels. Each leader sought to build a lasting state and

> **Khomeini, Ayatollah Ruhollah** [EYE-uh-TOH-lah Roo-hah-luh ko-MAY-nee] (1900–1989) Religious ruler of Iran following revolution of 1979 to expel the Pahlavi shah of Iran; emphasized religious purification; tried to eliminate western influences and establish purely Islamic government.

social order on the basis of what were believed to be Islamic precedents. Thus, each revivalist movement aimed at defending and restoring what its leaders believed to be the true beliefs, traditions, and institutions of Islamic civilization. The leaders of both movements sought to spread their revolutions to surrounding areas, both Muslim and infidel, and each believed he was setting in motion forces that would eventually sweep the entire globe.

Although proclaimed as an alternative path for development that could be followed by the rest of the emerging nations, Khomeini's revolution owed its initial success in seizing power to a combination of circumstances that was unique to Iran (Map 34.4). Like China, Iran had not been formally colonized by the European powers but rather had been reduced to a sphere of informal influence, divided between Great Britain and Russia. As a result, neither the bureaucratic nor the communication infrastructures that accompanied colonial takeovers were highly developed there. Nor did a substantial Western-educated middle class emerge. Thus, the impetus for "modernization" came suddenly and was imposed from above by the Pahlavi shahs. The initiatives taken by the second shah in particular, which were supported by Iran's considerable oil wealth, wrenched Iran out of the isolation and backwardness in which most of the nation lived until the mid-20th century. The shah had fled Iran in the early 1950s after a staunch nationalist leader named Mohammed Mosaddeq rose to power. But the shah was restored by a CIA-engineered coup in 1953, designed both to counter the growing influence of the Soviet-dominated Iranian communist party and ensure Anglo-American control over Iran's vast oil reserves. Once back in power, he tried to impose economic development and social change through government directives. Although advances occurred, the regime managed to alienate the great mass of the Iranian people in the process.

The shah's dictatorial and repressive regime deeply offended the emerging middle classes, whom he considered his strongest potential supporters. His flaunting of Islamic conventions and his neglect of Islamic worship and religious institutions enraged the *ayatollahs*, or religious experts. They also alienated the *mullahs*, or local prayer leaders and mosque attendants, who guided the religious and personal lives of the great majority of the Iranian population. The favoritism the shahs showed foreign investors and a handful of big Iranian entrepreneurs with personal connections to highly placed officials angered the smaller bazaar merchants, who had long maintained close links with the mullahs and other religious leaders. The shah's half-hearted land reform schemes alienated the land-owning classes without doing much to improve the condition of the rural poor. Even the urban workers, who benefited most from the boom in construction and light industrialization the shah's development efforts had stimulated, were dissatisfied. In the years before the 1979 revolution, a fall in oil prices resulted in an economic slump and widespread unemployment in urban areas such as the capital, Tehran.

Although he had treated his officers well, the shah had badly neglected the military rank-and-file, especially in the army. So when the crisis came in 1978, the shah found that few soldiers were prepared to defend his regime. His armies refused to fire on the growing crowds that demonstrated for his removal and the return of Khomeini, then in exile in Paris. Dying of cancer and disheartened by what he saw as betrayal by his people and by allies such as the United States, the shah fled without much of a fight. Khomeini's revolution triumphed over a regime that looked powerful but proved exceptionally vulnerable.

After coming to power, Khomeini, defying the predictions of most Western "experts" on Iranian affairs, followed through on his promises of radical change. Constitutional and leftist parties allied to the revolutionary movement were brutally repressed. Moderate leaders were replaced quickly by radical religious figures eager to obey Khomeini's every command. The "satanic" influences of the United States and western Europe were purged. At the same time, Iran also distanced itself from the atheistic communist world. Secular influences in law and government were supplanted by strict Islamic legal codes, which included such punishments as the amputation of limbs for theft and stoning for women caught in adultery. Veiling became obligatory for all women, and the career prospects for women of the educated middle classes, who had been among the most favored by the shah's reforms, suddenly were limited drastically (Figure 34.9).

Khomeini's planners also drew up grand schemes for land reform, religious education, and economic development that accorded with the dictates of Islam. Most of these measures came to little because soon after the revolution, Saddam Hussein, the military leader of neighboring Iraq, sought to take advantage of the turmoil in Iran by annexing its western, oil-rich provinces. The Iran–Iraq War that resulted swallowed up Iranian energies and resources for almost the entire decade after Khomeini came to power. The struggle became a highly personal vendetta for Khomeini, who was

FIGURE **34.9** Women played a vital role in the mass demonstrations that toppled the shah of Iran and brought Ayatollah Khomeini to power in 1979. In many ways women's support for political movements in the postcolonial period was a continuation of their active participation in earlier struggles against European colonial domination. But increasingly in the postcolonial era, women have organized not only to promote political change, but to force social and economic reforms intended to improve the quality of their own lives as women.

determined to destroy Saddam Hussein and punish the Iraqis. His refusal to negotiate peace caused heavy losses and untold suffering to the Iranian people. This suffering continued long after it was clear that the Iranians' aging military equipment and handful of allies were no match for Hussein's more advanced military hardware and an Iraqi war machine bankrolled by its oil-rich Arab neighbors, who were fearful that Khomeini's revolution might spread to their own countries.

As the support of the Western powers, including the United States (despite protestations of neutrality), for the Iraqis increased, the position of the isolated Iranians became increasingly intolerable. Hundreds of thousands of poorly armed and half-trained Iranian conscripts, including tens of thousands of untrained and nearly weaponless boys, died before Khomeini finally agreed to a humiliating armistice in 1988. Peace found revolutionary Iran in shambles. Few of its development initiatives had been pursued, and shortages in food, fuel, and the other necessities of life were widespread.

Iran's decade-long absorption in the war and its continuing isolation makes it impossible to assess the potential of the religious revivalist, anti-Western option for other postcolonial nations. What had seemed at first a viable path to independent development had become mired in brutal internal repression and misguided and failed development initiatives. By the 1990s, although control by Islamic clerics continued, more open elections began to occur in Iran, presenting new alternatives for the future. In the past decade, these trends have been reversed by the increasing hostility of the United States, which has greatly strengthened the hand of the religious hardliners and opened the way for the repression of moderate, pro-democracy forces through election reverses and political repression.

South Africa: The Apartheid State and Its Demise

South Africa was by no means the only area still under some form of colonial dominance decades after India gained its independence in 1947. Portugal, the oldest and long considered the weakest of the European colonizers, held onto Angola, Mozambique, and its other African possessions until the mid-1970s. Until 1980, Zimbabwe (formerly Southern Rhodesia) was run by white settlers, who had unilaterally declared their independence from Great Britain. Southwest Africa became fully free of South African control only in 1989, and some of the smaller islands in the West Indies and the Pacific remain under European or American rule to the present day.

By the 1970s, however, South Africa was by far the largest, most populous, richest, and most strategic area where most of the population had yet to be liberated from colonial domination. Since the 1940s, the white settlers, particularly the Dutch-descended Afrikaners, had solidified their internal control of the country under the leadership of the Nationalist party. In stages and through a series of elections in which the blacks, who made up the majority of South Africans, were not allowed to vote, the Nationalists won complete independence from Great Britain in 1960. From 1948, when the Nationalist party first came to power, the Afrikaners moved to institutionalize white supremacy and white minority rule by passing thousands of laws that, taken together, made up the system of apartheid (see Chapter 31) that dominated all aspects of South African life until the 1990s.

Apartheid was designed not only to ensure a monopoly of political power and economic dominance for the white minority, both British- and Dutch-descended, but also to impose a system of extreme segregation on all races of South Africa in all aspects of their lives. Separate and patently unequal facilities were established for different racial groups for recreation, education, housing, work, and medical care. Dating and sexual intercourse across racial lines were strictly prohibited; skilled and high-paying jobs were reserved for white workers; and nonwhites were required to carry passes that listed the parts of South Africa where they were allowed to work and live. If caught by the police without their passes or in areas where they were not permitted to travel, nonwhite South Africans were routinely given stiff jail sentences.

Spatial separation was also organized on a grander scale by the creation of numerous **homelands** within South Africa, each designated for the main ethnolinguistic or "tribal" groups within the black African population. Although touted by the Afrikaners as the ultimate solution to the racial "problem," the homelands scheme would have left the black African majority with a small portion of some of the poorest land in South Africa. Because the homelands were overpopulated and poverty-stricken, the white minority was guaranteed a ready supply of cheap black labor to work in their factories and mines and on their farms. Denied citizenship in South Africa proper, these laborers would have been forced eventually to return to the homelands, where they had left their wives and children while emigrating in search of work.

To maintain the blatantly racist and inequitable system of apartheid, the white minority had to build a police state and expend a large portion of the federal budget on a sophisticated and well-trained military establishment. Because of the land's great mineral wealth, the Afrikaner nationalists were able to find the resources to fund their garrison state for decades. Until the late 1980s, the government prohibited all forms of black protest and brutally repressed even nonviolent resistance. Black organizations such as the **African National Congress** were banned, and African leaders such as **Walter Sisulu** and **Nelson Mandela** were shipped off to maximum-security prisons. Other leaders, such as **Steve Biko**, one of the young organizers of the Black Consciousness movement, were murdered while in police custody.

Through spies and police informers, the regime tried to capitalize on personal and ethnic divisions within the black majority community. Favoritism was shown to some leaders and groups to keep them from uniting with others in all-out opposition to apartheid. With all avenues of constitutional negotiation and peaceful protest closed, many advocates of black majority rule in a multiracial society turned to guerrilla resistance from the 1960s onward. The South African government responded in the 1980s by declaring a state of emergency, which simply intensified the restrictions already in place in the garrison state. The government repeatedly justified its repression by labeling virtually all black protest as communist-inspired and playing on the racial fears of the white minority.

Through most of the 1970s and early 1980s, it appeared that the hardening hostility between the unyielding white minority and the frustrated black majority was building to a very violent upheaval. But from the late 1980s, countervailing forces were taking hold in South African society. An international boycott greatly weakened the South African economy. In addition, the South African army's costly and futile involvement in wars in neighboring Namibia and Angola seemed to presage never-ending struggles against black liberation movements within the country. Led by the courageous **F. W. de Klerk**, moderate Afrikaner leaders pushed for reforms that began to dismantle the system of apartheid. The release of key black political prisoners, such as the dramatic freeing of Nelson Mandela in 1990, signaled that at long last the leaders of the white majority were ready to negotiate the future of South African politics and society. Permission for peaceful mass demonstrations and ultimately the enfranchisement of all adult South Africans for the 1994 elections provided a way out of the dead end in which the nation was trapped under apartheid.

The well-run and remarkably participatory 1994 elections brought to power the African National Congress party, led by Nelson Mandela, who became the first black president of South Africa. Mandela proved to be one of the most skillful and respected political leaders on the world scene as well as a moderating force in the potentially volatile South African arena. The peaceful surrender of power by F. W. de Klerk's losing party, which was supported by most of the white minority, suggested that a pluralist democracy might well succeed in South Africa (Figure 34.10). But major obstacles remain. Bitter interethnic rivalries within the black majority community, which periodically flared into bloody battles between Zulus and Xhosas in 1990s, have yet to be fully resolved. Hard-line white supremacist organizations among the Afrikaners continue to defy the new regime. And the tasks of reforming the institutions and redistributing the wealth of South Africa in ways that will make for a just and equitable social order are formidable. Well into the 21st century, South Africa is likely to remain one of the most interesting and promising social experiments of an age in which communalism and ethnic hostility threatened to engulf much of the globe.

homelands Under apartheid, areas in South Africa designated for ethnolinguistic groups within the black African population; such areas tend to be overpopulated and poverty-stricken.

African National Congress Black political organization within South Africa; pressed for end to policies of apartheid; sought open democracy leading to black majority rule; until the 1990s declared illegal in South Africa.

Sisulu, Walter (1912–2003) Black African leader who, along with Nelson Mandela, opposed apartheid system in South Africa.

Mandela, Nelson (b. 1918) Long-imprisoned leader of the African National Congress party; worked with the ANC leadership and F. W. de Klerk's supporters to dismantle the apartheid system from the mid-1980s onward; in 1994, became the first black prime minister of South Africa after the ANC won the first genuinely democratic elections in the country's history.

Biko, Steve (1946–1977) An organizer of Black Consciousness movement in South Africa, in opposition to apartheid; murdered while in police custody.

de Klerk, F. W. White South African prime minister in the late 1980s and early 1990s. Working with Nelson Mandela and the African National Congress, de Klerk helped to dismantle the apartheid system and opened the way for a democratically elected government that represented all South Africans for the first time.

FIGURE **34.10** This photograph of a long line of newly enfranchised citizens waiting to vote in South Africa provides a striking contrast with the decreasing participation in elections in the United States and other older democracies in the West. For the first time, the Bantu-speaking peoples, coloreds, and Indians who make up the vast majority of South Africa's population were allowed to vote in free elections. Their determination to exercise their hard-won right to vote was demonstrated by the peoples' willingness to wait, often in stifling heat, for many hours in the long lines that stretched from polling stations throughout the country.

VISUALIZING THE PAST

Globalization and Postcolonial Societies

Although many of the areas colonized by the industrialized nations of the West had participated in long-distance trade from early times, colonial rule greatly intensified their integration into the capitalist-dominated world system. Colonization also brought more remote areas that had been only marginally affected by cross-cultural trade into the world system for the first time. As we have seen in Chapter 25 and the present chapter, new market linkages not only affected the elites and trading classes of African, Middle Eastern, and Asian societies, but they also increasingly involved the peasants, who made up the great majority of the population of colonial societies, as well as smaller numbers of workers in the towns and cities.

In the postcolonial era, this process of global market integration has accelerated steadily. One key feature of advancing globalization has been the specialized production of mineral and agricultural exports for foreign consumption. Another has been the growing proportion of uprooted farmers and urban laborers in postcolonial societies employed in factories that have very often been oppressive sweat shops manufacturing clothing,

(continued on next page)

household furnishings, audiovisual equipment, and other consumer goods for sale overseas, particularly in wealthy societies such as those in North America, western Europe, and Japan. These shifts have greatly increased trading links and economic independence between postcolonial societies and those that had formerly colonized them.

The pervasiveness of these connections in the daily lives of peoples around the globe can be readily seen in the shoes, clothing, and watches worn by the teacher and students in your class, and by the equipment and furnishings of your classrooms. Poll the class to determine where these items and other school supplies were produced. Discuss household and other personal items that were likely to have been manufactured, or at least assembled, in similar locales. Then consider the conditions under which the laborers who made these products were likely to have worked, and the international corporations that oversee and market these products.

> **QUESTIONS**
> - Who benefits the most from the profits made in the international marketing of goods from postcolonial societies?
> - How does the fact they are imported in massive quantities affect the wages and working conditions of American factory laborers?
> - What measures can be taken to improve the situation of both workers in emerging nations and those in the United States, or are the interests of the two irreconcilable?

Global Connections and Critical Themes

POSTCOLONIAL NATIONS IN THE COLD WAR WORLD ORDER

The years of independence for the nations that emerged from the colonial empires in Asia, the Middle East, and Africa have been filled with political and economic crises and social turmoil, and tensions between tradition and change. At the same time, it is important to put the recent history of these areas in a larger perspective. Most of the new nations that emerged from colonialism have been in existence for only a few decades. They came to independence with severe handicaps, many of which were a direct legacy of their colonial experiences. It is also important to remember that developed countries, such as the United States, took decades filled with numerous boundary disputes and outright wars to reach their current size and structure. Nearly a century after the original thirteen colonies broke from Great Britain and formed the United States, a civil war, the most costly war in the nation's history, was needed to preserve the union. If one takes into account the artificial nature of the emerging nations, many have held together rather well.

What is true in politics is true of all other aspects of the postcolonial experience of the African, Middle Eastern, and Asian peoples. With much lower populations and far fewer industrial competitors, as well as the capacity to draw on the resources of much of the rest of the world, European and North American nations had to struggle to industrialize and thereby achieve a reasonable standard of living for most of their people. Even with these advantages, the human cost in terms of horrific working conditions and urban squalor was enormous, and we are still paying the high ecological price. African, Middle Eastern, and Asian countries (and, as we saw in Chapter 28, this includes Japan) have had few or none of the West's advantages. Most of the emerging nations have begun the "great ascent" to development burdened by excessive and rapidly increasing populations that overwhelm the limited resources that developing nations often must export to earn the capital to buy food and machines. The emerging nations struggle to establish a place in the world market system that is structured in favor of the established industrial powers.

Despite the cultural dominance of the West, which was one of the great legacies and burdens of the colonial era, Asian, Middle Eastern, and African thinkers and artists have achieved a great deal. If much of this achievement has depended on Western models, one should not be surprised, given the educational backgrounds and personal experiences of the emerging nations' first generations of leaders. The challenge for the coming generations will be to find genuinely African, Middle Eastern, and Asian solutions to the problems that have stunted political and economic development in the postcolonial nations. The solutions arrived at are likely to vary a great deal, given the diversity of the nations and societies involved. They are also likely to be forged from a combination of Western influences and the ancient and distinguished traditions of civilized life that have been nurtured by African, Middle Eastern, and Asian peoples for millennia.

Further Readings

Much of the prolific literature on political and economic development in the emerging nations is focused on individual countries, and it is more helpful to know several cases in some depth than to try to master them all. Robert Heilbroner's writings, starting with *The Great Ascent* (1961), still provide the most sensible introduction to challenges to the new states in the early decades of independence. Peter Worsley's *The Third World* (1964) offers a provocative, if somewhat disjointed, supplement to Heilbroner's many works. Although focused mainly on South and Southeast Asia, Gunnar Myrdal's *Asian Drama*, 3 vols. (1968), is the best exploration in a single cultural area of the complexities of the challenges to development. A good overview of the history of postindependence in south Asia can be found in W. N. Brown, *The United States and India, Pakistan, and Bangladesh* (1984), despite its misleadingly Western-centric title, and especially Ramachandra Guha's *After Gandhi* (2007). Another reliable account of Indian politics is contained in Paul Brass, *The Politics of India Since Independence* (1990), in the New Cambridge History of India series. On development policy in India, see especially Guha and Francine R. Frankel, *India's Political Economy, 1947–1977* (1978).

Ali Mazrui and Michael Tidy, *Nationalism and New States in Africa* (1984), provides a good survey of developments throughout Africa. Also useful are S. A. Akintoye, *Emergent African States* (1976), and H. Bretton, *Power and Politics in Africa* (1973). Frederick Cooper's *Africa Since 1940: The Past of the Present* (2002) traces the struggles for nationhood and development into the first decade of the 21st century. For the Middle East, John Waterbury's *The Egypt of Nasser and Sadat* (1983) and Tim Mitchell's *Rule of Experts* (2002) provide detailed analyses of the politics of development.

On military coups, see Ruth First, *The Barrel of a Gun* (1971), and S. Decalo, *Coups and Army Rule in Africa* (1976). A fine analysis of the literature on the Iranian revolution is provided in Charles Kurzman's *The Unthinkable Revolution in Iran* (2004). Shaul Bakhash's *The Reign of the Ayatollahs* (1984) and R. K. Ramazani's *Revolutionary Iran* (1988) are among the more insightful of many books that have appeared about Iran since the revolution. Brian Bunting's *The Rise of the South African Reich* (1964) traces the rise of the apartheid regime in great (and polemical) detail, while Gail Gerhart's *Black Power in South Africa* (1978) is one of the better studies devoted to efforts to tear that system down. Nelson Mandela's *Long Walk to Freedom* (1994) is absolutely essential to understanding the latter processes. Among the many fine African, Middle Eastern, and Asian authors whose works are available in English, some of the best include (for Africa) Chinua Achebe, Wole Soyinka, and Ousmene Sembene; (for India) R. K. Narayan and V. S. Naipaul; (for Egypt) Nawal el Saadawi and Naguib Mahfouz; and (for Indonesia) Mochtar Lubis and P. A. Toer. For white perspectives on the South African situation, the fictional works of Nadine Gordimer and J. M. Coetzee are superb.

On MyHistoryLab

 Study and Review on MyHistoryLab

Critical Thinking Questions

1. How did the persisting legacies of the colonial era and the pervasive cold war rivalries and superpower interventions constrain political autonomy and socioeconomic development in the newly independent countries of Asia and Africa?

2. What factors account for the unprecedented increase in human populations worldwide, and why has that growth been much higher in developing than in industrialized societies?

3. Why have women in postcolonial societies lagged so far behind men in social status, opportunities for personal advancement, and the quality of their daily lives?

4. Which of the newly independent and developing nations do you think will be major political and economic powers in the later 21st century and why?

5. How well did experiences after decolonization position major African and Asian societies to deal with globalization?

Rebirth and Revolution: Nation-Building in East Asia and the Pacific Rim

35

Listen to Chapter 35 on MyHistoryLab

Well into young adulthood, Yun Ruo seemed to be a person blessed by good fortune. Although he grew up in post-1945 China, a nation wracked by revolutionary turmoil and state repression, Yun lived a life of relative privilege and security—until the late 1960s. His father, Liu Shaoqi, had long been one of the most prominent leaders of the Communist party, and his family was firmly ensconced in the elite strata of the People's Republic. Yun was a brilliant and hard-working student who in his late teens had gained admission into the highly competitive and prestigious Beijing Aeronautics Institute. In the late 1950s, he was rewarded for his academic accomplishments with the opportunity to further his technical training in the Soviet Union, which at the time was a major supporter of the struggling People's Republic of China.

LEARNING OBJECTIVES

35.1 What were the major factors that explain Japan's ability to emerge from devastating defeat to become a major industrial and economic power and key player in the world community of nations? p. 871

35.2 What sorts of political systems and economic policies predominated among the "little Tigers" in east and southeast Asia? p. 877

35.3 How did ideological extremism and totalitarianism in the People's Republic of China subvert efforts at economic development and result in widespread human suffering and environmental disasters? p. 882

35.4 How was it possible for the Vietnamese to liberate their homeland from Japanese, French and Chinese colonization efforts and defeat a massive intervention by the American superpower during decades dominated by civil war and devastating foreign aggression? p. 889

FIGURE **35.1** Mass demonstrations, such as the one in the photo that was staged in front of the Gate of Heavenly Peace in Beijing at the height of the Cultural Revolution in the mid-1960s, showed both the participants' adulation of Mao Zedong and their capacity to intimidate his political rivals.

869

Watch the Video Series on MyHistoryLab

Learn about some key topics related to this chapter with the *MyHistoryLab Video Series: Key Topics in World History*

In Russia, as in China, Yun went from one career achievement to the next, unaffected by the state's forcible mobilization of teachers, students, and other professionals into labor brigades for the Maoists' misguided 1958 Great Leap Forward campaign. But when the assault on the elite social strata broadened to doctors, government officials, scientists, and technicians during the Cultural Revolution of 1967–1970, Yun found himself caught up in persecution by the Red Guards and other political factions proclaiming their fanatical loyalty to Chairman Mao. In this more radical surge of anti-elitism in the People's Republic, intellectuals and party functionaries were not only sent into the countryside to labor among the peasants, but many were publicly purged, imprisoned, and killed (see Figure 35.1).

Reflecting the deep paranoia and widespread persecution of the times, Yun was branded an enemy of the revolution, ostensibly because he had fallen in love with a Russian woman while a student in the Soviet Union. Once Communist China's main backer, the Soviet Union had increasingly distanced itself from China beginning in the early 1960s. By the end of the decade Russia was denounced as antirevolutionary and a threat to the People's Republic. But Yun's romantic ties were largely a pretext to use him in a campaign of vilification against his father, Liu Shaoqi.

In response to political pressures surrounding the shifting Maoist stance toward the Soviets, Yun's family forbade him to marry his Russian lover. His family confiscated the couple's love letters, which had allowed them to sustain a long-distance relationship after Yun returned to China, and the letters were passed on to government functionaries. No less a personage than Jiang Qing (Mao's wife) branded Yun a spy, and he was later convicted of treason by a "people's court." Sentenced to eight years in prison, Yun was released in 1974, when the fervor of the Cultural Revolution had begun to fade. But his experiences in prison left him mentally unbalanced, and he died several years later of a lung disease that was probably contracted during his imprisonment. ■

The turmoil and uncertainty—and finally brutality—that enveloped Yun Ruo's life were dominant motifs throughout much of east and southeast Asia during the post–World War II era. Societies across both regions had been deeply disrupted, even devastated, by the Pacific war. Most of Japan's cities were smoldering ruins; its islands were occupied and ruled by the U.S. military, and its people were threatened by starvation, disease, homelessness, and utter despair. China, Vietnam, and Korea, all of which had been caught up in the war to varying degrees, were embroiled in civil wars that in Korea and Vietnam would prolong wartime privations and destruction for decades. The long civil war in China was decided by the victory of the Communists in 1949 and the flight of the Guomindang to Taiwan. But persecution of the fledgling regime's perceived enemies would continue through much of the following decade and, as we have seen through the experience of Yun Ruo, spread to loyal supporters of the revolution and across society at large by the late 1950s and 1960s.

By the 1980s a number of noncommunist nations on the **Pacific Rim**, including Japan, Korea, Singapore, Taiwan, Thailand, and Malaysia, had joined the ranks of developed nations. Their economic successes and political stability, as well as some of the challenges they have posed in recent decades for older developing societies, such as the United States, will be considered in the following chapter. By the 1980s both communist Vietnam and China had also begun to recover from foreign occupations, civil strife, and revolutionary turmoil. Since then, China in particular has emerged as a global economic power, and Vietnam has increasingly opened its tightly controlled society to the outside world. Altogether the nations of east Asia and the Pacific Rim have become major economic, and potentially political, players in the international arena of the early 21st century.

Pacific Rim Region including Japan, South Korea, Singapore, Hong Kong, Taiwan; typified by rapid growth rates, expanding exports, and industrialization; either Chinese or strongly influenced by Confucian values; considerable reliance on government planning and direction, limitations on dissent and instability.

1940 C.E.	1955 C.E.	1970 C.E.
1942 Japanese occupation of French Indochina **1945** Ho Chi Minh proclaims the Republic of Vietnam **1948** U.S.-sponsored Republic of (South) Korea established **1949** Communist victory in China; People's Republic of China established **1950–1951** Purge of the landlord class in China **1950–1953** Korean War **1952** U.S. occupation of Japan ends **1953** Beginning of China's first five-year plan **1954** French defeated at Dien Bien Phu; Geneva accords, French withdrawal from Vietnam; beginning of the Sino-Soviet split	**Mid–1950s** Buildup of U.S. advisors in South Vietnam **1957** "Let a Hundred Flowers Bloom" campaign in China **1958–1960** "Great Leap Forward" in China **1960** South Korean nationalist leader Syngman Rhee forced from office by student demonstrations **1963** Beginning of state family planning in China **1965–1968** Cultural Revolution in China **1965–1973** Direct U.S. military intervention in Vietnam **1968** Tet offensive in Vietnam	**1975** Communist victory in Vietnam; collapse of Republic of South Vietnam **1976** Deaths of Zhou Enlai and Mao Zedong; purge of Gang of Four **1994** Death of North Korean leader Kim Il-sung

EAST ASIA IN THE POSTWAR SETTLEMENTS

35.1 What were the the major factors that explain Japan's ability to emerge from devastating defeat to become a major industrial and economic power and key player in the world community of nations?

At the end of World War II a zone of reasonably stable noncommunist states developed along the Pacific Rim. Linked to the West, these nations maintained a Neo-Confucian emphasis on the importance of conservative politics and a strong state.

The victors in World War II had some reasonably clear ideas about how east Asia was to be restructured. Korea was divided between a Russian zone of occupation in the north and an American zone in the south. The island of **Taiwan** was restored to China, which in principle was ruled by a Guomindang government headed by Chiang Kai-shek. The United States regained the Philippines and pledged to grant independence quickly, although retaining some key military bases. The European powers sought to restore control over their colonies in Vietnam, Malaya, and Indonesia. Japan was occupied by American forces bent on introducing major changes that would prevent a recurrence of military aggression.

Not surprisingly, the Pacific regions of Asia did not quickly settle into agreed-upon patterns. A little more than a decade after the war's end, not only the Philippines but also Indonesia, Malaysia, Singapore, and Burma (later Myanmar) were independent, as part of the postwar tide of decolonization (Map 35.1). Taiwan was still ruled by Chiang Kai-shek, but the Chinese mainland was in the hands of a new and powerful communist regime. Chiang's nationalist regime claimed a mission to recover China, but in fact Taiwan was a separate republic. Korea remained divided but had undergone a brutal north–south conflict in which only U.S. intervention preserved South Korea's independence. Japan was one of the few Pacific regions where matters had proceeded somewhat according to plan, as the nation began to recover economically while accepting a very different political structure.

Japanese Recovery

Japan in 1945 was in shambles. Its cities were leveled, its factories destroyed or idle, its people impoverished and shocked by the fact of surrender and the trauma of bombing, including the atomic devastation of Hiroshima and Nagasaki. However, like the industrial nations of the West, Japan was capable of reestablishing a vigorous economy with surprising speed. Its

MAP 35.1 **The Pacific Rim Area by 1960** Geographic locations and political systems created new contacts and alignments.

Taiwan Island off Chinese mainland; became refuge for Nationalist Chinese regime under Chiang Kai-shek as Republic of China in 1948; successfully retained independence with aid of United States; rapidly industrialized after 1950s.

Read the Document on MyHistoryLab: The Constitution of Japan (1947)

Liberal Democratic Party Monopolized Japanese government from its formation in 1955 into the 1990s; largely responsible for the economic reconstruction of Japan.

Republic of Korea Southern half of Korea sponsored by United States following World War II; headed by nationalist Syngman Rhee; developed parliamentary institutions but maintained authoritarian government; defended by UN forces during Korean War; underwent industrialization and economic emergence after 1950s.

People's Democratic Republic of Korea Northern half of Korea dominated by U.S.S.R.; long headed by Kim Il-sung; attacked south in 1950 and initiated Korean War; retained independence as a communist state after the war.

occupation by U.S. forces, eager to reform Japan but also eager to avoid punitive measures, provided an opportunity for a new period of selective westernization.

The American occupation government, headed by General Douglas MacArthur, worked quickly to tear down Japan's wartime political structure. (The occupation lasted until 1952, a year after Japan signed a peace treaty with most of its wartime opponents.) Japan's military forces were disbanded, the police were decentralized, many officials were removed, and political prisoners were released. For the long run, American authorities pressed for a democratization of Japanese society by giving women the vote, encouraging labor unions, and abolishing Shintoism as a state religion. Several economic reforms were also introduced, breaking up landed estates for the benefit of small farmers—who quickly became politically conservative—and dissolving the holdings of the zaibatsu combines (see Chapter 28, p. 678), a measure that had little lasting effect as Japanese big business regrouped quickly.

A new constitution tried to cut through older limitations by making the parliament the supreme government body. Several civil liberties were guaranteed, along with gender equality in marriage and collective bargaining rights. Military forces with "war potential" were abolished forever, making Japan a unique major nation in its limited military strength. The emperor became merely a symbolic figurehead, without political power and with no claims to Shinto divinity. Even as Japan accepted many Western political and legal concepts, it inserted its own values into the new constitution. Thus, a 1963 law called for special social obligations to the elderly, in obvious contrast to Western approaches: "The elders shall be loved and respected as those who have for many years contributed toward the development of society, and a wholesome and peaceful life shall be guaranteed to them."

These new constitutional measures were embraced by the Japanese people, many of whom became avid opponents of any hint of military revival. Military power and responsibility in the region were retained by the United States, which long after the occupation period kept important bases in Japan. Many of the political features of the new constitution worked smoothly—in large part because the Japanese had experienced parliamentary and political party activity for extended periods in the pre–World War II decades. Two moderate parties merged in 1955 into the new **Liberal Democratic Party**, which monopolized Japan's government into the 1990s.

Japan became a genuine multiparty democracy but with unusual emphasis on one-party control in the interests of order and elite control. It granted women the vote, but women's conditions differed markedly from men's. In education, American occupation forces insisted on reducing the nationalism in textbooks and opening secondary schools to more social groups. These changes merged with existing Japanese enthusiasm for education, heightening the emphasis on school success. Japan developed one of the most meritocratic systems in the world, with students advanced to university training on the basis of rigorous examinations. But once the occupation ended, the government reasserted some traditional components in this education package, including careful controls over textbooks. In 1966, for example, the Ministry of Education attacked "egotistic" attitudes in Japan, which were producing "a feeling of spiritual hollowness and unrest." Schools in this situation should generate ethical discipline and group consciousness, touching base with more customary goals while preparing students for their role in Japan's expanding economy. As one conservative put it in the 1980s, "You have to teach tradition [to the children] whether they like it or not."

Korea: Intervention and War

Korea's postwar adjustment period was far more troubled than Japan's. The leaders of the great Allied powers during World War II had agreed in principle that Korea should be restored as an independent state. But the United States' eagerness to obtain Soviet help against Japan resulted in Soviet occupation of the northern part of the peninsula. As the cold war intensified, American and Soviet authorities could not agree on unification of the zones, and in 1948 the United States sponsored a **Republic of Korea** in the south, matched by a Soviet-dominated **People's Democratic Republic of Korea** in the north (Map 35.1). North Korea's regime drew on an earlier Korean Communist party founded in exile in the 1900s. North Korea quickly became a communist state with a Stalinist-style emphasis on the power of the leader, Kim Il-sung, and then his son after his death in 1994. The South Korean regime, bolstered by an ongoing American military presence, was headed by nationalist Syngman Rhee. Rhee's South Korea developed institutions that were parliamentary in form but maintained a strongly authoritarian tone.

In June 1950 North Korean forces attacked South Korea, hoping to impose unification on their own terms (Figure 35.2). The United States reacted quickly (after some confusing signals about

View the Closer Look on MyHistoryLab: The Korean War

FIGURE 35.2 The internationalization of the civil conflict between the regimes of North and South Korea in the late 1940s led to the flight of hundreds of thousands of refugees from one region to another. As this photo so starkly portrays, these migrations often occurred in the harsh winter season when many of those in flight died of the cold and hunger.

whether South Korea was inside the U.S. "defense perimeter"). President Truman insisted on drawing another line against communist aggression, and he orchestrated United Nations sponsorship of a largely American "police action" in support of South Korean troops. In the ensuing **Korean War**, under General MacArthur's leadership, Allied forces pushed North Korea back, driving on toward the Chinese border. This action roused concern on the part of China's communist regime, which sent "volunteers" to force American troops back toward the south. The front stabilized in 1952 near the original north–south border. The stalemate dragged on until 1953, when a new American administration was able to agree to an armistice.

Korea then continued its dual pattern of development. North Korea produced an unusually isolated version of one-man communist rule as Kim concentrated his powers over the only legal political party, the military, and the government. Even Soviet liberalization in the late 1980s brought little change. South Korea and the United States concluded a mutual defense treaty in 1954; American troop levels were reduced, but the South Korean army gained more sophisticated military equipment. The United States also poured economic aid into the country, initially to prevent starvation in a war-ravaged land. The political tenor of South Korea continued to be authoritarian. In 1961 army officers took over effective rule of the country, although sometimes a civilian government served as a front.

However, economic change began to gain ground in South Korea, ushering in a new phase of activity and international impact. Tensions between the two Koreas continued to run high, with many border clashes and sabotage, but outright warfare was avoided.

Korean War Fought from 1950 to 1953; North supported by U.S.S.R. and later People's Republic of China; South supported by United States and small international United Nations force; ended in stalemate and continued division of Korea.

Read the Document on MyHistoryLab: North and South Korean Accord (2000)

Emerging Stability in Taiwan, Hong Kong, and Singapore

Postwar adjustments in Taiwan involved yet another set of issues. As the communist revolutionary armies gained the upper hand in mainland China, between 1946 and 1948 the Guomindang (Nationalist) regime prepared to fall back on its newly reacquired island, which the communists could not threaten because they had no navy. The result was imposition over the Taiwanese majority of Chinese leadership plus a massive military force drawn from the mainland.

The authoritarian political patterns the nationalists had developed in China, centered on Chiang Kai-shek's personal control of the government, were amplified by the need to keep in check disaffected indigenous Taiwanese, who grew restive as Chinese migrants dominated political and economic life on the island. Hostility with the communist regime across the Taiwan Strait ran high. In 1955 and 1958, the communists bombarded two small islands controlled by the nationalists, Quemoy and Matsu, and wider conflict threatened as the United States backed up its ally. Tensions were defused when communist China agreed to fire on the islands only on alternate days, while U.S. ships supplied them on the off-days, thus salvaging national honor. Finally, the United States induced Chiang to renounce any intentions of attacking the mainland, and conflict eased into mutual bombardments of propaganda leaflets. During this period, as in South Korea, the United States gave economic aid to Taiwan, ending assistance only in the 1960s, when its growing prosperity seemed assured.

Two other participants in the economic advances of the Pacific Rim were distinguished by special ties to Britain. **Hong Kong** remained a British colony after World War II; only in the 1980s was an agreement reached between Britain and China for its 1997 return to the Chinese fold. Hong Kong gained increasing autonomy from direct British rule. Its Chinese population swelled at various points after 1946 as a result of flights from communist rule.

Singapore, at first part of Malaysia (see Map 35.1), retained a large British naval base until 1971, when Britain abandoned all pretense of power in east Asia. Singapore grew into a vigorous free port, and it became an independent nation in 1965.

Overall, by the end of the 1950s a certain stability had emerged in the political situation of many smaller east Asian nations. From the 1960s onward these same areas, combining Western contacts with important traditions of group loyalty, moved from impressive economic recovery to new international influence on the basis of manufacturing and trade.

Hong Kong British colony on Chinese mainland; major commercial center; agreement reached between Britain and People's Republic of China returned colony to China in 1997.

Japan, Incorporated: A Distinctive Political and Cultural Style

The chief emphasis of postwar Japanese politics lay in conservative stability. The Liberal Democratic Party held the reins of government from 1955 onward. This meant that Japan, uniquely among the democratic nations of the post-war world, had no experience with shifts in party administration until 1993. Changes in leadership, which at times were frequent, were handled through negotiations among the Liberal Democratic elite, not directly as a result of shifts in voter preference.

Clearly, this system revived many of the oligarchic features of Meiji Japan and the Japan of the 1920s. During the prosperous 1970s and 1980s, economic progress and the Liberal Democrats' willingness to consult opposition leaders about major legislation reinforced Japan's effective political unity. Only at the end of the 1980s, when several Liberal Democratic leaders were branded by corruption of various sorts, were new questions raised.

Post-War Politics and Culture

Japan's distinctive political atmosphere showed clearly in strong cooperation with business. The state set production and investment goals while actively lending public resources to encourage investment and limit imports. The government–business coordination to promote economic growth and export expansion prompted the half-admiring, half-derisory Western label "Japan, Incorporated."

The government actively campaigned to promote birth control and abortion, and population growth slowed. This was another product of the strong national tradition of state-sponsored discipline. As in politics and education, Japanese culture preserved important traditional elements, which provided aesthetic and spiritual satisfactions amid rapid economic change (Figure 35.3). Customary styles in poetry, painting, tea ceremonies, and flower arrangements continued. Each New Year's Day, for example, the emperor presided at a poetry contest, and masters of traditional arts were honored by being designated as Living National Treasures. Kabuki and Noh theater also flourished.

FIGURE **35.3** The blending of ancient Japanese culture (*kimonos*) and modern consumer goods (cellphones, backpacks, and thermoses) is evident in this photo of three young women dressed for an evening out on the town.

Japanese films and novels often recalled the country's earlier history. Japanese painters and architects participated actively in the "international style" pioneered in the West, but they often infused it with earlier Japanese motifs such as stylized nature painting. City orchestras played the works of Western composers and native compositions that incorporated passages played on the Japanese flute and zither.

Cultural combinations were not always smooth. Both before and after World War II, key intellectuals used art and literature to protest change, not merely to blend Western and traditional styles. The flamboyant postwar writer Hiraoka Kimitoke (pen name Yukio Mishima, 1925–1970) was a case in point. His novels and dramas, which began to appear in 1949, dealt with controversial themes such as homosexuality while also updating versions of the Noh plays. Although a passionate nationalist, he was too sickly for military service in World War II. But he later sought to foster cults of body building and Samurai discipline. At first he enjoyed many Western contacts and encouragement, but he came to hate Western ways. In 1968 he formed a private army with the intent of restoring Japanese ideals. After finishing a final major novel, Mishima performed his own ritual suicide in 1970. He wrote to an American friend shortly before his death, "I came to wish to sacrifice myself for this old beautiful tradition of Japan, which is disappearing very quickly day by day."

The Economic Surge: Japan Challenges the Superpowers for Economic Supremacy

Particularly after the mid-1950s, rapid economic growth made Japan's clearest mark internationally and commanded the most intense energies at home. By 1983 the total national product was equal to the combined totals of China, both Koreas, Taiwan, India, Pakistan, Australia, and Brazil. Per capita income, although still slightly behind that of the leading Western nations such as West Germany, had passed that of many countries, including Britain. Annual economic growth reached at least 10 percent regularly from the mid-1950s onward, surpassing the regular levels of every other nation during the 1960s and 1970s, as Japan became one of the top two or three economic powers in the world. Leading Japanese corporations, such as the great automobile manufacturers and electronic equipment producers, became known not simply for the volume of their international exports but for the high quality of their goods.

A host of factors fed this astounding economic performance. Active government encouragement was a major ingredient. Educational expansion played a major role as Japan began to turn out far more

FIGURE 35.4 Tokyo at night at the beginning of the 21st century epitomizes the resurgence of Asian economies following World War II.

engineers than did more populous competitors, such as the United States. Foreign policy also played a role. Japan was able to devote almost its whole capital to investment in productive technology, for its military expenses were negligible given its reliance on U.S. protection.

Japan's distinctive labor policies functioned well. Workers were organized mainly in company unions that were careful not to impair their companies' productivity. Leading corporations solidified this cooperation, which spurred zealous work from most employees. Social activities, including group exercise sessions before the start of the working day, promoted and expressed group loyalty, and managers took active interest in suggestions by employees. The Japanese system also ensured lifetime employment to an important part of the labor force, a policy aided by economic growth, low average unemployment rates, and an early retirement age. This network of policies and attitudes made Japanese labor seem both less class-conscious and less individualistic than labor forces in the advanced industrial nations of the West. It reflected older traditions of group solidarity in Japan, going back to feudal patterns.

Japanese management displayed a distinctive spirit, again as a result of adapting older traditions of leadership. There was more group consciousness, including a willingness to abide by collective decisions and less concern for quick personal profits than was characteristic of the West, particularly the United States. Few corporate bureaucrats changed firms, which meant that their efforts were concentrated on their company's success. Leisure life remained meager by Western standards, and many Japanese were reluctant to take regular vacations.

Japan's distinctiveness extended to family life, despite some features similar to the West's industrial experience. Japanese women, although increasingly well educated and experiencing an important decline in birth rates, did not follow Western patterns precisely. A feminist movement was confined to a small number of intellectuals. Within the family, women shared fewer leisure activities with their husbands, concentrating more heavily on domestic duties and intensive childrearing than was true in the West by the 1970s. In childrearing, conformity to group standards was emphasized far more than in the West or in communist China. A comparative study of nursery schools showed that Japanese teachers were bent on effacing their own authority in the interests of developing strong bonds between the children. Shame was directed toward nonconformist behaviors, a disciplinary approach the West had largely abandoned in the early 19th century. Japanese television game shows, superficially copied from those of the West, imposed elaborate, dishonoring punishment on losing contestants.

The nation had few lawyers, for it was assumed that people could make and abide by firm arrangements through mutual agreement. Psychiatrists reported far fewer problems of loneliness and individual alienation than in the West. Conversely, situations that promoted competition between individuals, such as university entrance tests, produced far higher stress levels than did analogous Western experiences. The Japanese had particular ways to relieve tension. Bouts of heavy drinking were more readily tolerated than in the West, seen as a time when normal codes of conduct could be suspended under the helpful eyes of friends. Businessmen and some politicians had recourse to traditional geisha houses for female-supplied cosseting, a normal and publicly accepted activity.

Japanese popular culture was not static, both because of ongoing attraction to Western standards and because of rapid urbanization and economic growth. The U.S. presence after World War II brought a growing fascination with baseball, and professional teams flourished. Japanese athletes began also to excel in such sports as tennis and golf. In the mid-1980s, the government, appalled to discover that a majority of Japanese children did not use chopsticks but preferred knives and forks in order to eat more rapidly, invested money to promote chopsticks training in the schools. This was a minor development, but it indicates the ongoing tension between change, with its Western connotations, and a commitment to Japanese identity (Figure 35.3). The veneration of old age was challenged by some youthful assertiveness and by the sheer cost of supporting the rapidly growing percentage of older people, for Japan relied heavily on family support for elders.

Other issues were associated with change. By the 1960s, pollution had become a serious problem as cities and industry expanded rapidly. Traffic police, for example, sometimes wore masks to protect their lungs. The government (eager to preempt a potential opposition issue) paid increasing attention to environmental issues after 1970. The 1990s brought some new questions to Japan. Mired in political corruption, the Liberal Democrats were replaced by shaky coalition governments. A severe economic recession caused widespread unemployment. Even as Japanese methods were being touted in the West as a basis for economic and social revitalization, some of the critical patterns of postwar development were at least temporarily disrupted.

THE PACIFIC RIM: MORE JAPANS?

35.2 What sorts of political systems and economic policies predominated among the "little Tigers" in east and southeast Asia?

> Economic and political developments in several nations and city-states on Asia's Pacific coast echoed important elements of Japan's 20th-century history. Political authoritarianism was characteristic of most Pacific Rim states, although there were periodic bows to parliamentary forms and protests from dissidents who wanted greater freedom.

South Korea was the most obvious example of the spread of new economic dynamism to other parts of the Pacific Rim (see Figure 35.5). The Korean government rested normally in the hands of a political strongman, usually from army ranks. Syngman Rhee was forced out of office by student demonstrations in 1960; a year later, a military general, Park Chung-hee, seized power. He retained his authority until his assassination in 1979 by his director of intelligence. Then another general seized power. Intense student protest, backed by wider popular support, pressed the military from power at the end of the 1980s. But a conservative politician won the ensuing general election, and it was not clear how much the political situation had changed. Opposition activity was possible in South Korea, although usually heavily circumscribed, and many leaders were jailed. There was some freedom of the press although it did not extend to publications from communist countries.

Development from the Top Down

As in postwar Japan, the South Korean government from the mid-1950s onward placed its primary emphasis on economic growth, which in this case started from a much lower base after the Korean War and previous Japanese exploitation. Huge industrial firms were created by a combination of government aid and active entrepreneurship. By the 1970s, when growth rates in Korea began to match those of Japan, Korea was competing successfully in the area of cheap consumer goods, as well as in steel and automobiles, in a variety of international markets. In steel, Korea's surge—based on the most up-to-date technology, a skilled engineering sector, and low wages—pushed past Japan's. The same held true in textiles, where Korean growth (along with that of Taiwan) erased almost one-third of the jobs held in the industry in Japan.

Hyundai Example of huge industrial groups that wield great power in modern South Korea; virtually governed Korea's southeastern coast; vertical economic organization with ships, supertankers, factories, schools, and housing units.

Huge industrial groups such as Daewoo and **Hyundai** resembled the great Japanese holding companies before and after World War II and wielded great political influence. For example, Hyundai was the creation of entrepreneur Chung Ju-yung, a modern folk hero who walked 150 miles to Seoul, South Korea's capital, from his native village to take his first job as a day laborer at age 16. By the 1980s, when Chung was in his 60s, his firm had 135,000 employees and 42 overseas offices throughout the world. Hyundai virtually governed Korea's southeastern coast. It built ships, including petroleum supertankers; it built thousands of housing units sold to low-paid workers at below-market rates; it built schools, a technical college, and an arena for the practice of the traditional Korean martial art Tae Kwon Do. With their lives carefully provided for, Hyundai workers responded in kind, putting in six-day weeks with three vacation days per year and participating in almost worshipful ceremonies when a fleet of cars was shipped abroad or a new tanker launched (Figure 35.6).

South Korea's rapid entry into the ranks of newly industrialized countries produced a host of more general changes. The population soared. By the 1980s more than 40 million people lived in a nation about the size of the state of Indiana, producing one of the highest population densities on earth: about 1000 people per square mile. This was one reason, even amid growing prosperity, why many Koreans emigrated. The government gradually began to encourage couples to limit their birth rates. Seoul expanded to embrace 9 million people; it developed intense air pollution and a hothouse atmosphere of deals and business maneuvers. Per capita income grew despite the population increase, rising almost 10 times from the early 1950s to the early 1980s, but to a level still only one-ninth that of Japan. Huge fortunes coexisted with widespread poverty in this setting, although the poor were better off than those of less developed nations.

Advances in Taiwan and the City-States

The Republic of China, as the government of Taiwan came to call itself, experienced a high rate of economic development. Productivity in both agriculture and industry increased rapidly, the former spurred by land reform that benefited small commercial farmers. The government concentrated increasingly on economic gains as its involvement in plans for military action against the mainland communist regime declined.

As in Japan and Korea, formal economic planning reached high levels, although allowing latitude for private business. Money was poured into education, and literacy rates and levels of technical training rose rapidly. The result was important cultural and economic change for the Taiwanese people. Traditional medical practices and ritualistic popular religion remained lively, but were expanded to allow simultaneous use of modern, Western-derived medicine and some of the urban entertainment forms popular elsewhere.

The assimilation of rapid change gave the Taiwanese government great stability despite a host of new concerns. The U.S. recognition of the People's Republic of China brought with it a steadily decreasing official commitment to Taiwan. In 1978 the United States severed diplomatic ties with the Taiwanese regime, although unofficial contacts—through the American Institute in Taiwan and the Coordination Council for North American Affairs, established by the republic in Washington—remained strong. The Taiwanese also built important regional contacts with other governments in eastern and southeastern Asia that facilitated trade. For example, Japan served as the nation's most important single trading partner, purchasing foodstuffs, manufactured textiles, chemicals, and other industrial goods.

Taiwan also developed some informal links with the communist regime in Beijing, although the latter continued to claim the island as part of its territory. The republic survived the death of Chiang Kai-shek and the accession of his son, **Chiang Ching-kuo**, in 1978. The young Chiang emphasized personal authority less than his father had, and he reduced somewhat the gap between mainland-born

FIGURE 35.5 As this photo of an ultramodern skyscraper in Hong Kong amply illustrates, some of the most innovative architecture of the age of globalization can be found in the great commercial centers along the Pacific Rim. The region also boasts one of the world's tallest buildings, a twin-tower office complex in the Malaysian capital of Kuala Lumpur.

Chiang Ching-kuo [jee-ahng jihn-kwoh] Son and successor of Chiang Kai-shek as ruler of Taiwanese government in 1978; continued authoritarian government; attempted to lessen gap between followers of his father and indigenous islanders.

FIGURE 35.6 Hyundai loading dock for export to the United States.

military personnel and native Taiwanese in government ranks. However, a strong authoritarian strain continued, and political diversity was not encouraged.

Conditions in the city-state of Singapore, although less tied to great power politics, resembled those in Taiwan in many ways. Prime Minister **Lee Kuan Yew** took office in 1965, when the area first gained independence, and held power for the next three decades. The government established tight controls over its citizens, going beyond anything attempted elsewhere in the Pacific Rim. Sexual behavior and potential economic corruption, as well as more standard aspects of municipal regulation and economic planning, were scrutinized carefully. The government proclaimed the necessity of unusual discipline and restraint because such a large population crowded into a limited space. One result was unusually low reported crime rates, and another was the near impossibility of serious political protest. The dominant People's Action party suppressed opposition movements. The authoritarian political style was rendered somewhat more palatable by extraordinarily successful economic development, based on a combination of government controls and initiatives and free enterprise. Already the world's fourth largest port, Singapore saw manufacturing and banking surpass shipping as sources of revenue. Electronics, textiles, and oil refining joined shipbuilding as major sectors. By the 1980s Singapore's population enjoyed the second highest per capita income in Asia. Educational levels and health conditions improved accordingly.

Finally, Hong Kong retained its status as a major world port and branched out as a center of international banking, serving as a bridge between the communist regime in China and the wider world. Export production combined high-speed technology with low wages and long hours for the labor force, yielding highly competitive results. Textiles and clothing formed 39 percent of total exports by the 1980s, but other sectors, including heavy industry, developed impressively as well. As in other Pacific Rim nations, a prosperous middle class emerged, with links to many other parts of the world, Western and Asian alike. In 1997, after careful negotiation with the British, Hong Kong was returned to China. The communist government promised to respect the territory's free market economic system and maintain democratic political rights, although the changeover raised questions for the future.

Lee Kuan Yew Ruler of Singapore from independence in 1959 through three decades; established tightly controlled authoritarian government; ruled through People's Action party to suppress political diversity.

Common Themes and New Problems

The Pacific Rim states had more in common than their rapid growth rates and expanding exports. They all stressed group loyalties against excessive individualism or protest, and in support of hard work. Confucian morality often was used, implicitly or explicitly, as part of this effort to cement group cohesion in factories and businesses. The Pacific Rim states also shared reliance on government

VISUALIZING THE PAST

Pacific Rim Growth

QUESTIONS

- The figures in the table can be used to illustrate the industrial emergence of the Pacific Rim (Japan, South Korea, Singapore, Hong Kong). Which countries most clearly have been undergoing an industrial revolution since the 1960s, and how can this be measured?
- How do the key Pacific Rim areas compare in growth to the neighboring "little tigers" Indonesia, Malaysia, and Thailand?
- Do the Philippines constitute another "little tiger"?
- How do Japanese patterns compare with the newer areas of the Pacific Rim, and how can this relationship be explained?

Indices of Growth and Change in the Pacific Rim: Gross National Product (GNP) 1965–1996

	Per Capita GNP East and Southeast Asia, annual growth rates (%)	
	1965	**1996**
China	8.5	6.7
Hong Kong	7.5	5.6
Indonesia	6.7	4.6
Japan	4.5	3.6
Korea (South)	8.9	7.3
Malaysia	6.8	4.1
Philippines	3.5	0.9
Singapore	8.3	6.3
Thailand	7.3	5.0
For comparison		
All preexisting industrial countries	3.0	2.2
United States	2.4	1.4
India	4.5	2.3

Social and Economic Data

	% labor force in agriculture		% population urban	
	1965	**1996**	**1965**	**1996**
China	78	72	17	31
Indonesia	66	55	41	82
Japan	20	7	71	78
Korea (South)	49	18	41	82
Malaysia	54	27	34	54
Thailand	80	64	13	20

NOTE: Growth at 2.3 percent per year doubles the category in 30 years; 7 percent per year doubles in 10 years.
Source: Adapted from World Bank, *World Development Indicators* (Washington, DC, 1998).

---

planning and direction amid limitations on dissent and instability. Of course, they benefited greatly from the expansion of the Japanese market for factory goods, such as textiles, as well as raw materials.

The dynamism of the Pacific Rim spilled over to neighboring parts of southeast Asia by the 1980s. "Little tigers" such as Indonesia, Malaysia, and Thailand began to experience rapid economic growth, along with the pollution problems that accompanied new manufacturing and larger cities.

However, the final years of the 20th century revealed unexpected weaknesses in this dynamic region. Growth faltered, unemployment rose, and currencies from South Korea to Indonesia took

THINKING HISTORICALLY

The Pacific Rim as a U.S. Policy Issue

ANY CHANGE IN THE POWER BALANCE between nations or larger civilizations results in a host of policy issues for all who are involved. The rise of the Pacific Rim economies posed some important questions for the West, particularly for the United States because of its military role in the Pacific as well as its world economic position. The United States had actively promoted economic growth in Japan, Korea, and Taiwan as part of its desire to discourage the spread of communism. Japan, for example, served as a major supplier for American forces fighting in Korea, and then Korea and Japan did the same during the long conflict in Vietnam. Japan and Thailand were major destinations for military personnel on R & R leaves during both wars. Although American aid was not solely responsible for Pacific Rim advances, and assistance tapered off by the 1960s, the United States took some satisfaction in demonstrating the vitality of noncommunist economies. The United States also was not eager to relinquish its military superiority in the region, which gave it a stake in Asian opinion.

Yet the threats posed by increasing Pacific Rim economic competition were real and growing. Japan seemed to wield a permanent balance-of-payments superiority; its exports to the United States regularly exceeded imports by the 1970s and 1980s, which contributed greatly to the United States' unfavorable overall trade balance. Japanese investment in American companies and real estate increased the United States' growing indebtedness to foreign nations. The symbolic problems were real as well. Japanese observers pointed out with some justice that Americans seemed more worried about Japanese investments than about larger British holdings in the United States, an imbalance that smacked of racism. Certainly, Americans found it harder to accept Asian competition than they did European, if only because it was less familiar. Japanese ability to gain near monopolies in key industries such as electronic recording systems as well as the growing Korean challenge in steel and automobiles meant or seemed to mean loss of jobs and perhaps a threat of more fundamental economic decline in years to come.

In the 1980s, several observers urged American imitation of the bases of Pacific Rim success: The United States should open more partnerships between government and private industry and do more economic planning, it should teach managers to commit themselves to group harmony rather than individual profit seeking, and it should build a new concord between management and labor, based on greater job security and cooperative social programs. Some firms in the United States did introduce certain Japanese management methods, including more consultation with workers, with some success.

Other observers, also concerned about long-term erosion of American power on the Pacific Rim, urged a more antagonistic stance. A few wanted the United States to pull out of costly Japanese and Korean military bases so that the Pacific Rim would be forced to shoulder more of its own defense costs. Others wanted to impose tariffs on Asian goods, at least until the Pacific Rim nations made it easier for American firms to compete in Asian markets. Aggrieved American workers sometimes smashed imported cars and threatened Asian immigrants, although many American consumers continued to prefer Pacific Rim products. The options were complex, and no clear change in U.S. policy emerged. As we shall see in the section that follows, by the late 1990s these and other economic concerns had become even more pronounced in America's evolving relationships with the People's Republic of China. In the case of mainland China, there was the added dimension of military rivalry. Some U.S. policymakers worried about China's growing nuclear arsenal and naval power, and warned that America was in danger of losing its century-long position of dominance in the Pacific.

> Asian leaders recognized the need for some change, but they did not welcome advice that seemed to ignore successful components from the past and threatened some of the privileges of established political and business elites.

Pacific Rim nations also faced choices about their orientation toward the West, particularly the United States. Questions that arose earlier about what Western patterns to copy and what to avoid continued to be important, as the Japanese concern about forks and chopsticks suggests. Added were issues about how to express pride and confidence in modern achievements against what were seen as Western tendencies to belittle and patronize. In 1988 the summer Olympic games were held in South Korea, a sign of Korea's international advance and a source of great national pride. During the games, Korean nationalism flared against the U.S. athletes and television commentators, based on their real or imagined tendencies to seek out faults in Korean society. South Korea, like Japan, continued to rely on Western markets and U.S. military assistance, but there was a clear desire to put the relationship on a more fully equal footing. This desire reflected widespread public opinion, and it could have policy implications.

The Pacific Rim crisis in 1998 raised a new set of questions. American leaders urged assistance to beleaguered economies such as those of South Korea and Indonesia, but they also, with

(continued on next page)

some self-satisfaction, tried to insist on introducing a more Western-style market economy. Asian leaders recognized the need for some change, but they did not welcome advice that seemed to ignore successful components from the past and threatened some of the privileges of established political and business elites.

QUESTIONS
- How great were the challenges posed by the Pacific Rim to the U.S. world position and well-being?
- What are the most likely changes in American and Pacific Rim relations over the next two decades?

a drastic hit. Many Western observers argued that this crisis could be resolved only by reducing the links between governments and major firms and introducing more free market competition. In essence, they contended that only a Western industrial model could be successful, and agencies such as the World Bank tried to insist on reforms in this direction as a condition for economic assistance. In the meantime, political pressures increased amid economic distress, and in 1998 the longtime authoritarian ruler of Indonesia was overturned in favor of pledges for future democracy. By 1999, however, economic growth rates in the region began to pick up. It was not clear that basic patterns had to be rethought.

MAO'S CHINA: VANGUARD OF WORLD REVOLUTION

35.3 How did ideological extremism and totalitarianism in the People's Republic of China subvert efforts at economic development and result in widespread human suffering and environmental disasters?

After their victory in the long civil war against the Guomindang in 1949, Chinese communists faced the formidable task of governing a vast nation in ruins. In their pursuit of economic development and social reform, the communists sought to build on the base they had established in the "liberated" zones during their struggle for power.

Just as he was convinced that he was on the verge of victory, Chiang Kai-shek's anticommunist crusade had been rudely interrupted by the Japanese invasion of the Chinese mainland (see Chapter 31). Obsessed with the communists, Chiang had done little to block the steady advance of Japanese forces in the early 1930s into Manchuria and the islands along China's coast. Even after the Japanese launched their assaults, aimed at conquering China, Chiang wanted to continue the struggle against the communists (Map 35.2).

Forced by his military commanders to concentrate on the Japanese threat, Chiang grudgingly formed a military alliance with the communists. Although he did all he could to undermine the alliance and continue the anticommunist struggle by underhanded means, for the next seven years the war against Japan took priority over the civil war in the contest for control of China.

Although it brought more suffering to the Chinese people, the Japanese invasion was enormously advantageous for the Communist party. The Japanese invaders captured much of the Chinese coast, where the cities were the centers of the business and mercantile backers of the Nationalists. Chiang's conventional military forces were pummeled by the superior air, land, and sea forces of the Japanese. The Nationalists' attempts to meet the Japanese in conventional battles led to disaster; their inability to defend the coastal provinces lowered their standing in the eyes of the Chinese people. Chiang's hasty and humiliating retreat to Chongqing (Map 35.2), in the interior of China, further eroded his reputation as the savior of the nation and rendered him more dependent than ever on his military allies, the rural landlords, and—perhaps most humiliating—foreign powers such as the United States.

The guerrilla warfare the communists waged against the Japanese armies proved far more effective than Chiang's conventional approach. With the Nationalist extermination offensives suspended, the communists used their anti-Japanese campaigns to extend their control over large areas of north China. By the end of World War II, the Nationalists controlled mainly the cities in the north; they had become (as Mao prescribed in his political writings) islands surrounded by a sea of revolutionary peasants.

MAP 35.2 **China in the Years of Japanese Occupation and Civil War, 1931–1949** The Chinese political map changed radically and often in the 1930s and 1940s due to civil wars and foreign invasions.

The communists' successes and their determination to fight the Japanese won them the support of most of China's intellectuals and many of the students who had earlier supported the Nationalists. By 1945 the balance of power within China was clearly shifting in the communists' favor. In the four-year civil war that followed, communist soldiers, who were well treated and fought for a cause, consistently routed the much-abused soldiers of the Nationalists, many of whom switched to the communist side. By 1949 it was over. Chiang and what was left of his armies fled to the island of Formosa, renamed Taiwan, and Mao proclaimed the establishment of the **People's Republic of China** in Beijing.

The Japanese invasion proved critical in the communist drive to victory. But equally important were the communists' social and economic reform programs, which eventually won the great majority of the peasantry, the students and intellectuals, and even many of the bureaucrats to their side. Whereas Chiang, whatever his intentions, was able to do little to improve the condition of the great mass of the people, Mao made uplifting the peasants the central element in his drive for power (Figure 35.7). Land reforms, access to education, and improved healthcare gave the peasantry a real stake in Mao's revolutionary movement and good reason to defend their soviets (or political-military bases) against both the Nationalists and the Japanese. In contrast to Chiang's armies, whose arrival meant theft, rape, and murder to China's villagers, Mao's soldiers were indoctrinated with the need to protect the peasantry and win their support. Lest they forget, harsh penalties were levied, such as execution for stealing an egg.

As guerrilla fighters, Mao's soldiers had a much better chance to survive and advance in the ranks than did the forcibly conscripted, brutally treated foot soldiers of the Nationalists. Mao and the commanders around him, such as **Lin Biao**, who had been trained at Chiang's Whampoa Academy in the 1920s, proved far more gifted—even in conventional warfare—than the often corrupt and inept Guomindang generals. Thus, although the importance of the Japanese invasion cannot be discounted, the communists won the mandate to govern China because they offered solutions to China's fundamental social and economic problems. Even more critically, they actually put their programs into action in the areas that came under their control. In a situation in which revolutionary changes appeared to be essential, the communists alone convinced the Chinese people that they had the leaders and the program that could improve their lives.

FIGURE **35.7** This propaganda poster features Mao Zedong as the friend and father of the people. Soldiers, peasants, women, children, and peoples from the many regions of China are pictured here joyously rallying to Mao's vision of a strong, just, and prosperous China.

Read the Document on MyHistoryLab: Mao Zedong, "From the Countryside to the City," 1949

The Communists Come to Power

The communists' long struggle for control had left the party with a strong political and military organization that was rooted in the **party cadres** (thoroughly indoctrinated party members) and the **People's Liberation Army**. The continuing importance of the army was indicated by the fact that most of China was administered by military officials for five years after the communists came to power. But the army remained clearly subordinate to the party. Cadre advisors were attached to military contingents at all levels, and the central committees of the party were dominated by nonmilitary personnel.

With this strong political framework in place, the communists moved quickly to assert China's traditional preeminence in East and much of southeast Asia. The Communist regime forcibly repressed potential secessionist movements in Inner Mongolia and Tibet, although resistance in the latter has erupted periodically and continues to the present day. In the early 1950s, the Chinese intervened militarily in the conflict between North and South Korea, an intervention that was critical in forcing the United States to settle for a stalemate and a lasting division of the peninsula. Refusing to accept a similar but far more lopsided two-nation outcome of the struggle in China itself, the communist leadership has periodically threatened to invade the Guomindang's refuge on Taiwan, often touching off international incidents. China also played an increasingly important role in the liberation struggle of the Vietnamese to the south, although that did not peak until the height of American involvement in the conflict in the 1960s.

By the late 1950s the close collaboration between the Soviet Union and China that marked the early years of Mao's rule had broken down. Border disputes, focusing on territories the Russians had seized

People's Republic of China Communist government of mainland China; proclaimed in 1949 following military success of Mao Zedong over forces of Chiang Kai-shek and the Guomindang.

Lin Biao [lihn byoo] (1907–1971) Chinese commander under Mao; trained at Chiang Kai-shek's Whampoa Academy in the 1920s.

party cadres Basis of China's communist government organization; cadre advisors were attached to military contingents at all levels.

People's Liberation Army Chinese Communist army; administered much of country under People's Republic of China.

during the period of Qing decline, and the Chinese refusal to play second fiddle to Russia, especially after Stalin was succeeded by the less imposing Khrushchev, were key factors behind the growing divisions between the two major communist regimes. These causes of the breakdown in collaboration worsened the differences resulting from the meager economic assistance provided by the Soviet "comrades." They also fed Mao's sense that with the passing of Stalin, he was the chief theoretician and leader of the communist world. In the early 1960s, the Chinese flexed their military and technological muscle by defeating India in a brief war that resulted from a border dispute. More startling, however, was the Chinese success in exploding the first nuclear device developed by a nonindustrial nation.

Planning for Economic Growth and Social Justice

On the domestic front, the new leaders of China moved with equal vigor, although with a good deal less success. Their first priority was to complete the social revolution in the rural areas that had been carried through to some extent in communist-controlled areas during the wars against the Japanese and Guomindang. Between 1950 and 1952, the landlord class and the large landholders, most of whom had been spared in the earlier stages of the revolution, were dispossessed and purged. Village tribunals, overseen by party cadre members, gave tenants and laborers a chance to get even for decades of oppression. Perhaps as many as three million people who were denounced as members of the exploitive landlord class were executed. At the same time, the property taken from the land-owning classes was distributed to peasants who had none or little. For a brief time at least, one of the central pledges of the communist revolutionaries was fulfilled: China became a land of peasant smallholders.

However, communist planners saw rapid industrialization, not peasant farmers, as the key to successful development. With the introduction of the first Stalinist-style five-year plan in 1953, the communist leaders turned away from the peasantry, which had brought them to power, to the urban workers as the hope for a new China. With little foreign assistance from either the West or the Soviet bloc, the state resorted to stringent measures to draw resources from the countryside to finance industrial growth. Some advances were made in industrialization, particularly in heavy industries such as steel. But the shift in direction had consequences that were increasingly unacceptable to Mao and his more radical supporters in the party. State planning and centralization were stressed, party bureaucrats greatly increased their power and influence, and an urban-based privileged class of technocrats began to develop. These changes, and the external threat to China posed by the U.S. intervention in Korea and continuing U.S.-China friction, led Mao and his followers to force a change of strategies in the mid-1950s.

Mao had long nurtured a deep hostility toward elitism, which he associated with the discredited Confucian system. He had little use for Lenin's vision of revolution from above, led by a disciplined cadre of professional political activists. He distrusted intellectuals, disliked specialization, and clung to his faith in the peasants rather than the workers as the repository of basic virtue and the driving force of the revolution. Acting to stem the trend toward an elitist, urban-industrial focus, Mao and his supporters pushed the **Mass Line** approach, beginning with the formation of agricultural cooperatives in 1955. In the following year, cooperatives became farming collectives that soon accounted for more than 90 percent of China's peasant population. The peasants had enjoyed their own holdings for less than three years. As had occurred earlier in the Soviet Union, the leaders of the revolution, who had originally given the land over to the mass of the peasants, later took it away from them through collectivization.

In 1957 Mao struck at the intellectuals through what may have been a miscalculation or perhaps a clever ruse. Announcing that he wanted to "let a hundred flowers bloom," Mao encouraged professors, artists, and other intellectuals to speak out on the course of development under communist rule. His request stirred up a storm of angry protest and criticism of communist schemes. Having flushed the critics into the open (if the campaign was indeed a ruse) or having been shocked by the vehemence of the response, the party struck with demotions, prison sentences, and banishment to hard labor on the collectives. The flowers rapidly wilted in the face of this betrayal.

The Great Leap Backward

With political opposition within the party and army apparently in check (or in prison), Mao and his supporters launched the **Great Leap Forward** in 1958. The programs of the Great Leap were a further effort to revitalize the flagging revolution by restoring its mass, rural base. Rather than huge

Mass Line Economic policy of Mao Zedong; led to formation of agricultural cooperatives in 1955; cooperatives became farming collectives in 1956.

Great Leap Forward Economic policy of Mao Zedong introduced in 1958; proposed industrialization of small-scale projects integrated into peasant communes; led to economic disaster; ended in 1960.

plants located in the cities, industrialization would be pushed through small-scale projects integrated into the peasant communes. Instead of the communes' surplus being siphoned off to build steel mills, industrial development would be aimed at producing tractors, cement for irrigation projects, and other manufactures needed by the peasantry. Enormous publicity was given to efforts to produce steel in "backyard" furnaces (Figure 35.8) that relied on labor rather than machine-intensive techniques. Mao preached the benefits of backwardness and the joys of mass involvement, and he looked forward to the withering away of the meddling bureaucracy. Emphasis was placed on self-reliance within the peasant communes. All aspects of the lives of their members were regulated and regimented by the commune leaders and the heads of the local labor brigades.

Within months after it was launched, all indicators suggested that the Great Leap Forward and rapid collectivization were leading to economic disaster. Peasant resistance to collectivization, the abuses of commune leaders, and the dismal output of the backyard factories combined with drought to turn the Great Leap into a giant step backward. The worst famine of the communist era spread across China. For the first time since 1949, China had to import large amounts of grain to feed its people, and the numbers of Chinese to feed continued to grow at an alarming rate. Hunger and starvation were compounded by severe damage to China's environment. A campaign to eradicate sparrows and other birds who fed on seeds led to a sharp increase in insect pests that proved far more ravaging. The need for fuel to fire the backyard furnaces accelerated the cutting of China's already depleted forests, and the widespread erosion of lands stripped of vegetation fouled river systems and further reduced the area that could be cultivated and harvested.

FIGURE **35.8** The famous backyard steel furnaces became a symbol of China's failed drive for self-sufficiency during the disastrous "Great Leap Forward" of the late 1950s.

Dismissing the fall in agricultural output and defiantly rejecting Western and United Nations proposals for family planning, Mao and like-thinking radicals charged that socialist China could care for its people, no matter how many they were. Birth control was seen as a symptom of capitalist selfishness and inability to provide a decent living for all of the people. Like those of India, China's birth rates were actually a good deal lower than those of many emerging nations. Also like India, however, the Chinese were adding people to a massive population base. At the time of the communist rise to power, China had approximately 550 million people. By 1965 this had risen to approximately 750 million. By the year 2000, China's population was approximately 1.3 billion.

In the face of the environmental degradation and overcrowding that this leap in population produced, even the party ideologues came around to the view that something must be done to curb the birth rate. Beginning in the mid-1960s, the government launched a nationwide family planning campaign designed to limit urban couples to two children and those in rural areas to one. By the early 1970s, these targets had been revised to two children for either urban or rural couples. By the 1980s, however, just one child per family was allowed. Although there is evidence of official excesses—undue pressure for women to have abortions, for example—these programs have greatly reduced the birth rate and have begun to slow China's overall population increase. But again, the base to which new births are added is already so large that China's population will not stabilize until well into the 21st century. By that time there will be far more people than now to educate, feed, house, and provide with productive work.

Advances made in the first decade of the new regime were lost through amateurish blunders, excesses of overzealous cadre leaders, and students' meddling. China's national productivity fell by as much as 25 percent. Population increase soon overwhelmed the stagnating productivity of the agricultural and industrial sectors. By 1960 it was clear that the Great Leap must be ended and a new course of development adopted. Mao lost his position as state chairman (although he remained the head of the party's Central Committee). The **pragmatists**, including Mao's old ally **Zhou Enlai**, along with **Liu Shaoqi** and **Deng Xiaoping**, came to power determined to restore state direction and market incentives at the local level.

pragmatists Chinese Communist politicians such as Zhou Enlai, Deng Xiaoping, and Liu Shaoqi; determined to restore state direction and market incentives at the local level; opposed Great Leap Forward.

 Read the Document on MyHistoryLab: China's One-Child Family Policy (1970s)

Zhou Enlai [joo ehn-LEYE] After Mao Zedong, the most important leader of the Communist party in China from the 1930s until his death in 1976; premier of China from 1954; notable as perhaps the most cosmopolitan and moderate of the inner circle of Communist leaders.

Liu Shaoqi [lyoh show-syee] Chinese Communist pragmatist; with Deng Xiaoping, came to power in 1959 after Mao was replaced; determined to restore state direction and market incentives at local level; purged in 1966 as Mao returned to power.

Deng Xiaoping [duhng shyoo-pihng] One of the more pragmatic, least ideological of the major Communist leaders of China; joined the party as a young man in the 1920s, survived the legendary Long March and persecution during the Cultural Revolution of the 1960s, and emerged as China's most influential leader in the early 1980s.

Jiang Qing [jee-AHNG chihng] (1914–1991) Wife of Mao Zedong; one of Gang of Four; opposed pragmatists and supported Cultural Revolution of 1965; arrested and imprisoned for life in 1976.

"Women Hold Up Half of the Heavens"

In Mao's struggles to renew the revolutionary fervor of the Chinese people, his wife, **Jiang Qing**, played an increasingly prominent role. Mao's reliance on her was consistent with the commitment to the liberation of Chinese women he had acted upon throughout his political career. As a young man he had been deeply moved by a newspaper story about a young girl who had committed suicide rather than be forced by her family to submit to the marriage they had arranged for her with a rich but very old man. From that point onward, women's issues and women's support for the communist movement became important parts of Mao's revolutionary strategy. Here he was drawing on a well-established revolutionary tradition, for women had been very active in the Taiping Rebellion of the mid-19th century, the Boxer revolt in 1900, and the 1911 revolution that had toppled the Manchu regime. One of the key causes taken up by the May Fourth intellectuals, who had a great impact on the youthful Mao Zedong, was women's rights. Their efforts put an end to footbinding. They also did much to advance campaigns to end female seclusion, win legal rights for women, and open educational and career opportunities to them.

The attempts by the Nationalists in the late 1920s and 1930s to reverse many of the gains made by women in the early revolution brought many women into the communist camp. Led by Chiang's wife, Madam Chiang Kai-shek, the Nationalist counteroffensive (like comparable movements in the fascist countries of Europe at the time) tried to return Chinese women to the home and hearth. Madam Chiang proclaimed a special Good Mother's Day and declared that for women, "virtue was more important than learning." She taught that it was immoral for a wife to criticize her husband (an ethical precept she herself ignored regularly).

The Nationalist campaign to restore Chinese women to their traditional domestic roles and dependence on men contrasted sharply with the communists' extensive employment of women to advance the revolutionary cause. Women served as teachers, nurses, spies, truck drivers, and laborers on projects ranging from growing food to building machine-gun bunkers. Although the party preferred to use them in these support roles, in moments of crisis women became soldiers on the front lines. Many won distinction for their bravery under fire. Some rose to become cadre leaders, and many were prominent in the anti-landlord campaigns and agrarian reform. Their contribution to the victory of the revolutionary cause bore out Mao's early dictum that the energies and talents of women had to be harnessed to the national cause because "women hold up half of the heavens."

As was the case in many other Asian and African countries, the victory of the revolution brought women legal equality with men—in itself a revolutionary development in a society such as China's. For example, women were given the right to choose their marriage partners without familial interference. But arranged marriages persist today, especially in rural areas, and the need to have party approval for all marriages is a new form of control. Since 1949 women have also been expected to work outside the home. Their opportunities for education and professional careers have improved greatly. As in other socialist states, however, openings for employment outside the home have proved to be a burden for Chinese women. Until the late 1970s, traditional attitudes toward childrearing and home care prevailed. As a result, women were required not only to hold down a regular job but also to raise a family, cook meals, clean, and shop, all without the benefit of the modern appliances available in Western societies.

Although many women held cadre posts at the middle and lower levels of the party and bureaucracy, the upper echelons of both were overwhelmingly controlled by men. The short-lived but impressive power amassed by Jiang Qing in the early 1970s ran counter to these overall trends, but Jiang Qing got to the top because she was married to Mao. She exercised power mainly in his name and was toppled soon after his death when she tried to rule in her own right.

DOCUMENT

Women in the Revolutionary Struggles for Social Justice

EVEN MORE THAN IN THE NATIONALIST movements in colonized areas, such as India and Egypt, women were drawn in large numbers into revolutionary struggles in areas such as China and Vietnam. The breakdown of the political and social systems weakened the legal and family restrictions that had subordinated women and limited their career choices. The collapse of the Confucian order also ushered in decades of severe crisis and brutal conflict in which women's survival depended on their assumption of radically new roles and their active involvement in revolutionary activities. The following quotations are taken from Vietnamese and Chinese revolutionary writings and interviews with women involved in revolutionary movements in each country. They express the women's goals, their struggle to be taken seriously in the uncharacteristic political roles they had assumed, and some of the many ways women found self-respect and redress for their grievances as a result of the changes wrought by the spread of the new social order.

> Women must first of all be masters of themselves. They must strive to become skilled workers . . . and, at the same time, they must strictly observe family planning. Another major question is the responsibility of husbands to help their wives look after children and other housework.

> We intellectuals had had little contact with the peasants and when we first walked through the village in our Chinese gowns or skirts the people would just stare at us and talk behind our backs. When the village head beat gongs to call out the women to the meeting we were holding for them, only men and old women came, but no young ones. Later we found out that the landlords and rich peasants had spread slanders among the masses saying "They are a pack of wild women. Their words are not for young brides to hear."

> Brave wives and daughters-in-law, untrammelled by the presence of their menfolk, could voice their own bitterness . . . encourage their poor sisters to do likewise, and thus eventually bring to the village-wide gatherings the strength of "half of China" as the more enlightened women, very much in earnest, like to call themselves. By "speaking pains to recall pains," the women found that they had as many if not more grievances than the men, and that given a chance to speak in public, they were as good at it as their fathers and husbands.

> In Chingtsun the work team found a woman whose husband thought her ugly and wanted to divorce her. She was very depressed until she learned that under the Draft Law [of the Communist party] she could have her own share of land. Then she cheered up immediately. "If he divorces me, never mind," she said. "I'll get my share and the children will get theirs. We can live a good life without him."

QUESTIONS

- On the basis of these quotations, identify the traditional roles and attitudes toward women (explored in earlier chapters on China and Vietnam) that women engaged in revolutionary movements in China and Vietnam have rejected. What do they believe is essential if women are to gain equality with men?
- How do the demands of the women supporting these revolutionary movements compare with those of women's rights advocates in the United States?

Mao's Last Campaign and the Fall of the Gang of Four

Having lost his position as head of state but still the most powerful and popular leader in the Communist party, Mao worked throughout the early 1960s to establish grassroots support for yet another renewal of the revolutionary struggle. He fiercely opposed the efforts of Deng Xiaoping and his pragmatist allies to scale back the communes, promote peasant production on what were in effect private plots, and push economic growth over political orthodoxy. By late 1965, Mao was convinced that his support among the students, peasants, and military was strong enough to launch what would turn out to be his last campaign, the **Cultural Revolution**. With mass student demonstrations paving the way, he launched an all-out assault on the "capitalist-roaders" in the party.

Waving "little red books" of Mao's pronouncements on all manner of issues, the infamous **Red Guard** student brigades publicly ridiculed and abused Mao's political rivals. Liu Shaoqi was killed, Deng Xiaoping was imprisoned, and Zhou Enlai was driven into seclusion. The aroused students and the rank and file of the People's Liberation Army were used to pull down the bureaucrats from their positions of power and privilege. College professors, plant managers, and the children of the bureaucratic elite were berated and forced to confess publicly their many crimes against "the people." Those who were not imprisoned or, more rarely, killed were forced to do manual labor on rural communes to enable them to understand the hardships endured by China's peasantry. In cities such as Shanghai, workers seized control of the factories and local bureaucracy. As Mao had hoped, the centralized state and technocratic elites that had grown steadily since the first revolution won power in 1949 were being torn apart by the rage of the people.

However satisfying for advocates of continuing revolution, such as Mao, it was soon clear that the Cultural Revolution threatened to return China to the chaos and vulnerability of the prerevolutionary era. The rank-and-file threat to the leaders of the People's Liberation Army eventually proved decisive in prompting countermeasures that forced Mao to call off the campaign by late 1968. The heads of the armed forces moved to bring the rank and file back into line; the student and worker movements were disbanded and in some cases forcibly repressed. By the early 1970s, Mao's old rivals had begun to surface again. For the next half decade, a hard-fought struggle was waged at the upper levels of the party and the army for control of the government. The reconciliation between China and the United States that was negotiated in the early 1970s suggested that, at least in foreign policy, the pragmatists were gaining the upper hand over the ideologues. Deng's growing role in policy formation from 1973 onward also represented a major setback for Jiang Qing, who led the notorious **Gang of Four** that increasingly contested power on behalf of the aging Mao.

The death in early 1976 of Zhou Enlai, who was second only to Mao in stature as a revolutionary hero and who had consistently backed the pragmatists, appeared to be a major blow to those whom the Gang of Four had marked out as "capitalist-roaders" and betrayers of the revolution. But Mao's death later in the same year cleared the way for an open clash between the rival factions. While the Gang of Four plotted to seize control of the government, the pragmatists acted in alliance with some of the more influential military leaders. The Gang of Four was arrested, and its supporters' attempts to foment popular insurrections were foiled easily. Later tried for their crimes against the people, Jiang Qing and the members of her clique were purged from the party and imprisoned for life after their death sentences were commuted.

Since the death of Mao, the pragmatists have been ascendant, and leaders such as Deng Xiaoping have opened China to Western influences and capitalist development, if not yet democratic reform. Under Deng and his allies, the farming communes were discontinued and private peasant production for the market was encouraged. Private enterprise has also been promoted in the industrial sector, and experiments have been made with such capitalist institutions as a stock exchange and foreign hotel chains.

Although it has become fashionable to dismiss the development schemes of the communist states as misguided failures, the achievements of the communist regime in China in the late 20th and early 21st centuries have been impressive. Despite severe economic setbacks, political turmoil, and a low level of foreign assistance, the communists have managed a truly revolutionary redistribution of the wealth of the country. China's very large population remains poor, but in education, healthcare, housing, working conditions, and the availability of food, most of it is far better off than it was in the prerevolutionary era. The Chinese have managed to provide a decent standard of living for a higher proportion of their people than perhaps any other large developing country. They have also

---

Cultural Revolution Movement initiated in 1965 by Mao Zedong to restore his dominance over pragmatists; used mobs to ridicule Mao's political rivals; campaign was called off in 1968.

Red Guard Student brigades utilized by Mao Zedong and his political allies during the Cultural Revolution to discredit Mao's political enemies.

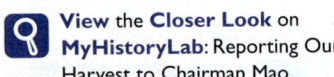
View the **Closer Look** on MyHistoryLab: Reporting Our Harvest to Chairman Mao

Gang of Four Jiang Qing and four political allies who attempted to seize control of Communist government in China from the pragmatists; arrested and sentenced to life imprisonment in 1976 following Mao Zedong's death.

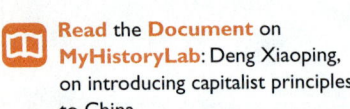
Read the **Document** on MyHistoryLab: Deng Xiaoping, on introducing capitalist principles to China

achieved higher rates of industrial and agricultural growth than neighboring India, with its mixed state–capitalist economy and democratic polity. The Chinese have done all of this with much less foreign assistance than most developing nations have had.

If the pragmatists remain in power and the champions of the market economy are right, China's growth in the 21st century should be even more impressive. But the central challenge for China's leaders will be to nurture that growth and the improved living standards without a recurrence of the economic inequities, social injustice, and environmental degradation that brought about the revolution in the first place. Environmental issues are particularly nettlesome. Although the excesses of the Maoist era have been renounced, China's recent leap in industrial production and energy output has been based largely on fossil fuels, particularly its abundant coal reserves. Unfortunately, China's coal is especially polluting and little of it has been "scrubbed" using the new (and expensive) technologies deployed in the Europe and North America. But China has also become one of the world's leading innovators and producers of solar, wind, and other non-fossil-fuel energy technologies. If the Chinese continue to be a leading proponent of what may well become a worldwide Green manufacturing and communications revolution, it could well recover its historic role as one of the premier technological civilizations of humankind.

COLONIALISM AND REVOLUTION IN VIETNAM

35.4 How was it possible for the Vietnamese to liberate their homeland from Japanese, French and Chinese colonization efforts and defeat a massive intervention by the American superpower during decades dominated by civil war and devastating foreign aggression?

The Vietnamese, as well as their neighbors in Laos and Cambodia, were brought under European colonial rule in the second half of the 19th century. As in China, the collapse of the Confucian system around which the Vietnamese had organized civilized life for nearly two millennia led to violent revolution and a search for a viable social and political order that brought a communist regime to power.

French interest in Vietnam reached back as far as the 17th century. Driven from Japan by the founders of the Tokugawa shogunate, French missionaries fell back on coastal Vietnam. Vietnam attracted them both because its Confucian elite seemed similar to that of the Japanese and because the continuing wars between rival dynastic houses in the Red River valley and central Vietnam gave the missionaries ample openings for their conversion efforts (Map 35.3). From this time onward, French rulers, who considered themselves the protectors of the Catholic missions overseas, took an interest in Vietnamese affairs. As the numbers of converts grew into the tens of thousands and French merchants began to trade at Vietnamese ports, the French stake in the region increased.

By the late 18th century, French involvement had become distinctly political as a result of the power struggles that convulsed the whole region. In the south, a genuine peasant rebellion, the **Tayson Rebellion**, toppled the Nguyen dynasty in the late 1770s. In the years that followed, the Trinh dynasty, the northern rival of the Nguyen, was also dethroned. The Tayson controlled most of the country, eliminated the Trinh, and all but wiped out the Nguyen. Seeing a chance to win influence in the ruling house, the French head of the Vietnam mission, the bishop of Adran, threw his support behind the one surviving prince of the southern house, **Nguyen Anh**.

Anh had fled into the Mekong wilderness with a handful of supporters, thus escaping death at the hands of the Tayson. With the arms and advice of the French, he rallied local support for the dynasty and soon fielded a large army. After driving the Tayson from the south, Nguyen Anh launched an invasion of rebels' strongholds in the north. His task of conquest was made easier by bitter quarrels between the Tayson leaders. By 1802 the Nguyen armies had prevailed, and Nguyen Anh had proclaimed himself the Gia Long emperor of Vietnam.

Gia Long made the old Nguyen capital at Hue in central Vietnam the imperial capital of a unified Vietnam. His French missionary allies were rewarded with a special place at court, and French traders were given greater access to the port of Saigon, which was rapidly emerging as the leading city of the Mekong River valley region in the south. The Nguyen dynasty was the first in centuries to rule all of Vietnam and the first to rule a Vietnamese

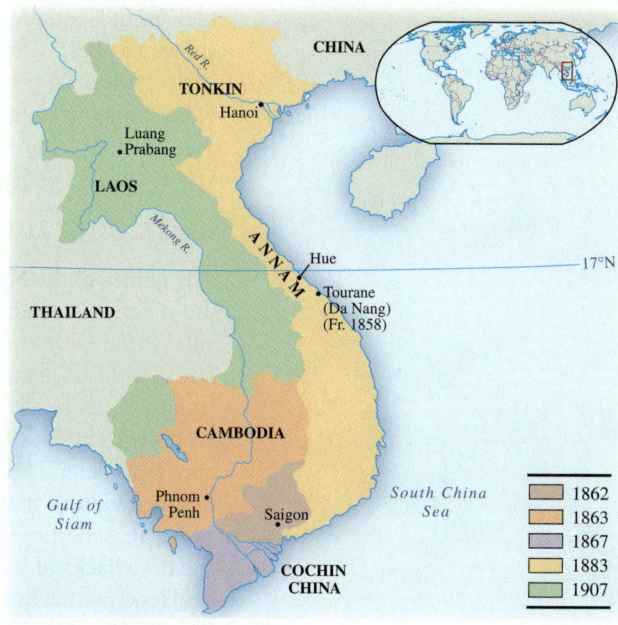

MAP **35.3 Vietnam: Divisions in the Nguyen and French Periods** Within decades of the unification of Vietnam under the Nguyen dynasty it was conquered piecemeal and again divided politically by French colonizers.

Tayson Rebellion Peasant revolution in southern Vietnam during the late 1770s; succeeded in toppling the Nguyen dynasty; subsequently unseated the Trinh dynasty of northern Vietnam.

Nguyen Anh [nwihn ahn] (1762–1820) Last surviving member of Nguyen dynasty following Tayson Rebellion in Vietnam; with French support retook southern Vietnam; drove Tayson from northern Vietnam by 1802; proclaimed himself emperor with capital at Hue; also known as Gia Long.

Minh Mang [min mäng] Second emperor of a united Vietnam; successor of Nguyen Anh; ruled from 1820 to 1841; sponsored emphasis of Confucianism; persecuted Catholics.

kingdom that included both the Red River and Mekong deltas. In fact, the Mekong region had only begun to be settled extensively by Vietnamese in the century or so before Gia Long rose to power.

Gia Long and his successors proved to be archtraditionalists deeply committed to strengthening Confucianism in Vietnam. Their capital at Hue was intended to be a perfect miniature of the imperial palace at Beijing. The dynasty patronized Confucian schools and built its administration around scholar-bureaucrats who were well versed in Confucian learning. The second emperor, **Minh Mang** (1820–1841), prided himself on his knowledge of the Confucian classics and his mastery of the Chinese script. He even had the audacity to criticize the brushwork of the reigning Chinese emperor, who was not any more Chinese than Minh Mang but was descended from Manchu nomads. All of this proved deeply disappointing to the French missionaries, who hoped to baptize Gia Long and then carry out through the Vietnamese the sort of top-down conversion that the Jesuits had hoped for ever since their arrival in Asia.

Things actually got much worse. Gia Long's ultra-Confucian successor, Minh Mang, came to see the Catholics as a danger to the dynasty. His persecution of the Vietnamese Catholic community not only enraged the missionaries but also contributed to the growing political and military intervention of the French government in the region. Pushed both by political pressures at home and military defeats in Europe, French adventurers and soldiers exploited quarrels with the Nguyen rulers to justify the piecemeal conquest of Vietnam and neighboring Cambodia and Laos beginning in the late 1840s (Map 35.3). By the 1890s, the whole of the country was under French control, and the Nguyen dynasty had been reduced to the status of puppet princes. In the decades that followed, the French concentrated on drawing revenue and resources from Vietnam while providing very little in return.

The French determination to make Vietnam a colony that was profitable for the homeland worsened social and economic problems that were already severe under the Nguyen rulers. Most of the densely packed peasant population of the north lacked enough land for a subsistence livelihood. French taxes and the burden of obligatory purchases by each village of set amounts of government-sold opium and alcohol drove many peasants into labor in the mines. Even larger numbers left their ancestral villages and migrated to the Mekong region to work on the plantations established there by French and Chinese entrepreneurs. Other migrants chose to become tenants on the great estates that had been carved out of sparsely settled frontier regions by Vietnamese and Chinese landlords.

Migration brought little relief. Plantation workers were paid little and were treated much like slave laborers. The unchecked demands of the Mekong landlords left their tenants with scarcely enough of the crops they grew to feed, clothe, and house their families. The exploitive nature of French colonialism in Vietnam was graphically revealed by the statistics the French themselves collected. These showed a sharp drop in the food consumed by the peasantry in all parts of the colony between the early 1900s and the 1930s, a drop that occurred despite the fact that Vietnam became one of the world's major rice-exporting areas.

Vietnamese Nationalism: Bourgeois Dead Ends and Communist Survival

The failure of the Nguyen rulers after Minh Mang to rally the forces of resistance against the French did much to discredit the dynasty. But from the 1880s into the first decades of the 20th century, guerrilla warfare was waged in various parts of the country in support of the "Save the King" movement. Because this resistance was localized and small, the French were able to crush it on a piecemeal basis. In any case, French control over the puppet emperors who remained on the throne at Hue left the rebels with little cause worth fighting for. The failure of the Nguyen and the Confucian bureaucratic classes to defend Vietnam against the French did much to discredit the old order in the eyes of the new generations that came of age in the early decades of French rule. Perhaps because it was imported rather than homegrown, the Vietnamese were quicker than the Chinese to reject Confucianism once the drawbacks of its inflexibility and past-oriented leanings were clear, and they did so with a good deal less trauma. But its demise left an ideological and institutional vacuum that the Vietnamese, again like the Chinese, would struggle for decades to fill.

In the early 20th century, a new Western-educated middle class, similar to that found in other colonial settings (see Chapters 25 and 29), was formed. It was made up mainly of the children of the traditional Confucian elite and the emerging landlord class in the Mekong region. Some, taking advantage of their parents' wealth, went to French schools and emerged speaking fluent French and with a taste for French fashions and frequent holiday jaunts to Paris and the French Riviera. Many of them went to work for the French as colonial administrators, bank managers, and even labor recruiters. Others pursued independent careers as lawyers, doctors, and journalists. Many who opted for French educations and French lifestyles were soon drawn into nationalist organizations. Like their counterparts elsewhere in the colonies, the members of these organizations initially concentrated on protesting French racism and discrimination, improving their own wages, and gaining access to positions in the colonial government held by French bureaucrats.

As in other colonies, nationalist newspapers and magazines proliferated. These became the focal point of an extended debate over the approach that should be taken toward winning freedom from French rule and, increasingly, what needed to be done to rebuild Vietnam as a whole. Because the French forcibly repressed all attempts to mount peaceful mass demonstrations or organize constitutional agitation, those who argued for violent resistance eventually gained the upper hand. In the early 1920s, the nationalist struggle was centered in the clandestine **Vietnamese Nationalist Party** (Vietnamese Quoc Dan Dong, or VNQDD), which was committed to violent revolution against the French colonizers. Although the VNQDD made some attempt to organize urban laborers and peasant villagers, the party members were drawn overwhelmingly from the children of the landlord elite and urban professional classes. Their secret codes and elaborate rituals proved little protection against the dreaded Sûreté, or French secret police. A series of failed uprisings, culminating in a 1929 attempt to spark a general revolution with the assassination of a much-hated French official in charge of labor recruitment, decimated the party. It was particularly hard hit by the ensuing French campaign of repression, execution, and imprisonment. From that point onward, the bourgeois nationalists were never again the dominant force in the struggle for independence.

The demise of the VNQDD left its major rival, the **Communist Party of Vietnam**, as the main focus of nationalist resistance in Vietnam. As in China and Korea, the communist wing of the nationalist movement had developed in Vietnam during the 1920s, often at the initiative of leaders in exile. By the late 1920s, the party was dominated by the charismatic young Nguyen Ai Quoc, who would later be known as **Ho Chi Minh**. Ho had discovered Marxism while studying in France and Russia during and after World War I. Disillusioned by his failure to gain a hearing for his plea for the Vietnamese right to self-determination at the post–World War I Paris Peace Conference, Ho dedicated himself to a revolutionary struggle to drive the French from Indochina.

In the early 1930s, the Communist party still held to the rigid but unrealistic orthodox vision of a revolution based on the urban working classes. Because the workers in Vietnam made up as small a percentage of the population as they had in China, the orthodox strategy made little headway. A sudden shift in the early 1930s to a peasant emphasis, in part to take advantage of widespread but not communist-inspired peasant uprisings in central Vietnam, led to a disaster almost as great as that which had overtaken the VNQDD a year before. French repression smashed the party hierarchy and drove most of the major communist leaders into exile. But the superior underground organization of the communists and the support they received from the Comintern helped them survive the French onslaught. When the French were weakened by the Japanese invasion of Indochina in 1941, the Vietnamese communists were ready to use the colonizers' setbacks to advance the struggle for national liberation.

The War of Liberation against the French

During World War II, operating out of bases in south China, the communist-dominated nationalist movement, known as the **Viet Minh**, established liberated areas throughout the northern Red River delta (Map 35.4). The abrupt end of Japanese rule left a vacuum in Vietnam, which only the Viet Minh was prepared to fill. Its programs for land reform and mass education had wide appeal among the hard-pressed

Vietnamese Nationalist Party English translation of the Vietnamese party name Quoc Dan Dong or VNQDD; active in 1920s as revolutionary force committed to violent overthrow of French colonialism.

Communist Party of Vietnam Originally a wing of nationalist movement; became primary nationalist party after decline of VNQDD in 1929; led in late 1920s by Nguyen Ai Quoc, alias Ho Chi Minh.

Read the Document on MyHistoryLab: Ho Chi Minh, "Equality!"

MAP 35.4 **North and South Vietnam** Vietnam was arbitrarily divided at the 17th parallel in 1954 due to the pressure of the great powers and over the objection of the Vietnamese communists who had led the war of liberation against the French.

CHAPTER 35 Rebirth and Revolution: Nation-Building in East Asia and the Pacific Rim **891**

Ho Chi Minh Also known as Nguyen Ai Quoc among other aliases; led Vietnamese Communist party in struggle for liberation from French and U.S. dominance and to unify north and south Vietnam.

Viet Minh Communist-dominated Vietnamese nationalist movement; operated out of base in southern China during World War II; employed guerrilla tactics similar to the Maoists in China.

 Read the Document on MyHistoryLab: Resolution Establishing the Viet Minh, 1941

Vo Minh Giap [vah-ah nwihn zap] One of the original and inner core of leaders of the Vietnamese Communist Party, Giap emerged as the chief military strategist of the guerilla wars against the French and Americans.

Dien Bien Phu Most significant victory of the Viet Minh over French colonial forces in 1954; gave the Viet Minh control of northern Vietnam.

 Read the Document on MyHistoryLab: Dwight D. Eisenhower, Dien Bien Phu (1954)

Ngo Dinh Diem [nyoh dihn DEE-ehm] Political leader of South Vietnam; established as president with United States support in the 1950s; opposed Communist government of North Vietnam; overthrown by military coup approved by United States.

Viet Cong Name given by Diem regime to communist guerrilla movement in southern Vietnam; reorganized with northern Vietnamese assistance as the National Liberation Front in 1958.

peasants of the north, where they had been propagated during the 1930s and especially during the war. The fact that the Viet Minh actually put their reform and community-building programs into effect in the areas they controlled won them very solid support among the rural population. The Viet Minh's efforts to provide assistance to the peasants during the terrible famine of 1944 and 1945 also convinced the much-abused Vietnamese people that here at last was a political organization genuinely committed to improving their lot.

Under the leadership of general **Vo Nguyen Giap**, the Viet Minh skillfully used guerrilla tactics similar to those devised by Mao in China (see Chapter 30). These offset the advantages that first the French and then the Japanese enjoyed in conventional firepower. With a strong base of support in much of the rural north and the hill regions, where they had won the support of key non-Vietnamese "tribal" peoples, the Viet Minh forces advanced triumphantly into the Red River delta as the Japanese withdrew. By August 1945, the Viet Minh were in control of Hanoi, where Ho Chi Minh proclaimed the establishment of the independent nation of Vietnam.

Although the Viet Minh had liberated much of the north, they had very little control in the south. In that part of Vietnam a variety of communist and bourgeois nationalist parties jostled for power. The French, eager to reclaim their colonial empire and put behind them their humiliations at the hands of the Nazis, were quick to exploit this turmoil. With British assistance, the French reoccupied Saigon and much of south and central Vietnam. In March 1946, they denounced the August declaration of Vietnamese independence and moved to reassert their colonial control over the whole of Vietnam and the rest of Indochina. An unsteady truce between the French and the Viet Minh quickly broke down. Soon Vietnam was consumed by a renewal of the Viet Minh's guerrilla war for liberation, as well as bloody infighting between the different factions of the Vietnamese.

After nearly a decade of indecisive struggle, the Viet Minh had gained control of much of the Vietnamese countryside, and the French, with increasing American financial and military aid, clung to the fortified towns. In 1954 the Viet Minh soundly defeated the French by capturing the giant fortress they had built at **Dien Bien Phu** in the mountain highlands hear the Laotian border. The victory gained international recognition at a 1954 conference in Geneva for an independent state—the Democratic Republic of Vietnam, in the north. At Geneva, elections throughout Vietnam were also promised in the treaty within two years to decide who should govern a reunited north and the still politically fragmented south (Map 35.4).

The War of Liberation against the United States

In Geneva, some hoped that free elections would eventually be held to determine who should govern a united Vietnam. However, this electoral contest never materialized. Like the rest of east Asia, Vietnam had become entangled in the cold war maneuvers of the United States and the Soviet Union. Despite very amicable cooperation between the Viet Minh and U.S. armed forces during the war against Japan, U.S. support for the French in the First Indochina War and the growing fame of Ho Chi Minh as a communist leader drove the two further and further apart. Anticommunist hysteria in the United States in the early 1950s fed the perception of influential American leaders that South Vietnam, like South Korea, must be protected from communist takeover.

The search for a leader to build a government in the south that the United States could prop up with economic and military assistance led to **Ngo Dinh Diem**. Diem appeared to have impeccable nationalist credentials. In fact, he had gone into exile rather than give up the struggle against the French. His sojourn in the United States in the 1940s and the fact that he was Catholic also recommended him to American politicians and clergy. Unfortunately, these same attributes would alienate him from the great majority of the Vietnamese people.

With U.S. backing, Diem was installed as the president of Vietnam. He tried to legitimatize his status in the late 1950s by holding rigged elections in the south, in which the communists were not permitted to run. Diem also mounted a series of campaigns to eliminate by force all possible political rivals. Because the communists posed the biggest threat (and were of the greatest concern to Diem's American backers), the suppression campaign increasingly focused on the communist cadres that remained in the south after Vietnam had been divided at Geneva. By the mid-1950s, the **Viet Cong** (as the Diem regime dubbed the communist resistance) were threatened with extermination. In response to this threat, the communist regime in the north began to send weapons,

FIGURE 35.9 April 30, 1975. As the victorious Viet Cong entered Saigon, a photographer captured the image of a lone woman hurrying along a road strewn with uniforms abandoned by former South Vietnamese soldiers fearful of being identified as having fought on the losing side.

advisors, and other resources to the southern cadres, which were reorganized as the National Liberation Front in 1960.

As guerrilla warfare spread and Diem's military responses expanded, both the United States and the North Vietnamese escalated their support for the warring parties. When Diem proved unable to stem the communist tide in the countryside, the United States authorized his generals to overthrow him and take direct charge of the war. When the Vietnamese military could make little headway, the United States stepped up its military intervention (Map 35.4).

From thousands of special advisors in the early 1950s, the overall U.S. commitment rose to nearly 500,000 men and women, who made up a massive force of occupation by 1968. But despite the loss of nearly 60,000 American lives and millions of Vietnamese casualties, the Americans could not defeat the communist movement. In part, their failure resulted from their very presence, which made it possible for the communists to convince the great majority of the Vietnamese people that they were fighting for their independence from yet another imperialist aggressor.

Although more explosives were dropped on tiny Vietnam, North and South, than in all of the theaters of World War II, and the United States resorted to chemical warfare against the very environment of the South Vietnamese they claimed to be trying to save, the communists would not yield. The Vietnamese emerged as the victors of the Vietnam or (from the Vietnamese perspective) Second Indochina War. In the early 1970s, U.S. diplomats negotiated an end to direct American involvement in the conflict. Without that support, the unpopular military regime in the south fell apart by 1975 (Figure 35.9). The communists united Vietnam under a single government for the first time since the late 1850s. But the nation they governed was shattered and impoverished by decades of civil war, revolution, and armed conflict with two major colonial powers and the most powerful nation of the second half of the 20th century.

After Victory: Salvaging Communism in an Era of Globalization

In the years since 1975 and the end of what was, for the Vietnamese, decades of wars for liberation, communist efforts to complete the revolution by rebuilding Vietnamese society made little headway in the early decades after they united the country. In part, this failure can be linked to Vietnam's isolation from much of the rest of the international community. This isolation resulted in part from pressures

FIGURE **35.10** By the mid-1990s, the failed efforts of the United States to isolate Vietnam gave way to increasing economic and diplomatic contacts. One example of American corporate penetration is depicted in this street scene from Hanoi in 1993. The opening of Vietnam to foreign investment, assistance, and tourism accelerated through the 1990s. In this atmosphere it has been possible to begin to heal the deep wounds and animosities generated by decades of warfare waged by the Vietnamese people against advanced industrial nations such as Japan, France, and the United States.

applied by a vengeful United States against relief from international agencies. It was increased by border clashes with China that were linked to ancient rivalries between the two countries. Deprived of assistance from abroad and faced with a shattered economy and a devastated environment at home, Vietnam's aging revolutionary leaders pushed hard-line Marxist-Leninist (and even Stalinist) political and economic agendas. Like their Chinese counterparts, they devoted their energies to persecuting old enemies (thus setting off mass migrations from what had been South Vietnam) and imposed a dictatorial regime that left little room for popular responses to government initiatives. In contrast to the Chinese in the past decade, however, the Vietnamese leadership also tried until the 1980s to maintain a highly centralized command economy. The rigid system that resulted stifled growth and, if anything, left the Vietnamese people almost as impoverished as they had been after a century of colonialism and decades of civil war.

By the late 1980s, the obvious failure of these approaches and the collapse of communist regimes throughout eastern Europe prompted measures aimed at liberalizing and expanding the market sector within the Vietnamese economy. The encouraging responses of Japanese and European corporations, eager to open up Vietnamese markets, have done much to stimulate growth in the Vietnamese economy. Growing investments by their industrial rivals have placed increasing pressure on American firms to move into the Vietnamese market (Figure 35.10). These trends have been strengthened by the genuine, and quite remarkable, willingness shown by Vietnamese leaders in the past decade to work with U.S. officials to resolve questions about prisoners of war and soldiers missing in action from the Vietnam War. But, like many other postcolonial nations, Vietnam has paid a high price for its efforts at integration into the globalizing economy. Many of its workers have had to endure the sweatshop conditions widely found in foreign factories, social inequality has increased markedly, and the free education system and other public services once provided by the communist state have declined or have entirely disappeared.

Global Connections and Critical Themes

EAST ASIA AND THE PACIFIC RIM IN THE CONTEMPORARY WORLD

In many respects, the recent histories of China and the peoples of Japan, Korea, and Vietnam, whose cultures were so profoundly affected by Chinese civilization, have been fundamentally different from those of much of the rest of Asia and Africa. Particularly in the past century, the experience of the Japanese has diverged significantly from those of other Asian and African peoples. The ethnically homogeneous, politically unified, and militarily adept Japanese not only were able to beat off Western imperialist advances against their island home but they have been one of the few non-Western peoples to achieve a high level of industrialization. Within decades of the forced "opening" of Japan by the United States in the 1850s, the island nation also became the only African or Asian country to join the ranks of the great powers. In imitation of its Western rivals, Japan embarked on its own campaign of imperialist expansion overseas. Although Korea was colonized early in the 20th century by its powerful Japanese neighbor, in the decades since World War II it has emerged as one of the leading industrial centers of the Pacific Rim. Since World War II, Taiwan and several other east Asian centers experienced rapid industrial advances, propelling the Pacific Rim to new importance in world affairs.

In contrast to industrialized Japan and to Korea in the past four decades or so, with their high standards of living and global economic power, China and Vietnam have had a good deal in common with the rest of the emerging nations. China and Vietnam suffered heavily from the assaults and exploitive terms of exchange imposed by imperialist powers, both Western and Japanese. Each has had to contend with underdevelopment, overpopulation, poverty, and environmental degradation. But unlike most of the rest of the formerly colonized peoples, the Chinese and the Vietnamese have had to deal with these awesome challenges in the midst of the collapse of the patterns of civilized life each had followed for thousands of years.

As disruptive as imperialist conquest and its effects were in the rest of the Asian and African worlds, most colonized peoples managed to preserve much of their precolonial cultures and modes of social organization. The defense and revival of traditional customs, religious beliefs, and social arrangements played a key role in their struggles for decolonization. This was not the case in China and Vietnam, where a combination of external aggression and internal upheavals discredited and destroyed the Confucian system that had long been synonymous with civilized life. With their traditional order in shambles, the peoples of China and Vietnam had no choice but to embark on full-scale revolutions that would clear away the rubble of the failed Confucian system. They needed to remove the obstacles posed by imperialist dominance and build new, viable states and societies.

In contrast to much of the rest of the colonized world, the countries of China and Vietnam derived few benefits from European domination, either informal or formal. Imperialist pressures eroded and smashed their political institutions rather than building up a bureaucratic grid and imparting political ideologies that could form the basis for nation-building. Both China and Vietnam already had the strong sense of identity, common language, and unifying polity that were among the major legacies of colonialism in other areas.

Because of economic development (in the Pacific Rim, and more recently in China and Vietnam) and the forces of revolution, east Asia has been fundamentally recast in the decades since World War II and has regained its longstanding importance in world affairs. The patterns of these transformations have varied. On the one hand, there has been a dynamic combination of industrialization and reform of the Pacific Rim in close connection to the West. On the other, the fluctuations of major revolutionary movements have been followed by the post-Maoist adoption of what one observer aptly dubbed "Market-Leninism" in China and Vietnam in recent decades. The legacy of earlier patterns in east Asia, including Confucianism, has similarly been redefined and utilized in different ways. But the themes of growing independence and self-assertion have been combined across east Asia in recent years with ongoing or new experiments in Western-style capitalism, replacing Confucianism as the state ideology and providing the philosophical basis for the new social order.

Revolution and economic change have combined to make east Asia a growing force in world affairs by the early 21st century—and largely independent of Western control in contrast to the previous period of imperialism. China's size and post-revolutionary economic surge, which has come to exceed even that of the rest of the Pacific Rim nations, has prompted some observers to wonder if the twenty-first century will be the "century of east Asia." China, Japan, and South Korea have become centers of multinational corporations, along with the West. East Asian exports, including toys like Pokemon, animated films, and South Korean soap operas are now staples of global consumer culture. Japanese, Korean, and more recently Chinese scientific capacity in areas like supercomputing have made them major global innovators, while China and Japan have come to play growing roles in space technology. China, Japan, and Korea have also become prominent participants in global athletic competitions. In various ways, including standard diplomatic and economic channels, the nations of east Asia have come to exert more influence in world affairs than ever before. Their growing predominance in all of these areas ensures that the peoples of east Asia will shape human history in the 21st century in major, perhaps transformative, ways.

Further Readings

The best account of late twentieth-century Japanese society and politics is E. O. Reischauer, *The Japanese* (1988). For recent history, see also M. Hane, *Modern Japan: A Historical Survey* (1992); William G. Beasley, *The Rise of Modern Japan* (1995); and Edward R. Beauchamp, ed., *Women and Women's Issues in Post World War II Japan* (1998).

Several novels and literary collections are accessible and useful. J. Tanizaki, *The Makioka Sisters* (1957), deals with a merchant family in the 1930s; see also H. Hibbett, ed., *Contemporary Japanese Literature: An Anthology of Fiction, Film, and Other Writing Since 1945* (1992). An important study of change, focusing on postwar rural society, is G. Bernstein, *Haruko's World: A Japanese Farm Woman and Her Community* (1983). Another complex 20th-century topic is assessed in R. Storry, *The Double Patriots: A Story of Japanese Nationalism* (1973).

On the Pacific Rim concept and its implications for the world economy, see David Aikman, *Pacific Rim: Area of Change, Area of Opportunity* (1986); Philip West et al., eds., *The Pacific Rim and the Western World: Strategic, Economic, and Cultural Perspectives* (1987); Stephen Haggard and Chung-In Moon, *Pacific Dynamics: The International Politics of Industrial Change* (1988); and Roland A. Morse et al., *Pacific Basin: Concept and Challenge* (1986). Vera Simone, *The Asian Pacific: Political and Economic Development in a Global Context* (1995), is a comparative survey of postcolonial state building and international cultural connections. Also see S. Ichimura, *The Political Economy of Japanese and Asian Development* (1998).

Excellent introductions to recent Korean history are Bruce Cumings, *The Two Koreas* (1984) and *Korea's Place in the Sun: A Modern History* (1997), and David Rees, *A Short History of Modern Korea* (1988). A variety of special topics are addressed in Marshal R. Pihl, ed., *Listening to Korea: Economic Transformation and Social Change* (1989). See also Paul Kuznet, *Economic Growth and Structure in the Republic of Korea* (1977), and Dennis McNamara, *The Colonial Origins of Korean Enterprise, 1910–1945* (1990).

For a fascinating exploration of cultural change and continuity in Taiwan regarding issues in health and medicine, see Arthur Kleinman, *Patients and Healers in the Context of Culture* (1979). On Singapore, Janet W. Salaff, *State and Family in Singapore* (1988), is an excellent study; see also R. N. Kearney, ed., *Politics and Modernization in South and Southeast Asia* (1975).

A good summary of the final stages of the civil war in China is provided in Lucien Bianco, *Origins of the Chinese Revolution,*

1915–1949 (1971). Perhaps the best overview of modern Chinese history from the Qing dynasty era through the Tiananmen Square massacres can be found in Jonathan D. Spence, *The Search for Modern China* (1990). Other useful accounts of the post-1949 era include Maurice Meisner, *Mao's China and After 1984* (1984); Michael Gasster, *China's Struggle to Modernize* (1987); and Immanuel C. Y. Hsu, *China Without Mao* (1983). On the pivotal period of the Cultural Revolution, see Roderick MacFarquhar, *The Origins of the Cultural Revolution*, 2 vols. (1974, 1983), and Lowell Dittmer, *Liu Shao-ch'i and the Chinese Cultural Revolution* (1974). For a highly critical assessment of the Maoist era, it is difficult to surpass Simon Leys, *Chinese Shadows* (1977). On cultural life in the postrevolutionary era, see the essays in R. MacFarquhar, ed., *The Hundred Flowers Campaign and the Chinese Intellectuals*, and Lois Wheeler Snow, *China on Stage* (1972). Elisabeth Croll, *Feminism and Socialism in China* (1978), remains by far the best single work on the position of women in revolutionary and Maoist China. Critical issues dealing with the environmental underpinnings of China's reemergence as a global power are covered in the Maoist era by Judith Shapiro's *Mao's War against Nature* (2001) and more broadly since 1949 in the works of Vaclav Smil, most recently *China's Environmental Crisis: An Enquiry into the Limits of National Development* (1993).

The first war of liberation in Vietnam is covered in Ellen J. Hammer, *The Struggle for Indochina, 1940–1955* (1966), and more recently Fredrik Logevall's *Embers of War: The Fall of an Empire and America's War in Vietnam* (2012). The best of many surveys of the second war, often called the American War in Vietnam, is Marilyn Young, *The Vietnam Wars, 1945–1990* (1989). Of a number of fine studies on the origins of American intervention in the area, two of the best are Patti Archimedes' *Why Vietnam?* (1980) and Lloyd Gardner's *Approaching Vietnam* (1988). On the conduct of the war, Jeffrey Race's *The War Comes to Long An* (1972); Eric Bergerud, *The Dynamics of Defeat: The Vietnam War in Hau Nghia Province* (1991); and Marc Jason Gilbert, ed., *Why the North Won the Vietnam War* (2002), are useful for the stress they place on the role of the Vietnamese in determining this conflict's course and ultimate outcome. Powerful firsthand accounts of the guerrilla war and U.S. combat include Mark Baker, *Nam* (1981); Philip Caputo, *A Rumor of War* (1977); Troung Nhu Tang, *A Viet Cong Memoir* (1985), and Bao Ninh, *The Sorrow of War* (1993).

On MyHistoryLab

 Study and Review on MyHistoryLab

Critical Thinking Questions

1. Discuss the ways in which the reemergence of China, Japan, and the "little tigers" of the Pacific Rim have decentered and reshaped the global economy in the decades since World War II.

2. Why has communism had a much greater appeal in the emerging nations of China and Vietnam that in most of the rest of the countries of the postcolonial world?

3. Were there any shared factors that help explain the dynamism of many east Asian nations by the late 20th/early 21st centuries? Were there any common factors that distinguished east Asia, despite major internal differences, from other world regions by the early 21st century?

4. What are some of the major contributions which the societies of east Asia have made to technological innovation in such key areas as communications, information gathering, entertainment, and transportation in recent decades?

5. Which of the states in the Pacific Rim do you think will play major roles in world history in the 21st century and why?

Power, Politics, and Conflict in World History, 1990–2014

36

Listen to Chapter 36 on MyHistoryLab

A human rights activist in Guatemala put the situation this way in the mid-1980s:

> If it were not for the international assistance, primarily from Americas Watch, Amnesty International, the World Council of Churches, solidarity organizations from democratic countries, Canadian organizations, organizations of Guatemalans working in the United States, Canada or Europe, without the moral and political help of those organizations, I believe we would have been dead many years ago, the army would not have permitted our organization to develop. . . . If you don't have the contacts, if the people who are doing the killing know that nobody is going to do anything if you disappear, then you disappear. . . . It was vital to have contacts so that information could go outside (Figure 36.1).

LEARNING OBJECTIVES

36.1 What were the main results of Gorbachev's policies in Russia, Central Asia, and east-central Europe? p. 898

36.2 What factors best explain why political democracy spread to additional regions from the late 20th century onward? p. 906

36.3 How do the former Yugoslavia and Rwanda compare with one another as cases of genocide? p. 908

36.4 What were the main limits to the U.S. exercise of power after the cold war? p. 911

FIGURE **36.1** During more than three decades of brutal civil conflict, 200,000 Guatemalans were killed or "disappeared," and more than a million were forced out of their homes. After a peace agreement was signed in 1996, a church commission headed by Bishop Juan José Gerardi investigated the atrocities committed during the civil war and issued a scathing report in which he found that 90 percent of the abuses had been committed by the government. Two days later, the 75-year-old bishop was bludgeoned to death. Here, throngs of mourners witness his funeral procession.

897

Watch the Video Series on MyHistoryLab

Learn about some key topics related to this chapter with the *MyHistoryLab Video Series: Key Topics in World History*

Many Central American regimes were repressive in the 1980s and at the beginning of the 1990s. Their hostility to communism and social revolution had earned them support from a conservative president in the United States. Free elections were impossible and many resistance figures were jailed or worse. But the situation changed. Local agitation for democracy would not cease. Instead, it spread in many parts of Latin America. Movement of people between countries played a key role, bringing opportunities for new contacts and for free expression. International human rights organizations took up the cause, organizing massive petition campaigns on behalf of victims. Church groups were active. Labor organizations, from the United States and elsewhere, chimed in, as did European Common Market (European Union) and United Nations human rights groups. Despite the power of the local military and the strength of U.S. policy, there was a new international counterweight, able to publicize abuse and prevent its concealment. Activities of local "death squads" received wide media attention, as did attacks on foreign Christian missionaries. Ultimately, these pressures forced the United States to change its policies, and fledgling democratic regimes began to take shape throughout the region.

Enthusiasm for international definitions of political rights had never run higher. There was a new force in world politics. At the same time, the force had clear limits. In some areas, particularly in conflict-torn regions of Africa, ruling groups resisted international criticism and made no effective effort to stop human rights abuses. How much was the world changing?

In the last two decades of the 20th century, global history took an abrupt turn. With the remarkably sudden collapse of the Soviet Union and the communist regimes of eastern Europe, the long and tense cold war came to an end. A larger current of expanding democracy provided a context for these developments as well. At the same time, a new set of regional conflicts complicated post–cold war politics, while the emergence of the United States as sole superpower had its own pluses and minuses. By 2008 limitations on the democratic current became more visible as well, further complicating the most recent phase of world history. ■

This chapter deals with the transition to a post–cold war framework, which provided some of the leading themes in world history from the mid-1980s well into the early 21st century. Political and diplomatic changes held center stage, along with a resurgence of terrorism. The end of the cold war redefined a central issue in the new world history period that had begun to open with World War I and its aftermath: What global power balance would replace 19th-century Western dominance? What political system or systems would replace the long hold of monarchies and empires? Political and diplomatic patterns were also involved, however, in the renewed process of globalization, which affected an even wider range of human activities, from culture to the environment. This wider process is taken up in the chapter that follows.

THE END OF THE COLD WAR

> Strains within the Soviet empire forced reforms that led to its downfall.

36.1 What were the main results of Gorbachev's policies in Russia, central Asia, and east-central Europe?

The cold war had lasted for 30 years when its context began to shift. The Russian empire had been expanding, off and on, for 500 years, interrupted only briefly by World War I and the initial phases of the Russian Revolution before it resumed its growth, to unprecedented levels. What could cause these two firmly established patterns, the cold war and the Russian empire, to change course dramatically?

1980 C.E.	1990 C.E.	2000 C.E.
1988 Soviet withdrawal from Afghanistan **1988–1991** Independence movements in eastern Europe and in minority states in Soviet Union **1989–1990** Collapse of Soviet Union and Warsaw Pact regimes	**1990** Iraqi invasion of Kuwait **1991** Breakup of Soviet Union; Yeltsin to power in Russia; civil wars begin in Yugoslavia; Slovenia and Croatia secede; First U.S.-Iraq War, Iraq defeated **1992** North American Free Trade Agreement (NAFTA) inaugurated; Bosnia withdraws from Yugoslavia; first World Environmental Conference in Brazil **1992–1993** UN-U.S. interventions in Somalia **1994** Mass genocide in Rwanda **1994** U.S. intervention in Haiti **1995** U.S.-NATO interventions in Bosnia **1997** Second World Environmental Conference, Kyoto, Japan **1998** Serbian assault on Albanians in Kosovo **1999** U.S.-NATO war against Yugoslavia; Putin becomes president of Russia	**2000** International Human Rights Conference, South Africa; Milosevic forced out as Serbian president; end of Yugoslav civil wars; emergence of China, India, Brazil as major economic forces **2000–2002** Second Intifada in Palestine and Israel **2001** Mass demonstrations against World Trade Organization in Genoa; terrorist attacks on World Trade Center and Pentagon; U.S.–led coalition topples Taliban regime in Afghanistan **2002** India and Pakistan mobilize armies over Kashmir dispute; euro becomes common currency in much of European Union **2003** U.S. and Great Britain bring down Saddam Hussein's government in Iraq **2004–2005** Democratic regimes begin in Georgia, Ukraine; new protests begin in central Asia **2008 ff.** Global economic crisis, fiscal pressures on European Union **2011-2012** Arab Spring revolts in Tunisia, Egypt, Libia, Syria, and Gulf States; tsunamis and Japan reactor disaster; tensions over Iran going nuclear; steep rise in the number and intensity of weather disruptions/arctic and world glacial meltdowns **2012** Return of Putin as Russian President; Kim Jong-un, son of Kim Jong-il, is new North Korean leader

Factors in Soviet Decline

Leadership was surely one component. After Stalin and then Khrushchev, Soviet leadership had turned conservative. Party bureaucrats, eager to protect the status quo, often advanced only mediocre people to top posts, men whose major leadership characteristic was their unwillingness to rock the boat. Many of these leaders then continued to hold power when their own aptitude declined with illness and age.

Of more general significance was the reassertion of initiative from some parts of the world surrounding the Soviet Union, despite continued pressures from the superpowers. The rise of Islamic fervor, evident in the Iranian Revolution of 1979, inevitably created anxiety in the Soviet Union with its large Muslim minority. To reduce this new threat, late in 1979 the Soviets invaded neighboring Afghanistan, hoping to set up a puppet regime that would protect Russian interests. The move drew widespread international disapproval. The war proved difficult, as Afghan guerrillas, with some backing from the United States, held their ground fiercely. Costs and casualties mounted, and the war—the first formal action the Soviets had indulged in since World War II—quickly proved unpopular at home.

At the same time, the success of western Europe's economy pushed communism into a defensive and retreating posture throughout eastern Europe. The attraction of Western institutions and consumer standards gained ground. Within the Soviet empire itself, a free trade union movement resumed in Poland, linked to the Catholic Church, and while it was repressed through Soviet-mandated martial law in 1981, the stress of keeping the lid on was likely to increase.

Changes in Chinese policy entered in. China, of course, had separated itself from Soviet tutelage in the 1960s. But in 1978 the Chinese regime made a choice to participate in the world economy and to admit more market forces and competitive free enterprise in the internal economy as well. There was no relaxation of political controls, and a democratic movement was vigorously quashed in 1989. But the Chinese economy now differed dramatically from that of the Soviet Union, and change was quickly rewarded, both with international investment and with rapid growth. The Soviets now had to contend not only with China's massive population but with its superior economic performance.

Finally, U.S. diplomatic policy tightened. While President Jimmy Carter hoped to reduce tensions in the late 1970s, he was a vigorous human rights advocate, particularly eager to point out Soviet deficiencies. American conservatives heightened their own opposition to the Soviet Union. A new strategic arms limitation agreement (SALT II) was negotiated in 1979 but quickly encountered resistance in the U.S. Senate. Then came the Soviet move into Afghanistan. President Carter reacted vigorously, claiming that the move was a "stepping stone to their possible control over much of the world's oil supplies" and, even more dramatically, the "gravest threat to world peace since World War II." American participation in the 1980 Moscow Olympics was cancelled.

Then, in 1980, the new, conservative president, Ronald Reagan, who had denounced the Soviet Union as an "evil empire," announced a massive increase in U.S. defense spending. The size of domestic programs declined relative to the federal budget as a whole, and some programs were cut outright (promoting, among other things, a surge in homelessness), but conservatives accepted a growing budget deficit in favor of the new military outlays. The president also announced a "Reagan doctrine" of assisting anticommunism anywhere, and followed it up with an invasion of a small, Marxist-controlled Caribbean island, Grenada, and support for anti-Marxist military action in Central America.

Read the **Document** on **MyHistoryLab**: Ronald Reagan, Speech to the House of Commons (1982)

These moves put new pressure on the Soviets, already stretched to the limit to maintain military and global competition with the United States and beset with an unpopular war and new regional pressures as well. The stage was set for the events that, initially promoted for quite different reasons, undid the cold war.

The Explosion of the 1980s and 1990s

From 1985 onward the Soviet Union entered a period of intensive reform, soon matched by new political movements in eastern Europe that effectively dismantled the Soviet empire. The initial trigger for this extraordinary and unanticipated upheaval lay in the deteriorating Soviet economic performance, intensified by the costs of military rivalry with the United States. There were reasons for pride in the Soviet system, and many observers believed that public attitudes by the 1980s were shaped much less by terror than by satisfaction with the Soviet Union's world prestige and the improvements the communist regime had fostered in education and welfare. But to a degree unperceived outside the Soviet Union, the economy was grinding to a standstill. Forced industrialization had produced extensive environmental deterioration throughout eastern Europe. According to Soviet estimates, half of all agricultural land was endangered by the late 1980s; more than 20 percent of Soviet citizens lived in regions of ecological disaster. Rates and severity of respiratory and other diseases increased, impairing both morale and economic performance. Infant mortality rates also rose in several regions, sometimes nearing the highest levels in the world.

More directly, industrial production began to stagnate and even drop as a result of rigid central planning, health problems, and poor worker morale. Growing inadequacy of housing and consumer goods resulted, further lowering motivation. As economic growth stopped, the percentage of resources allocated to military production escalated, toward a third of all national income. This reduced funds available for other investments or for consumer needs. At first only privately, younger leaders began to recognize that the system was near collapse.

The Age of Reform

Gorbachev, Mikhail U.S.S.R. premier after 1985; renewed attacks on Stalinism; urged reduction in nuclear armament; proclaimed policies of glasnost and perestroika.

Yet the Soviet system was not changeless, despite its heavy bureaucratization. Problems and dissatisfactions, although controlled, could provoke response beyond renewed repression. After a succession of leaders whose age or health precluded major initiatives, the Soviet Union in 1985 brought a new, younger official to the fore. **Mikhail Gorbachev** quickly renewed some of the earlier attacks on Stalinist rigidity and replaced some of the old-line party bureaucrats (Figure 36.2). He conveyed a new, more Western style, dressing in fashionable clothes (and accompanied by his stylish wife), holding relatively open press conferences, and even allowing the Soviet media to engage in active debate and report on problems as well as successes. Gorbachev also further altered the Soviet Union's

FIGURE 36.2 Early in his first administration, President Ronald Reagan referred to the Soviet Union as the "Evil Empire" and showed little interest in cooperating in any way with Moscow. After the accession of Mikhail Gorbachev, Reagan changed his attitude, and the two men worked closely to ease tensions between the two great powers.

modified cold war stance. He urged a reduction in nuclear armament, and in 1987 he negotiated a new agreement with the United States that limited medium-range missiles in Europe. He ended the war in Afghanistan, bringing Soviet troops home.

Internally, Gorbachev proclaimed a policy of **glasnost**, or openness, which implied new freedom to comment and criticize. He pressed particularly for a reduction in bureaucratic inefficiency and unproductive labor in the Soviet economy, encouraging more decentralized decision making and the use of some market incentives to stimulate greater output. The sweep of Gorbachev's reforms, as opposed to an undeniable new tone in Soviet public relations, remained difficult to assess. Strong limits on political freedom persisted, and it was unclear whether Gorbachev could cut through the centralized planning apparatus that controlled the main lines of the Soviet economy. There was also uncertainty about how well the new leader could balance reform and stability.

Indeed, questions about Gorbachev's prospects recalled many basic issues in Soviet history. In many ways Gorbachev's policies constituted a return to a characteristic ambivalence about the West. He reduced Soviet isolation while continuing to criticize aspects of Western political and social structure. Gorbachev clearly hoped to use some Western management techniques and was open to certain Western cultural styles without, however, intending to abandon basic control of the communist state. Western analysts wondered if the Soviet economy could improve worker motivation without embracing a Western-style consumerism or whether computers could be more widely introduced without allowing freedom for information exchange.

Gorbachev also sought to open the Soviet Union to fuller participation in the world economy, recognizing that isolation in a separate empire had restricted access to new technology and limited motivation to change. Although the new leadership did not rush to make foreign trade or investment too easy—considerable suspicion persisted—the economic initiatives brought symbolic changes, such as the opening of a McDonald's restaurant in Moscow and a whole array of new contacts between Soviet citizens and foreigners (Figure 36.3).

Gorbachev's initial policies did not quickly reform the Soviet economy, but they had immediate political effects, some of which the reform leader had almost certainly not anticipated. The keynote

glasnost Policy of openness or political liberation in Soviet Union put forward by Mikhail Gorbachev in the late 1980s.

FIGURE 36.3 After 14 years of negotiations between McDonald's executives and Soviet government officials, the first McDonald's restaurant opened in Moscow in 1990. Lines formed around the block to get a first taste of the famous fast food.

perestroika [pehr-uh-STROY-kuh] Policy of Mikhail Gorbachev calling for economic restructuring in the U.S.S.R. in the late 1980s; more leeway for private ownership and decentralized control in industry and agriculture.

of the reform program was **perestroika**, or economic restructuring, which Gorbachev translated into more leeway for private ownership and decentralized control in industry and agriculture. Farmers, for example, could now lease land for 50 years, with rights of inheritance, and industrial concerns were authorized to buy from either private or state operations. Foreign investment was encouraged. Gorbachev pressed for reductions in Soviet military commitments, particularly through agreements with the United States on troop reductions and limitations on nuclear weaponry, in order to free resources for consumer goods industries. He urged more self-help among the Soviets, including a reduction in drinking, arguing that he wanted to "rid public opinion of . . . faith in a 'good Tsar,' the all powerful center, the notion that someone can bring about order and organize perestroika from on high."

Politically, Gorbachev encouraged a new constitution in 1988, giving considerable power to a new parliament, the Congress of People's Deputies, and abolishing the Communist monopoly on elections. Important opposition groups developed both inside and outside the party, pressing Gorbachev between radicals who wanted a faster pace of reform and conservative hard-liners. Gorbachev himself was elected to a new, powerful presidency of the Soviet Union in 1990.

Reform amid continued economic stagnation provoked agitation among minority nationalities in the Soviet Union, from 1988 onward. Muslims and Armenian Christians rioted in the south, both against each other and against the central state. Baltic nationalist and other European minorities also stirred, some insisting on full independence, some only pressing for greater autonomy. Again, results of this diverse unrest were difficult to forecast, but some observers predicted the end of Soviet control of central Asia and the European borderlands.

Even social issues were given uncertain new twists. Gorbachev noted that Soviet efforts to establish equality between the sexes had burdened women with a combination of work and household duties. His solution—to allow women to "return to their purely womanly missions" of housework, childrearing, and "the creation of a good family atmosphere"—had a somewhat old-fashioned ring to it.

Dismantling the Soviet Empire

Gorbachev's new approach, including his desire for better relations with Western powers, prompted more definitive results outside the Soviet Union than within, as the smaller states of eastern Europe uniformly pushed for greater independence and internal reforms. Bulgaria moved for economic liberalization in 1987 but was held back by the Soviets; pressure resumed in 1989 as the party leader was ousted and free elections were arranged. Hungary changed leadership in 1988 and installed a noncommunist president. A new constitution and free elections were planned; the Communist party renamed itself Socialist. Hungary also reviewed its great 1956 rising, formally declaring it "a popular uprising... against an oligarchic system... which had humiliated the nation." Hungary moved rapidly toward a free-market economy. Poland installed a noncommunist government in 1988, and again moved quickly to dismantle the state-run economy. Prices rose rapidly as government subsidies were withdrawn. The Solidarity movement, born a decade before through a merger of noncommunist labor leaders and Catholic intellectuals, became the dominant political force. East Germany removed its communist government in 1989, expelling key leaders and moving rapidly toward unification with West Germany. The Berlin Wall was dismantled, and in 1990 noncommunists won a free election (Figure 36.4). German unification occurred later in 1990, a dramatic sign of the collapse of postwar Soviet foreign policy. Czechoslovakia installed a new government in 1989, headed by a playwright, and sought to introduce free elections and a more market-driven economy.

Although mass demonstrations played a key role in several of these political upheavals, only in Romania was there outright violence, as an exceptionally authoritarian communist leader was swept out by force. As in Bulgaria, the Communist party retained considerable power, although under new leadership, and reforms moved less rapidly than in Hungary and Czechoslovakia. The same held true for Albania, where the unreconstructed Stalinist regime was dislodged and a more flexible communist leadership installed.

New divergences in the nature and extent of reform in eastern Europe were exacerbated by clashes among nationalities, as in the Soviet Union. Change and uncertainty brought older attachments to the fore. Romanians and ethnic Hungarians clashed; Bulgarians attacked a Turkish minority left over from the Ottoman period. In 1991 the Yugoslavian communist regime, although not Soviet dominated, also came under attack, and a civil war boiled up from disputes among nationalities. Minority nationality areas, notably Slovenia, Croatia, and Bosnia-Herzegovina, proclaimed independence, but the national, Serbian-dominated army applied massive force to preserve the Yugoslav nation.

Amid this rapid and unexpected change, prospects for the future became unpredictable. Few of the new governments fully defined their constitutional structure, and amid innovation the range of new political parties almost compelled later consolidations. Like the Soviet Union itself, all the eastern

FIGURE **36.4** Breaching the Berlin Wall in 1989: West and East Germany meet.

European states suffered from sluggish production, massive pollution, and economic problems that might well lead to new political discontent.

With state controls and protection abruptly withdrawn by 1991, tensions over the first results of the introduction of the market economy in Poland brought rising unemployment and further price increases. These in turn produced growing disaffection from the Solidarity leadership. Diplomatic linkages among small states—a critical problem area between the two world wars—also had yet to be resolved.

The massive change in Soviet policy was clear. Gorbachev reversed postwar Russian imperialism, stating that "any nation has the right to decide its fate by itself." In several cases, notably Hungary, Soviet troops were rapidly withdrawn, and generally it seemed unlikely that a repressive attempt to reestablish an empire would be possible (Map 36.1). New contacts with Western nations, particularly in the European Economic Community (European Union), seemed to promise further realignment in the future.

Renewed Turmoil in the 1990s

The uncertainties of the situation within the Soviet Union were confirmed in the summer of 1991, when an attempted coup was mounted by military and police elements. Gorbachev's presidency and democratic decentralization were both threatened. Massive popular demonstrations, however, asserted the strong democratic current that had developed in the Soviet Union since 1986. The contrast with earlier Soviet history and the suppression of democracy in China two years before was striking.

In the aftermath of the attempted coup, Gorbachev's authority weakened. Leadership of the key republics, including the massive Russian Republic, became relatively stronger. The three Baltic states

MAP **36.1** Post–Soviet Union Russia, Eastern Europe, and Central Asia by 1991 With the collapse of the Soviet Union, the boundaries of eastern Europe and central Asia were substantially redrawn.

used the occasion to gain full independence though economic links with the Soviet Union remained. Other minority republics proclaimed independence as well, but Gorbachev struggled to win agreement on continued economic union and some other coordination. By the end of 1991 leaders of the major republics, including Russia's **Boris Yeltsin**, proclaimed the end of the Soviet Union, projecting a commonwealth of the leading republics, including the grain-rich Ukraine, in its stead. Amid the disputes Gorbachev fell from power, doomed by his attempts to salvage a presidency that depended on some survival of a greater Soviet Union. His leadership role was taken over by Boris Yeltsin, who as president of Russia and an early renouncer of communism now emerged as the leading, although quickly beleaguered, political figure. Yeltsin soon used force to bring Russia's parliament under some control.

Yeltsin, Boris Russian leader who stood up to coup attempt in 1991 that would have displaced Gorbachev; president of the Russian republic following dissolution of Soviet Union.

The former Soviet Union gave way to the loose Commonwealth of Independent States, which won tentative agreement from most of the now-independent republics. But tensions immediately surfaced about economic coordination amid rapid dismantling of state controls; about control of the military, where Russia—still by far the largest unit—sought predominance, including nuclear control amid challenges from the Ukraine and from Kazakhstan (two of the other republics with nuclear weaponry on their soil); and about relationships between the European-dominated republics, including Russia, and the cluster of central Asian states. How much unity might survive in the former Soviet Union was unclear. The fate of economic reform was also uncertain. Russian leaders hesitated to convert to a full market system lest transitional disruption further antagonize the population.

By the late 1990s, the leadership of Boris Yeltsin deteriorated as the economy performed badly, individual profiteers pulled in huge fortunes, and Yeltsin's health worsened. A bitter civil war broke out with the Muslim region of Chechnya: Terrorist acts by the rebels and brutal military repression seemed to feed each other. A new president, Vladimir Putin, was named in 1999, who vowed to clean up corruption and install more effective government controls over separate provinces. Putin

VISUALIZING THE PAST

Symbolism in the Breakdown of the Soviet Bloc

ALTHOUGH THE MAJORITY OF LATVIANS STRONGLY opposed the Soviet takeover of their government in 1939, for 50 years most had been afraid to express their views. After World War II, a strong nationalist resistance movement had arisen, but was harshly suppressed. Tens of thousands of Latvians were killed and many more were imprisoned or deported to Siberia. When, in the late 1980s, perestroika opened possibilities for change in the Soviet Union, Latvians were quick to act. They elected a new parliament that, in 1990, proclaimed its intention of beginning a transition to independence. Although Soviet hard-liners tried to crack down on Latvian independence advocates, the failed August 1991 coup in Moscow opened the door to Latvian independence. One of the first acts of the Latvians was to topple statues of Soviet leaders like this one of Lenin.

As part of the independence of the Baltic nation of Latvia, crowds toppled Soviet symbols—in this case, a giant statue of Lenin—in 1991.

QUESTIONS

- Imagine the toppled Lenin statue as it stood on the day it was erected. What do you think the Soviets intended to express to the Latvian people when they placed this statue?
- How do you think the Latvians who opposed Soviet rule might have viewed the meaning of the statue?
- What was the symbolism of toppling the statue?
- Why might it be one of the first acts of a people liberated from foreign occupation?

declared his commitment to democracy and a free press but also sponsored new attacks on dissident television stations and newspapers. Government repression restricted the activities of rival political parties, shaping the results of elections that returned ever-larger majorities to Putin's supporters. Many Russians seemed to agree that stronger measures were needed—why should a leader tolerate public criticism? Others longed for a return to the Soviet days of greater economic security and national glory. Reformists were able to voice their concerns, but Putin tightened his hold on the state and media, even attacking independent-minded business leaders. He also resisted appeals to compromise on the Chechnya revolt. Finishing his second term as president in 2008, Putin arranged still to serve as prime minister, and then was re-elected as president in 2012.

THE SPREAD OF DEMOCRACY

36.2 What factors best explain why political democracy spread to additional regions from the late 20th century onward?

A dramatic surge of democracy began in the 1970s, spreading further after 1989 with the fall of international communism. Important holdouts and regressions complicated the trend.

The end of the cold war was associated with another large trend in the world at the end of the 20th century: the spread of multiparty democracy with (reasonably) free elections.

Patterns of Change

Economic and political success in western Europe, including the drawing power of the Common Market, helped propel Spain, Portugal, and Greece to democratic systems in the mid-1970s, after long periods of authoritarian control. Then the democratic wave hit Latin America, backed by U.S. and western European support. Beginning with new regimes in Argentina and Brazil, authoritarian controls were replaced by free elections (see Chapter 33). The process continued through the 1990s, when literally all Latin American countries except Cuba were in the democratic camp. Revolutionaries in Central America accepted the system in the late 1980s; Paraguay was the final authoritarian regime to yield a decade later. In 2000 Mexico elected its first president from a party other than the PRI, the party that had monopolized control since the revolution.

Democratic systems gained ground in South Korea and Taiwan in the 1980s. In the Philippines, an authoritarian ruler was cast aside, amid considerable popular pressure, in favor of an elected government. Turkey also moved more decisively toward multiparty democracy, with both secular and Islamic parties involved. By this point, of course, the democratic current captured the Soviet bloc, with democratic systems winning out in most of east central Europe and in Russia itself.

While much of Africa remained authoritarian, democratic change spread to this region by the 1990s, headed with the triumph of democracy over apartheid in South Africa. After new assertions of military control, Nigeria, the continent's most populous country, turned to democracy in 1999, as did more than 20 other African nations. At this point also, a near-revolution toppled the authoritarian system in Indonesia and replaced it with competitive elections.

Another surge occurred in 2004–2005. Largely peaceful risings in Georgia and Ukraine replaced authoritarian leaders with democratic elections (against Russian opposition). Stirrings also occurred in former Soviet republics in central Asia, although in Uzbekistan they were brutally repressed.

Spurred in part by the American invasion of Iraq, which toppled a classic authoritarian regime and led to new elections, several Arab countries experimented with greater democracy. Openly contested local elections occurred in some cases, including Saudi Arabia. Kuwait granted the vote to women. Palestinians conducted an open election in their autonomous territory in Israel. These developments remained tentative, and key regimes, such as Egypt, continued to repress political opposition. Authoritarian systems predominated in most of the region.

Democracy and Its Limits

Never before had democracy spread so widely among so many otherwise different societies. Only China, North Korea, and parts of the Middle East and central Asia seemed to hold apart completely. In China the major democratic demonstration in Beijing in 1989 echoed the global democratic current but was brutally put down. The Chinese regimes vowed to couple rapid economic change with insistence on one-party rule, a major exception to democratic gains.

DOCUMENT

Democratic Protest and Repression in China

ON JUNE 4, 1989, CHINESE TROOPS marched on political protesters, many of them students, camped in Beijing's central Tiananmen Square. The protesters had been agitating for weeks for a more open, democratic system, as against communist one-party control. The military move caused hundreds of deaths and additional political imprisonments and exiles. It crushed the protest movement, differentiating China from the many other societies that were establishing new democracies at that time. (The imminent visit of Russia's democratizing president, Mikhail Gorbachev, was one spur to the protesters.) China continued, instead, its interesting experiment with authoritarian politics amid rapid economic change.

The following document, from a leading communist party official, Li Peng, establishes the kind of reasoning that, to the government, justified its later repression; it comes from a speech on Chinese television in mid-May. The document mixes some standard government claims about the nature of protest with some specific Chinese as well as communist traditions concerning politics and order.

> Comrades, in accordance with a decision made by the Standing Committee of the CPC Central Committee, the party Central Committee and the State Council have convened a meeting here of cadres from party, government, and army organs at the central and Beijing municipal levels, calling on everyone to mobilize in this emergency and to adopt resolute and effective measures to curb turmoil in a clear-cut manner, to restore normal order in society, and to maintain stability and unity in order to ensure the triumphant implementation of our reform and open policy and the program of socialist modernization [applause].
>
> The current situation in the capital is quite grim. The anarchic state is going from bad to worse. Law and discipline have been undermined. Prior to the beginning of May, the situation had begun to cool down as a result of great efforts. However, the situation has become more turbulent since the beginning of May. More and more students and other people have been involved in demonstrations. Many institutions of higher learning have come to a standstill. Traffic jams have taken place everywhere. The party and government leading organs have been affected, and public security has been rapidly deteriorating. All this has seriously disturbed and undermined the normal order of production, work, study, and everyday life of the people in the whole municipality. Some activities on the agenda for state affairs of the Sino-Soviet summit that attracted worldwide attention had to be canceled, greatly damaging China's international image and prestige.
>
> The activities of some of the students on hunger strike at Tiananmen Square have not yet been stopped completely. Their health is seriously deteriorating and some of their lives are still in imminent danger. In fact, a handful of persons are using the hunger strikes as hostages to coerce and force the party and the government to yield to their political demands. In this regard, they have not one iota of humanity [applause].
>
> The party and the government have, on one hand, taken every possible measure, to treat and rescue the fasting students. On the other hand, they have held several dialogues with representatives of the fasting students and have earnestly promised to continue to listen to their opinions in the future, in the hope that the students would stop their hunger strike immediately. But, the dialogues did not yield results as expected. The square is packed with extremely excited crowds who keep shouting demagogic slogans. Right now, representatives of the hunger striking students say that they can no longer control the situation. If we fail to promptly put an end to such a state of affairs and let it go unchecked, it will likely lead to serious consequences which none of us want to see.
>
> The situation in Beijing is still developing, and has already affected many other cities in the country. In many places, the number of demonstrators and protestors is increasing. In some places, there have been many incidents of people breaking into local party and government organs, along with beating, smashing, looting, burning, and other undermining activities that seriously violated the law. Some trains running on major railway lines have even been intercepted, causing communications to stop. Something has happened to our trunk line, the Beijing-Guangzhou line. Today, a train from Fuzhou was intercepted. The train was unable to move out for several hours.
>
> All these incidents demonstrate that we will have nationwide major turmoil if no quick action is taken to turn and stabilize the situation. Our nation's reforms and opening to the outside world, the cause of the modernization [program], and even the fate and future of the People's Republic of China, built by many revolutionary martyrs with their blood, are facing a serious threat [applause].
>
> Our party and government have pointed out time and time again that the vast numbers of young students are kindhearted, that subjectively they do not want turmoil, and that they have fervent patriotic spirit, wishing to push forward reform, develop democracy, and overcome corruption. This is also in line with the goals which the party and government have striven to accomplish. It should be said that many of the questions and views they raise have already exerted and will continue to exert positive influence on improving the work of the party and government. However, willfully using various forms of demonstrations, boycotts of class, and even hunger strikes to make petitions have damaged social stability and will not be beneficial to solving the problems....
>
> One important reason for us to take a clear-cut stand in opposing the turmoil and exposing the political conspiracy of a handful of people is to distinguish the masses of young students from the handful of people who incited the turmoil. For almost a month, we adopted an extremely tolerant and restrained attitude in handling the student unrest. No government in the world would be so tolerant. The reason that we were so tolerant was

(continued on next page)

out of our loving care for the masses of youths and students. We regard them as our own children and the future of China. We do not want to hurt good people, particularly not the young students. However, the handful of behind-the-scenes people, who were plotting and inciting the turmoil, miscalculated and took the tolerance as weakness on the part of the party and government. They continued to cook up stories to confuse and poison the masses, in an attempt to worsen the situation. This has caused the situation in the capital and many localities across the country to become increasingly acute. Under such circumstances, the CPC, as a ruling party and a government responsible to the people, is forced to take resolute and decisive measures to put an end to the turmoil [*applause*].

Comrades, our party is a party in power and our government is a people's government. To be responsible to our sacred motherland and to all people, we must adopt firm and resolute measures to end the turmoil swiftly, to maintain the leadership of the party as well as the socialist system. We believe that our actions will surely have the support of all members of the Communist Party and the Communist Youth League, as well as workers, peasants, intellectuals, democratic parties, people in various circles, and the broad masses [*applause*]. We believe that we will certainly have the backing of the People's Liberation Army [PLA], which is entrusted by the Constitution with guarding the country and the peaceful work of the people [*applause*]. At the same time, we also hope that the broad masses will fully support the PLA, the public security cadres, and the police in their efforts to maintain order in the capital [*applause*].

> **QUESTIONS**
> - Why does Li Peng object to the protest movement?
> - How does he try to persuade ordinary Chinese that the protest should cease?
> - What arguments reflect more distinctively Chinese traditions or communist values?
> - Why did the Chinese decide to repress political democracy?

Huge questions remained about democracy's future, even in other regions. The link to economic expectations—the sense that democracy was a precondition for freer markets and economic growth that supported many Latin American conversions and also Gorbachev's reforms in Russia—was an obvious vulnerability. What if the economy did not improve?

New uncertainties emerged after 2000. The United States voiced great support for the spread of democracy, but it also allied with authoritarian regimes—in Egypt, Pakistan, and Uzbekistan, for example—that promised cooperation against terrorism. Russia's retreat from full democracy, under President Putin, was an important development. Democratic systems struggled against poverty and social unrest in several Latin American countries, particularly in the Andes region. A new Venezuelan strongman, Hugo Chávez, recalled earlier populist authoritarians in Latin America. In 2007, however, popular vote rebuffed a Chávez effort to concentrate further power in his hands. Additional gains for democracy emerged in 2011–2012, in what was quickly called the Arab Spring. Risings in several countries, beginning with Tunisia but continuing in Egypt, Libya, and elsewhere, protested police authority and authoritarian politics. Massive demonstrations surged in several centers, while outright civil war broke out in Libya and Syria. Several longstanding rulers were toppled, amid great excitement. Results, however, were not entirely clear. Protests in several places were put down or opposed, in the case of Syria with great brutality as civil war raged for over two years. New elections in places in Egypt returned a strong Muslim majority, with questions about the ongoing commitment to democratic openness; then in 2013 a military regime unseated the Muslim group, amid ongoing tension in the streets. This was a story still being written. Interestingly, while the reelection of Putin in Russia saw new repression of opposition politicians, considerable public unrest suggested a growing desire for greater political freedom.

THE GREAT POWERS AND NEW DISPUTES

36.3 How do the former Yugoslavia and Rwanda compare with one another as cases of genocide?

> The collapse of the Soviet system created new, often bitter, regional disputes. Conflicts in other regions often led to massive bloodshed.

The end of the cold war framework highlighted certain regional rivalries. Many of them were not new, but they became more acute as the controlling influence of U.S.-Soviet rivalry disappeared. The surge of conflicts significantly constrained the spread of democracy.

The Former Soviet Empire

The Soviet Union, with its totalitarian government, opposition to religion, and emphasis on class rather than ethnic conflict, had kept a lid on hosts of potential internal disputes. When it collapsed, the lid came off. Ethnic and religious clashes occurred in several of the new nations. The Chechnya rising was a case in point within Russia itself. Armenia and Azerbaijan, now nations, conducted low-level warfare over disputed regions claimed by different ethnic groups. Disagreements between Czechs and Slovaks resulted in a split of Czechoslovakia, although in this instance the adjustment was peaceful.

The most important post-Soviet clash occurred in Yugoslavia (Map 36.2). Long-standing tensions divided different Slavic groups (Orthodox Serbs and Catholic Croats; Serbs and Muslim Bosnians) and also minority nationalities like Albanians. The communist regime had held the pieces together, particularly under Marshall Tito, who died in 1980. Amid Soviet collapse, two regions, more prosperous than the country as a whole, declared independence in 1991: Slovenia and Croatia. Serbians, eager to hold Yugoslavia together under their leadership, warred with Croatia but failed. Conflict spread to Bosnia, where Serbs attacked not only Croats but also Muslims. Brutal assaults on civilians caused massive deaths and were ultimately judged acts of genocide. After long hesitation, NATO intervened and protected a new nation in Bosnia-Herzegovina.

A second conflict developed at the end of the 1990s over the province of Kosovo. Albanian pressure for independence was met by Serbian resistance, again with acts of genocide under the label "ethnic cleansing." Again, NATO intervention, including air attacks, ended the violence and led to a new, more democratic regime in Serbia. Only ongoing military occupation, however, protected the peace. In the process, the federated nation of Serbia and Montenegro replaced the now defunct Yugoslavia, but Montenegro declared its own independence in 2007.

Read the Document on MyHistoryLab: The Balkan Proximity Peace Talks Agreement (1995)

MAP 36.2 **The Implosion of Yugoslavia, 1991–2008** During the decade after 2000 Kosovo became autonomous with ultimate plans for nationhood and Montenegro became a separate nation.

Endemic Conflicts

The end of the cold war did not cause several of the most troubling regional conflicts. However, the reduction of cold war tension and controls contributed to new regional latitude (Figure 36.5). The Middle East remained a trouble spot during the 1990s. Even before the end of the cold war, Iraq and Iran had conducted a long, casualty-filled war, with the ambitions of Iraq's dictatorial leader, Saddam Hussein, pitted against the Islamic revolutionary regime in Iran. Iraq prevailed, and then later, in 1990, invaded the small oil-rich state of Kuwait. This galvanized an international coalition of Western and moderate Arab states, which defeated Iraq in the 1991 **First U.S. Iraq War** while leaving Saddam Hussein in power. The United States maintained a large military presence in the Persian Gulf region, which drew criticism from many Arabs and Muslims.

Israeli–Palestinian tensions served as another Middle Eastern flashpoint. Israeli relations with the huge Palestinian minority deteriorated after the cold war ended, despite some promising peace moves in the mid-1990s. Although an autonomous Palestinian government was set up over two territories within Israel, tensions continued. Bitter violence between Israelis and Palestinians revived between 2001 and 2003. A wave of suicide bombings by Palestinians targeted Israeli civilians, while the Israeli government attacked Palestinian cities and refugee camps in turn. Concern

Read the Document on MyHistoryLab: George H.W. Bush Announces Action in the Persian Gulf (1991)

FIGURE 36.5 Image of the road to Baghdad after bombing in the Gulf War.

First U.S.-Iraq War 1991 war led by United States and various European and Middle Eastern allies, against Iraqi occupation of Kuwait. The war led to Iraqi withdrawal and a long confrontation with Iraq about armaments and political regime.

 Read the Document on MyHistoryLab: Israel-PLO Declaration of Principles on Interim Self-Government Arrangements (1993)

about possible nuclear weapons in Iran was another source of tension. Clearly, key issues in this complex region remain to be resolved.

Tensions between India and Pakistan also escalated, with various border clashes particularly around the disputed territory of Kashmir. By 2000 both countries had conducted tests of nuclear weapons. This was the most open case of nuclear dissemination, as the limited nuclear group of the cold war began to expand. Increased Hindu nationalism within India was matched by fiercer Muslim rhetoric in Pakistan. On another front: North Korea, also a nuclear power, periodically threatened aggression.

Ethnic and Other Conflicts: A New Surge

The upsurge of ethnic conflict in several areas constituted a striking new feature of the post–cold war scene. Ethnic rivalries were not new, of course, but several components helped explain the new and troubling outbreak. New levels of global interaction, for example, increased the potential for group identities to generate hostilities. Some groups clearly increased their investment in ethnic identity as a means of countering outside influences and global pressures.

Within Europe, a number of ethnic groups developed new opportunities for expression as the hold of the classic nation-state declined. The British government gave limited autonomy to Scottish and Welsh governments. France and Spain became more tolerant toward linguistic minorities such as the Bretons and the Catalans. During the 1990s, a number of European countries saw the rise of new political movements bent on reducing immigration in favor of protecting jobs and cultural identity for the majority national group. A National Front group in France won up to 10 percent of all votes during the mid-1990s, although it then fell back a bit. Austria generated a controversial right-wing national government rhetorically hostile to immigrants. Between 2001 and 2008, various leaders in Italy, the Netherlands, and France also discussed new barriers against immigrants. Violence against immigrant groups, such as Turks in Germany, flared recurrently as well.

In the 1990s a set of far bloodier conflicts broke out in central Africa, pitting tribal groups, the Hutus and the Tutsis, against each other particularly in the nation of Rwanda (Figure 36.6). Here, too, old rivalries blended with disputes over current power; the Tutsis had long ruled, but they were

Read the Document on MyHistoryLab: Alain Destexhe, from Rwanda and Genocide in the Twentieth Century

FIGURE **36.6** In the last decade of the 20th century, the specter of genocide returned to a century that had seen more examples of this extreme form of violence against whole peoples than any other period in world history. Genocide infected the Balkans and, as this picture shows, the nation of Rwanda in east central Africa.

outnumbered by resentful Hutus. Intervention from neighboring states like Uganda contributed to the confusion. Tremendous slaughter resulted, with hundreds of thousands killed and many more—over 2 million—driven from their homes. While outside powers, the Organization of African States, and the United Nations urged peace, there was no decisive outside intervention. Bloodshed finally ran its course, but ethnic disputes continued in central Africa, contributing to civil war in countries like Congo.

Ethnic and religious disputes were also involved in a number of other African trouble spots, including battles between government forces and various groups in Sudan, and warfare among military gangs in countries like Sierra Leone and Liberia. Violence frequently involved heavily armed children, or "boy soldiers." Sudanese conflicts resulted in over 2 million killed, and endemic warfare in the Congo (in which activities by neighboring states as well as internal ethnic struggle intensified the problems) killed almost the same number. Massive dislocations of refugees accompanied all these conflicts.

Clearly, ethnic tensions were leading not just to warfare, but to renewed acts of genocide that targeted whole populations of civilians, including women and children. Reactions from the world at large varied. In some instances, violence seemed sufficiently menacing to major powers that some intervention occurred, though never without great hesitation. No policies emerged that offered great promise of pushing back the potential for ethnic conflict.

THE UNITED STATES AS SOLE SUPERPOWER

36.4 What were the main limits to the U.S. exercise of power after the cold war?

> U.S. military power had no global rival by the 1990s, but a variety of reactions constrained American power. A new round of terrorism targeted the United States.

The decline of Russian power left the United States without a clear military competitor. Faced with economic problems, Russian leaders scaled back military expenses, which by 2001 totaled only 4 percent of American levels. Russia enjoyed some influence over neighboring states and retained a nuclear arsenal. Its role expanded in the 21st century as oil revenues fueled new prosperity. But its global military presence was greatly reduced. In contrast, U.S. military commitments remained high. By 2005 the nation was spending more on defense than the next 25 countries combined.

Read the Document on MyHistoryLab: François Mitterrand, Speech to the United Nations, 1990

FIGURE 36.7 In this cartoon from the *Ottawa Citizen*, Uncle Sam is portrayed as a vaudeville entertainer entirely absorbed in his act who is about to lose his place in the spotlight. In the wings, China waits to go on. The "fifteen minutes" is a reference to American artist Andy Warhol's much-quoted statement, "In the future everyone will be world-famous for fifteen minutes." What feelings toward the United States does this cartoon express?

(© 2005 Cam Cardow: The Ottawa Citizen and Political Cartoons.com.)

The United States and Other Power Centers

This level of American power obviously worried many (Figure 36.7). China increased its military arsenal, along with its growing power in the global economy. Periodic collaborations among powers like China, Russia, and Iran countered American interests, but they did not lead to permanent alignments. European countries, although allied with the United States, had their own concerns. Several nations discussed a joint military force independent of NATO, although on the whole European military outlays continued to decline.

The growth and success of the European Union (EU) sketched a potential counterweight to the United States. The new currency shared by most EU member states, the euro, surpassed the strength of the dollar. Expansion to 25 members was another key move. But an ambitious EU constitution that might provide more coordination in foreign affairs met widespread criticism in 2005 by nations concerned about their own independence of action. France and Holland voted nay, and the whole project was in doubt. The EU was a major economic force, but it was no match for American military strength. Between 1991 and 2008, American power provoked various resentments, but it was not unseated.

What was the United States to do with its world power? Americans debated how much they should try to police regional conflicts, often questioning the idea of serving as some kind of global enforcer. In 1993, for example, an American military intervention to halt civil strife in Somalia led to widespread resistance and loss of life, and the United States pulled out. At the same time, U.S. leaders clearly felt emboldened to tell other parts of the world how to organize their societies. Both business and political experts argued that the U.S. model of a free market economy should be widely adopted. U.S. leaders also worried about several medium-sized powers that had or might develop nuclear weapons or that might sponsor terrorism. Efforts to mobilize the world community against countries like Iran, Iraq, and North Korea had varying degrees of success, suggesting some limits to American influence if not its direct military strength.

The United States became increasingly suspicious of international agreements that might limit its sovereignty, particularly after George W. Bush became president in 2001. Treaties designed to protect the environment or prevent the use of land mines were rejected, despite wide international support. These gestures of independence provoked criticism in various parts of the world.

View the Closer Look on MyHistoryLab: World Trade Center, Sept. 11, 2001

FIGURE 36.8 At 10:05 on the morning of September 11, 2001, the south tower of the World Trade Center collapsed after having been hit by a hijacked commercial plane. The north tower, shown here in flames, collapsed less than half an hour later. This terrorist attack and the ensuing "War on Terror" changed the course of history, not just in the United States, but around the world, as terrorism became the focus of American foreign policy.

Anti-American Terrorism and Response

American interests had periodically been the targets of terrorist attacks since the 1960s. Hijacking of airplanes and other moves frequently expressed hostility to U.S. policies. But the massive attacks on the World Trade Center and the Pentagon by Islamic militants on September 11, 2001, created a new level of threat (Figure 36.8). The attacks reflected concern about specific U.S. policies in the Middle East, including support for authoritarian governments, the alliance with Israel, and the stationing of troops on "sacred ground" in Saudi Arabia. The terrorists were also hostile to wider U.S. power, or as they termed it, arrogance. Their response, hijacking airliners to crash into buildings that symbolized American financial and military might, killed about 3000 people. The terrorists regarded this as justifiable action against a nation they could not hope to fight by conventional means.

The attacks clearly altered U.S. policy and focused the administration on a war against terrorism. "War on Terror" was the new catchphrase, and a number of measures were taken, including heightened screening of international visitors. The problem dominated American foreign policy. A first response involved a military attack that successfully topped the Islamic fundamentalist regime in Afghanistan that had harbored the Al Qaeda group behind the September 11 attacks. World opinion largely supported this move. The United States established new military bases near several possible centers of terrorist activity (Map 36.3).

In 2003 U.S. focus turned to Iraq, which was accused of amassing dangerous weaponry and aiding terrorists.

THINKING HISTORICALLY

Terrorism, Then and Now

IN THE LAST YEARS OF THE 20TH CENTURY, terrorism became a major issue for the international media, the world's political and military leaders, and increasingly for civilians across the globe who became both targets and mass victims of increasingly indiscriminate violent assaults. For Americans terrorism on home soil arrived gradually as the initial, and largely failed, attempt to bomb the World Trade Center in New York City in 1993 faded from memory. By contrast, for much of the rest of the world, fear of and precautions against terrorist violence had become ongoing and a major concern as early as the late 1960s. From Basque separatists in Spain and Protestant and Catholic paramilitary units in Northern Ireland to Tamil suicide bombers in Sri Lanka and cult plotters in Japan, terrorism has become an ever-present menace in the lives of leaders and ordinary citizens alike over much of the globe.

This is particularly true in the growing conurbations where much of humanity has come to be concentrated. The well-coordinated and appallingly destructive attacks of September 11, 2001, on the World Trade Center in New York and the Pentagon in Washington, DC, brought these concerns and their vulnerability to terrorism home to Americans with mind-numbing force. Later terrorist attacks targeted commuter systems in Spain (2004) and Britain (2005).

Although current commentators often treat the late 20th-century global epidemic of terrorism as a phenomenon without historical precedent, in fact in the decades before World War I terrorist attacks were also a major concern and were carried out by dissident groups in many areas of the globe. From the capitals and metropolitan centers of Europe (especially those of tsarist Russia) and the United States to the port cities and imperial centers of the far-flung colonial empires of the great industrial powers, assassinations and bombs killed and maimed, disoriented societies, and challenged political regimes. But in critical ways—including the nature and causes espoused by terrorist groups, the targets they favored, and the amount of damage or numbers of casualties their attacks caused—terrorism in the 1880s or the early 1900s differed significantly from its counterpart in the 1970s or 1990s. An exploration of some of these key differences can tell us a great deal not only about the transformation of terrorists' motivations and operations, but also about key contrasts in terms of the global and local contexts in which each wave of terrorism occurred.

In both time periods, the main sources of terrorist assaults were small, secret, and highly politically motivated organizations.

> **Although current commentators often treat the late 20th-century global epidemic of terrorism as a phenomenon without historical precedent, in fact in the decades before World War I terrorist attacks were also a major concern and were carried out by dissident groups in many areas of the globe.**

In both the early 20th century and in the decades at its end, the main objective of the members of these organizations was to discredit, weaken, and ultimately overthrow political regimes that they believed were oppressive and supportive of exploitation at the national and international levels. Their operations were also designed to advertise the causes these extremist groups espoused and draw attention to injustices they believed could not be effectively addressed through less violent or less confrontational modes of protest. But in the pre–World War I era, most terrorists were driven either by (1) anarchist aspirations to destroy increasingly centralized states, (2) radical Marxist programs for workers to overthrow the capitalist world order, or (3) struggles for the liberation of colonized peoples, from Ireland to India. The most spectacular terrorist assault of the era was of the latter type: Bosnian Serb Gavril Princip's assassination of the Archduke Ferdinand and his wife, Sophie, which precipitated the crisis that led to World War I.

At the turn of the 21st century, by contrast, terrorist assaults have come mainly from sectarian extremists claiming affiliation with one of the world's great religious traditions—including Christianity, Hinduism, Judaism, and Islam—or from subnationalist groups, such as the Basques in Spain or Protestant and Catholic militias in Northern Ireland. Interethnic civil wars, such as those that have raged in Lebanon, Cyprus, Bosnia, and Sri Lanka in recent decades, have also proved to be major sources of terrorist activities. Periodically, radical environmentalists and groups opposing international institutions, such as the International Monetary Fund and World Trade Organization, that promote economic globalization have also resorted to terrorist tactics.

The targets terrorists select often tell us a good deal about the differing causes they espouse. Many of the regimes that anarchists struck at in the pre–World War I period—for example, the tsarist empire or the British Raj in India—were in fact autocratic, often indifferent to the oppressive living conditions of the great majority of their subjects and prone to respond to even peaceful protest with violent repression, including torture. Scholarly investigations of these and current causes of terrorist activities have made us aware of the frequent resort to terrorist tactics by bureaucrats, the military, and state officials who so vehemently condemn dissident violence. In fact, terrorist activities have often proved far less lethal and destructive than the violence employed by regimes in power. Although these discoveries do not justify violence, particularly that directed against innocent civilians, they help us to understand in part why terrorist groups resort to violence rather than trusting the state to carry through with reforms or to negotiate with them peacefully and in good faith.

In both time periods, terrorist acts were carried out mainly by young men. But in the decades at the turn of the 20th century, many of the operatives were middle-aged, and separatist activists in both eras have included young women. Targets differed significantly in each phase of the 20th century. In the decades before World War I, individuals—monarchs (and their spouses), government officials (including President McKinley of the United States), business tycoons, and colonial officials—were most often chosen, in part because of the propaganda value of striking at the powerful and wealthy. At times, bombs placed in public areas were used to instill mass panic and disrupt normal social life. In the case of anarchist and Marxist extremists, indiscriminate mass killings and widespread destruction in fashionable quarters of urban areas were seen as symbolic assaults on the bourgeois, capitalist global order.

At the turn of the 21st century, indiscriminate assaults on defenseless civilians have become the preferred tactic of terrorists in Ireland, Spain, Israel and the Palestinian territories, Sri Lanka, Japan, and other areas. Technological advances that allowed terrorist operatives to miniaturize bombs and automatic firearms contributed to this preference. But perhaps more critical were great advances in surveillance devices and the elaborate security measures taken to defend national and world leaders. Quite simply, it became more and more dangerous to target soldiers, police, and political leaders, and increasingly even economic magnates or religious figures. Contemporary theorists also argued that any member of a dominant society was an active agent of evil, and therefore a legitimate victim.

Technological change affected the nature of terrorist operations in other important ways. The spread of communications technologies such as the telephone and television, complex networks for delivering electric power and fuels like natural gas, and nuclear reactors and centers of scientific experimentation created a whole new range of what have often proved to be very vulnerable targets. Trains, buses, and airplanes have also become tempting objects for capture or destruction at the hands of hijackers and bombers. Finally, invention and scientific experimentation have made a whole new generation of terrorist weapons feasible, including gases like Sarin, which wreaked havoc on Tokyo's subways, toxic bacterial agents like anthrax, and miniaturized nuclear devices that, theoretically at least, can be packed in the proverbial suitcase and carried into the heart of major urban centers.

Between the 1970s and the 1990s, these shifts in science and technology greatly reduced the odds of success in operations aimed at well-defended leaders, government institutions, or military organizations. This situation turned unarmed civilians going about their daily lives into ever more tempting targets for terrorists with guns or bombs. The emergence of suicide bombers, particularly in the 1990s, made this pattern even more disturbing. Terrorist organizations were confident that these attacks would serve several purposes. To begin with, they dramatically publicized the grievances that inspired armed resistance. Highly lethal attacks on civilians were also seen to destabilize target societies and deprive citizens of the sense of security required to live productive and fulfilled lives. Both outcomes, in turn, were believed to discredit targeted political regimes. The dissident groups who launched the assaults hoped they would weaken governments in power to the point where they would either make major concessions or prove vulnerable to even more ambitious attempts to overthrow them.

These expected outcomes have very rarely come to pass. In fact, indiscriminate terrorist acts have usually outraged public and world opinion and obscured or distorted the causes that dissident groups were attempting to publicize. They have also greatly enhanced the latitude of retaliatory responses open to national governments and international agencies as well as public support for these measures. This has been true even in situations where large numbers of new civilian casualties occurred as a result. Equally critical, the terrorists' willingness to launch mass assaults on innocent civilians has tended to be equated with religious fanaticism or political radicalism that is so extreme as to preclude negotiation and even rational explanation. As a consequence, violent repression has very often been deemed the only viable response to the death and suffering visited upon innocent civilians by terrorist true believers.

These shifts in the nature and targets of terrorist assaults between the pre–World War I era and the last decades of the 20th century have in most instances greatly increased the cost in human lives and property. The magnitude of these losses has also been linked to the growing globalization of terrorist networks. This has meant a proliferation of complex linkages between dissident groups in different nations and regions, who are very often espousing radically different causes. Perhaps most sobering in this regard was the way in which the attacks on September 11, 2001, demonstrated the possibilities for well-funded and organized terrorist groups to turn highly advanced civilian technologies, embodied in modern passenger planes, into appallingly lethal weapons that could be aimed at innocent and unsuspecting civilian victims. The collapse of the World Trade Towers after each had been struck by hijacked airliners also revealed the vulnerability of even the most imposing modern buildings to this sort of assault. The nearly simultaneous crash of another airliner into the Pentagon demonstrated that even the headquarters of the world's most powerful military organization was not immune to terrorist attack. These events may mark a fundamental shift in the nature of violent protest and warfare that will be played out in the century to come.

QUESTIONS

- What are some of the specific technologies that have shaped changes in terrorist operations over the 20th century?
- What sorts of systems and devices have been used by states and military organizations to counter these shifts?
- In what instances have terrorist organizations been successful politically?
- Is terrorism likely to become the dominant mode of warfare in the 21st century?

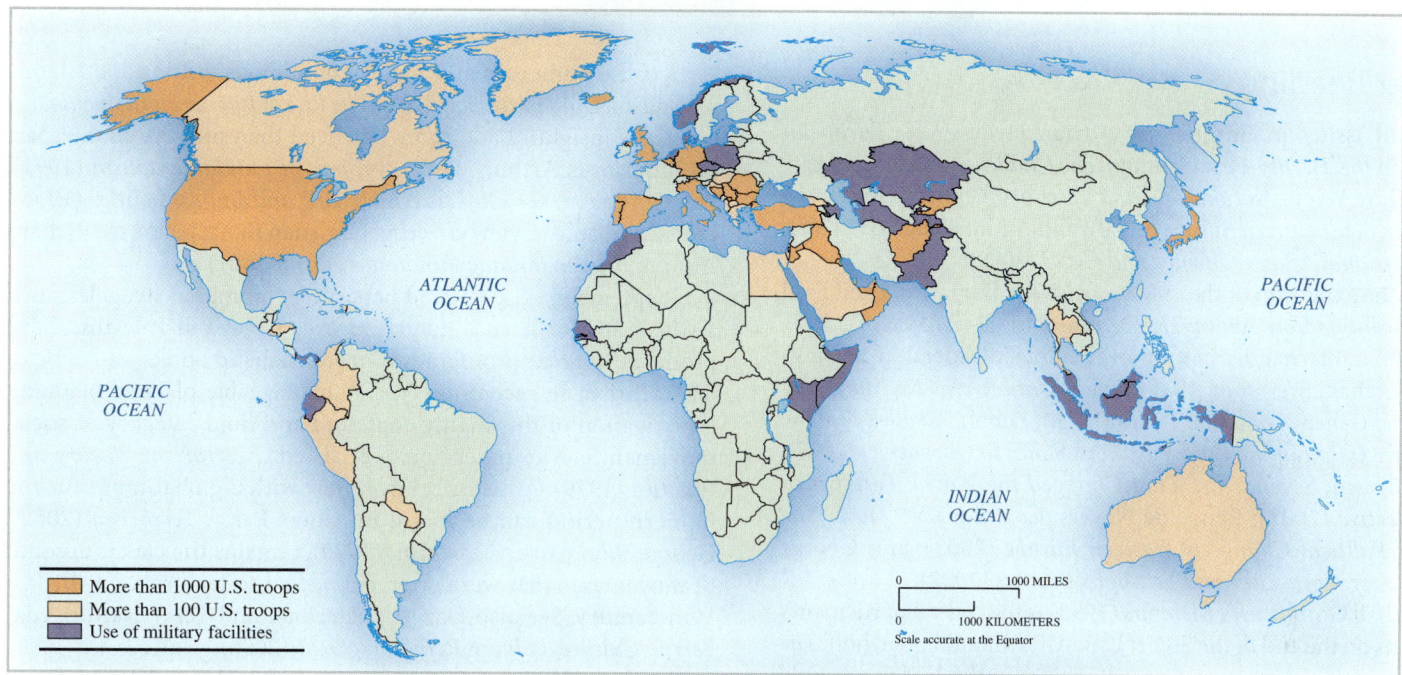

MAP 36.3 **Main U.S. Overseas Military Installations by 2007**

Evidence for these charges proved largely erroneous, and world opinion turned heavily against the American move, with millions of demonstrators protesting the impending war in February 2003. But the United States, joined by several allies, including Britain, invaded and quickly conquered the country. The ensuing occupation, however, was extremely troubled, as the United States had difficulty restoring order against a variety of insurgents. In 2009, with Iraq somewhat calmer, American attention turned back to Afghanistan and also to the growing strength of radical groups in Pakistan. American forces left Iraq in 2011, and were scheduled to leave Afghanistan in 2014. The wars proved costly and may have distracted United States' attention from other global issues.

Global Connections and Critical Themes

NEW GLOBAL STANDARDS, NEW DIVISIONS

The end of the cold war reduced divisions in the world and dramatically lowered the danger of all-out nuclear war. The larger spread of democracy also suggested new kinds of global linkages and agreements. A few optimistic observers argued that there would be an "end of history"—that democracy and peace would predominate, ending the contentious historical processes that had defined the human experience since the dawn of civilization.

But the escalation of regional conflicts, with their tragic violence and dislocation, argued against this kind of optimism. Democracy was spreading, but not winning everywhere, and peaceful solutions to many tensions seemed impossible to achieve. The emergence of the United States as the sole superpower also caused much ambivalence. On the one hand, the disproportion of American power gave the nation true global influence. On the other hand, reactions to this power, and American uses of it, raised new disputes. The United States did not in fact have the power to reshape the world. Its policies raised new tensions with segments of Islam. The military confrontation between the United States and terrorism was far different from that of the cold war, but the deep ideological roots of the hostilities seemed distressingly familiar to some observers.

Further Readings

On recent issues in Europe, see Adrian Hyde-Price, *European Security in the Twenty-First Century: The Challenge of Multipolarity* (2007); G. W. White, *Nationalism and Territory: Constructing Group Identity in Southeastern Europe* (2000); and Andrew Valls, ed., *Ethics in International Affairs: Themes and Cases* (2000).

For the explosion of the 1980s and 1990s, David Kotz and Fred Weir, *Revolution from Above: The Demise of the Soviet System* (1997), explores the internal dissolution of the Soviet leadership. See also Alexei Yurchak, *Everything Was Forever, Until It Was No More: The Last Soviet Generation* (2006); Vladislav M. Zubok, *A Failed Empire: The Soviet Union in the Cold War from Stalin to Gorbachev* (2007); Archie Brown, *Seven Years That Changed the World: Perestroika in Perspective* (2007); Renée de Nevers, *Comrades No More: The Seeds of Political Change in Eastern Europe* (2003); and George W. Breslauer, *Gorbachev and Yeltsin as Leaders* (2002).

Mikhail Gorbachev's *Memoirs* (1995) is the central participant's reflections on the end of the Soviet Union. Raymond L. Garthoff, *The Great Transition: American-Soviet Relations at the End of the Cold War* (1994), provides the foreign policy context. Karen Dawisha and Bruce Parrott, eds., *The Consolidation of Democracy in East-Central Europe* (1997), discusses recent experiences in the direction of democratization and includes a country-by-country survey.

Nanette Funk and Magda Mueller, *Gender Politics and Post-Communism: Reflections from Eastern Europe and the Former Soviet Union* (1993), deals with women's role in the transition. Tina Rosenberg, *The Haunted Land: Facing Europe's Ghosts After Communism* (1995), is an engaging narrative that explores the legacies of repression in Germany, Poland, and the Czech Republic. Also see Paul Hockenos, *Free to Hate: The Rise of the Right in Post-Communist Eastern Europe* (1994).

For a detailed, long-term historical perspective on the successive conflicts in the Balkans, see Misha Glenny, *The Balkans: Nationalism, War, and the Great Powers, 1804–1999* (2000); and Sabrina Ramet and Vjeran Pavlakovíc, eds., *Serbia Since 1989: Politics and Society under Milosevic and After* (2005). On the religious dimensions of the Yugoslavian wars, see the essays in Paul Mojzes, ed., *Religion and War in Yugoslavia* (1998). On the successive conflicts of the mid-1990s more specifically, see Misha Glenny, *The Fall of Yugoslavia* (1992); Laura Silber and Allan Little, *Yugoslavia: Death of a Nation* (1995); Tim Judah, *Kosovo: War and Revenge* (2000); and Noel Malcolm, *Kosovo* (1998). From the very substantial literature that has developed on the Rwanda crisis, Gérard Prunier, *The Rwanda Crisis: History of a Genocide* (1999), is one of the most detailed accounts, and Mahmood Mamdani, *When Victims Become Killers* (2001), is an interesting analysis of the conflict's larger political and philosophical implications. Levon Chorbajian and George Shirinian, *Studies in Comparative Genocide* (1999), is a good place to begin an exploration of the darker side of 20th-century history.

Of the numerous and highly contentious writings on Islamic revivalism, Dilip Hiro, *Holy Wars: The Rise of Islamic Fundamentalism* (1989), is insightful and more balanced than most. A counterpart on Judaism is Arthur Hertzberg, *Jewish Fundamentalism* (1991). For Hinduism, see Gurdas Ahuja, *BJP and Indian Politics* (1994). For a comparative view covering Christian movements, see Richard Antoun, *Understanding Fundamentalism* (2001).

September 11, 2001, and persisting communal struggles, such as those in Northern Ireland and over Israel and Palestine, have produced a great proliferation of journalistic books and articles on terrorism in recent decades. A manageable place to begin an investigation of this highly contested and fluid category of social movement is Alexander Yonan et al., eds., *Terrorism: Theory and Practice* (1979). A historical overview with a global range for the modern period can be found in Albert Parry, *Terrorism* (2002). George Woodcock, *Anarchism* (1970), remains the classic account of movements that were often connected to terrorism in the late 19th century. See also Daniel J. Sherman and Terry Nardin, eds., *Terror, Culture, Politics: Rethinking 9/11* (2006).

A very substantial literature has developed on the 1991 Persian Gulf War. The essays in Ibrahim Ibrahim, ed., *The Gulf Crisis* (1992) provide a good historical introduction to the conflict. Two of the better general accounts of the war itself are Lawrence Freedman and Efraim Karsh, *The Gulf Conflict, 1990–1991* (1993); and Michael Gordon and Bernard Trainor, *The General's War* (1995). An Arab viewpoint on the conflict is provided in Mohamed Heikal, *Illusions of Triumph* (1992), and a strong critique of the media coverage and technowar aspects of the conflict is the focus of *The Persian Gulf TV War* (1992) by Douglas Kellner.

For a provocative and detailed account of U.S. interventionism since the end of the cold war, a good place to begin is David Halberstam, *War in a Time of Peace* (2001). See also Charles Maier, *Among Empires: American Ascendancy and Its Predecessors* (2006). Less compellingly written, but useful for differing perspectives, is Lester Brune, *The United States and Post-Cold War Interventions* (1998). On specific flashpoints that provoked extensive international involvement and policy debate in the United States and elsewhere, some of the best work is on Somalia, including Mark Bowden's superb recounting of the mission in crisis in *Black Hawk Down* (1990) and Jonathan Stevenson's more policy-oriented *Losing Mogadishu* (1995).

Recent work includes *Congressional Quarterly, World at Risk: A Global Issues Sourcebook* (2002); Ronnie Lipshutz, *After Authority: War, Peace, and Global Politics in the 21st Century* (2000); Stanley Brunn, *11 September and Its Aftermath: The Geopolitics of Terror* (2004); Lee Harris, *Civilization and Its Enemies: The Next Stage of History* (2004); Ronald Glossop, *Confronting War: An Examination of Humanity's Most Pressing Problem* (2001); Barbara Walter and Jack Snyder, eds., *Civil Wars, Insecurity, and Intervention* (1999); and Immanuel Wallerstein, *The Decline of American Power: The U.S. in a Chaotic World* (2003).

On MyHistoryLab

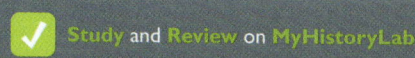

Critical Thinking Questions

1. What were the main causes of the end of the cold war?
2. Compare reactions to democracy in China and Latin America at the end of the 20th century. What caused the key differences?
3. Was there any dominant theme in the regional conflicts that surfaced after 1990?
4. Discuss the major continuities in Russian and in United States politics and policies from the cold war to the 1990s and 2000s.
5. Will some form of democracy become a global pattern? Why, or why not?

37

Globalization and Resistance

Listen to Chapter 37 on MyHistoryLab

LEARNING OBJECTIVES

37.1 What were the differences in the industrial map of the world in 2014, compared to 1950? p. 919

37.2 What caused the acceleration of globalization in the later 20th century? p. 922

37.3 How has globalization changed the human–environment relationship? p. 929

37.4 What were the main changes and continuities in religion in the contemporary period of world history? p. 932

37.5 What predictions about the future are particularly plausible, and why? p. 936

A recent movie about a family in Kerala (a state in southern India) makes the point inescapably. A baby girl is turned over to her "good" brother for care: He lives in the village and provides for her a simple, idyllic life. But when she enters college, she goes to the city to live with a childless aunt and uncle. They shower her with new clothes, including blue jeans, Western-style skirts, and cosmetics. She enters and wins a college beauty pageant. She gets in with a heavy-drinking, rowdy group of men and is disgraced—finally returning to the village where, in shame, she assumes the traditional costume.

By the early 21st century, Kerala had become a scene of quiet cultural struggle. Many residents worked abroad, mainly in the Persian Gulf. Television Channel V, the Indian version of MTV, piped in Japanese, Filipino, and Arab as well as Indian music, with disk jockeys—all women

FIGURE **37.1** Indian university students in New Delhi protest India's hosting of the Indian Miss World contest by burning contestants in effigy. Like these students, some Indian conservatives see beauty pageants as decadent imports from the West that are destructive of their culture's traditional values.

of Indian origin from Britain or North America—speaking English. All of this provided new levels of contact with the outside world. Growing interest in novel consumer standards formed part of this change. A word derived from lower-caste slang, *chetu*, came to mean "cool"—denoting jeans, cars, a new motorbike. But debate and opposition surfaced as well. A local Coca-Cola bottling plant, for example, was accused of contaminating the water.

Concern about beauty pageants formed part of the cultural mix. Beauty pageants had spread widely on the subcontinent after an Indian woman won the Miss Universe contest in the 1990s. Hindu nationalists, however, condemned the contests, arguing that "In India, the woman is not meant to be sold" (Figure 37.1). In Kerala, local officials attempted a compromise effort to hold a pageant in which women would be assessed for their beauty, but in traditional costume and with accompanying tests of knowledge of Keralan culture. In this case, the compromise failed because the women who wanted to be in beauty parades did not have the cultural knowledge, while those who had the knowledge shunned the beauty contest part. It was a confusing situation, with change and continuity warring for dominance and dividing the people of Kerala. ∎

The later 20th century saw renewed intensification of globalization. By the 1950s jet travel became increasingly routine. Several postwar agreements, such as the establishment of the International Monetary Fund, facilitated global economic contacts. Despite the cold war—and after all, both sides in this conflict had a global outlook—globalization gained ground after 1950, following the decades of partial retreat between the world wars.

But the end of the cold war unquestionably freed up new energy for global contacts. China, in 1978, and then Russia under Gorbachev opened to wider interactions. Another development both facilitated and reflected the latest surge of globalization: the expansion of industrial economies from their previous base in the West and the Pacific Rim to a host of additional countries. Although huge regional inequalities remained, essential industrialization itself globalized, and this encouraged still further contacts.

GLOBAL INDUSTRIALIZATION

37.1 What were the differences in the industrial map of the world in 2014, compared to 1950?

By the 1980s and 1990s, several key countries were able to go beyond earlier first steps, for example in import substitution, to expand industrial output and compete successfully in global export markets. In the case of China, previous experience with Mao Zedong's efforts at industrial growth, the "Great Leap Forward" after 1958, even though they had failed in the short run, provided similar impetus.

The countries involved were still in the "developing" category—Chinese leaders in the early 21st century like to call their country the world's largest developing economy, in contrast with the United States as the largest developed entry. They continued to take advantage of relatively low wages to help spur further growth. Many continued to host large number of foreign firms, seeking to take advantage of favorable pay scales and regulations. It was always possible that some future setbacks might reverse the patterns of the 1990s and early 2000s—skeptics warned, for example, of the burdens of unquestionably growing environmental pollution and the possibility of social unrest from the labor force amid potential resentments of a visibly growing, affluent middle class. But most observers anticipated further growth in most if not all of the newcomers. And there was no question that

> The decades on either side of 2000 saw a major reversal of the pattern of the first wave of industrialization in the 19th century. The share of industrial manufacturing in the economies of early industrializing nations in the West and Japan shrank while it spread and expanded rapidly in developing societies from China and India to Mexico, Brazil, and Turkey.

the rates of annual expansion, often at 10 percent or more a year, were propelling key economies toward the levels of the most established industrial nations, even though they had yet to reach that mark. Trajectories recalled the previous advance of the Pacific Rim, but over much larger stretches of territory and population ranges.

Mexico, Turkey, and Brazil, for example, began to enter the ranks of significant industrial exporters by the 1980s. Factory textiles in Turkey, for example, became competitive in world trade, with significant exports to nations such as Germany, the nation became the second most industrial country in the Middle East, after Israel. Brazil's steel industry exported successfully to the United States, and Brazilian and Korean steel combined to dent American production by the late 1970s. Governments in Mexico, Turkey, and Brazil eagerly backed industrial development, beginning their support in the 1920s (in Turkey's case) and the 1930s (in Brazil and Mexico). Government sponsorship of industry included carefully negotiated trade arrangements with other regions, active solicitation of foreign aid and investment, and support for technical training and infrastructure.

Brazil's computer industry was a striking success story: A nation well behind the world's industrial leaders deliberately fostered an industry capable of serving the nation's computer needs and so avoided yet another dependence on expensive imports. Governmental regulations protected this new Brazilian industry, and heavily supported computer engineers at the technical university in São Paulo constructed independent computer prototypes. Although the industry itself developed only in the 1970s, it clearly built on Brazil's earlier commitment to industrial growth and technological progress. The engineering group at São Paulo thus stemmed from earlier advances in university science and technology, including nuclear physics; Brazil by the 1970s was producing 3 percent of the scientific articles in international physics journals. Beginning in 1959 the government had supported computer research directly, in connection with the Brazilian navy. Training in advanced electronics expanded steadily. Imports of advanced Western military equipment spurred a growing interest in computers, and collaborative programs were developed with U.S. universities. By 1971 Brazil was ready to develop its own computer model, in partial imitation of European prototypes. A variety of small companies linked to the university center in São Paulo then developed to produce computers. Brazilian computer production depended on imports of microchips from other areas, including Japan; this was not an isolated national industry. But the Brazilian computer industry did demonstrate that prior technical progress, careful government sponsorship, and a growing awareness of production and export opportunities could cause a genuine industrial breakthrough even in an economy that was, in terms of overall standards, still struggling to industrialize.

Not surprisingly, this industrial surge provided Brazil with the highest annual economic growth rates in Latin America—over 6 percent per year by the 1960s and 1970s. Standards of living improved accordingly. By 1990, 22 percent of all Brazilians owned cars, 56 percent had television sets, and 63 percent had refrigerators. These levels were well below those in the advanced industrial nations, to be sure, but were actually higher than rates in eastern Europe.

Overall, industrialization in Mexico, Brazil, and Turkey showed a steady buildup during the later 20th century, followed by even more solid success after 2000. By this point, industrial expansion seemed to be self-sustaining, much as the Pacific Rim had achieved a few decades earlier. Slowing rates of population growth facilitated improvements in living standards as well. The result formed part of a picture of substantial global industrialization during this most recent phase of industrial history.

China and India

In broad outline, developments in the two giant nations of Asia were similar, with clear industrial breakthroughs by the 1990s. The result was an even more massive rebalancing of the world economy. At the same time, each nation carved out its own particular path.

China became one of the world's great industrial producers, replacing Japan as the number two in overall earnings behind the United States by 2010—but after several decades of experimentation and recovery. The nation's strategy shifted after Mao's death, in what amounted to a policy revolution as it embraced globalization for the first time. In 1978 China began to adopt a more flexible and conventional industrialization strategy. Exports were promoted, and foreign technical advice was eagerly sought. Despite China's commitment to communism, including considerable state planning and a fiercely authoritarian government, private business sectors were encouraged in agriculture and industry. Some rural industry persisted, but urban production was emphasized as China worked to recover familiarity with advanced technology. Economic growth rates boomed in the 1980s, and

China, thanks to its size, became a considerable industrial force. Not only factories but also roads and railroads expanded rapidly. By the 1990s the nation's economic output was growing by 10 percent per year. In 2003, China used a full half of the world's production of concrete, for factories, housing, and infrastructure expansion.

Industrial growth in China, as in other evolving economies, brought new wealth to many people. A new group of rich entrepreneurs surfaced in China, complete with symbols of high consumer standards, including television sets and tape recorders. Even many villagers enjoyed bicycles and other new products. Other industrial fruits were less palatable. Pollution levels in many countries surpassed those of the West and Japan. Chinese cities were choked with industrial gases, called the Yellow Dragon, and the chemical pollution of water sources was considerable. Industrial evolution had more than local pollution effects. By 2000 China's industrial advance, combined with its huge population, placed China in second position as a world contributor to the chemical emissions causing global warming. The growing use of coal for fuel (as China became the world's largest coal-mining nation) promised a further Chinese advance on this dubious achievement scale, as Chinese policy frankly placed economic growth ahead of environmental concerns.

China's expansion remained mixed. It depended heavily on cheap labor, plus continued pressure on the large peasant class. Hundreds of thousands of workers from the countryside took up industrial jobs without fully abandoning village ties. Multinational companies set up low-cost factory operations in China as in Mexico. Chinese exports were impressive, but they involved primarily inexpensive factory products like toys (China was filling almost half the U.S. toy market by the 1990s), as well as growing inroads in high technology. At the same time, however, China's rapid surge, combined with the growth of the Pacific Rim, caused some observers to wonder whether a vast new east Asian industrial complex was emerging, following Japan's initial lead. They noted that the area continued to emphasize modified Confucian values, which include hard work, discipline, loyalty, and education, along with forceful governments.

India's industrial growth was steadier than China's after World War II, but took a new turn slightly later, in the 1990s. Again, a government decision to loosen economic regulation in favor of more open competition was involved, although India had always had considerable private business. As in the other major cases of later 20th-century industrialization, finally, India's economy continued to display mixed signals.

With a liberalization of the economy after 1992, India increasingly added high-technology products, particularly software, exporting to both the industrial countries and southeast Asia. Using English-language as well as high-technology skills, India also entered the global service sector, with both Indian and multinational firms organizing operations that provided sales and telephone services to the entire English-speaking world. By the early 21st century, the country boasted a large middle class (80 million or more), complete with extensive consumer interests. Economic growth reached 9 percent per year.

Thus by 2000 it was increasingly clear that real industrial revolutions were underway in a number of new-old regimes. In China and India, the result began to return some of the world's traditional manufacturing powers to a lead position in the global economy, although on a far different basis from the strengths they had developed before the industrial era. Places like Brazil and Mexico gained a manufacturing position that was even more novel, from a historical standpoint.

Older Industrial Centers

The rise of industrial newcomers inevitably challenged older centers, most obviously the West and Japan. China and other regions took over many manufacturing staples, as their exports and export earnings expanded steadily. New competition also arose for resources. China and India increasingly turned to places like Africa in search of oil and other raw materials. This tended to drive prices up for all industrial countries and also created significant rivalries for the attention of African and Middle Eastern business and political leaders.

The older industrial centers retained great advantages. They still led in the export of some of the most high-technology products and also in services such as banking and finance. They also continued to profit from industrial designs, even though the actual fabrication might occur elsewhere. In 2011 the Chinese premier noted that he would be happiest when product labels, instead of saying "made in China" shifted to "created in China."

Inevitably, however, the relative growth rates of the older centers lagged, as the relative balance shifted. German growth—in a country that retained a significant high-tech manufacturing sector—was only a third of the Chinese rate, even in good times. Some countries also seemed to falter a bit, even aside from the changes in relative balance. The Japanese economy generated only sluggish growth from the 1990s onward. A global financial recession that began in 2008 also highlighted slow growth rates in much of Western Europe, while forecasts even for the United States were not robust. Many of the older centers faced painful choices about cutting back levels of welfare support, because their economies did not keep pace amid growing competition.

GLOBALIZATION: CAUSES AND PROCESSES

37.2 What caused the acceleration of globalization in the later 20th century?

> Globalization is a result of political, demographic, and cultural as well as technological changes. Economic globalization itself involves unprecedented interconnection among the world's peoples.

The spread of industrial economies not only contributed to the renewal of globalization; it also made the process less Western-centered than it had been previously, although regional imbalances persisted to some extent. Rapid globalization also spurred various types of resistance, both old and new. Different kinds of complexities resulted in global relationships.

What Globalization Means

globalization The increasing interconnectedness of all parts of the world, particularly in communication and commerce but also in culture and politics.

Globalization as a concept developed in the 1990s. At heart, it means the intensification of contacts among all major parts of the world, such that larger influences play a growing role in human life, from trade to culture to physical well-being. Even older kinds of interchange, like migration or disease, are partially redefined. Globalization means, also, the expansion of international influences, beyond familiar aspects like commerce or formal diplomacy to include political institutions, the environment, even elements of crime.

Globalization emerged, of course, from previous patterns of interregional contact. We have seen how connections among Africa, Asia, and Europe increased with the intercontinental network of the postclassical period. This was a move toward later globalization, but it was not globalization in itself. The whole world was not yet involved; levels of exchange increased but still had limited impact even on economic activity. Imitation of other societies increased, but not yet around standards that could be regarded as global. The expansion of the world religions came closest here, but none achieved full global standing. The early modern period intensified connections and did bring the whole world together for the first time. Cultural impacts were limited, however. International trading companies arose, but except in a few colonial settings they did not have the deep local effects that later, multinational companies would generate.

An initial version of globalization emerged in the later 19th century. It depended on dramatic new technologies, and also policy decisions, spearheaded by Western imperialist powers, to increase economic interdependence around the world. But this first surge did not bring uniform benefits, and the middle decades of the 20th century saw many societies attempt to limit their contacts with globalization. The United States remained an active economic participant, but tried to limit political involvement through the policy of isolation in the 1920s and 1930s. Japan and Germany strove to form their own economic systems, apart from fully global exchange. Under Stalin and later Mao Zedong, Russia and China pulled away culturally and economically.

By the later 20th century, however, forces of globalization again seized center stage. Technologies were crucial: From airplanes and radio on to satellite transmission and the Internet, the speed and volume of global communication and transportation moved ahead rapidly. Policy decisions entered in as well, for by the 21st century only a few small nations attempted isolation. Tentatively, growing numbers of people around the world became accustomed to global connections. The spread of English as a world language, although incomplete and often resented, was part of this connection. English served airline travel, many sports, and the early Internet as a common language. This encouraged and reflected other facets of global change.

Although globalization suggests growing uniformities around the world, it was still not, however, a uniform process. Different regions encountered globalization differently—by 2008 only about a third of the world's population had direct access to the Internet, and globalization was a remote force for many rural regions in south Asia or sub-Saharan Africa. Different regions also saw different patterns of benefit or harm. In some regions, globalization increased unemployment and economic dislocation; in many places, the process seemed to promote new levels of economic inequality (a pattern visible in the two past decades in the United States, Europe, India, and China). By the early 21st century several Latin American countries were questioning whether global trading patterns were bringing economic benefits to their regions or whether separate national economic policies might make more sense. Everywhere, furthermore, globalization challenges an established sense of identity, and many people resent this challenge deeply.

The New Technology

A globalization guru tells the following story. In 1988 a U.S. government official traveling to Chicago was assigned a limousine with a cellular phone. He was so delighted to have this novelty that he called his wife just to brag. Nine years later, in 1997, the same official was visiting a remote village in Côte d'Ivoire, in west Africa, that was accessible only by dugout canoe. As he prepared to leave, a Côte d'Ivoire official told him he had a call from Washington and handed him a cellular phone. Cellular phones, increasingly common, were among the key new communication devices that, by the 1990s, had made almost constant contact with other parts of the world feasible, and for some people unavoidable. Western Europe and east Asia led in the cellular phone revolution, but people in all parts of the world participated.

During the 1980s steady improvements in miniaturization made computers increasingly efficient. By the 1990s the amount of information that could be stored on microchips increased by more than 60 percent each year. Linkages among computers improved as well, starting with halting efforts in the 1960s mainly for defense purposes. Email was introduced in 1972. In 1990 a British software engineer working in Switzerland, Tim Berners, developed the World Wide Web, and the true age of the Internet was born. Almost instantaneous contact by computer became possible around the world, and with it came the capacity to send vast amounts of information, from text, to videos and other imagery, to music. While the Internet was not available to everyone—by 2012 only 35 percent of the world's population had access—it did provide global contacts for some otherwise fairly remote regions. In eastern Russia, for example, international mail service was agonizingly slow, telephone access often interrupted—but a student could sit at an Internet cafe in Vladivostok and communicate easily with friends in the United States or Brazil. By 2009, further development in computer-based networking included systems like Facebook and Twitter, which again could facilitate personal connections around the world.

Satellite linkages for television formed a final communications revolution, making simultaneous broadcasts possible around the world. A full quarter of the world's population now could, and sometimes did, watch the same sporting event—usually World Cup soccer or the Olympics—a phenomenon never before possible or even approachable in world history. Global technology gained new meaning.

Economic Globalization: Business Organization and Investment

Thanks in part to new technology, in part to more open political boundaries, international investment accelerated rapidly at the end of the 20th century. Stock exchanges featured holdings in Chinese utilities or Brazilian steel companies as well as the great corporations of the West and Japan. U.S. investments abroad multiplied rapidly, almost doubling in the first half of the 1970s. By the 1980s foreign operations were generating between 25 and 40 percent of all corporate profits in the United States. Japan's foreign investment rose 15-fold during the 1970s. During the 1980s Japanese car manufacturers set up factories in the United States, Europe, and other areas. German cars, French tires, German chemicals and pharmaceuticals, and Dutch petroleum all had substantial U.S. operations. At the end of the 1990s the German Volkswagen firm introduced an updated version of the automobile affectionately known as the "bug," whose initial design went back to Hitler's Germany. Its production facilities were entirely based in Mexico, but it was marketed in the United States and around the world.

Globalization in business involved rapid increases in exports and imports, the extension of business organization across political boundaries—resulting in **multinational corporations**—and division of labor on a worldwide basis (Map 37.1). Cars that were made in the United States were assembled from parts made in Japan, Korea, Mexico, and elsewhere. Japanese cars often had more

multinational corporations
Powerful companies, mainly from the West or Pacific Rim, with production as well as distribution operations in many different countries. Multinationals surged in the decades after World War II.

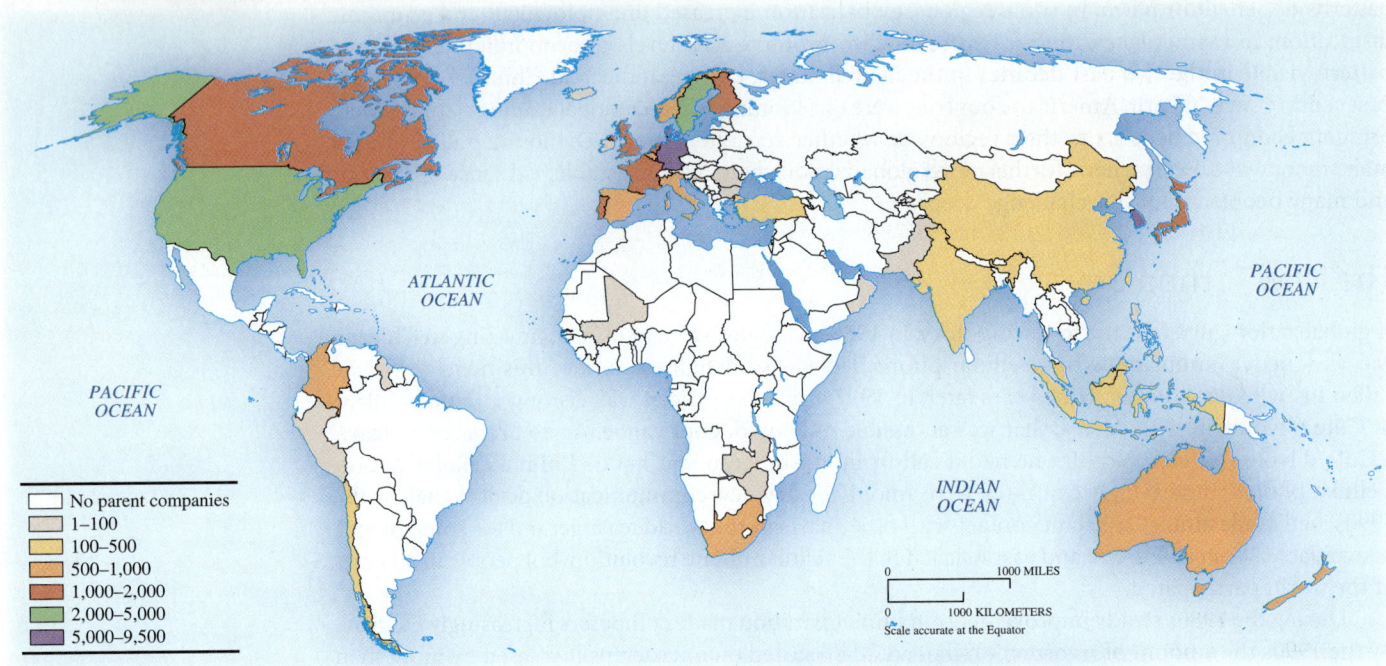

MAP 37.1 **Multinational Corporations in 2000** By the end of the 20th century, multinational companies had become a major force for economic change and political controversy over much of the world. As this map illustrates, these engines of globalization were especially prominent in mature industrial and more affluent societies, and much less in evidence in formerly colonized or communist countries.

American-made parts in them than Detroit products had. Firms set up operations not simply to produce closer to markets to save transportation costs; they also sought to reduce costs by looking for cheap labor and minimal environmental regulations. Computer boards were made by West Indian and African women. India developed a huge software industry, subcontracting for firms in the United States and western Europe. The linkages were dazzling.

International firms continued to seek cheap raw materials. For example, companies in Japan and the West competed for access to oil and minerals in the newly independent nations of central Asia after the collapse of the Soviet Union. China's rapid economic growth prompted active arrangements for oil supplies from Central Asia, Latin America and Africa, as well as the Middle East. International investments also followed interest rates. During the 1990s relatively attractive U.S. interest rates drew extensive investment from Europe, Japan, and the oil-rich regions in the Middle East.

While multinational corporations sometimes faced government regulation, many of them had more power, and far more resources, than the governments of most of the countries within which they operated. Thus, they could determine most aspects of labor and environmental policy. They could and did pull up stakes in one region if more attractive opportunities opened elsewhere, regardless of the impact on the workers and facilities they left behind. Early in the 21st century, for example, many multinationals pulled jobs from Mexico in favor of expansion to China or Vietnam, where wages were lower. Even clerical jobs were outsourced: Telephone services for many American companies, for example, were set up in India, where wages were lower and English was widely spoken. The spread of multinationals promoted industrial skills in many previously agricultural regions and depended on improvements in communications and transportation that could bring wider changes for the people of the lands in which they hired workers (Figure 37.2).

FIGURE 37.2 Change and continuity in rural India. New irrigation and electrification combine with traditional methods of tilling the soil as agricultural production rises.

American factories located in northern Mexico, designed to produce goods for sale back in the United States, showed the complexity of the new international economy. The owners of these factories unquestionably sought cheap labor and lax regulations. Their factories often leaked chemical waste. Wages were barely 10 percent of what U.S. workers would earn. Nonetheless, these factories often paid better than their Mexican counterparts. Many workers, including large numbers of women, found the labor policies more enlightened and the foremen better behaved in the foreign firms. A key question, not yet answerable, is whether the poverty-level wages for workers in such factories will improve and whether the industrial skills they learn will make possible a widening range of opportunities.

Efforts to tally the overall economic effects of globalization are complex and contested. Some parts of Africa lost traditional manufacturing jobs to new global competition, and in these regions, unemployment rates of 30 percent or more were common. Prostitution, including new international sex trafficking in women and children, and even the sale of body organs, showed the increasingly desperate poverty in some societies. Not only global competition but reductions in government services, in the name of free-market principles, contributed to new problems. In south and southeast Asia, rates of child labor rose, although the larger global patterns were different. On the other hand, new global opportunities permitted an increase in per capita income in places like China and India. Growth rates in several parts of Africa after 2000 were also encouraging.

It was clear that there were winners and losers in economic globalization, both among different parts of the world and within individual societies—even within industrial societies like the United States. Gaps widened between the poor and those with higher incomes. A growing middle class developed in Latin America, India, and China, but urban slums and exploited labor expanded as well.

Migration

Broad international patterns of migration had developed by the 1950s and 1960s, with the use of "guest workers" from Turkey and north Africa in Europe, for example. Here, patterns in the 1990s built clearly on previous trends. But easier travel, along with the continued gap between slowly growing populations in the industrial countries and rapidly growing populations in Latin America, Africa, and parts of Asia, maintained high levels of exchange. A few areas, including Italy, Greece, and Japan, had almost ceased internal population growth by the 1990s, which meant that new labor needs, particularly at the lower skill levels, had to be supplied by immigration.

Japan hoped to avoid too much influx by relying on high-technology solutions, but even here worker groups were brought in from the Philippines and southeast Asia. Migration into Europe and the United States was far more extensive, producing truly multinational populations in key urban and commercial centers. By 2000 at least 25 percent of all Americans, mostly people of color, came from households where English was not the first language. Ten percent of the French population in 2003 was Muslim (Figure 37.3). Here was an important source of tension, with local populations often fearing foreigners and worried about job competition. Here also was a new opportunity, not just for new laborers but for new cultural inspiration.

Migration was hardly new in world history. But new levels of migration from distant regions had novel qualities. So did the resulting mixture of migrants and locals in the cities of North America, western Europe, or the Persian Gulf states of the Middle East. So, finally, did the new facility of traveling back and forth: Many migrants, returning home to Turkey or India on vacation or permanently, brought back new styles and ideas, maintaining their own commitment to at least two different cultures.

Cultural Globalization

Thanks in part to global technologies and business organization, plus reduced political barriers, the pace of cultural exchange and contact around the world accelerated at the end of the 1990s. Much of this involved mass consumer goods, spread from the United States, western Europe, and Japan. But art shows, symphony exchanges, scientific conferences, and Internet contact increased as well. Music conductors and artists held posts literally around the world, sometimes juggling commitments among cities like Tokyo, Berlin, and Chicago within a single season. Science laboratories filled with researchers from around the world, collaborating (usually in English) with little regard for national origin.

The spread of fast-food restaurants from the United States, headed by McDonald's, formed one of the most striking international cultural influences from the 1970s onward. The company began

Read the Document on MyHistoryLab: Illegal Immigration Reform and Immigrant Responsibility Act of 1996

FIGURE 37.3 The mixtures of peoples and cultures that had become a prominent feature of world history by the end of the 20th century are wonderfully illustrated by this group of Muslim schoolchildren in a French school. By 2007, more than 10 percent of the French population was Islamic. In 2006, riots broke out in Islamic areas of French cities revealing tensions over the gap between opportunities available to immigrants and those available to the majority population.

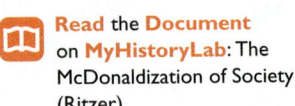

Read the Document on MyHistoryLab: The McDonaldization of Society (Ritzer)

in Illinois in 1955 and started its international career in 1967 with outlets in Canada and Puerto Rico. From then on, the company entered an average of two new nations per year and accelerated the pace in the 1990s. By 1998 it was operating in 109 countries overall. The company won quick success in Japan, where it gained its largest foreign audience; "makadonaldo" first opened in Tokyo's world famous Ginza, already known for cosmopolitan department stores, in 1971. McDonald's entry into the Soviet Union in 1990 was a major sign of the ending of cold war rivalries and the growing Russian passion for international consumer goods. The restaurants won massive patronage despite (by Russian standards) very high prices. Even in gourmet-conscious France, McDonald's and other fast-food outlets were winning 26 percent of all restaurant dining by the 1990s. Not everyone who patronized McDonald's really liked the food. Many patrons in Hong Kong, for example, said they went mainly to see and be seen and to feel part of the global world.

Cultural globalization obviously involved increasing exposure to American movies and television shows. Series like *Baywatch* won massive foreign audiences. Movie and amusement park icons like Mickey Mouse, and products and dolls derived from them, had international currency. Western beauty standards, based on the models and film stars, won wide exposure, expressed among other things in widely sought international beauty pageants. MTV spread Western images and sounds to youth audiences almost everywhere.

Holidays took on an international air. American-style Christmas trappings, including gift giving, lights, and Santa Claus, spread not only to countries of Christian background, like France, but also places like Muslim Istanbul. Northern Mexico picked up American Halloween trick-or-treating, as it displaced the more traditional Catholic observance of All Saints' Day. Muslim observance of Ramadan, the month of self-denial, began to include greeting cards and presents for children, a clear echo of new consumerism. The American jingle "happy birthday," with its implications about individualism and entertainment for children, was translated into virtually every language.

Consumer internationalization was not just American. Japanese rock groups gained wide audience. The Pokémon toy series, derived from Japanese cultural traditions, won a frenzied audience among American children in the 1990s, who for several years could not get enough. A Japanese soap opera heroine became the most admired woman in Muslim Iran. South Korea, historically hostile to Japan, proved open to popular Japanese music groups and cartoon animation, and anime also gained popularity in the United States. European popular culture, including fashion and music groups, gained large followings around the world as well. By the early 21st century, Korean popular culture, including music, gained ground rapidly throughout eastern Asia and began to penetrate the United States.

Dress was internationalized to an unprecedented extent. American-style blue jeans showed up almost everywhere. A major export item for Chinese manufacturing involved Western clothing pirated from famous brand names. A "Chinese market" in the cities of eastern Russia contained entirely Western-style items, mainly clothing and shoes.

The international expansion of middle-class consumerism also generated a global epidemic of obesity, particularly for children. Available foods increased along with more sedentary lives and entertainments, producing echoes in Shanghai and Bangalore of problems more obvious in Houston or Birmingham.

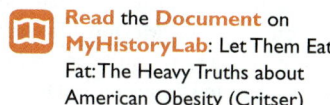

Read the Document on MyHistoryLab: Let Them Eat Fat: The Heavy Truths about American Obesity (Critser)

Cultural globalization roused extensive resistance. McDonald's became a symbol to attack by people eager to preserve local standards of food and culture; anti-McDonald's protests surged from France to South Korea. Efforts to adapt other forms of global consumer culture, like the beauty pageants, showed the interest in slowing or modifying this aspect of globalization. Some movements, at an extreme like the Taliban in Afghanistan, moved forcefully against any participation whatsoever. Contests over global culture became a standard part of life in many regions.

The penetration of cultural globalization varied—in part by wealth and urbanization, in part according to degrees of cultural tolerance. There were obvious resource limits, as in access to the Internet. Blending

DOCUMENT

Protests Against Globalization

IN DECEMBER 1999, A SERIES OF protests rocked Seattle on the occasion of a World Trade Organization (WTO) meeting designed to discuss further international tariff cuts in the interests of promoting global trade. The following passage was written by Jeffrey St. Clair, a radical journalist who is co-editor of the political newsletter *CounterPunch*. St. Clair describes the atmosphere of the Seattle protests and some of the groups involved. The Seattle protests foreshadowed a regular sequence of popular demonstrations at the meetings of such groups as the World Bank, which continue into the 21st century, involving many of the same groups and issues.

MONDAY

And the revolution will be started by: sea turtles. At noon about 2000 people massed at the United Methodist Church, the HQ of the grassroots [organizations], for a march to the convention center. It was Environment Day and the Earth Island Institute had prepared more than 500 sea turtle costumes for marchers to wear. The sea turtle became the prime symbol of the WTO's threats to environmental laws when a WTO tribunal ruled that the U.S. Endangered Species Act, which requires shrimp to be caught with turtle excluder devices, was an unfair trade barrier.

But the environmentalists weren't the only ones on the street Monday morning. In the first showing of a new solidarity, labor union members from the Steelworkers and the Longshoremen showed up to join the march. In fact, Steelworker Don Kegley led the march, alongside environmentalist Ben White. (White was later clubbed in the back of the head by a young man who was apparently angry that he couldn't do his Christmas shopping. The police pulled the youth away from White, but the man wasn't arrested. White played down the incident.) The throng of sea turtles and blue-jacketed union folk took off to the rhythm of a familiar chant that would echo down the streets of Seattle for days: "The people will never be divided!"

I walked next to Brad Spann, a Longshoreman from Tacoma, who hoisted up one of my favorite signs of the entire week: "Teamsters and Turtles Together at Last!" Brad winked at me and said, "What the hell do you think old Hoffa [former Teamster leader] thinks of that?"

The march, which was too fast and courteous for my taste, was escorted by motorcycle police and ended essentially in a cage, a protest pen next to a construction site near the convention center. A large stage had been erected there hours earlier and Carl Pope, the director of the Sierra Club, was called forth to give the opening speech. The Club is the nation's most venerable environmental group....

Standing near the stage I saw Brent Blackwelder, the head of Friends of the Earth. Behind his glasses and somewhat shambling manner, Blackwelder looks ever so professional. And he is by far the smartest of the environmental CEOs. But he is also the most radical politically, the most willing to challenge the tired complacency of his fellow green executives....

Blackwelder's speech was a good one, strong and defiant. He excoriated the WTO as a kind of global security force for transnational corporations whose mission is "to stuff unwanted products, like genetically engineered foods, down our throats." . . .

(continued on next page)

(continued from previous page)

After the speechifying most of the marchers headed back to the church. But a contingent of about 200 ended up in front of McDonald's where a group of French farmers had mustered to denounce U.S. policy on biotech foods. Their leader was José Bove, a sheep farmer from Millau in southwest France and a leader of Confederation Paysanne, a French environmental group. In August, Bove had been jailed in France for leading a raid on a McDonald's restaurant under construction in Larzac. At the time, he was already awaiting charges that he destroyed a cache of Novartis' genetically engineered corn. Bove said his raid on the Larzac McDonald's was promoted by the U.S. decision to impose a heavy tariff on Roquefort cheese in retaliation for the European Union's refusal to import American hormone-treated beef. Bove's act of defiance earned him the praise of Jacques Chirac and Friends of the Earth. Bove said he was prepared to start a militant worldwide campaign against "Frankenstein" foods. "These actions will only stop when this mad logic comes to a halt," Bove said. "I don't demand clemency but justice."

Bove showed up at the Seattle McDonald's with rounds of Roquefort cheese, which he handed out to the crowd. After listening to a rousing speech against the evils of Monsanto, and its bovine growth hormone and Roundup Ready soybeans, the crowd stormed the McDonald's breaking its windows and urging customers and workers to join the marchers on the streets. This was the first shot in the battle for Seattle.

Who were these direct action warriors on the front lines? Earth First, the Alliance for Sustainable Jobs and the Environment (the new enviro-steelworker alliance), the Ruckus Society (a direct action training center), Jobs with Justice, Rainforest Action Network, Food Not Bombs, Global Exchange, and a small contingent of Anarchists, the dreaded Black Bloc.

There was also a robust international contingent on the streets Tuesday morning: French farmers, Korean greens [environmentalists], Canadian wheat growers, Mexican environmentalists, Chinese dissidents, Ecuadorian anti-dam organizers, U'wa tribespeople from the Columbian rainforest, and British campaigners against genetically modified foods. Indeed earlier, a group of Brits had cornered two Monsanto lobbyists behind an abandoned truck carrying an ad for the *Financial Times*. They detained the corporate flacks long enough to deliver a stern warning about the threat of frankencrops to wildlife, such as the Monarch butterfly. Then a wave of tear gas wafted over them and the Monsanto men fled, covering their eyes with their neckties. . . .

As the march turned up toward the Sheraton and was beaten back by cops on horses, I teamed up with Etienne Vernet and Ronnie Cumming. Cumming is the head of one of the feistiest groups in the U.S., the PureFood Campaign, Monsanto's chief pain in the ass. Cumming hails from the oil town of Port Arthur, Texas. He went to Cambridge with another great foe of industrial agriculture, Prince Charles. Cumming was a civil rights organizer in Houston during the mid-sixties. "The energy here is incredible," Cumming said. "Black and white, labor and green, Americans, Europeans, Africans, and Asians arm in arm. It's the most hopeful I've felt since the height of the civil rights movement."

Vernet lives in Paris, where he is the leader of the radical green group EcoRopa. At that very moment the European delegates inside the convention were capitulating on a key issue: The EU, which had banned import of genetically engineered crops and hormone-treated beef, had agreed to a U.S. proposal to establish a scientific committee to evaluate the health and environmental risks of biotech foods, a sure first step toward undermining the moratorium. Still Vernet was in a jolly mood, lively and invigorated, if a little bemused by the decorous nature of the crowd. "Americans seem to have been out of practice in these things," he told me. "Everyone's so polite. The only things on fire are dumpsters filled with refuse." He pointed to a shiny black Lexus parked on Pine Street, which throngs of protesters had scrupulously avoided. In the windshield was a placard identifying it as belonging to a WTO delegate. "In Paris that car would be burning."

[David] Brower [environmental leader] was joined by David Foster, Director for District 11 of the United Steelworkers of America, one of the most articulate and unflinching labor leaders in America. Earlier this year, Brower and Foster formed an unlikely union, a coalition of radical environmentalists and Steelworkers called the Alliance for Sustainable Jobs and the Environment, which had just run an amusing ad in the *New York Times* asking, "Have You Heard the One about the Environmentalist and the Steelworker?" The groups had found they had a common enemy: Charles Hurwitz, the corporate raider. Hurwitz owned the Pacific Lumber company, the northern California timber firm that is slaughtering some of the last stands of ancient redwoods on the planet. At the same time, Hurwitz, who also controlled Kaiser Aluminum, had locked out 3000 Steelworkers at Kaiser's factories in Washington, Ohio, and Louisiana. "The companies that attack the environment most mercilessly are often also the ones that are the most anti-union," Foster told me. "More unites us than divides us."

I came away thinking that for all its promise this tenuous marriage might end badly. Brower, the master of ceremonies, isn't going to be around forever to heal the wounds and cover up the divisions. There are deep, inescapable issues that will, inevitably, pit Steelworkers, fighting for their jobs in an ever-tightening economy, against greens, defending dwindling species like sockeye salmon that are being killed off by hydrodams that power the aluminum plants that offer employment to steel workers. When asked about this potential both Brower and Foster danced around it skillfully. But it was a dance of denial. The tensions won't go away simply because the parties agree not to mention them in public. Indeed, they might even build, like a pressure cooker left unwatched. I shook the thought from my head. For this moment, the new, powerful solidarity was too seductive to let such broodings intrude for long.

From Alexander Cockburn, Jeffrey St. Clair, and Allan Sekula, *5 Days That Shook the World* (London: Verso, 2000), 16–21, 28, 29, 36–37.

QUESTIONS

- What were the principal groups involved in the globalization protests?
- Why did they feel such passion?
- Was this a global protest, or did different parts of the world have different issues?
- What were the key arguments of defenders of globalization who disapproved of this kind of protest and of its goals?

of global and local signals was another key development. Foreign models were often adapted to local customs. Thus foods in McDonald's in India (where the chain was not very popular in any event) included vegetarian items not found elsewhere. Comic books in Mexico, originally derived from U.S. models, took on Mexican cultural images, including frequent triumphs over "gringo" supermen. A host of combinations emerged. Cultural internationalization was a real development, but it was complex and incomplete.

Institutions of Globalization

On the whole, political institutions globalized less rapidly than technology or business, or even consumer culture. Many people worried about the gap between political supervision and control and the larger globalization process. UN activity accelerated a bit in the 1990s. With the end of the cold war, more diplomatic hotspots invited intervention by multinational military forces. UN forces tried to calm or prevent disputes in a number of parts of Africa, the Balkans, and the Middle East. Growing refugee populations called for UN humanitarian intervention, often aided by other international groups. UN conferences broadened their scope, dealing, for example, with gender and population control issues. While the results of the conferences were not always clear, a number of countries did incorporate international standards into domestic law. Women in many African countries, for example, were able to appeal to UN proclamations on gender equality as a basis for seeking new property rights in the courts. By 2001 the United Nations became increasingly active as well in encouraging assistance to stem the AIDS epidemic.

The World Health Organization also expanded its range directly. A threatened global outbreak of Severe Acute Respiratory Syndrome (SARS), after occurrences in east Asia and Canada in 2003, met with prompt controls under international guidance.

Another area of innovation involved international nongovernmental organizations (INGOs). Amnesty International, a London-based human rights agency, began in 1961. The 1970s saw a more rapid proliferation of humanitarian INGOs for human rights, labor, environmental, and other issues, often with networks of local affiliates. By the 1990s Internet-based petitions against torture, labor abuses, or the death penalty became standard fare, sometimes winning significant policy responses. The range of criteria for INGOs expanded steadily as well: Rape, for example, was internationally recognized as a war crime by the 1990s, a major innovation.

As more nations participated actively in international trade, the importance of organizations in this arena grew. The International Monetary Fund (IMF) and the World Bank had been founded after World War II to promote trade. Guided by the major industrial powers, these organizations offered loans and guidance to developing areas and also to regions that encountered temporary economic setbacks. Loans to Mexico and to southeast Asia during the 1990s, and again to several regions during the global recession after 2008, were intended to promote recovery from recessions that threatened to affect other areas. Loans were usually accompanied by requirements for economic reform, usually through reduced government spending, including social welfare spending, and the promotion of more open competition. These guidelines were not always welcomed by the regions involved. The IMF and the World Bank were widely viewed as primary promoters of the capitalist global economy.

Read the Document on MyHistoryLab: World Bank–Supported Day Care Programs in Uganda 1990s

Annual meetings of the heads of the seven leading industrial powers (four from Europe, two from North America, plus Japan) also promoted global trade and policies toward developing regions. After 2008, the global structure expanded to a Group of 20, including the rising economies of Asia and Latin America, an acknowledgment that leadership from the West plus Japan was no longer adequate. Finally, the regional economic arrangements that had blossomed from the 1950s onward gained growing importance as globalization accelerated. The European Union headed the list, but the North American Free Trade Agreement (NAFTA) and other regional consortiums in Latin America and east Asia also pushed for lower tariffs and greater economic coordination.

THE GLOBAL ENVIRONMENT

37.3 How has globalization changed the human–environment relationship?

Globalization generated unfamiliar environmental problems. These problems fed resistance to globalization and also efforts at corrective reform.

Human impact on the environment was not new, but the global level reached after the 1950s was unprecedented (Figure 37.4). Industrial competition, in the context of globalization and population explosion, increased the number of societies eager for economic growth regardless of environmental

CHAPTER 37 Globalization and Resistance **929**

FIGURE 37.4 This composite satellite image shows the regional impact of the human population on the planet. Regions where light burns brightest include much of Europe, Japan, and the United States—regions with a considerable amount of industry. Regions with excessive pollution because of petroleum extraction are also visible, particularly in the Middle East and areas of Russia, as are regions plagued by wild fires (Australia) and those that engage in slash-and-burn agriculture, particularly areas of the African and South American continents.

consequences. New technologies expanded global impact directly. Huge tankers periodically leaked massive amounts of oil into the oceans, affecting many regions. Tall smokestacks, designed to reduce local pollution in the American Midwest or the German Ruhr, spread acidity to the forests of Canada or Scandinavia. Multinationals, seeking loose environmental controls, often spilled chemicals. Above all, the pressure to expand production, in agriculture as well as industry, steadily cut into tropical rain forests, in places like Brazil, causing regional economic damage and contributing to global warming.

A key issue was the expansion of intensive industrial development goals. The Soviet Union and its satellites, pressing production during the cold war, had already caused extensive environmental damage, particularly in regions like central Asia. By the 1990s, China's headlong industrial drive raised new concerns. China's population of over a billion people was building on a resource base that was already severely depleted and degraded—including widespread water shortages. It was industrial growth that caused much of the smoke that enveloped many cities. Beijing planned to shut down manufacturing operations during the 2008 Olympics to provide a brief, internationally pleasant respite. The nation became the second greatest air polluter, after the United States, by 2001.

Equally alarming were reports on the ecological fallout of rapid development in southeast Asia, where multinationals based in Japan and in the newly industrialized countries of east Asia are extracting resources with abandon and where the rain forest is disappearing even more rapidly than in Brazil. Similar trends have been documented in sub-Saharan Africa, where imminent economic collapse and environmental demise are now routinely predicted.

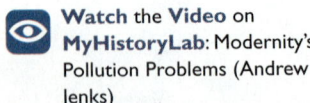

The general issues became abundantly clear in Mexico City, where oxygen is now widely sold by peddlers in the streets. A journalist, Marc Cooper, put it this way:

> The city's poised on the abyss of a world-class bio/technic disaster . . . its infrastructure is crumbling . . . the drinking water mixes with sewer effluent, many of the scars of the 1985 killer quake won't be healed before the next tremblor strikes. [And even then] Mexico City still beats the eternally depressed, sun-baked countryside.

Environmental Issues as Global Concerns

At the turn of the 21st century, environmental issues have emerged as focal points of public debate and government policy in most human societies (Figure 37.5). After a century of unprecedented levels of mechanized warfare, scientific experimentation, and the spread of industrialization, a wide variety of

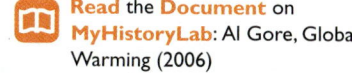

Read the Document on MyHistoryLab: Al Gore, Global Warming (2006)

FIGURE 37.5 In April 1986, nuclear chain reactions in the Chernobyl nuclear power plant in Ukraine (then part of the Soviet Union) leapt out of control, creating a fireball that blew the steel and concrete lid off of the reactor. Radioactive material was spewed into the open air and drifted across Europe. The area surrounding the plant, which is now closed, remains a contaminated wasteland. The Chernobyl catastrophe was unique, but it added to the larger environmental damage in many parts of the former Soviet Union.

complex and often interrelated environmental disruptions threaten not only humanity but all other life forms on the planet Earth.

Most scientists now agree that the greenhouse effect caused by the buildup in the atmosphere of excessive amounts of carbon dioxide and other heat-trapping gases has led to a substantial warming of the planet in recent decades. Some of the chief sources of the pollutants responsible for the atmospheric buildup are industrial wastes—including those resulting from energy production through the burning of fossil fuels like coal—and exhaust from millions of cars, trucks, and other machines run by internal combustion engines that burn petroleum. But other major sources of the greenhouse effect are both surprising and at present essential to the survival of large portions of humanity. Methane, another greenhouse gas, is introduced into the atmosphere in massive quantities as a by-product of the stew of fertilized soil and water in irrigated rice paddies, which feed a majority of the peoples of Asia, the world's most populous continent. Methane is also released by flatulent cattle, which produce milk and meat for human populations over much of the globe. Other gases have had equally alarming effects. Chlorofluorocarbons (CFCs), for example, which were once widely used in refrigeration, air conditioning, and spray cans, deplete the ozone layer, thereby removing atmospheric protection from the ultraviolet rays emanating from the sun.

If scientific predictions are correct, global warming will increasingly cause major shifts in temperatures and rainfall throughout much of the globe. Fertile and well-watered areas now highly productive in foods for humans and animals may well be overwhelmed by droughts and famine. If widely accepted computer simulations are correct, coastal areas at sea level—which from Bangladesh to the Netherlands to New Jersey are among the most densely populated in the world—are likely to be inundated. As climates are drastically altered, vegetation and wildlife in many areas will be radically altered. In Asia, the recent rapid melting of glaciers in the Himalayas threatens to deprive much of India and China of water for irrigation. Temperate forests may die off in many regions and be replaced by scrub, tropical vegetation, or desert flora. Some animal species may migrate or adapt and survive, but many, unable to adjust to such rapid climatic changes, will become extinct. In recent decades the extinction of species has clearly accelerated. In fact, in the 1990s and early 2000s, species have disappeared before they could even be put on the international endangered list.

CHAPTER 37 Globalization and Resistance

International discussions of environmental regulation increased from 1997 onward. A major conference in Kyoto, Japan, set limits on greenhouse gas emissions, in order to curtail global warming. It was not clear, however, whether these limits would have any effect. Many individual nations, including the United States between 2001 and 2009, opposed the limits proposed because of potential damage to national economies. Here was another area where global politics did not seem to be keeping pace with globalization. Some interest in sustainability movements and green design did gain ground in many different countries, including the United States, China, and the United Arab Emirates as well as countries like Germany and Japan, where environmental activism had an even larger pedigree. And there were a few local success stories, as in Mexico City where, by 2012, pollution control measures, particularly over vehicles, had measurably improved local environmental quality.

View the Closer Look on MyHistoryLab: Competing Visions: Global Warming, Good Science or Media Hype?

Disease

Changes in global contacts have usually involved disease, and globalization is no exception. Rapid international travel helped spread the AIDS epidemic from 1980 onward. Southern and eastern Africa were hit most severely, but AIDS also spread to the United States and western Europe. The epidemic took on even larger proportions in places like Brazil. By the early 21st century, rates of increase in parts of Asia and in Russia began to accelerate. These were regions that had initially felt relatively safe but where global contact ultimately brought new levels of contagion. The advent of SARS in 2003 raised fears of another global contagion. This is where the response of international organizations proved particularly essential.

The problem of contagious disease remained less severe than some of the earlier epidemics associated with global contacts, although some experts warned of even greater disease problems in the future. Environmental issues, newer on the global scale, may have replaced disease as the clearest downside of international connections.

Global health problems increasingly included disease patterns long characteristic of established industrial societies. Here, degenerative diseases, like heart disease and cancer, replaced older contagions as the leading source of mortality. These diseases accompanied growing life expectancy, but they were also hard to control. Global developments like rising rates of childhood obesity highlighted these health concerns, with no clear solutions in sight.

RESISTANCE AND ALTERNATIVES

37.4 What were the main changes and continuities in religion in the contemporary period of world history?

Accelerating globalization attracted a vigorous new protest movement, partly because of mounting environmental concerns. Meetings of the World Bank or of the industrial leaders were increasingly marked by huge demonstrations and some violence.

Globalization generated direct protest at the end of the 20th century. Nationalism and religion, overlapping globalization, provided alternative sets of loyalties.

Protest and Economic Uncertainties

A new anti-globalization protest movement began with massive protests in Seattle in 1999, and the protests continued at key gatherings thereafter. Protesters came from various parts of the world and raised a number of issues. Many people believed that rapid global economic development was threatening the environment. Others blasted the use of cheap labor by international corporations, which was seen as damaging labor conditions even in industrial nations. Rampant consumerism was another target.

Many critics claimed that globalization was working to the benefit of rich nations and the wealthy generally, rather than the bulk of the world's population. They pointed to figures that suggested growing inequalities of wealth, with the top quarter of the world's population growing richer during the 1990s while the rest of the people increasingly suffered (Figure 37.6). This division operated between regions, widening the gap between affluent nations and the more populous developing areas. It also operated within regions, including the United States and parts of western Europe, where income gaps were on the rise. Bitter disagreements increasingly divided the supporters and opponents of globalization.

932 PART VI The Newest Stage of World History: 1900–Present

FIGURE **37.6** The increasing gap between rich and poor is a controversial problem in the age of globalization. Here, contemporary workers and shoppers pass a homeless person on a Hong Kong sidewalk.

THINKING HISTORICALLY

How Much Historical Change?

AS THE COLD WAR DREW TO A CLOSE, a number of analysts, primarily in the United States, looked forward to dramatic shifts in human affairs. There were two related lines of argument. The "end of history" concept emphasized the new dominance of the democratic form of government. According to this view, the contest among political and economic systems, particularly between democracy and communism, was over; democracy would now sweep over the world. With this, the need for basic questioning about political institutions would also end: Democracy worked best, and it was here to stay. Further, the change in political structure also had implications for power rivalries. Some analysts contend that democracies never war on each other. Once the people control affairs of state through their votes, the selfishness and power trips that lead to war will end. Ordinary people understand the horror of war. They appreciate the common humanity they share with other democratic peoples. Just as democracy resolves internal conflicts through votes, democracies would come to resolve external conflicts through bargaining and compromise. They argue that, in the main, people do not vote for wars of aggression, at most sanctioning defense against attack.

Another argument, which might be combined with the democracy approach, focused on the spread of consumer capitalism around the world. As put forward by a U.S. journalist in a popular book called *The Lexus and the Olive Tree*, the consumer capitalism approach emphasized the benefits of a global economy. In this, everyone would gain access to greater material abundance and the wonders of consumerism, and no one would wish to jeopardize prosperity by waging war. Shared interests, rather than traditional disputes over limited resources, it is alleged, would carry the day. However, history suggests that capitalism is not necessarily compatible with democracy: The drive for material wealth has often led to corruption within democratic societies, sapping the effectiveness of their institutions. Even the greatest proponent of the idea that history will end in the triumph of capitalism, Harvard economist Francis Fukayama, has voiced concern that growing disparities of wealth even within the most prosperous capitalist nations might spark violent unrest that could derail the drive toward a free-market utopia.

> The "end of history" concept emphasized the new dominance of the democratic form of government.

This is a challenging kind of forecasting because it cannot easily be disproved—until the future does not correspond to the dramatic projections. The consumerism argument, particularly, has no precedent. At the same time, the predictions also could not be proved, for example, merely by pointing to some prior historical analogy. How, then, should they be assessed?

QUESTIONS
- Following the end of the cold war, did the world change as rapidly and fundamentally as these predictions implied?
- Did new systems spread as uniformly and consistently as the democracy and global consumerism arguments implied?
- How significant was the cold war's end in shaping global relationships?

Nationalism and New Religious Currents

Several trends ran counter to globalization as the 21st century began. Nationalism was one. While many nations were partially bypassed by globalization—many countries were much less powerful than the multinational corporations—nationalist resistance to globalization surfaced in many ways. Many countries opposed the erosion of traditions by global cultural patterns. The French government periodically resisted the incorporation of English words into the French language. Many Chinese families began to pay for private Confucian lessons for their children, to recall key cultural traditions lest global standards and materialism sweep everything else away. Many European countries tried to regulate the number of immigrants from Africa, Asia, and the West Indies, in the interest of preserving dominance for families and workers of European background. The United States rejected a wide variety of international treaties, including a provision for regulation against war crimes, because they might interfere with national sovereignty. China and other states periodically bristled against international criticism of internal policies concerning political prisoners.

Other individual nations tried to stand out against global trends, even aside from the few regimes, like North Korea, that were almost entirely isolated. The health ministry in Indonesia, for example, worked to prevent the World Health Organization from testing for outbreaks of new diseases. Several Latin American countries periodically opposed the efforts of international economic organizations to interfere with domestic economic policies in the interest of free trade.

It was religion, however, that posed the most interesting challenge to globalization in the final decades of the 20th century. Most religious movements were not necessarily opposed to globalization, but they tended to insist on their distinctiveness, against any uniform global culture. They also bred suspicions of the consumerism and sexuality highlighted in many manifestations of globalization, including films and tourism.

As communism collapsed in eastern Europe, many people returned to previous religious beliefs, including Orthodox Christianity. Protestant fundamentalists, often from the United States, were also busy in the region. Protestant fundamentalism also spread rapidly in parts of Latin America, such as Guatemala and Brazil. In India, Hindu fundamentalism surged by the 1990s, with Hindu nationalist politicians capturing the nation's presidency. In China, an intriguing spinoff from Buddhism, the Falun Gong, won wide support, despite brutal repression by the government.

Fundamentalism also gained ground in Islam, particularly in the Middle East and nearby parts of Africa and south central Asia. The Taliban, which followed a particular version of Islamic fundamentalism, gained control of the state in Afghanistan, initially in opposition to Soviet occupation, until the party was dislodged by the American invasion after the 2001 terrorist attack. Islamic fundamentalists argued for a return to religious law, opposing more secular governments in the region as well as the lures of global consumerism. Whether Christian, Hindu, or Islamic, fundamentalists tended to urge a return to the primacy of religion and religious laws and often opposed greater freedoms for women. Frequently, fundamentalists urged government support for religious values.

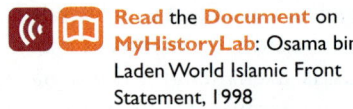

Read the Document on MyHistoryLab: Osama bin Laden World Islamic Front Statement, 1998

Religious fundamentalism ran counter to globalization in several ways, even though many religious leaders became adept at using new global technologies such as the Internet. It tended to appeal particularly to impoverished urban groups who seemed to be left behind in the global economy. Fundamentalism also tended to increase intolerance, even in religious traditions that had historically been reasonably open. Hindu fundamentalism, for example, was more fiercely exclusive than had been true in the past, while also more eager to seek support from the state. While some advocates of globalization assumed that religious traditionalism would decline, the balance was in fact unclear as the 21st century opened.

Religious differences contributed to many regional conflicts. Catholic, Serbian Orthodox, and Muslim clashes complicated the ethnic rivalries in the former Yugoslavia. Battles between Muslims and Christians occurred in Indonesia and the Sudan, and clashes between Hindus and Muslims intensified in India during the 1990s. Judaism and Islam, and Christianity as well, generated tensions not only in Israel but also in Lebanon. Antagonisms between Christian fundamentalists and other groups intensified political divisions within the United States. Clashes between Sunnis and Shiites, within Islam, contributed to Middle Eastern instability. In many areas, earlier patterns of tolerance were newly strained.

Religious-based terrorism aimed explicitly against globalization. The choice of the World Trade Center in New York as a target for the September 2001 attacks involved its symbolic role in international, and not just American, capitalism. A bloody bombing attack on a hotel in Bali, Indonesia, lashed out at Australian tourists and the consumerist lifestyle of an international resort. Reactions to terrorism, for example in generating new limitations on international travel, compounded the impact.

Most of the religious movements were not, of course, mainly terrorist, nor were they defined simply by opposition to globalization. Different strands of fundamentalism emerged: for example, many Iranian religious leaders, although eager to support religious law, regarded the Taliban in Afghanistan as crude and excessive. Many religious leaders were far more focused on local issues—like the secular regimes in the Middle East—than on global ones. Fundamentalists did, however, provide alternative identities and standards, compared to globalization. They generated debate within a large number of societies about what kind of future people should strive for.

Read the Document on MyHistoryLab: "America Enters a New Century with Terror," N. R. Kleinfield, *The New York Times*, 2001

VISUALIZING THE PAST

Two Faces of Globalization

EARLY IN THE 21ST CENTURY THE CITY OF DUBAI, in the United Arab Emirates, became a world commercial center, with banking, telecommunications, and other services. Many international corporations located regional offices there. The city was a beehive of construction, including work on the world's newest tallest skyscraper. Most of the buildings were in characteristic modern style, often designed by Western firms and often strikingly beautiful. This Arab center was becoming increasingly cosmopolitan, with little overt protest. But there was another face. Workers in Dubai, most of them immigrants from places like Pakistan, Palestine, and the Philippines, often had relatively low pay. Few were citizens, which limited their access to benefits such as higher education. While they wanted the work, for conditions in their host country were better than at home, they were not reaping the benefits of globalization in a way comparable to the citizens of Dubai, and their work was extremely physically challenging in a demanding climate.

QUESTIONS
- What does this picture say about globalization?
- There is an obvious side: the march of gleaming city centers in many parts of the world. A less obvious side is the people whose work built the global economy. The picture provides evidence about both sides.

TOWARD THE FUTURE

> Forecasts about the future use history, but in different ways. Key issues for the future emerge from recent trends and tensions.

37.5 What predictions about the future are particularly plausible, and why?

Human beings have always wanted to know what the future will hold. Various societies looked to the configurations of the stars for predictions, and astrology still has partisans in the contemporary world. Some societies generated beliefs in cycles, predicting that the future would repeat patterns already seen in the past; many Chinese scholars developed a cyclical approach. Still other societies assume that the future will differ from the past; from the Enlightenment onward, Western culture developed an additional belief in progress.

History suggests the futility of many efforts at forecasting. It has been estimated that well over half of the "expert" forecasts generated in the United States since World War II have been wrong. This includes predictions that by 2000 most Americans would be riding to and from work in some kind of airship, or that families would be replaced by promiscuous communes. Yet if history debunks forecasts, it also provides the basis for thinking about the future.

Projecting from Trends

The most obvious connection between history and the future involves the assessment of trends that are likely to continue at least for several decades. Thus we "know" that global population growth will slow up, because it is already slowing up. Many forecasts see stabilization by 2050, based on rapidly falling birth rates around the world. We also "know" that populations will become older; that is, the percentage of older citizens will increase. This is already happening in western Europe, the United States, and Japan and will occur elsewhere as birth rates drop. What we don't "know," of course, is how societies will react to the demands of the increasing numbers of older people, or how much the environment will have deteriorated by the time global population stabilizes. Even trend-based forecasts can be thrown off by unexpected events, like wars. In the 1930s experts "knew" that the American birth rate would fall, because it was already falling, but then war and prosperity created a totally unexpected baby boom, and the experts were wrong for at least two decades. Forecasts about the rise of Chinese or Indian economic power in coming decades also build on existing trends.

Trend-based forecasting is even chancier when the trends are already fragile. The late 20th century saw a genuine global spread of democracy, although admittedly not to every region. It was possible to venture predictions about the triumph of this form of government. But by 2002 it was hard to be confident that democracies were entirely secure in parts of Latin America or even in Russia. The hold of earlier, less democratic political traditions or the sheer pressure of economic stagnation might unseat the trend.

Forecasting is also complicated when two different trends are in play. The 20th century saw a fairly steady rise in consumerism, which spread to all parts of the world. The appeal of mass media, commercialized sports, and global fashions reaches across traditional boundaries. But the last 30 years have also seen a pronounced increase in religious interest, in many if not all parts of the world. Some people participate in both trends, but overall, the priorities are different. Is one of the two trends likely to predominate? Or should we think of the future in terms of division and tension among cultural interests?

Big Changes

Some analysts have looked at the world's future in terms of stark departures from its past. They argue that trend analysis is inadequate because we are on the verge of a major shift in framework. In the 1960s a "population bomb" analysis won considerable attention. The argument was that rapid population growth was about to overwhelm all other developments, leading to resource depletion, new wars over resources, and a world far different from what we had previously known. More recently, other forecasts, of dramatic climate change and of resource exhaustion, provide another dire picture of the world's future, in which other issues, like the fate of particular political systems, fade in importance.

Another scenario for a dramatically different future that has enjoyed recurrent popularity is the vision of a postindustrial world. Some pundits argue that computer technology, genetic engineering, and other technological advances are undermining the conditions of industrial society. Information, not production, becomes the key to economic growth and to social structures. The functions of cities shift from production to entertainment. Work will become more individualized and less time consuming, creating a new premium for expressive leisure. Here too, however, critics express doubts. Many parts of the world are not yet industrial, much less postindustrial. Work does not seem to be heading toward less routine; for example, computers promote repetitious activities as much as new creativity. As is always true with intriguing predictions of massive change, the jury is still out.

The Problem of the Contemporary Period

One of the reasons prediction is particularly difficult—although also compelling—is that world history has undergone so many fundamental changes during the past century. We know, for example, that the dominance of western Europe, for centuries a staple of world history, is a thing of the past, despite the continued vitality of the region. But what will replace it? Continued United States ascendancy, with military outposts in many parts of the world? Or the rise of China or east Asia? Or perhaps no single dominant region at all? We know there's a question about the world balance that will replace Western control, but the answer is unclear.

The same applies to conditions for women. Improvements in women's education plus the decline of the birth rate add up to significant changes for women around the world. The pace of change varies with the region, to be sure. Many regions also have given new legal and political rights to women. But is there a new model for women's roles that might be applicable around the world? Continued disputes about women's work roles, significant male backlash against change, and even disputes by women themselves about the relevance of an individualistic Western model for women's lives make forecasting difficult. We can assume continued change, but it's hard to pinpoint the results.

Global Connections and Critical Themes

CIVILIZATIONS AND GLOBAL FORCES

A key question for the future involves the fate of individual civilizations. World history has been shaped substantially by the characteristics of key civilizations for over 5000 years, granting that not everyone has been part of a major civilization and that in some cases civilizations are not easy to define. Some observers argue that, by the 21st century, the separate characteristics of civilizations are beginning to yield to homogenizing forces. Many scientists, athletes, and businesspeople feel more commitment to their professional interests than to their region of origin—which means that global professional identities can override civilizational loyalties. The downtowns of most cities around the world look very much alike. The same products, stores, and restaurants can be found in most urban areas. Globalization may be outpacing regional labels.

Yet we have also seen that globalization can falter, as it did in the middle decades of the 20th century. Even when it accelerates, as in the 1990s, it brings efforts to reassert separate identities. Even as it participates in the global economy, China remains distinctive, reflecting, for example, some of the political characteristics that were launched 3000 years ago. The Japanese easily move in global economics and culture, but with an emphasis on group identity measurably different from the personal goals emphasized in the United States. Major religions like Hinduism and Islam continue to mark their regions, and in some ways their influence seems to be on the rise.

World history has long been defined by a tension between regional features and larger connections. The specifics change, for example with shifts in technology and organizational capacity. But it may be premature to assume that some kind of global homogeneity is going to change the equation altogether.

Further Readings

For very different takes on the resurgence of globalization since 1989, see Thomas Friedman's cautious celebration in *The Lexus and the Olive Tree: Understanding Globalization* (2000), John Gray's more sober appraisal in *False Dawn* (2000), and Thomas Frank's lively critique in *One Market Under God* (2000). See also Joseph E. Stiglitz, *Making Globalization Work* (2006); Nathan M. Jensen, *Nation-States and the Multinational Corporation: A Political Economy of Foreign Direct Investment* (2006); Dimitris Stevis and Terry Boswell, *Globalization and Labor: Democratizing Global Governance* (2008); Peter Dicken, *Global Shift: Mapping the Changing Contours of the World Economy* (2007); Guillermo de la Dehesa, *What Do We Know About Globalization?: Issues of Poverty and Income Distribution* (2007); Daniel Cohen, *Globalization and its Enemies* (2006); Nelly P. Stromquist and Karen Monkman, eds., *Globalization and Education: Integration and Contestation across Cultures* (2000); Ernest Gundling and Anita Zanchettin, *Global Diversity: Winning Customers and Engaging Employees within World Markets* (2007); and Deen K. Chatterjee, ed., *Democracy in a Global World: Human Rights and Political Participation in the 21st Century* (2008).

Differing perspectives on the cultural ramifications of the new global economic order are provided by Peter Stearns, *Consumerism in World History* (2001); Walter LaFeber, *Michael Jordan and the New Global Capitalism* (2000); and the contributions to James Watson, ed., *Golden Arches East: McDonald's in East Asia* (1998). See also Lewis Solomon, *Multinational Corporations and the Emerging World Order* (1978); Stephen Rees, *American Films Abroad* (1997); Theodore von Laue, *The World Revolution of Westernization* (1997); Peter N. Stearns, *The Industrial Revolution in World History* (1998); and Bruce Mazlish and Ralph Buultjens, eds., *Conceptualizing Global History* (1993).

J. Luccassen and L. Luccassen, eds., *Migration, Migration, History, History: Old Paradigms and New Perspectives* (1997), is a recent comparative social history—in addition to an extensive bibliography it includes chapters on conceptual issues (periodization, definitions, etc.) and several regional historical case studies. Alistair Ager, *Refugees: Perspectives on the Experience of Forced Migration* (1998), is a useful survey. See also Patrick Manning, *Migration in World History* (2002).

For genuinely global perspectives on environmental issues, see Bill McKibben, *The End of Nature* (1999 ed.); Mark Hertsgaard, *Earth Odyssey* (1998); Jennifer Clapp and Peter Dauvergen, *Paths to a Green World: The Political Economy of the Global Environment* (2005); and Ramachandra Guha, *Environmentalism: A Global History* (2000). The best accounts of environmental degradation in key regions of the world include Susanna Hecht and Alexander Cockburn, *The Fate of the Forest* (1990), about Brazil; Judith Shapiro, *Mao's War against Nature* (2001); Vaclav Smil, *The Bad Earth* (1984) and *China's Environmental Crisis* (1993); Murray Feshback and Alfred Friendly Jr., *Ecocide in the USSR* (1992); Marc Reisner, *Cadillac Desert* (1993), about the United States; and Madhav Gadgil and Ramachandra Guha, *Ecology and Equity* (1995), about India.

For a good source about the movement for sustainable development, *Ecological Literacy: Education and the Transition to a Postmodern World* by David W. Orr (1992) and Andrés R. Edwards, *The Sustainability Revolution* (2005). Several serious books (as well as many more simplistic, popularized efforts) attempt to sketch the future of the world or the West. On the concept of the postindustrial society, see Daniel Bell, *The Coming of Post-Industrial Society* (1974). For other projections, consult R. L. Heilbroner, *An Inquiry into the Human Prospect* (1974); and L. Stavrianos, *The Promise of the Coming Dark Age* (1976).

On environment and resource issues, see D. H. Meadows and D. L. Meadows, *The Limits to Growth* (1974); Al Gore, *Earth in the Balance* (1992); and L. Herbert, *Our Synthetic Environment* (1962). M. ul Haq's *The Poverty Curtain: Choices for the Third World* (1976) and L. Solomon's *Multinational Corporations and the Emerging World Order* (1978) cover economic issues, in part from a non-Western perspective. On a leading social issue, see P. Huston, *Third World Women Speak Out* (1979).

On MyHistoryLab

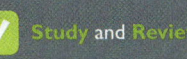 Study and Review on MyHistoryLab

Critical Thinking Questions

1. What are the main debates over the impact of globalization? Can some of the debates be resolved?
2. Compare interactions between religion and secular culture in the contemporary United States and the Middle East.
3. When did globalization begin? What are the main options in world history over the past two centuries, and what measurements work best?
4. Is nationalism declining or does it still serve important purposes? What kinds of evidence help answer this question?

PART VI AP® TEST PREP

MULTIPLE CHOICE QUESTIONS

1. By 1916, conflict on the Western Front
   a. had become a shifting game of rapid maneuvers with few major battles.
   b. left the French on the verge of victory after an easy triumph at Verdun.
   c. had resulted in victory for the British and French troops who pushed the exhausted enemy to the borders of Germany.
   d. had settled into a deadly stalemate in which hundreds of thousands of lives were expended for a few feet of trench.

2. Which of the following was included in the final set of treaties that ended World War I?
   a. A League of Nations, in which the United States came to play a critical role, was formed.
   b. Russia was rewarded for its service to the Allies by the grant of substantial territories in Poland and the Baltic republics.
   c. Germany was forced to accept blame for the war and to pay massive reparations to the victorious Allies.
   d. There were proposals to divide Austria-Hungary, but in the end the empire continued more or less as before.

3. By 1913, the British, who had begun to occupy Egypt in the 1880s,
   a. had granted full independence to Egypt.
   b. had eliminated resistance to their regime in Egypt.
   c. granted a constitution to Egyptian nationalists.
   d. had withdrawn from Egypt.

4. Which of the following statements concerning the leadership of the decolonization movement in India just prior to World War I is most correct?
   a. Leadership was assumed by more radical members of the Congress Party such as Tilak just before 1914.
   b. The Congress Party lost its leadership role to the Socialist Party, which was more willing to court the masses of the Indian peasantry.
   c. Tilak's removal and the repression campaigns against terrorists, along with British reforms, strengthened the hands of the Western-educated moderates in Congress.
   d. It is difficult, if not impossible, to identify leadership in the fragmented Congress Party of 1914.

5. Which of these is a reason that World War II proved to be disruptive to the colonial order imposed on Africa by European powers?
   a. African servicemen fought bravely for the British or French only to experience renewed racial discrimination once they returned home.
   b. The British, French, and Portuguese no longer wanted the expense and inconvenience of maintaining colonial empires.
   c. There was no need for anything produced in Africa during World War II, causing the colonial powers to lose interest in the colonies.
   d. Leaders such as Kwame Nkrumah had been against independence, but younger leaders eventually persuaded them to support independence.

World War I Losses			
	Dead	Wounded	Prisoner
Great Britain	947,000	2,122,000	192,000
France	1,385,000	3,044,000	446,000
Russia	1,700,000	4,950,000	500,000
Italy	460,000	947,000	530,000
United States	115,000	206,000	4,500
Germany	1,808,000	4,247,000	618,000
Austria–Hungary	1,200,000	3,620,000	200,000
Turkey	325,000	400,000	

Note: The number of known dead (round numbers) was placed at about 10 million and the wounded at about 20 million, distributed amoung chief combatants.

6. Based on this chart, which country suffered the highest number of casualties (dead and wounded) as a result of the carnage of World War I?
   a. Germany
   b. France
   c. Austria-Hungary
   d. Russia

7. The mid-1920s in western Europe could best be described as a period of
   a. war and destruction.
   b. stability and optimism.
   c. depression and unemployment.
   d. internal political unanimity.

8. What was the primary goal of Zapata's forces within the Mexican Revolution?
   a. the presidency for Zapata and political gains for his followers
   b. industrialization to provide employment for the peasants
   c. extension of the plantation economy in Oaxaca to provide more jobs for peasants
   d. sweeping land reform to benefit Mexican peasants

9. How did early Chinese Marxist philosophy differ from Lenin's?
   a. Chinese philosophers emphasized the role of the proletariat in the revolution.
   b. Chinese thinkers stressed the gradualist approach to political change.
   c. Sun Yat-sen taught that the revolution could only occur after the complete industrialization of China.
   d. The study circle at the University of Beijing saw the peasants as the vanguard of revolution.

10. What was Lenin's solution to Russian participation in World War I?
    a. He launched a massive offensive campaign that carried Russian forces deep within Germany.
    b. He immediately demanded that his British and French allies send humanitarian, economic, and military aid to the Eastern Front.
    c. He negotiated a peace treaty with the Germans and surrendered vast amounts of land on Russia's western border and also valuable resources.
    d. He successfully achieved a significant role at the Versailles peace negotiations.

CHAPTER 37 Globalization and Resistance

11. **What response did the Russian revolution provoke elsewhere in Europe?**
    a. Britain, France, the United States, and Japan all invaded Russia in reaction to the Bolshevik takeover, and in an effort to keep Russia in the war.
    b. Russia was immediately allied with Britain, France, and the United States against continued German aggression, though it contributed little to the war effort.
    c. France supported the revolution; Britain and the United States remained neutral.
    d. The government in Germany welcomed the communist success.

12. **Which of the following statements concerning warfare in the European theater during World War II is most accurate?**
    a. France mounted a fanatic defense of its home territories, only succumbing to the Nazi advance in 1944.
    b. By the summer of 1940, most of France lay in German hands, while a semi-fascist collaborative regime ruled in Vichy.
    c. British resistance crumbled before the air assaults of Germany, and an amphibious assault knocked the British from the war.
    d. From 1939 on, the chief resistance to the German advance was provided by American forces.

13. **Which of the following was NOT a result of the peace treaties signed following World War II?**
    a. The United States occupied Japan.
    b. Germany was divided into four zones of occupation.
    c. The Soviet Union took much of eastern Poland, while the Poles were compensated by receiving part of eastern Germany.
    d. German industrial power was destroyed.

14. **Which of the following statements concerning the creation of the state of Israel in 1948 is NOT correct?**
    a. Arab states bordering Israel attacked the new nation, but failed to defeat the Israelis.
    b. The United States supported the creation of Israel in 1948, but the Soviet Union opposed its formation.
    c. The partition of Palestine into Jewish and Arabic states was carried out in the United Nations.
    d. The Arab-Israeli war of 1948 created hundreds of thousands of Arab refugees from Palestine.

15. **Which of the following statements concerning Zionism following World War II is most accurate?**
    a. Zionists turned to violent attempts to eject the British from Palestine in response to the British attempts to limit immigration to the Middle East.
    b. The Zionist movement turned to peaceful demonstrations and boycotts on the model of the Indian nationalist movement and refused to participate in violence.
    c. The Zionist movement, frustrated by the failure to achieve an independent nation, weakened after World War II.
    d. The Zionist movement was eliminated after World War II by the combined action of the Palestinian Arabs and the British.

16. **Which of the following statements concerning the Algerian independence movement is most accurate?**
    a. Algeria won its independence from France in a peaceful movement led by white settlers in the colony.
    b. Decolonization in Algeria was violent, because white settlers resisted independence through the OAS supported by powerful elements within the French military.
    c. Independence in Algeria was achieved as a result of the military victory of the FLN over the French army.
    d. Unlike the rest of Africa, Algeria was never decolonized and remained a province of France.

17. **What was the solution to the division in India between Muslims and Hindus in 1947?**
    a. The British established a single government with a Hindu majority, but with specific offices reserved for Muslims.
    b. The government of India was divided between two houses of the Indian parliament, one for Muslims, one for Hindus.
    c. The British simply withdrew from India without any political settlement of the problem of religious division.
    d. The British decided to divide India into two nations: a Muslim Pakistan and a secular, but Hindu-dominated, India.

18. **Based on the map above, which of the following statements concerning the German government after World War II is most accurate?**
    a. Germany remained divided among three Western powers until 1980.
    b. During the cold war, France, Britain, and the United States merged their territories to form the Federal Republic of Germany.
    c. After World War II, the Weimar Republic was restored in Germany.
    d. Germany fell under the direct government of the Soviet Union along with the rest of eastern Europe.

19. Which of the following statements concerning U.S. military spending is most accurate?
    a. After World War II, U.S. military spending continuously declined.
    b. Under Democratic presidents, the percentage of U.S. resources devoted to the military increased while under Republican presidents, the same expenditures decreased.
    c. Heeding Eisenhower's warning of a growing "military-industrial complex," Republicans pushed for and obtained lower defense spending.
    d. Regardless of the party in political power, the percentage of the U.S. budget going to the military remained stable from the 1950s to the 1980s.

20. The creation of the welfare state in Europe
    a. was rejected by the majority of European parties on the grounds that their governments had done enough planning during the war.
    b. was partially adopted by European states, though most, such as the United Kingdom, would not go so far as to nationalize health care.
    c. was necessitated by the recurrence of economic conditions mirroring the Great Depression following World War II.
    d. resulted from the leftward shift of the political spectrum, such as with Britain's Labour party and the Communist–Socialist–Christian Democrat coalitions in France and Italy.

21. The European Economic Community is a good example of
    a. Europe's continued national strife.
    b. cooperation between European nations and a willingness to create a single European economy.
    c. the need for Europe to develop a single foreign policy independent of the United States.
    d. the continued economic dependence of the European nations on capital derived from the United States.

22. Which of the following was a right achieved by European women in the 20th century?
    a. the right to vote
    b. the right to attend religious services
    c. the right to work for wages
    d. payment equal to that of males for equal work

23. Despite the loosening of Soviet control over eastern Europe following Stalin's death, what aspects of Soviet domination continued to be enforced?
    a. single-party dominance and military alignment with the Soviet Union
    b. centralized economic planning
    c. total rejection of Catholicism
    d. agricultural collectivization

24. Which of the following statements concerning change in Latin America in the 20th century is most accurate?
    a. The region grappled with social justice, cultural autonomy, and economic security.
    b. While the Latin American economy remained relatively unchanged, the political and social order was revolutionized.
    c. The most significant change was the overthrow of the old social hierarchy based on race and color.
    d. The elites of Latin America today were recruited from the labor movements that accompanied industrialization throughout Latin America.

25. Which of the following statements most accurately describes the outcome of the Cuban revolution?
    a. Despite the successful overthrow of Batista, the revolutionary government failed to enact significant reforms in the plantation economy.
    b. The revolutionary government eventually announced its adoption of Marxist-Leninist leanings, broke off relations with the United States, and introduced sweeping socialist reforms.
    c. The largely liberal government that resulted from the revolution returned to the constitution of 1940 and closer relationships with the United States.
    d. After a brief sojourn in the United States, Batista was able to return to power with the support of the U.S. military.

26. Which of the following statements concerning military governments in Latin America after 1960 is most accurate?
    a. Military governments tended to favor labor and the working classes at the expense of the traditional oligarchy.
    b. Political repression and torture were often used to silence critics.
    c. None of the military governments was successful in introducing social or economic reforms.
    d. Military governments were uniformly surrogates for conservatives in Latin American society.

27. Which of the following statements concerning Latin American population is most accurate?
    a. Between 1950 and 1985, the Latin American population remained stagnant due to poor health conditions and constant internal warfare.
    b. Despite improvements, Latin America's population continued to increase more slowly than that of North America.
    c. Almost all population increase in Latin America can be attributed to immigration of European laborers.
    d. Since 1950, Latin American population has more than doubled, while North American population has grown more slowly.

28. Which of these reasons best explains the return of the United States to more aggressive policies, including direct military intervention following World War II?
    a. the desire to contain communism and the cold war
    b. the discovery of uranium in Mexico
    c. the increasing intervention of Japan into Latin American economies
    d. the alliance of many Latin American countries with fascist governments during the war

29. Why have ethnic rivalries and communal violence been endemic in decolonized African and Asian states?
    a. The level of civilization in Africa and Asia was more primitive at the time of colonization.
    b. Tribal life in Africa and Asia was traditionally more violent than other cultures.
    c. The introduction of slavery by whites in the late 19th century brutalized African and Asian culture.
    d. Europeans hastily colonized Africa and Asia and established boundaries without reference to ethnic groups or cultural homogeneity.

30. "Neocolonial economy" refers to
    a. Europe's conquest of new colonies in Africa and Asia.
    b. Japan's conquest of much of Asia during World War II.
    c. the global economy dominated by the industrial nations.
    d. the creation of colonies by India and the more advanced nations of Africa in the last several decades.

31. The Muslim Brotherhood embraced all of the following EXCEPT
    a. a fundamentalist approach to Islam.
    b. the promotion of trade unions.
    c. nonviolence.
    d. land reform.

32. Which is true about developments associated with the Green Revolution in India?
    a. The Green Revolution has greatly favored cultivators with the resources to invest in new seeds and fertilizer.
    b. The Green Revolution has decreased the gap between rich and poor people over much of rural India.
    c. The Green Revolution has contributed in major ways to the improvement of India's environment.
    d. The Green Revolution has had no impact whatsoever in India.

33. Which of the following methods was NOT used by the South African government to suppress dissent among the black population?
    a. arrest of opposition leaders
    b. favoritism shown to some leaders in order to divide opponents of apartheid
    c. use of spies and police informers
    d. use of state programs to improve the conditions of the black townships

34. According to the graph below, which area of the world has experienced the greatest population growth between 1930 and 2000?
    a. Europe
    b. Africa
    c. Latin America
    d. South Asia

35. Which of the following statements most accurately reflects the situation in Korea following the Korean War?
    a. North and South Korea were rapidly reunited under a single, authoritarian government controlled by the Soviet Union.
    b. North Korea threw off its ties with China and the Soviet Union and sought a closer relationship with the United States.
    c. Korea remained divided with relatively authoritarian governments in both halves of the divided nation, though over time North Korea remained authoritarian and South Korea became increasingly democratic.
    d. South Korea became fully democratic, but has continued to struggle economically since the war, moving closer to political neutrality during the cold war.

36. Americans introduced which of the following reforms to Japan during the occupation?
    a. They introduced industry to the Japanese economy.
    b. They abolished Shintoism as a state religion.
    c. They outlawed labor unions.
    d. They made the emperor a symbolic figurehead.

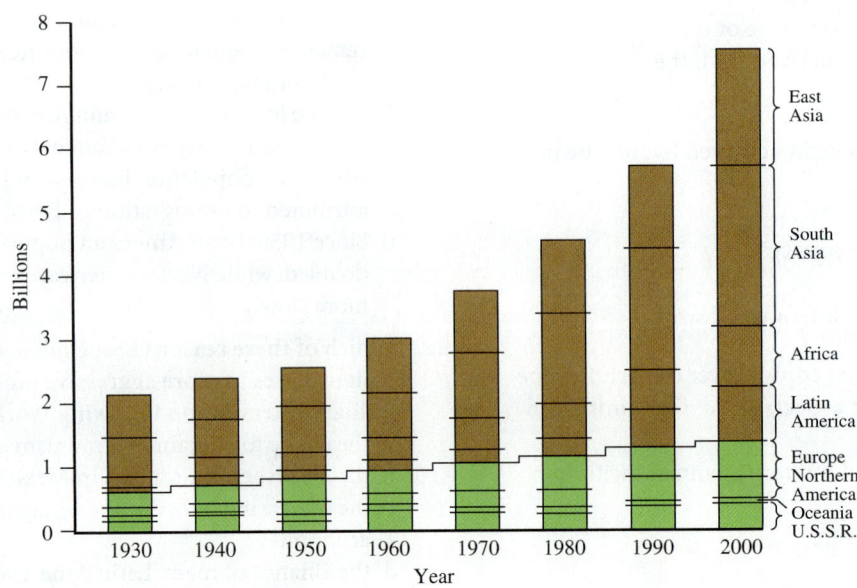

37. **Which of the following statements concerning the development of Japanese culture in the postwar era is most accurate?**
    a. Japanese culture shed its connections with the past and wholeheartedly embraced Western styles in literature, drama, and the arts.
    b. Japanese culture was defined by its conservatism and retention of old forms to the extent that Western forms, particularly in art and architecture, were unknown.
    c. Aside from interior decoration and film, Japanese contributions to world culture were not widespread.
    d. Buddhism and Shintoism were officially banned because of their association with Japan's imperialist past.

38. **By 1960, Mao lost his position as state chairman (although he remained the head of the party's Central Committee)**
    a. because of the general and catastrophic failure of the Great Leap Forward.
    b. following an assassination attempt by an opposition group.
    c. when he proposed the destruction of Buddhist monasteries throughout China.
    d. following the defeat of Chinese forces in Vietnam.

39. **During the 1980s, all of the following were typical of the Chinese government EXCEPT**
    a. encouragement of private market production for the peasantry.
    b. private enterprise within the industrial sector.
    c. domination by the "pragmatists."
    d. democratic reform.

40. **In which of the following ways were the preconditions for revolution in Vietnam NOT similar to those in China?**
    a. possession of a polity based on the Confucian system of China
    b. failure of imperial government to respond to foreign intervention leading to complete collapse of dynastic system
    c. actual colonization by a European power
    d. radical rather than gradualist solutions to reconstruction

41. **In what way was the early nationalist organization in Vietnam similar to other developing nations?**
    a. It was composed of a Western-educated middle class.
    b. It was modeled on the Marxism of the Communist Party of Russia.
    c. It was drawn almost entirely from the peasantry.
    d. Its goals were entirely peaceful.

42. **The term *perestroika* refers to**
    a. a new freedom to comment and criticize the Soviet government.
    b. economic restructuring and more leeway for private ownership.
    c. the Soviet space program.
    d. the establishment of a liberal democracy.

43. **Which of the following factors did NOT play a role in the demise of communism?**
    a. Soviet leadership
    b. reassertion of eastern European initiative
    c. western Europe's thriving Economy
    d. the steadfastness of Chinese policy

44. **All of the following were reforms of Mikhail Gorbachev EXCEPT**
    a. relaxation of media restrictions.
    b. the dividing of the Soviet Union into its original states.
    c. the reduction of nuclear arms.
    d. the ending of the Soviet-Afghani war.

45. **The end of the cold war was associated with what large trend in the world at the end of the 20th century?**
    a. the rapid industrialization of the third world
    b. the spread of multiparty democracy
    c. the ending of world hunger
    d. the dismantling of Western armed forces

46. **Terrorism in the late 20th and early 21st centuries**
    a. is similar to earlier terrorist activities in that it targets monarchs or high-profile individuals.
    b. is similar to earlier terrorist activities because of its adept use of technology to recruit membership.
    c. is the preferred weapon for some religious extremists and ethnic/national minorities.
    d. led to decolonization in Asia and the Middle East.

47. **This company has had the most striking international cultural influence since the 1970s.**
    a. Nike
    b. McDonald's
    c. Ford
    d. Sony

48. **Which of the following is NOT an issue raised against economic globalization?**
    a. It damages labor conditions in more developed countries through the use of cheap labor from abroad.
    b. It damages the environment, because industries can locate or relocate where environmental regulations are lax.
    c. Its pace is too slow; people would be better off if the globalization process was more rapid.
    d. It results in rampant consumerism and the loss of local craft and culture.

49. A major conference in Kyoto, Japan, the terms of which went into effect in 2005, set limits on
    a. greenhouse gas emissions.
    b. globalization.
    c. the use of weapons of mass destruction.
    d. religious fundamentalism.

50. By the end of the last century, what percentage of humanity consumed a staggering four-fifths of all marketed goods and services?
    a. four-fifths
    b. one-half
    c. two-thirds
    d. one-fifth

DOCUMENT-BASED QUESTION

 Read the Documents on MyHistoryLab

A practice document-based question for Part 6 is available on MyHistoryLab.

CONTINUITY AND CHANGE-OVER-TIME ESSAY

Analyze the demographic and environmental changes from 1914 to the present.

COMPARATIVE ESSAY

Analyze similarities and differences between the settlement of World War II and the Versailles Treaty that ended World War I.

PART VI

REVISITING
The Contemporary Period

This has been a period filled with dramatic events and many transformations. Sorting out the main points is not easy. There is ample opportunity to discuss short-term versus long-term change. Where, for example, does fascism or the Spanish Civil War fit the big picture? These were searing developments at the time, with important effects for several decades; but their durable mark is not easy to define.

CRITICAL THEMES

A key challenge is to identify the big themes beneath internal subperiods like the interwar decades or the cold war years. The advance of globalization, although not entirely steady, is an ongoing process through the period, although with intensification after 1950. A host of revolutions and independence movements offer individual features while also furthering the larger process of replacing older political and social systems with newer patterns. The burst of global industrialization in recent decades was prepared by earlier policies such as import substitution or even Japanese exploitation of Korean manufacturing. Beneath the surface, the population explosion had its own ramification on urbanism, migration, and environment.

The periodic, sometimes massive violence of the period calls for assessment. New technologies help explain mass slaughters, but what were the basic causes? Why did so many leaders, of formal states and internal factions alike, accept attacks on civilians? During the first decade of the 21st century some observers claimed that the rate of violence was declining, with very few outright wars and with resolutions of ethnic tensions in some places.

Handling cultural developments for the contemporary period is particularly tricky. Large patterns of change include the spread of Marxism, but then its ultimate retreat, but also global consumerism and the increasing global impact of science. The rate of cultural interaction increased greatly. But religious response proved to be an equally important theme. Outright religious change in Africa, for example, clearly superseded other global influences during the 20th century, and the same point applies to some other regions. Culture continued to serve regional identities, and the mixture of elements—including cultural clashes within as well as among several regions—was inherently complex.

There is always, finally, the question of when the contemporary period will end. At what point will the dominant themes of the past 120 years be replaced by new ones? Will environmental challenge, or new demographic patterns, or a new balance among major regional powers turn the tide, and usher in a definable new era? World history periods can last a long time, but not forever. Here's an obvious opportunity for creative debate.

CRITICAL THINKING QUESTIONS

1. Do the years 1900–2014 constitute a coherent period in world history? Is there an alternative periodization that would work better?
2. What were the main causes of the decline of monarchy and empire as forms of government during the contemporary period?
3. Compare the results of communist revolution in Russia and China.
4. Using the patterns of international contacts in the early 20th century as a base, what major changes marked the acceleration of globalization from the 1950s onward?
5. How did communist and Western leaders, respectively, explain the origins of the cold war? What kind of evidence would help in assessing their interpretations?

Credits

LITERARY CREDITS

PART I

Chapter 1 Map 1.1 and 1.2, W. H. McNeil, *A History of Human Community*, Third Edition 1990, pp. 9, 17. Pearson Education: Upper Saddle River, New Jersey.

Chapter 2 pp. 26–27, from J. M. Powis Smith, *The Origin and History of Hebrew Law* (Chicago: University of Chicago Press, 1931), pp. 181–183, 186, 190–193, 195, 199–200, 209–213. P. 36, Christian Jacq, *The Living Wisdom of Ancient Egypt*, Simon & Schuster 1999, page 107.

PART II

Chapter 3 By P. Lal, original by Kalidasa, from *Great Sanskrit Plays in Modern Translation*, copyright © 1964 by New Directions Publishing Corp. Reprinted by permission of New Directions Publishing Corp.

PART III

Chapter 7 From Selections from *The Arabian Nights* (Richard Burton Translation), The Book League of America, N.D., 1936.

Chapter 8 Khaldun, Ibn; *The Muqaddimah*. ©1958, 1967 by PUP. Reprinted by permission of Princeton University Press.

Chapter 9 Pp. 211–212, Soundjata ou l'Epopée du Manding, Tamsir Niane, Présence africaine, Paris, 1960.
P. 298, excerpts from a version collected among the Mandingo (Malinke) people of Guinea by the African scholar D. T. Niane, Sundiata: *An Epic of Old Mali* (1986).

Chapter 10 Vernadsky, ed., *Sourcebook for Russian History* copyright ©1972), Vol. I, p. 12-13. Used by permission of Yale University Press.

Chapter 11 German nun, James Harvey Robinson, *Readings in European History*, NY: Ginn & Company, 1906.

Chapter 12 Bernardino de Sahagún, *Florentine Codex: The General History of the Things of New Spain*.

Chapter 13 "The rain was over . . . from Tao (Dao) and from magic how to fly" from *Bright Moon, Perching Bird* © 1987 by J. P. Seaton. Reprinted by permission of Wesleyan University Press. www.wesleyan.edu/wespress

Chapter 14 P. 312, "Having come upon . . ." from Donald Keene, Ed., *Japanese Literature from the Earliest Era to the Nineteenth Century*, Grove Press, 1955. P. 324, "I myself often forget . . ." Troung Buu Lam, *Patterns of Vietnamese Response to Foreign Interventions, 1858–1900*, 1967, Yale Southeast Asia Studies Monographs. P. 328, "Kieu sensed a girl . . . ," "He said . . . ," "When evil strikes, you . . ." from: Nguyen Du, *The Tale of Kieu*, Translated and Annotated by Huynh Sanh Thông (New Haven: Yale University Press, 1983). P. 328, ". . . the picture of Kuei-feo, skillful thought the painter might be . . . ," "Now all is lost; for since she [the nun] cannot . . . , "She [a woman who was attracted . . ." from *The Tale of Genji, Part 1* by Lady Murasaki translated by Arthur Waley, Houghton Mifflin, 1929.

Chapter 15 From *The Story of the Mongols Whom We Call the Tartars* by Friar Giovanni Di Plano Carpini, translated by Erik Hildinger, Editor Adoph Caso, ©1996, Branden Publishing Company, pp. 50–52.

Chapter 16 P. 358, first column, Michael Dols "Ibn al-Wardi's Risalah Al-Naba An Al-Waba, A Translation of the a Major Source for the History of the Black Death in the Middle East" in *Near Eastern Numismatics, Iconography. Epigraphy and History: Studies in Honor of George C. Miles*, Ed. Dickran Kouymijian, (Beirut: American University of Beirut, 1974), 443–455. Reprinted by Permission of The American University of Beirut Press. Second column, *The Chronicle of Jean de Venette*, Richard A. Newhall, ed., Copyright © 1953, Columbia University Press. Reprinted with permission of the publisher.

PART IV

Chapter 19 P. 426, Stuart Stirling, *The Last Conquistador* (Stroud, Sutton, 1999), pp. 140–146. P. 511, *The War of Chupas* (London: Hakluyt Society, 1918), p. 59. P. 432, "The Broken Spears" by Miguel Leon-Portilla, Copyright © 1962, 1990 by Miguel Leon-Portilla. Expanded and Updated Edition © 1990, Miguel Leon-Portilla. Reprinted by permission of Beacon Press, Boston.

Chapter 20 C. Beazley and Edgard Prestage, eds. *The Chronicle of the Conquest of Guinea* written by Gomes Eannes de Azurara (London: Halyut Society, 1896) v. 1, chap. 25, p. 81.

Chapter 21 *Peter the Great From Imperial Russia: A Source Book, 1700–1917*, edited by Basil Dmytryshyn. Copyright Academic International Press, Gulf Breeze, Fla. Used by permission.

Chapter 23 Quoted in J. C. van Leur, *Indonesian Trade and Society*, 1955, W. Van Hoeve Ltd, p. 242.

PART V

Chapter 25 P. 591, Map 29.2 adapted from *A Short History of Indonesia* by Alis Zainu'ddin, copyright © 1970. Reproduced with permission of Greenwood Publishing Group, Inc., Westport, CT. Copyrighted by Pearson Education, Upper Saddle River, NJ.
P. 599, Ndabaningi Sithole, *African Nationalism*, Oxford University Press, 1968.

Chapter 26 *Life in the Argentine Republic in the Days of the Tyrants, or Civilization and Barbarism* (1868) by Domingo F. Sarmiento.

Chapter 27 *Sources of Chinese Tradition* by William T. deBary, copyright © 1960. Columbia University Press. Reprinted with permission from Columbia University Press.

Chapter 28 Pp. 768–769, excerpts from *Readings in Russian Civilization, Vol. I,* edited by T. Riha, University of Chicago Press, 1969. Reprinted by permission of The University of Chicago Press. P. 680, Excerpts from Japanese poem on personal conflicts, *Sources of Japanese Tradition, Volume One: From Earliest Times to 1600* (vol. 1), Wm. Theodore de Bary; Donald Keene; George Tanabe; and Paul Varley, eds. © 2001 Columbia University Press, Page 103. Reprinted with permission of the publisher.

PART VI

Chapter 29 P. 715 from *Nationalism* (1917) by Rabindranath Tagore. From: *Young India* (1926) by Mohandas Gandhi. P. 716, *Senghor: Selected Poems* translated by Reed and Wake © 1964. 5 lines from "Snow Upon Paris." By permission of Oxford University Press. From *Return to My Native Land* (1938) by Aimé Césaire.

Chapter 32 A Cold War Speech, United States President Dwight Eisenhower.

Chapter 33 P. 830, *Let Me Speak* by Domitilia Barrios de Chungara, edited by Mema Viezzer, *Monthly Review Press,* New York, 1978. Pp. 830–831, *I, Rigoberta Menchú*, Verso, London 1984, p. 251, editor Elisabeth Burgos Debray. P. 837, Poem, The United Fruit Co. © 2004 by City Lights Books. Preprinted by permission of City Lights Books.

Chapter 34 Stanza "I run around with them . . . And "jaw away the years." from poem by Chairil Anwar. Reprinted by permission from *The Complete Book of Poetry and Prose of Charil Anwar* edited by Burton Raffel, the State University of New York Press © 1970, State University of New York. All rights reserved.

Chapter 37 Pp. 927–928, Alexander Cockburn, Jeffrey St. Clair, and Allan Sekula, *5 Days That Shook the World* (London: Verso, 2000), 16–21, 28, 29, 36–37.

PHOTO CREDITS

PART I

P. 1 Bridgeman Art Library, London/SuperStock; **P. 2** Gianni Dagli Orti/Fine Arts/Corbis.
Chapter 1 Figure 1.1 Reeda Peel; **1.2** Art Resource, NY; **Visualizing the Past Image 1** Riedmiller/Caro/Alamy; **Image 2** Superstock/Superstock; **Images 3 & 4** Erich Lessing/Art Resource, NY; **1.3** Marion Bull/Alamy.

Chapter 2 Figure 2.1 Erich Lessing/Art Resource, NY; **2.2** University of Pennsylvania Museum of Archaeology and Anthropology, Philadelphia/Courtesy of the Penn Museum; **2.3** Scala/Art Resource, NY; **2.4** Ian Stewart/Shutterstock; **2.5** Asian Art & Archaeology, Inc./Corbis; **2.6** Werner Forman/Art Resource, NY; **2.7** Erich Lessing/Art Resource, NY.

PART I REVISITING

P. 46 DeAgostini/SuperStock.

PART II

P. 48 Robert Harding World Imagery; **P. 52** Dorling Kindersley.

Chapter 3 Figure 3.1 Art Archive, The/SuperStock; **3.2** Nancy McKenna/Photo Researchers, Inc.; **3.3** Graham Mulrooney/Alamy; **3.4** The Granger Collection; **3.5** Barney Burstein/Burstein Collection/Corbis; **3.6** The Granger Collection, NYC.

Chapter 4 Figure 4.1 David Gurr/Eye Ubiquitous/Corbis.; **4.2** Indian, (3rd century BC)/The Bridgeman Art Library Ltd./Alamy; **4.3** Smart-foto/Shutterstock; **4.4** PhotosIndia.com RM 20/Alamy; **4.3** Erich Lessing/Art Resource, NY.

Chapter 5 Figure 5.1 RMN-Grand Palais/Art Resource, NY; **5.2** Bridgeman-Giraudon/Art Resource, NY; **5.3** Bridgeman Art Library, London/SuperStock; **5.4** The British Museum; **5.5** Scala/Art Resource, NY; **5.6** Erich Lessing/Art Resource, NY.

Chapter 6 Figure 6.1 Mimmo Jodice/Fine Art/Corbis; **6.2** Erich Lessing/Art Resource, NY; **6.3** Sakamoto Photo Research Laboratory/Fine Art/Corbis; **6.4** Courtesy of the Penn Museum, Image #C 395 S8-G2844; **6.5** Bridgeman-Giraudon/Art Resource, NY.

PART II REVISITING

P. 145 Dorling Kindersley; **P. 146** Andy Sotiriou/Photodisc/Getty Images.

PART III

P. 149 Age Fotostock/SuperStock; **P. 150** British Library Board / Robana / Art Resource, NY.

Chapter 7 Figure 7.1 Ian Dagnall/Alamy; **7.2** Frederick Barry/Fine Art/Corbis; **7.3** Ursula Gahwiler/Robert Harding Picture Library Ltd/Alamy; **7.4** Werner Forman/Art Resource, NY; **7.5** The British Library Board; **7.6** Mohsin Raza/Corbis; **7.7** Bridgeman Art Library; **Visualizing the Past Image 1** Philip de Bay/Historical Picture Archive/Corbis; **Image 2** Terence Waeland/Alamy.; **Image 3** Pearson; **Image 4** Images & Stories/Alamy; **Image 5** Erich Lessing/Art Resource, NY.

Chapter 8 Figure 8.1 Heritage Images/Corbis; **8.2** Harvard Art Museums/Arthur M. Sackler Museum, Gift of John Goelet, formerly in the collection of Louis J. Cartier, 1958.76; **8.3** Digital Image © Museum Associates / LACMA. Licensed by Art Resource, NY; **8.4** The Granger Collection, NYC; **8.5** Ric Ergenbright/Corbis; **8.6** Pahari School (18th century) / British Library, London, UK / © British Library Board. All Rights Reserved / The Bridgeman Art Library.

Chapter 9 Figure 9.1 The Granger Collection New York; **9.2** George Steinmetz/Terra/Corbis; **Visualizing the Past Image 1** Bombaert Patrick/Alamy; **Image 2** Igor Alyukov/Shutterstock; **9.3** Brooklyn Museum L54.5 Collection of Robin B. Martin; **9.4** Werner Forman/Art Resource, NY; **9.5** Nick Greaves/Images of Africa Photobank/Alamy.

Chapter 10 Figure 10.1 Erich Lessing / Art Resource, NY; **10.2** B.O'Kane/Alamy; **Visualizing the Past** Erich Lessing/Art Resource, NY; **10.3** EvrenKalinbacak/Shutterstock; **10.4** Album/Art Resource, NY; **10.5** Gianni Dagli Orti / The Art Archive at Art Resource, NY.

Chapter 11 Figure 11.1 British Library/akg-images; **11.2** Snark / Art Resource, NY; **Visualizing the Past** RMN-Grand Palais/Art Resource, NY; **11.3** Bridgeman-Giraudon/Art Resource, NY; **11.4** The Art Archive at Art Resource, NY; **11.5** Elio Ciol/Fine Art/Corbis; **11.6** Ian Dagnall/Alamy; **11.7** akg-images/British Library/Newscom; **11.8** DeAgostini/SuperStock; **11.9** Snark/Art Resource, NY.

Chapter 12 Figure 12.1 Sucesores de Luis Covarrubias Duclaud, Sean Sprague/Mexicolore / The Bridgeman Art Library International; **12.2** SEF/Art Resource,

NY; **12.3** Scala / Art Resource, NY; **12.4** jejim/Shutterstock; **12.5** DeAgostini/SuperStock; **Visualizing the Past Image 1** Kevin Schafer/Corbis; **Image 2** Charles Lenars/Corbis; **12.6** Werner Forman/Art Resource, NY; **12.7** Chuck Pefley/Alamy.

Chapter 13 Figure 13.1 Eastphoto/Beijing Eastphoto stockimages Co.,Ltd/Alamy; **13.2** Image copyright © The Metropolitan Museum of Art. Image source: Art Resource, NY.; **13.3** Image copyright © The Metropolitan Museum of Art. Image source: Art Resource, NY; **13.4** The Granger Collection, NYC; **13.5** Art Archive, The/SuperStock; **13.6** Museum feur Asiatische Kunst, Staatliche Museen, Berlin, Germany/Juergen Lipe/Art Resource, NY; **Visualizing the Past** Library of Congress Prints and Photographs Division [LC-USZ62-49138] **13.7** Museum of Fine Arts, Boston.

Chapter 14 Figure 14.1 Art Archive, The/SuperStock; **14.2** DeA Picture Library/The Granger Collection; **14.3** Louis V. Ledoux and Asian Art/Department Funds/The Bridgeman Art Library; **14.4** Jon Arnold Images Ltd / Alamy; **14.5** The Nelson Atkins Museum of Art; **14.6** Free Agents Limited/Corbis; **14.7** Mr. and Mrs. Charles M. Endicott Fund/The Bridgeman Art Library; **14.8** David South/Alamy; **Visualizing the Past Image 1** The Granger Collection NYC; **Image 2** DeAgostini/SuperStock; **Image 3** akg-images/British Library/Newscom; **Image 4** Image copyright © The Metropolitan Museum of Art. Image source: Art Resource, NY.

Chapter 15 15.1 Scala/White Images / Art Resource, NY; **15.2** The Granger Collection, NYC; **15.3** The Granger Collection, NYC; **15.4** bpk, Berlin / Art Resource, NY; **15.5** The Granger Collection, NYC; **15.6** The Granger Collection, NYC; **15.7** De Agostini/Getty Images.

Chapter 16 Figure 16.1 The Granger Collection, NYC; **16.2** Scala/Art Resource, NY; **16.3** MasterLu/Fotolia; **16.4** The Granger Collection, NYC; **16.5** The Granger Collection, NYC.

PART III REVISITING

P. 374 Pascal Rateau/Shutterstock; **P. 375** Private Collection/akg-images; **P. 376** Image Asset Management Ltd. / Alamy.

PART IV

P. 377 "Departure for the Cape," King Manuel I of Portugal blessing Vasco da Gama and his expedition, c.1935, Anonymous / University of Witwatersrand, Johannesburg, South Africa/The Bridgeman Art Library; **P. 378** Model of the slave ship 'Brookes' used by William Wilberforce (1759-1833) in the House of Commons to demonstrate conditions on the middle passage, 18th century (wood) (see also 112029, 136291 and 135589) / © Wilberforce House, Hull City Museums and Art Galleries, UK/The Bridgeman Art Library.

Chapter 17 Figure 17.1 The Granger Collection, NYC; **17.2** The Granger Collection, NYC; **17.3** Art Resource, NY; **17.4** The Granger Collection, NYC; **17.5** The Granger Collection, NYC; **17.6** The Granger Collection, NYC; **17.7** National Gallery, London/Art Resource, NY; **17.8** V & A Images.

Chapter 18 Figure 18.1 V&A Images, London/Art Resource, NY; **18.2** The Granger Collection, NYC; **18.3** GL Archive/Alamy; **Visualizing the Past** RMN-Grand Palais/Art Resource, NY; **18.4** bpk, Berlin/National Portrait Gallery, London, Great Britain/Jochen Remmer/Art Resource, NY.

Chapter 19 Figure 19.1 Erich Lessing/Art Resource, NY; **19.2** The Granger Collection, NYC; **19.3** The Granger Collection, NYC; **19.4** The Granger Collection, NYC; **19.7** Erich Lessing/Art Resource; **19.8** INTERFOTO / Alamy; **19.9** Schalkwijk/Art Resource, NY; **19.10** The Granger Collection, NYC.

Chapter 20 Figure 20.1 Slaves on the West Coast of Africa, c.1833 (oil on canvas), Biard, Francois Auguste (1798–1882) / © Wilberforce House, Hull City Museums and Art Galleries, UK/The Bridgeman Art Library; **20.2** The Trustees of the British Museum/Art Resource, NY; **20.3** The British Library Board; **20.4** The Granger Collection, NYC; **20.5** The Metropolitan Museum of Art/Art Resource, NY; **20.6** The Granger Collection, NYC; **20.7** Michael Holford/British Library; **Visualizing the Past Image 1** Cary Wolinsky/Aurora Photos, Inc.; **Image 2** Tomborrw/Alamy; **20.8** UCLA Fowler Museum of Cultural History; **20.9** Museo Nacional del Virreinato, Tepotzotlan, Mexico/Schalkwijk/Art Resource, N.Y.; **20.10** The Granger Collection, New York.

Chapter 21 Figure 21.1 Tsar Ivan Alexeevich V (1666–96) (oil on panel), Russian School, (18th century)/State Russian Museum, St. Petersburg, Russia/The Bridgeman Art Library; **21.2** Gianni Dagli Orti/The Art Archive at Art Resource, NY; **21.3** akg-images; **21.4** Scala/Art Resource, NY; **Visualizing the Past** Sovfoto/Eastfoto; **21.5** Prisma Archivo/Alamy.

Chapter 22 Figure 22.1 V&A Images, London/Art Resource, NY; **22.2** Bettmann/Corbis; **22.3** The Mosque of Sultan Achmet at Constantinople, plate 2 from 'Views in the Ottoman Dominions', pub. by R. Bowyer, 1810 (aquatint), Mayer, Luigi (1755-1803) (after) / Private Collection / The Stapleton Collection/The Bridgeman Art Library; **22.4** Everett Collection Inc / Alamy; **22.5** Arthur Thevenart/Corbis; **22.6** Ullstein bild/The Granger Collection, NYC; **Visualizing the Past Image 1** Royal Collection Enterprises Ltd.; **Image 2** Royal Collection Enterprises Ltd.; **22.7** Scala/Art Resource, NY.

Chapter 23 Figure 23.1 The Arrival of Vasco da Gama (c.1469–1524) in Calcutta, 20th May 1498 (tapestry), Flemish School, (16th century) / Banco Nacional Ultramarino, Portugal / Giraudon/The Bridgeman Art Library; **23.2** Bry, Theodore de (1528–98) / Service Historique de la Marine, Vincennes, France / Lauros / Giraudon / The Bridgeman Art Library; **23.3** Berlin/Biblioteca Estense/Art Resource, NY; **23.4** S. Wells Williams, *The Middle Kingdom*, Vol. 1, (New York: Charles Scribner's Sons, 1882); **23.5** The Trustees of the British Museum/Art Resource, NY; **23.6** Matteo Ricci (1552-1610) and another Christian missionary to China, from 'China Illustrated' by Athanasius Kircher (1601–80) 1667 (later colouration), Dutch School, (17th century) / Private Collection / Giraudon/The Bridgeman Art Library; **Visualizing the Past Image 1** Michael K. Boss; **Image 2** Jan Adkins; **23.7** The Granger Collection, NYC; **23.8** Reunion des Musees Nationaux / Art Resource, NY.

PART IV REVISITING

P. 551 Philip Spruyt/Stapleton Collection/Corbis; **P. 552** Mary Evans Picture Library / Alamy; **P. 553** Jamie Marshall/Dorling Kindersly, Ltd.

PART V

P. 554 Marcello Saporetti/Direzione Civiche Raccolte d'Arte; **P. 555** Library of Congress Prints and Photographs Division[LC-USZC4-2758].

Chapter 24 Figure 24.1 The Granger Collection, NYC; **Visualizing the Past** The Trustees of the British Museum; **24.2** ullstein bild/The Granger Collection; **24.3** The Granger Collection, NYC; **24.4** National Gallery, London/Art Resource, NY; **24.5** The Philadelphia Museum of Art / Art Resource, NY.

Chapter 25 Figure 25.1 DeAgostini/SuperStock; **25.2** British Library; **25.3** Greenwich, London, Green Blackwall Collection/National Maritime Museum; **25.4** The Granger Collection, NYC; **25.5** Mary Evans Picture Library / Alamy; **25.6** North Wind Picture Archives/Alamy.

Chapter 26 Figure 26.1 Erich Lessing/Art Resource, NY; **26.2** Hisham Ibrahim/PhotoV/Alamy; **26.3** DeAgostini/Getty Images; **26.4** Bridgeman-Giraudon/Art Resource, NY; **26.5** Adoc-photos/Art Resource, NY; **Visualizing the Past Image 1** Everett Collection Historical/Alamy; **Image 2** Library of Congress Prints and Photographs Division Washington[LC-DIG-ppmsca-28721]; **26.6** The Granger Collection, NYC.

Chapter 27 Figure 27.1 The Granger Collection, NYC; **27.2** Bridgeman-Giraudon/Art Resource, NY; **27.3** Topical Press Agency/Stringer/Hulton Archive/Getty Images; **27.4** Erich Lessing/Art Resource, NY; **27.5** The Hongs of Canton—China Trade, c. 1850, Anonymous / Private Collection / © Taylor Gallery, London, UK/The Bridgeman Art Library; **27.6** The Granger Collection, NYC.

Chapter 28 Figure 28.1 Mary Evans Picture Library; **28.2** Keystone-Mast Collection, UCR/California Museum of Photography, University of California, Riverside; **28.3** Sovfoto/Eastfoto; **Visualizing the Past Image 1** Mary Evans Picture Library/Alamy; **Image 2** The Granger Collection, NYC.

PART V REVISITING

P. 690 Library of Congress Prints and Photographs Division[LC-DIG-stereo-1s02353]; **P. 691** Henry Guttmann/Hulton Archive/Getty Images; **P. 692** Fototeca Storica Nazionale/Getty PhotoDisc.

PART VI

P. 693 JoeFox/Alamy; **P. 694** Library of Congress; **P. 700** AP Photo/Hasan Jamali.

Chapter 29 Figure 29.1 Bettmann/Corbis; **29.2** Library of Congress Prints and Photographs Division [LC-USZC4-2950]; **Visualizing the Past** Imperial War Museum, London, UK / The Bridgeman Art Library; **29.3** Library of Congress Prints and Photographs Division[LC-USZC4-11161]; **29.4** Bettmann/Corbis; **29.5** The Granger Collection, NYC; **29.6** Library of Congress Prints and Photographs Division Washington, D.C.

Chapter 30 Figure 30. Sovfoto/Eastfoto; **30.2** Marcel Duchamp, Nude Descending a Staircase (No. 2), 1912. Oil on canvas, 57 7/8 x 35 1/8 inches (147 x 89.2cm), Photograph © The Philadelphia Museum of Art. The Louise and Walter Arensberg Collection, 1950/Art Resource, NY. Art © 2011 Artists Rights Society (ARS), New York/ADAGP, Paris/Succession Marcel Duchamp; **30.3** Neil Beer/Encyclopedia/Corbis; **30.4** Central Press/Stringer/Hulton Archive/Getty Images; **30.5** Bettmann/Corbis; **30.6** bpk, Berlin /Art Resource, NY; **30.7** Sovfoto/Eastfoto; **30.8** Everett Collection Inc/Alamy; **30.9** World History Archive/Alamy; **Visualizing the Past** John Bigelow Taylor/Art Resource, NY; **30.10** Sovfoto/Eastfoto.

Chapter 31 Figure 31.1 U.S. Marine Corps/AP Images; **31.2** ullstein bild/The Granger Collection, NYC; **31.3** AP Images; **31.4** The Image Works; **31.5** U.S. Army Photo; **31.6** ullstein bild / The Granger Collection, NYC; **Visualizing the Past Image 1** ullstein bild / The Granger Collection, NYC; **Image 2** Bettmann/Corbis; **Image 3** Bettmann/Corbis; **Image 4** Corbis Bettmann; **31.7** Keystone-France/Gamma-Keystone/Getty Images.

Chapter 32 Figure 32.1 The Granger Collection,NYC; **32.2** National Archives; **32.3** Anonymous/AP Images; **32.4** The Granger Collection, NYC; **32.5** Steve Northup/Time & Life Pictures/Getty Images; **32.6** Bettmann/Corbis; **32.7** The Granger Collection, NYC; **32.8** C. and M. History Pictures/Alamy; **32.9** Topham/The Image Works.

Chapter 33 Figure 33.1 Enrique Aracena/AP Images; **33.2** Bettmann/Corbis; **33.3** Alfredo Estrella/AFP/Newscom; **33.4** Gerardo Magallon/AFP/Getty Images; **Visualizing the Past Image 1** Tim Page/Corbis; **Image 2** Schalkwijk/Art Resource, NY; **33.5** Bettmann/Corbis; **33.6** Douglas Engle/AP Images; **33.7** Photo By Liu Zheng/Color China Photo/AP Images.

Chapter 34 Figure 34.1 Bettmann/Corbis; **34.2** Peter Turnley/Corbis; **34.4** Ladi Kirn/Alamy; **34.5** Bettmann/Corbis; **34.6** Bettmann/Corbis; **34.7** Stringer/AFP/Getty Images; **34.8** Bettmann/Corbis; **34.9** Bettmann/Corbis; **34.10** Peter Turnley/Corbis.

Chapter 35 Figure 35.1 Bettmann/Corbis; **35.2** Cpl. Walter Calmus/Historical/Corbis; **35.3** B.S.P.I./Terra/Corbis; **35.4** Kevin R. Morris/Bohemian Nomad Picturemakers/Corbis; **35.5** Walter Bibikow/Taxi/Getty Images; **35.6** Koichi Kamoshida/Stringer/Getty Images; **35.7** The Granger Collection, NYC; **35.8** Jacquet-Francillon/Stringer/AFP/Getty Images; **35.9** Jacques Pavlovsky/Sygma/Corbis; **35.10** Reuters/Corbis.

Chapter 36 Figure 36.1 Scott Sady/AP Images; **36.2** Bettmann/Corbis; **36.3** AlanWrigley/Alamy; **36.4** Kaiser/Caro/Alamy; **Visualizing the** Reuters/Corbis; **36.5** Peter Turnley/Turnley/Corbis; **36.6** © Peter Turnley/Corbis ; **36.7** Cagle Cartoons Inc; **36.8** AP Photo/Jerry Torrens.

Chapter 37 Figure 37.1 Ajit Kumar/AP Images; **37.2** Bettmann/Corbis; **37.3** Jacques Pavlovsky/Sygma/Corbis; **37.4** Yuri Arcurs/Insadco Photography/Alamy **37.5** Igor Kostin/Sygma/Corbis; **37.6** Justin Guariglia/National Geographic Stock; **Visualizing the Past** Rabih Moghrabi/AFP/Getty Images.

Index

Note: Page numbers followed by *f*, *m*, and *t* indicate figures, maps, and tables, respectively.

A

Abbasid era, 173–175, 174*m*, 177–179
  caliphs, 185–187, 192
  Christian crusades and, 187–188, 189
  commercial boom and agrarian expansion in, 175, 177, 179
  elite society in, 178
  imperial breakdown and agrarian disorder, 185
  imperial extravagance and succession disputes, 184–185
  Islamic conversion and Mawali acceptance in, 175
  Islamic learning in, 179
  nomadic incursions in, 187, 192
  peak of, 185*m*
  Persian literature in, 189–190
  religious trends and expansion, 191–192
  science achievements in and, 190
  women in, declining positions of, 186–187
Abbas the Great, 505
Abdallahi, Khalifa, 649, 650
Abd al-Rahman, 156–157
Abduh, Muhammad, 648
Abdul Hamid, 643
Abelard, Peter, 254
Absolute monarchy, 412*m*, 417, 418–419
Abu Bakr, 166–167
Abu Taleb, 503
Achebe, Chinua, 853
Afghanistan, 900, 901, 912, 915
Africa
  colonial expansion and, impact of, 401–402
  East Africa, Swahili coast of, 215–217, 216*m*
    cultures on, 216–217
    trading routes, 216, *m*2
  international contacts, in 1450, 365
  societies in
    artists and kings, 217–218, 220
    Central African kingdoms, 220
    elements in, common, 207
    Great Zimbabwe and, 221, 222*f*
    Kongo kingdom, 220–221
    Mwene Mutapa kingdom, 221
    stateless, 206
    with states, 206
  South Africa
    apartheid and, demise of, 864–865, 866*f*
    dominance, in European global order, 606–607
    mfecane and, 469
    white settlers and Africans in, 467–469
    Zulu and, 468–469
  trade in, 91, 91*m*
  during World War I, 710, 710*m*
  in World War II, 783–784, 785–788
Africa, rise and spread of Islam in, 204–223
  in Ethiopia, 208–209
  in Ghana, 209–210
  in grassland kingdoms, 209–214
  in North Africa, 207–208
  in Nubia, 208
  in Sudanic states, 210–214
  in Sudanic states in, 210–214
    city dwellers and villagers, 211, 212
    epic of Sundiata and, 212
    "Lion Prince" and, 211
    Mali Empire, 210–211
    political and social life in, 214
    Songhay, 213–214
  in Swahili coast of East Africa, 215–217, 216*m*
    cultures on, 216–217
    trading routes, 216, *m*2
Africa/Africans and Atlantic slave trade, 453–477
African art, 463, 465*m* 545*f*, 474*f*
African diaspora, 469–475
  abolition of slavery, 474–475
  Africans in Americas, 470
  American slave societies, 470, 472
  end of slave trade, 474–475
  Middle Passage and, 469, 471–472
  people and gods in exile, 472, 474
  slave lives in, 469
African National Congress, 865
African slave trade
  in Asante empire, 463–465
  in Dahomey, 465
  demographic patterns, 459
  in East Africa and Sudan, 465–467
  expansion of, 457–459
  organization of, 459–454
  politics and, 461, 462
  Portuguese and, 456–457, 456*m*
  slave exports from Africa, 458*t*
  slave imports into Americas, 458*t*
  society and, in historical perspective, 462–463
  through Atlantic System, 454–456
  timeline, 455
Afrikaner National Party, 787
Age of revolution, 562–563
  American Revolution, 565
  defined, 562–563
  French Revolution, 565–568, 567*m*
  Industrial and Atlantic revolutions compared, 580–581
  revolutions of 1848, 569–571
Agrarian, in Abbasid era, 175, 177, 179
Agrarian disorder, in Abbasid era, 185
Agrarian production, in Tang and Song eras, 300–301, 301*f*
Agriculture
  in Americas, 33–34
  Aztecs, 271
  change and, 15–16
  estate, 490
  Middle East and Mediterranean, classical, 111–112
  in Ming dynasty, 533
  Neolithic revolution and, 12–16
  Nomadic societies and, 16–18
  spread of, 3*m*
  in Tang and Song eras, 300–301, 301*f*
Ahmad, Muhammad, 649
Ajanta, cave temples at, 74–75, 74*f*
Akbar, 511–512
Akkadians, 25
Al-Afghani, Jamal al-Din, 648
Al-Din, Rashid, 331*f*
Alexander the Great, 77, 100–101, 100*m*
Al-Ghazali, 190, 191

I–1

Ali, 163
Ali, Muhammad, 645, 646–647
Allah, 162
Allende, Salvador, 832
Alliance for Progress, 837
Allies, cold war, 802–804
    Australia, 803
    Canada, 802–803
    New Zealand, 803
    United States, 803–804
Al-Mahdi, 184
Almohadis, 208
Amaru, Tupac, II, 450
American Civil War, 574
American Revolution, 565
Americas, 33–35
    Africans in, 470
    Chavin de Huantar and Andeans, 34–35
    in classical period, 122–125, 123*m*
        Maya peoples, 124–125
        valley of Mexico, 123–124
    colonial expansion and, impact of, 396–397
    Olmecs, 34, 34*f*
    political issues, in 1450, 363
    in postclassical period, 265–286
        Aztecs in (*See* Aztecs)
        civilized peoples in, 282
        culture patterns in, 283–284
        diversity in, 284
        Incas in (*See* Incas)
        population of, 282–283, 283*t*
        primitive peoples in, 282
        timeline, 267
        Toltecs in, 267–267
    slave imports into, 458*t*
    slave societies in, 470, 472
Amigos del país, 446
Amistad (slave ship), 475
Analects, 55, 64
Anarchists, 670
Andeans, 34–35, 276
Anglican church, 409
Anglo-American offensives, in World War II, 775–776
Anglo-Boer War, 607
Animal husbandry, 392
Anti-Chinese rioting, 561–562
Anwar, Chairil, 852–853
Apartheid, 787–788
Aquinas, Thomas, 254–255
Aquino, Corazon, 851, 852
Arabi, Ahmad, 648
Arabia, 158–181, 159*m*
    Abbasid rule in, 173–175, 174*m*, 177–179
    under Abu Bakr, 166–167

adversary empires, weakness of, 167–169
clans in, 160–161
conquests of, motives for, 167
environment of, 158–160, 160*f*
gender roles in, 172–173
Islam in, 156–181
    Abbasid era and, 174–175, 177–179
    Arabs and, 164–165
    elements in, universal, 165–166
    mosque as symbol of Islamic civilization, 171*f*, 176–177, 179
    Muhammad and, 163–166
    overview of, 157–158
    pre-Islamic Arabia and, 158–162, 159*m*
    timeline, 158
    Umayyads and, 166–173
marriage and family, 162
under Muhammad, 163–166
poets and neglected gods in, 162
succession and Sunni–Shi'a split in, 169
towns and long-distance trade in, 161
Umayyads in, 161, 169–171, 173
Arabian Nights, 195
Aragon, 361
Architecture
    in China, Vietnam influenced by, 325, 325*f*
    gothic, in western Europe, 256*f*
    Greek, 109, 110*f*
    Hellenistic, 109
    in Mughal empire, 512
Area of Darkness, An (Naipaul), 853
Arevalo, Juan José, 827
Argentina
    economy in, 624–625, 627, 633, 635
    in Great Depression, 756–757
Argentine Republic, 625
Ariel (Rodó), 636–637
Aristocrats, in Korea, 322
Aristotle, 107, 158
Armenian genocide, 711
Art
    African, 217–218, 220, 463, 465*m* 545*f*
    cave paintings, in Stone Age, 10*f*
    in China, 66, 67*m*
    Greek, 109, 110*f*
    Inca, 281, 281*f*
    India, classical, 86–87
    in Industrial Revolution, 578, 579*f*
    in Latin America, post-World War II, 827
    in Ming dynasty, 534
    in Mughal empire, 512, 513–515
    Persian Empire, 98–99
    religious, in western Europe, 255–256
    representations of women in, 11
    in Roaring Twenties, 731, 732*f*

    in Tang and song Song eras, 302, 303–306
    terra-cotta objects, 217, 218*f*
Artha, 82
The Art of War, 62–63
Aryans
    Braham culture, 77–78
    caste system, 77–78
    gods and goddesses, 78
    migrants, 31*m*, 32
    poetry, 18
    varnas, 77
Asante empire, 463
Asantehene, 463
Ashikaga Shogunate, 315
Ashikaga Takuaji, 315
Ashoka, 79, 79*m*, 80*f*
Asia
    British rule
        consolidation, 592–593
        in India, 591–592
    colonial expansion and, impact of, 401–402
    colonial society
        in India, 593–594
        in Java, 593–594
    Dutch advance on Java, 591
    east Asia, post-World War II
        Hong Kong, 875
        Japan, 871–877
        Korea, intervention and war, 872–873
        settlements, 871–877
        Singapore, stability in, 875
        Taiwan, stability in, 874
    European land empires in, 590–597, 590*m*
    social reform in colonies, 594, 596–597
    south Asia
        nationalism and, 848*m*, 849
        in World War II, 781–783
    southeast Asia
        Islam in, 200–202, 201*m*
        in World War II, 781–783
    transitions in age of global change, 520–543
        Japan, 538–542
        Ming dynasty, 529–538
        overseas expansion, Europe and China compared, 537–538
        timeline, 522
    Western education and, 595–596
    in World War II, 777*m*
Asian sea trading network, 522–529, 523*m*
    European tribute systems, 526–528
    expansion, pattern of, 527*m*

missionaries, in south and southeast Asia, 528–529
   Portuguese, 524–526
   zones, 523, 523*m*
Askia, 213
Assegais, 588
Atahuallpa, 398–399
Ataturk, 721
Atlantic Charter of 1941, 782
Atlantic revolutions, 580–581. *See also* Age of revolution
Atlantic System, 454–455. *See also* African slave trade
   creation of, 454–455
   slave trade through, 456–460
Attila the Hun, 131
Audiencia, 440
Augustine (Saint), 132
Aurangzeb, 513
Aurelius, Marcus, 101
Australia
   as cold war ally, 803
   Industrial Revolution in, 583
   in Roaring Twenties, 732, 734*m*
Austria, in Triple Alliance, 584
Authoritarianism, in Great Depression, 753–762
   in Argentina, 756–757
   in Brazil, 755–756
   fascism, 733–734, 753
   in Japan, 757–758, 758*m*
   in Latin America, 753–754, 755
   in Soviet Union, 758–762
   Spanish Civil War, 753
Axum, 28*f*, 119
Ayan, 179, 641
Ayatollahs (religious experts), 863
Ayllus, 276
Aztecs, 268–275
   agriculture of, 271
   behavior for people in different roles, 274–275
   calendar, 271, 271*f*
   conquest and, ideology of, 269–271
   economy of, 271–272
   Incas compared to, 281–282
   men's roles in, 274–275
   population of, 273, 275
   power of, rise to, 268–269
   religion of, 269–271, 270*f*
   social classes, 272–273, 273*f*
   social contract of, 269
   social transition of, 272–274
   technological constraints of, 273, 275
   tributes in, 275
   women's rights and roles in, 273, 274–275

B

Babur Muhammad (The Tiger), 493–494, 493*f*, 510, 511
Babylonians, 25
"Backyard" furnaces, 885, 885*f*
Bacon, Francis, 416
Bactria, 78
Baghdad
   as Abbasid capital, 174
   elite in, 178
Baibars, 342, 343
Ba Jin, 745
Bakufu, 315
Balance, Chinese tradition about, 55–56
Balboa, Vasco de, 396
Balfour Declaration, 722
Balkan nationalism, 284
Banana republics, 836
Bangladesh, 846, 848*m*
Banking, in western Europe, 258–259, 259*f*
Bankruptcy, Islamic heartlands, 647–648
Banner armies, 650
Baquaqua, Mahommah Gardo, 453–454
Barbudos (bearded rebels), 828–829, 829*f*
Batavia, 526
Batista, Fulgencio, 828
Batouala (Maran), 602
Battle of Algiers, The (Fanon), 724
Battle of Britain, 773
Battle of Isandhlwana, 587–588, 588*f*
Battle of Kulikova, 340
Battle of Siffin, 169
Battle of the Bulge, 776
Battle of the Coral Sea, 778
Battle of the River Zab, 173
Batu, 338
Bedouin culture, 159–160, 172–173. *See also* Arabia
Belisarius, 228, 229
Benedict of Nursia, 135
Benin, 218, 220
Beowulf, 256
Berke, 343
Berlin, revolution in, 570, 570*f*
Berlin Wall, 810, 903, 903*f*
Bernard of Clairvaux, 254
Bet Giorgis, 209*f*
Bhaktic cults, 199, 199*f*, 200
Bhutto, Benazir, 851, 852
Bian Liang, 287*f*
Biard, Auguste François, 453*f*
Biko, Steve, 865
Bistros, 681
Black Death, 261, 262*f*, 356, 358
Blitzkrieg, 772–775
Bodhisattvas, 133

Boer Republics, 607
Boers, 401
Bolívar, Simon, 616, 616*f*, 625–626
Bolsheviks, 671
Bonaparte, Napoleon, 567–568, 567*m*
Bourbon reforms, 447–449, 448*m*
Boxer Rebellion, 658, 658*f*
Boyars, 238, 481
Braham culture, 77–78
Brahma, 83
Brazil
   economy in, 627–628
   as first plantation colony, 441–443
      gold rush, 442–443
      sugar and slavery, 441–442
   in Great Depression, 755–756
   independence, 616–617
Britain
   colonial expansion and, impact of, 397, 399*f*, 400–401
   rule, in early colonial society
      consolidation, 592–593
      in India, 591–592
   in Triple Entente, 584
   West Indian slaveholding, 394
   in World War I, 710–711
   in World War II, 772–773
British Commonwealth of Nations, 732
British East India Company, 389, 401
British Raj, 592
Bronze Age, 15–16
Brookes (slave ship), 378
Bubonic plague, 356, 358
Buchan, John, 602
Buddha, 76, 78, 84–85
Buddhism, 76, 84–86, 85*m*
   dharma, 79, 82
   popularization of Chinese, 127
   spread of, in Asia, 85*m*
Bulgaria, 230
Bulgaroktonos, 230
Bungalow, 594
Bureaucracy, in China, 61
Bush, George W., 912
Bushi, 314
Buyids, 187
Byzantine, 230
Byzantine empire, 132
   Arab pressure and empire's defense, 228–229, 230
   art in, 228, 228*f*, 231, 232*f*
   decline of, 232–234
   under Justinian, 227–228, 228*m*
   politics in, 230–231
   power of, 225–226
   society in, 230–231
   women and power in, 229

C

Cabral, Pedro Alvares, 441
Caesar, 230
Caesar, Augustus, 101
Caesar, Julius, 101
Cairo, war protests in, 701–702, 701f
Calcutta, 401–402
Calendar systems
    Aztec, 271, 271f
Caliphs, 166, 214
    in Abbasid era, 185–187, 192
Calpulli, 272
Calvin, Jean, 409–410
Canada
    as cold war ally, 802–803
    Industrial Revolution in, 582–583
    in Roaring Twenties, 732, 734m
Candomblé, 439, 474
Canterbury Tales (Chaucer), 256
Canton, 533
Cape Colony, 401
Cape of Good Hope, 387
Capital cities
    Constantinople, 495, 496, 498f, 499–500
    Isfahan, 508, 508f
    Loango, 464f
    populations in Latin America, post-World War II, 839–840, 840t
Capitalism, 258–260
"Capitalist-roaders," 888
Captaincies, 441
Caravels (ships), 521
Cárdenas, Lázaro, 755
Caribbean, 428–431, 429m
Carlota, 612–613
Carolingians, 245
Carter, Jimmy, 900
Carthage, 101
Caste system, 77, 81, 82, 84, 85, 86, 87–90
Castile, 361
Castro, Fidel, 828–829, 829f
Çatal Hüyük, 15, 15f
Catherine the Great, 485, 487–489, 487f
Catholic Reformation, 410
Caudillos, 619
Causation, in historical perspective, 390
Cave temples at Ajanta, 74–75, 74f
Centralists, 619
Ceramics, in Korea, 321f
Césaire, Aimé, 716
Cetshwayo, 588
Cézanne, Paul, 579f
Chabi, 344, 345f
Chac, 270
Chaldiran, 504, 505
Chams, 327
Chan Buddhism, 293

Chan-Chan, 277
Chandragupta Maurya, 78–79
    Ashoka, 79, 79m
Chang'an, 291
Charlemagne, 245–247, 247f
Charles III, 447
Chartist movement, 570
Chavin de Huantar, 34–35
Chechnya revolt, 905, 906, 908–909
Chernobyl, 931f
Chetu (cool), 919
Chiang Ching-kuo, 878–879
Chiang Kai-shek, 747
Chichimecs, 18
Chimu, 277
China
    adaptation to Industrial Age, compared to Japan, 675
    early, 32–33
        ideographic symbols, 32
        Shang dynasty, 32–33, 33m
        Yellow River, 32, 33
        Zhou dynasty, 33, 33m
    global industrialization in, 920–921
    nationalist alternative, in Qing dynasty, 658–660
    overseas expansion, Europe compared to, 537–538
    revolution in, early 20th-century, 743–748, 746m
        Guomindang, 746–747
        Mao and peasant option, 747–748
        Marxism, 745–746
        May Fourth movement, 744–746
    transregional trade, in 1450, 354–355
    values in, exam questions and, 531
China, classical, 54–72
    compared to classical Mediterranean, 104
    compared to India, classical, 88
    complexities in, 71
    economy and society, 67–71
        Confucian social system, 68
        gender and family life, 70–71
        Han capital at Xi'an, 68–69, 69m
        trade and technology, 69, 70f
    Great Wall, 58, 58f
    overview of, 54–56
    patterns in, 56–60
        Han dynasty, 56, 59–60, 60m
        Qin dynasty, 56, 57–59, 57m
        Zhou dynasty, 56–57, 57m, 60m, 62–63
    politics, 60–63, 71
        bureaucracy, 61
        state functions, 61, 63
    religion and culture, 63–67

        art, 66, 67m
        Confucianism, 64–65
        Daoism, 65
        Legalism, 65
        literature, 65, 66
        math, 67
        science, 66
    ritual combat to real war, 62–63
    timeline, 56
China, in postclassical period, 287–307, 289m
    architecture in, 325, 325f
    cultural exports and, 325
    in east Asia, 308–330
        Japan, 310–319
        key centers of civilization in, 309m
        Korea, 319–322
        timeline, 310
        Vietnam, 322–329
    Golden Age of, 299–306
    Mongols, 331–350
    scholar-gentry elites in, 304, 306
    Song era, 296–306
    Sui era, 288–290
    Tang era, 290–296, 299–306
    timeline, 289
Chinampas, 271
Chinggis Khan, 191, 192, 332
    career of, early, 334–335
    death of, 338
    empire of, 332m, 333–338
Chongzhen, 538
Choson, 319
Christian crusades, 187–188, 189
Christianity
    Orthodox, 225, 226, 230, 231, 238, 239
    in postclassical period
        in eastern Europe, 232–234
        in Russia, 237
        in western Europe, 231–232
    in Rome, 102
Christos (God's anointed), 134
Chungara, Domitilia Barrios de, 830
Church
    in Latin America politics, 620
    and state, in Latin America, 439–441
Churchill, Winston, 770
Cicero, 107
Científicos, 633
Cities and towns
    Arabian long-distance trade, 161
    in Sudanic states, 211, 212
City-states, 24
Civilizations
    in crisis, 639–661
        Islamic heartlands, 644–650
        Ottoman empire, 641–644

Qing dynasty, 650–660
  timeline, 641
 defined, 22
 early, 7–20
  agriculture and, 15–16
  in Americas, 33–35
  centers of, 3*m*
  changes in, 4–5
  children and, daily life of, 6
  in China, 32–33
  in China, early, 23–25
  concepts of, 2, 4
  continuity in, 5–6
  defining, 17–19
  Egypt, 27–30
  Egyptian, 21–22
  historical perspective of, 18–19
  hunting and gathering, era of, 9–10
  in India, 30–32
  Neolithic Age, 12–14
  Nomadic societies and, 16–18
  overview of, 2
  Paleolithic Age, 10–12
  populations, spread of, 12*m*
  river valley, 30–37
  spread of, 22–23
  spread of civilizations, 22–23
  Tigris-Euphrates, 23–25
  timeline of, 4–5
 Nomadic societies, 17–18
Cixi, 658
Clans, in Arabia, 160–161
Classical civilization
 changes in, 49, 51
 China, 54–72
 concepts of, 49
 continuity in, 51–52, 53
 India, 74–93
 Middle East and Mediterranean, 94–116
 old age and, daily life of, 53
 overview of, 49
 timeline of, 52–53
 trends and societies, 53
Classical period, 117–148
 Africa and the Americas, similarities and differences between, 118–119
 Americas, 122–125, 123*m*
 Central and South America, civilizations of, 123*m*
 Han China, decline and fall in, 125–126, 128
 India, decline in, 128–129
 Japan and Northern Europe, 122
 Kush kingdom, developments in, 119, 119*f*, 122
 Maya peoples, 124–125
 Nomadic peoples and, 120–121
 religious geography, 136, 136*m*
 Roman Empire, decline and fall of, 129–133
 trade routes at end of, 121*m*
 Valley of Mexico, 123–124
 world religions, development and spread of, 133–137
Classic of Songs, 66
Clemenceau, Georges, 713
Clive, Robert, 592
Cloth, kent, 473
Clovis, 244
Coeur, Jacques, 259
Coffeehouses, 500
Cold war, 780–781, 791–820. *See also* Soviet Union
 allies, 802–804
  Australia, 803
  Canada, 802–803
  New Zealand, 803
  United States, 803–804
 end of, 898–906
  Berlin Wall and, 903, 903*f*
  Commonwealth of Independent States and, 905
  demonstrations in 1990s, 904–906, 905*f*
  genocide and, 910–911, 910*f*
  Gorbachev and, 900–902, 901*f*
  Middle East conflicts and, 909–910
  NATO intervention and, 909
  superpowers, 911–915
  timeline, 899
  Yeltsin and, 905
 overview of, 794–795
 rivalries, nationalism and, 853, 856
 timeline, 792–793
 western Europe, post-World War II, 793–802
Collectivization, 742, 743*f*
Colonial economies, in Latin America, 436–441
 haciendas and villages, 437
 industry and commerce, 437, 439
 silver discoveries, 436–437, 437*f*
 state and church, 439–441
Columbian Exchange, 391–393
 of animal husbandry, 392
 of crops, 391–392
 of disease, 391, 392*f*
 environmental impact of, 392–393
Columbus, Christopher, 387, 427, 428, 429, 438, 536
 expedition of, 398
Comintern (Communist International office), 742

Commerce
 commercialism, in western Europe, 357–359
 during 18th century, 422–423
 in Western transformation, 407–412
Commercial revolution, 412–415
 balance sheet, 414–415
 social protest, 413, 414
 world economy and, impact of, 413
Communism, 738–740, 741
Communist Party of Vietnam, 891
Compass, 351–352
Complimentary husbands, 302
Compradors, 653
Comte, Auguste, 621–622
Comunero Revolt, 450
Confucianism, 64–65
 in Song era, 298
Confucian social system, 68
Confucius, 54–55, 54*f*, 64–65, 66
Congress of Vienna, 568
Conquistadors, in Spanish/Portuguese conquest, 432, 434
Conservatives, 568
Constable, John, 578*f*
Constantine, 102, 130
Constantinople, 495, 496, 498*f*, 499–500
Consulado, 437
Consuls, 105
Consumption, in Industrial Revolution, 577
Contemporary period
 critical themes, 939
 critical thinking questions, 939
Convention People's Party (CPP), 785
Cook, Captain James, 608, 608*f*
Copernicus, Nicolaus, 415
Coptic Church, 133
Copts, 168
Córdoba, 156*f*, 157
Core nations, 394
Corinthian, 109
Cornfield, The (Constable), 578*f*
Cornwallis, Lord Charles, 594, 596
Coronado, Francisco Vázquez de, 432, 434
Corporatism, 755
Corregidores, 447
Corridos (ballads), 737
Cortés, Hernán, 431–432
Cossacks, 481
Cotton, 405, 405*f*
Council of Nicaea, 134
Council of the Indies, 440
CounterPunch (newsletter), 927–928
Creative Fellowship (Shcherbakov painting), 761*f*
Creoles, 445, 446, 614
Creole slaves, 470

Index I-5

Crimean War, 666–667
Cristeros, 738
Cromer, Lord, 720
Crops, Columbian Exchange of, 391–392
Cross-cultural exchange, Mongols and, 337–338
Crusades, 187
"Cry of the Excluded," 832f
Cuban revolution, 828–829, 831–833
Cubist movement, 731
Cultural globalization, 925–927
Cultural Revolution, 888
Culture
    bedouin, 159–160, 172–173
    in China, 63–67
        art, 66, 67m
        Confucianism, 64–65
        Daoism, 65
        Legalism, 65
        literature, 65, 66
        math, 67
        science, 66
    globalization, 925–927
    in Inca empire, 281, 281f
    India, classical, 76–78, 82–87
        arts, 86–87
        Buddhism, 76, 84–86, 85m
        cave temples at Ajanta, 74–75, 74f
        Hinduism, 82–84
        sciences, 86
        stupas, 86–87, 86f
    in Japan, post-World War II, 874–875
    in Kievan Rus', 237, 238
    in Latin America, after independence, 629
    Middle East, in 1450, 353–354
    Middle East and Mediterranean, classical, 107–110
    of Mongols, Chinese influence of, 344
    Nomadic societies, 17
    in Persia, Hellenistic influence on, 115
    in postcolonial nations, 852–853
    Renaissance, 359–360
    on Swahili coast of East Africa, 216–217
    Toltec, 267–268
    Western, post-World War II, 808–809
    in Western transformation, 407–412
        Catholic Reformation, 410, 410m
        Christian unity and, end of, 410–412
        Italian Renaissance, 407–408
        Northern Renaissance, 408
        Protestantism, 409–410, 410m
        technology and family, 409
Cuneiform, 23–24, 24f, 25f
Cunha, Euclides da, 628
Curacas (leaders), 278
Cuzco, 425–426

Cyril, 235
Cyrus the Great, 97
Czechoslovakia, 908–909

D

Dadu, 344
Da Gama, Vasco, 361, 362f, 520–521, 520f
Dahomey Kingdom, 465
Daimyos, 317
Damascus, 170
Damask, 188
Dao, 55–56
Daoism, 65
Darwin, Charles, 577–578
Death marches, 765f
De Beauvoir, Simone, 807
Decembrist uprising, 665
Declaration of the Rights of Man and the Citizen, 565
Decline and fall of civilizations, Ibn Khaldun on, 188
Decolonization, 781
    in Africa, 783–784, 785–788
    in Middle East, 788–789
    in south and southeast Asia, 781–783
Deism, 416
De Klerk, F. W., 865
De la Cruz, Sor Juana Inés, 440–441, 440f
De Las Casas, Bartolomé, 432f
Demak, 201
Democracy, 906–908
    in China, protest and repression, 907–908
    conflicts and, 908–911
    limits of, 906, 908
    patterns of change in, 906
Demographic transition, 219, 220
Demography, 218–220
Deng Xiaoping, 886
Dependency theory, 632
Descamisados (poor), 756
Descartes, René, 416
Description of the World (Polo), 346f
Deshima Island, 541
Destruction of the Philosophers, The (Al-Ghazali), 353
Developing nations, 631
Devi, 128–129
Dharma, 79, 82
Dhimmi, 170
Dhows, 175, 182–183, 182f
Díaz, Porfirio, 736
Dictatorships
    in Egypt, 857–861
    in Ghana, 856–857
    in World War II, 768, 769
Diderot, Denis, 420, 422
Dien Bien Phu, 892

Diet, 677
Diktat (dictated peace), 714
Din-i-Ilahi, 511
Dinshawai incident, 720–721, 721f
Diocletian, 102, 130
Direct democracy, 103, 105
Discourse between Muslim Sages, A, 190f
Disease
    Columbian Exchange of, 391, 392f
    globalization and, 932
Divine Comedy (Dante), 359f
Divorce, in Tang and Song eras, 302
Doric, 109
Douglass, Frederick, 471
Dreadnought (battleship), 705
Dreyfus, Alfred, 722
Du, Nguyen, 328
Dubai, 935
Du Bois, W. E. B., 726
Duchamp, Marcel, 732f
Duchy of Moscow, 479–480
Duma, 672
Dutch advance on Java, 591
Dutch East India Company, 389
Dutch Studies, 674
Dutch trading empire, 526, 527m
Dynamism, in western Europe, 356

E

Early modern period
    Africa/Africans and Atlantic slave trade, 453–477
    Asian transitions in age of global change, 520–543
    big changes, 380–381
    big concepts, 378
    biological exchange, 381
    contacts and their limits, 544–545
    continuity, 382
    critical themes, 546–547
    critical thinking questions, 547
    early Latin America, 425–452
    impact on daily life, work, 382
    major political units of the world, c. 1450, 379m
    major political units of the world, c. 1750, 379m
    Muslim empires, 493–519
    new empires, 381–382
    new global economy and proto-globalization, 380–381
    overview, changes in world map, 378
    Russia, 478–492
    timeline, 380–381
    transformation, 405–424
    trends and societies in, 382–383
    triggers for change, 378, 380

world economy, 384–404
East Africa, Swahili coast of, 215–217, 216*m*
   cultures on, 216–217
   trading routes, 216, *m*2
East Asia, post-World War II
   Hong Kong, 875
   Japan
      economic surge in, 875–877
      political and cultural style, 874
      recovery in, 871–872
   Korea, intervention and war, 872–873
   settlements, 871–877
   Singapore, stability in, 875
   Taiwan, stability in, 874
Eastern bloc, 794
Eastern Europe
   revolution in Russia and, 672–673
   in Roaring Twenties, 734–735, 735*m*
   Russia and, early modern period, 491
Eastern Europe, in postclassical era, 224–240
   Byzantine empire, 225–231, 228*m*, 233*m*
   Christianity and, 231–234
      decline of Byzantine empire and, 232–234
      schism in, 231–232
   end of, 239
   spread of civilization in, 235
      East Central borderlands, 235
      Kiev, 237, 238–239
      Kievan Rus', 237, 238
      slavic expansion, 235, 236*m*
      trade patterns, 236–237
   timeline, 226
   western Europe and, boundary problems between, 234
Eastern Front, 712
Econocide, 475
Economies
   Aztec, 271–272
   in China, 67–71
      Confucian social system, 68
      gender and family life, 70–71
      Han capital at Xi'an, 68–69, 69*m*
      trade and technology, 69, 70*f*
   in European global order, 604
   globalization and, 923–925, 927–928
   India, classical, 87–88
   in Japan, post-World War II, 875–877
   in Latin America, 620–628
      Argentina, 624–625, 627, 633, 635
      Brazilian empire, 627–628
      instability and foreign intervention, 622–624
      Mexico, 633
      Monroe Doctrine and, 620
      Panama Canal and, 635–637, 636*f*
      resurgence and liberal politics, 621–622
      stagnation, 621
      trade expansion, 630–631, 633
      United States' interest in, 635–637
   Middle East and Mediterranean, classical, 111–114
   in Russia, in Industrial Age, 665–667
   in Soviet Union, 759, 760–761
   in western Europe, 247–248
   in western Europe, post-World War II, 801–802, 801*f*
Edict of Nantes, 410
Edo, 539
Education, Western, 595–596
Effendi, 720
Egypt
   dictatorships in, 857–861
   early, 27–30
      Kush, 28, 28*f*
      Mesopotamia compared to, 29, 30
      pharaoh, 27
      pyramids, 27–28, 28*f*
   nationalism in
      revolt, in 1919, 723, 724–725
      rise of, 719–721, 720*m*
18th century
   reforms, in Latin America, 446–450
      Bourbon reforms, 447–449, 448*m*
      Marquis of Pombal, 449
      politics and trade, 446
      reforms, reactions, and revolts, 449–480
   Western transformation and, 420–423
      commerce, 422–423
      Enlightenment, 420–422
      innovation, 423
      instability, 424
      manufacturing, 422–423
      political patterns, 420
Einstein, Albert, 578
Eisenhower, Dwight, 817
Ejidos (communal holdings), 737
Elites
   in Abbasid era, 178
   in Baghdad, 178
   in historical perspective, 418
   in Japan
      gatekeeper, 326–327
      warrior, 311*m*, 314–319
   in Korea, 321–323
   in Mughal empire, 516
   scholar-gentry, in Tang and Song eras, 304, 306
   Sinification of, in Korea, 321–323
El Mina, 456
Emancipation of the serfs, 667

Emir, 214
Emperor, 246
Empress Wu, 294–295
Encomendero, 428
Encomienda, 428
Encyclopaedia Britannica, 422
Encyclopédie (Diderot), 420
Engineering in, in Tang and Song eras, 302, 304
English Civil War, 411
Enlightenment, 420–422
Environmental concerns
   of Arabia, 158–160, 160*f*
   of Columbian Exchange, 392–393
   globalization and, 929–932
      Chernobyl, 931*f*
      disease, 932
      as global concerns, 930–932
      global warming, 931–932
   in postcolonial nations, 850–851
Epic age, 31
Equiano, Olaudah, 471–472
Era of the Warring States, 57, 57*m*
Espanola, 398
Estado Novo (New State), 755
Estate agriculture, 490
Ethical systems, Hellenistic, 107
Ethiopia, 119, 208–209
Ethnocentrism, 364
Ethnocentrism, in historical perspective, 364
Eurasia, trade in, 91, 91*m*
Europe
   in Islamic heartlands, 648
   Japan's reunification and, 540, 541*m*
   in Ming dynasty, arrival of, 535
   Mongol retreat from, 341
   Mughal empire and, 512–513
   Northern Europe
      classical period, 122
      expeditions, 388–389, 389*f*, 391*m*
   overseas expansion, China compared to, 537–538
   in World War I, 704*m*, 707–710
   in World War II, 772, 773*m*
European global order, in Industrial Age, 587–611. *See also* World War I
   Asia, land empires in, 590–597, 590*m*
      British rule, 591–593
      colonial society, 593–594
      Dutch advance on Java, 591
      social reform in colonies, 594, 596–597
      Western education and, 595–596
   dominance in, patterns of, 601–609
      economic extraction, methods of, 604
      overseas possession s and, 601

European global order . . . (cont.)
    social relations between colonizers
        and colonies, 603
    South Africa, 606–607
    South Pacific tragedies, 607–609
    tropical dependencies, 601, 602
    white settler colonies, 604, 605–596
  end of (*See* World War II)
  partitioning, 1870-1914, 597–600
    of Africa, 598, 599, 599*m*
    colonial wars and European
        imperialism, 598–600
    resistance to, 600
    of southeast Asia and Pacific, 598,
        599, 600*m*
  timeline, 589
  tropical dependencies and, 601
European-style family, 409
European Union (EU)
  cold war, 798–799, 799*m*
  post-cold war, 911–912
Examination system, meritocracy and,
    291–292, 292*f*
Expansionist trends, in world economy, 396
Expeditions, Ming dynasty, 534*m*, 536

F

Fabrics, European, 405–406, 405*f*
Factories, 456, 524–525
Factory workers in Russia, in Industrial
    Age, 668–669
Facundo (Sarmiento), 625, 629
Families
  Arabian, 162
  aristocratic, in Korea, 322
  in China, 70–71
  in Song era, 301–302
  in Tang era, 301–302
  in Western transformation, 409
Family (Ba Jin), 745
Fanon, Frantz, 724
Fascio di combattimento (union for
    struggle), 733
Fascism, 733, 733–734, 753
Favelas, 840
Fazendas, 627
Federalists, 619
Feminine Mystique, The (Friedan), 807
Feminist movements, 575, 576
Feng shui, 351
Ferdinand, Archduke Franz, 706
Ferdinand of Aragon, 427, 428
"The First Emperor of the Han Dynasty
    Entering Guandang" (painting), 67*m*
First U.S. Iraq War, 909, 910
Five Classics, 65, 66
Five pillars, 166

Five-year plans, 760–761
*Florentine Codex: The General History of
    the Things of New Spain* (Sahagún),
    274–275
Flying money, 300
Footbinding, 303
*Former Great Dinner of the Modern
    Gargantua with His Family, The*, 566
Forum, 110*f*
1450, world in. *See* World power, in 1450
France. *See also* French Revolution
  in Triple Entente, 584
  women in workforce, 806
Francis I, 408
Frederick the Great, 420
Free Officers movement, 858
Free wage labor, 558
French Revolution, 565–568, 567*m*
  authoritarian phase of, 567–568
  in cartoons, 566
  Napoleon and, 567–568, 567*m*
  nationalism and, 566–567
  political movements, 568
  radical phase of, 566–567
Friedan, Betty, 807
Fujiwara, 313
Fukayama, Francis, 933
Fukuzawa Yukichi, 662–663
Fulani, 466
Fustian, 188

G

Galileo Galilei, 416
Galleons, 437
Gallipoli, 711
Gálvez, José de, 447
Gandhi, Indira, 843–845, 843*f*, 851
Gandhi, Mohandas, 715, 718–719
Gang of Four, 888
Garvey, Marcus, 726
Gatekeeper elites, in Japan, 326–327
Gauchos, 626
Gempei Wars, 315
Gender, in China, 70–71
Gender roles
  in bedouin culture, 172–173
  in historical perspective, 172–173
  in Latin America, 629–630
  in Latin America, post-World War II,
    838
  Mongols, Chinese culture and, 344
  in Mughal empire, 512, 516
  in Safavid dynasty, 508–509
Genocide
  Armenian, 711
  cold war and, 910–911, 910*f*
  in World War II, 775

Geometry, Hellenistic, 108
Germanic Kingdoms, 131*m*
Germany
  nationalism in, 574
  in Triple Alliance, 584
  unification of, 574, 575*m*
Gestapo, 752
Ghana, 209–210, 856–857
Glasnost, 901
Global connections and critical themes,
    222–223, 365
  Africa and African diaspora in world
    context, 476
  age of Eurasian proto-globalization, 542
  Americas and the world, 285
  China's world rule, 307
  civilizations and global forces, 937
  cold war and the world, 819
  early Islam and the world, 180
  east Asia and Pacific Rim in
    contemporary world, 894–895
  eastern Europe and the world, 240
  economic depression, authoritarian
    response, and democratic
    retreat, 762
  European-dominated early phase of
    globalization, 610
  Europe and the world, 424
  1450 and the world, 365
  gunpowder empires and restoration
    of Islamic bridge among
    civilizations, 518
  industrial Europe and the world, 585
  Islam as a bridge between two
    worlds, 202
  Latin American civilization and the
    world context, 451
  medieval Europe and the world, 263
  Mongol linkages, 349
  Muslim and Chinese retreat and shifting
    global balance, 660
  new global standards, new
    divisions, 915
  new Latin American nations and the
    world, 637
  in orbit of China (east Asian corner of
    the global system), 329
  persisting trends in world transformed
    by war, 789
  postcolonial nations in cold war world
    order, 867
  Russia and Japan in the world, 681
  Russia and the world, 492
  struggling toward future in global
    economy, 841
  world economy and the world, 403
  world war and global upheavals, 727

Globalization, 918–938
  cultural, 925–927
  Dubai and, 935
  economic, 923–925, 927–928
  environmental issues in, 929–932
    Chernobyl, 931f
    disease, 932
    as global concerns, 930–932
    global warming, 931–932
  future, predicting, 936–937
    big changes, 936–937
    contemporary period, problem of, 937
    projecting from trends, 936
  in historical perspective, 933
  institutions of, 929
  meaning of, 922–923
  migration and, 925
  multinational corporations and, 923–925, 924m
  nationalism and, 934
  postcolonial societies and, 866–867
  protests against, 927–928, 932
  religious conflicts, 934–935
  technology and, 923
  uncertainties, 932
Global warming, 931–932
Glorious Revolution, 419
Goa, 524
Godric, St., 241–242, 241f
Gods and goddesses
  Arabian, 162
  Aryan, 78
  Greco-Roman, 107
Golden Horde, 339
Golden Lotus, The (Ming), 534
Gold rush, in Brazil, 442–443
Golondrinas (swallows), 635
Good Neighbor Policy, 837
Gorbachev, Mikhail, 900–902, 901f
Gothic architecture, 256, 256f
Government
  industrial order in 1850-1900, 574–576
  in Latin America, 436–441
    haciendas and villages, 437
    industry and commerce, 437, 439
    silver discoveries, 436–437, 437f
    state and church, 439–441
  in western Europe, 249
Gran Colombia, 616
Grand Canal, 299
Great Depression, 748–764
  authoritarianism in, 753–762
    in Argentina, 756–757
    in Brazil, 755–756
    fascism, 733–734, 753
    in Japan, 757–758, 758m
    in Latin America, 753–754, 755
    in Soviet Union, 758–762
    Spanish Civil War, 753
  causation, 748–749
  debacle, 749–750
  Nazism, 751–753, 752f
  New Deal, 751
  response to, in western Europe, 750–751
  revolutions, early 20th-century, 736–748
    in China, 743–748
    in historical perspective, 741
    in Mexico, 736–738
    in Russia, 738–740, 739f, 741–742
  timeline, 731
Great Leap Forward, 884–886, 885f
Great Mosque at Córdoba, 156f, 157
Great Trek, 468
Great Wall, 58, 58f
Great Zimbabwe, 221, 222f
Greece, 99–101, 99m
  Alexander the Great, 100–101, 100m
  Hellenistic period, 100–101, 100m, 101, 107, 108, 114–115
  Olympic Games, 100
  Peloponnesian Wars, 100, 105
  Pericles, 100
  Philip of Macedonia, 100
  politics, 103, 105
Greek fire, 229
Greek Revolution, 568
Green movement, 798
Green Revolution, 861
Gregory VII, 252
Griots, 211, 212
Guaman Poma de Ayala, 433
Guanaham, 398
Guano, 621
Guatemala, post-World War II, 826, 827–828
Gubernia, 485
Guernica (Picasso), 754
Guevara, Ernesto "Che," 828
Guilds, 259
Guillotine, 566
Gulag Archipelago, The (Solzhenitsyn), 813
Gulf of Mexico, 34
GUM (Russian department stores), 729–730, 729f
Gunpowder empires, in historical perspective, 506–507
Guomindang, 746–747
Guptas, 79–80, 80m
Gurus, 83, 596
Gutenberg, Johannes, 409

H

Habsburg, Maximilian von, 624
Haciendas, in Latin America, 437
Hadiths, 171
Haganah, 788
Hagia Sophia, 227, 231f
Hajj, 166
Hajj (pilgrimage to Mecca), 204, 204f
Hammurabi, 25
  law code, 26–27
Han, 56, 59–60, 60m
  capital at Xi'an, 68–69, 69m
  decline and fall in, 125–126, 128
  Vietnam conquest and, 323–324, 323m
Hangzhou, 287–288
Hannibal, 101
Hanseatic League, 258
Haoles, 609
Hara-kiri, 314
Harappa, 30–32, 31m
Harsha, 128
Harun al-Rashid, 184–185
Harvey, William, 416
Hausa, 213
Hawaii, tragedies in, 608–609, 608f
Heian (Kyoto), 311–313
Hellenistic period, 100–101, 100m. *See also* Middle East and Mediterranean, classical
  architecture, 109
  cultural influence in Persia, 115
  ethical systems, 107
  geometry, 108
  Olympic Games, 95, 100
  science, 108
Henry the Navigator, 361, 362
Hercules, 107f
Hernández, José, 629
Herzl, Theodor, 722
Hidalgo, Father Miguel de, 615
Hideyoshi, Toyotomi, 539, 540f
High Middle Ages, 252, 253
Himalayas, 77
Hinduism, 82–84
  in Mughal empire, 511
  in south Asia, 197, 199
Hisako, Yoshizawa, 778–779
Hispaniola, 428
History of the World, 331f
History of the World (al-Din), 331f
Hitler, Adolf, 712, 775
Ho Chi Minh, 891, 892
Hojo, 315
Holocaust, 775
Holy Alliance, 665
Holy Roman emperors, 246
Home and the World, The (Tagore), 724
Homelands, 865
Homer, 109
Homo erectus, 10

Homo sapiens sapiens, 2, 10
Hong Kong, 874, 875
Hongwu, 529–531
Hong Xiuquan, 639–640
Hookahs (water pipes), 594
Huacas, 278
Huancavelica, 437
Huanghe River, 32, 33
Huerta, Victoriano, 737
Huitzilopochtli, 270
Hulegu, 191, 192
Humanism, 408
Human rights in, 20th century, 834–835
Humayan, 510, 511
Hundred Years' War, 249
Hungary, in Triple Alliance, 584
Hunting and gathering
   in Neolithic revolution, 13–14
   in Paleolithic Age, 9–10
Hussein (sherif of Mecca), 722
Hymn to Wisdom, 293–294
Hyundai, 877, 878, 879*f*

I

Iberian peninsula, in 1450, 361
Iberian society and tradition, Spanish/Portuguese conquest and, 428
Ibn Battuta, 211
Ibn Khaldun, 188
Icon, 230, 231
Ideographic symbols, 32
Ieyasu, Tokugawa, 539
Ifriqiya, 208
Iliad, 62, 109
Imams, 507
Imperial age of Japan, 310–314, 311*m*
Impis, 587–588
Inca (ruler), 276
Incas, 125, 276–282
   Andean societies in, 276
   archeological history of, 277
   Aztecs compared to, 281–282
   conquest and expansion, 276, 277–278
   cultural achievements of, 281, 281*f*
   expansion of, 276, 276*m*
   imperial rule in, techniques of, 278, 280–281
   power of, rise to, 276
   religion of, 276, 277–278
Inca socialism, 279, 280
India
   British rule, in Industrial Age, 591–592
   early, 30–32, 31*m*
      Aryan migrants, 32
      Harappa, 30–32
      literary epics, 32

   early colonial society in, 591–592
   global industrialization in, 921
   nationalism and, 716–717
   nationalism in, 861–862
   world economy in, 395
India, classical, 74–93
   caste system, 77, 81, 82, 84, 85, 86, 87–90
   China compared to, 88
   decline in, 128–129
   economy and society, 87–88
   geography and culture, 76–78
      Brahman culture, 77–78
      formative influences, 77
   influence of, 88–91
   overview of, 74–76
   patterns in, 78–80
      Guptas, 79–80, 80*m*
      Mauryan dynasty, 78–79
   politics, 80–81
   religion and culture, 82–87
      arts, 86–87
      Buddhism, 76, 84–86, 85*m*
      cave temples at Ajanta, 74–75, 74*f*
      Hinduism, 82–84
      sciences, 86
      stupas, 86–87, 86*f*
   timeline, 76
   trade in, 88, 91*m*
Indian Ocean, Ming expeditions and, 534*m*, 536
Indians
   defined, 266
   exploitation of, 435–436
Indian term, as insult, 630
Indies piece, 459
Indigenism, 737
Indigenous societies, in Latin America, 435–436
   Indians, exploitation of, 435–436
   population decline, 435, 435*f*
   workings of Spain's empire in America from Indian point of view, 433–434
Indra, 78
Indus River, 30. *See also* River valley
Industrial Age
   big changes, 558–559
   big concepts, 557
   causes of Industrial Revolution, 557
   civilizations, in crisis, 639–661
   contacts and their limits, 683–685
   continuity, 560
   critical themes, 685
   critical thinking questions, 686
   European global order, 587–611
   globalization, 559–560
   impact on daily life, leisure, 560
   Industrial Revolution, 561–586

   Latin America, consolidation of, 612–638
   major world empires, c. 1910, 556*m*
   overview of, 555
   political revolutions, 559–560
   Russia and Japan, 662–682
   societies and trends, 560
   timeline, 558–559
   triggers for change, 557
   world centers of industrialization, c. 1910, 556*m*
Industrialization
   global, 919–922
      in China, 920–921
      in India, 921
      older industrial centers, 921–922
   in Soviet Union, 761
Industrial Revolution, 561–586
   age of revolution and, 562–563
      American Revolution, 565
      defined, 562–563
      French Revolution, 565–568, 567*m*
      Industrial and Atlantic revolutions compared, 580–581
      revolutions of 1848, 569–571
   anti-Chinese rioting, 561–562
   change and, 563–564
   cultural transformations in, 576–579
      artistic expression, 578, 579*f*
      consumption and leisure, 577
      scientific knowledge, advances in, 577–578
   diplomatic tensions, World War I and, 583–585
      alliance system, 584
      Balkan nationalism, 584, 584*m*
      diplomacy and society, 584–585
   first phases of, 569–571
   industrial order in 1850-1900, 571–576, 571*m*
      government functions, 574–576
      industrial life, adjustments to, 572
      Italy and, unification of, 574, 574*m*
      political trends, 572, 573–574
      second industrial revolution, 572
   in Japan, 677–681
      effects of, social and diplomatic, 678–680
      modernization, 680–681
   timeline, 563
   in Western settler societies, 579, 581–583
      Australia, 583
      Canada, 582–583
      New Zealand, 583
      United States, 581–582
Inequalities in world economy, 394, 395
Integralists, 755
Intelligentsia, 670

Interesting Narrative: Biography of Mahommah G. Baquaqua, An (Baquaqua), 454
Invention, in Tang and Song eras, 302–304
Investiture, 252
Ionic, 109
Iran
   Islamic revolutionary regime in, 909
   nuclear weapons in, 910
   religious revivalism in, 862–864
Iraq
   First U.S. Iraq War, 909, 910
   terrorism and, 912, 915
Iron curtain, 794
"I Run Around with Them" (Anwar), 852–853
Isabella of Castile, 427, 428
Isandhlwana, 600
Isfahan, 508, 508*f*
Islam, 129
   architecture of, 215
   global expansions, patterns of, 193, 196–197
   Mongol assault on, 341, 342–343
   women and, 172–173
Islam, rise and spread of
   in Africa, 204–223
      in Ethiopia, 208–209
      in Ghana, 209–210
      in grassland kingdoms, 209–214
      in North Africa, 207–208
      in Nubia, 208
      in Sudanic states, 210–214
      in Sudanic states in, 210–214
      in Swahili coast of East Africa, 215–217, 216*m*
   in Arabia, 151*m*, 156–181, 168*m*
      Abbasid era and, 174–175, 177–179
      Arabs and, 164–165
      elements in, universal, 165–166
      mosque as symbol of Islamic civilization, 176–177
      Muhammad and, 163–166
      overview of, 157–158
      pre-Islamic Arabia and, 158–162, 159*m*
      timeline, 158
      Umayyads and, 166–173
   in middle and late Abbasid eras, 184–192, 185*m*
   in south Asia, 192–200
      accommodation patterns and, 197, 198–199
      challenge of, 197, 199
      conversion patterns and, 196–197, 198–199
      Hindu revival and, 197, 199
      Indian influences on, 195
      Muslim invasions, 194–196, 200
      political divisions and, 194
   in southeast Asia, 200–202, 201*m*
      conversion and, 201
      Sufi mystics and, 202
      trade contacts and, 201
Islamic heartlands
   decline and fall of, 644–650
      bankruptcy, 647–648
      European Intervention, 648
      Mahdist revolt in Sudan, 648–649
      Muhammad Ali, Westernization in Egypt and, 645, 646–647
      resistance, strategies of, 648
Ismâ'il, 504
Italian Renaissance. *See* Renaissance
Italy
   nationalism in, 574
   in Triple Alliance, 584
   unification of, 574, 574*m*
   in World War I, 707–710
Iturbide, Agustín de, 615
Ivan III (Ivan the Great), 480, 481, 482, 483
Ivan IV (Ivan the Terrible), 478–479, 478*f*, 481, 483

J

Janissaries, 497
Japan, 310–319
   classical period, 122
   decline of imperial power in, 313
   gatekeeper elites in, 326–327
   in Great Depression, 757–758, 758*m*
   Heian (Kyoto) as capital of, 311–313
   imperial age of, 310–314, 311*m*
   Nara crisis and, 311–312
   post–World War II
      economic surge in, 875–877
      political and cultural style, 874
      recovery in, 871–872
   reunification, in age of global change, 538–542
      Europeans and, 540, 541*m*
      isolation and, self-imposed, 540–542
      Tokugawa Shogunate, 539, 539*m*, 541
   warrior elites in, 311*m*, 314–319
   women in, 312, 312*f*, 313, 318
   world economy in, 395
   in World War II
      defeat of, 778–779
      invasion of China, 770–771
      Pearl Harbor, 776–778, 779
Japan, industrialization and, 673–681
   adaptation to, compared to China, 675
   expansion, 680*m*
   industrial revolution, 677–680
      effects of, social and diplomatic, 678–680
      modernization, 680–681
   isolation, 674, 675
   in Meiji state, 676–677
   shogunate, 673–674
   timeline, 664
   Western influence, 678
Jati, 77
Java
   colonial society in, 593–594
   Dutch advance on, 591
   early colonial society in, 593–594
Jerusalem, monk's visit to, 250–251
Jesuits, 410, 535, 535*f*, 540
Jesus of Nazareth, 134, 228*f*, 229*f*, 232*f*
Jiang Qing, 870, 886–887
Jihad, 167
   Mahdist revolt in Sudan, 648–649
Jin kingdom, 299
Jinnah, Muhammad Ali, 782
Jinshi, 292
Jizya, 170, 511
João VI, 617
Journal des Dames, 422
Juana, 398
Juárez, Benito, 612–613, 623, 623*f*
Judaism, 37
Junks, 300
Jurchens, 299
Justinian, 227–228, 228*m*
Juula, 210

K

Ka'ba, 161, 165*f*
Kabir, 199, 200
Kalidasa, 83
Kamasutra, 86
Kami, 310
Kangxi, 652
Karakorum, 338
Karbala, 169
Karma, 82
Kautilya, 81
Kent cloth, 473
Kenya African Union (KAU), 786
Kenyatta, Jomo, 786
Kepler, Johannes, 415, 415*f*, 416
Kerensky, Alexander, 738
Khadijah, 163
Khagan, 335
Khamsah, 186*f*
Khanates, 339
Khans, 333
Khartoum, 648, 649, 649*m*
Khayyam, Omar, 189

Khedives, 647
Khitans, 297
Khmers, 323, 327
Khoikhoi, 606
Khomeini, Ayatollah Ruhollah, 862–863, 864f
Khrushchev, Nikita, 815
Kiev, 236, 238–239
Kievan Rus', 237, 238
Kimonos, 875f
Kings, African, 217–218, 220
Knowledge of Kushite, 119
Koguryo, 320
Kong Fuzi. See Confucius
Kongo, 220–221
Korea, 319–322
    aristocratic families in, 322
    ceramics in, 321f
    Koryo collapse and, 322
    post–World War II, 872–873
    Sinification in, 320–323
        of elites, 321–323
        tribute system and, 320–322
    Tang alliances and conquest of, 320
    Yi dynasty in, 322
Korean War, 873
Koryo, 320–321, 322
Krises, 199
Kubilai Khan, 343–344, 344f
Kulaks, 672
Kuriltai, 335
Kush, 28, 28f
Kushans, 79
Kush kingdom, 119, 119f, 122

L

Lake Texcoco, 268–269, 269m
Land and Freedom Army, 786
Language
    Mandarin Chinese, 57
    Yoruba, 217–218
La Reforma, 623
Large Bathers, The (Cézanne), 579f
Las Casas, Bartolomé de, 431, 432f
Last Judgment: Apocalypse of Reichenau, 244f
Last Supper, 110f, 231
Lathi, 724
Latin America
    in Great Depression, 753–754, 755
    post–World War II, 821–842
        art and, 827
        Cuban revolution and, 828–829, 831–833
        democratic trends in, 833, 835
        Guatemala and, reform and U.S. intervention in, 826, 827–828
        human rights in, 20th century, 834–835
        literature in, 830–831
        Mexico and the PRI, 824
        population movements, 839–840, 840t
        radical options in 1950s, 825–831
        reform and military options in, 831–837
        social changes in, 837–841
        soldiers take power in, 831–833
        timeline, 823
        U.S. military interventions in, 835–837, 836m
        women's roles in, 838
Latin America, consolidation of, 612–638
    economies, 620–628
        Argentina, 624–625, 627, 633, 635
        Brazilian empire, 627–628
        instability and foreign intervention, 622–624
        Mexico, 633
        Monroe Doctrine and, 620
        Panama Canal and, 635–637, 636f
        resurgence and liberal politics, 621–622
        stagnation, 621
        trade expansion, 630–631, 633
        United States' interest in, 635–637
    political changes, 614–620
        caudillos, 619
        church and, 620
        independence struggles, 615–617
        issues in, 619
        liberal politics, 621–622
        political fragmentation, 618–619
        United States' interest in, 635–637
    societies, 628–637
        class patterns, 630
        cultural expression after independence, 629
        gender patterns, 629–630
        race patterns, 630
    timeline, 614
Latin America, in early modern period, 425–452
    Brazil, as first plantation colony, 441–443
        gold rush, 442–443
        sugar and slavery, 441–442
    colonial economies and governments, 436–441
        haciendas and villages, 437
        industry and commerce, 437, 439
        silver discoveries, 436–437, 437f
        state and church, 439–441
    18th-century reforms, 446–450
        Bourbon reforms, 447–449, 448m
        Marquis of Pombal, 449
        politics and trade, 446
        reforms, reactions, and revolts, 449–480
    indigenous societies, 435–436
        Indians, exploitation of, 435–436
        population decline, 435, 435f
        workings of Spain's empire in America from Indian point of view, 433–434
    multiracial societies, 443–445
        ratios of ethnic categories in Mexico and Peru, changing, 444–445
        sociedad de castas, 443–444, 445
    Spanish/Portuguese conquest, 427–435, 429m, 430m
        Caribbean and, 428–431, 429m
        chronology of, 428
        conquistadors, 432, 434
        in historical perspective, 438–439
        Iberian society and tradition, 428
        morality and, 434–435
        paths of, 431–432
    time line, 425–452
League of Nations, 714
Lee Kuan Yew, 879
Legalism, 65
Leisure, in Industrial Revolution, 577
Lepanto, 393
Lesotho, 469
Letrados, 439, 440
"Letter of Jamaica" (Bolívar), 625–626
Let Us Now Praise Famous Men, 749f
Lexus and the Olive Tree, The, 933
Liang Qichao, 659
Liao dynasty, 297
Liberal Democratic Party, 872
Liberals, 568
Liberation theology, 831
Li Bo, 304
Li Dazhao, 745
Life in the Argentine Republic in the Days of the Tyrants, or Civilization and Barbarism (Sarmiento), 626
Lin Biao, 883
Lineage, African, 849
Lin Zexu, 655–656
"Lion Prince," 211
Literary epics, 32
Literature
    in China, 65, 66
    Greek, 108–109
    in Latin America, post–World War II, 830–831
    Persian, in Abbasid era, 189–190
    religious, in western Europe, 255–256
    in Vietnam, 324–325

"Little red books," 888
Liu Shaoqi, 870, 886
Li Yuan, 290–291
Lloyd George, David, 713
Loango, 464f
Locke, John, 416
Long distance trade, with Mongols, 337–338
Long March, 746m, 747–748
Louis XIV, 417, 418–419
Louis XVI, 565
L'ouverture, Toussaint, 615
Luanda, 456, 457
Luo, 466
Luther, Martin, 409
Luzon, 527

M

Macao, 533
Machiavelli, Niccolo, 408
Madero, Francisco, 736
Madrasas (Islamic religious schools), 596
Magellan, Ferdinand, 387
Maghrib, 208
Magna Carta, 249
Mahabharata, 32, 62, 87, 766
Mahayana, 133
Mahdi, 649
Mahdist revolt in Sudan, 648–649
Mahmud II, 642
Mahmud of Ghazni, 196
Maipu, battle of, 617f
Malacca, 201
Mali Empire, 210–211
Mamluks, 192, 645
Mandarin Chinese, 57
Mandates, 722
Mandela, Nelson, 865
Mani, 221
Manifest destiny, 622
Manorialism, 243–244
Manufacturing, during 18th century, 422–423
Maori, in Polynesia, 363–364
Mao Zedong, 745, 747–748
Maran, René, 602
Marathon, 94
Marattas, 517
Maritime power, in world economy, 385–390, 391m
   Northern European expeditions, 388–389, 389f, 391m
   Portugal, 386–387, 388m
   Spain, 387, 388m
   technology, 386
Marquez, Gabriel García, 841
Marquis of Pombal, 449

Marriage
   Arabian, 162
   in Tang and Song eras, 302
Marshall Plan, 794, 795
Martel, Charles, 245
Martín Fierro (Hernández), 629
Marx, Karl, 575
Marxism, in China, 745–746
Mass consumerism, 422
Mass consumption items, in Roaring Twenties, 732
Mass leisure culture, 577
Mass Line, 884
Mataram, 591
Math, in China, 67
Mauryan dynasty, 78–79
Mawali, 170, 175
Maximilian, 612–613, 612f
Maya peoples, 124–125
May Fourth movement, 744–746
Mecca, 161
Medieval, 242
Medina, 161
Mediterranean, classical. *See* Middle East and Mediterranean, classical
Meeting of Cortés and Moctezuma, The (painting), 434f
Mehmed II, 496
Meiji, 676–677
Men
   Aztec, 274–275
   in Tang and Song eras, 302, 303
Menchú, Rigoberta, 830–831
Mercantilism, 394
Mercantilists, 524
Meritocracy, 291–292
Mesoamerica in postclassical period. *See under* Americas
Mesolithic Age, 12
Mesopotamia, 23, 23m, 27–30
   Egypt compared to, 29, 30
   in maps, 25–26, 26m
   Sumerians, 23–25
Mestizos, 395
Metalworking, 15–16
Metates, 273
Methodius, 235
Mexica, 268
Mexican-American War, 623
Mexican Constitution of 1917, 737
Mexican Revolution, 736–738
Mexico
   economy in, 633
   Lake Texcoco and, 268–269, 269m
   PRI and, 824
   ratios of ethnic categories in, changing, 444–445

Mexico City, 432
Mfecane, 469
Middle Ages, 242, 262. *See also* Postclassical period; western Europe
   High, 252, 253
Middle East
   conflicts, post-cold war, 909–910
   nationalism in, 719–721, 720m
      Egypt, 719–721, 720m
      Gandhi and, 718–719
      in India, 716–717
      mass movement, social foundations of, 717–718
      militant nationalism, rise of, 718
      revolt in Egypt, 723, 724–725
      war and nationalist movements in, 721–723
   social and cultural change, in 1450, 353–354
   world economy in, 395
   in World War II, 772, 773m
Middle East and Mediterranean, classical, 94–116. *See also* Hellenistic period
   art and architecture, 109, 110f
   comparative perspective of, 104
   economy and society, 111–114
      agriculture and trade, 111–112
      environmental consequences, 114
      slavery, 112, 113–114
   Greece, 99–101, 99m
      Alexander the Great, 100–101, 100m
      Olympic Games, 95, 100
      Peloponnesian Wars, 100, 105
      Pericles, 100
      Philip of Macedonia, 100
      politics, 103, 105
   literature, 108–109
   overview of, 94–96
   Persian Empire, 97–99, 97m
      art, 98–99
      Cyrus the Great, 97
      politics, 98, 110
      Zoroastrianism, 98
   religion and culture, 107–110
   Rome, 101–103
      complexities, 114–115
      fall of, 102, 114–115
      politics, 101, 105–106, 114–115
      Punic Wars, 101
      Roman republic, 101–102, 102m
      value crisis in, 113
   time line, 96
Middle Kingdom, 56
Middle Passage, 469, 471–472
Middle Stone Age. *See* Mesolithic Age
Midway Island, 778
Militant nationalism, 718

Index   I-13

Minamoto, 314–315
Minas Gerais, 442
Mindanao, 527
Ming dynasty, 348, 529–538
   agriculture in, 533
   art in, 534
   decline, 535, 536, 538
   Europeans in, arrival of, 535
   expansion, 534
   expeditions, 534*m*, 536
   Jesuits, 535, 535*f*, 540
   population in, 533
   retreat, 534
   scholar-gentry in, 529–533
   trade in, long-distance, 533–534
   Zheng He expeditions, 534, 534*m*, 536
Minh Mang, 890
Ministry of Rites, 291
Mira Bai, 199, 200
Missionaries, in south and southeast Asia, 528–529
Mita, 278, 384, 436
Moctezuma II, 269, 432
Modernization theory, 632
Moldboard, 244
Monarchies, in western Europe, 248
Mongol Imperium, 337–338
Mongols, 191, 192, 331–350. *See also* Chinggis Khan
   assaults
      on Islamic world, 336, 337, 340*m*, 341, 342–343
      on Khwarazm Empire, 331–332, 341
   in China, 343–349
      gender roles, 344
      Kubilai Khan and, 343–344, 344*f*
      scholar-gentry resistance, 345–346
      social policies, 345–346
      Timur-i Lang and, 348–349
      tolerance and cultural influences, 344
      Yuan and, fall of, 343, 346, 348
   conquest of, 336
   cross-cultural exchange and, 337–338
   division of, 338
   global exchange network of, 342, 342*m*
   incursions in, 341
   khanates of, 339, 340*m*
   movement of, 334*f*, 339–343
      assault on Islamic heartland, 341, 342–343
      retreat from Europe, 341
      in Russia, 339–341
   in Russia, end of, 479–480
   trade with, long distance, 337–338
   virtues and vices of, 337
   warriors, 335–336
   Monkey (Ming), 534

Monotheism, 37
Monroe Doctrine, 620
Monsoons, 77
Montagu-Chelmsford reforms, 719
Morality, Spanish/Portuguese conquest and, 434–435
Morley-Minto reforms, 718
Mosques, 171*f*, 176–177, 179
Mu'awiya, 169
Mubarak, Hosni, 860–861
Mughal empire, 496*m*, 510–517, 510*m*
   Akbar and, 511–512
   art and architecture in, 512, 513–515
   decline of, 516–517
   defined, 494, 495
   elite in, 516
   European contacts with, 512–513
   growth of, 510, 510*f*
   Hindu allies, 511
   politics in, 516
   religious syncretism in, 511
   social reform, 511–512
   trade in, 512
   women in, 512, 516
Muhammad, 163–166
Muhammad ibn Qasim, 194–195
Muhammad of Ghur, 196
Muhammad Shah, 331–332
Muhammad the Great, 213
Mullahs (local prayer leaders), 507, 863
Multinational corporations, 923–925, 924*m*
Multiracial societies, in Latin America, 443–445
   ratios of ethnic categories in Mexico and Peru, changing, 444–445
   sociedad de castas, 443–444, 445
Mumtaz Mahal, 516
Muqaddimah, The, 188
Murad, 645
Murasaki, Lady, 312–313, 313*f*
Muslim Brotherhood, 858–859
Muslim empires, 493–519, 496*m*
   Europe and, indifference to, 503
   gunpowder, global power and, 506–507
   Mughal, 496*m*, 510–517, 510*m*
   Ottoman, 495–503, 496*m*, 497*m*
   Safavid, 496*m*, 504–505, 504*m*, 507–510
   timeline, 494–495
Muslim invasions, in south Asia
   Muslim presence in India and, 200
   political divisions and, 194–195
   second wave of, 195–196
Muslim League, 782
Muslin, 188
Mussolini, Benito, 733, 734, 734*f*
Mvemba, Nzinga, 456
Mwene Mutapa, 221

N

Nabobs, 594
Nadir Khan Afshar, 510
Naipaul, V. S., 853
Napoleon, 567–568, 567*m*
Nara, 311–312
Nasser, Gamal Abdel, 858, 858*f*
Natal, 607
National Congress party, 717
Nationalism, 566–567, 843–856. *See also* Postcolonial nations
   in Africa, 845–846, 847*m*
   Balkan, 584, 584*m*
   cold war rivalries and, 853, 856
   French Revolution and, 566–567
   in Germany, 574
   in India, 861–862
   in Italy, 574
   military responses, 857–861
   Pakistan and, 848*m*, 854–855
   populists and one-party rule, 856–857
   south Asia and, 848*m*, 849
   in World War II
      in Africa, 783–784, 785–788
      in Middle East, 788–789
      in south and southeast Asia, 781–783
Nationalism (Tagore), 715
National Liberation Front (FLN), 786
National Socialist (Nazi) party, 768, 769
Nation-state, 419
Native Americans, 266
NATO, 909
Nawab, 592
Nazi blitzkrieg, 772–775
Nazi invasion of Poland, 771–772
Négritude, 726
Nehru, Jawaharlal, 851, 852
Neocolonial economy, 853, 855
Neo-Confucians, 298
Neo-Confucian thought, 298
   Japan's reunification and, 542
   of male dominance, assertion of, 302
Neolithic Age
   spread of agriculture and, 12–16
   tools, 15–16
Neolithic revolution, 13–14
Neruda, Pablo, 836–837
Nestorians, 168
New Deal, 751
New Economic Policy, 740
New feminism, 807
New France, 397
New Spain, 432
New Stone Age. *See* Neolithic Age
Newton, Isaac, 416
New world order, colonial expansion and, 403

New Zealand
  as cold war ally, 803
  Industrial Revolution in, 583
  in Roaring Twenties, 732, 734m
  tragedies in, 607–608
Nezhualcoyotl, 270–271
Ngo Dinh Diem, 892
Nguyen, 328
Nguyen Anh, 889, 890
Nicholas II, 708
1900–present, 729–764
  Africa, Middle East, and Asia in era of independence, 843–868
  authoritarianism, 753–762
  big changes, 697–699
  big concepts, 695–696
  cold war, Western society and eastern Europe in, 791–820
  continuity, 699–700
  critical themes, 939
  critical thinking questions, 940
  European global order
    World War I and crisis of, 701–728
  European world order
    World War II and end of, 765–790
  globalization and resistance, 918–938
  Great Depression, 748–764
  impact on daily life, emotions and behavior, 699–700
  Latin America, revolution and reaction, 821–842
  nation-building in east Asia and Pacific Rim, 869–896
  Nazism, 751–753, 752f
  1990–2014, 897–917
  overview, 694–695
  political map of the present-day world, 695m
  political map of the world in 1914, 695m
  revolutions, 736–748
  Roaring Twenties, 730–735
  societies and trends, 700
  timeline, 696–697, 731
  triggers for change, 696–697
1990–2014, 897–917
  cold war and, end of, 898–906
  democracy and, spread of, 906–908
  powers and disputes, 908–911
  United States as sole superpower, 911–915
Nirvana, 85
Nobili, Robert di, 528
Nobunaga, Oda, 538–539
No Longer at Ease (Achebe), 853
Nomadic societies, 16–18
  civilizations and, 17–18
  classical period and, 120–121
  culture and, 17
  early groups, 16–17
  Qin dynasty, 56, 57–59, 57m
  spread of agriculture and, 16–18
  Zhou dynasty, 56–57, 57m
North America, colonial expansion and, 397, 400
North American Free Trade Agreement (NAFTA), 929
North Atlantic Treaty Organization (NATO), 795
Northern Europe
  classical period, 122
  expeditions, 388–389, 389f, 391m
Northern Renaissance, 408
Notre-Dame, 256f
Nubia, 208
Nude Descending a Staircase, No. 2 (Duchamp), 732f
Nurhaci, 650
Nur Jahan, 516

O

Oba, 465
Oba, 221f
Obeah, 439, 474
Obregón, Alvaro, 737
Odyssey, 109
Oedipus complex, 108
Ogedei, 338
Old Believers, 483
Old Stone Age. *See* Paleolithic Age
Olmecs, 34, 34f
Olympic Games, 95, 100
One Hundred Years of Solitude (Marquez), 841
One-party rule, 856–857
Opium War, 652m, 655–657
Orejones, 281
Ormuz, 524
Orozco, José Clemente, 737
Orthodox Christianity, 225, 226, 230, 231, 238, 239
Ottoman empire, 495–503, 496m, 497m
  Constantinople and, 495, 496, 498f, 499–500
  decline, 501–502, 503
  decline and fall of, 641–644
    mapping, 651m
    reform and survival, 642–643
    repression and revolt, 643–644
  defined, 494
  expansion of, 495–496, 497m
  sultans, 498–499
  warfare and, 497–498
Ottoman Society for Union and Progress, 644
Overseas expansion, in historical perspective, 537–538
Oyo, 218

P

Pachacuti, 276
Pachisi, 513
Pacific Rim, post-World War II, 877–882
  countries in, 871, 871m
  development in, 877–878
  growth indices, 880
  Taiwan and, 878–879
  themes and problems in, 879, 880, 882
  as U.S. policy issue, 881–882
Padishah, 507
Paekche, 320, 320m
Paintings, in Mughal empire, 513–514
Pakistan, 30
  nationalism and, 848m, 854–855
Paleolithic Age
  human evolution, 9–10
  hunting and gathering, 9–10
  spread of the human species, 10, 11–12, 12m
  tools, 8–10, 12
Palmares, 474
Pamela (Richardson), 422
Pan, 197
Pan-African, 726
Panama Canal, 635–637, 636, 636f
Panchatantra, 86
Papa (father), 134
Parliamentary monarchy, 419
Parliaments, 249
Parthia, 102
Partition, 590
Partition of Poland, 488
Party cadres, 883
Party of the Institutionalized Revolution (PRI), 738
Pasteur, Louis, 572
Patriarchal societies, women in, 21f, 29–30
Paulistas, 442
Paul of Tarsus, 134
Pearl Harbor, 776–778, 776f, 777m, 779
Peasant option, Mao and, 747–748
Peasants
  in Russia, 481, 489–490
  Russian, in Industrial Age, 665–667, 668f
  in western Europe, 245, 245f
Pedro I, 617
Pedro II, 627f
Peloponnesian Wars, 100, 105
Peng, Li, 907–908
Peninsulares, 445, 446
People Made New, A (Liang Qichao), 659
People's Democratic Republic of Korea, 872

Index   I-15

People's Liberation Army, 883
People's Republic of China, 883
Perestroika, 902
Pericles, 100
Periplus of the Erythraean Sea, The, 216
Perón, Juan, 756–757, 824, 824f, 825
Perry, Matthew, 674, 678
Peru, 278m, 279, 281, 282, 444–445
Peter I (Peter the Great), 483–487, 484f
Peter III, 487, 491f
Petrarch, Francesco, 359
Pharaoh, 27
Pheidippides, 94, 94f
Philip of Macedonia, 100
Phoenicians, 37
Phúc, Ly Van, 308–309
Picasso, Pablo, 754
Pinochet, Augusto, 821f, 822
Pinsker, Leon, 722
Pipiltin, 272
Pizarro, Francisco, 396–397, 397f
Plassey, 592
Pochteca, 271
Poetry, Arabian, 162
Pogroms, 722
Poland, Nazi invasion of, 771–772
Polis, 103
Politburo, 762
Political organization
    African slave trade and, 461, 462
    Americas, in 1450, 363
    in China, 60–63, 71
        bureaucracy, 61
        state functions, 61, 63
    consuls, 105
    direct democracy, 103, 105
    during 18th century, 420
    18th-century reforms, in Latin America, 446
    Greece, 103, 105
    India, classical, 80–81
    industrial order in 1850-1900, 572, 573–574
    in Japan, post-World War II, 874
    in Latin America, 614–620
        caudillos, 619
        church and, 620
        democratic trends, 833, 835
        independence struggles, 615–617
        issues in, 619
        liberal politics, 621–622
        political fragmentation, 618–619
        United States' interest in, 635–637
    in Mughal empire, 516
    Persian Empire, 98, 110
    polis, 103
    political units of the world, 50m

Rome, 101, 105–106, 114–115
in Safavid dynasty, 505
Senate, 105
in Song era, 297
Sudanic states, 214
in western Europe, 244, 248
    post-World War I, 797–798
in Western transformation, 417–419
    absolute monarchies, 417, 418–419
    nation-state, 419
    parliamentary monarchies, 419
Polynesia, 125
    in 1450
        conquest in, 363
        Maorian achievements in, 363–364
    peoples of, 125
Polytheism, 24
Pope, 134
Popular Front, 750
Population
    of Aztecs, 273, 275
    trends, 357
    in Western transformation, 414m
Population revolution, 564
Populations
    of Africa, in historical perspective, 218–220
    of Americas, in historical perspective, 218–220
    demographic transition and, 219, 220
    demography and, 218–220
    explosion, nationalism and, 846–849, 850f
    in Latin America, post-World War II, 839–840, 840t
    in Ming dynasty, 533
    in New Spain, decline, 435, 435f
    in Pacific Rim, post-World War II, 880
Populism, in Argentina, 756–757
Populists, 856–857
Porteños, 616
Portugal
    African slave trade and, 456–457, 456m
    in Asian sea trading network, 524–526
    conquest, in Latin America (See Spanish/Portuguese conquest, in Latin America)
    maritime power in, 386–387, 388m
Positivism, 621
Postclassical period
    in Americas, 265–286
    big changes, 152
    big concepts, 150
    in China, 287–307
    contacts and their limits, 373–374
    continuity and limitations, 154
    critical themes, 374–375
    critical thinking questions, 376

eastern Europe in, 224–240
impact on daily life, women and, 154–154
Islam in, rise and spread of
    in Africa, 204–223
    in Arabia, 151m, 156–181, 168m
    in middle and late Abbasid eras, 184–192, 185m
    in south Asia, 192–200
    in southeast Asia, 200–202, 201m
main routes of Afro-Eurasian trade, c. 1250, 151m
overview of, 150
religion in, spread of, 151m
timeline, 152–153
transregional network, 153–154
trends and societies in early modern period, 155
triggers for change, 152
in western Europe, 241–264, 250m
Postcolonial nations. *See also* Nationalism
    cultural creativity and, 852–853
    dictatorships
        in Egypt, 857–861
        in Ghana, 856–857
    globalization and, 866–867
    India, 861–862
    internal conflicts and, 854–855
    Iran, 862–864
    neocolonialism and, 853, 856
    Pakistan, 848m, 854–855
    population explosion and, 846–849, 850f
    South Africa, 864–865, 866f
    south Asia, 848m, 849
    women and, subordination of, 851–852
Potosí, 436
Potosi silver mine, 384f
Potsdam Conference, 781
Pragmatists, 886
Predestination, 409
Presidencies, 593
Prester John, 341
Prester John (Buchan), 602
PRI (Party of the Institutionalized Revolution), 824, 825f
Primary products, 853
Prince, The (Machiavelli), 408
Princely States, 593
Prince of Wales (warship), 598f
Principia Mathematica (Newton), 416
Proletariat, 413
Protestantism, 409–410, 410m
Proto-globalization, 380, 423, 424, 533
Proto-industrialization, 564
Ptolemy, 108
Puck (magazine), 634

Pugachev, Emelian, 491, 491f
Pugachev rebellion, 487
Punic Wars, 101
Purdah, 512
Pure land Buddhism, 293
Putin, Vladimir, 905, 906
Puyi, 659
Pyramids, 27–28, 28f

Q

Qin dynasty, 56, 57–59, 57m
Qing dynasty, decline and fall of, 650–660
    bureaucratic breakdown, 654
    Chinese nationalist alternative and, 658–660
    economy in, 653
    mapping, 651, 652m
    Opium War, 652m, 655–657
    rebellion and failed reforms, 657–658
    society in, 653–655
Quetzalcoatl, 267
Queues (braided ponytails), 658
Quipu, 281
Quit India movement, 782
Qur'an, 163
Quraysh, 161
Qutb-ud-din Aibak, 196

R

Race, in Latin America, 630
Radicals, 568
Rajas, 195
Rajput, 128
Ramadan, 166
Ramahyana, 32
Ramayana, 766
Rebellion in the Backlands (Cunha), 628
Recopilación, 439, 440
Red Army, 740
Red Guard, 888
Red Heads, 504
Reform Bill of 1832, 568, 569–570
Reforms, reactions, and revolts, 449–480
Reincarnation, 84
Religion
    of Aztecs, 269–271, 270f
    in China, 63–67
        art, 66, 67m
        Confucianism, 64–65
        Daoism, 65
        Legalism, 65
        literature, 65, 66
        math, 67
        science, 66
    Christianity, 102
    globalization and, 934–935
    in Inca empire, 276, 277–278
    India, classical, 82–87
        arts, 86–87
        Buddhism, 76, 84–86, 85m
        cave temples at Ajanta, 74–75, 74f
        Hinduism, 82–84
        sciences, 86
        stupas, 86–87, 86f
    in Iran, revivalism of, 862–864
    Middle East and Mediterranean, classical, 107–110
    reform in western Europe, 252
    in Tang era, 293, 294–295
    terrorism and, 913–914, 934–935
    in western Europe, 255–256
        in art and literature, 255–256
        popular, 255
    world, classical period
        Christianity, increase of followers, 134–137
        Christianity and Buddhism compared, 133
        development and spread of, 133–137
        distribution of, 136m
Religious revivalism, 852
Renaissance, 359
    culture of, 359–360
    secular directions in, 359–360
Republic of Korea, 872
Return to My Native Land (Césaire), 716
Revisionism, 575, 576
Revolutions
    early 20th-century, 736–748
        in China, 743–748
        in historical perspective, 741
        in Mexico, 736–738
        in Russia, 671–672, 673f, 738–742, 739f
Rhodes, Cecil, 607
Ricci, Matteo, 535
Richard, King, 251f
Ridda Wars, 166
Rig-Veda, 78
Rio de Janeiro, 443
Rivera, Diego, 737
River valley, 30–37
    Americas, 33–35
    China, 32–33
    end of, 35–37
    heritage of, 35–36
    India, 30–32
    Judaism, 37
    new states and peoples, 36–37
Roaring Twenties, 730–735
    art in, 731, 732f
    Australia, 732, 734m
    British Commonwealth of Nations, 732
    Canada, 732, 734m
    eastern Europe, 734–735, 735m
    fascism, 733–734
    mass consumption items in, 732
    Mussolini, 733, 734, 734f
    New Zealand, 732, 734m
    Soviet Union, 734–735, 735m
    United States, 733
Rodó, José Enrique, 636
Roman baths, 52f
Romance of the Rose, The (Villon), 256
Romance of the West Chamber, 346
Roman Empire, decline and fall of, 129–133
    Attila the Hun and, 131
    causes of, 129–130
    patterns of, 131–132
    process of, 130
    results of, 132–133
    signs of, 129
Romanov, Alexis, 482, 483
Romanov dynasty, 482, 483
Roman republic, 101–102, 102m
Romanticism, 578
Rome, 101–103
    Christianity, 102
    complexities, 114–115
    fall of, 102, 114–115
    politics, 101, 105–106, 114–115
    Punic Wars, 101
    Roman republic, 101–102, 102m
    value crisis in, 113
Rosas, Juan Manuel de, 620
Rouseff, Dilma, 839f
Rowlatt Act, 719
Roy, Ram Mohun, 596
Royal African Company, 459
Rubaiyat (Khayyam), 189, 190
Ruo, Yun, 869–870
Rurik, 236–237
Russia, 237. *See also* Soviet Union
    Mongols in, 339–341
    revolution in, early 20th-century, 738–742, 739f
        liberalism to communism, 738–740
        Soviet experimentation, 741
        stabilization of communist regime, 740, 741
    in Triple Entente, 584
    tsars
        Catherine the Great, 485, 487–489, 487f
        expansionist politics under, 479–483, 482m
        Ivan III (Ivan the Great), 480, 481, 482, 483
        Ivan IV (Ivan the Terrible), 478–479, 478f, 481, 483

Russia (cont.)
    Peter I (Peter the Great), 483–487, 484f
    Peter III, 487, 491f
    Romanov dynasty, 483
  world economy in, 395
Russia, industrialization and, 664–673
  economic problems, 665–667
  expansion, 665, 666m
  factory workers in, 668–669
  peasants and, 665–667, 668f
  reform
    before, 665
    early industrialization and, 667–670
  revolution, 670–673
    eastern Europe and, 672–673
    of 1905, 671–672, 673f
    protests, 670–673
    road to, 670–671
    Russo-Japanese War, 671, 672, 672m
  social problems, 665–667
  timeline, 664
Russia, in early modern period, 478–492
  expansion, 479–483
    Mongol control and, end of, 479–480
    multinational empires and, 482
    patterns of, 481–482
    Romanov policy and, 483
    Time of Troubles and, 483
    under tsars, 479–483, 482m
  society in, history of, 489–491
    dependence, 491
    eastern Europe and, 491
    estate agriculture, 490
    serfdom, 489–490
    social unrest, 491
    trade, 490–491
  timeline, 480
  Westernization, first, 483–489, 488m
    Catherine the Great and, 485, 487–489, 487f
    meaning of, 485–487
    Peter the Great and, 483–487, 484m, 486m
Russia, in postclassical era
  Christianity and, 237
  spread of, in eastern Europe
    Kiev, 237, 238–239
    Kievan Rus', 237, 238
Russian Orthodoxy, 237
Russo-Japanese War, 671, 672, 672m

S

Sadat, Anwar, 860
Safavid dynasty, 496m, 504–505, 504m, 505, 507, 507–510
  commercial revival of, 507–508
  defined, 494
  demise of, 509–510
  gender roles, 508–509
  Isfahan, 508, 508f
  politics and war under shahs, 505
  state and religion, 505, 507
Sahara, 119
Sail al-Din, 504
Saint (title), 133
St. Augustine, Florida, 431f
St. Sophia, 229f, 231f
Saladin, 187, 250, 251f, 252
Saltwater slaves, 470
Samurai, 314
San, 606
Sandinista party, 833
Sandino, Augusto, 836
San Martín, José de, 616, 617, 617f
San Salvador, 398
Sanskrit, 77
Santa Anna, General Antonio López de, 620
Santa Cruz, Andrés, 619
Sarajevo, 706
Sarmiento, Domingo F., 625, 626
Sasanian empires, 163
Sati, 197, 512, 512f
Satyagraha, 719
Savages, 19
Schall, Adam, 535
Schism, 231–232
Scholar-gentry, 89
  in Ming dynasty, 529–533
    Hongwu, court politics and, 530–531
    revival of, 529–530
    social dominance, 531, 532
  Mongols and, Chinese influence of, 345–346
  in Tang and Song eras, 304, 306
Scholasticism, 255
School of National Learning, 542
Science
  in Abbasid era, 190
  in China, 66
  Hellenistic, 108
  in India, classical, 86
  in Industrial Revolution, 577–578
  in Tang and Song eras, 302, 303–304
Scientific Revolution, 415–417
  Bacon and, 416
  Copernicus and, 415
  Deism and, 416
  Galileo and, 416
  Harvey and, 416
  Kepler and, 415, 415f
  Locke and, 416
  Newton and, 416
Second industrial revolution, 572
Second Sex, The (de Beauvoir), 807

Secoton, Virginia, 400f
Secret Army Organization (OAS), 786
Self-determination, 713
Self-strengthening movement, 657
Selim III, 642
Seljuk Turks, 187
Senate, 105
Sendero Luminoso (Shining Path), 833
Senghor, Léopold Sédar, 715–716, 726
Sepoys, 591
Seppuku, 314
September 11, 2001 attacks, 912, 912f, 913–914, 935
Serfdom, in Russia, 489–490
Serfs, 243
Serra, Mancio, 425–426
Settlement colonies, 601
Seven Years War, 397
Shah, 504, 505
Shah-Nama, 189–190
Shakuntala, 83
Shamanistic beliefs, 338
Shang dynasty, 32–33, 33m, 62–63
Sharia, 214
Shaykhs, 161
Shi'a, 169
Shi class, 64, 68
Shi Huangdi, 56, 59f, 62–63
Shintoism, 122
Ships of Ming expeditions, 536
Shiva, 83, 84f
Shogunate, 673–674
Shoguns, 315
Shrivijaya, 200
Siddhartha Gautama. *See* Buddha
Sikhs, 517
Silla, 320, 320m
Silver
  discoveries, in Latin America, 436–437, 437f
  in new world economy, 384–385
  Potosi silver mine, 384f
Singapore, post-World War II, 875
Sinification, 320–323
  in Korea
    of elites, 321–323
    tribute system and, 320–322
  in Vietnam, 323–324
Sinified, 297
Sino-Japanese War, 680
Sisulu, Walter, 865
Slavery
  in Brazil, 441–442
  British West Indian slaveholding, 394
  Middle East and Mediterranean, classical, 112, 113–114
Slavic expansion in eastern Europe, 235, 236m

I-18 Index

Smith, Adam, 420
Snow upon Paris (Senghor), 716
Social class and organization
    African slave trade and, 462–463
    Aztec, 272–273, 273*f*
    in China, 67–71
        Confucian social system, 68
        gender and family life, 70–71
        Han capital at Xi'an, 68–69, 69*m*
        trade and technology, 69, 70*f*
    in European global order
        social reform in colonies, 594, 596–597
        social relations between colonizers and colonies, 603
    in India, classical, 87–88
    in Industrial Revolution, 584–585
    in Japan, in Industrial Age, 678–680
    in Latin America, 628–637, 630
        class patterns, 630
        cultural expression after independence, 629
        gender patterns, 629–630
        race patterns, 630
    in Latin America, post-World War II, 837–841
    Middle East, in 1450, 353–354
    Middle East and Mediterranean, classical, 111–114
    of Mongols, Chinese influence on, 345–346
    in postcolonial societies, 866–867
    in Qing dynasty, 653–655
    in Russia, early modern period, 489–491
        dependence, 491
        eastern Europe and, 491
        estate agriculture, 490
        serfdom, 489–490
        social unrest, 491
        trade, 490–491
    in Russia, in Industrial Age, 665–667
    in Song era, 301–302
    in Sudanic states, 214
    in Tang era, 301–302
    in western Europe, 257–258
        post-World War II, 804–805
Socialism, 574, 575
Socialist realism, 761, 761*f*
Social protest, in commercial revolution, 413, 414
Social question, 574, 575
Social values, in Song era, 305
Sociedad de castas, 443–444, 445
Socrates, 107–108
Soldaderas (women soldiers), 737
Solidarity, 811
Solzhenitsyn, Aleksandr, 813

Song era, 296–306, 297*m*
    agrarian production in, 300–301, 301*f*
    artistic creativity and accomplishment in, 302, 303–306
    Confucian thought in, 298
    decline of, 298–299
    divorce in, 302
    engineering in, 302, 304
    expansion in, commercial, 300
    family in, 301–302
    founding of, 296–297
    Golden Age of, 299–306
    Hangzhou as capital of, 287–288
    invention in, 302, 303–304
    male dominance in, Neo-Confucian, 302, 303
    marriage in, 302
    politics in, 297
    scholar-gentry elite in, 304, 306
    science and technology in, 302, 303–304
    social values in, 305
    society in, 301–302
    Southern Song era and, 299
    state and religion in, 293, 294–295
    Wang reforms in, 298–299
Songhay, 213, 213–214
Song of Roland, The, 256
Sons of Heaven, 57
Sophocles, 108
South Africa
    apartheid and, demise of, 864–865, 866*f*
    dominance, in European global order, 606–607
    mfecane and, 469
    white settlers and Africans in, 467–469
    Zulu and, 468–469
South Asia
    nationalism and, 848*m*, 849
    in World War II, 781–783
South Asia, Islam in, 192–200
    accommodation patterns and, 197, 198–199
    challenge of, 197, 199
    conversion patterns and, 196–197, 198–199
    Hindu revival and, 197, 199
    Indian influences on, 195
    Muslim invasions, 194–196, 200
        Muslim presence in India and, 200
        political divisions and, 194–195
        second wave of, 195–196
    political divisions and, 194
Southeast Asia
    Islam in, 200–202, 201*m*
        conversion and, 201
        Sufi mystics and, 202
        trade contacts and, 201
    in World War II, 781–783

Southern Song era, 299
South Pacific
    tragedies, 607–609
        Hawaii, 608–609, 608*f*
        New Zealand, 607–608
    in World War II, 777*m*
Soviet experimentation, 741
Soviet Union. *See also* Russia
    Armenia and Azerbaijan, disagreements between, 909
    Chechnya revolt and, 905, 906, 908–909
    conflicts in, 908–911
        endemic, 909–910
        ethnic and other, 910–911, 910*f*
    Czechs and Slovaks, disagreements between, 908–909
    decline, 899–900, 902–904, *m*72
    demonstrations in 1990s, 904–906, 905*f*
    economic policies in, 759, 760–761
    in Great Depression, 758–762
    industrialization and, 761
    Putin and, 905, 906
    reform, in 1980s and 1990s, 900–904
    in Roaring Twenties, 734–735, 735*m*
    Stalinism in, 758–759
    totalitarian rule and, 761–762
    Yeltsin and, 905
    Yugoslavia and, 909, 909*m*
Spain, maritime power in, 386–387, 388 *m*
Spanish-American War, 635–636
Spanish Civil War, 753
Spanish/Portuguese conquest, in Latin America, 427–435, 429*m*, 430*m*
    Caribbean and, 428–431, 429*m*
    chronology of, 428
    conquistadors, 432, 434
    in historical perspective, 438–439
    Iberian society and tradition, 428
    morality and, 434–435
    paths of, 431–432
Sphinx, 28*f*
Spiritual power, in western Europe, 244
Split inheritance, 277
Sputnik, 816
Sri Lanka, 848*m*, 855
Stalin, Joseph, 742
Stalinism, 758–759
State
    and church, in Latin America, 439–441
    functions, in China, 61, 63
    in Tang era, 293, 294–295
Stateless societies, 206
Steam-powered locomotive, 555
Stoics, 107
Stolypin reforms, 672
Stupas, 86–87, 86*f*

Index   I-19

Sudan, 28, 210–214
   city dwellers and villagers, 211, 212
   epic of Sundiata and, 212
   "Lion Prince" and, 211
   Mahdist revolt in, 648–649
   Mali Empire, 210–211
   political and social life in, 214
   Songhay, 213–214
Suez Canal, 648
Sufi mystics, 202
Sugar, in Brazil, 441–442
Sui dynasty, 128
Sui era, 288–290
Sukarno, 766–767
Suleymaniye, 499, 500f
Suleyman the Magnificent, 499, 511
Sultans, 187
   of Delhi, 196
   Ottoman, 498–499
Sumer, 23m
   Babylonian conquest, 25
   city-states, 24
   cuneiform, 23–24, 24f
   ziggurats, 24
Summas (highest works), 254, 255
Sundiata, 211, 212
Sunnis, 169
Sun Yat-sen, 658
Superpowers, 911–915
Supreme Soviet, 742
Suriname, 474
Swahili coast of East Africa, 215–217, 216m
   cultures on, 216–217
   trading routes, 216, m2
Swazi, 469
Swetham, Joseph, 421
Syncretism, 49
Syndicalism, 736

T

Taffeta, 188
Tagore, Rabindranath, 715
Taika reforms, 310
Taiping Rebellion, 639, 639f, 640
Taira, 314–315
Taiwan, 871, 872, 878–879
Taj Mahal, 515, 515f
Tale of Genji, The (Murasaki), 312–313, 313f, 328
Tale of Kieu, The (Du), 328
Tambos, 278
Tang era, 128, 290–296, 299–306
   agrarian production in, 300–301, 301f
   anti-Buddhist backlash in, 295
   artistic creativity in, 302, 303–306
   decline of, 295–296
   divorce in, 302
   emergence of, 290–291
   engineering in, 302, 304
   expansion in, commercial, 300
   family in, 301–302
   Golden Age of, 299–306
   invention in, 302, 303–304
   Korea and, alliances and conquest of, 320
   male dominance in, Neo-Confucian, 302, 303
   marriage in, 302
   meritocracy and examination system in, 291–292, 292f
   rebuilding, 291
   restoration of, 290–291
   scholar-gentry elite in, 304, 306
   science and technology in, 302, 303–304
   society in, 301–302
   state and religion in, 293, 294–295
Tangut tribes, 298
Tanzimat reforms, 643
Tatars, 239
Tayson Rebellion, 889, 890
Technocrat, 797
Technology
   in China, 69, 70f
   globalization and, 923
   in maritime power, 386
   in Tang and Song eras, 302, 303–304
   terrorism and, 914
   in Western transformation, 409
Tehran Conference, 780
Temple of the Sun, 278
Tenochtitlan, 265–266, 265f, 269, 269m
Teotihuacan, 123–124
Terakoya, 674
Terrorism, United States
   in historical perspective, 913–914
   Iraq and, 912, 915
   military installations, 915m
   response to, 912–915
   September 11, 2001 attacks, 912, 912f, 913–914, 935
Theology, in western Europe, 254–256
Thirty Years War, 410–411
Thousand and One Nights, The, 178, 185
Three estates, 249
Three-field system, 244
"Tierra y Libertad" (Land and Liberty), 737
Tigris-Euphrates civilization, 23–25
   Mesopotamia, 23, 23m
   Sumerians, 23–24, 23m
Tilak, B. G., 718
Timbuktu, 211, 213
Time of Troubles, 482, 483
Timur-i Lang, 348–349
Tlaloc, 270
Tokugawa Shogunate, 539, 539m, 541
Toltec culture, 267–268
Tools
   metal, discovery of, 15–16
   Neolithic Age, 15–16
   Paleolithic Age, 8–10, 12
   yucca-based fire-starter kits, 7f, 8
Topiltzin, 267
Totalitarian rule, in Soviet Union, 761–762
Totalitarian state, 752
Total war, 782
Trade
   Arabian long-distance, 161
   in China, 69
   Chinese transregional, in 1450, 354–355
   in eastern Europe, 236–237
   18th-century reforms, in Latin America, 446
   imbalances in world trade, 393–394
   in India, classical, 88, 91m
   in Latin America, 630–631, 633
   long-distance
      in Ming dynasty, 533–534
   long distance, with Mongols, 337–338
   Middle East and Mediterranean, classical, 111–112
   in Mughal empire, 512
   routes
      in western Europe, 257–259, 257m
   routes, classical period, 121m
   routes on Swahili coast of East Africa, 216, m2
   in Russia, early modern period, 490–491
   in southeast Asia, 201
Trade *econocide*, 475
Trans-Siberian railroad, 668
Trasformismo, 574
Treaty of Guadalupe-Hidalgo, 623
Treaty of Paris, 397
Treaty of Tordesillas, 439
Treaty of Westphalia, 411
Triangular trade, 460
Tribute ceremony, 308f
Tributes, 275, 320–322, 526–528
Trinh, 328
Triple Alliance, 584
Triple Entente, 584, 704m, 705, 710, 714
Tropical dependencies, 601, 602
Truman, Harry, 794
Trung sisters, 324
Tsar, defined, 230
Tsars, Russian
   Catherine the Great, 485, 487–489, 487f
   expansionist politics under, 479–483, 482m
   Ivan III (Ivan the Great), 480, 481, 482, 483

Ivan IV (Ivan the Terrible), 478–479, 478f, 481, 483
Peter I (Peter the Great), 483–487, 484f
Peter III, 487, 491f
Romanov dynasty, 483
Tumens, 335
Tutu, Osei, 463
Twantinsuyu, 276–282. *See also* Incas

U
Ulama, 190, 191
Ulyanov, Vladimir Ilyich, 671
Umayyad
    adversary empires and, weaknesses of, 167–169
    Arab conquests and, motives for, 167
    consolidation and division of, 166–167
    converts and, 170
    decline and fall of, 171–173
    dhimmi ("people of the book") and, 170
    family and gender roles in, 170–171
    imperium, 169–170
    Islam in, spread of, 168m, 169–173
    succession and the Sunni-Shi'a split, 169
Umma, 164
Union of Soviet Socialist Republics, 740
Unitarians, 624
"United Fruit Co., The" (Neruda), 836–837
United Fruit Company, 827–828
United Nations (UN), 780
United States
    as cold war ally, 803–804
    First U.S. Iraq War, 909, 910
    Industrial Revolution in, 581–582
    interventions in Latin America, post-World War II, 835–837, 836m
    Latin America and, 635–637
    Pacific Rim as policy issue, 881–882
    post-World War II, 800
    in Roaring Twenties, 733
    as sole superpower, 911–915
    terrorism and
        in historical perspective, 913–914
        Iraq and, 912, 915
        military installations, 915m
        response to, 912–915
        September 11, 2001 attacks, 912, 912f, 913–914
    women in workforce, 806
    World War I and, 709–710, 711–712, 714, 717
Untouchables, 77
Upanishads, 32, 78, 82–83
Urban II, 250
Urban surge, in western Europe, 247–248
Uthman, 169

V
Valdivia, Pedro de, 432, 434
Values
    in China, exam questions and, 531
    crisis in Rome, 113
Vargas, Getúlio, 755–756
Varnas, 77
Vassals, 248
Vedas, 32, 77
Vedic age, 31
Vergil, 109
Versailles, 417
Viceroyalties, 440
Viceroys, 440
Vichy, 772
Viet Cong, 892–893
Viet Minh, 891–892, 891m
Vietnam, 322–329
    Chams and, 327
    Chinese architecture in, 325, 325f
    Chinese cultural exports in, 325
    Han conquest, 323–324, 323m
    independence of, 325, 327
    Khmers and, 327
    literature in, 324–325
    Nguyen territories in, 328–329
    resistance against China, 324–325
    Sinification in, 323–324
    Trinh family in, 328–329
    women in, 323, 324–325, 327
Vietnamese Nationalist Party, 891
Vikings, 243
Villa, Pancho, 736
Villages
    in Latin America, 437
    Sudanic states, 211, 212
Vishnu, 83
Vivaldis, 361
Vizier, 499
Vladimir I, 224–225, 224f, 237
Vodun, 474
Vo Minh Giap, 892
Voortrekkers, 468
Voudon, 439

W
Wafd party, 723
Wang Anshi, 298–299
Wang Shugu, 54f
War, shift from ritual to real, 62–63
War of the Spanish Succession, 446
Warriors
    elites, in Japan, 311m, 314–319
    Mongol, 335–336
Warsaw Pact, 795
Water Margin, The (Ming), 534
Wayang shadow puppet plays, 766

Wazir, 175
Wealth of Nations (Smith), 420
Welfare state, 796–797, 797f
Western civilization, colonial expansion
    causation and, in historical perspective, 390
    conquerors, tactics and motives of, 398–399
    impact of, 401
Western Europe, 241–264
    civilization, in historical perspective, 253
    colonial expansion and, impact of, 402
    in 1450, 356–362
        colonial patterns in, 362
        dynamism in, 356
        expansion in, 361
        Iberian peninsula, 361
        imitation and commercial problems, 356, 357, 358
        Renaissance, 359–360
    in Middle Ages, 241–264, 250m
        Carolingian rulers in, 245
        under Charlemagne, 245–247, 246m, 247f
        decline of, 260–262
        development in, stages of, 243–253
        economic and urban surge in, 247–248
        expansionist impulse in, 249–250, 252
        government in, 249
        manorialism and, 243–244
        monarchies in, 248
        peasant labor in, 245, 245f
        political power in, 244, 248
        religious reform in, 252
        spiritual power in, 244
        timeline, 243
    in postclassical era, 253–260
        banking in, 258–259, 259f
        Christianity and, 231–232
        eastern Europe and, boundary problems between, 234
        economic changes in, 257–258
        religion in, 255–256
        social changes in, 257–258
        theology and, 254–256
        trade routes in, 257–259, 257m
        women in, 260
    post-World War II, 796–802
        cold war and, 793–804
        colonies of, 793–794
        diplomatic reform and, 798, 801
        economic expansion and, 801–802, 801f
        liberal democracy in, 796
        political stability and, 797–798
        resurgence of, 796–802

Western Europe (cont.)
    social structure of, 804–805
    timeline, 792–793
    United States and, 800
    welfare state and, 796–797, 797f
    Western culture and, 808–809
    women's revolution and, 805–807
Western Front, 707
Westernization, 632
  culture, post-World War II, 808–809
  in Egypt, Muhammad Ali and, 645, 646–647
  in Japan, industrialization and, 678
Western transformation, in early modern period, 405–424, 410m
  commerce, 407–412
  commercial revolution during, 412–415
    balance sheet, 414–415
    social protest, 413, 414
    world economy and, impact of, 413
  culture, 407–412
    Catholic Reformation, 410, 410m
    Christian unity and, end of, 410–412
    Italian Renaissance, 407–408
    Northern Renaissance, 408
    Protestantism, 409–410, 410m
    technology and family, 409
  during 18th century, 420–423
    commerce, 422–423
    Enlightenment, 420–422
    innovation, 423
    instability, 424
    manufacturing, 422–423
    political patterns, 420
  Northern Renaissance, 408
  political changes during, 417–419
    absolute monarchies, 412m, 417, 418–419
    nation-state, 419
    parliamentary monarchies, 419
  populations, 414m
  Scientific Revolution during, 415–417
    Bacon and, 416
    Copernicus and, 415
    Deism and, 416
    Galileo and, 416
    Harvey and, 416
    Kepler and, 415, 415f
    Locke and, 416
    Newton and, 416
  timeline, 407
  women in, 421
Whampoa Military Academy, 747
White, John, 400f
White Dominions, 601
White Lotus Society, 348
White racial supremacy, 603

Wilberforce, William, 475
William the Conqueror, 248
Witchcraft persecution, 414
Witte, Sergei, 669
Wollstonecraft, Mary, 422, 422f
Women
  in Abbasid era, declining positions of, 186–187
  Aztec, 273, 274–275
  in Byzantine Empire, 229
  in Cairo, war protests and, 701–702, 701f
  footbinding and, 303
  Islamic law and, 172–173
  in Japan, 312, 312f, 313, 318
  in Latin America, 629–630
  in Latin America, post-World War II, 838
  in Mughal empire, 512, 516
  in nationalist movement, 723–724
  in patriarchal societies, 21f, 29–30
  in postcolonial nations, 851–852
  representations of, in early art, 11
  revolution, post-World War II, 805–807
  in Tang and Song eras, 302, 303
  in Vietnam, 323, 324–325, 327
  in western Europe, 260
  in Western transformation, 421
World economy, 384–404
  in Asia, 395
  in China, 395
  colonial expansion and, impact of, 396–403
    on Africa, 401–402
    on Americas, 396–397
    on Asia, 401–402
    on British, 397, 399f, 400–401
    on new world order, 403
    on North America, 397, 400
    on Western civilization, 401
    on western Europe, 402
  Columbian Exchange, 391–393
    of animal husbandry, 392
    of crops, 391–392
    of disease, 391, 392f
    environmental impact of, 392–393
  commercial revolution and, 413
  expansionist trends in, 396
  imbalances in world trade, 393–394
  in India, 395
  international inequalities in, 394, 395
  in Japan, 395
  maritime power in, 385–390, 391m
    Northern European expeditions, 388–389, 389f, 391m
    Portugal, 386–387, 388m
    Spain, 387, 388m
    technology, 386

  in Middle East, 395
  in Russia, 395
World power, in 1450, 351–366
  Africa's international contacts and, 365
  Americas and, 363
  bubonic plague and, 356, 358
  China, transregional trade and, 354–355
  ethnocentrism and, in historical perspective, 364
  Middle East, 353–354
  Polynesia and, 363–364
  technology and, 365
  timeline, 353
  western Europe and, 356–362
World religions, classical period
  Christianity, increase of followers, 134–137
  Christianity and Buddhism compared, 133
  development and spread of, 133–137
  distribution of, 136m
  early Christianity, 134
World Trade Center, 912, 912f, 913–914, 935
World War I, 701–728
  Africa during, 710, 710m
  Britain's participation in, 710–711
  brutality of, 706–707, 715–716
  in Europe, 704m, 707–710
  factors leading up to, 704–706
  in Italy, 707–710
  losses, 712t
  in Middle East, 704m
  nationalism in, 714–726
    in Africa, liberation struggles of, 725–726
    British Empire and, 716, 717
    mass movement, social foundations of, 717–718
    Middle East and, 719–721, 720m
    women and, 723–724
  offensive warfare and, 712–713
  outbreak of, 706
  peace efforts, failed, 713–714
    League of Nations and, 714
    Paris peace conference, 713f
    Versailles Treaty, 714
  timeline, 703
  trench warfare in, 708, 715–716
  Triple Entente allies in, 704m, 705, 710, 714
  United States and, 709–710, 711–712, 714, 717
  Western Front in, 707
World War II, 765–790
  Anglo-American offensives in, 775–776
  Asia and Pacific in, 777m

beginning of, 770–772
    Japanese invasion of China, 770–771
    Nazi invasion of Poland, 771–772
British and, 772–773
causes of, 768, 769
cold war and, 780–781
dictators and, 768, 769
in Europe, 772, 773*m*
in historical perspective, 768–769
Hitler's war against Jews, 775
Japan in
    defeat of, 778–779
    Pearl Harbor, 776–778, 779
in Middle East, 772, 773*m*
nationalism and decolonization
    in Africa, 783–784, 785–788
    in Middle East, 788–789
    in south and southeast Asia, 781–783
Nazi blitzkrieg and, 772–775
post (*See also under* western Europe)
    East Asia settlements, 871–877
    Pacific Rim, 877–882
    People's Republic of China, 882–889
    politics and culture, 874–875
    timeline, 871
    Vietnam, 889–894
timeline, 767
World Zionist Organization, 722
Writing
    cuneiform, 23–24, 24*f*, 25*f*
    Sanskrit, 77
Wuzong, Emperor, 295

X

Xavier, Francis, 528
Xi'an, 68–69, 69*m*
Xionghu, 16–17
Xiongnu, 60
Xi Xia, 298
Xuanzong, 295–296
Xunzi, 62–63, 66

Y

Yalta Conference, 780
Yanas, 280
Yangdi, 289–290
Yang Guifei, 296, 296*f*
Yaroslav, 237, 238
Yellow peril, 681
Yellow River, 32, 33
Yellow Turbans, 126
Yeltsin, Boris, 905
Yi dynasty, 322
Yin/yang, 55–56
Yoruba, 217–218
Young India (Gandhi), 715
Yuan, 343, 346, 348
Yuan Shikai, 743
Yucca-based fire-starter kits, 7*f*, 8
Yukichi, Fukuzawa, 662–663
Yun Ruo, 869–870

Z

Zaghlul, Sa'd, 723
Zaibatsu, 678
Zakat, 165
Zapata, Emiliano, 736–737
Zapatistas, 824
Zemstvoes, 668
Zen Buddhism, 293
Zeng Guofan, 657
Zenj, 216
Zhao Kuangyin (Emperor Taizu), 296–297
Zhdanov, Andrey, 759–760
Zheng He, 355, 534, 534*m*, 536
Zhou dynasty, 33, 33*m*, 56–57, 57*m*, 60*m*, 62–63
Zhou Enlai, 886
Zhu Xi, 298
Zhu Yuanzhang, 348
Ziggurats, 24
Zionism, 722
Zoë, Empress, 229, 229*f*, 230
Zoroastrianism, 98
Zulu, 468–469, 468*f*, 587–588

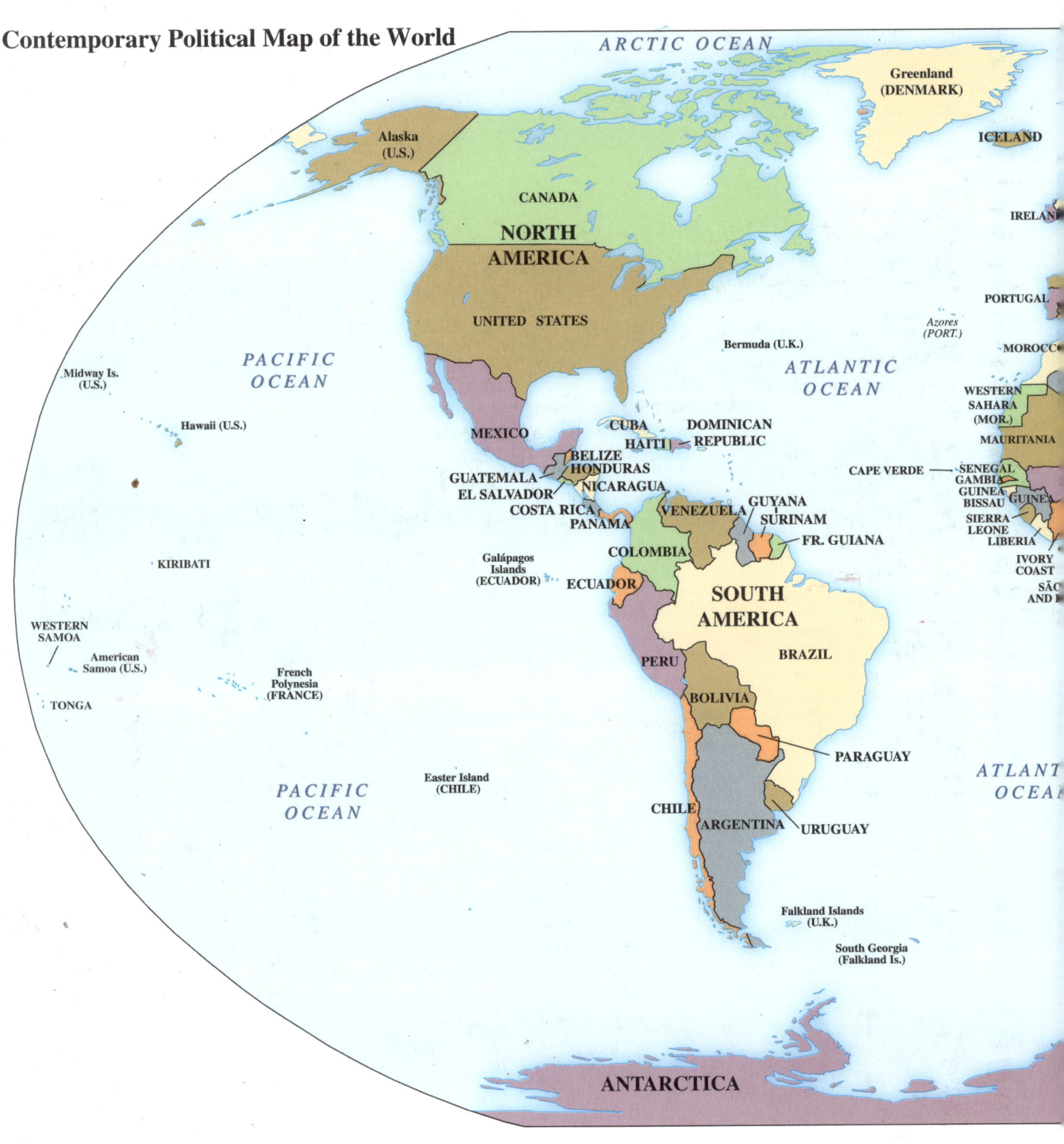

Contemporary Political Map of the World